P9-AFX-964

ALR
5th and 6th
TABLES

COVERING

ALR 5th Vols. 1–125
ALR 6th Vols. 1–104

TABLE OF CASES
S

By the Publisher's Editorial Staff

2015

Mat # 41584285

Library of Congress Catalog Card Number 92-75797

CONTENTS

TABLE OF CASES
S

7735 Hollywood Boulevard Venture v. Superior Court of Los Angeles County, 116 Cal. App. 3d 901, 172 Cal. Rptr. 528 (2d Dist. 1981)
43 ALR5th 207—§ 4, 29, 39

16809 Euclid Corp. v. Board of Zoning Appeals, Slip Op (1982 Ohio App.)
10 ALR5th 538—§ 7, 28

$62,200 in U.S. Currency, In re Forfeiture of, 531 So. 2d 352 (Fla. Dist. Ct. App. 1st Dist. 1988)
115 ALR5th 403—§ 8
116 ALR5th 325—§ 3

S., In Interest of, 648 S.W.2d 351 (Tex. App. Fort Worth 1983)
53 ALR5th 499—§ 2

S., In re, 29 N.Y.2d 206, 325 N.Y.S.2d 921, 275 N.E.2d 577 (1971)
101 ALR5th 351—§ 3

S., In re, 278 Pa. Super. 446, 420 A.2d 625 (1980)
5 ALR5th 550—§ 12
20 ALR5th 700—§ 2, 50
21 ALR5th 396—§ 4, 7, 18, 26, 33

S., In re, 556 P.2d 641 (Okla. Crim. 1976)
37 ALR5th 703—§ 3

S., In re, 575 S.W.2d 113 (Tex. Civ. App. Eastland 1978)
37 ALR5th 703—§ 3, 4

S., In re, 602 S.W.2d 402 (Tex. Civ. App. Amarillo 1980)
37 ALR5th 703—§ 3

S., In re Welfare of, 289 N.W.2d 137 (Minn. 1980)
37 ALR5th 703—§ 3

S., Re, 62 App. Div. 2d 1069, 403 N.Y.S.2d 802 (3d Dep't 1978)
1 ALR5th 469—§ 5, 7, 34

S., Re, 85 Misc. 2d 846, 380 N.Y.S.2d 620 (1976)
21 ALR5th 248—§ 3

S., Re, 579 A.2d 156 (Dist. Col. App. 1990)
1 ALR5th 874—§ 14

S., Re Guardianship of, 57 N.Y.2d 636, 454 N.Y.S.2d 61, 439 N.E.2d 870 (1982)

1 ALR5th 469—§ 5
S. v. A., 118 N.J. Super. 69, 285 A.2d 588 (1972)
53 ALR5th 375—§ 14

S. v. B., 102 Misc. 2d 650, 424 N.Y.S.2d 613 (1980)
21 ALR5th 396—§ 2, 3, 7, 18, 22, 29, 45
40 ALR5th 227—§ 43

S. v. H., 412 N.E.2d 1257 (Ind. App. 1980)
40 ALR5th 697—§ 4, 7 to 9, 22

S. v. S., 105 Wis. 2d 118, 312 N.W.2d 853 (App. 1981)
2 ALR5th 337—§ 2

S. v. S., 458 A.2d 707 (Del. Fam. Ct. 1982)
30 ALR5th 139—§ 6

S v. S, 608 S.W.2d 64 (Ky. Ct. App. 1980)
65 ALR5th 591—§ 2, 3

S. v. Sapega, 56 App. Div. 2d 841, 392 N.Y.S.2d 79 (2d Dep't 1977)
2 ALR5th 769—§ 3

S. v. Webb, 602 F. Supp. 2d 374 (D. Conn. 2009)
64 ALR6th 131—§ 2
89 ALR6th 1—§ 75

S.A., In re, 2005 SD 120, 708 N.W.2d 673 (S.D. 2005)
30 ALR6th 1—§ 4

S.A. v. E.J.P., 571 So. 2d 1187 (Ala. Civ. App. 1990)
89 ALR5th 195—§ 18
63 ALR6th 429—§ 3

S.A. v. K.F., 22 Misc. 3d 1115(A), 880 N.Y.S.2d 226 (Sup 2009)
81 ALR6th 1—§ 32

S.A. v. State, 654 N.E.2d 791 (Ind. App. 1995)
31 ALR5th 229—§ 28, 48.5

S.A. v. State, 654 N.E.2d 791, 103 Ed. Law Rep. 381 (Ind. Ct. App. 1995)
59 ALR6th 393—§ 8

S.A. v. State, 816 So. 2d 1201 (Fla. Dist. Ct. App. 4th Dist. 2002)
101 ALR5th 351—§ 9

S.A. v. Superior Court In and For County of Maricopa, 171 Ariz. 529, 831 P.2d 1297 (Ct. App. Div. 1 1992)
91 ALR5th 343—§ 22

Saab Cars USA, Inc. v. Avidan, 1991 WL 126041 (Conn. Super. Ct. 1991)
88 ALR5th 301—§ 27

Saacks v. City of New Orleans, 687 So. 2d 432 (La. Ct. App. 4th Cir. 1996)
19 ALR6th 217—§ 37

Saad v. Stanley Street Treatment and Resources, Inc., 1994 WL 846911 (D. Mass. 1994)
83 ALR5th 1—§ 13

Saad v. Village of Orland Park, 2012 WL 2721942 (N.D. Ill. 2012)
86 ALR6th 173—§ 6

Saafir, People ex rel. v. Mantello, 163 A.D.2d 824, 558 N.Y.S.2d 356 (4th Dep't 1990)
21 ALR6th 771—§ 21

Saakyan v. Modern Auto, Inc., 103 Cal. App. 4th 383, 126 Cal. Rptr. 2d 674 (2d Dist. 2002)
112 ALR5th 47—§ 11

Saal v. Board of Elections for Nassau County, 25 N.Y.2d 793, 303 N.Y.S.2d 657, 250 N.E.2d 707 (1969)
14 ALR6th 543—§ 7

Saal v. Board of Elections for Nassau County, 32 A.D.2d 800, 302 N.Y.S.2d 298 (2d Dep't 1969)
14 ALR6th 543—§ 44

Saala v. McFarland, 63 Cal. 2d 124, 45 Cal. Rptr. 144, 403 P.2d 400 (1965)
4 ALR5th 443—§ 5

Saar v. U.S. Dept. of Justice, 705 F. Supp. 999 (S.D. N.Y. 1989)
63 ALR6th 255—§ 30

Saari v. Silvers, 319 Mich. 591, 30 N.W.2d 286 (1948)
119 ALR5th 519—§ 2, 8

Saas v. Hindmarsh, 184 N.Y.S. 467 (App. Term 1920)
18 ALR6th 325—§ 42

Saasto v. Saasto, 211 A.D.2d 708, 621 N.Y.S.2d 660 (2d Dep't 1995)

3 ALR6th 447—§ 6, 12

Saathoff v. State, 891 S.W.2d 264 (Tex. Crim. App. 1994)
47 ALR6th 107—§ 3

Saathoff v. State, 991 P.2d 1280 (Alaska Ct. App. 1999)
24 ALR5th 132—§ 8

Saavedra v. Orange County Consolidated Transportation etc. Agency, 11 Cal. App. 4th 824, 14 Cal. Rptr. 2d 282 (4th Dist. 1992)
83 ALR5th 1—§ 3

Saavedra v. Schmidt, 96 S.W.3d 533 (Tex. App. Austin 2002)
100 ALR5th 1—§ 10
53 ALR6th 419—§ 5, 7, 10, 20, 44, 51
59 ALR6th 161—§ 41
60 ALR6th 193—§ 15

Saavedra v. State, 297 S.W.3d 342 (Tex. Crim. App. 2009)
97 ALR6th 567—§ 3, 5, 9

Saavedra v. State, 622 So. 2d 952, 18 FLW S317 (Fla. 1993)
51 ALR5th 425—§ 3, 4, 6, 9

Saavedra De Barreto v. Immigration and Naturalization Service, 427 F. Supp. 2d 51 (D. Conn. 2006)
31 ALR6th 1—§ 16

Saba v. Crater, 62 Cal. App. 4th 150, 72 Cal. Rptr. 2d 401 (4th Dist. 1998)
118 ALR5th 91—§ 29

Saba v. Gray, 111 Mich. App. 304, 314 N.W.2d 597 (1981)
42 ALR5th 221—§ 17

Sabados v. Kiraly, 258 Pa. Super. 532, 393 A.2d 486 (1978)
62 ALR5th 219—§ 10, 26

Sabag v. Continental South Dakota, 374 N.W.2d 349 (S.D. 1985)
10 ALR5th 663—§ 2, 3

Sabal Chase Homeowners Ass'n, Inc. v. Walt Disney World Co., 726 So. 2d 796 (Fla. Dist. Ct. App. 3d Dist. 1999)
5 ALR6th 497—§ 4

Saba Rug, Inc. v. Great American Ins. Companies, 678 N.Y.S.2d 629 (App. Div. 1st Dep't 1998)
16 ALR5th 412—§ 5

Sabastian v. Bible, 649 S.W.2d 593 (Tenn. Ct. App. 1983)
68 ALR5th 13—§ 10, 39

Sabat v. Fedders Corp., 75 N.J. 444, 383 A.2d 421 (1978)
15 ALR6th 633—§ 3, 12, 20, 25, 33

Sabatello v. Frescatore, 200 App. Div. 2d 939, 607 N.Y.S.2d 176 (3d Dep't 1994)
3 ALR5th 237—§ 4, 14

Sabatinelli v. Butler, 363 Mass. 565, 296 N.E.2d 190 (1973)
25 ALR5th 1—§ 6

Sabatini v. Marcuz, 122 Mich. App. 494, 332 N.W.2d 512 (1983)
24 ALR5th 1—§ 3, 10

Sabatino v. New York City Police Dept., 304 A.D.2d 399, 757 N.Y.S.2d 292 (1st Dep't 2003)
91 ALR6th 435—§ 63

Sabatino v. Sabatino, 1999 WL 436723 (Ohio Ct. App. 7th Dist. Mahoning County 1999)
109 ALR5th 1—§ 5, 9

Sabb v. South Carolina State University, 350 S.C. 416, 567 S.E.2d 231, 18 I.E.R. Cas. (BNA) 1602 (2002)
120 ALR5th 513—§ 2

Sabbatis v. Burkey, 166 Ohio App. 3d 739, 2006-Ohio-2395, 853 N.E.2d 329 (5th Dist. Tuscarawas County 2006)
66 ALR6th 351—§ 60

Sabbatis v. Burkey, 2007-Ohio-734, 2007 WL 543012 (Ohio Ct. App. 5th Dist. Tuscarawas County 2007)
66 ALR6th 351—§ 60

Sabedra v. State, 838 S.W.2d 761 (Tex. App. Corpus Christi 1992)
5 ALR5th 243—§ 50

Sabel v. Mead Johnson & Co., 737 F. Supp. 135, 31 Fed. Rules Evid. Serv. 67 (D.C. Mass. 1990)
29 ALR5th 534—§ 5, 7, 8, 10, 37

Sabelko v. City of Phoenix, 120 F.3d 161 (9th Cir. 1997)
62 ALR6th 359—§ 3, 4

Sabella v. Manor Care, 121 N.M. 596, 915 P.2d 901, 68 CCH EPD ¶ 44047 (1996)
51 ALR5th 163—§ 8

Sabella v. Wisler, 59 Cal. 2d 21, 27 Cal. Rptr. 689, 377 P.2d 889 (1963)
30 ALR5th 170—§ 4, 6, 9, 97

Sabeno v. Mitsubishi Motors Credit of America, Inc., 20 A.D.3d 466, 799 N.Y.S.2d 527, 57 U.C.C. Rep. Serv. 2d 931 (2d Dep't 2005)
88 ALR6th 533—§ 3

Saberg, In re, 87 Misc. 2d 848, 386 N.Y.S.2d 592 (N.Y. Fam. Ct. 1976)
46 ALR5th 735—§ 2

Sabes & Richman, Inc. v. Muenzer, 431 N.W.2d 916 (Minn. Ct. App. 1988)
12 ALR6th 1—§ 4, 9

Sabetay v. Sterling Drug, Inc., 69 N.Y.2d 329, 514 N.Y.S.2d 209, 506 N.E.2d 919, 2 I.E.R. Cas. (BNA) 150 (1987)
104 ALR5th 1—§ 3, 12
105 ALR5th 351—§ 3, 7

Sabghir v. Eagle Trace Community Ass'n, Inc., 1997 WL 33635315 (S.D. Fla. 1997)
51 ALR6th 533—§ 3

Sabhnani v. U.S., 131 S. Ct. 1000, 178 L. Ed. 2d 854 (2011)
66 ALR6th 635—§ 16

Sabia v. Niagara Mohawk Power Corp., 87 A.D.3d 1291, 930 N.Y.S.2d 160 (4th Dep't 2011)
98 ALR6th 231—§ 29, 31, 33

Sabin v. Sherman, 28 Kan. 289, 1882 WL 1035 (1882)
60 ALR6th 481—§ 4

Sabin v. Willamette-Western Corp., 276 Or. 1083, 557 P.2d 1344, 115 BNA LRRM 5036 (1976)
18 ALR5th 577—§ 38

Sabina v. Federal Bureau of Prisons, 2010 WL 972579 (D.S.C. 2010)
68 ALR6th 389—§ 6

Sabine Corp. v. ONG Western, Inc., 725 F. Supp. 1157, 11 U.C.C.R.S.2d 83, 107 OGR 292 (W.D. Okla. 1989)
55 ALR5th 1—§ 2, 16, 21, 24

Sabine Pilot Service, Inc. v. Hauck, 687 S.W.2d 733, 1 I.E.R. Cas. (BNA) 733, 119 L.R.R.M. (BNA) 2187, 102 Lab. Cas. (CCH) ¶ 55493 (Tex. 1985)
104 ALR5th 1—§ 3, 4, 8

Sabine River Authority, State ex rel. v. Lucius, 335 So. 2d 95 (La. App. 3d Cir. 1976)
8 ALR5th 653—§ 4

Sabini v. Artardi, 202 A.D.2d 568, 609 N.Y.S.2d 622 (2d Dep't 1994)
95 ALR6th 85—§ 7, 9

Sabino, In re Application of, 1998-Ohio-579, 81 Ohio St. 3d 98, 689 N.E.2d 555 (1998)
107 ALR5th 167—§ 19

Sabino v. Director, Division of Taxation, 17 N.J. Tax 29, 1997 WL 684208 (1997)
2 ALR6th 1—§ 55, 60

Sabino v. Director, Div. of Taxation, 14 N.J. Tax 501, 1995 WL 470127 (1995)
2 ALR6th 1—§ 55, 60

Sabino v. Director, Div. of Taxation, 296 N.J. Super. 269, 686 A.2d 1197, 1996 WL 754834 (App. Div. 1996)
2 ALR6th 1—§ 55, 60

Sabins v. McAllister, 116 Vt. 302, 76 A.2d 106 (1950)
62 ALR5th 219—§ 15, 31, 42

Sabiston's Adm'r v. Otis Elevator Co., 251 Ky. 222, 64 S.W.2d 588 (1933)
99 ALR5th 141—§ 15, 17, 18
115 ALR5th 1—§ 17
117 ALR5th 267—§ 5

Sable v. McGuire, 92 A.D.2d 805, 460 N.Y.S.2d 52 (1st Dep't 1983)
91 ALR6th 435—§ 151

Sable v. Unemployment Compensation Bd. of Review, 197 Pa. Super. 177, 177 A.2d 115 (1962)
75 ALR5th 339—§ 8

Sabo v. Hennelly & Grossfeld, 2005 WL 949802 (Cal. App. 2d Dist. 2005)
64 ALR6th 473—§ 8

Sabo v. State, 890 N.E.2d 803 (Ind. Ct. App. 2008)
63 ALR6th 351—§ 3

Sabol v. Walter Payton College Preparatory High School, 804 F. Supp. 2d 747, 275 Ed. Law Rep. 219, 90 A.L.R.6th 711 (N.D. Ill. 2011)
90 ALR6th 75—§ 44
90 ALR6th 235—§ 4

Sabolyk v. Morgan Guaranty Trust Company of New York, 1984 WL 1275, NO 84 CIV 3179 (S.D. N.Y. 1984)
56 ALR5th 565—§ 17, 21

Sabon v. People, 142 Colo. 323, 350 P.2d 576 (1960)
23 ALR6th 1—§ 3, 12

Sabot v. Sabot, 187 N.W.2d 59 (N.D. 1971)
10 ALR5th 191—§ 3
47 ALR5th 129—§ 11

Sabouri v. Ohio Bureau of Employment Services, 2000 WL 1620915 (S.D. Ohio 2000)
3 ALR6th 153—§ 6

Sabouri v. Ohio Dept. of Job & Family Serv., 145 Ohio App. 3d 651, 763 N.E.2d 1238 (10th Dist. Franklin County 2001)
3 ALR6th 153—§ 6

Sabourin v. Woish, 117 Vt. 94, 85 A.2d 493 (1952)
39 ALR6th 155—§ 15

Sabourin by Sabourin v. LBC, Inc., 731 F. Supp. 1151 (D.R.I. 1990)
75 ALR6th 1—§ 17

S. Abraham & Sons, Inc. v. Department of Treasury, 260 Mich. App. 1, 677 N.W.2d 31 (2003)
38 ALR6th 255—§ 4

Sabre Shipping Corp. v. American President Lines, Limited, 298 F. Supp. 1339 (S.D. N.Y. 1969)
17 ALR6th 1—§ 25

Sabrienia B., In re Interest of, 9 Neb. App. 888, 621 N.W.2d 836 (2001)
89 ALR5th 195—§ 17
61 ALR6th 521—§ 5, 30

Sabrina H., In re, 149 Cal. App. 4th 1403, 57 Cal. Rptr. 3d 863 (4th Dist. 2007)
66 ALR6th 269—§ 7

Sabrina W. v. Willman, 4 Neb. App. 149, 540 N.W.2d 364 (1995)
72 ALR5th 529—§ 20

Sabur v. Com., 2000 WL 781307 (Va. Ct. App. 2000)
80 ALR6th 599—§ 8

Saca v. Canas, 28 Misc. 3d 397, 903 N.Y.S.2d 861 (Sup 2010)
98 ALR6th 93—§ 46

Sacay v. Research Foundation of City University of New York, 44 F. Supp. 2d 496 (E.D.N.Y. 1999)
83 ALR5th 1—§ 3, 10

Saccente v. Laflamme, 33 Conn. L. Rptr. 490, 2002 WL 31687214 (Conn. Super. Ct. 2002)
79 ALR6th 487—§ 5

Saccente v. LaFlamme, 35 Conn. L. Rptr. 174, 2003 WL 21716586 (Conn. Super. Ct. 2003)
75 ALR6th 1—§ 5, 12

Sacchi v. Blodig, 215 Neb. 817, 341 N.W.2d 326 (1983)
23 ALR6th 697—§ 13

Sacchinelli v. State, 161 Ga. App. 763, 288 S.E.2d 894 (1982)
70 ALR5th 587—§ 16

Sacco v. Carothers, 257 Neb. 672, 601 N.W.2d 493 (1999)
111 ALR5th 1—§ 3, 20

Sacco v. City of Las Vegas, 2007 WL 2429151 (D. Nev. 2007)
70 ALR6th 513—§ 9
71 ALR6th 471—§ 5

Sacco v. Falke, 649 F.2d 634 (8th Cir. 1981)
71 ALR6th 335—§ 10

Sacco v. High Country Independent Press, Inc., 271 Mont. 209, 896 P.2d 411, 10 I.E.R. Cas. (BNA) 1041 (1995)
96 ALR5th 107—§ 3

Sacco v. Pataki, 114 F. Supp. 2d 264, 165 L.R.R.M. (BNA) 2487, 142 Lab. Cas. (CCH) ¶ 59130 (S.D. N.Y. 2000)
94 ALR5th 149—§ 5

Sacco v. Roupenian, 409 Mass. 25, 564 N.E.2d 386 (1990)
92 ALR6th 379—§ 22

Sacco v. Tate, 175 Misc. 2d 901, 672 N.Y.S.2d 618 (App. Term 1998)
74 ALR6th 505—§ 7, 10, 14, 20

Saccoccio v. Lange, 194 A.D.2d 794, 599 N.Y.S.2d 306 (2d Dep't 1993)
91 ALR6th 435—§ 123

Sacerdote, Re, 74 B.R. 487 (F. BC ED Pa. 1987)
23 ALR5th 241—§ 10

Sachem's Head Ass'n v. Board of Tax Review of Town of Guilford, 190 Conn. 627, 461 A.2d 995 (1983)
114 ALR5th 561—§ 10

Sachs, In re, 126 Wash. 343, 218 P. 209 (1923)
102 ALR5th 253—§ 4

Sachs v. Aluminum Co. of America, 167 F.2d 570, 77 U.S.P.Q. 649 (C.C.A. 6th Cir. 1948)
66 ALR6th 83—§ 20

Sachs v. Chiat, 281 Minn. 540, 162 N.W.2d 243 (1968)
103 ALR5th 157—§ 4

Sachs v. Commercial Ins. Co., 119 N.J. Super. 226, 290 A.2d 760 (1972)
19 ALR5th 533—§ 3, 17

Sachs v. Industrial Indem. Ins. Co., 1993 WL 93562 (C.D. Cal. 1993)
98 ALR5th 1—§ 7

Sachs v. Precision Products Co., 257 Or. 273, 476 P.2d 199 (1970)
55 ALR5th 1—§ 39

Sachs v. Sprague, 401 F. Supp. 2d 159, 63 Fed. R. Serv. 3d 607 (D. Mass. 2005)

---

43 ALR6th 1—§ 5
Sachs v. St. Paul Fire & Marine Ins. Co., 303 F. Supp. 1339 (D. D.C. 1969)
92 ALR5th 273—§ 10, 21
Sachs v. TWA Getaway Vacations, Inc., 125 F. Supp. 2d 1368 (S.D. Fla. 2000)
2 ALR5th 396—§ 27, 33
Sachs v. U.S., 412 F.2d 357 (8th Cir. 1969)
6 ALR6th 391—§ 5, 14, 17, 21
Sachs v. Walzer, 242 Ga. 742, 251 S.E.2d 302 (1978)
69 ALR5th 1—§ 5
Sachsenmaier v. Mittlestadt, 145 Wis. 2d 781, 429 N.W.2d 532 (Ct. App. 1988)
118 ALR5th 91—§ 16
Sachs et al. v. U.S., W. Div. No. C-75-247, CCH ¶ 14,942 (N.D. Ohio 1976)
60 ALR5th 459—§ 2
Sachs New York, Inc. v. Tully, 79 A.D.2d 1056, 435 N.Y.S.2d 172 (3d Dep't 1981)
38 ALR6th 255—§ 20
Sachtjen v. Sachtjen, 115 Wis. 2d 694, 339 N.W.2d 365 (Ct. App. 1983)
9 ALR5th 568—§ 19
Sachtjen, State ex rel. v. Festge, 25 Wis. 2d 128, 130 N.W.2d 457 (1964)
102 ALR5th 525—§ 19
Sackett v. E.P.A., 132 S. Ct. 1367, 182 L. Ed. 2d 367, 73 Env't. Rep. Cas. (BNA) 2121 (2012)
76 ALR6th 587—§ 1, 25
Sackett v. Farmers' State Bank of Boone, 209 Iowa 487, 228 N.W. 51 (1929)
88 ALR6th 533—§ 8
Sackett v. O'Brien, 43 Misc. 2d 476, 251 N.Y.S.2d 863 (1964)
62 ALR5th 219—§ 32, 43, 45
Sackett v. Roseman, 2003 WL 22349077 (Tenn. Ct. App. 2003)
52 ALR6th 433—§ 37
57 ALR6th 163—§ 38

Sackett v. U.S. E.P.A., 622 F.3d 1139, 71 Env't. Rep. Cas. (BNA) 2036 (9th Cir. 2010)
76 ALR6th 587—§ 1, 25
Sackler v. Sackler, 15 N.Y.2d 40, 255 N.Y.S.2d 83, 203 N.E.2d 481, 5 A.L.R.3d 664 (1964)
105 ALR5th 1—§ 5, 22
Sackman v. Liggett Group, Inc., 965 F. Supp. 391, Prod. Liab. Rep. (CCH) ¶ 15078 (E.D.N.Y. 1997)
36 ALR5th 541—§ 22
63 ALR5th 195—§ 6, 10
Sackman v. Thomas, 24 Wash. 660, 64 P. 819 (1901)
23 ALR6th 1—§ 21
Sacks v. Com., Unemployment Compensation Bd. of Review, 74 Pa. Commw. 31, 459 A.2d 461 (1983)
95 ALR5th 329—§ 19
Sacks v. Industrial Commission, 13 Ariz. App. 83, 474 P.2d 442 (Div. 1 1970)
80 ALR5th 417—§ 4
Sacks v. Loew's Theatres, Inc., 47 Misc. 2d 854, 263 N.Y.S.2d 253 (1965)
2 ALR5th 396—§ 3, 11
Sacks v. Mambu, 429 Pa. Super. 498, 632 A.2d 1333 (1993)
95 ALR6th 541—§ 34
Sacks v. Necaise, 991 So. 2d 615 (Miss. Ct. App. 2007)
94 ALR6th 431—§ 81, 88, 95, 97
Sacks v. Office of Foreign Assets Control, 466 F.3d 764 (9th Cir. 2006)
26 ALR6th 659—§ 60
Sacks v. Office of Foreign Assets Control, Dept. of Treasury, 127 S. Ct. 2033, 167 L. Ed. 2d 763 (U.S. 2007)
26 ALR6th 659—§ 60
Sacks v. Phillip Morris, Inc., 139 F.3d 892 (4th Cir. 1998)
73 ALR5th 75—§ 3
Sacks v. State, 172 Ind. App. 185, 360 N.E.2d 21 (1977)
55 ALR6th 157—§ 5
Sacramento & San Joaquin Drainage Dist. v. Goehring, 13 Cal. App. 3d 58, 91 Cal. Rptr. 375 (3d Dist. 1970)

49 ALR6th 205—§ 4, 40

Sacramento & San Joaquin Drainage Dist. v. Rector, 172 Cal. 385, 156 P. 506 (1916)

91 ALR5th 437—§ 12, 23

Sacramento Cable Television v. City of Sacramento, 234 Cal. App. 3d 232, 286 Cal. Rptr. 470, 19 Media L. Rep. (BNA) 1532 (3d Dist. 1991)

23 ALR6th 165—§ 3, 9

Sacramento, City of v. Drew, 207 Cal. App. 3d 1287, 255 Cal. Rptr. 704, 51 Ed. Law Rep. 998 (3d Dist. 1989)

106 ALR5th 523—§ 4, 39

Sacramento, City of v. State of California, 50 Cal. 3d 51, 266 Cal. Rptr. 139, 785 P.2d 522 (1990)

76 ALR6th 543—§ 7

Sacramento, City of v. State Water Resources Control Bd., 2 Cal. App. 4th 960, 3 Cal. Rptr. 2d 643 (3d Dist. 1992)

106 ALR5th 523—§ 44

Sacramento County Bd. of Sup'rs v. Sacramento Local Agency Formation Com'n (Citrus Heights Incorporation Project), 286 Cal. Rptr. 171 (App. 3d Dist. 1991)

106 ALR5th 523—§ 21

Sacramento County Deputy Sheriffs' Assn. v. County of Sacramento, 51 Cal. App. 4th 1468, 59 Cal. Rptr. 2d 834, 12 I.E.R. Cas. (BNA) 723 (3d Dist. 1996)

62 ALR5th 1—§ 2

91 ALR5th 585—§ 4, 9

18 ALR6th 1—§ 5, 30

Sacramento Municipal Utility Dist. v. Pacific Gas & Elec. Co., 72 Cal. App. 2d 638, 165 P.2d 741 (3d Dist. 1946)

44 ALR6th 259—§ 21

Sacramento Newspaper Guild, etc. v. Sacramento County Board of Supervisors, 263 Cal. App. 2d 41, 69 Cal. Rptr. 480 (3d Dist. 1968)

34 ALR5th 591—§ 3, 4, 6, 9

Sacramona v. Bridgestone/Firestone, Inc., 106 F.3d 444, Prod. Liab. Rep. (CCH) ¶ 14872, 46 Fed. R. Evid. Serv. 541 (1st Cir. 1997)

89 ALR5th 319—§ 17

102 ALR5th 99—§ 5

Sacramona v. Bridgestone/Firestone, Inc., 152 F.R.D. 428, 27 Fed. R. Serv. 3d 929 (D. Mass. 1993)

105 ALR5th 499—§ 4

Sacramona v. Bridgestone/Firestone, Inc., 152 F.R.D. 428, 27 Fed. R. Serv. 3d (LCP) 929 (D. Mass. 1993)

87 ALR5th 631—§ 33

Sacred Heart Healthcare System v. Com., 673 A.2d 1021 (Pa. Commw. Ct. 1996)

69 ALR5th 477—§ 5

Sadallah v. City of Utica, 383 F.3d 34 (2d Cir. 2004)

95 ALR6th 341—§ 64, 66

Saddle Brook, Township of v. A.B. Family Center, Inc., 307 N.J. Super. 16, 704 A.2d 81 (App. Div. 1998)

10 ALR5th 538—§ 7

Saddle Hills Community Ass'n v. Cavallari, 150 Ill. App. 3d 134, 103 Ill. Dec. 309, 501 N.E.2d 330 (2d Dist. 1986)

115 ALR5th 251—§ 21

Sade C., In re, 13 Cal. 4th 952, 55 Cal. Rptr. 2d 771, 920 P.2d 716 (1996)

92 ALR5th 379—§ 15

Sadek v. Job Service North Dakota, 420 N.W.2d 340 (N.D. 1988)

60 ALR5th 459—§ 2, 26

Sade Shoe Co. v. Oschin & Snyder, 162 Cal. App. 3d 1174, 209 Cal. Rptr. 124 (2d Dist. 1984)

71 ALR5th 491—§ 38, 41

Sade Shoe Co., Inc. v. Oschin & Snyder, 217 Cal. App. 3d 1509, 266 Cal. Rptr. 619 (2d Dist. 1990)

23 ALR5th 744—§ 8, 12

Sadie v. State, 488 So. 2d 1368 (Ala. Crim. App. 1986)

104 ALR5th 165—§ 5

S.A. Discount Liquor, Inc. v. Texas Alcoholic Beverage Com'n, 709 F.2d 291 (5th Cir. 1983)
116 ALR5th 149—§ 4, 9
Sadler v. Basin Elec. Power Co-op., 409 N.W.2d 87, 107 Lab. Cas. (CCH) P 55786 (N.D. 1987)
38 ALR6th 541—§ 11
Sadler v. Basin Electric Power Cooperative, 409 N.W.2d 87, 107 CCH LC ¶ 55786 (N.D. 1987)
17 ALR5th 1—§ 11
Sadler v. First Nat. Bank of Baldwin County, 267 Ga. 122, 475 S.E.2d 643 (1996)
62 ALR5th 219—§ 12, 32, 35
Sadler v. Loomis Co., 139 Md. App. 374, 776 A.2d 25 (2001)
121 ALR5th 365—§ 5
Sadler v. NCR Corp., 928 F.2d 48 (2d Cir. 1991)
37 ALR6th 1—§ 20
Sadler v. Rowland, 2004 WL 2061127 (D. Conn. 2004)
54 ALR6th 1—§ 10
Sadler v. Rowland, 2004 WL 2061518 (D. Conn. 2004)
54 ALR6th 1—§ 10, 12
Sadler v. State, 965 S.W.2d 389 (Mo. Ct. App. E.D. 1998)
31 ALR6th 49—§ 10
Sadlock v. Board of Ed. of Borough of Carlstadt in Bergen County, 137 N.J.L. 85, 58 A.2d 218 (N.J. Sup. Ct. 1948)
94 ALR5th 613—§ 7
Sadorus v. Wood, 230 A.2d 478 (Dist. Col. App. 1967)
21 ALR5th 82—§ 4
Sadowski v. McCormick, 2 F.3d 1157 (9th Cir. 1993)
53 ALR6th 81—§ 11
Sadowski v. McCormick, 785 F. Supp. 1417 (D. Mont. 1992)
53 ALR6th 81—§ 11
Sadowski v. Shevin, 345 So. 2d 330, 2 Media L. Rep. (BNA) 1822 (Fla. 1977)

53 ALR6th 491—§ 24
Sadowsky v. Anchor Packing Co., 201 Wis. 2d 816, 549 N.W.2d 286 (Ct. App. 1996)
63 ALR5th 331—§ 3, 17, 18
90 ALR5th 453—§ 53
Sadowy v. Sony Corp. of America, 496 F. Supp. 1071 (S.D. N.Y. 1980)
53 ALR6th 213—§ 9
Sadri v. Ulmer, 2007 WL 869192 (D. Haw. 2007)
68 ALR6th 229—§ 5
Sadrud-Din v. City of Chicago, 883 F. Supp. 270 (N.D. Ill. 1995)
90 ALR5th 273—§ 5, 6, 9, 14
Saechao v. Matsakoun, 78 Or. App. 340, 717 P.2d 165 (1986)
89 ALR5th 255—§ 3, 4
Saecker v. Thorie, 234 F.3d 1010 (7th Cir. 2000)
13 ALR6th 1—§ 4
14 ALR6th 1—§ 8
Saeed v. Warner-Lambert Co., 61 Fed. Appx. 740 (2d Cir. 2003)
7 ALR6th 563—§ 5
Saeger v. Zander, 2009 WL 1158845 (W.D. Wash. 2009)
73 ALR6th 281—§ 34
Saena v. Zenith Optical Co., 135 W. Va. 795, 65 S.E.2d 205 (1951)
122 ALR5th 515—§ 4
Saenz v. Lower Rio Grande Val. Chamber of Commerce, 296 S.W.2d 806 (Tex. Civ. App. San Antonio 1956)
94 ALR5th 149—§ 5
Saenz v. Roe, 526 U.S. 489, 119 S. Ct. 1518, 143 L. Ed. 2d 689, 61 Soc. Sec. Rep. Serv. 75 (1999)
70 ALR5th 377—§ 5
Saenz v. State, 632 S.W.2d 793 (Tex. App. Houston 14th Dist. 1982)
114 ALR5th 173—§ 9
1 ALR6th 371—§ 4
1 ALR6th 549—§ 25
Saenz v. Whitewater Voyages, Inc., 226 Cal. App. 3d 758, 276 Cal. Rptr. 672, 91 C.D.O.S. 165, 91 Daily Journal DAR 170 (1st Dist. 1990)

54 ALR5th 513—§ 3, 5
Saenz v. Williams, 232 F.3d 902 (10th Cir. 2000)
119 ALR5th 1—§ 3
Saenz Motors v. Big H. Auto Auction, Inc., 653 S.W.2d 521, 37 U.C.C.R.S. 696 (Tex. App. Corpus Christi 1983)
47 ALR5th 677—§ 3, 6
Saeta v. Superior Court, 117 Cal. App. 4th 261, 11 Cal. Rptr. 3d 610, 21 I.E.R. Cas. (BNA) 554 (2d Dist. 2004)
32 ALR6th 285—§ 3, 10
Saetz v. Langan, 1991 WL 12830 (D. Kan. 1991)
79 ALR5th 587—§ 3, 5
Saeuberlich v. Saeuberlich, 773 S.W.2d 170 (Mo. Ct. App. E.D. 1989)
120 ALR5th 229—§ 7, 8, 17
Saeuberlich v. Saeuberlich, 782 S.W.2d 78 (Mo. Ct. App. E.D. 1989)
82 ALR5th 389—§ 4
Saey v. Xerox Corp., 31 F. Supp. 2d 692 (E.D. Mo. 1998)
52 ALR5th 613—§ 4
Saez v. S & S Corrugated Paper Machinery Co., Inc., 302 N.J. Super. 545, 695 A.2d 740, Prod. Liab. Rep. (CCH) ¶ 15006 (App. Div. 1997)
18 ALR6th 629—§ 5, 29, 33
Safaie v. Jacuzzi Whirlpool Bath, Inc., 192 Cal. App. 4th 1160, 122 Cal. Rptr. 3d 344 (4th Dist. 2011)
83 ALR6th 143—§ 5
Safarets, Inc. v. Gannett Co., Inc., 80 Misc. 2d 109, 361 N.Y.S.2d 276 (Sup. Ct. 1974)
54 ALR5th 443—§ 8
69 ALR5th 645—§ 11
Safari Motor Coaches Inc. (Corwin), Matter of, 225 A.D.2d 921, 638 N.Y.S.2d 992 (3d Dep't 1996)
82 ALR5th 501—§ 5
Safari Motor Coaches, Inc. v. Corwin, 162 Misc. 2d 449, 617 N.Y.S.2d 289 (Sup. 1994)
88 ALR5th 301—§ 32

Safe Auto Ins. Co. v. School Dist. of Philadelphia, 872 A.2d 247, 197 Ed. Law Rep. 614 (Pa. Commw. Ct. 2005)
80 ALR6th 389—§ 22
Safecare Health Corp. v. Rimer, 620 So. 2d 161 (Fla. 1993)
97 ALR6th 83—§ 79
Safeco Ins. Co. v. Baker, 515 So. 2d 655 (La. App. 1987)
38 ALR5th 683—§ 3
Safeco Ins. Co. v. Costello, 799 F.2d 412, 21 Fed. Rules Evid. Serv. 672 (CA8 Mo. 1986)
6 ALR5th 297—§ 6, 34, 35
Safeco Ins. Co. v. Davis, 44 Wash. App. 161, 721 P.2d 550 (1986)
25 ALR5th 60—§ 4
Safeco Ins. Co. v. Ellinghouse, 223 Mont. 239, 725 P.2d 217 (1986)
14 ALR5th 242—§ 12
Safeco Ins. Co. v. Gipson, 619 S.W.2d 275 (Tex. Civ. App. Texarkana 1981)
58 ALR5th 535—§ 9
Safeco Ins. Co. v. Goldenberg, 435 N.W.2d 616 (Minn. Ct. App. 1989)
103 ALR5th 1—§ 4
Safeco Ins. Co. v. Guyton, 692 F.2d 551, 34 FR Serv. 2d 244 (CA9 Cal. 1982)
30 ALR5th 170—§ 78
Safeco Ins. Co. v. Hirschmann, 112 Wash. 2d 621, 773 P.2d 413 (1989)
30 ALR5th 170—§ 4, 84
Safeco Ins. Co. v. Houchins, 12 Cal. App. 3d 12, 90 Cal. Rptr. 414 (2d Dist. 1970)
31 ALR5th 116—§ 3, 6
Safeco Ins. Co. v. Howard, 782 S.W.2d 658 (Mo. App. 1989)
35 ALR5th 375—§ 3, 13, 14, 70, 82
Safeco Ins. Co. v. Leslie, 276 Or. 221, 554 P.2d 469 (1976)
35 ALR5th 375—§ 43, 93
Safeco Ins. Companies v. Blackmon, 851 So. 2d 532 (Ala. Civ. App. 2002)
112 ALR5th 509—§ 19

122 ALR5th 653—§ 2
13 ALR6th 209—§ 3, 12, 14, 41, 47
39 ALR6th 445—§ 3, 41
Safeco Ins. Companies v. Blackmon, 2002 WL 1143855 (Ala. Civ. App. 2002)
112 ALR5th 509—§ 2, 16
Safeco Ins. Co. of Am. v. Barnes, 133 Or. App. 390, 891 P.2d 682 (1995)
35 ALR5th 375—§ 57, 71
Safeco Ins. Co. of America v. Andrews, 915 F.2d 500 (9th Cir. 1990)
18 ALR5th 187—§ 4, 5
58 ALR5th 483—§ 5
Safeco Ins. Co. of America v. Burr, 127 S. Ct. 2201, 20 A.L.R. Fed. 2d 803 (U.S. 2007)
26 ALR6th 659—§ 21, 52
Safeco Ins. Co. of America v. Dain Bosworth Inc., 531 N.W.2d 867 (Minn. Ct. App. 1995)
66 ALR5th 135—§ 21
86 ALR6th 321—§ 13
89 ALR6th 409—§ 99
Safeco Ins. Co. of America v. Graybar Elec. Co., Inc., 59 So. 3d 649 (Ala. 2010)
81 ALR6th 363—§ 4, 15
Safeco Ins. Co. of America v. Hirschmann, 112 Wash. 2d 621, 773 P.2d 413 (1989)
37 ALR6th 657—§ 5
Safeco Ins. Co. of America v. Simmons, 642 F. Supp. 305 (N.D. Cal. 1986)
96 ALR5th 107—§ 7
99 ALR5th 301—§ 4
Safeco Ins. Co. of America v. Stariha, 346 N.W.2d 663 (Minn. Ct. App. 1984)
63 ALR5th 675—§ 3
Safeco Ins. Co. of America v. Wetherill, 622 F.2d 685 (3d Cir. 1980)
103 ALR5th 1—§ 4, 5
Safeco Insurance Co. v. Hale, 140 Cal. App. 3d 347, 189 Cal. Rptr. 463 (1st Dist. 1983)
35 ALR5th 375—§ 63

Safeco Surplus Lines Co. v. Employer's Reinsurance Corp., 11 Cal. App. 4th 1403, 15 Cal. Rptr. 2d 58, 92 C.D.O.S. 10297, 92 Daily Journal DAR 17241 (3d Dist. 1992)
14 ALR5th 695—§ 2
55 ALR5th 681—§ 6
Safeco Title Ins. Co. v. Gannon, 54 Wash. App. 330, 774 P.2d 30 (1989)
14 ALR5th 695—§ 25
Safeco Title Ins. Co. v. Reynolds, 452 So. 2d 45 (Fla. App. D2 1984)
19 ALR5th 786—§ 3
Safe Drinking Water, Citizens For v. San Diego City Council, 2002 WL 32353 (Cal. App. 4th Dist. 2002)
78 ALR6th 229—§ 6
Safeharbor Employer Services I, Inc. v. Cinto Velazquez, 860 So. 2d 984, 149 Lab. Cas. (CCH) ¶ 59794, 121 A.L.R.5th 769 (Fla. Dist. Ct. App. 1st Dist. 2003)
121 ALR5th 523—§ 3
Safelite Glass Corp. v. Fuller, 15 Kan. App. 2d 351, 807 P.2d 677, 6 BNA IER Cas. 417 (1991)
12 ALR5th 847—§ 6, 14
Safelite Glass Corp. v. Samuel, 771 So. 2d 44 (Fla. Dist. Ct. App. 4th Dist. 2000)
125 ALR5th 193—§ 4, 9, 10
Safety-Kleen Corp. v. Laidlaw Environmental Services, Inc., 1999 WL 601039 (N.D. Ill. 1998)
37 ALR6th 1—§ 15
Safety-Kleen Systems, Inc. v. McGinn, 233 F. Supp. 2d 121 (D. Mass. 2002)
36 ALR6th 537—§ 7
Safety Mut. Cas. Corp. v. Spears, Barnes, Baker, Wainio, Brown & Whaley, 104 N.C. App. 467, 409 S.E.2d 736 (1991)
41 ALR6th 1—§ 22
Safe Water Ass'n, Inc. v. City of Fond du Lac, 184 Wis. 2d 365, 516 N.W.2d 13 (Ct. App. 1994)
78 ALR6th 229—§ 9, 10

CASES CITED IN ALR5th and ALR6th

Safe Water Foundation of Texas v. City of Houston, 661 S.W.2d 190 (Tex. App. Houston 1st Dist. 1983)
78 ALR6th 229—§ 4

Safeway, Inc. v. Montana Petroleum Release Compensation Bd., 931 P.2d 1327 (Mont. 1997)
11 ALR5th 388—§ 4, 14

Safeway Ins. Co. v. Collins, 192 Ariz. 262, 963 P.2d 1085 (Ct. App. Div. 1 1998)
98 ALR6th 93—§ 34

Safeway Ins. Co. v. Holmes, 194 Ga. App. 160, 390 S.E.2d 52 (1989)
25 ALR5th 60—§ 3, 7

Safeway Ins. Co. v. Parker, 105 Ill. App. 2d 208, 245 N.E.2d 75 (1st Dist. 1969)
103 ALR5th 1—§ 6

Safeway Ins. Co. of Alabama, Inc. v. Amerisure Ins. Co., 707 So. 2d 218 (Ala. 1997)
23 ALR5th 75—§ 8

Safeway Managing General Agency for State and County Mut. Fire Ins. Co. v. Cooper, 952 S.W.2d 861 (Tex. App. Amarillo 1997)
33 ALR5th 121—§ 12

Safeway Stores v. City Council of City of San Mateo, 86 Cal. App. 2d 277, 194 P.2d 720 (1st Dist. 1948)
73 ALR5th 223—§ 2

Safeway Stores Inc. v. Bozeman, 394 S.W.2d 532 (Tex. Civ. App. Tyler 1965)
15 ALR6th 1—§ 4, 5, 9 to 11, 16

Safeway Stores, Inc. v. Broach, 654 S.W.2d 811 (Tex. App. Houston 14th Dist. 1983)
1 ALR6th 297—§ 8, 10

Safeway Stores, Inc. v. Certainteed Corp., 710 S.W.2d 544, 1 U.C.C. Rep. Serv. 2d (CBC) 1237 (Tex. 1986)
81 ALR5th 483—§ 3, 5

Safeway Stores, Inc. v. Cone, 2 Ariz. App. 151, 406 P.2d 869 (1965)
123 ALR5th 1—§ 14

Safeway Stores, Inc. v. Franchise Tax Board, 3 Cal. 3d 745, 91 Cal. Rptr. 616, 478 P.2d 48 (1970)
17 ALR6th 623—§ 7

Safeway Stores, Inc. v. Fuller, 189 Okla. 556, 118 P.2d 649 (1941)
2 ALR5th 1—§ 28

Safeway Stores, Inc. v. National Union Fire Ins. Co. of Pittsburgh, Pa., 64 F.3d 1282 (9th Cir. 1995)
22 ALR6th 113—§ 43, 50, 63

Safeway Stores, Inc. v. Nest-Kart, 21 Cal. 3d 322, 146 Cal. Rptr. 550, 579 P.2d 441 (1978)
42 ALR5th 159—§ 9

Safeway Stores, Inc. v. Rees, 152 Colo. 318, 381 P.2d 999 (1963)
1 ALR5th 1—§ 33

Safeway Stores, Inc. v. Sanders, 372 P.2d 1021 (Okla. 1962)
40 ALR5th 135—§ 2 to 4, 15

Safeway Stores, Inc. v. Scamardo, 673 S.W.2d 371 (Tex. App. Houston 1st Dist. 1984)
1 ALR6th 297—§ 8

Safeway Systems, Inc. v. Norberg, 115 R.I. 127, 341 A.2d 47 (1975)
89 ALR5th 493—§ 18

Safferstone v. Safferstone, 501 So. 2d 165, 12 FLW 376 (Fla. App. D3 1987)
49 ALR5th 441—§ 21

Saffir, In re, 264 A.D.2d 16, 703 N.Y.S.2d 30 (1st Dep't 2000)
44 ALR6th 75—§ 4, 6, 22, 25

Saffold v. City of Chicago, 775 F. Supp. 1126 (N.D. Ill. 1991)
89 ALR6th 1—§ 39

Saffold v. State, 570 So. 2d 727 (Ala. Crim. App. 1990)
72 ALR5th 109—§ 4

Saffold v. State, 850 So. 2d 574 (Fla. Dist. Ct. App. 2d Dist. 2003)
72 ALR6th 227—§ 23, 51, 59

Saffold, State ex rel. v. Schwarz, 2001 WI App 56, 241 Wis. 2d 253, 625 N.W.2d 333 (Ct. App. 2001)
85 ALR6th 229—§ 39

Saffold, State ex rel. v. Timmins, 22 Ohio St. 2d 63, 51 Ohio Op. 2d 95, 258 N.E.2d 112 (1970)
14 ALR6th 543—§ 31

Safford v. Boston & M. Railroad, 103 Mass. 583 (1870)
17 ALR5th 547—§ 38

Safford v. Vermont & C.R. Co., 60 Vt. 185, 14 A. 91 (1888)
102 ALR5th 253—§ 9

Safford Unified School Dist. No. 1 v. Redding, 129 S. Ct. 2633 (2009)
46 ALR6th 495—§ 45

Safie Enterprises, Inc. v. Nationwide Mut. Fire Ins. Co., 146 Mich. App. 483, 381 N.W.2d 747 (1985)
6 ALR5th 297—§ 6, 40, 49

Safier's, Inc. v. Bialer, 42 Ohio Ops. 209, 58 Ohio L. Abs. 292, 93 N.E.2d 734 (CP 1950)
12 ALR5th 847—§ 7, 12 to 14

Safine v. Sinnott, 15 Cal. App. 4th 614, 19 Cal. Rptr. 2d 52 (1st Dist. 1993)
13 ALR6th 1—§ 4

Safran v. Amato, 155 A.D.2d 653, 548 N.Y.S.2d 244 (2d Dep't 1989)
50 ALR6th 95—§ 10

Safransky v. State Personnel Bd., 62 Wis. 2d 464, 215 N.W.2d 379, 9 Fair Empl. Prac. Cas. (BNA) 1391, 7 Empl. Prac. Dec. (CCH) ¶ 9391 (1974)
96 ALR5th 391—§ 3, 5, 26

Saft America, Inc. v. Insurance Co. of North America, 155 Ga. App. 500, 271 S.E.2d 641 (1980)
16 ALR5th 412—§ 17

S.A.G., Matter of, 1998 WL 566824 (Minn. Ct. App. 1998)
84 ALR6th 427—§ 4, 16, 27

Sagamore Partners, Ltd., In re, 2012 WL 5463134 (Bankr. S.D. Fla. 2012)
86 ALR6th 411—§ 4

Sagan v. Com. of Pa., 542 F. Supp. 880 (W.D. Pa. 1982)
121 ALR5th 1—§ 57

Saganski, In re Admission of, 226 Wis. 2d 678, 595 N.W.2d 631 (1999)

107 ALR5th 167—§ 5, 12, 17

Sagar v. Sagar, 57 Mass. App. Ct. 71, 781 N.E.2d 54 (2003)
124 ALR5th 203—§ 10

Sagaser v. McCarthy, 176 Cal. App. 3d 288, 221 Cal. Rptr. 746 (5th Dist. 1986)
106 ALR5th 523—§ 36
63 ALR6th 1—§ 49, 63

Sage, Application of, 21 Wash. App. 803, 586 P.2d 1201 (Div. 3 1978)
103 ALR5th 255—§ 3, 8, 15, 19

Sage v. Boyd, 145 W. Va. 197, 113 S.E.2d 836 (1960)
97 ALR6th 375—§ 15

Sage v. Finney, 156 Mo. App. 30, 135 S.W. 996 (1911)
6 ALR6th 391—§ 5, 14, 17

Sage v. Hale, 75 Misc. 2d 256, 347 N.Y.S.2d 416 (1973)
6 ALR5th 883—§ 11

Sage v. Johnson, 437 N.W.2d 582 (Iowa 1989)
54 ALR5th 313—§ 2, 6, 25

Sage v. Northern P. R. Co., 62 Wash. 2d 6, 380 P.2d 856 (1963)
21 ALR5th 82—§ 3, 11

Sage v. Radiology and Diagnostic Services, L.L.C., 831 So. 2d 1053 (La. Ct. App. 1st Cir. 2002)
43 ALR6th 611—§ 43, 86

Sage v. Sage, 219 Ark. 853, 245 S.W.2d 398 (1952)
70 ALR5th 377—§ 5

Sage v. U.S., 974 F. Supp. 851 (E.D. Va. 1997)
80 ALR6th 469—§ 36, 39, 46, 48

Sage Enterprises, Inc., In re, 2006 WL 1722582 (Bankr. N.D. Ill. 2006)
23 ALR6th 457—§ 16

Sage, Estate of v. Sage, 515 So. 2d 1324, 12 FLW 2659 (Fla. App. D2 1987)
3 ALR5th 394—§ 4, 11

Sagehorn v. Phillips Petroleum Co., 648 S.W.2d 647 (Mo. App. 1983)
52 ALR5th 613—§ 3

Sagent Technology, Inc., Derivative Litigation, In re, 278 F. Supp. 2d 1079 (N.D. Cal. 2003)
43 ALR6th 1—§ 12, 16
Sager v. Renwick Park & Traffic Ass'n, 172 App. Div. 359, 159 N.Y.S. 4 (1916)
46 ALR5th 1—§ 31, 45
Sager v. Rivera, 1993 WL 356757 (N.Y. Sup 1993)
113 ALR5th 1—§ 7, 13
Sager v. St. Paul Fire & Marine Ins. Co., 461 S.W.2d 704 (Mo. 1971)
92 ALR5th 273—§ 3, 8
Sage Realty Corp. v. Kenbee Management-New York, Inc., 182 A.D.2d 480, 582 N.Y.S.2d 182 (1st Dep't 1992)
75 ALR5th 1—§ 2, 3
Sage Realty Corp. v. O'Cleireacain, 185 A.D.2d 188, 586 N.Y.S.2d 118 (1st Dep't 1992)
58 ALR5th 187—§ 9
Sage Realty Corp. v. Proskauer Rose LLP, 275 A.D.2d 11, 713 N.Y.S.2d 155 (1st Dep't 2000)
121 ALR5th 157—§ 21
Sagers v. Yellow Freight System, Inc., 529 F.2d 721, 12 Fair Empl. Prac. Cas. (BNA) 961, 11 Empl. Prac. Dec. (CCH) ¶ 10811, 38 A.L.R. Fed. 1 (5th Cir. 1976)
60 ALR6th 295—§ 60
Sage Street Associates v. Northdale Const. Co., 863 S.W.2d 438 (Tex. 1993)
73 ALR6th 571—§ 69
Saggese v. Kelley, 445 Mass. 434, 837 N.E.2d 699 (2005)
11 ALR6th 587—§ 10
Saggese v. Madison Mut. Ins. Co., 741 N.Y.S.2d 803 (App. Div. 4th Dep't 2002)
100 ALR5th 171—§ 3
Saggio v. Sprady, 475 F. Supp. 2d 203, 218 Ed. Law Rep. 234 (E.D. N.Y. 2007)
98 ALR6th 599—§ 68, 73, 76

Sag Harbor Port Associates v. Village of Sag Harbor, 21 F. Supp. 2d 179 (E.D.N.Y. 1998)
63 ALR5th 607—§ 11
Saginaw Prosecuting Attorney, State ex rel. v. Bobenal Investments, Inc., 111 Mich. App. 16, 314 N.W.2d 512 (1981)
92 ALR5th 593—§ 3, 5, 7, 9, 12
Sah v. Montanez, 2004 WL 352654 (Cal. App. 3d Dist. 2004)
3 ALR6th 153—§ 17, 18
Saha v. Aetna Casualty & Surety Co., 427 So. 2d 316 (Fla. App. D5 1983)
35 ALR5th 375—§ 8, 62
Saha v. Record, 177 A.D.2d 763, 575 N.Y.S.2d 986 (3d Dep't 1991)
16 ALR6th 1—§ 15
Sahagan v. Com., 25 Mass. App. Ct. 953, 518 N.E.2d 888 (1988)
12 ALR6th 645—§ 21
Sahagian, In re Marriage of, 70 Ill. App. 3d 562, 27 Ill. Dec. 28, 388 N.E.2d 991 (1st Dist. 1979)
49 ALR5th 441—§ 11, 14
Sahagian v. Murphy, 871 F.2d 714, 27 Fed. R. Evid. Serv. 899 (7th Cir. 1989)
51 ALR6th 1—§ 20
Sahara Gaming Corp. v. Culinary Workers Union Local 226, 984 P.2d 164, 139 Lab. Cas. (CCH) ¶ 58709 (Nev. 1999)
94 ALR5th 149—§ 8
Sahf v. Lake Havasu City Ass'n for the Retarded and Handicapped, 150 Ariz. 50, 721 P.2d 1177 (Ct. App. Div. 1 1986)
111 ALR5th 159—§ 5
23 ALR6th 697—§ 3
Sahlen & Assoc., Sec. Litig., In re, 773 F. Supp. 342, CCH Fed Secur L. Rep. ¶ 96931 (S.D. Fla. 1991)
48 ALR5th 389—§ 3
Sahlin v. American Cas. Co. of Reading, Pa., 103 Ariz. 57, 436 P.2d 606 (1968)
63 ALR5th 427—§ 2, 3, 10, 24

Sahm v. Poushter, 187 Misc. 486, 63 N.Y.S.2d 328 (1946)
  25 ALR5th 233—§ 19
Sah Quah, In re, 31 F. 327, 1 Alaska Fed. 136 (Alaska 1886)
  88 ALR6th 203—§ 91
Saia v. People of State of New York, 334 U.S. 558, 68 S. Ct. 1148, 92 L. Ed. 1574 (1948)
  122 ALR5th 593—§ 14
Saia Food Distributors and Club, Inc. v. SecurityLink from Ameritech, Inc., 902 So. 2d 46 (Ala. 2004)
  36 ALR6th 305—§ 9
Said v. Auto Club Ins. Ass'n, 152 Mich. App. 240, 393 N.W.2d 598 (1986)
  77 ALR5th 319—§ 4
Saide v. Stanton, 135 Ariz. 76, 659 P.2d 35 (1983)
  5 ALR5th 875—§ 3, 8, 23, 40
Saidel, In re, 22 A.D.3d 54, 800 N.Y.S.2d 563 (2d Dep't 2005)
  43 ALR6th 163—§ 50
Saidel, In re, 180 N.J. 359, 852 A.2d 132 (2004)
  43 ALR6th 163—§ 50
Saieg v. City of Dearborn, 641 F.3d 727 (6th Cir. 2011)
  70 ALR6th 513—§ 12
  71 ALR6th 471—§ 12
Saier v. Saier, 366 Mich. 515, 115 N.W.2d 279 (1962)
  3 ALR5th 590—§ 2, 22, 31
SAIF Corp. v. Batchelor, 130 Or. App. 414, 882 P.2d 615 (1994)
  112 ALR5th 509—§ 14
  13 ALR6th 209—§ 20
  39 ALR6th 445—§ 13, 36, 40
SAIF Corp. v. Campbell, 113 Or. App. 93, 830 P.2d 616 (1992)
  97 ALR5th 1—§ 17
  113 ALR5th 115—§ 10, 18, 33, 55, 56
SAIF Corp. v. Falconer, 154 Or. App. 511, 963 P.2d 50 (1998)
  112 ALR5th 509—§ 18, 27
  122 ALR5th 653—§ 5
  13 ALR6th 209—§ 7, 11, 35

39 ALR6th 445—§ 21, 42
SAIF Corp. v. Hukari, 113 Or. App. 475, 833 P.2d 1307 (1992)
  113 ALR5th 115—§ 10
SAIF Corp. v. Marin, 139 Or. App. 518, 913 P.2d 336 (1996)
  4 ALR5th 443—§ 5
SAIF Corp. v. Weathers, 151 Or. App. 510, 950 P.2d 405 (1997)
  82 ALR5th 149—§ 17
Sailer v. Wisconsin Real Estate Brokers' Board, 5 Wis. 2d 344, 92 N.W.2d 841 (1958)
  7 ALR5th 474—§ 89, 98, 155
Sail'er Inn, Inc. v. Kirby, 5 Cal. 3d 1, 95 Cal. Rptr. 329, 485 P.2d 529, 3 Fair Empl. Prac. Cas. (BNA) 550, 46 A.L.R.3d 351 (1971)
  116 ALR5th 149—§ 4
Sailfrog Software, Inc. v. Theonramp Group, Inc., 1998 WL 30100 (N.D. Cal. 1998)
  60 ALR5th 669—§ 6, 8
Sailling v. Morrell, 97 Neb. 454, 150 N.W. 195 (1914)
  54 ALR5th 649—§ 3
Sailor Music v. Mai Kai of Concord, Inc., 640 F. Supp. 629, 230 USPQ 860 (D.C. N.H. 1986)
  23 ALR5th 241—§ 30
Sailor Music v. Mai Kai of Concord, Inc., 640 F. Supp. 629, 230 U.S.P.Q. 860 (D.N.H. 1986)
  37 ALR6th 243—§ 3, 12, 19, 21, 53, 57, 59
Sain v. Sain, 426 So. 2d 853 (Ala. Civ. App. 1983)
  70 ALR5th 377—§ 3
Sain v. Sain, 517 S.E.2d 921 (N.C. Ct. App. 1999)
  34 ALR5th 447—§ 3
Saint v. Saint, 196 Kan. 330, 411 P.2d 683 (1966)
  49 ALR5th 441—§ 11
Saint Alphonsus Diversified Care, Inc. v. Mri Associates, LLP, 2006 WL 6011960 (Idaho Dist. Ct. 2006)
  70 ALR6th 209—§ 5, 62

Saint Alphonsus Regional Medical Center v. Bannon, 128 Idaho 41, 910 P.2d 155 (1995)
  16 ALR5th 262—§ 9
Saint Anne-Nackawic Pulp Co. v. Research-Cottrell, Inc., 788 F. Supp. 729 (S.D. N.Y. 1992)
  49 ALR5th 1—§ 3, 66
Saint Arnaud v. Chapdelaine Truck Ctr., 836 F. Supp. 41 (D.C. Mass. 1993)
  10 ALR5th 245—§ 22
Saint Bernard Ass'n of Educators v. Saint Bernard Parish Sch. Bd., 619 So. 2d 678 (La. App. 4th Cir. 1993)
  57 ALR5th 477—§ 6, 36
Saint George Greek Orthodox Church v. Laupmanis Assocs., PC, 204 Mich. App. 278, 514 N.W.2d 516 (1994)
  43 ALR5th 545—§ 47, 48
Saintha v. Mukasey, 129 S. Ct. 595, 172 L. Ed. 2d 455 (2008)
  46 ALR6th 495—§ 1
Saintha v. Mukasey, 516 F.3d 243 (4th Cir. 2008)
  46 ALR6th 495—§ 1
Saint John's Church in Wilderness v. Scott, 2012 COA 72, 296 P.3d 273 (Colo. App. 2012)
  86 ALR6th 577—§ 1, 15, 40
Saint-Pierre v. Saint-Pierre, 357 N.W.2d 250 (S.D. 1984)
  82 ALR5th 389—§ 2
  3 ALR6th 447—§ 5, 8
Saints and Sinners v. City of Providence, 172 F. Supp. 2d 348 (D.R.I. 2001)
  20 ALR6th 161—§ 4
  21 ALR6th 425—§ 10
  23 ALR6th 573—§ 8
Saintsing v. Steinbach Co., 1 N.J. Super. 259, 64 A.2d 99 (App. Div. 1949)
  11 ALR6th 351—§ 19
Saintsing v. Taylor, 57 N.C. App. 467, 291 S.E.2d 880 (1982)
  72 ALR6th 563—§ 25
Saitta v. Rivera, 264 A.D.2d 490, 694 N.Y.S.2d 164 (2d Dep't 1999)
  14 ALR6th 543—§ 43

S.A.J.C.H, In re, 36 S.W.3d 803 (Mo. Ct. App. W.D. 2001)
  10 ALR6th 173—§ 39
Saka v. Mann Theatres, 94 Nev. 137, 575 P.2d 1335, 24 U.C.C. Rep. Serv. (CBC) 174 (1978)
  77 ALR5th 429—§ 7
Sakala v. BAC Home Loans Servicing, LP, 2011 WL 719482 (D. Haw. 2011)
  86 ALR6th 411—§ 5
Sakamoto v. N. A. B. Trucking Co., 717 F.2d 1000, 37 FR Serv. 2d 637 (CA6 Tenn. 1983)
  12 ALR5th 195—§ 26
Sakas v. Jessee, 202 Ga. App. 838, 415 S.E.2d 670 (1992)
  11 ALR6th 587—§ 19
Sakata v. Cook, 2006 WL 164915 (Cal. App. 5th Dist. 2006)
  43 ALR6th 611—§ 10
  47 ALR6th 1—§ 19, 46
Sakeagak v. State, 952 P.2d 278 (Alaska Ct. App. 1998)
  73 ALR5th 383—§ 29
Sakellariadis v. Spanos, 163 Ill. App. 3d 1084, 115 Ill. Dec. 122, 517 N.E.2d 324 (2d Dist. 1987)
  76 ALR6th 31—§ 16
Sakkis v. Artisan Pictures, Inc., 2008 Copr. L. Dec. ¶ 29519, 2008 WL 683388 (C.D. Cal. 2008)
  76 ALR6th 289—§ 7
Sakolsky v. Coral Gables, 151 So. 2d 433 (Fla. 1963)
  26 ALR5th 736—§ 4, 5, 9
Sakosko v. Memorial Hosp., 167 Ill. App. 3d 842, 118 Ill. Dec. 818, 522 N.E.2d 273 (5th Dist. 1988)
  69 ALR5th 559—§ 2, 8, 19
Sakotas v. W.C.A.B., 80 Cal. App. 4th 262, 95 Cal. Rptr. 2d 153, 65 Cal. Comp. Cas. (MB) 366 (2d Dist. 2000)
  97 ALR5th 1—§ 2, 15, 26
  106 ALR5th 111—§ 9, 25
  108 ALR5th 1—§ 2, 29

Sakrel, Ltd. v. Roth, 582 N.Y.S.2d 492 (App. Div. 2d Dep't 1992)
2 ALR5th 553—§ 56

Saks & Co. v. City of Beverly Hills, 107 Cal. App. 2d 260, 237 P.2d 32 (2d Dist. 1951)
4 ALR6th 263—§ 37

Saktides v. Cooper, 742 F. Supp. 382 (W.D. Tex. 1990)
79 ALR5th 587—§ 3, 6, 8

S.A.L. v. S.Y./DCSE, 2006 WL 4043760 (Del. Fam. Ct. 2006)
30 ALR6th 483—§ 47

Saladeen v. Parker, 16 A.D.3d 737, 791 N.Y.S.2d 663 (3d Dep' 2005)
69 ALR6th 1—§ 5

Saladin v. Turner, 936 F. Supp. 1571, 20 A.D.D. 1329, 6 A.D. Cas. (BNA) 945 (N.D. Okla. 1996)
82 ALR5th 1—§ 2

Saladiner v. Polanco, 160 S.W.2d 537 (Tex. Civ. App. 1942)
58 ALR5th 535—§ 18

Saladini v. Righellis, 426 Mass. 231, 687 N.E.2d 1224 (1997)
72 ALR6th 385—§ 4, 10

Saladino, In re, 71 Ill. 2d 263, 16 Ill. Dec. 471, 375 N.E.2d 102 (1978)
80 ALR5th 597—§ 15, 19

Salafia v. Hanover Ins. Co., 2006 Mass. App. Div. 188, 2006 WL 3823927 (2006)
69 ALR6th 317—§ 42

Salahuddin v. State, 241 Ga. App. 168, 525 S.E.2d 422 (1999)
26 ALR5th 603—§ 6

Salamak v. Commonwealth Unemployment Compensation Bd. of Review, 91 Pa. Cmwlth. 493, 497 A.2d 951 (1985)
23 ALR5th 176—§ 2, 5, 33

Salamalekis v. Commissioner of Social Sec., 221 F.3d 828, 71 Soc. Sec. Rep. Serv. 29, Unempl. Ins. Rep. (CCH) ¶ 16405B, 2000 FED App. 238P (6th Cir. 2000)
105 ALR5th 499—§ 4

Salaman v. Bolt, 74 Cal. App. 3d 907, 141 Cal. Rptr. 841 (1st Dist. 1977)
27 ALR5th 764—§ 5

Salamar Builders Corp. v. Tuttle, 29 N.Y.2d 221, 325 N.Y.S.2d 933, 275 N.E.2d 585 (1971)
1 ALR5th 622—§ 17, 19

Salameh v. Spossey, 731 A.2d 649 (Pa. Commw. Ct. 1999)
110 ALR5th 329—§ 15

Salamey v. Aetna Casualty & Surety Co., 741 F.2d 874, 16 Fed. Rules Evid. Serv. 540 (CA6 Mich. 1984)
37 ALR5th 41—§ 51

Salamone v. Hollinger Intern., Inc., 347 Ill. App. 3d 837, 283 Ill. Dec. 245, 807 N.E.2d 1086, 32 Media L. Rep. (BNA) 1986 (1st Dist. 2004)
22 ALR6th 553—§ 6, 21, 36
52 ALR6th 271—§ 19

Salamone v. Wincaf Properties, Inc., 671 N.Y.S.2d 737 (App. Div. 1st Dep't 1998)
50 ALR5th 1—§ 4

Salamy v. State, 509 So. 2d 1201 (Fla. 1st DCA 1987)
99 ALR6th 397—§ 16

Salamy v. State, 509 So. 2d 1201 (Fla. Dist. Ct. App. 1st Dist. 1987)
61 ALR5th 1—§ 9, 10

Salanyder v. State, 18 Ala. App. 188, 90 So. 40 (1921)
45 ALR5th 591—§ 15

Salas, Ex parte, 724 S.W.2d 67 (Tex. Crim. 1987)
7 ALR5th 263—§ 2, 6

Salas, Re Marriage of, 447 N.E.2d 1176 (Ind. App. 1983)
17 ALR5th 366—§ 10

Salas v. Gamboa, 760 S.W.2d 838 (Tex. App. San Antonio 1988)
2 ALR5th 811—§ 3

Salas v. Hi-Tech Erectors, 168 Wash. 2d 664, 230 P.3d 583 (2010)
79 ALR6th 351—§ 14

Salas v. State, 246 So. 2d 621 (Fla. Dist. Ct. App. 3d Dist. 1971)
12 ALR6th 553—§ 22

Salas v. State, 385 S.W.2d 859 (Tex. Crim. 1965)
32 ALR5th 149—§ 22, 23, 32, 40
Salas v. State, 756 S.W.2d 832 (Tex. App. Corpus Christi 1988)
9 ALR5th 369—§ 11
Salas v. Texas Dept. of Protective and Regulatory Services, 71 S.W.3d 783 (Tex. App. El Paso 2002)
113 ALR5th 349—§ 22
12 ALR6th 417—§ 5
Salas v. Wang, 846 F.2d 897 (CA3 N.J. 1988)
2 ALR5th 811—§ 6
Salatino v. Pennsylvania Nurses Ass'n, 293 Pa. Super. 336, 439 A.2d 140 (1981)
120 ALR5th 351—§ 17
Salaymeh v. InterQual, Inc., 155 Ill. App. 3d 1040, 108 Ill. Dec. 578, 508 N.E.2d 1155 (5th Dist. 1987)
2 ALR6th 387—§ 3, 4, 11
Salazar v. BAC Home Loans Servicing, LP, 2012 WL 995296 (N.D. Tex. 2012)
86 ALR6th 411—§ 5
Salazar v. Buono, 129 S. Ct. 1313, 173 L. Ed. 2d 582 (2009)
46 ALR6th 495—§ 10
Salazar v. Buono, 130 S. Ct. 1803, 176 L. Ed. 2d 634 (2010)
56 ALR6th 679—§ 24
Salazar v. City of Albuquerque, 776 F. Supp. 2d 1217 (D.N.M. 2011)
95 ALR6th 341—§ 40
Salazar v. City of Santa Fe, 102 N.M. 172, 692 P.2d 1321 (Ct. App. 1983)
28 ALR6th 1—§ 13, 17, 24, 29, 31, 32, 67
Salazar v. Colorado Dept. of Corrections, 2011 WL 149279 (D. Colo. 2011)
64 ALR6th 1—§ 7
Salazar v. Freeport Overseas Service Co., 2000 WL 1099391 (E.D. La. 2000)
13 ALR6th 499—§ 10
36 ALR6th 203—§ 4

Salazar v. Furr's, Inc., 629 F. Supp. 1403 (D. N.M. 1986)
21 ALR5th 1—§ 9
53 ALR5th 219—§ 5, 10
Salazar v. Hill, 551 S.W.2d 518 (Tex. Civ. App. Corpus Christi 1977)
21 ALR5th 82—§ 3, 17
Salazar v. Lehman Bros. Bank, 2010 WL 3998047 (D. Ariz. 2010)
86 ALR6th 411—§ 5
Salazar v. Ramah Navajo Chapter, 132 S. Ct. 2181 (2012)
76 ALR6th 587—§ 31
Salazar v. Rodriguez, 371 F.2d 726 (10th Cir. 1967)
74 ALR5th 453—§ 4
Salazar v. Salazar, 582 So. 2d 374 (La. App. 4th Cir. 1991)
27 ALR5th 540—§ 3
Salazar v. Scotts Bluff County, 266 Neb. 444, 665 N.W.2d 659 (2003)
116 ALR5th 433—§ 6
Salazar v. State, 95 S.W.3d 501 (Tex. App. Houston 1st Dist. 2002)
26 ALR6th 511—§ 35
Salazar v. State, 298 S.W.3d 273 (Tex. App. Fort Worth 2009)
55 ALR6th 391—§ 24
Salazar v. State, 589 S.W.2d 412 (Tex. Crim. 1979)
26 ALR5th 1—§ 3, 5
Salazar v. State, 745 S.W.2d 385 (Tex. App. Fort Worth 1987)
20 ALR5th 398—§ 3
Salazar v. State, 795 S.W.2d 187 (Tex. Crim. 1990)
20 ALR5th 398—§ 15, 38
Salazar v. State, 818 S.W.2d 405 (Tex. Crim. 1991)
20 ALR5th 398—§ 7, 15, 38
Salazar v. State, 1998 OK CR 70, 973 P.2d 315 (Okla. Crim. App. 1998)
112 ALR5th 621—§ 5
Salazar v. State, 1998 OK CR 70, 1998 OK CR 70, 973 P.2d 315 (Okla. Crim. App. 1998)
20 ALR5th 177—§ 3

79 ALR5th 33—§ 52
Salazar v. State, 2003 WL 1746151 (Tex. App. Houston 1st Dist. 2003)
31 ALR6th 49—§ 4
Salazar v. State, 2004 WL 1123519 (Tex. App. Amarillo 2004)
7 ALR6th 487—§ 31
Salazar v. State, 2004 WL 2802508 (Tex. App. Dallas 2004)
84 ALR6th 293—§ 43
Salazar v. State, 2009 WL 1563554 (Tex. App. Austin 2009)
56 ALR6th 323—§ 7, 11
Salazar v. Whink Products Co., 881 P.2d 431, Prod. Liab. Rep. (CCH) ¶ 13946 (Colo. Ct. App. 1994)
69 ALR5th 137—§ 7
Salazar, People ex rel. v. Davidson, 79 P.3d 1221 (Colo. 2003)
114 ALR5th 387—§ 3, 5
34 ALR6th 643—§ 7, 11, 31, 33, 34
Salazar, State ex rel. v. Roybal, 125 N.M. 471, 1998 -NMCA- 093, 963 P.2d 548, 87 A.L.R.5th 767 (Ct. App. 1998)
86 ALR5th 637—§ 3
87 ALR5th 361—§ 22, 24
Salazar, State ex rel. v. The Cash Now Store, Inc., 31 P.3d 161 (Colo. 2001)
73 ALR6th 425—§ 2, 17
Salcedo v. Artuz, 107 F. Supp. 2d 405 (S.D. N.Y. 2000)
70 ALR5th 1—§ 11
Salcedo v. People, 999 P.2d 833 (Colo. 2000)
69 ALR5th 425—§ 4
Saldana, Ex parte, 2002 WL 91331 (Tex. App. Corpus Christi 2002)
7 ALR6th 487—§ 31
Saldana, Ex parte, 2010 WL 2789032 (Tex. App. Austin 2010)
74 ALR6th 373—§ 6
Saldana v. Erickson Landscaping & Const., 2005-Ohio-142, 2005 WL 89381 (Ohio Ct. App. 11th Dist. Geauga County 2005)
41 ALR6th 207—§ 27

Saldana v. Kmart Corp., 84 F. Supp. 2d 629 (D.V.I. 1999)
58 ALR5th 429—§ 3, 5
Saldana v. State, 33 S.W.3d 70 (Tex. App. Corpus Christi 2000)
63 ALR6th 351—§ 3
Saldana v. State, 2012 WL 3797611 (Tex. App. Austin 2012)
93 ALR6th 275—§ 10
Saldanha v. De Buono, 256 A.D.2d 935, 681 N.Y.S.2d 874 (3d Dep't 1998)
32 ALR5th 57—§ 13
Saldarriaga v. DeSantis Bros., 151 A.D.2d 270, 542 N.Y.S.2d 184 (1st Dep't 1989)
99 ALR5th 141—§ 16, 20
100 ALR5th 409—§ 13
Saldate v. Wilshire Credit Corp., 711 F. Supp. 2d 1126 (E.D. Cal. 2010)
81 ALR6th 161—§ 5
82 ALR6th 43—§ 5
Saldi v. Paul Revere Life Ins. Co., 224 F.R.D. 169 (E.D. Pa. 2004)
104 ALR6th 207—§ 12
Saldinger v. Santa Cruz County Superior Court, 2010 WL 3339512 (N.D. Cal. 2010)
64 ALR6th 131—§ 24
Saldivar v. State, 980 S.W.2d 475 (Tex. App. Houston 14th Dist. 1998)
29 ALR6th 1—§ 3
Saldiveri v. State, 217 Md. 412, 143 A.2d 70 (1958)
40 ALR6th 1—§ 3
Sale v. Allstate Ins. Co., 126 Ill. App. 3d 905, 81 Ill. Dec. 901, 467 N.E.2d 1023 (1st Dist. 1984)
6 ALR5th 297—§ 5, 7
Sale v. Leachman, 218 Ga. 834, 131 S.E.2d 185 (1963)
82 ALR5th 443—§ 2
83 ALR5th 375—§ 2
84 ALR5th 191—§ 2
Sale v. State, 8 So. 3d 330 (Ala. Crim. App. 2008)
83 ALR6th 465—§ 12

Sale City Peanut & Mill. Co. v. Planters & Citizens Bank, 107 Ga. App. 463, 130 S.E.2d 518 (1963)
104 ALR6th 485—§ 4, 6

Saleeby v. Safir, 289 A.D.2d 60, 734 N.Y.S.2d 139 (1st Dep't 2001)
91 ALR6th 435—§ 123

Saleeby v. State Bar, 39 Cal. 3d 547, 216 Cal. Rptr. 367, 702 P.2d 525 (1985)
106 ALR5th 523—§ 27

Sale Electric Supply, Inc. v. Emco, Inc., 385 So. 2d 873 (La. App. 2d Cir. 1980)
23 ALR5th 241—§ 5

Saleem v. New Jersey Dept. of Corrections, 2009 WL 910791 (N.J. Super. Ct. App. Div. 2009)
96 ALR6th 269—§ 43

Saleem v. State, 152 Ga. App. 552, 263 S.E.2d 490 (1979)
105 ALR5th 529—§ 11

Saleh v. New Jersey Dept. of Corrections, 2008 WL 4287157 (N.J. Super. Ct. App. Div. 2008)
56 ALR6th 553—§ 24

Salehpoor v. Shahinpoor, 358 F.3d 782, 185 Ed. Law Rep. 114, 149 Lab. Cas. (CCH) ¶ 59847 (10th Cir. 2004)
90 ALR6th 235—§ 37

Salem v. City of Sarasota, 2005 WL 1571883 (M.D. Fla. 2005)
62 ALR6th 413—§ 29
69 ALR6th 275—§ 5, 27

Salem v. Geraci, 27 A.D.3d 1175, 810 N.Y.S.2d 763 (4th Dep't 2006)
91 ALR6th 435—§ 34, 76

Salem v. Khalaf, 2003 WL 2002544 (Tex. App. Houston 1st Dist. 2003)
81 ALR6th 161—§ 5
82 ALR6th 43—§ 5

Salem v. Salem, 61 Ohio App. 3d 243, 572 N.E.2d 726 (9th Dist. Summit County 1988)
86 ALR6th 321—§ 5
90 ALR6th 451—§ 54

Salem v. State, 232 Ga. App. 886, 503 S.E.2d 62 (1998)
115 ALR5th 403—§ 3, 5
4 ALR6th 113—§ 16, 17
101 ALR6th 1—§ 32

Salembier v. Blackstone Valley Electric Co., 102 R.I. 399, 230 A.2d 872 (1967)
20 ALR5th 346—§ 12

Salem Church (Delaware) Associates v. New Castle County, 2006 WL 4782453 (Del. Ch. 2006)
68 ALR6th 229—§ 6

Salem, City of v. Harding, 121 Ohio St. 412, 7 Ohio L. Abs. 639, 169 N.E. 457 (1929)
54 ALR6th 201—§ 48

Salem, City of v. Lane & Bodley Co., 90 Ill. App. 560, 1900 WL 3224 (4th Dist. 1900)
81 ALR6th 363—§ 20

Salem Hosp. v. Commissioner of Public Welfare, 410 Mass. 625, 574 N.E.2d 385, 34 Soc. Sec. Rep. Serv. 80 (1991)
113 ALR5th 95—§ 3, 7

Salem-Keizer Ass'n of Classified Employees v. Salem-Keizer School Dist. 24J, 186 Or. App. 19, 61 P.3d 970, 173 Ed. Law Rep. 153, 172 L.R.R.M. (BNA) 2042, 112 A.L.R.5th 747 (2003)
112 ALR5th 263—§ 7

Salem-Keizer Sch. Dist. #24J v. Employment Dep't, 137 Or. App. 320, 904 P.2d 1082 (1995)
33 ALR5th 643—§ 19

Salemmo v. Dolan, 192 Pa. Super. 51, 159 A.2d 253 (1960)
5 ALR5th 875—§ 2, 6

Salem Radio Representatives, Inc. v. Can Tel Market Support Group, 1999 WL 1039708 (N.D. Tex. 1999)
79 ALR5th 587—§ 2

Salem Realty Co. v. Matera, 10 Mass. App. Ct. 571, 410 N.E.2d 716 (1980)
49 ALR6th 505—§ 5

Salem Realty Co. v. Matera, 384 Mass. 803, 426 N.E.2d 1160 (1981)
  56 ALR5th 1—§ 2, 3
  49 ALR6th 505—§ 5
Salem School Dist. 24J v. First State Ins. Co., 84 Or. App. 429, 734 P.2d 369, 38 Ed. Law Rep. 789 (1987)
  94 ALR5th 567—§ 15
Salem School Dist. 43-3 v. Puetz Const., Inc., 353 N.W.2d 51, 19 Ed. Law Rep. 401 (S.D. 1984)
  5 ALR6th 497—§ 5
Salemy v. Diab, 246 N.J. Super. 274, 587 A.2d 305, 14 U.C.C. Rep. Serv. 2d (CBC) 803 (App. Div. 1991)
  77 ALR5th 429—§ 4
Sale of Intoxicating Liquors, In re, 108 Iowa 368, 79 N.W. 260 (1899)
  56 ALR5th 171—§ 9, 30
Salerian v. Maryland State Bd. of Physicians, 176 Md. App. 231, 932 A.2d 1225 (2007)
  65 ALR6th 295—§ 12
Salerno v. Auto Owners Ins. Co., 2006 WL 2085467 (M.D. Fla. 2006)
  64 ALR6th 473—§ 8, 9
Salerno v. Corzine, 2007 WL 2159611 (D.N.J. 2007)
  73 ALR6th 281—§ 34
Salerno v. D'Alessandro, 623 N.Y.S.2d 305 (App. Div. 2d Dep't 1995)
  8 ALR5th 312—§ 8
Salerno v. LaBarr, 159 Pa. Commw. 99, 632 A.2d 1002 (1993)
  12 ALR6th 645—§ 61
Salerno v. Leica, Inc., 258 A.D.2d 896, 685 N.Y.S.2d 368 (4th Dep't 1999)
  85 ALR6th 323—§ 13
Salerno v. New Brunswick Fire Ins. Co., 72 Pa. D & C. 33 (1949)
  16 ALR5th 412—§ 20, 24
Salerno v. Philadelphia Newspapers, Inc., 377 Pa. Super. 83, 546 A.2d 1168, 15 Media L. Rep. (BNA) 2416 (1988)
  96 ALR5th 107—§ 8
Salerno v. Salerno, 241 N.J. Super. 536, 575 A.2d 532 (Ch. Div. 1990)

49 ALR6th 505—§ 41, 49
Sales v. Bacigalupi, 47 Cal. App. 2d 82, 117 P.2d 399 (1941)
  11 ALR5th 1—§ 10
Sales v. Guillory, 188 So. 2d 429 (La. App. 3d Cir. 1966)
  9 ALR5th 826—§ 6
Sales v. State, 199 Ga. App. 791, 406 S.E.2d 131, 102-113 Fulton County D R 12b (1991)
  22 ALR5th 1—§ 50
Sales v. State Farm Fire & Casualty Co., 849 F.2d 1383 (CA11 Ga. 1988)
  4 ALR5th 117—§ 2
Salesian Soc. v. Formigli Corp., 120 N.J. Super. 493, 295 A.2d 19 (Law Div. 1972)
  5 ALR6th 497—§ 7, 9, 11
Saleson v. Department of Registration & Education, 95 Ill. App. 2d 104, 237 N.E.2d 822 (1st Dist. 1968)
  7 ALR5th 474—§ 155, 171
Salestraq America, LLC v. Zyskowski, 635 F. Supp. 2d 1178 (D. Nev. 2009)
  76 ALR6th 289—§ 5
  77 ALR6th 543—§ 5, 7, 11
Salgado v. Atlantic Richfield Co., 823 F.2d 1322, 48 BNA FEP Cas. 546, 4 BNA IER Cas. 1240, 43 CCH EPD ¶ 37270 (CA9 Cal. 1987)
  21 ALR5th 1—§ 3
Salgado v. County of Los Angeles, 19 Cal. 4th 629, 20 Cal. 4th 22a, 80 Cal. Rptr. 2d 46, 967 P.2d 585 (1998)
  26 ALR5th 245—§ 33
Salgado v. Marquez, 356 Ill. App. 3d 1072, 293 Ill. Dec. 495, 828 N.E.2d 805 (2d Dist. 2005)
  14 ALR6th 543—§ 5, 50
Salgado v. State, 268 Ga. App. 18, 601 S.E.2d 417 (2004)
  19 ALR6th 115—§ 5, 13
Salgado v. State, 2001 WL 1512933 (Tex. App. Houston 1st Dist. 2001)
  34 ALR6th 1—§ 10

Saliba v. State, 475 N.E.2d 1181 (Ind. App. 1985)
59 ALR5th 749—§ 3
Salicos v. Louisiana State Racing Com., 482 So. 2d 117 (La. App. 4th Cir. 1986)
59 ALR5th 203—§ 14, 41
Salida v. McKinna, 16 Colo. 523, 27 P. 810 (1891)
49 ALR5th 685—§ 3
Saliem v. Glovsky, 132 Me. 402, 172 A. 4 (1934)
85 ALR6th 1—§ 53
Salien, In re Marriage of, 78 P.3d 498 (Kan. Ct. App. 2003)
21 ALR6th 351—§ 4
Salient Networks, Inc. v. Jones, 2004 WL 1470670 (Cal. App. 4th Dist. 2004)
22 ALR6th 387—§ 7, 38
Salierno v. Micro Stamping Co., 72 N.J. 205, 370 A.2d 3 (1977)
112 ALR5th 509—§ 18
39 ALR6th 445—§ 35
Salim v. Lee, 202 F. Supp. 2d 1122 (C.D. Cal. 2002)
76 ALR6th 289—§ 4, 5
77 ALR6th 543—§ 6, 13
Salimbene v. Merchants Mut. Ins. Co., 217 App. Div. 2d 991, 629 N.Y.S.2d 913 (4th Dep't 1995)
35 ALR5th 375—§ 43
Salimi v. Farmers Ins. Group, 684 P.2d 264, 1 I.E.R. Cas. (BNA) 1403, 116 L.R.R.M. (BNA) 3230, 106 Lab. Cas. (CCH) P 55727 (Colo. Ct. App. 1984)
38 ALR6th 541—§ 32
Salina, Kan., City of v. Maryland Cas. Co., 856 F. Supp. 1467 (D. Kan. 1994)
98 ALR5th 193—§ 16
105 ALR5th 95—§ 3
Salinas, In re, 130 Wash. App. 772, 124 P.3d 665 (Div. 3 2005)
56 ALR6th 553—§ 21
Salinas v. City of San Jose, 2010 WL 725803 (N.D. Cal. 2010)
56 ALR6th 467—§ 19, 20
Salinas v. Kahn, 2 Ariz. App. 181, 407 P.2d 120 (1965)
42 ALR5th 465—§ 3
Salinas v. State, 369 S.W.3d 176 (Tex. Crim. App. 2012)
86 ALR6th 577—§ 19, 58
Salinas v. State, 888 S.W.2d 93 (Tex. App. Corpus Christi 1994)
20 ALR5th 398—§ 3, 17, 25, 42, 55.5
Salinas v. Stillman, 25 Tex. 12 (1860)
19 ALR5th 622—§ 8, 11, 16
Salinas v. Stillman, 66 F. 677 (C.C.A. 5th Cir. 1894)
35 ALR6th 1—§ 27, 29
Salinas v. Texas, 2013 WL 2922119 (U.S. 2013)
86 ALR6th 577—§ 19, 58
Saline County Agricultural Asso. v. Great American Ins. Co., 144 Ill. App. 3d 394, 98 Ill. Dec. 951, 494 N.E.2d 1278 (5th Dist. 1986)
35 ALR5th 731—§ 2, 15
Salinero v. Pon, 124 Cal. App. 3d 120, 177 Cal. Rptr. 204 (1st Dist. 1981)
5 ALR6th 497—§ 7, 9
Salinsky v. Perma-Home Corp., 15 Mass. App. Ct. 193, 443 N.E.2d 1362 (1983)
122 ALR5th 1—§ 39
Salisbury, Ex parte, 98 Tex. Crim. 341, 265 S.W. 696 (1924)
76 ALR5th 485—§ 3, 17, 19
Salisbury v. Federal Home Loan Mortg. Corp., 2012 WL 3727545 (E.D. Tex. 2012)
86 ALR6th 411—§ 5
Salisbury v. Gourgas, 51 Mass. 442 (1845)
10 ALR5th 828—§ 4
Salisbury v. Housing Authority of City of Newport, 615 F. Supp. 1433 (E.D. Ky. 1985)
28 ALR6th 175—§ 12
Salisbury v. Salisbury, 83 App. Div. 2d 990, 443 N.Y.S.2d 528 (4th Dep't 1981)

38 ALR5th 69—§ 9
Salisbury v. State, 133 Ga. App. 964, 213 S.E.2d 90 (1975)
105 ALR5th 529—§ 11
Salisbury v. U.S., 690 F.2d 966, 11 Fed. R. Evid. Serv. 1409 (D.C. Cir. 1982)
23 ALR6th 521—§ 26
Salisbury v. Wal-Mart Stores Inc., 255 A.D.2d 95, 690 N.Y.S.2d 156 (3d Dep't 1999)
74 ALR5th 49—§ 40
Salisbury Cove Associates, Inc. v. Ind-con Design (1995), Ltd., 211 F. Supp. 2d 184 (D. Me. 2002)
78 ALR6th 151—§ 7
Salisbury Livestock Co. v. Colorado Cent. Credit Union, 793 P.2d 470, 12 U.C.C.R.S.2d 894 (Wyo. 1990)
25 ALR5th 696—§ 2, 3, 30, 36, 54
Salisbury Plumbing & Heating Co. v. Carpenter, 131 Ill. App. 3d 829, 86 Ill. Dec. 839, 476 N.E.2d 15 (5th Dist. 1985)
88 ALR5th 545—§ 2, 5, 6, 17
Salisbury, State ex rel. v. Vogel, 65 N.D. 137, 256 N.W. 404 (1935)
10 ALR5th 139—§ 12
Salistean v. State, 115 Neb. 838, 215 N.W. 107, 53 A.L.R. 1057 (1927)
14 ALR5th 89—§ 2
Saliterman v. Finney, 361 N.W.2d 175 (Minn. App. 1985)
12 ALR5th 847—§ 7, 14
Salk v. Alpine Ski Shop, Inc., 115 R.I. 309, 342 A.2d 622, 18 U.C.C. Rep. Serv. 335 (1975)
93 ALR5th 103—§ 12
Salkay v. Wainwright, 552 F.2d 151 (5th Cir. 1977)
117 ALR5th 513—§ 12
Salkeld v. V.R. Business Brokers, 192 Ill. App. 3d 663, 139 Ill. Dec. 595, 548 N.E.2d 1151 (2d Dist. 1989)
117 ALR5th 155—§ 10
Salkind v. Danilovic, 2005 WL 1273958 (Cal. App. 2d Dist. 2005)
48 ALR6th 1—§ 87

Sall v. Barber, 782 P.2d 1216, 16 Media L. R. 1700 (Colo. App. 1989)
54 ALR5th 443—§ 19
Sall v. Ellfeldt, 662 S.W.2d 517 (Mo. App. 1983)
9 ALR5th 746—§ 2, 3, 5, 21
Sall v. G.H. Miller & Co., 612 F. Supp. 1499 (D. Colo. 1985)
46 ALR6th 185—§ 9
Sallach v. Darvish, 655 S.W.2d 791 (Mo. Ct. App. E.D. 1983)
118 ALR5th 385—§ 14
Salladay v. Dodgeville, 85 Wis. 318, 55 N.W. 696 (1893)
15 ALR5th 119—§ 25
Sallam v. Nolan, 116 F.3d 466 (2d Cir. 1997)
82 ALR6th 281—§ 18
Sallee v. Mason, 714 N.E.2d 757, 15 I.E.R. Cas. (BNA) 1215 (Ind. Ct. App. 1999)
18 ALR5th 577—§ 57
Salley v. Board of Governors, University of North Carolina, Chapel Hill, N.C., 136 F.R.D. 417, 20 Fed. R. Serv. 3d 89 (M.D. N.C. 1991)
30 ALR6th 413—§ 13
Salley v. E. I. Du Pont de Nemours & Co., 966 F.2d 1011, 15 EBC 2057, 23 FR Serv. 3d 676 (CA5 La. 1992)
23 ALR5th 241—§ 37
Sallie v. State, 269 Ga. 446, 499 S.E.2d 897 (1998)
39 ALR5th 283—§ 44, 72, 77
Sallie v. State of N. C., 587 F.2d 636 (4th Cir. 1978)
117 ALR5th 513—§ 5
Sallie v. State of N.C., 587 F.2d 636 (4th Cir. 1978)
58 ALR6th 499—§ 19
Sallinger v. Mayer, 304 So. 2d 730 (La. App. 4th Cir. 1974)
8 ALR5th 312—§ 11
Sallings v. State, 789 S.W.2d 408 (Tex. App. Dallas 1990)
55 ALR5th 125—§ 3, 7
Sally M., In re, 2006 WL 2128573 (Cal. App. 4th Dist. 2006)

63 ALR6th 429—§ 13

Sally R. v. Stewart R., 151 Misc. 2d 307, 573 N.Y.S.2d 231 (Fam Ct. 1991)

57 ALR5th 389—§ 14

Salm v. Catherwood, 25 A.D.2d 697, 268 N.Y.S.2d 171 (3d Dep't 1966)

27 ALR6th 123—§ 7

Salman Ranch, Ltd. v. C.I.R., 132 S. Ct. 2100, 2012-1 U.S. Tax Cas. (CCH) ¶ 50325 (2012)

76 ALR6th 587—§ 34

Salmans v. Salmans, 643 S.W.2d 778 (Tex. App. San Antonio 1982)

59 ALR6th 433—§ 56

Salmine v. Knagin, 645 P.2d 148 (Alaska 1982)

112 ALR5th 47—§ 14
118 ALR5th 91—§ 33

Salmon v. Bank of America Corp., 2011 WL 2174554 (E.D. Wash. 2011)

86 ALR6th 411—§ 5

Salmon v. Bradshaw, 84 S.D. 500, 173 N.W.2d 281 (1969)

62 ALR5th 219—§ 12

Salmon v. Davis County, 916 P.2d 890, 289 Utah Adv. Rep. 3 (Utah 1996)

47 ALR5th 553—§ 10, 29

Salmon v. Delaware, L. & W. R. Co., 38 NJL 5 (1875)

17 ALR5th 547—§ 53, 59

Salmon v. Libby, McNeill & Libby, 219 Ill. 421, 76 N.E. 573 (1905)

2 ALR5th 1—§ 8

Salmon v. Parke, Davis & Co., 520 F.2d 1359 (CA4 N.C. 1975)

57 ALR5th 1—§ 3, 21, 23

Salmon v. Pearson & Associates, Inc., 214 Ga. App. 11, 446 S.E.2d 762 (1994)

117 ALR5th 23—§ 5, 12, 21

Salmon v. Salmon, 88 N.J. Super. 291, 212 A.2d 171 (1965)

53 ALR5th 375—§ 3

Salmon v. Salmon, 2006-Ohio-1557, 2006 WL 826328 (Ohio Ct. App. 9th Dist. Summit County 2006)

39 ALR6th 205—§ 4

Salmon v. Salmon, 2008-Ohio-2313, 2008 WL 2039078 (Ohio Ct. App. 9th Dist. Summit County 2008)

39 ALR6th 205—§ 4

Salmon v. Schwarz, 948 F.2d 1131 (10th Cir. 1991)

73 ALR6th 49—§ 35

Salmon v. State, 2 Md. App. 513, 235 A.2d 758 (1967)

43 ALR5th 1—§ 14

Salmon v. State, 249 Ga. App. 591, 549 S.E.2d 421 (2001)

115 ALR5th 403—§ 3, 5
116 ALR5th 325—§ 3
4 ALR6th 113—§ 14
101 ALR6th 1—§ 7

Salmons v. National Union Fire Ins. Co. of Pittsburgh, 2007 WL 2900352 (S.D. W. Va. 2007)

80 ALR6th 389—§ 25

Salmonte v. Eilertson, 526 So. 2d 179 (Fla. Dist. Ct. App. 1st Dist. 1988)

114 ALR5th 443—§ 2, 38

Saloga, In re Custody of, 96 Ill. App. 3d 661, 52 Ill. Dec. 128, 421 N.E.2d 991 (2d Dist. 1981)

6 ALR6th 229—§ 14, 22, 26

Salois v. Mutual of Omaha Ins. Co., 90 Wash. 2d 355, 581 P.2d 1349 (1978)

117 ALR5th 155—§ 12

Salone v. State, 652 N.E.2d 552 (Ind. App. 1995)

5 ALR5th 243—§ 35, 46

Salon Group, Inc. v. Salberg, R.I.C.O. Bus. Disp. Guide (CCH) ¶ 10236, 2002 WL 1058120 (N.D. Ill. 2002)

13 ALR6th 1—§ 4
15 ALR6th 427—§ 30

Salonia v. Samsol Homes, Inc., 119 A.D.2d 394, 507 N.Y.S.2d 186 (2d Dep't 1986)

17 ALR6th 1—§ 15

Salopek, In re, 137 N.M. 47, 2005-NMCA-016, 107 P.3d 1 (Ct. App. 2004)

87 ALR6th 495—§ 57, 67

Salpas v. State, 642 S.W.2d 71 (Tex. App. El Paso 1982)

61 ALR5th 1—§ 4, 14
Salpoglou v. Widder, 904 F. Supp. 34 (D.C. Mass. 1995)
12 ALR5th 1—§ 31
Salsbury v. Salsbury, 1999 WL 1338339 (Neb. Ct. App. 1999)
112 ALR5th 185—§ 10
Salsbury Laboratories, Inc. v. Merieux Laboratories, Inc., 735 F. Supp. 1555 (M.D. Ga. 1989)
14 ALR5th 242—§ 41
Salsitz v. Nasser, 208 F.R.D. 589 (E.D. Mich. 2002)
43 ALR6th 1—§ 5, 45
Salsman v. National Community Bank of Rutherford, 102 N.J. Super. 482, 246 A.2d 162, 5 U.C.C. Rep. Serv. 779 (Law Div. 1968)
91 ALR5th 89—§ 4
Salstein v. Ha-Lo Industries, Inc., 82 F. Supp. 2d 1080 (N.D. Cal. 1999)
104 ALR5th 1—§ 4
Salstrom v. Salstrom, 404 N.W.2d 848 (Minn. App. 1987)
9 ALR5th 568—§ 19
Salstrom v. State, 148 Ariz. 382, 714 P.2d 875 (Ct. App. Div. 2 1986)
98 ALR5th 445—§ 6
56 ALR6th 553—§ 6, 30
Salstrom v. Sumner, 959 F.2d 241 (9th Cir. 1992)
54 ALR6th 1—§ 7
Salter v. A. Fraser Pattillo, Jr., Inc., 519 So. 2d 930 (Ala. 1988)
6 ALR5th 883—§ 23
Salter v. Deaconess Family Medicine Center, 701 N.Y.S.2d 586 (App. Div. 4th Dep't 1999)
2 ALR5th 811—§ 34
Salter v. Johnson, 579 F.2d 1007, 10 Ohio Op. 3d 360 (6th Cir. 1978)
72 ALR6th 1—§ 9
Salter v. Leventhal, 337 Mass. 679, 151 N.E.2d 275 (1958)
81 ALR6th 161—§ 4
82 ALR6th 43—§ 4
Salter v. Nash, 2008 WL 4724267 (Mich. Ct. App. 2008)

57 ALR6th 163—§ 39
Salter v. State, 582 So. 2d 994 (La. App. 1st Cir. 1991)
52 ALR5th 1—§ 3
Salterini's Estate, In re, 7 Misc. 2d 497, 164 N.Y.S.2d 584 (Sur. Ct. 1957)
56 ALR5th 133—§ 5
Salters v. Town of Woodstock, 267 A.D.2d 720, 701 N.Y.S.2d 132 (3d Dep't 1999)
112 ALR5th 509—§ 5
13 ALR6th 209—§ 14
39 ALR6th 445—§ 39
Saltiel v. Olsen, 85 Ill. 2d 484, 55 Ill. Dec. 830, 426 N.E.2d 1204 (1981)
56 ALR5th 107—§ 6
Saltis v. A.B.B. Daimler Benz, 243 Ga. App. 603, 533 S.E.2d 772 (2000)
44 ALR5th 525—§ 9
Salt Lake City v. Davidson, 2000 UT App. 12, 994 P.2d 1283 (Utah Ct. App. 2000)
11 ALR5th 52—§ 10
Salt Lake City v. Industrial Comm'n, 104 Utah 436, 140 P.2d 644 (1943)
44 ALR5th 569—§ 10
Salt Lake City v. Johnson, 959 P.2d 1022 (Utah Ct. App. 1998)
91 ALR5th 343—§ 9
Salt Lake City v. Lopez, 935 P.2d 1259 (Utah Ct. App. 1997)
29 ALR5th 487—§ 3, 5, 12
Salt Lake City v. Roberts, 2002 UT 30, 44 P.3d 767 (Utah 2002)
95 ALR5th 229—§ 19
Salt Lake City v. Robinson, 2005 UT App 159, 2005 WL 775320 (Utah Ct. App. 2005)
37 ALR6th 357—§ 25
Salt Lake City v. Savage, 541 P.2d 1035 (Utah 1975)
72 ALR5th 1—§ 29
Salt Lake City v. Street, 2011 UT App 111, 251 P.3d 862 (Utah Ct. App. 2011)
84 ALR6th 293—§ 4, 19

Salt Lake City v. Tax Commission of Utah, 11 Utah 2d 359, 359 P.2d 397 (1961)
88 ALR6th 203—§ 5, 43, 54
Salt Lake City v. Trujillo, 854 P.2d 603, 214 Utah Adv. Rep. 21 (Utah App. 1993)
41 ALR5th 171—§ 13
Salt Lake City v. Venord, 2004 UT App 207, 2004 WL 1367933 (Utah Ct. App. 2004)
37 ALR6th 357—§ 59
Salt Lake City v. Womack, 747 P.2d 1039 (Utah 1987)
56 ALR6th 323—§ 7
Salt Lake City, Board of Education of v. Salt Lake Pressed-Brick Co., 13 Utah 211, 44 P. 709 (1896)
81 ALR6th 363—§ 22
Salt Lake City Corp. v. Confer, 674 P.2d 632, 1 A.D. Cas. (BNA) 504, 37 Fair Empl. Prac. Cas. (BNA) 283, 33 Empl. Prac. Dec. (CCH) ¶ 34284 (Utah 1983)
102 ALR5th 1—§ 6
Salt Lake City Corp. v. Kasler Corp., 842 F. Supp. 1380, 24 U.C.C. Rep. Serv. 2d 81 (D. Utah 1994)
89 ALR5th 319—§ 24
Salt Lake City Corp. v. Kasler Corp., 855 F. Supp. 1560, 24 U.C.C. Rep. Serv. 2d 518 (D. Utah 1994)
94 ALR6th 1—§ 36, 77
Salt Lake City Corp. v. Kasler Corp., 855 F. Supp. 1560, 24 U.C.C. Rep. Serv. 2d (CBC) 518 (D. Utah 1994)
49 ALR5th 1—§ 2, 8, 21, 48, 77
81 ALR5th 483—§ 5
Salt Lake City Southern R. Co. v. Utah State Tax Com'n, 1999 UT 90, 987 P.2d 594, 90 A.L.R.5th 789 (Utah 1999)
90 ALR5th 547—§ 5, 16
Salt Lake County v. Holliday Water Co., 2010 UT 45, 234 P.3d 1105 (Utah 2010)
78 ALR6th 229—§ 23

Saltou v. Dependable Ins. Co., 394 N.W.2d 629 (Minn. App. 1986)
6 ALR5th 297—§ 5, 6, 18
Salt River Pima-Maricopa Indian Comm. School v. State, 2001 WL 477029 (Ariz. Ct. App. Div. 1 2001)
78 ALR5th 533—§ 12
Salt River Project Agr. Imp. and Power Dist. v. Westinghouse Elec. Corp., 176 Ariz. 383, 861 P.2d 668, Prod. Liab. Rep. (CCH) ¶ 13562 (Ct. App. Div. 2 1993)
62 ALR6th 313—§ 10
Salt River Valley Water Users' Ass'n v. Cornum, 49 Ariz. 1, 63 P.2d 639 (1937)
8 ALR5th 177—§ 27
Saltz, In re, 33 A.D.2d 85, 305 N.Y.S.2d 293 (1st Dep't 1969)
49 ALR6th 505—§ 21, 23
Saltz v. State of Alaska, Dept. of Public Safety, Driver Imp. Bureau, 942 P.2d 1151, 109 A.L.R.5th 815 (Alaska 1997)
109 ALR5th 611—§ 6
Saltzman v. Heineman, 116 Ill. App. 2d 189, 253 N.E.2d 520 (1st Dist. 1969)
34 ALR5th 77—§ 5
Saltzman v. Saltzman, 124 N.H. 515, 475 A.2d 1 (1984)
87 ALR5th 1—§ 10
Salucco v. Alldredge, 17 Mass. L. Rptr. 498, 2004 WL 864459 (Mass. Super. Ct. 2004)
76 ALR6th 257—§ 8, 11
Salud v. Financial Sec. Ins. Co., Ltd., 7 Haw. App. 329, 763 P.2d 9 (1988)
63 ALR5th 675—§ 10
Salus v. Nevada ex rel. Bd. of Regents of Nevada System of Higher Educ., 2011 WL 4828821 (D. Nev. 2011)
90 ALR6th 235—§ 68
Salute v. Pitchess, 61 Cal. App. 3d 557, 132 Cal. Rptr. 345 (2d Dist. 1976)
91 ALR6th 435—§ 72

Salvador v. Atlantic Steel Boiler Co., 256 Pa. Super. 330, 389 A.2d 1148, 24 U.C.C.R.S. 627 (1978)
49 ALR5th 1—§ 44
50 ALR5th 327—§ 2

Salvador v. Atlantic Steel Boiler Co., 457 Pa. 24, 319 A.2d 903, 14 U.C.C.R.S. 1073 (1974)
50 ALR5th 327—§ 2 to 5

Salvador v. I. H. English of Phila., Inc., 224 Pa. Super. 377, 307 A.2d 398, 12 U.C.C.R.S. 769 (1973)
49 ALR5th 1—§ 44

Salvador v. Munoz, 193 So. 2d 442 (Fla. App. D3 1966)
20 ALR5th 1—§ 45, 60

Salvador C., In re, 2014 WL 1047949 (Cal. App. 1st Dist. 2014)
103 ALR6th 347—§ 10

Salvaggio v. Barnett, 248 S.W.2d 244 (Tex. Civ. App. Galveston 1952)
95 ALR5th 533—§ 3
124 ALR5th 203—§ 3, 9

Salvaggio v. Houston Independent School Dist., 752 S.W.2d 189 (Tex. App. Houston 14th Dist. 1988)
1 ALR6th 229—§ 9

Salvaggio v. North Dakota Dept. of Transp., 477 N.W.2d 195 (N.D. 1991)
92 ALR6th 295—§ 3, 12
95 ALR6th 1—§ 28
96 ALR6th 355—§ 36, 45

Salvamoser v. Pratt Inst., 150 App. Div. 2d 666, 541 N.Y.S.2d 540 (2d Dep't 1989)
43 ALR5th 207—§ 57

Salvati v. Blaw-Knox Food and Chemical Equipment, Inc., 130 Misc. 2d 626, 497 N.Y.S.2d 242 (Sup 1985)
13 ALR6th 355—§ 7, 40, 46

Salvation Army v. Mathews, 847 S.W.2d 751 (Ky. Ct. App. 1993)
33 ALR6th 251—§ 7

Salvation Army v. Security Roofing Co., 255 Ala. 349, 51 So. 2d 513 (1951)
91 ALR5th 1—§ 3

Salvato v. State, 814 P.2d 741 (Alaska App. 1991)
15 ALR5th 391—§ 45

Salvatore v. Harper Woods, 372 Mich. 14, 124 N.W.2d 780 (1963)
31 ALR5th 572—§ 2
33 ALR5th 205—§ 2, 6, 7

Salvatore v. State, 366 So. 2d 745 (Fla. 1978)
24 ALR6th 1—§ 18

Salvatori Corp. v. Rubin, 159 Ga. App. 369, 283 S.E.2d 326 (1981)
85 ALR6th 323—§ 29

Salver v. Com., 2010 WL 3927766 (Ky. Ct. App. 2010)
63 ALR6th 351—§ 3

Salvi v. Montgomery Ward & Co., 140 Ill. App. 3d 896, 95 Ill. Dec. 173, 489 N.E.2d 394, CCH Prod. Liab. Rep. ¶ 11084 (1st Dist. 1986)
15 ALR5th 119—§ 5

Salvitti v. Zoning Bd. of Adjustment of Kennedy Tp., 429 Pa. 330, 240 A.2d 534 (1968)
73 ALR5th 223—§ 9

Salvo v. Hewitt, Coleman & Associates, Inc., 274 S.C. 34, 260 S.E.2d 708 (1979)
13 ALR5th 289—§ 48

Salvo v. Ottaway Newspapers, Inc., 57 Mass. App. Ct. 255, 782 N.E.2d 535 (2003)
22 ALR6th 553—§ 8, 10, 16

Salvo v. Salem News Pub. Co., 4 Media L. R. 1856 (Mass. Dist. Ct. 1978)
19 ALR5th 1—§ 62, 104

Salvucci v. Gold Seal Rubber Co., 343 Mass. 120, 177 N.E.2d 578 (1961)
5 ALR5th 875—§ 2

Salyer, In Interest of, 44 Ill. App. 3d 854, 3 Ill. Dec. 648, 358 N.E.2d 1333 (3d Dist. 1977)
55 ALR5th 125—§ 3, 7

Salyer v. Clinchfield Coal Corp., 191 Va. 331, 61 S.E.2d 16 (1950)
86 ALR5th 295—§ 4

Salyer v. McLaughlin, 100 App. D.C. 29, 240 F.2d 891 (1957)

1 ALR5th 622—§ 10, 14, 17

Salzano v. First Nat. Stores, Inc., 268 App. Div. 993, 51 N.Y.S.2d 645 (1944)

1 ALR5th 1—§ 25, 30

Salzano v. Goulet, 39 Conn. L. Rptr. 166, 2005 WL 1154225 (Conn. Super. Ct. 2005)

47 ALR6th 1—§ 25

Salzano v. New York, 22 App. Div. 2d 656, 253 N.Y.S.2d 138 (1st Dep't 1964)

35 ALR5th 1—§ 3

Salzano v. North Jersey Media Group, Inc., 131 S. Ct. 1045, 178 L. Ed. 2d 864 (2011)

66 ALR6th 635—§ 27

Salzano v. North Jersey Media Group Inc., 201 N.J. 500, 993 A.2d 778, 38 Media L. Rep. (BNA) 1769 (2010)

66 ALR6th 635—§ 27

Salzarulo v. Salzarulo, 2004 WL 728907 (Conn. Super. Ct. 2004)

36 ALR6th 1—§ 18, 19

Salzman v. State, 591 So. 2d 1107, 17 FLW D 164 (Fla. App. D2 1992)

29 ALR5th 59—§ 35

Salzman & Salzman v. Home Ins. Co., 258 A.D.2d 455, 684 N.Y.S.2d 601 (2d Dep't 1999)

92 ALR5th 273—§ 19

Salzwedel v. Pinkley, 140 Or. 671, 15 P.2d 718 (1932)

125 ALR5th 1—§ 5

S.A.M., In Interest of, 703 S.W.2d 603 (Mo. Ct. App. S.D. 1986)

63 ALR6th 429—§ 3

S.A.M., In re, 826 So. 2d 1266 (Miss. 2002)

10 ALR6th 173—§ 2, 35

S.A.M., Matter of Welfare of, 570 N.W.2d 162 (Minn. Ct. App. 1997)

116 ALR5th 373—§ 3, 16

Sam v. Commonwealth, Unemployment Compensation Bd. of Review, 107 Pa. Cmwlth. 624, 528 A.2d 1067 (1987)

23 ALR5th 176—§ 19

Sam v. Delta Downs, Inc., 564 So. 2d 829 (La. App. 3d Cir. 1990)

35 ALR5th 731—§ 2, 18

Sam v. State, 771 S.W.2d 210 (Tex. App. Houston 1st Dist. 1989)

86 ALR5th 463—§ 5

Sam v. State, 1973 OK CR 264, 510 P.2d 978 (Okla. Crim. App. 1973)

85 ALR5th 471—§ 4, 7

Samadder v. Kramer, 138 Ohio App. 3d 111, 740 N.E.2d 685 (10th Dist. Franklin County 2000)

28 ALR5th 107—§ 5.5

Samanie v. Bourg, 434 So. 2d 149 (La. App. 5th Cir. 1983)

48 ALR5th 129—§ 19

50 ALR5th 1—§ 11

Samaniego v. City of Kodiak, 2 P.3d 78 (Alaska 2000)

52 ALR6th 623—§ 4

Samaniego v. State, 633 S.W.2d 915 (Tex. App. El Paso 1982)

49 ALR6th 343—§ 29

Samanski v. Otis Elevator Co., 216 A.D.2d 376, 628 N.Y.S.2d 170 (2d Dep't 1995)

115 ALR5th 1—§ 23

Samansky v. Rush-Presbyterian-St. Luke's Medical Center, 208 Ill. App. 3d 377, 153 Ill. Dec. 428, 567 N.E.2d 386 (1st Dist. 1990)

31 ALR5th 1—§ 12, 19

Samantar v. Yousuf, 130 S. Ct. 2278 (2010)

56 ALR6th 679—§ 26

Samantha B., In re, 2003 WL 22463987 (Cal. App. 2d Dist. 2003)

59 ALR6th 161—§ 6, 37

60 ALR6th 193—§ 21

Samantha P., Adoption of, 2013 WL 705814 (Cal. App. 2d Dist. 2013)

96 ALR6th 103—§ 3

Samara Bros., Inc. v. Wal-Mart Stores, Inc., 165 F.3d 120, 49 U.S.P.Q.2d 1260 (2d Cir. 1998)

76 ALR6th 289—§ 5

77 ALR6th 543—§ 9, 13

Samarah v. Danek Med., Inc., 70 F.
Supp. 2d 1196, Prod. Liab. Rep.
(CCH) ¶ 15708 (D. Kan. 1999)
26 ALR5th 628—§ 21, 24, 25
28 ALR5th 1—§ 3
57 ALR5th 1—§ 3, 6
Samaritan Center, Inc. v. Borough of
Englishtown, 294 N.J. Super. 437,
683 A.2d 611 (Law Div. 1996)
123 ALR5th 349—§ 6
Samaritan Found. v. Goodfarb, 176 Ariz.
497, 862 P.2d 870, 152 Ariz. Adv.
Rep. 14 (1993)
26 ALR5th 628—§ 3
27 ALR5th 76—§ 3
Samaritano v. Samaritano, 172 A.D.2d
817, 570 N.Y.S.2d 984 (2d Dep't
1991)
109 ALR5th 1—§ 2
Samarkand of Santa Barbara, Inc. v.
Santa Barbara County, 216 Cal.
App. 2d 341, 31 Cal. Rptr. 151 (2d
Dist. 1963)
1 ALR6th 1—§ 12
Samatar v. Clarridge, 2006 WL 355684
(S.D. Ohio 2006)
103 ALR6th 247—§ 11
Sam A. Tisci, Inc. v. State Farm Fire &
Casualty Co., 48 Ohio App. 3d 155,
548 N.E.2d 978 (Lucas Co. 1988)
1 ALR5th 817—§ 18
S. A. Maxwell Co. v. De Soto, Inc., 73
Ill. App. 3d 844, 29 Ill. Dec. 476,
392 N.E.2d 33 (1st Dist. 1979)
40 ALR5th 57—§ 4
Samayoa v. Ayers, 649 F.3d 919 (9th
Cir. 2011)
102 ALR6th 417—§ 32
Samba v. Delligard, 116 A.D.2d 563,
497 N.Y.S.2d 419 (2d Dep't 1986)
42 ALR6th 545—§ 20, 23
**43 ALR6th 375—§ 9, 10, 21, 22, 49,
50**
Samber v. Mullinax Ford E., 173 Ohio
App. 3d 585, 2007-Ohio-5778, 879
N.E.2d 814 (11th Dist. Lake County
2007)
66 ALR6th 351—§ 49, 51

Samborski v. West Valley Nuclear Ser-
vices, Co., Inc., 1999 WL 1293351
(W.D. N.Y. 1999)
82 ALR5th 1—§ 2
Sambou v. U.S., 2010 WL 3363034
(E.D. N.C. 2010)
68 ALR6th 1—§ 10
Sambs v. Nowak, 47 Wis. 2d 158, 177
N.W.2d 144 (1970)
64 ALR5th 519—§ 6
Samco Properties, Inc. v. Cheatham, 977
S.W.2d 469 (Tex. App. Houston
14th Dist. 1998)
7 ALR6th 1—§ 37
Samedan Oil Corp. v. Deer, 1995 WL
431307 (D.D.C. June 14, 1995)
57 ALR5th 753—§ 8
Samek v. Sanders, 788 So. 2d 872, 122
A.L.R.5th 743 (Ala. 2000)
122 ALR5th 205—§ 3, 4, 41
Samek v. State, 688 N.E.2d 1286 (Ind.
Ct. App. 1997)
40 ALR5th 113—§ 3
24 ALR6th 1—§ 29
Sament v. Hahnemann Medical College
& Hospital, 547 F.2d 1164 (E.D.
Pa) 413 F. Supp. 434, affd without
op (CA3 Pa. 1976)
28 ALR5th 107—§ 5
Samet v. Procter & Gamble Co., 2013
WL 3124647 (N.D. Cal. 2013)
92 ALR6th 141—§ 4, 5
Samet v. Procter & Gamble Company,
2013 WL 6491143 (N.D. Cal. 2013)
92 ALR6th 141—§ 4
Samett v. Whelan, 147 Colo. 41, 362
P.2d 559 (1961)
46 ALR5th 1—§ 13
Sam Finley, Inc. v. Russell, 75 Ga. App.
112, 42 S.E.2d 452 (1947)
25 ALR5th 568—§ 34
Sami v. U. S., 617 F.2d 755, 57 A.L.R.
Fed. 245 (D.C. Cir. 1979)
100 ALR5th 341—§ 6
Samide v. Roman Catholic Diocese of
Brooklyn, 5 A.D.3d 463, 773
N.Y.S.2d 116 (2d Dep't 2004)
27 ALR6th 565—§ 8

Samiento v. World Yacht Inc., 10
  N.Y.3d 70, 854 N.Y.S.2d 83, 883
  N.E.2d 990, 13 Wage & Hour Cas.
  2d (BNA) 587, 155 Lab. Cas.
  (CCH) ¶ 60569, 61 A.L.R.6th 649
  (2008)
  61 ALR6th 61—§ 14
Samii v. Baystate Medical Center, Inc.,
  8 Mass. App. 911, 395 N.E.2d 455
  (1979)
  3 ALR5th 146—§ 12
Sammamish Community Council v. City
  of Bellevue, 108 Wash. App. 46, 29
  P.3d 728 (Div. 1 2001)
  123 ALR5th 349—§ 7
Sammi Line Co. v. Altamar Navegacion
  S.A., 605 F. Supp. 72, 1985 AMC
  1790 (S.D. N.Y. 1985)
  60 ALR5th 669—§ 6
Sammons v. Broward Bank, 599 So. 2d
  1018 (Fla. App. D4 1992)
  25 ALR5th 696—§ 6
Sammons v. Cameron, 2005 WL
  1027509 (M.D. Fla. 2005)
  95 ALR6th 341—§ 14
Sammons v. Nabers, 186 Ga. 161, 197
  S.E. 284 (1938)
  36 ALR6th 387—§ 5
Sammons v. Pennsylvania State Police,
  931 A.2d 784 (Pa. Commw. Ct.
  2007)
  69 ALR6th 1—§ 14
Sammons v. Ridgeway, 293 A.2d 547
  (Del. Sup. 1972)
  16 ALR5th 1—§ 11, 14
Sammons v. Rotroff, 653 S.W.2d 740
  (Tenn. App. 1983)
  4 ALR5th 273—§ 18, 20, 34, 40, 41
Sammons v. Sibarco Stations, Inc., 10
  Or. App. 43, 497 P.2d 862 (1972)
  73 ALR5th 223—§ 8
Sammons v. Trust Co. of Florida, 102
  Fla. 711, 136 So. 442 (1931)
  86 ALR6th 411—§ 2
Samoila v. Unemployment Compensation Admr., 16 Conn. Supp. 333
  (1949)
  2 ALR5th 475—§ 15

Samolin v. Trans World Airlines, Inc.,
  20 A.D.2d 160, 245 N.Y.S.2d 628
  (3d Dep't 1963)
  107 ALR5th 441—§ 14
  109 ALR5th 161—§ 8
  20 ALR6th 641—§ 21
Samora v. State Farm Mut. Auto. Ins.
  Co., 119 N.M. 467, 892 P.2d 600
  (1995)
  40 ALR5th 603—§ 9
Sampang v. Detrick, 826 F. Supp. 174
  (W.D. Va. 1993)
  60 ALR6th 1—§ 90
Sampay v. Morton Salt Co., 395 So. 2d
  326, 24 A.L.R.4th 541 (La. 1981)
  6 ALR5th 883—§ 17, 20
Sampayo v. State, 625 S.W.2d 33 (Tex.
  App. San Antonio 1981)
  4 ALR5th 1—§ 2, 14
Samper v. University of Rochester
  Strong Memorial Hosp., 139 Misc.
  2d 580, 528 N.Y.S.2d 958, 47 Ed.
  Law Rep. 284 (Sup. Ct. 1987)
  83 ALR5th 1—§ 3
Sample, Re Estate of, 175 Mont. 93, 572
  P.2d 1232 (1977)
  1 ALR5th 965—§ 3, 5
Sample v. Chicago, B. & Q. R. Co., 233
  Ill. 564, 84 N.E. 643 (1908)
  15 ALR5th 119—§ 29
Sample v. Louisiana Oil Refining Corp.,
  162 La. 941, 111 So. 336 (1927)
  62 ALR5th 219—§ 7
Sample v. State, 601 N.E.2d 457 (Ind.
  Ct. App. 1st Dist. 1992)
  118 ALR5th 253—§ 14, 16
Sample v. Town of Verona, 94 Miss.
  264, 48 So. 2 (1909)
  5 ALR6th 1—§ 16, 33
Sample v. U.S., 178 F. Supp. 259 (D.C.
  Minn. 1959)
  27 ALR5th 174—§ 101
Samples v. City of Atlanta, 916 F.2d
  1548, 31 Fed. R. Evid. Serv. 1270
  (11th Cir. 1990)
  95 ALR6th 641—§ 5
Samples v. Geary, 292 S.W. 1066 (Mo.
  App. 1927)

For assistance, call 1-800-328-4880

54 ALR5th 393—§ 12
Samples v. Kouts, 954 S.W.2d 593 (Mo. Ct. App. W.D. 1997)
1 ALR6th 493—§ 14, 35
4 ALR6th 531—§ 3, 20
Samples v. Ohio State Racing Com., 25 Ohio Ops. 2d 265, 92 Ohio L. Abs. 481, 193 N.E.2d 552 (CP Ct. 1963)
59 ALR5th 203—§ 14, 47, 48
Samples v. Samples, 414 F. Supp. 773 (W.D. Okla. 1976)
52 ALR5th 221—§ 2
Samples v. State, 151 Ga. App. 179, 259 S.E.2d 178 (1979)
66 ALR5th 397—§ 4
Sampley v. Morris, 632 P.2d 837 (Utah 1981)
72 ALR6th 141—§ 14
Samply v. Integrity Ins. Co., 476 So. 2d 79 (Ala. 1985)
16 ALR6th 603—§ 6
Sampognaro v. Sampognaro, 222 La. 597, 63 So. 2d 11 (1953)
120 ALR5th 229—§ 4
Sampson, In re, 259 S.C. 471, 192 S.E.2d 859 (1972)
26 ALR6th 1—§ 7
Sampson, Re, 29 N.Y.2d 900, 328 N.Y.S.2d 686, 278 N.E.2d 918 (1972)
21 ALR5th 248—§ 3, 7
Sampson, Re, 65 Misc. 2d 658, 317 N.Y.S.2d 641 (1970)
21 ALR5th 248—§ 7
Sampson v. Administrator, Louisiana Office of Employment Sec., 439 So. 2d 458, 14 Ed. Law Rep. 416 (La. Ct. App. 2d Cir. 1983)
95 ALR5th 329—§ 6
Sampson v. Camperdown Cotton Mills, 64 F. 939 (C.C.D. S.C. 1894)
109 ALR5th 421—§ 5
Sampson v. Camperdown Cotton Mills, 82 F. 833 (C.C.D.S.C. 1897)
74 ALR5th 369—§ 10
Sampson v. City of Cedar Falls, 231 N.W.2d 609 (Iowa 1975)
122 ALR5th 337—§ 2, 3

Sampson v. Contillo, 55 A.D.3d 588, 865 N.Y.S.2d 634 (2d Dep't 2008)
64 ALR6th 249—§ 19
Sampson v. Conway, 386 F. Supp. 2d 173 (W.D. N.Y. 2005)
103 ALR6th 247—§ 20
Sampson v. Davis, 58 Fed. Appx. 217 (7th Cir. 2003)
119 ALR5th 1—§ 34
Sampson v. Department of Social & Health Services, 61 Wash. App. 488, 814 P.2d 204 (1991)
38 ALR5th 433—§ 15
Sampson v. Hughes, 147 Cal. 62, 81 P. 292 (1905)
25 ALR5th 391—§ 87
Sampson v. McAdoo, 47 Md. App. 602, 425 A.2d 1 (1981)
39 ALR5th 33—§ 12, 13
Sampson v. Sampson, 14 P.3d 272 (Alaska 2000)
38 ALR6th 313—§ 10
Sampson v. Sampson, 63 Me. 328, 1874 WL 3608 (1874)
76 ALR6th 31—§ 28
Sampson v. Sampson, 112 Wash. 1, 191 P. 840 (1920)
1 ALR5th 776—§ 2
Sampson v. Sampson, 223 Mass. 451, 112 N.E. 84 (1916)
23 ALR6th 1—§ 6
Sampson v. Sapoznik, 124 Cal. App. 2d 709, 269 P.2d 209 (1954)
50 ALR5th 653—§ 7
Sampson v. State, 31 P.3d 88 (Alaska 2001)
96 ALR6th 475—§ 5, 6
Sampson v. State, 478 N.W.2d 566 (N.D. 1991)
84 ALR6th 427—§ 13
Sampson v. Town of Salisbury, 441 F. Supp. 2d 271 (D. Mass. 2006)
68 ALR6th 229—§ 6
Sampson v. Veenboer, 252 Mich. 660, 234 N.W. 170 (1931)
98 ALR6th 1—§ 35

Sampson v. Washington Mut. Bank, 453
Fed. Appx. 863 (11th Cir. 2011)
81 ALR6th 161—§ 5
82 ALR6th 43—§ 7
Sampson v. W. F. Enterprises, Inc., 611
S.W.2d 333 (Mo. Ct. App. W.D.
1980)
91 ALR5th 1—§ 6
Sams v. Boston, 181 W. Va. 706, 384
S.E.2d 151, 6 A.L.R.5th 1033
(1989)
6 ALR5th 1—§ 28
16 ALR5th 650—§ 15
40 ALR5th 227—§ 12
Sams v. Brotherhood of Ry. and S. S.
Clerks, Sumter Lodge No. 6193,
233 F.2d 263, 38 L.R.R.M. (BNA)
2133, 30 Lab. Cas. (CCH) ¶ 69977
(4th Cir. 1956)
105 ALR5th 243—§ 13, 23
Sams v. Englewood Ready-Mix Corp.,
22 Ohio App. 2d 168, 51 Ohio Ops.
2d 315, 259 N.E.2d 507 (1969)
60 ALR5th 413—§ 5
Sams v. Ezy-Way Foodliner Co., 157
Me. 10, 170 A.2d 160 (1961)
1 ALR5th 1—§ 28
Sams v. Kendall Const. Co., 499 So. 2d
370 (La. Ct. App. 4th Cir. 1986)
47 ALR6th 303—§ 4
Sams v. Ohio Valley General Hospital
Asso., 413 F.2d 826 (CA4 W. Va.
1969)
28 ALR5th 107—§ 5, 9
Sams v. Olah, 225 Ga. 497, 169 S.E.2d
790 (1969)
105 ALR5th 243—§ 15
Sams v. Rhett, 27 S.C.L. 171, 2 McMul.
171, 1842 WL 2361 (Ct. App. Law
1842)
15 ALR6th 427—§ 4
Sams v. State, 239 Ga. App. 715, 521
S.E.2d 848 (1999)
29 ALR6th 1—§ 10
Sams v. State, 980 S.W.2d 294 (Mo.
1998)
37 ALR6th 357—§ 62
Sams v. U.S., 721 A.2d 945 (D.C. 1998)

16 ALR6th 329—§ 11
24 ALR6th 591—§ 9
Samsel v. Wheeler Trans. Servs., 246
Kan. 336, 789 P.2d 541 (1990)
26 ALR5th 245—§ 19
Sam's Furniture and Appliance Stores
of Olean, N.Y., Inc., In re, 1 U.C.C.
Rep. Serv. 422 (Bankr. W.D. Pa.
1962)
58 ALR6th 289—§ 5, 24
Samson, In re Marriage of, 245 Mont.
464, 802 P.2d 1241 (1990)
59 ALR6th 433—§ 52
Samson v. California, 126 S. Ct. 2193
(U.S. 2006)
16 ALR6th 767—§ 37
Samson v. California, 547 U.S. 843, 126
S. Ct. 2193, 165 L. Ed. 2d 250
(2006)
92 ALR6th 1—§ 7, 10
Samson v. Greenville Hosp. System, 295
S.C. 359, 368 S.E.2d 665, Prod.
Liab. Rep. (CCH) ¶ 11809, 5 U.C.C.
Rep. Serv. 2d (CBC) 1274 (1988)
75 ALR5th 229—§ 3
Samson v. Greenville Hosp. System, 297
S.C. 409, 377 S.E.2d 311, Prod.
Liab. Rep. (CCH) ¶ 12084 (1989)
64 ALR5th 333—§ 31
75 ALR5th 229—§ 8
Samson v. O'Hara, 239 So. 2d 151 (Fla.
Dist. Ct. App. 2d Dist. 1970)
64 ALR5th 1—§ 8
Samson v. Riesing, 62 Wis. 2d 698, 215
N.W.2d 662, 14 U.C.C. Rep. Serv.
618 (1974)
2 ALR5th 1—§ 73, 76, 81
89 ALR5th 319—§ 2
Samson v. Saginaw Professional Bldg.,
Inc., 393 Mich. 393, 224 N.W.2d
843 (1975)
43 ALR5th 207—§ 5, 81
Samson v. Southern Bell Tel. & Tel.
Co., 205 So. 2d 496 (La. Ct. App.
1st Cir. 1967)
97 ALR5th 1—§ 2, 5
106 ALR5th 111—§ 2
108 ALR5th 1—§ 2

Samson v. Trend Development Inc., 84
  Wash. App. 1066, 1997 WL 11977
  (Div. 1 1997)
  104 ALR6th 303—§ 8
Samson v. Trustees of Columbia University, 101 Misc. 146, 167 N.Y.S. 202
  (1917)
  46 ALR5th 581—§ 8
  47 ALR5th 1—§ 15, 22
Samson Sales, Inc. v. Honeywell, Inc.,
  12 Ohio St. 3d 27, 465 N.E.2d 392
  (1984)
  36 ALR6th 305—§ 10
Sams, State ex rel. v. Ohio Valley General Hospital Ass'n, 149 W. Va.
  229, 140 S.E.2d 457 (1965)
  28 ALR5th 107—§ 3, 5
Samstag v. McDonough., 1975 WL
  182931 (Ohio Ct. App. 8th Dist.
  Cuyahoga County 1975)
  99 ALR6th 1—§ 7
Samsung Electronics America, Inc. v.
  Federal Ins. Co., 202 S.W.3d 372,
  32 A.L.R.6th 835 (Tex. App. Dallas
  2006)
  32 ALR6th 505—§ 3 to 7
  49 ALR6th 169—§ 7
Sam Teague, Ltd. v. Hawai'i Civil
  Rights Com'n, 89 Haw. 269, 971
  P.2d 1104, 74 Empl. Prac. Dec.
  (CCH) ¶ 45721, 75 Empl. Prac.
  Dec. (CCH) ¶ 45721 (1999)
  99 ALR5th 1—§ 3
Samuel v. Braun Elevator Consultants,
  Inc., 204 A.D.2d 176, 612 N.Y.S.2d
  17 (1st Dep't 1994)
  115 ALR5th 1—§ 3
Samuel v. Curry County, 55 Or. App.
  653, 639 P.2d 687 (1982)
  28 ALR5th 107—§ 23
Samuel v. Ford Motor Co., 112 F. Supp.
  2d 460 (D. Md. 2000)
  38 ALR5th 683—§ 10
Samuel v. Hepworth, Nungester & Lez-
  amiz, Inc., 134 Idaho 84, 996 P.2d
  303 (2000)
  58 ALR6th 1—§ 5

Samuel v. Merrill Lynch Pierce Fenner
  & Smith, 771 F. Supp. 47, 60 Fair
  Empl. Prac. Cas. (BNA) 100 (S.D.
  N.Y. 1991)
  103 ALR5th 557—§ 5
Samuel v. Michaud, 980 F. Supp. 1381
  (D. Idaho 1996)
  95 ALR6th 341—§ 39
Samuel v. Porchia, 40 App. Div. 2d 697,
  336 N.Y.S.2d 387 (2d Dep't 1972)
  35 ALR5th 1—§ 7
Samuel v. Samuel, 64 A.D.3d 920, 881
  N.Y.S.2d 729 (3d Dep't 2009)
  100 ALR6th 1—§ 15
Samuel v. State, 222 So. 2d 3 (Fla. 1969)
  43 ALR5th 1—§ 13, 14
Samuel v. University of Pittsburgh, 395
  F. Supp. 1275 (W.D. Pa. 1975)
  49 ALR6th 93—§ 6
Samuel v. Vanderheiden, 277 Or. 239,
  560 P.2d 636 (1977)
  92 ALR6th 379—§ 20
Samuel v. Vicknair, 718 So. 2d 634 (La.
  Ct. App. 2d Cir. 1998)
  50 ALR5th 1—§ 12
Samuel v. Woodford, 2011 WL 1361533
  (C.D. Cal. 2011)
  101 ALR6th 207—§ 32
Samuel M. Feinberg Testamentary Trust
  v. Carter, 652 F. Supp. 1066, Fed.
  Sec. L. Rep. (CCH) ¶ 93172 (S.D.
  N.Y. 1987)
  43 ALR6th 1—§ 42
Samuel N. Zarpas, Inc. v. Morrow, 215
  F. Supp. 887 (D.C. N.J. 1963)
  14 ALR5th 695—§ 28
Samuelov v. Carnival Cruise Lines, Inc.,
  870 So. 2d 853 (Fla. 3d DCA 2003)
  82 ALR6th 175—§ 25
Samuel Roberts Noble Foundation, Inc.
  v. Vick, 840 P.2d 619 (Okla. 1992)
  33 ALR5th 1—§ 6
Samuels, In re, 176 B.R. 616, 32 Collier
  Bankr. Cas. 2d (MB) 1185 (Bankr.
  M.D. Fla. 1994)
  32 ALR6th 531—§ 35, 39

Samuels, In re Application of, 70 Ohio St. 3d 537, 1994-Ohio-257, 639 N.E.2d 1151 (1994)

108 ALR5th 289—§ 10

8 ALR6th 1—§ 16, 35

Samuels, In re Application of, 1994-Ohio-257, 70 Ohio St. 3d 537, 639 N.E.2d 1151 (1994)

107 ALR5th 167—§ 16

Samuels v. American Cyanamid Co., 130 Misc. 2d 175, 495 N.Y.S.2d 1006 (Sup. 1985)

57 ALR5th 1—§ 2, 4

Samuels v. Blue Cross of Greater Philadelphia, 405 Pa. Super. 476, 592 A.2d 1310 (1991)

63 ALR5th 427—§ 3, 17

Samuels v. Commonwealth, 1995 WL 452360 (Va. Ct. App. 1995)

88 ALR5th 121—§ 3, 18, 22, 27

Samuels v. Employment Sec. Dep't, 37 Wash. App. 409, 680 P.2d 764 (1984)

33 ALR5th 643—§ 9

Samuels v. Harrison, 195 N.Y.S.2d 882 (Sup. 1959)

1 ALR5th 622—§ 19

Samuels v. Health and Hospitals Corp. of City of New York, 591 F.2d 195 (2d Cir. 1979)

75 ALR5th 229—§ 6

Samuels v. Holland American Line-USA Inc., 656 F.3d 948, 2011 A.M.C. 2441, 86 Fed. R. Evid. Serv. 564, 82 A.L.R.6th 625 (9th Cir. 2011)

82 ALR6th 175—§ 24

Samuels v. Mitchell, 155 F.R.D. 195, 28 Fed. R. Serv. 3d 1434 (N.D. Cal. 1994)

66 ALR6th 83—§ 7

Samuels v. Mix, 22 Cal. 4th 1, 91 Cal. Rptr. 2d 273, 989 P.2d 701 (1999)

13 ALR6th 1—§ 4

14 ALR6th 1—§ 4

Samuels v. State, 253 A.2d 201 (Del. Sup. 1969)

39 ALR5th 283—§ 4

Samuelson v. Chicago, R. I. & P. R. Co., 287 Minn. 264, 178 N.W.2d 620 (1970)

17 ALR6th 1—§ 16

Samuelson v. Taylor, 160 Wash. 369, 295 P. 113 (1931)

30 ALR5th 571—§ 32, 72

Samuels-Wickham v. Department of Public Safety, 121 S.W.3d 829 (Tex. App. Fort Worth 2003)

112 ALR5th 621—§ 9

Sam Warren & Son Stone Co. v. Gruesser, 307 Ky. 98, 209 S.W.2d 817 (1948)

103 ALR5th 157—§ 4, 11

Sanabria-Casares v. Crabtree, 73 F.3d 370 (9th Cir. 1995)

62 ALR6th 517—§ 62

San Angelo Nat. Bank v. Fitzpatrick, 88 Tex. 213, 30 S.W. 1053 (1895)

91 ALR5th 437—§ 11

97 ALR5th 537—§ 48

San Angelo Pro Hockey Club, Inc., In re, 292 B.R. 118 (Bankr. N.D. Tex. 2003)

107 ALR5th 311—§ 3

San Antonio v. Aguilar, 670 S.W.2d 681 (Tex. App. San Antonio 1984)

34 ALR5th 591—§ 19

San Antonio v. Easley, 368 S.W.2d 683 (Tex. Civ. App. San Antonio 1963)

15 ALR5th 821—§ 13

San Antonio v. State, 195 S.W.2d 421 (Tex. Civ. App. 1946)

17 ALR5th 195—§ 22

San Antonio & A. P. R. Co. v. Adams, 66 S.W. 578 (Tex. Civ. App. 1902)

17 ALR5th 547—§ 44

San Antonio & A. P. R. Co. v. Moerbe, 189 S.W. 128 (Tex. Civ. App. 1916)

17 ALR5th 547—§ 79

San Antonio & A. P. R. Co. v. Wilson, 4 Tex. App. Civ. Cas. 565, 19 S.W. 910 (1892)

18 ALR5th 577—§ 3, 4

San Antonio Bldg. and Const. Trades Council v. Warrior Constructors, Inc., 466 S.W.2d 815, 78 L.R.R.M. (BNA) 2016, 65 Lab. Cas. (CCH) ¶ 11906 (Tex. Civ. App. San Antonio 1970)
110 ALR5th 111—§ 3

San Antonio, City of v. Guido Bros. Const. Co., 460 S.W.2d 155 (Tex. Civ. App. Beaumont 1970)
81 ALR6th 363—§ 5, 10

San Antonio, City of v. Heim, 932 S.W.2d 287, 12 I.E.R. Cas. (BNA) 264 (Tex. App. Austin 1996)
37 ALR6th 137—§ 3, 5

San Antonio, City of v. Hotels.com, 2007 WL 1541184 (W.D. Tex. 2007)
61 ALR6th 387—§ 6, 10

San Antonio, City of v. Hotels.com, 2008 WL 2486043 (W.D. Tex. 2008)
61 ALR6th 387—§ 45

San Antonio, City of v. Pfeiffer, 216 S.W. 207 (Tex. Civ. App. San Antonio 1919)
54 ALR6th 201—§ 8

San Antonio, City of v. Texas Waste Systems, Inc., 2007 WL 2042768 (Tex. App. San Antonio 2007)
86 ALR6th 173—§ 6

San Antonio, City of v. Wallace, 161 Tex. 41, 338 S.W.2d 153 (1960)
65 ALR5th 1—§ 8, 14

San Antonio Community Hosp. v. Southern California Dist. Council of Carpenters, 125 F.3d 1230, 156 L.R.R.M. (BNA) 2364 (9th Cir. 1997)
94 ALR5th 149—§ 5, 10

San Antonio Express News v. Dracos, 922 S.W.2d 242 (Tex. App. San Antonio 1996)
19 ALR5th 1—§ 48.5

San Antonio Independent School Dist. v. Rodriguez, 411 U.S. 1, 93 S. Ct. 1278, 36 L. Ed. 2d 16 (1973)
70 ALR5th 169—§ 2, 4, 6

110 ALR5th 293—§ 3
90 ALR6th 235—§ 2
San Antonio Press, Inc. v. Custom Bilt Machinery, 852 S.W.2d 64 (Tex. App. San Antonio 1993)
121 ALR5th 157—§ 16, 17

San Antonio River Authority v. Garrett Bros., 528 S.W.2d 266 (Tex. Civ. App. San Antonio 1975)
49 ALR6th 205—§ 32

San Antonio, Tex., City of v. Hotels.Com, 80 Fed. R. Evid. Serv. 1526 (W.D. Tex. 2009)
61 ALR6th 387—§ 29, 34

San Antonio, Tex., City of v. Hotels.Com, 2009 WL 3698481 (W.D. Tex. 2009)
61 ALR6th 387—§ 6, 35 to 37

San Antonio, Tex,, City of v. Hotels.com, L.P., 2007 WL 1541184 (W.D. Tex. 2007)
61 ALR6th 387—§ 34

San Bernardino County, Cal. v. California, 129 S. Ct. 2380 (2009)
46 ALR6th 495—§ 11

San Bernardino County Dep't of Public Social Services v. Superior Court, 232 Cal. App. 3d 188, 283 Cal. Rptr. 332, 19 Media L. R. 1545 (4th Dist. 1991)
39 ALR5th 103—§ 34, 37, 41, 42, 45

San Bernardino County Flood Control Dist. v. Superior Court of San Bernardino County, 269 Cal. App. 2d 514, 75 Cal. Rptr. 24 (4th Dist. 1969)
49 ALR5th 769—§ 12

San Bernardino County Sheriff's etc. Assn. v. Board of Supervisors, 7 Cal. App. 4th 602, 8 Cal. Rptr. 2d 658 (4th Dist. 1992)
106 ALR5th 523—§ 28

San Bernardino Valley Audubon Soc. v. Metropolitan Water Dist., 71 Cal. App. 4th 382, 83 Cal. Rptr. 2d 836 (4th Dist. 1999)
44 ALR6th 325—§ 30

San Bernardino Valley Audubon Society v. City of Moreno Valley, 44 Cal. App. 4th 593, 51 Cal. Rptr. 2d 897 (4th Dist. 1996)
44 ALR6th 325—§ 2, 31
San Bernardino Valley Audubon Society, Inc. v. County of San Bernardino, 155 Cal. App. 3d 738, 202 Cal. Rptr. 423 (4th Dist. 1984)
106 ALR5th 523—§ 36
Sanbonmatsu v. Boyer, 45 A.D.2d 249, 357 N.Y.S.2d 245, 16 Fair Empl. Prac. Cas. (BNA) 1650, 8 Empl. Prac. Dec. (CCH) ¶ 9704 (4th Dep't 1974)
123 ALR5th 411—§ 9, 17
Sanborn v. Brooker & Wake Property Management, 178 Ariz. 425, 874 P.2d 982, 162 Ariz. Adv. Rep. 40, 1 BNA WH Cas. 2d 1603 (App. 1994)
23 ALR5th 241—§ 42
Sanborn v. Com., 754 S.W.2d 534 (Ky. 1988)
24 ALR6th 1—§ 20
Sanborn v. Com., 892 S.W.2d 542 (Ky. 1994)
93 ALR5th 327—§ 4, 7, 9
Sanborn v. Commonwealth, 754 S.W.2d 534 (Ky. 1988)
10 ALR5th 700—§ 29
Sanborn v. Sanborn, 123 N.H. 740, 465 A.2d 888 (1983)
95 ALR5th 533—§ 3
Sanborn v. State, 513 So. 2d 1380, 12 FLW 2475 (Fla. App. D3 1987)
39 ALR5th 283—§ 4, 22
Sanborn v. Village of Enosburg Falls, 87 Vt. 479, 89 A. 746 (1914)
54 ALR6th 201—§ 10
Sanborn v. Wagner, 354 F. Supp. 291 (D.C. Md. 1973)
12 ALR5th 195—§ 32
Sanborn Plastics Corp. v. St. Paul Fire & Marine Ins. Co., 84 Ohio App. 3d 302, 616 N.E.2d 988 (11th Dist. Geauga County 1993)
88 ALR5th 493—§ 3
89 ALR5th 1—§ 8

Sanborn, State ex rel. v. Koscot Interplanetary, Inc., 212 Kan. 668, 512 P.2d 416 (1973)
48 ALR6th 511—§ 19
Sanches v. Carrollton-Farmers Branch Independent School Dist., 647 F.3d 156, 270 Ed. Law Rep. 417 (5th Cir. 2011)
98 ALR6th 599—§ 88
Sanches v. Morris, 802 So. 2d 755 (La. Ct. App. 5th Cir. 2001)
92 ALR5th 273—§ 7
9 ALR6th 467—§ 15
Sanchez (Sweeney), Claim of, 231 A.D.2d 778, 646 N.Y.S.2d 906 (3d Dep't 1996)
47 ALR5th 775—§ 5
Sanchez, In re, 577 F. Supp. 7 (S.D. N.Y. 1983)
66 ALR5th 111—§ 4
Sanchez, In re, 991 S.W.2d 507 (Tex. App. Corpus Christi 1999)
86 ALR6th 519—§ 7
Sanchez, In re Detention of, 2009 WL 3237757 (Ariz. Ct. App. Div. 2 2009)
78 ALR6th 417—§ 39
Sanchez, Matter of, 422 Mich. 758, 375 N.W.2d 353 (1985)
92 ALR5th 379—§ 10
Sanchez v. Abdel-Misih, 533 A.2d 1254 (Del. 1987)
95 ALR6th 85—§ 40
Sanchez v. Archdiocese of San Antonio, 873 S.W.2d 87 (Tex. App. 1994)
9 ALR5th 321—§ 4, 5
11 ALR5th 588—§ 4
51 ALR5th 747—§ 3
Sanchez v. Ayala, 2009 WL 1145349 (Cal. App. 3d Dist. 2009)
70 ALR6th 209—§ 57
Sanchez v. Bally's Total Fitness Corp., 68 Cal. App. 4th 62, 79 Cal. Rptr. 2d 902 (2d Dist. 1998)
61 ALR6th 147—§ 11
Sanchez v. Bay General Hospital, 116 Cal. App. 3d 776, 172 Cal. Rptr. 342 (4th Dist. 1981)

11 ALR5th 1—§ 4

Sanchez v. Bay Shores Medical Group, 75 Cal. App. 4th 946, 89 Cal. Rptr. 2d 634 (2d Dist. 1999)

95 ALR6th 541—§ 64

Sanchez v. Catherwood, 27 A.D.2d 678, 276 N.Y.S.2d 44 (3d Dep't 1967)

27 ALR6th 123—§ 7

Sanchez v. City of Los Angeles, 2010 WL 2569049 (C.D. Cal. 2010)

62 ALR6th 413—§ 35
86 ALR6th 173—§ 6

Sanchez v. City of Los Angeles, 2010 WL 2572615 (C.D. Cal. 2010)

86 ALR6th 173—§ 6

Sanchez v. City of Tucson, 191 Ariz. 128, 953 P.2d 168 (1998)

15 ALR5th 119—§ 46

Sanchez v. Davila, 2010 WL 728377 (D.P.R. 2010)

89 ALR6th 1—§ 57

Sanchez v. Derby, 230 Neb. 782, 433 N.W.2d 523 (1989)

72 ALR5th 529—§ 20

Sanchez v. Eagle Alloy Inc., 254 Mich. App. 651, 658 N.W.2d 510 (2003)

121 ALR5th 523—§ 3, 8

Sanchez v. Fernandez, 915 So. 2d 192 (Fla. Dist. Ct. App. 4th Dist. 2005)

66 ALR6th 269—§ 15

Sanchez v. Friesner, 477 So. 2d 66, 10 FLW 2441 (Fla. App. D3 1985)

53 ALR5th 287—§ 4, 11

Sanchez v. Guerrero, 885 S.W.2d 487 (Tex. App. El Paso 1994)

117 ALR5th 155—§ 6, 11

Sanchez v. Hialeah Police Dept., 357 Fed. Appx. 229 (11th Cir. 2009)

65 ALR6th 93—§ 29

Sanchez v. Johnson & Johnson Medical, 860 S.W.2d 503 (Tex. App. El Paso 1993)

11 ALR5th 88—§ 6
19 ALR5th 439—§ 3, 7

Sanchez v. Kelly, 5 Misc. 3d 1024(A), 799 N.Y.S.2d 164 (Sup 2004)

91 ALR6th 435—§ 133

Sanchez v. Kelly, 34 A.D.3d 252, 823 N.Y.S.2d 400 (1st Dep't 2006)

91 ALR6th 435—§ 133

Sanchez v. L.D.S. Social Services, 680 P.2d 753 (Utah 1984)

28 ALR6th 349—§ 37

Sanchez v. L.D.S. Social Servs., 680 P.2d 753 (Utah 1984)

61 ALR5th 151—§ 14

Sanchez v. Liberty, 42 N.Y.2d 876, 397 N.Y.S.2d 782, 366 N.E.2d 870 (1977)

24 ALR5th 200—§ 24, 26

Sanchez v. Liberty, 49 App. Div. 2d 507, 375 N.Y.S.2d 901 (3d Dep't 1975)

24 ALR5th 200—§ 26

Sanchez v. Life Care Ctrs., 855 P.2d 1256, 8 BNA IER Cas. 1101 (Wyo. 1993)

17 ALR5th 1—§ 5, 6

Sanchez v. Lippincott, 89 A.D.2d 372, 455 N.Y.S.2d 457 (4th Dep't 1982)

50 ALR6th 95—§ 4

Sanchez v. Martinez, 99 N.M. 66, 653 P.2d 897 (Ct. App. 1982)

8 ALR6th 549—§ 2

Sanchez v. Matta, 229 F.R.D. 649 (D.N.M. 2004)

66 ALR6th 83—§ 4

Sanchez v. McCray, 349 Fed. Appx. 479 (11th Cir. 2009)

65 ALR6th 93—§ 42

Sanchez v. Medicorp Health System, 270 Va. 299, 618 S.E.2d 331 (2005)

64 ALR6th 249—§ 3

Sanchez v. Memorial General Hosp., 110 N.M. 683, 798 P.2d 1069 (App. 1990)

12 ALR5th 658—§ 4, 9, 12, 13, 22, 33

Sanchez v. Mulvaney, 274 S.W.3d 708 (Tex. App. San Antonio 2008)

46 ALR6th 1—§ 31

Sanchez v. Murphy, 385 F. Supp. 1362 (D.C. Nev 1974)

4 ALR5th 273—§ 6

Sanchez v. New York, 25 App. Div. 2d 731, 268 N.Y.S.2d 732 (1st Dep't 1966)
57 ALR5th 689—§ 17

Sanchez v. O'Leary, 1993 WL 96117 (N.D. Ill. 1993)
65 ALR6th 93—§ 63

Sanchez v. Parker, 1995 WL 489146 (Del. Fam. Ct. 1995)
86 ALR6th 1—§ 50

Sanchez v. Puerto Rico Oil Co., 37 F.3d 712, 66 Fair Empl. Prac. Cas. (BNA) 148, 66 Empl. Prac. Dec. (CCH) ¶ 43439 (1st Cir. 1994)
51 ALR5th 1—§ 7
81 ALR5th 367—§ 21

Sanchez v. Rodriguez, 226 Cal. App. 2d 439, 38 Cal. Rptr. 110 (1964)
31 ALR5th 1—§ 14, 16
47 ALR5th 433—§ 3, 17

Sanchez v. Ryan, 315 Ill. App. 3d 1079, 248 Ill. Dec. 629, 734 N.E.2d 920 (1st Dist. 2000)
2 ALR5th 725—§ 10

Sanchez v. Sanchez, 777 F. Supp. 906 (D.C. N.M. 1991)
12 ALR5th 195—§ 36

Sanchez v. San Juan Concrete Co., 123 N.M. 537, 1997 -NMCA- 068, 943 P.2d 571 (Ct. App. 1997)
91 ALR5th 1—§ 3, 14

Sanchez v. Sirmons, 121 Misc. 2d 249, 467 N.Y.S.2d 757 (1983)
24 ALR5th 1—§ 9, 14

Sanchez v. South Hoover Hospital, 18 Cal. 3d 93, 132 Cal. Rptr. 657, 553 P.2d 1129 (1976)
19 ALR6th 475—§ 4

Sanchez v. State, 103 Nev. 166, 734 P.2d 726 (1987)
41 ALR5th 171—§ 17, 18, 22, 68

Sanchez v. State, 103 N.M. 25, 702 P.2d 345 (1985)
28 ALR5th 754—§ 5

Sanchez v. State, 582 S.W.2d 813 (Tex. Crim. App. 1979)
114 ALR5th 173—§ 4

Sanchez v. State, 600 So. 2d 1256 (Fla. Dist. Ct. App. 2d Dist. 1992)
46 ALR6th 241—§ 9

Sanchez v. State, 636 So. 2d 187, 19 FLW 986 (Fla. App. D3 1994)
45 ALR5th 1—§ 5, 32

Sanchez v. State, 692 N.W.2d 812, 16 A.L.R.6th 825 (Iowa 2005)
16 ALR6th 1—§ 38
16 ALR6th 131—§ 3

Sanchez v. State, 730 P.2d 328 (Colo. 1986)
48 ALR5th 659—§ 34

Sanchez v. State, 760 S.W.2d 731 (Tex. App. Corpus Christi 1988)
49 ALR6th 343—§ 24

Sanchez v. State, 797 S.W.2d 951 (Tex. App. Dallas 1990)
20 ALR5th 398—§ 25, 30, 53, 57

Sanchez v. State, 841 P.2d 85 (Wyo. 1992)
72 ALR5th 403—§ 10, 19

Sanchez v. State, 842 S.W.2d 732 (Tex. App. San Antonio 1992)
19 ALR6th 697—§ 4

Sanchez v. State, 931 S.W.2d 331 (Tex. App. San Antonio 1996)
117 ALR5th 513—§ 19

Sanchez v. State, 2010 WL 4237307 (Tex. App. Amarillo 2010)
99 ALR6th 397—§ 17

Sanchez v. Swinerton & Walberg Co., 47 Cal. App. 4th 1461, 55 Cal. Rptr. 2d 415 (2d Dist. 1996)
75 ALR5th 413—§ 3, 6, 8, 10, 11, 25

Sanchez v. The New Mexican, 106 N.M. 76, 738 P.2d 1321, 2 I.E.R. Cas. (BNA) 1427, 109 Lab. Cas. (CCH) ¶ 55918 (1987)
105 ALR5th 351—§ 3

Sanchez v. Turner, 2002 WL 1343754 (S.D. N.Y. 2002)
70 ALR6th 513—§ 11
71 ALR6th 471—§ 9

Sanchez v. Unemployment Appeals Comm'n, 665 So. 2d 1138, 21 FLW D95 (Fla. App. D5 1996)
33 ALR5th 643—§ 11.5

For assistance, call 1-800-328-4880

Sanchez v. Unemployment Ins. Appeals Board, 20 Cal. 3d 55, 141 Cal. Rptr. 146, 569 P.2d 740 (1977)
2 ALR5th 475—§ 2, 8, 11, 18
Sanchez v. U.S., 696 F.2d 213, 83-1 U.S. Tax Cas. (CCH) ¶ 9126, 35 U.C.C. Rep. Serv. 244, 51 A.F.T.R.2d 83-399 (2d Cir. 1982)
47 ALR6th 347—§ 5
Sanchez v. Vargo, 2014 WL 1165862 (E.D. Va. 2014)
102 ALR6th 637—§ 3, 5, 12, 13
Sanchez v. Wali, 2002 WL 44424 (Cal. App. 2d Dist. 2002)
95 ALR6th 85—§ 38
Sanchez v. Walls, 59 Ill. App. 3d 75, 16 Ill. Dec. 507, 375 N.E.2d 138 (2d Dist. 1978)
52 ALR5th 491—§ 14
Sanchez v. Wiley, 124 N.M. 47
33 ALR5th 303—§ 6
Sanchez By and Through DiFerdinando v. School Dist. 9-R, 902 P.2d 450, 23 A.D.D. 1266, 103 Ed. Law Rep. 838 (Colo. Ct. App. 1995)
66 ALR5th 1—§ 2, 47
Sanchez-Corea v. Bank of America, 38 Cal. 3d 892, 215 Cal. Rptr. 679, 701 P.2d 826 (1985)
18 ALR5th 307—§ 2
Sanchez Dieppa v. Rodriguez Pereira, 580 F. Supp. 735 (D.C. Puerto Rico 1984)
52 ALR5th 221—§ 29
Sanchez-Llamas v. Oregon, 2006 WL 1749688 (U.S. 2006)
16 ALR6th 767—§ 44
Sanchez-Rengifo v. U.S., 815 A.2d 351 (D.C. 2002)
71 ALR6th 1—§ 5
Sanchez Sepulveda v. Motorola Electronica De Puerto Rico, Inc., 988 F. Supp. 34 (D.P.R. 1997)
51 ALR5th 1—§ 5
Sanchez, State ex rel. v. Industrial Com'n of Ohio, 18 Ohio St. 3d 46, 479 N.E.2d 864 (1985)
31 ALR6th 199—§ 48

Sancken Associates, Inc. v. Stokes, 119 Ga. App. 282, 166 S.E.2d 924 (1969)
45 ALR5th 251—§ 23
Sanco Enterprises, Inc. v. Christian, 1972 OK 42, 495 P.2d 404 (Okla. 1972)
79 ALR6th 211—§ 7, 41
Sancourt Realty Corporation v. Dowling, 220 A.D. 660, 222 N.Y.S. 288 (1st Dep't 1927)
75 ALR5th 1—§ 3
Sanctions for Amato, In re, 2010-Ohio-67, 2010 WL 117709 (Ohio Ct. App. 8th Dist. Cuyahoga County 2010)
77 ALR6th 1—§ 7, 95
Sanctity of Human Life Network v. California Highway Patrol, 105 Cal. App. 4th 858, 129 Cal. Rptr. 2d 708 (3d Dist. 2003)
70 ALR6th 513—§ 5
71 ALR6th 471—§ 11
Sand v. Gold, 301 So. 2d 828 (Fla. App. D3 1974)
11 ALR5th 127—§ 29
Sand v. School Service Employees Union, Local 284, 402 N.W.2d 183 (Minn. Ct. App. 1987)
86 ALR6th 321—§ 10
91 ALR6th 171—§ 16
Sanda, Re Marriage of, 245 Ill. App. 3d 314, 184 Ill. Dec. 186, 612 N.E.2d 1346 (2d Dist. 1993)
17 ALR5th 366—§ 12
Sanda v. Coverson, 122 Ohio St. 238, 171 N.E. 89 (1930)
21 ALR6th 81—§ 5, 17
S & A Corp. v. Berger Co., 111 Ga. App. 39, 140 S.E.2d 509 (1965)
8 ALR6th 549—§ 8, 20
Sandage v. Studebaker Bros. Mfg. Co., 142 Ind. 148, 41 N.E. 380 (1895)
20 ALR6th 211—§ 22
Sandaker, State ex rel. v. Olson, 65 N.D. 561, 260 N.W. 586 (1935)
87 ALR6th 633—§ 3

Sandall v. Hoskins, 137 P.2d 819 (Utah 1943)
35 ALR5th 285—§ 4

Sandbach, People ex rel. v. Weber, 403 Ill. 331, 86 N.E.2d 202 (1949)
51 ALR5th 747—§ 3

Sandberg v. Burns, 198 Minn. 472, 270 N.W. 575 (1936)
46 ALR5th 1—§ 2, 22

Sandberg v. Cavanaugh Timber Co., 95 Wash. 556, 164 P. 200 (1917)
17 ALR5th 547—§ 30

Sandberg v. Commissioner of Public Safety, 2002 WL 338115 (Minn. Ct. App. 2002)
17 ALR6th 327—§ 12

Sandbom v. BASF Wyandotte, Corp., 674 So. 2d 349 (La. Ct. App. 1st Cir. 1996)
105 ALR5th 95—§ 13

Sandbulte v. Farm Bureau Mut. Ins. Co., 343 N.W.2d 457 (Iowa 1984)
121 ALR5th 365—§ 2

Sandburg-Schiller v. Rosello, 119 Ill. App. 3d 318, 74 Ill. Dec. 690, 456 N.E.2d 192 (1st Dist. 1983)
84 ALR5th 69—§ 19

S & C. Co. v. Horne, 218 Va. 124, 235 S.E.2d 456 (1977)
62 ALR5th 475—§ 3, 6

Sandefer v. State, 2005 WL 1903314 (Tex. App. Tyler 2005)
34 ALR6th 1—§ 10

Sandefur, Estate of v. Greenway, 898 S.W.2d 667, Fed. Sec. L. Rep. (CCH) ¶ 98761 (Mo. Ct. App. W.D. 1995)
14 ALR6th 491—§ 5

Sandel, State ex rel. v. New Mexico Public Utility Com'n, 1999-NMSC-019, 127 N.M. 272, 980 P.2d 55 (1999)
80 ALR6th 1—§ 2, 12, 74, 107

Sander v. Dow Chem. Co., 252 Ill. App. 3d 403, 191 Ill. Dec. 877, 624 N.E.2d 1255 (1st Dist. 1993)
3 ALR5th 237—§ 10

Sander v. Geib, Elston, Frost Professional Ass'n, 506 N.W.2d 107 (S.D. 1993)
26 ALR5th 245—§ 2, 30
93 ALR6th 123—§ 71, 73

Sander v. Missouri Real Estate Com., 710 S.W.2d 896 (Mo. App. 1986)
7 ALR5th 474—§ 92, 155, 159

Sanderford v. Lombard, 685 So. 2d 1162 (La. Ct. App. 4th Cir. 1996)
115 ALR5th 589—§ 5

Sanderlen v. State, 590 So. 2d 18 (Fla. Dist. Ct. App. 4th Dist. 1991)
85 ALR5th 1—§ 51

Sanderlin v. Central School Dist., 6 Or. App. 429, 487 P.2d 1399 (1971)
23 ALR5th 1—§ 20

Sanders, Ex parte, 659 So. 2d 1036 (Ala. Crim. App. 1995)
85 ALR5th 471—§ 4, 6

Sanders v. Acclaim Entertainment, Inc., 188 F. Supp. 2d 1264, 163 Ed. Law Rep. 224, Prod. Liab. Rep. (CCH) ¶ 16310 (D. Colo. 2002)
106 ALR5th 337—§ 3, 7

Sanders v. Alan White Co., 10 Ark. App. 322, 663 S.W.2d 939 (1984)
12 ALR5th 658—§ 4, 9, 17, 33

Sanders v. American Broadcasting Co., 28 Media L. Rep. (BNA) 1183, 1999 WL 1458129 (Cal. App. 2d Dist. 1999)
106 ALR5th 523—§ 31

Sanders v. Anchor Co., 12 N.C. App. 362, 183 S.E.2d 312 (1971)
6 ALR6th 1—§ 26, 58

Sanders v. Baucum, 929 F. Supp. 1028 (N.D. Tex. 1996)
5 ALR5th 530—§ 5, 6
12 ALR5th 195—§ 30
14 ALR5th 242—§ 16, 30

Sanders v. Blockbuster, Inc., 127 S.W.3d 382 (Tex. App. Beaumont 2004)
20 ALR6th 211—§ 4

Sanders v. Blunt, 357 So. 2d 620 (La. Ct. App. 1st Cir. 1978)
17 ALR6th 159—§ 28

Sanders v. Bratton, 258 A.D.2d 422, 685
N.Y.S.2d 722 (1st Dep't 1999)
114 ALR5th 283—§ 3, 10
Sanders v. Brown, 128 S. Ct. 2427 (U.S.
2008)
36 ALR6th 681—§ 4
Sanders v. Brown, 178 Ga. App. 447,
343 S.E.2d 722 (1986)
6 ALR5th 162—§ 3
Sanders v. Brown, 504 F.3d 903, 2007-2
Trade Cas. (CCH) ¶ 75888 (9th Cir.
2007)
36 ALR6th 681—§ 4
Sanders v. Campbell, 231 Mich. 592,
204 N.W. 767 (1925)
25 ALR5th 233—§ 3
Sanders v. Casa View Baptist Church,
134 F.3d 331, 77 Fair Empl. Prac.
Cas. (BNA) 51, 74 Empl. Prac. Dec.
(CCH) ¶ 45532 (5th Cir. 1998)
5 ALR5th 530—§ 3, 5
101 ALR5th 1—§ 8
Sanders v. Casa View Baptist Church,
898 F. Supp. 1169 (N.D. Tex. 1995)
99 ALR5th 445—§ 6
Sanders v. Charleston Consol. R. & L.
Co., 154 S.C. 220, 151 S.E. 438
(1930)
19 ALR5th 622—§ 40
Sanders v. Chicago Transit Authority,
220 Ill. App. 3d 505, 163 Ill. Dec.
260, 581 N.E.2d 211 (1st Dist.
1991)
64 ALR5th 519—§ 10
Sanders v. City of Bakersfield, 2009 WL
3300253 (E.D. Cal. 2009)
56 ALR6th 1—§ 22, 29
Sanders v. City of Carthage, 330 Mo.
844, 51 S.W.2d 529 (1932)
95 ALR5th 29—§ 6, 7
Sanders v. City of Fresno, 65 Fed. R.
Serv. 3d 960, 59 U.C.C. Rep. Serv.
2d 1209 (E.D. Cal. 2006)
56 ALR6th 467—§ 11, 12, 20
Sanders v. City of Fresno, 551 F. Supp.
2d 1149 (E.D. Cal. 2008)
45 ALR6th 1—§ 2, 9, 23, 25
52 ALR6th 623—§ 7

Sanders v. City of Seattle, 160 Wash. 2d
198, 156 P.3d 874 (2007)
70 ALR6th 513—§ 13
71 ALR6th 471—§ 9
Sanders v. CleanNet of Southern California, Inc., 135 Fed. Appx. 936
(9th Cir. 2005)
45 ALR6th 493—§ 3, 30
Sanders v. Cohen, 2009 WL 4421265
(S.D. Fla. 2009)
89 ALR6th 1—§ 118
Sanders v. Com., 2002 WL 1307445
(Ky. 2002)
101 ALR5th 187—§ 3
Sanders v. Coman, 864 F. Supp. 496
(E.D.N.C. 1994)
76 ALR5th 239—§ 2, 3, 5, 13, 15
Sanders v. Commonwealth, 244 Ky. 77,
50 S.W.2d 37 (1932)
24 ALR5th 465—§ 14, 103, 109
Sanders v. Commonwealth, 609 S.W.2d
690 (Ky. 1980)
55 ALR5th 125—§ 12
Sanders v. Davidson, 258 A.D. 1058, 17
N.Y.S.2d 627 (2d Dep't 1940)
4 ALR6th 263—§ 12
Sanders v. Day, 2008 WL 748170 (M.D.
Ga. 2008)
65 ALR6th 93—§ 25
Sanders v. Dunlop Tire Corp., 706 So.
2d 716 (Ala. Civ. App. 1996)
14 ALR5th 1—§ 14
Sanders v. Eilers, 217 So. 2d 205 (La.
App. 1st Cir. 1968)
9 ALR5th 826—§ 19
Sanders v. Emery, 317 S.C. 230, 452
S.E.2d 636 (Ct. App. 1994)
6 ALR6th 229—§ 24
Sanders v. Farmers' State Bank, 228
S.W. 635 (Tex. Civ. App. 1921)
20 ALR5th 229—§ 15
Sanders v. Federal Apartments Ltd. Part-
nership, 733 So. 2d 45 (La. Ct. App.
2d Cir. 1999)
56 ALR5th 1—§ 3
Sanders v. Florida Elections Commis-
sion, 407 So. 2d 1069 (Fla. Dist. Ct.
App. 4th Dist. 1981)

CASES CITED IN ALR5th and ALR6th

51 ALR6th 359—§ 31
Sanders v. Francis, 277 Or. 593, 561 P.2d 1003 (1977)
117 ALR5th 155—§ 10
Sanders v. Gardner, 7 F. Supp. 2d 151 (E.D. N.Y. 1998)
46 ALR6th 185—§ 3, 17
Sanders v. General American Life Ins. Co., 364 So. 2d 1373 (La. App. 3d Cir. 1978)
23 ALR5th 241—§ 15
Sanders v. Gray, Inc., 183 N.C. App. 490, 645 S.E.2d 229 (2007)
98 ALR6th 417—§ 4, 8
Sanders v. Griffin, 134 Ga. App. 689, 215 S.E.2d 720 (1975)
34 ALR5th 77—§ 7
Sanders v. Home Indem. Ins. Co., 594 So. 2d 1345 (La. App. 3d Cir. 1991)
23 ALR5th 241—§ 15
Sanders v. Johnson, 191 Fed. Appx. 240 (4th Cir. 2006)
71 ALR6th 1—§ 8
Sanders v. Johnson, 859 S.W.2d 329 (Tenn. App. 1993)
10 ALR5th 680—§ 5
20 ALR5th 1—§ 4, 38
Sanders v. Kennedy, 794 F.2d 478 (9th Cir. 1986)
89 ALR6th 1—§ 48
Sanders v. Kuna Joint School Dist., 125 Idaho 872, 876 P.2d 154, 92 Ed. Law Rep. 656 (Ct. App. 1994)
66 ALR5th 1—§ 3
Sanders v. Lakes, 270 Ky. 98, 109 S.W.2d 36 (1937)
91 ALR5th 1—§ 3, 4, 17
Sanders v. Lockyer, 365 F. Supp. 2d 1093, 2005-1 Trade Cas. (CCH) ¶ 74753 (N.D. Cal. 2005)
25 ALR6th 435—§ 2, 9, 10, 12, 13, 15, 41
Sanders v. Martin, 662 So. 2d 241 (Ala. 1995)
99 ALR6th 1—§ 5
Sanders v. McCaughey, 192 So. 2d 774 (Fla. App. D2 1966)
5 ALR5th 422—§ 3

Sanders v. Monical Machinery Co., 163 Mich. App. 689, 415 N.W.2d 276 (1987)
43 ALR5th 545—§ 42
119 ALR5th 121—§ 3, 6
125 ALR5th 193—§ 5
2 ALR6th 279—§ 4
Sanders v. Nabisco, Inc., 359 So. 2d 46 (Fla. App. D1 1978)
1 ALR5th 1—§ 10
Sanders v. Narcotics Anonymous World Services, Inc., 2009 WL 726321 (Cal. App. 4th Dist. 2009)
45 ALR6th 493—§ 52
Sanders v. O'Callaghan, 111 Iowa 574, 82 N.W. 969 (1900)
11 ALR5th 127—§ 4
Sanders v. Otis Elevator Co., 232 A.D.2d 327, 649 N.Y.S.2d 19 (1st Dep't 1996)
115 ALR5th 1—§ 2, 36
Sanders v. Park Towne, Ltd., 2 Kan. App. 2d 313, 578 P.2d 1131 (1978)
14 ALR5th 242—§ 31
Sanders v. Pennsylvania Bd. of Probation and Parole, 958 A.2d 582 (Pa. Commw. Ct. 2008)
75 ALR6th 181—§ 23
Sanders v. Prentice-Hall Corp., 178 F.3d 1296 (6th Cir. 1999)
93 ALR5th 1—§ 9
Sanders v. Prince, 304 S.C. 236, 403 S.E.2d 640 (1991)
12 ALR5th 195—§ 52
Sanders v. Putnam Comm. Hosp., 395 So. 2d 571 (Fla. App. D5 1981)
58 ALR5th 613—§ 8
Sanders v. Robertson, 954 So. 2d 493 (Miss. Ct. App. 2007)
30 ALR6th 413—§ 7
Sanders v. Rosen, 159 Misc. 2d 563, 605 N.Y.S.2d 805 (Sup 1993)
23 ALR6th 697—§ 14
Sanders v. Sanders, 1 Ark. App. 216, 615 S.W.2d 375 (1981)
21 ALR5th 396—§ 19, 21, 51
Sanders v. Sanders, 425 So. 2d 476 (Ala. Civ. App. 1983)

6 ALR6th 229—§ 15
Sanders v. Sanders, 452 N.E.2d 1057
  (Ind. Ct. App. 1st Dist. 1983)
71 ALR5th 99—§ 3
Sanders v. Sanders, 570 A.2d 1189 (Del.
  1990)
46 ALR5th 735—§ 6
Sanders v. Sanders, 2004 WL 206333
  (Ark. Ct. App. 2004)
39 ALR6th 205—§ 4
Sanders v. Sanders, 2010 WL 4056196
  (Tex. App. Fort Worth 2010)
77 ALR6th 293—§ 57
Sanders v. Shephard, 185 Ill. App. 3d
  719, 133 Ill. Dec. 712, 541 N.E.2d
  1150 (1st Dist. 1989)
32 ALR5th 31—§ 5, 7
Sanders v. Slater, 53 A.D.3d 716, 861
  N.Y.S.2d 461 (3d Dep't 2008)
102 ALR6th 153—§ 7
Sanders v. Smith, 83 N.M. 706, 496 P.2d
  1102 (Ct. App. 1972)
58 ALR6th 1—§ 5
59 ALR6th 1—§ 17
Sanders v. Spaulding & Perkins, Ltd., 82
  N.C. App. 680, 347 S.E.2d 866
  (1986)
14 ALR5th 242—§ 38
Sanders v. State, 40 S.W. 495 (Tex.
  Crim. App. 1897)
105 ALR5th 529—§ 11
Sanders v. State, 57 Md. App. 156, 469
  A.2d 476 (1984)
55 ALR6th 157—§ 72
Sanders v. State, 76 Ark. App. 104, 61
  S.W.3d 871 (2001)
23 ALR6th 307—§ 12
Sanders v. State, 160 Ind. App. 676, 313
  N.E.2d 551 (1974)
5 ALR5th 243—§ 34
Sanders v. State, 242 Ga. App. 743, 531
  S.E.2d 170 (2000)
105 ALR5th 529—§ 2
Sanders v. State, 252 Ga. App. 609, 556
  S.E.2d 505 (2001)
112 ALR5th 429—§ 13
Sanders v. State, 259 Ark. 329, 532
  S.W.2d 752 (1976)

35 ALR6th 127—§ 5
Sanders v. State, 264 Ark. 433, 572
  S.W.2d 397 (1978)
62 ALR6th 413—§ 42
Sanders v. State, 300 Ark. 25, 776
  S.W.2d 334 (1989)
110 ALR5th 329—§ 6
Sanders v. State, 312 Ark. 11, 846
  S.W.2d 651, 52 A.L.R.5th 939
  (1993)
52 ALR5th 655—§ 3
Sanders v. State, 317 Ark. 328, 878
  S.W.2d 391 (1994)
42 ALR5th 581—§ 10
Sanders v. State, 351 So. 2d 361 (Fla.
  Dist. Ct. App. 4th Dist. 1977)
99 ALR5th 557—§ 3
Sanders v. State, 662 So. 2d 1372 (Fla.
  Dist. Ct. App. 1st Dist. 1995)
9 ALR6th 633—§ 4, 33
13 ALR6th 603—§ 24
Sanders v. State, 675 S.W.2d 579 (Tex.
  App. Houston (14th Dist.) 1984)
7 ALR5th 263—§ 6
Sanders v. State, 713 N.E.2d 918 (Ind.
  Ct. App. 1999)
100 ALR5th 67—§ 17, 31
Sanders v. State, 790 S.W.2d 497 (Mo.
  Ct. App. E.D. 1990)
105 ALR5th 529—§ 30
Sanders v. State, 840 N.E.2d 319 (Ind.
  2006)
27 ALR6th 183—§ 35
Sanders v. State, 846 So. 2d 230 (Miss.
  Ct. App. 2002)
87 ALR6th 109—§ 50
Sanders v. State, 986 So. 2d 1230 (Ala.
  Crim. App. 2007)
40 ALR6th 355—§ 5
Sanders v. State, 1994 WL 111080
  (Tenn. Crim. App. 1994)
59 ALR5th 1—§ 2 to 4
Sanders v. State, 1997 WL 43664
  (Wash. Ct. App. Div. 3 1997)
59 ALR5th 535—§ 8
Sanders v. State, 2004 WL 100384 (Tex.
  App. Dallas 2004)

31 ALR6th 49—§ 4
Sanders v. State, 2004 WL 179188 (Tex. App. Eastland 2004)
73 ALR6th 49—§ 3, 6
Sanders v. State, 2006 WL 349693 (Ark. 2006)
29 ALR6th 237—§ 5, 25
Sanders v. State Farm Mut. Auto. Ins. Co., 516 So. 2d 1162 (La. App. 2d Cir. 1987)
26 ALR5th 401—§ 23, 30
Sanders v. State of S.C., 296 F. Supp. 563 (D.S.C. 1969)
90 ALR5th 225—§ 9
Sanders v. Texas Employers Ins. Asso., 775 S.W.2d 762 (Tex. App. El Paso 1989)
10 ALR5th 245—§ 9, 10
Sanders v. Travenol Laboratories, 1989 WL 108514 (Ark. Ct. App. 1989)
80 ALR5th 417—§ 4
Sanders v. Unemployment Compensation Bd. of Review, 739 A.2d 616 (Pa. Commw. Ct. 1999)
75 ALR5th 339—§ 8
Sanders v. United Distributors, Inc., 405 So. 2d 536 (La. App. 4th Cir. 1981)
14 ALR5th 537—§ 3
Sanders v. U.S., 130 F. Supp. 2d 447 (S.D. N.Y. 2001)
32 ALR5th 149—§ 7
Sanders v. U.S., 760 F.2d 869 (CA8 Mo. 1983)
45 ALR5th 109—§ 5
Sanders v. U.S. Congress, 399 F. Supp. 2d 1021 (E.D. Mo. 2005)
24 ALR6th 255—§ 3, 11, 13
Sanders v. Wallace, 817 S.W.2d 511 (Mo. App. 1991)
48 ALR5th 129—§ 8
50 ALR5th 1—§ 4, 15
Sanders v. Wallace, 884 S.W.2d 300 (Mo. App. 1994)
35 ALR5th 375—§ 3, 61, 118
Sanders v. Washington Metropolitan Area Transit Authority, 260 U.S. App. D.C. 359, 819 F.2d 1151, 2 BNA IER Cas. 287, 125 BNA

LRRM 2772, 43 CCH EPD ¶ 37105 (App. D.C. 1987)
53 ALR5th 219—§ 4, 11
Sanders v. Wausau Underwriters Ins. Co., 392 So. 2d 343 (Fla. Dist. Ct. App. 5th Dist. 1981)
66 ALR5th 269—§ 8
Sanders v. Whitfield, 1997 WL 778988 (Tenn. Ct. App. 1997)
7 ALR6th 357—§ 5
Sanders v. Wysocki, 631 So. 2d 1330 (La. Ct. App. 4th Cir. 1994)
92 ALR5th 273—§ 11
Sanders v. Yates, 215 Ga. 218, 109 S.E.2d 739 (1959)
20 ALR6th 211—§ 18, 22
Sanders Construction Co. v. San Joaquin First Fed. Sav. & Loan Assn., 136 Cal. App. 3d 387, 186 Cal. Rptr. 218 (5th Dist. 1982)
75 ALR5th 1—§ 3
Sanderson v. Allstate Ins. Co., 738 F. Supp. 432 (D.C. Colo. 1990)
2 ALR5th 449—§ 3
6 ALR5th 297—§ 51
Sanderson v. Eckerd Corp., 780 So. 2d 930 (Fla. Dist. Ct. App. 5th Dist. 2001)
79 ALR5th 409—§ 4
Sanderson v. Freedom Sav. & Loan Asso., 548 So. 2d 221, 14 FLW 383 (Fla. 1989)
25 ALR5th 97—§ 6, 10
Sanderson v. Greenland, 122 N.H. 1002, 453 A.2d 1285 (1982)
1 ALR5th 622—§ 6, 9, 19
38 ALR5th 737—§ 3, 11
Sanderson v. Holland, 39 Mo. App. 233, 1889 WL 1730 (1889)
108 ALR5th 385—§ 3
Sanderson v. International Flavors and Fragrances, Inc., 950 F. Supp. 981 (C.D. Cal. 1996)
63 ALR5th 195—§ 3, 7, 8
Sanderson v. Mark, 155 Or. App. 166, 962 P.2d 786 (1998)
92 ALR6th 379—§ 70, 74

Sanderson v. New Mexico State Racing Comm'n, 80 N.M. 200, 453 P.2d 370 (1969)
59 ALR5th 203—§ 10, 23, 49
Sanderson v. Ohio Edison Co., 69 Ohio St. 3d 582, 1994-Ohio-379, 635 N.E.2d 19 (1994)
16 ALR6th 491—§ 10
Sanderson v. Producers Commission Ass'n, 360 Mo. 571, 229 S.W.2d 563 (1950)
28 ALR6th 1—§ 4, 8, 13, 32, 55
Sanderson v. Town of Candia, 146 N.H. 598, 787 A.2d 167 (2001)
4 ALR6th 263—§ 3
Sanderson v. University of Tennessee, 1997 WL 718427 (Tenn. Ct. App. 1997)
83 ALR6th 195—§ 4
Sanderson Farms, Inc. v. Gatlin, 848 So. 2d 828 (Miss. 2003)
22 ALR6th 49—§ 5, 9
Sanders, State ex rel. v. Doyle, 187 Neb. 453, 191 N.W.2d 545 (1971)
15 ALR5th 692—§ 36
Sanders, U.S. ex rel. v. Rowe, 460 F. Supp. 1128 (N.D. Ill. 1978)
124 ALR5th 1—§ 5
S & F. Supply Co. v. Hunter, 527 P.2d 217 (Utah 1974)
52 ALR5th 491—§ 15
Sandgate School Dist. v. Cate, 178 Vt. 625, 2005 VT 88, 883 A.2d 774, 202 Ed. Law Rep. 215 (2005)
86 ALR6th 321—§ 6
91 ALR6th 171—§ 107
Sandgathe v. Jagger, 165 Or. App. 375, 996 P.2d 1001 (2000)
4 ALR5th 273—§ 6.5
S & G News, Inc. v. Southgate, 638 F. Supp. 1060 (E.D. Mich. 1986)
10 ALR5th 538—§ 3, 8, 19
Sandhaus, Recall of, 134 Wash. 2d 662, 953 P.2d 82 (1998)
114 ALR5th 1—§ 2, 17, 23, 28
S & H Computer Systems, Inc. v. SAS Institute, Inc., 568 F. Supp. 416, 222 USPQ 715 (M.D. Tenn. 1983)

38 ALR5th 1—§ 10, 12
S & H Marketing Group, Inc. v. Sharp, 951 S.W.2d 265 (Tex. App. Austin 1997)
1 ALR6th 1—§ 27
Sandick, In re Claim of, 197 App. Div. 2d 737, 602 N.Y.S.2d 944 (3d Dep't 1993)
33 ALR5th 643—§ 20
San Diego v. State Board of Equalization, 82 Cal. App. 2d 453, 186 P.2d 166 (1947)
56 ALR5th 171—§ 7, 30
San Diego Bldg. Trades Council, Millmen's Union, Local 2020 v. Garmon, 359 U.S. 236, 79 S. Ct. 773, 3 L. Ed. 2d 775, 43 L.R.R.M. (BNA) 2838, 37 Lab. Cas. (CCH) ¶ 65367 (1959)
108 ALR5th 253—§ 1, 2
110 ALR5th 111—§ 1, 2
120 ALR5th 351—§ 1, 2
San Diego, City of v. Superior Court, 137 Cal. App. 4th 21, 40 Cal. Rptr. 3d 26 (4th Dist. 2006)
89 ALR6th 565—§ 3
San Diego County, Cal. v. San Diego NORML, 129 S. Ct. 2380 (2009)
46 ALR6th 495—§ 11
San Diego, County of v. Commission on State Mandates, 2003 WL 22205626 (Cal. App. 4th Dist. 2003)
76 ALR6th 543—§ 4
San Diego, County of v. Gibson, 133 Cal. App. 2d 519, 284 P.2d 501 (4th Dist. 1955)
65 ALR5th 1—§ 2, 22
San Diego, County of v. Lamb, 63 Cal. App. 4th 845, 73 Cal. Rptr. 2d 912 (4th Dist. 1998)
106 ALR5th 523—§ 45
San Diego, County of v. Pointe Communities of San Diego, Inc., 2014 WL 295299 (Cal. App. 4th Dist. 2014)
104 ALR6th 1—§ 5

San Diego, County of v. San Diego
NORML, 165 Cal. App. 4th 798, 81
Cal. Rptr. 3d 461 (4th Dist. 2008)
46 ALR6th 495—§ 11
60 ALR6th 175—§ 5
San Diego, County of v. State, 164 Cal.
App. 4th 580, 79 Cal. Rptr. 3d 489
(4th Dist. 2008)
76 ALR6th 543—§ 15
San Diego, County of v. State of California, 15 Cal. 4th 68, 61 Cal. Rptr.
2d 134, 931 P.2d 312 (1997)
113 ALR5th 95—§ 8
76 ALR6th 543—§ 4
San Diego Gas & Electric Co. v. Daley,
205 Cal. App. 3d 1334, 253 Cal.
Rptr. 144 (4th Dist. 1988)
104 ALR5th 503—§ 4, 5
San Diego Gas & Electric Co. v. Superior Court, 13 Cal. 4th 893, 55 Cal.
Rptr. 2d 724, 920 P.2d 669 (1996)
88 ALR5th 641—§ 1
San Diego Home Solutions, Inc. v. Re-
contrust Co., 2008 WL 5209972
(S.D. Cal. 2008)
86 ALR6th 411—§ 5
San Diego Minutemen v. California
Business Transp. and Housing
Agency's Dept. of Transp., 570 F.
Supp. 2d 1229 (S.D. Cal. 2008)
70 ALR6th 513—§ 4
71 ALR6th 471—§ 6
San Diego Nat. Bank v. Aetna Casualty
& Surety Co., 807 F. Supp. 95 (S.D.
Cal. 1992)
18 ALR5th 187—§ 5
San Diego Professional Ass'n v. Supe-
rior Court of San Diego County, 58
Cal. 2d 194, 23 Cal. Rptr. 384, 373
P.2d 448, 97 A.L.R.2d 761 (1962)
66 ALR6th 83—§ 17, 20
Sandifer v. State, 88 P.3d 807 (Kan. Ct.
App. 2004)
29 ALR6th 1—§ 10
Sandifer v. U.S. Steel Corp., 134 S. Ct.
870, 187 L. Ed. 2d 729, 21 Wage &
Hour Cas. 2d (BNA) 1477, 164 Lab.
Cas. (CCH) ¶ 36197 (2014)

96 ALR6th 577—§ 33
Sandifer v. U.S. Steel Corp., 678 F.3d
590, 18 Wage & Hour Cas. 2d
(BNA) 1825, 162 Lab. Cas. (CCH)
¶ 36057 (7th Cir. 2012)
96 ALR6th 577—§ 33
Sandifer v. Womack, 230 So. 2d 212
(Miss. 1970)
86 ALR5th 637—§ 3
Sandifer Motors, Inc. v. City of Roeland
Park, 6 Kan. App. 2d 308, 628 P.2d
239 (1981)
54 ALR6th 201—§ 50
Sandifer Motors, Inc. v. Roeland Park, 6
Kan. App. 2d 308, 628 P.2d 239
(1981)
18 ALR5th 525—§ 2
S & I Investments v. Payless Flea Market, Inc., 10 So. 3d 699 (Fla. Dist.
Ct. App. 4th Dist. 2009)
71 ALR6th 249—§ 11
Sandin v. Conner, 515 U.S. 472, 115 S.
Ct. 2293, 132 L. Ed. 2d 418 (1995)
119 ALR5th 1—§ 13
96 ALR6th 269—§ 2, 22
Sanditen Investments, Limited v. Tom-
linson, 1968 OK 166, 447 P.2d 738
119 ALR5th 519—§ 9
S & L. Associates, Inc. v. Washington
Tp., 61 N.J. Super. 312, 160 A.2d
635 (App. Div. 1960)
73 ALR5th 223—§ 9
S. & L. Co. of Des Moines v. Wood, 323
F.2d 322 (8th Cir. 1963)
99 ALR5th 141—§ 20
Sandler v. Board of Adjustment, 113
N.J. Super. 333, 273 A.2d 775
(1971)
38 ALR5th 737—§ 3
Sandler v. Calcagni, 565 F. Supp. 2d
184, 36 Media L. Rep. (BNA) 2286
(D. Me. 2008)
54 ALR6th 99—§ 32
Sandler v. Eighth Judicial Dist. Court In
and For Clark County, 96 Nev. 622,
614 P.2d 10, 29 U.C.C. Rep. Serv.
(CBC) 1546 (1980)
89 ALR5th 577—§ 24

Sandler v. Green, 287 Mass. 404, 192 N.E. 39 (1934)
  81 ALR6th 161—§ 4
  82 ALR6th 43—§ 4
Sandler v. Lawn-A-Mat Chemical & Equipment Corp., 141 N.J. Super. 437, 358 A.2d 805 (App. Div. 1976)
  52 ALR5th 613—§ 3
Sandler v. Marconi Circuit Technology Corp., 814 F. Supp. 263, 20 U.C.C. Rep. Serv. 2d 1059 (E.D. N.Y. 1993)
  52 ALR6th 271—§ 5
Sandler v. New Jersey Realty Title Ins. Co., 66 N.J. Super. 597, 169 A.2d 735 (1961)
  19 ALR5th 786—§ 3
Sandler v. Silk, 292 Mass. 493, 198 N.E. 749 (1935)
  81 ALR6th 161—§ 3
  82 ALR6th 43—§ 3
Sandlin v. State, 542 S.E.2d 496 (Ga. 2001)
  38 ALR5th 433—§ 7
Sandlin v. Wilmington, 185 N.C. 257, 116 S.E. 733 (1923)
  25 ALR5th 568—§ 4
Sandlin's Adm'x v. Allen, 262 Ky. 355, 90 S.W.2d 350 (1936)
  14 ALR5th 557—§ 7, 20
Sand Livestock Systems, Inc. v. Svoboda, 17 Neb. App. 28, 756 N.W.2d 299 (2008)
  85 ALR6th 475—§ 4
Sandman Associates, L.L.C., In re, 251 B.R. 473 (W.D. Va. 2000)
  43 ALR6th 611—§ 27
S & M Brands, Inc. v. Caldwell, 131 S. Ct. 1601, 179 L. Ed. 2d 499 (2011)
  66 ALR6th 635—§ 42
S&M Brands, Inc. v. Caldwell, 614 F.3d 172, 2010-2 Trade Cas. (CCH) ¶ 77122 (5th Cir. 2010)
  66 ALR6th 635—§ 42
S & M Brands, Inc. v. Summers, 393 F. Supp. 2d 604, 2005-2 Trade Cas. (CCH) ¶ 75074 (M.D. Tenn. 2005)
  25 ALR6th 435—§ 4, 9, 10, 13, 23, 24, 27, 29, 35, 60, 61
S & M Brands, Inc. v. Summers, 420 F. Supp. 2d 840 (M.D. Tenn. 2006)
  25 ALR6th 435—§ 4
S & M Brands, Inc. v. Summers, 2005 WL 3160869 (M.D. Tenn. 2005)
  25 ALR6th 435—§ 4
S & M Brands, Inc. v. Summers, 2007 WL 1175630 (6th Cir. 2007)
  25 ALR6th 435—§ 9
S&M Golden Inc. v. Alarm Management II, L.L.C., 2006 WL 141847 (Mich. Ct. App. 2006)
  36 ALR6th 305—§ 14, 16
S & M Representatives, Inc. v. Hrga, 1997 WL 328004 (N.D. Tex. 1997)
  79 ALR5th 587—§ 3, 5, 8
S & M Rotogravure Service, Inc. v. Baer, 77 Wis. 2d 454, 252 N.W.2d 913 (1977)
  46 ALR5th 1—§ 30
Sandner, Inc. v. Centennial Ins. Co., 189 Ga. App. 277, 375 S.E.2d 611 (1988)
  8 ALR6th 549—§ 4, 20
Sandoe v. Lefta Associates, 559 A.2d 732 (D.C. 1988)
  5 ALR6th 497—§ 7, 9
Sandom v. Travelers Mortg. Services, Inc., 752 F. Supp. 1240, 54 Fair Empl. Prac. Cas. (BNA) 1259, 6 I.E.R. Cas. (BNA) 466, 30 Wage & Hour Cas. (BNA) 228, 56 Empl. Prac. Dec. (CCH) ¶ 40615 (D.N.J. 1990)
  105 ALR5th 351—§ 5
  10 ALR6th 531—§ 10
Sandoor Alex Telegdi v. A.M.R. Services Corp., 2000 WL 264333 (E.D. N.Y. 2000)
  121 ALR5th 365—§ 5
Sandor v. Ruffer, Ballan & Co., 309 F. Supp. 849, CCH Fed Secur L. Rep. ¶ 92563 (S.D. N.Y. 1970)
  52 ALR5th 491—§ 18

Sandor Development Co. v. Reitmeyer, 498 N.E.2d 1020 (Ind. Ct. App. 1st Dist. 1986)
75 ALR5th 1—§ 7, 14, 17

Sandoval v. American Bldg. Maintenance Industries, Inc., 2006 WL 6607858 (D. Minn. 2006)
79 ALR6th 351—§ 5

Sandoval v. Archdiocese of Denver, 8 P.3d 598, 147 Ed. Law Rep. 328 (Colo. Ct. App. 2000)
9 ALR5th 321—§ 9

Sandoval v. Birx, 767 P.2d 759 (Colo. App. 1988)
11 ALR5th 127—§ 4, 30

Sandoval v. People, 176 Colo. 414, 490 P.2d 1298 (1971)
78 ALR5th 567—§ 9

Sandoval v. Reno, 166 F.3d 225 (3d Cir. 1999)
31 ALR6th 1—§ 17

Sandoval v. Rizzuti Farms, Ltd., 2009 WL 2058145 (E.D. Wash. 2009)
79 ALR6th 351—§ 4

Sandoval v. Sandoval, 832 So. 2d 1221 (La. Ct. App. 3d Cir. 2002)
21 ALR6th 577—§ 21

Sandoval v. Southern California Enterprises, Inc., 98 Cal. App. 2d 240, 219 P.2d 928 (1950)
12 ALR5th 195—§ 10

Sandoval v. State, 689 So. 2d 1258 (Fla. Dist. Ct. App. 3d Dist. 1997)
57 ALR5th 141—§ 12

Sandoval v. Tharaldson Employee Management, 2009 WL 3877203 (C.D. Cal. 2009)
60 ALR6th 295—§ 42, 58

Sandoval v. Tharaldson Employee Management, Inc., 2010 WL 2486346 (C.D. Cal. 2010)
60 ALR6th 295—§ 42, 58

Sandoz, Inc. v. Employer's Liability Assur. Corp., 554 F. Supp. 257 (D.C. N.J. 1983)
14 ALR5th 695—§ 24

Sandra Cotton, Inc. v. Bank of New York, 64 B.R. 262 (W.D. N.Y. 1986)
81 ALR6th 161—§ 4
82 ALR6th 43—§ 4

Sandra L.G. v. Bouchey, 153 Misc. 2d 450, 576 N.Y.S.2d 767 (Fam. Ct. 1991)
103 ALR5th 255—§ 3

Sandra M. v. Jeremy M., 197 W. Va. 542, 476 S.E.2d 213 (1996)
40 ALR5th 227—§ 3
67 ALR5th 1—§ 12

S & R Associates, L.P. v. Shell Oil Co., 725 A.2d 431, 38 U.C.C. Rep. Serv. 2d 1197 (Del. Super. Ct. 1998)
81 ALR5th 483—§ 3, 5

S & R Co. of Kingston and Latona Trucking, Inc., Matter of Arbitration Between, 984 F. Supp. 95 (N.D. N.Y. 1997)
100 ALR5th 481—§ 10

Sandrini Brothers v. Agricultural Labor Relations Bd., 156 Cal. App. 3d 878, 203 Cal. Rptr. 304 (5th Dist. 1984)
73 ALR6th 571—§ 23, 67, 71

S & R Metals, Inc. v. C. Itoh & Co., 859 F.2d 814, 7 U.C.C.R.S.2d 61 (CA9 Cal. 1988)
38 ALR5th 191—§ 54

Sandroff v. Bakery and Confectionery Workers Union Local No. 3, 29 A.D.2d 585, 285 N.Y.S.2d 378 (3d Dep't 1967)
112 ALR5th 509—§ 18
39 ALR6th 445—§ 35

Sandrow v. Red Bandana Co., 2002 WL 1472332 (Pa. C.P. 2002)
107 ALR5th 311—§ 7

Sandry, In re Commitment of, 367 Ill. App. 3d 949, 306 Ill. Dec. 202, 857 N.E.2d 295 (2d Dist. 2006)
78 ALR6th 417—§ 75

Sands, Matter of, 22 B.R. 132, 6 Collier Bankr. Cas. 2d (MB) 1005 (Bankr. D. N.J. 1982)
32 ALR6th 531—§ 39

Sands v. Albert, 2002 WL 187387 (Cal. App. 2d Dist. 2002)

13 ALR6th 1—§ 4

Sands v. Albert, 2002 WL 187387 (Cal. App. 2d Dist. 2002), unpublished/noncitable

15 ALR6th 427—§ 28

Sands v. Andino, 404 Pa. Super. 238, 590 A.2d 761 (1991)

103 ALR5th 1—§ 14

Sands v. Arruda, 359 Mass. 591, 270 N.E.2d 826 (1971)

12 ALR6th 123—§ 8, 16

Sands v. Cooke, 368 S.W.2d 111 (Tex. Civ. App. San Antonio 1963)

35 ALR5th 1—§ 9

Sands v. Living Word Fellowship, 34 P.3d 955 (Alaska 2001)

109 ALR5th 541—§ 4, 6

Sands v. News America Pub., Inc., 237 A.D.2d 177, 655 N.Y.S.2d 18, 25 Media L. Rep. (BNA) 2055 (1st Dep't 1997)

19 ALR5th 1—§ 85, 103, 108, 110

Sands v. Sands, 157 Ariz. 322, 757 P.2d 126 (Ct. App. Div. 2 1988)

71 ALR5th 99—§ 3, 6

Sands v. Sears, Roebuck & Co., 438 F.2d 655 (CA6 Ky. 1971)

40 ALR5th 135—§ 2, 4, 15

Sands v. Statler Hilton Hotel, 40 App. Div. 2d 620, 336 N.Y.S.2d 529 (4th Dep't 1972)

33 ALR5th 205—§ 6

Sands v. Wainwright, 357 F. Supp. 1062 (M.D. Fla. 1973)

38 ALR6th 97—§ 8

Sandsberry v. International Ass'n of Machinists, 156 Tex. 340, 295 S.W.2d 412, 38 L.R.R.M. (BNA) 2478, 30 Lab. Cas. (CCH) ¶ 70131 (1956)

105 ALR5th 243—§ 13

S & S. Constr., Inc. v. Riss, 500 P.2d 1188 (Colo. App. 1972)

46 ALR5th 1—§ 22

S & S Cummins Corp. v. West Bay Builders, Inc., 159 Cal. App. 4th 765, 71 Cal. Rptr. 3d 828, 228 Ed. Law Rep. 856 (1st Dist. 2008)

73 ALR6th 571—§ 26, 47, 70

S & S Directional Boring And Cable Contractors, Inc. v. American Nat. Bank Of Minnesota, 961 So. 2d 1046 (Fla. Dist. Ct. App. 2d Dist. 2007)

32 ALR6th 419—§ 8

S & S Diversified Services, L.L.C. v. Arguello, 911 F. Supp. 498, 29 U.C.C. Rep. Serv. 2d 242 (D. Wyo. 1995)

76 ALR6th 31—§ 9

S & S. Diversified Services, L.L.C. v. Taylor, 897 F. Supp. 549, 49 Soc. Sec. Rep. Serv. 102 (D. Wyo. 1995)

86 ALR5th 527—§ 3, 8, 13, 15, 16

S & S, Inc. v. Meyer, 478 N.W.2d 857, 17 U.C.C.R.S.2d 137 (Iowa App. 1991)

37 ALR5th 459—§ 15

S & S Liquor Mart, Inc. v. Pastore, 497 A.2d 729, 12 Media L. Rep. (BNA) 1236 (R.I. 1985)

116 ALR5th 149—§ 5

S & S Pawn Shop Inc. v. City of Del City, 947 F.2d 432 (10th Cir. 1991)

16 ALR6th 219—§ 19, 21

Sands Point Academy v. Board of Ed. of City of New York, 63 Misc. 2d 276, 311 N.Y.S.2d 588 (Sup 1970)

115 ALR5th 183—§ 4, 21, 23

Sands Regent v. Valgardson, 105 Nev. 436, 777 P.2d 898, 5 BNA IER Cas. 381, 51 CCH EPD ¶ 39389 (1989)

21 ALR5th 1—§ 3, 7

Sands, Taylor & Wood Co. v. Quaker Oats Co., 978 F.2d 947, 24 U.S.P.Q.2d (BNA) 1001 (7th Cir. 1992)

114 ALR5th 129—§ 3, 4, 8

S & S Textiles Intern. v. Steve Weave, Inc., 48 U.C.C. Rep. Serv. 2d 899 (S.D. N.Y. 2002)

110 ALR5th 277—§ 3

S & S. Tobacco & Candy Co. v. Greater New York Mut. Ins. Co., 224 Conn. 313, 617 A.2d 1388 (1992)
1 ALR5th 817—§ 11

S & S Tobacco & Candy Co., Inc. v. Stop & Shop Companies, Inc., 815 F. Supp. 65 (D. Conn. 1992)
87 ALR6th 1—§ 64

Sandstone Inv. Co. v. City of Romulus, 1999 WL 33437837 (Mich. Ct. App. 1999)
118 ALR5th 91—§ 19, 25
2 ALR6th 279—§ 4

Sandstrom v. California Horse Racing Board, 31 Cal. 2d 401, 189 P.2d 17, 3 A.L.R.2d 90 (1948)
59 ALR5th 203—§ 3, 5, 23, 46, 48

Sandstrom v. Larsen, 59 Haw. 491, 583 P.2d 971, 1 A.L.R.4th 1009 (1978)
76 ALR5th 337—§ 23

Sandstrom on Behalf of Sandstrom v. Chemlawn Corp., 759 F. Supp. 84 (D. Conn. 1991)
111 ALR5th 159—§ 2

Sandt v. Mason, 208 Ga. 541, 67 S.E.2d 767, 29 L.R.R.M. (BNA) 2132, 20 Lab. Cas. (CCH) ¶ 66635 (1951)
105 ALR5th 243—§ 24

Sandusky v. Sandusky, 2001 WL 327898 (Tenn. Ct. App. 2001)
124 ALR5th 441—§ 15

Sandusky v. Smith, 2012 WL 4592635 (W.D. Ky. 2012)
90 ALR6th 235—§ 4

Sandusky Mall Co. v. Pet Corner, Inc., 1997 WL 177843 (Ohio Ct. App. 7th Dist. Mahoning County 1997)
75 ALR5th 1—§ 10

Sandutch v. Farrell, 319 Pa. Super. 589, 466 A.2d 701 (1983)
90 ALR6th 385—§ 12

Sandvik, In re, 2004 WL 3383656 (Bankr. D. N.D. 2004)
46 ALR6th 401—§ 9

S & W. Cabinets v. Consolidated Sch. Dist. No. 6, 901 S.W.2d 266 (Mo. App. 1995)
54 ALR5th 649—§ 3

S. & W. Const. Co. v. Bugge, 194 Miss. 822, 13 So. 2d 645, 146 A.L.R. 1190 (1943)
27 ALR5th 174—§ 6

S & W Trucks, Inc. v. Nelson Auction Service, Inc., 80 N.M. 423, 457 P.2d 220, 6 U.C.C. Rep. Serv. 830 (Ct. App. 1969)
35 ALR6th 437—§ 13

Sandy, In Re Disciplinary Proceedings Against, 208 Wis. 2d 375, 561 N.W.2d 327 (1997)
58 ALR5th 429—§ 6

Sandy v. Mouhot, 1 Ohio St. 3d 143, 1 Ohio B.R. 178, 438 N.E.2d 117 (1982)
31 ALR5th 499—§ 2, 6

Sandy v. U.S., 2008 WL 4865993 (E.D. N.Y. 2008)
68 ALR6th 1—§ 17

Sandy B. v. State, Dept. of Health & Social Services, Office of Children's Services, 216 P.3d 1180 (Alaska 2009)
61 ALR6th 521—§ 7, 16, 17, 21, 22, 28

Sandy River Coal Co. v. Champion Bridge Co., 243 Ky. 424, 48 S.W.2d 1062 (1932)
62 ALR5th 219—§ 10, 49, 59
111 ALR5th 313—§ 17

Sanem v. Home Ins. Co., 119 Wis. 2d 530, 350 N.W.2d 89 (1984)
50 ALR6th 95—§ 3

Sanfelice v. Dominick's Finer Foods, Inc., 899 F. Supp. 372, 69 BNA FEP Cas. 170 (N.D. Ill. 1995)
51 ALR5th 163—§ 7

Sanfelice v. Dominick's Finer Foods, Inc., 899 F. Supp. 372, 69 Fair Empl. Prac. Cas. (BNA) 170 (N.D. Ill. 1995)
20 ALR6th 1—§ 5

San Fernando Motors, Inc. v. Fowler, 17 Ariz. App. 357, 498 P.2d 169 (1972)
20 ALR5th 229—§ 5, 30, 34

Sanfilippo v. State Farm Mut. Auto. Ins. Co., 24 Ariz. App. 10, 535 P.2d 38 (1975)
8 ALR5th 825—§ 7
Sanford v. Bi-State Dev. Agency, 705 S.W.2d 572 (Mo. App. 1986)
16 ALR5th 1—§ 31, 35
Sanford v. Castleton Health Care Center, LLC, 813 N.E.2d 411 (Ind. Ct. App. 2004)
50 ALR6th 187—§ 8, 10, 15
Sanford v. Crittenden Memorial Hosp., 141 F.3d 882 (8th Cir. 1998)
5 ALR5th 875—§ 45
Sanford v. H.A.S., Inc., 136 F. Supp. 2d 1215 (M.D. Ala. 2001)
22 ALR6th 49—§ 4
Sanford v. Keer, 80 N.J. Eq. 240, 83 A. 225 (Ct. Err. & App. 1912)
119 ALR5th 519—§ 14
Sanford v. Poe (U.S. Reports Title: Adams Express Company v. Ohio State Auditor), 165 U.S. 194, 17 S. Ct. 305, 41 L. Ed. 683 (1897)
90 ALR5th 547—§ 3
Sanford v. Rockefeller, 40 A.D.2d 82, 337 N.Y.S.2d 688, 81 L.R.R.M. (BNA) 2815, 69 Lab. Cas. (CCH) ¶ 52935 (3d Dep't 1972)
63 ALR6th 1—§ 61
Sanford v. Sanford, 15 Md. App. 390, 290 A.2d 812 (1972)
118 ALR5th 513—§ 3, 9
Sanford v. Sanford, 19 Va. App. 241, 450 S.E.2d 185 (1994)
47 ALR5th 207—§ 3, 5
Sanford v. Sanford, 301 N.W.2d 118 (N.D. 1980)
4 ALR5th 403—§ 3, 4
Sanford v. Sanford, 508 So. 2d 516 (Fla. App. D4 1987)
49 ALR5th 441—§ 6, 17, 19
Sanford v. Shea, 103 Fed. Appx. 878 (6th Cir. 2004)
14 ALR6th 301—§ 3, 4
19 ALR6th 475—§ 4, 34
Sanford v. State, 75 Okla. Crim. 362, 131 P.2d 770 (1942)

105 ALR5th 529—§ 11
Sanford v. State, 76 Wis. 2d 72, 250 N.W.2d 348 (1977)
86 ALR5th 59—§ 5
Sanford v. State, 155 Miss. 295, 124 So. 353 (1929)
29 ALR5th 59—§ 3, 13
Sanford v. State, 342 Ark. 22, 25 S.W.3d 414 (2000)
78 ALR5th 197—§ 9, 16
31 ALR6th 49—§ 10
71 ALR6th 1—§ 5
Sanford v. State, 726 So. 2d 221 (Miss. Ct. App. 1998)
97 ALR6th 263—§ 4
Sanford v. Stiles, 456 F.3d 298, 211 Ed. Law Rep. 104 (3d Cir. 2006)
100 ALR6th 563—§ 21, 41
Sanford Home for Adults v. Local 6, IFHP, 665 F. Supp. 312, 126 L.R.R.M. (BNA) 3149, 111 Lab. Cas. (CCH) ¶ 11026 (S.D. N.Y. 1987)
66 ALR5th 611—§ 3
San Francisco v. Boyd, 17 Cal. 2d 606, 110 P.2d 1036 (1941)
65 ALR5th 1—§ 7
San Francisco & S. Ry. Co. v. Industrial Acci. Com., 201 Cal. 597, 258 P. 86 (1927)
61 ALR5th 375—§ 10
San Francisco Bay Guardian, Inc. v. Superior Court, 17 Cal. App. 4th 655, 21 Cal. Rptr. 2d 464, 93 C.D.O.S. 5763, 93 Daily Journal DAR 9751, 21 Media L. R. 1791 (1st Dist. 1993)
54 ALR5th 443—§ 9
San Francisco, Cal., City of v. Harman, 103 Fair Empl. Prac. Cas. (BNA) 1024, 2008 WL 1955817 (U.S. 2008)
36 ALR6th 681—§ 8
San Francisco, City and County of v. Ragland, 188 Cal. App. 3d 1375, 234 Cal. Rptr. 327 (1st Dist. 1987)
72 ALR6th 413—§ 6

San Francisco, City & County of v. Superior Court In and For City and County of San Francisco, 37 Cal. 2d 227, 231 P.2d 26, 25 A.L.R.2d 1418 (1951)
66 ALR6th 83—§ 10

San Francisco, City and County of v. Workers' Comp. Appeals Bd., 22 Cal. 3d 103, 148 Cal. Rptr. 626, 583 P.2d 151, 43 Cal. Comp. Cas. (MB) 984 (1978)
122 ALR5th 653—§ 2, 18

San Francisco, City & County of v. Superior Court In and For City and County of San Francisco, 37 Cal. 2d 227, 231 P.2d 26, 25 A.L.R.2d 1418 (1951)
64 ALR6th 655—§ 6

San Francisco Residence Club, Inc. v. Baswell-Guthrie, 2012 WL 4339316 (N.D. Ala. 2012)
82 ALR6th 281—§ 25

San Francisco Unified School Dist. v. San Francisco Classroom Teachers Assn., 222 Cal. App. 3d 146, 272 Cal. Rptr. 38, 61 Ed. Law Rep. 668 (1st Dist. 1990)
73 ALR6th 571—§ 70

San Francisco Unified School Dist. v. State of California, 131 Cal. App. 3d 54, 182 Cal. Rptr. 525, 3 Ed. Law Rep. 1057 (1st Dist. 1982)
106 ALR5th 523—§ 15

Sang v. Jefferson County Bd. of Educ., 652 So. 2d 310, 99 Ed. Law Rep. 663 (Ala. Civ. App. 1994)
85 ALR6th 323—§ 14

San Gabriel Tribune v. Superior Court, 143 Cal. App. 3d 762, 192 Cal. Rptr. 415 (2d Dist. 1983)
5 ALR6th 327—§ 3, 8, 9, 14
8 ALR6th 117—§ 5

San Gabriel Valley Water Co. v. Montebello, 84 Cal. App. 3d 757, 148 Cal. Rptr. 830 (2d Dist. 1978)
10 ALR5th 448—§ 6

Sangentini v. Mutual of America, 1990 WL 204190 (S.D. N.Y. 1990)
103 ALR5th 557—§ 5

Sanger v. Futch, 208 S.W. 681 (Tex. Civ. App. Austin 1918)
74 ALR5th 369—§ 8

San Geronimo Caribe Project, Inc. v. Acevedo-Vila, 687 F.3d 465, 89 A.L.R.6th 725 (1st Cir. 2012)
88 ALR6th 679—§ 12
89 ALR6th 1—§ 7, 10, 11, 14, 33, 57, 82

Sangineto v. Mamaroneck Union Free School Dist., 723 N.Y.S.2d 234 (App. Div. 2d Dep't 2001)
66 ALR5th 1—§ 6

Sangiolo v. Board of Aldermen of Newton, 57 Mass. App. Ct. 911, 783 N.E.2d 830 (2003)
4 ALR6th 263—§ 14

Sang Man Shin, In re, 206 P.3d 91 (Nev. 2009)
70 ALR6th 1—§ 22

Sangster v. Albertson's, Inc., 99 Wash. App. 156, 991 P.2d 674 (Div. 3 2000)
94 ALR5th 1—§ 4

Sangston v. Ridge Country Club, 35 F.3d 568 (7th Cir. 1994)
52 ALR6th 271—§ 19

Sanifill of Georgia, Inc. v. Roberts, 232 Ga. App. 510, 502 S.E.2d 343 (1998)
57 ALR5th 633—§ 4

Sanif, Inc. v. Iannotti, 119 A.D.2d 654, 500 N.Y.S.2d 798 (2d Dep't 1986)
36 ALR6th 305—§ 9

Sanitary and Imp. Dist. No. 145 of Douglas County v. Nye, 216 Neb. 354, 343 N.W.2d 753 (1984)
11 ALR6th 1—§ 4, 6

Sanitary and Improvement Dist. No. 32 of Sarpy County v. Continental Western Corp., 215 Neb. 843, 343 N.W.2d 314, 38 U.C.C. Rep. Serv. (CBC) 516 (1983)
89 ALR5th 577—§ 25

Sanitary and Improvement District No. 384 of Douglas County, In re, 259 Neb. 351, 609 N.W.2d 679 (2000)

49 ALR6th 205—§ 21, 41
Sanitary Dist. of Chicago v. Carr, 304 Ill. 120, 136 N.E. 479 (1922)
114 ALR5th 561—§ 12
Sanitary Dist. of Chicago v. Cook, 169 Ill. 184, 48 N.E. 461 (1897)
109 ALR5th 421—§ 8
Sanitary Dist. of Chicago v. Hanberg, 226 Ill. 480, 80 N.E. 1012
114 ALR5th 561—§ 12
Sanitary Dist. of Chicago v. Martin, 173 Ill. 243, 50 N.E. 201 (1898)
114 ALR5th 561—§ 13
Sanitary Dist. of Chicago v. Rhodes, 386 Ill. 269, 53 N.E.2d 869 (1944)
114 ALR5th 561—§ 13
Sanitary Grocery Co. v. Steinbrecher, 183 Va. 495, 32 S.E.2d 685 (1945)
10 ALR5th 371—§ 3, 13
San Jacinto Bldg. v. Brown, 79 S.W.2d 164 (Tex. Civ. App. Beaumont 1935)
6 ALR6th 391—§ 5
San Jacinto Sand Co. v. Southwestern Bell Tel. Co., 426 S.W.2d 338 (Tex. Civ. App. Houston 14th Dist. 1968)
111 ALR5th 313—§ 20
San Jacinto Sav. & Loan v. Kacal, 928 F.2d 697 (5th Cir. 1991)
95 ALR6th 341—§ 37
Sanjay, Inc. v. Duncan Constr. Co., 445 So. 2d 876 (Ala. 1983)
23 ALR5th 744—§ 11
Sanjines v. Ortwein and Associates, P.C., 984 S.W.2d 907 (Tenn. 1998)
37 ALR6th 511—§ 7, 8, 10, 16, 46
San Jose Charter of Hells Angels Motorcycle Club v. City of San Jose, 402 F.3d 962 (9th Cir. 2005)
16 ALR6th 767—§ 37
San Jose, City of v. Cigarettes Cheaper, Inc., 2004 WL 1559677 (Cal. App. 6th Dist. 2004)
66 ALR6th 315—§ 5 to 7
San Jose, City of v. State of California, 45 Cal. App. 4th 1802, 53 Cal. Rptr. 2d 521 (6th Dist. 1996)
76 ALR6th 543—§ 9

San Jose, City of v. Superior Court, 12 Cal. 3d 447, 115 Cal. Rptr. 797, 525 P.2d 701, 76 A.L.R.3d 1223 (1974)
25 ALR5th 568—§ 51
53 ALR5th 617—§ 2
San Jose, City of v. Superior Court, 32 Cal. App. 4th 330, 38 Cal. Rptr. 2d 205 (6th Dist. 1995)
113 ALR5th 1—§ 4, 12, 15
San Jose Police Officers Assn. v. City of San Jose, 199 Cal. App. 3d 1471, 245 Cal. Rptr. 728 (6th Dist. 1988)
91 ALR6th 435—§ 73
San Jose Safe Deposit Bank of Sav. v. Bank of Madera, 144 Cal. 574, 78 P. 5 (1904)
36 ALR6th 387—§ 6
San Jose Silicon Valley Chamber of Commerce Political Action Committee v. City of San Jose, 2006 WL 3832794 (N.D. Cal. 2006)
24 ALR6th 179—§ 20 to 22
San Jose Teachers Ass'n v. Allen, 144 Cal. App. 3d 627, 192 Cal. Rptr. 710, 52 A.L.R.4th 283 (1st Dist. 1983)
56 ALR5th 493—§ 23
Sanjuan v. IBP, Inc., 160 F.3d 1291, 14 I.E.R. Cas. (BNA) 972 (10th Cir. 1998)
86 ALR5th 397—§ 9
San Juan v. Leach, 278 A.D.2d 299, 717 N.Y.S.2d 334 (2d Dep't 2000)
93 ALR5th 47—§ 5
94 ALR5th 1—§ 3
Sanjuan v. Sanjuan, 68 A.D.3d 1093, 892 N.Y.S.2d 146 (2d Dep't 2009)
57 ALR6th 163—§ 24, 53
San Juan County v. No New Gas Tax, 160 Wash. 2d 141, 157 P.3d 831 (2007)
53 ALR6th 491—§ 18
San Juan Dupont Plaza Hotel Fire Litigation, In re, 687 F. Supp. 716 (D.P.R. 1988)
5 ALR6th 497—§ 3, 7, 9

San Juan Dupont Plaza Hotel Fire Litigation, In re, 789 F. Supp. 1212 (D.C. Puerto Rico 1992)
35 ALR5th 375—§ 3, 17
San Juan Dupont Plaza Hotel Fire Litigation, In re, 802 F. Supp. 624 (D.P.R. 1992)
98 ALR5th 1—§ 6, 7
San Juan Star v. Casiano Communications, Inc., 85 F. Supp. 2d 89, 2000-1 Trade Cas. (CCH) ¶ 72886 (D.P.R. 2000)
22 ALR6th 553—§ 16
San Juan-Torregosa v. Garcia, 80 S.W.3d 539 (Tenn. Ct. App. 2002)
95 ALR6th 479—§ 24
Sanjurjo v. Woods, 1998 WL 338203 (Tenn. Ct. App. 1998)
83 ALR5th 651—§ 4
Sankar v. Board of Education, 160 Mich. App. 470, 409 N.W.2d 213, 126 BNA LRRM 2092 (1987)
53 ALR5th 219—§ 4, 8
Sankar v. Federated Answering Service, 60 A.D.2d 951, 401 N.Y.S.2d 895 (3d Dep't 1978)
25 ALR6th 101—§ 26
Sankey v. Sankey, 51 Ala. App. 100, 282 So. 2d 924 (1973)
49 ALR5th 441—§ 11
Sankey v. State, 568 So. 2d 366 (Ala. App. 1990)
29 ALR5th 59—§ 3, 9
Sanko v. Rapho Tp., 6 Pa. Commw. 73, 293 A.2d 141 (1972)
63 ALR5th 607—§ 14
19 ALR6th 335—§ 21
Sanko S.S. Co., Ltd. v. Cook Industries, Inc., 495 F.2d 1260, 1973 A.M.C. 2088 (2d Cir. 1973)
67 ALR5th 179—§ 3
Sanko S.S. Co., Ltd. v. Galin, 1988 WL 96089 (S.D. N.Y. 1988)
98 ALR5th 353—§ 4
San Leandro Police Officers Asso. v. San Leandro, 55 Cal. App. 3d 553, 127 Cal. Rptr. 856 (1st Dist. 1976)
45 ALR5th 109—§ 6

San Leandro Teachers Ass'n v. Governing Bd. of San Leandro Unified School Dist., 46 Cal. 4th 822, 95 Cal. Rptr. 3d 164, 209 P.3d 73, 245 Ed. Law Rep. 364, 186 L.R.R.M. (BNA) 2949, 158 Lab. Cas. (CCH) ¶ 60818 (2009)
70 ALR6th 513—§ 17
71 ALR6th 471—§ 9
San Luis & Delta-Mendota Water Authority v. Salazar, 638 F.3d 1163, 72 Env't. Rep. Cas. (BNA) 2102 (9th Cir. 2011)
76 ALR6th 587—§ 25
San Luis Obispo Bay Properties, Inc. v. Pacific Gas & Elec. Co., 28 Cal. App. 3d 556, 104 Cal. Rptr. 733 (2d Dist. 1972)
67 ALR5th 179—§ 3
San Luis Obispo, County of v. Abalone Alliance, 178 Cal. App. 3d 848, 223 Cal. Rptr. 846 (2d Dist. 1986)
106 ALR5th 523—§ 5 to 7, 36
32 ALR6th 261—§ 6
San Luis Power & Water Co. v. State, 57 N.M. 734, 263 P.2d 398 (1953)
7 ALR5th 187—§ 7, 19
San Luis Valley Drainage Dist. No. 1 v. Stanley, 68 Colo. 393, 189 P. 855 (1920)
102 ALR5th 253—§ 4
San Manuel Copper Corp. v. Redmond, 8 Ariz. App. 214, 445 P.2d 162, 160 U.S.P.Q. 360 (1968)
85 ALR6th 1—§ 57
San Martin v. State, 705 So. 2d 1337 (Fla. 1997)
83 ALR6th 255—§ 15, 25
San Martin v. State, 995 So. 2d 247 (Fla. 2008)
102 ALR6th 417—§ 98
San Mateo County v. Jensen, 238 Cal. Rptr. 701 (App. 1st Dist. 1987)
106 ALR5th 523—§ 45
San Mateo, County of v. Bartole, 184 Cal. App. 2d 422, 7 Cal. Rptr. 569 (1st Dist. 1960)
53 ALR5th 1—§ 22, 31

San Mateo, County of v. City Council of Palo Alto, 168 Cal. App. 2d 220, 335 P.2d 1013 (1st Dist. 1959)
17 ALR5th 195—§ 7

San Mateo Planing Mill Co. v. Davenport Realty Co., 218 Cal. 702, 24 P.2d 787 (1933)
4 ALR5th 772—§ 12, 32

San Miguel Basin State Bank v. Oliver, 748 P.2d 1342 (Colo. App. 1987)
10 ALR5th 448—§ 5

Sanne v. State, 609 S.W.2d 762 (Tex. Crim. App. 1980)
83 ALR6th 465—§ 12, 66

Sannella v. Sannella, 993 S.W.2d 73 (Tenn. Ct. App. 1999)
36 ALR6th 1—§ 4, 6

Sanner v. Ford Motor Co., 144 N.J. Super. 1, 364 A.2d 43 (1976)
53 ALR5th 535—§ 14

Sanner v. Ford Motor Co., 154 N.J. Super. 407, 381 A.2d 805 (1977)
53 ALR5th 535—§ 14

Sanner v. Sanner, 46 S.W.2d 936 (Mo. App. 1932)
49 ALR5th 595—§ 3

San Nicolas v. U.S., 223 Ct. Cl. 223, 617 F.2d 246 (1980)
45 ALR5th 251—§ 6, 7

Sanone v. J. C. Penney Co., 17 Utah 2d 46, 404 P.2d 248 (1965)
63 ALR6th 495—§ 17

Sanor Sawmill, Inc., State ex rel. v. Indus. Comm., 101 Ohio St. 3d 199, 2004-Ohio-718, 803 N.E.2d 802 (2004)
31 ALR6th 199—§ 48

San Pedro Properties, Inc. v. Sayre & Toso, Inc., 203 Cal. App. 2d 750, 21 Cal. Rptr. 844 (2d Dist. 1962)
14 ALR5th 695—§ 28

Sans v. Monticello Ins. Co., 676 N.E.2d 1099 (Ind. Ct. App. 1997)
44 ALR5th 91—§ 13

Sans v. Monticello Ins. Co., 718 N.E.2d 814 (Ind. Ct. App. 1999)
44 ALR5th 91—§ 11, 13

Sans v. Ramsey Golf & Country Club, Inc., 29 N.J. 438, 149 A.2d 599, 68 A.L.R.2d 1323 (1959)
49 ALR6th 477—§ 4, 8

Sansbury v. Johnson, 134 N.Y.S. 130 (Sup. App. T 1911)
62 ALR5th 219—§ 29, 33

Sansevere v. United Parcel Service, Inc., 181 A.D.2d 521, 581 N.Y.S.2d 315 (1st Dep't 1992)
111 ALR5th 1—§ 8, 13

Sansom v. Sansom, 409 So. 2d 430 (Ala. App. 1981)
39 ALR5th 1—§ 4

Sanson v. General Motors Corp., 966 F.2d 618, 15 EBC 1943 (CA11 Ga. 1992)
14 ALR5th 537—§ 2

Sansone, Re, 99 B.R. 981 (F. BC CD Cal. 1989)
14 ALR5th 242—§ 53

Sansone v. National Food Stores, Inc., 352 S.W.2d 375 (Mo. App. 1961)
3 ALR5th 237—§ 15

Sansone, State ex rel. v. Wofford, 111 Mo. 526, 20 S.W. 236 (1892)
97 ALR5th 537—§ 68

Santa Ana Hospital Medical Center v. Belshe, 56 Cal. App. 4th 819, 65 Cal. Rptr. 2d 754 (3d Dist. 1997)
105 ALR5th 499—§ 4

Santa Barbara v. Modern Neon Sign Co., 189 Cal. App. 2d 188, 11 Cal. Rptr. 57 (2d Dist. 1961)
8 ALR5th 391—§ 2, 3, 6

Santa Barbara Beach Club, LLC v. Freeman, 2010 WL 1744950 (Cal. App. 2d Dist. 2010)
64 ALR6th 365—§ 4, 10, 11, 26, 35

Santa Barbara, County of v. David R., 200 Cal. App. 3d 98, 245 Cal. Rptr. 836 (1st Dist. 1988)
72 ALR6th 413—§ 7

Santa Barbara, County of v. Workers' Compensation Appeals Board, 53 Cal. App. 3d 820, 126 Cal. Rptr. 281, 40 Cal. Comp Cas. 794 (2d Dist. 1975)

48 ALR5th 473—§ 10, 14

Santacapita v. Town of Brookhaven, 202 App. Div. 2d 489, 609 N.Y.S.2d 55 (2d Dep't 1994)

24 ALR5th 200—§ 24, 41

Santa Clara, County of v. Perry, 18 Cal. 4th 435, 75 Cal. Rptr. 2d 738, 956 P.2d 1191 (1998)

87 ALR5th 361—§ 13

Santa Clara, County of v. Rucker, 2003 WL 22022026 (Cal. App. 6th Dist. 2003)

45 ALR6th 493—§ 57

Santa Clara, County of v. Superior Court, 2 Cal. App. 4th 1686, 5 Cal. Rptr. 2d 7, 92 C.D.O.S. 903, 92 Daily Journal DAR 1446 (6th Dist. 1992)

32 ALR5th 31—§ 3

Santa Clara, County of v. Superior Court, 170 Cal. App. 4th 1301, 89 Cal. Rptr. 3d 374, 37 Media L. Rep. (BNA) 1331 (6th Dist. 2009)

54 ALR6th 653—§ 8, 17, 28

Santa Clara, County of v. U.S. Fidelity and Guar. Co., 1993 WL 566443 (N.D. Cal. 1993)

88 ALR5th 493—§ 3

89 ALR5th 1—§ 13

Santacroce v. 40 W. 20th St., Inc., 9 A.D.2d 985, 194 N.Y.S.2d 541 (3d Dep't 1959)

107 ALR5th 441—§ 14

109 ALR5th 161—§ 17

20 ALR6th 641—§ 23

Santa Cruz v. Northwest Dade Community Health Center, Inc., 590 So. 2d 444 (Fla. 3d DCA 1991)

80 ALR6th 469—§ 36, 40, 55

Santa Cruz, City of v. Superior Court, 198 Cal. App. 3d 999, 244 Cal. Rptr. 105 (6th Dist. 1988)

16 ALR5th 605—§ 6, 12

Santa Cruz Irrigation Dist. v. Tucson, 108 Ariz. 152, 494 P.2d 24 (1972)

49 ALR5th 769—§ 3

Santa Fe v. Armijo, 96 N.M. 663, 634 P.2d 685, 70 OGR 579 (1981)

53 ALR5th 1—§ 25, 43

Santa Fe, City of v. Gamble-Skogmo, Inc., 73 N.M. 410, 389 P.2d 13 (1964)

72 ALR5th 607—§ 7

Santa Fe Springs Realty Corp. v. City of Westminster, 906 F. Supp. 1341 (C.D. Cal. 1995)

20 ALR6th 161—§ 4

21 ALR6th 425—§ 10

Santa Fe Trail Transp. Co., Re, 121 B.R. 794 (F. BC N.D. Ill. 1990)

27 ALR5th 76—§ 47

Santagata v. Woods, 84 A.D.3d 821, 921 N.Y.S.2d 868 (2d Dep't 2011)

91 ALR6th 435—§ 66, 138

Santa Maria v. Owens-Illinois, Inc., 808 F.2d 848, 6 Fed. R. Serv. 3d 1187 (1st Cir. 1986)

109 ALR5th 301—§ 18

13 ALR6th 355—§ 4, 27

Santa Monica Lumber & Mill Co. v. Hege, 119 Cal. 376, 51 P. 555 (1897)

46 ALR5th 1—§ 7

Santa Monica Police Officers Assn. v. Board of Administration, 69 Cal. App. 3d 96, 137 Cal. Rptr. 771 (2d Dist. 1977)

91 ALR5th 225—§ 5, 6

Santana, Matter of, 247 A.D.2d 107, 678 N.Y.S.2d 96 (1st Dep't 1998)

46 ALR6th 365—§ 5

Santana v. Cook County Bd. of Review, 679 F.3d 614, R.I.C.O. Bus. Disp. Guide (CCH) ¶ 12259, 95 A.L.R.6th 771 (7th Cir. 2012)

95 ALR6th 219—§ 27

95 ALR6th 341—§ 8

Santana v. Country-Wide Ins. Co., 675 N.Y.S.2d 817 (City Civ. Ct. 1998)

63 ALR5th 675—§ 10

64 ALR5th 475—§ 10

Santana v. New York City Transit Authority, 132 Misc. 2d 777, 505 N.Y.S.2d 775 (1986)

33 ALR5th 205—§ 9

For assistance, call 1-800-328-4880

Santana v. Prospect Hospital, 84 App.
Div. 2d 714, 444 N.Y.S.2d 6 (1st
Dep't 1981)
43 ALR5th 87—§ 7
Santana v. Rainbow Cleaners, 969 A.2d
653 (R.I. 2009)
80 ALR6th 469—§ 34, 36, 40, 41
Santana v. State, 677 So. 2d 1339 (Fla.
Dist. Ct. App. 3d Dist. 1996)
11 ALR6th 237—§ 12, 13
Santana v. Warden of PBSP, 2011 WL
3583411 (E.D. Cal. 2011)
81 ALR6th 505—§ 28
Santana Products, Inc. v. Bobrick Wash-
room Equipment, 14 F. Supp. 2d
710 (M.D. Pa. 1998)
81 ALR5th 41—§ 3
Santana Products, Inc. v. Bobrick Wash-
room Equipment, Inc., 69 F. Supp.
2d 678 (M.D. Pa. 1999)
17 ALR6th 1—§ 3, 26
Santangelo v. City of New York, 66
A.D.2d 880, 411 N.Y.S.2d 666 (2d
Dep' 1978)
75 ALR6th 1—§ 13
Santangelo v. New York, 66 App. Div.
2d 880, 411 N.Y.S.2d 666 (2d Dep't
1978)
38 ALR5th 107—§ 3
Santaniello v. Department of Professional Regulation/Board of Real
Estate, 432 So. 2d 82 (Fla. App. D2
1983)
7 ALR5th 474—§ 182
Santaniello v. Department of Professional Regulation/Board of Real
Estate, 432 So. 2d 84 (Fla. App. D2
1983)
7 ALR5th 474—§ 64
Santaniello v. Santaniello, 18 Kan. App.
2d 112, 850 P.2d 269 (1992)
69 ALR5th 1—§ 3, 4
Santantonio v. Westinghouse Broadcasting Co., 25 Cal. App. 4th 102, 30
Cal. Rptr. 2d 486 (2d Dist. 1994)
121 ALR5th 325—§ 3
125 ALR5th 193—§ 7
2 ALR6th 279—§ 4

34 ALR6th 431—§ 3, 18, 20
Santarelli v. BP America, 913 F. Supp.
324, Prod. Liab. Rep. (CCH)
¶ 14597 (M.D. Pa. 1996)
63 ALR5th 195—§ 3, 4
102 ALR5th 99—§ 3
Santaro v. Jack of Hearts Carpet Co.,
Inc., 6 Misc. 3d 1024(A), 800
N.Y.S.2d 356 (Sup 2005)
12 ALR6th 123—§ 11
Santa-Rosa v. Combo Records, 471 F.3d
224, 81 U.S.P.Q.2d 1221 (1st Cir.
2006)
76 ALR6th 289—§ 4
77 ALR6th 543—§ 4
Santa Rosa Health Care Corp. v. Garcia,
41 Tex. Sup. Ct. J. 535, 1998 WL
107928 (Tex. 1998)
59 ALR5th 535—§ 2
Santa Rosa Health Care Corp. v. Garcia,
964 S.W.2d 940 (Tex. 1998)
3 ALR5th 370—§ 3
12 ALR5th 149—§ 17, 28
Santa Rosa Junior College v. Workers'
Comp. Appeals Bd., 40 Cal. 3d 345,
220 Cal. Rptr. 94, 708 P.2d 673, 28
Ed. Law Rep. 909 (1985)
**15 ALR6th 633—§ 2, 3, 7, 9, 13, 17,
26, 49**
Santa Rosa Medical Center v. Spears,
709 S.W.2d 720 (Tex. App. San
Antonio 1986)
51 ALR5th 603—§ 2, 3, 6, 8, 11, 16
Santa Rosa Memorial Hospital v. Superior Court, 174 Cal. App. 3d 711,
220 Cal. Rptr. 236 (1st Dist. 1985)
69 ALR5th 559—§ 2, 6, 8, 15
Santee v. Santa Clara County Office of
Education, 220 Cal. App. 3d 702,
269 Cal. Rptr. 605, 60 Ed. Law Rep.
543 (6th Dist. 1990)
64 ALR5th 519—§ 4
Santee Portland Cement Co. v. Daniel
International Corp., 299 S.C. 269,
384 S.E.2d 693 (1989)
33 ALR5th 1—§ 8
Santellan v. Cockrell, 271 F.3d 190 (5th
Cir. 2001)

For assistance, call 1-800-328-4880

CASES CITED IN ALR5th and ALR6th

102 ALR6th 417—§ 25

Santelli v. Arean, 616 So. 2d 1154, 18 FLW D 1012 (Fla. App. D2 1993)

24 ALR5th 1—§ 5
26 ALR5th 245—§ 5, 7

Santeufemio v. State, 745 So. 2d 1002 (Fla. Dist. Ct. App. 2d Dist. 1999)

59 ALR5th 135—§ 10

Santha v. Mirel, 2003 WL 21327105 (Conn. Super. Ct. 2003)

52 ALR6th 433—§ 36

Santi v. Santi, 633 N.W.2d 312 (Iowa 2001)

86 ALR6th 1—§ 3, 54, 58

Santiago, In re, 308 A.D.2d 198, 763 N.Y.S.2d 498 (2d Dep't 2003)

43 ALR6th 163—§ 68
44 ALR6th 75—§ 27

Santiago v. 1370 Broadway Associates, L.P., 96 N.Y.2d 765, 725 N.Y.S.2d 599, 749 N.E.2d 168 (2001)

121 ALR5th 365—§ 5

Santiago v. City of Philadelphia, 435 F. Supp. 136 (E.D. Pa. 1977)

87 ALR6th 109—§ 95

Santiago v. City of Vineland, 2000 WL 1056438 (D.N.J. 2000)

83 ALR5th 1—§ 10

Santiago v. Clerk Magistrate of Clinton Dist. Court, 21 Mass. L. Rptr. 437, 2006 WL 2848120 (Mass. Super. Ct. 2006)

90 ALR6th 385—§ 5

Santiago v. E.W. Bliss Co., 2012 IL 111792, 362 Ill. Dec. 462, 973 N.E.2d 858 (Ill. 2012)

93 ALR6th 463—§ 43

Santiago v. E. W. Bliss Div., Gulf & Western Mfg. Co., 201 N.J. Super. 205, 492 A.2d 1089, CCH Prod. Liab. Rep. ¶ 10591 (1985)

9 ALR5th 1—§ 5, 7, 8

Santiago v. Fajardo, 70 F. Supp. 2d 72, 140 Ed. Law Rep. 150 (D.P.R. 1999)

41 ALR6th 391—§ 8

Santiago v. Greyhound Lines, Inc., 956 F. Supp. 144, 79 Fair Empl. Prac. Cas. (BNA) 651 (N.D. N.Y. 1997)

19 ALR6th 793—§ 11

Santiago v. Lloyd, 33 F. Supp. 2d 99 (D.P.R. 1998)

83 ALR5th 1—§ 3

Santiago v. New York City Housing Authority, 63 N.Y.2d 761, 480 N.Y.S.2d 321, 469 N.E.2d 839 (1984)

43 ALR5th 207—§ 56

Santiago v. Pinello, 647 F. Supp. 2d 239 (E.D. N.Y. 2009)

62 ALR6th 259—§ 8

Santiago v. Puerto Rico, 154 F.2d 811, 17 BNA LRRM 957 (CA1 Puerto Rico 1946)

38 ALR5th 39—§ 8

Santiago v. Sherwin Williams Co., 3 F.3d 546, Prod. Liab. Rep. (CCH) ¶ 13603, 24 Envtl. L. Rep. 20805 (1st Cir. 1993)

63 ALR5th 195—§ 6, 8
69 ALR5th 137—§ 11

Santiago v. State, 50 Md. App. 20, 435 A.2d 499 (1981)

125 ALR5th 281—§ 4

Santiago v. State, 644 N.W.2d 425 (Minn. 2002)

16 ALR6th 329—§ 5
24 ALR6th 591—§ 5, 12

Santiago v. State, 652 So. 2d 485 (Fla. Dist. Ct. App. 5th Dist. 1995)

70 ALR5th 587—§ 25

Santiago v. State, 669 So. 2d 334, 21 FLW D613 (Fla. App. D3 1996)

15 ALR5th 391—§ 5, 53

Santiago v. State, 832 So. 2d 783 (Fla. Dist. Ct. App. 4th Dist. 2002)

26 ALR6th 511—§ 51

Santiago v. Walls, 599 F.3d 749 (7th Cir. 2010)

65 ALR6th 93—§ 63

Santiesteban v. McGrath, 320 So. 2d 476 (Fla. Dist. Ct. App. 3d Dist. 1975)

2 ALR6th 279—§ 3
34 ALR6th 431—§ 3

Santigate v. Linsalata, 304 A.D.2d 639, 759 N.Y.S.2d 100 (2d Dep't 2003)
33 ALR6th 251—§ 11

Santillana v. Sivalingam, 2006 WL 45898 (Cal. App. 2d Dist. 2006)
96 ALR6th 503—§ 18

Santillanes, In re, 47 N.M. 140, 138 P.2d 503 (1943)
87 ALR6th 109—§ 38

Santillanes v. Property Management Servs., 110 Idaho 588, 716 P.2d 1360 (App. 1986)
45 ALR5th 251—§ 2, 6, 17, 31

Santilli v. Otis Elevator Co., 215 Cal. App. 3d 210, 263 Cal. Rptr. 496 (1st Dist. 1989)
64 ALR5th 119—§ 4

Santillo v. Chambersburg Engineering Co., 603 F. Supp. 211 (E.D. Pa. 1985)
13 ALR5th 289—§ 2, 16, 29

Santini v. American Media, Inc., 35 Media L. Rep. (BNA) 1699, 2005 WL 459195 (Cal. App. 2d Dist. 2005)
85 ALR6th 475—§ 5

Santini v. Witherell, 2005 WL 1953108 (Del. Super. Ct. 2005)
58 ALR6th 1—§ 5

Santistevan v. Santistevan, 768 So. 2d 79 (La. Ct. App. 5th Cir. 2000)
3 ALR6th 447—§ 6, 22

Santitoro v. Evans, 935 F. Supp. 733 (E.D. N.C. 1996)
51 ALR5th 271—§ 3

Santmier v. Santmier, 494 So. 2d 95 (Ala. Civ. App. 1986)
34 ALR5th 57—§ 3
93 ALR5th 327—§ 6

Santmyers v. Town of Oyster Bay, 10 Misc. 2d 614, 169 N.Y.S.2d 959 (Sup. Ct. 1957)
73 ALR5th 223—§ 8, 10

Santo, In re, 711 N.Y.S.2d 75 (App. Div. 3d Dep't 2000)
23 ALR5th 176—§ 29

Santobello v. New York, 404 U.S. 257, 92 S. Ct. 495, 30 L. Ed. 2d 427 (1971)
9 ALR6th 541—§ 6, 8, 10, 13, 15, 18, 19, 23, 29, 32

Santone v. State, 187 Ga. App. 789, 371 S.E.2d 428 (1988)
2 ALR6th 551—§ 5

Santoni v. Moodie, 53 Md. App. 129, 452 A.2d 1223 (1982)
47 ALR5th 433—§ 12

Santoni-Lorenzi v. F.W. Woolworth Co., 993 F.2d 1531 (1st Cir. 1993)
63 ALR6th 495—§ 42, 51

Santopietro v. Charlotte Hungerford Hosp., 2009 WL 3645403 (Conn. Super. Ct. 2009)
98 ALR6th 1—§ 45

Santora v. Schalabba, 2002-Ohio-2756, 2002 WL 1160202 (Ohio Ct. App. 8th Dist. Cuyahoga County 2002)
115 ALR5th 251—§ 65

Santore v. Wolf, 15 Misc. 3d 1109(A), 836 N.Y.S.2d 503 (Sup 2007)
97 ALR6th 83—§ 5, 7, 21

Santoro, In re, 594 N.W.2d 174 (Minn. 1999)
69 ALR5th 1—§ 6

Santoro, Petition of, 578 N.W.2d 369 (Minn. Ct. App. 1998)
86 ALR6th 1—§ 20, 64

Santoro v. American Airlines, Inc., 170 App. Div. 2d 206, 565 N.Y.S.2d 105 (1st Dep't 1991)
13 ALR5th 289—§ 47

Santoro v. Philadelphia, 59 Pa. Cmwlth. 114, 429 A.2d 113 (1981)
23 ALR5th 241—§ 44

Santoro v. Schulthess, 384 S.C. 250, 681 S.E.2d 897 (Ct. App. 2009)
81 ALR6th 469—§ 7

Santos, In re, 461 Mass. 565, 962 N.E.2d 726 (2012)
78 ALR6th 417—§ 38

Santos v. Bayley, 400 F. Supp. 784 (M.D. Pa. 1975)
35 ALR6th 127—§ 4

Santos v. Chrysler Corp., 430 Mass. 198, 715 N.E.2d 47, Prod. Liab. Rep. (CCH) ¶ 15593 (1999)
10 ALR5th 371—§ 11
59 ALR5th 733—§ 4

Santos v. Countrywide Home Loans, 2009 WL 3756337 (E.D. Cal. 2009)
104 ALR6th 485—§ 5

Santos v. Department of Motor Vehicles, 5 Cal. App. 4th 537, 7 Cal. Rptr. 2d 10 (1st Dist. 1992)
112 ALR5th 621—§ 3, 5

Santos v. Equitable Life Assur. Soc. of U.S., 220 A.D.2d 274, 632 N.Y.S.2d 110 (1st Dep't 1995)
63 ALR6th 495—§ 72

Santos v. George Washington University Hosp., 980 A.2d 1070 (D.C. 2009)
100 ALR6th 139—§ 37

Santos v. Greiner, 1999 WL 756473 (S.D. N.Y. 1999)
78 ALR5th 197—§ 13

Santos v. Sacks, 697 F. Supp. 275 (E.D. La. 1988)
78 ALR6th 151—§ 20

Santos v. Santos, 80 R.I. 5, 90 A.2d 771 (1952)
96 ALR5th 83—§ 2, 8, 9

Santos v. Scott Wetzel Services, 463 So. 2d 575, 10 FLW 436 (Fla. App. D1 1985)
12 ALR5th 658—§ 2, 4, 21, 33

Santos v. State Farm Mut. Auto. Ins. Co., 707 So. 2d 1181 (Fla. Dist. Ct. App. 2d Dist. 1998)
35 ALR5th 375—§ 50

Santos v. St. Vincent's Hosp. and Medical Center of New York, 8 Misc. 3d 193, 797 N.Y.S.2d 248 (Sup 2005)
100 ALR6th 139—§ 20

Santos v. Superior Court, 154 Cal. App. 3d 1178, 202 Cal. Rptr. 6 (1st Dist. 1984)
72 ALR5th 1—§ 29

Santos v. U.S., 461 F.3d 886 (7th Cir. 2006)
26 ALR6th 659—§ 59
36 ALR6th 681—§ 13

Santosa v. Chrysler Corp., 113 Wash. App. 1031, 2002 WL 31045305 (Div. 1 2002)
76 ALR6th 465—§ 4

Santoscoy v. State, 596 S.W.2d 896 (Tex. Crim. 1980)
13 ALR5th 1—§ 2, 22, 49

Santoscoy v. State, 596 S.W.2d 896 (Tex. Crim. App. 1980)
60 ALR6th 175—§ 7

Santosky v. Kramer, 455 U.S. 745, 71 L. Ed. 599, 102 S. Ct. 1388 (1982)
1 ALR5th 469—§ 2
15 ALR5th 692—§ 2

Santosky v. Kramer, 455 U.S. 745, 102 S. Ct. 1388, 71 L. Ed. 2d 599 (1982)
110 ALR5th 579—§ 2

Santos Y., In re, 92 Cal. App. 4th 1274, 112 Cal. Rptr. 2d 692 (2d Dist. 2001)
63 ALR6th 429—§ 5, 20

Santos Y., In re, 2001 WL 818896 (Cal. App. 2d Dist. 2001)
89 ALR5th 195—§ 2.5

Santoya, State ex rel. v. Edwards, 879 S.W.2d 775 (Mo. App. 1994)
58 ALR5th 535—§ 2, 10

Santoya, State ex rel. v. Edwards, 879 S.W.2d 775, 93 Ed. Law Rep. 428 (Mo. Ct. App. E.D. 1994)
80 ALR6th 389—§ 5

Santrade, Ltd. v. General Elec. Co., 150 F.R.D. 539, 27 U.S.P.Q.2d 1446 (E.D. N.C. 1993)
27 ALR5th 76—§ 8, 23, 44

Santry v. Richman, 6 Mass. App. 955, 383 N.E.2d 514 (1978)
23 ALR5th 241—§ 4

Santucci v. Chrysler Corp., 1995 WL 808713 (Mass. Super. Ct. 1995)
76 ALR6th 465—§ 5

Santucci v. Santucci, 1985 WL 9010 (Ohio Ct. App. 8th Dist. Cuyahoga County 1985)
124 ALR5th 441—§ 4, 8, 12
2 ALR6th 439—§ 12, 29

Santucci Const. Co. v. Baxter & Woodman, Inc., 151 Ill. App. 3d 547, 104 Ill. Dec. 474, 502 N.E.2d 1134 (2d Dist. 1986)
61 ALR6th 445—§ 21

Santy v. Bresee, 129 Ill. App. 3d 658, 84 Ill. Dec. 853, 473 N.E.2d 69 (4th Dist. 1984)
90 ALR5th 273—§ 3, 4, 12, 14

Sanvik v. Maher, 280 Minn. 113, 158 N.W.2d 206 (1968)
25 ALR5th 233—§ 12

Sanville v. State, 553 P.2d 1386 (Wyo. 1976)
57 ALR6th 83—§ 11

Sanwa Bank, Ltd. v. Kato, 734 So. 2d 557 (Fla. Dist. Ct. App. 5th Dist. 1999)
32 ALR6th 419—§ 24

Sanza v. Maryland State Board of Censors, 245 Md. 319, 226 A.2d 317 (1967)
13 ALR5th 567—§ 3

Sanzone v. National Elevator Inspection Service, Inc., 273 A.D.2d 94, 709 N.Y.S.2d 79 (1st Dep't 2000)
99 ALR5th 141—§ 1
115 ALR5th 1—§ 1

Saperstein v. Everett, 265 Mass. 195, 163 N.E. 757 (1928)
17 ALR5th 547—§ 25

SA-PG-Ocala, LLC v. Stokes, 935 So. 2d 1242 (Fla. Dist. Ct. App. 5th Dist. 2006)
50 ALR6th 187—§ 11

Sapiente v. Waltuch, 127 Conn. 224, 15 A.2d 417 (1940)
1 ALR5th 1—§ 26

Saponaro v. Com., 51 Va. App. 149, 655 S.E.2d 49 (2008)
68 ALR6th 527—§ 40

Sapp, Claim of, 75 Idaho 65, 266 P.2d 1027 (1954)
27 ALR6th 123—§ 15

Sapp v. City of Tallahassee, 348 So. 2d 363 (Fla. Dist. Ct. App. 1st Dist. 1977)
2 ALR5th 369—§ 2, 8, 9

90 ALR5th 273—§ 3, 4, 14

Sapp v. Coshatt, 245 Ga. App. 549, 538 S.E.2d 193 (2000)
11 ALR6th 1—§ 4, 6

Sapp v. Greif, 141 F.3d 1185 (10th Cir. 1998)
20 ALR6th 411—§ 12

Sapp v. Johnson, 184 Ga. App. 603, 362 S.E.2d 82 (1987)
62 ALR5th 537—§ 3

Sapp v. Key, 287 S.W.2d 775 (Mo. 1956)
5 ALR5th 875—§ 4, 8, 34, 36, 37

Sapp v. State, 690 So. 2d 581 (Fla. 1997)
38 ALR6th 97—§ 3, 14

Sapp v. State Farm Auto. Ins. Co., 272 S.C. 301, 251 S.E.2d 745 (1979)
77 ALR5th 319—§ 7
78 ALR5th 341—§ 11

Sapp v. State Farm Fire & Cas. Co., 226 Ga. App. 200, 486 S.E.2d 71 (1997)
8 ALR6th 549—§ 4, 20

Sappington v. Bartee, 195 F.3d 234 (5th Cir. 1999)
65 ALR6th 93—§ 15

Sappington v. Sutton, 501 P.2d 814 (Okla. 1972)
11 ALR5th 127—§ 4, 37, 45

Sappington v. U. S., 523 F.2d 858 (8th Cir. 1975)
97 ALR5th 201—§ 3

Sapp, State ex rel. v. Franklin Cty. Court of Appeals, 118 Ohio St. 3d 368, 2008-Ohio-2637, 889 N.E.2d 500 (2008)
45 ALR6th 493—§ 59

Sara B., In re, 203 App. Div.2d 747, 610 N.Y.S.2d 403 (3d Dep't 1994)
12 ALR6th 417—§ 10

Saracena v. Preisler, 180 A.D. 348, 167 N.Y.S. 871 (1st Dep't 1917)
75 ALR5th 1—§ 3

Saraceno v. Moore McCormack Lines, Inc., 26 App. Div. 2d 969, 274 N.Y.S.2d 717 (3d Dep't 1966)
26 ALR5th 127—§ 7

Saracina v. Cotoia, 417 Pa. 80, 208 A.2d 764 (1965)

97 ALR6th 375—§ 15
Saracino v. Davey & McConnell, Inc., 284 A.D. 913, 134 N.Y.S.2d 433 (3d Dep't 1954)

100 ALR5th 567—§ 8
Saracino v. Toms River Regional High School East, 2009 WL 3460680 (N.J. Super. Ct. App. Div. 2009)

75 ALR6th 109—§ 9
Sarafin v. Com., 62 Va. App. 385, 748 S.E.2d 641 (2013)

92 ALR6th 295—§ 16
96 ALR6th 355—§ 8, 34
Saragusa v. Chicago, 63 Ill. 2d 288, 348 N.E.2d 176 (1976)

45 ALR5th 109—§ 10
Sarah B., In re, 203 App. Div. 2d 747, 610 N.Y.S.2d 403 (3d Dep't 1994)

1 ALR5th 469—§ 40
Sarah B. v. Floyd B., 159 Cal. App. 4th 938, 71 Cal. Rptr. 3d 923 (Cal. App. 4th Dist. 2008)

57 ALR6th 163—§ 43
Sarah D., In re, 5 Cal. App. 4th 448, 6 Cal. Rptr. 2d 772, 92 C.D.O.S. 3101, 92 Daily Journal DAR 4868 (4th Dist. 1992)

20 ALR5th 534—§ 16
Sarah K., In re Interest of, 258 Neb. 52, 601 N.W.2d 780 (1999)

10 ALR6th 173—§ 37
Sarah Lawrence College v. City Council of City of Yonkers, 48 A.D.2d 897, 369 N.Y.S.2d 776 (2d Dep't 1975)

47 ALR6th 439—§ 7
Sara J., In re Adoption of, 123 P.3d 1017 (Alaska 2005)

63 ALR6th 429—§ 23, 25, 29
Sara K., In re, 611 A.2d 71 (Me. 1992)

113 ALR5th 349—§ 10
Sara K., Re, 611 A.2d 71 (Me. 1992)

1 ALR5th 469—§ 12, 14, 15
Sara Lee Corp. v. Carter, 129 N.C. App. 464, 500 S.E.2d 732 (1998)

48 ALR5th 473—§ 18
Saran C., Re Guardianship & Custody of, 156 App. Div. 2d 248, 548 N.Y.S.2d 509 (1st Dep't 1989)

20 ALR5th 534—§ 4
Saraniero v. Safeway, Inc., 540 F. Supp. 749, CCH Prod. Liab. Rep. ¶ 9673, 34 FR Serv. 2d 832 (D.C. Kan. 1982)

49 ALR5th 1—§ 40
Saranillio v. Silva, 78 Hawaii 1, 889 P.2d 685 (1995)

6 ALR5th 883—§ 7
Sarantopoulos v. State, 629 So. 2d 121 (Fla. 1993)

62 ALR6th 413—§ 39
Sara P. v. Richard T., 175 Misc. 2d 988, 670 N.Y.S.2d 964 (Fam. Ct. 1998)

70 ALR5th 377—§ 2, 5
Sarasota, City of v. Mikos, 374 So. 2d 458 (Fla. 1979)

114 ALR5th 561—§ 2, 4
Sarasota County School Dist. v. Sarasota Classified/Teachers Ass'n, 614 So. 2d 1143, 81 Ed. Law Rep. 666 (Fla. Dist. Ct. App. 2d Dist. 1993)

34 ALR6th 327—§ 6
Saratoga Bible Training Institute, Inc. v. Schuylerville Cent. School Dist., 18 F. Supp. 2d 178, 130 Ed. Law Rep. 127 (N.D. N.Y. 1998)

70 ALR6th 513—§ 17
71 ALR6th 471—§ 13
Saratoga Springs, City of v. Zoning Board of Appeals of the Town of Wilton, 279 A.D.2d 756, 719 N.Y.S.2d 178 (3d Dep't 2001)

64 ALR6th 365—§ 8
Sarauer v. Sarauer, 216 Wis. 2d 384, 576 N.W.2d 89 (Ct. App. 1998)

86 ALR6th 321—§ 13
90 ALR6th 451—§ 50
Saravia v. Makkos of Brooklyn, 694 N.Y.S.2d 393 (App. Div. 1st Dep't 1999)

38 ALR5th 107—§ 8
Sarbacher v. AmeriCold Realty Trust, 2011 WL 5520442 (D. Idaho 2011)

85 ALR6th 323—§ 88
Sarbro VII v. City of Binghamton, 270 A.D.2d 638, 704 N.Y.S.2d 358 (3d Dep't 2000)

12 ALR6th 123—§ 21
Sarchiz v. Clamdigger, Inc, 1983 WL 6831 (Ohio Ct. App. 6th Dist. Lucas County 1983)
74 ALR5th 49—§ 3, 10
Sardana, In re, 2011 WL 3299861 (B.A.P. 9th Cir. 2011)
86 ALR6th 411—§ 5
Sardella v. Hei Hotels No. 101 Inc., 715 N.Y.S.2d 748 (App. Div. 2d Dep't 2000)
55 ALR5th 463—§ 16
Sardinia v. Dellwood Foods, Inc., 69 Fair Empl. Prac. Cas. (BNA) 705, 67 Empl. Prac. Dec. (CCH) ¶ 43784, 1995 WL 640502 (S.D. N.Y. 1995)
73 ALR5th 1—§ 3, 5, 7
Sareen, In re Marriage of, 153 Cal. App. 4th 371, 62 Cal. Rptr. 3d 687 (3d Dist. 2007)
36 ALR6th 681—§ 7
52 ALR6th 433—§ 15
57 ALR6th 163—§ 40
66 ALR6th 269—§ 15
Sareen v. Sareen, 128 S. Ct. 1670, 170 L. Ed. 2d 357 (U.S. 2008)
36 ALR6th 681—§ 7
Sargeant v. Sargeant, 88 Nev. 223, 495 P.2d 618 (1972)
122 ALR5th 205—§ 16, 49
Sargeant v. Serrani, 866 F. Supp. 657 (D. Conn. 1994)
54 ALR6th 165—§ 7
Sargent, In re Adoption of, 28 Ohio Misc. 261, 57 Ohio Op. 2d 135, 57 Ohio Op. 2d 494, 272 N.E.2d 206 (C.P. 1970)
82 ALR5th 443—§ 4, 5, 8
83 ALR5th 375—§ 7
84 ALR5th 191—§ 7
Sargent v. Board of Ed. of Baltimore County, 49 Md. App. 577, 433 A.2d 1209 (1981)
83 ALR5th 103—§ 3, 26, 28, 31
84 ALR5th 249—§ 24

Sargent v. Browning-Ferris Industries, 167 Mich. App. 29, 421 N.W.2d 563, 131 L.R.R.M. (BNA) 2254, 108 Lab. Cas. (CCH) ¶ 10449 (1988)
110 ALR5th 111—§ 19
Sargent v. Central Nat. Bank & Trust Co. of Enid, Okl., 1991 OK 23, 809 P.2d 1298, 6 I.E.R. Cas. (BNA) 360, 121 Lab. Cas. (CCH) ¶ 56862 (Okla. 1991)
104 ALR5th 1—§ 3, 5, 6
Sargent v. City of Cincinnati, 25 Ohio N.P. (n.s.) 89, 1923 WL 2054 (C.P. 1923)
99 ALR6th 591—§ 4
Sargent v. Commissioner of Correction, 121 Conn. App. 725, 997 A.2d 609 (2010)
71 ALR6th 1—§ 12
Sargent v. Gagne, 121 Vt. 1, 147 A.2d 892 (1958)
62 ALR5th 219—§ 53
Sargent v. Idle, 212 Fed. Appx. 569 (7th Cir. 2006)
65 ALR6th 93—§ 22
Sargent v. Johnson, 601 F.2d 964 (CA8 Minn. 1979)
59 ALR5th 733—§ 3
Sargent v. New York Daily News, L.P., 42 A.D.3d 491, 840 N.Y.S.2d 101 (2d Dep't 2007)
48 ALR6th 243—§ 3
Sargent v. Sargent, 20 Va. App. 694, 460 S.E.2d 596 (1995)
57 ALR5th 389—§ 2
Sargent v. Sargent, 1997 ME 38, 691 A.2d 184 (Me. 1997)
86 ALR6th 321—§ 4
90 ALR6th 451—§ 49
Sargent v. State, 11 Ohio. 472 (1842)
14 ALR5th 89—§ 3, 11, 25, 30
Sargent v. State, 96 Ind. 63, 1884 WL 5320 (1884)
105 ALR5th 529—§ 11
Sargent v. State, 153 Ind. App. 430, 287 N.E.2d 795 (2d Dist. 1972)
23 ALR6th 307—§ 31

Sargent v. State Farm Mut. Auto. Ins. Co., 486 N.W.2d 14 (Minn. Ct. App. 1992)

75 ALR6th 235—§ 4, 10

Sargent Const. Co., Inc. v. State Auto. Ins. Co., 23 F.3d 1324 (8th Cir. 1994)

98 ALR5th 193—§ 10

Sarin v. Ochsner, 48 Mass. App. Ct. 421, 721 N.E.2d 932 (2000)

86 ALR6th 321—§ 12, 13

89 ALR6th 409—§ 42, 43

Sarin v. Samaritan Health Center, 176 Mich. App. 790, 440 N.W.2d 80 (1989)

28 ALR5th 107—§ 3

Saritejdiam, Inc. v. Excess Ins. Co., 971 F.2d 910 (CA2 N.Y. 1992)

22 ALR5th 579—§ 15

Sarivola v. Brookdale Hosp. and Medical Center, 204 A.D.2d 245, 612 N.Y.S.2d 151 (1st Dep't 1994)

64 ALR6th 249—§ 32

Sarkis v. Allstate Ins. Co., 863 So. 2d 210, 119 A.L.R.5th 611 (Fla. 2003)

119 ALR5th 121—§ 3, 11

Sarkis v. Harsco Corp., 332 A.2d 156 (Del. Super. Ct. 1975)

120 ALR5th 559—§ 10

Sarkisian Bros., Inc. v. Hartnett, 172 App. Div. 2d 895, 568 N.Y.S.2d 190, 30 BNA WH Cas. 405 (3d Dep't 1991)

5 ALR5th 470—§ 5, 6

10 ALR5th 337—§ 3

Sarkissian v. West Virginia University Bd. of Governors, 2008 WL 901722 (N.D. W. Va. 2008)

90 ALR6th 235—§ 71

Sarko v. Penn-Del Directory Co., 968 F. Supp. 1026, 25 A.D.D. 569, 7 A.D. Cas. (BNA) 1201 (E.D. Pa. 1997)

81 ALR5th 367—§ 4

Sarles, In re Marriage of, 143 Cal. App. 3d 24, 191 Cal. Rptr. 514 (4th Dist. 1983)

59 ALR6th 433—§ 46, 55

Sarl Louis Feraud Intern. v. Viewfinder, Inc., 489 F.3d 474, 35 Media L. Rep. (BNA) 1879, 83 U.S.P.Q.2d 1105 (2d Cir. 2007)

30 ALR6th 299—§ 25

Sarlo, Application of, 52 Misc. 2d 547, 276 N.Y.S.2d 41 (1966)

12 ALR5th 577—§ 2, 9

Sarlund v. Anderson, 205 F.3d 973 (7th Cir. 2000)

54 ALR5th 141—§ 5

Sarmiento, In re, 194 N.J. 164, 943 A.2d 839 (2008)

43 ALR6th 163—§ 68

Sarmiento v. Armour, 2005 WL 3019746 (S.D. Tex. 2005)

65 ALR6th 93—§ 58

Sarno v. Board of Firearms Permit Examiners, 1995 WL 643604 (Conn. Super. Ct. 1995)

91 ALR6th 435—§ 56

Sarno v. State, 424 So. 2d 829 (Fla. App. D3 1982)

18 ALR5th 1—§ 14, 24

Sarnovsky v. Snyder, Evans & Anderson, Inc., 38 Ohio App. 3d 33, 525 N.E.2d 826 (10th Dist. Franklin County 1987)

17 ALR6th 159—§ 8

Sarnovsky v. Snyder, Evans & Anderson, Inc., 38 Ohio App. 3d 33, 525 N.E.2d 826 (Franklin Co. 1987)

12 ALR5th 1—§ 2

Saro Corp. v. Waterman Broadcasting Corp., 595 So. 2d 87, 17 FLW D 319, 19 Media L. R. 2031 (Fla. App. D2 1992)

19 ALR5th 1—§ 172

Saroff v. Haun, 17 P.3d 943 (Kan. Ct. App. 2001)

47 ALR5th 129—§ 4

Saron v. State, 24 App. Div. 2d 771, 263 N.Y.S.2d 591 (1965)

43 ALR5th 87—§ 6

Sarosdy v. Sarosdy, 297 S.W.2d 852 (Tex. Civ. App. Dallas 1957)

53 ALR5th 375—§ 3

Sarpel v. Eflanli, 65 So. 3d 1080 (Fla. Dist. Ct. App. 4th Dist. 2011)
66 ALR6th 269—§ 15

Sarpel v. Eflanli, 2011 WL 2135575 (Fla. Dist. Ct. App. 4th Dist. 2011)
66 ALR6th 269—§ 15

Sarphie v. Rowe, 618 So. 2d 905 (La. Ct. App. 1st Cir. 1993)
66 ALR5th 591—§ 3

Sarr v. State, 2005 WY 67, 113 P.3d 1051 (Wyo. 2005)
30 ALR6th 1—§ 3, 6

Sarratore v. Longview Van Corp., 666 F. Supp. 1257, 2 I.E.R. Cas. (BNA) 922 (N.D. Ind. 1987)
104 ALR5th 1—§ 3 to 5, 8

Sarriera v. Axel Electronics, Inc., 25 A.D.2d 592, 267 N.Y.S.2d 84 (3d Dep't 1966)
41 ALR6th 207—§ 33

Sarro v. City of Sacramento, 78 F. Supp. 2d 1057, 81 Fair Empl. Prac. Cas. (BNA) 1142 (E.D. Cal. 1999)
94 ALR5th 1—§ 17, 19

Sarro v. Cornell Corrections, Inc., 248 F. Supp. 2d 52, 119 A.L.R.5th 593 (D.R.I. 2003)
119 ALR5th 1—§ 6, 8 to 10

Sarro v. Retail Store Employees Union, 155 Cal. App. 3d 206, 202 Cal. Rptr. 102 (1st Dist. 1984)
120 ALR5th 351—§ 29

Sarro v. Smith, 8 A.D.3d 395, 777 N.Y.S.2d 710 (2d Dep't 2004)
91 ALR6th 435—§ 151

Sarruf v. Miller, 90 Wash. 2d 880, 586 P.2d 466, 39 BNA FEP Cas. 366, 115 BNA LRRM 4221, 18 CCH EPD ¶ 8885 (1978)
51 ALR5th 1—§ 8

Sartain v. State, 10 Tex. App. 651 (Ct. App. 1881)
76 ALR5th 485—§ 3, 21

Sartain v. White, 588 So. 2d 204 (Miss. 1991)
86 ALR6th 321—§ 12
87 ALR6th 197—§ 76

Sartin v. Mazur, 237 Va. 82, 375 S.E.2d 741, 4 BNA IER Cas. 96 (1989)
1 ALR5th 401—§ 3

Sartin v. Sartin, 349 S.W.2d 705 (Mo. Ct. App. 1961)
26 ALR6th 331—§ 9

Sartin v. State, 51 Tex. Crim. 571, 103 S.W. 875 (1907)
50 ALR5th 467—§ 7, 8, 10

Sartor v. United Gas Public Service Co., 84 F.2d 436 (C.C.A. 5th Cir. 1936)
99 ALR5th 415—§ 3

Sartori v. Department of Revenue, 714 So. 2d 1136 (Fla. Dist. Ct. App. 5th Dist. 1998)
1 ALR6th 1—§ 16

Sartori v. Harnischfeger Corp., 432 N.W.2d 448 (Minn. 1988)
122 ALR5th 1—§ 12, 28, 33, 36
5 ALR6th 497—§ 3, 4, 7, 9

Sarvela, In re, 154 N.H. 426, 910 A.2d 1214 (2006)
101 ALR6th 455—§ 3

Sarver v. Com., 2005 WL 2044530 (Ky. 2005)
23 ALR6th 307—§ 38

Sarwar v. Sarwar, 117 S.W.3d 165, 118 A.L.R.5th 759 (Mo. Ct. App. W.D. 2003)
118 ALR5th 385—§ 14

Sarzillo v. Turner Const. Co., 101 N.J. 114, 501 A.2d 135 (1985)
11 ALR6th 351—§ 29

Sas, In re, 488 B.R. 178 (Bankr. D. Nev. 2013)
99 ALR6th 481—§ 34

Sas v. Strelecki, 110 N.J. Super. 14, 264 A.2d 247 (App. Div. 1970)
111 ALR5th 1—§ 8, 13

Sasco, Inc. v. Wells Fargo Alarm Services, Inc., 969 F. Supp. 535 (E.D. Mo. 1997)
36 ALR6th 305—§ 6, 14, 15

Sash v. City of New York, 2006 WL 2474874 (S.D. N.Y. 2006)
89 ALR6th 1—§ 105

Sash v. Dudley, 222 Fed. Appx. 95 (2d Cir. 2007)

52 ALR6th 1—§ 16
Sash v. Dudley, 2006 WL 997256 (S.D. N.Y. 2006)

52 ALR6th 1—§ 16
Sasiadek's Inc. v. City of Tucson, 159 Ariz. 164, 765 P.2d 566 (Ct. App. Div. 2 1988)

113 ALR5th 313—§ 17
Sasich v. City of Omaha, 216 Neb. 864, 347 N.W.2d 93 (1984)

66 ALR5th 135—§ 23
SAS Institute, Inc. v. S. & H Computer Systems, Inc., 605 F. Supp. 816, 225 USPQ 916 (M.D. Tenn. 1985)

38 ALR5th 1—§ 14
Saslow, In re Marriage of, 40 Cal. 3d 848, 221 Cal. Rptr. 546, 710 P.2d 346 (1985)

80 ALR5th 533—§ 8, 11
Sass v. Hanson, 5 Neb. App. 28, 554 N.W.2d 642 (1996)

11 ALR6th 1—§ 4, 10
Sass v. Spradlin, 66 Ill. App. 3d 976, 23 Ill. Dec. 670, 384 N.E.2d 464, 25 U.C.C. Rep. Serv. 1289 (2d Dist. 1978)

94 ALR6th 1—§ 2, 22, 42
Sass v. Spradlin, 66 Ill. App. 3d 976, 23 Ill. Dec. 670, 384 N.E.2d 464, 25 U.C.C.R.S. 1289 (2d Dist. 1978)

47 ALR5th 677—§ 5
Sassaman v. Heart City Toyota, 879 F. Supp. 901, 66 BNA FEP Cas. 1230 (N.D. Ind. 1994)

12 ALR5th 195—§ 33
Sasseen v. Community Hosp. Foundation, 159 Mich. App. 231, 406 N.W.2d 193 (1986)

58 ALR5th 613—§ 10
64 ALR6th 249—§ 34
Sassen v. Haegle, 125 Minn. 441, 147 N.W. 445 (1914)

109 ALR5th 421—§ 8
Sasser v. Beck, 65 N.C. App. 170, 308 S.E.2d 722 (1983)

55 ALR5th 463—§ 5, 14
Sasser v. Connery, 565 So. 2d 50 (Ala. 1990)

97 ALR6th 83—§ 34
Sasser v. Norris, 553 F.3d 1121 (8th Cir. 2009)

56 ALR6th 679—§ 22
Sasser v. Spartan Foods Systems, Inc., 452 So. 2d 475 (Ala. 1984)

62 ALR5th 219—§ 49
Sasser v. State, 338 Ark. 375, 993 S.W.2d 901 (1999)

83 ALR6th 465—§ 27, 33
Sasser v. U.S., 227 F.2d 358 (CA5 Fla. 1955)

41 ALR5th 171—§ 3
Sasso v. Koehler, 451 F. Supp. 933 (D. Md. 1978)

67 ALR5th 587—§ 11
15 ALR6th 427—§ 4
Sasso v. Ram Property Management, 431 So. 2d 204 (Fla. App. D1 1983)

12 ALR5th 658—§ 4, 20
Sasso v. Ram Property Management, 452 So. 2d 932 (Fla. 1984)

51 ALR5th 1—§ 4
Sasso v. Travel Dynamics, Inc., 844 F. Supp. 68 (D. Mass. 1994)

82 ALR6th 175—§ 6
Sasson, In re Estate of, 387 N.J. Super. 459, 904 A.2d 769 (App. Div. 2006)

21 ALR6th 351—§ 13, 14, 18, 20, 24, 27
Sassone v. Elder, 601 So. 2d 792 (La. App. 4th Cir. 1992)

19 ALR5th 1—§ 40
Sassoon v. Stynchombe, 654 F.2d 371 (5th Cir. 1981)

52 ALR6th 1—§ 10, 18
Sassoonian v. City of New York, 692 N.Y.S.2d 12 (App. Div. 1st Dep't 1999)

48 ALR5th 129—§ 8
Sassower, Matter of, 700 F. Supp. 100 (E.D. N.Y. 1988)

43 ALR6th 163—§ 63
Sastrom v. Mullaney, 1999 WL 1241246 (Conn. Super. Ct. 1999)

87 ALR5th 277—§ 39, 41
Sastrom v. Mullaney, 2000 WL 1838943 (Conn. Super. Ct. 2000)

---

87 ALR5th 277—§ 37
Satalino v. Satalino, No. 11440-86 (N.Y. Sup. Ct. Nassau Cty 1990)
36 ALR5th 377—§ 4
Satariano v. Sleight, 54 Cal. App. 2d 278, 129 P.2d 35 (1st Dist. 1942)
66 ALR5th 1—§ 25
Satawa v. Bd. of County Road Com'rs of Macomb County, 2011 WL 1515174 (E.D. Mich. 2011)
70 ALR6th 513—§ 5
Satawa v. Board of County Road Com'rs of Macomb County, 687 F. Supp. 2d 682 (E.D. Mich. 2009)
70 ALR6th 513—§ 5
71 ALR6th 471—§ 7
Satcher v. Honda Motor Co., Ltd., 855 F. Supp. 886 (S.D. Miss. 1994)
73 ALR5th 75—§ 12
Satcher v. Honda Motor Co., Ltd., 984 F.2d 135, Prod. Liab. Rep. (CCH) ¶ 13405 (5th Cir. 1993)
73 ALR5th 75—§ 12
Satcher v. Honda Motor Co., Ltd., 993 F.2d 56, Prod. Liab. Rep. (CCH) ¶ 13514 (5th Cir. 1993)
73 ALR5th 75—§ 12
Satcher v. Pruett, 126 F.3d 561 (4th Cir. 1997)
72 ALR5th 109—§ 4
102 ALR6th 417—§ 86
Satcher v. Wiser, 483 So. 2d 694 (Miss. 1986)
4 ALR5th 148—§ 13
4 ALR5th 210—§ 10
Satchwell v. LaQuinta Motor Inns, Inc., 532 So. 2d 1348 (Fla. Dist. Ct. App. 1st Dist. 1988)
17 ALR6th 453—§ 13
Sate v. Barnes, 32 S.C. 14, 10 S.E. 611 (1890)
54 ALR5th 743—§ 3
Sate v. Roesing, 2001 WL 951287 (Conn. Super. Ct. 2001)
111 ALR5th 239—§ 6
Sateren v. Sateren, 488 N.W.2d 631 (N.D. 1992)
10 ALR5th 191—§ 5

Sather, In re, 3 P.3d 403 (Colo. 2000)
102 ALR5th 253—§ 2, 5, 6, 10, 15, 18
Sather v. King, 2008 WL 170508 (Minn. Ct. App. 2008)
58 ALR6th 1—§ 5
60 ALR6th 1—§ 81
Sato v. Century 21 Ocean Shores Real Estate, 101 Wash. 2d 599, 681 P.2d 242 (1984)
117 ALR5th 155—§ 12
Sato v. Van Denburgh, 123 Ariz. 225, 599 P.2d 181 (1979)
7 ALR5th 852—§ 3, 9, 10, 18, 20
Satrap v. Pacific Gas & Electric Co., 42 Cal. App. 4th 72, 49 Cal. Rptr. 2d 348, 131 Lab. Cas. (CCH) ¶ 58111 (1st Dist. 1996)
106 ALR5th 523—§ 4, 14
Sattar v. Thomas, 2003 WL 21100664 (Conn. Super. Ct. 2003)
118 ALR5th 91—§ 30
Sattayarak v. State, 1994 OK CR 64, 887 P.2d 1326 (Okla. Crim. App. 1994)
35 ALR6th 127—§ 4
Satter v. Solem, 422 N.W.2d 425 (S.D. 1988)
38 ALR6th 97—§ 28
Satter v. Solem, 434 N.W.2d 725 (S.D. 1989)
38 ALR6th 97—§ 28
Satter v. Solem, 458 N.W.2d 762 (S.D. 1990)
38 ALR6th 97—§ 28
Satterfield v. Breeding Insulation Co., Inc., 2007 WL 1159416 (Tenn. Ct. App. 2007)
33 ALR6th 325—§ 12
Satterfield v. Crown Cork & Seal Co., Inc., 268 S.W.3d 190 (Tex. App. Austin 2008)
41 ALR6th 445—§ 15
Satterfield v. Lockheed Missiles and Space Co., Inc., 617 F. Supp. 1359 (D.S.C. 1985)
7 ALR6th 563—§ 5
Satterfield v. McLellan Stores Co., 215 N.C. 582, 2 S.E.2d 709 (1939)

52 ALR6th 271—§ 19
Satterfield v. Pappas, 67 N.C. App. 28, 312 S.E.2d 511 (1984)

12 ALR6th 123—§ 10
Satterfield v. Satterfield, 292 Or. 780, 643 P.2d 336 (1982)

48 ALR5th 473—§ 8
52 ALR5th 221—§ 20
Satterfield v. State, 256 Ga. 593, 351 S.E.2d 625 (1987)

97 ALR5th 201—§ 6
16 ALR6th 329—§ 4
24 ALR6th 591—§ 6, 12
Satterfield v. Texas Dept. of Public Safety, 221 S.W.3d 909 (Tex. App. Beaumont 2007)

91 ALR6th 435—§ 147
Satterfield v. Winston Industries, Inc., 553 So. 2d 61 (Ala. 1989)

86 ALR6th 321—§ 5
89 ALR6th 409—§ 62
Satterlee v. State, 1976 OK CR 88, 549 P.2d 104 (Okla. Crim. App. 1976)

85 ALR5th 471—§ 7
Satterlund v. Beal, 12 N.D. 122, 95 N.W. 518 (1903)

36 ALR6th 387—§ 5
Satterly v. Stiles, 409 S.W.2d 820 (Ky. 1966)

9 ALR5th 826—§ 6
Satterwhite v. Bocelato, 130 F. Supp. 825 (D.C. N.C. 1955)

27 ALR5th 174—§ 101
Satterwhite v. Jacobs, 26 S.W.3d 35 (Tex. App. Houston 1st Dist. 2000)

4 ALR5th 273—§ 27
Satterwhite v. State, 77 Tex. Crim. 130, 177 S.W. 959 (1915)

22 ALR5th 1—§ 9, 23, 55, 56
Satterwhite v. State, 359 So. 2d 816 (Ala. App. 1977)

42 ALR5th 581—§ 8, 19
Satterwhite v. State, 697 S.W.2d 774 (Tex. App. Corpus Christi 1985)

18 ALR5th 1—§ 15
Sattler v. City of Los Angeles, 121 Cal. App. 3d 511, 175 Cal. Rptr. 390 (2d Dist. 1981)

105 ALR5th 1—§ 3, 11
Sattler v. Northwest Tissue Center, 110 Wash. App. 689, 42 P.3d 440 (Div. 1 2002)

6 ALR6th 365—§ 6
Sattler v. Sattler, 284 S.C. 422, 327 S.E.2d 71 (S.C. 1985)

46 ALR5th 735—§ 3
Saturday Evening Post Co. v. Rumbleseat Press, Inc., 816 F.2d 1191, 2 U.S.P.Q.2d 1499, 1987-1 Trade Cas. (CCH) ¶ 67537 (7th Cir. 1987)

76 ALR6th 289—§ 7
Saturn Const. Co., Inc. v. Premier Roofing Co., Inc., 238 Conn. 293, 680 A.2d 1274 (1996)

60 ALR5th 669—§ 6
Satyshur v. General Motors Corp., 38 F. Supp. 2d 744 (N.D. Ind. 1999)

1 ALR5th 401—§ 3
Satz v. Corrections Corporations of America, Inc., 43 Fed. Appx. 64 (9th Cir. 2002)

119 ALR5th 1—§ 19 to 21
Satz v. Koplow, 397 N.E.2d 1082 (Ind. App. 1979)

12 ALR5th 195—§ 58, 66
Sauby v. City of Fargo, 2009 WL 2168942 (D.N.D. 2009)

60 ALR6th 295—§ 4, 6, 10, 18, 43, 50
Sauceda v. GMAC Mortg. Corp., 268 S.W.3d 135 (Tex. App. Corpus Christi 2008)

81 ALR6th 161—§ 3, 4
82 ALR6th 43—§ 3, 18
Sauceda v. Kerlin, 164 S.W.3d 892 (Tex. App. Corpus Christi 2005)

39 ALR6th 155—§ 16
Sauceda v. State, 2006 WL 488596 (Tex. App. Houston 1st Dist. 2006)

99 ALR6th 295—§ 9, 13
Saucedo v. State, 2003 WL 22298564 (Tex. App. San Antonio 2003)

41 ALR6th 141—§ 7
Saucedo, U.S. ex rel. v. Lane, 599 F. Supp. 337 (N.D. Ill. 1984)

49 ALR6th 343—§ 20

Saucer v. Willys-Overland, Inc., 49 F.2d 385 (D.C. Fla. 1931)
42 ALR5th 465—§ 3

Saucier v. Drs. Houston, Roy, Faust & Ewin, 446 So. 2d 877 (La. Ct. App. 4th Cir. 1984)
5 ALR6th 133—§ 14, 20
14 ALR6th 301—§ 4, 17
76 ALR6th 31—§ 46

Saucier v. Hayes Dairy Products, Inc., 373 So. 2d 102 (La. 1978)
56 ALR5th 1—§ 3, 8

Saucier v. Katz, 533 U.S. 194, 121 S. Ct. 2151, 150 L. Ed. 2d 272 (2001)
45 ALR6th 1—§ 3

Saucier v. Players Lake Charles, LLC, 751 So. 2d 312 (La. Ct. App. 3d Cir. 1999)
48 ALR5th 129—§ 18

Saucier v. State, 95 Miss. 226, 48 So. 840 (1909)
41 ALR5th 1—§ 3, 4

Saucier v. United States Fidelity & Guaranty Co., 765 F. Supp. 334 (S.D. Miss. 1991)
16 ALR5th 412—§ 20

Saucier's Case, 122 Me. 325, 119 A. 860 (1923)
80 ALR5th 417—§ 4

Saucon Valley School Dist. v. Robert O., 785 A.2d 1069, 160 Ed. Law Rep. 159, 115 A.L.R.5th 763 (Pa. Commw. Ct. 2001)
115 ALR5th 183—§ 3, 13, 26, 29

Sauczcuk v. Frankoski, 100 Conn. 700, 124 A. 719 (1924)
17 ALR5th 547—§ 14

Sauder v. Rayman, 800 So. 2d 355 (Fla. Dist. Ct. App. 4th Dist. 2001)
32 ALR6th 419—§ 16, 35

Saudi Arabian Airlines Corp. v. Dunn, 438 So. 2d 116 (Fla. App. D1 1983)
27 ALR5th 174—§ 92
40 ALR5th 603—§ 17

Saudi Basic Industries Corp. v. Mobil Yanbu Petrochemical Co., Inc., 866 A.2d 1 (Del. 2005)
82 ALR6th 1—§ 6, 22

Sauer v. Century Federal Sav. & Loan Ass'n of Long Island, 69 A.D.2d 495, 418 N.Y.S.2d 464 (2d Dep't 1979)
24 ALR6th 399—§ 20

Sauer v. Home Indem. Co., 841 P.2d 176 (Alaska 1992)
88 ALR5th 493—§ 4
89 ALR5th 1—§ 16

Sauer v. Wells Fargo Bank, N.A., 2013 WL 1824094 (W.D. Tex. 2013)
104 ALR6th 485—§ 5

Sauers v. Smits, 49 Wash. 557, 95 P. 1097 (1908)
84 ALR5th 619—§ 3
108 ALR5th 385—§ 8

Sauers v. Tibbs, 48 Ill. App. 3d 805, 6 Ill. Dec. 762, 363 N.E.2d 444, 22 U.C.C.R.S. 363 (4th Dist. 1977)
38 ALR5th 191—§ 2 to 5, 38

Sauer, State ex rel. v. Hellesvig, 376 N.W.2d 503 (Minn. App. 1985)
5 ALR5th 550—§ 42

Saugus Auto Theatre Corp. v. Munroe Realty Corp., 366 Mass. 310, 318 N.E.2d 615 (1974)
22 ALR5th 327—§ 2, 38

Saul v. Brunetti, 753 So. 2d 26 (Fla. 2000)
86 ALR6th 1—§ 98

Saul v. Brunetti, 2000 WL 65046 (Fla. 2000)
69 ALR5th 1—§ 4

Saul v. John D. & Catherine T. MacArthur Foundation, 499 So. 2d 917, 12 FLW 73 (Fla. App. D4 1986)
38 ALR5th 433—§ 56, 66

Saul v. State, 6 Md. App. 540, 252 A.2d 282 (1969)
72 ALR5th 529—§ 3, 5

Saul, Commonwealth ex rel. v. Saul, 175 Pa. Super. 540, 107 A.2d 182 (1954)
39 ALR5th 1—§ 3

Sauls v. Tangipahoa Parish School Bd., 273 So. 2d 899 (La. App. 1st Cir. 1973)
57 ALR5th 477—§ 31

CASES CITED IN ALR5th and ALR6th

Saulsberry v. Laboratory Corp. of America, 145 Lab. Cas. (CCH) ¶ 59450, 2001 WL 912824 (Tenn. Ct. App. 2001)
19 ALR6th 793—§ 8
Saulsberry v. State, 2004 WL 239767 (Tenn. Crim. App. 2004)
29 ALR6th 237—§ 4
Saulsbury v. State, 83 Okla. Crim. 7, 172 P.2d 440 (1946)
54 ALR6th 429—§ 24
Saulter v. State, 2013 WL 2313680 (Tenn. Crim. App. 2013)
97 ALR6th 263—§ 11
Saulters v. Anikst, 188 So. 2d 108 (La. App. 4th Cir. 1966)
9 ALR5th 826—§ 3
Saultz v. Funk, 64 Ohio App. 2d 29, 18 Ohio Op. 3d 19, 410 N.E.2d 1275 (8th Dist. Cuyahoga County 1979)
14 ALR6th 301—§ 4
Saum v. State, 200 Md. 85, 88 A.2d 562 (1952)
43 ALR5th 1—§ 8
Saums v. Saums, 610 S.W.2d 242 (Tex. Civ. App. El Paso 1980)
17 ALR5th 366—§ 10
Saunderlin v. E.I. DuPont Co., 102 N.J. 402, 508 A.2d 1095 (1986)
97 ALR5th 1—§ 5
106 ALR5th 111—§ 39
108 ALR5th 1—§ 43
Saunders, Application of, 295 F. Supp. 263 (D.V.I. 1968)
5 ALR6th 449—§ 4
Saunders, In re, 2 Cal. 3d 1033, 88 Cal. Rptr. 633, 472 P.2d 921 (1970)
79 ALR5th 419—§ 6, 9
Saunders, In re Marriage of, 496 N.E.2d 419 (Ind. Ct. App. 1st Dist. 1986)
26 ALR6th 331—§ 3, 22
Saunders v. Air Florida, Inc., 558 F. Supp. 1233 (D.D.C. 1983)
99 ALR5th 301—§ 8
Saunders v. Alamo Soil Conservation Dist., 545 S.W.2d 249 (Tex. Civ. App. San Antonio 1976)
111 ALR5th 313—§ 22

Saunders v. Bailey, 205 Ga. App. 808, 423 S.E.2d 688, 92 Fulton County D R 2238 (1992)
12 ALR5th 658—§ 17, 29
Saunders v. Baker, 122 Mo. App. 294, 99 S.W. 51 (1907)
74 ALR5th 369—§ 10
Saunders v. Berks Credit and Collections, Inc., 2002 WL 1497374 (E.D. Pa. 2002)
60 ALR6th 295—§ 56
Saunders v. Big Bros., Inc., 115 Misc. 2d 845, 454 N.Y.S.2d 787 (N.Y. City Civ. Ct. 1982)
85 ALR6th 323—§ 59
Saunders v. Callaway, 42 Wash. App. 29, 708 P.2d 652 (Div. 3 1985)
12 ALR6th 123—§ 5
Saunders v. Cariss, 224 Cal. App. 3d 905, 274 Cal. Rptr. 186 (4th Dist. 1990)
6 ALR5th 297—§ 40
121 ALR5th 365—§ 2
Saunders v. Com., 1 Va. App. 396, 339 S.E.2d 550 (1986)
116 ALR5th 373—§ 3, 11
Saunders v. Eyman, 600 F.2d 728 (9th Cir. 1977)
72 ALR5th 109—§ 4
79 ALR5th 419—§ 6
Saunders v. Firtel, 293 Conn. 515, 978 A.2d 487 (2009)
49 ALR6th 1—§ 48
Saunders v. H.K. Porter Co., Inc., 643 F. Supp. 198 (E.D. Va. 1986)
41 ALR6th 445—§ 5
Saunders v. Hunter, 980 F. Supp. 1236 (M.D. Fla. 1997)
10 ALR6th 531—§ 18
37 ALR6th 137—§ 15
Saunders v. Industrial Com'n, 189 Ill. 2d 623, 244 Ill. Dec. 948, 727 N.E.2d 247 (2000)
61 ALR5th 375—§ 4, 6
Saunders v. Knight, 2007 WL 3482047 (E.D. Cal. 2007)
101 ALR6th 207—§ 38

For assistance, call 1-800-328-4880

70

Saunders v. Lischkoff, 137 Fla. 826, 188
So. 815 (1939)
30 ALR5th 571—§ 12, 24
Saunders v. Mullen, 66 Iowa 728, 24
N.W. 529 (1885)
14 ALR5th 242—§ 26
Saunders v. New England Collapsible
Tube Co., 95 Conn. 40, 110 A. 538
(1920)
47 ALR5th 801—§ 3, 16
Saunders v. North Alabama Neurologi-
cal, P.A., 1999 WL 1046455 (Ala.
Civ. App. 1999)
85 ALR5th 353—§ 11
Saunders v. Packel, 436 F. Supp. 618
(E.D. Pa. 1977)
98 ALR5th 305—§ 14
Saunders v. Patseavouras, 808 F.2d 835
(4th Cir. 1986)
54 ALR6th 1—§ 8, 28
Saunders v. Port Authority of New York,
2004 WL 1077964 (S.D. N.Y. 2004)
83 ALR6th 399—§ 3
Saunders v. Post-Standard Pub. Co., 107
A.D. 84, 94 N.Y.S. 993 (4th Dep't
1905)
69 ALR5th 645—§ 3, 9
Saunders v. Saunders, 243 Wis. 94, 9
N.W.2d 629 (1943)
52 ALR5th 221—§ 24
Saunders v. Simms, 183 Cal. 167, 190
P. 806 (1920)
14 ALR5th 557—§ 3
Saunders v. State, 199 Md. 568, 87 A.2d
618 (1952)
43 ALR5th 1—§ 13
Saunders v. State, 319 So. 2d 118 (Fla.
App. D1 1975)
29 ALR5th 702—§ 4, 6, 7
Saunders v. State, 562 N.E.2d 729 (Ind.
Ct. App. 1990)
43 ALR6th 475—§ 16
Saunders v. State, 758 So. 2d 724 (Fla.
Dist. Ct. App. 2d Dist. 2000)
47 ALR6th 107—§ 26
Saunders v. Superior Court, 27 Cal. App.
4th 832, 33 Cal. Rptr. 2d 438 (2d
Dist. 1994)

115 ALR5th 709—§ 3
Saunders v. Sutton, 55 A. 652 (N.J. Sup.
Ct. 1903)
91 ALR6th 1—§ 47
Saunders v. Thorn Woode Partnership
L.P., 265 Ga. 703, 462 S.E.2d 135
(1995)
115 ALR5th 251—§ 6
Saunders v. VanPelt, 497 A.2d 1121
(Me. 1985)
52 ALR6th 271—§ 10
67 ALR6th 437—§ 4, 8, 16
Saunders, County of v. Moore, 182 Neb.
377, 155 N.W.2d 317 (1967)
38 ALR5th 737—§ 2
Saunders Properties v. Municipality of
Anchorage, 846 P.2d 135 (Alaska
1993)
1 ALR6th 1—§ 51, 71
Saupee v. Brown, 18 Pa. D & C. 588
(1932)
12 ALR5th 195—§ 43
Saupitty v. Yazoo Mfg. Co., 726 F.2d
657, CCH Prod. Liab. Rep. ¶ 9948
(CA10 Okla. 1984)
12 ALR5th 195—§ 24
Saur v. State, 918 S.W.2d 64 (Tex. App.
San Antonio 1996)
95 ALR6th 219—§ 13
Sauray v. City of New York, 261 A.D.2d
601, 690 N.Y.S.2d 716 (2d Dep't
1999)
2 ALR6th 429—§ 3
Saurel v. Sellick, 244 App. Div. 845,
279 N.Y.S. 323 (1935)
12 ALR5th 195—§ 42
Sauro v. Arena Co., 171 Conn. 168, 368
A.2d 58 (1976)
38 ALR5th 107—§ 7
Sauro v. Shea, 257 Pa. Super. 87, 390
A.2d 259 (1978)
125 ALR5th 403—§ 11
Saussy v. South F. R. R. Co., 22 Fla. 327
(1886)
25 ALR5th 391—§ 78
Sauter v. Bloyd, 2010 WL 5290422
(W.D. Ky. 2010)
89 ALR6th 1—§ 100

Sauter v. Federal Home Loan Bank of New York, 2009 WL 2424689 (D.N.J. 2009)
79 ALR6th 377—§ 40, 41
S_____ A_____ V_____, In Interest of, 798 S.W.2d 293 (Tex. App. Amarillo 1990)
40 ALR5th 227—§ 35
S.A.V., In Interest of, 837 S.W.2d 80 (Tex. 1992)
40 ALR5th 227—§ 35
73 ALR5th 185—§ 13
Savage, Matter of, 233 N.J. Super. 356, 558 A.2d 1357 (App. Div. 1989)
87 ALR5th 277—§ 2
Savage, Re Estate of, 650 S.W.2d 346, 39 A.L.R.4th 625 (Mo. App. 1983)
18 ALR5th 230—§ 3, 8
Savage v. Cochran (In re Estate of Savage), 259 Ill. App. 3d 328, 197 Ill. Dec. 575, 631 N.E.2d 797 (4th Dist. 1994)
14 ALR5th 242—§ 24
Savage v. Danek Medical, Inc., 31 F. Supp. 2d 980 (M.D. Fla. 1999)
57 ALR5th 1—§ 21
Savage v. Holiday Inn Corp., 603 F. Supp. 311, 37 BNA FEP Cas. 328, 118 BNA LRRM 3301, 40 CCH EPD ¶ 36122 (D.C. Nev 1985)
21 ALR5th 1—§ 3, 6, 11, 13
Savage v. Lincoln Ben. Life Co., 49 F. Supp. 2d 536 (E.D. Mich. 1999)
53 ALR6th 213—§ 9
Savage v. Martin G. (In re Kassandra B.), 3 Neb. App. 180, 524 N.W.2d 821 (1994)
61 ALR5th 151—§ 12, 15
Savage v. Otis Elevator Co., 136 N.J.L. 419, 56 A.2d 595 (N.J. Sup. Ct. 1948)
41 ALR6th 207—§ 28
Savage v. Prator, 921 So. 2d 51 (La. 2006)
69 ALR6th 207—§ 5
Savage v. Savage, 556 So. 2d 1213 (Fla. App. D2 1990)
49 ALR5th 441—§ 20
Savage v. Savage, 658 P.2d 1201 (Utah 1983)
9 ALR5th 568—§ 6
Savage v. Savage, 2010 WL 4673632 (Mich. Ct. App. 2010)
99 ALR6th 203—§ 16
102 ALR6th 153—§ 29
Savage v. Savage, 2014 WL 783463 (Conn. Super. Ct. 2014)
96 ALR6th 103—§ 3
Savage v. State, 83 Okla. Crim. 156, 174 P.2d 272 (1946)
105 ALR5th 529—§ 11
Savage v. State, 111 Tex. Crim. 437, 14 S.W.2d 848 (1929)
105 ALR5th 529—§ 11
Savage v. State, 114 S.W.3d 455 (Mo. Ct. App. E.D. 2003)
31 ALR6th 49—§ 7
Savage v. State, 252 Ga. App. 251, 556 S.E.2d 176 (2001)
96 ALR6th 355—§ 7, 25, 37, 60
Savage v. State, 274 Ga. 692, 558 S.E.2d 701 (2002)
3 ALR6th 543—§ 9
Savage v. State, 650 N.E.2d 1156 (Ind. App. 1995)
15 ALR5th 391—§ 30
Savage v. State, 2007 WL 538990 (Ark. 2007)
31 ALR6th 49—§ 11
Savage v. State, 2008 WL 726229 (Tex. App. Dallas 2008)
40 ALR6th 355—§ 3
Savage v. Third Judicial Dist. Court of State ex rel. County of Lyon, 125 Nev. 9, 200 P.3d 77 (2009)
76 ALR6th 543—§ 7
Savage v. Thompson, 22 Ariz. App. 59, 523 P.2d 110 (Ariz. App. 1974)
46 ALR5th 735—§ 3
Savage v. University State Bank of Champaign, 263 Ill. App. 457, 1931 WL 3172 (3d Dist. 1931)
109 ALR5th 421—§ 5
Savage v. U.S. Nat. Bank Ass'n, 19 A.3d 302 (Del. 2011)

86 ALR6th 411—§ 3

Savage Arms, Inc. v. Western Auto Supply Co., 18 P.3d 49, Prod. Liab. Rep. (CCH) ¶ 15837, Prod. Liab. Rep. (CCH) ¶ 16025, 13 A.L.R.6th 807 (Alaska 2001)

13 ALR6th 209—§ 49

13 ALR6th 355—§ 4, 7

Savage Indus. v. Utah State Tax Comm'n, 811 P.2d 664, 160 Utah Adv. Rep. 5 (Utah 1991)

33 ALR5th 509—§ 21

Savage Industries, Inc. v. Duke By and Through Duke, 598 So. 2d 856, Prod. Liab. Rep. (CCH) ¶ 13168 (Ala. 1992)

31 ALR5th 572—§ 3, 29

96 ALR5th 239—§ 22

Savage's Case, 257 Mass. 30, 153 N.E. 257 (1926)

4 ALR5th 443—§ 14

Savala v. Freedom Communications, Inc., 34 Media L. Rep. (BNA) 2241, 2006 WL 1738169 (Cal. App. 5th Dist. 2006)

85 ALR6th 475—§ 9

Savannah, F. & W. Ry. Co. v. Wainwright, 99 Ga. 255, 25 S.E. 622 (1896)

23 ALR6th 1—§ 8

Savannah News-Press, Div. Southeastern Newspapers Corp. v. Whetsell, 149 Ga. App. 233, 254 S.E.2d 151, 5 Media L. R. 1185 (1979)

44 ALR5th 193—§ 43

Savanna M., Interest of, 1998 WL 263371 (Conn. Super. Ct. 1998)

10 ALR6th 173—§ 26

Savant v. Lincoln Eng'g, 899 S.W.2d 120 (Mo. App. 1995)

9 ALR5th 102—§ 15

Savapolos v. State Dep't of Motor Vehicles, 1993 WL 7523 (Conn. Super. 1993)

52 ALR5th 655—§ 9

Savard v. Selby, 19 Ariz. App. 514, 508 P.2d 773 (1973)

18 ALR5th 474—§ 2, 4

Savarese v. Bye, 398 So. 2d 1276 (La. Ct. App. 4th Cir. 1981)

50 ALR6th 95—§ 4, 8

Savarin Corp. v. National Bank of Pakistan, 290 F. Supp. 285 (S.D. N.Y. 1968)

56 ALR5th 565—§ 45

Savarin Corp. v. National Bank of Pakistan, 447 F.2d 727 (CA2 N.Y. 1971)

13 ALR5th 465—§ 4, 17

Savas, Re Marriage of, 139 Ill. App. 3d 68, 93 Ill. Dec. 483, 486 N.E.2d 1318 (1st Dist. 1985)

17 ALR5th 366—§ 9

Savas v. Bednarz, 112 Wis. 2d 674, 333 N.W.2d 733, 1983 WL 161818 (App. 1983)

50 ALR5th 1—§ 6, 9

52 ALR5th 1—§ 8

Savas v. Savas, 127 A.D.2d 578, 511 N.Y.S.2d 378 (2d Dep't 1987)

26 ALR6th 331—§ 13

Savasta v. Com., Unemployment Compensation Bd. of Review, 44 Pa. Commw. 525, 403 A.2d 1375 (1979)

68 ALR5th 13—§ 19, 35

Savasta v. Savasta, 146 Misc. 2d 101, 549 N.Y.S.2d 544 (Fam. Ct. 1989)

3 ALR6th 447—§ 4, 7

Savattere v. Subin Associates, P.C., 261 A.D.2d 236, 690 N.Y.S.2d 229 (1st Dep't 1999)

9 ALR6th 285—§ 13

Savchuk v. Lomsen, 2008 WL 4371818 (E.D. Mich. 2008)

68 ALR6th 389—§ 3, 8

Save a Neighborhood Environment (SANE) v. City of Seattle, 101 Wash. 2d 280, 676 P.2d 1006 (1984)

73 ALR5th 223—§ 3, 7, 11

Save a Valuable Environment (SAVE) v. City of Bothell, 89 Wash. 2d 862, 576 P.2d 401, 8 Envtl. L. Rep. 20379 (1978)

73 ALR5th 223—§ 3

Save El Toro Assn. v. Days, 98 Cal. App. 3d 544, 159 Cal. Rptr. 577 (1st Dist. 1979)
106 ALR5th 523—§ 6

Save Immaculata/Dunblane, Inc. v. Immaculata Preparatory School, Inc., 514 A.2d 1152 (Dist. Col. App. 1986)
46 ALR5th 581—§ 23

Savell, In re Guardianship of, 876 So. 2d 308 (Miss. 2004)
49 ALR6th 505—§ 6

Savell v. Morrison, 929 So. 2d 414 (Miss. Ct. App. 2006)
100 ALR6th 1—§ 45

Savell v. State, 928 So. 2d 961 (Miss. Ct. App. 2006)
29 ALR6th 1—§ 10

Savelle v. Heilbrunn, 552 So. 2d 52 (La. Ct. App. 3d Cir. 1989)
93 ALR6th 123—§ 22, 63, 68

Save Mart Stores v. Workers' Comp. Appeals Bd., 3 Cal. App. 4th 720, 4 Cal. Rptr. 2d 597, 57 Cal. Comp. Cas. (MB) 89 (5th Dist. 1992)
106 ALR5th 111—§ 38

Save Our Forest Action Coalition Inc. v. City of Kingston, 246 A.D.2d 217, 675 N.Y.S.2d 451 (3d Dep't 1998)
73 ALR5th 223—§ 5

Save Our Forest & Ranchlands v. County of San Diego, 50 Cal. App. 4th 1757, 58 Cal. Rptr. 2d 708 (4th Dist. 1996)
106 ALR5th 523—§ 36

Save Our Neighborhoods v. St. John the Baptist Parish, 592 So. 2d 908 (La. Ct. App. 5th Cir. 1991)
73 ALR5th 223—§ 10

Save our Peninsula Committee v. Monterey County Board of Supervisors, 87 Cal. App. 4th 99, 104 Cal. Rptr. 2d 326 (6th Dist. 2001)
97 ALR5th 123—§ 31

Save Our Residential Environment v. City of West Hollywood, 9 Cal. App. 4th 1745, 12 Cal. Rptr. 2d 308 (2d Dist. 1992)
106 ALR5th 523—§ 36

Save Our Rural Environment v. Snohomish County, 99 Wash. 2d 363, 662 P.2d 816 (1983)
73 ALR5th 223—§ 3, 7, 11

Save Oxnard Shores v. California Coastal Com., 179 Cal. App. 3d 140, 224 Cal. Rptr. 425 (2d Dist. 1986)
106 ALR5th 523—§ 33

Savery v. State, 767 S.W.2d 242 (Tex. App. Beaumont 1989)
42 ALR5th 291—§ 6

Save Sunset Beach Coalition v. City and County of Honolulu, 102 Haw. 465, 78 P.3d 1 (2003)
66 ALR6th 83—§ 19

Save The Pine Bush, Inc. v. Common Council of City of Albany, 56 A.D.3d 32, 865 N.Y.S.2d 365 (3d Dep't 2008)
44 ALR6th 325—§ 3

Save the Pine Bush, Inc. v. Planning Bd. of City of Albany, 298 A.D.2d 806, 749 N.Y.S.2d 318 (3d Dep't 2002)
44 ALR6th 325—§ 16

Save the Welwood Murray Memorial Library Com. v. City Council, 215 Cal. App. 3d 1003, 263 Cal. Rptr. 896 (4th Dist. 1989)
106 ALR5th 523—§ 33

Savett v. Whirlpool Corp., 2012 WL 3780451 (N.D. Ohio 2012)
104 ALR6th 97—§ 14

Savidge v. Transcanada Power Marketing, Ltd., 2009 WL 6067019 (Mass. Super. Ct. 2009)
58 ALR6th 1—§ 5

Saville v. Houston County Healthcare Authority, 852 F. Supp. 1512, 92 Ed. Law Rep. 478, 66 Fair Empl. Prac. Cas. (BNA) 1821 (M.D. Ala. 1994)
86 ALR5th 1—§ 2, 12 to 14
90 ALR6th 235—§ 46

Saville v. Lee, 43 Ga. App. 263, 158 S.E. 441 (1931)
6 ALR6th 391—§ 3 to 5, 18

Saville Intern., Inc. v. Galanti Group, Inc., 107 Ill. App. 3d 799, 63 Ill. Dec. 578, 438 N.E.2d 509 (1st Dist. 1982)
67 ALR5th 179—§ 5, 6

Savina v. Sterling Drug, Inc., 247 Kan. 105, 795 P.2d 915, CCH Prod. Liab. Rep. ¶ 12552 (1990)
57 ALR5th 1—§ 3

Savin Hill Yacht Club Ass'n, Re, 246 Mass. 75, 140 N.E. 299 (1923)
22 ALR5th 327—§ 8, 58

Savini v. Kent Mach. Works, Inc., 525 F. Supp. 711 (E.D. Pa. 1981)
109 ALR5th 301—§ 3, 19
112 ALR5th 113—§ 24
13 ALR6th 355—§ 4, 27
18 ALR6th 629—§ 5, 15

Savino v. Murray, 82 F.3d 593 (4th Cir. 1996)
79 ALR5th 419—§ 4

Savino v. Robertson, 273 Ill. App. 3d 811, 210 Ill. Dec. 264, 652 N.E.2d 1240 (1st Dist. 1995)
55 ALR5th 529—§ 4
75 ALR6th 109—§ 15

Savino v. Savino, 110 A.D.2d 642, 487 N.Y.S.2d 378 (2d Dep't 1985)
70 ALR5th 377—§ 5

Saviske v. Corradino, 52 Conn. L. Rptr. 39, 2011 WL 2536461 (Conn. Super. Ct. 2011)
91 ALR6th 435—§ 12, 15, 38, 49, 96

Savitch v. Lange, 114 A.D.2d 372, 493 N.Y.S.2d 889 (2d Dep't 1985)
91 ALR6th 435—§ 122

Savitt v. City of Philadelphia, 557 F. Supp. 321 (E.D. Pa. 1983)
110 ALR5th 465—§ 2

Savka v. Smith, 58 Ill. App. 3d 12, 15 Ill. Dec. 579, 373 N.E.2d 1051 (3d Dist. 1978)
15 ALR5th 119—§ 3, 38

Savko v. Brooklyn & Queens Transit Corp., 166 Misc. 84, 1 N.Y.S.2d 489 (1937)
19 ALR5th 622—§ 3

Savoia v. F. W. Woolworth Co., 88 N.J. Super. 153, 211 A.2d 214, 14 A.L.R.3d 804 (1965)
40 ALR5th 807—§ 2

Savoie v. Grange Mut. Ins. Co., 67 Ohio St. 3d 500, 620 N.E.2d 809 (1993)
40 ALR5th 603—§ 9

Savoie v. Savoie, 482 So. 2d 23 (La. Ct. App. 5th Cir. 1986)
59 ALR6th 433—§ 76

Savory v. Haverhill, 132 Mass. 324 (1882)
57 ALR5th 689—§ 10

Savoy v. Action Products Co., Inc., 347 So. 2d 930 (La. Ct. App. 3d Cir. 1977)
3 ALR6th 355—§ 10

Savoy v. Cecil Perry Imp. Co., 691 So. 2d 692 (La. Ct. App. 3d Cir. 1997)
22 ALR6th 329—§ 32

Savoy v. Portserv Transp. Co., Inc., 721 So. 2d 54 (La. Ct. App. 5th Cir. 1998)
10 ALR5th 245—§ 21.5

Savoy v. Richard A. Carrier Trucking, Inc., 176 F.R.D. 10, 40 Fed. R. Serv. 3d (LCP) 350 (D. Mass. 1997)
26 ALR5th 628—§ 19

Savoy v. U.S., 981 A.2d 1208, 58 A.L.R.6th 775 (D.C. 2009)
58 ALR6th 215—§ 15

Savoy Medical Supply Co., Inc. v. F. & H Mfg. Corp., 776 F. Supp. 703 (E.D.N.Y. 1991)
14 ALR5th 695—§ 6, 26
88 ALR5th 493—§ 5
89 ALR5th 1—§ 10

S.A.W., In re Welfare of, 2007 WL 1322369 (Minn. Ct. App. 2007)
37 ALR6th 55—§ 6

S.A.W., Interest of, 228 Ga. App. 197, 491 S.E.2d 441 (1997)
20 ALR5th 534—§ 4

Sawabini v. Desenberg, 143 Mich. App. 373, 372 N.W.2d 559, 60 A.L.R.4th 37 (1985)
16 ALR6th 1—§ 5

Sawan, Inc. v. American Cyanamid Co., 211 Ga. 764, 88 S.E.2d 152 (1955)
93 ALR5th 103—§ 12, 13
Sawh v. Bridges, 120 A.D.2d 74, 507 N.Y.S.2d 632 (2d Dep't 1986)
121 ALR5th 157—§ 5
Sawh v. Schoen, 627 N.Y.S.2d 7 (App. Div. 1st Dep't 1995)
7 ALR5th 1—§ 33
Sawicki v. New Britain General Hosp., 302 Conn. 514, 29 A.3d 453 (2011)
92 ALR6th 379—§ 14
Sawka v. Prokopowycz, 104 Mich. App. 829, 306 N.W.2d 354 (1981)
84 ALR5th 619—§ 3, 6
94 ALR6th 431—§ 9, 17, 75, 76
Sawko v. Dominion Plaza One Condominium Ass'n No. 1-A, 218 Ill.App. 3d 521, 161 Ill. Dec. 263, 578 N.E.2d 621 (2d Dist. 1991)
60 ALR5th 647—§ 5, 7
Sawlani v. Mills, 830 N.E.2d 932 (Ind. Ct. App. 2005)
92 ALR6th 379—§ 12, 43, 68
Sawle v. Nicholson, 408 N.W.2d 173 (Minn. Ct. App. 1987)
16 ALR5th 650—§ 33
21 ALR5th 396—§ 66
67 ALR5th 1—§ 7
Sawtell v. Sawtell, 569 S.W.2d 286 (Mo. App. 1978)
49 ALR5th 441—§ 13
Sawtelle v. Farrell, 70 F.3d 1381 (1st Cir. 1995)
78 ALR6th 151—§ 7
Sawtelle v. Muncy, 116 Cal. 435, 48 P. 387 (1897)
64 ALR5th 163—§ 7, 16
Sawvel, In re Marriage of, 826 N.W.2d 515 (Iowa Ct. App. 2012)
96 ALR6th 103—§ 3
Sawyer, In Interest of, 234 Kan. 436, 672 P.2d 1093, 14 Ed. Law Rep. 1126 (1983)
70 ALR5th 169—§ 4, 23
Sawyer, In re, 953 A.2d 1019 (D.C. 2008)
43 ALR6th 163—§ 6

Sawyer v. Butler, 848 F.2d 582 (5th Cir. 1988)
78 ALR5th 197—§ 4
Sawyer v. Camp Dudley, 102 App. Div. 2d 914, 477 N.Y.S.2d 498, 38 U.C.C.R.S. 1287 (3d Dep't 1984)
49 ALR5th 1—§ 3, 72
Sawyer v. Church, 199 Misc. 1002, 106 N.Y.S.2d 653 (Sup. Ct. 1950)
91 ALR5th 225—§ 10, 41
Sawyer v. Churchill, 77 Vt. 273, 59 A. 1014 (1905)
58 ALR5th 387—§ 4
Sawyer v. Clement Mtarri, 33 Ark. App. 125, 806 S.W.2d 7 (App. 1991)
12 ALR5th 658—§ 4, 5, 17
Sawyer v. Comerci, 264 Va. 68, 563 S.E.2d 748 (2002)
108 ALR5th 385—§ 11
Sawyer v. Crouch, 2008 WL 5139847 (W.D. La. 2008)
65 ALR6th 93—§ 20
Sawyer v. Ewen, 122 Vt. 320, 173 A.2d 549 (1961)
5 ALR5th 875—§ 3, 23
Sawyer v. Green, 316 Fed. Appx. 715 (10th Cir. 2008)
89 ALR6th 1—§ 79
Sawyer v. Hart, 194 Mich. 399, 160 N.W. 572 (1916)
75 ALR6th 311—§ 61
Sawyer v. Head, Dependents of, 510 So. 2d 472 (Miss. 1987)
42 ALR6th 545—§ 18, 20
43 ALR6th 375—§ 4, 9, 19, 32
Sawyer v. Horne's Zoological Arena Co., 195 S.W. 537 (Mo. Ct. App. 1917)
74 ALR6th 505—§ 22
Sawyer v. Howard, 22 Vt. 538 (1850)
20 ALR5th 229—§ 4, 31
Sawyer v. Methodist Hospital, 522 F.2d 1102, 17 U.C.C. Rep. Serv. (CBC) 708 (6th Cir. 1975)
75 ALR5th 229—§ 8, 14
Sawyer v. Mortgage Electronic Registration Systems, Inc., 2010 WL 996768 (N.D. Tex. 2010)

86 ALR6th 411—§ 5

Sawyer v. Pacific Indem. Co., 141 Ga. App. 298, 233 S.E.2d 227 (1977)

108 ALR5th 1—§ 2, 35

113 ALR5th 115—§ 2, 9, 14, 37, 65

Sawyer v. Sandstrom, 615 F.2d 311 (5th Cir. 1980)

72 ALR5th 1—§ 8

Sawyer v. Sawyer, 181 Okla. 567, 75 P.2d 423 (1937)

3 ALR5th 237—§ 19

Sawyer v. State, 73 Okla. Crim. 186, 119 P.2d 256 (1941)

85 ALR5th 547—§ 7

Sawyer v. State, 100 Fla. 1603, 132 So. 188 (1931)

85 ALR5th 187—§ 4

Sawyer v. State, 127 Misc. 2d 295, 485 N.Y.S.2d 695 (1985)

50 ALR5th 1—§ 9

Sawyer v. State, 485 N.Y.S.2d 695 (Ct. Cl. 1985)

38 ALR5th 107—§ 11

Sawyer v. State, 663 P.2d 230 (Alaska App. 1983)

7 ALR5th 263—§ 7

Sawyer v. State, 810 S.W.2d 536 (Mo. Ct. App. E.D. 1991)

55 ALR6th 157—§ 4

Sawyer v. Sunset Mut. Life Ins. Co., 8 Cal. 2d 492, 66 P.2d 641 (1937)

87 ALR6th 319—§ 14

Sawyer v. Sweet, 33 Neb. 630, 50 N.W. 954 (1892)

60 ALR6th 481—§ 4, 24

Sawyer v. Tofany, 41 App. Div. 2d 583, 340 N.Y.S.2d 208 (4th Dep't 1973)

28 ALR5th 459—§ 3

Sawyer v. U.S., 224 F. Supp. 678 (E.D. La 1963)

1 ALR5th 163—§ 28, 30

Sawyer v. U.S., 436 F.2d 640 (2d Cir. 1971)

64 ALR5th 235—§ 5, 17

Sawyers v. Holder, 399 Fed. Appx. 313 (9th Cir. 2010)

76 ALR6th 587—§ 4

Sawyer's Will, Re, 102 Vt. 473, 150 A. 128 (1930)

19 ALR5th 622—§ 11, 24

Sax v. Votteler, 648 S.W.2d 661 (Tex. 1983)

71 ALR5th 307—§ 5

76 ALR6th 31—§ 41

Saxby v. F.B.I., 3 Fed. Appx. 60 (4th Cir. 2001)

70 ALR6th 361—§ 18

Saxe v. Commonwealth, Dep't of State, 73 Pa. Cmwlth. 589, 459 A.2d 445 (1983)

7 ALR5th 474—§ 41

Saxe v. State Farm Mut. Auto. Ins. Co., 955 S.W.2d 188 (Ky. Ct. App. 1997)

125 ALR5th 1—§ 5

Saxe Operating Corp. v. Industrial Commission of Wisconsin, 197 Wis. 552, 222 N.W. 781 (1929)

31 ALR6th 199—§ 8

Saxis S. S. Co. v. Multifacs Intern. Traders, Inc., 375 F.2d 577 (2d Cir. 1967)

67 ALR5th 179—§ 11

Saxton, In re Application of, 309 N.W.2d 298 (Minn. 1981)

40 ALR5th 697—§ 3, 5, 7 to 9, 11, 22, 27

Saxton v. Dodge, 57 Barb. 84, 1870 WL 7551 (N.Y. Gen. Term 1870)

85 ALR6th 1—§ 20

Saxton v. Pets Warehouse, Inc., 180 Misc. 2d 377, 691 N.Y.S.2d 872, 41 U.C.C. Rep. Serv. 2d 781 (App. Term 1999)

74 ALR6th 505—§ 7, 10, 20, 28

Saxton, State ex rel. v. Moore, 598 S.W.2d 586 (Mo. Ct. App. W.D. 1980)

72 ALR6th 141—§ 6, 10

Say & Say v. Castellano, 22 Cal. App. 4th 88, 27 Cal. Rptr. 2d 270 (2d Dist. 1994)

27 ALR6th 403—§ 15

Say & Say, Inc. v. Ebershoff, 20 Cal. App. 4th 1759, 25 Cal. Rptr. 2d 703 (2d Dist. 1993)
27 ALR6th 403—§ 15
45 ALR6th 493—§ 17

Saydell v. Geppetto's Pizza & Ribs Franchise Sys., 100 Ohio App. 3d 111, 652 N.E.2d 218 (Cuyahoga Co. 1994)
52 ALR5th 613—§ 3

Sayeedi v. Walser, 15 Misc. 3d 621, 835 N.Y.S.2d 840, 62 U.C.C. Rep. Serv. 2d 352 (N.Y. City Civ. Ct. 2007)
61 ALR6th 207—§ 6

Sayegh v. Sayegh, 777 So. 2d 1007 (Fla. Dist. Ct. App. 2d Dist. 2000)
49 ALR5th 441—§ 3

Sayers v. Artistic Kitchen Design LLC, 280 Ga. App. 223, 633 S.E.2d 619 (2006)
43 ALR6th 611—§ 33, 34, 72

Sayers v. Leon N. Weiner & Associates, Inc., 442 A.2d 98, 32 U.C.C.R.S. 1504 (Del. Super. Ct. 1981)
49 ALR5th 1—§ 57

Sayers v. Pyland, 139 Tex. 57, 161 S.W.2d 769, 140 A.L.R. 1164 (1942)
83 ALR6th 605—§ 5, 12

Sayes v. Safeco Ins. Co., 576 So. 2d 1071 (La. App. 3d Cir. 1991)
23 ALR5th 241—§ 14

Sayfie v. Gordon, 95 N.H. 182, 59 A.2d 483 (1948)
6 ALR6th 1—§ 17

Sayler v. Skutches, 2012 PA Super 23, 40 A.3d 135 (2012)
92 ALR6th 379—§ 105, 108

Sayles v. Foley, 38 R.I. 484, 96 A. 340 (1916)
40 ALR6th 99—§ 3

Sayles v. Hall, 210 Mass. 281, 96 N.E. 712 (1911)
25 ALR5th 233—§ 2, 12

Sayles v. Piccadilly Cafeterias, Inc., 242 Va. 328, 410 S.E.2d 632 (1991)
27 ALR5th 174—§ 91

Sayles v. Thompson, 99 Ill. 2d 122, 75 Ill. Dec. 446, 457 N.E.2d 440 (1983)
54 ALR6th 1—§ 3, 22, 26, 29
56 ALR6th 553—§ 3

Saylin v. California Ins. Guarantee Assn., 179 Cal. App. 3d 256, 224 Cal. Rptr. 493 (2d Dist. 1986)
14 ALR5th 695—§ 21

Saylor, Ex parte, 734 S.W.2d 55 (Tex. App. Houston 1st Dist. 1987)
51 ALR6th 1—§ 24

Saylor v. Black & Decker Mfg. Co., 258 Md. 605, 267 A.2d 81 (1970)
4 ALR5th 443—§ 4, 7

Saylor v. Green, 165 Pa. Commw. 249, 645 A.2d 318 (1994)
15 ALR6th 1—§ 5

Saylor v. Hall, 497 S.W.2d 218 (Ky. 1973)
75 ALR5th 413—§ 3
5 ALR6th 497—§ 12, 15

Saylor v. Mack, 27 Fed. Appx. 321 (6th Cir.2001)
31 ALR6th 1—§ 1

Saylor v. State, 185 Ga. App. 634, 365 S.E.2d 493 (1988)
59 ALR5th 615—§ 11

Saylor v. State, 719 So. 2d 266 (Ala. Crim. App. 1998)
5 ALR5th 243—§ 48

Saylor v. State, 765 N.E.2d 535 (Ind. 2002)
110 ALR5th 1—§ 2, 3

Saylor, State ex rel. v. Wilkes, 216 W. Va. 766, 613 S.E.2d 914, 96 Fair Empl. Prac. Cas. (BNA) 145, 22 I.E.R. Cas. (BNA) 1515, 151 Lab. Cas. (CCH) ¶ 60016 (2005)
22 ALR6th 49—§ 5

Sayre v. Rice, 132 Okla. 95, 269 P. 361 (1928)
25 ALR5th 568—§ 28

Sayre v. State, 471 N.E.2d 708 (Ind. App. 1984)
24 ALR5th 428—§ 16, 18

Sayres v. Commonwealth, 88 Pa. 291 (1879)
24 ALR5th 465—§ 33, 35

S.B., In re, 2004 WL 2457739 (Cal. App. 3d Dist. 2004)
38 ALR6th 1—§ 23
S.B. v. Saint James School, 959 So. 2d 72, 222 Ed. Law Rep. 444 (Ala. 2006)
91 ALR6th 409—§ 11
S.B. v. S.J.B., 258 N.J. Super. 151, 609 A.2d 124 (Ch. Div. 1992)
96 ALR5th 83—§ 3
S. B. v. State, 614 P.2d 786 (Alaska 1980)
69 ALR6th 579—§ 8
S.B. v. State, Dept. of Health & Social Services, Div. of Family & Youth Services, 61 P.3d 6 (Alaska 2002)
57 ALR6th 163—§ 13, 35
S.B. v. W.A., 2012 WL 5936035 (N.Y. Sup 2012)
82 ALR6th 1—§ 8, 10
S. B., 742 P.2d 935 (Colo. App. 1987)
21 ALR5th 396—§ 3, 9, 31
Sbado v. State, 264 Ark. 497, 572 S.W.2d 585 (1978)
5 ALR5th 243—§ 8
Sbarro Holding, Inc. v. Shien Tien Yuan, 111 Misc. 2d 910, 445 N.Y.S.2d 911 (Sup. 1981)
52 ALR5th 613—§ 4
S.B.C., Interest of, 952 S.W.2d 15 (Tex. App. San Antonio 1997)
39 ALR5th 1—§ 4
SBC Communications, Inc. v. F.C.C., 154 F.3d 226, 1998-2 Trade Cas. (CCH) ¶ 72256 (5th Cir. 1998)
62 ALR6th 517—§ 6, 18, 21, 38, 46
SBC Enterprises, Inc. v. City of South Burlington, 892 F. Supp. 578 (D. Vt. 1995)
63 ALR6th 1—§ 17, 20
S.B. Int'l, Inc. v. Union Bank of India, 783 S.W.2d 225, 11 U.C.C.R.S.2d 171 (Tex. App. Dallas 1989)
8 ALR5th 463—§ 10
53 ALR5th 667—§ 23
56 ALR5th 565—§ 13, 25, 28, 59
Sbitani, Matter of, 216 N.J. Super. 75, 522 A.2d 1041 (App. Div. 1987)

91 ALR6th 435—§ 110
Sbordy, State ex rel. v. Rowlett, 125 Fla. 562, 170 So. 311 (1936)
10 ALR5th 1—§ 3
S.B.R., In re Custody of, 43 Wash. App. 622, 719 P.2d 154 (Div. 1 1986)
89 ALR5th 195—§ 16
S.B.R. SVP-243-02, In re Civil Commitment of, 2008 WL 5274632 (N.J. Super. Ct. App. Div. 2008)
78 ALR6th 417—§ 42
SBT Holdings, LLC v. Town Of Westminster, 547 F.3d 28 (1st Cir. 2008)
68 ALR6th 229—§ 5
S.C., In re, 138 Cal. App. 4th 396, 41 Cal. Rptr. 3d 453 (3d Dist. 2006)
30 ALR6th 1—§ 4
S.C., Matter of, 264 Mont. 24, 869 P.2d 266 (1994)
12 ALR6th 417—§ 15
S.C., Matter of, 790 S.W.2d 766 (Tex. App. Austin 1990)
87 ALR6th 109—§ 93
S.C., Matter of Guardianship of, 246 N.J. Super. 414, 587 A.2d 1299 (App. Div. 1991)
116 ALR5th 559—§ 10
117 ALR5th 349—§ 11, 14
S.C., Re Guardianship of, 246 N.J. Super. 414, 587 A.2d 1299 (1991)
1 ALR5th 469—§ 25, 26, 33
S.C. v. J.T.C., 2010 WL 1265188 (Ala. Civ. App. 2010)
57 ALR6th 163—§ 40
60 ALR6th 193—§ 22
S.C. v. Monroe Woodbury Cent. School Dist., 2012 WL 2940020 (S.D. N.Y. 2012)
98 ALR6th 599—§ 20, 47, 50, 67, 74
S. C. v. State, 583 So. 2d 188 (Miss. 1991)
31 ALR5th 229—§ 2, 3, 10, 17, 28, 35, 45
Scacca v. Scacca, 694 So. 2d 1 (Ala. Civ. App. 1997)
102 ALR6th 153—§ 29

Scacchetti v. Gannett Co., 123 App. Div. 2d 497, 507 N.Y.S.2d 337, 13 Media L. R. 1396 (4th Dep't 1986)
44 ALR5th 193—§ 21, 50

Scacchi v. Montgomery, 365 Pa. 377, 75 A.2d 535 (1950)
42 ALR5th 1—§ 3

Scaccia v. New York State Div. of State Police, 138 App. Div. 2d 50, 530 N.Y.S.2d 309 (3d Dep't 1988)
51 ALR5th 603—§ 2

Scaccia v. Stamp, 700 F. Supp. 2d 219, 258 Ed. Law Rep. 167 (N.D. N.Y. 2010)
90 ALR6th 235—§ 49

Scaccia v. State Ethics Com'n, 431 Mass. 351, 727 N.E.2d 824 (2000)
35 ALR6th 1—§ 22

Scaccianoce v. Hixon Mfg. & Supply Co., 57 F.3d 582 (7th Cir. 1995)
73 ALR5th 75—§ 6

Scaduto v. State, 86 A.D.2d 682, 446 N.Y.S.2d 529, 2 Ed. Law Rep. 504 (3d Dep't 1982)
68 ALR5th 663—§ 4

Scaffide v. Fisher Foods, Inc., 1991 WL 232147 (Ohio Ct. App. 8th Dist. Cuyahoga County 1991)
74 ALR5th 49—§ 2, 3, 6

Scaffidi v. Fiserv, Inc., 2006 WL 2038348 (E.D. Wis. 2006)
22 ALR6th 49—§ 7, 8, 27

Scafide v. Bazzone, 962 So. 2d 585 (Miss. Ct. App. 2006)
98 ALR6th 1—§ 6

Scafidi v. Seiler, 225 N.J. Super. 576, 543 A.2d 95 (1988)
7 ALR5th 1—§ 22

Scafuri, Re Marriage of, 203 Ill. App. 3d 385, 149 Ill. Dec. 124, 561 N.E.2d 402 (2d Dist. 1990)
10 ALR5th 191—§ 2, 5

Scafuri v. DeMaso, 71 A.D.3d 755, 896 N.Y.S.2d 421 (2d Dep' 2010)
72 ALR6th 563—§ 8, 27

Scaggs v. GPCH-GP, Inc., 23 So. 3d 1080 (Miss. 2009)
100 ALR6th 139—§ 13

Scaglione v. Riverbay Corp., 279 A.D.2d 254, 719 N.Y.S.2d 37 (1st Dep't 2001)
99 ALR5th 141—§ 34

Scagnelli v. Whiting, 554 F. Supp. 77, 30 BNA FEP Cas. 1693 (M.D. N.C. 1982)
12 ALR5th 195—§ 36

Scainetti v. U.S. ex rel. Federal Bureau of Prisons, 2002 WL 31844920 (S.D. N.Y. 2002)
119 ALR5th 1—§ 55

SCA International, Inc. v. Garfield & Rosen, Inc., 337 F. Supp. 246, 10 U.C.C. Rep. Serv. (CBC) 1062 (D. Mass. 1971)
55 ALR5th 1—§ 2, 32

Scala v. American Laundry Machinery Co., 233 N.Y.S.2d 875 (Sup 1962)
104 ALR6th 97—§ 6

Scalamandre Silks, Inc. v. Fireman's Fund Ins. Co., 194 A.D.2d 421, 598 N.Y.S.2d 791 (1st Dep't 1993)
60 ALR5th 165—§ 5, 9

Scales v. Rapides Regional Medical Center, 2001-1147 La. App. 3 Cir. 2/6/2, 2002 WL 181989 (La. Ct. App. 3d Cir. 2002)
98 ALR5th 533—§ 22

Scales v. State, 64 Wis. 2d 485, 219 N.W.2d 286 (1974)
30 ALR6th 103—§ 20, 24, 30, 46

Scales v. State, 411 So. 2d 658 (La. Ct. App. 4th Cir. 1982)
104 ALR6th 1—§ 53

Scales v. State Farm Mut. Auto. Ins. Co., 119 N.C. App. 787, 460 S.E.2d 201 (1995)
41 ALR5th 91—§ 3

Scales v. St. Louis S. F. R. Co., 2 Kan. App. 2d 491, 582 P.2d 300 (1978)
33 ALR5th 205—§ 5, 7

Scales v. Tucker, 73 N.C. App. 696, 327 S.E.2d 306 (1985)
43 ALR5th 87—§ 2, 11

Scalf v. Berkel, Inc., 448 N.E.2d 1201, CCH Prod. Liab. Rep. ¶ 9618 (Ind. App. 1983)

30 ALR5th 1—§ 6, 7

Scalia v. Equitable Life Assur. Soc. of U.S., 263 A.D.2d 537, 693 N.Y.S.2d 218 (2d Dep't 1999)

100 ALR5th 293—§ 3

Scalice v. Kullen, 710 N.Y.S.2d 632 (App. Div. 2d Dep't 2000)

31 ALR5th 550—§ 3

Scaling v. Sutton, 167 S.W.2d 275 (Tex. Civ. App. Fort Worth 1942)

76 ALR5th 337—§ 20

Scalingi v. Scalingi, 65 N.J. 180, 320 A.2d 475 (1974)

17 ALR5th 366—§ 8

Scalise v. Bristol Hosp., 1995 WL 410751 (Conn. Super. Ct. 1995)

84 ALR5th 687—§ 4

Scalise v. National Utility Service, 120 F.2d 938 (CA5 Fla. 1941)

14 ALR5th 242—§ 44

23 ALR5th 744—§ 5

Scalisi v. Fund Asset Management, L.P., 380 F.3d 133, Fed. Sec. L. Rep. (CCH) ¶ 92892 (2d Cir. 2004)

43 ALR6th 1—§ 16, 26, 28

Scallan v. Mark Petroleum Corp., 303 So. 2d 498 (La. App. 2d Cir. 1974)

18 ALR5th 577—§ 9, 38, 58

23 ALR5th 241—§ 40

Scallon, Application of, 327 Or. 32, 956 P.2d 982 (1998)

108 ALR5th 289—§ 2, 11, 12

Scallon v. Hooper, 58 N.C. App. 551, 293 S.E.2d 843 (1982)

125 ALR5th 193—§ 7

34 ALR6th 431—§ 3

Scally v. Pacific Gas & Electric Co., 23 Cal. App. 3d 806, 100 Cal. Rptr. 501 (1st Dist. 1972)

9 ALR5th 102—§ 9, 11, 23

17 ALR5th 547—§ 13, 22

Scally v. W.T. Garratt & Co., 11 Cal. App. 138, 104 P. 325 (3d Dist. 1909)

7 ALR6th 1—§ 35

Scallywags, Inc., In re, 84 B.R. 303 (Bankr. D. Mass. 1988)

71 ALR5th 491—§ 20

Scalzo v. American Exp. Co., 185 Cal. App. 4th 91, 109 Cal. Rptr. 3d 638 (2d Dist. 2010)

85 ALR6th 475—§ 8

Scalzo v. Vincent, 279 A.D. 1141, 113 N.Y.S.2d 218 (4th Dep't 1952)

103 ALR5th 339—§ 6

Scamardella v. Illiano, 126 Md. App. 76, 727 A.2d 421 (1999)

56 ALR5th 1—§ 3

Scamardo v. Dunaway, 694 So. 2d 1041 (La. Ct. App. 5th Cir. 1997)

99 ALR5th 445—§ 7

Scambos v. Computer Management Services, Inc., 1998 WL 476256 (D. Md. 1998)

93 ALR5th 1—§ 9

Scampitilla v. State, 2009-Ohio-3403, 2009 WL 2030912 (Ohio Ct. App. 5th Dist. Richland County 2009)

64 ALR6th 1—§ 7, 9, 11

S. C. Anderson, Inc. v. Bank of America, 24 Cal. App. 4th 529, 30 Cal. Rptr. 2d 286 (5th Dist. 1994)

124 ALR5th 375—§ 6

Scandia Down Corp. v. Euroquilt, Inc., 772 F.2d 1423, 227 USPQ 138, 3 FR Serv. 3d 195 (CA7 Ill. 1985)

8 ALR5th 653—§ 3, 17

Scandinavian Health Spa, Inc. v. Ohio Civil Rights Comm., 64 Ohio App. 3d 480, 581 N.E.2d 1169, 63 Fair Empl. Prac. Cas. (BNA) 455 (8th Dist. Cuyahoga County 1990)

93 ALR5th 47—§ 4

94 ALR5th 1—§ 3

Scandinavian Satellite System, AS v. Prime TV Ltd., 291 F.3d 839, 62 U.S.P.Q.2d 1935 (D.C. Cir. 2002)

76 ALR6th 289—§ 2, 6

Scandinavian World Cruises (Bahamas) Ltd. v. Barone, 573 So. 2d 1036 (Fla. 3d DCA 1991)

82 ALR6th 175—§ 13

Scandinavian World Cruises, Ltd. v. Cronin, 509 So. 2d 1277, 12 FLW 1727 (Fla. App. D3 1987)

48 ALR5th 129—§ 20

Scandrett, State ex rel. v. Nelson, 240 Wis. 438, 3 N.W.2d 765 (1942)
73 ALR5th 223—§ 12

Scanga v. Family Practice Associates of Rockland, P.C., 302 A.D.2d 443, 753 N.Y.S.2d 744 (2d Dep't 2003)
95 ALR6th 541—§ 28

Scanio v. McFall, 877 S.W.2d 888 (Tex. App. Amarillo 1994)
110 ALR5th 371—§ 5

Scanlan, In re, 722 A.2d 42 (D.C. 1999)
45 ALR6th 175—§ 16

Scanlan v. Buffalo Public School System, 90 N.Y.2d 662, 665 N.Y.S.2d 51, 687 N.E.2d 1334, 122 Ed. Law Rep. 1034 (1997)
56 ALR5th 493—§ 23, 33

Scanlan v. Hoerth, 151 Ill. App. 582, 1909 WL 2325 (1st Dist. 1909)
75 ALR5th 1—§ 7

Scanlan v. Maryland Cas. Ins. Co., 203 Ill. App. 3d 340, 149 Ill. Dec. 23, 561 N.E.2d 301 (2d Dist. 1990)
77 ALR5th 319—§ 4
78 ALR5th 341—§ 6

Scanlan v. Miller, 1997 WL 769530 (Minn. Ct. App. 1997)
91 ALR6th 1—§ 46

Scanlan v. Rowinsky, 611 So. 2d 1092 (Ala. Civ. App. 1992)
53 ALR5th 375—§ 11

Scanlon v. Dewhurst, 197 S.W.2d 518 (Tex. Civ. App. San Antonio 1946)
76 ALR5th 337—§ 22

Scanlon v. Food Crafts, Inc., 2 Conn. Cir. 3, 193 A.2d 610, 1 U.C.C.R.S. 122 (1963)
2 ALR5th 1—§ 61

Scanlon v. General Motors Corp., Chevrolet Motor Division, 65 N.J. 582, 326 A.2d 673 (1974)
76 ALR6th 465—§ 11

Scanlon v. Herald Co., 201 A.D. 173, 194 N.Y.S. 663 (3d Dep't 1922)
15 ALR6th 633—§ 13, 17, 28, 34

Scanlon v. Kansas City, 336 Mo. 1058, 81 S.W.2d 939 (1935)
49 ALR5th 685—§ 6

Scanlon v. Scanlon, 29 N.J. Super. 317, 102 A.2d 656 (App. Div. 1954)
95 ALR5th 533—§ 3
124 ALR5th 203—§ 3, 7, 10

Scanlon v. Warren, 169 Ill. 142, 48 N.E. 410 (1897)
74 ALR5th 369—§ 14

Scanlon v. Wedger, 156 Mass. 462, 31 N.E. 642 (1892)
21 ALR6th 81—§ 11, 21

Scanlon's Estate, In re, 2 Misc. 2d 65, 150 N.Y.S.2d 511 (Sur. Ct. 1956)
102 ALR5th 253—§ 12, 14

Scannell, Re, 289 Or. 699, 617 P.2d 256 (1980)
9 ALR5th 193—§ 5, 12

Scannell v. Wolff, 86 Cal. App. 2d 489, 195 P.2d 536 (1st Dist. 1948)
28 ALR6th 175—§ 11

Scanscot Shipping Services GmbH v. Metales Tracomex LTDA, 617 F.3d 679, 2010 A.M.C. 2372 (2d Cir. 2010)
66 ALR6th 567—§ 3, 11, 21, 29

Scantlin v. City of Pevely, 741 S.W.2d 48 (Mo. Ct. App. E.D. 1987)
92 ALR5th 517—§ 10

Scappatura v. Baptist Hospital of Phoenix, 120 Ariz. 204, 584 P.2d 1195 (App. 1978)
28 ALR5th 107—§ 3, 13

Scarabino v. E. Liverpool City Hosp., 155 Ohio App. 3d 576, 2003-Ohio-7108, 802 N.E.2d 188 (7th Dist. Columbiana County 2003)
7 ALR6th 563—§ 11

Scarano v. Central R. Co. of N. J., 203 F.2d 510, 23 Lab. Cas. (CCH) ¶ 67540 (3d Cir. 1953)
85 ALR5th 353—§ 12

Scarano v. Schnoor, 158 Cal. App. 2d 612, 323 P.2d 178, 68 A.L.R.2d 416 (1st Dist. 1958)
30 ALR5th 571—§ 29

Scarberry v. Fidelity Mortg. of New York, 2012 WL 2522812 (D. Nev. 2012)
86 ALR6th 411—§ 5

Scarborough v. Brown Group, Inc., 972 F. Supp. 1112, 70 Empl. Prac. Dec. (CCH) ¶ 44724 (W.D. Tenn. 1997)
20 ALR6th 1—§ 9
Scarborough v. Granite School Dist., 531 P.2d 480 (Utah 1975)
64 ALR5th 519—§ 4
Scarborough v. Mississippi Dep't of Transp. Highway Dep't, 764 So. 2d 488 (Miss. Ct. App. 2000)
97 ALR5th 1—§ 2
Scarborough v. Mississippi Dept. of Transp. Highway Dept., 764 So. 2d 488 (Miss. Ct. App. 2000)
106 ALR5th 111—§ 2, 18, 20
108 ALR5th 1—§ 33
Scarborough v. Northern Assur. Co., 514 F. Supp. 337 (E.D. La 1981)
14 ALR5th 695—§ 18
Scarborough v. State, 50 Md. App. 276, 437 A.2d 672 (1981)
41 ALR6th 295—§ 12
Scarborough v. State, 261 So. 2d 475 (Miss. 1972)
109 ALR5th 611—§ 4
Scarbrough v. Dover Elevator Co., 232 Ga. App. 149, 500 S.E.2d 616 (1998)
99 ALR5th 141—§ 14
Scarbrough v. Johnson, 300 F.3d 302 (3d Cir. 2002)
31 ALR6th 49—§ 10
Scarbrough v. Watson, 140 Ala. 349, 37 So. 281 (1904)
45 ALR5th 109—§ 6
Scarbrow v. State Farm Mut. Auto. Ins. Co., 504 S.E.2d 860 (Va. 1998)
31 ALR5th 116—§ 3
Scarcella v. America Online, Inc., 11 Misc. 3d 19, 811 N.Y.S.2d 858 (App. Term 2005)
84 ALR6th 589—§ 4
Scarcia v. Maryland Cas. Co., 1988 WL 124570 (E.D. Pa. 1988)
88 ALR5th 493—§ 3
89 ALR5th 1—§ 18
Scardina v. Wood, 649 F. Supp. 793 (N.D. Ohio 1986)

71 ALR5th 307—§ 3
5 ALR6th 133—§ 15
14 ALR6th 301—§ 4
Scariano Bros., Inc. v. Backhaus, 359 So. 2d 1036 (La. App. 4th Cir. 1978)
20 ALR5th 229—§ 2, 11
Scaringe v. Holstein, 103 A.D.2d 880, 477 N.Y.S.2d 903, 38 U.C.C. Rep. Serv. 1595 (3d Dep't 1984)
83 ALR6th 1—§ 11, 15, 22, 39
Scarlercio v. Mazzuca, 2009 WL 3232990 (E.D. N.Y. 2009)
63 ALR6th 1—§ 55
Scarlet v. State, 766 So. 2d 1110 (Fla. 3d DCA 2000)
92 ALR6th 1—§ 8
Scarlett v. Barnes, 121 B.R. 578 (W.D. Mo. 1990)
64 ALR6th 473—§ 9, 20, 21
Scarlino, Claim of, 243 A.D.2d 800, 662 N.Y.S.2d 850 (3d Dep't 1997)
2 ALR5th 475—§ 4
Scarpulla v. Roscoe, 2002 WL 31174222 (Cal. App. 1st Dist. 2002)
111 ALR5th 313—§ 7
Scarrella v. Midwest Federal Sav. and Loan, 536 F.2d 1207, 21 Fed. R. Serv. 2d 1033 (8th Cir. 1976)
49 ALR6th 93—§ 3
Scarsellato v. Ford Motor Co., 1997 WL 28713 (E.D. Pa. 1997)
82 ALR5th 501—§ 2, 5, 7, 22, 26, 36, 37, 47 to 49
SCA Services, Inc. v. General Mill Supply Co., 129 Mich. App. 224, 341 N.W.2d 480 (1983)
56 ALR5th 757—§ 4
Scatamacchio v. W. Res. Care Sys., 161 Ohio App. 3d 230, 2005-Ohio-2690, 829 N.E.2d 1247 (7th Dist. Mahoning County 2005)
98 ALR6th 1—§ 18, 69
Scatena v. Connecticut State Police, 29 Conn. L. Rptr. 693, 2001 WL 812788 (Conn. Super. Ct. 2001)
114 ALR5th 283—§ 3, 4, 10
Scates v. State, 603 So. 2d 504, 17 FLW S. 467 (Fla. 1992)

27 ALR5th 593—§ 2, 28
Scates v. State, 603 So. 2d 504, 77 Ed. Law Rep. 596 (Fla. 1992)

113 ALR5th 597—§ 8
Scavetta v. King Soopers, Inc., 2012 WL 33259 (D. Colo. 2012)

76 ALR6th 587—§ 23
Scavone v. Scavone, 243 N.J. Super. 134, 578 A.2d 1230 (1990)

9 ALR5th 568—§ 11, 18
Scavone v. Volz, 34 App. Div. 2d 966, 313 N.Y.S.2d 948 (2d Dep't 1970)

2 ALR5th 553—§ 22
S.C.C., Re Welfare of, 452 N.W.2d 490 (Minn. App. 1990)

2 ALR5th 725—§ 17
S.C. Chimexim S.A. v. Velco Enterprises Ltd., 36 F. Supp. 2d 206 (S.D. N.Y. 1999)

88 ALR5th 545—§ 13, 15
SCD, In re Adoption of, 358 Ark. 51, 186 S.W.3d 225 (2004)

28 ALR6th 349—§ 23
SCDSS/Child Support Enforcement v. Carswell, 359 S.C. 424, 597 S.E.2d 859 (Ct. App. 2004)

18 ALR6th 97—§ 7
SCEcorp v. Superior Court, 3 Cal. App. 4th 673, 4 Cal. Rptr. 2d 372 (4th Dist. 1992)

71 ALR5th 491—§ 6
Sceifers v. State, 267 Ind. 687, 373 N.E.2d 131 (1978)

55 ALR6th 157—§ 92
Sceirine v. Densmore, 87 Nev. 9, 479 P.2d 779 (1971)

91 ALR6th 1—§ 52
Scelba v. Scelba, 342 S.C. 223, 535 S.E.2d 668 (Ct. App. 2000)

112 ALR5th 399—§ 4
Scelfo v. Rutgers University, 116 N.J. Super. 403, 282 A.2d 445 (1971)

44 ALR5th 193—§ 21
Scelta v. Delicatessen Support Services, Inc., 57 F. Supp. 2d 1327 (M.D. Fla. 1999)

93 ALR5th 47—§ 5
20 ALR6th 1—§ 5

Scentura Creations, Inc. v. Long, 325 Ill. App. 3d 62, 258 Ill. Dec. 469, 756 N.E.2d 451 (2d Dist. 2001)

48 ALR6th 511—§ 23
Schaad v. New York Life Ins. Co., 79 F. Supp. 463 (E.D. Tenn. 1948)

123 ALR5th 259—§ 6
Schaadt v. St. Jude Medical S.C., Inc., 2007 WL 978093 (D. Minn. 2007)

36 ALR6th 203—§ 4
Schaaf v. Highfield, 127 Wash. 2d 17, 896 P.2d 665 (1995)

44 ALR6th 1—§ 5, 19
Schaaf v. Kaufman, 2004 PA Super 129, 850 A.2d 655 (2004)

97 ALR6th 519—§ 4
Schaaf v. Lewis, 59 F.3d 176 (9th Cir. 1995)

51 ALR6th 1—§ 20
Schaaf v. Malave, 28 Ohio St. 3d 306, 503 N.E.2d 742 (1986)

5 ALR6th 133—§ 12
Schabarum v. California Legislature, 60 Cal. App. 4th 1205, 70 Cal. Rptr. 2d 745 (3d Dist. 1998)

9 ALR6th 177—§ 3, 31
Schaberg v. Alarm-Tech Sec. Systems, Inc., 13 Misc. 3d 134(A), 831 N.Y.S.2d 350 (App. Term 2006)

36 ALR6th 305—§ 8
Schachel v. Closet Concepts, Inc., 405 So. 2d 487, 217 U.S.P.Q. 502 (Fla. 3d DCA 1981)

85 ALR6th 1—§ 29
Schacht, In re, 228 A.D. 232, 239 N.Y.S. 516 (1st Dep't 1930)

25 ALR6th 1—§ 35
Schacht v. Ameritrust Co. N.A., 1994 WL 86229 (Ohio Ct. App. 8th Dist. Cuyahoga County 1994)

53 ALR6th 213—§ 7
Schacht v. Brown, 711 F.2d 1343, Fed. Sec. L. Rep. (CCH) ¶ 99160 (7th Cir. 1983)

23 ALR6th 457—§ 2
Schacht v. State, 154 Neb. 858, 50 N.W.2d 78 (1951)

76 ALR5th 1—§ 8, 14

Schachter v. U.S. Life Ins. Co. in City of New York, 77 Fed. Appx. 41 (2d Cir. 2003)
88 ALR6th 203—§ 45

Schacke v. State, 164 Ind. App. 153, 326 N.E.2d 856 (2d Dist. 1975)
57 ALR6th 445—§ 59

Schackow v. Medical-Legal Consulting Service, Inc., 46 Md. App. 179, 416 A.2d 1303, 15 A.L.R.4th 1239 (1980)
70 ALR5th 513—§ 4, 7, 10

Schacter v. Friendly Chevrolet Cadillac Toyota, Inc., 1996 WL 895464 (Tenn. Ct. App. 1996)
48 ALR6th 475—§ 3

Schad v. Borough of Mount Ephraim, 452 U.S. 61, 101 S. Ct. 2176, 68 L. Ed. 2d 671, 7 Media L. Rep. (BNA) 1426 (1981)
106 ALR5th 337—§ 2, 3
20 ALR6th 161—§ 4
21 ALR6th 425—§ 4, 10
23 ALR6th 573—§ 4, 14

Schad v. Mt. Ephraim, 452 U.S. 61, 68 L. Ed. 2d 671, 101 S. Ct. 2176, 7 Media L. R. 1426 (1981)
10 ALR5th 538—§ 1, 9

Schad v. Schriro, 454 F. Supp. 2d 897 (D. Ariz. 2006)
55 ALR6th 391—§ 7, 21, 24, 25
56 ALR6th 185—§ 39

Schade v. Diethrich, 158 Ariz. 1, 760 P.2d 1050 (1988)
85 ALR6th 323—§ 26

Schade v. Diethrich, 158 Ariz. 1, 760 P.2d 1050, 13 Ariz. Adv. Rep. 23 (1988)
27 ALR5th 1—§ 2 to 5, 8, 10, 13, 14

Schade v. Town of Wallkill, 235 A.D.2d 542, 652 N.Y.S.2d 756 (2d Dep't 1997)
91 ALR5th 225—§ 32

Schademann v. Casey, 194 Neb. 149, 231 N.W.2d 116 (1975)
28 ALR6th 1—§ 3, 8, 13, 32, 57

Schadewald v. Brule, 225 Mich. App. 26, 570 N.W.2d 788 (1997)

111 ALR5th 313—§ 7

Schadlick v. City of Concord, 108 N.H. 319, 234 A.2d 523 (1967)
73 ALR5th 223—§ 3, 7, 10

Schado v. Schado, 648 So. 2d 1169 (Ala. Civ. App. 1994)
59 ALR6th 433—§ 92

Schadt v. Brill, 173 Mich. 647, 139 N.W. 878 (1913)
25 ALR5th 123—§ 9

Schaecher v. Reinwein, 41 Ill. App. 3d 1055, 355 N.E.2d 351 (3d Dist. 1976)
97 ALR6th 83—§ 63

Schaefer, In re Disciplinary Action Against, 423 N.W.2d 680 (Minn. 1988)
96 ALR5th 23—§ 6

Schaefer, Matter of, 97 Misc. 2d 487, 411 N.Y.S.2d 977 (Fam. Ct. 1978)
26 ALR6th 451—§ 3, 9

Schaefer v. Allstate Ins. Co., 63 Ohio St. 3d 708, 590 N.E.2d 1242 (1992)
23 ALR5th 801—§ 4

Schaefer v. American Family Mut. Ins. Co., 192 Wis. 2d 768, 531 N.W.2d 585 (1995)
42 ALR5th 465—§ 2, 3

Schaefer v. Cerro Gordo County Abstract Co., 525 N.W.2d 844 (Iowa 1994)
71 ALR5th 491—§ 53

Schaefer v. City & County of Denver, 973 P.2d 717 (Colo. Ct. App. 1998)
74 ALR5th 439—§ 2, 3

Schaefer v. City of Bloomington, 309 Minn. 157, 244 N.W.2d 45 (1976)
12 ALR6th 645—§ 20

Schaefer v. Com., 13 Pa. Commw. 349, 318 A.2d 365, 14 U.C.C. Rep. Serv. 947 (1974)
94 ALR5th 247—§ 39

Schaefer v. Edward D. Jones & Co., 1996 S.D. 94, 552 N.W.2d 801 (1996)
14 ALR5th 242—§ 39

Schaefer v. Grausmall Restaurant Corp., 196 App. Div. 2d 692, 601 N.Y.S.2d 611, 54 A.L.R.5th 831 (1st Dep't 1993)
54 ALR5th 393—§ 7
Schaefer v. Larsen, 688 S.W.2d 430 (Tenn. App. 1984)
7 ALR5th 1—§ 19
Schaefer v. Las Cruces Public School Dist., 716 F. Supp. 2d 1052, 261 Ed. Law Rep. 299 (D.N.M. 2010)
98 ALR6th 599—§ 50, 56, 92
Schaefer v. Marchiano, 193 A.D.2d 664, 597 N.Y.S.2d 470 (2d Dep't 1993)
92 ALR6th 379—§ 21
Schaefer v. Mayor and Council of City of Athens, 120 Ga. App. 301, 170 S.E.2d 339 (1969)
64 ALR5th 519—§ 6, 16
Schaefer v. McCreary, 216 Neb. 739, 345 N.W.2d 821 (1984)
26 ALR5th 401—§ 7, 8, 20
Schaefer v. Merchants Nat'l Bank, 160 N.W.2d 318 (Iowa 1968)
36 ALR5th 395—§ 3, 11
37 ALR5th 237—§ 3, 12
Schaefer v. Miller, 322 Md. 297, 587 A.2d 491 (1991)
30 ALR5th 571—§ 2
35 ALR5th 145—§ 3
Schaefer v. Ohland, 105 N.Y.S.2d 935 (Sup. 1951)
42 ALR5th 53—§ 5, 32
Schaefer v. Publix Parking Systems, 226 Md. 150, 172 A.2d 508 (1961)
15 ALR6th 1—§ 4 to 6, 9, 10, 25
Schaefer v. Spokane-International Ry. Co., 110 Wash. 316, 188 P. 530 (1920)
12 ALR6th 645—§ 48
Schaefer v. Townsend, 215 F.3d 1031 (9th Cir. 2000)
34 ALR6th 643—§ 21
Schaefer v. Washington Times, Inc., 15 Media L. R. 1059 (D.C. Md. 1988)
19 ALR5th 1—§ 104
Schaefer v. Weber, 567 N.W.2d 29 (Minn. 1997)

87 ALR5th 361—§ 14
Schaefer v. Wickstead, 88 N.C. App. 468, 363 S.E.2d 653 (1988)
9 ALR5th 826—§ 3
Schaefer's Will, In re, 184 Misc. 811, 54 N.Y.S.2d 628 (1945)
56 ALR5th 133—§ 4
Schaeffer, Application of, 273 Or. 490, 541 P.2d 1400 (1975)
107 ALR5th 167—§ 16
3 ALR6th 49—§ 18
Schaeffer v. Burdette, 33 Ohio Misc. 2d 12, 514 N.E.2d 952 (C.P. 1986)
62 ALR5th 537—§ 3
Schaeffer v. Kansas Dept. of Transp., 227 Kan. 509, 608 P.2d 1309 (1980)
15 ALR6th 1—§ 4, 5, 9, 10
Schaeffer v. Lindsey, 41 Tenn. App. 600, 297 S.W.2d 801 (1956)
91 ALR5th 1—§ 3, 7, 11
Schaeffer v. Schaeffer, 101 Misc. 2d 118, 420 N.Y.S.2d 700 (1979)
5 ALR5th 550—§ 28
5 ALR5th 788—§ 2, 22
16 ALR5th 650—§ 39, 41
Schaeffer v. Woodhead, 63 Wash. App. 627, 821 P.2d 75 (Div. 3 1991)
74 ALR5th 49—§ 11
Schaefferkoetter v. Schaefferkoetter, 2003-Ohio-5529, 2003 WL 22359725 (Ohio Ct. App. 2d Dist. Greene County 2003)
59 ALR6th 433—§ 47
Schaeffer's Estate, In re, 52 Dauph. 45 (Pa. Orphans' Ct. 1942)
93 ALR5th 327—§ 4, 5, 7, 11, 30
Schaeffner, Petition of, 96 Misc. 2d 846, 410 N.Y.S.2d 44 (Sur. Ct. 1978)
111 ALR5th 1—§ 3
Schaer v. Brandeis University, 432 Mass. 474, 735 N.E.2d 373, 147 Ed. Law Rep. 247 (2000)
47 ALR5th 1—§ 15
Schaer v. City of New York, 2011 WL 1239836 (S.D. N.Y. 2011)
89 ALR6th 1—§ 60, 75
Schafer, In re, 315 B.R. 765 (Bankr. D. Colo. 2004)

53 ALR6th 159—§ 16

Schafer, In re, 455 B.R. 590 (B.A.P. 6th Cir. 2011)

77 ALR6th 273—§ 6, 7

Schafer, In re, 689 F.3d 601, Bankr. L. Rep. (CCH) P 82279 (6th Cir. 2012)

86 ALR6th 577—§ 9

Schafer, In re, 2012 WL 3553294 (6th Cir. 2012)

77 ALR6th 273—§ 7, 8

Schafer v. Ada County Assessor, 111 Idaho 870, 728 P.2d 394 (1986)

46 ALR5th 659—§ 12

Schafer v. Buckeye Union Ins. Co., 178 Ind. App. 70, 381 N.E.2d 519 (3d Dist. 1978)

104 ALR5th 331—§ 2

Schafer v. Ort, 202 Ind. 622, 177 N.E. 438 (1931)

75 ALR6th 311—§ 27

Schafer v. Ostmann, 172 Mo. App. 602, 155 S.W. 1102 (1913)

12 ALR5th 195—§ 10

Schafer v. Riedle, 481 N.W.2d 111 (Minn. App. 1992)

59 ALR5th 489—§ 12

Schafer v. Schafer, 95 Wash. 2d 78, 621 P.2d 721 (1980)

112 ALR5th 185—§ 3, 4, 7 to 9
120 ALR5th 229—§ 3, 5, 7, 9

Schafer v. Stevens, 352 S.W.2d 471 (Tex. Civ. App. Dallas 1961)

35 ALR5th 1—§ 5, 10

Schafer v. Superior Court, 180 Cal. App. 3d 305, 225 Cal. Rptr. 513 (4th Dist. 1986)

21 ALR6th 351—§ 14, 18

Schafer v. U.S., 656 A.2d 1185 (D.C. 1995)

57 ALR6th 445—§ 33

Schaff v. Bourland, 266 S.W. 843 (Tex. Civ. App. 1924)

40 ALR5th 1—§ 2, 3

Schaff v. Chateau Communities, Inc., 2004 WL 1908209 (Minn. Dist. Ct. 2004)

60 ALR6th 295—§ 48

Schaff v. Landers, 355 So. 2d 289 (La. App. 4th Cir. 1978)

23 ALR5th 241—§ 10, 42

Schaff v. Schaff, 446 N.W.2d 28 (N.D. 1989)

9 ALR6th 437—§ 12

Schaff v. State, 2003 MT 187, 316 Mont. 453, 73 P.3d 806 (2003)

19 ALR6th 411—§ 5

Schaff v. Stripling, 265 S.W. 264 (Tex. Civ. App. 1924)

40 ALR5th 1—§ 5

Schaffenacker v. State, 9 Ill. Ct. Cl. 250, 1936 WL 4552 (Ill. Ct. Cl. 1936)

40 ALR6th 99—§ 77

Schaffer v. A.O. Smith Harvestore Products, Inc., 1997 WL 746383 (Ohio Ct. App. 3d Dist. Auglaize County 1997)

5 ALR6th 497—§ 5

Schaffer v. Board of Educ. of City of St. Louis, 869 S.W.2d 163, 88 Ed. Law Rep. 1262, 148 L.R.R.M. (BNA) 2623 (Mo. Ct. App. E.D. 1993)

105 ALR5th 243—§ 17

Schaffer v. Bolz, 181 Neb. 509, 149 N.W.2d 334 (1967)

5 ALR5th 875—§ 36

Schaffer v. Clinton, 240 F.3d 878, 95 A.L.R.5th 715 (10th Cir. 2001)

95 ALR5th 459—§ 3

Schaffer v. Edward D. Jones & Co., 1996 SD 94, 552 N.W.2d 801 (S.D. 1996)

46 ALR6th 185—§ 4, 9, 17

Schaffer v. GTE, Inc., 2002 WL 1354703 (9th Cir. 2002)

99 ALR5th 1—§ 7

Schaffer v. Omaha, 197 Neb. 328, 248 N.W.2d 764 (1977)

30 ALR5th 549—§ 3

Schaffer v. State Board of Veterinary Medicine, 143 Ga. App. 68, 237 S.E.2d 510 (1977)

10 ALR5th 1—§ 3, 23

Schaffer v. Tennessee Dept. of Correction, 2011 WL 1842971 (Tenn. Ct. App. 2011)

96 ALR6th 269—§ 46

Schaffer v. Universal Rundle Corp., 397
F.2d 893 (5th Cir. 1968)
10 ALR6th 293—§ 7

Schaffer Associates v. Programs Ins.
Managers, Inc., 1997 WL 524136
(Conn. Super. Ct. 1997)
119 ALR5th 121—§ 3

Schaffer by Schaffer v. A.O. Smith Har-
vestore Products, Inc., 74 F.3d 722,
Prod. Liab. Rep. (CCH) ¶ 14477, 34
Fed. R. Serv. 3d 205, 1996 FED
App. 0040P (6th Cir. 1996)
5 ALR6th 497—§ 5

Schaffner v. Chicago & N. W. Transp.
Co., 129 Ill. 2d 1, 133 Ill. Dec. 432,
541 N.E.2d 643, 15 A.L.R.5th 1005
(1989)
15 ALR5th 119—§ 3, 5, 56, 61, 89

Schaffner v. Department of Employment
Sec., 140 Vt. 89, 436 A.2d 743
(1981)
95 ALR5th 329—§ 6

Schaffnit v. Danaher, 13 Conn. Supp.
101 (1944)
2 ALR5th 475—§ 15, 20

Schafke v. Chrysler Corp., 147 Mich.
App. 751, 383 N.W.2d 141, 47 BNA
FEP Cas. 1041 (1985)
12 ALR5th 508—§ 3

Schagger v. Pfeiffer, 244 A.D. 739, 278
N.Y.S. 949 (2d Dep't 1935)
108 ALR5th 385—§ 3

Schagrin v. Wilmington Medical Center,
Inc., 304 A.2d 61 (Del. Super. Ct.
1973)
58 ALR5th 613—§ 10

Schahrer v. Bell, 34 Ariz. 334, 271 P.
715 (1928)
60 ALR6th 481—§ 7

Schaidler v. Mercy Medical Center of
Oshkosh, Inc., 232 Wis. 2d 555,
2000 WI App. 32, 608 N.W.2d 436
(Ct. App. 1999)
87 ALR5th 277—§ 2, 44, 49

Schaill v. Tippecanoe County Sch.
Corp., 864 F.2d 1309 (CA7 Ind.
1988)
31 ALR5th 229—§ 15, 30

Schajer v. Northwestern Mut. Life Ins.
Co., 304 N.J. Super. 394, 701 A.2d
132 (Law Div. 1997)
67 ALR5th 513—§ 5

Schakel v. State, 513 P.2d 412 (Wyo.
1973)
31 ALR6th 523—§ 44, 45

Schalk v. State, 767 S.W.2d 441 (Tex.
App. Dallas 1988)
68 ALR5th 549—§ 3, 7

Schalk v. State, 823 S.W.2d 633, 21
U.S.P.Q.2d (BNA) 1838 (Tex.
Crim. App. 1991)
84 ALR5th 1—§ 3

Schalkenbach v. National Ventilating
Co., 129 A.D. 389, 113 N.Y.S. 352
(1st Dep't 1908)
85 ALR6th 1—§ 26

Schalko v. Schalko, 154 Wis. 2d 522,
454 N.W.2d 808 (Ct. App. 1990)
59 ALR6th 433—§ 79

Schallop v. New York State Dep't of
Law, 20 F. Supp. 2d 384 (N.D.N.Y.
1998)
83 ALR5th 1—§ 3, 10

Schamel v. St. Louis Arena Corp., 324
S.W.2d 375 (Mo. App. 1959)
38 ALR5th 107—§ 3

Schamel v. Textron-Lycoming, Div. of
Avco Corp., 1 F.3d 655, CCH Prod.
Liab. Rep. ¶ 13629 (CA7 Ind. 1993)
30 ALR5th 1—§ 34, 51

Schamoni v. Semler, 147 Or. 353, 31
P.2d 776 (1934)
18 ALR6th 325—§ 31, 53, 81

Schanafelt v. Seaboard Finance Co., 108
Cal. App. 2d 420, 239 P.2d 42
(1951)
12 ALR5th 195—§ 42

Schanback v. Schanback, 159 App. Div.
2d 498, 552 N.Y.S.2d 370 (2d Dep't
1990)
9 ALR5th 568—§ 9

Schandelmeier v. Winchester Western,
520 P.2d 70 (Alaska 1974)
86 ALR6th 321—§ 9
87 ALR6th 197—§ 50

Schanfield v. Sojitz Corp. of America, 258 F.R.D. 211 (S.D. N.Y. 2009)
67 ALR6th 341—§ 11

Schanke v. Manawa Community Nursing Center, Inc., 150 Wis. 2d 317, 442 N.W.2d 605 (Ct. App. 1989)
16 ALR6th 693—§ 20

Schanne v. Nationstar Mortg., LLC, 2011 WL 5119262 (W.D. Wash. 2011)
86 ALR6th 411—§ 5

Schantz, Ex parte, 26 N.D. 380, 144 N.W. 445 (1913)
76 ALR5th 485—§ 3, 17

Schaper v. City of Huntsville, 813 F.2d 709, 7 Fed. R. Serv. 3d 1464 (5th Cir. 1987)
89 ALR6th 1—§ 67

Schapira v. Connecticut Bank & Trust Co., 204 Conn. 450, 528 A.2d 367 (1987)
37 ALR5th 237—§ 3, 13

Schappe v. Com., Unemployment Compensation Bd. of Review, 38 Pa. Commw. 249, 392 A.2d 353 (1978)
95 ALR5th 329—§ 3

Schaps v. R.A. Transp. Services, Inc., 1987 WL 12178 (N.D. Ill. 1987)
9 ALR6th 285—§ 6

Scharen v. State, 249 P.3d 331 (Alaska Ct. App. 2011)
92 ALR6th 295—§ 38

Scharf v. Manson, 27 App. Div. 2d 613, 275 N.Y.S.2d 629 (3d Dep't 1966)
11 ALR5th 127—§ 4

Scharf v. Phillips, 391 So. 2d 223 (Fla. Dist. Ct. App. 3d Dist. 1980)
44 ALR6th 391—§ 5

Scharlack v. Richmond Memorial Hospital, 102 App. Div. 2d 886, 477 N.Y.S.2d 184 (2d Dep't 1984)
1 ALR5th 243—§ 2
2 ALR5th 811—§ 2

Scharrel v. Wal-Mart Stores, Inc., 949 P.2d 89 (Colo. Ct. App. 1997)
89 ALR5th 255—§ 2
15 ALR6th 1—§ 4, 10

Scharret v. City of Berkley, 249 Mich. App. 405, 642 N.W.2d 685 (2002)
118 ALR5th 1—§ 7, 11

Schartz v. D R B & M Real Estate Partnership, 5 Kan. App. 2d 625, 621 P.2d 1024 (1981)
25 ALR5th 123—§ 10
25 ALR5th 233—§ 19

Schartz v. Unified School Dist. No. 512, 953 F. Supp. 1208, 116 Ed. Law Rep. 645 (D. Kan. 1997)
51 ALR5th 1—§ 7

Schaser v. State Farm Ins. Co., 255 N.J. Super. 169, 604 A.2d 687 (1992)
33 ALR5th 587—§ 3

S. Chas. Gherardi & Sons, Inc. v. Glass, 32 App. Div. 2d 960, 303 N.Y.S.2d 220 (2d Dep't 1969)
2 ALR5th 553—§ 48

Schatz, Application of, 80 Wash. 2d 604, 497 P.2d 153 (1972)
5 ALR6th 449—§ 4

Schatz, In re Marriage of, 768 S.W.2d 607 (Mo. App. 1989)
49 ALR5th 441—§ 14

Schatz, In re Marriage of, 768 S.W.2d 607 (Mo. Ct. App. S.D. 1989)
39 ALR6th 205—§ 4

Schatz v. Abbott Laboratories, Inc., 51 Ill. 2d 143, 281 N.E.2d 323, 3 Envt. Rep. Cas. 1989, 2 ELR 20251 (1972)
25 ALR5th 568—§ 37

Schatz v. Zoning Hearing Bd. of Upper Dublin Tp., 21 Pa. Commw. 112, 343 A.2d 90 (1975)
47 ALR6th 439—§ 7

Schatz, State ex rel. v. McCaughtry, 2003 WI 80, 263 Wis. 2d 83, 664 N.W.2d 596 (2003)
85 ALR6th 229—§ 24, 37, 39

Schaub v. Cooper, 34 A.D.3d 268, 824 N.Y.S.2d 241 (1st Dep't 2006)
97 ALR6th 83—§ 35

Schaub v. Schaub, 117 La. 727, 42 So. 249 (1906)
101 ALR6th 455—§ 7

Schaubman v. Blum, 49 N.Y.2d 375, 426 N.Y.S.2d 230, 402 N.E.2d 1133 (1980)

16 ALR5th 390—§ 2

Schauder v. Pfeifer, 173 A.D.2d 598, 570 N.Y.S.2d 179 (2d Dep't 1991)

42 ALR6th 545—§ 8, 10, 18, 20

43 ALR6th 375—§ 4, 13, 49

Schauer v. DeNeveu Homeowners Ass'n, Inc., 194 Wis. 2d 62, 533 N.W.2d 470 (1995)

86 ALR6th 321—§ 4

Schauer v. Memorial Care Systems, 856 S.W.2d 437, 8 I.E.R. Cas. (BNA) 592 (Tex. App. Houston 1st Dist. 1993)

52 ALR6th 271—§ 5

Schauer v. Zellmann, 2001 WL 1530630 (Minn. Ct. App. 2001)

91 ALR6th 1—§ 8

Schauland v. Schmaltz, 252 Iowa 426, 107 N.W.2d 68 (1961)

91 ALR6th 1—§ 18, 20, 40, 41

Schaumann, Re, 243 Ga. 138, 252 S.E.2d 627 (1979)

9 ALR5th 193—§ 11, 33, 34

Schaumberg v. Schaumberg, 875 P.2d 598 (Utah Ct. App. 1994)

38 ALR6th 313—§ 7

Schaumburg v. Citizens for Better Environment, 444 U.S. 620, 63 L. Ed. 73, 100 S. Ct. 826 (1980)

7 ALR5th 455—§ 2

10 ALR5th 538—§ 2

Schaumburg, Village of v. Citizens for a Better Environment, 444 U.S. 620, 100 S. Ct. 826, 63 L. Ed. 2d 73 (1980)

72 ALR6th 513—§ 3

73 ALR6th 281—§ 23

Schaumburg, Village of v. Jeep Eagle Sales Corp., 285 Ill. App. 3d 481, 221 Ill. Dec. 679, 676 N.E.2d 200 (1st Dist. 1996)

103 ALR5th 445—§ 2, 3

31 ALR6th 333—§ 3

Schaus v. Rogowski, 161 A.D.2d 1204, 555 N.Y.S.2d 1018 (4th Dep't 1990)

91 ALR6th 435—§ 138

Schauss v. Garner, 590 P.2d 1316, 25 U.C.C.R.S. 1396 (Wyo. 1979)

61 ALR5th 525—§ 7, 24

Schawk, Inc. v. Donruss Trading Cards, Inc., 319 Ill. App. 3d 640, 253 Ill. Dec. 776, 746 N.E.2d 18, 43 U.C.C. Rep. Serv. 2d 1109 (1st Dist. 2001)

94 ALR5th 247—§ 37

Schayes v. T.D. Service Co. of Arizona, 2011 WL 1793161 (D. Ariz. 2011)

86 ALR6th 411—§ 5

Scheafer v. Herman, 172 Cal. 338, 155 P. 1084 (1916)

116 ALR5th 1—§ 58, 65

Scheafnocker v. Scheafnocker, 356 Pa. Super. 118, 514 A.2d 172 (1986)

5 ALR5th 550—§ 7

20 ALR5th 700—§ 22

Scheanette v. Riggins, 2006 WL 722212 (E.D. Tex. 2006)

54 ALR6th 99—§ 47

Schear v. Motel Management Corp., 61 Md. App. 670, 487 A.2d 1240 (1985)

2 ALR5th 369—§ 2, 6, 7

Schear v. Motel Management Corp. of America, 61 Md. App. 670, 487 A.2d 1240 (1985)

111 ALR5th 1—§ 5, 20

112 ALR5th 621—§ 3

Schearer v. Harber, 36 Ind. 536, 1871 WL 5281 (1871)

97 ALR6th 567—§ 4, 12

Schechter v. Boren, 535 F. Supp. 1 (W.D. Okla. 1980)

103 ALR5th 255—§ 3, 8, 11, 12

Schechter v. Com., Unemployment Compensation Bd. of Review, 89 Pa. Commw. 24, 491 A.2d 938 (1985)

25 ALR6th 101—§ 5

Schechter v. New Jersey Dept. of Law & Public Safety, Div. of Gaming Enforcement, 327 N.J. Super. 428, 743 A.2d 872 (App. Div. 2000)
13 ALR6th 499—§ 10, 22
37 ALR6th 137—§ 4

Schechter v. Schechter, 63 A.D.3d 817, 881 N.Y.S.2d 151 (2d Dep't 2009)
81 ALR6th 1—§ 24

Schechtman v. Lappin, 161 App. Div. 2d 118, 554 N.Y.S.2d 846 (1st Dep't 1990)
15 ALR5th 119—§ 5, 59, 64

Scheck v. Maryland Sec. Comm'r, 101 Md. App. 390, 646 A.2d 1092, CCH Blue Sky L. Rep. ¶ 73958 (1994)
58 ALR5th 293—§ 7

Scheckter v. Ryan, 161 A.D.2d 344, 555 N.Y.S.2d 99 (1st Dep't 1990)
91 ALR5th 485—§ 2, 9

Schedler v. Bayou Fabricators & Erectors, 340 So. 2d 673 (La. App. 4th Cir. 1976)
18 ALR5th 577—§ 38

Scheehle v. Justices of Supreme Court of State of Arizona, 203 Ariz. 520, 57 P.3d 379 (2002)
69 ALR6th 415—§ 36, 50, 52, 53

Scheehle v. Justices of the Supreme Court of the State of Arizona, 211 Ariz. 282, 120 P.3d 1092 (2005)
27 ALR6th 403—§ 14

Scheeler v. Bahr, 41 Wis. 2d 473, 164 N.W.2d 310 (1969)
65 ALR5th 105—§ 7

Scheer v. Syracuse, 53 Misc. 2d 80, 277 N.Y.S.2d 866 (1967)
48 ALR5th 473—§ 5, 16

Scheerer v. U.S. Atty. Gen., 513 F.3d 1244 (11th Cir. 2008)
62 ALR6th 517—§ 10, 33, 60

Scheffer, State ex rel. v. Justus, 85 Minn. 279, 88 N.W. 759 (1902)
95 ALR5th 1—§ 3, 11

Scheffler v. Scheffler, 453 So. 2d 960 (La. Ct. App. 5th Cir. 1984)
2 ALR6th 439—§ 36

Scheftel's Estate, Re, 156 Misc. 443, 281 N.Y.S. 957 (1935)
23 ALR5th 744—§ 3

Scheg v. Agway, Inc., 229 A.D.2d 963, 645 N.Y.S.2d 687 (4th Dep't 1996)
11 ALR5th 438—§ 13

Scheibe v. Brogan, 1995 WL 382752 (Neb. Ct. App. 1995)
64 ALR6th 473—§ 9

Scheibel v. Groeteka, 183 Ill. App. 3d 120, 131 Ill. Dec. 680, 538 N.E.2d 1236 (5th Dist. 1989)
26 ALR5th 401—§ 4, 16

Scheibel v. Scheibel, 204 Neb. 653, 284 N.W.2d 572 (1979)
9 ALR6th 437—§ 5, 9

Scheiber, In re, 168 Vt. 534, 724 A.2d 475 (1998)
19 ALR6th 335—§ 21

Scheiber v. I. Simon & Co., 25 App. Div. 2d 588, 267 N.Y.S.2d 44 (3d Dep't 1966)
26 ALR5th 127—§ 11

Scheiber v. St. John's Univ., 84 N.Y.2d 120, 615 N.Y.S.2d 332, 638 N.E.2d 977 (1994)
37 ALR5th 349—§ 8, 26

Scheidecker v. Arvig Enterprises, Inc., 122 F. Supp. 2d 1031, 6 Wage & Hour Cas. 2d (BNA) 999 (D. Minn. 2000)
99 ALR5th 1—§ 3

Scheidecker v. City of Napa, 1994 WL 589336 (N.D. Cal. 1994)
89 ALR6th 1—§ 113

Scheidecker v. Department of State, 242 App. Div. 119, 273 N.Y.S. 737 (1934)
7 ALR5th 474—§ 63

Scheidel v. Scheidel, 129 N.M. 223, 2000-NMCA-059, 4 P.3d 670 (Ct. App. 2000)
59 ALR6th 433—§ 61

Scheidel v. U.S., 2010 WL 3880873 (N.D. N.Y. 2010)
62 ALR6th 517—§ 26, 55
63 ALR6th 1—§ 26

Scheidler v. Brochstein, 73 S.W.2d 907 (Tex. Civ. App. Galveston 1934)
53 ALR6th 213—§ 14

Scheidler v. National Organization for Women, Inc., 126 S. Ct. 1264, 164 L. Ed. 2d 10, R.I.C.O. Bus. Disp. Guide (CCH) ¶ 11027 (U.S. 2006)
16 ALR6th 767—§ 19

Scheidt v. Denney, 644 So. 2d 813 (La. Ct. App. 1st Cir. 1994)
81 ALR5th 167—§ 5, 7

Scheifla v. Benchmark Management Corp., 270 A.D.2d 815, 705 N.Y.S.2d 749 (4th Dep't 2000)
99 ALR5th 141—§ 2, 10
100 ALR5th 409—§ 3, 12
115 ALR5th 1—§ 2

Schein v. Schein, 448 So. 2d 16 (Fla. App. D3 1984)
49 ALR5th 441—§ 21

Scheinberg v. Smith, 482 F. Supp. 529 (S.D. Fla. 1979)
77 ALR5th 1—§ 6

Scheinberg v. Smith, 659 F.2d 476 (5th Cir. 1981)
77 ALR5th 1—§ 3, 8, 14 to 17

Scheinblum v. Lauderdale County Bd. of Supervisors, 350 F. Supp. 2d 743 (S.D. Miss. 2004)
122 ALR5th 1—§ 9, 12

Scheiner v. New York City Health and Hospitals Corp., 1999 WL 771383 (S.D. N.Y. 1999)
89 ALR6th 1—§ 11, 48

Scheiner's Will, In re, 215 Iowa 1101, 247 N.W. 532 (1932)
31 ALR5th 499—§ 2

Scheinert v. Henderson, 800 F. Supp. 263 (E.D. Pa. 1992)
63 ALR6th 1—§ 5, 55

Scheinesohn v. Lemonek, 84 Ohio St. 424, 95 N.E. 913 (1911)
56 ALR5th 1—§ 3

Scheinfeld v. Muntz TV, Inc., 67 Ill. App. 2d 8, 214 N.E.2d 506 (1st Dist. 1966)
75 ALR5th 1—§ 7, 13, 17

Scheininger v. Department of Professional Regulation, Bd. of Medical Examiners, 443 So. 2d 387 (Fla. Dist. Ct. App. 1st Dist. 1983)
19 ALR6th 577—§ 10

Scheirman v. Coulter, 1980 OK 156, 624 P.2d 70, 30 U.C.C. Rep. Serv. 836 (Okla. 1980)
79 ALR6th 211—§ 9, 31

Schelbauer v. Butler Manufacturing Co., 35 Cal. 3d 442, 198 Cal. Rptr. 155, 673 P.2d 743, CCH Prod. Liab. Rep. ¶ 9925, 38 A.L.R.4th 566 (1984)
3 ALR5th 851—§ 7, 8

Scheldberger v. State, 204 Wis. 235, 235 N.W. 419 (1931)
54 ALR6th 429—§ 9

Schell v. Albrecht, 65 Ill. App. 3d 989, 22 Ill. Dec. 651, 383 N.E.2d 15 (3d Dist. 1978)
22 ALR5th 483—§ 22

Schell v. Eastern York School Dist., 92 Pa. Cmwlth. 333, 500 A.2d 896 (1985)
57 ALR5th 477—§ 30

Schell v. State, 72 Ga. App. 804, 35 S.E.2d 325 (1945)
81 ALR5th 563—§ 3, 5

Schell v. U. S., 423 F.2d 101 (7th Cir. 1970)
101 ALR5th 351—§ 2

Schellenberg v. Township of Bingham, 2009 WL 2245235 (W.D. Mich. 2009)
68 ALR6th 229—§ 6

Scheller v. Industrial Comm'n of Ariz, 134 Ariz. 418, 656 P.2d 1279 (App. 1982)
61 ALR5th 375—§ 5, 10

Schellhammer v. Schellhammer, 687 So. 2d 987 (Fla. Dist. Ct. App. 5th Dist. 1997)
47 ALR5th 129—§ 10

Schellhouse v. Norfolk & W. R. Co., 61 Ohio St. 3d 520, 575 N.E.2d 453 (1991)
18 ALR5th 525—§ 3

Schelp v. Cohen-Esrey Real Estate
Servs., 889 S.W.2d 848 (Mo. App.
1994)
43 ALR5th 207—§ 2, 3, 5, 36

Schelter v. Schelter, 206 App. Div. 2d
865, 614 N.Y.S.2d 853 (4th Dep't
1994)
49 ALR5th 595—§ 3

Scheman v. 1501 Broadway Corp., 127
N.Y.S.2d 600 (Sup. 1953)
42 ALR5th 53—§ 55

Schemansky v. California Pizza Kitchen,
Inc., 122 F. Supp. 2d 761 (E.D.
Mich. 2000)
94 ALR5th 1—§ 22, 24

Schemberg v. Progressive Cas. Ins. Co.,
709 F. Supp. 620 (E.D. Pa.1989)
103 ALR5th 1—§ 4, 17

Schemberg v. Progressive Casualty Ins.
Co., 709 F. Supp. 620 (E.D. Pa.
1989)
40 ALR5th 603—§ 4

Schembre v. Mid-America Transplant
Ass'n, 135 S.W.3d 527, 6 A.L.R.6th
711 (Mo. Ct. App. E.D. 2004)
6 ALR6th 365—§ 6, 7

Schemel v. General Motors Corp., 261
F. Supp. 134 (S.D. Ind. 1966)
93 ALR5th 103—§ 6

Schempp-Cook v. Cook, 455 N.W.2d
216 (N.D. 1990)
71 ALR5th 99—§ 3, 6

Schena v. Smiley, 488 Pa. 632, 413 A.2d
662, 107 L.R.R.M. (BNA) 2453, 89
Lab. Cas. (CCH) ¶ 12172 (1980)
120 ALR5th 351—§ 9

Schenburn v. Lehner Associates, Inc., 22
Mich. App. 534, 177 N.W.2d 699
(1970)
117 ALR5th 23—§ 15

Schenck, In re Conduct of, 318 Or. 402,
870 P.2d 185 (1994)
91 ALR5th 437—§ 15

Schenck v. Ebby Halliday Real Estate,
Inc., 803 S.W.2d 361 (Tex. App.
Fort Worth 1990)
115 ALR5th 709—§ 5

Schenck v. Kloster Cruise Ltd., 800 F.
Supp. 120, 1992 A.M.C. 2940
(D.N.J. 1992)
82 ALR6th 175—§ 6

Schenck v. Pelkey, 176 Conn. 245, 405
A.2d 665, 25 U.C.C. Rep. Serv.
(CBC) 416, 6 A.L.R.4th 481 (1978)
65 ALR5th 105—§ 11

Schenck v. Pro-Choice Network Of
Western New York, 519 U.S. 357,
117 S. Ct. 855, 137 L. Ed. 2d 1
(1997)
62 ALR6th 359—§ 4 to 6
70 ALR6th 513—§ 3, 5, 13
71 ALR6th 471—§ 3, 13

Schenck Tours, Inc., Re, 69 B.R. 906 (F.
BC ED N.Y. 1987)
12 ALR5th 630—§ 2

Schendel v. Hennepin County Medical
Center, 484 N.W.2d 803 (Minn. Ct.
App. 1992)
57 ALR5th 141—§ 14

Schendt v. Dewey, 246 Neb. 573, 520
N.W.2d 541 (1994)
5 ALR6th 133—§ 7, 14, 20
14 ALR6th 301—§ 15
19 ALR6th 475—§ 6
76 ALR6th 31—§ 50

Schendt v. Dewey, 252 Neb. 979, 568
N.W.2d 210 (1997)
19 ALR6th 475—§ 24

Schenebeck v. Sterling Drug, Inc., 423
F.2d 919 (CA8 Ark. 1970)
38 ALR5th 683—§ 5
57 ALR5th 1—§ 2, 3, 27

Schenectady (Schenectady Patrolmen's
Benev. Ass'n), Matter of City of,
138 A.D.2d 882, 526 N.Y.S.2d 259
(3d Dep't 1988)
31 ALR6th 433—§ 3

Schenectady v. State, 80 Misc. 2d 223,
363 N.Y.S.2d 76 (1975)
21 ALR5th 812—§ 3

Schenectady Chemicals, Inc. v. DeLuke
Sand & Gravel Co., 29 A.D.2d 800,
286 N.Y.S.2d 902 (3d Dep't 1968)
111 ALR5th 313—§ 17

Schenectady Intern. Inc. v. Employers Ins. of Wausau, 245 A.D.2d 754, 665 N.Y.S.2d 455 (3d Dep't 1997)
105 ALR5th 95—§ 5
Schenectady Sav. Bank v. Bartosik, 77 Misc. 2d 837, 353 N.Y.S.2d 706 (1974)
20 ALR5th 499—§ 15
Schenek v. FSI Futures, Inc., 1999 WL 33872 (S.D. N.Y. 1999)
60 ALR6th 295—§ 73
Schenekl v. State, 30 S.W.3d 412 (Tex. Crim. App. 2000)
47 ALR6th 107—§ 26
Schenher v. State, 38 Ala. App. 573, 90 So. 2d 234 (1956)
4 ALR5th 1—§ 4, 8, 10
Schenk, Re, 612 N.E.2d 1059 (Ind. 1993)
1 ALR5th 874—§ 9
Schenk v. HNA Holdings, Inc., 170 N.C. App. 555, 613 S.E.2d 503, 24 A.L.R.6th 919 (2005)
24 ALR6th 497—§ 10, 12
Schenkel v. Flaster, 54 Fed. Appx. 362, 49 U.C.C. Rep. Serv. 2d 1274 (3d Cir. 2002)
62 ALR6th 1—§ 49
Schenker v. Randle, 209 So. 2d 327 (La. App. 4th Cir. 1968)
16 ALR5th 1—§ 44
Schenley Industries, Inc. v. N.J. Wine & Spirit Wholesalers Ass'n, 272 F. Supp. 872 (D.N.J. 1967)
41 ALR6th 77—§ 9, 19
Schensul v. Community School Bd., 122 App. Div. 2d 56, 504 N.Y.S.2d 213 (2d Dep't 1986)
56 ALR5th 493—§ 33
Schentzel v. Philadelphia Nat. League Club, 173 Pa. Super. 179, 96 A.2d 181 (1953)
82 ALR6th 417—§ 2, 11
Scheper v. McKinnon, 177 Ohio App. 3d 820, 2008-Ohio-3964, 896 N.E.2d 208 (1st Dist. Hamilton County 2008)
86 ALR6th 321—§ 4, 12

87 ALR6th 197—§ 37
Schepps v. American Dist. Tel. Co. of Tex., 286 S.W.2d 684 (Tex. Civ. App. Dallas 1955)
36 ALR6th 305—§ 9
Schepps v. Howe, 665 P.2d 504 (Wyo. 1983)
8 ALR5th 312—§ 2, 3, 10, 11
Scher, In Matter of, 694 A.2d 845 (Del. 1997)
96 ALR5th 23—§ 3
Scher v. Sindel, 837 S.W.2d 350 (Mo. App. 1992)
4 ALR5th 273—§ 34
Scher v. W.C.A.B. (City of Philadelphia), 740 A.2d 741 (Pa. Commw. Ct. 1999)
15 ALR6th 633—§ 3, 12, 20, 25, 44
Scherbenske Excavating, Inc. v. North Dakota State Highway Dep't, 365 N.W.2d 485 (N.D. 1985)
67 ALR5th 179—§ 6
Scherbenske Excavating, Inc. v. North Dakota State Highway Dept., 365 N.W.2d 485 (N.D. 1985)
124 ALR5th 375—§ 3, 5
Schere v. Freehold, 119 N.J. Super. 433, 292 A.2d 35 (1972)
1 ALR5th 622—§ 19
Scherer, Appeal of, 199 Pa. Super. 49, 184 A.2d 502 (1962)
56 ALR5th 171—§ 4, 15, 30
Scherer v. Morrow, 401 F.2d 204 (7th Cir. 1968)
100 ALR5th 341—§ 6
Scherer v. Scherer, 249 Ga. 635, 292 S.E.2d 662 (1982)
77 ALR6th 293—§ 32
Scherer v. Waterbury, 2000 WL 254535 (Conn. Super. Ct. 2000)
87 ALR5th 277—§ 42
Scherer & Sons, Inc. v. International Ladies' Garment Workers' Union, Local 415, 142 So. 2d 290, 50 L.R.R.M. (BNA) 2216, 45 Lab. Cas. (CCH) ¶ 17615 (Fla. 1962)
120 ALR5th 351—§ 6

Scherf v. Myers, 258 N.W.2d 831 (S.D. 1977)

9 ALR6th 285—§ 12

Scherillo v. Dun & Bradstreet, Inc., 684 F. Supp. 2d 313 (E.D. N.Y. 2010)

84 ALR6th 589—§ 3

Schering-Plough Healthcare Products, Inc. v. Schwarz Pharma, Inc., 586 F.3d 500, 92 U.S.P.Q.2d 1545, 2009-2 Trade Cas. (CCH) ¶ 76798 (7th Cir. 2009)

92 ALR6th 141—§ 3

Schermbeck v. State, 690 S.W.2d 315 (Tex. App. Dallas 1985)

3 ALR5th 521—§ 6

Schermerhorn v. Department of Registration & Education, 185 Ill. App. 3d 883, 134 Ill. Dec. 42, 542 N.E.2d 42 (1st Dist. 1989)

7 ALR5th 474—§ 2, 154

Schermerhorn v. Local 1625 of Retail Clerks Intern. Ass'n, AFL-CIO, 141 So. 2d 269, 50 L.R.R.M. (BNA) 2055, 45 Lab. Cas. (CCH) ¶ 50523 (Fla. 1962)

105 ALR5th 243—§ 17

Schermerhorn v. Rosenberg, 73 A.D.2d 276, 426 N.Y.S.2d 274, 6 Media L. Rep. (BNA) 1376 (2d Dep't 1980)

13 ALR6th 111—§ 16

Scherr v. Abrahams, 1998 WL 299678 (N.D. Ill. 1998)

81 ALR5th 41—§ 6, 10

Scherr v. Handgun Permit Review Bd., 163 Md. App. 417, 880 A.2d 1137 (2005)

91 ALR6th 435—§ 12, 89

Scherr v. Hilton Hotels Corp., 168 Cal. App. 3d 908, 214 Cal. Rptr. 393, 11 Media L. Rep. (BNA) 2415 (2d Dist. 1985)

96 ALR5th 107—§ 7

99 ALR5th 301—§ 8

Scherrer v. City of Bella Villa, 2009 WL 440484 (E.D. Mo. 2009)

45 ALR6th 1—§ 8

52 ALR6th 623—§ 4, 6

Scherrer v. City of Bella Villa, 2009 WL 690186 (E.D. Mo. 2009)

95 ALR6th 641—§ 8

Scherrer v. Plaza Bowl Inv. Co., 277 S.W.2d 695 (Mo. App. 1955)

54 ALR5th 393—§ 10

Scherrer v. Seattle, 52 Wash. 4, 100 P. 144 (1909)

53 ALR5th 617—§ 7

Scherrer v. State, 294 Ark. 227, 742 S.W.2d 877 (1988)

57 ALR5th 141—§ 5

Schertz v. State, 380 N.W.2d 404 (Iowa 1985)

72 ALR5th 403—§ 12

Schertz v. Waupaca County, 683 F. Supp. 1551 (E.D. Wis. 1988)

98 ALR5th 305—§ 9

72 ALR6th 437—§ 13

Schetter v. Jordan, 294 So. 2d 130 (Fla. Dist. Ct. App. 4th Dist. 1974)

13 ALR6th 1—§ 4

Schetter v. Schetter, 239 So. 2d 51 (Fla. App. D4 1970)

51 ALR5th 603—§ 2, 4, 14

Schettino v. Roizman Development, Inc., 158 N.J. 476, 730 A.2d 797 (1999)

118 ALR5th 91—§ 1

121 ALR5th 325—§ 3, 4

125 ALR5th 193—§ 7

Scheuer v. District Court, In and For City and County of Denver, 684 P.2d 249 (Colo. 1984)

78 ALR6th 151—§ 6

Scheuerman v. Woronoff, 459 A.2d 957 (R.I. 1983)

46 ALR5th 735—§ 3, 4

Scheuermann v. Oscar Mayer Foods Corp., 515 N.W.2d 546 (Iowa Ct. App. 1994)

99 ALR6th 643—§ 10

Scheuler v. Aamco Transmissions, Inc., 1 Kan. App. 2d 525, 571 P.2d 48, 23 U.C.C. Rep. Serv. 30 (1977)

5 ALR5th 875—§ 48

93 ALR5th 103—§ 11, 12

Scheurer v. Trustees of Open Bible Church, 175 Ohio St. 163, 23 Ohio Ops. 2d 453, 192 N.E.2d 38 (1963)
8 ALR5th 1—§ 13, 38

Scheurer Hosp. v. Lancaster Pollard & Co., 2012 WL 3065347 (E.D. Mich. 2012)
78 ALR6th 151—§ 6

Scheurman v. Department of Transp., 434 Mich. 619, 456 N.W.2d 66 (1990)
12 ALR6th 645—§ 32
50 ALR6th 95—§ 8

Schevers v. State, 129 Idaho 573, 930 P.2d 603 (1996)
96 ALR6th 269—§ 22, 26

Schexnayder v. Colonial Penn Ins. Co., 405 So. 2d 1260 (La. Ct. App. 4th Cir. 1981)
42 ALR6th 545—§ 3, 8, 14, 26, 32
43 ALR6th 375—§ 3, 4, 15, 47

Schexnayder v. FED Ventures, 625 So. 2d 530 (La. App. 5th Cir. 1993)
44 ALR5th 91—§ 8, 13

Schexnayder v. Holbert, 714 So. 2d 680 (La. 1998)
59 ALR6th 433—§ 11, 56

Schexnayder v. Hyundai, 769 So. 2d 683 (La. Ct. App. 5th Cir. 2000)
48 ALR5th 129—§ 14
50 ALR5th 1—§ 7, 13

Schexnayder v. Mathews, 898 So. 2d 616 (La. Ct. App. 3d Cir. 2005)
92 ALR6th 379—§ 13

Schexnayder v. Schexnayder, 343 So. 2d 393 (La. Ct. App. 4th Cir. 1977)
108 ALR5th 359—§ 9
26 ALR6th 331—§ 8

Schexnayder v. Tarto, 722 So. 2d 1112 (La. Ct. App. 5th Cir. 1998)
11 ALR5th 127—§ 4
52 ALR5th 1—§ 8
96 ALR5th 107—§ 7, 10
99 ALR5th 301—§ 6

Schexnaydre v. M. W. Kellogg Co., 343 So. 2d 743 (La. App. 4th Cir. 1977)
10 ALR5th 245—§ 2, 9

Schexneider v. General American Tank Car Corp., 5 La. App. 84, 1926 WL 3395 (Orleans 1926)
41 ALR6th 207—§ 31

Schey v. Chrysler Corp., 228 Wis. 2d 483, 597 N.W.2d 457 (Ct. App. 1999)
88 ALR5th 301—§ 13

Schiaffo v. Helstoski, 492 F.2d 413 (3d Cir. 1974)
24 ALR6th 255—§ 4, 12, 14

Schiaroli v. Village of Ellenville, 111 A.D.2d 947, 490 N.Y.S.2d 43 (3d Dep't 1985)
90 ALR5th 273—§ 11

Schiavo v. John F. Kennedy Hosp., 258 N.J. Super. 380, 609 A.2d 781 (1992)
26 ALR5th 245—§ 27

Schiavo v. Owens-Corning Fiberglas Corp., 282 N.J. Super. 362, 660 A.2d 515, Prod. Liab. Rep. (CCH) ¶ 14281 (App. Div. 1995)
24 ALR6th 497—§ 7

Schiavo ex rel. Schindler v. Schiavo, 357 F. Supp. 2d 1378 (M.D. Fla. 2005)
95 ALR6th 479—§ 26, 28

Schiavo ex rel. Schindler v. Schiavo, 403 F.3d 1223 (11th Cir. 2005)
95 ALR6th 479—§ 26, 28

Schiavo ex rel. Schindler v. Schiavo, 403 F.3d 1289 (11th Cir. 2005)
95 ALR6th 479—§ 26, 29

Schiavone v. Schiavone, 273 A.D.2d 394, 710 N.Y.S.2d 924 (2d Dep't 2000)
91 ALR6th 435—§ 76

Schiavone Const. Co. v. Time, Inc., 847 F.2d 1069, 15 Media L. Rep. (BNA) 1417 (3d Cir. 1988)
54 ALR6th 165—§ 20

Schiavone Constr. Co. v. Time, Inc., 619 F. Supp. 684, 12 Media L. R. 1153 (D.C. N.J. 1985)
19 ALR5th 1—§ 2, 25, 103, 106, 135, 169

Schibuk v. New York State Tax Appeals Tribunal, 289 A.D.2d 718, 733 N.Y.S.2d 801 (3d Dep't 2001)
2 ALR6th 1—§ 70

Schibursky v. International Business Machines Corp., 820 F. Supp. 1169, 61 Fair Empl. Prac. Cas. (BNA) 1520, 64 Empl. Prac. Dec. (CCH) ¶ 42965 (D. Minn. 1993)
52 ALR6th 271—§ 15

Schick v. City of New Orleans, 49 F.2d 870 (C.C.A. 5th Cir. 1931)
88 ALR6th 203—§ 80

Schick v. Crucible Specialty Metals, 199 A.D.2d 810, 605 N.Y.S.2d 528 (3d Dep't 1993)
97 ALR5th 1—§ 2, 5
108 ALR5th 1—§ 30

Schick v. Ferolito, 167 N.J. 7, 767 A.2d 962 (2001)
75 ALR6th 109—§ 12

Schick v. Perry, 12 Utah 2d 173, 364 P.2d 116, 89 A.L.R.2d 986 (1961)
115 ALR5th 251—§ 16

Schick v. State, 570 N.E.2d 918 (Ind. Ct. App. 4th Dist. 1991)
79 ALR5th 419—§ 10

Schidlmeier, In re Petition of, 344 Pa. Super. 562, 496 A.2d 1249 (1985)
40 ALR5th 697—§ 12, 17

Schidzick v. Lear Siegler Inc., 222 A.D.2d 841, 635 N.Y.S.2d 323 (3d Dep't 1995)
102 ALR5th 99—§ 3

Schidzick v. Lear Siegler, Inc., 222 App. Div. 2d 841, 635 N.Y.S.2d 323 (3 Dep't 1995)
61 ALR5th 473—§ 8

Schieber v. City of Philadelphia, 1999 WL 482310 (E.D. Pa. 1999)
96 ALR5th 107—§ 8
99 ALR5th 301—§ 4, 15

Schieck, State ex rel. v. Hathaway, 493 P.2d 759 (Wyo. 1972)
9 ALR6th 177—§ 14

Schieffelin v. Goldsmith, 253 N.Y. 243, 170 N.E. 905 (1930)
97 ALR5th 537—§ 22

Schieffelin v. Henry, 123 Misc. 792, 206 N.Y.S. 172 (1924)
47 ALR5th 553—§ 4, 10, 25

Schieffer v. Catholic Archdiocese, 244 Neb. 715, 508 N.W.2d 907 (1993)
5 ALR5th 530—§ 6

Schieffer v. Catholic Archdiocese of Omaha, 244 Neb. 715, 508 N.W.2d 907 (1993)
101 ALR5th 1—§ 7, 8

Schiek v. Duluth Heating & Sheet Metal Supply Co., 53 F.R.D. 401 (D.C. Minn. 1971)
5 ALR5th 875—§ 25, 28

Schiernbeck v. Haight, 7 Cal. App. 4th 869, 9 Cal. Rptr. 2d 716 (4th Dist. 1992)
73 ALR6th 571—§ 70

Schieszler v. Ferrum College, 233 F. Supp. 2d 796, 172 Ed. Law Rep. 708 (W.D. Va. 2002)
100 ALR6th 563—§ 3

Schieszler v. Ferrum College, 236 F. Supp. 2d 602 (W.D. Va. 2002)
100 ALR6th 563—§ 4, 5, 44

Schieve v. Cincinnati & Suburban Bell Tel. Co., 71 Ohio L. Abs. 350, 126 N.E.2d 817 (Ct. App. 1st Dist. Hamilton County 1955)
52 ALR6th 271—§ 12

Schiff v. Attorney-General of State of N.Y., 4 Misc. 2d 1018, 163 N.Y.S.2d 151 (Sup. Ct. 1956)
58 ALR5th 293—§ 3

Schiff v. Director, Div. of Taxation, 15 N.J. Tax 370, 1995 WL 840763 (1995)
2 ALR6th 1—§ 64

Schiff v. Schiff, 2000 N.D. 113, 611 N.W.2d 191 (N.D. 2000)
20 ALR5th 534—§ 11

Schiffer v. State, 617 So. 2d 357 (Fla. Dist. Ct. App. 4th Dist. 1993)
115 ALR5th 509—§ 7, 9

Schifferle v. Catherwood, 33 App. Div. 2d 847, 305 N.Y.S.2d 911 (3d Dep't 1969)
47 ALR5th 775—§ 5

Schiffli Embroidery Workers Pension Fund v. Ryan, Beck & Co., 1994 WL 62124 (D.N.J. 1994)
72 ALR6th 563—§ 15, 20, 38

Schiffman, In re Marriage of, 28 Cal. 3d 640, 169 Cal. Rptr. 918, 620 P.2d 579 (1980)
40 ALR5th 697—§ 3, 9 to 11, 17

Schiffner v. Motorola, Inc., 297 Ill. App. 3d 1099, 232 Ill. Dec. 126, 697 N.E.2d 868, Prod. Liab. Rep. (CCH) ¶ 15319 (1st Dist. 1998)
32 ALR6th 505—§ 2

Schiff, State ex rel. v. Brennan, 99 N.M. 641, 662 P.2d 642 (1983)
13 ALR5th 118—§ 7

Schifrin v. Chenille Mfg. Co., 117 F.2d 92, 48 USPQ 225 (CA2 N.Y. 1941)
8 ALR5th 653—§ 3

Schilberg Integrated Metals v. Continental Cas. Co., 29 Conn. L. Rptr. 721, 2001 WL 459114 (Conn. Super. Ct. 2001)
105 ALR5th 95—§ 11

Schildkraut v. Bally's Casino New Orleans, LLC, 2004 WL 2348321 (E.D. La. 2004)
36 ALR6th 203—§ 6

S. Children, In re, 140 Misc. 2d 980, 532 N.Y.S.2d 192 (1988)
39 ALR5th 103—§ 45, 46

Schilke v. Bean, 232 Mont. 125, 755 P.2d 565 (1988)
10 ALR5th 828—§ 23

Schiller v. Lewis, 451 S.W.2d 544 (Tex. Civ. App. Houston (1st Dist.) 1970)
21 ALR5th 82—§ 3, 17

Schiller v. Mann, 44 A.D.2d 686, 353 N.Y.S.2d 816 (N.Y. App. Div. 1974)
46 ALR5th 735—§ 4

Schiller v. Orange Hall Corp., 144 Conn. 327, 130 A.2d 798 (1957)
15 ALR6th 1—§ 4, 5, 16

Schiller Park v. Chicago, 26 Ill. 2d 278, 186 N.E.2d 343 (1962)
53 ALR5th 1—§ 22, 32

Schiller Park, Village of v. City of Chicago, 26 Ill. 2d 278, 186 N.E.2d 343 (1962)
44 ALR6th 259—§ 7

Schillerstrom v. State, 180 Ariz. 468, 885 P.2d 156, 170 Ariz. Adv. Rep. 14 (App. 1994)
32 ALR5th 57—§ 20

Schillie v. Atchison, T. & S. F. R. Co., 222 F.2d 810 (CA8 Mo. 1955)
10 ALR5th 371—§ 3, 16

Schilling, In re, 251 F. 966 (N.D. Ohio 1918)
81 ALR6th 363—§ 26

Schilling, In re the Marriage of, 791 N.W.2d 711 (Iowa Ct. App. 2010)
100 ALR6th 1—§ 28

Schilling v. Bi-State Development Agency, 414 S.W.2d 818 (Mo. App. 1967)
9 ALR5th 826—§ 3

Schilling v. Cooper, 928 So. 2d 19 (La. Ct. App. 1st Cir. 2005)
75 ALR6th 1—§ 3

Schilling v. Schilling, 452 So. 2d 834 (Miss. 1984)
17 ALR5th 366—§ 16
49 ALR5th 441—§ 19

Schilling v. Schoenle, 782 S.W.2d 630 (Ky. 1990)
64 ALR5th 519—§ 6

Schilling v. United States Fidelity & Guaranty Co., 487 So. 2d 127 (La. App. 1st Cir. 1986)
48 ALR5th 129—§ 2, 4, 15, 20
50 ALR5th 1—§ 2
51 ALR5th 467—§ 2
52 ALR5th 1—§ 2

Schilling by Schilling, Estate of v. Blount, Inc., 152 Wis. 2d 608, 449 N.W.2d 56, Prod. Liab. Rep. (CCH) ¶ 12316 (Ct. App. 1989)
96 ALR5th 239—§ 25

Schilling Enterprises, LLC v. Superior Boat Works, Inc., 2006 WL 2577848 (N.D. Miss. 2006)
66 ALR6th 185—§ 10

For assistance, call 1-800-328-4880

Schillinger v. Brewer, 215 Mont. 333, 697 P.2d 919 (1985)
119 ALR5th 121—§ 4

Schimizzi v. Illinois Farmers Ins. Co., 928 F. Supp. 760 (N.D. Ind. 1996)
14 ALR5th 242—§ 12

Schimmel v. Merrill Lynch Pierce Fenner & Smith, Inc., 464 So. 2d 602 (Fla. Dist. Ct. App. 3d Dist. 1985)
46 ALR6th 185—§ 10

Schin v. State, 744 S.W.2d 370 (Tex. App. Dallas 1988)
72 ALR6th 141—§ 9

Schindele v. Nu-Car Carriers, Inc., 42 Md. App. 705, 402 A.2d 1307 (1979)
26 ALR5th 127—§ 11, 12

Schindler v. Austwell Farmers Co-op., 829 S.W.2d 283 (Tex. App. Corpus Christi 1992)
39 ALR6th 155—§ 16

Schindler v. Deal, 2012 WL 1110082 (N.D. Ga. 2012)
96 ALR6th 475—§ 9

Schindler v. Niche Media Holdings, LLC, 1 Misc. 3d 713, 772 N.Y.S.2d 781 (Sup 2003)
46 ALR6th 1—§ 39
49 ALR6th 1—§ 51

Schindler v. Orleans Regional Sec., 862 So. 2d 1032 (La. Ct. App. 4th Cir. 2003)
123 ALR5th 259—§ 3

Schindler v. State, 2009-Ohio-4008, 2009 WL 2487979 (Ohio Ct. App. 5th Dist. Richland County 2009)
64 ALR6th 1—§ 7, 9, 11

Schindler Corp. v. Ross, 625 So. 2d 94 (Fla. Dist. Ct. App. 3d Dist. 1993)
115 ALR5th 1—§ 13, 14

Schindler Elevator Corp. v. Carvalho, 895 So. 2d 1103 (Fla. Dist. Ct. App. 4th Dist. 2005)
63 ALR6th 495—§ 3

Schindler Elevator Corp. v. U.S. ex rel. Kirk, 131 S. Ct. 63, 177 L. Ed. 2d 1152 (2010)
66 ALR6th 635—§ 47

Schindler Elevator Corp. v. U.S. ex rel. Kirk, 131 S. Ct. 1885, 179 L. Ed. 2d 825, 32 I.E.R. Cas. (BNA) 252, 94 Empl. Prac. Dec. (CCH) ¶ 44175 (2011)
66 ALR6th 635—§ 47

Schindler Elevator Corp. v. Viera, 644 So. 2d 563 (Fla. Dist. Ct. App. 3d Dist. 1994)
100 ALR5th 409—§ 13

Schindley v. Northeast Texas Community College, 13 S.W.3d 62, 15 I.E.R. Cas. (BNA) 1807 (Tex. App. Texarkana 2000)
19 ALR5th 439—§ 7

Schine Enterprises, Inc. v. Real Estate Portfolio of New York, Inc., 32 A.D.2d 750, 300 N.Y.S.2d 638 (1st Dep't 1969)
67 ALR5th 179—§ 11

Schinkel v. Maxi-Holding, Inc., 30 Mass. App. Ct. 41, 565 N.E.2d 1219 (1991)
79 ALR5th 587—§ 4

Schinner v. Schinner, 143 Wis. 2d 81, 420 N.W.2d 381 (App. 1988)
9 ALR5th 568—§ 8

Schinzel v. Wilkerson, 110 Mich. App. 600, 313 N.W.2d 167 (1981)
118 ALR5th 1—§ 4, 7, 10, 11, 14

Schipper v. Levitt & Sons, Inc., 44 N.J. 70, 207 A.2d 314 (1965)
70 ALR5th 261—§ 2
74 ALR5th 523—§ 2
75 ALR5th 413—§ 2, 3, 37

Schipper v. Schipper, 46 Wis. 2d 303, 174 N.W.2d 474 (1970)
53 ALR5th 375—§ 17

Schiraldi v. AMPCO System Parking, 9 F. Supp. 2d 213 (W.D. N.Y. 1998)
51 ALR5th 163—§ 5

Schireson v. Walsh, 354 Ill. 40, 187 N.E. 921 (1933)
10 ALR5th 1—§ 2
32 ALR5th 57—§ 25

Schirmer v. Edwards, 2 F.3d 117 (5th Cir. 1993)

51 ALR6th 359—§ 15
65 ALR6th 441—§ 6
Schirmer v. Edwards, 608 So. 2d 948 (La. 1992)
51 ALR6th 359—§ 15
65 ALR6th 441—§ 15
Schirmer v. Fisher, 235 Cal. App. 3d 398, 286 Cal. Rptr. 590, 91 C.D.O.S. 8433, 91 Daily Journal DAR 12939 (4th Dist. 1991)
24 ALR5th 1—§ 55
Schiro v. Oriental Realty Co., 7 Wis. 2d 556, 97 N.W.2d 385 (1959)
10 ALR5th 371—§ 3, 7
Schiro v. State, 479 N.E.2d 556 (Ind. 1985)
78 ALR5th 197—§ 13
Schirtzinger v. Schirtzinger, 95 Ohio App. 31, 52 Ohio Op. 372, 117 N.E.2d 42 (2d Dist.Franklin County 1952)
55 ALR5th 557—§ 5
Schivarelli v. CBS, Inc., 333 Ill. App. 3d 755, 267 Ill. Dec. 321, 776 N.E.2d 693, 30 Media L. Rep. (BNA) 2268 (1st Dist. 2002)
52 ALR6th 271—§ 19
53 ALR6th 213—§ 5
Schjoll v. Town of Gilbert, 2009 WL 1066523 (D. Ariz. 2009)
95 ALR6th 341—§ 68
Schlachet v. Cleveland Clinic Found., 104 Ohio App. 3d 160, 661 N.E.2d 259 (8th Dist. Cuyahoga County 1995)
94 ALR6th 431—§ 41
Schlader v. Interstate Power Co., 591 N.W.2d 10 (Iowa 1999)
91 ALR5th 517—§ 3, 9
Schlaefer v. Schlaefer, 71 App. D.C. 350, 112 F.2d 177, 130 A.L.R. 1014 (1940)
52 ALR5th 221—§ 3, 32
Schlaeppi v. Delaware Trust Co., 525 A.2d 562 (Del. Ch. 1986)
37 ALR5th 237—§ 3, 5, 15
Schlaff v. Schlaff, 44 Mich. App. 465, 205 N.W.2d 194 (1973)

86 ALR6th 321—§ 12
90 ALR6th 451—§ 57
Schlafly v. Baumann, 341 Mo. 755, 108 S.W.2d 363 (1937)
7 ALR5th 187—§ 3
Schlamp v. Berner's Adm'r, 21 Ky. L. Rptr. 324, 51 S.W. 312 (Ky. 1899)
6 ALR6th 391—§ 5
Schland v. Key Airlines, Inc., 794 F. Supp. 1493, 124 CCH LC ¶ 10501 (D.C. Nev 1992)
14 ALR5th 242—§ 49
Schlang v. Key Airlines, Inc., 794 F. Supp. 1493, 124 Lab. Cas. (CCH) ¶ 10501 (D. Nev. 1992)
104 ALR5th 1—§ 3, 4, 9
Schlauch v. Hartford Accident & Indemnity Co., 146 Cal. App. 3d 926, 194 Cal. Rptr. 658 (3d Dist. 1983)
6 ALR5th 297—§ 40, 41, 43, 44, 49
Schlear, Matter of, 58 Pa. Commw. 241, 427 A.2d 751 (1981)
19 ALR6th 217—§ 43
Schleef v. Foodcraft Co., 165 N.Y.S. 209 (Sup. App. T 1917)
54 ALR5th 393—§ 2, 7
Schlegel v. Bank of America, N.A., 271 Va. 542, 628 S.E.2d 362, 59 U.C.C. Rep. Serv. 2d 797 (2006)
62 ALR6th 1—§ 7
Schlegel, Commonwealth ex rel. v. Bobb (1964) 36 Northum Leg J 136
124 ALR5th 203—§ 4
Schleidt v. Stamler, 106 A.D.2d 264, 482 N.Y.S.2d 481 (1st Dep't 1984)
11 ALR6th 1—§ 4, 6
Schleier v. Kaiser Foundation Health Plan of Mid-Atlantic States, Inc., 277 U.S. App. D.C. 415, 876 F.2d 174 (1989)
51 ALR5th 271—§ 4
Schlein v. Milford Hospital, Inc., 561 F.2d 427 (CA2 Conn. 1977)
28 ALR5th 107—§ 5
Schleininger v. Questor Corp., 153 Cal. App. 3d 762, 200 Cal. Rptr. 634 (5th Dist. 1984)
103 ALR6th 81—§ 15

For assistance, call 1-800-328-4880

Schleissner v. Provincetown, 27 Mass. App. 392, 538 N.E.2d 995 (1989)
25 ALR5th 568—§ 21

Schlem, In re, 308 A.D.2d 220, 763 N.Y.S.2d 558 (1st Dep't 2003)
44 ALR6th 75—§ 4, 27

Schlemmer v. Farmers Union Cent. Exchange, Inc., 397 N.W.2d 903, 45 BNA FEP Cas. 1172 (Minn. App. 1986)
51 ALR5th 1—§ 7

Schlemmer v. Provident Life & Acc. Ins. Co., 349 F.2d 682 (9th Cir. 1965)
6 ALR6th 391—§ 7

Schlender v. Andy Jansen Co., 1962 OK 156, 380 P.2d 523, 17 A.L.R.3d 412 (Okla. 1962)
70 ALR5th 261—§ 2, 3, 10, 18
74 ALR5th 523—§ 2, 3, 8
75 ALR5th 413—§ 2

Schlenz v. Castle, 132 Ill. App. 3d 993, 87 Ill. Dec. 571, 477 N.E.2d 697 (2d Dist. 1985)
54 ALR5th 575—§ 30

Schlesinger v. Chemical Bank, 707 So. 2d 868 (Fla. Dist. Ct. App. 4th Dist. 1998)
51 ALR5th 747—§ 3

Schlesinger v. ES & H, Inc., 2011 WL 3900577 (E.D. La. 2011)
102 ALR6th 1—§ 3, 13, 14

Schlesinger v. Teitelbaum, 475 F.2d 137, 1973 A.M.C. 2038 (3d Cir. 1973)
49 ALR6th 505—§ 18

Schlesinger v. U.S., 898 F. Supp. 2d 489 (E.D. N.Y. 2012)
103 ALR6th 247—§ 4

Schlesselman v. Gouge, 163 Colo. 312, 431 P.2d 35 (1967)
2 ALR5th 769—§ 3

Schlessinger v. Holland America, N.V., 120 Cal. App. 4th 552, 16 Cal. Rptr. 3d 5, 6 A.L.R.6th 765 (2d Dist. 2004)
6 ALR6th 659—§ 3

Schlessinger v. Schlessinger By and Through Schlessinger, 796 P.2d 1385 (Colo. 1990)
118 ALR5th 513—§ 8

Schleuter v. City of Fort Worth, 947 S.W.2d 920 (Tex. App. Fort Worth 1997)
67 ALR5th 431—§ 2, 3, 5, 6, 11

Schlicher v. (NFN) Peters, I & I, 103 F.3d 940 (10th Cir. 1996)
76 ALR5th 239—§ 2, 15

Schlicher v. Schlicher, 118 Wis. 2d 821, 346 N.W.2d 470 (Ct. App. 1984)
36 ALR6th 1—§ 15, 24, 26 to 28

Schlicht v. Wengert, 178 Md. 629, 15 A.2d 911 (1940)
25 ALR5th 233—§ 6
76 ALR5th 337—§ 14

Schlichtig v. Inacom Corp., 271 F. Supp. 2d 597 (D.N.J. 2003)
13 ALR6th 499—§ 16

Schlichtman v. New Jersey Highway Authority, 243 N.J. Super. 464, 579 A.2d 1275 (Law Div. 1990)
83 ALR6th 399—§ 8

Schlieman v. Gannett Minnesota Broadcasting, Inc., 33 Media L. Rep. (BNA) 1042, 2004 WL 1728514 (Minn. Ct. App. 2004)
42 ALR6th 353—§ 23

Schlier v. Milwaukee Elec. Tool Corp., 835 F. Supp. 839, Prod. Liab. Rep. (CCH) ¶ 13733 (E.D. Pa. 1993)
4 ALR6th 401—§ 7

Schliesman v. Fisher, 158 Cal. Rptr. 527 (App. 2d Dist. 1979)
84 ALR5th 619—§ 3

Schline v. Kine, 301 Pa. 586, 152 A. 845 (1930)
91 ALR5th 485—§ 5

Schlobohm v. Command Trucking Corp., 52 A.D.2d 844, 382 N.Y.S.2d 816 (2d Dep't 1976)
111 ALR5th 1—§ 3, 5, 13

Schlobohm v. Pepperidge Farm, Inc., 806 F.2d 578 (CA5 Tex. 1986)
60 ALR5th 669—§ 3, 7

Schlobohm v. Spa Petite, Inc., 326 N.W.2d 920 (Minn. 1982)
54 ALR5th 513—§ 3
61 ALR6th 147—§ 4, 7, 9

Schlobohm v. United Parcel Service, Inc., 248 Kan. 122, 804 P.2d 978 (1991)
10 ALR5th 371—§ 3, 4

Schlobohm, U.S. ex rel. v. Medical Center for Federal Prisoners, 453 F. Supp. 618 (S.D. Ill. 1978)
53 ALR6th 1—§ 7

Schlom v. Schlom, 149 Miss. 111, 115 So. 197 (1928)
119 ALR5th 445—§ 8, 14
120 ALR5th 229—§ 7, 14

Schloss v. Huber, 21 Misc. 28, 46 N.Y.S. 921 (1897)
13 ALR5th 169—§ 8

Schloss v. Sick Optic-Electronic, Inc., 1997 WL 487428 (N.D. Cal. 1997)
104 ALR5th 1—§ 3 to 5, 8

Schlossberg v. Solesbee, 844 F. Supp. 2d 1165, 94 A.L.R.6th 775 (D. Or. 2012)
94 ALR6th 431—§ 97
94 ALR6th 525—§ 3, 6

Schlosser, In re Marriage of, 241 Ill. App. 3d 49, 181 Ill. Dec. 496, 608 N.E.2d 569 (3d Dist. 1993)
49 ALR5th 441—§ 21

Schlosser v. Creamer, 263 Md. 583, 284 A.2d 220 (1971)
25 ALR5th 123—§ 10

Schlosser v. State, 2012 IL App (3d) 110115, 358 Ill. Dec. 359, 965 N.E.2d 430 (App. Ct. 3d Dist. 2012)
91 ALR6th 435—§ 108

Schlote v. Dawson, 676 N.W.2d 187 (Iowa 2004)
14 ALR6th 301—§ 19

Schlotfeldt v. Charter Hosp. of Las Vegas, 112 Nev. 42, 910 P.2d 271 (1996)
58 ALR5th 613—§ 10
64 ALR6th 249—§ 17

Schlotfelt v. Vinton Farmers' Supply Co., 252 Iowa 1102, 109 N.W.2d 695 (1961)
103 ALR5th 157—§ 4

Schloth v. Smith, 134 Ga. App. 529, 215 S.E.2d 292 (1975)
60 ALR6th 481—§ 4, 31, 45

Schlotz v. Hyundai Motor Co., 557 N.W.2d 613, Prod. Liab. Rep. (CCH) ¶ 14835 (Minn. Ct. App. 1997)
48 ALR5th 1—§ 4

Schlueter, In re Estate of, 994 P.2d 937 (Wyo. 2000)
47 ALR5th 523—§ 4

Schlueter v. Cleveland Bd. of Education, 12 Ohio Misc. 186, 40 Ohio Ops. 2d 427, 230 N.E.2d 364 (1960)
56 ALR5th 493—§ 7

Schlumberger Limited v. Superior Court, 115 Cal. App. 3d 386, 171 Cal. Rptr. 413 (2d Dist. 1981)
71 ALR6th 249—§ 4

Schlumberger Technology Corp. v. Dubno, 202 Conn. 412, 521 A.2d 569 (1987)
80 ALR6th 325—§ 4

Schlumberger Well Services, a Div. of Schlumberger Technology Corp. v. Blaker, 623 F. Supp. 1310 (S.D. Ind. 1985)
36 ALR6th 537—§ 4, 8

Schlumm v. Terrence J O'Hagan, PC, 173 Mich. App. 345, 433 N.W.2d 839 (1988)
4 ALR5th 273—§ 3, 4, 8, 34

Schlumpf v. Superior Court of Trinity County, 79 Cal. App. 3d 892, 145 Cal. Rptr. 190 (3d Dist. 1978)
5 ALR5th 550—§ 35
21 ALR5th 396—§ 2, 24, 60

Schlup v. Auburn Needleworks, Inc., 239 Neb. 854, 479 N.W.2d 440, 14 A.L.R.5th 963 (1992)
14 ALR5th 1—§ 3 to 5, 10

Schlup v. Delo, 513 U.S. 298, 115 S. Ct. 851, 130 L. Ed. 2d 808 (1995)
97 ALR6th 263—§ 13

Schluter v. Perrie, Buker, Stagg & Jones, P.C., 230 Ga. App. 776, 498 S.E.2d 543 (1998)

60 ALR6th 1—§ 86

Schmalfeldt v. Roe, 2008 WL 4756025 (W.D. Mich. 2008)

45 ALR6th 1—§ 8

Schmalhofer v. Schmalhofer, 2003 WL 22718271 (Tenn. Ct. App. 2003)

21 ALR6th 577—§ 16

Schmaltz v. Nissen, 431 N.W.2d 657, Prod. Liab. Rep. (CCH) ¶ 11969, 7 U.C.C. Rep. Serv. 2d 1061 (S.D. 1988)

88 ALR6th 1—§ 2, 8, 11, 16, 23, 112

Schmalz v. Hardy Salt Co., 739 S.W.2d 765, 110 Lab. Cas. (CCH) ¶ 56019 (Mo. Ct. App. E.D. 1987)

79 ALR6th 377—§ 3, 17, 40

Schmeck v. Shawnee, 232 Kan. 11, 651 P.2d 585 (1982)

15 ALR5th 119—§ 5, 10, 32, 46

Schmeet v. Schumacher, 137 N.W.2d 789 (N.D. 1965)

25 ALR5th 391—§ 87

Schmehl v. Wegelin, 592 Pa. 581, 927 A.2d 183 (2007)

86 ALR6th 1—§ 79

Schmeider v. Montefiore Hosp. and Medical Center, 122 A.D.2d 735, 511 N.Y.S.2d 608 (1st Dep't 1986)

6 ALR6th 311—§ 4

Schmeiser v. Trus Joist Corp., 273 Or. 120, 540 P.2d 998 (1975)

3 ALR5th 851—§ 17, 18

Schmeltz v. Rowen, 287 Mich. 657, 284 N.W. 597 (1938)

4 ALR5th 693—§ 5, 14

Schmeltzer, Matter of, 175 Mich. App. 666, 438 N.W.2d 866 (1989)

85 ALR5th 547—§ 3

Schmelzer v. Hilton Hotels Corp., 2007 WL 2789269 (S.D. N.Y. 2007)

76 ALR6th 395—§ 21

Schmer v. Hawkeye-Security Ins. Co., 194 Neb. 94, 230 N.W.2d 216 (1975)

23 ALR5th 241—§ 11

Schmerber v. California, 384 U.S. 757, 86 S. Ct. 1826, 16 L. Ed. 2d 908 (1966)

64 ALR5th 741—§ 2
74 ALR5th 319—§ 1
76 ALR5th 239—§ 8, 11
79 ALR6th 631—§ 2

Schmick v. State Farm Mut. Auto. Ins. Co., 103 N.M. 216, 704 P.2d 1092 (1985)

40 ALR5th 603—§ 8, 9

Schmid v. Fireman's Fund Ins. Co., Inc., 97 F. Supp. 2d 967 (D. Minn. 2000)

106 ALR5th 1—§ 12

Schmid v. Lovette, 154 Cal. App. 3d 466, 201 Cal. Rptr. 424, 16 Ed. Law Rep. 1313 (1st Dist. 1984)

106 ALR5th 523—§ 16

Schmid v. Milwaukee Elec. Tool Corp., 13 F.3d 76 (3d Cir. 1994)

102 ALR5th 99—§ 4
4 ALR6th 401—§ 4

Schmid v. Roehm GmbH, 544 F. Supp. 272 (D. Kan. 1982)

18 ALR6th 629—§ 13

Schmid v. Superior Court, 205 Cal. App. 3d 1244, 253 Cal. Rptr. 137 (3d Dist. 1988)

17 ALR6th 1—§ 27

Schmid v. Whitten, 114 S.C. 245, 103 S.E. 553 (1920)

58 ALR5th 387—§ 19

Schmidt, In re, 25 Ohio St. 3d 331, 496 N.E.2d 952 (1986)

113 ALR5th 349—§ 8

Schmidt, In re, 976 So. 2d 1267 (La. 2008)

44 ALR6th 75—§ 47

Schmidt, In re, 2002 WL 1060840 (Cal. App. 3d Dist. 2002)

100 ALR5th 1—§ 10

Schmidt, In re, 2002 WL 1747567 (Cal. App. 3d Dist. 2002)

53 ALR6th 419—§ 22, 44, 52, 58

Schmidt, In re Disciplinary Action Against, 586 N.W.2d 774 (Minn. 1998)

45 ALR6th 175—§ 26

Schmidt, In re Estate of, 638 P.2d 809 (Colo. App. 1981)

31 ALR5th 499—§ 5, 8, 13

Schmidt, Re Marriage of, 436 N.W.2d 99 (Minn. 1989)

5 ALR5th 550—§ 12
6 ALR5th 69—§ 7
20 ALR5th 700—§ 2
21 ALR5th 396—§ 2

Schmidt v. American Leasco, 139 Ariz. 509, 679 P.2d 532 (Ct. App. Div. 2 1983)

66 ALR6th 351—§ 51

Schmidt v. Atlas Erection Co., Inc., 487 So. 2d 112 (La. App. 4th Cir. 1986)

36 ALR5th 225—§ 3

Schmidt v. Bishop, 779 F. Supp. 321 (S.D. N.Y. 1991)

5 ALR5th 530—§ 3, 5, 6
9 ALR5th 321—§ 4, 12, 13
11 ALR5th 588—§ 4, 6, 7
101 ALR5th 1—§ 4

Schmidt v. Board of Adjustment of City of Newark, 9 N.J. 405, 88 A.2d 607 (1952)

73 ALR5th 223—§ 2, 7

Schmidt v. Capital Candy Co., 139 Minn. 378, 166 N.W. 502 (1918)

48 ALR5th 659—§ 19
21 ALR6th 81—§ 98

Schmidt v. Cenacle Convent, 86 Ill. App. 2d 150, 229 N.E.2d 413 (2d Dist. 1967)

8 ALR5th 1—§ 11, 48

Schmidt v. Central Hardware Co., 516 S.W.2d 556, 88 BNA LRRM 2675 (Mo. App. 1974)

14 ALR5th 242—§ 47

Schmidt v. Chicago C. R. Co., 239 Ill. 494, 88 N.E. 275 (1909)

19 ALR5th 622—§ 36, 44

Schmidt v. City of Chicago, 107 Ill. App. 64, 1903 WL 1393 (1st Dist. 1903)

111 ALR5th 579—§ 21, 24

Schmidt v. City of Duluth, 346 N.W.2d 671 (Minn. Ct. App. 1984)

18 ALR6th 195—§ 32

Schmidt v. Contra Costa County, 2006 WL 3412250 (N.D. Cal. 2006)

63 ALR6th 1—§ 60

Schmidt v. Cooper, 194 Kan. 403, 399 P.2d 888 (1965)

5 ALR5th 875—§ 4, 43

Schmidt v. Cornerstone Investments, Inc., 115 Wash. 2d 148, 795 P.2d 1143 (1990)

2 ALR6th 279—§ 16

Schmidt v. Fortner, 629 So. 2d 1036 (Fla. Dist. Ct. App. 4th Dist. 1993)

112 ALR5th 47—§ 17
119 ALR5th 121—§ 3, 6, 9
121 ALR5th 325—§ 3

Schmidt v. Genesee County Clerk, 127 Mich. App. 694, 339 N.W.2d 526 (1983)

114 ALR5th 1—§ 7
116 ALR5th 1—§ 40

Schmidt v. Gibbons, 101 Ariz. 222, 418 P.2d 378 (1966)

62 ALR6th 313—§ 10

Schmidt v. Gregorio, 25-305 La. App. 2 Cir. 10/27/93, 1993 WL 852155 (La. Ct. App. 2d Cir. 1993)

57 ALR5th 633—§ 3

Schmidt v. Greyhound Corp., 228 Md. 15, 177 A.2d 897 (1962)

16 ALR5th 1—§ 31

Schmidt v. Hedden, 38 A. 843 (N.J. Ch. 1897)

13 ALR5th 684—§ 2

Schmidt v. High-Five Erectors, 2004 WL 728111 (Minn. Ct. App. 2004)

122 ALR5th 1—§ 23

Schmidt v. Hinshaw, Culbertson, Moelmann, Hoban & Fuller, 75 Ill. App. 3d 516, 31 Ill. Dec. 357, 394 N.E.2d 559 (1st Dist. 1979)

58 ALR6th 1—§ 5, 17
60 ALR6th 1—§ 40

Schmidt v. Intermountain Health Care, 635 P.2d 99 (Utah 1981)

31 ALR5th 1—§ 29

Schmidt v. International Truck and Engine Corp., 2008 WL 4998375 (N.D. Ind. 2008)

68 ALR6th 331—§ 20, 27, 31, 39
Schmidt v. Johnson, 184 Neb. 643, 171 N.W.2d 64 (1969)
21 ALR5th 82—§ 3, 21
Schmidt v. Jomac, Inc., 196 Mont. 323, 639 P.2d 517 (1982)
86 ALR6th 321—§ 12
89 ALR6th 409—§ 64, 70, 71
Schmidt v. Kratzer, 402 Pa. 630, 168 A.2d 585 (1961)
5 ALR5th 875—§ 4
Schmidt v. Lieberum, 54 Pa. Super. 500 (1913)
62 ALR5th 219—§ 18, 45
Schmidt v. Magnetic Head Corp., 101 App. Div. 2d 268, 476 N.Y.S.2d 151 (2d Dep't 1984)
6 ALR5th 242—§ 19
Schmidt v. Manchester, 92 Conn. 551, 103 A. 654 (1918)
57 ALR5th 689—§ 10, 12, 15
Schmidt v. Midwest Family Mut. Ins. Co., 426 N.W.2d 870 (Minn. 1988)
23 ALR5th 801—§ 2, 4
Schmidt v. Modern Metals Foundry, Inc., 469 N.W.2d 320 (Minn. 1991)
90 ALR6th 425—§ 4
Schmidt v. Montgomery Kone, Inc., 69 F. Supp. 2d 706 (E.D. Pa. 1999)
11 ALR6th 447—§ 5
Schmidt v. Oaks, 2013 WL 4045775 (Minn. Ct. App. 2013)
98 ALR6th 231—§ 88
Schmidt v. Omaha Public Power Dist., 245 Neb. 776, 515 N.W.2d 756 (1994)
66 ALR5th 135—§ 21
Schmidt v. Parnes, 194 Ga. App. 622, 391 S.E.2d 459 (1990)
14 ALR6th 301—§ 3, 4, 14, 27
Schmidt v. Petty, 752 S.E.2d 690 (N.C. Ct. App. 2013)
94 ALR6th 431—§ 10
Schmidt v. Philadelphia Zoning Bd. of Adjustment, 382 Pa. 521, 114 A.2d 902 (1955)
73 ALR5th 223—§ 9

Schmidt v. Pine Lawn Memorial Park, 278 N.W.2d 180 (S.D. 1979)
54 ALR5th 681—§ 9
Schmidt v. Shearer, 26 Kan. App. 2d 760, 995 P.2d 381 (1999)
58 ALR5th 535—§ 10
Schmidt v. Smith, 1995 WL 146829 (Minn. Ct. App. 1995)
91 ALR6th 1—§ 41
Schmidt v. State, 60 Md. App. 86, 481 A.2d 241 (1984)
34 ALR6th 1—§ 12
Schmidt v. State, 198 Misc. 802, 100 N.Y.S.2d 504 (1950)
38 ALR5th 107—§ 7
Schmidt v. Superior Court, 48 Cal. 3d 370, 256 Cal. Rptr. 750, 769 P.2d 932 (1989)
96 ALR5th 485—§ 8
Schmidt v. U.S., 1996 OK 29, 912 P.2d 871 (Okla. 1996)
69 ALR6th 415—§ 41
Schmidt v. Vahjen, 143 App. Div. 479, 127 N.Y.S. 1038 (1911)
18 ALR5th 437—§ 6
Schmidt v. Washington Contractors Group, Inc., 1998 MT 194, 290 Mont. 276, 964 P.2d 34 (1998)
15 ALR6th 1—§ 9, 10, 13, 20
Schmidt v. Yardney Elec. Corp., 4 Conn. App. 69, 492 A.2d 512 (1985)
105 ALR5th 351—§ 3, 4, 6, 9
Schmidt v. Yardney Electric Corp., 4 Conn. App. 69, 492 A.2d 512 (1985)
53 ALR5th 219—§ 5
Schmidt and Schmidt, Re Marriage of, 108 Or. App. 110, 813 P.2d 1129 (1991)
10 ALR5th 191—§ 3, 7
Schmidtbauer v. Commissioner of Public Safety, 392 N.W.2d 668 (Minn. Ct. App. 1986)
63 ALR6th 1—§ 66
Schmidt, Commonwealth ex rel. v. Schmidt (1958) 8 Bucks Co LR 180
124 ALR5th 203—§ 4, 5

Schmidtkunz, State ex rel. v. Webb, 230 Wis. 390, 284 N.W. 6 (1939)
123 ALR5th 411—§ 35
Schmidt on Behalf of McNell v. Roberts, 74 N.Y.2d 513, 549 N.Y.S.2d 633, 548 N.E.2d 1284 (1989)
97 ALR5th 201—§ 7
Schmier v. Supreme Court, 78 Cal. App. 4th 703, 93 Cal. Rptr. 2d 580 (1st Dist. 2000)
105 ALR5th 499—§ 4
Schmier v. Supreme Court, 96 Cal. App. 4th 873, 117 Cal. Rptr. 2d 497 (1st Dist. 2002)
106 ALR5th 523—§ 7, 27
Schmier v. U.S. Court of Appeals for Ninth Circuit, 279 F 817 (9th Cir. 2002)
105 ALR5th 499—§ 4
Schmitt v. American Press, 42 S.W.2d 969 (Mo. App. 1931)
27 ALR5th 174—§ 3, 39
Schmitt v. City of Detroit, 395 F.3d 327, Unempl. Ins. Rep. (CCH) ¶ 17457B, 2005 FED App. 0023P (6th Cir. 2005)
16 ALR6th 767—§ 34
Schmitt v. City of Detroit, Mich., 126 S. Ct. 1143, 163 L. Ed. 2d 1000 (U.S. 2006)
16 ALR6th 767—§ 34
Schmitt v. Com., 547 S.E.2d 186 (Va. 2000)
79 ALR5th 33—§ 9
Schmitt v. Morgan, 98 A.D.2d 934, 471 N.Y.S.2d 365 (3d Dep't 1983)
15 ALR6th 241—§ 5
Schmitt v. State, 563 So. 2d 1095, 15 FLW D 1575 (Fla. App. D4 1990)
42 ALR5th 291—§ 25
Schmitt v. State, 590 So. 2d 404, 16 FLW S. 731 (Fla. 1991)
42 ALR5th 291—§ 3, 4, 6, 7, 10
Schmitt v. State, 968 N.E.2d 340 (Ind. Ct. App. 2012)
101 ALR6th 545—§ 4
Schmitt v. State, 2003 WL 22411210 (Tex. App. Tyler 2003)

19 ALR6th 697—§ 6
73 ALR6th 1—§ 7
Schmitt v. Woods, 73 Ill. App. 3d 498, 29 Ill. Dec. 498, 392 N.E.2d 55 (5th Dist. 1979)
11 ALR5th 259—§ 2, 3, 6, 37
Schmitter v. Kauffman, 274 N.W.2d 723 (Iowa 1979)
31 ALR5th 171—§ 3
Schmitz, In re Marriage of, 2014 WL 1877700 (Cal. App. 4th Dist. 2014)
100 ALR6th 1—§ 27
Schmitz v. Aston, 3 P.3d 1184 (Ariz. Ct. App. Div. 1 2000)
12 ALR5th 195—§ 6, 52
Schmitz v. Blanchard Valley OB-GYN, Inc., 63 Ohio App. 3d 756, 580 N.E.2d 55 (Hancock Co. 1989)
7 ALR5th 1—§ 30
Schmitz v. Bob Evans Farms, Inc., 120 Ohio App. 3d 264, 697 N.E.2d 1037 (8th Dist. Cuyahoga County 1997)
73 ALR5th 1—§ 5
Schmitz v. Crotty, 528 N.W.2d 112 (Iowa 1995)
58 ALR6th 1—§ 6
Schmitz v. Rinke, Noonan, Smoley, Deter, Colombo, Wiant, Von Korff and Hobbs, Ltd., 783 N.W.2d 733 (Minn. Ct. App. 2010)
60 ALR6th 1—§ 103
Schmitz v. Schmitz, 88 P.3d 1116 (Alaska 2004)
39 ALR6th 205—§ 7
Schmitz v. Schmitz, 255 Mont. 159, 841 P.2d 496 (1992)
30 ALR5th 139—§ 6
Schmitz v. Schmitz, 305 Pa. Super. 328, 451 A.2d 555 (1982)
52 ALR5th 221—§ 6, 32
Schmitz v. Schmitz, 351 N.W.2d 143 (S.D. 1984)
53 ALR5th 375—§ 16
Schmitz v. Schmitz, 801 S.W.2d 333 (Ky. Ct. App. 1990)
3 ALR6th 447—§ 3, 7
Schmitz v. State, 68 Wash. App. 486, 843 P.2d 1109 (1993)

45 ALR5th 109—§ 8
Schmitz v. U.S., 2012 WL 750446 (S.D. Ala. 2012)
103 ALR6th 247—§ 17
Schmitz v. Zilveti, 20 F.3d 1043 (9th Cir. 1994)
67 ALR5th 179—§ 3
Schmoll v. ACandS, Inc., 703 F. Supp. 868 (D. Or. 1988)
112 ALR5th 113—§ 30
Schmoll v. Chapman University, 70 Cal. App. 4th 1434, 83 Cal. Rptr. 2d 426, 133 Ed. Law Rep. 206, 75 Empl. Prac. Dec. (CCH) ¶ 45967 (4th Dist. 1999)
53 ALR6th 569—§ 5
Schmorrow v. Sentry Ins. Co., 138 Wis. 2d 31, 405 N.W.2d 672 (Ct. App. 1987)
48 ALR5th 129—§ 17
52 ALR5th 1—§ 7
99 ALR5th 141—§ 9 to 12, 14
115 ALR5th 1—§ 11, 12, 14
Schmoyer by Schmoyer v. Mexico Forge, Inc., 423 Pa. Super. 593, 621 A.2d 692, Prod. Liab. Rep. (CCH) ¶ 13582 (1993)
122 ALR5th 1—§ 4
Schmuck v. U.S., 489 U.S. 705, 109 S. Ct. 1443, 103 L. Ed. 2d 734 (1989)
66 ALR6th 351—§ 12
Schmucker v. Sibert, 18 Kan. 104, 1877 WL 947 (1877)
36 ALR6th 387—§ 7
Schmuckie v. Alvey, 758 S.W.2d 31, 8 U.C.C. Rep. Serv. 2d (CBC) 1110 (Ky. 1988)
61 ALR5th 525—§ 8
Schmunk v. State, 714 P.2d 724 (Wyo. 1986)
57 ALR5th 141—§ 6
Schmutz v. Bradford, 2013 WL 7156301 (Nev. 2013)
97 ALR6th 83—§ 4, 34
Schnabel v. Lui, 302 F.3d 1023, 53 Fed. R. Serv. 3d 641 (9th Cir. 2002)
70 ALR6th 209—§ 43, 57

Schnabel v. Tyler, 32 Conn. App. 704, 630 A.2d 1361 (1993)
12 ALR5th 195—§ 36, 39, 42, 67, 68
Schnaible v. City of Bismarck, 275 N.W.2d 859 (N.D. 1979)
107 ALR5th 311—§ 13
109 ALR5th 421—§ 12
Schnapps Shop, Inc. v. H. W. Wright & Co., Ltd., 377 F. Supp. 570, 1974-2 Trade Cas. (CCH) ¶ 75306 (D. Md. 1973)
41 ALR6th 77—§ 19
Schnarch v. Owen, 124 App. Div. 2d 372, 507 N.Y.S.2d 315 (3d Dep't 1986)
52 ALR5th 1—§ 4
Schnebly, Matter of Marriage of, 145 Or. App. 188, 930 P.2d 225 (1996)
102 ALR5th 395—§ 6
Schnebly v. Baker, 217 N.W.2d 708 (Iowa 1974)
2 ALR5th 811—§ 22, 32, 33
Schneckloth v. Bustamonte, 412 U.S. 218, 36 L. Ed. 2d 854, 93 S. Ct. 2041 (1973)
51 ALR5th 603—§ 2
Schneckloth v. Bustamonte, 412 U.S. 218, 93 S. Ct. 2041, 36 L. Ed. 2d 854 (1973)
15 ALR6th 515—§ 34
62 ALR6th 413—§ 3
67 ALR6th 531—§ 3
69 ALR6th 275—§ 3
Schnee v. Unemployment Compensation Bd. of Review, 701 A.2d 994 (Pa. Commw. Ct. 1997)
68 ALR5th 13—§ 22
Schneeloch v. Glastonbury Fitness & Wellness, Inc., 47 Conn. L. Rptr. 183, 2009 WL 416645 (Conn. Super. Ct. 2009)
61 ALR6th 147—§ 6
Schneemilch v. J.J. Shields, M.D., 2006 WL 2960684 (Mich. Ct. App. 2006)
92 ALR6th 379—§ 44
Schneider, In re, 271 B.R. 761 (Bankr. D. Vt. 2002)
32 ALR6th 531—§ 40

Schneider, In re, 710 N.E.2d 178 (Ind. 1999)

27 ALR6th 1—§ 14, 20

Schneider, In re, 951 A.2d 798 (D.C. 2008)

44 ALR6th 75—§ 6, 27

Schneider v. Amador County, 2013 WL 898054 (E.D. Cal. 2013)

86 ALR6th 173—§ 6

Schneider v. Ampliflo Corp., 148 Cal. App. 3d 637, 196 Cal. Rptr. 172 (2d Dist. 1983)

13 ALR5th 684—§ 4, 14

Schneider v. Biberger, 76 Wash. 504, 136 P. 701, 6 A.L.R. 1056 (1913)

80 ALR5th 533—§ 5

Schneider v. Brunk, 72 N.C. App. 560, 324 S.E.2d 922 (1985)

17 ALR6th 159—§ 11

Schneider v. Bulger, 194 S.W. 737 (Mo. Ct. App. 1917)

109 ALR5th 421—§ 3, 7, 10

Schneider v. Calabrese, 5 Pa. Commw. 444, 291 A.2d 326 (1972)

73 ALR5th 223—§ 9

Schneider v. Castle, 126 N.H. 174, 489 A.2d 127 (1985)

117 ALR5th 23—§ 6

Schneider v. Cessna Aircraft Co., 150 Ariz. 153, 722 P.2d 321, CCH Prod. Liab. Rep. ¶ 10743 (App. 1985)

29 ALR5th 534—§ 3, 10, 12, 32

Schneider v. Colegio de Abogados de Puerto Rico, 917 F.2d 620 (1st Cir. 1990)

73 ALR6th 281—§ 19, 20

Schneider v. Com., Dept. of Transp., Bureau of Driver Licensing, 790 A.2d 363 (Pa. Commw. Ct. 2002)

15 ALR6th 375—§ 15

Schneider v. Delo, 85 F.3d 335 (8th Cir. 1996)

70 ALR5th 1—§ 2, 7
72 ALR5th 109—§ 2
78 ALR5th 197—§ 2, 9
79 ALR5th 419—§ 2
80 ALR5th 55—§ 2
95 ALR5th 125—§ 2

Schneider v. Delo, 890 F. Supp. 791 (E.D. Mo. 1995)

79 ALR5th 419—§ 12

Schneider v. Delwood Center, Inc., 394 S.W.2d 671 (Tex. Civ. App. Austin 1965)

46 ALR5th 1—§ 3

Schneider v. Dorr, 3 Ohio Misc. 103, 32 Ohio Ops. 2d 391, 210 N.E.2d 311 (1965)

36 ALR5th 395—§ 10

Schneider v. Dumbarton Developers, Inc., 247 App. D.C. 217, 767 F.2d 1007 (1985)

9 ALR5th 933—§ 4, 8

Schneider v. Eckhoff, 188 Wis. 550, 206 N.W. 838 (1925)

25 ALR5th 233—§ 19

Schneider v. Fromm Laboratories, 262 Wis. 21, 53 N.W.2d 737 (1952)

90 ALR5th 619—§ 12, 17, 19, 21, 22

Schneider v. G. Guilliams, Inc., 976 S.W.2d 522 (Mo. Ct. App. E.D. 1998)

81 ALR5th 483—§ 3
121 ALR5th 157—§ 19, 21

Schneider v. Housewright, 668 F.2d 366 (8th Cir. 1981)

92 ALR6th 1—§ 3

Schneider v. Jacob, 86 Ky. 101, 5 S.W. 350 (1887)

61 ALR5th 739—§ 3

Schneider v. Keokuk Gas Service Co., 250 Iowa 37, 92 N.W.2d 439 (1958)

34 ALR5th 1—§ 3

Schneider v. Kirwan Financial Group, Inc., 127 S. Ct. 1267, 167 L. Ed. 2d 78, 40 Employee Benefits Cas. (BNA) 1288 (U.S. 2007)

26 ALR6th 659—§ 39

Schneider v. Lazarov, 216 Tenn. 1, 390 S.W.2d 197 (1965)

38 ALR5th 737—§ 2

Schneider v. Memorial Hosp. for Cancer and Allied Diseases, 100 A.D.2d 583, 473 N.Y.S.2d 524 (2d Dep't 1984)

92 ALR6th 379—§ 144, 154, 177, 182, 183

Schneider v. Middleswart, 457 N.W.2d 33 (Iowa App. 1990)

12 ALR5th 195—§ 8

Schneider v. Miller, 73 Ohio App. 3d 335, 597 N.E.2d 175, 18 U.C.C.R.S.2d 764 (Hancock Co. 1991)

47 ALR5th 677—§ 11, 19

Schneider v. National R. Passenger Corp., 987 F.2d 132 (CA2 Conn. 1993)

40 ALR5th 1—§ 8

Schneider v. Person, 34 Pa. D. & C.2d 10, 2 U.C.C. Rep. Serv. 37 (C.P. 1964)

89 ALR5th 319—§ 23

Schneider v. Plymouth State College, 744 A.2d 101, 141 Ed. Law Rep. 183 (N.H. 1999)

86 ALR5th 1—§ 9

Schneider v. Proctor & Gamble Mfg. Co., 411 So. 2d 669 (La. App. 4th Cir. 1982)

1 ALR5th 1—§ 19

Schneider v. Rabb, 100 S.W. 163 (Tex. Civ. App. 1906)

32 ALR5th 673—§ 7

Schneider v. Ramsey, 800 F. Supp. 815 (D.C. Minn. 1992)

10 ALR5th 538—§ 3, 8, 25

Schneider v. Revici, 817 F.2d 987, 22 Fed. R. Evid. Serv. 1493 (2d Cir. 1987)

108 ALR5th 385—§ 20
92 ALR6th 379—§ 158, 164

Schneider v. Rockefeller, 31 N.Y.2d 420, 340 N.Y.S.2d 889, 293 N.E.2d 67 (1972)

114 ALR5th 311—§ 4 to 6

Schneider v. Rockefeller, 38 A.D.2d 495, 331 N.Y.S.2d 270 (3d Dep't 1972)

114 ALR5th 311—§ 8

Schneider v. Schneider, 17 N.Y.2d 123, 269 N.Y.S.2d 107, 216 N.E.2d 318 (1966)

38 ALR5th 69—§ 4

Schneider v. Schneider, 142 N.J. Super. 512, 362 A.2d 61 (Ch. Div. 1976)

101 ALR6th 455—§ 12

Schneider v. Schneider, 178 Ohio App. 3d 264, 2008-Ohio-4495, 897 N.E.2d 706 (9th Dist. Lorain County 2008)

85 ALR6th 429—§ 3

Schneider v. Schneider, 408 Ill. App. 3d 192, 348 Ill. Dec. 881, 945 N.E.2d 650 (1st Dist. 2011)

81 ALR6th 1—§ 3

Schneider v. Schneider, 555 N.E.2d 196 (Ind. Ct. App. 3d Dist. 1990)

67 ALR5th 1—§ 34

Schneider v. Schneider, 704 S.W.2d 293 (Mo. App. 1986)

4 ALR5th 403—§ 3

Schneider v. Schneider, 824 S.W.2d 942 (Mo. App. 1992)

9 ALR5th 568—§ 24

Schneider v. Schneider, 2007 WL 2417145 (Minn. Ct. App. 2007)

30 ALR6th 483—§ 58

Schneider v. State, 3 A.3d 1098 (Del. 2010)

84 ALR6th 293—§ 19

Schneider v. State, 47 Ill. Ct. Cl. 268, 1994 WL 906661 (Ill. Ct. Cl. 1994)

12 ALR6th 645—§ 21

Schneider v. State, 269 Ark. 245, 599 S.W.2d 730 (1980)

92 ALR6th 1—§ 3, 5

Schneider v. State, 761 S.W.2d 292 (Mo. Ct. App. E.D. 1988)

31 ALR6th 49—§ 4

Schneider v. Susquehanna Radio Corp., 260 Ga. App. 296, 581 S.E.2d 603 (2003)

77 ALR6th 1—§ 35, 51, 55, 112

Schneider v. TRW, Inc., 938 F.2d 986, 6 I.E.R. Cas. (BNA) 1664, 119 Lab. Cas. (CCH) ¶ 56698 (9th Cir. 1991)

11 ALR6th 447—§ 4
19 ALR6th 1—§ 5

Schneider v. UNUM Life Ins. Co. of America, 149 F. Supp. 2d 169, 26 Employee Benefits Cas. (BNA) 1337 (E.D. Pa. 2001)
30 ALR6th 395—§ 3, 7

Schneider v. Wien & Malkin LLP., 5 Misc. 3d 1011(A), 798 N.Y.S.2d 713 (Sup 2004)
24 ALR6th 399—§ 7, 13, 23

Schneider ex rel. Schneider v. Erickson, 654 N.W.2d 144 (Minn. Ct. App. 2002)
75 ALR6th 109—§ 21

Schneiderman v. Rillen, 33 Misc. 3d 788, 930 N.Y.S.2d 855 (Sup 2011)
74 ALR6th 505—§ 3

Schneiderman v. Strelecki, 107 N.J. Super. 113, 257 A.2d 130 (App. Div. 1969)
111 ALR5th 1—§ 3, 5, 10, 13

Schneider Nat., Inc. v. Holland Hitch Co., 843 P.2d 561 (Wyo. 1992)
17 ALR6th 1—§ 7

Schneider, State ex rel. v. Kreiner, 83 Ohio St. 3d 203, 1998-Ohio-271, 699 N.E.2d 83 (1998)
32 ALR6th 285—§ 23, 26, 28, 47

Schneidman Heating v. New York Plumbers' Specialties Co., 238 A.D. 318, 264 N.Y.S. 146 (1st Dep't 1933)
106 ALR5th 475—§ 6

Schneidt v. Absey Motors, 248 N.W.2d 792, 21 U.C.C.R.S. 536 (N.D. 1976)
47 ALR5th 677—§ 20

Schneiker v. Gordon, 732 P.2d 603 (Colo. 1987)
75 ALR5th 1—§ 2, 7, 13, 21

Schneir v. Englewood Hospital Asso., 91 N.J. Super. 527, 221 A.2d 559 (1966)
28 ALR5th 107—§ 21

Schnell v. Schnell, 12 Neb. App. 321, 673 N.W.2d 578 (2003)
26 ALR6th 331—§ 5, 14

Schnell v. Spano, 120 A.D.2d 669, 502 N.Y.S.2d 263 (2d Dep't 1986)
91 ALR6th 435—§ 66

Schnellmann v. Southern Commercial & Savings Bank, 123 Mo. App. 188, 100 S.W. 575 (1907)
86 ALR5th 527—§ 3, 13, 15

Schnelting v. Coors Distributing Co. of Missouri, 729 S.W.2d 212, 2 I.E.R. Cas. (BNA) 1451, 125 L.R.R.M. (BNA) 3367, 110 Lab. Cas. (CCH) ¶ 56015 (Mo. Ct. App. E.D. 1987)
52 ALR6th 271—§ 9
53 ALR6th 213—§ 9

Schneph v. New York Post Corp., 16 N.Y.2d 1011, 265 N.Y.S.2d 897, 213 N.E.2d 309 (1965)
44 ALR5th 193—§ 14

Schneph v. New York Post Corp., 23 App. Div. 2d 822, 259 N.Y.S.2d 775 (1st Dep't 1965)
44 ALR5th 193—§ 14

Schnepp v. State, 84 Nev. 120, 437 P.2d 84 (1968)
58 ALR6th 215—§ 16

Schneps v. Sturm, 25 Misc. 168, 54 N.Y.S. 140 (1898)
54 ALR5th 393—§ 6

Schnetzler v. Cross, 688 So. 2d 445 (Fla. Dist. Ct. App. 1st Dist. 1997)
79 ALR5th 587—§ 3

Schnibbe v. Glenz, 245 N.Y. 388, 157 N.E. 504 (1927)
1 ALR6th 135—§ 28

Schniederjon v. Krupa, 130 Ill. App. 3d 656, 85 Ill. Dec. 845, 474 N.E.2d 805 (5th Dist. 1985)
11 ALR6th 587—§ 8, 16

Schniederjon v. Krupa, 162 Ill. App. 3d 192, 113 Ill. Dec. 189, 514 N.E.2d 1200 (5th Dist. 1987)
11 ALR6th 587—§ 4, 10, 18

Schnitger v. Backus, 10 Wash. App. 754, 519 P.2d 1315, 14 U.C.C. Rep. Serv. (CBC) 750 (Div. 1 1974)
77 ALR5th 429—§ 3

Schnitzer v. Nixon, 439 F.2d 940 (4th Cir. 1971)
3 ALR6th 355—§ 9

Schnitzler v. Reisch, 518 F. Supp. 2d 1098 (D.S.D. 2007)

73 ALR6th 281—§ 33

Schnoor v. Palisades Realty & Amusement Co., 112 NJL 506, 172 A. 43 (1934)

10 ALR5th 371—§ 3

Schnug v. Schnug, 203 Kan. 380, 454 P.2d 474 (1969)

36 ALR6th 387—§ 7

Schnulle v. Board of Fire and Police Com'rs of City of Elgin, 16 Ill. App. 3d 812, 306 N.E.2d 906 (2d Dist. 1974)

19 ALR6th 217—§ 9

Schock v. Sheppard, 7 Ohio App. 3d 45, 7 Ohio B.R. 48, 453 N.E.2d 1292 (Lucas Co. 1982)

32 ALR5th 31—§ 3

Schoeberlein v. Rohlfing, 383 N.W.2d 386 (Minn. Ct. App. 1986)

16 ALR5th 650—§ 28
67 ALR5th 1—§ 17
80 ALR5th 117—§ 11, 17, 30

Schoeffel, In re Marriage of, 268 Ill. App. 3d 839, 206 Ill. Dec. 59, 644 N.E.2d 827 (4th Dist. 1994)

6 ALR5th 1—§ 15, 27.5

Schoeffler v. Remington Arms, Inc., 339 So. 2d 52 (La. Ct. App. 3d Cir. 1976)

96 ALR5th 239—§ 25

Schoel v. Sikes Corp., 533 F.2d 930 (5th Cir. 1976)

81 ALR6th 161—§ 4
82 ALR6th 43—§ 4

Schoemaker v. Metropolitan Utilities Dist., 245 Neb. 967, 515 N.W.2d 675 (1994)

64 ALR5th 519—§ 16

Schoemer v. Hanes & Associates, Inc., 693 N.E.2d 1333 (Ind. Ct. App. 1998)

11 ALR5th 715—§ 14
18 ALR5th 577—§ 18

Schoen v. Boulder Stage Lines, Inc., 159 Colo. 531, 412 P.2d 905 (1966)

21 ALR5th 82—§ 4

Schoen v. Caterpillar Tractor Co., 103 Ill. App. 2d 197, 243 N.E.2d 31 (3d Dist. 1968)

1 ALR5th 401—§ 3

Schoen v. Cherokee County, 242 Ga. App. 501, 530 S.E.2d 226 (2000)

34 ALR5th 591—§ 18

Schoen v. Consumers United Group, Inc., 670 F. Supp. 367, 45 Fair Empl. Prac. Cas. (BNA) 1613, 2 I.E.R. Cas. (BNA) 1905 (D.D.C. 1986)

11 ALR6th 447—§ 11

Schoenbaum v. E.I. Dupont De Nemours and Co., 2009 Trade Cas. (CCH) ¶ 76837, 2009 WL 4782082 (E.D. Mo. 2009)

60 ALR6th 295—§ 45

Schoenberg v. Adler, 105 Wis. 645, 81 N.W. 1055 (1900)

74 ALR5th 369—§ 8

Schoenberg v. Shapolsky Publishers, Inc., 916 F. Supp. 333, 38 U.S.P.Q.2d 1856 (S.D. N.Y. 1996)

76 ALR6th 289—§ 3, 7
77 ALR6th 543—§ 3

Schoenborn v. Boeing Co. 19 CCH Avi 17913 (CA3 Pa. 1985)

72 ALR5th 299—§ 2, 38

Schoenborn v. State Farm Auto. Ins. Co., 495 N.W.2d 460 (Minn. Ct. App. 1993)

103 ALR5th 1—§ 5

Schoenborn v. Stryker Corp., 801 F. Supp. 2d 1098 (D. Or. 2011)

90 ALR6th 75—§ 17, 19, 24, 43

Schoeneman, In re, 777 A.2d 259 (D.C. 2001)

44 ALR6th 75—§ 25

Schoenenberger v. Hayman, 77 Pa. Cmwlth. 411, 465 A.2d 1335 (1983)

50 ALR5th 417—§ 2, 7

Schoeneweis v. Herrin, 110 Ill. App. 3d 800, 66 Ill. Dec. 513, 443 N.E.2d 36 (5th Dist. 1982)

8 ALR5th 312—§ 2, 11

Schoenfeld v. Ochsenhaut, 114 Misc. 2d
585, 452 N.Y.S.2d 173 (N.Y. City
Civ. Ct. 1982)
81 ALR6th 1—§ 51
Schoenfelder v. Winn & Jorgensen,
P.A., 704 So. 2d 136 (Fla. Dist. Ct.
App. 1st Dist. 1997)
15 ALR6th 633—§ 3, 10, 12, 29, 32
Schoenfield, In re, 608 F.2d 930, 5
Bankr. Ct. Dec. (CRR) 905, 21
C.B.C. 671, Bankr. L. Rep. (CCH)
¶ 67235 (2d Cir. 1979)
84 ALR5th 399—§ 3 to 5
Schoenhals v. Close, 451 S.W.2d 597
(Tex. Civ. App. Amarillo 1970)
25 ALR5th 123—§ 2
25 ALR5th 233—§ 2, 3
1 ALR6th 135—§ 12
Schoenhals v. Mains, 504 N.W.2d 233
(Minn. Ct. App. 1993)
109 ALR5th 541—§ 4, 6
Schoening v. Board of Ed. of City of
New York, 8 Misc. 2d 957, 169
N.Y.S.2d 711 (Sup. Ct. 1957)
56 ALR5th 493—§ 5
Schoenkerman's Estate, In re, 236 Wis.
311, 294 N.W. 810 (1940)
98 ALR5th 353—§ 3, 7
Schoenle v. Saunders, 1983 WL 413435
(Del. Super. Ct. 1983)
95 ALR6th 85—§ 39
Schoenrock v. Tappe, 419 N.W.2d 197
(S.D. 1988)
11 ALR6th 1—§ 4, 9
Schoensee v. Bennett, 228 Mich. App.
305, 577 N.W.2d 915 (1998)
17 ALR5th 366—§ 25
Schoenwald v. Farmers Coop. Assn.,
474 N.W.2d 519 (S.D. 1991)
13 ALR5th 289—§ 18
Schoenwetter v. State, 931 So. 2d 857
(Fla. 2006)
83 ALR6th 255—§ 25
Schoeny v. Lake, 13 So. 2d 109 (La. Ct.
App. 1st Cir. 1943)
36 ALR6th 387—§ 6
Schoer v. West Bend Mut. Ins. Co., 473
N.W.2d 73 (Minn. Ct. App. 1991)

66 ALR5th 269—§ 5
Schoettger v. American Nat. Property
and Cas. Co., 10 S.W.3d 566 (Mo.
Ct. App. W.D. 2000)
35 ALR5th 375—§ 10
Schoffstall v. Nationwide Mut. Ins. Co.,
58 Pa. D. & C.4th 14, 2002 WL
31951309 (C.P. 2002)
2 ALR6th 537—§ 3, 5
Schofield v. Bany, 175 Cal. App. 2d 534,
346 P.2d 891 (3d Dist. 1959)
111 ALR5th 313—§ 9
Schofield v. Cox Enters., 212 Ga. App.
354, 441 S.E.2d 693, 94 Fulton
County D R 1154 (1994)
27 ALR5th 174—§ 67
Schofield v. Frankel, 1995 WL 780937
(Conn. Super. Ct. 1995)
64 ALR5th 519—§ 6
Schofield v. Kinzell, 29 Utah 2d 427,
511 P.2d 149 (1973)
74 ALR5th 49—§ 21
Schofield v. Schofield, 777 P.2d 197
(Alaska 1989)
86 ALR6th 321—§ 13
90 ALR6th 451—§ 79
Schofield v. State, 861 So. 2d 1244 (Fla.
Dist. Ct. App. 2d Dist. 2003)
72 ALR6th 227—§ 61
Schofield v. Woolley, 98 Ga. 548, 25
S.E. 769 (1896)
67 ALR5th 587—§ 3
Schofs v. Warden, FCI, Lexington, 509
F. Supp. 78 (E.D. Ky. 1981)
53 ALR6th 1—§ 5
Scholastic Book Clubs, Inc., Appeal of,
260 Kan. 528, 920 P.2d 947, 71
A.L.R.5th 799 (1996)
71 ALR5th 671—§ 5
Scholastic Book Clubs, Inc. v. State Bd.
of Equalization, 207 Cal. App. 3d
734, 255 Cal. Rptr. 77, 51 Ed. Law
Rep. 569 (1st Dist. 1989)
71 ALR5th 671—§ 5
Scholastic Book Clubs, Inc. v. State,
Dep't of Treasury, Revenue Div.,
223 Mich. App. 576, 567 N.W.2d
692 (1997)

---

71 ALR5th 671—§ 5

Scholastic Bus Service, Inc. v. State Tax Commission, 116 App. Div. 2d 915, 498 N.Y.S.2d 278 (3d Dep't 1986)

33 ALR5th 509—§ 7

Scholastic Entertainment, Inc. v. Fox Entertainment Group, Inc., 336 F.3d 982, 67 U.S.P.Q.2d 1464 (9th Cir. 2003)

76 ALR6th 289—§ 7

Scholastic, Inc. v. Stouffer, 124 F. Supp. 2d 836, 57 U.S.P.Q.2d 1393 (S.D. N.Y. 2000)

76 ALR6th 289—§ 5

77 ALR6th 543—§ 13

Scholbrock v. City of New Hampton, 368 N.W.2d 195 (Iowa 1985)

54 ALR6th 201—§ 7, 11, 54, 66

SC Holdings, Inc. v. A.A.A. Realty Co., 935 F. Supp. 1354, 27 Envtl. L. Rep. 20120 (D.N.J. 1996)

17 ALR6th 1—§ 15

Scholes v. Hughes, 77 Tex. 482, 14 S.W. 148 (1890)

81 ALR6th 363—§ 20

Scholfield Bros., Inc. v. State Farm Mut. Auto. Ins. Co., 242 Kan. 848, 752 P.2d 661, 6 U.C.C. Rep. Serv. 2d 1588 (1988)

47 ALR6th 347—§ 8

Scholl, Appeal of, 292 Pa. 262, 141 A. 44 (1928)

22 ALR5th 327—§ 9

Scholl v. Baynes, 125 Misc. 114, 210 N.Y.S. 153 (App. Term 1925)

88 ALR6th 533—§ 9

Scholl v. Parsons, 655 So. 2d 1060 (Ala. Civ. App. 1995)

57 ALR5th 389—§ 2

102 ALR6th 153—§ 29

Scholl v. Scholl, 621 A.2d 808 (Del. Fam. Ct. 1992)

81 ALR6th 1—§ 3, 15

Schollenberger v. Sears, Roebuck & Co., 925 F. Supp. 1239, 17 A.D.D. 1303 (E.D. Mich. 1996)

1 ALR6th 297—§ 4, 14, 15

Schollian v. Ullo, 558 So. 2d 776 (La. App. 5th Cir. 1990)

10 ALR5th 448—§ 3

Scholl, People ex rel. v. Commissioner, New York City Dept. of Correction, 172 A.D.2d 432, 569 N.Y.S.2d 10 (1st Dep't 1991)

7 ALR6th 487—§ 1

Scholl, State ex rel. v. Anselmi, 640 P.2d 746 (Wyo. 1982)

93 ALR5th 1—§ 5

Scholtec v. Estate of Reeves, 327 S.C. 551, 490 S.E.2d 603 (Ct. App. 1997)

99 ALR6th 481—§ 65

Scholtes v. Signal Delivery Service, Inc., 548 F. Supp. 487, 115 L.R.R.M. (BNA) 5163 (W.D. Ark. 1982)

104 ALR5th 1—§ 3, 4

105 ALR5th 351—§ 3

Scholtes v. State, 691 S.W.2d 84 (Tex. App. Houston 1st Dist. 1985)

9 ALR6th 633—§ 8, 10, 21

Scholtz v. Northwestern Mut. Life Ins. Co., 100 F. 573 (C.C.A. 8th Cir. 1900)

12 ALR6th 123—§ 8

Scholz v. Metropolitan Pathologists, P.C., 851 P.2d 901 (Colo. 1993)

26 ALR5th 245—§ 17 to 19, 34

34 ALR6th 431—§ 4

Scholz v. Utica Mut. Ins. Co., 86 Misc. 2d 1090, 384 N.Y.S.2d 932 (1976)

23 ALR5th 241—§ 11

Schomas v. Farmers Auto. Asso., 14 Ill. App. 3d 598, 302 N.E.2d 196 (3d Dist. 1973)

43 ALR5th 149—§ 18

Schomburg v. Johnson, 2009 WL 799466 (D. Mass. 2009)

90 ALR6th 235—§ 9

Schomer v. Madigan, 120 Ill. App. 2d 107, 255 N.E.2d 620 (4th Dist. 1970)

62 ALR5th 537—§ 3

Schomer v. Smidt, 113 Cal. App. 3d 828, 170 Cal. Rptr. 662 (4th Dist. 1980)

---

12 ALR5th 195—§ 52
7 ALR6th 135—§ 3
Schommer v. State, 1998 WL 400910 (Tex. App. Dallas 1998)
43 ALR6th 475—§ 16
Schon v. Beeker, 94 N.C. App. 738, 381 S.E.2d 464 (1989)
66 ALR6th 351—§ 34
67 ALR6th 209—§ 49
Schonauer v. DCR Entertainment, Inc., 79 Wash. App. 808, 905 P.2d 392, 67 Empl. Prac. Dec. (CCH) ¶ 43821 (Div. 2 1995)
93 ALR5th 47—§ 4
94 ALR5th 1—§ 3
14 ALR6th 417—§ 3, 6
20 ALR6th 1—§ 5
Schonberger v. Serchuk, 1992 WL 183779 (S.D. N.Y. 1992)
46 ALR6th 185—§ 10
Schoneman, In re Marriage of, 13 Kan. App. 2d 536, 775 P.2d 194 (1989)
52 ALR5th 221—§ 7, 35
Schoneman, Matter of Marriage of, 13 Kan. App. 2d 536, 775 P.2d 194 (1989)
113 ALR5th 487—§ 8, 11, 12
Schonfield v. Turner, 75 Tex. 324, 12 S.W. 626 (1889)
6 ALR6th 391—§ 5, 11, 17, 18, 21
Schoning, Matter of Marriage of, 106 Or. App. 399, 807 P.2d 820 (1991)
59 ALR6th 433—§ 12, 55
Schonlau v. Price, 524 P.2d 311 (Colo. Ct. App. 1974)
19 ALR6th 217—§ 55
Schonts, In re Marriage of, 345 N.W.2d 145 (Iowa App. 1983)
48 ALR5th 473—§ 8
52 ALR5th 221—§ 7, 20, 31
Schonwald v. Tapp, 142 Conn. 719, 118 A.2d 302 (1955)
11 ALR5th 127—§ 24
Schonwetter v. Commissioner of Revenue, 316 N.W.2d 273 (Minn. 1982)
118 ALR5th 597—§ 19
School Asbestos Litigation, In re, 1991 WL 249789 (E.D. Pa. 1991)

63 ALR5th 195—§ 6
School Bd. v. Florida Publ. Co., 670 So. 2d 99, 21 FLW D500, 24 Media L. R. 1798 (Fla. App. D1 1996)
35 ALR5th 113—§ 14
School Bd. v. Florida Unemployment Appeals Com., 500 So. 2d 253, 11 FLW 2623 (Fla. App. D1 1986)
15 ALR5th 653—§ 5
School Bd. of Broward County v. Beharrie, 695 So. 2d 437, 119 Ed. Law Rep. 293 (Fla. Dist. Ct. App. 4th Dist. 1997)
68 ALR5th 663—§ 6
School Bd. of City of Norfolk v. U.S. Gypsum Co., 234 Va. 32, 360 S.E.2d 325, 41 Ed. Law Rep. 1142 (1987)
5 ALR6th 497—§ 7, 8
41 ALR6th 445—§ 6, 7, 29
School Bd. of Marshall v. State, 162 Tex. 9, 343 S.W.2d 247 (1961)
17 ALR5th 195—§ 37
School Bd. of Palm Beach County for Use and Ben. of Major Elec. Supplies of Stuart, Inc. v. Vincent J. Fasano, Inc., 417 So. 2d 1063 (Fla. 4th DCA 1982)
81 ALR6th 363—§ 4, 15
School Bd. of Parish of Livingston, La. v. Louisiana State Bd. of Elementary & Secondary Educ., 830 F.2d 563, 42 Ed. Law Rep. 57 (5th Cir. 1987)
110 ALR5th 293—§ 3
School Board v. Surette, 394 So. 2d 147 (Fla. App. D4 1981)
23 ALR5th 1—§ 8
School Board of Gary v. Claudio, 413 N.E.2d 628 (Ind. App. 1980)
23 ALR5th 1—§ 2, 3
School Board of Pardeeville Area School Dist. v. Bomber, 214 Wis. 2d 396, 571 N.W.2d 189, 122 Ed. Law Rep. 790 (Ct. App. 1997)
47 ALR5th 553—§ 6

School Committee of Boston v. Dever, 8
Mass. App. 920, 395 N.E.2d 900
(1979)
60 ALR5th 669—§ 5, 6
School Committee of Braintree v. Massachusetts Com. against Discrimination, 377 Mass. 424, 386 N.E.2d
1251, 21 BNA FEP Cas. 923, 19
CCH EPD ¶ 9110 (1979)
57 ALR5th 477—§ 27, 32
School Committee of Brockton v. Massachusetts Com. against Discrimination, 377 Mass. 392, 386 N.E.2d
1240, 21 BNA FEP Cas. 918, 19
CCH EPD ¶ 9089 (1979)
57 ALR5th 477—§ 32
School Committee of Brockton v. Massachusetts Commission Against
Discrimination, 377 Mass. 392, 386
N.E.2d 1240, 21 Fair Empl. Prac.
Cas. (BNA) 918, 19 Empl. Prac.
Dec. (CCH) ¶ 9089 (1979)
99 ALR5th 1—§ 4
School Com'rs of Mobile County, Board
of v. Ardis, 575 So. 2d 1125, 66 Ed.
Law Rep. 879 (Ala. Civ. App. 1990)
56 ALR5th 493—§ 3
Schoolcraft v. Schoolcraft, 851 S.W.2d
91 (Mo. Ct. App. E.D. 1993)
36 ALR6th 1—§ 31
Schoolcraft v. Schoolcraft, 869 S.W.2d
907 (Mo. Ct. App. E.D. 1994)
36 ALR6th 1—§ 5, 6
School Directors of Fox Chapel Area
School Dist., Board of v. Rossetti,
488 Pa. 125, 411 A.2d 486, 21
Empl. Prac. Dec. (CCH) ¶ 30540
(1979)
99 ALR5th 1—§ 3
School Dist., Appeal of, 347 Pa. 418, 32
A.2d 565 (1943)
57 ALR5th 477—§ 15
School Dist. v. Celotex Corp., 556 F.2d
883, 23 FR Serv. 2d 895 (CA8 Neb.
1977)
3 ALR5th 851—§ 2, 7
School Dist. v. Henderson, 146 Ark.
338, 226 S.W. 517 (1920)

17 ALR5th 195—§ 31
School Dist. v. Montana Dep't of Labor
& Indus., 217 Mont. 72, 702 P.2d
975 (1985)
33 ALR5th 643—§ 26
School Dist. v. Ochoa, 216 Neb. 191,
342 N.W.2d 665 (1984)
33 ALR5th 643—§ 28
School Dist. v. Roy, 4 Pa. Cmwlth. 237,
285 A.2d 550 (1971)
57 ALR5th 477—§ 29
School Dist. v. Rural Special School
Dist., 128 Ark. 383, 194 S.W. 241
(1917)
17 ALR5th 195—§ 31
School Dist. v. School Dist., 55 Neb.
716, 76 N.W. 420 (1898)
17 ALR5th 195—§ 31
School Dist. v. School Dist., 331 Mich.
523, 50 N.W.2d 150 (1951)
17 ALR5th 195—§ 2, 35
School Dist. v. Umberfield, 32 Colo.
App. 306, 512 P.2d 1166, 6 BNA
FEP Cas. 454, 6 CCH EPD ¶ 8848
(1973)
37 ALR5th 349—§ 12
School Dist. v. United States Fidelity &
Guaranty Co., 96 Kan. 499, 152 P.
668 (1915)
15 ALR5th 376—§ 3
School Dist. No. 1J, Multnomah County,
Or. v. ACandS, Inc., 5 F.3d 1255,
85 Ed. Law Rep. 1070, Prod. Liab.
Rep. (CCH) ¶ 13640, 26 Fed. R.
Serv. 3d 1428 (9th Cir. 1993)
5 ALR6th 497—§ 7
41 ALR6th 445—§ 6, 32
School Dist. No. 1, Multnomah County
v. Mission Ins. Co., 58 Or. App.
692, 650 P.2d 929, 6 Ed. Law Rep.
819 (1982)
94 ALR5th 567—§ 2, 7
School Dist. No. 1, Multnomah County
v. Nilsen, 17 Or. App. 601, 523 P.2d
1041, 16 Fair Empl. Prac. Cas.
(BNA) 1198, 8 Empl. Prac. Dec.
(CCH) ¶ 9649 (1974)
99 ALR5th 1—§ 4

School Dist. No. 1, Multnomah County v. Nilsen, 271 Or. 461, 534 P.2d 1135, 16 Fair Empl. Prac. Cas. (BNA) 1203, 9 Empl. Prac. Dec. (CCH) ¶ 10187 (1975)

14 ALR6th 417—§ 9

School Dist. No. 1, Village of Brown Deer v. Department of Industry, Labor and Human Relations, 62 Wis. 2d 370, 215 N.W.2d 373 (1974)

82 ALR5th 149—§ 2

84 ALR5th 249—§ 18

108 ALR5th 1—§ 18

School Dist. No. 11, Joint Counties of Archuleta and La Plata v. Umberfield, 32 Colo. App. 306, 512 P.2d 1166, 6 Fair Empl. Prac. Cas. (BNA) 454, 6 Empl. Prac. Dec. (CCH) ¶ 8848 (1973)

107 ALR5th 623—§ 7

School Dist. No. 27, Craig County v. Graham, 1915 OK 78, 45 Okla. 531, 146 P. 213 (1915)

81 ALR6th 363—§ 22

School Dist. of Beverly v. Geller, 50 Mass. App. Ct. 290, 737 N.E.2d 873, 148 Ed. Law Rep. 461, 16 I.E.R. Cas. (BNA) 1504 (2000)

112 ALR5th 263—§ 5

School Dist. of City of Grand Haven v. Grand Haven Ass'n of Educational Secretaries, 20 Empl. Prac. Dec. (CCH) ¶ 30117, 1979 WL 3873 (Mich. Cir. Ct. 1979)

107 ALR5th 623—§ 9

School Dist. of City of Independence, Mo., No. 30 v. U.S. Gypsum Co., 750 S.W.2d 442, 46 Ed. Law Rep. 1241, Prod. Liab. Rep. (CCH) ¶ 11717 (Mo. Ct. App. W.D. 1988)

24 ALR6th 497—§ 8

School Dist. of City of Independence, State ex rel. v. Jones, 653 S.W.2d 178, 12 Ed. Law Rep. 582 (Mo. 1983)

115 ALR5th 563—§ 3

School Dist. of City of Monessen v. Apostolou Associates, Inc., 761 A.2d 597 (Pa. Super. Ct. 2000)

56 ALR5th 757—§ 4

School Dist. of City of Pontiac v. Duncan, 2010 WL 182939 (U.S. 2010)

56 ALR6th 679—§ 39

School Dist. of City of Pontiac v. Secretary of U.S. Dept. of Educ., 584 F.3d 253, 249 Ed. Law Rep. 654, 74 Fed. R. Serv. 3d 1295 (6th Cir. 2009)

56 ALR6th 679—§ 39

School Dist. of City of York v. Lincoln Edison Charter School, 2001 WL 433382 (Pa. Commw. Ct. 2001)

78 ALR5th 533—§ 7

School Dist. of Ft. Smith v. Howe, 62 Ark. 481, 37 S.W. 717 (1896)

114 ALR5th 561—§ 19

School Dist. of Kansas City v. State, 317 S.W.3d 599, 259 Ed. Law Rep. 930 (Mo. 2010)

76 ALR6th 543—§ 3, 7

School Dist. of Omaha v. Omaha, 175 Neb. 21, 120 N.W.2d 267 (1963)

42 ALR5th 547—§ 1

School Dist. of Philadelphia v. Independence Charter School, 2001 WL 460109 (Pa. Commw. Ct. 2001)

78 ALR5th 533—§ 7

School Dist. of Philadelphia v. W.C.A.B. (Hennegan), 751 A.2d 729 (Pa. Commw. Ct. 2000)

86 ALR5th 295—§ 15

School Dist. of Wildwood v. State Bd. of Ed., 116 N.J.L. 572, 185 A. 664 (N.J. Sup. Ct. 1936)

123 ALR5th 411—§ 35

School District No. 1 v. ILHR Dept., 62 Wis.2d 370, 215 N.W.2d 373 (1974)

108 ALR5th 1—§ 39

Schooler, In re, 7 Ohio N.P. (n.s.) 276, 19 Ohio Dec. 465, 1908 WL 698 (C.P. 1908)

102 ALR5th 525—§ 47

Schooler v. Navarro County Memorial Hospital, 375 F. Supp. 841 (N.D. Tex. 1973)
28 ALR5th 107—§ 12

Schooley v. Board of Education, 50 Ohio St. 2d 67, 4 Ohio Ops. 3d 157, 362 N.E.2d 644 (1977)
57 ALR5th 477—§ 31

Schooley v. Schooley, 184 Iowa 835, 169 N.W. 56 (1918)
52 ALR5th 221—§ 15

Schooley v. Weatherby, 2008 WL 4823227 (Tex. App. Austin 2008)
95 ALR6th 541—§ 88

Schoolfield v. Brunton, 20 Colo. 139, 36 P. 1103 (1894)
19 ALR5th 622—§ 7, 11

School of Visual Arts v. Kuprewicz, 3 Misc. 3d 278, 771 N.Y.S.2d 804, 20 I.E.R. Cas. (BNA) 1488 (Sup 2003)
49 ALR6th 115—§ 7
52 ALR6th 271—§ 5
54 ALR6th 99—§ 43

School Trustees, Board of v. Evett, 482 N.E.2d 1173 (Ind. App. 1985)
57 ALR5th 477—§ 18

School Trustees, Board of v. Robertson, 637 N.E.2d 181 (Ind. App. 1994)
57 ALR5th 477—§ 27

School Union No. 37 v. Ms. C., 518 F.3d 31, 230 Ed. Law Rep. 498 (1st Cir. 2008)
59 ALR6th 111—§ 3

Schooner Dartmouth, Inc. v. Piper, 349 Mass. 347, 208 N.E.2d 214 (1965)
60 ALR5th 165—§ 15

Schoonmaker v. Wilbraham, 110 Mass. 134 (1872)
10 ALR5th 371—§ 3, 7, 11

Schoonmaker Homes-John Steinberg, Inc. v. Maybrook, 178 App. Div. 2d 722, 576 N.Y.S.2d 954 (3d Dep't 1991)
38 ALR5th 737—§ 3, 11

Schoonover v. Holden, 87 N.W. 737 (Iowa 1901)
108 ALR5th 385—§ 12

Schope v. State, 647 S.W.2d 675 (Tex. App. Houston (14th Dist.) 1982)
10 ALR5th 538—§ 19, 33

Schopen v. Rando, 343 Mass. 529, 179 N.E.2d 822 (1962)
6 ALR6th 1—§ 46, 47

Schopler v. Bliss, 903 F.2d 1373, 16 Fed. R. Serv. 3d 1199 (11th Cir. 1990)
120 ALR5th 483—§ 6

Schoppa Family v. Kupersmith, 54 Fed. Appx. 592 (5th Cir. 2002)
89 ALR6th 1—§ 38, 45

Schoppelrei v. Franklin University, 11 Ohio App. 2d 60, 40 Ohio Ops. 2d 228, 228 N.E.2d 334 (Franklin Co. 1967)
47 ALR5th 1—§ 19, 31

Schor v. Abbott Laboratories, 127 S. Ct. 1257, 167 L. Ed. 2d 75 (U.S. 2007)
26 ALR6th 659—§ 4

Schor v. Abbott Laboratories, 457 F.3d 608, 2006-2 Trade Cas. (CCH) ¶ 75354 (7th Cir. 2006)
26 ALR6th 659—§ 4

Schor v. City Of Chicago, 576 F.3d 775 (7th Cir. 2009)
86 ALR6th 173—§ 8

Schor v. North Braddock Borough, 801 F. Supp. 2d 369 (W.D. Pa. 2011)
89 ALR6th 1—§ 99

Schore v. Mueller, 290 Minn. 186, 186 N.W.2d 699 (1971)
5 ALR5th 875—§ 48

Schorer v. Schorer, 177 Wis. 2d 387, 501 N.W.2d 916 (App. 1993)
9 ALR5th 568—§ 12

Schorer v. Schorer, 177 Wis. 2d 387, 501 N.W.2d 916 (Ct. App. 1993)
16 ALR6th 693—§ 10
38 ALR6th 313—§ 7
39 ALR6th 205—§ 7

Schorno v. Schorno, 26 Wash. 2d 11, 172 P.2d 474 (1946)
6 ALR6th 229—§ 4, 22

Schorpp-Replogle v. New Jersey Mfrs. Ins. Co., 395 N.J. Super. 277, 928 A.2d 885 (App. Div. 2007)

99 ALR6th 643—§ 14

Schostag v. Cator, 151 Cal. 600, 91 P. 502 (1907)

120 ALR5th 125—§ 2, 8

121 ALR5th 1—§ 2

Schott v. Animagic Studios, LLC, 2004 WL 1813280 (Tenn. Ct. App. 2004)

43 ALR6th 611—§ 11, 49

Schott v. I-Flow Corp., 696 F. Supp. 2d 898, Prod. Liab. Rep. (CCH) ¶ 18381 (S.D. Ohio 2010)

90 ALR6th 75—§ 14, 16, 43

Schott v. Schott, 744 N.W.2d 85 (Iowa 2008)

61 ALR6th 1—§ 18

Schottel, Care and Treatment of v. State, 159 S.W.3d 836 (Mo. 2005)

78 ALR6th 417—§ 14, 24

Schottel, State ex rel. v. Harman, 208 S.W.3d 889 (Mo. 2006)

78 ALR6th 417—§ 14, 24

Schottenstein, Zox & Dunn, L.P.A. v. C.J. Mahan Constr. Co., L.L.C., 2009-Ohio-3616, 2009 WL 2196782 (Ohio Ct. App. 10th Dist. Franklin County 2009)

58 ALR6th 1—§ 5

59 ALR6th 1—§ 25

Schouboe v. Wyoming Dept. of Transp., 2010 WY 119, 238 P.3d 1246 (Wyo. 2010)

92 ALR6th 295—§ 7, 9, 31

93 ALR6th 207—§ 14, 31

96 ALR6th 355—§ 21, 37, 54, 61

Schouest v. Whitley, 927 F.2d 205 (5th Cir. 1991)

95 ALR5th 125—§ 4

Schouweiler v. Yancey Co., 101 Nev. 827, 712 P.2d 786 (1985)

118 ALR5th 91—§ 5

119 ALR5th 121—§ 3

125 ALR5th 193—§ 5

2 ALR6th 279—§ 4

Schovee v. Mikolasko, 356 Md. 93, 737 A.2d 578, 119 A.L.R.5th 809 (1999)

119 ALR5th 519—§ 2, 17, 24

Schowengerdt v. U.S., 944 F.2d 483, 7 I.E.R. Cas. (BNA) 462, 57 Empl. Prac. Dec. (CCH) ¶ 41054 (9th Cir. 1991)

96 ALR5th 391—§ 9, 12

Schrader v. Blackwell, 241 F.3d 783, 2001 FED App. 0048P (6th Cir. 2001)

120 ALR5th 1—§ 25

Schrader v. Carney, 180 A.D.2d 200, 586 N.Y.S.2d 687 (4th Dep't 1992)

62 ALR5th 537—§ 4, 6

Schrader v. Clark County, Wash., 2009 WL 5216983 (W.D. Wash. 2009)

68 ALR6th 229—§ 3, 8

Schrader v. E.G. & G., Inc., 953 F. Supp. 1160, 71 Empl. Prac. Dec. (CCH) ¶ 44998 (D. Colo. 1997)

20 ALR6th 1—§ 5

Schrader v. Eli Lilly and Co., 639 N.E.2d 258, 9 I.E.R. Cas. (BNA) 1830, 128 Lab. Cas. (CCH) ¶ 57756 (Ind. 1994)

53 ALR6th 213—§ 9

Schrader v. Great Plains Elec. Coop., 19 Kan. App. 2d 276, 868 P.2d 536 (1994)

8 ALR5th 177—§ 10.5

Schrader v. Huff, 8 Ohio App. 3d 111, 8 Ohio B.R. 146, 456 N.E.2d 587 (Summit Co. 1983)

48 ALR5th 659—§ 3, 7, 8

Schrader v. Royal Caribbean Cruise Line, Inc., 952 F.2d 1008, 21 Fed. R. Serv. 3d 918 (8th Cir. 1991)

82 ALR6th 175—§ 7

Schrader v. Scott, 8 Cal. App. 4th 1679, 11 Cal. Rptr. 2d 433, 92 C.D.O.S. 7350, 92 Daily Journal DAR 11913 (4th Dist. 1992)

7 ALR5th 852—§ 43

Schrader v. State, 2000 WL 1227866 (Tex. App. Austin 2000)

122 ALR5th 593—§ 9

For assistance, call 1-800-328-4880

Schrader by Schrader v. Board of Educ. of Taconic Hills Cent. School Dist., 249 A.D.2d 741, 671 N.Y.S.2d 785, 125 Ed. Law Rep. 789 (3d Dep't 1998)

86 ALR5th 1—§ 15

Schrader-Scalf v. CitiMortgage, Inc., 2013 WL 625745 (N.D. Tex. 2013)

86 ALR6th 411—§ 5

Schraeder v. Koopman, 190 Wis. 459, 209 N.W. 714 (1926)

11 ALR5th 127—§ 4

Schraff v. State, 544 P.2d 834 (Alaska 1975)

11 ALR5th 52—§ 2, 6

Schrage v. State Bd. of Elections, 88 Ill. 2d 87, 58 Ill. Dec. 451, 430 N.E.2d 483 (1981)

114 ALR5th 311—§ 3, 4, 6 to 8

Schrager v. New York University, 227 A.D.2d 189, 642 N.Y.S.2d 243 (1st Dep't 1996)

97 ALR6th 83—§ 68

Schram v. Albertson's, Inc., 146 Or. App. 415, 934 P.2d 483 (1997)

83 ALR5th 1—§ 8, 10

94 ALR5th 1—§ 3

Schram v. Burrillville Chevrolet, Inc., 728 A.2d 457 (R.I. 1999)

88 ALR5th 301—§ 33

Schram v. Commissioner of Public Safety, 359 N.W.2d 632 (Minn. Ct. App. 1984)

76 ALR5th 1—§ 5

Schramm v. County of Monroe, 325 Ill. App. 3d 760, 259 Ill. Dec. 472, 758 N.E.2d 880 (5th Dist. 2001)

17 ALR6th 1—§ 26

Schramm v. Long Island R.R., 857 F. Supp. 255 (E.D. N.Y. 1994)

50 ALR5th 1—§ 8, 12

51 ALR5th 467—§ 4

Schramm v. Physical Therapists Examining Board, 219 A.2d 846 (Dist. Col. App. 1966)

8 ALR5th 825—§ 9

Schrank v. Pennington County Bd. of Com'rs, 2000 S.D. 62, 610 N.W.2d 90 (S.D. 2000)

73 ALR5th 223—§ 3

Schranz v. I. L. Grossman, Inc., 90 Ill. App. 3d 507, 45 Ill. Dec. 654, 412 N.E.2d 1378, 30 U.C.C. Rep. Serv. (CBC) 1299 (1st Dist. 1980)

77 ALR5th 429—§ 8

Schranz & Bieber Co., Inc. v. Quayle, 201 Misc. 516, 106 N.Y.S.2d 887 (1951)

48 ALR5th 659—§ 3, 8

Schreck, Estate of, 47 Cal. App. 3d 693, 121 Cal. Rptr. 218 (2d Dist. 1975)

3 ALR5th 590—§ 26, 29

Schreck v. North Codorus Township, 126 Pa. Cmwlth. 407, 559 A.2d 1018 (1989)

50 ALR5th 417—§ 10

Schreck v. T & C Sanderson Farms, Inc., 37 P.3d 510 (Colo. Ct. App. 2001)

12 ALR6th 123—§ 18

Schreckengast v. Hammermills, Inc., 369 N.W.2d 809 (Iowa 1985)

106 ALR5th 111—§ 5

108 ALR5th 1—§ 14, 33

Schreffler v. Board of Ed. of Delmar School Dist., 506 F. Supp. 1300 (D. Del. 1981)

123 ALR5th 411—§ 56

Schreffler v. Board of Education, 506 F. Supp. 1300 (D.C. Del. 1981)

14 ALR5th 242—§ 49

Schreffler v. Chase, 245 Ill. 395, 92 N.E. 272 (1910)

23 ALR6th 1—§ 13

Schreib v. Walt Disney Co., 2006 WL 573008 (Ill. App. Ct. 1st Dist. 2006)

83 ALR6th 1—§ 11, 15, 28, 60

84 ALR6th 1—§ 26, 49

Schreiber v. Cestari, 40 App. Div. 2d 1025, 338 N.Y.S.2d 972 (2d Dep't 1972)

4 ALR5th 148—§ 4

4 ALR5th 210—§ 13

6 ALR5th 490—§ 6

Schreiber v. City of New York, 11 Misc. 551, 32 N.Y.S. 744 (Super. Ct. 1895)
54 ALR6th 201—§ 13, 66

Schreiber v. Kellogg, 1992 WL 309632 (E.D. Pa. 1992)
67 ALR6th 341—§ 6

Schreiber v. Kelsey, 62 Cal. App. 3d Supp. 45, 133 Cal. Rptr. 508 (App. Dep't Super. Ct. 1976)
78 ALR6th 97—§ 5, 33

Schreiber v. Lugar, 518 F.2d 1099 (7th Cir. 1975)
51 ALR6th 333—§ 3

Schreiber v. Moe, 596 F.3d 323 (6th Cir. 2010)
58 ALR6th 499—§ 30

Schreiber v. Multimedia of Ohio, Inc., 41 Ohio App. 3d 257, 535 N.E.2d 357 (Hamilton Co. 1987)
60 ALR5th 75—§ 7

Schreiber v. Philips Display Components Co., 692 F. Supp. 2d 747, 48 Employee Benefits Cas. (BNA) 2217, 187 L.R.R.M. (BNA) 3505, 159 Lab. Cas. (CCH) ¶ 10201 (E.D. Mich. 2010)
74 ALR6th 267—§ 5

Schreiber v. Rowe, 814 So. 2d 396 (Fla. 2002)
14 ALR6th 1—§ 4

Schreiber v. Rowe, 2003 WL 23273965 (W.D. Wis. 2003)
53 ALR6th 1—§ 13

Schreiber v. Rowe, 2004 WL 906418 (W.D. Wis. 2004)
71 ALR6th 335—§ 13

Schreiber v. Steris Corp., 2009 WL 4114632 (W.D. Pa. 2009)
85 ALR6th 323—§ 66

Schreiber v. Zimmer, 17 A.D.3d 342, 793 N.Y.S.2d 104 (2d Dep't 2005)
17 ALR6th 159—§ 59

Schreiber by Krueger v. Physicians Ins. Co. of Wisconsin, 217 Wis. 2d 94, 579 N.W.2d 730 (Ct. App. 1998)
4 ALR5th 148—§ 21

Schreiber, People ex rel. v. Warden of Queens House of Detention for Men, 282 A.D.2d 555, 723 N.Y.S.2d 96 (2d Dep't 2001)
7 ALR6th 487—§ 31

Schreibman v. Mason, 377 F.2d 99 (1st Cir. 1967)
32 ALR6th 531—§ 33

Schreibman v. Walter E. Heller & Co., 446 F. Supp. 141 (D.C. Puerto Rico 1978)
8 ALR5th 653—§ 10

Schreibman v. Walter E. Heller & Co. of Puerto Rico, 446 F. Supp. 141 (D.P.R. 1978)
32 ALR6th 531—§ 33

Schreidell v. Shoter, 500 So. 2d 228 (Fla. Dist. Ct. App. 3d Dist. 1986)
108 ALR5th 495—§ 2, 11

Schreier v. Schreier, 625 S.W.2d 644 (Mo. App. 1981)
17 ALR5th 366—§ 9

Schreifels v. Safeco Ins. Co., 45 Wash. App. 442, 725 P.2d 1022 (Div. 1 1986)
63 ALR5th 675—§ 3

Schreifels v. Schreifels, 47 Wash. 2d 409, 287 P.2d 1001 (1955)
95 ALR5th 533—§ 3 to 5
124 ALR5th 203—§ 3 to 5

Schreiner v. Lakeline Developers, 2003 WL 365967 (Tex. App. Austin 2003)
63 ALR6th 495—§ 73

Schreiner v. Schreiner, 217 Kan. 337, 537 P.2d 165 (1975)
26 ALR6th 331—§ 9

Schremp v. Haugh's Products, 1997 WL 760900 (Ohio Ct. App. 9th Dist.Lorain County 1997)
65 ALR5th 105—§ 7, 8, 18, 19

Schrempf v. State, 66 N.Y.2d 289, 496 N.Y.S.2d 973, 487 N.E.2d 883 (1985)
80 ALR6th 469—§ 61

Schrempp and Salerno v. Gross, 247 Neb. 685, 529 N.W.2d 764 (1995)
11 ALR6th 587—§ 19

Schrewe v. Sanders, 498 S.W.2d 775 (Mo. 1973)
19 ALR6th 217—§ 9

Schreyer v. State, 2005 WL 1793193 (Tex. App. Dallas 2005)
81 ALR6th 505—§ 54

Schriber v. Alameda County-East Bay Title Ins. Co., 156 Cal. App. 2d 700, 320 P.2d 82 (1st Dist. 1958)
36 ALR6th 387—§ 6

Schrieber v. Walker, 79 F. Supp. 2d 965 (N.D. Ind. 1999)
17 ALR6th 453—§ 13

Schrier v. Beltway Alarm Co., 73 Md. App. 281, 533 A.2d 1316 (1987)
36 ALR6th 305—§ 9, 21

Schrier v. Moore, 7 F.3d 1042 (8th Cir. 1993)
56 ALR6th 553—§ 27

Schrillo Co. v. Hartford Accident & Indemnity Co., 181 Cal. App. 3d 766, 226 Cal. Rptr. 717 (2d Dist. 1986)
14 ALR5th 695—§ 7, 22, 24

Schrimpf, In re Marriage of, 293 Ill. App. 3d 246, 227 Ill. Dec. 248, 687 N.E.2d 171 (5th Dist. 1997)
11 ALR6th 125—§ 4, 6, 7, 12, 26

Schrimsher v. Com., 190 S.W.3d 318, 27 A.L.R.6th 617 (Ky. 2006)
27 ALR6th 183—§ 15

Schriner v. Meginnis Ford Co., 228 Neb. 85, 421 N.W.2d 755, 3 I.E.R. Cas. (BNA) 129 (1988)
67 ALR6th 209—§ 10

Schriner v. Pennsylvania Power & Light Co., 348 Pa. Super. 177, 501 A.2d 1128, Prod. Liab. Rep. (CCH) ¶ 10811 (1985)
91 ALR5th 517—§ 8

Schriro v. Landrigan, 127 S. Ct. 1933, 167 L. Ed. 2d 836 (U.S. 2007)
26 ALR6th 659—§ 33

Schriro v. Smith, 126 S. Ct. 7, 163 L. Ed. 2d 6 (U.S. 2005)
16 ALR6th 767—§ 21

Schriro v. Summerlin, 542 U.S. 348, 124 S. Ct. 2519, 159 L. Ed. 2d 442 (2004)
102 ALR6th 637—§ 2, 6, 11

Schrock v. Federal Nat. Mortg. Ass'n, 2011 WL 3348227 (D. Ariz. 2011)
86 ALR6th 411—§ 5

Schrock v. Schrock, 89 N.C. App. 308, 365 S.E.2d 657 (1988)
20 ALR5th 700—§ 49
40 ALR5th 227—§ 13

Schrock v. Wyeth, Inc., 601 F. Supp. 2d 1262, Prod. Liab. Rep. (CCH) ¶ 18212 (W.D. Okla. 2009)
56 ALR6th 161—§ 3

Schroder v. Kansas State Highway Com., 199 Kan. 175, 428 P.2d 814 (1967)
1 ALR5th 163—§ 4, 16, 24, 32

Schroders, Inc. v. Hogan Systems, Inc., 137 Misc. 2d 738, 522 N.Y.S.2d 404, 4 U.C.C.R.S.2d 1397 (1987)
38 ALR5th 1—§ 9, 13

Schroeder, In re Marriage of, 215 Ill. App. 3d 156, 158 Ill. Dec. 721, 574 N.E.2d 834 (4th Dist. 1991)
49 ALR5th 441—§ 15

Schroeder v. Adkins, 149 W. Va. 400, 141 S.E.2d 352 (1965)
19 ALR5th 563—§ 11

Schroeder v. Auto Driveaway Co., 11 Cal. 3d 908, 114 Cal. Rptr. 622, 523 P.2d 662 (1974)
11 ALR5th 88—§ 3, 5
14 ALR5th 242—§ 4, 22, 40

Schroeder v. Board of Supervisors of Louisiana State University, 653 So. 2d 612, 99 Ed. Law Rep. 1158 (La. Ct. App. 1st Cir. 1995)
85 ALR5th 301—§ 13

Schroeder v. Brennan, 345 Ill. App. 87, 102 N.E.2d 164 (1951)
46 ALR5th 1—§ 47

Schroeder v. City of Baraboo, 93 Wis. 95, 67 N.W. 27 (1896)
54 ALR6th 201—§ 11, 25

Schroeder v. Colbert County, 66 Ala. 137 (1880)

45 ALR5th 109—§ 6

Schroeder v. Com., Dept. of Transp., 551 Pa. 243, 710 A.2d 23, Prod. Liab. Rep. (CCH) ¶ 15225 (1998)

102 ALR5th 99—§ 4

Schroeder v. Danielson, 37 Mass. App. 450, 640 N.E.2d 495 (1994)

37 ALR5th 237—§ 3, 6, 13

Schroeder v. Department of Motor Vehicles & Pub. Safety, 105 Nev. 179, 772 P.2d 1278 (1989)

28 ALR5th 459—§ 3

Schroeder v. District of Columbia Dept. of Employment Services, 479 A.2d 1281 (D.C. 1984)

26 ALR6th 111—§ 4

Schroeder v. Hudgins, 142 Ariz. 395, 690 P.2d 114 (Ct. App. Div. 1 1984)

64 ALR6th 473—§ 21

Schroeder v. Industrial Comm'n, 132 Ariz. 455, 646 P.2d 886 (App. 1982)

61 ALR5th 375—§ 5, 12

Schroeder v. Kreuter, 308 N.Y. 993, 127 N.E.2d 845 (1955)

63 ALR5th 607—§ 9

Schroeder v. Lester E. Cox Medical Center, Inc., 833 S.W.2d 411 (Mo. Ct. App. S.D. 1992)

109 ALR5th 397—§ 3, 8

Schroeder v. Memorial Medical Center, 1997 -NMSC- 046, 123 N.M. 719, 945 P.2d 449 (1997)

16 ALR5th 262—§ 15

Schroeder v. Northwest Community Hosp., 371 Ill. App. 3d 584, 308 Ill. Dec. 808, 862 N.E.2d 1011 (1st Dist. 2006)

64 ALR6th 249—§ 5

Schroeder v. Phillips Petroleum Co., 17 F.3d 1147, 17 Employee Benefits Cas. (BNA) 2519 (8th Cir. 1994)

85 ALR6th 323—§ 81

Schroeder v. Schroeder, 658 N.W.2d 909 (Minn. Ct. App. 2003)

100 ALR5th 1—§ 3.7

18 ALR6th 97—§ 34

Schroeder v. Smith, 21 A.D.3d 511, 800 N.Y.S.2d 224 (2d Dep't 2005)

14 ALR6th 543—§ 29

Schroeder v. State Farm Fire and Cas. Co., 770 F. Supp. 558 (D. Nev. 1991)

37 ALR6th 657—§ 4, 10

Schroeder v. State Farm Fire & Casualty Co., 770 F. Supp. 558 (D.C. Nev 1991)

30 ALR5th 170—§ 4, 83

Schroeder v. Syracuse Transit Corp., 9 App. Div. 2d 1012, 194 N.Y.S.2d 244 (4th Dep't 1959)

5 ALR5th 875—§ 48

Schroeder v. Taylor, 70 Wash. 2d 1, 422 P.2d 21 (1966)

9 ALR5th 826—§ 18

Schroeder v. Terra Energy, Ltd., 223 Mich. App. 176, 565 N.W.2d 887, 138 O.G.R. 361 (1997)

99 ALR5th 415—§ 3

Schroeder ex rel. Schroeder v. Maumee Bd. of Educ., 296 F. Supp. 2d 869, 184 Ed. Law Rep. 785 (N.D. Ohio 2003)

98 ALR6th 599—§ 4, 6, 22, 28, 94

Schroepfer v. Hudson, 214 Minn. 17, 7 N.W.2d 336 (1942)

40 ALR6th 99—§ 70

Schroeppel, Oswego County v. Spector, 43 Misc. 2d 290, 251 N.Y.S.2d 233 (1963)

8 ALR5th 391—§ 3, 7

Schroer, Estate of v. Stamco Supply, Inc., 19 Ohio App. 3d 34, 482 N.E.2d 975 (1st Dist. Hamilton County 1984)

111 ALR5th 207—§ 7, 11

Schroeter v. Lowers, 260 Cal. App. 2d 695, 67 Cal. Rptr. 270 (2d Dist. 1968)

97 ALR6th 375—§ 19

Schroetke v. Jackson-Church Co., 193 Mich. 616, 160 N.W. 383 (1916)

107 ALR5th 441—§ 13

20 ALR6th 641—§ 22

Schroth v. Schroth, 449 So. 2d 640 (La. App. 4th Cir. 1984)

5 ALR5th 550—§ 13

Schroyer v. McNeal, 323 Md. 275, 592 A.2d 1119 (1991)

74 ALR5th 49—§ 78

Schroyer v. Moore, 2007 WL 2492312 (S.D. Ohio 2007)

51 ALR6th 139—§ 3

Schrull v. Philadelphia Suburban Gas & Electric Co., 279 Pa. 473, 124 A. 141 (1924)

95 ALR5th 29—§ 3

Schrumpf v. Georgia International Life Ins. Co., 413 So. 2d 267 (La. App. 3d Cir. 1982)

43 ALR5th 657—§ 14

Schrupp v. Hanson, 306 Minn. 151, 235 N.W.2d 822 (1975)

93 ALR5th 621—§ 6, 8

Schryver v. Eriksen, 255 Ill. App. 3d 418, 194 Ill. Dec. 175, 627 N.E.2d 291 (1st Dist. 1993)

95 ALR6th 85—§ 56

Schubach v. Silver, 461 Pa. 366, 336 A.2d 328 (1975)

73 ALR5th 223—§ 6, 9

Schubach v. Zoning Bd. of Adjustment (Philadelphia), 440 Pa. 249, 270 A.2d 397 (1970)

73 ALR5th 223—§ 10

Schubbe v. Diesel Service Unit Co., 71 Or. App. 232, 692 P.2d 132, 119 L.R.R.M. (BNA) 2008 (1984)

86 ALR5th 397—§ 9

Schubert v. City of Springfield, 589 F.3d 496 (1st Cir. 2009)

64 ALR6th 131—§ 3, 22

Schubert v. City of Springfield, 602 F. Supp. 2d 254 (D. Mass. 2009)

64 ALR6th 131—§ 22, 35

Schubert v. DeBard, 398 N.E.2d 1339 (Ind. Ct. App. 1980)

91 ALR6th 435—§ 134

Schubert v. J. R. Clark Co., 49 Minn. 331, 51 N.W. 1103 (1892)

81 ALR5th 245—§ 3

Schubert v. Pleasant Glade Assembly of God, 129 S. Ct. 1003, 173 L. Ed. 2d 293 (2009)

46 ALR6th 495—§ 43

Schubert v. Tolivar, 905 S.W.2d 924 (Mo. Ct. App. E.D. 1995)

40 ALR5th 697—§ 17

87 ALR5th 361—§ 21

118 ALR5th 385—§ 7, 14

Schubiner v. West Bloomfield Township, 133 Mich. App. 490, 351 N.W.2d 214 (1984)

38 ALR5th 737—§ 3, 10

Schubring v. Schubring, 190 Mich. App. 468, 476 N.W.2d 434 (1991)

21 ALR6th 577—§ 11

Schuchart & Associates, Professional Engineers, Inc. v. Solo Serve Corp., 540 F. Supp. 928, 217 U.S.P.Q. 1227 (W.D. Tex. 1982)

76 ALR6th 289—§ 2, 4, 5

77 ALR6th 543—§ 2, 7, 12

Schuchmann v. Schuchmann, 768 So. 2d 614 (La. Ct. App. 3d Cir. 2000)

21 ALR6th 577—§ 3, 5

26 ALR6th 331—§ 3

Schuck v. John Morrell & Co., 529 N.W.2d 894 (S.D. 1995)

14 ALR5th 1—§ 10

Schuck v. Myers, 233 Cal. App. 2d 151, 43 Cal. Rptr. 215 (2d Dist. 1965)

32 ALR5th 673—§ 3

Schueck Steel, Inc. v. McCarthy Bros. Co., 289 Ark. 436, 717 S.W.2d 816 (1986)

102 ALR5th 647—§ 15

Schueler v. Madison, 49 Wis. 2d 695, 183 N.W.2d 116 (1971)

5 ALR5th 422—§ 6

Schueler v. Schueler, 460 So. 2d 1120 (La. Ct. App. 2d Cir. 1984)

59 ALR6th 433—§ 48, 66

Schuelke v. Quinn, 2009 WL 3321496 (Cal. App. 4th Dist. 2009)

58 ALR6th 1—§ 5

Schueller v. San Antonio & A.P. Ry. Co., 46 Tex. Civ. App. 444, 102 S.W. 922 (1907)

103 ALR5th 157—§ 4

Schuessler v. Benchmark Marketing and Consulting, Inc., 243 Neb. 425, 500 N.W.2d 529, 8 I.E.R. Cas. (BNA) 871, 127 Lab. Cas. (CCH) P 57658, 34 A.L.R.5th 907 (1993)

37 ALR6th 511—§ 3, 7, 8, 34, 50

Schuessler v. Benchmark Mktg. & Consulting, 243 Neb. 425, 500 N.W.2d 529 (1993)

34 ALR5th 699—§ 2, 3

Schuette v. Coalition to Defend Affirmative Action, Integration and Immigrant Rights and Fight for Equality By Any Means Necessary (BAMN), 134 S. Ct. 1623, 188 L. Ed. 2d 613, 303 Ed. Law Rep. 30, 97 Empl. Prac. Dec. (CCH) ¶ 45054 (2014)

96 ALR6th 577—§ 14

Schuette v. Department of Revenue, 326 Or. 213, 951 P.2d 690 (1997)

118 ALR5th 597—§ 23

Schuetzle v. Lineberger, 137 Wash. App. 1022, 2007 WL 575448 (Div. 1 2007)

70 ALR6th 209—§ 20, 29, 57

Schuetzle, State ex rel. v. Vogel, 537 N.W.2d 358, 66 A.L.R.5th 717 (N.D. 1995)

66 ALR5th 111—§ 4

Schuffenhauer v. Department of Employment Security, 86 Wash. 2d 233, 543 P.2d 343 (1975)

60 ALR5th 459—§ 2, 23

Schuffert v. Morgan, 777 So. 2d 87 (Ala. 2000)

17 ALR6th 159—§ 19

Schuhart v. State, 647 So. 2d 1049 (Fla. Dist. Ct. App. 5th Dist. 1994)

70 ALR6th 361—§ 29

Schuhmacher v. North Dakota Hosp. Ass'n, 528 N.W.2d 374 (N.D. 1995)

51 ALR5th 1—§ 7

Schuhs, In re Marriage of, 20 Kan. App. 2d 98, 883 P.2d 1225 (1994)

48 ALR5th 473—§ 8

52 ALR5th 221—§ 20

Schuisler v. Ames, 16 Ala. 73, 1849 WL 410 (1849)

75 ALR5th 1—§ 3

Schuitmaker v. Krieger, 2003 WL 1950238 (Mich. Ct. App. 2003)

119 ALR5th 121—§ 3, 6

121 ALR5th 325—§ 3

67 ALR6th 437—§ 14, 15, 18

Schuldt v. Chuckrow, 222 App. Div. 441, 226 N.Y.S. 220 (1928)

46 ALR5th 1—§ 22

Schuler v. Beers, 157 Ill. App. 3d 97, 109 Ill. Dec. 427, 510 N.E.2d 48 (1st Dist. 1987)

52 ALR5th 491—§ 6

Schuler v. Berger, 275 F. Supp. 120 (E.D. Pa. 1967)

6 ALR5th 534—§ 9

Schuler v. Hernandez, 202 Cal. App. 3d 1302, 249 Cal. Rptr. 550 (2d Dist. 1988)

17 ALR6th 1—§ 27

Schuler v. Hughes, 52 S.W.2d 453 (Mo. App. 1932)

12 ALR5th 195—§ 41

Schuler v. State, 2008 WY 47, 181 P.3d 929 (Wyo. 2008)

68 ALR6th 527—§ 37

Schuler v. Union News Co., 295 Mass. 350, 4 N.E.2d 465 (1936)

2 ALR5th 1—§ 54

Schuler v. University of Minnesota, 788 F.2d 510, 31 Ed. Law Rep. 770 (8th Cir. 1986)

90 ALR6th 235—§ 49

Schuler Homes of Oregon Inc. v. Department of Revenue, State, 19 Or. Tax 152, 2006 WL 373551 (Magistrate Div. 2006)

80 ALR6th 325—§ 8

Schulingkamp v. Bolton Ford, Inc., 163 So. 2d 161 (La. App. 4th Cir. 1964)

17 ALR5th 547—§ 2, 11, 13, 20, 25

Schulke, In re Marriage of, 40 Colo. App. 473, 579 P.2d 90 (1978)

124 ALR5th 203—§ 3

Schuller v. Hy-Vee Food Stores, Inc., 328 N.W.2d 328 (Iowa 1982)

For assistance, call 1-800-328-4880

10 ALR5th 371—§ 3, 5, 11

40 ALR5th 135—§ 2, 15

Schuller v. Schuller, 191 Neb. 266, 214 N.W.2d 617 (1974)

26 ALR6th 331—§ 3, 22

Schullman v. State Bar of California, 59 Cal. 2d 590, 30 Cal. Rptr. 834, 381 P.2d 658 (1963)

9 ALR5th 193—§ 33

Schulman v. Chase Manhattan Bank, 268 A.D.2d 174, 710 N.Y.S.2d 368 (2d Dep't 2000)

77 ALR6th 1—§ 8, 74, 75

Schulman v. Continental Ins., 239 A.D.2d 334, 657 N.Y.S.2d 1013 (2d Dep't 1997)

83 ALR5th 1—§ 3

Schulman v. Franklin and Marshall College, 371 Pa. Super. 345, 538 A.2d 49 (1988)

47 ALR5th 1—§ 31

Schulman v. Jacobowitz, 19 A.D.3d 574, 797 N.Y.S.2d 547 (2d Dep't 2005)

23 ALR6th 697—§ 12

Schulman v. Prudential Ins. Co. of Am., 226 A.D.2d 164, 640 N.Y.S.2d 112 (N.Y.A.D. 1 Dep't 1996)

59 ALR5th 535—§ 13

69 ALR5th 411—§ 4

Schulman v. Shaker Heights, 29 Ohio Ops. 2d 373, 94 Ohio L. Abs. 19, 196 N.E.2d 102 (App. Cuyahoga Co. 1964)

41 ALR5th 47—§ 12

Schulman v. Wolske & Blue Co., L.P.A., 125 Ohio App. 3d 365, 708 N.E.2d 753 (10th Dist. Franklin County 1998)

11 ALR6th 587—§ 26

Schulmeier v. Honorable Judges of Dist. Court of Tulsa County in the Fourteenth Judicial Dist., 1996 OK 103, 925 P.2d 63 (Okla. 1996)

97 ALR5th 537—§ 56

Schuloff v. Fields, 950 F. Supp. 66, 115 Ed. Law Rep. 882 (E.D. N.Y. 1997)

73 ALR6th 281—§ 29

Schuloff v. Murphy, 1997 WL 588876 (E.D. N.Y. 1997)

70 ALR6th 513—§ 17

71 ALR6th 471—§ 13

Schulpius, In re Commitment of, 2006 WI 1, 287 Wis. 2d 44, 707 N.W.2d 495 (2006)

78 ALR6th 417—§ 79

Schulstad v. Hudson Oil Co., 55 Or. App. 323, 637 P.2d 1334 (1981)

18 ALR5th 577—§ 38, 57

Schult, In re Marriage of, 2000 WL 962819 (Iowa Ct. App. 2000)

16 ALR6th 693—§ 10

Schultea v. City of Patton Village, 2006 WL 3063457 (S.D. Tex. 2006)

32 ALR6th 457—§ 3, 9

Schultheis v. Centennial Ins. Co., 108 Misc. 2d 725, 438 N.Y.S.2d 687 (1981)

14 ALR5th 695—§ 23

Schultheis v. Wohlleb, 231 A.D. 851, 246 N.Y.S. 485 (2d Dep't 1930)

76 ALR5th 337—§ 9

Schultz, Ex parte, 64 Nev. 264, 181 P.2d 585 (1947)

15 ALR5th 1—§ 4, 8

Schultz, Re, 36 Ohio Misc. 2d 14, 521 N.E.2d 525 (1987)

15 ALR5th 391—§ 52

Schultz v. Amica Mut. Ins. Co., 778 So. 2d 402 (Fla. Dist. Ct. App. 4th Dist. 2001)

104 ALR5th 331—§ 8

Schultz v. Ary, 175 F. Supp. 2d 959, 87 Fair Empl. Prac. Cas. (BNA) 744 (W.D. Mich. 2001)

3 ALR6th 153—§ 8

Schultz v. AT & T Wireless Services, Inc., a foreign corp., 376 F. Supp. 2d 685 (N.D. W. Va. 2005)

13 ALR6th 145—§ 7

Schultz v. BAC Home Loans Servicing, LP, 2011 WL 3684481 (D. Ariz. 2011)

86 ALR6th 411—§ 5

Schultz v. Burton-Moore Ford, Inc.,
2008 WL 2355588 (E.D. Mich.
2008)
67 ALR6th 209—§ 39
Schultz v. Champion Welding & Mfg.
Co., 230 N.Y. 309, 130 N.E. 304
(1921)
28 ALR6th 1—§ 3, 14, 35, 65
Schultz v. City of Cumberland, 228 F.3d
831 (7th Cir. 2000)
121 ALR5th 427—§ 7
20 ALR6th 161—§ 3, 4
23 ALR6th 573—§ 10, 13, 14
Schultz v. City of Milwaukee, 49 Wis.
254, 5 N.W. 342 (1880)
29 ALR6th 369—§ 41
Schultz v. Crystal River Three Participants, 686 So. 2d 1391 (Fla. Dist.
Ct. App. 5th Dist. 1997)
114 ALR5th 561—§ 12
Schultz v. Culbertson, 125 Wis. 169, 103
N.W. 234 (1905)
23 ALR6th 1—§ 12
Schultz v. Dellaire, 678 A.2d 46 (Me.
1996)
47 ALR5th 129—§ 11
Schultz v. Duitz, 253 Ky. 135, 69
S.W.2d 27, 92 A.L.R. 600 (1934)
44 ALR5th 1—§ 9, 19 to 21
Schultz v. Foster-Glocester Regional
School Dist., 755 A.2d 153, 146 Ed.
Law Rep. 256 (R.I. 2000)
25 ALR5th 784—§ 3
Schultz v. Frisby, 877 F.2d 6, 113 Lab.
Cas. (CCH) ¶ 56113 (7th Cir. 1989)
113 ALR5th 1—§ 12
Schultz v. Hennessy Industries, Inc., 222
Ill. App. 3d 532, 165 Ill. Dec. 56,
584 N.E.2d 235 (1st Dist. 1991)
76 ALR6th 465—§ 17
Schultz v. Heritage Mut. Ins. Co., 902 F.
Supp. 1051 (D.S.D. 1995)
75 ALR6th 235—§ 8, 26
Schultz v. Incorporated Village of Bell-
port, 2010 WL 3924751 (E.D. N.Y.
2010)
95 ALR6th 341—§ 35

Schultz v. Industrial Coils, Inc., 125
Wis. 2d 520, 373 N.W.2d 74, 103
Lab. Cas. (CCH) ¶ 55521 (Ct. App.
1985)
104 ALR5th 1—§ 3, 4, 13
Schultz v. Ingram, 38 N.C. App. 422,
248 S.E.2d 345 (1978)
50 ALR5th 653—§ 7
Schultz v. Mills Mut. Ins. Group, 474
N.W.2d 522 (S.D. 1991)
13 ALR5th 289—§ 18
Schultz v. Moerschel Products Co., 142
S.W.2d 106 (Mo. Ct. App. 1940)
80 ALR5th 417—§ 3
Schultz v. Mutch, 165 Cal. App. 3d 66,
211 Cal. Rptr. 445 (2d Dist. 1985)
2 ALR5th 811—§ 28
3 ALR5th 146—§ 18, 19, 24
4 ALR5th 210—§ 17
Schultz v. North American Ins. Group,
34 F. Supp. 2d 866 (W.D. N.Y.
1999)
36 ALR6th 203—§ 12
Schultz v. Piro, 40 Pa. Cmwlth. 395, 397
A.2d 484, 33 BNA FEP Cas. 892,
19 CCH EPD ¶ 9081 (1979)
51 ALR5th 1—§ 8
Schultz v. Reader's Digest Asso., 468 F.
Supp. 551, 4 Media L. R. 2356 (E.D.
Mich. 1979)
19 ALR5th 1—§ 101, 135
Schultz v. Richie, 148 Ill. App. 3d 903,
102 Ill. Dec. 289, 499 N.E.2d 1069
(4th Dist. 1986)
15 ALR5th 119—§ 3, 5, 32, 38
Schultz v. Roman Catholic Archdiocese,
95 N.J. 530, 472 A.2d 531 (1984)
5 ALR5th 530—§ 7
8 ALR5th 1—§ 4, 48
17 ALR5th 179—§ 5
Schultz v. Roman Catholic Archdiocese
of Newark, 95 N.J. 530, 472 A.2d
531 (1984)
101 ALR5th 1—§ 5
100 ALR6th 563—§ 54

Schultz v. Rural/Metro Corp. of New Mexico-Texas, 956 S.W.2d 757 (Tex. App. Houston 14th Dist. 1997)
12 ALR5th 1—§ 5

Schultz v. Schultz, 58 A.D.3d 616, 871 N.Y.S.2d 636 (2d Dep't 2009)
77 ALR6th 293—§ 22, 27, 28, 58

Schultz v. Schultz, 66 Wash. 2d 713, 404 P.2d 987 (1965)
53 ALR5th 375—§ 2, 15

Schultz v. Schultz, 133 Wis. 125, 113 N.W. 445 (1907)
52 ALR5th 221—§ 13

Schultz v. Schultz, 199 A.D.2d 1065, 606 N.Y.S.2d 480 (4th Dep't 1993)
70 ALR5th 377—§ 6

Schultz v. Schultz, 591 N.W.2d 212 (Iowa 1999)
99 ALR5th 637—§ 2, 3

Schultz v. Seiler Motor Car Co., 243 Ky. 459, 48 S.W.2d 1068 (1932)
109 ALR5th 421—§ 3

Schultz v. State, 82 Wis. 2d 737, 264 N.W.2d 245 (1978)
9 ALR6th 1—§ 6

Schultz v. State, 106 Md. App. 145, 664 A.2d 60 (1995)
90 ALR5th 453—§ 34

Schultz v. State, 894 N.E.2d 1110 (Ind. Ct. App. 2008)
69 ALR6th 579—§ 4

Schultz v. State Farm Ins. Co., 508 So. 2d 854 (La. Ct. App. 5th Cir. 1987)
66 ALR6th 185—§ 10

Schultz v. Subaru of America, Inc., 407 Mass. 1004, 553 N.E.2d 893 (1990)
60 ALR5th 669—§ 5

Schultz v. Sundberg, 759 F.2d 714 (9th Cir. 1985)
24 ALR6th 255—§ 5, 11, 13

Schultz v. Tampa Elec. Co., 704 So. 2d 605, 13 I.E.R. Cas. (BNA) 1439 (Fla. Dist. Ct. App. 2d Dist. 1997)
10 ALR6th 531—§ 7
13 ALR6th 499—§ 5

Schultz v. Tasche, 166 Wis. 561, 165 N.W. 292 (1917)
108 ALR5th 385—§ 3, 11

Schultz v. Thomas, 649 F. Supp. 620 (E.D. Wis 1986)
12 ALR5th 195—§ 39

Schultz v. Ti Ri Go Camp, 263 A.D. 850, 31 N.Y.S.2d 683 (2d Dep't 1941)
21 ALR6th 81—§ 4

Schultz v. U.S., 129 S. Ct. 742, 172 L. Ed. 2d 730 (2008)
46 ALR6th 495—§ 7

Schultz v. U.S., 203 F. Supp. 941 (E.D. N.Y. 1962)
123 ALR5th 1—§ 3

Schultz v. U.S., 529 F.3d 343, 50 Bankr. Ct. Dec. (CRR) 26, 59 Collier Bankr. Cas. 2d (MB) 1405, Bankr. L. Rep. (CCH) ¶ 81255 (6th Cir. 2008)
46 ALR6th 495—§ 7

Schultz v. Webster Groves Presbyterian Church, Asso., 726 S.W.2d 491 (Mo. App. 1987)
8 ALR5th 1—§ 4, 32, 48

Schultz by Schultz v. Eslick, 788 F.2d 558 (9th Cir. 1986)
62 ALR5th 475—§ 5, 14

Schultz Constr., Inc. v. Ross, 76 App. Div. 2d 151, 431 N.Y.S.2d 144, 92 CCH LC ¶ 55301 (3d Dep't 1980)
7 ALR5th 400—§ 7

Schultze v. Schultze, 66 S.W. 56 (Tex. Civ. App. 1901)
14 ALR5th 557—§ 24, 26, 29

Schultz' Estate, In re, 220 Or. 350, 348 P.2d 22, 81 A.L.R.2d 1121 (1959)
122 ALR5th 205—§ 2, 3, 10

Schulz v. Dreiling, 526 P.2d 1341 (Colo. App. 1974)
14 ALR5th 242—§ 29

Schulz v. Milam, 410 N.W.2d 845 (Minn. Ct. App. 1987)
86 ALR6th 321—§ 10
89 ALR6th 409—§ 50

Schulz v. Nienhuis, 152 Wis. 2d 434, 448 N.W.2d 655 (1989)
43 ALR5th 545—§ 14

Schulz v. Rockwell Mfg. Co., 108 Ill. App. 3d 113, 63 Ill. Dec. 867, 438 N.E.2d 1230 (2d Dist. 1982)
4 ALR6th 401—§ 4

Schulz v. Warren County Bd. of Sup'rs, 179 A.D.2d 118, 581 N.Y.S.2d 885 (3d Dep't 1992)
65 ALR5th 1—§ 2, 27

Schulz v. Ystad, 155 Wis. 2d 574, 456 N.W.2d 312 (1990)
11 ALR5th 259—§ 6, 8 to 10, 33, 35
112 ALR5th 185—§ 4, 5, 8
1 ALR6th 493—§ 4, 5, 15, 18
2 ALR6th 439—§ 8, 11, 21
3 ALR6th 641—§ 7, 20

Schulze, In re Marriage of, 60 Cal. App. 4th 519, 70 Cal. Rptr. 2d 488 (4th Dist. 1997)
17 ALR5th 366—§ 10

Schulze v. DeKalb County, 230 Ga. App. 305, 496 S.E.2d 273 (1998)
16 ALR5th 605—§ 11

Schulze v. Illinois State Police, 736 F. Supp. 193, 52 BNA FEP Cas. 1402, 54 CCH EPD ¶ 40073 (N.D. Ill. 1990)
51 ALR5th 1—§ 7

Schulze v. Jensen, 191 Neb. 253, 214 N.W.2d 591 (1974)
34 ALR5th 447—§ 3

Schulze v. Rapoport, 1994 WL 714331 (Minn. Ct. App. 1994)
11 ALR6th 1—§ 6

Schulze By and Through Schulze v. Haile, 840 S.W.2d 263 (Mo. Ct. App. W.D. 1992)
87 ALR5th 361—§ 8
72 ALR6th 413—§ 6

Schulz' Welfare, In re, 17 Wash. App. 134, 561 P.2d 1122 (Div. 1 1977)
92 ALR5th 379—§ 13

Schum v. Lawrenceburg Nat. Bank, 314 Ky. 297, 234 S.W.2d 962 (1950)
6 ALR6th 391—§ 5

Schumaat v. Mellies, 231 Mich. 277, 203 N.W. 990 (1925)
62 ALR5th 219—§ 18

Schumacher, In re Adoption of, 120 Ill. App. 3d 50, 75 Ill. Dec. 926, 458 N.E.2d 94 (2d Dist. 1983)
71 ALR5th 99—§ 3, 7

Schumacher v. Carl G. Neumann Dredging & Improvement Co., 206 Wis. 220, 239 N.W. 459 (1931)
70 ALR5th 261—§ 47

Schumacher v. City and Borough of Yakutat, 946 P.2d 1255 (Alaska 1997)
29 ALR6th 369—§ 29, 31

Schumacher v. City of New York, 166 N.Y. 103, 59 N.E. 773 (1901)
54 ALR6th 201—§ 13, 16, 35

Schumacher v. Cooper, 850 F. Supp. 438, 1994 AMC 2554 (D.C. S.C. 1994)
48 ALR5th 129—§ 6, 19

Schumacher v. Department of Professional Regulation, Div. of Real Estate, 611 So. 2d 75, 18 FLW D 138 (Fla. App. D4 1992)
7 ALR5th 474—§ 160

Schumacher v. Halverson, 467 F. Supp. 2d 939 (D. Minn. 2006)
45 ALR6th 1—§ 9
52 ALR6th 623—§ 7
62 ALR6th 413—§ 5, 29, 37

Schumacher v. Nix, 965 F.2d 1262 (3d Cir. 1992)
5 ALR6th 449—§ 5

Schumacher v. North British & Mercantile Ins. Co., 2 F.2d 509 (CA9 Wash. 1924)
37 ALR5th 41—§ 5

Schumacher v. Richards Shear Co., Inc., 59 N.Y.2d 239, 464 N.Y.S.2d 437, 451 N.E.2d 195 (1983)
13 ALR6th 355—§ 4, 30
18 ALR6th 629—§ 10, 16

Schumacher v. Schumacher, 67 S.D. 46, 288 N.W. 796 (1939)
40 ALR6th 99—§ 16
48 ALR6th 387—§ 4, 24

Schumacher v. Schumacher, 131 Wis. 2d 332, 388 N.W.2d 912 (1986)
3 ALR5th 394—§ 6, 8, 15

For assistance, call 1-800-328-4880

Schumacher v. Schumacher, 469 N.W.2d 793 (N.D. 1991)
10 ALR6th 293—§ 4, 8, 13
39 ALR6th 1—§ 10
Schumacher v. Schumacher, 1999 N.D. 149, 598 N.W.2d 131 (N.D. 1999)
51 ALR5th 241—§ 6
Schumacker v. Zoll, 2001 WL 1198641 (Ohio Ct. App. 6th Dist. Lucas County 2001)
32 ALR6th 285—§ 47
Schumaker v. Ivers, 238 N.W.2d 284, 18 U.C.C.R.S. 923 (S.D. 1976)
38 ALR5th 191—§ 3, 64
Schuman v. Bestrom, 214 Mont. 410, 693 P.2d 536 (1985)
58 ALR5th 669—§ 16
Schuman v. State, 106 Ark. 362, 153 S.W. 611 (1913)
54 ALR6th 429—§ 18
Schuman v. Vitale, 144 Pa. Commw. 560, 602 A.2d 390 (1992)
17 ALR6th 1—§ 9
Schumann v. Crofoot, 43 Or. App. 53, 602 P.2d 298 (1979)
9 ALR6th 285—§ 4, 14
Schumann v. Curry, 121 N.J. Eq. 439, 190 A. 628 (1937)
18 ALR5th 230—§ 3, 7
Schumann v. Schumann, 2005-Ohio-91, 2005 WL 77087 (Ohio Ct. App. 8th Dist. Cuyahoga County 2005)
77 ALR6th 293—§ 50, 54, 56, 58
Schumann v. State, 160 Misc. 2d 802, 610 N.Y.S.2d 987 (Ct. Cl. 1994)
106 ALR5th 1—§ 25
Schumer v. Holtzman, 60 N.Y.2d 46, 467 N.Y.S.2d 182, 454 N.E.2d 522 (1983)
42 ALR5th 581—§ 4
Schumm v. Board of Sup'rs of San Joaquin County, 140 Cal. App. 2d 874, 295 P.2d 934 (3d Dist. 1956)
63 ALR5th 607—§ 5
Schumm v. Schumm, 510 N.W.2d 13 (Minn. App. 1993)
53 ALR5th 375—§ 7

Schummer v. State, 657 So. 2d 3, 20 FLW D 701 (Fla. App. D1 1995)
29 ALR5th 59—§ 3
Schumpert v. Harvard Pilgrim Health Care of New England, Inc., 2000 WL 1273996 (R.I. Super. Ct. 2000)
107 ALR5th 311—§ 11
Schundler v. Paulsen, 340 N.J. Super. 319, 774 A.2d 585 (App. Div. 2001)
121 ALR5th 1—§ 59
63 ALR6th 1—§ 56
Schunk, Appeal of, 231 Minn. 219, 43 N.W.2d 104 (1950)
87 ALR6th 319—§ 4
Schunk v. U.S., 783 F. Supp. 72 (E.D. N.Y. 1992)
44 ALR6th 391—§ 5
Schupbach v. Continental Oil Co., 193 Kan. 401, 394 P.2d 1 (1964)
99 ALR5th 415—§ 4
Schuppe, In re, 1 A.D.2d 912, 149 N.Y.S.2d 535 (3d Dep't 1956)
19 ALR6th 217—§ 55
Schur v. Florida Birth-Related Neurological, 832 So. 2d 188 (Fla. Dist. Ct. App. 1st Dist. 2002)
111 ALR5th 459—§ 9
Schur v. Storage Technology Corp., 878 P.2d 51 (Colo. App. 1994)
17 ALR5th 1—§ 3
Schura v. Marymount Hosp., 2010-Ohio-5246, 2010 WL 4307691 (Ohio Ct. App. 8th Dist. Cuyahoga County 2010)
95 ALR6th 85—§ 20
Schure v. Commonwealth, Unemployment Compensation Bd. of Review, 68 Pa. Cmwlth. 490, 449 A.2d 825 (1982)
23 ALR5th 176—§ 5
Schuricht v. Hammen, 221 Mo. App. 389, 277 S.W. 944 (1925)
62 ALR5th 219—§ 25
Schuringa v. City of Chicago, 30 Ill. 2d 504, 198 N.E.2d 326 (1964)
78 ALR6th 229—§ 2, 4, 5, 9, 11
Schurk v. Christensen, 80 Wash. 2d 652, 497 P.2d 937 (1972)

49 ALR5th 685—§ 6

Schurmann v. Neau, 240 Wis. 2d 719

60 ALR5th 165—§ 3

Schurr v. Port Authority of New York
and New Jersey, 307 A.D.2d 837,
763 N.Y.S.2d 304 (1st Dep't 2003)

63 ALR6th 495—§ 15, 61, 62, 65

Schurtz v. Wescott, 286 Mich. 691, 282
N.W. 870 (1938)

90 ALR5th 619—§ 14, 23

Schusler v. Clark, 50 Pa. Super. 459
(1912)

11 ALR5th 88—§ 3

Schusse v. Pace Suburban Bus Div.,
Regional Transp. Authority, 2002
WL 1832230 (Ill. App. Ct. 1st Dist.
2002)

102 ALR5th 99—§ 7

Schussel v. Ladd Hairdressers, Inc., 736
So. 2d 776 (Fla. Dist. Ct. App. 4th
Dist. 1999)

112 ALR5th 47—§ 3

Schussler v. Schussler, 109 App. Div. 2d
875, 487 N.Y.S.2d 67 (2d Dep't
1985)

10 ALR5th 191—§ 6

Schuster, In re, 132 B.R. 604, 22 Bankr.
Ct. Dec. (CRR) 236, 25 Collier
Bankr. Cas. 2d (MB) 1611 (Bankr.
D. Minn. 1991)

2 ALR6th 195—§ 3, 4, 12

Schuster v. Altenberg, 144 Wis. 2d 223,
424 N.W.2d 159 (1988)

47 ALR5th 433—§ 8, 18
80 ALR6th 469—§ 7, 19, 28, 41

Schuster v. City of New York, 5 N.Y.2d
75, 180 N.Y.S.2d 265, 154 N.E.2d
534 (1958)

90 ALR5th 273—§ 4, 11

Schuster v. Douglas, 156 Neb. 484, 56
N.W.2d 618 (1953)

3 ALR5th 237—§ 16

Schuster v. Dragone Classic Motor Cars,
Inc., 98 F. Supp. 2d 441 (S.D. N.Y.
2000)

78 ALR6th 97—§ 8, 37

Schuster v. Municipal Court, 109 Cal.
App. 3d 887, 167 Cal. Rptr. 447 (4th
Dist. 1980)

51 ALR6th 359—§ 3, 28
53 ALR6th 491—§ 3

Schuster v. Puckett, 221 F.3d 1339 (7th
Cir. 2000)

119 ALR5th 1—§ 3

Schuster v. Schuster, 90 Wash. 2d 626,
585 P.2d 130 (1978)

65 ALR5th 591—§ 3

Schuster v. Schuster, 109 Wis. 2d 693,
326 N.W.2d 783 (Ct. App. 1982)

9 ALR5th 568—§ 19

Schusterman, Matter of, 108 B.R. 893,
22 Collier Bankr. Cas. 2d (MB) 418
(Bankr. D. Conn. 1989)

48 ALR6th 243—§ 24

Schuster's, Inc. v. Whitehead, 291 Ark.
180, 722 S.W.2d 862 (1987)

48 ALR5th 129—§ 20
50 ALR5th 1—§ 12

Schustrin v. Globe Indem. Co. of N. Y.,
44 N.J. Super. 462, 130 A.2d 897
(App. Div. 1957)

60 ALR5th 165—§ 3, 4, 8, 18
8 ALR6th 549—§ 10, 22

Schutkowski v. Carey, 725 P.2d 1057
(Wyo. 1986)

54 ALR5th 513—§ 3
92 ALR5th 473—§ 3, 15

Schutte v. Celotex Corp., 196 Mich.
App. 135, 492 N.W.2d 773, CCH
Prod. Liab. Rep. ¶ 13469 (1992)

38 ALR5th 683—§ 5

Schutter v. Williams, 1 West. L.J. 319, 1
Ohio Dec. Rep. 47, 1844 WL 2736
(Ohio Super. Ct. 1844)

97 ALR6th 567—§ 3, 5, 11

Schutterle v. Schutterle, 260 N.W.2d
341 (S.D. 1977)

3 ALR5th 394—§ 6, 8, 15
71 ALR6th 249—§ 4

Schuttler v. Ruark, 225 Ill. App. 3d 678,
167 Ill. Dec. 837, 588 N.E.2d 478
(2d Dist. 1992)

36 ALR5th 395—§ 3

Schutz v. Morris, 201 S.W.2d 144 (Tex. Civ. App. 1947)
14 ALR5th 242—§ 26

Schutz v. State, 275 Ind. 9, 413 N.E.2d 913 (1981)
24 ALR6th 1—§ 21

Schutz v. Thorne, 415 F.3d 1128, 35 Envtl. L. Rep. 20146 (10th Cir. 2005)
31 ALR6th 523—§ 5, 12

Schutze v. Springmeyer, 16 F. Supp. 2d 767 (S.D. Tex. 1998)
10 ALR5th 828—§ 10

Schutze v. Springmeyer, 989 F. Supp. 833 (S.D. Tex. 1998)
78 ALR6th 151—§ 22

Schuyler v. Ashcraft, 293 N.J. Super. 261, 680 A.2d 765 (App. Div. 1996)
40 ALR5th 227—§ 45, 47
67 ALR5th 1—§ 8
18 ALR6th 97—§ 34

Schuylkill Products, Inc. v. H. Rupert & Sons, Inc., 305 Pa. Super. 36, 451 A.2d 229 (1982)
87 ALR6th 319—§ 27

Schvaneveldt v. Idaho State Horse Racing Comm'n, 99 Idaho 131, 578 P.2d 673 (1978)
59 ALR5th 203—§ 48

Schwab v. Ariyoshi, 57 Haw. 348, 555 P.2d 1329 (1976)
27 ALR6th 403—§ 4, 5

Schwab v. Kelton, 405 So. 2d 1239 (La. App. 1st Cir. 1981)
25 ALR5th 123—§ 27

Schwab v. Matley, 164 Ariz. 421, 793 P.2d 1088 (1990)
62 ALR6th 313—§ 17

Schwab v. Zoning Bd. of Appeals, 154 Conn. 479, 226 A.2d 506 (1967)
38 ALR5th 357—§ 8

Schwabacher v. Herring, 35 Ala. App. 496, 48 So. 2d 574 (1950)
14 ALR5th 242—§ 23

Schwabe v. Porter, 174 Wis. 2d 600, 501 N.W.2d 470 (App. 1993)
22 ALR5th 464—§ 2

Schwabl v. St. Augustine's Church, of Rochester, 288 N.Y. 554, 42 N.E.2d 16 (1942)
8 ALR5th 1—§ 4, 36, 43

Schwab's Adoption, In re, 355 Pa. 534, 50 A.2d 504 (1947)
82 ALR5th 443—§ 3

Schwab, State ex rel. v. Riley, 417 S.W.2d 1 (Mo. 1967)
44 ALR6th 259—§ 12

Schwaiger v. Schwaiger, 392 So. 2d 1213 (Ala. App. 1981)
17 ALR5th 366—§ 15

Schwalb, In re, 347 B.R. 726, 60 U.C.C. Rep. Serv. 2d 755 (Bankr. D. Nev. 2006)
53 ALR6th 159—§ 28

Schwalben v. De Buono, 696 N.Y.S.2d 262 (App. Div. 3d Dep't 1999)
7 ALR5th 1—§ 22

Schwalm v. Beardsley, 106 Va. 407, 56 S.E. 135 (1907)
61 ALR5th 739—§ 3, 5

Schwamb v. Delta Air Lines, Inc., 516 So. 2d 452 (La. App. 1st Cir. 1987)
32 ALR5th 1—§ 2, 4
48 ALR5th 129—§ 20
50 ALR5th 1—§ 11
51 ALR5th 467—§ 7

Schwan v. CNH America LLC, 2006 WL 1215395 (D. Neb. 2006)
57 ALR6th 383—§ 11

Schwan v. CNH America LLC, 2007 WL 1345193 (D. Neb. 2007)
57 ALR6th 383—§ 8

Schwan v. Riverside Methodist Hosp., 6 Ohio St. 3d 300, 452 N.E.2d 1337 (1983)
71 ALR5th 307—§ 4
5 ALR6th 133—§ 12
76 ALR6th 31—§ 41

Schwanbeck v. Federal-Mogul Corp., 31 Mass. App. Ct. 390, 578 N.E.2d 789 (1991)
71 ALR5th 491—§ 25, 27

Schwander, In re Marriage of, 79 Cal. App. 3d 1013, 145 Cal. Rptr. 325 (2d Dist. 1978)

40 ALR5th 227—§ 1, 2

80 ALR5th 117—§ 35

Schwanebeck v. Calzado, 524 So. 2d 478, 13 FLW 1069 (Fla. App. D3 1988)

56 ALR5th 1—§ 3, 8

Schwan's Consumer Brands North America, Inc. v. Home Run Inn, Inc., 2005 WL 3434376 (D. Minn. 2005)

36 ALR6th 537—§ 45

Schwarcz v. Schwarcz, 378 Pa. Super. 170, 548 A.2d 556 (1988)

95 ALR5th 533—§ 5

124 ALR5th 203—§ 5, 7

Schware v. Board of Bar Exam. of State of N.M., 353 U.S. 232, 77 S. Ct. 752, 1 L. Ed. 2d 796, 64 A.L.R.2d 288 (1957)

3 ALR6th 49—§ 11, 13, 18

8 ALR6th 1—§ 23, 30

Schwarting, In re, 671 F.2d 1192 (8th Cir. 1982)

73 ALR6th 425—§ 11, 51

Schwartz, In re, 11 A.D.3d 168, 782 N.Y.S.2d 869 (2d Dep't 2004)

45 ALR6th 175—§ 16, 17

Schwartz, In re, 278 Ga. 216, 599 S.E.2d 184 (2004)

46 ALR6th 365—§ 7

Schwartz, In re, 802 A.2d 339 (D.C. 2002)

45 ALR6th 175—§ 16

Schwartz, In re, 870 So. 2d 982 (La. 2004)

43 ALR6th 163—§ 16

Schwartz, Matter of Disciplinary Proceedings Against, 193 Wis. 2d 157, 532 N.W.2d 450 (1995)

96 ALR5th 23—§ 6

Schwartz v. American College of Emergency Physicians, 215 F.3d 1140, 28 Media L. Rep. (BNA) 1929 (10th Cir. 2000)

16 ALR6th 1—§ 3, 32

Schwartz v. Banbury Woods Homeowners Ass'n, Inc., 196 N.C. App. 584, 675 S.E.2d 382, 81 A.L.R.6th 771 (2009)

81 ALR6th 469—§ 3, 6

Schwartz v. Bank of Hawaii Corp., 2012 WL 2504048 (D. Haw. 2012)

86 ALR6th 411—§ 5

Schwartz v. Bay Industries, Inc., 274 F. Supp. 2d 1041 (E.D. Wis. 2003)

20 ALR6th 1—§ 4

Schwartz v. Boston Hospital for Women, 422 F. Supp. 53 (S.D. N.Y. 1976)

42 ALR6th 301—§ 22, 23

Schwartz v. Broadcast Music, Inc., 130 F. Supp. 956 (D.C. N.Y. 1955)

56 ALR5th 1—§ 3

Schwartz v. Brucato, 57 App. Div. 202, 68 N.Y.S. 289 (1901)

18 ALR5th 437—§ 3

Schwartz v. California Claim Service, Ltd., 52 Cal. App. 2d 47, 125 P.2d 883 (1942)

12 ALR5th 195—§ 2

14 ALR5th 242—§ 2

Schwartz v. Catherwood, 27 A.D.2d 617, 275 N.Y.S.2d 898 (3d Dep't 1966)

68 ALR5th 13—§ 19

Schwartz v. City of Rosemead, 155 Cal. App. 3d 547, 202 Cal. Rptr. 400 (2d Dist. 1984)

106 ALR5th 523—§ 36

Schwartz v. Civil Service Commission of City of Chicago, 1 Ill. App. 2d 522, 117 N.E.2d 874 (1st Dist. 1954)

19 ALR6th 217—§ 53

Schwartz v. Com., 45 Va. App. 407, 611 S.E.2d 631 (2005)

66 ALR6th 83—§ 10

Schwartz v. Comcorp, Inc., 91 Ohio App. 3d 639, 633 N.E.2d 551 (8th Dist. Cuyahoga County 1993)

103 ALR5th 557—§ 4

Schwartz v. Commissioner of Public
Safety, 422 N.W.2d 761 (Minn.
App. 1988)
23 ALR5th 108—§ 4
Schwartz v. Commissioner of Public
Safety, 422 N.W.2d 761 (Minn. Ct.
App. 1988)
84 ALR6th 293—§ 16
Schwartz v. Department of State, 43
App. Div. 2d 826, 351 N.Y.S.2d
700 (1st Dep't 1974)
7 ALR5th 474—§ 142
Schwartz v. Douglas, 98 Wash. App.
836, 991 P.2d 665 (Div. 3 2000)
99 ALR6th 1—§ 6, 9, 11, 12
Schwartz v. Dover Public Schools, 180
N.J. Super. 222, 434 A.2d 645
(1981)
57 ALR5th 477—§ 31
Schwartz v. Employers' Group Assur-
ance Co., 192 So. 2d 912 (La. App.
4th Cir. 1966)
44 ALR5th 525—§ 11
Schwartz v. Estate of Greenspun, 110
Nev. 1042, 881 P.2d 638, 23 Media
L. Rep. (BNA) 1022 (1994)
112 ALR5th 47—§ 3, 5
119 ALR5th 121—§ 3, 6, 11
125 ALR5th 193—§ 7
2 ALR6th 279—§ 4
34 ALR6th 431—§ 3
Schwartz v. Fortune Magazine, 193
F.R.D. 144 (S.D. N.Y. 2000)
35 ALR5th 1—§ 8
Schwartz v. Furano, 2009 WL 296996
(Cal. App. 1st Dist. 2009)
100 ALR6th 281—§ 5
Schwartz v. Geico General Ins. Co., 712
So. 2d 773 (Fla. Dist. Ct. App. 4th
Dist. 1998)
16 ALR5th 262—§ 5
Schwartz v. Grossman, 173 N.W.2d 57
(Iowa 1969)
62 ALR5th 219—§ 2
Schwartz v. Hampton House Manage-
ment Corp., 14 A.D.2d 936, 221
N.Y.S.2d 286 (3d Dep't 1961)
83 ALR5th 103—§ 20, 28

84 ALR5th 249—§ 34
107 ALR5th 441—§ 26
109 ALR5th 161—§ 8, 9
20 ALR6th 641—§ 14
Schwartz v. Holycross, 83 Ind. App.
658, 149 N.E. 699 (1925)
25 ALR5th 123—§ 10
Schwartz v. Jones, 58 Misc. 2d 998, 297
N.Y.S.2d 275 (1969)
53 ALR5th 287—§ 3, 4
Schwartz v. Kelly, 140 Conn. 176, 99
A.2d 89 (1953)
116 ALR5th 149—§ 3, 10
41 ALR6th 77—§ 14, 16
Schwartz v. Khalsa, 482 Fed. Appx. 320
(10th Cir. 2012)
95 ALR6th 341—§ 6
Schwartz v. Leasametric, Inc., 224 N.J.
Super. 21, 539 A.2d 744 (App. Div.
1988)
52 ALR6th 271—§ 7
Schwartz v. Magyar House, Inc., 168
Cal. App. 2d 182, 335 P.2d 487 (2d
Dist. 1959)
23 ALR5th 744—§ 8
Schwartz v. McGraw-Edison Co., 14
Cal. App. 3d 767, 92 Cal. Rptr. 776,
66 A.L.R.3d 808 (2d Dist. 1971)
109 ALR5th 301—§ 18
112 ALR5th 113—§ 7, 30
13 ALR6th 355—§ 5, 33
Schwartz v. Metro Limo, Inc., 683 So.
2d 201 (Fla. 3d DCA 1996)
98 ALR6th 93—§ 12
Schwartz v. Meyer, 2001 WL 267284
(Minn. Ct. App. 2001)
113 ALR5th 1—§ 10
40 ALR6th 375—§ 27, 28
Schwartz v. Michigan Sugar Co., 106
Mich. App. 471, 308 N.W.2d 459,
115 L.R.R.M. (BNA) 4535, 1981
O.S.H. Dec. (CCH) ¶ 25584 (1981)
104 ALR5th 1—§ 5
Schwartz v. Novo Industri A/S, 119
F.R.D. 359, CCH Fed Secur L. Rep.
¶ 93738 (S.D. N.Y. 1988)
23 ALR5th 241—§ 17

Schwartz v. Paralyzed Veterans of Am., 930 F. Supp. 3 (D.C. Dist. Col. 1996)
17 ALR5th 1—§ 3
Schwartz v. Paul Tishman Co., 147 N.Y.S.2d 71 (Sup 1955)
99 ALR5th 141—§ 1
115 ALR5th 1—§ 1
Schwartz v. Peoples Gas Light & Coke Co., 35 Ill. App. 2d 25, 181 N.E.2d 826 (1st Dist. 1962)
84 ALR5th 69—§ 17
Schwartz v. Pinnacle Communications, 944 S.W.2d 427 (Tex. App. Houston 14th Dist. 1997)
64 ALR5th 163—§ 16
Schwartz v. Robin Hats, Inc., 9 A.D.2d 972, 193 N.Y.S.2d 689 (3d Dep't 1959)
107 ALR5th 441—§ 2, 14
109 ALR5th 161—§ 9
20 ALR6th 641—§ 3, 22
Schwartz v. Saiter, 40 La. Ann 264, 4 So. 77 (1888)
46 ALR5th 1—§ 46, 47
Schwartz v. Schwartz, 25 Misc. 2d 225, 205 N.Y.S.2d 34 (1960)
49 ALR5th 595—§ 3
Schwartz v. Schwartz, 38 Ill. App. 3d 959, 349 N.E.2d 567 (1st Dist. 1976)
17 ALR5th 366—§ 10
Schwartz v. Schwartz, 67 A.D.3d 989, 890 N.Y.S.2d 71 (2d Dep't 2009)
77 ALR6th 293—§ 59
Schwartz v. Schwartz, 90 A.D.2d 498, 454 N.Y.S.2d 747 (2d Dep't 1982)
7 ALR6th 411—§ 5, 22
Schwartz v. Schwartz, 153 Misc. 2d 789, 583 N.Y.S.2d 716 (Sup 1992)
81 ALR6th 1—§ 31
Schwartz v. Schwartz, 311 S.C. 303, 428 S.E.2d 748 (App. 1993)
40 ALR5th 227—§ 32, 34, 61
Schwartz v. Schwartz, 750 So. 2d 679 (Fla. Dist. Ct. App. 4th Dist. 1999)
9 ALR5th 568—§ 9

Schwartz v. State, 172 Tex. Crim. 326, 357 S.W.2d 393 (1962)
70 ALR5th 587—§ 5
Schwartz v. State, 177 Ind. App. 258, 379 N.E.2d 480 (1978)
55 ALR6th 391—§ 21
Schwartz v. Subaru of America, Inc., 851 F. Supp. 191 (E.D. Pa. 1994)
102 ALR5th 99—§ 6
Schwartz v. Tenenbaum, 6 App. Div. 2d 810, 174 N.Y.S.2d 1003 (2d Dep't 1958)
56 ALR5th 1—§ 3
Schwartz v. Unemployment Compensation Bd. of Review, 188 Pa. Super. 558, 149 A.2d 182 (1959)
95 ALR5th 329—§ 8
Schwartz v. Unger, 108 Misc. 2d 456, 437 N.Y.S.2d 641 (1981)
12 ALR5th 1—§ 22
Schwartz v. U.S. Dept. of Justice, 1995 WL 675462 (S.D. N.Y. 1995)
100 ALR5th 341—§ 11
Schwartz v. Welch, 890 F. Supp. 565 (S.D. Miss. 1995)
20 ALR6th 385—§ 3, 8
Schwartz v. Wenger, 267 Minn. 40, 124 N.W.2d 489 (1963)
51 ALR5th 603—§ 8
Schwartz v. Worrall Publications, Inc., 258 N.J. Super. 493, 610 A.2d 425, 20 Media L. R. 1661 (1992)
19 ALR5th 1—§ 40
Schwartz v. Zippy Mart, Inc., 470 So. 2d 720, 10 FLW 1134, 50 BNA FEP Cas. 464 (Fla. App. D1 1985)
51 ALR5th 163—§ 8
Schwartz v. Zulka, 70 N.J. Super. 256, 175 A.2d 465 (1961)
5 ALR5th 875—§ 3
Schwartz & Schwartz of Virginia, LLC v. Certain Underwriters at Lloyd's, London who Subscribed to Policy Number NC959, 677 F. Supp. 2d 890 (W.D. Va. 2009)
73 ALR6th 681—§ 3

Schwartz, Jaffee & Chas. D. Jaffee Co. v. O. B. Potter Properties, Inc., 182 N.Y.S. 685 (Sup. App. T 1920)
3 ALR5th 237—§ 24

Schwartzkopf v. Shannon the Cannon's Window & Other Works, Inc., 166 Or. App. 466, 998 P.2d 244 (2000)
60 ALR5th 669—§ 5

Schwartzman v. London & Lancashire Fire Ins. Co., Limited, of Liverpool, England, 318 Mo. 1089, 2 S.W.2d 593 (1927)
63 ALR5th 675—§ 7

Schwartzman v. Talking Water, LLC, 2011 WL 3497762 (E.D. Pa. 2011)
100 ALR6th 281—§ 3

Schwartzman v. Wilshinsky, 50 Cal. App. 4th 619, 57 Cal. Rptr. 2d 790 (2d Dist. 1996)
113 ALR5th 487—§ 5, 12

Schwartz, U.S. ex rel. v. TRW, Inc., 211 F.R.D. 388 (C.D. Cal. 2002)
23 ALR6th 521—§ 2

Schwarz v. Regents of University of California, 226 Cal. App. 3d 149, 276 Cal. Rptr. 470 (2d Dist. 1990)
96 ALR5th 107—§ 7

Schwarz v. Salt Lake Tribune, 2005 UT App 206, 2005 WL 1037843 (Utah Ct. App. 2005)
13 ALR6th 111—§ 4, 15

Schwarz v. Waterbury Public Market, Inc., 6 Conn. App. 429, 505 A.2d 1272 (1986)
15 ALR6th 1—§ 4, 5, 9, 10, 16

Schwarzbach, In re, 1989 WL 360742 (W.D. Tex. 1989)
46 ALR6th 401—§ 8

Schwarze v. Ridan Inv. Trust, Inc., 1991 A.M.C. 1728, 1991 WL 35874 (S.D. N.Y. 1991)
82 ALR6th 175—§ 14

Schwarzenegger v. Entertainment Merchants Ass'n, 130 S. Ct. 2398, 176 L. Ed. 2d 784 (2010)
56 ALR6th 679—§ 12

Schwarzkopf Development Corp. v. Ti-Coating, Inc., 800 F.2d 240, 231 U.S.P.Q. 47 (Fed. Cir. 1986)
85 ALR6th 1—§ 4

Schwarzman v. Schwarzman, 88 Misc. 2d 866, 388 N.Y.S.2d 993 (Sup 1976)
124 ALR5th 203—§ 13
81 ALR6th 1—§ 34

Schwarzschild v. Martin, 191 Conn. 316, 464 A.2d 774 (1983)
56 ALR5th 757—§ 3

Schwarzschild v. Welborne, 186 Va. 1052, 45 S.E.2d 152 (1947)
76 ALR5th 337—§ 20

Schwarz, State ex rel. v. Hamilton County Bd. of Elections, 173 Ohio St. 321, 19 Ohio Op. 2d 229, 181 N.E.2d 888 (1962)
14 ALR6th 543—§ 29

Schwasnick v. Fields, 2010 WL 2679935 (E.D. N.Y. 2010)
68 ALR6th 229—§ 8

Schwedt v. Department of Indus., Labor & Human Relations, 188 Wis. 2d 500, 525 N.W.2d 130 (App. 1994)
57 ALR5th 477—§ 30

Schwegmann v. Schwegmann, 441 So. 2d 316 (La. Ct. App. 5th Cir. 1983)
21 ALR6th 351—§ 4

Schwegmann Bank & Trust Co. of Jefferson v. Falkenberg, 931 F.2d 1081, 14 U.C.C. Rep. Serv. 2d (CBC) 795 (5th Cir. 1991)
76 ALR5th 289—§ 12

Schwegmann Bros. v. Calvert Distillers Corp., 341 U.S. 384, 71 S. Ct. 745, 95 L. Ed. 1035, 60 Ohio L. Abs. 81, 19 A.L.R.2d 1119 (1951)
41 ALR6th 77—§ 16

Schweibish v. Pontchartrain State Bank, 389 So. 2d 731, 30 U.C.C.R.S. 645 (La. App. 4th Cir. 1980)
8 ALR5th 463—§ 5, 10, 16
53 ALR5th 667—§ 19
56 ALR5th 565—§ 2, 28

Schweiger v. Empire Rollerdrome of
Brooklyn, 265 App. Div. 867, 37
N.Y.S.2d 753 (1942)
38 ALR5th 107—§ 5
Schweiger v. Hoch, 223 So. 2d 557 (Fla.
App. D4 1969)
12 ALR5th 847—§ 12
Schweiger v. Sanders, 449 So. 2d 681
(La. App. 5th Cir. 1984)
50 ALR5th 1—§ 7, 10
Schweihofer v. Zachary, 103 Mich. App.
792, 303 N.W.2d 896 (1981)
4 ALR6th 263—§ 22
Schweihs v. Burdick, 96 F.3d 917 (7th
Cir. 1996)
76 ALR6th 31—§ 35
Schweihs v. Davis, Friedman, Zavett,
Kane and MacRae, 344 Ill. App. 3d
493, 279 Ill. Dec. 380, 800 N.E.2d
448 (1st Dist. 2003)
49 ALR6th 505—§ 41
Schweisberger v. Weiner, 1995 WL
808866 (Ohio Ct. App. 5th Dist.
Stark County 1995)
98 ALR5th 533—§ 29
Schweiss v. Chrysler Motors Corp., 782
F. Supp. 88, 125 Lab. Cas. (CCH)
¶ 57402, 1992 O.S.H. Dec. (CCH)
¶ 29661 (E.D. Mo. 1992)
105 ALR5th 351—§ 5
Schweiss v. Sisters of Mercy, St. Louis,
Inc., 950 S.W.2d 537 (Mo. Ct. App.
E.D. 1997)
40 ALR5th 603—§ 22
Schweitzer, In re, 196 B.R. 620, 36 Collier Bankr. Cas. 2d (MB) 43 (Bankr.
M.D. Fla. 1996)
32 ALR6th 531—§ 39
Schweitzer, Matter of Marriage of, 132
Wash. 2d 318, 937 P.2d 1062 (1997)
105 ALR5th 499—§ 4
Schweitzer, Re, 409 N.Y.S.2d 964 (Jud
Ct. 1971)
15 ALR5th 923—§ 4, 6
Schweitzer v. Consolidated Rail Corp.,
65 B.R. 794, 15 Bankr. Ct. Dec.
(CRR) 882 (E.D. Pa. 1986)
18 ALR6th 629—§ 5, 9

Schweitzer v. Equitable Sav. & Loan
Ass'n, 98 Wash. 139, 167 P. 111
(1917)
18 ALR5th 307—§ 29
Schweitzer v. Estate of Halko, 231
Mont. 283, 751 P.2d 1064 (1988)
67 ALR5th 587—§ 2
11 ALR6th 1—§ 3
12 ALR6th 1—§ 3
13 ALR6th 1—§ 3, 4
14 ALR6th 1—§ 3
15 ALR6th 427—§ 12
Schweitzer v. Rockwell Intern., 402 Pa.
Super. 34, 586 A.2d 383, 61 Fair
Empl. Prac. Cas. (BNA) 1788
(1990)
20 ALR6th 1—§ 4
Schweitzer v. Rockwell Int'l, 586 A.2d
383 (Pa. Super. 1990)
51 ALR5th 163—§ 5
Schweizer, In re, 762 A.2d 34 (D.C.
2000)
45 ALR6th 175—§ 23, 25
Schweizer v. Mulvehill, 93 F. Supp. 2d
376 (S.D. N.Y. 2000)
9 ALR6th 285—§ 10
Schweizer Aircraft Corp. v. State Division of Human Rights, 48 N.Y.2d
294, 422 N.Y.S.2d 656, 397 N.E.2d
1323, 21 Empl. Prac. Dec. (CCH)
¶ 30510 (1979)
107 ALR5th 623—§ 7
Schweizer Aircraft Corp. v. State Div.
of Human Rights, 48 N.Y.2d 294,
422 N.Y.S.2d 656, 397 N.E.2d
1323, 21 CCH EPD ¶ 30510 (1979)
37 ALR5th 349—§ 11
Schwellinger v. Wisconsin Lawyers
Mut. Ins. Co., 192 Wis. 2d 763, 532
N.W.2d 469 (Ct. App. 1995)
92 ALR5th 273—§ 11
Schwencke v. Brown, 232 So. 2d 193
(Fla. App. D4 1970)
22 ALR5th 483—§ 3
Schwenk v. Boy Scouts of America, 275
Or. 327, 551 P.2d 465 (1976)
82 ALR5th 1—§ 13
83 ALR5th 467—§ 7

Schwen's, Inc., In re, 20 B.R. 638 (D. Minn. 1982)
107 ALR5th 311—§ 8

Schwerin v. H.C. Capwell Co., 140 Cal. App. 1, 34 P.2d 1050 (1st Dist. 1934)
63 ALR6th 495—§ 54

Schwertfeger v. Moorehouse, 569 So. 2d 322 (Ala. 1990)
14 ALR5th 242—§ 26

Schwetz v. Minnerly, 220 Cal. App. 3d 296, 269 Cal. Rptr. 417 (4th Dist. 1990)
33 ALR5th 1—§ 3
5 ALR6th 497—§ 9

Schwickert, Inc. v. Winnebago Seniors, Ltd., 661 N.W.2d 680 (Minn. Ct. App. 2003)
119 ALR5th 121—§ 4
120 ALR5th 559—§ 5

Schwickert, Inc. v. Winnebago Seniors, Ltd., 680 N.W.2d 79 (Minn. 2004)
120 ALR5th 559—§ 6
16 ALR6th 491—§ 4

Schwickert, Inc. v. Winnebago Seniors, Ltd., 680 N.W.2d 79, 2004 WL 1171399 (Minn. 2004)
119 ALR5th 121—§ 5

Schwier v. Bernstein, 734 So. 2d 531 (Fla. Dist. Ct. App. 4th Dist. 1999)
90 ALR5th 1—§ 32

Schwier v. Cox, 412 F. Supp. 2d 1266 (N.D. Ga. 2005)
48 ALR6th 181—§ 20, 21

Schwinden v. Burlington N., 213 Mont. 382, 691 P.2d 1351 (1984)
33 ALR5th 509—§ 23

Schwindt v. State, 596 N.E.2d 936 (Ind. Ct. App. 2d Dist. 1992)
97 ALR5th 537—§ 18

Schwindt v. Thompson, 249 App. Div. 639, 291 N.Y.S. 81 (1936)
27 ALR5th 174—§ 54

Schwing v. Bluebonnet Exp., Inc., 489 S.W.2d 279 (Tex. 1973)
80 ALR5th 533—§ 5

Schwing v. State, 633 P.2d 311 (Alaska Ct. App. 1981)

15 ALR5th 391—§ 32
92 ALR5th 35—§ 22
46 ALR6th 63—§ 6

Schwing, State ex rel. v. Fontelieu, 30 La. Ann. 1122, 1878 WL 8543 (1878)
97 ALR5th 537—§ 54

Schwinn v. Cook, 2004 UT App 372, 2004 WL 2361816 (Utah Ct. App. 2004)
16 ALR6th 653—§ 8

Schwinn Cycling and Fitness, Inc., In re, 313 B.R. 473, 54 U.C.C. Rep. Serv. 2d 645 (D. Colo. 2004)
53 ALR6th 159—§ 31, 32

Schwochert v. American Family Mut. Ins. Co., 139 Wis. 2d 335, 407 N.W.2d 525 (1987)
116 ALR5th 433—§ 13
125 ALR5th 193—§ 4

Schwochow v. Chung, 102 Ohio App. 3d 348, 657 N.E.2d 312 (Sandusky Co. 1995)
51 ALR5th 301—§ 3

Schy v. Hearst Pub. Co., 205 F.2d 750 (7th Cir. 1953)
94 ALR5th 149—§ 7

Schyman v. Department of Registration & Education, 9 Ill. App. 2d 504, 133 N.E.2d 551 (1st Dist. 1956)
10 ALR5th 1—§ 2, 3

Sciacca v. Sciacca, 173 Misc. 2d 756, 663 N.Y.S.2d 808 (Sup. Ct. 1997)
4 ALR5th 403—§ 3

Scialabba v. Cuellar de Osorio, 134 S. Ct. 2191 (2014)
96 ALR6th 577—§ 2, 3

Scialdo v. Cook, 53 A.D.3d 1090, 862 N.Y.S.2d 238 (4th Dep't 2008)
102 ALR6th 153—§ 22

Sciambra v. Graham News, 892 F.2d 411, 1990-1 CCH Trade Cases ¶ 68904, 15 FR Serv. 3d 945 (CA5 La. 1990)
23 ALR5th 241—§ 27

Sciandra v. Palmer, 174 Misc. 2d 959, 666 N.Y.S.2d 907 (Sup. Ct. 1997)
26 ALR5th 107—§ 8

Sciangula v. Mancuso, 204 A.D.2d 708, 612 N.Y.S.2d 645, Prod. Liab. Rep. (CCH) ¶ 13951 (2d Dep't 1994)
64 ALR5th 1—§ 29

Scianni v. Suriano, 2007 WL 506206 (N.J. Super. Ct. App. Div. 2007)
36 ALR6th 443—§ 6

Sciarra, In re, 175 B.R. 2 (Bankr. D. Conn. 1994)
86 ALR5th 527—§ 6, 13

Sciarrino v. City of Key West, Fla., 83 F.3d 364 (11th Cir. 1996)
70 ALR6th 513—§ 5
71 ALR6th 471—§ 7

Sciascia v. Riverpark Apartments, 3 Ohio App. 3d 164, 3 Ohio B.R. 188, 444 N.E.2d 40 (Franklin Co. 1981)
43 ALR5th 207—§ 25

Scientific Control Corp., Re, 80 F.R.D. 237, CCH Fed Secur L. Rep. ¶ 96481 (S.D. N.Y. 1978)
23 ALR5th 241—§ 19

Scientific Research, Inc. v. NIA Group, Inc., 96 N.Y.2d 20, 725 N.Y.S.2d 592, 749 N.E.2d 161 (2001)
121 ALR5th 365—§ 4

Scieszka v. State, 259 Ga. App. 486, 578 S.E.2d 149 (2003)
71 ALR6th 625—§ 28

Scifres v. Kraft, 916 S.W.2d 779 (Ky. Ct. App. 1996)
64 ALR5th 1—§ 12, 14

Scillia v. Szalai, 142 N.J. Eq. 92, 59 A.2d 435 (Ch. 1948)
76 ALR5th 337—§ 20
119 ALR5th 519—§ 26

Scimeca, Matter of, 265 Kan. 742, 962 P.2d 1080 (1998)
10 ALR5th 1—§ 48
58 ALR5th 429—§ 3
102 ALR5th 253—§ 6
26 ALR6th 1—§ 3
27 ALR6th 1—§ 3, 57

Scinto v. Marketcorp Properties, Inc., 3 Conn. L. Rptr. 412, 1991 WL 59714 (Conn. Super. Ct. 1991)
104 ALR6th 303—§ 12

Scinto v. Preston, 2005 WL 5967352 (E.D. N.C. 2005)
62 ALR6th 517—§ 35, 41, 43, 53

Scinto v. Sosin, 51 Conn. App. 222, 721 A.2d 552 (1998)
100 ALR5th 481—§ 3

Sciolaro v. Asch, 198 N.Y. 77, 91 N.E. 263 (1910)
100 ALR5th 409—§ 2

Sciortino v. Alfano, 435 So. 2d 1010 (La. App. 5th Cir. 1983)
52 ALR5th 1—§ 8

Sciortino v. Leach, 242 So. 2d 269 (La. App. 4th Cir. 1970)
46 ALR5th 581—§ 2

Sciortino v. Planning and Zoning Com'n of Trumbull, 1 Conn. L. Rptr. 419, 1990 WL 284346 (Conn. Super. Ct. 1990)
4 ALR6th 263—§ 13

Sciortino v. Songy, 198 So. 2d 422 (La. App. 4th Cir. 1967)
9 ALR5th 826—§ 7

Sciortino v. Winnebago County Housing Authority, 1996 WL 153687 (N.D. Ill. 1996)
105 ALR5th 351—§ 3, 4, 6

Scioscia, Matter of, 216 N.J. Super. 644, 524 A.2d 855, 1987-1 Trade Cas. (CCH) ¶ 67562 (App. Div. 1987)
63 ALR6th 1—§ 70

Scioto County Child Support Enforcement Agency, State ex rel. v. Adams, 1999 WL 597257 (Ohio Ct. App. 4th Dist. Scioto County 1999)
18 ALR6th 97—§ 17, 19

Scipio v. City of Steubenville, 2007 WL 654222 (S.D. Ohio 2007)
65 ALR6th 93—§ 29

Scipione v. Advance Stores Co., Inc., 2013 WL 646405 (M.D. Fla. 2013)
88 ALR6th 319—§ 45

Scire v. Board of Regents of University of State of N.Y., 23 A.D.2d 943, 259 N.Y.S.2d 930 (3d Dep't 1965)
19 ALR6th 577—§ 14

SCI-Sacramento, Inc. v. Superior Court (People), 54 Cal. App. 4th 654, 62 Cal. Rptr. 2d 868, 25 Media L. Rep. 1881 (3d Dist. 1997)

60 ALR5th 75—§ 11

SCJ, Inc. v. Davis, 2003 WL 123064 (Cal. App. 4th Dist. 2003)

64 ALR6th 365—§ 13, 26

Sclafani v. Spitzer, 734 F. Supp. 2d 288 (E.D. N.Y. 2010)

95 ALR6th 341—§ 67

SCM Chemicals, Inc. v. Wilkins, 106 Ohio St. 3d 43, 2005-Ohio-3676, 831 N.E.2d 417 (2005)

14 ALR6th 119—§ 85

SCM Corp. v. Berkel, Inc., 73 Cal. App. 3d 49, 140 Cal. Rptr. 559 (5th Dist. 1977)

112 ALR5th 113—§ 3

SCM Corp. v. Fisher Park Lane Co., 40 N.Y.2d 788, 390 N.Y.S.2d 398, 358 N.E.2d 1024 (1976)

56 ALR5th 757—§ 4

SCM Corp. v. Xerox Corp., 70 F.R.D. 508, 1976-2 CCH Trade Cases ¶ 61207, 1976-2 CCH Trade Cases ¶ 61208, 2 Fed. Rules Evid. Serv. 535 (D.C. Conn. 1976)

27 ALR5th 76—§ 45

SCM Land Co. v. Watkins & Faber, 732 P.2d 105 (Utah 1986)

12 ALR6th 123—§ 21

S.C.N., In the Matter of, 154 Wis. 2d 870, 455 N.W.2d 679 (Ct. App. 1990)

87 ALR5th 277—§ 8

Scoa Industries, Inc. v. Bracken, 374 A.2d 263 (Del. Sup. 1977)

18 ALR5th 577—§ 25

Scobee, In re Marriage of, 667 S.W.2d 467 (Mo. App. 1984)

53 ALR5th 375—§ 20

Scobey v. New York State Tax Com'n, 95 A.D.2d 905, 463 N.Y.S.2d 907 (3d Dep't 1983)

2 ALR6th 1—§ 39, 85, 94

Scobey v. Ross, 5 Ind. 445 (1854)

56 ALR5th 1—§ 3

Scobey v. State Tax Commission, 95 A.D.2d 905, 463 N.Y.S.2d 907 (3d Dep't 1983)

2 ALR6th 1—§ 38

Scobey v. Waters, 78 Tenn. 551, 1882 WL 4186 (1882)

6 ALR6th 391—§ 5

Scoby v. Vulcan-Hart Corp., 211 Ill. App. 3d 106, 155 Ill. Dec. 536, 569 N.E.2d 1147, Prod. Liab. Rep. (CCH) ¶ 12887 (4th Dist. 1991)

73 ALR5th 75—§ 3, 6, 11

S.C.O. Development Co. v. Consolidated Precast, Inc., 1993 WL 241529 (Conn. Super. Ct. 1993)

100 ALR5th 481—§ 3

Scofield v. State of Ill., 31 Ill. Ct. Cl. 540, 1977 WL 20646 (Ill. Ct. Cl. 1977)

12 ALR6th 645—§ 49

Scofield v. Tinnin, 171 F.2d 227, 37 AFTR 628 (CA5 Tex. 1948)

60 ALR5th 459—§ 2, 4, 5, 16

Scofield, Estate of v. C.I.R., T.C. Memo. 1980-470, T.C.M. (P-H) ¶ 80470, 41 T.C.M. (CCH) 227, 1980 WL 3844 (1980)

58 ALR5th 325—§ 4, 9

Scoggin v. Listerhill Employees Credit Union, 658 So. 2d 376 (Ala. 1995)

67 ALR6th 209—§ 44

Scoggins v. Curtiss & Taylor, 219 S.W.2d 451 (Tex. 1949)

31 ALR5th 572—§ 25

Scoggins v. Snap-On Tools, Inc., CCH Bus Fran Guide ¶ 10,203 (N.D. Ala. 1992)

52 ALR5th 613—§ 3

Scoggins v. State, 111 N.M. 122, 802 P.2d 631 (1990)

94 ALR5th 393—§ 6

Scoggins v. State, 258 Ark. 749, 528 S.W.2d 641 (1975)

51 ALR6th 219—§ 4

Scoggins v. Taylor, 248 S.W.2d 549 (Tex. Civ. App. Amarillo 1952)

83 ALR6th 605—§ 5

Scogin v. Nugen, 204 Kan. 568, 464 P.2d 166 (1970)

87 ALR5th 1—§ 8, 33

Scognamillo v. Olsen, 795 P.2d 1357 (Colo. App. 1990)

10 ALR5th 828—§ 2, 20

Scognamillo v. Olsen, 795 P.2d 1357 (Colo. Ct. App. 1990)

9 ALR6th 285—§ 15

SCO Group, Inc. v. Novell, Inc., 2004 WL 4737297 (D. Utah 2004)

76 ALR6th 289—§ 6

Scola v. County of Nassau, 230 A.D.2d 902, 646 N.Y.S.2d 852 (2d Dep't 1996)

7 ALR5th 1—§ 8

Scoma v. Chicago Bd. of Ed., 391 F. Supp. 452 (N.D. Ill. 1974)

70 ALR5th 169—§ 4, 6, 16

Sconce v. Interstate Com'n for Adult Offender Supervision, 2009 WL 579399 (D. Mont. 2009)

75 ALR6th 181—§ 3

Sconiers v. Fresno Unified School Dist., 2002 WL 31723098 (Cal. App. 5th Dist. 2002)

45 ALR6th 493—§ 63

Scope v. Fannelli, 639 So. 2d 141 (Fla. Dist. Ct. App. 5th Dist. 1994)

116 ALR5th 433—§ 2, 3, 7

Scopelliti v. Town of New Castle, 210 A.D.2d 308, 620 N.Y.S.2d 405 (2d Dep't 1994)

103 ALR5th 557—§ 5

Scope Pictures, of Missouri, Inc. v. City of Kansas City, 140 F.3d 1201 (8th Cir. 1998)

20 ALR6th 161—§ 3
21 ALR6th 425—§ 3, 5
23 ALR6th 573—§ 17
73 ALR6th 281—§ 14

Score v. American Family Mut. Ins. Co., 538 N.W.2d 206 (N.D. 1995)

40 ALR5th 603—§ 9

Score LLC v. City of Shoreline, 319 F. Supp. 2d 1224 (W.D. Wash. 2004)

20 ALR6th 161—§ 4
21 ALR6th 425—§ 10

23 ALR6th 573—§ 4, 14

Scotch Plains v. Westfield, 83 N.J. Super. 323, 199 A.2d 673 (1964)

17 ALR5th 195—§ 29
53 ALR5th 1—§ 7, 26, 38

Scotch Plains-Fanwood Bd. of Educ. v. Syvertsen, 251 N.J. Super. 566, 598 A.2d 1232 (1991)

34 ALR5th 591—§ 21
35 ALR5th 113—§ 13

Scothorn v. Kansas, 772 F.Supp. 556 (D.C. Kan. 1991)

81 ALR5th 167—§ 15

Scotia Associates v. Bond, 126 Misc. 2d 885, 484 N.Y.S.2d 479 (1985)

10 ALR5th 448—§ 4

Scotsman Group, Inc. v. Mid-America Distributors, Inc., 1994 WL 118458 (N.D. Ill. 1994)

63 ALR5th 1—§ 14

Scots Ventures v. Hayes Township, 212 Mich. App. 530, 537 N.W.2d 610 (1995)

1 ALR5th 622—§ 8

Scott, Estate of, 217 Cal. App. 2d 111, 31 Cal. Rptr. 438 (2d Dist. 1963)

3 ALR5th 590—§ 29

Scott, In re, 53 F.2d 89 (W.D. Mich. 1931)

32 ALR6th 531—§ 31

Scott, In re, 265 A.D.2d 777, 697 N.Y.S.2d 195 (3d Dep't 1999)

18 ALR6th 195—§ 15

Scott, In re, 2002 WL 1284281 (Bankr. M.D. N.C. 2002)

99 ALR6th 481—§ 27

Scott, In re Marriage of, 156 Cal. App. 3d 251, 202 Cal. Rptr. 716 (4th Dist. 1984)

59 ALR6th 433—§ 74

Scott, Re Marriage of, 85 Ill. App. 3d 773, 41 Ill. Dec. 547, 407 N.E.2d 1045 (2d Dist. 1980)

17 ALR5th 366—§ 11

Scott v. Allstate Ins. Co., 200 Ga. App. 296, 407 S.E.2d 492 (1991)

77 ALR5th 319—§ 19

Scott v. Alpha Beta Co., 104 Cal. App. 3d 305, 163 Cal. Rptr. 544, 20 A.L.R.4th 511 (2d Dist. 1980)
    83 ALR5th 589—§ 2, 4
    123 ALR5th 1—§ 10
Scott v. American Federation of State, County and Mun. Employees Council 79, 134 S. Ct. 1877, 37 I.E.R. Cas. (BNA) 1888 (2014)
    96 ALR6th 577—§ 11
Scott v. American Tobacco Co., 725 So. 2d 10 (La. Ct. App. 4th Cir. 1998)
    7 ALR6th 319—§ 4
Scott v. American Tobacco Co., 731 So. 2d 189 (La. 1999)
    7 ALR6th 319—§ 4
Scott v. Apgar, 238 La. 29, 113 So. 2d 457 (1959)
    39 ALR5th 33—§ 9
Scott v. Baker, 143 Ill. App. 151 (3d Dist. 1908)
    74 ALR5th 369—§ 8, 9
Scott v. Battle, 249 Ga. App. 618, 548 S.E.2d 124 (2001)
    8 ALR6th 439—§ 9
Scott v. Black, 95 W. Va. 48, 120 S.E. 167 (1923)
    62 ALR5th 219—§ 18
Scott v. Black and Decker, Inc., 717 F.2d 251 (5th Cir. 1983)
    4 ALR6th 401—§ 9
Scott v. Blanchet High School, 50 Wash. App. 37, 747 P.2d 1124, 43 Ed. Law Rep. 1187 (Div. 1 1987)
    86 ALR5th 1—§ 3, 10
Scott v. Board of Appeal of Wellesley, 356 Mass. 159, 248 N.E.2d 281 (1969)
    63 ALR5th 607—§ 15
Scott v. Board of Education, 61 Misc. 2d 333, 305 N.Y.S.2d 601 (1969)
    58 ALR5th 1—§ 12, 45
Scott v. Board of Election Com'rs of Newton, 346 Mass. 388, 193 N.E.2d 262 (1963)
    78 ALR6th 229—§ 18

Scott v. Borelli, 106 Ohio App. 3d 449, 666 N.E.2d 322 (10th Dist. Franklin County 1995)
    23 ALR6th 697—§ 6
Scott v. Brooklyn Hosp., 125 Misc. 2d 765, 480 N.Y.S.2d 270 (Sup 1984)
    93 ALR6th 123—§ 82, 86
Scott v. Burke, 55 Mass. App. Ct. 1103, 769 N.E.2d 342 (2002)
    58 ALR6th 1—§ 5
    60 ALR6th 1—§ 56
Scott v. Chope, 33 Neb. 41, 49 N.W. 940 (1891)
    19 ALR5th 622—§ 37, 51
Scott v. CIBA Vision Corp., 38 Cal. App. 4th 307, 44 Cal. Rptr. 2d 902, Prod. Liab. Rep. (CCH) ¶ 14351 (6th Dist. 1995)
    23 ALR6th 223—§ 3
Scott v. Citizens Bank of Americus, 188 Ga. App. 618, 373 S.E.2d 633, 8 U.C.C. Rep. Serv. 2d (CBC) 68 (1988)
    89 ALR5th 577—§ 12
Scott v. City of Dallas, 876 F. Supp. 852 (N.D. Tex. 1995)
    21 ALR6th 671—§ 13
Scott v. City of Laporte, 162 Ind. 34, 68 N.E. 278 (1903)
    122 ALR5th 337—§ 10
Scott v. City of Peoria, 2011 WL 673988 (C.D. Ill. 2011)
    65 ALR6th 93—§ 18
Scott v. Claiborne Elec. Co-op., 13 So. 2d 524 (La. Ct. App. 2d Cir. 1943)
    95 ALR5th 29—§ 3, 4
Scott v. Class, 532 N.W.2d 399 (S.D. 1995)
    45 ALR5th 591—§ 15
    99 ALR6th 295—§ 9
Scott v. Coady, 2008 WL 4891114 (E.D. La. 2008)
    89 ALR6th 1—§ 118
Scott v. Coastal Dragline Works, Inc., 525 So. 2d 695 (La. App. 1st Cir. 1988)
    26 ALR5th 401—§ 10

Scott v. Com., 29 Va. Cir. 324, 1992 WL 885029 (1992)
110 ALR5th 293—§ 3

Scott v. Com., 54 Va. App. 142, 676 S.E.2d 343 (2009)
75 ALR6th 181—§ 24, 25

Scott v. Commonwealth, 94 Ky. 511, 23 S.W. 219 (1893)
51 ALR5th 603—§ 4, 8, 11

Scott v. Continental Ins. Co., 44 Cal. App. 4th 24, 51 Cal. Rptr. 2d 566, 96 C.D.O.S. 2240, 96 Daily Journal DAR 3694 (4th Dist. 1996)
30 ALR5th 170—§ 86

Scott v. County of Los Angeles, 2003 WL 22078941 (Cal. App. 2d Dist. 2003)
17 ALR6th 563—§ 4

Scott v. Crowley County Correctional Facility, 76 Fed. Appx. 878 (10th Cir. 2003)
89 ALR6th 1—§ 100

Scott v. Crown, 765 P.2d 1043, 7 U.C.C.R.S.2d 464 (Colo. App. 1988)
37 ALR5th 459—§ 9

Scott v. Dennison, 739 F. Supp. 2d 342 (W.D. N.Y. 2010)
86 ALR6th 173—§ 14

Scott v. Department of Corrections, 1998 WL 1997674 (Mich. Ct. App. 1998)
29 ALR6th 237—§ 5

Scott v. Detroit, 107 Mich. App. 194, 309 N.W.2d 201 (1981)
13 ALR5th 289—§ 3

Scott v. District of Columbia, 184 A.2d 849 (Mun. Ct. App. D.C. 1962)
52 ALR6th 125—§ 14, 32, 46

Scott v. Dugger, 604 So. 2d 465, 17 FLW S. 545 (Fla. 1992)
20 ALR5th 177—§ 3

Scott v. Estes, 60 F. Supp. 2d 1260 (M.D. Ala. 1999)
20 ALR6th 1—§ 4

Scott v. Foltz, 1998 WL 918610 (Conn. Super. Ct. 1998)
125 ALR5th 133—§ 3

Scott v. Ford Motor Credit Co., 345 Md. 251, 691 A.2d 1320, 32 U.C.C. Rep. Serv. 2d (CBC) 646 (1997)
49 ALR5th 1—§ 16

Scott v. Glenn, 408 So. 2d 1167 (La. Ct. App. 4th Cir. 1981)
66 ALR5th 269—§ 7

Scott v. Glickman, 199 F.R.D. 174 (E.D.N.C. 2001)
51 ALR5th 603—§ 8

Scott v. Godwin, 147 S.W.3d 609, 21 I.E.R. Cas. (BNA) 1404 (Tex. App. Corpus Christi 2004)
10 ALR6th 531—§ 18
37 ALR6th 137—§ 3

Scott v. Graphic Center, 2011 WL 2279522 (Cal. App. 2d Dist. 2011)
83 ALR6th 143—§ 6

Scott v. Greenville Pharmacy, Inc., 212 S.C. 485, 48 S.E.2d 324, 11 A.L.R.2d 745 (1948)
44 ALR5th 393—§ 11

Scott v. Grinnell, 102 N.H. 490, 161 A.2d 179 (1960)
67 ALR6th 341—§ 16

Scott v. Gusman, 2011 WL 666851 (E.D. La. 2011)
89 ALR6th 1—§ 118

Scott v. Hall, 221 Ill. App. 115, 1921 WL 1733 (1st Dist. 1921)
85 ALR6th 1—§ 26

Scott v. Hammock, 870 P.2d 947 (Utah 1994)
93 ALR5th 327—§ 4, 6, 7, 28

Scott v. Hanson, 330 Fed. Appx. 490 (5th Cir. 2009)
65 ALR6th 93—§ 67

Scott v. Harris, 127 S. Ct. 1769, 167 L. Ed. 2d 686 (U.S. 2007)
26 ALR6th 659—§ 5

Scott v. Haverstraw Clay & Brick Co., 16 N.Y.S. 670 (Sup. 1891)
45 ALR5th 251—§ 6

Scott v. Hempfield Area School Dist., 164 Pa. Commw. 588, 643 A.2d 1140, 92 Ed. Law Rep. 583 (1994)
118 ALR5th 597—§ 9

Scott v. Hocker, 460 F.2d 303 (9th Cir. 1972)
  27 ALR6th 491—§ 3
Scott v. Hospital Service Dist. No. 1, 484 So. 2d 168 (La. App. 5th Cir. 1986)
  52 ALR5th 1—§ 8
Scott v. Housing Authority of City of Glennville, 223 Ga. App. 216, 477 S.E.2d 325 (1996)
  43 ALR5th 207—§ 4
Scott v. Hughes, 281 Kan. 642, 132 P.3d 889 (2006)
  42 ALR6th 545—§ 8, 20
Scott v. Hughes, 281 Kan. 642, 132 P.3d 889, 43 A.L.R.6th 789 (2006)
  43 ALR6th 375—§ 6, 11, 36
Scott v. Industrial Com., 122 Ariz. 169, 593 P.2d 919 (App. 1978)
  16 ALR5th 191—§ 2, 12, 14
Scott v. Insurance Co. of North America, 485 So. 2d 50 (La. 1986)
  115 ALR5th 589—§ 5
Scott v. Iverson, 120 Or. App. 538, 853 P.2d 302 (1993)
  10 ALR5th 680—§ 4
Scott v. Ives, 22 Misc. 749, 51 N.Y.S. 49 (1898)
  3 ALR5th 590—§ 15, 29
Scott v. Jackson, 38 A.D.3d 788, 832 N.Y.S.2d 611 (2d Dep't 2007)
  60 ALR6th 193—§ 5
Scott v. Jackson County, 244 Or. App. 484, 2011 WL 3124062 (2011)
  70 ALR6th 329—§ 12
Scott v. Joffee, 125 Mo. App. 573, 102 S.W. 1038 (1907)
  51 ALR5th 747—§ 3
  97 ALR5th 537—§ 44
Scott v. Johnson, 2003 WL 22298724 (Tex. App. San Antonio 2003)
  29 ALR6th 237—§ 16, 29
Scott v. Keever, 212 Kan. 719, 512 P.2d 346 (1973)
  14 ALR5th 695—§ 24
Scott v. Kelkris Associates, Inc., 2012 WL 1131360 (E.D. Cal. 2012)
  85 ALR6th 475—§ 10
Scott v. Kelley, 2012 WL 479896 (E.D. Ky. 2012)
  80 ALR6th 239—§ 15
Scott v. Kemper Ins. Co., 357 So. 2d 87 (La. App. 4th Cir. 1978)
  56 ALR5th 1—§ 8
Scott v. KeyCorp, 247 A.D.2d 722, 669 N.Y.S.2d 76 (3d Dep't 1998)
  18 ALR5th 307—§ 38
Scott v. K-Mart Store No. 3366, 144 A.D.2d 958, 534 N.Y.S.2d 42 (4th Dep't 1988)
  23 ALR6th 697—§ 13
Scott v. Labor & Industrial Relations Com., 757 S.W.2d 635 (Mo. App. 1988)
  15 ALR5th 391—§ 30
Scott v. Land Span Motor, Inc., 781 F. Supp. 1115 (D.S.C. 1991)
  99 ALR5th 65—§ 13
Scott v. Leigh, 355 S.W.2d 798 (Tex. Civ. App. Eastland 1962)
  30 ALR5th 571—§ 2, 8, 32
Scott v. Leonard, 119 Vt. 86, 119 A.2d 691 (1956)
  62 ALR5th 219—§ 21
Scott v. Lindsay, 2007 WL 2585072 (E.D. N.Y. 2007)
  46 ALR6th 63—§ 4 to 6, 10, 12
Scott v. Little, 617 A.2d 1025 (Me. 1992)
  57 ALR5th 141—§ 18
Scott v. Long Valley Farm Kentucky, Inc., 804 S.W.2d 15 (Ky. App. 1991)
  62 ALR5th 219—§ 16, 53
Scott v. Louisiana Creamery, Inc., 183 So. 2d 108 (La. App. 1st Cir. 1965)
  26 ALR5th 401—§ 27
Scott v. Macy, 402 F.2d 644 (D.C. Cir. 1968)
  96 ALR5th 391—§ 2, 7, 35
Scott v. Marshall County Bd. of Zoning Appeals, 696 N.E.2d 884 (Ind. Ct. App. 1998)
  4 ALR6th 263—§ 40
  77 ALR6th 393—§ 35, 60

Scott v. Mayflower Home Imp. Corp., 2001 WL 34136362 (N.J. Super. Ct. Law Div. 2001)
115 ALR5th 709—§ 4, 5
Scott v. McGaugh, 211 Kan. 323, 506 P.2d 1155 (1973)
3 ALR5th 1—§ 3, 40
Scott v. Min-Aqua Bats Water Ski Club, Inc., 79 Wis. 2d 316, 255 N.W.2d 536 (1977)
35 ALR5th 731—§ 7
Scott v. Montgomery County Bd. of Educ., 120 F.3d 262 (4th Cir. 1997)
100 ALR6th 563—§ 3, 5, 7, 12, 21, 30
Scott v. Moore, 98 Va. 668, 37 S.E. 342 (1900)
62 ALR5th 219—§ 5, 44
Scott v. Nassau County, 43 Misc. 2d 648, 252 N.Y.S.2d 135 (Sup 1964)
111 ALR5th 1—§ 26
Scott v. News-Herald, 25 Ohio St. 3d 243, 25 Ohio B.R. 302, 496 N.E.2d 699, 13 Media L. R. 1241 (1986)
44 ALR5th 193—§ 2, 29, 32, 50, 51
Scott v. Owings, 223 Pa. Super. 481, 302 A.2d 423 (1973)
76 ALR5th 337—§ 13
Scott v. Pacific Gas & Electric Co., 11 Cal. 4th 454, 46 Cal. Rptr. 2d 427, 904 P.2d 834, 11 I.E.R. Cas. (BNA) 161, 131 Lab. Cas. (CCH) ¶ 58045 (1995)
104 ALR5th 1—§ 3
105 ALR5th 351—§ 3
Scott v. Parker, 216 Ala. 321, 113 So. 495 (1927)
19 ALR5th 622—§ 29, 36, 49
Scott v. Petett, 63 Wash. App. 50, 816 P.2d 1229 (Div. 1 1991)
117 ALR5th 155—§ 3, 12
Scott v. Porter, 340 S.C. 158, 530 S.E.2d 389 (Ct. App. 2000)
12 ALR5th 195—§ 29
Scott v. Raines, 1962 OK CR 81, 373 P.2d 267 (Okla. Crim. App. 1962)
97 ALR5th 293—§ 2, 3

Scott v. Rapides Parish School Bd., 732 So. 2d 749, 135 Ed. Law Rep. 304 (La. Ct. App. 3d Cir. 1999)
66 ALR5th 1—§ 23
Scott v. Reedy, 5 Ohio Dec. Reprint 388, 1 WL Bull 331, 5 Am L. Rec 367 (1876)
9 ALR5th 933—§ 3, 8
Scott v. Regency Developers, Inc., 28 Conn. L. Rptr. 554, 2000 WL 1781846 (Conn. Super. Ct. 2000)
101 ALR5th 447—§ 5
Scott v. RKO Radio Pictures, Inc., 240 F.2d 87 (CA9 Cal. 1957)
38 ALR5th 39—§ 4
Scott v. Robertson, 583 P.2d 188 (Alaska 1978)
119 ALR5th 121—§ 3, 11
125 ALR5th 193—§ 5
Scott v. Romans, 2005 WL 1469371 (Cal. App. 6th Dist. 2005)
97 ALR6th 83—§ 168
Scott v. Ryan, 686 F.3d 1130 (9th Cir. 2012)
102 ALR6th 417—§ 3, 69
Scott v. Saint John's Church in the Wilderness, 2013 WL 799559 (U.S. 2013)
86 ALR6th 577—§ 1, 15, 40
Scott v. School Bd. of Alachua County, 324 F.3d 1246, 175 Ed. Law Rep. 88 (11th Cir. 2003)
66 ALR6th 493—§ 5, 8
Scott v. Scott, 45 So. 2d 878 (Fla. 1950)
32 ALR5th 673—§ 4
Scott v. Scott, 80 S.W.3d 447 (Ky. Ct. App. 2002)
86 ALR6th 1—§ 25
Scott v. Scott, 107 Nev. 837, 822 P.2d 654 (Nev 1991)
17 ALR5th 143—§ 3
Scott v. Scott, 121 Ariz. 492, 591 P.2d 980 (1979)
17 ALR5th 366—§ 9
Scott v. Scott, 154 Ga. 659, 115 S.E. 2 (1922)
71 ALR5th 99—§ 3, 6

Scott v. Scott, 223 Neb. 354, 389 N.W.2d 567 (1986)
70 ALR5th 377—§ 5
123 ALR5th 565—§ 22
7 ALR6th 411—§ 16, 44

Scott v. Scott, 227 Ga. App. 346, 489 S.E.2d 117 (1997)
95 ALR5th 533—§ 5
124 ALR5th 203—§ 5

Scott v. Scott, 401 So. 2d 92 (Ala. App. 1981)
17 ALR5th 366—§ 31

Scott v. Scott, 433 S.W.2d 631 (Ky. 1968)
4 ALR5th 403—§ 3

Scott v. Scott, 519 So. 2d 351 (La. Ct. App. 2d Cir. 1988)
59 ALR6th 433—§ 6, 36, 55

Scott v. Scott, 665 So. 2d 760 (La. Ct. App. 1st Cir. 1995)
65 ALR5th 591—§ 2, 3
95 ALR5th 533—§ 4
124 ALR5th 203—§ 4

Scott v. Scott, 2001 OK 9, 19 P.3d 273 (Okla. 2001)
69 ALR5th 1—§ 3

Scott v. Scott, 2002-Ohio-4974, 2002 WL 31105403 (Ohio Ct. App. 2d Dist. Greene County 2002)
11 ALR6th 125—§ 3, 26, 28

Scott v. Scott, 2004-Ohio-1405, 2004 WL 557316 (Ohio Ct. App. 10th Dist. Franklin County 2004)
59 ALR6th 433—§ 74, 99

Scott v. Scott, 2005 WL 1412453 (Ky. 2005)
53 ALR6th 419—§ 49

Scott v. Scott, 2008-Ohio-530, 2008 WL 351665 (Ohio Ct. App. 11th Dist. Trumbull County 2008)
39 ALR6th 205—§ 4

Scott v. Service Pipe Line Co., 159 Neb. 36, 65 N.W.2d 219 (1954)
27 ALR5th 174—§ 61

Scott v. Singleton, 378 So. 2d 885 (Fla. App. D1 1979)
15 ALR5th 692—§ 29, 34

Scott v. Sisters of St. Francis Health Services, Inc., 645 F. Supp. 1465, 42 BNA FEP Cas. 58 (N.D. Ill. 1986)
28 ALR5th 107—§ 35

Scott v. Somers, 42 Conn. L. Rptr. 657, 2007 WL 241067 (Conn. Super. Ct. 2007)
53 ALR6th 419—§ 16, 32, 49

Scott v. Somers, 97 Conn. App. 46, 903 A.2d 663 (2006)
59 ALR6th 161—§ 4, 41
60 ALR6th 193—§ 15

Scott v. Somers, 2006 WL 2865707 (Conn. Super. Ct. 2006)
53 ALR6th 419—§ 15, 46

Scott v. State, 7 A.3d 471 (Del. 2010)
72 ALR6th 1—§ 6

Scott v. State, 11 Misc. 3d 1059(A), 815 N.Y.S.2d 496 (Ct. Cl. 2006)
53 ALR6th 305—§ 15

Scott v. State, 29 Ala. App. 110, 192 So. 288 (1939)
57 ALR6th 445—§ 41

Scott v. State, 46 So. 3d 529 (Fla. 2009)
72 ALR6th 227—§ 51

Scott v. State, 55 S.W.3d 593 (Tex. Crim. App. 2001)
97 ALR5th 293—§ 2

Scott v. State, 61 Md. App. 599, 487 A.2d 1204 (1985)
103 ALR6th 507—§ 23

Scott v. State, 77 Ark. 455, 92 S.W. 241 (1906)
41 ALR5th 1—§ 3, 4

Scott v. State, 80 S.W.3d 306 (Tex. App. Fort Worth 2002)
99 ALR6th 295—§ 7

Scott v. State, 88 Nev. 682, 504 P.2d 10 (1972)
99 ALR6th 295—§ 10

Scott v. State, 90 Tex. Crim. 100, 233 S.W. 1097, 16 A.L.R. 1420 (1921)
26 ALR5th 1—§ 3, 5

Scott v. State, 108 Miss. 464, 66 So. 973 (1915)
81 ALR5th 563—§ 3, 8

Scott v. State, 165 S.W.3d 27 (Tex. App. Austin 2005)
32 ALR6th 1—§ 11
Scott v. State, 170 Ga. App. 409, 317 S.E.2d 282 (1984)
37 ALR5th 1—§ 3
Scott v. State, 178 Ga. App. 222, 343 S.E.2d 117 (1986)
19 ALR6th 115—§ 5, 10
Scott v. State, 207 So. 2d 493 (Fla. Dist. Ct. App. 2d Dist. 1968)
70 ALR5th 587—§ 3
Scott v. State, 213 Ga. App. 84, 444 S.E.2d 96 (1994)
103 ALR5th 463—§ 5
Scott v. State, 214 Ga. 154, 103 S.E.2d 545 (1958)
24 ALR5th 465—§ 23
Scott v. State, 218 Neb. 195, 352 N.W.2d 890 (1984)
97 ALR5th 1—§ 2
106 ALR5th 111—§ 2, 13
108 ALR5th 1—§ 2
Scott v. State, 230 Ga. App. 522, 496 S.E.2d 494 (1998)
26 ALR5th 1—§ 44
Scott v. State, 243 Ga. App. 383, 532 S.E.2d 141 (2000)
5 ALR5th 243—§ 31, 45, 46
Scott v. State, 281 Ga. 373, 637 S.E.2d 652 (2006)
32 ALR6th 1—§ 11
Scott v. State, 281 Ga. App. 813, 637 S.E.2d 751 (2006)
67 ALR6th 103—§ 5
Scott v. State, 337 So. 2d 1342 (Ala. Crim. App. 1976)
55 ALR5th 125—§ 3, 7, 12, 14, 22
Scott v. State, 347 Ark. 767, 67 S.W.3d 567 (2002)
15 ALR6th 515—§ 14
Scott v. State, 366 Md. 121, 782 A.2d 862 (2001)
15 ALR6th 515—§ 16, 22, 28, 34
Scott v. State, 374 So. 2d 316 (Ala. 1979)
29 ALR5th 59—§ 3, 55

Scott v. State, 406 So. 2d 100 (Fla. Dist. Ct. App. 3d Dist. 1981)
21 ALR6th 771—§ 5
Scott v. State, 501 So. 2d 1273 (Ala. Crim. App. 1986)
37 ALR5th 703—§ 5
Scott v. State, 521 A.2d 235 (Del. Sup. 1987)
39 ALR5th 283—§ 4, 64
Scott v. State, 618 So. 2d 1386 (Fla. Dist. Ct. App. 2d Dist. 1993)
115 ALR5th 509—§ 9, 15
Scott v. State, 788 N.W.2d 497 (Minn. 2010)
92 ALR6th 549—§ 7, 15
Scott v. State, 825 S.W.2d 521 (Tex. App. Dallas 1992)
4 ALR5th 1—§ 14, 15
Scott v. State, 2003 WL 21538033 (Del. Super. Ct. 2003)
122 ALR5th 439—§ 3
Scott v. State, 2004 WL 1277027 (Miss. 2004)
122 ALR5th 145—§ 23
Scott v. State, 2011 WL 5964349 (Fla. Dist. Ct. App. 4th Dist. 2011)
72 ALR6th 227—§ 24
Scott v. State Acc. Ins. Fund, 42 Or. App. 595, 600 P.2d 967 (1979)
11 ALR6th 351—§ 8
Scott v. State Bar Examining Committee, 220 Conn. 812, 601 A.2d 1021 (1992)
3 ALR6th 49—§ 4, 17
Scott v. Steelman, 953 S.W.2d 147 (Mo. Ct. App. S.D. 1997)
36 ALR5th 377—§ 3
Scott v. Strack, 164 F.3d 619 (2d Cir. 1998)
81 ALR6th 505—§ 30
Scott v. Sulzer Carbomedics, Inc., 141 F. Supp. 2d 154, 85 Fair Empl. Prac. Cas. (BNA) 1362, 143 Lab. Cas. (CCH) ¶ 34292 (D. Mass. 2001)
52 ALR6th 271—§ 5
Scott v. Swift & Co., 214 N.C. 580, 200 S.E. 21 (1938)
2 ALR5th 1—§ 3

Scott v. Sylvester, 225 Va. 304, 302 S.E.2d 30 (1983)

112 ALR5th 185—§ 4, 8

118 ALR5th 385—§ 4, 14

119 ALR5th 445—§ 3, 8 to 10

Scott v. Texas Dept. of Criminal Justice-Institutional Div., 2008 WL 4938265 (Tex. App. Corpus Christi 2008)

45 ALR6th 493—§ 12

Scott v. Texas State Bd. of Medical Examiners, 384 S.W.2d 686 (Tex. 1964)

19 ALR6th 577—§ 15

Scott v. Thor Corp., 283 A.D. 832, 128 N.Y.S.2d 909 (3d Dep't 1954)

104 ALR6th 97—§ 4

Scott v. Thornton, 104 Tenn. 547, 58 S.W. 236 (1900)

67 ALR5th 479—§ 7

Scott v. Times-Mirror Co., 181 Cal. 345, 184 P. 672, 12 A.L.R. 1007 (1919)

12 ALR5th 195—§ 48

Scott v. Topeka Performing Arts Center, Inc., 69 F. Supp. 2d 1325 (D. Kan. 1999)

104 ALR5th 1—§ 2, 3, 5

105 ALR5th 351—§ 2

Scott v. Total Renal Care, Inc., 2005 WL 1680677 (E.D. Mich. 2005)

10 ALR6th 531—§ 16

Scott v. Travis, 2007 WL 3124683 (E.D. La. 2007)

89 ALR6th 1—§ 117

Scott v. Universal Fidelity Corp., 1999 WL 684122 (N.D. Ill. 1999)

79 ALR5th 587—§ 6

Scott v. U.S., 392 A.2d 4 (Dist. Col. App. 1978)

11 ALR5th 218—§ 2, 9, 13

Scott v. U.S., 434 F.2d 11 (5th Cir. 1970)

76 ALR5th 485—§ 3, 8

Scott v. U.S., 559 A.2d 745 (D.C. 1989)

86 ALR6th 321—§ 13

Scott v. Vasquez, 2004 WL 746259 (C.D. Cal. 2004)

89 ALR6th 1—§ 27

Scott v. Village of Athens, 1 Ohio N.P. 94, 1 Ohio Dec. 84, 1894 WL 1370 (C.P. 1894)

114 ALR5th 561—§ 22

Scott v. Vought Aircraft Industries, Inc., 2007 WL 2983824 (Tenn. Workers' Comp. Panel 2007)

99 ALR6th 643—§ 17

Scott v. Wagoner, 400 S.E.2d 556, 14 A.L.R.5th 1031 (W. Va. 1990)

14 ALR5th 557—§ 2, 6, 16, 24

Scott v. Waldeck, 12 Neb. 5, 10 N.W. 413 (1881)

59 ALR5th 1—§ 5

Scott v. Watkins, 25 Colo. App. 340, 138 P. 432 (1914)

5 ALR5th 422—§ 3

Scott v. Watkins, 61 Colo. 244, 157 P. 3 (1916)

5 ALR5th 422—§ 3

Scott v. Watson, 278 Md. 160, 359 A.2d 548 (1976)

43 ALR5th 207—§ 5, 6, 36, 51

Scott v. W.C.A.B. (Jeanes Hosp.), 732 A.2d 29 (Pa. Commw. Ct. 1999)

97 ALR5th 1—§ 2, 4

106 ALR5th 111—§ 17, 19

108 ALR5th 1—§ 20

Scott v. Wellington, 2009 WL 5511175 (M.D. Pa. 2009)

68 ALR6th 331—§ 19, 21

Scott v. West, 64 Ky. 23, 1 Bush 23, 1866 WL 3507 (1866)

102 ALR5th 525—§ 44

Scott v. Western Intern. Surplus Sales, Inc., 267 Or. 512, 517 P.2d 661 (1973)

115 ALR5th 709—§ 2

117 ALR5th 155—§ 2, 5, 8

Scott v. Yurkewecz, 234 A.D.2d 673, 650 N.Y.S.2d 461 (3d Dep't 1996)

48 ALR5th 129—§ 15

50 ALR5th 1—§ 12

Scott & Williams, Inc. v. Board of Taxation, 117 N.H. 189, 372 A.2d 1305 (1977)

80 ALR6th 325—§ 21

Scott By and Through Scott v. Pacific West Mountain Resort, 119 Wash. 2d 484, 834 P.2d 6 (1992)

75 ALR6th 1—§ 4, 6, 9, 13, 22

Scott Co. of California v. Blount, Inc., 20 Cal. 4th 1103, 86 Cal. Rptr. 2d 614, 979 P.2d 974 (1999)

119 ALR5th 121—§ 5

34 ALR6th 431—§ 4

Scott Co. of California v. United States Fidelity & Guaranty Ins. Co., 107 Cal. App. 4th 197, 132 Cal. Rptr. 2d 89 (6th Dist. 2003)

81 ALR6th 363—§ 4

Scott Fetzer Co., Halex Div., State ex rel. v. Indus. Comm., 81 Ohio St. 3d 462, 1998-Ohio-457, 692 N.E.2d 195 (1998)

31 ALR6th 199—§ 46

Scott Galvanizing, Inc. v. Northwest EnviroServices, Inc., 63 Wash. App. 802, 822 P.2d 345 (1992)

23 ALR5th 241—§ 10

Scott-Groff Lumber Co. v. Independent School Dist., 112 Minn. 474, 128 N.W. 672 (1910)

54 ALR5th 649—§ 3

Scott-Huff Ins. Agency v. Sandusky, 318 Ark. 613, 887 S.W.2d 516 (1994)

8 ALR6th 549—§ 4

Scottish Heritable Trust, PLC v. Peat Marwick Main & Co., 81 F.3d 606, 35 FR Serv. 3d 284 (CA5 Tex. 1996)

48 ALR5th 389—§ 3

Scottish Rite Cathedral Ass'n of Los Angeles v. City of Los Angeles, 156 Cal. App. 4th 108, 67 Cal. Rptr. 3d 207 (2d Dist. 2007)

46 ALR6th 495—§ 8

Scottish Union & Nat. Ins. Co. v. Weeks Drug Co., 55 Tex. Civ. App. 263, 118 S.W. 1086 (1909)

16 ALR5th 412—§ 32, 34

Scott K., In re, 24 Cal. 3d 395, 155 Cal. Rptr. 671, 595 P.2d 105 (1979)

55 ALR5th 125—§ 2, 3, 5 to 7

Scotto v. Dilbert Bros., 263 A.D. 1016, 33 N.Y.S.2d 835 (2d Dep't 1942)

97 ALR6th 567—§ 4, 12

Scott Paper Co. v. Fort Howard Paper Co., 343 F. Supp. 229 (E.D. Wis. 1972)

104 ALR5th 523—§ 4

Scott Paper Co. v. Hughes, 628 So. 2d 638 (Ala. Civ. App. 1993)

99 ALR6th 643—§ 17

Scott, People ex rel. v. Cardet Intern., Inc., 24 Ill. App. 3d 740, 321 N.E.2d 386 (1st Dist. 1974)

63 ALR5th 1—§ 14

Scott, People ex rel. v. Grivetti, 50 Ill. 2d 156, 277 N.E.2d 881 (1971)

114 ALR5th 311—§ 4, 8

Scotts Bluff County v. State, 133 Neb. 508, 276 N.W. 185 (1937)

45 ALR5th 173—§ 5

Scottsboro, City of v. Johnson, 436 So. 2d 859 (Ala. 1983)

50 ALR6th 95—§ 5

Scott S., By Peter and Winifred S. v. Com., Dept. of Educ., 99 Pa. Commw. 57, 512 A.2d 790, 33 Ed. Law Rep. 1167 (1986)

115 ALR5th 183—§ 2, 3, 12, 18, 25

Scotts Co. LLC v. Liberty Mut. Ins. Co., 2007 WL 1723509 (S.D. Ohio 2007)

27 ALR6th 565—§ 2, 17

29 ALR6th 167—§ 3

Scottsdale v. Scottsdale Associated Merchants, Inc, 120 Ariz. 4, 583 P.2d 891 (1978)

8 ALR5th 391—§ 4

Scottsdale, City of v. Municipal Court of City of Tempe, 90 Ariz. 393, 368 P.2d 637 (1962)

92 ALR5th 517—§ 11

Scottsdale Healthcare, Inc. v. Arizona Health Care Cost Containment System Admin., 202 Ariz. 365, 45 P.3d 688 (Ct. App. Div. 1 2002)

113 ALR5th 95—§ 5, 8

Scottsdale Healthcare, Inc. v. Arizona Health Care Cost Containment System Admin., 206 Ariz. 1, 75 P.3d 91 (2003)
113 ALR5th 95—§ 8

Scottsdale Ins. Co. v. American Empire Surplus Lines Ins. Co., 811 F. Supp. 210 (D.C. Md. 1993)
14 ALR5th 695—§ 10, 25

Scottsdale Ins. Co. v. Orange Beach, 618 So. 2d 1323 (Ala. 1993)
14 ALR5th 695—§ 19

Scottsdale Ins. Co. v. Texas Sec. Concepts and Investigation, 173 F.3d 941 (5th Cir. 1999)
44 ALR5th 91—§ 4

Scottsdale Ins. Co. v. Tolliver, 2005 OK 93, 127 P.3d 611 (Okla. 2005)
69 ALR6th 415—§ 13, 51, 70

Scottsdale Ins. Co. v. Zimmerman & Kahanowitch, 2004 WL 1567763 (Cal. App. 2d Dist. 2004)
50 ALR6th 53—§ 4, 5
64 ALR6th 473—§ 8, 9

Scottsdale Pub., Inc. v. Superior Court of County of Maricopa, 159 Ariz. 72, 764 P.2d 1131, 10 Ariz. Adv. Rep. 16, 16 Media L. R. 1033 (App. 1988)
19 ALR5th 1—§ 98, 100, 101

Scott's Estate, In re, 150 Cal. App. 2d 590, 310 P.2d 46 (2d Dist. 1957)
112 ALR5th 399—§ 5

Scott's Liquid Gold-Inc. v. Lexington Ins. Co., 97 F. Supp. 2d 1226 (D. Colo. 2000)
23 ALR5th 75—§ 8

Scott, State ex rel. v. Cleveland, 112 Ohio St. 3d 324, 2006-Ohio-6573, 859 N.E.2d 923 (2006)
26 ALR6th 179—§ 8, 9

Scott, State ex rel. v. Uniroyal, Inc., 25 Ohio St. 3d 35, 494 N.E.2d 1122 (1986)
31 ALR6th 199—§ 47

Scotts Valley Circuits, Inc. v. Aetna Ins. Co., 1995 WL 854757 (Cal. Super. Ct. Trial Div. 1995)
89 ALR5th 1—§ 10

Scott Township, Appeal of, 31 Pa. Cmwlth. 505, 377 A.2d 826 (1977)
5 ALR5th 56—§ 3, 4, 15

Scott X, In re, 184 App. Div. 2d 866, 585 N.Y.S.2d 115 (3d Dep't 1992)
53 ALR5th 499—§ 3

Scoufos v. Fuller, 280 P.2d 720 (Okla. 1954)
32 ALR5th 673—§ 3, 6

Scouten v. Horace Mann Ins. Co., 765 F. Supp. 639 (D.C. Mont 1991)
40 ALR5th 603—§ 9

Scovel v. Pascagoula, 233 Miss. 198, 101 So. 2d 537 (1958)
5 ALR5th 875—§ 4

Scoville v. Trustees of Schools, 65 Ill. 523 (1872)
53 ALR5th 287—§ 3

S.C.P., In re Interest of, 2001 WL 803922 (Iowa Ct. App. 2001)
117 ALR5th 349—§ 11

SCQuARE Intern., Ltd. v. BBDO Atlanta, Inc., 455 F. Supp. 2d 1347 (N.D. Ga. 2006)
87 ALR6th 1—§ 68

Scranton v. Hutter, 40 A.D.2d 296, 339 N.Y.S.2d 708 (4th Dep't 1973)
69 ALR5th 1—§ 3, 5

Scranton-Averell, Inc. v. Hosler, 2000 WL 1753438 (Ohio Ct. App. 8th Dist. Cuyahoga County 2000)
107 ALR5th 311—§ 4

Scranton Lackawanna Trust Co. v. Bevan, 54 Lack. Jur. 99 (Pa. C.P. 1953)
49 ALR6th 505—§ 5

Scranton Times, L.P. v. Wilkes-Barre Pub. Co., 37 Media L. Rep. (BNA) 2428, 92 U.S.P.Q.2d 1269, 2009 WL 3100963 (M.D. Pa. 2009)
76 ALR6th 289—§ 5
77 ALR6th 543—§ 11

Screen Actors Guild, Inc. v. Cory, 91 Cal. App. 3d 111, 154 Cal. Rptr. 77 (2d Dist. 1979)
29 ALR6th 507—§ 10, 70

For assistance, call 1-800-328-4880

Screen Actors Guild, Inc. v. Magellan Pictures, Inc., 113 Lab. Cas. (CCH) ¶ 11777, 1989 WL 120199 (S.D. N.Y. 1989)
66 ALR5th 611—§ 3

Screven v. Drs. Gruskin & Lucas, P.C., 227 Ga. App. 756, 490 S.E.2d 422 (1997)
17 ALR6th 159—§ 6, 25

Scribner v. Ally Bank, N.A., 2012 WL 2999776 (D. Minn. 2012)
86 ALR6th 411—§ 5

Scribner v. Berry, 489 A.2d 8 (Me. 1985)
36 ALR5th 395—§ 3, 10, 12, 15

Scribner v. Gordon, 248 A.D. 925, 290 N.Y.S. 258 (3d Dep't 1936)
40 ALR6th 99—§ 28

Scribner v. Surapaneni, 2006 WL 3761976 (E.D. Tex. 2006)
89 ALR6th 701—§ 10

Scribner v. Waffle House, Inc., 14 F. Supp. 2d 873 (N.D. Tex. 1998)
12 ALR5th 195—§ 49
14 ALR5th 242—§ 42

Scribner v. Waffle House, Inc., 976 F. Supp. 439, 70 Empl. Prac. Dec. (CCH) ¶ 44640 (N.D. Tex. 1997)
12 ALR5th 195—§ 6, 49

Scrimpsher, In re, 17 B.R. 999 (Bankr. N.D. N.Y. 1982)
117 ALR5th 155—§ 3

Scripps Texas Newspapers, L.P. v. Belalcazar, 99 S.W.3d 829, 32 Media L. Rep. (BNA) 1050 (Tex. App. Corpus Christi 2003)
16 ALR6th 1—§ 3, 35
22 ALR6th 553—§ 8, 24

Scriven v. Scriven, 153 Neb. 655, 45 N.W.2d 760 (1951)
3 ALR5th 590—§ 6

Scrivener v. Com., 539 S.W.2d 291 (Ky. 1976)
99 ALR6th 295—§ 7, 20

Scrivener v. Sky's the Limit, Inc., 68 F. Supp. 2d 277 (S.D. N.Y. 1999)
92 ALR5th 473—§ 3, 15

Scrivener v. State, 441 N.E.2d 954 (Ind. 1982)
70 ALR6th 361—§ 15

Scriver v. Lister, 235 Ga. App. 487, 510 S.E.2d 59 (1998)
8 ALR6th 439—§ 6

Scrivner v. Hobson, 854 S.W.2d 148 (Tex. App. Houston 1st Dist. 1993)
71 ALR6th 249—§ 3

Scrivnor v. State, 113 Tex. Crim. 194, 20 S.W.2d 416 (1928)
97 ALR5th 293—§ 2, 3

Scroggin v. National Lumber Co., 41 Neb. 195, 59 N.W. 548 (1894)
46 ALR5th 1—§ 9

Scroggins v. Bill Furst Florist And Greenhouse, Inc., 2004-Ohio-79, 2004 WL 41716 (Ohio Ct. App. 2d Dist. Montgomery County 2004)
38 ALR6th 541—§ 24

Scroggins v. City of Topeka, Kan., 2 F. Supp. 2d 1362 (D. Kan. 1998)
70 ALR6th 513—§ 13
71 ALR6th 471—§ 11

Scroggins v. Dahne, 335 Md. 688, 645 A.2d 1160 (1994)
19 ALR5th 405—§ 3

Scroggins v. Davis, 346 Fed. Appx. 504 (11th Cir. 2009)
65 ALR6th 93—§ 61

Scroggins v. McDonough, 2009 WL 651804 (M.D. Fla. 2009)
71 ALR6th 625—§ 3, 19

Scroggins v. Sewerage & Water Bd., 533 So. 2d 132 (La. App. 4th Cir. 1988)
15 ALR5th 119—§ 16, 18

Scroggins v. State, 198 Ga. App. 29, 401 S.E.2d 13 (1990)
12 ALR5th 149—§ 12, 22
13 ALR5th 628—§ 4 to 6, 10

Scroggins v. State, 237 Ga. App. 122, 514 S.E.2d 252 (1999)
71 ALR5th 637—§ 7, 10
65 ALR6th 537—§ 43

Scroggins v. State, 312 Ark. 106, 848 S.W.2d 400 (1993)
8 ALR6th 265—§ 4

Scroggins v. State, 604 S.W.2d 699 (Mo. Ct. App. W.D. 1980)

72 ALR5th 109—§ 6
Scroggins v. State, 2001 WL 837946 (Tex. App. Austin 2001)

8 ALR6th 265—§ 10
Scroggins v. Templeton, 890 So. 2d 1017 (Ala. Civ. App. 2003)

100 ALR6th 1—§ 22
Scroggs v. Coast Community College Dist., 193 Cal. App. 3d 1399, 239 Cal. Rptr. 916 (4th Dist. 1987)

54 ALR5th 513—§ 4
Scronce v. Howard Bros. Discount Stores, Inc., 679 F.2d 1204 (5th Cir. 1982)

96 ALR5th 239—§ 10
Scruggins v. Jones, 207 Ky. 636, 269 S.W. 743 (1925)

2 ALR5th 1—§ 37
Scruggs v. Com., 566 S.W.2d 405 (Ky. 1978)

104 ALR5th 357—§ 6
Scruggs v. Haynes, 252 Cal. App. 2d 256, 60 Cal. Rptr. 355 (1st Dist. 1967)

12 ALR5th 195—§ 10
Scruggs v. International Indem. Co., 233 Ga. App. 772, 505 S.E.2d 267 (1998)

16 ALR6th 603—§ 5
Scruggs v. Meriden Bd. of Educ., 2007 WL 2318851 (D. Conn. 2007)

98 ALR6th 599—§ 16, 37, 55, 59
Scruggs v. Otteman, 640 P.2d 259 (Colo. App. 1981)

9 ALR5th 746—§ 3, 6
Scruggs v. State Farm Mut. Auto. Ins. Co., 62 P.3d 989 (Ariz. Ct. App. Div. 1 2003)

103 ALR5th 1—§ 6
Scruggs v. U.S., 959 F. Supp. 1537 (S.D. Fla. 1997)

64 ALR5th 235—§ 3
Scruggs v. Wal-Mart Stores, Inc., 2000 WL 371198 (Tenn. Sp. Workers' Comp. 2000)

86 ALR5th 295—§ 9
Scruggs & Echols v. City of Decatur, 155 Ala. 616, 46 So. 989 (1908)

81 ALR6th 363—§ 4, 5, 10
Scrum v. Davis, 141 Misc. 46, 251 N.Y.S. 746 (1931)

62 ALR5th 219—§ 39, 53
Scrutton v. Sacramento County, 275 Cal. App. 2d 412, 79 Cal. Rptr. 872 (3d Dist. 1969)

73 ALR5th 223—§ 5
S.C. Ryan, Inc. v. Lowe, 753 P.2d 580 (Wyo. 1988)

86 ALR6th 321—§ 6
S.C.S., In re, 2008 WL 1973570 (Tex. App. Dallas 2008)

57 ALR6th 163—§ 37
SCSC Corp. v. Allied Mut. Ins. Co., 515 N.W.2d 588 (Minn. Ct. App. 1994)

89 ALR5th 1—§ 10
SCSC Corp. v. Allied Mut. Ins. Co., 536 N.W.2d 305 (Minn. 1995)

48 ALR5th 355—§ 2, 4, 5
S.C., State in Interest of v. D.N.C., 639 So. 2d 426 (La. Ct. App. 2d Cir. 1994)

92 ALR5th 379—§ 16
12 ALR6th 417—§ 19
S.C., State of v. Katzenbach, 383 U.S. 301, 86 S. Ct. 803, 15 L. Ed. 2d 769 (1966)

62 ALR6th 517—§ 6, 7, 31, 70
Scucchi v. Woodruff, 503 S.W.2d 356 (Tex. Civ. App. 1973)

40 ALR5th 697—§ 2
Scudder v. Scudder, 55 Wash. 2d 454, 348 P.2d 225 (1960)

14 ALR5th 557—§ 6, 27, 28
Scudder v. Town of Greenwich, 127 Conn. 71, 14 A.2d 728 (1940)

90 ALR5th 619—§ 5
Scudella v. Illinois Farmers Ins. Co., 174 Ill. App. 3d 245, 123 Ill. Dec. 673, 528 N.E.2d 218 (1st Dist. 1988)

31 ALR5th 116—§ 3
Scuderi v. Niagara Mohawk Power Corp., 243 A.D.2d 1049, 663 N.Y.S.2d 912 (3d Dep't 1997)

98 ALR6th 231—§ 18, 31
Scugoza v. State, 949 S.W.2d 360 (Tex. App. San Antonio 1997)

---

57 ALR5th 315—§ 3, 5, 9, 11

Sculimbrene v. Reno, 158 F. Supp. 2d 8 (D.D.C. 2001)

42 ALR6th 353—§ 14

Scull v. Eilenberg, 94 N.J. Eq. 759, 121 A 788 (Ct. Err. & App. 1923)

119 ALR5th 519—§ 11

Scull v. Eilenberg, 119 A. 275 (N.J. Ch. 1922)

25 ALR5th 233—§ 19

Sculles v. American Environmental Products, Inc., 227 Ill. App. 3d 741, 169 Ill. Dec. 784, 592 N.E.2d 271 (1st Dist. 1992)

13 ALR5th 289—§ 34

Scullin Steel Co. v. Paccar, Inc., 708 S.W.2d 756, 1 U.C.C.R.S.2d 1172 (Mo. App. 1986)

37 ALR5th 459—§ 10

Scullin Steel Co. v. Whiteside, 682 S.W.2d 1 (Mo. Ct. App. E.D. 1984)

11 ALR6th 351—§ 23

Scullion v. Hackworth, 57 Del. 299, 199 A.2d 563 (Sup. 1964)

21 ALR5th 82—§ 3, 28

Scullion v. Wisconsin Power & Light Co., 241 Wis. 2d 49, 2001 WI App 31, 622 N.W.2d 770 (Ct. App. 2000)

91 ALR5th 517—§ 5

Scully, In re Claim of, 88 App. Div. 2d 689, 451 N.Y.S.2d 251 (3d Dep't 1982)

33 ALR5th 643—§ 12

Scully v. Director, Div. of Taxation, 19 N.J. Tax 553, 2001 WL 1677447 (2001)

2 ALR6th 1—§ 54

Scully v. Guardian Life Ins. Co., 2008 WL 723835 (N.J. Super. Ct. App. Div. 2008)

61 ALR6th 239—§ 19

Scully v. Otis Elevator Co., 2 Ill. App. 3d 185, 275 N.E.2d 905 (1st Dist. 1971)

63 ALR5th 285—§ 2, 3, 6

Scully v. Scully, 122 N.J. Super. 94, 299 A.2d 93 (Ch. Div. 1972)

101 ALR6th 455—§ 12

Scully v. Scully, 213 Neb. 857, 331 N.W.2d 801 (1983)

11 ALR5th 259—§ 8, 32

104 ALR5th 605—§ 3, 8

Scully v. U. S., 108 Ct. Cl. 310, 70 F. Supp. 239, 35 A.F.T.R. (P-H) ¶ 929 (1947)

60 ALR5th 459—§ 2, 3, 7, 12

Scurfield v. Federal Laboratories, 335 Pa. 145, 6 A.2d 559 (1939)

96 ALR5th 239—§ 31

Scurlock Oil Co. v. Smithwick, 724 S.W.2d 1 (Tex. 1986)

22 ALR5th 483—§ 2, 3

Scurry v. State, 490 So. 2d 223 (Fla. Dist. Ct. App. 2d Dist. 1986)

92 ALR5th 35—§ 25

Scurto v. Siegrist, 598 So. 2d 507 (La. Ct. App. 1st Cir. 1992)

11 ALR6th 587—§ 6, 8, 27

Scutti v. Daniel E. Adache & Associates Architects, P.A., 515 So. 2d 1023, 12 FLW 2456 (Fla. App. D4 1987)

60 ALR5th 669—§ 6

Scuzzaro v. Loma Linda University Medical Center, 2003 WL 22683416 (Cal. App. 4th Dist. 2003)

97 ALR6th 83—§ 126, 127, 132, 152, 160

S.C.W., Ex parte, 826 So. 2d 844 (Ala. 2001)

28 ALR6th 349—§ 30

Scyphers v. H & H Lumber, 237 Mont. 424, 774 P.2d 393 (1989)

63 ALR6th 187—§ 9

S.D., In re, 349 S.W.3d 76 (Tex. App. El Paso 2010)

69 ALR6th 1—§ 26

S.D., In re, 2010 WL 4676921 (Tex. App. El Paso 2010)

69 ALR6th 1—§ 20, 21

S.D., In the Interest of, 429 Pa. Super. 576, 633 A.2d 172 (1993)

50 ALR5th 581—§ 7, 20

S.D., Matter of, 402 N.W.2d 346 (S.D. 1987)

89 ALR5th 195—§ 11

S. D., Matter of, 549 P.2d 1190 (Alaska 1976)
6 ALR6th 161—§ 3

S.D. v. State, 650 So. 2d 198 (Fla. App. D3 1995)
31 ALR5th 229—§ 29, 45, 74

S.D. by D.D. v. Kishwaukee Community Hosp., 288 Ill. App. 3d 472, 224 Ill. Dec. 158, 681 N.E.2d 140 (2d Dist. 1997)
71 ALR5th 307—§ 19

SDDS, Inc. v. State, 2002 SD 90, 650 N.W.2d 1 (S.D. 2002)
49 ALR6th 205—§ 25, 29 to 31

S.D.G. v. Inventory Control Co., 178 N.J. Super. 411, 429 A.2d 394 (1981)
45 ALR5th 251—§ 2, 6, 21

S.D.G. v. State, 936 S.W.2d 371 (Tex. App. Houston 14th Dist. 1996)
79 ALR5th 237—§ 2

S.D.H., In re, 187 N.C. App. 813, 654 S.E.2d 83 (2007)
53 ALR6th 419—§ 41
57 ALR6th 163—§ 40

SDJ, Inc. v. City of Houston, 837 F.2d 1268 (5th Cir. 1988)
10 ALR5th 538—§ 5, 13, 19, 21, 24, 33, 34
67 ALR5th 431—§ 2, 4, 11
20 ALR6th 161—§ 3
21 ALR6th 425—§ 9
23 ALR6th 573—§ 3

SDJ, Inc. v. Houston, 636 F. Supp. 1359 (S.D. Tex. 1986)
8 ALR5th 391—§ 2, 3, 10

SDJ, Inc. v. Houston, 841 F.2d 107 (CA5 Tex. 1988)
10 ALR5th 538—§ 3

SDL Enterprises, Inc. v. DeReamer, 683 N.E.2d 1347 (Ind. Ct. App. 1997)
12 ALR5th 847—§ 5, 12

SDM, Matter of Paternity of, 882 P.2d 1217 (Wyo. 1994)
86 ALR5th 637—§ 3

S.D. Myers, Inc. v. City and County of San Francisco, 253 F.3d 461, 26 Employee Benefits Cas. (BNA) 1487, 85 Fair Empl. Prac. Cas. (BNA) 1802 (9th Cir. 2001)
8 ALR6th 667—§ 3, 5, 6, 12, 16

S.D. Myers, Inc. v. City and County of San Francisco, 336 F.3d 1174, 30 Employee Benefits Cas. (BNA) 2802 (9th Cir. 2003)
8 ALR6th 667—§ 5, 6, 16, 20

S.D. Myers, Inc. v. City and County of San Francisco, 2001 WL 664233
74 ALR5th 439—§ 3

S.D. Office Equipment Co., Inc. v. Philbrick, 668 N.Y.S.2d 426 (App. Div. 4th Dep't 1998)
63 ALR5th 607—§ 8

SDR Assocs. v. ARG Enters., 170 Ariz. 1, 821 P.2d 268, 99 Ariz. Adv. Rep. 24 (App. 1991)
13 ALR5th 169—§ 4, 11
45 ALR5th 251—§ 6, 7, 11, 25

S.D.S.-C., In re, 2009 WL 702777 (Tex. App. San Antonio 2009)
61 ALR6th 1—§ 13

S. D., State of v. Long, 465 F.2d 65 (8th Cir. 1972)
28 ALR6th 505—§ 12
29 ALR6th 1—§ 10

S.D. Warren Co. v. Maine Bd. of Environmental Protection, 126 S. Ct. 1843, 62 Env't. Rep. Cas. (BNA) 1257, 36 Envtl. L. Rep. 20089 (U.S. 2006)
16 ALR6th 767—§ 18

S.D. Warren Co. v. Vernon, 1997 ME 161, 697 A.2d 1280 (Me. 1997)
111 ALR5th 313—§ 9

S.E., In re Adoption of, 232 Mont. 31, 755 P.2d 27 (1988)
82 ALR5th 443—§ 4
83 ALR5th 375—§ 10, 12

S.E., Interest of, 296 Ill. App. 3d 412, 231 Ill. Dec. 248, 695 N.E.2d 1367 (3d Dist. 1998)
20 ALR5th 534—§ 17

Sea v. Seif, 831 A.2d 1288 (Pa. Commw. Ct. 2003)
   13 ALR6th 499—§ 29
   37 ALR6th 137—§ 17
Sea Air Support, Inc. v. Herrmann, 96 Nev. 574, 613 P.2d 413, 29 U.C.C. Rep. Serv. (CBC) 918 (1980)
   77 ALR5th 429—§ 7
Seaberry v. Smith, 527 So. 2d 1011 (La. App. 5th Cir. 1988)
   26 ALR5th 401—§ 28
Seablom v. Seablom, 348 N.W.2d 920 (N.D. 1984)
   47 ALR5th 129—§ 11
Seabloom v. Krier, 219 Minn. 362, 18 N.W.2d 88 (1945)
   22 ALR5th 327—§ 82
Seaboard A. L. R. Co. v. Marine Industries, Inc., 237 F. Supp. 10 (D.C. S.C. 1964)
   31 ALR5th 171—§ 17
Seaboard A. L. R. Co. v. Martin, 56 So. 2d 509 (Fla. 1952)
   42 ALR5th 465—§ 3
Seaboard A. L. Ry. v. Minor, 82 Fla. 492, 90 So. 611 (1921)
   17 ALR5th 547—§ 37
Seaboard C. L. R. Co. v. Blackmon, 129 Ga. App. 342, 199 S.E.2d 581 (1973)
   33 ALR5th 509—§ 5
Seaboard C. L. R. Co. v. Halks, 417 So. 2d 282 (Fla. App. D1 1982)
   12 ALR5th 195—§ 31
Seaboard Coast Line R. Co. v. Friddle, 290 So. 2d 85 (Fla. Dist. Ct. App. 4th Dist. 1974)
   15 ALR6th 1—§ 5
Seaboard Industries, Inc. v. Monaco, 258 Pa. Super. 170, 392 A.2d 738 (1978)
   92 ALR5th 273—§ 21
Seaboard Lumber Co. v. U.S., 308 F.3d 1283 (Fed. Cir. 2002)
   104 ALR6th 303—§ 13
Seaboard Nat. Bank v. Woesten, 176 Mo. 49, 75 S.W. 464 (1903)
   73 ALR6th 571—§ 46

Seaboard Shipping Corp., In re, 449 F.2d 132, 1971 A.M.C. 2145 (2d Cir. 1971)
   66 ALR6th 185—§ 9
Seaboard Tug & Barge, Inc. v. Rederi AB/Disa, 213 F.2d 772, 1954 A.M.C. 1498 (1st Cir. 1954)
   66 ALR6th 185—§ 2
Seabol, Ex parte, 782 So. 2d 212 (Ala. 2000)
   11 ALR6th 1—§ 4, 13
Seabourn v. Coronado Area Council, Boy Scouts of America, 257 Kan. 178, 891 P.2d 385 (1995)
   82 ALR5th 1—§ 13
   83 ALR5th 467—§ 7
Seabreak Homeowners Ass'n, Inc. v. Gresser, 517 A 263 (Del. Ch. 1986)
   115 ALR5th 251—§ 6, 28
Seabright v. Nesselrodt, 4 Va. Cir. 322, 1985 WL 306831 (1985)
   101 ALR5th 447—§ 3, 5, 12
Sea Bright, Bureau of v. State, Dept. of Educ., 242 N.J. Super. 225, 576 A.2d 331, 61 Ed. Law Rep. 643 (App. Div. 1990)
   110 ALR5th 293—§ 3
Seabrook v. Tra-Sea Corp., 119 N.H. 937, 410 A.2d 240 (1979)
   2 ALR5th 553—§ 47
Seabrook Island Property Owners Ass'n v. Marshland Trust, Inc., 358 S.C. 655, 596 S.E.2d 380 (Ct. App. 2004)
   115 ALR5th 251—§ 39
Seabrooks v. Cooper, 2008 WL 4414250 (D.S.C. 2008)
   65 ALR6th 93—§ 59
Seabury-Peterson v. Jhamb, 2011 ME 35, 15 A.3d 746 (Me. 2011)
   92 ALR6th 379—§ 60, 98, 113, 118
Sea Cabins on Ocean IV Homeowners Ass'n, Inc. v. City of North Myrtle Beach, 345 S.C. 418, 548 S.E.2d 595 (2001)
   55 ALR6th 635—§ 3, 5
Seach v. Armbruster, 725 N.E.2d 875 (Ind. Ct. App. 2000)
   95 ALR6th 85—§ 61

Seacoast Builders Corp. v. Rutgers, 358 N.J. Super. 524, 818 A.2d 455 (App. Div. 2003)
26 ALR6th 287—§ 15

Seafirst Center Ltd. Partnership v. Erickson, 127 Wash. 2d 355, 898 P.2d 299 (1995)
70 ALR6th 209—§ 38

Sea Food Co. v. Alves, 117 Miss. 1, 77 So. 857 (1917)
15 ALR5th 119—§ 51

Seaford Nylon Employees Council, Inc. v. E.I. duPont de Nemours & Co., 12 Del. J. Corp. L. 1200, 1986 WL 11533 (Del. Ch. 1986)
120 ALR5th 351—§ 6

Seaford School Dist. v. Delaware Dep't of Labor, 1989 WL 147425 (Del. Super)
51 ALR5th 1—§ 3

Sea-Gate, Inc. v. U.S., 1 Cl. Ct. 699 (1983)
84 ALR5th 399—§ 4, 13

Seagate Technology v. A. J. Kogyo Co., 219 Cal. App. 3d 696, 268 Cal. Rptr. 586 (1st Dist. 1990)
79 ALR5th 587—§ 8

Sea Girt Restaurant and Tavern Owners Ass'n, Inc. v. Borough of Sea Girt, New Jersey, 625 F. Supp. 1482 (D.N.J. 1986)
116 ALR5th 149—§ 4, 24

Seagle v. Cross, 680 S.E.2d 901 (N.C. Ct. App. 2009)
100 ALR6th 139—§ 11

Seago v. Horry County, 378 S.C. 414, 663 S.E.2d 38, 36 Media L. Rep. (BNA) 1875, 88 U.S.P.Q.2d 1520 (2008)
76 ALR6th 289—§ 7

Seagrave v. Dean, 908 So. 2d 41, 201 Ed. Law Rep. 790 (La. Ct. App. 1st Cir. 2005)
14 ALR6th 277—§ 6

Seagrave v. Price, 349 Ark. 433, 79 S.W.3d 339 (2002)
86 ALR6th 1—§ 85 to 87

Seagraves v. ABCO Mfg. Co., 118 Ga. App. 414, 164 S.E.2d 242 (1968)
22 ALR5th 464—§ 3

Seagren v. Peterson, 225 Neb. 747, 407 N.W.2d 790 (1987)
11 ALR6th 1—§ 4, 6
41 ALR6th 1—§ 20

Seagren v. Smith, 63 Cal. App. 2d 733, 147 P.2d 682, 61 U.S.P.Q. 330 (2d Dist. 1944)
85 ALR6th 1—§ 38

Seagroatt Floral Co., Inc., Matter of, 78 N.Y.2d 439, 576 N.Y.S.2d 831, 583 N.E.2d 287 (1991)
16 ALR6th 693—§ 5

Seagroves v. State, 282 Ala. 354, 211 So. 2d 486 (1968)
26 ALR6th 451—§ 9

Seagroves v. State, 726 So. 2d 738 (Ala. Crim. App. 1998)
34 ALR6th 1—§ 12

Sea Hawk Seafoods, Inc. v. Alyeska Pipeline Service Co., 206 F.3d 900 (9th Cir. 2000)
31 ALR5th 572—§ 53

S.E.A., Inc. v. Southside Leasing Co., 2000 WL 1449852 (Tenn. Ct. App. 2000)
2 ALR6th 195—§ 5, 9

Sea Island Bank v. First Bulloch Bank & Trust Co., 245 Ga. 715, 267 S.E.2d 12 (1980)
25 ALR5th 233—§ 8

Seal v. Marco's, Inc., 343 So. 2d 749 (La. App. 3d Cir. 1977)
18 ALR5th 577—§ 9, 49, 58
23 ALR5th 241—§ 40

Seal v. Mertz, 338 F. Supp. 945 (M.D. Pa. 1972)
58 ALR5th 1—§ 5, 9, 24, 26

Seal v. Morgan, 229 F.3d 567, 148 Ed. Law Rep. 34, 2000 FED App. 358P (6th Cir. 2000)
117 ALR5th 459—§ 4, 12

Seal v. Morgan, 229 F.3d 567, 148 Ed. Law Rep. 34, 2000 FED App. 0358P (6th Cir. 2000)
90 ALR6th 235—§ 58

Seal v. Pipeline, Inc., 731 F.2d 1194 (CA5 La. 1984)
56 ALR5th 1—§ 3

Sea-Land Service, Inc. v. County of Alameda, 12 Cal. 3d 772, 117 Cal. Rptr. 448, 528 P.2d 56 (1974)
108 ALR5th 189—§ 6

Sea-Land Services, Inc. v. Pepper Source, 941 F.2d 519, 1992 A.M.C. 1520 (7th Cir. 1991)
2 ALR6th 195—§ 14, 15

Sea-Land Services, Inc. v. Pepper Source, 993 F.2d 1309 (7th Cir. 1993)
2 ALR6th 195—§ 14, 15

Seal Beach Police Officers Assn., People ex rel. v. City of Seal Beach, 36 Cal. 3d 591, 205 Cal. Rptr. 794, 685 P.2d 1145, 120 L.R.R.M. (BNA) 2309 (1984)
106 ALR5th 523—§ 28

Seale v. Gulf, C. & S. F. R. Co., 65 Tex. 274 (1886)
17 ALR5th 547—§ 53

Seale v. Seale, 350 So. 2d 96 (Fla. App. D1 1977)
47 ALR5th 129—§ 10, 16

Seale v. State, 118 Tex. Crim. 324, 39 S.W.2d 58 (1931)
104 ALR5th 165—§ 11

Seale v. State, 857 N.E.2d 1048 (Ind. Ct. App. 2006)
26 ALR6th 511—§ 10

Sealed Appellant, In re, 77 F.3d 479 (5th Cir. 1996)
45 ALR6th 175—§ 12, 22

Sealed Appellant v. Sealed Appellee, 130 F.3d 695 (5th Cir. 1997)
68 ALR6th 1—§ 15

Sealed Case, In re, 99 F.3d 1175, 45 Fed. R. Evid. Serv. 1340 (D.C. Cir. 1996)
55 ALR6th 391—§ 21

Sealed Case, Re, 120 F.R.D. 66 (N.D. Ill. 1988)
28 ALR5th 1—§ 22

Sealed Case, Re, 237 U.S. App. D.C. 312, 737 F.2d 94, 1984-1 CCH Trade Cases ¶ 66062, 15 Fed. Rules Evid. Serv. 1811 (1984)
27 ALR5th 76—§ 41

Sealey v. Hicks, 309 Or. 387, 788 P.2d 435, CCH Prod. Liab. Rep. ¶ 12407 (1990)
30 ALR5th 1—§ 3, 6 to 8, 19

Sea Link Int'l, Inc. v. Osram Sylvania, Inc., 969 F. Supp. 781, 34 U.C.C. Rep. Serv. 2d 938 (S.D. Ga. 1997)
94 ALR5th 247—§ 12, 27, 32, 34, 42

Sealover v. Carey Canada, 793 F. Supp. 569, Prod. Liab. Rep. (CCH) ¶ 13210 (M.D. Pa. 1992)
24 ALR6th 497—§ 8

Seals v. Alabama, 2011 WL 2462583 (M.D. Ala. 2011)
93 ALR6th 1—§ 14

Seals v. Mitchell, 2011 WL 1399245 (N.D. Cal. 2011)
95 ALR6th 641—§ 9

Seals v. Seals, 22 Wash. App. 652, 590 P.2d 1301 (1979)
17 ALR5th 366—§ 37

Seals v. State, 634 S.W.2d 899 (Tex. App. San Antonio 1982)
7 ALR5th 263—§ 6

Seals v. State, 2000 WL 34251158 (Tex. App. Corpus Christi 2000)
47 ALR6th 107—§ 45

Sealy v. Vann, 122 A.D.2d 919, 505 N.Y.S.2d 952 (2d Dep't 1986)
14 ALR6th 543—§ 35

Seaman v. Fedourich, 16 N.Y.2d 94, 262 N.Y.S.2d 444, 209 N.E.2d 778 (1965)
56 ALR5th 171—§ 7, 26

Seaman v. Mann, 114 N.J. Eq. 408, 168 A. 833 (1933)
27 ALR5th 764—§ 3

Seaman v. State, 214 Ga. App. 878, 449 S.E.2d 526, 94 Fulton County D R 3302 (1994)
50 ALR5th 581—§ 5

Seaman v. State Farm Mut. Auto. Ins.
Co., 1991 WL 260369 (Tex. App.
Houston 1st Dist. 1991)
16 ALR6th 491—§ 5

Seaman v. Superior Court, 193 Cal. App.
3d 1279, 238 Cal. Rptr. 878 (5th
Dist. 1987)
83 ALR6th 465—§ 4, 6, 8, 14, 15, 55

Sea Management Service, Ltd. v. Club
Sea, Inc., 512 So. 2d 1025, 12 FLW
2108, 5 U.C.C.R.S.2d 424 (Fla.
App. D3 1987)
8 ALR5th 463—§ 4, 63
13 ALR5th 465—§ 27

Seaman Body Corp. v. Industrial Com.
of Wisc., 202 Wis. 13, 231 N.W.
251 (1930)
61 ALR5th 375—§ 5, 11

Seaman, People ex rel. v. Warden, 53
App. Div. 2d 848, 385 N.Y.S.2d
568 (1st Dep't 1976)
22 ALR5th 660—§ 17

Seamans v. Braun, 2000 WL 254559
(Conn. Super. Ct. 2000)
17 ALR6th 159—§ 35

Seamans v. Harris County Hosp. Dist.,
934 S.W.2d 393 (Tex. App. Houston 14th Dist. 1996)
6 ALR6th 365—§ 8

Seamans v. Seamans, 73 Ark. App. 27,
37 SW3d 693 (2001)
100 ALR5th 1—§ 15

Seamans v. Seamans, 73 Ark. App. 27,
37 S.W.3d 693 (2001)
100 ALR5th 1—§ 2, 3

Seamans v. Seamans, 73 Ark. App. 27,
37 S.W.3d 693 (Ark. App. 2001)
57 ALR6th 163—§ 4

Seamans, Estate of v. True, 247 Ga. 721,
279 S.E.2d 447 (1981)
62 ALR5th 219—§ 8, 42

Seaman Unified School Dist. No. 345 v.
Kansas Com'n on Human Rights,
26 Kan. App. 2d 521, 990 P.2d 155,
140 Ed. Law Rep. 772 (1999)
102 ALR5th 1—§ 5, 7

Seaman Unified School Dist. No. 345,
Shawnee County v. Casson Const.
Co., Inc., 3 Kan. App. 2d 289, 594
P.2d 241, 3 A.L.R.4th 1013 (1979)
47 ALR6th 303—§ 4

Seamar Shipping Corp. v. Kremikovtzi
Trade Ltd., 461 F. Supp. 2d 222,
2007 A.M.C. 156, 61 U.C.C. Rep.
Serv. 2d 298 (S.D. N.Y. 2006)
66 ALR6th 567—§ 21

Seamon v. Coccoma, 281 A.D.2d 824,
721 N.Y.S.2d 884 (3d Dep't 2001)
91 ALR6th 435—§ 123

Seamon v. Vaughan, 921 F.2d 1217, 13
EBC 1428, 18 FR Serv. 3d 1199
(CA11 Fla. 1991)
60 ALR5th 669—§ 8

Seamons v. Snow, 84 F.3d 1226, 109
Ed. Law Rep. 1103, 141 A.L.R.
Fed. 713 (10th Cir. 1996)
98 ALR6th 599—§ 12, 24, 25, 30, 71

Sean M., In re, 189 Ariz. 323, 942 P.2d
482 (Ct. App. Div. 1 1997)
78 ALR5th 489—§ 12
38 ALR6th 1—§ 5

Seanor, In re, 738 A.2d 282 (D.C. 1999)
44 ALR6th 75—§ 4

Sea Pines Plantation Co. v. Wells, 294
S.C. 266, 363 S.E.2d 891 (1987)
115 ALR5th 251—§ 22, 39

Seaquist v. Physicians Ins. Co. of Wisconsin, No. 94-1038 (Wis App.
1995)
43 ALR5th 545—§ 14

Sea Ranch II Owners Ass'n, Inc. v. Sea
Ranch II, Inc., 180 N.C. App. 226,
636 S.E.2d 332 (2006)
86 ALR6th 321—§ 13

Searcey v. Crim, 815 F.2d 1389, 38 Ed.
Law Rep. 929 (11th Cir. 1987)
70 ALR6th 513—§ 16
71 ALR6th 471—§ 12

Searches Conducted on March 5, 1980,
Matter of, 497 F. Supp. 1283 (E.D.
Wis. 1980)
85 ALR5th 471—§ 8

Search King Inc. v. Google Technology, Inc., 2003 WL 21464568 (W.D. Okla. 2003)
30 ALR6th 299—§ 24

Search of Certain Cell Phones, In re, 541 F. Supp. 2d 1 (D.D.C. 2008)
62 ALR6th 161—§ 12

Search of The Rayburn House Office Building Room Number 2113, In re, 432 F. Supp. 2d 100, 24 A.L.R.6th 845 (D.D.C. 2006)
24 ALR6th 255—§ 4, 8, 14, 43

Search Warrant, In re, 2003 WL 22095662 (D. Del. 2003)
81 ALR6th 257—§ 17, 20

Search Warrant for K-Sports Imports, Inc., Matter of, 163 F.R.D. 594 (C.D. Cal. 1995)
84 ALR5th 1—§ 3

Search Warrants Served on Home Health and Hospice Care, Inc., In re, 121 F.3d 700 (4th Cir. 1997)
81 ALR6th 257—§ 3, 4, 14

Searcy v. Bend Garage Co., 286 Or. 11, 592 P.2d 558 (1979)
66 ALR6th 351—§ 47

Searcy v. Chicago Transit Authority, 146 Ill. App. 3d 779, 100 Ill. Dec. 432, 497 N.E.2d 410 (1st Dist. 1986)
64 ALR5th 519—§ 11

Searcy v. City of Dayton, 38 F.3d 282 (CA6 Ohio. 1994)
36 ALR5th 1—§ 19

Searcy v. Hemet Unified School Dist., 177 Cal. App. 3d 792, 223 Cal. Rptr. 206, 30 Ed. Law Rep. 783 (4th Dist. 1986)
72 ALR5th 469—§ 2, 3, 10, 11, 20

Searcy v. Interurban Transp. Co., 189 La. 183, 179 So. 75 (1938)
108 ALR5th 495—§ 7

Seare, In re, 493 B.R. 158 (Bankr. D. Nev. 2013)
88 ALR6th 203—§ 45

Searer v. Wometco West Michigan TV, Inc., 7 Media L. R. 1639 (Mich. Cir. Ct. 1981)

19 ALR5th 1—§ 37

SeaRiver Maritime Financial Holdings, Inc. v. Mineta, 309 F.3d 662, 55 Env't. Rep. Cas. (BNA) 2004, 2002 A.M.C. 2409, 33 Envtl. L. Rep. 20199 (9th Cir. 2002)
62 ALR6th 517—§ 4, 5, 13, 14, 16, 18, 21, 36, 45, 46, 48, 58

SeaRiver Maritime, Inc. v. Industrial Medical Services, Inc., 983 F. Supp. 1287, 1998 A.M.C. 142 (N.D. Cal. 1997)
44 ALR6th 391—§ 4

Searle v. Cayuga Medical Center at Ithaca, 28 A.D.3d 834, 813 N.Y.S.2d 552 (3d Dep't 2006)
64 ALR6th 249—§ 19

Searle v. City of New Rochelle, 293 A.D.2d 735, 742 N.Y.S.2d 314, 114 A.L.R.5th 785 (2d Dep't 2002)
114 ALR5th 397—§ 9, 23

Searle v. Johnson, 646 P.2d 682 (Utah 1982)
94 ALR5th 455—§ 11

Searle v. Searle, 522 P.2d 697 (Utah 1974)
4 ALR5th 403—§ 3

Searle v. U.S., 1990 WL 266348 (4th Cir. 1990)
69 ALR6th 415—§ 54

Searle Pharmaceuticals, Inc. v. Department of Revenue, 117 Ill. 2d 454, 111 Ill. Dec. 603, 512 N.E.2d 1240 (1987)
33 ALR5th 509—§ 24

Searles v. Lum, 89 Mo. App. 235 (1901)
74 ALR5th 369—§ 10

Sears, Re Application of, 137 Cal. App. 308, 30 P.2d 571 (1934)
18 ALR5th 577—§ 8

Sears v. Curtis, 189 Ill. App. 420, 1914 WL 2907 (1st Dist. 1914)
75 ALR5th 1—§ 7, 13, 15

Sears v. Department of Treasury, 57 Mich. App. 218, 226 N.W.2d 63 (1974)
12 ALR5th 89—§ 7

Sears v. Mid-City Motors, Inc., 179 Neb. 100, 136 N.W.2d 428 (1965)
84 ALR5th 69—§ 12

Sears v. Olivarez, 28 S.W.3d 611 (Tex. App. Corpus Christi 2000)
54 ALR5th 575—§ 24
58 ALR5th 429—§ 3

Sears v. Ryder Truck Rental, Inc., 596 F. Supp. 1001, 41 Fair Empl. Prac. Cas. (BNA) 1347, 117 L.R.R.M. (BNA) 3237, 39 Empl. Prac. Dec. (CCH) ¶ 36008, 107 Lab. Cas. (CCH) ¶ 10041 (E.D. Mich. 1984)
123 ALR5th 411—§ 45

Sears v. Southworth, 563 P.2d 192 (Utah 1977)
45 ALR5th 173—§ 3

Sears v. State, 262 Ga. 805, 426 S.E.2d 553 (1993)
75 ALR5th 295—§ 10

Sears v. State, 270 Ga. 834, 514 S.E.2d 426 (1999)
39 ALR5th 283—§ 70
62 ALR5th 121—§ 7.5

Sears v. State, 457 N.E.2d 192 (Ind. 1983)
42 ALR5th 581—§ 5, 17

Sears v. State, 1974 OK CR 205, 528 P.2d 732 (Okla. Crim. App. 1974)
85 ALR5th 1—§ 11

Sears v. Superior Court of Calaveras County, 133 Cal. App. 704, 24 P.2d 842 (1933)
18 ALR5th 577—§ 8

Sears v. Upton, 130 S. Ct. 3259 (2010)
56 ALR6th 679—§ 42

Sears Commercial Sales v. Davis, 559 So. 2d 237 (Fla. Dist. Ct. App. 1st Dist. 1990)
63 ALR6th 187—§ 33

Sears' Estate, In re, 33 Misc. 141, 68 N.Y.S. 363 (Sur. Ct. 1900)
67 ALR6th 341—§ 23

Sears Mortg. Corp. v. Leeds Bldg. Products, Inc., 219 Ga. App. 349, 464 S.E.2d 907 (1995)
81 ALR6th 161—§ 4
82 ALR6th 43—§ 6

Sears, Roebuck and Co. v. Black, 708 S.W.2d 925, Prod. Liab. Rep. (CCH) ¶ 11056 (Tex. App. Eastland 1986)
104 ALR6th 97—§ 9

Sears, Roebuck & Co. v. Chandler, 152 Ga. App. 427, 263 S.E.2d 171 (1979)
40 ALR5th 135—§ 2 to 4, 14, 16
1 ALR6th 297—§ 4, 24

Sears, Roebuck & Co. v. City of Alexandria, 155 So. 2d 776 (La. Ct. App. 3d Cir. 1963)
73 ALR5th 223—§ 3, 8

Sears, Roebuck & Co. v. Davis, 234 So. 2d 695 (Fla. Dist. Ct. App. 3d Dist. 1970)
96 ALR5th 239—§ 15

Sears, Roebuck & Co. v. Donovan, 137 A.2d 716 (Mun Ct. App. Dist. Col. 1958)
40 ALR5th 135—§ 15

Sears, Roebuck and Co. v. Franchise Finance Corp. of America, 711 So. 2d 1189 (Fla. Dist. Ct. App. 2d Dist. 1998)
111 ALR5th 313—§ 22

Sears, Roebuck & Co. v. Geiger, 123 Fla. 446, 167 So. 658 (1936)
40 ALR5th 135—§ 6, 15 to 17

Sears Roebuck & Co. v. Glenwal Co., 325 F. Supp. 86 (S.D. N.Y. 1970)
75 ALR5th 595—§ 6

Sears, Roebuck & Co. v. Goldstone & Sudalter, 128 F.3d 10 (1st Cir. 1997)
50 ALR5th 301—§ 3

Sears, Roebuck & Co. v. Harris, 630 So. 2d 1018, CCH Prod. Liab. Rep. ¶ 13661 (Ala. 1993)
12 ALR5th 195—§ 24

Sears, Roebuck & Co. v. Hough, 421 S.W.2d 714 (Tex. Civ. App. Houston 14th Dist. 1967)
104 ALR6th 97—§ 9

Sears, Roebuck & Co. v. Industrial Commission, 79 Ill. 2d 59, 37 Ill. Dec. 341, 402 N.E.2d 231 (1980)
112 ALR5th 509—§ 18

13 ALR6th 209—§ 11, 13, 39

39 ALR6th 445—§ 46

Sears, Roebuck & Co. v. Johnson, 91 F.2d 332 (C.C.A. 10th Cir. 1937)

123 ALR5th 1—§ 17

Sears, Roebuck & Co. v. Jones, 303 S.W.2d 432 (Tex. Civ. App. Waco 1957)

33 ALR5th 303—§ 3, 13

Sears, Roebuck & Co. v. Kunze, 996 S.W.2d 416, Prod. Liab. Rep. (CCH) P 15650 (Tex. App. Beaumont 1999)

8 ALR6th 439—§ 15

Sears, Roebuck & Co. v. Kunze, 996 S.W.2d 416, Prod. Liab. Rep. (CCH) ¶ 15650 (Tex. App. Beaumont 1999)

12 ALR5th 195—§ 24

Sears Roebuck and Co. v. Manuilov, 742 N.E.2d 453 (Ind. 2001)

90 ALR5th 453—§ 9

Sears, Roebuck & Co. v. Metropolitan Engravers, Limited, 245 F.2d 67 (9th Cir. 1956)

39 ALR6th 155—§ 9

Sears, Roebuck & Co. v. Northumberland General Ins. Co., 617 F. Supp. 88 (N.D. Ill. 1985)

44 ALR5th 683—§ 12

Sears Roebuck and Co. v. Otis Elevator Co., 1989 WL 1558 (Minn. Ct. App. 1989)

63 ALR6th 495—§ 15

Sears, Roebuck & Co. v. Penn Cent. Co., 420 F.2d 560 (1st Cir. 1970)

84 ALR5th 69—§ 19, 21

Sears Roebuck & Co. v. Polchinski, 636 So. 2d 1369, 19 FLW D 1046 (Fla. App. D4 1994)

33 ALR5th 205—§ 4, 9

Sears, Roebuck & Co. v. Poling, 248 Iowa 582, 81 N.W.2d 462 (1957)

17 ALR5th 547—§ 4

Sears, Roebuck & Co. v. Reid, 132 Ga. App. 136, 207 S.E.2d 532 (1974)

123 ALR5th 1—§ 10, 14

Sears, Roebuck & Co. v. San Diego County Dist. Council of Carpenters, 436 U.S. 180, 98 S. Ct. 1745, 56 L. Ed. 2d 209, 98 L.R.R.M. (BNA) 2282, 83 Lab. Cas. (CCH) ¶ 10582 (1978)

108 ALR5th 253—§ 2, 15

110 ALR5th 111—§ 2

120 ALR5th 351—§ 2, 12

Sears, Roebuck and Co. v. Sears Realty Co., Inc., 932 F. Supp. 392 (N.D. N.Y. 1996)

114 ALR5th 129—§ 10

Sears, Roebuck & Co. v. State Tax Assessor, 561 A.2d 172 (Me. 1989)

81 ALR6th 97—§ 18

Sears, Roebuck & Co. v. Viera, 440 So. 2d 49 (Fla. App. D1 1983)

16 ALR5th 191—§ 8, 17

Sears, Roebuck and Co. v. Wholey, 370 Md. 38, 803 A.2d 482, 18 I.E.R. Cas. (BNA) 1313 (2002)

105 ALR5th 351—§ 8

Sears, Roebuck and Co. v. Wilson, 963 S.W.2d 166 (Tex. App. Fort Worth 1998)

63 ALR5th 1—§ 6

Searsy v. Commercial Trading Corp., 560 S.W.2d 637, Blue Sky L. Rep. (CCH) ¶ 71383, Fed. Sec. L. Rep. (CCH) ¶ 96276 (Tex. 1977)

28 ALR6th 281—§ 7, 11, 15

Sea Scaping Constr. Co. v. McAtee, 402 So. 2d 919 (Ala. 1981)

23 ALR5th 744—§ 11

Seaside Petroleum Co., Inc. v. Steve E. Rawl, Inc., 177 Ga. App. 341, 339 S.E.2d 601, 42 U.C.C. Rep. Serv. 1223 (1985)

94 ALR5th 247—§ 8, 14

Seaside Resorts, Inc. v. Club Car, Inc., 308 S.C. 47, 416 S.E.2d 655, 19 U.C.C. Rep. Serv. 2d 60 (Ct. App. 1992)

15 ALR5th 119—§ 5

89 ALR5th 319—§ 8, 12, 26

Seaside Village, Inc. v. Director of Revenue, 429 A.2d 980 (Del. 1981)

1 ALR6th 1—§ 54

14 ALR6th 119—§ 30

Seasongood v. Prager, 146 App. Div.
833, 131 N.Y.S. 771 (1911)

53 ALR5th 287—§ 3, 7, 12

Seastrunk v. Walker, 156 S.W.2d 996
(Tex. Civ. App. Waco 1941)

111 ALR5th 313—§ 9

Seat v. Seat, 227 S.W.2d 758 (Mo. App.
1950)

53 ALR5th 375—§ 30

Seaton v. Industrial Commission, 29
Ohio Op. 199, 13 Ohio Supp. 78,
1942 WL 3139 (C.P. 1942)

41 ALR6th 207—§ 2

Seaton v. Seaton, 971 F. Supp. 1188
(E.D. Tenn. 1997)

110 ALR5th 371—§ 6

23 ALR6th 697—§ 6

Seaton v. Sky Realty Co., 372 F. Supp.
1322 (N.D. Ill. 1972)

12 ALR5th 195—§ 32

Seaton v. Smith, 45 Kan. 43, 25 P. 222
(1890)

19 ALR5th 622—§ 2

Seaton v. State of Wyo. Highway
Com'n, Dist. No. 1, 784 P.2d 197
(Wyo. 1989)

112 ALR5th 621—§ 3, 6

Sea Trade Maritime Corp. v. Hellenic
Mut. War Risks Ass'n (Bermuda)
Ltd., 7 A.D.3d 289, 776 N.Y.S.2d
255 (App. Div. 1st Dep't 2004)

8 ALR6th 549—§ 4

Seattle v. Duncan, 44 Wash. App. 735,
723 P.2d 1156 (1986)

3 ALR5th 784—§ 2, 6, 10, 11, 13

Seattle v. Martin, 54 Wash. 2d 541, 342
P.2d 602 (1959)

8 ALR5th 391—§ 2, 3, 8

Seattle v. Webster, 115 Wash. 2d 635,
802 P.2d 1333, 7 A.L.R.5th 1100
(1990)

7 ALR5th 455—§ 3 to 6

Seattle v. Wright, 72 Wash. 2d 556, 433
P.2d 906 (1967)

52 ALR5th 655—§ 4

Seattle Affiliate of Oct. 22nd Coalition
to Stop Police Brutality, Repression
and Criminalization of a Generation
v. City of Seattle, 550 F.3d 788 (9th
Cir. 2008)

70 ALR6th 513—§ 3, 4

71 ALR6th 471—§ 3, 4

Seattle Ass'n of Credit Men v. Daniels,
15 Wash. 2d 393, 130 P.2d 892
(1942)

46 ALR5th 1—§ 23

Seattle Box Co., Inc. v. Industrial Crat-
ing & Packing, Inc., 731 F.2d 818,
221 U.S.P.Q. (BNA) 568 (Fed. Cir.
1984)

66 ALR5th 135—§ 15

Seattle, City of v. Barto, 31 Wash. 141,
71 P. 735 (1903)

16 ALR6th 219—§ 4, 13

Seattle, City of v. Box, 29 Wash. App.
109, 627 P.2d 584 (Div. 1 1981)

96 ALR5th 327—§ 7

Seattle, City of v. Buchanan, 90 Wash.
2d 584, 584 P.2d 918 (1978)

67 ALR5th 431—§ 2, 3, 9, 12

Seattle, City of v. $65,833.44 U.S. Cur-
rency, 125 Wash. App. 1043, 2005
WL 352082 (Div. 1 2005)

34 ALR6th 539—§ 4

Seattle, City of v. Drew, 70 Wash. 2d
405, 423 P.2d 522, 25 A.L.R.3d 827
(1967)

72 ALR5th 1—§ 2, 3

Seattle, City of v. Duncan, 44 Wash.
App. 735, 723 P.2d 1156 (Div. 1
1986)

7 ALR6th 233—§ 8

24 ALR6th 1—§ 11

Seattle, City of v. Fettig, 10 Wash. App.
773, 519 P.2d 1002 (Div. 1 1974)

24 ALR6th 1—§ 37

Seattle, City of v. Jarrett, 33 Wash. App.
525, 655 P.2d 1209 (Div. 1 1982)

95 ALR5th 229—§ 3

Seattle, City of v. Jones, 79 Wash. 2d
626, 488 P.2d 750 (1971)

72 ALR5th 1—§ 10, 12, 13, 30

Seattle, City of v. Lockhart, 85 Wash. App. 1064, 1997 WL 177414 (Div. 1 1997)
97 ALR6th 653—§ 25
Seattle, City of v. McCready, 131 Wash. 2d 266, 931 P.2d 156 (1997)
106 ALR5th 523—§ 34
Seattle, City of v. Mesiani, 110 Wash. 2d 454, 755 P.2d 775 (1988)
74 ALR5th 319—§ 2
Seattle, City of v. Messiani, 755 P.2d. 775 (Wash. 1988)
74 ALR5th 319—§ 3, 5, 9, 12
Seattle, City of v. Mighty Movers, Inc., 152 Wash. 2d 343, 96 P.3d 979 (2004)
70 ALR6th 513—§ 5
71 ALR6th 471—§ 5
Seattle, City of v. Nave, 62 Wash. 2d 446, 383 P.2d 491 (1963)
66 ALR5th 397—§ 16
Seattle, City of v. Orwick, 113 Wash. 2d 823, 784 P.2d 161 (1989)
71 ALR5th 1—§ 63
Seattle, City of v. Platt, 19 Wash. App. 904, 578 P.2d 873 (Div. 1 1978)
89 ALR6th 565—§ 10
Seattle, City of v. Pullman, 82 Wash. 2d 794, 514 P.2d 1059 (1973)
72 ALR5th 1—§ 3, 6
Seattle, City of v. Ratliff, 100 Wash. 2d 212, 667 P.2d 630 (1983)
62 ALR6th 259—§ 6
Seattle, City of v. $65,833.44 U.S. Currency, 2005 WL 352082 (Wash. Ct. App. Div. 1 2005)
4 ALR6th 113—§ 4
Seattle, City of v. Schurr, 76 Wash. App. 82, 881 P.2d 1063 (Div. 1 1994)
125 ALR5th 537—§ 2, 10
Seattle, City of v. Shepherd, 93 Wash. 2d 861, 613 P.2d 1158 (1980)
57 ALR6th 445—§ 40
Seattle, City of v. Slack, 113 Wash. 2d 850, 784 P.2d 494 (1989)
72 ALR5th 1—§ 10, 12, 30
Seattle, City of v. State, 12 Wash. App. 91, 527 P.2d 1404 (1974)
58 ALR5th 187—§ 29
Seattle, City of v. State, 54 Wash. 2d 139, 338 P.2d 126 (1959)
44 ALR6th 259—§ 15
Seattle, City of v. State, 59 Wash. 2d 150, 367 P.2d 123 (1961)
58 ALR5th 187—§ 29
Seattle Electric Co. v. Snoqualmie Falls Power Co., 40 Wash. 380, 82 P. 713 (1905)
58 ALR5th 387—§ 10
Seattle Endeavors, Inc. v. Mastro, 123 Wash. 2d 339, 868 P.2d 120, 33 U.S.P.Q.2d (BNA) 1851 (1994)
117 ALR5th 155—§ 12
Seattle-First Nat. Bank v. Rankin, 59 Wash. 2d 288, 367 P.2d 835 (1962)
7 ALR5th 1—§ 4
Seattle-First Nat. Bank v. Schriber, 282 Or. 625, 580 P.2d 1012, 24 U.C.C. Rep. Serv. (CBC) 359 (1978)
71 ALR5th 443—§ 7
Seattle-First Nat. Bank v. Tabert, 86 Wash. 2d 145, 542 P.2d 774 (1975)
73 ALR5th 75—§ 6, 8
Seattle-First Nat. Bank v. Westwood Lumber, Inc., 65 Wash. App. 811, 829 P.2d 1152, 18 U.C.C.R.S.2d 351 (1992)
18 ALR5th 307—§ 5, 16, 33
Seattle First Nat. Bank, N. A. v. Siebol, 64 Wash. App. 401, 824 P.2d 1252 (1992)
18 ALR5th 307—§ 6, 15, 19, 32
Seattle-First Nat'l Bank v. Federal Deposit Ins. Corp., 619 F. Supp. 1351, 42 U.C.C.R.S. 1378, 84 A.L.R. Fed 305 (W.D. Okla. 1985)
53 ALR5th 667—§ 2
Seattle-First Nat'l Bank v. Pacific Nat'l Bank, 22 Wash. App. 46, 587 P.2d 617, 25 U.C.C.R.S. 821 (1978)
45 ALR5th 389—§ 12, 16
Seattle Lighting Fixture Co. v. Broadway Cent. Market, Inc., 156 Wash. 189, 286 P. 43 (1930)
46 ALR5th 1—§ 3, 22

For assistance, call 1-800-328-4880

Seattle Northwest Securities Corp. v. SDG Holding Co., Inc., 61 Wash. App. 725, 812 P.2d 488 (Div. 1 1991)

47 ALR6th 255—§ 6

Seattle, Port of v. Rio, 16 Wash. App. 718, 559 P.2d 18 (1977)

34 ALR5th 591—§ 14

Seattle Pump Co., Inc. v. Traders and General Ins. Co., 93 Wash. App. 743, 970 P.2d 361 (Div. 1 1999)

116 ALR5th 247—§ 4

Seattle School Dist. No. 1 of King County v. State, 90 Wash. 2d 476, 585 P.2d 71 (1978)

110 ALR5th 293—§ 4

115 ALR5th 563—§ 2 to 4

Seattle Times Co. v. Ishikawa, 97 Wash. 2d 30, 640 P.2d 716, 8 Media L. R. 1041 (1982)

39 ALR5th 103—§ 38

Seattle Western Industries, Inc. v. David A. Mowat Co., 110 Wash. 2d 1, 750 P.2d 245 (1988)

124 ALR5th 375—§ 3, 5, 13

61 ALR6th 445—§ 11

Seaux v. Domingue, 509 So. 2d 536 (La. App. 3d Cir. 1987)

50 ALR5th 1—§ 11

Seaver v. Bradley, 179 Mass. 329, 60 N.E. 795 (1901)

63 ALR6th 495—§ 16

Seavey v. Meliak Mobile Court Inc., 246 A.D.2d 902, 667 N.Y.S.2d 822 (3d Dep't 1998)

74 ALR5th 49—§ 39

Seavey v. Northeast Utilities, 1994 WL 14533 (Conn. Super. Ct. 1994)

95 ALR5th 29—§ 9

Sea View Estates Beach Club, Inc. v. State Dep't of Natural Resources, 223 Wis. 2d 138, 588 N.W.2d 667 (Ct. App. 1998)

99 ALR5th 65—§ 18

Seavy v. State, 21 A.D.2d 445, 250 N.Y.S.2d 877 (4th Dep't 1964)

80 ALR6th 469—§ 28

Seavy and Jensen v. Industrial Commission, 523 P.2d 157 (Colo. Ct. App. 1974)

95 ALR5th 329—§ 17, 24

Seaward Constr. Co. v. Bradley, 817 P.2d 971 (Colo. 1991)

9 ALR5th 63—§ 6

Seaward Yacht Sales, Ltd. v. Murray Chris-Craft Cruisers, Inc., 701 F. Supp. 766, 1988-2 CCH Trade Cases ¶ 68337 (D.C. Or. 1988)

52 ALR5th 613—§ 3

Sea Watch Stores Ltd. Liability Co. v. Council of Unit Owners of Sea Watch Condominium, 115 Md. App. 5, 691 A.2d 750 (1997)

60 ALR5th 647—§ 5

Seaworth v. Pearson, 203 F.3d 1056, 82 Fair Empl. Prac. Cas. (BNA) 161, 77 Empl. Prac. Dec. (CCH) ¶ 46273, Unempl. Ins. Rep. (CCH) ¶ 16332B, 2000-1 U.S. Tax Cas. (CCH) ¶ 50244, 87 A.F.T.R.2d 2001-739 (8th Cir. 2000)

93 ALR5th 1—§ 2

Seay v. Chrysler Corp., 93 Wash. 2d 319, 609 P.2d 1382, 9 A.L.R.4th 625 (1980)

76 ALR6th 465—§ 4

Seay v. Commonwealth, 609 S.W.2d 128 (Ky. 1980)

39 ALR5th 283—§ 4, 22, 24

Seay v. General Elevator Co., 522 P.2d 1022 (Okla. 1974)

13 ALR5th 289—§ 28

Seay v. General Elevator Co., 1974 OK 63, 522 P.2d 1022 (Okla. 1974)

99 ALR5th 141—§ 3

115 ALR5th 1—§ 2, 3, 7, 8

117 ALR5th 267—§ 3

Seay v. Hutto, 483 Fed. Appx. 900 (5th Cir. 2012)

89 ALR6th 1—§ 10, 55

Seay v. Travelers Indem. Co., 730 S.W.2d 774 (Tex. App. Dallas 1987)

13 ALR5th 289—§ 2, 13, 20

Seay & Thomas v. Doyle, 331 Ill. App. 76, 72 N.E.2d 645 (1st Dist. 1947)
114 ALR5th 443—§ 30, 31

S. E. B., In re, 514 S.W.2d 948 (Tex. Civ. App. El Paso 1974)
114 ALR5th 173—§ 9

Sebago, Inc. v. Beazer East, Inc., 18 F. Supp. 2d 70, R.I.C.O. Bus. Disp. Guide (CCH) ¶ 9578 (D. Mass. 1998)
3 ALR5th 851—§ 14 to 16
57 ALR5th 1—§ 3

Sebago, Inc. v. Beazer East, Inc., 18 F. Supp. 2d 70, R.I.C.O. Bus. Disp. Guide (CCH) ¶ 9578, 37 U.C.C. Rep. Serv. 2d 963 (D. Mass. 1998)
83 ALR6th 1—§ 2, 27, 29, 73

Sebago, Inc. v. City of Alameda, 211 Cal. App. 3d 1372, 259 Cal. Rptr. 918, 16 Media L. R. 2377 (1st Dist. 1989)
10 ALR5th 538—§ 3, 6, 29

Sebago, Inc. v. City of Alameda, 211 Cal. App. 3d 1372, 259 Cal. Rptr. 918, 16 Media L. Rep. (BNA) 2377 (1st Dist. 1989)
20 ALR6th 161—§ 4
21 ALR6th 425—§ 12
23 ALR6th 573—§ 20

Sebastian, In re Adoption of, 25 Misc. 3d 567, 879 N.Y.S.2d 677 (Sur. Ct. 2009)
61 ALR6th 1—§ 11, 18

Sebastian v. Commonwealth, 623 S.W.2d 880 (Ky. 1981)
29 ALR5th 59—§ 6, 22, 31, 75, 88

Sebastian v. Sebastian, 524 N.E.2d 29 (Ind. Ct. App. 2d Dist. 1988)
21 ALR6th 577—§ 15, 23

Sebastian v. State, 726 N.E.2d 827 (Ind. Ct. App. 2000)
123 ALR5th 179—§ 4, 10

Sebastian v. Wood, 246 Iowa 94, 66 N.W.2d 841 (1954)
33 ALR5th 303—§ 3, 9, 15

Sebastien v. McKay, 649 So. 2d 711 (La. Ct. App. 3d Cir. 1994)
12 ALR6th 241—§ 5

Sebeck v. Plattdeutsche Volkfest Verein, 64 N.J.L. 624, 46 A. 631 (N.J. Ct. Err. & App. 1900)
21 ALR6th 81—§ 15, 17

Sebeck v. Plattdeutsche Volksfest Verein, 124 F. 11 (C.C.A. 2d Cir. 1903)
21 ALR6th 81—§ 17

Sebelius v. Cloer, 133 S. Ct. 1886 (2013)
86 ALR6th 577—§ 29

Sebeniecher v. Corl, 567 So. 2d 321 (Ala. Civ. App. 1990)
40 ALR5th 227—§ 33

Sebesta v. Kent Electronics Corp., 886 S.W.2d 459 (Tex. App. Houston 1st Dist. 1994)
7 ALR6th 563—§ 5

Sebetic v. Hagerty, 640 F. Supp. 1274, 41 Fair Empl. Prac. Cas. (BNA) 817 (E.D. Wis. 1986)
123 ALR5th 411—§ 4, 9 to 11

Sebree v. U.S., 567 F.2d 292 (CA5 Tex. 1978)
51 ALR5th 301—§ 3, 4, 10

Sebring Airport Authority v. McIntyre, 642 So. 2d 1072 (Fla. 1994)
114 ALR5th 561—§ 23

Sebring Airport Authority v. McIntyre, 783 So. 2d 238 (Fla. 2001)
114 ALR5th 561—§ 23

Sebro Packaging Corp. v. Liberty Mut. Fire Ins. Co., 69 F. Supp. 2d 642 (D.N.J. 1999)
37 ALR5th 41—§ 22

SEB S.A. v. Montgomery Ward & Co., Inc., 594 F.3d 1360, 93 U.S.P.Q.2d 1617 (Fed. Cir. 2010)
66 ALR6th 635—§ 32

S.E.C. v. American Bd. of Trade, Inc., 830 F.2d 431, Fed. Sec. L. Rep. (CCH) ¶ 93391 (2d Cir. 1987)
100 ALR6th 281—§ 7

S.E.C. v. Art Intellect, Inc., Fed. Sec. L. Rep. (CCH) ¶ 97314, 2013 WL 840048 (D. Utah 2013)
100 ALR6th 281—§ 9

S.E.C. v. Bass, Fed. Sec. L. Rep. (CCH) ¶ 97067, 2012 WL 5334743 (N.D. N.Y. 2012)

---

100 ALR6th 281—§ 9

S.E.C. v. Beacon Hill Asset Management LLC, 231 F.R.D. 134 (S.D. N.Y. 2004)

26 ALR6th 287—§ 38

S.E.C. v. Better Life Club of America, Inc., 995 F. Supp. 167, Fed. Sec. L. Rep. (CCH) ¶ 90162 (D.D.C. 1998)

100 ALR6th 281—§ 10

S.E.C. v. Blech, 501 Fed. Appx. 74, Fed. Sec. L. Rep. (CCH) ¶ 97078 (2d Cir. 2012)

100 ALR6th 281—§ 9

S.E.C. v. Brooks, Fed. Sec. L. Rep. (CCH) ¶ 90,537, 1999 WL 493052 (N.D. Tex. 1999)

100 ALR6th 281—§ 7

SEC v. Canadian Javelin, Ltd., 451 F. Supp. 594, CCH Fed Secur L. Rep. ¶ 96441, 25 FR Serv. 2d 1045 (D.C. Dist. Col. 1978)

26 ALR5th 628—§ 40

27 ALR5th 76—§ 36, 38

S.E.C. v. Chemical Trust, Fed. Sec. L. Rep. (CCH) ¶ 91291, 2000 WL 33231600 (S.D. Fla. 2000)

100 ALR6th 281—§ 7, 10, 13

S.E.C. v. Credit Bancorp, Ltd., 290 F.3d 80, 47 U.C.C. Rep. Serv. 2d 1467 (2d Cir. 2002)

100 ALR6th 281—§ 25

S.E.C. v. Credit Bancorp, Ltd., 386 F.3d 438, 55 U.C.C. Rep. Serv. 2d 74 (2d Cir. 2004)

100 ALR6th 281—§ 10

S.E.C. v. Diversified Corporate Consulting Group, 378 F.3d 1219 (11th Cir. 2004)

49 ALR6th 1—§ 8

S.E.C. v. Dowdell, 2002 WL 31357059 (W.D. Va. 2002)

100 ALR6th 281—§ 7

S.E.C. v. Dowdell, 2003 WL 25523590 (W.D. Va. 2003)

100 ALR6th 281—§ 9

S.E.C. v. Evolution Capital Advisors, LLC, 866 F. Supp. 2d 661, Fed. Sec. L. Rep. (CCH) ¶ 96616 (S.D. Tex. 2011)

100 ALR6th 281—§ 6

S.E.C. v. Evolution Capital Advisors, LLC, Fed. Sec. L. Rep. (CCH) ¶ 97708, 2013 WL 5670835 (S.D. Tex. 2013)

100 ALR6th 281—§ 9

S.E.C. v. Forma, 117 F.R.D. 516, 24 Fed. R. Evid. Serv. 300, 9 Fed. R. Serv. 3d 943 (S.D. N.Y. 1987)

71 ALR6th 249—§ 6

S.E.C. v. Gabelli, 653 F.3d 49 (2d Cir. 2011)

86 ALR6th 577—§ 36

S.E.C. v. Gen-See Capital Corp., Fed. Sec. L. Rep. (CCH) ¶ 95034, 2009 WL 57589 (W.D. N.Y. 2009)

100 ALR6th 281—§ 7

S.E.C. v. George, 426 F.3d 786, Fed. Sec. L. Rep. (CCH) ¶ 93540, 2005 FED App. 0415P (6th Cir. 2005)

100 ALR6th 281—§ 10

SEC v. Gulf & Western Industries, Inc., 518 F. Supp. 675, CCH Fed Secur L. Rep. ¶ 98233, 8 Fed. Rules Evid. Serv. 1436, 32 FR Serv. 2d 279 (DCDist Col. 1981)

26 ALR5th 628—§ 3

27 ALR5th 76—§ 3

28 ALR5th 1—§ 3

S.E.C. v. Haligiannis, 470 F. Supp. 2d 373, Fed. Sec. L. Rep. (CCH) ¶ 94146 (S.D. N.Y. 2007)

100 ALR6th 281—§ 9

S.E.C. v. Homa, Fed. Sec. L. Rep. (CCH) ¶ 91268, 2000 WL 1648929 (N.D. Ill. 2000)

100 ALR6th 281—§ 7

S.E.C. v. Illarramendi, Fed. Sec. L. Rep. (CCH) ¶ 96338, 2011 WL 2457734 (D. Conn. 2011)

100 ALR6th 281—§ 7, 13

S.E.C. v. Interlink Data Network of Los Angeles, Inc., 77 F.3d 1201, Fed. Sec. L. Rep. (CCH) ¶ 99048, 161 A.L.R. Fed. 709 (9th Cir. 1996)

102 ALR5th 253—§ 5, 6

S.E.C. v. Invest Better 2001, 2005 WL 2385452 (S.D. N.Y. 2005)

100 ALR6th 281—§ 9

S.E.C. v. JT Wallenbrock & Associates, 440 F.3d 1109, Fed. Sec. L. Rep. (CCH) ¶ 90711 (9th Cir. 2006)

100 ALR6th 281—§ 9

S.E.C. v. Life Partners, Inc., 87 F.3d 536, Fed. Sec. L. Rep. (CCH) ¶ 99256 (D.C. Cir. 1996)

28 ALR6th 281—§ 7, 10, 14, 25

S.E.C. v. Loomis, 2014 WL 1664930 (E.D. Cal. 2014)

100 ALR6th 281—§ 9

S.E.C. v. Mantria Corp., Fed. Sec. L. Rep. (CCH) ¶ 96510, 2011 WL 3439348 (D. Colo. 2011)

100 ALR6th 281—§ 9

S.E.C. v. Merrill Scott & Associates, Ltd., 505 F. Supp. 2d 1193 (D. Utah 2007)

100 ALR6th 281—§ 2

S.E.C. v. Merrill Scott & Associates, Ltd., 505 F. Supp. 2d 1193, Fed. Sec. L. Rep. (CCH) ¶ 94336 (D. Utah 2007)

100 ALR6th 281—§ 9

S.E.C. v. Merrill Scott & Associates, Ltd., 2007 WL 26981 (D. Utah 2007)

100 ALR6th 281—§ 28

S.E.C. v. Milan Capital Group, Inc., 2014 WL 2815590 (S.D. N.Y. 2014)

100 ALR6th 281—§ 9

S.E.C. v. Palmisano, 135 F.3d 860, Fed. Sec. L. Rep. (CCH) ¶ 90138, 147 A.L.R. Fed. 799 (2d Cir. 1998)

100 ALR6th 281—§ 9

S.E.C. v. Parrish, Fed. Sec. L. Rep. (CCH) ¶ 97035, 2012 WL 4378114 (D. Colo. 2012)

100 ALR6th 281—§ 9

SEC v. Research Automation Corp., 521 F.2d 585, 20 FR Serv. 2d 901 (CA2 N.Y. 1975)

8 ALR5th 653—§ 2, 3

S.E.C. v. Resource Development Intern., LLC, 487 F.3d 295 (5th Cir. 2007)

100 ALR6th 281—§ 5

S.E.C. v. Ross, 504 F.3d 1130, Fed. Sec. L. Rep. (CCH) ¶ 94451 (9th Cir. 2007)

100 ALR6th 281—§ 11

SEC v. Seahawk Deep Ocean Tech., 166 F.R.D. 268, 24 Media L. R. 1856, 35 FR Serv. 3d 360 (D.C. Conn. 1996)

60 ALR5th 75—§ 3, 6

S.E.C. v. U.S. Funding Corp., 2006 WL 995499 (D.N.J. 2006)

100 ALR6th 281—§ 9

S.E.C. v. Utsick, 373 Fed. Appx. 924, Fed. Sec. L. Rep. (CCH) ¶ 95706 (11th Cir. 2010)

100 ALR6th 281—§ 9

S.E.C. v. Vassallo, 2012 WL 1868559 (E.D. Cal. 2012)

100 ALR6th 281—§ 10, 12

S.E.C. v. Vassallo, Fed. Sec. L. Rep. (CCH) ¶ 97975, 2014 WL 2180116 (E.D. Cal. 2014)

100 ALR6th 281—§ 9

S.E.C. v. Vitesse Semiconductor Corp., 771 F. Supp. 2d 310 (S.D. N.Y. 2011)

66 ALR6th 83—§ 7

S.E.C. v. Watermark Financial Services Group, Inc., Fed. Sec. L. Rep. (CCH) ¶ 96736, 2012 WL 501450 (W.D. N.Y. 2012)

100 ALR6th 281—§ 9

S.E.C. v. W.J. Howey Co., 328 U.S. 293, 66 S. Ct. 1100, 90 L. Ed. 1244, 163 A.L.R. 1043 (1946)

28 ALR6th 281—§ 2, 7, 8, 10, 11

S.E.C. v. Wozniak, 1994 WL 24303 (N.D. Ill. 1994)

100 ALR6th 281—§ 29

Sechler v. Byrne, 4 Beaver Co. Leg J 176 (Pa. Com Pls 1942)

---

18 ALR5th 230—§ 8
Sechler v. State, 340 N.W.2d 759 (Iowa 1983)

76 ALR5th 1—§ 10
Sechler v. State College Area School Dist., 121 F. Supp. 2d 439, 149 Ed. Law Rep. 141 (M.D. Pa. 2000)

107 ALR5th 1—§ 3, 12, 16
Sechrest v. Baker, 816 F. Supp. 2d 1017 (D. Nev. 2011)

83 ALR6th 465—§ 33
Sechrest v. State, 101 Nev. 360, 705 P.2d 626 (1985)

124 ALR5th 1—§ 3
83 ALR6th 465—§ 7, 50
Sechrist v. Public Square Theatre Co., 54 Ohio App. 209, 7 Ohio Ops. 517, 23 Ohio L. Abs. 657, 6 N.E.2d 803 (Mahoning Co. 1936)

42 ALR5th 699—§ 6
Seckerson v. Sinclair, 24 N.D. 326, 140 N.W. 239 (1913)

25 ALR5th 391—§ 75
Seckinger v. Silvers, 104 Ga. App. 396, 121 S.E.2d 922 (1961)

46 ALR5th 1—§ 47
Second Chance Body Armor, Inc., In re, 417 B.R. 750 (Bankr. W.D. Mich. 2009)

83 ALR6th 1—§ 9, 25, 29, 91
94 ALR6th 1—§ 2, 8, 26, 30, 66
Second Continental, Inc. v. Atlanta E-Z Builders, Inc., 237 Ga. App. 304, 514 S.E.2d 846 (1999)

71 ALR5th 491—§ 55
Second Department in Hoerger, The v. Board of Education, 127 App. Div. 2d 88, 514 N.Y.S.2d 395 (2d Dep't 1987)

12 ALR5th 950—§ 6
Second Nat. Bank v. O.E. Merrill Co., 69 Wis. 501, 34 N.W. 514 (1887)

109 ALR5th 421—§ 5, 6, 8
Second Nat. Bank of Nashua v. Wood, 59 N.H. 407, 1879 WL 4257 (1879)

98 ALR5th 353—§ 3

Second Nat. Bank of Philadelphia v. Thompson, 141 N.J. Eq. 188, 56 A.2d 492 (Ch. 1947)

20 ALR6th 211—§ 11
Second Norwalk Corp. v. Planning and Zoning Commission of Town of Westport, 28 Conn. Supp. 426, 265 A.2d 332 (C.P. 1969)

73 ALR5th 223—§ 7, 11
4 ALR6th 263—§ 40
Second Reformed Church v. Board of Adjustment of Borough of Freehold, 30 N.J. Super. 338, 104 A.2d 703 (App. Div. 1954)

47 ALR6th 439—§ 4
Secor v. Harris, 18 Barb. 425, 1854 WL 5789 (N.Y. Gen. Term 1854)

16 ALR6th 1—§ 11
Secor v. Pioneer Foundry Co., 20 Mich. App. 30, 173 N.W.2d 780 (1969)

6 ALR6th 391—§ 4, 5, 8 to 10
Secord v. Cockburn, 747 F. Supp. 779, 18 Media L. R. 1209 (D.C. Dist. Col. 1990)

19 ALR5th 1—§ 66
Secord v. Fischetti, 236 A.D.2d 206, 653 N.Y.S.2d 551 (1st Dep't 1997)

8 ALR6th 339—§ 9
Secretary, Dept. of Revenue, State of La. v. GAP (Apparel), Inc., 886 So. 2d 459 (La. Ct. App. 1st Cir. 2004)

11 ALR6th 543—§ 6
Secretary, Kansas Dept. of Social and Rehabilitation Services, State ex rel. v. Keck, 266 Kan. 305, 969 P.2d 841 (1998)

86 ALR6th 321—§ 4, 7
90 ALR6th 451—§ 27
Secretary of Dept. of Transp., State ex rel. v. Regency Group, Inc., 598 A.2d 1123 (Del. Super. Ct. 1991)

117 ALR5th 23—§ 17
Secretary of Housing & Urban Development v. Layfield, 88 Cal. App. 3d Supp. 28, 152 Cal. Rptr. 342 (1978)

43 ALR5th 207—§ 9, 59

Secretary of Indiana Family and Social Services Admin. v. Planned Parenthood of Indiana, Inc., Medicare & Medicaid P 304345, 2013 WL 655224 (U.S. 2013)

86 ALR6th 577—§ 13

Secretary of Revenue v. Carolina Tel. & Tel. Co., 81 N.C. App. 240, 344 S.E.2d 46 (1986)

58 ALR5th 187—§ 19

Secretary of Social and Rehabilitation Services, State ex rel. v. King, 81 P.3d 461 (Kan. Ct. App. 2003)

86 ALR6th 321—§ 8, 11

90 ALR6th 451—§ 31, 97

Secretary of State v. Indiana State AFL-CIO, 175 Ind. App. 376, 371 N.E.2d 1343, 97 L.R.R.M. (BNA) 2690 (1978)

35 ALR6th 1—§ 25

Secretary of State v. McGucken, 244 Md. 70, 222 A.2d 693 (1966)

34 ALR6th 643—§ 29

Secretary of State of Md. v. Joseph H. Munson Co., Inc., 467 U.S. 947, 104 S. Ct. 2839, 81 L. Ed. 2d 786 (1984)

72 ALR6th 513—§ 3

73 ALR6th 281—§ 23

Secret Desires Lingerie, Inc. v. City of Atlanta, 266 Ga. 760, 470 S.E.2d 879 (1996)

20 ALR6th 161—§ 4

21 ALR6th 425—§ 12

23 ALR6th 573—§ 4

Secrist v. Board of Com'rs of Delaware County, 100 Ind. 59, 1885 WL 4211 (1885)

81 ALR6th 363—§ 4

Sector Enterprises, Inc. v. DiPalermo, 779 F. Supp. 236 (N.D.N.Y. 1991)

62 ALR5th 671—§ 5, 6

Secured Financial Solutions, LLC v. Winer, 2010 WL 334644 (Tenn. Ct. App. 2010)

68 ALR6th 331—§ 22

SecureInfo Corp. v. Telos Corp., 387 F. Supp. 2d 593, R.I.C.O. Bus. Disp. Guide (CCH) ¶ 10939 (E.D. Va. 2005)

87 ALR6th 1—§ 21

Securing Compensation by Lee Yit Kyau Pang, In re, 32 Hawaii 699 (1933)

28 ALR5th 547—§ 11

Securities and Exchange Commission v. Chenery Corp., 332 U.S. 194, 67 S. Ct. 1575, 91 L. Ed. 1995, 69 Pub. Util. Rep. (NS) 65 (1947)

80 ALR6th 1—§ 102

Securities and Exchange Commission v. Glenn W. Turner Enterprises, Inc., 474 F.2d 476, Fed. Sec. L. Rep. (CCH) ¶ 93748 (9th Cir. 1973)

28 ALR6th 281—§ 7, 10

Securities and Exchange Commission. Blank v. Talley Industries, Inc., 390 F. Supp. 1, CCH Fed Secur L. Rep. ¶ 94946, 20 FR Serv. 2d 610 (S.D. N.Y. 1975)

23 ALR5th 241—§ 20

Securities and Exchange Com'n v. Mantria Corp., Fed. Sec. L. Rep. (CCH) ¶ 96994, 2012 WL 3778286 (D. Colo. 2012)

100 ALR6th 281—§ 9

Securities Investor Protection Corp. v. BDO Seidman, LLP, 49 F. Supp. 2d 644 (S.D. N.Y. 1999)

48 ALR5th 389—§ 5

Securities Investor Protection Corp. v. BDO Seidman, L.L.P., 95 N.Y.2d 702, 723 N.Y.S.2d 750, 746 N.E.2d 1042 (2001)

48 ALR5th 389—§ 6

Securities Investor Protection Corp. v. R.D. Kushnir & Co., In re, 274 B.R. 768 (Bankr. N.D. Ill. 2002)

47 ALR6th 1—§ 17, 21

Securities Investor Protection Corp. v. R.D. Kushnir & Co., 246 B.R. 582 (Bankr. N.D. Ill. 2000)

28 ALR5th 1—§ 25.5

Securities Investor Protection Corp. v. Stratton Oakmont, Inc., 213 B.R. 433, 48 Fed. R. Evid. Serv. (LCP) 201 (Bankr. S.D. N.Y. 1997)
28 ALR5th 1—§ 25

Securities Investor Protection Corp. v. Stratton Oakmont, Inc., 234 B.R. 293 (Bankr. S.D. N.Y. 1999)
2 ALR6th 195—§ 3, 4

Securitron Magnalock Corp. v. Schnabolk, 65 F.3d 256, R.I.C.O. Bus. Disp. Guide (CCH) ¶ 8884, 42 Fed. R. Evid. Serv. 1388 (2d Cir. 1995)
104 ALR5th 523—§ 6
117 ALR5th 155—§ 12

Security America Corp. Secur. Litigation, Re, 750 F. Supp. 352, CCH Fed Secur L. Rep. ¶ 96231 (N.D. Ill. 1990)
23 ALR5th 241—§ 20

Security Bank v. Dalton, 803 S.W.2d 443 (Tex. App. Fort Worth 1991)
63 ALR5th 1—§ 7, 8

Security Bank & Trust Co. v. Bogard, 494 N.E.2d 965 (Ind. App. 1986)
18 ALR5th 307—§ 3, 15, 32

Security Ben. Asso. v. Daily New Pub. Co., 299 F. 445 (CA8 Neb. 1924)
45 ALR5th 739—§ 3

Security General Ins. Co., In re, 82 S.D. 47, 140 N.W.2d 676 (1966)
85 ALR6th 531—§ 28
87 ALR6th 319—§ 38

Security Ins. Co., Petition of, 258 La. 545, 246 So. 2d 858 (1971)
12 ALR5th 577—§ 12

Security Ins. Co., Petition of, 258 La. 561, 247 So. 2d 389 (1971)
12 ALR5th 577—§ 12

Security Ins. Co. v. Commercial Credit Equipment Corp., 399 So. 2d 31 (Fla. App. D3 1981)
30 ALR5th 170—§ 30

Security Ins. Co. v. Regional Transit Authority, 4 Ohio App. 3d 24, 446 N.E.2d 220 (8th Dist. Cuyahoga County 1982)
86 ALR6th 321—§ 4, 11
89 ALR6th 409—§ 38

Security Ins. Co. v. Webster, 357 So. 2d 741 (Fla. App. D4 1978)
23 ALR5th 241—§ 13

Security Ins. Co. of Hartford v. DeLaurentis, 202 Conn. 178, 520 A.2d 202 (1987)
103 ALR5th 1—§ 5

Security Ins. Co. of Hartford v. Trustmark Ins. Co., 218 F.R.D. 18 (D. Conn. 2003)
104 ALR6th 207—§ 18

Security Ins. Co. of Hartford v. Trustmark Ins. Co., 218 F.R.D. 29 (D. Conn. 2003)
104 ALR6th 207—§ 31

Security Ins. Co. of Hartford v. Trustmark Ins. Co., 2002 WL 32500873 (D. Conn. 2002)
39 ALR6th 391—§ 10, 14

Security Ins. Co. of Hartford v. Trustmark Ins. Co., 2002 WL 32500922 (D. Conn. 2002)
85 ALR6th 531—§ 7

Security Ins. Co. of New Haven, Conn. v. Hudgins, 87 Ga. App. 711, 75 S.E.2d 267 (1953)
115 ALR5th 589—§ 3

Security L. & T. Co. v. Willamette Steam Mills L. & M. Co., 99 Cal. 636, 34 P 321 (1893)
109 ALR5th 421—§ 3

Security Mut. Cas. Co. v. Century Cas. Co., 531 F.2d 974 (10th Cir. 1976)
94 ALR6th 341—§ 20

Security Mut. Ins. Co. v. Black & Decker Corp., 255 A.D.2d 771, 680 N.Y.S.2d 287 (3d Dep't 1998)
122 ALR5th 515—§ 4

Security Nat. Bank v. Belleville Livestock Com. Co., 619 F.2d 840 (CA10 Kan. 1979)
9 ALR5th 708—§ 9

Security Nat. Bank v. Bonnett, 623 P.2d 1061 (Okla. App. 1980)
10 ALR5th 448—§ 5

Security Nat. Bank v. Village Mall at Hillcrest, Inc., 85 Misc. 2d 771, 382 N.Y.S.2d 882 (1976)

4 ALR5th 772—§ 2

Security Nat'l Bank & Trust Co. v. Willim, 151 W. Va. 429, 153 S.E.2d 114 (1967)

36 ALR5th 395—§ 3

Security Nat. Trust v. Moore, 639 So. 2d 373 (La. Ct. App. 2d Cir. 1994)

61 ALR5th 525—§ 12

Security Pacific Finance Corp. v. Bishop, 109 Idaho 25, 704 P.2d 357 (Ct. App. 1985)

73 ALR6th 425—§ 10, 11, 27

Security Pacific Nat. Bank v. Chess, 58 Cal. App. 3d 555, 129 Cal. Rptr. 852, 19 U.C.C. Rep. Serv. (CBC) 544 (2d Dist. 1976)

77 ALR5th 429—§ 5

Security Professionals, Inc. By and Through Paikin v. Segall, 685 So. 2d 1381 (Fla. Dist. Ct. App. 4th Dist. 1997)

120 ALR5th 559—§ 10

Security Sav. & Loan Assn. v. Milton, 171 Ariz. 75, 828 P.2d 1216, 96 Ariz. Adv. Rep. 130 (App. 1991)

10 ALR5th 448—§ 5

Security Sav. Asso. v. Clifton, 755 S.W.2d 925 (Tex. App. Dallas 1988)

14 ALR5th 242—§ 4, 7, 24

Security Sewage Equipment Co. v. Mc-Ferren, 14 Ohio St. 2d 251, 43 O Ops. 2d 432, 237 N.E.2d 898 (1968)

55 ALR5th 1—§ 14

Security Southwest Life Ins. Co. v. Gomez, 768 S.W.2d 505 (Tex. App. El Paso 1989)

6 ALR6th 391—§ 7

Security State Bank v. Basin Petroleum Servs., 713 P.2d 1170, 42 U.C.C.R.S. 1724 (Wyo. 1986)

8 ALR5th 463—§ 4, 63
53 ALR5th 667—§ 26

Security State Bank v. Valley Wide Electric Supply Co., 752 S.W.2d 661 (Tex. App. Corpus Christi 1988)

14 ALR5th 242—§ 24

Security State Bank, Hartley, Iowa v. Ziegeldorf, 554 N.W.2d 884 (Iowa 1996)

16 ALR6th 693—§ 16

Security Trust Co. v. Clifford, 249 Mich. 215, 228 N.W. 719 (1930)

18 ALR5th 230—§ 3, 9

Security Trust Co. v. Graney, 89 Misc. 2d 290, 391 N.Y.S.2d 46 (1977)

13 ALR5th 684—§ 6, 20, 23, 25

Security Trust Corp. v. Estate of Fisher ex rel. Roy, 797 N.E.2d 789 (Ind. Ct. App. 2003)

28 ALR6th 281—§ 3, 4, 7, 10

Security Union Ins. Co. v. McClurkin, 35 S.W.2d 240 (Tex. Civ. App. Galveston 1930)

4 ALR6th 57—§ 2 to 4, 12, 13, 27, 37

Seda v. Board of Ed. of City of New York, 2 A.D.2d 666, 152 N.Y.S.2d 356 (1st Dep't 1956)

66 ALR5th 1—§ 12

Seda v. Sise, 231 A.D.2d 36, 661 N.Y.S.2d 76 (3d Dep't 1997)

97 ALR5th 201—§ 7

Sedalia #200 School Dist. v. Missouri Com. on Human Rights, 843 S.W.2d 928, 59 CCH EPD ¶ 41727 (Mo. App. 1992)

37 ALR5th 349—§ 2, 16

Sedalia No. 200 School Dist. v. Missouri Com'n on Human Rights, 843 S.W.2d 928, 80 Ed. Law Rep. 420, 59 Empl. Prac. Dec. (CCH) ¶ 41727 (Mo. Ct. App. W.D. 1992)

107 ALR5th 623—§ 5, 11

Sedar v. Knowlton Const. Co., 49 Ohio St. 3d 193, 551 N.E.2d 938, 59 Ed. Law Rep. 179 (1990)

5 ALR6th 497—§ 5

Sedberry v. Parsons, 232 N.C. 707, 62 S.E.2d 88 (1950)

119 ALR5th 519—§ 11
Sedberry v. Western Union Tel. Co., 9
So. 2d 73 (La. App. 2d Cir. 1942)
27 ALR5th 174—§ 88
Sedbrook v. Zimmerman Design Group,
Ltd., 190 Wis. 2d 14, 526 N.W.2d
758, Prod. Liab. Rep. (CCH)
¶ 14108 (Ct. App. 1994)
109 ALR5th 301—§ 4, 15
13 ALR6th 355—§ 4
Sedco Intern., S. A. v. Cory, 522 F.
Supp. 254, 9 Fed. R. Evid. Serv. 607
(S.D. Iowa 1981)
10 ALR6th 293—§ 11
Seddon v. Simpson, 816 So. 2d 915 (La.
Ct. App. 4th Cir. 2002)
125 ALR5th 537—§ 1
Sederes v. State, 776 S.W.2d 479 (Mo.
Ct. App. E.D. 1989)
80 ALR5th 55—§ 5
Sederholm v. Michigan Mut. Ins. Co.,
142 Mich. App. 372, 370 N.W.2d
357 (1985)
23 ALR5th 75—§ 9
Sedgwick v. Sedgwick, 50 Colo. 164,
114 P. 488 (1911)
101 ALR6th 455—§ 12
Sedgwick v. Stanton, 14 N.Y. 289, 1856
WL 6765 (1856)
35 ALR6th 1—§ 27
Sedgwick v. Tucker, 90 Ind. 271, 1883
WL 5620 (1883)
98 ALR5th 353—§ 3
Sedillo, In re, 84 N.M. 10, 498 P.2d
1353 (1972)
27 ALR6th 1—§ 5
Sedillo v. Flagstaff, 153 Ariz. 478, 737
P.2d 1377 (App. 1987)
5 ALR5th 875—§ 34
Sedillo v. Williams, 229 F.3d 1164 (10th
Cir. 2000)
119 ALR5th 1—§ 3
Sedlock, Re Marriage of, 69 Wash. App.
484, 849 P.2d 1243 (1993)
9 ALR5th 568—§ 12
Sedlock v. BIC Corp., 741 F. Supp. 175
(W.D. Mo. 1990)
14 ALR5th 47—§ 2, 3, 5

Sedlock v. BIC Corp., 926 F.2d 757
(CA8 Mo. 1991)
14 ALR5th 47—§ 2
Sedman v. Rijdes, 127 N.C. App. 700,
492 S.E.2d 620 (1997)
38 ALR5th 357—§ 4
Sedona Self Realization Group v.
Sun-Up Water Co., 123 Ariz. 168,
598 P.2d 987 (1979)
28 ALR5th 603—§ 18, 23
Sedotto v. Borg-Warner Protective Services Corp., 94 F. Supp. 2d 251, 141
Lab. Cas. (CCH) ¶ 34073 (D. Conn.
2000)
94 ALR5th 1—§ 3, 8
Sedule v. Capital School Dist., 425 F.
Supp. 552 (D. Del. 1976)
123 ALR5th 411—§ 2, 56
See v. Bridgeport Roman Catholic Dioc-
esan Corp., 20 Conn. L. Rptr. 271,
1997 WL 466498 (Conn. Super. Ct.
1997)
2 ALR6th 387—§ 3 to 5, 7, 8, 13
See v. Bridgeport Roman Catholic Dioc-
esan Corp., 1997 WL 466498
(Conn. Super. Ct. 1997)
101 ALR5th 1—§ 8
See v. City of Seattle, 387 U.S. 541, 87
S. Ct. 1737, 18 L. Ed. 2d 943 (1967)
18 ALR6th 1—§ 8
See v. Doe, 2010 WL 2555213 (U.S.
2010)
56 ALR6th 679—§ 26
Seeba, In re Marriage of, 480 N.E.2d
960 (Ind. Ct. App. 4th Dist. 1985)
55 ALR5th 557—§ 6
Seebacher v. Fitzgerald, Hodgman,
Cawthorne and King, P.C., 181
Mich. App. 642, 449 N.W.2d 673
(1989)
12 ALR6th 1—§ 16
Seeber v. Washington State Public Disclosure Commission, 96 Wash. 2d
135, 634 P.2d 303 (1981)
35 ALR6th 1—§ 20
SEECO, Inc. v. Hales, 341 Ark. 673, 22
S.W.3d 157 (2000)
57 ALR5th 753—§ 3

2 ALR6th 387—§ 3

Seedborg v. Lakewood Gardens Civic Asso., 105 Cal. App. 2d 449, 233 P. 2d 943 (1951)

49 ALR5th 685—§ 5

Seeder v. Zoros, 315 Ill. App. 60, 42 N.E.2d 134 (1942)

59 ALR5th 665—§ 12

See Dickerson v. U.S., 530 U.S. 428, 120 S. Ct. 2326, 147 L. Ed. 2d 405 (2000)

20 ALR6th 479—§ 2

See, e.g., In re Detention of Breedlove, 134 Wash. App. 1013, 2006 WL 2125782 (Div. 1 2006)

56 ALR6th 647—§ 2

Seef v. Ingalls Memorial Hosp., 311 Ill. App. 3d 7, 243 Ill. Dec. 806, 724 N.E.2d 115 (1st Dist. 1999)

3 ALR5th 146—§ 21

6 ALR5th 490—§ 12

7 ALR5th 1—§ 3

Seegars v. WIS-TV (Broadcasting Co. of South), 236 S.C. 355, 114 S.E.2d 502 (1960)

42 ALR5th 221—§ 17

Seeger v. Pettit, 77 Pa. 437, 1875 WL 13021 (1875)

109 ALR5th 421—§ 3

Seeger v. State, 2000 WL 1221508 (Minn. Ct. App. 2000)

30 ALR6th 483—§ 43

Seegert v. Zietlow, 95 Ohio App. 3d 451, 642 N.E.2d 697 (8th Dist. Cuyahoga County 1994)

87 ALR5th 361—§ 3, 9, 19

Seeglitz v. State, 500 N.E.2d 144 (Ind. 1986)

57 ALR6th 83—§ 9

Seegmiller v. KSL, Inc., 626 P.2d 968, 7 Media L. Rep. (BNA) 1012 (Utah 1981)

19 ALR5th 1—§ 100, 123

69 ALR5th 645—§ 6, 7

Seegott v. Great American Ins. Co., 1996 WL 417219 (Ohio Ct. App. 8th Dist. Cuyahoga County 1996)

88 ALR5th 493—§ 3

89 ALR5th 1—§ 10

See Harris v. Robert C. Groth, M.D., Inc., P.S., 99 Wash. 2d 438, 663 P.2d 113 (1983)

44 ALR5th 393—§ 2

Seehawer v. Magnecraft Electric Co., 714 F. Supp. 910, 15 FR Serv. 3d 846 (N.D. Ill. 1989)

21 ALR5th 1—§ 7, 14

Seehusen, In re, 273 B.R. 636 (Bankr. D. Colo. 2001)

32 ALR6th 531—§ 43

40 ALR6th 463—§ 32

Seekings v. Jimmy GMC of Tucson, Inc., 130 Ariz. 596, 638 P.2d 210, 32 U.C.C.R.S. 1450 (1981)

38 ALR5th 191—§ 41

Seelandt v. Seelandt, 24 Wis. 2d 73, 128 N.W.2d 66 (1964)

53 ALR5th 375—§ 36

Seelar v. East End Mantel & Tile Co., 58 Pa. Super. 119 (1914)

46 ALR5th 1—§ 2, 18

Seeley v. Killoran, 53 Minn. 290, 55 N.W. 132 (1893)

60 ALR6th 481—§ 4

Seeley v. Seymour, 190 Cal. App. 3d 844, 237 Cal. Rptr. 282 (1st Dist. 1987)

14 ALR5th 242—§ 2, 23

Seeley v. State, 782 N.E.2d 1052 (Ind. Ct. App. 2003)

113 ALR5th 517—§ 5

Seelig v. St. Paul Fire & Marine Ins. Co., 109 F. Supp. 277 (D.C. N.Y. 1953)

22 ALR5th 579—§ 23

Seeligson v. Lewis & Williams, 65 Tex. 215 (1885)

74 ALR5th 369—§ 8

Seely, Re Marriage of, 689 P.2d 1154 (Colo. App. 1984)

17 ALR5th 366—§ 12

Seely v. Board of Public Utilities of Kansas City, 143 Kan. 965, 57 P.2d 471 (1936)

95 ALR5th 29—§ 6

Seely v. Oklahoma Horse Racing Com., 743 P.2d 685 (Okla. App. 1987)

59 ALR5th 203—§ 14, 23
Seelye v. Harvey, 46 Cal. App. 448, 189 P. 311 (1920)

12 ALR5th 195—§ 10
Seelye v. Stephens, 979 F.2d 855 (9th Cir. 1992)

54 ALR6th 1—§ 18
Seeman v. Seeman, 251 A.D.2d 487, 674 N.Y.S.2d 423 (2d Dep't 1998)

3 ALR6th 447—§ 3, 11
Seemann v. Seemann, 225 Neb. 116, 402 N.W.2d 883 (1987)

10 ALR5th 191—§ 5
See N Ski Tours, Inc., In re Complaint of, 2000 WL 284265 (S.D. Ala. 2000)

92 ALR5th 473—§ 7
Seering v. Department of Social Services, 194 Cal. App. 3d 298, 239 Cal. Rptr. 422 (1st Dist. 1987)

85 ALR5th 595—§ 3, 8
Seese v. Volkswagenwerk A. G., 648 F.2d 833, CCH Prod. Liab. Rep. ¶ 8951, 8 Fed. Rules Evid. Serv. 45 (CA3 N.J. 1981)

29 ALR5th 534—§ 15, 39
Seested v. Post Printing & Publishing Co., 326 Mo. 559, 31 S.W.2d 1045 (1930)

12 ALR5th 195—§ 6, 48
See Strickland v. Washington, 466 U.S. 668, 104 S. Ct. 2052, 80 L. Ed. 2d 674 (1984)

19 ALR6th 411—§ 2
Seeton v. Adams, 17 Pa. D. & C.5th 341, 2010 WL 6309992 (Pa. C.P. 2010)

90 ALR6th 385—§ 5
Seeton v. Adams, 50 A.3d 268 (Pa. Commw. Ct. 2012)

90 ALR6th 385—§ 5
Seetransport Wiking Trader Schiffahrtsgesellschaft MBH & Co., Kommanditgesellschaft v. Navimpex Centrala Navala, 29 F.3d 79 (2d Cir. 1994)

88 ALR5th 545—§ 8
Seevers v. Potter, 248 Neb. 621, 537 N.W.2d 505 (1995)

11 ALR6th 1—§ 4, 10
Seewald, In re Marriage of, 22 P.3d 580 (Colo. App. 2001)

77 ALR6th 293—§ 20, 25
Seewald, In re Marriage of, 22 P.3d 580 (Colo. Ct. App. 2001)

3 ALR5th 394—§ 16
Sefick v. Gardner, 164 F.3d 370 (7th Cir. 1998)

70 ALR6th 513—§ 13

71 ALR6th 471—§ 7
Sefkow v. Sefkow, 427 N.W.2d 203 (Minn. 1988)

57 ALR5th 389—§ 21

70 ALR5th 377—§ 2, 4
Sefton v. Jew, 201 F. Supp. 2d 730 (W.D. Tex. 2001)

76 ALR6th 289—§ 5

77 ALR6th 543—§ 13
Sefton v. Pasadena Waldorf School, 219 Cal. App. 3d 359, 268 Cal. Rptr. 335 (2d Dist. 1990)

22 ALR5th 464—§ 4
Sefton v. State, 72 Nev. 106, 295 P.2d 385 (1956)

33 ALR5th 571—§ 4
S.E.G., Matter of Custody of, 521 N.W.2d 357 (Minn. 1994)

89 ALR5th 195—§ 7

63 ALR6th 429—§ 2, 19, 24
S.E.G., People in Interest of, 934 P.2d 920 (Colo. Ct. App. 1997)

58 ALR5th 669—§ 5, 29
S.E.G. v. R.A.G., 735 S.W.2d 164 (Mo. Ct. App. E.D. 1987)

62 ALR5th 591—§ 2, 6

99 ALR5th 475—§ 2, 5
Segal v. Carroll Furniture Co., 51 Ga. App. 164, 179 S.E. 775 (1935)

3 ALR6th 355—§ 4
Segal v. City of New York, 459 F.3d 207, 212 Ed. Law Rep. 21, 24 I.E.R. Cas. (BNA) 1640 (2d Cir. 2006)

41 ALR6th 391—§ 6
Segal v. National City Bank of N.Y., 269 A.D. 986, 58 N.Y.S.2d 261 (2d Dep't 1945)

108 ALR5th 593—§ 16

Segal v. Segal, 278 N.J. Super. 218, 650 A.2d 996 (App. Div. 1994)
81 ALR6th 1—§ 15

Segal v. State Farm General Ins. Co., 2001 WL 1297734 (Cal. App. 2d Dist. 2001)
114 ALR5th 397—§ 10

Segal v. U.S., 128 S. Ct. 2069 (U.S. 2008)
36 ALR6th 681—§ 49

Segal v. Zoning Hearing Bd. of Buckingham Tp., 771 A.2d 90 (Pa. Commw. Ct. 2001)
99 ALR5th 65—§ 25

Segal Co. v. Certain Underwriters at Lloyds, London, 798 N.Y.S.2d 30, 9 A.L.R.6th 787 (App. Div. 1st Dep't 2005)
9 ALR6th 437—§ 15
9 ALR6th 467—§ 13

Segall v. Segall, 632 So. 2d 76, 18 FLW D 2297 (Fla. App. D3 1993)
10 ALR5th 828—§ 19, 21

Segalla v. Planning Bd. of Town of Amenia, 204 A.D.2d 332, 611 N.Y.S.2d 287 (2d Dep't 1994)
4 ALR6th 263—§ 12, 25

Segar v. Garan, Inc., 388 So. 2d 164 (Miss. 1980)
14 ALR5th 1—§ 11

Segarra v. Mellerson, 675 So. 2d 980 (Fla. Dist. Ct. App. 3d Dist. 1996)
119 ALR5th 121—§ 3, 6
125 ALR5th 193—§ 5, 7
2 ALR6th 279—§ 4

Segars v. Bramlett, 245 Ga. 386, 265 S.E.2d 279 (1980)
116 ALR5th 1—§ 62

Segars v. McCormick, 2002 OK CIV APP 89, 55 P.3d 470 (Div. 1 2002)
70 ALR6th 209—§ 37, 42

Segars v. State, 409 So. 2d 1003 (Ala. App. 1982)
29 ALR5th 59—§ 3, 17

Segebart, Re, 61 Ohio Misc. 2d 428, 579 N.E.2d 796 (1989)
15 ALR5th 391—§ 5

Segel, In re Marriage of, 179 Cal. App. 3d 602, 224 Cal. Rptr. 591 (2d Dist. 1986)
110 ALR5th 371—§ 4

Seger v. Cornwell, 44 Misc. 2d 994, 255 N.Y.S.2d 744 (Sup 1964)
117 ALR5th 23—§ 17

Seger v. Seger, 780 N.E.2d 855 (Ind. Ct. App. 2002)
122 ALR5th 205—§ 16

Seger v. U. S., 199 Ct. Cl. 766, 469 F.2d 292 (1972)
25 ALR6th 265—§ 9

Segerson v. Conservation Com'n of Town of Redding, 1995 WL 41374 (Conn. Super. Ct. 1995)
4 ALR6th 263—§ 14

Seggebruch v. Industrial Commission, 288 Ill. 163, 123 N.E. 276 (1919)
40 ALR6th 99—§ 25

Sego v. Mains, 41 Colo. App. 1, 578 P.2d 1069 (1978)
25 ALR5th 1—§ 3

Sego, State ex rel. v. Kirkpatrick, 86 N.M. 359, 524 P.2d 975 (1974)
87 ALR6th 633—§ 7, 8

Segoviano v. Housing Authority, 143 Cal. App. 3d 162, 191 Cal. Rptr. 578 (5th Dist. 1983)
75 ALR6th 109—§ 11

Segrest v. Segrest, 574 So. 2d 821 (Ala. App. 1990)
49 ALR5th 441—§ 8

Segroves v. State, 629 So. 2d 967 (Fla. Dist. Ct. App. 5th Dist. 1993)
52 ALR6th 1—§ 3

Segs v. Consumers Min. Co., 167 Pa. Super. 308, 74 A.2d 688 (1950)
86 ALR5th 295—§ 3

Segui v. Margrill, 29 Fla. L. Weekly D183, 2004 WL 40512 (Fla. Dist. Ct. App. 5th Dist. 2004)
119 ALR5th 121—§ 6

Seguin v. Gallo, 21 Ohio App. 3d 163, 486 N.E.2d 1270 (8th Dist. Cuyahoga County 1985)
1 ALR6th 407—§ 14, 15

Seguna v. Maketa, 181 P.3d 399 (Colo. App. 2008)
91 ALR6th 435—§ 104
Segura v. Green Tree Servicing, LLC, 2011 WL 2462856 (E.D. Cal. 2011)
86 ALR6th 411—§ 5
Segura v. K-Mart Corp., 133 N.M. 192, 2003-NMCA-013, 62 P.3d 283 (Ct. App. 2002)
121 ALR5th 157—§ 2, 9
Segura v. Louisiana State Racing Com., 577 So. 2d 1031 (La. App. 4th Cir. 1991)
59 ALR5th 203—§ 23, 48, 52
Segura v. U.S., 468 U.S. 796, 82 L. Ed. 2d 599, 104 S. Ct. 3380 (1984)
19 ALR5th 470—§ 14
Seheult v. Jeffer, Mangels, Butler & Marmaro, 119 Cal. Rptr. 2d 229 (App. 2d Dist. 2002)
15 ALR6th 427—§ 20
Seheult v. Jeffer, Mangels, Butler & Marmaro, L.L.P., 2004 WL 2050763 (Cal. App. 2d Dist. 2004)
13 ALR6th 1—§ 4
Sehnert v. Schipper & Block, 168 Ill. App. 245, 1912 WL 2021 (2d Dist. 1912)
6 ALR6th 1—§ 7
Sehnert v. Schipper & Block, 193 Ill. App. 202, 1915 WL 2067 (2d Dist. 1915)
6 ALR6th 1—§ 26, 37, 39
Sehon, Stevenson & Co. v. Buckeye Union Ins. Co., 298 F. Supp. 1168 (S.D. W. Va. 1969)
30 ALR5th 170—§ 68
Sehremelis v. Farmers & Merchants Bank, 6 Cal. App. 4th 767, 7 Cal. Rptr. 2d 903, 17 U.C.C. Rep. Serv. 2d 831 (2d Dist. 1992)
104 ALR5th 459—§ 3
Seibel v. A.O. Smith Corp., 1998 WL 315067 (W.D. Wis. 1998)
98 ALR6th 417—§ 5
Seibel v. Colorado Real Estate Com., 34 Colo. App. 415, 530 P.2d 1290 (1974)

7 ALR5th 474—§ 151
Seiber v. State, 2002-Ohio-6816, 2002 WL 31771250 (Ohio Ct. App. 8th Dist. Cuyahoga County 2002)
53 ALR6th 305—§ 18
Seiber v. Wilder, 1994 WL 558969 (Ohio Ct. App. 2d Dist. Greene County 1994)
83 ALR5th 1—§ 3
Seibert v. Alt, 31 Fed. Appx. 309 (7th Cir. 2002)
89 ALR6th 1—§ 115
Seibert v. Amateur Athletic Union of U.S., Inc., 422 F. Supp. 2d 1033 (D. Minn. 2006)
22 ALR6th 49—§ 17
Seibert v. Briggs, 152 A.D.2d 900, 544 N.Y.S.2d 246 (N.Y. App. Div. 1989)
46 ALR5th 735—§ 1
Seibert v. General Motors Corp., 853 S.W.2d 773, Prod. Liab. Rep. (CCH) ¶ 13619 (Tex. App. Houston 14th Dist. 1993)
48 ALR5th 1—§ 2
93 ALR5th 103—§ 2
Seibert v. Mock, 510 N.E.2d 1373 (Ind. App. 1987)
7 ALR5th 841—§ 2
Seibert v. State, 923 So. 2d 460 (Fla. 2006)
58 ALR6th 499—§ 41
Seibert v. Vic Regnier Builders, 253 Kan. 540, 856 P.2d 1332 (1993)
31 ALR5th 550—§ 3, 4
Seibly v. Sunnyside, 178 Wash. 632, 35 P.2d 56 (1934)
25 ALR5th 391—§ 28, 87
Seibold v. Warehouse Leasing Associates, 7 Va. Cir. 56, 1981 WL 180509 (1981)
44 ALR6th 481—§ 45
Seibright v. State, 2 W. Va. 591, 1867 WL 1677 (1867)
57 ALR6th 445—§ 15
Seide v. Committee of Bar Examiners, 49 Cal. 3d 933, 264 Cal. Rptr. 361, 782 P.2d 602 (1989)

3 ALR6th 49—§ 14, 17

Seidel v. Albertson's, Inc., 1995 WL 82268 (D. Or. 1995)

82 ALR5th 1—§ 6

Seidel Belt Corp. v. Kennedy Photo Engraving, Inc., 153 N.Y.S.2d 951 (Sup. 1956)

42 ALR5th 53—§ 46

Seideman by Seideman v. County of Monroe, 185 A.D.2d 640, 585 N.Y.S.2d 909 (4th Dep't 1992)

29 ALR6th 369—§ 11, 43

Seidemann v. Bowen, 584 F.3d 104, 249 Ed. Law Rep. 638, 187 L.R.R.M. (BNA) 2257, 158 Lab. Cas. (CCH) ¶ 10100 (2d Cir. 2009)

73 ALR6th 281—§ 15

Seiden v. A. Silmac Glass Corp., 674 N.Y.S.2d 316 (App. Div. 1st Dep't 1998)

11 ALR5th 127—§ 29.5

Seiden v. National Commercial Bank & Trust Co., 57 Misc. 2d 132, 291 N.Y.S.2d 68 (City Ct. 1968)

123 ALR5th 1—§ 14

Seidl v. Greentree Mortg. Co., 30 F. Supp. 2d 1292 (D. Colo. 1998)

3 ALR6th 153—§ 25

68 ALR6th 331—§ 4, 17, 18

Seidl v. Trollhaugen, Inc., 305 Minn. 506, 232 N.W.2d 236 (1975)

75 ALR5th 583—§ 6

Seidlitz v. Seidlitz, 217 Wis. 2d 82, 578 N.W.2d 638 (Ct. App. 1998)

102 ALR5th 395—§ 4, 14

Seidman v. Central Bancorp, Inc., 16 Mass. L. Rptr. 383, 2003 WL 21528509 (Mass. Super. Ct. 2003)

37 ALR6th 1—§ 21

Seidman v. Fishburne-Hudgins Educational Foundation, Inc., 724 F.2d 413, 14 Fed. Rules Evid. Serv. 1715, 38 FR Serv. 2d 1157 (CA4 Va. 1984)

17 ALR5th 179—§ 4

Seidman v. Fishburne-Hudgins Educ. Foundation, Inc., 724 F.2d 413, 14 Fed. R. Evid. Serv. 1715, 38 Fed. R. Serv. 2d 1157 (4th Cir. 1984)

100 ALR6th 563—§ 5

Seidman v. Fishburne-Hudgins Educ. Found., Inc., 724 F.2d 413 (4th Cir. 1984)

101 ALR5th 619—§ 2

Seidman v. State, 847 So. 2d 1144 (Fla. Dist. Ct. App. 4th Dist. 2003)

28 ALR6th 281—§ 3, 20

Seierstad v. Serwold, 105 Wash. 2d 589, 716 P.2d 885 (1986)

29 ALR6th 507—§ 54

Seif v. Long Beach, 286 N.Y. 382, 36 N.E.2d 630 (1941)

47 ALR5th 553—§ 16, 23

Seifer v. PHE, Inc., 196 F. Supp. 2d 622 (S.D. Ohio 2002)

76 ALR6th 289—§ 5

77 ALR6th 543—§ 19

Seifer v. Schwimmer, 166 Misc. 329, 1 N.Y.S.2d 730 (Sup 1937)

81 ALR6th 1—§ 48

Seifert, Re Disciplinary Proceedings against, 149 Wis. 2d 832, 439 N.W.2d 578 (1989)

9 ALR5th 193—§ 25, 26, 31

Seifert v. Arlona Co., 205 A.D.2d 679, 613 N.Y.S.2d 643 (2d Dep't 1994)

74 ALR5th 49—§ 55, 62

Seifert v. California State Personnel Bd., 2007 WL 2323343 (Cal. App. 4th Dist. 2007)

87 ALR6th 1—§ 92

Seifert v. Seifert, 319 N.C. 367, 354 S.E.2d 506 (1987)

59 ALR6th 433—§ 66

Seifert v. Solem, 387 F.2d 925, 12 FR Serv. 2d 177 (CA7 Wis. 1967)

14 ALR5th 242—§ 32

Seifert v. Williams, 221 F.3d 1352 (10th Cir. 2000)

119 ALR5th 1—§ 3

Seiferth, Re, 309 N.Y. 80, 127 N.E.2d 820 (1955)

21 ALR5th 248—§ 3, 7

Seiffer v. Topsy's International, Inc., 70 F.R.D. 622, 22 FR Serv. 2d 259 (D.C. Kan. 1976)
23 ALR5th 241—§ 19

Seigal v. Merrick, 619 F.2d 160, CCH Fed Secur L. Rep. ¶ 97318 (CA2 N.Y. 1980)
23 ALR5th 241—§ 21

Seigel v. Merrill Lynch, Pierce, Fenner & Smith, Inc., 745 A.2d 301, 40 U.C.C. Rep. Serv. 2d 819 (D.C. 2000)
74 ALR5th 369—§ 19

Seigle v. Bromley, 22 Colo. App. 189, 124 P. 191 (1912)
93 ALR5th 621—§ 5, 7

Seigneur v. National Fitness Institute, Inc., 132 Md. App. 271, 752 A.2d 631 (2000)
61 ALR6th 147—§ 4, 8, 11

Seikbert, State ex rel. v. Wilkinson, 69 Ohio St. 3d 489, 1994-Ohio-39, 633 N.E.2d 1128 (1994)
9 ALR6th 541—§ 30

Seiler v. Levitz Furniture Co. of Eastern Region, Inc., 367 A.2d 999 (Del. 1976)
47 ALR6th 303—§ 5

Seiler v. Seiler, 48 Wis. 2d 400, 180 N.W.2d 627, 51 A.L.R.3d 455 (1970)
9 ALR5th 568—§ 8

Seiler v. State, 522 So. 2d 113 (Fla. Dist. Ct. App. 5th Dist. 1988)
57 ALR6th 445—§ 44

Seilkop v. Seilkop, 575 So. 2d 269, 16 FLW D 517 (Fla. App. D3 1991)
49 ALR5th 441—§ 17

Seimon v. Becton Dickinson & Co., 91 Ohio App. 3d 323, 632 N.E.2d 603 (Cuyahoga Co. 1993)
59 ALR5th 535—§ 8

Seipel, Re Estate of, 130 Cal. App. 273, 19 P.2d 808 (1933)
3 ALR5th 590—§ 19, 20

Seipp v. Chicago Transit Authority, 12 Ill. App. 3d 852, 299 N.E.2d 330 (1st Dist. 1973)
15 ALR5th 119—§ 3, 5, 32, 48

Seipp v. Stetson Ross Mach. Co., 32 Wash. App. 224, 646 P.2d 783 (Div. 1 1982)
13 ALR6th 355—§ 5, 41
18 ALR6th 629—§ 4, 19, 30

Seismic Explorations v. Dobray, 169 S.W.2d 739 (Tex. Civ. App. Galveston 1943)
24 ALR6th 747—§ 4

Seiter v. State, 719 S.W.2d 141 (Mo. Ct. App. E.D. 1986)
67 ALR6th 103—§ 13

Seith v. Commonwealth Elec. Co., 241 Ill. 252, 89 N.E. 425 (1909)
95 ALR5th 29—§ 3

Seith v. Wheaton, 89 Ill. App. 2d 446, 232 N.E.2d 173 (2d Dist. 1967)
5 ALR5th 422—§ 3

Seit-Olsen v. Reliance Appraisals, LLC, 2006 WL 1113936 (Mich. Ct. App. 2006)
44 ALR6th 1—§ 11

Seitz v. L. & R Industries, Inc. (Palco Products Division), 437 A.2d 1345 (R.I. 1981)
82 ALR5th 149—§ 2, 4, 16, 21, 30, 44, 65

Seitz v. Mark-O-Lite Sign Contractors, Inc., 210 N.J. Super. 646, 510 A.2d 319 (Law Div. 1986)
104 ALR6th 303—§ 15

Seitz v. Ohio State Medical Board, 24 Ohio App. 154, 5 Ohio L. Abs. 813, 157 N.E. 304 (4th Dist. Scioto County 1926)
19 ALR6th 577—§ 4

Seitz v. Seitz, 35 Wis. 2d 282, 151 N.W.2d 86 (1967)
31 ALR5th 572—§ 3, 13

Seitz v. Seitz, 471 So. 2d 612 (Fla. App. D3 1985)
49 ALR5th 441—§ 4, 19

Seitz v. State, 100 Or. App. 665, 788 P.2d 1004, 57 CCH EPD ¶ 41176 (1990)
20 ALR5th 677—§ 2, 4 to 6

Seitz v. Vogler, 289 Ill. App. 3d 1029, 225 Ill. Dec. 22, 682 N.E.2d 766 (2d Dist. 1997)
89 ALR5th 255—§ 5

Seitz v. Zac Smith & Co., Inc., 500 So. 2d 706 (Fla. Dist. Ct. App. 1st Dist. 1987)
70 ALR5th 261—§ 3, 5, 39
74 ALR5th 523—§ 2, 3, 9, 43
75 ALR5th 413—§ 2

Seitzinger v. American Red Cross, 1992 WL 361700 (E.D. Pa. 1992)
64 ALR5th 333—§ 3, 7
75 ALR5th 229—§ 14, 17

Seitz-Partridge v. Loyola University of Chicago, 409 Ill. App. 3d 76, 350 Ill. Dec. 150, 948 N.E.2d 219, 267 Ed. Law Rep. 851 (1st Dist. 2011)
83 ALR6th 195—§ 3, 18, 19

Seitz-Partridge v. Loyola University of Chicago, 2013 IL App (1st) 113409, 2013 WL 792835 (Ill. App. Ct. 1st Dist. 2013)
83 ALR6th 195—§ 4

SEIU Healthcare 775NW v. Gregoire, 168 Wash. 2d 593, 229 P.3d 774, 188 L.R.R.M. (BNA) 2238 (2010)
82 ALR6th 497—§ 3

Seivewright v. State, 7 P.3d 24 (Wyo. 2000)
90 ALR5th 453—§ 27
1 ALR6th 657—§ 4

Seiwert v. Spencer-Owen Community School Corp., 497 F. Supp. 2d 942, 223 Ed. Law Rep. 654 (S.D. Ind. 2007)
98 ALR6th 599—§ 22, 23, 89, 93

Seizer v. Sessions, 132 Wash. 2d 642, 940 P.2d 261 (1997)
124 ALR5th 537—§ 13

Seizure of $23,691.00 in U.S. Currency, Matter of, 273 Mont. 474, 905 P.2d 148 (1995)
104 ALR5th 229—§ 17
115 ALR5th 403—§ 7, 8
4 ALR6th 113—§ 18, 34

Seizure of $23,691.00 in U.S. Currency, Matter of, 273 Mont. 474, 905 P.2d 148 (1995)
34 ALR6th 539—§ 4

Seizure of Weapons Belonging to Smilovic, In re, 2006 WL 3543104 (N.J. Super. Ct. App. Div. 2006)
91 ALR6th 435—§ 64, 113

S.E.J., In re Civil Commitment of, 2008 WL 2466928 (N.J. Super. Ct. App. Div. 2008)
78 ALR6th 417—§ 68

Sekerak v. National City Bank, 342 F. Supp. 2d 701, 55 U.C.C. Rep. Serv. 2d 155 (N.D. Ohio 2004)
62 ALR6th 1—§ 23, 28

Sekeres, Ex parte, 646 So. 2d 640 (Ala. 1994)
79 ALR5th 587—§ 2

Sekerez v. Board of Sanitary Comm'rs etc., 160 Ind. App. 13, 309 N.E.2d 460 (1974)
41 ALR5th 47—§ 15

Sekhar v. U.S., 2013 WL 3196929 (U.S. 2013)
86 ALR6th 577—§ 25

Seklir v. Krizer, 48 Misc. 25, 96 N.Y.S. 74 (1905)
46 ALR5th 1—§ 16, 22

Sekora v. Industrial Com'n, 198 Ill. App. 3d 584, 144 Ill. Dec. 818, 556 N.E.2d 285 (2d Dist. 1990)
41 ALR6th 207—§ 30

S.E.L. v. J.W.W., 143 Misc. 2d 455, 541 N.Y.S.2d 675 (Fam. Ct. 1989)
95 ALR5th 533—§ 3, 7
124 ALR5th 203—§ 3

Selathia Nicole F., In re Commitment of Guardianship and Custody of, 243 A.D.2d 400, 663 N.Y.S.2d 183 (1st Dep't 1997)
20 ALR5th 534—§ 14

Selbst v. Touche Ross & Co., 587 F. Supp. 1015, 46 Fair Empl. Prac. Cas. (BNA) 669 (S.D. N.Y. 1984)
81 ALR5th 367—§ 4
103 ALR5th 557—§ 5

Selby v. Baker, 2002 WL 31264745 (Mich. Ct. App. 2002)
  18 ALR6th 325—§ 28
  54 ALR6th 593—§ 10
Selby v. Burgess, 289 Ark. 491, 712 S.W.2d 898 (1986)
  16 ALR6th 1—§ 23
Selby v. Danville Pepsi-Cola Bottling Co., Inc., 169 Ill. App. 3d 427, 119 Ill. Dec. 941, 523 N.E.2d 697 (4th Dist. 1988)
  74 ALR5th 49—§ 2, 6, 8, 12, 77
Selby v. New Line Cinema Corp., 96 F. Supp. 2d 1053, 54 U.S.P.Q.2d 1827 (C.D. Cal. 2000)
  76 ALR6th 289—§ 4
  77 ALR6th 543—§ 4
Selby v. Pepsico, Inc., 784 F. Supp. 750, 92 Daily Journal DAR 5732, 57 BNA FEP Cas. 500 (N.D. Cal. 1991)
  51 ALR5th 1—§ 7
Selby v. Savard, 134 Ariz. 222, 655 P.2d 342 (1982)
  44 ALR5th 193—§ 20
Selby v. Selby, 569 P.2d 539 (Okla. App. 1977)
  17 ALR5th 366—§ 10, 16
Selchert v. Selchert, 90 Wis. 2d 1, 280 N.W.2d 293 (App. 1979)
  9 ALR5th 568—§ 13
Selchert v. Selchert, 90 Wis. 2d 1, 280 N.W.2d 293 (Ct. App. 1979)
  38 ALR6th 313—§ 9
Selchert v. State, 420 N.W.2d 816, 4 A.L.R.5th 1129 (Iowa 1988)
  4 ALR5th 753—§ 4
Seld v. District of Columbia, 103 U.S. App. D.C. 71, 254 F.2d 774 (1958)
  45 ALR5th 173—§ 12
Selden v. Hiranaka, 1995 WL 705232 (Mass. Super. Ct. 1995)
  125 ALR5th 403—§ 10
  18 ALR6th 325—§ 29
Selden v. Sterling, 316 Ill. App. 455, 45 N.E.2d 329 (1942)
  28 ALR5th 107—§ 37

Seldin, Matter of, 147 A.D.2d 149, 541 N.Y.S.2d 573 (2d Dep't 1989)
  45 ALR6th 175—§ 24
Seldin v. Seldin, 55 Misc. 2d 187, 284 N.Y.S.2d 679 (Sup. Ct. 1967)
  99 ALR5th 475—§ 4, 8
Seldon v. Direct Response Technologies, Inc., 2004 WL 691222 (S.D. N.Y. 2004)
  3 ALR6th 153—§ 10
Seldon v. State, 151 Md. App. 204, 824 A.2d 999 (2003)
  115 ALR5th 477—§ 6
Select Creations, Inc. v. Paliafito America, Inc., 852 F. Supp. 740 (E.D. Wis. 1994)
  2 ALR6th 195—§ 3 to 5, 18
Select Designs, Ltd. v. Union Mut. Fire Ins. Co., 165 Vt. 69, 674 A.2d 798 (1996)
  98 ALR5th 1—§ 4
Selected Investments Corp. v. Spencer-Sedbrook, 1945 OK 340, 196 Okla. 565, 166 P.2d 764 (1945)
  73 ALR6th 571—§ 60
Selected Lands Corp. v. Speich, 702 S.W.2d 197 (Tex. App. Houston 1st Dist. 1985)
  119 ALR5th 519—§ 24
Selected Risks Ins. Co. v. Dierolf, 138 N.J. Super. 287, 350 A.2d 526 (Ch. Div. 1975)
  103 ALR5th 1—§ 10
Selected Risks Ins. Co. v. Schulz, 136 N.J. Super. 185, 345 A.2d 349 (App. Div. 1975)
  103 ALR5th 1—§ 4, 19
Selected Risks Ins. Co. v. Schulz, 140 N.J. Super. 555, 357 A.2d 31 (Ch Div. 1976)
  31 ALR5th 116—§ 5
Selected Risks Ins. Co. v. Thompson, 520 Pa. 130, 552 A.2d 1382 (1989)
  31 ALR5th 116—§ 5
Selective Ins. Co. v. J.B. Mouton & Sons, Inc., 954 F.2d 1075 (CA5 La. 1992)
  18 ALR5th 187—§ 5

Selective Ins. Co. of America v. Capo-ferri, 2010 WL 1028313 (N.J. Super. Ct. App. Div. 2010)

80 ALR6th 389—§ 22

Selective Service System v. Minnesota Public Interest Research Group, 468 U.S. 841, 104 S. Ct. 3348, 82 L. Ed. 2d 632, 18 Ed. Law Rep. 115 (1984)

62 ALR6th 517—§ 12, 16, 45, 46, 59

Select Lake City Theatre Operating Co. v. Central Nat. Bank, 277 F.2d 814 (CA7 Ill. 1960)

22 ALR5th 327—§ 8

Selectmen of Brookline v. Allen, 325 Mass. 482, 90 N.E.2d 903 (1950)

91 ALR5th 225—§ 10

Selectmen of Framingham, Board of v. Municipal Court of City of Boston, 373 Mass. 783, 369 N.E.2d 1145 (1977)

105 ALR5th 1—§ 4, 11

17 ALR6th 327—§ 29

Selevan v. New York Thruway Author-ity, 584 F.3d 82 (2d Cir. 2009)

83 ALR6th 399—§ 3, 4

Selevan v. New York Thruway Author-ity, 2011 WL 5974988 (N.D. N.Y. 2011)

83 ALR6th 399—§ 3, 5 to 7

Selevan v. New York Thruway Author-ity, 2013 WL 1223314 (2d Cir. 2013)

83 ALR6th 399—§ 3

Seley v. G. D. Searle & Co., 67 Ohio St. 2d 192, 21 Ohio Op. 3d 121, 423 N.E.2d 831 (1981)

38 ALR5th 683—§ 3, 7, 10

54 ALR5th 1—§ 2 to 4

57 ALR5th 1—§ 5, 25, 26, 31

Seley v. Unemployment Compensation Bd. of Review, 185 Pa. Super. 413, 138 A.2d 174 (1958)

60 ALR5th 459—§ 2, 12, 18

Self v. Allstate Ins. Co., 345 F. Supp. 191 (M.D. Fla. 1972)

51 ALR5th 701—§ 8, 9

Self v. American Legion Post No. 389, 29 Ohio App. 2d 189, 58 Ohio Op. 2d 328, 279 N.E.2d 889 (4th Dist. Washington County 1972)

21 ALR6th 81—§ 45, 50

Self v. Board of Review, 91 N.J. 453, 453 A.2d 170 (1982)

68 ALR5th 13—§ 9, 18, 31

Self v. Fugard, 518 So. 2d 727 (Ala. App. 1987)

15 ALR5th 692—§ 4, 27

Self v. Great Lakes Dredge & Dock Co., 832 F.2d 1540, 1988 A.M.C. 2278, 24 Fed. R. Evid. Serv. 949 (11th Cir. 1987)

66 ALR6th 185—§ 10

Self v. Lenertz Terminal, Inc., 854 S.W.2d 571, 8 BNA IER Cas. 710 (Mo. App. 1993)

3 ALR5th 746—§ 3

Self v. Maynor, 421 So. 2d 1279 (Ala. Civ. App. 1982)

86 ALR6th 321—§ 7

90 ALR6th 451—§ 51

Self v. State, 232 Ga. App. 735, 503 S.E.2d 625 (1998)

76 ALR5th 1—§ 2, 17

77 ALR5th 201—§ 2

79 ALR5th 237—§ 2

Self v. State, 504 So. 2d 810 (Fla. Dist. Ct. App. 2d Dist. 1987)

46 ALR6th 63—§ 2

Self v. Wisener, 226 Ark. 58, 287 S.W.2d 890, 37 L.R.R.M. (BNA) 2740, 30 Lab. Cas. (CCH) ¶ 69854 (1956)

105 ALR5th 243—§ 21

Selfe v. Smith, 397 So. 2d 348 (Fla. Dist. Ct. App. 1st Dist. 1981)

46 ALR5th 557—§ 6

62 ALR5th 537—§ 4

Selfe v. State, 8 Fulton County D. Rep. 358, 2008 WL 239846 (Ga. Ct. App. 2008)

33 ALR6th 373—§ 18

Selfe v. U.S., 778 F.2d 769, 86-1 U.S. Tax Cas. (CCH) ¶ 9115, 57 A.F.T.R.2d 86-464 (11th Cir. 1985)

118 ALR5th 597—§ 13

Selfridge v. Dollar General Corp., Inc.,
2000 OK CIV APP 86, 9 P.3d 695
(Okla. Civ. App. Div. 1 2000)

17 ALR5th 1—§ 6

Selfridge v. Morrison Cafeteria Co., 192
Ga. App. 469, 385 S.E.2d 137
(1989)

107 ALR5th 441—§ 38

109 ALR5th 161—§ 9

20 ALR6th 641—§ 10

Selfridge v. Paxton, 145 Cal. 713, 79 P.
425 (1905)

35 ALR5th 757—§ 5

Selfridge v. State, 723 P.2d 986 (Okla.
Crim. App. 1986)

77 ALR5th 201—§ 6

78 ALR5th 1—§ 21

Self Service Super Market, Inc. v. Harris, 3 N.Y.2d 615, 170 N.Y.S.2d
816, 148 N.E.2d 151 (1958)

45 ALR5th 251—§ 6

Self Towing, Inc. v. Brown Marine Services, Inc., 837 F.2d 1501 (11th Cir.
1988)

66 ALR6th 185—§ 13

Selgado v. Commercial Warehouse Co.,
86 N.M. 633, 526 P.2d 430 (App.
1974)

26 ALR5th 401—§ 8, 24

Selgado v. Commercial Warehouse Co.,
88 N.M. 579, 544 P.2d 719 (Ct.
App. 1975)

62 ALR5th 537—§ 3

Selig v. BMW of North America, Inc.,
832 S.W.2d 95, 1992-2 Trade Cas.
(CCH) ¶ 69891 (Tex. App. Houston
14th Dist. 1992)

76 ALR6th 465—§ 22

Selig v. Tribe, 30 Mass. L. Rptr. 94,
2012 WL 2913517 (Mass. Super.
Ct. 2012)

85 ALR6th 429—§ 23

Seligman v. Victor Talking Mach. Co.,
71 N.J. Eq. 697, 63 A. 1093 (Ch.
1906)

103 ALR5th 157—§ 4, 11

Seligman & Latz, Inc. v. Noonan, 201
Misc. 96, 104 N.Y.S.2d 35 (1951)

12 ALR5th 847—§ 12

Seligman & Latz of Pittsburgh, Inc. v.
Vernillo, 382 Pa. 161, 114 A.2d 672
(1955)

12 ALR5th 847—§ 17

Seligman-Hargis v. Hargis, 186 S.W.3d
582 (Tex. App. Dallas 2006)

52 ALR6th 433—§ 9

57 ALR6th 163—§ 9, 29

66 ALR6th 269—§ 16

Selinger Enterprises, Inc. v. Cassuto, 50
A.D.3d 766, 860 N.Y.S.2d 533 (2d
Dep't 2008)

47 ALR6th 1—§ 64

Selitte v. Pirolo, 2008 WL 5220297
(Conn. Super. Ct. 2008)

45 ALR6th 1—§ 9

Selivonik, In re, 164 Vt. 383, 670 A.2d
831 (1995)

36 ALR6th 475—§ 16

39 ALR6th 577—§ 11

Selke v. City of Waterloo, 1999 WL
711442 (Iowa Ct. App. 1999)

54 ALR6th 201—§ 49

Selko v. Home Ins. Co., 139 F.3d 146
(3d Cir. 1998)

92 ALR5th 273—§ 5

Selko v. Home Ins.Co., 1996 WL
397483 (E.D. Pa. 1996)

92 ALR5th 273—§ 5

Selkow v. W.C.A.B. (Anchor Davis-Jay
Box Co.), 662 A.2d 31 (Pa.
Commw. Ct. 1995)

108 ALR5th 1—§ 36

Selkowitz v. Litton Loan Servicing, LP,
2010 WL 3733928 (W.D. Wash.
2010)

104 ALR6th 485—§ 5

Sell, Re Marriage of, 451 N.W.2d 28
(Iowa App. 1989)

3 ALR5th 394—§ 6

Sell v. Bertsch & Co., 577 F. Supp.
1393, CCH Prod. Liab. Rep.
¶ 10081 (D.C. Kan. 1984)

9 ALR5th 1—§ 4

Sell v. Douglas Tp. Zoning Hearing Bd., 149 Pa. Commw. 425, 613 A.2d 162 (1992)
47 ALR6th 439—§ 3, 7

Sell v. Hotchkiss, 264 N.C. 185, 141 S.E.2d 259 (1965)
61 ALR5th 707—§ 17

Sell v. Mary Lanning Memorial Hosp. Ass'n, 243 Neb. 266, 498 N.W.2d 522 (1993)
96 ALR5th 107—§ 7

Sell v. Steller, 55 N.J. Eq. 530, 37 A. 1010 (Ct. Err. & App. 1897)
6 ALR6th 391—§ 7

Sell v. U.S., 539 U.S. 166, 123 S. Ct. 2174, 156 L. Ed. 2d 197, 188 A.L.R. Fed. 679 (2003)
78 ALR6th 229—§ 10

Sel-Lab Marketing, Inc. v. Dial Corp., 48 U.C.C. Rep. Serv. 2d 482 (S.D. N.Y. 2002)
110 ALR5th 277—§ 3, 4

Selland v. Perry, 905 F. Supp. 260, 67 Empl. Prac. Dec. (CCH) ¶ 43897 (D. Md. 1995)
96 ALR5th 391—§ 3, 8, 9

Selland Pontiac-GMC, Inc. v. King, 384 N.W.2d 490, 1 U.C.C.R.S.2d 463 (Minn. App. 1986)
55 ALR5th 1—§ 5, 37

Sellari v. W.C.A.B. (NGK Metals Corp.), 698 A.2d 1372 (Pa. Commw. Ct. 1997)
86 ALR5th 295—§ 14, 15

Sellars v. Florida Real Estate Com., 380 So. 2d 1052 (Fla. App. D1 1979)
7 ALR5th 474—§ 71

Sellars v. Southern Pacific Co., 33 Cal. App. 701, 166 P. 599 (1917)
10 ALR5th 371—§ 11, 17

Sellars v. Stauffer Communications, 9 Kan. App. 2d 573, 684 P.2d 450, 10 Media L. R. 2081 (1984)
19 ALR5th 1—§ 77, 135
44 ALR5th 193—§ 23

Selle v. Kleamenakis, 142 So. 2d 50 (La. Ct. App. 4th Cir. 1962)
103 ALR5th 157—§ 4

Selleck v. Janesville, 104 Wis. 570, 80 N.W. 944 (1899)
49 ALR5th 685—§ 3

Selleck v. Markell, 2008 WL 5352249 (Cal. App. 4th Dist. 2008)
72 ALR6th 563—§ 15, 34

Sellent-Repent Corp. v. Queens Borough Gas & Electric Co., 160 Misc. 920, 290 N.Y.S. 887 (1936)
8 ALR5th 653—§ 3

Sellers v. Abbeville, 458 So. 2d 592 (La. App. 3d Cir. 1984)
8 ALR5th 798—§ 3
10 ALR5th 245—§ 2, 20

Sellers v. A.H. Robins Co., 715 F.2d 1559 (CA11 Ala. 1983)
54 ALR5th 1—§ 2

Sellers v. Bank of America, Nat. Ass'n, 2012 WL 1853005 (N.D. Ga. 2012)
86 ALR6th 411—§ 5
104 ALR6th 485—§ 4, 7

Sellers v. Bell, 94 F. 801 (C.C.A. 5th Cir. 1899)
44 ALR6th 481—§ 26

Sellers v. Blackwell, 378 So. 2d 1106 (Ala. 1979)
36 ALR5th 395—§ 2, 3, 6
37 ALR5th 237—§ 2

Sellers v. Collins, 12 F.3d 1097 (5th Cir. 1993)
51 ALR6th 1—§ 27

Sellers v. Com., 41 Va. App. 268, 584 S.E.2d 452 (2003)
9 ALR6th 1—§ 8, 10

Sellers v. Hathaway, 36 A.D.2d 988, 321 N.Y.S.2d 62 (3d Dep't 1971)
42 ALR6th 545—§ 3, 8, 10, 18, 20
43 ALR6th 375—§ 3, 4, 11, 36

Sellers v. Hauch, 183 Mich. App. 1, 454 N.W.2d 150 (1990)
40 ALR6th 99—§ 11
42 ALR6th 61—§ 28

Sellers v. Lithium Corp., 94 N.C. App. 575, 380 S.E.2d 526 (1989)
99 ALR6th 643—§ 22

Sellers v. Philip's Barber Shop, 46 N.J. 340, 217 A.2d 121 (1966)

---

88 ALR6th 203—§ 51
Sellers v. Picou, 474 So. 2d 667 (Ala. 1985)
12 ALR5th 1—§ 18
Sellers v. Sebastian Cove Homeowners Ass'n, Inc., 250 Ga. App. 762, 552 S.E.2d 498 (2001)
115 ALR5th 251—§ 56
Sellers v. Seligman, 463 So. 2d 697 (La. Ct. App. 4th Cir. 1985)
97 ALR5th 359—§ 16
Sellers v. Sellers, 201 Wis. 2d 578, 549 N.W.2d 481 (Ct. App. 1996)
57 ALR5th 389—§ 14
76 ALR5th 191—§ 3
Sellers v. Sellers, 221 S.W.3d 43 (Tenn. Ct. App. 2006)
59 ALR6th 433—§ 20
Sellers v. Sellers, 555 So. 2d 1117 (Ala. Civ. App. 1989)
53 ALR5th 375—§ 17
Sellers v. Sellers, 638 So. 2d 481 (Miss. 1994)
53 ALR5th 375—§ 36
Sellers v. Sellers, 775 P.2d 1029 (Wyo. 1989)
47 ALR5th 129—§ 3
Sellers v. State, 300 Ark. 280, 778 S.W.2d 603 (1989)
7 ALR5th 758—§ 16
Sellers v. State, 362 S.C. 182, 607 S.E.2d 82 (2005)
8 ALR6th 265—§ 5
Sellers v. State, 809 P.2d 676 (Okla. Crim. App. 1991)
57 ALR5th 141—§ 11
Sellers v. State, 935 So. 2d 1207 (Ala. Crim. App. 2005)
25 ALR6th 227—§ 29
Sellers v. Trans World Airlines, Inc., 752 S.W.2d 413 (Mo. Ct. App. W.D. 1988)
86 ALR5th 295—§ 4, 18
Sellers v. U.S., 870 F.2d 1098 (6th Cir. 1989)
80 ALR6th 469—§ 22, 25
Sellers v. Ward, 135 F.3d 1333 (10th Cir. 1998)

72 ALR5th 109—§ 4
Sellery v. Cressey, 48 Cal. App. 4th 538, 55 Cal. Rptr. 2d 706 (2d Dist. 1996)
9 ALR5th 321—§ 3, 5
11 ALR5th 588—§ 4
Sellet v. United Artists Theaters, Inc., 251 A.D.2d 488, 674 N.Y.S.2d 426 (2d Dep't 1998)
74 ALR5th 49—§ 55, 62
Sellew v. Sellew, 675 S.W.2d 83 (Mo. App. 1984)
17 ALR5th 366—§ 21
Selley v. State, 237 Ga. App. 47, 514 S.E.2d 706 (1999)
65 ALR6th 537—§ 4
Selling v. Radford, 243 U.S. 46, 37 S. Ct. 377, 61 L. Ed. 585 (1917)
32 ALR6th 531—§ 3, 42, 43
Sellitto v. Litton Systems, Inc., 881 F. Supp. 932 (D.N.J. 1994)
7 ALR6th 563—§ 5
Sellman v. State, 47 Md. App. 510, 423 A.2d 974 (1981)
70 ALR5th 533—§ 3, 6
Sellmer v. Ruen, 115 Idaho 700, 769 P.2d 577 (1989)
40 ALR6th 99—§ 25
Sellon v. General Motors Corp., 521 F. Supp. 978 (D.C. Del. 1981)
6 ALR5th 883—§ 8
Sellon v. General Motors Corp., 571 F. Supp. 1094, 37 U.C.C. Rep. Serv. 1169 (D. Del. 1983)
49 ALR5th 1—§ 40
81 ALR5th 483—§ 2, 5
Sellon v. Manitou Springs, 745 P.2d 229 (Colo. 1987)
1 ALR5th 622—§ 16, 19, 34
2 ALR5th 553—§ 17
Sellors v. Concord, 329 Mass. 259, 107 N.E.2d 784 (1952)
53 ALR5th 1—§ 22, 31, 37, 47
Sells, Ex parte, 2000 WL 5060 (Tex. App. Houston 1st Dist. 2000)
15 ALR6th 375—§ 8, 16, 24
Sells' Estate, In re, 197 Iowa 696, 197 N.W. 922 (1924)

74 ALR5th 491—§ 3

Sellsted v. Washington Mut. Sav. Bank, 69 Wash. App. 852, 851 P.2d 716, 66 BNA FEP Cas. 267 (1993)

51 ALR5th 1—§ 7

Selm v. American States Ins. Co., 2001 WL 1103509 (Ohio Ct. App. 1st Dist. Hamilton County 2001)

98 ALR5th 193—§ 6

106 ALR5th 1—§ 8

Selma Foundry and Supply Co., Inc. v. Peoples Bank and Trust Co., 598 So. 2d 844 (Ala. 1992)

85 ALR5th 353—§ 11, 12

Selman v. Louisiana, 428 U.S. 906, 96 S. Ct. 3214, 49 L. Ed. 2d 1212 (1976)

62 ALR5th 121—§ 6

Selma Street & Suburban Ry. Co. v. Martin, 2 Ala. App. 537, 56 So. 601 (1911)

61 ALR5th 635—§ 3, 18

Selma University. Powell v. State, 600 So. 2d 1085 (Ala. App. 1992)

27 ALR5th 593—§ 25

Selmer, In re Disciplinary Action Against, 529 N.W.2d 684 (Minn. 1995)

25 ALR6th 1—§ 3, 32

26 ALR6th 1—§ 3

27 ALR6th 1—§ 3

Selmer, In re Disciplinary Action Against, 749 N.W.2d 30 (Minn. 2008)

43 ALR6th 163—§ 3

44 ALR6th 75—§ 3

45 ALR6th 175—§ 3

Selmer, In re Disciplinary Proceedings Against, 2009 WI 15, 761 N.W.2d 6 (Wis. 2009)

43 ALR6th 163—§ 48

Selmo v. Baratono, 28 Mich. App. 217, 184 N.W.2d 367 (1970)

62 ALR5th 537—§ 4

Selmon v. Hasbro Bradley, Inc., 669 F. Supp. 1267, 5 U.S.P.Q.2d 1278 (S.D. N.Y. 1987)

76 ALR6th 289—§ 4

77 ALR6th 543—§ 6

Selph v. Gottlieb's Financial Services, Inc., 35 F. Supp. 2d 564 (W.D. Mich. 1999)

94 ALR5th 1—§ 17, 21

20 ALR6th 1—§ 5

Selph v. North Wayne Community Unit School Dist. No. 200, 221 Ill. App. 3d 177, 163 Ill. Dec. 744, 581 N.E.2d 898, 70 Ed. Law Rep. 1190 (5th Dist. 1991)

66 ALR5th 1—§ 31

Selsor v. Shelby, 401 S.W.2d 169 (Mo. App. 1966)

25 ALR5th 233—§ 2, 3

Selsor v. Turnbull, 1997 OK CR 61, 947 P.2d 579 (Okla. Crim. App. 1997)

93 ALR6th 391—§ 6

Selsor v. Workman, 644 F.3d 984 (10th Cir. 2011)

93 ALR6th 391—§ 6

Selter v. Selter, 982 S.W.2d 764 (Mo. Ct. App. E.D. 1998)

2 ALR6th 439—§ 16, 44

Selts Inv. Co. v. Promoters of Federated Nations of World, 197 Wis. 476, 222 N.W. 812 (1929)

75 ALR5th 1—§ 7, 13

Seltzer, Application of, 11 A.D.2d 805, 205 N.Y.S.2d 218 (2d Dep't 1960)

124 ALR5th 203—§ 10

Seltzer v. Barnes, 182 Cal. App. 4th 953, 106 Cal. Rptr. 3d 290 (1st Dist. 2010)

64 ALR6th 365—§ 17, 26

Seltzer v. Kane, 242 A.D.2d 302, 660 N.Y.S.2d 740 (2d Dep't 1997)

91 ALR6th 435—§ 139

Seltzer v. Seltzer, 16 App. Div. 2d 836, 228 N.Y.S.2d 901 (1962)

38 ALR5th 69—§ 6

Selvage v. Robert Levis Chevrolet, Inc., 719 So. 2d 1088 (La. Ct. App. 5th Cir. 1998)

33 ALR5th 303—§ 3, 7

50 ALR5th 1—§ 6

52 ALR5th 1—§ 8

Selvage v. State, 29 Ala. App. 371, 196
So. 163 (1940)
104 ALR5th 357—§ 3
54 ALR6th 429—§ 9
Selver v. State, 568 So. 2d 1331 (Fla.
Dist. Ct. App. 4th Dist. 1990)
57 ALR5th 141—§ 3
Selvey v. Robertson, 468 S.W.2d 212
(Mo. Ct. App. 1971)
40 ALR6th 99—§ 16, 47
Selvidge v. McBeen, 230 Mont. 237,
750 P.2d 429 (1988)
14 ALR5th 242—§ 31
Selvig v. Caryl, 97 Wash. App. 220, 983
P.2d 1141 (Div. 1 1999)
12 ALR6th 645—§ 18
Selvog v. State, 895 S.W.2d 879 (Tex.
App. Texarkana 1995)
103 ALR6th 507—§ 14
Selvy v. Albany Police Department, 186
Misc. 2d 518, 719 N.Y.S.2d 463
(City Ct. 2000)
103 ALR5th 463—§ 3
59 ALR6th 311—§ 6
Selzer v. Berkowitz, 477 F. Supp. 686
(E.D. N.Y. 1979)
23 ALR5th 241—§ 39
Selzer v. Board of Educ. of City of New
York, 1993 WL 42787 (S.D. N.Y.
1993)
60 ALR6th 295—§ 60
Semaan v. State, 199 App. Div. 2d 884,
606 N.Y.S.2d 70 (3d Dep't 1993)
51 ALR5th 1—§ 8
Semachko v. Hopko, 35 Ohio App. 2d
205, 64 Ohio Op. 2d 316, 301
N.E.2d 560 (8th Dist. Cuyahoga
County 1973)
76 ALR5th 337—§ 20
Seman v. Lewis, 252 Mont. 508, 830
P.2d 1294 (1992)
86 ALR5th 527—§ 2, 7, 13
Semanko v. Minnesota Mut. Life Ins.
Co., 168 F. Supp. 2d 997 (D. Minn.
2000)
61 ALR6th 239—§ 8
Semasek v. Semasek, 331 Pa. Super. 1,
479 A.2d 1047 (1984)

4 ALR5th 403—§ 3
Semco Laser Technology, Inc. v. Jose
Yow & Associates, 2004 WL
434288 (Cal. App. 2d Dist. 2004)
47 ALR6th 303—§ 4
Semco Mfg., Inc. v. B-G Mechanical
Contractors, Inc., 1994 WL 171226
(Conn. Super. Ct. 1994)
119 ALR5th 121—§ 3
Semendinger v. Brittain, 770 P.2d 1270
(Colo. 1989)
53 ALR6th 1—§ 11
Semenetz v. Sherling & Walden, Inc., 7
N.Y.3d 194, 818 N.Y.S.2d 819, 851
N.E.2d 1170, Prod. Liab. Rep.
(CCH) ¶ 17478, 18 A.L.R.6th 887
(2006)
18 ALR6th 613—§ 5
18 ALR6th 629—§ 10
Semenza v. Alfano, 443 Pa. 201, 279
A.2d 29 (1971)
44 ALR5th 1—§ 3
Semerjian v. Stetson, 284 Mass. 510,
187 N.E. 829 (1933)
30 ALR5th 571—§ 32
Semetex Corp. v. UBAF Arab Am.
Bank, 853 F. Supp. 759, 24
U.C.C.R.S.2d 170 (S.D. N.Y. 1994)
53 ALR5th 667—§ 2
56 ALR5th 565—§ 21, 24, 41, 59
Semien v. Cain, 2008 WL 4556035
(E.D. Cal. 2008)
45 ALR6th 1—§ 33
Seminaris v. Landa, 662 A.2d 1350, Fed.
Sec. L. Rep. (CCH) ¶ 98844 (Del.
Ch. 1995)
43 ALR6th 1—§ 18
Seminatore v. Med. Mut. of Ohio, 136
Ohio App. 3d 758, 737 N.E.2d 1016
(8th Dist. Cuyahoga County 2000)
102 ALR5th 253—§ 2, 8
Seminole County v. City of Casselberry,
541 So. 2d 666 (Fla. Dist. Ct. App.
5th Dist. 1989)
97 ALR5th 123—§ 33
Seminole County v. Clayton, 665 So. 2d
363 (Fla. App. D5 1995)
10 ALR5th 448—§ 6

Seminole Pipeline Co. v. Broad Leaf Partners, Inc., 979 S.W.2d 730, 142 O.G.R. 338 (Tex. App. Houston 14th Dist. 1998)

103 ALR5th 379—§ 3, 7, 8

8 ALR6th 439—§ 3, 5, 14

Seminole Tribe of Florida v. Department of Children and Families, 959 So. 2d 761 (Fla. Dist. Ct. App. 4th Dist. 2007)

63 ALR6th 429—§ 2, 20, 23

Semkow, Claim of, 239 A.D.2d 759, 657 N.Y.S.2d 805 (3d Dep't 1997)

121 ALR5th 467—§ 3

Semler v. Knowling, 325 N.W.2d 395, 34 U.C.C.R.S. 1542 (Iowa 1982)

50 ALR5th 417—§ 10

Semler v. Ludeman, 2009 WL 2497697 (Minn. Ct. App. 2009)

96 ALR6th 269—§ 11

Semmelroth v. American Airlines, 448 F. Supp. 730 (E.D. Ill. 1978)

2 ALR5th 396—§ 2, 8

Semo Grain Co. v. Oliver Farms, Inc., 530 S.W.2d 256 (Mo. App. 1975)

55 ALR5th 1—§ 26, 28

Semore v. Pool, 217 Cal. App. 3d 1087, 266 Cal. Rptr. 280, 5 I.E.R. Cas. (BNA) 129, 5 I.E.R. Cas. (BNA) 672, 115 Lab. Cas. (CCH) ¶ 56232 (4th Dist. 1990)

104 ALR5th 1—§ 4

Semorile v. City of New York, 407 F. Supp. 2d 579 (S.D. N.Y. 2006)

89 ALR6th 1—§ 49

Semowich v. R.J. Reynolds Tobacco Co., 8 U.C.C.R.S.2d 976 (N.D. N.Y. 1988)

36 ALR5th 541—§ 15, 17, 20

Sem-Pak Corp. v. Com. Unemployment Compensation Bd. of Review, 93 Pa. Commw. 162, 501 A.2d 694 (1985)

68 ALR5th 13—§ 11

Sempione v. Provident Bank of Maryland, 75 F.3d 951, 29 U.C.C. Rep. Serv. 2d (CBC) 310 (4th Cir. 1996)

56 ALR5th 565—§ 47, 49

Semple v. Hope, 15 Ohio St. 3d 372, 474 N.E.2d 314 (1984)

87 ALR5th 1—§ 10, 14, 32

Semple v. Schwarz, 130 Mo. App. 65, 109 S.W. 633 (1908)

1 ALR6th 135—§ 17

Semple v. State, 271 Ga. 416, 519 S.E.2d 912, 86 A.L.R.5th 767 (1999)

86 ALR5th 463—§ 7, 9

Sempsrott v. State, 784 S.W.2d 198 (Mo. Ct. App. E.D. 1989)

70 ALR5th 1—§ 8

72 ALR5th 109—§ 5

Semsch v. Henry Mayo Newhall Memorial Hosp., 171 Cal. App. 3d 162, 216 Cal. Rptr. 913 (2d Dist. 1985)

26 ALR5th 245—§ 3, 32

Semsroth v. City of Wichita, 239 F.R.D. 630, 27 A.L.R.6th 705 (D. Kan. 2006)

27 ALR6th 565—§ 3, 9, 14

Semtner v. Group Health Service of Oklahoma, Inc., 129 F.3d 1390 (10th Cir. 1997)

43 ALR5th 657—§ 5

S.E.M. Villa II, Inc. v. Kinney, 66 Ohio St. 2d 67, 20 Ohio Ops. 3d 60, 419 N.E.2d 879 (1981)

34 ALR5th 529—§ 10

Sena v. Com., 417 Mass. 250, 629 N.E.2d 986 (1994)

101 ALR5th 515—§ 15

Sena v. Town of Greenfield, 91 N.Y.2d 611, 673 N.Y.S.2d 984, 696 N.E.2d 996 (1998)

29 ALR6th 369—§ 49

Sena v. Turner, 195 Cal. App. 2d 487, 15 Cal. Rptr. 857 (3d Dist. 1961)

35 ALR5th 1—§ 10

Senape v. Constantino, Medicare & Medicaid P 43094, 1995 WL 29502 (S.D. N.Y. 1995)

95 ALR6th 341—§ 16

Senator Mark Dayton, Office of v. Hanson, 127 S. Ct. 1145, 166 L. Ed. 2d 909 (U.S. 2007)

24 ALR6th 255—§ 10

Senator Mark Dayton, Office of v. Hanson, 127 S. Ct. 2018, 19 A.D. Cas. (BNA) 321, 100 Fair Empl. Prac. Cas. (BNA) 801, 12 Wage & Hour Cas. 2d (BNA) 961, 89 Empl. Prac. Dec. (CCH) ¶ 42826 (U.S. 2007)

26 ALR6th 659—§ 30

Sencer v. Carl's Markets, Inc., 45 So. 2d 671 (Fla. 1950)

2 ALR5th 1—§ 37

Senco of Florida, Inc. v. Clark, 473 F. Supp. 902 (M.D. Fla. 1979)

52 ALR5th 221—§ 27

Sendelbach v. Lockwood, 760 So. 2d 227 (Fla. Dist. Ct. App. 5th Dist. 2000)

24 ALR5th 200—§ 55

Sendelweck v. Kays, 1981 WL 6691 (Ohio Ct. App. 3d Dist. Union County 1981)

73 ALR5th 185—§ 10

Senders v. CNA Ins. Cos., 212 N.J. Super. 518, 515 A.2d 820 (1986)

7 ALR5th 143—§ 3, 6

Seneca Falls Greenhouse & Nursery v. Layton, 9 Va. App. 482, 389 S.E.2d 184 (1990)

72 ALR5th 529—§ 20

84 ALR5th 249—§ 2, 26

106 ALR5th 111—§ 16

Seneca Investments LLC, In re, 970 A.2d 259 (Del. Ch. 2008)

49 ALR6th 1—§ 38

Seneca Knitting Mills Corp. v. Wilkes, 120 A.D.2d 955, 502 N.Y.S.2d 844, 123 Lab. Cas. (CCH) ¶ 57131 (4th Dep't 1986)

7 ALR6th 563—§ 5

Seneca Nation of Indians v. New York, 126 S. Ct. 2351 (U.S. 2006)

16 ALR6th 767—§ 23

Seneca Nation of Indians v. New York, 382 F.3d 245, 34 Envtl. L. Rep. 20096 (2d Cir. 2004)

16 ALR6th 767—§ 23

Seneca One, LLC, In re, 22 Mass. L. Rptr. 111, 2007 WL 738944 (Mass. Super. Ct. 2007)

27 ALR6th 323—§ 20

Seneca One, LLC v. Hartford Life Ins. Co., 42 Conn. L. Rptr. 824, 2007 WL 611201 (Conn. Super. Ct. 2007)

27 ALR6th 323—§ 21

Senegal v. State, 2002 WL 480310 (Tex. App. Houston 14th Dist. 2002)

72 ALR6th 1—§ 4

Senegal, Republic of v. Brown Bros. Harriman & Co., 1989 WL 63085 (S.D. N.Y. 1989)

56 ALR5th 565—§ 33

Seneris v. Haas, 45 Cal. 2d 811, 291 P.2d 915, 53 A.L.R.2d 124 (1955)

1 ALR5th 269—§ 2, 17, 25

6 ALR5th 534—§ 6

Senesac v. Associates in Obstetrics & Gynecology, 141 Vt. 310, 449 A.2d 900 (1982)

42 ALR5th 1—§ 3, 10

Senesac v. Associates in Obstetrics and Gynecology, 141 Vt. 310, 449 A.2d 900 (1982)

97 ALR6th 519—§ 4

Senesac v. Employer's Vocational Resources, Inc., 324 Ill. App. 3d 380, 257 Ill. Dec. 705, 754 N.E.2d 363 (1st Dist. 2001)

125 ALR5th 457—§ 4

Senez v. Grumman Flxible Corp., 518 So. 2d 574 (La. App. 4th Cir. 1987)

48 ALR5th 129—§ 8, 13

Senft v. Ed Schuster & Co., 250 Wis. 406, 27 N.W.2d 464 (1947)

99 ALR5th 141—§ 31

Seng, In re Disciplinary Action Against, 462 N.W.2d 597 (Minn. 1990)

96 ALR5th 23—§ 6

Sengel v. Maddox, 31 Ohio Ops. 201 (CP 1945)

11 ALR5th 127—§ 4

Senger v. Minnesota Lawyers Mut. Ins. Co., 415 N.W.2d 364 (Minn. Ct. App. 1987)

92 ALR5th 273—§ 19

Senger v. Senger, 308 N.W.2d 395 (S.D. 1981)

17 ALR5th 366—§ 15

Sengpiel v. B.F. Goodrich Co., 156 F.3d 660, 22 Employee Benefits Cas. (BNA) 1817, 1998 FED App. 0293P (6th Cir. 1998)
74 ALR6th 267—§ 8

Sengstock, In re Custody of, 165 Wis. 2d 86, 477 N.W.2d 310 (Ct. App. 1991)
89 ALR5th 195—§ 4

Seng-Tiong Ho v. Taflove, 648 F.3d 489, 98 U.S.P.Q.2d 1935 (7th Cir. 2011)
76 ALR6th 289—§ 4
77 ALR6th 543—§ 8, 10, 14

Sengupta v. Wickwire, 124 P.3d 748 (Alaska 2005)
14 ALR6th 1—§ 5

Senior v. Zoning Commission of Town of New Canaan, 146 Conn. 531, 153 A.2d 415 (1959)
4 ALR6th 263—§ 54

Senior v. Zoning Com. of New Canaan, 146 Conn. 531, 153 A.2d 415 (1959)
1 ALR5th 622—§ 3, 17

Senior Cottages of America, LLC, In re, 482 F.3d 997, 48 Bankr. Ct. Dec. (CRR) 5 (8th Cir. 2007)
48 ALR6th 1—§ 4

Senior Tour Players 207 Management Co. LLC v. Golftown 207 Holding Co., LLC, 853 A.2d 124 (Del. Ch. 2004)
46 ALR6th 1—§ 9

Senkarik v. Attorney General, 357 Mass. 211, 257 N.E.2d 470 (1970)
73 ALR5th 223—§ 11

Senkier v. Hartford Life & Acc. Ins. Co., 948 F.2d 1050, 14 Employee Benefits Cas. (BNA) 2317 (7th Cir. 1991)
56 ALR5th 471—§ 3, 7

Senkinc v. Unemployment Compensation Bd. of Review, 144 Pa. Commw. 175, 601 A.2d 418 (1991)
75 ALR5th 339—§ 4, 8

Senkirik v. Royce, 192 Or. 583, 235 P.2d 886 (1951)
20 ALR5th 1—§ 45

Senn v. Buffalo Elec. Coop., 196 Wis. 2d 372, 539 N.W.2d 135 (Ct. App. 1995)
90 ALR5th 453—§ 53
91 ALR5th 517—§ 5

Senn v. J. S. Weeks & Co., 255 S.C. 585, 180 S.E.2d 336 (1971)
3 ALR5th 746—§ 4, 12

Senn v. Manchester Bank of St. Louis, 583 S.W.2d 119 (Mo. 1979)
14 ALR5th 242—§ 30

Senn v. Merrell-Dow Pharmaceuticals, Inc., 305 Or. 256, 751 P.2d 215, Prod. Liab. Rep. (CCH) ¶ 11729 (1988)
63 ALR5th 195—§ 3

Senn v. United Dominion Industries, Inc., 951 F.2d 806, 14 Employee Benefits Cas. (BNA) 2238, 139 L.R.R.M. (BNA) 2246, 120 Lab. Cas. (CCH) ¶ 11117 (7th Cir. 1992)
74 ALR6th 267—§ 5

Senna v. Cargill, Inc., 489 So. 2d 192, 11 FLW 1234 (Fla. App. D1 1986)
14 ALR5th 1—§ 2

Senn Blacktop, Inc. v. General Drivers and Helpers, Local 662, 74 L.R.R.M. (BNA) 2597, 63 Lab. Cas. (CCH) ¶ 11041, 1970 WL 7592 (Wis. Cir. Ct. 1970)
110 ALR5th 111—§ 20

Senneff v. Healy, 155 Iowa 82, 135 N.W. 27 (1912)
11 ALR6th 587—§ 6, 8

Senner v. Senner, 161 N.C. App. 78, 587 S.E.2d 675 (2003)
59 ALR6th 161—§ 33, 35
60 ALR6th 193—§ 13

Sennett v. National Healthcare Corp., 272 S.W.3d 237 (Mo. Ct. App. S.D. 2008)
50 ALR6th 187—§ 14, 16

Sennot v. Collet-Oser, 36 Ill. App. 3d 928, 344 N.E.2d 783 (1st Dist. 1976)
36 ALR5th 395—§ 2
37 ALR5th 237—§ 2, 13

Senn, State ex rel. v. Board of Elections of Cuyahoga County, 51 Ohio St. 2d 173, 5 Ohio Op. 3d 381, 367 N.E.2d 879 (1977)

14 ALR6th 543—§ 48

Senor T's Restaurant v. Industrial Commission of Arizona, 131 Ariz. 360, 641 P.2d 848 (1982)

61 ALR6th 61—§ 3

Senor T's Restaurant v. Industrial Com. of Arizona, 131 Ariz. 360, 641 P.2d 848 (1982)

16 ALR5th 191—§ 2, 12 to 14, 21

Sens v. Commissioner of Public Safety, 399 N.W.2d 602 (Minn. Ct. App. 1987)

92 ALR6th 295—§ 7, 19, 25
93 ALR6th 207—§ 6, 14, 16, 21, 31
96 ALR6th 355—§ 6, 9, 21, 41, 51

Sensat v. Lake Charles, 607 So. 2d 1069 (La. App. 3d Cir. 1992)

18 ALR5th 577—§ 45

Senseney v. Mississippi Power Co., 2005 WL 2851504 (Miss. Ct. App. 2005)

7 ALR6th 563—§ 5

Sensing v. Porter, 133 S. Ct. 338, 184 L. Ed. 2d 239 (2012)

86 ALR6th 577—§ 21

Senske v. Fairmont & Waseca Canning Co., 232 Minn. 350, 45 N.W.2d 640 (1951)

48 ALR5th 473—§ 5, 16

Sensk's Case, 247 Mass. 232, 141 N.E. 877 (1924)

16 ALR5th 191—§ 11

Senter v. B. F. Goodrich Co., 127 F. Supp. 705 (D. Colo. 1954)

39 ALR6th 155—§ 4

Senter v. Ross, 2007 WL 4224050 (D. Minn. 2007)

52 ALR6th 623—§ 4

Senter v. Tennessee Farmers Mut. Ins. Co., 702 S.W.2d 175 (Tenn. App. 1985)

35 ALR5th 1—§ 3

Sentex Systems, Inc. v. Hartford Acc. & Indem. Co., 93 F.3d 578, 39 U.S.P.Q.2d (BNA) 1860 (9th Cir. 1996)

98 ALR5th 1—§ 14

Sentinel v. Boggs, 177 Okla. 623, 61 P.2d 654 (1936)

25 ALR5th 568—§ 27

Sentinel Assoc. v. American Mfrs. Mut. Ins. Co., 804 F. Supp. 815 (E.D. Va. 1992)

30 ALR5th 170—§ 42, 85, 97

Sentinel Communications Co. v. Smith, 493 So. 2d 1048, 11 FLW 1484, 13 Media L. R. 1775 (Fla. App. D5 1986)

39 ALR5th 103—§ 16

Sentinel Communications Co. v. Watts, 936 F.2d 1189, 19 Media L. Rep. (BNA) 1097 (11th Cir. 1991)

70 ALR6th 513—§ 13
71 ALR6th 471—§ 6

Sentinel Fire Ins. Co. v. McRoberts, 50 Ga. App. 732, 179 S.E. 256 (1934)

116 ALR5th 247—§ 7

Sentinel Star Co. v. Edwards, 387 So. 2d 367, 6 Media L. R. 1603 (Fla. App. D5 1980)

39 ALR5th 103—§ 18

Sentinel, Town of v. Riley, 1935 OK 446, 171 Okla. 533, 43 P.2d 742 (1935)

92 ALR5th 517—§ 11, 12
101 ALR5th 287—§ 7, 12

Sentry Const. Corp. v. Revolation Enterprise, LLC, 2008 WL 5481405 (Conn. Super. Ct. 2008)

47 ALR6th 1—§ 25

Sentry Indem. Co. v. Hendricks Enterprises, 371 So. 2d 1105 (Fla. App. D4 1979)

20 ALR5th 229—§ 37

Sentry Indem. Co. v. Sharif, 156 Ga. App. 828, 280 S.E.2d 354 (1980)

116 ALR5th 247—§ 5

Sentry Ins. v. Marcella, 1991 WL 40353 (E.D. Pa. 1991)

103 ALR5th 1—§ 3

Sentry Ins. v. R.J. Weber Co., Inc., 2 F.3d 554, 28 U.S.P.Q.2d (BNA) 1397 (5th Cir. 1993)
98 ALR5th 1—§ 17

Sentry Ins. A Mut. Co. v. Flom's Corp., 818 F. Supp. 187 (E.D. Mich. 1993)
98 ALR5th 1—§ 20

Sentry Ins. Co. v. Grenga, 556 A.2d 998 (R.I. 1989)
23 ALR5th 75—§ 3

Sentry Ins. Co. v. S. & L. Home Heating Co., 91 Ill. App. 3d 687, 47 Ill. Dec. 102, 414 N.E.2d 1218 (1st Dist. 1980)
18 ALR5th 187—§ 5

Sentry Insurance Company v. Amsel, 36 N.Y.2d 291, 367 N.Y.S.2d 480 (1975)
55 ALR5th 747—§ 3

Sentry Select Ins. Co. v. Meyer, 2011 WL 1103333 (D. Nev. 2011)
72 ALR6th 563—§ 3, 9, 15, 20, 38

Seolas, In re, 140 B.R. 266, 15 Employee Benefits Cas. (BNA) 1371 (E.D. Cal. 1992)
73 ALR6th 571—§ 3, 64

Separation of Church and State Committee v. City of Eugene of Lane County, State of Or., 93 F.3d 617 (9th Cir. 1996)
107 ALR5th 1—§ 4, 7, 13, 18

Sepatis v. City and County of San Francisco, 217 F. Supp. 2d 992 (N.D. Cal. 2002)
101 ALR6th 207—§ 7, 15

Sepe v. Deemy, 9 Conn. App. 524, 520 A.2d 237 (1987)
50 ALR5th 1—§ 7, 15

Sepeda v. State, 301 S.W.3d 372 (Tex. App. Amarillo 2009)
72 ALR6th 227—§ 51

Sepro Corp. v. Florida Dept. of Environmental Protection, 839 So. 2d 781 (Fla. Dist. Ct. App. 1st Dist. 2003)
54 ALR6th 653—§ 11

Sepulvado v. General Fire & Casualty Co., 146 So. 2d 428 (La. App. 3d Cir. 1962)
6 ALR5th 883—§ 2
16 ALR5th 1—§ 14

Sepulvado v. Jindal, 134 S. Ct. 1789, 188 L. Ed. 2d 771 (2014)
96 ALR6th 577—§ 14, 46

Sepulvado v. Jindal, 729 F.3d 413 (5th Cir. 2013)
96 ALR6th 577—§ 14, 46

Sepulvado v. State, 395 So. 2d 858 (La. App. 2d Cir. 1981)
1 ALR5th 163—§ 2, 3, 27, 28, 30

Sepulvado, State ex rel. v. Rapides Parish School Board, 236 La. 482, 108 So. 2d 96 (1959)
57 ALR5th 477—§ 37

Sepulveda v. American Motors Sales Corp., 137 Misc. 2d 543, 521 N.Y.S.2d 387, 5 U.C.C. Rep. Serv. 2d 1365 (City Civ. Ct. 1987)
88 ALR5th 301—§ 26

Sepulveda v. State, 729 S.W.2d 954 (Tex. App. Corpus Christi 1987)
5 ALR6th 1—§ 7, 15, 60
55 ALR6th 599—§ 7

Sequa Corp. v. Aetna Cas. and Sur. Co., 1992 WL 147994 (Del. Super. Ct. 1992)
105 ALR5th 95—§ 5, 13

Sequa Corp. v. Aetna Cas. and Sur. Co., 1992 WL 179386 (Del. Super. Ct. 1992)
105 ALR5th 95—§ 5, 13

Sequa Corp. v. GBJ Corp., 156 F.3d 136 (2d Cir. 1998)
24 ALR6th 399—§ 13, 17

Sequa Corp. v. Lititech, Inc., 807 F. Supp. 653 (D. Colo. 1992)
57 ALR5th 633—§ 3, 5

Sequeira v. Sequeira, 105 A.D.3d 504, 963 N.Y.S.2d 102 (1st Dep't 2013)
99 ALR6th 203—§ 15

Sequoia Ins. Co. v. Superior Court, 13 Cal. App. 4th 1472, 16 Cal. Rptr. 2d 888, 8 I.E.R. Cas. (BNA) 458 (6th Dist. 1993)
104 ALR5th 1—§ 2 to 4, 10
105 ALR5th 351—§ 2

Sequoia Mfg. Co. v. Halec Constr. Co., 117 Ariz. 11, 570 P.2d 782 (App. 1977)

22 ALR5th 483—§ 9, 12

Sequoia Property and Equipment Ltd. Partnership v. U.S., 81 A.F.T.R.2d 98-2143, 1998 WL 471643 (E.D. Cal. 1998)

2 ALR6th 195—§ 4, 17

Seracuse Lawler & Partners, Inc. v. Copper Mountain, 654 P.2d 1328 (Colo. App. 1982)

31 ALR5th 664—§ 9

Serafin v. Pleasant Valley Wine Co., 98 A.D.2d 887, 470 N.Y.S.2d 874 (3d Dep't 1983)

100 ALR5th 567—§ 8

Serafin v. Seith, 284 Ill. App. 3d 577, 219 Ill. Dec. 794, 672 N.E.2d 302 (1st Dist. 1996)

98 ALR6th 417—§ 16

Serafini v. Blake, 167 Cal. App. 3d Supp. 11, 213 Cal. Rptr. 207, 9 Soc. Sec. Rep. Serv. 922 (App. Dep' Super. Ct. 1985)

69 ALR6th 317—§ 19

Serano v. State, 555 N.E.2d 487 (Ind. Ct. App. 1st Dist. 1990)

28 ALR6th 505—§ 37

Seraphin v. State, 706 So. 2d 913 (Fla. Dist. Ct. App. 4th Dist. 1998)

79 ALR5th 419—§ 4

Seravo v. Seravo, 525 A.2d 922 (R.I. 1987)

1 ALR5th 776—§ 2, 11

Serbian Eastern Orthodox Diocese for U. S. of America and Canada v. Milivojevich, 426 U.S. 696, 96 S. Ct. 2372, 49 L. Ed. 2d 151 (1976)

123 ALR5th 385—§ 17

Serbus, Re Estate of, 324 N.W.2d 381 (Minn. 1982)

3 ALR5th 394—§ 7, 14

Serdarevic v. Centex Homes, LLC, 2012 WL 4054161 (S.D. N.Y. 2012)

104 ALR6th 303—§ 18

Serdarevic v. Centex Homes, LLC, 2012 WL 5992744 (S.D. N.Y. 2012)

104 ALR6th 303—§ 18

Sere v. Group Hospitalization, Inc., 443 A.2d 33 (Dist. Col. App. 1982)

6 ALR5th 297—§ 9

Sereboff v. Mid Atlantic Medical Services, Inc., 126 S. Ct. 1869, 37 Employee Benefits Cas. (BNA) 1929 (U.S. 2006)

16 ALR6th 767—§ 26

Serefeas v. Nationwide Ins. Co., 338 Pa. Super. 587, 488 A.2d 48 (1985)

55 ALR5th 747—§ 3

Seres, In re, 437 B.R. 775 (Bankr. W.D. N.Y. 2010)

99 ALR6th 481—§ 26

Seretta Const., Inc. v. Great American Ins. Co., 869 So. 2d 676, 31 A.L.R.6th 737 (Fla. Dist. Ct. App. 5th Dist. 2004)

31 ALR6th 433—§ 5

Serge v. Matney, 165 W. Va. 801, 273 S.E.2d 818 (1980)

123 ALR5th 411—§ 11

Sergeant v. Watson Bros. Transp. Co., 244 Iowa 185, 52 N.W.2d 86 (1952)

12 ALR5th 195—§ 41

Sergent v. People, 177 Colo. 354, 497 P.2d 983 (1972)

55 ALR5th 125—§ 14, 25

Sergile v. New York City Health and Hospitals Corp., 175 A.D.2d 119, 571 N.Y.S.2d 814 (2d Dep't 1991)

71 ALR5th 307—§ 26

Sergio M., In re, 13 Cal. App. 4th 809, 16 Cal. Rptr. 2d 701 (6th Dist. 1993)

67 ALR5th 149—§ 3, 5

Serhofer v. Groman & Wolf, P.C., 203 A.D.2d 354, 610 N.Y.S.2d 294 (2d Dep't 1994)

60 ALR6th 1—§ 5

Serian v. State, 297 S.E.2d 889 (W. Va. 1982)

10 ALR5th 1—§ 15

Serigne v. Ivker, 669 So. 2d 1335 (La. App. 4th Cir. 1996)

47 ALR5th 433—§ 17

Serio v. Allstate Ins. Co., 210 N.J. Super. 167, 509 A.2d 273 (App. Div. 1986)

CASES CITED IN ALR5th and ALR6th

41 ALR6th 527—§ 5
Serio v. Brookhaven, 208 Miss. 620, 45 So. 2d 257 (1950)

14 ALR5th 89—§ 10, 15
Seritis v. Hotel & Restaurant Employees etc. Union, 167 Cal. App. 3d 78, 213 Cal. Rptr. 588, 37 BNA FEP Cas. 1501, 119 BNA LRRM 2497, 37 CCH EPD ¶ 35400, 103 CCH LC ¶ 11504 (1st Dist. 1985)

14 ALR5th 242—§ 50
Serlin Wine and Spirit Merchants, Inc. v. Healy, 512 F. Supp. 936, 1981-1 Trade Cas. (CCH) ¶ 63950 (D. Conn. 1981)

41 ALR6th 77—§ 3, 4, 13
Sermons v. State, 262 Ga. 286, 417 S.E.2d 144 (1992)

79 ALR5th 33—§ 9, 13
Sermor, Inc. v. U.S., 13 Cl. Ct. 1, 34 CCF ¶ 75342 (1987)

8 ALR5th 653—§ 3, 10, 13
Serna v. Goodno, 2006 WL 1985765 (Minn. Ct. App. 2006)

78 ALR6th 417—§ 5
Serna v. Kiger, 175 Ind. App. 566, 372 N.E.2d 1232 (1978)

3 ALR5th 1—§ 3, 4, 56
Serna v. New York State Urban Development Corp., 185 A.D.2d 562, 586 N.Y.S.2d 413, Prod. Liab. Rep. (CCH) ¶ 13471 (3d Dep't 1992)

99 ALR5th 141—§ 9
Serna v. State, 546 S.W.2d 788 (Mo. Ct. App. 1977)

43 ALR6th 475—§ 10
Serna, Inc. v. Harman, 742 F.2d 186, 39 U.C.C. Rep. Serv. 481 (5th Cir. 1984)

101 ALR5th 563—§ 4, 6
Serodino, Inc. v. Woods, 568 S.W.2d 610 (Tenn. 1978)

71 ALR5th 671—§ 3
Serota v. Kaplan, 127 App. Div. 2d 648, 511 N.Y.S.2d 667 (2d Dep't 1987)

35 ALR5th 1—§ 12
Seroyer v. Pfizer, Inc., 991 F. Supp. 1308 (M.D. Ala. 1997)

60 ALR6th 295—§ 53
Serpa v. Amaral, 635 A.2d 1196 (R.I. 1994)

64 ALR5th 519—§ 16
Serpas v. Collard Motors, 178 So. 261 (La. Ct. App., Orleans 1938)

91 ALR5th 1—§ 3, 11
Serpentfoot v. Salmon, 225 Ga. App. 478, 483 S.E.2d 927 (1997)

85 ALR6th 229—§ 4
Serra v. Lappin, 600 F.3d 1191, 159 Lab. Cas. (CCH) ¶ 35731 (9th Cir. 2010)

87 ALR6th 109—§ 35, 81
Serrano v. Burns, 248 Conn. 419, 727 A.2d 1276 (1999)

74 ALR5th 49—§ 73
Serrano v. Priest, 5 Cal. 3d 584, 96 Cal. Rptr. 601, 487 P.2d 1241, 41 A.L.R.3d 1187 (1971)

110 ALR5th 293—§ 4
Serrano v. Priest, 18 Cal. 3d 728, 135 Cal. Rptr. 345, 557 P.2d 929 (1976)

110 ALR5th 293—§ 4
Serrano v. Priest, 20 Cal. 3d 25, 141 Cal. Rptr. 315, 569 P.2d 1303, 7 Envtl. L. Rep. 20795 (1977)

106 ALR5th 523—§ 2, 3, 15
Serrano v. Riverside Dinette Products Co., 222 N.Y.S.2d 537 (Sup 1961)

3 ALR6th 355—§ 10
Serrano v. Underground Utilities Corp., 407 N.J. Super. 253, 970 A.2d 1054 (App. Div. 2009)

79 ALR6th 351—§ 4
Serrano v. Unruh, 32 Cal. 3d 621, 186 Cal. Rptr. 754, 652 P.2d 985 (1982)

106 ALR5th 523—§ 2, 15
Serrano v. World Savings Bank, FSB, 2011 WL 1668631 (N.D. Cal. 2011)

86 ALR6th 411—§ 5
Serrano ex rel. Serrano v. Massachusetts Dept. of Social Services, 22 Mass. L. Rptr. 501, 2007 WL 1631010 (Mass. Super. Ct. 2007)

103 ALR6th 461—§ 27

Serrano on California Condominium Homeowners Ass'n v. First Pacific Development, Ltd., 143 Wash. App. 521, 178 P.3d 1059 (Div. 1 2008)
  49 ALR6th 1—§ 70

Serratore v. American Port Services, Inc., 293 A.D.2d 464, 739 N.Y.S.2d 452 (2d Dep't 2002)
  52 ALR6th 271—§ 21

Serre, In re, 77 Ohio Misc. 2d 29, 665 N.E.2d 1185 (C.P. 1996)
  82 ALR5th 443—§ 4, 5
  83 ALR5th 375—§ 11

Serritella v. Plotkin, 89 Ill. App. 3d 739, 44 Ill. Dec. 931, 412 N.E.2d 7 (3d Dist. 1980)
  17 ALR5th 366—§ 11

Serritt v. State, 401 So. 2d 248 (Ala. App. 1981)
  7 ALR5th 263—§ 3

Serrmi Products, Inc. v. Insurance Co. of Pennsylvania, 201 Ga. App. 414, 411 S.E.2d 305 (1991)
  9 ALR6th 467—§ 19

Version v. Dairyland Ins. Co., 757 P.2d 1169 (Colo. App. 1988)
  33 ALR5th 121—§ 6, 15

Sertaut v. Crane Co., 142 Ill. App. 49, 1908 WL 1803 (1st Dist. 1908)
  97 ALR6th 567—§ 3, 5, 11

Sertik v. School Dist. of Pittsburgh, 136 Pa. Commw. 594, 584 A.2d 390, 65 Ed. Law Rep. 125 (1990)
  105 ALR5th 1—§ 3, 11

Servais v. Port of Bellingham, 127 Wash. 2d 820, 904 P.2d 1124 (1995)
  5 ALR6th 327—§ 3, 5
  8 ALR6th 117—§ 4

Servais v. T.J. Management of Minneapolis, Inc., 973 F. Supp. 885 (D. Minn. 1997)
  59 ALR5th 733—§ 3

Servantez v. Aguirre, 456 S.W.2d 467 (Tex. Civ. App. San Antonio 1970)
  122 ALR5th 205—§ 3, 21

Servbest Foods, Inc. v. Emessee Industries, Inc., 82 Ill. App. 3d 662, 37 Ill. Dec. 945, 403 N.E.2d 1, 29 U.C.C. Rep. Serv. 518 (1st Dist. 1980)
  101 ALR5th 563—§ 2, 3, 7, 9

Servedio v. Bratton, 268 A.D.2d 356, 702 N.Y.S.2d 264 (1st Dep't 2000)
  91 ALR6th 435—§ 121

Servedio v. U.S. Bank Nat. Ass'n, 46 So. 3d 1105 (Fla. 4th DCA 2010)
  86 ALR6th 411—§ 4

Service v. Newburyport Housing Authority, 63 Mass. App. Ct. 278, 825 N.E.2d 567 (2005)
  37 ALR6th 137—§ 4, 19

Service America Corp. v. County of San Diego, 15 Cal. App. 4th 1232, 19 Cal. Rptr. 2d 165 (4th Dist. 1993)
  90 ALR5th 547—§ 14, 15, 18, 22

Service by Medallion, Inc. v. Clorox Co., 44 Cal. App. 4th 1807, 52 Cal. Rptr. 2d 650, 152 L.R.R.M. (BNA) 2500 (6th Dist. 1996)
  108 ALR5th 253—§ 4, 6
  120 ALR5th 351—§ 5

Service Control Corp. v. Liberty Mutual Ins. Co., 54 Cal. Rptr. 2d 74
  88 ALR5th 493—§ 3
  89 ALR5th 1—§ 16

Service Corp. Intern. v. Fulmer, 883 So. 2d 621 (Ala. 2003)
  22 ALR6th 387—§ 12

Service Employee Intern. Union v. City of Los Angeles, 114 F. Supp. 2d 966 (C.D. Cal. 2000)
  46 ALR6th 465—§ 6
  70 ALR6th 513—§ 12

Service Employees International Union v. Hollywood Park, Inc., 149 Cal. App. 3d 745, 197 Cal. Rptr. 316 (2d Dist. 1983)
  95 ALR5th 1—§ 7

Service Employees Internat. Union v. Board of Trustees, 47 Cal. App. 4th 1661, 55 Cal. Rptr. 2d 484, 111 Ed. Law Rep. 431 (6th Dist. 1996)
  65 ALR5th 1—§ 11

Service Employees Internat. Union v. Superior Court, 112 Cal. App. 3d 712, 169 Cal. Rptr. 494 (4th Dist. 1980)

120 ALR5th 351—§ 17

Service Employees Intern. Union, Dist. 925, State ex rel. v. State Employment Relations Bd., 81 Ohio St. 3d 173, 689 N.E.2d 962, 158 L.R.R.M. (BNA) 2094 (1998)

65 ALR5th 1—§ 2

Service Life Ins. Co. v. Weinberg, 81 F.2d 359 (C.C.A. 7th Cir. 1936)

67 ALR5th 513—§ 4

Service Merchandise Co. Inc. v. Adams, 2001 WL 34384462 (Tenn. Ch. 2001)

29 ALR6th 507—§ 4, 56, 57

Service Merchandise, Inc. v. Johnson & Higgins of Georgia, Inc., 966 F.2d 1454 (6th Cir. 1992)

8 ALR6th 549—§ 4, 20

Service Oil Co. v. Rhodus, 179 Colo. 335, 500 P.2d 807 (1972)

8 ALR5th 391—§ 3, 5

Services to Children and Families, State ex rel. State Office for v. Blum, 175 Or. App. 447, 28 P.3d 1231 (2001)

113 ALR5th 349—§ 10, 15
116 ALR5th 559—§ 3

Services to Children and Families, State ex rel. State Office for v. Chapman, 169 Or. App. 168, 8 P.3d 243 (2000)

116 ALR5th 559—§ 9

Services to Children and Families, State ex rel. State Office for v. Frazier, 152 Or. App. 568, 955 P.2d 272 (1998)

122 ALR5th 385—§ 18

Services to Children and Families, State ex rel. State Office for v. Hammons, 170 Or. App. 287, 12 P.3d 983 (2000)

113 ALR5th 349—§ 13

Services to Children, State ex rel. State Office of v. Mendez, 162 Or. App. 601, 986 P.2d 670 (1999)

116 ALR5th 559—§ 3

Servidone Const. Corp. v. St. Paul Fire & Marine Ins. Co., 911 F. Supp. 560 (N.D.N.Y. 1995)

83 ALR5th 497—§ 5

Servidone Const. Corp. v. U.S., 931 F.2d 860, 37 Cont. Cas. Fed. (CCH) ¶ 76082 (Fed. Cir. 1991)

124 ALR5th 375—§ 2

Servies v. Servies, 524 So. 2d 678 (Fla. Dist. Ct. App. 1st Dist. 1988)

36 ALR6th 1—§ 13, 23, 27

Servin v. Servin, 345 N.W.2d 754 (Minn. 1984)

17 ALR5th 366—§ 15

Servis v. Com., 6 Va. App. 507, 371 S.E.2d 156 (1988)

64 ALR5th 637—§ 3

Serviss v. State, Dept. of Natural Resources, 721 N.E.2d 234 (Ind. 1999)

29 ALR6th 369—§ 11

Servomation Corp. v. Department of Revenue, 106 Wis. 2d 616, 317 N.W.2d 464 (1982)

69 ALR5th 477—§ 21

Servpro Industries, Inc. v. Schmidt, 905 F. Supp. 475 (N.D. Ill. 1995)

71 ALR5th 491—§ 35

Servpro Industries Inc. v. Schmidt, 1996 WL 400066 (N.D. Ill. 1996)

52 ALR5th 613—§ 3

Servpro Industries, Inc. v. Schmidt, 1997 WL 158316 (N.D. Ill. 1997)

71 ALR5th 491—§ 7

Serway v. Galentine, 75 Cal. App. 2d 86, 170 P.2d 32 (2d Dist. 1946)

86 ALR5th 637—§ 3

Sesco v. Dana World Trade Corp., 2002 WL 215015 (W.D. N.C. 2002)

105 ALR5th 243—§ 15

Sesma v. Cueto, 129 Cal. App. 3d 108, 181 Cal. Rptr. 12 (4th Dist. 1982)

3 ALR5th 146—§ 18

Sesow v. Swearingen, 552 P.2d 705, 19 U.C.C.R.S. 1160 (Okla. 1976)

49 ALR5th 1—§ 10

Sessa v. Riegle, 427 F. Supp. 760, 21 U.C.C. Rep. Serv. 745 (E.D. Pa. 1977)

88 ALR6th 1—§ 8, 9, 16, 23, 105

Sesselman v. Muhlenberg Hospital, 124 N.J. Super. 285, 306 A.2d 474 (1973)

1 ALR5th 269—§ 13, 25

Session, Matter of Disciplinary Proceedings Against, 205 Wis. 2d 116, 555 N.W.2d 120 (1996)

44 ALR6th 75—§ 4, 37, 39

Session v. Industrial Com. of Illinois, 124 Ill. App. 3d 715, 80 Ill. Dec. 22, 464 N.E.2d 887 (3d Dist. 1984)

14 ALR5th 1—§ 11

Sessions Payroll Management, Inc. v. Noble Const. Co., Inc., 84 Cal. App. 4th 671, 101 Cal. Rptr. 2d 127 (2d Dist. 2000)

124 ALR5th 575—§ 22

Sessions Tank Liners, Inc. v. Joor Mfg., Inc., 786 F. Supp. 1518, 92 Daily Journal DAR 9890, 1991-2 CCH Trade Cases ¶ 69688 (CD Cal. 1991)

23 ALR5th 241—§ 25

Sessoms v. State, 357 Md. 274, 744 A.2d 9 (2000)

22 ALR5th 1—§ 3

Sessums v. McFall, 551 So. 2d 178 (Miss. 1989)

51 ALR5th 603—§ 2

Sessums v. Northtown Limousines, 664 So. 2d 164 (Miss. 1995)

14 ALR5th 242—§ 29

Sestito, Estate of v. Silk, LLC, 2004 WL 574517 (Conn. Super. Ct. 2004)

47 ALR6th 1—§ 33

Setala v. J.C. Penney Co., 97 Haw. 484, 40 P.3d 886 (2002)

29 ALR6th 237—§ 4, 19

Set Aside Nomination of Fitzpatrick, In re Petition to, 822 A.2d 859 (Pa. Commw. Ct. 2003)

14 ALR6th 543—§ 14, 16

Setchel v. Hart County School Dist., 2009 WL 3757464 (M.D. Ga. 2009)

89 ALR6th 1—§ 86

SE Technologies, Inc. v. Summit Elec. Supply, Inc., 392 F. Supp. 2d 399, 63 Fed. R. Serv. 3d 255 (D. Conn. 2005)

64 ALR6th 473—§ 4

Seth, Adoption of, 29 Mass. App. Ct. 343, 560 N.E.2d 708 (1990)

122 ALR5th 385—§ 13

Seth v. Seth, 694 S.W.2d 459 (Tex. App. Fort Worth 1985)

82 ALR6th 1—§ 18

Setinc v. Masny, 185 Ill. App. 3d 15, 133 Ill. Dec. 71, 540 N.E.2d 937 (3d Dist. 1989)

118 ALR5th 513—§ 3, 15

Setliff v. Akins, 2000 SD 124, 616 N.W.2d 878, 16 I.E.R. Cas. (BNA) 1470, 142 Lab. Cas. (CCH) ¶ 59116 (S.D. 2000)

16 ALR6th 1—§ 29

Setliff v. E. I. Du Pont de Nemours & Co., 32 Cal. App. 4th 1525, 38 Cal. Rptr. 2d 763, Prod. Liab. Rep. (CCH) ¶ 14174 (3d Dist. 1995)

63 ALR5th 195—§ 7, 8
69 ALR5th 137—§ 11

Setliff v. Memorial Hosp. of Sheridan County, 850 F.2d 1384 (10th Cir. 1988)

95 ALR6th 341—§ 67

Setlur v. Setlur, 135 App. Div. 2d 873, 522 N.Y.S.2d 268 (3d Dep't 1987)

5 ALR5th 550—§ 36
21 ALR5th 396—§ 63

Seto v. Willits, 638 A.2d 258 (Pa. Super. 1994)

9 ALR5th 321—§ 4

Seton Hall College v. Calumet Const. Co., 81 N.J. Eq. 148, 88 A. 387 (1912)

4 ALR5th 772—§ 2, 16 to 18, 23

Setree v. Falkner, 50 N.E.2d 412 (Ohio Ct. App. 9th Dist. Summit County 1941)

61 ALR6th 61—§ 31

Setser v. Piazza, 644 So. 2d 1211 (Miss. 1994)

55 ALR5th 557—§ 5

Sette v. Benham, Blair & Affiliates, 70 Ohio App. 3d 651, 591 N.E.2d 871 (10th Dist. Franklin County 1991)
122 ALR5th 1—§ 2, 25
76 ALR6th 31—§ 46

Setter v. A.H. Robins Co., 748 F.2d 1328, CCH Prod. Liab. Rep. ¶ 10395 (CA8 Minn. 1984)
54 ALR5th 1—§ 2

Setterington v. Pontiac General Hosp., 223 Mich. App. 594, 568 N.W.2d 93 (1997)
64 ALR6th 249—§ 19
97 ALR6th 83—§ 61, 113, 114, 116

Settipalli v. Settipalli, 2005 WI App 8, 2004 WL 2792011 (Wis. Ct. App. 2004)
3 ALR6th 447—§ 5, 8

Settle v. Alison, 8 Ga. 201 (1850)
19 ALR5th 622—§ 5, 16

Settle v. Fluker, 978 F.2d 1063 (8th Cir. 1992)
13 ALR6th 1—§ 4
14 ALR6th 1—§ 4

Settle v. Galloway, 682 So. 2d 1032 (Miss. 1996)
71 ALR5th 99—§ 2, 3, 6

Settle v. Settle, 858 F. Supp. 610 (S.D. W. Va. 1994)
110 ALR5th 371—§ 4

Settle v. Tennessee Dept. of Correction, 276 S.W.3d 420 (Tenn. Ct. App. 2008)
96 ALR6th 269—§ 49

Settle By and Through Sullivan v. Beasley, 309 N.C. 616, 308 S.E.2d 288 (1983)
86 ALR5th 637—§ 3

Settlement & Audit of Auditors of Buckingham Township, In re Appeal from, 74 Pa. Cmwlth. 614, 460 A.2d 904 (1983)
41 ALR5th 47—§ 17

Settlement Capital Corp., In re, 1 Misc. 3d 446, 769 N.Y.S.2d 817 (Sup 2003)
27 ALR6th 323—§ 20

Settlement Capital Corp. v. State Farm Mut. Auto. Ins. Co., 646 N.W.2d 550 (Minn. Ct. App. 2002)
27 ALR6th 323—§ 12, 18, 21

Settlement Capital Corp. v. Yates, 12 Misc. 3d 1198(A), 824 N.Y.S.2d 770 (Sup 2006)
27 ALR6th 323—§ 22

Settlement Capital Corp. for Approval of Transfer of Structured Settlement Payment Rights of "Y," In re, 194 Misc. 2d 711, 756 N.Y.S.2d 728 (Sup 2003)
27 ALR6th 323—§ 3, 15, 16, 22

Settlement for Personal Injuries of Konicki, Matter of, 186 Wis. 2d 140, 519 N.W.2d 723 (Ct. App. 1994)
86 ALR6th 321—§ 4, 13
91 ALR6th 171—§ 41

Settlement Funding, LLC v. AXA Equitable Life Ins. Co., 2010 WL 3825735 (S.D. N.Y. 2010)
91 ALR6th 327—§ 13

Settlement Funding, LLC v. Travelers Cas. & Sur. Co., 41 Conn. L. Rptr. 876, 2006 WL 2605312 (Conn. Super. Ct. 2006)
27 ALR6th 323—§ 3, 22

Settlement Funding of New York, LLC, In re, 2 Misc. 3d 872, 774 N.Y.S.2d 635 (Sup 2003)
27 ALR6th 323—§ 13, 19

Settlement Funding of New York L.L.C., In re Petition of, 195 Misc. 2d 721, 761 N.Y.S.2d 816 (Sup 2003)
27 ALR6th 323—§ 22

Settlement Funding of New York, LLC v. Brown, 11 Misc. 3d 1059(A), 815 N.Y.S.2d 496 (Sup 2006)
27 ALR6th 323—§ 3, 22

Settlement Funding of New York LLC v. Kiezel, 12 Misc. 3d 1155(A), 819 N.Y.S.2d 213 (Sup 2006)
27 ALR6th 323—§ 22

Settlement Funding of New York, LLC
v. Transamerica Annuity Service
Corp., 11 Misc. 3d 1061(A), 816
N.Y.S.2d 701 (Sup 2006)
27 ALR6th 323—§ 21
Settlement Funding of New York, LLC,
1 Misc. 3d 910(A), In re, 781
N.Y.S.2d 628 (Sup 2003)
27 ALR6th 323—§ 3, 22
Settlement Funding of New York, LLC,
Petition of v. Allstate Settlement
Corp., 13 Misc. 3d 1245(A), 831
N.Y.S.2d 362 (Sup 2006)
27 ALR6th 323—§ 20
Settlement Funding of N.Y., LLC v.
Solivan, 8 Misc. 3d 1006(A), 801
N.Y.S.2d 781 (Sup 2005)
27 ALR6th 323—§ 22
Settlements of Betts, In re, 62 Ohio
Misc. 2d 30, 587 N.E.2d 997 (C.P.
1991)
49 ALR6th 505—§ 48
Settler v. Hopedale Medical Foundation,
80 Ill. App. 3d 1074, 36 Ill. Dec.
157, 400 N.E.2d 577 (3d Dist. 1980)
28 ALR5th 107—§ 3, 5
Settles v. Freeport, 132 Misc. 2d 240,
503 N.Y.S.2d 945 (1986)
23 ALR5th 1—§ 14
Settles v. Settles, 130 Ky. 797, 114 S.W.
303 (1908)
3 ALR5th 394—§ 6, 22
Settles v. State, 403 S.W.2d 417 (Tex.
Crim. 1966)
2 ALR5th 262—§ 6
Setty v. Koeneke, 148 A.D.2d 520, 538
N.Y.S.2d 857 (2d Dep't 1989)
26 ALR6th 331—§ 14
Setzer v. Boise Cascade Corp., 123 N.C.
App. 441, 473 S.E.2d 431 (1996)
90 ALR5th 453—§ 16
Setzer v. State, 29 Md. App. 347, 348
A.2d 866 (1975)
88 ALR5th 429—§ 7
Setzke v. Norris, 2009 WL 723244
(W.D. Ark. 2009)
63 ALR6th 351—§ 4
93 ALR6th 1—§ 5

Seumenicht v. Zoning Bd. of Appeals of
City of Rye, 217 A.D.2d 632, 629
N.Y.S.2d 784 (2d Dep't 1995)
63 ALR5th 607—§ 10
Seung v. Silverman, 288 B.R. 174 (E.D.
N.Y. 2003)
99 ALR6th 481—§ 20
Seureau v. Tanglewood Homes Asso.,
694 S.W.2d 119 (Tex. App. Houston (14th Dist.) 1985)
25 ALR5th 123—§ 2, 10
25 ALR5th 233—§ 2
Sevachko v. Com., 35 Va. App. 346, 544
S.E.2d 898 (2001)
9 ALR6th 363—§ 45
Sevario v. State ex rel. Dep't of Transp.
and Development, 752 So. 2d 221
(La. Ct. App. 1st Cir. 1999)
48 ALR5th 129—§ 8, 12, 16
52 ALR5th 1—§ 3, 9
Sevelis v. Sellers, 2005 WL 1160590
(Mich. Ct. App. 2005)
64 ALR6th 249—§ 36
Sevencan v. Herbert, 152 F. Supp. 2d
252 (E.D. N.Y. 2001)
100 ALR5th 171—§ 3, 8, 14, 16, 20
Sevencan v. Herbert, 316 F.3d 76 (2d
Cir. 2002)
100 ALR5th 171—§ 5, 17
Seven Gables Corp. v. Sterling Recre-
ation Organization Co., 686 F.
Supp. 1418 (W.D. Wash. 1988)
23 ALR5th 241—§ 25
Seven Hills v. Aryan Nations, 76 Ohio
St. 3d 304, 1996-Ohio-394, 667
N.E.2d 942 (1996)
113 ALR5th 1—§ 3, 4, 11
70 ALR6th 513—§ 6
71 ALR6th 471—§ 12
Seven-O Corp., In re, 289 S.W.3d 384
(Tex. App. Waco 2009)
72 ALR6th 563—§ 20, 35
Seventeen Hundred Peoria, Inc. v. Tulsa,
422 P.2d 840 (Okla. 1966)
63 ALR5th 517—§ 37
Sever v. Alaska Pulp Corp., 931 P.2d
354, 132 Lab. Cas. (CCH) ¶ 58182
(Alaska 1996)

CASES CITED IN ALR5th and ALR6th

2 ALR6th 387—§ 4
33 ALR6th 305—§ 4
Severance v. Healey, 50 N.H. 448, 1870
WL 3126 (1870)
10 ALR6th 31—§ 2
Severin v. U.S., 99 Ct. Cl. 435, 1943 WL
4198 (1943)
25 ALR6th 265—§ 1, 2, 4, 7, 8, 31
Severio P. v. Donald Y, 128 Misc. 2d
539, 490 N.Y.S.2d 439 (Fam. Ct.
1985)
16 ALR5th 650—§ 9
80 ALR5th 117—§ 14
Severn, Re Marriage of, 44 Colo. App.
109, 608 P.2d 381 (1980)
16 ALR5th 650—§ 16
Severn v. State, 2003 WL 22434125
(Tex. App. Amarillo 2003)
63 ALR6th 351—§ 3
Severson Agri-Service, Inc. v. Lander,
172 Wis. 2d 269, 493 N.W.2d 230
(Ct. App. 1992)
79 ALR6th 211—§ 2, 32
Severstal Sparrows Point, LLC v. Public
Service Com'n of Maryland, 194
Md. App. 601, 5 A.3d 713 (2010)
80 ALR6th 1—§ 3, 12, 58
Severtson v. Williams Construction Co.,
173 Cal. App. 3d 86, 220 Cal. Rptr.
400 (2d Dist. 1985)
60 ALR5th 669—§ 6
Sevey v. Knowles, 2003 WL 1872965
(N.D. Cal. 2003)
71 ALR6th 625—§ 29
Sevier v. Turner, 742 F.2d 262 (CA6
Tenn. 1984)
32 ALR5th 31—§ 3
Sevilla v. State, 111 App. Div. 2d 1046,
490 N.Y.S.2d 351 (3d Dep't 1985)
50 ALR5th 1—§ 4
Sevilla v. Stearns-Roger, Inc., 101 Cal.
App. 3d 608, 161 Cal. Rptr. 700 (4th
Dist. 1980)
122 ALR5th 1—§ 2, 36
Sevin, In re, 712 So. 2d 998 (La. Ct.
App. 5th Cir. 1998)
82 ALR5th 443—§ 2, 4, 8
83 ALR5th 375—§ 2, 7

84 ALR5th 191—§ 2 to 5
Sevin v. Louisiana Wildlife & Fisheries
Com., 283 So. 2d 690 (La. 1973)
50 ALR5th 703—§ 27
Sevion v. State, 620 N.E.2d 736 (Ind. Ct.
App. 4th Dist. 1993)
29 ALR6th 1—§ 10
Sevon, Re Marriage of, 117 Ill. App. 3d
313, 73 Ill. Dec. 41, 453 N.E.2d 866
(1st Dist. 1983)
11 ALR5th 259—§ 18
Sevrie v. Sevrie, 90 Misc. 2d 321, 394
N.Y.S.2d 389 (Fam. Ct. 1977)
55 ALR5th 557—§ 4, 8, 15
Sevruk v. Carr, 2002-Ohio-4707, 2002
WL 31008813 (Ohio Ct. App. 12th
Dist. Butler County 2002)
64 ALR6th 249—§ 17
S.E.W., In Interest of, 960 S.W.2d 954
(Tex. App. Texarkana 1998)
87 ALR5th 361—§ 19
Sewak v. Lockhart, 699 A.2d 755 (Pa.
Super. Ct. 1997)
84 ALR5th 487—§ 21
Sewall v. Duplessis, 2 Rob. 66 (La.
1842)
46 ALR5th 1—§ 47
Sewall v. Snook, 687 A.2d 234 (Me.
1996)
99 ALR5th 475—§ 15
Sewall's Falls Bridge v. Fisk & Nor-
cross, 23 N.H. 171 (1851)
31 ALR5th 171—§ 14, 26
Sewar v. Gagliardi Bros. Service, 51
N.Y.2d 752, 432 N.Y.S.2d 367, 411
N.E.2d 786 (1980)
23 ALR5th 1—§ 2
Sewar v. Gagliardi Bros. Service, 69
App. Div. 2d 281, 418 N.Y.S.2d
704 (4th Dep't 1979)
16 ALR5th 1—§ 16
Seward v. B.O.C. Div. of General Motors Corp., 805 F. Supp. 623, 16
Employee Benefits Cas. (BNA)
1029, 60 Fair Empl. Prac. Cas.
(BNA) 373, 60 Empl. Prac. Dec.
(CCH) ¶ 41911 (N.D. Ill. 1992)
79 ALR6th 377—§ 29, 32, 33

Seward v. County of Bernalillo, 61 N.M. 52, 294 P.2d 625 (1956)
13 ALR5th 444—§ 4

Seward v. Receivers of Seaboard Air Line Ry., 159 N.C. 241, 75 S.E. 34 (1912)
95 ALR5th 1—§ 10, 11

Seward County Board of Comm'rs v. Seward, 196 Neb. 266, 242 N.W.2d 849 (1976)
53 ALR5th 1—§ 22, 32, 37

Seward Park Housing Corp. v. Cohen, 287 A.D.2d 157, 734 N.Y.S.2d 42, 114 A.L.R.5th 789 (1st Dep't 2001)
114 ALR5th 443—§ 9, 24, 26

Seward, Town of v. Margules, 9 Alaska 354, 1938 WL 1186 (Terr. Alaska 1938)
44 ALR6th 259—§ 17

Sewell, Estate of, 487 Pa. 379, 409 A.2d 401 (1979)
37 ALR5th 237—§ 3

Sewell v. American Uniform Co., 759 S.W.2d 415 (Tenn. 1988)
4 ALR5th 443—§ 5

Sewell v. Bill Johnson Motors, Inc., 213 Ga. App. 853, 446 S.E.2d 239 (1994)
112 ALR5th 509—§ 18
39 ALR6th 445—§ 42

Sewell v. Brookbank, 119 Ariz. 422, 581 P.2d 267, 4 Media L. R. 1475 (App. 1978)
44 ALR5th 193—§ 31

Sewell v. City of New York, 182 A.D.2d 469, 583 N.Y.S.2d 255 (1st Dep't 1992)
91 ALR6th 435—§ 17, 59, 68, 140

Sewell v. Cohoes, 11 Hun. 626 (N.Y. 1877)
15 ALR5th 119—§ 85

Sewell v. Eubanks, 181 Ga. App. 545, 352 S.E.2d 802 (1987)
19 ALR5th 1—§ 43, 104, 110, 112

Sewell v. Gregory, 179 W. Va. 585, 371 S.E.2d 82 (1988)
33 ALR5th 1—§ 2

Sewell v. Henry Johnson Auto Body Shop, 274 A.D. 957, 83 N.Y.S.2d 795 (3d Dep't 1948)
41 ALR6th 207—§ 19

Sewell v. Hull/Storey Development, LLC, 241 Ga. App. 365, 526 S.E.2d 878 (1999)
31 ALR5th 550—§ 7
43 ALR5th 207—§ 82

Sewell v. Internal Medicine and Endocrine Associates, P.C., 600 So. 2d 242 (Ala. 1992)
124 ALR5th 623—§ 4

Sewell v. Nu Markets, Inc., 353 Mich. 553, 91 N.W.2d 861 (1958)
46 ALR5th 1—§ 23

Sewell v. Public Service Co., 832 P.2d 994 (Colo. App. 1991)
49 ALR5th 659—§ 2 to 4, 8

Sewell v. Southfield Public Schools, 456 Mich. 670, 576 N.W.2d 153, 125 Ed. Law Rep. 214, 66 A.L.R.5th 707 (1998)
66 ALR5th 1—§ 47

Sewell v. State, 238 Ga. 495, 233 S.E.2d 187 (1977)
94 ALR5th 497—§ 5, 7

Sewell v. State, 244 Ga. App. 449, 536 S.E.2d 173 (2000)
87 ALR5th 693—§ 3

Sewell v. State, 721 So. 2d 129 (Miss. 1998)
47 ALR5th 259—§ 7

Sewell v. Trib Publications, Inc., 276 Ga. App. 250, 622 S.E.2d 919, 204 Ed. Law Rep. 781 (2005)
22 ALR6th 553—§ 26

Sewell v. Wofford, 131 Ill. App. 3d 62, 86 Ill. Dec. 361, 475 N.E.2d 575 (1st Dist. 1985)
62 ALR5th 537—§ 3

Sewer v. Fat Albert's Warehouse, Inc., 235 A.D.2d 414, 652 N.Y.S.2d 102 (2d Dep't 1997)
1 ALR6th 297—§ 11, 14, 31

Sewerage Dist. No. 1 of Siloam Springs v. Black, 141 Ark. 550, 217 S.W. 813 (1920)

For assistance, call 1-800-328-4880

92 ALR5th 517—§ 2, 5, 11, 12
101 ALR5th 287—§ 13
Sewer Assessment for Passaic, In re, 54 NJL 156, 23 A. 517 (1891)
56 ALR5th 171—§ 10, 14, 16
Sewer Environmental Contractors, Inc. v. Goldin, 98 App. Div. 2d 606, 469 N.Y.S.2d 339, 26 BNA WH Cas. 929 (1st Dep't 1983)
10 ALR5th 337—§ 3, 9
Sewer Imp. Dist. No. 1 of City of Wynne v. Fiscus, 128 Ark. 250, 193 S.W. 521 (1917)
92 ALR5th 517—§ 11
Sewer Imp. Dist. No. 1 of Sheridan v. Jones, 199 Ark. 534, 134 S.W.2d 551 (1939)
92 ALR5th 517—§ 3, 11
101 ALR5th 287—§ 7
54 ALR6th 201—§ 47
Sexauer & Lemke v. Luke A. Burke & Sons Co., 228 N.Y. 341, 127 N.E. 329 (1920)
81 ALR6th 363—§ 4
Sexstone v. Rochester, 32 App. Div. 2d 737, 301 N.Y.S.2d 887 (4th Dep't 1969)
24 ALR5th 200—§ 22, 41
Sexton, In re, 16 B.R. 240, 33 U.C.C. Rep. Serv. 116 (Bankr. E.D. Tenn. 1981)
47 ALR6th 347—§ 4
Sexton v. Arkansas Supreme Court Committee on Professional Conduct, 299 Ark. 439, 774 S.W.2d 114, 9 A.L.R.5th 1032 (1989)
9 ALR5th 193—§ 2, 3, 6, 8, 10
Sexton v. City of Rock Hill, 107 S.C. 505, 93 S.E. 180 (1917)
12 ALR6th 645—§ 16
Sexton v. Continental Cas. Co., 1991 OK 84, 816 P.2d 1135 (Okla. 1991)
16 ALR6th 491—§ 4
Sexton v. IndyMac Bank, FSB, 2011 WL 4346367 (D. Nev. 2011)
86 ALR6th 411—§ 5

Sexton v. Louisiana Vacuum Services, Inc., 506 So. 2d 780 (La. App. 1st Cir. 1987)
48 ALR5th 129—§ 13, 14, 17
50 ALR5th 1—§ 9, 17
52 ALR5th 1—§ 7
Sexton v. Ohio State Lottery Com'n, 57 Ohio Misc. 2d 36, 566 N.E.2d 205 (C.P. 1989)
48 ALR6th 243—§ 22
Sexton v. Public Service Commission of City of New York, 180 A.D. 111, 167 N.Y.S. 493 (3d Dep't 1917)
80 ALR5th 417—§ 3
Sexton v. Public Service Com'n, 188 W. Va. 305, 423 S.E.2d 914 (1992)
101 ALR5th 287—§ 16
Sexton v. Scott County, 785 S.W.2d 814 (Tenn. 1990)
112 ALR5th 509—§ 2, 15
122 ALR5th 653—§ 2, 5
13 ALR6th 209—§ 2, 16, 31
39 ALR6th 445—§ 41
Sexton v. Security Ins. Co. of New Haven, Conn., 13 Pa. D. & C.2d 444, 1958 WL 5285 (C.P. 1958)
110 ALR5th 465—§ 4
Sexton v. Sexton, 32 Ohio App. 2d 344, 61 Ohio Ops. 2d 514, 291 N.E.2d 542 (Clermont Co. 1971)
34 ALR5th 447—§ 27
Sexton v. Sexton, 129 Iowa 487, 105 N.W. 314 (1905)
23 ALR6th 1—§ 4, 17, 26
Sexton v. Sexton, 433 S.W.2d 133 (Ky. 1968)
49 ALR5th 441—§ 20
Sexton v. Sexton, 1998 WL 566708 (Ark. Ct. App. 1998)
38 ALR6th 313—§ 9
Sexton v. Smith, 112 Ill. 2d 187, 97 Ill. Dec. 411, 492 N.E.2d 1284 (1986)
10 ALR5th 828—§ 21
Sexton v. South Portland, 499 A.2d 472 (Me. 1985)
1 ALR5th 622—§ 2
2 ALR5th 553—§ 30

For assistance, call 1-800-328-4880

Sexton v. Southwestern Auto Racing Asso., 75 Ill. App. 3d 338, 31 Ill. Dec. 133, 394 N.E.2d 49 (5th Dist. 1979)
54 ALR5th 513—§ 4

Sexton v. State, 775 So. 2d 923 (Fla. 2000)
110 ALR5th 1—§ 10

Sexton v. State, 997 So. 2d 1073 (Fla. 2008)
102 ALR6th 417—§ 18, 30

Sexton v. U.S., 132 F. Supp. 2d 967 (M.D. Fla. 2000)
64 ALR5th 235—§ 5, 17

Sexton Bros. Tire Co. v. Southern Burglar Alarm Co., 153 Ga. App. 413, 265 S.E.2d 335 (1980)
13 ALR5th 217—§ 14

Sexton Law Firm, P.A. v. Milligan, 329 Ark. 285, 948 S.W.2d 388, 134 Lab. Cas. (CCH) ¶ 58293 (1997)
39 ALR6th 155—§ 4

Sexton, People ex rel. v. Warden of Female Workhouse, 216 App. Div. 223, 215 N.Y.S. 116 (1926)
45 ALR5th 591—§ 15

Sexual Offender Reclassification Cases, In re, 126 Ohio St. 3d 322, 2010-Ohio-3753, 933 N.E.2d 801 (2010)
63 ALR6th 351—§ 3

Sexual-Offender Reclassification Cases, In re, 126 Ohio St. 3d 322, 2010-Ohio-3753, 933 N.E.2d 801 (2010)
64 ALR6th 1—§ 7, 9 to 11, 13

Seybert v. County of Imperial, 162 Cal. App. 2d 209, 327 P.2d 560 (4th Dist. 1958)
34 ALR5th 77—§ 3

Seybert v. Seybert, 2001-Ohio-7066, 2001 WL 1603089 (Ohio Ct. App. 11th Dist. Trumbull County 2001)
109 ALR5th 1—§ 10

Seybold v. Eisle, 154 Iowa 128, 134 N.W. 578 (1912)
25 ALR5th 391—§ 16, 88

Seybold v. Seybold, 191 Neb. 480, 216 N.W.2d 179 (1974)
17 ALR5th 366—§ 8, 15

Seydel v. Reuber, 254 Minn. 168, 94 N.W.2d 265 (1959)
5 ALR5th 875—§ 2, 29, 45

Seyle v. State, 584 P.2d 1081 (Wyo. 1978)
119 ALR5th 275—§ 7, 13

Seyler, In re Marriage of, 559 N.W.2d 7, 84 A.L.R.5th 399 (Iowa 1997)
84 ALR5th 399—§ 3, 5, 13, 19

Seyler v. Com., Unemployment Compensation Bd. of Review, 85 Pa. Commw. 392, 481 A.2d 1262 (1984)
95 ALR5th 329—§ 3

Seymour, Re Estate of, 93 N.M. 328, 600 P.2d 274 (1979)
3 ALR5th 590—§ 6, 15, 16

Seymour v. A.S. Abell Co., 557 F. Supp. 951, 9 Media L. R. 1098 (D.C. Md. 1983)
44 ALR5th 193—§ 20

Seymour v. Brunswick Corp., 655 So. 2d 892, Prod. Liab. Rep. (CCH) ¶ 14228 (Miss. 1995)
73 ALR5th 75—§ 12

Seymour v. Carcia, 24 Conn. App. 446, 589 A.2d 7 (1991)
14 ALR5th 242—§ 2
33 ALR5th 303—§ 2, 3, 6, 12

Seymour v. Carcia, 221 Conn. 473, 604 A.2d 1304, 26 A.L.R.5th 865 (1992)
26 ALR5th 401—§ 2, 3, 8, 30

Seymour v. Dalton Tp., 177 Mich. App. 403, 442 N.W.2d 655 (1989)
114 ALR5th 561—§ 28

Seymour v. Holcomb, 7 Misc. 3d 530, 790 N.Y.S.2d 858 (Sup 2005)
8 ALR6th 339—§ 3

Seymour v. Hug, 413 F. Supp. 2d 910 (N.D. Ill. 2005)
75 ALR6th 1—§ 3

Seymour v. Johnson, 2001 WL 1418778 (Cal. App. 2d Dist. 2001)
13 ALR6th 1—§ 4

Seymour v. Johnson, 2001 WL 1418778 (Cal. App. 2d Dist. 2001), unpublished/noncitable
15 ALR6th 427—§ 15

Seymour v. Lakeville Journal Co. LLC, 150 Fed. Appx. 103, 33 Media L. Rep. (BNA) 2409 (2d Cir. 2005)
22 ALR6th 553—§ 8, 21, 25

Seymour v. Nichols, 21 A.D.3d 1234, 801 N.Y.S.2d 426 (3d Dep't 2005)
91 ALR6th 435—§ 75, 121

Seymour v. Potlatch Forests, Inc., 94 Idaho 224, 486 P.2d 79 (1971)
68 ALR5th 13—§ 4, 22

Seymour v. Region One Bd. of Educ., 261 Conn. 475, 803 A.2d 318, 168 Ed. Law Rep. 368 (2002)
9 ALR6th 177—§ 54

Seymour v. Seymour, 89 N.M. 752, 557 P.2d 1101 (1976)
17 ALR5th 366—§ 12, 16

Seymour v. Sokolneck, 34 A.D.2d 1073, 312 N.Y.S.2d 323 (3d Dep't 1970)
107 ALR5th 441—§ 11
109 ALR5th 161—§ 9, 13
20 ALR6th 641—§ 18

Seymour v. State, 21 Ariz. App. 12, 515 P.2d 39 (Div. 2 1973)
71 ALR6th 335—§ 10, 13

Seymour v. State, 115 Tex. Crim. 348, 28 S.W.2d 549 (1930)
105 ALR5th 529—§ 11

Seymour v. State, 582 So. 2d 127 (Fla. Dist. Ct. App. 4th Dist. 1991)
115 ALR5th 509—§ 3, 7, 9

Seymour v. State, 949 P.2d 881 (Wyo. 1997)
1 ALR6th 549—§ 8

Seymour v. State Farm Mut. Ins. Co., 508 S.W.2d 572 (Ky. 1974)
9 ALR5th 826—§ 2, 3

Seymour v. Stotski, 82 Ohio App. 3d 87, 611 N.E.2d 454 (10th Dist. Franklin County 1992)
77 ALR5th 567—§ 2, 3

Seymour v. U.S., 129 S. Ct. 527, 172 L. Ed. 2d 355 (2008)
46 ALR6th 495—§ 31

Seymour v. Walker, 224 F.3d 542, 2000 FED App. 270P (6th Cir. 2000)
11 ALR5th 871—§ 5
57 ALR5th 315—§ 4

Seymour v. Walker, 224 F.3d 542, 2000 FED App. 0270P (6th Cir. 2000)
58 ALR6th 499—§ 22
71 ALR6th 1—§ 5

Seymour v. Warren, 179 N.Y. 1, 71 N.E. 260 (1904)
12 ALR6th 123—§ 4

Seymour Mfg. Co., Inc. v. Commercial Union Ins. Co., 665 N.E.2d 891 (Ind. 1996)
88 ALR5th 493—§ 4
89 ALR5th 1—§ 5
98 ALR5th 193—§ 23
105 ALR5th 95—§ 3

Seymour S. v. Glen S., 189 A.D.2d 765, 592 N.Y.S.2d 410 (2d Dep't 1993)
71 ALR5th 99—§ 3, 8

Seymour's Will, In re, 76 Misc. 371, 136 N.Y.S. 942 (Sur. Ct. 1912)
67 ALR6th 341—§ 23

Seymour Water Co. v. Lebline, 195 Ind. 481, 144 N.E. 30, 145 N.E. 764 (1924)
62 ALR5th 219—§ 51

S.F. v. M.D., 2000 WL 520686 (Md. Ct. Spec. App. 2000)
80 ALR5th 1—§ 7

S. F. v. State, 354 So. 2d 474 (Fla. Dist. Ct. App. 3d Dist. 1978)
72 ALR5th 1—§ 29

SFA Folio Collections, Inc. v. Bannon, 217 Conn. 220, 585 A.2d 666 (1991)
71 ALR5th 671—§ 8

SFA Folio Collections, Inc. v. Tracy, 73 Ohio St. 3d 119, 652 N.E.2d 693 (1995)
71 ALR5th 671—§ 5

SFBC Intern., Inc. Securities & Derivative Litigation, In re, 495 F. Supp. 2d 477 (D.N.J. 2007)
43 ALR6th 1—§ 4

S.F.E. ex rel. T.I.E., 981 P.2d 642 (Colo. Ct. App. 1998)
40 ALR5th 697—§ 7, 11, 13
58 ALR5th 669—§ 24

Sferra v. Mathew, 103 F. Supp. 2d 617 (E.D. N.Y. 2000)

13 ALR6th 1—§ 4, 6

Sferra, State ex rel. v. Girard, 2006-Ohio-1876, 2006 WL 988079 (Ohio Ct. App. 11th Dist. Trumbull County 2006)

26 ALR6th 179—§ 8

SF Hotel Co., L.P. v. Energy Investments, Inc., 985 F. Supp. 1032, 45 U.S.P.Q.2d (BNA) 1308 (D. Kan. 1997)

81 ALR5th 41—§ 3, 10

SFI, Inc. v. U.S. Fire Ins. Co., 634 F.2d 879 (5th Cir. 1981)

73 ALR6th 681—§ 4

S. Floridabanc Sav. Assn. v. Prof. Inv. of America, 77 Ohio App. 3d 435, 602 N.E.2d 677, 19 U.C.C. Rep. Serv. 2d 638 (8th Dist. Cuyahoga County 1991)

35 ALR6th 437—§ 9, 10, 12, 14, 17

S. Frederick P. v. Barbara P., 115 Misc. 2d 332, 454 N.Y.S.2d 202 (Fam. Ct. 1982)

80 ALR5th 117—§ 14

S.G. v. D.M., 171 Misc. 2d 169, 653 N.Y.S.2d 525 (Fam. Ct. 1996)

59 ALR5th 489—§ 12

Sgarlata v. City of Schenectady, 77 Misc. 2d 481, 353 N.Y.S.2d 603 (Sup 1974)

54 ALR6th 201—§ 9, 15, 25, 28, 45

Sgarlato, In re, 27 A.D.2d 738, 277 N.Y.S.2d 318 (2d Dep't 1967)

25 ALR6th 1—§ 34

S.G. ex rel. A.G. v. Sayreville Bd. of Educ., 333 F.3d 417, 178 Ed. Law Rep. 36 (3d Cir. 2003)

117 ALR5th 459—§ 3, 4, 6

S.G., Jr., Matter of, 935 S.W.2d 919 (Tex. App. San Antonio 1996)

103 ALR6th 137—§ 14, 19

S.G.K. v. K.S.K, 374 N.W.2d 525 (Minn. App. 1985)

1 ALR5th 776—§ 2, 9

S.G.K. v. State, 657 So. 2d 1246 (Fla. Dist. Ct. App. 1st Dist. 1995)

66 ALR5th 397—§ 22

Sgrignari v. Vallone, 1999 WL 367988 (Conn. Super. Ct. 1999)

111 ALR5th 313—§ 9

Sgro v. Getty Petroleum Corp., 854 F. Supp. 1164 (D.N.J. 1994)

107 ALR5th 311—§ 5

109 ALR5th 421—§ 5, 7

Sgro v. Howarth, 54 Ill. App. 2d 1, 203 N.E.2d 173 (4th Dist. 1964)

38 ALR5th 737—§ 2

Sgroe v. Wells Fargo Bank, N.A., 2013 WL 1739502 (E.D. Tex. 2013)

86 ALR6th 411—§ 5

S.H. v. B.L.H., 392 Pa. Super. 137, 572 A.2d 730 (1990)

1 ALR5th 776—§ 3

S.H. v. Calhoun County Dep't of Human Resources, 2001 WL 498979 (Ala. Civ. App. 2001)

89 ALR5th 195—§ 8

S.H. v. State, 598 So. 2d 320, 17 FLW D 1378 (Fla. App. D1 1992)

46 ALR5th 523—§ 4

Sha v. New York City Police Dept. Twentieth Precinct, Detectives, Officers Soe, 2005 WL 877852 (S.D. N.Y. 2005)

58 ALR6th 499—§ 45

Shaari v. Harvard Student Agencies, Inc., 427 Mass. 129, 691 N.E.2d 925, 26 Media L. Rep. (BNA) 1730 (1998)

19 ALR5th 1—§ 37.5

Shaban, In re Marriage of, 88 Cal. App. 4th 398, 105 Cal. Rptr. 2d 863 (4th Dist. 2001)

82 ALR6th 1—§ 11

Shabazz v. Odum, 591 F. Supp. 1513 (M.D. Pa. 1984)

89 ALR6th 1—§ 54

Shabazz v. Rochell, 73 Fed. Appx. 806 (6th Cir. 2003)

119 ALR5th 1—§ 12

Shabbona Creston Oil & Gas Corp. v. Doherty, 264 App. Div. 909, 35 N.Y.S.2d 839 (1942)

59 ALR5th 693—§ 5

Shabot v. East Ramapo School Dist.,
703 N.Y.S.2d 268, 142 Ed. Law
Rep. 468 (App. Div. 2d Dep't 2000)
66 ALR5th 1—§ 6

Shack v. Attorney General of State of
Pennsylvania, 776 F.2d 1170 (3d
Cir. 1985)
53 ALR6th 1—§ 14

Shackelford v. Central Bank of Mississippi, 354 So. 2d 253 (Miss. 1978)
23 ALR5th 241—§ 4
28 ALR5th 664—§ 4

Shackelford v. State, 486 N.E.2d 1014
(Ind. 1986)
72 ALR5th 109—§ 10

Shackelford v. State, 498 N.E.2d 382
(Ind. 1986)
99 ALR6th 295—§ 5

Shackford v. New England Tel. & Tel.
Co., 112 Me. 204, 91 A. 931 (1914)
8 ALR5th 177—§ 16

Shackil v. Lederle Laboratories, a Div.
of American Cyanamid Co., 116
N.J. 155, 561 A.2d 511, Prod. Liab.
Rep. (CCH) ¶ 12244 (1989)
63 ALR5th 195—§ 3, 4, 6

Shackleford v. Shackleford, 572 So. 2d
468 (Ala. Civ. App. 1990)
7 ALR6th 411—§ 4, 33

Shackleford v. State, 51 S.W.3d 125
(Mo. Ct. App. W.D. 2001)
31 ALR6th 49—§ 10

Shackleford v. United States Fidelity &
Guaranty Co., 219 So. 2d 243 (La.
App. 3d Cir. 1969)
9 ALR5th 826—§ 7

Shackman v. Daigle, 447 So. 2d 629 (La.
Ct. App. 4th Cir. 1984)
7 ALR6th 1—§ 6, 27

Shad v. Florida E. C. R. Co., 236 So. 2d
477 (Fla. App. D1 1970)
9 ALR5th 102—§ 19

Shada v. Title & Trust Co., 457 So. 2d
553, 9 FLW 2165 (Fla. App. D4
1984)
19 ALR5th 786—§ 3 to 6

SHAD Alliance v. Smith Haven Mall,
66 N.Y.2d 496, 498 N.Y.S.2d 99,
488 N.E.2d 1211 (1985)
70 ALR6th 513—§ 13
71 ALR6th 471—§ 9

SHAD Alliance v. Smith Haven Mall,
66 N.Y. 496, 498 N.Y.S.2d 99, 488
N.E.2d 1211 (1985)
52 ALR5th 195—§ 4

Shadday v. Omni Hotels Management
Corp., 2006 WL 693680 (S.D. Ind.
2006)
17 ALR6th 453—§ 13

Shadden v. Shadden, 11 So. 3d 761
(Miss. Ct. App. 2009)
60 ALR6th 193—§ 33

Shadders v. Brock, 101 Misc. 2d 11, 420
N.Y.S.2d 697 (Fam. Ct. 1979)
71 ALR5th 99—§ 3, 6

Shaddix v. Shaddix, 447 So. 2d 808
(Ala. Civ. App. 1984)
120 ALR5th 229—§ 7, 8, 18

Shaddock v. Walters, 55 N.Y.S.2d 635
(Sup 1945)
119 ALR5th 519—§ 12

Shaddox v. State, 594 S.W.2d 69 (Tex.
Crim. 1980)
29 ALR5th 59—§ 3

Shade v. Bay Counties Power Co., 152
Cal. 10, 92 P. 62 (1907)
95 ALR5th 29—§ 7

Shade v. Bowers, 29 Ohio Op. 2d 130,
93 Ohio L. Abs. 463, 199 N.E.2d
131 (C.P. 1962)
100 ALR5th 341—§ 9

Shade v. Kaiser, 2012-Ohio-4979, 2012
WL 5295844 (Ohio Ct. App. 2d
Dist. Montgomery County 2012)
95 ALR6th 85—§ 20, 65

Shader v. Railway Passenger Assur. Co.,
66 N.Y. 441, 1876 WL 11002
(1876)
100 ALR5th 617—§ 6, 9

Shades Ridge Holding Co., Inc. v. U.S.,
888 F.2d 725 (11th Cir. 1989)
2 ALR6th 195—§ 4

Shadle v. Pearce, 287 Pa. Super. 436,
430 A.2d 683 (1981)

17 ALR6th 159—§ 20
Shadler v. State, 761 So. 2d 279 (Fla. 2000)
19 ALR5th 470—§ 15
Shadoan v. Liberty Mut. Fire Ins. Co., 1994 OK CIV APP 182, 894 P.2d 1140 (Ct. App. Div. 1 1994)
118 ALR5th 91—§ 1
ShadowBird, Inc. v. Nicholson, 2004 WL 2862173 (Cal. App. 3d Dist. 2004)
64 ALR6th 365—§ 10, 26, 34, 35
Shadowood Associates v. Kirk, 170 Ga. App. 209, 316 S.E.2d 487 (1984)
43 ALR5th 207—§ 18
Shadrick v. Coker, 963 S.W.2d 726 (Tenn. 1998)
14 ALR6th 301—§ 4
19 ALR6th 475—§ 2, 4, 9, 15, 23
Shadwell v. Craigie, 361 S.C. 492, 605 S.E.2d 567, 14 A.L.R.6th 791 (Ct. App. 2004)
14 ALR6th 277—§ 13
14 ALR6th 301—§ 4, 13, 19
Shady Grove, Inc. v. Parish of Jefferson, 203 So. 2d 869, 32 A.L.R.3d 420 (La. App. 4th Cir. 1967)
63 ALR5th 607—§ 6
Shaeffer v. Collins, CCH Bus Fran Guide ¶ 7578 (E.D. Pa. 1980)
52 ALR5th 613—§ 3
Shaer Shoe Corp. v. Granite State Alarm, Inc., 110 N.H. 132, 262 A.2d 285 (1970)
36 ALR6th 305—§ 7
Shafaransky v. Cosmos Footwear Corp., 277 App. Div. 803, 96 N.Y.S.2d 706 (1950)
26 ALR5th 127—§ 7
Shafer v. H. B. Thomas Co., 53 N.J. Super. 19, 146 A.2d 483 (App. Div. 1958)
6 ALR6th 1—§ 3, 4
Shafer v. Kings Tire Service, Inc., 597 S.E.2d 302, 15 A.D. Cas. (BNA) 1088 (W. Va. 2004)
119 ALR5th 121—§ 4

Shafer v. Lamar Pub. Co., 621 S.W.2d 709, 7 Media L. R. 2049 (Mo. App. 1981)
44 ALR5th 193—§ 21, 44
Shafer v. Parke, Davis & Co., 192 Mich. 577, 159 N.W. 304 (1916)
40 ALR6th 99—§ 40
Shafer v. Shafer, 16 Neb. App. 170, 741 N.W.2d 173 (2007)
38 ALR6th 313—§ 10
Shafer v. Shafer, 1996 WL 456040 (Neb. Ct. App. 1996)
38 ALR6th 313—§ 5
Shafer v. State, 214 Tenn. 416, 381 S.W.2d 254 (1964)
68 ALR5th 343—§ 3, 14
Shafer v. State Employees' Retirement Bd., 696 A.2d 1186, 119 Ed. Law Rep. 1097 (Pa. 1997)
56 ALR5th 493—§ 14
Shafer Bros. Land Co. v. Universal Pictures Corp., 188 Wash. 33, 61 P.2d 593 (1936)
45 ALR5th 251—§ 7
Shaffer v. AMF, Inc., 842 F.2d 893, Prod. Liab. Rep. (CCH) ¶ 11730, 6 U.C.C. Rep. Serv. 2d 56 (6th Cir. 1988)
93 ALR5th 103—§ 12, 17, 21
Shaffer v. Brooklyn Park Garden Apartments, 311 Minn. 452, 250 N.W.2d 172, 20 U.C.C. Rep. Serv. (CBC) 1269 (1977)
77 ALR5th 429—§ 4
Shaffer v. Clinton, 54 F. Supp. 2d 1014 (D. Colo. 1999)
95 ALR5th 459—§ 2, 4
Shaffer v. Continental Cas. Co., 362 Fed. Appx. 627 (9th Cir. 2010)
60 ALR6th 295—§ 66
Shaffer v. Davidson, 445 P.2d 13, 5 U.C.C.R.S. 772 (Wyo. 1968)
61 ALR5th 525—§ 18
Shaffer v. Debbas, 17 Cal. App. 4th 33, 21 Cal. Rptr. 2d 110, 93 C.D.O.S. 5350, 93 Daily Journal DAR 9024 (4th Dist. 1993)
22 ALR5th 464—§ 2

Shaffer v. Fort Henry Surgical Associ-
ates, Inc., 215 W. Va. 453, 599
S.E.2d 876 (2004)
69 ALR6th 415—§ 43
Shaffer v. Jeffery, 915 P.2d 910 (Okla.
1996)
60 ALR5th 669—§ 4
Shaffer v. Liberty Life Assur. Co. of
Boston, 319 Ill. App. 3d 1048, 253
Ill. Dec. 837, 746 N.E.2d 285 (1st
Dist. 2001)
27 ALR6th 323—§ 11
Shaffer v. Lyme, 2011-Ohio-2204, 2011
WL 1782104 (Ohio Ct. App. 3d
Dist. Shelby County 2011)
90 ALR6th 451—§ 113
Shaffer v. National Can Corp., 565 F.
Supp. 909, 34 BNA FEP Cas. 172,
114 BNA LRRM 2941, 33 CCH
EPD ¶ 34184 (E.D. Pa. 1983)
21 ALR5th 1—§ 9
Shaffer v. National Can Corp., 565 F.
Supp. 909, 34 Fair Empl. Prac. Cas.
(BNA) 172, 114 L.R.R.M. (BNA)
2941, 33 Empl. Prac. Dec. (CCH)
¶ 34184 (E.D. Pa. 1983)
20 ALR6th 1—§ 4
Shaffer v. OhioHealth Corp., 2004-Ohio-
6523, 2004 WL 2806417 (Ohio Ct.
App. 10th Dist. Franklin County
2004)
10 ALR6th 531—§ 7
Shaffer v. Phoenix Ins. Co., 21 Pa. D. &
C.2d 79 (1959)
30 ALR5th 170—§ 84, 98
Shaffer v. Previews, Inc., 78 So. 2d 376
(Fla. 1955)
27 ALR5th 1—§ 3
Shaffer v. RWP Group, Inc., 169 F.R.D.
19 (E.D. N.Y. 1996)
121 ALR5th 157—§ 2
3 ALR6th 13—§ 16
Shaffer v. Saffle, 148 F.3d 1180 (10th
Cir. 1998)
76 ALR5th 239—§ 2, 5, 7, 11, 15, 22
Shaffer v. Shaffer, 2005-Ohio-3884,
2005 WL 1797739 (Ohio Ct. App.
3d Dist. Paulding County 2005)

21 ALR6th 577—§ 5
Shaffer v. Somerset Community Hospital, 205 Pa. Super. 419, 211 A.2d 49
(1965)
4 ALR5th 443—§ 12
Shaffer v. South State Machinery, Inc.,
995 F. Supp. 584 (W.D. Pa. 1998)
18 ALR6th 629—§ 4, 24
Shaffer v. Spangler, 144 Pa. 223, 22 A.
865 (1891)
6 ALR6th 391—§ 5, 11, 17, 19 to 21
Shaffer v. State, 68 Tex. Crim. 162, 151
S.W. 1061 (1912)
54 ALR6th 429—§ 7
Shaffer v. State, 162 P.3d 65 (Kan. Ct.
App. 2007)
99 ALR6th 295—§ 9, 19
Shaffer v. State, 184 S.W.3d 353 (Tex.
App. Fort Worth 2006)
54 ALR6th 593—§ 3
Shaffer v. State, 449 N.E.2d 1074 (Ind.
1983)
65 ALR6th 537—§ 18
Shaffer v. State, 640 P.2d 88, 31
A.L.R.4th 166 (Wyo. 1982)
34 ALR6th 1—§ 8
Shaffer v. State, 674 N.E.2d 1 (Ind. Ct.
App. 1996)
15 ALR5th 391—§ 39
Shaffer v. State Farm Fire & Cas. Co.,
120 Or. App. 70, 852 P.2d 245
(1993)
90 ALR6th 635—§ 26
Shaffer v. State Farm Mut. Auto. Ins.
Co., 246 Ga. App. 244, 540 S.E.2d
227 (2000)
115 ALR5th 589—§ 3
Shaffer v. Thull, 147 Neb. 947, 25
N.W.2d 755 (1947)
27 ALR5th 174—§ 78
Shaffer v. Victory Van Lines, Inc., 265
A.D.2d 543, 697 N.Y.S.2d 166 (2d
Dep't 1999)
11 ALR6th 447—§ 4
Shaffer ex rel. Shaffer v. Apfel, 229 F.3d
1153 (6th Cir. 2000)
122 ALR5th 205—§ 3, 10, 45

Shaffner v. City of Riverview, 154 Mich. App. 514, 397 N.W.2d 835 (1986)
17 ALR6th 1—§ 27

Shaffner v. City of Salem, 201 Or. 45, 268 P.2d 599 (1954)
73 ALR5th 223—§ 9

Shaffner v. Pinchback, 30 Ill. App. 355 (1st Dist. 1889)
74 ALR5th 369—§ 16

Shafii v. British Airways, 799 F. Supp. 292 (E.D. N.Y. 1992)
43 ALR5th 545—§ 31

Shafnaker v. Clayton, 680 So. 2d 1109 (Fla. Dist. Ct. App. 1st Dist. 1996)
71 ALR6th 249—§ 4

Shafouk Nor El Din Hamza v. Bourgeois, 493 So. 2d 112 (La. Ct. App. 5th Cir. 1986)
111 ALR5th 579—§ 4

Shafran v. Harley-Davidson, Inc., 2008 WL 763177 (S.D. N.Y 2008)
50 ALR6th 33—§ 6

Shafter-Wasco Irrig. Dist., Re, 55 Cal. App. 2d 484, 130 P.2d 755 (1942)
5 ALR5th 422—§ 3

Shah v. Liberty Mut. Ins. Co., 56 Mass. App. Ct. 903, 776 N.E.2d 1020 (2002)
69 ALR6th 317—§ 42

Shah v. Union College, 97 A.D.3d 949, 948 N.Y.S.2d 456, 281 Ed. Law Rep. 1171 (3d Dep't 2012)
83 ALR6th 195—§ 11, 18

Shaham v. Wheeler, 1996 WL 409364 (Conn. Super. Ct. 1996)
96 ALR5th 107—§ 7

Shahan, Re Estate of, 40 B.R. 608 (BC N.D. Tex. 1984)
16 ALR5th 262—§ 2, 35

Shahar v. Bowers, 114 F.3d 1097, 12 I.E.R. Cas. (BNA) 1582, 70 Empl. Prac. Dec. (CCH) P 44739 (11th Cir. 1997)
5 ALR6th 485—§ 6

Shahar v. Bowers, 114 F.3d 1097, 12 I.E.R. Cas. (BNA) 1582, 70 Empl. Prac. Dec. (CCH) ¶ 44739 (11th Cir. 1997)

96 ALR5th 391—§ 27

Shahawy v. Harrison, 875 F.2d 1529, 1989-1 CCH Trade Cases ¶ 68644 (CA11 Fla. 1989)
28 ALR5th 107—§ 5, 41

Shaheen v. Motion Industries, Inc., 880 S.W.2d 88 (Tex. App. Corpus Christi 1994)
38 ALR6th 541—§ 20

Shaheen v. U.S., 120 F. Supp. 574 (D.C. Ky. 1953)
45 ALR5th 251—§ 6

Shaheen & Co. v. Dickson, 207 Ga. App. 328, 427 S.E.2d 825 (1993)
75 ALR5th 1—§ 3, 14

Shaheen & Gordon v. Home Insurance Company, 13 N.H. 35, 719 A.2d 562 (1998)
92 ALR5th 273—§ 8

Shahid v. Campbell, 552 So. 2d 321, 14 FLW 2693 (Fla. App. D1 1989)
3 ALR5th 237—§ 11, 28

Shahid v. Moore, 2005 WL 2338859 (D.N.J. 2005)
55 ALR6th 391—§ 5

Shahinian v. McCormick, 59 Cal. 2d 554, 30 Cal. Rptr. 521, 381 P.2d 377 (1963)
34 ALR5th 77—§ 4, 9

Shahzad v. American Lung Ass'n, 184 Misc. 2d 156, 706 N.Y.S.2d 866 (Sup 2000)
85 ALR6th 323—§ 16

Shahzade v. C.J. Mabardy, Inc., 411 Mass. 788, 586 N.E.2d 3 (1992)
62 ALR5th 537—§ 6

Shahzade v. Gregory, 930 F. Supp. 673 (D.C. Mass. 1996)
9 ALR5th 321—§ 3

Shaida W., Matter of, 85 N.Y.2d 453, 626 N.Y.S.2d 35, 649 N.E.2d 1179 (1995)
5 ALR6th 193—§ 7, 12, 39

Shain v. City of Albany, 106 Cal. App. 3d 294, 165 Cal. Rptr. 69 (1st Dist. 1980)
2 ALR6th 279—§ 10

Shain v. Racine Raiders Football Club, Inc., 297 Wis. 2d 869, 2006 WI App 257, 726 N.W.2d 346 (Ct. App. 2006)

61 ALR6th 603—§ 6

Shainwald v. Shainwald, 302 S.C. 453, 395 S.E.2d 441 (Ct. App. 1990)

26 ALR6th 331—§ 5

Shaird v. Scully, 610 F. Supp. 442 (S.D. N.Y. 1985)

70 ALR5th 1—§ 5
79 ALR5th 419—§ 10

Shaker Bldg. Co. v. Federal Lime & Stone Co., 28 Ohio Misc. 246, 57 Ohio Op. 2d 486, 277 N.E.2d 584 (Mun. Ct. 1971)

75 ALR5th 1—§ 10

Shakiba P., Matter of, 181 A.D.2d 138, 587 N.Y.S.2d 300 (1st Dep't 1992)

5 ALR6th 193—§ 35, 39

Shakin v. Board of Medical Examiners, 254 Cal. App. 2d 102, 62 Cal. Rptr. 274, 23 A.L.R.3d 1398 (2d Dist. 1967)

54 ALR5th 575—§ 3
19 ALR6th 577—§ 4, 14

Shakkour v. Hamer, 368 Ill. App. 3d 627, 307 Ill. Dec. 49, 859 N.E.2d 49 (1st Dist. 2006)

74 ALR6th 1—§ 4 to 6, 14

Shakopee, In re, 295 N.W.2d 495 (Minn. 1980)

49 ALR5th 769—§ 5

Shakopee, City of v. Minnesota Valley Electric Cooperative, 303 N.W.2d 58 (Minn. 1981)

49 ALR5th 769—§ 7

Shakopee Housing Co. v. County of Scott, 1982 WL 1057 (Minn. Tax Ct. 1982)

56 ALR5th 171—§ 10, 28

Shakopee Mdewakanton Sioux (Dakota) Community v. Minnesota Campaign Finance & Public Disclosure Bd., 586 N.W.2d 406 (Minn. Ct. App. 1998)

24 ALR6th 179—§ 27

Shakur v. Bell, 447 F. Supp. 958 (S.D. N.Y. 1978)

53 ALR6th 1—§ 14

Shakur v. Coelho, 421 Fed. Appx. 132 (3d Cir. 2011)

89 ALR6th 1—§ 115, 117

Shalam v. KPMG LLP, 13 Misc. 3d 1205(A), 2006 WL 2589917 (N.Y. Sup 2006)

32 ALR6th 419—§ 17

Shalant v. Deutsch, 2004 WL 205837 (Cal. App. 2d Dist. 2004)

45 ALR6th 493—§ 32, 49, 52

Shaleen v. Central Coal & Coke Co., 127 Ark. 397, 192 S.W. 225 (1917)

109 ALR5th 421—§ 4, 6

Shalimar Ass'n v. D.O.C. Enterprises, Ltd., 142 Ariz. 36, 688 P.2d 682 (Ct. App. Div. 1 1984)

76 ALR5th 337—§ 2

Shalimar Contractors, Inc. v. American States Ins. Co., 975 F. Supp. 1450 (M.D. Ala. 1997)

98 ALR5th 193—§ 8
106 ALR5th 1—§ 8

Shallal v. Catholic Social Services of Wayne County, 455 Mich. 604, 566 N.W.2d 571, 13 I.E.R. Cas. (BNA) 218, 134 Lab. Cas. (CCH) ¶ 58304 (1997)

10 ALR6th 531—§ 10

Shallowhorn v. Stribling, 2008 WL 8007656 (C.D. Cal. 2008)

71 ALR6th 625—§ 19

Shamah v. Hellam Tp. Zoning Hearing Bd., 167 Pa. Commw. 610, 648 A.2d 1299 (1994)

4 ALR6th 263—§ 48

Shambach v. Bickhart, 577 Pa. 384, 845 A.2d 793 (2004)

75 ALR6th 311—§ 77

Shambaugh v. Lindsay, 445 N.E.2d 124 (Ind. App. 1983)

7 ALR5th 841—§ 4

Shamberg v. Lincoln, 174 Neb. 146, 116 N.W.2d 18 (1962)

63 ALR5th 607—§ 16

For assistance, call 1-800-328-4880

Shamberg v. State, 762 P.2d 488 (Alaska App. 1988)
31 ALR5th 229—§ 2, 3, 17, 31, 52, 65

Shamblin v. Albright, 278 Ark. 565, 647 S.W.2d 470 (1983)
97 ALR6th 83—§ 167

Shamblin v. Nationwide Mut. Ins. Co., 183 W. Va. 585, 396 S.E.2d 766 (1990)
51 ALR5th 701—§ 3, 8, 9

Shamblin v. State, 90 Okla. Crim. 33, 210 P.2d 197 (1949)
105 ALR5th 529—§ 22

Shamblin's Ready Mix, Inc. v. Eaton Corp., 873 F.2d 736, 13 FR Serv. 3d 925 (CA4 W. Va. 1989)
14 ALR5th 242—§ 26

Shamburger v. Behrens, 380 N.W.2d 659 (S.D. 1986)
6 ALR6th 311—§ 5

Shamburger v. Behrens, 418 N.W.2d 299 (S.D. 1988)
75 ALR5th 295—§ 7

Shamey v. Hickey, 433 A.2d 1111 (Dist. Col. App. 1981)
8 ALR5th 653—§ 3, 5, 12

Shamlin v. Commonwealth Edison Co., 1994 WL 148701 (N.D. Ill. 1994)
57 ALR5th 633—§ 3

Shamlin v. State, 23 Ark. App. 39, 743 S.W.2d 1 (1988)
62 ALR5th 629—§ 2, 5

Shamloo v. Lifespring, Inc., 713 F. Supp. 14 (D.C. Dist. Col. 1989)
11 ALR5th 588—§ 4

Shamoon v. Tombridge, 291 Ark. 222, 723 S.W.2d 827 (1987)
1 ALR5th 965—§ 5

Shamrock Cas. Co. v. Mack, 61 Misc. 2d 240, 305 N.Y.S.2d 525 (Sup. Ct. 1969)
79 ALR5th 289—§ 7

Shamrock Communications, Inc. v. Wilie, 2000 WL 1825501 (Tex. App. Austin 2000)
40 ALR6th 231—§ 6

Shamrock Dairy, Inc. v. International Brotherhood of Teamsters, etc. (1955, Ariz Super Ct) 28 CCH Lab Cas ¶ 69480
105 ALR5th 243—§ 21

Shamrock Hilton Hotel v. Caranas, 488 S.W.2d 151 (Tex. Civ. App. Houston (14th Dist.) 1972)
54 ALR5th 393—§ 3, 7

Shamrock Holdings, Inc. v. Arenson, 456 F. Supp. 2d 599 (D. Del. 2006)
46 ALR6th 1—§ 15
48 ALR6th 1—§ 35, 83

Shamrock Homebuilders, Inc. v. Cherokee Ins. Co., 486 S.W.2d 548 (Tenn. App. 1972)
30 ALR5th 170—§ 39

Shamrock Oil & Gas Co. v. Ethridge, 159 F. Supp. 693 (D. Colo. 1958)
2 ALR6th 195—§ 4

Shamsky v. Garan, Inc., 167 Misc. 2d 149, 632 N.Y.S.2d 930 (Sup 1995)
76 ALR6th 289—§ 5
77 ALR6th 543—§ 17

Shanafelt v. Allstate Ins. Co., 217 Mich. App. 625, 552 N.W.2d 671 (1996)
65 ALR5th 649—§ 3

Shanahan v. WITI-TV, Inc., 565 F. Supp. 219, 37 BNA FEP Cas. 1118, 115 BNA LRRM 4208, 32 CCH EPD ¶ 33872 (E.D. Wis 1982)
21 ALR5th 1—§ 3

Shanbaum v. Alliance Consulting Group, 26 A.D.3d 587, 808 N.Y.S.2d 834 (3d Dep't 2006)
20 ALR6th 729—§ 5
42 ALR6th 61—§ 4

Shand Morahan & Co., Inc. v. Rice, 160 A.D.2d 1078, 553 N.Y.S.2d 565 (3d Dep't 1990)
92 ALR5th 273—§ 15

Shane v. Commercial Cas. Ins. Co., 48 F. Supp. 151 (E.D. Pa. 1942)
110 ALR5th 465—§ 3

Shane v. Commissioner of Public Safety, 587 N.W.2d 639 (Minn. 1998)
92 ALR6th 295—§ 8, 9, 19
94 ALR6th 191—§ 4, 13

CASES CITED IN ALR5th and ALR6th

Shane v. Hobam, Inc, 332 F. Supp. 526 (E.D. Pa. 1971)
92 ALR5th 227—§ 4
112 ALR5th 113—§ 19

Shane v. Lowden, 232 Mo. App. 360, 106 S.W.2d 956 (1937)
40 ALR5th 1—§ 8

Shane v. Rhines, 672 P.2d 895 (Alaska 1983)
83 ALR5th 277—§ 3

Shaneeka Tysheeka J., In re, 722 N.Y.S.2d 258 (App. Div. 2d Dep't 2001)
1 ALR5th 469—§ 4

Shaneek Christal W., In re, 122 A.D.2d 215, 504 N.Y.S.2d 748 (2d Dep't 1986)
12 ALR6th 417—§ 7

Shaneek Christal W., Re, 122 App. Div. 2d 215, 504 N.Y.S.2d 748 (2d Dep't 1986)
1 ALR5th 469—§ 18

Shane PP, In re, 283 A.D.2d 725, 724 N.Y.S.2d 788 (3d Dep't 2001)
116 ALR5th 559—§ 3

Shanequa H., In re, 109 Ohio App. 3d 142, 671 N.E.2d 1113 (Lucas Co. 1996)
20 ALR5th 534—§ 4, 14

Shaner v. Greece Central School Dist. No. 1, 51 A.D.2d 662, 378 N.Y.S.2d 185 (4th Dep't 1976)
100 ALR6th 563—§ 8

Shaner v. Greece Cent. School Dist., 51 App. Div. 2d 662, 378 N.Y.S.2d 185 (4th Dep't 1976)
17 ALR5th 179—§ 3

Shaner v. Horizon Bancorp., 116 N.J. 433, 561 A.2d 1130, 52 BNA FEP Cas. 1475, 51 CCH EPD ¶ 39390 (1989)
12 ALR5th 508—§ 3
21 ALR5th 1—§ 3

Shaner v. Perry Tp., 775 A.2d 887 (Pa. Commw. Ct. 2001)
55 ALR6th 635—§ 4

Shaner v. State System of Higher Educ., 40 Pa. D. & C.4th 308, 1998 WL 1108422 (C.P. 1998)
75 ALR6th 1—§ 13

Shane T., In re, 544 A.2d 1295 (Me. 1988)
102 ALR5th 227—§ 3

Shaneyfelt v. State, 494 So. 2d 804 (Ala. Crim. App. 1986)
85 ALR5th 1—§ 42

Shangraw v. Shangraw, 61 A.D.3d 1302, 878 N.Y.S.2d 804 (3d Dep't 2009)
102 ALR6th 153—§ 25

Shank v. Administrative Committee of Wal-Mart Stores, Inc. Associates' Health and Welfare Plan, 128 S. Ct. 1651, 170 L. Ed. 2d 386, 43 Employee Benefits Cas. (BNA) 2696 (U.S. 2008)
36 ALR6th 681—§ 33

Shank v. County of Los Angeles, 139 Cal. App. 3d 152, 188 Cal. Rptr. 644 (2d Dist. 1983)
64 ALR5th 519—§ 6

Shank v. Government Employees Ins. Co., 390 So. 2d 903 (La. App. 3d Cir. 1980)
14 ALR5th 193—§ 8, 11

Shank v. Nexsen, 127 Ga. App. 684, 194 S.E.2d 586 (1972)
3 ALR5th 1—§ 61

Shank v. Sakal, 2007 WL 1381598 (D. Ariz. 2007)
95 ALR6th 341—§ 39

Shank-Jewella v. Diamond Gallery, 535 So. 2d 1207 (La. Ct. App. 2d Cir. 1988)
10 ALR5th 448—§ 4
75 ALR5th 1—§ 9, 13, 16

Shankle v. B-G Maintenance Management of Colorado, Inc., 163 F.3d 1230, 78 Fair Empl. Prac. Cas. (BNA) 1057, 74 Empl. Prac. Dec. (CCH) ¶ 45690 (10th Cir. 1999)
60 ALR5th 669—§ 5

Shankle v. State, 59 S.W.3d 756 (Tex. App. Austin 2001)
41 ALR6th 141—§ 7

Shankle v. Woodruff, 64 N.M. 88, 324 P.2d 1017 (1958)
  97 ALR5th 293—§ 2, 3
Shankles v. Director, TDCJ-ID, 877 F. Supp. 346 (E.D. Tex. 1995)
  63 ALR6th 1—§ 5, 38
Shanklin v. McCracken, 140 Mo. 348, 41 S.W. 898 (1897)
  23 ALR6th 1—§ 24
Shanklin v. Shanklin, 339 So. 2d 1262 (La. App. 1st Cir. 1976)
  17 ALR5th 143—§ 8
Shanks v. Com., 574 S.W.2d 688 (Ky. Ct. App. 1978)
  52 ALR6th 1—§ 27
Shanks v. Lowe, 364 Md. 538, 774 A.2d 411, 145 Lab. Cas. (CCH) ¶ 59462 (2001)
  61 ALR6th 61—§ 6, 7
Shanks v. Phillips, 55 S.W.2d 258 (Tenn. 1932)
  43 ALR5th 519—§ 5
Shanks v. Upjohn Co., 835 P.2d 1189, CCH Prod. Liab. Rep. ¶ 13229 (Alaska 1992)
  57 ALR5th 1—§ 3
Shanks v. Upjohn Co., 835 P.2d 1189, Prod. Liab. Rep. (CCH) ¶ 13229 (Alaska 1992)
  45 ALR6th 385—§ 5, 7, 8
Shanks v. Wolfenbarger, 387 F. Supp. 2d 740 (E.D. Mich. 2005)
  19 ALR6th 411—§ 9
Shanley v. Barnett, 168 Ill. App. 3d 799, 119 Ill. Dec. 592, 523 N.E.2d 60 (1st Dist. 1988)
  58 ALR6th 1—§ 5, 42
  60 ALR6th 1—§ 32
Shanley v. Callanan Industries, Inc., 54 N.Y.2d 52, 444 N.Y.S.2d 585, 429 N.E.2d 104 (1981)
  4 ALR5th 753—§ 4
Shanley, People on Complaint of v. Stowers, 259 A.D. 528, 19 N.Y.S.2d 921 (1st Dep't 1940)
  107 ALR5th 567—§ 14
Shanlian v. Faulk, 68 Wash. App. 320, 843 P.2d 535 (1992)

7 ALR5th 474—§ 126
Shannahan v. Gigray, 131 Idaho 664, 962 P.2d 1048 (1998)
  61 ALR5th 307—§ 3
Shannon, In re Marriage of, 2004 MT 25, 319 Mont. 357, 84 P.3d 645 (2004)
  86 ALR6th 321—§ 12
Shannon v. Central-Gaither Union School Dist., 133 Cal. App. 124, 23 P.2d 769 (1933)
  23 ALR5th 1—§ 2, 20
Shannon v. Civil Service Commission of Borough of Whitehall, 4 Pa. Commw. 492, 287 A.2d 858 (1972)
  19 ALR6th 217—§ 27
Shannon v. Com., 18 Va. App. 31, 441 S.E.2d 225 (1994)
  58 ALR6th 499—§ 70
Shannon v. Commonwealth, 767 S.W.2d 548 (Ky. 1988)
  7 ALR5th 758—§ 22
Shannon v. Cross, 245 Mich. 220, 222 N.W. 168 (1928)
  49 ALR6th 505—§ 33
Shannon v. Johnson, 2013 WL 1564223 (M.D. Tenn. 2013)
  90 ALR6th 385—§ 5
Shannon v. Kaiser Aluminum & Chemical Corp., 749 F.2d 689 (CA11 Fla. 1985)
  59 ALR5th 733—§ 3
Shannon v. Koehler, 2011 WL 10483363 (N.D. Iowa 2011)
  95 ALR6th 641—§ 8
Shannon v. Liberty Mut. Ins. Co., 236 A.D.2d 231, 653 N.Y.S.2d 335 (1st Dep't 1997)
  56 ALR5th 757—§ 3
Shannon v. Louisiana Real Estate Com., 250 So. 2d 425 (La. App. 1st Cir. 1971)
  7 ALR5th 474—§ 18, 100
Shannon v. McNulty, 718 A.2d 828 (Pa. Super. Ct. 1998)
  7 ALR5th 1—§ 10.5
Shannon v. Monasco, 632 S.W.2d 946 (Tex. App. Waco 1982)

14 ALR5th 242—§ 26

Shannon v. MTA Metro-North R.R., 269 A.D.2d 218, 704 N.Y.S.2d 208 (1st Dep't 2000)

7 ALR6th 563—§ 4

Shannon v. Planning Com'n of Town of Redding, 1997 WL 716463 (Conn. Super. Ct. 1997)

4 ALR6th 263—§ 12

Shannon v. Rado, 200 Ga. App. 495, 408 S.E.2d 441, 102-132 Fulton County D R 11B (1991)

19 ALR5th 1—§ 130

Shannon v. Samuel Langston Co, 379 F. Supp. 797 (W.D. Mich. 1974)

109 ALR5th 301—§ 3, 12

Shannon v. State, 631 S.W.2d 772 (Tex. App. Beaumont 1982)

68 ALR6th 527—§ 31

Shannon v. State, 753 So. 2d 148 (Fla. Dist. Ct. App. 3d Dist. 2000)

27 ALR6th 183—§ 34

Shannon v. State, 754 So. 2d 172 (Fla. Dist. Ct. App. 5th Dist. 2000)

38 ALR6th 439—§ 3

Shannon v. State, 942 S.W.2d 591 (Tex. Crim. App. 1996)

36 ALR5th 255—§ 18

Shannon v. St. Louis Bd. of Ed., 577 S.W.2d 949 (Mo. Ct. App. E.D. 1979)

11 ALR6th 351—§ 25

Shannon v. Texas General Indem. Co., 889 S.W.2d 662 (Tex. App. Houston 14th Dist. 1994)

108 ALR5th 1—§ 41
113 ALR5th 115—§ 2, 11, 21, 44, 53

Shannon v. Thornton, 155 Ga. App. 670, 272 S.E.2d 535 (1980)

17 ALR6th 159—§ 22

Shannon & Luchs Co. v. Tindal, 415 A.2d 805 (D.C. 1980)

114 ALR5th 443—§ 31

Shannondale, Inc. v. Jefferson County Planning and Zoning Com'n, 199 W. Va. 494, 485 S.E.2d 438 (1997)

4 ALR6th 263—§ 15

Shannon, Estate of v. Ahmed, 304 Ga. App. 380, 696 S.E.2d 408 (2010)

95 ALR6th 479—§ 12
97 ALR6th 83—§ 117, 137

Shannon H., In re, 2013 IL App (1st) 112441-U, 2013 WL 3148680 (Ill. App. Ct. 1st Dist. 2013)

103 ALR6th 247—§ 12

Shannon, People ex rel. v. Magee, 55 A.D. 195, 66 N.Y.S. 849 (3d Dep't 1900)

28 ALR6th 175—§ 11

Shannon Sales Co. v. Williams, 490 N.W.2d 436 (Minn. App. 1992)

23 ALR5th 744—§ 2, 5

Shanoski v. Miller, 2001 ME 139, 780 A.2d 275 (Me. 2001)

100 ALR5th 1—§ 13
59 ALR6th 161—§ 15

Shansab v. Homart Development Co., Inc., 205 Ga. App. 448, 422 S.E.2d 305 (1992)

74 ALR5th 49—§ 33

Shanteau, Estate of v. Shanteau, 510 N.E.2d 701, 4 U.C.C. Rep. Serv. 2d (CBC) 781 (Ind. Ct. App. 2d Dist. 1987)

71 ALR5th 443—§ 4, 8

Shante D. by Ada D. v. City of New York, 83 N.Y.2d 948, 615 N.Y.S.2d 317, 638 N.E.2d 962, 93 Ed. Law Rep. 272 (1994)

86 ALR5th 1—§ 15

Shantee Point, Inc., In re, 174 Vt. 248, 811 A.2d 1243 (2002)

47 ALR6th 439—§ 4

Shantelle W., Matter of, 185 A.D.2d 935, 587 N.Y.S.2d 393 (2d Dep't 1992)

122 ALR5th 385—§ 17
12 ALR6th 417—§ 11

Shapaka v. State Compensation Commissioner, 146 W. Va. 319, 119 S.E.2d 821 (1961)

41 ALR6th 207—§ 15

Shapell Industries, Inc. v. Governing Board, 1 Cal. App. 4th 218, 1 Cal. Rptr. 2d 818, 70 Ed. Law Rep. 1148 (6th Dist. 1991)
16 ALR6th 289—§ 6, 21

Shapera v. Levitt, 260 Pa. Super. 447, 394 A.2d 1011 (1978)
118 ALR5th 385—§ 14
124 ALR5th 441—§ 4, 7, 8

Shapero v. Fliegel, 191 Cal. App. 3d 842, 236 Cal. Rptr. 696 (2d Dist. 1987)
87 ALR5th 473—§ 4
13 ALR6th 1—§ 4
16 ALR6th 653—§ 8

Shapiro, Application of, 197 Misc. 241, 97 N.Y.S.2d 644 (Sup. Ct. 1949)
67 ALR5th 179—§ 3

Shapiro, Matter of, 90 A.D.2d 22, 455 N.Y.S.2d 604 (1st Dep't 1982)
45 ALR6th 175—§ 22

Shapiro, Matter of, 225 A.D.2d 215, 656 N.Y.S.2d 80 (4th Dep't 1996)
20 ALR6th 385—§ 16

Shapiro v. Amalgamated Trust & Sav. Bank, 283 Ill. App. 243, 1935 WL 3782 (1st Dist. 1935)
8 ALR6th 549—§ 11

Shapiro v. Burkons, 62 Ohio App. 2d 73, 16 Ohio Op. 3d 175, 404 N.E.2d 778 (8th Dist. Cuyahoga County 1978)
92 ALR6th 379—§ 47

Shapiro v. Butler, 709 N.Y.S.2d 687 (App. Div. 3d Dep't 2000)
10 ALR5th 828—§ 13

Shapiro v. Cadman Towers, Inc., 844 F. Supp. 116, 4 A.D.D. 595 (E.D.N.Y. 1994)
60 ALR5th 647—§ 7

Shapiro v. Catherwood, 36 A.D.2d 670, 318 N.Y.S.2d 254 (3d Dep't 1971)
68 ALR5th 13—§ 9, 25

Shapiro v. Central General Hosp., Inc., 181 App. Div. 2d 896, 581 N.Y.S.2d 430 (2d Dep't 1992)
28 ALR5th 107—§ 2

Shapiro v. City of Cambridge, 340 Mass. 652, 166 N.E.2d 208 (1960)
73 ALR5th 223—§ 12

Shapiro v. City of Glen Cove, 236 Fed. Appx. 645 (2d Cir. 2007)
58 ALR6th 499—§ 62

Shapiro v. City of Hartford, 4 Conn. App. 315, 494 A.2d 590 (1985)
12 ALR6th 645—§ 20

Shapiro v. City Stores Co. (Maison Blanche Division), 391 So. 2d 2 (La. Ct. App. 4th Cir. 1980)
63 ALR6th 495—§ 8, 14

Shapiro v. County of Nassau, 202 A.D.2d 358, 609 N.Y.S.2d 234 (1st Dep't 1994)
101 ALR5th 515—§ 15

Shapiro v. Glens Falls Ins. Co., 39 N.Y.2d 204, 383 N.Y.S.2d 263, 347 N.E.2d 624 (1976)
35 ALR5th 375—§ 17

Shapiro v. Glens Falls Ins. Co., 47 App. Div. 2d 856, 365 N.Y.S.2d 892 (2d Dep't 1975)
35 ALR5th 375—§ 3

Shapiro v. Good Samaritan Regional Hosp. Medical Center, 42 A.D.3d 443, 840 N.Y.S.2d 94 (2d Dep't 2007)
100 ALR6th 139—§ 37

Shapiro v. Grinspoon, 27 Mass. App. 596, 541 N.E.2d 359 (1989)
39 ALR5th 33—§ 9

Shapiro v. Hartford, 4 Conn. App. 315, 494 A.2d 590 (1985)
57 ALR5th 689—§ 2, 17

Shapiro v. Hotel Statler Corp., 132 F. Supp. 891 (D.C. Cal. 1955)
2 ALR5th 189—§ 3, 7

Shapiro v. Hu, 188 Cal. App. 3d 324, 233 Cal. Rptr. 470 (1st Dist. 1986)
8 ALR5th 312—§ 2 to 4, 9, 20

Shapiro v. Jefferson County, 278 Mont. 109, 923 P.2d 543 (1996)
62 ALR6th 259—§ 3

Shapiro v. Jones, 127 Misc. 2d 935, 487 N.Y.S.2d 707 (Sup 1985)
71 ALR6th 335—§ 5

Shapiro v. Long Island Lighting Co., 71 A.D.2d 671, 418 N.Y.S.2d 948, 27 U.C.C. Rep. Serv. (CBC) 445 (2d Dep't 1979)
81 ALR5th 483—§ 4

Shapiro v. Marstone Distributors, Inc., 40 App. Div. 2d 878, 337 N.Y.S.2d 928 (2d Dep't 1972)
42 ALR5th 53—§ 5, 13

Shapiro v. Massengill, 105 Md. App. 743, 661 A.2d 202 (1995)
105 ALR5th 351—§ 3
53 ALR6th 213—§ 4

Shapiro v. McCarthy, 279 Mass. 425, 181 N.E. 842 (1932)
97 ALR6th 375—§ 20

Shapiro v. McNeill, 92 N.Y.2d 91, 677 N.Y.S.2d 48, 699 N.E.2d 407 (1998)
50 ALR5th 301—§ 5

Shapiro v. New York City Police Dept., 201 A.D.2d 333, 607 N.Y.S.2d 320 (1st Dep't 1994)
91 ALR6th 435—§ 140

Shapiro v. Public Service Mut. Ins. Co., 19 Mass. App. Ct. 648, 477 N.E.2d 146 (1985)
88 ALR5th 493—§ 3
89 ALR5th 1—§ 18

Shapiro v. Public Service Mutual Ins. Co., 477 N.E.2d 146 (Mass. App. 1985)
117 ALR5th 155—§ 11

Shapiro v. Santa Fe Gaming Corp., 1998 WL 102677 (N.D. Ill. 1998)
81 ALR5th 41—§ 3

Shapiro v. Security Ins. Co., 256 Mass. 358, 152 N.E. 370 (1926)
16 ALR5th 412—§ 33

Shapiro v. Shapiro, 141 So. 2d 448 (La. App. 4th Cir. 1962)
28 ALR5th 46—§ 15

Shapiro v. State, 390 So. 2d 344 (Fla. 1980)
125 ALR5th 281—§ 11, 12

Shapiro v. Steinberg, 176 Mich. App. 683, 440 N.W.2d 9 (1989)
83 ALR5th 497—§ 6

Shapiro v. Stern, 2002 WL 47039 (Minn. Ct. App. 2002)
78 ALR6th 151—§ 7

Shapiro v. Sutherland, 64 Cal. App. 4th 1534, 76 Cal. Rptr. 2d 101 (2d Dist. 1998)
41 ALR5th 157—§ 4

Shapiro v. UJB Fin. Corp., 964 F.2d 272, CCH Fed Secur L. Rep. ¶ 96651, 23 FR Serv. 3d 24 (CA3 NJ)
48 ALR5th 389—§ 3, 5

Shapiro v. Wells Fargo Realty Advisors, 152 Cal. App. 3d 467, 199 Cal. Rptr. 613, 1 I.E.R. Cas. (BNA) 1803, 119 L.R.R.M. (BNA) 2520, 100 Lab. Cas. (CCH) ¶ 55454 (2d Dist. 1984)
104 ALR5th 1—§ 3

Shapiro v. Zoning Board of Adjustment, 377 Pa. 621, 105 A.2d 299 (1954)
26 ALR5th 736—§ 4

Shapiro, Bernstein & Co. v. Continental Record Co., 386 F.2d 426, 11 FR Serv. 2d 1207 (CA2 N.Y. 1967)
8 ALR5th 653—§ 3

Shapiro, Bernstein & Co. v. Veltin, 47 F. Supp. 648, 55 U.S.P.Q. 335 (W.D. La. 1942)
37 ALR6th 243—§ 6

Shapiro Bros. Shoe Co., Inc. v. Lewiston-Auburn Shoeworkers Protective Ass'n, 320 A.2d 247, 86 L.R.R.M. (BNA) 3176, 21 Wage & Hour Cas. (BNA) 925, 74 Lab. Cas. (CCH) ¶ 53385 (Me. 1974)
85 ALR6th 323—§ 4

Shapiro ex rel Ehrenpreis, In re v. Ehrenpreis, 108 Misc. 2d 495, 437 N.Y.S.2d 618 (N.Y. Fam. Ct. 1981)
46 ALR5th 735—§ 5

Shapiro-Gordon v. MCI Telecommunications Corp., 810 F. Supp. 574, 68 BNA FEP Cas. 281 (S.D. N.Y. 1993)
37 ALR5th 349—§ 2, 12

Shapiro, Lifschitz & Schram, P.C. v. Hazard, 24 F. Supp. 2d 66 (D.D.C. 1998)
41 ALR6th 1—§ 9

Shapiro, Lifschitz & Schram, P.C. v.
R.E. Hazard, Jr., 97 F. Supp. 2d 8
(D.D.C. 2000)
58 ALR6th 1—§ 5, 59
Shapley v. Bellows, 4 N.H. 347 (1828)
27 ALR5th 764—§ 3
Shapley v. Tex. Dep't of Human Re-
sources, 581 S.W.2d 250 (Tex. Civ.
App. El Paso 1979)
53 ALR5th 499—§ 6
Shapo v. Engle, 1999 WL 1045086
(N.D. Ill. 1999)
79 ALR5th 587—§ 2, 6
Shaquanna M., Re, 61 Conn. App. 592,
767 A.2d 155 (2001)
14 ALR5th 929—§ 3
Shara v. Moss, 52 Luz. L.R. 252 (Pa.
C.P. 1962)
69 ALR5th 219—§ 4
Sharbono v. Steve Lang & Son Loggers,
696 So. 2d 1382, 79 A.L.R.5th 733
(La. 1997)
79 ALR5th 201—§ 4, 5, 10, 14, 15
Sharbono v. Universal Underwriters Ins.
Co., 139 Wash. App. 383, 161 P.3d
406 (Div. 2 2007)
32 ALR6th 285—§ 12
Sharbutt-Ridge v. Ridge, 1998 WL
74306 (Va. Ct. App. 1998)
59 ALR6th 433—§ 9, 41
SHARE v. Commissioner of Revenue,
363 N.W.2d 47 (Minn. 1985)
69 ALR5th 477—§ 2, 4
Share v. Commonwealth, Unemployment Compensation Bd. of Review,
99 Pa. Cmwlth. 119, 512 A.2d 794
(1986)
41 ALR5th 123—§ 8
Shared Communications Services of
1800-80 JFK Blvd. Inc. v. Bell Atlantic Properties Inc., 692 A.2d 570
(Pa. Super. Ct. 1997)
2 ALR6th 387—§ 3
Sharer v. Hotel Corp. of America, 144
So. 2d 813 (Fla. 1962)
48 ALR6th 387—§ 18
Sharer v. Oregon, 481 F. Supp. 2d 1156
(D. Or. 2007)

32 ALR6th 457—§ 5
Sharer v. People, 96 Colo. 483, 44 P.2d
914 (1935)
108 ALR5th 593—§ 18
Shargal v. State Bd. of Examiners of
Psychologists, 135 N.H. 242, 604
A.2d 559 (1992)
67 ALR6th 437—§ 13, 19
Sharifi v. Young Bros., Inc., 835 S.W.2d
221 (Tex. App. Waco 1992)
7 ALR5th 444—§ 4
10 ALR5th 337—§ 3
Sharkey, In re, 272 B.R. 574 (Bankr. D.
N.J. 2001)
10 ALR6th 293—§ 5
Sharkey v. Chow, 84 A.D.3d 1719, 922
N.Y.S.2d 691 (4th Dep't 2011)
95 ALR6th 541—§ 96
Sharkey v. Portland Gas & Coke Co., 74
Or. 327, 144 P. 1152 (1914)
34 ALR5th 1—§ 3
Sharkey v. Sheets, 87 Cal. App. 99, 261
P. 1049 (1927)
9 ALR5th 102—§ 9, 22
Sharkey v. Sterling Drug, Inc., 600 So.
2d 701 (La. App. 1st Cir. 1992)
38 ALR5th 683—§ 2, 3, 7, 9
Sharkey v. Stryker Corp., 2013 WL
1149837 (D. Utah 2013)
90 ALR6th 75—§ 10, 19, 24, 43
Sharkey v. Thurston, 268 N.Y. 123, 196
N.E. 766 (1935)
28 ALR6th 175—§ 4
Sharkey's, Inc. v. City of Waukesha, 265
F. Supp. 2d 984 (E.D. Wis. 2003)
122 ALR5th 593—§ 2
Sharlin v. Neighborhood Theatre, Inc.,
209 Va. 718, 167 S.E.2d 334 (1969)
45 ALR5th 251—§ 6, 11
Sharlot v. Sharlot, 110 App. Div. 299,
494 N.Y.S.2d 238 (3d Dep't 1985)
52 ALR5th 221—§ 31
Sharma v. Hummer, 2001 WL 460281
(Ohio Ct. App. 6th Dist. Wood
County 2001)
100 ALR5th 341—§ 3
Sharma v. State, 800 So. 2d 1190 (Miss.
Ct. App. 2001)

For assistance, call 1-800-328-4880

2 ALR6th 551—§ 5

Sharma, State ex rel. v. Meyers, 803 S.W.2d 65 (Mo. Ct. App. W.D. 1990)

17 ALR6th 1—§ 27

Sharmba, In re, 2007 WL 1073770 (Bankr. D. Md. 2007)

61 ALR6th 207—§ 18

Sharon v. City of Newton, 437 Mass. 99, 769 N.E.2d 738, 165 Ed. Law Rep. 742 (2002)

75 ALR6th 1—§ 5, 12

Sharon v. Connecticut Fire Ins. Co., 270 So. 2d 900 (La. Ct. App. 1st Cir. 1972)

54 ALR6th 201—§ 57, 59, 62, 65, 73

Sharon v. Time, Inc., 575 F. Supp. 1162, 10 Media L. Rep. (BNA) 1146 (S.D. N.Y. 1983)

54 ALR6th 165—§ 18

Sharon B., Re, 72 N.Y.2d 394, 534 N.Y.S.2d 124, 530 N.E.2d 832 (1988)

8 ALR5th 653—§ 3, 11

Sharon B. v. Reverend S., 244 A.D.2d 878, 665 N.Y.S.2d 139 (4th Dep't 1997)

9 ALR5th 321—§ 11, 13

Sharon L. Batesole, Tonya Refro v. Ralph Smith d/b/a R & R Service Center, 1995 WL 458782 (Ohio Ct. App. 6th Dist. Sandusky County 1995)

88 ALR6th 1—§ 16, 23, 43

Sharon Motor Lodge, Inc. v. Tai, 2006 WL 697589 (Conn. Super. Ct. 2006)

32 ALR6th 285—§ 27

Sharon P. v. Arman, Ltd., 21 Cal. 4th 1181, 91 Cal. Rptr. 2d 35, 989 P.2d 121 (1999)

43 ALR5th 207—§ 77, 79

Sharon S. v. Superior Court, 31 Cal. 4th 417, 2 Cal. Rptr. 3d 699, 73 P.3d 554 (2003)

61 ALR6th 1—§ 9, 18, 23

Sharon S. v. Superior Court of California, San Diego County, 540 U.S. 1220, 124 S. Ct. 1510, 158 L. Ed. 2d 155 (2004)

61 ALR6th 1—§ 9, 18, 23

Sharon Steel Corp. v. Aetna Cas. and Sur. Co., 931 P.2d 127, 44 Env't. Rep. Cas. (BNA) 1745 (Utah 1997)

88 ALR5th 493—§ 3

89 ALR5th 1—§ 10

Sharon Steel Corp. v. VJR Co., 604 F. Supp. 420 (W.D. Pa. 1985)

7 ALR6th 563—§ 5

Sharp, Re Marriage of, 143 Cal. App. 3d 714, 192 Cal. Rptr. 97 (4th Dist. 1983)

9 ALR5th 568—§ 4, 11

Sharp v. Aarons, 101 Misc. 2d 323, 420 N.Y.S.2d 1013 (1979)

6 ALR5th 69—§ 5, 23

21 ALR5th 396—§ 25, 55

Sharp v. AMSCO Steel Co., 893 S.W.2d 742 (Tex. App. Austin 1995)

14 ALR6th 119—§ 74

Sharp v. Automobile Club of Southern California, 225 Cal. App. 2d 648, 37 Cal. Rptr. 585 (2d Dist. 1964)

14 ALR5th 242—§ 34

Sharp v. Broadway Nat'l Bank, 761 S.W.2d 141 (Tex. App. San Antonio 1988)

36 ALR5th 395—§ 2, 3, 10, 16

37 ALR5th 237—§ 2

Sharp v. Clearview Cable TV, Inc., 960 S.W.2d 424 (Tex. App. Austin 1998)

23 ALR6th 165—§ 35

Sharp v. Commonwealth, 849 S.W.2d 542 (Ky. 1993)

38 ALR5th 433—§ 2, 4

Sharp v. DePuy Orthopaedics, Inc., 2012 WL 2891182 (C.D. Cal. 2012)

96 ALR6th 1—§ 3

Sharp v. Employment Appeal Bd., 479 N.W.2d 280 (Iowa 1991)

68 ALR5th 13—§ 3, 16, 24

Sharp v. Federal Sav. & Loan Ins. Corp., 858 F.2d 1042 (CA5 La. 1988)

CASES CITED IN ALR5TH AND 6TH

21 ALR5th 292—§ 21, 25
Sharp v. Gray, York & Duffy, 2005 WL 713595 (Cal. App. 2d Dist. 2005)

85 ALR6th 475—§ 5
Sharp v. International Business Machines Corp., 927 S.W.2d 790 (Tex. App. Austin 1996)

14 ALR6th 119—§ 24, 73
Sharp v. J. C. Penney Co., 361 F.2d 722 (CA6 Tenn. 1966)

40 ALR5th 135—§ 3, 14
Sharp v. Kosmalski, 40 N.Y.2d 119, 386 N.Y.S.2d 72, 351 N.E.2d 721 (1976)

44 ALR5th 1—§ 31
Sharp v. Learned, 182 Miss. 333, 181 So. 142 (1938)

20 ALR6th 211—§ 13
Sharp v. Learned, 185 Miss. 872, 188 So. 302 (1939)

20 ALR6th 211—§ 22
Sharp v. Learned, 195 Miss. 201, 14 So. 2d 218 (1943)

20 ALR6th 211—§ 14
Sharp v. Leichus, 2006 WL 515532 (Fla. Cir. Ct. 2006)

56 ALR6th 161—§ 5
Sharp v. Longe, 2011 WL 489938 (D.S.C. 2011)

65 ALR6th 93—§ 59
Sharp v. McIntire, 23 Colo. 99, 46 P. 115 (1896)

97 ALR6th 567—§ 4, 14
Sharp v. Norfolk & W. Ry. Co., 72 Ohio St. 3d 307, 1995-Ohio-224, 649 N.E.2d 1219 (1995)

98 ALR6th 231—§ 103
Sharp v. Odom, 743 So. 2d 425 (Miss. Ct. App. 1999)

48 ALR5th 129—§ 5
Sharp v. Pennsylvania Army Nat. Guard, 2012 WL 3202939 (M.D. Pa. 2012)

95 ALR6th 341—§ 22
Sharp v. Sharp, 213 Ill. 332, 72 N.E. 1058 (1904)

76 ALR6th 31—§ 15
Sharp v. Sharp, 336 N.J. Super. 492, 765 A.2d 271 (App. Div. 2001)

90 ALR5th 1—§ 17
Sharp v. Sharp, 416 S.W.2d 691 (Mo. App. 1967)

55 ALR5th 647—§ 3
Sharp v. Sharp, 501 So. 2d 879 (La. App. 5th Cir. 1987)

11 ALR5th 259—§ 14, 18
Sharp v. Sharp, 516 S.W.2d 875 (Ky. 1974)

17 ALR5th 366—§ 11
Sharp v. State, 51 Ark. 147, 10 S.W. 228 (1888)

50 ALR5th 467—§ 6, 8
Sharp v. State, 203 Kan. 937, 457 P.2d 14 (1969)

39 ALR5th 283—§ 4
Sharp v. State, 908 S.W.2d 752 (Mo. Ct. App. E.D. 1995)

91 ALR5th 343—§ 31
Sharp v. State, 1999 WL 351060 (Tex. App. Texarkana 1999)

117 ALR5th 491—§ 7
Sharp v. Teague, 113 N.C. App. 589, 439 S.E.2d 792 (1994)

87 ALR5th 473—§ 4
11 ALR6th 1—§ 4, 7, 10
42 ALR6th 463—§ 3
Sharp v. Tinsley, 147 Colo. 84, 362 P.2d 859 (1961)

88 ALR5th 463—§ 4
Sharp v. Tulsa County Election Bd., 1994 OK 104, 890 P.2d 836, 98 Ed. Law Rep. 424 (Okla. 1994)

123 ALR5th 411—§ 2
Sharp v. W. & W. Trucking Co., 421 S.W.2d 213 (Mo. 1967)

27 ALR5th 174—§ 3, 37
Sharp v. W.H. Moore, Inc., 118 Idaho 297, 796 P.2d 506 (1990)

43 ALR5th 207—§ 4, 6, 76
Sharp v. Zoning Hearing Bd. of Tp. of Radnor, 157 Pa. Commw. 50, 628 A.2d 1223, 84 Ed. Law Rep. 1069 (1993)

73 ALR5th 223—§ 3, 4, 10
Sharp Bros. Contracting Co. v. American Hoist & Derrick Co., 714 S.W.2d 919 (Mo. App. 1986)

49 ALR5th 1—§ 59
Sharp Community Ambulance Service, Inc. v. Sharp, 582 So. 2d 778 (Fla. Dist. Ct. App. 1st Dist. 1991)
2 ALR6th 279—§ 9
Sharpe, Ex parte, 581 S.W.2d 183 (Tex. Crim. App. 1979)
68 ALR6th 527—§ 24
Sharpe, In re, 391 B.R. 117 (Bankr. N.D. Ala. 2008)
81 ALR6th 161—§ 5
82 ALR6th 43—§ 13
Sharpe, In re, 425 B.R. 620 (Bankr. N.D. Ala. 2010)
81 ALR6th 161—§ 5
82 ALR6th 43—§ 5
Sharpe v. Bestop, Inc., 314 N.J. Super. 54, 713 A.2d 1079, Prod. Liab. Rep. (CCH) ¶ 15281 (App. Div. 1998)
38 ALR5th 683—§ 8, 10
Sharpe v. Com., Unemployment Compensation Bd. of Review, 32 Pa. Commw. 10, 377 A.2d 1047 (1977)
18 ALR6th 195—§ 32
Sharpe v. Physicians Protective Trust Fund, 578 So. 2d 806, 16 FLW D 1139 (Fla. App. D1 1991)
18 ALR5th 474—§ 2, 4, 6
Sharpe v. Pugh, 286 N.C. 209, 209 S.E.2d 456 (1974)
47 ALR5th 433—§ 2, 9
Sharpe v. Robbins, 2009 WL 1811708 (D.N.J. 2009)
58 ALR6th 1—§ 5
60 ALR6th 1—§ 91
Sharpe v. South Carolina Dept. of Mental Health, 292 S.C. 11, 354 S.E.2d 778 (Ct. App. 1987)
80 ALR6th 469—§ 25
Sharpe v. State, 119 Ga. App. 222, 166 S.E.2d 645 (1969)
99 ALR6th 295—§ 16
Sharpe v. State, 272 Ga. 684, 531 S.E.2d 84 (2000)
16 ALR6th 329—§ 4
24 ALR6th 591—§ 6
Sharpe v. State, 547 So. 2d 334 (Fla. Dist. Ct. App. 1st Dist. 1989)

15 ALR6th 173—§ 19
Sharpe v. Trail, 902 P.2d 304, 43 A.L.R.5th 873 (Alaska 1995)
43 ALR5th 705—§ 12, 13, 22
Sharpe v. West Indian Co., Ltd., 118 F. Supp. 2d 646, 2001 A.M.C. 995 (D.V.I. 2000)
82 ALR6th 175—§ 22, 23
Sharp Electronics Corp. v. Branded Products, Inc., 604 F. Supp. 239, 1984-2 Trade Cas. (CCH) ¶ 66314 (S.D. N.Y. 1984)
22 ALR6th 49—§ 4
Sharp Electronics Corp. v. Lodgistix, Inc., 802 F. Supp. 370, 19 U.C.C. Rep. Serv. 2d 772 (D. Kan. 1992)
101 ALR5th 563—§ 4
Sharp ex rel. Gordon v. Case Corp., 227 Wis. 2d 1, 595 N.W.2d 380, Prod. Liab. Rep. (CCH) ¶ 15565 (1999)
30 ALR5th 1—§ 34
Sharples v. Roberts, 249 Kan. 286, 816 P.2d 390 (1991)
48 ALR5th 575—§ 2, 10
Sharpless, Appeal of, 140 Pa. 63, 21 A. 239 (1891)
98 ALR5th 353—§ 3
Sharpless v. Medford Monthly Meeting of Religious Soc. of Friends, 228 N.J. Super. 68, 548 A.2d 1157 (1988)
54 ALR5th 681—§ 8
Sharpless v. Sim, 209 S.W.3d 825 (Tex. App. Dallas 2006)
48 ALR6th 135—§ 5
Sharpless Separator Co. v. Brilhart, 129 Md. 82, 98 A. 484 (1916)
8 ALR5th 653—§ 3
Sharplin v. Casualty Reciprocal Exchange, 628 So. 2d 217 (La. Ct. App. 2d Cir. 1993)
56 ALR5th 407—§ 5, 6
Sharplin v. Sharplin, 465 So. 2d 1072 (Miss. 1985)
47 ALR5th 129—§ 10, 16
Sharplin v. State, 330 So. 2d 591 (Miss. 1976)
42 ALR5th 581—§ 6, 19

Sharplin v. State, 357 So. 2d 940 (Miss. 1978)
85 ALR5th 471—§ 6
Sharpnack v. Hoffinger Industries, Inc., 223 Ga. App. 833, 479 S.E.2d 435, Prod. Liab. Rep. (CCH) ¶ 14841 (1996)
65 ALR5th 105—§ 7, 8, 14
Sharpnack v. Hoffinger Industries, Inc., 231 Ga. App. 829, 499 S.E.2d 363 (1998)
101 ALR5th 61—§ 27
102 ALR5th 99—§ 10
Sharpness v. Grondfelt, 307 Ill. App. 3d 676, 240 Ill. Dec. 846, 718 N.E.2d 327 (2d Dist. 1999)
97 ALR6th 375—§ 16
Sharra v. Levine, 52 A.D.2d 1004, 383 N.Y.S.2d 440 (3d Dep't 1976)
27 ALR6th 123—§ 7
Sharsmith v. Hill, 764 P.2d 667 (Wyo. 1988)
58 ALR5th 613—§ 10
64 ALR6th 249—§ 19
97 ALR6th 83—§ 11, 26
Shartle's Estate, In re, 34 Ohio L. Abs. 203, 36 N.E.2d 534 (Ct. App. 2d Dist. Montgomery County 1940)
88 ALR6th 533—§ 19
Sharts v. Natelson, 118 N.M. 721, 885 P.2d 642 (1994)
13 ALR6th 1—§ 4
Sharyn's Jewelers, LLC v. Ipayment, Inc., 196 N.C. App. 281, 674 S.E.2d 732 (2009)
86 ALR6th 321—§ 11, 13
89 ALR6th 409—§ 20
Shasta, County of v. Caruthers, 31 Cal. App. 4th 1838, 38 Cal. Rptr. 2d 18 (3d Dist. 1995)
86 ALR5th 637—§ 3
Shasta Douglas Oil Co. v. Work, 212 Cal. App. 2d 618, 28 Cal. Rptr. 190 (3d Dist. 1963)
2 ALR6th 387—§ 4
Shatkin v. Buffalo General Hosp., 178 App. Div. 2d 934, 578 N.Y.S.2d 738 (4th Dep't 1991)

28 ALR5th 107—§ 4, 41
Shatkin v. St. Joseph Hosp., 168 App. Div. 2d 956, 564 N.Y.S.2d 908 (4th Dep't 1990)
28 ALR5th 107—§ 7
Shatner v. Atchison, 2013 WL 3771541 (S.D. Ill. 2013)
89 ALR6th 1—§ 61
Shattell v. Woodward, 17 Ind. 225, 1861 WL 2953 (1861)
81 ALR6th 363—§ 12
Shatterproof Glass v. James, 466 S.W.2d 873, 46 A.L.R.3d 968 (Tex. Civ. App. Fort Worth 1971)
48 ALR5th 389—§ 3
Shatto v. McNulty, 509 N.E.2d 897 (Ind. Ct. App. 1st Dist. 1987)
93 ALR5th 621—§ 15, 18
8 ALR6th 465—§ 18
Shattuck v. Hoegl (CA2 NY) 523 F.2d 509, 187 USPQ 1, 20 FR Serv. 2d 714) (held not control group member), and Hercules, Inc. v. Exxon Corp., 434 F. Supp. 136, 196 USPQ 401, 24 FR Serv. 2d 1343 (D.C. Del. 1977)
26 ALR5th 628—§ 14
Shattuck v. Klotzbach, 14 Mass. L. Rptr. 360, 2001 WL 1839720 (Mass. Super. Ct. 2001)
110 ALR5th 277—§ 3, 4
Shattuck v. Pennsylvania R. Co., 48 F.2d 346 (D.C. N.Y. 1931)
56 ALR5th 1—§ 3
Shattuck v. Pickwick Stages Corp., 135 Kan. 602, 11 P.2d 996 (1932)
49 ALR5th 685—§ 3
Shatz v. Dunn, 18 Ill. App. 3d 390, 309 N.E.2d 702, 14 U.C.C. Rep. Serv. (CBC) 441 (5th Dist. 1974)
75 ALR5th 559—§ 6
Shatzer v. State, 405 Md. 585, 954 A.2d 1118 (2008)
56 ALR6th 679—§ 16
Shaud v. Sugarloaf Tp. Sup'rs, 2008 WL 313849 (M.D. Pa. 2008)
86 ALR6th 173—§ 9, 12

Shaudys v. IMO Indus., 285 N.J. Super. 407, 667 A.2d 204 (App. Div. 1995)
4 ALR5th 443—§ 14

Shaughnessy, Matter of Estate of, 104 Wash. 2d 89, 702 P.2d 132 (1985)
80 ALR5th 597—§ 8

Shaughnessy v. Dolan, 1996 WL 1353074 (Mass. Super. Ct. 1996)
64 ALR6th 473—§ 9

Shaughnessy v. Mark Twain State Bank, 715 S.W.2d 944 (Mo. Ct. App. E.D. 1986)
71 ALR5th 443—§ 2, 7
75 ALR5th 559—§ 2

Shaughnessy v. Shaughnessy, 164 Ariz. 449, 793 P.2d 1116 (Ct. App. Div. 2 1990)
36 ALR6th 1—§ 15, 17, 25

Shaughnessy v. Shaughnessy, 1999 WL 692085 (Del. Fam. Ct. 1999)
123 ALR5th 565—§ 7, 21

Shaughnessy v. Shaughnessy, 2003 WL 898224 (Minn. Ct. App. 2003)
30 ALR6th 483—§ 3

Shauntz v. Schwegler Bros., Inc., 259 App. Div. 446, 20 N.Y.S.2d 198 (1940)
27 ALR5th 174—§ 66

Shaun ''X,'' In re, 643 N.Y.S.2d 703 (App. Div. 3d Dep't 1996)
1 ALR5th 776—§ 11

Shaurette v. Capitol Erecting Co., 23 Wis. 2d 538, 128 N.W.2d 34 (1964)
76 ALR6th 31—§ 39

Shaut v. Cannon, 526 S.E.2d 214 (N.C. Ct. App. 2000)
69 ALR5th 1—§ 6

Shaut v. Schauroth, 46 A.D. 450, 61 N.Y.S. 767 (4th Dep't 1899)
88 ALR6th 533—§ 19

Shaver v. Bell, 74 N.M. 700, 397 P.2d 723 (1964)
60 ALR5th 379—§ 2, 4

Shaver v. Clanton, 26 Cal. App. 4th 568, 31 Cal. Rptr. 2d 595 (4th Dist. 1994)
99 ALR6th 591—§ 9

Shaver v. F.W. Woolworth Co., 669 F. Supp. 243, 2 BNA IER Cas. 534 (E.D. Wis 1986)
53 ALR5th 219—§ 3, 11

Shaver v. Insurance Co. of North America, 817 S.W.2d 654 (Mo. App. 1991)
14 ALR5th 695—§ 6, 16

Shaver v. Memel, 186 W. Va. 325, 412 S.E.2d 519 (1991)
47 ALR5th 523—§ 4

Shaver v. Rotterdam, 22 App. Div. 2d, 253 N.Y.S.2d 893 (3d Dep't 1964)
38 ALR5th 107—§ 8

Shaver v. State, 199 Ga. App. 428, 405 S.E.2d 281 (1991)
71 ALR5th 637—§ 8

Shaver v. Wolske & Blue, 138 Ohio App. 3d 653, 742 N.E.2d 164, 11 A.D. Cas. (BNA) 245 (10th Dist. Franklin County 2000)
102 ALR5th 1—§ 5, 7

Shavers v. State, 985 S.W.2d 284 (Tex. App. Beaumont 1999)
58 ALR6th 499—§ 26

Shavitz v. City of High Point, 270 F. Supp. 2d 702, 179 Ed. Law Rep. 723 (M.D. N.C. 2003)
26 ALR6th 179—§ 3, 4, 6, 7, 13

Shavitz v. City of High Point, 630 S.E.2d 4, 209 Ed. Law Rep. 491 (N.C. Ct. App. 2006)
26 ALR6th 179—§ 16

Shaw, In re Complaint of, 668 F. Supp. 524, 1988 AMC 1433 (S.D. W. Va. 1987)
34 ALR5th 77—§ 7

Shaw, Matter of, 427 Mass. 764, 696 N.E.2d 126 (1998)
44 ALR6th 75—§ 27

Shaw, Re Marriage of, 47 Wash. App. 391, 735 P.2d 96 (1987)
21 ALR5th 396—§ 7, 30

Shaw v. AAA Engineering & Drafting, Inc., 213 F.3d 519, 16 I.E.R. Cas. (BNA) 513 (10th Cir. 2000)
105 ALR5th 351—§ 3, 4

Shaw v. Aetna Cas. & Sur. Ins. Co., 274 S.C. 281, 262 S.E.2d 903 (1980)
116 ALR5th 247—§ 6
Shaw v. Armontrout, 900 F.2d 123 (8th Cir. 1990)
111 ALR5th 491—§ 3, 4, 9
Shaw v. Armontrout, 900 F.2d 123 (CA8 Mo. 1990)
20 ALR5th 177—§ 3
Shaw v. Binghamton Lodge No. 852, B.P.O. Elks Home, Inc., 155 A.D.2d 805, 548 N.Y.S.2d 81 (3d Dep't 1989)
99 ALR5th 141—§ 18
Shaw v. Boise City, 1985 WL 11183 (D. Idaho 1985)
38 ALR6th 97—§ 29
Shaw v. Brown & Williamson Tobacco Corp., 973 F. Supp. 539 (D. Md. 1997)
49 ALR5th 1—§ 44
81 ALR5th 483—§ 3
Shaw v. Browning, 59 Wash. 2d 133, 367 P.2d 17 (1961)
5 ALR5th 875—§ 3, 41
Shaw v. Caldwell, 229 Ga. 87, 189 S.E.2d 684 (1972)
44 ALR5th 683—§ 32
Shaw v. Cassar, 558 F. Supp. 303 (E.D. Mich. 1983)
12 ALR5th 195—§ 32
Shaw v. Children's Medical Center of Dallas, 2002 WL 59258 (Tex. App. Dallas 2002)
64 ALR6th 249—§ 4
Shaw v. Christie, 160 S.W. 2d 989 (Tex. Civ. App. 1942)
44 ALR5th 1—§ 3, 21
Shaw v. City of Macon, 6 Ga. App. 306, 64 S.E. 1102 (1909)
12 ALR6th 645—§ 56
Shaw v. Consolidated Rail Corp., 74 A.D.2d 985, 426 N.Y.S.2d 182 (3d Dep't 1980)
52 ALR6th 271—§ 21
Shaw v. Continental Ins. Co., 108 Nev. 928, 840 P.2d 592 (1992)
75 ALR6th 235—§ 4

Shaw v. Davis, 55 Barb. 389, 1870 WL 7522 (N.Y. Gen. Term 1870)
44 ALR6th 481—§ 15
Shaw v. Delta Air Lines, Inc., 463 U.S. 85, 77 L. Ed. 2d 490, 103 S. Ct. 2890, 4 EBC 1593, 32 BNA FEP Cas. 121, 32 CCH EPD ¶ 33679 (1983)
51 ALR5th 271—§ 2
Shaw v. Dutton Berry Farm, 160 Vt. 594, 632 A.2d 18 (1993)
42 ALR6th 61—§ 28
Shaw v. Fidelity & Casualty Ins. Co., 582 So. 2d 919 (La. App. 2d Cir. 1991)
15 ALR5th 119—§ 5
Shaw v. Fisher, 113 S.C. 287, 102 S.E. 325 (1920)
88 ALR6th 203—§ 15
Shaw v. Fisk, 21 Wis. 368, 1867 WL 1698 (1867)
117 ALR5th 1—§ 3
Shaw v. Gathwright, 487 F. Supp. 459 (E.D. Va. 1980)
117 ALR5th 513—§ 33
Shaw v. General Motors Corp., 727 P.2d 387, Prod. Liab. Rep. (CCH) ¶ 11151, 1 U.C.C. Rep. Serv. 2d 76 (Colo. App. 1986)
83 ALR6th 1—§ 15, 26, 32, 40
Shaw v. Glickman, 45 Md. App. 718, 415 A.2d 625 (1980)
80 ALR6th 469—§ 5, 29
Shaw v. Globe Indem. Co., 134 So. 2d 609 (La. Ct. App. 2d Cir. 1961)
87 ALR5th 1—§ 10, 21
Shaw v. Greenwich Anesthesiology Associates, P.C., 137 F. Supp. 2d 48, 11 A.D. Cas. (BNA) 1354, 85 Fair Empl. Prac. Cas. (BNA) 937 (D. Conn. 2001)
51 ALR5th 1—§ 4
Shaw v. Hopkins, 338 So. 2d 961 (La. App. 4th Cir. 1976)
25 ALR5th 1—§ 5
Shaw v. Hospital Authority of Cobb County, 614 F.2d 946 (CA5 Ga. 1980)

28 ALR5th 107—§ 22

Shaw v. Housing Authority of City of Walla Walla, 75 Wash. App. 755, 880 P.2d 1006 (Div. 3 1994)

105 ALR5th 351—§ 3, 13

Shaw v. Hughes Aircraft Co., 83 Cal. App. 4th 1336, 100 Cal. Rptr. 2d 446 (4th Dist. 2000)

101 ALR5th 61—§ 3, 4

Shaw v. Hunt, 517 U.S. 899, 116 S. Ct. 1894, 135 L. Ed. 2d 207 (1996)

107 ALR5th 1—§ 2

Shaw v. Kaufman, 2009 WL 2952496 (Mich. Ct. App. 2009)

97 ALR6th 83—§ 38

Shaw v. Lubin, 6 A.D.2d 354, 177 N.Y.S.2d 1 (3d Dep't 1958)

25 ALR6th 101—§ 4, 10

Shaw v. Lumpkin, 241 S.W. 220 (Tex. Civ. App. Texarkana 1922)

73 ALR6th 571—§ 58

Shaw v. McGehee, 2007 WL 2461708 (W.D. Ky. 2007)

89 ALR6th 1—§ 101

Shaw v. M. Livingston & Co., 293 Ky. 575, 169 S.W.2d 612 (1943)

6 ALR6th 391—§ 5, 17, 21

Shaw v. Null, 397 S.W.2d 523 (Tex. Civ. App. Fort Worth 1965)

21 ALR5th 82—§ 3, 32

Shaw v. Owen, 229 Miss. 126, 90 So. 2d 179 (1956)

25 ALR5th 568—§ 33

Shaw v. People, 72 Colo. 142, 209 P. 812 (1922)

29 ALR5th 59—§ 25

Shaw v. Petersen, 169 Ariz. 559, 821 P.2d 220 (Ct. App. Div. 1 1991)

64 ALR5th 1—§ 15, 31

Shaw v. Premier Health and Fitness Center, Inc., 937 So. 2d 1204 (Fla. Dist. Ct. App. 1st Dist. 2006)

61 ALR6th 147—§ 12

Shaw v. Queen City Forging Co., 7 Ohio N.P. 254, 10 Ohio Dec. 107, 1900 WL 1222 (Super. Ct. 1900)

103 ALR5th 157—§ 15

Shaw v. Riverdell Hospital, 150 N.J. Super. 585, 376 A.2d 228 (Law Div. 1977)

37 ALR6th 511—§ 3, 7, 12, 39

Shaw v. Shaw, 227 Cal. App. 2d 159, 38 Cal. Rptr. 520 (2d Dist. 1964)

44 ALR5th 1—§ 21

Shaw v. Shaw, 451 S.E.2d 648 (N.C. App. 1995)

9 ALR5th 568—§ 3

Shaw v. Shaw (Miss) 603 So. 2d 287), and J. C. Penney Co. v. Blush, 356 So. 2d 590 (Miss. 1978)

32 ALR5th 715—§ 3

Shaw v. Smith, 964 P.2d 428 (Wyo. 1998)

21 ALR6th 351—§ 14, 15

Shaw v. Spencer, 57 Wash. 587, 107 P. 383 (1910)

46 ALR5th 1—§ 22

Shaw v. State, 12 Ala. App. 669, 67 So. 770 (1915)

105 ALR5th 529—§ 11

Shaw v. State, 42 S.W.2d 623 (Tex. Crim. App. 1931)

105 ALR5th 529—§ 11

Shaw v. State, 60 Ga. 246 (1878)

24 ALR5th 465—§ 41, 92

Shaw v. State, 104 Nev. 100, 753 P.2d 888 (1988)

12 ALR6th 267—§ 8

Shaw v. State, 166 Tex. Crim. 399, 313 S.W.2d 888 (1958)

54 ALR6th 429—§ 9

Shaw v. State, 201 Ga. App. 438, 411 S.E.2d 534 (1991)

98 ALR6th 455—§ 17

Shaw v. State, 253 Ga. 382, 320 S.E.2d 371 (1984)

6 ALR6th 533—§ 21

Shaw v. State, 282 A.2d 608 (Del. 1971)

19 ALR6th 697—§ 15

Shaw v. State, 304 Ark. 381, 802 S.W.2d 468 (1991)

39 ALR5th 283—§ 4, 58

Shaw v. State, 513 So. 2d 916 (Miss. 1987)

24 ALR5th 465—§ 2, 3, 25, 34
Shaw v. State, 622 S.W.2d 862 (Tex. Crim. 1981)

52 ALR5th 655—§ 4
Shaw v. State, 650 So. 2d 143 (Fla. Dist. Ct. App. 2d Dist. 1995)

117 ALR5th 513—§ 12
Shaw v. State, 663 So. 2d 8 (Fla. Dist. Ct. App. 2d Dist. 1995)

117 ALR5th 513—§ 12
Shaw v. State, 673 P.2d 781 (Alaska Ct. App. 1983)

97 ALR5th 293—§ 13
Shaw v. State, 710 So. 2d 182 (Fla. Dist. Ct. App. 3d Dist. 1998)

21 ALR6th 771—§ 10
Shaw v. State, 2003 WL 21263703 (Minn. Ct. App. 2003)

78 ALR6th 297—§ 46
Shaw v. State, 2009 WL 1896068 (Tex. App. Austin 2009)

69 ALR6th 579—§ 7, 16
Shaw v. State, 2010 WL 2612939 (Tenn. Crim. App. 2010)

99 ALR6th 295—§ 15
Shaw v. State, 2014 WL 3559389 (Ala. Crim. App. 2014)

99 ALR6th 295—§ 10
Shaw v. State, Dept. of Admin., 861 P.2d 566 (Alaska 1993)

97 ALR6th 263—§ 3
Shaw v. State, Dep't of Admin., Public Defender Agency, 816 P.2d 1358 (Alaska 1991)

4 ALR5th 273—§ 2
87 ALR5th 473—§ 6
Shaw v. State, Dept. of Admin., Public Defender Agency, 816 P.2d 1358 (Alaska 1991)

11 ALR6th 1—§ 10
Shaw v. Swift & Co., 351 Ill. App. 135, 114 N.E.2d 330 (1953)

2 ALR5th 1—§ 2, 3, 14
Shaw v. Topping, 142 N.Y.S.2d 490 (Sup. 1955)

41 ALR5th 47—§ 8

Shaw v. United States Fidelity & Guaranty Co., 101 F.2d 92 (CA3 N.J. 1938)

14 ALR5th 695—§ 23
Shaw v. Universal Life & Acci. Ins. Co., 123 S.W.2d 738 (Tex. Civ. App. 1938)

3 ALR5th 237—§ 5, 15, 22
Shaw v. Vannice, 96 Wash. 2d 532, 637 P.2d 241 (1981)

102 ALR5th 525—§ 5
Shaw v. Vermont Dist. Court, Unit No. 3, Franklin Circuit, 152 Vt. 1, 563 A.2d 636 (1989)

94 ALR6th 191—§ 7
Shaw v. Warren, 68 S.W.2d 588 (Tex. Civ. App. Eastland 1933)

15 ALR6th 241—§ 19
Shaw v. Waterbury, 46 Conn. 263 (1878)

57 ALR5th 689—§ 17
Shaw v. Wells Fargo Bank, N.A., 2013 WL 4829268 (S.D. Tex. 2013)

104 ALR6th 485—§ 5
Shaw v. Whitfield, 35 S.W.2d 1115 (Tex. Civ. App. El Paso 1931)

64 ALR5th 163—§ 16
Shaw v. Winters, 796 F.2d 1124 (CA9 Cal. 1986)

18 ALR5th 1—§ 26
Shaw v. Wood, 1991 WL 192523 (Tenn. Ct. App. 1991)

120 ALR5th 483—§ 5
Shaw v. Worley, 2007 WL 2461710 (W.D. Ky. 2007)

89 ALR6th 1—§ 100
Shaw v. Young, 87 Me. 271, 32 A. 897 (1895)

46 ALR5th 1—§ 16, 18
Shaw Cleaners & Dyers v. Des Moines Dress Club, 215 Iowa 1130, 245 N.W. 231, 86 A.L.R. 839 (1932)

104 ALR5th 523—§ 3, 4, 6, 8
Shawcross v. Pyro Products, Inc., 916 S.W.2d 342 (Mo. Ct. App. E.D. 1995)

105 ALR5th 351—§ 4, 5

Shawd v. Donohoe, 97 Ohio App. 252, 56 Ohio Ops. 36, 125 N.E.2d 368 (Franklin Co. 1954)

9 ALR5th 746—§ 3, 5, 21

Shaw Elec. Co. v. International Broth. Elec. Workers, Local Union No. 98, 418 Pa. 1, 208 A.2d 769, 51 Lab. Cas. (CCH) ¶ 51288 (1965)

110 ALR5th 111—§ 6

Shaw ex rel. Shaw v. Martin ex rel. Martin, 16 Mass. L. Rptr. 188, 2003 WL 21246198 (Mass. Super. Ct. 2003)

11 ALR6th 525—§ 7

Shawgo v. Spradlin, 701 F.2d 470, 1 I.E.R. Cas. (BNA) 164 (5th Cir. 1983)

123 ALR5th 411—§ 40, 42

Shaw Group, The v. Kulick, 915 So. 2d 796 (La. Ct. App. 1st Cir. 2005)

22 ALR6th 329—§ 29

Shawhan v. Langley, 249 Conn. 339, 732 A.2d 170 (1999)

116 ALR5th 433—§ 4, 13, 14

Shawmut Bank, N.A. v. Gilman, 1 Mass. L. Rptr. 2, 1993 WL 818758 (Mass. Super. Ct. 1993)

113 ALR5th 487—§ 12

Shawmut Bank, N.A. v. Miller, 415 Mass. 482, 614 N.E.2d 668, 21 U.C.C. Rep. Serv. 2d (CBC) 13 (1993)

71 ALR5th 443—§ 8

Shawmut Community Bank, N.A. v. Zagami, 411 Mass. 807, 586 N.E.2d 962 (1992)

63 ALR5th 1—§ 7

Shawmut Worcester County Bank v. First American Bank & Trust, 731 F. Supp. 57, 11 U.C.C. Rep. Serv. 2d 417 (D. Mass. 1990)

62 ALR6th 1—§ 29

Shawnee v. Bryant, 310 P.2d 754 (Okla. 1957)

25 ALR5th 568—§ 2, 43

Shawnee, City of v. Bryant, 1957 OK 25, 310 P.2d 754 (Okla. 1957)

92 ALR5th 517—§ 5, 12

101 ALR5th 287—§ 7

Shawnee Gas & Electric Co. v. Griffith, 96 Okla. 261, 222 P. 235 (1923)

8 ALR5th 177—§ 27

Shawnee Management Corp. v. Hamilton, 25 Va. App. 672, 492 S.E.2d 456 (1997)

3 ALR5th 907—§ 14

Shawnee-Tecumseh Traction Co. v. Griggs, 50 Okla. 566, 151 P. 230 (1915)

20 ALR5th 1—§ 2, 8, 14, 21, 31, 39, 43, 49

Shawnee Tp. Fire Dist. No. 1 v. Morgan, 221 Kan. 271, 559 P.2d 1141 (1977)

87 ALR5th 1—§ 8, 12, 14, 19, 31

Shawnn F., In re, 34 Cal. App. 4th 184, 40 Cal. Rptr. 2d 263 (5th Dist. 1995)

101 ALR5th 351—§ 7

Shaw's Supermarkets, Inc. v. Delgiacco, 410 Mass. 840, 575 N.E.2d 1115, 12 A.L.R.5th 1093 (1991)

12 ALR5th 658—§ 4, 9, 10, 28

Shaw Tank Cleaning Co. v. Texas Pipeline Co., 442 S.W.2d 851 (Tex. Civ. App. Amarillo 1969)

84 ALR5th 69—§ 17

Shay v. Palombaro, 229 A.D.2d 697, 645 N.Y.S.2d 888 (3d Dep't 1996)

17 ALR6th 159—§ 59

Shay v. Randall H. Hagner & Co., 34 A.2d 358 (Mun. Ct. App. D.C. 1943)

114 ALR5th 443—§ 28

Shay v. Randall H. Hagner & Co., 38 A.2d 617 (Mun. Ct. App. D.C. 1944)

114 ALR5th 443—§ 35

Shayeb v. Holland, 321 Mass. 429, 73 N.E.2d 731 (1947)

12 ALR6th 123—§ 18

Shayer v. Kirkpatrick, 541 F. Supp. 922 (W.D. Mo. 1982)

34 ALR6th 643—§ 34

Shaywitz v. Singing Oaks Day Camp, 8 Conn. App. 71, 510 A.2d 1013 (1986)

50 ALR5th 1—§ 4, 10

52 ALR5th 1—§ 8
Shazel v. State, 966 S.W.2d 414 (Tenn. 1998)

105 ALR5th 529—§ 31
S.H.C. v. Lu, 54 P.3d 174 (Wash. Ct. App. Div. 1 2002)

101 ALR5th 1—§ 8
Shchegol v. Rabinovich, 30 A.D.3d 311, 819 N.Y.S.2d 224 (1st Dep't 2006)

22 ALR6th 553—§ 18
Shea, Appeal of, 121 Pa. 302, 15 A. 629 (1888)

3 ALR5th 394—§ 7
Shea, In re, 308 A.D.2d 29, 760 N.Y.S.2d 492 (1st Dep't 2003)

44 ALR6th 75—§ 33
Shea, In re Marriage of, 1997 WL 146971 (Minn. Ct. App. 1997)

104 ALR6th 303—§ 17
Shea v. Board of Medical Examiners, 81 Cal. App. 3d 564, 146 Cal. Rptr. 653 (3d Dist. 1978)

10 ALR5th 1—§ 4
Shea v. Caritas Carney Hosp., Inc., 79 Mass. App. Ct. 530, 947 N.E.2d 99, 80 A.L.R.6th 767 (2011)

80 ALR6th 469—§ 11, 13, 23, 28
Shea v. Cassidy, 257 Ill. App. 557 (1930)

12 ALR5th 195—§ 8
Shea v. County of Sonoma, 2006 WL 3222306 (Cal. App. 1st Dist. 2006)

74 ALR6th 69—§ 3, 12, 13
Shea v. Esmay, 48 Misc. 2d 45, 264 N.Y.S.2d 181 (Sup 1965)

118 ALR5th 513—§ 3
Shea v. Hanna Mining Co., 397 N.W.2d 362, 51 BNA FEP Cas. 1088 (Minn. App. 1986)

14 ALR5th 537—§ 7
51 ALR5th 1—§ 8
Shea v. Johnson, 101 A.D.2d 1018, 476 N.Y.S.2d 706 (4th Dep't 1984)

111 ALR5th 1—§ 3, 13
Shea v. Oscor Medical Corp., 950 F. Supp. 246, Prod. Liab. Rep. (CCH) ¶ 14939 (N.D. Ill. 1996)

23 ALR6th 223—§ 3, 23, 24

Shea v. Phillips, 213 Ga. 269, 98 S.E.2d 552 (1957)

31 ALR5th 1—§ 2, 12
Shea v. Preservation Chicago, Inc., 206 Ill. App. 3d 657, 151 Ill. Dec. 749, 565 N.E.2d 20 (1st Dist. 1990)

43 ALR5th 207—§ 3, 4, 6, 13, 16, 25
Shea v. State, 46 Ga. App. 729, 169 S.E. 46 (1933)

5 ALR6th 1—§ 32
Shea v. State, 167 S.W.3d 98 (Tex. App. Waco 2005)

34 ALR6th 253—§ 4
Shea v. Valentine, 249 A.D. 556, 292 N.Y.S. 906 (1st Dep't 1937)

19 ALR6th 217—§ 54
Shea v. Volvo Cars of North America, Div. of Volvo North America Corp., 1991 WL 71109 (E.D. Pa. 1991)

88 ALR5th 301—§ 37
Shead v. Grissett, 566 S.W.2d 318, 24 U.C.C.R.S. 644 (Tex. Civ. App. Houston (1st Dist.) 1978)

49 ALR5th 1—§ 97
Sheaffer, In re Appeal of, 116 Ohio App. 3d 98, 686 N.E.2d 1382 (2d Dist. Montgomery County 1996)

7 ALR5th 474—§ 165
Sheaffer v. County of Chatham, 337 F. Supp. 2d 709 (M.D. N.C. 2004)

10 ALR6th 375—§ 15
Sheaffer v. Industrial Commission, 29 Wis. 2d 292, 139 N.W.2d 106, 52 Lab. Cas. (CCH) ¶ 51436 (1966)

61 ALR6th 61—§ 31
Sheahan v. Northeast Illinois Regional Commuter R.R. Corp., 146 Ill. App. 3d 116, 100 Ill. Dec. 114, 496 N.E.2d 1179 (1st Dist. 1986)

42 ALR5th 465—§ 3, 19
84 ALR5th 687—§ 2, 4
Sheahan v. Plagge, 255 Iowa 182, 121 N.W.2d 120 (1963)

40 ALR6th 99—§ 18
Shea Homes Ltd. Partnership v. UDR/ Pacific Los Alisos, 2006 WL 1779037 (Cal. App. 4th Dist. 2006)

64 ALR6th 365—§ 7, 24

For assistance, call 1-800-328-4880

Shea Homes Ltd. Partnership v. UDR/
Pacific Los Alisos, LP, 2007 WL
1207230 (Cal. App. 4th Dist. 2007)
64 ALR6th 365—§ 23, 34, 35
Shea-Kaiser-Lockheed-Healy, 73 Cal.
App. 3d 679, 140 Cal. Rptr. 884, 22
U.C.C. Rep. Serv. 607 (2d Dist.
1977)
94 ALR5th 247—§ 17, 27, 29, 41, 47
Shealy v. Aiken County, 341 S.C. 448,
535 S.E.2d 438 (2000)
97 ALR5th 1—§ 5
106 ALR5th 111—§ 6, 18, 25
108 ALR5th 1—§ 48
Shear, In re Estate of, 700 N.Y.S.2d 369
(Sur. Ct. 1999)
3 ALR5th 590—§ 7, 16
Shear v. Gabovitch, 43 Mass. App. Ct.
650, 685 N.E.2d 1168 (1997)
13 ALR5th 840—§ 6
Shear v. Shear, 1994 WL 110939 (Ohio
Ct. App. 8th Dist. Cuyahoga County
1994)
82 ALR5th 389—§ 3
Shearer v. Leuenberger, 256 Neb. 566,
591 N.W.2d 762 (1999)
36 ALR6th 475—§ 15
Shearer v. Mayer, 83 Mass. App. Ct.
1115, 982 N.E.2d 1226 (2013)
94 ALR6th 431—§ 10
Shearer v. Pacific Gas & Elec. Co., 43
Cal. App. 2d 306, 110 P.2d 690 (1st
Dist. 1941)
95 ALR5th 29—§ 3, 4
Shearer v. Reed, 286 Pa. Super. 188, 428
A.2d 635 (1981)
51 ALR5th 701—§ 9
Shearer v. Shearer, 73 N.Y.S.2d 337
(Sup 1947)
124 ALR5th 203—§ 14
Shearer v. State, 582 So. 2d 28, 16 FLW
D 1518 (Fla. App. D5 1991)
29 ALR5th 59—§ 59, 80
Shearin, In re, 166 N.J. 558, 766 A.2d
1146 (2001)
44 ALR6th 75—§ 4, 18, 24, 27
Shearin, In re, 172 N.J. 560, 799 A.2d
1284 (2002)

44 ALR6th 75—§ 18, 24
Shearin, In re, 764 A.2d 774 (D.C. 2000)
44 ALR6th 75—§ 18, 24, 27, 39
Shearin v. E.F. Hutton Group, 652 A.2d
578, 9 BNA IER Cas. 1317 (Del.
Ch. Ct. 1994)
52 ALR5th 405—§ 2, 4, 6
Shearin v. E.F. Hutton Group, Inc., 652
A.2d 578, 9 I.E.R. Cas. (BNA) 1317
(Del. Ch. 1994)
104 ALR5th 1—§ 3, 4, 12
105 ALR5th 351—§ 3, 8
Shearing v. Rochester, 51 Misc. 2d 436,
273 N.Y.S.2d 464 (1966)
25 ALR5th 568—§ 23
Shears v. State, 895 S.W.2d 456 (Tex.
App. Tyler 1995)
89 ALR5th 629—§ 9
Shearson, Hammill & Co. v. State Tax
Commission, 19 A.D.2d 245, 241
N.Y.S.2d 764 (3d Dep't 1963)
2 ALR6th 1—§ 90
Shearson Lehman Bros. v. Wasatch
Bank, 788 F. Supp. 1184, 18
U.C.C.R.S.2d 208 (D.C. Utah 1992)
45 ALR5th 389—§ 3, 4, 30, 32
Shearson Lehman Bros., Inc. v. Hedrich,
266 Ill. App. 3d 24, 203 Ill. Dec.
189, 639 N.E.2d 228, 9 I.E.R. Cas.
(BNA) 1826 (1st Dist. 1994)
104 ALR5th 1—§ 3
Shearson Lehman Bros., Inc. v. Wasatch
Bank, 139 F.R.D. 412 (D. Utah
1991)
57 ALR5th 633—§ 3
Shearson Lehman Hutton, Inc. v.
Tucker, 806 S.W.2d 914 (Tex. App.
Corpus Christi 1991)
12 ALR5th 195—§ 49
52 ALR6th 271—§ 18
Sheats v. Bowen, 318 F. Supp. 640 (D.C.
Del. 1970)
12 ALR5th 195—§ 4, 18, 47
Shebel ex rel. Shebel, Estate of v.
Yaskawa Elec. America, Inc., 713
N.E.2d 275, Prod. Liab. Rep. (CCH)
¶ 15562 (Ind. 1999)
30 ALR5th 1—§ 43

Shebester v. Triple Crown Insurers, 1992 OK 20, 826 P.2d 603, 17 U.C.C. Rep. Serv. 2d 295 (Okla. 1992)
47 ALR6th 347—§ 17
69 ALR6th 415—§ 15
Sheboygan, City of v. Aabrec, 128 Wis. 2d 561, 384 N.W.2d 368 (Ct. App. 1986)
86 ALR6th 321—§ 12
91 ALR6th 171—§ 98
Sheboygan, State ex rel. v. County Board of Sup'rs, 194 Wis. 456, 216 N.W. 144 (1928)
11 ALR5th 630—§ 2
Sheckles v. State, 501 N.E.2d 1053 (Ind. 1986)
79 ALR5th 237—§ 7
Shed Cafe v. Employment Division, 30 Or. App. 639, 567 P.2d 617 (1977)
95 ALR5th 329—§ 23
Shedd v. Bank of America, N.A., 2013 WL 4056359 (M.D. Ga. 2013)
104 ALR6th 485—§ 4
Shedd v. State, 350 So. 2d 1085 (Fla. Dist. Ct. App. 1st Dist. 1977)
57 ALR6th 445—§ 5
Shedd v. State, 358 So. 2d 1117 (Fla. Dist. Ct. App. 1st Dist. 1978)
103 ALR5th 463—§ 3
Sheddy v. JPMorgan Chase Bank, N.A., 2013 WL 5450288 (N.D. Tex. 2013)
96 ALR6th 125—§ 13
Shedlock v. Cudahy Packing Co., 134 Conn. 672, 60 A.2d 514 (1948)
41 ALR6th 207—§ 20
Shedrick v. Lathrop, 106 Vt. 311, 172 A. 630 (1934)
12 ALR5th 195—§ 43
Shedrick v. State, 10 Md. App. 579, 271 A.2d 773 (1970)
30 ALR6th 103—§ 30
Shedrick v. Trantolo and Trantolo, LLC, 2006 WL 2130403 (Conn. Super. Ct. 2006)
58 ALR6th 1—§ 5
59 ALR6th 1—§ 11

Sheedy v. Merrimack County Superior Court, 128 N.H. 51, 509 A.2d 144 (1986)
32 ALR5th 31—§ 7
Sheeham v. Superior Ambulance Co., Inc., 1997 WL 739407 (Conn. Super. Ct. 1997)
87 ALR5th 277—§ 46
Sheehan v. Atlanta International Ins. Co., 812 F.2d 465 (CA9 Cal. 1987)
6 ALR5th 297—§ 7
Sheehan v. Balasic, 46 Conn. App. 327, 699 A.2d 1036 (1997)
47 ALR5th 129—§ 8
Sheehan v. Board of Appeals of Saugus, 332 Mass. 188, 124 N.E.2d 253 (1955)
77 ALR6th 393—§ 69, 70
Sheehan v. Board of Fire and Police Com'rs of City of Des Plaines, 158 Ill. App. 3d 275, 108 Ill. Dec. 771, 509 N.E.2d 467 (1st Dist. 1987)
19 ALR6th 217—§ 55
Sheehan v. Bowden, 572 So. 2d 1211 (Ala. 1990)
48 ALR6th 511—§ 19
Sheehan v. De Witt, 153 Mont. 320, 456 P.2d 49 (1969)
12 ALR5th 195—§ 10
Sheehan v. El Johnan, Inc., 38 Mass. App. Ct. 975, 650 N.E.2d 819 (1995)
74 ALR5th 49—§ 2, 48, 50
Sheehan v. Hammond, 2 Cal. App. 371, 84 P. 340 (1905)
10 ALR5th 371—§ 3
Sheehan v. Menkes, 8 N.J. Misc. 867, 152 A. 326 (1930)
1 ALR5th 1—§ 4
Sheehan v. Morris Irrigation, Inc., 460 N.W.2d 413, 13 U.C.C.R.S.2d 145 (S.D. 1990)
49 ALR5th 1—§ 2, 8, 21
Sheehan v. Pantelidis, 6 A.D.3d 251, 774 N.Y.S.2d 336 (1st Dep't 2004)
47 ALR6th 303—§ 6

Sheehan v. Peveich, 574 F.3d 248, Bankr. L. Rep. (CCH) ¶ 81540, 77 A.L.R.6th 757 (4th Cir. 2009)
77 ALR6th 273—§ 6

Sheehan v. Sheehan, 51 N.J. Super. 276, 143 A.2d 874 (App. Div. 1958)
95 ALR5th 533—§ 5
124 ALR5th 203—§ 5

Sheehan v. Superior Ambulance Co., 1998 WL 951041 (Conn. Super. Ct. 1998)
87 ALR5th 277—§ 46

Sheehan v. Tobin, 326 Mass. 185, 93 N.E.2d 524, 18 Lab. Cas. (CCH) ¶ 65895 (1950)
94 ALR5th 149—§ 8, 9

Sheehan v. U.S., 822 F. Supp. 13 (D.C. Dist. Col. 1993)
50 ALR5th 1—§ 6
52 ALR5th 1—§ 9

Sheehan v. U.S., 896 F.2d 1168, 52 BNA FEP Cas. 334, 5 BNA IER Cas. 667, 52 CCH EPD ¶ 39687, 107 A.L.R. Fed 297 (CA9 Cal. 1990)
51 ALR5th 163—§ 6

Sheehan's Estate, In re, 290 Ill. App. 551, 9 N.E.2d 63 (1st Dist. 1937)
1 ALR6th 407—§ 7, 8, 15, 19

Sheehy v. Angerosa, 128 Misc. 2d 53, 488 N.Y.S.2d 371 (Sup 1985)
98 ALR5th 533—§ 22

Sheehy v. Ferda, 235 Mont. 63, 765 P.2d 722 (1988)
114 ALR5th 1—§ 28
116 ALR5th 1—§ 23

Sheehy v. Franchise Tax Bd., 84 Cal. App. 4th 280, 100 Cal. Rptr. 2d 760 (4th Dist. 2000)
73 ALR6th 571—§ 9, 43, 45

Sheehy v. Lipton Industries, Inc., 24 Mass. App. 188, 507 N.E.2d 781 (1987)
8 ALR5th 312—§ 4, 17

Sheehy v. New Century Mortg. Corp., 690 F. Supp. 2d 51 (E.D. N.Y. 2010)
58 ALR6th 1—§ 5, 17

Sheehy v. Quarterman, 2007 WL 667153 (W.D. Tex. 2007)
56 ALR6th 185—§ 37

Sheehy v. Sheehy, 325 So. 2d 12 (Fla. Dist. Ct. App. 2d Dist. 1975)
71 ALR5th 99—§ 6

Sheehy v. State, 2004 WL 1698327 (Tex. App. Corpus Christi 2004)
56 ALR6th 185—§ 37

Sheeks v. American Home Products Corp., 2004 WL 4056060 (Colo. Dist. Ct. 2004)
56 ALR6th 161—§ 3, 5

Sheeler v. U. S. Bank of Seminole, 283 So. 2d 566 (Fla. Dist. Ct. App. 4th Dist. 1973)
86 ALR5th 527—§ 9

Sheepscot Land Corp. v. Gregory, 383 A.2d 16 (Me. 1978)
86 ALR6th 321—§ 12

Sheeran v. Colpo, 460 A.2d 522, 114 BNA LRRM 3157, 98 CCH LC ¶ 10422 (Del. Sup. 1983)
12 ALR5th 195—§ 50

Sheeran v. Sheeran, 401 N.W.2d 111 (Minn. Ct. App. 1987)
26 ALR6th 331—§ 5

Sheerbonnet, Ltd. v. American Exp. Bank, Ltd., 951 F. Supp. 403 (S.D. N.Y. 1995)
62 ALR6th 1—§ 8

Sheerr v. Evesham Tp., 184 N.J. Super. 11, 445 A.2d 46 (Law Div. 1982)
49 ALR6th 205—§ 28, 42, 54
55 ALR6th 635—§ 4

Sheet Metal Workers Intern. Ass'n v. Carter, 133 Ga. App. 872, 212 S.E.2d 645, 89 L.R.R.M. (BNA) 3041, 75 Lab. Cas. (CCH) ¶ 53536 (1975)
120 ALR5th 351—§ 23

Sheet Metal Workers Intern. Ass'n v. Nichols, 89 Ariz. 187, 360 P.2d 204, 47 L.R.R.M. (BNA) 2856, 42 Lab. Cas. (CCH) ¶ 50176 (1961)
105 ALR5th 243—§ 11, 20

Sheet Metal Workers Intern. Ass'n, Local No. 162 v. Jason Mfg., Inc., 900 F.2d 1392, 134 L.R.R.M. (BNA) 2097, 115 Lab. Cas. (CCH) ¶ 10003 (9th Cir. 1990)

66 ALR5th 611—§ 10

Sheetmetal Workers' Intern. Ass'n, Local Union No. 223 v. Florida Heat & Power, Inc., 230 So. 2d 154, 73 L.R.R.M. (BNA) 2239 (Fla. 1970)

120 ALR5th 351—§ 33

Sheet Metal Workers Intern. Ass'n Local Union No. 420 v. Kinney Air Conditioning Co., 756 F.2d 742, 118 L.R.R.M. (BNA) 3398, 102 Lab. Cas. (CCH) ¶ 11417 (9th Cir. 1985)

66 ALR5th 611—§ 2, 5, 6, 10

Sheet Metal Workers Local No. 175 v. Walker, 236 S.W.2d 683, 28 L.R.R.M. (BNA) 2077, 20 Lab. Cas. (CCH) ¶ 66395 (Tex. Civ. App. Eastland 1951)

105 ALR5th 243—§ 16, 18

Sheets v. Agro-West, Inc., 104 Idaho 880, 664 P.2d 787 (App. 1983)

51 ALR5th 467—§ 2, 8

Sheets v. Armstrong, 307 Pa. 385, 161 A. 359 (1932)

53 ALR5th 1—§ 26, 50

Sheets v. Brethren Mut. Ins. Co., 342 Md. 634, 679 A.2d 540, 58 A.L.R.5th 883 (1996)

58 ALR5th 483—§ 3, 5

Sheets v. Dillon, 221 N.C. 426, 20 S.E.2d 344 (1942)

76 ALR5th 337—§ 8

Sheets v. Mullins, 109 F. Supp. 2d 879 (S.D. Ohio 2000)

90 ALR5th 273—§ 5

Sheets v. Ragsdale, 220 Va. 322, 257 S.E.2d 858 (1979)

64 ALR5th 163—§ 6

Sheets v. Rockwell Internatl. Corp., 68 Ohio App. 3d 345, 588 N.E.2d 271 (10th Dist. Franklin County 1990)

81 ALR5th 367—§ 5
11 ALR6th 447—§ 3, 6

Sheets v. Sheets, 22 App. Div. 2d 176, 254 N.Y.S.2d 320, 18 A.L.R.3d 1257 (1st Dep't 1964)

38 ALR5th 69—§ 4, 5, 8

Sheets v. State, 244 Ga. App. 304, 535 S.E.2d 312 (2000)

70 ALR5th 587—§ 24

Sheets v. State, 648 So. 2d 796 (Fla. Dist. Ct. App. 2d Dist. 1994)

92 ALR5th 35—§ 4

Sheets v. Teddy's Frosted Foods, Inc., 179 Conn. 471, 427 A.2d 385, 115 L.R.R.M. (BNA) 4626 (1980)

105 ALR5th 351—§ 3, 4, 9, 11

Sheets v. Winans, 285 S.W.2d 501 (Ky. 1955)

25 ALR5th 123—§ 9
76 ALR5th 337—§ 14

Sheetz v. Baltimore, 315 Md. 208, 553 A.2d 1281, 4 BNA IER Cas. 294 (1989)

23 ALR5th 108—§ 2

Sheetz v. Mayor and City Council of Baltimore, 315 Md. 208, 553 A.2d 1281, 4 I.E.R. Cas. (BNA) 294 (1989)

105 ALR5th 1—§ 4, 11

Sheetz, Inc. v. Bowles Rice McDavid Graff & Love, PLLC, 209 W. Va. 318, 547 S.E.2d 256 (2001)

58 ALR6th 1—§ 4
59 ALR6th 1—§ 17

Sheff v. O'Neill, 238 Conn. 1, 678 A.2d 1267, 111 Ed. Law Rep. 360 (1996)

9 ALR6th 177—§ 53

Sheff v. State, 329 So. 2d 270 (Fla. 1976)

61 ALR5th 1—§ 3, 5

Sheffer v. City of Harrisburg, 60 Pa. D. & C.2d 725, 1971 WL 14578 (C.P. 1971)

78 ALR6th 229—§ 20

Sheffer v. North American Ins. Co., 227 Mich. App. 723, 578 N.W.2d 691 (1998)

2 ALR6th 279—§ 3

Sheffer v. Willoughby, 163 Ill. 518, 45 N.E. 253 (1896)

2 ALR5th 1—§ 49

For assistance, call 1-800-328-4880

Sheffield v. Darby, 244 Ga. App. 437, 535 S.E.2d 776, 44 U.C.C. Rep. Serv. 2d 1046 (2000)

88 ALR6th 1—§ 11, 16, 29, 105

Sheffield v. Eli Lilly & Co, 144 Cal. App. 3d 583, 192 Cal. Rptr. 870 (1st Dist. 1983)

63 ALR5th 195—§ 8

Sheffield v. Goodyear Tire & Rubber Co., 2009 WL 2586619 (Wash. Ct. App. Div. 1 2009)

48 ALR6th 135—§ 4

Sheffield v. Heard, 92 So. 2d 295 (La. Ct. App. 2d Cir. 1957)

26 ALR6th 111—§ 4

Sheffield v. Paul T. Stone, Inc., 68 App. D.C. 378, 98 F.2d 250 (1938)

39 ALR5th 33—§ 12

Sheffield v. Runner, 163 Cal. App. 2d 48, 328 P.2d 828 (1st Dist. 1958)

42 ALR5th 1—§ 3

Sheffield v. Scott, 662 S.W.2d 674 (Tex. App. Houston (14th Dist.) 1983)

3 ALR5th 590—§ 16

Sheffield v. Sheffield, 405 So. 2d 1314 (Miss. 1981)

35 ALR5th 145—§ 14

Sheffield v. U. S., 397 A.2d 963 (D.C. 1979)

53 ALR6th 1—§ 7

Sheffield v. Zilis, 170 Ga. App. 62, 316 S.E.2d 493 (1984)

98 ALR5th 533—§ 20

Sheffield & Main v. Barber, 14 R.I. 263 (1883)

20 ALR5th 229—§ 11

Sheffield Assembly of God Church, Inc. v. American Ins. Co., 870 S.W.2d 926 (Mo. Ct. App. W.D. 1994)

100 ALR5th 481—§ 3

Sheffield Sav. Bank v. Klages, 294 N.W.2d 55 (Iowa 1980)

73 ALR6th 425—§ 9, 11, 15, 17, 52

Sheffield Services Co. v. Trowbridge, 211 P.3d 714 (Colo. App 2009)

46 ALR6th 1—§ 32

Sheffield Services Co. v. Trowbridge, 2009 WL 1477003 (Colo. App 2009)

47 ALR6th 1—§ 16

Sheffield Village v. Ohio Civil Rights Com'n, 2000 WL 727551 (Ohio Ct. App. 9th Dist. Lorain County 2000)

92 ALR6th 121—§ 4

Sheftel v. People, 111 Colo. 349, 141 P.2d 1018 (1943)

54 ALR6th 429—§ 10

Shegog v. Union Planters Bank, Nat. Ass'n, 332 F. Supp. 2d 945 (S.D. Miss. 2004)

22 ALR6th 49—§ 2, 4, 12

Shehane v. Station Casino, 27 Kan. App. 2d 257, 3 P.3d 551 (2000)

96 ALR5th 485—§ 10

Shehee v. Aetna Casualty & Surety Co., 122 F. Supp. 1 (D.C. La 1954)

44 ALR5th 91—§ 13

Shehu v. Creed, 2003 WL 23025573 (Conn. Super. Ct. 2003)

70 ALR6th 209—§ 55

Shehyn v. District of Columbia, 392 A.2d 1008 (Dist. Col. App. 1978)

45 ALR5th 173—§ 12

Sheik-Abdi v. McClellan, 37 F.3d 1240 (7th Cir. 1994)

58 ALR6th 499—§ 15

Sheikh v. Department of Public Safety, 904 P.2d 1103, 66 Empl. Prac. Dec. (CCH) ¶ 43746 (Utah Ct. App. 1995)

99 ALR5th 1—§ 3

Sheikh v. Sinha, 272 A.D.2d 465, 707 N.Y.S.2d 241 (2d Dep't 2000)

44 ALR6th 391—§ 5

Sheila L. on Behalf of Ronald M.M. v. Ronald P.M., 195 W. Va. 210, 465 S.E.2d 210 (1995)

5 ALR5th 788—§ 6
40 ALR5th 227—§ 4, 14, 15, 28, 32
80 ALR5th 117—§ 2

Sheila O. v. Superior Court, 125 Cal. App. 3d 812, 178 Cal. Rptr. 418 (1st Dist. 1981)

29 ALR5th 1—§ 3

37 ALR5th 703—§ 5
Sheils v. Bucks County Domestic Relations Section, 2013 WL 395488 (E.D. Pa. 2013)
88 ALR6th 203—§ 85
Sheils v. Jack Eckerd Corp., 560 So. 2d 361 (Fla. App. D2 1990)
12 ALR5th 1—§ 2
Sheils v. Murphy, 20 A.D.2d 927, 249 N.Y.S.2d 749 (2d Dep't 1964)
62 ALR5th 671—§ 16
Sheils v. State Tax Commission, 95 Misc. 2d 605, 407 N.Y.S.2d 823 (Sup 1978)
2 ALR6th 1—§ 41
Sheiner v. City of New York, 611 F. Supp. 172 (E.D. N.Y. 1985)
89 ALR6th 1—§ 48
Sheing v. Remington Arms Co., 48 Del. 591, 108 A.2d 364 (Super. Ct. 1954)
96 ALR5th 239—§ 27
Sheink v. Maine Dep't of Manpower Affairs, 423 A.2d 519 (Me. 1980)
95 ALR5th 329—§ 17
Sheipline v. Like, 28 Ohio St. 3d 308, 503 N.E.2d 744 (1986)
5 ALR6th 133—§ 12
Sheir v. Metropolitan Dade County, 375 So. 2d 1114 (Fla. App. D3 1979)
16 ALR5th 1—§ 31, 35
Shelanie v. National Fireworks Ass'n, 487 S.W.2d 921 (Ky. 1972)
21 ALR6th 81—§ 50
Shelby v. Slepekis, 687 S.W.2d 231 (Mo. Ct. App. W.D. 1985)
102 ALR5th 647—§ 18
Shelby v. State, 340 So. 2d 847 (Ala. Crim. App. 1976)
86 ALR5th 59—§ 7
87 ALR5th 181—§ 7
Shelby v. State, 2002 WL 31426618 (Tex. App. Houston 14th Dist. 2002)
99 ALR6th 295—§ 19
Shelby v. St. Luke's Episcopal Hosp., 1988 WL 28996 (S.D. Tex. 1988)
64 ALR5th 333—§ 7, 13, 31
75 ALR5th 229—§ 8, 14, 17

Shelby v. Union Life Ins. Co., 177 Ark. 737, 7 S.W.2d 778 (1928)
6 ALR6th 391—§ 5, 7
Shelby County, Ala. v. Holder, 2013 WL 3184629 (U.S. 2013)
86 ALR6th 519—§ 13
86 ALR6th 577—§ 22
Shelby County Commission v. Smith, 372 So. 2d 1092 (Ala. 1979)
106 ALR5th 523—§ 3, 28
Shelby County Housing Authority v. Thornell, 144 Ill. App. 3d 71, 98 Ill. Dec. 88, 493 N.E.2d 1109 (5th Dist. 1986)
23 ALR5th 140—§ 10, 12
Shelby Indus. Park, Inc. v. City of Shelbyville, 2008 WL 2018185 (S.D. Ind. 2008)
79 ALR6th 325—§ 5, 8, 14
Shelby Ins. Co. v. Kozak, 255 Va. 411, 497 S.E.2d 864 (1998)
5 ALR5th 875—§ 45
Shelby School v. Arizona State Bd. of Educ., 192 Ariz. 156, 962 P.2d 230, 128 Ed. Law Rep. 1254 (Ct. App. Div. 1 1998)
78 ALR5th 533—§ 5
Shelbyville Mut. Ins. Co. v. Sunbeam Leisure Products Co., 262 Ill. App. 3d 636, 199 Ill. Dec. 965, 634 N.E.2d 1319 (5th Dist. 1994)
102 ALR5th 99—§ 5
Shelden v. Platte Valley Sav., 794 P.2d 1083 (Colo. App. 1990)
31 ALR5th 664—§ 5
Sheldon v. Damle, 2004 WL 2075138 (R.I. Super. Ct. 2004)
64 ALR6th 249—§ 21
Sheldon v. Emergency Medicine Consultants, I, P.A., 43 S.W.3d 701 (Tex. App. Fort Worth 2001)
95 ALR6th 85—§ 46
Sheldon v. Flint & P.M. R. Co., 59 Mich. 172, 26 N.W. 507
8 ALR5th 1—§ 6
Sheldon v. Munford, Inc., 950 F.2d 403 (CA7 Ind. 1991)
40 ALR5th 57—§ 2, 4, 7

Sheldon v. Sheldon, 47 Wash. 2d 699, 289 P.2d 335 (1955)

5 ALR5th 863—§ 5

Sheldon v. State, 796 P.2d 831 (Alaska App. 1990)

49 ALR5th 639—§ 4

Sheldon v. Western Union Tel. Co., 51 Hun. 591, 4 N.Y.S. 526 (N.Y. 1889)

8 ALR5th 177—§ 2, 16

Sheldon and Sheldon, Re Marriage of, 82 Or. App. 621, 728 P.2d 946 (1986)

11 ALR5th 259—§ 6, 28

Sheldon Appel Co. v. Albert & Oliker, 47 Cal. 3d 863, 254 Cal. Rptr. 336, 765 P.2d 498 (1989)

66 ALR5th 135—§ 20

Sheldon Forwarding Co. v. Boston & M.R.R., 339 Mass. 679, 162 N.E.2d 288 (1959)

84 ALR5th 69—§ 14, 30

Shelko v. Board of Education, 97 N.J. 414, 478 A.2d 1187 (1984)

56 ALR5th 493—§ 34

Shell, In re, 295 B.R. 129 (Bankr. D. Alaska 2003)

46 ALR6th 401—§ 6

Shell v. King, 2004 WL 1749186 (Tenn. Ct. App. 2004)

48 ALR6th 1—§ 61, 87

49 ALR6th 1—§ 26

Shell v. Law, 935 S.W.2d 402 (Tenn. Ct. App. 1996)

77 ALR5th 201—§ 3

Shell v. Metropolitan Life Ins. Co., 183 W. Va. 407, 396 S.E.2d 174, 117 CCH LC ¶ 56516 (1990)

51 ALR5th 1—§ 7

Shell v. Northeast Utilities, 1997 WL 88216 (Conn. Super. Ct. 1997)

120 ALR5th 351—§ 33

Shell v. Union Oil Co., 489 So. 2d 569, CCH Prod. Liab. Rep. ¶ 11052, 1 U.C.C.R.S.2d 692 (Ala. 1986)

50 ALR5th 327—§ 5

Shell v. U.S., 448 F.3d 951 (7th Cir. 2006)

72 ALR6th 1—§ 14

81 ALR6th 257—§ 27

Shellaberger v. Fisher, 143 F. 937 (C.C.A. 8th Cir. 1906)

99 ALR5th 141—§ 3, 5, 6, 8

Shell Eastern Petroleum Products v. White, 68 F.2d 379 (App. D.C. 1933)

12 ALR6th 123—§ 10

Shellene v. Shellene, 52 Ill. App. 3d 889, 10 Ill. Dec. 667, 368 N.E.2d 153 (2d Dist. 1977)

36 ALR6th 1—§ 17, 23, 28

Sheller v. Cadillac Motor Div. of General Motors Corp., 1994 WL 396419 (E.D. Pa. 1994)

88 ALR5th 301—§ 19

Shelley v. City of Los Angeles, 36 Cal. App. 4th 692, 42 Cal. Rptr. 2d 529 (2d Dist. 1995)

83 ALR6th 143—§ 5

Shelley v. Creighton, 140 N.J. Eq. 603, 55 A.2d 646 (1947)

3 ALR5th 590—§ 15, 23

Shelley v. Kraemer, 334 U.S. 1, 68 S. Ct. 836, 92 L. Ed. 1161, 3 A.L.R.2d 441 (1948)

31 ALR5th 229—§ 2

76 ALR5th 337—§ 1

51 ALR6th 533—§ 4

Shelley v. Moir, 138 Wis. 2d 218, 405 N.W.2d 737 (App. 1987)

35 ALR5th 83—§ 4

Shelley v. State, 447 So. 2d 124 (Miss. 1984)

57 ALR6th 445—§ 29

Shelley v. United Air Lines, Inc., 84 Wash. App. 129, 925 P.2d 991 (Div. 1 1996)

63 ALR6th 495—§ 66

Shelley Electrical Co. v. Ross, 136 Kan. 244, 14 P.2d 638 (1932)

46 ALR5th 1—§ 22

Shelley Renea K, Matter of, 79 A.D.2d 1073, 436 N.Y.S.2d 99 (3d Dep't 1981)

6 ALR6th 161—§ 4

Shellman v. Com., 733 S.E.2d 242 (Va. 2012)

78 ALR6th 417—§ 25
Shellman v. JP Morgan Chase, N.A., 2012 WL 844132 (N.D. Ga. 2012)
86 ALR6th 411—§ 5
Shellman v. JP Morgan Chase, N.A., 2012 WL 844185 (N.D. Ga. 2012)
86 ALR6th 411—§ 5
Shell Offshore, Inc. v. FMP Operating Co., 1988 WL 125455 (E.D. La. 1988)
65 ALR5th 211—§ 20
Shell Oil Co. v. Board of Adjustment, 38 N.J. 403, 185 A.2d 201 (1962)
53 ALR5th 1—§ 25
Shell Oil Co. v. Capparelli, 648 F. Supp. 1052 (S.D. N.Y. 1986)
107 ALR5th 311—§ 5
Shell Oil Co. v. Christie, 125 Ariz. 38, 607 P.2d 21 (App. 1979)
22 ALR5th 483—§ 5
Shell Oil Co. v. Edwards, 263 Ala. 4, 81 So. 2d 535 (1955)
73 ALR5th 223—§ 5, 8
Shell Oil Co. v. Employers Ins. of Wausau, 69 Or. App. 179, 684 P.2d 622 (1984)
43 ALR5th 149—§ 3
Shell Oil Co. v. Gutierrez, 119 Ariz. 426, 581 P.2d 271 (App. 1978)
22 ALR5th 483—§ 5
Shell Oil Co. v. Haunchild, 203 Okla. 456, 223 P.2d 333 (1950)
11 ALR5th 438—§ 2, 8
Shell Oil Co. v. Hebble, 131 S. Ct. 822, 178 L. Ed. 2d 576 (2010)
66 ALR6th 635—§ 30
Shell Oil Co. v. Jackson County, 193 S.W.2d 268 (Tex. Civ. App. 1945)
31 ALR5th 171—§ 11, 12, 20, 30
Shell Oil Co. v. Par Four Partnership, 638 So. 2d 1050, 19 FLW D 1357 (Fla. App. D5 1994)
27 ALR5th 76—§ 36
Shell Oil Co. v. Winterthur Swiss Ins. Co., 12 Cal. App. 4th 715, 15 Cal. Rptr. 2d 815 (1st Dist. 1993)
88 ALR5th 493—§ 3, 8
89 ALR5th 1—§ 10

Shell Oil Co., People ex rel. v. Cicero, 11 Ill. App. 3d 900, 298 N.E.2d 9 (1st Dist. 1973)
38 ALR5th 737—§ 3, 8, 10
Shell Oil Products Co. LLC v. Mac's Shell Service, Inc., 129 S. Ct. 2789 (2009)
46 ALR6th 495—§ 3
Shell Oil Refinery, In re, 143 F.R.D. 105 (E.D. La 1992)
51 ALR5th 603—§ 2, 14
Shell Petroleum Corp. v. Jackson, 47 Ga. App. 667, 171 S.E. 171 (1933)
12 ALR6th 123—§ 10
Shell Petroleum Corp. v. Wilson, 178 Okla. 355, 65 P.2d 173 (1935)
17 ALR5th 547—§ 14, 20, 31
Shell Pipe Line Corp. v. Curtis, 1955 OK 212, 287 P.2d 681 (Okla. 1955)
111 ALR5th 313—§ 20
Shell's Super Store, Inc. v. Parker, 103 So. 2d 884 (Fla. App. 1958)
40 ALR5th 135—§ 10
Shellum v. Michigan Employment Sec. Com'n, 194 Mich. App. 474, 487 N.W.2d 490, 20 Media L. Rep. (BNA) 1907 (1992)
5 ALR6th 327—§ 8
8 ALR6th 117—§ 27
Shelly v. Hansen, 244 Cal. App. 2d 210, 53 Cal. Rptr. 20 (2d Dist. 1966)
13 ALR6th 1—§ 4
Shelly v. State, 95 Tenn. 152, 31 S.W. 492 (1895)
34 ALR5th 723—§ 4
Shelly Motors, Inc. v. Bortnick, 4 Hawaii App. 265, 664 P.2d 755, 36 U.C.C.R.S. 39 (1983)
47 ALR5th 677—§ 15
Shelnutt, In re, 694 A.2d 89 (D.C. 1997)
44 ALR6th 75—§ 13
Shelnutt, In re, 796 A.2d 672 (D.C. 2002)
44 ALR6th 75—§ 25, 27
Shelsey P., In re, 2002 WL 938268 (Cal. App. 1st Dist. 2002)
57 ALR6th 445—§ 43

Shelter Gen. Ins Co. v. Williams, 315 Ark. 409, 867 S.W.2d 457, 33 A.L.R.5th 787 (1993)
33 ALR5th 121—§ 6

Shelter Ins. Co. v. Hudson, 19 Ark. App. 296, 720 S.W.2d 326 (1986)
35 ALR5th 375—§ 9, 62

Shelter Ins. Companies v. Frohlich, 243 Neb. 111, 498 N.W.2d 74 (1993)
125 ALR5th 1—§ 14

Shelter Ins. Cos. v. Spence, 656 S.W.2d 36 (Tenn. App. 1983)
16 ALR5th 412—§ 35, 37

Shelter Mortgage Corp. v. Castle Mortgage Co., L.C., 117 Fed. Appx. 6 (10th Cir. 2004)
43 ALR6th 611—§ 21
47 ALR6th 1—§ 6, 54

Shelter Mut. Ins. Co. v. Barton, 822 So. 2d 1149 (Ala. 2001)
110 ALR5th 465—§ 11

Shelter Mut. Ins. Co. v. Smith, 300 Ark. 348, 779 S.W.2d 149 (1989)
35 ALR5th 375—§ 9, 64

Shelton v. Allen, 407 S.W.2d 832 (Tex. Civ. App. Waco 1966)
12 ALR6th 123—§ 7

Shelton v. American Ins. Co., 507 So. 2d 894 (Miss. 1987)
55 ALR5th 681—§ 9

Shelton v. Apex Surgical, LLC, 2009 WL 3837411 (W.D. Okla. 2009)
96 ALR6th 1—§ 34, 55

Shelton v. Atlantic C. L. R. Co., 88 Ga. App. 834, 78 S.E.2d 99 (1953)
58 ALR5th 535—§ 5

Shelton v. City of College Station, 754 F.2d 1251 (5th Cir. 1985)
89 ALR6th 1—§ 48

Shelton v. City of College Station, 780 F.2d 475 (5th Cir. 1986)
4 ALR6th 263—§ 19

Shelton v. Clevepak Container Corp., 752 S.W.2d 508 (Tenn. 1988)
12 ALR5th 658—§ 4, 11, 19, 28
14 ALR5th 1—§ 2, 14

Shelton v. Com., 229 Ky. 60, 16 S.W.2d 498 (1929)

108 ALR5th 593—§ 46

Shelton v. Com., 2003 WL 22977515 (Ky. Ct. App. 2003)
63 ALR6th 351—§ 3

Shelton v. Country Mut. Ins. Co., 161 Ill. App. 3d 652, 113 Ill. Dec. 426, 515 N.E.2d 235 (1st Dist. 1987)
75 ALR6th 235—§ 29

Shelton v. Doyal, 316 So. 2d 526 (La. Ct. App. 2d Cir. 1975)
95 ALR5th 329—§ 3

Shelton v. Evans, 292 Pa. Super. 228, 437 A.2d 18 (1981)
12 ALR5th 195—§ 64

Shelton v. Farkas, 30 Wash. App. 549, 635 P.2d 1109, 32 U.C.C.R.S. 1421 (1981)
38 ALR5th 191—§ 64

Shelton v. Firestone Tire & Rubber Co., 281 Ark. 100, 662 S.W.2d 473 (1983)
22 ALR5th 483—§ 24

Shelton v. Fiser, 340 Ark. 89, 8 S.W.3d 557 (2000)
71 ALR5th 307—§ 13

Shelton v. Flagstar Bank, F.S.B., 2012 WL 1231756 (S.D. Tex. 2012)
86 ALR6th 411—§ 5

Shelton v. Florida Real Estate Com., 120 So. 2d 191 (Fla. App. D2 1960)
7 ALR5th 474—§ 6, 155

Shelton v. Florida Real Estate Com., 121 So. 2d 711 (Fla. App. D2 1960)
7 ALR5th 474—§ 155

Shelton v. Gudmanson, 934 F. Supp. 1048 (W.D. Wis. 1996)
76 ALR5th 239—§ 2, 16

Shelton v. Hacelip, 167 Ala. 217, 51 So. 937 (1910)
30 ALR5th 571—§ 32

Shelton v. Hair, 939 So. 2d 685 (La. Ct. App. 3d Cir. 2006)
98 ALR6th 1—§ 5, 38

Shelton v. Industrial Com'n, 267 Ill. App. 3d 211, 204 Ill. Dec. 597, 641 N.E.2d 1216 (5th Dist. 1994)
86 ALR5th 295—§ 6

Shelton v. Jones, 1917 OK 368, 66 Okla.
83, 167 P 458 (1917)
109 ALR5th 421—§ 8
Shelton v. Morehead Memorial Hosp.,
318 N.C. 76, 347 S.E.2d 824 (1986)
69 ALR5th 559—§ 7, 9, 14, 17
Shelton v. O'Brien, 76 Ga. 820 (1886)
19 ALR5th 622—§ 5, 11, 27, 54
Shelton v. Phalen, 214 Kan. 54, 519 P.2d
754 (1974)
45 ALR5th 715—§ 2
27 ALR6th 123—§ 9
Shelton v. Sargent, 144 S.W.3d 113
(Tex. App. Fort Worth 2004)
92 ALR6th 379—§ 40, 54
Shelton v. Shelton, 119 Nev. 492, 78
P.3d 507 (2003)
59 ALR6th 433—§ 59
Shelton v. Shelton, 296 Ark. 212, 752
S.W.2d 758 (1988)
14 ALR5th 242—§ 49
Shelton v. Shelton, 571 So. 2d 1128
(Ala. Civ. App. 1990)
34 ALR5th 57—§ 3
Shelton v. Sloan, 127 N.M. 92, 1999-
NMCA-048, 977 P.2d 1012 (Ct.
App. 1999)
116 ALR5th 433—§ 3, 7
120 ALR5th 559—§ 11
Shelton v. Southern R. Co., 193 N.C.
670, 139 S.E. 232 (1927)
15 ALR5th 119—§ 15, 32, 81, 85
Shelton v. State, 44 Ark. App. 156, 870
S.W.2d 398 (1994)
69 ALR6th 1—§ 23
Shelton v. State, 131 Ga. App. 786, 206
S.E.2d 654 (1974)
105 ALR5th 529—§ 11
Shelton v. State, 214 Ga. App. 166, 447
S.E.2d 115 (1994)
28 ALR6th 505—§ 9
Shelton v. State, 287 Ark. 322, 699
S.W.2d 728, 56 A.L.R.4th 383
(1985)
34 ALR6th 1—§ 16
Shelton v. State, 445 So. 2d 844 (Miss.
1984)

72 ALR5th 403—§ 10
119 ALR5th 275—§ 8
Shelton v. State, 494 S.W.2d 851 (Tex.
Crim. 1973)
55 ALR5th 125—§ 3, 7
Shelton v. State, 744 A.2d 465 (Del.
2000)
102 ALR6th 417—§ 102
Shelton v. State, 1990 OK CR 34, 793
P.2d 866 (Okla. Crim. App. 1990)
16 ALR6th 329—§ 4
24 ALR6th 591—§ 4, 15
Shelton v. State, 2003 WL 1870529
(Tex. App. Dallas 2003)
33 ALR6th 91—§ 46
Shelton v. Stewart, 193 Va. 162, 67
S.E.2d 841 (1951)
58 ALR5th 387—§ 3
Shelton v. Torrington Co., 1998 WL
107995 (Tenn. Sp. Workers' Comp.
1998)
86 ALR5th 295—§ 4
Shelton v. Travelers Ins. Co., 289 So. 2d
255 (La. Ct. App. 1st Cir. 1973)
79 ALR5th 289—§ 3
Shelton v. U.S., 804 F. Supp. 1147 (E.D.
Mo. 1992)
19 ALR5th 563—§ 8, 12
84 ALR5th 619—§ 3, 7
Shelton v. Vinyard, 943 S.W.2d 727
(Mo. Ct. App. W.D. 1997)
48 ALR5th 659—§ 18
Shelton Ins. Agency v. St. Paul Mercury
Ins. Co., 848 S.W.2d 739 (Tex. App.
Corpus Christi 1993)
63 ALR5th 1—§ 10
Shelton Police Union, Inc. v. Voccola,
125 F. Supp. 2d 604 (D. Conn.
2001)
30 ALR6th 299—§ 27
Shelton, State ex rel. v. Sepe, 254 So. 2d
12 (Fla. Dist. Ct. App. 3d Dist.
1971)
85 ALR5th 471—§ 4
Sheltra v. Vermont Asbestos Group, 175
Vt. 499, 2003 VT 22, 820 A.2d 221
(2003)
41 ALR6th 445—§ 30

Shelvin v. Lykos, 741 S.W.2d 178 (Tex. App. Houston 1st Dist. 1987)

87 ALR5th 631—§ 35

Shemo, State ex rel. v. Mayfield Hts., 95 Ohio St. 3d 59, 2002-Ohio-1627, 765 N.E.2d 345 (2002)

49 ALR6th 205—§ 32

55 ALR6th 635—§ 3, 6

Shemwell v. Speck, 265 S.W.2d 468 (Ky. 1954)

73 ALR5th 223—§ 3, 9

Shenah v. Henderson, 106 Ariz. 399, 476 P.2d 854 (1970)

15 ALR5th 391—§ 30

92 ALR5th 35—§ 15

Shenandoah v. Halbritter, 366 F.3d 89 (2d Cir. 2004)

63 ALR6th 1—§ 38

Shenandoah Pub. House, Inc. v. Board of Sup'rs of Shenandoah County, 22 Media L. Rep. (BNA) 1177, 1993 WL 643358 (Va. Cir. Ct. 1993)

118 ALR5th 1—§ 4, 15

Shenandoah Pub. House, Inc. v. The Winchester City Council, 37 Va. Cir. 149, 1995 WL 1055895 (1995)

118 ALR5th 1—§ 4, 13

Shenango Valley Regional Charter School v. Hermitage School Dist., 756 A.2d 1191, 146 Ed. Law Rep. 790 (Pa. Commw. Ct. 2000)

78 ALR5th 533—§ 7

Shenango Valley Regional Charter School v. Hermitage School Dist., 2000 WL 1041230 (Pa. Commw. Ct. 2000)

78 ALR5th 533—§ 7

Sheneal W. Jr., In re, 45 Conn. Supp. 586, 728 A.2d 544, 23 Conn. L. Rptr. 698 (Super. Ct. Juv. Matters 1999)

10 ALR6th 173—§ 6

Shenk v. Commonwealth, State Real Estate Com., 107 Pa. Cmwlth. 48, 527 A.2d 629 (1987)

7 ALR5th 474—§ 34

Shenk v. Shenk, 100 Ohio App. 32, 59 Ohio Ops. 471, 135 N.E.2d 436 (Allen Co. 1954)

32 ALR5th 673—§ 3

Shenker v. Baltimore & O.R. Co., 374 U.S. 1, 10 L. Ed. 2d 709, 83 S. Ct. 1667 (1963)

40 ALR5th 1—§ 2

Shenkman v. O'Malley, 1 Misc. 2d 794, 147 N.Y.S.2d 87 (Sup 1955)

16 ALR6th 1—§ 6

Shepard v. Alden, 161 Minn. 135, 201 N.W. 537, 39 A.L.R. 1094 (1924)

109 ALR5th 421—§ 5, 16

Shepard v. Alexian Brothers Hosp., 33 Cal. App. 3d 606, 109 Cal. Rptr. 132, 12 U.C.C. Rep. Serv. (CBC) 1030 (1st Dist. 1973)

75 ALR5th 229—§ 8

Shepard v. Artuz, 2000 WL 423519 (S.D. N.Y. 2000)

33 ALR6th 1—§ 8

Shepard v. Bradford, 721 So. 2d 1049 (La. Ct. App. 3d Cir. 1998)

90 ALR5th 273—§ 13

Shepard v. City of Batesville, Mississippi, 2007 WL 108288 (N.D. Miss. 2007)

89 ALR6th 1—§ 48

Shepard v. Courtoise, 115 F. Supp. 2d 1142 (E.D. Mo. 2000)

94 ALR5th 149—§ 5, 10

Shepard v. Courtoise, 163 L.R.R.M. (BNA) 2638, 1999 WL 1336390 (E.D. Mo. 1999)

94 ALR5th 149—§ 4

Shepard v. Drucker & Falk, 63 N.C. App. 667, 306 S.E.2d 199 (1983)

43 ALR5th 207—§ 2, 4

Shepard v. Henderson, 1 Tenn. Crim. App. 694, 449 S.W.2d 726 (1969)

74 ALR5th 453—§ 3

Shepard v. Irving, 77 Fed. Appx. 615, 182 Ed. Law Rep. 92 (4th Cir. 2003)

83 ALR6th 195—§ 23

Shepard v. Keystone Ins. Co., 743 F. Supp. 429 (D. Md. 1990)

62 ALR5th 189—§ 2, 4

Shepard v. Leonard, 223 N.C. 110, 25 S.E.2d 445 (1943)
97 ALR5th 537—§ 15

Shepard v. Lopez-Barcenas, 200 Or. App. 692, 116 P.3d 254 (2005)
66 ALR6th 269—§ 16

Shepard v. Lopez-Barcenas, 200 Or. App. 692, 116 P.3d 254 (Or. 2005)
57 ALR6th 163—§ 40, 47

Shepard v. McGougan, 562 S.W.2d 678 (Mo. App. 1977)
9 ALR5th 826—§ 6

Shepard v. Milbank Mut. Ins. Co., 437 F. Supp. 744 (D.C. S.D. 1977)
35 ALR5th 375—§ 41, 57

Shepard v. Redford Community Hospital, 151 Mich. App. 242, 390 N.W.2d 239 (1986)
51 ALR5th 301—§ 20

Shepard v. Rhodes, 7 R.I. 470, 1863 WL 1434 (1863)
98 ALR5th 353—§ 4

Shepard v. Schurz Communications, Inc., 847 N.E.2d 219 (Ind. Ct. App. 2006)
22 ALR6th 553—§ 32

Shepard v. Shepard, 194 S.W.2d 319 (Mo. App. 1946)
1 ALR5th 776—§ 10

Shepard v. Sisters of Providence in Oregon, 89 Or. App. 579, 750 P.2d 500, 45 Ed. Law Rep. 341 (1988)
58 ALR5th 613—§ 10
64 ALR6th 249—§ 24

Shepard v. Sisters of Providence in Oregon, 102 Or. App. 196, 793 P.2d 1384, 61 Ed. Law Rep. 1400 (1990)
64 ALR6th 249—§ 24

Shepard v. Spaulding, 45 Mass. 416, 4 Met. 416, 1842 WL 4061 (1842)
109 ALR5th 421—§ 3

Shepard v. State, 500 N.E.2d 1172 (Ind. 1986)
103 ALR6th 347—§ 13

Shepard v. State Farm Mut. Auto. Ins. Co., 545 So. 2d 624 (La. App. 4th Cir. 1989)
23 ALR5th 241—§ 11

Shepard v. State Farm Mut. Auto. Ins. Co., 545 So. 2d 624 (La. Ct. App. 4th Cir. 1989)
115 ALR5th 589—§ 5

Shepard v. Superior Court, 76 Cal. App. 3d 16, 142 Cal. Rptr. 612 (1st Dist. 1977)
90 ALR5th 179—§ 14, 15, 17, 18
99 ALR5th 301—§ 3

Shepard v. U.S., 544 U.S. 13, 125 S. Ct. 1254, 161 L. Ed. 2d 205 (2005)
26 ALR6th 511—§ 2

Shepard v. U.S., 811 F. Supp. 98 (E.D. N.Y. 1993)
18 ALR6th 325—§ 28

Shepard v. Wal-Mart Stores, Inc., 226 Ga. App. 819, 487 S.E.2d 664 (1997)
40 ALR5th 135—§ 10
1 ALR6th 297—§ 11, 18, 21, 25

Shepard v. Wapello County, Iowa, 250 F. Supp. 2d 1112 (S.D. Iowa 2003)
37 ALR6th 137—§ 3, 15

Shepard-Patterson and Associates, Inc. v. Shepard, 1996 WL 195394 (E.D. Pa. 1996)
104 ALR6th 303—§ 18

Shepardson by Shepardson v. Town of Schodack, 83 N.Y.2d 894, 613 N.Y.S.2d 850, 636 N.E.2d 1383 (1994)
12 ALR6th 645—§ 22

Shepard's Pharmacy, Inc. v. Stop & Shop Companies, Inc., 37 Mass. App. Ct. 516, 640 N.E.2d 1112 (1994)
71 ALR5th 491—§ 10

Shephard v. Ouellette, 854 So. 2d 251 (Fla. Dist. Ct. App. 5th Dist. 2003)
70 ALR6th 209—§ 26, 29

Shephard v. Superior Court, 180 Cal. App. 3d 23, 225 Cal. Rptr. 328 (2d Dist. 1986)
70 ALR5th 1—§ 9

Shepherd, Ex parte, 565 So. 2d 241 (Ala. 1990)
5 ALR5th 550—§ 37

Shepherd v. American Home Mortg. Services, Inc., 71 U.C.C. Rep. Serv. 2d 589 (E.D. Cal. 2009)
86 ALR6th 411—§ 5

Shepherd v. Commonwealth, 240 Ky. 261, 42 S.W.2d 311 (1931)
41 ALR5th 1—§ 3

Shepherd v. Davies, 14 Kan. App. 2d 333, 789 P.2d 1190 (1990)
96 ALR6th 269—§ 41

Shepherd v. Davis, 1999 WL 632327 (Tenn. Crim. App. 1999)
88 ALR5th 463—§ 6

Shepherd v. Eagle Lincoln Mercury, Inc., 536 S.W.2d 92 (Tex. Civ. App. Eastland 1976)
67 ALR6th 209—§ 35

Shepherd v. Inhabitants of Chelsea, 86 Mass. 113, 4 Allen 113, 1862 WL 3685 (1862)
29 ALR6th 369—§ 41

Shepherd v. Johnson, 37 Fed. Appx. 340 (10th Cir. 2002)
119 ALR5th 1—§ 3

Shepherd v. Johnson, 535 S.W.2d 238 (Ky. 1976)
51 ALR6th 359—§ 39

Shepherd v. McGee, 986 F. Supp. 2d 1211, 37 I.E.R. Cas. (BNA) 148 (D. Or. 2013)
103 ALR6th 19—§ 4

Shepherd v. McGinnis, 257 Iowa 35, 131 N.W.2d 475 (1964)
42 ALR5th 1—§ 5

Shepherd v. Michelin Tire Corp., 6 F. Supp. 2d 1307 (N.D. Ala. 1997)
38 ALR5th 683—§ 3

Shepherd v. Miles & Sons, Inc., 10 Cal. App. 3d 7, 89 Cal. Rptr. 23 (5th Dist. 1970)
4 ALR5th 772—§ 2

Shepherd v. Morrison's Cafeteria Co., 29 Ala. App. 189, 194 So. 427 (1940)
6 ALR6th 1—§ 57

Shepherd v. Shepherd, 531 So. 2d 668 (Ala. Civ. App. 1988)
34 ALR5th 57—§ 3

Shepherd v. Shepherd, 891 N.E.2d 670 (Ind. Ct. App. 2008)
99 ALR6th 203—§ 15

Shepherd v. State, 51 Okla. Crim. 209, 300 P. 421 (1931)
11 ALR5th 497—§ 3, 8, 16

Shepherd v. State, 230 S.W.3d 738 (Tex. App. Houston 14th Dist. 2007)
58 ALR6th 499—§ 63

Shepherd v. State, 257 Ind. 229, 277 N.E.2d 165 (1971)
23 ALR6th 1—§ 5, 16

Shepherd v. State, 273 S.W.3d 681 (Tex. Crim. App. 2008)
58 ALR6th 499—§ 63

Shepherd v. State, 343 So. 2d 1349 (Fla. App. D1 1977)
11 ALR5th 52—§ 7

Shepherd v. State, 547 N.E.2d 839 (Ind. 1989)
37 ALR5th 515—§ 23

Shepherd v. State, 659 So. 2d 399, 20 FLW D 1684 (Fla. App. D2 1995)
29 ALR5th 59—§ 3

Shepherd v. State, 664 So. 2d 238 (Ala. Civ. App. 1995)
104 ALR5th 229—§ 7
115 ALR5th 403—§ 5
4 ALR6th 113—§ 6, 14, 30, 37
34 ALR6th 539—§ 4, 6, 10

Shepherd v. State, 690 N.E.2d 318 (Ind. Ct. App. 1997)
112 ALR5th 621—§ 3, 8
116 ALR5th 373—§ 3

Shepherd v. State, 915 S.W.2d 177 (Tex. App. Fort Worth 1996)
69 ALR6th 579—§ 7, 23

Shepherd v. State Auto Property & Casualty Ins. Co., 312 Ark. 502, 850 S.W.2d 324 (1993)
23 ALR5th 241—§ 11

Shepherd v. State, Dept. of Fish and Game, 897 P.2d 33 (Alaska 1995)
31 ALR6th 523—§ 52 to 54

Shepherd v. Summit Management Co., Inc., 726 So. 2d 686 (Ala. Civ. App. 1998)

19 ALR6th 1—§ 5
Shepherd v. Trevino, 575 F.2d 1110 (5th Cir. 1978)
10 ALR6th 31—§ 21
Shepherd v. Wilhelm, 41 Colo. App. 403, 591 P.2d 1039 (App. 1978)
99 ALR6th 1—§ 34
Shepherd Components, Inc. v. Brice Petrides-Donohue & Assoc., Inc., 473 N.W.2d 612 (Iowa 1991)
16 ALR5th 129—§ 3, 6
Shepherd Const. Co. v. Vaughn, 88 Ga. App. 285, 76 S.E.2d 647 (1953)
9 ALR5th 102—§ 9, 12, 13
25 ALR5th 568—§ 34
Shepherd Const. Co. v. Watson, 115 Ga. App. 224, 154 S.E.2d 388 (1967)
74 ALR5th 523—§ 3, 40
Shepherdstown Volunteer Fire Dep't v. State ex rel. State of West Virginia Human Rights Com'n, 172 W. Va. 627, 309 S.E.2d 342 (1983)
83 ALR5th 467—§ 2, 5
Shepley, Commonwealth ex rel. v. Szobocsan (1965) 84 Dauph Co 7
124 ALR5th 203—§ 4
Shepley, Commonwealth ex rel. v. Szobocsan (1965, Pa) 84 Dauph Co 7
124 ALR5th 203—§ 8
Shepp v. State, 87 Nev. 179, 484 P.2d 563 (1971)
29 ALR5th 59—§ 57, 88
65 ALR5th 407—§ 3, 19
Sheppard v. Board of Dentistry, 385 So. 2d 143 (Fla. App. D1 1980)
10 ALR5th 1—§ 33
Sheppard v. City of Gainesville Police Dep't, 490 So. 2d 972 (Fla. Dist. Ct. App. 1st Dist. 1986)
84 ALR5th 249—§ 20
Sheppard v. Com., 25 Va. App. 527, 489 S.E.2d 714 (1997)
82 ALR5th 103—§ 3, 5
116 ALR5th 479—§ 5
Sheppard v. Com., 250 Va. 379, 464 S.E.2d 131 (1995)
55 ALR5th 125—§ 3, 7

Sheppard v. Consolidated Edison Co., 2000 WL 33313540 (E.D. N.Y. 2000)
60 ALR6th 295—§ 9, 22, 42
Sheppard v. Consolidated Edison Co. of New York, Inc., 2002 WL 2003206 (E.D. N.Y. 2002)
60 ALR6th 295—§ 60
Sheppard v. Crow-Barker Paul No. 1 Ltd. Partnership, 192 Ariz. 539, 968 P.2d 612 (Ct. App. Div. 1 1998)
125 ALR5th 193—§ 4, 6
Sheppard v. Dun & Bradstreet, Inc., 71 F. Supp. 942 (D.C. N.Y. 1947)
45 ALR5th 739—§ 4
Sheppard v. Georgia Power Co., 66 Ga. App. 620, 18 S.E.2d 686 (1942)
104 ALR6th 97—§ 4
Sheppard v. Hood, 605 So. 2d 708 (La. App. 2d Cir. 1992)
15 ALR5th 692—§ 36
Sheppard v. Immanuel Baptist Church, 353 S.W.2d 212 (Ky. 1961)
8 ALR5th 1—§ 32, 47, 48
Sheppard v. Los Angeles, 172 Cal. App. 2d 338, 342 P.2d 282 (2d Dist. 1959)
21 ALR5th 82—§ 4
Sheppard v. Maxwell, 384 U.S. 333, 86 S. Ct. 1507, 16 L. Ed. 2d 600, 1 Media L. Rep. (BNA) 1220 (1966)
53 ALR6th 305—§ 46
55 ALR6th 157—§ 2, 57
Sheppard v. North River Ins. Co., 362 So. 2d 1212 (La. Ct. App. 4th Cir. 1978)
66 ALR5th 269—§ 3, 4
Sheppard v. Rhay, 73 Wash. 2d 734, 440 P.2d 422 (1968)
37 ALR5th 703—§ 3
Sheppard v. State, 235 Ga. 89, 218 S.E.2d 830 (1975)
98 ALR6th 455—§ 22
Sheppard v. State, 753 So. 2d 748 (Fla. Dist. Ct. App. 2d Dist. 2000)
92 ALR5th 35—§ 2, 19
Sheppard v. State of La. Bd. of Parole, 873 F.2d 761 (5th Cir. 1989)

89 ALR6th 1—§ 44

Sheppard v. Stephens, 8 Ky. LR (abstract) 603, 2 S.W. 548 (1887)

3 ALR5th 237—§ 20

Sheppard v. Welch, 2006 WL 3134869 (S.D. Ind. 2006)

89 ALR6th 1—§ 103

Sheppard-Pollack, Inc. v. Tully, 64 A.D.2d 296, 409 N.Y.S.2d 847 (3d Dep't 1978)

1 ALR6th 1—§ 29

14 ALR6th 119—§ 22

Shepperson v. Mosher Bros., 253 A.D. 852, 1 N.Y.S.2d 446 (3d Dep't 1938)

28 ALR6th 1—§ 12, 13, 39, 76

Sher, In re, 15 A.D.3d 123, 789 N.Y.S.2d 715 (2d Dep't 2005)

44 ALR6th 75—§ 27

Sher v. Johnson, 911 F.2d 1357 (9th Cir. 1990)

81 ALR5th 41—§ 2

Sher v. Leiderman, 181 Cal. App. 3d 867, 226 Cal. Rptr. 698 (6th Dist. 1986)

25 ALR5th 568—§ 51

Sher v. SAF Financial, Inc., 2011 WL 1529731 (D. Md. 2011)

66 ALR6th 83—§ 7

Sheraden v. Black, 107 N.M. 76, 752 P.2d 791 (App. 1988)

50 ALR5th 1—§ 15

Sherar v. B & E Convalescent Center, 49 Cal. App. 3d 227, 122 Cal. Rptr. 505 (2d Dist. 1975)

27 ALR5th 174—§ 3, 9

Sherard v. State, 244 Neb. 743, 509 N.W.2d 194 (1993)

79 ALR5th 201—§ 2, 5, 10, 12

Sheraton Corp. of America v. Korte Paper Co., Inc., 173 Ind. App. 407, 363 N.E.2d 1263 (1977)

86 ALR6th 321—§ 4

89 ALR6th 409—§ 49

Sherbeck v. Schaper, 232 Neb. 754, 442 N.W.2d 364 (1989)

11 ALR6th 1—§ 4, 13

Sherbert v. Verner, 374 U.S. 398, 83 S. Ct. 1790, 10 L. Ed. 2d 965, 9 Fair Empl. Prac. Cas. (BNA) 1152 (1963)

70 ALR5th 169—§ 2

93 ALR5th 1—§ 2, 4

116 ALR5th 233—§ 2

31 ALR6th 395—§ 2

Sherbunt, Matter of, 134 A.D.2d 723, 520 N.Y.S.2d 885 (3d Dep't 1987)

25 ALR6th 1—§ 55

26 ALR6th 1—§ 3, 7

27 ALR6th 1—§ 3

Sherbunt, Re, 134 App. Div. 2d 723, 520 N.Y.S.2d 885 (3d Dep't 1987)

9 ALR5th 193—§ 37

Sherburne v. Board of Dental Examiners, 13 Idaho 105, 88 P. 762 (1907)

32 ALR5th 57—§ 11

Sherburne Corp. v. Town of Sherburne, 124 Vt. 481, 207 A.2d 125 (1965)

107 ALR5th 311—§ 14

Sherburne County Social Services on behalf of Schafer v. Riedle, 481 N.W.2d 111 (Minn. App. 1992)

59 ALR5th 489—§ 4, 12, 15

Shere v. Davis, 95 Nev. 491, 596 P.2d 499 (1979)

5 ALR5th 875—§ 48

Shere v. Marshall Field & Co., 26 Ill. App. 3d 728, 327 N.E.2d 92 (1st Dist. 1974)

26 ALR5th 628—§ 4, 8

Shere v. State, 742 So. 2d 215 (Fla. 1999)

102 ALR6th 417—§ 74

Shereece B., In re, 231 Cal. App. 3d 613, 282 Cal. Rptr. 430, 91 C.D.O.S. 4901, 91 Daily Journal DAR 7526 (6th Dist. 1991)

61 ALR5th 151—§ 10

Sherelis v. State, 452 N.E.2d 411 (Ind. Ct. App. 3d Dist. 1983)

7 ALR6th 487—§ 10

Sherer v. Foodmaker, Inc., 921 F. Supp. 651, 68 CCH EPD ¶ 44192 (E.D. Mo. 1996)

12 ALR5th 508—§ 3

Sherez v. State of Hawai'i Dept. of
Educ., 396 F. Supp. 2d 1138, 204
Ed. Law Rep. 540 (D. Haw. 2005)
20 ALR6th 1—§ 7
Sherfey v. Bartley, 36 Tenn. 58 (1856)
11 ALR5th 127—§ 4
Sheridan, In re, 169 N.J. 221, 777 A.2d
298 (2001)
45 ALR6th 175—§ 6, 16, 18
Sheridan, In re, 422 Mass. 776, 665
N.E.2d 978 (1996)
78 ALR6th 417—§ 32
Sheridan, In re, 449 Mass. 1005, 867
N.E.2d 297 (2007)
44 ALR6th 75—§ 22, 31
Sheridan, In re, 680 A.2d 439 (D.C.
1996)
44 ALR6th 75—§ 18, 35, 37
Sheridan, In re, 798 A.2d 516 (D.C.
2002)
45 ALR6th 175—§ 24
Sheridan, Petition of, 412 Mass. 599,
591 N.E.2d 193 (1992)
78 ALR6th 417—§ 5
Sheridan v. Cabot Corp., 113 Fed. Appx.
444 (3d Cir. 2004)
16 ALR6th 143—§ 5
Sheridan v. Catering Management, Inc.,
252 Neb. 825, 566 N.W.2d 110
(1997)
90 ALR5th 453—§ 39
Sheridan v. Forest Hills Public Schools,
247 Mich. App. 611, 637 N.W.2d
536 (2001)
93 ALR5th 47—§ 13
Sheridan v. Gardner, 347 Mass. 8, 196
N.E.2d 303 (1964)
63 ALR6th 1—§ 60
Sheridan v. Glen Alden Coal Co., 160
Pa. Super. 115, 50 A.2d 540 (1947)
4 ALR5th 443—§ 12
Sheridan v. Great Atlantic & Pacific Tea
Co., 353 Pa. 11, 44 A.2d 280, 162
A.L.R. 946 (1945)
6 ALR6th 1—§ 28, 47, 61
Sheridan v. Greenberg, 391 So. 2d 234
(Fla. Dist. Ct. App. 3d Dist. 1980)
60 ALR5th 165—§ 3, 10

Sheridan v. Horn & Hardart Baking Co.,
366 Pa. 485, 77 A.2d 362 (1951)
83 ALR5th 589—§ 2, 4
123 ALR5th 1—§ 8
Sheridan v. Kurz, 314 Mich. 10, 22
N.W.2d 52 (1946)
25 ALR5th 233—§ 3
Sheridan v. Planning Bd. of City of
Stamford, 159 Conn. 1, 266 A.2d
396 (1969)
73 ALR5th 223—§ 5
Sheridan v. Salem, 14 Or. 328, 12 P. 925
(1886)
15 ALR5th 119—§ 85
Sheridan v. Sheridan, 174 Misc. 2d 249,
663 N.Y.S.2d 797 (Sup 1997)
124 ALR5th 441—§ 3, 4, 8
2 ALR6th 439—§ 5, 13, 31
Sheridan v. State, 239 Ark. 322, 389
S.W.2d 232 (1965)
76 ALR5th 485—§ 17
Sheridan Healthcorp, Inc. v. Amko, 993
So. 2d 167 (Fla. Dist. Ct. App. 4th
Dist. 2008)
70 ALR6th 209—§ 24
Sheridan Mobile Village, Inc. v. Larsen,
78 Ohio App. 3d 203, 604 N.E.2d
217 (Lawrence Co. 1992)
8 ALR5th 653—§ 3
Sheridan Rd. Baptist Church v. Department of Educ., 426 Mich. 462, 396
N.W.2d 373 (1986)
8 ALR5th 875—§ 3
Sheridan Rd. Baptist Church v. Department of Education, 132 Mich. App.
1, 348 N.W.2d 263 (1984)
8 ALR5th 875—§ 3, 4
Sheridan Transp. Co. v. U.S., 897 F.2d
795, 1990 A.M.C. 2978 (5th Cir.
1990)
66 ALR6th 185—§ 10
Sheriff v. Codd, 83 Misc. 2d 625, 373
N.Y.S.2d 254 (Sup 1975)
91 ALR6th 435—§ 139
Sheriff, Clark County v. Benson, 89
Nev. 160, 509 P.2d 554 (1973)
4 ALR5th 1—§ 2

Sheriff, Clark County v. Frank, 103 Nev. 160, 734 P.2d 1241 (1987)
49 ALR5th 639—§ 3
Sheriff, Clark County v. Medberry, 96 Nev. 202, 606 P.2d 181 (1980)
39 ALR5th 283—§ 4, 75
Sheriff, Clark County v. Warner, 112 Nev. 1234, 926 P.2d 775 (1996)
53 ALR6th 81—§ 12
55 ALR6th 391—§ 7
56 ALR6th 185—§ 10, 13, 15, 20, 31, 32
Sheriff of Fayette v. Buckner, 11 Ky. 126 (1822)
20 ALR5th 229—§ 31
Sheriff, Washoe County v. Middleton, 112 Nev. 956, 921 P.2d 282 (1996)
33 ALR5th 571—§ 3
Sheriff, Washoe County, Nev. v. Encoe, 110 Nev. 1317, 885 P.2d 596 (1994)
70 ALR5th 461—§ 2, 3
Sherill (State Report Title: Matter of Sherrill, In re v. O'Brien), 188 N.Y. 185, 81 N.E. 124 (1907)
114 ALR5th 311—§ 5, 7
Sherkow v. Glacier Ice Co., 95 Wis. 2d 743, 293 N.W.2d 182 (March 21, 1980, Wis App. Dist. I)
20 ALR5th 1—§ 8, 14, 41
Sherle, Matter of Guardianship of, 683 P.2d 78 (Okla. Ct. App. Div. 4 1984)
69 ALR5th 1—§ 3, 4
Sherlock v. Quality Control Equipment Co., Inc., 79 F.3d 731, Prod. Liab. Rep. (CCH) ¶ 14556 (8th Cir. 1996)
92 ALR5th 227—§ 10, 11
Sherlock v. State, 632 S.W.2d 604 (Tex. Crim. App. 1982)
6 ALR6th 533—§ 4
Sherman, Application of, 107 N.Y.S.2d 905 (Sup 1951)
81 ALR6th 1—§ 47
Sherman, Ex parte, 81 Okla. Crim. 41, 159 P.2d 755 (1945)
54 ALR5th 743—§ 4
Sherman v. Byrd, 83 F.3d 428 (9th Cir. 1996)
98 ALR5th 305—§ 9

101 ALR6th 207—§ 26
Sherman v. Cabildo Const. Co., 490 So. 2d 1386 (La. 1986)
115 ALR5th 589—§ 12
Sherman v. Carlin, 46 Ohio App. 3d 149, 546 N.E.2d 433 (8th Dist. Cuyahoga County 1988)
75 ALR5th 1—§ 10
Sherman v. Carr, 8 R.I. 431 (1867)
47 ALR5th 553—§ 7, 20
Sherman v. Champlain Transp. Co., 31 Vt. 162, 1858 WL 3045 (1858)
85 ALR6th 1—§ 22
Sherman v. City of Tempe, 202 Ariz. 339, 45 P.3d 336 (2002)
29 ALR6th 343—§ 1
Sherman v. Com., 55 Va. 677, 14 Gratt. 677, 1858 WL 3966 (1858)
105 ALR5th 529—§ 11
Sherman v. Concourse Realty Corp., 47 App. Div. 2d 134, 365 N.Y.S.2d 239 (2d Dep't 1975)
43 ALR5th 207—§ 3, 39
Sherman v. District of Columbia Com. on Licensure to Practice Healing Art, 476 A.2d 667 (Dist. Col. App. 1984)
10 ALR5th 1—§ 19
Sherman v. First Financial Planners, Inc., 41 S.W.3d 633 (Mo. Ct. App. E.D. 2001)
97 ALR5th 1—§ 21
106 ALR5th 111—§ 27
108 ALR5th 1—§ 30
Sherman v. International Publications, 214 A.D. 437, 212 N.Y.S. 478 (1st Dep't 1925)
16 ALR6th 1—§ 21
Sherman v. Kaiser, 664 A.2d 221 (Pa. Commw. Ct. 1995)
28 ALR6th 175—§ 20
Sherman v. Kane, 86 N.Y. 57, 1881 WL 12959 (1881)
91 ALR6th 1—§ 8
Sherman v. Kraft General Foods, Inc., 272 Ill. App. 3d 833, 209 Ill. Dec. 530, 651 N.E.2d 708 (4th Dist. 1995)

93 ALR5th 269—§ 3, 5

Sherman v. Millhon, 1992 WL 142368 (Ohio Ct. App. 10th Dist. Franklin County 1992)

94 ALR6th 431—§ 29

Sherman v. Physical Therapists Examining Board, 208 A.2d 728 (Dist. Col. App. 1965)

8 ALR5th 825—§ 9

Sherman v. Platte County, 642 P.2d 787 (Wyo. 1982)

74 ALR5th 49—§ 16

Sherman v. Prudential-Bache Securities Inc., 732 F. Supp. 541 (E.D. Pa. 1989)

19 ALR6th 1—§ 7

Sherman v. Sherman, 1993 WL 479792 (Conn. Super. Ct. 1993)

59 ALR6th 433—§ 91

Sherman v. Smith, 89 F.3d 1134 (4th Cir. 1996)

77 ALR6th 251—§ 5

Sherman v. State, 20 Okla. Crim. 306, 202 P. 521 (1921)

24 ALR6th 747—§ 49

Sherman v. State, 114 Nev. 998, 965 P.2d 903 (1998)

79 ALR5th 33—§ 60

Sherman v. State, 170 Ark. 148, 279 S.W. 353 (1926)

93 ALR5th 327—§ 4, 9

Sherman v. State, 626 S.W.2d 520 (Tex. Crim. App. 1981)

120 ALR5th 351—§ 26

Sherman v. State, 2009 Ark. 275, 308 S.W.3d 614 (2009)

92 ALR6th 1—§ 4

Sherman v. St. Barnabas Hosp., 535 F. Supp. 564, 115 L.R.R.M. (BNA) 5133 (S.D. N.Y. 1982)

104 ALR5th 1—§ 3

105 ALR5th 351—§ 3

Sherman v. Stryker Corp., 2009 WL 2241664 (C.D. Cal. 2009)

90 ALR6th 75—§ 37, 40

Sherman v. Sunsong America, Inc., 485 F. Supp. 2d 1070 (D. Neb. 2007)

84 ALR6th 1—§ 4, 29, 62

Sherman v. Town of Brentwood, 112 N.H. 122, 290 A.2d 47 (1972)

4 ALR6th 263—§ 10

Sherman v. U.S., 356 U.S. 369, 2 L. Ed. 848, 78 S. Ct. 819 (1958)

9 ALR5th 464—§ 2

Sherman v. Westbrook Zoning Board of Appeals, 16 Conn. L. Rptr. 395, 1996 WL 176352 (Conn. Super. Ct. 1996)

77 ALR6th 393—§ 40, 91

Sherman & Sons Co. v. Princess Shirt Waist Mfg. Co., 213 App. Div. 140, 210 N.Y.S. 100 (1925)

5 ALR5th 56—§ 4, 10

Sherman, City of v. Henry, 928 S.W.2d 464, 11 I.E.R. Cas. (BNA) 1569 (Tex. 1996)

123 ALR5th 411—§ 7

Sherman-Colonial Realty Corp. v. Goldsmith, 155 Conn. 175, 230 A.2d 568 (1967)

2 ALR5th 553—§ 44

38 ALR5th 737—§ 3, 6

Sherman, Estate of v. Millhon, 104 Ohio App. 3d 614, 662 N.E.2d 1098 (10th Dist. Franklin County 1995)

94 ALR6th 431—§ 23

Sherman Simon Enterprises, Inc. v. Lorac Service Corp., 724 S.W.2d 13 (Tex. 1987)

63 ALR5th 1—§ 10

Sherman Treaters, Ltd. v. Ahlbrandt, 115 F.R.D. 519 (D.C. Dist. Col. 1987)

23 ALR5th 241—§ 36

Shermer v. Cornelius, 278 S.E.2d 349 (W. Va. 1981)

16 ALR5th 650—§ 26

21 ALR5th 396—§ 71

Shero v. Home Show U.S.A., Ltd., 193 A.D.2d 1072, 598 N.Y.S.2d 408, 21 U.C.C. Rep. Serv. 2d (CBC) 664 (4th Dep't 1993)

81 ALR5th 483—§ 4

Sherr v. Northport-East Northport Union
Free School Dist., 672 F. Supp. 81,
42 Ed. Law Rep. 1103 (E.D.N.Y.
1987)
94 ALR5th 613—§ 3, 6, 8, 9
Sherrad v. State, 167 Tex. Crim. 119,
318 S.W.2d 900 (1958)
34 ALR5th 125—§ 4
Sherrard v. Sherrard, 175 N.W.2d 411
(Iowa 1970)
47 ALR5th 129—§ 11
Sherrell v. Chesapeake, O. & S. W. R.
Co., 89 Ky. 302, 12 S.W. 465 (1889)
58 ALR5th 535—§ 8
Sherrell v. State, 622 So. 2d 1233 (Miss.
1993)
57 ALR5th 141—§ 2, 3, 6
Sherrell By and Through Wooden v.
City of Longview, 683 F. Supp.
1108 (E.D. Tex. 1987)
90 ALR5th 273—§ 8, 10
Sherrick v. Simon Property Group, Inc.,
133 Wash. App. 1038, 2006 WL
1846446 (Div. 1 2006)
30 ALR6th 413—§ 13, 15
Sheriff-Goslin Co. v. Cawood, 91 Mich.
App. 204, 283 N.W.2d 691, 27
U.C.C. Rep. Serv. 497 (1979)
91 ALR5th 89—§ 4
Sherrill v. Royal Industries, Inc., 526
F.2d 507 (8th Cir. 1975)
73 ALR5th 75—§ 3, 8
Sherrill v. Sherrill, 639 So. 2d 794 (La.
Ct. App. 2d Cir. 1994)
59 ALR6th 433—§ 11, 55, 63
Sherrill & La Follette v. Herring, 78
Ariz. 332, 279 P.2d 907 (1955)
**28 ALR6th 1—§ 13, 25, 29, 31, 36,
64**
Sherrin v. Bose, 608 So. 2d 364 (Ala.
1992)
94 ALR6th 111—§ 14
Sherrod v. Bird, 155 S.W.2d 422 (Tex.
Civ. App. 1941)
58 ALR5th 535—§ 5, 18
Sherrod v. Furniture Center, 769 F.
Supp. 1021 (W.D. Tenn. 1991)
57 ALR5th 633—§ 3

Sherrod v. Municipality of Anchorage,
Water/Sewer Refuse Utility, 803
P.2d 874 (Alaska 1990)
125 ALR5th 1—§ 5
Sherrod v. Piedmont Aviation, Inc., 516
F. Supp. 46 (E.D. Tenn. 1978)
12 ALR5th 195—§ 7, 71
Sherrod v. Sherrod, 448 So. 2d 1234
(Fla. App. D1 1984)
53 ALR5th 375—§ 8
Sherrod v. State, 484 So. 2d 1279 (Fla.
Dist. Ct. App. 4th Dist. 1986)
33 ALR6th 407—§ 46
Sherrod v. Wix, 849 S.W.2d 780 (Tenn.
App. 1992)
17 ALR5th 366—§ 28
Sherrouse Realty Co. v. Marine, 46 So.
2d 156 (La. App. 2d Cir. 1950)
25 ALR5th 123—§ 2, 3
Sherry, In re Adoption of, 107 Ohio
App. 3d 830, 669 N.E.2d 551 (9th
Dist.Medina County 1995)
61 ALR5th 151—§ 8
Sherry, In re Adoption of, 435 Mass.
331, 757 N.E.2d 1097 (2001)
10 ALR6th 173—§ 24
Sherry v. Diercks, 29 Wash. App. 433,
628 P.2d 1336 (Div. 1 1981)
41 ALR6th 1—§ 19
Sherry v. Roseville Tel. Co., 2002 WL
31098066 (Cal. App. 3d Dist. 2002)
10 ALR6th 375—§ 7
Sherry v. Salvo, 205 Wis. 2d 14, 555
N.W.2d 402 (Ct. App. 1996)
87 ALR5th 277—§ 2
Sherry Ann F. v. Bennett S., 131 Misc.
2d 854, 502 N.Y.S.2d 383 (1986)
40 ALR5th 227—§ 43
Sherry H. v. Probate Court, 177 Conn.
93, 411 A.2d 931 (1979)
103 ALR5th 255—§ 4
Sherwin v. Indianapolis Colts, Inc., 752
F. Supp. 1172, 119 CCH LC
¶ 10754 (N.D. N.Y. 1990)
33 ALR5th 619—§ 3
Sherwin v. Levine, 48 App. Div. 2d 733,
367 N.Y.S.2d 868 (3d Dep't 1975)
33 ALR5th 643—§ 17

Sherwin v. Sherwin, 1994 WL 16508 (Conn. Super. Ct. 1994)

124 ALR5th 441—§ 4, 15

1 ALR6th 493—§ 21

2 ALR6th 439—§ 11, 19, 26, 51

3 ALR6th 641—§ 28

Sherwin Alumina L.P. v. AluChem, Inc., 512 F. Supp. 2d 957, 62 U.C.C. Rep. Serv. 2d 319 (S.D. Tex. 2007)

104 ALR6th 303—§ 16

Sherwinski v. State, 1991 WL 154767 (Tex. App. Dallas 1991)

42 ALR6th 237—§ 12

Sherwin-Williams Co. v. Commissioner Of Revenue, 438 Mass. 71, 778 N.E.2d 504 (2002)

11 ALR6th 543—§ 5, 17, 19, 21

Sherwin-Williams Co. v. Department of Revenue, 329 Or. 599, 996 P.2d 500 (2000)

80 ALR6th 325—§ 16

Sherwin Williams Co. v. Feld Bros. & Co., 139 Miss. 21, 103 So. 795 (1925)

3 ALR5th 237—§ 13, 15

Sherwin-Williams Co. v. Indiana Dept. of State Revenue, 673 N.E.2d 849 (Ind. Tax Ct. 1996)

80 ALR6th 325—§ 16

Sherwin-Williams Co. v. Johnson, 989 S.W.2d 710 (Tenn. Ct. App. 1998)

80 ALR6th 325—§ 16

81 ALR6th 97—§ 14

Sherwin-Williams Co. v. Perry Co., 424 S.W.2d 940 (Tex. Civ. App. Austin 1968)

69 ALR5th 137—§ 3, 4, 6

Sherwin-Williams Co. v. Smith, 253 Miss. 769, 179 So. 2d 263 (1965)

4 ALR5th 772—§ 59, 60

Sherwin-Williams Co. v. Tax Appeals Tribunal of Dept. of Taxation and Finance of State of New York, 12 A.D.3d 112, 784 N.Y.S.2d 178 (3d Dep't 2004)

11 ALR6th 543—§ 5

Sherwin-Williams Paint Co. v. Card, 449 S.W.2d 317 (Tex. Civ. App. San Antonio 1970)

21 ALR5th 82—§ 3, 17, 19

Sherwood v. Bellevue Dodge, Inc., 35 Wash. App. 741, 669 P.2d 1258 (Div. 1 1983)

117 ALR5th 155—§ 6, 12

Sherwood v. Danbury Hosp., 252 Conn. 193, 746 A.2d 730 (2000)

14 ALR6th 301—§ 3, 5, 7, 11, 28

Sherwood v. Huber & Huber Motor Exp. Co., 286 Ky. 775, 151 S.W.2d 1007, 135 A.L.R. 263 (1941)

88 ALR6th 533—§ 11

Sherwood v. Jackson, 126 Cal. App. 441, 14 P.2d 861 (1932)

12 ALR5th 195—§ 12

Sherwood v. Microsoft Corp., 2003-2 Trade Cas. (CCH) ¶ 74109, 2003 WL 21780975 (Tenn. Ct. App. 2003)

35 ALR6th 245—§ 6, 10, 15

Sherwood v. Oregon Dep't of Transp., 170 Or. App. 66, 11 P.3d 664 (2000)

89 ALR5th 255—§ 3

Sherwood v. South, 29 S.W.2d 805 (Tex. Civ. App. San Antonio 1930)

67 ALR5th 587—§ 10

Sherwood v. State, 261 Ark. N-140, 1977 WL 636 (1977)

1 ALR6th 549—§ 15

Sherwood v. State, 271 So. 2d 21 (Fla. Dist. Ct. App. 3d Dist. 1972)

24 ALR6th 747—§ 40

Sherwood v. State, 784 N.E.2d 946 (Ind. Ct. App. 2003)

99 ALR6th 295—§ 21

Sherwood v. Superior Court of Orange County, 24 Cal. 3d 183, 154 Cal. Rptr. 917, 593 P.2d 862 (1979)

49 ALR5th 639—§ 3

Sherwood School Dist. 88J v. Washington County Educ. Service Dist., 167 Or. App. 372, 6 P.3d 518, 146 Ed. Law Rep. 879 (2000)

110 ALR5th 293—§ 3

Sherwood Village Co-op. A. Inc. v. Had-
Ten Estates Corp., 53 Misc. 2d 27,
277 N.Y.S.2d 877 (Sup. Ct. 1967)
100 ALR5th 481—§ 3
Sheryl S., In re, 3 Conn. L. Rptr. 448,
1991 WL 61396 (Conn. Super. Ct.
Juv. Matters 1991)
56 ALR6th 553—§ 26
Sheshunoff v. Sheshunoff, 172 S.W.3d
686 (Tex. App. Austin 2005)
77 ALR6th 293—§ 56
Sheskey v. Sheskey, 16 Mass. App. 159,
450 N.E.2d 187 (1983)
9 ALR5th 568—§ 23
Shesler v. Carlson, 2010 WL 2803091
(E.D. Wis. 2010)
68 ALR6th 389—§ 22
Shetler v. Ohio Bur. of Emp. Serv.,
2002-Ohio-3232, 2002 WL
31975087 (Ohio Ct. Cl. 2002)
14 ALR6th 277—§ 6
Shetsky, State ex rel. v. Utecht, 228
Minn. 44, 36 N.W.2d 126, 6
A.L.R.2d 988 (1949)
59 ALR5th 135—§ 3, 5, 14
Shetter v. Rochelle, 2 Ariz. App. 358,
409 P.2d 74 (1965)
30 ALR5th 571—§ 2, 40
Shetters v. State, 1994 WL 16196525
(Alaska Ct. App. 1994)
65 ALR6th 537—§ 40, 72
Shettle v. Shearer, 425 N.E.2d 739 (Ind.
Ct. App. 1981)
91 ALR6th 435—§ 134
Shetty v. Palm Beach Radiation Oncol-
ogy Associates-Sunderam K.
Shetty, M.D., P.A., 915 So. 2d 1233
(Fla. Dist. Ct. App. 4th Dist. 2005)
22 ALR6th 387—§ 4, 38
Shew v. Hartnett, 121 Wash. 1, 208 P.
60 (1922)
100 ALR5th 409—§ 5, 9
Shewan v. State, 396 So. 2d 1133 (Fla.
Dist. Ct. App. 5th Dist. 1980)
51 ALR6th 1—§ 4
Sheward v. Magit, 106 Cal. App. 2d 163,
234 P.2d 708 (1951)
12 ALR5th 195—§ 10

Sheward v. Virtue, 20 Cal. 2d 410, 126
P.2d 345 (1942)
3 ALR6th 355—§ 9
Shewbart v. State, 33 Ala. App. 195, 32
So. 2d 241 (1947)
24 ALR6th 747—§ 17
Shewfelt v. Alaska, 4 Fed. Appx. 328
(9th Cir. 2001)
65 ALR6th 537—§ 48, 53
Shewmake v. Alejaudro, 466 So. 2d 711
(La. Ct. App. 4th Cir. 1985)
42 ALR6th 545—§ 18, 26
43 ALR6th 375—§ 4, 21, 49
Shewmaker v. Etter, 644 N.E.2d 922
(Ind. Ct. App. 2d Dist. 1994)
85 ALR5th 353—§ 2, 12
Shewmaker v. Minchew, 504 F. Supp.
156 (D.D.C. 1980)
38 ALR6th 541—§ 18
Sheyenne Valley Lumber Co. v. Nokle-
berg, 319 N.W.2d 120 (N.D. 1982)
49 ALR5th 1—§ 10
S. H. Harmon Lumber Co. v. Brown,
165 Cal. 193, 131 P. 368 (1913)
46 ALR5th 1—§ 46
Shibuya v. Architects Hawaii Ltd., 65
Haw. 26, 647 P.2d 276 (1982)
5 ALR6th 497—§ 3, 10
Shick v. Shirey, 691 A.2d 511 (Pa.
Super. 1997)
52 ALR5th 405—§ 3
Shideler v. Dwyer, 275 Ind. 270, 417
N.E.2d 281 (1981)
12 ALR6th 1—§ 4, 6, 8, 14
Shieh, In re, 17 Cal. App. 4th 1154, 21
Cal. Rptr. 2d 886 (2d Dist. 1993)
45 ALR6th 493—§ 20, 21, 26, 40
Shieh, In re, 738 A.2d 814 (D.C. 1999)
43 ALR6th 163—§ 3, 63
Shiel v. U.S., 515 A.2d 405 (Dist. Col.
App. 1986)
3 ALR5th 521—§ 15
Shield v. California Pool Service, Inc.,
515 S.W.2d 342 (Tex. Civ. App.
Houston 1st Dist. 1974)
65 ALR5th 105—§ 12

Shield v. State, 744 So. 2d 564 (Fla. Dist. Ct. App. 1st Dist. 1999)
9 ALR6th 633—§ 35

Shields, Ex parte, 371 S.W.2d 395 (Tex. Crim. App. 1963)
76 ALR5th 485—§ 15

Shields, Ex parte, 2010 WL 1509293 (Tex. App. Waco 2010)
103 ALR6th 137—§ 14, 18

Shields v. Board of Adjustment of Mansfield Tp., 133 N.J. Super. 418, 337 A.2d 54 (App. Div. 1975)
63 ALR5th 607—§ 11

Shields v. Buchholz, 515 So. 2d 1379 (Fla. Dist. Ct. App. 4th Dist. 1987)
5 ALR6th 133—§ 7, 18
14 ALR6th 301—§ 4

Shields v. Dretke, 122 Fed. Appx. 133 (5th Cir. 2005)
103 ALR6th 247—§ 17

Shields v. Easterling, 676 So. 2d 293 (Miss. 1996)
21 ALR5th 82—§ 36

Shields v. Garrison, 91 Wash. App. 381, 957 P.2d 805 (Div. 2 1998)
7 ALR5th 113—§ 3

Shields v. Gerhart, 155 Vt. 141, 582 A.2d 153 (1990)
75 ALR5th 619—§ 5

Shields v. GNB Technologies, Inc., 768 So. 2d 774 (La. Ct. App. 2d Cir. 2000)
14 ALR5th 1—§ 12

Shields v. Kimble, 2010 Ark. App. 479, 2010 WL 2195447 (2010)
59 ALR6th 161—§ 13, 17, 22

Shields v. Kleiner, 93 A.D.3d 710, 940 N.Y.S.2d 134 (2d Dep't 2012)
95 ALR6th 541—§ 7

Shields v. Madigan, 5 Misc. 3d 901, 783 N.Y.S.2d 270 (Sup 2004)
8 ALR6th 339—§ 3

Shields v. Norfolk & C. R. Co., 129 N.C. 1, 39 S.E. 582 (1901)
17 ALR5th 547—§ 53

Shields v. Outboard Marine Corp., 776 F. Supp. 1579, Prod. Liab. Rep. (CCH) ¶ 13101, 1993 A.M.C. 1215 (M.D. Ga. 1991)
73 ALR5th 75—§ 11

Shields v. Pennsylvania General Ins. Co., 488 So. 2d 1252 (La. App. 4th Cir. 1986)
30 ALR5th 170—§ 53

Shields v. Prendergast, 36 N.C. App. 633, 244 S.E.2d 475, 24 U.C.C. Rep. Serv. (CBC) 644 (1978)
71 ALR5th 443—§ 12

Shields v. School of Law of Hofstra University, 77 App. Div. 2d 867, 431 N.Y.S.2d 60 (2d Dep't 1980)
47 ALR5th 1—§ 15, 17, 23, 32

Shields v. Singleton, 15 Cal. App. 4th 1611, 19 Cal. Rptr. 2d 459 (2d Dist. 1993)
43 ALR6th 1—§ 5

Shields v. South Carolina Dep't of Highways & Public Transp., 303 S.C. 439, 401 S.E.2d 185 (App. 1991)
15 ALR5th 119—§ 3, 15

Shields v. Sta-Fit, Inc., 79 Wash. App. 584, 903 P.2d 525 (Div. 3 1995)
61 ALR6th 147—§ 4

Shields v. State, 104 Ala. 35, 16 So. 85 (1894)
85 ALR5th 261—§ 4

Shields v. State, 187 Wis. 448, 204 N.W. 486, 40 A.L.R. 945 (1925)
80 ALR5th 255—§ 3, 35

Shields v. State, 608 S.W.2d 924 (Tex. Crim. App. 1980)
68 ALR6th 527—§ 18

Shields v. State, 757 S.W.2d 247 (Mo. Ct. App. E.D. 1988)
72 ALR5th 109—§ 5

Shields v. State, 820 S.W.2d 831 (Tex. App. Waco 1991)
20 ALR5th 398—§ 53

Shields v. Unum Provident Corp., 2007 WL 764298 (S.D. Ohio 2007)
47 ALR6th 255—§ 12

Shields v. Upham, 597 S.W.2d 502 (Tex. Civ. App. El Paso 1980)

14 ALR6th 543—§ 16

Shields v. Van Kelton Amusement Corp., 228 N.Y. 396, 127 N.E. 261 (1920)

38 ALR5th 107—§ 8

Shields v. Wainwright, 813 F.2d 1123 (CA11 Fla. 1987)

39 ALR5th 283—§ 4

Shields v. Welshire Development Co., 37 Del. Ch. 439, 144 A.2d 759 (1958)

25 ALR5th 123—§ 3

115 ALR5th 251—§ 6, 8, 25

Shields v. Westmoreland County, 253 Pa. 271, 98 A. 572 (1916)

10 ALR5th 139—§ 5

Shields on Behalf of Sundstrand Corp. v. Erickson, 710 F. Supp. 686, Fed. Sec. L. Rep. (CCH) ¶ 94392, R.I.C.O. Bus. Disp. Guide (CCH) ¶ 7187 (N.D. Ill. 1989)

43 ALR6th 1—§ 9, 16, 18

Shielee v. Hill, 47 Wash. 2d 362, 287 P.2d 479 (1955)

100 ALR5th 409—§ 2

Shiels v. Byrd, 168 A.D. 112, 153 N.Y.S. 728 (1st Dep't 1915)

109 ALR5th 421—§ 3

Shifflett v. Baltimore County, 247 Md. 151, 230 A.2d 310 (1967)

8 ALR5th 391—§ 3, 7, 11

Shiffman, Application of, 35 App. Div. 2d 709, 314 N.Y.S.2d 823 (1st Dep't 1970)

28 ALR5th 107—§ 3

Shiflett v. M. Timberlake, Inc., 205 Va. 406, 137 S.E.2d 908 (1964)

83 ALR5th 589—§ 6

123 ALR5th 1—§ 10

Shiflett v. State, 262 Ala. 337, 78 So. 2d 805 (1955)

24 ALR5th 465—§ 43, 45

Shigemura v. U.S., 726 F.2d 380 (8th Cir. 1984)

52 ALR6th 1—§ 10

Shigoto Far East Importers, Ltd. v. Republic Nat. Bank, 176 App. Div. 2d 654, 575 N.Y.S.2d 308 (1st Dep't 1991)

23 ALR5th 744—§ 7

Shikany v. Blue Cross & Blue Shield, 134 Mich. App. 603, 350 N.W.2d 910 (1984)

6 ALR5th 297—§ 9

Shikoh v. Murff, 257 F.2d 306 (2d Cir. 1958)

82 ALR6th 1—§ 18

Shillaire, Matter of, 597 A.2d 913 (D.C. 1991)

43 ALR6th 163—§ 48

Shilling v. Bethany, 552 P.2d 94 (Okla. App. 1976)

1 ALR5th 622—§ 13

Shillington Borough Annexation, 73 Pa. D & C. 596 (1949)

17 ALR5th 195—§ 15, 21

Shima, In re Marriage of, 360 N.W.2d 827 (Iowa 1985)

47 ALR5th 129—§ 11

Shimanovsky v. General Motors Corp., 181 Ill. 2d 112, 229 Ill. Dec. 513, 692 N.E.2d 286 (1998)

102 ALR5th 99—§ 3

Shimbori v. Coelho, 18 Cal. App. 2d 641, 64 P.2d 479 (1937)

35 ALR5th 285—§ 4

Shimek v. Janesko, 188 Ark. 418, 66 S.W.2d 626 (1933)

60 ALR6th 481—§ 4

Shimek v. State, 610 So. 2d 632, R.I.C.O. Bus. Disp. Guide (CCH) ¶ 8191 (Fla. Dist. Ct. App. 1st Dist. 1992)

89 ALR5th 629—§ 8

Shimkus, State ex rel. v. Sondalle, 239 Wis. 2d 327, 2000 WI App 238, 620 N.W.2d 409 (Ct. App. 2000)

29 ALR6th 237—§ 2, 4, 8, 14, 26

Shimman v. Frank, 625 F.2d 80, 104 BNA LRRM 2440, 89 CCH LC ¶ 12153 (CA6 Ohio. 1980)

12 ALR5th 195—§ 10

Shimniok v. State, 197 Miss. 179, 19 So. 2d 760 (1944)
103 ALR6th 35—§ 5
Shimsky v. Ford Motor Co., 170 F.R.D. 125 (E.D. Pa. 1997)
82 ALR5th 501—§ 44
88 ALR5th 301—§ 37
Shin v. Massachusetts Inst. of Technology, 19 Mass. L. Rptr. 570, 2005 WL 1869101 (Mass. Super. Ct. 2005)
100 ALR6th 563—§ 3, 6, 8, 10, 11, 37, 38, 40
Shinabarger v. Phillips, 370 Mich. 135, 121 N.W.2d 693 (1963)
20 ALR5th 1—§ 5, 30, 60
Shinall v. State, 199 So. 2d 251 (Miss. 1967)
70 ALR5th 587—§ 3
Shinault v. McLennan County, 330 S.W.2d 486 (Tex. Civ. App. 1959)
22 ALR5th 327—§ 64, 68
Shinault v. State, 668 N.E.2d 274 (Ind. App. 1996)
49 ALR5th 717—§ 4
50 ALR5th 581—§ 7
Shinbone v. Randolph County, 56 Ala. 183 (1876)
45 ALR5th 109—§ 6
Shindelus v. Sevcik, 211 Minn. 432, 1 N.W.2d 399 (1941)
2 ALR5th 1—§ 8
Shindle v. State, 731 P.2d 582 (Alaska Ct. App. 1987)
69 ALR6th 579—§ 8, 17
Shine v. Shine, 189 S.W. 403 (Mo. Ct. App. 1916)
124 ALR5th 203—§ 15
26 ALR6th 331—§ 13
Shine v. Vega, 429 Mass. 456, 709 N.E.2d 58 (1999)
100 ALR6th 477—§ 9
Shiner v. Moriarty, 706 A.2d 1228 (Pa. Super. Ct. 1998)
14 ALR5th 242—§ 42
Shingles v. Com., Unemployment Compensation Bd. of Review, 99 Pa. Commw. 417, 513 A.2d 575 (1986)

80 ALR6th 635—§ 8
Shinholster v. Akron Auto. Ass'n, Inc., 711 F. Supp. 357, 50 Fair Empl. Prac. Cas. (BNA) 1272 (N.D. Ohio 1989)
19 ALR6th 1—§ 7
Shinholster v. Annapolis Hosp., 255 Mich. App. 339, 660 N.W.2d 361 (2003)
108 ALR5th 385—§ 3
Shinn, In re, 195 Cal. App. 2d 683, 16 Cal. Rptr. 165 (4th Dist. 1961)
70 ALR5th 169—§ 4, 25, 29, 30
6 ALR6th 161—§ 5
Shinn v. Stemler, 163 Pa. Super. 363, 61 A.2d 777 (1948)
91 ALR5th 485—§ 5
Shinn v. St. James Mercy Hospital, 675 F. Supp. 94 (W.D. N.Y. 1987)
47 ALR5th 433—§ 5, 11
S.H. Invest. & Dev. Corp. v. Kincaid, 495 So. 2d 768, 11 FLW 1834 (Fla. App. D5 1986)
11 ALR5th 88—§ 3
Shipan v. Slivka, 1982 WL 2309 (Ohio Ct. App. 8th Dist. Cuyahoga County 1982)
103 ALR5th 417—§ 6
Shipka v. Helvig, 405 N.W.2d 248 (Minn. Ct. App. 1987)
6 ALR6th 311—§ 3
Shipkowski v. U.S. Steel Corp., 585 F. Supp. 66, 116 L.R.R.M. (BNA) 3166 (E.D. Pa. 1983)
21 ALR6th 671—§ 4
Shipley v. Bankers Life & Cas. Co., 1962 OK 264, 377 P.2d 571 (Okla. 1962)
99 ALR5th 141—§ 15
Shipley v. City of Spearfish, 89 S.D. 559, 235 N.W.2d 911 (1975)
54 ALR6th 201—§ 22
Shipley v. Lexington Ins. Co., 2007 WL 2810996 (E.D. La. 2007)
62 ALR6th 227—§ 3
Shipley v. New Castle County, 975 A.2d 764 (Del. 2009)
86 ALR6th 321—§ 13

88 ALR6th 385—§ 54
Shipley v. State, 570 A.2d 1159 (Del. 1990)

29 ALR6th 1—§ 8
Shipley v. State, 620 N.E.2d 710 (Ind. Ct. App. 3d Dist. 1993)

77 ALR5th 201—§ 13
Shipley Baking Co. v. Stiles, 17 Ark. App. 72, 703 S.W.2d 465 (1986)

95 ALR5th 329—§ 6
Shipley Co., Inc. v. Clark, 728 F. Supp. 818 (D. Mass. 1990)

79 ALR5th 587—§ 4
Shipman, In re, 125 Wash. 2d 683, 886 P.2d 1127 (1995)

114 ALR5th 1—§ 23, 25, 26
Shipman v. Craig Ayers Chevrolet, Inc., 541 P.2d 876, 17 U.C.C.R.S. 1169 (Okla. App. 1975)

14 ALR5th 242—§ 25
Shipman v. Du Pre, 222 S.C. 475, 73 S.E.2d 716 (1952)

50 ALR5th 703—§ 37
Shipman v. Employers Mut. Liability Ins. Co., 105 Ga. App. 487, 125 S.E.2d 72 (1962)

99 ALR6th 643—§ 17
Shipman v. Glenn, 314 S.C. 327, 443 S.E.2d 921, 3 A.D. Cas. (BNA) 714, 91 Ed. Law Rep. 692, 9 I.E.R. Cas. (BNA) 991 (Ct. App. 1994)

10 ALR6th 375—§ 17
Shipman v. Jennings Firearms, Inc., 791 F.2d 1532 (11th Cir. 1986)

88 ALR5th 1—§ 4 to 6
Shipman v. Johnson, 89 Ga. App. 620, 80 S.E.2d 717 (1954)

9 ALR5th 102—§ 10
Shipman v. Kruck, 267 Va. 495, 593 S.E.2d 319 (2004)

12 ALR6th 1—§ 4
Shipman v. Seiwell, 101 Pa. Super. 95 (1931)

20 ALR5th 229—§ 21
Shipman v. Stone, 28 Ohio C.D. 504 (Ohio Cir. Ct. 1907)

75 ALR5th 1—§ 10

Shipman, Denny, Rhame & Co. v. Portland Const. Co., 64 Or. 1, 128 P. 989 (1913)

23 ALR5th 744—§ 3
Shipner v. Eastern Air Lines, Inc., 868 F.2d 401 (11th Cir. 1989)

85 ALR6th 323—§ 112
Shipp v. Baptist Memorial Hosp., 1995 WL 381750 (Tenn. Sp. Workers' Comp. 1995)

86 ALR5th 295—§ 21
Shipp v. Davis, 48 Ill. App. 3d 463, 6 Ill. Dec. 187, 362 N.E.2d 822 (3d Dist. 1977)

28 ALR6th 175—§ 20
Shipp v. Eklecco L.L.C., 10 A.D.3d 515, 781 N.Y.S.2d 524 (1st Dep't 2004)

63 ALR6th 495—§ 73
Shipp v. McMahon, 54 Fed. Appx. 413 (5th Cir. 2002)

86 ALR6th 173—§ 10
Shipp v. McMahon, 234 F.3d 907 (5th Cir. 2000)

86 ALR6th 173—§ 1, 9, 10
Shipp v. O'Dowd, 454 S.W.2d 845 (Tex. Civ. App. Waco 1970)

33 ALR5th 1—§ 17
Shipp v. Todd, 568 F.2d 133 (9th Cir. 1978)

68 ALR6th 1—§ 4
Shippan Point Ass'n, Inc. v. McManus, 34 Conn. App. 209, 641 A.2d 144, 76 A.L.R.5th 735 (1994)

76 ALR5th 337—§ 14
Shippee v. Zoning Bd. of Appeals of Town of Old Lyme, 39 Conn. Supp. 436, 466 A.2d 328 (Super. Ct. Appellate Sess. 1983)

64 ALR6th 601—§ 24
Shippen v. Bowen, 122 U.S. 575, 30 L. Ed. 1172, 7 S. Ct. 1283 (1887)

50 ALR5th 417—§ 5
Shippen v. Parrott, 506 N.W.2d 82 (S.D. 1993)

11 ALR5th 588—§ 4
Shippen v. Parrott, 1996 S.D. 105, 553 N.W.2d 503 (1996)

12 ALR5th 195—§ 11

Shippen Township v. Portage Township, 133 Pa. Cmwlth. 142, 575 A.2d 157 (1990)
31 ALR5th 171—§ 5

Shippers Exp. v. Chapman, 364 So. 2d 1097 (Miss. 1978)
23 ALR6th 697—§ 11

Shippers Transport of Georgia v. Stepp, 265 Ark. 365, 578 S.W.2d 232 (1979)
12 ALR5th 658—§ 4, 17, 22

Shipping Corp. of India Ltd. v. Jaldhi Overseas Pte Ltd., 585 F.3d 58, 2009 A.M.C. 2409, 70 U.C.C. Rep. Serv. 2d 352 (2d Cir. 2009)
66 ALR6th 567—§ 2, 4, 11, 21

Shippley v. Gremmels, 192 Iowa 801, 185 N.W. 922 (1921)
14 ALR5th 242—§ 23

Shippy v. Hollopeter, 304 N.W.2d 118 (S.D. 1981)
62 ALR5th 219—§ 6, 22

Shirazi v. Childtime Learning Center, Inc., 2009 OK 13, 204 P.3d 75, 105 Fair Empl. Prac. Cas. (BNA) 1587 (Okla. 2009)
69 ALR6th 415—§ 43

Shirck v. Thomas, 486 F.2d 691 (7th Cir. 1973)
41 ALR6th 391—§ 10

Shirey v. State, 1974 OK CR 55, 520 P.2d 701 (Okla. Crim. App. 1974)
9 ALR6th 1—§ 8
54 ALR6th 429—§ 27

Shirey v. Woods, 118 Ga. App. 851, 165 S.E.2d 891 (1968)
21 ALR5th 82—§ 4

Shirk v. Bowling, Inc., 2001 WI 36, 242 Wis. 2d 153, 624 N.W.2d 375 (2001)
86 ALR6th 321—§ 6, 13
91 ALR6th 171—§ 19

Shirk v. Kelsey, 246 Ill. App. 3d 1054, 186 Ill. Dec. 913, 617 N.E.2d 152 (1st Dist. 1993)
2 ALR5th 769—§ 3
35 ALR5th 145—§ 6

Shirk v. Shirk, 186 Kan. 32, 348 P.2d 840 (1960)
3 ALR5th 237—§ 20

Shirk v. Shirk, 190 Kan. 14, 372 P.2d 556 (1962)
3 ALR5th 237—§ 20

Shirk v. Village of Alger, 2009-Ohio-6028, 2009 WL 3806291 (Ohio Ct. App. 3d Dist. Hardin County 2009)
54 ALR6th 201—§ 26

Shirley, In re, 184 B.R. 613, 34 Collier Bankr. Cas. 2d (MB) 143 (Bankr. N.D. Ga. 1995)
32 ALR6th 531—§ 39
40 ALR6th 463—§ 18

Shirley v. Aetna Casualty & Surety Co., 256 So. 2d 462 (La. App. 2d Cir. 1972)
40 ALR5th 603—§ 21

Shirley v. Armstrong, 2003 WL 22230334 (Cal. App. 3d Dist. 2003)
76 ALR6th 395—§ 27

Shirley v. Danziger, 252 A.D.2d 969, 676 N.Y.S.2d 369 (4th Dep't 1998)
76 ALR6th 31—§ 14

Shirley v. Retail Store Emp. Union, 225 Kan. 470, 592 P.2d 433, 101 L.R.R.M. (BNA) 2844, 86 Lab. Cas. (CCH) ¶ 11509 (1979)
120 ALR5th 351—§ 10

Shirley v. Shirley, 600 So. 2d 284 (Ala. App. 1992)
17 ALR5th 366—§ 12, 16
49 ALR5th 441—§ 15

Shirley v. State, 148 Ga. App. 96, 251 S.E.2d 57 (1978)
86 ALR5th 59—§ 8

Shirley v. Unemployment Compensation Bd. of Review, 198 Pa. Super. 296, 181 A.2d 709 (1962)
95 ALR5th 329—§ 5

Shirley v. Venaglia, 86 N.M. 721, 527 P.2d 316 (1974)
10 ALR5th 448—§ 4

Shirley Cloak & Dress Co. v. Arnold, 92 Ga. App. 885, 90 S.E.2d 622 (1955)
14 ALR5th 193—§ 13, 15

Shirley Silk Co. v. American Silk Mills, 260 A.D. 572, 23 N.Y.S.2d 254 (1st Dep't 1940)
67 ALR5th 179—§ 3

Shirokey v. Marth, 63 Ohio St. 3d 113, 585 N.E.2d 407 (1992)
89 ALR6th 1—§ 64, 94, 103

Shirvani v. Capital Investing Corp., Inc., 112 F.R.D. 389 (D. Conn. 1986)
47 ALR6th 255—§ 5

Shirvanion v. State, 64 A.D.3d 1113, 883 N.Y.S.2d 639 (3d Dep't 2009)
65 ALR6th 93—§ 30

Shisinday v. Johnson, 234 F.3d 28 (5th Cir. 2000)
87 ALR6th 109—§ 86

Shister v. City of New York, 63 A.D.3d 1032, 882 N.Y.S.2d 224 (2d Dep't 2009)
93 ALR6th 123—§ 23, 39

Shivangi v. Dean Witter Reynolds, Inc., 107 F.R.D. 313, CCH Fed Secur L. Rep. ¶ 92426 (S.D. Miss. 1985)
52 ALR5th 491—§ 3

Shively v. Green Local School Dist. Bd. of Educ., 579 Fed. Appx. 348 (6th Cir. 2014)
98 ALR6th 599—§ 23

Shively v. Green Local School Dist. Bd. of Educ., 2013 WL 774643 (N.D. Ohio 2013)
98 ALR6th 599—§ 7, 29, 35, 65, 81, 95

Shively v. Green Local School Dist. Bd. of Educ., 2014 WL 4211100 (6th Cir. 2014)
98 ALR6th 599—§ 24

Shively v. Pickens, 346 So. 2d 1314 (La. Ct. App. 3d Cir. 1977)
15 ALR6th 1—§ 4, 10, 14

Shively v. Stewart, 65 Cal. 2d 475, 55 Cal. Rptr. 217, 421 P.2d 65, 28 A.L.R.3d 1431 (1966)
57 ALR6th 445—§ 2
65 ALR6th 295—§ 4, 13, 19

Shiver v. Apalachee Pub. Co., 425 So. 2d 1173, 9 Media L. R. 1053 (Fla. App. D1 1983)

54 ALR5th 443—§ 11

Shiver v. Burkett, 74 Ga. App. 1195, 39 S.E.2d 431 (1946)
35 ALR5th 285—§ 3

Shiver v. State, 327 So. 2d 251 (Fla. App. D4 1976)
6 ALR5th 733—§ 2, 12

Shiver v. Waites, 408 So. 2d 502 (Ala. 1981)
12 ALR5th 195—§ 12

Shivers v. Good Shepherd Hospital, Inc., 427 S.W.2d 104 (Tex. Civ. App. Tyler 1968)
65 ALR5th 357—§ 5, 6

Shivers v. Liberty Mut. Ins. Co., 75 Ga. App. 409, 43 S.E.2d 429 (1947)
83 ALR5th 103—§ 2, 20, 25, 26
84 ALR5th 249—§ 2, 25

Shivers v. State, 258 Ga. App. 253, 573 S.E.2d 494 (2002)
114 ALR5th 235—§ 9

Shives v. Chamberlain, 168 Or. 676, 126 P.2d 28 (1942)
30 ALR5th 571—§ 5

Shiv-Ram, Inc. v. McCaleb, 2003 WL 23025586 (Ala. 2003)
3 ALR6th 355—§ 4

S.H.J. v. State Dep't of Revenue, 682 So. 2d 1354 (Ala. Civ. App. 1995)
12 ALR5th 89—§ 4, 10

Shkolnick v. American Family Mut. Ins. Co., 2 Neb. App. 61, 506 N.W.2d 356 (1993)
40 ALR5th 603—§ 19

Shkolnikov v. JPMorgan Chase Bank, 2012 WL 6553988 (N.D. Cal. 2012)
86 ALR6th 411—§ 5

S. H. Kress & Co. v. Ferguson, 60 S.W.2d 817 (Tex. Civ. App. 1933)
1 ALR5th 1—§ 43
2 ALR5th 1—§ 60

S. H. Kress & Co. v. Self, 22 Ariz. App. 230, 526 P.2d 754 (Div. 1 1974)
100 ALR5th 341—§ 4

Shlachtman v. Mitrani, 508 So. 2d 494, 12 FLW 1423 (Fla. App. D3 1987)
23 ALR5th 241—§ 10

Shlahtichman v. 1-800-Contacts, Inc., 131 S. Ct. 1007, 178 L. Ed. 2d 828 (2011)

66 ALR6th 635—§ 13

Shlahtichman v. 1-800 Contacts, Inc., 615 F.3d 794 (7th Cir. 2010)

66 ALR6th 635—§ 13

Shlien v. Board of Regents, University of Nebraska, 263 Neb. 465, 640 N.W.2d 643, 162 Ed. Law Rep. 551 (2002)

54 ALR6th 99—§ 50

Shlomchik v. Richmond 103 Equities Co., 763 F. Supp. 732, CCH Fed Secur L. Rep. ¶ 96124 (S.D. N.Y. 1991)

23 ALR5th 241—§ 18

SHLP Associates v. State, 692 N.Y.S.2d 421 (App. Div. 2d Dep't 1999)

13 ALR5th 169—§ 3

Shmueli v. Corcoran Group, 9 Misc. 3d 589, 802 N.Y.S.2d 871 (Sup 2005)

40 ALR6th 295—§ 2, 5

91 ALR6th 409—§ 5

Shoaf v. Bland, 208 Ga. 709, 69 S.E.2d 258 (1952)

1 ALR6th 135—§ 8, 39

Shoaf v. Palatine Ins. Co., 127 N.C. 308, 37 S.E. 451 (1900)

87 ALR6th 319—§ 56

Shober v. Commonwealth, State Real Estate Com., 62 Pa. Cmwlth. 110, 435 A.2d 284 (1981)

7 ALR5th 474—§ 160

Shochat v. Weisz, 757 F. Supp. 189, CCH Fed Secur L. Rep. ¶ 96020 (E.D. N.Y. 1991)

7 ALR5th 852—§ 4, 41

Shochet v. Arkansas Bd. of Law Examiners, 335 Ark. 176, 979 S.W.2d 888 (1998)

107 ALR5th 167—§ 5, 16, 21

8 ALR6th 1—§ 12

Shock v. Holt Lumber Co., 107 W. Va. 259, 148 S.E. 73 (1929)

111 ALR5th 313—§ 17

Shock v. Wheeling Pipe Line, Inc., 270 Ark. 57, 603 S.W.2d 446 (App. 1980)

12 ALR5th 658—§ 4, 9, 20, 23, 28, 33

Shocker Const. Co. v. State, 619 P.2d 1378 (Utah 1980)

124 ALR5th 375—§ 14

Shockey v. Shields, 272 Or. 226, 536 P.2d 424 (1975)

98 ALR6th 231—§ 66

Shockey v. Winfield, 97 Ohio App. 3d 409, 646 N.E.2d 911 (4th Dist. Ross County 1994)

66 ALR5th 237—§ 6

Shockley, Interest of, 611 A.2d 508 (Del. Fam. Ct. 1992)

21 ALR5th 396—§ 64

Shockley v. Christopher, 180 Ala. 140, 60 So. 317 (1912)

36 ALR6th 387—§ 5

Shockley v. Director, Div. of Child Support Enforcement, Mo. Dep't of Social Services, 980 S.W.2d 173 (Mo. Ct. App. E.D. 1998)

99 ALR5th 65—§ 24

Shockley v. State, 585 S.W.2d 645 (Tenn. Crim. App. 1978)

86 ALR5th 59—§ 8

Shockley v. Whitehead, 2014 WL 1254113 (Del. Super. Ct. 2014)

98 ALR6th 93—§ 20

Shocrylas v. Worcester State College, 2009 WL 3298126 (D. Mass. 2009)

90 ALR6th 235—§ 50

Shoecraft v. Catholic Social Services Bureau, Inc., 222 Neb. 574, 385 N.W.2d 448 (1986)

61 ALR5th 151—§ 12

28 ALR6th 349—§ 39 to 41

Shoeder's Auto Center, Inc. v. Teschner, 166 Wis. 2d 198, 479 N.W.2d 203 (Ct. App. 1991)

79 ALR6th 211—§ 41, 47

Shoemaker, In re, 2 Pa. Super. 27, 1896 WL 4299 (1896)

37 ALR6th 511—§ 22

Shoemaker, Matter of Estate of, 22 Kan. App. 2d 444, 917 P.2d 897 (1996)
56 ALR5th 133—§ 5

Shoemaker v. Barberton, 36 Ohio L. Abs. 539, 44 N.E.2d 477 (App. Summit Co. 1940)
15 ALR5th 119—§ 83

Shoemaker v. Handel, 619 F. Supp. 1089 (D.C. N.J. 1985)
59 ALR5th 203—§ 2, 43

Shoemaker v. Harris, 214 Cal. App. 4th 1210, 155 Cal. Rptr. 3d 76 (2013)
93 ALR6th 1—§ 30

Shoemaker v. Longo, 186 A.D.2d 979, 588 N.Y.S.2d 441 (4th Dep't 1992)
14 ALR6th 543—§ 21, 30

Shoemaker v. Myers, 2 Cal. App. 4th 1407, 4 Cal. Rptr. 2d 203, 57 Cal. Comp Cas. 45, 92 C.D.O.S. 828, 92 Daily Journal DAR 1384, 7 BNA IER Cas. 175, 126 CCH LC ¶ 57473 (3d Dist. 1992)
19 ALR5th 439—§ 2, 8

Shoemaker v. Myers, 52 Cal. 3d 1, 276 Cal. Rptr. 303, 801 P.2d 1054, 6 I.E.R. Cas. (BNA) 1, 20 A.L.R.5th 1016 (1990)
20 ALR5th 677—§ 2, 3
82 ALR5th 149—§ 2

Shoemaker v. Ragland, 202 Iowa 947, 211 N.W. 564 (1926)
86 ALR6th 411—§ 2

Shoemaker v. Rush-Presbyterian-St. Luke's Medical Center, 187 Ill. App. 3d 1040, 135 Ill. Dec. 446, 543 N.E.2d 1014 (1st Dist. 1989)
123 ALR5th 1—§ 12

Shoemaker v. Shoemaker, 275 Neb. 112, 745 N.W.2d 299, 70 A.L.R.6th 713(2008)
70 ALR6th 209—§ 3, 64

Shoemaker v. South Bend Spark-Arrester Co., 135 Ind. 471, 35 N.E. 280 (1893)
85 ALR6th 1—§ 44, 61

Shoemaker v. State, 52 Md. App. 463, 451 A.2d 127 (1982)
111 ALR5th 239—§ 6

Shoemaker v. State, 228 Md. 462, 180 A.2d 682 (1962)
40 ALR6th 1—§ 3

Shoemaker v. State, 971 S.W.2d 178, 127 Ed. Law Rep. 1117 (Tex. App. Beaumont 1998)
68 ALR6th 527—§ 18

Shoemaker v. St. Joseph Hosp. and Health Care Center, 56 Wash. App. 575, 784 P.2d 562 (Div. 2 1990)
96 ALR5th 107—§ 6

Shoemaker v. Whistler's Estate, 513 S.W.2d 10 (Tex. 1974)
3 ALR5th 1—§ 3, 4, 57
80 ALR5th 533—§ 5

Shoen v. Shoen, 5 F.3d 1289, 93 C.D.O.S. 7213, 93 Daily Journal DAR 12263, 21 Media L. R. 1961, 26 FR Serv. 3d 1117 (CA9 Ariz. 1993)
60 ALR5th 75—§ 7

Shoenfeld v. Fontek, 67 Misc. 2d 481, 324 N.Y.S.2d 487 (1971)
44 ALR5th 1—§ 13

Shoenfeld v. Shoenfeld, 168 A.D.2d 674, 563 N.Y.S.2d 500 (2d Dep't 1990)
9 ALR5th 568—§ 9
3 ALR6th 447—§ 3, 7

Shoenfelt v. Donna Belle Loan & Inv. Co., 1935 OK 579, 172 Okla. 346, 45 P.2d 507 (1935)
73 ALR6th 571—§ 17

Shoff v. Shoff, 179 Ill. App. 3d 178, 128 Ill. Dec. 280, 534 N.E.2d 462 (5th Dist. 1989)
118 ALR5th 385—§ 20

Shoffner Industries, Inc. v. W. B. Lloyd Const. Co., 42 N.C. App. 259, 257 S.E.2d 50 (1979)
61 ALR6th 445—§ 4

Shofner v. Baptist Healthcare Affiliates, Inc., 2003 WL 22025906 (Ky. Ct. App. 2003)
64 ALR6th 249—§ 4

Shofner v. Jackson, 2007 WL 1002492 (Tenn. Ct. App. 2007)
42 ALR6th 463—§ 20

Shofner v. Red Food Stores (Tennessee), Inc., 970 S.W.2d 468 (Tenn. Ct. App. 1997)
31 ALR5th 550—§ 3, 4

Shofstall v. Allied Van Lines, Inc., 455 F. Supp. 351 (N.D. Ill. 1978)
48 ALR5th 389—§ 3, 5
52 ALR5th 491—§ 3

Shofstall v. Hollins, 110 Ariz. 88, 515 P.2d 590 (1973)
110 ALR5th 293—§ 3

Shohatee v. Jackson, 257 Fed. Appx. 968 (6th Cir. 2007)
65 ALR6th 537—§ 45, 58

Shohatee v. Jackson, 2006 WL 1109234 (E.D. Mich. 2006)
65 ALR6th 537—§ 58

Shohfi v. Shohfi, 277 A.D. 390, 100 N.Y.S.2d 497 (2d Dep't 1950)
36 ALR6th 387—§ 5

Shohola Falls Trails End Property Owners Ass'n, Inc. v. Zoning Hearing Bd. of Shohola Tp., Pike County, Pa., 679 A.2d 1335 (Pa. Commw. Ct. 1996)
73 ALR5th 223—§ 3, 11

Shoichi Otsuki v. Shigeru Date Yamauchi, 93 Colo. 458, 26 P.2d 805 (1933)
46 ALR6th 185—§ 13

Sholar v. U. S. Fire Ins. Co., 261 So. 2d 327 (La. Ct. App. 1st Cir. 1972)
87 ALR5th 1—§ 10, 19, 33

Sholer v. State ex rel. Dep't of Public Safety, 945 P.2d 469 (Okla. 1995)
2 ALR5th 725—§ 12

Sholer v. State ex rel. Dept. of Public Safety, 2006 OK CIV APP 145, 149 P.3d 1040 (Div. 4 2006)
35 ALR6th 1—§ 28, 30

Sholes v. Agency Rent-A-Car, Inc., 76 Ohio App. 3d 349, 601 N.E.2d 634 (Cuyahoga Co. 1991)
17 ALR5th 1—§ 4

ShoLodge, Inc. v. Travelers Indem. Co. of Illinois, 168 F.3d 256, 49 U.S.P.Q.2d (BNA) 1694, 1999 FED App. 43P (6th Cir. 1999)

98 ALR5th 1—§ 12

Sholtis v. American Cyanamid Co., 238 N.J. Super. 8, 568 A.2d 1196, Prod. Liab. Rep. (CCH) ¶ 12361 (App. Div. 1989)
63 ALR5th 195—§ 4

Sholtis v. City of Fresno, 2009 WL 4030674 (E.D. Cal. 2009)
89 ALR6th 1—§ 113
101 ALR6th 207—§ 35

Sholty v. Carruth, 126 Ariz. 458, 616 P.2d 918 (App. 1980)
40 ALR5th 227—§ 23

Shomaker v. George Washington University, 669 A.2d 1291, 106 Ed. Law Rep. 726 (D.C. 1995)
97 ALR6th 83—§ 108, 109, 113

Shontz v. Iowa Employment Sec. Commission, 248 N.W.2d 88 (Iowa 1976)
68 ALR5th 13—§ 13, 23

Shook v. Ackert, 152 Or. App. 224, 952 P.2d 1044 (1998)
29 ALR5th 487—§ 3

Shook v. Hertz Corp., 349 A.2d 874 (Del. Super. Ct. 1975)
16 ALR6th 491—§ 4

Shook v. Shook, 651 So. 2d 6 (Ala. Civ. App. 1994)
40 ALR5th 227—§ 35
80 ALR5th 117—§ 4, 5

Shook v. State, 27 Ill. Ct. Cl. 29, 1969 WL 8212 (Ill. Ct. Cl. 1969)
53 ALR6th 305—§ 18

Shook v. State, 221 Ga. App. 151, 470 S.E.2d 535 (1996)
34 ALR6th 539—§ 3

Shook v. State, 948 N.E.2d 870 (Ind. Ct. App. 2011)
77 ALR6th 197—§ 5

Shooltz v. Shooltz, 27 Va. App. 264, 498 S.E.2d 437 (1998)
9 ALR5th 568—§ 9

Shoop v. Shoop, 58 S.D. 593, 237 N.W. 904 (1931)
47 ALR5th 129—§ 7, 11

Shoopman v. Travelers Ins. Co., 518 P.2d 1108 (Okla. 1974)

21 ALR5th 82—§ 3, 12

Shooshanian v. Wagner, 672 P.2d 455, 37 U.C.C. Rep. Serv. 55 (Alaska 1983)

89 ALR5th 319—§ 10, 23

Shooting Point, L.L.C. v. Wescoat, 265 Va. 256, 576 S.E.2d 497 (2003)

111 ALR5th 313—§ 5

Shopco Distribution Co., Inc. v. Commanding General of Marine Corps Base, Camp Lejeune, North Carolina, 885 F.2d 167 (4th Cir. 1989)

70 ALR6th 513—§ 11

71 ALR6th 471—§ 9

Shopco Group, The v. Springdale, 66 Ohio App. 3d 702, 586 N.E.2d 145 (1st Dist. Hamilton County 1990)

55 ALR6th 635—§ 5

Shope v. Industrial Commission, 17 Ariz. App. 23, 495 P.2d 148 (Div. 1 1972)

84 ALR5th 249—§ 14

106 ALR5th 111—§ 18, 21, 26

108 ALR5th 1—§ 27

Shoppes Ltd. Partnership v. Conn, 829 So. 2d 356 (Fla. Dist. Ct. App. 5th Dist. 2002)

32 ALR6th 419—§ 32

Shop Rite Foods, Inc. v. Upjohn Co., 619 S.W.2d 574, CCH Prod. Liab. Rep. ¶ 9105 (Tex. Civ. App. Amarillo 1981)

3 ALR5th 851—§ 14 to 16

Shor v. Schneider, 1990 WL 67924 (Ohio Ct. App. 1st Dist. Hamilton County 1990)

17 ALR6th 159—§ 34, 36

Shorb by Shorb v. Airco, Inc., 644 F. Supp. 923, Prod. Liab. Rep. (CCH) ¶ 11264 (E.D. Pa. 1986)

112 ALR5th 113—§ 4

18 ALR6th 629—§ 5, 15

Shore, In re Estate of, 605 So. 2d 951 (Fla. 4th DCA 1992)

87 ALR6th 495—§ 27, 71, 77

Shore, In re Marriage of, 135 Ohio App. 3d 374, 734 N.E.2d 395 (8th Dist. Cuyahoga County 1999)

95 ALR5th 533—§ 4

124 ALR5th 203—§ 4, 14

Shore v. Farmer, 515 S.E.2d 495 (N.C. Ct. App. 1999)

35 ALR5th 1—§ 11

Shore v. Stonington, 187 Conn. 147, 444 A.2d 1379 (1982)

9 ALR5th 969—§ 3

Shore Acres Nursing Home v. Sturms, 439 So. 2d 988 (Fla. App. D1 1983)

12 ALR5th 658—§ 2

Shore Block Corp. v. Lakeview Apartments, 377 F.2d 835, 67-2 USTC ¶ 9492 (CA3 N.J. 1967)

4 ALR5th 772—§ 80, 81, 86, 96

Shorehaven in Manhasset, Inc. v. Great Neck Estates, 22 N.Y.S.2d 944 (Sup. 1940)

2 ALR5th 553—§ 68

Shoreline, City of v. Club for Free Speech Rights, 109 Wash. App. 696, 36 P.3d 1058 (Div. 1 2001)

20 ALR6th 161—§ 3

21 ALR6th 425—§ 9

23 ALR6th 573—§ 13

Shoreline School Dist. No. 412, State ex rel. v. Superior Court for King County, Juvenile Court, 55 Wash. 2d 177, 346 P.2d 999 (1959)

70 ALR5th 169—§ 25

6 ALR6th 161—§ 5, 15

Shorenstein v. Pacific Ins. Co., 216 A.D.2d 122, 628 N.Y.S.2d 641 (1st Dep't 1995)

92 ALR5th 273—§ 19

Shores v. Chip Steak Co., 130 Cal. App. 2d 620, 279 P.2d 591 (2d Dist. 1955)

85 ALR6th 1—§ 29

Shores v. Senior Manor Nursing Center, Inc., 164 Ill. App. 3d 503, 115 Ill. Dec. 946, 518 N.E.2d 471 (5th Dist. 1988)

93 ALR5th 269—§ 3, 8

105 ALR5th 351—§ 4

Shores v. Shores, 670 F. Supp. 774 (E.D. Tenn. 1987)

5 ALR5th 788—§ 10, 15

20 ALR5th 700—§ 8, 63
Shores v. Spann, 557 S.W.2d 67 (Tenn. App. 1977)
50 ALR5th 417—§ 2
Shores v. Troglin, 260 Ga. App. 696, 580 S.E.2d 659 (2003)
11 ALR6th 1—§ 4, 6
Shore, Shirley & Co. v. Kelley, 40 Ohio App. 3d 10, 531 N.E.2d 333 (Cuyahoga Co. 1988)
12 ALR5th 195—§ 4, 66
Shorewood v. Steinberg, 174 Wis. 2d 191, 496 N.W.2d 57 (1993)
10 ALR5th 448—§ 6
Shorey v. Lincoln Pulp & Paper Co., 511 A.2d 1076 (Me. 1986)
37 ALR5th 645—§ 2, 3, 7, 8, 11, 12
Shorr v. Professional Photographers of America, Inc., 1997 Mass. App. Div. 61, 1997 WL 271757 (1997)
119 ALR5th 121—§ 4, 5
2 ALR6th 279—§ 20, 21
34 ALR6th 431—§ 4, 5
Shors v. Branch, 221 Mont. 390, 720 P.2d 239 (1986)
10 ALR5th 448—§ 3
Short, In re, 205 App. Div. 2d 99, 617 N.Y.S.2d 866 (2d Dep't 1994)
1 ALR5th 874—§ 9
Short, In re, 2010 WL 4736209 (Bankr. D. Md. 2010)
99 ALR6th 481—§ 56, 58, 76
Short, In re Marriage of, 698 P.2d 1310 (Colo. 1985)
95 ALR5th 533—§ 3
124 ALR5th 203—§ 3, 6, 7, 9
Short v. Boss, 198 Wis. 586, 225 N.W. 197 (1929)
31 ALR5th 572—§ 25
Short v. Bridwell, 1992 WL 178665 (E.D. La. 1992)
97 ALR5th 473—§ 13
Short v. Central Louisiana Electric Co., 36 So. 2d 658 (La. App. 2d Cir. 1948)
46 ALR5th 423—§ 3, 12
Short v. City of Birmingham, 393 So. 2d 518 (Ala. Crim. App. 1981)

72 ALR5th 1—§ 14, 30
Short v. Commissioner of Public Safety, 422 N.W.2d 40 (Minn. Ct. App. 1988)
93 ALR6th 207—§ 14, 16
96 ALR6th 355—§ 51
Short v. Commonwealth, 291 Ky. 604, 165 S.W.2d 177 (1942)
81 ALR5th 563—§ 5
Short v. Downs, 36 Colo. App. 109, 537 P.2d 754 (1975)
28 ALR5th 497—§ 3, 7
35 ALR5th 145—§ 3
108 ALR5th 385—§ 19
Short v. Greensboro, 15 N.C. App. 135, 189 S.E.2d 560 (1972)
57 ALR5th 689—§ 14
Short v. Jones, 1980 OK 87, 613 P.2d 452 (Okla. 1980)
85 ALR5th 671—§ 5
Short v. Miller, 166 Ga. App. 265, 304 S.E.2d 434 (1983)
27 ALR5th 174—§ 80
Short v. Morrison, 159 La. 193, 105 So. 286 (1925)
101 ALR6th 455—§ 6
Short v. Motor Vehicle Acc. Indemnification Corp., 42 Misc. 2d 682, 248 N.Y.S.2d 664 (Sup. Ct. 1964)
103 ALR5th 1—§ 5, 7, 12
Short v. Otis Elevator Co., 502 So. 2d 1100, Prod. Liab. Rep. (CCH) ¶ 11449 (La. Ct. App. 4th Cir. 1987)
99 ALR5th 141—§ 14
115 ALR5th 1—§ 9 to 11
117 ALR5th 267—§ 4, 20, 24, 28
Short v. Philadelphia, B. & W. R. Co., 23 Del. 108, 7 Penne 108, 76 A. 363 (1908)
42 ALR5th 465—§ 3
Short v. Plantation Management Corp., 299 La. App. 1 Cir. 12/27/00, 2000 WL 1874228 (La. Ct. App. 1st Cir. 2000)
87 ALR5th 277—§ 50
Short v. Prime Care Medical-WV, 2008 WL 780637 (S.D. W. Va. 2008)
65 ALR6th 93—§ 46

For assistance, call 1-800-328-4880

Short v. Safeco Ins. Co. of Am., 864 S.W.2d 361 (Mo. App. 1993)
  43 ALR5th 149—§ 13, 15

Short v. Short, 730 F. Supp. 1037 (D.C. Colo. 1990)
  14 ALR5th 929—§ 2, 3

Short v. State, 586 A.2d 1203 (Del. 1991)
  85 ALR6th 641—§ 5

Short v. State, 929 S.W.2d 13 (Tex. Crim. App. 1996)
  105 ALR5th 529—§ 12

Short v. State, 995 S.W.2d 948 (Tex. App. Fort Worth 1999)
  45 ALR5th 767—§ 12

Short v. State, 1999 OK CR 15, 980 P.2d 1081 (Okla. Crim. App. 1999)
  83 ALR6th 255—§ 9, 12

Short v. State, 1999 OK CR 15, 1999 OK CR 15, 980 P.2d 1081 (Okla. Crim. App. 1999)
  79 ALR5th 33—§ 53

Short v. State, 2009 WY 52, 205 P.3d 195, 70 A.L.R.6th 745 (Wyo. 2009)
  70 ALR6th 361—§ 31

Short v. U.S., 245 F. Supp. 591 (D.C. Del. 1965)
  27 ALR5th 174—§ 3, 4, 104

Short v. U.S., 908 F. Supp. 227 (D. Vt. 1995)
  48 ALR5th 575—§ 14

Shortall v. Puget Sound Bridge & Dredging Co., 45 Wash. 290, 88 P. 212 (1907)
  11 ALR5th 715—§ 3

Short Bros., PLC v. U.S., 65 Fed. Cl. 695 (2005)
  104 ALR6th 303—§ 13

Short Clove Assocs. v. Ilana Realty, Inc., 154 B.R. 21 (S.D. N.Y. 1993)
  39 ALR5th 33—§ 12

Shorten v. State, 751 S.W.2d 262 (Tex. App. Beaumont 1988)
  11 ALR5th 497—§ 3, 12, 17, 19, 23

Shorter v. Drury, 103 Wash. 2d 645, 695 P.2d 116 (1985)
  3 ALR5th 721—§ 4, 7

  108 ALR5th 385—§ 9, 18

Shorter v. Lawson, 403 F. Supp. 2d 703 (N.D. Ind. 2005)
  89 ALR6th 1—§ 115

Shorter v. State, 946 So. 2d 815 (Miss. Ct. App. 2007)
  43 ALR6th 475—§ 8, 21

Shorter's Estate, In re, 444 A.2d 954 (D.C. 1982)
  86 ALR6th 321—§ 4
  90 ALR6th 451—§ 90

Shortes v. State, 193 Ga. App. 859, 389 S.E.2d 354 (1989)
  5 ALR5th 243—§ 62

Short, Estate of v. Commissioner, 68 TC 184 (F. 1977)
  31 ALR5th 499—§ 3

Shorthose v. Shorthose, 319 Ill. App. 355, 49 N.E.2d 280 (3d Dist. 1943)
  101 ALR6th 455—§ 13

Shorthouse, Ex parte, 640 S.W.2d 924 (Tex. Crim. 1982)
  29 ALR5th 1—§ 3

Short On Cash.Net of New Castle, Inc. v. Department of Financial Institutions, 811 N.E.2d 819 (Ind. Ct. App. 2004)
  29 ALR6th 461—§ 6

Shortridge v. Deel, 224 Va. 589, 299 S.E.2d 500 (1983)
  15 ALR5th 692—§ 4, 8

Shorts v. Gambino, 570 So. 2d 209 (La. App. 5th Cir. 1990)
  12 ALR5th 1—§ 25

Shortt v. City of Chicago, 160 Ill. App. 3d 933, 112 Ill. Dec. 607, 514 N.E.2d 3 (1st Dist. 1987)
  64 ALR5th 519—§ 10, 20

Short Term Housing, Inc. v. Department of State, 176 App. Div. 2d 619, 575 N.Y.S.2d 61 (1st Dep't 1991)
  7 ALR5th 474—§ 183

Shortz v. Farrell, 327 Pa. 81, 193 A. 20 (1937)
  8 ALR5th 653—§ 3, 7
  58 ALR5th 449—§ 2, 8, 9

Shortz v. Yetter, 38 Pa. D. & C. 291, 1940 WL 2486 (C.P. 1940)

---

32 ALR6th 531—§ 37
Shotkin v. Cohen, 163 So. 2d 330 (Fla. App. D3 1964)
8 ALR5th 653—§ 3
Shotkin, State ex rel. v. Buchanan, 149 So. 2d 574, 98 A.L.R.2d 683 (Fla. Dist. Ct. App. 3d Dist. 1963)
76 ALR5th 485—§ 3, 18
Shotkoski v. Standard Chemical Mfg. Co., 195 Neb. 22, 237 N.W.2d 92, 18 U.C.C. Rep. Serv. 328 (1975)
88 ALR6th 1—§ 20, 110
Shotmeyer v. New Jersey Realty Title Ins. Co., 195 N.J. 72, 948 A.2d 600 (2008)
70 ALR6th 209—§ 16, 26
Shotthafer, In re Compensation of, 169 Or. App. 556, 2000 WL 1224816 (2000)
84 ALR5th 249—§ 14
Shotto v. Laub, 632 F. Supp. 516 (D. Md. 1986)
22 ALR6th 49—§ 4, 11
Shotts v. OP Winter Haven, Inc., 988 So. 2d 639 (Fla. Dist. Ct. App. 2d Dist. 2008)
50 ALR6th 187—§ 8, 12
Shouey ex rel. Litz v. Duck Head Apparel Co., Inc., 49 F. Supp. 2d 413, Prod. Liab. Rep. (CCH) ¶ 15594 (M.D. Pa. 1999)
14 ALR5th 47—§ 3
Shoultz v. McPheeters, 79 Ind. 373, 1881 WL 6822 (1881)
97 ALR5th 537—§ 18
Shoultz v. State, 735 N.E.2d 818 (Ind. Ct. App. 2000)
66 ALR6th 397—§ 6
65 ALR6th 93—§ 19
Shoup v. Holman, 81 Ohio App. 3d 127, 610 N.E.2d 502 (9th Dist. Summit County 1991)
86 ALR6th 321—§ 4, 12
87 ALR6th 197—§ 73
Shoup v. Shoup, 257 Pa. Super. 263, 390 A.2d 814 (1978)
95 ALR5th 533—§ 4
124 ALR5th 203—§ 4

Shovak v. Long Island Commercial Bank, 50 A.D.3d 1118, 858 N.Y.S.2d 660 (2d Dep't 2008)
46 ALR6th 185—§ 12
Shovelin v. Central New Mexico Elec. Co-op., Inc., 115 N.M. 293, 850 P.2d 996, 8 I.E.R. Cas. (BNA) 654, 38 A.L.R.5th 819 (1993)
104 ALR5th 1—§ 3, 4, 13
Shovelin v. Central N.M. Elec Coop., 115 N.M. 293, 850 P.2d 996, 8 BNA IER Cas. 654, 38 A.L.R.5th 819 (1993)
38 ALR5th 39—§ 9
Shover v. Iowa Lutheran Hospital, 252 Iowa 706, 107 N.W.2d 85 (1961)
26 ALR5th 401—§ 4, 7 to 9, 18, 27
Shovlin v. University of Medicine and Dentistry of New Jersey (UMDNJ), 50 F. Supp. 2d 297, 136 Ed. Law Rep. 328 (D.N.J. 1998)
41 ALR6th 391—§ 18
Showalter v. Rinard, 752 F. Supp. 963 (D.C. Or. 1990)
6 ALR5th 297—§ 45
Showell v. Atkins, 483 A.2d 1113 (Del. Sup. 1984)
9 ALR5th 826—§ 11
Showell v. State, 886 A.2d 1278 (Del. 2005)
79 ALR6th 125—§ 18
Showen, State ex rel. v. O'Brien, 89 W. Va. 634, 109 S.E. 830 (1921)
49 ALR5th 595—§ 4
Showers v. Laughlin, 497 So. 2d 361 (La. App. 3d Cir. 1986)
48 ALR5th 129—§ 20
Showers v. Spangler, 957 F. Supp. 584 (M.D. Pa. 1997)
50 ALR5th 703—§ 37, 40
Show-Me Restoration Services v. Harlan, 778 S.W.2d 350 (Mo. App. 1989)
8 ALR5th 653—§ 3
Showmethemoney Check Cashers, Inc. v. Williams, 342 Ark. 112, 27 S.W.3d 361 (2000)
29 ALR6th 461—§ 8

Shows v. Freeman, 230 So. 2d 63 (Miss. 1969)
58 ALR5th 1—§ 7, 25
Shows v. Jamison Bedding, Inc., 671 F.2d 927, 33 FR Serv. 2d 1488 (CA5 Miss. 1982)
48 ALR5th 129—§ 12, 14
50 ALR5th 1—§ 3, 11
Shows v. Morgan, 40 F. Supp. 2d 1345 (M.D. Ala. 1999)
100 ALR5th 341—§ 7
Shows v. Shows, 345 So. 2d 975 (La. Ct. App. 2d Cir. 1977)
36 ALR6th 1—§ 3, 26, 28
Shpikula v. State, 68 S.W.3d 212 (Tex. App. Houston 1st Dist. 2002)
55 ALR6th 513—§ 8, 12
Shpritzman v. Strong, 248 A.D.2d 524, 670 N.Y.S.2d 50 (2d Dep't 1998)
62 ALR5th 537—§ 4
Shqeirat v. U.S. Airways Group, Inc., 515 F. Supp. 2d 984 (D. Minn. 2007)
54 ALR6th 99—§ 23
Shrader v. Holland, 186 W. Va. 687, 414 S.E.2d 448 (1992)
30 ALR5th 699—§ 6
Shrader v. Life General Sec. Ins. Co., 588 So. 2d 1309 (La. Ct. App. 2d Cir. 1991)
115 ALR5th 589—§ 12
Shrader v. Monforte, 622 N.Y.S.2d 362 (App. Div. 3d Dep't 1995)
6 ALR5th 242—§ 10
Shrader v. State, 101 Nev. 499, 706 P.2d 834 (1985)
24 ALR5th 428—§ 19
Shrader v. State, 159 Ga. App. 522, 284 S.E.2d 37 (1981)
112 ALR5th 429—§ 13
Shrauger v. Shrauger, 146 App. Div. 2d 955, 537 N.Y.S.2d 84 (3d Dep't 1989)
17 ALR5th 366—§ 10
Shreiner v. Cummins, 63 Pa. 374, 1869 WL 7692 (1869)
98 ALR5th 353—§ 3

Shreve v. Duke Power Co., 97 N.C. App. 648, 389 S.E.2d 444 (1990)
53 ALR6th 213—§ 10
Shreve v. Faris, 144 W. Va. 819, 111 S.E.2d 169 (1959)
26 ALR5th 401—§ 4, 33
Shreve v. Jessamine County Fiscal Court, 453 F.3d 681, 2006 FED App. 0235P (6th Cir. 2006)
65 ALR6th 93—§ 29
Shreveport v. Bernstein, 391 So. 2d 1331 (La. App. 2d Cir. 1980)
10 ALR5th 448—§ 6
Shreveport v. Kleowdis, 408 So. 2d 956 (La. App. 2d Cir. 1981)
30 ALR5th 494—§ 2, 4
Shreveport v. Pupillo, 390 So. 2d 941 (La. App. 2d Cir. 1980)
10 ALR5th 448—§ 6
Shreveport Armature & Electric Works, Inc. v. Harwell, 172 So. 463 (La. App. 1937)
46 ALR5th 1—§ 45
Shreveport Long Leaf Lumber Co. v. Parker, 144 So. 153 (La. App. 1932)
46 ALR5th 1—§ 7
Shreves v. Radiology Associates, Inc., 1994 WL 682525 (Del. Super. Ct. 1994)
57 ALR5th 1—§ 14
Shriner v. Minnesota, 129 S. Ct. 1001, 173 L. Ed. 2d 292 (2009)
46 ALR6th 495—§ 6
Shriner v. Simmons, 483 S.W.2d 324 (Tex. Civ. App. San Antonio 1972)
102 ALR5th 227—§ 4
Shriners Hospitals for Crippled Children v. St. Jude Children's Research Hospital, Inc., 629 S.W.2d 767 (Tex. Civ. App. Dallas 1981)
1 ALR5th 965—§ 3, 5
Shrink Missouri Government PAC v. Adams, 5 F. Supp. 2d 734 (E.D. Mo. 1998)
24 ALR6th 179—§ 6
Shrink Missouri Government PAC v. Adams, 161 F.3d 519 (8th Cir. 1998)

For assistance, call 1-800-328-4880

24 ALR6th 179—§ 3, 4
Shrink Missouri Government PAC v. Adams, 204 F.3d 838 (8th Cir. 2000)

24 ALR6th 179—§ 4
Shrink Missouri Government PAC v. Maupin, 71 F.3d 1422 (8th Cir. 1995)

53 ALR6th 491—§ 20, 22
Shrink Missouri Government PAC v. Maupin, 892 F. Supp. 1246 (E.D. Mo. 1995)

53 ALR6th 491—§ 20, 22
Shrink Missouri Government PAC v. Maupin, 922 F. Supp. 1413 (E.D. Mo. 1996)

24 ALR6th 179—§ 24, 26
Shriver v. Baskin-Robbins Ice Cream Co., 145 F.R.D. 112 (D.C. Colo. 1992)

26 ALR5th 628—§ 18
27 ALR5th 76—§ 14
Shriver v. Carlin & Fulton Co., 155 Md. 51, 141 A. 434 (1928)

100 ALR5th 409—§ 2
Shriver v. Shriver, 7 Ohio App. 2d 169, 36 Ohio Op. 2d 308, 219 N.E.2d 300 (3d Dist. Union County 1966)

71 ALR5th 99—§ 6
Shroades, State ex rel. v. Henry, 187 W. Va. 723, 421 S.E.2d 264 (1992)

69 ALR5th 559—§ 2, 7, 9
Shropshire v. State, 12 Ark. 190, 1851 WL 449 (1851)

85 ALR5th 471—§ 2
Shrout v. Black Clawson Co., 689 F. Supp. 774, 46 BNA FEP Cas. 1339, 3 BNA IER Cas. 492, 46 CCH EPD ¶ 37994 (S.D. Ohio 1988)

12 ALR5th 195—§ 33, 68
Shrout v. Black Clawson Co., 689 F. Supp. 774, 46 Fair Empl. Prac. Cas. (BNA) 1339, 3 I.E.R. Cas. (BNA) 492, 46 Empl. Prac. Dec. (CCH) ¶ 37994 (S.D. Ohio 1988)

20 ALR6th 1—§ 4
Shrout v. Lewis, 147 Kan. 592, 77 P.2d 973 (1938)

40 ALR6th 99—§ 19
Shroyer v. McCarthy, 769 S.W.2d 156 (Mo. Ct. App. W.D. 1989)

95 ALR6th 85—§ 22
Shroyer v. Sokol, 191 Colo. 32, 550 P.2d 309 (1976)

13 ALR6th 661—§ 26
Shrum v. Atlantic Crushed Coke Co., 186 Pa. Super. 377, 142 A.2d 792 (1958)

100 ALR5th 567—§ 5
Shrv Teletype Coin Exchange, Inc. v. Commercial Union Ins. Co., 191 So. 2d 208 (La. App. 2d Cir. 1966)

55 ALR5th 681—§ 6
Shryock, Commonwealth ex rel. v. Dietz (1952) 68 Montg Co LR 309

124 ALR5th 203—§ 4
Shubat v. Sutter County Assessment Appeals Bd., 13 Cal. App. 4th 794, 17 Cal. Rptr. 2d 1 (3d Dist. 1993)

90 ALR5th 547—§ 2, 5, 8, 14, 15, 23
Shubert, Matter of, 677 N.Y.S.2d 815 (App. Div. 3d Dep't 1998)

68 ALR5th 13—§ 19
Shubert v. State, 518 S.W.2d 326 (Mo. Ct. App. 1975)

70 ALR5th 1—§ 7, 8
72 ALR5th 109—§ 7
Shubert v. W.C.A.B. (C.M. American), 110 Pa. Commw. 137, 531 A.2d 1189 (1987)

82 ALR5th 149—§ 2, 4, 48
Shubin v. William Lyon Homes, Inc., 84 Cal. App. 4th 1041, 101 Cal. Rptr. 2d 390 (1st Dist. 2000)

60 ALR5th 669—§ 5
Shubov, In re, 25 A.D.3d 33, 802 N.Y.S.2d 437 (1st Dep't 2005)

46 ALR6th 365—§ 8
87 ALR6th 1—§ 89
Shubutidze, In re, 2001 WL 233400 (Ohio Ct. App. 8th Dist. Cuyahoga County 2001)

19 ALR6th 697—§ 6
Shuck v. City of Sioux Falls, 79 S.D. 505, 113 N.W.2d 849 (1962)

54 ALR6th 201—§ 11

Shuck v. Keefe, 205 Iowa 365, 218 N.W. 31 (1928)

20 ALR5th 1—§ 6, 38, 45

Shuda v. Williams, 2008 WL 4661455 (D. Neb. 2008)

95 ALR6th 341—§ 46

Shue v. State, 129 Ga. App. 757, 201 S.E.2d 174 (1973)

61 ALR5th 1—§ 3, 9

Shue v. State, 366 So. 2d 387 (Fla. 1978)

62 ALR5th 121—§ 8

Shufelt v. Beaudoin, 116 A.D.2d 422, 501 N.Y.S.2d 532 (3d Dep't 1986)

88 ALR6th 203—§ 50

Shufelt v. Department of Employment & Training, 148 Vt. 163, 531 A.2d 894 (1987)

2 ALR5th 475—§ 8

Shuff v. Fulte, 344 Ill. App. 157, 100 N.E.2d 502 (3d Dist. 1951)

55 ALR5th 557—§ 5

Shufflebarger by Oktavec v. Shufflebarger, 460 So. 2d 982 (Fla. Dist. Ct. App. 3d Dist. 1984)

2 ALR6th 439—§ 48

Shuford v. Asheville Oil Co., 243 N.C. 636, 91 S.E.2d 903 (1956)

76 ALR5th 337—§ 20

Shuford v. McIntosh, 104 N.C. App. 201, 408 S.E.2d 747 (1991)

41 ALR5th 771—§ 2 to 4

Shugar v. Pat Walker Figure Perfection Salons Intern., 541 S.W.2d 511 (Tex. Civ. App. Eastland 1976)

76 ALR6th 395—§ 5

Shugart v. State, 32 S.W.3d 355 (Tex. App. Waco 2000)

3 ALR5th 521—§ 17
57 ALR5th 141—§ 4

Shuggars v. Brake, 248 Md. 38, 234 A.2d 752 (1967)

62 ALR5th 219—§ 10

Shulansky v. Rodriguez, 44 Conn. Supp. 72, 669 A.2d 638, Blue Sky L. Rep. (CCH) ¶ 74097 (Super Ct. 1994)

58 ALR5th 293—§ 4

Shulenberger v. Shulenberger, 15 Phila. 237 (1987)

72 ALR5th 249—§ 14

Shulenberger v. Shulenberger, 1987 Phil Cty Rptr. (Pa. 1987)

16 ALR5th 650—§ 30
20 ALR5th 700—§ 44

Shuler v. School Board, 366 So. 2d 1184 (Fla. App. D1 1978)

47 ALR5th 553—§ 16

Shuler v. Shuler, 371 So. 2d 588 (Fla. Dist. Ct. App. 1st Dist. 1979)

71 ALR5th 99—§ 3, 6

Shuler v. Wainwright, 341 F. Supp. 1061 (M.D. Fla. 1972)

102 ALR5th 327—§ 3

Shuler v. Wainwright, 491 F.2d 1213 (5th Cir. 1974)

102 ALR5th 327—§ 2, 3, 6

Shulgan v. Noetzel, 2008 WL 1730091 (E.D. Wash. 2008)

45 ALR6th 1—§ 7, 25

Shull v. Shepherd, 63 Wash. 2d 503, 387 P.2d 767 (1963)

69 ALR5th 219—§ 4

Shulman v. Miskell, 200 U.S. App. D.C. 1, 626 F.2d 173 (App. D.C. 1980)

61 ALR5th 307—§ 3

Shulman v. Safir, 249 A.D.2d 10, 670 N.Y.S.2d 838 (1st Dep't 1998)

91 ALR6th 435—§ 63, 123

Shulman v. Washington Hospital Center, 222 F. Supp. 59 (D.C. Dist. Col. 1963)

28 ALR5th 107—§ 3, 5

Shulman v. Washington Hospital Center, 319 F. Supp. 252 (D.C. Dist. Col. 1970)

28 ALR5th 107—§ 5, 18

Shultes v. Carr, 127 A.D.2d 916, 512 N.Y.S.2d 276 (3d Dep't 1987)

91 ALR5th 1—§ 3

Shult Homes Corp. v. Maurice, 348 So. 2d 1217 (Fla. App. D4 1977)

23 ALR5th 241—§ 47

Shults, In re, 97 B.R. 874 (Bankr. N.D. Tex. 1989)

83 ALR6th 605—§ 5

Shults v. Champion Int'l Corp., 821 F. Supp. 517 (E.D. Tenn. 1992)

For assistance, call 1-800-328-4880

25 ALR5th 568—§ 37

Shults v. State, 575 S.W.2d 29 (Tex. Crim. 1979)

4 ALR5th 1—§ 15

Shults v. State, 696 S.W.2d 126 (Tex. App. Dallas 1985)

6 ALR5th 652—§ 2, 3

Shults v. U.S., 995 F. Supp. 1270 (D. Kan. 1998)

86 ALR5th 693—§ 3, 4

Shultz v. Barko Hydraulics, Inc., a Div. of Pettibone Corp., 832 F. Supp. 142, 27 Fed. R. Serv. 3d 1055 (W.D. Pa. 1993)

102 ALR5th 99—§ 4

Shultz v. Linden-Alimak, Inc., 734 P.2d 146, Prod. Liab. Rep. (CCH) ¶ 11222, 3 U.C.C. Rep. Serv. 2d 1385 (Colo. Ct. App. 1986)

117 ALR5th 267—§ 13, 14, 22, 23

Shultz v. Rice, 809 F.2d 643, 22 Fed. Rules Evid. Serv. 224 (CA10 Kan. 1986)

11 ALR5th 1—§ 20

Shultz v. Ritterbusch, 1913 OK 462, 38 Okla. 478, 134 P. 961 (1913)

73 ALR6th 571—§ 46

Shultz v. Shultz, 1998 WL 463480 (Wash. Ct. App. Div. 1 1998)

80 ALR5th 487—§ 3, 16

Shultz v. State, 811 P.2d 1322 (Okla. Crim. 1991)

42 ALR5th 291—§ 6, 22

Shultz v. State, 1986 OK CR 34, 715 P.2d 485 (Okla. Crim. App. 1986)

54 ALR6th 429—§ 25

Shultz v. State, 1991 OK CR 57, 811 P.2d 1322 (Okla. Crim. App. 1991)

111 ALR5th 239—§ 11

65 ALR6th 537—§ 13, 62

Shultz v. W.C.A.B. (Leroy Roofing Co.), 154 Pa. Commw. 34, 621 A.2d 1239 (1993)

63 ALR6th 1—§ 5, 64

Shulz v. Griffith, 103 Iowa 150, 72 N.W. 445 (1897)

11 ALR5th 127—§ 4

Shumaker, In re, 124 B.R. 820 (Bankr. D. Mont. 1991)

77 ALR6th 273—§ 4

Shumaker v. Johnson, 571 So. 2d 991 (Ala. 1990)

6 ALR6th 311—§ 5

Shumaker v. U.S., 714 F. Supp. 154 (M.D. N.C. 1988)

30 ALR5th 571—§ 18, 73

Shuman v. City of Ft. Wayne, 127 Ind. 109, 26 N.E. 560 (1891)

16 ALR6th 219—§ 5, 17, 19

Shuman v. City of Philadelphia, 470 F. Supp. 449, 19 Empl. Prac. Dec. (CCH) ¶ 9248 (E.D. Pa. 1979)

123 ALR5th 411—§ 7, 56

Shuman v. Laverne Farmers Coop., 809 P.2d 76, CCH Prod. Liab. Rep. ¶ 12928 (Okla. App. 1991)

14 ALR5th 242—§ 22

Shuman v. Mashburn, 137 Ga. App. 231, 223 S.E.2d 268, 85 A.L.R.3d 741 (1976)

64 ALR5th 1—§ 14

Shuman v. Mayor & Aldermen of Savannah, 180 Ga. App. 427, 349 S.E.2d 239 (1986)

50 ALR6th 95—§ 7

Shumate, Matter of, 647 N.E.2d 321 (Ind. 1995)

96 ALR5th 23—§ 6

Shumate v. Lycan, 675 N.E.2d 749 (Ind. App. 1997)

54 ALR5th 513—§ 3

Shumate v. Newland, 75 F. Supp. 2d 1076 (N.D. Cal. 1999)

87 ALR5th 693—§ 4

Shumate v. Pacific Ins. Co., 162 F.3d 1174 (10th Cir. 1998)

92 ALR5th 273—§ 9

Shumsky v. Eisenstein, 96 N.Y.2d 164, 726 N.Y.S.2d 365, 750 N.E.2d 67 (2001)

11 ALR6th 1—§ 4, 6

Shumsky v. Eisenstein, 96 N.Y.2d 164, 2001 WL 499224 (2001)

87 ALR5th 473—§ 4

Shumway, In re Estate of, 198 Ariz. 323

3 ALR5th 590—§ 17

Shumway v. Kelley, 60 A.D.3d 1457, 876 N.Y.S.2d 299 (4th Dep't 2009)

44 ALR6th 545—§ 9

Shumway v. United Parcel Service, Inc., 118 F.3d 60, 74 Fair Empl. Prac. Cas. (BNA) 26, 70 Empl. Prac. Dec. (CCH) ¶ 44788 (2d Cir. 1997)

71 ALR5th 257—§ 5

Shunk v. State, 164 Ind. App. 21, 326 N.E.2d 644 (1975)

35 ALR6th 1—§ 20

Shunk v. State, 924 P.2d 879, 113 Ed. Law Rep. 957 (Utah 1996)

64 ALR5th 519—§ 4

Shupak v. New York Life Ins. Co., 780 F. Supp. 1328 (D.C. Mont 1991)

6 ALR5th 297—§ 40, 49

Shupe, In re Marriage of, 276 Mont. 409, 916 P.2d 744, 67 A.L.R.5th 679 (1996)

40 ALR5th 227—§ 3, 21
67 ALR5th 1—§ 23

Shupe v. Antelope County, 157 Neb. 374, 59 N.W.2d 710 (1953)

74 ALR5th 523—§ 3

Shupe v. Bell, 127 Ind. App. 292, 141 N.E.2d 351 (1957)

102 ALR5th 227—§ 6

Shupe & Yost, Inc. v. Fallon Nat. Bank of Nevada, 109 Nev. 99, 847 P.2d 720, 20 U.C.C. Rep. Serv. 2d 1298 (1993)

91 ALR5th 89—§ 5

Shuping v. Barber, 89 N.C. App. 242, 365 S.E.2d 712 (1988)

100 ALR5th 341—§ 5

Shuptrine v. McDougal Littell, 535 F. Supp. 2d 892 (E.D. Tenn. 2008)

76 ALR6th 289—§ 5
77 ALR6th 543—§ 9

Shuqin v. Rafoth, 2009 WL 3834009 (W.D. Pa. 2009)

83 ALR6th 195—§ 7

Shurlow Tile & Carpet, Inc. v. Dahlmann Bldg. Co., 54 Mich. App. 180, 220 N.W.2d 732 (1974)

23 ALR5th 744—§ 2

Shurpin v. Elmhirst, 148 Cal. App. 3d 94, 195 Cal. Rptr. 737 (2d Dist. 1983)

70 ALR5th 261—§ 51

Shurtliff v. Northwest Pools, Inc., 120 Idaho 263, 815 P.2d 461 (Ct. App. 1991)

117 ALR5th 155—§ 5

Shurtliff v. Oregon Short Line R. Co., 66 Utah 161, 241 P. 1058 (1925)

42 ALR6th 545—§ 6, 8, 10, 18
43 ALR6th 375—§ 4, 13, 36

Shur-Value Stamps v. Phillips Petroleum Co., 50 F.3d 592, 26 U.C.C.R.S.2d 27 (CA8 Ark. 1995)

49 ALR5th 1—§ 2

Shuster v. BAC Home Loans Servicing, LP, 211 Cal. App. 4th 505, 149 Cal. Rptr. 3d 749 (2d Dist. 2012)

86 ALR6th 411—§ 5

Shuster v. Buckley, 5 Conn. App. 473, 500 A.2d 240 (1985)

11 ALR6th 1—§ 4, 5

Shuster v. California Auto Dealers Exchange, Inc., 2007-1 Trade Cas. (CCH) ¶ 75703, 2007 WL 763165 (Cal. App. 4th Dist. 2007)

83 ALR6th 143—§ 7

Shuster v. South Broward Hosp. Dist. Physicians' Professional Liability Ins. Trust, 591 So. 2d 174, 17 FLW S. 4, 18 A.L.R.5th 1023 (Fla. 1992)

18 ALR5th 474—§ 2, 4, 5, 7

Shutan v. Bloomenthal, 371 Ill. 244, 20 N.E.2d 570 (1939)

18 ALR6th 325—§ 50, 53

Shute v. Moon Lake Electric Ass'n, 899 F.2d 999 (CA10 Utah 1990)

49 ALR5th 659—§ 3, 4

Shute v. Princeton, 58 Minn. 337, 59 N.W. 1050 (1894)

25 ALR5th 391—§ 91

Shute v. Shute, 158 Vt. 242, 607 A.2d 890 (1992)

40 ALR5th 227—§ 13

Shute v. State, 36 Ga. 87, 1867 WL 1470 (1867)

102 ALR5th 525—§ 52

Shutes v. Cheney, 123 Cal. App. 2d 256, 266 P.2d 902, 101 U.S.P.Q. 90 (1st Dist. 1954)
85 ALR6th 1—§ 18

Shutt v. Kaufman's, Inc., 165 Colo. 175, 438 P.2d 501 (1968)
1 ALR6th 297—§ 4, 13, 28

Shutt v. Sandoz Crop Protection Corp., 944 F.2d 1431, 91 Daily Journal DAR 12018, 57 BNA FEP Cas. 144, 56 CCH EPD ¶ 40869 (CA9 Wash. 1991)
51 ALR5th 1—§ 7

Shutt v. Shutt, 133 Misc. 2d 81, 506 N.Y.S.2d 611 (Sup. Ct. 1986)
55 ALR5th 557—§ 5

Shutta v. Radio Corp. of America, 73 Lack. Jur. 5 (Pa. C.P. 1971)
68 ALR5th 13—§ 33, 40

Shutters, In Interest of, 56 Ill. App. 3d 184, 13 Ill. Dec. 198, 370 N.E.2d 1225 (2d Dist. 1977)
9 ALR6th 1—§ 10

Shuttlesworth v. City of Birmingham, 382 U.S. 87, 86 S. Ct. 211, 15 L. Ed. 2d 176 (1965)
72 ALR5th 1—§ 3
52 ALR6th 125—§ 15

Shuttlesworth v. City of Birmingham, Ala., 394 U.S. 147, 89 S. Ct. 935, 22 L. Ed. 2d 162 (1969)
80 ALR5th 255—§ 5, 6
118 ALR5th 213—§ 11

Shuttleworth, Ex parte, 410 So. 2d 896 (Ala. 1981)
92 ALR5th 379—§ 7

Shuttleworth v. Catholic Family Services, 439 So. 2d 1292 (Ala. Civ. App. 1983)
61 ALR5th 151—§ 5

Shuttleworth v. Conti Const. Co., Inc., 193 N.J. Super. 469, 475 A.2d 48 (App. Div. 1984)
50 ALR6th 95—§ 4

Shuttleworth v. McGee, 47 Tex. Civ. App. 604, 105 S.W. 823 (1907)
87 ALR5th 473—§ 3

Shuttleworth v. State, 469 N.E.2d 1210 (Ind. App. 1984)
12 ALR5th 909—§ 2, 5

Shuttleworth, Ruloff and Giordano, P.C. v. Nutter, 493 S.E.2d 364 (Va. 1997)
28 ALR5th 420—§ 3

Shutts v. Siehl, 109 Ohio App. 145, 10 Ohio Op. 2d 363, 164 N.E.2d 443 (2d Dist. Montgomery County 1959)
108 ALR5th 385—§ 7

Shwary v. Cranetrol Corp., 88 Mich. App. 264, 276 N.W.2d 882 (1979)
13 ALR5th 289—§ 3

Shy v. State, 234 Ga. 816, 218 S.E.2d 599 (1975)
98 ALR6th 455—§ 22

Shydler v. Shydler, 114 Nev. 192, 954 P.2d 37 (1998)
102 ALR5th 395—§ 6

Siah v. State, 1992 OK CR 59, 837 P.2d 485 (Okla. Crim. App. 1992)
100 ALR6th 535—§ 3

Siano v. Haber, 40 F. Supp. 2d 516, 83 Fair Empl. Prac. Cas. (BNA) 1733 (S.D. N.Y. 1999)
11 ALR6th 447—§ 6

Siao-Pao v. Connolly, 564 F. Supp. 2d 232 (S.D. N.Y. 2008)
86 ALR6th 173—§ 14

Sias v. General Motors Corp., 372 Mich. 542, 127 N.W.2d 357 (1964)
53 ALR6th 213—§ 8

Sias v. State, 539 So. 2d 22 (Fla. Dist. Ct. App. 2d Dist. 1989)
1 ALR6th 549—§ 31

Sias ex rel. Mabry v. Wal-Mart Stores, Inc., 137 F. Supp. 2d 699 (S.D. W. Va. 2001)
118 ALR5th 513—§ 3, 11

Siau v. Rapides Parish School Bd., 264 So. 2d 372 (La. Ct. App. 3d Cir. 1972)
66 ALR5th 1—§ 20

Sibely & Morrison v. Tutt, 16 S.C. Eq. 320, McMul. Eq. 320, 1841 WL 2304 (Ct. App. Eq. 1841)

77 ALR6th 293—§ 39, 42
Sibert v. State Farm Fire & Cas. Co.,
1999 WL 33453993 (Mich. Ct. App.
1999)
119 ALR5th 121—§ 3, 6
2 ALR6th 279—§ 4
Sibertzeff, In re, 694 N.Y.S.2d 817 (App.
Div. 3d Dep't 1999)
68 ALR5th 13—§ 22, 33
Sibilrud v. Minneapolis & St. L. R. Co.,
29 Minn. 58, 11 N.W. 146 (1882)
17 ALR5th 547—§ 44, 51
Sibiski v. Cuomo, 2010 WL 3984706
(E.D. N.Y. 2010)
95 ALR6th 341—§ 64, 66
Sibley v. Adams, 56 Ala. App. 572, 324
So. 2d 287 (1975)
14 ALR5th 242—§ 23
Sibley v. Board of Supervisors of La.
State Univ., 477 So. 2d 1094 (La.
1985)
26 ALR5th 245—§ 10, 16, 27
Sibley v. Board of Supervisors of Loui-
siana State University, 462 So. 2d
149 (La. 1985)
26 ALR5th 245—§ 10, 16
Sibley v. Kaiser Foundation Health Plan
of Texas, 998 S.W.2d 399 (Tex.
App. Texarkana 1999)
19 ALR6th 1—§ 7
Sibley v. National City Mortg. Co., 560
Fed. Appx. 825 (11th Cir. 2014)
104 ALR6th 485—§ 4, 7
Sibley v. Sibley, 286 S.W.2d 657 (Tex.
Civ. App. Dallas 1955)
66 ALR5th 135—§ 10
Sibley v. Superior Court of Los Angeles
County, 16 Cal. 3d 442, 128 Cal.
Rptr. 34, 546 P.2d 322 (1976)
28 ALR5th 664—§ 9
Sibley v. Unifirst Bank for Sav. Through
Resolution Trust Corp., 699 So. 2d
1214 (Miss. 1997)
82 ALR5th 149—§ 64
84 ALR5th 249—§ 42
Sibley v. U.S. Dept. of Educ., 111 F.3d
133 (7th Cir. 1997)
88 ALR6th 203—§ 70

Sibley v. Waffle, 16 N.Y. 180, 1857 WL
7096 (1857)
64 ALR6th 655—§ 4
Sibley v. Wells, 462 A.2d 27 (Me. 1983)
1 ALR5th 622—§ 19
Sibley on Behalf of Sheppard, People ex
rel. v. Sheppard, 54 N.Y.2d 320,
445 N.Y.S.2d 420, 429 N.E.2d 1049
(1981)
69 ALR5th 1—§ 3, 5
86 ALR6th 1—§ 66
Sibrava v. W.C.A.B. (Trans World Airlines), 113 Pa. Commw. 286, 537
A.2d 75 (1988)
97 ALR5th 1—§ 4
106 ALR5th 111—§ 19
108 ALR5th 1—§ 27
Sicairos v. NDEX West, LLC, 2009 WL
385855 (S.D. Cal. 2009)
86 ALR6th 411—§ 5
Sicaras v. City of Hartford, 44 Conn.
App. 771, 692 A.2d 1290 (1997)
79 ALR6th 377—§ 20, 41
Siccardi v. State, 59 N.J. 545, 284 A.2d
533, 51 A.L.R.3d 494 (1971)
91 ALR6th 435—§ 89
Siciliano v. Capitol City Shows, Inc.,
124 N.H. 719, 475 A.2d 19 (1984)
96 ALR5th 107—§ 6
Siciliano v. Scheyer, 150 App. Div. 2d
460, 541 N.Y.S.2d 69 (2d Dep't
1989)
1 ALR5th 622—§ 19
Siciliano v. Vose, 834 F.2d 29 (1st Cir.
1987)
72 ALR5th 403—§ 11, 15
Sicinski v. Will County Police Dept.
Merit Com'n, 131 Ill. App. 3d 966,
87 Ill. Dec. 106, 476 N.E.2d 808 (3d
Dist. 1985)
19 ALR6th 217—§ 20
Sick v. Levine, 53 A.D.2d 727, 384
N.Y.S.2d 49 (3d Dep't 1976)
25 ALR6th 101—§ 26
SICK, Inc. v. Motion Control Corp., 50
U.C.C. Rep. Serv. 2d 1021 (D.
Minn. 2003)
39 ALR6th 155—§ 5

Sicking v. Sicking, 2000 OK CIV APP
32, 996 P.2d 471 (Div. 1 1999)
86 ALR6th 1—§ 27

Sicking v. State Medical Bd., 62 Ohio
App. 3d 387, 575 N.E.2d 881 (10th
Dist. Franklin County 1991)
19 ALR6th 577—§ 8

Sickler v. Pope, 326 N.W.2d 86 (N.D.
1982)
98 ALR5th 665—§ 4

Sickles v. Cabot Corp., 379 N.J. Super.
100, 877 A.2d 267, 2005-2 Trade
Cas. (CCH) ¶ 74858 (App. Div.
2005)
35 ALR6th 245—§ 3, 4, 11

Sickly v. Board of Comm'rs, 83 Kan.
740, 112 P. 621 (1911)
56 ALR5th 171—§ 7, 18

Sickmen v. Birzon, Szczepanowski &
Quinn, 276 A.D.2d 689, 716
N.Y.S.2d 581 (2d Dep't 2000)
11 ALR6th 587—§ 25

Sicpa North America, Inc. v. Donaldson
Enterprises, Inc., 179 N.J. Super.
56, 430 A.2d 262 (1981)
26 ALR5th 628—§ 27
28 ALR5th 1—§ 17
51 ALR5th 603—§ 2

Sicuranza v. Northwest Florida Blood
Center, Inc., 582 So. 2d 54, Prod.
Liab. Rep. (CCH) ¶ 12922 (Fla.
Dist. Ct. App. 1st Dist. 1991)
64 ALR5th 333—§ 7
75 ALR5th 229—§ 14

Sidak v. Pinnacle Telemarketing Ltd.,
182 F. Supp. 2d 873 (D. Neb. 2002)
94 ALR5th 1—§ 4

Sidarma Societa Italiana Di Armamento
Spa, Venice v. Holt Marine Indus-
tries, Inc., 515 F. Supp. 1302, 1981
A.M.C. 2729, 1982 A.M.C. 3000
(S.D. N.Y. 1981)
67 ALR5th 179—§ 2, 7, 11

Sidco Products Marketing, Inc. v. Gulf
Oil Corp., 858 F.2d 1095, Prod.
Liab. Rep. (CCH) ¶ 11960, 7 U.C.C.
Rep. Serv. 2d 711 (5th Cir. 1988)
94 ALR6th 1—§ 2, 4, 16, 64

Sid Dillon Chevrolet-Oldsmobile-Pon-
tiac, Inc. v. Sullivan, 251 Neb. 722,
559 N.W.2d 740 (1997)
44 ALR5th 619—§ 3

Siddiqui v. Illinois Dep't of Professional
Regulation, 307 Ill. App. 3d 753,
240 Ill. Dec. 736, 718 N.E.2d 217
(4th Dist. 1999)
10 ALR5th 1—§ 5, 7

Siddle v. City of Cambridge, Ohio, 761
F. Supp. 503 (S.D. Ohio 1991)
90 ALR5th 273—§ 2, 3, 5, 6, 9

Siddon v. M. H. Fishman Co., Inc., 65
A.D.2d 832, 409 N.Y.S.2d 830 (3d
Dep't 1978)
**74 ALR5th 49—§ 2, 22, 63, 64, 68,
79**

Sidell v. Structured Settlement Investments, LP, 2009 WL 103518 (D.
Conn. 2009)
68 ALR6th 331—§ 39

Sidelnik v. American States Ins. Co.,
914 S.W.2d 689 (Tex. App. Austin
1996)
2 ALR5th 922—§ 4

Siden v. U.S., 9 F.2d 241 (CA8 Minn.
1925)
41 ALR5th 171—§ 13, 15, 77, 107

Siderius, Inc. v. Wallace Co., 583
S.W.2d 852, 27 U.C.C.R.S. 191
(Tex. Civ. App. Tyler 1979)
8 ALR5th 463—§ 4, 13, 63

Siderpali, S.P.A. v. Judal Industries,
Inc., 833 F. Supp. 1023, 23 U.C.C.
Rep. Serv. 2d 214 (S.D. N.Y. 1993)
39 ALR6th 155—§ 4

Sider Ventures & Services Corp., In re,
31 B.R. 522 (F. BC S.D. N.Y.1983)
27 ALR5th 719—§ 7

Sides v. Duke University, 74 N.C. App.
331, 328 S.E.2d 818, 24 Ed. Law
Rep. 1033, 1 I.E.R. Cas. (BNA)
512, 120 L.R.R.M. (BNA) 2091,
103 Lab. Cas. (CCH) ¶ 55512
(1985)
104 ALR5th 1—§ 3, 4, 7

Sides v. Pittman, 167 Miss. 751, 150 So.
211 (1933)

47 ALR5th 129—§ 10
Sides v. Reid, 35 N.C. App. 235, 241 S.E.2d 110 (1978)
    86 ALR6th 321—§ 5, 13
    89 ALR6th 409—§ 14
Sidewinder Marine, Inc. v. Nescher, 440 F. Supp. 680, 200 U.S.P.Q. 327 (N.D. Cal. 1976)
    85 ALR6th 1—§ 25
Sidman v. Director, Div. of Taxation, 19 N.J. Tax 484, 2001 WL 1055469 (Super. Ct. App. Div. 2001)
    118 ALR5th 597—§ 10, 18
Sidney v. Allen, 114 N.C. App. 138, 441 S.E.2d 561 (1994)
    14 ALR6th 301—§ 5, 7, 23
    19 ALR6th 475—§ 3, 5, 6
Sidney v. Allen, 338 N.C. 670, 453 S.E.2d 182 (1994)
    19 ALR6th 475—§ 6
Sidney v. Stout, 79 Ohio Misc. 2d 79, 671 N.E.2d 341 (Mun. Ct. 1996)
    84 ALR6th 293—§ 30
Sidney, City of v. Thompson, 118 Ohio App. 512, 26 Ohio Op. 2d 18, 196 N.E.2d 112 (2d Dist. Shelby County 1962)
    92 ALR6th 295—§ 5
Sidney Coal Co., Inc. v. Kirk, 364 S.W.3d 168 (Ky. 2012)
    99 ALR6th 643—§ 19
Sidney Coal Co., Inc./Rockhouse Energy Mining Co. v. Slone, 2007 WL 3122281 (Ky. Ct. App. 2007)
    99 ALR6th 643—§ 17
Sidney Philip Gilbert Associates (Taisei Const. Corp.), Matter of, 213 A.D.2d 281, 624 N.Y.S.2d 824 (1st Dep't 1995)
    67 ALR5th 179—§ 11
Sidoti Chiropractic Center v. Prudential Ins. Co., 2006 WL 848230 (N.J. Super. Ct. App. Div. 2006)
    80 ALR6th 389—§ 22
Sidway v. American Mortg. Co., 222 Ill. 270, 78 N.E. 561 (1906)
    24 ALR6th 399—§ 8, 17

Sidwell v. Griggsville Community School Dist. 4, 208 Ill. App. 3d 296, 152 Ill. Dec. 961, 566 N.E.2d 838, 65 Ed. Law Rep. 829 (4th Dist. 1991)
    66 ALR5th 1—§ 42
Sidwell v. Griggsville Community Unit School Dist. No. 4, 146 Ill. 2d 467, 167 Ill. Dec. 1055, 588 N.E.2d 1185, 73 Ed. Law Rep. 485 (1992)
    66 ALR5th 1—§ 42
Sidwell v. Horseshoe Entertainment Ltd. Partnership, 811 So. 2d 229 (La. Ct. App. 2d Cir. 2002)
    97 ALR5th 1—§ 9
    106 ALR5th 111—§ 11
    108 ALR5th 1—§ 18
Sidwell v. Sidwell, 28 Ill. App. 3d 580, 328 N.E.2d 595 (4th Dist. 1975)
    17 ALR5th 366—§ 12
Sieben v. Sieben, 231 Kan. 372, 646 P.2d 1036 (1982)
    18 ALR5th 525—§ 3
Sieber v. Frink, 7 Colo. 148, 2 P. 901 (1883)
    62 ALR5th 219—§ 52
Sieber v. Laawe, 33 N.J. Super. 115, 109 A.2d 470 (Law Div. 1954)
    73 ALR5th 223—§ 11
Sieber v. Rose, 2012 WL 3038645 (D. Md. 2012)
    99 ALR6th 481—§ 27
Sieber v. White, 366 P.2d 755 (Okla. 1961)
    62 ALR5th 219—§ 21, 31
Sieber v. Zoning Bd. of Appeals, 16 Mass. App. 985, 454 N.E.2d 108 (1983)
    2 ALR5th 553—§ 47
Siebern v. Government Emp. Ins. Co., 33 A.D.2d 1026, 308 N.Y.S.2d 268 (2d Dep't 1970)
    103 ALR5th 1—§ 5
Siebern v. Missouri-Illinois Tractor & Equipment Co., 711 S.W.2d 935, CCH Prod. Liab. Rep. ¶ 11007 (Mo. App. 1986)
    29 ALR5th 534—§ 20, 42

For assistance, call 1-800-328-4880

Siebert, Ex parte, 555 So. 2d 780 (Ala. 1989)
37 ALR5th 515—§ 5, 9
Siebert v. Fowler, 637 P.2d 255 (Wyo. 1981)
43 ALR5th 87—§ 2, 10
Siebert v. Severino, 97 F. Supp. 2d 882 (C.D. Ill. 2000)
6 ALR5th 733—§ 16
Siebert v. Severino, 256 F.3d 648 (7th Cir. 2001)
67 ALR6th 531—§ 28
Siebert, People ex rel. v. Board of Police Comrs., 20 Hun. 333 (N.Y. 1880)
10 ALR5th 139—§ 3
Siebold, Ex parte, 100 U.S. 371, 25 L. Ed. 717, 1879 WL 16559 (1879)
34 ALR6th 643—§ 5, 8, 16
Sieck v. Trueblood, 29 Colo. App. 432, 485 P.2d 134 (1971)
11 ALR6th 351—§ 4, 6
Siecker v. Unemployment Compensation Board of Review, 194 Pa. Super. 181, 166 A.2d 68 (1960)
45 ALR5th 715—§ 5
Siedel v. Snider, 241 Iowa 1227, 44 N.W.2d 687 (1950)
61 ALR5th 707—§ 21
Siedle v. National Ass'n of Securities Dealers, Inc., 248 F. Supp. 2d 1140 (M.D. Fla. 2002)
106 ALR5th 309—§ 3
Siedlecki v. Arabia, 699 So. 2d 1040 (Fla. Dist. Ct. App. 4th Dist. 1997)
118 ALR5th 91—§ 19
125 ALR5th 193—§ 9
Siedler v. Jacobson, 86 Misc. 2d 1010, 383 N.Y.S.2d 833 (App. Term 1976)
88 ALR5th 545—§ 2, 16
Siedler v. Waln, 266 Pa. 361, 109 A. 643, 8 A.L.R. 1363 (1920)
111 ALR5th 313—§ 3
Siefert v. Alexander, 608 F.3d 974 (7th Cir. 2010)
65 ALR6th 503—§ 4
Siegal, Application of, 153 N.Y.S.2d 673 (Sup. Ct. 1956)

66 ALR5th 611—§ 3
Siegal v. Aircoa, Inc., 499 So. 2d 1232 (La. App. 4th Cir. 1986)
18 ALR5th 577—§ 27
Sieg Co. v. Kelly, 568 N.W.2d 794 (Iowa 1997)
16 ALR6th 693—§ 16
Siegel, Ex parte, 263 Mo. 375, 173 S.W. 1 (1914)
5 ALR6th 1—§ 33
Siegel, In re Marriage of, 26 Cal. App. 3d 88, 102 Cal. Rptr. 613 (4th Dist. 1972)
49 ALR5th 441—§ 3
Siegel, Re Marriage of, 123 Ill. App. 3d 710, 79 Ill. Dec. 219, 463 N.E.2d 773 (1st Dist. 1984)
17 ALR5th 366—§ 10
Siegel v. Alexander, 477 So. 2d 1345 (Miss. 1985)
21 ALR5th 396—§ 3, 19, 21, 54
Siegel v. City of Chicago, 127 Ill. App. 2d 84, 261 N.E.2d 802 (1st Dist. 1970)
73 ALR5th 223—§ 3, 11
Siegel v. Committee of Bar Examiners, 10 Cal. 3d 156, 110 Cal. Rptr. 15, 514 P.2d 967 (1973)
107 ALR5th 167—§ 5, 17
3 ALR6th 49—§ 10
Siegel v. Holson Co., 768 F. Supp. 444 (S.D. N.Y. 1991)
79 ALR5th 587—§ 4
Siegel v. Knott, 316 Mass. 526, 55 N.E.2d 889 (1944)
81 ALR6th 161—§ 2, 4
82 ALR6th 43—§ 2, 16
Siegel v. Kranis, 29 A.D.2d 477, 288 N.Y.S.2d 831 (2d Dep't 1968)
87 ALR5th 473—§ 4
11 ALR6th 1—§ 4
Siegel v. Leer, Inc., 156 Wis. 2d 621, 457 N.W.2d 533 (Ct. App. 1990)
124 ALR5th 575—§ 17
Siegel v. Levy Organization Dev. Co., 182 Ill. App. 3d 859, 131 Ill. Dec. 340, 538 N.E.2d 715 (1st Dist. 1989)

---

39 ALR5th 33—§ 3

Siegel v. Levy Organization Development Co., Inc., 153 Ill. 2d 534, 180 Ill. Dec. 300, 607 N.E.2d 194 (1992)

115 ALR5th 709—§ 2

117 ALR5th 155—§ 2, 10

Siegel v. Meyer, 319 Ill. App. 102, 48 N.E.2d 595 (1943)

27 ALR5th 764—§ 3

Siegel v. Norwegian Cruise Line, 2001 WL 1905983 (D.N.J. 2001)

82 ALR6th 175—§ 6

Siegel v. Portland General Electric Co., 79 Or. App. 47, 717 P.2d 1245 (1986)

8 ALR5th 177—§ 2, 7

Siegel v. Salisbury, 379 F. Supp. 317 (W.D. Pa. 1974)

92 ALR5th 593—§ 3, 5, 8, 11

Siegel v. Siegel, 122 Misc. 2d 932, 472 N.Y.S.2d 272 (Sup 1984)

95 ALR5th 533—§ 3, 8

124 ALR5th 203—§ 3, 13

Siegel v. Siegel, 575 So. 2d 1267, 16 FLW S. 140 (Fla. 1991)

20 ALR5th 700—§ 54

21 ALR5th 396—§ 2

Siegel v. St. Vincent Charity Hospital & Health Center, 35 Ohio App. 3d 143, 520 N.E.2d 249 (Cuyahoga Co. 1987)

28 ALR5th 107—§ 18

Siegel v. Sun Printing & Publishing Ass'n, 130 Misc. 18, 223 N.Y.S. 549 (Sup 1927)

16 ALR6th 1—§ 36

Siegel v. Time Warner Inc., 496 F. Supp. 2d 1111 (C.D. Cal. 2007)

85 ALR6th 1—§ 3

Siegel v. Wank, 183 A.D.2d 158, 589 N.Y.S.2d 934 (3d Dep't 1992)

17 ALR6th 159—§ 47

Siegel Trading Co., Inc. v. Coral Ridge Nat. Bank, 328 So. 2d 476, 18 U.C.C. Rep. Serv. 1257 (Fla. Dist. Ct. App. 4th Dist. 1976)

91 ALR5th 89—§ 4

Sieger v. Sieger, 37 A.D.3d 585, 829 N.Y.S.2d 649 (2d Dep't 2007)

81 ALR6th 1—§ 28

Sieger v. Wisconsin Personnel Com'n, 181 Wis. 2d 845, 512 N.W.2d 220, 17 Employee Benefits Cas. (BNA) 2201 (Ct. App. 1994)

57 ALR5th 477—§ 13, 27, 48

Sieger v. Zak, 60 A.D.3d 661, 874 N.Y.S.2d 535, 66 A.L.R.6th 711 (2d Dep' 2009)

66 ALR6th 83—§ 9

Siegert v. Crook County, 246 Or. App. 500, 266 P.3d 170 (2011)

77 ALR6th 393—§ 73

Siegert v. Gilley, 500 U.S. 226, 111 S. Ct. 1789, 114 L. Ed. 2d 277, 6 I.E.R. Cas. (BNA) 705 (1991)

41 ALR6th 391—§ 14

95 ALR6th 341—§ 2, 25

Siegfried v. Everhart, 55 Ohio App. 351, 9 Ohio Ops. 85, 23 Ohio L. Abs. 361, 9 N.E.2d 891 (Summit Co. 1936)

11 ALR5th 127—§ 4

Siegfried v. South Bethlehem Borough, 27 Pa. Super. 456, 1905 WL 3613 (1905)

54 ALR6th 201—§ 3

Siegler v. Batdorff, 63 Ohio App. 2d 76, 17 Ohio Ops. 3d 260, 408 N.E.2d 1383 (Cuyahoga Co. 1979)

23 ALR5th 140—§ 11

Siegler v. Counties Contracting & Const. Co., 203 Pa. Super. 568, 202 A.2d 127 (1964)

75 ALR5th 413—§ 3, 49

Siegler v. Robinson, 600 S.W.2d 382 (Tex. Civ. App. Houston (1st Dist. 1980)

45 ALR5th 251—§ 5, 6, 12

Siegman v. Columbia Pictures Entertainment, Inc., 576 A.2d 625, Fed. Sec. L. Rep. (CCH) ¶ 94796 (Del. Ch. 1989)

37 ALR6th 1—§ 17

Siegman v. Palomar Medical Technologies, Inc., 24 Del. J. Corp. L. 284, 1998 WL 409352 (Del. Ch. 1998)
124 ALR5th 575—§ 15

Siegman for Siegman v. Columbia Pictures Entertainment, Inc., Fed. Sec. L. Rep. (CCH) ¶ 97397, 1993 WL 10969 (Del. Ch. 1993)
37 ALR6th 1—§ 17

Siegner v. Interstate Production Credit Assn., 109 Or. App. 417, 820 P.2d 20 (1991)
18 ALR5th 307—§ 24, 32

Siegrist v. Carrillo, 112 Ariz. 218, 540 P.2d 690 (1975)
76 ALR5th 1—§ 3

Siegwald v. Curry, 40 Ohio App. 2d 313, 69 Ohio Op. 2d 293, 319 N.E.2d 381 (10th Dist. Franklin County 1974)
109 ALR5th 611—§ 6

Sielicki v. New York Yankees, 388 So. 2d 25 (Fla. Dist. Ct. App. 1st Dist. 1980)
112 ALR5th 365—§ 10

Sieloff v. Stryker Corp., 2012 WL 5835396 (D. Ariz. 2012)
90 ALR6th 75—§ 11, 29, 31, 33, 40, 44

Siembab v. Siembab, 284 A.D. 652, 134 N.Y.S.2d 437 (4th Dep't 1954)
118 ALR5th 513—§ 3, 9

Siemen v. Alden, 34 Ill. App. 3d 961, 341 N.E.2d 713, 18 U.C.C. Rep. Serv. 884 (2d Dist. 1975)
4 ALR6th 401—§ 15

Siemen v. Alden, 34 Ill. App. 3d 961, 341 N.E.2d 713, 18 U.C.C.R.S. 884 (2d Dist. 1975)
9 ALR5th 1—§ 5, 8

Siemens Energy & Automation, Inc. v. Medina, 719 So. 2d 312, Prod. Liab. Rep. (CCH) ¶ 15324 (Fla. Dist. Ct. App. 3d Dist. 1998)
86 ALR5th 215—§ 2

Siemer v. Quizno's Franchise Co. LLC, 2010 WL 3238840 (N.D. Ill. 2010)
60 ALR6th 295—§ 13

Siemianowski v. Bushey, 1990 WL 131537 (Ohio Ct. App. 7th Dist. Mahoning County 1990)
125 ALR5th 403—§ 14
18 ALR6th 325—§ 13, 28

Siemieniec v. Lutheran Gen. Hosp., 117 Ill. 2d 230, 111 Ill. Dec. 302, 512 N.E.2d 691 (1987)
89 ALR5th 255—§ 5, 6, 8

Siemientkowski v. State Farm Ins. Co., 2005-Ohio-4295, 2005 WL 1994486 (Ohio Ct. App. 8th Dist. Cuyahoga County 2005)
90 ALR6th 635—§ 3, 31

Siemion v. Rumfelt, 825 P.2d 896 (Alaska 1992)
97 ALR6th 375—§ 6, 24, 27, 30

Siemon v. Stoughton, 184 Conn. 547, 440 A.2d 210 (1981)
22 ALR5th 1—§ 44
80 ALR5th 55—§ 5

Siena v. Microsoft Corp., 796 A.2d 461, 2002-1 Trade Cas. (CCH) ¶ 73666 (R.I. 2002)
35 ALR6th 245—§ 4, 11, 15

Sienkiewicz v. Sienkiewicz, 178 Conn. 675, 425 A.2d 116 (1979)
52 ALR5th 221—§ 26

Sienkiewicz v. Smith, 97 Wash. 2d 711, 649 P.2d 112 (1982)
58 ALR5th 387—§ 20

Sier v. Jacobs Persinger & Parker, 276 A.D.2d 401, 714 N.Y.S.2d 283 (1st Dep't 2000)
94 ALR5th 1—§ 3, 10
14 ALR6th 417—§ 6

Sieren v. American Family Financial Services, Inc., 356 N.W.2d 408 (Minn. App. 1984)
14 ALR5th 242—§ 25

Siering v. Bronson, 564 So. 2d 247, 15 FLW D 1866 (Fla. App. D5 1990)
25 ALR5th 123—§ 2
25 ALR5th 233—§ 2, 3

Sierra v. Employment Appeal Bd., 508 N.W.2d 719 (Iowa 1993)
68 ALR5th 13—§ 8, 9, 39

Sierra v. Romprey, 165 F. Supp. 483 (D.N.H. 1958)
110 ALR5th 465—§ 25

Sierra v. Schwegmann Giant Supermarkets, Inc., 487 So. 2d 151 (La. App. 4th Cir. 1986)
50 ALR5th 1—§ 12

Sierra Blanca Sales Co. v. Newco Industries, Inc., 84 N.M. 524, 505 P.2d 867 (App. 1972)
14 ALR5th 242—§ 32

Sierra Club v. California Coastal Com., 12 Cal. App. 4th 602, 15 Cal. Rptr. 2d 779 (1st Dist. 1993)
106 ALR5th 523—§ 36

Sierra Club v. Contra Costa County, 10 Cal. App. 4th 1212, 13 Cal. Rptr. 2d 182 (1st Dist. 1992)
106 ALR5th 523—§ 36

Sierra Club v. El Paso Gold Mines, Inc., 421 F.3d 1133, 61 Env't. Rep. Cas. (BNA) 1274, 35 Envtl. L. Rep. 20175 (10th Cir. 2005)
16 ALR6th 767—§ 18

Sierra Club v. Gilroy City Council, 222 Cal. App. 3d 30, 271 Cal. Rptr. 393 (6th Dist. 1990)
44 ALR6th 325—§ 19

Sierra Club Foundation v. Graham, 72 Cal. App. 4th 1135, 85 Cal. Rptr. 2d 726 (1st Dist. 1999)
14 ALR5th 242—§ 54

Sierra Creek Ranch, Inc. v. J. I. Case, 97 Nev. 457, 634 P.2d 458, 32 U.C.C. Rep. Serv. 777 (1981)
101 ALR5th 563—§ 8

Sierra Dev., Ex parte, 652 So. 2d 251 (Ala. 1994)
42 ALR5th 221—§ 2

Sierra Diesel Injection Service v. Burroughs Corp., 648 F. Supp. 1148, 3 U.C.C.R.S.2d 646 (D.C. Nev 1986)
49 ALR5th 1—§ 52

Sierra Foods v. Williams, 107 Nev. 574, 816 P.2d 466, 19 A.L.R.5th 1043 (1991)
19 ALR5th 622—§ 2, 8, 17

Sierra Fria Corp. v. Donald J. Evans, P.C., 127 F.3d 175, 38 Fed. R. Serv. 3d 1288 (1st Cir. 1997)
58 ALR6th 1—§ 5

Sierra-Melendez v. Brown, 410 So. 2d 258 (La. Ct. App. 4th Cir. 1982)
50 ALR6th 95—§ 5, 8

Sierra Nat. Bank v. Brown, 18 Cal. App. 3d 98, 95 Cal. Rptr. 742 (1st Dist. 1971)
11 ALR5th 88—§ 2, 5

Sierra Nevada SW Enterprises, Ltd. v. Douglas County, 2011 WL 1304472 (D. Nev. 2011)
68 ALR6th 229—§ 8

Sierra Pacific Power Co. v. Anderson, 77 Nev. 68, 358 P.2d 892 (1961)
20 ALR5th 1—§ 8, 14, 45, 62

Sierra Screw Products v. Azusa Greens, Inc., 88 Cal. App. 3d 358, 151 Cal. Rptr. 799 (2d Dist. 1979)
49 ALR6th 477—§ 11

Sierra Trading Post, Inc., In re, 996 P.2d 1144 (Wyo. 2000)
96 ALR5th 485—§ 10, 13

Sierra Vista Hospital v. Superior Court of San Luis Obispo County, 248 Cal. App. 2d 359, 56 Cal. Rptr. 387 (2d Dist. 1967)
26 ALR5th 628—§ 20, 22, 23
27 ALR5th 76—§ 12, 33

Sierzega v. U. S. Steel Corp., 204 Pa. Super. 531, 205 A.2d 696 (1964)
86 ALR5th 295—§ 4

Siesta Hills Neighborhood Ass'n v. City of Albuquerque, 124 N.M. 670, 1998-NMCA-028, 954 P.2d 102 (Ct. App. 1998)
4 ALR6th 263—§ 48

Siesta Manor, Inc. v. Community Federal Sav. and Loan Ass'n, 716 S.W.2d 835 (Mo. Ct. App. E.D. 1986)
81 ALR6th 161—§ 5
82 ALR6th 43—§ 17

Sieteski v. Dibiase, 242 A.D.2d 753, 661 N.Y.S.2d 314 (3d Dep't 1997)
45 ALR5th 767—§ 10

Sietins v. Joseph, 238 F. Supp. 2d 366 (D. Mass. 2003)
101 ALR5th 515—§ 24, 25

Sievers v. Hannah, 296 Ill. 593, 130 N.E. 361 (1921)
75 ALR6th 311—§ 29, 56, 76

Sievers v. U.S., 194 F. Supp. 608 (D.C. Or. 1961)
27 ALR5th 174—§ 95

Sieverson v. Allied Stores Corp., 97 Or. App. 315, 776 P.2d 38, 4 I.E.R. Cas. (BNA) 785, 124 Lab. Cas. (CCH) ¶ 57173 (1989)
105 ALR5th 351—§ 3, 10

Siewerth v. Charleston, 89 Ill. App. 2d 64, 231 N.E.2d 644 (1st Dist. 1967)
11 ALR5th 127—§ 18, 21

Sifakis, In re Claim of, 133 App. Div. 2d 511, 519 N.Y.S.2d 433 (3d Dep't 1987)
33 ALR5th 643—§ 28

Sifers v. Exxon Corp., 338 So. 2d 763 (La. App. 4th Cir. 1976)
18 ALR5th 577—§ 9, 38, 58

Sifers v. Horen, 385 Mich. 195, 188 N.W.2d 623 (1971)
78 ALR6th 151—§ 21

Sifford v. State, 505 S.W.2d 866 (Tex. Crim. App. 1974)
104 ALR5th 357—§ 6

Sigafus v. St. Louis Post-Dispatch, L.L.C., 109 S.W.3d 174 (Mo. Ct. App. E.D. 2003)
22 ALR6th 553—§ 27, 32

Sigal v. Manufacturers Light & Heat Co., 450 Pa. 228, 299 A.2d 646 (1973)
111 ALR5th 313—§ 20

Sigal v. Miller, 25 S.W. 1012 (Tex. Civ. App. 1894)
19 ALR5th 622—§ 8, 24

Sigall, State ex rel. v. Aetna Cleaning Contractors of Cleveland, Inc., 45 Ohio St. 2d 308, 74 Ohio Op. 2d 471, 345 N.E.2d 61 (1976)
65 ALR5th 1—§ 8, 14

Sigel v. New Jersey Mfrs. Ins. Co., 328 N.J. Super. 293, 745 A.2d 602 (App. Div. 2000)
66 ALR5th 269—§ 12

Sigesmund v. Sigesmund, 115 Cal. App. 2d 628, 252 P.2d 713 (2d Dist. 1953)
95 ALR5th 533—§ 5
124 ALR5th 203—§ 5

Siggelkow v. State, 648 P.2d 611 (Alaska 1982)
57 ALR5th 141—§ 13

Siggers v. Renner, 37 Fed. Appx. 138 (6th Cir. 2002)
65 ALR6th 93—§ 59

Sightes v. Barker, 684 N.E.2d 224 (Ind. Ct. App. 1997)
86 ALR6th 1—§ 89, 91

Sigler v. LeVan, 485 F. Supp. 185 (D. Md. 1980)
23 ALR6th 521—§ 23

Sigler v. Mutual Ben. Life Ins. Co., 506 F. Supp. 542 (S.D. Iowa 1981)
6 ALR5th 297—§ 10, 33
51 ALR6th 495—§ 4 to 6

Sigler v. State, 700 N.E.2d 809 (Ind. Ct. App. 1998)
12 ALR6th 267—§ 5

Sigler v. State, 2009-Ohio-2010, 2009 WL 1145232 (Ohio Ct. App. 5th Dist. Richland County 2009)
63 ALR6th 351—§ 3

Sigler & Sigler, In re Marriage of, 133 Or. App. 68, 889 P.2d 1323 (1995)
57 ALR5th 389—§ 2

Sigler, State on Behalf of v. Sigler, 85 Wash. App. 329, 932 P.2d 710 (Div. 3 1997)
118 ALR5th 385—§ 7, 16

Sigma Construction Co., Inc. v. Guilford County Bd. of Education, 547 S.E.2d 178 (N.C. Ct. App. 2001)
34 ALR5th 591—§ 3

Sigma Delta, LLC v. George, 2007 WL 4590097 (E.D. La. 2007)
47 ALR6th 255—§ 3

Sigman v. Gove, 169 Ga. App. 580, 314 S.E.2d 238, 10 Media L. R. 1896 (1984)

19 ALR5th 1—§ 104

Sigman Meat Co. v. Industrial Claim Appeals Office, 761 P.2d 265 (Colo. App. 1988)

36 ALR5th 225—§ 3

Sigma Reproductive Health Center v. State, 297 Md. 660, 467 A.2d 483 (1983)

3 ALR5th 521—§ 3

Sigmen v. Arizona Dep't of Real Estate, 169 Ariz. 383, 819 P.2d 969, 83 Ariz. Adv. Rep. 18 (App. 1991)

7 ALR5th 474—§ 112

Sigmoil Resources, N.V. v. Pan Ocean Oil Corp. (Nigeria), 234 A.D.2d 103, 650 N.Y.S.2d 726 (1st Dep' 1996)

66 ALR6th 567—§ 2, 11, 15, 18

Sigmon v. Brank, 826 F.2d 1060 (4th Cir. 1987)

99 ALR6th 481—§ 75

Sigmon v. Com., 200 Va. 258, 105 S.E.2d 171 (1958)

97 ALR5th 201—§ 7

Sigmon v. County of Tompkins, 113 Misc. 2d 655, 449 N.Y.S.2d 621 (1982)

12 ALR5th 1—§ 2, 5

Sigmon v. Womack, 158 Ga. App. 47, 279 S.E.2d 254 (1981)

52 ALR6th 271—§ 19

Sigmond v. Liberty Lines Transit, Inc., 689 N.Y.S.2d 239, 135 Ed. Law Rep. 218 (App. Div. 2d Dep't 1999)

16 ALR5th 1—§ 22

23 ALR5th 1—§ 17

Signad, Inc. v. Billboards Ltd., Inc., 1989 WL 128393 (Tex. App. Houston 14th Dist. 1989)

94 ALR5th 455—§ 9

Signaigo v. Begun, 234 Mich. 246, 207 N.W. 799 (1926)

25 ALR5th 123—§ 27

25 ALR5th 233—§ 3, 12

SIGNAL Corp. v. Keane Federal Systems, Inc., 265 Va. 38, 574 S.E.2d 253 (2003)

14 ALR6th 491—§ 5

Signal Peak Enterprises of Texas, Inc. v. Bettina Investments, Inc., 138 S.W.3d 915, 8 A.L.R.6th 761 (Tex. App. Dallas 2004)

8 ALR6th 399—§ 11

8 ALR6th 439—§ 8, 9

Signature Development Companies, Inc. v. Royal Ins. Co. of America, 230 F.3d 1215 (10th Cir. 2000)

14 ALR5th 695—§ 16

Signature Pharmacy, Inc. v. Soares, 717 F. Supp. 2d 1276 (M.D. Fla. 2010)

81 ALR6th 257—§ 17

Sign-A-Way, Inc. v. Mechtronics Corp., 12 F. Supp. 2d 132 (D. Mass. 1998)

2 ALR6th 195—§ 3, 5, 11

Sign-O-Lite Signs, Inc. v. DeLaurenti Florists, Inc., 64 Wash. App. 553, 825 P.2d 714 (Div. 1 1992)

115 ALR5th 709—§ 2

117 ALR5th 155—§ 2, 8, 12

Signorelli v. Jones, 483 So. 2d 672 (La. App. 5th Cir. 1986)

48 ALR5th 129—§ 12

Signs v. Brewington, 2009 WL 1693833 (Mich. App. 2009)

57 ALR6th 163—§ 40, 43

Sigsbee v. Swathwood, 419 N.E.2d 789 (Ind. Ct. App. 3d Dist. 1981)

75 ALR5th 1—§ 7, 13

Siguel v. Trustees of Tufts College, 52 Fair Empl. Prac. Cas. (BNA) 697, 53 Empl. Prac. Dec. (CCH) ¶ 39775, 1990 WL 29199 (D. Mass. 1990)

57 ALR5th 633—§ 3

Sigurdson v. Carl Bolander & Sons, 532 N.W.2d 225, 4 AD Cas. 852 (Minn. 1995)

51 ALR5th 1—§ 3

Siirila v. Barrios, 398 Mich. 576, 248 N.W.2d 171 (1976)

2 ALR5th 811—§ 2

4 ALR5th 148—§ 2

4 ALR5th 210—§ 2
6 ALR5th 490—§ 2
7 ALR5th 1—§ 2
Siker v. Siker, 225 Wis. 2d 522, 593 N.W.2d 830 (Ct. App. 1999)
16 ALR6th 693—§ 10
Sikes v. Heritage Oaks West Retirement Village, 238 S.W.3d 807 (Tex. App. Waco 2007)
50 ALR6th 187—§ 14
Sikes v. Seaboard C. L. R. Co., 429 So. 2d 1216 (Fla. App. D1 1983)
15 ALR5th 119—§ 5, 10
Sikes v. State, 247 Ga. App. 855, 545 S.E.2d 73 (2001)
73 ALR6th 1—§ 5
Sikes v. State, 711 So. 2d 250 (Fla. Dist. Ct. App. 4th Dist. 1998)
100 ALR5th 67—§ 45
Sikora v. AFD Industries, Inc., 319 F. Supp. 2d 872 (N.D. Ill. 2004)
115 ALR5th 1—§ 35
117 ALR5th 267—§ 8
Sikora v. AFD Industries, Inc., 2004 WL 848186 (N.D. Ill. 2004)
117 ALR5th 267—§ 8
Sikora v. Gibbs, 132 Ohio App. 3d 770, 726 N.E.2d 540, 111 A.L.R. 5th 685 (10th Dist. Franklin County 1999)
111 ALR5th 1—§ 11, 16
Sikora v. Plain Dealer Pub. Co., 2003-Ohio-3218, 2003 WL 21419279 (Ohio Ct. App. 8th Dist. Cuyahoga County 2003)
22 ALR6th 553—§ 4, 18, 32
Silagy v. State, 105 N.J. Super. 507, 253 A.2d 478 (1969)
13 ALR5th 444—§ 3, 4
Silagy v. Thompson, 1991 WL 18418 (N.D. Ill. 1991)
21 ALR6th 1—§ 4
Silagy, United States ex rel. v. Peters, 713 F. Supp. 1246 (C.D. Ill. 1989)
59 ALR5th 1—§ 3, 5, 6
Silagy, U.S. ex rel. v. Peters, 713 F. Supp. 1246 (C.D. Ill. 1989)
21 ALR6th 1—§ 4

Silak v. Hudson & M. R. Co., 114 NJL 428, 176 A. 674 (1935)
31 ALR5th 572—§ 29
Silano v. Board of Educ. of City of Bridgeport, 52 Conn. Supp. 42, 23 A.3d 104, 269 Ed. Law Rep. 606 (Super. Ct. 2011)
98 ALR6th 599—§ 22, 84
Silas v. Silas, 300 So. 2d 522 (La. Ct. App. 2d Cir. 1974)
120 ALR5th 229—§ 14
Silas v. State, 1999 WL 73983 (Alaska Ct. App. 1999)
7 ALR6th 233—§ 12
Silbaugh v. Strang, Inc., 242 Wis. 2d 473, 2001 WI App 75, 625 N.W.2d 361 (Ct. App. 2001)
5 ALR6th 497—§ 4, 5
Silbaugh v. Strang, Inc., 2000 WL 19807 (Wis. Ct. App. 2000)
5 ALR6th 497—§ 4
Silber, Matter of, 226 A.D.2d 50, 652 N.Y.S.2d 43 (2d Dep't 1996)
45 ALR6th 175—§ 4
Silber v. Seidler, 19 Misc. 2d 516, 188 N.Y.S.2d 111 (1959)
11 ALR5th 127—§ 37
Silberberg v. Lynberg, 186 F. Supp. 2d 157 (D. Conn. 2002)
101 ALR5th 515—§ 13
Silberfein, Matter of, 212 A.D.2d 907, 622 N.Y.S.2d 819 (3d Dep't 1995)
43 ALR6th 163—§ 6
Silberman v. Brown, 34 Ohio Ops. 295, 48 Ohio L. Abs. 97, 72 N.E.2d 267 (CP 1946)
14 ALR5th 557—§ 9, 14, 29
Silberman v. Com., 738 A.2d 508 (Pa. Commw. Ct. 1999)
14 ALR6th 119—§ 16
Silberman's Will, In re, 23 N.Y.2d 98, 295 N.Y.S.2d 478, 242 N.E.2d 736 (1968)
36 ALR5th 395—§ 3, 6, 10
37 ALR5th 237—§ 11
Silberstang v. Lomenzo, 37 App. Div. 2d 826, 325 N.Y.S.2d 297 (1st Dep't 1971)

7 ALR5th 474—§ 131

Silberstein v. Advance Magazine Publishers, Inc., 988 F. Supp. 391, 72 Empl. Prac. Dec. (CCH) ¶ 45167 (S.D. N.Y. 1997)

20 ALR6th 1—§ 7

Silberstein v. Berwald, 460 S.W.2d 707 (Mo. 1970)

95 ALR6th 541—§ 27

Silberstein v. City of Dayton, 440 F.3d 306, 24 I.E.R. Cas. (BNA) 153, 87 Empl. Prac. Dec. (CCH) ¶ 42384, 152 Lab. Cas. (CCH) ¶ 60160, 2006 FED App. 0083P (6th Cir. 2006)

89 ALR6th 1—§ 48

Silberstein v. Kitrick, 35 Cal. App. 91, 169 P. 250 (1917)

4 ALR5th 772—§ 107

Silbert v. Keton, 29 S.W.2d 824 (Tex. Civ. App. Waco 1930)

75 ALR5th 1—§ 3

Silbert v. Lakeview Educ. Assn., 187 Mich. App. 21, 466 N.W.2d 333 (1991)

12 ALR5th 950—§ 3

Silbert v. Ramsey, 301 Md. 96, 482 A.2d 147 (1984)

64 ALR5th 769—§ 4

Silbert v. State, 12 Md. App. 516, 280 A.2d 55 (1971)

85 ALR5th 547—§ 7

Silbowitz v. Lepper, 32 A.D.2d 520, 299 N.Y.S.2d 564 (1st Dep't 1969)

94 ALR5th 149—§ 8

Silbowitz v. Lepper, 32 App. Div. 2d 520, 299 N.Y.S.2d 564 (1st Dep't 1969)

44 ALR5th 193—§ 5

Silchia v. MCI Telecommunications Corp., 942 F. Supp. 1369, 153 L.R.R.M. (BNA) 2934 (D. Colo. 1996)

17 ALR5th 1—§ 6

Silcott v. Oglesby, 721 S.W.2d 290 (Tex. 1986)

103 ALR6th 461—§ 15

Siler v. 146 Montague Assocs., 652 N.Y.S.2d 315 (App. Div. 2d Dep't 1997)

50 ALR5th 1—§ 9, 11
54 ALR5th 379—§ 5

Siler v. Department of Employment Sec., 192 Ill. App. 3d 971, 140 Ill. Dec. 109, 549 N.E.2d 760 (1st Dist. 1989)

95 ALR5th 329—§ 5, 10, 16

Siler v. Guillotte, 410 So. 2d 1265 (La. App. 3d Cir. 1982)

1 ALR5th 163—§ 12, 15

Siler v. Gunn, 117 Ga. App. 325, 160 S.E.2d 427 (1968)

46 ALR6th 185—§ 7

Siler v. Marshall, 251 Md. 342, 247 A.2d 385 (1968)

39 ALR5th 33—§ 2 to 4

Siler v. State, 2005 WY 73, 115 P.3d 14 (Wyo. 2005)

9 ALR6th 1—§ 17

Sileven, Re Contempt of, 219 Neb. 34, 361 N.W.2d 189 (1985)

8 ALR5th 875—§ 2, 3, 6

Sileven v. Tesch, 212 Neb. 880, 326 N.W.2d 850 (1982)

8 ALR5th 875—§ 2, 3, 6

Silhan v. Allstate Ins. Co., 236 F. Supp. 2d 1303 (N.D. Fla. 2002)

101 ALR5th 61—§ 3, 9, 11, 12

Silica Products Liability Litigation, In re, 398 F. Supp. 2d 563 (S.D. Tex. 2005)

57 ALR6th 383—§ 13

Silicone Gel Breast Implants Products Liability Litigation, In re, 887 F. Supp. 1455 (N.D. Ala. 1995)

70 ALR6th 209—§ 23

Silicon Electro-Physics, Inc., In re, 116 B.R. 44, 12 U.C.C. Rep. Serv. 2d 232 (Bankr. W.D. Pa. 1990)

47 ALR6th 347—§ 5, 13

Silicon Graphics Inc. Securities Litigation, In re, 183 F.3d 970, Fed. Sec. L. Rep. (CCH) ¶ 90610, 44 Fed. R. Serv. 3d 1311 (9th Cir. 1999)

43 ALR6th 1—§ 12, 24, 26, 43

Silides v. Thomas, 559 P.2d 80 (Alaska 1977)

14 ALR6th 543—§ 53

Silinovich v. Vogt, 194 A.D.2d 1030, 599 N.Y.S.2d 694 (3d Dep't 1993)

91 ALR6th 435—§ 66, 121

Silinsky v. State-Wide Ins. Co., 30 A.D.2d 1, 289 N.Y.S.2d 541 (2d Dep't 1968)

125 ALR5th 1—§ 10

Silks v. State, 92 Nev. 91, 545 P.2d 1159 (1976)

51 ALR6th 219—§ 4

Silkworth v. Ryder Truck Rental, Inc., 70 Md. App. 264, 520 A.2d 1124, 2 I.E.R. Cas. (BNA) 1015, 13 O.S.H. Cas. (BNA) 1474, 1986-1987 O.S.H. Dec. (CCH) ¶ 27816 (1987)

104 ALR5th 1—§ 3, 5, 8

Sille v. McCann Constr. Specialties Co., 265 Ill. App. 3d 1051, 202 Ill. Dec. 808, 638 N.E.2d 676, CCH Prod. Liab. Rep. ¶ 14051, 25 U.C.C.R.S.2d 1128 (1st Dist. 1994)

49 ALR5th 1—§ 42

Sillery v. Board of Medicine, 145 Mich. App. 681, 378 N.W.2d 570 (1985)

97 ALR5th 419—§ 8

Sillett v. State, 393 So. 2d 53 (Fla. Dist. Ct. App. 2d Dist. 1981)

21 ALR6th 771—§ 31

Silliphant v. City of Beverly Hills, 195 Cal. App. 3d 1239, 241 Cal. Rptr. 356 (2d Dist. 1987)

43 ALR5th 545—§ 12

Sill Properties, Inc. v. CMAG, Inc., 219 Cal. App. 2d 42, 33 Cal. Rptr. 155 (5th Dist. 1963)

107 ALR5th 311—§ 10

Sills v. Oakland General Hosp., 220 Mich. App. 303, 559 N.W.2d 348 (1996)

5 ALR6th 133—§ 4, 6

14 ALR6th 301—§ 4

19 ALR6th 475—§ 2, 4, 7, 24

Sills v. Walworth County Land Management Committee, 254 Wis. 2d 538, 2002 WI App 111, 648 N.W.2d 878 (Ct. App. 2002)

4 ALR6th 263—§ 46

Silo v. CHW Medical Foundation, 103 Cal. Rptr. 2d 825, 84 Fair Empl. Prac. Cas. (BNA) 1632, 17 I.E.R. Cas. (BNA) 402 (App. 3d Dist. 2001)

106 ALR5th 523—§ 14

Silo v. CHW Medical Foundation, 2002 WL 31160871 (Cal. App. 3d Dist. 2002)

107 ALR5th 623—§ 8

Silo v. Ridge, 728 A.2d 394 (Pa. Commw. Ct. 1999)

89 ALR6th 1—§ 63

Silong v. U.S., 2007 WL 2535126 (E.D. Cal. 2007)

43 ALR6th 327—§ 3

Silsbee v. Herron, 484 S.W.2d 154 (Tex. Civ. App. Beaumont 1972)

38 ALR5th 737—§ 2

Silsby v. Ownit Mortg. Solutions, Inc., 2011 WL 4346384 (D. Nev. 2011)

86 ALR6th 411—§ 5

Silsby v. Ownit Mortg. Solutions, Inc., 2012 WL 1813054 (D. Nev. 2012)

86 ALR6th 411—§ 5

Silton v. Altman, 1984 WL 3139 (D. Mass. 1984)

22 ALR6th 113—§ 84

Silva v. Adams, 2010 WL 331754 (C.D. Cal. 2010)

81 ALR6th 505—§ 22

Silva v. American Federation of State, County and Municipal Employees, 231 F.3d 691 (10th Cir. 2000)

69 ALR6th 415—§ 54

Silva v. Autos of Amboy, 267 N.J. Super. 546, 632 A.2d 291 (App. Div. 1993)

23 ALR5th 241—§ 48

Silva v. Bieluch, 351 F.3d 1045, 20 I.E.R. Cas. (BNA) 1130 (11th Cir. 2003)

95 ALR6th 341—§ 63

Silva v. F. W. Woolworth Co., 28 Cal. App. 2d 649, 83 P.2d 76 (1938)
  2 ALR5th 189—§ 2, 3, 5, 7
Silva v. Hodge, 583 So. 2d 231 (Ala. 1991)
  13 ALR5th 289—§ 6, 18
Silva v. Industrial Acci. Com., 68 Cal. App. 510, 229 P. 870 (1924)
  26 ALR5th 127—§ 11
Silva v. Kaiser Permanente, 59 F. Supp. 2d 597 (N.D. Tex. 1999)
  51 ALR5th 271—§ 3
Silva v. Martin Lumber Co., 2003 WL 22496233 (Tenn. Workers' Comp. Panel 2003)
  121 ALR5th 523—§ 3, 7
Silva v. New York Life Ins. Co., 2001 WL 100325 (Conn. Super. Ct. 2001)
  2 ALR6th 387—§ 3 to 5, 8
Silva v. Saxon Mortg. Services Inc., 2012 WL 2450709 (E.D. Cal. 2012)
  86 ALR6th 411—§ 5
Silva v. Silva, 142 Idaho 900, 136 P.3d 371, 26 A.L.R.6th 837 (Ct. App. 2006)
  26 ALR6th 331—§ 24, 40
Silva v. Southwest Florida Blood Bank, Inc., 578 So. 2d 503 (Fla. App. D2 1991)
  12 ALR5th 1—§ 6
Silva v. Southwest Florida Blood Bank, Inc., 601 So. 2d 1184 (Fla. 1992)
  75 ALR5th 229—§ 2
Silva v. Spohn Health System Corp., 951 S.W.2d 91 (Tex. App. Corpus Christi 1997)
  40 ALR5th 1—§ 3
Silva v. State, 113 Nev. 1365, 951 P.2d 591 (1997)
  32 ALR6th 1—§ 11
Silva v. State, 152 Tex. Crim. 545, 215 S.W.2d 887 (1948)
  5 ALR5th 243—§ 49
Silva v. State, 344 So. 2d 559 (Fla. 1977)
  65 ALR5th 407—§ 3, 11, 16, 17
  68 ALR5th 343—§ 3, 4, 9
Silva v. State, 800 S.W.2d 912 (Tex. App. San Antonio 1990)

Silva v. State, 933 S.W.2d 715 (Tex. App. San Antonio 1996)
  16 ALR6th 329—§ 5
  24 ALR6th 591—§ 4, 12
Silva v. Stevens, 156 Vt. 94, 589 A.2d 852 (1991)
  8 ALR5th 312—§ 4, 10
Silva v. Tucker, 500 A.2d 947 (R.I. 1985)
  5 ALR5th 788—§ 2
  40 ALR5th 227—§ 2
  80 ALR5th 117—§ 2, 14
Silva v. Wilcox, 223 P.3d 127 (Colo. App. 2009)
  79 ALR6th 351—§ 14
Silva v. Woodford, 279 F.3d 825 (9th Cir. 2002)
  102 ALR6th 417—§ 3, 12, 24
Silvan v. Sylvan, 267 N.J. Super. 578, 632 A.2d 528 (App. Div. 1993)
  11 ALR6th 125—§ 7, 8, 13, 17, 18
Silvan W. v. Briggs, 309 Fed. Appx. 216 (10th Cir. 2009)
  62 ALR6th 161—§ 6
Silva-Pearson v. BAC Home Loans Servicing, LP, 2011 WL 2633406 (N.D. Cal. 2011)
  86 ALR6th 411—§ 5
Silvas v. Ghiatas, 954 S.W.2d 50 (Tex. App. San Antonio 1997)
  97 ALR6th 83—§ 18
Silvas v. GMAC Mortg., LLC, 2009 WL 4573234 (D. Ariz. 2009)
  86 ALR6th 411—§ 5
Silvas v. South Bay Community Services, 2003 WL 23419 (Cal. App. 4th Dist. 2003)
  80 ALR6th 469—§ 57, 60
Silveira v. Las Gallinas Valley Sanitary Dist., 54 Cal. App. 4th 980, 63 Cal. Rptr. 2d 244 (1st Dist. 1997)
  106 ALR5th 523—§ 43
Silveira v. Silveira, 630 So. 2d 204, 18 FLW D 2593 (Fla. App. D4 1993)
  38 ALR5th 69—§ 9
Silver v. Apfel, 286 A.D.2d 725, 730 N.Y.S.2d 456 (2d Dep't 2001)

17 ALR6th 159—§ 58
Silver v. Castle Memorial Hospital, 53 Hawaii 475, 53 Hawaii 563, 497 P.2d 564, 1972 CCH Trade Cases ¶ 74016 (1972)
28 ALR5th 107—§ 3, 41
Silver v. Downs, 493 Pa. 50, 425 A.2d 359 (1981)
47 ALR5th 553—§ 10
Silver v. First Nat. Bank of Hillsborough, 108 N.H. 390, 236 A.2d 493 (1967)
81 ALR6th 161—§ 4
82 ALR6th 43—§ 4
Silver v. Klehr, Harrison, Harvey, Branzburg & Ellers, LLP, 2004 WL 1699269 (E.D. Pa. 2004)
64 ALR6th 473—§ 11
Silver v. Los Angeles County Metropolitan Transportation Authority, 79 Cal. App. 4th 338, 94 Cal. Rptr. 2d 287 (2d Dist. 2000)
106 ALR5th 523—§ 18
Silver v. Mount Hebron Cemetery, 64 N.Y.S.2d 274 (Sup 1946)
81 ALR6th 1—§ 47
Silver v. New York C. R. Co., 329 Mass. 14, 105 N.E.2d 923 (1952)
10 ALR5th 371—§ 3, 4, 14
Silver v. Queen's Hospital, 63 Hawaii 430, 629 P.2d 1116, 1981-2 CCH Trade Cases ¶ 64443 (1981)
28 ALR5th 107—§ 4, 13, 18
Silver v. Reagan, 67 Cal. 2d 452, 62 Cal. Rptr. 424, 432 P.2d 26 (1967)
114 ALR5th 387—§ 3
Silver v. Silver, 36 N.Y.2d 324, 367 N.Y.S.2d 777, 327 N.E.2d 816 (1975)
46 ALR5th 735—§ 2
Silver v. Silver, 100 App. Div. 2d 543, 473 N.Y.S.2d 240 (2d Dep't 1984)
20 ALR5th 700—§ 27
21 ALR5th 396—§ 3, 13, 20, 49
Silver v. Sloop Silver Cloud, 259 F. Supp. 187, 1967 A.M.C. 737, 3 U.C.C. Rep. Serv. 971 (S.D. N.Y. 1966)

48 ALR6th 475—§ 4
Silver v. Starrett, 176 Misc. 2d 511, 674 N.Y.S.2d 915 (Sup 1998)
21 ALR6th 351—§ 5, 14, 15, 20, 21
Silver v. State, 147 Ga. 162, 93 S.E. 145 (1917)
31 ALR6th 523—§ 25, 29, 32, 33, 36, 55
Silver v. State, 420 Md. 415, 23 A.3d 867 (2011)
70 ALR6th 329—§ 18
Silver v. U.S., 726 A.2d 191 (D.C. 1999)
6 ALR5th 733—§ 15
68 ALR6th 115—§ 28, 37, 40
Silvera v. Connecticut Dept. of Corrections, 726 F. Supp. 2d 183 (D. Conn. 2010)
86 ALR6th 173—§ 10, 14
Silvera v. Home Depot U.S.A., Inc., 189 F. Supp. 2d 304 (D. Md. 2002)
7 ALR6th 563—§ 5
Silverberg v. Dillon, 73 A.D.2d 838, 423 N.Y.S.2d 760 (4th Dep't 1979)
91 ALR6th 435—§ 68, 140
Silverberg v. People's Bank, 23 Fed. Appx. 46 (2d Cir. 2001)
60 ALR6th 295—§ 5, 74
Silverberg v. Schwartz, 75 App. Div. 2d 817, 427 N.Y.S.2d 480 (2d Dep't 1980)
28 ALR5th 420—§ 6
Silver by Silver v. Cooper, 199 A.D.2d 255, 604 N.Y.S.2d 968, 87 Ed. Law Rep. 1037 (2d Dep't 1993)
72 ALR5th 469—§ 15
Silver City and Silver City Police Officers Ass'n, Matter of Arbitration Between Town of, 115 N.M. 628, 857 P.2d 28 (1993)
66 ALR5th 611—§ 2, 9
Silver Creations, Ltd. v. United Parcel Service, 133 N.J. Super. 543, 337 A.2d 641, 16 U.C.C. Rep. Serv. (CBC) 1299, 88 A.L.R.3d 1093 (Law Div. 1975)
71 ALR5th 443—§ 13

Silverdale Hotel Associates v. Lomas & Nettleton Co., 36 Wash. App. 762, 677 P.2d 773 (1984)

18 ALR5th 307—§ 29

Silver Eagle Co. v. National Union Fire Ins. Co., 246 Or. 398, 423 P.2d 944, 40 A.L.R.3d 1432 (1967)

14 ALR5th 695—§ 24

Silver Falls Timber Co. v. Eastern & Western Lumber Co., 149 Or. 126, 40 P.2d 703 (1935)

17 ALR5th 547—§ 3, 22, 34, 35

Silverhart v. Mount Zion Hospital, 20 Cal. App. 3d 1022, 98 Cal. Rptr. 187, 54 A.L.R.3d 250 (1st Dist. 1971)

65 ALR5th 357—§ 3

Silver Hills Country Club v. Sobieski, 55 Cal. 2d 811, 13 Cal. Rptr. 186, 361 P.2d 906, Blue Sky L. Rep. (CCH) ¶ 70550, 87 A.L.R.2d 1135 (1961)

28 ALR6th 281—§ 7, 8, 12

Silver Leaf, L.L.C., In re, 31 Del. J. Corp. L. 326, 2005 WL 2045641 (Del. Ch. 2005)

49 ALR6th 1—§ 50, 81

Silverman, Ex parte, 69 Ohio App. 128, 23 Ohio Op. 555, 37 Ohio L. Abs. 199, 42 N.E.2d 87 (1st Dist. Hamilton County 1942)

76 ALR5th 485—§ 15, 19

Silverman, In re, 155 B.R. 362 (Bankr. E.D. N.C. 1993)

117 ALR5th 155—§ 3

Silverman, In re Claim of, 82 App. Div. 2d 955, 440 N.Y.S.2d 771 (3d Dep't 1981)

33 ALR5th 643—§ 12

Silverman v. Benmor Coats, Inc., 61 N.Y.2d 299, 473 N.Y.S.2d 774, 461 N.E.2d 1261 (1984)

56 ALR5th 757—§ 2

Silverman v. Berkson, 141 N.J. 412, 661 A.2d 1266, CCH Blue Sky L. Rep. ¶ 74055 (1995)

58 ALR5th 293—§ 6, 7

Silverman v. CBS, Inc., 675 F. Supp. 870, 6 U.S.P.Q.2d 1975 (S.D. N.Y. 1988)

23 ALR5th 241—§ 36

Silverman v. Charmac, Inc., 414 So. 2d 892 (Ala. 1982)

104 ALR6th 303—§ 16

Silverman v. City of New York, 28 Misc. 2d 20, 211 N.Y.S.2d 560 (App. Term 1961)

66 ALR5th 1—§ 26

Silverman v. City of New York, 56 N.Y.2d 608, 450 N.Y.S.2d 480, 435 N.E.2d 1095, 44 Fair Empl. Prac. Cas. (BNA) 316 (1982)

14 ALR6th 417—§ 8

Silverman v. City of New York, 2001 WL 218943 (E.D. N.Y. 2001)

89 ALR6th 1—§ 88

Silverman v. Clark, 35 A.D.3d 1, 822 N.Y.S.2d 9 (1st Dep't 2006)

52 ALR6th 271—§ 5

Silverman v. New Rochelle Hospital, 98 App. Div. 2d 774, 469 N.Y.S.2d 488 (2d Dep't 1983)

33 ALR5th 205—§ 5, 30

Silverman v. New York Univ. Sch. of Law, 193 App. Div. 2d 411, 597 N.Y.S.2d 314 (1st Dep't 1993)

47 ALR5th 1—§ 23, 32

Silverman v. Pitterman, 574 So. 2d 275 (Fla. Dist. Ct. App. 3d Dist. 1991)

46 ALR6th 185—§ 7

Silverman v. Progressive Broadcasting, Inc., 125 N.M. 500, 1998-NMCA-107, 964 P.2d 61 (Ct. App. 1998)

38 ALR6th 541—§ 3, 5

Silverman v. Silverman, 91 App. Div. 2d 609, 456 N.Y.S.2d 408 (2d Dep't 1982)

47 ALR5th 207—§ 20

Silver Meadows Properties v. Biney, Slip Op. No. 1556 (Ohio App. Portage Co. 1986)

38 ALR5th 433—§ 2

Silvern v. Silvern, 252 So. 2d 865 (Fla. Dist. Ct. App. 3d Dist. 1971)

84 ALR5th 399—§ 3, 9, 13

Silver Plume v. Hudson, 151 Colo. 394,
380 P.2d 59 (1963)
7 ALR5th 187—§ 2
Silvers v. Brodeur, 682 N.E.2d 811 (Ind.
Ct. App. 1997)
12 ALR6th 1—§ 4, 5
Silvers v. Erie Ins. Group, 2005-Ohio-
2504, 2005 WL 1205560 (Ohio Ct.
App. 3d Dist. Hancock County
2005)
90 ALR6th 635—§ 27
Silvers v. Horace Mann Ins. Co., 324
N.C. 289, 378 S.E.2d 21 (1989)
75 ALR6th 235—§ 30
Silvers v. Wesson, 122 Cal. App. 2d
902, 266 P.2d 169 (1st Dist. 1954)
97 ALR6th 83—§ 42
Silvers v. Wesson, 122 Cal. App. 2d
902, 266 P.2d 169 (1954)
48 ALR5th 575—§ 11
Silvers' Estate, Re, 24 Misc. 2d 939, 201
N.Y.S.2d 415 (1960)
14 ALR5th 557—§ 3
Silverside Home Mart, Inc. v. Hall, 345
A.2d 427 (Del. Super. Ct. 1975)
46 ALR5th 1—§ 47
Silverstar Enterprises, Inc. v. Aday, 537
F. Supp. 236, 218 U.S.P.Q. 142
(S.D. N.Y. 1982)
76 ALR6th 289—§ 2
Silverstein v. Gwinnett Hospital Authority, 861 F.2d 1560 (CA11 Ga. 1988)
28 ALR5th 107—§ 4, 5, 8
Silverstein v. Keane, 19 N.J. 1, 115 A.2d
1 (1955)
12 ALR6th 123—§ 4
Silverstein v. Marine Midland Trust Co.,
1 App. Div. 2d 1037, 152 N.Y.S.2d
30 (2d Dep't 1956)
14 ALR5th 242—§ 24
Silverstein v. Microsystems Software,
Inc., 57 Mass. App. Ct. 1114, 785
N.E.2d 428 (2003)
120 ALR5th 559—§ 9
Silverstein v. Penguin Putnam, Inc., 522
F. Supp. 2d 579, 85 U.S.P.Q.2d
1559 (S.D. N.Y. 2007)
76 ALR6th 289—§ 4

77 ALR6th 543—§ 12
Silverstein v. R.H. Macy & Co., 266
A.D. 5, 40 N.Y.S.2d 916 (1st Dep't
1943)
93 ALR5th 103—§ 1, 12
76 ALR6th 395—§ 19
Silverstein v. Silverstein, 748 P.2d 1004
(Okla. App. 1987)
49 ALR5th 441—§ 20
Silverstein v. Silverstein, 1987 OK CIV
APP 87, 748 P.2d 1004 (Ct. App.
Div. 1 1987)
3 ALR6th 447—§ 6, 8
Silverstein v. Sisters of Charity of Leav-
enworth Health Services Corp., 38
Colo. App. 286, 559 P.2d 716, 1
A.D. Cas. (BNA) 8, 14 Fair Empl.
Prac. Cas. (BNA) 1066, 13 Empl.
Prac. Dec. (CCH) ¶ 11500 (1976)
106 ALR5th 523—§ 14
Silverstein v. Town of Alexandria, 150
N.H. 679, 843 A.2d 963 (2004)
91 ALR6th 435—§ 143
Silverthorne v. U.S., 400 F.2d 627 (9th
Cir. 1968)
55 ALR6th 157—§ 32, 57
Silves v. King, 93 Wash. App. 873, 970
P.2d 790, 79 A.L.R.5th 771 (Div. 1
1999)
79 ALR5th 409—§ 3
Silvester v. American Broadcasting
Companies, Inc., 839 F.2d 1491, 15
Media L. Rep. (BNA) 1138 (11th
Cir. 1988)
42 ALR6th 353—§ 17
Silvester v. American Broadcasting
Cos., 839 F.2d 1491, 15 Media L.
R. 1138 (CA11 Fla. 1988)
19 ALR5th 1—§ 2, 59
Silvestre v. Bell Atlantic Corp., 973 F.
Supp. 475 (D.N.J. 1997)
51 ALR5th 1—§ 7
11 ALR6th 447—§ 6
19 ALR6th 1—§ 7
Silvestre v. De Loaiza, 12 Misc. 3d 492,
820 N.Y.S.2d 440 (Sup 2006)
32 ALR6th 419—§ 23

Silvestri v. General Motors Corp., 210
F.3d 240 (4th Cir. 2000)
39 ALR5th 267—§ 5
Silvestri v. General Motors Corp., 271
F.3d 583, 51 Fed. R. Serv. 3d 694
(4th Cir. 2001)
102 ALR5th 99—§ 6
Silvestri-Gagliardoni, Re Marriage of,
186 Ill. App. 3d 46, 134 Ill. Dec.
106, 542 N.E.2d 106 (1st Dist.
1989)
16 ALR5th 650—§ 34
Silvestrone v. Edell, 701 So. 2d 90 (Fla.
Dist. Ct. App. 5th Dist. 1997)
87 ALR5th 473—§ 2
Silvestrone v. Edell, 721 So. 2d 1173
(Fla. 1998)
12 ALR6th 1—§ 7
13 ALR6th 1—§ 4
14 ALR6th 1—§ 4
Silvey v. Kaiser, 173 S.W.2d 63 (Mo.
1943)
88 ALR5th 463—§ 9, 13
Silvey v. Silvey, 634 So. 2d 138 (Ala.
App. 1993)
9 ALR5th 568—§ 9
Silvey v. State, 485 So. 2d 790 (Ala.
App. 1986)
7 ALR5th 263—§ 3
Silvia, Ex parte, 123 Cal. 293, 55 P. 988
(1899)
52 ALR5th 221—§ 12
Silvia v. Zayre Corp., 233 So. 2d 856
(Fla. App. D3 1970)
12 ALR5th 195—§ 40
Silvius v. Mordoff, 183 Cal. 628, 192 P.
289 (1920)
13 ALR5th 684—§ 13
Silz, State ex rel. v. Indus. Comm., 2004-
Ohio-4100, 2004 WL 1752863
(Ohio Ct. App. 10th Dist. Franklin
County 2004)
31 ALR6th 199—§ 80
Simaee v. Levi, 22 A.D.3d 559, 802
N.Y.S.2d 493 (2d Dep't 2005)
43 ALR6th 611—§ 65
Simaitis v. Flood, 182 Conn. 24, 437
A.2d 828 (1980)

42 ALR6th 61—§ 11
Simakis v. District Court of Fifth Judi-
cial for Eagle County, 194 Colo.
436, 577 P.2d 3 (1978)
70 ALR6th 361—§ 31
Simas v. First Citizens' Federal Credit
Union, 63 F. Supp. 2d 110, 15 I.E.R.
Cas. (BNA) 922 (D. Mass. 1999)
105 ALR5th 351—§ 3, 4, 7
53 ALR6th 213—§ 11
Simat v. Trytten, 2010 WL 2572621
(Minn. Ct. App. 2010)
91 ALR6th 1—§ 3
Simat Corp. v. Arizona Health Care Cost
Containment System, 203 Ariz. 454,
56 P.3d 28 (2002)
118 ALR5th 463—§ 16
Simboli v. State, 728 So. 2d 792 (Fla.
Dist. Ct. App. 5th Dist. 1999)
100 ALR5th 67—§ 12
Simbraw, Inc. v. U.S., 367 F.2d 373
(CA3 Pa. 1966)
8 ALR5th 653—§ 3
Simburg, Ketter, Sheppard & Purdy,
L.L.P. v. Olshan, 97 Wash. App.
901, 109 Wash. App. 436, 988 P.2d
467 (Div. 1 1999)
13 ALR6th 1—§ 4
16 ALR6th 653—§ 7
Simchuk v. Angel Island Community
Ass'n, 253 Mont. 221, 833 P.2d 158
(1992)
50 ALR5th 1—§ 4
52 ALR5th 1—§ 9
Simcoe v. Huszar, 10 Pa. D. & C.3d 298,
27 U.C.C.R.S. 627 (1979)
62 ALR5th 137—§ 5
Simeon v. State, 778 So. 2d 455 (Fla.
Dist. Ct. App. 4th Dist. 2001)
66 ALR5th 397—§ 8
Simeon v. T. Smith & Son, Inc., 852
F.2d 1421 (CA5 La. 1988)
52 ALR5th 1—§ 3
Simeone v. Girard City Bd. of Edn., 171
Ohio App. 3d 633, 2007-Ohio-1775,
872 N.E.2d 344, 222 Ed. Law Rep.
362 (11th Dist. Trumbull County
2007)

For assistance, call 1-800-328-4880

57 ALR6th 383—§ 3, 16

Simeone v. Simeone, 525 Pa. 392, 581 A.2d 162 (1990)

3 ALR5th 394—§ 5, 8, 9

Simeone v. Smith, 204 Va. 860, 134 S.E.2d 281 (1964)

56 ALR5th 133—§ 4

Simeon, Inc. v. Cox, 655 So. 2d 156 (Fla. Dist. Ct. App. 5th Dist. 1995)

21 ALR6th 671—§ 4

Simeon, Inc. v. Cox, 671 So. 2d 158 (Fla. 1996)

21 ALR6th 671—§ 4, 5

Simera v. Simera, 638 So. 2d 901 (Ala. Civ. App. 1993)

86 ALR6th 321—§ 4

90 ALR6th 451—§ 23

Simerka v. Pridemore, 380 Mich. 250, 156 N.W.2d 509 (1968)

4 ALR5th 443—§ 3, 6

Simeth, In re, 40 Cal. App. 3d 982, 115 Cal. Rptr. 617 (2d Dist. 1974)

92 ALR5th 379—§ 10

Simic v. State ex rel. Dept. of Public Safety, 2006 OK CIV APP 8, 129 P.3d 177, 206 Ed. Law Rep. 1013 (Div. 2 2005)

18 ALR6th 519—§ 8

Simics v. Sharpe, 1991 WL 86196 (Conn. Super, May 13, 1991)

50 ALR5th 417—§ 2

Simien v. Medical Protective Co., 11 So. 3d 1206 (La. Ct. App. 3d Cir. 2009)

97 ALR6th 83—§ 120, 147

Simien v. S. S. Kresge Co., 566 F.2d 551 (5th Cir. 1978)

86 ALR5th 215—§ 8

Simitar Entertainment, Inc. v. Silva Entertainment, Inc., 44 F. Supp. 2d 986 (D. Minn. 1999)

8 ALR5th 653—§ 3

Sim Kar Lighting Fixture Co. v. Genlyte, Inc., 906 F. Supp. 967 (D.N.J. 1995)

104 ALR5th 1—§ 3

Simkin v. Vinci, 215 So. 2d 404 (La. App. 4th Cir. 1968)

13 ALR5th 169—§ 7

Simkins v. Davenport, 232 N.W.2d 561 (Iowa 1975)

15 ALR5th 821—§ 7

Simkins v. Moses H. Cone Memorial Hospital, 323 F.2d 959 (CA4 N.C. 1963)

28 ALR5th 107—§ 5, 35

Simkins-Hallin Lumber Co. v. Simonson, 214 Mont. 36, 692 P.2d 424 (1984)

10 ALR5th 448—§ 8

Simkins Industries, Inc. v. Highlands Ins. Co., 795 So. 2d 169 (Fla. Dist. Ct. App. 3d Dist. 2001)

119 ALR5th 121—§ 3, 12

Simkins Industries, Inc. v. Lexington Ins. Co., 42 Md. App. 396, 401 A.2d 181 (1979)

37 ALR5th 41—§ 26, 51

Simko v. Town of Highlands, 276 Fed. Appx. 39 (2d Cir. 2008)

67 ALR6th 531—§ 21, 23, 25, 37

Simkus v. State, 296 Md. 718, 464 A.2d 1055 (1983)

124 ALR5th 1—§ 5

Simmerman v. Department of Transp., 167 Ga. App. 383, 307 S.E.2d 4 (1983)

22 ALR5th 327—§ 26, 58, 62

Simmermon v. Dryvit Systems, Inc., 196 N.J. 316, 953 A.2d 478 (2008)

50 ALR6th 281—§ 6

Simmerock, State ex rel. v. Brackmann, 714 S.W.2d 938 (Mo. App. 1986)

6 ALR5th 883—§ 2

Simmers v. American Cyanamid Corp., 394 Pa. Super. 464, 576 A.2d 376 (1990)

109 ALR5th 301—§ 2, 3, 14

18 ALR6th 629—§ 3, 5, 25

Simmers v. Depoy, 212 Va. 447, 184 S.E.2d 776 (1971)

9 ALR5th 826—§ 3

Simmers v. State, 943 P.2d 1189 (Wyo. 1997)

38 ALR5th 433—§ 7

Simmerson v. Herringdine, 166 Ga. 143, 142 S.E. 687 (1928)

36 ALR6th 387—§ 4
Simmonds v. Abbott, 169 Fed. Appx. 840 (5th Cir. 2006)
63 ALR6th 1—§ 29
Simmonds v. Abbott, 2004 WL 5016170 (S.D. Tex. 2004)
63 ALR6th 1—§ 5, 34
Simmonds v. Com., 2000 WL 1377128 (Va. Ct. App. 2000)
92 ALR6th 171—§ 32
Simmonds v. Credit Suisse Securities (USA) LLC, 638 F.3d 1072 (9th Cir. 2011)
66 ALR6th 635—§ 28
76 ALR6th 587—§ 51
Simmonds v. Cuomo, 59 App. Div. 2d 621, 398 N.Y.S.2d 169 (2d Dep't 1977)
7 ALR5th 474—§ 189
Simmonds v. New York & N. E. R. Co., 52 Conn. 264 (1884)
17 ALR5th 547—§ 38, 77
Simmonds v. TDCJ, 2010 WL 654498 (Tex. App. Waco 2010)
89 ALR6th 1—§ 54
Simmonds v. Virgin Islands, 2010 WL 1813502 (V.I. 2010)
62 ALR6th 413—§ 38
Simmonds-Hewett v. Keaton, 626 So. 2d 249 (Fla. Dist. Ct. App. 4th Dist. 1993)
111 ALR5th 579—§ 2
Simmons, In re Marriage of, 636 S.W.2d 351 (Mo. Ct. App. E.D. 1982)
7 ALR6th 411—§ 3, 34
Simmons, Re, 65 Wash. 2d 88, 395 P.2d 1013 (1964)
10 ALR5th 139—§ 12
Simmons, Re, 112 App. Div. 2d 806, 492 N.Y.S.2d 308 (4th Dep't 1985)
12 ALR5th 577—§ 14
Simmons v. Aiken, 100 App. Div. 2d 769, 474 N.Y.S.2d 41 (1st Dep't 1984)
16 ALR5th 262—§ 58
Simmons v. Albany Boys Club, Inc., 80 Misc. 2d 19, 362 N.Y.S.2d 113 (1974)

49 ALR5th 1—§ 61
Simmons v. Balcarran, 105 A.D.2d 639, 481 N.Y.S.2d 701 (1st Dep't 1984)
69 ALR5th 1—§ 3, 4
Simmons v. Bank of Mississippi, 593 So. 2d 40 (Miss. 1992)
107 ALR5th 311—§ 11
109 ALR5th 421—§ 3
Simmons v. Beazel, 125 Ind. 362, 25 N.E. 344 (1890)
31 ALR5th 499—§ 15
Simmons v. Berry, 779 So. 2d 910 (La. Ct. App. 1st Cir. 2000)
90 ALR5th 453—§ 12
Simmons v. Board of Comm'rs, 624 So. 2d 935 (La. App. 2d Cir. 1993)
25 ALR5th 568—§ 47
Simmons v. Bonhotel, 40 Conn. App. 278, 670 A.2d 874 (1996)
41 ALR6th 207—§ 2
Simmons v. Bowersox, 235 F.3d 1124 (8th Cir. 2001)
10 ALR5th 700—§ 8
79 ALR5th 33—§ 10
Simmons v. Byrd, 192 Ind. 274, 136 N.E. 14 (1922)
56 ALR6th 523—§ 4
Simmons v. Calcasieu Community Center Playground Dist. #2, 524 So. 2d 775 (La. App. 3d Cir. 1988)
50 ALR5th 1—§ 3
Simmons v. Carnival Cruise Lines, 2003 A.M.C. 454, 2003 WL 21204631 (E.D. N.Y. 2003)
82 ALR6th 175—§ 6
Simmons v. Carter, 576 N.E.2d 1278 (Ind. App. 1991)
8 ALR5th 653—§ 5
Simmons v. Chemol Corp., 137 N.C. App. 319, 528 S.E.2d 368, 10 A.D. Cas. (BNA) 1646 (2000)
7 ALR6th 563—§ 18
Simmons v. City of Evanston, 1992 WL 25712 (N.D. Ill. 1992)
90 ALR5th 273—§ 5, 9
Simmons v. City of Paris, Tex., 378 F.3d 476 (5th Cir. 2004)
59 ALR6th 311—§ 3, 30

Simmons v. City of Toledo, 4 Ohio C.D.
69, 1890 WL 367 (Ohio Cir. Ct.
1890)
95 ALR5th 29—§ 3
Simmons v. City Stores Co., 412 F.2d
897 (5th Cir. 1969)
63 ALR6th 495—§ 44
Simmons v. Clemco Industries, 368 So.
2d 509, 25 U.C.C.R.S. 1088 (Ala.
1979)
49 ALR5th 1—§ 44
50 ALR5th 327—§ 10
Simmons v. Com., 238 Va. 200, 380
S.E.2d 656 (1989)
116 ALR5th 479—§ 2, 5
Simmons v. Com., Unemployment
Compensation Bd. of Review, 129
Pa. Commw. 315, 565 A.2d 829
(1989)
95 ALR5th 329—§ 10
Simmons v. Custom-Bilt Cabinet & Supply Co., 509 So. 2d 663 (La. App.
3d Cir. 1987)
48 ALR5th 129—§ 2, 3
50 ALR5th 1—§ 2
51 ALR5th 467—§ 2
52 ALR5th 1—§ 2
Simmons v. Danhauer & Associates,
LLC, 2010 WL 4238856 (D.S.C.
2010)
61 ALR6th 207—§ 10
Simmons v. Director, TDCJ-CID, 2006
WL 1004879 (E.D. Tex. 2006)
55 ALR6th 391—§ 19
Simmons v. District of Columbia Armory Bd., 656 A.2d 1155 (Dist. Col.
App. 1995)
45 ALR5th 173—§ 12
Simmons v. East Nassau Medical Group,
P.C., 260 A.D.2d 463, 688 N.Y.S.2d
209 (2d Dep't 1999)
92 ALR6th 379—§ 62, 114
Simmons v. Egwu, 662 N.E.2d 657 (Ind.
App. 1996)
47 ALR5th 433—§ 13
Simmons v. F. W. Woolworth Co., 163
Cal. App. 2d 709, 329 P.2d 999 (4th
Dist. 1958)

63 ALR6th 495—§ 77
Simmons v. Galvin, 131 S. Ct. 412, 178
L. Ed. 2d 321 (2010)
66 ALR6th 635—§ 17
Simmons v. Galvin, 575 F.3d 24 (1st
Cir. 2009)
66 ALR6th 635—§ 17
Simmons v. Gerace, 377 So. 2d 407 (La.
Ct. App. 2d Cir. 1979)
95 ALR5th 329—§ 12
Simmons v. Ghaderi, 49 Cal. Rptr. 3d
342 (Cal. App. 2d Dist. 2006)
32 ALR6th 285—§ 29
Simmons v. Gillespie, 2008 WL
3925157 (C.D. Ill. 2008)
64 ALR6th 131—§ 41
Simmons v. Hartford Ins. Co., 786 F.
Supp. 574 (E.D. La. 1992)
96 ALR5th 107—§ 7, 10
99 ALR5th 301—§ 4
Simmons v. Insurance Co. of North
America, 17 P.3d 56 (Alaska 2001)
66 ALR5th 269—§ 3
Simmons v. John L. Roper Lumber Co.,
174 N.C. 220, 93 S.E. 736 (1917)
17 ALR5th 547—§ 36
Simmons v. Justice, 87 F. Supp. 2d 524,
1 A.L.R.6th 785 (W.D. N.C. 2000)
1 ALR6th 407—§ 9, 17
Simmons v. Lennon, 139 Md. App. 15,
773 A.2d 1064, 91 A.L.R.5th 653
(2001)
91 ALR5th 89—§ 7, 9
Simmons v. Lincoln, 176 Neb. 71, 125
N.W.2d 63 (1963)
5 ALR5th 422—§ 6
Simmons v. Lockhart, 626 F. Supp. 872
(E.D. Ark. 1985)
7 ALR5th 758—§ 4
Simmons v. Miller, 261 Va. 561, 544
S.E.2d 666 (2001)
111 ALR5th 207—§ 7
Simmons v. Mississippi Transp. Com'n,
717 So. 2d 300 (Miss. 1998)
93 ALR6th 363—§ 3

Simmons v. Mobil Oil Corp., 29 F.3d 505, 94 C.D.O.S. 5430, 94 Daily Journal DAR 9979 (CA9 Ariz. 1994)

52 ALR5th 613—§ 1, 2

Simmons v. Monarch Mach. Tool Co., Inc., 413 Mass. 205, 596 N.E.2d 318, Prod. Liab. Rep. (CCH) ¶ 13264, 18 U.C.C. Rep. Serv. 2d (CBC) 420 (1992)

64 ALR5th 119—§ 3

Simmons v. Morgan Stanley Smith Barney, LLC, 2012 WL 6725844 (S.D. Cal. 2012)

86 ALR6th 519—§ 5

Simmons v. Mullen, 231 Pa. Super. 199, 331 A.2d 892 (1974)

72 ALR5th 529—§ 19

Simmons v. New York, 168 App. Div. 2d 230, 562 N.Y.S.2d 119 (1st Dep't 1990)

43 ALR5th 207—§ 60

Simmons v. New York City Police Dept. License Div., 35 A.D.3d 748, 825 N.Y.S.2d 768 (2d Dep't 2006)

91 ALR6th 435—§ 25, 68, 85

Simmons v. Norfolk & Western Ry. Co., 734 F. Supp. 230 (W.D. Va. 1990)

7 ALR6th 563—§ 3

Simmons v. Poe, 47 F.3d 1370, 31 Fed. R. Serv. 3d 451 (4th Cir. 1995)

74 ALR6th 69—§ 3, 12

Simmons v. Provident Mut. Life Ins. Co., 496 So. 2d 243 (Fla. App. D3 1986)

56 ALR5th 471—§ 2, 4, 8

Simmons v. Prudential Ins. Co., 641 F. Supp. 675, 7 EBC 2140 (D.C. Colo. 1986)

6 ALR5th 297—§ 3, 4, 9, 18

Simmons v. Reid, 31 S.C. 389, 9 S.E. 1058 (1889)

27 ALR5th 764—§ 6, 10, 11

Simmons v. Rhodes & Jamieson, Ltd., 46 Cal. 2d 190, 293 P.2d 26 (1956)

60 ALR5th 413—§ 4 to 6

Simmons v. Saltz, 9 Pa. D. & C.2d 605, 1957 WL 6446 (C.P. 1957)

17 ALR6th 159—§ 9

Simmons v. Simmons, 74 N.C. App. 725, 329 S.E.2d 723 (1985)

120 ALR5th 229—§ 7, 22

Simmons v. Simmons, 98 Ark. App. 12, 249 S.W.3d 843 (2007)

77 ALR6th 293—§ 11, 42

Simmons v. Simmons, 159 App. Div. 2d 775, 551 N.Y.S.2d 997 (3d Dep't 1990)

9 ALR5th 568—§ 24

Simmons v. Simmons, 208 Ky. 614, 271 S.W. 679 (1925)

95 ALR5th 533—§ 5

124 ALR5th 203—§ 5

Simmons v. Simmons, 244 Conn. 158, 708 A.2d 949 (1998)

3 ALR6th 447—§ 6, 8

Simmons v. Simmons, 453 So. 2d 631 (La. Ct. App. 3d Cir. 1984)

59 ALR6th 433—§ 77

Simmons v. Simmons, 486 N.W.2d 788 (Minn. App. 1992)

47 ALR5th 207—§ 4, 11

Simmons v. Simmons, 507 So. 2d 939 (Ala. Civ. App. 1986)

21 ALR6th 577—§ 5

Simmons v. Simmons, 568 S.W.2d 169 (Tex. Civ. App. Dallas 1978)

80 ALR5th 533—§ 5

Simmons v. Simmons, 600 So. 2d 305 (Ala. App. 1992)

17 ALR5th 143—§ 5

Simmons v. Simmons, 649 So. 2d 799 (La. App. 2d Cir. 1995)

51 ALR5th 241—§ 2 to 4, 6

Simmons v. Simmons, 698 So. 2d 947 (Fla. Dist. Ct. App. 4th Dist. 1997)

5 ALR5th 788—§ 7

Simmons v. Simmons, 773 P.2d 602 (Colo. App. 1988)

4 ALR5th 972—§ 3

Simmons v. Simmons, 773 P.2d 602 (Colo. Ct. App. 1988)

110 ALR5th 371—§ 6

Simmons v. Simmons, 900 S.W.2d 682 (Tenn. 1995)

For assistance, call 1-800-328-4880

71 ALR5th 99—§ 3, 7
86 ALR6th 1—§ 28
Simmons v. South Carolina, 512 U.S. 154, 114 S. Ct. 2187, 129 L. Ed. 2d 133 (1994)
83 ALR6th 255—§ 30
Simmons v. South Carolina Farm Bureau Mut. Ins. Co., 301 S.C. 267, 391 S.E.2d 560 (1990)
125 ALR5th 1—§ 5, 10
Simmons v. Southern Energy Homes, Inc., 783 So. 2d 636 (La. Ct. App. 3d Cir. 2001)
101 ALR5th 447—§ 6
Simmons v. Southern Pac. Transportation Co., 62 Cal. App. 3d 341, 133 Cal. Rptr. 42 (1st Dist. 1976)
15 ALR6th 1—§ 4, 10, 23
Simmons v. Sowela Technical Institute, 470 So. 2d 913 (La. App. 3d Cir. 1985)
46 ALR5th 581—§ 2
47 ALR5th 1—§ 2, 15
Simmons v. State, 17 Misc. 3d 394, 843 N.Y.S.2d 794 (Ct. Cl. 2007)
53 ALR6th 305—§ 12
Simmons v. State, 25 So. 3d 638 (Fla. 1st DCA 2009)
77 ALR6th 197—§ 4
Simmons v. State, 105 So. 3d 475, 102 A.L.R.6th 791 (Fla. 2012)
102 ALR6th 417—§ 3, 12, 15, 32
Simmons v. State, 151 Fla. 778, 10 So. 2d 436 (1942)
46 ALR5th 499—§ 3
Simmons v. State, 164 Ga. App. 643, 298 S.E.2d 313 (1982)
62 ALR6th 413—§ 41
Simmons v. State, 262 Ga. 674, 424 S.E.2d 274 (1993)
33 ALR6th 407—§ 11, 12
Simmons v. State, 266 Ga. 223, 466 S.E.2d 205, 96 Fulton County D R 618 (1996)
24 ALR5th 465—§ 11, 42, 43, 46
Simmons v. State, 291 Ga. 705, 733 S.E.2d 280 (2012)
93 ALR6th 275—§ 26

Simmons v. State, 375 So. 2d 870 (Fla. Dist. Ct. App. 1st Dist. 1979)
31 ALR6th 49—§ 4
Simmons v. State, 511 S.W.2d 308 (Tex. Crim. 1974)
26 ALR5th 765—§ 13
Simmons v. State, 568 So. 2d 1192 (Miss. 1990)
5 ALR5th 243—§ 61
Simmons v. State, 574 So. 2d 1046 (Ala. App. 1990)
15 ALR5th 391—§ 45
Simmons v. State, 625 So. 2d 975, 18 FLW D 2285 (Fla. App. D2 1993)
15 ALR5th 391—§ 45
Simmons v. State, 748 P.2d 996 (Okla. Crim. 1988)
22 ALR5th 1—§ 9, 17
Simmons v. State, 754 So. 2d 618 (Miss. Ct. App. 2000)
100 ALR5th 67—§ 43
Simmons v. State, 797 So. 2d 1134 (Ala. Crim. App. 1999)
83 ALR6th 255—§ 9, 20
Simmons v. State, 803 So. 2d 787 (Fla. Dist. Ct. App. 1st Dist. 2001)
104 ALR5th 357—§ 9
Simmons v. State, 805 So. 2d 452 (Miss. 2001)
58 ALR6th 499—§ 19
Simmons v. State, 899 P.2d 931 (Alaska Ct. App. 1995)
6 ALR6th 533—§ 11, 21
Simmons v. State, 913 So. 2d 19 (Fla. 2d DCA 2005)
92 ALR6th 1—§ 8
Simmons v. State, 944 So. 2d 317 (Fla. 2006)
33 ALR6th 373—§ 10
Simmons v. State, 1955 OK CR 89, 286 P.2d 296 (Okla. Crim. App. 1955)
27 ALR6th 491—§ 4
Simmons v. State, 2004 WL 187411 (Tex. App. Tyler 2004)
26 ALR6th 511—§ 4, 25

Simmons v. St. Clair Memorial Hosp.,
332 Pa. Super. 444, 481 A.2d 870
(1984)
64 ALR6th 249—§ 15

Simmons v. Stewart, 198 Ky. 330, 248
S.W. 892 (1923)
55 ALR5th 557—§ 5

Simmons v. Stryker Corp., 2008 WL
4936982 (D.N.J. 2008)
90 ALR6th 75—§ 29

Simmons v. Templeton, 684 So. 2d 529
(La. Ct. App. 4th Cir. 1996)
79 ALR5th 587—§ 3, 8

Simmons v. Timek, 2007 WL 4556955
(D.N.J. 2007)
65 ALR6th 93—§ 26

Simmons v. Trinity Industries, 528 So.
2d 1337, 13 FLW 1832 (Fla. App.
D1 1988)
12 ALR5th 658—§ 4, 10, 16, 17

Simmons v. Tuomey Regional Medical
Center, 341 S.C. 32, 533 S.E.2d 312
(2000)
64 ALR6th 249—§ 13

Simmons v. Tuomey Regional Medical
Center, 1998 WL 57450 (S.C.App.)
58 ALR5th 613—§ 3

Simmons v. U.S., 120 F. Supp. 641
(M.D. Pa. 1954)
62 ALR6th 517—§ 59

Simmons v. U.S., 390 U.S. 377, 88 S.
Ct. 967, 19 L. Ed. 2d 1247 (1968)
66 ALR5th 373—§ 2
102 ALR6th 365—§ 1, 2

Simmons v. U.S., 805 F.2d 1363 (CA9
Wash. 1986)
11 ALR5th 588—§ 4
12 ALR5th 546—§ 3, 4

Simmons v. U.S., 841 F. Supp. 748
(W.D. La 1993)
31 ALR5th 1—§ 2, 20, 21

Simmons v. Ware, 920 S.W.2d 438
(Tex. App. Amarillo 1996)
54 ALR5th 443—§ 15, 19

Simmons v. Whittington, 444 So. 2d
1357 (La. Ct. App. 2d Cir. 1984)
64 ALR5th 1—§ 5, 15, 30, 31

Simmons v. Wilder, 6 N.C. App. 179,
169 S.E.2d 480 (1969)
6 ALR5th 883—§ 2, 7

Simmons v. Yurchak, 28 Mass. App. Ct.
371, 551 N.E.2d 539 (1990)
57 ALR5th 141—§ 2, 14

Simmons Auto Sales, Inc. v. Royal Motor Co., Inc., 489 So. 2d 518 (Ala.
1986)
66 ALR6th 351—§ 27, 47

Simmons Co. v. Hardin, 75 Ga. App.
420, 43 S.E.2d 553 (1947)
3 ALR6th 355—§ 4

Simmons First Nat. Bank v. PAPCO,
Inc., 592 F. Supp. 719 (E.D. Ark.
1983)
13 ALR5th 289—§ 29

Simmons Foods, Inc. v. Hill's Pet Nutri-
tion, Inc., 2001 WL 1327107 (8th
Cir. 2001)
94 ALR5th 247—§ 5

Simmons Foods, Inc. v. Willis, 191
F.R.D. 625, 46 Fed. R. Serv. 3d 962
(D. Kan. 2000)
71 ALR6th 249—§ 4

Simmons Ford, Inc. v. Consumers Union
of U.S., Inc., 516 F. Supp. 742, 7
Media L. Rep. (BNA) 1776 (S.D.
N.Y. 1981)
54 ALR6th 165—§ 4, 6

Simmons Hardware Co. v. Baker, 140
Mich. 123, 103 N.W. 529 (1905)
16 ALR5th 548—§ 5

Simmons-Harris v. Goff, 86 Ohio St. 3d
1, 711 N.E.2d 203, 135 Ed. Law
Rep. 596 (1999)
78 ALR5th 133—§ 3, 6, 7, 9, 11, 12

Simmons-Harris v. Zelman, 54 F. Supp.
2d 725, 137 Ed. Law Rep. 275 (N.D.
Ohio 1999)
78 ALR5th 133—§ 3

Simmons-Harris v. Zelman, 72 F. Supp.
2d 834, 140 Ed. Law Rep. 243, 78
A.L.R.5th 623 (N.D. Ohio 1999)
78 ALR5th 133—§ 3, 6, 7, 9, 11, 12

Simmons-Harris v. Zelman, 2000 WL
1816079 (6th Cir. 2000)
78 ALR5th 133—§ 3

Simmons Oil Corp. v. Wells Fargo Bank, N.A., 1998 MT 129, 289 Mont. 119, 960 P.2d 291 (1998)
27 ALR6th 183—§ 17, 46

Simmons, People ex rel. v. Sheridan, 98 Misc. 2d 328, 414 N.Y.S.2d 83 (Sup. Ct. 1979)
69 ALR5th 1—§ 3

Simmons, State ex rel. v. Peca, 799 S.W.2d 426 (Tex. App. El Paso 1990)
51 ALR5th 603—§ 2, 15

Simms v. Camp Concrete Co., 156 Ga. App. 771, 275 S.E.2d 357 (1980)
21 ALR5th 82—§ 4

Simms v. County Court of Kanawha County, 134 W. Va. 867, 61 S.E.2d 849 (1950)
51 ALR6th 287—§ 7, 9

Simms v. Exeter Architectural Products, Inc., 868 F. Supp. 677 (M.D. Pa. 1994)
39 ALR6th 1—§ 6, 10, 13

Simms v. Farris, 657 F. Supp. 119 (E.D. Ky. 1987)
116 ALR5th 149—§ 4

Simms v. Farris, 840 F.2d 18, 1988-1 Trade Cas. (CCH) ¶ 67912 (6th Cir. 1988)
41 ALR6th 77—§ 22

Simms v. Gafney, 227 S.W.2d 848 (Tex. Civ. App. 1950)
30 ALR5th 571—§ 3

Simms v. Lakewood Village Property Owners Ass'n, 895 S.W.2d 779 (Tex. App. Corpus Christi 1995)
25 ALR5th 123—§ 14, 22, 23

Simms v. Los Angeles County, 35 Cal. 2d 303, 217 P.2d 936 (1950)
107 ALR5th 311—§ 11

Simms v. State, 127 S.W.3d 924 (Tex. App. Corpus Christi 2004)
71 ALR6th 1—§ 15
71 ALR6th 625—§ 15, 19, 29

Simms v. State, 409 Md. 722, 976 A.2d 1012 (2009)
72 ALR6th 227—§ 50

Simms v. St. Nicholas Ave. Hotel Co., 187 A.D.2d 373, 589 N.Y.S.2d 485 (1st Dep't 1992)
17 ALR6th 453—§ 13

Simms v. Webb, 219 Kan. 675, 549 P.2d 570 (1976)
9 ALR5th 826—§ 3

Simms v. William Simms Hardware, 216 Minn. 283, 12 N.W.2d 783 (1943)
62 ALR5th 219—§ 21, 46

Simms v. William Simms Hardware (State Report Title: Simms v. Fagan), 216 Minn. 283, 12 N.W.2d 783 (1943)
91 ALR6th 1—§ 21

Simo v. Home Health & Hospice Care, 906 F. Supp. 714, 11 A.D.D. 1105, 5 A.D. Cas. (BNA) 1461 (D.N.H. 1995)
99 ALR5th 65—§ 9

Simoes v. Simoes, 790 So. 2d 1221 (Fla. Dist. Ct. App. 3d Dist. 2001)
112 ALR5th 399—§ 4

Simon, In re, 71 B.R. 65 (Bankr. N.D. Ohio 1987)
99 ALR6th 481—§ 83

Simon, In re, 170 B.R. 999 (Bankr. S.D. Ill. 1994)
99 ALR6th 481—§ 83

Simon, In re Marriage of, 856 P.2d 47 (Colo. Ct. App. 1993)
109 ALR5th 1—§ 3

Simon v. Adm'r of Employment Sec., 281 So. 2d 165 (La. Ct. App. 4th Cir. 1973)
68 ALR5th 13—§ 13, 27

Simon v. American Crescent Elevator Co., 767 So. 2d 64 (La. Ct. App. 4th Cir. 2000)
51 ALR5th 467—§ 3

Simon v. Auburn, Bd. of Zoning Appeals, 519 N.E.2d 205 (Ind. App. 1988)
35 ALR5th 113—§ 4, 10

Simon v. Auler, 155 Ill. App. 3d 1000, 108 Ill. Dec. 525, 508 N.E.2d 1102 (4th Dist. 1987)

17 ALR5th 366—§ 9
Simon v. Becherer, 7 A.D.3d 66, 775 N.Y.S.2d 313 (1st Dep't 2004)

43 ALR6th 1—§ 5, 11
Simon v. Bridewell, 950 S.W.2d 439 (Tex. App. Waco 1997)

86 ALR6th 519—§ 4
Simon v. Calvert, 289 So. 2d 567 (La. Ct. App. 3d Cir. 1974)

118 ALR5th 385—§ 3, 10, 21
Simon v. Chicago, M. & St. P. Ry., 45 N.D. 251, 177 N.W. 107 (1920)

56 ALR5th 1—§ 4, 8
Simon v. City of Naperville, 88 F. Supp. 2d 872 (N.D. Ill. 2000)

93 ALR5th 47—§ 5

94 ALR5th 1—§ 3, 8
Simon v. Com., 55 Pa. Commw. 225, 422 A.2d 1229 (1980)

1 ALR6th 1—§ 42
Simon v. Commissioner of Revenue, 1983 WL 1845 (Minn. Tax Ct. 1983)

118 ALR5th 597—§ 29
Simon v. Crowley Industries, Inc., 287 So. 2d 549, 73 CCH LC ¶ 53292 (La. App. 3d Cir. 1973)

18 ALR5th 577—§ 35, 41
Simon v. Drake Constr. Co., 87 Ohio App 3d 23, 621 N.E.2d 837 (8th Dist. Cuyahoga County 1993)

47 ALR6th 303—§ 4
Simon v. Epps, 2007 WL 4292498 (N.D. Miss. 2007)

98 ALR6th 455—§ 14
Simon v. Ford Motor Co., 282 So. 2d 126 (La. 1973)

23 ALR5th 75—§ 8
Simon v. Henrichson, 394 S.W.2d 249 (Tex. Civ. App. Corpus Christi 1965)

76 ALR5th 337—§ 12
Simon v. Hulse, 12 La. App. 450, 124 So. 845 (1929)

16 ALR5th 548—§ 3
Simon v. Maldonado, 65 So. 3d 8 (Fla. 3d DCA 2011)

97 ALR6th 83—§ 63

Simon v. Mann, 373 F. Supp. 2d 1196, 10 A.L.R.6th 767 (D. Nev. 2005)

10 ALR6th 265—§ 16

10 ALR6th 293—§ 4, 5, 14
Simon v. Maricopa Medical Center, 225 Ariz. 55, 234 P.3d 623 (Ct. App. Div. 1 2010)

100 ALR6th 139—§ 44
Simon v. Morehouse Sch. of Medicine, 908 F. Supp. 959 (N.D. Ga. 1995)

51 ALR5th 163—§ 5
Simon v. Morehouse School of Medicine, 908 F. Supp. 959, 105 Ed. Law Rep. 1067 (N.D. Ga. 1995)

20 ALR6th 1—§ 4
Simon v. Needham, 311 Mass. 560, 42 N.E.2d 516, 141 A.L.R. 688 (1942)

1 ALR5th 622—§ 4, 14, 17
Simon v. New Jersey Asphalt & Paving Co., 123 N.J.L. 232, 8 A.2d 256 (N.J. Sup. Ct. 1939)

79 ALR5th 201—§ 4, 5, 10, 16
Simon v. Pronational Ins. Co., 2007 WL 4893477 (S.D. Fla. 2007)

104 ALR6th 207—§ 16
Simon v. Pronational Ins. Co., 2007 WL 4893478 (S.D. Fla. 2007)

86 ALR6th 519—§ 7
Simon v. Republic of Iraq, 529 F.3d 1187 (D.C. Cir. 2008)

46 ALR6th 495—§ 29
Simon v. R. H. H. Steel Laundry, Inc., 25 N.J. Super. 50, 95 A.2d 446 (County Ct. 1953)

83 ALR5th 103—§ 19, 26, 28

84 ALR5th 249—§ 25
Simon v. Safelite Glass Corp., 128 F.3d 68, 75 Fair Empl. Prac. Cas. (BNA) 147, 73 Empl. Prac. Dec. (CCH) ¶ 45344 (2d Cir. 1997)

99 ALR5th 65—§ 11
Simon v. Sargent, 346 F. Supp. 277 (D. Mass. 1972)

72 ALR5th 607—§ 5, 6
Simon v. Schenectady North Congregation of Jehovah's Witnesses, 132 App. Div. 2d 313, 522 N.Y.S.2d 343 (3d Dep't 1987)

For assistance, call 1-800-328-4880

8 ALR5th 1—§ 11, 26, 56
Simon v. Shearson Lehman Bros., Inc.,
625 895 F.2d 1304 (CA11 Ga. 1990)
14 ALR5th 242—§ 49
Simon v. Simon, 35 Mass. App. Ct. 705,
625 N.E.2d 564 (1994)
12 ALR6th 123—§ 15
Simon v. Simon, 170 Misc. 420, 10
N.Y.S.2d 577 (1939)
35 ALR5th 757—§ 3
Simon v. Smith & Nephew, Inc., 13
CIV. 1909 PAE, 2013 WL 6244525
(S.D.N.Y. Dec. 3, 2013)
96 ALR6th 1—§ 19
Simon v. Smith & Nephew, Inc., 990 F.
Supp. 2d 395, Prod. Liab. Rep.
(CCH) P 19288 (S.D. N.Y. 2013)
96 ALR6th 1—§ 30, 31
Simon v. State, 31 Tex. Crim. 186, 20
S.W. 399 (1892)
34 ALR5th 723—§ 4
Simon v. State, 279 Ga. App. 844, 632
S.E.2d 723 (2006)
34 ALR6th 253—§ 4
Simon v. State, 679 So. 2d 617 (Miss.
1996)
70 ALR5th 587—§ 25
Simon v. State, 1986 WL 9856 (Tex.
App. Houston 14th Dist. 1986)
76 ALR5th 1—§ 16
Simon v. St. Elizabeth Medical Center,
3 Ohio Ops. 3d 164, 355 N.E.2d 903
(CP 1976)
26 ALR5th 245—§ 23, 27
Simon v. Toshiba America, 2010 WL
1757956 (N.D. Cal. 2010)
60 ALR6th 295—§ 68
Simon v. Town of Kennebunkport, 417
A.2d 982, 21 A.L.R.4th 465 (Me.
1980)
15 ALR6th 1—§ 4, 8 to 11, 24
Simon v. Toye Bros. Yellow Cab Co.,
152 So. 606 (La. App. 1934)
20 ALR5th 1—§ 13, 29
Simon v. U.S., 438 F. Supp. 759 (S.D.
Fla. 1977)
7 ALR5th 1—§ 13, 18

Simon & Schuster, Inc. v. Members of
New York State Crime Victims Bd.,
502 U.S. 105, 112 S. Ct. 501, 116
L. Ed. 2d 476, 19 Media L. Rep.
(BNA) 1609 (1991)
70 ALR6th 513—§ 3
71 ALR6th 471—§ 3
Simonca v. Mukasey, 2008 WL 5113757
(E.D. Cal. 2008)
72 ALR6th 563—§ 9, 15, 28
Simonds v. New York State Teachers'
Retirement System, 42 A.D.2d 470,
349 N.Y.S.2d 140 (3d Dep't 1973)
91 ALR5th 225—§ 12
Simonds v. Simonds, 229 S.C. 376, 93
S.E.2d 107 (1956)
101 ALR6th 455—§ 13
Simone v. Crans, 891 F. Supp. 112 (S.D.
N.Y. 1994)
48 ALR5th 129—§ 5, 14
50 ALR5th 1—§ 17
Simone v. McKee, 142 Cal. App. 2d
307, 298 P.2d 667 (1st Dist. 1956)
14 ALR5th 242—§ 38
46 ALR6th 185—§ 7
Simone v. Sabo, 37 Cal. 2d 253, 231
P.2d 19 (1951)
18 ALR6th 325—§ 2, 12
Simoneau v. Pacific E. R. Co., 159 Cal.
494, 115 P. 320 (1911)
42 ALR5th 465—§ 5
Simoneau v. South Bend Lathe, Inc., 130
N.H. 466, 543 A.2d 407, Prod. Liab.
Rep. (CCH) ¶ 11833 (1988)
18 ALR6th 629—§ 10
Simonelli v. Anderson Concrete Co., 99
Ohio App. 3d 254, 650 N.E.2d 488,
11 BNA IER Cas. 236 (Franklin Co.
1994)
52 ALR5th 405—§ 3, 6
Simonelli v. Anderson Concrete Co., 99
Ohio App. 3d 254, 650 N.E.2d 488,
11 I.E.R. Cas. (BNA) 236 (10th
Dist. Franklin County 1994)
7 ALR6th 563—§ 5
Simonetti v. Rinshed-Mason Co., 41
Mich. App. 446, 200 N.W.2d 354
(1972)

69 ALR5th 137—§ 7

Simonian v. Donoian, 96 Cal. App. 2d 259, 215 P.2d 119 (1950)

44 ALR5th 1—§ 2, 10, 20, 27

Simonian v. Patterson, 27 Cal. App. 4th 773, 32 Cal. Rptr. 2d 722, 94 C.D.O.S. 6322, 94 Daily Journal DAR 11458 (2d Dist. 1994)

44 ALR5th 1—§ 2

Simon II Litigation, In re, 211 F.R.D. 86 (E.D. N.Y. 2002)

7 ALR6th 233—§ 20

7 ALR6th 319—§ 4, 5

Simon II Litigation, In re, 407 F.3d 125, 7 A.L.R.6th 797 (2d Cir. 2005)

7 ALR6th 233—§ 20

7 ALR6th 319—§ 4, 5

Simon Neustadt Family Center, Inc. v. Bludworth, 97 N.M. 500, 641 P.2d 531 (App. 1982)

7 ALR5th 143—§ 2

Simonoff v. McPhee & Sons, Ltd., 25 Conn. L. Rptr. 678, 1999 WL 1081371 (Conn. Super. Ct. 1999)

104 ALR6th 1—§ 38

Simonoko v. Stop & Shop, Inc., 376 Mass. 929, 383 N.E.2d 505 (1978)

1 ALR6th 297—§ 4, 25

Simonoko v. Stop & Shop, Inc., 383 N.E.2d 505 (Mass. 1978)

40 ALR5th 135—§ 15

Simon Property Group, Inc. v. Benson, 278 Ga. App. 277, 628 S.E.2d 697 (2006)

29 ALR6th 507—§ 57

Simon Property Group, Inc. v. Taubman Centers, Inc., 240 F. Supp. 2d 642, 37 A.L.R.6th 707 (E.D. Mich. 2003)

37 ALR6th 1—§ 7

Simon Property Group, Inc. v. Taubman Centers, Inc., 261 F. Supp. 2d 919 (E.D. Mich. 2003)

37 ALR6th 1—§ 8

Simon Property Group L.P. v. mySimon, Inc., 194 F.R.D. 639, 47 Fed. R. Serv. 3d 247 (S.D. Ind. 2000)

27 ALR6th 565—§ 13

Simons, In re, 34 A.D.3d 136, 822 N.Y.S.2d 254 (1st Dep't 2006)

45 ALR6th 175—§ 24

Simons, In re Commitment of, 213 Ill. 2d 523, 290 Ill. Dec. 610, 821 N.E.2d 1184 (2004)

20 ALR6th 607—§ 3, 7

38 ALR6th 439—§ 12

Simons v. Bellinger, 643 F.2d 774 (D.C. Cir. 1980)

40 ALR6th 463—§ 3

Simons v. Blue Cross & Blue Shield, 144 App. Div. 2d 28, 536 N.Y.S.2d 431 (1st Dep't 1989)

19 ALR5th 533—§ 5

Simons v. Canty, 195 Conn. 524, 488 A.2d 1267 (1985)

13 ALR6th 661—§ 13

Simons v. City of Austin, 921 S.W.2d 524 (Tex. App. Austin 1996)

50 ALR5th 1—§ 14

Simons v. Fagan, 62 Neb. 287, 87 N.W. 21 (1901)

88 ALR6th 533—§ 19

Simons v. Fahnestock, 1938 OK 264, 182 Okla. 460, 78 P.2d 388 (1938)

90 ALR5th 619—§ 16

Simons v. Federal Bar Bldg. Corp., 275 A.2d 545 (D.C. 1971)

75 ALR5th 1—§ 3, 5

Simons v. Georgiade, 55 N.C. App. 483, 286 S.E.2d 596 (1982)

28 ALR5th 497—§ 4

Simons v. Longbranch Farms, Inc., 345 S.C. 277, 547 S.E.2d 500 (Ct. App. 2001)

40 ALR6th 99—§ 18

Simons v. Mercedes-Benz of North America, Inc., 1996 WL 103796 (E.D. Pa. 1996)

88 ALR5th 301—§ 20

Simons v. Monier, 29 Barb. 419 (N.Y. 1859)

25 ALR5th 391—§ 27, 30

Simons v. New Britain Trust Co., 80 Conn. 263, 67 A. 883 (1907)

12 ALR6th 123—§ 5

Simons v. Schiek's Inc., 275 Minn. 132, 145 N.W.2d 548 (1966)
86 ALR6th 321—§ 7
87 ALR6th 197—§ 31
Simons v. Steverson, 88 Cal. App. 4th 693, 106 Cal. Rptr. 2d 193 (2d Dist. 2001)
78 ALR6th 151—§ 28
Simonsen v. Hendricks Sodding & Landscaping Inc., 5 Neb. App. 263, 558 N.W.2d 825 (1997)
104 ALR5th 1—§ 3, 8
Simonsen v. Swenson, 104 Neb. 224, 177 N.W. 831, 9 A.L.R. 1250 (1920)
3 ALR5th 370—§ 2
Simonson v. Simonson, 128 Ill. App. 2d 39, 262 N.E.2d 326 (1st Dist. 1970)
53 ALR5th 375—§ 5
Simonson v. Simonson, 292 N.W.2d 12 (Minn. 1980)
99 ALR5th 475—§ 2
Simonson v. United Press International, Inc., 500 F. Supp. 1261, 6 Media L. R. 2313 (E.D. Wis 1980)
44 ALR5th 193—§ 2, 17, 50
Simonson v. White, 220 Mont. 14, 713 P.2d 983 (1986)
10 ALR5th 680—§ 3
Simons Solomon v. Walgreen Co., 975 F.2d 1086, 8 BNA IER Cas. 34, 123 CCH LC ¶ 57154 (CA5 Miss. 1992)
17 ALR5th 1—§ 8
Simonton v. State, 44 Fla. 289, 31 So. 821 (1902)
97 ALR5th 537—§ 67
Simopoulos v. Com., 221 Va. 1059, 277 S.E.2d 194 (1981)
77 ALR5th 1—§ 3
Simopoulos v. Virginia, 462 U.S. 506, 103 S. Ct. 2532, 76 L. Ed. 2d 755 (1983)
5 ALR6th 423—§ 6
Simos v. State, 53 Wis. 2d 493, 192 N.W.2d 877 (1972)
102 ALR5th 327—§ 5
Simpkins, In re, 599 N.W.2d 170 (Minn. Ct. App. 1999)

115 ALR5th 509—§ 16
Simpkins v. Disney, 416 Pa. Super. 243, 610 A.2d 1062 (1992)
6 ALR5th 1—§ 10
Simpkins v. Simpkins, 595 So. 2d 493 (Ala. App. 1991)
17 ALR5th 366—§ 31
Simpkins v. Snow, 139 N.H. 735, 661 A.2d 772 (1995)
57 ALR5th 141—§ 17
105 ALR5th 1—§ 3, 16
Simpkins v. State, 268 Ga. 219, 486 S.E.2d 833 (1997)
79 ALR5th 33—§ 10, 42, 57
Simpkins v. State, 395 So. 2d 625 (Fla. App. D1 1981)
39 ALR5th 283—§ 4, 41
Simpleville Music v. Mizell, 451 F. Supp. 2d 1293, 81 U.S.P.Q.2d 1581 (M.D. Ala. 2006)
37 ALR6th 243—§ 53, 55 to 57
SimplexGrinnell LP v. Integrated Systems & Power, Inc., 642 F. Supp. 2d 167, 2009-1 Trade Cas. (CCH) ¶ 76588 (S.D. N.Y. 2009)
76 ALR6th 289—§ 5
77 ALR6th 543—§ 11
Simplex Machine Tool Corp. v. Swind Machinery Co., 16 Misc. 2d 85, 144 N.Y.S.2d 595 (1955)
56 ALR5th 757—§ 3
Simplot, Estate of v. C.I.R., 112 T.C. 130, Tax Ct. Rep. Dec. (RIA) 112.13, 1999 WL 152610 (1999)
16 ALR6th 693—§ 12
Simply Fresh Fruit, Inc. v. Continental Ins. Co., 94 F.3d 1219 (9th Cir. 1996)
98 ALR5th 1—§ 18, 21
Simply Lite Food Corp. v. Aetna Cas. & Sur. Co. of America, 245 A.D.2d 500, 666 N.Y.S.2d 714 (2d Dep't 1997)
98 ALR5th 1—§ 23
Simpsen v. Madison General Hospital Ass'n, 48 Wis. 2d 498, 180 N.W.2d 586 (1970)
38 ALR6th 399—§ 5, 8

Simpson, Ex parte, 77 S.W.3d 894 (Tex. App. Tyler 2002)
7 ALR6th 487—§ 31

Simpson, Ex parte, 136 S.W.3d 660 (Tex. Crim. App. 2004)
122 ALR5th 145—§ 23

Simpson, Ex parte, 736 S.W.2d 939 (Tex. App. Beaumont 1987)
32 ALR5th 31—§ 3

Simpson, Guardianship of, 67 Cal. App. 4th 914, 68 Cal. App. 4th 986b, 79 Cal. Rptr. 2d 389 (4th Dist. 1998)
51 ALR5th 241—§ 5

Simpson, In re, 959 So. 2d 836 (La. 2007)
49 ALR6th 505—§ 17, 21

Simpson v. Alaska State Com. for Human Rights, 423 F. Supp. 552, 13 BNA FEP Cas. 1779, 13 CCH EPD ¶ 11391 (D.C. Alaska 1976)
51 ALR5th 1—§ 2, 8

Simpson v. Anthony Auto Sales, Inc., 32 F. Supp. 2d 405 (W.D. La. 1998)
66 ALR6th 351—§ 28
67 ALR6th 209—§ 25

Simpson v. Atherton, 210 F.3d 390 (10th Cir. 2000)
37 ALR6th 357—§ 67

Simpson v. Balboa Ins. Co., 2009 WL 1291275 (S.D. Miss. 2009)
96 ALR6th 125—§ 3

Simpson v. Breckenridge, 32 Pa. 287, 1858 WL 8004 (1858)
77 ALR6th 293—§ 41

Simpson v. Buck, 971 S.W.2d 856 (Mo. Ct. App. W.D. 1998)
71 ALR5th 99—§ 8

Simpson v. Burrows, 90 F. Supp. 2d 1108 (D. Or. 2000)
7 ALR6th 135—§ 10

Simpson v. Caddo Parish School Bd., 540 So. 2d 997 (La. App. 2d Cir. 1989)
23 ALR5th 1—§ 14

Simpson v. Cain, 217 S.W.2d 92 (Tex. Civ. App. 1948)
58 ALR5th 535—§ 5, 18

Simpson v. Camelot Music, 220 Wis. 2d 357, 582 N.W.2d 504 (Ct. App. 1998)
86 ALR6th 321—§ 6

Simpson v. Cenarrusa, 130 Idaho 609, 944 P.2d 1372 (1997)
106 ALR5th 523—§ 21
112 ALR5th 1—§ 2
24 ALR6th 255—§ 3, 5, 11, 17

Simpson v. Chesterfield County Bd. of Sup'rs, 404 F.3d 276 (4th Cir. 2005)
30 ALR6th 459—§ 3, 5, 7

Simpson v. City of Houston, 260 S.W.2d 94 (Tex. Civ. App. Galveston 1953)
19 ALR6th 217—§ 55

Simpson v. City of Muskogee, 879 P.2d 1269 (Okla. App. 1994)
15 ALR5th 119—§ 5, 16, 52

Simpson v. City of Muskogee, 1994 OK CIV APP 103, 879 P.2d 1269 (Ct. App. Div. 1 1994)
62 ALR6th 313—§ 6

Simpson v. City of Pickens, Miss., 887 F. Supp. 126 (S.D. Miss. 1995)
57 ALR5th 689—§ 2

Simpson v. City of Tulsa, 1980 OK CIV APP 50, 620 P.2d 921 (Okla. Ct. App. Div. 2 1980)
108 ALR5th 1—§ 26

Simpson v. Com., 13 Va. App. 604, 414 S.E.2d 407 (1992)
85 ALR5th 671—§ 7

Simpson v. Commonwealth, 889 S.W.2d 781 (Ky. 1994)
39 ALR5th 283—§ 4, 60

Simpson v. Coosa Valley Production Credit Asso., 495 So. 2d 1029 (Ala. 1986)
10 ALR5th 828—§ 33

Simpson v. Dail, 2010 WL 3835137 (E.D. N.C. 2010)
72 ALR6th 141—§ 8

Simpson v. Davidson & Case Lumber Co., 150 Okla. 132, 300 P. 631 (1931)
46 ALR5th 1—§ 24

Simpson v. Davis, 219 Kan. 584, 549 P.2d 950 (1976)

7 ALR6th 357—§ 8, 32

Simpson v. Department of Corrections, 2003 WL 22240633 (Mich. Ct. App. 2003)

119 ALR5th 121—§ 3

121 ALR5th 325—§ 3

Simpson v. Emery, 134 Me. 213, 183 A. 842 (1936)

109 ALR5th 421—§ 3

Simpson v. Farmers Ins. Co., Inc., 225 Kan. 508, 592 P.2d 445 (1979)

77 ALR5th 319—§ 3

78 ALR5th 341—§ 3, 11

Simpson v. Fillichio, 560 So. 2d 331, 15 FLW D 1119 (Fla. App. D4 1990)

22 ALR5th 327—§ 58

Simpson v. Frontier Community Credit Union, 810 S.W.2d 147 (Tenn. 1991)

36 ALR5th 225—§ 3, 7

Simpson v. Georgia State Bank, 159 Ga. App. 310, 283 S.E.2d 278 (1981)

86 ALR5th 527—§ 2, 3

Simpson v. Glen Aubrey Fire Co., 86 App. Div. 2d 909, 448 N.Y.S.2d 261 (3d Dep't 1982)

36 ALR5th 225—§ 3

Simpson v. Hanover Ins. Co., 588 A.2d 1183 (Me. 1991)

23 ALR5th 75—§ 3

Simpson v. Hatteras Island Gallery Restaurant, Inc., 109 N.C. App. 314, 427 S.E.2d 131, CCH Prod. Liab. Rep. ¶ 13576, 20 U.C.C.R.S.2d 84 (1993)

2 ALR5th 1—§ 15

Simpson v. Iowa Dep't of Job Service, 327 N.W.2d 775 (Iowa App. 1982)

33 ALR5th 643—§ 17

Simpson v. JAMS/Endispute, LLC, 2006 WL 2076028 (Cal. App. 1st Dist. 2006)

69 ALR6th 513—§ 4

Simpson v. Jeanerette Sugar Co., Inc., 667 So. 2d 1087 (La. Ct. App. 3d Cir. 1995)

22 ALR6th 329—§ 34

Simpson v. Kane, 2010 WL 5479868 (W.D. N.C. 2010)

65 ALR6th 93—§ 59

Simpson v. Matthews, 339 Ill. App. 3d 322, 274 Ill. Dec. 25, 790 N.E.2d 401 (5th Dist. 2003)

17 ALR6th 1—§ 27

Simpson v. Midland-Ross Corp., 823 F.2d 937, 44 BNA FEP Cas. 418, 43 CCH EPD ¶ 37234 (CA6 Mich. 1987)

51 ALR5th 1—§ 7

Simpson v. Moore, 367 S.C. 587, 627 S.E.2d 701, 56 A.L.R.6th 767 (2006)

56 ALR6th 185—§ 33

Simpson v. Motorists Mut. Ins. Co., 494 F.2d 850 (7th Cir. 1974)

110 ALR5th 465—§ 31

Simpson v. Murkowski, 129 P.3d 435, 37 Employee Benefits Cas. (BNA) 2237 (Alaska 2006)

87 ALR6th 633—§ 3

Simpson v. Norris, 490 F.3d 1029 (8th Cir. 2007)

36 ALR6th 681—§ 22

Simpson v. North Collins Cent. School Dist., 56 A.D.2d 166, 392 N.Y.S.2d 107, 95 L.R.R.M. (BNA) 2083 (4th Dep't 1977)

112 ALR5th 263—§ 3, 4

Simpson v. O'Sullivan, 2010 WL 4608741 (E.D. N.Y. 2010)

95 ALR6th 341—§ 54

Simpson v. Phillips Pipe Line Co., 603 S.W.2d 307 (Tex. Civ. App. Beaumont 1980)

111 ALR5th 313—§ 24

Simpson v. Pittsburgh Corning Corp., 901 F.2d 277, Prod. Liab. Rep. (CCH) ¶ 12442 (2d Cir. 1990)

24 ALR6th 497—§ 3

41 ALR6th 445—§ 33

Simpson v. Reed, 186 Ga. App. 297, 367 S.E.2d 563 (1988)

50 ALR5th 1—§ 6

Simpson v. Revco Drug Centers, Inc., 702 S.W.2d 482 (Mo. App. 1985)

12 ALR5th 195—§ 40

Simpson v. Rourke, 13 Misc. 230, 34 N.Y.S. 11 (1895)

54 ALR5th 393—§ 7

Simpson v. Simpson, 29 N.C. App. 14, 222 S.E.2d 747 (1976)

36 ALR5th 395—§ 3, 6

Simpson v. Simpson, 108 So. 2d 632 (Fla. App. D2 1959)

14 ALR5th 557—§ 6, 9, 13

Simpson v. Simpson, 232 So. 2d 249 (Fla. App. D1 1970)

60 ALR5th 379—§ 2, 5

Simpson v. Simpson, 679 S.W.2d 39 (Tex. App. Dallas 1984)

9 ALR5th 568—§ 13

Simpson v. Simpson, 680 So. 2d 1085, 21 FLW D2161 (Fla. App. D4 1996)

57 ALR5th 389—§ 20, 21

Simpson v. Simpson's Ex'rs, 94 Ky. 586, 23 S.W. 361 (1893)

3 ALR5th 394—§ 5, 7, 22

Simpson v. Smith, 34 Ohio Misc. 2d 7, 517 N.E.2d 276 (Mun. Ct. 1987)

78 ALR6th 97—§ 11, 26

Simpson v. Specialty Retail Concepts, 908 F. Supp. 323 (M.D. N.C. 1995)

48 ALR5th 389—§ 3

Simpson v. Spencer, 372 F. Supp. 2d 140 (D. Mass. 2005)

56 ALR6th 185—§ 39

Simpson v. State, 111 Ala. 6, 20 So. 572 (1896)

81 ALR5th 563—§ 3

Simpson v. State, 144 Ga. App. 657, 242 S.E.2d 265 (1978)

94 ALR5th 497—§ 5, 7

Simpson v. State, 159 Ga. App. 235, 283 S.E.2d 91 (1981)

109 ALR5th 99—§ 8

Simpson v. State, 269 Ind. 495, 381 N.E.2d 1229 (1978)

72 ALR5th 529—§ 2

Simpson v. State, 289 Ga. 685, 715 S.E.2d 142 (2011)

101 ALR6th 331—§ 12

Simpson v. State, 505 So. 2d 1378 (Fla. Dist. Ct. App. 1st Dist. 1987)

73 ALR5th 383—§ 63

Simpson v. State, 506 N.E.2d 473 (Ind. 1987)

9 ALR6th 1—§ 10

Simpson v. State, 668 S.W.2d 915 (Tex. App. Houston (1st Dist.) 1984)

4 ALR5th 1—§ 38

Simpson v. State, 712 So. 2d 1 (Fla. Dist. Ct. App. 2d Dist. 1997)

15 ALR5th 391—§ 30

Simpson v. State, 772 S.W.2d 276 (Tex. App. Amarillo 1989)

15 ALR5th 391—§ 39

Simpson v. State, 990 S.W.2d 693 (Mo. Ct. App. E.D. 1999)

105 ALR5th 529—§ 19

Simpson v. State, 1983 OK CR 158, 672 P.2d 303 (Okla. Crim. App. 1983)

124 ALR5th 1—§ 3

Simpson v. State ex rel. Department of Transp. & Dev., 636 So. 2d 608 (La. App. 1st Cir. 1994)

50 ALR5th 1—§ 3, 12

52 ALR5th 1—§ 8, 9

Simpson v. State Mut. Life Assurance Co., 135 Vt. 554, 382 A.2d 198 (1977)

43 ALR5th 657—§ 2, 3

Simpson v. Tennant, 871 S.W.2d 301 (Tex. App. Houston 14th Dist. 1994)

93 ALR5th 327—§ 4, 7, 17, 30

Simpson v. Thorslund, 151 Wash. App. 276, 211 P.3d 469 (Div. 1 2009)

70 ALR6th 209—§ 5, 12, 25, 57

Simpson v. Times-Journal, Inc., 170 Ga. App. 175, 316 S.E.2d 795 (1984)

106 ALR5th 475—§ 10

Simpson v. Unemployment Compensation Bd. of Review, 29 Pa. Commw. 245, 370 A.2d 432 (1977)

68 ALR5th 13—§ 2, 5, 39

Simpson v. Unemployment Ins. Comp. Appeals Bd., 187 Cal. App. 3d 342, 231 Cal. Rptr. 690 (2d Dist. 1986)

106 ALR5th 523—§ 17

For assistance, call 1-800-328-4880

Simpson v. U.S., 576 A.2d 1336 (D.C. 1990)
71 ALR6th 1—§ 11

Simpson v. Weeks, 530 F. Supp. 196 (E.D. Ark. 1977)
12 ALR5th 195—§ 36

Simpson v. Widger, 311 N.J. Super. 379, 709 A.2d 1366, 35 U.C.C. Rep. Serv. 2d 837 (App. Div. 1998)
88 ALR6th 1—§ 8, 14, 29, 105

Simpson v. Williams Rural High School Dist., 153 S.W.2d 852 (Tex. Civ. App. Amarillo 1941)
98 ALR5th 353—§ 3

Simpson v. Wolf Ridge Corp., 486 So. 2d 418 (Ala. 1986)
40 ALR5th 1—§ 3

Simpson v. Zoning Bd. of Appeals of City of Milford, 1995 WL 476786 (Conn. Super. Ct. 1995)
4 ALR6th 263—§ 12

Simpson County Steeplechase Ass'n v. Roberts, 898 S.W.2d 523 (Ky. App. 1995)
14 ALR5th 242—§ 49

Simpson, Estate of v. C.I.R., T.C. Memo. 1994-207, T.C.M. (RIA) ¶ 94207, 67 T.C.M. (CCH) 2938 (1994)
16 ALR6th 693—§ 14

Simpson Props. v. Oexco, Inc., 916 P.2d 853, 29 U.C.C.R.S.2d 748 (Okla. App. 1996)
49 ALR5th 1—§ 10

Simpson's Food Fair, Inc. v. City of Evansville, 149 Ind. App. 387, 272 N.E.2d 871, 46 A.L.R.3d 1077 (Div. 1 1971)
90 ALR5th 273—§ 3, 4, 15

Simpson Timber Co. v. Department of Revenue, 13 Or. Tax 315, 1995 WL 412427 (1995)
74 ALR6th 1—§ 7

Simpson Timber Co. v. Department of Revenue, 326 Or. 370, 953 P.2d 366 (1998)
74 ALR6th 1—§ 7

Simrin v. Simrin, 233 Cal. App. 2d 90, 43 Cal. Rptr. 376 (5th Dist. 1965)
93 ALR5th 327—§ 2, 3, 11

Sims, In re, 17 A.D.3d 905, 793 N.Y.S.2d 292 (3d Dep't 2005)
25 ALR6th 101—§ 5

Sims, In re, 59 B.R. 651 (Bankr. N.D. Ala. 1986)
47 ALR6th 347—§ 14

Sims, In re, 308 Ill. App. 3d 311, 241 Ill. Dec. 763, 719 N.E.2d 1166 (4th Dist. 1999)
6 ALR6th 483—§ 7

Sims, In re, 665 N.E.2d 584 (Ind. 1996)
1 ALR5th 874—§ 9

Sims, In re, 861 A.2d 1 (D.C. 2004)
43 ALR6th 163—§ 59

Sims v. Agosta, 1996 WL 72610 (Ohio Ct. App. 5th Dist. Fairfield County 1996)
97 ALR6th 375—§ 20

Sims v. American Cas. Co., 131 Ga. App. 461, 206 S.E.2d 121 (1974)
93 ALR6th 463—§ 42
94 ALR6th 111—§ 14

Sims v. American Casualty Co., 131 Ga. App. 461, 206 S.E.2d 121 (1974)
13 ALR5th 289—§ 2 to 4, 13, 18

Sims v. American Hardware Mut. Ins. Co., 429 So. 2d 21 (Fla. Dist. Ct. App. 2d Dist. 1982)
78 ALR5th 341—§ 4

Sims v. Besaw's Cafe, 165 Or. App. 180, 997 P.2d 201, 81 Fair Empl. Prac. Cas. (BNA) 1411 (2000)
82 ALR5th 1—§ 6

Sims v. Block, 94 Ill. App. 2d 215, 236 N.E.2d 572 (2d Dist. 1968)
74 ALR5th 49—§ 2, 3, 77

Sims v. Bradley, 309 Ky. 626, 218 S.W.2d 641 (1949)
4 ALR6th 263—§ 11

Sims v. Brown, 425 F.3d 560 (9th Cir. 2005)
102 ALR6th 417—§ 34

Sims v. Brown & Root Indus. Services, Inc., 889 F. Supp. 920, 70 Fair Empl. Prac. Cas. (BNA) 501 (W.D. La. 1995)
94 ALR5th 1—§ 4, 9

Sims v. Buena Vista School Dist., 138 Mich. App. 426, 360 N.W.2d 211 (1984)
6 ALR5th 297—§ 10

Sims v. Century Kiest Apartments, 567 S.W.2d 526 (Tex. Civ. App. Dallas 1978)
23 ALR5th 140—§ 6

Sims v. Charness, 86 Cal. App. 4th 884, 103 Cal. Rptr. 2d 619 (2d Dist. 2001)
11 ALR6th 587—§ 4, 16, 18

Sims v. City of Broadview Heights, 41 F.3d 1507 (6th Cir. 1994)
103 ALR5th 445—§ 5

Sims v. Clarendon Nat. Ins. Co., 336 F. Supp. 2d 1311 (S.D. Fla. 2004)
22 ALR6th 49—§ 4, 13, 16

Sims v. Cockrell, 2002 WL 1315797 (N.D. Tex. 2002)
7 ALR6th 169—§ 12

Sims v. Colfax Community School Dist., 307 F. Supp. 485 (S.D. Iowa 1970)
58 ALR5th 1—§ 3, 9, 20, 22, 52

Sims v. Collection Div. of Utah State Tax Com'n, 841 P.2d 6 (Utah 1992)
82 ALR5th 103—§ 3
105 ALR5th 1—§ 3, 14

Sims v. Com., 2000 WL 1364196 (Ky. Ct. App. 2000)
36 ALR5th 161—§ 17.5

Sims v. Davis, 388 S.W.2d 752 (Tex. Civ. App. Houston 1965)
112 ALR5th 621—§ 4, 7

Sims v. Div. of Utah State Tax Com., 841 P.2d 6, 198 Utah Adv. Rep. 5 (Utah 1992)
12 ALR5th 89—§ 3, 7, 16

Sims v. General Motors Corp., 751 P.2d 357, Prod. Liab. Rep. (CCH) ¶ 11700 (Wyo. 1988)
29 ALR5th 534—§ 2
48 ALR5th 1—§ 34

96 ALR5th 107—§ 8

Sims v. Hall, 357 S.C. 288, 592 S.E.2d 315 (Ct. App. 2003)
58 ALR6th 1—§ 5, 29

Sims v. Ham, 275 S.C. 369, 271 S.E.2d 316 (1980)
60 ALR6th 481—§ 4

Sims v. Hays, 521 So. 2d 730 (La. App. 2d Cir. 1988)
23 ALR5th 241—§ 3

Sims v. Health Midwest Physician Services Corp., 196 F.3d 915, 81 Fair Empl. Prac. Cas. (BNA) 1658, 77 Empl. Prac. Dec. (CCH) ¶ 46302 (8th Cir. 1999)
94 ALR5th 1—§ 3

Sims v. Hendrickson, 2002 WL 1988154 (Cal. App. 1st Dist. 2002)
22 ALR6th 387—§ 7, 36

Sims v. Johnson, 41 Fed. Appx. 149 (10th Cir. 2002)
119 ALR5th 1—§ 3

Sims v. Kiro, Inc., 20 Wash. App. 229, 580 P.2d 642, 4 Media L. Rep. (BNA) 1149 (Div. 1 1978)
34 ALR6th 431—§ 4, 22

Sims v. Mack Truck Corp., 488 F. Supp. 592, 206 U.S.P.Q. (BNA) 11 (E.D. Pa. 1980)
104 ALR5th 523—§ 4, 5

Sims v. Monumental General Ins. Co., 960 F.2d 478 (5th Cir. 1992)
51 ALR6th 495—§ 5

Sims v. Oakwood Mobile Homes, Inc., 27 N.C. App. 25, 217 S.E.2d 737 (1975)
61 ALR5th 473—§ 9

Sims v. Parke Davis & Co., 334 F. Supp. 774, 20 Wage & Hour Cas. (BNA) 270, 66 Lab. Cas. (CCH) ¶ 32576, 15 Fed. R. Serv. 2d 709 (E.D. Mich. 1971)
87 ALR6th 109—§ 24, 63, 91

Sims v. Rea Const. Co., 25 N.C. App. 472, 213 S.E.2d 398 (1975)
99 ALR6th 1—§ 19

Sims v. Rickets, 35 Ind. 181, 1871 WL 4951 (1871)

87 ALR6th 495—§ 21, 37, 64
Sims v. Roberts, 188 Ark. 1030, 68 S.W.2d 1001 (1934)
87 ALR6th 495—§ 44, 78
Sims v. Selvage, 499 So. 2d 325 (La. App. 1st Cir. 1986)
56 ALR5th 1—§ 3
Sims v. Silvey, 246 So. 2d 394 (La. App. 1971)
48 ALR5th 575—§ 2, 5
Sims v. Sims, 121 N.C. 297, 28 S.E. 407 (1897)
32 ALR5th 673—§ 7
Sims v. Sims, 290 S.C. 190, 348 S.E.2d 835 (S.C. 1986)
46 ALR5th 735—§ 2, 6
Sims v. Sims, 422 So. 2d 618 (La. Ct. App. 3d Cir. 1982)
120 ALR5th 229—§ 7, 13
21 ALR6th 577—§ 20
Sims v. Sims, 515 So. 2d 1 (Ala. Civ. App. 1987)
82 ALR5th 389—§ 2, 4
Sims v. Singletary, 155 F.3d 1297 (11th Cir. 1998)
79 ALR5th 33—§ 63
Sims v. Stanton, 706 F.3d 954 (9th Cir. 2013)
96 ALR6th 577—§ 11
Sims v. State, 51 Ala. App. 183, 283 So. 2d 635 (Crim. App. 1973)
28 ALR6th 505—§ 9, 11
Sims v. State, 169 Tex. Crim. 466, 334 S.W.2d 818 (1960)
108 ALR5th 593—§ 50
Sims v. State, 207 Ga. App. 353, 427 S.E.2d 842 (1993)
109 ALR5th 99—§ 9
Sims v. State, 242 Ga. App. 460, 530 S.E.2d 212 (2000)
29 ALR6th 1—§ 10
Sims v. State, 243 Ga. 83, 252 S.E.2d 501 (1979)
79 ALR5th 237—§ 3
Sims v. State, 251 Ga. 877, 311 S.E.2d 161 (1984)
93 ALR5th 527—§ 15

Sims v. State, 296 Ga. App. 461, 675 S.E.2d 241 (2009)
67 ALR6th 103—§ 5, 10
Sims v. State, 299 Ga. App. 871, 683 S.E.2d 911 (2009)
84 ALR6th 293—§ 35
Sims v. State, 333 Ark. 405, 969 S.W.2d 657 (1998)
67 ALR5th 361—§ 6, 11
Sims v. State, 391 S.W.2d 63 (Tex. Crim. App. 1965)
72 ALR5th 1—§ 3
Sims v. State, 425 So. 2d 563 (Fla. Dist. Ct. App. 4th Dist. 1982)
62 ALR5th 1—§ 3, 10, 15
Sims v. State, 428 So. 2d 162 (Ala. Crim. App. 1982)
79 ALR5th 237—§ 11
Sims v. State, 589 So. 2d 970 (Fla. App. D1 1991)
7 ALR5th 263—§ 4
Sims v. State, 602 So. 2d 1253 (Fla. 1992)
79 ALR5th 33—§ 17, 72
Sims v. State, 637 So. 2d 21, 19 FLW D 1059 (Fla. App. D4 1994)
15 ALR5th 391—§ 5, 7
Sims v. State, 754 So. 2d 657 (Fla. 2000)
21 ALR6th 1—§ 6, 10, 15, 19
22 ALR6th 19—§ 7
Sims v. State, 768 S.W.2d 863 (Tex. App. Texarkana 1989)
47 ALR5th 259—§ 2
Sims v. State, 833 S.W.2d 281 (Tex. App. Houston 14th Dist. 1992)
2 ALR6th 551—§ 21
Sims v. State, 2000 WL 175107 (Tex. App. Dallas 2000)
99 ALR6th 295—§ 13
Sims v. State, 2000 WL 567069 (Tex. App. Dallas 2000)
3 ALR6th 543—§ 11
Sims v. State Dept. of Public Welfare of State of Tex., 438 F. Supp. 1179 (S.D. Tex. 1977)
36 ALR6th 475—§ 10

Sims v. Thornburgh, 1991 WL 30954 (D. Kan. 1991)
54 ALR6th 1—§ 14
Sims v. Unicor Mortgage, 1998 WL 34016832 (N.D. Miss. 1998)
13 ALR6th 145—§ 11
Sims v. Union Assur. Soc., 129 F. 804 (CC Ga. 1903)
16 ALR5th 412—§ 23, 40
Sims v. U.S., 963 A.2d 147 (D.C. 2008)
64 ALR6th 131—§ 31
Sims v. Washex Machinery Corp., 932 S.W.2d 559, Prod. Liab. Rep. (CCH) ¶ 14392 (Tex. App. Houston 1st Dist. 1995)
104 ALR6th 97—§ 6, 8
Sims v. Western Steel Co., 551 F.2d 811, 194 USPQ 71 (CA10 Utah 1977)
6 ALR5th 883—§ 17
Sims v. Williams, 441 S.W.2d 385 (Mo. Ct. App. 1969)
107 ALR5th 311—§ 14
Sims v. Willoughby, 179 Ga. App. 2, 345 S.E.2d 626 (1986)
64 ALR5th 1—§ 21, 29
Sims v. Wyrick, 552 F. Supp. 748 (W.D. Mo. 1982)
12 ALR6th 267—§ 4
Simsbury-Avon Preservation Society, LLC v. Metacon Gun Club, Inc., 37 Conn. L. Rptr. 726, 2004 WL 2094933 (Conn. Super. Ct. 2004)
43 ALR6th 611—§ 57
Simsirdag v. U.S., 315 F.2d 230 (CA5 La. 1963)
34 ALR5th 125—§ 14, 36
Simson's Estate, Re, 123 N.J. Eq. 388, 196 A. 451 (1938)
3 ALR5th 590—§ 2, 35
Simuel v. U.S., 2009 WL 902054 (D. Md. 2009)
73 ALR6th 1—§ 5, 7
Simzer v. Simzer, 514 So. 2d 372, 12 FLW 2142 (Fla. App. D2 1987)
49 ALR5th 441—§ 20
Sina v. Sina, 402 N.W.2d 573 (Minn. Ct. App. 1987)

95 ALR5th 533—§ 4, 7, 9
124 ALR5th 203—§ 4, 14
Sinai Memorial Chapel v. Dudler, 231 Cal. App. 3d 190, 282 Cal. Rptr. 263 (1st Dist. 1991)
81 ALR6th 1—§ 52
Sinatra v. National X-Ray Products Corp., 26 N.J. 546, 141 A.2d 28 (1958)
93 ALR6th 463—§ 4
Sincavage v. Superior Court, 42 Cal. App. 4th 224, 49 Cal. Rptr. 2d 615 (1st Dist. 1996)
85 ALR5th 471—§ 2, 7
Sincerely Yours, Inc. v. Cooper, 130 S. Ct. 1688, 176 L. Ed. 2d 180 (2010)
56 ALR6th 679—§ 32
Sinclair, Application of, 33 Misc. 2d 226, 225 N.Y.S.2d 668 (Sup. Ct. 1962)
103 ALR5th 1—§ 7
Sinclair, Matter of, 517 A.2d 309 (D.C. 1986)
44 ALR6th 75—§ 4
Sinclair v. Bloom, 1995 WL 348127 (N.D. Ill.)
50 ALR5th 301—§ 5
Sinclair v. City of Ecorse, 561 F. Supp. 2d 804 (E.D. Mich. 2008)
68 ALR6th 229—§ 8
Sinclair v. Coughlin, 128 App. Div. 2d 883, 513 N.Y.S.2d 806 (2d Dep't 1987)
9 ALR5th 451—§ 3, 5
Sinclair v. Dunagan, 905 F. Supp. 208 (D.N.J. 1995)
57 ALR5th 689—§ 6
Sinclair v. Fotomat Corp., 140 Cal. App. 3d 217, 189 Cal. Rptr. 393 (2d Dist. 1983)
115 ALR5th 709—§ 3
Sinclair v. Justice, 414 So. 2d 826 (La. App. 4th Cir. 1982)
46 ALR5th 1—§ 25
Sinclair v. Okata, 874 F. Supp. 1051 (D.C. Alaska 1994)
11 ALR5th 127—§ 18, 46

CASES CITED IN ALR5TH AND 6TH

Sinclair v. Perma-Maid Co., 345 Pa. 280, 26 A.2d 924 (1942)
27 ALR5th 174—§ 48

Sinclair v. Sinclair, 136 App. Div. 2d 694, 524 N.Y.S.2d 53 (2d Dep't 1988)
9 ALR5th 568—§ 20

Sinclair v. Sinclair, 204 Kan. 240, 461 P.2d 750 (1969)
124 ALR5th 203—§ 9

Sinclair v. Sinclair, 392 P.2d 750 (Okla. 1964)
53 ALR5th 375—§ 16

Sinclair v. State, 278 Md. 243, 363 A.2d 468 (1976)
42 ALR5th 581—§ 11, 18, 19

Sinclair v. State, 2007 WL 189457 (Tenn. Crim. App. 2007)
69 ALR6th 579—§ 4

Sinclair v. State ex rel. McShane, 99 So. 2d 238 (Fla. Dist. Ct. App. 1st Dist. 1957)
76 ALR5th 485—§ 15, 19

Sinclair v. U.S., 388 A.2d 1201 (Dist. Col. App. 1978)
39 ALR5th 283—§ 4, 32

Sinclair Refining Co. v. Bennett, 123 F.2d 884 (CA6 Tenn. 1941)
5 ALR5th 1—§ 2, 16
11 ALR5th 438—§ 7

Sinclair Refining Co. v. Fuller, 190 Ark. 426, 79 S.W.2d 736 (1935)
53 ALR6th 213—§ 8

Sincoff v. Liberty Mut. Fire Ins. Co., 11 N.Y.2d 386, 230 N.Y.S.2d 13, 183 N.E.2d 899 (1962)
30 ALR5th 170—§ 110

Sincox v. Blackwell, 525 F. Supp. 96 (W.D. La 1981)
4 ALR5th 273—§ 2

Sindell v. Abbott Laboratories, 26 Cal. 3d 588, 163 Cal. Rptr. 132, 607 P.2d 924, 2 A.L.R.4th 1061 (1980)
63 ALR5th 195—§ 2 to 6, 8
69 ALR5th 137—§ 11

Sindell v. Gibson, Dunn & Crutcher, 54 Cal. App. 4th 1457, 63 Cal. Rptr. 2d 594 (2d Dist. 1997)
87 ALR5th 473—§ 5
13 ALR6th 1—§ 4

Sindler v. William M. Bailey Co., 348 Mass. 589, 204 N.E.2d 717 (1965)
62 ALR5th 219—§ 25, 42

Sindorf v. Jacron Sales Co., 27 Md. App. 53, 341 A.2d 856 (1975)
19 ALR5th 1—§ 114

Sinex v. Wallis, 611 A.2d 31 (Del. Super. Ct. 1991)
60 ALR5th 165—§ 14

Singarella v. Boston, 330 Mass. 257, 112 N.E.2d 809 (1953)
16 ALR5th 548—§ 7

Singelmann, State ex rel. v. Morrison, 57 So. 2d 238 (La. Ct. App., Orleans 1952)
107 ALR5th 1—§ 3, 9, 16, 19, 20
26 ALR6th 145—§ 3

Singer, In re, 290 A.D.2d 197, 738 N.Y.S.2d 38 (1st Dep't 2002)
43 ALR6th 163—§ 3, 41
44 ALR6th 75—§ 3
45 ALR6th 175—§ 3

Singer, In re, 302 A.D.2d 179, 752 N.Y.S.2d 655 (1st Dep't 2002)
45 ALR6th 175—§ 14

Singer v. A. Krasne, Inc., 34 N.Y.S.2d 236 (Sup. App. T 1941)
2 ALR5th 1—§ 2, 23

Singer v. American Airlines Federal Credit Union, 2006 WL 3093759 (N.D. Cal. 2006)
60 ALR6th 295—§ 52

Singer v. BAC Home Loan Servicing, LP, 2011 WL 2940733 (D. Ariz. 2011)
86 ALR6th 411—§ 5

Singer v. BFS Capital, 2005 WL 3589424 (Ohio C.P. 2005)
77 ALR6th 1—§ 120

Singer v. Bossingham, 152 Minn. 111, 188 N.W. 155 (1922)
3 ALR5th 146—§ 27
6 ALR5th 534—§ 7, 19

Singer v. Bulk Petroleum Corp., 9 F. Supp. 2d 916, 47 Env't. Rep. Cas. (BNA) 1501 (N.D. Ill. 1998)

For assistance, call 1-800-328-4880

301

11 ALR5th 388—§ 7

11 ALR5th 438—§ 7

Singer v. Commodities Corp., 292 N.J. Super. 391, 678 A.2d 1165 (App. Div. 1996)

60 ALR5th 669—§ 3

Singer v. Dungan, 1992 WL 884986 (Va. Cir. Ct. 1992)

2 ALR6th 387—§ 3, 4

Singer v. Hara, 11 Wash. App. 247, 522 P.2d 1187 (Div. 1 1974)

81 ALR5th 1—§ 2, 3, 5, 6, 8, 9, 11, 13

Singer v. Highland Park, 31 Ill. App. 3d 1071, 335 N.E.2d 585 (2d Dist. 1975)

1 ALR5th 622—§ 17

Singer v. James, 130 Md. 382, 100 A. 642 (1917)

90 ALR5th 619—§ 7, 17

93 ALR5th 621—§ 7, 10

Singer v. Land Rover North America, Inc., 955 F. Supp. 359 (D.N.J. 1997)

88 ALR5th 301—§ 35

Singer v. National Bond & Invest. Co., 218 Ala. 375, 118 So. 561 (1928)

19 ALR5th 622—§ 36, 49

Singer v. Oken, 193 Misc. 1058, 87 N.Y.S.2d 686 (1949)

44 ALR5th 393—§ 26

Singer v. Shannon & Luchs Co., 670 F. Supp. 1024 (D.C. Dist. Col. 1987)

10 ALR5th 448—§ 2, 5

Singer v. Singer, 52 App. Div. 2d 774, 382 N.Y.S.2d 793 (1st Dep't 1976)

38 ALR5th 69—§ 4

Singer v. Singer, 79 App. Div. 2d 680, 433 N.Y.S.2d 864 (2d Dep't 1980)

21 ALR5th 396—§ 19, 61

Singer v. Singer, 175 A.D.2d 328, 572 N.Y.S.2d 415 (3d Dep't 1991)

70 ALR5th 377—§ 7

Singer v. Singer, 636 A.2d 422 (Dist. Col. App. 1994)

44 ALR5th 1—§ 2

Singer v. State, 63 N.J. 319, 307 A.2d 94 (1973)

87 ALR5th 277—§ 35

Singer v. U.S., 126 Ct. Cl. 417, 115 F. Supp. 166 (1953)

45 ALR5th 251—§ 6

Singer v. U.S. Civil Service Com'n, 429 U.S. 1034, 97 S. Ct. 725, 50 L. Ed. 2d 744, 14 Fair Empl. Prac. Cas. (BNA) 203, 13 Empl. Prac. Dec. (CCH) ¶ 11310 (1977)

96 ALR5th 391—§ 14, 15

Singer v. U.S. Civil Service Com'n, 530 F.2d 247, 12 Fair Empl. Prac. Cas. (BNA) 208, 11 Empl. Prac. Dec. (CCH) ¶ 10630 (9th Cir. 1976)

81 ALR5th 1—§ 3

96 ALR5th 391—§ 5, 14, 15, 24

Singer v. Wadman, 595 F. Supp. 188, 21 Ed. Law Rep. 65 (D. Utah 1982)

101 ALR5th 515—§ 25

Singer v. Zabelin, 24 N.Y.S.2d 962 (City Ct. 1941)

2 ALR5th 1—§ 37, 70

Singer Asset Finance Co., L.L.C. v. State, Dept. of Treasury, Div. of State Lottery, 314 N.J. Super. 106, 714 A.2d 317 (App. Div. 1998)

48 ALR6th 243—§ 10

Singer by Singer v. School Dist. of Philadelphia, 99 Pa. Commw. 553, 513 A.2d 1108, 34 Ed. Law Rep. 520 (1986)

66 ALR5th 1—§ 47

Singer Co. v. County of Kings, 46 Cal. App. 3d 852, 121 Cal. Rptr. 398 (5th Dist. 1975)

1 ALR6th 1—§ 31

14 ALR6th 119—§ 12

Singer Co., Link Simulation Systems Div. v. Baltimore Gas and Elec. Co., 79 Md. App. 461, 558 A.2d 419, 9 U.C.C. Rep. Serv. 2d 41 (1989)

97 ALR6th 1—§ 2, 5, 21

Singer Housing Co. v. Seven Lakes Venture, 466 F. Supp. 369, 27 Fed. R. Serv. 2d 530 (D. Colo. 1979)

88 ALR6th 533—§ 17

Singer Hutner Levine Seeman & Stuart v. Louisiana State Bar Ass'n, 378 So. 2d 423, 6 A.L.R.4th 1244 (La. 1979)
83 ALR5th 497—§ 10

Singer Management Consultants, Inc. v. Milgram, 650 F.3d 223, 99 U.S.P.Q.2d 1180 (3d Cir. 2011)
76 ALR6th 587—§ 12

Singer Sewing Mach. Co. v. Stockton, 171 Miss. 209, 157 So. 366 (1934)
13 ALR5th 217—§ 3

Singer Shop-Rite, Inc. v. Rangel, 174 N.J. Super. 442, 416 A.2d 965 (1980)
12 ALR5th 195—§ 10

Singh, In re, 710 N.Y.S.2d 164 (App. Div. 3d Dep't 2000)
23 ALR5th 176—§ 29

Singh, Re, 149 Misc. 2d 365, 565 N.Y.S.2d 395 (1990)
12 ALR5th 577—§ 10

Singh v. Allstate Ins. Co., 63 Cal. App. 4th 135, 73 Cal. Rptr. 2d 546 (4th Dist. 1998)
4 ALR6th 509—§ 8

Singh v. Boodhoo, 17 A.D.3d 345, 791 N.Y.S.2d 842 (2d Dep't 2005)
18 ALR6th 325—§ 28

Singh v. City of Sacramento, 2010 WL 1178543 (Cal. App. 3d Dist. 2010)
66 ALR6th 315—§ 3, 20

Singh v. Furuta, 59 Cal. App. 2d 695, 139 P.2d 664 (1943)
27 ALR5th 174—§ 3, 26

Singh v. Krueger, 39 Kan. App. 2d 637, 183 P.3d 1 (2008)
58 ALR6th 1—§ 5
60 ALR6th 1—§ 89

Singh v. Lipworth, 132 Cal. App. 4th 40, 33 Cal. Rptr. 3d 178 (3d Dist. 2005)
45 ALR6th 493—§ 46

Singh v. Maheshwari, 2002 WL 54648 (Cal. App. 4th Dist. 2002)
79 ALR6th 377—§ 38

Singh v. Prunty, 142 F.3d 1157 (9th Cir. 1998)
12 ALR6th 267—§ 4

Singh v. Saint Clair's Nursing Center, Inc., 2004 WL 1615992 (Cal. App. 3d Dist. 2004)
45 ALR6th 493—§ 46

Singh v. Singh, 81 Ohio App. 3d 376, 611 N.E.2d 347 (Cuyahoga Co. 1992)
11 ALR5th 88—§ 3

Singh v. Singh, 213 Conn. 637, 569 A.2d 1112 (1990)
34 ALR5th 723—§ 4

Singh v. State Farm Mut. Auto. Ins. Co., 860 P.2d 1193 (Alaska 1993)
23 ALR5th 241—§ 11

Singh v. U.S. Bank Home Mortg., 2013 WL 3192938 (S.D. Tex. 2013)
104 ALR6th 485—§ 5

Singh v. Wells Fargo Bank, 2013 WL 1787157 (N.D. Cal. 2013)
86 ALR6th 411—§ 5

Singha v. BAC Home Loans Servicing, LP, 2011 WL 7678684 (E.D. Tex. 2011)
86 ALR6th 411—§ 5

Singhaviroj v. Fairfield Bd. of Educ., 2007 WL 2200374 (Conn. Super. Ct. 2007)
32 ALR6th 457—§ 8

Singing River Tire Shop v. Stone, 21 So. 2d 580 (Miss. 1945)
113 ALR5th 313—§ 4

Singiser, In re, 288 A.D.2d 553, 732 N.Y.S.2d 650 (3d Dep't 2001)
44 ALR6th 75—§ 21

Singla v. New York State Dept. of Health, 229 A.D.2d 798, 646 N.Y.S.2d 421 (3d Dep't 1996)
65 ALR6th 295—§ 4

Singletary v. Benton, 693 So. 2d 1119 (Fla. Dist. Ct. App. 4th Dist. 1997)
6 ALR6th 483—§ 7

Singletary v. Bullard, 701 So. 2d 590 (Fla. Dist. Ct. App. 5th Dist. 1997)
6 ALR6th 483—§ 7

Singletary v. Carpenter, 705 So. 2d 110 (Fla. Dist. Ct. App. 2d Dist. 1998)
6 ALR6th 483—§ 7

Singletary v. Costello, 665 So. 2d 1099
(Fla. 4th DCA 1996)
78 ALR6th 229—§ 9

Singletary v. Costello, 665 So. 2d 1099
(Fla. Dist. Ct. App. 4th Dist. 1996)
66 ALR5th 111—§ 3

Singletary v. Reilly, 452 F.3d 868 (D.C.
Cir. 2006)
21 ALR6th 771—§ 10

Singletary v. Singletary, 2013 Ark. 506,
431 S.W.3d 234 (2013)
102 ALR6th 153—§ 21

Singletary v. South Carolina Dep't of
Educ., 447 S.E.2d 231 (S.C. App.
1994)
10 ALR5th 680—§ 5

Singletary v. Southeastern Freight Lines,
Inc., 832 F. Supp. 1552 (N.D. Ga.
1993)
110 ALR5th 465—§ 2, 29

Singletary v. State, 290 So. 2d 116 (Fla.
4th DCA 1974)
92 ALR6th 1—§ 3

Singletary v. Storey, 711 So. 2d 221
(Fla. Dist. Ct. App. 5th Dist. 1998)
6 ALR6th 483—§ 7

Singleton, In re, 2004 WL 2830698
(Bankr. M.D. N.C. 2004)
32 ALR6th 531—§ 28

Singleton v. Airco, Inc., 169 Ga. App.
662, 314 S.E.2d 680 (1984)
57 ALR5th 1—§ 3, 18

Singleton v. Bank of Monticello, 113
Ga. 527, 38 S.E. 947 (1901)
74 ALR5th 369—§ 9, 14

Singleton v. Carter, 74 Fed. Appx. 536
(6th Cir. 2003)
29 ALR6th 1—§ 10

Singleton v. Cecil, 133 F.3d 631, 13
I.E.R. Cas. (BNA) 987, 13 I.E.R.
Cas. (BNA) 1344 (8th Cir. 1998)
123 ALR5th 411—§ 23

Singleton v. Cecil, 176 F.3d 419, 14
I.E.R. Cas. (BNA) 1793 (8th Cir.
1999)
123 ALR5th 411—§ 23

Singleton v. Charlebois Const. Co., 690
S.W.2d 845 (Mo. Ct. App. W.D.
1985)
74 ALR5th 523—§ 3, 13

Singleton v. Christ the Servant Evangelical Lutheran Church, 541 N.W.2d
606 (Minn. Ct. App. 1996)
108 ALR5th 495—§ 4, 18
109 ALR5th 541—§ 11

Singleton v. Chung Sun Suhr M.D.,
1989 WL 54383 (Ohio Ct. App. 8th
Dist. Cuyahoga County 1989)
95 ALR6th 541—§ 31

Singleton v. City of Newburgh, 1 F.
Supp. 2d 306 (S.D. N.Y. 1998)
65 ALR6th 93—§ 20

Singleton v. Crown Cent. Petroleum
Corp., 713 S.W.2d 115 (Tex. App.
Houston (1st Dist.) 1985)
22 ALR5th 483—§ 3

Singleton v. Cushman, 117 Ind. App.
183, 70 N.E.2d 642 (1947)
69 ALR5th 219—§ 4

Singleton v. Davis, 95 Mich. App. 182,
290 N.W.2d 117 (1980)
23 ALR5th 75—§ 9
120 ALR5th 559—§ 6

Singleton v. D. T. Vance Mica Co., 235
N.C. 315, 69 S.E.2d 707 (1952)
86 ALR5th 295—§ 4

Singleton v. Endell, 316 Ark. 133, 870
S.W.2d 742 (1994)
111 ALR5th 491—§ 3, 9

Singleton v. Foreman, 435 F.2d 962 (5th
Cir. 1970)
9 ALR6th 285—§ 7

Singleton v. Gulf Coast Truck Service,
409 So. 2d 377 (La. App. 4th Cir.
1982)
18 ALR5th 577—§ 9, 26, 38, 58

Singleton v. International Ass'n of Machinists, Dist. 141, Local Lodge No.
1747, 240 Va. 403, 397 S.E.2d 856,
135 L.R.R.M. (BNA) 2966, 121
Lab. Cas. (CCH) ¶ 56868 (1990)
105 ALR5th 243—§ 11

Singleton v. New York Underwriters Ins. Co., 739 F.2d 198 (5th Cir. 1984)
17 ALR6th 1—§ 15

Singleton v. Norris, 319 F.3d 1018 (8th Cir. 2003)
111 ALR5th 491—§ 7

Singleton v. Olin Mathieson Chemical Corp., 131 So. 2d 329 (La. Ct. App. 3d Cir. 1961)
96 ALR5th 239—§ 27

Singleton v. Singleton, 68 Cal. App. 2d 681, 157 P.2d 886 (1945)
12 ALR5th 195—§ 64

Singleton v. State, 33 Ala. App. 536, 35 So. 2d 375 (1948)
118 ALR5th 253—§ 3, 7

Singleton v. State, 143 Ga. App. 387, 238 S.E.2d 743 (1977)
95 ALR5th 229—§ 28

Singleton v. State, 146 Ga. App. 72, 245 S.E.2d 473 (1978)
95 ALR5th 229—§ 28

Singleton v. State, 168 Ga. App. 555, 309 S.E.2d 867 (1983)
33 ALR5th 571—§ 4

Singleton v. State, 193 Ga. App. 778, 389 S.E.2d 269 (1989)
55 ALR6th 391—§ 21

Singleton v. State, 240 Ga. App. 240, 522 S.E.2d 734 (1999)
56 ALR6th 185—§ 20

Singleton v. State, 256 Ark. 756, 510 S.W.2d 283 (1974)
117 ALR5th 513—§ 27

Singleton v. State, 266 Ga. App. 795, 598 S.E.2d 80 (2004)
28 ALR6th 505—§ 7, 9

Singleton v. State, 313 S.C. 75, 437 S.E.2d 53 (1993)
111 ALR5th 491—§ 3, 4, 7, 8

Singleton v. State, 344 So. 2d 911 (Fla. Dist. Ct. App. 3d Dist. 1977)
124 ALR5th 1—§ 3

Singleton v. State, 396 So. 2d 1050 (Ala. 1981)
1 ALR5th 317—§ 4

Singleton v. State, 860 So. 2d 1017 (Fla. Dist. Ct. App. 3d Dist. 2003)
11 ALR6th 237—§ 10

Singleton v. State, 921 P.2d 636, 75 A.L.R.5th 701 (Alaska Ct. App. 1996)
75 ALR5th 295—§ 21

Singleton v. St. Charles Parish, 833 So. 2d 486 (La. Ct. App. 5th Cir. 2002)
38 ALR6th 541—§ 9

Singleton v. Stegall, 580 So. 2d 1242 (Miss. 1991)
4 ALR5th 273—§ 42, 47

Singleton v. Stokes Motors, Inc., 595 S.E.2d 461 (S.C. 2004)
117 ALR5th 155—§ 12

Singleton v. Wells Fargo Bank, N.A., 2013 WL 5423917 (N.D. Miss. 2013)
96 ALR6th 125—§ 22

Singleton v. Younger Bros., Inc., 247 So. 2d 273 (La. Ct. App. 4th Cir. 1971)
41 ALR6th 207—§ 31

Singleton Sheet Metal Works, Inc. v. Martin, 680 P.2d 1288 (Colo. Ct. App. 1983)
89 ALR5th 493—§ 18

Singley v. Norman, 202 Ark. 532, 150 S.W.2d 947 (1941)
74 ALR5th 369—§ 8

Singley v. U.S., 533 A.2d 245 (Dist. Col. App. 1987)
4 ALR5th 1—§ 2, 17, 34

Singsaas v. Diederich, 307 Minn. 153, 238 N.W.2d 878 (1976)
14 ALR5th 695—§ 16

Sinha v. Ambach, 91 A.D.2d 703, 457 N.Y.S.2d 603 (3d Dep't 1982)
65 ALR6th 295—§ 6

Sinha v. Dabezies, 590 So. 2d 795 (La. App. 1991)
47 ALR5th 433—§ 14

Sinicrope v. Keller Industries, Inc., 1997 WL 115841 (D. Mass. 1997)
81 ALR5th 245—§ 10

Sink v. Easter, 288 N.C. 183, 217 S.E.2d 532 (1975)

5 ALR5th 422—§ 3, 4

Sink v. Meadow Wood Country Estates, Inc., 18 Conn. App. 569, 559 A.2d 725 (1989)

104 ALR6th 303—§ 17

Sink v. Sink, 721 S.W.2d 108 (Mo. Ct. App. E.D. 1986)

59 ALR6th 433—§ 61

Sink v. Sumrell, 41 N.C. App. 242, 254 S.E.2d 665 (1979)

9 ALR5th 826—§ 19

Sinka v. Northern Commercial Co., 491 P.2d 116, 9 U.C.C.R.S. 1350 (Alaska 1971)

49 ALR5th 1—§ 40, 106

Sinker v. Sweeney, 89 N.Y.2d 485, 655 N.Y.S.2d 842, 678 N.E.2d 454 (1997)

18 ALR6th 195—§ 34

Sinkevich v. Cenkus, 24 A.D.2d 903, 264 N.Y.S.2d 979 (2d Dep't 1965)

111 ALR5th 1—§ 8, 9, 13

Sinkfield v. Strong, 34 Ohio Misc. 2d 19, 517 N.E.2d 1051 (Mun. Ct. 1987)

63 ALR5th 1—§ 4

Sinko v. Bethlehem Steel Co., 104 Pa. Super. 357, 159 A. 230 (1932)

41 ALR6th 207—§ 19

Sinks, In re Marriage of, 204 Cal. App. 3d 586, 251 Cal. Rptr. 379 (4th Dist. 1988)

36 ALR6th 1—§ 15, 24

Sinks v. Caughey, 890 N.E.2d 34 (Ind. Ct. App. 2008)

97 ALR6th 375—§ 5, 7

Sinks v. State, 44 Ark. App. 1, 864 S.W.2d 879 (1993)

4 ALR5th 1—§ 14

Sinn v. Burd, 486 Pa. 146, 404 A.2d 672 (1979)

96 ALR5th 107—§ 6, 8

Sinnott, In re, 176 Vt. 596, 845 A.2d 373 (2004)

27 ALR6th 1—§ 21

Sinnott v. Schumacher, 45 Cal. App. 46, 187 P. 105 (1919)

15 ALR5th 376—§ 3

Sinns v. State, 248 Ga. 385, 283 S.E.2d 479 (1981)

31 ALR5th 704—§ 16

Sinochem Intern. Co. Ltd. v. Malaysia Intern. Shipping Corp., 127 S. Ct. 1184, 167 L. Ed. 2d 15, 2007 A.M.C. 609 (U.S. 2007)

26 ALR6th 659—§ 30

Sinon v. Zoning Bd. of Appeals of Town of Shelter Island, 117 A.D.2d 606, 497 N.Y.S.2d 952 (2d Dep't 1986)

63 ALR5th 607—§ 13

Sinopoli v. North River Ins. Co., 244 N.J. Super. 245, 581 A.2d 1368 (1990)

35 ALR5th 375—§ 31

Sinor v. National Casualty Co., 633 So. 2d 720 (La. App. 1st Cir. 1993)

50 ALR5th 1—§ 3

52 ALR5th 1—§ 3

Sinquefield v. Clay County, Ga., 2005 WL 2217440 (M.D. Ga. 2005)

95 ALR6th 341—§ 14

Sinquefield v. Sears Roebuck and Co., 209 Ill. App. 3d 595, 154 Ill. Dec. 325, 568 N.E.2d 325 (1st Dist. 1991)

112 ALR5th 113—§ 2

Sinquefield v. Yates, 197 So. 2d 395, CCH Prod. Liab. Rep. ¶ 9226 (La. App. 3d Cir. 1967)

61 ALR5th 473—§ 3

Sinram v. Gertz Dept. Stores, 207 N.Y.S.2d 306 (App. Term 1960)

63 ALR6th 495—§ 77

Sinsabaugh v. Heinerscheid, 428 N.W.2d 476 (Minn. App. 1988)

53 ALR5th 375—§ 5

Sinsky v. Gatien, 2000 WL 1226616 (Ohio Ct. App. 9th Dist. Summit County 2000)

13 ALR6th 1—§ 4

14 ALR6th 1—§ 4

Sinthasomphone by Sinthasomphone, Estate of v. City of Milwaukee, 785 F. Supp. 1343 (E.D. Wis. 1992)

90 ALR5th 273—§ 5, 6, 14

Sintic v. Cvelbar, 1996 WL 649137 (Ohio App. 11 Dist, Lake County)
50 ALR5th 417—§ 5

Sintra, Inc. v. City of Seattle, 131 Wash. 2d 640, 935 P.2d 555 (1997)
2 ALR6th 279—§ 20
49 ALR6th 205—§ 54

Sinwellan Corp. v. Farmers Bank of Delaware, 345 A.2d 430, 18 U.C.C.R.S. 178 (Del. Super. 1975)
23 ALR5th 744—§ 2

Siok v. Turner, 2012 WL 3058656 (Va. Cir. Ct. 2012)
99 ALR6th 481—§ 9

Siordia v. Circuit City Stores, Inc., 2005 WL 1368083 (9th Cir. 2005)
13 ALR6th 145—§ 14

Sioux City Bridge Co. v. Dakota County, Neb., 260 U.S. 441, 43 S. Ct. 190, 67 L. Ed. 340, 28 A.L.R. 979 (1923)
32 ALR6th 457—§ 2

Sioux City Police Officers' Ass'n v. City of Sioux City, 495 N.W.2d 687, 10 I.E.R. Cas. (BNA) 1858, 144 L.R.R.M. (BNA) 2433 (Iowa 1993)
123 ALR5th 411—§ 4, 13

Sioux Falls, City of v. Miller, 1996 SD 132, 555 N.W.2d 368 (S.D. 1996)
10 ALR6th 375—§ 3

Sipari v. Villa Olivia Country Club, 63 Ill. App. 3d 985, 20 Ill. Dec. 610, 380 N.E.2d 819 (1st Dist. 1978)
54 ALR5th 513—§ 6

Sipary v. State, 91 P.3d 296 (Alaska Ct. App. 2004)
27 ALR6th 183—§ 19

Sipco, Inc. v. Director of Revenue, 875 S.W.2d 539 (Mo. 1994)
89 ALR5th 493—§ 7

Sipe, In re, 44 Kan. App. 2d 584, 239 P.3d 871 (2010)
78 ALR6th 417—§ 70, 85

Sipe v. Countrywide Bank, 690 F. Supp. 2d 1141 (E.D. Cal. 2010)
86 ALR6th 411—§ 5

Sipe v. McKenna, 88 Cal. App. 2d 1001, 200 P.2d 61 (2d Dist. 1948)
36 ALR6th 387—§ 9, 10

Sipe v. State, 690 N.E.2d 779 (Ind. Ct. App. 1998)
70 ALR6th 361—§ 31, 32
72 ALR6th 141—§ 18

Sipes v. Board of Mun. and Zoning Appeals, 99 Md. App. 78, 635 A.2d 86 (1994)
47 ALR6th 439—§ 3, 8

Sipes v. General Motors Corp., 946 S.W.2d 143 (Tex. App. Texarkana 1997)
39 ALR5th 267—§ 5

Siporin v. Carrington, 200 Ariz. 97, 23 P.3d 92, Blue Sky L. Rep. (CCH) ¶ 74255 (Ct. App. Div. 1 2001)
28 ALR6th 281—§ 3, 7, 10, 14

Sipos v. Desel, 1995 WL 785023 (Conn. Super. Ct. 1995)
8 ALR6th 549—§ 7

Sipp v. Commonwealth, Pennsylvania State Horse Racing Com., 77 Pa. Cmwlth. 561, 466 A.2d 296 (1983)
59 ALR5th 203—§ 14, 51

Sipp v. State, 936 So. 2d 326 (Miss. 2006)
42 ALR6th 237—§ 5
55 ALR6th 157—§ 94

Sipper v. Urban, 22 Cal. 2d 138, 137 P.2d 425 (1943)
7 ALR5th 474—§ 66

Sippin v. McClintock, 2001 WL 649516 (Conn. Super. Ct. 2001)
119 ALR5th 519—§ 20

Sipple v. Laclede Gaslight Co., 125 Mo. App. 81, 102 S.W. 608 (1907)
34 ALR5th 1—§ 3

Siracusa v. Inch Corp., 164 Misc. 820, 298 N.Y.S. 878 (1937)
46 ALR5th 1—§ 47

Siragusa v. State, 122 Tex. Crim. 263, 54 S.W.2d 107 (1932)
41 ALR5th 171—§ 66

Siravo By and Through Siravo v. Florida Birth-Related Neurological Injury Compensation Ass'n, 667 So. 2d 971 (Fla. Dist. Ct. App. 4th Dist. 1996)
111 ALR5th 459—§ 9

Sircar v. New Masa Partners, LLC, 2004
WL 2668702 (Cal. App. 2d Dist.
2004)
36 ALR6th 387—§ 10
Sireci v. Moore, 825 So. 2d 882 (Fla.
2002)
110 ALR5th 1—§ 2, 3
Sireci v. State, 587 So. 2d 450 (Fla.
1991)
20 ALR5th 177—§ 3, 8
91 ALR5th 343—§ 17
Sireci v. State, 908 So. 2d 321 (Fla.
2005)
72 ALR6th 227—§ 51
Sirek v. Fairfield Snowbowl, 166 Ariz.
183, 800 P.2d 1291, 72 Ariz. Adv.
Rep. 63 (App. 1990)
54 ALR5th 513—§ 4
Sires v. Luke, 544 F. Supp. 1155, 34
U.C.C. Rep. Serv. 533 (S.D. Ga.
1982)
94 ALR6th 1—§ 22, 42
Siriano v. Beth Israel Hosp. Ctr., 161
Misc. 2d 512, 614 N.Y.S.2d 700
(Sup. 1994)
20 ALR5th 398—§ 9
Sirigiano v. Otis Elevator Co., 118
A.D.2d 920, 499 N.Y.S.2d 486 (3d
Dep't 1986)
115 ALR5th 1—§ 9, 10, 13, 14
Sirigiano v. Otis Elevator Co., 118 App.
Div. 2d 920, 499 N.Y.S.2d 486 (3d
Dep't 1986)
51 ALR5th 467—§ 10, 12
Siripongs v. Calderon, 35 F.3d 1308 (9th
Cir. 1994)
38 ALR6th 97—§ 11
Sirman v. Com., Unemployment Com-
pensation Bd. of Review, 35 Pa.
Commw. 334, 385 A.2d 1052
(1978)
68 ALR5th 13—§ 8, 35
Sirmans v. State, 244 Ga. App. 252, 534
S.E.2d 862 (2000)
45 ALR6th 435—§ 11
Sirohi v. Lee, 634 N.Y.S.2d 119 (App.
Div. 1st Dep't 1995)
46 ALR5th 581—§ 3, 25

Sirone v. Distefano, 67 So. 2d 150 (La.
App. 1st Cir. 1953)
46 ALR5th 1—§ 22, 43
Sirott v. Latts, 6 Cal. App. 4th 923, 8
Cal. Rptr. 2d 206 (2d Dist. 1992)
67 ALR5th 587—§ 2
87 ALR5th 473—§ 5
11 ALR6th 1—§ 3
12 ALR6th 1—§ 3
13 ALR6th 1—§ 3 to 5
14 ALR6th 1—§ 3
15 ALR6th 427—§ 3
Siroty v. Nelson, 75 N.Y.2d 957, 556
N.Y.S.2d 4, 555 N.E.2d 256, 7
A.L.R.5th 1196 (1990)
7 ALR5th 976—§ 2, 3
Siruta v. Hesston Corp., 232 Kan. 654,
659 P.2d 799 (1983)
42 ALR5th 221—§ 3, 8, 27
73 ALR5th 75—§ 6
Sisbarro v. Warden, Massachusetts State
Penitentiary, 592 F.2d 1 (1st Cir.
1979)
56 ALR6th 553—§ 25
Sisco v. American Family Mut. Ins. Co.,
806 S.W.2d 409 (Mo. 1991)
24 ALR5th 766—§ 7
31 ALR5th 116—§ 6
Sisco v. City of Huntsville, 220 Ala. 59,
124 So. 95 (1929)
54 ALR6th 201—§ 7, 42
Sisco v. Empiregas, Inc. of Belle Mina,
286 Ala. 72, 237 So. 2d 463 (1970)
12 ALR5th 847—§ 5, 11, 12
Sisco v. Fabrication Technologies, Inc.,
350 F. Supp. 2d 932, 95 Fair Empl.
Prac. Cas. (BNA) 208 (D. Wyo.
2004)
20 ALR6th 1—§ 4
Sisco v. Iowa-Illinois Gas & Electric
Co., 368 N.W.2d 853 (Iowa App.
1985)
8 ALR5th 177—§ 2, 3
Sisk v. Richards, 130 S.W.2d 1076 (Tex.
Civ. App. Galveston 1939)
76 ALR5th 337—§ 14

Sisk v. Sanditen Investments, Ltd., 1983 OK CIV APP 17, 662 P.2d 317 (Ct. App. Div. 1 1983)
119 ALR5th 121—§ 4, 5, 9

Sisk v. Sears, Roebuck & Co., 959 F. Supp. 337 (E.D. La. 1996)
4 ALR6th 401—§ 5, 9

Sisk v. Sears, Roebuck & Co., 1996 WL 736967 (E.D. La. 1996)
4 ALR6th 401—§ 9

Sisk v. State, 232 Md. 155, 192 A.2d 108 (1963)
116 ALR5th 373—§ 3, 7

Sisk v. State, 236 Md. 589, 204 A.2d 684 (1964)
116 ALR5th 373—§ 3, 7

Sisk v. Valley Forge Ins. Co., 640 S.W.2d 844, 33 A.L.R.4th 566 (Tenn. Ct. App. 1982)
116 ALR5th 247—§ 4

Siskind v. Newton-John, 1987 Copr. L. Dec. P 26113, 1987 WL 11701 (S.D. N.Y. 1987)
37 ALR6th 243—§ 45

Siskron v. Temel-Peck Enterprises, Inc., 26 N.C. App. 387, 216 S.E.2d 441 (1975)
46 ALR5th 1—§ 16

Sisk, State ex rel. v. Sisk, 222 P.3d 1019 (Kan. Ct. App. 2010)
86 ALR6th 321—§ 4, 12
90 ALR6th 451—§ 38

Sisler v. Courier-News Co., 199 N.J. Super. 307, 489 A.2d 704 (1985)
19 ALR5th 1—§ 34, 104, 110, 123

Sisneros v. Nix, 95 F.3d 749 (8th Cir. 1996)
56 ALR6th 553—§ 3, 40

Sisneroz v. Polanco, 126 N.M. 779, 1999 -NMCA- 039, 975 P.2d 392 (Ct. App. 1999)
17 ALR5th 366—§ 33
87 ALR5th 361—§ 21

Sisneroz v. Polanco, 126 N.M. 779, 1999-NMCA-039, 975 P.2d 392 (Ct. App. 1999)
72 ALR6th 413—§ 6

Sissel v. Smith, 242 Ga. 595, 250 S.E.2d 463 (1978)
1 ALR6th 135—§ 3, 5, 11

Sisseton Educ. Ass'n v. Sisseton School Dist. No. 54-8, 516 N.W.2d 301, 91 Ed. Law Rep. 328 (S.D. 1994)
34 ALR6th 327—§ 4

Sissman, In re, 274 A.D.2d 738, 710 N.Y.S.2d 731 (3d Dep't 2000)
27 ALR6th 1—§ 22

Sisson, In re Marriage of, 170 Or. App. 480, 13 P.3d 152 (2000)
69 ALR5th 1—§ 3, 6

Sisson, In re Marriage of, 2000 WL 1533075 (Or. Ct. App. 2000)
71 ALR5th 99—§ 4

Sisson v. Triplett, 428 N.W.2d 565, 12 A.L.R.5th 980 (Minn. 1988)
12 ALR5th 89—§ 5, 7, 8

Sisson, People ex rel. v. Sisson, 271 N.Y. 285, 2 N.E.2d 660 (1936)
124 ALR5th 203—§ 8

Sisters of Charity Health Systems, Inc. v. Raikes, 1998 WL 566085 (Ky. 1998)
69 ALR5th 559—§ 2

Sisters of Charity of Cincinnati, Ohio v. Bernalillo County, 93 N.M. 42, 596 P.2d 255 (1979)
14 ALR6th 119—§ 14, 54

Sisters of Charity of Providence v. Nichols, 157 Mont. 106, 483 P.2d 279 (1971)
16 ALR5th 262—§ 2, 35, 54

Sisti v. Barker, 70 Ill. App. 3d 734, 27 Ill. Dec. 154, 388 N.E.2d 1117 (2d Dist. 1979)
26 ALR5th 401—§ 25

Sisti v. Merrill, Lynch, Pierce, Fenner & Smith, 1991 WL 575874 (E.D. Va. 1991)
67 ALR5th 179—§ 6

Sistler v. Liberty Mut. Ins. Co., 558 So. 2d 1106 (La. 1990)
48 ALR5th 129—§ 12, 17

Sisto v. Housing & Redevelopment Authority, 258 Minn. 391, 104 N.W.2d 529 (1960)

41 ALR5th 47—§ 7, 18

Sisto v. Levine, 50 A.D.2d 701, 375 N.Y.S.2d 444 (3d Dep't 1975)

27 ALR6th 123—§ 7

Sistok v. Kalispell Regional Hospital, 251 Mont. 38, 823 P.2d 251

69 ALR5th 559—§ 13

Sistrunk v. Audubon Park Natatorium, Inc., 164 So. 667 (La. App. 1935)

10 ALR5th 371—§ 5, 6

Sistrunk v. City of Strongsville, 99 F.3d 194, 1996 FED App. 0342P (6th Cir. 1996)

70 ALR6th 513—§ 10
71 ALR6th 471—§ 13

Sistrunk v. Lyons, 646 F.2d 64 (3d Cir. 1981)

7 ALR6th 487—§ 1

Sistrunk v. Vaughn, 96 F.3d 666 (3d Cir. 1996)

70 ALR5th 1—§ 9

Sita v. Danek Medical, Inc., 43 F. Supp. 2d 245, Prod. Liab. Rep. (CCH) ¶ 15634 (E.D.N.Y. 1999)

9 ALR5th 1—§ 6

Sitarek v. Montgomery, 32 Wash. 2d 794, 203 P.2d 1062 (1949)

40 ALR5th 1—§ 4

Site for Library, Re, 254 Minn. 358, 95 N.W.2d 112 (1959)

22 ALR5th 327—§ 9

Site for Library in City of Minneapolis, In re, 254 Minn. 358, 95 N.W.2d 112 (1959)

107 ALR5th 311—§ 11
109 ALR5th 421—§ 12

Siteman v. City of Allentown, 695 A.2d 888 (Pa. Commw. Ct. 1997)

28 ALR6th 175—§ 15

Sites v. State, 300 Md. 702, 481 A.2d 192 (1984)

109 ALR5th 611—§ 3

Sit, Estate of v. Dighello Bros. Auto Sales, 2000 WL 288466 (Conn. Super. Ct. 2000)

96 ALR5th 107—§ 7

Sitka v. Construction & General Laborers, 644 P.2d 227, 26 BNA WH Cas. 360, 100 CCH LC ¶ 55436 (Alaska 1982)

7 ALR5th 444—§ 2, 3

Sitkin Converting, Inc. v. Com., Unemployment Compensation Bd. of Review, 11 Pa. Commw. 604, 314 A.2d 534 (1974)

68 ALR5th 13—§ 4, 39

Sitkin Smelting and Refining, Inc., In re, 639 F.2d 1213, 30 U.C.C. Rep. Serv. 1566 (5th Cir. 1981)

44 ALR6th 441—§ 9
48 ALR6th 475—§ 14

Sitler v. Sitler, 266 A.D.2d 202, 697 N.Y.S.2d 316 (2d Dep't 1999)

36 ALR6th 1—§ 32, 33

Sitomer v. Half Hollow Hills Cent. School Dist., 133 App. Div. 2d 748, 520 N.Y.S.2d 37 (2d Dep't 1987)

33 ALR5th 619—§ 4

Sitomer v. North River Savings Bank, 196 Misc. 870, 95 N.Y.S.2d 402 (City Ct. 1949)

86 ALR5th 527—§ 7, 12

Sitowsky v. Sitowsky, 9 Misc. 2d 528, 173 N.Y.S.2d 626 (1957)

35 ALR5th 757—§ 3

Sitterly v. Matthews, 2000 -NMCA-037, 2 P.3d 871 (N.M. Ct. App. 2000)

62 ALR5th 219—§ 21

Sitton v. Print Direction, Inc., 312 Ga. App. 365, 718 S.E.2d 532 (2011)

87 ALR6th 1—§ 71

Sitton v. Print Direction, Inc., 2011 WL 4469712 (Ga. Ct. App. 2011)

68 ALR6th 331—§ 39

Sitz v. Department of State Police, 443 Mich. 744, 506 N.W.2d 209 (1993)

74 ALR5th 319—§ 2, 3

Sitzes v. Raidt, 335 S.W.2d 690 (Mo. App. 1960)

35 ALR5th 285—§ 8

Sitzman v. National Life & Acc. Ins. Co., 133 Ind. App. 578, 182 N.E.2d 448 (Div. 1 1962)

100 ALR5th 293—§ 6
Siva v. 1138 LLC, 2007-Ohio-4667, 2007 WL 2634007 (Ohio Ct. App. 10th Dist. Franklin County 2007)
47 ALR6th 1—§ 53
Sivak v. State, 112 Idaho 197, 731 P.2d 192 (1986)
12 ALR6th 267—§ 12
Sivak v. State, 134 Idaho 641, 8 P.3d 636 (2000)
12 ALR6th 267—§ 12
Sivaslian v. Rawlins, 88 A.D.2d 703, 451 N.Y.S.2d 307 (3d Dep't 1982)
92 ALR5th 473—§ 3, 16
Sive v. Hasso, 2003 WL 329564 (Cal. App. 4th Dist. 2003)
88 ALR6th 533—§ 11
Siver v. Rockingham Memorial Hosp., 48 F. Supp. 2d 608 (W.D. Va. 1999)
86 ALR5th 693—§ 4, 8
SI V, LLC v. FMC Corp., 223 F. Supp. 2d 1059 (N.D. Cal. 2002)
100 ALR5th 481—§ 10
Sivsa Entertainment v. World Intern. Network, 2004 WL 1895080 (Cal. App. 2d Dist. 2004)
49 ALR6th 1—§ 10, 30
Siwek v. Van Wart, 67 Misc. 2d 593, 324 N.Y.S.2d 839 (Sup 1971)
14 ALR6th 543—§ 23
Siwiec v. Financial Resources, Inc., 375 N.J. Super. 212, 867 A.2d 485 (App. Div. 2005)
86 ALR6th 321—§ 6
88 ALR6th 385—§ 22
Siwik v. Siwik, 89 Mich. App. 603, 280 N.W.2d 610 (1979)
15 ALR5th 692—§ 2, 26
Six v. Delo, 94 F.3d 469 (8th Cir. 1996)
102 ALR6th 417—§ 103
Sixberry v. Sixberry, 540 N.E.2d 95 (Ind. App. 1989)
6 ALR5th 1—§ 16
21 ALR5th 396—§ 9, 18, 33
Six Cos. of California v. Joint Highway Dist., 311 U.S. 180, 85 L. Ed. 114, 61 S. Ct. 186 (1940)
15 ALR5th 376—§ 3

Sixkiller v. Summers, 1984 OK 14, 680 P.2d 360 (Okla. 1984)
118 ALR5th 513—§ 3, 11
Six Six One Middle Turnpike Associates v. Planning and Zoning Com'n Town of Mansfield, 1999 WL 370543 (Conn. Super. Ct. 1999)
73 ALR5th 223—§ 13
Six, State ex rel. v. Industrial Com'n, 21 Ohio App. 3d 22, 486 N.E.2d 125 (10th Dist. Franklin County 1984)
31 ALR6th 199—§ 44
Sixteenth of September Planning Committee, Inc. v. City and County of Denver, Colo., 474 F. Supp. 1333 (D. Colo. 1979)
80 ALR5th 255—§ 3, 19
Sixth Angel Shepherd Rescue, Inc. v. Bengal, 448 Fed. Appx. 252 (3d Cir. 2011)
77 ALR6th 393—§ 95
Sixth Angel Shepherd Rescue Inc. v. West, 790 F. Supp. 2d 339 (E.D. Pa. 2011)
77 ALR6th 393—§ 81, 83, 86, 93
Sixth Angel Shepherd Rescue, Inc. v. West, 2012 WL 1385009 (3d Cir. 2012)
77 ALR6th 393—§ 17, 81, 83, 86, 93
Sixty Enterprises, Inc. v. Roman & Ciro, Inc., 601 So. 2d 234, 1992-1 Trade Cas. (CCH) ¶ 69832 (Fla. Dist. Ct. App. 3d Dist. 1992)
26 ALR6th 249—§ 4
Size, Inc. v. Network Solutions, Inc., 255 F. Supp. 2d 568, 66 U.S.P.Q.2d 1636 (E.D. Va. 2003)
40 ALR6th 295—§ 3
Sizemore, Ex parte, 9 Okla. Crim. 376, 131 P. 1108 (1913)
102 ALR5th 525—§ 10
Sizemore v. Myers, 327 Or. 114, 957 P.2d 155 (1998)
28 ALR6th 439—§ 17, 18
Sizemore v. Raxter, 73 N.C. App. 531, 327 S.E.2d 258 (1985)
9 ALR5th 826—§ 14

CASES CITED IN ALR5th and ALR6th

Sizemore v. Sizemore, 77 Ohio App. 3d 733, 603 N.E.2d 1032 (Montgomery Co. 1991)
28 ALR5th 46—§ 9, 10
Sizemore v. State, 530 N.E.2d 736 (Ind. 1988)
86 ALR5th 59—§ 5
Sizemore v. State, 2002 WL 31151371 (Ala. Crim. App. 2002)
108 ALR5th 593—§ 38
Sizemore v. State Workmen's Compensation Com'r, 160 W. Va. 407, 235 S.E.2d 473 (1977)
41 ALR6th 207—§ 21
Sizemore v. West Jefferson General Hospital, 260 So. 2d 800 (La. Ct. App. 4th Cir. 1972)
97 ALR5th 419—§ 11
Sizemore Secur. International, Inc. v. Lee, 161 Ga. App. 332, 287 S.E.2d 782 (1982)
12 ALR5th 195—§ 57
Sizzler Restaurants Intern., Inc., In re, 225 B.R. 466 (Bankr. C.D. Cal. 1998)
52 ALR5th 613—§ 3
S.J., In re, 2005-Ohio-4945, 2005 WL 2291892 (Ohio Ct. App. 9th Dist. Summit County 2005)
27 ALR6th 183—§ 13, 16
S.J., Re, 233 Ill. App. 3d 88, 174 Ill. Dec. 259, 598 N.E.2d 456 (2d Dist. 1992)
20 ALR5th 534—§ 4, 15, 17
S.J. v. L.T., 727 P.2d 789 (Alaska 1986)
6 ALR5th 69—§ 5, 24, 25
S.J.A., In re, 272 S.W.3d 678 (Tex. App. Dallas 2008)
52 ALR6th 433—§ 3, 37
57 ALR6th 163—§ 14, 36, 40, 42
60 ALR6th 193—§ 25
S.J.A.J. v. First Things First, Ltd., 239 Wis. 2d 233, 2000 WI App. 233, 619 N.W.2d 307 (Ct. App. 2000)
87 ALR5th 277—§ 2
S. J. Amoroso Constr. Co. v. Lazovich & Lazovich, 810 P.2d 775 (Nev 1991)

14 ALR5th 242—§ 40
S.J.B., In re Adoption of, 294 Ark. 598, 745 S.W.2d 606 (1988)
61 ALR5th 151—§ 14, 15
S.J.C., Interest of, 234 Ga. App. 491, 507 S.E.2d 226 (1998)
20 ALR5th 534—§ 14
S. J. C. Cambridgeport Sav. Bank v. Boersner, 413 Mass. 432, 597 N.E.2d 1017 (1992)
18 ALR5th 307—§ 32
S.J. Groves & Sons Co. v. Aerospatiale Helicopter Corp., 374 N.W.2d 431, Prod. Liab. Rep. (CCH) ¶ 10684, 42 U.C.C. Rep. Serv. (CBC) 100 (Minn. 1985)
72 ALR5th 299—§ 48
S.J. Groves & Sons Co. v. Midwest Steel Erection Co. Inc., 666 F. Supp. 129 (N.D. Ill. 1986)
81 ALR6th 363—§ 4
S.J.L.S. v. T.L.S., 265 S.W.3d 804 (Ky. Ct. App. 2008)
61 ALR6th 1—§ 10, 19, 26
Sjodin v. Commissioner of Public Safety, 401 N.W.2d 422 (Minn. Ct. App. 1987)
17 ALR6th 327—§ 42
Sjogren v. Metropolitan Property and Cas. Ins. Co., 703 A.2d 608, 66 A.L.R.5th 755 (R.I. 1997)
66 ALR5th 269—§ 11
Sjoland v. Carter, 2003 SD 66, 664 N.W.2d 48 (S.D. 2003)
98 ALR6th 93—§ 57
Sjolund v. Carlson, 511 N.W.2d 818 (S.D. 1994)
57 ALR5th 389—§ 4, 5
118 ALR5th 385—§ 7, 8, 14
S.J.S., In re, 4 Okla. Trib. 466, 1995 WL 1074094 (Chey.-Arap. D. Ct. 1995)
102 ALR5th 227—§ 4
S.J.S. v. B.R., 949 So. 2d 941 (Ala. Civ. App. 2006)
28 ALR6th 349—§ 17
S.J.T., In Interest of, 475 So. 2d 951 (Fla. Dist. Ct. App. 1st Dist. 1985)
92 ALR5th 379—§ 5

S.J.T., Inc. v. Richmond County, 263
Ga. 267, 430 S.E.2d 726 (1993)
20 ALR6th 161—§ 3
21 ALR6th 425—§ 9
23 ALR6th 573—§ 7, 13
S. K., In re, 647 A.2d 952 (Pa. Super.
1994)
**31 ALR5th 229—§ 3, 17, 52, 54, 60,
63, 69**
S.K. v. Anoka-Hennepin Independent
School Dist. No. 11, 399 F. Supp.
2d 963, 205 Ed. Law Rep. 180 (D.
Minn. 2005)
90 ALR6th 235—§ 12
Skaar v. Wisconsin Dept. of Revenue,
61 Wis. 2d 93, 211 N.W.2d 642
(1973)
2 ALR6th 1—§ 8
Skagen v. Shoaf, 86 Wash. App. 1080,
1997 WL 360863 (Div. 1 1997)
86 ALR6th 321—§ 11
Skaggs v. Carr, 178 Ky. 849, 200 S.W.
27 (1918)
62 ALR5th 219—§ 20, 31, 43
Skaggs v. Com., 803 S.W.2d 573 (Ky.
1990)
95 ALR5th 125—§ 4
Skaggs v. Commonwealth, 694 S.W.2d
672 (Ky. 1985)
10 ALR5th 700—§ 29
Skaggs v. Parker, 27 F. Supp. 2d 952
(W.D. Ky. 1998)
10 ALR5th 700—§ 4, 34
20 ALR6th 479—§ 23
Skaggs v. Parker, 230 F.3d 876 (6th Cir.
2000)
78 ALR5th 197—§ 3, 9
Skaggs v. Sanky, 2012 WL 243329 (D.
Neb. 2012)
75 ALR6th 181—§ 4, 6
77 ALR6th 197—§ 14
Skaggs v. Senior Services of Cent. Illinois, Inc., 355 Ill. App. 3d 1120,
291 Ill. Dec. 435, 823 N.E.2d 1021
(4th Dist. 2005)
17 ALR6th 1—§ 27
Skaggs v. Yunck, 10 Or. App. 536, 500
P.2d 1230 (1972)

56 ALR5th 133—§ 4
Skaggs v. Zinken, 293 Minn. 392, 196
N.W.2d 290 (1972)
21 ALR6th 81—§ 3, 64
Skaggs-Ferrell v. State, 287 Ga. App.
872, 652 S.E.2d 891 (2007)
72 ALR6th 1—§ 4
Skagit Pacific Corp., In re, 316 B.R. 330,
43 Bankr. Ct. Dec. (CRR) 218, 55
U.C.C. Rep. Serv. 2d 162 (B.A.P.
9th Cir. 2004)
53 ALR6th 159—§ 28
Skaja v. Andrews Hotel Co., 281 Minn.
417, 161 N.W.2d 657 (1968)
17 ALR6th 1—§ 24, 25
Skalbeck v. Agristor Leasing, 384
N.W.2d 209 (Minn. App. 1986)
5 ALR5th 56—§ 4, 11
Skaling v. Aetna Ins. Co., 742 A.2d 282
(R.I. 1999)
23 ALR5th 75—§ 9
Skalky v. Department of State, 83 App.
Div. 2d 848, 441 N.Y.S.2d 748 (2d
Dep't 1981)
7 ALR5th 474—§ 189
Skamania County v. Woodall, 16 P.3d
701 (Wash. Ct. App. Div. 2 2001)
38 ALR5th 737—§ 3
Skamfer v. Germain, 158 Wis. 2d 730,
463 N.W.2d 881 (Ct. App. 1990)
87 ALR5th 277—§ 37
Skandia America Reinsurance Corp. v.
Schenck, 441 F. Supp. 715 (S.D.
N.Y. 1977)
23 ALR5th 241—§ 45
87 ALR6th 319—§ 37
Skandia Coal & Lumber Co. v. Rockford
Metal Products Co., 332 Ill. App.
584, 76 N.E.2d 247 (2d Dist. 1947)
98 ALR5th 353—§ 3
Skar v. City of Lincoln, Neb., 599 F.2d
253 (8th Cir. 1979)
81 ALR5th 167—§ 12
Skaria v. State, 110 Misc. 2d 711, 442
N.Y.S.2d 838 (1981)
43 ALR5th 207—§ 6, 39, 40
Skarpeletzos v. Counes & Raptis Corp.,
228 N.Y. 46, 126 N.E. 268 (1920)

28 ALR5th 547—§ 19

S. K. Barnes, Inc. v. Valiquette, 23 Wash. App. 702, 597 P.2d 941 (Div. 3 1979)

31 ALR6th 433—§ 4

Skechers U.S.A., Inc. v. Tomlinson, 132 S. Ct. 551, 181 L. Ed. 2d 410 (2011)

76 ALR6th 587—§ 48

Skeels v. Paulus, 32 Ohio Op. 334, 44 Ohio L. Abs. 529, 17 Ohio Supp. 71 (C.P. 1945)

75 ALR6th 311—§ 26

Skeels v. State, 300 Ark. 285, 779 S.W.2d 146 (1989)

31 ALR6th 49—§ 10

Skeen v. Monsanto Co., 569 F. Supp. 232 (S.D. Tex. 1983)

5 ALR6th 497—§ 7

Skeen v. Skeen, 190 S.W. 1118 (Tex. Civ. App. 1916)

32 ALR5th 673—§ 3

Skeen v. State, 505 N.W.2d 299 (Minn. 1993)

110 ALR5th 293—§ 3

Skeens v. Miller, 331 Md. 331, 628 A.2d 185, 118 A.L.R. 1276 (1993)

56 ALR5th 1—§ 2, 3, 8

Skeens v. Paterno, 60 Md. App. 48, 480 A.2d 820 (1984)

58 ALR5th 669—§ 8, 23

Skeen, State ex rel. v. Tunnell, 768 S.W.2d 765 (Tex. App. Tyler 1989)

47 ALR5th 259—§ 2

Skees v. Kentucky Unemployment Ins. Com'n, 347 S.W.3d 467 (Ky. Ct. App. 2011)

80 ALR6th 635—§ 7

Skeete v. Ming, 2010 WL 2836996 (Ariz. Ct. App. Div. 1 2010)

60 ALR6th 193—§ 16

Skeffington v. Bradley, 366 Mich. 552, 115 N.W.2d 303 (1962)

97 ALR6th 83—§ 6

Skelgas Co. v. Industrial Com., 400 Ill. 322, 79 N.E.2d 501 (1948)

10 ALR5th 245—§ 17

Skelly v. Heidemann, 26 F.3d 132 (9th Cir. 1994)

88 ALR6th 203—§ 85

Skelly v. Westminster School Dist. of Orange County, 103 Cal. 652, 37 P. 643 (1894)

81 ALR6th 363—§ 22

Skelton v. B. C. Land Co., 256 Ark. 961, 513 S.W.2d 919 (1974)

33 ALR5th 509—§ 19

Skelton v. Doble, 347 N.W.2d 81 (Minn. Ct. App. 1984)

91 ALR6th 1—§ 3, 5

Skelton v. Pri-Cor, Inc., 963 F.2d 100 (6th Cir. 1991)

119 ALR5th 1—§ 5, 20, 25

Skelton v. Schenetzky, 82 Ind. App. 432, 144 N.E. 144 (1924)

62 ALR5th 219—§ 39

Skelton v. Skelton, 490 A.2d 1204 (Me. 1985)

49 ALR5th 441—§ 9

Skelton v. Sudge, 455 So. 2d 38 (Ala. App. 1984)

16 ALR5th 650—§ 18

Skene v. Fileccia, 213 Mich. App. 1, 539 N.W.2d 531 (1995)

38 ALR5th 107—§ 4, 10

Skerston v. Industrial Com'n, 146 Ill. App. 3d 544, 99 Ill. Dec. 812, 496 N.E.2d 505 (3d Dist. 1986)

40 ALR6th 99—§ 18

Sketo v. Brown, 559 So. 2d 381 (Fla. 1st DCA 1990)

86 ALR6th 1—§ 63

Sketo v. Brown, 559 So. 2d 381 (Fla. Dist. Ct. App. 1st Dist. 1990)

69 ALR5th 1—§ 3, 4

Skevin, Matter of, 157 A.D.2d 107, 554 N.Y.S.2d 725 (2d Dep't 1990)

45 ALR6th 175—§ 4

Skevofilax v. Quigley, 586 F. Supp. 532 (D.C. N.J. 1984)

36 ALR5th 1—§ 2, 18

Skewes v. Ocean Radiology Associates, 2011 WL 1087249 (Conn. Super. Ct. 2011)

92 ALR6th 379—§ 12

Skewes v. Ocean Radiology Associates, 2011 WL 7715895 (Conn. Super. Ct. 2011)
92 ALR6th 379—§ 12
SKF USA Inc. v. International Trade Com'n, 423 F.3d 1307, 27 Int'l Trade Re. (BNA) 1705, 78 U.S.P.Q.2d 1045 (Fed. Cir. 2005)
16 ALR6th 767—§ 43
SKF USAm Inc. v. International Trade Com'n, 2006 WL 1725647 (U.S. 2006)
16 ALR6th 767—§ 43
Skibo v. Shamrock Co., Ltd., 504 S.E.2d 188 (W. Va. 1998)
20 ALR5th 1—§ 16
50 ALR5th 1—§ 11
Skic v. Beverage Transp., 407 N.W.2d 488 (Minn. Ct. App. 1987)
95 ALR5th 329—§ 25
Skidis v. Industrial Com'n, 309 Ill. App. 3d 720, 243 Ill. Dec. 94, 722 N.E.2d 1163 (5th Dist. 1999)
97 ALR5th 1—§ 2
106 ALR5th 111—§ 2, 25, 28
108 ALR5th 1—§ 2, 4, 6, 29
Skidmore v. Fuller, 59 Wash. 2d 818, 370 P.2d 975 (1962)
114 ALR5th 1—§ 16, 20, 24
Skidmore v. Gateway Western Ry. Co., 333 Ill. App. 3d 947, 267 Ill. Dec. 196, 776 N.E.2d 333 (5th Dist. 2002)
105 ALR5th 499—§ 4
Skidmore v. Grueninger, 506 F.2d 716, 1976 A.M.C. 1103 (5th Cir. 1975)
12 ALR6th 241—§ 3
Skidmore v. Skidmore, 257 Ala. 570, 60 So. 2d 473 (1952)
101 ALR6th 455—§ 12
Skidmore v. Warburg Dillon Read LLC, 2001 WL 504876 (S.D. N.Y. 2001)
72 ALR6th 563—§ 12
Skidmore & Hall v. Rottman, 5 Ohio St. 3d 210, 450 N.E.2d 684 (1983)
87 ALR5th 473—§ 4
12 ALR6th 1—§ 16
13 ALR6th 1—§ 4, 5

14 ALR6th 1—§ 5
Skiff v. Colchester Bd. of Educ., 514 F. Supp. 2d 284, 225 Ed. Law Rep. 877 (D. Conn. 2007)
41 ALR6th 391—§ 15, 22
Skiff-Murray v. Murray, 305 A.D.2d 751, 760 N.Y.S.2d 564 (3d Dep't 2003)
112 ALR5th 399—§ 4
Skil Corp. v. Korzen, 32 Ill. 2d 249, 204 N.E.2d 738 (1965)
114 ALR5th 561—§ 4
Skil Corp. v. Lugsdin, 168 Ga. App. 754, 309 S.E.2d 921 (1983)
4 ALR6th 401—§ 3, 4, 8, 12
Skiles v. Gloeckner, 645 So. 2d 109, 19 FLW D 2381 (Fla. App. D5 1994)
6 ALR5th 1—§ 14
20 ALR5th 700—§ 45, 54
Skiles v. Security State Bank, 1 Neb. App. 360, 494 N.W.2d 355, 20 U.C.C. Rep. Serv. 2d (CBC) 512 (1992)
76 ALR5th 289—§ 9
Skiles v. State, 516 S.W.2d 75 (Tenn. 1974)
69 ALR6th 1—§ 21
Skill v. Martinez, 91 F.R.D. 498 (D.C. N.J. 1981)
25 ALR5th 343—§ 2
54 ALR5th 1—§ 4, 12
Skillen, In re, 2004 WL 764675 (Bankr. N.D. Iowa 2004)
2 ALR6th 195—§ 4, 12
Skillern & Sons, Inc. v. Stewart, 379 S.W.2d 687 (Tex. Civ. App. Fort Worth 1964)
12 ALR5th 195—§ 41
Skillicorn v. State, 22 S.W.3d 678 (Mo. 2000)
78 ALR5th 197—§ 5
80 ALR5th 55—§ 7
Skilling v. U.S., 130 S. Ct. 2896 (2010)
56 ALR6th 679—§ 11, 16, 32
Skilling v. U.S., 2010 WL 2518587 (U.S. 2010)
56 ALR6th 679—§ 21

Skillings v. Allen, 143 Minn. 323, 173 N.W. 663, 5 A.L.R. 922 (1919)

3 ALR5th 370—§ 2, 3

Skillings v. Allen, 148 Minn. 88, 180 N.W. 916 (1921)

3 ALR5th 370—§ 3

Skillings v. Illinois, 121 F. Supp. 2d 1235 (C.D. Ill. 2000)

25 ALR6th 435—§ 7, 68

Skinker v. Smith, 48 Mo. App. 91 (1892)

27 ALR5th 764—§ 4

Skinner, In re Detention of, 122 Wash. App. 620, 94 P.3d 981 (Div. 1 2004)

78 ALR6th 417—§ 79, 80

Skinner v. Anderson, 38 Ill. 2d 455, 231 N.E.2d 588 (1967)

5 ALR6th 497—§ 12

76 ALR6th 31—§ 41

Skinner v. Braum's Ice Cream Store, 890 P.2d 922 (Okla. 1995)

27 ALR5th 174—§ 7

Skinner v. Coleman-Nincic Urology Clinic, P.A., 156 Ga. App. 638, 275 S.E.2d 724 (1980)

31 ALR5th 1—§ 2, 33

48 ALR5th 575—§ 7, 13

Skinner v. Coleman-Nincic Urology Clinic, P.A., 165 Ga. App. 280, 300 S.E.2d 319 (1983)

31 ALR5th 1—§ 27

Skinner v. Grant, 12 Vt. 456, 1840 WL 2529 (1840)

108 ALR5th 495—§ 15

Skinner v. Henderson, 556 S.W.2d 730 (Mo. App. 1977)

25 ALR5th 123—§ 22

Skinner v. Missouri, 215 Fed. Appx. 555 (8th Cir. 2007)

89 ALR6th 1—§ 118

Skinner v. Motor Vehicles Div., 107 Or. App. 529, 812 P.2d 46 (1991)

28 ALR5th 459—§ 3

Skinner v. Railway Labor Executives' Ass'n, 489 U.S. 602, 109 S. Ct. 1402, 103 L. Ed. 2d 639, 4 I.E.R. Cas. (BNA) 224, 130 L.R.R.M. (BNA) 2857, 13 O.S.H. Cas. (BNA) 2065, 49 Empl. Prac. Dec. (CCH)

¶ 38791, 111 Lab. Cas. (CCH) ¶ 11001, 1989 O.S.H. Dec. (CCH) ¶ 28476 (1989)

13 ALR5th 628—§ 3

74 ALR5th 319—§ 1

76 ALR5th 239—§ 2, 14, 16

87 ALR5th 631—§ 2, 3

96 ALR5th 485—§ 2, 6, 8

18 ALR6th 1—§ 1

Skinner v. Reed, 265 S.W.2d 850 (Tex. Civ. App. Eastland 1954)

73 ALR5th 223—§ 10

Skinner v. Reed-Prentice Division Package Machinery Co., 70 Ill. 2d 1, 15 Ill. Dec. 829, 374 N.E.2d 437 (1977)

17 ALR6th 1—§ 27

Skinner v. Roach, 2007 WL 2579951 (N.D. Miss. 2007)

65 ALR6th 93—§ 67

Skinner v. Sillas, 58 Cal. App. 3d 591, 130 Cal. Rptr. 91 (2d Dist. 1976)

28 ALR5th 459—§ 3

Skinner v. Skinner, 252 Ga. 512, 314 S.E.2d 897 (1984)

7 ALR6th 411—§ 5, 36

Skinner v. Skinner, 509 So. 2d 867 (Miss. 1987)

47 ALR5th 129—§ 10

Skinner v. State, 16 Md. App. 116, 293 A.2d 828 (1972)

31 ALR5th 760—§ 6, 7

Skinner v. State, 83 Nev. 380, 432 P.2d 675 (1967)

36 ALR5th 255—§ 24, 32

Skinner v. State, 270 Ind. 52, 383 N.E.2d 307 (1978)

57 ALR6th 313—§ 7

Skinner v. State, 607 A.2d 1170 (Del. Sup. 1992)

39 ALR5th 283—§ 4, 55, 70

Skinner v. State, 784 S.W.2d 873 (Mo. App. 1990)

18 ALR5th 804—§ 3, 7, 11, 19

Skinner v. State, 837 S.W.2d 718 (Tex. App. Fort Worth 1992)

31 ALR5th 704—§ 8

Skinner v. State, 1996 WL 227404 (Tex. App. Houston 1st Dist. 1996)

34 ALR6th 1—§ 12

Skinner, People ex rel. v. Caudill Rowlett Scott, 172 Ill. App. 3d 790, 122 Ill. Dec. 774, 527 N.E.2d 146 (2d Dist. 1988)

76 ALR6th 31—§ 16

Skinner, People ex rel. v. Graham, 170 Ill. App. 3d 417, 120 Ill. Dec. 612, 524 N.E.2d 642 (4th Dist. 1988)

76 ALR6th 31—§ 16

Skipper v. Skipper, 290 S.C. 412, 351 S.E.2d 153 (S.C. 1986)

46 ALR5th 735—§ 6

Skipper v. Skipper, 654 So. 2d 1181, 20 FLW D 723 (Fla. App. D3 1995)

17 ALR5th 143—§ 3

Skipwith, In re, 14 Misc. 2d 325, 180 N.Y.S.2d 852 (Dom. Rel. Ct. 1958)

6 ALR6th 161—§ 12

Skipworth by Williams v. Lead Industries Ass'n, Inc., 547 Pa. 224, 690 A.2d 169, Prod. Liab. Rep. (CCH) ¶ 14914, 69 A.L.R.5th 693 (1997)

63 ALR5th 195—§ 4, 6, 7

69 ALR5th 137—§ 11

Skiris v. City of Port Washington, 223 Wis. 51, 269 N.W. 556, 109 A.L.R. 599 (1936)

29 ALR6th 369—§ 27

Skitt v. Bickmeyer, 299 N.Y. 567, 85 N.E.2d 792 (1949)

38 ALR5th 107—§ 6, 9

Skiver v. State, 37 Ark. App. 146, 826 S.W.2d 309 (1992)

27 ALR6th 183—§ 35

57 ALR6th 445—§ 29, 55

Skjonsby v. Ness, 221 N.W.2d 70 (N.D. 1974)

12 ALR5th 195—§ 52

Sklar v. Clough, 2007 WL 2049698 (N.D. Ga. 2007)

34 ALR6th 253—§ 5, 12, 15

Sklar v. Southcombe, 194 Md. 626, 72 A.2d 11 (1950)

52 ALR5th 155—§ 5, 6, 8, 10

Skobinsky, In re, 167 B.R. 45 (E.D. Pa. 1994)

32 ALR6th 531—§ 39

40 ALR6th 463—§ 18

Skogen v. Murray, 2007 MT 104, 337 Mont. 139, 157 P.3d 1143 (2007)

41 ALR6th 1—§ 9

86 ALR6th 321—§ 11, 13

88 ALR6th 385—§ 64, 66

Skoglund v. Blankenship, 134 Ill. App. 3d 628, 89 Ill. Dec. 695, 481 N.E.2d 47 (1st Dist. 1985)

47 ALR5th 433—§ 13

Skokie v. Walton on Dempster, Inc., 119 Ill. App. 3d 299, 74 Ill. Dec. 791, 456 N.E.2d 293 (1st Dist. 1983)

8 ALR5th 391—§ 5

Skokie Town House Builders, Inc., People ex rel. v. Morton Grove, 16 Ill. 2d 183, 157 N.E.2d 33 (1959)

38 ALR5th 737—§ 2 to 4

Skokos v. Corradini, 900 P.2d 539 (Utah Ct. App. 1995)

9 ALR6th 177—§ 56

Skoller v. Short, 35 N.Y.S.2d 68 (City Ct. 1942)

111 ALR5th 1—§ 9, 13

Skolnick v. Doria, 1994 WL 445088 (N.D. Ill. 1994)

89 ALR6th 1—§ 110

Skolnick v. State, 275 Ind. 461, 417 N.E.2d 1103 (1981)

105 ALR5th 529—§ 31

Skomo, In re Marriage of, 94 P.3d 738 (Kan. Ct. App. 2004)

59 ALR6th 161—§ 33, 35

Skomo v. Skomo, 2004 PA Super 53, 844 A.2d 1256 (2004)

60 ALR6th 193—§ 15

Skonberg v. Owens-Corning Fiberglas Corp., 215 Ill. App. 3d 735, 159 Ill. Dec. 359, 576 N.E.2d 28, CCH Prod. Liab. Rep. ¶ 12910 (1st Dist. 1991)

25 ALR5th 343—§ 2

38 ALR5th 683—§ 5

Skonieczny v. Churchman, 23 Del. 226, 7 Penne 226, 78 A. 634 (1905)

42 ALR5th 465—§ 3

Skonieczny v. City of Eastlake, 2002-Ohio-5152, 2002 WL 31160574 (Ohio Ct. App. 11th Dist. Lake County 2002)
9 ALR6th 177—§ 49

Skorczynski's Will, Re, 256 Wis. 300, 41 N.W.2d 301 (1950)
14 ALR5th 557—§ 3

Skorek v. Przybylo, 256 Ill. App. 3d 288, 195 Ill. Dec. 274, 628 N.E.2d 738 (1st Dist. 1993)
50 ALR5th 301—§ 3, 5

Skoros v. City of New York, 437 F.3d 1, 206 Ed. Law Rep. 525 (2d Cir. 2006)
26 ALR6th 659—§ 15

Skoros v. City of New York, N.Y., 127 S. Ct. 1245, 167 L. Ed. 2d 74, 217 Ed. Law Rep. 28 (U.S. 2007)
26 ALR6th 659—§ 15

Skotak v. Vic Tanny Intern., Inc., 203 Mich. App. 616, 513 N.W.2d 428 (1994)
61 ALR6th 147—§ 3, 4, 16

Skotak v. Vic Tanny Int'l, 203 Mich. App. 616, 513 N.W.2d 428 (1994)
54 ALR5th 513—§ 3

Skouras v. Phyllis Realty Co., 261 A.D.2d 389, 689 N.Y.S.2d 235 (2d Dep't 1999)
31 ALR5th 550—§ 10

Skov v. Wicker, 272 Kan. 240, 32 P.3d 1122 (2001)
86 ALR6th 1—§ 77

Skrabak v. Skrabak, 108 Md. App. 633, 673 A.2d 732 (1996)
9 ALR5th 568—§ 14

Skrabalak v. Rock, 208 App. Div. 2d 1100, 617 N.Y.S.2d 912 (3d Dep't 1994)
28 ALR5th 664—§ 5

Skrable v. St. Vincent Infirmary, 57 Ark. App. 164, 943 S.W.2d 236, 12 I.E.R. Cas. (BNA) 1530 (1997)
105 ALR5th 351—§ 3, 12

Skrantz v. Skrantz, 617 So. 2d 206 (La. App. 3d Cir. 1993)
9 ALR5th 568—§ 10

Skreen v. Rauk, 224 Minn. 96, 27 N.W.2d 869 (1947)
40 ALR6th 99—§ 23

Skrha, In re, 98 Ohio App. 3d 487, 648 N.E.2d 908 (Cuyahoga Co. 1994)
21 ALR5th 396—§ 3, 7, 18, 37

Skripek v. Bergamo, 200 N.J. Super. 620, 491 A.2d 1336 (1985)
28 ALR5th 497—§ 6, 8

Skrove v. Heiraas, 303 N.W.2d 526 (N.D. 1981)
23 ALR5th 241—§ 41

Skrupky v. Elbert, 189 Wis. 2d 31, 526 N.W.2d 264 (App. 1994)
12 ALR5th 630—§ 5

Skuaskai v. Philadelphia & Reading Coal & Iron Co., 104 Pa. Super. 25, 159 A. 47 (1932)
80 ALR5th 417—§ 3

Skudnov v. Cabinet for Health and Family Services, 2013 WL 1403492 (W.D. Ky. 2013)
90 ALR6th 385—§ 5

Skuffeeda v. St. Vincent Hosp. and Medical Center, 77 Or. App. 477, 714 P.2d 235 (1986)
19 ALR6th 475—§ 4, 19, 20

Skvarla v. Park, 62 N.C. App. 482, 303 S.E.2d 354 (1983)
62 ALR5th 219—§ 41, 42

Sky D., In re, 138 N.H. 543, 643 A.2d 529 (1994)
61 ALR5th 151—§ 12

Skydell v. Gelb, 177 A.D.2d 437, 576 N.Y.S.2d 281 (1st Dep't 1991)
91 ALR5th 485—§ 6

Skye, Succession of, 417 So. 2d 1221 (La. Ct. App. 3d Cir. 1982)
74 ALR5th 491—§ 5, 7

Sky Harbor Air Service, Inc. v. Reams, 491 Fed. Appx. 875, R.I.C.O. Bus. Disp. Guide (CCH) ¶ 12247 (10th Cir. 2012)
95 ALR6th 341—§ 6

Skylar P., In re, 2006 WL 3030182 (Cal. App. 5th Dist. 2006)
61 ALR6th 521—§ 3

Skyleasing, LLC v. Tejas Avco Inc., 2006 WL 2290852 (Tex. App. Houston 14th Dist. 2006)

22 ALR6th 387—§ 4, 20

Skyles v. State Farm Fire & Cas. Co., 210 So. 2d 609 (La. Ct. App. 2d Cir. 1968)

6 ALR6th 1—§ 3

Skyline Air Service, Inc. v. G.L. Capps Co., 916 F.2d 977, Prod. Liab. Rep. (CCH) ¶ 12645, 18 Fed. R. Serv. 3d (LCP) 650 (5th Cir. 1990)

72 ALR5th 299—§ 5, 38

Skyline Intern. Development v. Citibank, F.S.B., 302 Ill. App. 3d 79, 236 Ill. Dec. 68, 706 N.E.2d 942, 37 U.C.C. Rep. Serv. 2d 708 (1st Dist. 1998)

62 ALR6th 1—§ 2, 8, 22, 23

Skyline Intern. Development v. Citibank, F.S.B., 302 Ill. App. 3d 79, 236 Ill. Dec. 68, 706 N.E.2d 942, 37 U.C.C. Rep. Serv. 2d (CBC) 708 (1st Dist. 1998)

63 ALR5th 1—§ 8

Skyline Partners LLC v. Easley, 2000 WL 1028483 (Tex. App. Austin 2000)

49 ALR6th 1—§ 77

Skyrider, Matter of, 1991 A.M.C. 1956, 1990 WL 192479 (D. Haw. 1990)

92 ALR5th 473—§ 2, 7

Skyywalker Records, Inc. v. Navarro, 739 F. Supp. 578, 17 Media L. R. 2073 (S.D. Fla. 1990)

30 ALR5th 718—§ 4

S.L., In re, 2004 WL 1418077 (Mo. Ct. App. S.D. 2004)

122 ALR5th 385—§ 18

S.L., In re, 2006 WL 477772 (Cal. App. 6th Dist. 2006)

63 ALR6th 429—§ 7

S.L., State ex rel., 1999 UT App. 390, 995 P.2d 17 (Utah Ct. App. 1999)

20 ALR5th 534—§ 14

Slabaugh v. State Farm Fire & Cas. Co., 2013 WL 4777206 (S.D. Ind. 2013)

104 ALR6th 97—§ 9

Slabaugh v. State Farm Fire & Cas. Co., 2014 WL 1767088 (S.D. Ind. 2014)

104 ALR6th 97—§ 9

Slabotsky v. State Dep't of Health, 108 Conn. 88, 142 A. 477 (1928)

32 ALR5th 57—§ 3

Slaby v. Fairbridge, 3 F. Supp. 2d 22 (D.D.C. 1998)

63 ALR5th 1—§ 14

Slack v. Crawford, 131 F.2d 101 (CA5 Ga. 1942)

30 ALR5th 571—§ 34

Slack v. Fleet, 242 So. 2d 650 (La. App. 1970)

47 ALR5th 433—§ 4, 17

Slack v. Havens, 522 F.2d 1091, 11 Fair Empl. Prac. Cas. (BNA) 27, 10 Empl. Prac. Dec. (CCH) ¶ 10343 (9th Cir. 1975)

99 ALR5th 1—§ 2

Slack v. Slack, 641 So. 2d 1059 (La. Ct. App. 2d Cir. 1994)

26 ALR6th 331—§ 13

Slade v. Com., 155 Va. 1099, 156 S.E. 388 (1931)

54 ALR6th 429—§ 13

Slade v. Dennis, 594 P.2d 898 (Utah 1979)

58 ALR5th 669—§ 5, 20

Slade v. Metropolitan Life Ins. Co., 255 A.D.2d 130, 679 N.Y.S.2d 390 (1st Dep't 1998)

52 ALR6th 271—§ 15

Slade v. Montgomery, 577 So. 2d 887 (Ala. 1991)

15 ALR5th 119—§ 5, 15, 19, 32, 40, 59, 80

Slade v. New Hanover County Board of Education, 10 N.C. App. 287, 178 S.E.2d 316 (1971)

16 ALR5th 1—§ 16

23 ALR5th 1—§ 2, 20

Slade v. Slade, 81 N.M. 462, 468 P.2d 627 (1970)

111 ALR5th 159—§ 4

Slade v. State, 267 Ga. 868, 485 S.E.2d 726 (1997)

99 ALR6th 295—§ 10

Slade v. State, 270 Ga. 305, 509 S.E.2d 618 (1998)

72 ALR6th 1—§ 7

Slade v. Vernon, 110 N.C. App. 422, 429 S.E.2d 744 (1993)

49 ALR5th 717—§ 3

Slade v. Whitco Corp., 811 F. Supp. 71 (N.D. N.Y. 1993)

50 ALR5th 1—§ 4

51 ALR5th 467—§ 3

Sladky v. Lomax, 43 Ohio App. 3d 4, 538 N.E.2d 1089 (Summit Co. 1988)

7 ALR5th 852—§ 10, 23, 24

Slagel v. State, 766 P.2d 355 (Okla. Crim. 1988)

9 ALR5th 464—§ 4, 9

Slager v. Commonwealth Edison Co., 230 Ill. App. 3d 894, 172 Ill. Dec. 427, 595 N.E.2d 1097 (1st Dist. 1992)

40 ALR5th 1—§ 5

Slagle v. Clarion County, Pa., 98 Fair Empl. Prac. Cas. (BNA) 384, 2006 WL 993484 (U.S. 2006)

16 ALR6th 767—§ 7

Slagle v. County of Clarion, 435 F.3d 262, 97 Fair Empl. Prac. Cas. (BNA) 386, 87 Empl. Prac. Dec. (CCH) ¶ 42212 (3d Cir. 2006)

16 ALR6th 767—§ 7

Slagle v. State, 145 Ohio Misc. 2d 98, 2008-Ohio-593, 884 N.E.2d 109 (C.P. 2008)

63 ALR6th 351—§ 3

64 ALR6th 1—§ 9, 11

Slagle v. White Castle Systems, Inc., 79 Ohio App. 3d 210, 607 N.E.2d 45 (Franklin Co. 1992)

40 ALR5th 1—§ 2, 6

Slagle's Estate, Appeal of, 294 Pa. 442, 144 A. 426 (1928)

87 ALR6th 495—§ 41, 74, 76, 80, 82

Slaid v. Evergreen Indem., Ltd., 745 So. 2d 793, Prod. Liab. Rep. (CCH) ¶ 15690 (La. Ct. App. 2d Cir. 1999)

61 ALR5th 473—§ 9

Slaiman v. Allstate Ins. Co., 617 A.2d 873 (R.I. 1992)

23 ALR5th 801—§ 4

Slakman v. State, 272 Ga. 662, 533 S.E.2d 383 (2000)

24 ALR5th 465—§ 11

Slane v. Jerry Scott Drilling Co., 918 F.2d 123 (CA10 Okla. 1990)

10 ALR5th 680—§ 5

Slane v. Mariah Boats, Inc., 164 F.3d 1065, 14 I.E.R. Cas. (BNA) 1291 (7th Cir. 1999)

86 ALR5th 397—§ 9, 10

Slaney v. Westwood Auto, Inc., 366 Mass. 688, 322 N.E.2d 768, 89 A.L.R.3d 433 (1975)

115 ALR5th 709—§ 2

117 ALR5th 155—§ 2

Slansky v. Nebraska State Patrol, 268 Neb. 360, 685 N.W.2d 335 (2004)

63 ALR6th 351—§ 3

64 ALR6th 1—§ 2, 5, 7, 9

66 ALR6th 1—§ 3, 12, 14, 16

67 ALR6th 1—§ 2

93 ALR6th 1—§ 35

Slansky v. Slansky, 150 Vt. 438, 553 A.2d 152 (1988)

4 ALR5th 972—§ 3

Slapikas v. Llorente, 766 So. 2d 440 (Fla. Dist. Ct. App. 4th Dist. 2000)

12 ALR6th 1—§ 4, 6

13 ALR6th 1—§ 4

14 ALR6th 1—§ 5

Slappy v. Georgia Power Co., 109 Ga. App. 850, 137 S.E.2d 537 (1964)

95 ALR5th 29—§ 6, 7

Slaseman v. Com., Unemployment Compensation Bd. of Review, 80 Pa. Commw. 582, 472 A.2d 276 (1984)

80 ALR6th 635—§ 12

Slate, In re Marriage of, 181 Ill. App. 3d 110, 129 Ill. Dec. 844, 536 N.E.2d 894 (1st Dist. 1989)

5 ALR6th 193—§ 37

Slate, Re Marriage of, 181 Ill. App. 3d 110, 129 Ill. Dec. 844, 536 N.E.2d 894 (1st Dist. 1989)

21 ALR5th 396—§ 14, 18, 19, 26, 48, 67

Slater, Application of, 180 Misc. 798, 41 N.Y.S.2d 11 (County Ct. 1943)

75 ALR6th 311—§ 15, 26, 29, 48

Slater, In re, 627 A.2d 508 (D.C. 1993)

43 ALR6th 163—§ 39

Slater, Matter of, 156 A.D.2d 89, 554 N.Y.S.2d 11 (1st Dep't 1990)

44 ALR6th 75—§ 4

Slater, Re Marriage of, 100 Cal. App. 3d 241, 160 Cal. Rptr. 686 (1st Dist. 1979)

9 ALR5th 568—§ 7

Slater v. Bank of America, N.A., 2012 WL 2997880 (S.D. W. Va. 2012)

86 ALR6th 411—§ 5

Slater v. Farmland Mut. Ins. Co., 334 N.W.2d 728 (Iowa 1983)

13 ALR5th 289—§ 10

Slater v. Jacobs, 56 Ill. App. 3d 636, 14 Ill. Dec. 1, 371 N.E.2d 1054 (1st Dist. 1977)

23 ALR5th 241—§ 42, 49

Slater v. Lawyers' Mutual Ins. Co., 227 Cal. App. 3d 1415, 278 Cal. Rptr. 479 (2d Dist. 1991)

14 ALR5th 695—§ 21

92 ALR5th 273—§ 7

Slater v. McKinna, 997 P.2d 1196 (Colo. 2000)

119 ALR5th 1—§ 3, 4, 63

54 ALR6th 1—§ 14

Slater v. Mexican Nat. R. Co., 194 U.S. 120, 24 S. Ct. 581, 48 L. Ed. 900 (1904)

66 ALR5th 135—§ 42

Slater v. Olson, 230 Iowa 1005, 299 N.W. 879 (1941)

101 ALR6th 431—§ 15

Slater v. Pennsylvania Power Co., 383 Pa. Super. 509, 557 A.2d 368 (1989)

91 ALR5th 517—§ 3

Slater v. Slater, 310 Ill. 454, 142 N.E. 177 (1923)

3 ALR5th 394—§ 6, 7, 16

Slater v. Textron, Inc., 214 Cal. App. 3d 967, 262 Cal. Rptr. 812, 56 CCH EPD ¶ 40824 (4th Dist. 1989)

12 ALR5th 195—§ 34

Slater v. United States Fidelity & Guaranty Co., 379 Mass. 801, 400 N.E.2d 1256 (1980)

30 ALR5th 170—§ 49

Slatmeyer v. Industrial Commission of Ohio, 115 Ohio St. 654, 4 Ohio L. Abs. 381, 155 N.E. 484 (1926)

31 ALR6th 199—§ 22

Slaton, Ex parte, 484 S.W.2d 102 (Tex. Crim. App. 1972)

99 ALR6th 295—§ 7

Slaton, Ex parte, 680 So. 2d 909 (Ala. 1996)

77 ALR5th 201—§ 21

78 ALR5th 1—§ 49

Slaton v. Chicago, M. & S. P. R. Co., 97 Wash. 441, 166 P. 644 (1917)

17 ALR5th 547—§ 53

Slaton v. Slaton, 336 Ark. 211, 983 S.W.2d 951 (1999)

7 ALR6th 411—§ 21, 43

Slaton v. Slaton, 987 S.W.2d 180 (Tex. App. Houston 14th Dist. 1999)

80 ALR5th 533—§ 3 to 5

Slaton v. Vansickle, 1994 OK 39, 872 P.2d 929, Prod. Liab. Rep. (CCH) ¶ 13881 (Okla. 1994)

89 ALR5th 255—§ 2

96 ALR5th 239—§ 18

Slattery, Ex parte, 3 Ark. 484, 1841 WL 322 (1841)

102 ALR5th 525—§ 22

Slattery, In re, 766 A.2d 561 (D.C. 2001)

45 ALR6th 175—§ 6

Slattery v. Board of Firearms Permit Examiners, 1996 WL 410707 (Conn. Super. Ct. 1996)

91 ALR6th 435—§ 39

Slattery v. City of New York, 179 Misc. 2d 740, 686 N.Y.S.2d 683 (Sup. Ct. 1999)

74 ALR5th 439—§ 2, 3

Slattery v. O'Meara, 120 Conn. 465, 181 A. 610 (1935)

27 ALR5th 174—§ 59

Slattery v. Standard Sanitary Mfg. Co., 111 Pa. Super. 341, 170 A. 719 (1934)

3 ALR5th 907—§ 10

Slaught v. Bencomo Roofing Co., 25 Cal. App. 4th 744, 30 Cal. Rptr. 2d 618 (2d Dist. 1994)

100 ALR5th 481—§ 3

Slaughter v. American Arbitration Ass'n, 2011 WL 2174403 (D. Nev. 2011)

69 ALR6th 513—§ 5

Slaughter v. American Casualty Co., 37 F.3d 385 (CA8 Ark. 1994)

21 ALR5th 292—§ 2, 10, 22

Slaughter v. Anderson, 673 F. Supp. 929 (N.D. Ill. 1987)

89 ALR6th 1—§ 113

Slaughter v. Brigham Young University, 514 F.2d 622 (CA10 Utah 1975)

47 ALR5th 1—§ 15, 16, 18, 25, 27, 33

Slaughter v. Coke County, 34 Tex. Civ. App. 598, 79 S.W. 863 (1904)

59 ALR5th 1—§ 5, 6

Slaughter v. Daniels, 127 S.W.2d 317 (Tex. Civ. App. 1939)

39 ALR5th 33—§ 3, 4

Slaughter v. Friedman, 32 Cal. 3d 149, 185 Cal. Rptr. 244, 649 P.2d 886 (1982)

120 ALR5th 483—§ 4

Slaughter v. Holsomback, 166 Miss. 643, 147 So. 318 (1933)

91 ALR5th 1—§ 3, 17

Slaughter v. Rotan, 1994 WL 514873 (Del. Ch. 1994)

83 ALR5th 651—§ 2, 5

Slaughter v. Slaughter, 264 N.C. 732, 142 S.E.2d 683 (1965)

21 ALR6th 81—§ 62

Slaughter v. Slaughter, 321 Mich. 590, 32 N.W.2d 847 (1948)

21 ALR6th 577—§ 23, 24

Slaughter v. St. Anthony Community Hosp., 206 A.D.2d 513, 615 N.Y.S.2d 61 (2d Dep't 1994)

86 ALR5th 693—§ 14
97 ALR5th 419—§ 10

Slaughter v. State, 240 Ga. App. 758, 525 S.E.2d 130 (1999)

29 ALR6th 1—§ 14

Slaughter v. State, 257 Ga. 104, 355 S.E.2d 660 (1987)

16 ALR6th 329—§ 4
24 ALR6th 591—§ 6

Slaughter v. State, 424 So. 2d 1365 (Ala. App. 1982)

7 ALR5th 758—§ 11

Slaughter v. State, 1997 OK CR 78, 950 P.2d 839 (Okla. Crim. App. 1997)

16 ALR5th 152—§ 3
18 ALR5th 804—§ 5, 10, 11
79 ALR5th 33—§ 9

Slaughter v. State, 2001 WL 193767 (Tex. App. Austin 2001)

111 ALR5th 239—§ 7

Slaughter v. State, 2005 OK CR 2, 105 P.3d 832 (Okla. Crim. App. 2005)

92 ALR6th 549—§ 6

Slaughter v. State, 2005 OK CR 6, 108 P.3d 1052 (Okla. Crim. App. 2005)

92 ALR6th 549—§ 7
97 ALR6th 263—§ 17

Slaughter v. Van Winkle, 213 Cal. 573, 2 P.2d 789 (1931)

12 ALR5th 195—§ 43

Slaughter-House Cases, 83 U.S. 36, 21 L. Ed. 394, 1872 WL 15386 (1872)

87 ALR6th 109—§ 2
88 ALR6th 203—§ 2, 51

Slauson Partnership v. Ochoa, 112 Cal. App. 4th 1005, 5 Cal. Rptr. 3d 668 (2d Dist. 2003)

64 ALR6th 365—§ 3, 24, 34

Slavcoff v. Harrisburg Polyclinic Hospital, 375 F. Supp. 999 (M.D. Pa. 1974)

28 ALR5th 107—§ 5

Slaven v. BP America, Inc., 958 F. Supp. 1472, 1997 A.M.C. 2580 (C.D. Cal. 1997)

17 ALR6th 1—§ 25

Slaven v. Com., 962 S.W.2d 845 (Ky. 1997)

3 ALR6th 269—§ 9, 24

27 ALR6th 183—§ 31

Slaven v. Slaven, 22 Ohio Op. 230, 35 Ohio L. Abs. 268, 8 Ohio Supp. 70 (C.P. 1941)

84 ALR5th 399—§ 3, 7

Slavens v. William C. Haas Co., 563 S.W.2d 157 (Mo. App. 1978)

18 ALR5th 577—§ 9, 17, 41

Slavenski v. Breg, Inc., 2011 WL 2709108 (D. Or. 2011)

90 ALR6th 75—§ 17, 19, 24, 43

Slavich v. Knox, 750 So. 2d 301 (La. Ct. App. 4th Cir. 1999)

97 ALR6th 83—§ 5, 62

Slavik v. Slavik, 1982 WL 4997 (Ohio Ct. App. 9th Dist. Lorain County 1982)

11 ALR6th 125—§ 26, 28

Slavin, In re, 911 A.2d 822 (D.C. 2006)

44 ALR6th 75—§ 27

Slavin, In re, 940 A.2d 112 (D.C. 2007)

45 ALR6th 175—§ 12

Slavin v. City of Tucson, 17 Ariz. App. 16, 495 P.2d 141 (Div. 2 1972)

50 ALR6th 95—§ 8, 10

Slavin v. Francis H. Leggett & Co., 114 NJL 421, 177 A. 120 (1935)

1 ALR5th 1—§ 49

Slavin v. Kay, 108 So. 2d 462 (Fla. 1958)

70 ALR5th 261—§ 3, 37, 39

74 ALR5th 523—§ 3, 4, 9, 15, 32, 38, 40, 41, 43, 45

Slavin v. Levine, 111 A.D.2d 381, 489 N.Y.S.2d 362 (2d Dep't 1985)

77 ALR6th 393—§ 69

Slavin v. McCann Plumbing Co., 73 So. 2d 902 (Fla. 1954)

74 ALR5th 523—§ 3

Slavit Furniture Co. v. Eisenberg, 129 N.Y.S.2d 18 (Sup 1954)

12 ALR6th 123—§ 5, 7

Slavkin v. State Bar, 49 Cal. 3d 894, 264 Cal. Rptr. 131, 782 P.2d 270 (1989)

1 ALR5th 874—§ 14

9 ALR5th 193—§ 18, 19, 28, 30

Slavsky v. Himmelheber, 2002 WL 1938973 (Cal. App. 1st Dist. 2002)

42 ALR6th 463—§ 12

Slawick v. Detroit Newspaper Agency, 2001 WL 664568 (Mich. Ct. App. 2001)

53 ALR6th 213—§ 10

Slawik v. Folsom, 410 A.2d 512 (Del. Sup. 1979)

10 ALR5th 139—§ 5

Slawski v. Com., Dep't of Social Services, 2000 WL 558631 (Va. Ct. App. 2000)

90 ALR5th 1—§ 46 to 48

Slawski v. Com., Dep't of Social Services, Div. of Child Support Enforcement ex rel. Sheehan, 29 Va. App. 721, 514 S.E.2d 773 (1999)

90 ALR5th 1—§ 49

Slay v. Louisiana Energy and Power Authority, 473 So. 2d 51 (La. 1985)

114 ALR5th 561—§ 12

Slay v. Old Southern Life Ins. Co., 498 So. 2d 1129 (La. App. 3d Cir. 1986)

23 ALR5th 241—§ 15

Slay v. Old Southern Life Ins. Co., 498 So. 2d 1129 (La. Ct. App. 3d Cir. 1986)

123 ALR5th 259—§ 3

Slay v. State, 347 So. 2d 730 (Fla. Dist. Ct. App. 1st Dist. 1977)

15 ALR6th 173—§ 15

Slaymaker v. Warren, 224 A.D. 229, 229 N.Y.S. 505 (1st Dep't 1928)

19 ALR6th 217—§ 16

Slayton v. Com., 1989 WL 641935 (Va. Ct. App. 1989)

35 ALR6th 497—§ 23, 37

Slayton v. Jordan, 42 App. D.C. 421 (App. D.C. 1914)

75 ALR5th 1—§ 3

Slayton v. Michigan Host, Inc., 122 Mich. App. 411, 332 N.W.2d 498, 43 BNA FEP Cas. 1164, 32 CCH EPD ¶ 33663 (1983)

20 ALR5th 677—§ 2, 5

Slayton v. Michigan Host, Inc., 144
Mich. App. 535, 376 N.W.2d 664,
43 BNA FEP Cas. 1847, 39 CCH
EPD ¶ 35844, 122 CCH LC ¶ 57034
(1985)
    20 ALR5th 677—§ 5
    38 ALR5th 433—§ 64
Slayton v. Michigan Host, Inc., 144
Mich. App. 535, 376 N.W.2d 664,
43 Fair Empl. Prac. Cas. (BNA)
1847, 39 Empl. Prac. Dec. (CCH)
¶ 35844, 122 Lab. Cas. (CCH)
¶ 57034 (1985)
    14 ALR6th 417—§ 8
Slayton v. Pomona Unified School Dist.,
161 Cal. App. 3d 538, 207 Cal. Rptr.
705, 20 Ed. Law Rep. 1192 (2d Dist.
1984)
    106 ALR5th 523—§ 5 to 7, 15
Slayton v. Slayton, 55 Ala. App. 351,
315 So. 2d 588 (Civ. App. 1975)
    98 ALR5th 353—§ 3, 7
Slayton v. State, 633 S.W.2d 934 (Tex.
App. Fort Worth 1982)
    81 ALR5th 1—§ 3
Slazas v. Industrial Com'n of State of
Colo., 660 P.2d 513 (Colo. Ct. App.
1983)
    68 ALR5th 13—§ 5, 27
Sleavin v. Greenwich Gynecology and
Obstetrics, P.C., 6 Conn. App. 340,
505 A.2d 436 (1986)
    6 ALR6th 311—§ 3, 5
Sledge, Ex parte, 391 S.W.3d 104 (Tex.
Crim. App. 2013)
    97 ALR6th 263—§ 4
Sledge v. City of Fort Lauderdale, 497
So. 2d 1231 (Fla. Dist. Ct. App. 1st
Dist. 1986)
    86 ALR5th 295—§ 17
Sledge v. Continental Casualty Co., 639
So. 2d 805 (La. App. 2d Cir. 1994)
    50 ALR5th 1—§ 9
Sledge v. Dawson State Jail, 2003 WL
21751246 (N.D. Tex. 2003)
    119 ALR5th 1—§ 18, 19, 21
Sledge v. Sledge, 630 So. 2d 461 (Ala.
Civ. App. 1993)

    76 ALR5th 191—§ 3
Sledge v. State, 677 N.E.2d 82 (Ind. Ct.
App. 1997)
    2 ALR6th 551—§ 5, 12
Sledge v. State, 2005 WL 2572364
(Tenn. Crim. App. 2005)
    83 ALR6th 465—§ 6, 24, 33
Sledziewski v. Cioffi, 137 A.D.2d 186,
528 N.Y.S.2d 913 (3d Dep't 1988)
    98 ALR5th 533—§ 20
Sleek v. State, 499 N.E.2d 751 (Ind.
1986)
    90 ALR5th 225—§ 4
    124 ALR5th 1—§ 5
Sleeman v. Oakland County, 2007 WL
1343403 (E.D. Mich. 2007)
    45 ALR6th 1—§ 6, 23
Sleeper v. Laconia, 60 N.H. 201 (1990)
    61 ALR5th 739—§ 3
Sleeper v. Massachusetts Bonding &
Ins. Co., 283 Mass. 511, 186 N.E.
778 (1933)
    57 ALR5th 591—§ 5
Sleeper Farms v. Agway, Inc., 211 F.
Supp. 2d 197 (D. Me. 2002)
    22 ALR6th 49—§ 4
Sleepy Creek Club, Inc. v. Lawrence, 29
N.C. App. 547, 225 S.E.2d 167
(1976)
    119 ALR5th 519—§ 7, 8
Sleepy Hollow Development Co. v.
South Park Civic Club, 524 S.W.2d
604 (Tex. Civ. App. Houston 1st
Dist. 1975)
    115 ALR5th 251—§ 8, 14
Slemmer, Appeal of, 58 Pa. 155, 1868
WL 7228 (1868)
    85 ALR6th 1—§ 54
Slemp v. City of North Miami, 545 So.
2d 256 (Fla. 1989)
    54 ALR6th 201—§ 7
Slemp v. City of Tulsa, 1929 OK 419,
139 Okla. 76, 281 P. 280 (1929)
    44 ALR6th 259—§ 3
Slenker, Re, 424 N.E.2d 1005 (Ind.
1981)
    1 ALR5th 874—§ 15

Slentz v. American Airlines, Inc., 817 S.W.2d 366 (Tex. App. Austin 1991)
14 ALR5th 662—§ 2, 16, 19

Sletten v. Briggs, 448 N.W.2d 607 (N.D. 1989)
19 ALR6th 577—§ 10

Slevin v. Amex Life Assur. Co., 695 F. Supp. 712 (E.D. N.Y. 1988)
15 ALR5th 92—§ 2, 3, 6, 8

Slidell v. Valentine, 298 N.W.2d 599 (Iowa 1980)
40 ALR5th 227—§ 8, 23

Slide Mountain Realty Co. v. State, 61 Misc. 2d 708, 306 N.Y.S.2d 519 (Ct. Cl. 1969)
49 ALR6th 205—§ 4, 18, 54

Slider v. Myers, 557 So. 2d 1111 (La. Ct. App. 2d Cir. 1990)
83 ALR5th 277—§ 3, 7

Sligar v. Bartlett, 916 P.2d 1383 (Okla. 1996)
36 ALR5th 255—§ 18, 19, 30

Sliger v. Stokes, 953 S.W.2d 208 (Tenn. Ct. App. 1997)
68 ALR5th 13—§ 19, 34

Sligh v. Johnson, 288 S.C. 364, 342 S.E.2d 620 (Ct. App. 1986)
77 ALR5th 201—§ 3

SLI Intern. Corp. v. Crystal, 236 Conn. 156, 671 A.2d 813 (1996)
17 ALR6th 623—§ 19

Slimak v. Department of Rehabilitation and Correction, 85 Fair Empl. Prac. Cas. (BNA) 1765, 2001 WL 664638 (Ohio Ct. App. 10th Dist. Franklin County 2001)
107 ALR5th 623—§ 11

Slim and Shorty v. State, 123 Ark. 583, 186 S.W. 308 (1916)
66 ALR5th 397—§ 5
54 ALR6th 429—§ 20, 29

Sliman's Printing, Inc. v. Velo Internatl., 2005-Ohio-173, 2005 WL 100963 (Ohio Ct. App. 5th Dist. Stark County 2005)
47 ALR6th 1—§ 59

Slimp v. Department of Liquor Control, 239 Conn. 599, 687 A.2d 123 (1996)
41 ALR6th 77—§ 3, 4

Slimp v. State, Dept. of Liquor Control, 1995-2 Trade Cas. (CCH) ¶ 71200, 1995 WL 870976 (Conn. Super. Ct. 1995)
116 ALR5th 149—§ 4

Slindee v. Fritch Investments, LLC, 760 N.W.2d 903 (Minn. Ct. App. 2009)
91 ALR6th 1—§ 39

SL Industries, Inc. v. American Motorists Ins. Co., 128 N.J. 188, 607 A.2d 1266 (1992)
58 ALR5th 483—§ 3

Sliney v. State, 699 So. 2d 662 (Fla. 1997)
7 ALR6th 233—§ 9

Slinger Drainage, Inc. v. E.P.A., 244 F.3d 967 (D.C. Cir. 2001)
105 ALR5th 499—§ 4

Slingerland v. Binns, 56 N.J. Eq. 413, 39 A. 712 (1898)
4 ALR5th 772—§ 66

Slingerland v. Sherer, 46 Minn. 422, 49 N.W. 237 (1891)
36 ALR6th 387—§ 5

Slingerland v. Slingerland, 115 Minn. 270, 132 N.W. 326 (1911)
3 ALR5th 394—§ 6, 7, 22

Slinkard v. Hunter, 209 Ind. 475, 199 N.E. 560 (1936)
60 ALR6th 481—§ 4

Slipka v. Chase Home Finance, LLC, 2011 WL 1343340 (D. Minn. 2011)
86 ALR6th 411—§ 5

Slivenik v. Dukes, 1996 WL 75695 (Ohio Ct. App. 8th Dist. Cuyahoga County 1996)
87 ALR5th 277—§ 33

Sliwinski v. Duncan, 608 A.2d 730 (Del. 1992)
34 ALR6th 431—§ 16, 20, 21

Slizyk v. Smilack, 825 So. 2d 428 (Fla. 4th DCA 2002)
86 ALR6th 411—§ 5

S.L.J. v. R.J., 778 S.W.2d 239 (Mo. Ct. App. E.D. 1989)
  95 ALR5th 533—§ 5
  124 ALR5th 203—§ 5, 8
S.L.M., In re, 97 S.W.3d 224 (Tex. App. Amarillo 2002)
  112 ALR5th 185—§ 4, 8
S.L.M., In re, 207 S.W.3d 288 (Tenn. Ct. App. 2006)
  52 ALR6th 433—§ 22
  57 ALR6th 163—§ 40, 48
  66 ALR6th 269—§ 15
S.L.M. ex rel. Musick v. Dorel Juvenile Group, Inc., 514 Fed. Appx. 389, Prod. Liab. Rep. (CCH) ¶ 19051 (4th Cir. 2013)
  103 ALR6th 81—§ 20
Sloan., In re, 320 F.3d 1073 (10th Cir. 2003)
  69 ALR6th 415—§ 54
Sloan v. Anderson, 160 Okla. 180, 18 P.2d 274 (1932)
  20 ALR5th 1—§ 8, 16
Sloan v. City of Moultrie, 61 Ga. App. 885, 7 S.E.2d 760 (1940)
  66 ALR5th 397—§ 4
Sloan v. Com., Dept. of Transp., Bureau of Driver Licensing, 822 A.2d 105 (Pa. Commw. Ct. 2003)
  15 ALR6th 375—§ 15
Sloan v. Delo, 54 F.3d 1371 (8th Cir. 1995)
  95 ALR5th 125—§ 4
Sloan v. Donoghue, 20 Cal. 2d 607, 127 P.2d 922 (1942)
  62 ALR6th 143—§ 8
Sloan v. Estelle, 710 F.2d 229 (5th Cir. 1983)
  70 ALR5th 1—§ 5
  95 ALR5th 125—§ 3
Sloan v. Florida-Vanderbilt Development Corp., 22 Ariz. App. 572, 529 P.2d 726 (Div. 1 1974)
  86 ALR6th 321—§ 7
  88 ALR6th 385—§ 60, 61
Sloan v. F. W. Woolworth Co., 193 Ill. App. 620 (1915)
  2 ALR5th 1—§ 35

Sloan v. Iverson, 385 S.W.2d 178 (Ky. 1964)
  21 ALR5th 82—§ 2
Sloan v. Lemon, 413 U.S. 825, 93 S. Ct. 2982, 37 L. Ed. 2d 939 (1973)
  78 ALR5th 133—§ 2, 3, 5
Sloan v. Metropolitan Health Council, Inc., 516 N.E.2d 1104 (Ind. App. 1987)
  51 ALR5th 271—§ 3
Sloan v. Miller Bldg. Corp., 119 N.C. App. 162, 458 S.E.2d 30 (1995)
  17 ALR6th 715—§ 4
Sloan v. People, 65 Colo. 456, 176 P. 481 (1918)
  57 ALR6th 445—§ 59
Sloan v. Phoenix of Hartford Ins. Co., 46 Mich. App. 46, 207 N.W.2d 434 (1973)
  37 ALR5th 41—§ 17, 22
Sloan v. Robinson, 145 Wash. App. 1033, 2008 WL 2623967 (Div. 3 2008)
  86 ALR6th 321—§ 12
  88 ALR6th 385—§ 15
Sloan v. School Dist. of Greenville County, 342 S.C. 515, 537 S.E.2d 299 (Ct. App. 2000)
  51 ALR6th 333—§ 9
Sloan v. State, 168 Tenn. 573, 79 S.W.2d 1021, 97 A.L.R. 1505 (1935)
  125 ALR5th 537—§ 32
Sloan v. State, 172 Ga. App. 620, 323 S.E.2d 834 (1984)
  117 ALR5th 513—§ 6
Sloan v. State, 779 S.W.2d 580 (Mo. 1989)
  70 ALR5th 1—§ 4, 9
Sloan v. Urban Title Services, Inc., 770 F. Supp. 2d 227 (D.D.C. 2011)
  82 ALR6th 281—§ 24
Sloan v. U.S., 527 A.2d 1277 (Dist. Col. App. 1987)
  15 ALR5th 391—§ 5
Sloane v. Ruiz, 2009 WL 1024237 (S.D. N.Y. 2009)
  95 ALR6th 341—§ 17

For assistance, call 1-800-328-4880

Sloane v. Smith, 351 F. Supp. 1299 (M.D. Pa. 1972)
48 ALR6th 181—§ 11

Sloat v. Matheny, 625 P.2d 1031 (Colo. 1981)
8 ALR5th 312—§ 11

Sloat v. Rochester Taxicab Co., 177 App. Div. 57, 163 N.Y.S. 904 (1917)
16 ALR5th 191—§ 2, 5, 6, 20

Sloboda, In re, 157 N.J. 16, 722 A.2d 925 (1999)
27 ALR6th 1—§ 56

Sloboda v. State, 747 S.W.2d 20, 46 Ed. Law Rep. 464 (Tex. App. San Antonio 1988)
114 ALR5th 173—§ 7

Slobodkina v. Village of Great Neck, 285 A.D. 908, 138 N.Y.S.2d 28 (2d Dep't 1955)
92 ALR5th 517—§ 5, 12
101 ALR5th 287—§ 14

Slocum v. City of Claremore, 2009 WL 2835399 (N.D. Okla. 2009)
87 ALR6th 1—§ 42, 68

Slocum v. Daigre, 504 So. 2d 671 (La. Ct. App. 3d Cir. 1987)
117 ALR5th 23—§ 14

Slocum v. Donahue, 44 Mass. App. Ct. 937, 693 N.E.2d 179 (1998)
17 ALR6th 1—§ 27

Slocum v. Hammond, 346 N.W.2d 485 (Iowa 1984)
69 ALR5th 219—§ 3, 9
21 ALR6th 351—§ 4

Slocum v. State, 757 So. 2d 1246 (Fla. Dist. Ct. App. 4th Dist. 2000)
29 ALR6th 1—§ 10

Slocum v. Webb, 375 So. 2d 125 (La. Ct. App. 3d Cir. 1979)
42 ALR6th 353—§ 23

Slocum on Behalf of Nathan A. v. Joseph B, 183 A.D.2d 102, 588 N.Y.S.2d 930 (3d Dep't 1992)
86 ALR5th 637—§ 3

Slodowski v. Slodowski, 156 N.J. Super. 376, 383 A.2d 1188 (Ch. Div. 1978)
85 ALR5th 353—§ 24

Slohoda v. United Parcel Service, Inc., 207 N.J. Super. 145, 504 A.2d 53 (App. Div. 1986)
123 ALR5th 411—§ 60

Sloin v. Lavine, 11 N.J. Misc. 899, 168 A. 849 (1933)
44 ALR5th 1—§ 3, 4, 23

Sloma v. Pfluger, 125 Ill. App. 2d 347, 261 N.E.2d 323 (2d Dist. 1970)
27 ALR5th 174—§ 72

Slominski v. Employment Div., 77 Or. App. 142, 711 P.2d 215 (1985)
33 ALR5th 643—§ 19

Slone v. Meko, 2013 WL 979104 (E.D. Ky. 2013)
89 ALR6th 1—§ 99

Sloop v. London, 27 N.C. App. 516, 219 S.E.2d 502 (1975)
81 ALR6th 161—§ 4
82 ALR6th 43—§ 20

Slope County, By and Through Bd. of County Com'rs v. Consolidation Coal Co., 277 N.W.2d 124 (N.D. 1979)
125 ALR5th 147—§ 27

Slosberg, In re, 758 A.2d 521 (D.C. 2000)
45 ALR6th 175—§ 22

Sloss v. Case Western Reserve University, 23 Ohio App. 3d 46, 23 Ohio B.R. 90, 491 N.E.2d 339 (Cuyahoga Co. 1985)
4 ALR5th 443—§ 12, 27

Sloss v. General Motors Acceptance Corp., 48 Cal. App. 2d 574, 120 P.2d 85 (1941)
14 ALR5th 242—§ 25

Sloss v. Greenberger, 396 Pa. 353, 152 A.2d 910 (1959)
40 ALR5th 135—§ 4, 10

Sloss v. Industrial Commission, 121 Ariz. 10, 588 P.2d 303 (1978)
97 ALR5th 1—§ 5
106 ALR5th 111—§ 18, 26, 27
108 ALR5th 1—§ 33
112 ALR5th 509—§ 10
13 ALR6th 209—§ 16, 28
39 ALR6th 445—§ 22

Slossen v. Burlington, C. R. & N. R. Co., 60 Iowa 215, 14 N.W. 244 (1882)
17 ALR5th 547—§ 51, 56

Sloss-Sheffield Steel & Iron Co. v. Allred, 247 Ala. 499, 25 So. 2d 179 (1945)
52 ALR5th 155—§ 8, 10

Slotkin v. Saul Rosoff, M.D., P.C., 2003 WL 139984 (Cal. App. 2d Dist. 2003)
95 ALR6th 85—§ 6, 21

Slotterback By and Through Slotterback v. Interboro School Dist., 766 F. Supp. 280, 68 Ed. Law Rep. 599 (E.D. Pa. 1991)
70 ALR6th 513—§ 16
71 ALR6th 471—§ 8

Slottow v. American Cas. Co. of Reading, Pennsylvania, 10 F.3d 1355 (9th Cir. 1993)
22 ALR6th 113—§ 11, 62, 69

Slough v. J. I. Case Co., 8 Kan. App. 2d 104, 650 P.2d 729, CCH Prod. Liab. Rep. ¶ 9425 (1982)
14 ALR5th 242—§ 36

Slough v. State, 279 S.W.3d 409 (Tex. App. Eastland 2009)
68 ALR6th 527—§ 33

Slough v. Telb, 644 F. Supp. 2d 978 (N.D. Ohio 2009)
64 ALR6th 131—§ 2

Slough v. U.S., 2012 WL 1969398 (U.S. 2012)
76 ALR6th 587—§ 21

Sloup v. Loeffler, 2008 WL 3978208 (E.D. N.Y. 2008)
86 ALR6th 173—§ 1, 5

Slovak v. Adams, 141 Ohio App. 3d 838, 753 N.E.2d 910 (6th Dist. Lucas County 2001)
8 ALR6th 549—§ 2, 5, 7

Slover v. Equitable Variable Life Ins. Co., 443 F. Supp. 2d 1272 (N.D. Okla. 2006)
61 ALR6th 239—§ 16, 32

Slover v. Oregon State Bd. of Clinical Social Workers, 144 Or. App. 565, 927 P.2d 1098 (1996)
67 ALR6th 437—§ 26

Slover v. Union Bank, 115 Tenn. 347, 89 S.W. 399 (1905)
76 ALR6th 31—§ 12

Slovick v. Koca (In re Koca), 264 Ill. App. 3d 291, 201 Ill. Dec. 240, 636 N.E.2d 672 (1st Dist. 1993)
53 ALR5th 375—§ 5, 9, 10

Slow Development Co. v. Coulter, 88 Ariz. 122, 353 P.2d 890 (1960)
15 ALR5th 119—§ 5, 59, 75
15 ALR6th 1—§ 4, 5, 9, 10, 12, 16

Slowe v. Pike Creek Court Club, Inc., 2008 WL 5115035 (Del. Super. Ct. 2008)
61 ALR6th 147—§ 4, 5, 13, 17

S.L.P., In re, 123 S.W.3d 685 (Tex. App. Fort Worth 2003)
57 ALR6th 163—§ 41

S.L.P., In re Interest of, 230 Neb. 635, 432 N.W.2d 826 (1988)
116 ALR5th 559—§ 5

S. L. R., Matter of Adoption of, 196 Mont. 411, 640 P.2d 886 (1982)
82 ALR5th 443—§ 4, 5
83 ALR5th 375—§ 10
84 ALR5th 191—§ 7

S.L. Rowland Const. Co. v. Beall Pipe & Tank Corp., 14 Wash. App. 297, 540 P.2d 912 (Div. 1 1975)
124 ALR5th 375—§ 16

Sluka v. State, 717 P.2d 394 (Alaska App. 1986)
38 ALR5th 433—§ 11

Slum Clearance, in City of Detroit, In re, 332 Mich. 485, 52 N.W.2d 195 (1952)
107 ALR5th 311—§ 13

Slusher v. Furlong, 29 Fed. Appx. 490 (10th Cir. 2002)
43 ALR6th 475—§ 10

Slusher v. Oeder, 16 Ohio App. 3d 432, 476 N.E.2d 714 (12th Dist. Warren County 1984)
44 ALR5th 1—§ 11
99 ALR5th 445—§ 4

Slusher v. Ospital, 777 P.2d 437, 111 Utah Adv. Rep. 18 (Utah 1989)

22 ALR5th 483—§ 8 to 10, 12
Slusher v. Samu, 2008 WL 791959 (D. Colo. 2008)
68 ALR6th 389—§ 6
Slusher v. Slusher, 31 Ark. App. 28, 786 S.W.2d 843 (1990)
6 ALR5th 1—§ 17
40 ALR5th 227—§ 12, 14
Slusher v. State, Dept. of Commerce, 354 So. 2d 450 (Fla. Dist. Ct. App. 1st Dist. 1978)
26 ALR6th 111—§ 4
Sluss v. Com., 381 S.W.3d 215 (Ky. 2012)
88 ALR6th 319—§ 3
Slusser ex rel. Slusser v. Life Care Centers of America, Inc., 977 So. 2d 662 (Fla. Dist. Ct. App. 4th Dist. 2008)
50 ALR6th 187—§ 10
Slutsky-Peltz Plumbing & Heating Co., Inc. v. Vincennes Community School Corp., 556 N.E.2d 344, 61 Ed. Law Rep. 263 (Ind. Ct. App. 1990)
31 ALR6th 433—§ 7, 11
Slwooko v. State, 139 P.3d 593 (Alaska Ct. App. 2006)
32 ALR6th 1—§ 11
Slycord v. Horn, 179 Iowa 936, 162 N.W. 249, 7 A.L.R. 1285 (1917)
40 ALR6th 99—§ 32
Slygh, In re, 244 B.R. 410 (Bankr. N.D. Ohio 2000)
105 ALR5th 499—§ 4
Slyter v. State, 246 Miss. 402, 149 So. 2d 489 (1963)
96 ALR5th 523—§ 3
S.M., In re, 207 S.W.3d 421 (Tex. App. Fort Worth 2006)
30 ALR6th 1—§ 4
S.M., Interest of, 169 Ga. App. 364, 312 S.E.2d 829 (1983)
20 ALR5th 534—§ 5, 16
S.M., People ex rel., 7 P.3d 1021 (Colo. Ct. App. 2000)
87 ALR5th 361—§ 5

S.M. v. R.B., 261 Mont. 522, 862 P.2d 1166, 87 Ed. Law Rep. 280 (1993)
86 ALR5th 1—§ 12
S.M. v. State, 597 So. 2d 950, 17 FLW D 1023 (Fla. App. D1 1992)
46 ALR5th 523—§ 4
S.M. v. State, 665 So. 2d 355, 21 FLW D122 (Fla. App. D1 1995)
15 ALR5th 391—§ 45
Smack Apparel Co. v. Board of Sup'rs of Louisiana State University and Agr. and Mechanical College, 129 S. Ct. 2759 (2009)
46 ALR6th 495—§ 52
Smail v. Douglas County, 210 Ga. App. 830, 437 S.E.2d 824 (1993)
90 ALR5th 273—§ 3, 4, 14
Small v. Baker, 605 S.W.2d 401 (Tex. Civ. App. Beaumont 1980)
63 ALR5th 1—§ 3
Small v. Beverly Bank, 936 F.2d 945, CCH Bankr L. Rptr. ¶ 74068 (CA7 Ill. 1991)
27 ALR5th 719—§ 11
Small v. Burleigh County, 239 N.W.2d 823 (N.D. 1976)
86 ALR6th 321—§ 12
91 ALR6th 171—§ 96
Small v. Com., 617 S.W.2d 61 (Ky. Ct. App. 1981)
85 ALR5th 471—§ 2, 4, 13
Small v. Desselle, 520 So. 2d 1167 (La. Ct. App. 3d Cir. 1987)
60 ALR6th 481—§ 4
Small v. Federal Home Loan Mortg. Corp., 2012 WL 715823 (W.D. Mo. 2012)
96 ALR6th 125—§ 14
Small v. Harper, 638 S.W.2d 24 (Tex. App. Houston 1st Dist. 1982)
69 ALR5th 219—§ 3, 4, 7 to 9
Small v. HCF of Perrysburg, Inc., 159 Ohio App. 3d 66, 2004-Ohio-5757, 823 N.E.2d 19 (6th Dist. Wood County 2004)
50 ALR6th 187—§ 9, 11
Small v. King, 915 P.2d 1192 (Wyo. 1996)

60 ALR5th 165—§ 9
8 ALR6th 549—§ 4
Small v. Lorillard Tobacco Co., Inc., 94
    N.Y.2d 43, 698 N.Y.S.2d 615, 720
    N.E.2d 892 (1999)
7 ALR6th 319—§ 5
Small v. Morrison, 185 N.C. 577, 118
    S.E. 12, 31 A.L.R. 1135 (1923)
118 ALR5th 513—§ 2
125 ALR5th 133—§ 2
Small v. Oneita Indus., 442 S.E.2d 213
    (S.C. App. 1994)
12 ALR5th 658—§ 17, 24, 33
Small v. Oneita Indus., 459 S.E.2d 306
    (S.C. 1995)
12 ALR5th 658—§ 9
Small v. Pangle, 60 Ill. 2d 510, 328
    N.E.2d 285 (1975)
34 ALR5th 529—§ 3
Small v. Rockfeld, 66 N.J. 231, 330
    A.2d 335, 87 A.L.R.3d 829 (1974)
118 ALR5th 513—§ 7
Small v. Small, 93 N.C. App. 614, 379
    S.E.2d 273 (1989)
77 ALR6th 293—§ 4, 62
Small v. Small, 227 A.D.2d 949, 643
    N.Y.S.2d 842 (4th Dep't 1996)
3 ALR6th 447—§ 6, 18
Small v. Smith, 16 Cal. App. 3d 450, 94
    Cal. Rptr. 136 (2d Dist. 1971)
7 ALR5th 474—§ 162
Small v. Springs Industries, Inc., 292
    S.C. 481, 357 S.E.2d 452, 2 BNA
    IER Cas. 266, 106 CCH LC ¶ 55766
    (1987)
17 ALR5th 1—§ 12
Small v. State, 132 Idaho 327, 971 P.2d
    1151 (Ct. App. 1998)
83 ALR6th 465—§ 33
Small v. State, 667 So. 2d 299 (Fla. Dist.
    Ct. App. 1st Dist. 1995)
73 ALR5th 383—§ 5
Small v. State, 977 S.W.2d 771 (Tex.
    App. Fort Worth 1998)
1 ALR6th 371—§ 4
Small v. Strain, 2001 WL 1631341 (E.D.
    La. 2001)
65 ALR6th 93—§ 47

Small v. Travelers Indem. Co., 243 So.
    2d 862 (La. App. 1st Cir. 1971)
9 ALR5th 826—§ 6
Small v. U.S., 586 F. Supp. 2d 417
    (D.S.C. 2007)
71 ALR6th 1—§ 8
Small v. Wegner, 267 S.W.2d 26, 50
    A.L.R.2d 170 (Mo. 1954)
3 ALR5th 146—§ 8
Small v. Whittick, 2010 WL 3881303
    (D.N.J. 2010)
65 ALR6th 93—§ 58
Small v. Zelin, 152 App. Div. 2d 690,
    544 N.Y.S.2d 27 (2d Dep't 1989)
50 ALR5th 1—§ 12
Smallbone, In re, 16 Cal. 2d 532, 106
    P.2d 873, 131 A.L.R. 222 (1940)
52 ALR5th 221—§ 15
Smaller Mfrs. Council v. Council of City
    of Pittsburgh, 85 Pa. Commw. 533,
    485 A.2d 73, 1 I.E.R. Cas. (BNA)
    1354, 117 L.R.R.M. (BNA) 2828
    (1984)
120 ALR5th 351—§ 22
Small, Estate of v. Southland Life Ins.
    Co., 797 S.W.2d 74 (Tex. App.
    Houston (14th Dist.) 1990)
6 ALR5th 297—§ 9
Smalley, In re, 62 Ohio App. 3d 435,
    575 N.E.2d 1198 (8th Dist. Cuya-
    hoga County 1989)
28 ALR6th 505—§ 9
Smalley v. American Can Co., 428
    N.W.2d 390 (Minn. 1988)
99 ALR6th 643—§ 17
Smalley v. Fast Fare, Inc., 4 I.E.R. Cas.
    (BNA) 105, 117 Lab. Cas. (CCH)
    ¶ 56424, 1988 WL 220237 (D.S.C.
    1988)
105 ALR5th 351—§ 3, 4, 6
Smalley v. JHA-Markleysburg Inc., 3
    Pa. D. & C.5th 471, 2007 WL
    5323786 (Pa. C.P. 2007)
50 ALR6th 187—§ 13, 21
Smalley v. Parks, 108 S.W.3d 138 (Mo.
    Ct. App. S.D. 2003)
122 ALR5th 205—§ 3

For assistance, call 1-800-328-4880

Smalley v. State, 546 So. 2d 720 (Fla. 1989)
83 ALR6th 255—§ 6

Smalls v. State, Unemployment Appeals Com'n, 485 So. 2d 1 (Fla. Dist. Ct. App. 2d Dist. 1985)
121 ALR5th 467—§ 3

Smalls v. Weed, 293 S.C. 364, 360 S.E.2d 531 (App. 1987)
44 ALR5th 683—§ 13

Smallwood, Ex parte, 811 So. 2d 537 (Ala. 2001)
59 ALR6th 433—§ 7, 61

Smallwood v. American Trading & Transp. Co., 868 F. Supp. 280, 1995 A.M.C. 560 (N.D. Cal. 1994)
122 ALR5th 205—§ 3, 14

Smallwood v. Central Peninsula General Hosp., 151 P.3d 319 (Alaska 2006)
69 ALR6th 317—§ 4

Smallwood v. Dick, 114 Idaho 860, 761 P.2d 1212 (1988)
5 ALR5th 875—§ 2, 14, 23, 25, 26, 45

Smallwood v. Florida Dep't of Commerce, 350 So. 2d 121 (Fla. Dist. Ct. App. 4th Dist. 1977)
68 ALR5th 13—§ 4, 16, 19, 27

Smallwood v. Gibson, 191 F.3d 1257 (10th Cir. 1999)
79 ALR5th 33—§ 36

Smallwood v. Pettit-Galloway Co., 187 Ark. 379, 59 S.W.2d 1031 (1933)
50 ALR5th 417—§ 6

Smallwood v. Smallwood, 811 So. 2d 535 (Ala. Civ. App. 2000)
59 ALR6th 433—§ 61

Smallwood v. State, 343 Md. 97, 680 A.2d 512 (1996)
13 ALR5th 628—§ 6, 9

Smallwood v. State, 607 S.W.2d 911 (Tex. Crim. App. 1979)
57 ALR6th 445—§ 55

Smallwood v. State, 907 P.2d 217 (Okla. Crim. App. 1995)
79 ALR5th 33—§ 2, 63, 65

Smallwood v. U.S., 68 F.2d 244 (C.C.A. 5th Cir. 1933)
62 ALR6th 413—§ 23

Smallwood v. Warden, Md. Penitentiary, 205 F. Supp. 325 (D. Md. 1962)
101 ALR5th 187—§ 5

Smallwood, U.S. ex rel. v. Lavalle, 377 F. Supp. 1148 (E.D. N.Y. 1974)
33 ALR6th 1—§ 12, 20

Smaltz v. Boyce, 109 Mich. 382, 69 N.W. 21 (1896)
25 ALR5th 391—§ 88

Smart v. American Country Ins. Co., 2002 WL 318283 (Conn. Super. Ct. 2002)
2 ALR6th 279—§ 32
34 ALR6th 431—§ 21

Smart v. City of New York, 2009 WL 862281 (S.D. N.Y. 2009)
65 ALR6th 93—§ 21

Smart v. Goord, 21 F. Supp. 2d 309 (S.D. N.Y. 1998)
54 ALR6th 1—§ 4, 16

Smart v. Hardesty, 238 Ind. 218, 149 N.E.2d 547 (1958)
40 ALR6th 99—§ 18

Smart v. Los Angeles, 112 Cal. App. 3d 232, 169 Cal. Rptr. 174 (2d Dist. 1980)
25 ALR5th 568—§ 51

Smart v. Smart, 59 N.C. App. 533, 297 S.E.2d 135 (1982)
82 ALR5th 389—§ 3

Smart v. Smart, 94 Ill. App. 3d 791, 50 Ill. Dec. 587, 419 N.E.2d 695 (3d Dist. 1981)
70 ALR5th 377—§ 2 to 5

Smart v. State, 652 So. 2d 448 (Fla. Dist. Ct. App. 3d Dist. 1995)
100 ALR5th 67—§ 12

SmarTalk Teleservices Securities, Inc. Litigation, In re, 124 F. Supp. 2d 505 (S.D. Ohio 2000)
48 ALR5th 389—§ 3

Smart Chevrolet Co. v. Davis, 262 Ark. 500, 558 S.W.2d 147 (1977)
89 ALR5th 319—§ 22

Smart Farm Co. v. Promak, 257 Mich. 684, 241 N.W. 813 (1932)

1 ALR6th 135—§ 9
Smartfoods, Inc. v. Northbrook Property and Cas. Co., 35 Mass. App. Ct. 239, 618 N.E.2d 1365 (1993)
98 ALR5th 1—§ 4, 7
Smartfoods, Inc. v. Northbrook Property & Casualty Co., 35 Mass. App. 239, 618 N.E.2d 1365 (1993)
14 ALR5th 695—§ 6
Smart Indus. Corp., Mfg. v. Superior Court ex rel. County of Yuma, 876 P.2d 1176, 162 Ariz. Adv. Rep. 13 (Ariz. App. 1994)
6 ALR5th 242—§ 10
Smartix Intern. Corp. v. Garrubbo, Romankow & Capese, P.C., 2009 WL 857467 (S.D. N.Y. 2009)
58 ALR6th 1—§ 5
60 ALR6th 1—§ 65
Smart, State ex rel. v. City of Big Timber, 528 P.2d 688 (Mont 1974)
49 ALR5th 769—§ 17
Smartt v. Clifton, 1997 WL 1774874 (S.D. Ohio 1997)
90 ALR6th 235—§ 9
Smartt v. Lamar Oil Co., 623 P.2d 73 (Colo. App. 1980)
63 ALR5th 285—§ 5, 8
Smathers v. Board of Chosen Freeholders of Atlantic County, 113 N.J.L. 281, 174 A. 336 (N.J. Sup. Ct. 1934)
35 ALR6th 1—§ 27, 35
Smaul v. Irvington General Hospital, 108 N.J. 474, 530 A.2d 1251 (1987)
42 ALR5th 727—§ 2, 4
S.M.E., In re Welfare of, 2007 WL 2244693 (Minn. Ct. App. 2007)
38 ALR6th 1—§ 13
Smeal v. Olson, 263 Neb. 900, 644 N.W.2d 550 (2002)
97 ALR6th 375—§ 5
Smebak, Matter of, 160 Mich. App. 122, 408 N.W.2d 117 (1987)
113 ALR5th 349—§ 6
Smebak, Re, 160 Mich. App. 122, 408 N.W.2d 117 (1987)
1 ALR5th 469—§ 13

SMEC, Inc., In re, 160 B.R. 86 (M.D. Tenn. 1993)
13 ALR6th 1—§ 4, 6
Smedberg v. Connecticut Dept. of Transp., 425 F. Supp. 2d 262 (D. Conn. 2006)
32 ALR6th 457—§ 10
Smedes-Jardine & Co. v. Romero, 376 So. 2d 333 (La. App. 3d Cir. 1979)
35 ALR5th 285—§ 13
45 ALR5th 251—§ 4, 6
Smedley, Matter of Marriage of, 60 Or. App. 249, 653 P.2d 267 (1982)
59 ALR6th 433—§ 56
Smedley v. Discount Drug Mart, Inc., 190 Ohio App. 3d 684, 2010-Ohio-5665, 943 N.E.2d 1078 (12th Dist. Fayette County 2010)
69 ALR6th 317—§ 22
Smedley v. Temple Drilling Co., 782 F.2d 1357 (CA5 La. 1986)
5 ALR5th 56—§ 3, 4, 15
Smedley v. Tripp, 2010 WL 3892251 (M.D. Ala. 2010)
65 ALR6th 93—§ 29
Smedt v. Hain Celestial Group, Inc., 2013 WL 4455495 (N.D. Cal. 2013)
92 ALR6th 141—§ 5
Smeets v. Genesee County Clerk, 193 Mich. App. 628, 484 N.W.2d 770 (1992)
116 ALR5th 1—§ 30
SME Industries, Inc. v. Thompson, Ventulett, Stainback and Associates, Inc., 2001 UT 54, 28 P.3d 669 (Utah 2001)
61 ALR6th 445—§ 11
Smelcer v. Rippetoe, 24 Tenn. App. 516, 147 S.W.2d 109 (1940)
62 ALR5th 219—§ 25, 27, 51
Smelko By and Through Smelko v. Brinton, 241 Kan. 763, 740 P.2d 591 (1987)
48 ALR5th 129—§ 2, 6
50 ALR5th 1—§ 2
51 ALR5th 467—§ 2
52 ALR5th 1—§ 8
89 ALR5th 255—§ 3, 4

Smelser v. Southern R. Co., 148 F. Supp. 891 (D.C. Tenn. 1956)
14 ALR5th 557—§ 6
Smeltzley v. Nicholson Mfg. Co., 18 Cal. 3d 932, 136 Cal. Rptr. 269, 559 P.2d 624, 85 A.L.R.3d 121 (1977)
93 ALR6th 463—§ 10
Smethurst v. Proprietors Ind. Cong. Church, 148 Mass. 261, 19 N.E. 387 (1889)
8 ALR5th 1—§ 16, 45
S.M.F., In re Adoption of, 2004 WL 2804892 (Tenn. Ct. App. 2004)
28 ALR6th 349—§ 23
Smid, In re Estate of, 2008 SD 82, 756 N.W.2d 1 (S.D. 2008)
87 ALR6th 495—§ 33, 56, 74, 76, 80, 82
Smigiel v. State, 439 So. 2d 239 (Fla. Dist. Ct. App. 5th Dist. 1983)
6 ALR6th 533—§ 21
SMI Industries Canada Ltd. v. Caelter Industries, Inc., 586 F. Supp. 808, 223 U.S.P.Q. 742 (N.D. N.Y. 1984)
72 ALR6th 563—§ 15, 20, 29
Smiley v. California Institute of Technology, 2012 WL 3038590 (Cal. App. 2d Dist. 2012)
90 ALR6th 235—§ 72
Smiley v. Holm, 285 U.S. 355, 52 S. Ct. 397, 76 L. Ed. 795 (1932)
34 ALR6th 643—§ 3, 5, 7, 10, 14
Smiley v. Manchester Ins. & Indem. Co., 71 Ill. 2d 306, 16 Ill. Dec. 487, 375 N.E.2d 118 (1978)
10 ALR5th 828—§ 20
Smiley v. McCaughtry, 495 F. Supp. 2d 948 (E.D. Wis. 2007)
35 ALR6th 127—§ 4
Smiley v. Nelson, 805 So. 2d 870 (Fla. Dist. Ct. App. 2d Dist. 2001)
2 ALR6th 279—§ 4
Smiley v. Sincoff, 958 F.2d 498 (2d Cir. 1992)
11 ALR6th 587—§ 9
Smiley v. State, 606 So. 2d 213 (Ala. Crim. App. 1992)
55 ALR5th 125—§ 12, 14, 24

Smiley's Too, Inc. v. Denver Post Corp., 935 P.2d 39, 24 Media L. Rep. (BNA) 2272 (Colo. Ct. App. 1996)
19 ALR5th 1—§ 37.5
S. M., Inc. v. Wise, 373 So. 2d 868 (Ala. App. 1979)
16 ALR5th 191—§ 3
Smirl v. Bridewell, 932 S.W.2d 743 (Tex. App. Waco 1996)
6 ALR5th 242—§ 24
Smith, Application of, 8 N.J. Super. 573, 73 A.2d 761 (County Ct. 1950)
10 ALR6th 31—§ 33, 34
Smith, Application of, 381 Pa. 223, 112 A.2d 625, 55 A.L.R.2d 420 (1955)
43 ALR5th 545—§ 26
Smith, Ex parte, 17 Okla. Crim. 578, 190 P. 1092 (1920)
76 ALR5th 485—§ 3, 10
Smith, Ex parte, 232 Mo. App. 521, 119 S.W.2d 65 (1938)
97 ALR5th 537—§ 72
Smith, Ex parte, 441 S.W.2d 544 (Tex. Crim. App. 1969)
72 ALR5th 607—§ 3, 6, 7
Smith, Ex parte, 548 S.W.2d 410 (Tex. Crim. App. 1977)
97 ALR5th 293—§ 4
Smith, Ex parte, 624 S.W.2d 671 (Tex. App. Beaumont 1981)
13 ALR5th 118—§ 8, 16
Smith, Ex parte, 2003 WL 1145475 (Ala. 2003)
110 ALR5th 1—§ 19
122 ALR5th 145—§ 7, 10, 24
Smith, Ex parte, 2006 WL 3691244 (Tex. Crim. App. 2006)
97 ALR6th 263—§ 16
Smith, Ex parte, 2010 WL 4148528 (Ala. 2010)
98 ALR6th 455—§ 4
Smith, In re, 5 B.R. 92, 6 Bankr. Ct. Dec. (CRR) 506, 2 Collier Bankr. Cas. 2d (MB) 481 (Bankr. D. D.C. 1980)
32 ALR6th 531—§ 10
90 ALR6th 1—§ 9
Smith, In re, 7 Cal. 3d 362, 102 Cal. Rptr. 335, 497 P.2d 807 (1972)

36 ALR5th 161—§ 19
Smith, In re, 11 Vet. App. 379 (1998)

43 ALR6th 163—§ 37
Smith, In re, 16 Md. App. 209, 295 A.2d 238 (1972)

77 ALR5th 1—§ 2
Smith, In re, 16 Ohio App. 3d 75, 474 N.E.2d 632 (2d Dist. Miami County 1984)

86 ALR5th 637—§ 3
Smith, In re, 25 N.M. 48, 176 P. 819, 3 A.L.R. 83 (1918)

111 ALR5th 491—§ 3, 4, 9
Smith, In re, 42 Wash. 2d 188, 254 P.2d 464 (1953)

26 ALR6th 1—§ 28
Smith, In re, 48 A.D.3d 72, 848 N.Y.S.2d 353, 45 A.L.R.6th 785 (2d Dep't 2007)

45 ALR6th 175—§ 7, 9, 17, 19, 21, 23
Smith, In re, 59 B.R. 298 (Bankr. E.D. Pa. 1986)

81 ALR6th 161—§ 5

82 ALR6th 43—§ 13
Smith, In re, 96 F. 832 (W.D. Tex. 1899)

44 ALR6th 481—§ 10
Smith, In re, 112 Cal. App. 3d 956, 169 Cal. Rptr. 564, 15 A.L.R.4th 1223 (2d Dist. 1980)

6 ALR6th 483—§ 4
Smith, In re, 119 B.R. 757, 20 Bankr. Ct. Dec. (CRR) 1682, 24 Collier Bankr. Cas. 2d (MB) 355, Bankr. L. Rep. (CCH) ¶ 73633 (Bankr. E.D. Cal. 1990)

99 ALR6th 481—§ 17, 61, 69, 71
Smith, In re, 131 B.R. 959 (Bankr. E.D. Mich. 1991)

3 ALR6th 447—§ 3, 7
Smith, In re, 142 Ohio App. 3d 16, 753 N.E.2d 930 (8th Dist. Cuyahoga County 2001)

101 ALR5th 351—§ 9
Smith, In re, 148 Cal. App. 4th 1115, 56 Cal. Rptr. 3d 341 (6th Dist. 2007)

59 ALR6th 433—§ 78, 79

Smith, In re, 270 S.W.3d 783 (Tex. App. Waco 2008)

45 ALR6th 493—§ 3
Smith, In re, 296 A.D.2d 803, 745 N.Y.S.2d 618 (3d Dep't 2002)

106 ALR5th 297—§ 3
Smith, In re, 316 Or. 646, 853 P.2d 282 (1993)

20 ALR5th 534—§ 8
Smith, In re, 762 P.2d 1193 (Wyo. 1988)

61 ALR5th 375—§ 5, 9
Smith, In re, 866 F.2d 576, Bankr. L. Rep. (CCH) ¶ 72640 (3d Cir. 1989)

63 ALR5th 1—§ 7

117 ALR5th 155—§ 10
Smith, In re, 886 A.2d 75 (D.C. 2005)

45 ALR6th 175—§ 6, 16, 24
Smith, In re, 2008-Ohio-3234, 2008 WL 2581667 (Ohio Ct. App. 3d Dist. Allen County 2008)

37 ALR6th 55—§ 8, 9, 11, 17

38 ALR6th 1—§ 29

63 ALR6th 351—§ 3

64 ALR6th 1—§ 9, 11
Smith, In re Claim of, 89 App. Div. 2d 684, 453 N.Y.S.2d 800 (3d Dep't 1982)

33 ALR5th 643—§ 24
Smith, In re Compensation of, 54 Or. App. 261, 634 P.2d 809 (1981)

36 ALR5th 225—§ 3
Smith, In re Custody of, 137 Wash. 2d 1, 969 P.2d 21 (1998)

69 ALR5th 1—§ 5
Smith, In re Marriage of, 7 P.3d 1012 (Colo. Ct. App. 1999)

87 ALR5th 361—§ 20
Smith, In re Marriage of, 77 Ill. App. 3d 858, 33 Ill. Dec. 332, 396 N.E.2d 859 (2d Dist. 1979)

88 ALR6th 203—§ 31, 84
Smith, In re Marriage of, 90 Cal. App. 4th 74, 108 Cal. Rptr. 2d 537 (5th Dist. 2001)

27 ALR5th 540—§ 4
Smith, In re Marriage of, 122 Ill. App. 3d 213, 77 Ill. Dec. 637, 460 N.E.2d 1201 (4th Dist. 1984)

For assistance, call 1-800-328-4880

49 ALR5th 441—§ 21

Smith, In re Marriage of, 225 Cal. App. 3d 469, 274 Cal. Rptr. 911, 90 C.D.O.S. 8492 (1st Dist. 1990)

17 ALR5th 143—§ 2, 7, 9

Smith, In re Marriage of, 264 Mont. 306, 871 P.2d 884 (1994)

38 ALR6th 313—§ 8, 14

Smith, In re Marriage of, 501 N.W.2d 558 (Iowa App. 1993)

57 ALR5th 389—§ 2

Smith, In re Marriage of, 756 N.W.2d 48 (Iowa Ct. App. 2008)

100 ALR6th 1—§ 10

Smith, In re Marriage of, 817 P.2d 641 (Colo. App. 1991)

30 ALR5th 139—§ 3, 8

48 ALR5th 473—§ 9

Smith, In re Marriage of, 817 P.2d 641 (Colo. Ct. App. 1991)

109 ALR5th 1—§ 5

Smith, In re Petition of, 82 N.C. App. 107, 345 S.E.2d 423 (1986)

45 ALR5th 767—§ 2, 3

Smith, Matter of, 176 B.R. 221 (Bankr. N.D. Ala. 1995)

16 ALR5th 855—§ 5

Smith, Matter of, 189 Ariz. 144, 939 P.2d 422 (1997)

96 ALR5th 23—§ 2, 3

97 ALR5th 457—§ 2, 3, 5 to 7

Smith, Matter of, 572 N.E.2d 1280 (Ind. 1991)

26 ALR6th 1—§ 7

Smith, Matter of Marriage of, 100 Wash. 2d 319, 669 P.2d 448 (1983)

59 ALR6th 433—§ 6

Smith, Petition of, 114 N.J. Super. 421, 276 A.2d 868 (App. Div. 1971)

116 ALR5th 1—§ 29, 39, 42

Smith, Re, 76 B.R. 426 (F. BC ED Pa. 1987)

10 ALR5th 448—§ 5

Smith, Re, 119 B.R. 714 (F. BC D.C. N.D. 1990)

16 ALR5th 262—§ 2, 29

Smith, Re Estate of, 200 Cal. 654, 254 P. 567 (1927)

14 ALR5th 557—§ 3, 4, 9, 24

Smith, Re Marriage of, 162 Ill. App. 3d 792, 114 Ill. Dec. 622, 516 N.E.2d 777 (5th Dist. 1987)

9 ALR5th 568—§ 5

Smith v. 2001 South Dixie Highway, Inc., 872 So. 2d 992 (Fla. Dist. Ct. App. 4th Dist. 2004)

117 ALR5th 155—§ 5.5

Smith v. Abercrombie, 235 Ga. 741, 221 S.E.2d 802 (1975)

13 ALR6th 661—§ 6, 9, 11, 16

Smith v. Abshire, 786 F.2d 1166 (6th Cir. 1986)

51 ALR6th 1—§ 30

Smith v. ABS Industries, Inc., 890 F.2d 841, 11 Employee Benefits Cas. (BNA) 2242, 133 L.R.R.M. (BNA) 2001, 113 Lab. Cas. (CCH) ¶ 11685 (6th Cir. 1989)

74 ALR6th 267—§ 2, 3

Smith v. A. C. & S., Inc., 843 F.2d 854 (CA5 La. 1988)

6 ALR5th 162—§ 11

Smith v. Ach, 32 Ohio N.P. (n.s.) 57, 1934 WL 1922 (C.P. 1934)

101 ALR5th 287—§ 14

Smith v. Addy, 343 Fed. Appx. 806 (3d Cir. 2009)

65 ALR6th 93—§ 22

Smith v. Adler's Millinery, Inc., 122 NJL 236, 4 A.2d 782 (1939)

8 ALR5th 798—§ 4

Smith v. ADM Feed Corp., 456 N.W.2d 378, 54 CCH EPD ¶ 40231, 12 A.L.R.5th 1040 (Iowa 1990)

12 ALR5th 508—§ 3

Smith v. Aetna Casualty & Surety Co., 128 So. 2d 235 (La. App. 2d Cir. 1961)

26 ALR5th 401—§ 2, 10

Smith v. Aggregate Supply Co., 214 Ga. 20, 102 S.E.2d 539 (1958)

99 ALR6th 591—§ 10

Smith v. AirTouch Cellular of Georgia, Inc., 244 Ga. App. 71, 534 S.E.2d 832 (2000)

50 ALR6th 281—§ 4, 24

Smith v. Akstein, 408 F. Supp. 2d 1309 (N.D. Ga. 2005)

20 ALR6th 1—§ 5

Smith v. Alaskan Fur Co., 325 S.W.2d 740 (Mo. 1959)

83 ALR5th 589—§ 6

123 ALR5th 1—§ 5

Smith v. Allen-Bradley Co., 371 F. Supp. 698 (W.D. Va. 1974)

5 ALR6th 497—§ 7

Smith v. Allendale Mut. Ins. Co., 79 Mich. App. 351, 261 N.W.2d 561 (1977)

13 ALR5th 289—§ 18

Smith v. Allendale Mut. Ins. Co., 410 Mich. 685, 303 N.W.2d 702 (1981)

13 ALR5th 289—§ 2, 18

Smith v. Allstate Ins. Co., 224 Tenn. 423, 456 S.W.2d 654 (1970)

78 ALR5th 341—§ 4

Smith v. Allstate Ins. Co., 241 Va. 477, 403 S.E.2d 696 (1991)

35 ALR5th 375—§ 11, 121

Smith v. Allwright, 321 U.S. 649, 64 S. Ct. 757, 88 L. Ed. 987, 151 A.L.R. 1110 (1944)

120 ALR5th 125—§ 6

Smith v. Alum Rock Union Elementary School Dist., 6 Cal. App. 4th 1651, 8 Cal. Rptr. 2d 399, 92 C.D.O.S. 4687, 92 Daily Journal DAR 7404 (6th Dist. 1992)

51 ALR5th 1—§ 8

Smith v. Amedisys Inc., 298 F.3d 434, 89 Fair Empl. Prac. Cas. (BNA) 874 (5th Cir. 2002)

20 ALR6th 1—§ 5

Smith v. American Cystoscope Makers, 44 Wash. 2d 202, 266 P.2d 792 (1954)

48 ALR5th 575—§ 7

Smith v. American Employers' Ins. Co., 102 N.H. 530, 163 A.2d 564 (1960)

13 ALR5th 289—§ 3

Smith v. American Family Mut. Ins. Co., 294 N.W.2d 751, 20 A.L.R.4th 1 (N.D. 1980)

6 ALR5th 297—§ 25

14 ALR5th 242—§ 12

89 ALR5th 255—§ 5

Smith v. American Greetings Corp., 304 Ark. 596, 804 S.W.2d 683, 6 I.E.R. Cas. (BNA) 1039, 121 Lab. Cas. (CCH) P 56815 (1991)

38 ALR6th 541—§ 3

Smith v. American Greetings Corp., 304 Ark. 596, 804 S.W.2d 683, 6 I.E.R. Cas. (BNA) 1039, 121 Lab. Cas. (CCH) ¶ 56815 (1991)

125 ALR5th 457—§ 2

7 ALR6th 563—§ 3, 5

10 ALR6th 375—§ 3

11 ALR6th 447—§ 3

19 ALR6th 1—§ 3

20 ALR6th 1—§ 3

21 ALR6th 671—§ 3

Smith v. American Honda Motor Co., 846 F. Supp. 1217 (M.D. Pa. 1994)

48 ALR5th 1—§ 2, 12

Smith v. American Motors Sales Corp., 215 Ill. App. 3d 951, 159 Ill. Dec. 477, 576 N.E.2d 146, Prod. Liab. Rep. (CCH) ¶ 12908 (1st Dist. 1991)

93 ALR5th 103—§ 24

Smith v. American Transitional Hospitals, Inc., 330 F. Supp. 2d 1358 (S.D. Ga. 2004)

24 ALR6th 549—§ 13

Smith v. Ames Dept. Stores, Inc., 988 F. Supp. 827 (D.N.J. 1997)

114 ALR5th 129—§ 9

Smith v. AMLI Realty Co., 614 N.E.2d 618 (Ind. Ct. App. 1993)

76 ALR6th 395—§ 14

Smith v. Anderson, 402 F.3d 718, 2005 FED App. 0109P (6th Cir. 2005)

102 ALR6th 417—§ 23

Smith v. Anderson, 451 N.W.2d 108 (N.D. 1990)

26 ALR5th 401—§ 5, 7, 24, 30

Smith v. Anderson-Tulley Co., 608 F. Supp. 1143 (S.D. Miss. 1985)
27 ALR5th 174—§ 3, 33

Smith v. Angel Guardian Home, 263 A.D.2d 476, 692 N.Y.S.2d 724 (2d Dep't 1999)
36 ALR6th 203—§ 12

Smith v. Anheuser-Busch Brewing Co., Inc., 346 So. 2d 125 (Fla. Dist. Ct. App. 1st Dist. 1977)
53 ALR6th 213—§ 9

Smith v. Anheuser-Busch, Inc., 599 A.2d 320, 16 U.C.C. Rep. Serv. 2d 595 (R.I. 1991)
93 ALR5th 103—§ 8, 14

Smith v. Arbella Mut. Ins. Co., 49 Mass. App. Ct. 53, 725 N.E.2d 1080 (2000)
86 ALR6th 321—§ 13
91 ALR6th 171—§ 45

Smith v. Archbishop of St. Louis, 632 S.W.2d 516 (Mo. App. 1982)
50 ALR5th 1—§ 5
51 ALR5th 467—§ 8
52 ALR5th 1—§ 8

Smith v. Argonne Holdings, L.L.C., 110 Wash. App. 1021, 2002 WL 191992 (Div. 3 2002)
111 ALR5th 313—§ 13

Smith v. Arizona, 128 S. Ct. 466, 169 L. Ed. 2d 326 (U.S. 2007)
36 ALR6th 681—§ 46

Smith v. Arkansas State Highway Emp., Local 1315, 441 U.S. 463, 99 S. Ct. 1826, 60 L. Ed. 2d 360, 101 L.R.R.M. (BNA) 2091 (1979)
72 ALR6th 513—§ 4

Smith v. Armontrout, 857 F.2d 1228 (8th Cir. 1988)
111 ALR5th 491—§ 3

Smith v. Armour Pharmaceutical Co., 838 F. Supp. 1573, 27 FR Serv. 3d 1360, 7 FLW Fed D 607 (S.D. Fla. 1993)
51 ALR5th 603—§ 2, 4, 14

Smith v. Armstrong, 968 F. Supp. 40 (D. Conn. 1996)
98 ALR5th 445—§ 5

Smith v. Arnold, 564 So. 2d 873 (Ala. 1990)
81 ALR5th 167—§ 16

Smith v. Arthur Andersen LLP, 421 F.3d 989, 45 Bankr. Ct. Dec. (CRR) 58, Fed. Sec. L. Rep. (CCH) ¶ 93,341 (9th Cir. 2005)
23 ALR6th 457—§ 5, 8

Smith v. Arthur C. Baue Funeral Home, 370 S.W.2d 249, 54 L.R.R.M. (BNA) 2158, 48 Lab. Cas. (CCH) ¶ 50912 (Mo. 1963)
75 ALR5th 619—§ 3

Smith v. Artus, 2009 WL 1726301 (W.D. N.Y. 2009)
55 ALR6th 391—§ 5

Smith v. Asarco Inc., 627 S.W.2d 946 (Tenn. 1982)
86 ALR5th 295—§ 4

Smith v. Ashmore, 68 Wash. 2d 473, 413 P.2d 651 (1966)
52 ALR5th 155—§ 8

Smith v. Associated Pipe Line Contractors, Inc., 357 F. Supp. 493 (W.D. La 1972)
27 ALR5th 174—§ 74

Smith v. Atkins, 565 F. Supp. 721 (D. Kan. 1983)
55 ALR6th 157—§ 101

Smith v. Atkinson, 98 F. Supp. 2d 1334 (M.D. Ala. 2000)
101 ALR5th 61—§ 26

Smith v. Atkinson, 771 So. 2d 429 (Ala. 2000)
101 ALR5th 61—§ 3, 5, 13, 24 to 26
102 ALR5th 99—§ 8

Smith v. Atlantic Coast Line R. Co., 212 S.C. 332, 47 S.E.2d 725 (1948)
122 ALR5th 205—§ 3, 14

Smith v. Atlantic Mut. Ins. Co., 151 Wis. 2d 542, 444 N.W.2d 465 (App. 1989)
40 ALR5th 603—§ 6, 9

Smith v. Avatar Properties, Inc., 714 So. 2d 1103 (Fla. Dist. Ct. App. 5th Dist. 1998)
99 ALR5th 65—§ 10

Smith v. Avemco Ins. Co., 157 Ga. App. 531, 278 S.E.2d 112 (1981)
30 ALR5th 170—§ 93

Smith v. Ayrault, 71 Mich. 475, 39 N.W. 724 (1888)
85 ALR6th 1—§ 42

Smith v. Bakewell, 2010 WL 4178877 (D. Neb. 2010)
81 ALR6th 505—§ 54

Smith v. Bank of America N.A., 2011 WL 1578508 (D. Ariz. 2011)
86 ALR6th 411—§ 5

Smith v. Bank of America, N.A., 2012 WL 4320845 (N.D. Miss. 2012)
86 ALR6th 411—§ 5

Smith v. Barber, 316 F. Supp. 2d 992, 188 Ed. Law Rep. 323 (D. Kan. 2004)
90 ALR6th 235—§ 16

Smith v. Barker, 368 Pa. Super. 472, 534 A.2d 533 (1987)
51 ALR5th 467—§ 7

Smith v. Barney, 101 A.D.3d 1499, 957 N.Y.S.2d 766 (3d Dep't 2012)
102 ALR6th 153—§ 23

Smith v. Batchelor, 832 P.2d 467, 185 Utah Adv. Rep. 7, 30 BNA WH Cas. 1586, 121 CCH LC ¶ 35639 (Utah 1992)
18 ALR5th 577—§ 57

Smith v. Baule, 260 N.W.2d 850 (Iowa 1977)
98 ALR6th 93—§ 14

Smith v. Bauman, 2009 WL 3271329 (W.D. Okla. 2009)
89 ALR6th 1—§ 115

Smith v. Beard, 56 Wyo. 375, 110 P.2d 260 (1941)
19 ALR5th 563—§ 2, 14, 17, 18, 24
30 ALR5th 571—§ 2

Smith v. Belle Bonfils Memorial Blood Center, 1998 WL 684332 (Colo. Ct. App. 1998)
64 ALR5th 333—§ 8

Smith v. Bentley, 70 Ga. App. 13, 27 S.E.2d 252 (1943)
62 ALR5th 219—§ 5, 43, 46

Smith v. Bentley, 493 F. Supp. 916 (E.D. Ark. 1980)
5 ALR6th 423—§ 5

Smith v. Berghuis, 543 F.3d 326 (6th Cir. 2008)
56 ALR6th 679—§ 22

Smith v. Berry Co., 1997 WL 83144 (E.D. La. 1997)
79 ALR5th 587—§ 3

Smith v. Beseler, 2011 WL 6813226 (M.D. Fla. 2011)
80 ALR6th 239—§ 3, 5, 8

Smith v. BIC Corp., 121 F.R.D. 235 (E.D. Pa. 1988)
14 ALR5th 47—§ 2

Smith v. BIC Corp., 869 F.2d 194, 16 Media L. R. 1286, 10 U.S.P.Q.2d 1052, 13 FR Serv. 3d 181 (CA3 Pa. 1989)
14 ALR5th 47—§ 2

Smith v. Binder, 20 Mass. App. Ct. 21, 477 N.E.2d 606 (1985)
102 ALR5th 253—§ 13

Smith v. Black & Decker (U.S.), Inc., 272 Ill. App. 3d 451, 209 Ill. Dec. 135, 650 N.E.2d 1108, Prod. Liab. Rep. (CCH) ¶ 14255 (3d Dist. 1995)
4 ALR6th 401—§ 5

Smith v. Blackwell, 14 Kan. App. 2d 158, 791 P.2d 1343 (1989)
51 ALR5th 701—§ 8

Smith v. Blackwell, 250 S.C. 170, 156 S.E.2d 867 (1967)
9 ALR5th 826—§ 19

Smith v. Blair, 521 P.2d 581 (Wyo. 1974)
5 ALR5th 875—§ 4

Smith v. Board of Appeals of Salem, 313 Mass. 622, 48 N.E.2d 620 (1943)
73 ALR5th 223—§ 9

Smith v. Board of Com'rs of Roads & Revenues of Hall County, 244 Ga. 133, 259 S.E.2d 74 (1979)
65 ALR5th 1—§ 17

Smith v. Board of County Com'rs, 2008 MT 263N, 2008 WL 2898225 (Mont. 2008)
47 ALR6th 439—§ 21

Smith v. Board of County Com'rs of Howard County, 252 Md. 280, 249 A.2d 708 (1969)
  73 ALR5th 223—§ 11
Smith v. Board of Directors, Hosp. Dist. No. 1, Pinal County, 148 Ariz. 598, 716 P.2d 55 (Ct. App. Div. 2 1985)
  60 ALR6th 481—§ 4, 25, 36
Smith v. Board of Election Com'rs for City of Chicago, 587 F. Supp. 1136 (N.D. Ill. 1984)
  121 ALR5th 1—§ 30
Smith v. Board of Review, Dep't of Labor, State of N.J., 281 N.J. Super. 426, 658 A.2d 310 (App. Div. 1995)
  95 ALR5th 329—§ 12
Smith v. Bordelove, 63 Mich. App. 384, 234 N.W.2d 535 (1975)
  1 ALR6th 407—§ 11, 19
Smith v. Borg-Warner Automotive Diversified Transmission Products Corp., 2000 WL 1006619 (S.D. Ind. 2000)
  3 ALR6th 13—§ 28
Smith v. Borough of Dunmore, 516 Fed. Appx. 194 (3d Cir. 2013)
  95 ALR6th 341—§ 17
Smith v. Borough of Pottstown, 1997 WL 381778 (E.D. Pa. 1997)
  95 ALR6th 341—§ 68
Smith v. Boscov's Dep't Store, 192 App. Div. 2d 949, 596 N.Y.S.2d 575 (3d Dep't 1993)
  56 ALR5th 1—§ 3
Smith v. Botsford General Hosp., 126 S. Ct. 1912 (U.S. 2006)
  16 ALR6th 767—§ 22
Smith v. Botsford General Hosp., 419 F.3d 513, 2005 FED App. 0355P (6th Cir. 2005)
  16 ALR6th 767—§ 22
Smith v. Bounds, 610 F. Supp. 597 (E.D. N.C. 1985)
  98 ALR5th 445—§ 2
Smith v. Bounds, 657 F. Supp. 1322 (E.D. N.C. 1985)
  98 ALR5th 445—§ 2

Smith v. Bounds, 813 F.2d 1299 (4th Cir. 1987)
  98 ALR5th 445—§ 2
Smith v. Bounds, 841 F.2d 77, 10 Fed. R. Serv. 3d 971 (4th Cir. 1988)
  98 ALR5th 445—§ 2
Smith v. Bowers, 463 S.W.2d 222 (Tex. Civ. App. Waco 1970)
  83 ALR5th 651—§ 3
Smith v. Boyett, 908 P.2d 508 (Colo. 1995)
  19 ALR6th 475—§ 2 to 4, 9
Smith v. BP America, Inc., 522 Fed. Appx. 859 (11th Cir. 2013)
  102 ALR6th 1—§ 38, 42, 43
Smith v. Bradford, 76 Va. 758, 1882 WL 6066 (1882)
  87 ALR6th 495—§ 62
Smith v. Bramhall, 563 S.W.2d 238 (Tex. 1978)
  14 ALR5th 557—§ 2, 3
Smith v. Bramwell, 146 Or. 611, 31 P.2d 647 (1934)
  10 ALR6th 293—§ 16
Smith v. Brewer, 149 S.W.2d 262 (Tex. Civ. App. El Paso 1941)
  73 ALR6th 571—§ 12, 17, 56
Smith v. Brooks, 394 Pa. Super. 327, 575 A.2d 926 (1990)
  50 ALR5th 1—§ 4
  52 ALR5th 1—§ 9
Smith v. Brown, 139 Pa. Commw. 304, 590 A.2d 816 (1991)
  14 ALR6th 543—§ 54
Smith v. Brown & Williamson Tobacco Corp., 108 F. Supp. 2d 12 (D.D.C. 2000)
  36 ALR5th 541—§ 15
Smith v. Brown & Williamson Tobacco Corp., 174 F.R.D. 90 (W.D. Mo. 1997)
  7 ALR6th 319—§ 5
Smith v. Brown-Forman Distillers Corp., 196 Cal. App. 3d 503, 241 Cal. Rptr. 916, 2 I.E.R. Cas. (BNA) 1516, 118 Lab. Cas. (CCH) ¶ 56593 (2d Dist. 1987)
  86 ALR5th 397—§ 3, 15

104 ALR5th 1—§ 3, 13
Smith v. Buchanan, 291 Ky. 44, 163
S.W.2d 5, 145 A.L.R. 813 (1942)
19 ALR5th 351—§ 15
Smith v. Buffalo Times, 124 Misc. 495,
209 N.Y.S. 225 (Sup 1925)
108 ALR5th 495—§ 5, 13
Smith v. Burden Constr. Co., 379 So. 2d
1135 (La. App. 2d Cir. 1980)
18 ALR5th 577—§ 38, 58
Smith v. Burgess, 72 N.C. App. 340, 324
S.E.2d 53 (1985)
15 ALR5th 692—§ 36
Smith v. Butler, 19 Md. App. 467, 311
A.2d 813, 13 U.C.C. Rep. Serv. 838
(1973)
89 ALR5th 319—§ 7
Smith v. Butler, 72 Ark. 350, 80 S.W.
580 (1904)
20 ALR5th 229—§ 26, 29
Smith v. Butler Mfg. Co., 230 Neb. 734,
433 N.W.2d 493 (1988)
33 ALR5th 1—§ 16
Smith v. Butler Mountain Estates Property Owners Ass'n, Inc., 324 N.C.
80, 375 S.E.2d 905 (1989)
115 ALR5th 251—§ 6, 27
Smith v. Butterick, 769 So. 2d 1056 (Fla.
Dist. Ct. App. 2d Dist. 2000)
62 ALR5th 537—§ 4, 6, 9
Smith v. Caggiano, 12 Mass. App. Ct.
41, 421 N.E.2d 473 (1981)
115 ALR5th 709—§ 2
117 ALR5th 155—§ 2, 8
Smith v. Cain, 132 S. Ct. 627, 181 L. Ed.
2d 571 (2012)
76 ALR6th 587—§ 21
Smith v. Calgon Carbon Corp., 917 F.2d
1338, 5 I.E.R. Cas. (BNA) 1542,
117 Lab. Cas. (CCH) ¶ 56503 (3d
Cir. 1990)
105 ALR5th 351—§ 3, 4, 11
Smith v. California, 361 U.S. 147, 4 L.
Ed. 2d 205, 80 S. Ct. 215 (1959)
59 ALR5th 749—§ 2
Smith v. Campbell, 781 F. Supp. 521
(M.D. Tenn. 1991)
72 ALR5th 403—§ 19

Smith v. Campbell & Facciolla, Inc., 202
Cal. App. 2d 134, 20 Cal. Rptr. 606
(3d Dist. 1962)
75 ALR5th 595—§ 3, 9
Smith v. Canevary, 553 So. 2d 1312, 14
FLW 2867 (Fla. App. D3 1989)
21 ALR5th 82—§ 2, 4
Smith v. Capps, 414 So. 2d 102 (Ala.
Civ. App. 1982)
48 ALR6th 387—§ 12
Smith v. Carlos, 215 Mo. App. 488, 247
S.W. 468 (1923)
2 ALR5th 1—§ 58
Smith v. Carrier Air Conditioning, 21
Ark. App. 162, 730 S.W.2d 509
(1987)
12 ALR5th 658—§ 2, 4, 33
Smith v. Cayuga Lake Cement Co., 107
App. Div. 524, 95 N.Y.S. 236
(1905)
27 ALR5th 764—§ 3, 7
Smith v. Celotex Corp., 387 Pa. Super.
340, 564 A.2d 209 (1989)
24 ALR6th 497—§ 13
Smith v. Central V. R. Co., 80 Vt. 208,
67 A. 535 (1907)
17 ALR5th 547—§ 53, 81
Smith v. Chaffee, 181 Minn. 322, 232
N.W. 515 (1930)
9 ALR6th 285—§ 14
Smith v. Chaney Brooks Realty, 10 Ha-
waii App. 250, 865 P.2d 170, 10
BNA IER Cas. 1111 (1994)
52 ALR5th 405—§ 3
Smith v. Chaney Brooks Realty, Inc., 10
Haw. App. 250, 865 P.2d 170, 10
I.E.R. Cas. (BNA) 1111 (1994)
104 ALR5th 1—§ 3 to 5, 13
Smith v. Chapman, 115 Ariz. 211, 564
P.2d 900 (1977)
33 ALR5th 303—§ 2, 4, 7, 9, 26
Smith v. Chapman, 436 F. Supp. 58
(W.D. Tex. 1977)
23 ALR5th 241—§ 5
Smith v. Charnes, 728 P.2d 1287 (Colo.
1986)
93 ALR6th 207—§ 14, 18, 26
96 ALR6th 355—§ 24, 37, 54

Smith v. Chase Home Finance, LLC, 2011 WL 4017956 (E.D. Tex. 2011)
86 ALR6th 411—§ 5

Smith v. Chase Manhattan Bank, USA, 2011 WL 1327916 (D. Minn. 2011)
86 ALR6th 411—§ 5

Smith v. Chatfield, 797 S.W.2d 508 (Mo. App. 1990)
18 ALR5th 211—§ 4

Smith v. Chenoweth, 14 Daly. 166 (N.Y. 1887)
27 ALR5th 764—§ 7

Smith v. Chicago, 92 Ill. App. 3d 247, 48 Ill. Dec. 125, 416 N.E.2d 20 (1st Dist. 1980)
57 ALR5th 689—§ 8

Smith v. Chicago Housing Authority, 36 Ill. App. 3d 967, 344 N.E.2d 536 (1st Dist. 1976)
43 ALR5th 207—§ 3, 22, 25, 29, 47

Smith v. Children's Hospital Medical Center, 1985 WL 8861 (Ohio Ct. App. 1st Dist. Hamilton County 1985)
5 ALR6th 133—§ 15
14 ALR6th 301—§ 4, 15

Smith v. Children's Hosp. Medical Center, 28 Ohio St. 3d 303, 503 N.E.2d 741 (1986)
5 ALR6th 133—§ 12

Smith v. Childs, 112 N.C. App. 672, 437 S.E.2d 500 (1993)
60 ALR6th 1—§ 34

Smith v. Choy Yin, 30 Haw. 948, 1929 WL 3029 (1929)
15 ALR6th 241—§ 19

Smith v. Christus Saint Michaels Health System, 496 Fed. Appx. 468 (5th Cir. 2012)
95 ALR6th 541—§ 92

Smith v. Chrysler Motors Corp., 1990 WL 65700 (E.D. Pa. 1990)
88 ALR5th 301—§ 22

Smith v. CIGNA HealthPlan of Arizona, 203 Ariz. 173, 52 P.3d 205, 19 I.E.R. Cas. (BNA) 41, 170 L.R.R.M. (BNA) 2884, 147 Lab. Cas. (CCH) ¶ 59642, 120 A.L.R.5th 757 (Ct. App. Div. 2 2002)
120 ALR5th 351—§ 17

Smith v. C.I.R., T.C. Memo. 1999-368, T.C.M. (RIA) ¶ 99368, 78 T.C.M. (CCH) 745 (1999)
16 ALR6th 693—§ 12

Smith v. City and County of Denver, 2008 WL 724629 (D. Colo. 2008)
45 ALR6th 1—§ 4, 22, 24

Smith v. City Council of Alexandria, 74 Va. 208, 33 Gratt. 208, 1880 WL 6149 (1880)
54 ALR6th 201—§ 7

Smith v. City of Ann Arbor, 303 Mich. 476, 6 N.W.2d 752
93 ALR5th 621—§ 4

Smith v. City of Arkadelphia, 336 Ark. 42, 984 S.W.2d 392 (1999)
38 ALR5th 737—§ 10

Smith v. City of Birmingham, 42 Ala. App. 467, 168 So. 2d 35 (1964)
72 ALR5th 1—§ 28

Smith v. City of Chester, 842 F. Supp. 147, 89 Ed. Law Rep. 100 (E.D. Pa. 1994)
72 ALR5th 469—§ 2

Smith v. City of Cumming, 212 F.3d 1332, 28 Media L. Rep. (BNA) 1959 (11th Cir. 2000)
84 ALR6th 89—§ 3, 4, 7, 11

Smith v. City of Dallas, 404 S.W.2d 839 (Tex. Civ. App. Dallas 1966)
64 ALR5th 519—§ 7

Smith v. City of East Point, 183 Ga. App. 659, 359 S.E.2d 692, 3 I.E.R. Cas. (BNA) 153 (1987)
78 ALR5th 1—§ 10

Smith v. City of East Point, 189 Ga. App. 454, 376 S.E.2d 215 (1988)
78 ALR5th 1—§ 10

Smith v. City of Elyria, 857 F. Supp. 1203 (N.D. Ohio 1994)
90 ALR5th 273—§ 2, 4 to 6, 8, 10, 14

Smith v. City of Evanston, 260 Ill. App. 3d 925, 197 Ill. Dec. 810, 631 N.E.2d 1269 (1st Dist. 1994)
5 ALR5th 875—§ 4, 23, 44

Smith v. City of Fort Lauderdale, Fla., 177 F.3d 954 (11th Cir. 1999)
7 ALR5th 455—§ 3
Smith v. City of Gainesville, 93 So. 2d 105 (Fla. 1957)
63 ALR6th 1—§ 66
Smith v. City of Gulfport, 949 So. 2d 844 (Miss. Ct. App. 2007)
54 ALR6th 201—§ 26
Smith v. City of Hemet, 394 F.3d 689 (9th Cir. 2005)
65 ALR6th 93—§ 29
Smith v. City of Houston, 960 S.W.2d 326 (Tex. App. Houston 14th Dist. 1997)
64 ALR5th 519—§ 17
Smith v. City of Jackson, 792 So. 2d 335 (Miss. Ct. App. 2001)
97 ALR5th 1—§ 5
106 ALR5th 111—§ 27
Smith v. City of Lowell, 334 Mass. 516, 136 N.E.2d 186 (1956)
91 ALR5th 225—§ 8
Smith v. City of New York, 66 A.D.2d 946, 411 N.Y.S.2d 424 (3d Dep't 1978)
42 ALR6th 61—§ 17
Smith v. City of New York, 66 N.Y. 295, 1876 WL 12228 (1876)
54 ALR6th 201—§ 13, 46, 66
Smith v. City of New York, 2005 WL 1026551 (S.D. N.Y. 2005)
89 ALR6th 1—§ 29, 55, 57
Smith v. City of Oakland, 2007 WL 2288328 (N.D. Cal. 2007)
101 ALR6th 207—§ 5
Smith v. City of Philadelphia, 2009 WL 792341 (E.D. Pa. 2009)
95 ALR6th 341—§ 58
Smith v. City of Salem, Ohio, 378 F.3d 566, 94 Fair Empl. Prac. Cas. (BNA) 273, 87 Empl. Prac. Dec. (CCH) ¶ 42173, 88 Empl. Prac. Dec. (CCH) ¶ 42173, 2004 FED App. 0262A (6th Cir. 2004)
96 ALR6th 189—§ 5
Smith v. City of Shelbyville, 462 N.E.2d 1052 (Ind. Ct. App. 1st Dist. 1984)

4 ALR6th 263—§ 3
Smith v. City of Tuscaloosa, 601 So. 2d 1136 (Ala. Crim. App. 1992)
119 ALR5th 379—§ 3
Smith v. City of Unadilla, 510 F. Supp. 2d 1335 (M.D. Ga. 2007)
95 ALR6th 341—§ 61
Smith v. Civil Service Commission of City of Chicago, 343 Ill. App. 267, 98 N.E.2d 602 (1st Dist. 1951)
19 ALR6th 217—§ 55
Smith v. Clark, 189 F. Supp. 2d 548 (S.D. Miss. 2002)
34 ALR6th 643—§ 7
Smith v. Clark, 468 So. 2d 138 (Ala. 1985)
86 ALR6th 321—§ 7, 12, 13
88 ALR6th 385—§ 56, 57
Smith v. Clarke Hardware Co., 100 Ga. 163, 28 S.E. 73 (1897)
96 ALR5th 239—§ 26
Smith v. Clay, 239 Ga. 220, 236 S.E.2d 346 (1977)
62 ALR5th 219—§ 8
Smith v. Claybrook, 349 So. 2d 1087 (Ala. 1977)
85 ALR5th 671—§ 3, 6
Smith v. Clearwater, 383 So. 2d 681, 19 A.L.R.4th 745 (Fla. App. D2 1980)
1 ALR5th 622—§ 19
2 ALR5th 553—§ 82
Smith v. Cleburne County Hospital, 667 F. Supp. 644 (E.D. Ark. 1987)
12 ALR5th 195—§ 36
Smith v. Cleburne County Hospital, 870 F.2d 1375 (CA8 Ark. 1989)
28 ALR5th 107—§ 16
Smith v. Clements, 45 Ala. App. 435, 231 So. 2d 759 (Ala. Civ. App. 1970)
35 ALR5th 1—§ 9
Smith v. Cobb County-Kennestone Hosp. Authority, 262 Ga. 566, 423 S.E.2d 235 (1992)
71 ALR5th 307—§ 4, 5, 10
Smith v. Cockrell, 311 F.3d 661 (5th Cir. 2002)
122 ALR5th 145—§ 4, 6, 11

For assistance, call 1-800-328-4880

Smith v. Cole, 270 App. Div. 675, 62 N.Y.S.2d 226 (1946)
59 ALR5th 203—§ 48

Smith v. Coleman Co., Prod. Liab. Rep. (CCH) ¶ 18378, 71 U.C.C. Rep. Serv. 2d 131(M.D. Ala. 2010)
84 ALR6th 1—§ 11, 24, 60

Smith v. Colonial Ins. Co. of Calif., 2000-Ohio-1866, 2000 WL 1373964 (Ohio Ct. App. 3d Dist. Defiance County 2000)
75 ALR6th 235—§ 5

Smith v. Colorado Interstate Gas Co., 794 F. Supp. 1035, 64 Fair Empl. Prac. Cas. (BNA) 685, 59 Empl. Prac. Dec. (CCH) ¶ 41621 (D. Colo. 1992)
20 ALR6th 1—§ 7

Smith v. Com., 219 Va. 455, 248 S.E.2d 135 (1978)
28 ALR6th 505—§ 9

Smith v. Com., 280 Va. 178, 694 S.E.2d 578 (2010)
78 ALR6th 417—§ 39

Smith v. Com., 282 S.W.2d 618 (Ky. 1955)
108 ALR5th 593—§ 46

Smith v. Com., 307 S.W.2d 201 (Ky. 1957)
108 ALR5th 593—§ 34

Smith v. Com., 563 S.W.2d 494 (Ky. Ct. App. 1978)
81 ALR5th 563—§ 3, 6

Smith v. Com., 684 A.2d 647 (Pa. Commw. Ct. 1996)
2 ALR6th 1—§ 37

Smith v. Com., 707 S.W.2d 342 (Ky. 1986)
104 ALR5th 229—§ 11, 16
4 ALR6th 113—§ 13
101 ALR6th 1—§ 6, 29

Smith v. Com., 734 S.W.2d 437 (Ky. 1987)
70 ALR5th 587—§ 5

Smith v. Com., 2011 WL 4407486 (Ky. Ct. App. 2011)
99 ALR6th 295—§ 9, 16

Smith v. Commonwealth, 19 Va. App. 594, 453 S.E.2d 572 (1995)
34 ALR5th 125—§ 31

Smith v. Commonwealth, 134 Va. 589, 113 S.E. 707, 24 A.L.R. 1286 (1922)
10 ALR5th 139—§ 5

Smith v. Commonwealth, 737 S.W.2d 683 (Ky. 1987)
7 ALR5th 758—§ 13, 18

Smith v. Commonwealth, Crime Victim's Compensation Bd., 92 Pa. Cmwlth. 148, 498 A.2d 489 (1985)
15 ALR5th 391—§ 31

Smith v. Commonwealth Land Title Ins. Co., 177 Cal. App. 3d 625, 223 Cal. Rptr. 339 (2d Dist. 1986)
19 ALR5th 786—§ 8

Smith v. Commonwealth, Pennsylvania State Horse Racing Com., 72 Pa. Cmwlth. 421, 456 A.2d 727 (1983)
59 ALR5th 203—§ 18, 60

Smith v. Commonwealth, State Real Estate Com., 69 Pa. Cmwlth. 107, 450 A.2d 301 (1982)
7 ALR5th 474—§ 2, 7, 12

Smith v. Commonwealth, Unemployment Compensation Board of Review, 57 Pa. Cmwlth. 173, 425 A.2d 1198 (1981)
2 ALR5th 475—§ 8

Smith v. Community Bd. No. 14, 128 Misc. 2d 944, 491 N.Y.S.2d 584 (Sup 1985)
26 ALR6th 145—§ 3

Smith v. Community Lending, Inc., 773 F. Supp. 2d 941 (D. Nev. 2011)
81 ALR6th 161—§ 5
82 ALR6th 43—§ 5

Smith v. Com., Unemployment Compensation Bd. of Review., 35 Pa. Commw. 14, 384 A.2d 1023 (1978)
18 ALR6th 195—§ 28

Smith v. Com., Unemployment Compensation Bd. of Review, 81 Pa. Commw. 131, 473 A.2d 235 (1984)
68 ALR5th 13—§ 5, 27

Smith v. Congregation of St. Rose, 265
Wis. 393, 61 N.W.2d 896 (1953)
  8 ALR5th 1—§ 31, 45
Smith v. Conley, 109 Ohio St. 3d 141,
2006-Ohio-2035, 846 N.E.2d 509
(2006)
  13 ALR6th 1—§ 4
Smith v. Connecticut Light and Power
Co., 73 Conn. App. 619, 808 A.2d
1171 (2002)
  108 ALR5th 1—§ 33
Smith v. Connecticut Light and Power
Co., 73 Conn. App. 619, 2002 WL
31521557 (2002)
  106 ALR5th 111—§ 13
Smith v. Connecticut Racquetball Club,
32 Conn. L. Rptr. 283, 2002 WL
1446633 (Conn. Super. Ct. 2002)
  61 ALR6th 147—§ 10
Smith v. Consolidated School Dist. No.
2, 408 S.W.2d 50 (Mo. 1966)
  66 ALR5th 1—§ 39
Smith v. Continental Ins. Co., 63 Tenn.
App. 48, 469 S.W.2d 138 (1971)
  115 ALR5th 589—§ 3
Smith v. Convenience Store Distributing Co., 583 N.E.2d 735 (Ind. 1992)
  31 ALR5th 572—§ 2
  33 ALR5th 205—§ 2, 4, 13
Smith v. Cooley, 5 Daly. 401 (N.Y.C.P.
1874)
  67 ALR5th 179—§ 5
Smith v. Copeland, 2009 WL 2223926
(N.D. Ga. 2009)
  100 ALR6th 281—§ 18
Smith v. Copiah County, 239 F. 425
(D.C. Miss. 1916)
  15 ALR5th 376—§ 5
Smith v. Copley Press, Inc., 140 Ill. App.
3d 613, 94 Ill. Dec. 785, 488 N.E.2d
1032, 12 Media L. R. 1775 (4th
Dist. 1986)
  44 ALR5th 193—§ 24
Smith v. Copley Press, Inc., 140 Ill. App.
3d 613, 94 Ill. Dec. 785, 488 N.E.2d
1032, 12 Media L. Rep. (BNA)
1775 (4th Dist. 1986)
  7 ALR6th 135—§ 7

Smith v. Corrections Corp. of America,
5 Fed. Appx. 443 (6th Cir. 2001)
  119 ALR5th 1—§ 13, 14
Smith v. Corrigan, 100 NJL 267, 126 A.
680 (1924)
  35 ALR5th 145—§ 7
Smith v. Cote, 128 N.H. 231, 513 A.2d
341 (1986)
  49 ALR5th 685—§ 3, 9
Smith v. Cotter, 107 Nev. 267, 810 P.2d
1204 (1991)
  87 ALR5th 277—§ 24
Smith v. Cotton, 50 Ark. App. 100, 902
S.W.2d 240 (1995)
  40 ALR5th 227—§ 21
Smith v. Coughlin, 727 F. Supp. 834
(S.D. N.Y. 1989)
  95 ALR6th 341—§ 25
Smith v. County of Albemarle, Va., 895
F.2d 953 (4th Cir. 1990)
  107 ALR5th 1—§ 4, 5, 11, 19
  70 ALR6th 513—§ 11
  71 ALR6th 471—§ 13
Smith v. County of Fresno (California
Academy of Sciences), 268 Cal.
Rptr. 351 (App. 5th Dist. 1990)
  106 ALR5th 523—§ 20
Smith v. County of Los Angeles, 24 Cal.
App. 4th 990, 29 Cal. Rptr. 2d 680,
94 C.D.O.S. 3167, 94 Daily Journal
DAR 5909 (2d Dist. 1994)
  10 ALR5th 538—§ 4
Smith v. County of Los Angeles, 214
Cal. App. 3d 266, 262 Cal. Rptr.
754 (2d Dist. 1989)
  25 ALR5th 568—§ 51
Smith v. Courter, 575 S.W.2d 199 (Mo.
App. 1978)
  35 ALR5th 145—§ 38
Smith v. Cox, 247 Ga. 563, 277 S.E.2d
512 (1981)
  12 ALR6th 123—§ 19
Smith v. Crose, 2006 WL 2591075
(D.N.J. 2006)
  68 ALR6th 389—§ 15
Smith v. Crouse, 413 F.2d 979 (10th Cir.
1969)
  101 ALR5th 351—§ 7, 9

Smith v. Crown Financial Services of
America, 111 Nev. 277, 890 P.2d
769 (1995)
125 ALR5th 193—§ 8
Smith v. Crump, 223 Ga. App. 52, 476
S.E.2d 817, 96 Fulton County D R
3553 (1996)
51 ALR5th 467—§ 8
52 ALR5th 1—§ 3
Smith v. Cruz, 161 A.D.2d 938, 557
N.Y.S.2d 509 (3d Dep't 1990)
92 ALR6th 379—§ 22
Smith v. CSK Auto, Inc., 204 P.3d 1001
(Alaska 2009)
79 ALR6th 377—§ 10
Smith v. Cumberland County Agr. Society, 163 N.C. 346, 79 S.E. 632
(1913)
88 ALR6th 679—§ 6
Smith v. Cumberland County Board of
Education, 241 N.C. 305, 84 S.E.2d
903 (1954)
23 ALR5th 1—§ 12
Smith v. Cumberland Group, Ltd., 455
Pa. Super. 276, 687 A.2d 1167
(1997)
100 ALR5th 481—§ 10
Smith v. Cummings, 445 F.3d 1254
(10th Cir. 2006)
54 ALR6th 1—§ 8
Smith v. Curry, 580 F.3d 1071 (9th Cir.
2009)
66 ALR6th 635—§ 22
Smith v. Cutrer & Jefferson, 2002 WL
87485 (Tex. App. Houston 14th
Dist. 2002)
9 ALR6th 285—§ 4
13 ALR6th 1—§ 4
14 ALR6th 1—§ 4
Smith v. Cutson, 188 A.D.2d 1034, 591
N.Y.S.2d 674 (4th Dep't 1992)
95 ALR6th 85—§ 22
Smith v. Cutter Biological, Inc., a Div.
of Miles Inc., 72 Haw. 416, 823
P.2d 717, Prod. Liab. Rep. (CCH)
¶ 13056 (1991)
63 ALR5th 195—§ 4, 8
64 ALR5th 333—§ 4, 6, 11, 31

75 ALR5th 229—§ 10, 18
Smith v. Cybex Intern., 2002 WL
31082162 (Mich. Ct. App. 2002)
76 ALR6th 395—§ 8
Smith v. Dacotah Cotton Mills, Inc., 31
N.C. App. 687, 230 S.E.2d 772
(1976)
11 ALR6th 351—§ 4
Smith v. Daffin, 115 Fla. 418, 155 So.
658 (1934)
35 ALR6th 1—§ 28
Smith v. Daily Mail Pub. Co., 443 U.S.
97, 61 L. Ed. 2d 399, 99 S. Ct. 2667,
5 Media L. R. 1305 (1979)
39 ALR5th 103—§ 53
Smith v. Dallas Ry. & Terminal Co., 250
S.W.2d 256 (Tex. Civ. App. Waco
1952)
87 ALR5th 1—§ 12, 31
Smith v. Daneshjoo, 2002-Ohio-4338,
2002 WL 1941160 (Ohio Ct. App.
2d Dist. Montgomery County 2002)
92 ALR6th 379—§ 96, 101
Smith v. Daniels, 2010 WL 4882950
(N.D. Ga. 2010)
65 ALR6th 93—§ 21
Smith v. DataCard Corp., 9 F. Supp. 2d
1067, 75 Empl. Prac. Dec. (CCH)
¶ 45977, 76 Empl. Prac. Dec.
(CCH) ¶ 45977, 139 Lab. Cas.
(CCH) ¶ 33947 (D. Minn. 1998)
83 ALR5th 1—§ 11, 15
94 ALR5th 1—§ 17, 21
52 ALR6th 271—§ 9
Smith v. Datachem, Inc., 540 So. 2d
1282 (La. Ct. App. 5th Cir. 1989)
22 ALR6th 329—§ 6
Smith v. D.C. Rental Accommodations
Com., 411 A.2d 612 (Dist. Col.
App. 1979)
23 ALR5th 140—§ 6
Smith v. Decatur School Dist., 2011
Ark. App. 126, 2011 WL 549057
(2011)
104 ALR6th 303—§ 8
Smith v. Deep River Planning and Zoning Com'n, 1998 WL 345399
(Conn. Super. Ct. 1998)

4 ALR6th 263—§ 9
Smith v. Deering, 880 F. Supp. 816
(S.D. Ga. 1994)
81 ALR6th 257—§ 3, 5, 21
Smith v. Delano, 179 Mo. App. 242, 166
S.W. 852 (1914)
12 ALR5th 195—§ 10
Smith v. Delaware, L. & W. R. Co., 89
NJL 654, 99 A. 325 (1916)
17 ALR5th 547—§ 53
Smith v. Delta Tau Delta, Inc., 9 N.E.3d
154, 305 Ed. Law Rep. 406 (Ind.
2014)
100 ALR6th 365—§ 11
Smith v. Department of Ins., 507 So. 2d
1080, Prod. Liab. Rep. (CCH)
¶ 11363 (Fla. 1987)
103 ALR5th 379—§ 10
Smith v. Department of Motor Vehicles,
1 Cal. App. 3d 499, 81 Cal. Rptr.
800 (1st Dist. 1969)
109 ALR5th 611—§ 5
Smith v. Department of Public Health,
428 Mich. 540, 410 N.W.2d 749
(1987)
75 ALR5th 619—§ 3
Smith v. Department of Registration &
Ed., 412 Ill. 332, 106 N.E.2d 722
(1952)
28 ALR6th 175—§ 12
Smith v. Department of Revenue, Motor
Vehicle Div., 793 P.2d 611 (Colo.
App. 1990)
2 ALR5th 725—§ 10
Smith v. Department of State, 3 App.
Div. 2d 954, 162 N.Y.S.2d 528 (3d
Dep't 1957)
7 ALR5th 474—§ 155
Smith v. DeVincent, 322 So. 2d 257 (La.
Ct. App. 2d Cir. 1975)
83 ALR5th 651—§ 3
Smith v. Dewey, 214 Neb. 605, 335
N.W.2d 530 (1983)
5 ALR6th 133—§ 7
14 ALR6th 301—§ 5, 7, 23
Smith v. Dillard Dep't Stores, Inc., 139
Ohio App. 3d 525, 744 N.E.2d 1198
(8th Dist. Cuyahoga County 2000)

99 ALR5th 65—§ 5
Smith v. Dillard Dept. Stores, Inc., 139
Ohio App. 3d 525, 744 N.E.2d 1198
(8th Dist. Cuyahoga County 2000)
10 ALR6th 375—§ 7
Smith v. Director, Div. of Taxation, 7
N.J. Tax 187 (1984)
2 ALR6th 1—§ 56
Smith v. Director, Div. of Taxation, 108
N.J. 19, 527 A.2d 843 (1987)
2 ALR6th 1—§ 53
Smith v. District of Columbia, 399 A.2d
213 (D.C. 1979)
53 ALR6th 213—§ 8
Smith v. Dixon Ford Tractor Co., 160
Ga. App. 885, 288 S.E.2d 599, 33
U.C.C.R.S. 1384 (1982)
49 ALR5th 1—§ 22
Smith v. Dodge & Bliss Co., 59 N.J. Eq.
584, 44 A. 639 (1899)
4 ALR5th 772—§ 68
Smith v. Doe, 538 U.S. 84, 123 S. Ct.
1140, 155 L. Ed. 2d 164 (2003)
51 ALR6th 139—§ 2, 6, 13
63 ALR6th 351—§ 3
Smith v. Doe, 538 U.S. 84, 123 S.Ct.
1140, 155 L.Ed.2d 164 (2003)
63 ALR6th 351—§ 3
Smith v. Doe, 538 U.S. 84, 123 S. Ct.
1140, 155 L. Ed. 2d 164 (2003)pp
63 ALR6th 351—§ 3
Smith v. Dow, 178 Iowa 108, 159 N.W.
654 (1916)
19 ALR5th 622—§ 31, 39, 49
Smith v. Dretke, 157 Fed. Appx. 747
(5th Cir. 2005)
87 ALR6th 109—§ 32, 81
Smith v. Duckworth, 680 F. Supp. 299
(N.D. Ind. 1987)
124 ALR5th 1—§ 5
Smith v. Dugan & Meyers Const. Co.,
Inc., 18 Ohio Misc. 2d 5, 480
N.E.2d 830 (C.P. 1984)
100 ALR5th 481—§ 3
Smith v. Eagleton, 455 F. Supp. 403
(W.D. Mo. 1978)
24 ALR6th 255—§ 3, 11, 13

Smith v. Eakes, 212 N.C. 382, 193 S.E.
393 (1937)
83 ALR6th 605—§ 7
Smith v. Eastern New Mexico Medical
Center, 72 F.3d 138 (10th Cir. 1995)
32 ALR6th 457—§ 4, 6
Smith v. Eaton Corp., 195 F. Supp. 2d
1079, 88 Fair Empl. Prac. Cas.
(BNA) 142 (N.D. Iowa 2002)
93 ALR5th 47—§ 21
Smith v. Ebasco Constructors, Inc., 1988
WL 44143 (D.N.J. 1988)
13 ALR6th 499—§ 22
Smith v. Edwards, 2000 WL 709005
(S.D. N.Y. 2000)
125 ALR5th 497—§ 4
Smith v. Elenges, 156 Mich. App. 260,
401 N.W.2d 342 (1986)
43 ALR5th 545—§ 53, 84
Smith v. Eli Lilly & Co., 137 Ill. 2d 222,
148 Ill. Dec. 22, 560 N.E.2d 324,
Prod. Liab. Rep. (CCH) ¶ 12590
(1990)
63 ALR5th 195—§ 4
Smith v. Elmwood Medical Center, 720
So. 2d 1222 (La. Ct. App. 5th Cir.
1998)
38 ALR6th 399—§ 15
Smith v. Elo, 23 Fed. Appx. 310 (6th
Cir. 2001)
72 ALR6th 141—§ 9
Smith v. Employer's Liability Assur.
Corp., 217 Pa. Super. 31, 268 A.2d
200 (1970)
103 ALR5th 1—§ 3
Smith v. Employment Div., 34 Or. App.
623, 579 P.2d 310 (1978)
47 ALR5th 775—§ 5
Smith v. Emporium Mercantile Co., 190
Minn. 294, 251 N.W. 265 (1933)
40 ALR5th 135—§ 2 to 4, 14
1 ALR6th 297—§ 4, 14
Smith v. Endell, 860 F.2d 1528 (9th Cir.
1988)
124 ALR5th 1—§ 5
Smith v. Epps, 326 Fed. Appx. 764 (5th
Cir. 2009)
89 ALR6th 1—§ 54

Smith v. Erickson, 884 F.2d 1108 (8th
Cir. 1989)
56 ALR6th 553—§ 5, 7, 40
Smith v. E. R. Squibb & Sons, Inc., 405
Mich. 79, 273 N.W.2d 476, 26
U.C.C. Rep. Serv. (CBC) 330
(1979)
57 ALR5th 1—§ 2, 3
Smith v. Ethyl Corp., 417 F. Supp. 669
(S.D. Tex. 1976)
48 ALR5th 473—§ 13
Smith v. Executive Club, Ltd., 458 A.2d
32, 48 A.L.R.4th 147 (Dist. Col.
App. 1983)
12 ALR5th 195—§ 10
Smith v. Eyerly Motors, Inc., 269 Or.
613, 525 P.2d 1013 (1974)
48 ALR5th 1—§ 25
Smith v. Fair Employment & Housing
Com., 12 Cal. 4th 1143, 51 Cal.
Rptr. 2d 700, 913 P.2d 909 (1996)
10 ALR6th 513—§ 3 to 5
Smith v. Fairfax Hosp., 1998 WL
841501 (Va. Ct. App. 1998)
86 ALR5th 295—§ 4
Smith v. Falke, 474 So. 2d 1044 (Miss.
1985)
6 ALR5th 883—§ 26
Smith v. Fall River Joint Union High
School Dist., 118 Cal. App. 673, 5
P.2d 930 (1931)
23 ALR5th 1—§ 14
Smith v. FDC Corp., 109 N.M. 514, 787
P.2d 433, 52 BNA FEP Cas. 245, 53
CCH EPD ¶ 39872 (1990)
51 ALR5th 1—§ 7
Smith v. Federal Surety Co., 60 S.D.
100, 243 N.W. 664 (1932)
5 ALR5th 132—§ 15
Smith v. Federated Metals Corp., 235
Mo. App. 297, 133 S.W.2d 1112
(1939)
86 ALR5th 295—§ 4
Smith v. Fenner, 399 Pa. 633, 161 A.2d
150 (1960)
6 ALR5th 883—§ 7
Smith v. Fergus County, 39 P.2d 193
(Mont 1934)

---

35 ALR5th 285—§ 3, 15
Smith v. Fernandez, 520 So. 2d 654 (Fla. Dist. Ct. App. 3d Dist. 1988)
82 ALR5th 443—§ 4
Smith v. Fields, 268 A.D.2d 579, 702 N.Y.S.2d 364 (2d Dep't 2000)
17 ALR6th 159—§ 54
Smith v. Fine, 351 Mo. 1179, 175 S.W.2d 761 (1943)
27 ALR5th 174—§ 63
Smith v. Finstad, 247 Ga. 603, 277 S.E.2d 736 (1981)
71 ALR5th 99—§ 7
Smith v. Firestone Tire & Rubber Co., 755 F.2d 129, 17 Fed. Rules Evid. Serv. 752 (CA8 Mo. 1985)
47 ALR5th 395—§ 11
Smith v. Fireworks by Girone, Inc., 180 N.J. 199, 850 A.2d 456 (2004)
21 ALR6th 81—§ 44
Smith v. First Bank of Childersburg, 501 So. 2d 1228 (Ala. App. 1987)
9 ALR5th 708—§ 3
Smith v. First Union Mortg. Corp., 1999 WL 1081362 (E.D. Pa. 1999)
60 ALR6th 295—§ 56
Smith v. First Union Nat. Bank, 202 F.3d 234, 81 Fair Empl. Prac. Cas. (BNA) 1391, 5 Wage & Hour Cas. 2d (BNA) 1511, 77 Empl. Prac. Dec. (CCH) ¶ 46211 (4th Cir. 2000)
94 ALR5th 1—§ 27
Smith v. Fisher, 965 So. 2d 205 (Fla. Dist. Ct. App. 4th Dist. 2007)
45 ALR6th 493—§ 4
Smith v. Fitton & Pittman, Inc., 264 S.C. 129, 212 S.E.2d 925 (1975)
75 ALR5th 413—§ 3, 8, 49
Smith v. Fluor Corp., 514 So. 2d 1227 (Miss. 1987)
122 ALR5th 1—§ 2, 10, 16, 30, 35
5 ALR6th 497—§ 4
Smith v. Fonda, 265 App. Div. 977, 38 N.Y.S.2d 740 (1942)
27 ALR5th 174—§ 66
Smith v. Foote's Dixie Dandy, Inc., 941 F. Supp. 807, 70 Empl. Prac. Dec. (CCH) ¶ 44759 (E.D. Ark. 1995)

20 ALR6th 1—§ 4
Smith v. Ford Motor Co., 882 F. Supp. 770, 42 Fed. R. Evid. Serv. 466 (N.D. Ind. 1995)
84 ALR5th 69—§ 14, 17, 26
Smith v. Ford Motor Co., 1990 WL 301520 (Mar 17, 1990, W.D. Mo)
51 ALR5th 163—§ 4, 5
Smith v. Foret, 734 So. 2d 922 (La. Ct. App. 1st Cir. 1999)
80 ALR6th 389—§ 27
Smith v. Fraternal Order of Eagles, 39 Ohio App. 3d 97, 529 N.E.2d 477 (9th Dist. Summit County 1987)
74 ALR5th 49—§ 3
Smith v. Friendship Village of Dublin, Ohio, Inc., 2001-Ohio-1272, 92 Ohio St. 3d 503, 751 N.E.2d 1010, 12 A.D. Cas. (BNA) 258 (2001)
103 ALR5th 557—§ 4
Smith v. Frisch's Big Boy, Inc., 208 So. 2d 310 (Fla. Dist. Ct. App. 2d Dist. 1968)
111 ALR5th 1—§ 4, 13
Smith v. Frye, 488 F.3d 263, 26 I.E.R. Cas. (BNA) 106, 90 Empl. Prac. Dec. (CCH) ¶ 43056, 154 Lab. Cas. (CCH) ¶ 60411 (4th Cir. 2007)
73 ALR6th 281—§ 31
Smith v. Funk, 141 Okla. 188, 284 P. 638 (1930)
14 ALR5th 557—§ 6, 7, 26
Smith v. Galland and Associates, Inc., 24 Wash. App. 632, 602 P.2d 1197 (Div. 3 1979)
117 ALR5th 155—§ 12
Smith v. Ganz, 219 Neb. 432, 363 N.W.2d 526 (1985)
11 ALR6th 1—§ 4
Smith v. Garrett, 2006 WL 3791951 (E.D. Ark. 2006)
70 ALR6th 361—§ 9
Smith v. Gateway, Inc., 2002 WL 1728615 (Tex. App. Austin 2002)
22 ALR6th 49—§ 4
Smith v. General Apartment Co., 133 Ga. App. 927, 213 S.E.2d 74 (1975)
43 ALR5th 207—§ 2, 34

Smith v. General Cas. Ins. Co., 2000 WI
127, 619 N.W.2d 882 (Wis. 2000)
77 ALR5th 319—§ 7
78 ALR5th 341—§ 7
79 ALR5th 289—§ 7
Smith v. General Casualty Ins. Co., 230
Wis. 2d 411, 601 N.W.2d 844 (Ct.
App. 1999)
77 ALR5th 319—§ 7
78 ALR5th 341—§ 6
79 ALR5th 289—§ 7
Smith v. General Electric, 1996 WL
24762 (E.D.Pa.)
81 ALR5th 367—§ 39
Smith v. General Life Ins. Co., 592 So.
2d 1021 (Ala. 1992)
14 ALR5th 242—§ 2
Smith v. General Motors Corp., 1995
WL 1055810 (Va. Cir. Ct. 1995)
88 ALR5th 301—§ 23
Smith v. Gentilotti, 371 Mass. 839, 359
N.E.2d 953, 20 U.C.C. Rep. Serv.
(CBC) 1222 (1977)
71 ALR5th 443—§ 17
Smith v. Gentiva Health Services (USA)
Inc., 296 F. Supp. 2d 758 (E.D.
Mich. 2003)
36 ALR6th 203—§ 3
Smith v. Georgia Granite Corp., 186 Ga.
634, 198 S.E. 772, 119 A.L.R. 550
(1938)
48 ALR5th 473—§ 23
Smith v. Gerrish, 256 Mass. 183, 152
N.E. 318 (1926)
2 ALR5th 1—§ 58
Smith v. Gibson, 197 F.3d 454 (10th Cir.
1999)
102 ALR6th 417—§ 37
Smith v. Gilman, 38 Ill. App. 393 (1890)
10 ALR5th 371—§ 5
Smith v. Glowacki, 122 Ill. App. 2d 336,
258 N.E.2d 591 (4th Dist. 1970)
5 ALR5th 422—§ 3
Smith v. GMAC Mortg. Corp., 2007 WL
2593148 (W.D. N.C. 2007)
96 ALR6th 125—§ 4
Smith v. Goetzman, 720 So. 2d 39 (La.
Ct. App. 1st Cir. 1998)

52 ALR5th 1—§ 8
Smith v. Goguen, 415 U.S. 566, 94 S.
Ct. 1242, 39 L. Ed. 2d 605 (1974)
31 ALR6th 333—§ 9, 11, 12
Smith v. Goins, 994 So. 2d 591 (La. Ct.
App. 3d Cir. 2008)
74 ALR6th 209—§ 15
Smith v. Golden Eagle Ins. Co., 69 Cal.
App. 4th 1371, 82 Cal. Rptr. 2d 300
(4th Dist. 1999)
39 ALR6th 155—§ 4
Smith v. Gonzales, 222 F.3d 1220 (10th
Cir. 2000)
63 ALR6th 255—§ 2
Smith v. Goodwill Industries of West
Michigan, Inc., 243 Mich. App. 438,
622 N.W.2d 337, 6 Wage & Hour
Cas. 2d (BNA) 1284 (2000)
99 ALR5th 1—§ 3
Smith v. Goodyear Tire & Rubber Co.,
600 F. Supp. 1561, Prod. Liab. Rep.
(CCH) ¶ 10603 (D. Vt. 1985)
62 ALR5th 537—§ 4
Smith v. Goodyear Tire & Rubber Co.,
856 F. Supp. 1347 (W.D. Mo. 1994)
52 ALR5th 613—§ 3
Smith v. Grab, 705 A.2d 894 (Pa. Super.
Ct. 1997)
92 ALR6th 379—§ 65
Smith v. Graham, 161 A.D. 803, 147
N.Y.S. 773 (4th Dep't 1914)
1 ALR6th 135—§ 19
Smith v. Graham, 161 App. Div. 803,
147 N.Y.S. 773 (1914)
25 ALR5th 233—§ 19
Smith v. Gray Concrete Pipe Co., 267
Md. 149, 297 A.2d 721 (1972)
33 ALR5th 303—§ 4, 11
Smith v. Gray Concrete Pipe Co., Inc.,
267 Md. 149, 297 A.2d 721 (1972)
69 ALR6th 415—§ 15
Smith v. Great American Restaurants,
Inc., 969 F.2d 430, 59 BNA FEP
Cas. 646, 59 CCH EPD ¶ 41636, 36
Fed. Rules Evid. Serv. 345 (CA7 Ill.
1992)
23 ALR5th 241—§ 2

Smith v. Great Am. Ins. Co., 29 N.Y.2d 116, 324 N.Y.S.2d 15, 272 N.E.2d 528 (1971)
79 ALR5th 289—§ 8, 16
Smith v. Greenville Products Co., 185 Mich. App. 512, 462 N.W.2d 789 (1990)
4 ALR5th 585—§ 15
Smith v. Greer, 22 Tenn. 118, 3 Hum. 118, 1842 WL 1891 (1842)
77 ALR6th 293—§ 42
Smith v. Greyhound Lines, Inc., 614 F. Supp. 558, 117 L.R.R.M. (BNA) 2253 (W.D. Pa. 1984)
53 ALR6th 213—§ 9
Smith v. Griswold, 15 Hun. 273 (N.Y. Gen. Term 1878)
61 ALR5th 635—§ 12
Smith v. Grobet File Co. of America, Inc., 20 I.E.R. Cas. (BNA) 718, 2003 WL 22047869 (S.D. N.Y. 2003)
13 ALR6th 499—§ 10, 21
Smith v. Groose, 205 F.3d 1045 (8th Cir. 2000)
121 ALR5th 551—§ 15
Smith v. Groose, 998 F.2d 1439 (8th Cir. 1993)
79 ALR5th 419—§ 4
Smith v. Grumman-Olsen Corp., 913 F. Supp. 1077 (E.D. Tenn. 1995)
23 ALR6th 697—§ 5
Smith v. GTE Corp., 236 F.3d 1292 (11th Cir. 2001)
56 ALR5th 107—§ 4
Smith v. GTE N. Inc. (In re Smith), 170 B.R. 111 (BC N.D. Ohio 1994)
14 ALR5th 242—§ 52
Smith v. Guerre, 159 S.W. 417 (Tex. Civ. App. Amarillo 1913)
71 ALR6th 249—§ 7
Smith v. Guilford Bd. of Educ., 226 Fed. Appx. 58 (2d Cir. 2007)
98 ALR6th 599—§ 19, 49, 59, 70, 84
Smith v. Gwinnett County, 248 Ga. 882, 286 S.E.2d 739 (1982)
7 ALR5th 187—§ 13, 14, 17

Smith v. Haden, 872 F. Supp. 1040 (D.D.C. 1994)
58 ALR6th 1—§ 5
59 ALR6th 1—§ 5
Smith v. Hall, 2005 ND 215, 707 N.W.2d 247 (N.D. 2005)
18 ALR6th 97—§ 41
30 ALR6th 483—§ 20
Smith v. Hallahan, 75 N.H. 534, 78 A. 122 (1910)
11 ALR5th 127—§ 4
Smith v. Hall's Estate, 215 Kan. 262, 524 P.2d 684 (1974)
111 ALR5th 1—§ 6, 9, 13
Smith v. Hamm, 314 Ky. 339, 235 S.W.2d 437 (1950)
20 ALR5th 1—§ 6, 31, 55
Smith v. Hanson, 228 App. Div. 634, 238 N.Y.S. 86 (1929)
2 ALR5th 1—§ 41
Smith v. Hardrick, 266 Ga. 54, 464 S.E.2d 198 (1995)
67 ALR6th 103—§ 5, 13
Smith v. Hardy, 228 S.C. 112, 88 S.E.2d 865 (1955)
12 ALR5th 195—§ 26
Smith v. Harrington, 2013 WL 1196892 (N.D. Cal. 2013)
98 ALR6th 599—§ 37
Smith v. Hartford Acc. & Indem. Co., 399 So. 2d 1193 (La. Ct. App. 3d Cir. 1981)
61 ALR5th 473—§ 9
Smith v. Hartrampf, 105 Ga. App. 40, 123 S.E.2d 417 (1961)
20 ALR5th 229—§ 4, 11
Smith v. Hartrampf, 106 Ga. App. 603, 127 S.E.2d 814 (1962)
20 ALR5th 229—§ 4, 11
Smith v. Hawkeye-Security Ins. Co., 842 F. Supp. 1373 (D. Kan. 1994)
110 ALR5th 465—§ 8, 31
Smith v. Haworth, 53 Mo. 88, 1873 WL 7943 (1873)
97 ALR5th 537—§ 81
Smith v. Hawthorne, 2006 ME 19, 892 A.2d 433 (Me. 2006)

27 ALR6th 183—§ 45
Smith v. Hayes, 2005-Ohio-2961, 2005 WL 1394779 (Ohio Ct. App. 10th Dist. Franklin County 2005)
70 ALR6th 183—§ 3
Smith v. Haynsworth, 472 S.E.2d 612 (S.C. 1996)
50 ALR5th 301—§ 3, 6, 9
Smith v. Haynsworth, Marion, McKay & Geurard, 322 S.C. 433, 472 S.E.2d 612 (1996)
58 ALR6th 1—§ 5, 16
Smith v. Hendrix, 265 S.C. 417, 219 S.E.2d 312 (1975)
60 ALR6th 481—§ 4, 18
Smith v. Hennepin Technical Center, 1988 WL 53400 (D. Minn. 1988)
83 ALR5th 1—§ 12, 13
Smith v. Henry Ford Hosp., 219 Mich. App. 555, 557 N.W.2d 154 (1996)
95 ALR6th 85—§ 22
Smith v. Herco, Inc., 900 S.W.2d 852 (Tex. App. Corpus Christi 1995)
117 ALR5th 23—§ 5, 13, 17, 18
Smith v. Heritage Salmon, Inc., 180 F. Supp. 2d 208 (D. Me. 2002)
13 ALR6th 499—§ 25
36 ALR6th 203—§ 3
Smith v. Higgins, 2006 WL 2053400 (Minn. Ct. App. 2006)
91 ALR6th 1—§ 9
Smith v. Highmore Farm Ltd Partnership, 489 N.W.2d 908 (S.D. 1992)
35 ALR5th 285—§ 5
Smith v. Higinbothom, 187 Md. 115, 48 A.2d 754 (1946)
51 ALR6th 359—§ 9
53 ALR6th 491—§ 13
Smith v. Hillerich & Bradsby Co., 253 S.W.2d 629 (Ky. 1952)
66 ALR5th 611—§ 10
Smith v. H. J. Landreneau Bldg. Contractor, Inc., 426 So. 2d 1360 (La. App. 3d Cir. 1983)
33 ALR5th 1—§ 13
Smith v. HMO Great Lakes, 852 F. Supp. 669 (N.D. Ill. 1994)
51 ALR5th 271—§ 3

Smith v. Hobbs, 848 S.W.2d 662 (1993 Tenn. App)
59 ALR5th 191—§ 5
Smith v. Hobby Lobby Stores, Inc., 968 F. Supp. 1356 (W.D. Ark. 1997)
81 ALR5th 41—§ 3
Smith v. Holloway Sportswear, Inc., 704 So. 2d 420 (La. Ct. App. 3d Cir. 1997)
19 ALR5th 439—§ 8
Smith v. Holtz, 210 F.3d 186 (3d Cir. 2000)
56 ALR6th 185—§ 31
63 ALR6th 255—§ 4, 7, 10, 24, 29, 30
Smith v. Holtz, 531 U.S. 880, 121 S. Ct. 192, 148 L. Ed. 2d 133 (2000)
56 ALR6th 185—§ 31
Smith v. Hooper, 89 N.H. 36, 192 A. 496 (1937)
68 ALR5th 599—§ 4
Smith v. Hope Mining Co. of St. Louis, 18 Mont. 432, 45 P. 632 (1896)
62 ALR5th 219—§ 52
Smith v. Hornblower & Weeks-Hemphill Noyes, Inc., 86 A.D.2d 865, 447 N.Y.S.2d 311 (2d Dep't 1982)
46 ALR6th 185—§ 10
Smith v. Hospital Authority of Terrell County, 161 Ga. App. 657, 288 S.E.2d 715 (1982)
58 ALR5th 613—§ 7
Smith v. Hough, 2010 WL 3855290 (M.D. Ga. 2010)
65 ALR6th 93—§ 70
Smith v. Houston, 244 Ga. 113, 259 S.E.2d 93 (1979)
82 ALR5th 389—§ 7
Smith v. Hovey, 72 Misc. 2d 48, 338 N.Y.S.2d 259 (1972)
2 ALR5th 553—§ 48
Smith v. Howard, 489 So. 2d 1037 (La. App. 1st Cir. 1986)
43 ALR5th 207—§ 3, 55
Smith v. Howard Johnson Co., Inc., 1993-Ohio-229, 67 Ohio St. 3d 28, 615 N.E.2d 1037 (1993)
102 ALR5th 99—§ 9

Smith v. Hubbard, 253 Minn. 215, 91 N.W.2d 756 (1958)
  12 ALR5th 195—§ 10
Smith v. Hubbell, 142 Mich. 637, 106 N.W. 547 (1906)
  54 ALR5th 649—§ 4
Smith v. Hub Mfg. Inc., 634 F. Supp. 1505, Prod. Liab. Rep. (CCH) ¶ 11125 (N.D.N.Y. 1986)
  65 ALR5th 105—§ 8, 13, 23
  81 ALR5th 245—§ 7
  90 ALR5th 179—§ 4
Smith v. Hughes Aircraft Co., 22 F.3d 1432 (9th Cir. 1993)
  88 ALR5th 493—§ 3, 7
  89 ALR5th 1—§ 10
  97 ALR5th 359—§ 18
Smith v. Hull, 659 N.E.2d 185 (Ind. Ct. App. 1995)
  108 ALR5th 385—§ 8
Smith v. Huntsville Times Co., Inc., 888 So. 2d 492, 32 Media L. Rep. (BNA) 1776 (Ala. 2004)
  22 ALR6th 553—§ 27, 32
Smith v. Hurley, 121 Ariz. 164, 589 P.2d 38 (Ct. App. Div. 1 1978)
  118 ALR5th 91—§ 33
Smith v. Hussmann Refrigerator Co., 658 S.W.2d 948 (Mo. App. 1983)
  61 ALR5th 375—§ 5, 10
Smith v. Idaho Com'n on Redistricting, 136 Idaho 542, 38 P.3d 121 (2001)
  106 ALR5th 523—§ 23
Smith v. Idaho Peterbilt, Inc., 106 Idaho 846, 683 P.2d 882 (App. 1984)
  18 ALR5th 577—§ 37, 38
Smith v. I-Flow Corp., 753 F. Supp. 2d 744 (N.D. Ill. 2010)
  90 ALR6th 75—§ 43
Smith v. Illinois Farmers Ins. Co., 455 N.W.2d 499 (Minn. Ct. App. 1990)
  55 ALR5th 747—§ 3
Smith v. IMG Worldwide, Inc., 437 F. Supp. 2d 297 (E.D. Pa. 2006)
  52 ALR6th 271—§ 18
Smith v. Indiana Dept. of Correction, 861 N.E.2d 1271 (Ind. Ct. App. 2007)

  96 ALR6th 269—§ 5, 10, 38
Smith v. Industrial Com'n, 134 Colo. 454, 306 P.2d 254 (1957)
  40 ALR6th 99—§ 84
Smith v. Ingersoll-Rand Co., 214 F.3d 1235 (10th Cir. 2000)
  12 ALR5th 195—§ 20
Smith v. Insurance Co. of North America, 411 N.E.2d 638 (Ind. App. 1980)
  25 ALR5th 391—§ 42
Smith v. International Paper Co., 87 F.3d 245 (8th Cir. 1996)
  110 ALR5th 277—§ 3
Smith v. Invacare Corp., 2004 WL 2164891 (Conn. Super. Ct. 2004)
  54 ALR6th 619—§ 43
Smith v. Iowa Jewish Senior Life Center, 161 F. Supp. 2d 991 (S.D. Iowa 2001)
  52 ALR6th 271—§ 4
Smith v. Iron County, 692 F.2d 685 (10th Cir. 1982)
  65 ALR6th 93—§ 42
Smith v. Ironwood Management, 2011 WL 5531027 (Cal. App. 2d Dist. 2011)
  83 ALR6th 143—§ 6
Smith v. I.R.S., 94-2 U.S. Tax Cas. (CCH) ¶ 50503, 75 A.F.T.R.2d 95-2253, 1994 WL 512426 (S.D. N.Y. 1994)
  124 ALR5th 537—§ 9
Smith v. ITT Corp., 918 F. Supp. 304, 68 Empl. Prac. Dec. (CCH) ¶ 44156 (D. Ariz. 1995)
  94 ALR5th 1—§ 18, 22
Smith v. Jack Dyer & Assocs., 633 So. 2d 694 (La. App. 1st Cir. 1993)
  51 ALR5th 467—§ 11
Smith v. Jansen, 85 Misc. 2d 81, 379 N.Y.S.2d 254 (Sup 1975)
  63 ALR6th 1—§ 56
Smith v. Jay Apartments, Inc., 33 A.D.2d 624, 304 N.Y.S.2d 737 (3d Dep't 1969)
  99 ALR5th 141—§ 10, 13, 14
  100 ALR5th 409—§ 12

---

115 ALR5th 1—§ 13, 14
Smith v. J. C. Penney Co., 260 Iowa 573, 149 N.W.2d 794 (1967)
15 ALR6th 1—§ 4, 6, 9, 10, 26
Smith v. Jefferson County Bd. of School Com'rs, 641 F.3d 197, 268 Ed. Law Rep. 37, 31 I.E.R. Cas. (BNA) 1424 (6th Cir. 2011)
76 ALR6th 587—§ 15
Smith v. Jefferson Pilot Financial Ins. Co., 245 F.R.D. 45 (D. Mass. 2007)
47 ALR6th 255—§ 17
Smith v. John Deere Co., 83 Ohio App. 3d 398, 614 N.E.2d 1148 (Franklin Co. 1993)
25 ALR5th 696—§ 45
Smith v. Johnson, 219 Mass. 142, 106 N.E. 604 (1914)
6 ALR6th 1—§ 60, 76
Smith v. Johnson, 415 So. 2d 291 (La. App. 2d Cir. 1982)
15 ALR5th 692—§ 11
Smith v. Johnson, 440 F.3d 262 (5th Cir. 2006)
22 ALR6th 19—§ 7
Smith v. Johnston, 591 P.2d 1260 (Okla. 1978)
33 ALR5th 1—§ 2
Smith v. Jones, 43 Misc. 2d 350, 250 N.Y.S.2d 955 (Fam. Ct. 1964)
122 ALR5th 205—§ 3, 32
Smith v. Jones, 113 Ill. 2d 126, 100 Ill. Dec. 560, 497 N.E.2d 738 (1986)
48 ALR6th 243—§ 10
Smith v. Jones, 155 Misc. 2d 254, 587 N.Y.S.2d 506 (Fam. Ct. 1992)
69 ALR5th 1—§ 3, 6
71 ALR5th 99—§ 3
Smith v. Joseph, 31 U.C.C. Rep. Serv. 1560 (D.C. Super. Ct. 1981)
101 ALR5th 563—§ 8, 9
Smith v. J.P. Morgan Chase Bank N/A, 2010 WL 4622209 (S.D. Tex. 2010)
104 ALR6th 485—§ 5
Smith v. J.P. Morgan Chase Bank N/A, 2011 WL 11196 (S.D. Tex. 2011)
104 ALR6th 485—§ 5

Smith v. JPMorgan Chase Bank, N.A., 2011 WL 6217783 (E.D. Tex. 2011)
96 ALR6th 125—§ 14
Smith v. Jung, 241 So. 2d 874 (Fla. Dist. Ct. App. 3d Dist. 1970)
62 ALR5th 475—§ 3, 4
Smith v. Kahler Corp., 297 Minn. 272, 211 N.W.2d 146 (1973)
10 ALR5th 371—§ 2, 3
Smith v. Kang, 37 Ohio St. 3d 170, 524 N.E.2d 506 (1988)
5 ALR6th 133—§ 8
Smith v. Kansas City Southern Ry. Co., 846 So. 2d 980 (La. Ct. App. 3d Cir. 2003)
111 ALR5th 529—§ 4
Smith v. Karen S. Reisig, M.D., Inc., 686 P.2d 285 (Okla. 1984)
42 ALR5th 1—§ 3
Smith v. Kauffman, 212 Va. 181, 183 S.E.2d 190 (1971)
118 ALR5th 513—§ 9
Smith v. Kavanaugh, Pierson & Talley, 513 So. 2d 1138 (La. 1987)
66 ALR6th 83—§ 6
Smith v. Kavanaugh, Pierson & Talley, Succession of, 513 So. 2d 1138 (La. 1987)
51 ALR5th 603—§ 2, 8, 10
Smith v. Kavanaugh, Pierson and Talley, Succession of, 565 So. 2d 990 (La. Ct. App. 1st Cir. 1990)
87 ALR5th 473—§ 4
Smith v. Keller, 151 Wis. 2d 264, 444 N.W.2d 396 (Ct. App. 1989)
125 ALR5th 193—§ 10
Smith v. Keller Ladder Co., 275 N.J. Super. 280, 645 A.2d 1269, Prod. Liab. Rep. (CCH) ¶ 14033 (App. Div. 1994)
81 ALR5th 245—§ 2, 6
Smith v. Kelley, 228 A.D.2d 831, 643 N.Y.S.2d 764 (3d Dep't 1996)
111 ALR5th 159—§ 9
Smith v. Kelly, 664 F. Supp. 131 (S.D. N.Y. 1987)
59 ALR5th 135—§ 8

Smith v. Kelso, 863 F.2d 1564 (11th Cir. 1989)

24 ALR6th 591—§ 12

Smith v. Kemp, 664 F. Supp. 500 (M.D. Ga. 1987)

20 ALR5th 177—§ 4

Smith v. Kentucky State Fair Bd., 816 S.W.2d 911 (Ky. Ct. App. 1991)

116 ALR5th 433—§ 3, 5

Smith v. Keystone Wood Products Co., 32 F.2d 261 (D.C. Pa. 1927)

19 ALR5th 622—§ 49

Smith v. King, 106 Wash. 2d 443, 772 P.2d 796 (1986)

39 ALR5th 33—§ 8, 11

Smith v. King, 615 So. 2d 69 (Ala. 1993)

81 ALR5th 167—§ 4

Smith v. Kings Entertainment Co., 99 Ohio App. 3d 1, 649 N.E.2d 1252 (1st Dist. Hamilton County 1994)

96 ALR5th 107—§ 3

98 ALR5th 609—§ 23

Smith v. Klein, 23 Ohio App. 3d 146, 492 N.E.2d 852 (8th Dist. Cuyahoga County 1985)

53 ALR6th 213—§ 4

Smith v. Klemm, 118 NJL 471, 193 A. 790 (1937)

26 ALR5th 127—§ 3, 11

Smith v. Kmart Corp., 177 F.3d 19 (1st Cir. 1999)

50 ALR5th 1—§ 12

52 ALR5th 1—§ 3, 9

Smith v. Knight, 608 S.W.2d 165 (Tex. 1980)

13 ALR6th 1—§ 4

Smith v. Knowles, 281 N.W.2d 653 (Minn. 1979)

7 ALR5th 1—§ 2, 3

Smith v. Kohl's Dept. Store, Inc., 2001 WL 681766 (Mich. Ct. App. 2001)

1 ALR6th 297—§ 4, 14

Smith v. Kouri, 2010 WL 2228423 (C.D. Cal. 2010)

101 ALR6th 207—§ 39

Smith v. Kurtzman, 106 Ill. App. 3d 712, 62 Ill. Dec. 419, 436 N.E.2d 1 (1st Dist. 1982)

5 ALR6th 133—§ 14, 20

14 ALR6th 301—§ 15

76 ALR6th 31—§ 46

Smith v. Landfair, 194 Ohio App. 3d 468, 2011-Ohio-3043, 956 N.E.2d 915 (9th Dist. Summit County 2011)

79 ALR6th 487—§ 19

Smith v. Lane, 358 Ill. App. 3d 1126, 295 Ill. Dec. 497, 832 N.E.2d 947 (5th Dist. 2005)

79 ALR6th 487—§ 17

Smith v. Langford, 271 Ga. 221, 518 S.E.2d 884, 97 A.L.R.5th 767 (1999)

97 ALR5th 537—§ 23

Smith v. Lapidus, 208 Md. 273, 118 A.2d 373 (1955)

5 ALR5th 422—§ 6

Smith v. Ledford, 2006 WL 1431666 (W.D. N.C. 2006)

89 ALR6th 1—§ 100

Smith v. Legal Helpers Debt Resolution, LLC, 2011 WL 5166494 (W.D. Wash. 2011)

90 ALR6th 1—§ 6, 16

Smith v. Lenchner, 204 Pa. Super. 500, 205 A.2d 626, 2 U.C.C. Rep. Serv. (CBC) 436 (1964)

75 ALR5th 559—§ 6

Smith v. Levine, 911 S.W.2d 427 (Tex. App. San Antonio 1995)

8 ALR5th 312—§ 4

Smith v. Lewis, 499 So. 2d 1350 (La. App. 5th Cir. 1986)

27 ALR5th 174—§ 3, 4, 26

48 ALR5th 129—§ 12

Smith v. LG Electronics U.S.A., Inc., 83 U.C.C. Rep. Serv. 2d 92 (N.D. Cal. 2014)

104 ALR6th 97—§ 14

Smith v. Liberty Mut. Ins. Co., 130 N.H. 117, 536 A.2d 164 (1987)

1 ALR5th 132—§ 2, 7, 19

Smith v. Liberty Mut. Ins. Co., 449 F. Supp. 928 (M.D. N.C. 1978)

13 ALR5th 289—§ 3

For assistance, call 1-800-328-4880

Smith v. Liburdi, 26 Conn. App. 254, 600 A.2d 17 (1991)
53 ALR6th 1—§ 5

Smith v. Life Investors Ins. Co. Of America, 2009 WL 3756911 (W.D. Pa. 2009)
68 ALR6th 297—§ 4

Smith v. Lightning Bolt Productions, Inc., 861 F.2d 363 (2d Cir. 1988)
9 ALR6th 285—§ 13

Smith v. Lightning Bolt Productions, Inc., 861 F.2d 363 (CA2 N.Y. 1988)
14 ALR5th 242—§ 2, 5, 28, 40

Smith v. Lincoln Park Public School, 2004 WL 1124467 (Mich. Ct. App. 2004)
100 ALR6th 563—§ 11, 41

Smith v. Lit Bros., 174 Pa. Super. 102, 100 A.2d 390 (1953)
63 ALR6th 495—§ 72

Smith v. Litten, 256 Va. 573, 507 S.E.2d 77, 78 Fair Empl. Prac. Cas. (BNA) 1092 (1998)
81 ALR5th 367—§ 34

Smith v. Lockheed Propulsion Co., 247 Cal. App. 2d 774, 56 Cal. Rptr. 128, 29 A.L.R.3d 538 (4th Dist. 1967)
103 ALR5th 157—§ 4

Smith v. Loeffler, 20 Ohio App. 3d 66, 484 N.E.2d 185 (9th Dist. Summit County 1984)
5 ALR6th 133—§ 15

Smith v. Lomax, 45 F.3d 402, 67 Fair Empl Prac. Cas. (BNA) 1005, 66 Empl. Prac. Dec. (CCH) ¶ 43456 (11th Cir. 1995)
83 ALR5th 1—§ 5

Smith v. Lombard, 480 So. 2d 1077 (La. Ct. App. 4th Cir. 1986)
74 ALR6th 209—§ 7

Smith v. Lomenzo, 33 App. Div. 2d 874, 307 N.Y.S.2d 774 (4th Dep't 1969)
7 ALR5th 474—§ 177

Smith v. Los Angeles Bookbinders Union No. 63, 133 Cal. App. 2d 486, 284 P.2d 194 (2d Dist. 1955)
94 ALR5th 149—§ 7, 8

Smith v. Louis Berkman Co., 894 F. Supp. 1084 (W.D. Ky. 1995)
53 ALR5th 535—§ 15

Smith v. Louisiana Farm Bureau Cas. Ins. Co., 603 So. 2d 199 (La. Ct. App. 3d Cir. 1992)
115 ALR5th 589—§ 5

Smith v. Louisiana Farm Bureau Mut. Ins. Co., 440 So. 2d 801 (La. App. 1st Cir. 1983)
48 ALR5th 129—§ 14, 15

Smith v. Louisiana Health & Human Resources Admin., 637 So. 2d 1177 (La. App. 4th Cir. 1994)
26 ALR5th 245—§ 27

Smith v. Louisiana State Police, 2007 WL 2903299 (E.D. La. 2007)
56 ALR6th 467—§ 7, 9, 15, 20

Smith v. Louisiana State Police, 2009 WL 411553 (E.D. La. 2009)
45 ALR6th 1—§ 11
52 ALR6th 623—§ 9

Smith v. Louisville Ladder Co., 237 F.3d 515 (5th Cir. 2001)
81 ALR5th 245—§ 6

Smith v. Lowe's Home Centers, Inc., 2005 WL 1071680 (W.D. Tex. 2005)
8 ALR6th 439—§ 4, 18

Smith v. Lowe's Home Centers, Inc., 2005 WL 1533108 (W.D. Tex. 2005)
8 ALR6th 439—§ 18

Smith v. Lowe's Home Centers, Inc., 2005 WL 1902544 (W.D. Tex. 2005)
8 ALR6th 439—§ 18

Smith v. Lucas County Children Services Bd., 1992 WL 388952 (Ohio Ct. App. 6th Dist. Lucas County 1992)
82 ALR5th 389—§ 5

Smith v. Ly, 470 So. 2d 326 (La. App. 5th Cir. 1985)
33 ALR5th 1—§ 15

Smith v. MacArthur Surgical Clinic, 610 So. 2d 245 (La. App. 3d Cir. 1992)
31 ALR5th 1—§ 26

Smith v. Macomber, 28 R.I. 248, 66 A. 570 (1907)

12 ALR5th 195—§ 58, 60

Smith v. Mallick, 60 U.C.C. Rep. Serv. 2d 884 (D.D.C. 2006)

35 ALR6th 437—§ 3, 4

Smith v. Mallinckrodt Chemical Works, 212 Mo. App. 158, 251 S.W. 155 (1923)

30 ALR5th 571—§ 8, 14

Smith v. Maloney, 55 Mass. App. Ct. 1112, 772 N.E.2d 1098 (2002)

96 ALR6th 269—§ 17

Smith v. Maloney, 735 F. Supp. 39 (D. Mass. 1990)

85 ALR5th 261—§ 3

Smith v. Malouf, 722 So. 2d 490 (Miss. 1998)

61 ALR5th 151—§ 13

Smith v. Manausa, 385 F. Supp. 443 (E.D. Ky. 1974)

52 ALR5th 491—§ 13

Smith v. Margerum, 21 Pa. C.C. 209 (Pa. C.P. 1898)

111 ALR5th 313—§ 20

Smith v. Marion County Dep't of Public Welfare, 635 N.E.2d 1144 (Ind. Ct. App. 2d Dist. 1994)

92 ALR5th 379—§ 5

Smith v. Mark Dodge, Inc., 934 So. 2d 375 (Ala. 2006)

22 ALR6th 387—§ 29

Smith v. Marquross, 276 S.W.3d 926, 65 U.C.C. Rep. Serv. 2d 831 (Tenn. Ct. App. 2008)

61 ALR6th 207—§ 3

Smith v. Martin Mills, Inc., 701 So. 2d 680 (La. Ct. App. 3d Cir. 1997)

14 ALR5th 1—§ 8

Smith v. Maryland, 442 U.S. 735, 99 S. Ct. 2577, 61 L. Ed. 2d 220 (1979)

9 ALR5th 553—§ 4
78 ALR5th 309—§ 4, 7
18 ALR6th 1—§ 2, 7
25 ALR6th 201—§ 2
94 ALR6th 579—§ 2

Smith v. Maschner, 899 F.2d 940 (10th Cir. 1990)

89 ALR6th 1—§ 117, 118

Smith v. Massey, 235 F.3d 1259 (10th Cir. 2000)

102 ALR6th 417—§ 6, 20

Smith v. Masterson, 538 F. Supp. 2d 653 (S.D. N.Y. 2008)

86 ALR6th 173—§ 14

Smith v. Matthews, 793 F. Supp. 998 (D. Kan. 1992)

85 ALR5th 261—§ 3

Smith v. Matthews, 907 N.E.2d 1076 (Ind. Ct. App. 2009)

89 ALR6th 1—§ 61

Smith v. Maxfield, 9 Misc. 42, 29 N.Y.S. 63 (1894)

13 ALR5th 169—§ 9

Smith v. McClung, 201 N.C. 648, 161 S.E. 91 (1931)

11 ALR6th 695—§ 46

Smith v. McCotter, 786 F.2d 697 (5th Cir. 1986)

31 ALR6th 49—§ 4

Smith v. McCoy, 58 S.D. 256, 235 N.W. 661 (1931)

46 ALR5th 1—§ 39

Smith v. McDaniel, 2009 WL 2152325 (D. Nev. 2009)

56 ALR6th 185—§ 20

Smith v. McDonald, 713 F. Supp. 871 (M.D. N.C. 1988)

12 ALR5th 195—§ 52

Smith v. McDonald, 869 F. Supp. 918 (D. Kan. 1994)

6 ALR6th 483—§ 5

Smith v. McDougall, 65 Ohio App. 152, 18 Ohio Op. 351, 29 N.E.2d 441 (6th Dist. Lucas County 1940)

11 ALR6th 695—§ 10, 15

Smith v. McDuffee, 72 Or. 276, 142 P. 558 (1914)

65 ALR5th 407—§ 3

Smith v. McFerron, 540 N.E.2d 1273 (Ind. Ct. App. 1989)

97 ALR6th 375—§ 5, 7

Smith v. McGee, 2007 WL 4191725 (S.D. Miss. 2007)

65 ALR6th 93—§ 63

Smith v. McLaughlin, 1984 WL 14219 (Ohio Ct. App. 6th Dist. Lucas County 1984)
17 ALR6th 159—§ 40

Smith v. McMillan, 841 S.W.2d 172 (Ky. 1992)
5 ALR5th 875—§ 48

Smith v. McNamara, 395 F.2d 896, 4 A.L.R. Fed. 335 (10th Cir. 1968)
100 ALR6th 335—§ 6

Smith v. McNulty, 293 F.2d 924 (CA5 Fla. 1961)
12 ALR5th 195—§ 13

Smith v. Meadows Mills, Inc., 60 F. Supp. 2d 911, Prod. Liab. Rep. (CCH) ¶ 15649 (E.D. Wis. 1999)
109 ALR5th 301—§ 4, 21
112 ALR5th 113—§ 6
13 ALR6th 355—§ 4, 20

Smith v. Mehaffy, 30 P.3d 727 (Colo. Ct. App. 2000)
13 ALR6th 1—§ 4, 6

Smith v. Menet, 175 Ill. App. 3d 714, 125 Ill. Dec. 249, 530 N.E.2d 277 (2d Dist. 1988)
97 ALR6th 83—§ 19, 29

Smith v. Mensing, 86 Or. App. 285, 739 P.2d 595 (1987)
12 ALR6th 1—§ 4

Smith v. Mercy Hosp., 597 So. 2d 114 (La. Ct. App. 4th Cir. 1992)
82 ALR5th 149—§ 2, 5, 53
97 ALR5th 1—§ 20
108 ALR5th 1—§ 17

Smith v. MERS, 2011 WL 4469148 (E.D. Mich. 2011)
86 ALR6th 411—§ 5

Smith v. Methodist Hospitals of Memphis, 995 S.W.2d 584 (Tenn. Ct. App. 1999)
17 ALR6th 1—§ 13

Smith v. Metropolitan Dade County, 338 So. 2d 878 (Fla. 3d DCA 1976)
95 ALR6th 85—§ 21

Smith v. Metropolitan Life Ins. Co., 550 F. Supp. 896 (N.D. Ill. 1982)
6 ALR5th 297—§ 5, 10

Smith v. Miami Farmers' Mut. Fire Ins. Co., 125 Kan. 10, 262 P. 552 (1928)
87 ALR6th 319—§ 60

Smith v. Michigan Basic Property Ins. Assn., 441 Mich. 181, 490 N.W.2d 864 (1992)
1 ALR5th 817—§ 12

Smith v. Michigan State University, 1998 WL 1989867 (Mich. Ct. App. 1998)
102 ALR5th 1—§ 5, 7

Smith v. Midland Brake, Inc., a Div. of Echlin, Inc., 138 F.3d 1304, 98 A.D. Cas. (BNA) 1560, 72 Empl. Prac. Dec. (CCH) ¶ 45248 (10th Cir. 1998)
99 ALR5th 65—§ 9

Smith v. Milford, 89 Conn. 24, 92 A. 675 (1914)
10 ALR5th 371—§ 11

Smith v. Miliken, 247 Ga. 369, 276 S.E.2d 35 (1981)
14 ALR5th 242—§ 18

Smith v. Miller, 249 Md. 390, 239 A.2d 900 (1968)
38 ALR5th 357—§ 14

Smith v. Miller Brewing Co. Health Benefits Program, 860 F. Supp. 855 (M.D. Ga. 1994)
23 ALR5th 241—§ 37

Smith v. Millers Mut. Ins. Co., 419 So. 2d 59 (La. Ct. App. 2d Cir. 1982)
8 ALR6th 549—§ 5

Smith v. Milliken & Co., 189 Ga. App. 897, 377 S.E.2d 916 (1989)
12 ALR5th 508—§ 3

Smith v. Mimnaugh, 105 Mich. App. 209, 306 N.W.2d 454 (1981)
72 ALR5th 469—§ 2

Smith v. Mission Associates Ltd. Partnership, 225 F. Supp. 2d 1293 (D. Kan. 2002)
7 ALR6th 135—§ 4

Smith v. Mitchell, 6 Ga. 458 (1849)
19 ALR5th 622—§ 58

Smith v. Mitchell, 348 F.3d 177, 2003 FED App. 0381P (6th Cir. 2003)
102 ALR6th 417—§ 11, 31

Smith v. Mitchell, 624 F.3d 1235 (9th Cir. 2010)
76 ALR6th 587—§ 28

Smith v. Mitlof, 130 F. Supp. 2d 578 (S.D. N.Y. 2001)
66 ALR6th 185—§ 9

Smith v. Mitre Corp., 949 F. Supp. 943, 69 Empl. Prac. Dec. (CCH) ¶ 44506, 37 Fed. R. Serv. 3d 54 (D. Mass. 1997)
105 ALR5th 351—§ 3, 6, 9

Smith v. Moffat, 73 Cal. App. 3d 86, 140 Cal. Rptr. 566 (4th Dist. 1977)
5 ALR5th 875—§ 3, 23

Smith v. Monongahela Power Co., 189 W. Va. 237, 429 S.E.2d 643 (1993)
17 ALR6th 1—§ 26

Smith v. Monroe, 1 S.W.2d 358 (Tex. Civ. App. 1927)
32 ALR5th 673—§ 7

Smith v. Monro Muffler Brake, Inc., 713 N.Y.S.2d 581 (App. Div. 4th Dep't 2000)
52 ALR5th 1—§ 4

Smith v. Monsanto Co., 9 F. Supp. 2d 1113 (E.D. Mo. 1998)
52 ALR5th 1—§ 8

Smith v. Montgomery Ward & Co., 232 So. 2d 195 (Fla. Dist. Ct. App. 4th Dist. 1970)
1 ALR6th 297—§ 4, 26

Smith v. Montgomery Ward & Co., Inc., 567 F. Supp. 1331, 32 Fair Empl. Prac. Cas. (BNA) 995, 114 L.R.R.M. (BNA) 3678, 115 L.R.R.M. (BNA) 4283, 33 Empl. Prac. Dec. (CCH) ¶ 34155 (D. Colo. 1983)
125 ALR5th 457—§ 3

Smith v. Moore, 220 N.C. 165, 16 S.E.2d 701 (1941)
27 ALR5th 174—§ 58

Smith v. Moore, 749 A.2d 132 (D.C. 2000)
96 ALR6th 269—§ 41

Smith v. Morales, 2008 WL 4909630 (Minn. Ct. App. 2008)
52 ALR6th 623—§ 8

Smith v. Morris, Manning & Martin, LLP, 264 Ga. App. 24, 589 S.E.2d 840 (2003)
9 ALR6th 285—§ 7, 9, 13

Smith v. Moughan, 442 So. 2d 338 (Fla. App. D5 1983)
47 ALR5th 129—§ 10

Smith v. M. Spiegel & Sons, Inc., 31 App. Div. 2d 819, 298 N.Y.S.2d 47 (2d Dep't 1969)
38 ALR5th 737—§ 3, 10

Smith v. Mullin, 379 F.3d 919 (10th Cir. 2004)
102 ALR6th 417—§ 24

Smith v. Murphy, 267 A.D. 468, 46 N.Y.S.2d 774 (3d Dep't 1944)
80 ALR6th 635—§ 9

Smith v. Nace, 824 A.2d 416 (Pa. Commw. Ct. 2003)
91 ALR6th 435—§ 26, 68, 101

Smith v. National City Mortg., 2010 WL 3338537 (W.D. Tex. 2010)
104 ALR6th 485—§ 5

Smith v. National Indem. Co., 57 Wis. 2d 706, 205 N.W.2d 365 (1973)
29 ALR5th 469—§ 4

Smith v. National Life & Acci. Ins. Co., 351 So. 2d 217 (La. App. 4th Cir. 1977)
23 ALR5th 241—§ 12, 15

Smith v. Nationstar Mortg., LLC, 2010 WL 4539520 (E.D. Mich. 2010)
86 ALR6th 411—§ 5

Smith v. Nationwide Mut. Ins. Co., 107 Ohio App. 3d 769, 669 N.E.2d 512 (Shelby Co. 1995)
40 ALR5th 603—§ 9

Smith v. Nationwide Mut. Ins. Co., 306 So. 2d 385 (La. App. 3d Cir. 1975)
23 ALR5th 241—§ 15

Smith v. Navistar Intern. Transp. Corp., 737 F. Supp. 1446, Prod. Liab. Rep. (CCH) ¶ 11983 (D. Md. 1988)
13 ALR6th 355—§ 5, 32
18 ALR6th 629—§ 11

Smith v. Nelson, 149 Colo. 200, 368 P.2d 566 (1962)
25 ALR5th 233—§ 12, 19, 20, 24

Smith v. Neumann, 289 Ill. App. 3d
1056, 225 Ill. Dec. 168, 682 N.E.2d
1245 (2d Dist. 1997)
92 ALR5th 273—§ 5, 25

Smith v. Neville, 539 N.W.2d 679 (S.D.
1995)
64 ALR5th 519—§ 11

Smith v. New Jersey, 2013 WL 3658786
(D.N.J. 2013)
95 ALR6th 641—§ 8

Smith v. Newsome, 815 F.2d 1386 (11th
Cir. 1987)
64 ALR5th 671—§ 13, 14

Smith v. New York, 68 N.Y. 552 (1877)
7 ALR5th 187—§ 2, 17

Smith v. New York, 2006 WL 1725665
(U.S. 2006)
16 ALR6th 767—§ 25

Smith v. New York City Health and
Hospitals Corp., 211 A.D.2d 483,
621 N.Y.S.2d 319 (1st Dep't 1995)
81 ALR5th 167—§ 4, 7

Smith v. New York City Health & Hospitals Corp., 284 A.D.2d 121, 726
N.Y.S.2d 89 (1st Dep't 2001)
121 ALR5th 157—§ 18

Smith v. New York City Housing Authority, 689 N.Y.S.2d 237 (App.
Div. 2d Dep't 1999)
43 ALR5th 207—§ 25

Smith v. New York Life Ins. Co., 579
F.2d 1267 (5th Cir. 1978)
116 ALR5th 247—§ 5

Smith v. Nichols, 270 Ga. 550, 512
S.E.2d 279 (1999)
85 ALR6th 229—§ 10

Smith v. Nickoloff, 283 Mich. 188, 277
N.W. 880 (1938)
76 ALR5th 337—§ 14

Smith v. Norman, 586 S.W.2d 84 (Mo.
App. 1979)
45 ALR5th 251—§ 6 to 8

Smith v. Normant, 13 Tenn. 271, 5 Yer.
271, 1833 WL 1201 (Ct. Err. &
App. 1833)
97 ALR5th 537—§ 30

Smith v. North Dakota Workers Compensation Bureau, 2000 N.D. 51,
608 N.W.2d 250 (N.D. 2000)
20 ALR5th 346—§ 12

Smith v. O'Connell, 986 F. Supp. 73
(D.R.I. 1997)
101 ALR5th 1—§ 4

Smith v. O'Connell, 997 F. Supp. 226
(D.R.I. 1998)
5 ALR5th 530—§ 6.5

Smith v. O'Donnell, 5 P.2d 690 (Cal.
App. 2d Dist. 1931)
64 ALR5th 235—§ 7

Smith v. Officers & Directors of Kart-N-
Karry, Inc., 346 So. 2d 313 (La.
App. 1977)
40 ALR5th 1—§ 2, 7

Smith v. Ogden & N. W. R. Co., 33 Utah
129, 93 P. 185 (1907)
17 ALR5th 547—§ 53, 56

Smith v. Oglesby, 33 S.C. 194, 11 S.E.
687 (1890)
87 ALR6th 495—§ 58

Smith v. Oklahoma Publication Co.,
2008 WL 1840751 (N.D. Okla.
2008)
95 ALR6th 341—§ 22, 43

Smith v. Old Warson Dev. Co., 479
S.W.2d 795 (Mo. 1972)
8 ALR5th 312—§ 11

Smith v. Olger, 2008 WL 5111900
(W.D. Mich. 2008)
89 ALR6th 1—§ 29

Smith v. Olympic Bank, 103 Wash. 2d
418, 693 P.2d 92, 40 U.C.C. Rep.
Serv. 519 (1985)
117 ALR5th 155—§ 12

Smith v. O'Neal, 850 S.W.2d 797 (Tex.
App. Houston 14th Dist. 1993)
18 ALR6th 325—§ 11, 22, 36, 57, 74

Smith v. Orkin Exterminating Co., 540
So. 2d 363, 13 A.L.R.5th 962 (La.
App. 1st Cir. 1989)
13 ALR5th 217—§ 2, 5

Smith v. Ortho Pharmaceutical Corp.,
770 F. Supp. 1561 (N.D. Ga. 1991)
29 ALR5th 534—§ 2
54 ALR5th 1—§ 30

Smith v. Overhead Door Corp. of Texas, 859 S.W.2d 151 (Mo. Ct. App. W.D. 1993)
93 ALR6th 463—§ 7
Smith v. Owen, 75 Tenn. 53 (1881)
67 ALR5th 587—§ 3
Smith v. Painter, 408 S.W.2d 785 (Tex. Civ. App. Eastland 1966)
69 ALR5th 1—§ 5
Smith v. Palace Transp. Co., 142 Misc. 93, 253 N.Y.S. 87 (Mun. Ct. 1931)
61 ALR5th 635—§ 6, 21
Smith v. Paoli Popcorn Co., 260 Neb. 460, 618 N.W.2d 452 (2000)
101 ALR5th 563—§ 4, 5
Smith v. Paris Intern. Corp., 267 A.D.2d 223, 699 N.Y.S.2d 490 (2d Dep't 1999)
99 ALR5th 1—§ 3
Smith v. Park, 31 Minn. 70, 16 N.W. 490 (1883)
109 ALR5th 421—§ 5, 6, 13, 17
Smith v. Parker, 25 Ill. App. 2d 530, 167 N.E.2d 19 (2d Dist. 1960)
102 ALR5th 647—§ 21
Smith v. Parker, 508 So. 2d 1262, 12 FLW 1300 (Fla. App. D5 1987)
53 ALR5th 287—§ 3, 12
Smith v. Paslode Corp., 799 F. Supp. 960, Prod. Liab. Rep. (CCH) ¶ 13365, 19 U.C.C. Rep. Serv. 2d (CBC) 394 (E.D. Mo. 1992)
12 ALR5th 1—§ 6
64 ALR5th 333—§ 3, 7, 31
75 ALR5th 229—§ 3, 8, 14, 17
Smith v. Pass, 95 N.C. App. 243, 382 S.E.2d 781 (1989)
15 ALR5th 119—§ 5, 14
Smith v. Paterson, 88 App. Div. 2d 917, 450 N.Y.S.2d 577 (2d Dep't 1982)
7 ALR5th 474—§ 187
Smith v. Pathmark Stores, Inc., 1998 WL 309916 (E.D. Pa. 1998)
83 ALR5th 1—§ 10
Smith v. Patterson, 159 N.C. 138, 74 S.E. 923 (1912)
58 ALR5th 535—§ 5

Smith v. Payne, 41 Media L. Rep. (BNA) 1299, 2012 WL 6712041 (N.D. Cal. 2012)
85 ALR6th 475—§ 4, 6
Smith v. Pearre, 96 Md. App. 376, 625 A.2d 349 (1993)
84 ALR5th 619—§ 6
97 ALR6th 83—§ 15
Smith v. Penbridge Associates, Inc., 440 Pa. Super. 410, 655 A.2d 1015, 26 U.C.C. Rep. Serv. 2d 273 (1995)
89 ALR5th 319—§ 19
Smith v. Pennsylvania Bd. of Probation and Parole, 546 Pa. 115, 683 A.2d 278 (1996)
29 ALR6th 237—§ 4, 15, 27
Smith v. Pennsylvania Power & Light Co., 50 Pa. D. & C. 581, 1944 WL 2281 (C.P. 1944)
95 ALR5th 29—§ 6
Smith v. Penta, 81 N.J. 65, 405 A.2d 350 (1979)
120 ALR5th 125—§ 14
Smith v. Perkins, 246 Ark. 427, 439 S.W.2d 275 (1969)
19 ALR5th 622—§ 2
Smith v. Perlmutter, 145 Ill. App. 3d 783, 99 Ill. Dec. 783, 496 N.E.2d 358 (3d Dist. 1986)
108 ALR5th 385—§ 7
Smith v. Phillips, 455 U.S. 209, 71 L. Ed. 2d 78, 102 S. Ct. 940 (1982)
3 ALR5th 963—§ 5, 6
Smith v. Phillips, 2010 WL 1221436 (Tenn. Ct. App. 2010)
79 ALR6th 487—§ 28
Smith v. Piedmont Airlines, Inc., 728 F. Supp. 914 (S.D. N.Y. 1989)
32 ALR5th 1—§ 7
Smith v. Pinkerton's Sec. and Investigations, 146 N.C. App. 278, 552 S.E.2d 682 (2001)
107 ALR5th 441—§ 14
Smith v. Pinkerton's Sec. and Investigations, 146 N.C. App. 278, 552 S.E.2d 682, 109 A.L.R.5th 759 (2001)
109 ALR5th 161—§ 4, 19

20 ALR6th 641—§ 23
Smith v. Pinner, 68 Ariz. 115, 201 P.2d 741 (1948)
39 ALR6th 155—§ 4
Smith v. Pinner, 891 F.2d 784 (10th Cir. 1989)
99 ALR5th 65—§ 13
Smith v. Pitchford, 219 Ill. App. 3d 152, 161 Ill. Dec. 767, 579 N.E.2d 24 (5th Dist. 1991)
11 ALR5th 127—§ 4, 12, 37
Smith v. Plati, 258 F.3d 1167, 155 Ed. Law Rep. 1090, 29 Media L. Rep. (BNA) 2305 (10th Cir. 2001)
30 ALR6th 299—§ 12
Smith v. Pocono Country Place Property Owners Ass'n, 686 F. Supp. 1053 (M.D. Pa. 1987)
19 ALR5th 1—§ 44
44 ALR5th 193—§ 42
Smith v. Polar Cia de Navegacion, Ltda, 15 Misc. 2d 301, 181 N.Y.S.2d 368 (1958)
56 ALR5th 757—§ 3
Smith v. Pollack Co., 9 La. App. 432, 121 So. 240 (1928)
1 ALR5th 401—§ 2, 7
Smith v. Pollock Co., 3 La. App. 125 (1925)
1 ALR5th 401—§ 3, 6
Smith v. Portland Traction Co., 220 Or. 215, 349 P.2d 286 (1960)
10 ALR5th 371—§ 6
Smith v. Positive Productions, 419 F. Supp. 2d 437 (S.D. N.Y. 2005)
42 ALR6th 1—§ 14
Smith v. Post-Tensioned Systems, Inc., 537 S.W.2d 144, 19 U.C.C.R.S. 844 (Tex. Civ. App. Fort Worth 1976)
49 ALR5th 1—§ 10
Smith v. Powell, 109 Ill. App. 3d 814, 65 Ill. Dec. 383, 441 N.E.2d 175 (4th Dist. 1982)
104 ALR5th 331—§ 2, 5
Smith v. Price, 74 N.C. App. 413, 328 S.E.2d 811 (1985)
2 ALR5th 301—§ 7
2 ALR5th 337—§ 2, 7

Smith v. Price, 315 N.C. 523, 340 S.E.2d 408 (1986)
2 ALR5th 301—§ 7
2 ALR5th 337—§ 7
Smith v. Price, 616 F.2d 1371 (5th Cir. 1980)
123 ALR5th 411—§ 56
Smith v. Printup, 254 Kan. 315, 866 P.2d 985 (1993)
103 ALR5th 379—§ 7
Smith v. Privette, 128 N.C. App. 490, 495 S.E.2d 395, 13 I.E.R. Cas. (BNA) 1228, 72 Empl. Prac. Dec. (CCH) ¶ 45165 (1998)
5 ALR5th 530—§ 5
101 ALR5th 1—§ 4
Smith v. Prudential Securities Inc., 846 F. Supp. 978 (M.D. Fla. 1994)
67 ALR5th 179—§ 3, 11
Smith v. Pullan, 1999 WL 1442002 (Del. Super. Ct. 1999)
116 ALR5th 433—§ 4
Smith v. Pust, 19 Cal. App. 4th 263, 23 Cal. Rptr. 2d 364 (4th Dist. 1993)
99 ALR5th 445—§ 7
Smith v. Putnam, 145 App. Div. 2d 383, 535 N.Y.S.2d 725 (1st Dep't 1988)
39 ALR5th 33—§ 10
Smith v. QHG of Dothan, Inc., 872 So. 2d 197 (Ala. Civ. App. 2003)
63 ALR6th 187—§ 6
Smith v. Quarles Drilling Co., 741 So. 2d 829 (La. Ct. App. 3d Cir. 1999)
90 ALR6th 425—§ 8
Smith v. Rabago, 672 S.W.2d 38 (Tex. App. Houston (14th Dist.) 1984)
11 ALR5th 259—§ 3, 28, 29
Smith v. Radisson Suite Hotel New Orleans, 650 So. 2d 333 (La. Ct. App. 5th Cir. 1995)
80 ALR5th 417—§ 3
Smith v. Raleigh Dist. of North Carolina Conference of United Methodist Church, 63 F. Supp. 2d 694 (E.D. N.C. 1999)
123 ALR5th 385—§ 7, 8
Smith v. Raparot, 101 R.I. 565, 225 A.2d 666 (1967)

6 ALR5th 883—§ 7

Smith v. Rasmussen, 249 F.3d 755, 74 Soc. Sec. Rep. Serv. 20, 56 Fed. R. Evid. Serv. 1369 (8th Cir. 2001)

6062 ALR6th 7—§ 10, 12

Smith v. Ray, 409 Fed. Appx. 641 (4th Cir. 2011)

101 ALR6th 207—§ 1

Smith v. R.B. Jones of St. Louis, Inc., 672 S.W.2d 185 (Mo. Ct. App. E.D. 1984)

8 ALR6th 549—§ 12

Smith v. Reese, 221 A.2d 439 (D.C. 1966)

86 ALR6th 321—§ 11

91 ALR6th 171—§ 35

Smith v. Regents of University of California, 4 Cal. 4th 843, 16 Cal. Rptr. 2d 181, 844 P.2d 500, 80 Ed. Law Rep. 248 (1993)

73 ALR6th 281—§ 5

Smith v. Reitman, 389 F.2d 303 (D.C. Cir. 1967)

11 ALR6th 695—§ 44, 49, 53

18 ALR6th 325—§ 29

Smith v. Reliance Ins. Co. of Illinois, 1-888 La. App. 5 Cir. 1/15/02, 2002 WL 55972 (La. Ct. App. 5th Cir. 2002)

97 ALR5th 359—§ 13

Smith v. Reliance Ins. Co. of Illinois, 807 So. 2d 1010 (La. Ct. App. 5th Cir. 2002)

98 ALR5th 193—§ 16

Smith v. Reliance Ins. Co. of Illinois, 807 So. 2d 1010, 32 Envtl. L. Rep. 20478 (La. Ct. App. 5th Cir. 2002)

105 ALR5th 95—§ 3

Smith v. Richards, 38 U.S. 26, 10 L. Ed. 42 (1839)

8 ALR5th 312—§ 4

Smith v. Richardson, 277 Ala. 389, 171 So. 2d 96 (1965)

49 ALR5th 685—§ 3

Smith v. Richardson, 347 F. Supp. 265 (S.D. W. Va. 1972)

122 ALR5th 205—§ 3, 10, 45

Smith v. Rickards, 149 Cal. App. 2d 648, 308 P.2d 758 (3d Dist. 1957)

8 ALR5th 312—§ 4

Smith v. Roberts, 265 S.W.2d 915 (Tex. Civ. App. 1954)

58 ALR5th 535—§ 5, 19

Smith v. Robertson, 106 Ky. 472, 50 S.W. 852 (1899)

34 ALR5th 651—§ 4

Smith v. Robson, 2001 WL 1464773 (V.I. Terr. Ct. 2001)

70 ALR6th 209—§ 57

Smith v. Rogers, 16 Ga. 479, 1854 WL 1643 (1854)

44 ALR6th 481—§ 8

Smith v. Roosevelt County, 242 Mont. 27, 788 P.2d 895 (1990)

66 ALR5th 135—§ 9

Smith v. Rose, 760 F.2d 102 (6th Cir. 1985)

89 ALR6th 1—§ 77

Smith v. Roussel, 554 So. 2d 776 (La. App. 5th Cir. 1989)

50 ALR5th 1—§ 3, 6, 9, 10

Smith v. Ruberg, 167 Mich. App. 13, 421 N.W.2d 557 (1988)

24 ALR5th 1—§ 56

Smith v. Rural Mut. Ins. Co., 20 Wis. 2d 592, 123 N.W.2d 496 (1963)

112 ALR5th 621—§ 5, 6

Smith v. Russell, 456 So. 2d 462, 9 FLW 359, 11 Media L. R. 1275 (Fla. 1984)

44 ALR5th 193—§ 21

Smith v. Sabine Royalty Corp., 556 S.W.2d 365 (Tex. Civ. App. Amarillo 1977)

65 ALR5th 211—§ 2, 6, 8, 11

Smith v. Safeway Stores, Inc., 206 A.2d 264 (D.C. 1965)

1 ALR6th 297—§ 3, 4, 31

Smith v. Safeway Stores, Inc., 206 A.2d 264 (Dist. Col. App. 1965)

40 ALR5th 135—§ 2, 12

Smith v. Saget, 258 A.D.2d 641, 685 N.Y.S.2d 793 (2d Dep't 1999)

19 ALR5th 405—§ 3

Smith v. San Joaquin Light & Power
Corp., 59 Cal. App. 647, 211 P. 843
(1st Dist. 1922)
95 ALR5th 29—§ 6
Smith v. Sante Volpe, Inc., 1992 WL
19938 (Del. Super. Ct. 1992)
125 ALR5th 193—§ 5, 6
Smith v. Sapienza, 115 App. Div. 2d
723, 496 N.Y.S.2d 538 (2d Dep't
1985)
11 ALR5th 127—§ 5
Smith v. Sayles, 637 S.W.2d 714 (Mo.
App. 1982)
20 ALR5th 1—§ 16
33 ALR5th 303—§ 3, 11
Smith v. School Administrative Dist.
No. 58, 582 A.2d 247, 64 Ed. Law
Rep. 160 (Me. 1990)
64 ALR5th 519—§ 3
Smith v. School Dist. of Philadelphia,
158 F. Supp. 2d 599 (E.D. Pa. 2001)
105 ALR5th 499—§ 4
Smith v. Schulte, 671 So. 2d 1334 (Ala.
1995)
103 ALR5th 379—§ 6, 7
Smith v. Scott Lewis Chevrolet, Inc.,
843 S.W.2d 9 (Tenn. Ct. App. 1992)
115 ALR5th 709—§ 5
Smith v. Seamless Rubber Co., 111
Conn. 365, 150 A. 110, 69 A.L.R.
856 (1930)
11 ALR6th 351—§ 20, 27
Smith v. Sears Roebuck & Co., 84
S.W.2d 414 (Mo. Ct. App. 1935)
123 ALR5th 1—§ 6
Smith v. Sears, Roebuck & Co., 117
S.W.2d 658 (Mo. Ct. App. 1938)
83 ALR5th 589—§ 5
123 ALR5th 1—§ 7
Smith v. Sears, Roebuck & Co., 191 W.
Va. 563, 447 S.E.2d 255 (1994)
35 ALR5th 375—§ 3, 44, 50
Smith v. Sears, Roebuck and Co., 276 F.
Supp. 2d 603 (S.D. Miss. 2003)
8 ALR6th 399—§ 4
Smith v. Secretary, Dept. of Corrections,
572 F.3d 1327 (11th Cir. 2009)
92 ALR6th 549—§ 4, 24

Smith v. Secretary, Dept. of Corrections,
2007 WL 2302207 (M.D. Fla. 2007)
92 ALR6th 549—§ 3, 24
Smith v. Secretary of Health, Ed. and
Welfare, 431 F.2d 1241 (5th Cir.
1970)
122 ALR5th 205—§ 2, 3, 10, 38
Smith v. Secretary of New Mexico Dept.
of Corrections, 50 F.3d 801 (10th
Cir. 1995)
55 ALR6th 391—§ 6
Smith v. Seene, 2004 WL 406978 (Cal.
App. 4th Dist. 2004)
45 ALR6th 493—§ 67
Smith v. Seiber, 127 Ill. App. 3d 950, 82
Ill. Dec. 697, 469 N.E.2d 231 (5th
Dist. 1984)
12 ALR5th 195—§ 6, 31
Smith v. Selco Products, Inc., 96 N.C.
App. 151, 385 S.E.2d 173, CCH
Prod. Liab. Rep. ¶ 12349 (1989)
47 ALR5th 395—§ 2, 7
Smith v. Seven Points, 608 F. Supp. 458
(E.D. Tex. 1985)
12 ALR5th 195—§ 35
Smith v. Sex Offender Registry Bd., 65
Mass. App. Ct. 803, 844 N.E.2d 680
(2006)
64 ALR6th 1—§ 5
93 ALR6th 1—§ 41
Smith v. Shankman, 208 Cal. App. 2d
177, 25 Cal. Rptr. 195 (1st Dist.
1962)
2 ALR5th 769—§ 4
31 ALR5th 572—§ 9
Smith v. Shelby Ins. Co. of Shelby Ins.
Group, 936 S.W.2d 261 (Tenn. Ct.
App. 1996)
56 ALR5th 407—§ 4
Smith v. Shell Chemical Co., 333 F.
Supp. 2d 579 (M.D. La. 2004)
69 ALR6th 513—§ 3
Smith v. Shell Oil Co., 746 F.2d 1087
(CA5 La. 1984)
52 ALR5th 1—§ 8
Smith v. Sheppard, 301 A.D.2d 913, 754
N.Y.S.2d 122 (3d Dep't 2003)
115 ALR5th 251—§ 55

81 ALR6th 469—§ 4

Smith v. Shining Rock Golf Community, LLC, 2007 WL 2110958 (Mass. Super. Ct. 2007)

47 ALR6th 1—§ 51

Smith v. SHN Consulting Engineers & Geologists, Inc., 89 Cal. App. 4th 638, 107 Cal. Rptr. 2d 424 (1st Dist. 2001)

61 ALR6th 445—§ 26

Smith v. Silberman, 586 So. 2d 467 (Fla. Dist. Ct. App. 3d Dist. 1991)

84 ALR5th 399—§ 3, 12, 13

Smith v. Silver Cross Hosp., 312 Ill. App. 3d 210, 244 Ill. Dec. 722, 726 N.E.2d 697 (1st Dist. 2000)

58 ALR5th 535—§ 21

Smith v. Simmons, 4 Kan. App. 2d 60, 602 P.2d 546 (1979)

86 ALR5th 637—§ 6

Smith v. Simmons, 65 Fed. Appx. 250 (10th Cir. 2003)

63 ALR6th 1—§ 53

Smith v. Simpson, 648 P.2d 677 (Colo. App. 1982)

12 ALR5th 195—§ 13
52 ALR5th 1—§ 8

Smith v. Simpson, 2007 WL 4215622 (W.D. Ky. 2007)

52 ALR6th 1—§ 32

Smith v. Sioux City, 119 Iowa 50, 93 N.W. 81 (1903)

20 ALR5th 1—§ 36, 48

Smith v. Skagit County, 75 Wash. 2d 715, 453 P.2d 832 (1969)

73 ALR5th 223—§ 10

Smith v. Smathers, 372 So. 2d 427 (Fla. 1979)

12 ALR6th 523—§ 7, 14

Smith v. Smith, 1 Wis. 2d 174, 83 N.W.2d 672 (1957)

53 ALR5th 375—§ 31

Smith v. Smith, 30 Del. 283, 7 Boyce 283, 105 A. 833 (Super. Ct. 1919)

101 ALR6th 455—§ 3

Smith v. Smith, 40 Or. App. 257, 594 P.2d 1292 (1979)

67 ALR5th 1—§ 22

Smith v. Smith, 71 N.C. App. 242, 322 S.E.2d 393 (1984)

3 ALR6th 447—§ 5, 19

Smith v. Smith, 77 Ind. 80, 1881 WL 6628 (1881)

23 ALR6th 1—§ 10

Smith v. Smith, 79 Md. App. 650, 558 A.2d 798 (1989)

120 ALR5th 229—§ 7, 14
124 ALR5th 441—§ 3, 8

Smith v. Smith, 81 Ind. App. 566, 142 N.E. 128 (Div. 1 1924)

118 ALR5th 513—§ 3

Smith v. Smith, 89 Ariz. 84, 358 P.2d 183 (1960)

28 ALR5th 46—§ 14

Smith v. Smith, 90 Ariz. 190, 367 P.2d 230 (1961)

124 ALR5th 203—§ 8, 9

Smith v. Smith, 104 N.C. App. 788, 411 S.E.2d 197 (1991)

9 ALR5th 568—§ 15, 16

Smith v. Smith, 108 So. 2d 761 (Fla. 1959)

69 ALR5th 219—§ 3

Smith v. Smith, 111 N.C. App. 460, 433 S.E.2d 196 (1993)

39 ALR6th 205—§ 7

Smith v. Smith, 113 Mich. App. 148, 317 N.W.2d 324 (1982)

30 ALR5th 139—§ 4, 8

Smith v. Smith, 115 Cal. App. 2d 92, 251 P.2d 720 (1952)

50 ALR5th 653—§ 4

Smith v. Smith, 125 Mich. App. 164, 335 N.W.2d 657 (1983)

32 ALR5th 673—§ 4

Smith v. Smith, 125 N.H. 336, 480 A.2d 158 (1984)

55 ALR5th 647—§ 3

Smith v. Smith, 133 Ariz. 384, 651 P.2d 1209 (App. 1982)

34 ALR5th 447—§ 13

Smith v. Smith, 150 Ill. App. 3d 34, 103 Ill. Dec. 785, 501 N.E.2d 1323 (3d Dist. 1986)

49 ALR5th 441—§ 18

Smith v. Smith, 162 A.D.2d 346, 557 N.Y.S.2d 22 (1st Dep't 1990)
124 ALR5th 537—§ 3, 4, 9
Smith v. Smith, 172 Colo. 516, 474 P.2d 619 (1970)
53 ALR5th 375—§ 14
Smith v. Smith, 175 Misc. 2d 189, 668 N.Y.S.2d 336 (Fam. Ct. 1998)
5 ALR5th 788—§ 10
Smith v. Smith, 177 Wis. 2d 128, 501 N.W.2d 850 (Ct. App. 1993)
76 ALR5th 191—§ 3
Smith v. Smith, 190 W. Va. 402, 438 S.E.2d 582 (1993)
59 ALR6th 433—§ 31, 91
Smith v. Smith, 197 W. Va. 505, 475 S.E.2d 881 (1996)
39 ALR6th 205—§ 7
Smith v. Smith, 198 Misc. 400, 98 N.Y.S.2d 802 (1950)
52 ALR5th 221—§ 32
Smith v. Smith, 226 N.C. 544, 39 S.E.2d 458 (1946)
32 ALR5th 673—§ 2
Smith v. Smith, 278 N.W.2d 155 (S.D. 1979)
4 ALR6th 401—§ 4
Smith v. Smith, 295 Ky. 50, 173 S.W.2d 813 (1943)
87 ALR6th 495—§ 70
Smith v. Smith, 307 Pa. Super. 544, 453 A.2d 1020 (1982)
70 ALR5th 377—§ 3
Smith v. Smith, 336 N.C. 575, 444 S.E.2d 420 (1994)
39 ALR6th 205—§ 7
Smith v. Smith, 340 Ill. App. 636, 92 N.E.2d 358 (1st Dist. 1950)
124 ALR5th 203—§ 15
Smith v. Smith, 349 So. 2d 529 (Miss. 1977)
14 ALR5th 557—§ 6, 14, 29
Smith v. Smith, 359 S.C. 393, 597 S.E.2d 188 (Ct. App. 2004)
11 ALR6th 125—§ 3
Smith v. Smith, 419 A.2d 1035 (Me. 1980)

11 ALR6th 125—§ 4, 6 to 8
36 ALR6th 1—§ 18, 22, 26
Smith v. Smith, 419 S.E.2d 232 (S.C. App. 1992)
17 ALR5th 366—§ 10
Smith v. Smith, 440 So. 2d 1095 (Ala. App. 1983)
17 ALR5th 366—§ 15
Smith v. Smith, 443 So. 2d 43 (Ala. Civ. App. 1983)
120 ALR5th 229—§ 7, 22
124 ALR5th 441—§ 12, 16
Smith v. Smith, 445 A.2d 666 (Dist. Col. App. 1982)
17 ALR5th 366—§ 21
Smith v. Smith, 448 So. 2d 381 (Ala. Civ. App. 1984)
26 ALR6th 331—§ 9
Smith v. Smith, 458 A.2d 711 (Del. Fam. Ct. 1983)
59 ALR6th 433—§ 55
Smith v. Smith, 470 So. 2d 1252 (Ala. App. 1985)
17 ALR5th 366—§ 28
Smith v. Smith, 473 S.W.2d 299 (Tex. Civ. App. Texarkana 1971)
80 ALR5th 533—§ 5
Smith v. Smith, 497 S.W.2d 418 (Ky. 1973)
69 ALR5th 219—§ 6
Smith v. Smith, 508 N.W.2d 222 (Minn. Ct. App. 1993)
5 ALR5th 550—§ 6
6 ALR5th 69—§ 3
21 ALR5th 396—§ 65
67 ALR5th 1—§ 19
Smith v. Smith, 517 So. 2d 274 (La. App. 1st Cir. 1987)
21 ALR5th 396—§ 19, 50
Smith v. Smith, 528 So. 2d 1055 (La. Ct. App. 5th Cir. 1988)
101 ALR6th 455—§ 4
Smith v. Smith, 544 S.W.2d 888 (Mo. Ct. App. 1976)
21 ALR6th 577—§ 12
Smith v. Smith, 558 S.W.2d 785 (Mo. Ct. App. 1977)

84 ALR5th 399—§ 3 to 5, 13
Smith v. Smith, 561 S.W.2d 714, 26
A.L.R.4th 1181 (Mo. App. 1978)
49 ALR5th 441—§ 12
Smith v. Smith, 578 So. 2d 1342 (Ala.
Civ. App. 1991)
34 ALR5th 57—§ 3
53 ALR5th 375—§ 17
Smith v. Smith, 579 P.2d 841 (Okla.
App. 1978)
4 ALR5th 403—§ 3, 14
Smith v. Smith, 594 N.E.2d 825 (Ind.
App. 1992)
21 ALR5th 396—§ 58
Smith v. Smith, 599 So. 2d 1182 (Ala.
Civ. App. 1991)
95 ALR5th 533—§ 3
99 ALR5th 475—§ 14
124 ALR5th 203—§ 3, 6
26 ALR6th 331—§ 3, 9
Smith v. Smith, 607 So. 2d 122 (Miss.
1992)
49 ALR5th 441—§ 2, 15
Smith v. Smith, 612 So. 2d 713 (Fla.
Dist. Ct. App. 2d Dist. 1993)
84 ALR5th 399—§ 3, 12, 13
Smith v. Smith, 614 So. 2d 394 (Miss.
1993)
34 ALR5th 57—§ 3
53 ALR5th 375—§ 17
Smith v. Smith, 637 S.E.2d 662 (Ga.
2006)
24 ALR6th 549—§ 33
Smith v. Smith, 653 A.2d 1259 (Pa.
Super. 1995)
9 ALR5th 568—§ 10
Smith v. Smith, 676 N.E.2d 388 (Ind. Ct.
App. 1997)
109 ALR5th 1—§ 3
Smith v. Smith, 683 S.W.2d 651 (Mo.
App. 1984)
49 ALR5th 441—§ 11
Smith v. Smith, 724 S.W.2d 541 (Mo.
App. 1986)
17 ALR5th 366—§ 30
Smith v. Smith, 737 So. 2d 641 (Fla.
Dist. Ct. App. 1st Dist. 1999)

76 ALR5th 191—§ 3
Smith v. Smith, 793 N.E.2d 282, 120
A.L.R.5th 739 (Ind. Ct. App. 2003)
120 ALR5th 229—§ 7, 23
Smith v. Smith, 797 S.W.2d 879 (Mo.
App. 1990)
44 ALR5th 1—§ 3
Smith v. Smith, 830 F.2d 11 (CA2 N.Y.
1987)
9 ALR5th 321—§ 9, 11, 13
12 ALR5th 546—§ 4, 5
Smith v. Smith, 1994 WL 45449 (Tenn.
Ct. App. 1994)
11 ALR6th 125—§ 20
Smith v. Smith, 1994 WL 814265 (Del.
Fam. Ct. 1994)
11 ALR6th 125—§ 18, 20
Smith v. Smith, 1996 WL 17188 (Tenn.
Ct. App. 1996)
86 ALR6th 1—§ 25, 28
Smith v. Smith, 1997 WL 723297 (Neb.
Ct. App. 1997)
59 ALR5th 489—§ 6
Smith v. Smith, 1998 OK CIV APP 71,
963 P.2d 24 (Okla. Civ. App. Div. 3
1998)
51 ALR5th 241—§ 6
Smith v. Smith, 1999 WL 1059692
(Tenn. Ct. App. 1999)
11 ALR6th 125—§ 3, 4, 6, 21
Smith v. Smith, 1999 WL 1488950
(Ohio Ct. App. 11th Dist. Trumbull
County 1999)
109 ALR5th 1—§ 5, 9, 10
Smith v. Smith, 2001 WL 242562 (Tenn.
Ct. App. 2001)
59 ALR6th 433—§ 78
Smith v. Smith, 2002 WL 31777836
(Tex. App. Beaumont 2002)
57 ALR6th 163—§ 40
Smith v. Smith, 2003-Ohio-1478, 2003
WL 1524636 (Ohio Ct. App. 9th
Dist. Summit County 2003)
18 ALR6th 97—§ 33
Smith v. Smith, 2013 WL 3154999 (Ala.
Civ. App. 2013)
90 ALR6th 451—§ 66

Smith v. Sneed, 638 So. 2d 1252 (Miss. 1994)

   4 ALR5th 273—§ 11, 26

   11 ALR6th 1—§ 4

Smith v. Sno Eagles Snowmobile Club, Inc., 823 F.2d 1193 (7th Cir. 1987)

   98 ALR6th 231—§ 14, 15, 39, 94, 97

Smith v. Snowden Tp., 348 Pa. 187, 34 A.2d 515 (1943)

   19 ALR5th 622—§ 32, 37, 47

Smith v. South Carolina Election Com'n, 874 F. Supp. 2d 483 (D.S.C. 2012)

   104 ALR6th 547—§ 20

Smith v. South Dakota, 2011 WL 500027 (D.S.D. 2011)

   65 ALR6th 329—§ 4

Smith v. Southeastern Properties, Ltd., 776 S.W.2d 106 (Tenn. Ct. App. 1989)

   94 ALR6th 111—§ 13

Smith v. Southern Pacific Transp. Co., 467 So. 2d 70 (La. App. 4th Cir. 1985)

   48 ALR5th 129—§ 15

Smith v. Southwest Florida Blood Bank, Inc., 578 So. 2d 501 (Fla. App. D2 1991)

   12 ALR5th 1—§ 6

Smith v. Spence & Spence, Attorneys, 80 N.C. App. 636, 343 S.E.2d 256 (1986)

   18 ALR6th 195—§ 38

Smith v. Spencer, 81 N.J. Eq. 389, 87 A. 158 (1913)

   25 ALR5th 233—§ 19

Smith v. Spisak, 130 S. Ct. 676 (2010)

   56 ALR6th 679—§ 16

Smith v. Spokane County, 89 Wash. App. 340, 948 P.2d 1301 (Div. 3 1997)

   106 ALR5th 523—§ 44

Smith v. Squire Homes, Inc., 38 A.D.2d 879, 329 N.Y.S.2d 243, 10 U.C.C. Rep. Serv. (CBC) 312 (4th Dep't 1972)

   61 ALR5th 473—§ 3

   84 ALR5th 69—§ 19

Smith v. Stacy, 198 W. Va. 498, 482 S.E.2d 115 (1996)

   87 ALR5th 473—§ 4

   11 ALR6th 1—§ 7

   13 ALR6th 1—§ 4

   15 ALR6th 427—§ 8

Smith v. Stanford Research Institute, 212 Cal. App. 2d 750, 28 Cal. Rptr. 481 (1st Dist. 1963)

   58 ALR5th 535—§ 7

Smith v. Stark, 67 N.Y.2d 693, 499 N.Y.S.2d 922, 490 N.E.2d 841, Prod. Liab. Rep. (CCH) ¶ 10944 (1986)

   65 ALR5th 105—§ 3

Smith v. State, 7 So. 3d 473 (Fla. 2009)

   71 ALR6th 625—§ 29

Smith v. State, 9 Tenn. 228, 1 Yer. 228, 1829 WL 488 (Ct. Err. & App. 1829)

   37 ALR6th 511—§ 18

Smith v. State, 15 S.W.2d 618 (Tex. Crim. App. 1929)

   105 ALR5th 529—§ 11

Smith v. State, 20 Md. App. 577, 318 A.2d 568 (1974)

   124 ALR5th 1—§ 4, 7

Smith v. State, 23 So. 3d 1277 (Fla. 2d DCA 2010)

   92 ALR6th 549—§ 4

Smith v. State, 26 Ill. Ct. Cl. 290, 1969 WL 8162 (Ill. Ct. Cl. 1969)

   53 ALR6th 305—§ 4

Smith v. State, 30 Ark. App. 111, 783 S.W.2d 72 (1990)

   7 ALR5th 758—§ 14, 22

Smith v. State, 33 Ark. App. 37, 801 S.W.2d 655 (1990)

   11 ALR5th 1—§ 14

   11 ALR5th 831—§ 2

   57 ALR5th 141—§ 3

Smith v. State, 33 Tex. Crim. 513, 27 S.W. 137 (1894)

   50 ALR5th 467—§ 7, 10

Smith v. State, 36 Ala. App. 209, 55 So. 2d 202 (1951)

   24 ALR6th 747—§ 17

Smith v. State, 36 S.W.3d 908 (Tex. App. Houston 1st Dist. 2001)
89 ALR5th 629—§ 9

Smith v. State, 37 Ala. App. 116, 64 So. 2d 620 (1953)
99 ALR6th 113—§ 10

Smith v. State, 44 Tex. Crim. 137, 68 S.W. 995 (1902)
46 ALR5th 499—§ 3

Smith v. State, 49 Misc. 2d 985, 268 N.Y.S.2d 873 (Ct. Cl. 1966)
49 ALR6th 205—§ 18, 33, 54

Smith v. State, 50 Ark. 545, 8 S.W. 941 (1888)
50 ALR5th 467—§ 6

Smith v. State, 50 Md. App. 638, 440 A.2d 406 (1982)
97 ALR5th 293—§ 3, 14
71 ALR6th 335—§ 13

Smith v. State, 51 Md. App. 408, 443 A.2d 985 (1982)
56 ALR5th 385—§ 3

Smith v. State, 54 Ala. App. 237, 307 So. 2d 47 (Crim App. 1975)
50 ALR5th 467—§ 9

Smith v. State, 59 Ohio St. 350, 52 N.E. 826 (1898)
29 ALR5th 59—§ 7, 48

Smith v. State, 68 Ark. App. 106, 3 S.W.3d 712 (1999)
8 ALR6th 265—§ 16

Smith v. State, 72 Ga. 114, 1883 WL 2839 (1883)
54 ALR6th 429—§ 9

Smith v. State, 75 So. 3d 205 (Fla. 2011)
92 ALR6th 549—§ 4, 24

Smith v. State, 79 Okla. Crim. 151, 152 P.2d 279 (1944)
19 ALR5th 823—§ 2, 9, 11

Smith v. State, 83 P.3d 12 (Alaska Ct. App. 2004)
84 ALR6th 293—§ 25

Smith v. State, 92 Tex. Crim. 589, 245 S.W. 237 (1922)
105 ALR5th 529—§ 11

Smith v. State, 95 Ga. 472, 20 S.E. 291 (1894)
54 ALR6th 429—§ 17

Smith v. State, 95 Miss. 786, 49 So. 945 (1909)
101 ALR6th 499—§ 18

Smith v. State, 106 N.M. 368, 743 P.2d 124 (App. 1987)
45 ALR5th 173—§ 6

Smith v. State, 107 Ala. 139, 18 So. 306 (1895)
103 ALR6th 35—§ 16

Smith v. State, 110 Nev. 1094, 881 P.2d 649 (1994)
79 ALR5th 33—§ 9, 27, 55

Smith v. State, 112 Nev. 1269, 927 P.2d 14 (1996)
118 ALR5th 253—§ 19

Smith v. State, 113 Tex. Crim. 212, 18 S.W.2d 1068 (1929)
29 ALR5th 59—§ 3, 13

Smith v. State, 122 Ga. App. 470, 177 S.E.2d 485 (1970)
81 ALR5th 563—§ 3

Smith v. State, 126 Idaho 106, 878 P.2d 805 (Ct. App. 1994)
85 ALR5th 547—§ 2

Smith v. State, 127 Ga. App. 468, 193 S.E.2d 921 (1972)
19 ALR5th 823—§ 3, 7

Smith v. State, 139 Ga. App. 129, 227 S.E.2d 911 (1976)
43 ALR5th 1—§ 14
50 ALR5th 581—§ 2

Smith v. State, 141 Ga. App. 720, 234 S.E.2d 385 (1977)
72 ALR5th 529—§ 6
9 ALR6th 1—§ 6

Smith v. State, 145 Ala. 17, 40 So. 957 (1906)
50 ALR5th 467—§ 6

Smith v. State, 146 Idaho 822, 203 P.3d 1221 (2009)
63 ALR6th 351—§ 3

Smith v. State, 147 Ga. App. 549, 249 S.E.2d 353 (1978)
13 ALR5th 1—§ 2

Smith v. State, 148 Ga. App. 634, 252 S.E.2d 62 (1979)

15 ALR5th 391—§ 18
Smith v. State, 159 Ga. App. 349, 283
    S.E.2d 324 (1981)
104 ALR5th 165—§ 3
Smith v. State, 159 Md. App. 1, 857
    A.2d 1224 (2004)
50 ALR6th 1—§ 3, 8
Smith v. State, 160 Ga. App. 26, 285
    S.E.2d 749 (1981)
6 ALR5th 733—§ 2, 16
99 ALR6th 397—§ 17
Smith v. State, 160 Tex. Crim. 438, 272
    S.W.2d 104 (1954)
46 ALR5th 499—§ 3
Smith v. State, 165 S.W.3d 361 (Tex.
    Crim. App. 2005)
97 ALR6th 263—§ 16
Smith v. State, 167 S.W.3d 44 (Tex.
    App. Waco 2005)
55 ALR6th 391—§ 22
56 ALR6th 185—§ 23
Smith v. State, 182 So. 2d 461 (Fla. Dist.
    Ct. App. 2d Dist. 1966)
103 ALR5th 463—§ 5
Smith v. State, 187 Ind. 253, 118 N.E.
    954 (1918)
57 ALR6th 445—§ 15
Smith v. State, 195 Ga. App. 486, 393
    S.E.2d 743 (1990)
124 ALR5th 1—§ 5
Smith v. State, 198 Ind. 156, 152 N.E.
    803 (1926)
23 ALR6th 1—§ 4, 15
Smith v. State, 204 Ga. App. 576, 420
    S.E.2d 29 (1992)
18 ALR6th 519—§ 4
Smith v. State, 206 Ga. App. 184, 424
    S.E.2d 864 (1992)
86 ALR5th 59—§ 3 to 5
Smith v. State, 212 Miss. 497, 54 So. 2d
    739 (1951)
85 ALR5th 471—§ 6, 10
Smith v. State, 214 Ind. 169, 13 N.E.2d
    562 (1938)
13 ALR5th 1—§ 44
Smith v. State, 227 Ark. 332, 299
    S.W.2d 52 (1957)

54 ALR6th 429—§ 9, 27
Smith v. State, 229 Ga. 727, 194 S.E.2d
    82 (1972)
88 ALR6th 203—§ 62
Smith v. State, 231 Ga. App. 677, 499
    S.E.2d 663 (1998)
11 ALR5th 871—§ 5
Smith v. State, 232 Ga. App. 458, 501
    S.E.2d 622 (1998)
47 ALR5th 259—§ 3, 12, 14 to 16
Smith v. State, 233 Miss. 503, 102 So.
    2d 699 (1958)
41 ALR5th 171—§ 87
Smith v. State, 234 Ga. App. 586, 506
    S.E.2d 406 (1998)
12 ALR6th 267—§ 5
24 ALR6th 1—§ 21
Smith v. State, 236 Ga. App. 548, 512
    S.E.2d 19 (1999)
58 ALR6th 215—§ 7
Smith v. State, 237 Ind. 532, 146 N.E.2d
    86 (1957)
87 ALR6th 109—§ 31, 75
Smith v. State, 239 Ga. 477, 238 S.E.2d
    116 (1977)
54 ALR5th 575—§ 32
Smith v. State, 247 Ga. 612, 277 S.E.2d
    678, 18 A.L.R.4th 1144 (1981)
58 ALR5th 749—§ 6
Smith v. State, 248 Ala. 363, 27 So. 2d
    495 (1946)
20 ALR6th 479—§ 13
Smith v. State, 248 Ga. 507, 284 S.E.2d
    406 (1981)
53 ALR6th 81—§ 5
Smith v. State, 249 Ga. 801, 294 S.E.2d
    525 (1982)
98 ALR6th 455—§ 32
Smith v. State, 252 Ind. 425, 249 N.E.2d
    493 (1969)
20 ALR6th 479—§ 3
Smith v. State, 253 Ga. 536, 322 S.E.2d
    492 (1984)
1 ALR6th 657—§ 4
Smith v. State, 255 Ga. App. 580, 565
    S.E.2d 904 (2002)
57 ALR6th 445—§ 36

Smith v. State, 262 Ga. App. 614, 585 S.E.2d 888 (2003)

58 ALR6th 215—§ 11

Smith v. State, 264 Ga. 87, 441 S.E.2d 241, 94 Fulton County D R 1056 (1994)

55 ALR5th 125—§ 3, 8

Smith v. State, 267 Ga. 363, 478 S.E.2d 379 (1996)

86 ALR5th 59—§ 4, 5

Smith v. State, 267 Ga. 372, 477 S.E.2d 827 (1996)

16 ALR6th 329—§ 6
24 ALR6th 591—§ 6

Smith v. State, 267 Ind. 167, 368 N.E.2d 1154 (1977)

99 ALR6th 295—§ 5

Smith v. State, 267 S.W.3d 829 (Mo. Ct. App. E.D. 2008)

69 ALR6th 1—§ 10

Smith v. State, 268 Ga. 196, 486 S.E.2d 819 (1997)

58 ALR5th 749—§ 8

Smith v. State, 269 Ga. 72, 495 S.E.2d 280 (1998)

39 ALR5th 283—§ 56

Smith v. State, 270 Ga. 240, 510 S.E.2d 1 (1998)

10 ALR5th 700—§ 4

Smith v. State, 270 Ind. 93, 383 N.E.2d 324 (1978)

72 ALR5th 109—§ 9

Smith v. State, 272 Ind. 34, 395 N.E.2d 789 (1979)

36 ALR5th 255—§ 11

Smith v. State, 275 Ind. 642, 419 N.E.2d 743 (1981)

34 ALR6th 1—§ 12

Smith v. State, 277 Ga. 213, 586 S.E.2d 639 (2003)

98 ALR6th 455—§ 32

Smith v. State, 279 Ark. 68, 648 S.W.2d 490 (1983)

3 ALR6th 269—§ 24

Smith v. State, 287 Ga. 391, 697 S.E.2d 177 (2010)

74 ALR6th 373—§ 3, 9

Smith v. State, 292 So. 2d 69 (Fla. Dist. Ct. App. 3d Dist. 1974)

65 ALR5th 623—§ 9

Smith v. State, 294 Ga. App. 692, 670 S.E.2d 191 (2008)

71 ALR6th 1—§ 15

Smith v. State, 317 A.2d 20 (Del. 1974)

55 ALR6th 157—§ 76

Smith v. State, 318 Ark. 142, 883 S.W.2d 837 (1994)

39 ALR5th 283—§ 4, 40

Smith v. State, 320 So. 2d 420 (Fla. App. D2 1975)

34 ALR5th 125—§ 9

Smith v. State, 329 S.C. 280, 494 S.E.2d 626 (1997)

31 ALR6th 49—§ 10

Smith v. State, 330 So. 2d 59 (Fla. App. D1 1976)

14 ALR5th 89—§ 7, 11

Smith v. State, 344 A.2d 251 (Del. 1975)

100 ALR6th 535—§ 3

Smith v. State, 383 So. 2d 991 (Fla. Dist. Ct. App. 5th Dist. 1980)

99 ALR5th 557—§ 3, 10

Smith v. State, 399 So. 2d 70 (Fla. Dist. Ct. App. 5th Dist. 1981)

58 ALR6th 499—§ 30

Smith v. State, 408 N.E.2d 614 (Ind. App. 1980)

53 ALR5th 499—§ 2

Smith v. State, 409 So. 2d 455 (Ala. Crim. App. 1981)

86 ALR5th 59—§ 5

Smith v. State, 413 N.E.2d 652, 6 Media L. R. 2344 (Ind. App. 1980)

42 ALR5th 291—§ 25

Smith v. State, 419 So. 2d 563 (Miss. 1982)

58 ALR6th 499—§ 38, 97

Smith v. State, 432 N.E.2d 1363 (Ind. 1982)

59 ALR5th 1—§ 4, 6

Smith v. State, 438 So. 2d 896 (Fla. Dist. Ct. App. 2d Dist. 1983)

109 ALR5th 99—§ 6

For assistance, call 1-800-328-4880

Smith v. State, 445 So. 2d 227 (Miss. 1984)
83 ALR6th 465—§ 5, 6
Smith v. State, 455 N.E.2d 606 (Ind. 1983)
103 ALR6th 507—§ 14
Smith v. State, 460 So. 2d 343 (Ala. App. 1984)
7 ALR5th 758—§ 11
Smith v. State, 465 N.E.2d 702 (Ind. 1984)
72 ALR5th 109—§ 4
Smith v. State, 465 So. 2d 603, 10 FLW 729 (Fla. App. D3 1985)
55 ALR5th 125—§ 14, 23
Smith v. State, 470 So. 2d 1365 (Ala. Crim. App. 1985)
56 ALR6th 323—§ 7
Smith v. State, 475 N.E.2d 27 (Ind. 1985)
99 ALR6th 295—§ 13
Smith v. State, 475 So. 2d 633 (Ala. Crim. App. 1985)
37 ALR5th 703—§ 3
Smith v. State, 491 N.E.2d 193 (Ind. 1986)
116 ALR5th 373—§ 3, 5
Smith v. State, 502 N.E.2d 122 (Ind. Ct. App. 2d Dist. 1986)
119 ALR5th 379—§ 8
Smith v. State, 502 S.W.2d 814 (Tex. Crim. 1973)
24 ALR5th 465—§ 22, 40
Smith v. State, 506 N.E.2d 31 (Ind. 1987)
11 ALR5th 497—§ 6
Smith v. State, 510 P.2d 793 (Alaska 1973)
62 ALR5th 1—§ 9, 15
Smith v. State, 513 So. 2d 1367 (Fla. Dist. Ct. App. 1st Dist. 1987)
46 ALR6th 241—§ 15
Smith v. State, 513 S.W.2d 407 (Mo. 1974)
19 ALR6th 411—§ 19
Smith v. State, 515 So. 2d 149 (Ala. Crim. App. 1987)

74 ALR5th 319—§ 13
Smith v. State, 515 So. 2d 182, 12 FLW 541 (Fla. 1987)
10 ALR5th 700—§ 7, 30
Smith v. State, 517 So. 2d 1072 (La. App. 3d Cir. 1987)
42 ALR5th 1—§ 10
Smith v. State, 530 S.W.2d 827 (Tex. Crim. App. 1975)
11 ALR5th 831—§ 8
68 ALR5th 343—§ 3
Smith v. State, 532 So. 2d 50 (Fla. Dist. Ct. App. 2d Dist. 1988)
113 ALR5th 597—§ 3
Smith v. State, 549 N.E.2d 1101 (Ind. Ct. App. 1990)
65 ALR6th 537—§ 8, 12, 72
Smith v. State, 550 So. 2d 174 (Fla. Dist. Ct. App. 1st Dist. 1989)
9 ALR6th 633—§ 42
Smith v. State, 565 N.E.2d 1059 (Ind. 1991)
78 ALR6th 297—§ 35, 38, 62
Smith v. State, 584 So. 2d 1107 (Fla. App. D2 1991)
7 ALR5th 263—§ 7
Smith v. State, 589 So. 2d 423 (Fla. Dist. Ct. App. 2d Dist. 1991)
46 ALR6th 241—§ 8
Smith v. State, 589 So. 2d 798 (Ala. App. 1991)
27 ALR5th 593—§ 2
Smith v. State, 595 S.W.2d 120 (Tex. Crim. App. 1980)
93 ALR5th 527—§ 4
Smith v. State, 598 P.2d 1389 (Wyo. 1979)
85 ALR5th 547—§ 7
Smith v. State, 598 So. 2d 1063 (Fla. 1992)
113 ALR5th 597—§ 8
Smith v. State, 602 So. 2d 470 (Ala. Crim. App. 1992)
9 ALR6th 1—§ 17
Smith v. State, 606 So. 2d 174 (Ala. Crim. App. 1992)
114 ALR5th 173—§ 7

Smith v. State, 616 So. 2d 368 (Ala. App. 1992)
27 ALR5th 593—§ 2

Smith v. State, 628 S.W.2d 393 (Mo. Ct. App. E.D. 1982)
43 ALR6th 475—§ 12

Smith v. State, 639 So. 2d 543 (Ala. Crim. App. 1993)
93 ALR5th 527—§ 15
9 ALR6th 1—§ 10

Smith v. State, 643 So. 2d 709 (Fla. Dist. Ct. App. 4th Dist. 1994)
15 ALR6th 173—§ 14

Smith v. State, 650 P.2d 904 (Okla. Crim. App. 1982)
70 ALR5th 1—§ 4

Smith v. State, 658 N.E.2d 910 (Ind. Ct. App. 1995)
110 ALR5th 329—§ 5, 6

Smith v. State, 661 So. 2d 358 (Fla. Dist. Ct. App. 1st Dist. 1995)
88 ALR5th 67—§ 11

Smith v. State, 664 So. 2d 72 (Fla. Dist. Ct. App. 3d Dist. 1995)
21 ALR6th 771—§ 31

Smith v. State, 664 So. 2d 1047, 20 FLW D2647 (Fla. App. D2 1995)
15 ALR5th 391—§ 45

Smith v. State, 674 S.W.2d 634 (Mo. App. 1984)
8 ALR5th 713—§ 4, 8

Smith v. State, 675 S.W.2d 300 (Tex. App. Houston 1st Dist. 1984)
54 ALR6th 429—§ 9

Smith v. State, 677 So. 2d 1240 (Ala. Crim. App. 1995)
78 ALR5th 1—§ 23
90 ALR5th 453—§ 44

Smith v. State, 686 N.E.2d 1264 (Ind. 1997)
79 ALR5th 33—§ 40

Smith v. State, 687 So. 2d 875 (Fla. Dist. Ct. App. 2d Dist. 1997)
23 ALR6th 307—§ 44

Smith v. State, 690 So. 2d 733 (Fla. Dist. Ct. App. 4th Dist. 1997)
21 ALR6th 771—§ 5

Smith v. State, 698 So. 2d 1166 (Ala. Crim. App. 1997)
70 ALR5th 587—§ 24

Smith v. State, 713 N.E.2d 338 (Ind. Ct. App. 1999)
84 ALR5th 1—§ 13
62 ALR6th 161—§ 10

Smith v. State, 718 N.E.2d 794 (Ind. Ct. App. 1999)
118 ALR5th 253—§ 16

Smith v. State, 727 So. 2d 147 (Ala. Crim. App. 1998)
9 ALR6th 1—§ 17
35 ALR6th 127—§ 5
98 ALR6th 455—§ 27

Smith v. State, 734 N.E.2d 706 (Ind. Ct. App. 2000)
76 ALR5th 239—§ 19

Smith v. State, 739 So. 2d 545 (Ala. Crim. App. 1999)
29 ALR5th 59—§ 79

Smith v. State, 742 So. 2d 352 (Fla. Dist. Ct. App. 5th Dist. 1999)
7 ALR5th 263—§ 7

Smith v. State, 745 So. 2d 922 (Ala. Crim. App. 1999)
3 ALR6th 269—§ 24

Smith v. State, 754 S.W.2d 310 (Tex. App. Houston 1st Dist. 1988)
109 ALR5th 611—§ 3

Smith v. State, 765 N.E.2d 578 (Ind. 2002)
121 ALR5th 551—§ 4, 5, 7, 15

Smith v. State, 771 So. 2d 1189 (Fla. Dist. Ct. App. 5th Dist. 2000)
23 ALR6th 307—§ 8

Smith v. State, 773 P.2d 139 (Wyo. 1989)
36 ALR5th 255—§ 18
59 ALR5th 1—§ 3 to 6

Smith v. State, 779 N.E.2d 111 (Ind. Ct. App. 2002)
4 ALR6th 1—§ 10

Smith v. State, 784 S.W.2d 855 (Mo. Ct. App. E.D. 1990)
79 ALR5th 419—§ 3, 7

For assistance, call 1-800-328-4880

Smith v. State, 788 So. 2d 1131 (Fla. Dist. Ct. App. 2d Dist. 2001)
21 ALR6th 771—§ 5

Smith v. State, 789 S.W.2d 172 (Mo. Ct. App. E.D. 1990)
79 ALR5th 419—§ 9, 10

Smith v. State, 789 S.W.2d 350 (Tex. App. Amarillo 1990)
34 ALR6th 1—§ 12

Smith v. State, 795 So. 2d 788 (Ala. Crim. App. 2000)
83 ALR6th 255—§ 9

Smith v. State, 797 S.W.2d 243 (Tex. App. Corpus Christi 1990)
55 ALR5th 125—§ 3, 4, 7, 8
58 ALR6th 499—§ 46

Smith v. State, 829 S.W.2d 885 (Tex. App. Houston 1st Dist. 1992)
7 ALR6th 487—§ 20

Smith v. State, 835 So. 2d 927 (Miss. 2002)
56 ALR6th 185—§ 25

Smith v. State, 837 So. 2d 567 (Fla. Dist. Ct. App. 4th Dist. 2003)
21 ALR6th 771—§ 5

Smith v. State, 838 So. 2d 413 (Ala. Crim. App. 2002)
103 ALR6th 35—§ 23

Smith v. State, 839 So. 2d 489 (Miss. 2003)
2 ALR6th 551—§ 16

Smith v. State, 840 So. 2d 404 (Fla. 4th DCA 2003)
78 ALR6th 1—§ 13

Smith v. State, 840 S.W.2d 689 (Tex. App. Fort Worth 1992)
66 ALR5th 135—§ 44

Smith v. State, 854 So. 2d 684 (Fla. Dist. Ct. App. 2d Dist. 2003)
72 ALR6th 227—§ 11

Smith v. State, 859 S.W.2d 463 (Tex. App. Fort Worth 1993)
75 ALR5th 295—§ 18

Smith v. State, 861 N.E.2d 742 (Ind. Ct. App. 2007)
26 ALR6th 511—§ 27, 50

Smith v. State, 866 S.W.2d 760 (Tex. App. Houston (1st Dist.) 1993)
10 ALR5th 538—§ 10

Smith v. State, 869 So. 2d 425 (Miss. Ct. App. 2004)
69 ALR6th 1—§ 23

Smith v. State, 889 N.E.2d 836 (Ind. Ct. App. 2008)
79 ALR6th 1—§ 34, 35

Smith v. State, 908 So. 2d 273 (Ala. Crim. App. 2000)
83 ALR6th 255—§ 17

Smith v. State, 919 A.2d 539 (Del. 2006)
63 ALR6th 351—§ 3

Smith v. State, 919 S.W.2d 96 (Tex. Crim. App. 1996)
79 ALR5th 33—§ 42

Smith v. State, 931 So. 2d 790 (Fla. 2006)
92 ALR6th 549—§ 3, 24

Smith v. State, 949 S.W.2d 333 (Tex. App. Tyler 1996)
54 ALR5th 141—§ 3

Smith v. State, 957 A.2d 2 (Del. 2008)
103 ALR6th 35—§ 7

Smith v. State, 962 S.W.2d 178 (Tex. App. Houston 1st Dist. 1998)
103 ALR5th 463—§ 7

Smith v. State, 968 So. 2d 1054 (Fla. Dist. Ct. App. 5th Dist. 2007)
33 ALR6th 91—§ 38

Smith v. State, 968 S.W.2d 452 (Tex. App. Amarillo 1998)
24 ALR5th 465—§ 117

Smith v. State, 972 S.W.2d 551 (Mo. Ct. App. S.D. 1998)
71 ALR6th 1—§ 6

Smith v. State, 976 A.2d 172 (Del. 2009)
99 ALR6th 295—§ 8, 15

Smith v. State, 982 N.E.2d 393 (Ind. Ct. App. 2013)
93 ALR6th 275—§ 4

Smith v. State, 998 So. 2d 516 (Fla. 2008)
83 ALR6th 255—§ 27

Smith v. State, 1973 OK CR 243, 509 P.2d 1391 (Okla. Crim. App. 1973)

65 ALR6th 537—§ 8, 14, 47, 55, 62
Smith v. State, 1981 OK CR 41, 626 P.2d 1357 (Okla. Crim. App. 1981)
99 ALR6th 295—§ 5
Smith v. State, 1987 OK CR 75, 736 P.2d 531 (Okla. Crim. App. 1987)
9 ALR6th 1—§ 17
Smith v. State, 1993 OK CR 50, 863 P.2d 465 (Okla. Crim. App. 1993)
68 ALR6th 527—§ 33
Smith v. State, 1995 WL 316867 (Tex. App. Dallas 1995)
15 ALR6th 515—§ 10
Smith v. State, 1996 OK CR 13, 915 P.2d 927 (Okla. Crim. App. 1996)
24 ALR6th 1—§ 21
Smith v. State, 1999 WL 494991 (Alaska Ct. App. 1999)
85 ALR5th 547—§ 8
Smith v. State, 2000 WL 329024 (Ohio Ct. App. 10th Dist. Franklin County 2000)
53 ALR6th 305—§ 8
Smith v. State, 2000 WL 681033 (Ala. Crim. App. 2000)
85 ALR5th 471—§ 7
Smith v. State, 2000 WL 962751 (Tex. App. Austin 2000)
119 ALR5th 379—§ 2
Smith v. State, 2000 WL 1868419 (Ala. Crim. App. 2000)
3 ALR6th 269—§ 18, 25
Smith v. State, 2001 WL 931178 (Tex. App. Houston 14th Dist. 2001)
58 ALR6th 215—§ 5
Smith v. State, 2001 WL 1635948 (Tex. App. El Paso 2001)
67 ALR6th 103—§ 10, 15
Smith v. State, 2002 WL 193200 (Tex. App. Dallas 2002)
71 ALR6th 1—§ 5
Smith v. State, 2002 WL 799860 (Tex. App. Tyler 2002)
84 ALR6th 293—§ 17, 33
Smith v. State, 2002 WL 32341877 (Tex. App. Eastland 2002)
67 ALR6th 103—§ 5, 10

Smith v. State, 2004 WL 639643 (Tex. App. Dallas 2004)
31 ALR6th 49—§ 4
Smith v. State, 2004 WL 989827 (Tenn. Crim. App. 2004)
29 ALR6th 237—§ 4
Smith v. State, 2004 WL 1118621 (Miss. 2004)
122 ALR5th 145—§ 22
Smith v. State, 2005 WL 1405791 (Tex. App. Dallas 2005)
67 ALR6th 103—§ 5, 10
Smith v. State, 2005 WY 113, 119 P.3d 411 (Wyo. 2005)
82 ALR6th 373—§ 6, 10
Smith v. State, 2006 WL 1791681 (Tex. App. Fort Worth 2006)
97 ALR6th 653—§ 29
Smith v. State, 2007 WL 336879 (Miss. Ct. App. 2007)
26 ALR6th 511—§ 28
Smith v. State, 2009-1765 La. App. 1 Cir. 3/26/10, 2010 WL 1173071 (La. Ct. App. 1st Cir. 2010)
63 ALR6th 351—§ 4
Smith v. State, 2009-Ohio-4441, 2009 WL 2751267 (Ohio Ct. App. 5th Dist. Richland County 2009)
64 ALR6th 1—§ 7, 9, 11
Smith v. State, 2010 OK CR 24, 245 P.3d 1233 (Okla. Crim. App. 2010)
102 ALR6th 417—§ 25
Smith v. State, 2010 WL 3928485 (Tex. App. Houston 1st Dist. 2010)
81 ALR6th 505—§ 54
Smith v. State, 2012 WL 2914178 (Tenn. Ct. App. 2012)
91 ALR6th 435—§ 89
Smith v. State, Dept. of Health and Hospitals, 676 So. 2d 543 (La. 1996)
94 ALR6th 431—§ 63
Smith v. State ex rel. Dept. of Public Safety, 2004 OK 22, 89 P.3d 1062 (Okla. 2004)
15 ALR6th 375—§ 21
Smith v. State ex rel. Osborne, 121 Fla. 241, 163 So. 524 (1935)
91 ALR6th 435—§ 72, 129

Smith v. State Farm Fire and Cas. Co., 2007 WL 1459379 (S.D. Miss. 2007)

37 ALR6th 657—§ 7

Smith v. State Farm Fire and Cas. Co., 2007 WL 1459381 (S.D. Miss. 2007)

37 ALR6th 657—§ 7

Smith v. State Farm Mut. Auto. Ins. Co., 122 Ga. App. 430, 177 S.E.2d 195 (1970)

41 ALR6th 527—§ 5

Smith v. State Indus. Com'n, 1938 OK 167, 182 Okla. 433, 78 P.2d 288 (1938)

40 ALR6th 99—§ 19

Smith v. State Lottery Com'n of Indiana, 812 N.E.2d 1066 (Ind. Ct. App. 2004)

48 ALR6th 243—§ 20

Smith v. State of Cal., 336 F.2d 530 (9th Cir. 1964)

63 ALR6th 1—§ 60

Smith v. Steuben County Highway Dep't., 199 A.D. 2d 590, 604 N.Y.S. 2d 352 (3d Dep't 1993)

106 ALR5th 111—§ 23
108 ALR5th 1—§ 6

Smith v. Stevens, 313 Ark. 534, 855 S.W.2d 323 (1993)

10 ALR5th 680—§ 5

Smith v. Stewart, 233 Kan. 904, 667 P.2d 358, 36 U.C.C. Rep. Serv. 1141 (1983)

89 ALR5th 319—§ 10, 21

Smith v. Stewart, 268 Ark. 766, 596 S.W.2d 346, 9 A.L.R.4th 1185 (Ct. App. 1980)

69 ALR5th 219—§ 4

Smith v. St. Francis Hosp., Inc., 676 P.2d 279 (Okla. App. 1983)

58 ALR5th 613—§ 10

Smith v. St. Francis Hosp., Inc., 1983 OK CIV APP 58, 676 P.2d 279 (Ct. App. Div. 1 1983)

64 ALR6th 249—§ 13

Smith v. St. Joseph Ry., Light, Heat & Power Co., 310 Mo. 469, 276 S.W. 607 (1925)

70 ALR5th 261—§ 3, 23

Smith v. St. Lawrence County Sup'rs, 148 N.Y. 187, 42 N.E. 592 (1896)

114 ALR5th 311—§ 5, 12

Smith v. St. Louis S. F. R. Co., 214 S.W.2d 443 (Mo. App. 1948)

17 ALR5th 547—§ 36, 38

Smith v. St. Mary's Hospital, 23 A.D.2d 929, 259 N.Y.S.2d 373 (3d Dep't 1965)

48 ALR6th 387—§ 4

Smith v. Stoley, 2009 WL 3233825 (W.D. Mich. 2009)

89 ALR6th 1—§ 77

Smith v. Stoner, 594 F. Supp. 1091, 35 CCH EPD ¶ 34799 (N.D. Ind. 1984)

12 ALR5th 195—§ 38

Smith v. St. Paul Fire & Marine Ins. Co., 353 N.W.2d 130 (Minn. 1984)

60 ALR5th 239—§ 4, 18

Smith v. St. Regis Corp., 850 F. Supp. 1296, 146 BNA LRRM 2101 (S.D. Miss. 1994)

19 ALR5th 439—§ 3

Smith v. Strickland, 442 S.E.2d 207 (S.C. App. 1994)

2 ALR5th 449—§ 3, 4

Smith v. Stryker Corp., 2011 WL 445646 (Mich. Ct. App. 2011)

90 ALR6th 75—§ 42

Smith v. St. Tammany Parish School Bd., 448 F.2d 414 (5th Cir. 1971)

66 ALR6th 493—§ 1

Smith v. Sturm, Ruger & Co., Inc., 39 Wash. App. 740, 695 P.2d 600, 59 A.L.R.4th 89 (Div. 3 1985)

96 ALR5th 239—§ 6
117 ALR5th 155—§ 12

Smith v. Superintendent, 73 Mass. App. Ct. 1104, 896 N.E.2d 60 (2008)

89 ALR6th 1—§ 61

Smith v. Superior Court, 10 Cal. App. 4th 1033, 13 Cal. Rptr. 2d 133 (4th Dist. 1992)

9 ALR6th 285—§ 5

Smith v. Superior Court, 151 Cal. App. 3d 491, 198 Cal. Rptr. 829 (2d Dist. 1984)

101 ALR5th 61—§ 16

102 ALR5th 99—§ 9

Smith v. Superior Court, 2004 WL 1194707 (Cal. App. 4th Dist. 2004)

45 ALR6th 493—§ 10, 18, 36

Smith v. Superior Court of San Mateo County, 68 Cal. App. 3d 457, 137 Cal. Rptr. 348 (1st Dist. 1977)

5 ALR5th 550—§ 23

Smith v. Swope, 91 F.2d 260 (C.C.A. 9th Cir. 1937)

76 ALR5th 485—§ 15, 18

Smith v. Syd's, Inc., 570 N.E.2d 126 (Ind. App. 1991)

5 ALR5th 875—§ 3

Smith v. Tang, 926 S.W.2d 716 (Mo. Ct. App. E.D. 1996)

95 ALR6th 85—§ 3, 18

100 ALR6th 139—§ 3

Smith v. Taylor County Pub. Co., 443 So. 2d 1042 (Fla. App. D1 1983)

54 ALR5th 443—§ 2, 11

Smith v. Taylor County Pub. Co., Inc., 443 So. 2d 1042 (Fla. Dist. Ct. App. 1st Dist. 1983)

13 ALR6th 111—§ 4

Smith v. Teel, 2008 OK CIV APP 7, 175 P.3d 960 (Div. 1 2007)

46 ALR6th 1—§ 25

Smith v. Telophase Nat. Cremation Soc., 471 So. 2d 163, 10 FLW 1496 (Fla. App. D2 1985)

12 ALR5th 195—§ 68

Smith v. Teunis, 16 Va. Cir. 135, 1989 WL 646535 (1989)

99 ALR5th 445—§ 3

Smith v. Texaco, Inc., 232 Ill. App. 3d 463, 173 Ill. Dec. 776, 597 N.E.2d 750 (1st Dist. 1992)

17 ALR6th 1—§ 27

Smith v. Texas, 127 S. Ct. 1686, 167 L. Ed. 2d 632 (U.S. 2007)

26 ALR6th 659—§ 54

Smith v. Texas, 881 S.W.2d 727 (Tex. App. Houston (1st Dist.) 1994)

36 ALR5th 255—§ 8

Smith v. Thompson, 584 S.W.2d 253 (Tenn. Crim. App. 1979)

88 ALR5th 463—§ 10, 11

Smith v. Thornburgh, 1991 WL 31101 (D. Kan. 1991)

54 ALR6th 1—§ 14

Smith v. Timken Mercy Medical Center, 1983 WL 6373 (Ohio Ct. App. 5th Dist. Stark County 1983)

64 ALR6th 249—§ 32

Smith v. Tipps Engineering & Supply Co., 231 Ark. 952, 333 S.W.2d 483 (1960)

6 ALR5th 883—§ 8

Smith v. Tipton, 284 S.W.2d 100 (Ky. App. 1955)

35 ALR5th 285—§ 4

Smith v. Tolley, 960 F.Supp. 977 (E.D.Va. 1997)

66 ALR5th 397—§ 3, 4, 9, 12, 25

Smith v. Topeff, 2003 WL 22234900 (Minn. Ct. App. 2003)

23 ALR6th 697—§ 14

Smith v. Tower Loan of Mississippi, Inc., 216 F.R.D. 338 (S.D. Miss. 2003)

60 ALR6th 295—§ 23, 35, 54

Smith v. Town of Snowmass Village, 919 P.2d 868 (Colo. Ct. App. 1996)

125 ALR5th 193—§ 5

2 ALR6th 279—§ 6, 9

34 ALR6th 431—§ 4

Smith v. Town of St. Johnsbury, 150 Vt. 351, 554 A.2d 233 (1988)

73 ALR5th 223—§ 4, 10

28 ALR6th 439—§ 16

Smith v. Trattler, 681 So. 2d 961 (La. Ct. App. 5th Cir. 1996)

96 ALR5th 107—§ 7

Smith v. Travelers Indem. Co., 343 F. Supp. 605 (M.D.N.C. 1972)

92 ALR5th 273—§ 10

Smith v. Travelers Indem. Co. of Rhode Island, 374 So. 2d 708 (La. Ct. App. 1st Cir. 1979)

50 ALR6th 95—§ 10

For assistance, call 1-800-328-4880

Smith v. Travelers Ins. Co., 438 F.2d 373 (6th Cir. 1971)
115 ALR5th 589—§ 10
123 ALR5th 259—§ 5

Smith v. Travelers Mortg. Services, 699 F. Supp. 1080, 48 Fair Empl. Prac. Cas. (BNA) 590, 3 I.E.R. Cas. (BNA) 1706, 48 Empl. Prac. Dec. (CCH) ¶ 38573, 115 Lab. Cas. (CCH) ¶ 56291 (D.N.J. 1988)
105 ALR5th 351—§ 3
13 ALR6th 499—§ 27
36 ALR6th 203—§ 4

Smith v. Trosclair, 321 So. 2d 514 (La. 1975)
69 ALR5th 1—§ 3, 5

Smith v. Tudor Constr., 637 So. 2d 666 (La. App. 2d Cir. 1994)
14 ALR5th 1—§ 5, 11

Smith v. Turner, 238 Cal. App. 2d 141, 47 Cal. Rptr. 582 (2d Dist. 1965)
52 ALR5th 491—§ 7

Smith v. Tygrett, 302 S.W.2d 604 (Ky. 1956)
76 ALR5th 337—§ 9

Smith v. Union Bank & Trust Asso., 15 Cal. App. 3d 413, 93 Cal. Rptr. 282 (2d Dist. 1971)
4 ALR5th 772—§ 12, 34

Smith v. Union Labor Life Ins. Co., 620 A.2d 265, 8 BNA IER Cas. 434 (Dist. Col. App. 1993)
17 ALR5th 1—§ 3

Smith v. Union Nat'l. Life Ins. Co., 286 F. Supp. 2d 782 (S.D. Miss. 2003)
8 ALR6th 549—§ 13

Smith v. Union P. R. Co., 214 Kan. 128, 519 P.2d 1101 (1974)
59 ALR5th 1—§ 3 to 6

Smith v. Union Supply Co., 675 P.2d 333, 37 U.C.C. Rep. Serv. (CBC) 795 (Colo. Ct. App. 1983)
81 ALR5th 483—§ 5

Smith v. United Technologies, Essex Group, Inc., Wire & Cable Div., 240 Kan. 562, 731 P.2d 871, 42 CCH EPD ¶ 36884 (1987)
12 ALR5th 195—§ 32

Smith v. Universal Elec. Const. Co., 30 S.W.3d 435 (Tex. App. Tyler 2000)
27 ALR5th 174—§ 4, 36

Smith v. Universal Underwriters Ins. Co., 732 F.2d 129 (CA11 Ga. 1984)
13 ALR5th 289—§ 18

Smith v. Universal Underwriters Ins. Co., 752 F.2d 1535 (CA11 Ga. 1985)
13 ALR5th 289—§ 2, 13, 18

Smith v. University Diagnostic Medical Imaging, P.C., 43 A.D.3d 344, 842 N.Y.S.2d 9 (1st Dep't 2007)
92 ALR6th 379—§ 34

Smith v. University of Idaho, 67 Idaho 22, 170 P.2d 404 (1946)
11 ALR6th 351—§ 8

Smith v. Urethane Installations, Inc., 492 A.2d 1266, 41 U.C.C.R.S. 733 (Me. 1985)
49 ALR5th 1—§ 3, 87

Smith v. U.S., 94 U.S. 97, 24 L. Ed. 32 (1876)
105 ALR5th 529—§ 11

Smith v. U.S., 157 F. 721 (C.C.A. 8th Cir. 1907)
88 ALR6th 203—§ 89

Smith v. U.S., 170 Fed. Appx. 971 (7th Cir. 2006)
71 ALR6th 1—§ 5

Smith v. U.S., 385 F.2d 34 (5th Cir. 1967)
55 ALR6th 157—§ 47

Smith v. U.S., 392 F. Supp. 654 (N.D. Ohio 1975)
7 ALR5th 1—§ 6

Smith v. U.S., 470 A.2d 315 (D.C. 1983)
70 ALR6th 361—§ 32

Smith v. U.S., 522 A.2d 1274 (D.C. 1987)
23 ALR6th 307—§ 42

Smith v. U.S., 666 A.2d 1216 (D.C. 1995)
7 ALR6th 233—§ 3, 5

Smith v. U.S., 684 A.2d 307 (D.C. 1996)
88 ALR5th 121—§ 7, 32

Smith v. U.S., 896 F. Supp. 1183 (M.D. Fla. 1995)
119 ALR5th 1—§ 10, 11, 28

Smith v. U.S., 1954-2 C.B. 225, 348 U.S. 147, 75 S. Ct. 194, 99 L. Ed. 192, 54-2 U.S. Tax Cas. (CCH) ¶ 9715, 46 A.F.T.R. (P-H) P 968 (1954)
65 ALR6th 359—§ 5

Smith v. U.S., 2010 WL 430768 (S.D. Fla. 2010)
56 ALR6th 553—§ 32

Smith v. U.S., 2013 WL 2154004 (D. Mass. 2013)
90 ALR6th 385—§ 5

Smith v. U.S. Nat. Bank of Galveston, 767 S.W.2d 820 (Tex. App. Texarkana 1989)
63 ALR5th 1—§ 7

Smith v. U.S. Postal Service, 69 S.W.3d 926 (Mo. Ct. App. S.D. 2002)
121 ALR5th 467—§ 2, 3

Smith v. Vallejo General Hospital, 170 Cal. App. 3d 450, 216 Cal. Rptr. 189 (1st Dist. 1985)
28 ALR5th 107—§ 8

Smith v. Vavoulis, 373 Fed. Appx. 965 (11th Cir. 2010)
65 ALR6th 93—§ 46

Smith v. Venezian Lamp Co., 5 App. Div. 2d 12, 168 N.Y.S.2d 764 (3d Dep't 1957)
8 ALR5th 798—§ 3, 4

Smith v. Vernon Parish School Bd., 442 So. 2d 1319, 15 Ed. Law Rep. 627 (La. Ct. App. 3d Cir. 1983)
66 ALR5th 1—§ 16

Smith v. Verson Allsteel Press Co., 74 Ill. App. 3d 818, 30 Ill. Dec. 562, 393 N.E.2d 598, CCH Prod. Liab. Rep. ¶ 8657 (1st Dist. 1979)
10 ALR5th 371—§ 17

Smith v. Vicorp, Inc., 107 F.3d 816, 37 Fed. R. Serv. 3d (LCP) 145 (10th Cir. 1997)
63 ALR5th 285—§ 7

Smith v. Video Lottery Consultants, Inc., 260 Mont. 54, 858 P.2d 11, 1993-2 Trade Cas. (CCH) ¶ 70375 (1993)
83 ALR6th 419—§ 9

Smith v. Village of Henderson, 54 A.D. 26, 66 N.Y.S. 347 (4th Dep't 1900)
12 ALR6th 645—§ 5

Smith v. Vilvarajah, 57 S.W.3d 839 (Ky. Ct. App. 2000)
12 ALR6th 241—§ 4

Smith v. Vining, 407 So. 2d 1048 (Fla. App. D3 1981)
14 ALR5th 242—§ 38

Smith v. Virginia Military Institute, 2010 WL 2132240 (W.D. Va. 2010)
90 ALR6th 235—§ 53

Smith v. Virginia Transit Co., 206 Va. 951, 147 S.E.2d 110 (1966)
16 ALR5th 1—§ 4, 6

Smith v. Visa U.S.A., Inc., 2005 WL 1936336 (Minn. Dist. Ct. 2005)
35 ALR6th 245—§ 6, 16

Smith v. Voisine, 650 A.2d 1350 (Me. 1994)
64 ALR5th 519—§ 12

Smith v. Volk, 85 Ohio App. 347, 40 Ohio Op. 231, 53 Ohio L. Abs. 432, 86 N.E.2d 30 (2d Dist. Montgomery County 1948)
115 ALR5th 251—§ 5

Smith v. Wachovia, 2009 WL 1948829 (N.D. Cal. 2009)
86 ALR6th 411—§ 5

Smith v. Waller, 1997 WL 412537 (Tenn. Ct. App. 1997)
60 ALR5th 669—§ 6

Smith v. Wal-Mart Stores, Inc., 128 N.C. App. 282, 495 S.E.2d 149, 83 A.L.R.5th 811 (1998)
83 ALR5th 589—§ 2, 6
123 ALR5th 1—§ 4

Smith v. Wal-Mart Stores, Inc., 967 S.W.2d 198 (Mo. Ct. App. E.D. 1998)
15 ALR5th 119—§ 32, 51, 59
83 ALR5th 589—§ 2, 6
123 ALR5th 1—§ 6

Smith v. Ward, 47 S.D. 243, 197 N.W. 684 (1924)
121 ALR5th 1—§ 52

Smith v. Warden, New Hampshire State Prison, 2008 DNH 28, 2008 WL 282263 (D.N.H. 2008)
54 ALR6th 1—§ 23
56 ALR6th 553—§ 41

Smith v. Ware, 13 Johns. 257, 1816 WL 1179 (N.Y. Sup 1816)
98 ALR5th 353—§ 8

Smith v. Warren, 225 A.D. 601, 233 N.Y.S. 627 (1st Dep't 1929)
19 ALR6th 217—§ 15

Smith v. Washington, 716 N.E.2d 607 (Ind. Ct. App. 1999)
30 ALR5th 571—§ 40
84 ALR5th 619—§ 5
108 ALR5th 385—§ 8

Smith v. Washington County, 241 Or. 380, 406 P.2d 545 (1965)
73 ALR5th 223—§ 2, 11

Smith v. Washington Metropolitan Area Transit Authority, 184 Fed. Appx. 311 (4th Cir. 2006)
63 ALR6th 495—§ 61

Smith v. Washington Metropolitan Area Transit Authority, 290 F.3d 201 (4th Cir. 2002)
63 ALR6th 495—§ 61, 62

Smith v. Washington Metropolitan Area Transit Authority, 2004 WL 5298831 (D. Md. 2004)
63 ALR6th 495—§ 61

Smith v. W.C.A.B. (Dept. of Labor and Industry), 159 Pa. Commw. 171, 632 A.2d 1033 (1993)
106 ALR5th 111—§ 19
108 ALR5th 1—§ 46

Smith v. Weaver, 225 Neb. 569, 407 N.W.2d 174 (1987)
47 ALR5th 433—§ 5, 14

Smith v. Webber, 282 S.W.2d 346 (Ky. 1955)
5 ALR5th 875—§ 23, 32

Smith v. Weber County Sch. Dist., 877 P.2d 1276, 243 Utah Adv. Rep. 14 (Utah App. 1994)

23 ALR5th 1—§ 9

Smith v. Weinstein, 578 F. Supp. 1297, 222 U.S.P.Q. 381 (S.D. N.Y. 1984)
76 ALR6th 289—§ 4
77 ALR6th 543—§ 12

Smith v. Wembley Industries, Inc., 490 So. 2d 1107 (La. Ct. App. 4th Cir. 1986)
43 ALR6th 1—§ 13

Smith v. West, 498 So. 2d 1168 (La. App. 3d Cir. 1986)
38 ALR5th 107—§ 4

Smith v. Western Preferred Casualty Co., 424 So. 2d 375 (La. App. 2d Cir. 1982)
33 ALR5th 121—§ 4, 37, 43

Smith v. Westinghouse Elec. Corp., 1987 OK 3, 732 P.2d 466 (Okla. 1987)
122 ALR5th 1—§ 2, 10, 32

Smith v. White, 3 A.D.2d 869, 161 N.Y.S.2d 440 (3d Dep't 1957)
80 ALR5th 417—§ 3

Smith v. Williams, 277 Ga. 778, 596 S.E.2d 112 (2004)
31 ALR6th 49—§ 15

Smith v. Williams, 422 S.W.2d 168 (Tex. 1967)
119 ALR5th 519—§ 18

Smith v. Williams, 1994 WL 1031188 (Va. Cir. Ct. 1994)
101 ALR5th 447—§ 10

Smith v. Wilson, 90 So. 3d 51 (Miss. 2012)
86 ALR6th 1—§ 60, 61

Smith v. Winhall Planning Comm'n, 140 Vt. 178, 436 A.2d 760 (1981)
38 ALR5th 737—§ 2

Smith v. Winn Dixie Stores of Louisiana, Inc., 389 So. 2d 900 (La. Ct. App. 4th Cir. 1980)
123 ALR5th 1—§ 14

Smith v. Winter Park Software Inc., 504 So. 2d 523 (Fla. Dist. Ct. App. 5th Dist. 1987)
113 ALR5th 487—§ 4

Smith v. Winter Place LLC, 447 Mass.
363, 851 N.E.2d 417, 12 Wage &
Hour Cas. 2d (BNA) 139, 153 Lab.
Cas. (CCH) ¶ 60252 (2006)
61 ALR6th 61—§ 18

Smith v. Wisconsin, 127 S. Ct. 1005,
166 L. Ed. 2d 713 (U.S. 2007)
26 ALR6th 659—§ 37

Smith v. Wisconsin Physicians Service,
152 Wis. 2d 25, 447 N.W.2d 371
(App. 1989)
45 ALR5th 173—§ 4

Smith v. Wm. Wrigley Jr. Co., 2010 WL
2401149 (S.D. Fla. 2010)
60 ALR6th 295—§ 52, 70

Smith v. Workers' Compensation
Comm'r, 179 W. Va. 782, 373
S.E.2d 495 (1988)
26 ALR5th 127—§ 3, 7, 10

Smith v. Workman, 550 F.3d 1258 (10th
Cir. 2008)
102 ALR6th 417—§ 3, 23

Smith v. Workmen's Compensation Appeal Bd. (Donegal Industries, Inc.),
131 Pa. Cmwlth. 240, 569 A.2d
1049 (1990)
14 ALR5th 1—§ 2

Smith v. Worn, 93 Cal. 206, 28 P. 944
(1892)
62 ALR5th 219—§ 13, 42

Smith v. Wright, 195 Minn. 589, 263
N.W. 903 (1935)
83 ALR6th 605—§ 5

Smith v. Wrigley, 908 N.E.2d 354 (Ind.
Ct. App. 2009)
85 ALR6th 229—§ 5

Smith v. Wyeth, Inc., 2008 WL 2677051
(W.D. Ky. 2008)
56 ALR6th 161—§ 3

Smith v. Xerox Corp., 866 F.2d 135,
CCH Prod. Liab. Rep. ¶ 12062
(CA5 La. 1989)
53 ALR5th 535—§ 3 to 5, 7, 8

Smith v. Yeager, 459 F.2d 124 (3d Cir.
1972)
74 ALR5th 453—§ 4

Smith v. YMCA of Benton Harbor/Saint
Joseph, 216 Mich. App. 552, 550
N.W.2d 262 (1996)
75 ALR6th 1—§ 15

Smith v. York, 90 Ohio Misc. 2d 55, 696
N.E.2d 682 (Ct. Cl. 1998)
48 ALR5th 575—§ 3

Smith & Burnetti, PA v. Faulk, 677 So.
2d 404, 21 FLW D1694 (Fla. App.
D2 1996)
53 ALR5th 287—§ 4, 12

Smith & Egge Mfg. Co. v. Webster, 87
Conn. 74, 86 A. 763 (1913)
85 ALR6th 1—§ 53

Smith & Hitt Constr. Co. v. Fowler, 466
So. 2d 896 (Miss. 1985)
61 ALR5th 525—§ 7

Smith and Sanders, Inc. v. Peery, 473
So. 2d 423 (Miss. 1985)
10 ALR5th 245—§ 23
82 ALR5th 149—§ 1, 5, 27, 29, 42, 64

Smith and Smith, In re Marriage of, 103
Or. App. 614, 798 P.2d 717 (1990)
47 ALR5th 129—§ 12

Smith, Bell & Hauck, Inc. v. Cullins,
123 Vt. 96, 183 A.2d 528 (1962)
12 ALR5th 847—§ 6

Smithberg v. Merico, Inc., 575 F. Supp.
80, 38 Fair Empl. Prac. Cas. (BNA)
1868 (C.D. Cal. 1983)
81 ALR5th 367—§ 33

Smith-Bozarth v. Coalition Against
Rape and Abuse, Inc., 329 N.J.
Super. 238, 747 A.2d 322 (App.
Div. 2000)
13 ALR6th 499—§ 22

Smith by Smith v. Professional Painting,
Inc., 202 A.D.2d 263, 608 N.Y.S.2d
641 (1st Dep't 1994)
103 ALR5th 339—§ 8

Smith-Caronia v. U.S., 714 A.2d 764
(D.C. 1998)
70 ALR6th 513—§ 11
71 ALR6th 471—§ 5

Smith County Education Asso. v. Anderson, 676 S.W.2d 328 (Tenn. 1984)
34 ALR5th 591—§ 3, 6

Smith-Dobben v. Dobben, 886 N.E.2d 118 (Ind. Ct. App. 2008)
99 ALR6th 203—§ 15
102 ALR6th 153—§ 19
Smith-Douglass, Div. of Borden Chemical, Borden Inc. v. Kornegay, 70 N.C. App. 264, 318 S.E.2d 895 (1984)
15 ALR6th 241—§ 24
Smitheal v. Smitheal, 518 S.W.2d 842 (Tex. Civ. App. Fort Worth 1975)
15 ALR5th 692—§ 4
Smith/Enron Cogeneration Ltd. Partnership, Inc. v. Smith Cogeneration Intern., Inc., 198 F.3d 88 (2d Cir. 1999)
100 ALR5th 481—§ 13, 14
Smitherman v. Morris Plan Bank of Greensboro, 211 N.C. 65, 188 S.E. 645 (1936)
81 ALR6th 161—§ 4
82 ALR6th 43—§ 4
Smithers v. Metro-Goldwyn-Mayer Studios, Inc., 139 Cal. App. 3d 643, 189 Cal. Rptr. 20 (2d Dist. 1983)
14 ALR5th 242—§ 32
Smithers v. State, 826 So. 2d 916 (Fla. 2002)
20 ALR6th 479—§ 3, 23
Smith ex rel. Lanham v. Greene County School Dist., 100 F. Supp. 2d 1354, 145 Ed. Law Rep. 368 (M.D. Ga. 2000)
58 ALR5th 1—§ 42
Smith ex rel. Smith v. Bryco Arms, 2001 -NMCA- 090, 33 P.3d 638 (N.M. Ct. App. 2001)
96 ALR5th 239—§ 6
Smith ex rel. Smith v. Siegelman, 322 F.3d 1290 (11th Cir. 2003)
36 ALR6th 475—§ 3, 13
Smith ex rel. Stephan v. AF & L Ins. Co., 147 S.W.3d 767 (Mo. Ct. App. E.D. 2004)
30 ALR6th 395—§ 8
Smith ex rel. Strickland v. Jones, 183 N.C. App. 643, 645 S.E.2d 198 (2007)

86 ALR6th 321—§ 12
Smithey v. Hansberger, 189 Ariz. 103, 938 P.2d 498 (Ct. App. Div. 1 1996)
42 ALR6th 545—§ 3, 8, 20
43 ALR6th 375—§ 3, 4, 6, 13, 49
Smith Family Trust v. Hudson Bd. of Zoning & Bldg. Appeals, 2009-Ohio-2557, 2009 WL 1539065 (Ohio Ct. App. 9th Dist. Summit County 2009)
84 ALR6th 133—§ 14
Smithfield v. Fanning, 602 A.2d 939 (R.I. 1992)
53 ALR5th 1—§ 12, 13, 39
Smithfield Peat Co. v. Scott-Lee Constr. Co., 525 A.2d 495 (R.I. 1987)
4 ALR5th 772—§ 44
Smithhart v. AAA Contracting Co., 260 So. 2d 8 (La. App. 1st Cir. 1972)
13 ALR5th 289—§ 22
Smithhart v. State, 591 N.E.2d 149 (Ind. App. 1992)
48 ALR5th 659—§ 17, 22
SmithKline Beckman Corp. Securities Litigation, In re, 751 F. Supp. 525, Fed. Sec. L. Rep. (CCH) ¶ 95,686 (E.D. Pa. 1990)
60 ALR6th 295—§ 73
SmithKline Beckman Corp. Secur. Litigation, Re, 751 F. Supp. 525, CCH Fed Secur L. Rep. ¶ 95686 (E.D. Pa. 1990)
23 ALR5th 241—§ 2, 20
Smithkline Beecham Corp. v. Apotex Corp., 194 F.R.D. 624 (N.D. Ill. 2000)
27 ALR5th 76—§ 35
SmithKline Beecham Corp. v. Apotex Corp., 232 F.R.D. 467 (E.D. Pa. 2005)
66 ALR6th 83—§ 19
SmithKline Beecham Corp. v. Doe, 903 S.W.2d 347, 10 I.E.R. Cas. (BNA) 1487, 130 Lab. Cas. (CCH) ¶ 57980 (Tex. 1995)
19 ALR6th 793—§ 10

Smithline v. Ghessi, 25 App. Div. 2d 841, 270 N.Y.S.2d 103 (1st Dep't 1966)

4 ALR5th 443—§ 5

Smith Materials Corp., In re, 108 B.R. 784 (Bankr. M.D. Fla. 1989)

107 ALR5th 311—§ 13

Smith-Moore Body Co. v. Heil Co., 603 F. Supp. 354, 40 U.C.C. Rep. Serv. 898 (E.D. Va. 1985)

89 ALR5th 319—§ 23

Smith Office Service, Inc. v. Kelley, 762 P.2d 791, 7 U.C.C.R.S.2d 528 (Colo. App. 1988)

23 ALR5th 744—§ 8

Smith Oil Co. v. Logan, 180 Okla. 474, 71 P.2d 766 (1937)

76 ALR5th 337—§ 20

Smith on Behalf of Smith v. City of Kenner, 428 So. 2d 1171 (La. Ct. App. 5th Cir. 1983)

90 ALR5th 273—§ 4, 7, 14

Smith, on Behalf of Smith v. Severn, 1996 WL 19455 (N.D. Ill. 1996)

90 ALR6th 235—§ 30

Smith, People ex rel. v. McClellan, 133 Misc. 280, 232 N.Y.S. 9 (Sup 1928)

102 ALR5th 525—§ 23

Smithpeters v. Prudential Ins. Co. of America, 18 Tenn. App. 628, 81 S.W.2d 392 (1934)

67 ALR5th 513—§ 5

Smith-Pfeffer v. Superintendent of the Walter E. Fernald State School, 404 Mass. 145, 533 N.E.2d 1368, 51 Ed. Law Rep. 1035, 4 I.E.R. Cas. (BNA) 289 (1989)

105 ALR5th 351—§ 3, 8

Smiths v. McConathy, 11 Mo. 517, 1848 WL 4031 (1848)

93 ALR5th 621—§ 4, 8

Smith's Adm'r v. Price, 252 Ky. 806, 68 S.W.2d 422 (1934)

87 ALR6th 495—§ 5, 42, 54

Smith's Appeal, 115 Pa. 319, 8 A. 582 (1887)

3 ALR5th 394—§ 10

Smith-Scharff Paper Co. v. P.N. Hirsch & Co. Stores, Inc., 754 S.W.2d 928, 7 U.C.C.R.S.2d 38 (Mo. App. 1988)

37 ALR5th 459—§ 16

Smith's Estate, In re, 226 Wis. 556, 277 N.W. 141 (1938)

98 ALR5th 353—§ 4, 8

Smith's Estate, Matter of, 82 Wis. 2d 667, 264 N.W.2d 239 (1978)

86 ALR6th 321—§ 4, 12

90 ALR6th 451—§ 121

Smith's Ex'x v. Washington City, V.M. & G.S.R. Co., 74 Va. 617, 33 Gratt. 617, 1880 WL 6113 (1880)

36 ALR6th 387—§ 5, 8

Smith's Food King No. 1 v. Hornwood, 108 Nev. 666, 836 P.2d 1241 (1992)

84 ALR5th 399—§ 3, 4, 12

Smith's Marriage, Matter of, 23 Or. App. 450, 543 P.2d 313 (1975)

26 ALR6th 331—§ 13

Smithson v. Cessna Aircraft Co., 665 S.W.2d 439 (Tex. 1984)

7 ALR6th 1—§ 11, 38

Smithson v. Nordstrom, Inc., 63 Or. App. 423, 664 P.2d 1119, 118 L.R.R.M. (BNA) 3019 (1983)

21 ALR6th 671—§ 4

Smithson v. Smithson, 986 S.W.2d 939 (Mo. Ct. App. S.D. 1999)

10 ALR5th 191—§ 6

11 ALR5th 259—§ 28

Smithson v. State, 275 Ga. App. 591, 621 S.E.2d 783 (2005)

50 ALR6th 455—§ 24

Smithsonian Institution v. Meech, 169 U.S. 398, 42 L. Ed. 793, 18 S. Ct. 396A (1898)

3 ALR5th 590—§ 27

Smith, State ex rel. v. Board of County Comm'rs, 125 Kan. 379, 264 P. 84 (1928)

56 ALR5th 171—§ 5, 26

Smith, State ex rel. v. Bohannan, 101 Ariz. 520, 421 P.2d 877 (1966)

10 ALR5th 139—§ 4

For assistance, call 1-800-328-4880

Smith, State ex rel. v. District Court of Ninth Judicial Dist., 112 Mont. 506, 118 P.2d 141 (1941)

12 ALR5th 577—§ 3, 11

Smith, State ex rel. v. Duncan, 134 Kan. 85, 4 P.2d 443 (1931)

56 ALR5th 171—§ 5, 18

Smith, State ex rel. v. Endicott, 185 Wis. 2d 919, 520 N.W.2d 292 (Ct. App. 1994)

46 ALR6th 63—§ 5

Smith, State ex rel. v. Indus. Comm., 99 Ohio St. 3d 90, 2003-Ohio-2452, 789 N.E.2d 189 (2003)

31 ALR6th 199—§ 99

Smith, State ex rel. v. Lazar Elec. & Const., Inc., 789 N.E.2d 189 (2003)

31 ALR6th 199—§ 99

Smith, State ex rel. v. Martinez, 2011-NMSC-043, 150 N.M. 703, 265 P.3d 1276 (2011)

87 ALR6th 633—§ 6

Smith, State ex rel. v. Neal, 25 Wash. 264, 65 P. 188 (1901)

56 ALR5th 171—§ 6, 10, 18

Smith, State ex rel. v. Smith, 75 Ohio St. 3d 418, 662 N.E.2d 366 (1996)

61 ALR5th 151—§ 14

Smith, State ex rel. v. Smith, 631 So. 2d 252 (Ala. App. 1993)

17 ALR5th 143—§ 3

Smith, Succession of v. Kavanaugh, Pierson and Talley, 565 So. 2d 990 (La. Ct. App. 1st Cir. 1990)

12 ALR6th 1—§ 4, 5

Smith-Tyler v. Bank of America, N.A., 992 F. Supp. 2d 1277 (N.D. Ga. 2014)

104 ALR6th 485—§ 4, 7

Smith, United States ex rel. v. Fairman, 769 F.2d 386 (7th Cir. 1985)

95 ALR5th 611—§ 4

Smith, U.S. ex rel. v. Baldi, 344 U.S. 561, 73 S. Ct. 391, 97 L. Ed. 549 (1953)

111 ALR5th 491—§ 3

Smith, U.S. ex rel. v. Dowd, 271 F.2d 292 (7th Cir. 1959)

87 ALR6th 109—§ 31, 75

Smith, U.S. ex rel. v. Yeager, 336 F. Supp. 1287 (D.N.J. 1971)

20 ALR6th 479—§ 24

Smith, U.S. ex rel. v. Yeager, 451 F.2d 164 (3d Cir. 1971)

20 ALR6th 479—§ 24

Smith-Victor Corp. v. Sylvania Elec. Products, Inc., 242 F. Supp. 302, 146 U.S.P.Q. (BNA) 701 (N.D. Ill. 1965)

104 ALR5th 523—§ 3 to 5

Smith v, Smith, 1990 WL 166983 (Ohio Ct. App. 2d Dist. Montgomery County 1990)

81 ALR6th 655—§ 3, 6

Smitley v. Cigna Corp., 640 F. Supp. 397, 51 BNA FEP Cas. 407 (D.C. Kan. 1986)

21 ALR5th 1—§ 3
51 ALR5th 1—§ 7

Smits v. E-Z Por Corp., 365 N.W.2d 352 (Minn. Ct. App. 1985)

122 ALR5th 515—§ 5

Smitty's Super Markets, Inc. v. Retail Store Employees Local 322, 637 S.W.2d 148, 116 L.R.R.M. (BNA) 3393, 97 Lab. Cas. (CCH) ¶ 10205 (Mo. Ct. App. S.D. 1982)

120 ALR5th 351—§ 10

Smizer v. Community Mennonite Early Learning Center, 538 Fed. Appx. 711, 300 Ed. Law Rep. 60, 120 Fair Empl. Prac. Cas. (BNA) 1106, 97 Empl. Prac. Dec. (CCH) ¶ 44935 (7th Cir. 2013)

103 ALR6th 19—§ 4

S.M.M., In Interest of, 558 N.W.2d 405 (Iowa 1997)

37 ALR6th 55—§ 8, 16
38 ALR6th 1—§ 29

Smoak v. Seaboard C. L. R. Co., 259 S.C. 632, 193 S.E.2d 594 (1972)

12 ALR5th 195—§ 27

Smock, In re, 5 N.J. Super. 495, 68 A.2d 508 (Law Div. 1949)

60 ALR6th 481—§ 4

Smock v. American Equity Ins. Co., 748 N.E.2d 432 (Ind. Ct. App. 2001)
44 ALR5th 91—§ 11, 13

Smock v. State, 766 N.E.2d 401 (Ind. Ct. App. 2002)
58 ALR6th 499—§ 56, 99

Smoke v. State, Dep't of Pensions and Sec., 378 So. 2d 1149 (Ala. Civ. App. 1979)
92 ALR5th 379—§ 5

Smoketree-Lake Murray, Ltd. v. Mills Concrete Construction Co., 234 Cal. App. 3d 1724, 286 Cal. Rptr. 435 (4th Dist. 1991)
77 ALR6th 251—§ 4

Smokey, Inc. v. Pany Inv. Co., 276 A.2d 741 (Del. 1971)
102 ALR5th 647—§ 20

Smolarz v. Colon Tp., 2005 WL 927144 (Mich. Ct. App. 2005)
19 ALR6th 335—§ 16

Smolder v. State, 671 So. 2d 757 (Ala. Crim. App. 1995)
32 ALR6th 1—§ 11

Smolicz ex rel. Koestner v. Cantor Fitzgerald, LP, 28 A.D.3d 857, 812 N.Y.S.2d 694 (3d Dep't 2006)
20 ALR6th 729—§ 10

Smollet v. Skatying Development Corp., 793 F.2d 547 (CA3 V.I. 1986)
38 ALR5th 107—§ 9, 10

Smolnikar v. Royal Caribbean Cruises Ltd., 787 F. Supp. 2d 1308, 2011 A.M.C. 2941 (S.D. Fla. 2011)
82 ALR6th 175—§ 26

Smolow v. Hafer, 867 A.2d 767 (Pa. Commw. Ct. 2005)
29 ALR6th 507—§ 3, 16, 31

Smolsky v. Governor's Office of Admin., 990 A.2d 173 (Pa. Commw. Ct. 2010)
85 ALR6th 229—§ 22

Smolsky v. Pennsylvania General Assembly, 34 A.3d 316 (Pa. Commw. Ct. 2011)
85 ALR6th 229—§ 46

Smoltz v. Peterson, 204 Mich. App. 136, 514 N.W.2d 199 (1994)
23 ALR5th 75—§ 8

Smook v. Minnehaha County, 457 F.3d 806 (8th Cir. 2006)
26 ALR6th 659—§ 35

Smook v. Minnehaha County, S.D., 127 S. Ct. 1885, 167 L. Ed. 2d 386 (U.S. 2007)
26 ALR6th 659—§ 35

Smoot, Re, 134 B.R. 960, 26 CBC2d 565 (F. BC N.D. Ala. 1991)
14 ALR5th 242—§ 53

Smoot v. Dingess, 160 W. Va. 558, 236 S.E.2d 468 (1977)
32 ALR5th 31—§ 3
97 ALR5th 537—§ 19

Smoot v. Lund, 13 Utah 2d 168, 369 P.2d 933 (1962)
39 ALR6th 155—§ 4

Smoot v. Smoot, 233 Va. 435, 357 S.E.2d 728 (1987)
109 ALR5th 1—§ 10

Smoot v. Smoot, 604 N.E.2d 618 (Ind. App. 1992)
28 ALR5th 46—§ 9

Smoot v. State Farm Mut. Auto. Ins. Co., 299 F.2d 525, 5 FR Serv. 2d 856 (CA5 Ga. 1962)
18 ALR5th 474—§ 2

S. Morantz, Inc. v. Hang & Shine Ultrasonics, Inc., 79 F. Supp. 2d 537 (E.D. Pa. 1999)
81 ALR5th 41—§ 6

Smothers v. Butler, 78 Ill. App. 3d 1018, 34 Ill. Dec. 337, 398 N.E.2d 12 (1st Dist. 1979)
31 ALR5th 1—§ 12, 19

Smothers v. Com., 2003 WL 22975690 (Ky. Ct. App. 2003)
125 ALR5th 357—§ 6
7 ALR6th 233—§ 9

Smothers v. Gibson, 778 F.2d 470 (8th Cir. 1985)
85 ALR5th 261—§ 3, 7

Smothers v. State, 614 S.W.2d 20 (Mo. Ct. App. W.D. 1981)
80 ALR5th 55—§ 10

Smoyer v. Birmingham Area Chamber of Commerce, 517 So. 2d 585 (Ala. 1987)
70 ALR5th 261—§ 2
74 ALR5th 523—§ 2
75 ALR5th 413—§ 2
SMP Sales Management, Inc. v. Fleet Credit Corp., 960 F.2d 557 (CA5 La. 1992)
27 ALR5th 719—§ 4, 13
S.M.S. Textile Mills, Inc. v. Brown, Jacobson, Tillinghast, Lahan and King, P.C., 32 Conn. App. 786, 631 A.2d 340 (1993)
87 ALR5th 473—§ 4
11 ALR6th 1—§ 4, 9
Smuck v. National Management Corp., 540 N.W.2d 669, 11 I.E.R. Cas. (BNA) 33 (Iowa Ct. App. 1995)
104 ALR5th 1—§ 3, 4, 12
Smucker v. Grinberg, 27 Pa. Super. 531 (1905)
75 ALR5th 1—§ 3
Smullyan v. SIBJET S.A., 201 App. Div. 2d 335, 607 N.Y.S.2d 316 (1st Dep't 1994)
56 ALR5th 757—§ 2, 3
Smusch v. Kohn, 22 Misc. 344, 49 N.Y.S. 176 (App. Term 1898)
109 ALR5th 421—§ 5, 13
Smuzynski v. East S. L. R. Co., 230 Mo. App. 1095, 93 S.W.2d 1058 (1936)
16 ALR5th 1—§ 25
S.M.W. v. J.M.C. (In re J.C.), 679 So. 2d 256 (Ala. Civ. App. 1996)
20 ALR5th 534—§ 18
Smyles v. Hastings, 22 N.Y. 217 (1860)
62 ALR5th 219—§ 6
Smyre v. Progressive Sec. Ins. Co., 726 So. 2d 984 (La. Ct. App. 5th Cir. 1998)
33 ALR5th 121—§ 4
Smyth, Matter of Extradition of, 826 F. Supp. 316 (N.D. Cal. 1993)
23 ALR6th 521—§ 13
Smyth v. Anderson, 238 Ga. 343, 232 S.E.2d 835 (1977)
36 ALR5th 395—§ 3, 6, 22, 23

Smyth v. Carter, 845 N.E.2d 219 (Ind. Ct. App. 2006)
29 ALR6th 507—§ 16, 31, 33
Smyth v. Cooksey, 108 F.3d 1380 (7th Cir. 1997)
52 ALR6th 1—§ 5
Smyth v. Hanig, 163 Misc. 59, 296 N.Y.S. 260 (App. Term 1937)
75 ALR5th 1—§ 4, 13, 19
Smyth v. Lubbers, 398 F. Supp. 777 (W.D. Mich. 1975)
31 ALR5th 229—§ 8, 22, 25, 32, 78
105 ALR5th 1—§ 3, 11
Smyth v. Pillsbury Co., 914 F. Supp. 97, 11 I.E.R. Cas. (BNA) 585, 131 Lab. Cas. (CCH) ¶ 58104 (E.D. Pa. 1996)
92 ALR5th 15—§ 3
68 ALR6th 331—§ 35, 41
Smyth v. Thomas, 198 Kan. 250, 424 P.2d 498 (1967)
36 ALR5th 395—§ 4, 12
Smyth v. USAA Property & Casualty Ins. Co., 5 Cal. App. 4th 1470, 7 Cal. Rptr. 2d 694 (2d Dist. 1992)
4 ALR6th 509—§ 8
Smyth v. USAA Property & Casualty Ins. Co., 5 Cal. App. 4th 1470, 7 Cal. Rptr. 2d 694, 92 C.D.O.S. 3755, 92 Daily Journal DAR 5898 (2d Dist. 1992)
35 ALR5th 375—§ 3, 18
Smyth County Community Hosp. v. Town of Marion, 259 Va. 328, 527 S.E.2d 401 (2000)
34 ALR5th 529—§ 11
Smythe v. American Red Cross Blood Services Northeastern New York Region, 797 F. Supp. 147 (N.D.N.Y. 1992)
64 ALR5th 333—§ 3, 8, 21, 22
Smythe v. Phoenix, 63 Idaho 585, 123 P.2d 1010 (1942)
60 ALR5th 459—§ 2, 6
Smythe v. Schacht, 93 Cal. App. 2d 315, 209 P.2d 114 (1949)
11 ALR5th 127—§ 3, 12, 28, 49
Smyth's Estate, Re, 155 Misc. 775, 281 N.Y.S. 260 (1935)

For assistance, call 1-800-328-4880

3 ALR5th 590—§ 27
Smyth's Estate, Re, 246 App. Div. 820, 284 N.Y.S. 470 (1936)

3 ALR5th 590—§ 27
S.N., In Interest of, 500 N.W.2d 32 (Iowa 1993)

117 ALR5th 349—§ 4
S.N., Interest of, 500 N.W.2d 32 (Iowa 1993)

1 ALR5th 469—§ 15, 28, 42
Snaider v. Mano Hoffner Fur Corp., 269 A.D. 271, 55 N.Y.S.2d 285 (1st Dep't 1945)

67 ALR5th 179—§ 3
Snake River Venture v. Board of County Comm'rs, 616 P.2d 744 (Wyo. 1980)

38 ALR5th 737—§ 2
Snaman v. Donahoe's, Inc., 307 Pa. 282, 161 A. 68 (1932)

19 ALR5th 622—§ 32, 40
Snap-Drape, Inc. v. C.I.R., 98 F.3d 194, 21 Employee Benefits Cas. (BNA) 2963, 96-2 U.S. Tax Cas. (CCH) ¶ 50564, 45 Fed. R. Evid. Serv. (LCP) 1129, 78 A.F.T.R.2d (P-H) ¶ 96-6930 (5th Cir. 1996)

66 ALR5th 135—§ 19
Snapir, Commonwealth ex rel. v. Snapir, 196 Pa. Super. 38, 173 A.2d 694 (1961)

53 ALR5th 375—§ 32, 34
Snap-N-Pops, Inc. v. Browning, 432 F. Supp. 360 (E.D. Va. 1977)

48 ALR5th 659—§ 7, 8, 17
Snap-on Business Solutions Inc. v. O'Neil & Associates, Inc., 708 F. Supp. 2d 669 (N.D. Ohio 2010)

76 ALR6th 289—§ 4, 5
77 ALR6th 543—§ 6, 19
95 ALR6th 57—§ 8, 10
Snap-On Business Solutions Inc. v. O'Neil & Associates, Inc., 2010 WL 2650875 (N.D. Ohio 2010)

95 ALR6th 57—§ 3
Snap-on Tools Corp. v. Vetter, 838 F. Supp. 468 (D. Mont. 1993)

22 ALR6th 49—§ 8, 9

Snapp v. State Farm Fire & Casualty Co., 206 Cal. App. 2d 827, 24 Cal. Rptr. 44 (2d Dist. 1962)

1 ALR5th 817—§ 20
30 ALR5th 170—§ 6
Snapperman v. Levine, 50 A.D.2d 1029, 377 N.Y.S.2d 281 (3d Dep't 1975)

75 ALR5th 339—§ 6
Snare & Triest Co. v. Friedman, 169 F. 1 (C.C.A. 3d Cir. 1909)

1 ALR6th 407—§ 11, 19
Snashall v. Jewell, 228 Or. 130, 363 P.2d 566 (1961)

115 ALR5th 251—§ 4, 13
119 ALR5th 519—§ 18
Snavely, In re Adoption of, 2000 WL 1597977 (Ohio Ct. App. 2d Dist. Greene County 2000)

28 ALR6th 349—§ 4
Snavely v. Dollison, 61 Ohio App. 2d 140, 15 Ohio Op. 3d 244, 400 N.E.2d 415 (8th Dist. Cuyahoga County 1979)

109 ALR5th 611—§ 6
Snavely v. Perpetual Federal Sav. Bank, 306 S.C. 348, 412 S.E.2d 382 (1991)

5 ALR6th 497—§ 7, 9, 10
Snavely Co., Inc. v. Laurel Lake Retirement Community, Inc., 1999 WL 980646 (Ohio Ct. App. 8th Dist. Cuyahoga County 1999)

100 ALR5th 481—§ 10
Snawder v. Cohen, 5 F.3d 1012 (CA6 Ky. 1993)

47 ALR5th 433—§ 5
Snawder v. Cohen, 749 F. Supp. 1473, 13 U.C.C. Rep. Serv. 2d (CBC) 744 (W.D. Ky. 1990)

50 ALR5th 327—§ 7
57 ALR5th 1—§ 25
Snawder v. Cohen, 804 F. Supp. 910 (W.D. Ky. 1992)

47 ALR5th 433—§ 16
SNB Bank and Trust v. Kensey, 145 Mich. App. 765, 378 N.W.2d 594 (1985)

86 ALR5th 527—§ 9

---

86 ALR6th 321—§ 11
89 ALR6th 409—§ 65
Snead v. H. E. Butt Grocery Co., 397 S.W.2d 332 (Tex. Civ. App. Waco 1965)
83 ALR5th 589—§ 6
Snead v. State, 913 So. 2d 724 (Fla. Dist. Ct. App. 5th Dist. 2005)
28 ALR6th 505—§ 18
Snead v. Waite, 306 Ky. 587, 208 S.W.2d 749 (1948)
2 ALR5th 1—§ 57
Sneary v. Director of Revenue, 865 S.W.2d 342, 27 A.L.R.5th 959 (Mo. 1993)
27 ALR5th 794—§ 3
Sneath v. Express Messenger, 881 P.2d 453 (Colo. App. 1994)
63 ALR6th 187—§ 51
Sneath v. Popiolek, 135 Mich. App. 17, 352 N.W.2d 331 (1984)
97 ALR6th 653—§ 2, 16
Sneberger v. BTI Americas, Inc., 1998 WL 826992 (E.D. Pa. 1998)
79 ALR5th 587—§ 3, 5, 8
Sneddon v. Hotwire, Inc., 2005 WL 1593593 (N.D. Cal. 2005)
61 ALR6th 387—§ 41
Snedegar v. Midwestern Indem. Co., 44 Ohio App. 3d 64, 541 N.E.2d 90 (10th Dist. Franklin County 1988)
66 ALR5th 269—§ 3
Snediker v. County of Orange, 58 N.Y.2d 647, 458 N.Y.S.2d 517, 444 N.E.2d 981 (1982)
31 ALR5th 572—§ 44
33 ALR5th 205—§ 28
Snediker v. County of Orange, 89 App. Div. 2d 560, 452 N.Y.S.2d 111 (2d Dep't 1982)
31 ALR5th 572—§ 44
33 ALR5th 205—§ 28
Snee v. Carter-Wallace, Inc., 145 Lab. Cas. (CCH) ¶ 59438, 2001 WL 849734 (E.D. Pa. 2001)
53 ALR6th 213—§ 9

Sneed, Matter of Disciplinary Proceedings Against, 176 Wis. 2d 126, 499 N.W.2d 668 (1993)
43 ALR6th 163—§ 26
Sneed v. Beaverson, 395 P.2d 414 (Okla. 1964)
2 ALR5th 1—§ 57
Sneed v. Dixon, 2007 WL 1202243 (N.D. Tex. 2007)
65 ALR6th 93—§ 16
Sneed v. Hanly, 22 F. Cas. 712
67 ALR5th 587—§ 4
Sneed v. Johnson, 600 F.3d 607 (6th Cir. 2010)
102 ALR6th 417—§ 6
Sneed v. People, 38 Mich. 248 (1878)
12 ALR5th 909—§ 3
Sneed v. PNC Bank, Nat. Ass'n, 2011 WL 7429423 (D. Colo. 2011)
86 ALR6th 411—§ 5
Sneed v. State, 85 So. 3d 298, 97 A.L.R.6th 777 (Miss. Ct. App. 2012)
97 ALR6th 263—§ 15, 194
Sneed v. State, 235 Ind. 198, 130 N.E.2d 32 (1955)
57 ALR6th 445—§ 59
Sneed v. State, 955 S.W.2d 451 (Tex. App. Houston 14th Dist. 1997)
38 ALR5th 433—§ 49
Sneed v. Stovall, 22 S.W.3d 277 (Tenn. Ct. App. 1999)
11 ALR5th 1—§ 7, 21
Sneeze v. National Super Markets, Inc., 429 So. 2d 211 (La. Ct. App. 1st Cir. 1983)
123 ALR5th 1—§ 3
Sneh v. Bank of New York Mellon, 2012 WL 5519690 (D. Minn. 2012)
86 ALR6th 411—§ 5
Sneider v. Kimberly-Clark Corp., 91 F.R.D. 1, 33 FR Serv. 2d 449 (N.D. Ill. 1980)
26 ALR5th 628—§ 31, 33
Sneij v. Department of Professional Regulation, Bd. of Medical Examiners, 454 So. 2d 795 (Fla. Dist. Ct. App. 3d Dist. 1984)

19 ALR6th 577—§ 13

Snell v. Allianz Life Ins. Co. of North
America, 2000 WL 1336640 (D.
Minn. 2000)

105 ALR5th 499—§ 3

Snell v. Bangor Steam Navigation Co.,
30 Me. 337 (1849)

19 ALR5th 622—§ 34, 38, 47, 49

Snell v. Bell Helicopter Textron, 107
F.3d 744, 97 C.D.O.S. 1187, 97
Daily Journal DAR 1793, CCH
Prod. Liab. Rep. ¶ 14876 (CA9 Cal.
1997)

53 ALR5th 535—§ 3, 7

Snell v. City Of York, Pennsylvania, 564
F.3d 659 (3d Cir. 2009)

70 ALR6th 513—§ 7

71 ALR6th 471—§ 11

Snell v. Johnson County School Dist.
No. 1, 2004 WY 19, 86 P.3d 248,
185 Ed. Law Rep. 1063 (Wyo.
2004)

60 ALR6th 481—§ 4

Snell v. Levitt, 110 N.Y. 595, 18 N.E.
370, 1 LRA 414 (1888)

62 ALR5th 219—§ 5, 53

Snell v. Montana-Dakota Utilities Co.,
198 Mont. 56, 643 P.2d 841, 32 Fair
Empl. Prac. Cas. (BNA) 193 (1982)

17 ALR6th 563—§ 4, 11

Snell v. Salem Ave. Assoc., 111 Ohio
App. 3d 23, 675 N.E.2d 555 (2d
Dist. Montgomery County 1996)

75 ALR5th 1—§ 10, 13, 14, 20

Snell v. State, 658 So. 2d 1165 (Fla.
Dist. Ct. App. 2d Dist. 1995)

21 ALR6th 771—§ 6

Snell v. Village of University Park, 185
Ill. App. 3d 973, 134 Ill. Dec. 49,
542 N.E.2d 49 (1st Dist. 1989)

12 ALR6th 645—§ 55

Snell v. Wyman, 281 F. Supp. 853 (S.D.
N.Y. 1968)

48 ALR5th 473—§ 3

Snellen v. Brazoria County, 224 S.W.2d
305 (Tex. Civ. App. Galveston
1949)

44 ALR6th 259—§ 27

Snellen v. State Farm Fire & Casualty
Co., 675 F. Supp. 1064 (W.D. Ky.
1987)

1 ALR5th 817—§ 12

Snellgrose, In re, 432 Pa. 158, 247 A.2d
596 (1968)

95 ALR5th 533—§ 4

124 ALR5th 203—§ 4

Snellgrove v. State, 569 N.E.2d 337
(Ind. 1991)

20 ALR6th 479—§ 3

Snelling v. Fall Mountain Regional
School Dist., 2001 DNH 57, 2001
WL 276975 (D.N.H. 2001)

98 ALR6th 599—§ 16, 17, 50, 75

Snelling v. State, 123 P.3d 1096 (Alaska
Ct. App. 2005)

26 ALR6th 511—§ 26

Snelling v. State, 2009-Ohio-4558, 2009
WL 2841382 (Ohio Ct. App. 5th
Dist. Richland County 2009)

64 ALR6th 1—§ 7, 9, 11

Snelling & Snelling, Inc. v. Armel, Inc.,
360 F. Supp. 1319, 179 USPQ 699
(W.D. La 1973)

14 ALR5th 242—§ 41, 44

Snellings v. Snellings, 272 Ala. 254, 130
So. 2d 363 (1961)

55 ALR5th 557—§ 10

Snelson v. Com., Unemployment Compensation Bd. of Review, 93 Pa.
Commw. 539, 502 A.2d 734 (1985)

18 ALR6th 195—§ 34

Snevily v. Read, 9 Watts 396, 1840 WL
3773 (Pa. 1840)

98 ALR5th 353—§ 4

S.N. Golden Estates, Inc. v. Continental
Cas. Co., 293 N.J. Super. 395, 680
A.2d 1114 (App. Div. 1996)

98 ALR5th 193—§ 15

106 ALR5th 1—§ 7

S.N.H., In re, 300 Ga. App. 321, 685
S.E.2d 290 (2009)

103 ALR6th 247—§ 17

Sniadach v. Family Finance Corp. of
Bay View, 395 U.S. 337, 89 S. Ct.
1820, 23 L. Ed. 2d 349, 19 Wage &
Hour Cas. (BNA) 5 (1969)

---

86 ALR5th 527—§ 12
Snider v. Allstate Ins. Co., 135 Wis. 2d 546, 401 N.W.2d 183 (Ct. App. 1986)
86 ALR6th 321—§ 11, 12
91 ALR6th 171—§ 25
Snider v. Bob Heinlin Concrete Const. Co., 506 N.E.2d 77 (Ind. Ct. App. 1st Dist. 1987)
70 ALR5th 261—§ 2, 3, 5, 38, 42, 46
74 ALR5th 523—§ 2 to 4, 10, 41
75 ALR5th 413—§ 2
Snider v. Grodetz, 442 So. 2d 344 (Fla. 5th DCA 1983)
81 ALR6th 469—§ 7
Snider v. Grodetz, 442 So. 2d 344 (Fla. Dist. Ct. App. 5th Dist. 1983)
83 ALR5th 651—§ 7
Snider v. Harvey, 215 Pa. 538, 64 A. 687 (1906)
74 ALR5th 369—§ 8, 14
Snider v. Lewis, 150 Ind. App. 30, 276 N.E.2d 160 (1971)
12 ALR5th 195—§ 66
Snider v. Lillie, 131 Ohio App. 3d 444, 722 N.E.2d 1036 (1st Dist. Hamilton County 1997)
86 ALR5th 637—§ 3
Snider v. Peyton, 384 F.2d 521 (4th Cir. 1967)
111 ALR5th 491—§ 3, 9
Snider v. Snider, 302 S.W.2d 621 (Ky. 1957)
53 ALR5th 375—§ 14
Snider v. Snider, 375 So. 2d 591 (Fla. App. D3 1979)
17 ALR5th 366—§ 2, 14
Snider v. Snider, 474 So. 2d 1374 (La. Ct. App. 2d Cir. 1985)
21 ALR5th 396—§ 3, 15, 19, 22, 23, 71
40 ALR5th 227—§ 21
67 ALR5th 1—§ 12
Snider v. Snider, 2001 WL 32670 (Va. Ct. App. 2001)
109 ALR5th 1—§ 3
Snider v. State, 71 Okla. Crim. 98, 108 P.2d 552 (1940)

108 ALR5th 593—§ 11
Snider v. State, 119 Tex. Crim. 584, 44 S.W.2d 998 (1931)
29 ALR5th 59—§ 3, 53
Snider v. State, 119 Tex. Crim. 635, 44 S.W.2d 997 (1931)
29 ALR5th 59—§ 3, 53
Snider v. State ex rel. Oklahoma Real Estate Com'n, 1999 OK 55, 987 P.2d 1204 (Okla. 1999)
7 ALR5th 474—§ 148
Snider v. Unemployment Compensation Board of Review, 204 Pa. Super. 538, 205 A.2d 658 (1964)
23 ALR5th 176—§ 20
Snider v. Wimberly, 357 Mo. 491, 209 S.W.2d 239 (1948)
112 ALR5th 621—§ 7
Snider's Case, 334 Mass. 65, 134 N.E.2d 16 (1956)
36 ALR5th 225—§ 14
Sniecinski v. Blue Cross & Blue Shield of Michigan, 2001 WL 717456 (Mich. Ct. App. 2001)
99 ALR5th 1—§ 3
Sniegowski v. Bureau of Unemployment Compensation, 11 Ohio App. 2d 73, 228 N.E.2d 679 (1966 Ohio App)
60 ALR5th 459—§ 2, 20
Snipes v. Carr, 526 So. 2d 591 (Ala. Civ. App. 1988)
69 ALR5th 1—§ 3, 5
Snipes v. Jackson, 69 N.C. App. 64, 316 S.E.2d 657 (1984)
7 ALR5th 852—§ 23, 25, 27
Snipes v. State, 651 So. 2d 108 (Fla. Dist. Ct. App. 2d Dist. 1995)
124 ALR5th 1—§ 3
Snisky v. Whisenhunt, 44 Ark. App. 13, 864 S.W.2d 875 (1993)
40 ALR5th 227—§ 2
Snitowsky v. NBC Subsidiary (WMAQ-TV), Inc., 297 Ill. App. 3d 304, 231 Ill. Dec. 465, 696 N.E.2d 761, 127 Ed. Law Rep. 935, 26 Media L. Rep. (BNA) 2265 (1st Dist. 1998)
19 ALR5th 1—§ 92

Snively v. Record Publishing Co., 185 Cal. 565, 198 P. 1 (1921)

44 ALR5th 193—§ 21

Snively, Commonwealth ex rel. v. Snively, 206 Pa. Super. 278, 212 A.2d 905 (1965)

39 ALR5th 1—§ 4

S.N. Mart, Ltd. v. Maurices Inc., 234 Neb. 343, 451 N.W.2d 259 (1990)

75 ALR5th 1—§ 7, 13, 14, 17

Snoddy, Ex parte, 487 So. 2d 860 (Ala. 1986)

42 ALR5th 221—§ 10, 18

Snoddy v. American Nat. Bank, 88 Tenn. 573, 13 S.W. 127 (1890)

74 ALR5th 369—§ 8

Snoddy v. Teepak, Inc., 198 Ill. App. 3d 966, 145 Ill. Dec. 64, 556 N.E.2d 682 (1st Dist. 1990)

17 ALR6th 1—§ 27

Snodgrass v. Baumgart, 25 Kan. App. 2d 812, 974 P.2d 604 (1999)

91 ALR5th 1—§ 6

Snodgrass v. Headco Industries, Inc., 640 S.W.2d 147 (Mo. App. 1982)

12 ALR5th 195—§ 49

Snodgrass v. Headco Industries, Inc., 640 S.W.2d 147 (Mo. Ct. App. W.D. 1982)

53 ALR6th 213—§ 12

Snodgrass v. Rissler & McMurry Co., 903 P.2d 1015 (Wyo. 1995)

112 ALR5th 47—§ 6

116 ALR5th 433—§ 13

118 ALR5th 91—§ 2, 19

Snodgrass v. Snodgrass, 90 Ohio App. 441, 48 Ohio Ops. 111, 107 N.E.2d 155 (Belmont Co. 1951)

31 ALR5th 499—§ 8, 11, 13, 18

Snodgrass v. Snodgrass, 297 S.W.3d 878 (Ky. Ct. App. 2009)

86 ALR6th 321—§ 13

90 ALR6th 451—§ 86

Snodgrass v. State, 67 Tex. Crim. 615, 150 S.W. 162 (1912)

10 ALR6th 31—§ 54

Snodgrass v. State Farm Mut. Auto. Ins. Co., 15 Kan. App. 2d 153, 804 P.2d 1012 (1991)

51 ALR5th 701—§ 13

Snohomish County v. Hinds, 61 Wash. App. 371, 810 P.2d 84 (1991)

17 ALR5th 195—§ 16

Snohomish County v. State, 97 Wash. 2d 646, 648 P.2d 430 (1982)

53 ALR5th 1—§ 23, 41

Snoke v. Staff Leasing, Inc., 43 F. Supp. 2d 1317 (M.D. Fla. 1998)

93 ALR5th 47—§ 13

123 ALR5th 411—§ 61

Snook v. City of Anaconda, 26 Mont. 128, 66 P. 756 (1901)

12 ALR6th 645—§ 3

Snook v. Hall, 33 A.D.2d 876, 307 N.Y.S.2d 679 (4th Dep't 1969)

26 ALR6th 331—§ 4

Snook v. Herrmann, 161 N.W.2d 185 (Iowa 1968)

40 ALR6th 99—§ 29

Snook v. Sierra Pacific Mortg. Co., Inc., 2011 WL 4402507 (D. Nev. 2011)

86 ALR6th 411—§ 5

Snook v. Snetzer, 25 Ohio St. 516, 1874 WL 105 (1874)

20 ALR6th 211—§ 26

Snook v. State, 34 Ohio App. 60, 170 N.E. 444 (2d Dist. Franklin County 1929)

101 ALR6th 499—§ 15

Snoparsky v. Baer, 439 Pa. 140, 266 A.2d 707 (1970)

63 ALR5th 195—§ 3

Snortland v. Crawford, 306 N.W.2d 614 (N.D. 1981)

51 ALR6th 359—§ 7

Snover v. City of Starke, Florida, 398 Fed. Appx. 445 (11th Cir. 2010)

84 ALR6th 89—§ 3

Snow, Ex parte, 508 So. 2d 266 (Ala. 1987)

86 ALR5th 637—§ 3

Snow, Ex parte, 764 So. 2d 531 (Ala. 1999)

95 ALR6th 85—§ 38
Snow v. Amherst County Bd. of Zoning Appeals, 248 Va. 404, 448 S.E.2d 606 (1994)

38 ALR5th 737—§ 2
Snow v. C.I.T. Corp. of South, Inc., 278 Ark. 554, 647 S.W.2d 465, 36 U.C.C.R.S. 145 (1983)

38 ALR5th 191—§ 2, 49
Snow v. Commonwealth, Unemployment Compensation Bd. of Review, 95 Pa. Cmwlth. 259, 505 A.2d 383 (1986)

33 ALR5th 643—§ 23
Snow v. Crosby, 851 So. 2d 222 (Fla. Dist. Ct. App. 3d Dist. 2003)

11 ALR6th 237—§ 9
Snow v. Durham County Com'rs, 112 N.C. 335, 17 S.E. 176 (1893)

81 ALR6th 363—§ 24
Snow v. Grillo, 2004 WL 2958685 (N.D. Ill. 2004)

89 ALR6th 1—§ 69
Snow v. Gulf States Utilities Co., 492 So. 2d 31 (La. Ct. App. 1st Cir. 1986)

95 ALR5th 29—§ 6, 7
Snow v. Harnischfeger Corp., 12 F.3d 1154, Prod. Liab. Rep. (CCH) ¶ 13776, 1993 WL 530680 (1st Cir. 1993)

122 ALR5th 1—§ 28
Snow v. Holistic Health, 2010-1347 La. App. 1 Cir. 2/11/11, 2011 WL 767065 (La. Ct. App. 1st Cir. 2011)

85 ALR6th 323—§ 71
Snow v. Industrial Commission, 172 Colo. 133, 470 P.2d 852 (1970)

107 ALR5th 441—§ 15
20 ALR6th 641—§ 23
Snow v. Irion, 2005 UT App 521, 127 P.3d 1222 (Utah Ct. App. 2005)

93 ALR6th 123—§ 66
Snow v. Johnston, 197 Ga. 146, 28 S.E.2d 270 (1943)

73 ALR5th 223—§ 11
Snow v. Metropolitan Transit Authority, 323 Mass. 21, 80 N.E.2d 49 (1948)

63 ALR6th 495—§ 42
Snow v. Mikenas, 373 Mass. 809, 370 N.E.2d 1001 (1977)

49 ALR6th 505—§ 4
Snow v. Ridgeview Medical Center, 128 F.3d 1201, 8 A.D. Cas. (BNA) 343, 75 Fair Empl. Prac. Cas. (BNA) 185 (8th Cir. 1997)

51 ALR5th 1—§ 7
Snow v. Ruden, McClosky, Smith, Schuster & Russell, P.A., 896 So. 2d 787, 22 I.E.R. Cas. (BNA) 873, 36 A.L.R.6th 845 (Fla. Dist. Ct. App. 2d Dist. 2005)

36 ALR6th 203—§ 4
Snow v. Snow, 189 Or. App. 189, 74 P.3d 1137 (2003)

59 ALR6th 161—§ 43
60 ALR6th 193—§ 23
Snow v. Snow, 369 N.W.2d 581 (Minn. Ct. App. 1985)

16 ALR5th 650—§ 35
20 ALR5th 700—§ 2, 25
67 ALR5th 1—§ 8
Snow v. State, 11 Tex. App. 99, 1881 WL 9624 (Ct. App. 1881)

97 ALR5th 537—§ 35
Snow v. State, 423 So. 2d 220 (Ala. 1982)

37 ALR5th 703—§ 3
Snow v. State, 800 So. 2d 472 (Miss. 2001)

98 ALR6th 455—§ 22
Snow v. State, 875 So. 2d 188 (Miss. 2004)

122 ALR5th 145—§ 22
Snow v. State, 994 S.W.2d 737 (Tex. App. Corpus Christi 1999)

29 ALR6th 1—§ 10
Snow v. State, 2004 OK CR 10, 87 P.3d 626 (Okla. Crim. App. 2004)

122 ALR5th 145—§ 9
Snow v. Van Dam, 291 Mass. 477, 197 N.E. 224 (1935)

25 ALR5th 123—§ 9
25 ALR5th 233—§ 12
119 ALR5th 519—§ 4, 14, 15

Snow v. Villacci, 2000 ME 127, 754 A.2d 360 (Me. 2000)

7 ALR6th 1—§ 2, 37

Snow v. WRS Group, Inc., 73 Fed. Appx. 2, 56 Fed. R. Serv. 3d 300 (5th Cir. 2003)

54 ALR6th 99—§ 36

Snowball v. State, 2013 WL 6506172 (Idaho Ct. App. 2013)

97 ALR6th 263—§ 13, 24

Snowbarger v. M. F. A. Central Co-op., 349 S.W.2d 224 (Mo. 1961)

11 ALR6th 351—§ 20

Snowden v. Anne Arundel County, 295 Md. 429, 456 A.2d 380 (1983)

47 ALR5th 553—§ 4, 10, 20

Snowden v. CheckPoint Check Cashing, 290 F.3d 631, R.I.C.O. Bus. Disp. Guide (CCH) ¶ 10250 (4th Cir. 2002)

13 ALR6th 145—§ 11

Snowden v. Handgun Permit Review Bd. of Maryland Dept. of Public Safety and Correctional Services, 45 Md. App. 464, 413 A.2d 295 (1980)

91 ALR6th 435—§ 61, 66

Snowden v. McGuire, 2 Cranch CC 6, 22 F. Cas. 736, No 13150 (F. CC Dist. Col. 1810)

19 ALR5th 622—§ 3, 17

Snowden v. Osborne, 269 So. 2d 858 (Miss. 1972)

12 ALR5th 195—§ 10

Snowden v. Pearl River Broadcasting Corp., 251 So. 2d 405 (La. Ct. App. 1st Cir. 1971)

40 ALR6th 231—§ 5, 8

Snowden v. State, 449 So. 2d 332 (Fla. App. D5 1984)

7 ALR5th 263—§ 4

Snowden v. State, 574 So. 2d 960 (Ala. Crim. App. 1990)

77 ALR5th 201—§ 5
78 ALR5th 1—§ 21

Snowden v. State, 677 A.2d 33 (Del. 1996)

29 ALR5th 487—§ 3

Snowhite v. State, Use of Tennant, 243 Md. 291, 221 A.2d 342, 19 A.L.R.3d 1155 (1966)

91 ALR5th 1—§ 3, 10, 19

Snow Lake Shores Property Owners Corp. v. Smith, 610 So. 2d 357 (Miss. 1992)

111 ALR5th 313—§ 20

Snowmass Am. Corp. v. Schoenheit, 524 P.2d 645 (Colo. Ct. App. 1974)

115 ALR5th 251—§ 6

Snowney v. Harrah's Entertainment, Inc., 35 Cal. 4th 1054, 29 Cal. Rptr. 3d 33, 112 P.3d 28 (2005)

16 ALR6th 767—§ 12

Snow, Nuffer, Engstrom & Drake v. Tanasse, 1999 UT 49, 980 P.2d 208 (Utah 1999)

64 ALR6th 473—§ 8

S.N.R., In re Welfare of, 617 N.W.2d 77 (Minn. Ct. App. 2000)

89 ALR5th 195—§ 3

S.N.R., In re Welfare of, 617 N.W.2d 77(Minn. Ct. App. 2000)

63 ALR6th 429—§ 3

Snug Club, Inc. v. State, 1976 OK CR 31, 545 P.2d 1301 (Okla. Crim. App. 1976)

103 ALR6th 137—§ 15

Snug Harbor, Ltd. v. Zurich Ins., 968 F.2d 538 (CA5 Tex. 1992)

14 ALR5th 695—§ 4, 28

Snug Harbor Realty Co. v. First Nat'l Bank, 54 N.J. 95, 253 A.2d 545 (1969)

45 ALR5th 389—§ 18

Snug Harbor Realty Co. v. First Nat'l Bank, 105 N.J. Super. 572, 253 A.2d 581, 6 U.C.C.R.S. 689 (1969)

45 ALR5th 389—§ 18

SNW, State ex rel. v. Mitchell, 800 So. 2d 809 (La. 2001)

10 ALR6th 173—§ 2

Snyder, Ex parte, 81 Okla. Crim. 34, 159 P.2d 752 (1945)

54 ALR5th 743—§ 4

Snyder, In re, 102 Pa. Commw. 165, 516 A.2d 788 (1986)

14 ALR6th 543—§ 4

Snyder, In re Complaint of, 276 Or. 897, 559 P.2d 1273 (1976)

26 ALR6th 1—§ 8

Snyder, In re Marriage of, 739 P.2d 923 (Colo. App. 1987)

48 ALR5th 473—§ 8

52 ALR5th 221—§ 2, 4, 20, 21

Snyder v. Ag Trucking, Inc., 57 F.3d 484, 131 Lab. Cas. (CCH) ¶ 58061, 1995 FED App. 0184P (6th Cir. 1995)

53 ALR6th 213—§ 5

Snyder v. Alternate Energy Inc., 2008 WL 1701744 (N.Y. City Civ. Ct. 2008)

30 ALR6th 413—§ 5

Snyder v. Ambrose, 266 Ill. App. 3d 163, 203 Ill. Dec. 319, 639 N.E.2d 639 (2d Dist. 1994)

75 ALR5th 1—§ 7, 14

Snyder v. American Ass'n of Blood Banks, 144 N.J. 269, 676 A.2d 1036 (1996)

64 ALR5th 333—§ 2, 3, 6, 40, 41

Snyder v. American Ass'n of Blood Banks, 282 N.J. Super. 23, 659 A.2d 482 (App. Div. 1995)

1 ALR5th 431—§ 12

Snyder v. American Beverage Ass'n, 134 S. Ct. 61, 187 L. Ed. 2d 26 (2013)

94 ALR6th 239—§ 10 to 12

96 ALR6th 577—§ 12, 21

Snyder v. Ash, 72 Ohio App. 3d 795, 596 N.E.2d 518 (5th Dist. Stark County 1991)

125 ALR5th 403—§ 12

Snyder v. Bank One, Kentucky, N.A., 113 F.3d 774, 32 U.C.C. Rep. Serv. 2d (CBC) 614 (7th Cir. 1997)

61 ALR5th 525—§ 5, 22, 24

Snyder v. Baumecker, 708 F. Supp. 1451 (D.C. N.J. 1989)

4 ALR5th 273—§ 2, 34

Snyder v. Bopp, 240 App. Div. 989, 268 N.Y.S. 269 (1933)

19 ALR5th 622—§ 36, 47

Snyder v. Boston Whaler, Inc., 892 F. Supp. 955, 27 U.C.C. Rep. Serv. 2d (CBC) 898 (W.D. Mich. 1994)

81 ALR5th 483—§ 5

Snyder v. Boy Scouts of America, Inc., 205 Cal. App. 3d 1318, 253 Cal. Rptr. 156 (3d Dist. 1988)

9 ALR5th 321—§ 3, 8, 11 to 13, 15

12 ALR5th 546—§ 2 to 4

Snyder v. Case, 259 Neb. 621, 611 N.W.2d 409 (2000)

75 ALR6th 235—§ 11

Snyder v. CBS, 204 App. Div. 2d 252, 612 N.Y.S.2d 147 (1st Dep't 1994)

51 ALR5th 1—§ 7

Snyder v. C.I.R., 93 T.C. 529, Tax Ct. Rep. (CCH) 46137, Tax Ct. Rep. Dec. (P-H) 93.43, 1989 WL 129656 (1989)

16 ALR6th 693—§ 14

Snyder v. City of Philadelphia, 129 Pa. Commw. 89, 564 A.2d 1036, Prod. Liab. Rep. (CCH) ¶ 12270 (1989)

96 ALR5th 239—§ 5

Snyder v. City of Topeka, 884 F. Supp. 1504 (D. Kan. 1995)

89 ALR6th 1—§ 48

Snyder v. Commissioner of Public Safety, 496 N.W.2d 858 (Minn. Ct. App. 1993)

92 ALR6th 295—§ 14

94 ALR6th 191—§ 4, 15

96 ALR6th 355—§ 17, 36

Snyder v. Commissioner of Public Safety, 744 N.W.2d 19 (Minn. Ct. App. 2008)

92 ALR6th 295—§ 7, 25

96 ALR6th 355—§ 17, 36, 46

Snyder v. Commonwealth, Unemployment Compensation Board of Review, 36 Pa. Cmwlth. 102, 387 A.2d 517 (1978)

2 ALR5th 475—§ 3

Snyder v. Contemporary Obstetrics & Gynecology, P.C., 258 Neb. 643, 605 N.W.2d 782 (2000)

7 ALR5th 1—§ 3

Snyder v. Cook, 688 P.2d 496 (Utah 1984)
41 ALR5th 47—§ 5, 8, 12

Snyder v. Farnam Companies, Inc., 792 F. Supp. 2d 712, 74 U.C.C. Rep. Serv. 2d 592 (D.N.J. 2011)
83 ALR6th 1—§ 6, 11, 14, 31, 35, 85
84 ALR6th 1—§ 2, 5, 7, 11, 13, 28, 51

Snyder v. First Fed Sav & Loan Ass'n, 90 S.D. 440, 241 N.W.2d 725 (1976)
20 ALR5th 499—§ 3

Snyder v. Foote, 822 P.2d 1353 (Alaska 1991)
11 ALR5th 1—§ 16

Snyder v. Freeman, 300 N.C. 204, 266 S.E.2d 593 (1980)
111 ALR5th 207—§ 11

Snyder v. General Electric Co., 47 Wash. 2d 60, 287 P.2d 108 (1955)
63 ALR5th 285—§ 6

Snyder v. Guardian Automotive Products, Inc., 288 F. Supp. 2d 868 (N.D. Ohio 2003)
12 ALR6th 241—§ 5

Snyder v. Innis, 2009 WI App 27, 316 Wis. 2d 411, 763 N.W.2d 559 (Ct. App. 2009)
96 ALR6th 103—§ 3

Snyder v. I.R.S., 596 F. Supp. 240, 84-2 U.S. Tax Cas. (CCH) ¶ 9894, 40 Fed. R. Serv. 2d 496, 54 A.F.T.R.2d 84-6425 (N.D. Ind. 1984)
62 ALR6th 517—§ 68

Snyder v. Isaly Dairy Co., 79 Ohio L. Abs. 289, 155 N.E.2d 235 (App. Mahoning Co. 1957)
2 ALR5th 1—§ 25

Snyder v. Jessie, 164 App. Div. 2d 405, 565 N.Y.S.2d 924 (4th Dep't 1990)
5 ALR5th 1—§ 12, 14

Snyder v. Lehigh V. R. Co., 245 F.2d 112 (CA3 Pa. 1957)
33 ALR5th 205—§ 7

Snyder v. Louisiana, 128 S. Ct. 1203, 170 L. Ed. 2d 175 (U.S. 2008)
36 ALR6th 681—§ 32

Snyder v. Louisiana, 2007 WL 843815 (U.S. 2007)
26 ALR6th 659—§ 37

Snyder v. Love, 2006 MT 317, 335 Mont. 49, 153 P.3d 571 (2006)
98 ALR6th 417—§ 5

Snyder v. Lovercheck, 992 P.2d 1079 (Wyo. 1999)
33 ALR6th 305—§ 7

Snyder v. Major, 789 F. Supp. 646 (S.D. N.Y., 1992)
60 ALR5th 239—§ 2, 5, 29

Snyder v. Major, 818 F. Supp. 68 (S.D. N.Y. 1993)
60 ALR5th 239—§ 12, 15

Snyder v. Medical Service Corp. of Eastern Washington, 145 Wash. 2d 233, 35 P.3d 1158, 12 A.D. Cas. (BNA) 1155, 18 I.E.R. Cas. (BNA) 1267 (2001)
10 ALR6th 375—§ 7

Snyder v. Mekhjian, 125 N.J. 328, 593 A.2d 318 (1991)
12 ALR5th 149—§ 2

Snyder v. Mekhjian, 244 N.J. Super. 281, 582 A.2d 307, Prod. Liab. Rep. (CCH) ¶ 12686 (App. Div. 1990)
12 ALR5th 149—§ 15
64 ALR5th 333—§ 13, 14, 19, 32 to 34

Snyder v. Millersville University, 2008 WL 5093140 (E.D. Pa. 2008)
49 ALR6th 115—§ 4

Snyder v. Minneapolis, 441 N.W.2d 781 (Minn. 1989)
24 ALR5th 200—§ 5

Snyder v. Morristown Cent. School Dist. No. 1, 167 A.D.2d 678, 563 N.Y.S.2d 258, 64 Ed. Law Rep. 1161 (3d Dep't 1990)
66 ALR5th 1—§ 6

Snyder v. Murray City Corp., 159 F.3d 1227 (10th Cir. 1998)
30 ALR6th 459—§ 7

Snyder v. Murray City Corp., 902 F. Supp. 1455 (D. Utah 1995)
26 ALR6th 145—§ 3

Snyder v. Murray City Corp., 2003 UT 13, 73 P.3d 325 (Utah 2003)

26 ALR6th 145—§ 4

Snyder v. National Union Fire Ins. Co., 688 F. Supp. 932 (S.D. N.Y. 1988)

60 ALR5th 239—§ 29

Snyder v. Nationwide Mut. Ins. Co., 373 Pa. Super. 294, 541 A.2d 19 (1988)

103 ALR5th 1—§ 15

Snyder v. O'Bannon, 191 F.3d 456 (7th Cir. 1999)

93 ALR5th 1—§ 6

Snyder v. Pantaleo, 143 Conn. 290, 122 A.2d 21 (1956)

42 ALR5th 1—§ 3

Snyder v. P., C. & S. L. R. Co., 11 W. Va. 14 (1877)

17 ALR5th 547—§ 53, 54, 59

Snyder v. Phelps, 130 S. Ct. 1737, 176 L. Ed. 2d 211 (2010)

56 ALR6th 679—§ 12

Snyder v. Phelps, 131 S. Ct. 1207, 179 L. Ed. 2d 172, 39 Media L. Rep. (BNA) 1353 (2011)

66 ALR6th 635—§ 12

Snyder v. Phelps, 533 F. Supp. 2d 567, 36 Media L. Rep. (BNA) 1516, 40 A.L.R.6th 735 (D. Md. 2008)

40 ALR6th 375—§ 3, 20 to 26

Snyder v. Phelps, 580 F.3d 206, 37 Media L. Rep. (BNA) 2377 (4th Cir. 2009)

56 ALR6th 679—§ 12
66 ALR6th 635—§ 12

Snyder v. Phelps, 2006 WL 3081106 (D. Md. 2006)

40 ALR6th 375—§ 18, 19

Snyder v. Phelps, 2007 WL 3071412 (D. Md. 2007)

40 ALR6th 375—§ 17 to 19

Snyder v. Plankenhorn, 398 Pa. 540, 159 A.2d 209 (1960)

76 ALR5th 337—§ 20

Snyder v. Poplett, 98 Ill. App. 3d 359, 53 Ill. Dec. 761, 424 N.E.2d 396 (4th Dist. 1981)

93 ALR5th 327—§ 3, 7, 13, 17, 33

Snyder v. Portland Traction Co., 182 Or. 344, 185 P.2d 563 (1947)

111 ALR5th 1—§ 8, 10, 13

Snyder v. Roach Bros. Realtors, 17 Pa. D. & C.4th 60, 1992 WL 557661 (C.P. 1992)

27 ALR6th 465—§ 7

Snyder v. San Francisco Feed & Grain, 230 Mont. 16, 748 P.2d 924 (1987)

112 ALR5th 509—§ 2, 12
122 ALR5th 653—§ 2, 7
13 ALR6th 209—§ 7, 24, 27
39 ALR6th 445—§ 40

Snyder v. Scheerer, 190 W. Va. 64, 436 S.E.2d 299 (1993)

6 ALR6th 229—§ 8, 22, 24

Snyder v. Shuttleworth, 5 Ohio App. 137, 27 Ohio C.D. 234, 1916 WL 826 (4th Dist. Hocking County 1916)

122 ALR5th 205—§ 3, 10

Snyder v. Snyder, 27 Ohio App. 3d 1, 27 Ohio B.R. 1, 499 N.E.2d 320 (Cuyahoga Co. 1985)

47 ALR5th 207—§ 6

Snyder v. Snyder, 170 Mich. App. 801, 429 N.W.2d 234 (1988)

99 ALR5th 475—§ 4

Snyder v. Snyder, 579 So. 2d 671 (Ala. Civ. App. 1991)

1 ALR6th 493—§ 5, 11, 17, 18
7 ALR6th 411—§ 4, 5, 22

Snyder v. Snyder, 2007 WL 894415 (D. Minn. 2007) (applying, in part, Minnesota law)

30 ALR6th 483—§ 4

Snyder v. State, 15 Ark. App. 277, 692 S.W.2d 273 (1985)

57 ALR6th 83—§ 6

Snyder v. State, 90 Okla. Crim. 116, 210 P.2d 787 (1949)

105 ALR5th 529—§ 11

Snyder v. State, 92 Idaho 175, 438 P.2d 920 (1968)

15 ALR5th 821—§ 16

Snyder v. State, 103 Nev. 275, 738 P.2d 1303 (1987)

55 ALR5th 125—§ 14, 22

51 ALR6th 1—§ 20
Snyder v. State, 201 Ga. App. 66, 410 S.E.2d 173 (1991)

79 ALR5th 419—§ 9
Snyder v. State, 332 Ark. 279, 965 S.W.2d 121 (1998)

36 ALR5th 161—§ 24
38 ALR6th 1—§ 15
Snyder v. State, 538 N.E.2d 961 (Ind. Ct. App. 4th Dist. 1989)

74 ALR5th 319—§ 13
116 ALR5th 479—§ 2, 5
Snyder v. State, 661 P.2d 638 (Alaska Ct. App. 1983)

6 ALR6th 533—§ 17
Snyder v. State, 893 So. 2d 488 (Ala. Crim. App. 2003)

71 ALR6th 625—§ 21
83 ALR6th 255—§ 22
Snyder v. State, 912 P.2d 1127 (Wyo. 1996)

36 ALR5th 161—§ 3, 7, 9
63 ALR6th 351—§ 3
93 ALR6th 1—§ 5
Snyder v. State, 2000 WL 717081 (Tex. App. El Paso 2000)

101 ALR5th 619—§ 7
Snyder v. State, 2005 WL 2313676 (Tex. App. El Paso 2005)

71 ALR6th 335—§ 13
Snyder v. Sumner, 960 F.2d 1448 (9th Cir. 1992)

51 ALR6th 1—§ 24
52 ALR6th 1—§ 3
Snyder v. Viani, 112 Nev. 568, 916 P.2d 170 (1996)

56 ALR5th 783—§ 2, 4
Snyder v. Western Union Tel. Co., 277 S.W. 362 (Mo. App. 1925)

27 ALR5th 174—§ 63
Snyder v. Whittaker Corp., 839 F.2d 1085, CCH Prod. Liab. Rep. ¶ 11708, 1988 AMC 2534, 24 Fed. Rules Evid. Serv. 1217 (CA5 Tex. 1988)

42 ALR5th 465—§ 2, 7, 13
Snyder v. Woxo, Inc., 185 Neb. 545, 177 N.W.2d 281 (1970)

73 ALR6th 571—§ 15, 55
Snyder v. Zoning Bd. of Westerly, 98 R.I. 139, 200 A.2d 222 (1964)

2 ALR5th 553—§ 66
Snyder Constr. Co., Re, 65 App. Div. 2d 633, 409 N.Y.S.2d 278 (3d Dep't 1978)

7 ALR5th 400—§ 7
SnyderGeneral Corp. v. Century Indem. Co., 113 F.3d 536, 45 Env't. Rep. Cas. (BNA) 1222, 27 Envtl. L. Rep. 21326 (5th Cir. 1997)

88 ALR5th 493—§ 3
89 ALR5th 1—§ 10
SnyderGeneral Corp. v. Continental Ins. Co., 133 F.3d 373, 28 Envtl. L. Rep. 20607 (5th Cir. 1998)

89 ALR5th 1—§ 10
Snyder Industries, Inc. v. Otto, 212 Neb. 40, 321 N.W.2d 77 (1982)

18 ALR6th 195—§ 27
Snyderman v. Isaacs, 31 Ill. 2d 192, 201 N.E.2d 106 (1964)

1 ALR6th 229—§ 23
Snyder's Estate, In re, 71 Pa. D. & C.2d 353, 1975 WL 16718 (C.P. 1975)

87 ALR6th 495—§ 28, 30, 54, 72, 76
Snyder's Estate, Re, 375 Pa. 185, 100 A.2d 67 (1953)

3 ALR5th 394—§ 8, 10
Snyders Smart Shop, Inc. v. Santi, Inc., 590 S.W.2d 167 (Tex. Civ. App. Corpus Christi 1979)

63 ALR5th 1—§ 14
Snype v. New York City, 2006 WL 1441013 (S.D. N.Y. 2006)

89 ALR6th 1—§ 113
S.O., In re Petition of, 795 P.2d 254 (Colo. 1990)

61 ALR5th 151—§ 13
S.O., Interest of, 483 N.W.2d 602 (Iowa 1992)

20 ALR5th 534—§ 16
So v. Land Base, LLC, 2010 WL 3075641 (C.D. Cal. 2010)

72 ALR6th 563—§ 9, 13, 15, 25

Soam Corp. v. Trane Co., 202 A.D.2d 162, 608 N.Y.S.2d 177 (1st Dep't 1994)

24 ALR6th 399—§ 4, 18

Soap v. Carter, 632 F.2d 872 (CA10 Okla. 1980)

32 ALR5th 149—§ 74

Soap v. State, 1977 OK CR 133, 562 P.2d 889 (Okla. Crim. App. 1977)

54 ALR6th 429—§ 7

Soaper v. Hope Industries, Inc., 309 S.C. 438, 424 S.E.2d 493, 20 U.C.C. Rep. Serv. 2d 101 (1992)

89 ALR5th 319—§ 21

Sobeck & Associates, Inc. v. B & R Investments No. 24, 215 Cal. App. 3d 861, 264 Cal. Rptr. 156 (6th Dist. 1989)

104 ALR6th 1—§ 31

Sobel v. Board of Pharmacy (In re Sobel), 130 Or. App. 374, 882 P.2d 606 (1994)

32 ALR5th 57—§ 13

Sobel v. Higgins, 188 A.D.2d 286, 590 N.Y.S.2d 883 (1st Dep't 1992)

88 ALR6th 203—§ 67

Sobelman v. Mark, 9 Conn. L. Rptr. 127, 1993 WL 182397 (Conn. Super. Ct. 1993)

116 ALR5th 433—§ 4, 14

Sobh v. Frederick & Herrud, Inc., 189 Mich. App. 24, 472 N.W.2d 8 (1991)

97 ALR5th 1—§ 15

106 ALR5th 111—§ 10, 12

108 ALR5th 1—§ 18, 37

Sobieske v. Preslar, 755 So. 2d 410 (Miss. 2000)

26 ALR6th 331—§ 17

Sobieski, In re, 246 Ind. 222, 204 N.E.2d 353 (1965)

102 ALR5th 525—§ 21

Sobieski v. Sobieski, 2000 WI App 233, 239 Wis. 2d 232, 619 N.W.2d 307 (Ct. App. 2000)

86 ALR6th 321—§ 12

90 ALR6th 451—§ 116

Sobik's Sandwich Shops, Inc. v. Davis, 371 So. 2d 709 (Fla. App. D4 1979)

6 ALR5th 883—§ 2

Sobik's Sandwich Shops, Inc. v. Davis, 371 So. 2d 709 (Fla. Dist. Ct. App. 4th Dist. 1979)

17 ALR6th 1—§ 26, 28

Sobin, In re, 649 A.2d 589 (D.C. 1994)

3 ALR6th 49—§ 13, 16

Sobin v. Guarnaccia, 256 A.D.2d 457, 682 N.Y.S.2d 93 (2d Dep't 1998)

12 ALR5th 1—§ 19

Sobin v. M. Frisch and Sons, 108 N.J. Super. 99, 260 A.2d 228 (App. Div. 1969)

23 ALR6th 697—§ 12

SOB, Inc. v. County of Benton, 317 F.3d 856 (8th Cir. 2003)

20 ALR6th 161—§ 3

21 ALR6th 425—§ 9

23 ALR6th 573—§ 13

Sobley v. Southern Natural Gas Co., 302 F.3d 325 (5th Cir. 2002)

123 ALR5th 259—§ 4

Sobo, In re, 905 A.2d 158 (D.C. 2006)

44 ALR6th 75—§ 4

Sobol v. E. P. Dutton, Inc., 112 F.R.D. 99 (S.D. N.Y. 1986)

28 ALR5th 1—§ 5

Sobol v. E.P. Dutton, Inc., 112 F.R.D. 99 (S.D. N.Y. 1986)

47 ALR6th 255—§ 6

Sobol v. Perez, 289 F. Supp. 392 (E.D. La. 1968)

83 ALR5th 497—§ 6

Sobota v. Williard, 247 Or. 151, 427 P.2d 758 (1967)

46 ALR6th 241—§ 29, 34

Sobotor v. Prudential Property & Cas. Ins. Co., 200 N.J. Super. 333, 491 A.2d 737 (App. Div. 1984)

8 ALR6th 549—§ 19

Sobotta v. Carlson, 65 Ill. App. 3d 752, 22 Ill. Dec. 465, 382 N.E.2d 855 (3d Dist. 1978)

11 ALR5th 127—§ 42

Sobus v. Contiguglia, 113 A.D.2d 1027, 494 N.Y.S.2d 589 (4th Dep't 1985)

---

91 ALR6th 435—§ 75
Soca v. State, 656 So. 2d 536, 20 FLW
D 1363 (Fla. App. D3 1995)
19 ALR5th 470—§ 3, 9, 15
Socha v. Cudahy Packing Co., 105 Neb.
691, 181 N.W. 706, 13 A.L.R. 513
(1921)
41 ALR6th 207—§ 27
Socha v. Metz, 385 Pa. 632, 123 A.2d
837 (1956)
42 ALR6th 545—§ 18
43 ALR6th 375—§ 9, 15, 47
Socha for State Senate Committee v.
Cleveland Plain Dealer, 1979 WL
210043 (Ohio Ct. App. 8th Dist.
Cuyahoga County 1979)
51 ALR6th 359—§ 13
Sochor v. State, 580 So. 2d 595, 16 FLW
S. 297 (Fla. 1991)
39 ALR5th 283—§ 4, 77
Sochor v. State, 619 So. 2d 285 (Fla.
1993)
65 ALR6th 359—§ 3
83 ALR6th 255—§ 27
Sochor v. State, 883 So. 2d 766 (Fla.
2004)
21 ALR6th 1—§ 4
Social and Rehabilitation Services, State
Department of v. Paillet, 27 Kan.
App. 2d 295
69 ALR5th 1—§ 3
Social and Rehabilitation Services,
State, Dept. of v. Paillet, 270 Kan.
646, 16 P.3d 962 (2001)
86 ALR6th 1—§ 33, 77
Socialist Party v. Uhl, 155 Cal. 776, 103
P. 181 (1909)
120 ALR5th 125—§ 2
121 ALR5th 1—§ 2, 9, 49, 50
Socialist Workers Party v. Associated
Press, 8 Media L. R. 1554 (N.Y.
Sup. 1982)
19 ALR5th 1—§ 162
Social Secur. Admin., etc. v. Employers
Mut. Liability Ins. Co., 234 Md.
493, 199 A.2d 918 (1964)
5 ALR5th 132—§ 3, 13

Social Services, Department of v. Pritchett, 296 S.C. 517, 374 S.E.2d 500
(App. 1988)
20 ALR5th 534—§ 4
Social Services Div. of Child Support
Enforcement, State ex rel. Depart-
ment of v. Kost, 964 S.W.2d 528
(Mo. Ct. App. W.D. 1998)
34 ALR5th 447—§ 4
Social Services etc., Petition of Depart-
ment of, 391 Mass. 113, 461 N.E.2d
186 (1984)
61 ALR5th 151—§ 9
Social Services in Interest of A.E.V.,
People, Department of, 782 P.2d
858 (Colo. Ct. App. 1989)
89 ALR5th 195—§ 7
Social Services of State ex rel. Wolf,
Department of v. McCarty, 506
N.W.2d 144 (S.D. 1993)
90 ALR5th 453—§ 22
Social Services on Behalf of Children
C., Department of v. Richard C.,
674 N.Y.S.2d 53 (App. Div. 2d
Dep't 1998)
27 ALR5th 540—§ 3
Social Services on behalf of Gary Z.,
Department of v. Burton H., 151
Misc. 2d 400, 572 N.Y.S.2d 839
(Fam Ct. 1991)
46 ALR5th 735—§ 2
Social Services on Behalf of Troy C.,
Department of v. Janice T., 137
A.D.2d 527, 524 N.Y.S.2d 267 (2d
Dep't 1988)
87 ALR5th 631—§ 30
Social Services, State Department of v.
White, 606 So. 2d 31 (La. App. 5th
Cir. 1992)
57 ALR5th 389—§ 16
Social Services to Dispense with Con-
sent to Adoption, Petitions of De-
partment of, 20 Mass. App. 689,
482 N.E.2d 535 (1985)
1 ALR5th 469—§ 22

Social Services to Dispense With Consent to Adoption, Petitions of Department of, 20 Mass. App. Ct. 689, 482 N.E.2d 535 (1985)

116 ALR5th 559—§ 7, 13

Social Servs., Div. of Child Support Enforcement ex rel. Comptroller of Virginia, Department of v. Skeens, 442 S.E.2d 432 (Va. App. 1994)

34 ALR5th 447—§ 4

Social Welfare, Department of v. Miller, 157 Vt. 92, 595 A.2d 288 (1991)

77 ALR5th 201—§ 6

Social Welfare of State, Department of v. Gardiner, 94 Cal. App. 2d 431, 210 P.2d 855 (4th Dist. 1949)

63 ALR6th 1—§ 36, 64

Sociedad Espanola de Auxilio Mutuo y Beneficencia v. Morales, 129 S. Ct. 898, 173 L. Ed. 2d 107 (2009)

46 ALR6th 495—§ 24

Societa Italiana di Mutua Beneficenza v. Burr, 71 F.2d 496 (C.C.A. 9th Cir. 1934)

109 ALR5th 421—§ 5, 13

Society for Animal Rights, Inc. v. Mahwah Tp., 138 N.J. Super. 322, 350 A.2d 544 (Law Div. 1975)

77 ALR6th 393—§ 7

Society for Individual Rights, Inc. v. Hampton, 63 F.R.D. 399, 11 Fair Empl. Prac. Cas. (BNA) 1243, 6 Empl. Prac. Dec. (CCH) ¶ 8934 (N.D. Cal. 1973)

96 ALR5th 391—§ 5, 15, 17

Society for Seamen's Children ex rel. Juda J. v. Jennifer J., 208 App. Div. 2d 849, 617 N.Y.S.2d 843 (2d Dep't 1994)

20 ALR5th 534—§ 5, 16

Society Ins. v. Town of Franklin, 233 Wis. 2d 207

14 ALR5th 695—§ 26

Society Nat. Bank v. Pemberton, 63 Ohio Misc. 26, 17 Ohio Op. 3d 342, 409 N.E.2d 1073, 30 U.C.C. Rep. Serv. 76 (Mun. Ct. 1979)

88 ALR6th 1—§ 5, 7, 8, 11, 15, 26, 102

Society of Jesus of New England v. Com., 441 Mass. 662, 808 N.E.2d 272 (2004)

123 ALR5th 385—§ 17

Society of Lloyd's v. Ashenden, 233 F.3d 473 (7th Cir. 2000)

88 ALR5th 545—§ 15

Society of New York Hospital v. Malsky, 88 Misc. 2d 832, 390 N.Y.S.2d 512 (App. Term 1976)

63 ALR5th 427—§ 3, 26

Society of Plastics Industry, Inc. v. City of New York, 68 Misc. 2d 366, 326 N.Y.S.2d 788, 3 Env't. Rep. Cas. (BNA) 1370 (Sup 1971)

94 ALR6th 239—§ 12, 17

Society of Plastics Industry, Inc. v. County of Suffolk, 77 N.Y.2d 761, 570 N.Y.S.2d 778, 573 N.E.2d 1034, 21 Envtl. L. Rep. 21413 (1991)

115 ALR5th 563—§ 3

Society of Professional Journalists v. Secretary of Labor, 616 F. Supp. 569, 11 Media L. R. 2474 (D.C. Utah 1985)

39 ALR5th 103—§ 23

Society of Professional Journalists v. Sexton, 283 S.C. 563, 324 S.E.2d 313, 11 Media L. Rep. (BNA) 1334 (1984)

118 ALR5th 1—§ 4, 14, 15, 27 to 29

Society of Roman Catholic Church of Diocese of Lafayette, Inc. v. Interstate Fire & Cas. Co., 126 F.3d 727 (5th Cir. 1997)

60 ALR5th 165—§ 15

Society of Separationists, Inc. v. Whitehead, 870 P.2d 916 (Utah 1993)

26 ALR6th 145—§ 3

30 ALR6th 459—§ 7

S.O.C., Inc. v. County of Clark, 152 F.3d 1136, 26 Media L. Rep. (BNA) 2199 (9th Cir. 1998)

70 ALR6th 513—§ 6

71 ALR6th 471—§ 4

S.O.C., Inc. v. Mirage Casino-Hotel, 117 Nev. 403, 23 P.3d 243 (2001)
70 ALR6th 513—§ 7
71 ALR6th 471—§ 13
Sockloff v. Burstein, 177 App. Div. 471, 164 N.Y.S. 262 (1917)
45 ALR5th 251—§ 6
Sockow v. Whitmore, 1984 WL 1230 (N.D. Ill. 1984)
89 ALR5th 255—§ 5, 6
Sockwell, Ex parte, 675 So. 2d 38 (Ala. 1995)
15 ALR6th 319—§ 4
Sockwell v. Lucas & Jenkins, 71 Ga. App. 765, 32 S.E.2d 201 (1944)
6 ALR6th 1—§ 5
Sockwell v. Phelps, 20 F.3d 187 (CA5 La. 1994)
14 ALR5th 242—§ 54
Sockwell v. State, 675 So. 2d 4 (Ala. Crim. App. 1993)
15 ALR6th 319—§ 4
Socony Mobil Co. v. Southwestern Bell Tel. Co., 518 S.W.2d 257 (Tex. Civ. App. Corpus Christi 1974)
34 ALR5th 1—§ 9
Socony Mobil Oil Co. v. Continental Oil Co., 335 F.2d 438 (10th Cir. 1964)
65 ALR5th 211—§ 3, 45
Socony Mobil Oil Co. v. Superior Court for Providence County, 97 R.I. 396, 198 A.2d 44 (1964)
26 ALR6th 249—§ 9
Socony-Vacuum Oil Co. v. Bailey, 202 Misc. 364, 109 N.Y.S.2d 799 (1952)
28 ALR5th 603—§ 15, 17
Socony-Vacuum Oil Co. v. C. M. Johnston & Sons Sand & Gravel Co., 103 F.2d 275 (CA8 Mo. 1939)
16 ALR5th 548—§ 5
Socorro v. Orleans Levee Bd., 561 So. 2d 739 (La. App. 4th Cir. 1990)
51 ALR5th 467—§ 2, 3
52 ALR5th 1—§ 2
Soda v. Baird, 411 Pa. Super. 80, 600 A.2d 1274 (1991)
92 ALR6th 379—§ 74

Soday v. Mall Snacks, Inc., 374 So. 2d 138 (La. App. 1st Cir. 1979)
11 ALR5th 715—§ 31, 32, 46, 56
23 ALR5th 241—§ 40
Sodders v. Sodders, 210 Neb. 276, 313 N.W.2d 927 (1981)
27 ALR5th 540—§ 3, 12
Soden, Re Marriage of, 251 Kan. 225, 834 P.2d 358 (1992)
17 ALR5th 143—§ 5, 8
Soden v. Starkman, 218 So. 2d 763 (Fla. App. D3 1969)
12 ALR5th 195—§ 12
Soder v. Chenot, 2007 WL 4556670 (M.D. Pa. 2007)
86 ALR6th 173—§ 8
Soderbeck v. Burnett County, Wis., 752 F.2d 285, 40 Fed. R. Serv. 2d 1470 (7th Cir. 1985)
123 ALR5th 411—§ 22
Soderberg v. McKinney, 44 Cal. App. 4th 1760, 52 Cal. Rptr. 2d 635 (2d Dist. 1996)
44 ALR6th 1—§ 5, 15
Soderholm v. Massachusetts State Lottery Com'n, 2001 WL 34048065 (Mass. Super. Ct. 2001)
48 ALR6th 243—§ 18
Soderling v. Hickok, 409 N.W.2d 73 (Minn. Ct. App. 1987)
86 ALR6th 321—§ 10
87 ALR6th 197—§ 12, 56
Sod Farm Associates v. Springfield Tp. Planning Bd., 297 N.J. Super. 584, 688 A.2d 1058 (App. Div. 1996)
1 ALR5th 622—§ 8
Sodomsky v. Pennsylvania, 129 S. Ct. 2776 (2009)
46 ALR6th 495—§ 38
Sodorff, Estate of v. United Southern Assur. Co., 980 F. Supp. 1004 (W.D. Ark. 1997)
43 ALR5th 149—§ 7.5, 16
Sody v. Sody, 32 Md. App. 644, 363 A.2d 568 (1976)
17 ALR5th 366—§ 9

For assistance, call 1-800-328-4880

Soeder's Estate, In re, 7 Ohio App. 2d
271, 36 Ohio Op. 2d 404, 220
N.E.2d 547 (8th Dist. Cuyahoga
County 1966)
93 ALR5th 327—§ 3 to 5, 18, 23
Soehle v. State, 60 Wis. 2d 72, 208
N.W.2d 341 (1973)
68 ALR5th 343—§ 3
Soenksen v. Cincinnati Milacron Co.,
slip op, No. 81 (October 23, 1984,
F. N.D. Ill.)
30 ALR5th 1—§ 51
Soergel, In re Marriage of, 154 Wis. 2d
564, 453 N.W.2d 624 (1990)
71 ALR5th 99—§ 3, 7
Soesbe v. Lines, 180 Iowa 943, 164
N.W. 129 (1917)
14 ALR5th 242—§ 4, 24
Soet v. State, 381 N.W.2d 285 (S.D.
1986)
107 ALR5th 567—§ 10
Sofa Gallery, Inc. v. Stratford Co., 872
F.2d 259 (CA8 Minn. 1989)
40 ALR5th 57—§ 2, 6
Sofer v. State of N.C. Hertford Police
Dept., 935 F.2d 1287 (4th Cir. 1991)
89 ALR6th 1—§ 113
Sofia Bros. v. General Reinsurance
Corp., 153 Misc. 6, 274 N.Y.S. 565
(Sup 1934)
87 ALR6th 319—§ 38
Sofia Shipping Co., Ltd. v. Amoco
Transport Co., 628 F. Supp. 116,
1986 A.M.C. 2163 (S.D. N.Y. 1986)
67 ALR5th 179—§ 2, 3
Sofie v. Fibreboard Corp., 112 Wash. 2d
636, 771 P.2d 711, Prod. Liab. Rep.
(CCH) ¶ 12169 (1989)
103 ALR5th 379—§ 7
Sofman v. Denham Food Service, Inc.,
37 N.J. 304, 181 A.2d 168, 1
U.C.C.R.S. 93 (1962)
1 ALR5th 1—§ 41
2 ALR5th 189—§ 7
Sofo v. Egan, 57 App. Div. 2d 841, 394
N.Y.S.2d 43 (2d Dep't 1977)
2 ALR5th 553—§ 48

Sofranko v. Ridley Tp., Zoning Bd. of
Adjustment, 35 Pa. D. & C.2d 689,
1964 WL 6481 (C.P. 1964)
47 ALR6th 439—§ 16
Sofranko v. Stefan, 80 A.D.3d 814, 914
N.Y.S.2d 361 (3d Dep't 2011)
102 ALR6th 153—§ 23
Softel Computers, Inc. v. Grosky, 183
A.D.2d 527, 584 N.Y.S.2d 2 (1st
Dep't 1992)
79 ALR5th 587—§ 4
Softman Products Co., LLC v. Adobe
Systems, Inc., 171 F. Supp. 2d 1075,
45 U.C.C. Rep. Serv. 2d 945 (C.D.
Cal. 2001)
106 ALR5th 309—§ 4
Softsolutions, Inc. v. Brigham Young
University, 2000 UT 46, 1 P.3d
1095 (Utah 2000)
60 ALR5th 669—§ 6
Software Design & Application, Ltd. v.
Hoefer & Arnett, Inc., 49 Cal. App.
4th 472, 56 Cal. Rptr. 2d 756, 30
U.C.C. Rep. Serv. 2d 898 (1st Dist.
1996)
62 ALR6th 1—§ 2, 18, 20
Software Design & Application, Ltd. v.
Price Waterhouse, 49 Cal. App. 4th
464, 57 Cal. Rptr. 2d 36, 96
C.D.O.S. 7054, 96 Daily Journal
DAR 11449 (1st Dist. 1996)
48 ALR5th 389—§ 3, 6
Soft Water Utilities, Inc. v. LeFevre, 159
Ind. App. 529, 308 N.E.2d 395,
Blue Sky L. Rep. (CCH) ¶ 71120
(1st Dist. 1974)
2 ALR6th 387—§ 4
Soft Water Utilities, Inc. v. Le Fevre,
261 Ind. 260, 301 N.E.2d 745
(1973)
86 ALR6th 321—§ 5, 6, 9 to 12
Sogg v. American Airlines, 193 App.
Div. 2d 153, 603 N.Y.S.2d 21, 3 AD
Cas. 1195, 63 CCH EPD ¶ 42872
(1st Dep't 1993)
51 ALR5th 1—§ 6, 7
Sogg v. Nevada State Bank, 832 P.2d
781 (Nev 1992)

3 ALR5th 394—§ 23

Soghomonian v. U.S., 82 F. Supp. 2d 1134, 2000-1 U.S. Tax Cas. (CCH) ¶ 50146

19 ALR5th 786—§ 3

Sohaey v. Van Cura, 240 Ill. App. 3d 266, 180 Ill. Dec. 359, 607 N.E.2d 253 (2d Dist. 1992)

66 ALR5th 135—§ 21

115 ALR5th 709—§ 2

117 ALR5th 155—§ 2

Sohi v. Ohio State Dental Bd., 130 Ohio App. 3d 414, 720 N.E.2d 187 (1st Dist. Hamilton County 1998)

10 ALR5th 1—§ 5, 21

Sohn v. Brockington, 371 So. 2d 1089 (Fla. App. D1 1979)

56 ALR5th 1—§ 2, 3, 8

Sohn v. Waterson, 84 U.S. 596, 21 L. Ed. 737, 1873 WL 15949 (1873)

76 ALR6th 31—§ 2, 13

Sohns v. Pederson, 354 N.W.2d 852, 39 U.C.C.R.S. 514 (Minn. App. 1984)

49 ALR5th 1—§ 102

Soho Plaza Corp. v. Nationwide Mut. Ins. Co., 244 A.D.2d 184, 664 N.Y.S.2d 23 (1st Dep't 1997)

22 ALR6th 113—§ 33

Soichet v. Toracinta, 111 F.3d 124 (2d Cir. 1997)

98 ALR5th 305—§ 9

Soileau v. Chet & Kennys Auto Parts, Inc., 337 So. 2d 604 (La. Ct. App. 4th Cir. 1976)

107 ALR5th 441—§ 47

109 ALR5th 161—§ 9

20 ALR6th 641—§ 23

Soileau v. United States Fidelity & Guaranty Co., 158 So. 2d 397 (La. App. 3d Cir. 1963)

26 ALR5th 401—§ 10

Soil Enrichment Materials Corp. v. Zoning Bd. of Appeals, 15 Ill. App. 3d 432, 304 N.E.2d 521 (3d Dist. 1973)

38 ALR5th 357—§ 3, 14

Soil Remediation Co. v. Nu-Way Envtl., 476 S.E.2d 149 (S.C. 1996)

60 ALR5th 669—§ 3

Sokaogon Chippewa Community (Mole Lake Band of Lake Superior Chippewas) v. Schenck, S.C., 287 Wis. 2d 132, 2005 WI App 193, 703 N.W.2d 383 (Ct. App. 2005)

39 ALR6th 155—§ 4

Sokol v. Bob McKinnon Chevrolet, Inc., 307 So. 2d 404 (La. App. 4th Cir. 1975)

23 ALR5th 241—§ 48

Sokol v. Mortimer, 81 Ill. App. 2d 55, 225 N.E.2d 496 (1st Dist. 1967)

35 ALR5th 1—§ 4

71 ALR6th 249—§ 11

Sokol v. Sofokles, 136 App. Div. 2d 535, 523 N.Y.S.2d 155 (2d Dep't 1988)

61 ALR5th 307—§ 6, 7, 10

Sokol v. University Hospital, Inc., 402 F. Supp. 1029 (D.C. Mass. 1975)

28 ALR5th 107—§ 5

Sokol and Co. v. Atlantic Mut. Ins. Co., 430 F.3d 417 (7th Cir. 2005)

49 ALR6th 169—§ 5

Sokolinski v. Municipal Council of Woodbridge Tp., 192 N.J. Super. 101, 469 A.2d 96, 15 Ed. Law Rep. 289 (App. Div. 1983)

4 ALR6th 263—§ 9, 21

Sokolove v. City of Rehoboth Beach, DE, 2005 WL 1800007 (D. Del. 2005)

51 ALR6th 359—§ 16

Sokolow v. County of San Mateo, 213 Cal. App. 3d 231, 261 Cal. Rptr. 520, 62 Empl. Prac. Dec. (CCH) ¶ 42404 (1st Dist. 1989)

106 ALR5th 523—§ 28

Sokolowski, Re Marriage of, 232 Ill. App. 3d 535, 173 Ill. Dec. 701, 597 N.E.2d 675 (1st Dist. 1992)

3 ALR5th 394—§ 6, 7

Sokolsky v. Kuhn, 405 So. 2d 975 (Fla. 1981)

52 ALR5th 221—§ 16

Sola v. Bidwell, 980 S.W.2d 60 (Mo. Ct. App. W.D. 1998)

17 ALR5th 366—§ 13

For assistance, call 1-800-328-4880

59 ALR6th 433—§ 4, 46

Sol Abrahams & Son Const. Co. v. Osterholm, 136 S.W.2d 86 (Mo. App. 1940)

46 ALR5th 1—§ 23

Soland v. Evert, 2011 WL 6015170 (Minn. Ct. App. 2011)

91 ALR6th 1—§ 51

Solano, County of v. Delancy, 264 Cal. Rptr. 721 (App. 1st Dist. 1989)

101 ALR5th 61—§ 20

Solantic, LLC v. City of Neptune Beach, 410 F.3d 1250 (11th Cir. 2005)

70 ALR6th 513—§ 3

71 ALR6th 471—§ 3

Solar Enterprises, Inc. v. Polich, 12 Media L. R. 1844 (Minn. Dist. Ct. 1985)

19 ALR5th 1—§ 152

Solar Kinetics Corp. v. Joseph T. Ryerson & Son, Inc., 488 F. Supp. 1237, 29 U.C.C.R.S. 85 (D.C. Conn. 1980)

38 ALR5th 191—§ 2, 54

Solberg v. Superior Court, 19 Cal. 3d 182, 137 Cal. Rptr. 460, 561 P.2d 1148 (1977)

91 ALR5th 437—§ 4

Solboro Knitting Mills v. International Ladies Garment Workers Union, Local 107, 90 Lab. Cas. (CCH) ¶ 12376, 1980 WL 27627 (N.Y. Sup 1980)

120 ALR5th 351—§ 6

Soldal v. Cook County, Ill., 506 U.S. 56, 113 S. Ct. 538, 121 L. Ed. 2d 450 (1992)

98 ALR5th 305—§ 3

Soldano v. Soldano, 66 App. Div. 2d 839, 411 N.Y.S.2d 395 (2d Dep't 1978)

2 ALR5th 337—§ 2

Soldiers', Sailors', Marines' and Airmen's Club, Inc. v. Carlton Regency Corp., 30 Misc. 3d 352, 911 N.Y.S.2d 774 (Sup 2010)

99 ALR6th 591—§ 9

Soldiers', Sailors', Marines' and Airmen's Club Inc. v. Carlton Regency Corp., 95 A.D.3d 687, 945 N.Y.S.2d 40 (1st Dep't 2012)

99 ALR6th 591—§ 9

Soldinger v. Northwest Airlines, Inc., 51 Cal. App. 4th 345, 58 Cal. Rptr. 2d 747, 72 Fair Empl. Prac. Cas. (BNA) 1261, 153 L.R.R.M. (BNA) 3050 (2d Dist. 1996)

107 ALR5th 623—§ 5 to 7

19 ALR6th 1—§ 3, 11

Soldo v. City of Los Angeles, 2003 WL 21742322 (Cal. App. 2d Dist. 2003)

19 ALR6th 217—§ 52

Sole v. Wyner, 127 S. Ct. 2188 (U.S. 2007)

26 ALR6th 659—§ 12

Sol E. Feldman Furs Inc. v. Jewelers Protection Services Ltd., 134 A.D.2d 171, 520 N.Y.S.2d 760 (1st Dep't 1987)

36 ALR6th 305—§ 14

Solem v. Helm, 463 U.S. 277, 103 S. Ct. 3001, 77 L. Ed. 2d 637 (1983)

12 ALR5th 89—§ 6

89 ALR5th 539—§ 4

Soler v. G & U, Inc., 801 F. Supp. 1056, 1 BNA WH Cas. 2d 192, 122 CCH LC ¶ 35671 (S.D. N.Y. 1992)

23 ALR5th 241—§ 41

Solers, Inc. v. Hartford Cas. Ins. Co., 146 F. Supp. 2d 785 (E.D. Va. 2001)

98 ALR5th 1—§ 4

Solers, Inc. v. Hartford Cas. Ins. Co., 2002 WL 1289740 (4th Cir. 2002)

98 ALR5th 1—§ 4

Solerwitz, In re, 575 A.2d 287 (D.C. 1990)

44 ALR6th 75—§ 19, 46

Soles v. City of Vidalia, 92 Ga. App. 839, 90 S.E.2d 249 (1955)

72 ALR5th 1—§ 6

Soles v. Gonzales, 2007 WL 1675922 (Cal. App. 2d Dist. 2007)

97 ALR6th 375—§ 4, 23

Soley v. Ampudia, 183 F.2d 277, 19 A.L.R.2d 689 (5th Cir. 1950)

94 ALR5th 149—§ 3, 5, 9

Solheim v. Hastings Housing Co., 151 Neb. 264, 37 N.W.2d 212 (1949)

48 ALR6th 387—§ 9, 10

Solich v. Wheeling, 543 F. Supp. 576 (W.D. Pa. 1982)

64 ALR6th 249—§ 17

Soliday v. Haycock Tp., 785 A.2d 139 (Pa. Commw. Ct. 2001)

97 ALR5th 123—§ 12

Solid Waste Auth. v. Parker, 622 So. 2d 1010, 18 FLW D 1273 (Fla. App. D4 1993)

10 ALR5th 448—§ 6

Solimena v. State, Dep't of Business Regulation, etc., 402 So. 2d 1240 (Fla. App. D3 1981)

59 ALR5th 203—§ 6, 9, 42, 48

Solimene v. B. Grauel & Co., 399 Mass. 790, 507 N.E.2d 662, CCH Prod. Liab. Rep. ¶ 11407 (1987)

51 ALR5th 467—§ 13

Solimini v. Thomas, 293 Ill. App. 3d 430, 227 Ill. Dec. 875, 688 N.E.2d 356 (2d Dist. 1997)

17 ALR6th 1—§ 26

Solin v. O'Melveny & Myers, LLP, 89 Cal. App. 4th 451, 107 Cal. Rptr. 2d 456 (2d Dist. 2001)

71 ALR6th 249—§ 4

Solina v. U.S., 709 F.2d 160 (CA2 N.Y. 1983)

19 ALR5th 351—§ 5, 11, 13, 16

Solis, In re, 124 Ohio App. 3d 547, 706 N.E.2d 839 (8th Dist. Cuyahoga County 1997)

101 ALR5th 351—§ 8

Solis v. Cindy's Total Care, Inc., 2011 WL 6013844 (S.D. N.Y. 2011)

79 ALR6th 351—§ 10

Solis v. City of Columbus, 319 F. Supp. 2d 797 (S.D. Ohio 2004)

59 ALR6th 311—§ 31

Solis v. EMC Mortgage, 2012 WL 2949787 (Cal. App. 2d Dist. 2012)

86 ALR6th 411—§ 5

Solis v. Evins, 951 S.W.2d 44 (Tex. App. Corpus Christi 1997)

60 ALR5th 669—§ 4

Solis v. Fresno Police Dept., 2011 WL 3568889 (E.D. Cal. 2011)

86 ALR6th 173—§ 8

Solis v. Prince George's County, 153 F. Supp. 2d 793 (D. Md. 2001)

101 ALR5th 515—§ 13

Solis v. State, 647 S.W.2d 95 (Tex. App. San Antonio 1983)

32 ALR5th 149—§ 5, 56, 58

Solis v. State, 851 P.2d 1296 (Wyo. 1993)

49 ALR6th 343—§ 3, 20

Solis v. State, 1988 WL 75758 (Tex. App. Houston 14th Dist. 1988)

104 ALR5th 165—§ 15

Solis v. State, 2002 WL 1480890 (Tex. App. Houston 1st Dist. 2002)

73 ALR6th 49—§ 3, 4

Solis v. Superior Court of Monterey County, 63 Cal. 2d 774, 48 Cal. Rptr. 169, 408 P.2d 945 (1966)

41 ALR5th 171—§ 16 to 19, 21, 72

Solis v. Tea, 468 A.2d 1276 (Del. 1983)

46 ALR5th 735—§ 2, 4

Solis-Avila v. State, 830 P.2d 191, 41 A.L.R.5th 883 (Okla. Crim. 1992)

41 ALR5th 171—§ 38, 40, 107, 117

Soliva v. Shand, Morahan & Co., 345 S.E.2d 33 (W. Va. 1986)

14 ALR5th 695—§ 23

Soliz v. State, 832 N.E.2d 1022 (Ind. Ct. App. 2005)

26 ALR6th 511—§ 26

Solk v. Department of State, 286 App. Div. 178, 142 N.Y.S.2d 251 (1955)

7 ALR5th 474—§ 125

Sollars v. City of Albuquerque, 794 F. Supp. 360 (D.N.M. 1992)

96 ALR5th 107—§ 7

98 ALR5th 609—§ 19, 20

Sollay v. Sollay Foundation & Drilling, Inc., 389 So. 2d 834, 26 BNA WH Cas. 1016 (La. App. 3d Cir. 1980)

18 ALR5th 577—§ 58

Sollenbarger v. Mountain States Tel. & Tel. Co., 121 F.R.D. 417, 1988-2 Trade Cas. (CCH) ¶ 68301 (D.N.M. 1988)
50 ALR6th 281—§ 27

Solles v. Israel, 868 F.2d 242 (7th Cir. 1989)
56 ALR6th 185—§ 34

Sollid, In re, 32 Wash. App. 349, 647 P.2d 1033 (1982)
37 ALR5th 237—§ 3, 11, 13

Solmica of Gulf Coast, Inc. v. Braggs, 285 Ala. 396, 232 So. 2d 638 (1970)
27 ALR5th 174—§ 72

Solmitz v. Maine School Administrative Dist. No. 59, 495 A.2d 812, 26 Ed. Law Rep. 702 (Me. 1985)
70 ALR6th 513—§ 17
71 ALR6th 471—§ 13

Soloco, Inc. v. Dupree, 758 So. 2d 851 (La. Ct. App. 3d Cir. 2000)
59 ALR5th 733—§ 3

Solo Cup Co. v. International Broth. of Pulp, Sulphite and Paper Mill Workers, AFL-CIO, 237 Md. 143, 205 A.2d 213 (1964)
120 ALR5th 351—§ 28

Solo Cup Co. v. Pate, 528 P.2d 300 (Okla. 1974)
10 ALR5th 245—§ 12

Solodky v. Wilson, 474 So. 2d 1231 (Fla. Dist. Ct. App. 5th Dist. 1985)
9 ALR6th 285—§ 5

Solof v. City of Chattanooga, 180 Tenn. 296, 174 S.W.2d 471 (1943)
16 ALR6th 219—§ 29

Solof v. Heitner, 125 N.Y.S.2d 67 (Sup. 1953)
25 ALR5th 233—§ 19

Soloff v. Board of Educ. of City of New York, 90 A.D.2d 829, 455 N.Y.S.2d 832, 7 Ed. Law Rep. 975 (2d Dep't 1982)
64 ALR5th 519—§ 16

Soloman v. State, 143 Ga. App. 449, 238 S.E.2d 573 (1977)
55 ALR5th 125—§ 3, 6, 8

Soloman v. State, 252 Ga. App. 787, 556 S.E.2d 914 (2001)
114 ALR5th 173—§ 8, 9

Soloman v. State, 741 So. 2d 1211 (Fla. Dist. Ct. App. 5th Dist. 1999)
70 ALR5th 1—§ 9

Soloman Ltd. v. Biederman and Co., Inc., 177 A.D.2d 350, 576 N.Y.S.2d 118 (1st Dep't 1991)
88 ALR5th 545—§ 2, 16

Solomen v. Redwood Advisory Co., 183 F. Supp. 2d 748, 99 A.L.R.5th 1 (E.D. Pa. 2002)
99 ALR5th 1—§ 2, 3

Solomon v. Carrasco, 2012 WL 3744666 (E.D. Cal. 2012)
89 ALR6th 1—§ 117

Solomon v. Catherwood, 28 A.D.2d 618, 279 N.Y.S.2d 989 (3d Dep't 1967)
25 ALR6th 101—§ 11

Solomon v. Central Trust Co., N.A., 63 Ohio St. 3d 35, 584 N.E.2d 1185, 36 A.L.R.5th 873 (1992)
36 ALR5th 395—§ 4, 18, 20

Solomon v. City of Denver, 12 Colo. App. 179, 55 P. 199 (1898)
16 ALR6th 219—§ 5

Solomon v. Congregation B'nai Jeshurum, 49 How. Pr. 263, 1875 WL 9464 (N.Y.C.P. 1875)
81 ALR6th 1—§ 45

Solomon v. Congregation Tiffereth Israel of Revere, 344 Mass. 755, 183 N.E.2d 492 (1962)
81 ALR6th 1—§ 45

Solomon v. Continental Ins. Co., 122 N.J. Super. 125, 299 A.2d 413 (1972)
35 ALR5th 375—§ 22

Solomon v. Duke University, 850 F. Supp. 372, 6 A.D.D. 1258, 91 Ed. Law Rep. 575, 145 L.R.R.M. (BNA) 2959 (M.D. N.C. 1993)
7 ALR6th 563—§ 5

Solomon v. Findley, 167 Ariz. 409, 808 P.2d 294 (Ariz. 1991)
46 ALR5th 735—§ 3

Solomon v. Guardian Life Ins. Co. of
America, 1996 WL 741888 (E.D.
Pa. 1996)
  61 ALR6th 239—§ 11
Solomon v. Guardian Life Ins. Co. of
America, 1997 WL 611586 (E.D.
Pa. 1997)
  61 ALR6th 239—§ 11
Solomon v. Hall, 767 S.W.2d 158 (Tenn.
Ct. App. 1988)
  98 ALR6th 1—§ 15
Solomon v. Harman, 107 Ariz. 426, 489
P.2d 236 (1971)
  84 ALR5th 687—§ 3, 4
Solomon v. Massachusetts Mut. Life Ins.
Co., 47 Pa. D. & C.4th 36, 2000 WL
33116006 (C.P. 2000)
  61 ALR6th 239—§ 42
Solomon v. Norwest Mortg. Corp., 245
Ga. App. 875, 538 S.E.2d 783
(2000)
  81 ALR6th 161—§ 4
  82 ALR6th 43—§ 4
Solomon v. School Committee of Boston, 395 Mass. 12, 478 N.E.2d 137
(1985)
  57 ALR5th 477—§ 14, 35
Solomon v. Shuell, 435 Mich. 104, 457
N.W.2d 669 (1990)
  111 ALR5th 1—§ 2, 3, 5 to 8, 11, 17
Solomon v. Skinner, 458 So. 2d 962 (La.
App. 4th Cir. 1984)
  50 ALR5th 1—§ 12
Solomon v. Solomon, 5 Ill. App. 2d 297,
125 N.E.2d 675 (1955)
  40 ALR5th 697—§ 2
Solomon v. Solomon, 118 Md. App. 96,
701 A.2d 1199 (1997)
  5 ALR5th 550—§ 23
  21 ALR5th 396—§ 4
Solomon v. Solomon, 187 Miss. 22, 192
So. 10 (1939)
  83 ALR6th 605—§ 5
Solomon v. Solomon, 319 Ill. App. 618,
49 N.E.2d 807 (1st Dist. 1943)
  71 ALR5th 99—§ 6
Solomon v. State, 247 Ga. 27, 277
S.E.2d 1 (1980)

71 ALR6th 1—§ 9
Solomon v. State, 323 Ark. 178, 913
S.W.2d 288 (1996)
  98 ALR6th 455—§ 29
Solomon v. Walsh, 2012 WL 4450974
(M.D. Pa. 2012)
  89 ALR6th 1—§ 61
Solomon v. Warren, 540 F.2d 777 (CA5
Fla. 1976)
  **42 ALR5th 465—§ 2, 7, 13, 15, 17,
18**
Solomon and Solomon, P.C. v. Ellis, 130
S. Ct. 3333 (2010)
  56 ALR6th 679—§ 3
Solomon & Son v. Thomas, 45 Luz. L.R.
269 (Pa. C.P. 1955)
  89 ALR5th 319—§ 10
Solomon L., Re, 190 Cal. App. 3d 1106,
236 Cal. Rptr. 2 (4th Dist. 1987)
  20 ALR5th 534—§ 4, 15
Solondz Bros. Lumber Co. v. Piperato,
28 N.J. Super. 414, 101 A.2d 33
(1953)
  4 ALR5th 772—§ 24, 59, 69
Solonoski by Solonoski v. Yuhas, 657
A.2d 137 (Pa. Commw. Ct. 1995)
  46 ALR5th 557—§ 3
  62 ALR5th 537—§ 3
So-Lo Oil Co., Inc. v. Total Petroleum,
Inc., 968 F.2d 21 (10th Cir. 1992)
  26 ALR6th 249—§ 16
So-Lo Oil Co., Inc. v. Total Petroleum,
Inc., 1992 OK 71, 832 P.2d 14,
1992-1 Trade Cas. (CCH) ¶ 69854
(Okla. 1992)
  26 ALR6th 249—§ 9
Solo Serve Co. v. Howell, 35 S.W.2d
474 (Tex. Civ. App. 1931)
  40 ALR5th 135—§ 7
Solow v. City of New York, 49 A.D.2d
414, 375 N.Y.S.2d 356 (1st Dep't
1975)
  73 ALR5th 223—§ 13
Solow v. Levittown Arena, Inc., 24
N.Y.2d 812, 300 N.Y.S.2d 590, 248
N.E.2d 445 (1969)
  38 ALR5th 107—§ 10

Solow v. Liebman, 175 A.D.2d 120, 572 N.Y.S.2d 19 (2d Dep't 1991)
111 ALR5th 313—§ 12

Solow v. New York, 49 App. Div. 2d 414, 375 N.Y.S.2d 356 (1st Dep't 1975)
1 ALR5th 622—§ 17, 19, 28

Solow v. U.S., 282 F. Supp. 900 (E.D. Pa. 1968)
27 ALR5th 174—§ 101

Solow v. W.R. Grace & Co., 597 N.Y.S.2d 361 (App. Div. 1st Dep't 1993)
6 ALR5th 242—§ 10, 24

Solt v. Walker, 1996 WL 363438 (Ohio Ct. App. 5th Dist. Fairfield County 1996)
111 ALR5th 313—§ 5

Solter v. P. M. Place Stores Co., 748 S.W.2d 919, 29 BNA WH Cas. 805, 109 CCH LC ¶ 55905 (Mo. App. 1988)
18 ALR5th 577—§ 27, 52

Soltero v. OneWest Bank FSB, 2013 WL 1878932 (D. Ariz. 2013)
86 ALR6th 411—§ 5

Soltis v. State, 188 App. Div. 2d 201, 594 N.Y.S.2d 433 (3d Dep't 1993)
48 ALR5th 129—§ 20

Solutec Corp., Inc. v. Agnew, 88 Wash. App. 1067, 1997 WL 794496 (Div. 3 1997)
36 ALR6th 537—§ 4, 21, 40

Solutia Inc. v. FMC Corp., 385 F. Supp. 2d 324 (S.D. N.Y. 2005)
48 ALR6th 1—§ 36, 45, 49, 54, 78

Solvex Corp. v. Freeman, 459 F. Supp. 440, 199 USPQ 726 (W.D. Va. 1977)
23 ALR5th 241—§ 23, 32

Soma Enterprises, Inc. v. State, DOT & Dev., 584 So. 2d 1243 (La. App. 2d Cir. 1991)
22 ALR5th 327—§ 58, 60

Soma Medical Intern. v. Standard Chartered Bank, 196 F.3d 1292 (10th Cir. 1999)
81 ALR5th 41—§ 3

Somekh v. Ipswich House, Inc., 81 A.D.2d 662, 438 N.Y.S.2d 362 (2d Dep't 1981)
114 ALR5th 443—§ 44

Some Other Place, Inc., In re, 1995 WL 230559 (Bankr. N.D. Ill. 1995)
107 ALR5th 311—§ 3

Somer v. Johnson, 704 F.2d 1473, 13 Fed. R. Evid. Serv. 123 (11th Cir. 1983)
6 ALR6th 311—§ 5

Somers v. Camarco Contractors, Inc., 24 Misc. 2d 673, 205 N.Y.S.2d 724 (1960)
8 ALR5th 391—§ 3

Somers v. SAIF Corp., 77 Or. App. 259, 712 P.2d 179 (1986)
107 ALR5th 441—§ 21
109 ALR5th 161—§ 11
112 ALR5th 509—§ 2, 18
122 ALR5th 653—§ 2
13 ALR6th 209—§ 3, 13, 20
20 ALR6th 641—§ 22
39 ALR6th 445—§ 3, 36

Somers v. Somers, 326 Pa. Super. 556, 474 A.2d 630 (1984)
99 ALR5th 475—§ 13

Somers & Schefiliti, P.C. v. Pine Corp., 1990 WL 290142 (Conn. Super. Ct. 1990)
118 ALR5th 91—§ 30

Somers Construction Co., Inc. v. Southeastern Pennsylvania Transportation Authority, 20 Phila. Co. Rptr. 238, 1990 WL 902393 (Pa. C.P. 1990)
124 ALR5th 375—§ 5, 8

Somerset v. Montgomery County Bd. of Appeals, 245 Md. 52, 225 A.2d 294 (1966)
2 ALR5th 553—§ 62, 93

Somerset Capital Corp., In re, 264 B.R. 788, 38 Bankr. Ct. Dec. (CRR) 49 (Bankr. D. Mass. 2001)
32 ALR6th 531—§ 18

Somerset Sav. Bank v. Chicago Title Ins. Co., 420 Mass. 422, 649 N.E.2d 1123 (1995)

CASES CITED IN ALR5th and ALR6th

19 ALR5th 786—§ 3, 5
Somers Lumber Co. v. Kaufman, 102 NJL 601, 133 A. 200 (1926)
4 ALR5th 772—§ 69
Somerstein Caterers of Lawrence, Inc. v. Insurance Co. of State of Pennsylvania, 692 N.Y.S.2d 369 (App. Div. 1st Dep't 1999)
16 ALR5th 412—§ 5
Somir v. Weiss, 271 A.D.2d 433, 705 N.Y.S.2d 648 (2d Dep't 2000)
125 ALR5th 403—§ 10
Somma v. Gracey, 15 Conn. App. 371, 544 A.2d 668 (1988)
10 ALR5th 828—§ 2, 37
58 ALR6th 1—§ 5, 12, 45
60 ALR6th 1—§ 76
Sommer, In re, 2008 WL 704401 (Bankr. N.D. Ohio 2008)
99 ALR6th 481—§ 13
Sommer v. Federal Signal Corp., 79 N.Y.2d 540, 583 N.Y.S.2d 957, 593 N.E.2d 1365 (1992)
36 ALR6th 305—§ 14, 15
Sommer v. Kridel, 74 N.J. 446, 378 A.2d 767 (1977)
75 ALR5th 1—§ 2, 7, 13 to 16, 18
Sommer v. Monga, 35 Mass. App. Ct. 761, 626 N.E.2d 16 (1994)
112 ALR5th 399—§ 8
Sommer v. Oak Brook Park District Bd. of Park Com'r, 1996 WL 422152 (N.D. Ill. 1996)
105 ALR5th 351—§ 3 to 6
Sommer v. Sommer, 108 Wisc. 2d 586, 323 N.W.2d 144 (App. 1982)
59 ALR5th 489—§ 9, 10
Sommer v. Sommer, 176 A.D.2d 1022, 575 N.Y.S.2d 178 (3d Dep't 1991)
16 ALR6th 693—§ 10
Sommer v. Sommer, 508 So. 2d 773 (Fla. Dist. Ct. App. 5th Dist. 1987)
80 ALR5th 117—§ 3, 19
Sommer v. Sommer, 2001 ND 191, 636 N.W.2d 423 (N.D. 2001)
110 ALR5th 237—§ 2

Sommer v. Taylorville, 59 Ill. App. 3d 765, 16 Ill. Dec. 924, 375 N.E.2d 1031 (5th Dist. 1978)
5 ALR5th 875—§ 3
Sommerfield v. Helmick, 57 Cal. App. 4th 315, 67 Cal. Rptr. 2d 51 (3d Dist. 1997)
91 ALR6th 435—§ 73
Sommerfield v. Sommerfield, 154 Wis. 2d 840, 454 N.W.2d 55 (App. 1990)
9 ALR5th 568—§ 9
Sommers v. Baltimore, 215 Md. 1, 135 A.2d 625 (1957)
2 ALR5th 553—§ 11
Sommers v. Com., Unemployment Compensation Bd. of Review, 56 Pa. Commw. 275, 424 A.2d 619 (1981)
95 ALR5th 329—§ 25
Sommers v. Iowa Civil Rights Com'n, 337 N.W.2d 470, 1 A.D. Cas. (BNA) 442, 47 Fair Empl. Prac. Cas. (BNA) 1217, 33 Empl. Prac. Dec. (CCH) ¶ 34260 (Iowa 1983)
96 ALR6th 189—§ 9, 11, 14, 22
Sommers v. McKinney, 287 N.J. Super. 1, 670 A.2d 99 (App. Div. 1996)
50 ALR5th 301—§ 3
60 ALR6th 1—§ 57
Sommers v. Sisters of Charity of Providence, 277 Or. 549, 561 P.2d 603 (1977)
31 ALR5th 1—§ 20
Sommers v. Sommers, 169 So. 2d 496 (Fla. App. D3 1964)
49 ALR5th 441—§ 20
Sommers v. Sommers, 183 So. 2d 744 (Fla. App. D3 1966)
49 ALR5th 441—§ 20
Sommers v. Sommers, 2003 ND 77, 660 N.W.2d 586 (N.D. 2003)
102 ALR5th 395—§ 6
Sommers v. Thomas, 251 Minn. 461, 88 N.W.2d 191 (1958)
86 ALR6th 321—§ 11, 12
87 ALR6th 197—§ 68

Sommers Drug Stores Co. Employee Profit Sharing Trust v. Corrigan Enterprises, Inc., 793 F.2d 1456, 7 Employee Benefits Cas. (BNA) 1782 (5th Cir. 1986)

16 ALR6th 693—§ 20

Sommers' Estate, In re, 200 Misc. 1013, 104 N.Y.S.2d 453 (Sur. Ct. 1951)

87 ALR6th 495—§ 46, 48, 56, 82

Sommervold v. Grevlos, 518 N.W.2d 733 (S.D. 1994)

111 ALR5th 529—§ 3, 5

Somoza v. St. Vincent's Hosp. & Medical Ctr., 192 App. Div. 2d 429, 596 N.Y.S.2d 789 (1st Dep't 1993)

7 ALR5th 1—§ 22

Sompolski v. Miller, 239 Ill. App. 3d 1087, 180 Ill. Dec. 932, 608 N.E.2d 54 (1st Dist. 1992)

99 ALR6th 1—§ 11

Somppi v. Commissioner, TC Memo 1984-190, PH TCM ¶ 84190, 47 CCH TCM 1519 (1984)

44 ALR5th 1—§ 2

Somuah v. Flachs, 352 Md. 241, 721 A.2d 680 (1998)

83 ALR5th 497—§ 4

Son v. Hartford Ice Cream Co., 102 Conn. 696, 129 A. 778 (1925)

13 ALR5th 217—§ 13

Sonaggera v. Dayton Tire & Rubber Co., 627 P.2d 452 (Okla. App. 1981)

3 ALR5th 907—§ 3

Sonara v. Star Casualty Ins. Co., 603 So. 2d 661, 17 FLW D 1897 (Fla. App. D3 1992)

23 ALR5th 241—§ 11

Soncheray H., In re, 42 Conn. App. 664, 680 A.2d 1363 (1996)

20 ALR5th 534—§ 4, 16

Soncrant v. Soncrant, Inc., 59 Mich. App. 287, 229 N.W.2d 419 (1975)

28 ALR6th 1—§ 2, 3, 12, 13, 48, 67

Sondheim v. Gilbert, 117 Ind. 71, 18 N.E. 687 (1888)

74 ALR5th 369—§ 9, 14, 22

Sondheimer v. Georgetown University, 1987 WL 14618 (D.D.C. 1987)

82 ALR5th 1—§ 7

Sondrol v. Placid Oil Co., 23 F.3d 1341, 129 O.G.R. 227 (8th Cir. 1994)

99 ALR5th 415—§ 3

Soneeya v. Spencer, 851 F. Supp. 2d 228 (D. Mass. 2012)

89 ALR6th 701—§ 16

Soneff v. Harlan, 712 P.2d 1084 (Colo. App. 1985)

14 ALR5th 242—§ 6, 7, 23

Sonenstahl v. L.E.L.S., Inc., 372 N.W.2d 1 (Minn. Ct. App. 1985)

32 ALR6th 285—§ 28

Sonenthal v. Harry Weinstein & Son, 14 N.J. Misc. 368, 185 A. 917 (1936)

2 ALR5th 1—§ 2, 4

Sones v. Thompson Furniture Co., 163 Pa. Super. 392, 62 A.2d 116 (1948)

8 ALR5th 798—§ 2

Sonfield v. Burleson, 543 So. 2d 488 (La. Ct. App. 4th Cir. 1989)

67 ALR6th 209—§ 40

Song v. Ignacio, 68 F.3d 481 (9th Cir. 1995)

94 ALR5th 537—§ 6

Song v. Ives Laboratories, Inc., 957 F.2d 1041, 59 BNA FEP Cas. 1072, 58 CCH EPD ¶ 41306 (CA2 N.Y. 1992)

12 ALR5th 508—§ 3

Song v. Ives Laboratories, Inc., a Div. of American Home Products Corp., 735 F. Supp. 550, 59 Fair Empl. Prac. Cas. (BNA) 1065, 53 Empl. Prac. Dec. (CCH) ¶ 39867 (S.D. N.Y. 1990)

103 ALR5th 557—§ 5

Songster v. Beard, 2014 WL 3731459 (E.D. Pa. 2014)

102 ALR6th 637—§ 4, 11

Soniat v. State Farm Mut. Auto. Ins. Co., 340 So. 2d 1097 (La. App. 4th Cir. 1976)

23 ALR5th 241—§ 11

Sonic Engineering, Inc. v. Konover Const. Co. South, 51 U.C.C. Rep. Serv. 2d 844 (Conn. Super. Ct. 2003)

53 ALR6th 159—§ 14, 16

Sonin v. Massachusetts Turnpike Authority, 61 Mass. App. Ct. 287, 2004 WL 1238211, 122 A.L.R.5th 725 (2004)

122 ALR5th 1—§ 12

Sonkin & Melena Co., L.P.A. v. Zaransky, 83 Ohio App. 3d 169, 614 N.E.2d 807 (8th Dist.Cuyahoga County 1992)

56 ALR5th 1—§ 3

Sonley v. Sonley, 115 A.D.3d 1071, 981 N.Y.S.2d 861 (3d Dep't 2014)

100 ALR6th 1—§ 24

Sonlin ex rel. Sonlin v. Abington Memorial Hosp., 2000 PA Super 44, 748 A.2d 213 (Pa. Super. Ct. 2000)

96 ALR5th 107—§ 8

Sonne v. Community Medical Associates, Inc., 2011 WL 2553378 (Ky. Ct. App. 2011)

95 ALR6th 541—§ 5

Sonneland v. City of Spokane, 4 Wash. App. 865, 484 P.2d 421 (Div. 3 1971)

73 ALR5th 223—§ 8

Sonneman v. Knight, 790 P.2d 702, 47 A.L.R.5th 965 (Alaska 1990)

47 ALR5th 775—§ 3 to 5, 9

Sonnenberg v. Farmington Township, 39 Mich. App. 446, 197 N.W.2d 853 (1972)

47 ALR5th 553—§ 10

Sonnenburg v. Grohskopf, 144 Wis. 2d 62, 422 N.W.2d 925 (Ct. App. 1988)

116 ALR5th 433—§ 4, 6

Sonnenreich v. Philip Morris Inc., 929 F. Supp. 416, CCH Prod. Liab. Rep. ¶ 14647, 9 FLW Fed D 814 (S.D. Fla. 1996)

36 ALR5th 541—§ 19, 22

Sonners, Re Claim of, 133 App. Div. 2d 491, 519 N.Y.S.2d 283 (3d Dep't 1987)

23 ALR5th 176—§ 15

Sonnier, Ex parte, 707 So. 2d 635 (Ala. 1997)

14 ALR6th 301—§ 6, 13, 20, 21

19 ALR6th 475—§ 5
98 ALR6th 1—§ 34

Sonnier v. Amalgamated Local 148, 2006 WL 241507 (Cal. App. 2d Dist. 2006)

54 ALR6th 99—§ 6

Sonnier v. Chisholm-Ryder Co., Inc., 909 S.W.2d 475, Prod. Liab. Rep. (CCH) ¶ 14343 (Tex. 1995)

122 ALR5th 1—§ 2, 25, 27

Sonnier v. County of Los Angeles, 2002 WL 31217252 (Cal. App. 2d Dist. 2002)

30 ALR6th 483—§ 22

Sonnier v. Field, 2007 WL 576655 (W.D. Pa. 2007)

95 ALR6th 641—§ 4

Sonnier v. Ramsey, 424 S.W.2d 684 (Tex. Civ. App. Houston 1st Dist. 1968)

62 ALR5th 537—§ 3

Sonnier v. Reed, 532 So. 2d 344 (La. App. 3d Cir. 1988)

50 ALR5th 1—§ 12

Sonntag v. Whippletree Village Partnership, 207 Ill. App. 3d 892, 152 Ill. Dec. 780, 566 N.E.2d 467 (1st Dist. 1990)

43 ALR5th 705—§ 20

Sonny H. B., Matter of, 672 N.Y.S.2d 579 (App. Div. 4th Dep't 1998)

20 ALR5th 534—§ 14

Sonoma, County of v. Commission on State Mandates, 84 Cal. App. 4th 1264, 101 Cal. Rptr. 2d 784, 149 Ed. Law Rep. 207 (1st Dist. 2000)

110 ALR5th 293—§ 3

Sonoma, County of v. Grant W., 187 Cal. App. 3d 1439, 232 Cal. Rptr. 471 (1st Dist. 1986)

77 ALR5th 201—§ 4

Sonoma, County of v. Santa Rosa, 102 Cal. 426, 36 P. 810 (1894)

11 ALR5th 630—§ 7

Sonoran Desert Investigations, Inc. v. Miller, 213 Ariz. 274, 141 P.3d 754 (Ct. App. Div. 2 2006)

62 ALR6th 313—§ 17

Sons v. Commercial Union Assur. Companies, 433 So. 2d 842 (La. Ct. App. 3d Cir. 1983)
48 ALR5th 129—§ 18
51 ALR5th 467—§ 7
87 ALR5th 1—§ 9, 10, 15, 32

Sonsini v. Memorial Hosp. for Cancer and Diseases, 693 N.Y.S.2d 17 (App. Div. 1st Dep't 1999)
69 ALR5th 559—§ 13

Sons of Confederate Veterans, Inc. v. Glendening, 954 F. Supp. 1099 (D. Md. 1997)
8 ALR6th 639—§ 3, 10
66 ALR6th 493—§ 24

Sons of Confederate Veterans, Inc. ex rel. Griffin v. Commission of Virginia Dept. of Motor Vehicles, 288 F.3d 610, 8 A.L.R.6th 797 (4th Cir. 2002)
8 ALR6th 549—§ 31
8 ALR6th 639—§ 3, 8
66 ALR6th 493—§ 24

Sonsteng v. Dominican Sisters of Ontario, Inc., 630 F. Supp. 2d 1253 (D. Or. 2009)
94 ALR6th 431—§ 11, 13

Sontag v. State, 841 S.W.2d 889 (Tex. App. Corpus Christi 1992)
109 ALR5th 611—§ 3
27 ALR6th 183—§ 32
32 ALR6th 1—§ 4

Sonus Networks, Inc, Shareholder Derivative Litigation, In re, 499 F.3d 47 (1st Cir. 2007)
43 ALR6th 1—§ 5, 26

Sonus-USA, Inc. v. Thomas W. Lyons, Inc., 966 So. 2d 992 (Fla. Dist. Ct. App. 5th Dist. 2007)
32 ALR6th 419—§ 35

Sony BMG Music Entertainment v. Tenenbaum, 660 F.3d 487, 100 U.S.P.Q.2d 1161 (1st Cir. 2011)
76 ALR6th 587—§ 15, 18

Sony Computer Entertainment America, Inc. v. Great American Ins. Co., 229 F.R.D. 632 (N.D. Cal. 2005)
26 ALR6th 287—§ 34

Sony Corp. of America v. American Exp. Co., 115 Misc. 2d 1060, 455 N.Y.S.2d 227, 35 U.C.C. Rep. Serv. 558 (City Civ. Ct. 1982)
91 ALR5th 89—§ 3, 6

Sony Gaming Networks and Customer Data Sec. Breach Litigation, In re, 903 F. Supp. 2d 942 (S.D. Cal. 2012)
91 ALR6th 409—§ 8

Sony PS3 Other OS Litigation, In re, 828 F. Supp. 2d 1125 (N.D. Cal. 2011)
88 ALR6th 1—§ 29, 65

Soohoo v. State, 737 So. 2d 1108 (Fla. Dist. Ct. App. 4th Dist. 1999)
9 ALR5th 464—§ 9

Soo L. R. R. Co. v. B. J. Carney & Co., 797 F. Supp. 1472 (D.C. Minn. 1992)
11 ALR5th 438—§ 13

Soos v. Superior Court in and for County of Maricopa, 182 Ariz. 470, 897 P.2d 1356 (Ct. App. Div. 1 1994)
77 ALR5th 567—§ 5

Sooy v. Petrolane Steel Gas, Inc., 218 Mont. 418, 708 P.2d 1014 (1985)
98 ALR6th 93—§ 17
104 ALR6th 1—§ 53

Sopchak v. Tacoma, 189 Wash. 518, 66 P.2d 302 (1937)
53 ALR5th 617—§ 8

Soper v. First Sec. Ins. Co. of America, 148 A.2d 580 (Mun. Ct. App. D.C. 1959)
16 ALR6th 491—§ 5

Soper v. Hoben, 195 F.3d 845, 139 Ed. Law Rep. 807, 1999 FED App. 0375P (6th Cir. 1999)
98 ALR6th 599—§ 46, 78

Soper's Estate, Matter of, 598 S.W.2d 528 (Mo. Ct. App. S.D. 1980)
87 ALR6th 495—§ 15, 39, 54, 64, 80, 82

Sophia G.L., In re, 229 Ill. 2d 143, 321 Ill. Dec. 748, 890 N.E.2d 470 (2008)
57 ALR6th 163—§ 35

Sophia G.L., In re, 229 Ill. 2d 143, 321 Ill. Dec. 748, 890 N.E.2d 470 (Ill. 2008)
57 ALR6th 163—§ 13, 43

Sopkin v. Premier Pontiac, Inc., 539 P.2d 1393 (Okla. App. 1975)
14 ALR5th 242—§ 25

Sopronyi v. Asztalos, 60 Ohio L. Abs. 137, 101 N.E.2d 161 (App. Montgomery Co. 1949)
45 ALR5th 251—§ 9

Sorah, In re, 203 B.R. 620 (Bankr. E.D. Ky. 1996)
38 ALR6th 313—§ 4

Soranno's Gasco, Inc. v. Morgan, 874 F.2d 1310 (9th Cir. 1989)
89 ALR6th 1—§ 5, 22, 46

Soratsavong v. Haskell, 133 Wash. App. 77, 134 P.3d 1172 (Div. 1 2006)
42 ALR6th 463—§ 12

Sorbee Intern. Ltd. v. Chubb Custom Ins. Co., 1999 PA Super 178, 735 A.2d 712 (Pa. Super. Ct. 1999)
98 ALR5th 1—§ 13

Sorber v. American Motorists Ins. Co., 451 Pa. Super. 507, 680 A.2d 881 (1996)
75 ALR6th 235—§ 4, 26

Sorbonne Apartments Co. v. Kranz, 96 Misc. 2d 396, 409 N.Y.S.2d 83, 410 N.Y.S.2d 768 (1978)
42 ALR5th 53—§ 9

Sorce v. Rinehart, 69 Wis. 2d 631, 230 N.W.2d 645 (1975)
39 ALR5th 33—§ 8, 10

Sorchini v. City of Covina, 250 F.3d 706 (9th Cir. 2001)
105 ALR5th 499—§ 4

Sordelet v. Golsteyn, 697 N.E.2d 943 (Ind. Ct. App. 1998)
70 ALR5th 377—§ 2, 4

Soren v. Ezelle, 737 F. Supp. 49 (M.D. Tenn. 1990)
31 ALR5th 116—§ 3

Sorensen, In re, 157 Vt. 651, 596 A.2d 924 (1991)
45 ALR6th 175—§ 18

Sorensen v. City of Omaha, Public Safety/Fire Div., 230 Neb. 286, 430 N.W.2d 696 (1988)
107 ALR5th 441—§ 6
109 ALR5th 161—§ 2, 5, 13, 16
20 ALR6th 641—§ 13

Sorensen v. Comm Tek, Inc., 118 Idaho 664, 799 P.2d 70, 5 BNA IER Cas. 1301 (1990)
17 ALR5th 1—§ 3

Sorensen v. Goldman, 837 P.2d 266 (Colo. Ct. App. 1992)
40 ALR6th 99—§ 70

Sorensen v. Hutson, 175 Cal. App. 2d 817, 346 P.2d 785 (4th Dist. 1959)
34 ALR5th 77—§ 3, 8

Sorensen v. Sigelman, 2003 WL 21744077 (Cal. App. 4th Dist. 2003)
13 ALR6th 1—§ 4
14 ALR6th 1—§ 5

Sorensen v. Sorensen, 769 P.2d 820, 102 Utah Adv. Rep. 14 (Utah App. 1989)
4 ALR5th 403—§ 3, 11

Sorensen v. Sorensen, 839 P.2d 774, 183 Utah Adv. Rep. 13 (Utah 1992)
4 ALR5th 403—§ 11

Sorensen v. State, 478 S.W.2d 532 (Tex. Crim. 1972)
55 ALR5th 125—§ 3, 6, 7

Sorensen v. State, Dep't of Revenue, 836 P.2d 29 (Mont 1992)
12 ALR5th 89—§ 4, 7

Sorensen, State ex rel. v. Baird, 201 Or. 240, 269 P.2d 535 (1954)
102 ALR5th 525—§ 22

Sorenson, In re Marriage of, 127 Ill. App. 3d 967, 82 Ill. Dec. 906, 469 N.E.2d 440 (5th Dist. 1984)
84 ALR5th 399—§ 3, 13, 14

Sorenson v. Allied Products Corp., 706 N.E.2d 1097, Prod. Liab. Rep. (CCH) ¶ 15478, 109 A.L.R.5th 771 (Ind. Ct. App. 1999)
109 ALR5th 301—§ 3, 7
13 ALR6th 355—§ 4, 39

Sorenson v. Beers, 585 P.2d 458 (Utah 1978)
81 ALR6th 161—§ 5
82 ALR6th 43—§ 19
Sorenson v. Connelly, 36 Colo. App. 168, 536 P.2d 328 (1975)
39 ALR5th 33—§ 2
Sorenson v. Department of Labor & Industries, 12 Wash. 2d 355, 121 P.2d 978 (1942)
26 ALR5th 127—§ 7
Sorenson v. Fio Rito, 90 Ill. App. 3d 368, 45 Ill. Dec. 714, 413 N.E.2d 47 (1st Dist. 1980)
58 ALR6th 1—§ 5
60 ALR6th 1—§ 11
Sorenson v. Keith Uddenberg, Inc., 65 Wash. App. 474, 828 P.2d 650 (Div. 1 1992)
74 ALR5th 49—§ 3, 16
Sorenson v. National Transp. Safety Bd., 684 F.2d 683, 10 Fed. R. Evid. Serv. 1590 (10th Cir. 1982)
51 ALR6th 219—§ 4
Sorenson v. Pavlikowski, 94 Nev. 440, 581 P.2d 851, 2 A.L.R.4th 277 (1978)
13 ALR6th 1—§ 4
15 ALR6th 427—§ 28
Sorenson v. Safety Flate, Inc., 306 Minn. 300, 235 N.W.2d 848 (1975)
59 ALR5th 733—§ 4
Sorenson v. State, 2001 WL 830709 (Alaska Ct. App. 2001)
106 ALR5th 397—§ 4
Sorenson v. St. Paul Ramsey Medical Center, 457 N.W.2d 188 (Minn. 1990)
6 ALR5th 490—§ 14
Sorenson v. Switzer, 37 N.D. 536, 164 N.W. 136 (1917)
25 ALR5th 391—§ 87, 91, 99
Sorenson v. Tenuta, 62 Ohio App. 3d 696, 577 N.E.2d 408 (Franklin Co. 1989)
52 ALR5th 491—§ 2
Sorenson v. U.S., 539 F. Supp. 865 (S.D. N.Y. 1982)

53 ALR6th 1—§ 14
Sorenson v. Wright, 268 N.W.2d 203 (Iowa 1978)
98 ALR5th 665—§ 6
Sorenson, People ex rel. v. Randolph, 99 Cal. App. 3d 183, 160 Cal. Rptr. 69 (1st Dist. 1979)
92 ALR5th 593—§ 5, 7 to 9, 12
Sorey v. Kellett, 849 F.2d 960 (CA5 Miss. 1988)
33 ALR5th 619—§ 7
Sorey v. Sorey, 1998 ME 217, 718 A.2d 568 (Me. 1998)
102 ALR5th 395—§ 14
Sorey v. State, 419 So. 2d 810 (Fla. App. D3 1982)
39 ALR5th 283—§ 4, 17, 18
Sorg v. Crandall, 233 Ill. 79, 84 N.E. 181 (1908)
46 ALR5th 1—§ 2, 46, 47
Sorg v. Motor Vehicle Acc. Indemnification Corp., 30 A.D.2d 540, 291 N.Y.S.2d 385 (2d Dep't 1968)
103 ALR5th 1—§ 7
Sorge v. Wright's Knitwear Corp., 832 F. Supp. 118, 8 I.E.R. Cas. (BNA) 1274, 128 Lab. Cas. (CCH) ¶ 57696, 1994 O.S.H. Dec. (CCH) ¶ 30,324 (E.D. Pa. 1993)
105 ALR5th 351—§ 4, 5
Sorgenfrei v. Carnival Corp., 727 F. Supp. 2d 1354, 2011 A.M.C. 552 (S.D. Fla. 2010)
82 ALR6th 175—§ 6
Soria v. Sierra Pacific Airlines, Inc., 111 Idaho 594, 726 P.2d 706 (1986)
22 ALR5th 483—§ 9
Soria v. Sierra Pacific Airlines, Inc., 114 Idaho 1, 752 P.2d 603 (1987)
12 ALR5th 195—§ 31
Soriano v. Gillespie, 857 So. 2d 64 (Miss. Ct. App. 2003)
86 ALR6th 321—§ 11
89 ALR6th 409—§ 26
Soriano v. Greenfield, 131 NJL 401, 36 A.2d 750 (1944)
30 ALR5th 571—§ 35

Soriano v. State, 527 So. 2d 1367 (Ala. Crim. App. 1988)
32 ALR5th 149—§ 32

Sorich v. U.S., 129 S. Ct. 1308, 173 L. Ed. 2d 645 (2009)
46 ALR6th 495—§ 39

Sorichetti by Sorichetti v. City of New York, 65 N.Y.2d 461, 492 N.Y.S.2d 591, 482 N.E.2d 70 (1985)
90 ALR5th 273—§ 3, 4, 9

Sorina v. Armstrong, 51 Ohio App. 3d 113, 554 N.E.2d 943 (6th Dist. Lucas County 1988)
84 ALR5th 619—§ 6

Sorin Equipment Co., Inc. v. The Firm, Inc., 323 S.C. 359, 474 S.E.2d 819 (Ct. App. 1996)
76 ALR6th 289—§ 5
77 ALR6th 543—§ 5

Sorini, Re, 220 Mont. 459, 717 P.2d 7 (1986)
7 ALR5th 474—§ 2, 157, 159

Sorisio v. Lenox, Inc., 701 F. Supp. 950 (D. Conn. 1988)
117 ALR5th 155—§ 12

Sorlie v. Ness, 323 N.W.2d 841 (N.D. 1982)
111 ALR5th 207—§ 5, 8

Sorlie v. School Dist., 205 Mont. 22, 667 P.2d 400 (1983)
56 ALR5th 493—§ 5

Sormani v. Orange County Community College, 240 A.D.2d 724, 659 N.Y.S.2d 507, 119 Ed. Law Rep. 625 (2d Dep't 1997)
94 ALR5th 1—§ 18, 22

Sorokolit v. Rhodes, 37 Tex. Sup. Ct. Jour 680 (Tex. 1994)
28 ALR5th 497—§ 11

Sorokwasz v. Kaiser, 549 So. 2d 1209, 14 FLW 2453 (Fla. App. D3 1989)
28 ALR5th 664—§ 9

Soros v. Board of Appeals, 50 Misc. 2d 205, 269 N.Y.S.2d 796 (1966)
2 ALR5th 553—§ 39

Sorosky v. Burroughs Corp., 37 BNA FEP Cas. 1510, 119 BNA LRRM 2785 (CD Cal. 1985)

21 ALR5th 1—§ 3

Sorrell v. IMS Health Inc., 131 S. Ct. 2653, 67 A.L.R.6th 755 (U.S. 2011)
66 ALR6th 635—§ 12
67 ALR6th 629—§ 2 to 4, 6

Sorrell v. Norfolk Southern Ry. Co., 170 S.W.3d 35 (Mo. Ct. App. E.D. 2005)
26 ALR6th 659—§ 38

Sorrell v. Ohio Dept. of Natural Resources, Div. of Parks and Recreation, 40 Ohio St. 3d 141, 532 N.E.2d 722 (1988)
98 ALR6th 231—§ 17, 22

Sorrell v. State, 315 Md. 224, 554 A.2d 352 (1989)
57 ALR6th 313—§ 7

Sorrells v. Egleston Children's Hosp. at Emory University, Inc., 222 Ga. App. 229, 474 S.E.2d 60 (1996)
64 ALR6th 249—§ 5

Sorrells v. M.Y.B. Hospitality Ventures of Asheville, 334 N.C. 669, 435 S.E.2d 320 (1993)
96 ALR5th 107—§ 3, 4

Sorrells v. State, 667 So. 2d 142 (Ala. Crim. App. 1994)
15 ALR5th 391—§ 5

Sorrells v. U.S., 287 U.S. 435, 77 L. Ed. 413, 53 S. Ct. 210, 86 A.L.R. 249 (1932)
9 ALR5th 464—§ 2

Sorrells, State ex rel. v. Mosier Tree Service, 69 Ohio St. 2d 341, 23 Ohio Op. 3d 312, 432 N.E.2d 197 (1982)
31 ALR6th 199—§ 78

Sorrels v. Texas Bank & Trust Co., 597 F.2d 997 (CA5 Tex. 1979)
14 ALR5th 242—§ 30

Sorrentino v. Cunningham, 111 Ind. App. 212, 39 N.E.2d 473 (1942)
25 ALR5th 233—§ 6
76 ALR5th 337—§ 23

Sorrentino v. Shaffer, 125 App. Div. 2d 956, 510 N.Y.S.2d 46 (4th Dep't 1986)
7 ALR5th 474—§ 95, 106

Sorrentino v. Sorrentino, 248 N.Y. 626, 162 N.E. 551 (1928)
118 ALR5th 513—§ 3

Sorrow, In re, 279 B.R. 363 (Bankr. M.D. Ga. 2000)
99 ALR6th 481—§ 10

Sortino v. Chiavaroli, 59 A.D.2d 644, 398 N.Y.S.2d 385 (4th Dep't 1977)
14 ALR6th 543—§ 33

Sosa v. Beverly Hills Racquet Club, Ltd., 1998 WL 2016590 (Mich. Ct. App. 1998)
61 ALR6th 147—§ 12

Sosa v. Board of Managers of Val Verde Memorial Hospital, 437 F.2d 173 (CA5 Tex. 1971)
28 ALR5th 107—§ 5, 11 to 13

Sosa v. Dretke, 133 Fed. Appx. 114 (5th Cir. 2005)
83 ALR6th 465—§ 4, 27

Sosa v. Dretke, 2004 WL 1124949 (W.D. Tex. 2004)
83 ALR6th 465—§ 27

Sosa v. M/V Lago Izabal, 736 F.2d 1028, 1986 AMC 1426 (CA5 Tex. 1984)
48 ALR5th 129—§ 2
50 ALR5th 1—§ 2
51 ALR5th 467—§ 2
52 ALR5th 1—§ 2

Sosa v. Paulos, 924 P.2d 357, 299 Utah Adv. Rep. 26 (Utah 1996)
24 ALR5th 1—§ 9

Sosbee v. State, 155 Ga. App. 196, 270 S.E.2d 367 (1980)
29 ALR5th 59—§ 8

Sosebee v. State, 257 Ga. 298, 357 S.E.2d 562 (1987)
71 ALR5th 637—§ 13

S.O.S., Inc. v. Payday, Inc., 886 F.2d 1081, 12 U.S.P.Q.2d 1241 (CA9 Cal. 1989)
38 ALR5th 1—§ 8, 10, 15

Soskin v. Reinertson, 257 F. Supp. 2d 1320 (D. Colo. 2003)
113 ALR5th 95—§ 3

Soskin v. Reinertson, 353 F.3d 1242 (10th Cir. 2004)
113 ALR5th 95—§ 3

Sosnoff v. Jackman, 45 A.D.3d 568, 845 N.Y.S.2d 391 (2d Dep't 2007)
93 ALR6th 123—§ 56

Sosnoski, Commonwealth ex rel. v. Sosnoski (1965) 37 Northum Leg J 176
124 ALR5th 203—§ 4

Sosnowski v. Wright Medical Technology, Inc., Prod. Liab. Rep. (CCH) ¶ 18809, 2012 WL 1030485 (N.D. Ill. 2012)
96 ALR6th 1—§ 31, 42, 47

Sossamon v. Lone Star State of Texas, 560 F.3d 316 (5th Cir. 2009)
56 ALR6th 679—§ 9
66 ALR6th 635—§ 47

Sossamon v. State, 31 Ark. App. 131, 789 S.W.2d 738 (1990)
41 ALR5th 171—§ 12, 32, 68

Sossamon v. Texas, 130 S. Ct. 3319 (2010)
56 ALR6th 679—§ 9

Sossamon v. Texas, 131 S. Ct. 1651, 179 L. Ed. 2d 700 (2011)
66 ALR6th 635—§ 47

Sossamon v. Williams, 270 Fed. Appx. 323 (5th Cir. 2008)
89 ALR6th 1—§ 55

Sostre, In re, 2010 WL 455392 (Cal. App. 4th Dist. 2010)
63 ALR6th 351—§ 3

Sostre v. Swift, 603 A.2d 809 (Del. Sup. 1992)
6 ALR5th 534—§ 18
31 ALR5th 1—§ 2, 12

Sosunova v. Regents of University of California, 11 Cal. Rptr. 2d 130 (App. 2d Dist. 1992)
17 ALR6th 159—§ 3

Sotel v. City of New York, 81 Misc. 344, 142 N.Y.S. 361 (Sup 1913)
54 ALR6th 201—§ 13, 15

Sotelo, In re Adoption of, 130 Ill. App. 3d 398, 85 Ill. Dec. 685, 474 N.E.2d 413 (3d Dist. 1985)
92 ALR5th 379—§ 9

Sotelo v. DirectRevenue, LLC, 384 F. Supp. 2d 1219 (N.D. Ill. 2005)
87 ALR6th 1—§ 68

Sotelo v. Interstate Financial Corp., 224 S.W.3d 517 (Tex. App. El Paso 2007)
81 ALR6th 161—§ 5
82 ALR6th 43—§ 5

Sotelo v. Old Republic Life Ins., 2006 WL 2632563 (N.D. Cal. 2006)
104 ALR6th 207—§ 21

Sotelo v. State, 273 Ind. 694, 408 N.E.2d 1215 (1980)
95 ALR5th 125—§ 5, 6

Sotelo v. Washington Mut. Ins. Co., 734 A.2d 421 (Pa. Super. Ct. 1999)
23 ALR5th 75—§ 6

Sothras v. Employment Division, 48 Or. App. 69, 616 P.2d 524 (1980)
25 ALR6th 101—§ 17

Sotirakis v. United Service Auto. Ass'n, 106 Nev. 123, 787 P.2d 788 (1990)
110 ALR5th 465—§ 2, 5

Soto v. 2101 Realty Co., 699 N.Y.S.2d 107 (App. Div. 2d Dep't 1999)
43 ALR5th 207—§ 39, 47

Soto v. Adams Elevator Equipment Co., 941 F.2d 543, 56 BNA FEP Cas. 1270, 30 BNA WH Cas. 857, 57 CCH EPD ¶ 40937, 119 CCH LC ¶ 35530 (CA7 Ill. 1991)
23 ALR5th 241—§ 41

Soto v. Artuz, 78 Fed. Appx. 760 (2d Cir. 2003)
29 ALR6th 1—§ 14

Soto v. Com., 139 S.W.3d 827 (Ky. 2004)
7 ALR6th 233—§ 5
27 ALR6th 183—§ 11, 15

Soto v. Dickey, 744 F.2d 1260 (7th Cir. 1984)
65 ALR6th 93—§ 59

Soto v. Dolgen Corp., 665 So. 2d 1086 (Fla. App. D4 1995)
5 ALR5th 875—§ 23.5

Soto v. El Paso Natural Gas Co., 942 S.W.2d 671 (Tex. App. El Paso 1997)
93 ALR5th 47—§ 22
94 ALR5th 1—§ 8

Soto v. Henessy, 2010 WL 4919485 (N.D. Cal. 2010)
101 ALR6th 207—§ 32, 37

Soto v. Royal Globe Ins. Co., 184 Cal. App. 3d 420, 229 Cal. Rptr. 192 (4th Dist. 1986)
6 ALR5th 297—§ 7, 8, 43
96 ALR5th 107—§ 7, 11

Soto v. State, 671 S.W.2d 43 (Tex. Crim. 1984)
31 ALR5th 704—§ 2, 8

Soto v. State, 727 So. 2d 1044 (Fla. Dist. Ct. App. 2d Dist. 1999)
21 ALR6th 771—§ 5

Soto v. State, 837 S.W.2d 401 (Tex. App. Dallas 1992)
32 ALR5th 149—§ 56

Soto v. Texas, 2001 WL 42969 (Tex. App. Austin 2001)
6 ALR6th 533—§ 21

Soto v. U.S. Lines, Inc., 608 F. Supp. 904 (S.D. N.Y. 1985)
17 ALR6th 1—§ 27

Soto v. Vacco, 208 F.3d 204 (2d Cir. 2000)
100 ALR5th 171—§ 3, 14

Soto v. Vandeventer, 56 N.M. 483, 245 P.2d 826, 35 A.L.R.2d 1190 (1952)
80 ALR5th 533—§ 3 to 5

Soto v. Workers' Comp. Appeals Bd., 46 Cal. App. 4th 1356, 54 Cal. Rptr. 2d 446, 61 Cal. Comp. Cas. (MB) 578 (2d Dist. 1996)
79 ALR5th 201—§ 5, 10

Sotolongo v. State, 530 So. 2d 514 (Fla. Dist. Ct. App. 2d Dist. 1988)
113 ALR5th 517—§ 19
73 ALR6th 49—§ 15

Sotomayer v. New Haven Parking Auth., 2000 WL 1023212 (Conn. Super. Ct. 2000)
100 ALR5th 409—§ 6

Sotomayor v. Medifast, Inc., 28 A.D.3d 309, 814 N.Y.S.2d 103 (1st Dep't 2006)
48 ALR6th 1—§ 43

Soto-Ruphuy v. Yates, 687 S.W.2d 19 (Tex. App. San Antonio 1984)

5 ALR5th 788—§ 2, 5, 21

Sotto v. State, 701 So. 2d 309 (Ala. Crim. App. 1997)

70 ALR5th 587—§ 24

Soucek v. Banham, 503 N.W.2d 153 (Minn. Ct. App. 1993)

61 ALR5th 635—§ 22
91 ALR5th 545—§ 11

Soucek v. Banham, 524 N.W.2d 478 (Minn. Ct. App. 1994)

61 ALR5th 635—§ 3, 10

Soucie v. Hess, 2005 WL 1432262 (Minn. Ct. App. 2005)

91 ALR6th 1—§ 52

Soucy, Appeal of, 139 N.H. 110, 649 A.2d 60 (1994)

12 ALR6th 523—§ 12

Soucy v. City of Manchester, 78 N.H. 591, 98 A. 518 (1916)

54 ALR6th 201—§ 66

Souder v. Cannon, 235 S.W.3d 841 (Tex. App. Fort Worth 2007)

81 ALR6th 363—§ 4, 15

Souder v. Commonwealth, 719 S.W.2d 730 (Ky. 1986)

5 ALR5th 243—§ 52

Souder v. Owens-Corning Fiberglas Corp., 939 F.2d 647, CCH Prod. Liab. Rep. ¶ 12861, 20 FR Serv. 3d 1314 (CA8 Minn. 1991)

63 ALR5th 195—§ 3

Souder v. State, 147 Ga. App. 431, 249 S.E.2d 146 (1978)

55 ALR5th 125—§ 20, 24

Souder v. State, 301 Ga. App. 348, 687 S.E.2d 594 (2009)

71 ALR6th 1—§ 17

Soufane v. Wu, 2009 WL 3789979 (Mich. Ct. App. 2009)

64 ALR6th 249—§ 37

Soufflas v. Zimmer, Inc., 474 F. Supp. 2d 737, 62 U.C.C. Rep. Serv. 2d 590 (E.D. Pa. 2007)

89 ALR6th 337—§ 12 to 14, 19, 21, 23, 26

Soukoian v. Cadillac Taxi Co., 68 Cal. App. 604, 229 P. 1015 (1924)

31 ALR5th 572—§ 15

Soukop v. ConAgra, Inc., 264 Neb. 1015, 653 N.W.2d 655 (2002)

8 ALR6th 465—§ 20

Soulas v. Troy Donut University, Inc., 9 Ohio App. 3d 339, 460 N.E.2d 310 (10th Dist. Franklin County 1983)

10 ALR6th 293—§ 6

Soule, In re Estate of, 248 Neb. 878, 540 N.W.2d 118, 74 A.L.R.5th 783 (1995)

74 ALR5th 491—§ 3, 6

Soule v. General Motors Corp., 8 Cal. 4th 548, 34 Cal. Rptr. 2d 607, 882 P.2d 298, Prod. Liab. Rep. (CCH) ¶ 14046 (1994)

73 ALR5th 75—§ 6, 15, 17

Soule v. Soule, 252 A.D.2d 768, 676 N.Y.S.2d 701 (3d Dep't 1998)

123 ALR5th 565—§ 25

Soule v. Stuyvesant Ins. Co., 116 N.H. 595, 364 A.2d 883 (1976)

77 ALR5th 319—§ 3
78 ALR5th 341—§ 5

Soule v. Town of Perinton, 152 N.Y.S.2d 734 (Sup. Ct. 1956)

73 ALR5th 223—§ 9

Soules v. Cadam, Inc., 2 Cal. App. 4th 390, 3 Cal. Rptr. 2d 6, 92 C.D.O.S. 370, 66 BNA FEP Cas. 587, 121 CCH LC ¶ 56881 (2d Dist. 1991)

51 ALR5th 1—§ 5

Soulia v. O'Brien, 94 F. Supp. 764 (D. Mass. 1950)

95 ALR5th 611—§ 3
53 ALR6th 81—§ 9

Soulisak, In re, 227 B.R. 77 (Bankr. E.D. Va. 1998)

25 ALR6th 323—§ 4
32 ALR6th 531—§ 39

Soulliere v. St. Joseph's Mercy of Macomb, 2001 WL 1335951 (Mich. Ct. App. 2001)

64 ALR6th 249—§ 38

Soundgarden v. Eikenberry, 123 Wash. 2d 750, 871 P.2d 1050, 22 Media L. R. 2385, 30 A.L.R.5th 869 (1994)

30 ALR5th 718—§ 3

Sound of Market Street, Inc. v. Continental Bank International, 819 F.2d 384, 4 U.C.C.R.S.2d 175 (CA3 Pa. 1987)

53 ALR5th 667—§ 2
56 ALR5th 565—§ 3, 4, 10, 39

Sound Timber Co. v. Danaher Lumber Co., 112 Wash. 314, 192 P. 941 (1920)

17 ALR5th 547—§ 37

Souran v. Souran, 80 Misc. 2d 476, 363 N.Y.S.2d 511 (Dist. Ct. 1975)

120 ALR5th 229—§ 7, 22

Sourdiff v. Texas Roadhouse Holdings, LLC, 2011 WL 7560647 (N.D. N.Y. 2011)

88 ALR6th 319—§ 45, 52

Souris River Tel. Mut. Aid Corp. v. State, 162 N.W.2d 685 (N.D. 1968)

58 ALR5th 187—§ 42

Sours v. Goodrich, 674 P.2d 995 (Colo. App. 1983)

20 ALR5th 1—§ 2, 3, 26

Sours v. Norris, 782 F.2d 106 (8th Cir. 1986)

56 ALR6th 553—§ 23

Sousa v. BP Oil, RICO Bus Disp Guide (CCH) ¶ 8986 (D.C. Mass. 1995)

49 ALR5th 1—§ 101

Sousa v. Chaset, 519 A.2d 1132 (R.I. 1987)

48 ALR5th 575—§ 2, 6, 9

Sousa v. Providence Subaru Co., 668 A.2d 331 (R.I. 1995)

10 ALR5th 245—§ 10

Sousa v. Soares, 1997 WL 535259 (Conn. Super. Ct. 1997)

96 ALR5th 107—§ 7
99 ALR5th 301—§ 9

Sousa v. U. S., 400 A.2d 1036 (D.C. 1979)

16 ALR6th 329—§ 11

Sousa v. U.S., 400 A.2d 1036 (D.C. 1979)

24 ALR6th 591—§ 9

Sousaris v. Miller, 92 Haw. 534, 993 P.2d 568 (Haw. Ct. App. 1998)

64 ALR5th 475—§ 3

Soussa v. Department of Motor Vehicles of State, 2006 WL 3317792 (Cal. App. 2d Dist. 2006)

34 ALR6th 623—§ 11

Soutar v. St. Clair County Election Com'n, 334 Mich. 258, 54 N.W.2d 425 (1952)

121 ALR5th 1—§ 37

South v. Gomez, 211 F.3d 1275 (9th Cir. 2000)

89 ALR6th 701—§ 9

South v. National R. R. Passenger Corp. (AMTRAK), 290 N.W.2d 819 (N.D. 1980)

15 ALR6th 1—§ 4, 5, 9

South v. Peters, 89 F. Supp. 672 (N.D. Ga. 1950)

68 ALR6th 489—§ 10

South v. Peters, 339 U.S. 276, 70 S. Ct. 641, 94 L. Ed. 834 (1950)

68 ALR6th 489—§ 10

South v. State, 111 Neb. 383, 196 N.W. 684 (1923)

54 ALR6th 429—§ 11

South v. Toledo Edison Co., 32 Ohio App. 3d 24, 513 N.E.2d 800, 45 Fair Empl. Prac. Cas. (BNA) 422 (6th Dist. Lucas County 1986)

12 ALR5th 508—§ 4
51 ALR5th 1—§ 7
81 ALR5th 367—§ 5

South 41 Lumber Co. v. Gibson, 438 S.W.2d 343 (Ky. 1969)

3 ALR5th 907—§ 9, 11, 12

South African Airways v. New York State Division of Human Rights, 64 Misc. 2d 707, 315 N.Y.S.2d 651 (Sup 1970)

108 ALR5th 189—§ 7

Southall v. Gabel, 28 Ohio App. 2d 295, 57 Ohio Ops. 2d 451, 277 N.E.2d 230 (Franklin Co. 1971)

12 ALR5th 1—§ 27

Southall v. Kingsville Timber Co., 168 So. 2d 424 (La. App. 3d Cir. 1964)

36 ALR5th 225—§ 3

Southall v. U.S., 716 A.2d 183 (D.C. 1998)

For assistance, call 1-800-328-4880

15 ALR5th 391—§ 5
South American Minerals & Merchandise Corp. v. Lewis, 337 Mass. 298, 149 N.E.2d 385 (1958)
56 ALR5th 757—§ 3
Southampton v. Platt, 55 App. Div. 2d 603, 389 N.Y.S.2d 625 (2d Dep't 1976)
45 ALR5th 109—§ 16
Southampton Civic Club v. Couch, 159 Tex. 464, 322 S.W.2d 516 (1958)
1 ALR6th 135—§ 3, 29
Southampton Civic Club v. Foxworth, 550 S.W.2d 152 (Tex. Civ. App. Houston 14th Dist. 1977)
1 ALR6th 135—§ 3, 30
Southampton, Town of v. Equus Assocs., 201 App. Div. 2d 210, 615 N.Y.S.2d 714 (2d Dep't 1994)
38 ALR5th 357—§ 7
Southard, In re Adoption of, 358 Pa. 386, 57 A.2d 904 (1948)
82 ALR5th 443—§ 3
84 ALR5th 191—§ 6
Southard v. Biddle, 305 S.W.2d 762 (Ky. 1957)
38 ALR5th 357—§ 16
Southard v. Com., Unemployment Compensation Bd. of Review, 88 Pa. Commw. 578, 490 A.2d 952 (1985)
68 ALR5th 13—§ 17, 19, 39
Southard v. Lester, 260 Fed. Appx. 611, 2008 A.M.C. 1467 (4th Cir. 2008)
66 ALR6th 185—§ 22
Southard v. Southard, 239 S.W.3d 172 (Mo. Ct. App. E.D. 2007)
100 ALR6th 1—§ 34
Southard v. Visa U.S.A. Inc., 734 N.W.2d 192, 2007-1 Trade Cas. (CCH) ¶ 75756 (Iowa 2007)
35 ALR6th 245—§ 10, 16
Southard v. Visa U.S.A., Inc., 2004 WL 3030028 (Iowa Dist. Ct. 2004)
35 ALR6th 245—§ 6
Southard By and Through Southard v. Miles, 714 P.2d 891 (Colo. 1986)
5 ALR6th 133—§ 17

South Atlantic Packers Ass'n, Inc., In re, 30 B.R. 836, 36 U.C.C. Rep. Serv. 1040 (Bankr. D. S.C. 1983)
107 ALR5th 311—§ 8
South Atlantic S.S. Co. v. Munkacsy, 37 Del. 580, 187 A. 600 (Sup. 1936)
10 ALR5th 371—§ 4, 5
South Bay Expressway, L.P., In re, 434 B.R. 589 (Bankr. S.D. Cal. 2010)
81 ALR6th 363—§ 3, 9, 25
South Bay Expressway, L.P., In re, 455 B.R. 732, 55 Bankr. Ct. Dec. (CRR) 32 (Bankr. S.D. Cal. 2011)
81 ALR6th 363—§ 9, 25
South Bend, City of v. Bowman, 434 N.E.2d 104 (Ind. Ct. App. 3d Dist. 1982)
72 ALR5th 1—§ 10
South Bend Clinic, Inc. v. Kistner, 769 N.E.2d 591 (Ind. Ct. App. 2002)
92 ALR6th 379—§ 60, 81
South Blvd. Video & News, Inc. v. Charlotte Zoning Bd. of Adjustment, 129 N.C. App. 282, 498 S.E.2d 623 (1998)
20 ALR6th 161—§ 3
21 ALR6th 425—§ 3
South Boston Allied War Veterans Council v. City of Boston, 875 F. Supp. 891 (D. Mass. 1995)
82 ALR5th 1—§ 3
72 ALR6th 513—§ 2
South Boston Allied War Veterans Council v. Massachusetts Com'n against Discrimination, 1994 WL 879961 (Mass. Super. Ct. 1994)
82 ALR5th 1—§ 3
South Boston Allied War Veterans Council v. Zobel, 830 F. Supp. 643 (D. Mass. 1993)
82 ALR5th 1—§ 3
Southbridge Towers, Inc. v. Rovics, 76 Misc. 2d 396, 350 N.Y.S.2d 62 (App. Term 1973)
114 ALR5th 443—§ 17, 40
Southbridge, Town of v. Massachusetts Coalition of Police,, 51 Mass. App. Ct. 1101, 751 N.E.2d 934 (2001)

112 ALR5th 263—§ 21

South Brunswick Associates v. Township Council of Tp. of Monroe, 285 N.J. Super. 377, 667 A.2d 1 (Law Div. 1994)

4 ALR6th 263—§ 27

South Brunswick, Township of v. State Agriculture Development Committee, 352 N.J. Super. 361, 800 A.2d 202 (App. Div. 2002)

8 ALR6th 465—§ 52

South Burlington v. American Fidelity Co., 125 Vt. 348, 215 A.2d 508 (1965)

30 ALR5th 699—§ 1 to 3, 6

South Burlington School Dist. v. Calcagni-Frazier-Zajchowski Architects, Inc., 138 Vt. 33, 410 A.2d 1359, 28 U.C.C. Rep. Serv. (CBC) 1382 (1980)

81 ALR5th 483—§ 3, 5

South Burlington School Dist. v. Goodrich, 135 Vt. 601, 382 A.2d 220 (1977)

33 ALR5th 1—§ 10

South Carolina v. Gathers, 490 U.S. 805, 109 S. Ct. 2207, 104 L. Ed. 2d 876 (1989)

79 ALR5th 33—§ 2

South Carolina Coin Operators Ass'n v. Beasley, 320 S.C. 183, 464 S.E.2d 103 (1995)

87 ALR6th 633—§ 7, 8

South Carolina Department of Social Services v. Humphreys, 297 S.C. 118, 374 S.E.2d 922 (Ct. App. 1988)

12 ALR6th 417—§ 7, 8

South Carolina Department of Social Services v. Smith, 311 S.C. 426, 429 S.E.2d 807 (1993)

12 ALR6th 417—§ 7

South Carolina Dept. of Health and Environmental Control v. Kennedy, 289 S.C. 73, 344 S.E.2d 859 (Ct. App. 1986)

88 ALR6th 203—§ 70

South Carolina Dep't of Mental Health v. State, 301 S.C. 75, 390 S.E.2d 185 (1990)

46 ALR5th 735—§ 2

South Carolina Dep't of Social Services v. Bess, 327 S.C. 523, 489 S.E.2d 671 (Ct. App. 1997)

90 ALR5th 1—§ 45

South Carolina Dept. of Social Services v. Broome, 307 S.C. 48, 413 S.E.2d 835 (1992)

12 ALR6th 417—§ 18

South Carolina Dep't of Social Services v. Humphreys, 297 S.C. 118, 374 S.E.2d 922 (App. 1988)

1 ALR5th 469—§ 8, 18, 37

South Carolina Dept. of Social Services v. Humphreys, 297 S.C. 118, 374 S.E.2d 922 (Ct. App. 1988)

110 ALR5th 579—§ 14

South Carolina Dep't of Social Services v. McDow, 276 S.C. 509, 280 S.E.2d 208 (1981)

1 ALR5th 469—§ 2

South Carolina Dep't of Social Services v. Vanderhorst, 287 S.C. 554, 340 S.E.2d 149 (1986)

92 ALR5th 379—§ 7

South Carolina Dep't of Social Servs. v. Smith, 429 S.E.2d 807 (S.C. 1993)

1 ALR5th 469—§ 16.5, 37

South Carolina Dep't of Social Servs. ex rel. Sallie M. H. v. James C. D., 119 Misc. 2d 649, 464 N.Y.S.2d 942 (Fam Ct. 1983)

46 ALR5th 735—§ 2

South Carolina Electric & Gas Co. v. Public Service Com., 275 S.C. 487, 272 S.E.2d 793 (1980)

41 ALR5th 783—§ 4

South Carolina Employment Sec. Com'n, Ex parte, 332 S.C. 286, 504 S.E.2d 345 (Ct. App. 1998)

75 ALR5th 339—§ 6

South Carolina Equipment, Inc. v. Sheedy, 120 Wis. 2d 119, 353 N.W.2d 63 (App. 1984)

23 ALR5th 744—§ 2, 5

South Carolina Farm Bureau Marketing Ass'n v. South Carolina State Ports Authority, 278 S.C. 198, 293 S.E.2d 854 (1982)

65 ALR5th 1—§ 2, 20

South Carolina Ins. Co. v. Coody, 813 F. Supp. 1570 (M.D. Ga. 1993)

14 ALR5th 695—§ 6, 26

88 ALR5th 493—§ 4

89 ALR5th 1—§ 10

South Carolina Ins. Co. v. Smith, 67 N.C. App. 632, 313 S.E.2d 856 (1984)

43 ALR5th 149—§ 3

South Carolina Medical Malpractice Joint Underwriting Ass'n v. Froelich, 297 S.C. 400, 377 S.E.2d 306 (1989)

83 ALR5th 497—§ 5

South Carolina Medical Malpractice Liability Ins. Joint Underwriting Ass'n v. Ferry, 291 S.C. 460, 354 S.E.2d 378 (1987)

60 ALR5th 239—§ 27

South Carolina Nat. Bank v. S. & L. Invest. Partnership, 419 S.E.2d 243 (S.C. App. 1992)

10 ALR5th 448—§ 5

South Carolina Nat'l Bank v. Stone, 749 F. Supp. 1419, CCH Fed Secur L. Rep. ¶ 95453 (D.C. S.C. 1990)

23 ALR5th 241—§ 19

South Carolina. Oehler v. Clinton, 282 S.C. 25, 317 S.E.2d 445 (1984)

21 ALR5th 396—§ 9

South Carolina Pipeline Corp. v. Lone Star Steel Co., 345 S.C. 151, 546 S.E.2d 654, 2001 WL 506498 (2001)

122 ALR5th 1—§ 11

South Carolina Public Service Authority v. Summers, 282 S.C. 148, 318 S.E.2d 113 (1984)

114 ALR5th 561—§ 21

South Carolina Real Estate Com. v. Boineau, 267 S.C. 574, 230 S.E.2d 440 (1976)

7 ALR5th 474—§ 22, 49, 109

South Carolina Second Injury Fund v. Liberty Mut. Ins. Co., 353 S.C. 117, 576 S.E.2d 199 (Ct. App. 2003)

112 ALR5th 509—§ 18

20 ALR6th 641—§ 22

South Carolina. Smoak v. Wright (In re Wright), 443 S.E.2d 920 (S.C. App. 1994)

5 ALR5th 550—§ 23

South Carolina State Conference of Branches of Nat. Ass'n for Advancement of Colored People, Inc. v. Riley, 533 F. Supp. 1178 (D.S.C. 1982)

34 ALR6th 643—§ 34

South Carolina State Highway Dept. v. Booker, 260 S.C. 245, 195 S.E.2d 615 (1973)

66 ALR6th 83—§ 18

South Carolina State Highway Dep't v. J. W. Conder Co., 262 S.C. 318, 204 S.E.2d 381 (1974)

36 ALR5th 255—§ 18

South Carolina State Highway Dep't v. Wilson, 254 S.C. 360, 175 S.E.2d 391 (1970)

15 ALR5th 821—§ 3, 6, 11

South Carolina State Law Enforcement Div. v. Crook, 273 S.C. 285, 255 S.E.2d 846 (1979)

1 ALR5th 317—§ 4

South Carolina Tax Commission v. Metropolitan Life Ins. Co., 266 S.C. 34, 221 S.E.2d 522 (1975)

104 ALR5th 331—§ 6, 8

29 ALR6th 507—§ 18, 25, 27, 70

South Carolina Tax Commission v. York Elec. Co-op., Inc., 275 S.C. 326, 270 S.E.2d 626 (1980)

29 ALR6th 507—§ 3, 16, 19

South Carolina Tax Com'n v. Gaston Copper Recycling Corp., 316 S.C. 163, 447 S.E.2d 843, 22 Media L. Rep. (BNA) 2211 (1994)

8 ALR6th 117—§ 25

South Cent. Bell v. Milton J. Womack & Associates, Inc., 744 So. 2d 635 (La. Ct. App. 1st Cir. 1998)

28 ALR5th 603—§ 18, 21

South Cent. Bell Tel. Co. v. Barthelemy, 643 So. 2d 1240, 36 A.L.R.5th 689 (La. 1994)

36 ALR5th 133—§ 4

South Cent. Bell Tel. Co. v. Celauro, 735 S.W.2d 228 (Tenn. 1987)

58 ALR5th 187—§ 15

South Cent. Bell Tel. Co. v. Gaines Petroleum Co., 499 So. 2d 521 (La. App. 2d Cir. 1986)

5 ALR5th 1—§ 2 to 4, 8, 13

South Cent. Bell Tel. Co. v. Olsen, 669 S.W.2d 649 (Tenn. 1984)

58 ALR5th 187—§ 28

South Cent. Bell Tel. Co. v. Texaco, Inc., 418 So. 2d 531 (La. 1982)

11 ALR5th 438—§ 2, 3

South Cent. Bell Telephone Co. v. Barthelemy, 643 So. 2d 1240, 36 A.L.R.5th 689 (La. 1994)

50 ALR6th 261—§ 10, 11

South Cent. Bell Telephone Co. v. Ka-Jon Food Stores of Louisiana, Inc., 644 So. 2d 368, 39 Env't. Rep. Cas. (BNA) 1895 (La. 1994)

105 ALR5th 95—§ 18

Southcenter Joint Venture v. National Democratic Policy Committee, 113 Wash. 2d 413, 780 P.2d 1282 (1989)

52 ALR5th 195—§ 2 to 4

South Central Bell Tel. Co. v. Tennessee Public Service Com., 675 S.W.2d 718 (Tenn. App. 1984)

41 ALR5th 783—§ 2, 4

South Central Bell Tel. Co. v. Traigle, 367 So. 2d 1143 (La. 1978)

58 ALR5th 187—§ 19, 41

South Central Bell Telephone Co. v. Sumrall, 414 So. 2d 876 (La. Ct. App. 4th Cir. 1982)

18 ALR6th 195—§ 34

South Central Coast Regional Com. v. Charles A. Pratt Construction Co., 128 Cal. App. 3d 830, 180 Cal. Rptr. 555 (5th Dist. 1982)

38 ALR5th 737—§ 3

South Central Regional Medical Center v. Pickering, 749 So. 2d 95 (Miss. 1999)

59 ALR5th 535—§ 8

South Cheyenne Water and Sewer Dist. v. Stundon, 483 P.2d 240 (Wyo. 1971)

54 ALR6th 201—§ 7, 11, 28

South Dakota v. Neville, 459 U.S. 553, 103 S. Ct. 916, 74 L. Ed. 2d 748 (1983)

74 ALR5th 319—§ 1

South Dakota Dep't of Pub. Safety ex rel. Melgaard v. Haddenham, 339 N.W.2d 786 (S.D. 1983)

48 ALR5th 659—§ 4, 7, 9, 12

South Dakota Dept. of Social Services, People ex rel., 2011 SD 8, 795 N.W.2d 39 (S.D. 2011)

63 ALR6th 429—§ 25

South Dakota Dept. of Social Services, People ex rel., 2011 SD 8, 2011 WL 727570 (S.D. 2011)

63 ALR6th 429—§ 25

South Dakota Dept. of Social Services in Interest of C.H., People ex rel., 510 N.W.2d 119 (S.D. 1993)

6 ALR6th 161—§ 21

South Dakota Farm Bureau, Inc. v. Hazeltine, 340 F.3d 583, 33 Envtl. L. Rep. 20260, 125 A.L.R.5th 665 (8th Cir. 2003)

125 ALR5th 147—§ 3, 29, 30

South Dakota Microsoft Antitrust Litigation, In re, 2003 SD 19, 657 N.W.2d 668, 2003-1 Trade Cas. (CCH) ¶ 73962 (S.D. 2003)

35 ALR6th 245—§ 6

South Dakota Real Estate Com. v. Haggar, 446 N.W.2d 66 (S.D. 1989)

7 ALR5th 474—§ 162

South Dakota State Cement Plant Com'n v. Wausau Underwriters Ins. Co., 2000 SD 116, 616 N.W.2d 397, 31 Envtl. L. Rep. 20094 (S.D. 2000)

98 ALR5th 193—§ 7

South Discount Foods, Inc. v. Retail
   Clerks Union Local 1552, 14 Ohio
   Misc. 188, 43 Ohio Op. 2d 418, 235
   N.E.2d 143 (C.P. 1968)
   120 ALR5th 351—§ 10
Southeast Alabama Gas Dist. v. City of
   Dothan, 279 Ala. 667, 189 So. 2d
   350 (1966)
   58 ALR5th 187—§ 13
Southeast Alaska Conservation Council
   v. U.S. Army Corps of Engineers,
   486 F.3d 638, 64 Env't. Rep. Cas.
   (BNA) 1581 (9th Cir. 2007)
   36 ALR6th 681—§ 18
   46 ALR6th 495—§ 18
Southeast Alaska Const. Co., Inc. v.
   State, Dept. of Transp. and Public
   Facilities, 791 P.2d 339 (Alaska
   1990)
   124 ALR5th 375—§ 15
Southeast Alaska Constr. Co. v. State,
   DOT & Public Facilities, 791 P.2d
   339 (Alaska 1990)
   15 ALR5th 376—§ 3
Southeast Coal Co. v. Combs, 760
   S.W.2d 83 (Ky. 1988)
   25 ALR5th 568—§ 3
South-East Coal Co. v. Consolidation
   Coal Co., 434 F.2d 767, 75 BNA
   LRRM 2634, 64 CCH LC ¶ 11285,
   1970 CCH Trade Cases ¶ 73391
   (CA6 Ky. 1970)
   9 ALR5th 102—§ 18
South-East Coal Co. v. Dingus, 352
   S.W.2d 190 (Ky. 1961)
   86 ALR5th 295—§ 7
Southeast Consultants, Inc. v. O'Pry,
   199 Ga. App. 125, 404 S.E.2d 299
   (1991)
   117 ALR5th 23—§ 5
Southeastern Associates, Inc. v. First
   Georgia Bank, 362 So. 2d 967 (Fla.
   App. D1 1978)
   8 ALR5th 653—§ 3
Southeastern Color Lithographers, Inc.
   v. Graphic Arts Mut. Ins. Co., 164
   Ga. App. 70, 296 S.E.2d 378 (1982)
   18 ALR5th 187—§ 5

Southeastern Colo. Water Conservancy
   Dist. v. Cache Creek Mining Trust,
   854 P.2d 167 (Colo. 1993)
   5 ALR5th 422—§ 3
Southeastern Elevator Co. v. Phelps, 70
   Ga. App. 331, 28 S.E.2d 85 (1943)
   13 ALR5th 289—§ 16, 28
   115 ALR5th 1—§ 17, 20
Southeastern Fair Ass'n v. Ford, 64 Ga.
   App. 871, 14 S.E.2d 139 (1941)
   54 ALR5th 393—§ 8
Southeastern Fidelity Ins. Co. v. Gann,
   340 So. 2d 429 (Miss. 1976)
   16 ALR5th 412—§ 7
Southeastern Fire Ins. Co. v. Walton,
   256 N.C. 345, 123 S.E.2d 780
   (1962)
   5 ALR5th 422—§ 3, 4
Southeastern Freight Lines v. City of
   Hartsville, 313 S.C. 466, 443 S.E.2d
   395 (1994)
   17 ALR6th 1—§ 6
Southeastern Greyhound Lines v. Hard-
   en's Adm'x, 281 Ky. 345, 136
   S.W.2d 42 (1940)
   58 ALR5th 535—§ 5
Southeastern Greyhound Lines, etc. v.
   Grimes, 385 S.W.2d 189 (Ky. 1964)
   16 ALR5th 1—§ 30
Southeastern Hosp. Supply Corp. v.
   Clifton & Singer, 110 N.C. App.
   652, 430 S.E.2d 470 (1993)
   11 ALR6th 1—§ 4
Southeastern Housing Foundation v.
   Smith, 380 S.C. 621, 670 S.E.2d
   680 (Ct. App. 2008)
   58 ALR6th 1—§ 5, 14
Southeastern, Inc. v. Doty, 481 P.2d 144
   (Okla. 1971)
   5 ALR5th 422—§ 3, 4
Southeastern Kentucky Baptist Hosp.,
   Inc. v. Gaylor, 756 S.W.2d 467 (Ky.
   1988)
   23 ALR6th 697—§ 6
Southeastern Land Fund, Inc. v. Real
   Estate World, Inc., 237 Ga. 227, 227
   S.E.2d 340 (1976)
   39 ALR5th 33—§ 3, 9

Southeastern Medical Supply, Inc. v. Boyles, Moak & Brickell Insurance, Inc., 822 So. 2d 323, 3 A.L.R.6th 693 (Miss. Ct. App. 2002)

3 ALR6th 13—§ 9

Southeastern Mun. Supply Co. v. Citizens First Nat'l Bank, 432 So. 2d 753, 36 U.C.C.R.S. 189 (Fla. App. D5 1983)

45 ALR5th 389—§ 17

Southeastern Pennsylvania Transp. Authority v. Caremarkpcs Health, L.P., 254 F.R.D. 253 (E.D. Pa. 2008)

64 ALR6th 655—§ 13

Southeastern Pennsylvania Transp. Authority v. Com., Unemployment Compensation Bd. of Review, 96 Pa. Commw. 38, 506 A.2d 974 (1986)

18 ALR6th 195—§ 6

Southeastern Pennsylvania Transp. Authority v. Com., Unemployment Compensation Bd. of Review, 106 Pa. Commw. 16, 525 A.2d 458 (1987)

95 ALR5th 329—§ 4

Southeastern Pennsylvania Transp. Authority v. W.C.A.B. (McDowell), 730 A.2d 562 (Pa. Commw. Ct. 1999)

44 ALR5th 569—§ 17

Southeastern Promotions, Ltd. v. Conrad, 420 U.S. 546, 95 S. Ct. 1239, 43 L. Ed. 2d 448, 1 Media L. Rep. (BNA) 1140 (1975)

70 ALR6th 513—§ 3
71 ALR6th 471—§ 3

Southeastern Sec. Ins. Co. v. Empire Banking Co., 230 Ga. App. 755, 498 S.E.2d 282 (1998)

8 ALR6th 549—§ 3

Southeastern Sec. Ins. Co. v. Hotle, 222 Ga. App. 161, 473 S.E.2d 256 (1996)

81 ALR5th 367—§ 32, 39

Southeastern United Medigroup, Inc. v. Hughes, 952 S.W.2d 195 (Ky. 1997)

5 ALR6th 327—§ 9, 14

8 ALR6th 117—§ 33

Southeast First Nat. Bank of Satellite Beach v. Atlantic Telec, Inc., 389 So. 2d 1032, 30 U.C.C. Rep. Serv. (CBC) 1629 (Fla. Dist. Ct. App. 5th Dist. 1980)

77 ALR5th 429—§ 7

Southeast Furniture Co. v. Barrett, 24 Utah 2d 24, 465 P.2d 346 (1970)

33 ALR5th 587—§ 5

Southeast Land Development Associates, L.P. v. District of Columbia, 2005 WL 3211458 (D.D.C. 2005)

21 ALR6th 261—§ 4, 6, 8, 41

Southeast Title & Ins. Co. v. Thompson, 231 So. 2d 201 (Fla. 1970)

33 ALR5th 121—§ 4

Southeast Warren Community School Dist. v. Department of Public Instruction, 285 N.W.2d 173 (Iowa 1979)

115 ALR5th 563—§ 3

South End Imp. Co. v. Harden, 52 A. 1127 (N.J. Ch. 1902)

4 ALR5th 772—§ 55

Southerland v. Gourd, 269 F. Supp. 2d 48 (E.D. N.Y. 2003)

24 ALR6th 1—§ 11

Southerland v. Northeast Datsun, Inc., 659 S.W.2d 889, 38 U.C.C. Rep. Serv. 78 (Tex. App. El Paso 1983)

47 ALR5th 677—§ 3
89 ALR5th 319—§ 17, 24

Southerland v. Smith, 142 B.R. 980, 6 FLW Fed D 328 (M.D. Fla. 1992)

55 ALR5th 647—§ 6

Southerland v. State, 176 Ind. 493, 96 N.E. 583 (1911)

105 ALR5th 529—§ 21

Southerland v. Streeter, 41 So. 2d 708 (La. Ct. App. 2d Cir. 1949)

111 ALR5th 313—§ 5

Southerland v. Thigpen, 784 F.2d 713 (5th Cir. 1986)

5 ALR6th 485—§ 8

Southerland v. Wal-Mart Stores, Inc., 848 P.2d 68 (Okla. App. 1993)

40 ALR5th 135—§ 3, 15

Southern v. Board of Trustees, 318 F. Supp. 355 (N.D. Tex. 1970)
58 ALR5th 1—§ 5, 10, 13
Southern v. Glenn, 568 So. 2d 281 (Miss. 1990)
59 ALR6th 433—§ 49
Southern v. Glenn, 677 S.W.2d 576 (Tex. App. San Antonio 1984)
59 ALR6th 433—§ 4, 15 to 17, 47
Southern Air Transport, Inc. v. Post-Newsweek Stations, Florida, Inc., 568 So. 2d 927 (Fla. Dist. Ct. App. 3d Dist. 1990)
42 ALR6th 353—§ 20
Southern Air Transport, Inc. v. Post-Newsweek Stations, Inc., 568 So. 2d 927, 15 FLW D 1290 (Fla. App. D3 1990)
19 ALR5th 1—§ 2, 143
Southern American Ins. Co. v. Dobson, 441 So. 2d 1185 (La. 1983)
2 ALR5th 922—§ 5
52 ALR5th 451—§ 3, 7
Southern American Ins. Co. v. E.W. Corrigan Const. Co., 1991 WL 149981 (N.D. Ill. 1991)
62 ALR5th 1—§ 2
Southern Amusement Corp. v. Summers, 23 Ala. App. 595, 129 So. 489 (1930)
10 ALR5th 371—§ 12, 21
Southern Bell Tel. and Tel. Co. v. Beard, 597 So. 2d 873 (Fla. Dist. Ct. App. 1st Dist. 1992)
8 ALR6th 117—§ 35
Southern Bell Tel. & Tel. Co. v. Cherokee, Inc., 297 S.C. 206, 375 S.E.2d 347 (App. 1988)
28 ALR5th 603—§ 21
Southern Bell Tel. & Tel. Co. v. City of Spartanburg, 285 S.C. 495, 331 S.E.2d 333 (1985)
58 ALR5th 187—§ 37, 42
Southern Bell Tel. & Tel. Co. v. Clayton, 266 N.C. 687, 147 S.E.2d 195 (1966)
58 ALR5th 187—§ 2, 20

Southern Bell Tel. and Tel. Co. v. Coastal Transmission Service, Inc., 167 Ga. App. 611, 307 S.E.2d 83 (1983)
104 ALR5th 523—§ 4, 6
Southern Bell Tel. & Tel. Co. v. Com., 266 S.W.2d 308 (Ky. 1954)
122 ALR5th 337—§ 14
Southern Bell Tel. & Tel. Co. v. Conyers Toyota, Inc., 190 Ga. App. 792, 380 S.E.2d 296 (1989)
8 ALR5th 177—§ 2, 3
Southern Bell Tel. & Tel. Co. v. Deason, 632 So. 2d 1377, 19 FLW S. 119, 27 A.L.R.5th 829 (Fla. 1994)
26 ALR5th 628—§ 17
27 ALR5th 76—§ 8, 23, 37
Southern Bell Tel. & Tel. Co. v. Don Hammond, Inc., 198 Ga. App. 517, 402 S.E.2d 112 (1991)
28 ALR5th 603—§ 2
Southern Bell Tel. & Tel. Co. v. Hamm, 409 S.E.2d 775, 9 A.L.R.5th 1131 (S.C. 1991)
9 ALR5th 553—§ 3, 4, 6
Southern Bell Tel. & Tel. Co. v. McCook, 355 So. 2d 1166 (Fla. 1977)
80 ALR5th 417—§ 3, 4
Southern Bell Tel. & Tel. Co. v. Nineteen Hundred One Collins Corp., 83 So. 2d 865 (Fla. 1955)
63 ALR6th 1—§ 53
Southern Bell Tel. & Tel. Co. v. Odom, 9 Ga. App. 246, 70 S.E. 1116 (1910)
8 ALR5th 177—§ 16
Southern Bell Tel. & Tel. Co. v. Roper, 438 So. 2d 1046 (Fla. App. D3 1983)
10 ALR5th 663—§ 3
Southern Bell Tel. & Tel. Co. v. Sharara, 167 Ga. App. 665, 307 S.E.2d 129 (1983)
13 ALR5th 217—§ 2, 6 to 8
Southern Bell Tel. & Tel. Co. v. Town of Surfside, 186 So. 2d 777 (Fla. 1966)
58 ALR5th 187—§ 38

Southern Bell Tel. & Tel. Co. v. Whiddon, 108 Ga. App. 106, 132 S.E.2d 237 (1963)

8 ALR5th 177—§ 8

Southern Bell Tel. & Tel. Co. v. Woodstock, Inc., 34 Ill. App. 3d 86, 339 N.E.2d 423 (1st Dist. 1975)

88 ALR5th 545—§ 6, 22

Southern Burlington County N.A.A.C.P. v. Mount Laurel Tp., 67 N.J. 151, 336 A.2d 713 (1975)

123 ALR5th 349—§ 6
22 ALR6th 295—§ 4

Southern Burlington County N.A.A.C.P. v. Mount Laurel Tp., 92 N.J. 158, 456 A.2d 390 (1983)

123 ALR5th 349—§ 6
22 ALR6th 295—§ 4, 6, 11, 14, 15

Southern Burlington County NAACP v. Mt. Laurel, 92 N.J. 158, 456 A.2d 390 (1983)

1 ALR5th 622—§ 32

Southern Cal. Edison Co. v. F.E.R.C., 603 F.3d 996 (D.C. Cir. 2010)

80 ALR6th 1—§ 85, 89

Southern California Edison Co. v. Lynch, 307 F.3d 794, 54 Fed. R. Serv. 3d 286 (9th Cir. 2002)

80 ALR6th 1—§ 16

Southern California Edison Co. v. Peevey, 31 Cal. 4th 781, 3 Cal. Rptr. 3d 703, 74 P.3d 795 (2003)

80 ALR6th 1—§ 29

Southern California Electric Co. v. McDonald, 178 Cal. 386, 173 P. 760 (1918)

4 ALR5th 772—§ 77, 92, 94

Southern California First Nat'l Bank v. Olsen, 41 Cal. App. 3d 234, 116 Cal. Rptr. 4 (2d Dist. 1974)

58 ALR5th 325—§ 2, 3, 8

Southern California IBEW-NECA Trust Funds v. Standard Indus. Elec. Co., 247 F.3d 920, 25 Employee Benefits Cas. (BNA) 2537 (9th Cir. 2001)

81 ALR6th 363—§ 15, 17

Southern Cal. Permanente Medical Group v. Bozinovski, 148 Cal. App. 3d 503, 196 Cal. Rptr. 150, 37 U.C.C. Rep. Serv. 7 (2d Dist. 1983)

91 ALR5th 89—§ 6

Southern Cal. Rapid Transit Dist. v. Superior Court, 30 Cal. App. 4th 713, 36 Cal. Rptr. 2d 665, 10 I.E.R. Cas. (BNA) 162 (2d Dist. 1994)

105 ALR5th 351—§ 3, 6, 9, 12

Southern Cal. Underground Contractors, Inc. v. City of San Diego, 108 Cal. App. 4th 533, 133 Cal. Rptr. 2d 527 (4th Dist. 2003)

28 ALR6th 175—§ 18

Southern Cal. White Trucks v. Teresinski, 190 Cal. App. 3d 1393, 236 Cal. Rptr. 159 (2d Dist. 1987)

6 ALR5th 883—§ 2

Southern Co. v. Graham, 271 Ark. 223, 607 S.W.2d 677, CCH Prod. Liab. Rep. ¶ 8879 (1980)

5 ALR5th 1—§ 2, 13

Southern Co. v. Hamburg, 220 Ga. App. 834, 470 S.E.2d 467 (1996)

52 ALR6th 271—§ 18
85 ALR6th 323—§ 108

Southern Const. Co. v. U. S., 176 Ct. Cl. 1339, 364 F.2d 439 (1966)

25 ALR6th 265—§ 5

Southern Co-op. Development Fund v. Driggers, 696 F.2d 1347 (11th Cir. 1983)

123 ALR5th 349—§ 4

Southern Co. Services, Inc. v. F.E.R.C., 416 F.3d 39 (D.C. Cir. 2005)

80 ALR6th 1—§ 100

Southern Cotton Oil Division v. Childress, 237 Ark. 909, 377 S.W.2d 167 (1964)

41 ALR6th 207—§ 27

Southern County Mut. Ins. Co. v. Bryant, 385 So. 2d 1286 (La. Ct. App. 3d Cir. 1980)

111 ALR5th 1—§ 8
112 ALR5th 621—§ 6

Southern Energy Homes, Inc. v. Ard, 772 So. 2d 1131, 2000-1 Trade Cas. (CCH) ¶ 72930 (Ala. 2000)
22 ALR6th 387—§ 11

Southern Energy Homes, Inc. v. Kennedy, 774 So. 2d 540 (Ala. 2000)
22 ALR6th 387—§ 9, 30, 37

Southern Entertainment Co. v. Boynton Beach, 736 F. Supp. 1094 (S.D. Fla. 1990)
10 ALR5th 538—§ 3, 4, 8, 16

Southern Exp. v. Green, 26 Va. App. 439, 495 S.E.2d 500 (1998)
20 ALR5th 346—§ 14

Southern Exp. Co. v. Texarkana Water Co., 54 Ark. 131, 15 S.W. 361 (1891)
70 ALR5th 261—§ 10

Southern Express Co. v. Malone, 16 Ala. App. 414, 78 So. 408 (1918)
14 ALR5th 242—§ 46

Southern Farm Bureau Cas. Ins. Co. v. Brewer, 507 So. 2d 369 (Miss. 1987)
79 ALR5th 289—§ 8, 14

Southern Farm Bureau Cas. Ins. Co. v. Craven, 79 Ark. App. 423, 89 S.W.3d 369 (2002)
110 ALR5th 465—§ 33

Southern Farm Bureau Cas. Ins. Co. v. Easter, 345 Ark. 273, 45 S.W.3d 380 (2001)
41 ALR6th 527—§ 4, 7, 9

Southern Farm Bureau Cas. Ins. Co. v. Fields, 262 Ark. 144, 553 S.W.2d 278 (1977)
80 ALR6th 389—§ 3, 9

Southern Farm Bureau Cas. Ins. Co. v. Kimball, 552 S.W.2d 207 (Tex. Civ. App. Waco 1977)
66 ALR5th 269—§ 8

Southern Farm Bureau Cas. Ins. Co. v. Pettie, 54 Ark. App. 79, 924 S.W.2d 828 (1996)
3 ALR5th 1—§ 40
42 ALR6th 545—§ 3, 29
43 ALR6th 375—§ 3, 5, 22, 50

Southern Farm Bureau Cas. Ins. Co. v. Sonnier, 396 So. 2d 996 (La. Ct. App. 3d Cir. 1981)
125 ALR5th 1—§ 5

Southern Farm Bureau Casualty Ins. Co. v. Gooding, 263 Ark. 435, 565 S.W.2d 421 (1978)
6 ALR5th 611—§ 3, 6, 11

Southern Farm Bureau Life Ins. Co. v. Cowger, 295 Ark. 250, 748 S.W.2d 332 (1988)
23 ALR5th 241—§ 12

Southern Floridabanc Federal Sav. & Loan Asso. v. Buscemi, 529 So. 2d 303, 13 FLW 1643 (Fla. App. D4 1988)
13 ALR5th 684—§ 2

Southern Gas Corp. v. Brooks, 50 Tenn. App. 1, 359 S.W.2d 570 (1961)
34 ALR5th 1—§ 5, 7

Southern General Ins. Co. v. Holt, 200 Ga. App. 759, 409 S.E.2d 852 (1991)
6 ALR5th 297—§ 41, 44, 49

Southern General Ins. Co. v. National Union Fire Ins. Co. of Pittsburgh, 218 Ga. App. 400, 461 S.E.2d 574 (1995)
125 ALR5th 1—§ 5

Southern Grocery Stores, Inc. v. Donehoo, 59 Ga. App. 212, 200 S.E. 335 (1939)
2 ALR5th 1—§ 35

Southern Guaranty Ins. Co. v. Ash, 192 Ga. App. 24, 383 S.E.2d 579 (1989)
26 ALR5th 628—§ 17, 27
27 ALR5th 76—§ 8, 10

Southern Guaranty Ins. Co. v. Dean, 252 Miss. 69, 172 So. 2d 553 (1965)
16 ALR5th 412—§ 7

Southern Guaranty Ins. Co. v. Duncan, 131 Ga. App. 761, 206 S.E.2d 672 (1974)
35 ALR5th 375—§ 5, 23

Southern Guar. Ins. Co. v. Cotton States Mut. Ins. Co., 176 Ga. App. 140, 335 S.E.2d 598 (1985)
105 ALR5th 499—§ 4

Southern Guar. Ins. Co. of Georgia v. Saxon, 190 Ga. App. 652, 379 S.E.2d 577 (1989)

41 ALR6th 527—§ 7

Southern Home Ins. Co. v. Putnal, 57 Fla. 199, 49 So. 922 (1909)

16 ALR5th 412—§ 31

Southern Idaho Production Credit Ass'n v. Ruiz, 105 Idaho 140, 666 P.2d 1151 (1983)

86 ALR6th 321—§ 11

88 ALR6th 385—§ 17

Southern Ill. Clinic v. Human Rights Comm'n, 274 Ill. App. 3d 840, 211 Ill. Dec. 193, 654 N.E.2d 655 (5th Dist. 1995)

51 ALR5th 1—§ 7

Southern Illinoisan v. Department of Public Health, 2004 WL 1303565 (Ill. App. Ct. 5th Dist. 2004)

118 ALR5th 1—§ 18

Southern Illinoisan, a Div. of Lee Enterprises, Inc. v. Department of Public Health, 319 Ill. App. 3d 979, 254 Ill. Dec. 361, 747 N.E.2d 401 (5th Dist. 2001)

118 ALR5th 1—§ 4, 18, 20

Southern Illinois Contracting Co. v. Launtz, 169 Ill. App. 87 (1912)

46 ALR5th 1—§ 45

Southern Illinois Laborers Dist. Council of Labors Intern. Union of North America v. Special Mine Services, Inc., 754 F. Supp. 645, 117 Lab. Cas. (CCH) ¶ 10507 (S.D. Ill. 1990)

94 ALR5th 149—§ 4

Southern Illinois Stone Co. v. Universal Engineering Corp., 592 F.2d 446, 25 U.C.C. Rep. Serv. 1336 (8th Cir. 1979)

89 ALR5th 319—§ 2, 9

Southern Indiana Gas and Elec. Co. v. Indiana Dept. of State Revenue, 804 N.E.2d 877 (Ind. Tax Ct. 2004)

80 ALR6th 325—§ 16

Southern Indus. v. Chumney, 613 So. 2d 74, 18 FLW D369 (Fla. App. D1 1993)

63 ALR5th 163—§ 13

Southern Industrial Banking Corp., Re, 35 B.R. 643 (F. BC ED Tenn. 1983)

27 ALR5th 76—§ 30, 36

Southern Ins. Co. v. Domino of California, Inc., 173 Cal. App. 3d 619, 219 Cal. Rptr. 112 (2d Dist. 1985)

30 ALR5th 170—§ 99

Southern Ins. Underwriters, Inc. v. Ray, 188 Ga. App. 469, 373 S.E.2d 236 (1988)

115 ALR5th 589—§ 4

Southern Land and Resources Co., Inc. v. Dobbs, 467 So. 2d 652 (Miss. 1985)

81 ALR6th 161—§ 4

82 ALR6th 43—§ 4

Southern Lead Corporation v. Glass, 103 Fla. 657, 138 So. 59 (1931)

85 ALR6th 1—§ 24

Southern Life & Health Ins. Co. v. Turner, 586 So. 2d 854 (Ala. 1991)

14 ALR5th 242—§ 34

Southern Life & Health Ins. Co. v. Williams, 230 Ala. 681, 163 So. 321 (1935)

87 ALR6th 319—§ 60

Southern Maryland Agricultural Asso. v. Bituminous Casualty Corp., 539 F. Supp. 1295 (D.C. Md. 1982)

14 ALR5th 695—§ 28

Southern Massachusetts Broadcasters, Inc. v. Duchaine, 26 Mass. App. Ct. 497, 529 N.E.2d 887 (1988)

107 ALR5th 311—§ 14

109 ALR5th 421—§ 5, 17

Southern Med. Health Sys. v. Vaughn, 130 CCH LC ¶ 57979 (Ala. 1995)

34 ALR5th 699—§ 5

Southern Message Service, Inc. v. Commercial Union Ins. Co., 647 So. 2d 398 (La. Ct. App. 2d Cir. 1994)

90 ALR5th 453—§ 12

Southern Methodist University v. Evans, 131 Tex. 333, 115 S.W.2d 622 (1938)

46 ALR5th 581—§ 2

47 ALR5th 1—§ 2

Southern Mississippi Planning & Development Dist., Inc. v. Robertson, 660 F. Supp. 1057 (S.D. Miss. 1986)
  76 ALR6th 289—§ 5
  77 ALR6th 543—§ 11
Southern Mut. Life Ins. Co. v. Montague, 8 Ky.L.Rptr. 579, 84 Ky. 653, 2 S.W. 443, 4 Am.St.Rep. 218 (1887)
  63 ALR5th 427—§ 3, 29
Southern Nat. Bank v. Curtis, 36 S.W. 911 (Tex. Civ. App. 1896)
  53 ALR5th 287—§ 3, 10
Southern Nevada Homebuilders Ass'n v. Clark County, 121 Nev. 446, 117 P.3d 171 (2005)
  28 ALR6th 439—§ 19
Southern Ohio Correctional Facility, In re, 24 Fed. Appx. 520 (6th Cir. 2001)
  60 ALR6th 295—§ 10, 13, 51
Southern Pac. Co. v. Barnes, 3 Ariz. App. 483, 415 P.2d 579 (1966)
  15 ALR6th 1—§ 4, 10, 22
Southern Pac. Co. v. Bogert, 250 U.S. 483, 39 S. Ct. 533, 63 L. Ed. 1099 (1919)
  10 ALR6th 293—§ 15
Southern Pac. Co. v. Globe Indem. Co., 21 F.2d 288 (CA2 N.Y. 1927)
  15 ALR5th 376—§ 4
Southern Pac. Co. v. Harris, 80 Nev. 426, 395 P.2d 767 (1964)
  15 ALR6th 1—§ 4, 9, 10
Southern Pac. Co. v. Martinez, 270 F. 770 (C.C.A. 9th Cir. 1921)
  62 ALR6th 313—§ 3
Southern Pac. Co. v. State of Ariz. ex rel. Sullivan, 325 U.S. 761, 65 S. Ct. 1515, 89 L. Ed. 1915, 59 Pub. Util. Rep. (NS) 211 (1945)
  98 ALR5th 167—§ 4
Southern Pac. Co. v. Stevenson, 218 S.W. 151 (Tex. Civ. App. 1920)
  40 ALR5th 1—§ 4
Southern Pac. Co. v. Watkins, 83 Nev. 471, 435 P.2d 498 (1967)
  15 ALR6th 1—§ 4, 5, 10, 22

Southern Pacific Transp. Co. v. Chabert, 973 F.2d 441 (CA5 La. 1992)
  23 ALR5th 241—§ 42
Southern Pacific Transp. Co. v. Lueck, 111 Ariz. 560, 535 P.2d 599 (1975)
  12 ALR5th 195—§ 6, 26, 27
Southern Pacific Transp. Co. v. Maliska, 1999 WL 354507 (Tex. App. Beaumont 1999)
  90 ALR5th 453—§ 24
Southern Pacific Transp. Co. v. The Tug Capt. Vick, 443 F. Supp. 722 (E.D. La 1977)
  31 ALR5th 171—§ 16
Southern Pacific Transp. Co. v. Tug Capt. Vick, 443 F. Supp. 722, 1979 A.M.C. 1404 (E.D. La. 1977)
  66 ALR6th 185—§ 4
Southern Pac. R. R. Co. v. Mitchell, 80 Ariz. 50, 292 P.2d 827 (1956)
  19 ALR5th 622—§ 2
  31 ALR5th 572—§ 22
Southern R. Co. v. American Peanut Corp., 158 Va. 359, 164 S.E. 261 (1932)
  17 ALR5th 547—§ 37, 38
Southern R. Co. v. Birch, 185 F.2d 44 (CA5 Ga. 1950)
  17 ALR5th 547—§ 45, 52, 53
Southern R. Co. v. Black Diamond Collieries, Inc., 9 Tenn. App. 225 (1928)
  31 ALR5th 171—§ 15, 17
Southern R. Co. v. Clariday, 124 Ga. 958, 53 S.E. 461 (1906)
  20 ALR5th 1—§ 4, 11, 14, 43
Southern R. Co. v. Coltex, Inc., 282 S.C. 321, 318 S.E.2d 284 (App. 1984)
  45 ALR5th 227—§ 6
Southern R. Co. v. Darwin, 156 Ala. 311, 47 So. 314 (1908)
  17 ALR5th 547—§ 46, 51, 59
Southern R. Co. v. Dickens, 161 Ala. 144, 49 So. 766 (1909)
  17 ALR5th 547—§ 36, 53
Southern R. Co. v. Everett, 211 Ala. 61, 99 So. 82 (1924)
  17 ALR5th 547—§ 53

Southern R. Co. v. Johnston, 22 Ala. App. 629, 118 So. 680 (1928)
17 ALR5th 547—§ 53

Southern R. Co. v. Lawson, 174 Ga. App. 101, 329 S.E.2d 288 (1985)
58 ALR5th 535—§ 7, 8, 21

Southern R. Co. v. Lefan, 195 Ala. 295, 70 So. 249 (1915)
10 ALR5th 371—§ 3, 4, 19

Southern R. Co. v. Madden, 235 F.2d 198 (CA4 S.C. 1956)
5 ALR5th 875—§ 2, 23

Southern R. Co. v. McLellan, 80 Miss. 700, 32 So. 283 (1902)
10 ALR5th 371—§ 3, 4

Southern R. Co. v. Minor, 196 Ga. App. 183, 395 S.E.2d 845 (1990)
9 ALR5th 102—§ 17

Southern R. Co. v. Patterson, 105 Va. 6, 52 S.E. 694 (1906)
17 ALR5th 547—§ 60

Southern R. Co. v. Power Fuel Co., 152 F. 917 (CA4 S.C. 1907)
17 ALR5th 547—§ 68

Southern R. Co. v. Routh, 161 Ky. 196, 170 S.W. 520 (1914)
25 ALR5th 568—§ 3

Southern R. Co. v. Scott, 215 Ga. 739, 113 S.E.2d 459 (1960)
17 ALR5th 547—§ 37, 54

Southern R. Co. v. Slade, 192 Ala. 568, 68 So. 867 (1915)
17 ALR5th 547—§ 43, 46, 53, 59

Southern R. Co. v. Taylor, 76 Ga. App. 745, 47 S.E.2d 77 (1948)
17 ALR5th 547—§ 36

Southern R. Co. v. Thompson, 129 Ga. 367, 58 S.E. 1044 (1907)
17 ALR5th 547—§ 52

Southern R. Co. v. White, 108 Ga. 201, 33 S.E. 952 (1899)
51 ALR5th 603—§ 4

Southern Rock Products Co. v. Board of Zoning Adjustment of City of Trussville, 282 Ala. 186, 210 So. 2d 419 (1968)
103 ALR5th 157—§ 12

Southern Ry. Co. v. A. O. Smith Corp., 134 Ga. App. 219, 213 S.E.2d 903 (1975)
17 ALR6th 1—§ 16

Southern Ry. Co. v. Foote Mineral Co., 384 F.2d 224 (6th Cir. 1967)
105 ALR5th 499—§ 4

Southern Ry. Co. v. Parnell, 142 Ala. 146, 37 So. 925 (1904)
61 ALR5th 635—§ 15

Southern Ry. Co. v. Taylor, 812 S.W.2d 577 (Tenn. 1991)
33 ALR5th 509—§ 5

Southern Ry. Co. v. Waldrup, 76 Ga. App. 356, 45 S.E.2d 775 (1947)
94 ALR6th 111—§ 9

Southern Ry. News Co. v. Fidelity & Cas. Co. of New York, 26 Ky. L. Rptr. 1217, 83 S.W. 620 (Ky. 1904)
16 ALR6th 491—§ 10

Southern Sawmill Co. v. Ducote, 120 La. 1052, 46 So. 20 (1908)
8 ALR5th 653—§ 4

Southern Scales, Inc. v. Aronov Ins., Inc., 608 So. 2d 724 (Ala. 1992)
60 ALR5th 165—§ 9

Southern Silica Min. & Mfg. Co. v. Hoefer, 215 S.C. 480, 56 S.E.2d 321 (1949)
45 ALR5th 251—§ 6

Southern Solvents, Inc. v. Canal Ins. Co., 894 F. Supp. 430 (M.D. Fla.1995)
88 ALR5th 493—§ 3

Southern States Fire Ins. Co. v. Hand-Jordan Co., 112 Miss. 565, 73 So. 578 (1917)
87 ALR6th 319—§ 54

Southern States Henry Co-operative, Inc. v. U.S., 4 Cl. Ct. 370 (1984)
27 ALR5th 719—§ 2, 11

Southern States Landfill, Inc. v. Walton County, 259 Ga. 673, 386 S.E.2d 358 (1989)
47 ALR6th 439—§ 7

Southern States Power Co. v. Clark, 118 Fla. 521, 159 So. 881 (1935)
10 ALR5th 371—§ 3, 7

Southern Sur. Co. of New York v. Fortson, 46 Ga. App. 265, 167 S.E. 335 (1933)

116 ALR5th 247—§ 5

Southern Surety Co. v. York Tire Service, 209 Iowa 104, 227 N.W. 606 (1929)

46 ALR5th 1—§ 47

Southern Tank Equip. Co. v. Zartic, Inc., 221 Ga. App. 503, 471 S.E.2d 587, 96 Fulton County D R 2190, 30 U.C.C.R.S.2d 54 (1996)

49 ALR5th 1—§ 3

Southern Transit Co., Inc. v. Collums, 333 Ark. 170, 966 S.W.2d 906 (1998)

86 ALR6th 321—§ 12

Southern Union Co. v. U.S., 132 S. Ct. 2344 (2012)

76 ALR6th 587—§ 36, 52

Southern United Fire Ins. Co. v. Willingham, 739 So. 2d 503 (Ala. Civ. App. 1999)

33 ALR5th 121—§ 36

Southern Utilities Co. v. Davis, 83 Fla. 366, 92 So. 683 (1922)

42 ALR5th 465—§ 3

Southern Volkswagen, Inc. v. Centrix Financial, LLC, 357 F. Supp. 2d 837, 2005-1 Trade Cas. (CCH) ¶ 74699 (D. Md. 2005)

52 ALR6th 271—§ 6

Southern Win-Dor, Inc. v. RLI Ins. Co., 925 So. 2d 884 (Miss. Ct. App. 2005)

104 ALR6th 1—§ 26

South Euclid v. Ostendorf-Morris Co., 24 Ohio Misc. 259, 53 Ohio Ops. 2d 153, 260 N.E.2d 843 (1970)

63 ALR5th 517—§ 9, 46

South Euclid Fraternal Order of Police, Lodge 80 v. D'Amico, 13 Ohio App. 3d 46, 13 Ohio B.R. 49, 468 N.E.2d 735 (Cuyahoga Co. 1983)

57 ALR5th 477—§ 38

South Fayette v. Boy's Home, 31 Pa. Cmwlth. 254, 376 A.2d 663 (1977)

53 ALR5th 1—§ 15, 30, 57

South Fayette v. Commonwealth, 477 Pa. 574, 385 A.2d 344 (1978)

53 ALR5th 1—§ 12, 41

South Federal St. Associates v. Iron Fireman Mfg. Co., 23 Misc. 2d 1070, 201 N.Y.S.2d 579 (Sup 1960)

20 ALR6th 211—§ 35

Southfield Western, Inc. v. City of Southfield, 146 Mich. App. 585, 382 N.W.2d 187 (1985)

90 ALR5th 547—§ 14, 16

South Florida Free Beaches, Inc. v. City of Miami, Fla., 734 F.2d 608 (11th Cir. 1984)

71 ALR6th 283—§ 5, 28

South Florida Regional Planning Council v. Florida Division of State Planning, 370 So. 2d 447 (Fla. Dist. Ct. App. 1st Dist. 1979)

47 ALR6th 439—§ 12

South Fulton Medical Center, Inc. v. Poe, 224 Ga. App. 107, 480 S.E.2d 40 (1996)

58 ALR5th 613—§ 12

Southfund Partners III v. Sears, Roebuck and Co., 57 F. Supp. 2d 1369 (N.D. Ga. 1999)

8 ALR5th 312—§ 13, 17

Southgate Community Sch. Dist. v. West Side Constr. Co., 399 Mich. 72, 247 N.W.2d 884, 20 U.C.C.R.S. 1202 (1976)

49 ALR5th 1—§ 43, 48

South Gibson School Bd. v. Sollman, 768 N.E.2d 437 (Ind. 2002)

117 ALR5th 459—§ 11

South Hadley v. Director of Div. of Employment Sec., 389 Mass. 399, 450 N.E.2d 596 (1983)

33 ALR5th 643—§ 24

South Hampton Co. v. Stinnes Corp., 733 F.2d 1108, 38 U.C.C. Rep. Serv. (CBC) 1137 (5th Cir. 1984)

63 ALR5th 1—§ 14

South Jefferson General Hospital, Inc. v. Connors, 341 So. 2d 637 (La. App. 4th Cir. 1977)

35 ALR5th 757—§ 3

South Jersey Catholic School Teachers Organization v. St. Teresa of the Infant Jesus Church Elementary School, 150 N.J. 575, 696 A.2d 709, 119 Ed. Law Rep. 1035, 155 L.R.R.M. (BNA) 2972 (1997)
123 ALR5th 385—§ 12

South Lake Tahoe, City of v. California Tahoe Regional Planning Agency, 625 F.2d 231 (9th Cir. 1980)
115 ALR5th 563—§ 3

Southland Broadcasting Co. v. Tracy, 210 Miss. 836, 50 So. 2d 572 (1951)
33 ALR5th 303—§ 3, 9, 10

Southland Capital Corp. v. Clark, 526 S.W.2d 278 (Tex. Civ. App. Waco 1975)
23 ALR5th 241—§ 10

Southland Corp. v. Ashland Oil, Inc., 696 F. Supp. 994, 28 Envt. Rep. Cas. 1805, 19 ELR 20733 (D.C. N.J. 1988)
8 ALR5th 312—§ 9, 13

Southland Corp. v. Keating, 465 U.S. 1, 79 L. Ed. 2d 1, 104 S. Ct. 852 (1984)
60 ALR5th 669—§ 2, 3

Southland Corp. v. Welch, 33 Va. App. 633, 536 S.E.2d 443 (2000)
3 ALR5th 907—§ 8

Southland Corp., The v. Comptroller of The Treasury, 1999 WL 33290788 (Md. Tax Ct. 1999)
17 ALR6th 623—§ 3

Southland Hills Imp. Ass'n of Baltimore County, Inc. v. Raine, 220 Md. 213, 151 A.2d 734 (1959)
47 ALR6th 439—§ 10

Southland Ins. Co., In re, 535 So. 2d 648, 13 FLW 2755 (Fla. App. D1 1988)
44 ALR5th 683—§ 22

Southland Mechanical Constructors Corp. v. Nixen, 119 Cal. App. 3d 417, 173 Cal. Rptr. 917 (4th Dist. 1981)
87 ALR5th 473—§ 5
13 ALR6th 1—§ 4
14 ALR6th 1—§ 5

Southland Mobile Home Corp. v. Winders, 262 Ark. 693, 561 S.W.2d 280 (1978)
102 ALR5th 647—§ 4, 6

Southland Royalty Co. v. Federal Power Commission, 543 F.2d 1134 (5th Cir. 1976)
65 ALR5th 211—§ 37

Southland Sweet Potato Curing & Storage Ass'n v. Beck, 221 S.W. 656 (Tex. Civ. App. Dallas 1920)
85 ALR6th 1—§ 36

Southland Title Corp. v. Superior Court, 231 Cal. App. 3d 530, 282 Cal. Rptr. 425, 91 C.D.O.S. 4880, 91 Daily Journal DAR 7393 (2d Dist. 1991)
19 ALR5th 786—§ 4, 5, 7

Southlanes Bowl, Inc. v. Lumbermen's Mut. Ins. Co., 46 Mich. App. 758, 208 N.W.2d 569 (1973)
37 ALR5th 41—§ 17, 22

South Louisiana Grain Services, Inc. v. Bergland, 590 F.2d 1204 (D.C. Cir. 1978)
62 ALR6th 517—§ 49

South Lyme Property Owners Ass'n., Inc. v. Town of Old Lyme, 539 F. Supp. 2d 524 (D. Conn. 2008)
68 ALR6th 229—§ 7
89 ALR6th 1—§ 50

South Macomb Disposal Authority v. American Ins. Co., 225 Mich. App. 635, 572 N.W.2d 686 (1997)
97 ALR5th 473—§ 3, 9

South Macomb Disposal Authority v. National Surety Corp., 239 Mich. App. 344, 608 N.W.2d 814 (2000)
88 ALR5th 493—§ 3
89 ALR6th 1—§ 5

Southmark Corp. v. Trotter, Smith & Jacobs, 212 Ga. App. 454, 442 S.E.2d 265 (1994)
85 ALR5th 353—§ 2, 11

South Miami v. Alvin, 189 So. 2d 386 (Fla. App. D3 1966)
1 ALR5th 622—§ 17

Southminster, Inc. v. Justus, 119 N.C. App. 669, 459 S.E.2d 793 (1995)

69 ALR5th 477—§ 6

South Newton Tp. Electors v. South Newton Tp. Sup'r, Bouch, 575 Pa. 670, 838 A.2d 643 (2003)

13 ALR6th 661—§ 13

South Norwalk Trust Co. v. St. John, 92 Conn. 168, 101 A. 961 (1917)

3 ALR5th 590—§ 11, 15, 17

South of Ann Drive, Re, 34 App. Div. 2d 412, 312 N.Y.S.2d 66 (2d Dep't 1970)

8 ALR5th 391—§ 3

South Orangetown Kitchen Workers Ass'n v. South Orangetown Central School Dist. of Towns of Orangetown and Clarkstown, 101 Misc. 2d 1016, 422 N.Y.S.2d 597 (Sup. Ct. 1979)

65 ALR5th 1—§ 2, 8

South Pierre Associates v. Meyers, 12 Misc. 3d 955, 820 N.Y.S.2d 485 (N.Y. City Civ. Ct. 2006)

24 ALR6th 399—§ 3, 8, 17

South Portland v. State, 476 A.2d 690 (Me. 1984)

11 ALR5th 630—§ 10

Southridge Capital Management, LLC v. Twin City Fire Ins. Co., 2006 WL 2730312 (Conn. Super. Ct. 2006)

20 ALR6th 411—§ 14

South Santa Clara Val. Water Conservation Dist. v. Johnson, 231 Cal. App. 2d 388, 41 Cal. Rptr. 846 (1st Dist. 1964)

116 ALR5th 373—§ 3

South Shore Bank v. Stewart Title Guaranty Co., 688 F. Supp. 803, 28 Envt. Rep. Cas. 1391 (D.C. Mass. 1988)

12 ALR5th 630—§ 2

South Shore Baseball, LLC v. DeJesus, 982 N.E.2d 1076 (Ind. Ct. App. 2013)

82 ALR6th 417—§ 4

South Shore Baseball, LLC v. DeJesus, 2013 WL 587476 (Ind. Ct. App. 2013)

82 ALR6th 417—§ 4, 11

South Shore Homes Ass'n, Inc. v. Holland Holiday's, 219 Kan. 744, 549 P.2d 1035 (1976)

25 ALR5th 233—§ 14
76 ALR5th 337—§ 2, 19
81 ALR6th 469—§ 6

South Shore Hospital v. Easton, 441 So. 2d 161 (Fla. App. D3 1983)

6 ALR5th 883—§ 7

Southside Baptist Church v. Drennen, 362 So. 2d 854 (Ala. 1978)

36 ALR5th 395—§ 3, 12

Southside Internists Group PC Money Purchase Pension Plan v. Janus Capital Corp., 741 F. Supp. 1536, 12 Employee Benefits Cas. (BNA) 2162, Fed. Sec. L. Rep. (CCH) ¶ 96079 (N.D. Ala. 1990)

22 ALR6th 49—§ 4, 11

Southside Utilities, Inc. v. Abante Corp., 54 Va. Cir. 288, 2000 WL 33595090 (2000)

81 ALR6th 363—§ 4

Southstar Corp. v. St. Paul Surplus Lines Ins. Co., 42 S.W.3d 187 (Tex. App. Corpus Christi 2001)

98 ALR5th 1—§ 24

South Sutter, LLC v. LJ Sutter Partners, L.P., 193 Cal. App. 4th 634, 2011 WL 900583 (3d Dist. 2011)

64 ALR6th 365—§ 6

South Texas Coaches, Inc. v. Eastland, 101 S.W.2d 878 (Tex. Civ. App. 1937)

12 ALR5th 195—§ 26

South Texas Tel. Co. v. Tabb, 52 Tex. Civ. App. 213, 114 S.W. 448 (1908)

8 ALR5th 177—§ 16

South Texas Tire Test Fleet, Inc. v. Long, 594 S.W.2d 540 (Tex. Civ. App. San Antonio 1979)

50 ALR5th 653—§ 9

SouthTrust Bank v. Ford, 835 So. 2d 990 (Ala. 2002)

22 ALR6th 387—§ 11, 28

SouthTrust Bank v. Jones, Morrison, Womack & Dearing, P.C., 2005 WL 628876 (Ala. Civ. App. 2005)

11 ALR6th 1—§ 4, 7

Southtrust Bank and Right Equipment Co. of Pinellas County, Inc. v. Export Ins. Services, Inc., 190 F. Supp. 2d 1304 (M.D. Fla. 2002)

8 ALR6th 549—§ 14

SouthTrust Bank of Tuscaloosa County, N.A., Ex parte, 619 So. 2d 1356, 42 A.L.R.5th 825 (Ala. 1993)

42 ALR5th 221—§ 20

Southtrust Bank of Tuskegee, Ex parte, 469 So. 2d 103 (Ala. 1985)

42 ALR5th 221—§ 5

South Union, Ltd. v. George Parker & Associates, 29 Ohio App. 3d 197, 504 N.E.2d 1131 (10th Dist. Franklin County 1985)

47 ALR6th 303—§ 12

Southwell, Matter of Marriage of, 119 Or. App. 366, 851 P.2d 599, 82 Ed. Law Rep. 936 (1993)

57 ALR5th 389—§ 11, 12

Southwell v. Mallery, Stern & Warford, 194 Cal. App. 3d 140, 239 Cal. Rptr. 371 (2d Dist. 1987)

16 ALR6th 1—§ 35

Southwell v. University of Incarnate Word, 974 S.W.2d 351, 128 Ed. Law Rep. 1294 (Tex. App. San Antonio 1998)

46 ALR5th 581—§ 5, 23

Southwest Airlines Co. v. BoardFirst, L.L.C., 2007 WL 4823761 (N.D. Tex. 2007)

95 ALR6th 57—§ 2, 7, 8, 10

Southwest Airlines Co. v. Bullock, 784 S.W.2d 563 (Tex. App. Austin 1990)

113 ALR5th 313—§ 6

Southwest Airlines Co. v. Farechase, Inc., 318 F. Supp. 2d 435 (N.D. Tex. 2004)

87 ALR6th 1—§ 22, 84

Southwest Architectural Products, Inc. v. Smith, 4 Va. App. 474, 358 S.E.2d 745, 28 Wage & Hour Cas. (BNA) 1096 (1987)

48 ALR6th 387—§ 9

63 ALR6th 187—§ 32

Southwest Bank v. Information Support Concepts, Inc., 85 S.W.3d 462 (Tex. App. Fort Worth 2002)

104 ALR5th 459—§ 3

Southwest Bank & Trust Co. v. Calmark Asset Management, Inc., 694 S.W.2d 199 (Tex. App. Dallas 1985)

86 ALR5th 527—§ 2, 3, 11

Southwest Community Health Services, Presbyterian Hosp. Div. v. Safeco Ins. Co., 108 N.M. 570, 775 P.2d 1287 (1989)

16 ALR5th 262—§ 31

Southwest Concrete Products v. Gosh Construction Corp., 51 Cal. 3d 701, 274 Cal. Rptr. 404, 798 P.2d 1247, 13 U.C.C. Rep. Serv. 2d 985 (1990)

73 ALR6th 571—§ 8, 9, 32, 77

Southwest Delaware County Municipal Authority v. Aston Tp., 413 Pa. 526, 198 A.2d 867, 15 A.L.R.3d 836 (1964)

114 ALR5th 561—§ 19

Southwest Development Group, Inc. v. Blue Cross of California, 2005 WL 40035 (Cal. App. 4th Dist. 2005)

22 ALR6th 387—§ 4, 48

Southwestern Bank v. Renfro, 208 Ga. App. 487, 430 S.E.2d 860 (1993)

61 ALR5th 525—§ 24

Southwestern Bell Tel. Co. v. Baker, 650 S.W.2d 467 (Tex. App. Houston (14th Dist.) 1983)

12 ALR5th 195—§ 31

Southwestern Bell Tel. Co. v. Batten, 688 S.W.2d 61 (Mo. App. 1985)

28 ALR5th 603—§ 19

Southwestern Bell Tel. Co. v. Calvert, 479 S.W.2d 697 (Tex. Civ. App. Austin 1972)

58 ALR5th 187—§ 20, 33

Southwestern Bell Tel. Co. v. Davis, 582 S.W.2d 191 (Tex. Civ. App. Waco 1979)

52 ALR5th 155—§ 5

For assistance, call 1-800-328-4880

Southwestern Bell Tel. Co. v. Nationwide Independent Directory Service, Inc., 371 F. Supp. 900, 182 USPQ 193 (W.D. Ark. 1974)
23 ALR5th 241—§ 32
Southwestern Bell Tel. Co. v. Parker Pest Control, Inc., 737 P.2d 1186 (Okla. 1987)
23 ALR5th 241—§ 10
Southwestern Bell Tel. Co. v. Rawlings Mfg. Co., 359 S.W.2d 393 (Mo. App. 1962)
28 ALR5th 603—§ 4, 6, 16, 17
Southwestern Bell Tel. Co. v. Roberts, 182 Ark. 211, 31 S.W.2d 302 (1930)
27 ALR5th 174—§ 61, 75
Southwestern Bell Tel. Co. v. Thomas, 554 S.W.2d 672 (Tex. 1977)
80 ALR5th 533—§ 3, 5
Southwestern Bell Telephone Co., In re, 2007 WL 817637 (Mo. P.S.C. 2007)
36 ALR6th 149—§ 4
Southwestern Bell Telephone Co. v. General Cable Industries, Inc., 966 S.W.2d 166 (Tex. App. El Paso 1998)
17 ALR6th 1—§ 7
Southwestern Bell Telephone Co. v. Oklahoma Corp. Com'n, 1994 OK 38, 873 P.2d 1001 (Okla. 1994)
28 ALR6th 175—§ 6, 18
Southwestern Bell Telephone Co. v. State Commission of Revenue and Taxation, 168 Kan. 227, 212 P.2d 363 (1949)
89 ALR5th 493—§ 18
Southwestern Bell Telephone Co. v. Travelers Indem. Co., 252 Ark. 400, 479 S.W.2d 232 (1972)
70 ALR5th 261—§ 3
Southwestern Community Action Council, Inc. v. Community Services Administration, 462 F. Supp. 289, 19 Empl. Prac. Dec. (CCH) ¶ 9258 (S.D. W. Va. 1978)
123 ALR5th 411—§ 4
Southwestern Const. Co., Inc. v. Liberto, 385 So. 2d 633 (Ala. 1980)

76 ALR5th 337—§ 19
103 ALR5th 157—§ 4
Southwestern Elec. Power Co. v. Grant, 73 S.W.3d 211, 47 U.C.C. Rep. Serv. 2d 38 (Tex. 2002)
97 ALR6th 1—§ 20
Southwestern Elec. Power Co. v. Public Utility Com'n, 2011 WL 5299490 (Tex. App. Amarillo 2011)
80 ALR6th 1—§ 14
Southwestern Energy Co. v. Eickenhorst, 955 F. Supp. 1078, 42 U.S.P.Q.2d 1824 (W.D. Ark. 1997)
36 ALR6th 537—§ 1, 4
Southwestern Gas, Light & Power Co. v. Jay, 275 S.W. 735 (Tex. Civ. App. El Paso 1925)
112 ALR5th 113—§ 30
Southwestern Greyhound Lines, Inc. v. Rogers, 267 P.2d 572 (Okla. 1954)
12 ALR5th 195—§ 5, 17
Southwestern Invest. Co. v. Neeley, 452 S.W.2d 705 (Tex. 1970)
14 ALR5th 242—§ 4
Southwestern Invest. Co. v. Neeley, 455 S.W.2d 785 (Tex. Civ. App. Fort Worth 1970)
14 ALR5th 242—§ 26
Southwestern Sewer Co. v. Morris, 26 S.W.2d 311 (Tex. Civ. App. Amarillo 1930)
92 ALR5th 517—§ 11
101 ALR5th 287—§ 14
Southwestern Sur. Ins. Co. v. Stein Double Cushion Tire Co., 180 S.W. 1165 (Tex. Civ. App. Dallas 1915)
87 ALR6th 319—§ 27
Southwest Express Co. v. Interstate Commerce Com., 670 F.2d 53 (CA5 1982)
8 ALR5th 653—§ 3
Southwest Factories, Inc. v. Eaton, 1969 OK 77, 453 P.2d 1021 (Okla. 1969)
86 ALR5th 295—§ 15
Southwest Florida Heart Group, P.A., In re, 346 B.R. 897 (Bankr. M.D. Fla. 2006)
23 ALR6th 457—§ 4

Southwest Florida Production Credit Ass'n v. Schirow, 388 So. 2d 338, 30 U.C.C. Rep. Serv. (CBC) 268 (Fla. Dist. Ct. App. 4th Dist. 1980)

61 ALR5th 525—§ 7

Southwest Florida Tele-Communications, Inc., In re, 195 B.R. 504 (Bankr. M.D. Fla. 1996)

66 ALR6th 83—§ 5

Southwest Forest Indus. v. Industrial Comm'n, 96 Ariz. 91, 392 P.2d 506 (1964)

47 ALR5th 801—§ 2, 3, 12

Southwest Forest Industries, Inc. v. Sutton, 868 F.2d 352, 4 BNA IER Cas. 160, 130 BNA LRRM 2600 (CA10 Kan. 1989)

14 ALR5th 242—§ 4

Southwest Marine, Inc. v. Triple A Mach. Shop, Inc., 720 F. Supp. 805, 36 Cont. Cas. Fed. (CCH) ¶ 75806, R.I.C.O. Bus. Disp. Guide (CCH) ¶ 7428 (N.D. Cal. 1989)

115 ALR5th 709—§ 3

Southwest Mississippi Elec. Power Ass'n v. Harried, 773 So. 2d 365 (Miss. Ct. App. 2000)

95 ALR5th 29—§ 3

Southwest Natural Gas Co. v. Oklahoma Portland Cement Co., 102 F.2d 630 (C.C.A. 10th Cir. 1939)

94 ALR5th 247—§ 40

Southwest Ohio Regional Transit Auth. v. Amalgamated Transit Union, Local 627, 91 Ohio St. 3d 108, 2001-Ohio-294, 742 N.E.2d 630, 166 L.R.R.M. (BNA) 2873 (2001)

112 ALR5th 263—§ 2, 39

Southwest Ohio Regional Transit Auth. v. Amalgamated Transit Union, Local 627, 131 Ohio App. 3d 751, 723 N.E.2d 645, 160 L.R.R.M. (BNA) 2743 (1st Dist. Hamilton County 1998)

112 ALR5th 263—§ 66

Southwest Ohio Regional Transit Authority v. Amalgamated Transit Union, Local 627, 1994 WL 525543 (Ohio Ct. App. 1st Dist. Hamilton County 1994)

112 ALR5th 263—§ 46

Southwest Oregon Dairy Herd Improv. Asso. v. Morgan, 17 Or. App. 300, 521 P.2d 1308 (1974)

60 ALR5th 459—§ 2, 9, 15

Southwest Petroleum Co. v. Logan, 180 Okla. 477, 71 P.2d 759 (1937)

76 ALR5th 337—§ 20

Southwest Petroleum Co. v. Logan, 1937 OK 473, 180 Okla. 477, 71 P.2d 759 (1937)

119 ALR5th 519—§ 4

Southwest Ranches Homeowners Ass'n, Inc. v. Broward County, 502 So. 2d 931 (Fla. Dist. Ct. App. 4th Dist. 1987)

73 ALR5th 223—§ 3, 10

Southwest Supermarkets, LLC, In re, 325 B.R. 417, 44 Bankr. Ct. Dec. (CRR) 231 (Bankr. D. Ariz. 2005)

23 ALR6th 457—§ 17

Southwest Voter Registration Educ. Project v. Shelley, 344 F.3d 914 (9th Cir. 2003)

104 ALR6th 547—§ 12

Southwick v. Southwick, 214 A.D.2d 987, 627 N.Y.S.2d 497 (4th Dep't 1995)

104 ALR5th 605—§ 4, 8
123 ALR5th 565—§ 31

Southwick v. State, 701 S.W.2d 927 (Tex. App. Houston 1st Dist. 1985)

94 ALR5th 497—§ 5

Southwick v. Univ. Hosp., Inc., 2006-Ohio-1376, 2006 WL 744297 (Ohio Ct. App. 1st Dist. Hamilton County 2006)

92 ALR6th 379—§ 85

South Wind Motel v. Ohio Civil Rights Com., 24 Ohio App. 3d 209, 24 Ohio B.R. 386, 494 N.E.2d 1158, 46 BNA FEP Cas. 1259 (Franklin Co. 1985)

For assistance, call 1-800-328-4880

37 ALR5th 349—§ 11

South Wind Motel v. Ohio Civil Rights Com'n, 24 Ohio App. 3d 209, 494 N.E.2d 1158, 46 Fair Empl. Prac. Cas. (BNA) 1259 (10th Dist. Franklin County 1985)

107 ALR5th 623—§ 7

Southwinds Farm, Inc. v. Albertson, 664 So. 2d 13, 11 I.E.R. Cas. (BNA) 280, 133 Lab. Cas. (CCH) ¶ 58230 (Fla. Dist. Ct. App. 3d Dist. 1995)

118 ALR5th 91—§ 26

Southwind Shipping Co., S.A., Complaint of, 709 F. Supp. 79, 1989 A.M.C. 1088 (S.D. N.Y. 1989)

64 ALR5th 475—§ 10

South Windsor, Town of v. South Windsor Police Union Local 1480, 255 Conn. 800, 770 A.2d 14, 169 L.R.R.M. (BNA) 2551 (2001)

112 ALR5th 263—§ 17

South Windsor, Town of v. South Windsor Police Union, Local 1480, Council 15, AFSCME, AFL-CIO, 41 Conn. App. 649, 677 A.2d 464, 156 L.R.R.M. (BNA) 3143 (1996)

112 ALR5th 263—§ 25

Southwire Co. v. American Arbitration Ass'n, 248 Ga. App. 226, 545 S.E.2d 681 (2001)

69 ALR6th 513—§ 5

Southwire Co. v. Essex Group, Inc., 570 F. Supp. 643, 219 USPQ 1053, 37 FR Serv. 2d 318 (N.D. Ill. 1983)

28 ALR5th 1—§ 19

Southwire Co. v. George, 266 Ga. 739, 470 S.E.2d 865 (1996)

83 ALR5th 103—§ 3, 24, 28
84 ALR5th 249—§ 38

Southwood v. Carlson, 704 N.E.2d 163 (Ind. Ct. App. 1999)

5 ALR5th 422—§ 3

Southworth v. Board of Regents of University of Wisconsin System, 307 F.3d 566, 170 Ed. Law Rep. 122 (7th Cir. 2002)

73 ALR6th 281—§ 5

Southworth v. City of Seattle, 145 Wash. 138, 259 P. 26 (1927)

92 ALR5th 517—§ 3

Southworth v. Southworth, 168 Mass. 511, 47 N.E. 93 (1897)

47 ALR5th 129—§ 11, 14

Southworth v. State, 913 P.2d 444 (Wyo. 1996)

28 ALR6th 505—§ 7, 16

South W. R. Co. v. Paulk, 24 Ga. 356 (1858)

58 ALR5th 535—§ 5

Soutiere v. Soutiere, 163 Vt. 265, 657 A.2d 206 (1995)

57 ALR5th 315—§ 2

Souza v. Corvick, 441 F.2d 1013 (D.C. Cir. 1970)

30 ALR5th 170—§ 42, 85, 97
56 ALR5th 407—§ 14

Souza v. Erie Strayer Co., 557 A.2d 1226 (R.I. 1989)

93 ALR6th 463—§ 32

Souza v. Fred Carries Contracts, Inc., 191 Ariz. 247, 955 P.2d 3 (Ct. App. Div. 2 1997)

102 ALR5th 99—§ 3

Souza v. Lauppe, 59 Cal. App. 4th 865, 69 Cal. Rptr. 2d 494 (3d Dist. 1997)

8 ALR6th 465—§ 18

Souza v. Superior Court, 193 Cal. App. 3d 1304, 238 Cal. Rptr. 892 (6th Dist. 1987)

5 ALR5th 550—§ 3
16 ALR5th 650—§ 7, 9, 13
67 ALR5th 1—§ 3

S.O.V. v. People in Interest of M.C., 914 P.2d 355 (Colo. 1996)

86 ALR5th 637—§ 3

Sova v. Apple Vacations, 984 F. Supp. 1136, 1998 A.M.C. 419 (S.D. Ohio 1997)

2 ALR5th 396—§ 5, 6

Sova Drugs v. Barnes, 661 So. 2d 393, 20 FLW D 2304 (Fla. App. D5 1995)

12 ALR5th 1—§ 12

Sovary v. Los Angeles Police Dep't, City of Los Angeles, 222 Cal. Rptr. 504 (App. 2d Dist. 1986)
90 ALR5th 273—§ 3, 4, 8, 14

Sovereen v. Meadows, 595 P.2d 852 (Utah 1979)
86 ALR6th 321—§ 11

Sovereign Bank v. BJ's Wholesale Club, Inc., 395 F. Supp. 2d 183 (M.D. Pa. 2005)
51 ALR6th 311—§ 2

Sovereign Bank v. BJ's Wholesale Club, Inc., 427 F. Supp. 2d 526 (M.D. Pa. 2006)
51 ALR6th 311—§ 11

Sovereign Bank v. BJ's Wholesale Club, Inc., 533 F.3d 162, 51 A.L.R.6th 657 (3d Cir. 2008)
51 ALR6th 311—§ 3, 4, 7, 13

Sovereign Camp of Woodmen of the World v. Boehme, 44 Tex. Civ. App. 159, 97 S.W. 847 (1906)
97 ALR5th 537—§ 39

Sovereign Healthcare of Tampa, LLC v. Estate of Huerta ex rel. Huerta, 14 So. 3d 1033 (Fla. Dist. Ct. App. 2d Dist. 2009)
50 ALR6th 187—§ 13

Sovie v. Aetna Life and Cas. Co., 127 A.D.2d 995, 513 N.Y.S.2d 44 (4th Dep't 1987)
103 ALR5th 1—§ 33

Soviero v. U.S., 967 F.2d 791 (CA2 N.Y. 1992)
39 ALR5th 87—§ 2

Sovik v. Healing Network, 244 A.D.2d 985, 665 N.Y.S.2d 997 (4th Dep't 1997)
19 ALR5th 1—§ 94, 96, 180

Sovine v. Teater, 47 Ohio App. 2d 254, 1 Ohio Op. 3d 299, 1 Ohio Op. 3d 316, 353 N.E.2d 880 (10th Dist.Franklin County 1976)
65 ALR5th 1—§ 2, 25

Sowa v. Sodolak, 398 S.W.2d 653 (Tex. Civ. App. Eastland 1965)
21 ALR5th 82—§ 3, 33

Sowarby v. Russell, 4 Abb. Pr. N.S. 238, 29 N.Y. Super. Ct. 322, 1868 WL 5781 (1868)
86 ALR6th 411—§ 2

Sowards v. Loudon County, Tenn., 203 F.3d 426, 16 I.E.R. Cas. (BNA) 213, 140 Lab. Cas. (CCH) ¶ 58838, 2000 FED App. 0046P, 123 A.L.R.5th 783 (6th Cir. 2000)
123 ALR5th 411—§ 22

Sowards v. Sowards, 96 Wash. App. 1026, 1999 WL 450921 (Div. 2 1999)
86 ALR6th 321—§ 13
90 ALR6th 451—§ 115

Sowder v. Sowder, 179 Neb. 29, 136 N.W.2d 231 (1965)
49 ALR5th 441—§ 12

Sowders v. M.W. Kellogg Co., 663 S.W.2d 644 (Tex. App. Houston 1st Dist. 1983)
5 ALR6th 497—§ 7, 9

Sowders v. M.W. Kellogg Co., 663 S.W.2d 644 (Tex. App. Houston 1st Dist.1983)
5 ALR6th 497—§ 4

Sowell v. Bausch & Lomb, Inc., 230 A.D.2d 77, 656 N.Y.S.2d 16, Prod. Liab. Rep. (CCH) ¶ 15001 (1st Dep't 1997)
23 ALR6th 223—§ 3

Sowell v. Clark, 151 N.C. App. 723, 567 S.E.2d 200 (2002)
119 ALR5th 121—§ 4
2 ALR6th 279—§ 16

Sowell v. Collins, 557 F. Supp. 2d 843 (S.D. Ohio 2008)
102 ALR6th 417—§ 37

Sowell v. Hyatt Corp., 623 A.2d 1221, 20 U.C.C.R.S.2d 1232 (Dist. Col. App. 1993)
1 ALR5th 1—§ 37, 41

Sowell v. Morgan, 2011 WL 7404718 (N.D. Ohio 2011)
103 ALR6th 247—§ 5

Sowell v. Trotter, 69 Ohio Misc. 7, 23 Ohio Ops. 3d 75, 430 N.E.2d 480 (1981)

24 ALR5th 200—§ 27
Sowemimo v. D.A.O.R. Sec., Inc., 43 F. Supp. 2d 477, 82 Fair Empl. Prac. Cas. (BNA) 1155 (S.D. N.Y. 1999)
83 ALR5th 1—§ 10, 12
94 ALR5th 1—§ 8
Sower v. State, 382 So. 2d 1257 (Fla. Dist. Ct. App. 1st Dist. 1980)
114 ALR5th 173—§ 7
Sowers v. Dixie Shell Homes of America, Inc., 762 So. 2d 186 (La. Ct. App. 2d Cir. 2000)
101 ALR5th 447—§ 7
Sowers v. Fasttrack Coatings Co., 1994 WL 470198 (E.D. Pa. 1994)
69 ALR5th 137—§ 13
Sowers v. Howard, 346 Mo. 10, 139 S.W.2d 897 (1940)
27 ALR5th 174—§ 67
Sowers v. May, 338 P.2d 160 (Okla. 1959)
33 ALR5th 205—§ 9
Sowers v. Ohio Civil Rights Comm'n, 20 Ohio Misc. 115, 49 Ohio Ops. 2d 203, 252 N.E.2d 463, 2 BNA FEP Cas. 240, 2 CCH EPD ¶ 10124, 61 CCH LC ¶ 9360 (1969)
37 ALR5th 349—§ 5, 20
Sowers v. Powhatan County, Virginia, 347 Fed. Appx. 898 (4th Cir. 2009)
68 ALR6th 229—§ 6, 8
Sowers v. State, 146 Ga. App. 701, 247 S.E.2d 225 (1978)
116 ALR5th 479—§ 6
Sowers v. State, 416 N.E.2d 466 (Ind. Ct. App. 2d Dist. 1981)
113 ALR5th 517—§ 14
Sowers v. State, 724 N.E.2d 588 (Ind. 2000)
66 ALR5th 373—§ 5
104 ALR5th 165—§ 4
Sowers v. Tsamolias, 23 Kan. App. 2d 270, 929 P.2d 188 (1996)
71 ALR5th 99—§ 3, 7
Sowers v. Tsamolias, 262 Kan. 717, 941 P.2d 949 (1997)
71 ALR5th 99—§ 7

Soza, In re, 542 F.3d 1060, Bankr. L. Rep. (CCH) ¶ 81316, 74 A.L.R.6th 759 (5th Cir. 2008)
74 ALR6th 549—§ 4
Soza v. William Ziering, Inc., 2002 WL 1482553 (Cal. App. 5th Dist. 2002)
14 ALR6th 417—§ 3, 6
Sozzi v. Levine, 52 A.D.2d 694, 382 N.Y.S.2d 383 (3d Dep't 1976)
68 ALR5th 13—§ 9
S.P. v. Collier High School, 319 N.J. Super. 452, 725 A.2d 1142, 133 Ed. Law Rep. 183 (App. Div. 1999)
23 ALR5th 1—§ 12
S.P. v. State, 705 So. 2d 124 (Fla. Dist. Ct. App. 2d Dist. 1998)
15 ALR5th 391—§ 4
Space v. Division of Employment Sec., Dep't of Labor and Industry, 60 N.J. Super. 380, 159 A.2d 131 (App. Div. 1960)
60 ALR5th 459—§ 2, 12, 21
Space v. Farm Family Mut. Ins. Co., 235 A.D.2d 797, 652 N.Y.S.2d 357 (3d Dep't 1997)
97 ALR5th 359—§ 13
Space Leasing Associates v. Atlantic Bldg. Systems, Inc., 144 Ga. App. 320, 241 S.E.2d 438, 23 U.C.C. Rep. Serv. (CBC) 642 (1977)
33 ALR5th 1—§ 10
81 ALR5th 483—§ 4
Spacemaker, Inc. v. Borochoff Properties, Inc., 112 Ga. App. 512, 145 S.E.2d 740 (1965)
45 ALR5th 251—§ 2, 6, 19
Space Needle v. Kamla, 105 Wash. App. 123, 19 P.3d 461 (Div. 1 2001)
99 ALR5th 141—§ 2, 15 to 17
115 ALR5th 1—§ 2
Space Technology Development Corp. v. Boeing Co., 209 Fed. Appx. 236 (4th Cir. 2006)
43 ALR6th 611—§ 56
Spada v. Pauley, 149 Mich. App. 196, 385 N.W.2d 746 (1986)
86 ALR5th 637—§ 3

Spada v. Planning and Zoning Commission of Town of Stratford, 159 Conn. 192, 268 A.2d 376 (1970)
73 ALR5th 223—§ 5, 11

Spadaccini v. Dolan, 63 A.D.2d 110, 407 N.Y.S.2d 840 (1st Dep't 1978)
6 ALR6th 311—§ 5

Spadafora v. Nolan Corp., 66 N.Y.S.2d 127 (Sup 1946)
103 ALR5th 157—§ 11

Spadaro v. City of Rialto, 2007 WL 1747981 (Cal. App. 4th Dist. 2007)
45 ALR6th 435—§ 11

Spade v. Lynn & B.R. Co., 168 Mass. 285, 47 N.E. 88 (1897)
96 ALR5th 107—§ 6

Spaduccino v. John G. Hayes & Co., 180 App. Div. 37, 167 N.Y.S. 483 (1917)
28 ALR5th 547—§ 18

Spaduccino v. John G. Hayes & Co., 223 N.Y. 681, 119 N.E. 1078 (1918)
28 ALR5th 547—§ 14

Spady v. America's Servicing Co., 2012 WL 1884115 (S.D. Tex. 2012)
86 ALR6th 411—§ 5

Spaeder v. Tabak, 170 Pa. Super. 392, 85 A.2d 654 (1952)
62 ALR5th 219—§ 21, 39

Spaeth v. Union Oil Co., 762 F.2d 865, 84 OGR 556 (CA10 Okla. 1985)
14 ALR5th 242—§ 4 to 6, 26

Spaeth, State ex rel. v. Eddy Furniture Co., 386 N.W.2d 901 (N.D. 1986)
68 ALR5th 13—§ 13, 37

Spafford v. Coats, 118 Ill. App. 3d 566, 74 Ill. Dec. 211, 455 N.E.2d 241 (2d Dist. 1983)
69 ALR5th 219—§ 3, 6

Spafford v. Crescent Credit Corp., 497 So. 2d 160 (Ala. App. 1986)
23 ALR5th 241—§ 7

Spagnolia v. U.S., 598 F. Supp. 683 (W.D. N.Y. 1984)
123 ALR5th 1—§ 12

Spagnolo v. Spagnolo, 20 Va. App. 736, 460 S.E.2d 616 (1995)
47 ALR5th 207—§ 18

Spahr v. F.W. Woolworth Co., 1993 WL 330993 (Tenn. Ct. App. 1993)
63 ALR6th 495—§ 38, 39, 45

Spahr v. Secco, 330 F.3d 1266 (10th Cir. 2003)
22 ALR6th 49—§ 4

Spain, Ex parte, 589 S.W.2d 132 (Tex. Crim. 1979)
42 ALR5th 581—§ 2, 3, 14, 21

Spain v. Aetna Life Ins. Co., 11 F.3d 129, 93 C.D.O.S. 8936, 93 Daily Journal DAR 15230, 17 EBC 2239 (CA9 Cal. 1993)
56 ALR5th 737—§ 6

Spain v. Brown & Williamson Tobacco Corp., 230 F.3d 1300, Prod. Liab. Rep. (CCH) ¶ 15937 (11th Cir. 2000)
36 ALR5th 541—§ 20, 22

Spain v. Holland, 483 So. 2d 318 (Miss. 1986)
21 ALR6th 577—§ 5

Spain v. Valley Forge Ins. Co., 152 Ariz. 189, 731 P.2d 84 (1986)
40 ALR5th 603—§ 4, 5

Spainerman Gallery, Profit Sharing Plan v. Merritt, 49 U.C.C. Rep. Serv. 2d 809 (S.D. N.Y. 2003)
88 ALR6th 533—§ 13

Spainhour v. B. Aubrey Huffman & Associates, Ltd., 237 Va. 340, 377 S.E.2d 615 (1989)
117 ALR5th 23—§ 2, 3, 6, 18

Spakes v. State, 913 S.W.2d 597 (Tex. Crim. 1996)
54 ALR5th 141—§ 3, 8, 10

Spalding v. Ewing, 149 Pa. 375, 24 A. 219 (1892)
35 ALR6th 1—§ 28, 30, 34

Spalding v. Zatz, 70 So. 3d 692 (Fla. 5th DCA 2011)
97 ALR6th 83—§ 74

Spalding County v. East Enterprises, Inc., 232 Ga. 887, 209 S.E.2d 215 (1974)
38 ALR5th 737—§ 3

Spalding Sports Worldwide, Inc., In re, 203 F.3d 800, 53 U.S.P.Q.2d (BNA) 1747 (Fed. Cir. 2000)
27 ALR5th 76—§ 36

Spallino, Matter of, 218 A.D.2d 431, 638 N.Y.S.2d 948 (1st Dep't 1996)
45 ALR6th 175—§ 22, 24

Span v. Ely, 8 Hun. 255 (N.Y. 1876)
3 ALR5th 370—§ 9

Spancrete, Inc. v. Ronald E. Frazier & Associates, P.A., 630 So. 2d 1197 (Fla. Dist. Ct. App. 3d Dist. 1994)
61 ALR6th 445—§ 4

Spaneas v. Travelers Indem. Co., 423 Mass. 352, 668 N.E.2d 325 (1996)
117 ALR5th 441—§ 4

Spangenberg, Re Estate of, 561 So. 2d 315, 15 FLW 728 (Fla. App. D2 1990)
3 ALR5th 394—§ 6

Spangenberg v. Verner, 321 Ill. App. 3d 429, 254 Ill. Dec. 319, 747 N.E.2d 359 (5th Dist. 2001)
92 ALR5th 473—§ 2

Spangler v. City and County of San Francisco, 84 Cal. 12, 23 P. 1091 (1890)
54 ALR6th 201—§ 13, 41, 45

Spangler v. Collins, 2012 WL 1340366 (S.D. Ohio 2012)
75 ALR6th 181—§ 11

Spangler v. Glover, 50 Wash. 2d 473, 313 P.2d 354 (1957)
94 ALR5th 149—§ 6

Spangler v. Schaus, 106 R.I. 795, 264 A.2d 161 (1970)
62 ALR5th 219—§ 16

Spangler v. State, 233 Neb. 790, 448 N.W.2d 145 (1989)
112 ALR5th 509—§ 2
13 ALR6th 209—§ 21, 25, 37

Spangler v. State, 2009-Ohio-3178, 2009 WL 1856784 (Ohio Ct. App. 11th Dist. Lake County 2009)
63 ALR6th 351—§ 3
64 ALR6th 1—§ 13

Spangler v. Unemployment Appeals Com'n, 632 So. 2d 98 (Fla. Dist. Ct. App. 5th Dist. 1994)
68 ALR5th 13—§ 8, 35

Spangler, State ex rel. v. Board of Elections of Cuyahoga County, 7 Ohio St. 3d 20, 455 N.E.2d 1009 (1983)
74 ALR6th 209—§ 25

Spanier v. Huntington, 19 Misc. 2d 979, 188 N.Y.S.2d 381 (1959)
1 ALR5th 622—§ 19

Spanierman v. Hughes, 576 F. Supp. 2d 292, 238 Ed. Law Rep. 170, 156 Lab. Cas. (CCH) ¶ 60690, 49 A.L.R.6th 699 (D. Conn. 2008)
49 ALR6th 115—§ 3, 4
103 ALR6th 19—§ 4

Spanish Council of York, Inc. v. Pennsylvania Human Relations Com'n, 879 A.2d 391, 14 A.L.R.6th 779 (Pa. Commw. Ct. 2005)
14 ALR6th 263—§ 6
14 ALR6th 277—§ 5

Spanish Fork City v. Bryan, 1999 UT App 61, 975 P.2d 501 (Utah Ct. App. 1999)
23 ALR6th 307—§ 39

Spanish. Hernandez v. Erlenbusch, 368 F. Supp. 752 (D.C. Or. 1973)
12 ALR5th 195—§ 32

Spanks-El v. Finley, 1987 WL 10307 (N.D. Ill. 1987)
18 ALR6th 775—§ 3

Spann, In re, 711 A.2d 1262 (D.C. 1998)
45 ALR6th 175—§ 12

Spann, Matter of, 235 A.D.2d 718, 653 N.Y.S.2d 41 (3d Dep't 1997)
43 ALR6th 163—§ 51

Spann v. Abraham, 36 S.W.3d 452 (Tenn. Ct. App. 1999)
99 ALR5th 1—§ 7

Spann v. AOL Time Warner Inc., 35 Employee Benefits Cas. (BNA) 1648, 2005 WL 1330937 (S.D. N.Y. 2005)
60 ALR6th 295—§ 32, 62

Spann v. Bees, 23 Md. App. 313, 327 A.2d 801 (1974)

72 ALR5th 529—§ 3, 20

Spann v. First Nat. Bank of Montgomery, 240 Ala. 539, 200 So. 554 (1941)

111 ALR5th 159—§ 3, 13

1 ALR6th 407—§ 8

Spann v. Industrial Com., 181 Colo. 153, 508 P.2d 385 (1973)

46 ALR5th 659—§ 2, 4, 8, 17

Spann v. Irwin Memorial Blood Centers, 34 Cal. App. 4th 644, 40 Cal. Rptr. 2d 360 (1st Dist. 1995)

64 ALR5th 333—§ 3, 7, 13, 14

75 ALR5th 229—§ 14, 17

Spann v. Robinson Property Group, L.P., 970 F. Supp. 564 (N.D. Miss. 1997)

64 ALR5th 205—§ 10

Spann v. Spann, 852 P.2d 826 (Okla. App. 1992)

30 ALR5th 139—§ 3

Spann v. Spann, 1992 OK CIV APP 150, 852 P.2d 826 (Okla. Ct. App. Div. 1 1992)

109 ALR5th 1—§ 5

Spann v. State, 426 So. 2d 492 (Ala. Crim. App. 1982)

52 ALR5th 559—§ 3

Spann v. State, 440 So. 2d 1224 (Ala. Crim. App. 1983)

92 ALR6th 295—§ 19

Spannaus v. Larkin, Hoffman, Daly, and Lindgren, Ltd., 368 N.W.2d 395 (Minn. Ct. App. 1985)

58 ALR6th 1—§ 38

Spano v. McAvoy, 589 F. Supp. 423 (N.D.N.Y. 1984)

101 ALR5th 61—§ 1

Spano v. Orange County Independent Corp., 243 A.D. 537, 275 N.Y.S. 818 (2d Dep't 1934)

16 ALR6th 1—§ 15

Spanos v. Skouras Theatres Corp., 235 F. Supp. 1 (S.D. N.Y. 1964)

83 ALR5th 497—§ 4

Spanos v. Skouras Theatres Corp., 364 F.2d 161 (2d Cir. 1966)

83 ALR5th 497—§ 4

32 ALR6th 531—§ 42, 43

Spar, Matter of, 100 A.D.2d 71, 473 N.Y.S.2d 192 (1st Dep't 1984)

40 ALR6th 463—§ 36

Spar v. Obwoya, 369 A.2d 173 (Dist. Col. App. 1977)

43 ALR5th 207—§ 2, 5, 39

Sparagon v. Native American Publishers, Inc., 1996 S.D. 3, 542 N.W.2d 125 (S.D. 1996)

19 ALR5th 1—§ 38

44 ALR5th 193—§ 5

Sparano v. Southland Corp., 1995 WL 470267 (N.D. Ill. 1995)

79 ALR5th 587—§ 3, 8

Spar Gas, Inc. v. McCune, 908 S.W.2d 400 (Tenn. Ct. App. 1995)

67 ALR5th 587—§ 9

87 ALR5th 473—§ 2

12 ALR6th 1—§ 4, 11

Spargo v. Civil Service Com'n, 50 Mass. App. Ct. 1106, 737 N.E.2d 23 (2000)

19 ALR6th 217—§ 46

Spark v. MBNA Corp., 157 F. Supp. 2d 330, R.I.C.O. Bus. Disp. Guide (CCH) ¶ 10128 (D. Del. 2001)

60 ALR6th 295—§ 54

Sparkman v. Atlantic City, 237 N.J. Super. 623, 568 A.2d 917 (1990)

47 ALR5th 553—§ 10, 25

Sparkman v. Etter, 249 Ark. 93, 458 S.W.2d 129 (1970)

45 ALR5th 251—§ 6, 12

107 ALR5th 311—§ 9

109 ALR5th 421—§ 5, 16

Sparks, Matter of Disciplinary Proceedings Against, 167 Wis. 2d 747, 482 N.W.2d 653 (1992)

45 ALR6th 175—§ 26

Sparks v. Alabama Power Co., 679 So. 2d 678 (Ala. 1996)

95 ALR5th 29—§ 3, 4

Sparks v. Bank of Georgia, 110 Ga. App. 98, 138 S.E.2d 86 (1964)

104 ALR5th 459—§ 7

Sparks v. Barnes, 755 So. 2d 718 (Fla. Dist. Ct. App. 2d Dist. 1999)

118 ALR5th 91—§ 28, 30

Sparks v. Berntsen, 19 Cal. 2d 308, 121 P.2d 497 (1942)
19 ALR5th 622—§ 4, 12

Sparks v. Boone, 560 S.W.2d 236, 99 A.L.R.3d 566 (Ky. App. 1977)
19 ALR5th 1—§ 89, 93, 104
54 ALR5th 443—§ 16

Sparks v. Caldwell, 104 N.M. 475, 723 P.2d 244 (1986)
59 ALR6th 433—§ 47

Sparks v. City of Atlanta, 496 F. Supp. 770 (N.D. Ga. 1980)
95 ALR6th 341—§ 59

Sparks v. City of Pella, 258 Iowa 187, 137 N.W.2d 909 (1965)
54 ALR6th 201—§ 47, 49

Sparks v. Com., 721 S.W.2d 726 (Ky. Ct. App. 1986)
19 ALR6th 411—§ 19

Sparks v. Consolidated Aluminum Co., 679 S.W.2d 348 (Mo. Ct. App. E.D. 1984)
81 ALR5th 245—§ 6

Sparks v. East, 202 Iowa 718, 210 N.W. 969 (1926)
52 ALR5th 221—§ 15

Sparks v. Metropolitan Atlanta Rapid Transit Authority, 223 Ga. App. 768, 478 S.E.2d 923 (1996)
63 ALR6th 495—§ 43, 49

Sparks v. Norris, 2010 WL 3761841 (W.D. Ark. 2010)
72 ALR6th 141—§ 16

Sparks v. Owens-Illinois, Inc., 32 Cal. App. 4th 461, 38 Cal. Rptr. 2d 739 (1st Dist. 1995)
73 ALR5th 75—§ 6, 18

Sparks v. Republic Nat. Life Ins. Co., 132 Ariz. 529, 647 P.2d 1127 (1982)
63 ALR5th 427—§ 3, 24

Sparks v. Southwest Community Hosp. & Medical Center, Inc., 195 Ga. App. 858, 395 S.E.2d 68 (1990)
38 ALR6th 399—§ 17

Sparks v. Sparks, 233 P.3d 1091 (Alaska 2010)
81 ALR6th 655—§ 6

Sparks v. Sparks, 1988 WL 37886 (Ohio Ct. App. 2d Dist. Clark County 1988)
109 ALR5th 1—§ 8

Sparks v. State, 25 Ark. App. 190, 756 S.W.2d 911 (1988)
47 ALR6th 107—§ 48

Sparks v. State, 96 Nev. 26, 604 P.2d 802 (1980)
39 ALR5th 283—§ 4, 31

Sparks v. State, 104 Nev. 316, 759 P.2d 180 (1988)
94 ALR5th 393—§ 7

Sparks v. State, 108 Tex. Crim. 367, 300 S.W. 938 (1927)
29 ALR5th 59—§ 3, 13

Sparks v. State, 121 Ga. App. 115, 173 S.E.2d 239 (1970)
89 ALR6th 565—§ 17, 20

Sparks v. State, 450 So. 2d 188 (Ala. Crim. App. 1984)
85 ALR5th 471—§ 2, 6, 11, 12

Sparks v. State, 537 N.E.2d 1179 (Ind. 1989)
97 ALR5th 293—§ 4
83 ALR6th 465—§ 32

Sparks v. State, 626 S.W.2d 187 (Tex. App. Fort Worth 1981)
5 ALR5th 243—§ 50

Sparks v. State, 2001 WL 42285 (Tex. App. Dallas 2001)
88 ALR5th 67—§ 3

Sparks v. Sterling Doubleday Enterprises, LP., 300 A.D.2d 467, 752 N.Y.S.2d 79 (2d Dep't 2002)
82 ALR6th 417—§ 4, 7

Sparks v. St. Paul Ins. Co., 100 N.J. 325, 495 A.2d 406 (1985)
92 ALR5th 273—§ 2, 7, 13
21 ALR6th 515—§ 3

Sparks v. Thurmond, 171 Ga. App. 138, 319 S.E.2d 46 (1984)
19 ALR5th 1—§ 60, 135
44 ALR5th 193—§ 21, 44

Sparks v. Tulane Medical Center Hosp. and Clinic, 546 So. 2d 138 (La. 1989)
82 ALR5th 149—§ 2

---

83 ALR5th 103—§ 2, 3, 5, 28

84 ALR5th 249—§ 2, 7, 25, 48

Sparks Milling Co. v. Industrial Com., 293 Ill. 350, 127 N.E. 737 (1920)

47 ALR5th 801—§ 2, 9

Sparler v. Fireman's Ins. Co., 360 Pa. Super. 597, 521 A.2d 433 (1987)

40 ALR5th 603—§ 4, 9

Sparlin v. BAC Home Loans Servicing, L.P., 2011 WL 2695645 (Ariz. Ct. App. Div. 2 2011)

86 ALR6th 411—§ 5

Sparling v. Hoffman Const. Co., Inc., 864 F.2d 635, R.I.C.O. Bus. Disp. Guide (CCH) ¶ 7095 (9th Cir. 1988)

10 ALR6th 293—§ 11

Sparrow v. Dixie Leaf Tobacco Co., 232 N.C. 589, 61 S.E.2d 700 (1950)

111 ALR5th 313—§ 17

Sparrow v. Forsyth County Board of Education, 19 N.C. App. 383, 198 S.E.2d 762 (1973)

23 ALR5th 1—§ 15

Sparrow v. Sparrow, 231 La. 966, 93 So. 2d 232 (1957)

69 ALR5th 219—§ 9

Sparrow v. Toyota of Florence, Inc., 302 S.C. 418, 396 S.E.2d 645 (App. 1990)

11 ALR5th 88—§ 4

Sparrow Chisholm Co. v. Boston, 327 Mass. 64, 97 N.E.2d 172 (1951)

22 ALR5th 327—§ 25

Sparrow, People ex rel. v. Lucas, 159 N.Y.S. 218 (Sup 1916)

102 ALR5th 525—§ 42

Sparta, City of v. Brooks, 179 Wis. 2d 506, 508 N.W.2d 77 (Ct. App. 1993)

97 ALR6th 653—§ 29

Spartalis v. State Bd. for Professional Medical Conduct, 205 A.D.2d 940, 613 N.Y.S.2d 759 (3d Dep't 1994)

19 ALR6th 577—§ 10, 12

Spartanburg v. Bull, 266 S.C. 168, 222 S.E.2d 491 (1976)

10 ALR5th 448—§ 6

Spartan Petroleum Co., Inc. v. Federated Mut. Ins. Co., 162 F.3d 805 (4th Cir. 1998)

14 ALR5th 695—§ 6, 28

Spartin v. District of Columbia Dept. of Employment Services, 584 A.2d 564 (D.C. 1990)

106 ALR5th 111—§ 8, 14, 23, 39

108 ALR5th 1—§ 29

Sparwick Contracting, Inc. v. Tomasco Corp., 335 N.J. Super. 73, 761 A.2d 90 (App. Div. 2000)

31 ALR6th 433—§ 10

Spatafore v. Yale University, 239 Conn. 408, 684 A.2d 1155 (1996)

11 ALR6th 351—§ 24

Spataro v. Kloster Cruise, Ltd., 894 F.2d 44, 1990 A.M.C. 936 (2d Cir. 1990)

82 ALR6th 175—§ 6

Spates v. Manson, 644 F.2d 80 (2d Cir. 1981)

98 ALR5th 445—§ 6

Spates v. Republic Ins. Co., 756 S.W.2d 88 (Tex. App. San Antonio 1988)

62 ALR5th 189—§ 2, 4

Spaugh v. City of Charlotte, 239 N.C. 149, 79 S.E.2d 748 (1954)

97 ALR5th 537—§ 47

Spaugh v. City of Winston-Salem, 249 N.C. 194, 105 S.E.2d 610 (1958)

101 ALR5th 287—§ 7

Spaulding, In re, 694 N.Y.S.2d 813 (App. Div. 3d Dep't 1999)

68 ALR5th 13—§ 34

Spaulding v. Albertson's, Inc., 610 So. 2d 721 (Fla. Dist. Ct. App. 1st Dist. 1992)

79 ALR5th 201—§ 10, 12

Spaulding v. Albin, 63 Vt. 148, 21 A. 530 (1891)

23 ALR6th 1—§ 7

Spaulding v. Cameron, 127 Cal. App. 2d 698, 274 P.2d 177 (1954)

25 ALR5th 568—§ 51

Spaulding v. Chicago & N. R. Co., 30 Wis. 110 (1872)

17 ALR5th 547—§ 52 to 54

Spaulding v. Christakos, 269 A.D. 909, 56 N.Y.S.2d 372 (2d Dep't 1945)
123 ALR5th 1—§ 14

Spaulding v. Honeywell Intern., Inc., 184 N.C. App. 317, 646 S.E.2d 645 (2007)
46 ALR6th 1—§ 22

Spaulding v. Hussain, 229 N.J. Super. 430, 551 A.2d 1022 (App. Div. 1988)
58 ALR6th 1—§ 5
60 ALR6th 1—§ 53

Spaulding v. Mingo County Bd. of Educ., 206 W. Va. 559, 526 S.E.2d 525, 144 Ed. Law Rep. 420 (1999)
48 ALR5th 129—§ 4
50 ALR5th 1—§ 9

Spaulding v. Rovner, 47 Conn. L. Rptr. 544, 2009 WL 1175555 (Conn. Super. Ct. 2009)
64 ALR6th 249—§ 27

Spaulding v. Spaulding, 460 A.2d 1360 (Me. 1983)
40 ALR5th 227—§ 44, 52, 55

Spaulding v. State, 195 Ga. App. 420, 394 S.E.2d 111 (1990)
24 ALR6th 1—§ 33

Spaulding v. State Farm Mut. Ins. Co., 262 S.C. 95, 202 S.E.2d 653 (1974)
78 ALR5th 341—§ 4
79 ALR5th 289—§ 7

Spaulding v. White, 173 Ill. 127, 50 N.E. 224 (1898)
76 ALR6th 31—§ 26

Spaulding Mfg. Co. v. Board of Com'rs of La Plata County, 63 Colo. 438, 168 P. 34 (1917)
88 ALR6th 533—§ 19

Spaur v. Owens-Corning Fiberglas Corp., 510 N.W.2d 854, Prod. Liab. Rep. (CCH) ¶ 13808 (Iowa 1994)
24 ALR6th 497—§ 3

Spayd, Appeal of, 31 Pa. D. & C. 496 (C.P. 1937)
62 ALR5th 671—§ 17

Spaziani v. Millar, 215 Cal. App. 2d 667, 30 Cal. Rptr. 658 (4th Dist. 1963)
13 ALR5th 684—§ 10, 15

Spaziano v. Lucky Stores, Inc., 69 Cal. App. 4th 106, 81 Cal. Rptr. 2d 378, 78 Fair Empl. Prac. Cas. (BNA) 1516 (2d Dist. 1999)
99 ALR5th 1—§ 4

Spaziano v. Seminole County, 726 So. 2d 772 (Fla. 1999)
83 ALR6th 465—§ 76

Spaziano v. State, 429 So. 2d 1344 (Fla. 2d DCA 1983)
103 ALR6th 137—§ 3, 6

Speagle v. Nationwide Mut. Fire Ins. Co., 138 Ga. App. 384, 226 S.E.2d 459 (1976)
35 ALR5th 1—§ 7
84 ALR5th 69—§ 18

Speagle v. State, 217 Ga. App. 577, 458 S.E.2d 852 (1995)
55 ALR5th 125—§ 2, 3, 7

Speake v. Grantham, 317 F. Supp. 1253 (S.D. Miss. 1970)
31 ALR5th 229—§ 36, 37, 75

Speake v. Tofte, 327 F. Supp. 200 (D.D.C. 1971)
42 ALR6th 353—§ 27

Speaker v. Cates Co., 879 S.W.2d 811 (Tenn. 1994)
43 ALR5th 207—§ 33, 36

Speaker v. State, 740 S.W.2d 486 (Tex. App. Houston 1st Dist. 1987)
15 ALR6th 319—§ 6

Speakman v. Mayor & Council of Borough of North Plainfield, 8 N.J. 250, 84 A.2d 715 (1951)
73 ALR5th 223—§ 2, 5, 8, 10

Speakman v. Tatem, 48 N.J. Eq. 136, 21 A. 466 (Ch. 1891)
87 ALR6th 495—§ 17, 56

Speakman Co. v. Harper Buffing Mach. Co., Inc., 583 F. Supp. 273, 38 U.C.C. Rep. Serv. 469 (D. Del. 1984)
89 ALR5th 319—§ 20, 23, 24

Speaks v. Rouse Co. of Georgia, 172 Ga. App. 9, 321 S.E.2d 774 (1984)
74 ALR5th 49—§ 11, 16

Spear v. Farwell, 5 Cal. App. 2d 111, 42 P.2d 391 (2d Dist. 1935)
86 ALR5th 527—§ 3, 11, 13, 15, 18

Spear v. Griffith, 86 Ill. 552, 1877 WL 9774 (1877)
98 ALR5th 353—§ 7

Spear v. Hoffses, 128 Me. 409, 148 A. 146 (1929)
25 ALR5th 391—§ 3, 4

Spear v. Marshall, 95 Utah 62, 79 P.2d 15 (1938)
60 ALR6th 481—§ 4, 23

Spear v. Sowders, 33 F.3d 576, 1994 FED App. 293P (6th Cir. 1994)
85 ALR5th 261—§ 6, 13

Spear v. Sowders, 71 F.3d 626, 1995 FED App. 366P (6th Cir. 1995)
85 ALR5th 261—§ 3, 4, 6, 13

Spear v. Spear, 101 Misc. 2d 341, 421 N.Y.S.2d 277 (Sup 1979)
91 ALR5th 485—§ 5

Spear v. Wineman, 335 Mich. 287, 55 N.W.2d 833 (1952)
6 ALR6th 1—§ 3, 4, 6

Spearing Tool and Mfg. Co., In re, 412 F.3d 653, Bankr. L. Rep. (CCH) ¶ 80317, 56 U.C.C. Rep. Serv. 2d 807, 95 A.F.T.R.2d 2005-2890, 2005 FED App. 0271P (6th Cir. 2005)
28 ALR6th 461—§ 3

Spearman v. J & S. Farms, Inc., 755 F. Supp. 137 (D.C. S.C. 1990)
14 ALR5th 242—§ 21, 22

Spearman v. State, 694 S.W.2d 216 (Tex. App. Houston (1st Dist.) 1985)
5 ALR5th 243—§ 2

Spearman v. State, 694 S.W.2d 216 (Tex. App. Houston 1st Dist. 1985)
103 ALR6th 507—§ 20

Spearman v. State Farm Fire & Casualty Co., 185 Cal. App. 3d 1105, 230 Cal. Rptr. 264 (2d Dist. 1986)
6 ALR5th 297—§ 7, 33

Spearman v. University City Public School Dist., 617 S.W.2d 68 (Mo. 1981)

66 ALR5th 1—§ 46

Spearman v. U.S., 860 F. Supp. 1234 (E.D. Mich. 1994)
72 ALR6th 1—§ 5

Spearman v. Wilson, 44 Ga. 473 (1871)
67 ALR5th 179—§ 9

Spears, In re, 250 Mich. App. 349, 645 N.W.2d 718 (2002)
38 ALR6th 1—§ 10

Spears, In re, 964 So. 2d 293 (La. 2007)
46 ALR6th 365—§ 8

Spears v. Albertson's, Inc., 848 So. 2d 1176 (Fla. Dist. Ct. App. 1st Dist. 2003)
52 ALR6th 271—§ 18
53 ALR6th 213—§ 8

Spears v. Cooper, 2009 WL 838179 (E.D. Tenn. 2009)
45 ALR6th 1—§ 33

Spears v. People, 220 Ill. 72, 77 N.E. 112 (1906)
54 ALR6th 429—§ 7

Spears v. Rountree Oldsmobile-Cadillac Co., 653 So. 2d 182, 69 Fair Empl. Prac. Cas. (BNA) 109 (La. Ct. App. 2d Cir. 1995)
83 ALR5th 1—§ 3
94 ALR5th 1—§ 18, 24

Spears v. Ryan, 2009 WL 2998937 (D. Ariz. 2009)
102 ALR6th 417—§ 101

Spears v. Spears, 148 So. 2d 564 (Fla. App. D1 1963)
47 ALR5th 129—§ 10

Spears v. Spears, 339 Ark. 162, 3 S.W.3d 691 (1999)
118 ALR5th 513—§ 3

Spears v. Spears, 2008 WL 4182384 (Ky. Ct. App. 2008)
102 ALR6th 153—§ 22

Spears v. State, 38 Md. App. 700, 382 A.2d 616 (1978)
107 ALR5th 567—§ 10

Spears v. State, 41 Tex. Crim. 527, 56 S.W. 347 (1899)
24 ALR5th 465—§ 11, 74

Spears v. State, 92 Miss. 613, 46 So. 166 (1908)
81 ALR5th 563—§ 3
Spears v. State, 264 Ark. 83, 568 S.W.2d 492 (1978)
57 ALR5th 141—§ 12
Spears v. State, 280 Ark. 577, 660 S.W.2d 913 (1983)
70 ALR6th 361—§ 31
Spears v. State, 412 N.E.2d 81 (Ind. Ct. App. 4th Dist. 1980)
66 ALR5th 397—§ 13
Spears v. State, 801 S.W.2d 571 (Tex. App. Fort Worth 1990)
58 ALR6th 499—§ 37
Spears v. State, 1994 WL 44854 (Tex. App. Dallas 1994)
21 ALR6th 1—§ 4
Spears v. State Bar of Cal., 211 Cal. 183, 294 P. 697, 72 A.L.R. 923 (1930)
105 ALR5th 217—§ 6
107 ALR5th 167—§ 16
3 ALR6th 49—§ 6, 19
Spears v. Unisys Corp., 1995 WL 871152 (E.D. Mich. 1995)
59 ALR5th 461—§ 3
Spears v. U.S., 129 S. Ct. 840, 172 L. Ed. 2d 596 (2009)
46 ALR6th 495—§ 49
Spears v. U.S., 221 F. Supp. 990 (E.D. Okla. 1963)
1 ALR5th 163—§ 19
Spears v. Voss Chevrolet, Inc., 1986 WL 14772 (Ohio Ct. App. 2d Dist. Montgomery County 1986)
66 ALR6th 351—§ 56
Spebar v. City of Hammond, 2010 WL 2952999 (N.D. Ind. 2010)
58 ALR6th 499—§ 49
Spece v. Erie Ins. Group, 2004 PA Super 154, 850 A.2d 679 (2004)
37 ALR6th 657—§ 16
Specht v. Gaines, 65 Ga. App. 782, 16 S.E.2d 507 (1941)
11 ALR6th 695—§ 15, 32
Specht v. Jensen, 832 F.2d 1516, 24 Fed. Rules Evid. Serv. 124 (CA10 Colo. 1987)

12 ALR5th 195—§ 68
Specht v. Jensen, 853 F.2d 805, 26 Fed. R. Evid. Serv. (LCP) 718 (10th Cir. 1988)
66 ALR5th 135—§ 5
Specht v. Netscape Communications Corp., 150 F. Supp. 2d 585, 45 U.C.C. Rep. Serv. 2d 1 (S.D. N.Y. 2001)
95 ALR6th 57—§ 9
Specht v. Netscape Communications Corp., 306 F.3d 17, 48 U.C.C. Rep. Serv. 2d 761 (2d Cir. 2002)
106 ALR5th 309—§ 4
95 ALR6th 57—§ 9
Specht v. Waterbury Co., 70 Misc. 404, 127 N.Y.S. 137 (1911)
25 ALR5th 391—§ 41
Special Abrasives, Inc., Re, 26 B.R. 399, 35 U.C.C.R.S. 1307 (F. BC ED Mich. 1983)
9 ALR5th 708—§ 11
Special Counsel for Discipline Nebraska Supreme Court, State ex rel. v. Shapiro, 266 Neb. 328, 665 N.W.2d 615 (2003)
25 ALR6th 1—§ 24
Special Docket No. 73958, In re, 115 Ohio St. 3d 425, 2007-Ohio-5268, 875 N.E.2d 596 (2007)
41 ALR6th 445—§ 17
Special Docket No. 73958, In re, 2008-Ohio-4444, Prod. Liab. Rep. (CCH) ¶ 18092, 2008 WL 4068212 (Ohio Ct. App. 8th Dist. Cuyahoga County 2008)
41 ALR6th 445—§ 18, 20
Special Grand Jury Investigating Medicaid Fraud & Nursing Homes, In re, 38 Ohio App. 3d 161, 528 N.E.2d 598 (Franklin Co. 1987)
29 ALR5th 1—§ 2
Special Investigation No. 258, In re, 55 Md. App. 119, 461 A.2d 34 (1983)
33 ALR5th 453—§ 4

Special Investigations, Bureau of v. Coalition of Public Safety, 430 Mass. 601, 722 N.E.2d 441, 164 L.R.R.M. (BNA) 2247 (2000)
112 ALR5th 263—§ 65

Specialized Waste Systems, Inc. v. State, 126 S.W.3d 530 (Tex. App. Houston 1st Dist. 2003)
69 ALR6th 1—§ 3
70 ALR6th 1—§ 3

Special Products Mfg., Inc. v. Douglass, 159 App. Div. 2d 847, 553 N.Y.S.2d 506, 5 BNA IER Cas. 335 (3d Dep't 1990)
12 ALR5th 847—§ 9

Special Prosecutors, State ex rel. v. Judges, Court of Common Pleas, 55 Ohio St. 2d 94, 9 Ohio Ops. 3d 88, 378 N.E.2d 162 (1978)
5 ALR5th 422—§ 7

Special Purpose Accounts Receivable Co-op Corp. v. Prime One Capital Co., 125 F. Supp. 2d 1093 (S.D. Fla. 2000)
71 ALR5th 491—§ 11

Special Souvenirs, Inc. v. Town of Wayne, 56 F. Supp. 2d 1062 (E.D. Wis. 1999)
20 ALR6th 161—§ 4
21 ALR6th 425—§ 4
23 ALR6th 573—§ 4

Special's Trading Co. v. International Consumer Corp., 679 So. 2d 369 (Fla. Dist. Ct. App. 4th Dist. 1996)
2 ALR6th 279—§ 8

Special Tax School Dist. No. 1 of Palm Beach County v. Smith, 61 Fla. 782, 54 So. 376 (1911)
81 ALR6th 363—§ 22

Specialty Healthcare Management, Inc. v. St. Mary Parish Hosp., 220 F.3d 650 (5th Cir. 2000)
60 ALR5th 669—§ 6

Specialty Malls v. City of Tampa, 916 F. Supp. 1222 (M.D. Fla. 1996)
10 ALR5th 538—§ 7

Specialty Retailers, Inc. v. DeMoranville, 933 S.W.2d 490, 74 Fair Empl. Prac. Cas. (BNA) 1795 (Tex. 1996)
11 ALR6th 447—§ 6

Specialty Tires of America, Inc. v. CIT Group/Equipment Financing, Inc., 82 F. Supp. 2d 434, 40 U.C.C. Rep. Serv. 2d 691 (W.D. Pa. 2000)
104 ALR6th 303—§ 5

Speck v. Abell-Howe Co., 839 S.W.2d 623 (Mo. App. 1992)
9 ALR5th 102—§ 17

Speck v. Bowling, 892 S.W.2d 309 (Ky. Ct. App. 1995)
87 ALR5th 1—§ 14, 24, 33

Speck v. Federal Land Bank of Omaha, 494 N.W.2d 628 (S.D. 1993)
81 ALR6th 161—§ 5
82 ALR6th 43—§ 9

Speck v. Speck, 42 Ga. App. 517, 156 S.E. 706 (1931)
14 ALR5th 929—§ 6

Speck v. State, 34 Ala. App. 325, 41 So. 2d 198 (1949)
66 ALR5th 397—§ 4, 9, 19

Speck v. Unemployment Compensation Bd. of Review, 680 A.2d 27 (Pa. Commw. Ct. 1996)
80 ALR6th 635—§ 3

Specking v. Specking, 528 S.W.2d 448 (Mo. Ct. App. 1975)
55 ALR5th 557—§ 4

Speckman v. Speckman, 15 Ohio App. 283 (1921)
3 ALR5th 394—§ 7

Specktor v. Commissioner of Revenue, 308 N.W.2d 806 (Minn. 1981)
118 ALR5th 597—§ 29

Spector v. K-Mart Corp., 99 App. Div. 2d 605, 471 N.Y.S.2d 711 (3d Dep't 1984)
6 ALR5th 883—§ 11

Spector v. Konover, 57 Conn. App. 121, 747 A.2d 39 (2000)
70 ALR6th 209—§ 49

Spector v. Mermelstein, 485 F.2d 474 (CA2 N.Y. 1973)

10 ALR5th 828—§ 41
Spector v. Sidhu, 2004 WL 350682 (N.D. Tex. 2004)
14 ALR6th 687—§ 3
Spector v. Spector, 23 Ariz. App. 131, 531 P.2d 176 (1975)
17 ALR5th 366—§ 11
Spector v. State, 746 S.W.2d 946 (Tex. App. Austin 1988)
4 ALR5th 1—§ 17, 24
Spector v. Torenberg, 852 F. Supp. 201 (S.D. N.Y. 1994)
60 ALR5th 669—§ 6
67 ALR5th 179—§ 5, 6, 8, 11
Spectrum Arena, Inc., In re, 330 F. Supp. 125 (E.D. Pa. 1971)
114 ALR5th 561—§ 2, 23
Spectrum Arena Ltd. Partnership v. Com., 951 A.2d 1226 (Pa. Commw. Ct. 2008)
80 ALR6th 1—§ 70
Spectrum Automotive Finishes, Inc. v. Westbank Body Works, Inc., 27 So. 3d 875 (La. Ct. App. 5th Cir. 2009)
58 ALR6th 289—§ 32
Spectrum Creations, L.P. v. Carolyn Kinder Intern., LLC, 514 F. Supp. 2d 934 (W.D. Tex. 2007)
76 ALR6th 289—§ 5
77 ALR6th 543—§ 15
Spectrum Health Continuing Care Group v. Anna Marie Bowling Irrecoverable Trust Dated June 27, 2002, 410 F.3d 304, 2005 FED App. 0260P (6th Cir. 2005)
69 ALR6th 317—§ 7
Spectrum Stores, Inc. v. Citgo Petroleum Corp., 132 S. Ct. 366, 181 L. Ed. 2d 233 (2011)
76 ALR6th 587—§ 15
Spectrum Stores, Inc. v. Citgo Petroleum Corp., 632 F.3d 938, 2011-1 Trade Cas. (CCH) ¶ 77328 (5th Cir. 2011)
76 ALR6th 587—§ 15
Speece v. Leaseway Transp. Corp., 721 F. Supp. 144, 48 BNA FEP Cas. 1127, 49 CCH EPD ¶ 38849 (N.D. Ohio 1988)

51 ALR5th 1—§ 7
SpeechNow.org v. Federal Election Com'n, 599 F.3d 686 (D.C. Cir. 2010)
65 ALR6th 503—§ 9, 10, 13
66 ALR6th 635—§ 17
Speed v. American Workman, 199 S.C. 187, 18 S.E.2d 732 (1942)
14 ALR5th 242—§ 34
Speed v. Avis Rent-A-Car, 172 A.D.2d 267, 568 N.Y.S.2d 90 (1st Dep't 1991)
102 ALR5th 99—§ 3
Speed v. Eluma International, Inc., 757 S.W.2d 794 (Tex. App. Dallas 1988)
14 ALR5th 242—§ 40
Speed v. Scott, 787 So. 2d 626 (Miss. 2001)
21 ALR6th 671—§ 5
Speed v. State, 240 N.W.2d 901 (Iowa 1976)
33 ALR5th 619—§ 4
Speed v. State, 270 Ga. 688, 512 S.E.2d 896 (1999)
22 ALR5th 1—§ 3
79 ALR5th 33—§ 3
83 ALR6th 255—§ 9
Speedee Cash of Alabama, Inc., Ex parte, 806 So. 2d 389 (Ala. 2001)
29 ALR6th 461—§ 10
Speedee Mart Inc. v. Stovall, 664 S.W.2d 174 (Tex. App. Amarillo 1983)
75 ALR5th 1—§ 3
Speedee Oil Change No. 2, Inc. v. National Union Fire Ins. Co., 444 So. 2d 1304 (La. App. 4th Cir. 1984)
10 ALR5th 828—§ 11
Speed Fastners, Inc. v. Newsom, 382 F.2d 395, 4 U.C.C. Rep. Serv. 681 (10th Cir. 1967)
50 ALR5th 327—§ 5
93 ALR5th 103—§ 12, 14
Speedway/SuperAmerica, L.L.C. v. Phillips Truck Stop, Inc., 782 So. 2d 255, 2000-2 Trade Cas. (CCH) ¶ 73080 (Ala. 2000)

26 ALR6th 249—§ 8, 13

Speedway, Town of v. Dugan, 228 Ind. 701, 94 N.E.2d 542 (1950)

92 ALR5th 517—§ 3 to 5, 11, 13
101 ALR5th 287—§ 14

Speedy v. State, 611 S.W.2d 253 (Mo. Ct. App. E.D. 1980)

70 ALR5th 1—§ 8
95 ALR5th 125—§ 7, 9

Speedy Mulch LLC v. Gadd, 2006 WL 462361 (S.D. Ohio 2006)

89 ALR6th 1—§ 119

Speener, State ex rel. v. Gudmanson, 2000 WI App 78, 234 Wis. 2d 461, 610 N.W.2d 136 (Ct. App. 2000)

85 ALR6th 229—§ 10

Speer v. Colon, 155 S.W.3d 60 (Mo. 2005)

99 ALR6th 203—§ 12

Speer v. Dealy, 242 Neb. 542, 495 N.W.2d 911 (1993)

99 ALR5th 445—§ 3

Speer v. Farm Bureau Mut. Ins. Co., Inc., 43 Kan. App. 2d 520, 226 P.3d 558 (2010)

80 ALR6th 389—§ 11

Speer v. Olson, 367 So. 2d 207 (Fla. 1978)

97 ALR5th 123—§ 5

Speer v. Presbyterian Children's Home & Serv. Agency, 824 S.W.2d 589, 63 BNA FEP Cas. 483 (Tex. App. Dallas 1991)

37 ALR5th 349—§ 8, 26

Speer v. State, 109 S.W.2d 1150 (Tex. Civ. App. Galveston 1937)

19 ALR6th 577—§ 4, 6

Speer v. U. S., 512 F. Supp. 670 (N.D. Tex. 1981)

44 ALR5th 393—§ 5
81 ALR5th 167—§ 8

Speering v. State, 763 S.W.2d 801 (Tex. App. Texarkana 1988)

9 ALR5th 369—§ 2

Speers v. Delaware Harness Racing Com., 449 A.2d 205 (Del. 1982)

59 ALR5th 203—§ 35, 49

Speers v. Speers, 108 Mich. App. 543, 310 N.W.2d 455 (1981)

6 ALR6th 229—§ 16

Speetjens v. Larson, 401 F. Supp. 2d 600 (S.D. Miss. 2005)

22 ALR6th 49—§ 4

Spegon v. Catholic Bishop of Chicago, 175 F.3d 544, 5 Wage & Hour Cas. 2d (BNA) 457, 137 Lab. Cas. (CCH) ¶ 33866 (7th Cir. 1999)

23 ALR5th 241—§ 41

Spegon v. Catholic Bishop of Chicago, 989 F. Supp. 984, 4 Wage & Hour Cas. 2d (BNA) 568, 135 Lab. Cas. (CCH) ¶ 33683 (N.D. Ill. 1998)

23 ALR5th 241—§ 41

Spehar, Re Estate of, 140 Mont. 76, 367 P.2d 563 (1961)

3 ALR5th 590—§ 40

Speicher v. Dalkon Shield Claimants Trust, 943 F. Supp. 554, CCH Prod. Liab. Rep. ¶ 14803 (E.D. Pa. 1996)

54 ALR5th 1—§ 22

Speichler v. Board of Co-op. Educational Services, Second Supervisory Dist., 90 N.Y.2d 110, 659 N.Y.S.2d 199, 681 N.E.2d 366, 119 Ed. Law Rep. 614 (1997)

56 ALR5th 493—§ 33

Speidel v. Weiner, 129 N.J. Eq. 434, 19 A.2d 875 (Ct. Err. & App. 1941)

76 ALR5th 337—§ 20

Speier v. Renaissance at Victoria Farms, L.L.C., 2002 WL 31188559 (Va. Cir. Ct. 2002)

114 ALR5th 397—§ 9

Speigel v. Southern Bell Tel. & Tel. Co., 341 So. 2d 832 (Fla. Dist. Ct. App. 3d Dist. 1977)

111 ALR5th 579—§ 27

Speight v. Albano Cleaners, Inc., 21 F. Supp. 2d 560, 79 Fair Empl Prac. Cas. (BNA) 141, 75 Empl. Prac. Dec. (CCH) ¶ 45932 (E.D. Va. 1998)

83 ALR5th 1—§ 5

Speight v. Albano Cleaners, Inc., 21 F. Supp. 2d 560, 79 Fair Empl. Prac. Cas. (BNA) 141, 75 Empl. Prac. Dec. (CCH) ¶ 45932 (E.D. Va. 1998)
20 ALR6th 1—§ 4

Speight v. U.S., 671 A.2d 442 (Dist. Col. App. 1996)
50 ALR5th 581—§ 9

Speights v. Arkansas Sav. & Loan Asso., 239 Ark. 587, 393 S.W.2d 228 (1965)
4 ALR5th 772—§ 2

Speights v. Forbes, 206 N.C. App. 762, 699 S.E.2d 139 (2010)
99 ALR6th 1—§ 19

Speights v. Rockwood, 451 So. 2d 1275 (La. Ct. App. 3d Cir. 1984)
16 ALR5th 650—§ 23
67 ALR5th 1—§ 17

Speights v. State, 554 So. 2d 20, 14 FLW 2849 (Fla. App. D1 1989)
27 ALR5th 593—§ 14

Speights v. State, 668 So. 2d 316, 21 FLW D472 (Fla. App. D4 1996)
47 ALR5th 259—§ 12

Speiginer v. Ben Bennett, Inc., 2013 WL 285686 (Cal. App. 4th Dist. 2013)
96 ALR6th 503—§ 64

Speigle v. First Nat. Bank of Nevada, 2011 WL 4346365 (D. Nev. 2011)
86 ALR6th 411—§ 5

Speir v. City of Brooklyn, 139 N.Y. 6, 34 N.E. 727 (1893)
21 ALR6th 81—§ 32

Speir v. U. S., 206 Ct. Cl. 828, 513 F.2d 638 (1975)
49 ALR6th 205—§ 19, 54

Speirs, In re Marriage of, 956 P.2d 622 (Colo. Ct. App. 1997)
3 ALR6th 447—§ 5, 11

Speiser v. Schmidt, 387 Pa. Super. 30, 563 A.2d 927 (1989)
74 ALR6th 549—§ 12

Spelina v. Sporry, 279 Ill. App. 376 (1935)
12 ALR5th 195—§ 8

Spell, In re, 355 S.C. 655, 587 S.E.2d 104 (2003)
119 ALR5th 191—§ 3

Spell v. Bible Baptist Church, Inc., 166 Ga. App. 22, 303 S.E.2d 156 (1983)
47 ALR5th 1—§ 4, 5

Spell v. McDaniel, 604 F. Supp. 641 (E.D. N.C. 1985)
5 ALR5th 875—§ 4, 17, 23, 25, 27, 37, 47

Speller ex rel. Miller v. Sears, Roebuck and Co., 100 N.Y.2d 38, 760 N.Y.S.2d 79, 790 N.E.2d 252, Prod. Liab. Rep. (CCH) ¶ 16609 (2003)
122 ALR5th 515—§ 3

Spellis v. Lawn, 200 Cal. App. 3d 1075, 246 Cal. Rptr. 385 (4th Dist. 1988)
110 ALR5th 371—§ 5

Spellman, In re, 4 A.D.2d 215, 164 N.Y.S.2d 182 (1st Dep't 1957)
27 ALR6th 1—§ 57

Spellman, In re, 685 A.2d 1171 (D.C. 1996)
45 ALR6th 175—§ 24

Spellman v. Bankers' Trust, 6 F.2d 799 (CA2 N.Y. 1925)
56 ALR5th 1—§ 3

Spellman v. Bizal, 755 So. 2d 1013 (La. Ct. App. 4th Cir. 2000)
42 ALR6th 463—§ 11

Spellman v. Dyer, 186 Mass. 176, 71 N.E. 295 (1904)
11 ALR5th 127—§ 31

Spellman v. Katz, 2009 WL 418302 (Del. Ch. 2009)
49 ALR6th 1—§ 3, 59, 80

Spellman v. Mount, 696 P.2d 510 (Okla. App. 1984)
4 ALR5th 148—§ 3
4 ALR5th 210—§ 13

Spellman v. State, 469 So. 2d 695 (Ala. Crim. App. 1985)
37 ALR5th 703—§ 3

Spellman v. State, 500 So. 2d 110 (Ala. App. 1986)
22 ALR5th 1—§ 37

Spellmeyer v. Weyerhaeuser Corp., 14 Wash. App. 642, 544 P.2d 107 (Div. 1 1975)
76 ALR6th 465—§ 4

Spells v. Spells, 250 Pa. Super. 168, 378 A.2d 879 (1977)
95 ALR5th 533—§ 4
124 ALR5th 203—§ 4

Speltz Grain & Coal Co. v. Rush, 236 Minn. 1, 51 N.W.2d 641 (1952)
25 ALR5th 391—§ 101

Spence v. Cooke, 222 Wis. 2d 530, 587 N.W.2d 904 (Ct. App. 1998)
85 ALR6th 229—§ 37

Spence v. Durham, 283 N.C. 671, 198 S.E.2d 537 (1973)
95 ALR5th 533—§ 5
124 ALR5th 203—§ 5

Spence v. Flynt, 816 P.2d 771, 19 Media L. R. 1129, 19 A.L.R.5th 911 (Wyo. 1991)
19 ALR5th 1—§ 40

Spence v. Hamm, 226 Ga. App. 357, 487 S.E.2d 9 (1997)
67 ALR6th 341—§ 3

Spence v. Industrial N.D.T., 731 So. 2d 473 (La. Ct. App. 2d Cir. 1999)
36 ALR5th 225—§ 3, 13, 15

Spence v. Johnson, 80 F.3d 989 (5th Cir. 1996)
1 ALR6th 657—§ 4
12 ALR6th 267—§ 5, 12

Spence v. Johnson, 142 Ga. 267, 82 S.E. 646 (1914)
45 ALR5th 739—§ 4

Spence v. JPMorgan Chase Bank, N.A., 2011 WL 4733445 (W.D. Mo. 2011)
86 ALR6th 411—§ 5

Spence v. Kuznia, 307 Mich. 219, 11 N.W.2d 865 (1943)
25 ALR5th 123—§ 3
76 ALR5th 337—§ 23

Spence v. Maier, 137 NJL 284, 59 A.2d 609 (1948)
27 ALR5th 174—§ 54

Spence v. Maryland Casualty Co., 803 F. Supp. 649, 62 BNA FEP Cas. 131, 61 CCH EPD ¶ 42276 (W.D. N.Y. 1992)
51 ALR5th 1—§ 7

Spence v. Miles Lab., 810 F. Supp. 952 (E.D. Tenn. 1992)
30 ALR5th 1—§ 3, 7, 27, 30

Spence v. Miles Laboratories, Inc., 37 F.3d 1185, 1994 FED App. 352P (6th Cir. 1994)
30 ALR5th 1—§ 19, 47.5
75 ALR5th 229—§ 2

Spence v. Price, 48 Idaho 121, 279 P. 1092 (1929)
17 ALR5th 547—§ 30

Spence v. Spence, 287 A.D.2d 447, 731 N.Y.S.2d 66 (2d Dep't 2001)
3 ALR6th 447—§ 6, 14

Spence v. State, 198 Cal. App. 2d 332, 18 Cal. Rptr. 302 (2d Dist. 1961)
45 ALR5th 173—§ 5

Spence v. State, 321 Md. 526, 583 A.2d 715 (1991)
3 ALR6th 269—§ 9, 24

Spence v. State, 795 S.W.2d 743 (Tex. Crim. App. 1990)
1 ALR6th 657—§ 4

Spence v. State of Wash., 418 U.S. 405, 94 S. Ct. 2727, 41 L. Ed. 2d 842 (1974)
31 ALR6th 333—§ 9 to 11, 14

Spence v. Stewart, 705 So. 2d 996 (Fla. 4th DCA 1998)
86 ALR6th 1—§ 8, 80, 98

Spence v. Stewart, 705 So. 2d 996 (Fla. Dist. Ct. App. 4th Dist. 1998)
71 ALR5th 99—§ 3, 4, 7

Spence v. Terry, 215 Neb. 810, 340 N.W.2d 884 (1983)
116 ALR5th 1—§ 54

Spence v. U.S., 370 A.2d 1351 (Dist. Col. App. 1977)
41 ALR5th 171—§ 3, 32, 50, 51, 63, 77, 95, 107

Spence v. Wrobleski, 603 S.W.2d 91 (Mo. App. 1980)
62 ALR5th 219—§ 11, 30

Spence-Chapin Services to Families & Children, State ex rel. v. Tedeno, 101 Misc. 2d 485, 421 N.Y.S.2d 297 (1979)
40 ALR5th 697—§ 3, 6, 15, 22
Spenceley v. Spenceley, 1999 WL 1062513 (Fla. Dist. Ct. App. 4th Dist. 1999)
76 ALR5th 191—§ 3
Spencer, In re, 168 N.J. 169, 773 A.2d 692 (2001)
44 ALR6th 75—§ 31
Spencer, Re Estate of, 232 N.W.2d 491 (Iowa 1975)
3 ALR5th 590—§ 15
Spencer v. A-1 Crane Serv., 880 S.W.2d 938 (Tenn. 1994)
33 ALR5th 205—§ 5, 9
Spencer v. Aetna Life & Cas. Ins. Co., 227 Kan. 914, 611 P.2d 149 (1980)
69 ALR6th 415—§ 5
Spencer v. Barrow, 752 So. 2d 135 (Fla. Dist. Ct. App. 2d Dist. 2000)
112 ALR5th 47—§ 19
119 ALR5th 121—§ 2, 3, 9
Spencer v. Burglass, 337 So. 2d 596 (La. App. 1976)
61 ALR5th 307—§ 4, 12
Spencer v. Byrd, 917 F. Supp. 368, 69 Fair Empl. Prac. Cas. (BNA) 906 (M.D. N.C. 1995)
100 ALR5th 341—§ 8
Spencer v. Chesapeake Paperboard Co., 186 Md. 522, 47 A.2d 385 (1946)
41 ALR6th 207—§ 2
Spencer v. Childers, 307 Mich. 145, 11 N.W.2d 837 (1943)
25 ALR5th 233—§ 12
Spencer v. City of Bristow, 2007 OK CIV APP 67, 165 P.3d 361 (Div. 2 2007)
54 ALR6th 201—§ 7, 11, 13, 17, 23
Spencer v. City of Philadelphia, 2012 WL 1111141 (W.D. Pa. 2012)
95 ALR6th 341—§ 14
Spencer v. Civil Service Com'n, 173 W. Va. 153, 313 S.E.2d 430 (1984)
19 ALR6th 217—§ 27

Spencer v. Com., 143 Va. 531, 129 S.E. 351 (1925)
101 ALR6th 499—§ 15
Spencer v. Com., 240 Va. 78, 393 S.E.2d 609 (1990)
90 ALR5th 453—§ 52
99 ALR6th 113—§ 7
Spencer v. Commonwealth, 238 Va. 295, 384 S.E.2d 785 (1989)
37 ALR5th 515—§ 4, 11
Spencer v. Commonwealth, 554 S.W.2d 355 (Ky. 1977)
39 ALR5th 283—§ 4, 63
Spencer v. Community Hospital of Evanston, 87 Ill. App. 3d 214, 42 Ill. Dec. 272, 408 N.E.2d 981 (1st Dist. 1980)
28 ALR5th 107—§ 3, 14
Spencer v. Community Hospital of Evanston, 393 F. Supp. 1072 (N.D. Ill. 1975)
28 ALR5th 107—§ 5
Spencer v. Dawson, 2006 WL 3253574 (N.D. Ill. 2006)
65 ALR6th 93—§ 19
Spencer v. DHI Mortg. Co., Ltd., 642 F. Supp. 2d 1153 (E.D. Cal. 2009)
81 ALR6th 161—§ 5
82 ALR6th 43—§ 21
86 ALR6th 411—§ 5
Spencer v. Gaylord Container Corp., 693 So. 2d 818 (La. Ct. App. 1st Cir. 1997)
79 ALR5th 201—§ 14
Spencer v. Gedney, 45 Idaho 64, 260 P. 699 (1927)
25 ALR5th 391—§ 15
Spencer v. Hill, 2003 WL 25279367 (D. Or. 2003)
68 ALR6th 527—§ 41
Spencer v. Lighthouse, 114 App. Div. 591, 99 N.Y.S. 1015 (1906)
62 ALR5th 219—§ 39
Spencer v. Maverick, 146 S.W.2d 819 (Tex. Civ. App. San Antonio 1941)
76 ALR5th 337—§ 3

Spencer v. McGill, 87 Ohio App. 3d 267, 622 N.E.2d 7 (8th Dist. Cuyahoga County 1993)
  13 ALR6th 1—§ 4
  15 ALR6th 427—§ 20
Spencer v. Montana C. R. Co., 11 Mont. 164, 27 P. 681 (1891)
  17 ALR5th 547—§ 53
Spencer v. Murray, 18 F.3d 229 (4th Cir. 1994)
  72 ALR5th 109—§ 6
Spencer v. Nesto, 46 Conn. Supp. 566, 764 A.2d 224
  43 ALR5th 207—§ 3
Spencer v. O'Connor, 707 N.E.2d 1039 (Ind. Ct. App. 1999)
  78 ALR5th 489—§ 3
  63 ALR6th 351—§ 3
Spencer v. Old Stein Grill, 194 F. Supp. 274 (D.C. Dist. Col. 1961)
  4 ALR5th 772—§ 50
Spencer v. People, 163 Colo. 182, 429 P.2d 266 (1967)
  68 ALR5th 343—§ 3, 5
Spencer v. Poole, 207 Ga. 155, 60 S.E.2d 371 (1950)
  119 ALR5th 519—§ 14
Spencer v. Small, 693 N.Y.S.2d 727 (App. Div. 3d Dep't 1999)
  51 ALR5th 241—§ 3
  70 ALR5th 377—§ 7
Spencer v. Spencer, 61 N.C. App. 535, 301 S.E.2d 411 (1983)
  93 ALR5th 327—§ 7, 11
Spencer v. Spencer, 70 N.C. App. 159, 319 S.E.2d 636 (1984)
  17 ALR5th 366—§ 12
Spencer v. Spencer, 132 Ill. App. 2d 740, 270 N.E.2d 72 (1st Dist. 1971)
  124 ALR5th 203—§ 7
Spencer v. Spencer, 165 Neb. 675, 87 N.W.2d 212 (1957)
  14 ALR5th 557—§ 4, 9, 11, 15, 16
Spencer v. Spencer, 230 A.D.2d 645, 646 N.Y.S.2d 674 (1st Dep't 1996)
  38 ALR6th 313—§ 10

Spencer v. Spencer, 479 N.W.2d 293 (Iowa 1991)
  12 ALR5th 195—§ 52
Spencer v. Spencer, 494 A.2d 1279 (Dist. Col. App. 1985)
  38 ALR5th 69—§ 3 to 5
Spencer v. Spencer, 684 N.E.2d 500 (Ind. Ct. App. 1997)
  6 ALR6th 229—§ 3, 23
  26 ALR6th 331—§ 25
Spencer v. Spencer, 1998 ME 252, 720 A.2d 1159 (Me. 1998)
  110 ALR5th 237—§ 2, 3, 5, 7
Spencer v. State, 76 Md. App. 71, 543 A.2d 851 (1988)
  54 ALR6th 429—§ 20
Spencer v. State, 264 Kan. 4, 954 P.2d 1088 (1998)
  93 ALR5th 683—§ 3
Spencer v. State, 286 Ga. 483, 689 S.E.2d 823 (2010)
  64 ALR6th 131—§ 33
Spencer v. State, 293 Ga. App. 450, 667 S.E.2d 223 (2008)
  71 ALR6th 1—§ 5
Spencer v. State, 501 S.W.2d 799 (Tenn. 1973)
  78 ALR5th 567—§ 5
Spencer v. State, 611 So. 2d 16, 18 FLW D 85 (Fla. App. D3 1992)
  45 ALR5th 591—§ 18
Spencer v. State, 623 So. 2d 1211 (Fla. Dist. Ct. App. 4th Dist. 1993)
  9 ALR6th 541—§ 22
Spencer v. State, 842 So. 2d 52 (Fla. 2003)
  110 ALR5th 1—§ 17, 19
Spencer v. State, 889 So. 2d 868 (Fla. Dist. Ct. App. 2d Dist. 2004)
  71 ALR6th 1—§ 4
Spencer v. State, 925 P.2d 994 (Wyo. 1996)
  55 ALR6th 391—§ 23
Spencer v. Steinbrecher, 152 W. Va. 490, 164 S.E.2d 710 (1968)
  14 ALR5th 242—§ 25

For assistance, call 1-800-328-4880

Spencer v. Sutterfield, 66 Fed. Appx. 569 (6th Cir. 2003)
81 ALR6th 257—§ 3, 10

Spencer v. Talabock, 370 So. 2d 684 (La. Ct. App. 4th Cir. 1979)
6 ALR6th 229—§ 8, 22, 26

Spencer v. Tax Appeals Tribunal of State of N.Y., 251 A.D.2d 764, 674 N.Y.S.2d 158 (3d Dep't 1998)
2 ALR6th 1—§ 50, 98

Spencer v. Time Warner Cable, 278 A.D.2d 622, 717 N.Y.S.2d 711 (3d Dep't 2000)
106 ALR5th 111—§ 34
108 ALR5th 1—§ 22

Spencer v. Ulreich, 2009 WL 765493 (Ariz. Ct. App. Div. 2 2009)
97 ALR6th 375—§ 21

Spencer v. World Vision, Inc., 132 S. Ct. 96, 181 L. Ed. 2d 25, 113 Fair Empl. Prac. Cas. (BNA) 704 (2011)
76 ALR6th 587—§ 12

Spencer v. World Vision, Inc., 633 F.3d 723, 111 Fair Empl. Prac. Cas. (BNA) 619, 94 Empl. Prac. Dec. (CCH) ¶ 44082 (9th Cir. 2011)
76 ALR6th 587—§ 12

Spencer Creek Pollution Control Asso. v. Organic Fertilizer Co., 264 Or. 557, 505 P.2d 919 (1973)
25 ALR5th 568—§ 32

Spencer, State ex rel. v. Baker, 212 Ind. 44, 7 N.E.2d 984 (1937)
97 ALR5th 537—§ 81

Spencer, State ex rel. v. Marion Circuit Court, 212 Ind. 54, 7 N.E.2d 993 (1937)
97 ALR5th 537—§ 81

Spengel v. Kantor, 736 S.W.2d 51 (Mo. Ct. App. E.D. 1987)
92 ALR6th 379—§ 23

Spengler v. ADT Sec. Services, Inc., 505 F.3d 456 (6th Cir. 2007)
36 ALR6th 305—§ 3

Spengler v. Kaufman & Wilkinson, 46 Mo. App. 644 (1891)
52 ALR5th 221—§ 17

Spenser v. Deutsche Bank, 2011 WL 4574894 (W.D. Wash. 2011)
86 ALR6th 411—§ 5

Spenser v. Spenser, 128 Misc. 2d 298, 488 N.Y.S.2d 565 (N.Y. Fam. Ct. 1985)
46 ALR5th 735—§ 2

Spenzierato v. Our Lady Monte Virgine Soc. of Mut. Ben. of East Orange, N.J., 112 N.J.L. 93, 169 A. 831 (N.J. Ct. Err. & App. 1934)
21 ALR6th 81—§ 44

Spera v. Audiotape Corp., 1 Conn. App. 629, 474 A.2d 481 (1984)
45 ALR5th 251—§ 7

Spera v. Fleming, Hovenkamp & Grayson, P.C., 25 S.W.3d 863 (Tex. App. Houston 14th Dist. 2000)
124 ALR5th 575—§ 2, 8

Spera v. Samsung Electronics America, Inc., 83 U.C.C. Rep. Serv. 2d 394 (D.N.J. 2014)
104 ALR6th 97—§ 13, 14

Spera v. State, 467 So. 2d 329 (Fla. Dist. Ct. App. 2d Dist. 1985)
6 ALR6th 533—§ 3
27 ALR6th 491—§ 4

Sperandeo v. Denny's, Inc., 683 So. 2d 743 (La. Ct. App. 5th Cir. 1996)
48 ALR5th 129—§ 15

Sperduto v. Sperduto, 145 App. Div. 2d 476, 535 N.Y.S.2d 433 (2d Dep't 1988)
17 ALR5th 366—§ 10, 11

Sperling v. Allstate Indem. Co., 182 Vt. 521, 2007 VT 126, 944 A.2d 210 (2007)
90 ALR6th 635—§ 29

Sperling v. State, 924 S.W.2d 722 (Tex. App. Amarillo 1996)
82 ALR6th 373—§ 3, 7, 16

Sperman v. Codd, 62 A.D.2d 1062, 404 N.Y.S.2d 137 (2d Dep't 1978)
91 ALR6th 435—§ 39

Spern v. Time, Inc., 324 F. Supp. 1201 (W.D. Pa. 1971)
108 ALR5th 495—§ 14

Spero v. Zoning Bd. of Appeals of Town of Guilford, 217 Conn. 435, 586 A.2d 590 (1991)

4 ALR6th 263—§ 40

Speroni S.p.A. v. Perceptron, Inc., 12 Fed. Appx. 355 (6th Cir. 2001)

121 ALR5th 403—§ 3

Sperow v. Carter, 8 Pa. D. & C.2d 635 (C.P. 1957)

84 ALR5th 69—§ 5, 7, 9, 14, 22, 25

Sperr v. Ramsey County, 429 N.W.2d 315 (Minn. App. 1988)

38 ALR5th 107—§ 9

Sperry v. Florida, 373 U.S. 379, 10 L. Ed. 2d 428, 83 S. Ct. 1322, 137 USPQ 578 (1963)

27 ALR5th 76—§ 42

Sperry v. Hurd, 267 Mo. 628, 185 S.W. 170 (1916)

14 ALR5th 242—§ 18

Sperry v. ITT Commercial Finance Corp., 799 S.W.2d 871, 14 U.C.C. Rep. Serv. 2d 319 (Mo. Ct. App. W.D. 1990)

58 ALR6th 289—§ 2, 26

Sperry v. ITT Commercial Finance Corp., 799 S.W.2d 871, 14 U.C.C.R.S.2d 319 (Mo. App. 1990)

25 ALR5th 696—§ 4

Sperry v. Smith, 694 P.2d 581 (Utah 1984)

86 ALR6th 321—§ 4
91 ALR6th 171—§ 104

Sperry v. Sperry, 530 So. 2d 1043, 13 FLW 2067 (Fla. App. D2 1988)

5 ALR5th 550—§ 35

Sperry v. State of Fla. ex rel. Florida Bar, 373 U.S. 379, 83 S. Ct. 1322, 10 L. Ed. 2d 428, 137 U.S.P.Q. 578 (1963)

32 ALR6th 531—§ 3 to 5, 8, 9, 19, 27, 34, 40 to 43

Sperry & Hutchinson Co. v. Department of Revenue, 270 Or. 329, 527 P.2d 729 (1974)

74 ALR6th 1—§ 4, 10, 17

Sperry & Hutchinson Co. v. Mattson, 64 Utah 214, 228 P. 755 (1924)

14 ALR6th 119—§ 31

Sperry-New Holland, a Div. of Sperry Corp. v. Prestage, 617 So. 2d 248, Prod. Liab. Rep. (CCH) ¶ 13437 (Miss. 1993)

73 ALR5th 75—§ 3, 12

Sperry Rand Corp. v. A-T-0, Inc., 447 F.2d 1387, 171 USPQ 775 (CA4 Va. 1971)

14 ALR5th 242—§ 41

Sperry Rand Corp. v. Hill, 356 F.2d 181, 23 A.L.R.3d 853 (1st Cir. 1966)

16 ALR6th 1—§ 21

Sperte v. Shaffer, 111 App. Div. 2d 856, 490 N.Y.S.2d 592 (2d Dep't 1985)

7 ALR5th 474—§ 131

Spetalieri v. Kavanaugh, 36 F. Supp. 2d 92 (N.D. N.Y. 1998)

84 ALR6th 89—§ 17
95 ALR6th 341—§ 57

Spevack v. Belnat Realty Corp., 17 Misc. 2d 341, 191 N.Y.S.2d 63 (Sup 1959)

99 ALR5th 141—§ 11, 12, 14
115 ALR5th 1—§ 11, 12

Spevack v. Breitman, 68 N.Y.S.2d 663 (Sup. App. T 1947)

42 ALR5th 53—§ 55

Speyer v. Barry, 588 A.2d 1147 (Dist. Col. App. 1991)

53 ALR5th 1—§ 28, 57

SPGGC, LLC v. Ayotte, 488 F.3d 525, 46 A.L.R.6th 687 (1st Cir. 2007)

46 ALR6th 437—§ 4, 11

SPGGC, LLC v. Blumenthal, 505 F.3d 183 (2d Cir. 2007)

46 ALR6th 437—§ 3 to 5, 10, 11

Sphere Drake Ins. Co. v. 72 Centre Ave. Corp., 238 A.D.2d 574, 657 N.Y.S.2d 65 (2d Dep't 1997)

44 ALR5th 91—§ 13

Sphere Drake Ins. Co. v. Block 7206 Corp., 237 A.D.2d 427, 655 N.Y.S.2d 86 (2d Dep't 1997)

44 ALR5th 91—§ 9

Sphere Drake Ins. Co. v. Litchfield, 313 S.C. 471, 438 S.E.2d 275 (App. 1993)

44 ALR5th 91—§ 2, 3, 5, 9, 10

Sphere Drake Ins. Co. v. P.B.L. Entertainment, 52 F.3d 22 (CA2 N.Y. 1995)

44 ALR5th 91—§ 9

Sphere Drake Ins. Co. v. Y.L. Realty Co., 990 F. Supp. 240 (S.D. N.Y. 1997)

98 ALR5th 193—§ 8

106 ALR5th 1—§ 3

Sphere Drake Ins. Co., PLC v. Block 7206 Corp., 705 N.Y.S.2d 623 (App. Div. 2d Dep't 2000)

44 ALR5th 91—§ 9

Sphere Drake Ins. Ltd. v. American General Life Ins. Co., 376 F.3d 664 (7th Cir. 2004)

39 ALR6th 391—§ 5

Sphere Drake Ins., P.L.C. v. Shoney's, Inc., 923 F. Supp. 1481 (M.D. Ala. 1996)

44 ALR5th 91—§ 11

Sphere Drake, P.L.C. v. 101 Variety, Inc., 35 F. Supp. 2d 421 (E.D. Pa. 1999)

44 ALR5th 91—§ 9, 14

Sphinx Intern., Inc. v. National Union Fire Ins. Co. of Pittsburgh, Pa, 226 F. Supp. 2d 1326 (M.D. Fla. 2002)

22 ALR6th 113—§ 21

Sphinx Intern., Inc. v. National Union Fire Ins. Co. of Pittsburgh, Pa., 412 F.3d 1224, 23 I.E.R. Cas. (BNA) 70, 14 A.L.R.6th 871 (11th Cir. 2005)

14 ALR6th 543—§ 57

14 ALR6th 687—§ 5, 6, 8

22 ALR6th 113—§ 4

Sphnix Enterprises, Inc. v. Santa Cruz, 561 So. 2d 1348 (Fla. App. D1 1990)

16 ALR5th 191—§ 7, 16

Spica v. International Ladies Garment Workers' Union, 420 Pa. 427, 218 A.2d 579, 61 L.R.R.M. (BNA) 2649, 53 Lab. Cas. (CCH) ¶ 51477 (1966)

120 ALR5th 351—§ 6

Spicer v. American Home Assur. Co., 292 F. Supp. 27 (N.D. Ga. 1967)

88 ALR6th 533—§ 19

Spicer v. Beaman Bottling Co., 937 S.W.2d 884, 72 Fair Empl. Prac. Cas. (BNA) 1202 (Tenn. 1996)

83 ALR5th 1—§ 11

Spicer v. Benson, 1996 WL 11094 (N.D. Ill. 1996)

68 ALR6th 389—§ 7, 14, 17

Spicer v. Chicago Bd. Options Exch., 844 F. Supp. 1226 (N.D. Ill. 1993)

23 ALR5th 241—§ 20

Spicer v. Chicago Bd. Options Exchange, Inc., 844 F. Supp. 1226 (N.D. Ill. 1993)

60 ALR6th 295—§ 71

Spicer v. Collins, 9 F. Supp. 2d 673 (E.D. Tex. 1998)

89 ALR6th 1—§ 61

Spicer v. State, 115 Tex. Crim. 110, 28 S.W.2d 810 (1930)

23 ALR6th 1—§ 7

Spicer v. State, 898 So. 2d 984 (Fla. Dist. Ct. App. 5th Dist. 2005)

29 ALR6th 237—§ 4, 7

Spicer v. Terhune, 57 Fed. Appx. 732 (9th Cir. 2003)

89 ALR6th 701—§ 10

Spickler v. Flynn, 494 A.2d 1369 (Me. 1985)

8 ALR5th 653—§ 3

Spicola v. New York, 132 S. Ct. 400, 181 L. Ed. 2d 257 (2011)

76 ALR6th 587—§ 21

Spidell v. Jenkins, 111 Idaho 857, 727 P.2d 1285, 3 U.C.C. Rep. Serv. 2d (CBC) 161 (Ct. App. 1986)

23 ALR5th 241—§ 4

77 ALR5th 523—§ 3

Spiegal v. Fireman's Fund Ins. Co., 680 So. 2d 690 (La. App. 4th Cir. 1996)

50 ALR5th 1—§ 4

52 ALR5th 1—§ 3, 9

Spiegel, In re, 172 N.J. 74, 796 A.2d 246 (2002)

43 ALR6th 163—§ 68

Spiegel v. Adirondack Park Agency, 662 F. Supp. 2d 243 (N.D. N.Y. 2009)

68 ALR6th 229—§ 6

Spiegel v. Flemming, 181 F. Supp. 185, 13 Ohio Op. 2d 225, 89 Ohio L. Abs. 562 (N.D. Ohio 1960)

122 ALR5th 205—§ 3, 10

Spiegel v. Saks 34th St., 43 Misc. 2d 1065, 252 N.Y.S.2d 852 (App. Term 1964)

93 ALR5th 103—§ 12

Spiegel v. Sharp Electronics Corp., 125 Ill. App. 3d 897, 81 Ill. Dec. 238, 466 N.E.2d 1040, 38 U.C.C.R.S. 1624 (1st Dist. 1984)

50 ALR5th 327—§ 9

Spiegel v. Thomas, Mann & Smith, P.C., 811 S.W.2d 528 (Tenn. 1991)

28 ALR5th 420—§ 2, 4

Spiegel v. University of South Florida, 555 So. 2d 428, 58 Ed. Law Rep. 408 (Fla. Dist. Ct. App. 2d Dist. 1989)

41 ALR6th 391—§ 17

Spiegelman v. Victory Memorial Hosp., 392 Ill. App. 3d 826, 331 Ill. Dec. 792, 911 N.E.2d 1022 (1st Dist. 2009)

64 ALR6th 249—§ 5, 9

Spiegla v. Hull, 128 S. Ct. 441, 169 L. Ed. 2d 308 (U.S. 2007)

36 ALR6th 681—§ 9

Spiegla v. Hull, 481 F.3d 961, 25 I.E.R. Cas. (BNA) 1508, 89 Empl. Prac. Dec. (CCH) ¶ 42770, 154 Lab. Cas. (CCH) ¶ 60383 (7th Cir. 2007)

36 ALR6th 681—§ 9

Spieker v. Westgo, Inc., 479 N.W.2d 837, CCH Prod. Liab. Rep. ¶ 13018, 17 U.C.C.R.S.2d 1130 (N.D. 1992)

49 ALR5th 1—§ 44

50 ALR5th 327—§ 2

Spielman v. Manufacturers Hanover Trust Co., 60 N.Y.2d 221, 469 N.Y.S.2d 69, 456 N.E.2d 1192, 37 U.C.C.R.S. 1 (1983)

45 ALR5th 389—§ 33

Spielman v. State, 298 Md. 602, 471 A.2d 730 (1984)

92 ALR5th 35—§ 25

Spielter v. North German Lloyd S. S. Co., 232 App. Div. 104, 249 N.Y.S. 358 (1931)

19 ALR5th 622—§ 36, 40

Spier v. American University of Caribbean, 3 Ohio App. 3d 28, 3 Ohio B.R. 29, 443 N.E.2d 1021 (Hamilton Co. 1981)

46 ALR5th 581—§ 15, 25

Spier v. Baker, 120 Cal. 370, 52 P. 659 (1898)

120 ALR5th 125—§ 2, 3, 20, 21

121 ALR5th 1—§ 2

Spier v. Barker, 35 N.Y.2d 444, 363 N.Y.S.2d 916, 323 N.E.2d 164, 80 A.L.R.3d 1025 (1974)

62 ALR5th 537—§ 4

Spierling v. First American Home Health Services, Inc., 1999 PA Super 222, 737 A.2d 1250, 16 I.E.R. Cas. (BNA) 308, 105 A.L.R.5th 727 (Pa. Super. Ct. 1999)

105 ALR5th 351—§ 3, 4, 6, 9

Spiers v. Maples, 970 S.W.2d 166 (Tex. App. Fort Worth 1998)

122 ALR5th 205—§ 3, 34

Spiers v. Sydnor, 3 Fed. Appx. 176 (4th Cir. 2001)

101 ALR5th 515—§ 13

Spies v. Rock Industries, Inc., 39 A.D.2d 723, 331 N.Y.S.2d 847 (2d Dep't 1972)

85 ALR6th 323—§ 54

Spies v. Rosenstock, 87 Md. 14, 39 A. 268 (1898)

74 ALR5th 369—§ 16

Spiess v. Johnson, 89 Or. App. 289, 748 P.2d 1020 (1988)

99 ALR5th 445—§ 4

Spieth, Re Estate of, 181 Neb. 11, 146 N.W.2d 746 (1966)

3 ALR5th 394—§ 11

Spiewak v. Ackerman, 88 A.D.3d 1191, 932 N.Y.S.2d 207 (3d Dep't 2011)

100 ALR6th 1—§ 27

For assistance, call 1-800-328-4880

Spiewak v. Board of Education, 90 N.J. 63, 447 A.2d 140 (1982)
56 ALR5th 493—§ 34

Spiewak v. Board of Education, 180 N.J. Super. 312, 434 A.2d 1105 (1981)
57 ALR5th 477—§ 29

Spiezio v. American General Finance, Inc., 204 Ga. App. 350, 419 S.E.2d 149 (1992)
81 ALR6th 161—§ 5
82 ALR6th 43—§ 19

Spike v. Sellett, 102 Ill. App. 3d 270, 58 Ill. Dec. 565, 430 N.E.2d 597 (3d Dist. 1981)
4 ALR5th 148—§ 25
6 ALR5th 534—§ 2, 22

Spiker v. Hoogeboom, 628 P.2d 177 (Colo. App. 1981)
104 ALR6th 1—§ 11

Spikes v. State, 460 N.E.2d 954 (Ind. 1984)
37 ALR5th 703—§ 4

Spiking v. Consolidated R. & P. Co., 33 Utah 313, 93 P. 838 (1908)
42 ALR5th 465—§ 3

Spikler v. Lincoln, 238 Neb. 188, 469 N.W.2d 546, CCH Prod. Liab. Rep. ¶ 12932 (1991)
30 ALR5th 1—§ 3, 6, 7

Spiller v. Mackereth, 334 So. 2d 859 (Ala. 1976)
10 ALR5th 448—§ 7

Spiller v. Spiller, 21 S.W.3d 451 (Tex. App. San Antonio 2000)
45 ALR6th 493—§ 15, 20, 65

Spiller v. State, 68 Tex. Crim. 195, 150 S.W. 1164 (1912)
5 ALR5th 243—§ 62

Spillers v. Slaughter, 325 F. Supp. 550 (M.D. Fla. 1971)
121 ALR5th 1—§ 3

Spillers v. State, 145 Ga. App. 809, 245 S.E.2d 54 (1978)
1 ALR5th 938—§ 3

Spillers v. State, 272 Ark. 212, 613 S.W.2d 387 (1981)
7 ALR5th 758—§ 13
9 ALR6th 1—§ 6

Spillett v. Clear Lake Boating & Amusement Co., 155 N.W. 822 (Iowa 1916)
12 ALR5th 195—§ 42

Spillios v. Green, 137 Ariz. 443, 671 P.2d 421 (Ct. App. Div. 2 1983)
80 ALR5th 533—§ 5

Spillman v. Parker, 332 So. 2d 573, 83 A.L.R.3d 796 (La. Ct. App. 4th Cir. 1976)
103 ALR5th 255—§ 3, 19

Spillyards v. Abboud, 278 Ill. App. 3d 663, 215 Ill. Dec. 218, 662 N.E.2d 1358 (1st Dist. 1996)
43 ALR6th 1—§ 23, 53

Spilotro v. State, ex rel. Nevada Gaming Com'n, 99 Nev. 187, 661 P.2d 467 (1983)
63 ALR6th 1—§ 5, 14

Spinal Dimensions, Inc. v. Chepenuk, 16 Misc. 3d 1121(A), 847 N.Y.S.2d 905 (Sup 2007)
36 ALR6th 537—§ 17, 22

Spinale v. U.S. Dept. of Agriculture, 621 F. Supp. 2d 112 (S.D. N.Y. 2009)
95 ALR6th 341—§ 6

Spinden v. Johnson & Johnson, 177 N.J. Super. 605, 427 A.2d 597, CCH Prod. Liab. Rep. ¶ 8942 (1981)
54 ALR5th 1—§ 2, 4

Spindler v. Spindler, 207 Wis. 2d 327, 558 N.W.2d 645 (Ct. App. 1996)
38 ALR6th 313—§ 3, 10

Spindler Realty Corp. v. Monning, 243 Cal. App. 2d 255, 53 Cal. Rptr. 7 (2d Dist. 1966)
38 ALR5th 737—§ 3, 10

Spindulys v. Los Angeles Olympic Organizing Com., 175 Cal. App. 3d 206, 220 Cal. Rptr. 565 (2d Dist. 1985)
9 ALR6th 177—§ 38

Spinella, In re, 168 App. Div. 2d 816, 564 N.Y.S.2d 234 (3d Dep't 1990)
23 ALR5th 176—§ 8

Spinella v. Director, Div. of Taxation, 13 N.J. Tax 305, 1993 WL 310740 (1993)

2 ALR6th 1—§ 64

Spinelli, Claim of, 250 A.D.2d 920, 672 N.Y.S.2d 512 (3d Dep't 1998)

25 ALR6th 101—§ 21

Spinelli, Claim of, 672 N.Y.S.2d 512 (App. Div. 3d Dep't 1998)

46 ALR5th 659—§ 11, 17

Spinelli v. Golda, 6 N.J. 68, 77 A.2d 233 (1950)

66 ALR5th 135—§ 20

Spinelli v. U.S., 393 U.S. 410, 89 S. Ct. 584, 21 L. Ed. 2d 637 (1969)

67 ALR5th 361—§ 2
73 ALR6th 49—§ 8

Spingola v. Village of Granville, 39 Fed. Appx. 978 (6th Cir. 2002)

122 ALR5th 593—§ 2, 5
70 ALR6th 513—§ 13
71 ALR6th 471—§ 7

Spinks, Matter of Adoption of, 32 N.C. App. 422, 232 S.E.2d 479 (1977)

103 ALR5th 255—§ 3, 19

Spinks v. American Mfg. Co., 243 App. Div. 828, 278 N.Y.S. 66 (1935)

26 ALR5th 127—§ 11

Spinks v. Orleans County, 2011 WL 2491001 (W.D. N.Y. 2011)

77 ALR6th 393—§ 75

Spinks v. State, 564 So. 2d 1043 (Ala. App. 1990)

27 ALR5th 593—§ 25

Spinnaker Softward Corp. v. Nicholson, 495 N.W.2d 441 (Minn. App. 1993)

23 ALR5th 241—§ 21

Spinnell v. Quigley, 56 Wash. App. 799, 785 P.2d 1149 (1990)

44 ALR5th 1—§ 3, 20

Spinney's Adm'x v. O. V. Hooker & Son, 92 Vt. 146, 102 A. 53 (1917)

9 ALR5th 102—§ 9, 13, 16

Spino v. Cioffi, 1996 WL 92208 (Conn. Super. Ct. 1996)

91 ALR6th 435—§ 96

Spino v. John S. Tilley Ladder Co., 548 Pa. 286, 696 A.2d 1169, Prod. Liab. Rep. (CCH) ¶ 14991 (1997)

81 ALR5th 245—§ 4

Spinosa v. Weinstein, 168 App. Div. 2d 32, 571 N.Y.S.2d 747 (2d Dep't 1991)

35 ALR5th 145—§ 4

Spinrad v. Gasser, 652 N.Y.S.2d 156 (App. Div. 3d Dep't 1997)

52 ALR5th 1—§ 8

Spinx Oil Co. v. Federated Mut. Ins. Co., 427 S.E.2d 649 (S.C. 1993)

14 ALR5th 695—§ 4

Spire v. Malito, 99 Cal. App. 3d Supp. 16, 160 Cal. Rptr. 698, 45 Cal. Comp Cas. 93 (1979)

48 ALR5th 473—§ 20

Spires v. Casterline, 4 Misc. 3d 428, 778 N.Y.S.2d 259 (Sup 2004)

43 ALR6th 611—§ 17, 51, 52
49 ALR6th 1—§ 41

Spires v. Edgar, 513 S.W.2d 372 (Mo. 1974)

81 ALR6th 161—§ 5
82 ALR6th 43—§ 5

Spires v. Lawless, 493 S.W.2d 65, 69 A.L.R.3d 762 (Mo. Ct. App. 1973)

81 ALR6th 161—§ 4
82 ALR6th 43—§ 16

Spires v. Middlesex & Monmouth Electric Light, Heat & Power Co., 70 N.J.L. 355, 57 A. 424 (N.J. Sup. Ct. 1904)

95 ALR5th 29—§ 3, 4

Spires v. Mt. Vernon Mills, Columbia Division, 277 S.C. 300, 286 S.E.2d 379 (1982)

86 ALR5th 295—§ 7

Spires v. State, 10 So. 3d 477 (Miss. 2009)

76 ALR6th 1—§ 20

Spirko v. Com., 480 S.W.2d 169 (Ky. 1972)

61 ALR5th 1—§ 4, 13

Spirnak v. Com., Unemployment Compensation Bd. of Review, 125 Pa. Commw. 354, 557 A.2d 451 (1989)

95 ALR5th 329—§ 14

Spiro v. Pence, 566 N.Y.S.2d 1010 (City Ct. 1991)

2 ALR5th 396—§ 16

Spiropoulos v. Unemployment Compensation Bd. of Review, 654 A.2d 642 (Pa. Commw. Ct. 1995)
10 ALR6th 531—§ 19

Spirtas Co. v. Federal Ins. Co., 481 F. Supp. 2d 993 (E.D. Mo. 2007)
34 ALR6th 345—§ 36

Spirtas Co. v. Federal Ins. Co., 521 F.3d 833 (8th Cir. 2008)
34 ALR6th 345—§ 36

Spirtos, In re Estate of, 2005 WL 527401 (Cal. App. 4th Dist. 2005)
45 ALR6th 493—§ 40

Spitaleri v. Metro Regional Transit Authority, 67 Ohio App. 2d 57, 21 Ohio Ops. 3d 367, 426 N.E.2d 183 (Summit Co. 1980)
57 ALR5th 477—§ 9

Spitalieri v. Spitalieri, 593 N.Y.S.2d 172 (Sup. 1993)
52 ALR5th 221—§ 4, 18, 19

Spitz v. Holland, 243 Ga. 9, 252 S.E.2d 406 (1979)
69 ALR5th 1—§ 4

Spitz v. Maxwell, 186 Misc. 159, 59 N.Y.S.2d 593 (1945)
44 ALR5th 1—§ 11, 24

Spitzak v. Hylands, Ltd., 500 N.W.2d 154 (Minn. App. 1993)
43 ALR5th 207—§ 8, 37, 56

Spitzel v. U.S., 146 Ct. Cl. 399 (1959)
45 ALR5th 251—§ 7

Spitzer, In re, 845 A.2d 1137 (D.C. 2004)
44 ALR6th 75—§ 4, 25

Spitzer v. Commonwealth, 233 Va. 7, 353 S.E.2d 711 (1987)
29 ALR5th 59—§ 29

Spitzer v. Haims & Co., 217 Conn. 532, 587 A.2d 105 (1991)
10 ALR5th 828—§ 3

Spitzer v. Lewark, 259 N.C. 50, 129 S.E.2d 620 (1963)
53 ALR5th 375—§ 37

Spitzer, People ex rel. v. La Salle County, 20 Ill. 2d 18, 169 N.E.2d 521 (1960)
65 ALR5th 1—§ 10

Spitzer, State ex rel. v. Daicel Chemical Industries, Ltd., 42 A.D.3d 301, 840 N.Y.S.2d 8, 2007-2 Trade Cas. (CCH) ¶ 75780 (1st Dep't 2007)
35 ALR6th 245—§ 5

Spitzli v. Minson, 231 Va. 12, 341 S.E.2d 170 (1986)
10 ALR5th 828—§ 29

Spivack, Shulman & Goldman v. Foremost Liquor Store, Inc., 124 Ill. App. 3d 676, 80 Ill. Dec. 388, 465 N.E.2d 500 (1st Dist. 1984)
58 ALR6th 1—§ 5, 42

Spivak v. Sachs, 16 N.Y.2d 163, 263 N.Y.S.2d 953, 211 N.E.2d 329 (1965)
83 ALR5th 497—§ 3

Spivak v. Sachs, 21 A.D.2d 348, 250 N.Y.S.2d 666 (1st Dep't 1964)
83 ALR5th 497—§ 3

Spivak v. State Tax Com'n of State of N.Y., 135 A.D.2d 940, 522 N.Y.S.2d 349 (3d Dep't 1987)
2 ALR6th 1—§ 97

Spivey v. Furtado, 242 Cal. App. 2d 259, 51 Cal. Rptr. 362 (1st Dist. 1966)
2 ALR6th 439—§ 18, 20, 49, 54

Spivey v. Getz Exterminators, Inc., 224 Ga. 427, 162 S.E.2d 409 (1968)
85 ALR6th 323—§ 71

Spivey v. Head, 207 F.3d 1263 (11th Cir. 2000)
102 ALR5th 327—§ 7

Spivey v. Keller, 2004-Ohio-6667, 2004 WL 2849023 (Ohio Ct. App. 3d Dist. Allen County 2004)
86 ALR6th 1—§ 60, 61

Spivey v. Platon, 29 Ark. 603, 1874 WL 1203 (1874)
23 ALR6th 1—§ 24

Spivey v. Sellers, 185 Ga. App. 241, 363 S.E.2d 856 (1987)
54 ALR5th 313—§ 3, 17

Spivey v. State, 12 So. 3d 880 (Fla. 5th DCA 2009)
78 ALR6th 417—§ 29, 39

Spivey v. State, 170 Ga. App. 196, 316 S.E.2d 822 (1984)

76 ALR5th 1—§ 19
Spivey v. State, 253 Ga. 187, 319 S.E.2d 420 (1984)

83 ALR6th 465—§ 27, 41, 46
Spivey v. State, 274 Ga. App. 834, 619 S.E.2d 346 (2005)

33 ALR6th 373—§ 13
Spivey v. State, 531 So. 2d 965, 13 FLW 602 (Fla. 1988)

15 ALR5th 391—§ 41
Spivey v. Super Valu, 575 So. 2d 876 (La. App. 2d Cir. 1991)

44 ALR5th 525—§ 4
50 ALR5th 1—§ 12
Spivey v. Trader, 620 So. 2d 212 (Fla. Dist. Ct. App. 4th Dist. 1993)

13 ALR6th 1—§ 4
15 ALR6th 427—§ 18
Spivey v. Vaughn, 182 Ga. App. 91, 354 S.E.2d 870 (1987)

34 ALR5th 77—§ 9
Splaine v. Eastern Dog Club, 306 Mass. 381, 28 N.E.2d 450, 129 A.L.R. 427 (1940)

68 ALR5th 599—§ 15, 16
Splawn v. Lextaj Corp., NV, 197 A.D.2d 479, 603 N.Y.S.2d 41 (1st Dep't 1993)

17 ALR6th 453—§ 12, 14
Spleas v. Milwaukee & Suburban Transport Corp., 21 Wis. 2d 635, 124 N.W.2d 593 (1963)

26 ALR5th 401—§ 7, 8, 20
Splendore v. Guglielmo, 205 Misc. 941, 129 N.Y.S.2d 374 (1954)

44 ALR5th 1—§ 11
Split Rock Development Co., LLC v. Hoey Outdoor Advertising, Inc., 2004 WL 2662523 (Minn. Ct. App. 2004)

12 ALR6th 123—§ 6
Split Rock Hardwoods, Inc. v. Lumber Liquidators, Inc., 2002 WI 66, 253 Wis. 2d 238, 646 N.W.2d 19 (2002)

86 ALR6th 321—§ 13
S.P.M., Matter of Adoption of, 266 Mont. 269, 880 P.2d 297 (1994)

82 ALR5th 443—§ 4

83 ALR5th 375—§ 4
Spock v. U.S., 464 F. Supp. 510 (S.D. N.Y. 1978)

23 ALR6th 521—§ 12
Spohrer v. Town of Oyster Bay, 29 Misc. 2d 366, 219 N.Y.S.2d 376 (Sup. Ct. 1961)

63 ALR5th 607—§ 4, 12
Spokane Arcade, Inc. v. City of Spokane, 75 F.3d 663, 24 Media L. Rep. (BNA) 1475 (9th Cir. 1996)

20 ALR6th 161—§ 3
21 ALR6th 425—§ 3
23 ALR6th 573—§ 17
Spokane, City of v. Badeaux, 20 Wash. App. 731, 581 P.2d 1088 (Div. 3 1978)

96 ALR6th 355—§ 24
Spokane, City of v. Beck, 130 Wash. App. 481, 123 P.3d 854 (Div. 3 2005)

92 ALR6th 295—§ 36
Spokane, City of v. Canyon Greens, LLC, 107 Wash. App. 1005, 2001 WL 772498 (Div. 3 2001)

49 ALR6th 477—§ 12
Spokane, City of v. United Nat. Ins.Co., 190 F. Supp. 2d 1209 (E.D. Wash. 2002)

105 ALR5th 95—§ 3
Spokane, City of v. Williams, 157 Wash. 120, 288 P. 258 (1930)

44 ALR6th 259—§ 7
Spokane County Health Dist. v. Brockett, 120 Wash. 2d 140, 839 P.2d 324 (1992)

23 ALR6th 307—§ 28
Spokane I. R. Co. v. U.S., 72 F.2d 440 (CA9 Idaho 1934)

17 ALR5th 547—§ 36, 53
Spokane Merchants' Asso. v. Olmstead, 80 Idaho 166, 327 P.2d 385 (1958)

23 ALR5th 744—§ 11
Spokane Research & Defense Fund v. City of Spokane, 96 Wash. App. 568, 983 P.2d 676 (Div. 3 1999)

5 ALR6th 327—§ 3
8 ALR6th 117—§ 3, 11

Spolar v. Datsopoulos, 2003 MT 54, 314
Mont. 364, 66 P.3d 284 (2003)
12 ALR6th 1—§ 13
15 ALR6th 427—§ 10

Spomer v. Spomer, 580 P.2d 1146 (Wyo.
1978)
50 ALR5th 653—§ 3

Sponco Mfg., Inc. v. Alcover, 656 So.
2d 629 (Fla. Dist. Ct. App. 3d Dist.
1995)
102 ALR5th 99—§ 3, 6

Sponick v. City of Detroit Police Dep't,
49 Mich. App. 162, 211 N.W.2d
674 (1973)
91 ALR5th 585—§ 14

Sponick v. City of Detroit Police Dept.,
49 Mich. App. 162, 211 N.W.2d
674 (1973)
19 ALR6th 217—§ 4

Sponseller v. Meltebeke, 280 Or. 361,
570 P.2d 974, 22 U.C.C.R.S. 1182
(1977)
49 ALR5th 1—§ 87

Spool Stockyards Co. v. Chicago, R. I.
& P. R. Co., 353 F.2d 263 (5th Cir.
1965)
111 ALR5th 313—§ 17

Spoon v. American Agriculturalist, Inc.,
103 A.D.2d 929, 478 N.Y.S.2d 174,
44 Fair Empl. Prac. Cas. (BNA) 69
(3d Dep't 1984)
103 ALR5th 557—§ 5

Spoon v. American Agriculturalist, Inc.,
120 App. Div. 2d 857, 502 N.Y.S.2d
296 (1986)
51 ALR5th 163—§ 7

Spoonamore v. Armstrong World Industries, Inc., 105 F. Supp. 2d 928 (S.D.
Ind. 1999)
30 ALR5th 1—§ 26.5

Spooner v. EEN, Inc., 2010 Copr. L.
Dec. ¶ 29941, 2010 WL 1930239
(D. Me. 2010)
76 ALR6th 289—§ 6

Spooner v. National Elevator Inspection
Services, Inc., 161 Misc. 2d 73, 613
N.Y.S.2d 339 (Sup 1994)
99 ALR5th 141—§ 1

115 ALR5th 1—§ 1

Spooner v. Sears, Roebuck and Co., 161
A.D.2d 103, 554 N.Y.S.2d 540 (1st
Dep't 1990)
4 ALR6th 401—§ 5, 9

Spooner v. State Farm Mut. Auto. Ins.
Co., 709 So. 2d 1157 (Ala. 1997)
6 ALR5th 297—§ 7

Spooner v. West Baton Rouge Parish
School Bd., 709 F. Supp. 705, 53
Ed. Law Rep. 69 (M.D. La. 1989)
63 ALR6th 1—§ 60

Spoone, State ex rel. v. Morristown, 222
Tenn. 21, 431 S.W.2d 827 (1968)
17 ALR5th 195—§ 6

Spooney v. State, 844 So. 2d 615 (Ala.
Crim. App. 2001)
26 ALR6th 511—§ 33

Spoor-Lasher Co. v. Aetna Casualty &
Surety Co., 39 N.Y.2d 875, 386
N.Y.S.2d 221, 352 N.E.2d 139
(1976)
18 ALR5th 187—§ 5

Sporborg v. State, 226 App. Div. 113,
234 N.Y.S. 476 (1929)
**1 ALR5th 163—§ 4, 6, 10, 16, 21,
24, 32**

Sporio v. W.C.A.B. (Songer Const.),
553 Pa. 44, 717 A.2d 525 (1998)
100 ALR5th 567—§ 5

Sporkin v. Stafford Township, 227 N.J.
Super. 569, 548 A.2d 218 (1988)
1 ALR5th 622—§ 16

Sporn v. MCA Records, Inc., 58 N.Y.2d
482, 462 N.Y.S.2d 413, 448 N.E.2d
1324 (1983)
40 ALR6th 295—§ 2

Spors v. Stoll, 684 N.Y.S.2d 372 (App.
Div. 4th Dep't 1998)
48 ALR5th 129—§ 8, 9

Sport O'Kings Farms v. Thomas, 1990
OK CIV APP 75, 797 P.2d 1016
(Ct. App. Div. 4 1990)
40 ALR6th 99—§ 45

Sports Authority Michigan, Inc. v. Just-
balls, Inc., 97 F. Supp. 2d 806 (E.D.
Mich. 2000)
81 ALR5th 41—§ 6

Sports Bench, Inc. v. McPherson, 509 N.E.2d 233 (Ind. App. 1987)
25 ALR5th 97—§ 3

Sports Courts of Omaha, Ltd. v. Brower, 248 Neb. 272, 534 N.W.2d 317, 26 U.C.C. Rep. Serv. 2d (CBC) 1272 (1995)
66 ALR5th 135—§ 6

Sports, Inc. v. Sportshop, Inc., 14 Kan. App. 2d 141, 783 P.2d 1318 (1989)
56 ALR5th 565—§ 52

Sportsman Store of Lake Charles, Inc. v. Sonitrol Sec. Systems of Calcasieu, Inc., 725 So. 2d 74 (La. Ct. App. 3d Cir. 1998)
36 ALR6th 305—§ 10, 14, 15

Sportsmen's Boating Corp. v. Hensley, 192 Conn. 747, 474 A.2d 780 (1984)
117 ALR5th 155—§ 5, 12

Sports Page, Inc. v. First Union Management, Inc., 438 N.W.2d 428 (Minn. Ct. App. 1989)
85 ALR5th 353—§ 12

Sportswear, Inc., 70 Misc. 2d 898, 335 N.Y.S.2d 306 (1972)
8 ALR5th 653—§ 3, 12

Sporty's Farm L.L.C. v. Sportsman's Market, Inc., 202 F.3d 489, 53 U.S.P.Q.2d (BNA) 1570 (2d Cir. 2000)
96 ALR5th 1—§ 5

Spositi v. Federal Nat. Mortg. Ass'n, 2011 WL 5977319 (E.D. Tex. 2011)
86 ALR6th 411—§ 5

Sposito Associates, Inc. v. Maneely Catering, Inc., 1992 WL 75942 (Conn. Super. Ct. 1992)
116 ALR5th 433—§ 14

Spoto v. Hayward Mfg. Co., 2 Conn. App. 663, 482 A.2d 91 (1984)
65 ALR5th 105—§ 14

Spott v. Otis Elevator Co., 601 So. 2d 1355 (La. 1992)
13 ALR5th 289—§ 28
100 ALR5th 409—§ 2
115 ALR5th 1—§ 24, 25
117 ALR5th 267—§ 9

Spotts v. Reidell, 345 Pa. Super. 37, 497 A.2d 630 (1985)
98 ALR6th 1—§ 25

Spotts v. Spotts, 355 So. 2d 228 (Fla. App. D1 1978)
28 ALR5th 46—§ 11, 12
49 ALR5th 441—§ 13

Spotts v. Unemployment Compensation Board of Review, 176 Pa. Super. 484, 109 A.2d 212 (1954)
2 ALR5th 475—§ 3

Spradley v. Martin, 897 F. Supp. 560 (M.D. Fla. 1995)
89 ALR6th 1—§ 63, 118

Spradlin, In re Interest of, 214 Neb. 834, 336 N.W.2d 563 (1983)
113 ALR5th 349—§ 4

Spradlin v. City of Fulton, 1998 WL 37620 (Mo. Ct. App. W.D. 1998)
54 ALR6th 653—§ 33

Spradlin v. State Farm Mut. Auto. Ins., 650 So. 2d 1383 (Miss. 1995)
41 ALR5th 91—§ 4

Spradling v. Blackburn, 919 F. Supp. 969, 70 Fair Empl. Prac. Cas. (BNA) 1082, 69 Empl. Prac. Dec. (CCH) ¶ 44308 (S.D. W. Va. 1996)
79 ALR6th 377—§ 40

Spradling v. Harris, 13 Kan. App. 2d 595, 778 P.2d 365 (1989)
71 ALR5th 99—§ 3, 6
86 ALR6th 1—§ 34

Spradling v. State, 628 S.W.2d 123 (Tex. App. Beaumont 1981)
26 ALR5th 1—§ 2, 3, 22

Spradling v. State, 865 S.W.2d 806 (Mo. Ct. App. S.D. 1993)
31 ALR6th 49—§ 10

Spradling v. State, 2004 WL 2463204 (Tex. App. Texarkana 2004)
17 ALR6th 757—§ 4

Spragg v. Shore Care, 293 N.J. Super. 33, 679 A.2d 685 (App. Div. 1996)
81 ALR5th 367—§ 36
14 ALR6th 417—§ 8, 9

Spragg v. State, 292 Ga. App. 37, 663 S.E.2d 389 (2008)
57 ALR6th 313—§ 3

For assistance, call 1-800-328-4880

Spraggins v. Elvidge, 192 Mont. 8, 625
P.2d 1151 (1981)
27 ALR6th 183—§ 46
Spragins v. Jiffy Food Stores, Inc., 492
S.W.2d 719 (Tex. Civ. App. Fort
Worth 1973)
123 ALR5th 1—§ 14
Sprague v. Atchison T. & S. F. R. Co.,
70 Kan. 359, 78 P. 828 (1904)
17 ALR5th 547—§ 55
Sprague v. Brodus, 245 Iowa 90, 60
N.W.2d 850 (1953)
51 ALR5th 603—§ 2
Sprague v. Equifax, Inc., 166 Cal. App.
3d 1012, 213 Cal. Rptr. 69 (2d Dist.
1985)
11 ALR5th 88—§ 5
14 ALR5th 242—§ 34
Sprague v. Fauver, 71 Cal. App. 2d 333,
162 P.2d 865 (1945)
45 ALR5th 251—§ 6
Sprague v. Frank J. Sanders Lincoln
Mercury, Inc., 120 Cal. App. 3d
412, 174 Cal. Rptr. 608 (5th Dist.
1981)
11 ALR5th 88—§ 2, 5
Sprague v. General Motors Corp., 133
F.3d 388, 21 Employee Benefits
Cas. (BNA) 2267, 39 Fed. R. Serv.
3d 788, 1998 FED App. 0004P (6th
Cir. 1998)
74 ALR6th 267—§ 8
Sprague v. Ireland, 36 Tex. 654, 1872
WL 7341 (1872)
36 ALR6th 387—§ 7, 10
Sprague v. Rooney, 104 Mo. 349, 16
S.W. 505 (1891)
58 ALR5th 387—§ 20
Sprague v. State, 34 Ohio App. 354, 8
Ohio L. Abs. 231, 171 N.E. 259 (4th
Dist. Scioto County 1930)
102 ALR5th 525—§ 22, 24
Sprague v. State, 590 P.2d 410 (Alaska
1979)
99 ALR5th 557—§ 2, 15
Sprague v. Sumitomo Forestry Co., Ltd.,
104 Wash. 2d 751, 709 P.2d 1200,
42 U.C.C. Rep. Serv. 202 (1985)

101 ALR5th 563—§ 7
Sprague v. Thorn Americas, Inc., 129
F.3d 1355, 75 Fair Empl. Prac. Cas.
(BNA) 1111, 72 Empl. Prac. Dec.
(CCH) ¶ 45104, 39 Fed. R. Serv. 3d
(LCP) 706 (10th Cir. 1997)
28 ALR5th 1—§ 20
Sprague v. Walter, 656 A.2d 890 (Pa.
Super. 1995)
12 ALR5th 195—§ 48
Sprague-Cappel by Cappel v. Sprague,
852 S.W.2d 361 (Mo. Ct. App. E.D.
1993)
1 ALR6th 493—§ 13, 34
72 ALR6th 413—§ 6
Sprague-Dawley, Inc. v. Moore, 37 Wis.
2d 689, 155 N.W.2d 579 (1968)
60 ALR5th 459—§ 2, 21
Sprague, Levinson & Thall v. Advest,
Inc., 623 F. Supp. 11 (E.D. Pa.
1985)
46 ALR6th 185—§ 10
Spraker v. Watts, 41 A.D.3d 953, 837
N.Y.S.2d 754 (3d Dep't 2007)
99 ALR6th 203—§ 14, 15
102 ALR6th 153—§ 19, 21
Spranger v. State, 650 N.E.2d 1117 (Ind.
1995)
83 ALR6th 465—§ 4, 19, 20
Sprangers v. Interactive Technologies,
Inc, 394 N.W.2d 498 (Minn. App.
1986)
52 ALR5th 491—§ 2
Spratling v. Spratling, 720 S.W.2d 936
(Ky. Ct. App. 1986)
59 ALR6th 433—§ 66
Spratt, Matter of, 170 Mich. App. 719,
428 N.W.2d 754 (1988)
113 ALR5th 349—§ 6
Spratt v. Duke Power Co., 65 N.C. App.
457, 310 S.E.2d 38 (1983)
61 ALR5th 375—§ 5, 7
Spray v. Ammerman, 66 Ill. 309 (1872)
61 ALR5th 635—§ 3, 4
Spray v. Board of Medical Examiners,
50 Or. App. 311, 624 P.2d 125
(1981)
19 ALR6th 577—§ 15

65 ALR6th 295—§ 12
Spray v. Board of Medical Examiners, 51 Or. App. 773, 627 P.2d 25 (1981)
39 ALR5th 103—§ 29
Spray v. Continental Casualty Co., 86 Or. App. 156, 739 P.2d 40 (1987)
51 ALR5th 701—§ 11
Sprayberry v. First Nat. Bank, 465 So. 2d 1111 (Ala. 1984)
15 ALR6th 241—§ 13, 14
Spray-Rite Service Corp. v. Monsanto Co., 684 F.2d 1226, 1982-2 CCH Trade Cases ¶ 64808, 11 Fed. Rules Evid. Serv. 226, 34 FR Serv. 2d 698 (CA7 Ill. 1982)
23 ALR5th 241—§ 2
Spree.Com Corp., In re, 295 B.R. 762, 41 Bankr. Ct. Dec. (CRR) 156 (Bankr. E.D. Pa. 2003)
125 ALR5th 1—§ 4
Sprenger v. Public Service Com'n of Maryland, 400 Md. 1, 926 A.2d 238 (2007)
64 ALR6th 601—§ 44, 51
Sprenger v. Trout, 375 N.J. Super. 120, 866 A.2d 1035 (App. Div. 2005)
78 ALR6th 97—§ 2, 5, 7, 12
Sprenger, Grubb & Associates, Inc. v. City of Hailey, 127 Idaho 576, 903 P.2d 741 (1995)
4 ALR6th 263—§ 40
Sprewell v. NYP Holdings, Inc., 1 Misc. 3d 847, 772 N.Y.S.2d 188, 32 Media L. Rep. (BNA) 2338 (Sup 2003)
22 ALR6th 553—§ 7, 20, 35
Spriggs Enterprises, Ex parte, 879 So. 2d 587 (Ala. Civ. App. 2003)
86 ALR6th 321—§ 4, 7, 13
91 ALR6th 171—§ 2, 56
Spring v. Constantino, 168 Conn. 563, 362 A.2d 871 (1975)
4 ALR5th 273—§ 8, 31
Spring v. Inhabitants of Williamstown, 186 Mass. 479, 71 N.E. 949 (1904)
12 ALR6th 645—§ 50
Springdale v. Fleming, 191 Ark. 1058, 89 S.W.2d 602 (1936)
58 ALR5th 387—§ 6

Springdale, City of v. Duncan, 240 Ark. 716, 401 S.W.2d 747 (1966)
114 ALR5th 561—§ 5
Springdale, Village of v. Freeman, 25 Ohio Op. 2d 462, 93 Ohio L. Abs. 379, 196 N.E.2d 471 (C.P. 1963)
89 ALR6th 565—§ 27, 31, 33
Springer, Ex parte, 619 So. 2d 1267 (Ala. 1992)
37 ALR6th 357—§ 2, 4, 25
Springer, In re, 338 B.R. 515 (Bankr. N.D. Ga. 2005)
99 ALR6th 481—§ 70
Springer, In re Marriage of, 538 N.W.2d 897 (Iowa Ct. App. 1995)
82 ALR5th 389—§ 3
Springer v. Collins, 586 F.2d 329 (4th Cir. 1978)
72 ALR5th 109—§ 4 to 6
Springer v. Emerson Elec. Co., 1995 WL 546937 (Ohio Ct. App. 8th Dist. Cuyahoga County 1995)
81 ALR5th 245—§ 8
Springer v. Fitton Ctr. for Creative Arts, 2005-Ohio-3624, 16 A.D. Cas. (BNA) 1731, 2005 WL 1670788 (Ohio Ct. App. 12th Dist. Butler County 2005)
7 ALR6th 563—§ 18
10 ALR6th 375—§ 7
Springer v. George, 403 Pa. 563, 170 A.2d 367 (1961)
7 ALR6th 1—§ 6, 30
Springer v. Government Emp. Ins. Co., Inc., 311 So. 2d 36 (La. Ct. App. 4th Cir. 1975)
79 ALR5th 289—§ 4, 12, 13
Springer v. Haugeberg, Rueter, Stone & Gowell, P.C., 124 Or. App. 2, 860 P.2d 912 (1993)
60 ALR6th 1—§ 52
Springer v. Pearson, 96 Idaho 477, 531 P.2d 567 (1975)
6 ALR6th 1—§ 63
Springer v. Rosauer, 31 Wash. App. 418, 641 P.2d 1216 (Div. 3 1982)
38 ALR6th 541—§ 32

For assistance, call 1-800-328-4880

Springer v. Seaman, 658 F. Supp. 1502 (D.C. Me. 1987)
45 ALR5th 109—§ 6

Springer v. Serge Elevator Co., Inc., 211 A.D.2d 673, 621 N.Y.S.2d 637 (2d Dep't 1995)
99 ALR5th 141—§ 34

Springer v. Springer, 107 Wis. 2d 742, 321 N.W.2d 366 (Ct. App. 1982)
38 ALR6th 313—§ 4

Springer v. State, 102 Ga. 447, 30 S.E. 971 (1897)
29 ALR5th 59—§ 37, 46

Springer v. State, 2005 WL 2850257 (Minn. Ct. App. 2005)
19 ALR6th 411—§ 9

Springer, State ex rel. v. One 1940 Mercury 5-Passenger Coupe, 1950 OK 236, 203 Okla. 428, 223 P.2d 121 (1950)
105 ALR5th 1—§ 3, 9

Springett v. Iowa District Court, 2002 WL 31882912 (Iowa Ct. App. 2002)
78 ALR6th 417—§ 25

Springfield v. Civil Service Com., 403 Mass. 612, 532 N.E.2d 636 (1988)
29 ALR5th 1—§ 4

Springfield v. San Diego Unified Port Dist., 950 F. Supp. 1482 (S.D. Cal. 1996)
70 ALR6th 513—§ 14
71 ALR6th 471—§ 4

Springfield v. State, 481 So. 2d 975 (Fla. Dist. Ct. App. 4th Dist. 1986)
72 ALR5th 1—§ 29

Springfield v. State, 860 P.2d 435 (Wyo. 1993)
90 ALR5th 453—§ 27

Springfield v. Talladega City Bd. of Educ., 628 So. 2d 704 (Ala. Civ. App. 1993)
56 ALR5th 493—§ 37

Springfield v. Tracy, 105 Ohio App. 3d 187, 663 N.E.2d 962 (2d Dist. Clark County 1995)
114 ALR5th 561—§ 22

Springfield v. Ushman, 71 Ill. App. 3d 112, 27 Ill. Dec. 308, 388 N.E.2d 1357 (4th Dist. 1979)
48 ALR5th 659—§ 2

Springfield Armory v. City of Columbus, 29 F.3d 250 (CA6 Ohio. 1994)
29 ALR5th 664—§ 4, 5, 9

Springfield Armory v. City of Columbus, 805 F. Supp. 489 (S.D. Ohio 1992)
29 ALR5th 664—§ 2, 4, 5

Springfield, City of v. Industrial Com'n, 214 Ill. App. 3d 301, 158 Ill. Dec. 23, 573 N.E.2d 836 (4th Dist. 1991)
113 ALR5th 115—§ 6, 47, 64

Springfield, City of v. Industrial Com'n, 291 Ill. App. 3d 734, 226 Ill. Dec. 198, 685 N.E.2d 12 (4th Dist. 1997)
108 ALR5th 1—§ 6

Springfield, City of v. Rexnord Corp., 196 F.R.D. 7 (D. Mass. 2000)
27 ALR5th 76—§ 35

Springfield C. R. Co. v. Welsh, 155 Ill. 511, 40 N.E. 1034 (1895)
19 ALR5th 622—§ 52

Springfield ex rel. Bd. of Public Utilities of Springfield, Mo., City of v. Brechbuhler, 895 S.W.2d 583 (Mo. 1995)
44 ALR6th 259—§ 22

Springfield Fire & Marine Ins. Co. v. J. T. Wilson Co., 67 F.2d 426 (CA6 Ky. 1933)
16 ALR5th 412—§ 8
37 ALR5th 41—§ 3

Springfield, Illinois Police Dept., City of v. Industrial Com'n, 328 Ill. App. 3d 448, 262 Ill. Dec. 641, 766 N.E.2d 261 (4th Dist. 2002)
112 ALR5th 509—§ 20
13 ALR6th 209—§ 3, 11, 24, 48
39 ALR6th 445—§ 21

Springfield N. O. Nelson Company, Inc. v. Mapes, 1983 WL 2422 (Ohio Ct. App. 2d Dist. Clark County 1983)
107 ALR5th 311—§ 14

Springfield Oil Services, Inc. v. Costello, 941 F. Supp. 45, 33 U.C.C. Rep. Serv. 2d (CBC) 1164 (E.D. Pa. 1996)
76 ALR5th 289—§ 8, 9
Springfield Rare Coin Galleries, Inc. v. Johnson, 115 Ill. 2d 221, 104 Ill. Dec. 743, 503 N.E.2d 300 (1986)
108 ALR5th 189—§ 4, 6
Springfield, State ex rel. City of v. Cox, 327 Mo. 152, 36 S.W.2d 102 (1931)
111 ALR5th 579—§ 27
Spring Hill Cemetery, Inc. v. Lindsey, 162 Tenn. 420, 37 S.W.2d 111 (1931)
54 ALR5th 681—§ 3, 15
Spring Hill Civic Ass'n, Inc. v. Richard, 526 So. 2d 211 (Fla. Dist. Ct. App. 5th Dist. 1988)
115 ALR5th 251—§ 15
Springhill Nursing Homes, Inc. v. Mc-Curdy, 898 So. 2d 694 (Ala. 2004)
50 ALR6th 187—§ 16
Spring Lake Park, State, City of v. Seekon, 392 N.W.2d 624 (Minn. Ct. App. 1986)
34 ALR6th 1—§ 9
Spring Motors Distributors v. Ford Motor Co., 98 N.J. 555, 489 A.2d 660, CCH Prod. Liab. Rep. ¶ 10528, 40 U.C.C.R.S. 1184 (1985)
49 ALR5th 1—§ 48
Spring Motors Distributors, Inc. v. Ford Motor Co., 191 N.J. Super. 22, 465 A.2d 530, 37 U.C.C. Rep. Serv. 62 (App. Div. 1983)
84 ALR6th 1—§ 25, 37
Spring Motors Distributors, Inc. v. Ford Motor Co., 191 N.J. Super. 22, 465 A.2d 530, 37 U.C.C. Rep. Serv. (CBC) 62 (App. Div. 1983)
81 ALR5th 483—§ 5
Springs, In re, 358 B.R. 236 (Bankr. M.D. N.C. 2006)
32 ALR6th 531—§ 28
Springs v. Atlantic Refining Co., 205 N.C. 444, 171 S.E. 635, 110 A.L.R. 474 (1933)

109 ALR5th 421—§ 3, 8
Springs v. Commonwealth, 198 Ky. 258, 248 S.W. 535 (1923)
81 ALR5th 563—§ 3, 5
Springs Industries, Inc. v. Gasson, 923 F. Supp. 823 (D.S.C. 1996)
79 ALR5th 587—§ 4
Springs Mills, Inc. v. Carolina Underwear Co., 87 App. Div. 2d 524, 448 N.Y.S.2d 10, 33 U.C.C.R.S. 597 (1st Dep't 1982)
49 ALR5th 1—§ 29
Springsteen v. Plaza Roller Dome, Inc., 602 F. Supp. 1113, 225 U.S.P.Q. 1008 (M.D. N.C. 1985)
37 ALR6th 243—§ 54
Spring Val. Coal Co. v. Donaldson, 123 Ill. App. 196, 1905 WL 2342 (2d Dist. 1905)
75 ALR6th 1—§ 15
Spring Valley, Re, 189 Misc. 324, 71 N.Y.S.2d 848 (1947)
17 ALR5th 195—§ 10
Springville Banking Co. v. Burton, 10 Utah 2d 100, 349 P.2d 157 (1960)
15 ALR5th 821—§ 19
Sprinkle v. Burlington Northern R. Co., 236 Mont. 383, 769 P.2d 1261 (1989)
17 ALR6th 1—§ 15
Sprinkle v. Davis-Noland-Merrill Grain Co., 354 S.W.2d 34 (Mo. Ct. App. 1962)
40 ALR6th 99—§ 66, 78
Sprinkle v. Sprinkle, 441 So. 2d 974 (Ala. App. 1983)
17 ALR5th 366—§ 16
Sprinkle v. State, 92 Tex. Crim. 590, 244 S.W. 1004 (1922)
105 ALR5th 529—§ 11
Sprint Communications Co. v. Kelly, 642 A.2d 106 (Dist. Col. App. 1994)
58 ALR5th 187—§ 39
Sprint Communications Co. v. State Bd. of Equalization, 40 Cal. App. 4th 1254, 47 Cal. Rptr. 2d 399 (1st Dist. 1995)
1 ALR6th 1—§ 3

Sprouse v. Skinner, 155 Ga. 119, 116 S.E. 606 (1923)
6 ALR6th 391—§ 5, 17, 18
Sprouse v. State, 242 Ga. 831, 252 S.E.2d 173 (1979)
5 ALR5th 243—§ 2
105 ALR5th 529—§ 18
Sprovero v. Miller, 404 So. 2d 793 (Fla. Dist. Ct. App. 3d Dist. 1981)
52 ALR6th 271—§ 18
Sprowl v. Dooley, 2007 WL 1330447 (Tex. App. Dallas 2007)
58 ALR6th 1—§ 5
59 ALR6th 1—§ 10
60 ALR6th 1—§ 72
Sprowl v. Eddy, 547 N.E.2d 865 (Ind. Ct. App. 1st Dist. 1989)
104 ALR5th 331—§ 6
Sprowl v. Ward, 441 So. 2d 898 (Ala. 1983)
7 ALR6th 357—§ 3, 9, 18, 29
Spruce Creek Development Co., of Ocala, Inc. v. Drew, 746 So. 2d 1109 (Fla. Dist. Ct. App. 5th Dist. 1999)
118 ALR5th 91—§ 16
125 ALR5th 193—§ 4, 5
Spruce Manor Enterprises v. Borough of Bellmawr, 315 N.J. Super. 286, 717 A.2d 1008 (Law Div. 1998)
21 ALR6th 261—§ 24, 31, 32
Spruell v. Administrator of Division of Employment Sec. of Dep't of Labor, 158 So. 2d 364 (La. Ct. App. 2d Cir. 1963)
68 ALR5th 13—§ 13, 35
Spruell v. Allied Meadows Corp., 117 Idaho 277, 787 P.2d 263 (1990)
95 ALR5th 329—§ 25
Spruell v. Georgia Automatic Gas Appliance Co., 84 Ga. App. 657, 67 S.E.2d 178 (1951)
34 ALR5th 1—§ 4
Spruyt v. Spruyt, 115 N.M. 405, 851 P.2d 1072, 55 A.L.R.5th 885 (App. 1993)
55 ALR5th 647—§ 4

Spruytte v. Govorchin, 961 F. Supp. 1094 (W.D. Mich. 1997)
89 ALR6th 1—§ 55, 115
Spruytte v. Walters, 753 F.2d 498 (6th Cir. 1985)
89 ALR6th 1—§ 54
Spry v. Carnival Cruise Lines, 951 F.2d 362 (9th Cir. 1991)
82 ALR6th 175—§ 13
Spry v. State, 396 Md. 682, 914 A.2d 1182 (2007)
52 ALR6th 125—§ 3, 24, 44
Spry v. State, 750 So. 2d 123 (Fla. Dist. Ct. App. 2d Dist. 2000)
46 ALR6th 241—§ 34
Spry, Estate of v. Batey, 804 N.E.2d 250 (Ind. Ct. App. 2004)
13 ALR6th 1—§ 4
15 ALR6th 427—§ 27
S.P.S. v. State, 2010 WL 668884 (Tex. App. Austin 2010)
69 ALR6th 1—§ 12
SPS Industries, Inc. v. Atlantic Steel Co., 186 Ga. App. 94, 366 S.E.2d 410, 6 U.C.C.R.S.2d 122 (1988)
37 ALR5th 459—§ 4
Spuhler, In re, 2012 WL 5193776 (Bankr. N.D. Ohio 2012)
99 ALR6th 481—§ 69
Spulak v. K Mart Corp., 664 F. Supp. 1395, 2 BNA IER Cas. 1816 (D.C. Colo. 1985)
51 ALR5th 1—§ 8
Spunaugle v. State, 1997 OK CR 47, 946 P.2d 246 (Okla. Crim. App. 1997)
16 ALR6th 329—§ 3
24 ALR6th 591—§ 3, 4, 15
Spurgeon, Matter of Marriage of, 119 Or. App. 59, 849 P.2d 1132 (1993)
26 ALR6th 331—§ 6, 19
Spurgeon v. Board of Comrs., 181 Kan. 1008, 317 P.2d 798 (1957)
8 ALR5th 391—§ 3, 4, 7
Spurgeon v. Julius Blum, Inc., 816 F. Supp. 1317 (C.D. Ill. 1993)
73 ALR5th 75—§ 6
Spurgers v. State, 576 S.W.2d 830 (Tex. Crim. 1978)

34 ALR5th 125—§ 15

Spurlin v. Paul Brown Agency, Inc., 80 N.M. 306, 454 P.2d 963 (1969)

121 ALR5th 365—§ 2

Spurlin v. State, 228 Ga. 763, 187 S.E.2d 856 (1972)

99 ALR6th 295—§ 10, 16

Spurling, Application of, 595 A.2d 1062 (Me. 1991)

105 ALR5th 217—§ 8

Spurlock v. Begley, 2008 WL 5429542 (Ky. Ct. App. 2008)

43 ALR6th 611—§ 28

Spurlock v. Brown, 91 Tenn. 241, 18 S.W. 868 (1892)

3 ALR5th 394—§ 8

Spurlock v. Schwegmann Bros. Giant Supermarket, 475 So. 2d 20 (La. App. 4th Cir. 1985)

60 ALR5th 379—§ 2, 8

Spurlock v. Texas Dept. of Protective and Regulatory Services, 904 S.W.2d 152 (Tex. App. Austin 1995)

113 ALR5th 349—§ 4
116 ALR5th 559—§ 6
117 ALR5th 349—§ 10

Spur Products Corp. v. Stoel Rives LLP, 143 Idaho 812, 153 P.3d 1158 (2007)

41 ALR6th 1—§ 8

Spurr v. La Salle Constr. Co., 385 F.2d 322 (CA7 Ill. 1967)

15 ALR5th 119—§ 5, 59, 71, 85, 86

Spurs v. State, 850 S.W.2d 611 (Tex. App. Tyler 1993)

104 ALR5th 229—§ 9
115 ALR5th 403—§ 8
34 ALR6th 539—§ 4
101 ALR6th 1—§ 5, 28, 46, 48

S.P.W., In re, 707 S.W.2d 814 (Mo. Ct. App. W.D. 1986)

113 ALR5th 349—§ 12
122 ALR5th 385—§ 3, 19
12 ALR6th 417—§ 11

SPX Corp. v. Doe, 253 F. Supp. 2d 974 (N.D. Ohio 2003)

3 ALR6th 153—§ 21

Spychala v. G.D. Searle & Co., 705 F. Supp. 1024 (D.N.J. 1988)

54 ALR5th 1—§ 17
57 ALR5th 1—§ 5, 26, 31

Square v. State, 145 Tex. Crim. 219, 167 S.W.2d 192 (1942)

97 ALR5th 293—§ 2, 3

Square D Co. v. C.J. Kern Contractors, Inc., 314 N.C. 423, 334 S.E.2d 63 (1985)

5 ALR6th 497—§ 4, 9

Square D Co. v. Kentucky Bd. of Tax Appeals, 415 S.W.2d 594 (Ky. 1967)

17 ALR6th 623—§ 28

Square Deal Fruit Co. v. Florida Industrial Com., 42 So2d 276 (Fla. 1949)

60 ALR5th 459—§ 2, 6

Squaw Valley Development Co. v. Goldberg, 375 F.3d 936, 58 Env't. Rep. Cas. (BNA) 2013, 34 Envtl. L. Rep. 20051 (9th Cir. 2004)

86 ALR6th 173—§ 1, 5

Squeglia v. Squeglia, 234 Conn. 259, 661 A.2d 1007 (1995)

118 ALR5th 513—§ 11
125 ALR5th 133—§ 3

Squibb v. Squibb, 190 Cal. App. 2d 766, 12 Cal. Rptr. 346 (2d Dist. 1961)

83 ALR6th 605—§ 5

Squibb-Mathieson Intern. Corp. v. St. Paul Mercury Ins. Co., 44 Misc. 2d 835, 254 N.Y.S.2d 586 (Sup 1964)

87 ALR6th 319—§ 9

Squiciari v. Brenner, 276 A.D.2d 689, 714 N.Y.S.2d 355 (2d Dep't 2000)

93 ALR6th 123—§ 99, 100

Squilla v. W.C.A.B. (Marple Tp.), 146 Pa. Commw. 23, 606 A.2d 539 (1992)

82 ALR5th 149—§ 4, 36, 61

Squire v. Com., 214 Va. 260, 199 S.E.2d 534 (1973)

102 ALR5th 525—§ 14

Squire v. Sumner Rhubarb Growers' Ass'n, 184 F.2d 94, 39 A.F.T.R. (P-H) ¶ 1020 (9th Cir. 1950)

60 ALR5th 459—§ 2, 9, 15

Squires v. Board of County Road Comrs., 378 Mich. 613, 147 N.W.2d 65 (1967)
3 ALR5th 746—§ 8
Squires v. Dugger, 794 F. Supp. 1568 (M.D. Fla. 1992)
94 ALR5th 393—§ 13
95 ALR5th 611—§ 3
Squires v. Fithian's Adm'r, 27 Mo. 134 (1858)
46 ALR5th 1—§ 7
Squires v. Republic Ins. Co., 572 F.2d 560 (6th Cir. 1978)
116 ALR5th 247—§ 7
Squires v. Sierra Nev. Educ. Found., 107 Nev. 902, 823 P.2d 256 (1991)
46 ALR5th 581—§ 4, 5, 12, 13, 16, 18
Squires v. Squires, 12 Ohio App. 3d 138, 12 Ohio B.R. 460, 468 N.E.2d 73 (Preble Co. 1983)
20 ALR5th 700—§ 2
40 ALR5th 227—§ 3
Squires v. Unemployment Compensation Board of Review, 172 Pa. Super. 424, 94 A.2d 172 (1953)
2 ALR5th 475—§ 11
Squire, Sanders & Dempsey, L.L.P. v. Givaudan Flavors Corp., 127 Ohio St. 3d 161, 2010-Ohio-4469, 937 N.E.2d 533, 71 A.L.R.6th 717 (2010)
71 ALR6th 249—§ 2, 11
Squires ex rel. Squires v. Goodwin, 2011 WL 5374754 (D. Colo. 2011)
75 ALR6th 1—§ 12
Squires Gate, Inc. v. County of Monmouth, 247 N.J. Super. 1, 588 A.2d 824 (App. Div. 1991)
97 ALR5th 123—§ 1
Squires III, Inc. v. National Union Fire Ins. Co., 593 So. 2d 272, 17 FLW D 261 (Fla. App. D5 1992)
37 ALR5th 41—§ 6
Squitieri v. City of New York, 248 A.D.2d 201, 669 N.Y.S.2d 589 (1st Dep't 1998)
102 ALR5th 99—§ 6

Squyres v. F.D.I.C., 1992 WL 167487 (N.D. Tex. 1992)
56 ALR5th 565—§ 31
Squyres v. Nationwide Housing Systems, Inc., 715 So. 2d 538 (La. Ct. App. 3d Cir. 1998)
101 ALR5th 447—§ 4, 13
S.R., In re, 157 Vt. 417, 599 A.2d 364 (1991)
6 ALR6th 161—§ 21
S.R., In re, 671 N.W.2d 533 (Iowa App. 2003)
116 ALR5th 559—§ 3
S.R., Interest of, 735 P.2d 53, 54 Utah Adv. Rep. 21 (Utah 1987)
20 ALR5th 534—§ 4, 6, 16
S. R., People in Interest of, 323 N.W.2d 885 (S.D. 1982)
89 ALR5th 195—§ 15
S.R. v. Inova Healthcare Services, 49 Va. Cir. 119, 1999 WL 797192 (1999)
87 ALR6th 1—§ 84
S.R. v. M.R., 401 N.W.2d 221 (Iowa App. 1986)
5 ALR5th 550—§ 2
20 ALR5th 700—§ 2
21 ALR5th 396—§ 2
40 ALR5th 227—§ 2
67 ALR5th 1—§ 2, 3
S. R. v. S. M. R., 709 S.W.2d 910 (Mo. App. 1986)
17 ALR5th 366—§ 12
Sragowicz v. Sragowicz, 603 So. 2d 1323 (Fla. Dist. Ct. App. 3d Dist. 1992)
71 ALR5th 99—§ 8
Srail v. RJF Internatl. Corp., 126 Ohio App. 3d 689, 711 N.E.2d 264 (8th Dist. Cuyahoga County 1998)
81 ALR5th 367—§ 42
S.R.B., In re, 2008-Ohio-6340, 2008 WL 5104690 (Ohio Ct. App. 2d Dist. Miami County 2008)
65 ALR6th 1—§ 23
S.R.B., Interest of, 760 P.2d 49 (Kan. App. 1988)
20 ALR5th 534—§ 4, 16, 17

SRC Holdings Corp., In re, 2005 WL 2240352 (D. Minn. 2005)
  22 ALR6th 113—§ 32
  34 ALR6th 345—§ 20, 33
SR Condominiums, LLC v. K.C. Const., Inc., 176 P.3d 866 (Colo. App. 2007)
  86 ALR6th 321—§ 13
  88 ALR6th 385—§ 90
Srebnik v. State, 245 N.J. Super. 344, 585 A.2d 950 (App. Div. 1991)
  96 ALR5th 107—§ 7
SRE Carlsbad, Inc. v. Kerr-McGee Coal Corp., 56 F.3d 67 (7th Cir. 1995)
  101 ALR5th 61—§ 5
Sreshta v. Kaydan, 1999 WL 285047 (Ohio Ct. App. 8th Dist. Cuyahoga County 1999)
  17 ALR6th 159—§ 3, 22, 30, 56
S. R. Fowle & Son v. Atlantic C. L. R. Co., 147 N.C. 491, 61 S.E. 262 (1908)
  17 ALR5th 547—§ 14
S.R.H., In Interest of, 15 Kan. App. 2d 415, 809 P.2d 1 (1991)
  92 ALR5th 379—§ 5
SRH, Inc. v. IFC Credit Corp., 275 Ga. App. 18, 619 S.E.2d 744 (2005)
  39 ALR6th 629—§ 4, 5
SR Inter. Business Ins. Co., Ltd. v. World Trade Center Properties, LLC, 375 F. Supp. 2d 238 (S.D. N.Y. 2005)
  47 ALR6th 1—§ 19, 22
S.R.J., In re, 176 Ga. App. 685, 337 S.E.2d 444 (1985)
  113 ALR5th 349—§ 10, 11
  117 ALR5th 349—§ 12
S.R.J., Re, 176 Ga. App. 685, 337 S.E.2d 444 (1985)
  1 ALR5th 469—§ 12, 29
S.R.L. v. State, 733 P.2d 885 (Okla. Crim. 1987)
  37 ALR5th 703—§ 5
Sroka v. Halliday, 39 R.I. 119, 97 A. 965 (1916)
  21 ALR6th 81—§ 44

Sroka v. Halliday, 41 R.I. 322, 103 A. 799 (1918)
  21 ALR6th 81—§ 44
S.R.P., In re, 2009-Ohio-11, 2009 WL 18001 (Ohio Ct. App. 12th Dist. Butler County 2009)
  64 ALR6th 1—§ 7, 18
S.R.S., Application of, 225 Neb. 759, 408 N.W.2d 272 (1987)
  28 ALR6th 349—§ 39, 40, 42
S.R.S., In re Application of, 225 Neb. 759, 408 N.W.2d 272 (1987)
  61 ALR5th 151—§ 8, 11, 12
S.R.T., In re, 2006 WL 397946 (Tex. App. San Antonio 2006)
  52 ALR6th 433—§ 9
  57 ALR6th 163—§ 32
S.R. Weinstock & Assocs., Inc., 223 Ct. Cl. 677, 27 CCF ¶ 80283 (1980)
  8 ALR5th 653—§ 3
S.S., Application of, 130 N.J. Super. 21, 324 A.2d 611 (County Ct. 1974)
  91 ALR6th 435—§ 93
S.S., In re, 37 Cal. App. 4th 543, 43 Cal. Rptr. 2d 768, 95 C.D.O.S. 6192, 95 Daily Journal DAR 10512 (1st Dist. 1995)
  15 ALR5th 391—§ 45
S.S., In re, 281 Ga. App. 781, 637 S.E.2d 151 (2006)
  30 ALR6th 1—§ 4, 7
S.S., In re, 665 N.W.2d 442 (Iowa Ct. App. 2003)
  113 ALR5th 349—§ 4
  117 ALR5th 349—§ 3
S.S., In re, 2009 WL 161333 (Ohio App. 2 Dist. 2009)
  57 ALR6th 163—§ 39
S.S., In re Adoption of, 167 Ill. 2d 250, 212 Ill. Dec. 590, 657 N.E.2d 935 (1995)
  89 ALR5th 195—§ 6
  63 ALR6th 429—§ 3
S.S. v. Eastern Kentucky University, 532 F.3d 445, 234 Ed. Law Rep. 612 (6th Cir. 2008)
  98 ALR6th 599—§ 55

S.S. v. Madison County Dept. of Human Resources, 2004 WL 1178368 (Ala. Civ. App. 2004)
122 ALR5th 385—§ 15, 19
S.S. v. State, 816 So. 2d 225 (Fla. Dist. Ct. App. 5th Dist. 2002)
101 ALR5th 351—§ 9
S.S. v. Wakefield, 764 P.2d 70 (Colo. 1988)
54 ALR5th 575—§ 19
S.S.A., In re, 319 S.W.3d 796 (Tex. App. El Paso 2010)
69 ALR6th 1—§ 9
S. S. Kresge Co. v. Fader, 116 Ohio St. 718, 5 Ohio L. Abs. 381, 158 N.E. 174, 58 A.L.R. 132 (1927)
123 ALR5th 1—§ 12, 14
S. S. Kresge Co. v. McCallion, 58 F.2d 931 (C.C.A. 8th Cir. 1932)
63 ALR6th 495—§ 37
S. S. Kresge Co. v. Prescott, 435 S.W.2d 203 (Tex. Civ. App. Texarkana 1968)
12 ALR5th 195—§ 42
S. S. Kresge Co. v. Ruby, 348 So. 2d 484 (Ala. 1977)
12 ALR5th 195—§ 63
S. S. Kresge Co. of Mich. v. Winkelman Realty Co., 260 Wis. 372, 50 N.W.2d 920 (1952)
111 ALR5th 313—§ 5
S. S. Kresge Co., State ex rel. v. Howard, 357 Mo. 302, 208 S.W.2d 247 (1947)
1 ALR6th 229—§ 26
S.T., In Interest of, 201 Ga. App. 37, 410 S.E.2d 312 (1991)
122 ALR5th 385—§ 3
S.T., In re, 161 Vt. 639, 641 A.2d 120 (1994)
34 ALR6th 1—§ 16
S.T., State in the Interest of, 928 P.2d 393 (Utah Ct. App. 1996)
6 ALR6th 161—§ 21
S.T. v. State Department of Human Resources, 579 So. 2d 640 (Ala. Civ. App. 1991)
117 ALR5th 349—§ 11

S.T. v. State Dep't of Human Resources, 579 So. 2d 640 (Ala. App. 1991)
1 ALR5th 469—§ 26, 33
Staats v. McKinnon, 206 S.W.3d 532 (Tenn. Ct. App. 2006)
53 ALR6th 419—§ 9
57 ALR6th 163—§ 41, 47
60 ALR6th 193—§ 16
Staats v. McKinnon, 924 So. 2d 82 (Fla. Dist. Ct. App. 1st Dist. 2006)
57 ALR6th 163—§ 41
60 ALR6th 193—§ 16
Stabak v. ISS Intern., 248 A.D.2d 814, 670 N.Y.S.2d 242 (3d Dep't 1998)
19 ALR5th 439—§ 8
Stabenow v. Jacobsen, 234 Wis. 2d 151, 2000 WI App 71, 610 N.W.2d 512 (Ct. App. 2000)
96 ALR5th 107—§ 8
Stabenow v. State, 495 N.E.2d 197 (Ind. App. 1986)
19 ALR5th 470—§ 12
Staber v. Fidler, 65 N.Y.2d 529, 493 N.Y.S.2d 288, 482 N.E.2d 1204 (1985)
14 ALR6th 543—§ 34
Stabile, People ex rel. v. Warden of City Prison of City of New York, 139 A.D. 488, 124 N.Y.S. 341 (1st Dep't 1910)
103 ALR6th 137—§ 4
Stabilus, Div. of Fichtel & Sachs Industries, Inc. v. Haysnworth, Baldwin, Johnson & Greaves, 1992 WL 68563 (E.D. Pa. 1992)
57 ALR5th 633—§ 3, 5
Stablein v. Stablein, 59 Wash. 2d 465, 368 P.2d 174 (1962)
5 ALR5th 863—§ 5
Stacey v. Insurance Corp. of Ireland, 189 Ill. App. 3d 229, 136 Ill. Dec. 697, 545 N.E.2d 221, 5 I.E.R. Cas. (BNA) 1848, 119 Lab. Cas. (CCH) ¶ 56680 (1st Dist. 1989)
85 ALR6th 323—§ 17
Stacey v. State, 79 Okla. Crim. 417, 155 P.2d 736 (1945)
104 ALR5th 357—§ 6

Staceyville Community Nursing Home v. Department of Inspections & Appeals, 528 N.W.2d 557, 46 A.L.R.5th 947 (Iowa 1995)
46 ALR5th 821—§ 2, 4, 5

Stach v. Sears, Roebuck and Co., 102 Ill. App. 3d 397, 57 Ill. Dec. 879, 429 N.E.2d 1242 (1st Dist. 1981)
63 ALR6th 495—§ 37, 41

Stach v. Stach, 83 Md. App. 36, 573 A.2d 409 (1990)
82 ALR5th 389—§ 3

Stachniak v. Hayes, 989 F.2d 914, 38 Fed. R. Evid. Serv. 446 (7th Cir. 1993)
95 ALR6th 641—§ 9

Stachowski v. Town of Cicero, 425 F.3d 1075, 23 I.E.R. Cas. (BNA) 897, 151 Lab. Cas. (CCH) ¶ 60091 (7th Cir. 2005)
89 ALR6th 1—§ 88

Stachura v. Truszkowski, 763 F.2d 211 (CA6 Mich. 1985)
12 ALR5th 195—§ 36, 38

Stack v. Boyle, 342 U.S. 1, 72 S. Ct. 1, 96 L. Ed. 3 (1951)
7 ALR6th 487—§ 2

Stack v. City of Portsmouth, 52 N.H. 221, 1872 WL 4368 (1872)
23 ALR6th 1—§ 8

Stack v. Hanover Ins. Co., 57 Ala. App. 504, 329 So. 2d 561 (Civ. App. 1976)
56 ALR5th 407—§ 7

Stack v. Killian, 96 F.3d 159, 1996 FED App. 305P (6th Cir. 1996)
68 ALR5th 549—§ 3, 4

Stack v. Midwood Chayim Aruchim Dialysis Associates, Inc., 54 A.D.3d 935, 864 N.Y.S.2d 121 (2d Dep't 2008)
48 ALR6th 1—§ 40

Stack v. State Farm Mut. Auto. Ins. Co., 507 So. 2d 617 (Fla. Dist. Ct. App. 3d Dist. 1987)
42 ALR6th 545—§ 13
43 ALR6th 375—§ 3, 5, 16, 40

Stack v. Wapner, 244 Pa. Super. 278, 368 A.2d 292 (1976)
1 ALR5th 243—§ 2, 5

Stack, Commonwealth ex rel. v. Stack, 141 Pa. Super. 147, 15 A.2d 76 (1940)
124 ALR5th 203—§ 15

Stack, Estate of v. Venzke, 485 N.E.2d 907 (Ind. Ct. App. 1985)
87 ALR6th 495—§ 33, 77

Stackhouse, In re, 1991 WL 37940 (Ohio Ct. App. 4th Dist.Athens County 1991)
57 ALR5th 141—§ 22

Stackhouse v. New York City Health & Hosp. Corp., 577 N.Y.S.2d 833 (App. Div. 1st Dep't 1992)
52 ALR5th 1—§ 8

Stackhouse v. Stackhouse, 1997 WL 451471 (Ohio Ct. App. 2d Dist. Clark County 1997)
39 ALR6th 205—§ 5

Stackhouse v. Zaretsky, 2006 PA Super 108, 900 A.2d 383 (2006)
77 ALR6th 293—§ 4, 23, 25, 45

Stackiewicz v. Nissan Motor Corp., 100 Nev. 443, 686 P.2d 925 (1984)
48 ALR5th 129—§ 17
51 ALR5th 467—§ 3

Stackrow v. New York Property Ins. Underwriter's Ass'n, 115 A.D.2d 883, 496 N.Y.S.2d 794 (3d Dep't 1985)
23 ALR6th 697—§ 13

Stacks, Re, 406 So. 2d 979 (Ala. App. 1981)
15 ALR5th 692—§ 33

Stacks v. F & S Petroleum Co., Inc., 6 Ark. App. 327, 641 S.W.2d 726, 35 U.C.C. Rep. Serv. 376 (1982)
94 ALR5th 247—§ 3, 5, 18, 32

Stacy, In re, 193 B.R. 31, 28 Bankr. Ct. Dec. (CRR) 951 (Bankr. D. Or. 1996)
32 ALR6th 531—§ 39

Stacy, In re, 223 B.R. 132 (N.D. Ill. 1998)
18 ALR5th 230—§ 5

Stacy v. Aetna Casualty & Surety Co, 334 F. Supp. 1216 (N.D. Miss. 1971)

13 ALR5th 289—§ 3

Stacy v. Aetna Casualty & Surety Co., 484 F.2d 289, 17 FR Serv. 2d 955 (CA5 Miss. 1973)

13 ALR5th 289—§ 18

Stacy v. Greenberg, 14 N.J. 262, 102 A.2d 48 (1954)

42 ALR6th 545—§ 3, 8, 20

43 ALR6th 375—§ 3, 4, 13, 38

Stacy v. LSI Corp., 544 Fed. Appx. 93, 120 Fair Empl. Prac. Cas. (BNA) 1103, 97 Empl. Prac. Dec. (CCH) ¶ 44956 (3d Cir. 2013)

96 ALR6th 189—§ 2, 14

Stacy v. LSI Corp., 2012 WL 4039851 (E.D. Pa. 2012)

96 ALR6th 189—§ 5, 14

Stacy v. Merchants Bank, 144 Vt. 515, 482 A.2d 61 (1984)

18 ALR5th 307—§ 6, 21, 32

Stacy v. Parker, 63 Tex. Civ. App. 129, 132 S.W. 532 (1910)

6 ALR6th 391—§ 5, 17, 21

Stacy v. Petty, 362 So. 2d 810 (La. Ct. App. 3d Cir. 1978)

60 ALR5th 165—§ 3, 11

Stacy v. Ross, 798 So. 2d 1275 (Miss. 2001)

86 ALR6th 1—§ 35

Stacy v. Shoney's, Inc., 142 F.3d 436 (6th Cir. 1998)

93 ALR5th 47—§ 16

94 ALR5th 1—§ 4, 9

Stacy v. Williams, 253 Ky. 353, 69 S.W.2d 697 (1934)

108 ALR5th 385—§ 3

Stad v. Grace Downs Model & Air Career School, 65 Misc. 2d 1095, 319 N.Y.S.2d 918 (1941)

46 ALR5th 581—§ 24

Stadheim, In re Marriage of, 170 Ill. App. 3d 19, 120 Ill. Dec. 373, 523 N.E.2d 1284 (1st Dist. 1988)

77 ALR6th 293—§ 22, 24, 30

Stadler v. Cross, 295 N.W.2d 552 (Minn. 1980)

89 ALR5th 255—§ 2

Stadt v. Fox News Network LLC, 719 F. Supp. 2d 312, 38 Media L. Rep. (BNA) 2461, 96 U.S.P.Q.2d 1115 (S.D. N.Y. 2010)

76 ALR6th 289—§ 4, 5

77 ALR6th 543—§ 5, 6, 12

Stadt v. State, 182 S.W.3d 360 (Tex. Crim. App. 2005)

84 ALR6th 427—§ 26

Staecker v. Hitachi Seiki U.S.A., Inc., 1998 WL 30698 (N.D. Ill. 1998)

73 ALR5th 75—§ 3, 6

Staefa Control-System Inc. v. St. Paul Fire & Marine Ins. Co., 847 F. Supp. 1460 (N.D. Cal. 1994)

89 ALR5th 1—§ 10

97 ALR5th 473—§ 9

98 ALR5th 193—§ 12

106 ALR5th 1—§ 2

Staehler v. Beuthin, 206 Wis. 2d 610, 557 N.W.2d 487 (Ct. App. 1996)

125 ALR5th 193—§ 2, 5, 6

Staehli's Estate, In re, 86 Ill. App. 3d 1, 41 Ill. Dec. 243, 407 N.E.2d 741 (1st Dist. 1980)

122 ALR5th 205—§ 3, 26, 51

Staehr v. Alm, 269 Fed. Appx. 888 (11th Cir. 2008)

43 ALR6th 1—§ 5, 12, 16, 20, 32

Stael v. Stael, 1993 WL 267484 (Minn. Ct. App. 1993)

30 ALR6th 413—§ 12

Stafeil, Re Marriage of, 169 Ill. App. 3d 630, 120 Ill. Dec. 92, 523 N.E.2d 1003 (1st Dist. 1988)

5 ALR5th 550—§ 25

Staff v. State Farm Mut. Ins. Co., 87 Ohio App. 3d 440, 622 N.E.2d 434 (8th Dist.Cuyahoga County 1993)

63 ALR5th 675—§ 3

Staffel v. San Antonio School Board of Education, 201 S.W. 413 (Tex. Civ. App. San Antonio 1918)

94 ALR5th 613—§ 7

Staffier v. Sandoz Pharmaceuticals Corp., 888 F. Supp. 287 (D.C. Mass. 1995)

51 ALR5th 1—§ 3

Staffney v. Fireman's Fund Ins. Co., 91 Mich. App. 745, 284 N.W.2d 277 (1979)

13 ALR5th 289—§ 3

Staff of Idaho Real Estate Com. v. Parkinson, 100 Idaho 96, 593 P.2d 1000 (1979)

7 ALR5th 474—§ 121

Staffon v. Lyon, 110 Mich. 260, 68 N.W. 151 (1896)

54 ALR5th 649—§ 4

Stafford, In re, 36 Wash. 2d 108, 216 P.2d 746 (1950)

26 ALR6th 1—§ 7

Stafford, In re Application of, 193 Kan. 120, 392 P.2d 140 (1964)

53 ALR5th 375—§ 40

Stafford v. Bacon, 1 Hill 532, 2 Hill 353, 25 Wend. 384, 1841 WL 3938 (N.Y. Sup 1841)

98 ALR5th 353—§ 3, 7

Stafford v. Baton Rouge, 403 So. 2d 733, 25 BNA WH Cas. 1208 (La. 1981)

18 ALR5th 577—§ 11

Stafford v. Correction Reception Ctr., 2004-Ohio-7085, 2004 WL 2985232 (Ohio Ct. Cl. 2004)

53 ALR6th 305—§ 38

Stafford v. Dickison, 46 Haw. 52, 374 P.2d 665 (1962)

86 ALR6th 321—§ 11

Stafford v. Drury Inns, Inc., 165 S.W.3d 494 (Mo. Ct. App. E.D. 2005)

17 ALR6th 453—§ 8

Stafford v. E.I. Dont De Nemours & Co., 1996 WL 659023 (Del. Super. Ct. 1996)

86 ALR5th 295—§ 18

Stafford v. Food World, Inc., 31 N.C. App. 213, 228 S.E.2d 756 (1976)

123 ALR5th 1—§ 9

Stafford v. Fred Wolferman, Inc., 307 S.W.2d 468 (Mo. 1957)

83 ALR5th 589—§ 5

123 ALR5th 1—§ 16

Stafford v. Greater Cleveland Regional Transit Authority, 1993 WL 536089 (Ohio Ct. App. 8th Dist. Cuyahoga County 1993)

66 ALR5th 611—§ 9

Stafford v. Intrav, Inc., 16 F.3d 1228, 1994 A.M.C. 939 (8th Cir. 1994)

2 ALR5th 396—§ 28

Stafford v. Intrav, Inc., 841 F. Supp. 284, 1994 AMC 934 (E.D. Mo. 1993)

2 ALR5th 396—§ 25 to 27

Stafford v. Intrav, Inc., 841 F. Supp. 284, 1994 A.M.C. 934 (E.D. Mo. 1993)

82 ALR6th 175—§ 27

Stafford v. Mingo County Court, 58 W. Va. 88, 51 S.E. 2 (1905)

27 ALR6th 403—§ 20

60 ALR6th 481—§ 4, 30

Stafford v. Molinoff, 228 A.D.2d 662, 645 N.Y.S.2d 313 (2d Dep't 1996)

24 ALR6th 549—§ 3

Stafford v. Neurological Medicine, Inc., 811 F.2d 470 (8th Cir. 1987)

98 ALR6th 1—§ 52, 60

Stafford v. New York C. R. Co., 80 Pa. Super. 408 (1923)

17 ALR5th 547—§ 36, 53

Stafford v. Nipp, 502 So. 2d 702 (Ala. 1987)

54 ALR5th 1—§ 3, 5

Stafford v. Northeast Utilities, 1997 WL 88192 (Conn. Super. Ct. 1997)

120 ALR5th 351—§ 33

Stafford v. Postal Tel. & Cable Co., 58 Ga. App. 213, 198 S.E. 117 (1938)

13 ALR5th 217—§ 6

Stafford v. Puro, 63 F.3d 1436, 2 BNA WH Cas. 2d 1451, 130 CCH LC ¶ 57970 (CA7 Ill. 1995)

14 ALR5th 242—§ 42

18 ALR5th 577—§ 38

Stafford v. Radford Community Hosp., 908 F. Supp. 1369, 11 ADD 949, 67 CCH EPD ¶ 43963 (W.D. Va. 1995)

51 ALR5th 1—§ 7

Stafford v. Richardson, 15 Wend. 302 (N.Y. Sup. Ct. 1836)

67 ALR5th 587—§ 6

Stafford v. Sibley, Lindsay & Curr Co., 280 A.D. 495, 114 N.Y.S.2d 177 (4th Dep't 1952)

63 ALR6th 495—§ 45, 56

Stafford v. Stacey, 115 Misc. 2d 291, 453 N.Y.S.2d 992 (Fam. Ct. 1982)

67 ALR5th 1—§ 22

Stafford v. Stafford, 18 Wash. 2d 775, 140 P.2d 545 (1943)

52 ALR5th 221—§ 3, 13

Stafford v. Stafford, 27 Misc. 2d 9, 203 N.Y.S.2d 935 (Sup 1960)

112 ALR5th 185—§ 10

Stafford v. Stafford, 161 Vt. 580, 641 A.2d 348 (1993)

34 ALR6th 253—§ 15

Stafford v. Stafford, 618 S.W.2d 578 (Ky. App. 1981)

53 ALR5th 375—§ 5, 9

Stafford v. Stafford, 726 S.W.2d 14 (Tex. 1987)

4 ALR5th 972—§ 7

Stafford v. State Election Bd., 1950 OK 135, 203 Okla. 132, 218 P.2d 617 (1950)

121 ALR5th 1—§ 44, 47

Stafford v. St. Clair's Hospital, 19 Misc. 2d 710, 189 N.Y.S.2d 351 (Sup 1959)

24 ALR6th 721—§ 10

Stafford v. True Temper Sports, 123 F.3d 291 (5th Cir. 1997)

7 ALR6th 563—§ 18

Stafford v. Ward, 59 F.3d 1025 (10th Cir. 1995)

94 ALR5th 393—§ 10

Stafford Trading, Inc. v. Lovely, 2007 WL 611252 (N.D. Ill. 2007)

26 ALR6th 287—§ 22
66 ALR6th 83—§ 8, 9

Stage, In re, 85 B.R. 880 (BC M.D. Fla. 1988)

44 ALR5th 1—§ 3, 19, 21

Stage, In re Application of, 81 Ohio St. 3d 554, 692 N.E.2d 993 (1998)

83 ALR5th 497—§ 5

Stage, In re Application of, 81 Ohio St. 3d 554, 1998-Ohio-338, 692 N.E.2d 993 (1998)

8 ALR6th 1—§ 13

Stagebrush Promotions, Inc., In re, 98 Pa. Commw. 634, 512 A.2d 776 (1986)

4 ALR6th 263—§ 4, 46, 51

Stage Door Development, Inc. v. Broadcast Music, Inc., 698 So. 2d 787 (Ala. Civ. App. 1997)

8 ALR5th 653—§ 3

Stager v. Harrington, 27 Kan. 414 (1882)

33 ALR5th 205—§ 30

Stager v. Schneider, 494 A.2d 1307 (D.C. 1985)

108 ALR5th 385—§ 12, 13
94 ALR6th 431—§ 11

Stagg v. City Products Corp., 339 So. 2d 362 (La. App. 1976)

40 ALR5th 135—§ 7, 17

Staggs v. Sparks, 286 Ky. 398, 150 S.W.2d 690 (1941)

95 ALR5th 533—§ 5
124 ALR5th 203—§ 5

Staggs v. Staggs, 250 Iowa 938, 96 N.W.2d 736 (1959)

95 ALR5th 533—§ 5
124 ALR5th 203—§ 5

Stagikas v. Saxon Mortg. Services, Inc., 795 F. Supp. 2d 129 (D. Mass. 2011)

86 ALR6th 411—§ 4

Stagner v. Board of Review of Oklahoma Employment Sec. Com'n, 1990 OK CIV APP 15, 792 P.2d 94 (Okla. Ct. App. Div. 3 1990)

95 ALR5th 329—§ 25

Stagner v. Friendswood Development Co., Inc., 620 S.W.2d 103 (Tex. 1981)

63 ALR5th 1—§ 3

St. Agnes Hospital v. Jaeckel, 616 F. Supp. 426 (E.D. Wis 1985)

16 ALR5th 262—§ 40

Stahel v. Brown, 422 So. 2d 1291 (La. Ct. App. 4th Cir. 1982)

103 ALR5th 255—§ 3, 19

Staheli v. Smith, 548 So. 2d 1299 (Miss. 1989)
  19 ALR5th 1—§ 87
  44 ALR5th 193—§ 33
Staheli's Will, In re, 57 N.Y.S.2d 185 (Sur. Ct. 1945)
  56 ALR5th 133—§ 4
Stahl v. Board of Finance, 62 N.J. Super. 562, 163 A.2d 396 (1960)
  56 ALR5th 171—§ 10, 17
Stahl v. Patrick, 206 Minn. 413, 288 N.W. 854 (1939)
  40 ALR6th 99—§ 29
Stahl v. Sentry Ins., 180 Wis. 2d 299, 509 N.W.2d 320 (Ct. App. 1993)
  2 ALR6th 279—§ 14
Stahl v. Southeastern X-Ray, 427 So. 2d 1089 (Fla. Dist. Ct. App. 1st Dist. 1983)
  63 ALR6th 187—§ 34
Stahl v. Stahl, 115 Neb. 882, 215 N.W. 131 (1927)
  3 ALR5th 394—§ 6, 7, 22
Stahl v. State, 328 Ark. 106, 940 S.W.2d 880 (1997)
  105 ALR5th 529—§ 14
Stahl v. State, 749 S.W.2d 826 (Tex. Crim. App. 1988)
  99 ALR6th 113—§ 20
Stahl v. Utah Transit Auth., 618 P.2d 480 (Utah 1980)
  45 ALR5th 173—§ 3
Stahl v. Wal-Mart Stores, Inc., 47 F. Supp. 2d 783 (S.D. Miss. 1998)
  102 ALR5th 99—§ 3
  121 ALR5th 157—§ 9
Stahle v. State, 970 S.W.2d 682 (Tex. App. Dallas 1998)
  29 ALR6th 1—§ 10
Stahmann v. Maryland Casualty Co., 44 N.M. 289, 101 P.2d 1021, 128 A.L.R. 556 (1940)
  16 ALR6th 491—§ 4
Stahn v. Fairmont Nat. Bank, 367 N.W.2d 784 (S.D. 1985)
  125 ALR5th 147—§ 18, 24
Stahovic v. Rajchel, 122 Wis. 2d 370, 363 N.W.2d 243 (Ct. App. 1984)
  116 ALR5th 1—§ 67
Stainback v. Stainback, 11 Va. App. 13, 396 S.E.2d 686 (1990)
  2 ALR6th 195—§ 10, 14
Staines v. State, 659 S.W.2d 50 (Tex. App. Houston 14th Dist. 1983)
  111 ALR5th 239—§ 4
Stainless Specialty Mfg. Co. v. Industrial Com. of Arizona, 144 Ariz. 12, 695 P.2d 261 (1985)
  26 ALR5th 127—§ 2
Staino v. Com., Pennsylvania State Horse Racing Com'n, 98 Pa. Commw. 461, 512 A.2d 75 (1986)
  64 ALR5th 769—§ 4, 6
Stair v. Calhoun, 2009 WL 792189 (E.D. N.Y. 2009)
  48 ALR6th 1—§ 31
  78 ALR6th 151—§ 7
Stair v. Gilbert, 209 Ky. 243, 272 S.W. 732 (1925)
  23 ALR6th 697—§ 4
Stair v. Phoenix Presentations, Inc., 116 Ohio App. 3d 500, 688 N.E.2d 582 (12th Dist. Butler County 1996)
  51 ALR5th 1—§ 7
Stajos v. City of Lansing, 221 Mich. App. 223, 561 N.W.2d 116 (1997)
  48 ALR5th 659—§ 3, 7, 17
Staklinski v. Pyramid Elec. Co., 6 N.Y.2d 159, 188 N.Y.S.2d 541, 160 N.E.2d 78, 37 Lab. Cas. (CCH) ¶ 65506 (1959)
  112 ALR5th 263—§ 77
Staklinski v. Pyramid Electric Co., 6 App. Div. 2d 565, 180 N.Y.S.2d 20, 36 CCH LC ¶ 65226 (1st Dep't 1958)
  56 ALR5th 757—§ 3
Stalcup, In re Estate of, 627 S.W.2d 364 (Tenn. App. 1981)
  58 ALR5th 325—§ 4, 9
Stalcup v. Orthotic & Prosthetic Lab, Inc., 989 S.W.2d 654 (Mo. Ct. App. E.D. 1999)
  12 ALR5th 1—§ 10

Stalder v. Board of Medical Examiners, 37 Or. App. 853, 588 P.2d 659 (1978)

10 ALR5th 1—§ 7, 18

Staley v. AC&S, Inc., 2006-Ohio-7033, Prod. Liab. Rep. (CCH) ¶ 17667, 2006 WL 3833883 (Ohio Ct. App. 12th Dist. Butler County 2006)

41 ALR6th 445—§ 18

Staley v. Brown, 244 Miss. 825, 146 So. 2d 739 (1962)

20 ALR5th 229—§ 2, 28

Staley v. Jones, 108 F. Supp. 2d 777 (W.D. Mich. 2000)

29 ALR5th 487—§ 3

Staley v. Jones, 2001 WL 91611 (6th Cir. 2001)

29 ALR5th 487—§ 3, 7

Staley v. Lower Merion Tp., 69 Montg. 407 (Pa. C.P. 1953)

4 ALR6th 263—§ 12

Staley v. Sagel, 841 P.2d 379 (Colo. Ct. App. 1992)

93 ALR5th 621—§ 8

Staley v. State, 633 N.E.2d 314 (Ind. Ct. App. 1st Dist. 1994)

66 ALR5th 397—§ 13, 21

Staley v. State, 851 So. 2d 805 (Fla. 2d DCA 2003)

78 ALR6th 1—§ 22

Staley v. State, 887 S.W.2d 885 (Tex. Crim. App. 1994)

75 ALR5th 295—§ 33

Staley v. Taylor, 165 Or. App. 256, 994 P.2d 1220 (2000)

11 ALR5th 88—§ 4

Stalker v. Drake, 91 Kan. 142, 136 P. 912 (1913)

12 ALR5th 195—§ 66

Stalker v. Luria, 217 A.D.2d 294, 634 N.Y.S.2d 874 (3d Dep't 1995)

23 ALR6th 697—§ 14

Stalker v. Stalker, 88 A.D.3d 1177, 932 N.Y.S.2d 202 (3d Dep't 2011)

100 ALR6th 1—§ 45

Stall v. Professional Divers of New Orleans, Inc., 739 So. 2d 1005, 5 Wage & Hour Cas. 2d (BNA) 1129 (La. Ct. App. 5th Cir. 1999)

11 ALR5th 715—§ 22, 26

Stall v. State, 570 So. 2d 257 (Fla. 1990)

58 ALR6th 385—§ 37

Stallard v. State, 6 Md. App. 560, 252 A.2d 267 (1969)

85 ALR5th 547—§ 8

Stallard v. State, 209 Tenn. 13, 348 S.W.2d 489 (1961)

16 ALR6th 329—§ 7
24 ALR6th 591—§ 10

Stallcup, Re Marriage of, 97 Cal. App. 3d 294, 158 Cal. Rptr. 679 (3d Dist. 1979)

10 ALR5th 191—§ 2

Stallcup v. Coscarart, 79 Ariz. 42, 282 P.2d 791 (1955)

18 ALR6th 325—§ 2, 55

Stallcup v. Taylor, 62 Tenn. App. 407, 463 S.W.2d 416 (1970)

62 ALR5th 537—§ 3

Stalley v. State, 91 Nev. 671, 541 P.2d 658 (1975)

39 ALR5th 283—§ 4

Stalling v. State, 90 Tex. Crim. 310, 234 S.W. 914 (1921)

26 ALR5th 1—§ 3

Stallings v. Angelica Uniform Co., 388 So. 2d 942 (Ala. 1980)

17 ALR5th 547—§ 13

Stallings v. Bagley, 561 F. Supp. 2d 821 (N.D. Ohio 2008)

102 ALR6th 417—§ 41, 46

Stallings v. Daniels, 159 N.C. App. 467, 583 S.E.2d 428 (2003)

54 ALR6th 653—§ 30

Stallings v. Gunter, 99 N.C. App. 710, 394 S.E.2d 212 (1990)

14 ALR6th 301—§ 5, 7, 8, 23, 24
19 ALR6th 475—§ 5, 6

Stallings v. State, 255 Ind. 365, 264 N.E.2d 618 (1970)

28 ALR6th 505—§ 9

Stallings v. U.S. Electronics Inc., 707 N.Y.S.2d 9 (App. Div. 1st Dep't 2000)
73 ALR5th 1—§ 7

Stallings & Sons, Inc., Ex parte, 670 So. 2d 861 (Ala. 1995)
100 ALR5th 481—§ 6
22 ALR6th 387—§ 54

Stallion v. Morris, 546 So. 2d 563 (La. App. 1st Cir. 1989)
50 ALR5th 1—§ 9

Stallman v. Bell, 235 Cal. App. 3d 740, 286 Cal. Rptr. 755 (2d Dist. 1991)
125 ALR5th 193—§ 3 to 6, 9
2 ALR6th 279—§ 11
34 ALR6th 431—§ 20

Stallnacker v. State, 19 Ark. App. 9, 715 S.W.2d 883 (1986)
38 ALR5th 433—§ 11

Stallone v. Northwest Airlines, Inc., 247 A.D.2d 832, 668 N.Y.S.2d 832 (4th Dep't 1998)
21 ALR6th 671—§ 4, 8

Stalls v. Penny, 62 N.C. App. 511, 302 S.E.2d 912 (1983)
57 ALR6th 83—§ 5

Stallworth v. AmSouth Bank of Alabama, 709 So. 2d 458 (Ala. 1997)
43 ALR6th 1—§ 33

Stallworth v. Hazel, 167 Mich. App. 345, 421 N.W.2d 685 (1988)
86 ALR6th 321—§ 12, 13
90 ALR6th 451—§ 94

Stallworth v. State, 2005 WL 2092667 (Tex. App. Beaumont 2005)
47 ALR6th 107—§ 48, 67

Stalnaker v. General Motors Corp., 972 F. Supp. 335 (D. Md. 1996)
48 ALR5th 1—§ 10

Stalnaker v. GM Corp., 934 F. Supp. 179 (D.C. Md. 1996)
48 ALR5th 1—§ 6, 12

Stalnaker v. Only One Dollar, Inc., 188 W. Va. 744, 426 S.E.2d 536, 8 I.E.R. Cas. (BNA) 1763, 125 Lab. Cas. (CCH) ¶ 57353 (1992)
53 ALR6th 213—§ 9

Staloch v. Belsaas, 271 Minn. 315, 136 N.W.2d 92 (1965)
16 ALR5th 1—§ 26, 43

Stam v. Cannon, 176 N.W.2d 794 (Iowa 1970)
3 ALR5th 1—§ 3, 4, 22, 41
33 ALR5th 205—§ 23

Stam v. Mack, 984 S.W.2d 747 (Tex. App. Texarkana 1999)
22 ALR5th 483—§ 9

Staman v. Lipman, 641 So. 2d 453 (Fla. Dist. Ct. App. 1st Dist. 1994)
66 ALR5th 591—§ 3

St. Amant v. Aetna Cas. and Sur. Co., 499 So. 2d 322 (La. Ct. App. 1st Cir. 1986)
78 ALR5th 341—§ 4
79 ALR5th 289—§ 3

St. Amant v. Thompson, 390 U.S. 727, 88 S. Ct. 1323, 20 L. Ed. 2d 262, 1 Media L. R. 1586 (1968)
44 ALR5th 193—§ 21
54 ALR5th 443—§ 2

St. Amant v. Thompson, 390 U.S. 727, 88 S. Ct. 1323, 20 L. Ed. 2d 262, 1 Media L. Rep. (BNA) 1586 (1968)
40 ALR6th 231—§ 2
42 ALR6th 353—§ 2, 19

St. Amant v. Travelers Ins. Co., 233 So. 2d 23 (La. App. 4th Cir. 1970)
9 ALR5th 826—§ 3

Stamas v. County of Madera, 2010 WL 1416866 (E.D. Cal. 2010)
86 ALR6th 173—§ 5

Stamat v. Merry, 78 Ill. App. 3d 445, 33 Ill. Dec. 808, 397 N.E.2d 141 (1st Dist. 1979)
5 ALR5th 875—§ 4

Stamatiou v. El Greco Studios, Inc., 935 S.W.2d 701 (Mo. Ct. App. W.D. 1996)
8 ALR5th 653—§ 3

Stamatis v. Bechtel Power Corp., 184 Mont. 64, 601 P.2d 403 (1979)
20 ALR5th 346—§ 12

Stambaugh v. International Harvester Co., 102 Ill. 2d 250, 80 Ill. Dec. 28, 464 N.E.2d 1011 (1984)

42 ALR5th 221—§ 20

Stambaugh v. International Harvester Co., 106 Ill. App. 3d 1, 61 Ill. Dec. 888, 435 N.E.2d 729, CCH Prod. Liab. Rep. ¶ 9307, 35 A.L.R.4th 414 (5th Dist. 1982)

12 ALR5th 195—§ 22

48 ALR5th 129—§ 4

Stambovsky v. Ackley, 169 App. Div. 2d 254, 572 N.Y.S.2d 672 (1stDep't)

8 ALR5th 312—§ 19

50 ALR5th 417—§ 5, 9

Stamey, Ex parte, 776 So. 2d 85 (Ala. 2000)

22 ALR6th 387—§ 9, 34

Stamford Athletic Club v. Union Trust Co., 1997 WL 155376 (Conn. Super. Ct. 1997)

91 ALR5th 89—§ 9

Stamford Wallpaper Co., Inc. v. TIG Ins., 138 F.3d 75, 46 Env't. Rep. Cas. (BNA) 1889, 28 Envtl. L. Rep. 20584 (2d Cir. 1998)

89 ALR5th 1—§ 6

Stamler v. Willis, 287 F. Supp. 734 (N.D. Ill. 1968)

24 ALR6th 255—§ 3, 11, 13

Stamm v. Wilder Travel Trailers, 44 Ill. App. 3d 530, 3 Ill. Dec. 215, 358 N.E.2d 382, 20 U.C.C.R.S. 1142 (1976)

38 ALR5th 191—§ 2 to 5, 43

Stammer v. Mulvaney, 264 Wis. 244, 58 N.W.2d 671 (1953)

50 ALR5th 417—§ 10

Stamp v. Hagerman, 181 Mich. App. 332, 448 N.W.2d 849 (1989)

119 ALR5th 121—§ 3

125 ALR5th 193—§ 5, 7

Stamper, In re, 2000 WL 222017 (Ohio Ct. App. 5th Dist. Richland County 2000)

82 ALR5th 389—§ 3

Stamper v. Adams, 165 F.3d 36 (9th Cir. 1998)

46 ALR6th 63—§ 5

Stamper v. Allstate Ins. Co., 115 Idaho 237, 766 P.2d 707 (1988)

78 ALR5th 341—§ 4

Stamper v. Charlotte-Mecklenburg Bd. of Ed., 143 N.C. App. 172, 544 S.E.2d 818, 152 Ed. Law Rep. 832 (2001)

7 ALR6th 563—§ 16

Stamper v. Commonwealth, 220 Va. 260, 257 S.E.2d 808 (1979)

37 ALR5th 515—§ 4

Stamper v. Hiteshew, 797 P.2d 784, 54 BNA FEP Cas. 209, 60 CCH EPD ¶ 42026 (Colo. App. 1990)

51 ALR5th 163—§ 5

Stamper v. Hyundai Motor Co., 699 N.E.2d 678 (Ind. Ct. App. 1998)

111 ALR5th 529—§ 6

Stamper v. State, 662 P.2d 82 (Wyo. 1983)

19 ALR5th 823—§ 4, 8

Stampfes v. Action Appraisers, 88 Wash. App. 1063, 1997 WL 783944 (Div. 1 1997)

44 ALR6th 1—§ 5, 18

Stamps v. Century Electric Co., 225 S.W.2d 493 (Mo. App. 1949)

47 ALR5th 801—§ 2, 8, 11

Stamps v. Johns, 597 F. Supp. 2d 1, 56 A.L.R.6th 845 (D.D.C. 2009)

56 ALR6th 553—§ 12, 28

Stamps v. State, 603 S.W.2d 59 (Mo. Ct. App. E.D. 1980)

70 ALR5th 587—§ 11

Stamps v. State, 620 So. 2d 1033, 18 FLW D 1586 (Fla. App. D2 1993)

27 ALR5th 593—§ 19

Stamsen v. Barrett, 135 Ga. App. 156, 217 S.E.2d 320 (1975)

17 ALR5th 547—§ 14

Stamulis, In re Claim of, 176 App. Div. 2d 426, 574 N.Y.S.2d 417 (3d Dep't 1991)

23 ALR5th 176—§ 26

Stan v. Constitution State Service Co., 168 Or. App. 92

61 ALR5th 375—§ 3

Stan v. Constitution State Service Co., 168 Or. App. 92, 9 P.3d 119 (2000)
41 ALR6th 207—§ 30

Stana v. School Dist. of City of Pittsburgh, 775 F.2d 122, 28 Ed. Law Rep. 53 (3d Cir. 1985)
89 ALR6th 1—§ 52

Stanage v. State, 674 N.E.2d 214 (Ind. Ct. App. 1996)
27 ALR6th 183—§ 21, 35, 37

Stanavich v. General Acc. Ins. Co. of America, 229 A.D.2d 872, 645 N.Y.S.2d 657 (3d Dep't 1996)
65 ALR5th 649—§ 5

Stanback v. Parke, Davis & Co., 657 F.2d 642, CCH Prod. Liab. Rep. ¶ 9048 (CA4 Va. 1981)
57 ALR5th 1—§ 4

Stanbridge, In re Detention of, 356 Ill. Dec. 797, 962 N.E.2d 482 (Ill. 2011)
78 ALR6th 417—§ 38

Stanbridge, In re Detention of, 408 Ill. App. 3d 553, 350 Ill. Dec. 556, 948 N.E.2d 1063 (4th Dist. 2011)
78 ALR6th 417—§ 38

Stanbro v. Baptist Home Asso., etc., 172 Colo. 572, 475 P.2d 23, 45 A.L.R.3d 606 (1970)
34 ALR5th 529—§ 3

Stanbury v. Larsen, 803 P.2d 349 (Wyo. 1990)
23 ALR5th 241—§ 4

Stancher v. Wyoming Valley Improv. Co., 33 Pa. D. & C.2d 513 (1964)
28 ALR5th 547—§ 3, 15

Stancil, In re Custody of, 10 N.C. App. 545, 179 S.E.2d 844 (1971)
53 ALR5th 375—§ 42

Stancil v. Brock, 108 N.C. App. 745, 425 S.E.2d 446 (1993)
5 ALR6th 193—§ 10, 42

Stancil v. K.S.B. Inv. & Management Co., 62 Ohio App. 3d 765, 577 N.E.2d 452 (Cuyahoga Co. 1991)
43 ALR5th 207—§ 23

Stancliff v. State, 852 S.W.2d 639 (Tex. App. Houston 14th Dist. 1993)
9 ALR6th 633—§ 8

13 ALR6th 603—§ 44

Stancraft Corp., In re, 39 B.R. 748, 10 Collier Bankr. Cas. 2d (MB) 1061 (Bankr. E.D. Va. 1984)
72 ALR6th 563—§ 38

Stancuna v. Town of Wallingford, 487 F. Supp. 2d 15 (D. Conn. 2007)
68 ALR6th 229—§ 8

Standage v. Standage, 147 Ariz. 473, 711 P.2d 612 (Ct. App. Div. 1 1985)
2 ALR6th 195—§ 3, 10

Standal v. Armstrong Cork Co., 356 N.W.2d 380 (Minn. Ct. App. 1984)
18 ALR6th 629—§ 3, 5, 14

Standard v. Buckner, 561 S.W.2d 329 (Ky. Ct. App. 1977)
37 ALR6th 511—§ 8, 14

Standard v. Meadors, 347 F. Supp. 908, 11 U.C.C.R.S. 760 (N.D. Ga. 1972)
50 ALR5th 327—§ 7

Standard Acc. Ins. Co. v. Cloutier, 92 N.H. 449, 32 A.2d 684, 147 A.L.R. 626 (1943)
57 ALR5th 591—§ 5

Standard Acc. Ins. Co. v. Pennsylvania Car Co., 15 S.W.2d 1081 (Tex. Civ. App. 1929)
58 ALR5th 535—§ 5, 18

Standard Acc. Ins. Co. v. Stanaland, 285 S.W. 878 (Tex. Civ. App. Galveston 1926)
41 ALR6th 207—§ 31

Standard & Poor's Corp. v. Commodity Exchange, Inc., 541 F. Supp. 1273, 8 Media L. R. 1755, 220 USPQ 522, 69 A.L.R. Fed 883 (S.D. N.Y. 1982)
39 ALR5th 103—§ 3, 10

Standard Bank & Trust Co. v. Village of Oak Lawn, 61 Ill. App. 3d 174, 18 Ill. Dec. 516, 377 N.E.2d 1152 (1st Dist. 1978)
47 ALR6th 439—§ 7, 8

Standard Bleachery & Printing Co. v. Board of Review of Unemployment Compensation Commission, 132 N.J.L. 318, 40 A.2d 558 (N.J. Sup. Ct. 1945)
68 ALR5th 13—§ 9, 23

Standard Brands, Inc. v. Zumpe, 264 F. Supp. 254, 152 U.S.P.Q. 731 (E.D. La. 1967)
36 ALR6th 537—§ 7, 36

Standard Brass & Mfg. Co. v. Maryland Casualty Co., 153 So. 2d 475 (La. App. 4th Cir. 1963)
5 ALR5th 132—§ 5

Standard Chartered Bank PLC v. Ayala International Holdings (U.S.), Inc., 111 F.R.D. 76 (S.D. N.Y. 1986)
51 ALR5th 603—§ 2, 5, 11

Standard Chartered PLC v. Price Waterhouse, 190 Ariz. 6, 945 P.2d 317 (Ct. App. Div. 1 1996)
48 ALR5th 389—§ 3

Standard Chtd. P.L.C. v. Price Waterhouse, 229 Ariz. Adv. Rep. 26 (Ariz. App. 1996)
48 ALR5th 389—§ 3, 6

Standard Combustion Co. v. Farr, 9 Ohio Dec. Rep. 509, 14 W.L.B. 201, 1885 WL 3781 (Ohio C.P. 1885)
85 ALR6th 1—§ 24

Standard Dental Mfg Co v. National Tooth Co, 95 F. 291 (C.C.E.D. Pa. 1899)
85 ALR6th 1—§ 38

Standard Electric Supply Co. v. Norfolk & Dedham Mut. Fire Ins. Co., 1 Mass. App. 762, 307 N.E.2d 11 (1973)
30 ALR5th 170—§ 2, 4, 9, 79

Standard Equipment Co., Inc. v. Albertson, 35 N.C. App. 144, 240 S.E.2d 499 (1978)
86 ALR6th 321—§ 13
89 ALR6th 409—§ 90

Standard Finance Co., Ltd. v. Ellis, 3 Haw. App. 614, 657 P.2d 1056, 35 U.C.C. Rep. Serv. (CBC) 864 (1983)
42 ALR5th 137—§ 3
89 ALR5th 577—§ 4, 9

Standard Fire Ins. Co. v. Blakeslee, 54 Wash. App. 1, 771 P.2d 1172 (Div. 2 1989)
60 ALR5th 239—§ 4, 10

Standard Fire Ins. Co. v. Chester O'Donley & Associates, Inc., 972 S.W.2d 1 (Tenn. Ct. App. 1998)
49 ALR6th 169—§ 7

Standard Fire Ins. Co. v. Kent & Associates, Inc., 232 Ga. App. 419, 501 S.E.2d 858 (1998)
122 ALR5th 1—§ 15

Standard Fire Ins. Co. v. Knowles, 133 S. Ct. 1345, 185 L. Ed. 2d 439 (2013)
86 ALR6th 577—§ 27

Standard Fire Ins. Co. v. Peoples Church of Fresno, 985 F.2d 446 (9th Cir. 1993)
98 ALR5th 1—§ 7

Standard Fire Ins. Co. v. Smithhart, 183 Ky. 679, 211 S.W. 441, 5 A.L.R. 972 (1919)
9 ALR6th 363—§ 14

Standard Fire Ins. Co. v. Stephenson, 963 S.W.2d 81 (Tex. App. Beaumont 1997)
6 ALR5th 297—§ 8

Standard Fire Ins. Co. v. Wagner, 2006 WL 1787580 (M.D. Pa. 2006)
75 ALR6th 235—§ 26

Standard Fruit and Vegetable Co., Inc. v. Johnson, 985 S.W.2d 62 (Tex. 1998)
96 ALR5th 107—§ 8
98 ALR5th 609—§ 26

Standard Furnace Co. v. Lorincz, 106 Pa. Super. 116, 161 A. 573 (1932)
91 ALR5th 485—§ 6

Standard Furniture Mfg. Co. v. Reed, 572 So. 2d 389, 14 A.L.R.5th 1020 (Ala. 1990)
14 ALR5th 537—§ 3

Standard Guaranty Ins. Co. v. Quanstrom, 555 So. 2d 828, 15 FLW S23 (Fla. 1990)
56 ALR5th 107—§ 5

Standard Ins. Co. v. Anderson, 227 Miss. 397, 86 So. 2d 298 (1956)
16 ALR5th 412—§ 7, 24

Standard Jury Instructions-Civil Cases, 613 So. 2d 1316, 18 FLW S. 111 (Fla. 1993)

22 ALR5th 464—§ 2

Standard Knitting, Ltd. v. Outside Design, Inc., 2000 WL 804434 (E.D. Pa. 2000)

81 ALR5th 41—§ 6

Standard Life & Acc. Ins. Co. v. Jones, 94 Ala. 434, 10 So. 530 (1892)

100 ALR5th 617—§ 6, 9

Standard Life Ins. Co. v. Veal, 354 So. 2d 239 (Miss. 1977)

14 ALR5th 242—§ 12

Standard Lumber & Mfg. Co. v. Deposit Guaranty Bank & Trust Co., 169 Miss. 120, 152 So. 639 (1934)

4 ALR5th 693—§ 9, 14

Standard Management, Inc. v. Kekona, 98 Haw. 95, 43 P.3d 232 (Ct. App. 2001)

45 ALR6th 493—§ 2, 16, 19, 26, 41

Standard Marine Ins. Co. v. Peck, 140 Colo. 56, 342 P.2d 661 (1959)

48 ALR5th 659—§ 17, 19, 46

Standard Mortg. Corp. v. Wells, 865 So. 2d 93 (La. Ct. App. 4th Cir. 2002)

86 ALR6th 411—§ 4

Standard Motor Car Co. v. St. Amant, 18 La. App. 298, 134 So. 279 (1931)

47 ALR5th 677—§ 7, 9

Standard Motor Car Co. v. St. Amant, 18 La. App. 304, 138 So. 461 (1931)

47 ALR5th 677—§ 9

Standard Mut. Ins. Co. v. Boyd, 452 N.E.2d 1074 (Ind. App. 1983)

16 ALR5th 412—§ 20

Standard Mut. Ins. Co. v. Kidd, 136 F. Supp. 2d 950 (S.D. Ind. 2001)

35 ALR5th 375—§ 14

Standard Mut. Ins. Co. v. Petreikis, 183 Ill. App. 3d 272, 131 Ill. Dec. 771, 538 N.E.2d 1327 (4th Dist. 1989)

16 ALR6th 491—§ 23

Standard Oil Co. v. Burleson, 117 F.2d 412 (CA5 Fla. 1941)

60 ALR5th 379—§ 2, 6

Standard Oil Co. v. Gentry, 241 Ala. 62, 1 So. 2d 29 (1941)

60 ALR5th 379—§ 2, 3, 5

Standard Oil Co. v. Midgett, 116 F.2d 562 (CA4 N.C. 1941)

17 ALR5th 547—§ 13, 20, 26, 27

Standard Oil Co. v. Payne, 220 Mich. 663, 190 N.W. 769 (1922)

17 ALR5th 547—§ 64

Standard Oil Co. v. R. L. Pitcher Co., 289 F. 678 (CA1 Me. 1923)

17 ALR5th 547—§ 7

Standard Oil Co. v. Tallahassee, 183 F.2d 410 (CA5 Fla. 1950)

8 ALR5th 391—§ 3, 9

Standard Oil Co. of Cal. v. State Bd. of Equalization, 232 Cal. App. 2d 91, 42 Cal. Rptr. 543 (3d Dist. 1965)

107 ALR5th 311—§ 9

Standard Oil Co. of Louisiana v. Reddick, 202 Ark. 393, 150 S.W.2d 612 (1941)

20 ALR6th 211—§ 19, 32

Standard Packaging Corp. v. Commissioner of Revenue, 288 N.W.2d 234 (Minn. 1979)

89 ALR5th 493—§ 4

Standard Packaging Corp. v. Julian Goodrich Architects, Inc., 136 Vt. 376, 392 A.2d 402 (1978)

104 ALR6th 1—§ 16

Standard Premium Corp. v. Hirschorn, 50 Misc.2d 687, 290 N.Y.S.2d 276 (1968)

75 ALR5th 559—§ 7

Standard Premium Plan Corp. v. Hirschorn, 56 Misc. 2d 687, 290 N.Y.S.2d 226, 5 U.C.C. Rep. Serv. (CBC) 163 (City Civ. Ct. 1968)

71 ALR5th 443—§ 23

Standard Products Co., Inc. v. Wooldridge & Co., Ltd., 214 Va. 476, 201 S.E.2d 801 (1974)

39 ALR6th 155—§ 11

Standard Roller Bearing Co. v. Crucible Steel Co. of America, 71 N.J. Eq. 61, 63 A. 546 (Ch. 1906)

20 ALR6th 211—§ 18, 34

Standard Sav. Ass'n v. Greater New Canaan Missionary Baptist Church, Inc., 786 S.W.2d 774 (Tex. App. Houston 14th Dist. 1990)
73 ALR6th 571—§ 86

Standard Sewing Mach. Co. v. Leslie, 118 F. 557 (C.C.A. 7th Cir. 1902)
85 ALR6th 1—§ 22

Standard Structural Steel Co. v. Bethlehem Steel Corp., 597 F. Supp. 164, 40 U.C.C.R.S. 1245 (D.C. Conn. 1984)
30 ALR5th 170—§ 7, 19, 86, 88, 105

Standard Supply Co., Inc. v. Reliance Ins. Co., 49 N.C. App. 616, 272 S.E.2d 394 (1980)
8 ALR6th 549—§ 4

Standard Theatres, Inc. v. State, Dep't of Transp., Div. of Highways, 118 Wis. 2d 730, 349 N.W.2d 661 (1984)
10 ALR5th 448—§ 6

Standefer v. Standefer, 2001 OK 37, 26 P.3d 104 (Okla. 2001)
109 ALR5th 1—§ 8

Standiford v. Standiford, 89 Md. App. 326, 598 A.2d 495 (1991)
33 ALR5th 205—§ 5, 6

Standing Rock Sioux Tribe v. Janklow, 2000 DSD 10, 103 F. Supp. 2d 1146 (D.S.D. 2000)
1 ALR6th 1—§ 22

Standish v. American Mfrs. Mut. Ins. Co., 698 A.2d 599 (Pa. Super. Ct. 1997)
33 ALR5th 587—§ 5

Standish v. Department of Revenue, Motor Vehicle Div., 235 Kan. 900, 683 P.2d 1276 (1984)
28 ALR5th 459—§ 4, 5

Standish v. Sotavento Corp., 58 Conn. App. 789, 755 A.2d 910 (2000)
50 ALR5th 301—§ 5

Standish v. Unemployment Compensation Bd. of Review, 189 Pa. Super. 471, 151 A.2d 842 (1959)
95 ALR5th 329—§ 25

Standke v. B. E. Darby & Sons, Inc., 291 Minn. 468, 193 N.W.2d 139 (1971)
44 ALR5th 193—§ 18

Standlee v. St. Paul Fire & Marine Ins. Co., 107 Idaho 899, 693 P.2d 1101 (Ct. App. 1984)
60 ALR5th 239—§ 4, 9, 26, 27

Standley v. Johnson, 276 So. 2d 77 (Fla. App. D1 1973)
27 ALR5th 174—§ 3, 4, 37

Standley v. Town of Woodfin, 362 N.C. 328, 661 S.E.2d 728 (2008)
40 ALR6th 419—§ 7

Standley v. Town of Woodfin, 650 S.E.2d 618 (N.C. Ct. App. 2007)
40 ALR6th 419—§ 7

St. Andrew Associates, Application of, 57 Misc. 2d 1079, 294 N.Y.S.2d 188 (1968)
12 ALR5th 577—§ 2, 11

St. Andrews Park, Inc. v. U.S. Dept. of Army Corps of Engineers, 299 F. Supp. 2d 1264 (S.D. Fla. 2003)
26 ALR6th 287—§ 38

St. Andrews Public Service Dist. v. Charleston, 294 S.C. 92, 362 S.E.2d 877 (1987)
17 ALR5th 195—§ 41

St. Andrews Public Service Dist. Com'n v. Commissioners of Public Works of City of Charleston, 289 S.C. 68, 344 S.E.2d 857 (Ct. App. 1986)
44 ALR6th 259—§ 13

Standridge v. Alabama Power Co., 418 So. 2d 84 (Ala. 1982)
15 ALR5th 119—§ 5, 15, 32, 33, 51, 59, 85, 93

Standridge v. State, 37 Ark. App. 153, 826 S.W.2d 303 (1992)
66 ALR5th 373—§ 2, 4

St. Andrie v. St. Andrie, 473 So. 2d 140 (La. App. 3d Cir. 1985)
5 ALR5th 550—§ 16
20 ALR5th 700—§ 24

Standun, Inc. v. Fireman's Fund Ins. Co., 62 Cal. App. 4th 882, 73 Cal. Rptr. 2d 116 (2d Dist. 1998)
88 ALR5th 493—§ 3

89 ALR5th 1—§ 6

Stanek v. Lake County, 60 Ill. App. 3d 357, 17 Ill. Dec. 597, 376 N.E.2d 743 (2d Dist. 1978)
77 ALR6th 393—§ 58

Stanely v. State, 89 P.3d 662 (Kan. Ct. App. 2004)
19 ALR6th 411—§ 5

Stanfield v. Forrest Five to Five Dollar Stores, 95 Ga. App. 739, 99 S.E.2d 167 (1957)
40 ALR5th 135—§ 10

Stanfield v. F. W. Woolworth Co., 143 Kan. 117, 53 P.2d 878 (1936)
2 ALR5th 1—§ 57

Stanfield v. Hay, 849 S.W.2d 551 (Ky. Ct. App. 1992)
66 ALR5th 237—§ 3, 5, 6

Stanfield v. Laccoarce, 284 Or. 651, 588 P.2d 1271 (1978)
27 ALR5th 174—§ 63

Stanfield v. Stanfield, 435 S.W.2d 690 (Mo. Ct. App. 1968)
95 ALR5th 533—§ 5
124 ALR5th 203—§ 5

Stanfield v. State, 718 S.W.2d 734 (Tex. Crim. App. 1986)
108 ALR5th 593—§ 46

Stanfield v. W.C. McBride, Inc., 149 Kan. 567, 88 P.2d 1002 (1939)
20 ALR5th 229—§ 2

Stanfill, In re, 984 S.W.2d 925 (Tenn. Ct. App. 1998)
20 ALR5th 534—§ 14

Stanfill v. Real Estate Div., 35 Or. App. 549, 581 P.2d 980 (1978)
7 ALR5th 474—§ 81

Stanford v. Brooks, 298 S.W.2d 268 (Tex. Civ. App. Fort Worth 1957)
25 ALR5th 123—§ 10

Stanford v. Caesars Entertainment, Inc., 430 F. Supp. 2d 749, 80 U.S.P.Q.2d 1349 (W.D. Tenn. 2006)
76 ALR6th 289—§ 4
77 ALR6th 543—§ 18

Stanford v. Murphy, 63 Ga. 410, 1879 WL 2547 (1879)
23 ALR6th 1—§ 22

Stanford v. Parker, 266 F.3d 442, 2001 FED App. 0334P (6th Cir. 2001)
102 ALR6th 417—§ 6

Stanford v. Parker, 822 So. 2d 886 (Miss. 2002)
86 ALR6th 321—§ 5
87 ALR6th 197—§ 20

Stanford v. Parker, 949 S.W.2d 616 (Ky. Ct. App. 1996)
96 ALR6th 269—§ 24

Stanford v. Stanford, 567 So. 2d 371 (Ala. App. 1990)
49 ALR5th 441—§ 13

Stanford v. State, 272 Ga. 267, 528 S.E.2d 246 (2000)
71 ALR6th 625—§ 29

Stanford v. Sylvain, 2007 WL 1062080 (Tenn. Ct. App. 2007)
52 ALR6th 433—§ 2
57 ALR6th 163—§ 47

Stanford v. Tennessee Val. Authority, 18 F.R.D. 152 (M.D. Tenn. 1955)
49 ALR6th 205—§ 6

Stanford Ranch, Inc. v. Maryland Cas. Co., 89 F.3d 618 (9th Cir. 1996)
97 ALR5th 473—§ 19

Stang v. Com., Unemployment Compensation Bd. of Review, 52 Pa. Commw. 555, 415 A.2d 1288 (1980)
68 ALR5th 13—§ 2, 8, 39

Stanger, In re, 385 B.R. 758 (Bankr. D. Idaho 2008)
100 ALR6th 251—§ 3, 22

Stanger v. Epler, 382 Pa. 411, 115 A.2d 197 (1955)
44 ALR5th 1—§ 3, 21, 28

Stanger v. Smith & Nephew, Inc., 401 F. Supp. 2d 974 (E.D. Mo. 2005)
89 ALR6th 337—§ 7, 10, 11, 15, 16, 18

Stanger v. State, 545 N.E.2d 1105 (Ind. Ct. App. 1st Dist. 1989)
85 ALR5th 547—§ 6

Stangle's Welfare, In re, 311 Minn. 518, 247 N.W.2d 419 (1976)
12 ALR6th 417—§ 19

Stanhope, In re, 76 B.R. 165 (Bankr. D. Mont. 1987)
44 ALR6th 481—§ 8

Stanish v. Polish Roman Catholic Union, 484 F.2d 713 (CA7 Ind. 1973)
18 ALR5th 307—§ 30

Stanislaus, County of v. Assessment Appeals Bd., 213 Cal. App. 3d 1445, 262 Cal. Rptr. 439 (5th Dist. 1989)
90 ALR5th 547—§ 8

Staniszeski v. Walker, 550 So. 2d 19, 14 FLW 1742 (Fla. App. D2 1989)
11 ALR5th 127—§ 16

Stanko v. Cruz, 2008 WL 4849025 (D. Minn. 2008)
62 ALR6th 517—§ 54

Stanko v. Rios, 2009 WL 1303969 (D. Minn. 2009)
62 ALR6th 517—§ 54

Stankunas v. Stankunas, 133 N.H. 643, 582 A.2d 280 (1990)
55 ALR5th 647—§ 4

Stankus v. Anthem Cas. Ins. Group, 2001 WL 273183 (Conn. Super. Ct. 2001)
103 ALR5th 1—§ 5

Stan Lee Trading, Inc. v. Holtz, 649 F. Supp. 577, 22 Fed. R. Evid. Serv. 210 (C.D. Cal. 1986)
73 ALR6th 571—§ 69

Stanley, In re Marriage of, 411 N.W.2d 698 (Iowa App. 1987)
36 ALR5th 377—§ 4

Stanley v. American Fire & Casualty Co., 361 So. 2d 1030 (Ala. 1978)
35 ALR5th 375—§ 2, 3, 10, 70, 71, 74 to 76, 80, 83

Stanley v. Bouck, 107 Wis. 225, 83 N.W. 298 (1900)
27 ALR5th 764—§ 9

Stanley v. Central Garden and Pet Corp., 2012 WL 4127619 (D. Md. 2012)
84 ALR6th 1—§ 29, 52

Stanley v. City of Baytown, Texas, 2005 WL 2757370 (S.D. Tex. 2005)
45 ALR6th 1—§ 9

Stanley v. Cobb, 624 F. Supp. 536 (E.D. Tenn. 1986)
16 ALR6th 603—§ 3, 6

Stanley v. Georgia, 394 U.S. 557, 89 S. Ct. 1243, 22 L. Ed. 2d 542 (1969)
42 ALR5th 291—§ 2, 6, 12
94 ALR5th 497—§ 2

Stanley v. Greenfield, 207 Ga. 390, 61 S.E.2d 818, 21 A.L.R.2d 1256 (1950)
25 ALR5th 233—§ 19

Stanley v. Illinois, 405 U.S. 645, 31 L. Ed. 2d 551, 92 S. Ct. 1208 (1972)
61 ALR5th 151—§ 2, 3

Stanley v. Illinois, 405 U.S. 645, 92 S. Ct. 1208, 31 L. Ed. 2d 551 (1972)
28 ALR6th 349—§ 2

Stanley v. John H. Rion & Associates, 2001 WL 1103326 (Ohio Ct. App. 2d Dist. Greene County 2001)
13 ALR6th 1—§ 4
14 ALR6th 1—§ 4

Stanley v. Kawakami, 127 Cal. App. 2d 277, 273 P.2d 709 (1st Dist. 1954)
97 ALR6th 375—§ 19

Stanley v. Lockhart, 941 F.2d 707 (8th Cir. 1991)
70 ALR5th 1—§ 6

Stanley v. Mast, 1988 WL 112858 (Ohio Ct. App. 8th Dist. Cuyahoga County 1988)
5 ALR6th 133—§ 8

Stanley v. McCarver, 208 Ariz. 219, 92 P.3d 849 (2004)
94 ALR6th 431—§ 11

Stanley v. McDaniel, 128 Idaho 343, 913 P.2d 76, 3 BNA WH Cas. 2d 422 (App. 1996)
23 ALR5th 241—§ 41

Stanley v. Motor Vehicle Acc. Indemnification Corp., 20 A.D.2d 877, 248 N.Y.S.2d 630 (1st Dep't 1964)
103 ALR5th 1—§ 5, 8

Stanley v. Mueller, 222 Or. 194, 350 P.2d 880 (1960)
18 ALR5th 230—§ 11

Stanley v. Planning & Zoning Com'n of City of New London, 4 Conn. L. Rptr. 491, 1991 WL 172828 (Conn. Super. Ct. 1991)

4 ALR6th 263—§ 15

Stanley v. Planning & Zoning Com'n of Trumbull, 1997 WL 381573 (Conn. Super. Ct. 1997)

73 ALR5th 223—§ 3, 5, 11

Stanley v. Richmond, 35 Cal. App. 4th 1070, 41 Cal. Rptr. 2d 768, 95 C.D.O.S. 4598, 95 Daily Journal DAR 8016 (1st Dist. 1995)

50 ALR5th 301—§ 3

Stanley v. Schiavi Mobile Homes, Inc., 462 A.2d 1144, CCH Prod. Liab. Rep. ¶ 9694 (Me. 1983)

61 ALR5th 473—§ 9

Stanley v. Schriro, 2006 WL 2816541 (D. Ariz. 2006)

32 ALR6th 1—§ 9

Stanley v. Schumpert, 117 La. 255, 41 So. 565 (1906)

30 ALR5th 571—§ 57

Stanley v. Secretary of Health, Ed. and Welfare, 356 F. Supp. 793 (W.D. Mo. 1973)

122 ALR5th 205—§ 3, 10, 38

Stanley v. South Carolina State Highway Dept., 249 S.C. 230, 153 S.E.2d 687 (1967)

50 ALR6th 95—§ 9

Stanley v. Stanley, 112 Ind. 143, 13 N.E. 261 (1887)

23 ALR6th 1—§ 10, 19

Stanley v. Stanley, 251 S.W.2d 365 (Mo. App. 1952)

12 ALR5th 195—§ 10

Stanley v. State, 97 Ga. App. 828, 104 S.E.2d 591 (1958)

29 ALR5th 59—§ 56

Stanley v. State, 313 Md. 50, 542 A.2d 1267 (1988)

47 ALR5th 259—§ 2

Stanley v. State, 324 Ark. 310, 920 S.W.2d 835 (1996)

99 ALR6th 295—§ 16

Stanley v. State, 501 So. 2d 90 (Fla. Dist. Ct. App. 1st Dist. 1987)

13 ALR6th 603—§ 12

Stanley v. State, 587 So. 2d 1258 (Ala. Crim. App. 1991)

21 ALR6th 771—§ 5

Stanley v. State, 2001 WL 1092814 (Ark. Ct. App. 2001)

68 ALR6th 527—§ 38

Stanley v. State, Dep't of Human Resources, 567 So. 2d 310 (Ala. Civ. App. 1990)

40 ALR5th 227—§ 31
78 ALR5th 465—§ 2
80 ALR5th 117—§ 4

Stanley v. Stuart, 89 Fed. Appx. 481 (5th Cir. 2004)

89 ALR6th 1—§ 54

Stanley v. Sullivan, 71 Wis. 585, 37 N.W. 801 (1888)

52 ALR5th 221—§ 13

Stanley v. Superior Court, 206 Cal. App. 4th 265, 141 Cal. Rptr. 3d 675, 103 A.L.R.6th 689 (2d Dist. 2012)

103 ALR6th 137—§ 2, 7, 41

Stanley v. Trinchard, 500 F.3d 411, 48 Bankr. Ct. Dec. (CRR) 266 (5th Cir. 2007)

64 ALR6th 473—§ 20

Stanley v. U. S., 239 F. Supp. 973 (N.D. Ohio 1965)

64 ALR5th 235—§ 3, 5, 17

Stanley v. Whiteville Lumber Co., 184 N.C. 302, 114 S.E. 385 (1922)

24 ALR6th 747—§ 8, 12, 14

Stanley v. Winn Correctional Center, 2010 WL 2710391 (W.D. La. 2010)

89 ALR6th 1—§ 118

Stanley v. Wyeth, Inc., 991 So. 2d 31, Prod. Liab. Rep. (CCH) ¶ 18025 (La. Ct. App. 1st Cir. 2008)

56 ALR6th 161—§ 5

Stanley Children, In re, 1990 WL 160374 (Ohio Ct. App. 12th Dist. Butler County 1990)

9 ALR6th 437—§ 4, 5, 9, 14

Stanley F. v. Marlene F., 144 Misc. 2d 235, 544 N.Y.S.2d 291 (Fam. Ct. 1989)

20 ALR5th 700—§ 8, 9, 40, 55
21 ALR5th 396—§ 3, 8, 18, 22, 31
80 ALR5th 117—§ 30

Stanley Industries, Inc. v. W.M. Barr & Co., 784 F. Supp. 1570, 6 FLW Fed D 17 (S.D. Fla. 1992)

27 ALR5th 697—§ 2, 4, 13

Stanley L. and Carolyn M. Watkins Trust v. Lacosta, 2004 MT 144, 321 Mont. 432, 92 P.3d 620 (2004)

15 ALR6th 427—§ 12, 13

Stanley L. Wiles, In re, 107 S.W.3d 228 (Mo. 2003)

44 ALR6th 75—§ 3

Stanley, State ex rel. v. Davis, 569 S.W.2d 202 (Mo. Ct. App. 1978)

72 ALR6th 141—§ 5

Stanley Steamer Int'l Inc. v. Frazier, 1984 WL 4279 (Ohio Ct. App. Pickaway Cnty 1984)

52 ALR5th 613—§ 3

Stanley Stores v. Chavana, 909 S.W.2d 554 (Tex. App. Corpus Christi 1995)

51 ALR5th 1—§ 7

Stanley Works v. Globemaster, Inc., 400 F. Supp. 1325, 187 U.S.P.Q. 80 (D. Mass. 1975)

85 ALR6th 1—§ 62

Stanley Works v. Hackett, 122 Conn. 547, 190 A. 743 (1937)

17 ALR6th 623—§ 2

Stanley Works v. New Britain Redevelopment Agency, 155 Conn. 86, 230 A.2d 9 (1967)

66 ALR6th 83—§ 18

St. Ann v. American Ins. Cos., 206 So. 2d 817 (La. App. 4th Cir. 1968)

27 ALR5th 174—§ 76

St. Ann v. Palisi, 495 F.2d 423 (5th Cir. 1974)

90 ALR6th 235—§ 61

Stannard v. Wilcox & Gibbs Sewing Mach. Co., 118 Md. 151, 84 A. 335 (1912)

52 ALR6th 271—§ 13

Stannik v. Bellingham-Whatcom County Dist. Bd. of Health, 48 Wash. App. 160, 737 P.2d 1054 (1987)

24 ALR5th 200—§ 24, 31, 41

Stano v. Butterworth, 51 F.3d 942 (11th Cir. 1995)

82 ALR5th 591—§ 8

Stano v. Dugger, 883 F.2d 900 (11th Cir. 1989)

82 ALR5th 591—§ 8

Stano v. Dugger, 901 F.2d 898 (11th Cir. 1990)

82 ALR5th 591—§ 8

Stano v. State, 520 So. 2d 278 (Fla. 1988)

72 ALR5th 109—§ 7

Stanolind Pipe Line Co. v. Jenkins, 194 Okla. 334, 151 P.2d 422 (1944)

7 ALR5th 187—§ 7

Stansberry v. McDowell, 186 S.W. 757 (Mo. Ct. App. 1916)

81 ALR6th 161—§ 4
82 ALR6th 43—§ 1, 6

Stansberry v. Stansberry, 580 P.2d 147 (Okla. 1978)

4 ALR5th 403—§ 3
49 ALR5th 441—§ 19

Stansbury v. Hover, 366 So. 2d 918 (La. App. 1st Cir. 1978)

34 ALR5th 77—§ 4, 7

Stansbury v. Stansbury, 1999 WL 668742 (Ohio Ct. App. 5th Dist. Licking County 1999)

18 ALR6th 97—§ 3, 6, 33

Stansel v. Rahman, 2000 WL 210444 (Tex. App. Houston 1st Dist. 2000)

98 ALR6th 1—§ 31, 55

Stansell v. American Radiator Co., 163 Mich. 528, 128 N.W. 789 (1910)

7 ALR5th 187—§ 17

Stansell v. Roach, 147 Tenn. 183, 246 S.W. 520, 29 A.L.R. 143 (1923)

35 ALR6th 1—§ 27, 29

Stansfield v. Dunne, 16 Ariz. 153, 141 P. 736 (1914)

3 ALR5th 237—§ 4, 15

Stanske v. Wazee Elec. Co., 690 P.2d 1291 (Colo. Ct. App. 1984)
122 ALR5th 1—§ 15

Stanske v. Wazee Elec. Co., 722 P.2d 402 (Colo. 1986)
122 ALR5th 1—§ 2, 15, 27

Stan's Lumber, Inc. v. Fleming, 196 Wis. 2d 554, 538 N.W.2d 849, 28 U.C.C. Rep. Serv. 2d 801 (Ct. App. 1995)
118 ALR5th 91—§ 2, 25

Stant v. Lamberson, 103 Ind. App. 411, 8 N.E.2d 115 (1937)
55 ALR5th 557—§ 6

St. Anthony Medical Center, Inc. v. Smith, 592 N.E.2d 732 (Ind. App. 1992)
26 ALR5th 245—§ 2, 17, 28

St. Anthony's Hosp., Inc. v. Lewis, 652 So. 2d 386 (Fla. Dist. Ct. App. 2d Dist. 1995)
98 ALR5th 533—§ 22, 23

St. Anthony's Medical Center v. Metze, 23 S.W.3d 692 (Mo. Ct. App. E.D. 2000)
16 ALR5th 262—§ 4

Stanton, Ex parte, 545 So. 2d 58 (Ala. 1989)
79 ALR5th 201—§ 2 to 4

Stanton v. Abbey, 874 S.W.2d 493 (Mo. Ct. App. E.D. 1994)
57 ALR5th 389—§ 2
76 ALR5th 191—§ 4

Stanton v. Arizona Life Coalition, 129 S. Ct. 56, 172 L. Ed. 2d 24 (2008)
46 ALR6th 495—§ 10

Stanton v. Carlson Sales, Inc., 45 Conn. Supp. 531, 728 A.2d 534 (Super Ct. 1998)
9 ALR5th 1—§ 3

Stanton v. Continental Casualty Co., 197 Cal. App. 3d 821, 243 Cal. Rptr. 147 (2d Dist. 1988)
6 ALR5th 297—§ 25

Stanton v. Federal Nat. Mortg. Ass'n, 2010 WL 707346 (W.D. Mich. 2010)
86 ALR6th 411—§ 5

Stanton v. Gibbins, 103 Mo. App. 264, 77 S.W. 95 (1903)
36 ALR6th 387—§ 6

Stanton v. Graham, 2008 WL 4443283 (W.D. Wis. 2008)
75 ALR6th 181—§ 6

Stanton v. Gulf Oil Corp., 232 S.C. 148, 101 S.E.2d 250 (1957)
119 ALR5th 519—§ 11

Stanton v. Johnson, 127 Ill. App. 2d 114, 262 N.E.2d 162 (1st Dist. 1970)
40 ALR6th 99—§ 70

Stanton v. Larry Fowler Trucking, 863 F. Supp. 908 (E.D. Ark. 1994)
23 ALR5th 241—§ 37

Stanton v. Lloyd Hammond Produce Farms, 400 Mich. 135, 253 N.W.2d 114 (1977)
40 ALR6th 99—§ 11

Stanton v. Manhattan East Suite Hotels, 2002 WL 31641127 (S.D. N.Y. 2002)
63 ALR6th 495—§ 66

Stanton v. Mattson, 175 Neb. 767, 123 N.W.2d 844 (1963)
73 ALR6th 571—§ 14, 15, 47

Stanton v. Nat. Fuel Gas Co., 1 Pa. D. & C.4th 223, 4 U.C.C. Rep. Serv. 2d 378 (C.P. 1987)
97 ALR6th 1—§ 2, 5, 24

Stanton v. National R.R. Passenger Corp., 849 F. Supp. 1524 (M.D. Ala. 1994)
121 ALR5th 157—§ 3

Stanton v. Nationwide Mut. Ins. Co., 68 Ohio St. 3d 111, 623 N.E.2d 1197 (1993)
57 ALR5th 591—§ 4

Stanton v. Panish, 28 Cal. 3d 107, 167 Cal. Rptr. 584, 615 P.2d 1372 (1980)
106 ALR5th 523—§ 23

Stanton v. Republic Bank of South Chicago, 144 Ill. 2d 472, 163 Ill. Dec. 524, 581 N.E.2d 678 (1991)
13 ALR5th 840—§ 6
16 ALR6th 693—§ 17

Stanton v. Sims, 134 S. Ct. 3, 187 L. Ed.
2d 341 (2013)
96 ALR6th 577—§ 11
Stanton v. Stanton, 30 Utah 2d 315, 517
P.2d 1010 (1974)
112 ALR5th 185—§ 4, 6, 10
Stanton v. Stanton, 213 Ga. 545, 100
S.E.2d 289, 66 A.L.R.2d 1401
(1957)
55 ALR5th 647—§ 4
95 ALR5th 533—§ 5
124 ALR5th 203—§ 5, 13
Stanton v. Stanton, 631 So. 2d 242 (Ala.
Civ. App. 1993)
21 ALR6th 577—§ 12
Stanton v. State, 70 Tex. Crim. 519, 158
S.W. 994 (1913)
24 ALR5th 465—§ 32, 41
Stanton v. State, 88 Tex. Crim. 465, 227
S.W. 1104 (1921)
105 ALR5th 529—§ 11
Stanton v. State, 344 Ark. 589, 42
S.W.3d 474 (2001)
23 ALR6th 307—§ 40
Stanton v. State, 648 So. 2d 638 (Ala.
Crim. App. 1994)
37 ALR5th 515—§ 2, 3
110 ALR5th 329—§ 5, 6
Stanton v. State, 686 P.2d 587 (Wyo.
1984)
68 ALR6th 1—§ 5
Stanton v. State, 747 S.W.2d 914 (Tex.
App. Dallas 1988)
38 ALR6th 97—§ 7
Stanton v. State, 953 S.W.2d 832 (Tex.
App. Amarillo 1997)
109 ALR5th 611—§ 4
Stanton v. Westbrook, 598 S.W.2d 331
(Tex. Civ. App. Houston 14th Dist.
1980)
92 ALR6th 379—§ 7
Stanton, City of v. Cox, 207 Cal. App.
3d 1557, 255 Cal. Rptr. 682 (4th
Dist. 1989)
10 ALR5th 538—§ 2, 8
Stanush v. Aetna Life Ins. Co., 538
S.W.2d 648 (Tex. Civ. App. San
Antonio 1976)

23 ALR5th 241—§ 15
Stanziale v. Skiba, 2008 WL 4150302
(Conn. Super. Ct. 2008)
49 ALR6th 1—§ 58, 60
Stanzione v. Pascevich, 431 N.E.2d 847
(Ind. App. 1982)
14 ALR5th 242—§ 38
Staph v. Sheldon, 2009-Ohio-122, 2009
WL 94545 (Ohio Ct. App. 8th Dist.
Cuyahoga County 2009)
47 ALR6th 303—§ 4
Stapleford v. Houghton, 185 Ariz. 560,
917 P.2d 703 (1996)
91 ALR5th 343—§ 12
Staples, Re, 259 Or. 406, 486 P.2d 1281
(1971)
9 ALR5th 193—§ 5, 8, 28, 30, 33, 36
Staples v. A. P. Green Fire Brick Co.,
307 S.W.2d 457 (Mo. 1957)
100 ALR5th 567—§ 5
Staples v. Bangor Hydro-Electric Co.,
561 A.2d 499, 4 I.E.R. Cas. (BNA)
918 (Me. 1989)
38 ALR6th 541—§ 9
Staples v. Bangor Hydro-Electric Co.,
629 A.2d 601, 8 I.E.R. Cas. (BNA)
1153 (Me. 1993)
38 ALR6th 541—§ 9
52 ALR6th 271—§ 18
Staples v. Bernabucci, 119 Conn. 443,
177 A. 380 (1935)
10 ALR5th 371—§ 3, 11
Staples v. CBL & Associates, Inc., 15
S.W.3d 83 (Tenn. 2000)
31 ALR5th 550—§ 4, 10
Staples v. City of Milwaukee, 142 F.3d
383, 13 I.E.R. Cas. (BNA) 1527
(7th Cir. 1998)
32 ALR6th 457—§ 13
Staples v. City of Somerville, 176 Mass.
237, 57 N.E. 380 (1900)
81 ALR6th 363—§ 22
Staples v. Henderson Jersey Farms, 181
So. 48 (La. Ct. App. 2d Cir. 1938)
40 ALR6th 99—§ 31
Staples v. Langley, 148 Colo. 498, 366
P.2d 861 (1961)
5 ALR5th 875—§ 48

Staples v. Washington, 125 A.2d 322
(Mun. Ct. App. D.C. 1956)
11 ALR6th 695—§ 11, 27

Stapleton, Application of, 257 A.D.
1072, 14 N.Y.S.2d 552 (2d Dep't
1939)
14 ALR6th 543—§ 22

Stapleton, Re, 243 Kan. 146, 753 P.2d
1278 (1988)
9 ALR5th 193—§ 16

Stapleton v. Clerk for City of Inkster,
311 F. Supp. 1187 (E.D. Mich.
1970)
121 ALR5th 1—§ 46

Stapleton v. First Sec. Bank, 219 Mont.
323, 711 P.2d 1364, 42 U.C.C. Rep.
Serv. 493 (1985)
91 ALR5th 89—§ 6

Stapleton v. Gunn, 69 S.W.2d 1104 (Mo.
Ct. App. 1934)
63 ALR6th 187—§ 27

Stapleton v. Nyhan, 3 Mass. L. Rptr.
423, 1995 WL 809921 (Mass.
Super. Ct. 1995)
116 ALR5th 1—§ 63, 64, 67

Stapleton v. Stapleton, 118 Wis. 2d 819,
346 N.W.2d 469 (Ct. App. 1984)
7 ALR6th 411—§ 3, 9, 31
86 ALR6th 321—§ 4
90 ALR6th 451—§ 39

Stapleton v. State, 790 So. 2d 897 (Miss.
Ct. App. 2001)
99 ALR6th 295—§ 9

Stapley v. Stapley, 15 Ariz. App. 64, 485
P.2d 1181 (Div. 1 1971)
124 ALR5th 203—§ 8, 9

Starace v. Inner Circle Qonexions, 198
App. Div. 2d 493, 604 N.Y.S.2d
179 (2d Dep't 1993)
50 ALR5th 1—§ 10

Star Bank, N.A. v. Laker, 637 N.E.2d
805 (Ind. 1994)
14 ALR5th 242—§ 21, 22

Starbird v. County of San Benito, 122
Cal. App. 3d 657, 176 Cal. Rptr.
149 (1st Dist. 1981)
106 ALR5th 523—§ 35

Star Broadcasting, Inc. v. Reed Smith,
LLP, 2010 WL 1474359 (4th Cir.
2010)
60 ALR6th 1—§ 22

Star Broadcasting Inc. v. Reed Smith
Ltd. Liability Partnership, 2009 WL
482833 (E.D. Va. 2009)
58 ALR6th 1—§ 5

Starbucks Employee Gratuity Litigation,
In re, 264 F.R.D. 67 (S.D. N.Y.
2009)
61 ALR6th 61—§ 21

Starcher v. Wingard, 16 Fed. Appx. 383
(6th Cir. 2001)
31 ALR6th 49—§ 10

Starck v. Foley, 209 Ky. 332, 272 S.W.
890, 41 A.L.R. 756 (1925)
25 ALR5th 233—§ 3

Starczewski v. Mulvey, 2000 WL
33170921 (Mass. Super. Ct. 2000)
58 ALR6th 1—§ 5
60 ALR6th 1—§ 70

Staren & Co. v. Shapiro, 3 Ill. App. 3d
417, 279 N.E.2d 470 (1st Dist.
1972)
91 ALR5th 485—§ 5

Starfish Condominium Ass'n v.
Yorkridge Service Corp., Inc., 295
Md. 693, 458 A.2d 805 (1983)
101 ALR5th 447—§ 3, 11

Starfish Condominium Asso. v.
Yorkridge Service Corp., 295 Md.
693, 458 A.2d 805 (1983)
8 ALR5th 312—§ 11

Star Fuel Marts, LLC v. Sam's East,
Inc., 362 F.3d 639, 2004-1 Trade
Cas. (CCH) ¶ 74338 (10th Cir.
2004)
26 ALR6th 249—§ 2, 12

Stargate Software Intern., Inc. v. Rumph,
224 Ga. App. 873, 482 S.E.2d 498,
R.I.C.O. Bus. Disp. Guide (CCH)
¶ 9239 (1997)
87 ALR6th 1—§ 88

Stariha, In re Marriage of, 509 N.E.2d
1117 (Ind. App. 1987)
32 ALR5th 31—§ 3

Starinieri v. Unemployment Compensation Bd. of Review, 447 Pa. 256, 289 A.2d 726 (1972)
23 ALR5th 176—§ 2, 4, 5, 14

Stark v. Advanced Magnetics, Inc., 50 Mass. App. Ct. 226, 736 N.E.2d 434 (2000)
85 ALR6th 1—§ 3, 59

Stark v. Allis-Chalmers & Northwest Roads, Inc., 2 Wash. App. 399, 467 P.2d 854 (Div. 1 1970)
10 ALR5th 371—§ 3, 5, 11
64 ALR5th 119—§ 4

Stark v. Anderson, 748 So. 2d 838 (Miss. Ct. App. 1999)
70 ALR5th 377—§ 4

Stark v. Chock Full O'Nuts, 77 Misc. 2d 553, 356 N.Y.S.2d 403, 14 U.C.C.R.S. 51 (1974)
2 ALR5th 189—§ 2, 4, 9, 10

Stark v. Com., Unemployment Compensation Bd. of Review, 48 Pa. Commw. 422, 409 A.2d 968 (1980)
95 ALR5th 329—§ 3

Stark v. Hoff Lithograph Co., 79 A.D.2d 780, 434 N.Y.S.2d 826 (3d Dep't 1980)
15 ALR6th 633—§ 6, 16, 24, 33

Stark v. Mercantile Bank, N.A., 29 Kan. App. 2d 717, 33 P.3d 609 (2000)
98 ALR6th 417—§ 4, 12

Stark v. National Research & Design Corp., 33 N.J. Super. 315, 110 A.2d 143 (App. Div. 1954)
75 ALR5th 1—§ 12, 15

Stark v. Robar, 339 Mich. 145, 63 N.W.2d 606 (1954)
25 ALR5th 123—§ 3
119 ALR5th 519—§ 15, 28

Stark v. State, 316 So. 2d 586 (Fla. Dist. Ct. App. 4th Dist. 1975)
107 ALR5th 567—§ 10

Stark v. State, 489 N.E.2d 43 (Ind. 1986)
116 ALR5th 373—§ 3, 6

Stark v. State Indus. Acc. Commission, 103 Or. 80, 204 P. 151 (1922)
41 ALR6th 207—§ 27

Stark v. Visa U.S.A. Inc., 2004-2 Trade Cas. (CCH) ¶ 74555, 2004 WL 1879003 (Mich. Cir. Ct. 2004)
35 ALR6th 245—§ 6, 16

Stark Co. v. National Guardian Sec. Services, 1990 WL 112110 (E.D. Pa. 1990)
36 ALR6th 305—§ 14, 15

Stark County v. Ferguson, 2 Ohio App. 3d 72, 440 N.E.2d 816 (5th Dist. Stark County 1981)
9 ALR6th 177—§ 48

Stark County Agr. Soc. v. Brenner, 122 Ohio St. 560, 8 Ohio L. Abs. 385, 172 N.E. 659 (1930)
21 ALR6th 81—§ 45

Stark Cty. Bar Assn. v. Hare, 99 Ohio St. 3d 310, 2003-Ohio-3651, 791 N.E.2d 966 (2003)
26 ALR6th 1—§ 25

Stark Cty. Bar Assn. v. Watterson, 103 Ohio St. 3d 322, 2004-Ohio-4776, 815 N.E.2d 386 (2004)
25 ALR6th 1—§ 31

Starke v. Pewaukee, 85 Wis. 2d 272, 270 N.W.2d 219 (1978)
51 ALR5th 747—§ 3, 4

Starke v. Town of Smithtown, 155 A.D.2d 526, 547 N.Y.S.2d 383 (2d Dep't 1989)
82 ALR6th 417—§ 4, 15

Starke v. Village of Pewaukee, 85 Wis. 2d 272, 270 N.W.2d 219 (1978)
86 ALR6th 321—§ 4

Starkenstein v. Merrill Lynch Pierce Fenner & Smith, Inc., 572 F. Supp. 189, CCH Fed Secur L. Rep. ¶ 99519 (M.D. Fla. 1983)
14 ALR5th 242—§ 2, 4, 24

Starkenstein v. Merrill Lynch Pierce Fenner & Smith Inc., 572 F. Supp. 189, Fed. Sec. L. Rep. (CCH) ¶ 99519 (M.D. Fla. 1983)
46 ALR6th 185—§ 9

Starkes v. U. S., 427 A.2d 437 (D.C. App.1981)
81 ALR5th 563—§ 3, 7 to 9

Starkey v. Dameron, 92 Colo. 420, 21 P.2d 1112 (1933)
12 ALR5th 195—§ 31

Starkey v. Unemployment Ins. Appeal Bd., 340 A.2d 165 (Del. Super. Ct. 1975)
95 ALR5th 329—§ 16

Starkey v. Wyrick, 555 F.2d 1352 (8th Cir. 1977)
28 ALR6th 505—§ 9

Starkey, Kelly, Blaney & White v. Estate of Nicolaysen, 172 N.J. 60, 796 A.2d 238 (2002)
49 ALR6th 505—§ 28

Starkins v. Bateman, 150 Ariz. 537, 724 P.2d 1206 (App. 1986)
12 ALR5th 195—§ 3, 49

Star-Kist Foods, Inc. v. U.S., 8 Ct. Int'l Trade 305, 600 F. Supp. 212, 6 Int'l Trade Rep. (BNA) 1584 (1984)
23 ALR6th 521—§ 24

Stark Liquidation Co. v. Florists' Mut. Ins. Co., 243 S.W.3d 385, 49 A.L.R.6th 741 (Mo. Ct. App. E.D. 2007)
49 ALR6th 169—§ 7, 8

Starks v. Commercial Union Ins. Co., 501 So. 2d 1214 (Ala. 1987)
13 ALR5th 289—§ 6, 18

Starks v. Director of Div. of Employment Sec., 391 Mass. 640, 462 N.E.2d 1360 (1984)
95 ALR5th 329—§ 12

Starks v. Easterling, 2014 WL 4347593 (M.D. Tenn. 2014)
102 ALR6th 637—§ 11

Starks v. State, 74 Ark. App. 366, 49 S.W.3d 122 (2001)
58 ALR6th 499—§ 22, 100, 109

Starks v. State, 283 Ga. 164, 656 S.E.2d 518 (2008)
42 ALR6th 237—§ 3

Stark Street Properties, Inc. v. Teufel, 277 Or. 649, 562 P.2d 531 (1977)
51 ALR5th 603—§ 2

Starkville v. Harrison, 418 So. 2d 51 (Miss. 1982)
46 ALR5th 423—§ 3, 16

Starkville, City of v. 4-County Elec. Power Ass'n, 819 So. 2d 1216 (Miss. 2002)
104 ALR6th 303—§ 18

Starkweather v. Patel, 34 Conn. App. 395, 641 A.2d 809 (1994)
14 ALR6th 301—§ 11, 28

Starkweather v. Shaffer, 262 Or. 198, 497 P.2d 358 (1972)
46 ALR6th 185—§ 7

Starlets Intern., Inc. v. Christensen, 106 Nev. 732, 801 P.2d 1343, 15 A.L.R.5th 1118 (1990)
20 ALR6th 161—§ 3
21 ALR6th 425—§ 7
23 ALR6th 573—§ 19

Starlets Int'l, Inc. v. Christensen, 106 Nev. 732, 801 P.2d 1343, 15 A.L.R.5th 1118 (1990)
15 ALR5th 900—§ 2, 3, 7, 8

Starlight Intern. Inc. v. Herlihy, 186 F.R.D. 626 (D. Kan. 1999)
70 ALR6th 209—§ 53

Starling v. Davis, 121 Ga. App. 428, 174 S.E.2d 214 (1970)
68 ALR5th 599—§ 2

Starling v. Jephunneh Lawrence & Associates, 495 A.2d 1157 (D.C. 1985)
86 ALR6th 321—§ 6, 10, 12, 13
89 ALR6th 409—§ 93

Starling v. Seaboard Coast Line R. Co., 533 F. Supp. 183 (S.D. Ga. 1982)
63 ALR5th 195—§ 4

Starling v. State, 301 Ark. 603, 786 S.W.2d 114 (1990)
24 ALR5th 465—§ 15, 16, 19, 33, 34, 37

Star Markets, Ltd. v. Texaco, Inc., 945 F. Supp. 1344 (D. Haw. 1996)
117 ALR5th 155—§ 12

St. Arnaud v. Chapdelaine Truck Center, Inc., 836 F. Supp. 41 (D. Mass. 1993)
82 ALR5th 149—§ 2

Starnes, Ex parte, 993 S.W.2d 685 (Tex. App. Houston 14th Dist. 1999)
89 ALR5th 629—§ 3, 7, 9 to 11

Starnes v. First American Nat. Bank, 723 S.W.2d 113 (Tenn. App. 1986)
18 ALR5th 307—§ 2

Starnes v. General Electric Co., 201 F. Supp. 2d 549 (M.D. N.C. 2002)
10 ALR6th 375—§ 7

Starnes v. Williams, 232 F.3d 902 (10th Cir. 2000)
119 ALR5th 1—§ 3

Starns v. Starns, 176 La. 610, 146 So. 165 (1933)
101 ALR6th 455—§ 11

Starns v. U.S., 923 F.2d 34 (CA4 Va. 1991)
26 ALR5th 245—§ 30, 35

Star of Detroit Line, Inc. v. Comerica Bank, 1999 WL 33454888 (Mich. Ct. App. 1999)
2 ALR6th 279—§ 5

Staropoli, In re, 185 N.J. 401, 886 A.2d 1055 (2005)
43 ALR6th 163—§ 68
44 ALR6th 75—§ 27

Star Pub. Co. v. Jackson, 115 Ind. App. 221, 58 N.E.2d 202 (1944)
113 ALR5th 115—§ 1, 6, 49, 58

Star Pub. Co. v. Martin, 47 Del. 585, 95 A.2d 465 (1953)
91 ALR5th 485—§ 6

Starr, In re, 101 B.R. 274 (Bankr. E.D. Okla. 1988)
99 ALR6th 481—§ 42

Starr, In re, 123 B.R. 314 (Bankr. S.D. Ill. 1991)
99 ALR6th 481—§ 14, 31

Starr v. Allegheny General Hospital, 305 Pa. Super. 215, 451 A.2d 499 (1982)
35 ALR5th 145—§ 16

Starr v. Beckley Newspapers Corp., 157 W. Va. 447, 201 S.E.2d 911 (1974)
44 ALR5th 193—§ 21

Starr v. Campos, 134 Ariz. 254, 655 P.2d 794 (App. 1982)
33 ALR5th 303—§ 2, 7, 26

Starr v. Commonwealth Unemployment Compensation Board of Review, 10 Pa. Cmwlth. 265, 309 A.2d 837 (1973)

23 ALR5th 176—§ 24

Starr v. Corley, 662 F. Supp. 219 (N.D. Ohio 1987)
110 ALR5th 371—§ 2

Starr v. Fregosi, 370 F.2d 15 (CA5 Ga. 1966)
48 ALR5th 575—§ 3

Starr v. Gorman, 136 N.J. Eq. 105, 40 A.2d 564 (Ct. Err. & App. 1945)
69 ALR5th 1—§ 4

Starr v. Koppers Co., 398 S.W.2d 827 (Tex. Civ. App. San Antonio 1965)
69 ALR5th 137—§ 9

Starr v. Liftchild, 40 Barb. 541 (NY, Sup. Ct. 1863)
47 ALR5th 1—§ 29

Starr v. Mooslin, 14 Cal. App. 3d 988, 92 Cal. Rptr. 583 (2d Dist. 1971)
58 ALR6th 1—§ 4

Starr v. Pearle Vision, Inc., 54 F.3d 1548, 32 Fed. R. Serv. 3d 816 (10th Cir. 1995)
21 ALR6th 671—§ 5, 6
38 ALR6th 541—§ 9

Starr v. State, 297 Ark. 26, 759 S.W.2d 535 (1988)
20 ALR5th 177—§ 7

Starr v. State, 564 S.W.2d 335 (Mo. App. 1978)
59 ALR5th 1—§ 5, 6

Starr v. State Bd. of Medicine, 720 A.2d 183 (Pa. Commw. Ct. 1998)
65 ALR6th 295—§ 19

Starr v. Stiles, 2 Ariz. 436, 19 P. 225 (1888)
6 ALR5th 883—§ 26

Starr v. Thompson, 96 N.C. App. 369, 385 S.E.2d 535 (1989)
83 ALR5th 651—§ 2, 5

Starr v. Washington State Dept. of Employment Sec., 130 Wash. App. 541, 123 P.3d 513 (Div. 2 2005)
25 ALR6th 101—§ 15

Starr Elec. Co., Inc. v. Basic Const. Co., 586 F. Supp. 964 (M.D. N.C. 1982)
100 ALR5th 481—§ 10

Starrels v. First Nat. Bank of Chicago, 870 F.2d 1168, Fed. Sec. L. Rep. (CCH) ¶ 94354 (7th Cir. 1989)
43 ALR6th 1—§ 45, 47

Starrett v. Connolly, 150 A.D. 859, 135 N.Y.S. 325 (2d Dep't 1912)
102 ALR5th 525—§ 22

Starrett v. Iberia Airlines of Spain, 756 F. Supp. 292, 53 Fair Empl. Prac. Cas. (BNA) 1776 (S.D. Tex. 1989)
96 ALR5th 107—§ 8

Starrett v. Pier Foundry, 488 N.W.2d 273 (Minn. 1992)
4 ALR5th 443—§ 3, 10

Starrett v. Shepard, 606 P.2d 1247 (Wyo. 1980)
8 ALR5th 653—§ 3

Starrett v. Starrett, 703 S.W.2d 544 (Mo. Ct. App. E.D. 1985)
59 ALR6th 433—§ 33

Starrett City, Inc. v. Jace, 137 Misc. 2d 328, 524 N.Y.S.2d 130 (App. Term 1987)
114 ALR5th 443—§ 14

Starrett Corp., In re, 92 F.2d 375 (C.C.A. 3d Cir. 1937)
32 ALR6th 531—§ 11

Starr Fireworks v. West Adams County Fire Dep't, 903 P.2d 1202 (Colo. App. 1995)
48 ALR5th 659—§ 3

Starr Street in Borough of Queens, In re, 73 Misc. 380, 131 N.Y.S. 71 (Sup 1911)
109 ALR5th 421—§ 3, 12

Star Safety, Inc., In re, 39 B.R. 755, 40 U.C.C. Rep. Serv. 1105 (Bankr. D. N.D. 1984)
47 ALR6th 347—§ 4, 9

Star Satellite, Inc. v. City of Biloxi, 779 F.2d 1074 (5th Cir. 1986)
121 ALR5th 427—§ 2, 15

Star Scientific Inc. v. Beales, 278 F.3d 339 (4th Cir. 2002)
25 ALR6th 435—§ 4, 18, 24, 29, 30

Star Scientific Inc. v. Carter, 61 U.S.P.Q.2d 1252, 2001 WL 1112673 (S.D. Ind. 2001)
25 ALR6th 435—§ 18

Star Service & Petroleum Co. v. Administrative Hearing Commission, 623 S.W.2d 237 (Mo. 1981)
1 ALR6th 1—§ 5

Star Service & Petroleum Co., Inc. v. State ex rel. Galanos, 518 So. 2d 126 (Ala. Civ. App. 1986)
26 ALR6th 249—§ 6, 9, 15

Starsky Roy K., Re, 150 App. Div. 2d 685, 541 N.Y.S.2d 558 (2d Dep't 1989)
1 ALR5th 469—§ 18

Star-Telegram v. Doe, 23 Media L. R. 2492 (Tex. 1995)
40 ALR5th 787—§ 6

Star-Telegram, Inc. v. Walker, 834 S.W.2d 54, 20 Media L. R. 1379 (Tex. 1992)
40 ALR5th 787—§ 6

Star Tribune v. Board of Educ., 507 N.W.2d 869, 22 Media L. R. 1445 (Minn. App. 1993)
34 ALR5th 591—§ 2, 6, 9, 16
35 ALR5th 113—§ 2

Startzell v. City of Philadelphia, Pennsylvania, 533 F.3d 183 (3d Cir. 2008)
70 ALR6th 513—§ 3, 13
71 ALR6th 471—§ 3, 11

Star Vector Corp. v. Town of Windham, 146 N.H. 490, 776 A.2d 138 (2001)
19 ALR6th 335—§ 20

Stasel v. Com., 278 S.W.2d 727 (Ky. 1955)
24 ALR6th 747—§ 49

Stasiak v. Schindler Elevator Corp., 1994 WL 527967 (Ohio Ct. App. 5th Dist. Richland County 1994)
99 ALR5th 141—§ 34
115 ALR5th 1—§ 35
117 ALR5th 267—§ 8, 16

Stassi v. Boone, 2003 WL 21436995 (Tex. Dist. Ct. 2003)
60 ALR6th 295—§ 71

Stasz v. Schwab, 121 Cal. App. 4th 420, 17 Cal. Rptr. 3d 116 (2d Dist. 2004)
69 ALR6th 513—§ 4

Statchuk v. Warden, Maryland Peniten-
tiary, 53 Md. App. 680, 455 A.2d
1000 (1983)
53 ALR6th 1—§ 11
Statco Wireless, LLC v. Southwestern
Bell Wireless, LLC, 80 Ark. App.
284, 95 S.W.3d 13 (2003)
36 ALR6th 537—§ 1
State Board of—see name of party
State Department of—see name of party
State, Dept. of—see name of party
State ex rel.—see name of party
State ex rel. Board of—see name of
party
State ex rel. Dept. of—see name of party
State ex rel. The—see name of party
State in Interest of—see name of party
State, In Interest of Goodman, 531 P.2d
478 (Utah 1975)
66 ALR5th 397—§ 10, 25
State, In Interest of M.L., 965 P.2d 551,
85 A.L.R. 5th 761 (Utah Ct. App.
1998)
20 ALR5th 534—§ 14
85 ALR5th 547—§ 3
State, In re, 632 N.W.2d 225 (Minn.
2001)
37 ALR6th 357—§ 61, 67
State in the Interest of—see name of
party
State of—see name of party
State, Petition of, 597 A.2d 1 (Del. 1991)
79 ALR5th 33—§ 9
State, Petition of, 2014 WL 4253359
(N.H. 2014)
102 ALR6th 637—§ 4, 6
State v. 3M Nat. Advertising Co., Inc.,
139 N.H. 360, 653 A.2d 1092
(1995)
107 ALR5th 311—§ 6
State v. , 155 N.C. App. 294, 573 S.E.2d
721 (2002)
32 ALR6th 385—§ 4
State v. 192 Coin-Operated Video Game
Machines, 338 S.C. 176, 525 S.E.2d
872 (2000)
6 ALR6th 533—§ 19

State v. 392 S. 600 E., 886 P.2d 534, 253
Utah Adv. Rep. 30 (Utah 1994)
1 ALR5th 375—§ 4
State v. $1970, 43 Conn. Supp. 203, 648
A.2d 917 (1994)
6 ALR5th 711—§ 6.5
State v. 1978 Chevrolet Auto., VIN No.
1L69U8J314191, 17 Kan. App. 2d
144, 835 P.2d 1376 (1992)
104 ALR5th 229—§ 10, 12
4 ALR6th 113—§ 6, 30, 39
34 ALR6th 539—§ 3, 6, 8
101 ALR6th 1—§ 3, 23, 28, 60, 68
State v. 1982 Chevrolet Custom Deluxe
Truck, 776 P.2d 573 (Okla. App.
1989)
6 ALR5th 652—§ 2, 3
State v. 1985 Chevy PU, 797 S.W.2d
682 (Tex. App. Fort Worth 1990)
6 ALR5th 711—§ 5
State v. $2,200.00 in U.S. Currency,
1993 OK CIV APP 22, 851 P.2d
1081 (Okla. Ct. App. Div. 2 1993)
104 ALR5th 229—§ 10
State v. $2,434.00 Cash, 461 N.W.2d
346 (Iowa Ct. App. 1990)
104 ALR5th 229—§ 4
115 ALR5th 403—§ 5
101 ALR6th 1—§ 19, 29, 39, 49
State v. $4097 in U. S. Currency, 773
S.W.2d 674 (Tex. App. Fort Worth
1989)
6 ALR5th 711—§ 5
State v. $7379.54 U.S. Currency, 80
Conn. App. 471, 844 A.2d 220
(2003)
101 ALR6th 1—§ 3, 23, 26, 28
State v. $8,000.00 U.S. Currency, 827
So. 2d 634 (La. Ct. App. 3d Cir.
2002)
115 ALR5th 403—§ 2, 7
101 ALR6th 1—§ 7, 23, 28, 56, 62
State v. $8,353.00 U. S. Currency, 809
S.W.2d 344 (Tex. App. Austin
1991)
6 ALR5th 711—§ 5

State v. $10,000 Seized from Mary Patrick, 562 N.W.2d 192 (Iowa Ct. App. 1997)
115 ALR5th 403—§ 10
116 ALR5th 325—§ 6
101 ALR6th 1—§ 5, 23, 30, 42, 56, 60

State v. $11,014.00, 820 S.W.2d 783 (Tex. 1991)
104 ALR5th 229—§ 9
116 ALR5th 325—§ 4
101 ALR6th 1—§ 22, 45, 56, 60, 61

State v. 17,515.00 in Cash Money, 2003 ND 168, 670 N.W.2d 826 (N.D. 2003)
4 ALR6th 113—§ 24
101 ALR6th 1—§ 42

State v. $29,177.00 U.S. Currency, 638 So. 2d 653 (La. Ct. App. 3d Cir. 1994)
104 ALR5th 229—§ 6, 13
116 ALR5th 325—§ 3
101 ALR6th 1—§ 24

State v. $31,400, 828 S.W.2d 112 (Tex. App. Houston 1st Dist. 1992)
104 ALR5th 229—§ 9
101 ALR6th 1—§ 5

State v. $36,560.00 in U.S. Currency, 289 N.J. Super. 237, 673 A.2d 810 (App. Div. 1996)
104 ALR5th 229—§ 4
115 ALR5th 403—§ 5
101 ALR6th 1—§ 3, 13, 34, 46

State v. $217,590.00 in U.S. Currency, 18 S.W.3d 631 (Tex. 2000)
101 ALR6th 1—§ 7, 56

State v. $435,000.00, 842 S.W.2d 642 (Tex. 1992)
6 ALR5th 711—§ 5

State v. Aaron, 2003-Ohio-5159, 2003 WL 22232343 (Ohio Ct. App. 9th Dist. Summit County 2003)
33 ALR6th 91—§ 45

State v. Ababa, 101 Haw. 209, 65 P.3d 156, 124 A.L.R.5th 711 (2003)
124 ALR5th 1—§ 4

State v. Abbatto, 64 N.J.L. 658, 47 A. 10 (N.J. Ct. Err. & App. 1900)

97 ALR6th 567—§ 3, 7, 9
State v. Abbink, 260 Neb. 211, 616 N.W.2d 8 (2000)
113 ALR5th 1—§ 2, 12, 15
State v. Abbott, 5 Conn. App. 441, 499 A.2d 437 (1985)
109 ALR5th 99—§ 11
State v. Abbott, 79 Haw. 317, 901 P.2d 1296 (Ct. App. 1995)
9 ALR6th 541—§ 16
State v. Abbott, 79 Haw. 317, 901 P.2d 1296 (Haw. Ct. App. 1995)
12 ALR5th 149—§ 14
87 ALR5th 631—§ 35
State v. Abbott, 87 S.C. 466, 70 S.E. 6 (1911)
76 ALR5th 485—§ 5
State v. Abbott, 277 Kan. 161, 83 P.3d 794 (2004)
23 ALR6th 307—§ 44
State v. Abbott, 356 N.W.2d 677 (Minn. 1984)
124 ALR5th 1—§ 5
State v. Abbott, 571 S.W.2d 809 (Mo. App. 1978)
55 ALR5th 125—§ 12, 18, 23
State v. Abbott, 634 So. 2d 911 (La. Ct. App. 4th Cir. 1994)
102 ALR5th 327—§ 4
State v. Abdelnoor, 273 N.J. Super. 321, 641 A.2d 1102 (App. Div. 1994)
43 ALR6th 475—§ 21
State v. Abdo, 518 N.W.2d 223 (S.D. 1994)
26 ALR5th 378—§ 8.5
State v. Abdullah, 357 S.C. 344, 592 S.E.2d 344 (Ct. App. 2004)
79 ALR6th 1—§ 39, 55
State v. Abell, 2003 UT 20, 70 P.3d 98, 116 A.L.R.5th 735 (Utah 2003)
116 ALR5th 479—§ 5
State v. Abellano, 50 Haw. 384, 441 P.2d 333 (1968)
69 ALR6th 207—§ 10
State v. Abellano, 50 Hawaii 384, 441 P.2d 333 (1968)
6 ALR5th 733—§ 26

State v. Abernathy, 265 Ark. 218, 577 S.W.2d 591 (1979)

57 ALR5th 141—§ 5, 7, 9

State v. Abislaiman, 437 So. 2d 181 (Fla. App. D3 1983)

59 ALR5th 615—§ 12

State v. Able, 65 Mo. 357, 1877 WL 9157 (1877)

97 ALR5th 537—§ 24

State v. Ableman, 134 N.J. Super. 517, 342 A.2d 228 (App. Div. 1975)

97 ALR5th 201—§ 6

State v. Abner, 889 So. 2d 52 (Ala. Crim. App. 2004)

92 ALR6th 171—§ 16

State v. Abner, 2006-Ohio-4510, 2006 WL 2522384 (Ohio Ct. App. 2d Dist. Montgomery County 2006)

103 ALR6th 247—§ 4

State v. Abney, Ohio App. Case No 1137, Slip Opinion (Greene Co. 1981)

45 ALR5th 1—§ 2, 5, 7, 12, 23, 29

State v. Abraham, 2008 WL 5046837 (N.J. Super. Ct. App. Div. 2008)

80 ALR6th 239—§ 22

State v. Abrahamson, 328 N.W.2d 213 (N.D. 1982)

28 ALR6th 505—§ 9

State v. Abram, 353 So. 2d 1019 (La. 1977)

61 ALR5th 1—§ 2

State v. Abrams, 67 Ohio Op. 2d 121, 322 N.E.2d 339 (Ct. App. 1st Dist. Butler County 1974)

88 ALR5th 121—§ 14, 26, 28

State v. Abrams, 471 S.E.2d 716 (S.C. App. 1996)

50 ALR5th 581—§ 7, 9

State v. Abrams, 1999 WL 957652 (Ohio Ct. App. 2d Dist. Montgomery County 1999)

41 ALR6th 141—§ 5

State v. Absher, 34 N.C. App. 197, 237 S.E.2d 749 (1977)

45 ALR5th 1—§ 5, 8, 12, 23, 25, 29

State v. Absher, 220 N.C. 126, 16 S.E.2d 656 (1941)

67 ALR5th 637—§ 5, 11

State v. Accardo, 466 So. 2d 549 (La. App. 5th Cir. 1985)

5 ALR5th 243—§ 45

State v. Accetturo, 261 N.J. Super. 487, 619 A.2d 272 (Law Div. 1992)

60 ALR5th 39—§ 3 to 6, 11, 12

State v. Aceto, 2004 MT 247, 323 Mont. 24, 100 P.3d 629, 19 A.L.R.6th 905 (2004)

19 ALR6th 577—§ 17

19 ALR6th 697—§ 11

State v. Acevedo, 2009 WL 2357163 (Ariz. Ct. App. Div. 2 2009)

79 ALR6th 1—§ 75

State v. A.C.H., 710 N.W.2d 587 (Minn. Ct. App. 2006)

68 ALR6th 1—§ 12

69 ALR6th 1—§ 23

State v. Acheson, 75 Wash. App. 151, 877 P.2d 217 (Div. 2 1994)

38 ALR6th 1—§ 14, 17

State v. Acker, 26 Utah 2d 104, 485 P.2d 1038 (1971)

72 ALR5th 607—§ 3, 4, 6, 7

State v. Ackerman, 90 Wash. App. 477, 953 P.2d 816 (Div. 3 1998)

38 ALR5th 433—§ 8, 16

State v. Ackerman, 144 N.C. App. 452, 551 S.E.2d 139 (2001)

103 ALR6th 507—§ 8

State v. Ackerman, 380 N.W.2d 922 (Minn. Ct. App. 1986)

73 ALR5th 615—§ 7

State v. Ackerman, 499 N.W.2d 882 (N.D. 1993)

122 ALR5th 439—§ 7

State v. Acklin, 71 N.C. App. 261, 321 S.E.2d 532 (1984)

26 ALR5th 1—§ 3, 28

State v. Ackward, 281 Kan. 2, 128 P.3d 382 (2006)

20 ALR6th 479—§ 3, 9

State v. Acosta, 125 Ariz. 146, 608 P.2d 83 (Ct. App. Div. 1 1980)

110 ALR5th 329—§ 5

State v. Acquin, 187 Conn. 647, 448 A.2d 163 (1982)

 70 ALR5th 587—§ 6, 19

 32 ALR6th 1—§ 11

 101 ALR6th 331—§ 12

State v. Acquisto, 463 A.2d 122 (R.I. 1983)

 49 ALR5th 639—§ 5

State v. Acree, 121 Ariz. 94, 588 P.2d 836 (1978)

 3 ALR6th 269—§ 4, 7, 10, 23, 30, 32

State v. Acrey, 97 Wash. App. 784, 988 P.2d 17 (Div. 1 1999)

 105 ALR5th 499—§ 4

State v. Adames, 2006-Ohio-1839, 2006 WL 962611 (Ohio Ct. App. 8th Dist. Cuyahoga County 2006)

 26 ALR6th 511—§ 19

State v. Adams, 13 A.3d 1162 (Del. Super. Ct. 2008)

 92 ALR6th 171—§ 18

State v. Adams, 18 Ariz. App. 292, 501 P.2d 561 (1972)

 41 ALR5th 171—§ 17, 68

State v. Adams, 35 Kan. App. 2d 439, 131 P.3d 556 (2006)

 23 ALR6th 307—§ 38, 44

 26 ALR6th 511—§ 25

State v. Adams, 39 Ohio St. 3d 186, 529 N.E.2d 1264 (1988)

 63 ALR5th 417—§ 4

State v. Adams, 51 S.W.3d 94 (Mo. Ct. App. E.D. 2001)

 78 ALR6th 297—§ 46

State v. Adams, 57 Or. App. 725, 646 P.2d 37 (1982)

 69 ALR6th 1—§ 33

State v. Adams, 64 Hawaii 568, 645 P.2d 308 (1982)

 13 ALR5th 1—§ 2

State v. Adams, 76 Haw. 408, 879 P.2d 513 (1994)

 9 ALR6th 541—§ 6

State v. Adams, 85 Kan. 435, 116 P. 608 (1911)

 81 ALR5th 563—§ 3

State v. Adams, 103 Ohio St. 3d 508, 2004-Ohio-5845, 817 N.E.2d 29 (2004)

 21 ALR6th 1—§ 4

 71 ALR6th 625—§ 18, 20

State v. Adams, 109 Ariz. 556, 514 P.2d 477 (1973)

 85 ALR5th 1—§ 42

State v. Adams, 125 N.J. Super. 587, 312 A.2d 642 (App. Div. 1973)

 125 ALR5th 281—§ 10

State v. Adams, 131 Wash. App. 1032, 2006 WL 302761 (Div. 3 2006)

 78 ALR6th 1—§ 59

State v. Adams, 142 Idaho 305, 127 P.3d 208 (Ct. App. 2005)

 92 ALR6th 295—§ 8

 95 ALR6th 1—§ 6, 8, 10, 18, 27

State v. Adams, 145 Ariz. 566, 703 P.2d 510 (Ct. App. Div. 2 1985)

 20 ALR6th 479—§ 9

State v. Adams, 148 Wash. App. 231, 198 P.3d 1057 (Div. 3 2009)

 50 ALR6th 353—§ 4, 25

State v. Adams, 187 N.C. App. 676, 654 S.E.2d 711 (2007)

 67 ALR6th 103—§ 6

State v. Adams, 189 Ariz. 235, 941 P.2d 908 (Ct. App. Div. 1 1997)

 15 ALR5th 391—§ 21

State v. Adams, 197 Ariz. 569, 5 P.3d 903 (Ct. App. Div. 1 2000)

 104 ALR5th 165—§ 2, 3

State v. Adams, 224 N.J. Super. 669, 541 A.2d 262 (App. Div. 1988)

 28 ALR6th 245—§ 6

State v. Adams, 284 Mont. 25, 943 P.2d 955 (1997)

 73 ALR6th 49—§ 21

State v. Adams, 291 S.C. 132, 352 S.E.2d 483 (1987)

 1 ALR6th 549—§ 15

 2 ALR6th 551—§ 15

State v. Adams, 299 N.C. 699, 264 S.E.2d 46 (1980)

 39 ALR5th 283—§ 4, 39

State v. Adams, 331 N.C. 317, 416 S.E.2d 380 (1992)
57 ALR6th 445—§ 58

State v. Adams, 354 S.C. 361, 580 S.E.2d 785 (Ct. App. 2003)
72 ALR6th 141—§ 12

State v. Adams, 355 So. 2d 917 (La. 1978)
97 ALR5th 293—§ 4, 8

State v. Adams, 446 So. 2d 355 (La. Ct. App. 3d Cir. 1984)
79 ALR5th 237—§ 10

State v. Adams, 470 S.E.2d 366 (S.C. 1996)
47 ALR5th 259—§ 2, 10, 12, 16

State v. Adams, 481 A.2d 718 (R.I. 1984)
1 ALR6th 657—§ 5

State v. Adams, 839 S.W.2d 740 (Mo. App. 1992)
18 ALR5th 1—§ 3

State v. Adams, 864 S.W.2d 31 (Tenn. 1993)
73 ALR5th 383—§ 2, 5, 6, 20

State v. Adams, 909 So. 2d 5 (La. Ct. App. 4th Cir. 2005)
16 ALR6th 329—§ 4
24 ALR6th 591—§ 4

State v. Adams, 1988 WL 27280 (Tenn. Crim. App. 1988)
76 ALR5th 1—§ 11

State v. Adams, 1991 WL 216874 (Ohio Ct. App. 3d Dist. Union County 1991)
107 ALR5th 567—§ 3

State v. Adams, 1992 WL 36198 (Ohio Ct. App. 2d Dist. Clark County 1992)
103 ALR5th 347—§ 26

State v. Adams, 1998 WL 389066 (Tenn. Crim. App. 1998)
73 ALR5th 383—§ 5

State v. Adams, 2004-Ohio-3199, 2004 WL 1380494 (Ohio Ct. App. 7th Dist. Mahoning County 2004)
122 ALR5th 593—§ 5, 8, 9

State v. Adams, 2005-Ohio-1548, 2005 WL 736672 (Ohio Ct. App. 6th Dist. Sandusky County 2005)
26 ALR6th 511—§ 19

State v. Adams, 2011-Ohio-5361, 2011 WL 4923522 (Ohio Ct. App. 7th Dist. Mahoning County 2011)
79 ALR6th 1—§ 87

State v. Adamson, 72 Ohio St. 3d 431, 1995-Ohio-199, 650 N.E.2d 875 (1995)
23 ALR6th 1—§ 3, 16

State v. Adamson, 136 Ariz. 250, 665 P.2d 972 (1983)
41 ALR5th 171—§ 17, 68, 72, 78, 104
57 ALR5th 141—§ 5

State v. Adkins, 136 Ohio App. 3d 765, 737 N.E.2d 1021 (3d Dist. Hancock County 2000)
89 ALR5th 629—§ 8

State v. Adkins, 161 Ohio App. 3d 114, 2005-Ohio-2577, 829 N.E.2d 729 (4th Dist. Athens County 2005)
26 ALR6th 511—§ 19

State v. Adkins, 176 W. Va. 613, 346 S.E.2d 762 (1986)
19 ALR5th 470—§ 3

State v. Adkins, 702 So. 2d 1115 (La. Ct. App. 3d Cir. 1997)
91 ALR5th 343—§ 20, 21

State v. Adkins, 786 S.W.2d 642 (Tenn. 1990)
99 ALR6th 113—§ 10

State v. Adkins, 2000 WL 1713708 (Ohio Ct. App. 6th Dist. Erie County 2000)
84 ALR6th 293—§ 15

State v. Adler, 92 S.W.3d 397 (Tenn. 2002)
68 ALR6th 1—§ 3
69 ALR6th 1—§ 3
70 ALR6th 1—§ 3, 25

State v. Adler, 189 Ariz. 280, 942 P.2d 439 (1997)
59 ALR5th 135—§ 11

State v. Advertiser Co., 257 Ala. 423, 59 So. 2d 576 (1952)

89 ALR5th 493—§ 14
State v. Aesoph, 2002 SD 71, 647 N.W.2d 743 (S.D. 2002)
28 ALR6th 505—§ 9
State v. Aetna Cas. and Sur. Co., 155 A.D.2d 740, 547 N.Y.S.2d 452 (3d Dep't 1989)
88 ALR5th 493—§ 5
89 ALR5th 1—§ 18
State v. Afana, 233 P.3d 879 (Wash. 2010)
56 ALR6th 1—§ 6, 38
State v. Afanador, 134 N.J. 162, 631 A.2d 946, 30 A.L.R.5th 744 (1993)
30 ALR5th 121—§ 2, 3, 7
State v. Affsprung, 115 N.M. 546, 854 P.2d 873 (Ct. App. 1993)
114 ALR5th 173—§ 3, 5
State v. AFSCME, Council 4, Local 387, AFL-CIO, 252 Conn. 467, 747 A.2d 480, 164 L.R.R.M. (BNA) 2242 (2000)
112 ALR5th 263—§ 32
State v. AFSCME, Council 4, Local 2663, AFL-CIO, 59 Conn. App. 793, 758 A.2d 387, 169 L.R.R.M. (BNA) 2292 (2000)
112 ALR5th 263—§ 62
State v. AFSCME, Council 31, AFL-CIO, 321 Ill. App. 3d 1038, 255 Ill. Dec. 371, 749 N.E.2d 472 (5th Dist. 2001)
112 ALR5th 263—§ 33
State v. Age, 38 Or. App. 501, 590 P.2d 759 (1979)
99 ALR5th 557—§ 10, 12
State v. Agent, 101 N.J. Super. 190, 243 A.2d 846 (1968)
11 ALR5th 52—§ 5
State v. Aggarwal, 31 Ohio App. 3d 32, 507 N.E.2d 1167 (1st Dist. Hamilton County 1986)
70 ALR6th 1—§ 5
State v. Agnesi, 92 N.J.L. 53, 104 A. 299 (N.J. Sup. Ct. 1918)
97 ALR6th 567—§ 3, 6, 9
State v. Agoney, 608 P.2d 762 (Alaska 1980)

34 ALR6th 1—§ 11
State v. Agosto, 101 Haw. 45, 61 P.3d 556 (Ct. App. 2003)
96 ALR6th 355—§ 33
State v. Agrabante, 73 Hawaii 179, 830 P.2d 492, 15 A.L.R.5th 974 (1992)
15 ALR5th 39—§ 9
18 ALR5th 1—§ 4, 11
State v. Agren, 28 Wash. App. 1, 622 P.2d 388 (1980)
5 ALR5th 243—§ 21
State v. Aguallo, 318 N.C. 590, 350 S.E.2d 76 (1986)
38 ALR5th 433—§ 2, 11, 19
State v. Agubata, 92 N.C. App. 651, 375 S.E.2d 702 (1989)
7 ALR6th 169—§ 8
State v. Agubata, 94 N.C. App. 710, 381 S.E.2d 191 (1989)
7 ALR6th 169—§ 8
19 ALR6th 115—§ 13
State v. Aguelera, 326 Mo. 1205, 33 S.W.2d 901 (1930)
32 ALR5th 149—§ 5, 29, 32, 33
State v. Ague-Masters, 138 Wash. App. 86, 156 P.3d 265 (Div. 2 2007)
45 ALR6th 643—§ 13
State v. Aguilar, 210 Ariz. 51, 107 P.3d 377 (Ct. App. Div. 1 2005)
30 ALR6th 1—§ 4, 7
State v. Aguilar, 2007 WL 5210596 (Ariz. Ct. App. Div. 1 2007)
92 ALR6th 295—§ 19
93 ALR6th 207—§ 13, 26
96 ALR6th 355—§ 5, 26, 36, 37, 49
State v. Aguilar-Gonzalez, 2010 WL 2450576 (Ariz. Ct. App. Div. 1 2010)
92 ALR6th 171—§ 32
State v. Aguillard, 567 So. 2d 674 (La. App. 5th Cir. 1990)
3 ALR5th 521—§ 2, 5
State v. Aguirre, 73 Wash. App. 682, 871 P.2d 616 (Div. 1 1994)
101 ALR6th 431—§ 3
State v. Aguirre, 84 N.M. 376, 503 P.2d 1154 (1972)

28 ALR5th 754—§ 4, 7
State v. Ahakuelo, 683 P.2d 400 (Hawaii App. 1984)
7 ALR5th 263—§ 4
State v. Ahearn, 137 Vt. 253, 403 A.2d 696 (1979)
98 ALR5th 445—§ 4
State v. Ahearn, 307 N.C. 584, 300 S.E.2d 689 (1983)
73 ALR5th 383—§ 6
State v. Ahern, 227 N.W.2d 164 (Iowa 1975)
68 ALR5th 343—§ 3
122 ALR5th 439—§ 7
State v. Ahmed, 924 P.2d 679 (Mont 1996)
54 ALR5th 743—§ 9
State v. A House and 1.37 Acres of Real Property located at 392 South 600 East, Nephi, 886 P.2d 534 (Utah 1994)
124 ALR5th 509—§ 5
State v. Aicklen, 767 So. 2d 116 (La. Ct. App. 4th Cir. 2000)
58 ALR6th 499—§ 41
State v. Aiken, 73 N.C. App. 487, 326 S.E.2d 919 (1985)
80 ALR5th 55—§ 11
State v. Aikins, 261 Kan. 346, 932 P.2d 408 (1997)
16 ALR6th 329—§ 4
19 ALR6th 115—§ 7
24 ALR6th 591—§ 4, 12, 15
State v. Ailport, 412 N.W.2d 35 (Minn. App. 1987)
41 ALR5th 171—§ 7, 31, 32, 41, 93, 100, 108, 114, 121, 133
State v. Ainslie, 103 Wash. App. 1
29 ALR5th 487—§ 3, 8, 11, 12
State v. Aitken, 79 Wash. App. 890, 905 P.2d 1235 (1995)
125 ALR5th 537—§ 12, 19
State v. Akahi, 92 Haw. 148, 988 P.2d 667 (Haw. Ct. App. 1999)
72 ALR5th 403—§ 3
State v. Akala, 2003 WL 21085381 (Del. Super. Ct. 2003)
102 ALR6th 279—§ 13

State v. Akers, 88 Wash. App. 891, 946 P.2d 1222 (Div. 1 1997)
27 ALR5th 593—§ 31.5
State v. Akers, 119 N.H. 161, 400 A.2d 38, 12 A.L.R.4th 667 (1979)
74 ALR6th 181—§ 6
State v. Akers, 136 Wash. 2d 641, 965 P.2d 1078 (1998)
27 ALR5th 593—§ 31.5
State v. Akers, 877 S.W.2d 147 (Mo. Ct. App. S.D. 1994)
105 ALR5th 529—§ 13
State v. Akers, 1999 WL 731066 (Ohio Ct. App. 4th Dist. Lawrence County 1999)
85 ALR5th 595—§ 14
State v. Akin, 77 Wash. App. 575, 892 P.2d 774 (Div. 1 1995)
113 ALR5th 597—§ 3
State v. Akins, 2009 WL 3925179 (Tenn. Crim. App. 2009)
78 ALR6th 297—§ 57
State v. Alabama Metallurgical Corp., 446 So. 2d 41 (Ala. Civ. App. 1984)
89 ALR5th 493—§ 8
State v. Alaska Civil Liberties Union, 978 P.2d 597 (Alaska 1999)
35 ALR6th 1—§ 3, 21, 23
State v. Alaska Continental Development Corp., 630 P.2d 977 (Alaska 1980)
10 ALR5th 448—§ 6
State v. Albanese, 2006 WL 2194118 (Del. Super. Ct. 2006)
96 ALR6th 355—§ 38
State v. Albano, 2001 WL 273054 (Minn. Ct. App. 2001)
92 ALR6th 295—§ 7, 8, 14, 25
96 ALR6th 355—§ 24
State v. Albaugh, 133 Idaho 587, 990 P.2d 753 (Ct. App. 1999)
56 ALR6th 323—§ 13
State v. Albee, 118 Or. App. 212, 847 P.2d 858 (1993)
6 ALR6th 533—§ 22
69 ALR6th 207—§ 9, 12
State v. Alberico, 116 N.M. 156, 861 P.2d 192 (1993)

90 ALR5th 453—§ 15
State v. Alberigo, 109 Ariz. 294, 508 P.2d 1156 (1973)
54 ALR5th 141—§ 8
State v. Albert, 115 Ariz. 354, 565 P.2d 534 (App. 1977)
43 ALR5th 1—§ 6
State v. Albert, 312 N.C. 567, 324 S.E.2d 233 (1985)
104 ALR5th 357—§ 4
54 ALR6th 429—§ 11
State v. Albert, 430 So. 2d 1279 (La. Ct. App. 1st Cir. 1983)
103 ALR6th 137—§ 15
State v. Alberto, 665 So. 2d 614 (La. Ct. App. 5th Cir. 1995)
102 ALR5th 327—§ 3
24 ALR6th 1—§ 19
State v. Albertson, 93 Idaho 640, 470 P.2d 300 (1970)
72 ALR5th 607—§ 3, 6, 7
State v. Albrecht, 242 Mont. 403, 791 P.2d 760 (1990)
79 ALR5th 419—§ 6
State v. Albrecht, 465 N.W.2d 107 (Minn. App. 1991)
19 ALR5th 470—§ 12
State v. Albright, 96 Wis. 2d 122, 291 N.W.2d 487 (1980)
72 ALR5th 403—§ 12, 15
State v. Albright & Wood, Inc., 268 Ala. 607, 109 So. 2d 844 (1959)
30 ALR5th 494—§ 29
State v. Albritton, 160 N.C. App. 708, 2003 WL 22387894 (2003)
68 ALR6th 527—§ 39
State v. Albritton, 610 So. 2d 209 (La. Ct. App. 3d Cir. 1992)
104 ALR5th 229—§ 6
115 ALR5th 403—§ 8
116 ALR5th 325—§ 3
4 ALR6th 113—§ 43
34 ALR6th 539—§ 3, 4
101 ALR6th 1—§ 21, 23, 28, 50, 57
State v. Alcantaro, 407 So. 2d 922 (Fla. App. D1 1981)
54 ALR5th 141—§ 3 to 5, 7, 8, 10

State v. Alcorn, 741 S.W.2d 135 (Tenn. Crim. App. 1987)
19 ALR6th 115—§ 5, 7, 10
State v. Alden Mills, 202 La. 416, 12 So. 2d 204 (1943)
76 ALR6th 31—§ 11
State v. Alderete, 95 N.M. 691, 625 P.2d 1208 (Ct. App. 1980)
70 ALR6th 361—§ 27, 31
State v. Alderman, 285 So. 2d 193 (La. 1973)
50 ALR5th 703—§ 35, 38
State v. Alderman, 289 Wis. 2d 218, 2006 WI App 20, 709 N.W.2d 111 (Ct. App. 2005)
43 ALR6th 475—§ 10
State v. Aldrich, 135 Wash. App. 1017, 2006 WL 2988485 (Div. 1 2006)
69 ALR6th 579—§ 4
State v. Aldridge, 120 Ohio App. 3d 122, 697 N.E.2d 228 (2d Dist. Montgomery County 1997)
91 ALR5th 343—§ 39
102 ALR5th 327—§ 5, 6
State v. Aldridge, 212 Ala. 660, 103 So. 835, 39 A.L.R. 1470 (1925)
28 ALR6th 175—§ 4, 12, 21
State v. Aldridge, 534 S.E.2d 629 (N.C. Ct. App. 2000)
57 ALR5th 141—§ 4
State v. Aldridge, 1997 WL 291245 (Tenn. Crim. App. 1997)
76 ALR5th 1—§ 12
State v. Alectus, 2011 WL 2496318 (N.J. Super. Ct. App. Div. 2011)
74 ALR6th 373—§ 9
State v. Alegrand, 130 Conn. App. 652, 23 A.3d 1250 (2011)
74 ALR6th 373—§ 13
State v. Alejo, 723 A.2d 762 (R.I. 1999)
69 ALR6th 1—§ 23
State v. Aleman, 210 Ariz. 232, 109 P.3d 571 (Ct. App. Div. 2 2005)
101 ALR6th 331—§ 10
State v. Aleman, 809 So. 2d 1056 (La. Ct. App. 5th Cir. 2002)
11 ALR6th 237—§ 15

State v. Alen, 616 So. 2d 452, 20
A.L.R.5th 961 (Fla. 1993)

20 ALR5th 398—§ 3, 28, 29, 61

63 ALR5th 375—§ 5, 6

State v. Alewine, 474 S.W.2d 848 (Mo.
1971)

124 ALR5th 1—§ 4

State v. Alexander, 12 Kan. App. 2d 1,
732 P.2d 814 (1987)

63 ALR5th 417—§ 3, 5

State v. Alexander, 16 N.C. App. 95, 191
S.E.2d 395 (1972)

84 ALR6th 427—§ 10

State v. Alexander, 24 Kan. App. 2d
817, 953 P.2d 685 (1998)

7 ALR5th 73—§ 3

State v. Alexander, 26 Kan. App. 2d
192, 981 P.2d 761 (1999)

62 ALR5th 1—§ 3

State v. Alexander, 56 P.3d 780 (Idaho
Ct. App. 2002)

106 ALR5th 397—§ 5

State v. Alexander, 64 Wash. App. 147,
822 P.2d 1250 (1992)

38 ALR5th 433—§ 3

State v. Alexander, 64 Wash. App. 147,
822 P.2d 1250 (Div. 1 1992)

40 ALR6th 1—§ 4, 24

State v. Alexander, 118 So. 3d 1138 (La.
Ct. App. 5th Cir. 2013)

98 ALR6th 455—§ 5

State v. Alexander, 124 Md. App. 258,
721 A.2d 275 (1998)

58 ALR6th 499—§ 39

State v. Alexander, 136 N.J. 563, 643
A.2d 996 (1994)

30 ALR5th 121—§ 4

State v. Alexander, 138 Idaho 18, 56
P.3d 780 (Ct. App. 2002)

113 ALR5th 517—§ 4

State v. Alexander, 215 La. 245, 40 So.
2d 232 (1949)

9 ALR6th 1—§ 17

State v. Alexander, 252 La. 564, 211 So.
2d 650 (1968)

72 ALR5th 529—§ 3, 7

State v. Alexander, 320 So. 2d 610 (La.
App. 4th Cir. 1975)

59 ALR5th 489—§ 2

State v. Alexander, 337 So. 2d 1111 (La.
1976)

103 ALR5th 463—§ 3

State v. Alexander, 1983 WL 8910 (Ohio
Ct. App. 1st Dist. Hamilton
County1983)

85 ALR5th 1—§ 24

State v. Alexander, 2004-Ohio-3861,
2004 WL 1630491 (Ohio Ct. App.
8th Dist. Cuyahoga County 2004)

72 ALR6th 1—§ 7

State v. Alexander, 2004-Ohio-5525,
2004 WL 2340039 (Ohio Ct. App.
7th Dist. Carroll County 2004)

32 ALR6th 171—§ 17, 20, 22

33 ALR6th 1—§ 21

State v. Alexander, No. 80 (March 6,
1981, Ct. App. Ohio, 7th App. Dist.
Mahoning Co.)

39 ALR5th 283—§ 14, 46

State v. Alexander, Slip Op. No. 51093
(Ohio App. Cuyahoga Co. 1986)

38 ALR5th 433—§ 30, 37

State v. Alexandre, 2003 WL 21387159
(Me. Super. Ct. 2003)

38 ALR6th 97—§ 10

State v. Alfaro, 127 Ariz. 578, 623 P.2d
8 (1980)

92 ALR6th 1—§ 3

State v. Alfieri, 132 Ohio App. 3d 69,
724 N.E.2d 477 (1st Dist. Hamilton
County 1998)

64 ALR5th 671—§ 7

State v. Alford, 225 So. 2d 582 (Fla.
Dist. Ct. App. 2d Dist. 1969)

96 ALR5th 327—§ 3

State v. Alford, 298 N.C. 465, 259
S.E.2d 242 (1979)

67 ALR6th 531—§ 27

State v. Alford, 970 S.W.2d 944 (Tenn.
1998)

92 ALR5th 35—§ 25

State v. Alford, 2010-Ohio-4130, 2010
WL 3442398 (Ohio Ct. App. 8th
Dist. Cuyahoga County 2010)

99 ALR6th 295—§ 13
State v. Alfred, 510 So. 2d 93 (La. Ct. App. 1st Cir. 1987)
99 ALR6th 295—§ 9, 16
State v. Alger, 31 Wash. App. 244, 640 P.2d 44 (Div. 1 1982)
28 ALR6th 505—§ 9
State v. Ali, 119 Ohio App. 3d 766, 696 N.E.2d 285 (8th Dist. Cuyahoga County 1997)
104 ALR5th 229—§ 4
115 ALR5th 403—§ 8
116 ALR5th 325—§ 3
4 ALR6th 113—§ 25, 31
34 ALR6th 539—§ 5, 7, 9
101 ALR6th 1—§ 6, 51
State v. Ali, 613 N.W.2d 796 (Minn. Ct. App. 2000)
4 ALR5th 1—§ 19
State v. Ali, 855 N.W.2d 235 (Minn. 2014)
102 ALR6th 637—§ 2
State v. Aligah, 1988 WL 128101 (Minn. Ct. App. 1988)
39 ALR6th 257—§ 46
State v. Alihodzic, 32 Conn. L. Rptr. 705, 2002 WL 31045981 (Conn. Super. Ct. 2002)
84 ALR6th 293—§ 15
State v. Alioto, 588 So. 2d 17 (Fla. Dist. Ct. App. 5th Dist. 1991)
28 ALR6th 505—§ 11, 34
58 ALR6th 439—§ 3
State v. Alires, 246 Kan. 635, 792 P.2d 1019 (1990)
39 ALR5th 283—§ 4, 19
State v. Allberry, 1991 WL 13736 (Ohio Ct. App. 4th Dist. Hocking County 1991)
92 ALR6th 295—§ 8, 34, 38
95 ALR6th 1—§ 5, 6, 8, 10, 11, 13, 26
State v. Alldredge, 73 Wash. App. 171, 868 P.2d 183 (Div. 2 1994)
85 ALR5th 1—§ 2, 22, 33
State v. Allen, 2 Hawaii App. 606, 638 P.2d 338 (1981)
59 ALR5th 615—§ 4

State v. Allen, 14 N.C. App. 485, 188 S.E.2d 568 (1972)
66 ALR5th 397—§ 9
State v. Allen, 16 Or. App. 456, 518 P.2d 1332 (1974)
84 ALR6th 427—§ 4, 13
State v. Allen, 23 Idaho 772, 131 P. 1112 (1913)
104 ALR5th 357—§ 6
54 ALR6th 429—§ 9
State v. Allen, 50 N.C. App. 173, 272 S.E.2d 785 (1980)
98 ALR6th 455—§ 18
State v. Allen, 69 Ohio App. 3d 366, 590 N.E.2d 1272 (Hamilton Co. 1990)
38 ALR5th 433—§ 3
State v. Allen, 80 N.C. App. 549, 342 S.E.2d 571 (1986)
22 ALR5th 1—§ 13, 30, 33, 42, 54
State v. Allen, 89 Or. App. 167, 747 P.2d 384 (1987)
39 ALR5th 283—§ 4, 75
State v. Allen, 91 N.M. 759, 581 P.2d 22 (Ct. App. 1978)
88 ALR5th 429—§ 4
State v. Allen, 94 Wash. 2d 860, 621 P.2d 143 (1980)
39 ALR5th 283—§ 4, 20
State v. Allen, 100 Iowa 7, 69 N.W. 274 (1896)
104 ALR5th 357—§ 8
State v. Allen, 109 Wis. 2d 697, 327 N.W.2d 723 (Ct. App. 1982)
57 ALR6th 313—§ 3
State v. Allen, 122 Or. App. 587, 858 P.2d 176 (1993)
15 ALR5th 391—§ 39
State v. Allen, 128 N.H. 390, 514 A.2d 1263 (1986)
7 ALR5th 758—§ 9
State v. Allen, 141 N.C. App. 610, 541 S.E.2d 490 (2000)
98 ALR6th 455—§ 16, 29
State v. Allen, 145 Vt. 593, 496 A.2d 168 (1985)
29 ALR5th 702—§ 4, 6

State v. Allen, 157 Ariz. 165, 755 P.2d 1153 (1988)
    38 ALR5th 433—§ 8, 9
    71 ALR5th 637—§ 5
State v. Allen, 159 Neb. 314, 66 N.W.2d 830 (1954)
    50 ALR5th 703—§ 16
State v. Allen, 163 Kan. 374, 183 P.2d 458 (1947)
    33 ALR6th 353—§ 5
State v. Allen, 193 N.C. App. 375, 667 S.E.2d 295 (2008)
    67 ALR6th 103—§ 5, 10
State v. Allen, 198 Or. App. 392, 108 P.3d 651 (2005)
    26 ALR6th 511—§ 36
State v. Allen, 204 La. 513, 15 So. 2d 870 (1943)
    111 ALR5th 491—§ 3, 9
State v. Allen, 212 N.J. Super. 276, 514 A.2d 879 (Law Div. 1986)
    119 ALR5th 379—§ 11
State v. Allen, 260 Kan. 107, 917 P.2d 848 (1996)
    15 ALR5th 391—§ 45
    87 ALR6th 1—§ 42
State v. Allen, 266 S.C. 175, 222 S.E.2d 287 (1976)
    24 ALR6th 591—§ 6
State v. Allen, 269 S.C. 233, 237 S.E.2d 64 (1977)
    52 ALR6th 1—§ 25
State v. Allen, 276 So. 2d 868 (La. 1973)
    102 ALR6th 279—§ 11
State v. Allen, 278 Mont. 326, 925 P.2d 470 (1996)
    11 ALR6th 237—§ 12, 13
State v. Allen, 283 Kan. 372, 153 P.3d 488 (2007)
    30 ALR6th 373—§ 4
State v. Allen, 301 Or. 35, 717 P.2d 1178 (1986)
    26 ALR5th 603—§ 2, 4, 7
State v. Allen, 304 N.W.2d 203 (Iowa 1981)
    34 ALR5th 723—§ 3

State v. Allen, 334 N.J. Super. 133, 756 A.2d 1087 (Law Div. 2000)
    22 ALR5th 261—§ 4, 13
State v. Allen, 346 N.C. 731, 488 S.E.2d 188 (1997)
    24 ALR5th 465—§ 43
State v. Allen, 431 S.E.2d 563 (S.C. 1993)
    52 ALR5th 655—§ 3
State v. Allen, 482 N.W.2d 228 (Minn. Ct. App. 1992)
    73 ALR5th 383—§ 6
State v. Allen, 488 S.E.2d 294 (N.C. Ct. App. 1997)
    57 ALR5th 141—§ 13
State v. Allen, 539 So. 2d 1232 (La. 1989)
    42 ALR5th 581—§ 6, 19
State v. Allen, 548 So. 2d 762 (Fla. Dist. Ct. App. 1st Dist. 1989)
    96 ALR5th 327—§ 3
State v. Allen, 646 N.E.2d 965 (Ind. Ct. App. 2d Dist. 1995)
    89 ALR5th 629—§ 3
    97 ALR5th 201—§ 2, 6, 7
State v. Allen, 647 So. 2d 428 (La. Ct. App. 2d Cir. 1994)
    73 ALR5th 383—§ 5
State v. Allen, 665 N.W.2d 440 (Iowa Ct. App. 2003)
    72 ALR6th 1—§ 9
State v. Allen, 684 S.W.2d 417 (Mo. App. 1984)
    22 ALR5th 1—§ 39
State v. Allen, 692 S.W.2d 651 (Tenn. Crim. App. 1985)
    111 ALR5th 1—§ 8
State v. Allen, 800 S.W.2d 82 (Mo. App. 1990)
    26 ALR5th 1—§ 4, 25, 26, 33
State v. Allen, 944 S.W.2d 580 (Mo. Ct. App. W.D. 1997)
    105 ALR5th 529—§ 2
State v. Allen, 954 S.W.2d 414 (Mo. Ct. App. E.D. 1997)
    37 ALR6th 357—§ 46, 47, 63, 67
State v. Allen, 994 P.2d 728 (N.M. 1999)

39 ALR5th 283—§ 59
79 ALR5th 33—§ 48
State v. Allen, 1993 WL 4123 (Minn. Ct. App. 1993)
73 ALR5th 383—§ 5
State v. Allen, 1998 MT 293, 292 Mont. 1, 970 P.2d 81 (1998)
56 ALR6th 323—§ 7
State v. Allen, 2006-Ohio-30, 2006 WL 29114 (Ohio Ct. App. 5th Dist. Licking County 2006)
47 ALR6th 107—§ 37
State v. Allen, 2009-Ohio-2036, 2009 WL 1156697 (Ohio Ct. App. 8th Dist. Cuyahoga County 2009)
71 ALR6th 1—§ 8
State v. Allen, No. 51051 (October 9, 1990, Ct. App. Ohio, 8th App. Dist. Cuyahoga Co.)
39 ALR5th 283—§ 14, 45
State v. Allert, 117 Wash. 2d 156, 815 P.2d 752 (1991)
113 ALR5th 597—§ 3, 8
State v. Allery, 101 Wash. 2d 591, 682 P.2d 312 (1984)
58 ALR5th 749—§ 6
State v. Alliance Village, Inc., 592 S.W.2d 687 (Tex. Civ. App. Corpus Christi 1979)
34 ALR5th 529—§ 4
State v. Allie, 147 Ariz. 320, 710 P.2d 430 (1985)
72 ALR5th 403—§ 15
63 ALR6th 1—§ 5, 36, 55
State v. Allison, 142 Wash. App. 1048, 2008 WL 257337 (Div. 3 2008)
43 ALR6th 475—§ 6
State v. Allison, 330 Mo. 773, 51 S.W.2d 51, 85 A.L.R. 471 (1932)
11 ALR5th 497—§ 3, 5, 11, 14, 15
State v. Allo, 510 So. 2d 14 (La. Ct. App. 5th Cir. 1987)
95 ALR5th 229—§ 26
State v. Allo, 525 So. 2d 664 (La. App. 5th Cir. 1988)
45 ALR5th 591—§ 18
State v. Allocco, 162 Vt. 59, 644 A.2d 835 (1994)

58 ALR6th 439—§ 30
State v. Allred, 505 S.E.2d 153 (N.C. Ct. App. 1998)
39 ALR5th 283—§ 23
State v. Allum, 2005 MT 150, 327 Mont. 363, 114 P.3d 233 (2005)
24 ALR6th 1—§ 51
State v. Almeda, 211 Conn. 441, 560 A.2d 389 (1989)
5 ALR5th 243—§ 2, 6
State v. Almly, 216 Ariz. 41, 162 P.3d 680 (Ct. App. Div. 1 2007)
70 ALR6th 361—§ 4, 19
State v. Alonzo, 675 So. 2d 266 (La. 1996)
103 ALR5th 463—§ 3
State v. Alsay, 847 So. 2d 144 (La. Ct. App. 2d Cir. 2003)
117 ALR5th 407—§ 4
State v. Alshaif, 2012 WL 540740 (N.C. Ct. App. 2012)
74 ALR6th 373—§ 23
State v. Also, 11 Ariz. App. 227, 463 P.2d 122 (Div. 1 1969)
72 ALR5th 607—§ 3, 4
State v. Alspach, 524 N.W.2d 665 (Iowa 1994)
93 ALR5th 327—§ 3, 7, 25
101 ALR5th 619—§ 9
20 ALR6th 479—§ 3
State v. Alsteen, 108 Wis. 2d 723, 324 N.W.2d 426 (1982)
86 ALR5th 59—§ 4, 6
State v. Alston, 88 N.J. 211, 440 A.2d 1311 (1981)
18 ALR6th 1—§ 2
State v. Alston, 91 N.C. App. 707, 373 S.E.2d 306 (1988)
24 ALR5th 428—§ 2, 7, 13
State v. Alston, 111 N.C. App. 416, 432 S.E.2d 385 (1993)
27 ALR5th 593—§ 2, 24
State v. Alston, 295 N.C. 629, 247 S.E.2d 898 (1978)
31 ALR6th 465—§ 22
State v. Alston, 310 N.C. 399, 312 S.E.2d 470 (1984)

33 ALR6th 353—§ 3, 6
State v. Alston, 341 N.C. 198, 461 S.E.2d 687 (1995)
57 ALR5th 141—§ 3
79 ALR5th 33—§ 66
State v. Alsup, 75 Wash. App. 128, 876 P.2d 935 (Div. 1 1994)
27 ALR6th 183—§ 28, 30
State v. Alsup, 140 Mo. App. 194, 123 S.W. 1011 (1909)
97 ALR5th 537—§ 41
State v. Alt, 469 N.W.2d 732 (Minn. App. 1991)
19 ALR5th 470—§ 12
41 ALR5th 171—§ 68, 86, 90, 95, 107, 108, 117, 119
State v. Alt, 504 N.W.2d 38 (Minn. Ct. App. 1993)
90 ALR5th 453—§ 36
State v. Alt, 529 N.W.2d 727 (Minn. Ct. App. 1995)
15 ALR5th 391—§ 31, 39
86 ALR5th 59—§ 2, 5
88 ALR5th 429—§ 2
State v. Altamirano, 2008-2083 La. App. 1 Cir. 3/27/09, 2009 WL 838360 (La. Ct. App. 1st Cir. 2009)
75 ALR6th 541—§ 12
State v. Altayeb, 126 Conn. App. 383, 11 A.3d 1122, 72 A.L.R.6th 737 (2011)
72 ALR6th 437—§ 6
State v. Alterio, 154 Conn. 23, 220 A.2d 451 (1966)
89 ALR6th 565—§ 20
State v. Altgilbers, 109 N.M. 453, 786 P.2d 680 (App. 1989)
38 ALR5th 433—§ 11, 13
State v. Altick, 82 Ohio App. 3d 240, 611 N.E.2d 863 (Ohio App. Montgomery Co. 1992)
27 ALR5th 593—§ 8
State v. Altig, 243 Or. 138, 412 P.2d 25 (1966)
57 ALR6th 445—§ 49
State v. Altman, 107 Ariz. 93, 482 P.2d 460 (1971)
1 ALR6th 549—§ 8

State v. Alton, 139 Mont. 479, 365 P.2d 527 (1961)
99 ALR6th 295—§ 16
State v. Altum, 47 Wash. App. 495, 735 P.2d 1356 (Div. 2 1987)
73 ALR5th 383—§ 49
State v. Alvarado, 56 Wash. App. 454, 783 P.2d 1106 (Div. 1 1989)
4 ALR6th 599—§ 8, 16
State v. Alvarado, 226 Neb. 195, 410 N.W.2d 118 (1987)
20 ALR5th 398—§ 2, 7, 34, 56
47 ALR5th 259—§ 2
State v. Alvarado, 260 Ga. 563, 397 S.E.2d 550, 1990 WL 176611 (1990)
2 ALR6th 551—§ 4
State v. Alvarado, 961 S.W.2d 136 (Tenn. Crim. App. 1996)
28 ALR6th 505—§ 9
State v. Alvarez, 9 Kan. App. 2d 371, 678 P.2d 1132 (1984)
29 ALR5th 59—§ 3
State v. Alvarez, 93 N.M. 761, 605 P.2d 1160 (App. 1978)
9 ALR5th 464—§ 7
State v. Alvarez, 110 Or. App. 230, 822 P.2d 1207 (1991)
38 ALR5th 433—§ 11
State v. Alvarez, 138 Idaho 747, 69 P.3d 167 (Ct. App. 2003)
99 ALR6th 295—§ 11
State v. Alvarez, 776 So. 2d 1060 (Fla. Dist. Ct. App. 3d Dist. 2001)
58 ALR6th 215—§ 5
State v. Alvarez, 2009 WL 1506900 (N.J. Super. Ct. App. Div. 2009)
65 ALR6th 537—§ 22
State v. Alvarez-Garcia, 86 Wash. App. 1043, 1997 WL 305234 (Div. 2 1997)
75 ALR6th 541—§ 15
State v. Alvarino, 585 So. 2d 1094, 16 FLW D 2375 (Fla. App. D3 1991)
27 ALR5th 593—§ 25
State v. Alvidrez, 271 Kan. 143, 20 P.3d 1264 (2001)

42 ALR6th 237—§ 5
State v. Amabile, 2006 WL 853199 (N.J. Super. Ct. App. Div. 2006)
79 ALR6th 125—§ 16
102 ALR6th 279—§ 30
State v. Amarillas, 141 Ariz. 620, 688 P.2d 628 (1984)
45 ALR5th 591—§ 3
State v. Amarillo, 198 Conn. 285, 503 A.2d 146 (1986)
39 ALR5th 283—§ 3, 59
93 ALR5th 527—§ 3
State v. Amaro, 448 A.2d 1257 (R.I. 1982)
64 ALR5th 671—§ 8
State v. Amaya, 227 Mont. 390, 739 P.2d 955 (1987)
56 ALR6th 185—§ 39
State v. Ambaye, 616 N.W.2d 256 (Minn. 2000)
69 ALR6th 1—§ 21
State v. Ambrose, 598 P.2d 354 (Utah 1979)
103 ALR6th 137—§ 3, 4
State v. Amburgy, 122 Ohio App. 3d 277, 701 N.E.2d 728 (12th Dist. Warren County 1997)
78 ALR6th 599—§ 4, 17
State v. Amend, 250 P.3d 541 (Alaska Ct. App. 2011)
69 ALR6th 579—§ 8, 17
State v. American Banking Ins. Co., 263 N.J. Super. 124, 622 A.2d 261 (1993)
1 ALR5th 317—§ 4
State v. American Book Co., 69 Kan. 1, 76 P. 411 (1904)
23 ALR5th 744—§ 5
State v. Americk, 42 Wash. 2d 504, 256 P.2d 278 (1953)
23 ALR6th 1—§ 19
State v. Ameritech Corp., 185 Wis. 2d 686, 517 N.W.2d 705 (App. 1994)
54 ALR5th 631—§ 4
State v. Amerman, 84 Md. App. 461, 581 A.2d 19 (1990)
112 ALR5th 429—§ 6

State v. Ames, 109 Idaho 373, 707 P.2d 484 (Ct. App. 1985)
94 ALR5th 393—§ 7
State v. Amezola, 49 Wash. App. 78, 741 P.2d 1024 (Div. 1 1987)
85 ALR5th 1—§ 44
State v. Amick, 173 Neb. 770, 114 N.W.2d 893 (1962)
102 ALR5th 525—§ 65
State v. Amilcar, 2008-Ohio-6918, 2008 WL 5423263 (Ohio Ct. App. 10th Dist. Franklin County 2008)
71 ALR6th 1—§ 24
State v. Amiotte, 124 Wash. App. 1040, 2004 WL 2931060 (Div. 1 2004)
26 ALR6th 511—§ 25
State v. Amo, 76 Wash. App. 129, 882 P.2d 1188 (Div. 3 1994)
113 ALR5th 597—§ 8
State v. Amorin, 61 Haw. 356, 604 P.2d 45 (1979)
55 ALR6th 513—§ 11
State v. Amoroso, 1999 UT App 60, 975 P.2d 505 (Utah Ct. App. 1999)
116 ALR5th 149—§ 23
State v. Amos, 347 N.W.2d 498 (Minn. 1984)
8 ALR5th 713—§ 5
State v. Amos, 1999 WL 1531344 (Tenn. Crim. App. 1999)
100 ALR5th 67—§ 10, 41
State v. Amphy, 259 La. 161, 249 So. 2d 560 (1971)
70 ALR5th 587—§ 3
State v. A.M.R., 27 P.3d 678, 2001 WL 849794 (Wash. Ct. App. Div. 1 2001)
92 ALR5th 35—§ 25
State v. Amundson, 69 Wis. 2d 554, 230 N.W.2d 775 (1975)
1 ALR5th 938—§ 5
State v. Amundson, 108 Ohio App. 3d 438, 670 N.E.2d 1083 (12th Dist. Clermont County 1996)
85 ALR5th 1—§ 15, 24
State v. Amundson, 712 N.W.2d 560 (Minn. Ct. App. 2006)
26 ALR6th 511—§ 32, 44

50 ALR6th 455—§ 8
State v. Anair, 499 A.2d 152 (Me. 1985)
52 ALR6th 125—§ 44
State v. Anaya, 111 Or. App. 204, 826 P.2d 27 (1992)
34 ALR5th 125—§ 15, 26
State v. Anaya, 238 N.J. Super. 31, 568 A.2d 1208 (1990)
27 ALR5th 593—§ 7
State v. Anaya, 438 A.2d 892 (Me. 1981)
58 ALR5th 749—§ 4
State v. Ancar, 508 So. 2d 943 (La. App. 4th Cir. 1987)
9 ALR5th 369—§ 2, 15
State v. Anchorage, 805 P.2d 971 (Alaska 1991)
5 ALR5th 875—§ 23
State v. Anders, 596 So. 2d 463, 17 FLW D 695 (Fla. App. D4 1992)
18 ALR5th 1—§ 2, 12, 13
State v. Andersen, 213 Neb. 695, 331 N.W.2d 507 (1983)
34 ALR6th 1—§ 8
State v. Andersen-Conway, 2007 MT 281, 339 Mont. 439, 171 P.3d 678 (2007)
38 ALR6th 1—§ 6
State v. Anderson, 1 Neb. App. 914, 511 N.W.2d 174 (1993)
57 ALR5th 141—§ 11
State v. Anderson, 11 Ohio St. 2d 252, 40 Ohio Op. 2d 217, 228 N.E.2d 312 (1967)
29 ALR6th 237—§ 4, 9
State v. Anderson, 16 Conn. App. 346, 547 A.2d 1368 (1988)
5 ALR5th 243—§ 2, 50
State v. Anderson, 16 Ohio App. 3d 251, 16 Ohio B.R. 275, 475 N.E.2d 492 (Hamilton Co. 1984)
5 ALR5th 243—§ 46
State v. Anderson, 18 N.D. 149, 118 N.W. 22 (1908)
120 ALR5th 125—§ 2
121 ALR5th 1—§ 2
State v. Anderson, 31 Wash. App. 352, 641 P.2d 728 (Div. 1 1982)

83 ALR5th 277—§ 11
State v. Anderson, 57 N.C. App. 602, 292 S.E.2d 163 (1982)
55 ALR6th 391—§ 21
State v. Anderson, 76 N.C. App. 434, 333 S.E.2d 762 (1985)
34 ALR5th 125—§ 30, 35
45 ALR5th 1—§ 5, 10, 21
State v. Anderson, 84 Ohio App. 218, 39 Ohio Op. 265, 53 Ohio L. Abs. 318, 85 N.E.2d 412 (2d Dist. Franklin County 1948)
66 ALR5th 397—§ 9
State v. Anderson, 88 Wash. App. 541, 945 P.2d 1147 (Div. 2 1997)
21 ALR6th 771—§ 20
State v. Anderson, 94 Wash. 2d 176, 616 P.2d 612 (1980)
7 ALR5th 758—§ 6
State v. Anderson, 102 Ariz. 295, 428 P.2d 672 (1967)
28 ALR6th 505—§ 8
State v. Anderson, 111 N.C. 689, 16 S.E. 316 (1892)
105 ALR5th 529—§ 20
State v. Anderson, 117 P.3d 762 (Alaska Ct. App. 2005)
38 ALR6th 97—§ 25
State v. Anderson, 118 N.M. 284, 881 P.2d 29 (1994)
90 ALR5th 453—§ 15
38 ALR6th 439—§ 5
State v. Anderson, 119 Iowa 711, 94 N.W. 208 (1903)
42 ALR5th 547—§ 5
State v. Anderson, 119 P.3d 19 (Kan. Ct. App. 2005)
26 ALR6th 511—§ 25
State v. Anderson, 147 Ariz. 346, 710 P.2d 456 (1985)
9 ALR6th 633—§ 4, 15
15 ALR6th 173—§ 48
State v. Anderson, 160 Wis. 2d 307, 466 N.W.2d 201 (Ct. App. 1991)
62 ALR6th 413—§ 39
State v. Anderson, 185 Ariz. 454, 916 P.2d 1170 (Ct. App. Div. 1 1996)

51 ALR6th 219—§ 4
State v. Anderson, 186 N.J. Super. 174, 451 A.2d 1326 (1982)
7 ALR5th 263—§ 5, 7
State v. Anderson, 194 Ga. App. 139, 390 S.E.2d 68 (1989)
104 ALR5th 229—§ 12
115 ALR5th 403—§ 8
101 ALR6th 1—§ 16
State v. Anderson, 204 Neb. 186, 281 N.W.2d 743 (1979)
103 ALR6th 347—§ 8, 13
State v. Anderson, 209 Conn. 622, 553 A.2d 589 (1989)
124 ALR5th 1—§ 5
State v. Anderson, 210 Ariz. 327, 111 P.3d 369 (2005)
21 ALR6th 1—§ 4
State v. Anderson, 215 Or. 72, 332 P.2d 884 (1958)
19 ALR5th 823—§ 16
State v. Anderson, 230 Wis. 2d 121, 600 N.W.2d 913 (Ct. App. 1999)
27 ALR6th 183—§ 2, 13, 18, 34
State v. Anderson, 233 Wis. 2d 274, 2000 WI App 47, 610 N.W.2d 229 (Ct. App. 2000)
47 ALR6th 107—§ 21
State v. Anderson, 239 P.3d 114 (Kan. Ct. App. 2010)
68 ALR6th 115—§ 11
State v. Anderson, 247 Minn. 469, 78 N.W.2d 320 (1956)
9 ALR6th 1—§ 16, 18
State v. Anderson, 254 La. 1107, 229 So. 2d 329 (1969)
124 ALR5th 1—§ 4
State v. Anderson, 275 N.C. 168, 166 S.E.2d 49 (1969)
72 ALR5th 607—§ 3, 12
State v. Anderson, 288 Wis. 2d 83, 2005 WI App 238, 707 N.W.2d 159 (Ct. App. 2005)
30 ALR6th 1—§ 4
State v. Anderson, 304 Or. 139, 743 P.2d 715 (1987)
19 ALR5th 470—§ 3

74 ALR5th 319—§ 3
State v. Anderson, 308 N.W.2d 42 (Iowa 1981)
103 ALR6th 507—§ 20, 30
State v. Anderson, 322 N.C. 22, 366 S.E.2d 459 (1988)
59 ALR5th 749—§ 4
State v. Anderson, 322 S.C. 89, 470 S.E.2d 103 (1996)
99 ALR6th 113—§ 13
State v. Anderson, 332 So. 2d 452 (La. 1976)
28 ALR6th 505—§ 14
State v. Anderson, 333 So. 2d 919 (La. 1976)
54 ALR6th 429—§ 7
State v. Anderson, 336 N.W.2d 123 (N.D. 1983)
83 ALR5th 277—§ 9
84 ALR5th 487—§ 19, 25
State v. Anderson, 350 N.C. 152, 513 S.E.2d 296 (1999)
1 ALR6th 657—§ 4
State v. Anderson, 356 N.W.2d 453 (Minn. Ct. App. 1984)
84 ALR6th 427—§ 8
State v. Anderson, 370 N.W.2d 703 (Minn. App. 1985)
5 ALR5th 243—§ 2, 41, 50, 58
State v. Anderson, 384 S.W.2d 591 (Mo. 1964)
77 ALR5th 201—§ 21
State v. Anderson, 388 N.W.2d 784 (Minn. Ct. App. 1986)
58 ALR6th 499—§ 30
State v. Anderson, 390 So. 2d 878 (La. 1980)
95 ALR5th 611—§ 3
State v. Anderson, 405 N.W.2d 527 (Minn. App. 1987)
15 ALR5th 391—§ 13
State v. Anderson, 415 N.W.2d 57 (Minn. App. 1987)
43 ALR5th 1—§ 13
State v. Anderson, 427 N.W.2d 316, 48 Ed. Law Rep. 649 (N.D. 1988)
70 ALR5th 169—§ 8, 11

For assistance, call 1-800-328-4880

State v. Anderson, 434 A.2d 6 (Me. 1981)

85 ALR5th 187—§ 9, 13

State v. Anderson, 440 So. 2d 205 (La. Ct. App. 3d Cir. 1983)

78 ALR5th 1—§ 57

State v. Anderson, 517 N.W.2d 208 (Iowa 1994)

93 ALR5th 527—§ 17

State v. Anderson, 573 N.W.2d 872 (Wis. Ct. App. 1997)

15 ALR5th 391—§ 43

State v. Anderson, 603 So. 2d 776 (La. Ct. App. 1st Cir. 1992)

99 ALR6th 295—§ 7

State v. Anderson, 636 N.W.2d 26 (Iowa 2001)

119 ALR5th 275—§ 8, 11

State v. Anderson, 679 S.E.2d 165 (N.C. Ct. App. 2009)

57 ALR6th 1—§ 3, 7, 8, 19

State v. Anderson, 784 So. 2d 666 (La. Ct. App. 1st Cir. 2001)

47 ALR6th 107—§ 48, 65, 71

State v. Anderson, 929 P.2d 1107 (Utah 1996)

70 ALR5th 533—§ 2

State v. Anderson, 1990 WL 50740 (Tenn. Crim. App. 1990)

56 ALR6th 323—§ 11

State v. Anderson, 1991 WL 90856 (Minn. Ct. App. 1991)

73 ALR5th 383—§ 5, 32

State v. Anderson, 1991 WL 126648 (Minn. Ct. App. 1991)

73 ALR5th 383—§ 3

State v. Anderson, 1996 WL 665902 (Minn. Ct. App. 1996)

32 ALR6th 171—§ 6, 21

33 ALR6th 1—§ 22

State v. Anderson, 1997 WL 600042 (Wash. Ct. App. Div. 3 1997)

68 ALR5th 343—§ 3

State v. Anderson, 1998 OK CR 67, 972 P.2d 32 (Okla. Crim. App. 1998)

76 ALR6th 1—§ 5, 6

State v. Anderson, 1998 WL 74261 (Minn. Ct. App. 1998)

31 ALR6th 465—§ 11, 26, 27, 34

State v. Anderson, 1998 WL 531854 (Minn. Ct. App. 1998)

69 ALR5th 425—§ 5

State v. Anderson, 1999 WL 486982 (Minn. Ct. App. 1999)

87 ALR5th 1—§ 11

State v. Anderson, 2000 SD 45, 608 N.W.2d 644 (S.D. 2000)

29 ALR6th 1—§ 8

State v. Anderson, 2001 -NMCA- 027, 24 P.3d 327 (N.M. Ct. App. 2001)

29 ALR5th 487—§ 13

State v. Anderson, 2001 WL 1729141 (Del. Super. Ct. 2001)

47 ALR6th 423—§ 2

State v. Anderson, 2002 WL 1968814 (Minn. Ct. App. 2002)

45 ALR6th 337—§ 7

69 ALR6th 579—§ 8, 18

State v. Anderson, 2006 WI 77, 291 Wis. 2d 673, 717 N.W.2d 74 (2006)

65 ALR6th 537—§ 19

State v. Anderson, 2006 WL 1985778 (Minn. Ct. App. 2006)

84 ALR6th 293—§ 15

State v. Anderson, 2008 WL 114360 (N.J. Super. Ct. App. Div. 2008)

99 ALR6th 295—§ 5

State v. Anderson, 2009 WL 1515258 (Minn. Ct. App. 2009)

50 ALR6th 455—§ 36

State v. Anderson, No. 9277 (September 6, 1979, Ct. App. Ohio, 9th App. Dist. Summit Co.)

39 ALR5th 283—§ 14, 56

State v. Anderson, No. 52160, Slip Op. (Ohio App. Cuyahoga Co. 1987)

45 ALR5th 591—§ 9

State v. Andre, 121 Wash. App. 1027, 2004 WL 938563 (Div. 1 2004)

27 ALR6th 183—§ 35

State v. Andree, 90 Wash. App. 917, 954 P.2d 346 (Div. 1 1998)

6 ALR5th 733—§ 15

State v. Andrei, 574 A.2d 295 (Me. 1990)
 65 ALR5th 407—§ 2, 3, 20
State v. Andreias, 2011-Ohio-5030, 2011 WL 4529116 (Ohio Ct. App. 6th Dist. Erie County 2011)
 74 ALR6th 373—§ 18
State v. Andren, 347 N.W.2d 846 (Minn. Ct. App. 1984)
 73 ALR5th 383—§ 5
State v. Andren, 358 N.W.2d 428 (Minn. Ct. App. 1984)
 31 ALR6th 49—§ 8
State v. Andretta, 61 N.J. 544, 296 A.2d 644 (1972)
 95 ALR5th 471—§ 2, 3, 11, 14
State v. Andrews, 52 N.C. App. 26, 277 S.E.2d 857 (1981)
 24 ALR5th 132—§ 3, 9
State v. Andrews, 123 N.M. 95, 934 P.2d 289 (N.M.App. 1997)
 66 ALR5th 397—§ 16
State v. Andrews, 131 N.C. App. 371, 507 S.E.2d 305 (1998)
 93 ALR5th 327—§ 32
State v. Andrews, 171 Wis. 2d 217, 491 N.W.2d 504 (App. 1992)
 27 ALR5th 593—§ 15
State v. Andrews, 187 Kan. 458, 357 P.2d 739 (1960)
 93 ALR5th 327—§ 32
State v. Andrews, 201 Wis. 2d 383, 549 N.W.2d 210, 51 A.L.R.5th 833 (1996)
 51 ALR5th 375—§ 7, 10
State v. Andrews, 306 N.C. 144, 291 S.E.2d 581 (1982)
 29 ALR5th 59—§ 58, 69, 76, 84
State v. Andrews, 337 So. 2d 1175 (La. 1976)
 84 ALR6th 427—§ 4
State v. Andrews, 369 So. 2d 1049 (La. 1979)
 72 ALR5th 529—§ 8
State v. Andrews, 371 S.W.2d 324 (Mo. 1963)
 70 ALR5th 587—§ 3

State v. Andrews, 393 N.W.2d 76 (S.D. 1986)
 5 ALR5th 243—§ 59
State v. Andrews, 907 P.2d 967 (Mont 1995)
 5 ALR5th 243—§ 56
State v. Andrews, 2007 SD 29, 730 N.W.2d 416 (S.D. 2007)
 47 ALR6th 107—§ 4
State v. Andrews, 2008 WL 3413306 (Ariz. Ct. App. Div. 2 2008)
 71 ALR6th 1—§ 8
State v. Andrial, 150 N.J. Super. 198, 375 A.2d 292 (Law Div. 1977)
 57 ALR6th 313—§ 7
State v. Andrial, 203 N.J. Super. 1, 495 A.2d 878 (App. Div. 1985)
 57 ALR6th 313—§ 7
State v. Anello, 2007-Ohio-4822, 2007 WL 2713802 (Ohio Ct. App. 5th Dist. Stark County 2007)
 67 ALR6th 531—§ 29
State v. Anez, 108 Ohio Misc. 2d 18, 738 N.E.2d 491 (C.P. 2000)
 117 ALR5th 491—§ 2, 6
State v. Ange, 72 N.C. App. 524, 324 S.E.2d 887 (1985)
 86 ALR5th 59—§ 5
State v. Angel, 173 W. Va. 620, 319 S.E.2d 388 (1984)
 124 ALR5th 1—§ 3
State v. Angelo, 3 N.J. Misc. 1014, 130 A. 458 (Sup. Ct. 1925)
 33 ALR6th 407—§ 5
State v. Angelone, 67 Wash. App. 555, 837 P.2d 656 (Div. 2 1992)
 70 ALR6th 361—§ 4
 72 ALR6th 141—§ 3, 10
State v. Angelos, 86 Wash. App. 253, 936 P.2d 52 (Div. 1 1997)
 58 ALR6th 499—§ 12
State v. Angelos, 2003 UT App 162, 2003 WL 21281931 (Utah Ct. App. 2003)
 78 ALR6th 1—§ 3
State v. Angeski, 2005 WL 3289447 (Minn. Ct. App. 2005)

78 ALR6th 599—§ 6

State v. Angulo, 2007-Ohio-525, 2007 WL 404349 (Ohio Ct. App. 5th Dist. Muskingum County 2007)

26 ALR6th 511—§ 4

State v. Angus, 2006-Ohio-4455, 2006 WL 2474512 (Ohio Ct. App. 10th Dist. Franklin County 2006)

45 ALR6th 435—§ 10
70 ALR6th 329—§ 18

State v. Anhalt, 630 N.W.2d 658 (Minn. Ct. App. 2001)

50 ALR6th 455—§ 8, 19

State v. Anicker, 217 Kan. 314, 536 P.2d 1355 (1975)

24 ALR5th 465—§ 13, 115, 116, 120

State v. Anim, 2000 WL 136095 (Minn. Ct. App. 2000)

43 ALR6th 475—§ 6

State v. A.N.J., 98 N.J. 421, 487 A.2d 324 (1985)

69 ALR6th 1—§ 22

State v. Annadale, 329 N.C. 557, 406 S.E.2d 837 (1991)

22 ALR5th 1—§ 4, 5, 14, 28, 31, 44, 45

State v. Annor, 2010-Ohio-5423, 2010 WL 4512832 (Ohio Ct. App. 12th Dist. Butler County 2010)

71 ALR6th 1—§ 8

State v. Annunziato, 145 Conn. 124, 139 A.2d 612 (1958)

102 ALR5th 525—§ 44

State v. Anonymous (1971-2), 6 Conn. Cir. Ct. 372, 274 A.2d 897 (App. Div. 1971)

113 ALR5th 1—§ 10

State v. Anonymous (1971-7), 6 Conn. Cir. Ct. 462, 275 A.2d 825 (1971)

67 ALR6th 209—§ 26

State v. Anonymous (1972-4), 6 Conn. Cir. Ct. 667, 298 A.2d 52 (1972)

52 ALR6th 125—§ 14

State v. Anonymous (1973-5), 30 Conn. Supp. 197, 308 A.2d 251 (Super Ct. 1973)

85 ALR5th 1—§ 11

State v. Anonymous (1976-9), 33 Conn. Supp. 93, 363 A.2d 772 (C.P. 1976)

52 ALR6th 125—§ 31, 51

State v. Anonymous (1984-1), 40 Conn. Supp. 20, 480 A.2d 600 (Super. Ct. 1984)

85 ALR5th 1—§ 24
18 ALR6th 1—§ 2, 5, 13
27 ALR6th 491—§ 3

State v. Anonymous (1986-1), 40 Conn. Supp. 498, 516 A.2d 156 (Super Ct. 1986)

64 ALR5th 671—§ 4

State v. Ansari, 2004 UT App 326, 100 P.3d 231 (Utah Ct. App. 2004)

33 ALR6th 373—§ 4, 5, 7, 8

State v. Anselmo, 558 P.2d 1325 (Utah 1977)

103 ALR6th 507—§ 20

State v. Anthony, 24 Conn. App. 195, 588 A.2d 214 (1991)

3 ALR5th 521—§ 3

State v. Anthony, 257 Kan. 1003, 898 P.2d 1109 (1995)

16 ALR6th 329—§ 4
19 ALR6th 115—§ 4, 7, 10
24 ALR6th 591—§ 4, 12, 15

State v. Anthony, 354 N.C. 372, 555 S.E.2d 557 (2001)

83 ALR6th 255—§ 15

State v. Anthony, 759 S.E.2d 712 (N.C. Ct. App. 2014)

99 ALR6th 295—§ 9

State v. Anthony, 817 S.W.2d 299 (Tenn. 1991)

39 ALR5th 283—§ 2, 4, 18

State v. Anthony, 837 S.W.2d 941 (Mo. App. 1992)

27 ALR5th 593—§ 7, 12

State v. Anthony, 1997 WL 629983 (Ohio Ct. App. 10th Dist. Franklin County 1997)

90 ALR5th 453—§ 17
10 ALR6th 463—§ 4
103 ALR6th 247—§ 18

State v. Anthony D.B., 237 Wis. 2d 1, 2000 WI 94, 614 N.W.2d 435 (2000)

87 ALR5th 277—§ 2
State v. Antoine, 1997 N.D. 100, 564 N.W.2d 637 (N.D. 1997)
72 ALR5th 403—§ 11, 15
State v. Antone, 62 Haw. 346, 615 P.2d 101, 9 A.L.R.4th 342 (1980)
80 ALR5th 55—§ 3
State v. Antonelli, 2003 WL 21699977 (Tex. App. Dallas 2003)
51 ALR6th 359—§ 28
State v. Antrican, 1986 WL 712 (Ohio Ct. App. 2d Dist. Montgomery County 1986)
85 ALR5th 1—§ 15
State v. Anzaldua, 675 S.W.2d 806 (Tex. App. Corpus Christi 1984)
70 ALR6th 1—§ 7
State v. Anzalone, 1983 WL 5785 (Ohio Ct. App. 8th Dist. Cuyahoga County 1983)
102 ALR5th 525—§ 19
State v. A.O., 2009 WL 232415 (N.J. Super. Ct. App. Div. 2009)
69 ALR6th 579—§ 11
State v. Apanovitch, 33 Ohio St. 3d 19, 514 N.E.2d 394 (1987)
57 ALR5th 141—§ 2, 3, 14
State v. Apanovitch, 113 Ohio App. 3d 591, 681 N.E.2d 961 (8th Dist. Cuyahoga County 1996)
94 ALR5th 393—§ 13
State v. Apelt, 176 Ariz. 349, 861 P.2d 634 (1993)
57 ALR5th 141—§ 7
83 ALR5th 541—§ 2, 3
State v. Apodaca, 85 Or. App. 128, 735 P.2d 1264 (1987)
64 ALR5th 637—§ 4
58 ALR6th 499—§ 87
State v. Apodaca, 166 Ariz. 274, 801 P.2d 1177, 64 Ariz. Adv. Rep. 72 (App. 1990)
34 ALR5th 125—§ 30
State v. Aponte, 249 Conn. 735, 738 A.2d 117 (1999)
82 ALR6th 373—§ 7, 19, 20

State v. Applegate, 68 Ohio St. 3d 348, 1994-Ohio-356, 626 N.E.2d 942 (1994)
58 ALR6th 499—§ 30
State v. Applegate, 266 Kan. 1072, 976 P.2d 936 (1999)
15 ALR5th 391—§ 15
State v. Applegate, 2005 WL 564158 (Tenn. Crim. App. 2005)
26 ALR6th 511—§ 33
State v. Appleton, 297 A.2d 363 (Me. 1972)
41 ALR5th 171—§ 16
113 ALR5th 517—§ 3
State v. Applewhite, 1989 WL 138965 (Minn. Ct. App. 1989)
73 ALR5th 383—§ 31
State v. Apportionment Com'n, 125 N.J. 375, 593 A.2d 710 (1991)
56 ALR5th 171—§ 12, 26
State v. Apprendi, 159 N.J. 7, 731 A.2d 485 (1999)
22 ALR5th 261—§ 3
State v. Apt, 244 N.W.2d 801 (Iowa 1976)
18 ALR5th 1—§ 2, 10
State v. Aquino, 149 N.C. App. 172, 560 S.E.2d 552 (2002)
29 ALR6th 1—§ 10
49 ALR6th 343—§ 32
State v. Aquino-Cervantes, 88 Wash. App. 699, 945 P.2d 767 (Div. 2 1997)
66 ALR6th 83—§ 21
State v. Araiza, 124 Idaho 82, 856 P.2d 872 (1993)
20 ALR5th 398—§ 25
State v. Araki, 82 Haw. 474, 923 P.2d 891 (1996)
18 ALR6th 1—§ 5, 9
State v. Arana, 165 Or. App. 454, 998 P.2d 688 (2000)
112 ALR5th 429—§ 12
State v. Araujo, 36 Kan. App. 2d 747, 144 P.3d 66 (2006)
30 ALR6th 1—§ 4, 7
State v. Arbino, 83 Ohio Misc. 2d 12, 677 N.E.2d 1273 (Mun. Ct. 1996)

58 ALR6th 499—§ 48
State v. Archer, 1927-NMSC-002, 32
N.M. 319, 255 P. 396 (1927)
101 ALR6th 499—§ 15
State v. Archible, 25 N.C. App. 95, 212
S.E.2d 44 (1975)
38 ALR6th 97—§ 17
State v. Archuletta, 28 Utah 2d 255, 501
P.2d 263 (1972)
99 ALR6th 295—§ 5
State v. Archuletta, 85 Haw. 512, 946
P.2d 620 (Haw. Ct. App. 1997)
71 ALR5th 285—§ 3
State v. Arculeo, 29 Kan. App. 2d 962,
36 P.3d 305 (2001)
74 ALR6th 69—§ 3, 5
State v. Ard, 332 S.C. 370, 505 S.E.2d
328 (1998)
79 ALR5th 33—§ 47
State v. Arellano, 801 S.W.2d 128 (Tex.
App. San Antonio 1990)
70 ALR6th 1—§ 6
State v. Arena, 46 Haw. 315, 379 P.2d
594, 20 A.L.R.3d 450 (1963)
84 ALR6th 427—§ 27
State v. Arend, 2001 WL 436218 (Minn.
Ct. App. 2001)
34 ALR6th 1—§ 8
State v. Arias, 283 N.J. Super. 269, 661
A.2d 850 (Law Div. 1992)
58 ALR6th 499—§ 110
State v. Arillo, 122 N.H. 107, 441 A.2d
1163 (1982)
5 ALR5th 243—§ 59
State v. Arlington, 265 Mont. 127, 875
P.2d 307 (1994)
38 ALR5th 433—§ 29
State v. Arlington, 875 P.2d 307 (Mont
1994)
5 ALR5th 243—§ 60, 61
State v. Armbrust, 274 Kan. 1089, 59
P.3d 1000 (2002)
33 ALR6th 91—§ 6
63 ALR6th 351—§ 3
State v. Armendariz, 234 Neb. 170, 449
N.W.2d 555 (1989)
41 ALR5th 171—§ 12

State v. Armenta, 2002-Ohio-6110, 2002
WL 31502090 (Ohio Ct. App. 12th
Dist. Warren County 2002)
58 ALR6th 215—§ 13
State v. Armentor, 649 So. 2d 1187 (La.
Ct. App. 3d Cir. 1995)
88 ALR5th 121—§ 3, 36
State v. Armijo, 90 N.M. 614, 566 P.2d
1152 (App. 1977)
28 ALR5th 754—§ 2
State v. Armijo, 123 N.M. 690, 1997
-NMCA- 080, 944 P.2d 919,
R.I.C.O. Bus. Disp. Guide (CCH)
¶ 9349 (Ct. App. 1997)
89 ALR5th 629—§ 6
State v. Arms, 1998 WL 114356 (Ohio
Ct. App. 6th Dist. Lucas County
1998)
84 ALR6th 293—§ 31
State v. Armstead, 85 Ohio App. 3d 247,
619 N.E.2d 513 (Allen Co. 1993)
27 ALR5th 593—§ 2
State v. Armstead, 103 Miss. 790, 60 So.
778 (1913)
88 ALR6th 203—§ 15, 68
State v. Armstead, 385 So. 2d 241 (La.
1980)
27 ALR6th 491—§ 3
State v. Armstrong, 38 Or. App. 219,
589 P.2d 1174 (1979)
28 ALR6th 505—§ 10
State v. Armstrong, 44 Or. App. 219,
605 P.2d 736 (1980)
92 ALR5th 35—§ 7
State v. Armstrong, 103 Ohio App. 3d
416, 659 N.E.2d 844 (Lorain Co.
1995)
50 ALR5th 581—§ 7
State v. Armstrong, 106 Wash. 2d 547,
723 P.2d 1111 (1986)
73 ALR5th 383—§ 5
State v. Armstrong, 144 Wash. App.
1044, 2008 WL 2239518 (Div. 2
2008)
45 ALR6th 643—§ 9
State v. Armstrong, 150 Wis. 2d 949,
444 N.W.2d 67 (Ct. App. 1989)
72 ALR5th 403—§ 19

State v. Armstrong, 179 W. Va. 435, 369
S.E.2d 870 (1988)
1 ALR6th 657—§ 4

State v. Armstrong, 189 Mont. 407, 616
P.2d 341 (1980)
93 ALR5th 527—§ 17

State v. Armstrong, 203 Mo. 554, 102
S.W. 503 (1907)
5 ALR6th 1—§ 61

State v. Armstrong, 209 Wis. 2d 82, 562
N.W.2d 926 (Ct. App. 1997)
69 ALR6th 579—§ 5

State v. Armstrong, 223 Wis. 2d 331,
588 N.W.2d 606 (1999)
38 ALR6th 97—§ 18

State v. Armstrong, 240 Kan. 446, 731
P.2d 249 (1987)
55 ALR6th 391—§ 10
56 ALR6th 185—§ 10

State v. Armstrong, 282 Minn. 39, 162
N.W.2d 357 (1968)
72 ALR5th 1—§ 10

State v. Armstrong, 287 N.C. 60, 212
S.E.2d 894 (1975)
62 ALR5th 121—§ 3

State v. Armstrong, 555 S.W.2d 640
(Mo. App. 1977)
29 ALR5th 59—§ 7

State v. Armstrong, 756 So. 2d 533 (La.
Ct. App. 5th Cir. 2000)
97 ALR5th 293—§ 3

State v. Armstrong, 1998 WL 229592
(Wash. Ct. App. Div. 2 1998)
73 ALR5th 383—§ 48

State v. Armstrong, 2004-Ohio-5635,
2004 WL 2376467 (Ohio Ct. App.
11th Dist. Trumbull County 2004)
103 ALR6th 247—§ 5, 20

State v. Armstrong, 2004 WI App 125,
683 N.W.2d 93 (Wis. Ct. App.
2004)
125 ALR5th 497—§ 4

State v. Arnall, 603 S.W.2d 111 (Mo. Ct.
App. S.D. 1980)
1 ALR6th 549—§ 8

State v. Arnett, 38 Wash. App. 527, 686
P.2d 500 (1984)
39 ALR5th 283—§ 4

State v. Arnold, 98 Conn. App. 492, 909
A.2d 581 (2006)
27 ALR6th 491—§ 3

State v. Arnold, 115 Or. App. 258, 838
P.2d 74 (1992)
85 ALR5th 1—§ 24

State v. Arnold, 118 Or. App. 64, 846
P.2d 418 (1993)
38 ALR5th 433—§ 3

State v. Arnold, 133 Or. App. 647, 893
P.2d 1050 (1995)
38 ALR5th 433—§ 3

State v. Arnold, 147 N.C. App. 670, 557
S.E.2d 119 (2001)
68 ALR6th 115—§ 46 to 48, 52

State v. Arnold, 284 N.C. 41, 199 S.E.2d
423 (1973)
104 ALR5th 357—§ 6
54 ALR6th 429—§ 9, 11

State v. Arnold, 421 A.2d 932 (Me.
1980)
41 ALR5th 171—§ 6, 10, 16

State v. Arnold, 2003-Ohio-6818, 2003
WL 22956425 (Ohio Ct. App. 9th
Dist. Wayne County 2003)
23 ALR6th 307—§ 12

State v. Arnoldi, 176 Ariz. 236, 860 P.2d
503, 136 Ariz. Adv. Rep. 42 (App.
1993)
7 ALR5th 263—§ 3

State v. Arntzen, 1996 WL 341654
(Alaska Ct. App. 1996)
60 ALR5th 1—§ 2, 8

State v. Aronhalt, 99 Wash. App. 302,
994 P.2d 248 (Div. 3 2000)
39 ALR5th 283—§ 70

State v. Arp, 274 N.J. Super. 379, 644
A.2d 149 (Law Div. 1994)
39 ALR5th 283—§ 4, 58

State v. Arpan, 277 N.W.2d 597 (S.D.
1979)
124 ALR5th 1—§ 4

State v. Arpin, 188 Conn. 183, 448 A.2d
1334 (1982)
106 ALR5th 397—§ 4

State v. Arredondo, 111 Ariz. 141, 526
P.2d 163 (1974)

---

9 ALR6th 1—§ 15

State v. Arreola, 93 Or. App. 680, 763 P.2d 748 (1988)

109 ALR5th 99—§ 3

State v. Arrington, 375 S.W.2d 186 (Mo. 1964)

54 ALR6th 429—§ 5

State v. Arrone, 2006-Ohio-4144, 2006 WL 2335574 (Ohio Ct. App. 2d Dist. Greene County 2006)

35 ALR6th 127—§ 5

State v. Arroyo, 284 Conn. 597, 935 A.2d 975 (2007)

30 ALR6th 1—§ 3, 7

39 ALR6th 257—§ 34

State v. Arroyo, 2005 WL 3710667 (N.J. Super. Ct. App. Div. 2006)

33 ALR6th 91—§ 36

State v. Arstone, 1992 WL 90146 (Ohio Ct. App. 8th Dist. Cuyahoga County 1992)

80 ALR6th 599—§ 11

State v. Arteaga, 2013 WL 1776691 (Ariz. Ct. App. Div. 2 2013)

94 ALR6th 191—§ 7

State v. Arthun, 274 Mont. 82, 906 P.2d 216 (1995)

23 ALR6th 307—§ 31, 38

State v. Arthur, 244 N.C. 582, 94 S.E.2d 646 (1956)

41 ALR5th 1—§ 3, 4, 8

State v. Arthur, 287 N.J. Super. 147, 670 A.2d 592 (App. Div. 1996)

62 ALR5th 1—§ 2

State v. Arthur, 296 S.C. 495, 374 S.E.2d 291 (1988)

20 ALR5th 177—§ 3

State v. Artis, 316 N.C. 507, 342 S.E.2d 847 (1986)

73 ALR5th 383—§ 9

State v. Artis, 325 N.C. 278, 384 S.E.2d 470 (1989)

57 ALR5th 141—§ 2, 7

State v. Artrip, 112 N.M. 87, 811 P.2d 585 (Ct. App. 1991)

95 ALR5th 229—§ 32

State v. Arundell, 278 N.J. Super. 202, 650 A.2d 845 (Law Div. 1994)

121 ALR5th 551—§ 8, 12

State v. Arvel, 481 So. 2d 691 (La. Ct. App. 1st Cir. 1985)

124 ALR5th 1—§ 5

State v. Arviso, 1999 UT App 381, 993 P.2d 894 (Utah Ct. App. 1999)

75 ALR6th 541—§ 15

State v. Arvizo, 233 Neb. 327, 444 N.W.2d 921 (1989)

15 ALR5th 391—§ 35

92 ALR5th 35—§ 7

State v. Arwood, 46 Or. App. 653, 612 P.2d 763 (1980)

70 ALR6th 361—§ 3, 4

71 ALR6th 335—§ 3

State v. A.S., 622 So. 2d 1127, 18 FLW D 1787 (Fla. App. D1 1993)

46 ALR5th 523—§ 4, 8

State v. A.S., 2007 WL 1541926 (N.J. Super. Ct. App. Div. 2007)

39 ALR6th 257—§ 47

State v. Asbell, 57 Kan. 398, 46 P. 770 (1896)

11 ALR5th 497—§ 3, 6, 12, 13

State v. Asfoor, 75 Wis. 2d 411, 249 N.W.2d 529 (1977)

33 ALR6th 407—§ 12

State v. Ash, 23 Utah 2d 14, 456 P.2d 154 (1969)

78 ALR5th 567—§ 10

State v. Ashby, 567 N.W.2d 21 (Minn. 1997)

57 ALR5th 141—§ 13

State v. Ashby, 2008 MT 83, 342 Mont. 187, 179 P.3d 1164 (2008)

46 ALR6th 241—§ 6, 9 to 11, 20

State v. Ashcraft, 859 P.2d 60 (Wash. App. 1993)

38 ALR5th 433—§ 11

State v. Ashe, 425 A.2d 191 (Me. 1981)

9 ALR6th 1—§ 17

State v. Ashelman, 137 Ariz. 460, 671 P.2d 901 (1983)

124 ALR5th 1—§ 5

State v. Asher, 112 Ohio App. 3d 646, 679 N.E.2d 1147 (1st Dist. Hamilton County 1996)

For assistance, call 1-800-328-4880

3 ALR6th 269—§ 5, 8
State v. Asher, 246 S.W. 911 (Mo. 1922)
97 ALR5th 293—§ 3 to 6
State v. Asherman, 193 Conn. 695, 478 A.2d 227 (1984)
1 ALR6th 657—§ 4, 13
State v. Ashley, 616 S.W.2d 556 (Mo. Ct. App. W.D. 1981)
1 ALR6th 549—§ 8
State v. Ashley, 701 So. 2d 338 (Fla. 1997)
64 ALR5th 671—§ 4
State v. Ashley, 2006-Ohio-2016, 2006 WL 1062879 (Ohio Ct. App. 11th Dist. Lake County 2006)
26 ALR6th 511—§ 19
State v. Ashman, 123 Tenn. 654, 135 S.W. 325 (1911)
31 ALR6th 523—§ 7, 10, 46, 47
State v. Ashworth, 170 W. Va. 205, 292 S.E.2d 615 (1982)
34 ALR5th 125—§ 3
State v. A.S.J., 2010 WL 773617 (Minn. Ct. App. 2010)
69 ALR6th 1—§ 5
State v. Askew, 2005-Ohio-3194, 2005 WL 1491503 (Ohio Ct. App. 5th Dist. Stark County 2005)
62 ALR6th 161—§ 3
State v. Aspili, 105 Haw. 251, 96 P.3d 271 (2004)
63 ALR6th 351—§ 3
State v. Astalos, 160 N.J. Super. 407, 390 A.2d 144 (Law Div. 1978)
114 ALR5th 173—§ 11
State v. Astello, 602 N.W.2d 190 (Iowa Ct. App. 1999)
29 ALR6th 1—§ 10
State v. Aston, 2006-Ohio-3773, 2006 WL 2042929 (Ohio Ct. App. 11th Dist. Lake County 2006)
26 ALR6th 511—§ 4, 19
State v. Astorga, 26 Ariz. App. 133, 546 P.2d 1142 (Div. 2 1976)
7 ALR6th 169—§ 3, 7
8 ALR6th 265—§ 3
State v. Atchison, 15 Neb. App. 422, 730 N.W.2d 115 (2007)

33 ALR6th 373—§ 17
State v. Aten, 130 Wash. 2d 640, 927 P.2d 210 (1996)
33 ALR5th 571—§ 3
96 ALR5th 523—§ 3
State v. Atherton, 106 Wash. App. 783, 24 P.3d 1123 (Div. 1 2001)
19 ALR6th 697—§ 5, 17
State v. Atkins, 182 Wis. 2d 509, 514 N.W.2d 878 (Ct. App. 1994)
72 ALR5th 403—§ 15
State v. Atkins, 292 S.W. 422 (Mo. 1926)
104 ALR5th 357—§ 3
State v. Atkins, 349 N.C. 62, 505 S.E.2d 97 (1998)
10 ALR5th 700—§ 3
State v. Atkins, 1989 WL 52659 (Minn. Ct. App. 1989)
19 ALR6th 697—§ 6
State v. Atkins, 1994 WL 81524 (Tenn. Crim. App. 1994)
55 ALR5th 423—§ 6
State v. Atkinson, 46 Conn. Supp. 130, 741 A.2d 991 (Super Ct. 1999)
5 ALR5th 243—§ 47
State v. Atkinson, 215 Kan. 139, 523 P.2d 737 (1974)
88 ALR5th 121—§ 3, 37
State v. Atkinson, 458 A.2d 1200 (Me. 1983)
78 ALR5th 567—§ 9
State v. Atlas, 224 Mont. 92, 728 P.2d 421 (1986)
85 ALR5th 187—§ 20
State v. Atley, 564 N.W.2d 817 (Iowa 1997)
55 ALR6th 391—§ 21, 23
State v. Attaway, 117 N.M. 141, 870 P.2d 103 (1994)
85 ALR5th 1—§ 23, 49
State v. Atterton, 81 Wash. App. 470, 915 P.2d 535 (Div. 1 1996)
84 ALR5th 487—§ 19
State v. Atti, 127 N.J.L. 39, 21 A.2d 603 (N.J. Sup. Ct. 1941)
5 ALR6th 1—§ 3, 40

State v. Attmore, 92 N.C. App. 385, 374 S.E.2d 649 (1988)
   72 ALR5th 109—§ 4, 5

State v. Atwood, 171 Ariz. 576, 832 P.2d 593 (1992)
   79 ALR5th 33—§ 9, 39
   86 ALR5th 463—§ 2, 4, 7, 10

State v. Atwood, 250 N.C. 141, 108 S.E.2d 219, 86 A.L.R.2d 602 (1959)
   11 ALR5th 497—§ 3, 9, 16

State v. Atwood, 602 N.W.2d 775 (Iowa 1999)
   84 ALR6th 427—§ 10, 19

State v. Auble, 754 P.2d 935 (Utah 1988)
   57 ALR5th 141—§ 3

State v. Aubrey, 609 So. 2d 1183 (La. Ct. App. 3d Cir. 1992)
   70 ALR5th 587—§ 21

State v. Aucoin, 278 A.2d 395 (Me. 1971)
   72 ALR5th 1—§ 3

State v. Aucoin, 756 S.W.2d 705 (Tenn. Crim. 1988)
   31 ALR5th 704—§ 2

State v. Auge, 2002-Ohio-3061, 2002 WL 1312668 (Ohio Ct. App. 10th Dist. Franklin County 2002)
   70 ALR6th 1—§ 23

State v. Auger, 124 Vt. 50, 196 A.2d 562 (1963)
   76 ALR5th 1—§ 5, 14

State v. August, 719 So. 2d 536 (La. Ct. App. 4th Cir. 1998)
   16 ALR6th 329—§ 4
   24 ALR6th 591—§ 4, 14

State v. Augustine, 449 So. 2d 78 (La. Ct. App. 4th Cir. 1984)
   4 ALR6th 599—§ 16

State v. Augustine, 458 N.W.2d 859 (Iowa App. 1990)
   3 ALR5th 784—§ 10, 20

State v. Augustine, 458 N.W.2d 859 (Iowa Ct. App. 1990)
   7 ALR6th 233—§ 9

State v. Aukes, 192 Wis. 2d 338, 531 N.W.2d 382 (Ct. App. 1995)
   70 ALR6th 361—§ 32

State v. Aukes, 2001 WL 23000 (Iowa Ct. App. 2001)
   112 ALR5th 429—§ 15

State v. Auld, 2 N.J. 426, 67 A.2d 175 (1949)
   33 ALR6th 353—§ 3

State v. Ault, 150 Ariz. 459, 724 P.2d 545 (1986)
   19 ALR5th 470—§ 3, 13
   17 ALR6th 327—§ 31, 40

State v. Auman, 386 N.W.2d 818 (Minn. App. 1986)
   11 ALR5th 52—§ 10

State v. Aune, 1999 WL 672678 (Minn. Ct. App. 1999)
   30 ALR6th 483—§ 15

State v. Auringer, 335 N.J. Super. 94, 761 A.2d 102 (App. Div. 2000)
   65 ALR6th 329—§ 4, 6

State v. Ausmus, 336 Or. 493, 85 P.3d 864 (2004)
   52 ALR6th 125—§ 13, 18

State v. Austad, 197 Mont. 70, 641 P.2d 1373 (1982)
   100 ALR6th 535—§ 3

State v. Austex, Ltd., 35 Tex. Sup. Ct. Jour 300 (Tex. 1992)
   7 ALR5th 113—§ 5

State v. Austex, Ltd., 862 S.W.2d 1 (Tex. App. Austin 1991)
   7 ALR5th 113—§ 5

State v. Austin, 74 Conn. App. 802, 813 A.2d 1060 (2003)
   4 ALR6th 599—§ 13

State v. Austin, 111 N.C. App. 590, 432 S.E.2d 881 (1993)
   47 ALR5th 259—§ 2, 5

State v. Austin, 124 Ariz. 231, 603 P.2d 502 (1979)
   72 ALR6th 1—§ 4

State v. Austin, 160 Tex. 348, 331 S.W.2d 737 (1960)
   36 ALR5th 657—§ 4

State v. Austin, 258 La. 273, 246 So. 2d 12 (1971)
   55 ALR6th 157—§ 21

State v. Austin, 320 N.C. 276, 357 S.E.2d 641 (1987)
57 ALR5th 141—§ 6

State v. Austin, 584 P.2d 853 (Utah 1978)
62 ALR5th 1—§ 6, 14

State v. Austin, 585 N.W.2d 241 (Iowa 1998)
59 ALR5th 135—§ 5

State v. Austin, 641 A.2d 56 (R.I. 1994)
103 ALR6th 347—§ 25

State v. Austin, 689 S.W.2d 136 (Mo. Ct. App. S.D. 1985)
71 ALR6th 335—§ 22

State v. Austin, 900 So. 2d 867 (La. Ct. App. 5th Cir. 2005)
55 ALR6th 157—§ 26

State v. Austin, 2007 ND 30, 727 N.W.2d 790 (N.D. 2007)
84 ALR6th 263—§ 8

State v. Austin, No. 6314 (December 5, 1980, Ct. App. Ohio, 2nd App. Dist. Montgomery Co.)
39 ALR5th 283—§ 14, 57, 68

State v. Austin, No. 45267 (July 28, 1983, Ct. App. Ohio, 8th App. Dist. Cuyahoga Co.)
39 ALR5th 283—§ 14, 71

State v. Austria, 55 Haw. 565, 524 P.2d 290 (1974)
6 ALR6th 533—§ 17

State v. Autheman, 47 Idaho 328, 274 P. 805, 62 A.L.R. 195 (1929)
28 ALR5th 754—§ 6

State v. Avant, 1993 WL 481408 (Ohio Ct. App. 3d Dist. Marion County 1993)
99 ALR6th 295—§ 9

State v. Avena, 281 N.J. Super. 327, 657 A.2d 883 (App. Div. 1995)
90 ALR6th 385—§ 7

State v. Avery, 120 S.W.3d 196, 3 A.L.R.6th 809 (Mo. 2003)
3 ALR6th 543—§ 6

State v. Avery, 130 P.3d 959 (Alaska Ct. App. 2006)
26 ALR6th 511—§ 26

State v. Avery, 213 Wis. 2d 228, 570 N.W.2d 573 (Ct. App. 1997)
125 ALR5th 497—§ 4

State v. Avery, 215 Wis. 2d 45, 571 N.W.2d 907 (Ct. App. 1997)
41 ALR6th 295—§ 2, 5, 7

State v. Avery, 295 Wis. 2d 489, 2006 WI App 156, 719 N.W.2d 799 (Ct. App. 2006)
41 ALR6th 295—§ 5, 7

State v. Avery, 315 N.C. 1, 337 S.E.2d 786 (1985)
110 ALR5th 329—§ 6

State v. Avery, 333 S.C. 284, 509 S.E.2d 476 (1998)
16 ALR6th 329—§ 4
24 ALR6th 591—§ 6

State v. Avery, 2004-Ohio-4165, 2004 WL 1770566 (Ohio Ct. App. 3d Dist. Union County 2004)
97 ALR6th 263—§ 30

State v. A.V.G., 2010 WL 935357 (Minn. Ct. App. 2010)
69 ALR6th 1—§ 33

State v. Avila, 803 N.W.2d 128 (Iowa Ct. App. 2011)
74 ALR6th 373—§ 13

State v. Avnayim, 1 Conn. Cir. Ct. 348, 24 Conn. Supp. 7, 185 A.2d 295 (App. Div. 1962)
66 ALR5th 397—§ 3, 4, 13

State v. Awkal, 76 Ohio St. 3d 324, 667 N.E.2d 960 (1996)
57 ALR5th 141—§ 3

State v. Ayala, 2011 WI App 6, 331 Wis. 2d 171, 793 N.W.2d 511 (Ct. App. 2010)
79 ALR6th 1—§ 45

State v. Ayer, 136 N.H. 191, 612 A.2d 923 (1992)
102 ALR5th 447—§ 4

State v. Ayers, 198 Kan. 467, 426 P.2d 21 (1967)
39 ALR5th 283—§ 4

State v. Ayers, 207 Or. App. 668, 143 P.3d 251 (2006)
70 ALR6th 361—§ 6

State v. Ayers, 257 Ga. App. 117, 570 S.E.2d 603 (2002)
116 ALR5th 479—§ 5
State v. Ayers, 2011-Ohio-4719, 2011 WL 4346678 (Ohio Ct. App. 12th Dist. Warren County 2011)
99 ALR6th 295—§ 13
State v. Aynes, 715 N.E.2d 945 (Ind. Ct. App. 1999)
29 ALR6th 1—§ 9
State v. Ayudkya, 96 N.C. App. 606, 386 S.E.2d 604 (1989)
3 ALR6th 269—§ 25
State v. Azar, 539 So. 2d 1222 (La. 1989)
70 ALR5th 647—§ 2, 3
87 ALR6th 1—§ 3, 5, 6
State v. Aziz, 1994 WL 78349 (Ohio Ct. App. 8th Dist. Cuyahoga County 1994)
88 ALR5th 121—§ 2, 19, 28
State v. Baba, 2002 WL 31440791 (Conn. Super. Ct. 2002)
75 ALR6th 443—§ 8
State v. Babayan, 106 Nev. 155, 787 P.2d 805 (1990)
49 ALR5th 639—§ 3
State v. Babb, 125 Idaho 934, 877 P.2d 905 (1994)
54 ALR6th 429—§ 25
State v. Babin, 637 So. 2d 814 (La. App. 1st Cir. 1994)
36 ALR5th 161—§ 3
State v. Babineaux, 22 Ariz. App. 322, 526 P.2d 1277 (1974)
31 ALR5th 704—§ 16, 18
State v. Babst, 104 Ohio St. 167, 135 N.E. 525 (1922)
51 ALR6th 359—§ 27
State v. Baby, 2008 WL 1734610 (Md. 2008)
33 ALR6th 353—§ 3, 4, 6
State v. Baca, 120 N.M. 383, 902 P.2d 65 (1995)
28 ALR5th 754—§ 5, 8
39 ALR5th 283—§ 77
57 ALR5th 141—§ 3, 7

27 ALR6th 183—§ 39
State v. Baca, 172 Ariz. 1, 832 P.2d 933 (Ct. App. Div. 1 1992)
37 ALR6th 357—§ 24
State v. Baca, 1997-NMSC-018, 123 N.M. 124, 934 P.2d 1053 (1997)
108 ALR5th 593—§ 50
State v. Baccino, 282 A.2d 869, 49 A.L.R.3d 973 (Del. Super. 1971)
31 ALR5th 229—§ 2, 3, 17, 62
State v. Bachelor, 6 Neb. App. 426, 575 N.W.2d 625 (1998)
67 ALR6th 103—§ 3, 23
State v. Bachman, 61 Haw. 71, 595 P.2d 287 (1979)
50 ALR6th 353—§ 54
State v. Bachman, 61 Hawaii 71, 595 P.2d 287 (1979)
1 ALR5th 938—§ 2, 3
State v. Backlund, 2003 ND 184, 672 N.W.2d 431 (N.D. 2003)
33 ALR6th 373—§ 6, 9 to 11, 13
63 ALR6th 351—§ 3
State v. Backus, 881 S.W.2d 591, 93 Ed. Law Rep. 1068 (Tex. App. Austin 1994)
18 ALR6th 519—§ 8
State v. Bacon, 114 N.H. 306, 319 A.2d 636 (1974)
1 ALR6th 549—§ 8
State v. Bacon, 326 N.C. 404, 390 S.E.2d 327 (1990)
31 ALR5th 704—§ 2, 8
28 ALR6th 505—§ 7, 13
State v. Bacon, 337 N.C. 66, 446 S.E.2d 542 (1994)
83 ALR6th 255—§ 9
State v. Bacon, 733 A.2d 50 (Vt. 1999)
73 ALR5th 383—§ 41
State v. Bader, 148 N.H. 265, 808 A.2d 12 (2002)
12 ALR6th 267—§ 5
State v. Badessa, 869 A.2d 61 (R.I. 2005)
70 ALR6th 1—§ 5
State v. Badger, 229 N.J. Super. 288, 551 A.2d 207 (Law Div. 1988)

100 ALR6th 535—§ 3
State v. Badley, 1995 WL 662109 (Ohio App. 8 Dist.)

50 ALR5th 581—§ 9, 19
State v. Baer, 2001 WI App 224, 247 Wis. 2d 991, 635 N.W.2d 28 (Ct. App. 2001)

84 ALR6th 293—§ 38
State v. Baez, 238 N.J. Super. 93, 569 A.2d 268 (1990)

27 ALR5th 593—§ 22
State v. Baez, 530 So. 2d 405 (Fla. Dist. Ct. App. 3d Dist. 1988)

125 ALR5th 281—§ 11
State v. Bagemehl, 213 Kan. 210, 515 P.2d 1104, 62 A.L.R.3d 103 (1973)

34 ALR5th 125—§ 8
State v. Bagley, 52 Conn. L. Rptr. 284, 2011 WL 3587391 (Conn. Super. Ct. 2011)

84 ALR6th 293—§ 19
State v. Bagley, 164 Wis. 2d 255, 474 N.W.2d 761, 17 A.L.R.5th 1072 (App. 1991)

17 ALR5th 837—§ 3
State v. Bagley, 844 So. 2d 688 (Fla. 3d DCA 2003)

103 ALR6th 347—§ 20
State v. Bagshaw, 141 Idaho 257, 108 P.3d 404 (Ct. App. 2004)

38 ALR6th 97—§ 29
State v. Bailey, 32 Conn. App. 773, 631 A.2d 333 (1993)

39 ALR6th 257—§ 42, 47
State v. Bailey, 64 Ohio App. 3d 379, 581 N.E.2d 1104 (Wood Co. 1989)

1 ALR5th 346—§ 5, 7
State v. Bailey, 71 Ohio St. 3d 443, 644 N.E.2d 314 (1994)

87 ALR5th 597—§ 15
State v. Bailey, 76 N.C. App. 610, 334 S.E.2d 266 (1985)

76 ALR5th 1—§ 10
State v. Bailey, 77 Wash. App. 732, 893 P.2d 681 (1995)

50 ALR5th 703—§ 7, 12
State v. Bailey, 85 W. Va. 165, 101 S.E. 169 (1919)

59 ALR5th 135—§ 4, 13
State v. Bailey, 94 Or. App. 767, 767 P.2d 114 (1989)

24 ALR5th 132—§ 5, 7
State v. Bailey, 120 Ariz. 399, 586 P.2d 648 (App. 1978)

42 ALR5th 547—§ 7
State v. Bailey, 144 Vt. 86, 475 A.2d 1045 (1984)

40 ALR5th 113—§ 4
State v. Bailey, 159 W. Va. 167, 220 S.E.2d 432 (1975)

78 ALR5th 567—§ 7
State v. Bailey, 276 S.C. 32, 274 S.E.2d 913 (1981)

55 ALR5th 125—§ 12
State v. Bailey, 321 Wis. 2d 350, 2009 WI App 140, 773 N.W.2d 488 (Ct. App. 2009)

55 ALR6th 1—§ 26
State v. Bailey, 457 So. 2d 94 (La. Ct. App. 4th Cir. 1984)

84 ALR6th 427—§ 14
State v. Bailey, 500 So. 2d 843 (La. Ct. App. 1st Cir. 1986)

57 ALR6th 83—§ 5
State v. Bailey, 639 So. 2d 860 (La. Ct. App. 5th Cir. 1994)

6 ALR6th 533—§ 17
27 ALR6th 491—§ 3
State v. Bailey, 664 So. 2d 665 (La. App. 3d Cir. 1995)

24 ALR5th 465—§ 6, 23, 41.5
State v. Bailey, 713 So. 2d 588 (La. Ct. App. 5th Cir. 1998)

109 ALR5th 99—§ 5
State v. Bailey, 839 S.W.2d 657 (Mo. Ct. App. W.D. 1992)

72 ALR6th 1—§ 4
State v. Bailey, 1991 WL 190294 (Del. Super. Ct. 1991)

21 ALR6th 1—§ 5, 6
State v. Bailey, 1991 WL 225795 (Tenn. Crim. 1991)

52 ALR5th 655—§ 2, 6
State v. Bailey, 2002-Ohio-6740, 2002 WL 31750242 (Ohio Ct. App. 10th Dist. Franklin County 2002)

CASES CITED IN ALR5th and ALR6th

69 ALR6th 1—§ 27
State v. Baillie, 62 N.D. 705, 245 N.W. 466 (1932)
    116 ALR5th 1—§ 35
State v. Bain, 130 Mont. 90, 295 P.2d 241 (1956)
    8 ALR5th 825—§ 6
State v. Bain, 176 Mont. 23, 575 P.2d 919 (1978)
    78 ALR5th 567—§ 7
State v. Baird, 83 Wash. App. 477, 922 P.2d 157 (Div. 1 1996)
    73 ALR5th 383—§ 27
State v. Baity, 140 Wash. 2d 1, 991 P.2d 1151 (2000)
    117 ALR5th 491—§ 3
State v. Baker, 4 Kan. App. 2d 340, 606 P.2d 120 (1980)
    9 ALR6th 1—§ 19
State v. Baker, 46 Or. App. 79, 610 P.2d 840 (1980)
    39 ALR6th 257—§ 19
State v. Baker, 48 S.D. 636, 205 N.W. 666 (1925)
    98 ALR6th 455—§ 28
State v. Baker, 62 Or. App. 835, 662 P.2d 365 (1983)
    55 ALR6th 513—§ 5
State v. Baker, 87 Or. App. 285, 742 P.2d 633 (1987)
    50 ALR5th 467—§ 7, 9
State v. Baker, 112 N.C. App. 410, 435 S.E.2d 812 (1993)
    2 ALR6th 551—§ 32
State v. Baker, 137 Ohio App. 3d 628, 739 N.E.2d 819 (12th Dist. Clinton County 2000)
    3 ALR6th 269—§ 5, 8
State v. Baker, 150 Wash. 82, 272 P. 80 (1928)
    16 ALR6th 329—§ 4
State v. Baker, 154 Vt. 411, 579 A.2d 479 (1990)
    7 ALR5th 73—§ 2, 3
State v. Baker, 165 Or. App. 565, 998 P.2d 700 (2000)
    42 ALR5th 547—§ 6

State v. Baker, 169 W. Va. 357, 287 S.E.2d 497 (1982)
    117 ALR5th 513—§ 5
    71 ALR6th 1—§ 8
State v. Baker, 180 W. Va. 233, 376 S.E.2d 127 (1988)
    68 ALR5th 343—§ 12, 13
State v. Baker, 197 Ga. App. 1, 397 S.E.2d 554 (1990)
    47 ALR6th 107—§ 19
State v. Baker, 216 Ga. App. 66, 453 S.E.2d 115 (1995)
    67 ALR5th 361—§ 3, 7
State v. Baker, 238 Ga. App. 802, 521 S.E.2d 24 (1999)
    28 ALR6th 505—§ 30
State v. Baker, 251 S.C. 108, 160 S.E.2d 556 (1968)
    27 ALR6th 491—§ 4
State v. Baker, 288 So. 2d 52 (La. 1973)
    16 ALR6th 329—§ 3, 4
    19 ALR6th 115—§ 3
    24 ALR6th 591—§ 3, 4
State v. Baker, 293 S.W.2d 900 (Mo. 1956)
    99 ALR6th 113—§ 5, 19, 22
State v. Baker, 312 N.C. 34, 320 S.E.2d 670 (1984)
    55 ALR6th 157—§ 112
State v. Baker, 336 N.C. 58, 441 S.E.2d 551, 44 A.L.R.5th 873 (1994)
    44 ALR5th 651—§ 5
State v. Baker, 598 S.W.2d 540 (Mo. App. 1980)
    54 ALR5th 141—§ 3, 9, 10
State v. Baker, 627 A.2d 835, 26 A.L.R.5th 795 (R.I. 1993)
    26 ALR5th 1—§ 4, 34
State v. Baker, 636 S.W.2d 902 (Mo. 1982)
    70 ALR5th 587—§ 13
State v. Baker, 639 S.W.2d 617 (Mo. Ct. App. S.D. 1982)
    33 ALR6th 407—§ 55, 56
State v. Baker, 720 So. 2d 767 (La. Ct. App. 2d Cir. 1998)
    101 ALR5th 187—§ 17

For assistance, call 1-800-328-4880

State v. Baker, 850 S.W.2d 944 (Mo. Ct. App. E.D. 1993)
 38 ALR6th 97—§ 29
State v. Baker, 956 S.W.2d 8 (Tenn. Crim. App. 1997)
 111 ALR5th 239—§ 11
State v. Baker, 1992 WL 114324 (Del. Super. Ct. 1992)
 16 ALR6th 329—§ 4
 24 ALR6th 591—§ 6, 12
State v. Baker, 2001 WL 1558352(Del. C.P. 2001)
 92 ALR6th 295—§ 13
State v. Baker, 2002 WL 562839 (Mo. Ct. App. S.D. 2002)
 109 ALR5th 99—§ 2
 112 ALR5th 429—§ 2
 114 ALR5th 235—§ 2
State v. Baker, 2009-Ohio-2340, 2009 WL 1396435 (Ohio Ct. App. 9th Dist. Summit County 2009)
 58 ALR6th 499—§ 30
State v. Baker, 2010 UT 18, 2010 WL 841271 (Utah 2010)
 55 ALR6th 1—§ 30, 40
State v. Bakke, 44 Wash. App. 830, 723 P.2d 534 (Div. 1 1986)
 64 ALR5th 637—§ 3
State v. Bakker, 262 N.W.2d 538 (Iowa 1978)
 68 ALR5th 343—§ 3, 13
State v. Balanza, 93 Haw. 279
 68 ALR5th 299—§ 4
State v. Balberdi, 90 Haw. 16, 975 P.2d 773 (Haw. Ct. App. 1999)
 85 ALR5th 1—§ 15
State v. Baldenegro, 188 Ariz. 10, 932 P.2d 275 (Ct. App. Div. 2 1996)
 58 ALR6th 385—§ 8
State v. Baldon, 672 N.W.2d 335 (Iowa Ct. App. 2003)
 71 ALR6th 1—§ 14
State v. Baldridge, 152 P.3d 688 (Kan. Ct. App. 2007)
 37 ALR6th 357—§ 45
State v. Baldwin, 125 N.C. App. 530, 482 S.E.2d 1 (1997)

State v. Baldwin, 130 N.M. 705, 2001-NMCA-063, 30 P.3d 394 (Ct. App. 2001)
 119 ALR5th 379—§ 8
State v. Baldwin, 150 Wash. 2d 448, 78 P.3d 1005 (2003)
 125 ALR5th 537—§ 2, 24, 48, 49
State v. Baldwin, 184 Ariz. 267, 908 P.2d 483 (Ct. App. Div. 1 1995)
 113 ALR5th 1—§ 2 to 4, 12, 15
State v. Baldwin, 192 Mont. 521, 629 P.2d 222 (1981)
 11 ALR6th 237—§ 4, 8, 12
State v. Baldwin, 224 Conn. 347, 618 A.2d 513 (1993)
 55 ALR6th 391—§ 21
State v. Baldwin, 388 So. 2d 664 (La. 1980)
 10 ALR5th 700—§ 3
State v. Baldwin, 388 So. 2d 679 (La. 1980)
 54 ALR5th 141—§ 4 to 6, 8, 10
State v. Balfa, 506 So. 2d 1369 (La. Ct. App. 3d Cir. 1987)
 83 ALR6th 465—§ 5, 62
State v. Ball, 141 N.J. 142, 661 A.2d 251, R.I.C.O. Bus. Disp. Guide (CCH) ¶ 8881 (1995)
 89 ALR5th 629—§ 3, 8 to 10
 58 ALR6th 385—§ 20, 34
State v. Ball, 164 W. Va. 588, 264 S.E.2d 844 (1980)
 52 ALR5th 655—§ 2, 4
State v. Ball, 226 Conn. 265, 627 A.2d 892 (1993)
 17 ALR5th 837—§ 3
 70 ALR6th 513—§ 9
 71 ALR6th 471—§ 5
State v. Ball, 381 N.J. Super. 545, 887 A.2d 174 (App. Div. 2005)
 71 ALR6th 1—§ 5
State v. Ball, 622 S.W.2d 285 (Mo. App. 1981)
 23 ALR5th 672—§ 6
State v. Ball, 748 So. 2d 1249 (La. Ct. App. 2d Cir. 1999)

7 ALR5th 263—§ 7

State v. Ball, 1981 WL 9809 (Ohio Ct. App. 1st Dist.Hamilton County 1981)

57 ALR5th 141—§ 3

State v. Ball, 2000 WL 288651 (Ohio Ct. App. 7th Dist. Jefferson County 2000)

6 ALR6th 533—§ 21

State v. Ball, 2000 WL 1785031 (Conn. Super. Ct. 2000)

17 ALR5th 837—§ 3

State v. Ball, 2002-Ohio-360, 2002 WL 121926 (Ohio Ct. App. 5th Dist. Stark County 2002)

63 ALR6th 351—§ 3

State v. Ball, 2004-Ohio-2586, 2004 WL 1125193 (Ohio Ct. App. 6th Dist. Erie County 2004)

98 ALR6th 455—§ 25

State v. Ballard, 333 N.C. 515, 428 S.E.2d 178 (1993)

83 ALR5th 541—§ 3, 6

State v. Ballard, 439 A.2d 1375 (R.I. 1982)

39 ALR5th 283—§ 4, 71

State v. Ballard, 855 S.W.2d 557 (Tenn. 1993)

85 ALR5th 595—§ 8

State v. Ballard, 1994 WL 47683 (Ohio Ct. App. 3d Dist. Auglaize County 1994)

117 ALR5th 407—§ 4

State v. Ballay, 757 So. 2d 115 (La. Ct. App. 5th Cir. 2000)

54 ALR6th 429—§ 18

State v. Ballenger, 123 N.C. App. 179, 472 S.E.2d 572 (1996)

12 ALR5th 89—§ 4

State v. Ballett, 756 So. 2d 587 (La. Ct. App. 4th Cir. 2000)

39 ALR5th 283—§ 55

State v. Ballinger, 19 Ariz. App. 32, 504 P.2d 955 (Div. 1 1973)

7 ALR6th 169—§ 11

State v. Ballinger, 99 N.M. 707, 663 P.2d 366 (Ct. App. 1983)

57 ALR5th 141—§ 8

State v. Ballinger, 2002-Ohio-2146, 2002 WL 962835 (Ohio Ct. App. 8th Dist. Cuyahoga County 2002)

3 ALR6th 543—§ 12

State v. Ballom, 562 So. 2d 1073 (La. App. 4th Cir. 1990)

45 ALR5th 1—§ 2, 4, 5, 7, 11, 18

State v. Ballos, 230 Wis. 2d 495, 602 N.W.2d 117 (Ct. App. 1999)

125 ALR5th 357—§ 6

7 ALR6th 233—§ 9

State v. Ballou, 127 Vt. 1, 238 A.2d 658 (1968)

50 ALR5th 703—§ 2, 15

State v. Ball, Slip Op. No. 48275 (Ohio App. Cuyahoga Co. 1984)

38 ALR5th 433—§ 30, 37

State v. Ballweg, 2003 ND 153, 670 N.W.2d 490 (N.D. 2003)

73 ALR6th 49—§ 41

State v. Balser, 460 So. 2d 74 (La. Ct. App. 1st Cir. 1984)

85 ALR5th 261—§ 5

State v. Baltier, 109 Ariz. 96, 505 P.2d 556 (1973)

34 ALR5th 125—§ 9

State v. Baltzell, 175 Ariz. 437, 857 P.2d 1291 (Ct. App. Div. 1 1992)

92 ALR5th 35—§ 18

State v. Baltzell, 857 P.2d 1291, 129 Ariz. Adv. Rep. 20 (Ariz. App. 1992)

15 ALR5th 391—§ 33, 40

State v. Balwanz, 2004-Ohio-1534, 2004 WL 609602 (Ohio Ct. App. 7th Dist. Belmont County 2004)

34 ALR6th 539—§ 4

State v. Bane, 2008 WL 2406233 (Ariz. Ct. App. Div. 1 2008)

56 ALR6th 185—§ 41

State v. Banet, 140 Conn. 118, 98 A.2d 530 (1953)

57 ALR6th 445—§ 30

State v. Bankey, 2005-Ohio-5878, 2005 WL 2933680 (Ohio Ct. App. 6th Dist. Wood County 2005)

26 ALR6th 511—§ 19

State v. Banks, 14 Kan. App. 2d 393, 790 P.2d 962 (1990)
125 ALR5th 537—§ 44

State v. Banks, 31 Ohio App. 3d 57, 31 Ohio B.R. 97, 508 N.E.2d 986 (Franklin Co. 1986)
24 ALR5th 465—§ 2, 5, 34, 36

State v. Banks, 59 Conn. App. 145, 754 A.2d 859 (2000)
56 ALR5th 385—§ 3

State v. Banks, 181 Wis. 2d 364, 514 N.W.2d 421 (Ct. App. 1993)
45 ALR6th 337—§ 31

State v. Banks, 204 N.C. 233, 167 S.E. 851 (1933)
51 ALR5th 603—§ 2

State v. Banks, 271 S.W.3d 90 (Tenn. 2008)
83 ALR6th 255—§ 17

State v. Banks, 322 N.C. 753, 370 S.E.2d 398 (1988)
81 ALR6th 505—§ 12

State v. Banks, 328 Wis. 2d 766, 2010 WI App 107, 790 N.W.2d 526 (Ct. App. 2010)
69 ALR6th 579—§ 5, 16

State v. Banks, 358 N.W.2d 133 (Minn. App. 1984)
29 ALR5th 59—§ 6, 58, 79

State v. Banks, 564 S.W.2d 947 (Tenn. 1978)
37 ALR5th 515—§ 21

State v. Banks, 800 So. 2d 28 (La. Ct. App. 4th Cir. 2001)
19 ALR6th 115—§ 4, 9, 10

State v. Banks, 1987 WL 17624 (Ohio Ct. App. 8th Dist. Cuyahoga County 1987)
11 ALR6th 237—§ 16

State v. Banks, 1991 WL 227028 (Ohio Ct. App. 2d Dist. Montgomery County 1991)
107 ALR5th 567—§ 10

State v. Banks, 2002-Ohio-3341, 2002 WL 1379943 (Ohio Ct. App. 10th Dist. Franklin County 2002)
3 ALR6th 269—§ 5, 14, 22, 25

State v. Bankston, 99 Wash. App. 266, 992 P.2d 1041 (Div. 3 2000)
83 ALR5th 277—§ 25
84 ALR5th 487—§ 3

State v. Bannie, 2000 WL 1146142 (Minn. Ct. App. 2000)
85 ALR5th 1—§ 15, 23

State v. Bantley, 44 Conn. 537 (1877)
50 ALR5th 467—§ 6, 8

State v. Banusik, 84 N.J.L. 640, 64 A. 994 (N.J. Ct. Err. & App. 1906)
97 ALR6th 567—§ 3, 7, 9

State v. Barajas, 115 Wis. 2d 696, 339 N.W.2d 366 (Ct. App. 1983)
88 ALR6th 203—§ 84

State v. Baranski, 2005-Ohio-4956, 2005 WL 2296644 (Ohio Ct. App. 4th Dist. Scioto County 2005)
51 ALR6th 1—§ 23

State v. Barb, 1996 WL 325335 (Ohio Ct. App. 8th Dist. Cuyahoga County 1996)
43 ALR6th 475—§ 21

State v. Barbee, 370 N.W.2d 603 (Iowa App. 1985)
39 ALR5th 283—§ 10, 66

State v. Barber, 42 Conn. App. 589, 681 A.2d 348 (1996)
119 ALR5th 379—§ 7

State v. Barber, 179 Or. App. 674, 41 P.3d 455 (2002)
29 ALR6th 1—§ 10

State v. Barber, 317 N.C. 502, 346 S.E.2d 441 (1986)
93 ALR5th 327—§ 3, 9, 26
101 ALR5th 619—§ 3

State v. Barber, 1994 WL 47681 (Ohio Ct. App. 2d Dist. Montgomery County 1994)
38 ALR6th 97—§ 29

State v. Barbour, 243 N.C. 265, 90 S.E.2d 388 (1955)
12 ALR6th 389—§ 5

State v. Barboza, 57 Wash. App. 822, 790 P.2d 647 (Div. 1 1990)
58 ALR6th 499—§ 25

State v. Barcheski, 181 N.J. Super. 34, 436 A.2d 550 (App. Div. 1981)

102 ALR5th 525—§ 75

State v. Barcia, 228 N.J. Super. 267, 549 A.2d 491 (Law Div. 1988)

82 ALR5th 103—§ 3

State v. Barcia, 235 N.J. Super. 311, 562 A.2d 246 (App. Div. 1989)

82 ALR5th 103—§ 3

State v. Barclay, 398 A.2d 794 (Me. 1979)

114 ALR5th 173—§ 7

State v. Barclays Bank of New York, N.A., 76 N.Y.2d 533, 561 N.Y.S.2d 697, 563 N.E.2d 11, 12 U.C.C. Rep. Serv. 2d 1120 (1990)

91 ALR5th 89—§ 2, 3

State v. Barczak, 562 A.2d 140 (Me. 1989)

41 ALR5th 171—§ 16, 26, 27

State v. Barden, 356 N.C. 316, 572 S.E.2d 108 (2002)

29 ALR6th 1—§ 10

83 ALR6th 255—§ 3, 5, 9, 15, 19

State v. Bare, 197 N.C. App. 461, 677 S.E.2d 518 (2009)

63 ALR6th 351—§ 3

State v. Bare, 677 S.E.2d 518 (N.C. Ct. App. 2009)

57 ALR6th 1—§ 4, 18, 19

State v. Barefield, 47 Wash. App. 444, 735 P.2d 1339 (Div. 1 1987)

52 ALR6th 1—§ 34

72 ALR6th 141—§ 9

State v. Barefield, 110 Wash. 2d 728, 756 P.2d 731 (1988)

52 ALR6th 1—§ 34

70 ALR6th 361—§ 11

State v. Barfield, 23 N.C. App. 619, 209 S.E.2d 809 (1974)

4 ALR5th 1—§ 4, 10

85 ALR5th 1—§ 50

State v. Barfield, 298 N.C. 306, 259 S.E.2d 510 (1979)

83 ALR6th 465—§ 12, 50

State v. Bargas-Perez, 117 Or. App. 510, 844 P.2d 931 (1992)

34 ALR5th 125—§ 14

State v. Barger, 78 Ohio App. 3d 451, 605 N.E.2d 409 (Hancock Co. 1992)

52 ALR5th 655—§ 3

State v. Barger, 84 Ohio App. 3d 409, 616 N.E.2d 1176 (Clermont Co. 1992)

27 ALR5th 593—§ 7

State v. Barger, 167 Ariz. 563, 810 P.2d 191 (App. 1990)

57 ALR5th 141—§ 9

State v. Barger, 511 N.W.2d 632 (Iowa App. 1993)

12 ALR5th 89—§ 4

State v. Barger, 612 S.W.2d 485 (Tenn.Crim.App. 1980)

81 ALR5th 563—§ 3, 5, 8, 10, 11

State v. Barile, 54 Conn. App. 866, 738 A.2d 709 (1999)

38 ALR5th 433—§ 7

State v. Barile, 267 Conn. 576, 839 A.2d 1281 (2004)

101 ALR6th 545—§ 13

State v. Barker, 128 Ohio App. 3d 233, 714 N.E.2d 447 (6th Dist. Fulton County 1998)

6 ALR5th 733—§ 16, 17

66 ALR5th 397—§ 25

70 ALR6th 329—§ 14

74 ALR6th 505—§ 3

State v. Barker, 252 Kan. 949, 850 P.2d 885 (1993)

74 ALR5th 319—§ 2, 5 to 12

State v. Barker, 531 S.E.2d 228 (N.C. Ct. App. 2000)

72 ALR5th 607—§ 7

State v. Barker, 628 So. 2d 168 (La. Ct. App. 2d Cir. 1993)

9 ALR6th 1—§ 17

State v. Barker, 705 N.W.2d 768 (Minn. 2005)

26 ALR6th 511—§ 44

State v. Barker, 768 N.E.2d 425 (Ind. 2002)

110 ALR5th 1—§ 2, 3, 20

State v. Barker, 2009-Ohio-2774, 2009 WL 1653013 (Ohio Ct. App. 2d Dist. Montgomery County 2009)

64 ALR6th 1—§ 9, 11
State v. Barker, 2010-Ohio-5744, 2010 WL 4867675 (Ohio Ct. App. 2d Dist. Montgomery County 2010)

65 ALR6th 359—§ 3
State v. Barkley, 108 Or. App. 756, 817 P.2d 1328, 1991 WL 176312 (1991)

92 ALR5th 35—§ 16
State v. Barkley, 315 Or. 420, 846 P.2d 390 (1993)

38 ALR5th 433—§ 18
92 ALR5th 35—§ 16
State v. Barkley, 412 So. 2d 1380 (La. 1982)

11 ALR6th 237—§ 13
State v. Barlow, 107 Utah 292, 153 P.2d 647 (1944)

22 ALR6th 1—§ 4, 7, 9, 11
State v. Barlow, 152 Wash. App. 1027, 2009 WL 2999144 (Div. 3 2009)

78 ALR6th 297—§ 41
State v. Barlow, 792 So. 2d 63 (La. Ct. App. 3d Cir. 2001)

117 ALR5th 407—§ 4
State v. Barmeier, 878 So. 2d 411 (Fla. Dist. Ct. App. 3d Dist. 2004)

58 ALR6th 499—§ 45
State v. Barmon, 67 Or. App. 369, 679 P.2d 888 (1984)

32 ALR6th 1—§ 4
State v. Barnard, 346 N.C. 95, 484 S.E.2d 382 (1997)

54 ALR6th 429—§ 17
State v. Barnard, 645 S.E.2d 780 (N.C. Ct. App. 2007)

35 ALR6th 127—§ 22
State v. Barnard, 678 S.W.2d 448 (Mo. Ct. App. S.D. 1984)

71 ALR6th 335—§ 14
State v. Barnd, 85 Ohio App. 3d 254, 619 N.E.2d 518 (3d Dist.Hancock County 1993)

57 ALR5th 141—§ 4
State v. Barnes, 25 Ohio St. 3d 203, 495 N.E.2d 922 (1986)

29 ALR6th 1—§ 10
State v. Barnes, 48 La. Ann. 460, 19 So. 251 (1895)

104 ALR5th 357—§ 8
State v. Barnes, 54 N.J. 1, 252 A.2d 398 (1969)

58 ALR6th 215—§ 12
State v. Barnes, 85 Wash. App. 638, 932 P.2d 669 (Div. 2 1997)

89 ALR5th 629—§ 10, 11
State v. Barnes, 116 N.C. App. 311, 447 S.E.2d 478 (1994)

29 ALR6th 1—§ 10
State v. Barnes, 124 Ariz. 586, 606 P.2d 802 (1980)

29 ALR6th 1—§ 10
State v. Barnes, 141 Tenn. 469, 212 S.W. 100 (1919)

118 ALR5th 253—§ 3
State v. Barnes, 154 N.C. App. 111, 572 S.E.2d 165 (2002)

9 ALR6th 1—§ 17
29 ALR6th 1—§ 10
State v. Barnes, 289 S.W. 562 (Mo. 1926)

81 ALR5th 563—§ 3, 5
State v. Barnes, 345 N.C. 184, 481 S.E.2d 44 (1997)

16 ALR6th 329—§ 4
24 ALR6th 591—§ 6, 14
State v. Barnes, 390 So. 2d 1243 (Fla. App. D1 1980)

59 ALR5th 615—§ 3, 7, 12
State v. Barnes, 559 A.2d 136 (R.I. 1989)

39 ALR5th 283—§ 4, 63
State v. Barnes, 595 So. 2d 22 (Fla. 1992)

7 ALR5th 263—§ 4
State v. Barnes, 597 So. 2d 1109 (La. App. 2d Cir. 1992)

11 ALR5th 497—§ 5
State v. Barnes, 598 S.W.2d 179 (Mo. Ct. App. S.D. 1980)

74 ALR5th 643—§ 3
State v. Barnes, 618 N.W.2d 805 (Minn. Ct. App. 2000)

50 ALR6th 455—§ 12, 24, 28
State v. Barnes, 721 So. 2d 923 (La. Ct. App. 1st Cir. 1998)

79 ALR6th 125—§ 4

State v. Barnes, 753 So. 2d 605 (Fla. Dist. Ct. App. 2d Dist. 2000)

113 ALR5th 597—§ 8

State v. Barnes, 859 P.2d 1387 (Idaho 1993)

24 ALR5th 132—§ 3, 8

State v. Barnes, 954 S.W.2d 760 (Tenn. Crim. App. 1997)

5 ALR5th 243—§ 49
1 ALR6th 657—§ 15

State v. Barnes, 980 S.W.2d 314 (Mo. Ct. App. W.D. 1998)

5 ALR5th 243—§ 47

State v. Barnes, Slip Op. No. CA84-05-041 (Ohio App. Clermont Co. 1985)

38 ALR5th 433—§ 7, 15

State v. Barnett, 16 P.3d 74 (Wash. Ct. App. Div. 3 2001)

72 ALR5th 403—§ 3

State v. Barnett, 36 Wash. App. 560, 675 P.2d 626 (Div. 1 1984)

92 ALR5th 35—§ 25

State v. Barnett, 147 N.H. 334, 789 A.2d 629 (2001)

69 ALR6th 579—§ 4

State v. Barnett, 480 A.2d 791 (Me. 1984)

85 ALR5th 187—§ 9

State v. Barnett, 543 N.W.2d 774 (N.D. 1996)

24 ALR6th 1—§ 7

State v. Barnett, 909 S.W.2d 423 (Tenn. 1995)

83 ALR5th 541—§ 2, 3, 7

State v. Barnett, 980 S.W.2d 297 (Mo. 1998)

91 ALR5th 343—§ 21, 32

State v. Barnett, 1994 WL 567551 (Ohio Ct. App. 2d Dist. Montgomery County 1994)

34 ALR6th 1—§ 10

State v. Barnette, 2004-Ohio-7211, 2004 WL 3090228 (Ohio Ct. App. 7th Dist. Mahoning County 2004)

11 ALR6th 237—§ 10

State v. Barney, 92 Idaho 581, 448 P.2d 195 (1968)

51 ALR6th 359—§ 28

State v. Barney, 2008 UT App 250, 189 P.3d 1277 (Utah Ct. App. 2008)

70 ALR6th 361—§ 18

State v. Barnhart, 127 W. Va. 545, 33 S.E.2d 857 (1945)

108 ALR5th 593—§ 11

State v. Barnhart, 587 S.W.2d 308 (Mo. App. 1979)

11 ALR5th 497—§ 2, 5

State v. Barnhart, 850 P.2d 473 (Utah Ct. App. 1993)

92 ALR6th 295—§ 7, 8, 13, 19, 25
93 ALR6th 207—§ 4, 6, 28
96 ALR6th 355—§ 6, 26, 28, 36, 44, 49, 60

State v. Barnholtz, 287 S.W.2d 808 (Mo. 1956)

54 ALR6th 429—§ 11, 29

State v. Baron, 156 Ohio App. 3d 241, 2004-Ohio-747, 805 N.E.2d 173 (8th Dist. Cuyahoga County 2004)

63 ALR6th 351—§ 3

State v. Barone, 288 N.J. Super. 102, 671 A.2d 1096 (App. Div. 1996)

121 ALR5th 551—§ 2, 14

State v. Barone, 852 S.W.2d 216, 38 A.L.R.5th 897 (Tenn. 1993)

38 ALR5th 433—§ 5, 6

State v. Barr, 23 Del. 340, 7 Penne. 340, 79 A. 730 (Gen. Sess. 1909)

5 ALR6th 1—§ 69

State v. Barr, 28 Mo. App. 84 (1887)

87 ALR5th 715—§ 4

State v. Barr, 90 S.D. 9, 237 N.W.2d 888 (1976)

24 ALR5th 428—§ 3

State v. Barr, 98 Nev. 428, 651 P.2d 649 (1982)

59 ALR5th 615—§ 4, 12

State v. Barr, 99 Wash. 2d 75, 658 P.2d 1247 (1983)

15 ALR5th 391—§ 30
92 ALR5th 35—§ 13

State v. Barr, 126 Vt. 112, 223 A.2d 462 (1966)

28 ALR5th 754—§ 6

State v. Barr, 2001 WL 767006 (Tenn. Crim. App. 2001)
125 ALR5th 537—§ 49, 52

State v. Barr, 2007 WL 329215 (Minn. Ct. App. 2007)
26 ALR6th 511—§ 29

State v. Barragan-Sierra, 219 Ariz. 276, 196 P.3d 879 (Ct. App. Div. 1 2008)
75 ALR6th 541—§ 3, 7

State v. Barrager, 78 P.3d 497 (Kan. Ct. App. 2003)
23 ALR6th 307—§ 44

State v. Barras, 20 So. 3d 1100 (La. Ct. App. 1st Cir. 2009)
84 ALR6th 293—§ 9, 38

State v. Barraza, 110 N.M. 45, 791 P.2d 799 (App. 1990)
44 ALR5th 651—§ 3

State v. Barrenechea, 2009 WL 2525457 (N.J. Super. Ct. App. Div. 2009)
71 ALR6th 1—§ 24

State v. Barret, 151 La. 52, 91 So. 543 (1922)
45 ALR5th 591—§ 15

State v. Barrett, 45 Ohio App. 2d 20, 74 Ohio Op. 2d 64, 340 N.E.2d 418 (6th Dist. Wood County 1975)
89 ALR6th 565—§ 28, 30, 34

State v. Barrett, 138 Idaho 290, 62 P.3d 214 (Ct. App. 2003)
58 ALR6th 499—§ 45

State v. Barrett, 205 Conn. 437, 534 A.2d 219 (1987)
124 ALR5th 1—§ 5

State v. Barrett, 408 So. 2d 903 (La. 1981)
123 ALR5th 221—§ 3

State v. Barrett, 683 So. 2d 331 (La. Ct. App. 1st Cir. 1996)
59 ALR6th 393—§ 3

State v. Barrett, 864 P.2d 1078, 152 Ariz. Adv. Rep. 37 (Ariz. App. 1993)
15 ALR5th 391—§ 22

State v. Barrett, 2004-Ohio-5530, 2004 WL 2340658 (Ohio Ct. App. 12th Dist. Butler County 2004)
30 ALR6th 103—§ 34

57 ALR6th 83—§ 5

State v. Barrington, 198 Mo. 23, 95 S.W. 235 (1906)
98 ALR6th 455—§ 26

State v. Barrios, 2010 WL 5071177 (N.J. Super. Ct. App. Div. 2010)
74 ALR6th 373—§ 18, 22

State v. Barron, 137 N.H. 29, 623 A.2d 216 (1993)
41 ALR5th 171—§ 55, 58, 129, 134

State v. Barron, 214 N.J. Super. 46, 518 A.2d 484 (App. Div. 1986)
113 ALR5th 517—§ 7

State v. Barron, 465 S.W.2d 523, 49 A.L.R.3d 1176 (Mo. 1971)
45 ALR5th 531—§ 9

State v. Barron, 2000 WL 739427 (Ohio Ct. App. 10th Dist. Franklin County 2000)
79 ALR6th 125—§ 5, 8

State v. Barron, 2005-Ohio-6108, 2005 WL 3072914 (Ohio Ct. App. 5th Dist. Perry County 2005)
89 ALR6th 565—§ 29, 33

State v. Barros, 24 A.3d 1158 (R.I. 2011)
69 ALR6th 579—§ 4

State v. Barros, 2012 WL 1365801 (N.J. Super. Ct. App. Div. 2012)
74 ALR6th 373—§ 23

State v. Barroso, 328 S.C. 268, 493 S.E.2d 854 (1997)
37 ALR5th 319—§ 10

State v. Barroso, 762 So. 2d 206 (La. Ct. App. 5th Cir. 2000)
11 ALR6th 237—§ 12, 13

State v. Barsness, 102 Idaho 210, 628 P.2d 1044 (1981)
87 ALR5th 1—§ 5, 10, 14, 32

State v. Barsness, 473 N.W.2d 325 (Minn. Ct. App. 1991)
73 ALR5th 383—§ 5
113 ALR5th 597—§ 3, 4, 8

State v. Barstad, 93 Wash. App. 553, 970 P.2d 324 (Div. 3 1999)
7 ALR5th 758—§ 7, 12

State v. Bartee, 894 S.W.2d 34 (Tex. App. San Antonio 1994)

57 ALR6th 445—§ 25
State v. Bartis, 1997 WL 771021 (Ohio Ct. App. 10th Dist. Franklin County 1997)

78 ALR5th 489—§ 3
State v. Bartlett, 35 Wis. 287, 1874 WL 3379 (1874)

97 ALR5th 537—§ 4
State v. Bartlett, 74 Wash. App. 580, 875 P.2d 651 (Div. 1 1994)

73 ALR5th 383—§ 5
State v. Bartlett, 199 Neb. 471, 259 N.W.2d 917 (1977)

72 ALR6th 1—§ 14
State v. Bartlett, 1997 WL 269188 (Ohio Ct. App. 11th Dist. Trumbull County 1997)

45 ALR6th 435—§ 29
State v. Bartlette, 2003 WL 21743483 (Minn. Ct. App. 2003)

114 ALR5th 173—§ 6
1 ALR6th 371—§ 6
State v. Bartley, 304 Mo. 58, 263 S.W. 95 (1924)

34 ALR5th 723—§ 4
State v. Bartley, 329 So. 2d 431 (La. 1976)

65 ALR5th 407—§ 3
State v. Bartley, 782 So. 2d 29 (La. Ct. App. 5th Cir. 2001)

27 ALR5th 593—§ 36
34 ALR5th 125—§ 18
23 ALR6th 679—§ 6
State v. Bartnick, 436 N.W.2d 647 (Iowa App. 1988)

18 ALR5th 804—§ 7, 11
State v. Barto, 202 Wis. 329, 232 N.W. 553 (1930)

26 ALR6th 1—§ 25
27 ALR6th 1—§ 4
State v. Barton, 119 Idaho 114, 803 P.2d 1020 (App. 1991)

52 ALR5th 559—§ 6, 11
State v. Barton, 2003 WL 22481107 (Minn. Ct. App. 2003)

84 ALR6th 293—§ 15, 38
State v. Bartram, 925 S.W.2d 227 (Tenn. 1996)

65 ALR5th 407—§ 3, 5, 12
State v. Barts, 316 N.C. 666, 343 S.E.2d 828 (1986)

55 ALR6th 157—§ 73
State v. Bartusek, 383 N.W.2d 582 (Iowa 1986)

2 ALR5th 725—§ 14
State v. Baruth, 47 Wash. 283, 91 P. 977 (1907)

50 ALR5th 467—§ 3, 5 to 7
State v. Barwick, 66 Wash. App. 706, 833 P.2d 421 (Div. 3 1992)

97 ALR6th 653—§ 30
State v. Barzacchini, 96 Ohio App. 3d 440, 645 N.E.2d 137 (6th Dist. Lucas County 1994)

81 ALR6th 257—§ 20
State v. Basden, 339 N.C. 288, 451 S.E.2d 238 (1994)

79 ALR5th 33—§ 68, 72
State v. Basham, 84 S.D. 250, 170 N.W.2d 238 (1969)

12 ALR5th 909—§ 4, 9
State v. Baskerville, 616 S.W.2d 839 (Mo. 1981)

29 ALR6th 1—§ 18
State v. Baskett, 111 Mo. 271, 19 S.W. 1097 (1892)

46 ALR5th 499—§ 3
State v. Bass, 53 N.C. App. 40, 280 S.E.2d 7 (1981)

15 ALR5th 391—§ 50
State v. Bass, 93 N.H. 172, 37 A.2d 7 (1944)

24 ALR6th 747—§ 36
State v. Bass, 186 La. 139, 171 So. 829 (1936)

11 ALR5th 497—§ 3, 12, 16, 19
State v. Bass, 320 N.W.2d 824 (Iowa 1982)

70 ALR6th 361—§ 19
71 ALR6th 335—§ 5, 16
State v. Bass, 349 N.W.2d 498 (Iowa 1984)

93 ALR5th 527—§ 5
State v. Bass, 451 So. 2d 986 (Fla. App. D2 1984)

For assistance, call 1-800-328-4880

18 ALR5th 1—§ 20
State v. Bassett, 97 Wash. App. 737, 987
P.2d 119 (Div. 2 1999)
36 ALR5th 161—§ 27
33 ALR6th 91—§ 22
State v. Bassett, 215 Ariz. 600, 161 P.3d
1264 (Ct. App. Div. 1 2007)
71 ALR6th 625—§ 14
State v. Bassett, 447 A.2d 371 (R.I.
1982)
102 ALR5th 327—§ 6
State v. Bassett, 1999 MT 109, 294
Mont. 327, 982 P.2d 410 (1999)
58 ALR6th 499—§ 88
State v. Basson, 105 Wash. 2d 314, 714
P.2d 1188 (1986)
29 ALR6th 1—§ 10
State v. Basta, 966 P.2d 260 (Utah Ct.
App. 1998)
40 ALR5th 113—§ 4
State v. Basten, 217 Wis. 2d 290, 577
N.W.2d 387 (Ct. App. 1998)
111 ALR5th 529—§ 4
State v. Basting, 572 N.W.2d 281 (Minn.
1997)
67 ALR6th 103—§ 5, 11
State v. Baston, 85 Ohio St. 3d 418, 709
N.E.2d 128 (1999)
9 ALR5th 369—§ 19.5
State v. Basu, 2005 ME 74, 875 A.2d
686 (Me. 2005)
62 ALR6th 161—§ 11
State v. Basurto, 15 Kan. App. 2d 264,
807 P.2d 162 (1991)
104 ALR5th 165—§ 12
State v. Bateman, 48 Or. App. 357, 616
P.2d 1206 (1980)
39 ALR5th 283—§ 4, 45
State v. Bates, 48 Ohio St. 2d 315, 2
Ohio Ops. 3d 453, 358 N.E.2d 584
(1976)
11 ALR5th 497—§ 3, 25, 27
State v. Bates, 84 Haw. 211, 933 P.2d
48 (1997)
58 ALR6th 385—§ 22, 41
State v. Bates, 84 Haw. 211, 933 P.2d
48 (Haw. 1997)

89 ALR5th 629—§ 9
State v. Bates, 105 Minn. 440, 117 N.W.
844 (1908)
102 ALR5th 525—§ 65
State v. Bates, 120 N.M. 1060, 902 P.2d
1060 (Ct. App. 1995)
74 ALR5th 319—§ 5 to 11
State v. Bates, 203 Or. App. 245, 125
P.3d 42 (2005)
71 ALR6th 625—§ 37
State v. Bates, 305 N.W.2d 426 (Iowa
1981)
8 ALR5th 391—§ 4
State v. Bates, 333 N.C. 523, 428 S.E.2d
693 (1993)
83 ALR5th 541—§ 3, 6
State v. Bates, 343 N.C. 564, 473 S.E.2d
269 (1996)
70 ALR5th 587—§ 25
State v. Bates, 363 So. 2d 469 (La. 1978)
50 ALR5th 703—§ 16
State v. Bates, 689 N.W.2d 479 (Iowa
Ct. App. 2004)
70 ALR6th 361—§ 7
State v. Bates, 711 So. 2d 281 (La. Ct.
App. 2d Cir. 1997)
9 ALR6th 541—§ 4
State v. Bates, 804 S.W.2d 868 (Tenn.
1991)
37 ALR5th 515—§ 5, 7, 9
State v. Bates, 1987 WL 15817 (Ohio
Ct. App. 9th Dist. Medina County
1987)
18 ALR6th 519—§ 20
State v. Bates, 2003 ME 67, 822 A.2d
1129 (Me. 2003)
23 ALR6th 1—§ 15
State v. Bates, 2004-Ohio-2260, 2004
WL 957665 (Ohio Ct. App. 5th Dist.
Ashland County 2004)
70 ALR6th 1—§ 23
State v. Bates, 2005-Ohio-967, 2005 WL
519010 (Ohio Ct. App. 5th Dist.
Ashland County 2005)
70 ALR6th 1—§ 23
State v. Bates, 2005 WL 1521940 (Tenn.
Crim. App. 2005)

26 ALR6th 511—§ 22

State v. Bateson, 25 Kan. App. 2d 90, 958 P.2d 44 (1998)

7 ALR5th 73—§ 5, 11

State v. Batey, 2003 WL 1337834 (Tenn. Crim. App. 2003)

78 ALR6th 297—§ 39, 61

State v. Batin, 2005-Ohio-36, 2005 WL 30543 (Ohio Ct. App. 5th Dist. Stark County 2005)

26 ALR6th 511—§ 43

State v. Batista, 106 Ariz. Adv. Rep. 52 (Ariz. App. 1992)

20 ALR5th 398—§ 8, 12, 34, 36, 53

State v. Batista, 116 Wash. 2d 777, 808 P.2d 1141 (1991)

73 ALR5th 383—§ 41

State v. Batiste, 371 So. 2d 1164 (La. 1979)

62 ALR5th 121—§ 6

State v. Batiste, 445 So. 2d 1323 (La. Ct. App. 5th Cir. 1984)

28 ALR6th 245—§ 7

State v. Batson, 73 Haw. 236, 831 P.2d 924 (1992)

118 ALR5th 253—§ 9, 11, 16

State v. Batt, 2010 WI App 155, 330 Wis. 2d 159, 793 N.W.2d 104 (Ct. App. 2010)

84 ALR6th 293—§ 27

State v. Battest, 295 N.W.2d 739 (S.D. 1980)

5 ALR5th 243—§ 60

55 ALR6th 157—§ 62

State v. Battista, 31 Conn. App. 497, 626 A.2d 769 (1993)

57 ALR5th 315—§ 3, 9, 12

State v. Battle, 32 S.W.3d 193 (Mo. Ct. App. E.D. 2000)

3 ALR6th 543—§ 6

State v. Battle, 39 Conn. App. 742, 667 A.2d 1288 (1995)

39 ALR6th 257—§ 4, 5

State v. Battle, 61 N.C. App. 87, 300 S.E.2d 276 (1983)

39 ALR5th 283—§ 4, 19

State v. Battle, 1993 WL 303253 (Ohio Ct. App. 9th Dist. Summit County 1993)

77 ALR5th 201—§ 21

State v. Battles, 585 S.W.2d 213 (Mo. App. 1979)

54 ALR5th 141—§ 6, 8

State v. Batts, 195 P.3d 144 (Alaska Ct. App. 2008)

42 ALR6th 237—§ 5

State v. Batty, 109 Or. App. 62, 819 P.2d 732 (1991)

57 ALR5th 141—§ 7, 9

27 ALR6th 183—§ 17

State v. Batungbacal, 81 Haw. 123, 913 P.2d 49 (1996)

72 ALR6th 141—§ 12

State v. Baucom, 340 S.C. 339, 531 S.E.2d 922, 97 A.L.R.5th 685 (2000)

97 ALR5th 293—§ 17

State v. Baudler, 349 N.W.2d 493 (Iowa 1984)

7 ALR5th 263—§ 3

State v. Bauer, 98 Wash. App. 870, 991 P.2d 668 (Div. 2 2000)

72 ALR6th 1—§ 16

State v. Bauer, 99 Ohio App. 3d 505, 651 N.E.2d 46 (10th Dist. Franklin County 1994)

74 ALR5th 319—§ 11

State v. Bauer, 123 Wis. 2d 444, 368 N.W.2d 59 (Ct. App. 1985)

93 ALR5th 527—§ 4, 9

State v. Bauer, 127 Wis. 2d 401, 379 N.W.2d 895 (App. 1985)

6 ALR5th 733—§ 2, 16

State v. Bauer, 127 Wis. 2d 401, 379 N.W.2d 895 (Ct. App. 1985)

58 ALR6th 499—§ 62

State v. Bauer, 138 Wis. 2d 527, 406 N.W.2d 171 (Ct. App. 1987)

45 ALR6th 435—§ 3

State v. Bauer, 324 N.W.2d 320 (Iowa 1982)

102 ALR5th 447—§ 4

State v. Bauer, 337 N.W.2d 209 (Iowa 1983)

71 ALR6th 283—§ 7
State v. Bauer, 598 N.W.2d 352 (Minn. 1999)
27 ALR6th 183—§ 6
State v. Bauman, 98 Or. App. 316, 779 P.2d 185 (1989)
38 ALR5th 433—§ 19
State v. Baumann, 616 N.W.2d 771 (Minn. Ct. App. 2000)
17 ALR6th 327—§ 14
State v. Baumgartner, 2008-Ohio-1275, 2008 WL 746928 (Ohio Ct. App. 1st Dist. Hamilton County 2008)
55 ALR6th 513—§ 8
State v. Baumruk, 85 S.W.3d 644 (Mo. 2002)
100 ALR6th 535—§ 3
State v. Bautista-Martinez, 207 Or. App. 520, 142 P.3d 511 (2006)
26 ALR6th 511—§ 27
State v. Bawdon, 386 N.W.2d 484 (S.D. 1986)
38 ALR5th 433—§ 3
State v. Baxley, 656 So. 2d 973 (La. 1995)
63 ALR6th 1—§ 38
State v. Baxter, 357 So. 2d 271 (La. 1978)
75 ALR5th 295—§ 27
State v. Bay, 130 Ohio App. 3d 772, 721 N.E.2d 421 (1st Dist. Hamilton County 1998)
66 ALR5th 397—§ 19
State v. Baye, 197 Wis. 2d 956, 543 N.W.2d 868 (Ct. App. 1995)
1 ALR6th 549—§ 16
State v. Bayless, 48 Ohio St. 2d 73, 2 Ohio Op. 3d 249, 357 N.E.2d 1035 (1976)
32 ALR6th 171—§ 3
33 ALR6th 1—§ 3, 6
State v. Baynard, 4 N.C. App. 645, 167 S.E.2d 514 (1969)
46 ALR6th 241—§ 4
State v. Bays, 87 Ohio St. 3d 15, 716 N.E.2d 1126 (1999)
20 ALR5th 177—§ 11

State v. Bays, 90 Wash. App. 731, 954 P.2d 301 (Div. 2 1998)
105 ALR5th 499—§ 4
State v. Bays, 159 Ohio App. 3d 469, 2005-Ohio-47, 824 N.E.2d 167 (2d Dist. Greene County 2005)
122 ALR5th 145—§ 7, 12.5
State v. Baysinger, 28 N.C. App. 300, 220 S.E.2d 831 (1976)
99 ALR6th 295—§ 21
State v. Baze, 164 Wash. App. 1003, 2011 WL 4436658 (Div. 1 2011)
99 ALR6th 295—§ 13
State v. Bazinet, 372 A.2d 1036 (Me. 1977)
55 ALR6th 157—§ 4, 11
State v. Bazis, 190 Neb. 586, 210 N.W.2d 919 (1973)
42 ALR6th 237—§ 4
State v. B.C., 139 Wash. App. 1032, 2007 WL 1822403 (Div. 2 2007)
38 ALR6th 1—§ 13
State v. Beach, 102 N.M. 642, 699 P.2d 115 (1985)
41 ALR5th 171—§ 68
State v. Beach, 119 Idaho 837, 810 P.2d 1123 (1991)
7 ALR5th 263—§ 7
State v. Beach, 329 S.W.2d 712 (Mo. 1959)
118 ALR5th 253—§ 17
State v. Beachboard, 1993 WL 350169 (Tenn. Crim. App. 1993)
73 ALR5th 383—§ 6, 32
State v. Beal, 147 P.3d 1095 (Kan. Ct. App. 2006)
26 ALR6th 511—§ 25
State v. Beal, 602 S.W.2d 22 (Mo. Ct. App. E.D. 1980)
99 ALR6th 295—§ 5, 21
State v. Beale, 324 N.C. 87, 376 S.E.2d 1 (1989)
64 ALR5th 671—§ 4
State v. Beam, 109 Idaho 616, 710 P.2d 526 (1985)
16 ALR6th 329—§ 3
19 ALR6th 115—§ 3

24 ALR6th 591—§ 3
41 ALR6th 295—§ 9
State v. Beam, 226 S.W.3d 392 (Tex. 2007)
69 ALR6th 1—§ 13
State v. Beam, 325 N.C. 217, 381 S.E.2d 327 (1989)
112 ALR5th 429—§ 3
State v. Bean, 49 Del. 247, 113 A.2d 875 (Super. Ct. 1955)
57 ALR6th 445—§ 48
State v. Bean, 153 Wis. 2d 774, 452 N.W.2d 586 (Ct. App. 1989)
123 ALR5th 221—§ 3
State v. Bean, 174 Ariz. 544, 851 P.2d 843 (Ct. App. Div. 1 1992)
58 ALR5th 669—§ 8
State v. Bean, 239 N.W.2d 556 (Iowa 1976)
6 ALR6th 533—§ 17
State v. Beard, 194 W. Va. 740, 461 S.E.2d 486 (1995)
90 ALR5th 453—§ 26
9 ALR6th 363—§ 37
10 ALR6th 463—§ 4, 8
State v. Beard, 574 N.W.2d 87 (Minn. Ct. App. 1998)
73 ALR5th 383—§ 5
State v. Beasley, 126 Wash. App. 670, 109 P.3d 849 (Div. 2 2005)
19 ALR6th 697—§ 6
State v. Beasley, 1999 WL 100001 (Ohio Ct. App. 5th Dist. Stark County 1999)
63 ALR6th 351—§ 3
State v. Beasley, 2013 WL 6818153 (Mo. Ct. App. E.D. 2013)
94 ALR6th 525—§ 7
State v. Beason, 653 So. 2d 1274 (La. Ct. App. 2d Cir. 1995)
84 ALR6th 427—§ 17, 21
State v. Beatty, 64 N.C. App. 511, 308 S.E.2d 65 (1983)
16 ALR5th 390—§ 3
State v. Beatty, 347 N.C. 555, 495 S.E.2d 367 (1998)
39 ALR5th 283—§ 20

State v. Beauchamp, 2011 WI 27, 333 Wis. 2d 1, 796 N.W.2d 780 (2011)
76 ALR6th 587—§ 21
State v. Beaudet, 53 Conn. 536, 4 A. 237 (1886)
11 ALR5th 831—§ 5
State v. Beaudoin, 503 A.2d 1289 (Me. 1986)
15 ALR5th 391—§ 28
State v. Beaudoin, 600 A.2d 1097 (Me. 1991)
103 ALR6th 137—§ 17
State v. Beaudry, 53 Wis. 2d 148, 191 N.W.2d 842 (1971)
80 ALR5th 597—§ 2, 15, 16
State v. Beaulieu, 82 Conn. App. 856, 848 A.2d 500 (2004)
40 ALR6th 1—§ 28
State v. Beaulieu, 550 A.2d 68 (Me. 1988)
84 ALR6th 293—§ 35
State v. Beaulieu, 2006 WL 852139 (Minn. Ct. App. 2006)
33 ALR6th 91—§ 45
State v. Beaumier, 480 A.2d 1367 (R.I. 1984)
58 ALR6th 499—§ 69
State v. Beavers, 173 Wis. 2d 305, 498 N.W.2d 912 (Ct. App. 1992)
73 ALR5th 383—§ 67
State v. Beavers, 394 So. 2d 1218 (La. 1981)
54 ALR5th 575—§ 17
State v. Beavers, 591 S.W.2d 215 (Mo. Ct. App. W.D. 1979)
70 ALR5th 587—§ 8, 10
State v. Beavers, 859 P.3d 9 (Utah Ct. App. 1993)
79 ALR6th 1—§ 46
State v. Beavers, 1998 WL 12685 (Ohio Ct. App. 2d Dist. Clark County 1998)
19 ALR6th 697—§ 4
State v. Beavers, 2009-Ohio-4214, 2009 WL 2579501 (Ohio Ct. App. 10th Dist. Franklin County 2009)
71 ALR6th 1—§ 8

State v. Bebb, 108 Wash. 2d 515, 740 P.2d 829 (1987)
98 ALR5th 445—§ 2, 4

State v. Bebel, 383 N.W.2d 724 (Minn. Ct. App. 1986)
109 ALR5th 611—§ 3

State v. Becerill, 124 Ariz. 535, 606 P.2d 25 (Ct. App. Div. 2 1979)
82 ALR5th 359—§ 2
83 ALR5th 277—§ 2
84 ALR5th 487—§ 2

State v. Beck, 5 Conn. Cir. Ct. 587, 259 A.2d 149, 44 A.L.R.3d 1014 (App. Div. 1969)
66 ALR5th 397—§ 3, 4, 12

State v. Beck, 23 Wash. App. 640, 598 P.2d 400 (Div. 1 1979)
105 ALR5th 529—§ 8

State v. Beck, 42 Wash. App. 12, 707 P.2d 1380 (Div. 1 1985)
92 ALR6th 295—§ 36

State v. Beck, 163 N.C. App. 469, 594 S.E.2d 94 (2004)
3 ALR6th 543—§ 6, 11

State v. Beck, 763 So. 2d 506 (Fla. Dist. Ct. App. 4th Dist. 2000)
113 ALR5th 597—§ 8

State v. Beck, 849 S.W.2d 668 (Mo. Ct. App. E.D. 1993)
1 ALR6th 549—§ 3, 24
7 ALR6th 169—§ 3
8 ALR6th 265—§ 3

State v. Beckenbach, 136 Vt. 557, 397 A.2d 79 (1978)
9 ALR6th 1—§ 17

State v. Becker, 80 Wash. App. 364, 908 P.2d 903 (1996)
27 ALR5th 593—§ 6, 17

State v. Becker, 132 Wash. 2d 54, 935 P.2d 1321 (1997)
27 ALR5th 593—§ 5, 21

State v. Becker, 458 N.W.2d 604 (Iowa 1990)
92 ALR6th 171—§ 3, 5

State v. Beckert, 137 N.J.L. 562, 61 A.2d 213 (N.J. Sup. Ct. 1948)
77 ALR6th 393—§ 34, 40

State v. Beckham, 105 N.C. App. 214, 412 S.E.2d 114 (1992)
28 ALR6th 505—§ 6, 8

State v. Beckham, 334 S.C. 302, 513 S.E.2d 606 (1999)
23 ALR5th 672—§ 10
6 ALR6th 533—§ 21

State v. Beckley, 192 Wis. 367, 212 N.W. 792 (1927)
116 ALR5th 1—§ 65

State v. Beckley, 2004-Ohio-2977, 2004 WL 1277358 (Ohio Ct. App. 8th Dist. Cuyahoga County 2004)
33 ALR6th 91—§ 5
34 ALR6th 171—§ 16

State v. Beckman, 284 Mont. 459, 944 P.2d 756 (1997)
69 ALR6th 1—§ 13

State v. Beckman, 547 So. 2d 210, 14 FLW 1621 (Fla. App. D5 1989)
42 ALR5th 291—§ 6

State v. Beckman, 2003 WL 22774394 (Minn. Ct. App. 2003)
4 ALR6th 1—§ 4

State v. Bedard, 120 Idaho 869, 820 P.2d 1226 (1991)
87 ALR5th 1—§ 14

State v. Beddard, 35 N.C. App. 212, 241 S.E.2d 83 (1978)
112 ALR5th 429—§ 3

State v. Bedker, 74 Wash. App. 87, 871 P.2d 673 (Div. 1 1994)
73 ALR5th 383—§ 5, 26

State v. Bednar, 2006 WL 1765251 (N.J. Super. Ct. App. Div. 2006)
79 ALR6th 1—§ 40

State v. Bednarz, 179 Wis. 2d 460, 507 N.W.2d 168 (Ct. App. 1993)
57 ALR5th 315—§ 2, 3, 11

State v. Bedoni, 161 Ariz. 480, 779 P.2d 355 (Ct. App. Div. 1 1989)
108 ALR5th 593—§ 38

State v. Beebe, 67 Or. App. 738, 680 P.2d 11 (1984)
22 ALR5th 261—§ 2, 4 to 6

State v. Beebe, 244 Kan. 48, 766 P.2d 158 (1988)

37 ALR5th 515—§ 2, 12

State v. Beechum, 251 Kan. 194, 833 P.2d 988 (1992)

92 ALR5th 35—§ 28

State v. Beecraft, 2007 WI App 19, 298 Wis. 2d 551, 727 N.W.2d 375 (Ct. App. 2006)

87 ALR6th 109—§ 44

State v. Beede, 119 N.H. 620, 406 A.2d 125 (1979)

61 ALR5th 1—§ 3, 7
58 ALR6th 499—§ 85

State v. Beeken, 7 Neb. App. 438, 585 N.W.2d 865 (1998)

106 ALR5th 397—§ 2, 4
78 ALR6th 297—§ 42

State v. Beeman, 25 Ariz. App. 83, 541 P.2d 409 (Div. 1 1975)

72 ALR5th 607—§ 3, 5

State v. Beermann, 231 Neb. 380, 436 N.W.2d 499 (1989)

39 ALR6th 257—§ 23, 27
40 ALR6th 1—§ 16
103 ALR6th 507—§ 27

State v. Beeson, 569 N.W.2d 107 (Iowa 1997)

54 ALR5th 141—§ 3 to 5, 9

State v. Begay, 1998 -NMSC- 029, 125 N.M. 541, 964 P.2d 102 (1998)

20 ALR5th 398—§ 5, 33.5

State v. Begley, 956 S.W.2d 471 (Tenn. 1997)

90 ALR5th 453—§ 23

State v. Behar, 39 Or. App. 503, 592 P.2d 1056 (1979)

99 ALR5th 557—§ 3, 10

State v. Behn, 375 N.J. Super. 409, 868 A.2d 329 (App. Div. 2005)

92 ALR6th 549—§ 12

State v. Behrens, 86 Wash. App. 1067, 1997 WL 345214 (Div. 2 1997)

19 ALR6th 697—§ 6

State v. Behrens, 204 Neb. 785, 285 N.W.2d 513 (1979)

15 ALR5th 391—§ 5
46 ALR6th 241—§ 6

State v. Beine, 162 S.W.3d 483 (Mo. 2005)

71 ALR6th 283—§ 6

State v. Beishline, 920 S.W.2d 622 (Mo. Ct. App. W.D. 1996)

57 ALR6th 445—§ 40

State v. Bejar, 104 N.M. 138, 717 P.2d 591 (App. 1985)

7 ALR5th 263—§ 6

State v. Belanus, 144 Vt. 166, 475 A.2d 227 (1984)

9 ALR6th 633—§ 4, 5, 13
15 ALR6th 173—§ 19

State v. Belcher, 25 Utah 2d 37, 475 P.2d 60 (1970)

37 ALR6th 357—§ 8, 67

State v. Belcher, 111 Ariz. 580, 535 P.2d 1297 (1975)

21 ALR6th 771—§ 5

State v. Belcher, 146 Ariz. 380, 706 P.2d 392 (App. 1985)

1 ALR5th 938—§ 4
8 ALR5th 713—§ 10

State v. Belcher, 183 S.W.3d 443 (Tex. App. Houston 14th Dist. 2005)

71 ALR6th 625—§ 4, 39

State v. Belcher, 317 S.W.3d 101 (Mo. Ct. App. S.D. 2010)

72 ALR6th 227—§ 23, 51

State v. Belcher, 805 S.W.2d 245 (Mo. App. 1991)

39 ALR5th 283—§ 4

State v. Belcourt, 425 A.2d 1224 (R.I. 1981)

101 ALR6th 299—§ 6

State v. Belfry, 416 N.W.2d 811 (Minn. Ct. App. 1987)

92 ALR5th 35—§ 2

State v. Belgarde, 1998 MT 152, 289 Mont. 287, 962 P.2d 571 (1998)

24 ALR6th 1—§ 38
35 ALR6th 127—§ 5

State v. Belgarde, 1998 M.T. 152, 962 P.2d 571 (Mont. 1998)

40 ALR5th 113—§ 4

State v. Beliveau, 52 Conn. App. 475, 727 A.2d 737 (1999)

32 ALR6th 1—§ 9
State v. Belk, 199 Or. App. 382, 111 P.3d 801 (2005)
26 ALR6th 511—§ 27
State v. Belken, 633 N.W.2d 786 (Iowa 2001)
38 ALR6th 439—§ 8
State v. Belknap, 2004-Ohio-5636, 2004 WL 2376443 (Ohio Ct. App. 11th Dist. Portage County 2004)
71 ALR6th 1—§ 17
State v. Bell, 28 So. 3d 502 (La. Ct. App. 4th Cir. 2009)
79 ALR6th 1—§ 40
State v. Bell, 55 N.J. 239, 260 A.2d 849 (1970)
29 ALR5th 59—§ 69, 88
State v. Bell, 62 Wis. 2d 534, 215 N.W.2d 535 (1974)
91 ALR5th 437—§ 16
State v. Bell, 69 S.W.3d 171, 24 A.L.R.6th 979 (Tenn. 2002)
24 ALR6th 747—§ 12, 20
State v. Bell, 83 Wash. 2d 383, 518 P.2d 696 (1974)
13 ALR5th 1—§ 2
State v. Bell, 87 N.C. App. 626, 362 S.E.2d 288 (1987)
3 ALR6th 269—§ 25
State v. Bell, 149 Wash. App. 1058, 2009 WL 1110881 (Div. 1 2009)
78 ALR6th 1—§ 28, 51
State v. Bell, 188 Conn. 406, 450 A.2d 356 (1982)
39 ALR5th 283—§ 3, 15, 18
State v. Bell, 189 W. Va. 448, 432 S.E.2d 532 (1993)
29 ALR6th 1—§ 14
State v. Bell, 195 N.J. Super. 49, 477 A.2d 1272 (App. Div. 1984)
67 ALR5th 361—§ 3
State v. Bell, 270 N.C. 25, 153 S.E.2d 741 (1967)
4 ALR6th 577—§ 5
State v. Bell, 273 Kan. 49, 41 P.3d 783 (2002)
3 ALR6th 543—§ 8

State v. Bell, 346 So. 2d 1090 (La. 1977)
83 ALR6th 465—§ 31
State v. Bell, 377 So. 2d 275 (La. 1979)
79 ALR5th 419—§ 18
State v. Bell, 404 So. 2d 974 (La. 1981)
29 ALR5th 59—§ 58
State v. Bell, 572 N.W.2d 910 (Iowa 1997)
18 ALR5th 542—§ 3
State v. Bell, 589 P.2d 517 (Hawaii 1978)
49 ALR5th 639—§ 4
State v. Bell, 639 So. 2d 856 (La. App. 5th Cir. 1994)
38 ALR5th 433—§ 3
State v. Bell, 716 S.E.2d 268 (N.C. Ct. App. 2011)
79 ALR6th 1—§ 49
State v. Bell, 1997 WL 317425 (Ohio Ct. App. 4th Dist. Scioto County 1997)
99 ALR6th 295—§ 16
State v. Bell, 2000 ND 58, 608 N.W.2d 232 (N.D. 2000)
105 ALR5th 529—§ 11
State v. Bell, 2002-Ohio-2182, 2002 WL 987536 (Ohio Ct. App. 3d Dist. Marion County 2002)
29 ALR6th 237—§ 4, 9
State v. Bellotti, 383 N.W.2d 308 (Minn. App. 1986)
38 ALR5th 433—§ 3, 11
State v. Bellows, 72 Wash. 2d 264, 432 P.2d 654 (1967)
68 ALR5th 343—§ 3, 14
State v. Bellows, 596 N.W.2d 509 (Iowa 1999)
29 ALR5th 487—§ 9
State v. Bellville, 705 N.W.2d 506 (Iowa Ct. App. 2005)
78 ALR6th 1—§ 26
State v. Belnavis, 311 N.J. Super. 195, 709 A.2d 805 (App. Div. 1998)
27 ALR5th 593—§ 20, 22
State v. Belote, 213 Kan. 291, 516 P.2d 159 (1973)
84 ALR5th 487—§ 3

For assistance, call 1-800-328-4880

State v. Belser, 945 S.W.2d 776 (Tenn. Crim. App. 1996)
27 ALR6th 183—§ 45

State v. Belton, 318 N.C. 141, 347 S.E.2d 755 (1986)
39 ALR5th 283—§ 4, 62, 67

State v. Beltran, 246 Conn. 268, 717 A.2d 168 (1998)
70 ALR5th 587—§ 25

State v. Beltran-Felix, 922 P.2d 30 (Utah Ct. App. 1996)
91 ALR5th 343—§ 3, 16

State v. Beltz, 2006 WL 1627913 (Alaska Ct. App. 2006)
63 ALR6th 351—§ 3

State v. Belyea, 160 N.H. 298, 999 A.2d 1080 (2010)
78 ALR6th 1—§ 43, 59, 61

State v. Bember, 183 Conn. 394, 439 A.2d 387 (1981)
101 ALR5th 187—§ 16

State v. Benallie, 1997 S.D. 118, 570 N.W.2d 236 (S.D. 1997)
68 ALR5th 343—§ 3

State v. Benbow, 169 N.C. App. 613, 610 S.E.2d 297 (2005)
15 ALR6th 375—§ 19

State v. Bencomo, 109 N.M. 724, 790 P.2d 521 (Ct. App. 1990)
15 ALR6th 173—§ 19

State v. Bender, 24 Ohio App. 3d 131, 493 N.E.2d 552 (9th Dist. Lorain County 1985)
80 ALR6th 599—§ 10

State v. Bender, 598 So. 2d 629 (La. App. 3d Cir. 1992)
12 ALR5th 909—§ 7

State v. Bendlin, 221 Wis. 2d 598, 586 N.W.2d 700 (Ct. App. 1998)
30 ALR6th 103—§ 6, 15, 22, 24, 55

State v. Benefiel, 131 Idaho 226, 953 P.2d 976 (1998)
18 ALR6th 519—§ 19
56 ALR6th 323—§ 7

State v. Benenati, 203 Ariz. 235, 52 P.3d 804 (Ct. App. Div. 2 2002)
26 ALR6th 511—§ 5, 27

State v. Bengtson, 230 Or. 19, 367 P.2d 363, 96 A.L.R.2d 150 (1961)
64 ALR6th 655—§ 11

State v. Benitez, 157 Conn. 384, 254 A.2d 564 (1969)
32 ALR6th 1—§ 4

State v. Benjamin, 124 N.C. App. 734, 478 S.E.2d 651 (1996)
50 ALR5th 581—§ 6, 7

State v. Benjamin, 345 S.C. 470, 549 S.E.2d 258 (2001)
121 ALR5th 551—§ 14

State v. Benjamin, 478 S.E.2d 651 (N.C. App. 1996)
50 ALR5th 581—§ 6, 9, 12, 19

State v. Benner, 284 A.2d 91 (Me. 1971)
23 ALR6th 1—§ 15

State v. Bennet, 2011 WL 1045646 (Tenn. Crim. App. 2011)
92 ALR6th 1—§ 4

State v. Bennett, 36 Wash. App. 176, 672 P.2d 772 (1983)
46 ALR5th 499—§ 2, 3, 5

State v. Bennett, 142 Idaho 166, 125 P.3d 522 (2005)
55 ALR6th 391—§ 24

State v. Bennett, 150 Ohio App. 3d 450, 2002-Ohio-6651, 782 N.E.2d 101 (1st Dist. Hamilton County 2002)
58 ALR6th 385—§ 3, 5, 8

State v. Bennett, 154 Wash. App. 202, 224 P.3d 849 (Div. 1 2010)
63 ALR6th 351—§ 3

State v. Bennett, 171 Conn. 47, 368 A.2d 184 (1976)
28 ALR6th 505—§ 9

State v. Bennett, 204 Neb. 28, 281 N.W.2d 216 (1979)
32 ALR6th 1—§ 11

State v. Bennett, 205 Mont. 117, 666 P.2d 747 (1983)
59 ALR5th 615—§ 3, 4, 12

State v. Bennett, 223 P.3d 837 (Kan. Ct. App. 2010)
103 ALR6th 347—§ 13

State v. Bennett, 328 S.C. 251, 493 S.E.2d 845 (1997)

33 ALR5th 571—§ 4
67 ALR6th 103—§ 9, 10
State v. Bennett, 481 So. 2d 971 (Fla. Dist. Ct. App. 5th Dist. 1986)
114 ALR5th 173—§ 7
State v. Bennett, 503 N.W.2d 42 (Iowa Ct. App. 1993)
1 ALR6th 657—§ 4
State v. Bennett, 517 So. 2d 1115 (La. Ct. App. 1st Cir. 1987)
19 ALR6th 115—§ 4, 9, 10
State v. Bennett, 520 So. 2d 635 (Fla. 4th DCA 1988)
78 ALR6th 599—§ 4, 5
State v. Bennett, 591 So. 2d 783 (La. App. 4th Cir. 1991)
38 ALR5th 433—§ 2, 26
State v. Bennett, 880 So. 2d 165 (La. Ct. App. 2d Cir. 2004)
71 ALR6th 1—§ 6
State v. Bennett, 2000 UT 34, 999 P.2d 1 (Utah 2000)
99 ALR6th 295—§ 7
State v. Bennett, 2011 WL 3557533 (N.J. Super. Ct. App. Div. 2011)
99 ALR6th 295—§ 5
State v. Bennett, No. 50432 (April 17, 1986, Ct. App. Ohio, 8th App. Dist. Cuyahoga Co.)
39 ALR5th 283—§ 14, 23
State v. Bennis, 457 N.W.2d 843 (S.D. 1990)
50 ALR5th 467—§ 5
State v. Benny, 20 N.J. 238, 119 A.2d 155 (1955)
5 ALR6th 1—§ 25, 27, 40
State v. Beno, 116 Wis. 2d 122, 341 N.W.2d 668 (1984)
24 ALR6th 255—§ 5, 7, 15
State v. Beno, 1999 WL 1577 (Ohio Ct. App. 9th Dist. Medina County 1998)
54 ALR6th 593—§ 4
State v. Benoit, 21 Kan. App. 2d 184, 898 P.2d 653 (1995)
38 ALR6th 97—§ 22
State v. Benoit, 117 R.I. 69, 363 A.2d 207 (1976)

99 ALR6th 113—§ 16
State v. Benoit, 131 Vt. 631, 313 A.2d 387 (1973)
15 ALR5th 391—§ 50
92 ALR5th 35—§ 10
State v. Benson, 124 N.H. 767, 474 A.2d 576 (1984)
5 ALR5th 243—§ 59
19 ALR5th 823—§ 3, 7
State v. Benson, 198 Neb. 14, 251 N.W.2d 659 (1977)
114 ALR5th 173—§ 3, 7
35 ALR6th 497—§ 27
State v. Benson, 645 S.W.2d 423 (Tenn. Crim. App. 1983)
55 ALR6th 391—§ 20
State v. Benson, 983 P.2d 225 (Idaho Ct. App. 1999)
55 ALR5th 125—§ 3, 5
State v. Benson, 2004 WL 2266801 (Tenn. Crim. App. 2004)
26 ALR6th 511—§ 25, 27
State v. Bentlage, 192 Ariz. 117, 961 P.2d 1065 (Ct. App. Div. 2 1998)
68 ALR5th 343—§ 3, 4, 17
State v. Bentley, 155 Mont. 383, 472 P.2d 864 (1970)
99 ALR6th 295—§ 13
State v. Bentley, 201 Wis. 2d 303, 548 N.W.2d 50 (1996)
31 ALR6th 49—§ 10
State v. Bentley, 692 So. 2d 1207 (La. Ct. App. 5th Cir. 1997)
32 ALR6th 1—§ 4
State v. Bentley, 739 N.W.2d 296 (Iowa 2007)
30 ALR6th 1—§ 6
36 ALR6th 681—§ 13
State v. Bentley Bootery, 128 N.J.L. 555, 27 A.2d 620 (N.J. Sup. Ct. 1942)
55 ALR6th 157—§ 11
State v. Benton, 136 Ohio App. 3d 801, 737 N.E.2d 1046 (6th Dist. Ottawa County 2000)
24 ALR6th 1—§ 32

State v. Benvenuto, 2000-Ohio-1674, 2000 WL 327228 (Ohio Ct. App. 3d Dist. Auglaize County 2000)
11 ALR6th 237—§ 10
State v. Berard, 154 Vt. 306, 576 A.2d 118, 14 A.L.R.5th 1080 (1990)
14 ALR5th 913—§ 3
State v. Berardinelli, 95 Or. App. 364, 769 P.2d 235 (1989)
41 ALR5th 171—§ 55
State v. Berberian, 122 R.I. 693, 411 A.2d 308 (1980)
87 ALR5th 1—§ 12
State v. Berberian, 459 A.2d 928 (R.I. 1983)
79 ALR5th 1—§ 2, 6, 8
State v. Berberich, 248 Kan. 854, 811 P.2d 1192 (1991)
12 ALR5th 89—§ 4, 7
State v. Berenyi, 1997 WL 576357 (Ohio Ct. App. 3d Dist.Paulding County 1997)
58 ALR5th 749—§ 4
State v. Berg, 76 Ariz. 96, 259 P.2d 261 (1953)
5 ALR5th 875—§ 31
State v. Berge, 25 Wash. App. 433, 607 P.2d 1247 (1980)
7 ALR5th 758—§ 6, 13
State v. Berge, 130 Ariz. 135, 634 P.2d 947 (1981)
67 ALR5th 361—§ 3, 4, 6
State v. Bergen, 121 Ohio App. 3d 459, 700 N.E.2d 345 (1st Dist. Hamilton County 1997)
6 ALR5th 733—§ 18
State v. Berger, 212 Ariz. 473, 134 P.3d 378 (2006)
26 ALR6th 659—§ 54
State v. Berger, 285 N.W.2d 533 (N.D. 1979)
41 ALR5th 171—§ 63, 68
State v. Bergerson, 671 N.W.2d 197 (Minn. Ct. App. 2003)
78 ALR6th 297—§ 8, 41, 67
State v. Bergin, 214 Conn. 657, 574 A.2d 164 (1990)
81 ALR6th 257—§ 16

State v. Bergman, 558 N.E.2d 1111 (Ind. Ct. App. 1990)
70 ALR6th 1—§ 21
State v. Berini, 167 Vt. 565, 701 A.2d 1055 (1997)
109 ALR5th 611—§ 6
State v. Berker, 112 R.I. 624, 314 A.2d 11 (1974)
89 ALR6th 565—§ 10
State v. Berkins, 2 Wash. App. 910, 471 P.2d 131 (Div. 1 1970)
57 ALR6th 83—§ 11
State v. Berky, 214 Ga. App. 174, 447 S.E.2d 147 (1994)
116 ALR5th 373—§ 4
State v. Berlin, 46 Wash. App. 587, 731 P.2d 548 (Div. 1 1987)
85 ALR5th 1—§ 40
State v. Berlow, 284 N.J. Super. 356, 665 A.2d 404 (Law Div. 1995)
66 ALR5th 397—§ 12
58 ALR6th 499—§ 22
State v. Berman, 50 Wash. App. 125, 747 P.2d 492 (Div. 1 1987)
57 ALR6th 445—§ 22
State v. Bermudez, 2010 WL 2990292 (N.J. Super. Ct. App. Div. 2010)
79 ALR6th 1—§ 69
State v. Bernal, 122 P.3d 42 (Kan. Ct. App. 2005)
30 ALR6th 1—§ 3, 4, 6, 7
State v. Bernard, 121 Wash. App. 1005, 2004 WL 792453 (Div. 2 2004)
125 ALR5th 537—§ 5, 36, 39
State v. Bernard, 608 So. 2d 966 (La. 1992)
79 ALR5th 33—§ 2, 9, 11, 23, 25, 56
State v. Bernardy, 25 Wash. App. 146, 605 P.2d 791 (Div. 1 1980)
79 ALR5th 419—§ 10
State v. Bernath, 3 Ohio App. 3d 229, 444 N.E.2d 439 (6th Dist. Fulton County 1981)
62 ALR6th 413—§ 10, 12, 23, 41
State v. Berndt, 138 Ariz. 41, 672 P.2d 1311 (1983)
31 ALR5th 704—§ 16

State v. Bernhardt, 245 N.J. Super. 210, 584 A.2d 854 (1991)
28 ALR5th 459—§ 3
State v. Bernie, 472 So. 2d 1243, 10 FLW 1551 (Fla. App. D2 1985)
19 ALR5th 470—§ 3, 12
State v. Bernier, 486 A.2d 147 (Me. 1985)
99 ALR5th 557—§ 12
State v. Berres, 130 P.3d 149 (Kan. Ct. App. 2006)
25 ALR6th 379—§ 3, 5, 11
State v. Berrill, 196 W. Va. 578, 474 S.E.2d 508, 112 Ed. Law Rep. 487 (1996)
94 ALR5th 455—§ 14
State v. Berry, 51 N.C. App. 97, 275 S.E.2d 269 (1981)
99 ALR6th 295—§ 8
State v. Berry, 72 Ohio St. 3d 354, 650 N.E.2d 433 (1995)
70 ALR5th 1—§ 8
State v. Berry, 74 Or. App. 224, 702 P.2d 82 (1985)
92 ALR5th 35—§ 30
State v. Berry, 92 S.W.3d 823 (Mo. Ct. App. S.D. 2003)
67 ALR6th 531—§ 4, 6, 18
State v. Berry, 92 Wash. App. 1056, 1998 WL 758894 (Div. 1 1998)
63 ALR6th 1—§ 5
State v. Berry, 124 N.H. 203, 470 A.2d 881 (1983)
56 ALR6th 185—§ 37
State v. Berry, 133 Ariz. 264, 650 P.2d 1246 (Ct. App. Div. 1 1982)
97 ALR5th 201—§ 3, 6
State v. Berry, 165 W. Va. 783, 271 S.E.2d 776 (1980)
109 ALR5th 611—§ 6
State v. Berry, 176 W. Va. 291, 342 S.E.2d 259 (1986)
24 ALR5th 465—§ 7, 15 to 17
State v. Berry, 223 Kan. 102, 573 P.2d 584 (1977)
4 ALR5th 1—§ 4, 7, 10
State v. Berry, 324 So. 2d 822 (La. 1975)

93 ALR5th 327—§ 4, 7, 28
State v. Berry, 391 So. 2d 406 (La. 1980)
10 ALR5th 700—§ 2, 3, 9, 16, 17
24 ALR6th 747—§ 43
State v. Berry, 609 S.W.2d 948 (Mo. 1980)
93 ALR5th 527—§ 9
State v. Berry, 1993 WL 425370 (Ohio Ct. App. 8th Dist. Cuyahoga County 1993)
79 ALR5th 33—§ 63
State v. Berry, 2003 WL 1855099 (Tenn. Crim. App. 2003)
110 ALR5th 1—§ 15
State v. Bertke, 1988 WL 83491 (Ohio Ct. App. 1st Dist. Hamilton County 1988)
35 ALR6th 361—§ 7
State v. Bertrand, 133 N.H. 843, 587 A.2d 1219 (1991)
103 ALR6th 137—§ 4
State v. Bertul, 664 P.2d 1181 (Utah 1983)
111 ALR5th 1—§ 2, 5, 9, 35
State v. Berube, 107 Wash. App. 1035, 2001 WL 873853 (Div. 2 2001)
16 ALR6th 329—§ 4
19 ALR6th 115—§ 4
24 ALR6th 591—§ 9, 13
State v. Berube, 669 A.2d 170 (Me. 1995)
84 ALR6th 427—§ 21, 26
99 ALR6th 113—§ 18
State v. Beserra, 2010 WL 2211073 (Ariz. Ct. App. Div. 1 2010)
68 ALR6th 527—§ 42
State v. Beshears, 112 Wash. App. 1028, 2002 WL 1399121 (Div. 2 2002)
71 ALR6th 625—§ 29
State v. Beson, 179 Wis. 2d 504, 508 N.W.2d 76 (Ct. App. 1993)
99 ALR6th 295—§ 9, 21
State v. Besso, 72 Wis. 2d 335, 240 N.W.2d 895 (1976)
32 ALR5th 149—§ 50 to 52, 55
State v. Best, 8 N.J. Misc. 271, 150 A. 44 (Quar. Sess. 1930)

103 ALR5th 463—§ 7

State v. Best, 31 N.C. App. 250, 229 S.E.2d 581 (1976)

13 ALR5th 1—§ 4, 15

State v. Best, 232 N.C. 575, 61 S.E.2d 612 (1950)

29 ALR5th 59—§ 84, 89

State v. Best, 292 N.C. 294, 233 S.E.2d 544 (1977)

13 ALR5th 1—§ 2, 22, 25

State v. Best, 342 N.C. 502, 467 S.E.2d 45 (1996)

20 ALR5th 177—§ 3, 7

State v. Best, 713 S.E.2d 556 (N.C. Ct. App. 2011)

71 ALR6th 1—§ 14

State v. Betcher, 1992 WL 231657 (Minn. Ct. App. 1992)

15 ALR6th 515—§ 27

State v. Bethea, 173 N.C. App. 43, 617 S.E.2d 687 (2005)

102 ALR6th 279—§ 30

State v. Bethea, 243 N.J. Super. 280, 579 A.2d 341 (1990)

27 ALR5th 593—§ 32

State v. Bethel, 569 S.W.2d 270 (Mo. Ct. App. 1978)

1 ALR6th 549—§ 3, 4, 9

State v. Bethune, 121 N.J. 137, 578 A.2d 364 (1990)

39 ALR6th 257—§ 23, 27, 47, 49
40 ALR6th 1—§ 9, 12

State v. Bethune, 207 Ga. App. 340, 427 S.E.2d 795 (1993)

99 ALR5th 557—§ 3, 9, 10

State v. Bettenhausen, 460 N.W.2d 394, 2 A.L.R.5th 1127 (N.D. 1990)

2 ALR5th 725—§ 2, 5, 6, 8, 13, 20

State v. Betterton, 527 So. 2d 743 (Ala. Crim. App. 1986)

114 ALR5th 173—§ 9

State v. Bettin, 295 N.W.2d 542 (Minn. 1980)

83 ALR5th 277—§ 17

State v. Bettis, 2005-Ohio-2917, 2005 WL 1385220 (Ohio Ct. App. 12th Dist. Butler County 2005)

34 ALR6th 253—§ 13

State v. Betts, 21 Ohio Misc. 175, 49 Ohio Op. 2d 22, 50 Ohio Op. 2d 351, 252 N.E.2d 866 (Mun. Ct. 1969)

72 ALR5th 607—§ 3

State v. Betts, 71 Ariz. 362, 227 P.2d 749 (1951)

41 ALR5th 1—§ 3, 4, 8

State v. Betz, 815 So. 2d 627 (Fla. 2002)

114 ALR5th 173—§ 6
123 ALR5th 179—§ 7, 9

State v. Beugli, 126 Or. App. 290, 868 P.2d 766 (1994)

29 ALR5th 1—§ 2

State v. Beveridge, 112 N.C. App. 688, 436 S.E.2d 912 (1993)

50 ALR5th 581—§ 6, 7, 14, 20

State v. Bews, 177 Ariz. 334, 868 P.2d 347 (Ct. App. Div. 2 1993)

87 ALR5th 597—§ 11

State v. Bey, 85 Ohio St. 3d 487, 709 N.E.2d 484 (1999)

72 ALR5th 403—§ 15

State v. Bey, 112 N.J. 45, 548 A.2d 846 (1988)

55 ALR6th 157—§ 5, 29

State v. Bey, 129 N.J. 557, 610 A.2d 814 (1992)

63 ALR6th 1—§ 36

State v. Bey, 161 N.J. 233, 736 A.2d 469 (1999)

78 ALR5th 197—§ 3
71 ALR6th 249—§ 8

State v. Bey, 270 Kan. 544, 17 P.3d 322, 9 A.L.R.6th 807 (2001)

9 ALR6th 633—§ 14, 55
9 ALR6th 693—§ 12
13 ALR6th 603—§ 13
14 ALR6th 517—§ 9

State v. Beyers, 1996 WL 368241 (Wash. Ct. App. Div. 3 1996)

68 ALR5th 343—§ 17

State v. Beynon, 484 N.W.2d 898 (S.D. 1992)

27 ALR6th 183—§ 7

For assistance, call 1-800-328-4880

State v. B.G.S., 2011 WL 1743914
(Minn. Ct. App. 2011)
68 ALR6th 1—§ 17
State v. Bhat, 127 S.W.3d 435 (Tex.
App. Dallas 2004)
69 ALR6th 1—§ 9
State v. Biancamano, 284 N.J. Super.
654, 666 A.2d 199, 104 Ed. Law
Rep. 776 (App. Div. 1995)
59 ALR6th 393—§ 3
State v. Bias, 171 W. Va. 687, 301
S.E.2d 776 (1983)
95 ALR5th 125—§ 3
State v. Bias, 352 So. 2d 1011 (La. 1977)
9 ALR6th 1—§ 19
State v. Bible, 175 Ariz. 549, 858 P.2d
1152 (1993)
57 ALR5th 141—§ 9
82 ALR5th 67—§ 3
90 ALR5th 453—§ 28
54 ALR6th 429—§ 5, 11
98 ALR6th 455—§ 3
99 ALR6th 113—§ 3
102 ALR6th 279—§ 3
State v. Biby, 142 Wash. App. 1011,
2007 WL 4446938 (Div. 3 2007)
99 ALR6th 295—§ 11
State v. Bice, 115 Or. App. 482, 839
P.2d 244 (1992)
112 ALR5th 429—§ 10
State v. Bicek, 429 N.W.2d 289 (Minn.
Ct. App. 1988)
73 ALR5th 383—§ 5
State v. Bickel, 1994 WL 370022 (Ohio
Ct. App. 5th Dist. Holmes County
1994)
102 ALR6th 279—§ 32
State v. Bickell, 941 S.W.2d 767 (Mo.
Ct. App. E.D. 1997)
105 ALR5th 529—§ 31
State v. Bickford, 2011 WL 43317 (N.J.
Super. Ct. App. Div. 2011)
84 ALR6th 293—§ 43
State v. Bickham, 2009-825 La. App. 1
Cir. 10/23/09, 2009 WL 3453677
(La. Ct. App. 1st Cir. 2009)
55 ALR6th 1—§ 25

92 ALR6th 171—§ 14
State v. Bickman, 285 N.J. Super. 365,
666 A.2d 1386 (App. Div. 1995)
41 ALR5th 171—§ 108, 116
State v. Bidegain, 88 N.M. 466, 541 P.2d
971 (1975)
116 ALR5th 479—§ 5
State v. Biebinger, 585 N.W.2d 384
(Minn. 1998)
32 ALR6th 171—§ 8, 15, 18, 21, 22
33 ALR6th 1—§ 19, 20
State v. Bienvenu, 260 La. 1023, 258 So.
2d 72 (1972)
41 ALR5th 171—§ 10, 54, 78
State v. Bierstock, 195 Or. App. 514, 98
P.3d 771 (2004)
69 ALR6th 1—§ 12
State v. Biezer, 947 S.W.2d 540 (Mo. Ct.
App. E.D. 1997)
87 ALR5th 693—§ 2, 4
State v. Bigbee, 885 S.W.2d 797 (Tenn.
1994)
37 ALR5th 515—§ 2, 10
79 ALR5th 33—§ 65, 70
State v. Biggerstaff, 17 Mont. 510, 43 P.
709 (1896)
10 ALR5th 700—§ 4, 40
State v. Biggs, 13 Conn. App. 12, 534
A.2d 1217 (1987)
93 ALR5th 527—§ 4
State v. Biggs, 16 Wash. App. 221, 556
P.2d 247 (1976)
51 ALR5th 375—§ 7, 9
State v. Biggs, 292 N.C. 328, 233 S.E.2d
512 (1977)
9 ALR6th 1—§ 17
State v. Bigham, 119 S.C. 368, 112 S.E.
332 (1922)
54 ALR6th 429—§ 11
State v. Bigley, 202 N.W.2d 56 (Iowa
1972)
55 ALR6th 157—§ 4, 21
State v. Bigsby, 2000 WL 775580 (Tenn.
Crim. App. 2000)
4 ALR5th 1—§ 38
State v. Bilancio, 318 N.J. Super. 408,
724 A.2d 278 (App. Div. 1999)

50 ALR6th 455—§ 3, 8, 19
State v. Bilbo, 719 So. 2d 1134 (La. Ct. App. 1st Cir. 1998)
39 ALR5th 283—§ 67
State v. Bilbrey, 858 S.W.2d 911 (Tenn. Crim. 1993)
45 ALR5th 591—§ 5
State v. Billie, 497 So. 2d 889 (Fla. Dist. Ct. App. 2d Dist. 1986)
44 ALR6th 325—§ 2
State v. Billiot, 370 So. 2d 539 (La. 1979)
78 ALR5th 197—§ 10
State v. Bilotta, 522 So. 2d 300 (Ala. Civ. App. 1988)
115 ALR5th 403—§ 5
101 ALR6th 1—§ 29
State v. Binegar, 1992 WL 129323 (Ohio App. Washington Co. 1992)
52 ALR5th 655—§ 3
State v. Bines, 8 N.C. App. 1, 173 S.E.2d 605 (1970)
81 ALR5th 563—§ 3
State v. Binford, 90 Wash. 2d 370, 582 P.2d 863 (1978)
46 ALR5th 523—§ 10
State v. Bingham, 124 Idaho 698, 864 P.2d 144 (1993)
27 ALR6th 183—§ 15, 32
State v. Bingham, 132 Wash. App. 1054, 2006 WL 1217236 (Div. 1 2006)
92 ALR6th 1—§ 8
State v. Bingham, 406 N.W.2d 567 (Minn. Ct. App. 1987)
73 ALR5th 383—§ 28, 32
State v. Bingman, 1999 WL 254419 (Ohio Ct. App. 5th Dist. Licking County 1999)
78 ALR5th 489—§ 10
State v. Binion, 900 S.W.2d 702 (Tenn. Crim. App. 1994)
74 ALR5th 319—§ 14
State v. Binion, 947 S.W.2d 867 (Tenn. Crim. App. 1996)
39 ALR6th 257—§ 14
State v. Binn, 208 N.J. Super. 443, 506 A.2d 67 (App. Div. 1986)

70 ALR6th 361—§ 31, 32
State v. Binns, 194 N.W.2d 756 (N.D. 1972)
114 ALR5th 173—§ 9
123 ALR5th 179—§ 4
State v. Bintzler, 220 Wis. 2d 714, 583 N.W.2d 673 (Ct. App. 1998)
24 ALR6th 1—§ 7
State v. Bior, 2010 WL 5541184 (Del. Super. Ct. 2010)
78 ALR6th 297—§ 15, 39, 57, 68
State v. Birbiglia, 149 La. 4, 88 So. 533 (1920)
16 ALR6th 329—§ 4
24 ALR6th 591—§ 4, 14
State v. Birbiglia, 155 La. 597, 99 So. 462 (1924)
76 ALR5th 485—§ 3, 16
State v. Birch, 1987 WL 13473 (Ohio Ct. App. 5th Dist. Stark County 1987)
99 ALR6th 295—§ 13
State v. Birchfield, 2007 WL 1437235 (N.J. Super. Ct. App. Div. 2007)
33 ALR6th 373—§ 17
State v. Bird, 2 Wash. 2d 286, 97 P.2d 1076 (1940)
50 ALR5th 703—§ 15
State v. Bird, 59 Or. App. 74, 650 P.2d 949 (1982)
26 ALR5th 603—§ 4
State v. Bird, 81 Ohio St. 3d 582, 692 N.E.2d 1013 (1998)
13 ALR5th 628—§ 5
State v. Bird Head, 225 Neb. 822, 408 N.W.2d 309 (1987)
85 ALR5th 471—§ 7
85 ALR5th 547—§ 2, 8
State v. Birdsong, 66 Wash. App. 534, 832 P.2d 533 (Div. 1 1992)
61 ALR5th 1—§ 2, 9
State v. Birge, 263 Neb. 77, 638 N.W.2d 529 (2002)
9 ALR6th 541—§ 12
15 ALR6th 173—§ 28
State v. Birgen, 33 Wash. App. 1, 651 P.2d 240 (Div. 1 1982)

56 ALR5th 385—§ 4
State v. Birkestrand, 239 N.W.2d 353 (Iowa 1976)
113 ALR5th 517—§ 12
State v. Birkla, 126 Idaho 498, 887 P.2d 43 (Ct. App. 1994)
32 ALR6th 1—§ 11
State v. Birnbach, 184 La. 215, 165 So. 717 (1936)
13 ALR5th 118—§ 14
State v. Birnel, 89 Wash. App. 459, 949 P.2d 433 (Div. 3 1998)
34 ALR6th 1—§ 12
State v. Biros, 78 Ohio St. 3d 426, 678 N.E.2d 891 (1997)
9 ALR5th 369—§ 14
State v. Birtha, 669 So. 2d 513 (La. Ct. App. 4th Cir. 1996)
71 ALR6th 1—§ 8
State v. Bisaccia, 58 N.J. 586, 279 A.2d 675 (1971)
103 ALR5th 463—§ 3
State v. Bishop, 14 Kan. App. 2d 223, 786 P.2d 1152 (1990)
97 ALR6th 653—§ 15
State v. Bishop, 22 Mo. App. 435, 1886 WL 5107 (1886)
97 ALR5th 537—§ 10
State v. Bishop, 43 Wash. App. 17, 714 P.2d 1199 (Div. 2 1986)
28 ALR6th 245—§ 3
State v. Bishop, 63 Wash. App. 15, 816 P.2d 738 (1991)
38 ALR5th 433—§ 3, 19
State v. Bishop, 134 Wash. App. 133, 139 P.3d 363 (Div. 3 2006)
70 ALR6th 361—§ 42
State v. Bishop, 157 Or. App. 33, 967 P.2d 1241 (1998)
26 ALR5th 378—§ 13
State v. Bishop, 228 N.C. 371, 45 S.E.2d 858, 21 L.R.R.M. (BNA) 2202, 14 Lab. Cas. (CCH) ¶ 64238 (1947)
105 ALR5th 243—§ 24
State v. Bishop, 240 Kan. 647, 732 P.2d 765 (1987)
39 ALR5th 283—§ 4, 41

State v. Bishop, 343 N.C. 518, 472 S.E.2d 842 (1996)
79 ALR5th 33—§ 63
State v. Bishop, 346 N.C. 365, 488 S.E.2d 769 (1997)
57 ALR5th 141—§ 7
State v. Bisner, 2001 UT 99, 37 P.3d 1073 (Utah 2001)
12 ALR6th 267—§ 5
State v. Bissantz, 3 Ohio App. 3d 108, 444 N.E.2d 92 (12th Dist. Clermont County 1982)
9 ALR6th 363—§ 43
State v. Biter, 49 Del. 503, 119 A.2d 894 (Super. Ct. 1955)
67 ALR6th 209—§ 25
State v. Bitt, 118 Idaho 584, 798 P.2d 43 (1990)
72 ALR5th 1—§ 3
State v. Bittner, 209 Iowa 109, 227 N.W. 601 (1929)
73 ALR5th 615—§ 3, 6, 9
State v. Bittner, 359 N.W.2d 121 (S.D. 1984)
58 ALR6th 499—§ 27
State v. Bjerke, 697 A.2d 1069 (R.I. 1997)
84 ALR6th 293—§ 31
State v. Bjorkaryd-Bradbury, 792 A.2d 1082 (Me. 2002)
116 ALR5th 479—§ 5
State v. Bjorklund, 79 Conn. App. 535, 830 A.2d 1141 (2003)
72 ALR6th 437—§ 18
State v. Bjorklund, 258 Neb. 432, 604 N.W.2d 169 (2000)
3 ALR5th 963—§ 6
37 ALR5th 515—§ 17
79 ALR5th 33—§ 40
State v. Bjornaas, 88 Minn. 301, 92 N.W. 980 (1903)
108 ALR5th 593—§ 23
State v. Bjornson, 378 N.W.2d 4 (Minn. Ct. App. 1985)
66 ALR5th 135—§ 23
State v. Black, 36 Or. App. 613, 585 P.2d 44 (1978)

109 ALR5th 99—§ 12
State v. Black, 50 S.W.3d 778 (Mo. 2001)

110 ALR5th 1—§ 2, 19
State v. Black, 54 N.J.L. 446, 24 A. 489 (N.J. Sup. Ct. 1892)

5 ALR6th 1—§ 4, 12
65 ALR6th 441—§ 4
State v. Black, 80 Or. App. 12, 721 P.2d 842 (1986)

84 ALR6th 293—§ 18
State v. Black, 86 Wash. App. 791, 938 P.2d 362 (Div. 1 1997)

82 ALR5th 359—§ 2
83 ALR5th 277—§ 2, 10
84 ALR5th 487—§ 2
State v. Black, 111 N.C. App. 284, 432 S.E.2d 710 (1993)

85 ALR5th 595—§ 7
State v. Black, 124 Ohio App. 3d 419, 706 N.E.2d 407 (1st Dist. Hamilton County 1997)

1 ALR6th 549—§ 12
State v. Black, 188 Wis. 2d 639, 526 N.W.2d 132 (1994)

64 ALR5th 671—§ 15
State v. Black, 260 Ark. 864, 545 S.W.2d 617 (1977)

95 ALR5th 229—§ 2, 22
State v. Black, 291 N.W.2d 208 (Minn. 1980)

93 ALR5th 327—§ 7, 29
State v. Black, 328 N.C. 191, 400 S.E.2d 398 (1991)

14 ALR5th 89—§ 36
State v. Black, 924 S.W.2d 912 (Tenn. Crim. App. 1995)

66 ALR5th 397—§ 13, 17, 22
State v. Black, 1995 WL 567069 (Tenn. Crim. App. 1995)

83 ALR5th 541—§ 7
State v. Black, 2000 ME 211, 763 A.2d 109 (Me. 2000)

6 ALR5th 733—§ 12
State v. Blackburn, 63 Ohio Misc. 2d 211, 620 N.E.2d 319 (Mun. Ct. 1993)

74 ALR5th 319—§ 6, 8, 10, 11
State v. Blackburn, 214 Wis. 2d 372, 571 N.W.2d 695 (Ct. App. 1997)

71 ALR6th 335—§ 5
State v. Blackburn, 251 Kan. 787, 840 P.2d 497 (1992)

39 ALR5th 283—§ 4, 58
State v. Blackburn, 2005-Ohio-4710, 2005 WL 2174614 (Ohio Ct. App. 5th Dist. Fairfield County 2005)

72 ALR6th 227—§ 49
State v. Black Elk, 1993 WL 459824 (Minn. Ct. App. 1993)

73 ALR5th 383—§ 6
State v. Blackman, 93 N.C. App. 207, 377 S.E.2d 290 (1989)

29 ALR6th 1—§ 10
State v. Blackmon, 78 S.W.3d 322 (Tenn. Crim. App. 2001)

43 ALR6th 475—§ 16
State v. Blackmon, 184 Ariz. 196, 908 P.2d 10 (Ct. App. Div. 1 1995)

91 ALR5th 343—§ 30
State v. Blackmon, 1992 WL 2945 (Ohio Ct. App. 9th Dist. Summit County 1992)

99 ALR6th 295—§ 13
State v. Blacknall, 2009 WL 3430114 (N.J. Super. Ct. App. Div. 2009)

56 ALR6th 185—§ 44
State v. Blackshaw, 2005-Ohio-5203, 2005 WL 2401629 (Ohio Ct. App. 8th Dist. Cuyahoga County 2005)

56 ALR6th 185—§ 39
State v. Blackshire, 10 Haw. App. 123, 861 P.2d 736 (1993)

81 ALR6th 505—§ 34
State v. Blackson, 865 So. 2d 272 (La. Ct. App. 2d Cir. 2004)

28 ALR6th 505—§ 9
State v. Blackstock, 314 N.C. 232, 333 S.E.2d 245 (1985)

98 ALR6th 455—§ 27
103 ALR6th 507—§ 20, 28
State v. Blackwell, 120 Wash. 2d 822, 845 P.2d 1017 (1993)

71 ALR5th 1—§ 56

State v. Blackwell, 135 N.C. App. 729, 522 S.E.2d 313 (1999)
9 ALR6th 541—§ 3, 32

State v. Blackwell, 459 S.W.2d 268 (Mo. 1970)
68 ALR5th 343—§ 3, 12

State v. Blackwood, 2000 WL 1672343 (Tenn. Crim. App. 2000)
3 ALR6th 543—§ 8

State v. Blackwood, No. 11548 (July 5, 1984, Ct. App. Ohio, 8th App. Dist. Summit Co.)
39 ALR5th 283—§ 14, 31

State v. Blades, 225 Conn. 609, 626 A.2d 273 (1993)
58 ALR6th 499—§ 51

State v. Blades, 928 S.W.2d 371 (Mo. Ct. App. S.D. 1996)
43 ALR6th 475—§ 16

State v. Bladow, 1989 WL 100641 (Minn. Ct. App. 1989)
73 ALR5th 383—§ 28

State v. Blagajevic, 21 Ohio App. 3d 297, 488 N.E.2d 495 (8th Dist. Cuyahoga County 1985)
71 ALR6th 1—§ 6

State v. Blaine, 148 Vt. 272, 531 A.2d 933 (1987)
93 ALR6th 207—§ 6
95 ALR6th 1—§ 26

State v. Blair, 17 Neb. App. 611, 767 N.W.2d 143 (2009)
69 ALR6th 1—§ 21

State v. Blair, 34 Ohio App. 3d 6, 516 N.E.2d 240 (8th Dist. Cuyahoga County 1986)
3 ALR6th 269—§ 5, 8, 14, 29

State v. Blair, 70 Ohio App. 3d 774, 592 N.E.2d 854 (2d Dist. Clark County 1990)
77 ALR5th 201—§ 21
38 ALR6th 439—§ 5, 8

State v. Blair, 145 S.W.3d 633 (Tenn. Crim. App. 2004)
8 ALR6th 265—§ 17

State v. Blair, 298 S.W.3d 38 (Mo. Ct. App. W.D. 2009)
69 ALR6th 579—§ 4

State v. Blair, 435 So. 2d 124 (Ala. Civ. App. 1983)
104 ALR5th 229—§ 7
115 ALR5th 403—§ 5
101 ALR6th 1—§ 17, 29, 35

State v. Blair, 638 S.W.2d 739 (Mo. 1982)
55 ALR5th 125—§ 3, 7

State v. Blair, 1997 WL 800854 (Ohio Ct. App. 4th Dist. Meigs County 1997)
81 ALR6th 505—§ 10

State v. Blaisdell, 20 N.D. 622, 127 N.W. 720 (1910)
120 ALR5th 125—§ 2
121 ALR5th 1—§ 2, 49, 58

State v. Blaisdell, 34 N.D. 321, 159 N.W. 401 (1910)
14 ALR6th 543—§ 5

State v. Blaise, 2009 WL 4981851 (Ariz. Ct. App. Div. 1 2009)
103 ALR6th 35—§ 6

State v. Blake, 83 N.C. App. 77, 349 S.E.2d 78 (1986)
3 ALR5th 784—§ 20

State v. Blake, 106 Conn. App. 345, 942 A.2d 496 (2008)
38 ALR6th 439—§ 4

State v. Blake, 113 N.H. 115, 305 A.2d 300 (1973)
33 ALR6th 1—§ 6, 24

State v. Blake, 197 W. Va. 700, 478 S.E.2d 550 (1996)
72 ALR5th 403—§ 2, 3

State v. Blake, 209 Kan. 196, 495 P.2d 905 (1972)
45 ALR5th 531—§ 7
100 ALR6th 535—§ 3

State v. Blakely, 230 So. 2d 698 (Fla. Dist. Ct. App. 2d Dist. 1970)
65 ALR5th 407—§ 11, 17

State v. Blakeney, 137 Vt. 495, 408 A.2d 636 (1979)
5 ALR5th 243—§ 47

State v. Blakley, 90 N.M. 744, 568 P.2d 270 (Ct. App. 1977)
32 ALR6th 385—§ 5

State v. Blakney, 197 Mont. 131, 641 P.2d 1045 (1982)
124 ALR5th 1—§ 5

State v. Blalock, 150 Wis. 2d 688, 442 N.W.2d 514 (Ct. App. 1989)
1 ALR6th 549—§ 16

State v. Blamer, 2001 WL 109130 (Ohio Ct. App. 5th Dist. Knox County 2001)
1 ALR6th 657—§ 4, 14

State v. Blancett, 24 N.M. 433, 174 P. 207 (1918)
73 ALR5th 615—§ 3, 7

State v. Blancett, 1918-NMSC-091, 24 N.M. 433, 174 P. 207 (1918)
103 ALR6th 35—§ 10

State v. Blanchard, 100 S.W.3d 226 (Tenn. Crim. App. 2002)
70 ALR6th 1—§ 22

State v. Blanchard, 315 N.W.2d 427 (Minn. 1982)
57 ALR5th 141—§ 3

State v. Blanchard, 786 So. 2d 701 (La. 2001)
41 ALR6th 141—§ 7

State v. Blanche, 696 N.W.2d 351 (Minn. 2005)
16 ALR6th 329—§ 4
24 ALR6th 591—§ 5, 12

State v. Blanchette, 35 Kan. App. 2d 686, 134 P.3d 19 (2006)
30 ALR6th 1—§ 4

State v. Blanco, 2000 WI App 119, 237 Wis. 2d 395, 614 N.W.2d 512 (Ct. App. 2000)
79 ALR6th 1—§ 57

State v. Bland, 33 Kan. App. 2d 412, 103 P.3d 492 (2004)
71 ALR6th 249—§ 3

State v. Bland, 103 P.3d 492 (Kan. Ct. App. 2004)
125 ALR5th 537—§ 43

State v. Blane, 985 So. 2d 384 (Ala. 2007)
70 ALR6th 1—§ 15

State v. Blanford, 306 N.W.2d 93 (Iowa 1981)
96 ALR5th 327—§ 3

State v. Blank, 955 So. 2d 90 (La. 2007)
35 ALR6th 127—§ 5

State v. Blank, 2005-Ohio-2642, 2005 WL 1252550 (Ohio Ct. App. 10th Dist. Franklin County 2005)
70 ALR6th 1—§ 5

State v. Blankenship, 38 Ohio St. 3d 116, 526 N.E.2d 816 (1988)
39 ALR5th 283—§ 14, 71

State v. Blankenship, 77 Ohio App. 3d 324, 602 N.E.2d 311 (Franklin Co. 1991)
32 ALR5th 149—§ 22, 23, 37

State v. Blankenship, 115 Ohio App. 3d 512, 685 N.E.2d 831 (12th Dist. Butler County 1996)
70 ALR5th 1—§ 6

State v. Blankenship, 757 S.W.2d 354 (Tenn. Crim. App. 1988)
78 ALR6th 599—§ 4, 8

State v. Blankenship, Slip Op. No. 9-192 (Ohio App. Lake Co. 1982)
38 ALR5th 433—§ 48

State v. Blankinship, 127 Ariz. 507, 622 P.2d 66 (Ct. App. Div. 2 1980)
65 ALR6th 537—§ 4

State v. Blanton, 166 N.J. Super. 62, 398 A.2d 1328 (App. Div. 1979)
66 ALR5th 397—§ 4, 22

State v. Blanton, 173 Ariz. 517, 844 P.2d 1167 (Ct. App. Div. 1 1992)
15 ALR5th 391—§ 30
92 ALR5th 35—§ 13, 25

State v. Blanton, 2002-Ohio-1794, 2002 WL 538869 (Ohio Ct. App. 2d Dist. Montgomery County 2002)
73 ALR6th 1—§ 7

State v. Blase, 208 Kan. 969, 494 P.2d 1224 (1972)
32 ALR6th 531—§ 43

State v. Blassingame, 149 Wis. 2d 400, 439 N.W.2d 645 (Ct. App. 1989)
101 ALR6th 331—§ 8, 22

State v. Blaurock, 143 N.J. Super. 476, 363 A.2d 909 (App. Div. 1976)
114 ALR5th 235—§ 4

State v. Blaylock, 2011-Ohio-4865, 2011 WL 4424935 (Ohio Ct. App. 2d Dist. Montgomery County 2011)
74 ALR6th 69—§ 6

State v. Blazak, 114 Ariz. 199, 560 P.2d 54 (1977)
12 ALR6th 267—§ 8

State v. Blazina, 174 Wash. App. 906, 301 P.3d 492 (Div. 2 2013)
95 ALR6th 219—§ 5

State v. Bleau, 139 Vt. 305, 428 A.2d 1097 (1981)
29 ALR5th 59—§ 3, 14

State v. Bledsoe, 538 So. 2d 94 (Fla. Dist. Ct. App. 3d Dist. 1989)
113 ALR5th 597—§ 8

State v. Bledsoe, 2004-Ohio-4764, 2004 WL 2002855 (Ohio Ct. App. 5th Dist. Stark County 2004)
26 ALR6th 511—§ 18

State v. Bleed, 2005 WL 949229 (Minn. Ct. App. 2005)
26 ALR6th 511—§ 16, 32

State v. Bletsch, 281 Conn. 5, 912 A.2d 992 (2007)
39 ALR6th 577—§ 4

State v. Blevins, 13 Conn. App. 413, 536 A.2d 1002 (1988)
55 ALR5th 423—§ 4

State v. Blevins, 36 Ohio App. 3d 147, 521 N.E.2d 1105 (10th Dist. Franklin County 1987)
43 ALR6th 475—§ 16

State v. Blevins, 128 Ariz. 64, 623 P.2d 853 (App. 1981)
26 ALR5th 1—§ 3

State v. Blevins, 128 Ariz. 64, 623 P.2d 853 (Ct. App. Div. 1 1981)
84 ALR6th 427—§ 19

State v. Blevins, 231 W. Va. 135, 744 S.E.2d 245 (2013)
102 ALR6th 365—§ 30

State v. Blews, 148 Ga. App. 73, 251 S.E.2d 10 (1978)
103 ALR5th 463—§ 3

State v. Bleyl, 435 A.2d 1349 (Me. 1981)
29 ALR6th 1—§ 10

State v. Blickem, 2001 WL 138768 (Minn. Ct. App. 2001)
84 ALR6th 293—§ 21

State v. Blier, 113 Ariz. 501, 557 P.2d 1058 (1976)
22 ALR5th 660—§ 11

State v. Blinkinsop, 2010 WL 3119396 (Minn. Ct. App. 2010)
69 ALR6th 579—§ 8, 23

State v. Bliss, 153 Wash. App. 197, 222 P.3d 107 (Div. 2 2009)
55 ALR6th 1—§ 6, 40

State v. Block, 170 Wis. 2d 676, 489 N.W.2d 715 (1992)
50 ALR5th 467—§ 6

State v. Blocker, 46 Conn. App. 734, 700 A.2d 1186 (1997)
5 ALR5th 243—§ 50

State v. Blocker, 205 S.C. 303, 31 S.E.2d 908 (1944)
33 ALR5th 571—§ 4

State v. Blohm, 281 N.W.2d 651 (Minn. 1979)
39 ALR6th 257—§ 47
40 ALR6th 1—§ 33

State v. Bloom, 90 N.M. 192, 561 P.2d 465 (1977)
116 ALR5th 479—§ 6

State v. Bloom, 516 N.W.2d 159 (Minn. 1994)
38 ALR6th 439—§ 12

State v. Bloom, 1996 WL 33092 (Minn. Ct. App. 1996)
77 ALR5th 201—§ 6

State v. Bloom, 2009-Ohio-1371, 2009 WL 794304 (Ohio Ct. App. 1st Dist. Hamilton County 2009)
65 ALR6th 1—§ 26

State v. Bloomer, 156 Ariz. 276, 751 P.2d 592 (App. 1987)
45 ALR5th 767—§ 14

State v. Bloomquist, 2000 WL 1493799 (Minn. Ct. App. 2000)
85 ALR5th 1—§ 16

State v. Bloss, 62 Haw. 147, 613 P.2d 354 (1980)
72 ALR5th 1—§ 18

State v. Blouvet, 965 S.W.2d 489 (Tenn. Crim. App. 1997)

39 ALR5th 283—§ 17, 18

State v. Blow, 123 N.J. 472, 588 A.2d 821 (1991)

27 ALR5th 593—§ 29

State v. Blue Thunder, 466 N.W.2d 613 (S.D. 1991)

124 ALR5th 1—§ 3

State v. Blydenburgh, 595 S.W.2d 759 (Mo. Ct. App. W.D. 1980)

70 ALR5th 587—§ 19

State v. Blye, 130 S.W.3d 776 (Tenn. 2004)

93 ALR6th 275—§ 8

State v. Blythman, 201 Neb. 285, 267 N.W.2d 525 (1978)

78 ALR6th 417—§ 24, 29

State v. Boales, 2005 WL 517538 (Tenn. Crim. App. 2005)

26 ALR6th 511—§ 25, 27

State v. Board of County Comrs., 642 P.2d 456 (Wyo. 1982)

11 ALR5th 630—§ 6

State v. Board of Educ. of City of Duluth, 158 Minn. 459, 197 N.W. 964 (1924)

56 ALR6th 523—§ 4

State v. Board of Elections of Trumbull County, 1983 WL 6088 (Ohio Ct. App. 11th Dist. Trumbull County 1983)

14 ALR6th 543—§ 48

State v. Board of Police Com'rs of Trenton, 66 N.J.L. 173, 48 A. 1006 (N.J. Sup. Ct. 1901)

19 ALR6th 217—§ 26

State v. Bobadilla, 709 N.W.2d 243 (Minn. 2006)

30 ALR6th 1—§ 4, 7

State v. Bobbitt, 415 So. 2d 724 (Fla. 1982)

67 ALR5th 637—§ 3, 7

State v. Bob Chambers Ford, Inc., 522 A.2d 362, 3 U.C.C.R.S.2d 625 (Me. 1987)

49 ALR5th 1—§ 38

State v. Bobkiewicz, 20 Or. App. 479, 532 P.2d 256 (1975)

7 ALR5th 758—§ 17

State v. Bobo, 724 S.W.2d 760 (Tenn. Crim. App. 1981)

51 ALR6th 1—§ 18

State v. Boccelli, 105 Ariz. 495, 467 P.2d 740 (1970)

9 ALR5th 464—§ 3, 4, 9

State v. Bocharski, 22 P.3d 43 (Ariz. 2001)

40 ALR5th 113—§ 3

State v. Bock, 229 Minn. 449, 39 N.W.2d 887 (1949)

22 ALR5th 1—§ 4, 9, 34, 54, 56

State v. Bock, 490 N.W.2d 116 (Minn. Ct. App. 1992)

73 ALR5th 383—§ 21, 41

State v. Bockman, 11 Neb. App. 273, 648 N.W.2d 786 (2002)

93 ALR6th 275—§ 19

101 ALR6th 299—§ 4

103 ALR6th 347—§ 26

State v. Bodden, 166 Wis. 219, 164 N.W. 1009 (1917)

109 ALR5th 421—§ 3

State v. Bodden, 661 S.E.2d 23 (N.C. Ct. App. 2008)

30 ALR6th 1—§ 6

State v. Boddie, 170 Ohio App. 3d 590, 2007-Ohio-626, 868 N.E.2d 699 (8th Dist. Cuyahoga County 2007)

69 ALR6th 1—§ 10

State v. Boddie, 683 So. 2d 1246 (La. Ct. App. 3d Cir. 1996)

20 ALR5th 398—§ 65

State v. Bodley, 394 So. 2d 584 (La. 1981)

68 ALR5th 343—§ 3

State v. Bodoh, 220 Wis. 2d 102, 582 N.W.2d 440 (Ct. App. 1998)

124 ALR5th 657—§ 8

State v. Bodoh, 226 Wis. 2d 718, 595 N.W.2d 330 (1999)

124 ALR5th 657—§ 1, 2, 4, 8

State v. Bodyke, 126 Ohio St. 3d 266, 2010-Ohio-2424, 933 N.E.2d 753 (2010)

64 ALR6th 1—§ 7, 9 to 13, 19
State v. Bodyke, 2008-Ohio-6387, 2008
WL 5148003 (Ohio Ct. App. 6th
Dist. Huron County 2008)
63 ALR6th 351—§ 3
State v. Boeglin, 100 N.M. 127, 666
P.2d 1274 (Ct. App. 1983)
124 ALR5th 1—§ 5
State v. Boeglin, 105 N.M. 247, 731
P.2d 943 (1987)
24 ALR6th 1—§ 17
State v. Boehme, 71 Wash. 2d 621, 430
P.2d 527 (1967)
77 ALR5th 201—§ 16
78 ALR5th 1—§ 10
State v. Boethin, 109 P.3d 461 (Wash.
Ct. App. Div. 2 2005)
122 ALR5th 439—§ 7
State v. Boffer, 158 Wis. 2d 655, 462
N.W.2d 906 (Ct. App. 1990)
92 ALR5th 35—§ 25
State v. Bogan, 183 Ariz. 506, 905 P.2d
515 (Ct. App. Div. 1 1995)
90 ALR5th 453—§ 28
State v. Bogan, 774 N.W.2d 676 (Iowa
2009)
59 ALR6th 393—§ 13
State v. Bogan, Slip Op. No. 45084
(Ohio App. Cuyahoga Co. 1983)
38 ALR5th 433—§ 26, 37
State v. Bogart, 57 Wash. App. 353, 788
P.2d 14 (Div. 3 1990)
9 ALR6th 541—§ 11
State v. Bogenreif, 465 N.W.2d 777, 5
A.L.R.5th 1078 (S.D. 1991)
5 ALR5th 243—§ 28, 61
54 ALR6th 429—§ 27
State v. Boggess, 110 Wis. 2d 309, 328
N.W.2d 878 (Ct. App. 1982)
28 ALR6th 505—§ 9
State v. Boggess, 115 Wis. 2d 443, 340
N.W.2d 516 (1983)
58 ALR6th 499—§ 33
State v. Boggs, 16 Wash. App. 682, 559
P.2d 11 (Div. 2 1977)
124 ALR5th 1—§ 4

State v. Bogris, 26 Idaho 587, 144 P. 789
(1914)
32 ALR5th 149—§ 3, 29
State v. Bohan, 72 Wash. App. 335, 864
P.2d 26 (Div. 1 1993)
103 ALR5th 463—§ 8
State v. Bohanan, 220 Kan. 121, 551
P.2d 828 (1976)
34 ALR6th 1—§ 12
State v. Bohannon, 62 Wash. App. 462,
814 P.2d 694 (1991)
42 ALR5th 291—§ 10
State v. Bohannon, 62 Wash. App. 462,
814 P.2d 694 (Div. 2 1991)
111 ALR5th 239—§ 6
State v. Bohe, 447 N.W.2d 277 (N.D.
1989)
83 ALR5th 277—§ 9, 11
84 ALR5th 487—§ 21
State v. Bohl, 317 N.W.2d 790 (N.D.
1982)
46 ALR6th 241—§ 4, 41
State v. Bohlman, 2006 WL 915765
(Minn. Ct. App. 2006)
34 ALR6th 253—§ 3, 4
State v. Bohuk, 269 N.J. Super. 581, 636
A.2d 105 (App. Div. 1994)
94 ALR5th 393—§ 4
State v. Boissineau, 1997 WL 610611
(Wash. Ct. App. Div. 2 1997)
73 ALR5th 383—§ 5
State v. Boisvert, 40 Conn. App. 420,
671 A.2d 834 (1996)
74 ALR5th 319—§ 4 to 11
State v. Bojorquez, 111 Ariz. 549, 535
P.2d 6, 78 A.L.R.3d 1135 (1975)
75 ALR5th 295—§ 21
State v. Bojorquez-Ochoa, 112 Wash.
App. 1007, 2002 WL 1290180 (Div.
1 2002)
43 ALR6th 475—§ 21
State v. Boka, 2006 WL 13165 (N.J.
Super. Ct. App. Div. 2006)
26 ALR6th 511—§ 17
State v. Bolan, 27 Ohio St. 2d 15, 56
Ohio Op. 2d 8, 271 N.E.2d 839
(1971)

51 ALR6th 219—§ 4
State v. Boland, 115 Wash. 2d 571, 800 P.2d 1112 (1990)

62 ALR5th 1—§ 2, 3, 9, 12, 15
State v. Bolander, 1998 WL 505691 (Tex. App. Houston 1st Dist. 1998)

48 ALR6th 243—§ 21
State v. Bolanos, 58 Conn. App. 365, 753 A.2d 943 (2000)

84 ALR6th 293—§ 4, 14, 37
State v. Bolanos, 743 S.W.2d 442 (Mo. Ct. App. W.D. 1987)

22 ALR5th 1—§ 4, 6, 56
87 ALR5th 181—§ 4
State v. Bolden, 257 La. 60, 241 So. 2d 490 (1970)

86 ALR5th 59—§ 3
State v. Bolden, 680 So. 2d 6 (La. Ct. App. 3d Cir. 1996)

90 ALR5th 453—§ 12
State v. Bolden, 1999 WL 330272 (Neb. Ct. App. 1999)

71 ALR6th 625—§ 31
State v. Bolder, 635 S.W.2d 673 (Mo. 1982)

99 ALR6th 295—§ 9, 13
State v. Boldra, 292 Minn. 491, 195 N.W.2d 578 (1972)

84 ALR6th 427—§ 4
State v. Boldridge, 274 Kan. 795, 57 P.3d 8 (2002)

29 ALR6th 1—§ 10
State v. Boldt, 40 Wash. App. 798, 700 P.2d 1186 (Div. 2 1985)

71 ALR5th 1—§ 63
State v. Bolduc, 822 A.2d 184 (R.I. 2003)

99 ALR6th 113—§ 17
State v. Bolen, 142 Wash. 653, 254 P. 445 (1927)

66 ALR5th 135—§ 33
State v. Boleyn, 328 So. 2d 95 (La. 1976)

54 ALR5th 141—§ 3 to 5, 9
State v. Bolin, 128 Ohio App. 3d 58, 713 N.E.2d 1092 (8th Dist. Cuyahoga County 1998)

70 ALR5th 1—§ 5
State v. Bolin, 922 S.W.2d 870 (Tenn. 1996)

85 ALR5th 595—§ 8
State v. Boling, 131 Wash. App. 329, 127 P.3d 740 (Div. 3 2006)

48 ALR6th 135—§ 14
State v. Boling, 806 S.W.2d 202 (Tenn. Crim. App. 1990)

93 ALR5th 327—§ 3, 4, 7, 9, 26
State v. Boling, 1990 WL 160296 (Tenn. Crim. App. 1990)

11 ALR6th 237—§ 15
State v. Bolle, 201 S.W.2d 158 (Mo. 1947)

102 ALR6th 279—§ 33
State v. Bollig, 232 Wis. 2d 561, 2000 WI 6, 605 N.W.2d 199 (2000)

9 ALR6th 633—§ 3 to 5, 13, 27, 29, 31
9 ALR6th 693—§ 3, 5
10 ALR6th 265—§ 3, 8, 9
12 ALR6th 389—§ 3
13 ALR6th 603—§ 3
14 ALR6th 517—§ 3
15 ALR6th 173—§ 3
State v. Bollig, 2000 WI 6, 232 Wis. 2d 561, 605 N.W.2d 199 (2000)

51 ALR6th 139—§ 11
State v. Bolsinger, 699 P.2d 1214 (Utah 1985)

124 ALR5th 1—§ 3
State v. Bolt, 142 Ariz. 260, 689 P.2d 519 (1984)

19 ALR5th 470—§ 3, 14
State v. Bolton, 111 N.M. 28, 801 P.2d 98 (Ct. App. 1990)

116 ALR5th 479—§ 6
State v. Bolton, 182 Ariz. 290, 896 P.2d 830 (1995)

79 ALR5th 33—§ 39, 40
State v. Bolton, 548 So. 2d 345 (La. Ct. App. 4th Cir. 1989)

64 ALR5th 741—§ 3
State v. Bomar, 199 Ariz. 472, 19 P.3d 613 (Ct. App. Div. 1 2001)

46 ALR6th 63—§ 17
State v. Bond, 52 Wash. App. 326, 759 P.2d 1220 (Div. 1 1988)

83 ALR5th 277—§ 9

State v. Bond, 237 Wis. 2d 633, 2000 WI App 118, 614 N.W.2d 552 (Ct. App. 2000)

29 ALR6th 1—§ 5

State v. Bonefield, 37 Wash. App. 878, 683 P.2d 1129 (Div. 3 1984)

84 ALR5th 487—§ 19

State v. Boneventure, 374 So. 2d 1238 (La. 1979)

112 ALR5th 429—§ 13

State v. Bonfanti, 157 Vt. 625, 603 A.2d 365 (1991)

92 ALR5th 35—§ 25

State v. Bongalis, 180 W. Va. 584, 378 S.E.2d 449 (1989)

75 ALR5th 295—§ 25

State v. Bonham, 28 P.3d 303, 97 A.L.R.5th 673 (Alaska Ct. App. 2001)

97 ALR5th 201—§ 3, 6

State v. Boniface, 26 Ariz. App. 118, 546 P.2d 843 (Div. 1 1976)

103 ALR5th 463—§ 3

State v. Bonilla, 131 Conn. App. 388, 28 A.3d 1005, 2011 WL 3903354 (2011)

69 ALR6th 207—§ 4, 9

State v. Bonilla, 1999 -NMCA- 096, 985 P.2d 168 (N.M. Ct. App. 1999)

18 ALR5th 1—§ 6, 15

State v. Bonnell, 75 Haw. 124, 856 P.2d 1265, 8 I.E.R. Cas. (BNA) 1226 (1993)

91 ALR5th 585—§ 9
18 ALR6th 1—§ 3, 5, 18

State v. Bonner, 241 Or. 404, 406 P.2d 160 (1965)

19 ALR5th 823—§ 15

State v. Bonner, 252 La. 200, 210 So. 2d 319 (1968)

16 ALR6th 329—§ 4
24 ALR6th 591—§ 4, 14

State v. Bonney, 427 A.2d 467 (Me. 1981)

4 ALR5th 1—§ 4
45 ALR5th 767—§ 9

State v. Bonnie, 135 Or. App. 314, 898 P.2d 1356 (1995)

15 ALR5th 391—§ 13

State v. Bonny, 25 Utah 2d 117, 477 P.2d 147 (1970)

37 ALR6th 357—§ 53

State v. Bono, 103 Wis. 2d 654, 309 N.W.2d 400 (Ct. App. 1981)

105 ALR5th 529—§ 20

State v. Boobar, 637 A.2d 1162 (Me. 1994)

101 ALR5th 619—§ 9

State v. Booher, 54 Ohio App. 3d 1, 560 N.E.2d 786 (Defiance Co. 1988)

12 ALR5th 909—§ 5
42 ALR5th 581—§ 7

State v. Booher, 78 N.M. 76, 428 P.2d 478 (App. 1967)

50 ALR5th 703—§ 15

State v. Booker, 63 Ohio App. 3d 459, 579 N.E.2d 264 (Montgomery Co. 1989)

19 ALR5th 470—§ 3

State v. Booker, 250 N.C. 272, 108 S.E.2d 426 (1959)

57 ALR6th 445—§ 27

State v. Booker, 286 Wis. 2d 747, 2005 WI App 182, 704 N.W.2d 336 (Ct. App. 2005)

27 ALR6th 183—§ 31

State v. Boone, 15 Conn. App. 34, 544 A.2d 217 (1988)

45 ALR5th 531—§ 1

State v. Boone, 40 Md. App. 41, 388 A.2d 150 (1978)

53 ALR6th 1—§ 7

State v. Boone, 108 Ohio App. 3d 233, 670 N.E.2d 527 (1st Dist. Hamilton County 1995)

23 ALR6th 307—§ 12

State v. Boone, 293 N.C. 702, 239 S.E.2d 459 (1977)

11 ALR6th 237—§ 11

State v. Boone, 307 N.C. 198, 297 S.E.2d 585 (1982)

44 ALR5th 651—§ 5, 6

State v. Boone, 444 A.2d 438 (Me. 1982)

9 ALR6th 633—§ 4, 5, 23
10 ALR6th 265—§ 16
State v. Boone, 820 P.2d 930 (Utah Ct. App. 1991)
98 ALR6th 455—§ 25
State v. Boone, 908 S.W.2d 165 (Mo. Ct. App. E.D. 1995)
80 ALR5th 55—§ 5
State v. Bootes, 2011-Ohio-1605, 2011 WL 1225589 (Ohio Ct. App. 10th Dist. Franklin County 2011)
69 ALR6th 1—§ 10
State v. Booth, 124 Or. App. 282, 862 P.2d 518 (1993)
38 ALR5th 433—§ 11
State v. Booth, 202 Neb. 692, 276 N.W.2d 673 (1979)
12 ALR6th 553—§ 13, 22, 30
35 ALR6th 497—§ 13
State v. Booth, 250 Conn. 611, 737 A.2d 404 (1999)
16 ALR6th 329—§ 4
24 ALR6th 591—§ 4, 12
State v. Booth, 670 N.W.2d 209 (Iowa 2003)
97 ALR6th 653—§ 2, 23
State v. Boothe, 689 S.E.2d 600 (N.C. Ct. App. 2010)
57 ALR6th 1—§ 4
State v. Booton, 85 Idaho 51, 375 P.2d 536 (1962)
108 ALR5th 593—§ 16
State v. Booton, 114 N.H. 750, 329 A.2d 376 (1974)
55 ALR6th 157—§ 16, 18
State v. Boppre, 234 Neb. 922, 453 N.W.2d 406 (1990)
57 ALR5th 141—§ 9
State v. Boratto, 80 N.J. 506, 404 A.2d 604 (1979)
41 ALR5th 1—§ 3
State v. Borbon, 146 Ariz. 392, 706 P.2d 718 (1985)
79 ALR5th 419—§ 10
State v. Borchard, 24 Ohio App. 2d 95, 53 Ohio Op. 2d 254, 264 N.E.2d 646 (4th Dist. Athens County 1970)

71 ALR6th 283—§ 12
State v. Bordelon, 141 La. 611, 75 So. 429 (1917)
85 ALR5th 471—§ 2, 4
State v. Bordelon, 600 So. 2d 678 (La. 1992)
72 ALR5th 529—§ 14
State v. Borden, 455 N.W.2d 482 (Minn. App. 1990)
42 ALR5th 291—§ 19, 39
State v. Boren, 654 S.W.2d 547 (Tex. App. Waco 1983)
6 ALR5th 711—§ 5
State v. Boretsky, 186 N.J. 271, 894 A.2d 659 (2006)
28 ALR6th 505—§ 31
State v. Borges, 10 Ohio App. 3d 158, 10 Ohio B.R. 211, 460 N.E.2d 1147 (Lake Co. 1983)
50 ALR5th 703—§ 3, 5, 9
State v. Bormann, 279 Neb. 320, 777 N.W.2d 829 (2010)
81 ALR6th 505—§ 55
State v. Born, 280 Minn. 306, 159 N.W.2d 283, 33 A.L.R.3d 919 (1968)
19 ALR5th 823—§ 9, 11
67 ALR6th 103—§ 5, 10
State v. Borne, 691 So. 2d 1281 (La. Ct. App. 4th Cir. 1997)
96 ALR5th 485—§ 14
State v. Borough, 287 Minn. 482, 178 N.W.2d 897 (1970)
37 ALR6th 357—§ 69
State v. Borras, 399 So. 2d 212 (La. 1981)
7 ALR6th 487—§ 1
State v. Borrelli, 227 Conn. 153, 629 A.2d 1105 (1993)
57 ALR5th 315—§ 3, 5 to 8, 11
State v. Borsheim, 140 Wash. App. 357, 165 P.3d 417 (Div. 1 2007)
42 ALR6th 237—§ 11
State v. Boscarino, 204 Conn. 714, 529 A.2d 1260 (1987)
55 ALR5th 423—§ 10
State v. Boss, 195 Neb. 467, 238 N.W.2d 639 (1976)

66 ALR5th 397—§ 3

State v. Boss, 2005 UT App 520, 127 P.3d 1236 (Utah Ct. App. 2005)

84 ALR6th 427—§ 6

State v. Bost, 317 Or. 538, 857 P.2d 132 (1993)

85 ALR5th 1—§ 27

State v. Bostick, 253 S.C. 205, 169 S.E.2d 608 (1969)

81 ALR5th 563—§ 3

State v. Bostick, 715 So. 2d 298 (Fla. Dist. Ct. App. 4th Dist. 1998)

113 ALR5th 597—§ 8

State v. Boston, 46 Ohio St. 3d 108, 545 N.E.2d 1220 (1989)

38 ALR5th 433—§ 3, 8, 11, 19, 26
72 ALR5th 529—§ 15

State v. Boston, 170 Ariz. 315, 823 P.2d 1323, 94 Ariz. Adv. Rep. 56 (App. 1991)

20 ALR5th 398—§ 2, 9, 12, 38

State v. Boston, 226 Iowa 429, 278 N.W. 291 (1938)

8 ALR5th 825—§ 6

State v. Boston, 910 S.W.2d 306 (Mo. Ct. App. W.D. 1995)

110 ALR5th 329—§ 16

State v. Boston & M. R. R., 99 N.H. 66, 105 A.2d 751 (1954)

17 ALR5th 547—§ 36, 85

State v. Boswell, 30 Kan. App. 2d 9, 37 P.3d 40 (2001)

26 ALR6th 511—§ 14, 32

State v. Boswell, 52 Or. App. 535, 628 P.2d 763 (1981)

92 ALR5th 35—§ 7

State v. Boswell, 131 Ga. App. 657, 206 S.E.2d 682 (1974)

6 ALR6th 533—§ 17

State v. Botelho, 638 N.W.2d 770 (Minn. Ct. App. 2002)

50 ALR6th 455—§ 3, 7, 8, 12, 19, 41

State v. Botos, 2005-Ohio-3504, 2005 WL 1606416 (Ohio Ct. App. 12th Dist. Butler County 2005)

26 ALR6th 511—§ 19

State v. Botsch, 44 Ohio App. 3d 59, 541 N.E.2d 489 (6th Dist. Ottawa County 1989)

47 ALR6th 107—§ 22

State v. Botta, 27 Ohio St. 2d 196, 56 Ohio Ops. 2d 119, 271 N.E.2d 776 (1971)

29 ALR5th 59—§ 7, 48, 62

State v. Bouchard, 31 Wash. App. 381, 639 P.2d 761 (1982)

38 ALR5th 433—§ 3

State v. Boucher, 207 Conn. 612, 541 A.2d 865 (1988)

52 ALR5th 655—§ 9

State v. Boucher, 376 A.2d 478 (Me. 1977)

55 ALR6th 157—§ 4, 8

State v. Bouchier, 159 Ariz. 346, 767 P.2d 233, 25 Ariz. Adv. Rep. 28 (App. 1989)

36 ALR5th 161—§ 19

State v. Boudreau, 1990 WL 61279 (Minn. Ct. App. 1990)

84 ALR6th 293—§ 21

State v. Boudreaux, 304 So. 2d 343 (La. 1974)

41 ALR5th 171—§ 85

State v. Boudreaux, 454 So. 2d 1293 (La. Ct. App. 3d Cir. 1984)

9 ALR6th 1—§ 20

State v. Boudreaux, 741 So. 2d 860 (La. Ct. App. 3d Cir. 1999)

15 ALR5th 391—§ 21

State v. Bound, 2004-Ohio-7097, 2004 WL 2988294 (Ohio Ct. App. 5th Dist. Guernsey County 2004)

97 ALR6th 263—§ 24

State v. Bourassa, 137 Vt. 62, 399 A.2d 507 (1979)

81 ALR5th 563—§ 3, 5

State v. Bourgeois, 388 So. 2d 359 (La. 1980)

90 ALR5th 225—§ 4

State v. Bourland, 99 Wash. App. 1048, 2000 WL 241095 (Div. 2 2000)

89 ALR6th 565—§ 20

State v. Bourne, 233 Kan. 166, 660 P.2d 565 (1983)

39 ALR5th 283—§ 4, 41

State v. Bouse, 199 Or. 676, 264 P.2d 800 (1953)

24 ALR5th 465—§ 2, 115

State v. Boushee, 284 N.W.2d 423 (N.D. 1979)

112 ALR5th 429—§ 6

State v. Bousum, 12 Neb. App. 401, 674 N.W.2d 802 (2004)

9 ALR6th 633—§ 5

9 ALR6th 693—§ 13

State v. Bousum, 2003 SD 58, 663 N.W.2d 257 (S.D. 2003)

56 ALR6th 185—§ 39

State v. Boutch, 60 Wis. 2d 397, 210 N.W.2d 751 (1973)

34 ALR5th 125—§ 3, 8

State v. Boutilier, 426 A.2d 876 (Me. 1981)

84 ALR6th 427—§ 20

State v. Boutin, 1996 WL 56505 (Minn. Ct. App. 1996)

73 ALR5th 383—§ 29

State v. Bowden, 538 So. 2d 83 (Fla. Dist. Ct. App. 2d Dist. 1989)

114 ALR5th 173—§ 8, 9

State v. Bowditch, 364 N.C. 335, 700 S.E.2d 1 (2010)

63 ALR6th 351—§ 3

State v. Bowe, 52 Ohio App. 3d 112, 557 N.E.2d 139 (9th Dist. Summit County 1988)

17 ALR6th 327—§ 31, 36

58 ALR6th 499—§ 81

State v. Bowe, 77 Hawaii 51, 881 P.2d 538, 48 A.L.R.5th 907 (1994)

48 ALR5th 555—§ 3

State v. Bowen, 12 Wash. App. 604, 531 P.2d 837 (1975)

45 ALR5th 591—§ 15

State v. Bowen, 254 Kan. 618, 867 P.2d 1024 (1994)

55 ALR6th 157—§ 7, 114

State v. Bowen, 274 Ga. 1, 547 S.E.2d 286 (2001)

47 ALR6th 107—§ 36

State v. Bowen, 340 Or. 487, 135 P.3d 272 (2006)

71 ALR6th 625—§ 3, 29

State v. Bowen, 444 So. 2d 1009 (Fla. Dist. Ct. App. 1st Dist. 1984)

62 ALR6th 413—§ 22, 42

State v. Bowens, 535 S.E.2d 870 (N.C. Ct. App. 2000)

24 ALR5th 428—§ 19

State v. Bowens, 722 N.E.2d 368 (Ind. Ct. App. 2000)

12 ALR6th 267—§ 4

State v. Bowens, 1998 WL 553049 (Ohio Ct. App. 11th Dist. Ashtabula County 1998)

29 ALR6th 237—§ 4, 9, 24

State v. Bower, 73 Wash. 2d 634, 440 P.2d 167 (1968)

28 ALR6th 505—§ 9

35 ALR6th 127—§ 5

State v. Bower, 135 Idaho 554, 21 P.3d 491 (Ct. App. 2001)

58 ALR6th 499—§ 14

State v. Bower, 2009-Ohio-201, 2009 WL 119833 (Ohio Ct. App. 4th Dist. Ross County 2009)

63 ALR6th 351—§ 3

State v. Bowers, 178 Minn. 589, 228 N.W. 164 (1929)

5 ALR5th 243—§ 62

State v. Bowers, 218 Kan. 736, 545 P.2d 303 (1976)

24 ALR6th 747—§ 21

State v. Bowers, 239 Kan. 417, 721 P.2d 268 (1986)

124 ALR5th 657—§ 2, 3, 7

State v. Bowers, 498 N.W.2d 202 (S.D. 1993)

3 ALR5th 521—§ 3

State v. Bowers, 909 So. 2d 1038 (La. Ct. App. 2d Cir. 2005)

9 ALR6th 1—§ 17

State v. Bowersmith, 224 Neb. 6, 395 N.W.2d 527 (1986)

35 ALR6th 127—§ 15

State v. Bowie, 813 So. 2d 377 (La. 2002)

12 ALR6th 267—§ 5

State v. Bowker, 713 P.2d 494 (Kan. Ct. App. 1986)

114 ALR5th 173—§ 9

State v. Bowles, 28 Kan. App. 2d 488, 18 P.3d 250 (2001)

106 ALR5th 397—§ 5

113 ALR5th 517—§ 5

State v. Bowles, 530 N.W.2d 521 (Minn. 1995)

60 ALR5th 39—§ 4 to 8, 11, 13

State v. Bowley, 232 Neb. 771, 442 N.W.2d 215 (1989)

84 ALR6th 293—§ 4, 41

State v. Bowlin, 2010 WL 1957517 (N.C. Ct. App. 2010)

57 ALR6th 1—§ 14

State v. Bowling, 163 Ariz. 22, 785 P.2d 591 (Ct. App. Div. 2 1989)

72 ALR5th 1—§ 2

State v. Bowman, 36 Wash. App. 798, 678 P.2d 1273 (Div. 1 1984)

56 ALR5th 385—§ 3, 4

86 ALR5th 59—§ 2, 5

87 ALR5th 181—§ 2

88 ALR5th 429—§ 2

State v. Bowman, 60 Or. App. 184, 653 P.2d 254, 7 Ed. Law Rep. 453 (1982)

70 ALR5th 169—§ 7, 8

State v. Bowman, 124 Idaho 936, 866 P.2d 193 (Ct. App. 1993)

66 ALR5th 397—§ 6, 9, 10, 25

State v. Bowman, 252 Kan. 883, 850 P.2d 236 (1993)

82 ALR5th 359—§ 5

84 ALR5th 487—§ 29

State v. Bowman, 349 N.C. 459, 509 S.E.2d 428 (1998)

79 ALR5th 33—§ 52

State v. Bowman, 588 A.2d 728 (Me. 1991)

41 ALR6th 295—§ 5

State v. Bowman, 945 P.2d 153 (Utah Ct. App. 1997)

20 ALR5th 398—§ 42

State v. Bowman, 1990 WL 209806 (Ohio Ct. App. 3d Dist. Crawford County 1990)

70 ALR6th 361—§ 32

State v. Bowser, 272 N.J. Super. 582, 640 A.2d 884 (Law Div. 1993)

7 ALR5th 263—§ 4

State v. Bowshier, 1992 WL 288780 (Ohio Ct. App. 2d Dist. Clark County 1992)

30 ALR6th 103—§ 3, 8, 19, 21, 32, 45

State v. Box, 89 Ohio App. 3d 614, 626 N.E.2d 996 (Ohio App. Cuyahoga Co. 1993)

39 ALR5th 283—§ 14, 71

State v. Boyanovsky, 304 Or. 131, 743 P.2d 711 (1987)

74 ALR5th 319—§ 2, 3

State v. Boyce, 44 Wash. App. 724, 723 P.2d 28 (Div. 1 1986)

117 ALR5th 407—§ 4

State v. Boyce, 194 Neb. 538, 233 N.W.2d 912 (1975)

42 ALR5th 581—§ 13

State v. Boyce, 1998 ME 219, 718 A.2d 1097 (Me. 1998)

85 ALR5th 547—§ 6

State v. Boyce, 2006-Ohio-2048, 2006 WL 1085603 (Ohio Ct. App. 4th Dist. Washington County 2006)

26 ALR6th 511—§ 19

State v. Boyd, 9 P.3d 1273 (Kan. Ct. App. 2000)

45 ALR5th 591—§ 4

State v. Boyd, 27 Wash. App. 719, 620 P.2d 135 (Div. 1 1980)

93 ALR5th 527—§ 15

State v. Boyd, 29 Wash. App. 584, 629 P.2d 930 (Div. 1 1981)

24 ALR6th 1—§ 12

State v. Boyd, 31 N.C. App. 328, 229 S.E.2d 229 (1976)

35 ALR6th 127—§ 8

State v. Boyd, 38 S.W.3d 155 (Tex. Crim. App. 2001)

29 ALR5th 1—§ 3

State v. Boyd, 90 Ohio Misc. 2d 20, 695 N.E.2d 843 (Mun. Ct. 1998)
68 ALR5th 343—§ 3, 8

State v. Boyd, 150 Wash. 326, 272 P. 964 (1928)
54 ALR6th 429—§ 13

State v. Boyd, 177 N.C. App. 165, 628 S.E.2d 796 (2006)
81 ALR6th 505—§ 34

State v. Boyd, 206 Kan. 597, 481 P.2d 1015 (1971)
68 ALR5th 343—§ 3, 12

State v. Boyd, 281 Kan. 70, 127 P.3d 998 (2006)
16 ALR6th 329—§ 4
24 ALR6th 591—§ 4, 12

State v. Boyd, 288 S.C. 206, 341 S.E.2d 144 (App. 1986)
7 ALR5th 263—§ 3

State v. Boyd, 295 Conn. 707, 992 A.2d 1071 (2010)
62 ALR6th 161—§ 28

State v. Boyd, 321 N.C. 574, 364 S.E.2d 118 (1988)
86 ALR5th 59—§ 3, 4

State v. Boyd, 548 So. 2d 1265 (La. App. 2d Cir. 1989)
18 ALR5th 1—§ 2, 3

State v. Boyd, 615 So. 2d 786 (Fla. Dist. Ct. App. 2d Dist. 1993)
58 ALR6th 499—§ 25

State v. Boyd, 797 S.W.2d 589 (Tenn. 1990)
83 ALR6th 255—§ 12

State v. Boyd, 1995 WL 12462 (Ohio Ct. App. 8th Dist. Cuyahoga County 1995)
88 ALR5th 121—§ 2

State v. Boyd, 2008 WL 3287240 (N.J. Super. Ct. App. Div. 2008)
99 ALR6th 295—§ 13

State v. Boyd, 2013 WL 1976082 (N.J. Super. Ct. App. Div. 2013)
99 ALR6th 295—§ 13

State v. Boyea, 171 Vt. 401, 765 A.2d 862 (2000)
84 ALR6th 293—§ 14, 29

State v. Boyer, 124 Wash. App. 593, 102 P.3d 833 (Div. 3 2004)
78 ALR6th 297—§ 53

State v. Boyer, 342 N.W.2d 497 (Iowa 1984)
34 ALR5th 125—§ 31

State v. Boyett, 32 N.C. 336, 10 Ired. 336, 1849 WL 1403 (1849)
5 ALR6th 1—§ 40

State v. Boykin, 112 Ariz. 109, 538 P.2d 383 (1975)
106 ALR5th 523—§ 17

State v. Boykin, 285 Minn. 276, 172 N.W.2d 754 (1969)
58 ALR6th 439—§ 8

State v. Boykin, 307 N.C. 87, 296 S.E.2d 258 (1982)
16 ALR6th 329—§ 5
24 ALR6th 591—§ 6, 14

State v. Boykins, 173 W. Va. 761, 320 S.E.2d 134 (1984)
93 ALR5th 527—§ 4

State v. Boykins, 1980 WL 353034 (Ohio Ct. App. 1st Dist. Hamilton County 1980)
19 ALR6th 697—§ 13, 14

State v. Boyle, 44 Del. 414, 61 A.2d 121 (Gen. Sess. 1948)
70 ALR5th 587—§ 10

State v. Boyle, 49 Nev. 386, 248 P. 48 (1926)
24 ALR6th 747—§ 43
54 ALR6th 429—§ 13, 29

State v. Boyle, 168 Ind. App. 643, 344 N.E.2d 302 (1st Dist. 1976)
75 ALR5th 1—§ 7, 13

State v. Boyle, 207 Kan. 833, 486 P.2d 849 (1971)
55 ALR5th 125—§ 12, 14, 23

State v. Boyle, 326 So. 2d 225 (Fla. Dist. Ct. App. 2d Dist. 1976)
114 ALR5th 173—§ 8

State v. Boyle, 793 So. 2d 1281 (La. Ct. App. 2d Cir. 2001)
84 ALR6th 293—§ 32

State v. Boyle, 1991 WL 208063 (Ohio Ct. App. 5th Dist. Richland County 1991)

For assistance, call 1-800-328-4880

7 ALR6th 487—§ 31
State v. Boynton, 556 So. 2d 428 (Fla. 4th DCA 1989)
92 ALR6th 295—§ 30
95 ALR6th 1—§ 5, 11, 29
State v. Boys, 302 S.C. 545, 397 S.E.2d 529 (1990)
16 ALR6th 329—§ 4
24 ALR6th 591—§ 6
State v. Boysaw, 99 Conn. App. 358, 913 A.2d 1112 (2007)
63 ALR6th 351—§ 3
State v. Brabson, 976 S.W.2d 182 (Tex. Crim. App. 1998)
23 ALR5th 108—§ 3
State v. Bracey, 202 Wis. 2d 648, 551 N.W.2d 63 (Ct. App. 1996)
99 ALR6th 295—§ 5
State v. Bracht, 1997 SD 136, 573 N.W.2d 176 (S.D. 1997)
9 ALR6th 541—§ 14
State v. Brackett, 547 So. 2d 272 (Fla. Dist. Ct. App. 2d Dist. 1989)
113 ALR5th 597—§ 8
State v. Bracy, 145 Ariz. 520, 703 P.2d 464 (1985)
93 ALR5th 527—§ 22
State v. Bracy, 1999 WL 787644 (Minn. Ct. App. 1999)
50 ALR6th 455—§ 12, 28
State v. Braden, 98 Ohio St. 3d 354, 2003-Ohio-1325, 785 N.E.2d 439 (2003)
3 ALR6th 543—§ 12
State v. Braden, 867 S.W.2d 750 (Tenn. Crim. App. 1993)
7 ALR5th 758—§ 11
76 ALR5th 1—§ 9
State v. Braden, 2003-Ohio-2949, 2003 WL 21321457 (Ohio Ct. App. 10th Dist. Franklin County 2003)
21 ALR6th 1—§ 4
State v. Bradfield, 973 S.W.2d 937 (Tenn. Crim. App. 1997)
99 ALR6th 295—§ 13
State v. Bradford, 129 Ohio App. 3d 128, 717 N.E.2d 376 (8th Dist. Cuyahoga County 1998)

70 ALR6th 1—§ 5
State v. Bradford, 223 Neb. 908, 395 N.W.2d 495 (1986)
70 ALR5th 1—§ 5
State v. Bradford, 368 So. 2d 317 (Ala. App. 1979)
13 ALR5th 1—§ 21
State v. Bradford, 434 S.W.2d 497 (Mo. 1968)
57 ALR6th 83—§ 11
State v. Bradford, 618 N.W.2d 782 (Minn. 2000)
58 ALR6th 499—§ 41, 112
State v. Bradford, 700 So. 2d 1046 (La. Ct. App. 2d Cir. 1997)
59 ALR5th 135—§ 3
State v. Bradford, 2010-Ohio-1784, 2010 WL 1632318 (Ohio Ct. App. 4th Dist. Adams County 2010)
67 ALR6th 531—§ 4, 6, 16, 20, 22
State v. Bradley, 3 Ohio St. 2d 38, 32 Ohio Op. 2d 21, 209 N.E.2d 215 (1965)
98 ALR6th 455—§ 22
State v. Bradley, 17 Wash. App. 916, 567 P.2d 650 (1977)
3 ALR5th 784—§ 2, 10
State v. Bradley, 17 Wash. App. 916, 567 P.2d 650 (Div. 2 1977)
111 ALR5th 1—§ 3, 5, 8, 29
State v. Bradley, 31 Mo. App. 308, 1888 WL 1755 (1888)
102 ALR5th 525—§ 61
State v. Bradley, 42 Ohio St. 3d 136, 538 N.E.2d 373 (1989)
10 ALR5th 700—§ 33
72 ALR5th 109—§ 5
State v. Bradley, 51 Or. App. 569, 626 P.2d 403 (1981)
2 ALR5th 262—§ 2, 4, 5
State v. Bradley, 163 W. Va. 148, 255 S.E.2d 356 (1979)
124 ALR5th 1—§ 5
State v. Bradley, 164 Vt. 346, 670 A.2d 811 (1995)
19 ALR6th 697—§ 4
State v. Bradley, 171 Wis. 2d 349, 493 N.W.2d 271 (Ct. App. 1992)

99 ALR6th 295—§ 19
State v. Bradley, 236 Neb. 371, 461 N.W.2d 524 (1990)

31 ALR5th 704—§ 8
State v. Bradley, 254 Iowa 211, 116 N.W.2d 439 (1962)

19 ALR5th 823—§ 9
State v. Bradley, 262 Mont. 194, 864 P.2d 787 (1993)

76 ALR5th 1—§ 4, 9
State v. Bradley, 431 N.W.2d 317 (S.D. 1988)

57 ALR5th 141—§ 2, 3
State v. Bradley, 578 P.2d 1267 (Utah 1978)

119 ALR5th 379—§ 8, 9
State v. Bradley, 1987 WL 17303 (Ohio Ct. App. 4th Dist. Scioto County 1987)

77 ALR5th 201—§ 21
State v. Bradley, 1994 WL 50656 (Ohio Ct. App. 8th Dist. Cuyahoga County 1994)

99 ALR6th 295—§ 9
State v. Bradley, 1997 WL 691510 (Ohio Ct. App. 2d Dist. Champaign County 1997)

107 ALR5th 567—§ 10, 11, 18
State v. Bradley, 1998 WL 321306 (Ohio Ct. App. 2d Dist. Montgomery County 1998)

78 ALR5th 489—§ 3, 6
State v. Bradley, 2003-Ohio-5914, 2003 WL 22501501 (Ohio Ct. App. 5th Dist. Richland County 2003)

1 ALR6th 371—§ 5
State v. Bradley, 2005-Ohio-6533, 2005 WL 3346082 (Ohio Ct. App. 2d Dist. Champaign County 2005)

99 ALR6th 295—§ 7, 12
State v. Bradshaw, 26 S.W.3d 461 (Mo. Ct. App. W.D. 2000)

45 ALR5th 767—§ 8, 9
State v. Bradshaw, 81 S.W.3d 14 (Mo. Ct. App. W.D. 2002)

103 ALR6th 347—§ 20
State v. Bradshaw, 193 W. Va. 519, 457 S.E.2d 456 (1995)

20 ALR6th 479—§ 3, 13

23 ALR6th 1—§ 15
State v. Bradshaw, 680 P.2d 1036 (Utah 1984)

62 ALR6th 413—§ 29
State v. Brady, 66 Ariz. 365, 189 P.2d 198 (1948)

99 ALR6th 113—§ 4
State v. Brady, 105 Ariz. 592, 469 P.2d 77 (1970)

85 ALR5th 1—§ 38
State v. Brady, 130 Wis. 2d 443, 388 N.W.2d 151 (1986)

19 ALR5th 470—§ 3
State v. Brady, 169 Ariz. 447, 819 P.2d 1033, 98 Ariz. Adv. Rep. 32 (App. 1991)

15 ALR5th 391—§ 39
State v. Brady, 237 N.C. 675, 75 S.E.2d 791 (1953)

57 ALR6th 445—§ 43
State v. Brady, 290 A.2d 322 (Del. Super. Ct. 1972)

72 ALR5th 607—§ 3
State v. Brady, 569 So. 2d 110 (La. Ct. App. 4th Cir. 1990)

58 ALR6th 499—§ 26
State v. Brady, 585 So. 2d 524 (La. 1991)

58 ALR6th 499—§ 26
State v. Brady, 655 P.2d 1132 (Utah 1982)

105 ALR5th 529—§ 25
State v. Bragan, 920 S.W.2d 227 (Tenn. Crim. App. 1995)

57 ALR5th 141—§ 3
State v. Bragg, 2004-Ohio-1943, 2004 WL 831023 (Ohio Ct. App. 5th Dist. Licking County 2004)

24 ALR6th 549—§ 6
State v. Bragg, 2006-Ohio-1903, 2006 WL 1000335 (Ohio Ct. App. 10th Dist. Franklin County 2006)

32 ALR6th 171—§ 16, 19, 21

33 ALR6th 1—§ 10
State v. Brake, 796 So. 2d 522 (Fla. 2001)

35 ALR6th 361—§ 3, 6, 7, 9

State v. Bramson, 94 Or. App. 374, 765 P.2d 824 (1988)
  64 ALR5th 637—§ 3
  58 ALR6th 499—§ 80
State v. Brana, 127 N.J. 64, 601 A.2d 1160 (1992)
  27 ALR5th 593—§ 29
State v. Branch, 298 N.W.2d 173 (S.D. 1980)
  34 ALR6th 1—§ 10
State v. Branch, 301 N.J.Super 307, 693 A.2d 1272 (N.J.Super.A.D. 1997)
  66 ALR5th 397—§ 5, 22
State v. Brand, 157 Ohio App. 3d 451, 2004-Ohio-1490, 811 N.E.2d 1156 (1st Dist. Hamilton County 2004)
  30 ALR6th 103—§ 3, 20, 24, 35
State v. Brand, 2000 WL 299497 (Ohio Ct. App. 1st Dist. Hamilton County 2000)
  10 ALR6th 463—§ 4
State v. Brandenburg, 38 N.J. Super. 561, 120 A.2d 59 (1956)
  14 ALR5th 89—§ 8
State v. Brandenburg, 153 Wash. App. 944, 223 P.3d 1259 (Div. 3 2009)
  55 ALR6th 1—§ 38, 40
State v. Brander, 2004 MT 150, 321 Mont. 484, 92 P.3d 1173 (2004)
  84 ALR6th 293—§ 13, 14, 33
State v. Brandon, 20 N.C. App. 262, 201 S.E.2d 234 (1973)
  58 ALR6th 215—§ 7
State v. Brandt, 110 Idaho 341, 715 P.2d 1011 (App. 1986)
  7 ALR5th 263—§ 4
State v. Brandt, 135 Idaho 205, 16 P.3d 302 (Ct. App. 2000)
  98 ALR5th 445—§ 4
State v. Brandt, 467 S.W.2d 948 (Mo. 1971)
  50 ALR5th 467—§ 3, 9
State v. Brann, 1999 ME 113, 736 A.2d 251 (Me. 1999)
  81 ALR6th 505—§ 31
State v. Branning, 85 Fla. 61, 95 So. 237 (1923)

  97 ALR5th 537—§ 38
State v. Brannon, 741 N.W.2d 823 (Iowa Ct. App. 2007)
  73 ALR6th 49—§ 19, 66
State v. Brannon, 971 So. 2d 511 (La. Ct. App. 3d Cir. 2007)
  84 ALR6th 263—§ 4
State v. Branscomb, 638 S.W.2d 306 (Mo. Ct. App. E.D. 1982)
  79 ALR5th 237—§ 11
State v. Branson, 154 P.3d 556 (Kan. Ct. App. 2007)
  26 ALR6th 511—§ 25
State v. Branstetter, 107 S.W.3d 465 (Mo. Ct. App. W.D. 2003)
  37 ALR6th 357—§ 3, 10, 13, 28
State v. Brantley, 236 Kan. 379, 691 P.2d 26 (1984)
  45 ALR5th 767—§ 2, 19
State v. Brasch, 118 Ohio App. 3d 659, 693 N.E.2d 1134 (12th Dist. Warren County 1997)
  70 ALR6th 1—§ 5
State v. Brasel, 538 S.W.2d 325 (Mo. 1976)
  61 ALR5th 1—§ 3, 5
State v. Braskamp, 87 Iowa 588, 54 N.W. 532 (1893)
  56 ALR5th 171—§ 12, 24
State v. Brass, 632 So. 2d 819 (La. App. 4th Cir. 1994)
  7 ALR5th 263—§ 7
State v. Braswell, 194 Conn. 297, 481 A.2d 413 (1984)
  70 ALR6th 361—§ 39
State v. Braswell, 312 N.C. 553, 324 S.E.2d 241 (1985)
  58 ALR6th 499—§ 23
State v. Brauch, 133 Idaho 215, 984 P.2d 703 (1999)
  99 ALR6th 397—§ 17
State v. Brauch, 984 P.2d 703 (Idaho 1999)
  61 ALR5th 1—§ 3, 9
State v. Brauer, 16 Neb. App. 257, 743 N.W.2d 655 (2007)
  56 ALR6th 323—§ 7, 11

State v. Braun, 185 Wis. 2d 152, 516 N.W.2d 740 (1994)
105 ALR5th 529—§ 31

State v. Braun, 253 Kan. 141, 853 P.2d 686 (1993)
59 ALR5th 135—§ 3, 5, 12

State v. Braverman, 348 So. 2d 1183 (Fla. Dist. Ct. App. 3d Dist. 1977)
14 ALR6th 517—§ 13

State v. Bravo, 139 N.M. 93, 2006-NMCA-019, 128 P.3d 1070 (Ct. App. 2005)
28 ALR6th 505—§ 19
32 ALR6th 1—§ 11

State v. Bravo, 158 Ariz. 364, 762 P.2d 1318 (1988)
96 ALR5th 523—§ 3

State v. Brawley, 347 So. 2d 238 (La. 1977)
6 ALR6th 533—§ 19

State v. Braxton, 294 N.C. 446, 242 S.E.2d 769 (1978)
55 ALR5th 125—§ 3, 10

State v. Braxton, 352 N.C. 158, 531 S.E.2d 428 (2000)
110 ALR5th 1—§ 2, 3, 14, 15

State v. Bray, 738 So. 2d 962 (Fla. Dist. Ct. App. 2d Dist. 1999)
106 ALR5th 377—§ 4

State v. Bray, 1995 WL 356359 (Neb. Ct. App. 1995)
103 ALR6th 347—§ 13

State v. Brazil, 2007 WI App 203, 2007 WL 2089375 (Wis. Ct. App. 2007)
28 ALR6th 505—§ 9

State v. Breazile, 189 Or. App. 138, 74 P.3d 1099 (2003)
38 ALR6th 97—§ 8

State v. Brecht, 157 Mont. 264, 485 P.2d 47 (1971)
19 ALR5th 470—§ 6

State v. Breckenridge, 4 Wash. App. 328, 481 P.2d 26 (Div. 1 1971)
68 ALR5th 343—§ 2, 3, 13

State v. Breeden, 374 N.W.2d 560 (Minn. Ct. App. 1985)
109 ALR5th 611—§ 3

State v. Breeze, 379 S.C. 538, 665 S.E.2d 247 (Ct. App. 2008)
55 ALR6th 391—§ 21

State v. Breeze, 2001 UT App 200, 424 Utah Adv. Rep. 24, 2001 WL 721389 (Utah Ct. App. 2001)
92 ALR5th 35—§ 17

State v. Breffeihl, 130 La. 904, 58 So. 763 (1912)
5 ALR6th 1—§ 39

State v. Brehm, 27 Ohio St. 2d 239, 56 Ohio Ops. 2d 145, 272 N.E.2d 122 (1971)
4 ALR5th 1—§ 7

State v. Brehmer, 211 Neb. 29, 317 N.W.2d 885 (1982)
3 ALR6th 269—§ 4, 8, 9, 23, 24, 29

State v. Brehmer, 281 Minn. 156, 160 N.W.2d 669 (1968)
84 ALR6th 427—§ 4

State v. Brenan, 772 So. 2d 64 (La. 2000)
94 ALR5th 497—§ 2, 3, 5, 6

State v. Brenke, 1996 WL 665890 (Minn. Ct. App. 1996)
73 ALR5th 383—§ 32

State v. Brennan, 115 N.J. Super. 400, 279 A.2d 900 (1971)
45 ALR5th 591—§ 15

State v. Brent, 137 N.J. 107, 644 A.2d 583 (1994)
39 ALR5th 283—§ 4, 66

State v. Brentlinger, 1983 WL 3704 (Ohio Ct. App. 10th Dist. Franklin County 1983)
43 ALR6th 475—§ 10

State v. Breshears, 98 Or. App. 105, 779 P.2d 158 (1989)
69 ALR6th 275—§ 32

State v. Bressman, 236 Kan. 296, 689 P.2d 901 (1984)
119 ALR5th 379—§ 2

State v. Bresson, 51 Ohio St. 3d 123, 554 N.E.2d 1330 (1990)
117 ALR5th 491—§ 2, 6

State v. Brett, 126 Wash. 2d 136, 892 P.2d 29 (1995)
39 ALR5th 283—§ 4, 77

State v. Bretz, 185 Mont. 253, 605 P.2d 974 (1979)
22 ALR5th 660—§ 11, 20

State v. Brewer, 7 Or. App. 158, 490 P.2d 202 (1971)
57 ALR6th 445—§ 59

State v. Brewer, 48 Ohio St. 3d 50, 549 N.E.2d 491 (1990)
12 ALR5th 909—§ 12
57 ALR5th 141—§ 5, 9

State v. Brewer, 247 N.W.2d 205 (Iowa 1976)
10 ALR5th 700—§ 2, 18, 39

State v. Brewer, 875 S.W.2d 298 (Tenn. Crim. App. 1993)
81 ALR5th 563—§ 3, 6

State v. Brewer, 932 S.W.2d 1 (Tenn. Crim. App. 1996)
24 ALR6th 1—§ 18

State v. Brewer, 1999 M.T. 369, 989 P.2d 407 (Mont. 1999)
15 ALR5th 391—§ 45

State v. Brewer, 2003-Ohio-701, 2003 WL 352771 (Ohio Ct. App. 11th Dist. Lake County 2003)
69 ALR6th 1—§ 27

State v. Brewington, 352 N.C. 489, 532 S.E.2d 496 (2000)
29 ALR6th 1—§ 8
83 ALR6th 255—§ 15

State v. Brewington, 687 S.E.2d 319 (N.C. Ct. App. 2009)
57 ALR6th 1—§ 4

State v. Brewster, 157 Ohio App. 3d 342, 2004-Ohio-2722, 811 N.E.2d 162 (1st Dist. Hamilton County 2004)
79 ALR6th 1—§ 39, 57

State v. Brewster, 164 W. Va. 173, 261 S.E.2d 77 (1979)
95 ALR5th 611—§ 3

State v. Brewster, 429 N.J. Super. 387, 58 A.3d 1234 (App. Div. 2013)
97 ALR6th 263—§ 11

State v. Brewster, 601 So. 2d 1289 (Fla. Dist. Ct. App. 5th Dist. 1992)
87 ALR5th 631—§ 14

State v. Brewster, 836 S.W.2d 9 (Mo. Ct. App. E.D. 1992)
32 ALR6th 1—§ 9

State v. Brewster, 2004-Ohio-2993, 2004 WL 1284008 (Ohio Ct. App. 1st Dist. Hamilton County 2004)
79 ALR6th 1—§ 57

State v. Briand, 130 N.H. 650, 547 A.2d 235 (1988)
58 ALR5th 749—§ 9

State v. Briceno, 33 Wash. App. 101, 651 P.2d 1093 (1982)
56 ALR5th 385—§ 3, 4

State v. Brick, 163 Wash. App. 1029, 2011 WL 4389893 (Div. 1 2011)
82 ALR6th 373—§ 4, 6, 7, 17

State v. Bricker, 321 Md. 86, 581 A.2d 9 (1990)
72 ALR5th 529—§ 9

State v. Briden, 179 Wash. App. 1040, 2014 WL 812469 (Div. 3 2014)
101 ALR6th 331—§ 12

State v. Brider, 386 So. 2d 818 (Fla. App. D2 1980)
9 ALR5th 464—§ 3

State v. Bridewell, 306 Or. 231, 759 P.2d 1054 (1988)
58 ALR6th 499—§ 85

State v. Bridge, 60 Ohio App. 3d 76, 573 N.E.2d 762 (6th Dist. Lucas County 1989)
81 ALR5th 563—§ 3, 7, 8, 10

State v. Bridgeforth, 357 N.W.2d 393 (Minn. App. 1984)
5 ALR5th 243—§ 28

State v. Bridges, 109 La. 530, 33 So. 589 (1903)
19 ALR5th 351—§ 16

State v. Bridges, 398 S.W.2d 1 (Mo. 1966)
13 ALR5th 1—§ 2, 4

State v. Bridges, 513 A.2d 1365 (Me. 1986)
67 ALR6th 531—§ 23

State v. Bridges, 1995 WL 764998 (Tenn. Crim. App)
50 ALR5th 581—§ 3, 5, 7, 9, 11, 13, 19, 22

State v. Bridges, 2006-Ohio-6280, 2006 WL 3446221 (Ohio Ct. App. 8th Dist. Cuyahoga County 2006)
26 ALR6th 511—§ 7
State v. Bridgett, 3 Conn. Cir. Ct. 206, 210 A.2d 182 (App. Div. 1965)
9 ALR6th 633—§ 5
15 ALR6th 173—§ 31
State v. Bridwell, 592 P.2d 520 (Okla. 1979)
10 ALR5th 1—§ 26
State v. Bridwell, 1979 OK 37, 592 P.2d 520 (Okla. 1979)
19 ALR6th 577—§ 5, 9
State v. Brierly, 109 Ariz. 310, 509 P.2d 203 (1973)
77 ALR5th 201—§ 21
90 ALR5th 225—§ 5
State v. Briggins, 11 Wash. App. 687, 524 P.2d 496 (Div. 3 1974)
117 ALR5th 513—§ 5
State v. Briggs, 137 N.C. App. 125, 526 S.E.2d 678 (2000)
38 ALR6th 97—§ 17
State v. Briggs, 140 N.C. App. 484, 536 S.E.2d 858 (2000)
116 ALR5th 479—§ 5
State v. Briggs, 179 Conn. 328, 426 A.2d 298 (1979)
39 ALR5th 283—§ 3
State v. Briggs, 214 Wis. 2d 281, 571 N.W.2d 881 (Ct. App. 1997)
27 ALR6th 183—§ 46
State v. Briggs, 343 S.W.3d 106 (Tenn. Crim. App. 2010)
84 ALR6th 427—§ 29
State v. Briggs, 740 S.W.2d 399 (Mo. App. 1987)
5 ALR5th 243—§ 22
State v. Briggs, 756 A.2d 731 (R.I. 2000)
28 ALR6th 505—§ 9
State v. Briggs, 787 A.2d 479 (R.I. 2001)
104 ALR5th 357—§ 7
State v. Briggs, 934 A.2d 811 (R.I. 2007)
70 ALR6th 1—§ 5
State v. Bright, 78 N.C. App. 239, 337 S.E.2d 87 (1985)

31 ALR5th 760—§ 4
State v. Bright, 320 N.C. 491, 358 S.E.2d 498 (1987)
38 ALR5th 433—§ 13
State v. Bright, 860 So. 2d 196 (La. Ct. App. 5th Cir. 2003)
92 ALR6th 171—§ 14
State v. Bright, 2008 WL 2964335 (N.J. Super. Ct. App. Div. 2008)
55 ALR6th 157—§ 5
State v. Brighter, 60 Haw. 318, 589 P.2d 527 (1979)
60 ALR5th 1—§ 10
62 ALR6th 413—§ 29
State v. Brigman, 201 N.C. 793, 161 S.E. 727 (1931)
119 ALR5th 275—§ 14
State v. Brillon, 2008 VT 35, 955 A.2d 1108 (Vt. 2008)
46 ALR6th 495—§ 13
State v. Brim, 298 N.W.2d 73 (S.D. 1980)
56 ALR6th 185—§ 39
State v. Brimmer, 876 S.W.2d 75 (Tenn. 1994)
79 ALR5th 33—§ 7, 63
83 ALR6th 255—§ 17
State v. Briner, 253 Mont. 158, 831 P.2d 1365 (1992)
18 ALR5th 1—§ 10
State v. Brinker, 128 Wash. 319, 222 P. 615 (1924)
105 ALR5th 529—§ 28
State v. Brinkley, 354 Mo. 337, 189 S.W.2d 314 (1945)
41 ALR5th 1—§ 3
State v. Brinkley, 354 Mo. 1051, 193 S.W.2d 49 (1946)
8 ALR5th 775—§ 6
97 ALR5th 293—§ 6
State v. Brinkman, 168 Ohio App. 3d 245, 2006-Ohio-3868, 859 N.E.2d 595 (6th Dist. Wood County 2006)
26 ALR6th 511—§ 19
State v. Brinks, 87 Wash. App. 1021, 1997 WL 469864 (Div. 1 1997)
45 ALR6th 643—§ 14

State v. Brinks, 1997 WL 469864 (Wash. Ct. App. Div. 1 1997)
60 ALR5th 1—§ 2, 5
State v. Brinson, 337 N.C. 764, 448 S.E.2d 822 (1994)
8 ALR5th 775—§ 5
State v. Brintzenhofe, 1999 WL 292195 (Ohio Ct. App. 9th Dist. Summit County 1999)
78 ALR5th 489—§ 3, 10
State v. Brisco, 84 Conn. App. 120, 852 A.2d 746 (2004)
39 ALR6th 257—§ 35, 41
State v. Briscoe, 892 S.W.2d 355 (Mo. Ct. App. W.D. 1995)
1 ALR6th 549—§ 3, 5
State v. Briscoeray, 95 Wash. App. 167, 974 P.2d 912 (Div. 1 1999)
7 ALR6th 233—§ 5
State v. Brissenden, 23 N.C. App. 730, 209 S.E.2d 539 (1974)
85 ALR5th 1—§ 33
State v. Bristor, 236 Kan. 313, 691 P.2d 1 (1984)
109 ALR5th 611—§ 3
State v. Britt, 93 N.C. App. 126, 377 S.E.2d 79 (1989)
38 ALR5th 433—§ 19
State v. Britt, 203 Wis. 2d 25, 553 N.W.2d 528 (Ct. App. 1996)
60 ALR5th 39—§ 3, 5, 7, 11, 13
State v. Britt, 235 S.C. 395, 111 S.E.2d 669 (1959)
16 ALR6th 329—§ 7
24 ALR6th 591—§ 6
State v. Britt, 237 Neb. 163, 465 N.W.2d 466 (1991)
117 ALR5th 513—§ 3
State v. Britton, 443 So. 2d 6 (La. App. 5th Cir. 1983)
29 ALR5th 59—§ 76
State v. Broach, 2001-Ohio-8745, 2001 WL 1887776 (Ohio Ct. App. 1st Dist. Hamilton County 2001)
99 ALR6th 295—§ 9
State v. Broad, 61 Haw. 187, 600 P.2d 1379 (1979)

95 ALR5th 229—§ 32
State v. Broaddus, 3 S.W.3d 919 (Tex. Crim. App. 1999)
41 ALR6th 295—§ 4
State v. Broaddus, 2010-Ohio-490, 2010 WL 541043 (Ohio Ct. App. 2d Dist. Montgomery County 2010)
55 ALR6th 1—§ 26
State v. Broadhurst, 184 Or. 178, 196 P.2d 407 (1948)
55 ALR5th 125—§ 12, 19, 22
State v. Broadnax, 98 Wash. 2d 289, 654 P.2d 96 (1982)
50 ALR5th 581—§ 2
State v. Broadway, 269 Ark. 215, 599 S.W.2d 721 (1980)
41 ALR5th 171—§ 36, 38, 93, 111, 113
State v. Broberg, 342 Md. 544, 677 A.2d 602 (1996)
91 ALR5th 343—§ 25
State v. Brochu, 237 A.2d 418 (Me. 1967)
104 ALR5th 165—§ 11
State v. Brock, 110 Ohio App. 3d 656, 675 N.E.2d 18 (3d Dist. Shelby County 1996)
20 ALR5th 398—§ 6.5
State v. Brock, 294 Or. 15, 653 P.2d 543 (1982)
41 ALR5th 171—§ 8, 55, 63, 66, 72, 88, 114, 116, 120, 134
State v. Brockenshire, 26 Kan. App. 2d 902, 995 P.2d 905 (2000)
98 ALR5th 445—§ 4
State v. Brockett, 471 So. 2d 867 (La. Ct. App. 2d Cir. 1985)
9 ALR6th 1—§ 17
State v. Brockington, 89 N.J. Super. 423, 215 A.2d 362 (App. Div. 1965)
71 ALR6th 335—§ 10
State v. Brockman, 231 Wis. 634, 283 N.W. 338 (1939)
106 ALR5th 397—§ 3
State v. Brocuglio, 64 Conn. App. 93, 779 A.2d 793 (2001)
45 ALR6th 643—§ 19
62 ALR6th 413—§ 38

State v. Brodigan, 37 Nev. 492, 143 P.
238 (1914)
120 ALR5th 125—§ 2
121 ALR5th 1—§ 2, 16
State v. Brogan, 272 Mont. 156, 900
P.2d 284 (1995)
50 ALR5th 703—§ 27
State v. Brogan, 453 So. 2d 325 (La. Ct.
App. 3d Cir. 1984)
72 ALR5th 109—§ 5
State v. Brom, 8 Or. App. 598, 494 P.2d
434 (1972)
58 ALR6th 439—§ 16
State v. Bromley, 117 Vt. 228, 88 A.2d
833 (1952)
52 ALR5th 655—§ 3
State v. Bronson, 55 Conn. App. 717,
740 A.2d 458 (1999)
40 ALR6th 1—§ 13
State v. Bronson, 242 Neb. 931, 496
N.W.2d 882 (1993)
32 ALR6th 1—§ 11
State v. Bronson, 267 Neb. 103, 672
N.W.2d 244, 125 A.L.R.5th 759
(2003)
125 ALR5th 497—§ 4
72 ALR6th 227—§ 57
State v. Bronston, 7 Wis. 2d 627, 97
N.W.2d 504 (1959)
5 ALR5th 243—§ 2, 51, 61
State v. Brooke, 565 N.E.2d 754 (Ind.
1991)
7 ALR5th 263—§ 6
State v. Brooks, 9 West. L.J. 109, 1 Ohio
Dec. Rep. 407, 1851 WL 2665
(Ohio C.P. 1851)
81 ALR5th 563—§ 3
State v. Brooks, 16 Wash. App. 535, 557
P.2d 362 (1976)
11 ALR5th 497—§ 3, 5, 12, 32
State v. Brooks, 23 Ariz. App. 463, 534
P.2d 271 (1975)
45 ALR5th 173—§ 8
State v. Brooks, 43 Wash. App. 560, 718
P.2d 837 (1986)
**31 ALR5th 229—§ 2, 3, 17, 43, 58,
62, 67**

State v. Brooks, 46 Kan. App. 2d 601,
265 P.3d 1175 (2011)
87 ALR6th 1—§ 42
State v. Brooks, 73 Wash. 2d 653, 440
P.2d 199 (1968)
84 ALR6th 427—§ 27
State v. Brooks, 75 Ohio St. 3d 148, 661
N.E.2d 1030 (1996)
79 ALR5th 33—§ 68
State v. Brooks, 92 Mo. 542, 5 S.W. 257
(1887)
16 ALR5th 152—§ 7, 14
State v. Brooks, 99 Wash. App. 1016,
2000 WL 124684 (Div. 1 2000)
7 ALR6th 233—§ 5, 9
State v. Brooks, 116 N.M. 309, 862 P.2d
57 (Ct. App. 1993)
92 ALR5th 35—§ 25
51 ALR6th 219—§ 4
State v. Brooks, 120 Wash. App. 1041,
2004 WL 439979 (Div. 2 2004)
7 ALR6th 233—§ 7
State v. Brooks, 126 Ariz. 395, 616 P.2d
70 (App. 1980)
42 ALR5th 581—§ 11
State v. Brooks, 127 Ariz. 130, 618 P.2d
624 (Ct. App. Div. 1 1980)
124 ALR5th 1—§ 3
State v. Brooks, 148 Md. App. 374, 812
A.2d 342 (2002)
58 ALR6th 499—§ 76, 115
State v. Brooks, 162 Vt. 26, 643 A.2d
226 (1993)
90 ALR5th 453—§ 25
State v. Brooks, 167 Conn. 281, 355
A.2d 67 (1974)
7 ALR6th 169—§ 8
State v. Brooks, 177 P.3d 428 (Kan. Ct.
App. 2008)
63 ALR6th 1—§ 5, 53
State v. Brooks, 185 S.W.3d 265 (Mo.
Ct. App. W.D. 2006)
32 ALR6th 1—§ 10, 11
State v. Brooks, 206 Kan. 418, 479 P.2d
893 (1971)
37 ALR6th 357—§ 69

State v. Brooks, 222 Kan. 432, 565 P.2d 241 (1977)

39 ALR5th 283—§ 4, 17, 18

State v. Brooks, 235 S.C. 344, 111 S.E.2d 686 (1959)

88 ALR5th 429—§ 5, 6

State v. Brooks, 275 Or. 171, 550 P.2d 440 (1976)

95 ALR5th 229—§ 16

State v. Brooks, 337 N.C. 132, 446 S.E.2d 579 (1994)

97 ALR5th 201—§ 3, 4

State v. Brooks, 348 So. 2d 417 (Fla. App. D1 1977)

29 ALR5th 59—§ 5, 22, 31

State v. Brooks, 499 So. 2d 741 (La. App. 3d Cir. 1986)

45 ALR5th 531—§ 7

State v. Brooks, 505 So. 2d 245 (La. Ct. App. 3d Cir. 1987)

77 ALR5th 201—§ 10

State v. Brooks, 693 S.E.2d 204 (N.C. Ct. App. 2010)

57 ALR6th 1—§ 22, 25

State v. Brooks, 734 So. 2d 1232 (La. Ct. App. 1st Cir. 1999)

90 ALR5th 453—§ 12

State v. Brooks, 810 S.W.2d 627 (Mo. Ct. App. E.D. 1991)

86 ALR5th 59—§ 2, 4, 5
87 ALR5th 181—§ 2
88 ALR5th 429—§ 2

State v. Brooks, 833 P.2d 362 (Utah Ct. App. 1992)

72 ALR5th 403—§ 11 to 13, 15

State v. Brooks, 889 So. 2d 1064 (La. Ct. App. 5th Cir. 2004)

26 ALR6th 511—§ 3, 28

State v. Brooks, 909 S.W.2d 854 (Tenn. Crim. App. 1995)

78 ALR5th 567—§ 5
27 ALR6th 183—§ 10, 35

State v. Brooks, 960 S.W.2d 479 (Mo. 1997)

98 ALR6th 455—§ 11

State v. Brooks., 1976 WL 190847 (Ohio Ct. App. 8th Dist. Cuyahoga County 1976)

103 ALR6th 347—§ 16

State v. Brooks, 1986 WL 2677 (Ohio Ct. App. 8th Dist. Cuyahoga County 1986)

85 ALR5th 1—§ 7

State v. Brooks, 1994 WL 466032 (Del. Super. Ct. 1994)

61 ALR5th 1—§ 7

State v. Brooks, 1995 WL 390935 (Ohio Ct. App. 10th Dist. Franklin County 1995)

17 ALR6th 327—§ 40

State v. Brooks, 2001-Ohio-1950, 2001 WL 1617194 (Ohio Ct. App. 5th Dist. Ashland County 2001)

34 ALR6th 1—§ 7

State v. Brooks, 2003 WL 22039323 (Minn. Ct. App. 2003)

7 ALR6th 233—§ 9

State v. Brooks, 2007 WL 1248491 (Del. C.P. 2007)

58 ALR6th 215—§ 12

State v. Brooks, 2008-Ohio-3723, 2008 WL 2876619 (Ohio Ct. App. 9th Dist. Medina County 2008)

70 ALR6th 329—§ 14

State v. Brooks, 2008 WL 726809 (Del. Super. Ct. 2008)

56 ALR6th 553—§ 18

State v. Brooks, 2009 WL 3430018 (N.J. Super. Ct. App. Div. 2009)

69 ALR6th 579—§ 11

State v. Brooks, 2010 WI App 71, 325 Wis. 2d 400, 786 N.W.2d 488 (Ct. App. 2010)

93 ALR6th 275—§ 23

State v. Brooks, 2010 WL 481212 (Tenn. Crim. App. 2010)

57 ALR6th 83—§ 6, 7

State v. Brookshire, 355 S.W.2d 333 (Mo. App. 1962)

6 ALR5th 733—§ 2, 5, 16

State v. Broom, 40 Ohio St. 3d 277, 533 N.E.2d 682 (1988)

39 ALR5th 283—§ 14, 60, 77

State v. Broom, 121 Or. 202, 253 P. 1044 (1927)
105 ALR5th 529—§ 20
State v. Broome, 136 N.C. App. 82, 523 S.E.2d 448 (1999)
43 ALR6th 475—§ 21
State v. Brosius, 154 Wash. App. 714, 225 P.3d 1049 (Div. 2 2010)
64 ALR6th 1—§ 12, 20
State v. Brosnan, 221 Conn. 788, 608 A.2d 49 (1992)
24 ALR6th 1—§ 40
State v. Brossoit, 2005 WL 1269091 (Minn. Ct. App. 2005)
84 ALR6th 427—§ 10
State v. Brothers, 12 Or. App. 435, 507 P.2d 398 (1973)
50 ALR6th 455—§ 34
State v. Brothers, 828 S.W.2d 414 (Tenn. Crim. App. 1991)
84 ALR6th 293—§ 33
State v. Brotherton, 2008 MT 119, 342 Mont. 511, 182 P.3d 88, 46 A.L.R.6th 629 (2008)
46 ALR6th 241—§ 11
State v. Brotman, 1991 WL 138421 (Del. Super. Ct. 1991)
30 ALR6th 103—§ 25, 27, 34, 48
State v. Broucher, 388 A.2d 907 (Me. 1978)
102 ALR6th 365—§ 2
State v. Brouillette, 465 So. 2d 124 (La. Ct. App. 4th Cir. 1985)
104 ALR5th 165—§ 12
27 ALR6th 491—§ 3
State v. Broussard, 202 La. 458, 12 So. 2d 218 (1942)
101 ALR6th 499—§ 19
103 ALR6th 35—§ 26
State v. Broussard, 517 So. 2d 1000 (La. Ct. App. 3d Cir. 1987)
109 ALR5th 611—§ 3
State v. Broussard, 560 So. 2d 694 (La. Ct. App. 3d Cir. 1990)
68 ALR5th 343—§ 3, 13
State v. Browder, 486 P.2d 925 (Alaska 1971)

82 ALR6th 317—§ 15, 17
State v. Brower, 2009 UT App 143, 2009 WL 1496818 (Utah Ct. App. 2009)
55 ALR6th 1—§ 6
State v. Brown, 5 Kan. App. 2d 149, 613 P.2d 387 (1980)
7 ALR6th 169—§ 12
State v. Brown, 8 Or. App. 72, 491 P.2d 1193 (1971)
50 ALR5th 467—§ 9
State v. Brown, 9 Or. App. 137, 495 P.2d 304 (1972)
29 ALR6th 1—§ 10
State v. Brown, 12 Ohio St. 3d 147, 12 Ohio B.R. 186, 465 N.E.2d 889 (1984)
39 ALR5th 283—§ 14, 41, 47
State v. Brown, 13 Neb. App. 359, 693 N.W.2d 559 (2005)
57 ALR6th 83—§ 6
State v. Brown, 14 Conn. App. 605, 543 A.2d 750 (1988)
19 ALR5th 470—§ 3, 12
State v. Brown, 16 Del. 380, 2 Marvel 380, 36 A. 458 (Ct. of Oyer & Terminer 1896)
64 ALR6th 655—§ 4
State v. Brown, 18 S.W.3d 482 (Mo. Ct. App. E.D. 2000)
38 ALR6th 97—§ 13
State v. Brown, 20 Ohio App. 3d 36, 484 N.E.2d 215 (1st Dist. Hamilton County 1984)
62 ALR5th 1—§ 3, 12, 14
State v. Brown, 21 N.C. App. 552, 204 S.E.2d 861 (1974)
5 ALR5th 243—§ 6
State v. Brown, 27 Wash. App. 639, 620 P.2d 529 (Div. 3 1980)
93 ALR5th 527—§ 4
State v. Brown, 28 Or. 147, 41 P. 1042 (1895)
101 ALR6th 499—§ 14
State v. Brown, 33 Conn. Supp. 515, 356 A.2d 913 (Super Ct. Appellate Sess. 1976)
66 ALR5th 397—§ 10

State v. Brown, 36 Wash. App. 166, 672
P.2d 1268 (Div. 1 1983)
65 ALR5th 623—§ 6, 9

State v. Brown, 45-138 La. App. 2 Cir.
10/15/09, 2009 WL 3301387 (La.
Ct. App. 2d Cir. 2009)
56 ALR6th 1—§ 23

State v. Brown, 50 Wash. App. 405, 748
P.2d 276 (Div. 1 1988)
79 ALR5th 1—§ 6

State v. Brown, 53 S.W.3d 264 (Tenn.
Crim. App. 2000)
52 ALR6th 1—§ 5
72 ALR6th 141—§ 5

State v. Brown, 55 Wash. App. 738, 780
P.2d 880 (Div. 2 1989)
73 ALR5th 383—§ 6

State v. Brown, 65 Ohio App. 3d 322,
583 N.E.2d 1331 (11th Dist. Portage
County 1989)
83 ALR5th 277—§ 3, 19, 29

State v. Brown, 71 N.J. 578, 367 A.2d
417 (1976)
15 ALR6th 173—§ 28

State v. Brown, 79 Ohio App. 3d 445,
607 N.E.2d 540 (12th Dist. Clermont County 1992)
72 ALR6th 141—§ 10

State v. Brown, 82 Conn. App. 678, 846
A.2d 943 (2004)
15 ALR6th 173—§ 53

State v. Brown, 84 Ohio App. 3d 414,
616 N.E.2d 1179 (8th Dist. Cuyahoga County 1992)
72 ALR5th 109—§ 5

State v. Brown, 85 Ohio App. 3d 716,
621 N.E.2d 447 (3d Dist. Van Wert
County 1993)
27 ALR5th 593—§ 17
83 ALR5th 277—§ 9
84 ALR5th 487—§ 21, 25

State v. Brown, 90 Ohio App. 3d 674,
630 N.E.2d 397 (Portage Co. 1993)
30 ALR5th 683—§ 2, 14

State v. Brown, 95 Iowa 381, 64 N.W.
277 (1895)
93 ALR5th 327—§ 3, 4, 7, 9

State v. Brown, 99 Ohio App. 3d 604,
651 N.E.2d 470 (10th Dist. Franklin
County 1994)
79 ALR6th 125—§ 5

State v. Brown, 103 S.C. 437, 88 S.E. 21
(1916)
81 ALR5th 563—§ 3, 7, 8

State v. Brown, 103 S.W.3d 923 (Mo.
Ct. App. W.D. 2003)
108 ALR5th 593—§ 5.5

State v. Brown, 108 S.C. 490, 95 S.E. 61
(1918)
16 ALR6th 329—§ 4, 7

State v. Brown, 109 Or. App. 636, 820
P.2d 878 (1991)
106 ALR5th 397—§ 5

State v. Brown, 110 Ohio App. 57, 12
Ohio Ops. 2d 227, 168 N.E.2d 419
(Summit Co. 1953)
14 ALR5th 89—§ 2

State v. Brown, 111 Wash. 2d 124, 761
P.2d 588 (1988)
84 ALR5th 487—§ 25

State v. Brown, 112 P.3d 963 (Kan. Ct.
App. 2005)
26 ALR6th 511—§ 25

State v. Brown, 113 Wash. 2d 520, 782
P.2d 1013, 80 A.L.R.4th 989 (1989)
82 ALR5th 359—§ 2, 4
83 ALR5th 277—§ 2, 11
84 ALR5th 487—§ 2, 18, 21, 25

State v. Brown, 116 N.M. 705, 866 P.2d
1172 (Ct. App. 1993)
105 ALR5th 529—§ 2, 15

State v. Brown, 119 Wash. App. 1073,
2004 WL 27207 (Div. 2 2004)
**125 ALR5th 537—§ 2, 11, 15, 24, 40
to 43, 49**

State v. Brown, 121 R.I. 422, 399 A.2d
1222 (1979)
19 ALR6th 697—§ 3, 9

State v. Brown, 123 Wash. App. 1053,
2004 WL 2378421 (Div. 1 2004)
45 ALR6th 643—§ 11

State v. Brown, 125 N.H. 346, 480 A.2d
901 (1984)
70 ALR6th 361—§ 29

CASES CITED IN ALR5th and ALR6th

State v. Brown, 127 Wash. 2d 749, 903
P.2d 459 (1995)
7 ALR6th 233—§ 3, 6
State v. Brown, 128 N.H. 606, 517 A.2d
831 (1986)
73 ALR5th 615—§ 3, 7, 9
State v. Brown, 132 Wash. 2d 529, 940
P.2d 546 (1997)
87 ALR5th 181—§ 6
State v. Brown, 141 Wash. App. 1019,
2007 WL 3195199 (Div. 2 2007)
75 ALR6th 443—§ 12
State v. Brown, 150 N.C. 867, 64 S.E.
775 (1909)
102 ALR5th 525—§ 13
State v. Brown, 156 N.C. App. 217, 575
S.E.2d 72 (2003)
38 ALR6th 439—§ 4
State v. Brown, 157 N.H. 555, 953 A.2d
1174 (2008)
70 ALR6th 361—§ 26, 30, 33
State v. Brown, 163 Conn. 52, 301 A.2d
547 (1972)
7 ALR6th 169—§ 8
State v. Brown, 168 Ohio App. 3d 314,
2006-Ohio-4174, 859 N.E.2d 1017
(11th Dist. Trumbull County 2006)
33 ALR6th 407—§ 49, 50
State v. Brown, 169 Conn. 692, 364
A.2d 186 (1975)
10 ALR6th 31—§ 10
State v. Brown, 170 N.J. 138, 784 A.2d
1244 (2001)
19 ALR6th 115—§ 4, 7, 10
State v. Brown, 170 Ohio App. 3d 235,
2007-Ohio-179, 866 N.E.2d 584 (2d
Dist. Montgomery County 2007)
55 ALR6th 391—§ 21
State v. Brown, 173 P.3d 612 (Kan.
2007)
30 ALR6th 1—§ 3, 7
State v. Brown, 181 Kan. 375, 312 P.2d
832 (1957)
39 ALR5th 283—§ 4
State v. Brown, 188 N.J. Super. 656, 458
A.2d 165 (Law Div. 1983)
4 ALR5th 1—§ 4, 7

68 ALR5th 299—§ 3, 4, 6
State v. Brown, 191 Wis. 2d 361, 530
N.W.2d 70 (Ct. App. 1995)
81 ALR6th 505—§ 11
State v. Brown, 200 Or. App. 427, 115
P.3d 254 (2005)
46 ALR6th 241—§ 39
State v. Brown, 216 N.J. 508, 83 A.3d
45 (2014)
99 ALR6th 397—§ 13
State v. Brown, 219 N.J. Super. 412, 530
A.2d 402 (Law Div. 1987)
24 ALR6th 591—§ 6
State v. Brown, 225 Neb. 418, 405
N.W.2d 600 (1987)
28 ALR6th 505—§ 9
State v. Brown, 227 N.J. Super. 429, 547
A.2d 743 (1988)
27 ALR5th 593—§ 3, 6, 7, 9, 12
State v. Brown, 230 Kan. 499, 638 P.2d
912 (1982)
22 ALR5th 1—§ 6, 49
State v. Brown, 245 Kan. 604, 783 P.2d
1278 (1989)
4 ALR5th 1—§ 4, 7
State v. Brown, 247 N.C. 539, 101
S.E.2d 418 (1958)
29 ALR5th 59—§ 3, 69, 76
State v. Brown, 258 Neb. 330, 603
N.W.2d 419 (1999)
84 ALR6th 427—§ 10, 27
State v. Brown, 279 Conn. 493, 903
A.2d 169 (2006)
71 ALR6th 1—§ 5
State v. Brown, 282 N.J. Super. 538, 660
A.2d 1221 (App. Div. 1995)
18 ALR6th 1—§ 5, 30
29 ALR6th 1—§ 4
State v. Brown, 297 Or. 404, 687 P.2d
751 (1984)
90 ALR5th 453—§ 19
State v. Brown, 298 Wis. 2d 548, 2007
WI App 19, 727 N.W.2d 373 (Ct.
App. 2006)
69 ALR6th 579—§ 6
State v. Brown, 306 Or. 599, 761 P.2d
1300 (1988)

7 ALR5th 73—§ 5
State v. Brown, 310 Or. 347, 800 P.2d 259 (1990)
57 ALR5th 141—§ 3
65 ALR6th 359—§ 10
State v. Brown, 311 N.J. Super. 273, 709 A.2d 845 (Law Div. 1997)
34 ALR5th 723—§ 3
State v. Brown, 325 N.C. 427, 383 S.E.2d 910 (1989)
83 ALR6th 465—§ 18, 23, 68, 78
State v. Brown, 340 So. 2d 1306 (La. 1976)
28 ALR6th 505—§ 9
State v. Brown, 341 So. 2d 1 (La. 1976)
62 ALR5th 121—§ 6
State v. Brown, 356 Ark. 460, 156 S.W.3d 722 (2004)
15 ALR6th 515—§ 33
State v. Brown, 368 So. 2d 961 (La. 1978)
99 ALR6th 295—§ 7
State v. Brown, 370 So. 2d 547 (La. 1979)
37 ALR5th 1—§ 3
69 ALR5th 425—§ 4, 5, 9
State v. Brown, 389 S.C. 84, 697 S.E.2d 622 (Ct. App. 2010)
81 ALR6th 505—§ 39
State v. Brown, 397 N.W.2d 689 (Iowa 1986)
16 ALR6th 329—§ 4
24 ALR6th 591—§ 4, 12
State v. Brown, 408 So. 2d 846 (Fla. Dist. Ct. App. 2d Dist. 1982)
68 ALR5th 343—§ 3
State v. Brown, 444 So. 2d 1346 (La. App. 2d Cir. 1984)
42 ALR5th 581—§ 5
State v. Brown, 449 S.W.2d 664 (Mo. 1970)
8 ALR5th 713—§ 5, 14
State v. Brown, 466 N.W.2d 702 (Iowa App. 1990)
34 ALR5th 125—§ 14
State v. Brown, 486 A.2d 595 (R.I. 1985)
89 ALR5th 629—§ 3, 7

58 ALR6th 385—§ 40
State v. Brown, 488 A.2d 1217 (R.I. 1985)
101 ALR6th 331—§ 17
State v. Brown, 522 So. 2d 1110 (La. Ct. App. 1st Cir. 1988)
9 ALR6th 1—§ 17
State v. Brown, 539 So. 2d 532 (Fla. Dist. Ct. App. 3d Dist. 1989)
109 ALR5th 99—§ 3
State v. Brown, 558 So. 2d 1054, 15 FLW 660 (Fla. App. D2 1990)
55 ALR5th 125—§ 3, 7
State v. Brown, 562 So. 2d 408 (Fla. Dist. Ct. App. 2d Dist. 1990)
72 ALR5th 1—§ 2, 29
State v. Brown, 562 So. 2d 868 (La. 1990)
57 ALR5th 141—§ 6
State v. Brown, 564 So. 2d 136 (Fla. Dist. Ct. App. 2d Dist. 1990)
85 ALR5th 1—§ 2
State v. Brown, 579 So. 2d 375, 16 FLW D 1317 (Fla. App. D4 1991)
27 ALR5th 593—§ 16
State v. Brown, 579 So. 2d 376, 16 FLW D 1319 (Fla. App. D4 1991)
27 ALR5th 593—§ 16
State v. Brown, 585 So. 2d 1211 (La. 1991)
99 ALR6th 295—§ 7
State v. Brown, 594 So. 2d 372 (La. Ct. App. 1st Cir. 1991)
99 ALR6th 295—§ 21
State v. Brown, 606 So. 2d 586 (La. App. 5th Cir. 1992)
27 ALR5th 593—§ 7, 9, 12
State v. Brown, 620 So. 2d 508 (La. Ct. App. 4th Cir. 1993)
101 ALR5th 187—§ 5
State v. Brown, 643 S.W.2d 68 (Mo. Ct. App. W.D. 1982)
96 ALR6th 269—§ 11
State v. Brown, 648 So. 2d 872 (La. 1995)
27 ALR5th 593—§ 3, 6, 7, 10, 12

State v. Brown, 660 So. 2d 123 (La. Ct.
App. 2d Cir. 1995)
73 ALR5th 383—§ 5
State v. Brown, 664 S.W.2d 318 (Tenn.
Crim. App. 1983)
9 ALR6th 1—§ 17
State v. Brown, 694 So. 2d 435 (La. Ct.
App. 5th Cir. 1997)
55 ALR6th 157—§ 65
99 ALR6th 113—§ 7, 22
State v. Brown, 698 S.W.2d 9 (Mo. Ct.
App. E.D. 1985)
9 ALR6th 1—§ 6
State v. Brown, 699 S.W.2d 512 (Mo.
Ct. App. E.D. 1985)
42 ALR6th 237—§ 4
State v. Brown, 708 S.W.2d 140 (Mo.
1986)
19 ALR5th 470—§ 12
State v. Brown, 717 So. 2d 625 (Fla.
Dist. Ct. App. 5th Dist. 1998)
113 ALR5th 597—§ 8
State v. Brown, 719 So. 2d 146 (La. Ct.
App. 2d Cir. 1998)
90 ALR5th 453—§ 12
38 ALR6th 439—§ 5
State v. Brown, 733 So. 2d 1282 (La. Ct.
App. 4th Cir. 1999)
17 ALR6th 327—§ 12
State v. Brown, 746 So. 2d 643 (La. Ct.
App. 4th Cir. 1999)
99 ALR6th 113—§ 11, 17
State v. Brown, 750 So. 2d 262 (La. Ct.
App. 5th Cir. 1999)
19 ALR5th 470—§ 12
State v. Brown, 771 P.2d 1093 (Utah Ct.
App. 1989)
84 ALR5th 487—§ 21
State v. Brown, 782 So. 2d 646 (La. Ct.
App. 4th Cir. 2001)
30 ALR6th 483—§ 44
State v. Brown, 784 S.W.2d 903 (Mo.
App. 1990)
3 ALR5th 784—§ 13, 16, 20
State v. Brown, 793 So. 2d 422 (La. Ct.
App. 4th Cir. 2001)
99 ALR6th 295—§ 5, 10, 19

State v. Brown, 801 S.W.2d 474 (Mo.
Ct. App. S.D. 1990)
23 ALR6th 307—§ 40
State v. Brown, 814 S.W.2d 304 (Mo.
Ct. App. W.D. 1991)
55 ALR6th 513—§ 5
State v. Brown, 824 S.W.2d 924 (Mo.
App. 1992)
39 ALR5th 283—§ 4
State v. Brown, 836 S.W.2d 530 (Tenn.
1992)
31 ALR6th 465—§ 3, 15, 29
State v. Brown, 871 S.W.2d 492 (Tenn.
Crim. App. 1993)
39 ALR6th 257—§ 18
State v. Brown, 902 S.W.2d 278 (Mo.
1995)
72 ALR5th 109—§ 5
State v. Brown, 948 P.2d 337 (Utah
1997)
10 ALR6th 463—§ 3, 4, 8
State v. Brown, 958 S.W.2d 574 (Mo.
Ct. App. W.D. 1997)
20 ALR5th 398—§ 3
State v. Brown, 966 S.W.2d 332 (Mo.
Ct. App. W.D. 1998)
47 ALR5th 259—§ 3, 4, 16
State v. Brown, 974 S.W.2d 630 (Mo.
Ct. App. S.D. 1998)
105 ALR5th 529—§ 13
State v. Brown, 998 S.W.2d 531 (Mo.
1999)
70 ALR5th 587—§ 25
9 ALR6th 1—§ 22
State v. Brown., 1977 WL 201487 (Ohio
Ct. App. 8th Dist. Cuyahoga County
1977)
19 ALR6th 697—§ 14
State v. Brown, 1980 WL 352548 (Ohio
Ct. App. 2d Dist. Montgomery
County 1980)
99 ALR6th 295—§ 7
State v. Brown, 1993 WL 129325 (Ohio
Ct. App. 9th Dist. Summit County
1993)
72 ALR5th 1—§ 31
State v. Brown, 1993 WL 500567 (Minn.
Ct. App. 1993)

57 ALR5th 141—§ 3
State v. Brown, 1994 WL 705378 (Minn. Ct. App. 1994)
19 ALR6th 697—§ 8
State v. Brown, 1996 WL 74698 (Ohio App. 2 Dist.)
50 ALR5th 581—§ 3, 7, 9
State v. Brown, 1996 WL 474012 (Tenn. Crim. App. 1996)
99 ALR6th 295—§ 5, 19
State v. Brown, 1997 WL 219117 (Ohio Ct. App. 5th Dist. Stark County 1997)
92 ALR6th 549—§ 26, 42
State v. Brown, 1998 WL 827566 (Ohio Ct. App. 8th Dist. Cuyahoga County 1998)
32 ALR6th 171—§ 3, 5, 11, 22
33 ALR6th 1—§ 3, 5
State v. Brown, 2000 WL 528636 (Conn. Super. Ct. 2000)
52 ALR6th 125—§ 11, 46
State v. Brown, 2001-Ohio-3175, 2001 WL 103958 (Ohio Ct. App. 7th Dist. Mahoning County 2001)
21 ALR6th 1—§ 4
State v. Brown, 2001 WL 741639 (Ga. Ct. App. 2001)
42 ALR5th 291—§ 17
State v. Brown, 2002-Ohio-5455, 2002 WL 31261718 (Ohio Ct. App. 12th Dist. Warren County 2002)
71 ALR6th 1—§ 9
State v. Brown, 2003 MT 166, 316 Mont. 310, 71 P.3d 1215 (2003)
11 ALR6th 237—§ 16
State v. Brown, 2003-Ohio-4762, 2003 WL 22077854 (Ohio Ct. App. 10th Dist. Franklin County 2003)
125 ALR5th 537—§ 39, 51
State v. Brown, 2004-Ohio-4058, 2004 WL 1730132 (Ohio Ct. App. 2d Dist. Montgomery County 2004)
97 ALR6th 653—§ 29
State v. Brown, 2004 WL 193092 (Minn. Ct. App. 2004)
98 ALR6th 455—§ 29

State v. Brown, 2004 WL 424257 (Conn. Super. Ct. 2004)
62 ALR6th 161—§ 27
State v. Brown, 2004 WL 2083925 (Tenn. Crim. App. 2004)
26 ALR6th 511—§ 25, 27
State v. Brown, 2006-Ohio-1905, 2006 WL 1009007 (Ohio Ct. App. 9th Dist. Summit County 2006)
26 ALR6th 511—§ 18
State v. Brown, 2006-Ohio-6267, 2006 WL 3446238 (Ohio Ct. App. 8th Dist. Cuyahoga County 2006)
30 ALR6th 1—§ 3, 4, 6, 7
State v. Brown, 2007-Ohio-5016, 2007 WL 2773848 (Ohio Ct. App. 10th Dist. Franklin County 2007)
69 ALR6th 1—§ 21
State v. Brown, 2009 WL 3246603 (Tenn. Crim. App. 2009)
56 ALR6th 1—§ 3, 18
State v. Brown, 2010 Ark. 483, 2010 WL 5059593 (2010)
69 ALR6th 1—§ 25
State v. Brown, 2011 WL 887785 (Ariz. Ct. App. Div. 1 2011)
84 ALR6th 427—§ 4
State v. Brown, 2012 WL 360290 (N.J. Super. Ct. App. Div. 2012)
99 ALR6th 397—§ 3, 7
State v. Brown, 2013-Ohio-1099, 988 N.E.2d 924 (Ohio Ct. App. 11th Dist. Lake County 2013)
103 ALR6th 247—§ 6
State v. Browne, 84 Conn. App. 351, 854 A.2d 13 (2004)
84 ALR6th 427—§ 4, 13
State v. Browne, 86 N.J. Super. 217, 206 A.2d 591 (1965)
44 ALR5th 193—§ 4, 34
State v. Brownell, 696 S.W.2d 362 (Tenn. Crim. App. 1985)
93 ALR5th 527—§ 15
State v. Browning, 28 N.C. App. 376, 221 S.E.2d 375 (1976)
67 ALR5th 637—§ 5, 9

State v. Brownlee, 2009-Ohio-5396, 2009 WL 3246841 (Ohio Ct. App. 2d Dist. Greene County 2009)
77 ALR6th 197—§ 5

State v. Brown, No. 52098, Slip Op. (Ohio App. Cuyahoga Co. 1987)
45 ALR5th 591—§ 3

State v. Brownson, 157 Wis. 2d 404, 459 N.W.2d 877 (Ct. App. 1990)
88 ALR6th 203—§ 17, 65

State v. Brownson, 189 Wis. 2d 493, 527 N.W.2d 400 (Ct. App. 1994)
88 ALR6th 203—§ 66

State v. Brubaker, 184 Mont. 294, 602 P.2d 974 (1979)
38 ALR5th 433—§ 36

State v. Bruce, 95 Ohio App. 3d 169, 642 N.E.2d 12 (Butler Co. 1994)
15 ALR5th 391—§ 5, 48

State v. Bruce, 126 Vt. 367, 231 A.2d 107 (1967)
52 ALR5th 655—§ 3

State v. Bruce, 556 So. 2d 129 (La. App. 5th Cir. 1990)
29 ALR5th 59—§ 58

State v. Bruce, 655 S.W.2d 66 (Mo. Ct. App. E.D. 1983)
62 ALR5th 629—§ 4

State v. Bruce, 779 P.2d 646 (Utah 1989)
82 ALR5th 359—§ 3, 5
83 ALR5th 277—§ 9, 11
84 ALR5th 487—§ 21
103 ALR6th 347—§ 15

State v. Bruckner, 151 Wis. 2d 833, 447 N.W.2d 376 (App. 1989)
42 ALR5th 291—§ 8, 14, 18

State v. Bruckner, 151 Wis. 2d 833, 447 N.W.2d 376 (Ct. App. 1989)
74 ALR6th 69—§ 19

State v. Brude, 222 N.W.2d 296 (N.D. 1974)
2 ALR5th 725—§ 13

State v. Bruggeman, 152 P.3d 689 (Kan. Ct. App. 2007)
84 ALR6th 293—§ 33

State v. Brumage, 435 N.W.2d 337 (Iowa 1989)
71 ALR5th 1—§ 41

State v. Brumfield, 358 S.E.2d 801 (W. Va. 1987)
39 ALR5th 283—§ 4, 75

State v. Brumfield, 737 So. 2d 660 (La. 1998)
20 ALR5th 177—§ 3

State v. Brumley, 1996 WL 210767 (Ohio Ct. App. 11th Dist. Portage County 1996)
65 ALR6th 359—§ 8

State v. Brummall, 51 S.W.3d 113 (Mo. Ct. App. W.D. 2001)
3 ALR6th 543—§ 9

State v. Brunell, 150 Vt. 388, 554 A.2d 242 (1988)
32 ALR6th 1—§ 10

State v. Bruner, 143 W. Va. 755, 105 S.E.2d 140 (1958)
20 ALR6th 479—§ 15

State v. Brunner, 211 Kan. 596, 507 P.2d 233 (1973)
30 ALR6th 103—§ 19, 25

State v. Bruno, 119 Idaho 199, 804 P.2d 928 (Ct. App. 1990)
24 ALR6th 1—§ 7

State v. Bruno, 427 So. 2d 1174 (La. 1983)
27 ALR6th 491—§ 3

State v. Brunori, 22 Conn. App. 431, 578 A.2d 139 (1990)
23 ALR6th 307—§ 46

State v. Bruns, 1998 WL 412451 (Ohio Ct. App. 2d Dist. Montgomery County 1998)
78 ALR5th 489—§ 3, 6

State v. Brunson, 103 Haw. 180, 80 P.3d 1001 (2003)
55 ALR6th 157—§ 4, 65

State v. Brunson, 180 N.C. App. 188, 636 S.E.2d 202 (2006)
67 ALR6th 103—§ 10

State v. Brunt, 53 Ohio Misc. 1, 7 Ohio Op. 3d 76, 371 N.E.2d 852 (Mun. Ct. 1977)
93 ALR5th 493—§ 3

State v. Brunzo, 248 Neb. 176, 532 N.W.2d 296 (1995)

32 ALR6th 1—§ 11

State v. Brust, 94 Or. App. 416, 765 P.2d 1246 (1988)

112 ALR5th 429—§ 11

State v. Brusven, 327 N.W.2d 591 (Minn. 1982)

73 ALR5th 383—§ 5

State v. Bruton, 27 Ohio App. 3d 362, 27 Ohio B.R. 457, 501 N.E.2d 651 (Cuyahoga Co. 1985)

43 ALR5th 777—§ 2, 4

State v. Bruyere, 751 A.2d 1285 (R.I. 2000)

98 ALR5th 445—§ 3

State v. Bruyette, 158 Vt. 21, 604 A.2d 1270 (1992)

68 ALR5th 343—§ 3, 13

State v. Bryan, 40 Wash. App. 366, 698 P.2d 1084 (Div. 2 1985)

28 ALR6th 505—§ 8

State v. Bryan, 67 N.C. App. 558, 313 S.E.2d 613 (1984)

15 ALR5th 391—§ 7

State v. Bryan, 227 So. 2d 221 (Fla. App. D2 1969)

42 ALR5th 581—§ 4

State v. Bryan, 259 Kan. 143, 910 P.2d 212 (1996)

29 ALR5th 487—§ 4

State v. Bryant, 95 Neb. 129, 145 N.W. 266 (1914)

95 ALR5th 533—§ 5
124 ALR5th 203—§ 5
6 ALR6th 229—§ 8, 22

State v. Bryant, 121 P.3d 1003 (Kan. Ct. App. 2005)

92 ALR6th 1—§ 6

State v. Bryant, 127 Idaho 24, 896 P.2d 350 (Ct. App. 1995)

94 ALR5th 393—§ 7

State v. Bryant, 163 N.C. App. 478, 594 S.E.2d 202 (2004)

93 ALR6th 1—§ 35

State v. Bryant, 178 N.C. App. 742, 632 S.E.2d 599 (2006)

33 ALR6th 91—§ 5, 11, 37

State v. Bryant, 217 N.J. Super. 72, 524 A.2d 1291 (1987)

39 ALR5th 283—§ 4, 23, 25

State v. Bryant, 337 N.C. 298, 446 S.E.2d 71 (1994)

57 ALR5th 141—§ 10

State v. Bryant, 347 So. 2d 227 (La. 1977)

62 ALR5th 121—§ 6

State v. Bryant, 351 So. 2d 1188 (La. 1977)

79 ALR5th 237—§ 11

State v. Bryant, 359 N.C. 554, 614 S.E.2d 479 (2005)

33 ALR6th 91—§ 5
34 ALR6th 171—§ 16
93 ALR6th 1—§ 35

State v. Bryant, 670 A.2d 776 (R.I. 1996)

24 ALR6th 549—§ 6

State v. Bryant, 2001 WI App 41, 241 Wis. 2d 554, 624 N.W.2d 865 (Ct. App. 2001)

81 ALR6th 505—§ 10

State v. Bryant, 2005-Ohio-3352, 2005 WL 1532617 (Ohio Ct. App. 6th Dist. Lucas County 2005)

26 ALR6th 511—§ 19

State v. Bryant, 2007 WL 2706474 (Neb. Ct. App. 2007)

72 ALR6th 227—§ 57

State v. Bryant, 2008 VT 39, 950 A.2d 467 (Vt. 2008)

45 ALR6th 643—§ 5, 14

State v. Brydon, 626 S.W.2d 443 (Mo. Ct. App. W.D. 1981)

119 ALR5th 275—§ 2

State v. Bryson, 78 Ohio App. 3d 702, 605 N.E.2d 1284 (11th Dist. Ashtabula County 1992)

69 ALR6th 207—§ 9, 10, 18

State v. Buccini, 167 Ariz. 550, 810 P.2d 178 (1991)

75 ALR6th 443—§ 3, 25

State v. Buch, 83 Haw. 308, 926 P.2d 599 (Haw. 1996)

46 ALR5th 499—§ 3

State v. Buchanan, 8 Or. App. 150, 493 P.2d 184 (1972)

34 ALR5th 125—§ 6, 13

State v. Buchanan, 108 N.C. App. 338, 423 S.E.2d 819 (1992)

15 ALR5th 391—§ 5

State v. Buchanan, 178 Wis. 2d 441, 504 N.W.2d 400 (App. 1993)

50 ALR5th 581—§ 2, 3, 7, 9, 14, 20

State v. Buchanan, 353 N.C. 332, 543 S.E.2d 823 (2001)

32 ALR6th 1—§ 8, 10

State v. Buchanan, 431 N.W.2d 542 (Minn. 1988)

9 ALR6th 1—§ 22

State v. Buchanan, 432 S.W.2d 342 (Mo. 1968)

103 ALR5th 463—§ 3

State v. Buchanan, 463 So. 2d 660 (La. Ct. App. 4th Cir. 1985)

80 ALR6th 599—§ 8

State v. Buchanan, 2001 WL 477122 (Minn. Ct. App. 2001)

47 ALR6th 423—§ 4

State v. Buck, 139 Vt. 310, 428 A.2d 1090 (1981)

66 ALR5th 397—§ 25

State v. Buck, 210 Wis. 2d 115, 565 N.W.2d 168 (Ct. App. 1997)

30 ALR6th 103—§ 59

State v. Buckles, 1999 MT 79, 294 Mont. 95, 979 P.2d 177 (1999)

55 ALR6th 391—§ 18
56 ALR6th 185—§ 37

State v. Bucklew, 973 S.W.2d 83 (Mo. 1998)

79 ALR5th 33—§ 25

State v. Buckley, 2011 WL 5353083 (Ariz. Ct. App. Div. 2 2011)

97 ALR6th 263—§ 5

State v. Buckman, 18 Fla. 267, 1881 WL 2967 (1881)

10 ALR6th 31—§ 47

State v. Buckman, 259 Neb. 924, 613 N.W.2d 463 (2000)

32 ALR6th 1—§ 5

State v. Buckman, 267 Neb. 505, 675 N.W.2d 372 (2004)

125 ALR5th 497—§ 4

72 ALR6th 227—§ 51

State v. Buckmeir, 902 S.W.2d 418 (Tenn. Crim. App. 1995)

73 ALR5th 383—§ 29

State v. Buckner, 472 So. 2d 1228, 26 Ed. Law Rep. 903 (Fla. Dist. Ct. App. 2d Dist. 1985)

70 ALR5th 169—§ 7

State v. Buckner, 1989 WL 144909 (Tenn. Crim. App. 1989)

72 ALR5th 529—§ 2

State v. Buckner, 1995 WL 479600 (Minn. Ct. App. 1995)

73 ALR5th 383—§ 6, 32

State v. Buckwald, 2000 WL 1859845 (Ohio Ct. App. 9th Dist. Lorain County 2000)

29 ALR6th 237—§ 24

State v. Budden, 226 Kan. 150, 595 P.2d 1138 (1979)

52 ALR5th 655—§ 5

State v. Buddenhagen, 149 P.3d 25 (Kan. Ct. App. 2006)

26 ALR6th 511—§ 25

State v. Buddhu, 264 Conn. 449, 825 A.2d 48 (2003)

6 ALR6th 533—§ 19

State v. Budgetts, 771 S.W.2d 902 (Mo. Ct. App. W.D. 1989)

123 ALR5th 221—§ 10

State v. Budke, 372 N.W.2d 799 (Minn. Ct. App. 1985)

59 ALR6th 393—§ 10

State v. Buehler, 206 Or. App. 167, 136 P.3d 64 (2006)

26 ALR6th 511—§ 27

State v. Buell, 22 Ohio St. 3d 124, 22 Ohio B.R. 203, 489 N.E.2d 795 (1986)

39 ALR5th 283—§ 14

State v. Buell, No. 11626 (November 15, 1984, Ct. App. Ohio, 9th App. Dist. Summit Co.)

39 ALR5th 283—§ 14, 79

State v. Buff, 34 S.W.3d 856 (Mo. Ct. App. E.D. 2000)

105 ALR5th 529—§ 13

State v. Buffington, 20 Kan. 599 (1878)

For assistance, call 1-800-328-4880

51 ALR5th 603—§ 3, 14
State v. Bufford, 1997 WL 122781 (Tenn. Crim. App. 1997)
73 ALR5th 383—§ 4
State v. Buford, 65 N.M. 51, 331 P.2d 1110, 82 A.L.R.2d 787 (1958)
6 ALR5th 733—§ 25
69 ALR6th 207—§ 22
State v. Buford, 820 P.2d 1381 (Utah Ct. App. 1991)
67 ALR5th 361—§ 2 to 4
State v. Buford, 907 S.W.2d 316 (Mo. Ct. App. E.D. 1995)
23 ALR6th 307—§ 38
State v. Bugger, 25 Utah 2d 404, 483 P.2d 442 (1971)
92 ALR6th 295—§ 12
93 ALR6th 207—§ 4
96 ALR6th 355—§ 44
State v. Buggs, 219 Kan. 203, 547 P.2d 720 (1976)
39 ALR5th 283—§ 4, 15, 17, 18, 36, 41, 70
State v. Buhl, 269 N.J. Super. 344, 635 A.2d 562 (App. Div. 1994)
39 ALR5th 283—§ 4
97 ALR5th 201—§ 3
70 ALR6th 361—§ 32
State v. Buhl, 1998 WL 40493 (Minn. Ct. App. 1998)
6 ALR6th 533—§ 19
State v. Buhl, 2012 WL 4902683 (Conn. Super. Ct. 2012)
81 ALR6th 257—§ 18
State v. Buhrman, 1997 WL 566154 (Ohio Ct. App. 2d Dist. Greene County 1997)
24 ALR6th 1—§ 21
State v. Bulgin, 120 Idaho 878, 820 P.2d 1235 (App. 1991)
51 ALR5th 375—§ 3, 4
State v. Bulhoes, 430 A.2d 1274 (R.I. 1981)
24 ALR5th 428—§ 6, 7
State v. Bull, 268 N.J. Super. 504, 634 A.2d 101 (App. Div. 1993)
22 ALR5th 1—§ 6, 9

State v. Bullcoming, 2010-NMSC-007, 147 N.M. 487, 226 P.3d 1 (2010)
66 ALR6th 635—§ 16
State v. Buller, 517 N.W.2d 711 (Iowa 1994)
81 ALR5th 563—§ 3
State v. Bullin, 150 N.C. App. 631, 564 S.E.2d 576 (2002)
78 ALR6th 297—§ 39, 57
State v. Bull Inv. Group, Inc., 32 Conn. Supp. 279, 351 A.2d 879, Blue Sky L. Rep. (CCH) ¶ 71279 (Super. Ct. 1974)
48 ALR6th 511—§ 17, 19
State v. Bullock, 26 Ariz. App. 149, 546 P.2d 1158 (Div. 2 1976)
71 ALR6th 1—§ 5
State v. Bullock, 135 Or. App. 303, 899 P.2d 709 (1995)
15 ALR5th 391—§ 39
State v. Bullock, 272 Mont. 361, 901 P.2d 61 (1995)
59 ALR5th 615—§ 3, 4, 12
76 ALR5th 563—§ 2, 3
45 ALR6th 643—§ 16, 19
State v. Bullock, 311 So. 2d 242 (La. 1975)
11 ALR5th 218—§ 2
State v. Bullock, 320 N.C. 780, 360 S.E.2d 689 (1987)
38 ALR5th 433—§ 11, 13
State v. Bullock, 329 So. 2d 733 (La. 1976)
11 ALR5th 218—§ 6
State v. Bullock, 576 So. 2d 453 (La. 1991)
29 ALR5th 702—§ 4, 11
State v. Bullock, 651 S.W.2d 173 (Mo. Ct. App. E.D. 1983)
86 ALR5th 59—§ 3, 4
State v. Bullock, 699 P.2d 753 (Utah 1985)
37 ALR6th 357—§ 53
State v. Bumgarner, 147 N.C. App. 409, 556 S.E.2d 324 (2001)
3 ALR6th 543—§ 8
State v. Bumpers, 270 N.C. 521, 155 S.E.2d 173 (1967)

55 ALR5th 125—§ 12

State v. Bunch, 2005-Ohio-3309, 2005 WL 1523844 (Ohio Ct. App. 7th Dist. Mahoning County 2005)

19 ALR6th 115—§ 5

24 ALR6th 591—§ 6, 10, 14

State v. Bundy, 91 Ariz. 325, 372 P.2d 329, 99 A.L.R.2d 808 (1962)

29 ALR5th 59—§ 44

State v. Bundy, 684 P.2d 58 (Utah 1984)

119 ALR5th 275—§ 8

State v. Bunker, 436 A.2d 413 (Me. 1981)

39 ALR5th 283—§ 4, 67

State v. Bunn, 66 N.C. App. 187, 310 S.E.2d 792 (1984)

15 ALR5th 391—§ 5

State v. Bunner, 234 Neb. 879, 453 N.W.2d 97 (1990)

103 ALR6th 507—§ 31

State v. Bunting, 187 N.J. Super. 506, 455 A.2d 531, 41 A.L.R.4th 808 (App. Div. 1983)

116 ALR5th 373—§ 3, 5

State v. Bunting, 2006 WL 1994573 (Tenn. Crim. App. 2006)

26 ALR6th 511—§ 22, 25

State v. Bunton, 1989 WL 121145 (Ohio Ct. App. 1st Dist. Hamilton County 1989)

70 ALR6th 361—§ 19

State v. Bunyard, 281 Kan. 392, 133 P.3d 14 (2006)

32 ALR6th 385—§ 3

State v. Bunyard, 281 Kan. 392, 133 P.3d 14, 33 A.L.R.6th 751 (2006)

33 ALR6th 353—§ 4

State v. Burak, 12 Conn. App. 613, 533 A.2d 237 (1987)

39 ALR5th 283—§ 3

State v. Burak, 201 Conn. 517, 518 A.2d 639 (1986)

12 ALR6th 267—§ 5

State v. Burch, 65 Wash. App. 828, 830 P.2d 357 (Div. 1 1992)

70 ALR5th 587—§ 21

State v. Burch, 70 N.C. App. 444, 320 S.E.2d 28 (1984)

62 ALR6th 413—§ 49

State v. Burch, 545 So. 2d 279, 14 FLW 382 (Fla. App. D4 1989)

27 ALR5th 593—§ 3, 6, 7, 10, 12 to 14, 23, 31

State v. Burch, 939 S.W.2d 525 (Mo. Ct. App. W.D. 1997)

67 ALR6th 103—§ 20

State v. Burchett, 107 Ariz. 185, 484 P.2d 181 (1971)

39 ALR5th 283—§ 3, 59

State v. Burchett, 526 So. 2d 303 (La. App. 3d Cir. 1988)

37 ALR5th 319—§ 3

State v. Burdeau, 2003 MT 201N, 317 Mont. 530, 77 P.3d 553 (2003)

125 ALR5th 537—§ 1

State v. Burdette, 259 Neb. 679, 611 N.W.2d 615 (2000)

32 ALR6th 1—§ 11

State v. Burdette, 2008 WL 4635849 (Neb. Ct. App. 2008)

72 ALR6th 227—§ 57

State v. Burdgess, 434 So. 2d 1062 (La. 1983)

37 ALR5th 515—§ 3

State v. Burdick, 186 Or. App. 460, 63 P.3d 1190 (2003)

28 ALR6th 505—§ 6, 32

State v. Burdin, 924 S.W.2d 82 (Tenn. 1996)

65 ALR5th 187—§ 2, 3, 7

State v. Burgan, 1997 WL 28242 (Ohio Ct. App. 9th Dist. Summit County 1997)

57 ALR6th 313—§ 3

State v. Burge, 195 Conn. 232, 487 A.2d 532 (1985)

22 ALR5th 1—§ 5, 7, 17, 31, 42

State v. Burge, 362 So. 2d 1371 (La. 1978)

62 ALR5th 121—§ 6

State v. Burgess, 74 N.C. 272, 1876 WL 2591 (1876)

57 ALR6th 445—§ 60

State v. Burgess, 457 S.W.2d 680 (Mo. 1970)

41 ALR5th 1—§ 3, 4, 8

State v. Burgess, 477 S.W.2d 105 (Mo. 1972)

53 ALR6th 81—§ 7

State v. Burgess, 543 So. 2d 1332 (La. 1989)

51 ALR6th 359—§ 28

State v. Burgess, 780 S.W.2d 688 (Mo. Ct. App. S.D. 1989)

86 ALR5th 59—§ 3, 5, 6

State v. Burgess, 800 S.W.2d 743 (Mo. 1990)

99 ALR6th 113—§ 16

State v. Burgess, 2001 ME 117, 776 A.2d 1223 (Me. 2001)

78 ALR6th 599—§ 8

State v. Burgos, 7 Conn. App. 265, 508 A.2d 795 (1986)

113 ALR5th 517—§ 10
27 ALR6th 491—§ 3

State v. Burgos, 613 So. 2d 588 (Fla. Dist. Ct. App. 4th Dist. 1993)

113 ALR5th 597—§ 8

State v. Burk, 49 S.W.3d 207 (Mo. Ct. App. W.D. 2001)

105 ALR5th 529—§ 13

State v. Burk, 101 N.M. 263, 680 P.2d 980 (App. 1984)

11 ALR5th 218—§ 2

State v. Burke, 51 Conn. App. 328, 723 A.2d 327 (1998)

101 ALR5th 187—§ 9

State v. Burke, 73 Ohio St. 3d 399, 1995-Ohio-290, 653 N.E.2d 242 (1995)

24 ALR6th 1—§ 21

State v. Burke, 92 Wash. 2d 474, 598 P.2d 395 (1979)

50 ALR5th 703—§ 15

State v. Burke, 110 Idaho 621, 717 P.2d 1039 (App. 1986)

41 ALR5th 171—§ 26, 95

State v. Burke, 110 Idaho 621, 717 P.2d 1039 (Ct. App. 1986)

1 ALR6th 549—§ 19

State v. Burke, 183 Wis. 2d 433, 516 N.W.2d 21 (Ct. App. 1994)

67 ALR6th 209—§ 21

State v. Burke, 225 Neb. 625, 408 N.W.2d 239 (1987)

42 ALR5th 291—§ 4, 10

State v. Burke, 235 Mont. 165, 766 P.2d 254 (1988)

99 ALR5th 557—§ 10

State v. Burke, 342 N.C. 113, 463 S.E.2d 212 (1995)

83 ALR6th 465—§ 4, 5, 13

State v. Burke, 343 N.C. 129, 469 S.E.2d 901 (1996)

57 ALR5th 141—§ 3

State v. Burke, 362 N.J. Super. 55, 826 A.2d 808, 120 A.L.R.5th 749 (App. Div. 2003)

120 ALR5th 337—§ 2, 4

State v. Burke, 574 A.2d 1217 (R.I. 1990)

3 ALR6th 269—§ 20

State v. Burke, 2000 ND 25, 606 N.W.2d 108 (N.D. 2000)

103 ALR6th 247—§ 9

State v. Burke, 2005-Ohio-7020, 2005 WL 3557641 (Ohio Ct. App. 10th Dist. Franklin County 2005)

83 ALR6th 465—§ 19, 70

State v. Burke, 2006-Ohio-1026, 2006 WL 541240 (Ohio Ct. App. 10th Dist. Franklin County 2006)

83 ALR6th 465—§ 70

State v. Burke, 2010-Ohio-1433, 2010 WL 1254292 (Ohio Ct. App. 8th Dist. Cuyahoga County 2010)

55 ALR6th 1—§ 6

State v. Burkett, 179 Ariz. 109, 876 P.2d 1144 (Ct. App. Div. 1 1993)

70 ALR6th 361—§ 11

State v. Burkett, 357 N.W.2d 632 (Iowa 1984)

93 ALR5th 327—§ 3, 7, 15
12 ALR6th 267—§ 12

State v. Burkhalter, 211 La. 342, 30 So. 2d 112 (1947)

24 ALR5th 465—§ 5, 33, 34

State v. Burkholder, 12 Ohio St. 3d 205, 12 Ohio B.R. 269, 466 N.E.2d 176 (1984)

19 ALR5th 470—§ 3, 5

State v. Burkholder, 12 Ohio St. 3d 205, 466 N.E.2d 176 (1984)

92 ALR6th 1—§ 3

State v. Burkholder, 1983 WL 2505 (Ohio Ct. App. 2d Dist. Montgomery County 1983)

92 ALR6th 1—§ 3

State v. Burkins, 94 Wash. App. 677, 973 P.2d 15 (Div. 1 1999)

73 ALR5th 383—§ 29

State v. Burkins, 1998 WL 549432 (Wash. Ct. App. Div. 1 1998)

73 ALR5th 383—§ 29

State v. Burkitt, 89 Ohio App. 3d 214, 624 N.E.2d 210 (2d Dist. Clark County 1993)

89 ALR5th 629—§ 8, 12

State v. Burmaster, 710 So. 2d 274 (La. Ct. App. 3d Cir. 1998)

35 ALR6th 127—§ 5

State v. Burnau, 642 S.W.2d 621 (Mo. 1982)

48 ALR5th 659—§ 7, 32

State v. Burnett, 4 Kan. App. 2d 412, 607 P.2d 88 (1980)

78 ALR5th 567—§ 7

State v. Burnett, 47 W. Va. 731, 35 S.E. 983 (1900)

97 ALR5th 537—§ 10

State v. Burnett, 93 Ohio St. 3d 419, 2001-Ohio-1581, 755 N.E.2d 857, 107 A.L.R.5th 821 (2001)

107 ALR5th 697—§ 2 to 4, 6

State v. Burnett, 368 Ark. 625, 249 S.W.3d 141 (2007)

69 ALR6th 1—§ 5

State v. Burnett, 768 So. 2d 783 (La. Ct. App. 2d Cir. 2000)

41 ALR6th 141—§ 7

State v. Burnett, 970 S.W.2d 412 (Mo. Ct. App. W.D. 1998)

108 ALR5th 593—§ 20

State v. Burnett, 2010 WL 611498 (Wash. Ct. App. Div. 2 2010)

55 ALR6th 1—§ 6, 39

State v. Burnette, 22 N.C. App. 29, 205 S.E.2d 357 (1974)

29 ALR5th 59—§ 14

State v. Burnette, 158 N.C. App. 716, 582 S.E.2d 339 (2003)

23 ALR6th 307—§ 44

55 ALR6th 391—§ 23

State v. Burney, 288 Conn. 548, 954 A.2d 793 (2008)

40 ALR6th 1—§ 22

State v. Burney, 302 N.C. 529, 276 S.E.2d 693, 7 Media L. Rep. (BNA) 1411 (1981)

32 ALR6th 171—§ 21

State v. Burnham, 427 A.2d 969 (Me. 1981)

27 ALR6th 183—§ 23, 36

State v. Burnight, 132 Idaho 654, 978 P.2d 214 (1999)

74 ALR5th 453—§ 5

State v. Burnison, 247 Kan. 19, 795 P.2d 32, 17 A.L.R.5th 1084 (1990)

17 ALR5th 851—§ 2, 3

State v. Burns, 23 Conn. App. 602, 583 A.2d 1296 (1990)

19 ALR6th 115—§ 5, 7, 10

State v. Burns, 85 Wash. App. 1082, 1997 WL 206066 (Div. 2 1997)

15 ALR6th 515—§ 10

State v. Burns, 112 S.W.3d 451 (Mo. Ct. App. W.D. 2003)

55 ALR6th 391—§ 5, 7

56 ALR6th 185—§ 23

State v. Burns, 142 Ariz. 531, 691 P.2d 297 (1984)

73 ALR5th 581—§ 2, 5

State v. Burns, 661 So. 2d 842 (Fla. 5th DCA 1995)

81 ALR6th 505—§ 6

State v. Burns, 661 So. 2d 842 (Fla. Dist. Ct. App. 5th Dist. 1995)

58 ALR6th 215—§ 10

State v. Burns, 723 So. 2d 1013 (La. Ct. App. 4th Cir. 1998)

106 ALR5th 377—§ 3

113 ALR5th 597—§ 7

State v. Burns, 979 S.W.2d 276 (Tenn. 1998)

79 ALR5th 33—§ 58

98 ALR6th 455—§ 11

State v. Burns, 2006-Ohio-693, 2006 WL 349610 (Ohio Ct. App. 8th Dist. Cuyahoga County 2006)
71 ALR6th 1—§ 5

State v. Burns, 2006-Ohio-2666, 2006 WL 1461074 (Ohio Ct. App. 2d Dist. Greene County 2006)
26 ALR6th 511—§ 4

State v. Burns, 2013 WL 149908 (Conn. App. Ct. 2013)
84 ALR6th 293—§ 15

State v. Burnside, 113 Idaho 65, 741 P.2d 352 (App. 1987)
41 ALR5th 171—§ 3, 10

State v. Burnside, 2009-Ohio-2653, 2009 WL 1598781 (Ohio Ct. App. 7th Dist. Mahoning County 2009)
69 ALR6th 1—§ 27

State v. Burr, 147 N.H. 102, 782 A.2d 914 (2001)
45 ALR6th 435—§ 15, 18, 28

State v. Burr, 195 N.J. 119, 948 A.2d 627 (2008)
65 ALR6th 537—§ 19, 22, 25, 41, 73, 74

State v. Burr, 392 N.J. Super. 538, 921 A.2d 1135 (App. Div. 2007)
65 ALR6th 537—§ 25

State v. Burr, 1999 ND 143, 598 N.W.2d 147 (N.D. 1999)
63 ALR6th 351—§ 3

State v. Burrell, 71 Ohio App. 3d 507, 594 N.E.2d 1059 (6th Dist. Wood County 1991)
70 ALR6th 329—§ 14

State v. Burrell, 89 Ohio App. 3d 737, 627 N.E.2d 605 (Summit Co. 1993)
38 ALR5th 433—§ 3

State v. Burrell, 2008-Ohio-1785, 2008 WL 1700417 (Ohio Ct. App. 3d Dist. Allen County 2008)
66 ALR6th 351—§ 11, 35
67 ALR6th 209—§ 40

State v. Burri, 87 Wash. 2d 175, 550 P.2d 507 (1976)
71 ALR5th 1—§ 50

State v. Burris, 131 Ariz. 563, 643 P.2d 8 (App. 1982)
32 ALR5th 149—§ 74, 99

State v. Burrough, 85 P.3d 737 (Kan. Ct. App. 2004)
26 ALR6th 511—§ 28

State v. Burroughs, 328 S.C. 489, 492 S.E.2d 408 (Ct. App. 1997)
38 ALR5th 433—§ 28

State v. Burrows, 142 Wash. App. 1008, 2007 WL 4296369 (Div. 1 2007)
64 ALR6th 1—§ 7

State v. Burrows, 295 N.W.2d 100 (Minn. 1980)
83 ALR5th 277—§ 13

State v. Burrows, 2007 WL 4296369 (Wash. Ct. App. Div. 1 2007)
33 ALR6th 91—§ 5

State v. Burrows, No. 3907 (January 22, 1986, Ct. App. Ohio, 9th App. Dist. Lorain Co.)
39 ALR5th 283—§ 14, 73

State v. Burrus, 151 Ariz. 581, 729 P.2d 935 (1986)
51 ALR6th 1—§ 24
52 ALR6th 1—§ 18, 30

State v. Burrus, 344 N.C. 79, 472 S.E.2d 867 (1996)
57 ALR5th 141—§ 7

State v. Burse, 600 S.W.2d 250 (Tenn. Crim. 1979)
29 ALR5th 59—§ 3, 17

State v. Burss, 316 Or. 1, 848 P.2d 596 (1993)
70 ALR6th 361—§ 19

State v. Burt, 17 S.D. 7, 94 N.W. 409 (1903)
119 ALR5th 275—§ 13

State v. Burt, 24 Wash. App. 867, 605 P.2d 342 (Div. 2 1979)
29 ALR6th 1—§ 10

State v. Burt, 60 Ariz. Adv. Rep. 48 (Ariz. App. 1990)
54 ALR5th 141—§ 3 to 5, 11

State v. Burt, 249 N.W.2d 651 (Iowa 1977)
55 ALR6th 157—§ 9

State v. Burton, 101 Wash. 2d 1, 676 P.2d 975 (1984)

82 ALR5th 359—§ 4

84 ALR5th 487—§ 21, 25

State v. Burton, 112 Wis. 2d 560, 334 N.W.2d 263 (1983)

33 ALR5th 205—§ 5, 13, 17

State v. Burton, 119 N.C. App. 625, 460 S.E.2d 181 (1995)

16 ALR6th 329—§ 6

24 ALR6th 591—§ 6, 14

State v. Burton, 121 Or. App. 508, 855 P.2d 1124 (1993)

103 ALR5th 463—§ 3

State v. Burton, 155 Wash. App. 1006, 2010 WL 918078 (Div. 3 2010)

57 ALR6th 445—§ 28

State v. Burton, 302 S.C. 494, 397 S.E.2d 90 (1989)

50 ALR5th 467—§ 2, 8, 9

State v. Burton, 556 N.W.2d 600 (Minn. App. 1996)

50 ALR5th 581—§ 3, 5, 7, 16, 24

State v. Burton, 727 So. 2d 518 (La. Ct. App. 4th Cir. 1998)

16 ALR6th 329—§ 4

24 ALR6th 591—§ 4, 14

State v. Burton, 751 S.W.2d 440 (Tenn. Crim. 1988)

42 ALR5th 581—§ 14

State v. Burton, 800 P.2d 817 (Utah Ct. App. 1990)

57 ALR6th 445—§ 20

State v. Burton, 808 N.W.2d 755 (Iowa Ct. App. 2011)

97 ALR6th 653—§ 19

State v. Burton, 1994 WL 29885 (Ohio App. Warren Co. 1994)

52 ALR5th 655—§ 3

State v. Burton, 1996 WL 315824 (Tenn. Crim. App. 1996)

73 ALR5th 383—§ 25

State v. Burton, 2000 WL 1132771 (Ohio Ct. App. 6th Dist. Wood County 2000)

9 ALR6th 541—§ 29

State v. Burtzlaff, 493 N.W.2d 1 (S.D. 1992)

58 ALR5th 749—§ 6, 10

State v. Burwell, 2001 WL 1607012 (Minn. Ct. App. 2001)

113 ALR5th 597—§ 8

State v. Busacker, 154 Or. App. 528, 962 P.2d 723 (1998)

47 ALR6th 107—§ 19

State v. Busby, 653 So. 2d 140 (La. Ct. App. 3d Cir. 1995)

102 ALR5th 327—§ 9

24 ALR6th 1—§ 43

State v. Busch, 76 Ohio St. 3d 613, 669 N.E.2d 1125 (1996)

71 ALR5th 1—§ 26

State v. Buscham, 360 N.J. Super. 346, 823 A.2d 71 (App. Div. 2003)

39 ALR6th 257—§ 19, 47

40 ALR6th 1—§ 25

State v. Buscher, 45 Wash. App. 141, 724 P.2d 411 (Div. 1 1986)

71 ALR5th 1—§ 36

State v. Bush, 34 Wash. App. 121, 659 P.2d 1127 (1983)

15 ALR5th 391—§ 7

State v. Bush, 174 Or. App. 280, 25 P.3d 368 (2001)

103 ALR5th 463—§ 3

State v. Bush, 185 Wis. 2d 716, 519 N.W.2d 645 (App. 1994)

22 ALR5th 660—§ 15

State v. Bush, 260 N.W.2d 226 (S.D. 1977)

72 ALR5th 529—§ 7

State v. Bush, 942 S.W.2d 489 (Tenn. 1997)

32 ALR6th 1—§ 11

State v. Buss, 76 Wash. App. 780, 887 P.2d 920 (Div. 1 1995)

93 ALR5th 327—§ 3, 9

101 ALR5th 619—§ 3

State v. Bussard, 494 S.W.2d 401 (Mo. Ct. App. 1973)

37 ALR6th 357—§ 25

State v. Bussart, 29 Kan. App. 2d 996, 35 P.3d 281 (2001)

26 ALR6th 511—§ 25

State v. Bustos-Anaya, 131 Wash. App. 1026, 2006 WL 226718 (Div. 2 2006)
49 ALR6th 343—§ 14

State v. Butchek, 121 Or. 141, 253 P. 367 (1927)
24 ALR5th 465—§ 62, 63, 69

State v. Butenhoff, 392 N.W.2d 619 (Minn. Ct. App. 1986)
73 ALR5th 383—§ 4

State v. Buterbaugh, 1999 WL 717268 (Ohio Ct. App. 10th Dist. Franklin County 1999)
89 ALR6th 565—§ 20, 27

State v. Butler, 11 Ohio St. 2d 23, 40 Ohio Op. 2d 43, 227 N.E.2d 627, 21 A.L.R.3d 102 (1967)
89 ALR6th 565—§ 13, 20

State v. Butler, 53 Wash. App. 214, 766 P.2d 505 (Div. 1 1989)
38 ALR5th 433—§ 14, 15
73 ALR5th 383—§ 5

State v. Butler, 75 Wash. App. 47, 876 P.2d 481 (Div. 1 1994)
73 ALR5th 383—§ 3

State v. Butler, 79 Tenn. 418, 1883 WL 3731 (1883)
98 ALR5th 353—§ 3

State v. Butler, 108 S.W.3d 845 (Tenn. 2003)
92 ALR6th 295—§ 19
95 ALR6th 1—§ 5, 8, 25
96 ALR6th 355—§ 9, 25, 26, 36, 47

State v. Butler, 126 Wash. App. 741, 109 P.3d 493 (Div. 2 2005)
50 ALR6th 353—§ 11, 22, 23

State v. Butler, 129 Conn. App. 833, 21 A.3d 583 (2011)
72 ALR6th 227—§ 51

State v. Butler, 132 La. 597, 61 So. 682 (1913)
105 ALR5th 529—§ 11

State v. Butler, 205 N.W. 842 (Iowa 1925)
29 ALR5th 59—§ 10

State v. Butler, 296 Conn. 62, 2010 WL 1657697 (2010)
55 ALR6th 1—§ 26

State v. Butler, 331 N.C. 227, 415 S.E.2d 719 (1992)
5 ALR5th 243—§ 6, 9

State v. Butler, 496 So. 2d 916 (Fla. Dist. Ct. App. 2d Dist. 1986)
70 ALR6th 361—§ 7, 43

State v. Butler, 626 S.W.2d 6 (Tenn. 1981)
83 ALR5th 277—§ 28
84 ALR5th 487—§ 22

State v. Butler, 674 A.2d 925 (Me. 1996)
19 ALR6th 697—§ 4

State v. Butler, 676 S.W.2d 809 (Mo. 1984)
65 ALR5th 407—§ 3, 11
58 ALR6th 499—§ 21, 102

State v. Butler, 900 S.W.2d 305 (Tenn. Crim. App. 1994)
73 ALR5th 383—§ 4

State v. Butler, 2002-Ohio-774, 2002 WL 253853 (Ohio Ct. App. 5th Dist. Stark County 2002)
64 ALR6th 1—§ 29

State v. Butler, 2004 WL 1732321 (Tenn. Crim. App. 2004)
26 ALR6th 511—§ 25, 33

State v. Butler, 2006-Ohio-5919, 2006 WL 3234024 (Ohio Ct. App. 8th Dist. Cuyahoga County 2006)
71 ALR6th 335—§ 7

State v. Butler, 2007-Ohio-485, 2007 WL 353881 (Ohio Ct. App. 5th Dist. Stark County 2007)
26 ALR6th 511—§ 19

State v. Butterfield, 128 Or. App. 1, 874 P.2d 1339 (1994)
118 ALR5th 253—§ 9

State v. Butterfield, 784 P.2d 153 (Utah 1989)
32 ALR6th 171—§ 4
33 ALR6th 1—§ 20

State v. Butterfield, 2001 UT 59, 27 P.3d 1133 (Utah 2001)
38 ALR6th 439—§ 5

State v. Buttner, 489 So. 2d 970 (La. Ct. App. 4th Cir. 1986)
101 ALR5th 187—§ 3

99 ALR6th 295—§ 9, 15

State v. Butts, 938 S.W.2d 924 (Mo. Ct. App. S.D. 1997)

80 ALR5th 55—§ 8, 9

State v. Butzin, 404 N.W.2d 819 (Minn. Ct. App. 1987)

29 ALR6th 1—§ 10

State v. Butzke, 7 Neb. App. 360, 584 N.W.2d 449 (1998)

51 ALR5th 425—§ 3, 5

State v. Buyers Service Co., Inc., 292 S.C. 426, 357 S.E.2d 15 (1987)

119 ALR5th 191—§ 3

State v. Buzzard, 4 Ark. 18, 1842 WL 331 (1842)

33 ALR6th 407—§ 4, 5

State v. Buzzard, 112 Ohio St. 3d 451, 2007-Ohio-373, 860 N.E.2d 1006 (2007)

67 ALR6th 531—§ 2

State v. Buzzard, 163 Ohio App. 3d 591, 2005-Ohio-5270, 839 N.E.2d 469 (3d Dist. Crawford County 2005)

62 ALR6th 413—§ 2
69 ALR6th 275—§ 2

State v. Buzzell, 617 A.2d 1016 (Me. 1992)

69 ALR6th 579—§ 4

State v. Byas, 648 So. 2d 37 (La. Ct. App. 4th Cir. 1994)

17 ALR6th 327—§ 21

State v. Bybee, 115 Idaho 541, 768 P.2d 804 (App. 1989)

15 ALR5th 391—§ 45

State v. Bybee, 134 Ohio App. 3d 395, 731 N.E.2d 232 (1st Dist. Hamilton County 1999)

45 ALR6th 435—§ 9

State v. Byerly, 1998 WL 637689 (Ohio Ct. App. 11th Dist. Portage County 1998)

58 ALR6th 499—§ 30

State v. Byerly, 2003-Ohio-6911, 2003 WL 22971723 (Ohio Ct. App. 5th Dist. Richland County 2003)

3 ALR6th 543—§ 10

State v. Byers, 95 Or. App. 139, 768 P.2d 414 (1989)

5 ALR5th 243—§ 10

State v. Byers, 2008-Ohio-5051, 2008 WL 4416519 (Ohio Ct. App. 7th Dist. Columbiana County 2008)

64 ALR6th 1—§ 7, 9

State v. Bynum, 680 S.W.2d 156 (Mo. 1984)

110 ALR5th 329—§ 5

State v. Byrd, 30 Wash. App. 794, 638 P.2d 601 (Div. 1 1981)

79 ALR5th 419—§ 10

State v. Byrd, 39 N.C. App. 659, 251 S.E.2d 712 (1979)

42 ALR6th 237—§ 11

State v. Byrd, 50 N.C. App. 736, 275 S.E.2d 522 (1981)

55 ALR6th 157—§ 26

State v. Byrd, 60 N.C. App. 740, 300 S.E.2d 16 (1983)

109 ALR5th 99—§ 4

State v. Byrd, 83 Wash. App. 509, 922 P.2d 168 (1996)

27 ALR5th 593—§ 19, 36

State v. Byrd, 97 P.3d 528 (Kan. Ct. App. 2004)

8 ALR6th 265—§ 17

State v. Byrd, 145 Ohio App. 3d 318, 762 N.E.2d 1043 (1st Dist. Hamilton County 2001)

97 ALR6th 263—§ 22

State v. Byrd, 448 N.W.2d 29 (Iowa 1989)

105 ALR5th 529—§ 11, 25

State v. Byrd, 2003-Ohio-7168, 2003 WL 23094775 (Ohio Ct. App. 9th Dist. Lorain County 2003)

27 ALR6th 183—§ 17, 35

State v. Byrge, 1999 WL 142078 (Wis. Ct. App. 1999)

70 ALR5th 1—§ 9

State v. Byrne, 149 Vt. 224, 542 A.2d 276 (1988)

50 ALR5th 703—§ 2, 15

State v. Byrne, 261 Wis. 2d 878, 2003 WI App 67, 659 N.W.2d 507 (Ct. App. 2003)

30 ALR6th 373—§ 16

State v. Byrns, 911 P.2d 981 (Utah Ct. App. 1995)
 97 ALR5th 201—§ 2, 4
State v. Bystrom, 279 Minn. 206, 156 N.W.2d 234 (1968)
 17 ALR6th 757—§ 4
State v. Cababag, 9 Haw. App. 496, 850 P.2d 716 (1993)
 57 ALR5th 315—§ 2, 3, 5, 6, 8, 9, 11
State v. Cabalceta, 174 W. Va. 240, 324 S.E.2d 383 (1984)
 1 ALR6th 549—§ 20
State v. Caballero, 396 So. 2d 1210 (Fla. Dist. Ct. App. 3d Dist. 1981)
 72 ALR5th 1—§ 29
State v. Cabana, 315 N.J. Super. 84, 716 A.2d 576 (Law Div. 1997)
 68 ALR5th 299—§ 3
State v. Cabiness, 273 S.C. 56, 254 S.E.2d 291 (1979)
 85 ALR5th 547—§ 8
State v. Cabodi, 18 N.M. 513, 138 P. 262 (1914)
 32 ALR5th 149—§ 5, 7, 21 to 23, 31, 32, 73, 74, 76
State v. Cabral, 8 Haw. App. 506, 810 P.2d 672 (1991)
 118 ALR5th 253—§ 5, 9
State v. Cabral, 77 Haw. 216, 883 P.2d 638 (Ct. App. 1994)
 118 ALR5th 253—§ 5
 97 ALR6th 539—§ 7
State v. Cabral, 160 P.3d 481 (Kan. Ct. App. 2007)
 79 ALR6th 1—§ 22, 82
State v. Cabral, 228 Kan. 741, 619 P.2d 1163 (1980)
 39 ALR5th 283—§ 4, 58
State v. Cabral, 785 P.2d 1314 (Hawaii 1990)
 7 ALR5th 263—§ 4
State v. Cabrera, 387 N.J. Super. 81, 903 A.2d 427 (App. Div. 2006)
 32 ALR6th 1—§ 10
State v. Cabrera, 2000 WL 33113956 (Del. Super. Ct. 2000)
 81 ALR6th 505—§ 5

State v. Cabrera-Pena, 361 S.C. 372, 605 S.E.2d 522 (2004)
 27 ALR6th 183—§ 7, 34
State v. Cada, 129 Idaho 224, 923 P.2d 469 (Ct. App. 1996)
 60 ALR5th 1—§ 7
 67 ALR6th 531—§ 9
 69 ALR6th 275—§ 5, 6, 8
State v. Cadotte, 542 N.W.2d 834 (Iowa 1996)
 55 ALR5th 125—§ 2, 12, 15
State v. Caekaert, 1999 M.T. 147, 295 Mont. 42, 983 P.2d 332 (1999)
 88 ALR5th 121—§ 22, 31
State v. Caez, 81 N.J. Super. 315, 195 A.2d 496 (App. Div. 1963)
 72 ALR5th 1—§ 3
State v. Cafe Erotica, Inc., 269 Ga. 486, 500 S.E.2d 574 (1998)
 20 ALR6th 161—§ 4
 21 ALR6th 425—§ 10
 23 ALR6th 573—§ 6
State v. Caffey, 445 S.W.2d 642 (Mo. 1969)
 37 ALR6th 357—§ 69
State v. Caffey, 1980 WL 353858 (Ohio Ct. App. 10th Dist. Franklin County 1980)
 19 ALR6th 697—§ 12
State v. Cage, 703 So. 2d 1280 (La. 1997)
 38 ALR6th 97—§ 8
State v. Cager, 732 So. 2d 97, 94 A.L.R.5th 705 (La. Ct. App. 4th Cir. 1999)
 94 ALR5th 393—§ 12
State v. Caha, 184 Neb. 70, 165 N.W.2d 362 (1969)
 34 ALR6th 1—§ 12
State v. Cahill, 186 N.W.2d 587 (Iowa 1971)
 119 ALR5th 275—§ 7
State v. Cahill, 196 Iowa 486, 194 N.W. 191 (1923)
 54 ALR5th 141—§ 7
State v. Cahoon, 59 Wash. App. 606, 799 P.2d 1191 (Div. 3 1990)

58 ALR6th 499—§ 9
State v. Caibaiosai, 122 Wis. 2d 587, 363 N.W.2d 574 (1985)
47 ALR6th 107—§ 5
State v. Caillet, 518 So. 2d 1062 (La. App. 1st Cir. 1987)
6 ALR5th 733—§ 2, 5, 22
State v. Caillet, 518 So. 2d 1062 (La. Ct. App. 1st Cir. 1987)
68 ALR6th 115—§ 61
State v. Cain, 31 S.W.2d 559 (Mo. App. 1930)
41 ALR5th 171—§ 3, 10
State v. Cain, 79 N.C. App. 35, 338 S.E.2d 898 (1986)
5 ALR5th 243—§ 8
State v. Cain, 152 Ariz. 479, 733 P.2d 676 (App. 1987)
5 ALR5th 243—§ 5
State v. Cain, 297 S.C. 497, 377 S.E.2d 556 (1988)
12 ALR6th 267—§ 5
State v. Cain, 400 N.W.2d 582 (Iowa 1987)
30 ALR6th 103—§ 43
State v. Cain, 697 N.W.2d 127 (Iowa Ct. App. 2005)
55 ALR6th 513—§ 11
81 ALR6th 505—§ 20
State v. Cain, 1992 WL 3008 (Tenn. Crim. App. 1992)
1 ALR6th 549—§ 19
State v. Cain, 2006-Ohio-1779, 2006 WL 903592 (Ohio Ct. App. 3d Dist. Union County 2006)
26 ALR6th 511—§ 19
State v. Cairnes, 126 Wash. App. 1032, 2005 WL 713320 (Div. 1 2005)
45 ALR6th 643—§ 6
State v. Cairo, 74 R.I. 377, 60 A.2d 841 (1948)
65 ALR5th 407—§ 3, 14
State v. Calcagno, 120 N.J. Super. 536, 295 A.2d 366 (App. Div. 1972)
51 ALR6th 219—§ 4
State v. Caldera, 66 Wash. App. 548, 832 P.2d 139 (1992)

45 ALR5th 1—§ 5, 10, 17
State v. Calderilla, 34 Or. App. 1007, 580 P.2d 578 (1978)
92 ALR5th 35—§ 24
State v. Calderon, 233 Kan. 87, 661 P.2d 781 (1983)
37 ALR6th 357—§ 69
State v. Calderon, 2010-Ohio-2807, 2010 WL 2499657 (Ohio Ct. App. 9th Dist. Medina County 2010)
70 ALR6th 1—§ 4
State v. Caldwell, 2 Tyl. 212 (Vt. 1802)
66 ALR5th 397—§ 6, 11
State v. Caldwell, 20 Ariz. App. 331, 512 P.2d 863 (Div. 2 1973)
106 ALR5th 397—§ 4
State v. Caldwell, 53 N.C. App. 1, 279 S.E.2d 852 (1981)
109 ALR5th 99—§ 8
State v. Caldwell, 154 Wis. 2d 683, 454 N.W.2d 13 (Ct. App. 1990)
66 ALR5th 397—§ 8
State v. Caldwell, 283 S.C. 350, 322 S.E.2d 662 (1984)
85 ALR5th 187—§ 9
State v. Caldwell, 616 So. 2d 713 (La. App. 3d Cir. 1993)
18 ALR5th 1—§ 3, 14
State v. Caldwell, 1995 WL 656743 (Wis App)
50 ALR5th 581—§ 9, 23
State v. Caldwell, 2003 ME 85, 828 A.2d 765 (Me. 2003)
78 ALR6th 1—§ 14
State v. Caldwell, 2009 WL 2596084 (Minn. Ct. App. 2009)
65 ALR6th 537—§ 23
State v. Calero, 2011 WL 9325 (N.J. Super. Ct. App. Div. 2010)
74 ALR6th 373—§ 4
State v. Calhoun, 479 So. 2d 241 (Fla. Dist. Ct. App. 4th Dist. 1985)
91 ALR5th 585—§ 2, 10
State v. Calhoun, 657 S.E.2d 424 (N.C. Ct. App. 2008)
30 ALR6th 1—§ 3

State v. Calhoun, 669 So. 2d 1359 (La.
Ct. App. 1st Cir. 1996)
73 ALR5th 383—§ 5
63 ALR6th 351—§ 4
State v. Calhoun, 694 So. 2d 909 (La.
1997)
41 ALR6th 141—§ 7, 8
State v. Calhoun, 2002-Ohio-3371, 2002
WL 1401543 (Ohio Ct. App. 11th
Dist. Lake County 2002)
31 ALR6th 49—§ 10
State v. Caliguri, 99 Wash. 2d 501, 664
P.2d 466 (1983)
56 ALR5th 385—§ 6
97 ALR5th 201—§ 3, 6, 7
State v. Call, 75 Wash. App. 866, 880
P.2d 571 (Div. 3 1994)
88 ALR5th 121—§ 22, 27
State v. Call, 349 N.C. 382, 508 S.E.2d
496 (1998)
97 ALR6th 567—§ 3, 9
State v. Callaghan, 33 Or. App. 49, 576
P.2d 14 (1978)
41 ALR5th 171—§ 6, 12
State v. Callahan, 93 N.C. App. 579, 378
S.E.2d 812 (1989)
57 ALR6th 313—§ 5
State v. Callahan, 155 Vt. 571, 587 A.2d
970 (1991)
7 ALR5th 73—§ 2, 3
State v. Callahan, 1997 WL 199059
(Tenn. Crim. App. 1997)
69 ALR6th 579—§ 4
State v. Callaway, 154 Mo. 91, 55 S.W.
444 (1900)
24 ALR5th 465—§ 35
State v. Callaway, 2003 WL 21947602
(Kan. Ct. App. 2003)
9 ALR6th 541—§ 12
State v. Calle, 125 Wash. 2d 769, 888
P.2d 155 (1995)
56 ALR5th 385—§ 6
State v. Callender, 444 N.W.2d 768
(Iowa Ct. App. 1989)
99 ALR6th 113—§ 14
State v. Calmese, 628 S.W.2d 382 (Mo.
Ct. App. E.D. 1982)

28 ALR6th 505—§ 9
State v. Calor, 585 A.2d 1385 (Me.
1991)
84 ALR5th 487—§ 21
State v. Calvert, 211 Kan. 174, 505 P.2d
1110 (1973)
22 ALR5th 1—§ 5, 6, 49
State v. Calvillo, 2009 WL 6547609
(N.M. Ct. App. 2009)
71 ALR6th 1—§ 8
State v. Calvin, 209 La. 257, 24 So. 2d
467 (1945)
124 ALR5th 657—§ 8
67 ALR6th 103—§ 4, 23
State v. Camargo, 112 Ariz. 50, 537 P.2d
920 (1975)
109 ALR5th 99—§ 8
75 ALR6th 541—§ 15, 17
State v. Cambra, 9 Haw. App. 160, 828
P.2d 295 (1992)
9 ALR6th 633—§ 13
10 ALR6th 265—§ 5
State v. Cameron, 100 N.J. 586, 498
A.2d 1217 (1985)
31 ALR6th 395—§ 8
State v. Cameron, 129 Ohio App. 3d
457, 717 N.E.2d 1186 (9th Dist.
Lorain County 1998)
15 ALR5th 391—§ 30
State v. Cameron, 203 Ind. 526, 181
N.E. 160 (1932)
102 ALR5th 525—§ 3
State v. Cameron, 721 A.2d 493 (Vt.
1998)
22 ALR5th 1—§ 52
State v. Cameron, 2007-Ohio-6066,
2007 WL 3377237 (Ohio Ct. App.
8th Dist. Cuyahoga County 2007)
78 ALR6th 297—§ 37, 52
State v. Caminiti, 613 So. 2d 141, 18
FLW D 431 (Fla. App. D4 1993)
18 ALR5th 1—§ 20
State v. Camino, 118 Ariz. 89, 574 P.2d
1308 (App. 1977)
59 ALR5th 135—§ 3
State v. Camino, 118 Ariz. 89, 574 P.2d
1308 (Ct. App. Div. 2 1977)

57 ALR6th 313—§ 8
State v. Cammack, 1997 WL 104913 (Minn. Ct. App. 1997)

69 ALR6th 579—§ 8, 35
State v. Camp, 579 So. 2d 763, 16 FLW D 1113 (Fla. App. D5 1991)

29 ALR5th 59—§ 35, 80, 89
State v. Camp, 590 N.W.2d 115 (Minn. 1999)

12 ALR6th 553—§ 23
State v. Camp, 596 So. 2d 1055, 17 FLW S. 230 (Fla. 1992)

29 ALR5th 59—§ 35, 80, 89
State v. Campanponi, 424 So. 2d 163 (Fla. Dist. Ct. App. 3d Dist. 1983)

125 ALR5th 281—§ 9, 10
State v. Campbell, 14 N.C. App. 633, 188 S.E.2d 754 (1972)

78 ALR5th 567—§ 8
State v. Campbell, 15 Wash. App. 98, 547 P.2d 295 (Div. 1 1976)

58 ALR6th 499—§ 39
State v. Campbell, 42 W. Va. 246, 24 S.E. 875 (1896)

59 ALR5th 135—§ 4, 13
State v. Campbell, 43 Or. App. 979, 607 P.2d 745 (1979)

122 ALR5th 439—§ 3
State v. Campbell, 67 N.D. 581, 274 N.W. 844 (1937)

108 ALR5th 593—§ 18
State v. Campbell, 68 Ohio App. 3d 688, 589 N.E.2d 452 (1st Dist. Hamilton County 1990)

84 ALR6th 293—§ 32
State v. Campbell, 69 Ohio St. 3d 38, 630 N.E.2d 339 (1994)

82 ALR5th 67—§ 3
State v. Campbell, 74 Ohio App. 3d 352, 598 N.E.2d 1244 (Hamilton Co. 1991)

26 ALR5th 603—§ 4
State v. Campbell, 85 Ohio App. 3d 510, 620 N.E.2d 150 (Warren Co. 1993)

15 ALR5th 391—§ 22
State v. Campbell, 90 Ohio St. 3d 320, 738 N.E.2d 1178 (2000)

78 ALR5th 197—§ 10
State v. Campbell, 112 Wash. 2d 186, 770 P.2d 620 (1989)

21 ALR6th 1—§ 5
State v. Campbell, 115 Ohio App. 3d 319, 685 N.E.2d 308 (7th Dist. Columbiana County 1996)

2 ALR5th 725—§ 16
State v. Campbell, 128 Or. App. 592, 876 P.2d 799 (1994)

99 ALR5th 557—§ 3, 4
State v. Campbell, 133 N.C. App. 531, 515 S.E.2d 732 (1999)

93 ALR5th 527—§ 15
29 ALR6th 1—§ 10
State v. Campbell, 146 Mont. 251, 405 P.2d 978, 22 A.L.R.3d 824 (1965)

73 ALR5th 615—§ 3, 6, 9
State v. Campbell, 178 Mont. 15, 582 P.2d 783 (1978)

27 ALR6th 183—§ 32
State v. Campbell, 190 Neb. 22, 206 N.W.2d 53 (1973)

39 ALR6th 257—§ 17, 23, 24
State v. Campbell, 217 Kan. 756, 539 P.2d 329 (1975)

110 ALR5th 329—§ 5
State v. Campbell, 219 Mont. 194, 711 P.2d 1357 (1985)

86 ALR5th 463—§ 5, 8
State v. Campbell, 239 Neb. 14, 473 N.W.2d 420 (1991)

46 ALR5th 499—§ 3
State v. Campbell, 247 Neb. 517, 527 N.W.2d 868 (1995)

15 ALR5th 391—§ 13
State v. Campbell, 265 Or. 82, 506 P.2d 163 (1973)

40 ALR6th 317—§ 7, 10, 13, 15
State v. Campbell, 294 Wis.2d 100, 718 N.W.2d 649, 2006 WI 99 (Wis. 2006)

57 ALR6th 163—§ 37
State v. Campbell, 306 Or. 157, 759 P.2d 1040 (1988)

62 ALR5th 1—§ 2
5 ALR6th 385—§ 3

State v. Campbell, 311 N.C. 386, 317 S.E.2d 391 (1984)
77 ALR5th 201—§ 10, 26
State v. Campbell, 326 N.W.2d 350 (Iowa 1982)
55 ALR5th 125—§ 12, 14, 22
State v. Campbell, 367 N.W.2d 454 (Minn. 1985)
124 ALR5th 1—§ 5
State v. Campbell, 1989 WL 51587 (Tenn. Crim. App. 1989)
103 ALR6th 507—§ 8, 14
State v. Campbell, 1989 WL 128899 (Ohio Ct. App. 4th Dist. Ross County 1989)
53 ALR6th 1—§ 14
State v. Campbell, 1989 WL 153899 (Tenn. Crim. App. 1989)
79 ALR5th 237—§ 2
State v. Campbell, 1995 WL 472142 (Ohio Ct. App. 2d Dist. Clark County 1995)
55 ALR6th 513—§ 8
State v. Campbell, 2003-Ohio-3201, 2003 WL 21415147 (Ohio Ct. App. 1st Dist. Hamilton County 2003)
125 ALR5th 497—§ 4
State v. Campbell, 2009 WL 1509108 (Ariz. Ct. App. Div. 2 2009)
56 ALR6th 1—§ 20
State v. Campbell, 2010-Ohio-128, 2010 WL 174105 (Ohio Ct. App. 9th Dist. Summit County 2010)
69 ALR6th 1—§ 29
State v. Campbell County School Dist., 2001 WY 19, 19 P.3d 518, 151 Ed. Law Rep. 634 (Wyo. 2001)
115 ALR5th 183—§ 3, 22
State v. Campbell County School Dist., 2001 WY 90, 32 P.3d 325, 157 Ed. Law Rep. 366 (Wyo. 2001)
110 ALR5th 293—§ 4
9 ALR6th 177—§ 54
State v. Campion, 353 N.W.2d 573 (Minn. App. 1984)
57 ALR5th 141—§ 13
State v. Campisi, 64 N.J. 120, 313 A.2d 193 (1973)

7 ALR6th 487—§ 31
State v. Camplese, 2006-Ohio-3403, 2006 WL 1816026 (Ohio Ct. App. 11th Dist. Ashtabula County 2006)
26 ALR6th 511—§ 19
State v. Campos, 61 N.M. 392, 301 P.2d 329 (1956)
55 ALR6th 157—§ 4
State v. Campos, 2010 WL 1610710 (Wash. Ct. App. Div. 3 2010)
55 ALR6th 1—§ 12
State v. Camuso, 1999 WL 1009828 (Ohio Ct. App. 7th Dist. Mahoning County 1999)
9 ALR6th 541—§ 6
State v. Canaan, 265 Kan. 835, 964 P.2d 681,82 A.L.R.5th 675 (1998)
82 ALR5th 67—§ 3, 8
State v. Canady, 80 Haw. 469, 911 P.2d 104 (App. 1996)
57 ALR5th 141—§ 3
State v. Canady, 234 Wis. 2d 261
15 ALR5th 391—§ 7
State v. Canales, 281 Conn. 572, 916 A.2d 767 (2007)
28 ALR6th 505—§ 14
State v. Canas, 597 N.W.2d 488 (Iowa 1999)
45 ALR5th 767—§ 12, 22
58 ALR6th 499—§ 66
State v. Canbaz, 270 Neb. 559, 705 N.W.2d 221 (2005)
72 ALR6th 1—§ 6
State v. Cancel, 256 N.J. Super. 430, 607 A.2d 199 (App. Div. 1992)
117 ALR5th 407—§ 4
State v. Cancel, 275 Conn. 1, 878 A.2d 1103 (2005)
65 ALR6th 537—§ 40
State v. Candela, 2009-Ohio-4096, 2009 WL 2488027 (Ohio Ct. App. 11th Dist. Ashtabula County 2009)
64 ALR6th 1—§ 9
State v. Canedo-Astorga, 79 Wash. App. 518, 903 P.2d 500 (Div. 2 1995)
19 ALR6th 115—§ 4, 7
State v. Canelo, 139 N.H. 376, 653 A.2d 1097 (1995)

67 ALR5th 361—§ 2, 3, 10, 12
State v. Canerdy, 132 Vt. 131, 315 A.2d 237 (1974)
78 ALR5th 1—§ 52
State v. Canez, 202 Ariz. 133, 42 P.3d 564 (2002)
21 ALR6th 1—§ 4
State v. Canez, 205 Ariz. 620, 74 P.3d 932 (2003)
122 ALR5th 145—§ 7, 12, 16, 22
State v. Canha, 159 Wash. App. 1044, 2011 WL 240680 (Div. 3 2011)
78 ALR6th 297—§ 41
State v. Cannell, 2005-Ohio-5769, 2005 WL 2840639 (Ohio Ct. App. 12th Dist. Butler County 2005)
18 ALR6th 519—§ 8
State v. Cannon, 130 Wash. 2d 313, 922 P.2d 1293 (1996)
90 ALR5th 453—§ 43
State v. Cannon, 192 Ariz. 236, 963 P.2d 315 (Ct. App. Div. 1 1998)
119 ALR5th 379—§ 12
State v. Cannon, 253 Ga. App. 445, 559 S.E.2d 76 (2002)
1 ALR6th 371—§ 3, 4
State v. Cannon, 326 N.C. 37, 387 S.E.2d 450 (1990)
11 ALR6th 237—§ 3, 11
State v. Cannon, 336 S.C. 335, 520 S.E.2d 317 (1999)
55 ALR5th 125—§ 3
State v. Cannuli, 143 N.H. 149, 722 A.2d 450 (1998)
6 ALR6th 533—§ 3, 21
State v. Cano, 64 Utah 87, 228 P. 563 (1924)
32 ALR5th 149—§ 22, 23, 29, 34
State v. Cansler, 54 Conn. App. 819, 738 A.2d 1095 (1999)
39 ALR6th 257—§ 4, 42
40 ALR6th 1—§ 5
State v. Cantelupe, 2000 WL 875356 (Ohio Ct. App. 7th Dist. Harrison County 2000)
92 ALR6th 171—§ 14

State v. Canter, 2009-Ohio-4837, 2009 WL 2941524 (Ohio Ct. App. 10th Dist. Franklin County 2009)
55 ALR6th 1—§ 7, 22, 29
State v. Cantlebarry, 69 Ohio App. 3d 216, 590 N.E.2d 342 (10th Dist. Franklin County 1990)
3 ALR6th 269—§ 5, 8
State v. Cantrell, 151 Vt. 130, 558 A.2d 639 (1989)
57 ALR5th 141—§ 11
State v. Cantrell, 1990 WL 103642 (Tenn. Crim. App. 1990)
88 ALR5th 121—§ 32
State v. Cantrell, 2010 WL 919314 (Idaho Ct. App. 2010)
55 ALR6th 1—§ 4
State v. Cantu, 144 P.3d 758 (Kan. 2006)
26 ALR6th 511—§ 25
State v. Cantu, 750 P.2d 591, 73 Utah Adv. Rep. 74 (Utah 1988)
20 ALR5th 398—§ 3, 8
State v. Cantu, 778 P.2d 517, 114 Utah Adv. Rep. 3 (Utah 1989)
20 ALR5th 398—§ 29, 59
State v. Canty, 278 N.J. Super. 80, 650 A.2d 391 (App. Div. 1994)
105 ALR5th 529—§ 1
State v. Canty, 1990 WL 121109 (Ohio Ct. App. 9th Dist.Lorain County 1990)
64 ALR5th 637—§ 3
State v. Capawanna, 118 NJL 429, 193 A. 902 (1937)
5 ALR5th 243—§ 2, 19, 48
State v. Capone, 2004-Ohio-4679, 2004 WL 1949423 (Ohio Ct. App. 2d Dist. Montgomery County 2004)
70 ALR6th 1—§ 19
State v. Capper, 539 N.W.2d 361 (Iowa 1995)
33 ALR5th 571—§ 5
State v. Capps, 61 N.C. App. 225, 300 S.E.2d 819 (1983)
51 ALR6th 1—§ 20
52 ALR6th 1—§ 5
State v. Capps, 97 N.M. 453, 641 P.2d 484 (1982)

114 ALR5th 173—§ 9
State v. Caraballo, 62 Haw. 309, 615 P.2d 91 (1980)
19 ALR6th 697—§ 14
State v. Carangelo, 151 N.J. Super. 138, 376 A.2d 596 (1977)
41 ALR5th 171—§ 8, 81, 107, 108, 116, 135
State v. Carangelo, 151 N.J. Super. 138, 376 A.2d 596 (Law Div. 1977)
27 ALR6th 491—§ 3
State v. Carawan, 80 N.C. App. 151, 341 S.E.2d 96 (1986)
52 ALR5th 655—§ 2, 8
State v. Carbajal, 868 P.2d 1044, 156 Ariz. Adv. Rep. 31 (Ariz. App. 1994)
15 ALR5th 391—§ 5, 21, 22
State v. Carbone, 172 Conn. 242, 374 A.2d 215 (1977)
6 ALR6th 533—§ 21
State v. Card, 121 Idaho 425, 825 P.2d 1081 (1991)
79 ALR5th 33—§ 40, 56
State v. Cardall, 1999 UT 51, 982 P.2d 79 (Utah 1999)
98 ALR6th 455—§ 29
State v. Cardany, 35 Conn. App. 728, 646 A.2d 291 (1994)
39 ALR6th 257—§ 3
State v. Cardell, 180 Or. App. 104, 41 P.3d 1111 (2002)
89 ALR6th 565—§ 3
State v. Cardell, 318 N.J. Super. 175, 723 A.2d 111 (App. Div. 1999)
29 ALR5th 487—§ 3, 8, 14
State v. Carden, 50 Wash. 2d 15, 308 P.2d 675 (1957)
29 ALR5th 59—§ 7
State v. Cardenas, 26 Kan. App. 2d 135, 980 P.2d 594 (1999)
19 ALR5th 470—§ 12
State v. Cardenas, 129 Wash. 2d 1, 914 P.2d 57 (1996)
73 ALR5th 383—§ 41, 54
State v. Cardenas, 2009 WL 4981845 (Ariz. Ct. App. Div. 1 2009)
55 ALR6th 1—§ 33

State v. Carder, 9 Ohio St. 2d 1, 38 Ohio Ops. 2d 1, 222 N.E.2d 620 (1966)
55 ALR5th 125—§ 3, 9
State v. Cardwell, 1996 WL 509521 (Wash. Ct. App. Div. 1 1996)
85 ALR5th 1—§ 47
State v. Carey, 30 Conn. App. 346, 620 A.2d 201 (1993)
21 ALR6th 771—§ 12
State v. Carey, 136 Me. 47, 1 A.2d 341 (1938)
102 ALR5th 525—§ 34
State v. Carey, 256 La. 990, 240 So. 2d 733 (1970)
102 ALR5th 525—§ 72
State v. Carey, 290 A.2d 839 (Me. 1972)
36 ALR5th 255—§ 24, 33
State v. Carey, 417 A.2d 979 (Me. 1980)
15 ALR6th 1—§ 11
State v. Carey, 2013 ME 83, 77 A.3d 471 (Me. 2013)
103 ALR6th 137—§ 15
State v. Cargill, 312 N.J. Super. 13, 711 A.2d 318 (App. Div. 1998)
97 ALR5th 201—§ 6
State v. Cargille, 507 So. 2d 1254 (La. Ct. App. 3d Cir. 1987)
79 ALR6th 125—§ 4, 5, 18
State v. Carillo, 122 R.I. 392, 407 A.2d 491 (1979)
82 ALR5th 67—§ 3, 8 to 10
State v. Carl, 310 Minn. 365, 246 N.W.2d 192 (1976)
45 ALR6th 337—§ 31
State v. Carl B., 171 W. Va. 774, 301 S.E.2d 864 (1983)
92 ALR5th 379—§ 5
State v. Carle, 2007-Ohio-5376, 2007 WL 2909750 (Ohio Ct. App. 11th Dist. Ashtabula County 2007)
35 ALR6th 361—§ 15, 20
State v. Carlino, 373 N.J. Super. 377, 861 A.2d 849 (App. Div. 2004)
50 ALR6th 455—§ 34
State v. Carlino, 2007 WL 1687551 (N.J. Super. Ct. App. Div. 2007)
35 ALR6th 361—§ 20

State v. Carlson, 45 Conn. Supp. 461, 720 A.2d 886 (Super Ct. 1998)

90 ALR5th 453—§ 6

State v. Carlson, 66 Wash. App. 909, 833 P.2d 463 (Div. 1 1992)

49 ALR6th 93—§ 5

State v. Carlson, 80 Wash. App. 116, 906 P.2d 999 (Div. 2 1995)

90 ALR5th 453—§ 43

State v. Carlson, 101 Idaho 598, 618 P.2d 776 (1980)

103 ALR5th 463—§ 5

State v. Carlson, 134 Idaho 389, 3 P.3d 67 (Ct. App. 2000)

98 ALR6th 455—§ 32

State v. Carlson, 134 Idaho 471, 4 P.3d 1122 (Ct. App. 2000)

112 ALR5th 429—§ 10

State v. Carlson, 258 N.W.2d 253 (N.D. 1977)

37 ALR6th 357—§ 47, 62, 67

State v. Carlson, 260 Neb. 815, 619 N.W.2d 832 (2000)

9 ALR6th 633—§ 13, 25

13 ALR6th 603—§ 36

15 ALR6th 173—§ 49

State v. Carlson, 261 Wis. 2d 97, 2003 WI 40, 661 N.W.2d 51, 117 A.L.R.5th 615 (2003)

117 ALR5th 1—§ 4

State v. Carlson, 267 N.W.2d 170 (Minn. 1978)

28 ALR6th 505—§ 9

State v. Carlson, 302 Mont. 508, 15 P.3d 893 (2000)

117 ALR5th 407—§ 3

State v. Carlson, 318 N.W.2d 308 (N.D. 1982)

32 ALR6th 1—§ 11

State v. Carlson, 363 S.C. 586, 611 S.E.2d 283 (Ct. App. 2005)

65 ALR6th 537—§ 40, 72

State v. Carlson, 399 N.W.2d 625 (Minn. Ct. App. 1987)

109 ALR5th 611—§ 3

State v. Carlson, 548 N.W.2d 138 (Iowa 1996)

58 ALR6th 499—§ 51

State v. Carlson, 560 P.2d 26 (Alaska 1977)

7 ALR5th 263—§ 7

State v. Carlson, 762 N.E.2d 121 (Ind. Ct. App. 2002)

114 ALR5th 173—§ 10

State v. Carlson, No. 53234, Slip Op., June 18, 1987 (Ohio App. Cuyahoga Co. 1987)

45 ALR5th 591—§ 16

State v. Carlton, 233 Or. 296, 378 P.2d 557 (1963)

29 ALR5th 59—§ 3, 29

State v. Carlton, 276 Ga. 693, 583 S.E.2d 1 (2003)

70 ALR6th 361—§ 14

State v. Carlton S. C.-B. (In the Interest of Carlton S.C.-B.), 1995 WL 737219 (Wis App)

50 ALR5th 581—§ 3, 7, 14, 19

State v. Carlyle, 19 Wash. App. 450, 576 P.2d 408 (Div. 1 1978)

97 ALR5th 293—§ 18

State v. Carmichael, 35 Ohio St. 2d 1, 64 Ohio Ops. 2d 1, 298 N.E.2d 568 (1973)

37 ALR5th 703—§ 3

State v. Carmichael, 405 A.2d 732 (Me. 1979)

5 ALR5th 243—§ 2, 21

State v. Carmouche, 508 So. 2d 792 (La. 1987)

37 ALR5th 515—§ 3, 10

State v. Carmouche, 872 So. 2d 1020 (La. 2002)

122 ALR5th 145—§ 9

State v. Carney, 2000 WL 1335770 (Tenn. Crim. App. 2000)

24 ALR6th 1—§ 21

State v. Carol M.D., 89 Wash. App. 77, 948 P.2d 837 (Div. 3 1997)

38 ALR5th 433—§ 8

State v. Caron, 155 Vt. 492, 586 A.2d 1127 (1990)

9 ALR6th 1—§ 22

State v. Caron, 334 A.2d 495 (Me. 1975)

92 ALR6th 1—§ 3
State v. Carothers, 2006 SD 100, 724
N.W.2d 610 (S.D. 2006)
32 ALR6th 1—§ 11
State v. Carpenter, 24 Wash. App. 41,
599 P.2d 1 (Div. 1 1979)
70 ALR6th 361—§ 29
State v. Carpenter, 69 S.W.3d 568
(Tenn. Crim. App. 2001)
97 ALR5th 201—§ 3
State v. Carpenter, 83 Ohio App. 3d 842,
615 N.E.2d 1103 (12th Dist. Cler-
mont County 1992)
23 ALR6th 1—§ 16
State v. Carpenter, 155 Vt. 59, 580 A.2d
497 (1990)
5 ALR5th 243—§ 47
State v. Carpenter, 250 Neb. 427, 551
N.W.2d 518 (1996)
66 ALR6th 351—§ 9
State v. Carpenter, 334 N.W.2d 137
(Iowa 1983)
26 ALR5th 1—§ 3, 33
State v. Carpenter, 1996 WL 601628
(Minn. Ct. App. 1996)
73 ALR5th 383—§ 17
State v. Carpenter, No. 2977 (August 20,
1980, Ct. App. Ohio, 9th App. Dist.
Lorain Co.)
39 ALR5th 283—§ 14, 60
State v. Carr, 95 N.M. 755, 626 P.2d 292
(App. 1981)
**13 ALR5th 1—§ 2, 13, 22, 23, 29,
33, 36, 42, 45, 46, 50**
State v. Carr, 95 N.M. 755, 626 P.2d 292
(Ct. App. 1981)
27 ALR6th 183—§ 15, 35
State v. Carr, 169 Wash. 56, 13 P.2d 497
(1932)
57 ALR6th 445—§ 8
State v. Carr, 173 Ohio App. 3d 436,
2007-Ohio-5466, 878 N.E.2d 1077,
2007 A.M.C. 2892 (5th Dist. Perry
County 2007)
47 ALR6th 107—§ 28
State v. Carr, 215 Or. App. 306, 170
P.3d 563 (2007)
70 ALR6th 513—§ 17

71 ALR6th 471—§ 11
State v. Carr, 261 Ga. 845, 413 S.E.2d
192, 103-35 Fulton County D R 21
(1992)
47 ALR5th 259—§ 4
State v. Carr, 262 Ga. 893, 427 S.E.2d
273, 93 Fulton County D R 1169
(1993)
47 ALR5th 259—§ 4
State v. Carr, 373 So. 2d 657 (Fla. 1979)
5 ALR5th 422—§ 3
State v. Carr, 530 So. 2d 579 (La. Ct.
App. 1st Cir. 1988)
65 ALR5th 407—§ 3
124 ALR5th 1—§ 5
State v. Carr, 1993 WL 188025 (Ohio
Ct. App. 3d Dist.Shelby County
1993)
57 ALR5th 141—§ 13
State v. Carr, 1997 ME 221, 704 A.2d
353 (Me. 1997)
28 ALR6th 505—§ 9
101 ALR6th 331—§ 17
State v. Carrasco-Calderon, 2008 WL
5377923 (Ariz. Ct. App. Div. 1
2008)
49 ALR6th 343—§ 3, 12
State v. Carraway, 251 Ga. App. 469,
554 S.E.2d 602 (2001)
55 ALR6th 513—§ 8
State v. Carreon, 117 Wash. App. 1050,
2003 WL 21518822 (Div. 1 2003)
101 ALR6th 331—§ 10
State v. Carreon, 210 Ariz. 54, 107 P.3d
900 (2005)
21 ALR6th 1—§ 4
State v. Carriere, 545 N.W.2d 773 (N.D.
1996)
62 ALR5th 1—§ 4, 13, 15
State v. Carriger, 123 Ariz. 335, 599
P.2d 788 (1979)
82 ALR5th 67—§ 3
State v. Carriker, 24 N.C. App. 91, 210
S.E.2d 98 (1974)
1 ALR6th 549—§ 30, 32, 33
State v. Carrillo, 26 Ariz. App. 113, 546
P.2d 838 (1976)
61 ALR5th 1—§ 3 to 5

State v. Carrillo, 115 N.C. App. 674, 446 S.E.2d 379 (1994)
39 ALR5th 283—§ 4, 72

State v. Carrillo, 125 Or. App. 52, 865 P.2d 379 (1993)
15 ALR5th 391—§ 39
92 ALR5th 35—§ 16

State v. Carrillo, 597 N.W.2d 497 (Iowa 1999)
9 ALR6th 541—§ 28

State v. Carrion-Collazo, 221 N.J. Super. 103, 534 A.2d 21 (App. Div. 1987)
99 ALR6th 295—§ 12, 15

State v. Carr, No. 43524 (December 3, 1981, Ct. App. Ohio, 8th App. Dist. Cuyahoga Co.)
39 ALR5th 283—§ 14, 32, 71

State v. Carroll, 4 Haw. App. 573, 670 P.2d 1290 (1983)
72 ALR6th 141—§ 9

State v. Carroll, 17 N.C. App. 691, 195 S.E.2d 306 (1973)
96 ALR6th 269—§ 31

State v. Carroll, 54 Ohio App. 2d 160, 8 Ohio Ops. 3d 285, 376 N.E.2d 596 (Erie Co. 1977)
10 ALR5th 1—§ 2, 40, 56

State v. Carroll, 97 Conn. 598, 117 A. 694 (1922)
102 ALR5th 525—§ 25

State v. Carroll, 110 R.I. 532, 294 A.2d 187 (1972)
9 ALR6th 633—§ 5
12 ALR6th 389—§ 7
13 ALR6th 603—§ 41

State v. Carroll, 123 N.W.2d 659 (N.D. 1963)
85 ALR5th 187—§ 7, 8

State v. Carroll, 131 N.H. 179, 552 A.2d 69 (1988)
4 ALR6th 599—§ 12, 28

State v. Carroll, 138 N.H. 687, 645 A.2d 82 (1994)
48 ALR5th 555—§ 4
29 ALR6th 1—§ 10

State v. Carroll, 225 Minn. 384, 31 N.W.2d 44 (1948)

State v. Carroll, 383 Md. 438, 859 A.2d 1138 (2004)
52 ALR5th 655—§ 3, 5

State v. Carroll, 383 Md. 438, 859 A.2d 1138 (2004)
50 ALR6th 455—§ 12

State v. Carroll, 855 S.W.2d 128, 83 Ed. Law Rep. 1175 (Tex. App. Austin 1993)
18 ALR6th 519—§ 8

State v. Carroll, 2008 WL 4224681 (Minn. Ct. App. 2008)
57 ALR6th 83—§ 19

State v. Carroll, 2010 WI 8, 322 Wis. 2d 299, 778 N.W.2d 1 (2010)
62 ALR6th 161—§ 14, 23

State v. Carr-Poindexter, 2005-Ohio-1571, 2005 WL 737371 (Ohio Ct. App. 2d Dist. Montgomery County 2005)
79 ALR6th 1—§ 69

State v. Carruth, 947 P.2d 690 (Utah Ct. App. 1997)
78 ALR5th 567—§ 3

State v. Carruth, 1999 UT 107, 993 P.2d 869 (Utah 1999)
78 ALR5th 567—§ 3

State v. Carruthers, 1999 WL 1530153 (Tenn. Crim. App. 1999)
21 ALR6th 1—§ 6

State v. Carsey, 295 Or. 32, 664 P.2d 1085 (1983)
55 ALR5th 125—§ 6, 15, 22

State v. Carson, 2005 WL 2512116 (N.J. Super. Ct. App. Div. 2005)
26 ALR6th 511—§ 17

State v. Carstensen, 1991 WL 270665 (Ohio Ct. App. 2d Dist. Miami County 1991)
84 ALR6th 293—§ 27

State v. Cartagena, 140 Wis. 2d 59, 409 N.W.2d 386 (App. 1987)
14 ALR5th 89—§ 25, 33

State v. Carter, 54 Or. App. 852, 636 P.2d 460 (1981)
60 ALR5th 1—§ 2, 5
45 ALR6th 643—§ 19

State v. Carter, 54 So. 3d 1093 (La. 2011)
99 ALR6th 397—§ 11

State v. Carter, 56 Wash. App. 217, 783 P.2d 589 (Div. 1 1989)
86 ALR6th 321—§ 13
State v. Carter, 64 Ohio St. 3d 218, 594 N.E.2d 595 (1992)
50 ALR5th 467—§ 9
State v. Carter, 69 N.J. 420, 354 A.2d 627 (1976)
24 ALR6th 1—§ 20
State v. Carter, 74 N.C. App. 437, 328 S.E.2d 607 (1985)
1 ALR6th 657—§ 14
State v. Carter, 89 Ohio St. 3d 593, 734 N.E.2d 345 (2000)
70 ALR5th 1—§ 11
State v. Carter, 89 Ohio St. 3d 593, 2000-Ohio-172, 734 N.E.2d 345 (2000)
21 ALR6th 1—§ 4
State v. Carter, 101 Or. App. 281, 790 P.2d 1152 (1990)
59 ALR5th 615—§ 4, 9
State v. Carter, 106 Wash. App. 1029, 2001 WL 567694 (Div. 2 2001)
16 ALR6th 329—§ 4
19 ALR6th 115—§ 4
24 ALR6th 591—§ 9, 13
State v. Carter, 122 N.C. App. 332, 470 S.E.2d 74 (1996)
57 ALR6th 445—§ 55
State v. Carter, 132 Or. App. 461, 889 P.2d 354 (1995)
112 ALR5th 429—§ 12
State v. Carter, 142 Vt. 588, 458 A.2d 1112 (1983)
119 ALR5th 379—§ 8
State v. Carter, 153 N.C. App. 200, 569 S.E.2d 33 (2002)
34 ALR6th 1—§ 12
State v. Carter, 244 Ga. App. 560, 536 S.E.2d 230 (2000)
6 ALR5th 711—§ 6
State v. Carter, 246 Neb. 953, 524 N.W.2d 763 (1994)
90 ALR5th 453—§ 39
State v. Carter, 255 Neb. 591, 586 N.W.2d 818 (1998)

78 ALR5th 1—§ 31, 63
90 ALR5th 453—§ 39
State v. Carter, 285 Mont. 449, 948 P.2d 1173 (1997)
66 ALR5th 397—§ 25
State v. Carter, 293 Minn. 102, 196 N.W.2d 607 (1972)
29 ALR5th 59—§ 6, 11, 15
State v. Carter, 424 N.E.2d 158 (Ind. App. 1981)
52 ALR5th 655—§ 3
State v. Carter, 451 S.W.2d 340 (Mo. 1970)
84 ALR6th 427—§ 4
State v. Carter, 537 N.W.2d 804 (Iowa Ct. App. 1995)
68 ALR5th 343—§ 3, 5
State v. Carter, 572 S.W.2d 430 (Mo. 1978)
70 ALR5th 587—§ 3
State v. Carter, 578 P.2d 1275 (Utah 1978)
9 ALR6th 363—§ 2
State v. Carter, 602 N.W.2d 818 (Iowa 1999)
103 ALR6th 507—§ 10, 28
State v. Carter, 636 S.W.2d 183 (Tenn. 1982)
34 ALR5th 125—§ 26
State v. Carter, 641 S.W.2d 54 (Mo. 1982)
66 ALR6th 83—§ 11
State v. Carter, 682 S.E.2d 416 (N.C. Ct. App. 2009)
55 ALR6th 1—§ 6
State v. Carter, 762 So. 2d 662 (La. Ct. App. 4th Cir. 2000)
38 ALR5th 433—§ 20
58 ALR5th 749—§ 6
State v. Carter, 773 So. 2d 268 (La. Ct. App. 4th Cir. 2000)
4 ALR5th 1—§ 32
State v. Carter, 888 P.2d 629 (Utah 1995)
79 ALR5th 33—§ 9, 13, 42, 52
State v. Carter, 889 S.W.2d 231 (Tenn. Crim. App. 1994)

92 ALR6th 295—§ 8, 19
95 ALR6th 1—§ 5 to 6, 27
State v. Carter, 901 P.2d 335 (Wash. App. 1995)
43 ALR5th 1—§ 13
State v. Carter, 955 S.W.2d 548 (Mo. 1997)
79 ALR5th 33—§ 40
99 ALR6th 295—§ 15
State v. Carter, 1995 WL 809483 (Ohio App. 5 Dist.)
50 ALR5th 581—§ 6, 20
State v. Carter, 1997 WL 9273 (Wash. Ct. App. Div. 2 1997)
73 ALR5th 383—§ 57
State v. Carter, 1997 WL 90632 (Tenn. Crim. App. 1997)
73 ALR5th 383—§ 29
State v. Carter, 2003 WL 22213225 (Tenn. Crim. App. 2003)
115 ALR5th 477—§ 4
State v. Carter, 2004-Ohio-39, 2004 WL 35458 (Ohio Ct. App. 5th Dist. Coshocton County 2004)
43 ALR6th 475—§ 24
State v. Carter, 2004-Ohio-3372, 2004 WL 1445079 (Ohio Ct. App. 1st Dist. Hamilton County 2004)
122 ALR5th 145—§ 7, 22
State v. Carter, 2005 MT 87, 326 Mont. 427, 114 P.3d 1001 (2005)
30 ALR6th 1—§ 4, 5, 7
State v. Carter, 2005-Ohio-291, 2005 WL 174806 (Ohio Ct. App. 10th Dist. Franklin County 2005)
72 ALR6th 1—§ 7
State v. Carter, 2005 WL 1307807 (Tenn. Crim. App. 2005)
26 ALR6th 511—§ 9, 22
State v. Carter, 2006 WL 2714443 (Tenn. Crim. App. 2006)
99 ALR6th 295—§ 7
State v. Carter, 2007-Ohio-5259, 2007 WL 2852157 (Ohio Ct. App. 5th Dist. Richland County 2007)
43 ALR6th 475—§ 6

State v. Carter, 2008-Ohio-6955, 2008 WL 5423554 (Ohio Ct. App. 8th Dist. Cuyahoga County 2008)
72 ALR6th 1—§ 5
State v. Carter, No. 1644, No. 1647 (March 9, 1982, Ct. App. Ohio, 2nd App. Dist. Clark)
39 ALR5th 283—§ 14, 17
State v. Cartledge, 76 Ohio App. 3d 145, 601 N.E.2d 157 (Cuyahoga Co. 1991)
50 ALR5th 581—§ 2
State v. Cartwright, 17 S.W.3d 149 (Mo. Ct. App. E.D. 2000)
29 ALR5th 487—§ 12
State v. Cartwright, 200 Mont. 91, 650 P.2d 758 (1982)
42 ALR6th 237—§ 4
State v. Caruolo, 524 A.2d 575 (R.I. 1987)
29 ALR6th 1—§ 10
State v. Caruthers, 22 Kan. App. 2d 910, 924 P.2d 1278 (1996)
70 ALR5th 533—§ 3, 7
State v. Carver, 113 Wash. 2d 591, 781 P.2d 1308 (1989)
40 ALR5th 227—§ 33, 43
67 ALR5th 1—§ 20
State v. Carver, 753 S.E.2d 397 (N.C. Ct. App. 2013)
96 ALR6th 355—§ 24, 37
State v. Carwile, 615 So. 2d 748 (Fla. Dist. Ct. App. 2d Dist. 1993)
118 ALR5th 253—§ 10
State v. Cary, 49 N.J. 343, 230 A.2d 384 (1967)
95 ALR5th 471—§ 2, 3, 11
State v. Cary, 53 N.J. 256, 250 A.2d 15 (1969)
95 ALR5th 471—§ 3
State v. Cary, 56 N.J. 16, 264 A.2d 209 (1970)
95 ALR5th 471—§ 3
State v. Cary, 99 N.J. Super. 323, 239 A.2d 680 (Law Div. 1968)
95 ALR5th 471—§ 2, 3
State v. Cary, 331 N.J. Super. 236, 751 A.2d 620 (App. Div. 2000)

93 ALR5th 327—§ 4, 24
101 ALR5th 619—§ 5
State v. Casada, 825 N.E.2d 936 (Ind. Ct. App. 2005)
33 ALR6th 91—§ 11, 36
State v. Casado, 42 Conn. App. 371, 680 A.2d 981 (1996)
9 ALR6th 633—§ 7, 41, 46
State v. Casby, 348 N.W.2d 736 (Minn. 1984)
9 ALR6th 363—§ 54
State v. Cascone, 195 Conn. 183, 487 A.2d 186 (1985)
64 ALR6th 655—§ 18
State v. Casconi, 94 Or. App. 457, 766 P.2d 397 (1988)
91 ALR5th 585—§ 11
State v. Case, 4 Neb. App. 885, 553 N.W.2d 173 (1996)
90 ALR5th 453—§ 39
20 ALR6th 479—§ 3
State v. Case, 100 N.M. 714, 676 P.2d 241 (1984)
54 ALR5th 575—§ 5
State v. Case, 103 N.M. 574, 711 P.2d 19 (Ct. App. 1985)
27 ALR6th 183—§ 15
State v. Casey, 59 N.C. App. 99, 296 S.E.2d 473 (1982)
37 ALR5th 1—§ 4
State v. Casey, 129 P.3d 582 (Kan. 2006)
26 ALR6th 511—§ 25, 29
State v. Casey, 325 S.C. 447, 481 S.E.2d 169 (Ct. App. 1997)
88 ALR5th 67—§ 6
State v. Casey, 876 P.2d 138 (Idaho 1994)
17 ALR5th 837—§ 3
State v. Casey, 1992 WL 9539 (Ohio Ct. App. 6th Dist. Lucas County 1992)
99 ALR6th 295—§ 13
State v. Cash Totalling $15,156.00, 623 So. 2d 114 (La. Ct. App. 1st Cir. 1993)
104 ALR5th 229—§ 6, 14
116 ALR5th 325—§ 5
4 ALR6th 113—§ 17, 19

101 ALR6th 1—§ 5, 12, 47
State v. Cash Totalling $15,156.00, 623 So. 2d 114 (La. Ct. App. 1st Cir. 1993)
34 ALR6th 539—§ 9
State v. Casiano, 55 Conn. App. 582, 740 A.2d 435 (1999)
32 ALR6th 1—§ 11
State v. Casillas, 279 Neb. 820, 782 N.W.2d 882 (2010)
57 ALR6th 83—§ 12
State v. Casino Mktg. Group, 491 N.W.2d 882 (Minn. 1992)
44 ALR5th 619—§ 2, 3
State v. Casipe, 5 Hawaii App. 210, 686 P.2d 28 (1984)
32 ALR5th 149—§ 72, 73, 76, 78, 79
State v. Caslavka, 531 N.W.2d 102 (Iowa 1995)
57 ALR6th 445—§ 8
State v. Cass, 55 N.C. App. 291, 285 S.E.2d 337 (1982)
32 ALR6th 1—§ 9
State v. Cassady, 243 N.W.2d 581 (Iowa 1976)
113 ALR5th 517—§ 20
State v. Cassell, 280 Mont. 397, 932 P.2d 478 (1996)
69 ALR6th 579—§ 4
State v. Cassell, 602 P.2d 410 (Alaska 1979)
32 ALR6th 1—§ 4
State v. Cassell, 2011-Ohio-23, 2011 WL 96183 (Ohio Ct. App. 2d Dist. Clark County 2011)
64 ALR6th 1—§ 12
State v. Cassidy, 567 N.W.2d 707 (Minn. 1997)
19 ALR6th 697—§ 13
State v. Cassill-Skilton, 122 Wash. App. 652, 94 P.3d 407 (Div. 2 2004)
78 ALR6th 1—§ 28, 32, 35, 37, 42, 48, 58
State v. Castagna, 170 Conn. 80, 364 A.2d 200 (1976)
11 ALR5th 497—§ 3, 16
State v. Castaneda, 150 Ariz. 382, 724 P.2d 1 (1986)

55 ALR5th 125—§ 14, 26
72 ALR5th 109—§ 9
State v. Castaneda, 245 P.3d 550, 126
   Nev. Adv. Op. No. 45 (Nev. 2010)
71 ALR6th 283—§ 13, 14
State v. Castanedo, 523 So. 2d 1253
   (Fla. Dist. Ct. App. 3d Dist. 1988)
113 ALR5th 597—§ 8
State v. Casteel, 137 Wis. 2d 648, 405
   N.W.2d 83 (Ct. App. 1987)
123 ALR5th 221—§ 5, 6
State v. Castellano, 162 Ariz. 461, 784
   P.2d 287 (Ct. App. Div. 2 1989)
55 ALR6th 513—§ 12
State v. Castellano, 506 N.W.2d 641
   (Minn. Ct. App. 1993)
113 ALR5th 1—§ 2 to 4, 12, 15
State v. Castelli, 92 Conn. 58, 101 A.
   476 (1917)
24 ALR6th 591—§ 4
State v. Casteneda, 1997 WL 154100
   (Wash. Ct. App. Div. 2 1997)
73 ALR5th 383—§ 5
State v. Castillo, 149 N.M. 536, 2011-
   NMCA-046, 252 P.3d 760 (Ct. App.
   2011)
68 ALR6th 527—§ 8
State v. Castillo, 156 Ariz. 323, 751 P.2d
   983 (App. 1987)
20 ALR5th 398—§ 3, 19, 24, 25, 33,
   34, 42
State v. Castillo, 486 So. 2d 565, 11
   FLW 113 (Fla. 1986)
63 ALR5th 375—§ 5, 6
State v. Castillo, 1993 WL 355903
   (Minn. Ct. App. 1993)
73 ALR5th 383—§ 3
State v. Castillo, 2004 WL 1149497
   (Tenn. Crim. App. 2004)
81 ALR6th 505—§ 30
State v. Castillo, 2010 WL 346254
   (Minn. Ct. App. 2010)
73 ALR6th 49—§ 54
State v. Castillo, 2012-NMCA-116, 290
   P.3d 727 (N.M. Ct. App. 2012)
101 ALR6th 545—§ 9

State v. Castillo-Sanchez, 127 N.M. 540,
   1999-NMCA-085, 984 P.2d 787
   (Ct. App. 1999)
49 ALR6th 343—§ 19, 26
State v. Castle, 285 Mont. 363, 948 P.2d
   688 (1997)
27 ALR6th 183—§ 17, 32
State v. Castle, 2005-Ohio-5423, 2005
   WL 2562598 (Ohio Ct. App. 10th
   Dist. Franklin County 2005)
26 ALR6th 511—§ 19
State v. Casto, 22 Kan. App. 2d 152, 912
   P.2d 772 (1996)
15 ALR5th 391—§ 11
State v. Castonguay, 240 A.2d 747 (Me.
   1968)
97 ALR5th 201—§ 3
State v. Castor, 257 Neb. 572, 599
   N.W.2d 201 (1999)
56 ALR6th 185—§ 6
State v. Castrejon, 635 S.E.2d 520 (N.C.
   Ct. App. 2006)
19 ALR6th 115—§ 10
27 ALR6th 183—§ 15
State v. Castro, 141 Wash. App. 485,
   170 P.3d 78 (Div. 3 2007)
101 ALR6th 545—§ 5
State v. Castro, 238 N.J. Super. 482, 570
   A.2d 40 (App. Div. 1990)
58 ALR6th 499—§ 8
State v. Castro, 1995 WL 558782 (Ohio
   Ct. App. 2d Dist. Montgomery
   County 1995)
43 ALR6th 475—§ 6
State v. Catalino, 316 Mo. 1152, 295
   S.W. 568 (1927)
97 ALR5th 537—§ 18
State v. Catanese, 368 So. 2d 975 (La.
   1979)
90 ALR5th 453—§ 12
State v. Catchings, 440 So. 2d 153 (La.
   Ct. App. 4th Cir. 1983)
88 ALR5th 121—§ 36
State v. Catch the Bear, 352 N.W.2d 640
   (S.D. 1984)
51 ALR5th 603—§ 2

State v. Cater, 2003-Ohio-2789, 2003 WL 21255929 (Ohio Ct. App. 6th Dist. Williams County 2003)
95 ALR6th 1—§ 10, 34

State v. Cathey, 32 Wis. 2d 79, 145 N.W.2d 100 (1966)
101 ALR5th 187—§ 10

State v. Catlin, 392 A.2d 27 (Me. 1978)
29 ALR6th 1—§ 5

State v. Catoe, 78 N.C. App. 167, 336 S.E.2d 691 (1985)
119 ALR5th 379—§ 3

State v. Caton, 163 Wash. App. 659, 260 P.3d 946 (Div. 2 2011)
93 ALR6th 1—§ 36

State v. Caton, 174 Wash. 2d 239, 273 P.3d 980 (2012)
93 ALR6th 1—§ 36

State v. Catterall, 5 Wash. App. 373, 486 P.2d 1167 (1971)
34 ALR5th 125—§ 8, 9

State v. Caudill, 75 Ohio App. 3d 322, 599 N.E.2d 395 (10th Dist.Franklin County 1991)
59 ALR5th 749—§ 2, 4

State v. Caudill, 109 Idaho 222, 706 P.2d 456 (1985)
16 ALR6th 329—§ 4
24 ALR6th 591—§ 4

State v. Caughron, 855 S.W.2d 526 (Tenn. 1993)
37 ALR5th 515—§ 10

State v. Cauich-Ake, 1998 WL 244247 (Wash. Ct. App. Div. 2 1998)
73 ALR5th 383—§ 6

State v. Caulfield, 722 N.W.2d 304 (Minn. 2006)
30 ALR6th 1—§ 3, 6

State v. Caulley, 132 Ohio App. 3d 706, 725 N.E.2d 1229 (10th Dist. Franklin County 1999)
26 ALR5th 765—§ 7

State v. Caulley, 2002-Ohio-1078, 2002 WL 392191 (Ohio Ct. App. 10th Dist. Franklin County 2002)
65 ALR6th 537—§ 4

State v. Causby, 269 N.C. 747, 153 S.E.2d 467 (1967)
46 ALR6th 241—§ 4

State v. Causby, 683 S.E.2d 262 (N.C. Ct. App. 2009)
57 ALR6th 1—§ 23

State v. Cavanaugh, 23 Conn. App. 667, 583 A.2d 1311 (1990)
19 ALR6th 115—§ 3, 5, 7, 13

State v. Cavegn, 356 N.W.2d 671 (Minn. 1984)
114 ALR5th 235—§ 5

State v. Cavness, 80 Haw. 460, 911 P.2d 95 (Haw. Ct. App. 1996)
68 ALR5th 299—§ 4

State v. Cayouette, 25 Conn. App. 384, 594 A.2d 1020 (1991)
39 ALR6th 257—§ 37

State v. Cayton, 175 Wis. 2d 626, 502 N.W.2d 284 (Ct. App. 1993)
9 ALR6th 541—§ 10

State v. Cazares, 44 Or. App. 621, 606 P.2d 688 (1980)
39 ALR5th 283—§ 4, 66

State v. Cazes, 875 S.W.2d 253 (Tenn. 1994)
9 ALR5th 369—§ 13
10 ALR5th 700—§ 30, 37
104 ALR5th 357—§ 6
1 ALR6th 657—§ 4
54 ALR6th 429—§ 11, 13

State v. C.E., 2010-Ohio-1743, 2010 WL 1610489 (Ohio Ct. App. 8th Dist. Cuyahoga County 2010)
70 ALR6th 1—§ 3, 5

State v. Cecil, 173 W. Va. 27, 311 S.E.2d 144 (1983)
58 ALR6th 499—§ 49
71 ALR6th 1—§ 5

State v. Cecil, 221 W. Va. 495, 655 S.E.2d 517 (2007)
48 ALR6th 135—§ 8

State v. Cedrington, 725 So. 2d 565 (La. Ct. App. 5th Cir. 1998)
16 ALR6th 329—§ 4
24 ALR6th 591—§ 4, 14

State v. Ceglowski, 103 Wash. App. 346, 12 P.3d 160 (Div. 2 2000)
24 ALR5th 428—§ 6, 7

State v. Cejer, 1992 WL 55455 (Ohio Ct. App. 8th Dist. Cuyahoga County 1992)
80 ALR6th 599—§ 10

State v. Celestine, 91 So. 3d 573 (La. Ct. App. 3d Cir. 2012)
103 ALR6th 247—§ 9

State v. Celestine, 443 So. 2d 1091 (La. 1983)
77 ALR5th 201—§ 3

State v. Celestine, 540 So. 2d 1208 (La. Ct. App. 3d Cir. 1989)
19 ALR6th 411—§ 13

State v. Celmer, 80 N.J. 405, 404 A.2d 1 (1979)
102 ALR5th 525—§ 4

State v. Cemper, 209 Neb. 376, 307 N.W.2d 820 (1981)
18 ALR6th 1—§ 5, 23

State v. Central Computer Services, Inc., 349 So. 2d 1160, 91 A.L.R.3d 274 (Ala. 1977)
36 ALR5th 133—§ 3

State v. Cephas, 637 A.2d 20 (Del. 1994)
97 ALR5th 1—§ 7
106 ALR5th 111—§ 10, 14 to 17, 26, 27, 39
108 ALR5th 1—§ 29

State v. Cephus, 241 N.C. 562, 86 S.E.2d 70 (1955)
14 ALR5th 89—§ 34

State v. Cerda, 957 A.2d 382(R.I. 2008)
67 ALR6th 103—§ 5

State v. Cerilli, 222 Conn. 556, 610 A.2d 1130 (1992)
93 ALR5th 527—§ 20

State v. Cermak, 344 N.W.2d 833 (Minn. 1984)
73 ALR5th 383—§ 5, 6

State v. Cerny, 248 S.W.2d 844 (Mo. 1952)
97 ALR5th 293—§ 3, 10

State v. Cervantes, 62 Wash. App. 695, 814 P.2d 1232 (1991)
32 ALR5th 149—§ 51

State v. C.G., 101 Wash. App. 1053, 2000 WL 1009028 (Div. 2 2000)

59 ALR6th 393—§ 3

State v. Chacon, 146 Idaho 520, 198 P.3d 749 (Ct. App. 2008)
104 ALR6th 303—§ 14

State v. Chacon, 962 P.2d 48 (Utah 1998)
79 ALR5th 419—§ 21

State v. Chacon, 2013 WL 4609602 (Ariz. Ct. App. Div. 1 2013)
98 ALR6th 455—§ 11
102 ALR6th 279—§ 8

State v. Chadderton, 119 Wash. 2d 390, 832 P.2d 481 (1992)
73 ALR5th 383—§ 2, 3, 5, 40, 49, 54

State v. Chaffin, 324 So. 2d 369 (La. 1975)
114 ALR5th 235—§ 4

State v. Chairs, 106 So. 3d 1232 (La. Ct. App. 5th Cir. 2012)
98 ALR6th 455—§ 14
103 ALR6th 35—§ 7

State v. Chaisson, 123 N.H. 17, 458 A.2d 95 (1983)
29 ALR5th 59—§ 3, 81

State v. Chamberlain, 112 N.M. 723, 819 P.2d 673 (1991)
83 ALR6th 465—§ 4, 36

State v. Chamberlain, 137 N.H. 414, 628 A.2d 704 (1993)
85 ALR5th 595—§ 2, 7

State v. Chamberlin, 872 S.W.2d 615 (Mo. Ct. App. W.D. 1994)
66 ALR5th 397—§ 13, 21

State v. Chambers, 1 N.C.A. 1929, 1992 WL 296370 (1992)
2 ALR6th 169—§ 3, 5

State v. Chambers, 36 Kan. App. 2d 228, 138 P.3d 405, 30 A.L.R.6th 695 (2006)
30 ALR6th 373—§ 3, 15, 19
44 ALR6th 301—§ 4
51 ALR6th 139—§ 3, 6
63 ALR6th 351—§ 3

State v. Chambers, 87 Iowa 1, 53 N.W. 1090 (1893)
119 ALR5th 275—§ 13

State v. Chambers, 92 N.C. App. 230, 374 S.E.2d 158 (1988)
39 ALR5th 283—§ 4, 60
State v. Chambers, 134 Wash. App. 853, 142 P.3d 668 (Div. 2 2006)
30 ALR6th 1—§ 4, 7
State v. Chambers, 533 P.2d 876 (Utah 1975)
68 ALR6th 1—§ 4
State v. Chambers, 709 P.2d 339 (Utah 1985)
15 ALR5th 391—§ 22
State v. Chambers, 891 S.W.2d 93 (Mo. 1994)
83 ALR6th 255—§ 2, 15
State v. Chambers, 998 S.W.2d 85 (Mo. Ct. App. W.D. 1999)
5 ALR5th 243—§ 49
103 ALR6th 507—§ 4
State v. Chambers, 1993 WL 90416 (Tenn. Crim. App. 1993)
73 ALR5th 383—§ 5
State v. Chambers, 2010-Ohio-3559, 2010 WL 3004031 (Ohio Ct. App. 12th Dist. Brown County 2010)
64 ALR6th 1—§ 18
State v. Chambliss, 752 So. 2d 114 (Fla. Dist. Ct. App. 5th Dist. 2000)
1 ALR6th 371—§ 4
State v. Champa, 494 A.2d 102 (R.I. 1985)
3 ALR5th 521—§ 9, 10
State v. Champagne, 381 So. 2d 482 (La. 1980)
110 ALR5th 329—§ 5, 12
State v. Champion, 171 N.C. App. 716, 615 S.E.2d 366 (2005)
30 ALR6th 1—§ 3
State v. Champion, 413 N.W.2d 161 (Minn. Ct. App. 1987)
113 ALR5th 597—§ 8
State v. Champion, 533 N.W.2d 40 (Minn. 1995)
29 ALR6th 1—§ 9
State v. Champlain, 307 Wis. 2d 232, 2008 WI App 5, 744 N.W.2d 889 (Ct. App. 2007)

71 ALR6th 625—§ 3, 10, 30
State v. Champlain Cable Corp., 147 Vt. 436, 520 A.2d 596 (1986)
50 ALR5th 653—§ 14
State v. Chance, 19 P.3d 490 (Wash. Ct. App. Div. 2 2001)
29 ALR5th 487—§ 11.7
State v. Chance, 719 S.W.2d 108 (Mo. App. 1986)
34 ALR5th 125—§ 9
State v. Chance, 778 S.W.2d 457 (Tenn. Crim. 1989)
36 ALR5th 255—§ 18, 30
State v. Chancey, 2000 WL 193235 (Ohio Ct. App. 8th Dist. Cuyahoga County 2000)
19 ALR6th 697—§ 18
State v. Chandler, 252 Kan. 797, 850 P.2d 803 (1993)
5 ALR5th 243—§ 45, 48
State v. Chandler, 267 S.C. 138, 226 S.E.2d 553 (1976)
41 ALR5th 171—§ 8, 86, 98, 108, 115, 120, 122, 130, 136
State v. Chandler, 681 S.E.2d 565 (N.C. Ct. App. 2009)
57 ALR6th 1—§ 4, 13, 19
State v. Chandler, 2003-Ohio-6037, 2003 WL 22671580 (Ohio Ct. App. 8th Dist. Cuyahoga County 2003)
71 ALR6th 1—§ 5
State v. Chaney, 141 Ariz. 295, 686 P.2d 1265 (1984)
56 ALR6th 185—§ 26
State v. Chaney, 169 Ohio App. 3d 246, 2006-Ohio-5288, 862 N.E.2d 559 (3d Dist. Seneca County 2006)
98 ALR6th 455—§ 25
102 ALR6th 279—§ 23
State v. Chaney, 261 N.W.2d 674 (S.D. 1978)
92 ALR6th 295—§ 3
93 ALR6th 207—§ 3
96 ALR6th 355—§ 3
State v. Chaney, 1988 WL 86940 (Ohio Ct. App. 8th Dist. Cuyahoga County 1988)
99 ALR6th 295—§ 9

State v. Chang, 2001 WL 536975 (Minn. Ct. App. 2001)

69 ALR6th 579—§ 8, 27

State v. Chanoine, 2009 WL 4254456 (N.J. Super. Ct. App. Div. 2009)

71 ALR6th 1—§ 5

State v. Chapdelaine, 2010-Ohio-2683, 2010 WL 2349199 (Ohio Ct. App. 11th Dist. Lake County 2010)

65 ALR6th 1—§ 6, 9

State v. Chapman, 20 Conn. App. 205, 565 A.2d 259 (1989)

52 ALR6th 1—§ 3

70 ALR6th 361—§ 7

State v. Chapman, 33 Conn. App. 205, 635 A.2d 290 (1993)

55 ALR6th 157—§ 65

State v. Chapman, 97 Ohio App. 3d 687, 647 N.E.2d 504 (Hamilton Co. 1994)

55 ALR5th 125—§ 7

State v. Chapman, 122 Wash. App. 1034, 2004 WL 1616701 (Div. 2 2004)

125 ALR5th 497—§ 4

State v. Chapman, 358 A.2d 387 (Me. 1976)

19 ALR6th 697—§ 6

State v. Chapman, 367 So. 2d 808 (La. 1979)

7 ALR5th 263—§ 4

State v. Chapman, 454 S.E.2d 317, 47 A.L.R.5th 871 (S.C. 1995)

47 ALR5th 259—§ 2, 6

State v. Chapman, 805 So. 2d 906 (Fla. Dist. Ct. App. 2d Dist. 2001)

106 ALR5th 377—§ 4

113 ALR5th 597—§ 8

State v. Chapman, 921 P.2d 446 (Utah 1996)

72 ALR5th 1—§ 32

State v. Chapman, 1997 WL 602944 (Tenn. Crim. App. 1997)

90 ALR5th 453—§ 23

State v. Chappel, 149 Mont. 114, 423 P.2d 47 (1967)

9 ALR6th 1—§ 19

State v. Chappell, 24 N.C. App. 656, 211 S.E.2d 828 (1975)

28 ALR6th 505—§ 9

State v. Chappell, 97 Ohio App. 3d 515, 646 N.E.2d 1191 (Cuyahoga Co. 1994)

38 ALR5th 433—§ 7

State v. Chapple, 462 S.W.2d 707 (Mo. 1971)

18 ALR5th 856—§ 4

State v. Chapple, 2008-Ohio-1157, 2008 WL 697409 (Ohio Ct. App. 2d Dist. Montgomery County 2008)

35 ALR6th 361—§ 9, 10, 15, 20

State v. Chaput, 43 Or. App. 831, 604 P.2d 435 (1979)

56 ALR6th 323—§ 5

State v. Charboneau, 116 Idaho 129, 774 P.2d 299 (1989)

24 ALR5th 465—§ 42, 43

26 ALR5th 603—§ 3

State v. Charboneau, 323 Or. 38, 913 P.2d 308 (1996)

27 ALR6th 183—§ 17, 32

State v. Charest, 424 A.2d 718 (Me. 1981)

82 ALR5th 359—§ 6

84 ALR5th 487—§ 24

State v. Charles, 16 So. 3d 1166 (La. 2009)

58 ALR6th 439—§ 39

State v. Charles, 264 Ga. App. 874, 592 S.E.2d 518 (2003)

79 ALR6th 1—§ 40, 82

State v. Charles, 377 So. 2d 344 (La. 1979)

3 ALR5th 963—§ 2

State v. Charles, 572 S.W.2d 193 (Mo. Ct. App. 1978)

70 ALR5th 587—§ 3

State v. Charles, 602 So. 2d 15 (La. App. 3d Cir. 1992)

55 ALR5th 125—§ 20, 23

State v. Charles, 1997 WL 3197 (Wash. Ct. App. Div. 2 1997)

73 ALR5th 383—§ 29

State v. Charles E. Lohman, 1985 WL 10425 (Ohio Ct. App. 7th Dist. Carroll County 1985)
1 ALR6th 549—§ 25

State v. Charlesworth, 151 Or. App. 100, 951 P.2d 153 (1997)
97 ALR5th 201—§ 3
9 ALR6th 363—§ 38

State v. Charo, 156 Ariz. 561, 754 P.2d 288, 6 Ariz. Adv. Rep. 10 (1988)
57 ALR5th 141—§ 3

State v. Chase, 15 Or. App. 369, 515 P.2d 1337 (1973)
80 ALR6th 599—§ 5, 8

State v. Chase, 55 Ohio St. 2d 237, 9 Ohio Op. 3d 180, 378 N.E.2d 1064 (1978)
96 ALR5th 327—§ 3

State v. Chase, 329 So. 2d 434 (La. 1976)
55 ALR5th 125—§ 3, 12, 14

State v. Chase, 343 N.W.2d 695 (Minn. Ct. App. 1984)
73 ALR5th 383—§ 5, 31

State v. Chase, 588 A.2d 120 (R.I. 1991)
2 ALR5th 262—§ 4 to 6

State v. Chase, 2004 MT 375, 325 Mont. 64, 103 P.3d 1060 (2004)
23 ALR6th 307—§ 38, 44

State v. Chasse, 2000 ME 90, 750 A.2d 586 (Me. 2000)
99 ALR6th 295—§ 9

State v. Chattley, 650 A.2d 948 (Me. 1994)
15 ALR5th 391—§ 5

State v. Chaussee, 72 Wash. App. 704, 866 P.2d 643 (Div. 3 1994)
45 ALR6th 643—§ 13

State v. Chavarria, 1996 WL 665926 (Minn. Ct. App. 1996)
79 ALR6th 1—§ 88

State v. Chavers, 2005-Ohio-714, 2005 WL 418033 (Ohio Ct. App. 9th Dist. Wayne County 2005)
46 ALR6th 241—§ 10

State v. Chavez, 82 N.M. 569, 484 P.2d 1279 (App. 1971)

State v. Chavez, 98 N.M. 61, 644 P.2d 1050 (Ct. App. 1982)
5 ALR5th 243—§ 34
17 ALR6th 327—§ 40

State v. Chavez, 102 N.M. 279, 694 P.2d 927 (App. 1985)
21 ALR5th 275—§ 5

State v. Chavez, 2005 UT App 363, 2005 WL 2045798 (Utah Ct. App. 2005)
29 ALR6th 237—§ 4, 6

State v. Chavez, 2011 UT App 17, 246 P.3d 1219 (Utah Ct. App. 2011)
74 ALR6th 373—§ 18

State v. Chavez-Inzunza, 145 Ariz. 362, 701 P.2d 858 (Ct. App. Div. 2 1985)
35 ALR6th 497—§ 21

State v. Chavis, 540 S.E.2d 404 (N.C. Ct. App. 2000)
101 ALR5th 187—§ 6, 9

State v. Chavis, 2003-Ohio-512, 2003 WL 231265 (Ohio Ct. App. 10th Dist. Franklin County 2003)
3 ALR6th 269—§ 25

State v. Chears, 231 Kan. 161, 643 P.2d 154 (1982)
39 ALR5th 283—§ 4, 41
99 ALR6th 113—§ 4

State v. Cheatham, 134 Idaho 565, 6 P.3d 815 (2000)
20 ALR6th 479—§ 3

State v. Cheatham, 458 S.W.2d 336 (Mo. 1970)
81 ALR5th 563—§ 8

State v. Cheatham, 519 So. 2d 188 (La. Ct. App. 4th Cir. 1987)
68 ALR5th 343—§ 3

State v. Cheathon, 682 So. 2d 823 (La. Ct. App. 2d Cir. 1996)
93 ALR5th 527—§ 4

State v. Chee, 74 Ariz. 402, 250 P.2d 985 (1952)
41 ALR5th 1—§ 3, 4, 8

State v. Cheek, 100 Or. App. 501, 786 P.2d 1305, R.I.C.O. Bus. Disp. Guide (CCH) ¶ 7435 (1990)
89 ALR5th 629—§ 3

State v. Cheek, 351 N.C. 48, 520 S.E.2d 545 (1999)

9 ALR6th 1—§ 17

State v. Cheeks, 258 Kan. 581, 908 P.2d 175 (1995)

24 ALR5th 465—§ 79

State v. Cheers, 79 Ohio App. 3d 322, 607 N.E.2d 115 (6th Dist. Lucas County 1992)

58 ALR6th 499—§ 73

State v. Cheers, 102 Wis. 2d 367, 306 N.W.2d 676 (1981)

103 ALR6th 347—§ 13

State v. Cheeseboro, 346 S.C. 526, 552 S.E.2d 300 (2001)

27 ALR6th 183—§ 35

State v. Cheever, 295 Kan. 229, 284 P.3d 1007 (2012)

96 ALR6th 577—§ 17

State v. Chelson, 104 N.J. Super. 508, 250 A.2d 445 (County Ct. 1969)

69 ALR6th 1—§ 33

State v. Chem, 1995 WL 389237 (Minn. Ct. App. 1995)

42 ALR6th 237—§ 5

State v. Chemequip Sales, Inc., 69 Ohio App. 3d 236, 590 N.E.2d 355 (Ohio App. Summit Co. 1990)

11 ALR5th 388—§ 8

State v. Chenette, 151 Vt. 237, 560 A.2d 365 (1989)

79 ALR6th 125—§ 5

State v. Cheney, 116 Idaho 917, 782 P.2d 40 (Ct. App. 1989)

92 ALR6th 295—§ 3, 7 to 8, 11
95 ALR6th 1—§ 26
96 ALR6th 355—§ 3, 23, 35

State v. Chenoweth, 160 Wash. 2d 454, 158 P.3d 595 (2007)

73 ALR6th 49—§ 3

State v. Chenoweth, 163 Ind. 94, 71 N.E. 197 (1904)

118 ALR5th 253—§ 18

State v. Cheris, 153 Ind. App. 451, 287 N.E.2d 777 (1972)

15 ALR5th 821—§ 8, 9

State v. Cherry, 154 N.C. 624, 70 S.E. 294 (1911)

59 ALR5th 135—§ 4, 14

State v. Cherry, 154 N.J. Super. 157, 381 A.2d 49 (App. Div. 1977)

39 ALR6th 257—§ 15
40 ALR6th 1—§ 5, 8

State v. Chesher, 2001 WL 524063 (Tenn. Crim. App. 2001)

7 ALR6th 233—§ 9

State v. Chesire, 756 N.W.2d 49 (Iowa Ct. App. 2008)

71 ALR6th 1—§ 8

State v. Chesley, 2004 MT 165, 322 Mont. 26, 92 P.3d 1212 (2004)

68 ALR6th 1—§ 4

State v. Chesnel, 1999 ME 120, 734 A.2d 1131 (Me. 1999)

16 ALR6th 329—§ 15
24 ALR6th 591—§ 10

State v. Chestnut, 643 S.W.2d 343 (Tenn. Crim. 1982)

59 ALR5th 1—§ 4 to 6

State v. Chestnut, 718 So. 2d 312 (Fla. Dist. Ct. App. 5th Dist. 1998)

106 ALR5th 377—§ 3

State v. Chetcuti, 173 Conn. 165, 377 A.2d 263 (1977)

39 ALR5th 283—§ 3

State v. Chevalier, 458 So. 2d 507 (La. Ct. App. 4th Cir. 1984)

9 ALR6th 1—§ 17

State v. Chezem, 125 Or. App. 341, 865 P.2d 1307 (1993)

113 ALR5th 517—§ 5

State v. Chiapetta, 513 A.2d 831 (Me. 1986)

70 ALR6th 513—§ 11
71 ALR6th 471—§ 11

State v. Chiaverini, 2001 WL 256104 (Ohio Ct. App. 6th Dist. Lucas County 2001)

70 ALR6th 1—§ 5

State v. Chiavetta, 737 N.W.2d 325 (Iowa Ct. App. 2007)

30 ALR6th 103—§ 21

State v. Chichester, 31 Neb. 325, 47 N.W. 934 (1891)

5 ALR6th 1—§ 34

State v. Chichester, 48 Wash. App. 257, 738 P.2d 329 (Div. 3 1987)
65 ALR5th 407—§ 3, 9, 16

State v. Chief, 2011 WL 2201249 (Ariz. Ct. App. Div. 1 2011)
96 ALR6th 355—§ 24, 37

State v. Chiellini, 557 A.2d 1195 (R.I. 1989)
9 ALR5th 369—§ 2, 14, 17

State v. Chiello, 1995 R.I. Super. 415, 1995 WL 941448 (R.I. Super. Ct. 1995)
67 ALR5th 431—§ 4, 13

State v. Child, 1999 ME 198, 743 A.2d 230 (Me. 1999)
5 ALR5th 243—§ 15
19 ALR5th 823—§ 18

State v. Childers (1973) 13 Or App 622, 511 P2d 447
114 ALR5th 173—§ 10

State v. Childers, 196 La. 554, 199 So. 640 (1940)
9 ALR6th 363—§ 40

State v. Childers, 197 La. 715, 2 So. 2d 189 (1941)
97 ALR5th 293—§ 4

State v. Childers, 358 S.C. 614, 595 S.E.2d 872 (Ct. App. 2004)
3 ALR6th 543—§ 6

State v. Childers, 801 S.W.2d 442 (Mo. App. 1990)
5 ALR5th 243—§ 7

State v. Childers, 853 S.W.2d 332 (Mo. Ct. App. W.D. 1993)
19 ALR6th 115—§ 6, 8, 14

State v. Chiles, 53 Wash. App. 452, 767 P.2d 597 (Div. 2 1989)
95 ALR5th 229—§ 25

State v. Chiles, 680 N.W.2d 380 (Iowa Ct. App. 2004)
71 ALR6th 1—§ 21

State v. China, 150 N.C. App. 469, 564 S.E.2d 64 (2002)
58 ALR6th 499—§ 47

State v. Chincio, 60 Haw. 104, 588 P.2d 408 (1978)
9 ALR6th 541—§ 10

State v. Chinn, 85 Ohio St. 3d 548, 709 N.E.2d 1166 (1999)
79 ALR5th 33—§ 62

State v. Chinn, 229 La. 984, 87 So. 2d 315 (1955)
98 ALR6th 455—§ 13

State v. Chio Hang Saechao, 195 Or. App. 581, 98 P.3d 1144 (2004)
30 ALR6th 1—§ 4, 7

State v. Chippewa Cable Co., 48 Wis. 2d 341, 180 N.W.2d 714 (1970)
88 ALR5th 641—§ 3, 6

State v. Chirra, 79 N.J. Super. 270, 191 A.2d 308 (Law Div. 1963)
71 ALR6th 335—§ 10

State v. Chitwood, 730 N.W.2d 210 (Iowa Ct. App. 2007)
33 ALR6th 91—§ 45

State v. Chlebowski, 1992 WL 114505 (Ohio Ct. App. 8th Dist. Cuyahoga County 1992)
124 ALR5th 657—§ 7

State v. Choi, 2007 WL 445445 (N.J. Super. Ct. App. Div. 2007)
69 ALR6th 579—§ 11

State v. Choice Tobacco, Inc., 2004 WL 1434542 (Me. Super. Ct. 2004)
25 ALR6th 435—§ 58

State v. Choinacki, 324 N.J. Super. 19, 734 A.2d 324 (App. Div. 1999)
30 ALR6th 103—§ 8, 17

State v. Chong, 121 N.H. 860, 435 A.2d 538 (1981)
51 ALR6th 359—§ 24

State v. Chrisco, 26 Kan. App. 2d 816, 995 P.2d 401 (1999)
106 ALR5th 377—§ 4

State v. Chrisco, 232 Wis. 2d 557, 2000 WI App 32, 608 N.W.2d 437 (Ct. App. 1999)
4 ALR6th 599—§ 16

State v. Chrisicos, 148 N.H. 546, 813 A.2d 513 (2002)
81 ALR6th 505—§ 20

State v. Chrisman, 75 A.D.3d 1057, 905 N.Y.S.2d 414 (4th Dep't 2010)
78 ALR6th 417—§ 42

State v. Christen, 1997 ME 213, 704 A.2d 335 (Me. 1997)

50 ALR6th 353—§ 45, 48

State v. Christensen, 18 Wash. 2d 7, 137 P.2d 512, 146 A.L.R. 1302 (1943)

60 ALR5th 459—§ 2, 10, 17

State v. Christensen, 100 Idaho 631, 603 P.2d 586 (1979)

37 ALR5th 703—§ 3

State v. Christensen, 129 Ariz. 32, 628 P.2d 580 (1981)

57 ALR5th 141—§ 3

State v. Christensen, 131 Idaho 143, 953 P.2d 583 (1998)

45 ALR6th 643—§ 14

State v. Christensen, 244 Mont. 312, 797 P.2d 893 (1990)

19 ALR5th 470—§ 6

State v. Christensen, 414 N.W.2d 843 (Iowa Ct. App. 1987)

102 ALR5th 447—§ 4, 16

State v. Christensen (In re C.C.), 907 P.2d 241 (Okla. App. 1995)

53 ALR5th 499—§ 5

State v. Christensen, 953 P.2d 583 (Idaho 1998)

60 ALR5th 1—§ 4

State v. Christensen, 1999 WL 100871 (Wash. Ct. App. Div. 2 1999)

73 ALR5th 383—§ 6, 32

State v. Christensen, 2011 WL 2176656 (Tex. App. Dallas 2011)

92 ALR6th 295—§ 3
93 ALR6th 207—§ 3
94 ALR6th 191—§ 3

State v. Christenson, 181 Or. App. 345, 45 P.3d 511 (2002)

58 ALR6th 499—§ 80

State v. Christian, 35 Or. App. 339, 581 P.2d 132 (1978)

87 ALR5th 597—§ 15

State v. Christian, 95 Wash. 2d 655, 628 P.2d 806 (1981)

61 ALR5th 1—§ 4, 7

State v. Christian, 723 N.W.2d 453 (Iowa Ct. App. 2006)

93 ALR6th 275—§ 4

State v. Christiana, 249 La. 247, 186 So. 2d 580 (1966)

29 ALR5th 59—§ 84

State v. Christiansen, 515 N.W.2d 110 (Minn. Ct. App. 1994)

109 ALR5th 611—§ 3

State v. Christiansen, 2010 MT 197, 357 Mont. 379, 239 P.3d 949 (2010)

92 ALR6th 295—§ 14

State v. Christianson, 97 Wash. App. 1087, 1999 WL 1033554 (Div. 1 1999)

125 ALR5th 497—§ 4

State v. Christie, 91 N.J. Super. 420, 221 A.2d 20 (1966)

45 ALR5th 531—§ 7

State v. Christie, 243 Iowa 1199, 53 N.W.2d 887 (1952)

79 ALR5th 237—§ 3

State v. Christley, 2009-Ohio-6635, 2009 WL 4856800 (Ohio Ct. App. 8th Dist. Cuyahoga County 2009)

63 ALR6th 303—§ 22

State v. Christoffersen, 756 N.W.2d 230 (Iowa Ct. App. 2008)

84 ALR6th 293—§ 27

State v. Christopher, 20 Wash. App. 755, 583 P.2d 638 (Div. 1 1978)

56 ALR6th 185—§ 13

State v. Christopher, 176 N.W.2d 777 (Iowa 1970)

26 ALR5th 1—§ 3, 41

State v. Christopher, 258 Wis. 2d 300, 2002 WI App 261, 653 N.W.2d 772 (Ct. App. 2002)

15 ALR6th 375—§ 22

State v. Christopher, 2002 WI App 261, 258 Wis. 2d 300, 653 N.W.2d 772 (Ct. App. 2002)

84 ALR6th 293—§ 38

State v. Christopherson, 36 Wis. 2d 574, 153 N.W.2d 631 (1967)

108 ALR5th 593—§ 11, 23

State v. Chryst, 320 N.W.2d 721 (Minn. 1982)

67 ALR6th 209—§ 21

State v. Chrzanowski, 180 Ohio App. 3d 324, 2008-Ohio-6993, 905 N.E.2d 266 (11th Dist. Portage County 2008)

57 ALR6th 83—§ 12

State v. Chu, 2002-Ohio-2673, 2002 WL 1308353 (Ohio Ct. App. 8th Dist. Cuyahoga County 2002)

11 ALR6th 237—§ 13

State v. Chubb Corp., 239 N.J. Super. 257, 570 A.2d 1313 (Ch. Div. 1989)

29 ALR6th 507—§ 14

State v. Chubbuck, 406 A.2d 282 (Me. 1979)

84 ALR5th 487—§ 21, 24

State v. Chudzik, 2004-Ohio-2788, 2004 WL 1192124 (Ohio Ct. App. 11th Dist. Ashtabula County 2004)

57 ALR6th 83—§ 7

State v. Chukes, 2003 UT App 155, 71 P.3d 624 (Utah Ct. App. 2003)

125 ALR5th 537—§ 2, 15, 17
80 ALR6th 599—§ 7

State v. Chumley, 122 Wash. App. 1011, 2004 WL 1444915 (Div. 1 2004)

33 ALR6th 91—§ 45

State v. Church, 538 So. 2d 993 (La. 1989)

74 ALR5th 319—§ 2, 3

State v. Church, 1995 WL 413412 (Del. Super. Ct. 1995)

85 ALR5th 1—§ 24

State v. Chvala, 271 Wis. 2d 115, 2004 WI App 53, 678 N.W.2d 880 (Ct. App. 2004)

9 ALR6th 177—§ 18, 19
24 ALR6th 255—§ 6, 8, 14

State v. Chyo Chiagk, 92 Mo. 395, 4 S.W. 704 (1887)

32 ALR5th 149—§ 50, 51, 71

State v. Cianci, 496 A.2d 139, 11 Media L. R. 2403 (R.I. 1985)

16 ALR5th 152—§ 4

State v. Cianflone, 98 Conn. 454, 120 A. 347 (1923)

16 ALR6th 329—§ 4
24 ALR6th 591—§ 4

State v. Cibrian, 96 Wash. App. 1028, 1999 WL 458974 (Div. 1 1999)

8 ALR6th 265—§ 7

State v. Cichowicz, 1992 WL 52573 (Ohio Ct. App. 11th Dist. Ashtabula County 1992)

69 ALR6th 207—§ 9, 10, 18

State v. Cimini, 53 Wash. 268, 101 P. 891 (1909)

32 ALR5th 149—§ 67

State v. Cinel, 646 So. 2d 309 (La. 1994)

42 ALR5th 291—§ 3, 10

State v. Cinel, 660 So. 2d 887 (La. App. 4th Cir. 1995)

51 ALR5th 603—§ 2

State v. Cinotti, 2007 WL 108345 (N.J. Super. Ct. App. Div. 2007)

84 ALR6th 293—§ 27

State v. Ciskie, 110 Wash. 2d 263, 751 P.2d 1165 (1988)

57 ALR5th 315—§ 1 to 3, 6 to 9, 12

State v. Citta, 265 N.J. Super. 208, 625 A.2d 1162 (Law Div. 1990)

59 ALR5th 615—§ 3, 7, 12

State v. City of Anchorage, 513 P.2d 1104 (Alaska 1973)

85 ALR5th 547—§ 3

State v. City of Austin, 160 Tex. 348, 331 S.W.2d 737 (1960)

122 ALR5th 337—§ 14

State v. City of Baltimore, 141 Md. 344, 118 A. 753 (1922)

95 ALR5th 29—§ 4

State v. City of Beaumont, 161 S.W.2d 344 (Tex. Civ. App. Beaumont 1942)

114 ALR5th 561—§ 4

State v. City of Columbia, 115 S.C. 108, 104 S.E. 337 (1920)

114 ALR5th 561—§ 23

State v. City of Concordia, 78 Kan. 250, 96 P. 487 (1908)

92 ALR5th 517—§ 3

State v. City of Hudson, 231 Minn. 127, 42 N.W.2d 546 (1950)

114 ALR5th 561—§ 8

State v. City of Port Orange, 650 So. 2d 1 (Fla. 1994)
97 ALR5th 123—§ 13
State v. City of San Antonio, 147 Tex. 1, 209 S.W.2d 756 (1948)
114 ALR5th 561—§ 6
State (State University of New York) v. Civil Service Employees Ass'n, 148 App. Div. 2d 790, 538 N.Y.S.2d 641 (3d Dep't 1989)
56 ALR5th 757—§ 3
State v. C.L., 148 N.M. 837, 2010-NMCA-050, 242 P.3d 404 (Ct. App. 2010)
68 ALR6th 1—§ 17
State v. Clabaugh, 346 N.W.2d 448 (S.D. 1984)
24 ALR6th 1—§ 11
State v. Clabo, 905 S.W.2d 197 (Tenn. Crim. App. 1995)
73 ALR5th 383—§ 5, 24
State v. Claborn, 1994 OK CR 8, 870 P.2d 169 (Okla. Crim. App. 1994)
87 ALR6th 109—§ 68
State v. Clabourne, 142 Ariz. 335, 690 P.2d 54 (1984)
9 ALR6th 1—§ 17
State v. Clah, 124 N.M. 6, 1997-NMCA-091, 946 P.2d 210 (Ct. App. 1997)
46 ALR6th 63—§ 9
State v. Claiborne, 483 So. 2d 1301 (La. Ct. App. 4th Cir. 1986)
99 ALR6th 295—§ 5, 9
State v. Claiborne, 1997 WL 24792 (Ohio Ct. App. 2d Dist. Montgomery County 1997)
84 ALR6th 293—§ 15
State v. Clancy, 30 Mont. 529, 77 P. 312 (1904)
91 ALR5th 437—§ 4, 9, 10, 15, 17, 23, 25
97 ALR5th 537—§ 18
State v. Clappes, 117 Wis. 2d 277, 344 N.W.2d 141 (1984)
30 ALR6th 103—§ 8, 19, 34, 43
State v. Clappes, 136 Wis. 2d 222, 401 N.W.2d 759 (1987)
9 ALR6th 1—§ 17

State v. Clark, 5 Conn. Cir. Ct. 699, 261 A.2d 294 (App. Div. 1969)
118 ALR5th 253—§ 9, 16
State v. Clark, 28 Utah 2d 272, 501 P.2d 274 (1972)
37 ALR6th 357—§ 8
State v. Clark, 34 Wash. App. 173, 659 P.2d 554 (1983)
56 ALR5th 385—§ 3, 4
State v. Clark, 36 Nev. 472, 135 P. 1083 (1913)
54 ALR6th 429—§ 20
State v. Clark, 38 Ohio St. 3d 252, 527 N.E.2d 844 (1988)
10 ALR5th 700—§ 31
20 ALR5th 177—§ 3, 8, 11
65 ALR6th 537—§ 4, 47
State v. Clark, 63 Ohio App. 3d 52, 577 N.E.2d 1141 (8th Dist. Cuyahoga County 1989)
104 ALR5th 229—§ 4
4 ALR6th 113—§ 44
101 ALR6th 1—§ 41, 49
State v. Clark, 75 Wash. App. 827, 880 P.2d 562 (1994)
36 ALR5th 161—§ 9
State v. Clark, 75 Wash. App. 827, 880 P.2d 562 (Div. 1 1994)
41 ALR6th 141—§ 7
State v. Clark, 76 Wash. App. 150, 883 P.2d 333 (Div. 1 1994)
113 ALR5th 597—§ 8
State v. Clark, 80 N.M. 91, 451 P.2d 995 (App. 1969)
39 ALR5th 283—§ 3
State v. Clark, 80 N.M. 340, 455 P.2d 844 (1969)
28 ALR5th 754—§ 2, 3, 8
State v. Clark, 83 Haw. 289, 926 P.2d 194 (Haw. 1996)
57 ALR5th 315—§ 3, 11
State v. Clark, 83 N.M. 484, 493 P.2d 969 (Ct. App. 1971)
104 ALR5th 357—§ 6
State v. Clark, 87 Wash. App. 1059, 1997 WL 568024 (Div. 2 1997)
92 ALR6th 171—§ 4

State v. Clark, 101 Ohio App. 3d 389, 655 N.E.2d 795 (8th Dist. Cuyahoga County 1995)
90 ALR5th 453—§ 17
State v. Clark, 104 N.J. Super. 67, 248 A.2d 559 (1968)
50 ALR5th 467—§ 6, 9
State v. Clark, 104 N.M. 434, 1986-NMCA-058, 722 P.2d 685 (Ct. App. 1986)
102 ALR6th 365—§ 20
State v. Clark, 104 Wash. App. 1001, 2001 WL 6723 (Div. 3 2001)
106 ALR5th 397—§ 4
State v. Clark, 105 N.M. 10, 727 P.2d 949 (Ct. App. 1986)
61 ALR5th 1—§ 2, 4, 11
State v. Clark, 105 N.M. 10, 1986-NMCA-095, 727 P.2d 949 (Ct. App. 1986)
99 ALR6th 397—§ 17
State v. Clark, 107 N.C. App. 184, 419 S.E.2d 188 (1992)
57 ALR5th 141—§ 8
State v. Clark, 115 Idaho 1056, 772 P.2d 263 (App. 1989)
5 ALR5th 243—§ 45
State v. Clark, 124 Idaho 308, 859 P.2d 344 (Ct. App. 1993)
60 ALR5th 1—§ 2, 8
State v. Clark, 143 Wash. 2d 731, 24 P.3d 1006 (2001)
72 ALR6th 437—§ 6, 17
State v. Clark, 161 N.C. App. 316, 588 S.E.2d 66 (2003)
28 ALR6th 505—§ 16
State v. Clark, 165 N.C. App. 279, 598 S.E.2d 213 (2004)
30 ALR6th 1—§ 3, 6
State v. Clark, 170 Wash. App. 166, 283 P.3d 1116 (Div. 1 2012)
101 ALR6th 417—§ 8
State v. Clark, 171 Or. App. 1, 14 P.3d 626 (2000)
24 ALR6th 1—§ 33
State v. Clark, 218 Kan. 726, 544 P.2d 1372 (1976)
101 ALR6th 299—§ 6, 9

State v. Clark, 222 Kan. 65, 563 P.2d 1028 (1977)
72 ALR6th 141—§ 9
State v. Clark, 296 N.W.2d 359 (Minn. 1980)
84 ALR5th 487—§ 21
94 ALR5th 393—§ 10, 14
State v. Clark, 324 N.C. 146, 377 S.E.2d 54 (1989)
30 ALR6th 103—§ 11, 14, 26, 58
32 ALR6th 1—§ 11
State v. Clark, 338 So. 2d 690 (La. 1976)
86 ALR5th 59—§ 3
State v. Clark, 351 N.W.2d 532 (Iowa 1984)
7 ALR5th 263—§ 5
State v. Clark, 372 So. 2d 1218 (La. 1979)
95 ALR5th 229—§ 25
State v. Clark, 423 A.2d 1151 (R.I. 1980)
82 ALR5th 67—§ 3, 7
State v. Clark, 475 A.2d 418 (Me. 1984)
9 ALR6th 1—§ 17
State v. Clark, 492 So. 2d 862 (La. 1986)
10 ALR5th 700—§ 16, 20
State v. Clark, 538 So. 2d 500, 14 FLW 337 (Fla. App. D3 1989)
45 ALR5th 1—§ 2, 5, 9, 21, 28
State v. Clark, 574 S.W.2d 452 (Mo. Ct. App. 1978)
70 ALR5th 587—§ 4
State v. Clark, 638 So. 2d 225 (La. App. 3d Cir. 1994)
31 ALR5th 704—§ 4
State v. Clark, 675 P.2d 557 (Utah 1983)
55 ALR6th 157—§ 4, 17
State v. Clark, 724 So. 2d 653 (Fla. Dist. Ct. App. 5th Dist. 1999)
113 ALR5th 597—§ 8
State v. Clark, 745 So. 2d 1116 (Fla. Dist. Ct. App. 4th Dist. 1999)
113 ALR5th 597—§ 3
State v. Clark, 783 P.2d 68, 121 Utah Adv. Rep. 48 (Utah App. 1989)
34 ALR5th 125—§ 18
State v. Clark, 846 S.W.2d 750 (Mo. Ct. App. E.D. 1993)

37 ALR6th 357—§ 71
State v. Clark, 851 So. 2d 1055 (La. 2003)
98 ALR6th 455—§ 14
State v. Clark, 924 So. 2d 282 (La. Ct. App. 5th Cir. 2006)
38 ALR6th 439—§ 11
State v. Clark, 1982 WL 6502 (Ohio Ct. App. 6th Dist.Ottawa County 1982)
66 ALR5th 373—§ 5
State v. Clark, 1988 WL 50506 (Ohio Ct. App. 4th Dist.Pike County 1988)
57 ALR5th 141—§ 2, 13
State v. Clark, 1989 WL 36697 (Ohio Ct. App. 8th Dist. Cuyahoga County 1989)
88 ALR5th 121—§ 2, 10, 24, 28
State v. Clark, 1995 WL 44582 (Del. Super. Ct. 1995)
57 ALR5th 141—§ 3
State v. Clark, 1999 -NMSC- 035, 128 N.M. 119, 990 P.2d 793 (1999)
79 ALR5th 33—§ 3
State v. Clark, 2000 M.T. 40, 997 P.2d 107 (Mont. 2000)
2 ALR5th 725—§ 12, 13
State v. Clark, 2003-Ohio-6689, 2003 WL 22931358 (Ohio Ct. App. 11th Dist. Ashtabula County 2003)
71 ALR6th 1—§ 8
State v. Clark, 2003 WL 21789648 (Minn. Ct. App. 2003)
78 ALR6th 297—§ 37
State v. Clark, 2004-Ohio-334, 2004 WL 144238 (Ohio Ct. App. 11th Dist. Portage County 2004)
71 ALR6th 1—§ 5
State v. Clark, 2004-Ohio-5964, 2004 WL 2535271 (Ohio Ct. App. 8th Dist. Cuyahoga County 2004)
3 ALR6th 543—§ 8
State v. Clark, 2005-Ohio-1324, 2005 WL 678565 (Ohio Ct. App. 1st Dist. Hamilton County 2005)
35 ALR6th 361—§ 7, 9, 10, 15, 21
State v. Clark, 2005 WL 3710959 (N.J. Super. Ct. App. Div. 2006)
26 ALR6th 511—§ 28

State v. Clark, 2006-Ohio-4212, 2006 WL 2347877 (Ohio Ct. App. 12th Dist. Clermont County 2006)
51 ALR6th 139—§ 6
State v. Clark, 2010-Ohio-2383, 2010 WL 2162649 (Ohio Ct. App. 6th Dist. Williams County 2010)
71 ALR6th 1—§ 6
State v. Clarke, 3 Del. 557, 3 Harr. 557, 1840 WL 3673 (Ct. of Oyer & Terminer 1840)
5 ALR6th 1—§ 41
State v. Clarke, 24 Conn. App. 541, 590 A.2d 468 (1991)
3 ALR5th 521—§ 3, 5
State v. Clarke, 198 N.J. Super. 219, 486 A.2d 935 (App. Div. 1985)
93 ALR5th 683—§ 4
State v. Clarke, 203 N.J. 166, 1 A.3d 607 (2010)
78 ALR6th 1—§ 7, 8
State v. Clarke, 448 A.2d 1208 (R.I. 1982)
16 ALR6th 329—§ 13
24 ALR6th 591—§ 9
State v. Clarke, 2001 WL 1255793 (Ohio Ct. App. 12th Dist. Butler County 2001)
122 ALR5th 439—§ 9
State v. Clarkston, 963 S.W.2d 705 (Mo. Ct. App. W.D. 1998)
96 ALR5th 523—§ 3
17 ALR6th 757—§ 3, 8
State v. Clary, 73 Ohio App. 3d 42, 596 N.E.2d 554 (Franklin Co. 1991)
38 ALR5th 433—§ 26
State v. Clausen, 697 So. 2d 1066 (La. Ct. App. 4th Cir. 1997)
50 ALR5th 581—§ 9
State v. Clausmier, 154 Ind. 599, 57 N.E. 541 (1900)
100 ALR5th 341—§ 3, 5
State v. Claussen, 522 N.W.2d 196 (S.D. 1994)
74 ALR5th 319—§ 4
State v. Claussen, 2007 WL 91652 (Neb. Ct. App. 2007)
45 ALR6th 435—§ 3

State v. Clay, 7 Wash. App. 631, 501 P.2d 603 (Div. 1 1972)
114 ALR5th 235—§ 4
55 ALR6th 157—§ 10

State v. Clay, 145 Wash. App. 1040, 2008 WL 2721282 (Div. 1 2008)
94 ALR6th 579—§ 6

State v. Clay, 297 N.C. 555, 256 S.E.2d 176 (1979) (disapproved of by, State v. Davis, 305 N.C. 400, 290 S.E.2d 574 (1982)) and (disapproved of by, State v. Jones, 72 N.C. App. 610, 325 S.E.2d 309 (1985)) and (disapproved of by, State v. McAvoy on other grounds, 331 N.C. 583, 417 S.E.2d 489 (1992))
28 ALR6th 505—§ 9

State v. Clay, 332 Or. 327, 29 P.3d 1101 (2001)
26 ALR6th 179—§ 15

State v. Clay, 779 S.W.2d 673 (Mo. Ct. App. W.D. 1989)
70 ALR5th 587—§ 21

State v. Clay, 780 So. 2d 269 (Fla. Dist. Ct. App. 5th Dist. 2001)
113 ALR5th 597—§ 8

State v. Clay, 975 S.W.2d 121 (Mo. 1998)
83 ALR6th 255—§ 12, 15, 25

State v. Clay, 2000 WL 202083 (Ohio Ct. App. 9th Dist. Summit County 2000)
78 ALR5th 489—§ 10

State v. Clay, 2009-Ohio-2725, 2009 WL 1629669 (Ohio Ct. App. 8th Dist. Cuyahoga County 2009)
56 ALR6th 1—§ 15, 24, 35

State v. Clayborn, 125 Ohio St. 3d 450, 2010-Ohio-2123, 928 N.E.2d 1093 (2010)
64 ALR6th 1—§ 4

State v. Clayborn, 2011-Ohio-1890, 2011 WL 1483914 (Ohio Ct. App. 10th Dist. Franklin County 2011)
64 ALR6th 1—§ 9

State v. Clayborne, 1996 WL 315811 (Tenn. Crim. App. 1996)
57 ALR5th 141—§ 3, 6

State v. Claybrook, 193 Ariz. 588, 975 P.2d 1101 (Ct. App. Div. 1 1998)
119 ALR5th 379—§ 8

State v. Claybrook, 198 Wis. 2d 386, 542 N.W.2d 237 (Ct. App. 1995)
72 ALR5th 403—§ 15

State v. Clayton, 84 Wash. App. 318, 927 P.2d 258, 114 Ed. Law Rep. 668 (Div. 3 1996)
27 ALR5th 593—§ 25

State v. Clayton, 658 P.2d 624 (Utah 1983)
26 ALR5th 603—§ 4

State v. Clayton, 823 S.W.2d 17 (Mo. App. 1991)
26 ALR5th 1—§ 4, 33

State v. Clayton, 995 S.W.2d 468 (Mo. 1999)
101 ALR6th 331—§ 12

State v. Clayton, 2010 WL 3001418 (N.C. Ct. App. 2010)
57 ALR6th 1—§ 27

State v. Claytor, 108 Wash. App. 1036, 2001 WL 1226537 (Div. 1 2001)
7 ALR6th 233—§ 5

State v. Cleator, 71 Wash. App. 217, 857 P.2d 306 (Div. 1 1993)
66 ALR5th 373—§ 4, 5

State v. Cleland, 246 Mont. 165, 803 P.2d 1093 (1990)
71 ALR6th 1—§ 6

State v. Clement, 153 Wis. 2d 287, 450 N.W.2d 789 (App. 1989)
28 ALR5th 754—§ 4, 7

State v. Clement, 1995 WL 390795 (Ohio Ct. App. 10th Dist. Franklin County 1995)
29 ALR6th 237—§ 4, 9, 21

State v. Clements, 52 Or. App. 309, 628 P.2d 433 (1981)
55 ALR6th 391—§ 19

State v. Clements, 108 N.M. 13, 765 P.2d 1195 (Ct. App. 1988)
19 ALR6th 697—§ 17, 20

State v. Clements, 925 S.W.2d 224 (Tenn. 1996)
42 ALR5th 547—§ 4, 5

State v. Clements, 1992 WL 297266 (Ohio Ct. App. 10th Dist. Franklin County 1992)
34 ALR6th 1—§ 12

State v. Clemmons, 81 Wash. App. 1003, 1996 WL 146721 (Div. 1 1996)
91 ALR5th 585—§ 2, 3, 12

State v. Clemmons, 100 N.C. App. 286, 396 S.E.2d 616 (1990)
87 ALR5th 597—§ 3, 10

State v. Clemmons, 150 So. 2d 231 (Fla. 1963)
93 ALR5th 493—§ 14

State v. Clemons, 27 Ariz. App. 193, 552 P.2d 1208 (1976)
55 ALR5th 125—§ 3, 5, 7

State v. Clemons, 82 Ohio St. 3d 438, 696 N.E.2d 1009 (1998)
79 ALR5th 33—§ 40

State v. Clemons, 251 Kan. 473, 836 P.2d 1147 (1992)
47 ALR5th 259—§ 15
28 ALR6th 505—§ 9

State v. Clepper, 399 N.W.2d 574 (Minn. Ct. App. 1987)
34 ALR6th 1—§ 10

State v. Cleveland, 101 Haw. 96, 63 P3d 404 (2003)
57 ALR6th 83—§ 5

State v. Cleveland, 630 So. 2d 1365 (La. Ct. App. 2d Cir. 1994)
99 ALR6th 295—§ 5

State v. Cleveland, 2004 WL 236762 (Minn. Ct. App. 2004)
59 ALR6th 311—§ 11

State v. Clevenger, 69 Wash. 2d 136, 417 P.2d 626 (1966)
55 ALR5th 125—§ 3, 9

State v. Cliff, 116 Idaho 921, 782 P.2d 44 (Ct. App. 1989)
82 ALR6th 373—§ 4, 7, 16

State v. Clifton, 125 N.C. App. 471, 481 S.E.2d 393 (1997)
97 ALR5th 293—§ 2

State v. Clifton, 150 Wis. 2d 673, 443 N.W.2d 26 (Ct. App. 1989)
99 ALR6th 295—§ 5

State v. Clifton, 302 S.C. 431, 396 S.E.2d 831 (Ct. App. 1990)
109 ALR5th 99—§ 9

State v. Clinding, 92 N.C. App. 555, 374 S.E.2d 891 (1989)
39 ALR5th 283—§ 4, 18

State v. Cline, 122 R.I. 297, 405 A.2d 1192 (1979)
9 ALR6th 1—§ 22
55 ALR6th 157—§ 9

State v. Cline, 238 Wis. 2d 447, 2000 WI App 186, 617 N.W.2d 907 (Ct. App. 2000)
38 ALR6th 97—§ 28

State v. Cline, 275 Mont. 46, 909 P.2d 1171 (1996)
90 ALR5th 453—§ 14

State v. Cline, 617 N.W.2d 277 (Iowa 2000)
19 ALR5th 470—§ 15

State v. Cline, 696 S.E.2d 554 (N.C. Ct. App. 2010)
58 ALR6th 499—§ 48

State v. Cline, 1998 -NMCA- 154, 966 P.2d 785 (N.M. Ct. App. 1998)
65 ALR5th 407—§ 3, 5, 7, 11

State v. Clinkscales, 231 S.C. 650, 99 S.E.2d 663 (1957)
24 ALR5th 465—§ 51

State v. Clinton, 48 Wash. App. 671, 741 P.2d 52 (Div. 1 1987)
73 ALR5th 383—§ 3

State v. Clinton, 181 Ariz. 299, 890 P.2d 74 (Ct. App. Div. 1 1995)
92 ALR5th 35—§ 3

State v. Clinton, 890 P.2d 74, 184 Ariz. Adv. Rep. 6 (Ariz. App. 1995)
15 ALR5th 391—§ 5

State v. Cloksey, 37 Tenn. 482, 5 Sneed 482, 1858 WL 2776 (1858)
5 ALR6th 1—§ 28

State v. Cloninger, 37 N.C. App. 22, 245 S.E.2d 192 (1978)
1 ALR6th 549—§ 15, 16

State v. Clontz, 4 N.C. App. 667, 167 S.E.2d 520 (1969)

---

125 ALR5th 537—§ 23
State v. Close, 267 Mont. 44, 881 P.2d 1312 (1994)
55 ALR6th 391—§ 5
State v. Closser, 687 S.W.2d 657 (Mo. Ct. App. S.D. 1985)
70 ALR6th 361—§ 3, 29
71 ALR6th 335—§ 3
72 ALR6th 141—§ 3
State v. Closson, 1996 WL 219156 (Wash. Ct. App. Div. 1 1996)
73 ALR5th 383—§ 23
State v. Cloud, 91 Ohio App. 3d 366, 632 N.E.2d 932 (Cuyahoga Co. 1993)
50 ALR5th 581—§ 7, 20
State v. Cloud, 319 So. 2d 793 (La. 1975)
17 ALR6th 327—§ 23
State v. Cloukey, 486 A.2d 143 (Me. 1985)
116 ALR5th 479—§ 3
State v. Cloverdale, 1999 WL 517410 (Del. Super. Ct. 1999)
119 ALR5th 379—§ 7
State v. Clowes, 310 Or. 686, 801 P.2d 789 (1990)
3 ALR5th 521—§ 2, 3
State v. Clum, 216 Or. App. 1, 171 P.3d 980 (2007)
34 ALR6th 171—§ 13
38 ALR6th 1—§ 26
State v. C.M., 746 So. 2d 410 (Ala. Crim. App. 1999)
36 ALR5th 161—§ 3, 27
25 ALR6th 227—§ 11, 18
37 ALR6th 55—§ 8
63 ALR6th 351—§ 3, 4
State v. C.M., 1999 WL 274903 (Ala. Crim. App. 1999)
78 ALR5th 489—§ 3
State v. C.M.B. III Enterprises, Inc., 734 N.E.2d 653 (Ind. Ct. App. 2000)
7 ALR5th 474—§ 29.5, 176
State v. Coates, 17 Wash. App. 415, 563 P.2d 208 (Div. 1 1977)
84 ALR6th 427—§ 4

State v. Coauette, 601 N.W.2d 443 (Minn. Ct. App. 1999)
11 ALR6th 525—§ 4, 5, 10
State v. Cobb, 21 N.C. App. 66, 202 S.E.2d 801 (1974)
113 ALR5th 517—§ 8
State v. Cobb, 22 Or. App. 510, 539 P.2d 1140 (1975)
34 ALR6th 1—§ 12
State v. Cobb, 30 Kan. App. 2d 544, 43 P.3d 855 (2002)
20 ALR6th 479—§ 9, 13
State v. Cobb, 115 Ariz. 484, 566 P.2d 285 (1977)
24 ALR6th 1—§ 17
State v. Cobb, 251 Conn. 285, 743 A.2d 1 (1999)
24 ALR6th 747—§ 24
93 ALR6th 391—§ 20
State v. Cobb, 403 N.W.2d 329 (Minn. Ct. App. 1987)
97 ALR5th 293—§ 2
State v. Cobb, 931 S.W.2d 904 (Mo. Ct. App. W.D. 1996)
84 ALR6th 293—§ 43
State v. Cobb, 1991 WL 71910 (Tenn. Crim. App. 1991)
84 ALR6th 293—§ 34
State v. Cobb, 2007-Ohio-1885, 2007 WL 1165863 (Ohio Ct. App. 4th Dist. Scioto County 2007)
26 ALR6th 511—§ 31
State v. Cobb, 2007-Ohio-5614, 2007 WL 3052540 (Ohio Ct. App. 11th Dist. Portage County 2007)
43 ALR6th 475—§ 21
State v. Cobb, 2008-Ohio-5210, 2008 WL 4456995 (Ohio Ct. App. 12th Dist. Butler County 2008)
43 ALR6th 475—§ 8
State v. Cobbins, 66 N.C. App. 616, 311 S.E.2d 653 (1984)
26 ALR5th 1—§ 3, 28
State v. Coberly, 233 Kan. 100, 661 P.2d 383 (1983)
39 ALR5th 283—§ 4, 58
State v. Cobos, 93 Wash. App. 1008, 1998 WL 954608 (Div. 3 1998)

4 ALR6th 599—§ 19
71 ALR6th 625—§ 29
State v. Coburn, 82 Idaho 437, 354 P.2d 751 (1960)
76 ALR5th 1—§ 6
State v. Coburn, 165 Mont. 488, 530 P.2d 442 (1974)
19 ALR5th 470—§ 6
State v. Coburn, 221 N.J. Super. 586, 535 A.2d 531 (App. Div. 1987)
28 ALR6th 505—§ 31
State v. Coburn, 294 N.W.2d 57 (Iowa 1980)
26 ALR5th 765—§ 7, 11, 16, 18, 23
48 ALR5th 473—§ 2, 10, 11
State v. Coburne, 10 Wash. App. 298, 518 P.2d 747 (Div. 2 1973)
86 ALR5th 463—§ 9
State v. Coccomo, 177 N.J. Super. 575, 427 A.2d 131 (Law Div. 1980)
116 ALR5th 479—§ 5
State v. Cochran, 81 P.3d 1275 (Kan. Ct. App. 2004)
1 ALR6th 549—§ 7, 36
State v. Cochran, 135 Ga. App. 47, 217 S.E.2d 181 (1975)
43 ALR5th 1—§ 3, 13
State v. Cochran, 172 W. Va. 715, 310 S.E.2d 476 (1983)
3 ALR6th 269—§ 22
State v. Cochran, 275 Ga. App. 185, 620 S.E.2d 444 (2005)
50 ALR6th 455—§ 36
State v. Cochran, 425 A.2d 999 (Me. 1981)
29 ALR6th 1—§ 10
State v. Cochrane, 294 Or. 12, 653 P.2d 549 (1982)
41 ALR5th 171—§ 2
State v. Cockerham, 24 N.C. 204, 2 Ired. 204 (1842)
76 ALR5th 485—§ 3, 11
State v. Cockerham, 155 N.C. App. 729, 574 S.E.2d 694 (2003)
28 ALR6th 505—§ 9
State v. Cockrell, 131 Mont. 254, 309 P.2d 316 (1957)

90 ALR6th 385—§ 19
State v. Cockrell, 858 S.W.2d 825 (Mo. Ct. App. E.D. 1993)
108 ALR5th 593—§ 46
State v. Cockshutt, 59 Ohio App. 3d 87, 571 N.E.2d 464 (1st Dist. Hamilton County 1989)
33 ALR6th 1—§ 12
State v. Coconino County Superior Court, Div. II, 139 Ariz. 422, 678 P.2d 1386 (1984)
49 ALR5th 639—§ 4
State v. Cody, 248 Neb. 683, 539 N.W.2d 18 (1995)
67 ALR6th 531—§ 27
State v. Cody, 272 Kan. 564, 35 P.3d 800 (2001)
26 ALR6th 511—§ 14, 32
State v. Cody, 522 S.E.2d 777 (N.C. Ct. App. 1999)
5 ALR5th 243—§ 53
State v. Coe, 86 Wash. App. 841, 939 P.2d 715 (Div. 2 1997)
92 ALR5th 35—§ 30
State v. Coe, 101 Wash. 2d 772, 684 P.2d 668 (1984)
84 ALR5th 487—§ 21
State v. Coen, 203 Or. App. 92, 125 P.3d 761 (2005)
30 ALR6th 103—§ 35
State v. Coen, 382 N.W.2d 703 (Iowa App. 1985)
39 ALR5th 283—§ 10, 64
State v. Coffer, 54 N.C. App. 78, 282 S.E.2d 492 (1981)
39 ALR5th 283—§ 4, 71
State v. Coffey, 205 Wis. 2d 739, 557 N.W.2d 257 (Ct. App. 1996)
28 ALR6th 245—§ 6
State v. Coffey, 326 N.C. 268, 389 S.E.2d 48 (1990)
57 ALR5th 141—§ 5
State v. Coffin, 29 Or. App. 819, 565 P.2d 391 (1977)
94 ALR5th 393—§ 5
State v. Cofield, 80 P.3d 1201 (Kan. Ct. App. 2003)

37 ALR6th 357—§ 23
State v. Cofield, 324 N.C. 452, 379 S.E.2d 834 (1989)
44 ALR5th 651—§ 5
State v. Cogar, 2005-Ohio-6062, 2005 WL 3047523 (Ohio Ct. App. 5th Dist. Holmes County 2005)
46 ALR6th 241—§ 43
State v. Coggins, 210 S.C. 242, 42 S.E.2d 240 (1947)
54 ALR6th 429—§ 3, 20
State v. Cohen, 105 N.J.L. 529, 147 A. 325 (N.J. Sup. Ct. 1929)
57 ALR6th 445—§ 15
State v. Cohen, 143 Wash. 464, 255 P. 910 (1927)
104 ALR5th 357—§ 6
54 ALR6th 429—§ 11
State v. Cohen, 191 Ariz. 471, 957 P.2d 1014 (Ct. App. Div. 1 1998)
85 ALR5th 1—§ 37
State v. Cohen, 549 So. 2d 884 (La. Ct. App. 2d Cir. 1989)
114 ALR5th 173—§ 7
State v. Cohen, 667 So. 2d 438 (Fla. Dist. Ct. App. 2d Dist. 1996)
113 ALR5th 597—§ 8
State v. Cohen, 2007-Ohio-4546, 2007 WL 2482605 (Ohio Ct. App. 2d Dist. Montgomery County 2007)
32 ALR6th 385—§ 5
State v. Cohron, 597 So. 2d 251, 17 FLW S. 129 (Fla. 1992)
7 ALR5th 263—§ 7
State v. Cokeley, 159 W. Va. 664, 226 S.E.2d 40 (1976)
104 ALR5th 357—§ 8
State v. Coker, 746 S.W.2d 167 (Tenn. 1987)
67 ALR5th 361—§ 3, 4, 9
State v. Colabianchi, 1989 WL 62932 (Ohio App. 4 Dist. 1989)
54 ALR5th 141—§ 2, 10
State v. Colasurdo, 214 N.J. Super. 185, 518 A.2d 768 (App. Div. 1986)
24 ALR6th 1—§ 38
State v. Colbert, 257 Kan. 896, 896 P.2d 1089 (1995)

93 ALR6th 275—§ 10
State v. Colbert, 615 So. 2d 32 (La. App. 3d Cir. 1993)
36 ALR5th 255—§ 7
State v. Colbert, 949 S.W.2d 932 (Mo. Ct. App. W.D. 1997)
39 ALR5th 283—§ 15.5
State v. Colbert, 1981 WL 2792 (Ohio Ct. App. 2d Dist. Montgomery County 1981)
99 ALR6th 295—§ 5
State v. Colbert, 2006 WL 2388951 (N.J. Super. Ct. App. Div. 2006)
26 ALR6th 511—§ 17
State v. Colby, 140 Vt. 638, 443 A.2d 456 (1982)
45 ALR5th 591—§ 15
State v. Cole, 71 S.W.3d 163 (Mo. 2002)
110 ALR5th 1—§ 3, 15
State v. Cole, 128 Wash. 2d 262, 906 P.2d 925 (1995)
106 ALR5th 397—§ 4
State v. Cole, 160 W. Va. 804, 238 S.E.2d 849 (1977)
52 ALR5th 655—§ 4
State v. Cole, 204 N.J. Super. 618, 499 A.2d 1030 (1985)
29 ALR5th 59—§ 7, 22
State v. Cole, 226 Mont. 377, 744 P.2d 526 (1987)
29 ALR5th 59—§ 3, 14
State v. Cole, 238 Kan. 370, 710 P.2d 25 (1985)
45 ALR5th 767—§ 2, 15
State v. Cole, 252 Or. 146, 448 P.2d 523 (1968)
38 ALR6th 97—§ 29
State v. Cole, 264 Wis. 2d 520, 2003 WI 112, 665 N.W.2d 328 (2003)
33 ALR6th 407—§ 5, 6
State v. Cole, 270 N.C. 382, 154 S.E.2d 506 (1967)
50 ALR5th 467—§ 4
State v. Cole, 294 N.C. 304, 240 S.E.2d 355 (1978)
50 ALR5th 703—§ 26

State v. Cole, 304 S.C. 47, 403 S.E.2d 117, 7 A.L.R.5th 998 (1991)

7 ALR5th 73—§ 2, 3

State v. Cole, 338 S.C. 97, 525 S.E.2d 511 (2000)

3 ALR6th 543—§ 10

State v. Cole, 354 Mo. 181, 188 S.W.2d 43 (1945)

70 ALR5th 587—§ 4

102 ALR6th 279—§ 32

State v. Cole, 395 So. 2d 628 (Fla. Dist. Ct. App. 1st Dist. 1981)

112 ALR5th 429—§ 14

State v. Cole, 594 N.W.2d 197 (Minn. Ct. App. 1999)

71 ALR5th 637—§ 7, 9

State v. Cole, 645 S.W.2d 417 (Tenn. Crim. 1982)

29 ALR5th 59—§ 3, 14

State v. Cole, 706 S.W.2d 917 (Mo. App. 1986)

55 ALR5th 125—§ 3, 7

State v. Cole, 1997 ME 112, 695 A.2d 1180 (Me. 1997)

81 ALR5th 563—§ 7

State v. Cole, 2005 WL 2620926 (N.J. Super. Ct. App. Div. 2005)

26 ALR6th 511—§ 28

State v. Cole, 2010 WL 7797175 (Vt. 2010)

73 ALR6th 49—§ 4

State v. Coleman, 10 Neb. App. 337, 630 N.W.2d 686 (2001)

4 ALR6th 599—§ 9, 10, 23, 26

State v. Coleman, 102 Haw. 556, 78 P.3d 369 (Ct. App. 2003)

27 ALR6th 183—§ 13, 31, 40

State v. Coleman, 122 Ariz. 130, 593 P.2d 684 (Ct. App. Div. 2 1978)

81 ALR5th 563—§ 3

State v. Coleman, 224 Kan. 447, 580 P.2d 1329 (1978)

65 ALR5th 623—§ 9

State v. Coleman, 254 La. 264, 223 So. 2d 402 (1969)

76 ALR5th 1—§ 10

State v. Coleman, 373 N.W.2d 777 (Minn. 1985)

57 ALR6th 445—§ 21

State v. Coleman, 552 So. 2d 471 (La. Ct. App. 4th Cir. 1989)

99 ALR6th 295—§ 9

State v. Coleman, 582 S.W.2d 335 (Mo. Ct. App. W.D. 1979)

70 ALR5th 587—§ 3

State v. Coleman, 743 S.E.2d 62 (N.C. Ct. App. 2013)

97 ALR6th 653—§ 20

State v. Coleman, 756 So. 2d 1218 (La. Ct. App. 2d Cir. 2000)

38 ALR6th 439—§ 5

State v. Coleman, 780 So. 2d 1004 (Fla. Dist. Ct. App. 4th Dist. 2001)

113 ALR5th 597—§ 3

State v. Coleman, 865 S.W.2d 455 (Tenn. 1993)

39 ALR5th 283—§ 4, 18

State v. Coleman, 1992 WL 1962 (Tenn. Crim. App. 1992)

67 ALR5th 361—§ 2 to 4, 8

State v. Coleman, 1997 WL 798300 (Ohio Ct. App. 10th Dist.Franklin County 1997)

64 ALR5th 671—§ 3

State v. Coleman, 2001 UT App 281, 34 P.3d 790 (Utah Ct. App. 2001)

37 ALR6th 357—§ 57, 67

State v. Coleman, 2002-Ohio-2387, 2002 WL 999304 (Ohio Ct. App. 8th Dist. Cuyahoga County 2002)

97 ALR6th 653—§ 30

State v. Coleman, 2007-Ohio-1573, 2007 WL 969428 (Ohio Ct. App. 7th Dist. Mahoning County 2007)

34 ALR6th 1—§ 2, 8

55 ALR6th 513—§ 2

56 ALR6th 323—§ 2

57 ALR6th 83—§ 2

58 ALR6th 215—§ 2

State v. Cole, No. 45388 (April 14, 1983, Ct. App. Ohio, 8th App. Dist. Cuyahoga Co.)

39 ALR5th 283—§ 14, 76

State v. Coley, 158 Ariz. 471, 763 P.2d
535 (Ct. App. Div. 2 1988)
88 ALR5th 121—§ 32
State v. Collard, 414 N.W.2d 733 (Minn.
Ct. App. 1987)
97 ALR6th 653—§ 29
State v. Collard, 951 P.2d 56 (Mont.
1997)
50 ALR5th 581—§ 9
State v. Collentine, 39 Wis. 2d 325, 159
N.W.2d 50 (1968)
80 ALR5th 597—§ 15
State v. Collett, 526 S.W.2d 920 (Mo.
Ct. App. 1975)
12 ALR6th 267—§ 5
State v. Collier, 270 So. 2d 451 (Fla.
Dist. Ct. App. 4th Dist. 1972)
85 ALR5th 1—§ 11
State v. Collier, 919 P.2d 376 (Mont
1996)
15 ALR5th 391—§ 53
State v. Collier, 1992 WL 92958 (Tenn.
Crim. App. 1992)
57 ALR5th 141—§ 4, 9
State v. Collier, 1998 WL 42487 (Tenn.
Crim. App. 1998)
90 ALR5th 453—§ 23
State v. Collier, 1998 WL 398211 (Ohio
Ct. App. 8th Dist. Cuyahoga County
1998)
90 ALR5th 453—§ 17
10 ALR6th 463—§ 4, 6, 8
State v. Collier, 2005-Ohio-944, 2005
WL 516525 (Ohio Ct. App. 12th
Dist. Butler County 2005)
26 ALR6th 511—§ 19
State v. Collier, 2006-Ohio-2605, 2006
WL 1431412 (Ohio Ct. App. 10th
Dist. Franklin County 2006)
72 ALR6th 227—§ 41, 48
State v. Collins, 38 Conn. App. 247, 661
A.2d 612 (1995)
36 ALR5th 255—§ 29
State v. Collins, 42 S.W.3d 736 (Mo. Ct.
App. W.D. 2001)
105 ALR5th 529—§ 22
State v. Collins, 46 Wash. App. 636, 731
P.2d 1157 (Div. 1 1987)

9 ALR6th 541—§ 3, 11
State v. Collins, 50 Wash. 2d 740, 314
P.2d 660 (1957)
24 ALR6th 747—§ 27
State v. Collins, 69 Wash. 268, 124 P.
903 (1912)
10 ALR6th 31—§ 46
State v. Collins, 69 Wash. App. 110, 847
P.2d 528 (Div. 3 1993)
73 ALR5th 383—§ 32
State v. Collins, 76 Wash. App. 496, 886
P.2d 243 (1995)
57 ALR5th 141—§ 12
State v. Collins, 80 N.M. 499, 458 P.2d
225 (1969)
54 ALR5th 681—§ 16, 22
State v. Collins, 87 So. 3d 857 (La. Ct.
App. 2d Cir. 2010)
97 ALR6th 653—§ 6
State v. Collins, 122 Wis. 2d 320, 363
N.W.2d 229 (Ct. App. 1984)
124 ALR5th 1—§ 3
State v. Collins, 139 Ariz. 434, 679 P.2d
80 (App. 1983)
50 ALR5th 581—§ 2
State v. Collins, 186 W. Va. 1, 409
S.E.2d 181 (1990)
3 ALR6th 269—§ 22
State v. Collins, 288 So. 2d 602 (La.
1974)
45 ALR5th 531—§ 3, 9
State v. Collins, 317 So. 2d 846 (Fla.
App. D2 1975)
41 ALR5th 171—§ 54
State v. Collins, 370 So. 2d 533 (La.
1979)
20 ALR5th 177—§ 3
28 ALR6th 505—§ 34
State v. Collins, 470 So. 2d 553 (La.
App. 1st Cir. 1985)
42 ALR5th 581—§ 4
State v. Collins, 546 So. 2d 1246 (La.
Ct. App. 1st Cir. 1989)
102 ALR6th 365—§ 20
State v. Collins, 763 So. 2d 618 (La. Ct.
App. 2d Cir. 1999)
38 ALR6th 439—§ 4

State v. Collins, 768 So. 2d 674 (La. Ct. App. 2d Cir. 2000)

6 ALR5th 733—§ 15

State v. Collins, 787 So. 2d 391 (La. Ct. App. 4th Cir. 2001)

71 ALR6th 1—§ 15

State v. Collins, 986 S.W.2d 13 (Tenn. Crim. App. 1998)

73 ALR5th 383—§ 5

118 ALR5th 253—§ 7, 16, 25

State v. Collins, 1991 WL 254636 (Ohio Ct. App. 12th Dist. Butler County 1991)

81 ALR6th 505—§ 6

State v. Collins, 1997 WL 605081 (Ohio Ct. App. 3d Dist. Union County 1997)

78 ALR5th 489—§ 10

State v. Collins, 2005-Ohio-2812, 2005 WL 1339157 (Ohio Ct. App. 9th Dist. Summit County 2005)

24 ALR6th 549—§ 6

State v. Collins, 2006 WL 3359199 (N.J. Super. Ct. App. Div. 2006)

26 ALR6th 511—§ 17

State v. Collins, 2007-Ohio-3578, 2007 WL 2019528 (Ohio Ct. App. 6th Dist. Lucas County 2007)

99 ALR6th 295—§ 13

State v. Collins, 2010 WL 2367304 (N.C. Ct. App. 2010)

57 ALR6th 1—§ 23

State v. Colombo, 4 Conn. Cir. Ct. 671, 238 A.2d 806 (App. Div. 1967)

84 ALR6th 427—§ 4

State v. Colomy, 407 A.2d 1115 (Me. 1979)

5 ALR5th 243—§ 39

State v. Colon, 2001 WL 51669 (Conn. Super. Ct. 2001)

69 ALR6th 579—§ 4

State v. Colonna, 97 Utah Adv R 20, 766 P.2d 1062 (1988)

57 ALR5th 141—§ 12

State v. Colonna, 766 P.2d 1062, 97 Utah Adv. Rep. 20 (Utah 1988)

18 ALR5th 1—§ 16, 22

State v. Colosimo, 122 Nev. 950, 142 P.3d 352, 33 A.L.R.6th 785 (2006)

33 ALR6th 373—§ 6, 7, 9, 10, 13, 14

State v. Colquitt, 133 Wash. App. 789, 137 P.3d 892 (Div. 2 2006)

78 ALR6th 1—§ 19

State v. Colter, 1987 WL 31687 (Ohio Ct. App. 5th Dist. Holmes County 1987)

43 ALR6th 475—§ 16

State v. Coltrane, 307 N.C. 511, 299 S.E.2d 199 (1983)

52 ALR5th 559—§ 2

State v. Comardelle, 942 So. 2d 1126 (La. Ct. App. 5th Cir. 2006)

69 ALR6th 1—§ 23

State v. Combs, 62 Ohio St. 3d 278, 581 N.E.2d 1071 (1991)

79 ALR5th 33—§ 66, 68

State v. Combs, 100 Ohio App. 3d 90, 652 N.E.2d 205 (1st Dist. Hamilton County 1994)

79 ALR5th 419—§ 10

State v. Combs, 102 Wash. App. 949, 10 P.3d 1101 (Div. 3 2000)

4 ALR6th 1—§ 10

State v. Combs, 330 So. 2d 560 (Fla. App. D1 1976)

34 ALR5th 125—§ 7

State v. Comeaux, 252 La. 481, 211 So. 2d 620 (1968)

65 ALR5th 407—§ 3, 16

70 ALR5th 587—§ 3

94 ALR5th 537—§ 5

State v. Comeaux, 514 So. 2d 84 (La. 1987)

20 ALR5th 177—§ 3

State v. Comeaux, 699 So. 2d 16 (La. 1997)

20 ALR5th 177—§ 3, 9

State v. Comer, 165 Ariz. 413, 799 P.2d 333, 66 Ariz. Adv. Rep. 18 (1990)

7 ALR5th 758—§ 13

State v. Comer, 2002 UT App 219, 51 P.3d 55 (Utah Ct. App. 2002)

58 ALR6th 499—§ 3, 76

State v. Comes, 144 Vt. 103, 472 A.2d 1253 (1984)

34 ALR6th 1—§ 10
State v. Communication Equipment & Contracting Co., Inc., 335 So. 2d 123 (Ala. Civ. App. 1976)
113 ALR5th 313—§ 9
State v. Community Finance & Thrift Corp., 334 S.W.2d 559 (Tex. Civ. App. Austin 1960)
73 ALR6th 571—§ 57
State v. Compton, 104 N.M. 683, 726 P.2d 837 (1986)
51 ALR5th 603—§ 2, 4
State v. Compton, 1953-NMSC-036, 57 N.M. 227, 257 P.2d 915 (1953)
101 ALR6th 499—§ 14
State v. Compton, 1997 WL 691444 (Ohio Ct. App. 3d Dist. Union County 1997)
78 ALR5th 489—§ 10
State v. Comstock, 145 Vt. 503, 494 A.2d 135 (1985)
78 ALR5th 1—§ 51
State v. Conant, 124 Me. 198, 126 A. 838 (1924)
52 ALR5th 655—§ 4, 5
State v. Conatser, 958 S.W.2d 357 (Tenn. Crim. App. 1997)
113 ALR5th 517—§ 15
State v. Conaway, 319 N.W.2d 35 (Minn. 1982)
92 ALR6th 1—§ 5
103 ALR6th 347—§ 13
State v. Conaway, 339 N.C. 487, 453 S.E.2d 824 (1995)
79 ALR5th 33—§ 13, 47, 67, 73
83 ALR6th 255—§ 15
State v. Concannon, 25 Wash. 327, 65 P. 534 (1901)
54 ALR6th 429—§ 7
State v. Condley, 904 So. 2d 881 (La. Ct. App. 5th Cir. 2005)
24 ALR6th 591—§ 4, 14
State v. Condon, 152 Ohio App. 3d 629, 2003-Ohio-2335, 789 N.E.2d 696 (1st Dist. Hamilton County 2003)
101 ALR5th 187—§ 17
State v. Condon, 1997 WL 259791 (Minn. Ct. App. 1997)

73 ALR5th 383—§ 31
State v. Condron, 1998 WL 135817 (Ohio Ct. App. 2d Dist. Montgomery County 1998)
41 ALR6th 141—§ 5
State v. Cone, 665 S.W.2d 87 (Tenn. 1984)
72 ALR5th 529—§ 7
State v. Conger, 434 N.W.2d 406 (Iowa App. 1988)
29 ALR5th 59—§ 6, 36
State v. Conger, 483 So. 2d 1100 (La. Ct. App. 4th Cir. 1986)
99 ALR6th 295—§ 5
State v. Conger, 652 N.W.2d 704 (Minn. 2002)
69 ALR6th 579—§ 8
State v. Conifer Enterprises, Inc., 82 Wash. 2d 94, 508 P.2d 149 (1973)
40 ALR6th 317—§ 4, 6, 8, 10
State v. Conkel, 2009-Ohio-2852, 2009 WL 1682006 (Ohio Ct. App. 10th Dist. Franklin County 2009)
64 ALR6th 1—§ 7, 9, 11, 45
State v. Conklin, 79 Wash. 2d 805, 489 P.2d 1130 (1971)
108 ALR5th 593—§ 10
State v. Conklin, 115 N.H. 331, 341 A.2d 770 (1975)
38 ALR6th 97—§ 29
State v. Conklin, 249 Neb. 727, 545 N.W.2d 101 (1996)
33 ALR6th 407—§ 3, 12, 14
State v. Conkling, 2005 WL 375492 (Me. Super. Ct. 2005)
34 ALR6th 1—§ 12
State v. Conley, 31 Conn. App. 548, 627 A.2d 436 (1993)
12 ALR6th 553—§ 29, 34
State v. Conley, 168 W. Va. 694, 285 S.E.2d 454 (1981)
9 ALR6th 541—§ 29
State v. Conley, 1998 ND 5, 574 N.W.2d 569 (N.D. 1998)
38 ALR6th 97—§ 16
State v. Conley, 1999 WL 797191 (Ohio Ct. App. 3d Dist. Allen County 1999)

78 ALR5th 489—§ 9

State v. Conlogue, 474 A.2d 167 (Me. 1984)

22 ALR5th 1—§ 2

State v. Connell, 478 So. 2d 1176 (Fla. Dist. Ct. App. 2d Dist. 1985)

102 ALR5th 327—§ 2, 8

State v. Connelly, 143 Wis. 2d 500, 421 N.W.2d 859 (Ct. App. 1988)

92 ALR5th 35—§ 22

State v. Connelly, 194 Conn. 589, 483 A.2d 1085 (1984)

1 ALR5th 375—§ 3

6 ALR5th 652—§ 2, 11

State v. Conner, 22 Neb. 265, 34 N.W. 499 (1887)

56 ALR6th 523—§ 10

State v. Conners, 90 Wash. App. 48, 950 P.2d 519 (Div. 3 1998)

27 ALR5th 593—§ 36

State v. Conners, 125 N.J. Super. 500, 311 A.2d 764 (County Ct. 1973)

111 ALR5th 1—§ 27

State v. Conners, 129 N.J. Super. 476, 324 A.2d 85 (App. Div. 1974)

111 ALR5th 1—§ 27

State v. Conners, 994 P.2d 44 (Nev. 2000)

50 ALR5th 581—§ 5

State v. Connery, 441 N.W.2d 651 (N.D. 1989)

34 ALR6th 1—§ 10

State v. Connick, 5 Neb. App. 176, 557 N.W.2d 713 (1996)

18 ALR6th 519—§ 4, 11

State v. Connolly, 133 Vt. 565, 350 A.2d 364 (1975)

50 ALR5th 703—§ 15

State v. Connor, 252 S.W. 713 (Mo. 1923)

98 ALR6th 455—§ 20

99 ALR6th 113—§ 18

State v. Connor, 292 Conn. 483, 973 A.2d 627 (2009)

99 ALR6th 295—§ 13

State v. Connor, 1982 WL 4494 (Ohio Ct. App. 10th Dist. Franklin County 1982)

31 ALR6th 199—§ 25

State v. Connor, 2011 WL 2478223 (N.J. Super. Ct. App. Div. 2011)

69 ALR6th 579—§ 38

State v. Connors, 1985 WL 6613 (Ohio Ct. App. 8th Dist. Cuyahoga County 1985)

88 ALR5th 121—§ 14, 36

State v. Conover, 1994 WL 476235 (Ohio Ct. App. 12th Dist. Butler County 1994)

46 ALR6th 241—§ 26

State v. Conroy, 131 Ariz. 528, 642 P.2d 873 (Ct. App. Div. 1 1982)

3 ALR6th 269—§ 23

State v. Conroy, 194 Conn. 623, 484 A.2d 448 (1984)

104 ALR5th 357—§ 3

State v. Constant, 2009-Ohio-3936, 2009 WL 2425842 (Ohio Ct. App. 11th Dist. Lake County 2009)

72 ALR6th 227—§ 42, 60

State v. Constanza, 157 La. 411, 102 So. 507 (1924)

98 ALR6th 455—§ 11

State v. Continental Cas. Co., 121 Idaho 938, 829 P.2d 528, 74 Ed. Law Rep. 347 (1992)

94 ALR5th 567—§ 14

State v. Continental Cas. Co., 126 Idaho 178, 879 P.2d 1111, 94 Ed. Law Rep. 548 (1994)

94 ALR5th 567—§ 14

State v. Contreras, 92 Wash. App. 307, 966 P.2d 915 (Div. 2 1998)

71 ALR6th 1—§ 5

State v. Contreras, 134 N.M. 503, 2003-NMCA-129, 79 P.3d 1111 (Ct. App. 2003)

84 ALR6th 293—§ 4, 8, 15, 27

State v. Contreras, 180 Ariz. 450, 885 P.2d 138 (Ct. App. Div. 1 1994)

91 ALR5th 343—§ 35

State v. Conway, 193 N.J. Super. 133, 472 A.2d 588 (1984)

For assistance, call 1-800-328-4880

49 ALR5th 619—§ 2, 6
State v. Conway, 2005-Ohio-6377, 2005
WL 3220243 (Ohio Ct. App. 10th
Dist. Franklin County 2005)
21 ALR6th 1—§ 4
State v. Conyers, 413 A.2d 1264 (Del.
Super. Ct. 1979)
117 ALR5th 513—§ 7
State v. Cooey, 46 Ohio St. 3d 20, 544
N.E.2d 895 (1989)
39 ALR5th 283—§ 14
State v. Cook, 31 Wash. App. 165, 639
P.2d 863 (Div. 1 1982)
54 ALR6th 1—§ 27
State v. Cook, 48 N.C. App. 685, 269
S.E.2d 743 (1980)
16 ALR6th 329—§ 6
24 ALR6th 591—§ 6, 14
State v. Cook, 65 Ohio St. 3d 516, 605
N.E.2d 70 (1992)
17 ALR5th 851—§ 3
39 ALR5th 283—§ 14
State v. Cook, 83 Ohio St. 3d 404, 700
N.E.2d 570 (1998)
36 ALR5th 161—§ 3
78 ALR5th 489—§ 3, 9, 10
State v. Cook, 83 Ohio St. 3d 404, 1998-
Ohio-291, 700 N.E.2d 570 (1998)
37 ALR6th 55—§ 8, 9, 11
63 ALR6th 351—§ 3
64 ALR6th 1—§ 9
State v. Cook, 84 Wash. 2d 342, 525
P.2d 761 (1974)
62 ALR6th 259—§ 11
State v. Cook, 115 Ariz. 146, 564 P.2d
97 (App. 1977)
59 ALR5th 135—§ 3
State v. Cook, 115 Ariz. 188, 564 P.2d
877 (1977)
17 ALR6th 327—§ 40
State v. Cook, 123 Wash. App. 1060,
2004 WL 2430123 (Div. 1 2004)
7 ALR6th 169—§ 8
State v. Cook, 149 Ohio App. 3d 422,
2002-Ohio-4812, 777 N.E.2d 882
(2d Dist. Montgomery County
2002)
34 ALR6th 253—§ 3, 13

State v. Cook, 179 N.J. 533, 847 A.2d
530 (2004)
69 ALR6th 579—§ 11
State v. Cook, 213 So. 2d 18 (Fla. App.
D3 1968)
43 ALR5th 1—§ 14
State v. Cook, 215 La. 163, 39 So. 2d
898 (1949)
16 ALR6th 329—§ 4
24 ALR6th 591—§ 4
State v. Cook, 224 Kan. 132, 578 P.2d
257 (1978)
9 ALR6th 1—§ 17
State v. Cook, 286 Kan. 766, 187 P.3d
1283 (2008)
63 ALR6th 351—§ 3
State v. Cook, 300 N.J. Super. 476, 693
A.2d 483 (App. Div. 1996)
88 ALR5th 121—§ 2
State v. Cook, 330 N.J. Super. 395, 750
A.2d 91 (App. Div. 2000)
7 ALR5th 263—§ 7
49 ALR5th 639—§ 4
72 ALR6th 141—§ 9
102 ALR6th 365—§ 5, 15
State v. Cook, 345 So. 2d 29 (La. 1977)
55 ALR5th 125—§ 3, 9
State v. Cook, 460 So. 2d 1075 (La. App.
2d Cir. 1984)
34 ALR5th 125—§ 3, 16
State v. Cook, 485 So. 2d 606 (La. App.
4th Cir. 1986)
45 ALR5th 531—§ 7
State v. Cook, 594 S.E.2d 819, 124
A.L.R.5th 829 (N.C. Ct. App. 2004)
124 ALR5th 657—§ 3, 7
State v. Cook, 782 S.W.2d 762 (Mo.
App. 1989)
59 ALR5th 1—§ 3 to 6
State v. Cook, 830 S.W.2d 474 (Mo. Ct.
App. E.D. 1992)
105 ALR5th 529—§ 13
State v. Cook, 854 S.W.2d 579 (Mo. Ct.
App. S.D. 1993)
114 ALR5th 173—§ 7
State v. Cook, 1995 WL 507618 (Minn.
Ct. App. 1995)

For assistance, call 1-800-328-4880

73 ALR5th 383—§ 5

State v. Cooke, 1992 WL 233254 (Ohio Ct. App. 11th Dist. Lake County 1992)

78 ALR5th 567—§ 10

State v. Cooke, 1997 WL 428332 (Wash. Ct. App. Div. 1 1997)

58 ALR5th 749—§ 6

State v. Cooke, 2006 WL 2620533 (Del. Super. Ct. 2006)

93 ALR6th 275—§ 20

State v. Cookman, 324 Or. 19, 920 P.2d 1086 (1996)

42 ALR5th 291—§ 12

State v. Cooks, 642 So. 2d 23 (Fla. 5th DCA 1994)

100 ALR6th 535—§ 4

State v. Cooks, 861 S.W.2d 769 (Mo. Ct. App. E.D. 1993)

117 ALR5th 513—§ 23

State v. Cookson, 2003 ME 136, 837 A.2d 101 (Me. 2003)

24 ALR6th 549—§ 29

State v. Cool, 119 Wash. App. 1023, 2003 WL 22708906 (Div. 2 2003)

79 ALR6th 325—§ 12

State v. Cooley, 62 Minn. 183, 64 N.W. 379 (1895)

114 ALR5th 561—§ 22

State v. Cooley, 260 La. 768, 257 So. 2d 400 (1972)

65 ALR5th 407—§ 3

State v. Cooley, 342 S.C. 63, 536 S.E.2d 666 (2000)

3 ALR6th 543—§ 9

State v. Cooley, 457 A.2d 352 (Del. 1983)

101 ALR6th 331—§ 8

State v. Cooley, 1994 WL 570254 (Ohio Ct. App. 1st Dist. Hamilton County 1994)

85 ALR5th 1—§ 23

State v. Coolidge, 915 S.W.2d 820 (Tenn. Crim. App. 1995)

102 ALR5th 525—§ 11

State v. Coon, 124 Wash. App. 1053, 2004 WL 2988625 (Div. 2 2004)

19 ALR6th 697—§ 4

State v. Coon, 136 Wash. App. 1031, 2006 WL 3783594 (Div. 2 2006)

26 ALR6th 511—§ 41

State v. Coon, 974 P.2d 386, 95 A.L.R.5th 729 (Alaska 1999)

90 ALR5th 453—§ 3

95 ALR5th 471—§ 2, 17

State v. Cooney, 271 Mont. 42, 894 P.2d 303 (1995)

29 ALR5th 487—§ 3

State v. Cooney, 284 Mont. 500, 945 P.2d 891 (1997)

2 ALR5th 725—§ 9.5

State v. Coons, 886 S.W.2d 699 (Mo. Ct. App. S.D. 1994)

37 ALR6th 357—§ 67

State v. Cooper, 9 Conn. App. 15, 514 A.2d 758 (1986)

35 ALR6th 497—§ 12, 27

State v. Cooper, 54 N.J. 330, 255 A.2d 232 (1969)

97 ALR5th 201—§ 3

State v. Cooper, 65 Conn. App. 551, 783 A.2d 100 (2001)

97 ALR5th 201—§ 3

State v. Cooper, 71 Ohio App. 3d 471, 594 N.E.2d 713 (Scioto Co. 1991)

48 ALR5th 659—§ 5, 6, 10, 11

State v. Cooper, 117 Wis. 2d 30, 344 N.W.2d 194 (Ct. App. 1983)

84 ALR6th 427—§ 4

State v. Cooper, 119 Idaho 654, 809 P.2d 515 (Ct. App. 1991)

30 ALR6th 103—§ 43

State v. Cooper, 126 N.M. 500, 1998-NMCA-180, 972 P.2d 1 (Ct. App. 1998)

71 ALR6th 1—§ 15

State v. Cooper, 146 Mont. 336, 406 P.2d 691 (1965)

108 ALR5th 593—§ 10, 24

State v. Cooper, 151 N.J. 326, 700 A.2d 306 (1997)

26 ALR5th 603—§ 6

39 ALR5th 283—§ 55

State v. Cooper, 205 Minn. 333, 285 N.W. 903, 4 L.R.R.M. (BNA) 827, 1 Lab. Cas. (CCH) ¶ 18374, 122 A.L.R. 727 (1939)
113 ALR5th 1—§ 4, 7, 14

State v. Cooper, 211 N.J. Super. 1, 510 A.2d 681 (App. Div. 1986)
97 ALR5th 201—§ 6

State v. Cooper, 212 S.C. 61, 46 S.E.2d 545 (1948)
83 ALR6th 465—§ 74

State v. Cooper, 253 P.3d 798 (Kan. Ct. App. 2011)
72 ALR6th 227—§ 6

State v. Cooper, 410 N.J. Super. 43, 979 A.2d 792 (App. Div. 2009)
102 ALR6th 417—§ 25

State v. Cooper, 617 A.2d 1011 (Me. 1992)
9 ALR6th 1—§ 19

State v. Cooper, 811 S.W.2d 786 (Mo. Ct. App. W.D. 1991)
85 ALR5th 547—§ 8

State v. Cooper, 1997-NMSC-058, 124 N.M. 277, 949 P.2d 660 (1997)
45 ALR6th 337—§ 24

State v. Cooper, 2004-Ohio-6428, 2004 WL 2757193 (Ohio Ct. App. 1st Dist. Hamilton County 2004)
33 ALR6th 91—§ 44

State v. Cooper, 2009 WL 2778035 (N.J. Super. Ct. App. Div. 2009)
99 ALR6th 295—§ 16

State v. Cooper, 2014-Ohio-817, 2014 WL 888382 (Ohio Ct. App. 8th Dist. Cuyahoga County 2014)
99 ALR6th 295—§ 9

State v. Coots, 1997 WL 803125 (Ohio Ct. App. 9th Dist. Wayne County 1997)
29 ALR6th 237—§ 22

State v. Cootz, 110 Idaho 807, 718 P.2d 1245 (Ct. App. 1986)
55 ALR5th 125—§ 17, 26
124 ALR5th 1—§ 5

State v. Cope, 250 Mont. 387, 819 P.2d 1280 (1991)
103 ALR5th 463—§ 10

State v. Copeland, 86 N.C. 691, 1882 WL 2857 (1882)
57 ALR6th 445—§ 11

State v. Copeland, 124 N.H. 90, 467 A.2d 238 (1983)
124 ALR5th 1—§ 5
32 ALR6th 1—§ 5

State v. Copeland, 130 Wash. 2d 244, 922 P.2d 1304 (1996)
40 ALR5th 113—§ 3
90 ALR5th 453—§ 43

State v. Copeland, 255 La. 91, 229 So. 2d 710 (1969)
70 ALR5th 587—§ 3

State v. Copeland, 530 So. 2d 526 (La. 1988)
10 ALR5th 700—§ 4

State v. Copeland, 631 So. 2d 1223 (La. Ct. App. 5th Cir. 1994)
58 ALR6th 499—§ 98

State v. Copeland, 928 S.W.2d 828 (Mo. 1996)
28 ALR6th 505—§ 7, 9

State v. Copeland, 2005 WL 2008177 (Tenn. Crim. App. 2005)
21 ALR6th 1—§ 4

State v. Copenny, 888 S.W.2d 450 (Tenn. Crim. 1993)
7 ALR5th 263—§ 4

State v. Copher, 395 So. 2d 635 (Fla. Dist. Ct. App. 2d Dist. 1981)
107 ALR5th 567—§ 11

State v. Copley, 1978 WL 218044 (Ohio Ct. App. 8th Dist. Cuyahoga County 1978)
19 ALR6th 697—§ 18

State v. Coppenburg, 33 SCL 273 (1847)
29 ALR5th 59—§ 3, 37

State v. Coppens, 2011 WI App 114, 336 Wis. 2d 475, 801 N.W.2d 349 (Ct. App. 2011)
84 ALR6th 293—§ 17, 21, 27

State v. Coppersmith, 231 Mo. App. 711, 105 S.W.2d 991 (1937)
29 ALR5th 59—§ 7

State v. Copple, 218 Neb. 837, 359 N.W.2d 782 (1984)

9 ALR6th 633—§ 13

13 ALR6th 603—§ 21

State v. Corbett, 15 Or. App. 470, 516 P.2d 487 (1973)

60 ALR5th 1—§ 8

45 ALR6th 643—§ 9

State v. Corbett, 309 N.C. 382, 307 S.E.2d 139 (1983)

86 ALR5th 463—§ 9

State v. Corbett, 339 N.C. 313, 451 S.E.2d 252 (1994)

28 ALR6th 505—§ 11

State v. Corbett, 339 N.C. 313, 451 S.E.2d 252 (1996)

57 ALR5th 141—§ 3

State v. Corbett, 618 A.2d 222 (Me. 1992)

27 ALR5th 593—§ 28

State v. Corbidge, 78 P.3d 497 (Kan. Ct. App. 2003)

8 ALR6th 265—§ 15

State v. Corbin, 15 Or. App. 536, 516 P.2d 1314 (1973)

58 ALR6th 499—§ 41

State v. Corbin, 22 Or. App. 505, 539 P.2d 1113 (1975)

58 ALR6th 499—§ 41

State v. Corbin, 194 Ohio App. 3d 720, 2011-Ohio-3491, 957 N.E.2d 849 (6th Dist. Wood County 2011)

93 ALR6th 275—§ 4

State v. Corbin, 2008 MT 146, 343 Mont. 211, 184 P.3d 287 (2008)

46 ALR6th 241—§ 13

State v. Corbisier, 2006 WI App 56, 290 Wis. 2d 511, 712 N.W.2d 87 (Ct. App. 2006)

84 ALR6th 293—§ 7, 43

State v. Corbitt, 720 S.E.2d 29 (N.C. Ct. App. 2011)

79 ALR6th 1—§ 14, 39

State v. Corcoran, 186 Wis. 2d 616, 522 N.W.2d 226 (Ct. App. 1994)

87 ALR6th 1—§ 13, 16 to 18, 22

State v. Cord, 103 Wash. 2d 361, 693 P.2d 81 (1985)

73 ALR6th 49—§ 43, 65

State v. Corder, 460 N.W.2d 733 (S.D. 1990)

29 ALR6th 1—§ 10

State v. Cordova, 128 N.M. 390, 1999-NMCA-144, 993 P.2d 104 (Ct. App. 1999)

10 ALR6th 463—§ 3

State v. Corella, 79 Haw. 255, 900 P.2d 1322 (Ct. App. 1995)

27 ALR6th 183—§ 7, 40

State v. Corey, 2001 S.D. 53, 624 N.W.2d 841 (S.D. 2001)

90 ALR5th 453—§ 22

State v. Coria, 39 Or. App. 507, 592 P.2d 1057 (1979)

32 ALR5th 149—§ 29, 52, 67

88 ALR5th 121—§ 36

State v. Coria, 105 Wash. App. 51, 17 P.3d 1278 (Div. 2 2001)

57 ALR6th 445—§ 3

State v. Coria, 120 Wash. 2d 156, 839 P.2d 890 (1992)

72 ALR5th 607—§ 7

State v. Coria, 146 Wash. 2d 631, 48 P.3d 980 (2002)

57 ALR6th 445—§ 12

State v. Corley, 13 S.C. 1 (1880)

14 ALR5th 89—§ 25, 26, 28

State v. Cormier, 141 Me. 307, 43 A.2d 819 (1945)

52 ALR5th 655—§ 5

State v. Cormier, 438 So. 2d 1269 (La. Ct. App. 3d Cir. 1983)

76 ALR5th 563—§ 2, 4, 5

State v. Cormier, 535 A.2d 913 (Me. 1987)

3 ALR5th 963—§ 4

State v. Cornelison, 538 N.W.2d 864 (Iowa App. Jun 27, 1995)

54 ALR5th 141—§ 3 to 5, 10

State v. Cornell, 491 N.W.2d 668 (Minn. App. 1992)

50 ALR5th 581—§ 2

State v. Cornish, 568 P.2d 360 (Utah 1977)

78 ALR5th 567—§ 3

State v. Cornwell, 149 Ohio App. 3d
212, 2002-Ohio-5178, 776 N.E.2d
572 (7th Dist. Mahoning County
2002)
122 ALR5th 593—§ 2, 8, 9
State v. Coron, 411 So. 2d 237 (Fla. Dist.
Ct. App. 3d Dist. 1982)
72 ALR5th 1—§ 29
State v. Corpus-Ruiz, 127 Or. App. 666,
874 P.2d 90 (1994)
113 ALR5th 517—§ 11
State v. Corpuz, 49 Or. App. 811, 621
P.2d 604 (1980)
26 ALR5th 1—§ 3
State v. Corra, 88 Or. App. 339, 745
P.2d 786 (1987)
62 ALR6th 413—§ 39
State v. Corrado, 113 N.J.L. 53, 172 A.
571 (N.J. Ct. Err. & App. 1934)
98 ALR6th 455—§ 32
State v. Correa, 5 Hawaii App. 644, 706
P.2d 1321 (1985)
39 ALR5th 283—§ 4, 18
State v. Correia, 600 A.2d 279 (R.I.
1991)
1 ALR6th 657—§ 4
State v. Corrolla, 113 Conn. 103, 154 A.
152 (1931)
78 ALR5th 567—§ 10
State v. Corsi, 86 N.J. 172, 430 A.2d 210
(1981)
41 ALR6th 295—§ 9
State v. Corsi, 686 N.W.2d 215 (Iowa
2004)
26 ALR6th 511—§ 35
State v. Corson, 1992 WL 52574 (Ohio
Ct. App. 11th Dist. Ashtabula
County 1992)
69 ALR6th 207—§ 9, 10, 18
State v. Cort, 766 A.2d 260 (N.H. 2000)
90 ALR5th 453—§ 48
State v. Cortes, 84 So. 3d 733 (La. Ct.
App. 3d Cir. 2012)
102 ALR6th 621—§ 3
State v. Cortez, 102 Wash. App. 1019,
2000 WL 1250755 (Div. 2 2000)
44 ALR6th 301—§ 6

State v. Cortez, 191 Neb. 800, 218
N.W.2d 217 (1974)
72 ALR5th 109—§ 6
State v. Cortez, 705 So. 2d 676 (Fla.
Dist. Ct. App. 3d Dist. 1998)
72 ALR5th 1—§ 29
State v. Cortman, 251 Or. 566, 446 P.2d
681 (1968)
85 ALR5th 1—§ 42
State v. Cory, 156 Ariz. 27, 749 P.2d 936
(App. 1987)
36 ALR5th 161—§ 8, 12, 19
State v. Cosey, 1988 WL 32982 (Ohio
Ct. App. 3d Dist. Marion County
1988)
77 ALR5th 201—§ 23
State v. Cosgro, 2008 ME 64, 945 A.2d
1221 (Me. 2008)
63 ALR6th 351—§ 3
State v. Coss, 53 Or. 462, 101 P. 193
(1909)
104 ALR5th 357—§ 7
State v. Costa, 11 S.W.3d 670 (Mo. Ct.
App. W.D. 1999)
71 ALR5th 637—§ 3
103 ALR6th 247—§ 7
State v. Costa Gonzales, 126 Wis. 2d
515, 376 N.W.2d 869 (App. 1985)
45 ALR5th 591—§ 14
State v. Costantino, 107 R.I. 215, 266
A.2d 33 (1970)
82 ALR6th 317—§ 8, 11, 22
State v. Costanzo, 94 Or. App. 516, 766
P.2d 415 (1988)
7 ALR5th 73—§ 1, 3
State v. Costello, 138 N.H. 587, 643
A.2d 531 (1994)
36 ALR5th 161—§ 3
33 ALR6th 91—§ 6
63 ALR6th 351—§ 3
State v. Costello, 252 S.W. 727 (Mo.
1923)
54 ALR6th 429—§ 9
State v. Costin, 168 Vt. 175, 720 A.2d
866 (1998)
91 ALR5th 585—§ 8

State v. Cote, 126 N.H. 514, 493 A.2d
1170 (1985)
104 ALR5th 165—§ 8
State v. Cote, 129 Conn. App. 842, 21
A.3d 589 (2011)
72 ALR6th 227—§ 51
State v. Cote, 444 A.2d 34 (Me. 1982)
34 ALR5th 125—§ 37
State v. Cothran, 115 S.W.3d 513 (Tenn.
Crim. App. 2003)
15 ALR6th 515—§ 4, 14, 27
State v. Cotten, 75 Wash. App. 669, 879
P.2d 971 (Div. 2 1994)
55 ALR5th 125—§ 3
68 ALR5th 343—§ 3
State v. Cotter, 262 Wis. 168, 54 N.W.2d
43, 41 A.L.R.2d 222 (1952)
33 ALR5th 205—§ 5
State v. Cotterell, 2008 MT 409, 347
Mont. 231, 198 P.3d 254 (2008)
45 ALR6th 643—§ 18
State v. Cottman Transmissions Systems, Inc., 86 Md. App. 714, 587
A.2d 1190 (1991)
78 ALR6th 97—§ 4
State v. Cottman Transmission Systems,
Inc., 75 Md. App. 647, 542 A.2d
859, 15 Media L. R. 1644 (1988)
39 ALR5th 103—§ 3, 9
State v. Cotton, 55 Haw. 138, 516 P.2d
709 (1973)
72 ALR5th 607—§ 3, 4, 6
State v. Cotton, 77 Conn. App. 749, 825
A.2d 189 (2003)
102 ALR5th 447—§ 22
State v. Cotton, 318 N.C. 663, 351
S.E.2d 277 (1987)
**22 ALR5th 1—§ 2, 5, 8, 9, 13, 16,
19, 20, 22, 23, 32, 33, 35, 40, 41,
45**
State v. Cottrell, 45 W. Va. 837, 32 S.E.
162 (1899)
85 ALR5th 471—§ 11
State v. Cottrell, 215 Or. App. 276, 168
P.3d 1200 (2007)
84 ALR6th 293—§ 31
State v. Cottrell, 910 S.W.2d 814 (Mo.
App. 1995)

37 ALR5th 515—§ 10
State v. Cottrell, Slip Op. No. 51576
(Ohio App. Cuyahoga Co. 1987)
38 ALR5th 433—§ 7, 8, 23
State v. Coubal, 248 Wis. 247, 21
N.W.2d 381 (1946)
63 ALR6th 1—§ 36
State v. Couch, 635 P.2d 89 (Utah 1981)
39 ALR5th 283—§ 2, 4, 64
State v. Coudotte, 7 N.D. 109, 72 N.W.
913 (1897)
73 ALR5th 615—§ 3, 6, 9
State v. Coulter, 67 S.W.3d 3 (Tenn.
Crim. App. 2001)
58 ALR6th 499—§ 16
State v. Coulverson, 2002 -Ohio- 1324,
2002 WL 433633 (Ohio Ct. App.
10th Dist. Franklin County 2002)
95 ALR5th 125—§ 3
State v. Council 4, AFSCME, 27 Conn.
App. 635, 608 A.2d 718 (1992)
112 ALR5th 263—§ 64
State v. Council, 335 S.C. 1, 515 S.E.2d
508 (1999)
90 ALR5th 453—§ 21
10 ALR6th 463—§ 3 to 5
State v. Council of Hammonton, 38 NJL
430 (1876)
47 ALR5th 553—§ 20
State v. Counort, 69 Wash. 361, 124 P.
910 (1912)
70 ALR5th 169—§ 25
State v. Counterman, 8 Ariz. App. 526,
448 P.2d 96 (1968)
55 ALR6th 391—§ 7
State v. Countryman, 572 N.W.2d 553
(Iowa 1997)
9 ALR6th 1—§ 17
32 ALR6th 1—§ 11
State v. Counts, 99 Wash. 2d 54, 659
P.2d 1087 (1983)
17 ALR6th 327—§ 31
State v. Counts, 783 S.W.2d 181 (Mo.
App. 1990)
2 ALR5th 725—§ 13
State v. Courchesne, 296 Conn. 622, 998
A.2d 1 (2010)

---

93 ALR6th 391—§ 25

State v. Courtier, 166 Or. App. 514, 997 P.2d 894 (2000)

33 ALR6th 407—§ 11

State v. Courtright, 66 Ohio St. 35, 63 N.E. 590 (1902)

41 ALR5th 1—§ 3

State v. Couture, 194 Conn. 530, 482 A.2d 300 (1984)

49 ALR5th 639—§ 4

State v. Covarrubias, 244 Neb. 366, 507 N.W.2d 248 (1993)

20 ALR5th 398—§ 21

State v. Covell, 157 N.J. 554, 725 A.2d 675 (1999)

35 ALR6th 361—§ 22

State v. Covender, 1997 WL 802947 (Ohio Ct. App. 9th Dist. Lorain County 1997)

24 ALR6th 1—§ 29

State v. Covert, 160 Wash. App. 1019, 2011 WL 692912 (Div. 3 2011)

101 ALR6th 331—§ 12

State v. Covey, 2000 WL 638951 (Ohio Ct. App. 6th Dist. Lucas County 2000)

45 ALR6th 435—§ 9

State v. Covington, 169 La. 939, 126 So. 431 (1930)

104 ALR5th 357—§ 5
54 ALR6th 429—§ 22

State v. Covington, 315 N.C. 352, 338 S.E.2d 310 (1986)

3 ALR6th 269—§ 12

State v. Covington, 904 P.2d 209, 274 Utah Adv. Rep. 22 (Utah App. 1995)

43 ALR5th 1—§ 13

State v. Cowans, 87 Ohio St. 3d 68, 717 N.E.2d 298 (1999)

81 ALR5th 563—§ 2

State v. Coward, 54 N.C. App. 488, 283 S.E.2d 536 (1981)

78 ALR5th 567—§ 5

State v. Cowhig, 604 So. 2d 1233, 17 FLW S. 601 (Fla. 1992)

29 ALR5th 59—§ 35

State v. Cowperthwaite, 354 A.2d 173 (Me. 1976)

18 ALR6th 519—§ 4

State v. Cox, 6 N.C. App. 18, 169 S.E.2d 134 (1969)

54 ALR6th 429—§ 7

State v. Cox, 12 Or. App. 215, 505 P.2d 360 (1973)

61 ALR5th 1—§ 4, 5
71 ALR6th 335—§ 10

State v. Cox, 36 Conn. App. 463, 652 A.2d 520 (1994)

55 ALR6th 513—§ 8, 12

State v. Cox, 82 Idaho 150, 351 P.2d 472 (1960)

50 ALR5th 467—§ 5, 7

State v. Cox, 87 Or. App. 443, 742 P.2d 694 (1987)

93 ALR5th 327—§ 3, 7, 9, 11
101 ALR5th 619—§ 2

State v. Cox, 91 N.H. 137, 16 A.2d 508 (1940)

80 ALR5th 255—§ 4, 8, 9, 35

State v. Cox, 110 Ariz. 603, 522 P.2d 29 (1974)

67 ALR5th 361—§ 3, 4, 9

State v. Cox, 172 Minn. 226, 215 N.W. 189 (1927)

98 ALR6th 455—§ 6

State v. Cox, 219 Or. App. 319, 182 P.3d 259 (2008)

33 ALR6th 91—§ 20

State v. Cox, 221 S.C. 1, 68 S.E.2d 624 (1951)

24 ALR5th 465—§ 44

State v. Cox, 266 Mont. 110, 879 P.2d 662 (1994)

55 ALR6th 391—§ 5

State v. Cox, 325 N.W.2d 181 (N.D. 1982)

57 ALR6th 445—§ 38

State v. Cox, 326 S.C. 440, 484 S.E.2d 108 (Ct. App. 1997)

15 ALR5th 391—§ 41

State v. Cox, 575 P.2d 121 (Okla. Crim. App. 1978)

71 ALR5th 1—§ 56

CASES CITED IN ALR5th and ALR6th

State v. Cox, 787 P.2d 4 (Utah Ct. App. 1990)
86 ALR5th 59—§ 3 to 5
State v. Cox, 2000 WL 1562920 (Tenn. Crim. App. 2000)
7 ALR6th 233—§ 3, 5
State v. Cox, 2009-Ohio-1625, 2009 WL 891790 (Ohio Ct. App. 5th Dist. Coshocton County 2009)
56 ALR6th 323—§ 7
State v. Coyle, 119 N.J. 194, 574 A.2d 951 (1990)
61 ALR5th 1—§ 3
State v. Coyle, 567 A.2d 870 (Del. Super. Ct. 1989)
90 ALR5th 225—§ 2
96 ALR5th 327—§ 2
109 ALR5th 611—§ 2, 3
124 ALR5th 1—§ 2, 5
57 ALR6th 83—§ 4
State v. Coyne, 69 Ohio App. 2d 63, 23 Ohio Op. 3d 68, 430 N.E.2d 473 (1st Dist. Clermont County 1980)
67 ALR6th 209—§ 39
State v. Cozzens, 241 Neb. 565, 490 N.W.2d 184 (1992)
3 ALR5th 521—§ 3
State v. C.P.H., 707 N.W.2d 699 (Minn. Ct. App. 2006)
68 ALR6th 1—§ 9
69 ALR6th 1—§ 22
State v. Crabtree, 248 Kan. 33, 805 P.2d 1 (1991)
22 ALR5th 787—§ 4
State v. Crabtree, 655 S.W.2d 173 (Tenn. Crim. App. 1983)
64 ALR5th 637—§ 3
97 ALR5th 201—§ 8
State v. Craft, 32 N.C. App. 357, 232 S.E.2d 282 (1977)
99 ALR5th 557—§ 3, 4
State v. Craft, 85 Ariz. 143, 333 P.2d 728 (1958)
98 ALR6th 455—§ 24
State v. Craft, 200 W. Va. 496, 490 S.E.2d 315 (1997)
22 ALR5th 660—§ 4

State v. Crager, 116 Ohio St. 3d 369, 2007-Ohio-6840, 879 N.E.2d 745 (2007)
38 ALR6th 439—§ 3
State v. Crager, 164 Ohio App. 3d 816, 2005-Ohio-6868, 844 N.E.2d 390 (3d Dist. Marion County 2005)
30 ALR6th 1—§ 3, 6
State v. Craig, 19 Ohio App. 2d 29, 48 Ohio Op. 2d 28, 249 N.E.2d 75 (3d Dist. Seneca County 1969)
72 ALR5th 607—§ 3
State v. Craig, 33 S.W.3d 597 (Mo. Ct. App. E.D. 2000)
3 ALR6th 543—§ 6
State v. Craig, 110 Ohio St. 3d 306, 2006-Ohio-4571, 853 N.E.2d 621 (2006)
21 ALR6th 1—§ 4
State v. Craig, 117 Idaho 983, 793 P.2d 215 (1990)
7 ALR5th 263—§ 7
State v. Craig, 237 N.J. Super. 407, 568 A.2d 100 (App. Div. 1989)
32 ALR6th 1—§ 5
State v. Craig, 254 Kan. 575, 867 P.2d 1013, 34 A.L.R.5th 929 (1994)
34 ALR5th 723—§ 4
State v. Craig, 340 So. 2d 191 (La. 1976)
62 ALR5th 121—§ 6
State v. Craig, 490 N.W.2d 795 (Iowa 1992)
40 ALR5th 113—§ 3
53 ALR6th 81—§ 13
State v. Craig, 699 So. 2d 865 (La. 1997)
99 ALR6th 113—§ 19
State v. Craig, 1998 WL 263991 (Wash. Ct. App. Div. 3 1998)
73 ALR5th 383—§ 65
State v. Craighead, 44 La. Ann. 968, 11 So. 629 (1892)
105 ALR5th 529—§ 11
State v. Crail, 97 Haw. 170, 35 P.3d 197 (2001)
23 ALR6th 307—§ 38
State v. Crain, 124 N.M. 84
39 ALR5th 283—§ 70

State v. Cram, 84 Me. 271, 24 A. 853 (1892)

102 ALR5th 525—§ 20

State v. Cram, 157 Vt. 466, 600 A.2d 733 (1991)

3 ALR5th 521—§ 14

State v. Cram, 2002 UT 37, 46 P.3d 230 (Utah 2002)

103 ALR6th 137—§ 15, 18

State v. Cramer, 174 Ariz. 522, 851 P.2d 147 (Ct. App. Div. 2 1992)

78 ALR5th 309—§ 5

State v. Crampton, 30 Or. App. 779, 568 P.2d 680 (1977)

1 ALR5th 317—§ 6

State v. Crandall, 39 Wash. App. 849, 697 P.2d 250 (Div. 3 1985)

62 ALR6th 413—§ 2
67 ALR6th 531—§ 2
69 ALR6th 275—§ 2

State v. Crandell, 604 So. 2d 123 (La. App. 2d Cir. 1992)

42 ALR5th 581—§ 3

State v. Crane, 260 Kan. 208, 918 P.2d 1256 (1996)

91 ALR5th 343—§ 17

State v. Craney, 347 N.W.2d 668 (Iowa 1984)

66 ALR6th 83—§ 11

State v. Craney, 381 A.2d 630 (Me. 1978)

28 ALR6th 505—§ 9

State v. Crank, 666 S.W.2d 91 (Tex. 1984)

10 ALR5th 1—§ 34, 58

State v. Crannell, 750 A.2d 1002 (Vt. 2000)

85 ALR5th 1—§ 44

State v. Cravalho, 120 Haw. 255, 203 P.3d 675 (Ct. App. 2009)

78 ALR6th 1—§ 35

State v. Crawford, 21 Kan. App. 2d 859, 908 P.2d 638 (1995)

106 ALR5th 377—§ 4

State v. Crawford, 29 N.C. App. 117, 223 S.E.2d 534 (1976)

68 ALR5th 343—§ 3, 12

State v. Crawford, 60 Ohio App. 3d 61, 573 N.E.2d 784 (Sandusky Co. 1989)

5 ALR5th 243—§ 62

State v. Crawford, 66 W. Va. 114, 66 S.E. 110 (1909)

67 ALR5th 637—§ 5

State v. Crawford, 91 Or. App. 597, 756 P.2d 68 (1988)

103 ALR6th 347—§ 5, 11

State v. Crawford, 104 N.C. App. 591, 410 S.E.2d 499 (1991)

4 ALR6th 599—§ 16, 29

State v. Crawford, 120 S.W.3d 508 (Tex. App. Dallas 2003)

114 ALR5th 173—§ 8

State v. Crawford, 159 Wash. 2d 86, 147 P.3d 1288 (2006)

31 ALR6th 49—§ 10

State v. Crawford, 188 Neb. 378, 196 N.W.2d 915 (1972)

118 ALR5th 253—§ 3, 25

State v. Crawford, 223 Kan. 127, 573 P.2d 982 (1977)

78 ALR5th 1—§ 57

State v. Crawford, 275 Kan. 492, 67 P.3d 115 (2003)

84 ALR6th 293—§ 12, 14, 29

State v. Crawford, 472 S.E.2d 920 (N.C. 1996)

57 ALR5th 141—§ 2, 3

State v. Crawford, 619 So. 2d 828 (La. Ct. App. 1st Cir. 1993)

9 ALR6th 1—§ 17

State v. Crawford, 672 So. 2d 197 (La. Ct. App. 3d Cir. 1996)

99 ALR6th 113—§ 5

State v. Crawford, 727 So. 2d 589 (La. Ct. App. 1st Cir. 1998)

27 ALR5th 593—§ 7

State v. Crawford, 914 S.W.2d 390 (Mo. Ct. App. E.D. 1996)

99 ALR6th 295—§ 13

State v. Crawford, 1988 WL 10045 (Tenn. Crim. App. 1988)

99 ALR6th 295—§ 19

State v. Crawford, 1993 WL 302388 (Ohio Ct. App. 8th Dist.Cuyahoga County 1993)
57 ALR5th 141—§ 9
State v. Crawford, 1993 WL 384506 (Ohio App. 8 Dist.)
50 ALR5th 581—§ 7, 19
State v. Crawford, 1998 WL 812499 (Ohio Ct. App. 2d Dist. Montgomery County 1998)
74 ALR5th 453—§ 5
State v. Crawford, No. 42187 (October 30, 1980, Ct. App. Ohio, 8th App. Dist. Cuyahoga Co.)
39 ALR5th 283—§ 14, 22
State v. Crawley, 61 Wash. App. 29, 808 P.2d 773 (1991)
19 ALR5th 470—§ 3, 12
State v. Crawley, 2009 WL 143030 (Del. Super. Ct. 2009)
71 ALR6th 1—§ 6
State v. Craycraft, 704 So. 2d 593 (Fla. Dist. Ct. App. 4th Dist. 1997)
64 ALR5th 637—§ 5
State v. Crayton, 344 So. 2d 771 (Ala. App. 1977)
21 ALR5th 812—§ 6
State v. Crea, 119 Idaho 352, 806 P.2d 445 (1991)
9 ALR5th 369—§ 3, 5
State v. Crea, 305 Minn. 342, 233 N.W.2d 736 (1975)
60 ALR5th 1—§ 8
State v. Creach, 77 Wash. 2d 194, 461 P.2d 329 (1969)
45 ALR6th 337—§ 19
State v. Creamer, 528 So. 2d 667 (La. App. 2d Cir. 1988)
32 ALR5th 31—§ 3
State v. Creason, 33 Kan. App. 2d 114, 98 P.3d 985, 2 A.L.R.6th 709(2004)
2 ALR6th 169—§ 3, 5
State v. Creason, 123 N.C. App. 495, 473 S.E.2d 771 (1996)
12 ALR5th 89—§ 4
State v. Credit Bureau of Laredo, Inc., 530 S.W.2d 288 (Tex. 1975)
54 ALR5th 631—§ 3

State v. Creech, 111 N.M. 490, 806 P.2d 1080 (App. 1991)
50 ALR5th 703—§ 38
State v. Creech, 111 N.M. 490, 806 P.2d 1080 (Ct. App. 1991)
18 ALR6th 519—§ 5
State v. Creech, 229 N.C. 662, 51 S.E.2d 348 (1949)
24 ALR5th 465—§ 44
State v. Creegan, 123 Wash. App. 718, 99 P.3d 897 (Div. 3 2004)
28 ALR6th 505—§ 9
State v. Creekmore, 55 Wash. App. 852, 783 P.2d 1068 (Div. 1 1989)
73 ALR5th 383—§ 5
State v. Cremeans, 62 W. Va. 134, 57 S.E. 405 (1907)
11 ALR5th 831—§ 4, 9
State v. Crenshaw, 548 So. 2d 223, 14 FLW 421, 1 A.L.R.5th 1075 (Fla. 1989)
1 ALR5th 375—§ 3
6 ALR5th 652—§ 2, 5, 7, 17
State v. Crenshaw, 2008-Ohio-4859, 2008 WL 4356104 (Ohio Ct. App. 8th Dist. Cuyahoga County 2008)
62 ALR6th 413—§ 18, 38
State v. Crepeault, 167 Vt. 209, 704 A.2d 778 (1997)
42 ALR5th 581—§ 7
State v. Crepeault, 704 A.2d 778 (Vt. 1997)
42 ALR5th 581—§ 6
State v. Cresie, 93 Ohio App. 3d 67, 637 N.E.2d 935 (1st Dist. Hamilton County 1993)
70 ALR6th 1—§ 5
State v. Crespin, 94 N.M. 486, 612 P.2d 716 (App. 1980)
47 ALR5th 259—§ 2
State v. Cress, 1993 WL 14267 (Minn. Ct. App. 1993)
113 ALR5th 597—§ 3
State v. Cressey, 137 N.H. 402, 628 A.2d 696 (1993)
85 ALR5th 595—§ 7
State v. Crevina, 110 N.J. Super. 571, 266 A.2d 319 (Law Div. 1970)

65 ALR5th 407—§ 3, 5, 11
State v. Crews, 110 N.M. 723, 799 P.2d 592, R.I.C.O. Bus. Disp. Guide (CCH) ¶ 7616 (Ct. App. 1989)

89 ALR5th 629—§ 8
State v. Crews, 607 S.W.2d 759 (Mo. App. 1980)

39 ALR5th 283—§ 4
State v. Cribb, 310 S.C. 518, 426 S.E.2d 306 (1992)

76 ALR5th 1—§ 3, 5
State v. Cribbs, 29 Kan. App. 2d 919, 34 P.3d 76 (2001)

9 ALR6th 1—§ 17
State v. Crider, 21 Ohio App. 3d 268, 487 N.E.2d 911 (9th Dist. Summit County 1984)

55 ALR6th 157—§ 26
State v. Crietello, 197 Iowa 772, 197 N.W. 902 (1924)

54 ALR6th 429—§ 18
State v. Criger, 151 Kan. 176, 98 P.2d 133 (1940)

11 ALR5th 497—§ 3, 27, 28
State v. Crims, 540 N.W.2d 860 (Minn. Ct. App. 1995)

33 ALR6th 353—§ 4
State v. Crisanti, 220 Ga. App. 705, 470 S.E.2d 314 (1996)

125 ALR5th 281—§ 14
State v. Crisp, 19 N.C. App. 456, 199 S.E.2d 155 (1973)

106 ALR5th 397—§ 8
State v. Criss, 2000 WL 46105 (Ohio Ct. App. 9th Dist. Summit County 2000)

78 ALR5th 489—§ 9, 10
State v. Crissman, 31 Ohio App. 2d 170, 60 Ohio Op. 2d 279, 287 N.E.2d 642 (7th Dist. Columbiana County 1971)

39 ALR6th 257—§ 19
55 ALR6th 157—§ 24
State v. Crist, 80 Wash. App. 511, 909 P.2d 1341 (1996)

17 ALR5th 111—§ 3
State v. Crist, 150 Wash. App. 1001, 2009 WL 1178472 (Div. 1 2009)

78 ALR6th 1—§ 28, 42, 51
State v. Crist, 281 N.W.2d 657 (Minn. 1979)

18 ALR5th 1—§ 28
State v. Crites, 277 Mo. 194, 209 S.W. 863 (1919)

35 ALR6th 1—§ 16, 27
State v. Crocker, 409 N.W.2d 840 (Minn. 1987)

39 ALR5th 283—§ 3
State v. Crocker, 2005 WL 3678059 (Me. Super. Ct. 2005)

79 ALR6th 1—§ 25, 42
State v. Crockett, 801 S.W.2d 712 (Mo. Ct. App. E.D. 1990)

109 ALR5th 99—§ 5
State v. Crofton, 110 Wash. App. 1054, 2002 WL 374129 (Div. 2 2002)

33 ALR6th 91—§ 3, 42
63 ALR6th 351—§ 3
State v. Crofton, 144 Wash. App. 1047, 2008 WL 2231821 (Div. 1 2008)

63 ALR6th 351—§ 3
State v. Crom, 222 Neb. 273, 383 N.W.2d 461 (1986)

74 ALR5th 319—§ 5
116 ALR5th 479—§ 5
State v. Cromer, 186 S.W.3d 333 (Mo. Ct. App. W.D. 2005)

78 ALR6th 297—§ 9, 22, 80
State v. Cromwell, 157 Wash. 2d 529, 140 P.3d 593 (2006)

26 ALR6th 511—§ 42
State v. Cromwell, 211 Ariz. 181, 119 P.3d 448 (2005)

21 ALR6th 1—§ 4
State v. Cromwell, 253 Kan. 495, 856 P.2d 1299 (1993)

19 ALR6th 697—§ 10
State v. Cronin, 2001 WL 34013570 (N.H. Super. Ct. 2001)

122 ALR5th 439—§ 4, 8
State v. Crook, 253 La. 961, 221 So. 2d 473 (1969)

86 ALR5th 59—§ 3
State v. Crooks, 378 N.W.2d 722 (Iowa Ct. App. 1985)

90 ALR5th 225—§ 4

State v. Crosby, 927 P.2d 638 (Utah 1996)

90 ALR5th 453—§ 51

10 ALR6th 463—§ 4

State v. Cross, 23 Or. App. 536, 543 P.2d 48 (1975)

122 ALR5th 439—§ 4

State v. Cross, 31 Ohio App. 3d 28, 508 N.E.2d 172 (2d Dist. Greene County 1986)

66 ALR6th 351—§ 4

67 ALR6th 209—§ 21

State v. Cross, 58 Ohio St. 2d 482, 12 Ohio Ops. 3d 396, 391 N.E.2d 319 (1979)

54 ALR5th 141—§ 2 to 7

State v. Cross, 156 Wash. 2d 580, 132 P.3d 80 (2006)

83 ALR6th 255—§ 15

State v. Cross, 487 So. 2d 1056 (Fla. 1986)

92 ALR6th 1—§ 8

State v. Cross, 487 So. 2d 1056, 11 FLW 193 (Fla. 1986)

19 ALR5th 470—§ 5

State v. Cross, 673 S.E.2d 167 (N.C. Ct. App. 2009)

57 ALR6th 313—§ 7

State v. Crossen, 10 Or. App. 442, 499 P.2d 1357 (1972)

28 ALR6th 505—§ 9

State v. Crosswell, 223 Conn. 243, 612 A.2d 1174 (1992)

57 ALR6th 445—§ 15, 43

State v. Crouch, 339 Mo. 847, 98 S.W.2d 550 (1936)

54 ALR6th 429—§ 10

State v. Crowder, 80 P.3d 76 (Kan. Ct. App. 2003)

99 ALR6th 295—§ 15

State v. Crowder, 248 Mont. 169, 810 P.2d 299 (1991)

106 ALR5th 397—§ 5

State v. Crowe, 258 S.C. 258, 188 S.E.2d 379 (1972)

16 ALR6th 329—§ 4

24 ALR6th 591—§ 6

State v. Crowell, 773 So. 2d 871 (La. Ct. App. 4th Cir. 2000)

19 ALR6th 115—§ 4, 9, 10

State v. Crowl, 119 Wash. App. 1033, 2003 WL 22794534 (Div. 2 2003)

35 ALR6th 361—§ 17, 20

State v. Crowley, 220 Kan. 532, 552 P.2d 971 (1976)

82 ALR5th 359—§ 5

83 ALR5th 277—§ 9, 10

84 ALR5th 487—§ 3

State v. Crowley, 571 S.W.2d 460 (Mo. Ct. App. 1978)

9 ALR6th 1—§ 7

State v. Crowley, 1998 ME 187, 714 A.2d 834 (Me. 1998)

112 ALR5th 429—§ 6

State v. Crum, 1998 WL 818055 (Ohio Ct. App. 5th Dist. Stark County 1998)

63 ALR6th 351—§ 3

State v. Crumble, 2003 WL 734525 (Wash. Ct. App. Div. 2 2003)

7 ALR6th 233—§ 5

State v. Crumley, 128 Ariz. 302, 625 P.2d 891 (1981)

14 ALR5th 89—§ 11

State v. Crummy, 107 N.C. App. 305, 420 S.E.2d 448 (1992)

104 ALR5th 357—§ 3, 4, 9

54 ALR6th 429—§ 3, 5, 7

State v. Crump, 589 S.W.2d 328 (Mo. Ct. App. E.D. 1979)

99 ALR6th 295—§ 5

State v. Cruse, 112 Kan. 486, 212 P. 81 (1923)

24 ALR5th 465—§ 107

State v. Cruse, 2002-Ohio-3259, 2002 WL 1377826 (Ohio Ct. App. 10th Dist. Franklin County 2002)

83 ALR6th 465—§ 64

State v. Crutchfield, 318 Md. 200, 567 A.2d 449 (1989)

34 ALR6th 1—§ 11

State v. Cruz, 15 Kan. App. 2d 476, 809 P.2d 1233 (1991)

18 ALR6th 1—§ 4, 5
State v. Cruz, 28 Conn. App. 575, 611
A.2d 457 (1992)
23 ALR6th 307—§ 45
State v. Cruz, 56 Conn. App. 763, 746
A.2d 196 (2000)
38 ALR5th 433—§ 15
40 ALR6th 1—§ 9
State v. Cruz, 121 Or. App. 241, 855
P.2d 191 (1993)
94 ALR6th 191—§ 7
State v. Cruz, 137 Ariz. 541, 672 P.2d
470 (1983)
16 ALR6th 329—§ 4
19 ALR6th 115—§ 4, 7, 10
24 ALR6th 591—§ 4, 12
State v. Cruz, 175 Ariz. 395, 857 P.2d
1249, 144 Ariz. Adv. Rep. 26
(1993)
20 ALR5th 398—§ 25, 26
State v. Cruz, 218 Ariz. 149, 181 P.3d
196 (2008)
71 ALR6th 625—§ 10, 11, 19
State v. Cruz, 582 So. 2d 20 (Fla. Dist.
Ct. App. 5th Dist. 1991)
114 ALR5th 235—§ 3
State v. Cruz, 594 A.2d 1082 (Me. 1991)
33 ALR5th 571—§ 3
State v. Cruz Const. Co., Inc., 279 N.J.
Super. 241, 652 A.2d 741 (App.
Div. 1995)
105 ALR5th 499—§ 4
State v. Cruz-Mata, 138 Ariz. 370, 674
P.2d 1368 (1983)
32 ALR6th 1—§ 11
State v. Cruz-Meza, 2003 UT 32, 76
P.3d 1165 (Utah 2003)
27 ALR6th 183—§ 4
State v. Crystal B., 2001 -NMCA- 010,
24 P.3d 771 (N.M. Ct. App. 2000)
**31 ALR5th 229—§ 17, 20, 25.5, 27,
42, 64.5**
State v. C.S. Jackson & Co., 137 La.
931, 69 So. 751 (1915)
81 ALR6th 363—§ 26
State v. Cuesta, 68 Conn. App. 470, 791
A.2d 686 (2002)
81 ALR6th 505—§ 30

State v. Cuevas, 281 N.W.2d 627 (Iowa
1979)
59 ALR5th 1—§ 3, 4, 6
State v. Cuevas, 288 N.W.2d 525 (Iowa
1980)
54 ALR6th 429—§ 13
State v. Cugliata, 372 A.2d 1019 (Me.
1977)
57 ALR5th 141—§ 2, 5
State v. Culbertson, 29 Or. App. 363,
563 P.2d 1224 (1977)
99 ALR5th 557—§ 3
State v. Culbertson, 214 Kan. 884, 522
P.2d 391 (1974)
1 ALR6th 549—§ 15
State v. Culbertson, 2008 WL 65327
(Tenn. Crim. App. 2008)
38 ALR6th 97—§ 5
State v. Culbreath, 30 S.W.3d 309
(Tenn. 2000)
18 ALR5th 1—§ 41
State v. Culkin, 791 S.W.2d 803 (Mo.
App. 1990)
22 ALR5th 1—§ 13, 14, 32, 38
State v. Cullen, 14 Wash. 2d 105, 127
P.2d 257 (1942)
97 ALR5th 293—§ 3
State v. Cullen, 646 S.W.2d 850 (Mo.
App. 1982)
7 ALR5th 263—§ 6
State v. Cullison, 147 P.3d 1090 (Kan.
2006)
26 ALR6th 511—§ 25
State v. Culmo, 43 Conn. Supp. 46, 642
A.2d 90 (1993)
29 ALR5th 487—§ 3, 8, 11
State v. Culmsee, 91 Or. App. 63, 754
P.2d 11 (1988)
95 ALR5th 229—§ 19
State v. Culp, 900 S.W.2d 707 (Tenn.
Crim. 1994)
54 ALR5th 141—§ 3 to 5, 8
State v. Culp, 1997 WL 97870 (Tenn.
Crim. 1997)
54 ALR5th 141—§ 8
State v. Culpepper, 302 N.C. 179, 273
S.E.2d 686 (1981)

85 ALR5th 187—§ 12

State v. Culton, 273 N.W.2d 200 (S.D. 1979)

74 ALR5th 453—§ 2, 5

State v. Cumming, 365 So. 2d 153 (Fla. 1978)

50 ALR5th 703—§ 27

State v. Cummings, 46 Conn. App. 661, 701 A.2d 663 (1997)

29 ALR5th 487—§ 3, 6, 11, 12

State v. Cummings, 120 Ariz. 69, 583 P.2d 1389 (App. 1978)

15 ALR5th 391—§ 2, 7

State v. Cummings, 206 Mo. 613, 105 S.W. 649 (1907)

5 ALR6th 1—§ 60

State v. Cummings, 242 Kan. 84, 744 P.2d 858 (1987)

26 ALR5th 603—§ 4

State v. Cummings, 326 N.C. 298, 389 S.E.2d 66 (1990)

57 ALR5th 141—§ 3, 7
24 ALR6th 1—§ 21

State v. Cummings, 332 N.C. 487, 422 S.E.2d 692 (1992)

31 ALR5th 704—§ 9, 18

State v. Cummings, 353 N.C. 281, 543 S.E.2d 849 (2001)

110 ALR5th 1—§ 15

State v. Cummings, 748 So. 2d 388, 113 A.L.R.5th 761 (Fla. Dist. Ct. App. 5th Dist. 2000)

113 ALR5th 597—§ 3, 4, 8

State v. Cummings, 2002-Ohio-213, 2002 WL 57979 (Ohio Ct. App. 9th Dist. Summit County 2002)

17 ALR6th 327—§ 29

State v. Cummings, 2007-Ohio-4970, 2007 WL 2757752 (Ohio Ct. App. 12th Dist. Butler County 2007)

56 ALR6th 185—§ 37

State v. Cummins, 257 Mont. 491, 850 P.2d 952 (1993)

71 ALR5th 1—§ 52

State v. Cumpton, 2000 -NMCA- 033, 1 P.3d 429 (N.M. Ct. App. 2000)

26 ALR5th 1—§ 4

State v. Cunigan, 2000 WL 1369901 (Ohio Ct. App. 2d Dist. Montgomery County 2000)

43 ALR6th 475—§ 21

State v. Cunningham, 17 Ariz. App. 314, 497 P.2d 821 (1972)

4 ALR5th 1—§ 17, 23

State v. Cunningham, 144 Wis. 2d 272, 423 N.W.2d 862 (1988)

28 ALR6th 505—§ 9

State v. Cunningham, 344 N.C. 341, 474 S.E.2d 772 (1996)

50 ALR5th 467—§ 9
115 ALR5th 509—§ 2

State v. Cunningham, 972 S.W.2d 16 (Tenn. Crim. App. 1998)

102 ALR5th 525—§ 27

State v. Cunningham, No. 48558 (January 31, 1985, Ct. App. Ohio, 8th App. Dist. Cuyahoga Co.)

39 ALR5th 283—§ 14, 15

State v. Cuno, 869 S.W.2d 285 (Mo. Ct. App. E.D. 1994)

111 ALR5th 1—§ 3, 5, 7

State v. Cuny, 534 N.W.2d 52 (S.D. 1995)

84 ALR6th 293—§ 27

State v. Cupp, 2006-Ohio-1808, 2006 WL 925174 (Ohio Ct. App. 2d Dist. Montgomery County 2006)

25 ALR6th 227—§ 13
41 ALR6th 141—§ 5

State v. Curcio, 191 Conn. 27, 463 A.2d 566 (1983)

82 ALR5th 389—§ 3

State v. Curd, 2009-Ohio-3814, 2009 WL 2356874 (Ohio Ct. App. 11th Dist. Lake County 2009)

63 ALR6th 351—§ 3

State v. Cure, 93 So. 3d 1268 (La. 2012)

92 ALR6th 171—§ 16

State v. Curevich, 1998 WL 401720 (Tenn. Crim. App. 1998)

73 ALR5th 383—§ 5

State v. Curlew, 459 A.2d 160 (Me. 1983)

33 ALR5th 571—§ 3

For assistance, call 1-800-328-4880

State v. Curley, 253 S.C. 513, 171 S.E.2d 699 (1970)
  68 ALR5th 343—§ 3
State v. Curley, 691 So. 2d 618 (Fla. Dist. Ct. App. 5th Dist. 1997)
  51 ALR6th 219—§ 4
State v. Curley, 2007 WL 1247976 (Minn. Ct. App. 2007)
  37 ALR6th 357—§ 3, 71
State v. Curls, 90 P.3d 378 (Kan. Ct. App. 2004)
  23 ALR6th 307—§ 44
State v. Currens, 55 Ohio Misc. 2d 3, 563 N.E.2d 57 (Mun. Ct. 1989)
  47 ALR6th 107—§ 12
State v. Currie, 150 Ariz. 59, 721 P.2d 1186 (App. 1986)
  15 ALR5th 391—§ 31
State v. Currie, 400 N.W.2d 361 (Minn. App. 1987)
  5 ALR5th 243—§ 2, 50
State v. Currington, 113 Idaho 538, 746 P.2d 997 (Ct. App. 1987)
  56 ALR6th 185—§ 10
State v. Curry, 29 Kan. App. 2d 392, 28 P.3d 1019 (2001)
  23 ALR6th 307—§ 31, 44
State v. Curry, 187 Ariz. 623, 931 P.2d 1133 (Ct. App. Div. 1 1996)
  54 ALR5th 575—§ 16
  85 ALR5th 595—§ 8, 9
State v. Curry, 262 La. 280, 263 So. 2d 36 (1972)
  70 ALR5th 587—§ 3
State v. Curry, 436 N.W.2d 371 (Iowa Ct. App. 1988)
  112 ALR5th 621—§ 5
State v. Curry, 1993 WL 256967 (Ohio Ct. App. 11th Dist. Ashtabula County 1993)
  43 ALR6th 475—§ 21
State v. Curry, 2002-Ohio-2260, 2002 WL 973069 (Ohio Ct. App. 8th Dist. Cuyahoga County 2002)
  27 ALR6th 491—§ 3
State v. Curtin, 175 W. Va. 318, 332 S.E.2d 619 (1985)

  1 ALR6th 549—§ 20
  62 ALR6th 413—§ 43
State v. Curtis, 7 N.C. App. 707, 173 S.E.2d 613 (1970)
  9 ALR6th 1—§ 17
State v. Curtis, 42 Kan. App. 2d 132, 209 P.3d 753 (2009)
  92 ALR6th 1—§ 6
State v. Curtis, 298 N.W.2d 807 (S.D. 1980)
  39 ALR5th 283—§ 4, 72
State v. Curtis, 681 So. 2d 1287 (La. App. 4th Cir. 1996)
  50 ALR5th 581—§ 7
State v. Curtis, 964 S.W.2d 604 (Tenn. Crim. App. 1997)
  113 ALR5th 517—§ 7
State v. Curtiss, 114 Mont. 232, 135 P.2d 361 (1943)
  54 ALR6th 429—§ 9
State v. Curtiss, 242 P.3d 1281 (Kan. Ct. App. 2010)
  64 ALR6th 131—§ 5
State v. Curto, 73 Ohio App. 3d 16, 595 N.E.2d 1038 (9th Dist. Summit County 1991)
  62 ALR6th 413—§ 29
State v. Cushman, 451 S.W.2d 17 (Mo. 1970)
  72 ALR5th 607—§ 3, 6, 7, 12
State v. Custodio, 62 Haw. 1, 607 P.2d 1048 (1980)
  85 ALR5th 261—§ 3, 5
State v. Cuthrell, 233 N.C. 274, 63 S.E.2d 549 (1951)
  85 ALR5th 187—§ 7, 8
State v. Cutler, 2000-Ohio-2587, 2000 WL 1617820 (Ohio Ct. App. 7th Dist. Jefferson County 2000)
  29 ALR6th 237—§ 4, 9, 21
State v. Cutro, 37 Conn. App. 534, 657 A.2d 239 (1995)
  95 ALR5th 229—§ 2, 19
State v. Cvorovic, 158 Wis. 2d 630, 462 N.W.2d 897 (Ct. App. 1990)
  93 ALR5th 683—§ 4
State v. Cyr, 389 A.2d 834 (Me. 1978)

CASES CITED IN ALR5th and ALR6th

54 ALR6th 593—§ 11
State v. Cyr, 611 A.2d 64 (Me. 1992)
20 ALR6th 479—§ 3
State v. Czajka, 101 Ohio App. 3d 564, 656 N.E.2d 9 (Cuyahoga Co. 1995)
5 ALR5th 243—§ 45, 47
State v. Czartorsky, 2009 WL 1228442 (N.J. Super. Ct. App. Div. 2009)
90 ALR6th 385—§ 5
State v. Czechowicz, 146 Wis. 2d 873, 433 N.W.2d 34 (Ct. App. 1988)
84 ALR6th 293—§ 30
State v. Czmowski, 393 N.W.2d 72 (S.D. 1986)
84 ALR6th 293—§ 27
State v. $10,000 Seized from Mary Patrick, 562 N.W.2d 192 (Iowa Ct. App. 1997)
34 ALR6th 539—§ 4, 6, 8
State v. $11,014.00, 820 S.W.2d 783 (Tex. 1991)
34 ALR6th 539—§ 8, 9
State v. $29,177.00 U.S. Currency, 638 So. 2d 653 (La. Ct. App. 3d Cir. 1994)
34 ALR6th 539—§ 9
State v. D.A., 2009-Ohio-3103, 2009 WL 1819446 (Ohio Ct. App. 8th Dist. Cuyahoga County 2009)
70 ALR6th 1—§ 5
State v. Dabney, 77 Okla. Crim. 331, 141 P.2d 303 (1943)
95 ALR5th 1—§ 3, 11
State v. Dabney, 181 Neb. 263, 147 N.W.2d 768 (1967)
53 ALR6th 81—§ 5
State v. Dace, 333 N.W.2d 812 (S.D. 1983)
5 ALR5th 243—§ 39
State v. Dacey, 138 Vt. 491, 418 A.2d 856 (1980)
119 ALR5th 379—§ 8
State v. Dacons, 5 Ohio App. 3d 112, 449 N.E.2d 507 (10th Dist. Franklin County 1982)
3 ALR6th 269—§ 3, 5
State v. Dagley, 793 S.W.2d 420 (Mo. Ct. App. W.D. 1990)

84 ALR6th 427—§ 6
State v. Dahl, 139 Wash. 2d 678, 990 P.2d 396 (1999)
71 ALR5th 637—§ 7, 8
State v. Dahl, 185 Or. App. 149, 57 P.3d 965 (2002)
26 ALR6th 179—§ 14
State v. Dahl, 336 Or. 481, 87 P.3d 650 (2004)
26 ALR6th 179—§ 6, 11, 14
State v. Dahlgren, 627 S.W.2d 53 (Mo. 1982)
84 ALR6th 427—§ 14
State v. Dahlheimer, 804 N.W.2d 314 (Iowa Ct. App. 2011)
96 ALR6th 355—§ 24, 39, 52
State v. Dahms, 252 Mont. 1, 825 P.2d 1214 (1992)
97 ALR5th 201—§ 6
State v. Daigle, 701 So. 2d 685 (La. App. 3 Cir. 1997)
66 ALR5th 397—§ 6, 8
State v. Dailey, 93 Wash. 2d 454, 610 P.2d 357 (1980)
71 ALR5th 1—§ 56
State v. Dailey, 2010-Ohio-4816, 2010 WL 3836204 (Ohio Ct. App. 3d Dist. Logan County 2010)
62 ALR6th 161—§ 16
State v. Dais, 22 N.C. App. 379, 206 S.E.2d 759 (1974)
98 ALR6th 455—§ 12, 30
State v. Dakins, 209 Wis. 2d 84, 562 N.W.2d 927 (Ct. App. 1997)
68 ALR5th 343—§ 5
State v. Dakota, 300 Minn. 12, 217 N.W.2d 748 (1974)
34 ALR6th 1—§ 11
State v. D'Alexander, 496 So. 2d 1007 (Fla. Dist. Ct. App. 2d Dist. 1986)
113 ALR5th 597—§ 8
State v. Dalglish, 131 Ariz. 133, 639 P.2d 323 (1982)
7 ALR5th 758—§ 13
State v. Dall, 305 A.2d 270 (Me. 1973)
29 ALR5th 59—§ 3, 8

State v. Dallmann, 441 N.W.2d 912 (N.D. 1989)
    68 ALR5th 549—§ 3
State v. Dalpiaz, 151 Ohio App. 3d 257, 2002-Ohio-7346, 783 N.E.2d 976 (11th Dist. Portage County 2002)
    104 ALR5th 165—§ 14
State v. Dalrymple, 80 N.M. 492, 458 P.2d 96 (App. 1969)
    41 ALR5th 171—§ 6, 66, 90, 116, 136
State v. Dalsen, 444 N.W.2d 582 (Minn. Ct. App. 1989)
    73 ALR5th 383—§ 57
State v. Dalton, 185 N.C. 606, 115 S.E. 881 (1923)
    105 ALR5th 529—§ 24
State v. Daly, 4 Haw. App. 52, 659 P.2d 83 (1983)
    68 ALR6th 527—§ 26
State v. Daly, 14 Kan. App. 2d 310, 789 P.2d 1203 (1990)
    117 ALR5th 407—§ 4
State v. Daly, 202 Neb. 217, 274 N.W.2d 557 (1979)
    114 ALR5th 173—§ 3, 7
State v. Daly, 210 Mo. 664, 109 S.W. 53 (1908)
    50 ALR5th 467—§ 6, 8
    78 ALR5th 1—§ 34
State v. Dalzell, 2010 WL 1256045 (Ariz. Ct. App. Div. 2 2010)
    55 ALR6th 1—§ 41
State v. Dam, 111 Or. App. 15, 825 P.2d 286 (1992)
    32 ALR5th 149—§ 62, 85
State v. Damask, 936 S.W.2d 565 (Mo. 1996)
    82 ALR5th 103—§ 5
State v. Damaske, 212 Wis. 2d 169, 567 N.W.2d 905 (Ct. App. 1997)
    9 ALR6th 633—§ 55
State v. Dambrell, 120 Idaho 532, 817 P.2d 646 (1991)
    16 ALR6th 329—§ 4
    24 ALR6th 591—§ 4
State v. Damico, 513 S.W.2d 351 (Mo. 1974)

    37 ALR5th 515—§ 5
    23 ALR6th 1—§ 15
State v. Damm, 62 S.D. 123, 252 N.W. 7, 104 A.L.R. 430 (1933)
    119 ALR5th 275—§ 13
State v. Dammeron, 719 So. 2d 1151 (La. Ct. App. 5th Cir. 1998)
    71 ALR6th 1—§ 5
State v. Dammons, 159 N.C. App. 284, 583 S.E.2d 606 (2003)
    125 ALR5th 537—§ 15, 22, 29
State v. Damofle, 89 Or. App. 620, 750 P.2d 518 (1988)
    30 ALR5th 683—§ 2
State v. Damon, 18 Ariz. App. 421, 502 P.2d 1360 (Div. 2 1972)
    125 ALR5th 281—§ 11
State v. Dampier, 862 S.W.2d 366 (Mo. Ct. App. S.D. 1993)
    1 ALR6th 549—§ 5
State v. Damron, 213 W. Va. 8, 576 S.E.2d 253 (2002)
    72 ALR6th 141—§ 9, 18
State v. Damron, 1998 ND 71, 575 N.W.2d 912 (N.D. 1998)
    6 ALR6th 533—§ 22
State v. Damuth, 135 Minn. 76, 160 N.W. 196 (1916)
    5 ALR5th 243—§ 26
State v. Dana, 84 Wash. App. 166, 926 P.2d 344 (Div. 1 1996)
    35 ALR6th 361—§ 5, 7, 12, 15, 20, 21
State v. Dancy, 2012 WL 538952 (Minn. Ct. App. 2012)
    92 ALR6th 171—§ 16
State v. D'Andrea, 1998 WL 251829 (Wash. Ct. App. Div. 1 1998)
    71 ALR5th 637—§ 7
State v. Dane, 89 Wash. App. 226, 948 P.2d 1326 (Div. 2 1997)
    85 ALR5th 261—§ 4, 6
State v. Danek, 118 N.M. 8, 878 P.2d 326, Blue Sky L. Rep. (CCH) ¶ 74009 (1994)
    66 ALR5th 135—§ 37
State v. Dangelo, 182 Iowa 1253, 166 N.W. 587 (1918)

98 ALR6th 455—§ 5

State v. D'Angelo, 605 A.2d 68 (Me. 1992)

74 ALR5th 319—§ 13

State v. Dangerfield, 32 N.C. App. 608, 233 S.E.2d 663 (1977)

11 ALR5th 831—§ 13, 15, 19

State v. Danh, 500 N.W.2d 506 (Minn. Ct. App. 1993)

46 ALR6th 63—§ 13

State v. Daniel, 97 Ohio App. 3d 548, 647 N.E.2d 174 (10th Dist. Franklin County 1994)

85 ALR5th 595—§ 3

State v. Daniel, 109 Or. App. 680, 820 P.2d 901 (1991)

92 ALR5th 35—§ 26

State v. Daniel, 132 Idaho 701, 979 P.2d 103 (1999)

119 ALR5th 379—§ 6

State v. Daniel, 255 N.C. 717, 122 S.E.2d 704 (1961)

89 ALR6th 565—§ 13

State v. Daniel, 297 So. 2d 417 (La. 1974)

70 ALR5th 587—§ 3

State v. Daniel, 574 N.W.2d 333 (Iowa 1998)

18 ALR5th 542—§ 3

State v. Daniel, 903 So. 2d 644 (La. Ct. App. 2d Cir. 2005)

69 ALR6th 1—§ 17, 27

State v. Daniel, 1990 WL 237188 (Ohio App. 11 Dist., Trumbull County, Dec. 31, 1990)

60 ALR5th 75—§ 12

State v. Daniel, 2007 WL 1174905 (Tenn. Crim. App. 2007)

92 ALR6th 1—§ 4

State v. Daniels, 14 Ohio App. 3d 41, 14 Ohio B.R. 45, 469 N.E.2d 1338 (Hamilton Co. 1984)

5 ALR5th 243—§ 59

State v. Daniels, 26 Ohio App. 3d 101, 26 Ohio B.R. 276, 498 N.E.2d 227 (Hamilton Co. 1985)

4 ALR5th 1—§ 4, 7

State v. Daniels, 46 N.J. 428, 217 A.2d 610 (1966)

103 ALR5th 463—§ 3

State v. Daniels, 59 N.C. App. 63, 295 S.E.2d 508 (1982)

5 ALR5th 243—§ 6, 11

State v. Daniels, 66 Mo. 192, 1877 WL 8760 (1877)

97 ALR5th 537—§ 48

State v. Daniels, 92 Ohio App. 3d 473, 636 N.E.2d 336 (1st Dist. Hamilton County 1993)

16 ALR6th 329—§ 4

19 ALR6th 115—§ 5

24 ALR6th 591—§ 6, 10, 14

State v. Daniels, 92 Ohio App. 3d 473, 636 N.E.2d 336 (1st Dist.Hamilton County 1993)

85 ALR5th 471—§ 2, 7

85 ALR5th 547—§ 7

State v. Daniels, 106 Wash. App. 571, 23 P.3d 1125 (Div. 1 2001)

80 ALR6th 599—§ 8

State v. Daniels, 188 N.J. 486, 909 A.2d 722 (2006)

26 ALR6th 511—§ 17

State v. Daniels, 222 Neb. 850, 388 N.W.2d 446 (1986)

39 ALR6th 257—§ 42, 47

40 ALR6th 1—§ 28

State v. Daniels, 226 Mont. 80, 734 P.2d 188 (1987)

57 ALR5th 315—§ 11

State v. Daniels, 346 So. 2d 672 (La. 1977)

62 ALR6th 259—§ 13

State v. Daniels, 641 S.W.2d 488 (Mo. App. 1982)

54 ALR5th 141—§ 3 to 5, 8, 10

State v. Daniels, 2002 UT 2, 40 P.3d 611 (Utah 2002)

99 ALR6th 295—§ 16

State v. Daniels, 2003 MT 30, 314 Mont. 208, 64 P.3d 1045 (2003)

79 ALR6th 125—§ 4

State v. Danielson, 276 Minn. 428, 150 N.W.2d 567 (1967)

---

59 ALR5th 1—§ 3, 4, 6
State v. Danikas, 11 S.W.3d 782 (Mo. Ct. App. W.D. 1999)
24 ALR5th 465—§ 36, 39
State v. Dankworth, 672 P.2d 148 (Alaska Ct. App. 1983)
24 ALR6th 255—§ 5, 7, 13
State v. Dann, 206 Ariz. 371, 79 P.3d 58 (2003)
122 ALR5th 145—§ 7, 9, 23
State v. Dann, 702 A.2d 105 (Vt. 1997)
48 ALR5th 659—§ 7
State v. Dannels, 226 Mont. 80, 734 P.2d 188 (1987)
29 ALR6th 1—§ 10
30 ALR6th 103—§ 58
45 ALR6th 337—§ 30
State v. Danny A., 536 A.2d 1136 (Me. 1988)
18 ALR5th 856—§ 4
State v. Dansinger, 521 A.2d 685 (Me. 1987)
3 ALR5th 521—§ 2, 9, 10
State v. Danskin, 122 N.H. 817, 451 A.2d 396 (1982)
55 ALR6th 157—§ 6, 65
State v. Dantonio, 18 N.J. 570, 115 A.2d 35, 49 A.L.R.2d 460 (1955)
18 ALR6th 613—§ 3
State v. Daophin, 533 So. 2d 761 (Fla. 1988)
2 ALR6th 551—§ 5
State v. Dapice, 1989 WL 122542 (Ohio Ct. App. 9th Dist. Summit County 1989)
70 ALR5th 491—§ 2
State v. Darby, 1996 SD 127, 556 N.W.2d 311 (S.D. 1996)
32 ALR6th 1—§ 11
State v. Darga, 30 Ohio App. 3d 54, 506 N.E.2d 266 (10th Dist. Franklin County 1985)
18 ALR6th 519—§ 20
State v. Dario, 106 Ohio App. 3d 232, 665 N.E.2d 759 (Hamilton Co. 1995)
29 ALR5th 487—§ 3

State v. Darkis, 129 N.M. 547, 2000-NMCA-085, 10 P.3d 871 (Ct. App. 2000)
2 ALR6th 551—§ 25
State v. Darmsteder, 1985 WL 7871 (Ohio Ct. App. 2d Dist. Montgomery County 1985)
72 ALR5th 1—§ 30
State v. Darnell, 49 Or. App. 461, 619 P.2d 1321 (1980)
20 ALR5th 534—§ 2
State v. Darrah, 446 S.W.2d 745 (Mo. 1969)
72 ALR5th 607—§ 3
State v. Darrin, 325 N.W.2d 110 (Iowa 1982)
21 ALR5th 275—§ 1
State v. Darst, 1997 WL 567939 (Ohio Ct. App. 4th Dist. Athens County 1997)
34 ALR6th 1—§ 12
State v. Dartez, 124 N.M. 455, 1998-NMCA-009, 952 P.2d 450 (Ct. App. 1997)
79 ALR6th 125—§ 4
State v. Darveaux, 318 N.W.2d 44 (Minn. 1982)
83 ALR5th 277—§ 29
84 ALR5th 487—§ 22
State v. Datwyler, 2006 WL 163418 (Minn. Ct. App. 2006)
26 ALR6th 511—§ 26
State v. Dauenhauer, 85 Wash. App. 1037, 1997 WL 138904 (Div. 3 1997)
16 ALR6th 329—§ 11
24 ALR6th 591—§ 9, 13
State v. Daugherty, 94 Wash. 2d 263, 616 P.2d 649 (1980)
60 ALR5th 1—§ 2, 6
State v. Daugherty, 744 S.W.2d 849 (Mo. Ct. App. S.D. 1988)
101 ALR6th 417—§ 8
State v. Daughtery, 563 So. 2d 1171 (La. Ct. App. 1st Cir. 1990)
86 ALR5th 463—§ 10
State v. Daughtry, 340 N.C. 488, 459 S.E.2d 747 (1995)

32 ALR6th 1—§ 11

State v. Daughtry, 505 So. 2d 537 (Fla. Dist. Ct. App. 4th Dist. 1987)

106 ALR5th 377—§ 3

State v. Dauphin, 2009 WL 162005 (Vt. 2009)

92 ALR6th 295—§ 7

96 ALR6th 355—§ 7

State v. Dauzat, 843 So. 2d 526 (La. Ct. App. 3d Cir. 2003)

5 ALR6th 1—§ 70

State v. Davenport, 116 Ohio App. 3d 6, 686 N.E.2d 531 (12th Dist. Warren County 1996)

69 ALR6th 1—§ 27

State v. Davenport, 399 So. 2d 201 (La. 1981)

24 ALR6th 1—§ 20

State v. Davenport, 771 So. 2d 837 (La. Ct. App. 2d Cir. 2000)

106 ALR5th 377—§ 4

State v. Davenport, 801 So. 2d 380 (La. Ct. App. 2d Cir. 1999)

15 ALR6th 515—§ 14

State v. Davenport, 2007 WL 1582659 (Tenn. Crim. App. 2007)

33 ALR6th 91—§ 30, 45

State v. Davi, 504 N.W.2d 844 (S.D. 1993)

24 ALR5th 465—§ 14, 88, 109

State v. David, 130 Ga. App. 872, 204 S.E.2d 773 (1974)

125 ALR5th 281—§ 9

State v. David G.K., 2001 WL 687610 (Wis. Ct. App. 2001)

91 ALR5th 343—§ 12, 31

State v. Davido, 89 Wash. App. 1036, 1998 WL 85710 (Div. 1 1998)

79 ALR6th 1—§ 30

State v. Davidson, 26 Wash. App. 623, 613 P.2d 564 (Div. 1 1980)

102 ALR5th 525—§ 72

State v. Davidson, 44 Wis. 2d 177, 170 N.W.2d 755 (1969)

58 ALR6th 499—§ 57

State v. Davidson, 77 N.C. App. 540, 335 S.E.2d 518 (1985)

39 ALR5th 283—§ 4, 18

State v. Davidson, 131 N.C. App. 276, 506 S.E.2d 743, Blue Sky L. Rep. (CCH) ¶ 74171 (1998)

27 ALR6th 491—§ 3

State v. Davidson, 136 Kan. 406, 15 P.2d 404 (1932)

105 ALR5th 1—§ 3

State v. Davidson, 225 N.J. Super. 1, 541 A.2d 700 (1988)

15 ALR5th 391—§ 11, 38

State v. Davidson, 2002 WL 1482720 (Tenn. Crim. App. 2002)

8 ALR6th 265—§ 28

State v. Davidson, 2003-Ohio-1448, 2003 WL 1509931 (Ohio Ct. App. 10th Dist. Franklin County 2003)

70 ALR6th 1—§ 5

State v. Davidson, 2003-Ohio-2993, 2003 WL 21350310 (Ohio Ct. App. 5th Dist. Stark County 2003)

38 ALR6th 97—§ 28

State v. Davie, 80 Ohio St. 3d 311, 1997-Ohio-341, 686 N.E.2d 245 (1997)

3 ALR6th 269—§ 5, 8

State v. Davies, 1986 WL 657 (Ohio Ct. App. 1st Dist. Hamilton County 1986)

85 ALR5th 1—§ 11

State v. Davila, 203 N.J. 97, 999 A.2d 1116 (2010)

79 ALR6th 1—§ 14, 17, 21

State v. Davino, 1990 WL 289572 (Conn. Super. Ct. 1990)

103 ALR5th 463—§ 3

State v. Davis, 4 Ohio App. 3d 199, 447 N.E.2d 139 (9th Dist. Medina County 1982)

27 ALR6th 183—§ 38

State v. Davis, 6 Wash. 2d 696, 108 P.2d 641 (1940)

111 ALR5th 491—§ 3

State v. Davis, 11 P.3d 1177 (Kan. Ct. App. 2000)

50 ALR5th 581—§ 7, 9, 19

State v. Davis, 14 Nev. 439 (1880)

54 ALR5th 141—§ 3, 4, 7

State v. Davis, 27 Wash. App. 498, 618
  P.2d 1034 (1980)
    1 ALR5th 938—§ 6
State v. Davis, 32 Conn. App. 21, 628
  A.2d 11 (1993)
    55 ALR6th 157—§ 4
State v. Davis, 33 N.C. App. 262, 234
  S.E.2d 762 (1977)
    5 ALR5th 243—§ 2, 11, 24
State v. Davis, 41 Or. App. 249, 597
  P.2d 1280 (1979)
    99 ALR5th 557—§ 3, 12
State v. Davis, 51 Or. App. 827, 627
  P.2d 492 (1981)
    45 ALR6th 643—§ 4
State v. Davis, 53 Wash. App. 502, 768
  P.2d 499 (1989)
    42 ALR5th 291—§ 6
State v. Davis, 54 N.C. App. 596, 284
  S.E.2d 139
    81 ALR5th 563—§ 3, 5
State v. Davis, 57 Or. App. 322, 644
  P.2d 623 (1982)
    66 ALR6th 351—§ 64
State v. Davis, 62 Ohio St. 3d 326, 581
  N.E.2d 1362 (1991)
    57 ALR5th 141—§ 12
State v. Davis, 64 Ohio App. 3d 334, 581
  N.E.2d 604 (12th Dist. Preble
  County 1989)
    85 ALR5th 595—§ 2, 3, 8, 10
State v. Davis, 76 Conn. App. 653, 820
  A.2d 1122 (2003)
    39 ALR6th 257—§ 4
State v. Davis, 77 N.C. 483 (1877)
    11 ALR5th 831—§ 5, 6
State v. Davis, 80 Ohio App. 3d 277, 609
  N.E.2d 174 (8th Dist. Cuyahoga
  County 1992)
    78 ALR6th 297—§ 41
State v. Davis, 86 Wash. App. 414, 937
  P.2d 1110 (Div. 2 1997)
    61 ALR5th 1—§ 5
    58 ALR6th 499—§ 54
State v. Davis, 91 N.J. Super. 470, 221
  A.2d 47 (1966)
    23 ALR5th 672—§ 5

State v. Davis, 93 P.3d 745 (Kan. Ct.
  App. 2004)
    8 ALR6th 265—§ 18
State v. Davis, 93 Wash. App. 648, 970
  P.2d 336 (Div. 2 1999)
    27 ALR5th 593—§ 7, 21, 31
State v. Davis, 101 N.C. App. 12, 398
  S.E.2d 645 (1990)
    44 ALR5th 651—§ 5
    86 ALR5th 59—§ 4
    103 ALR6th 507—§ 22
State v. Davis, 106 Or. App. 546, 809
  P.2d 125 (1991)
    43 ALR5th 1—§ 13
    103 ALR5th 463—§ 3
State v. Davis, 115 Ariz. 3, 562 P.2d
  1370 (App. 1977)
    59 ALR5th 135—§ 3
State v. Davis, 116 N.J. 341, 561 A.2d
  1082 (1989)
    66 ALR6th 83—§ 4
State v. Davis, 116 Ohio St. 3d 404,
  2008-Ohio-2, 880 N.E.2d 31 (2008)
    38 ALR6th 439—§ 4
State v. Davis, 116 Wash. App. 81, 64
  P.3d 661 (Div. 1 2003)
    7 ALR6th 233—§ 5
State v. Davis, 117 Wash. App. 702, 72
  P.3d 1134 (Div. 1 2003)
    125 ALR5th 357—§ 6
    7 ALR6th 233—§ 9
State v. Davis, 126 P.3d 1132 (Kan. Ct.
  App. 2006)
    26 ALR6th 511—§ 25
State v. Davis, 129 P.3d 582 (Kan. 2006)
    26 ALR6th 511—§ 25
State v. Davis, 133 Or. App. 467, 891
  P.2d 1373 (1995)
    99 ALR5th 557—§ 3
State v. Davis, 154 La. 295, 97 So. 449
  (1923)
    81 ALR5th 563—§ 3, 5
State v. Davis, 155 Vt. 417, 584 A.2d
  1146 (1990)
    11 ALR6th 237—§ 9, 12
State v. Davis, 159 Ga. App. 537, 284
  S.E.2d 51 (1981)

54 ALR5th 575—§ 30
State v. Davis, 168 N.C. App. 321, 608 S.E.2d 74 (2005)

83 ALR6th 465—§ 18, 21, 69, 78
State v. Davis, 195 W. Va. 79, 464 S.E.2d 598 (1995)

116 ALR5th 479—§ 5
State v. Davis, 199 W. Va. 84, 483 S.E.2d 84, 66 A.L.R.5th 783 (1996)

66 ALR5th 397—§ 5
State v. Davis, 210 S.W.3d 229, 53 A.L.R.6th 617 (Mo. Ct. App. W.D. 2006)

53 ALR6th 1—§ 11
State v. Davis, 214 Neb. 474, 334 N.W.2d 450 (1983)

39 ALR6th 257—§ 19, 23, 24
State v. Davis, 217 S.W. 87 (Mo. 1919)

54 ALR6th 429—§ 10
State v. Davis, 231 Neb. 878, 438 N.W.2d 772 (1989)

103 ALR6th 347—§ 15
State v. Davis, 240 Wis. 2d 15, 2000 WI App 270, 622 N.W.2d 1 (Ct. App. 2000)

50 ALR6th 455—§ 12, 20, 34, 38, 40
State v. Davis, 244 N.J. Super. 180, 581 A.2d 1333 (App. Div. 1990)

107 ALR5th 567—§ 2, 3, 18
State v. Davis, 253 N.C. 86, 116 S.E.2d 365 (1960)

54 ALR6th 429—§ 11, 13
State v. Davis, 255 Kan. 357, 874 P.2d 1156 (1994)

83 ALR5th 277—§ 11
84 ALR5th 487—§ 3, 19
State v. Davis, 272 N.C. 111, 157 S.E.2d 622 (1967)

89 ALR6th 565—§ 33, 35
State v. Davis, 284 Mo. 695, 225 S.W. 707 (1920)

54 ALR6th 429—§ 21
State v. Davis, 295 Or. 227, 666 P.2d 802 (1983)

58 ALR6th 499—§ 78
State v. Davis, 297 N.C. 566, 256 S.E.2d 184 (1979)

55 ALR5th 423—§ 3
State v. Davis, 302 N.C. 370, 275 S.E.2d 491 (1981)

24 ALR5th 132—§ 3, 13
State v. Davis, 305 N.C. 400, 290 S.E.2d 574 (1982)

28 ALR6th 505—§ 9
State v. Davis, 309 S.C. 326, 422 S.E.2d 133 (1992)

72 ALR5th 403—§ 3
67 ALR6th 103—§ 9
State v. Davis, 313 Or. 246, 834 P.2d 1008 (1992)

19 ALR5th 470—§ 3, 7
State v. Davis, 325 N.C. 607, 386 S.E.2d 418 (1989)

73 ALR5th 383—§ 4, 5
State v. Davis, 328 N.W.2d 301 (Iowa 1982)

39 ALR5th 283—§ 10
State v. Davis, 340 N.C. 1, 455 S.E.2d 627 (1995)

39 ALR5th 283—§ 4, 77
State v. Davis, 349 N.C. 1, 506 S.E.2d 455 (1998)

24 ALR6th 549—§ 3, 30
83 ALR6th 255—§ 22
State v. Davis, 353 N.C. 1, 539 S.E.2d 243 (2000)

83 ALR6th 255—§ 7
State v. Davis, 354 S.C. 348, 580 S.E.2d 778 (Ct. App. 2003)

73 ALR6th 49—§ 65
State v. Davis, 371 S.C. 170, 638 S.E.2d 57 (2006)

30 ALR6th 1—§ 3
State v. Davis, 375 S.C. 12, 649 S.E.2d 178 (Ct. App. 2007)

77 ALR6th 197—§ 4
State v. Davis, 375 So. 2d 69 (La. 1979)

92 ALR6th 1—§ 5
State v. Davis, 393 N.W.2d 179 (Minn. 1986)

84 ALR6th 293—§ 19
State v. Davis, 419 S.E.2d 820 (S.C. App. 1992)

18 ALR5th 1—§ 40

State v. Davis, 422 S.E.2d 133 (S.C. 1992)
20 ALR5th 177—§ 3
State v. Davis, 446 N.W.2d 785 (Iowa 1989)
28 ALR6th 505—§ 9
State v. Davis, 464 So. 2d 195 (Fla. Dist. Ct. App. 3d Dist. 1985)
113 ALR5th 597—§ 4
State v. Davis, 504 N.W.2d 767, 63 A.L.R.5th 837 (Minn. 1993)
63 ALR5th 375—§ 4, 5, 7
State v. Davis, 539 S.E.2d 243 (N.C. 2000)
79 ALR5th 33—§ 5
State v. Davis, 540 N.W.2d 88 (Minn. Ct. App. 1995)
19 ALR5th 823—§ 11
73 ALR5th 383—§ 9
67 ALR6th 103—§ 5, 14
State v. Davis, 547 S.W.2d 482 (Mo. Ct. App. 1976)
68 ALR5th 343—§ 3
State v. Davis, 556 So. 2d 1104 (Fla. 1990)
44 ALR6th 325—§ 12
State v. Davis, 556 S.W.2d 45 (Mo. 1977)
70 ALR5th 587—§ 3
State v. Davis, 564 S.W.2d 876 (Mo. 1978)
45 ALR5th 591—§ 5, 7, 11
State v. Davis, 580 So. 2d 1046 (La. Ct. App. 3d Cir. 1991)
104 ALR5th 229—§ 6
116 ALR5th 325—§ 10
4 ALR6th 113—§ 40
34 ALR6th 539—§ 9
101 ALR6th 1—§ 6, 8, 22, 24, 29, 41, 49
State v. Davis, 590 S.W.2d 418 (Mo. App. 1979)
29 ALR5th 59—§ 17
State v. Davis, 607 S.W.2d 149 (Mo. 1980)
29 ALR5th 59—§ 7, 34, 39
State v. Davis, 619 So. 2d 517, 18 FLW D 1434 (Fla. App. D4 1993)

46 ALR5th 523—§ 4
State v. Davis, 624 S.W.2d 72 (Mo. App. 1981)
39 ALR5th 283—§ 4, 63, 67
56 ALR5th 385—§ 5
State v. Davis, 637 So. 2d 1012 (La. 1994)
37 ALR5th 515—§ 23, 26
State v. Davis, 654 S.W.2d 688 (Tenn. Crim. 1983)
13 ALR5th 567—§ 3 to 5
State v. Davis, 668 So. 2d 323 (Fla. App. D3 1996)
39 ALR5th 283—§ 18
State v. Davis, 689 P.2d 5 (Utah 1984)
57 ALR6th 445—§ 19
State v. Davis, 689 S.W.2d 743 (Mo. App. 1985)
5 ALR5th 243—§ 34, 59
State v. Davis, 706 S.W.2d 96 (Tenn. Crim. App. 1985)
86 ALR5th 59—§ 5
State v. Davis, 720 So. 2d 220, 26 Media L. Rep. (BNA) 2457 (Fla. 1998)
60 ALR5th 75—§ 3, 7
State v. Davis, 729 S.E.2d 128 (N.C. Ct. App. 2012)
79 ALR6th 1—§ 45
State v. Davis, 735 S.W.2d 854 (Tenn. Crim. App. 1987)
29 ALR6th 1—§ 10
State v. Davis, 745 S.W.2d 249 (Mo. Ct. App. S.D. 1988)
93 ALR5th 1—§ 7
State v. Davis, 768 So. 2d 201 (La. Ct. App. 5th Cir. 2000)
17 ALR6th 327—§ 7
State v. Davis, 787 P.2d 517, 128 Utah Adv. Rep. 15 (Utah App. 1990)
12 ALR5th 89—§ 5, 8
State v. Davis, 830 S.W.2d 469 (Mo. App. 1992)
47 ALR5th 259—§ 2, 12
State v. Davis, 867 S.W.2d 539 (Mo. Ct. App. W.D. 1993)
87 ALR5th 181—§ 8

State v. Davis, 963 S.W.2d 317 (Mo. Ct. App. W.D. 1997)
47 ALR5th 259—§ 15

State v. Davis, 965 P.2d 525 (Utah Ct. App. 1998)
68 ALR5th 343—§ 3, 16

State v. Davis, 1980 WL 352786 (Ohio Ct. App. 1st Dist. Hamilton County 1980)
19 ALR6th 697—§ 4

State v. Davis, 1983 WL 6586 (Ohio Ct. App. 12th Dist. Madison County 1983)
62 ALR6th 413—§ 43

State v. Davis, 1990 WL 3308 (Minn. Ct. App. 1990)
88 ALR5th 121—§ 2, 22, 35

State v. Davis, 1990 WL 75294 (Ohio Ct. App. 7th Dist. Mahoning County 1990)
38 ALR6th 439—§ 4

State v. Davis, 1994 WL 450138 (Ohio Ct. App. 2d Dist. Darke County 1994)
98 ALR6th 455—§ 12

State v. Davis, 1995 WL 131864 (Neb. Ct. App. 1995)
85 ALR5th 1—§ 24

State v. Davis, 1998 WL 283064 (Tenn. Crim. App. 1998)
73 ALR5th 383—§ 3

State v. Davis, 1999 WL 886981 (Minn. Ct. App. 1999)
17 ALR6th 327—§ 12

State v. Davis, 2002-Ohio-2368, 2002 WL 1000405 (Ohio Ct. App. 2d Dist. Montgomery County 2002)
11 ALR6th 237—§ 13

State v. Davis, 2003-Ohio-1363, 2003 WL 1394308 (Ohio Ct. App. 8th Dist. Cuyahoga County 2003)
69 ALR6th 1—§ 10

State v. Davis, 2004 WL 2583893 (Tenn. Crim. App. 2004)
95 ALR6th 641—§ 8

State v. Davis, 2005-Ohio-188, 2005 WL 110438 (Ohio Ct. App. 8th Dist. Cuyahoga County 2005)

State v. Davis, 2006-Ohio-4005, 2006 WL 2218583 (Ohio Ct. App. 2d Dist. Montgomery County 2006)
26 ALR6th 511—§ 31

State v. Davis, 2008-Ohio-6841, 2008 WL 5381695 (Ohio Ct. App. 5th Dist. Licking County 2008)
71 ALR6th 625—§ 12, 18, 28

State v. Davis, 2009-Ohio-2881, 2009 WL 1710759 (Ohio Ct. App. 8th Dist. Cuyahoga County 2009)
71 ALR6th 1—§ 12

State v. Davis, 2009-Ohio-5888, 2009 WL 3689308 (Ohio Ct. App. 5th Dist. Richland County 2009)
58 ALR6th 499—§ 30

State v. Davis, 2009 WL 1349985 (Ariz. Ct. App. Div. 1 2009)
56 ALR6th 1—§ 11, 32

State v. Davis, 2011 WL 2085900 (Del. Super. Ct. 2011)
74 ALR6th 373—§ 13, 22

State v. Davis, No. 9383 (December 31, 1979, Ct. App. Ohio, 9th App. Dist. Summit Co.)
39 ALR5th 283—§ 14, 65

State v. Davis, No. 42610 (September 24, 1981, Ct. App. Ohio, 8th App. Dist. Cuyahoga Co.)
39 ALR5th 283—§ 14, 55

State v. Davison, 116 Wash. 2d 917, 809 P.2d 1374 (1991)
15 ALR5th 391—§ 5

State v. Davison, 280 Ga. 84, 623 S.E.2d 500 (2005)
32 ALR6th 1—§ 11

State v. Davison, 689 S.E.2d 510 (N.C. Ct. App. 2009)
57 ALR6th 1—§ 22

State v. Davisson, 196 Ind. 451, 148 N.E. 401 (1925)
97 ALR5th 537—§ 57

State v. Davisson, 624 N.W.2d 292 (Minn. Ct. App. 2001)
69 ALR6th 1—§ 21

State v. Davlin, 263 Neb. 283, 639 N.W.2d 631 (2002)

101 ALR5th 187—§ 17
State v. Davolt, 207 Ariz. 191, 84 P.3d 456 (2004)
38 ALR6th 439—§ 12
State v. Davy, 100 N.C. App. 551, 397 S.E.2d 634 (1990)
73 ALR5th 383—§ 10, 28, 57, 66
State v. Daw, 94 Or. App. 370, 765 P.2d 241 (1988)
27 ALR6th 491—§ 4
State v. Dawkins, 32 S.C. 17, 10 S.E. 772 (1890)
14 ALR5th 89—§ 3, 17
19 ALR5th 622—§ 21
State v. Dawley, 201 Ariz. 285, 34 P.3d 394 (Ct. App. Div. 2 2001)
92 ALR6th 295—§ 13, 20
93 ALR6th 207—§ 15
96 ALR6th 355—§ 50
State v. Daws, 104 Ohio App. 3d 448, 662 N.E.2d 805 (2d Dist.Montgomery County 1994)
58 ALR5th 749—§ 6, 8
State v. Dawson, 23 Conn. App. 720, 583 A.2d 1326 (1991)
84 ALR6th 427—§ 4
State v. Dawson, 146 Wash. App. 1068, 2008 WL 4411539 (Div. 3 2008)
79 ALR6th 1—§ 7, 26, 66
State v. Dawson, 195 Wis. 2d 161, 536 N.W.2d 119 (Ct. App. 1995)
79 ALR5th 1—§ 14
State v. Dawson, 233 Mont. 345, 761 P.2d 352 (1988)
58 ALR6th 499—§ 53
State v. Dawson, 681 A.2d 407 (Del. Super. Ct. 1995)
56 ALR5th 385—§ 2 to 4
State v. Dawson, 681 So. 2d 1206 (Fla. Dist. Ct. App. 3d Dist. 1996)
18 ALR5th 1—§ 25
State v. Dawson, 985 S.W.2d 941 (Mo. Ct. App. W.D. 1999)
29 ALR5th 487—§ 7
74 ALR6th 69—§ 13
81 ALR6th 257—§ 18

State v. Dawson, 1984 WL 4651 (Ohio Ct. App. 10th Dist. Franklin County 1984)
43 ALR6th 475—§ 16, 18, 21
State v. Dawson, 1999 MT 171, 295 Mont. 212, 983 P.2d 916 (1999)
45 ALR6th 337—§ 29
State v. Day, 72 Ohio App. 3d 82, 593 N.E.2d 456 (4th Dist. Ross County 1991)
98 ALR5th 445—§ 4
State v. Day, 94 N.M. 753, 617 P.2d 142 (1980)
83 ALR5th 277—§ 11
State v. Day, 96 Wash. 2d 646, 638 P.2d 546 (1981)
52 ALR5th 655—§ 5
State v. Day, 148 Ariz. 490, 715 P.2d 743 (1986)
94 ALR5th 393—§ 5
State v. Day, 216 N.J. Super. 33, 522 A.2d 1019 (App. Div. 1987)
103 ALR6th 507—§ 22
State v. Day, 263 S.W.3d 891 (Tenn. 2008)
84 ALR6th 293—§ 42
State v. Day, 2010 WL 2861852 (Del. Super. Ct. 2010)
72 ALR6th 1—§ 18
State v. Daymus, 90 Ariz. 294, 367 P.2d 647 (1961)
83 ALR5th 277—§ 9
State v. Dayton, 535 S.W.2d 469 (Mo. Ct. App. 1976)
101 ALR5th 187—§ 5
State v. Dazhan, 15 Or. App. 300, 516 P.2d 92 (1973)
5 ALR5th 243—§ 50, 59
State v. Deal, 271 Kan. 483, 23 P.3d 840 (2001)
32 ALR6th 1—§ 11
State v. Deal, 578 So. 2d 994 (La. Ct. App. 4th Cir. 1991)
6 ALR6th 533—§ 21
State v. Deal, 740 N.W.2d 755 (Minn. 2007)
37 ALR6th 511—§ 3, 9, 21, 23

State v. Deal, 2010-Ohio-4490, 2010 WL 3722554 (Ohio Ct. App. 8th Dist. Cuyahoga County 2010)
63 ALR6th 1—§ 55

State v. Dean, 76 S.W.3d 352 (Tenn. Crim. App. 2001)
93 ALR6th 275—§ 4

State v. Dean, 84 Or. App. 108, 733 P.2d 105 (1987)
95 ALR6th 1—§ 16

State v. Dean, 87 Wash. App. 1037, 1997 WL 524029 (Div. 1 1997)
22 ALR6th 533—§ 5

State v. Dean, 105 N.M. 5, 727 P.2d 944 (Ct. App. 1986)
92 ALR5th 35—§ 22

State v. Dean, 105 Wis. 2d 390, 314 N.W.2d 151 (Ct. App. 1981)
79 ALR6th 125—§ 8, 22

State v. Dean, 205 Or. App. 661, 135 P.3d 364 (2006)
26 ALR6th 511—§ 27

State v. Dean, 246 Neb. 869, 523 N.W.2d 681 (1994)
90 ALR5th 453—§ 39

State v. Dean, 270 Neb. 972, 708 N.W.2d 640 (2006)
72 ALR6th 227—§ 57

State v. Dean, 2002-Ohio-4088, 2002 WL 1824982 (Ohio Ct. App. 8th Dist. Cuyahoga County 2002)
70 ALR6th 1—§ 4

State v. DeAngelis, 116 S.W.3d 396 (Tex. App. El Paso 2003)
9 ALR6th 363—§ 46

State v. DeAngelis, 329 N.J. Super. 178, 747 A.2d 289 (App. Div. 2000)
15 ALR5th 391—§ 51

State v. Deangelo, 113 Or. App. 192, 830 P.2d 630 (1992)
18 ALR5th 1—§ 35

State v. DeAngelo, 197 N.J. 478, 963 A.2d 1200, 185 L.R.R.M. (BNA) 3057, 157 Lab. Cas. (CCH) ¶ 60747, 49 A.L.R.6th 729 (2009)
49 ALR6th 153—§ 4

State v. Dean, No. 45518 (June 2, 1983, Ct. App. Ohio, 8th App. Dist, Cuyahoga Co.)
39 ALR5th 283—§ 14

State v. Deans, 356 N.W.2d 674 (Minn. 1984)
22 ALR5th 1—§ 19, 61

State v. Deardurff, 186 Neb. 92, 180 N.W.2d 890 (1970)
39 ALR6th 257—§ 19, 23, 26

State v. Dearing, 513 So. 2d 232 (Fla. Dist. Ct. App. 3d Dist. 1987)
76 ALR5th 485—§ 15

State v. DeArman, 54 Wash. App. 621, 774 P.2d 1247 (1989)
19 ALR5th 884—§ 4

State v. Deases, 518 N.W.2d 784 (Iowa 1994)
38 ALR6th 97—§ 26

State v. DeBaere, 356 N.W.2d 301 (Minn. 1984)
86 ALR5th 59—§ 6

State v. De Berry, 75 W. Va. 632, 84 S.E. 508 (1915)
57 ALR6th 445—§ 55

State v. Debevec, 1992 WL 52575 (Ohio Ct. App. 11th Dist. Ashtabula County 1992)
69 ALR6th 207—§ 9, 10, 18

State v. DeBlanc, 549 So. 2d 1287 (La. Ct. App. 3d Cir. 1989)
68 ALR5th 343—§ 3

State v. DeBlanco, 1998 WL 400564 (Ohio Ct. App. 10th Dist. Franklin County 1998)
79 ALR6th 125—§ 4

State v. Debler, 856 S.W.2d 641 (Mo. 1993)
9 ALR6th 1—§ 20
83 ALR6th 255—§ 15, 17

State v. Debnam, 23 Or. App. 433, 542 P.2d 939 (1975)
72 ALR5th 1—§ 15

State v. DeBooy, 2000 UT 32, 996 P.2d 546 (Utah 2000)
74 ALR5th 319—§ 3, 6
82 ALR5th 103—§ 4
116 ALR5th 479—§ 5, 6

State v. DeBorde, 121 N.M. 601, 915 P.2d 906 (App. 1996)

52 ALR5th 559—§ 2, 6, 8, 11

State v. Deboue, 496 So. 2d 394 (La. Ct. App. 4th Cir. 1986)

16 ALR6th 329—§ 4

24 ALR6th 591—§ 4, 14

State v. Debra A.E., 188 Wis. 2d 111, 523 N.W.2d 727 (1994)

85 ALR5th 471—§ 7

State v. DeCastro, 342 N.C. 667, 467 S.E.2d 653 (1996)

83 ALR6th 255—§ 15, 30

State v. Decato, 165 N.H. 294, 75 A.3d 1131, 100 A.L.R.6th 803 (2013)

100 ALR6th 535—§ 3, 51

State v. Decay, 798 So. 2d 1057 (La. Ct. App. 5th Cir. 2001)

71 ALR6th 1—§ 3

72 ALR6th 1—§ 3

State v. Decenso, 5 Hawaii App. 127, 681 P.2d 573 (1984)

39 ALR5th 283—§ 70

State v. Dechand, 13 Or. App. 530, 511 P.2d 430 (1973)

29 ALR5th 59—§ 59, 88

State v. Deck, 136 S.W.3d 481 (Mo. 2004)

83 ALR6th 255—§ 12, 22

State v. Deck, 994 S.W.2d 527 (Mo. 1999)

70 ALR5th 587—§ 25

83 ALR6th 255—§ 4, 13, 15, 17

98 ALR6th 455—§ 11

State v. Deckard, 18 S.W.3d 495 (Mo. Ct. App. S.D. 2000)

3 ALR6th 543—§ 10

State v. Decker, 119 Ariz. 195, 580 P.2d 333 (1978)

122 ALR5th 439—§ 3

State v. Decker, 258 Wis. 177, 45 N.W.2d 98 (1950)

35 ALR6th 1—§ 18, 20

State v. DeClue, 805 S.W.2d 253 (Mo. Ct. App. S.D. 1991)

85 ALR5th 547—§ 2

State v. DeConingh, 400 So. 2d 998 (Fla. Dist. Ct. App. 3d Dist. 1981)

25 ALR6th 379—§ 3, 5, 18, 23

State v. Decorso, 1999 UT 57, 993 P.2d 837 (Utah 1999)

6 ALR6th 533—§ 21

State v. DeCoteau, 1999 ND 77, 592 N.W.2d 579 (N.D. 1999)

58 ALR6th 499—§ 76

State v. DeCroce, 1994 WL 102252 (Ohio App. Geauga Co. 1994)

52 ALR5th 655—§ 3

State v. Decuir, 599 So. 2d 358 (La. Ct. App. 3d Cir. 1992)

28 ALR6th 505—§ 7, 9

State v. Dedonado, 99 Wash. App. 251, 991 P.2d 1216 (Div. 1 2000)

15 ALR5th 391—§ 46

State v. Dedrick, 24 Conn. App. 518, 589 A.2d 1241 (1991)

3 ALR5th 784—§ 2

State v. Dedrick, 132 N.H. 218, 564 A.2d 423 (1989)

29 ALR6th 1—§ 9

State v. Deem, 1987 WL 13056 (Ohio Ct. App. 12th Dist. Butler County 1987)

57 ALR6th 83—§ 6

State v. Deeno Parlapiano, 1999 WL 797053 (Ohio Ct. App. 3d Dist. Auglaize County 1999)

78 ALR5th 489—§ 9

State v. Dees, 14 N.C. App. 110, 187 S.E.2d 433 (1972)

57 ALR6th 445—§ 54

State v. Deese, 127 N.C. App. 536, 491 S.E.2d 682 (1997)

73 ALR5th 383—§ 3

State v. Deese, 136 N.C. App. 413, 524 S.E.2d 381 (2000)

32 ALR6th 1—§ 11

State v. DeFiore, 64 Ohio App. 2d 115, 18 Ohio Op. 3d 90, 411 N.E.2d 837 (1st Dist. Hamilton County 1979)

85 ALR5th 1—§ 2, 24, 53

50 ALR6th 455—§ 3

State v. Defley, 395 So. 2d 759 (La. 1981)

44 ALR5th 193—§ 48, 52

State v. DeFusco, 224 Conn. 627, 620 A.2d 746 (1993)
    62 ALR5th 1—§ 2 to 4, 11, 12, 14, 15

State v. De George, 171 Mont. 531, 560 P.2d 138 (1976)
    10 ALR5th 139—§ 12

State v. DeGidio, 277 Minn. 218, 152 N.W.2d 179 (1967)
    108 ALR5th 593—§ 57

State v. Degourville, 41 Conn. App. 772, 678 A.2d 485 (1996)
    19 ALR5th 470—§ 13

State v. De Hart, 38 Mont. 211, 99 P. 438 (1909)
    104 ALR5th 357—§ 3
    54 ALR6th 429—§ 9

State v. Deherrera, 965 P.2d 501 (Utah Ct. App. 1998)
    82 ALR5th 103—§ 3

State v. Dehler, 2009-Ohio-5059, 2009 WL 3068999 (Ohio Ct. App. 11th Dist. Trumbull County 2009)
    64 ALR6th 1—§ 7, 9, 11

State v. Dehn, 2005 WL 2739301 (Minn. Ct. App. 2005)
    26 ALR6th 511—§ 26

State v. Deitz, 120 Idaho 755, 819 P.2d 1155 (Ct. App. 1991)
    97 ALR5th 293—§ 17

State v. de la Beckwith, 344 So. 2d 360 (La. 1977)
    97 ALR5th 201—§ 3, 4

State v. Delaboin, 2008-Ohio-4093, 2008 WL 3522313 (Ohio Ct. App. 8th Dist. Cuyahoga County 2008)
    81 ALR6th 505—§ 17

State v. DeLaBruere, 154 Vt. 237, 577 A.2d 254, 8 A.L.R.5th 1097 (1990)
    8 ALR5th 875—§ 2, 3, 6

State v. Delacruz, 2004 WL 193058 (Minn. Ct. App. 2004)
    32 ALR6th 171—§ 5, 22
    33 ALR6th 1—§ 23

State v. Delahunt, 121 R.I. 565, 401 A.2d 1261 (1979)
    101 ALR5th 351—§ 9

State v. Delaney, 187 W. Va. 212, 417 S.E.2d 903 (1992)
    119 ALR5th 275—§ 8

State v. De La Paz, 106 Idaho 924, 684 P.2d 326 (Ct. App. 1984)
    79 ALR5th 419—§ 4

State v. de la Paz, 1989 WL 109329 (Minn. Ct. App. 1989)
    71 ALR6th 335—§ 10

State v. Delarosa-Flores, 59 Wash. App. 514, 799 P.2d 736 (Div. 3 1990)
    73 ALR5th 383—§ 3

State v. De Lay, 87 Ohio L. Abs. 449, 181 N.E.2d 706 (Ct. App. 10th Dist. Franklin County 1959)
    109 ALR5th 421—§ 12

State v. DelCastillo, 411 N.W.2d 602 (Minn. Ct. App. 1987)
    19 ALR6th 697—§ 5, 18

State v. Delebreau, 2006 WI App 1, 288 Wis. 2d 659, 707 N.W.2d 580 (Ct. App. 2005)
    84 ALR6th 293—§ 25

State v. Deleon, 230 Conn. 351, 645 A.2d 518 (1994)
    37 ALR5th 515—§ 2, 4

State v. Delgado, 327 N.J. Super. 137, 742 A.2d 990 (App. Div. 2000)
    71 ALR5th 637—§ 13

State v. Delgado, 411 So. 2d 7 (La. 1982)
    122 ALR5th 439—§ 5

State v. Delgado, 825 S.W.2d 744 (Tex. App. Houston (14th Dist.) 1992)
    7 ALR5th 263—§ 7

State v. Delgado, 2010 WL 4642989 (N.J. Super. Ct. App. Div. 2010)
    74 ALR6th 373—§ 4

State v. Delgros, 104 Ohio App. 3d 531, 662 N.E.2d 858 (Trumbull Co. 1995)
    18 ALR5th 804—§ 4

State v. Delisle, 137 N.H. 549, 630 A.2d 767 (1993)
    90 ALR5th 225—§ 5

State v. Delisle, 162 Vt. 293, 648 A.2d 632 (1994)
    56 ALR6th 185—§ 43

State v. Delisle, 648 A.2d 632 (Vt. 1994)
40 ALR5th 113—§ 4

State v. Delker, 35 Wash. App. 346, 666 P.2d 896 (Div. 1 1983)
83 ALR5th 277—§ 25

State v. Delling, 152 Idaho 122, 267 P.3d 709 (2011)
86 ALR6th 577—§ 15, 30

State v. Dellinger, 79 S.W.3d 458 (Tenn. 2002)
110 ALR5th 1—§ 3, 8, 15, 20, 25
41 ALR6th 295—§ 15

State v. Dell Intern., Inc., 922 So. 2d 1257 (La. Ct. App. 1st Cir. 2006)
30 ALR6th 341—§ 3

State v. Dellorfano, 128 N.H. 628, 517 A.2d 1163 (1986)
38 ALR6th 97—§ 13

State v. Delmonico, 2005-Ohio-2902, 2005 WL 1384383 (Ohio Ct. App. 11th Dist. Ashtabula County 2005)
71 ALR6th 1—§ 4

State v. Deloch, 628 S.W.2d 954 (Mo. Ct. App. E.D. 1982)
57 ALR6th 83—§ 18

State v. Delore, 381 So. 2d 455 (La. 1980)
9 ALR6th 1—§ 4

State v. DeLuca, 168 N.J. 626, 775 A.2d 1284 (2001)
25 ALR6th 201—§ 3, 4

State v. DeLuca, 325 N.J. Super. 376, 739 A.2d 455 (App. Div. 1999)
25 ALR6th 201—§ 3

State v. DeMagistris, 714 A.2d 567 (R.I. 1998)
73 ALR6th 49—§ 32

State v. DeMarco, 174 N.J. Super. 411, 416 A.2d 949 (Law Div. 1980)
69 ALR6th 1—§ 5

State v. Demarr, 2003 WL 21946726 (Tenn. Ct. App. 2003)
28 ALR6th 349—§ 27

State v. Demars, 1993 WL 76895 (Ohio Ct. App. 8th Dist. Cuyahoga County 1993)
85 ALR5th 187—§ 15

State v. DeMasi, 34 Conn. App. 46, 640 A.2d 138 (1994)
52 ALR5th 559—§ 4, 13

State v. DeMatteo, 134 N.H. 296, 591 A.2d 1323 (1991)
108 ALR5th 593—§ 11

State v. DeMatteo, 186 Conn. 696, 443 A.2d 915 (1982)
29 ALR6th 1—§ 10

State v. Demeritt, 148 N.H. 435, 813 A.2d 393 (2002)
84 ALR6th 427—§ 17

State v. Demoret, 132 P.3d 958 (Kan. 2006)
26 ALR6th 511—§ 25

State v. Demoss, 2002-Ohio-1193, 2002 WL 360581 (Ohio Ct. App. 2d Dist. Champaign County 2002)
7 ALR6th 233—§ 5

State v. Demosthene, 78 Ohio App. 3d 421, 604 N.E.2d 1383 (3d Dist. Allen County 1992)
46 ALR6th 241—§ 16, 25

State v. Dempsey, 22 Ohio St. 2d 219, 51 Ohio Ops. 2d 306, 259 N.E.2d 745 (1970)
4 ALR5th 1—§ 4, 7, 11

State v. Dempsey, 26 Mont. 504, 68 P. 1114 (1902)
105 ALR5th 529—§ 11

State v. Dempsey, 88 Wash. App. 918, 947 P.2d 265 (Div. 3 1997)
11 ALR5th 52—§ 11

State v. Demry, 260 Minn. 173, 109 N.W.2d 587 (1961)
108 ALR5th 593—§ 27

State v. Denby, 35 Conn. App. 609, 646 A.2d 909 (1994)
37 ALR5th 319—§ 3

State v. Dendy, 520 N.W.2d 411 (Minn. Ct. App. 1994)
92 ALR5th 35—§ 2, 30
59 ALR6th 311—§ 3

State v. DeNegris, 153 Conn. 5, 212 A.2d 894 (1965)
6 ALR6th 533—§ 13

State v. Denison, 607 N.W.2d 796 (Minn. Ct. App. 2000)

22 ALR5th 1—§ 3

State v. De Nistor, 143 Ariz. 407, 694 P.2d 237 (1985)

9 ALR6th 633—§ 15, 21, 53
15 ALR6th 173—§ 19

State v. Denmon, 595 S.W.2d 769 (Mo. Ct. App. W.D. 1980)

70 ALR5th 587—§ 3

State v. Denney, 4 Wash. App. 604, 483 P.2d 141 (Div. 3 1971)

108 ALR5th 593—§ 38

State v. Denney, 101 P.3d 1257 (Kan. 2004)

125 ALR5th 497—§ 3

State v. Denney, 152 Wash. App. 665, 218 P.3d 633 (Div. 2 2009)

81 ALR6th 505—§ 45

State v. Denney, 278 Kan. 643, 101 P.3d 1257 (2004)

72 ALR6th 227—§ 7

State v. Dennis, 16 Wash. App. 417, 558 P.2d 297 (Div. 2 1976)

28 ALR6th 505—§ 17

State v. Dennis, 79 Ohio St. 3d 421, 683 N.E.2d 1096 (1997)

79 ALR5th 33—§ 42

State v. Dennis, 189 Conn. 429, 456 A.2d 333 (1983)

103 ALR6th 347—§ 13

State v. Dennis, 250 La. 125, 194 So. 2d 720 (1967)

99 ALR6th 295—§ 16

State v. Dennis, 337 S.C. 275, 523 S.E.2d 173 (1999)

16 ALR6th 329—§ 15
24 ALR6th 591—§ 6, 14

State v. Dennis, 622 S.W.2d 404 (Mo. Ct. App. S.D. 1981)

108 ALR5th 593—§ 55

State v. Dennis, 1995 WL 695091 (Ohio Ct. App. 3d Dist.Marion County 1995)

57 ALR5th 141—§ 12

State v. Dennis, 2005-Ohio-1530, 2005 WL 736150 (Ohio Ct. App. 10th Dist. Franklin County 2005)

19 ALR6th 697—§ 6

State v. Dennison, 2008 MT 344, 346 Mont. 295, 194 P.3d 704 (2008)

57 ALR6th 1—§ 2

State v. Denny, 27 Ariz. App. 354, 555 P.2d 111 (1976)

24 ALR5th 465—§ 24 to 26

State v. Denny, 120 Wis. 2d 614, 357 N.W.2d 12 (Ct. App. 1984)

16 ALR6th 329—§ 4
24 ALR6th 591—§ 4

State v. Denny, 294 N.C. 294, 240 S.E.2d 437 (1978)

55 ALR6th 157—§ 76

State v. Densmore, 165 Wash. App. 1014, 2011 WL 6315145 (Div. 1 2011)

80 ALR6th 239—§ 3, 11

State v. Dent, 322 So. 2d 543 (Fla. 1975)

34 ALR5th 125—§ 8

State v. Denton, 58 Wash. App. 251, 792 P.2d 537 (Div. 1 1990)

38 ALR6th 97—§ 11

State v. Denton, 387 So. 2d 578 (La. 1980)

59 ALR5th 615—§ 3, 12

State v. Denue, 18 Or. App. 594, 526 P.2d 455 (1974)

50 ALR5th 703—§ 15

State v. Depaoli, 835 P.2d 162 (Utah 1992)

92 ALR5th 35—§ 2, 21

State v. DePastino, 228 Conn. 552, 638 A.2d 578 (1994)

39 ALR6th 257—§ 4, 42

State v. DePina, 21 Ohio App. 3d 91, 486 N.E.2d 1155 (9th Dist. Medina County 1984)

39 ALR5th 283—§ 14, 66
86 ALR5th 59—§ 5

State v. DePina, 810 A.2d 768 (R.I. 2002)

3 ALR6th 543—§ 8

State v. DePue, 237 Mont. 428, 774 P.2d 386 (1989)

38 ALR6th 97—§ 5

State v. Deputy, 19 Del. 19, 3 Penne. 19, 50 A. 176 (Gen. Sess. 1900)

119 ALR5th 275—§ 2
State v. Deputy, 644 A.2d 411 (Del. Super. Ct. 1994)

21 ALR6th 1—§ 4, 15, 19, 21
State v. Deputy, 1999 WL 743921 (Del. Super. Ct. 1999)

71 ALR6th 625—§ 40
State v. DeRango, 229 Wis. 2d 1, 599 N.W.2d 27 (Ct. App. 1999)

42 ALR5th 291—§ 13.5
State v. Derango, 236 Wis. 2d 721

42 ALR5th 291—§ 13.5, 25, 30
State v. Derby, 2007 WL 1470154 (Minn. Ct. App. 2007)

73 ALR6th 49—§ 54
State v. Derenzy, 89 S.W.3d 472 (Mo. 2002)

1 ALR6th 549—§ 31
State v. Derison, 2011-Ohio-1570, 2011 WL 1197640 (Ohio Ct. App. 8th Dist. Cuyahoga County 2011)

69 ALR6th 1—§ 29
State v. Derouchie, 153 Vt. 29, 568 A.2d 416 (1989)

38 ALR5th 433—§ 26
State v. Derouin, 778 So. 2d 1186 (La. Ct. App. 3d Cir. 2001)

97 ALR5th 293—§ 3
State v. Derrickson, 31 Del. 342, 114 A. 286 (Gen. Sess. 1921)

107 ALR5th 567—§ 11
State v. Derrow, 981 S.W.2d 776 (Tex. App. Houston 1st Dist. 1998)

68 ALR5th 343—§ 3, 17
State v. Derschon, 206 Or. App. 574, 138 P.3d 30 (2006)

30 ALR6th 1—§ 3, 6
State v. Derubeis, 2005-Ohio-4179, 2005 WL 1939668 (Ohio Ct. App. 8th Dist. Cuyahoga County 2005)

26 ALR6th 511—§ 25
State v. Derugen, 110 Ohio App. 3d 408, 674 N.E.2d 719 (3d Dist. Marion County 1996)

70 ALR6th 1—§ 5
State v. DeRuyck, 2002 WL 1363869 (Minn. Ct. App. 2002)

113 ALR5th 597—§ 8
State v. DeSanto, 172 N.J. Super. 27, 410 A.2d 704 (App. Div. 1980)

65 ALR5th 623—§ 6, 9
State v. Desbiens, 2008-Ohio-3375, 2008 WL 2627638 (Ohio Ct. App. 2d Dist. Montgomery County 2008)

63 ALR6th 351—§ 3
State v. Deschampe, 332 N.W.2d 18 (Minn. 1983)

73 ALR5th 383—§ 5
State v. Desdunes, 576 So. 2d 520 (La. Ct. App. 4th Cir. 1990)

108 ALR5th 593—§ 27
State v. Deshazo, 2008 MT 131, 343 Mont. 77, 183 P.3d 47 (2008)

46 ALR6th 241—§ 15
State v. DeShields, 1992 WL 245582 (Del. Super. Ct. 1992)

21 ALR6th 1—§ 4, 5
State v. DeSilva, 64 Haw. 40, 636 P.2d 728 (1981)

79 ALR5th 237—§ 3
State v. De Simone, 60 N.J. 319, 288 A.2d 849 (1972)

43 ALR5th 1—§ 13
State v. Desjardins, 110 N.H. 511, 272 A.2d 599 (1970)

57 ALR6th 83—§ 6
State v. Deskins, 234 Kan. 529, 673 P.2d 1174 (1983)

74 ALR5th 319—§ 5 to 7, 9, 11
State v. DesLaurier, 32 Conn. App. 553, 630 A.2d 119 (1993)

33 ALR5th 571—§ 3
State v. DesLaurier, 230 Conn. 572, 646 A.2d 108 (1994)

30 ALR6th 103—§ 3, 8, 43
State v. Deslovers, 40 R.I. 89, 100 A. 64 (1917)

32 ALR5th 149—§ 29, 52, 71, 74, 77, 82, 95
State v. De Smidt, 151 Wis. 2d 324, 444 N.W.2d 420 (App. 1989)

19 ALR5th 470—§ 3, 12
State v. DeSmidt, 155 Wis. 2d 119, 454 N.W.2d 780 (1990)

79 ALR6th 125—§ 8

State v. Desmond, 593 So. 2d 965 (La. Ct. App. 4th Cir. 1992)
64 ALR5th 741—§ 3

State v. Desnoyers, 2002-NMSC-031, 132 N.M. 756, 55 P.3d 968 (2002)
124 ALR5th 1—§ 3

State v. DeSocio, 2008 WL 544513 (Conn. Super. Ct. 2008)
75 ALR6th 443—§ 5, 18, 19

State v. Desote, 2003-Ohio-6311, 2003 WL 22784920 (Ohio Ct. App. 3d Dist. Putnam County 2003)
34 ALR6th 171—§ 20

State v. Dess, 201 Mont. 456, 655 P.2d 149 (1982)
66 ALR5th 373—§ 2, 4, 6

State v. De Stasio, 49 N.J. 247, 229 A.2d 636 (1967)
45 ALR5th 591—§ 15

State v. Deters, 128 Ohio App. 3d 329, 714 N.E.2d 972 (1st Dist. Hamilton County 1998)
47 ALR6th 107—§ 22

State v. Detter, 298 N.C. 604, 260 S.E.2d 567 (1979)
77 ALR5th 201—§ 6, 10
78 ALR5th 1—§ 3, 5, 13, 15, 32, 33, 41, 43, 45, 46, 53, 54

State v. Deutsch, 34 N.J. 190, 168 A.2d 12 (1961)
9 ALR6th 633—§ 5, 11
12 ALR6th 389—§ 8

State v. Deutsch, 229 N.J. Super. 374, 551 A.2d 991 (1988)
39 ALR5th 283—§ 4

State v. Deutschmann, 392 S.W.2d 279 (Mo. 1965)
59 ALR5th 1—§ 5, 6

State v. De Vane, 166 N.C. 281, 81 S.E. 293 (1914)
105 ALR5th 529—§ 24

State v. Devaney, 705 N.W.2d 507 (Iowa Ct. App. 2005)
70 ALR6th 361—§ 40

State v. Devenow, 253 La. 796, 220 So. 2d 78 (1969)
80 ALR6th 599—§ 8

State v. Dever, 64 Ohio St. 3d 401, 596 N.E.2d 436 (1992)
38 ALR5th 433—§ 3, 7, 8, 11, 19, 26

State v. Devereaux, 20 Or. App. 358, 531 P.2d 749 (1975)
84 ALR6th 427—§ 26

State v. DeVerney, 592 N.W.2d 837 (Minn. 1999)
20 ALR5th 398—§ 5
24 ALR6th 591—§ 5, 12

State v. Devine, 9 Or. App. 424, 496 P.2d 51 (1972)
114 ALR5th 173—§ 9
1 ALR6th 371—§ 4

State v. Devine, 168 Vt. 566, 719 A.2d 861 (1998)
56 ALR6th 185—§ 37
84 ALR6th 427—§ 19

State v. Devine, 307 Or. 341, 768 P.2d 913 (1989)
104 ALR5th 165—§ 4

State v. Devine, 719 A.2d 861 (Vt. 1998)
40 ALR5th 113—§ 3

State v. Devitt, 215 Tenn. 146, 384 S.W.2d 26 (1964)
29 ALR5th 59—§ 3

State v. Devlin, 251 Mont. 278, 825 P.2d 185 (1991)
5 ALR5th 243—§ 45

State v. Devore, 134 Idaho 344, 2 P.3d 153 (Ct. App. 2000)
99 ALR5th 557—§ 9

State v. DeWald, 463 N.W.2d 741 (Minn. 1990)
6 ALR6th 533—§ 3, 17, 19

State v. De Wees, 2 Ohio App. 2d 343, 31 Ohio Ops. 2d 519, 208 N.E.2d 558 (Lucas Co. 1965)
48 ALR5th 659—§ 32

State v. De Wees, 6 Ohio St. 2d 153, 35 Ohio Ops. 2d 222, 216 N.E.2d 624 (1966)
48 ALR5th 659—§ 32

State v. Dewey, 93 Wash. App. 50, 966 P.2d 414 (Div. 2 1998)
86 ALR5th 59—§ 5

State v. De Witt, 177 Conn. 637, 419 A.2d 861 (1979)
39 ALR5th 283—§ 3, 23
State v. DeWitt, 184 Ariz. 464, 910 P.2d 9 (1996)
64 ALR5th 637—§ 5
State v. DeWitt, 674 N.W.2d 683 (Iowa Ct. App. 2003)
125 ALR5th 537—§ 39, 40
State v. DeWitt, 910 P.2d 9, 208 Ariz. Adv. Rep. 23 (Ariz. 1996)
19 ALR5th 470—§ 12
State v. Dexter, 269 N.W.2d 721 (Minn. 1978)
3 ALR6th 269—§ 22, 24
State v. Dey, 798 S.W.2d 210 (Mo. App. 1990)
52 ALR5th 655—§ 3
State v. Dezaine, 141 Vt. 335, 449 A.2d 913 (1982)
50 ALR5th 703—§ 15
State v. D.G., 157 N.J. 112, 723 A.2d 588 (1999)
71 ALR5th 637—§ 7, 9
State v. Dhaemers, 276 Minn. 332, 150 N.W.2d 61 (1967)
55 ALR5th 125—§ 10
State v. Dial, 122 N.C. App. 298, 470 S.E.2d 84 (1996)
55 ALR6th 157—§ 21
State v. Dial, 405 S.C. 247, 746 S.E.2d 495 (Ct. App. 2013)
99 ALR6th 113—§ 9
State v. Diamond, 1991 WL 230050 (Ohio App. Portage Co. 1991)
52 ALR5th 655—§ 3
State v. Diana, 24 Wash. App. 908, 604 P.2d 1312 (1979)
1 ALR5th 938—§ 2, 3
State v. Diana, 24 Wash. App. 908, 604 P.2d 1312 (Div. 3 1979)
50 ALR6th 353—§ 49
State v. Dias, 62 Haw. 52, 609 P.2d 637 (1980)
99 ALR6th 397—§ 3, 4
State v. Dias, 284 Ga. App. 10, 642 S.E.2d 925 (2007)

103 ALR6th 347—§ 16
State v. Diaz, 39 Conn. Supp. 392, 466 A.2d 318 (Super. Ct. Appellate Sess. 1983)
55 ALR6th 391—§ 15
State v. Diaz, 69 Conn. App. 187, 793 A.2d 1204 (2002)
19 ALR6th 115—§ 5, 7, 10
State v. Diaz, 100 Haw. 210, 58 P.3d 1257 (2002)
18 ALR6th 1—§ 2, 5, 20
State v. Diaz, 122 N.M. 384, 925 P.2d 4 (Ct. App. 1996)
55 ALR5th 125—§ 6, 7
State v. Diaz, 142 Ariz. 119, 688 P.2d 1011 (1984)
7 ALR5th 263—§ 4
State v. Diaz, 308 N.J. Super. 504, 706 A.2d 264 (App. Div. 1998)
91 ALR5th 585—§ 4
State v. Diaz, 615 So. 2d 1336 (La. 1993)
15 ALR5th 391—§ 5
State v. Diaz, 654 A.2d 1195 (R.I. 1995)
32 ALR6th 1—§ 11
State v. Diaz, 803 N.W.2d 128 (Iowa Ct. App. 2011)
74 ALR6th 373—§ 13
State v. Dibello, 115 Utah Adv R 20, 780 P.2d 1221 (1989)
57 ALR5th 141—§ 9
State v. Dibello, 780 P.2d 1221, 115 Utah Adv. Rep. 20 (Utah 1989)
37 ALR5th 515—§ 9
State v. Diblasio, 2002-Ohio-2466, 2002 WL 724598 (Ohio Ct. App. 5th Dist. Licking County 2002)
10 ALR6th 463—§ 4, 8
State v. Dick, 69 S.W.3d 612 (Tex. App. Tyler 2001)
49 ALR6th 205—§ 3, 15
State v. Dick, 419 N.W.2d 828 (Minn. App. 1988)
38 ALR5th 433—§ 49
State v. Dick, 1997 WL 656305 (Ohio Ct. App. 12th Dist. Warren County 1997)
43 ALR6th 475—§ 10

State v. Dickens, 187 Ariz. 1, 926 P.2d 468 (1996)

21 ALR6th 1—§ 4

State v. Dickens, 1992 WL 333645 (Ohio Ct. App. 12th Dist.Clermont County 1992)

57 ALR5th 141—§ 7

State v. Dickens, 1999 WL 562125 (Ohio Ct. App. 12th Dist. Clermont County 1999)

78 ALR5th 489—§ 9

State v. Dickerson, 72 N.J. Super. 459, 179 A.2d 33 (App. Div. 1962)

9 ALR6th 633—§ 5

12 ALR6th 389—§ 7

15 ALR6th 173—§ 38

State v. Dickerson, 77 Ohio St. 34, 82 N.E. 969 (1907)

81 ALR5th 563—§ 3

State v. Dickerson, 142 Idaho 514, 129 P.3d 1263 (Ct. App. 2006)

34 ALR6th 171—§ 9, 14

State v. Dickerson, 298 A.2d 761 (Del. 1972)

93 ALR6th 391—§ 5

State v. Dickerson, 579 So. 2d 472 (La. Ct. App. 3d Cir. 1991)

19 ALR6th 115—§ 4, 9, 10

State v. Dickerson, 760 So. 2d 503 (La. Ct. App. 5th Cir. 2000)

103 ALR6th 137—§ 16

State v. Dickerson, 789 S.W.2d 566 (Tenn. Crim. App. 1990)

85 ALR5th 595—§ 6, 8

State v. Dickinson, 23 Ohio App. 2d 259, 52 Ohio Op. 2d 414, 263 N.E.2d 253 (5th Dist. Stark County 1970)

64 ALR5th 671—§ 8

State v. Dickinson, 1997 WL 593804 (Ohio Ct. App. 3d Dist. Union County 1997)

78 ALR5th 489—§ 10

State v. Dickson, 10 Conn. App. 462, 523 A.2d 935 (1987)

5 ALR5th 243—§ 2, 11

State v. Dickson, 337 S.W.3d 733, 82 A.L.R.6th 677 (Mo. Ct. App. S.D. 2011)

82 ALR6th 373—§ 4, 7

State v. Diecidue, 2007 ME 137, 931 A.2d 1077 (Me. 2007)

33 ALR6th 91—§ 20

63 ALR6th 351—§ 4

State v. Diener, 706 S.W.2d 582 (Mo. App. 1986)

3 ALR5th 521—§ 9, 12

State v. Diercks, 674 S.W.2d 72 (Mo. App. 1984)

45 ALR5th 1—§ 5, 12, 23

State v. Dierlamm, 189 La. 544, 180 So. 135 (1938)

46 ALR5th 499—§ 3

State v. Diesen, 1998 MT 163, 290 Mont. 55, 964 P.2d 712 (1998)

47 ALR6th 107—§ 3

State v. Diesen, 2000 MT 1, 297 Mont. 459, 992 P.2d 1287 (2000)

47 ALR6th 107—§ 14

State v. Dieter, 1998 WL 767854 (Ohio Ct. App. 3d Dist. Seneca County 1998)

92 ALR6th 171—§ 14

State v. Diggs, 272 Kan. 349, 34 P.3d 63 (2001)

12 ALR6th 267—§ 8

State v. Diggs, 715 So. 2d 692 (La. Ct. App. 4th Cir. 1998)

103 ALR5th 463—§ 3

State v. Digilormo, 505 So. 2d 1154 (La. App. 3d Cir. 1987)

6 ALR5th 733—§ 21

State v. Digilormo, 505 So. 2d 1154 (La. Ct. App. 3d Cir. 1987)

68 ALR6th 115—§ 28, 38

State v. Dillihay, 127 N.J. 42, 601 A.2d 1149 (1992)

27 ALR5th 593—§ 4, 29

State v. Dillingham., 1980 WL 354551 (Ohio Ct. App. 8th Dist. Cuyahoga County 1980)

31 ALR6th 465—§ 14

State v. Dillon, 24 Or. App. 695, 546 P.2d 1090 (1976)

5 ALR5th 243—§ 6

State v. Dillon, 41 S.W.3d 479 (Mo. Ct. App. E. D. 2000)

104 ALR5th 229—§ 11, 12

State v. Dillon, 41 S.W.3d 479 (Mo. Ct. App. E.D. 2000)

4 ALR6th 113—§ 4
101 ALR6th 1—§ 44, 48

State v. Dillon, 51 Or. App. 729, 626 P.2d 959 (1981)

15 ALR5th 391—§ 39

State v. Dillon, 242 Kan. 410, 748 P.2d 856 (1988)

9 ALR6th 633—§ 14
12 ALR6th 389—§ 4

State v. Dillon, 292 Or. 172, 637 P.2d 602 (1981)

15 ALR5th 391—§ 2, 5, 6, 11, 40
92 ALR5th 35—§ 2, 11, 17, 20

State v. Dillon, 529 N.W.2d 387 (Minn. Ct. App. 1995)

92 ALR5th 35—§ 22

State v. Dillon, 1991 WL 65120 (Ohio Ct. App. 9th Dist.Summit County 1991)

57 ALR5th 141—§ 10

State v. Dillon, 2007 SD 77, 738 N.W.2d 57 (S.D. 2007)

58 ALR6th 499—§ 27

State v. DiLorenzo, 181 Neb. 59, 146 N.W.2d 791 (1966)

102 ALR5th 525—§ 17

State v. Dilosa, 849 So. 2d 657 (La. Ct. App. 1st Cir. 2003)

19 ALR6th 115—§ 4, 9, 10

State v. Dimeo, 2010 WL 5646047 (Conn. Super. Ct. 2010)

69 ALR6th 579—§ 4

State v. Dinkel, 34 Or. App. 375, 579 P.2d 245 (1978)

39 ALR5th 283—§ 16

State v. Dinkel, 49 Or. App. 917, 621 P.2d 626 (1980)

39 ALR5th 283—§ 4, 15, 16, 24

State v. Dinkins, 319 S.C. 415, 462 S.E.2d 59 (1995)

90 ALR5th 453—§ 21

State v. Dinsmore, 182 Or. App. 505, 49 P.3d 830 (2002)

84 ALR6th 427—§ 24

State v. Dion, 154 Vt. 420, 578 A.2d 101 (1990)

66 ALR5th 397—§ 6

State v. Dion, 2007 ME 87, 928 A.2d 746 (Me. 2007)

28 ALR6th 505—§ 11

State v. Dionne, 1 Conn. Cir. Ct. 395, 24 Conn. Supp. 59, 186 A.2d 561 (App. Div. 1962)

89 ALR6th 565—§ 31, 33

State v. DiPietro, 2009 ME 12, 964 A.2d 636 (Me. 2009)

92 ALR6th 171—§ 14

State v. Diprete, 1996 WL 936879 (R.I. Super. Ct. 1996)

90 ALR5th 453—§ 20
10 ALR6th 463—§ 4, 8

State v. DiRosa, 520 So. 2d 1244 (La. Ct. App. 5th Cir. 1988)

102 ALR5th 525—§ 44

State v. Dishman, 915 S.W.2d 458 (Tenn. Crim. App. 1995)

83 ALR5th 277—§ 9

State v. Dishon, 297 N.J. Super. 254, 687 A.2d 1074 (App. Div. 1997)

80 ALR5th 469—§ 4
38 ALR6th 439—§ 13

State v. Dishon, No. 1507 (August 4, 1981, Ct. App. Ohio, 2nd App. Dist. Clark Co.)

39 ALR5th 283—§ 14, 19

State v. Dispoto, 383 N.J. Super. 205, 891 A.2d 633 (App. Div. 2006)

32 ALR6th 1—§ 8

State v. District Court of Eighth Judicial Dist., In and For Cascade County, 176 Mont. 257, 577 P.2d 849 (1978)

17 ALR6th 327—§ 36
35 ALR6th 127—§ 17
58 ALR6th 499—§ 4

State v. District Court of Second Judicial Dist., 30 Mont. 547, 77 P. 318 (1904)

91 ALR5th 437—§ 4

State v. District Court of Sixth Judicial District in and for Park County, 67 Mont. 164, 215 P. 240 (1923)
44 ALR6th 259—§ 6

State v. District Court of Watonwan County, 140 Minn. 398, 168 N.W. 130 (1918)
40 ALR6th 99—§ 32

State v. Ditter, 232 Neb. 600, 441 N.W.2d 622 (1989)
11 ALR6th 237—§ 4

State v. Ditton, 2009 MT 10N, 350 Mont. 558, 213 P.3d 787 (2009)
78 ALR6th 599—§ 10

State v. Di Ventura, 187 N.J. Super. 165, 453 A.2d 1354 (App. Div. 1982)
97 ALR5th 201—§ 6

State v. Dix, 282 N.C. 490, 193 S.E.2d 897 (1973)
39 ALR5th 283—§ 4

State v. Dixon, 5 Or. App. 113, 481 P.2d 629 (1971)
55 ALR6th 157—§ 62

State v. Dixon, 15 Ariz. App. 62, 485 P.2d 1179 (Div. 2 1971)
42 ALR6th 237—§ 12

State v. Dixon, 72 Conn. App. 852, 806 A.2d 1153 (2002)
12 ALR6th 267—§ 5

State v. Dixon, 126 Ariz. 613, 617 P.2d 779 (App. 1980)
7 ALR5th 263—§ 7

State v. Dixon, 153 Ariz. 151, 735 P.2d 761 (1987)
44 ALR5th 651—§ 5

State v. Dixon, 223 Neb. 316, 389 N.W.2d 307 (1986)
10 ALR6th 265—§ 13, 16
13 ALR6th 603—§ 15, 20, 25

State v. Dixon, 226 Ariz. 545, 250 P.3d 1174 (2011)
71 ALR6th 625—§ 3, 10, 29

State v. Dixon, 237 Neb. 630, 467 N.W.2d 397 (1991)
72 ALR6th 1—§ 7

State v. Dixon, 655 S.W.2d 547 (Mo. Ct. App. E.D. 1983)
29 ALR6th 1—§ 4

State v. Dixon, 957 S.W.2d 532 (Tenn. 1997)
39 ALR5th 283—§ 3, 71

State v. Dixon, 969 S.W.2d 252 (Mo. Ct. App. W.D. 1998)
55 ALR5th 423—§ 3

State v. Dixon, 1986 WL 13571 (Tenn. Crim. 1986)
52 ALR5th 655—§ 2, 6

State v. Dixon, 2010 WL 3419231 (Tex. App. Corpus Christi 2010)
62 ALR6th 161—§ 4, 18

State v. Dixon, No. 49432 (November 21, 1985, Ct. App. Ohio, 8th App. Dist. Cuyahoga Co.)
39 ALR5th 283—§ 14, 57

State v. Dixson, 80 Mont. 181, 260 P. 138 (1927)
23 ALR6th 1—§ 15, 21

State v. Dixson, 87 Or. App. 1, 740 P.2d 1224 (1987)
62 ALR5th 1—§ 2

State v. Dizon, 47 Haw. 444, 390 P.2d 759 (1964)
102 ALR5th 447—§ 6, 12

State v. D.J., 132 Wash. App. 1055, 2006 WL 1217215 (Div. 1 2006)
59 ALR6th 393—§ 7

State v. D.K., 113 Wash. App. 1013, 2002 WL 1880766 (Div. 2 2002)
38 ALR6th 1—§ 14

State v. D.M., 2013 WL 1845596 (Del. Fam. Ct. 2013)
89 ALR6th 261—§ 29, 32

State v. D.M.Z., 830 P.2d 314, 184 Utah Adv. Rep. 84 (Utah App. 1992)
37 ALR5th 703—§ 3

State v. Doan, 1 Neb. App. 484, 498 N.W.2d 804 (1993)
85 ALR5th 595—§ 6

State v. Dobbins, 67 Wash. App. 15, 834 P.2d 646 (1992)
27 ALR5th 593—§ 8, 9

State v. Dobbins, 2003-Ohio-4644, 2003 WL 22049145 (Ohio Ct. App. 5th Dist. Fairfield County 2003)

125 ALR5th 537—§ 51

State v. Dobbs, 2010-Ohio-3649, 2010 WL 3064368 (Ohio Ct. App. 2d Dist. Greene County 2010)

65 ALR6th 1—§ 4

State v. Dobies, 147 Ohio App. 3d 568, 2001-Ohio-8823, 771 N.E.2d 867 (11th Dist. Lake County 2001)

63 ALR6th 351—§ 3

State v. Dobsinski, 2007 WL 738688 (Minn. Ct. App. 2007)

78 ALR6th 599—§ 6

State v. Dobson, 2010-Ohio-279, 2010 WL 334900 (Ohio Ct. App. 2d Dist. Miami County 2010)

64 ALR6th 1—§ 7

State v. Dobyns, 55 Wash. App. 609, 779 P.2d 746 (Div. 1 1989)

112 ALR5th 429—§ 10

State v. Dockery, 2000 WL 1839132 (Tenn. Crim. App. 2000)

55 ALR6th 513—§ 8

State v. Dodd, 28 Wis. 2d 643, 137 N.W.2d 465 (1965)

4 ALR5th 1—§ 14

State v. Dodd, 53 Wash. App. 178, 765 P.2d 1337 (1989)

46 ALR5th 499—§ 2, 5

State v. Dodd, 419 So. 2d 333 (Fla. 1982)

92 ALR6th 1—§ 8

State v. Dodd, 871 S.W.2d 496 (Tenn. Crim. 1993)

34 ALR5th 723—§ 4

State v. Dodd, 1999 WL 689408 (Tenn. Crim. App. 1999)

99 ALR6th 295—§ 13

State v. Dodge, 397 A.2d 588 (Me. 1979)

3 ALR6th 269—§ 22

State v. Dodson, 110 Wash. App. 112, 39 P.3d 324 (Div. 3 2002)

103 ALR5th 463—§ 3
45 ALR6th 643—§ 11

State v. Dodson, 195 N.W.2d 684 (Iowa 1972)

28 ALR6th 505—§ 7, 13

State v. Dodson, 452 N.W.2d 610 (Iowa Ct. App. 1989)

85 ALR5th 595—§ 5

State v. Dodson, 2009 MT 419, 354 Mont. 28, 221 P.3d 687 (2009)

51 ALR6th 1—§ 15, 18
70 ALR6th 361—§ 5, 19
72 ALR6th 141—§ 9

State v. Doe, 95 N.M. 302, 621 P.2d 519 (Ct. App. 1980)

101 ALR5th 351—§ 3

State v. Doe, 115 Wis. 2d 700, 341 N.W.2d 419 (App. 1983)

33 ALR5th 453—§ 4

State v. Doe, 117 N.H. 259, 372 A.2d 279 (1977)

69 ALR6th 1—§ 23

State v. Doe, 130 Idaho 811, 948 P.2d 166, 122 Ed. Law Rep. 820 (Ct. App. 1997)

59 ALR6th 393—§ 9

State v. Doe, 137 Idaho 519, 50 P.3d 1014 (2002)

26 ALR6th 451—§ 3, 10

State v. Doe, 140 Idaho 873, 103 P.3d 967 (Ct. App. 2004)

30 ALR6th 1—§ 4, 7

State v. Doe, 218 S.C. 520, 63 S.E.2d 303 (1951)

50 ALR5th 467—§ 6, 9

State v. Doehrer, 200 Conn. 642, 513 A.2d 58 (1986)

35 ALR6th 127—§ 5

State v. Doerr, 193 Ariz. 56, 969 P.2d 1168 (1998)

21 ALR6th 1—§ 4

State v. Dohlman, 725 N.W.2d 428 (Iowa 2006)

53 ALR6th 305—§ 18

State v. Doile, 7 Kan. App. 2d 722, 648 P.2d 262 (1982)

33 ALR6th 407—§ 20

State v. Dolack, 216 Kan. 622, 533 P.2d 1282 (1975)

97 ALR5th 201—§ 2
71 ALR6th 335—§ 10

State v. Dolan, 58 W. Va. 263, 52 S.E. 181 (1905)

59 ALR5th 135—§ 4, 13

State v. Dolbeare, 140 N.H. 84, 663 A.2d 85 (1995)
70 ALR6th 361—§ 3, 33
State v. Dolcater, 2009 WL 1682132 (Ariz. Ct. App. Div. 1 2009)
92 ALR6th 1—§ 3
State v. Dolce, 92 Ohio App. 3d 687, 637 N.E.2d 51 (6th Dist. Huron County 1993)
79 ALR6th 125—§ 28
State v. Doliner, 96 N.J. 236, 475 A.2d 552 (1984)
79 ALR6th 125—§ 10
State v. Doll, 1999 WL 228137 (Minn. Ct. App. 1999)
32 ALR6th 171—§ 15, 22
State v. Dollard, 2008 WL 4137985 (Del. Super. Ct. 2008)
71 ALR6th 1—§ 7
State v. Dolliver, 150 Minn. 155, 184 N.W. 848 (1921)
24 ALR6th 747—§ 17, 46
State v. Domangue, 350 So. 2d 599 (La. 1977)
98 ALR6th 455—§ 25
State v. Domangue, 649 So. 2d 1034 (La. App. 1st Cir. 1994)
50 ALR5th 703—§ 9
State v. Domicz, 188 N.J. 285, 907 A.2d 395 (2006)
62 ALR6th 413—§ 18, 31
State v. Domicz, 377 N.J. Super. 515, 873 A.2d 630 (App. Div. 2005)
15 ALR6th 515—§ 32
State v. Dominguez, 115 N.M. 445, 853 P.2d 147 (App. 1993)
20 ALR5th 398—§ 2, 10
47 ALR5th 259—§ 2
State v. Dominguez, 128 N.H. 288, 512 A.2d 1112 (1986)
7 ALR5th 758—§ 8
State v. Dominguez, 521 So. 2d 340 (Fla. Dist. Ct. App. 2d Dist. 1988)
65 ALR5th 407—§ 3, 16
State v. Dominguez, 732 So. 2d 36 (Fla. Dist. Ct. App. 2d Dist. 1999)
113 ALR5th 597—§ 8

State v. Dominguez, 1999 UT App 343, 992 P.2d 995 (Utah Ct. App. 1999)
92 ALR5th 35—§ 25
State v. Dominguez-Ramirez, 563 N.W.2d 245 (Minn. 1997)
49 ALR6th 343—§ 3, 8, 11, 14, 24
State v. Domingus, 234 Neb. 267, 450 N.W.2d 668 (1990)
19 ALR6th 411—§ 21
State v. Dominic, 117 N.H. 573, 376 A.2d 124 (1977)
52 ALR6th 125—§ 11, 18, 44
State v. Dominie, 134 N.C. App. 445, 518 S.E.2d 32 (1999)
34 ALR6th 1—§ 8
State v. Dominy, 1997 WL 284591 (Tenn. Crim. App. 1997)
124 ALR5th 657—§ 8
State v. Don, 318 N.W.2d 801 (Iowa 1982)
55 ALR5th 125—§ 3, 7
State v. Donaghe, 172 Wash. 2d 253, 256 P.3d 1171 (2011)
78 ALR6th 417—§ 14
State v. Donahue, 141 Conn. 656, 109 A.2d 364 (1954)
72 ALR5th 529—§ 2
State v. Donahue, 585 S.W.2d 160 (Mo. Ct. App. W.D. 1979)
70 ALR5th 587—§ 3
State v. Donald, 57 Ohio St. 2d 73, 11 Ohio Ops. 3d 242, 386 N.E.2d 1341 (1979)
39 ALR5th 283—§ 14, 44
State v. Donald, 614 S.W.2d 66 (Tenn. Crim. 1980)
3 ALR5th 963—§ 6
State v. Donaldson, 112 P.3d 99 (Kan. 2005)
9 ALR6th 1—§ 17
State v. Donatelli, 2010 ME 43, 995 A.2d 238 (Me. 2010)
92 ALR6th 171—§ 14
State v. Donato, 20 P.3d 5 (Idaho 2001)
62 ALR5th 1—§ 3
State v. Donato, 516 A.2d 880 (R.I. 1986)

46 ALR5th 735—§ 2

State v. Donato, 2001 WL 200149 (Idaho 2001)

62 ALR5th 1—§ 3

State v. Donery, 131 Wash. App. 667, 128 P.3d 1262 (Div. 2 2006)

71 ALR6th 625—§ 11, 20, 29

State v. Donkers, 170 Ohio App. 3d 509, 2007-Ohio-1557, 867 N.E.2d 903 (11th Dist. Portage County 2007)

71 ALR6th 1—§ 8

State v. Donlay, 253 Kan. 132, 853 P.2d 680, 26 A.L.R.5th 854 (1993)

26 ALR5th 378—§ 4, 9

125 ALR5th 537—§ 2, 13

State v. Donnell, 353 Mo. 878, 184 S.W.2d 1008 (1945)

97 ALR5th 293—§ 3, 5

State v. Donnell, 849 S.W.2d 733 (Mo. Ct. App. S.D. 1993)

57 ALR6th 83—§ 5

State v. Donner, 13 Neb. App. 85, 690 N.W.2d 181 (2004)

15 ALR6th 375—§ 23

State v. Donner, 243 N.W.2d 850 (Iowa 1976)

66 ALR5th 397—§ 4

State v. Donohoe, 126 Idaho 989, 895 P.2d 590 (Ct. App. 1995)

11 ALR6th 237—§ 18

State v. Donohue, 2 N.J. 381, 67 A.2d 152 (1949)

24 ALR5th 465—§ 11, 88

State v. Donovan, 116 Ariz. 209, 568 P.2d 1107 (App. 1977)

4 ALR5th 1—§ 2, 17, 32

State v. Donovan, 120 N.H. 603, 419 A.2d 1102 (1980)

45 ALR5th 591—§ 12

55 ALR6th 157—§ 66

State v. Donovan, 305 Or. 332, 751 P.2d 1109 (1988)

2 ALR5th 262—§ 2, 4, 5

State v. Donovan, 2004 ME 81, 853 A.2d 772 (Me. 2004)

72 ALR6th 227—§ 23

State v. Dontigney, 215 Conn. 646, 577 A.2d 1032, 11 A.L.R.5th 1053 (1990)

11 ALR5th 497—§ 2, 3, 11

State v. Don Wood Buick, Olds, Pontiac, Cadillac, GMC Truck, Inc., 113 Ohio App. 3d 358, 680 N.E.2d 1269 (4th Dist. Athens County 1996)

66 ALR6th 351—§ 38

State v. Dooley, 380 N.W.2d 582 (Minn. App. 1986)

39 ALR5th 283—§ 3

State v. Dooley, 549 S.W.2d 677 (Mo. App. 1977)

34 ALR5th 125—§ 8

State v. Doolittle, 22 Conn. Supp. 32, 158 A.2d 858 (Super. Ct. 1960)

96 ALR6th 269—§ 31

State v. Doolittle, 189 Conn. 183, 455 A.2d 843 (1983)

93 ALR5th 527—§ 4

State v. Dooms, 280 Mo. 84, 217 S.W. 43 (1919)

81 ALR5th 563—§ 2, 3, 11

State v. Dopkowski, 325 Md. 671, 602 A.2d 1185 (1992)

70 ALR5th 533—§ 6, 7

State v. Dopp, 129 Idaho 597, 930 P.2d 1039 (Ct. App. 1996)

55 ALR6th 391—§ 7

State v. Doppler, 590 N.W.2d 627 (Minn. 1999)

78 ALR5th 197—§ 4, 14

79 ALR5th 419—§ 10

State v. Doran, 5 Ohio St. 3d 187, 5 Ohio BR 404, 449 N.E.2d 1295 (1983)

18 ALR5th 1—§ 7, 16

State v. Dorantes, 331 S.W.3d 370 (Tenn. 2011)

97 ALR6th 539—§ 4

State v. Doray, 359 A.2d 613 (Me. 1976)

54 ALR6th 593—§ 9

State v. Dore, 79 Ohio App. 3d 466, 607 N.E.2d 553 (3d Dist. Seneca County 1992)

103 ALR5th 463—§ 5

State v. Doren, 654 N.W.2d 137 (Minn. Ct. App. 2002)

1 ALR6th 371—§ 4
92 ALR6th 171—§ 16
State v. Doriguzzi, 334 N.J. Super. 530, 760 A.2d 336 (App. Div. 2000)
90 ALR5th 453—§ 49
State v. Dorisio, 189 W. Va. 788, 434 S.E.2d 707 (1993)
23 ALR5th 672—§ 5
State v. Dorman, 30 Wash. App. 351, 633 P.2d 1340 (Div. 1 1981)
57 ALR6th 445—§ 4
State v. Dorn, 145 Vt. 606, 496 A.2d 451 (1985)
16 ALR5th 390—§ 2, 3
State v. Dorn, 1989 WL 135712 (Del. Super. Ct. 1989)
111 ALR5th 239—§ 8, 9
State v. Dorsey, 44 Or. App. 721, 607 P.2d 204 (1980)
39 ALR5th 283—§ 4, 61
State v. Dorsey, 118 N.H. 844, 395 A.2d 855 (1978)
3 ALR5th 521—§ 6
State v. Dorsey, 224 Kan. 152, 578 P.2d 261 (1978)
39 ALR5th 283—§ 4
State v. Dorsey, 593 So. 2d 1372 (La. App. 5th Cir. 1992)
34 ALR5th 125—§ 19
State v. Dorsey, 706 S.W.2d 478 (Mo. Ct. App. E.D. 1986)
111 ALR5th 1—§ 8, 38
State v. Dorsey, 731 P.2d 1085 (Utah 1986)
4 ALR6th 599—§ 16
State v. Dorsey, 1998 WL 196182 (Ohio Ct. App. 8th Dist. Cuyahoga County 1998)
99 ALR6th 295—§ 13
State v. D'Orsi, 113 N.J. Super. 527, 274 A.2d 586 (App. Div. 1971)
33 ALR6th 407—§ 77
State v. Dorson, 62 Haw. 377, 615 P.2d 740 (1980)
122 ALR5th 439—§ 7
State v. Dorval, 144 N.H. 455, 743 A.2d 836 (1999)

38 ALR6th 97—§ 23
State v. Dosch, 2008 SD 21, 747 N.W.2d 142 (S.D. 2008)
38 ALR6th 439—§ 4
State v. Doss, 522 So. 2d 1274 (La. App. 5th Cir. 1988)
45 ALR5th 531—§ 3, 9
State v. Dossett, 851 S.W.2d 750 (Mo. Ct. App. W.D. 1993)
66 ALR5th 397—§ 21
State v. Doss, Slip Opinion for Cases No. 40773, 40774, 40776 (Ohio App. Cuyahoga Co. 1980)
41 ALR5th 171—§ 16, 27
State v. Dost, 695 N.W.2d 506 (Iowa Ct. App. 2005)
56 ALR6th 323—§ 11
State v. Doster, 157 N.C. 634, 73 S.E. 111 (1911)
102 ALR5th 525—§ 13
State v. Doster, 247 Or. 336, 427 P.2d 413 (1967)
29 ALR5th 59—§ 3, 29
State v. Dotson, 635 S.W.2d 373 (Mo. App. 1982)
34 ALR5th 125—§ 8
State v. Dotson, 1988 WL 13561 (Tenn. Crim. App. 1988)
35 ALR6th 127—§ 14
State v. Dotson, 2002 WL 31370471 (Tenn. Crim. App. 2002)
102 ALR6th 279—§ 13
State v. Doucet, 443 So. 2d 777 (La. Ct. App. 3d Cir. 1983)
84 ALR6th 427—§ 21, 23
State v. Doucette, 143 Vt. 573, 470 A.2d 676 (1983)
6 ALR6th 533—§ 7
State v. Doucette, 398 A.2d 36 (Me. 1978)
32 ALR5th 149—§ 4, 45
State v. Dougherty, 8 Or. App. 267, 493 P.2d 1383 (1972)
61 ALR5th 1—§ 3 to 5
State v. Dougherty, 358 Mo. 734, 216 S.W.2d 467 (1949)
26 ALR5th 1—§ 4, 51

State v. Doughty, 359 N.W.2d 439 (Iowa 1984)

39 ALR5th 283—§ 10, 56

State v. Douglas, 66 Ohio App. 3d 788, 586 N.E.2d 1096 (Greene Co. 1989)

36 ALR5th 161—§ 5

State v. Douglas, 82 Or. App. 222, 728 P.2d 548 (1986)

46 ALR6th 241—§ 16, 31

State v. Douglas, 97 Idaho 878, 555 P.2d 1145 (1976)

71 ALR6th 1—§ 10

State v. Douglas, 204 N.J. Super. 265, 498 A.2d 364 (App. Div. 1985)

55 ALR5th 125—§ 7

State v. Douglas, 260 Or. 60, 488 P.2d 1366 (1971)

28 ALR6th 505—§ 9

State v. Douglas, 274 Kan. 96, 49 P.3d 446 (2002)

3 ALR6th 543—§ 8

State v. Douglas, 312 Mo. 373, 278 S.W. 1016 (1925)

108 ALR5th 593—§ 16

State v. Douglas, 359 S.C. 187, 597 S.E.2d 1 (Ct. App. 2004)

28 ALR6th 505—§ 9

State v. Douglas, 501 N.W.2d 694 (Minn. Ct. App. 1993)

73 ALR5th 383—§ 22

State v. Douglas, 541 So. 2d 285, 6 A.L.R.5th 1157 (La. App. 3d Cir. 1989)

6 ALR5th 652—§ 2, 3

State v. Douglas, 541 So. 2d 285, 6 A.L.R.5th 1157 (La. Ct. App. 3d Cir. 1989)

115 ALR5th 403—§ 8
34 ALR6th 539—§ 5
101 ALR6th 1—§ 49

State v. Douglas, 2001 WL 99558 (Tenn. Crim. App. 2001)

7 ALR6th 233—§ 4

State v. Douglas, 2004-Ohio-3605, 2004 WL 1520022 (Ohio Ct. App. 8th Dist. Cuyahoga County 2004)

33 ALR6th 91—§ 6
63 ALR6th 351—§ 3

State v. Douglass, 7 Iowa 413, 7 Clarke 413, 1858 WL 275 (1858)

5 ALR6th 1—§ 40

State v. Douglas S., 42 Wash. App. 138, 709 P.2d 817 (1985)

43 ALR5th 1—§ 11, 15

State v. Douglas S., 42 Wash. App. 138, 709 P.2d 817 (Div. 3 1985)

122 ALR5th 439—§ 8

State v. Doust, 285 Minn. 336, 173 N.W.2d 337 (1969)

103 ALR5th 463—§ 3

State v. Douty, 92 Wash. 2d 930, 603 P.2d 373 (1979)

86 ALR5th 637—§ 2, 3, 6

State v. Dow, 126 N.H. 205, 489 A.2d 650 (1985)

7 ALR5th 758—§ 4, 15, 16

State v. Dow, 256 Mont. 126, 844 P.2d 780 (1992)

17 ALR6th 327—§ 37, 39

State v. Dow, 392 A.2d 532 (Me. 1978)

50 ALR5th 703—§ 2, 15

State v. Dowe, 197 Wis. 2d 848, 541 N.W.2d 218 (App. 1995)

12 ALR5th 89—§ 4

State v. Dowling, 204 Iowa 977, 216 N.W. 271 (1927)

52 ALR5th 655—§ 3

State v. Dowling, 387 So. 2d 1165 (La. 1980)

65 ALR5th 407—§ 3, 17

State v. Downes, 19 Or. App. 401, 528 P.2d 110 (1974)

114 ALR5th 173—§ 7, 12

State v. Downey, 53 Wash. App. 543, 768 P.2d 502 (Div. 1 1989)

58 ALR6th 499—§ 61

State v. Downey, 206 N.J. Super. 382, 502 A.2d 1171 (App. Div. 1986)

57 ALR5th 141—§ 2, 3
29 ALR6th 1—§ 10

State v. Downey, 237 N.J. Super. 4, 566 A.2d 822 (App. Div. 1989)

57 ALR5th 141—§ 7, 9

State v. Downey, 242 N.J. Super. 367, 576 A.2d 945 (Law Div. 1988)

68 ALR5th 299—§ 4
State v. Downey, 683 S.E.2d 791 (N.C. Ct. App. 2009)
57 ALR6th 1—§ 4
State v. Downey, 945 S.W.2d 102, 74 A.L.R.5th 729 (Tenn. 1997)
74 ALR5th 319—§ 2, 4, 5, 11
State v. Downing, 66 N.C. App. 686, 311 S.E.2d 702 (1984)
66 ALR5th 397—§ 4, 6, 14
State v. Downing, 109 Ariz. 456, 511 P.2d 638 (1973)
87 ALR5th 181—§ 4
State v. Downing, 240 Mont. 215, 783 P.2d 412 (1989)
34 ALR5th 125—§ 8
State v. Downing, 2004-Ohio-5952, 2004 WL 2535422 (Ohio Ct. App. 9th Dist. Summit County 2004)
83 ALR6th 465—§ 39
State v. Downs, 168 Wash. 664, 13 P.2d 1 (1932)
22 ALR5th 1—§ 6
State v. Doyle, 735 P.2d 733 (Alaska 1987)
10 ALR5th 448—§ 2, 6
State v. Doyle, 918 P.2d 141, 291 Utah Adv. Rep. 7 (Utah App. 1996)
43 ALR5th 1—§ 13
State v. Doyle, 2004 WL 1434503 (Me. Super. Ct. 2004)
45 ALR6th 337—§ 7
State v. Doyle, 2006 WI App 244, 724 N.W.2d 703 (Wis. Ct. App. 2006)
27 ALR6th 183—§ 31
State v. Doyon, 416 A.2d 130 (R.I. 1980)
56 ALR5th 385—§ 4
State v. Dozier, 163 W. Va. 192, 255 S.E.2d 552 (1979)
58 ALR5th 749—§ 7
State v. Dozier, 949 So. 2d 502 (La. Ct. App. 4th Cir. 2006)
26 ALR6th 511—§ 28
State v. Dozier, No. 6022 (May 6, 1980, Ct. App. Ohio, 2nd App. Dist. Montgomery Co.)
39 ALR5th 283—§ 14

State v. D.P., 2008 WL 2898336 (Del. Fam. Ct. 2008)
47 ALR6th 423—§ 4
State v. D.R., 84 Wash. App. 832, 930 P.2d 350, 115 Ed. Law Rep. 522 (Div. 3 1997)
59 ALR6th 393—§ 9
State v. Drach, 268 Kan. 636
42 ALR5th 581—§ 16
State v. Drain, 1995 WL 765169 (Ohio Ct. App. 10th Dist. Franklin County 1995)
28 ALR6th 245—§ 6
30 ALR6th 103—§ 3
State v. Drake, 128 Iowa 539, 105 N.W. 54 (1905)
54 ALR6th 429—§ 7
State v. Drake, 139 N.H. 662, 662 A.2d 265 (1995)
31 ALR5th 229—§ 17, 28
State v. Drake, 733 So. 2d 33 (La. Ct. App. 2d Cir. 1999)
55 ALR6th 513—§ 4
State v. Drake, 1993 WL 274342 (Ohio Ct. App. 5th Dist. Morrow County 1993)
116 ALR5th 373—§ 3, 16
State v. Drane, 137 Wash. App. 1024, 2007 WL 592560 (Div. 2 2007)
103 ALR6th 507—§ 4
State v. Draughon, 2004-Ohio-320, 2004 WL 117632 (Ohio Ct. App. 10th Dist. Franklin County 2004)
24 ALR6th 549—§ 6
State v. Dravenstott, 138 S.W.3d 186 (Mo. Ct. App. W.D. 2004)
28 ALR6th 505—§ 11
State v. Draves, 18 Or. App. 248, 524 P.2d 1225 (1974)
7 ALR5th 758—§ 6, 14
State v. Drayton, 321 N.C. 512, 364 S.E.2d 121 (1988)
73 ALR5th 383—§ 28, 29
State v. Dreger, 97 Minn. 221, 106 N.W. 904 (1906)
102 ALR5th 525—§ 17
State v. Dreher, 166 La. 924, 118 So. 85 (1928)

---

70 ALR5th 587—§ 3
State v. Dreher, 302 N.J. Super. 408, 695 A.2d 672 (App. Div. 1997)

49 ALR5th 639—§ 5
State v. Dreifurst, 204 Neb. 378, 282 N.W.2d 51 (1979)

66 ALR5th 397—§ 10
State v. Drennan, 101 P.3d 1218 (Kan. 2004)

3 ALR6th 543—§ 8
State v. Dresbach, 122 Ohio App. 3d 647, 702 N.E.2d 513 (10th Dist. Franklin County 1997)

6 ALR5th 733—§ 7, 16, 17
State v. Dressel, 241 Kan. 426, 738 P.2d 830 (1987)

22 ALR5th 1—§ 5, 19
State v. Drew, 89 N.H. 54, 192 A. 629 (1937)

94 ALR5th 613—§ 7, 8
State v. Drews, 23 Ohio Misc. 370, 51 Ohio Ops. 2d 395, 261 N.E.2d 357 (1970)

52 ALR5th 655—§ 3
State v. Drexel, 74 Neb. 776, 105 N.W. 174 (1905)

120 ALR5th 125—§ 2, 3, 8
121 ALR5th 1—§ 2, 9, 14
State v. Drexel, 1990 WL 34437 (Ohio Ct. App. 4th Dist. Highland County 1990)

11 ALR6th 237—§ 12, 14
State v. Driscoll, 137 Vt. 89, 400 A.2d 971 (1979)

6 ALR6th 533—§ 15
State v. Driver, 143 Or. App. 17, 923 P.2d 1272 (1996)

33 ALR6th 91—§ 6
State v. Drobel, 815 P.2d 724, 164 Utah Adv. Rep. 64 (Utah App. 1991)

32 ALR5th 149—§ 29, 32
State v. Droste, 83 Ohio St. 3d 36, 1887-Ohio-97, 1998-Ohio-182, 697 N.E.2d 620 (1998)

18 ALR6th 519—§ 17
State v. Drown, 148 Vt. 311, 532 A.2d 575 (1987)

119 ALR5th 379—§ 11

State v. Drown, 2007 ME 142, 937 A.2d 157 (Me. 2007)

79 ALR6th 1—§ 78
State v. Drowne, 436 So. 2d 916 (Fla. Dist. Ct. App. 4th Dist. 1983)

85 ALR5th 1—§ 16
State v. Druktenis, 135 N.M. 223, 2004-NMCA-032, 86 P.3d 1050 (Ct. App. 2004)

63 ALR6th 351—§ 3
93 ALR6th 1—§ 5
State v. Drum, 143 Wash. App. 608, 181 P.3d 18 (Div. 2 2008)

78 ALR6th 1—§ 3, 56
State v. Drum, 168 Wash. 2d 23, 225 P.3d 237 (2010)

78 ALR6th 1—§ 20
State v. Drummer, 54 Wash. App. 751, 775 P.2d 981 (Div. 1 1989)

73 ALR5th 383—§ 4, 41
State v. Drummer, 750 So. 2d 360 (La. Ct. App. 4th Cir. 1999)

4 ALR5th 1—§ 7
State v. Drummond, 111 Ohio St. 3d 14, 2006-Ohio-5084, 854 N.E.2d 1038 (2006)

32 ALR6th 171—§ 16, 20, 21
33 ALR6th 1—§ 8
71 ALR6th 1—§ 15
State v. Drummy, 18 Conn. App. 303, 557 A.2d 574 (1989)

3 ALR5th 521—§ 14
State v. Dry, 152 N.C. 813, 67 S.E. 1000 (1910)

103 ALR6th 137—§ 15
State v. D.S., Sr., 2010 WL 2089662 (N.J. Super. Ct. App. Div. 2010)

65 ALR6th 537—§ 22
State v. D. T. W., 425 So. 2d 1383 (Fla. App. D1 1983)

31 ALR5th 229—§ 2, 3, 17, 18, 38, 53, 54
State v. Duarte, 93 Wash. App. 1047, 1999 WL 7832 (Div. 2 1999)

88 ALR5th 121—§ 22, 33
State v. Dubany, 184 Neb. 337, 167 N.W.2d 556 (1969)

57 ALR6th 83—§ 6

95 ALR6th 1—§ 28

State v. Dube, 598 A.2d 742 (Me. 1991)

40 ALR6th 1—§ 4

State v. Dube, 655 A.2d 338 (Me. 1995)

58 ALR6th 499—§ 42

State v. Dubina, 164 Conn. 95, 318 A.2d 95 (1972)

39 ALR5th 283—§ 3, 59

State v. Dubish, 234 Kan. 708, 675 P.2d 877 (1984)

5 ALR5th 243—§ 62

State v. Dubois, 80 P.3d 1201 (Kan. Ct. App. 2003)

24 ALR6th 549—§ 6

State v. Dubois, 556 So. 2d 1295 (La. Ct. App. 5th Cir. 1990)

102 ALR5th 525—§ 65

State v. Dubose, 155 Wash. App. 1042, 2010 WL 1756369 (Div. 1 2010)

99 ALR6th 113—§ 10, 13

State v. Dubose, 174 Ohio App. 3d 637, 2007-Ohio-7217, 884 N.E.2d 75 (7th Dist. Mahoning County 2007)

33 ALR6th 1—§ 11

State v. DuBray, 298 N.W.2d 811 (S.D. 1980)

93 ALR6th 207—§ 14, 20, 26

96 ALR6th 355—§ 24, 37, 59, 60

State v. DuBray, 2003 MT 255, 317 Mont. 377, 77 P.3d 247 (2003)

12 ALR6th 267—§ 8

State v. Ducally, 896 A.2d 723 (R.I. 2006)

27 ALR6th 183—§ 4

State v. Ducheneaux, 2003 SD 131, 671 N.W.2d 841 (S.D. 2003)

50 ALR6th 353—§ 48

State v. Duckett, 2005 WL 2777378 (Tenn. Crim. App. 2005)

26 ALR6th 511—§ 22, 25, 33

State v. Dudas, 2008-Ohio-3262, 2008 WL 2582523 (Ohio Ct. App. 11th Dist. Lake County 2008)

71 ALR6th 1—§ 11

State v. Dudgeon, 13 Ariz. App. 464, 477 P.2d 750 (Div. 2 1970)

41 ALR5th 171—§ 17, 58, 68, 90, 107, 108

85 ALR5th 1—§ 42

State v. Dudgeon, 146 Wash. App. 216, 189 P.3d 240 (Div. 2 2008)

56 ALR6th 647—§ 6

State v. Dudley, 819 S.W.2d 51 (Mo. Ct. App. S.D. 1991)

12 ALR6th 553—§ 6, 7, 29, 36

State v. Dudley, 847 P.2d 424 (Utah Ct. App. 1993)

114 ALR5th 173—§ 7

State v. Dudley, 984 So. 2d 11 (La. Ct. App. 1st Cir. 2007)

79 ALR6th 125—§ 29

State v. Dudley, 2010-Ohio-3240, 2010 WL 2706318 (Ohio Ct. App. 2d Dist. Montgomery County 2010)

64 ALR6th 1—§ 7, 9, 12

State v. Dudoit, 90 Haw. 262, 978 P.2d 700 (Haw. 1999)

7 ALR5th 263—§ 4

State v. Duelley, 2000 WL 955532 (Ohio Ct. App. 1st Dist. Hamilton County 1999)

7 ALR6th 233—§ 3, 6

State v. Duemke, 352 N.W.2d 427 (Minn. Ct. App. 1984)

92 ALR6th 295—§ 14, 25

93 ALR6th 207—§ 6, 28

96 ALR6th 355—§ 9, 37

State v. Duerr, 8 Ohio App. 3d 396, 457 N.E.2d 834 (1st Dist. Hamilton County 1982)

124 ALR5th 1—§ 3

29 ALR6th 1—§ 10

State v. Duestrow, 137 Mo. 44, 38 S.W. 554 (1897)

54 ALR6th 429—§ 9

State v. Dufault, 540 A.2d 355 (R.I. 1988)

71 ALR6th 335—§ 16

State v. Duff, 171 N.C. App. 662, 615 S.E.2d 373 (2005)

67 ALR6th 103—§ 6, 8

State v. Duffy, 112 R.I. 276, 308 A.2d 796 (1973)

103 ALR6th 347—§ 15

State v. Duffy, 146 N.H. 648, 778 A.2d 415 (2001)

81 ALR6th 505—§ 64

State v. Dufield, 131 N.H. 35, 549 A.2d 1205 (1988)

7 ALR5th 758—§ 7, 22

State v. Dufour, 63 Ind. 567, 1878 WL 6170 (1878)

97 ALR5th 537—§ 81

State v. Duganitz, 76 Ohio App. 3d 363, 601 N.E.2d 642 (8th Dist. Cuyahoga County 1991)

88 ALR5th 121—§ 35

State v. Dugar, 643 So. 2d 870 (La. Ct. App. 3d Cir. 1994)

70 ALR5th 1—§ 4

24 ALR6th 1—§ 52

State v. Dugas, 683 So. 2d 1253 (La. Ct. App. 3d Cir. 1996)

88 ALR5th 67—§ 3

State v. Duggan, 291 Minn. 422, 192 N.W.2d 185 (1971)

72 ALR5th 1—§ 30

State v. Duke, 360 N.C. 110, 623 S.E.2d 11 (2005)

83 ALR6th 255—§ 9

State v. Duke, 625 So. 2d 325 (La. Ct. App. 3d Cir. 1993)

73 ALR5th 383—§ 5

State v. Duker, 2007 WL 3105900 (Del. Super. Ct. 2007)

37 ALR6th 55—§ 8

38 ALR6th 1—§ 17, 25

State v. Dukes, 110 N.C. App. 695, 431 S.E.2d 209 (1993)

28 ALR6th 505—§ 8

State v. Dukes, 209 Conn. 98, 547 A.2d 10 (1988)

19 ALR5th 470—§ 3

State v. Dukes, 234 Ga. App. 343, 507 S.E.2d 147 (1998)

123 ALR5th 221—§ 2

State v. Dukes, 609 So. 2d 1144 (La. Ct. App. 2d Cir. 1992)

106 ALR5th 397—§ 5

115 ALR5th 477—§ 5

State v. Dukette, 127 N.H. 540, 506 A.2d 699 (1986)

93 ALR5th 527—§ 2

94 ALR5th 393—§ 2

95 ALR5th 611—§ 2

101 ALR5th 187—§ 2

102 ALR5th 327—§ 2

24 ALR6th 1—§ 3

53 ALR6th 81—§ 3

55 ALR6th 391—§ 3, 7

56 ALR6th 185—§ 3

State v. Dula, 67 N.C. App. 748, 313 S.E.2d 899 (1984)

15 ALR5th 391—§ 7

State v. Dulaney, 493 N.W.2d 787 (Iowa 1992)

40 ALR5th 113—§ 3

State v. Dulany, 781 S.W.2d 52 (Mo. 1989)

11 ALR5th 871—§ 7

State v. Dumaine, 162 Ariz. 392, 783 P.2d 1184 (1989)

101 ALR5th 187—§ 9

State v. Dumars, 33 Kan. App. 2d 735, 108 P.3d 448 (2005)

23 ALR6th 307—§ 38

State v. Dumas, 700 So. 2d 1223 (Fla. 1997)

26 ALR5th 1—§ 3

State v. Dumont, 3 Or. App. 189, 471 P.2d 847 (1970)

80 ALR6th 599—§ 5

State v. Dumont, 146 Vt. 252, 499 A.2d 787 (1985)

119 ALR5th 379—§ 8

State v. Dunavant, 250 Or. 570, 444 P.2d 1 (1968)

6 ALR6th 533—§ 14

State v. Dunbar, 117 Wash. 2d 587, 817 P.2d 1360 (1991)

7 ALR5th 758—§ 9, 13

State v. Dunbar, 356 So. 2d 956 (La. 1978)

17 ALR6th 327—§ 23

State v. Dunbar, 772 A.2d 533 (Vt. 2001)

14 ALR5th 89—§ 3

19 ALR5th 622—§ 3

State v. Duncan, 28 N.C. 236 (1846)
11 ALR5th 831—§ 4, 13

State v. Duncan, 82 Mont. 170, 266 P. 400 (1928)
46 ALR5th 499—§ 3

State v. Duncan, 146 Wash. 2d 166, 43 P.3d 513 (2002)
78 ALR6th 599—§ 1

State v. Duncan, 185 Neb. 227, 175 N.W.2d 3 (1970)
89 ALR6th 565—§ 13

State v. Duncan, 605 N.W.2d 745 (Minn. Ct. App. 2000)
71 ALR6th 283—§ 30

State v. Duncan, 802 So. 2d 533 (La. 2001)
1 ALR6th 657—§ 7, 9

State v. Duncan, 866 S.W.2d 510 (Mo. Ct. App. W.D. 1993)
78 ALR6th 297—§ 70

State v. Duncan, 894 So. 2d 817 (Fla. 2004)
83 ALR6th 255—§ 27

State v. Duncan, 2008 MT 148, 343 Mont. 220, 183 P.3d 111 (2008)
56 ALR6th 185—§ 14

State v. Duncan, 2008-Ohio-6802, 2008 WL 5341012 (Ohio Ct. App. 6th Dist. Fulton County 2008)
63 ALR6th 351—§ 3
64 ALR6th 1—§ 9

State v. Duncan, Slip Opinion for Cases No. 73 CR 117, 73 CR 118, 73 CR 119, 73 CR 120, 73 CR 121, 73 CR 122 (Ohio App. Wood Co. 1974)
41 ALR5th 171—§ 58

State v. Dunham, 154 Ohio St. 63, 42 Ohio Op. 133, 93 N.E.2d 286 (1950)
118 ALR5th 253—§ 9
6 ALR6th 161—§ 10

State v. Dunham, 1996 WL 33082 (Minn. Ct. App. 1996)
73 ALR5th 383—§ 33
44 ALR6th 301—§ 2, 5

State v. Dunlap, 57 N.C. App. 175, 290 S.E.2d 744 (1982)
70 ALR6th 361—§ 3, 7

State v. Dunlap, 148 Wash. App. 1011, 2009 WL 82358 (Div. 2 2009)
51 ALR6th 139—§ 11

State v. Dunlap, 187 Ariz. 441, 930 P.2d 518 (Ct. App. Div. 1 1996)
27 ALR6th 183—§ 33

State v. Dunlap, 2013 WL 5539583 (Ariz. Ct. App. Div. 2 2013)
97 ALR6th 263—§ 18

State v. Dunn, 44 Idaho 636, 258 P. 553 (1927)
55 ALR5th 125—§ 12, 18, 23

State v. Dunn, 132 Wash. App. 1056, 2006 WL 1231424 (Div. 2 2006)
68 ALR6th 527—§ 32

State v. Dunn, 162 W. Va. 63, 246 S.E.2d 245 (1978)
116 ALR5th 373—§ 4

State v. Dunn, 223 Kan. 545, 575 P.2d 530 (1978)
39 ALR5th 283—§ 4, 7

State v. Dunn, 233 Kan. 411, 662 P.2d 1286 (1983)
23 ALR6th 307—§ 3, 8, 19, 35

State v. Dunn, 243 Kan. 414, 758 P.2d 718 (1988)
8 ALR5th 713—§ 14
11 ALR5th 871—§ 9

State v. Dunn, 308 Md. 147, 517 A.2d 772 (1986)
70 ALR5th 533—§ 3

State v. Dunn, 442 So. 2d 1166 (La. Ct. App. 3d Cir. 1983)
112 ALR5th 429—§ 13

State v. Dunn, 478 So. 2d 659 (La. App. 2d Cir. 1985)
14 ALR5th 913—§ 4

State v. Dunn, 709 So. 2d 852 (La. Ct. App. 2d Cir. 1998)
5 ALR5th 243—§ 51

State v. Dunn, 831 So. 2d 862 (La. 2002)
122 ALR5th 145—§ 3, 7, 9, 13, 16, 22

State v. Dunn, 2004-Ohio-2249, 2004 WL 950404 (Ohio Ct. App. 9th Dist. Wayne County 2004)
56 ALR6th 185—§ 37

State v. Dunn, 2005-Ohio-1270, 2005 WL 663001 (Ohio Ct. App. 9th Dist. Lorain County 2005)
24 ALR6th 549—§ 6
State v. Dunn, 2007 MT 296, 340 Mont. 31, 172 P.3d 110 (2007)
62 ALR6th 413—§ 29
State v. Dunning, 81 Or. App. 296, 724 P.2d 924 (1986)
109 ALR5th 99—§ 11
State v. Dunnington, 157 La. 369, 102 So. 478 (1924)
66 ALR5th 397—§ 25
State v. Duntz, 223 Conn. 207, 613 A.2d 224 (1992)
19 ALR5th 470—§ 12
State v. Dunwoody, 231 Mo. 48, 132 S.W. 227 (1910)
5 ALR6th 1—§ 60
State v. Dupepe, 631 So. 2d 20 (La. Ct. App. 4th Cir. 1994)
112 ALR5th 185—§ 10
124 ALR5th 441—§ 8
3 ALR6th 641—§ 30
State v. Dupier, 118 P.3d 1039 (Alaska 2005)
31 ALR6th 523—§ 10, 12
State v. Dupigney, 295 Conn. 50, 988 A.2d 851 (2010)
72 ALR6th 227—§ 51
State v. Dupont, 2007-1094 La. App. 1 Cir. 12/21/07, 2007 WL 4465604 (La. Ct. App. 1st Cir. 2007)
94 ALR6th 525—§ 9
State v. Dupre, 200 Mont. 165, 650 P.2d 1381 (1982)
32 ALR6th 1—§ 11
State v. Dupree, 164 Or. App. 413, 992 P.2d 472 (1999)
18 ALR5th 1—§ 28
State v. Dupuis, 159 Me. 100, 188 A.2d 688 (1963)
108 ALR5th 593—§ 44
State v. Dupuy, 118 N.H. 848, 395 A.2d 851 (1978)
3 ALR5th 521—§ 6
State v. Dupuy, 319 So. 2d 299 (La. 1975)

65 ALR5th 407—§ 3, 16
State v. Duque, 2005-Ohio-4187, 2005 WL 1939411 (Ohio Ct. App. 3d Dist. Seneca County 2005)
24 ALR6th 549—§ 6
State v. Duran, 96 N.M. 364, 630 P.2d 763 (1981)
56 ALR6th 185—§ 23
State v. Duran, 105 N.M. 231, 731 P.2d 374 (Ct. App. 1986)
72 ALR5th 403—§ 18
State v. Duran, 126 N.M. 60
29 ALR5th 487—§ 14
State v. Durand, 461 So. 2d 1090 (La. Ct. App. 4th Cir. 1984)
109 ALR5th 99—§ 8
27 ALR6th 491—§ 3
State v. Durand, 569 P.2d 1107 (Utah 1977)
55 ALR5th 125—§ 3, 8
State v. Durben, 2009-Ohio-3977, 2009 WL 2457800 (Ohio Ct. App. 5th Dist. Coshocton County 2009)
64 ALR6th 1—§ 7, 9, 11
State v. Durbin, 646 So. 2d 1035 (La. App. 5th Cir. 1994)
7 ALR5th 263—§ 4
State v. Durbin, 1988 WL 72460 (Ohio Ct. App. 12th Dist.Butler County 1988)
64 ALR5th 637—§ 2, 3
State v. Durgin, 328 N.W.2d 507 (Iowa 1983)
48 ALR5th 659—§ 21
State v. Durham, 231 Wis. 2d 720, 2000 WI App 1, 605 N.W.2d 663 (Ct. App. 1999)
4 ALR6th 599—§ 14
State v. Durham, 418 S.W.2d 23 (Mo. 1967)
97 ALR5th 293—§ 4
State v. Durham, 676 S.W.2d 86 (Mo. Ct. App. S.D. 1984)
97 ALR5th 293—§ 2
State v. Durham, 822 S.W.2d 453 (Mo. Ct. App. E.D. 1991)
97 ALR5th 201—§ 3

State v. Durkin, 1992 WL 52576 (Ohio Ct. App. 11th Dist. Ashtabula County 1992)
69 ALR6th 207—§ 9, 10, 18

State v. Durocher, 2007 WI App 216, 305 Wis. 2d 656, 739 N.W.2d 491 (Ct. App. 2007)
84 ALR6th 293—§ 18, 26, 34

State v. Duroseau, 2010 WL 4608249 (N.J. Super. Ct. App. Div. 2010)
74 ALR6th 373—§ 8, 22

State v. Durr, 58 Ohio St. 3d 86, 568 N.E.2d 674 (1991)
10 ALR5th 700—§ 31
55 ALR6th 157—§ 105

State v. Durrant, 244 Kan. 522, 769 P.2d 1174 (1989)
12 ALR5th 89—§ 5

State v. Dusenberry, 112 Mo. 277, 20 S.W. 461 (1892)
101 ALR6th 499—§ 15
102 ALR6th 279—§ 33

State v. Dussell, 1993 WL 204626 (Ohio Ct. App. 8th Dist. Cuyahoga County 1993)
56 ALR6th 185—§ 39

State v. Dutton, 1997 WL 219789 (Wash. Ct. App. Div. 2 1997)
71 ALR5th 637—§ 7

State v. Duvall, 747 So. 2d 793 (La. Ct. App. 1st Cir. 1999)
79 ALR5th 419—§ 21

State v. Duvall, 1997 WL 361698 (Ohio Ct. App. 11th Dist. Portage County 1997)
65 ALR5th 623—§ 3

State v. Dwenger, 168 Ind. App. 90, 341 N.E.2d 776 (1976)
15 ALR5th 119—§ 32, 46

State v. Dwyer, 28 Kan. App. 2d 238, 14 P.3d 1186 (2000)
15 ALR6th 515—§ 15

State v. Dwyer, 181 Wis. 2d 826, 512 N.W.2d 233 (Ct. App. 1994)
62 ALR6th 259—§ 13

State v. Dye, 207 N.C. App. 473, 700 S.E.2d 135 (2010)
98 ALR6th 455—§ 24

State v. Dye, 298 S.E.2d 898 (W. Va. 1982)
3 ALR5th 963—§ 5

State v. Dye, 371 N.W.2d 47 (Minn. Ct. App. 1985)
73 ALR5th 383—§ 3

State v. Dye, 946 S.W.2d 783 (Mo. Ct. App. E.D. 1997)
26 ALR6th 451—§ 10

State v. Dye, 1993 WL 157728 (Ohio Ct. App. 3d Dist. Crawford County 1993)
51 ALR6th 1—§ 5

State v. Dyer, 200 P.3d 38 (Kan. Ct. App. 2009)
69 ALR6th 1—§ 5

State v. Dyer, 245 Neb. 385, 513 N.W.2d 316 (1994)
38 ALR5th 433—§ 26, 29
28 ALR6th 505—§ 8

State v. Dyer, 371 A.2d 1079 (Me. 1977)
70 ALR5th 1—§ 5

State v. Dyer, 371 A.2d 1086 (Me. 1977)
54 ALR5th 141—§ 3, 4, 10

State v. Dyer, 438 N.W.2d 716 (Minn. Ct. App. 1989)
114 ALR5th 235—§ 3

State v. Dyer, 551 N.W.2d 320 (Iowa 1996)
105 ALR5th 529—§ 11

State v. Dyess, 124 Wis. 2d 525, 370 N.W.2d 222 (1985)
84 ALR6th 427—§ 27

State v. Dykes, 471 N.W.2d 846 (Iowa 1991)
104 ALR5th 229—§ 4
115 ALR5th 403—§ 5
4 ALR6th 113—§ 22
34 ALR6th 539—§ 4
101 ALR6th 1—§ 28

State v. Dykes, 816 So. 2d 179 (Fla. Dist. Ct. App. 1st Dist. 2002)
58 ALR6th 215—§ 12

State v. Dymond, 248 Ga. App. 582, 546 S.E.2d 69 (2001)
74 ALR5th 319—§ 6

For assistance, call 1-800-328-4880

State v. Dyreson, 17 P.3d 668 (Wash. Ct. App. Div. 3 2001)
60 ALR5th 1—§ 3

State v. Dyson, 518 N.E.2d 812 (Ind. App. 1988)
2 ALR5th 725—§ 13

State v. Dzama, 2011-Ohio-2634, 2011 WL 2175472 (Ohio Ct. App. 9th Dist. Summit County 2011)
70 ALR6th 1—§ 4

State v. Dzubak, 2002-Ohio-6261, 2002 WL 31501567 (Ohio Ct. App. 11th Dist. Geauga County 2002)
84 ALR6th 293—§ 22

State v. E., 360 So. 2d 148 (Fla. App. D1 1978)
31 ALR5th 229—§ 3, 17, 52

State v. $8,000.00 U.S. Currency, 827 So. 2d 634 (La. Ct. App. 3d Cir. 2002)
4 ALR6th 113—§ 4, 39

State v. $11,014.00, 820 S.W.2d 783 (Tex. 1991)
4 ALR6th 113—§ 18, 19, 28, 39

State v. Eagan, 115 Wis. 417, 91 N.W. 984 (1902)
75 ALR6th 311—§ 15, 28

State v. Eagle, 196 Ariz. 188, 994 P.2d 395 (2000)
39 ALR5th 283—§ 41

State v. Eagle, 992 P.2d 1122 (Ariz. Ct. App. Div. 1 1998)
20 ALR5th 398—§ 3, 8

State v. Eagle, 2004-Ohio-3255, 2004 WL 1397966 (Ohio Ct. App. 9th Dist. Wayne County 2004)
24 ALR6th 549—§ 10

State v. Eagle Hawk, 411 N.W.2d 120 (S.D. 1987)
70 ALR5th 461—§ 2, 5

State v. Ealy, 530 So. 2d 1309 (La. Ct. App. 2d Cir. 1988)
28 ALR6th 505—§ 7

State v. Earhart, 2004-Ohio-4791, 2004 WL 2008236 (Ohio Ct. App. 1st Dist. Hamilton County 2004)
71 ALR6th 625—§ 25

State v. Earle, 120 Ohio App. 3d 457, 698 N.E.2d 440 (11th Dist. Lake County 1997)
45 ALR5th 1—§ 18

State v. Earley, 2002-Ohio-4112, 2002 WL 1832911 (Ohio Ct. App. 2d Dist. Montgomery County 2002)
114 ALR5th 173—§ 7

State v. Earls, 97 Wash. App. 1066, 1999 WL 969612 (Div. 1 1999)
9 ALR6th 541—§ 24

State v. Earls, 214 N.J. 564, 70 A.3d 630, 94 A.L.R.6th 785 (2013)
94 ALR6th 525—§ 22
94 ALR6th 579—§ 2 to 4

State v. Earls, 1998 WL 15896 (Tenn. Crim. App. 1998)
73 ALR5th 383—§ 4

State v. Earnest, 1996 WL 63878 (Tenn. Crim. App. 1996)
73 ALR5th 383—§ 29

State v. Eary, 235 Neb. 254, 454 N.W.2d 685 (1990)
109 ALR5th 99—§ 11

State v. Easley, 662 S.W.2d 248 (Mo. 1983)
22 ALR5th 1—§ 6

State v. Eason, 67 N.C. App. 460, 313 S.E.2d 221 (1984)
73 ALR5th 383—§ 9

State v. Eason, 245 Wis. 2d 206, 2001 WI 98, 629 N.W.2d 625 (2001)
2 ALR6th 169—§ 3, 5
50 ALR6th 455—§ 10, 18, 27

State v. Eason, 328 N.C. 409, 402 S.E.2d 809 (1991)
85 ALR5th 187—§ 7, 14
9 ALR6th 1—§ 17

State v. Eason, 336 N.C. 730, 445 S.E.2d 917 (1994)
63 ALR5th 375—§ 2, 6

State v. Eason, 786 A.2d 365, 9 A.L.R.6th 801 (R.I. 2001)
9 ALR6th 541—§ 32
9 ALR6th 633—§ 5, 26, 43, 44
13 ALR6th 603—§ 10

State v. East, 345 N.C. 535, 481 S.E.2d 652 (1997)

57 ALR5th 141—§ 7
State v. East, 743 P.2d 1211 (Utah 1987)
56 ALR6th 323—§ 7
State v. Easter, 172 W. Va. 338, 305 S.E.2d 294 (1983)
124 ALR5th 1—§ 5
State v. Easter, 661 S.W.2d 644 (Mo. App. 1983)
49 ALR5th 639—§ 5
State v. Easterling, 119 N.C. App. 22, 457 S.E.2d 913 (1995)
39 ALR5th 283—§ 4, 32
44 ALR5th 651—§ 5
32 ALR6th 1—§ 4
State v. Easterling, 300 N.C. 594, 268 S.E.2d 800 (1980)
83 ALR6th 465—§ 6, 52
State v. Easthope, 668 P.2d 528 (Utah 1983)
55 ALR6th 157—§ 4, 17
State v. Easton, 169 Misc. 2d 282, 647 N.Y.S.2d 904 (Sup 1995)
2 ALR6th 195—§ 4, 14
79 ALR6th 125—§ 23
State v. Eastridge, 2002-Ohio-6999, 2002 WL 31828956 (Ohio Ct. App. 9th Dist. Summit County 2002)
23 ALR6th 307—§ 44
71 ALR6th 1—§ 11
State v. Eaton, 20 Wash. App. 351, 582 P.2d 517 (1978)
5 ALR5th 243—§ 59
State v. Eaton, 82 Wash. App. 723, 919 P.2d 116 (Div. 1 1996)
56 ALR5th 385—§ 4
State v. Eaton, 101 Nev. 705, 710 P.2d 1370 (1985)
96 ALR5th 107—§ 3, 8
99 ALR5th 301—§ 3
State v. Eaton, 568 S.W.2d 541 (Mo. Ct. App. 1978)
93 ALR5th 527—§ 15
94 ALR5th 393—§ 17
State v. Eberhart, 2002-Ohio-1140, 2002 WL 397744 (Ohio Ct. App. 1st Dist. Hamilton County 2002)
56 ALR6th 323—§ 7

State v. Eberly, 271 Neb. 893, 716 N.W.2d 671 (2006)
58 ALR6th 499—§ 39
State v. Ebey, 491 So. 2d 498 (La. App. 3d Cir. 1986)
19 ALR5th 470—§ 3, 12
State v. Eby, 342 So. 2d 1087 (Fla. Dist. Ct. App. 2d Dist. 1977)
78 ALR5th 197—§ 3
95 ALR5th 125—§ 4
State v. Echevarrieta, 621 P.2d 709 (Utah 1980)
62 ALR6th 413—§ 31
State v. Echeverria, 85 Wash. App. 777, 934 P.2d 1214 (Div. 3 1997)
88 ALR5th 121—§ 22, 26, 35
State v. Echols, 203 Conn. 385, 524 A.2d 1143 (1987)
22 ALR5th 1—§ 4, 13, 17, 40
State v. Echols, 382 S.W.3d 266 (Tenn. 2012)
101 ALR6th 331—§ 8, 12
State v. Echols, 793 P.2d 1066 (Alaska Ct. App. 1990)
71 ALR5th 1—§ 58
State v. Eckart, 2000 WL 1146145 (Minn. Ct. App. 2000)
71 ALR6th 335—§ 26
State v. Ecker, 311 So. 2d 104 (Fla. 1975)
72 ALR5th 1—§ 2, 3, 5, 25, 29
State v. Eckman, 86 Wash. App. 1028, 1997 WL 287628 (Div. 1 1997)
9 ALR6th 541—§ 5
State v. Eckroth, 238 So. 2d 75 (Fla. 1970)
4 ALR5th 1—§ 4
State v. EDB, 638 So. 2d 1108 (La. Ct. App. 2d Cir. 1994)
69 ALR6th 1—§ 20
State v. Edelman, 1999 S.D. 52, 593 N.W.2d 419, 85 A.L.R.5th 783 (S.D. 1999)
85 ALR5th 595—§ 3, 8
90 ALR5th 453—§ 22
State v. Edelstein, 146 Wash. 221, 262 P. 622 (1927)

97 ALR5th 293—§ 3

State v. Edgecombe, 275 So. 2d 740 (La. 1973)

87 ALR5th 181—§ 5

State v. Edgell, 153 Or. App. 108, 956 P.2d 988 (1998)

19 ALR5th 470—§ 15

State v. Edgerton, 100 Iowa 63, 69 N.W. 280 (1896)

50 ALR5th 467—§ 6, 8, 9

State v. Edgington, 99 N.M. 715, 663 P.2d 374, 11 Ed. Law Rep. 301 (Ct. App. 1983)

70 ALR5th 169—§ 6

State v. Edgman, 447 N.E.2d 1091 (Ind. Ct. App. 4th Dist. 1983)

111 ALR5th 1—§ 5 to 7, 13

State v. Edmison, 398 N.W.2d 584 (Minn. Ct. App. 1986)

73 ALR5th 383—§ 5

State v. Edmondson, 112 N.M. 654, 818 P.2d 855 (Ct. App. 1991)

97 ALR5th 293—§ 2, 3, 9, 18, 19

State v. Edmonson, 113 Idaho 230, 743 P.2d 459 (1987)

62 ALR5th 1—§ 2, 4

State v. Edmonson, 257 Neb. 468, 598 N.W.2d 450 (1999)

103 ALR5th 463—§ 3

State v. Edmunds, 229 Wis. 2d 67, 598 N.W.2d 290 (Ct. App. 1999)

121 ALR5th 551—§ 5, 13

State v. Edmundson, 1991 WL 207314 (Ohio Ct. App. 2d Dist. Montgomery County 1991)

85 ALR5th 1—§ 50

State v. Edney, 145 Idaho 694, 183 P.3d 782, 55 A.L.R.6th 705 (Ct. App. 2008)

55 ALR6th 391—§ 22

State v. Edrozo, 578 N.W.2d 719 (Minn. 1998)

34 ALR6th 1—§ 10
69 ALR6th 579—§ 8, 18

State v. Edson, 209 Wis. 2d 82, 562 N.W.2d 926 (Ct. App. 1997)

69 ALR6th 579—§ 5

State v. Edson, 329 Or. 127, 985 P.2d 1253 (1999)

15 ALR5th 391—§ 5

State v. Edward C., 531 A.2d 672 (Me. 1987)

18 ALR5th 856—§ 4

State v. Edward Charles L., 183 W. Va. 641, 398 S.E.2d 123 (1990)

38 ALR5th 433—§ 13

State v. Edwards, 13 S.C. 30, 1880 WL 5604 (1880)

103 ALR6th 137—§ 3

State v. Edwards, 15 Wash. App. 848, 552 P.2d 1095 (1976)

14 ALR5th 89—§ 6, 13

State v. Edwards, 27 N.C. App. 369, 219 S.E.2d 249 (1975)

80 ALR5th 469—§ 3, 5

State v. Edwards, 28 N.J. 292, 146 A.2d 209 (1958)

5 ALR5th 243—§ 62

State v. Edwards, 31 S.W.3d 73 (Mo. Ct. App. W.D. 2000)

7 ALR6th 233—§ 3, 5

State v. Edwards, 36 La. Ann. 863, 1884 WL 7911 (1884)

105 ALR5th 529—§ 11

State v. Edwards, 36 S.W.3d 22 (Mo. Ct. App. W.D. 2000)

60 ALR5th 1—§ 3

State v. Edwards, 51 Wash. App. 763, 755 P.2d 821 (1988)

56 ALR5th 385—§ 3, 4

State v. Edwards, 70 N.C. App. 317, 319 S.E.2d 613 (1984)

41 ALR5th 171—§ 121, 134
85 ALR5th 1—§ 50

State v. Edwards, 73 N.C. App. 599, 327 S.E.2d 16 (1985)

19 ALR5th 351—§ 12

State v. Edwards, 75 N.C. App. 588, 331 S.E.2d 183 (1985)

17 ALR5th 125—§ 7

State v. Edwards, 84 Wash. App. 5, 924 P.2d 397 (Div. 2 1996)

79 ALR5th 1—§ 2, 6, 14

State v. Edwards, 92 Wash. App. 156, 961 P.2d 969 (Div. 1 1998)
7 ALR5th 758—§ 6
State v. Edwards, 95 W. Va. 599, 122 S.E. 272 (1924)
10 ALR6th 31—§ 26
State v. Edwards, 96 Haw. 224, 30 P.3d 238 (2001)
124 ALR5th 1—§ 3
State v. Edwards, 96 Hawaii 224, 30 P.3d 238 (2001)
96 ALR5th 327—§ 3
State v. Edwards, 98 Wis. 2d 367, 297 N.W.2d 12 (1980)
27 ALR6th 491—§ 3, 5
State v. Edwards, 109 Idaho 501, 708 P.2d 906 (Ct. App. 1985)
102 ALR5th 327—§ 9
24 ALR6th 1—§ 19
State v. Edwards, 111 Ariz. 357, 529 P.2d 1174 (1974)
124 ALR5th 1—§ 3
State v. Edwards, 130 P.3d 148 (Kan. Ct. App. 2006)
26 ALR6th 511—§ 25
State v. Edwards, 141 N.M. 491, 2007-NMCA-043, 157 P.3d 56 (Ct. App. 2007)
41 ALR6th 141—§ 7
State v. Edwards, 149 Or. App. 702, 945 P.2d 553 (1997)
103 ALR5th 463—§ 3
State v. Edwards, 173 S.C. 161, 175 S.E. 277 (1934)
104 ALR5th 357—§ 8
54 ALR6th 429—§ 13
State v. Edwards, 229 Wis. 2d 733, 600 N.W.2d 54 (Ct. App. 1999)
4 ALR6th 599—§ 16
State v. Edwards, 278 Neb. 55, 767 N.W.2d 784 (2009)
65 ALR6th 359—§ 9
State v. Edwards, 279 N.W.2d 9 (Iowa 1979)
9 ALR6th 541—§ 3
State v. Edwards, 287 Minn. 83, 177 N.W.2d 40 (1970)

72 ALR5th 607—§ 3, 6
State v. Edwards, 287 So. 2d 518 (La. 1973)
70 ALR5th 587—§ 3
State v. Edwards, 299 Conn. 419, 11 A.3d 116 (2011)
69 ALR6th 579—§ 4
State v. Edwards, 380 N.W.2d 503 (Minn. Ct. App. 1986)
22 ALR5th 1—§ 4, 40, 44, 52, 56
94 ALR5th 393—§ 8
55 ALR6th 391—§ 9
State v. Edwards, 485 N.W.2d 911 (Minn. 1992)
7 ALR6th 233—§ 5
State v. Edwards, 509 So. 2d 1161 (Fla. Dist. Ct. App. 5th Dist. 1987)
70 ALR6th 361—§ 33
State v. Edwards, 581 So. 2d 232, 16 FLW D 1563 (Fla. App. D4 1991)
27 ALR5th 593—§ 17
State v. Edwards, 589 N.W.2d 807 (Minn. Ct. App. 1999)
32 ALR6th 1—§ 5
State v. Edwards, 750 So. 2d 893 (La. 1999)
38 ALR6th 439—§ 4
State v. Edwards, 752 So. 2d 395 (La. Ct. App. 1st Cir. 2000)
89 ALR5th 539—§ 5, 5.5
State v. Edwards, 760 N.W.2d 209 (Iowa Ct. App. 2008)
80 ALR6th 599—§ 8
State v. Edwards, 868 S.W.2d 682 (Tenn. Crim. 1993)
38 ALR5th 433—§ 30
State v. Edwards, 1991 WL 102729 (Ohio Ct. App. 2d Dist. Clark County 1991)
54 ALR6th 593—§ 3
State v. Edwards, 1991 WL 165819 (Tenn. Crim. App. 1991)
57 ALR5th 141—§ 7
State v. Edwards, 1996 WL 488805 (Ohio App. 5 Dist.)
50 ALR5th 581—§ 7, 9, 11, 20

State v. Edwards, 2000-1246 La. 6/1/01, 2001 WL 587484 (La. 2001)

89 ALR5th 539—§ 5.5

State v. Edwards, 2002-Ohio-267, 2002 WL 63191 (Ohio Ct. App. 2d Dist. Greene County 2002)

125 ALR5th 537—§ 15

80 ALR6th 599—§ 6

State v. Edwards, 2003-Ohio-571, 2003 WL 257383 (Ohio Ct. App. 6th Dist. Lucas County 2003)

43 ALR6th 475—§ 8

State v. Edwardsen, 146 Wis. 2d 198, 430 N.W.2d 604 (Ct. App. 1988)

121 ALR5th 551—§ 13

State v. Eff, 2002-Ohio-2559, 2002 WL 1041855 (Ohio Ct. App. 8th Dist. Cuyahoga County 2002)

104 ALR5th 165—§ 7

72 ALR6th 1—§ 4

State v. Egan, 37 Conn. App. 213, 655 A.2d 802 (1995)

51 ALR5th 603—§ 2

State v. Egana, 703 So. 2d 223 (La. Ct. App. 4th Cir. 1997)

99 ALR6th 295—§ 7

State v. Eged, 48 Conn. App. 283, 709 A.2d 39 (1998)

39 ALR6th 257—§ 4

State v. Egger, 8 Neb. App. 740, 601 N.W.2d 785 (1999)

38 ALR5th 433—§ 24

State v. Eggersgluess, 483 N.W.2d 94 (Minn. Ct. App. 1992)

47 ALR6th 423—§ 4

97 ALR6th 653—§ 31

State v. Eggleston, 109 Ohio App. 3d 217, 671 N.E.2d 1325 (2d Dist. Montgomery County 1996)

74 ALR5th 319—§ 5 to 7

State v. Egwaoje, 156 Ariz. 28, 749 P.2d 937 (App. 1988)

15 ALR5th 391—§ 45

State v. Ehli, 2004 ND 125, 681 N.W.2d 808 (N.D. 2004)

4 ALR6th 1—§ 10

State v. Ehnert, 160 Wis. 2d 464, 466 N.W.2d 237 (Ct. App. 1991)

112 ALR5th 429—§ 6

State v. Eib, 716 S.W.2d 304 (Mo. App. 1986)

9 ALR5th 464—§ 6, 8

State v. Eichhorn, 47 Ohio App. 2d 227, 1 Ohio Ops. 3d 301, 353 N.E.2d 861 (Franklin Co. 1975)

41 ALR5th 171—§ 2, 16

State v. Eicholz, 999 S.W.2d 738 (Mo. Ct. App. W. D. 1999)

104 ALR5th 229—§ 12

State v. Eichorn, 143 Ariz. 609, 694 P.2d 1223 (App. 1984)

41 ALR5th 171—§ 17, 19, 30, 68, 72, 105, 107

State v. Eidson, 73 Or. App. 719, 700 P.2d 285 (1985)

32 ALR6th 1—§ 8

State v. Eighinger, 931 S.W.2d 835 (Mo. Ct. App. W.D. 1996)

70 ALR5th 587—§ 17

State v. Eighteen Thousand Six Hundred Sixty-Three Dollars and Twenty-Five Cents ($18,663.25) Cash, 2000 OK CIV APP 102, 11 P.3d 1253 (Div. 4 2000)

115 ALR5th 403—§ 8

116 ALR5th 325—§ 10

4 ALR6th 113—§ 7

101 ALR6th 1—§ 29

State v. Eighteen Thousand Six Hundred Sixty-Three Dollars and Twenty-Five Cents ($18,663.25) Cash, 2000 OK CIV APP 102, 11 P.3d 1253 (Okla. Civ. App. Div. 4 2000)

104 ALR5th 229—§ 10

State v. Eight Judicial Dist. Court, In and For State, Clark County, 101 Nev. 658, 708 P.2d 1022 (1985)

72 ALR5th 607—§ 4, 6, 9

State v. Eilts, 23 Wash. App. 39, 596 P.2d 1050 (Div. 1 1979)

92 ALR5th 35—§ 2, 7

State v. Eisenberg, 29 Wis. 2d 233, 138 N.W.2d 235 (1965)

80 ALR5th 597—§ 15, 18

State v. Eisenberg, 48 Wis. 2d 364, 180 N.W.2d 529 (1970)

63 ALR6th 1—§ 60

State v. Eisenshank, 10 Wash. App. 921, 521 P.2d 239 (Div. 2 1974)

71 ALR6th 283—§ 1

State v. Eitel, 227 So. 2d 489 (Fla. 1969)

72 ALR5th 607—§ 4, 7, 9, 11

State v. Elam, 108 N.M. 268, 771 P.2d 597 (App. 1989)

41 ALR5th 171—§ 6

State v. Elder, 77 S.D. 540, 95 N.W.2d 592 (1959)

21 ALR5th 275—§ 6, 7

State v. Elder, 130 Wash. 612, 228 P. 1016 (1924)

54 ALR6th 429—§ 3

State v. Elder, 697 S.W.2d 359 (Tenn. Crim. App. 1985)

73 ALR5th 383—§ 22

State v. Elder, 815 P.2d 1341, 167 Utah Adv. Rep. 5 (Utah App. 1991)

55 ALR5th 125—§ 14, 23

State v. Elder, 1998 WL 233390 (Ohio Ct. App. 12th Dist. Butler County 1998)

78 ALR5th 489—§ 3

State v. Eldredge, 180 Vt. 278, 2006 VT 80, 910 A.2d 816 (2006)

45 ALR6th 435—§ 16, 25

State v. Eldridge, 134 N.H. 118, 588 A.2d 1222 (1991)

7 ALR5th 758—§ 13

State v. Eldridge, 951 S.W.2d 775 (Tenn. Crim. App. 1997)

53 ALR6th 81—§ 5

State v. Eleneki, 92 Haw. 562, 993 P.2d 1191 (Haw. 2000)

85 ALR5th 1—§ 18

State v. Elersic, 2002-Ohio-2945, 2002 WL 1270599 (Ohio Ct. App. 11th Dist. Lake County 2002)

12 ALR6th 267—§ 5

State v. Eleven Thousand Five Hundred Sixty-Six ($11,566.00) Dollars, 1996 OK CIV APP 67, 919 P.2d 34 (Ct. App. Div. 1 1996)

4 ALR6th 113—§ 4, 14, 37, 39

101 ALR6th 1—§ 62

State v. Eleven Thousand Five Hundred Sixty-Six ($11,566.00) Dollars, 1996 OK CIV APP 67, 919 P.2d 34 (Okla. Ct. App. Div. 1 1996)

104 ALR5th 229—§ 10, 12

State v. Eleven Thousand Three Hundred Forty-Six Dollars & No Cents in United States Currency, 777 P.2d 65, 1 A.L.R.5th 1057 (Wyo. 1989)

1 ALR5th 346—§ 9

State v. Elias, 2010 WL 1478909 (Tex. App. El Paso 2010)

55 ALR6th 1—§ 6

State v. Elim, 303 Wis. 2d 746, 2007 WI App 162, 735 N.W.2d 193 (Ct. App. 2007)

69 ALR6th 579—§ 13

State v. Eling, 355 N.W.2d 286 (Minn. 1984)

101 ALR6th 331—§ 17

State v. Elison, 2000 MT 288, 302 Mont. 228, 14 P.3d 456 (2000)

34 ALR6th 1—§ 5

56 ALR6th 323—§ 7

State v. Elisondo, 97 Idaho 425, 546 P.2d 380 (1976)

72 ALR5th 109—§ 5, 6

State v. Elkhill, 715 So. 2d 327 (Fla. Dist. Ct. App. 2d Dist. 1998)

85 ALR5th 1—§ 27

State v. Elkins, 148 Ohio App. 3d 370, 2002-Ohio-2914, 773 N.E.2d 593 (10th Dist. Franklin County 2002)

26 ALR6th 511—§ 18, 35

State v. Elkins, 1997 WL 619791 (Ohio Ct. App. 3d Dist. Union County 1997)

78 ALR5th 489—§ 10

State v. Elkwisni, 384 N.J. Super. 351, 894 A.2d 1180 (App. Div. 2006)

34 ALR6th 1—§ 9

State v. Ellefson, 2007 WL 1120554 (Minn. Ct. App. 2007)

58 ALR6th 499—§ 28

State v. Ellenbecker, 159 Wis. 2d 91, 464 N.W.2d 427 (App. 1990)

19 ALR5th 884—§ 2, 4

CASES CITED IN ALR5TH AND 6TH

State v. Ellerbe, 217 La. 639, 47 So. 2d
30 (1950)
  24 ALR5th 132—§ 5, 12
State v. Ellerson, 125 Ariz. 249, 609
P.2d 64 (1980)
  59 ALR5th 135—§ 3
State v. Elliot, 11 N.H. 540, 1841 WL
1890 (1841)
  109 ALR5th 421—§ 5
State v. Elliott, 35 So. 3d 247 (La. 2010)
  84 ALR6th 293—§ 15, 38
State v. Elliott, 69 N.C. App. 89, 316
S.E.2d 632 (1984)
  86 ALR5th 463—§ 9
State v. Elliott, 126 Idaho 323, 882 P.2d
978 (Ct. App. 1994)
  19 ALR6th 697—§ 2, 4, 21
State v. Elliott, 344 N.C. 242, 475 S.E.2d
202 (1996)
  57 ALR5th 315—§ 2
State v. Elliott, 459 S.W.2d 526 (Mo. Ct.
App. 1970)
  72 ALR5th 607—§ 6
State v. Elliott, 879 S.W.2d 381 (Tex.
App. Waco 1994)
  18 ALR6th 519—§ 10
State v. Elliott, 1992 WL 355302 (Ohio
Ct. App. 6th Dist. Wood County
1992)
  1 ALR6th 371—§ 4
State v. Elliott, 1997 WL 4504 (Wash.
App. Div. 3)
  50 ALR5th 581—§ 7
State v. Elliott, 2002 MT 26, 308 Mont.
227, 43 P.3d 279 (2002)
  27 ALR6th 183—§ 28, 30
State v. Elliott, 2003-Ohio-4962, 2003
WL 22149321 (Ohio Ct. App. 1st
Dist. Hamilton County 2003)
  125 ALR5th 497—§ 4
State v. Elliott, 2006-Ohio-4508, 2006
WL 2520336 (Ohio Ct. App. 1st
Dist. Hamilton County 2006)
  72 ALR6th 227—§ 48
State v. Elliott, 2010-Ohio-241, 2010
WL 320479 (Ohio Ct. App. 8th Dist.
Cuyahoga County 2010)
  55 ALR6th 1—§ 3, 11

State v. Ellis, 21 Wash. App. 123, 584
P.2d 428 (Div. 2 1978)
  85 ALR5th 1—§ 18, 32
State v. Ellis, 48 Wash. App. 333, 738
P.2d 1085 (Div. 1 1987)
  81 ALR5th 563—§ 8
State v. Ellis, 88 Wash. App. 1069, 1998
WL 2770 (Div. 3 1998)
  84 ALR6th 293—§ 4, 15
State v. Ellis, 90 P.3d 379 (Kan. Ct. App.
2004)
  26 ALR6th 511—§ 29
State v. Ellis, 95 N.M. 427, 622 P.2d
1047 (Ct. App. 1980)
  54 ALR6th 1—§ 30
State v. Ellis, 117 Ariz. 329, 572 P.2d
791 (1977)
  19 ALR6th 411—§ 14
State v. Ellis, 120 N.M. 709, 905 P.2d
747 (Ct. App. 1995)
  92 ALR5th 35—§ 11
State v. Ellis, 172 Ariz. 549, 838 P.2d
1310, 108 Ariz. Adv. Rep. 28 (App.
1992)
  15 ALR5th 391—§ 13
State v. Ellis, 200 N.C. 77, 156 S.E. 157
(1930)
  103 ALR6th 137—§ 15
State v. Ellis, 208 Kan. 59, 490 P.2d 364
(1971)
  37 ALR6th 357—§ 31, 69
State v. Ellis, 208 Neb. 379, 303 N.W.2d
741 (1981)
  82 ALR5th 359—§ 3, 5
  84 ALR5th 487—§ 24
State v. Ellis, 214 Neb. 172, 333 N.W.2d
391 (1983)
  7 ALR5th 263—§ 2, 3
State v. Ellis, 280 N.J. Super. 533, 656
A.2d 25 (App. Div. 1995)
  57 ALR5th 315—§ 3, 12
State v. Ellis, 487 So. 2d 752 (La. Ct.
App. 3d Cir. 1986)
  99 ALR6th 295—§ 21
State v. Ellis, 639 S.W.2d 420 (Mo. App.
1982)
  5 ALR5th 243—§ 51

State v. Ellis, 669 A.2d 752 (Me. 1996)
87 ALR5th 693—§ 4

State v. Ellis, 715 So. 2d 364 (Fla. Dist. Ct. App. 5th Dist. 1998)
113 ALR5th 597—§ 8

State v. Ellis, 756 So. 2d 418 (La. Ct. App. 1st Cir. 1999)
93 ALR5th 327—§ 28

State v. Ellis, 2004-Ohio-3108, 2004 WL 1352916 (Ohio Ct. App. 8th Dist. Cuyahoga County 2004)
66 ALR6th 351—§ 17

State v. Ellison, 13 Conn. L. Rptr. 470, 1995 WL 55006 (Conn. Super. Ct. 1995)
92 ALR6th 1—§ 3

State v. Ellison, 26 Ariz. App. 547, 550 P.2d 101 (Div. 1 1976)
121 ALR5th 551—§ 4, 14

State v. Ellison, 79 Conn. App. 591, 830 A.2d 812 (2003)
40 ALR6th 1—§ 10, 22, 27

State v. Ellison, 213 Ariz. 116, 140 P.3d 899 (2006)
21 ALR6th 1—§ 4

State v. Elmore, 205 N.J. Super. 373, 500 A.2d 1089 (App. Div. 1985)
96 ALR5th 327—§ 3

State v. Elmore, 1998 WL 573407 (Tenn. Crim. App. 1998)
73 ALR5th 383—§ 5

State v. Elmore, 2005-Ohio-5940, 2005 WL 2981797 (Ohio Ct. App. 5th Dist. Licking County 2005)
71 ALR6th 625—§ 28, 29

State v. Elsinore Shore Associates, 249 N.J. Super. 403, 592 A.2d 604 (App. Div. 1991)
29 ALR6th 507—§ 16, 42, 44, 68

State v. Elson, 116 Conn. App. 196, 975 A.2d 678 (2009)
67 ALR6th 103—§ 4

State v. El-Tabech, 234 Neb. 831, 453 N.W.2d 91 (1990)
72 ALR5th 403—§ 19

State v. El-Tabech, 259 Neb. 509, 610 N.W.2d 737 (2000)
97 ALR6th 263—§ 17

State v. El-Tabech, 269 Neb. 810, 696 N.W.2d 445 (2005)
72 ALR6th 227—§ 51

State v. Elton, 680 P.2d 727 (Utah 1984)
46 ALR5th 499—§ 2, 3

State v. Eluska, 724 P.2d 514 (Alaska 1986)
50 ALR5th 703—§ 22

State v. Elvin, 481 N.W.2d 571 (Minn. Ct. App. 1992)
73 ALR5th 383—§ 35

State v. Elwell, 380 A.2d 1016 (Me. 1977)
85 ALR5th 187—§ 8, 14

State v. Ely, 708 A.2d 1332 (Vt. 1997)
29 ALR5th 1—§ 3

State v. Embry, 563 So. 2d 147, 15 FLW 1500 (Fla. App. D2 1990)
18 ALR5th 1—§ 12

State v. Embry, 593 So. 2d 327, 17 FLW D 554 (Fla. App. D2 1992)
18 ALR5th 1—§ 12

State v. Emerick, 170 Ohio App. 3d 647, 2007-Ohio-1334, 868 N.E.2d 742 (2d Dist. Montgomery County 2007)
72 ALR6th 227—§ 48

State v. Emerick, 2011-Ohio-5543, 2011 WL 5137200 (Ohio Ct. App. 2d Dist. Montgomery County 2011)
72 ALR6th 227—§ 48

State v. Emerson, 10 Wash. App. 235, 517 P.2d 245 (1973)
18 ALR5th 1—§ 28

State v. Emerson, 43 Wash. 2d 5, 259 P.2d 406 (1953)
57 ALR6th 445—§ 3

State v. Emerson, 149 Vt. 171, 541 A.2d 466 (1987)
84 ALR5th 487—§ 24

State v. Emerson, 375 N.W.2d 256 (Iowa 1985)
58 ALR6th 499—§ 59
100 ALR6th 535—§ 3

State v. Emery, 230 N.W.2d 521 (Iowa 1975)
55 ALR5th 423—§ 6

State v. Emery, 357 A.2d 878 (Me. 1976)
54 ALR6th 429—§ 27

State v. Emmons, 57 Ohio App. 2d 173, 11 Ohio Op. 3d 173, 386 N.E.2d 838 (2d Dist. Montgomery County 1978)
57 ALR6th 445—§ 43

State v. Emmons, 72 Iowa 265, 33 N.W. 672 (1887)
45 ALR5th 591—§ 14

State v. Emmons, 173 Vt. 492, 788 A.2d 24 (2001)
92 ALR6th 295—§ 32
93 ALR6th 207—§ 26
96 ALR6th 355—§ 29

State v. Emond, 163 Ariz. 138, 786 P.2d 989, 44 Ariz. Adv. Rep. 13 (App. 1989)
42 ALR5th 291—§ 6

State v. Emonds, 11 Ohio Op. 258, 26 Ohio L. Abs. 410, 3 Ohio Supp. 207, 1938 WL 1564 (C.P. 1938)
92 ALR5th 35—§ 15

State v. Emonds, 11 Ohio Ops. 258, 26 Ohio L. Abs. 410 (CP 1938)
15 ALR5th 391—§ 30

State v. Emory, 643 S.W.2d 24 (Mo. App. 1982)
5 ALR5th 243—§ 57

State v. Emrick, 129 Vt. 475, 282 A.2d 821 (1971)
36 ALR5th 255—§ 7

State v. Endo, 83 Haw. 87, 924 P.2d 581 (Ct. App. 1996)
27 ALR6th 491—§ 4

State v. Engel, 249 N.J. Super. 336, 592 A.2d 572 (1991)
19 ALR5th 470—§ 3

State v. Engel, 465 N.W.2d 787 (S.D. 1991)
67 ALR5th 361—§ 3, 4, 6

State v. Engel, 859 S.W.2d 822 (Mo. Ct. App. W.D. 1993)
68 ALR5th 343—§ 3
42 ALR6th 237—§ 8

State v. Engelking, 117 P.3d 150 (Kan. Ct. App. 2005)
26 ALR6th 511—§ 25

State v. Engelking, 149 P.3d 25 (Kan. Ct. App. 2006)
26 ALR6th 511—§ 25

State v. Engels, 2 N.J. Super. 126, 64 A.2d 897 (1949)
50 ALR5th 703—§ 41

State v. English, 62 Minn. 402, 64 N.W. 1136 (1895)
104 ALR5th 357—§ 8

State v. Engweiler, 118 Or. App. 132, 846 P.2d 1163 (1993)
57 ALR5th 141—§ 6

State v. Ennis, 99 N.M. 117, 654 P.2d 570 (App. 1982)
15 ALR5th 391—§ 31

State v. Ennis, 212 Or. App. 240, 158 P.3d 510 (2007)
30 ALR6th 1—§ 3, 6

State v. Ennis, 334 N.W.2d 827 (N.D. 1983)
112 ALR5th 429—§ 17

State v. Ennis, 676 So. 2d 196 (La. Ct. App. 4th Cir. 1996)
17 ALR6th 327—§ 7

State v. Enoch, 1996 WL 278220 (Minn. Ct. App. 1996)
33 ALR6th 1—§ 6, 12

State v. Enriquez, 2012 WL 723077 (Ariz. Ct. App. Div. 1 2012)
101 ALR6th 331—§ 12

State v. Ensley, 240 Ind. 472, 164 N.E.2d 342 (1960)
15 ALR5th 821—§ 9, 11

State v. Ensley, 956 S.W.2d 502 (Tenn. Crim. App. 1996)
16 ALR6th 329—§ 15
24 ALR6th 591—§ 10

State v. Enstice, 573 So. 2d 340 (Fla. Dist. Ct. App. 5th Dist. 1990)
111 ALR5th 239—§ 4

State v. Epperson, 571 S.W.2d 260 (Mo. 1978)
58 ALR6th 499—§ 52, 56, 98

State v. Eppinette, 838 So. 2d 189 (La. Ct. App. 2d Cir. 2003)
47 ALR6th 107—§ 26, 63, 72

State v. Eppinger, 74 Ohio App. 3d 503, 599 N.E.2d 709 (Cuyahoga Co. 1991)

50 ALR5th 581—§ 2

State v. Epps, 284 N.J. Super. 373, 665 A.2d 412 (Law Div. 1995)

49 ALR5th 639—§ 4

State v. Epstein, 25 R.I. 131, 55 A. 204 (1903)

97 ALR6th 567—§ 4, 10

State v. Erbacher, 8 Kan. App. 2d 169, 651 P.2d 973 (1982)

97 ALR6th 653—§ 14

State v. Erbele, 554 N.W.2d 448 (N.D. 1996)

92 ALR6th 295—§ 3
96 ALR6th 355—§ 3

State v. Erby, 735 S.W.2d 148 (Mo. App. 1987)

39 ALR5th 283—§ 4, 55

State v. Erickson, 93 Mont. 466, 19 P.2d 227 (1933)

82 ALR6th 497—§ 80

State v. Erickson, 101 Wis. 2d 224, 303 N.W.2d 850 (App. 1981)

50 ALR5th 703—§ 2, 35

State v. Erickson, 241 N.W.2d 854 (N.D. 1976)

84 ALR6th 427—§ 26

State v. Erickson, 496 N.W.2d 555 (N.D. 1993)

62 ALR5th 1—§ 2

State v. Erickson, 610 N.W.2d 335 (Minn. 2000)

104 ALR5th 357—§ 3, 4, 7, 9
54 ALR6th 429—§ 9, 11

State v. Erickson, 674 N.W.2d 684 (Iowa Ct. App. 2003)

45 ALR6th 643—§ 7

State v. Erickson K., 132 N.M. 258, 2002-NMCA-058, 46 P.3d 1258 (Ct. App. 2002)

21 ALR6th 771—§ 5

State v. Erickstad, 2000 ND 202, 620 N.W.2d 136 (N.D. 2000)

54 ALR6th 593—§ 12

State v. Ericson, 2011 ME 28, 13 A.3d 777 (Me. 2011)

84 ALR6th 263—§ 5

State v. Erkins, 2012-Ohio-5372, 2012 WL 5870516 (Ohio Ct. App. 1st Dist. Hamilton County 2012)

103 ALR6th 347—§ 20

State v. Erlewein, 755 N.E.2d 700 (Ind. Ct. App. 2001)

97 ALR5th 537—§ 29

State v. Ernest, 200 Neb. 615, 264 N.W.2d 677 (1978)

59 ALR5th 135—§ 10

State v. Ervin, 38 N.C. App. 261, 248 S.E.2d 91 (1978)

115 ALR5th 403—§ 8
4 ALR6th 113—§ 16
101 ALR6th 1—§ 3

State v. Ervin, 835 S.W.2d 905 (Mo. 1992)

83 ALR6th 255—§ 17, 27

State v. Ervin, 979 S.W.2d 149, 96 A.L.R.5th 755 (Mo. 1998)

96 ALR5th 523—§ 3

State v. Erving, 558 A.2d 703 (Me. 1989)

50 ALR5th 703—§ 15

State v. Erwin, 848 S.W.2d 476 (Mo. 1993)

78 ALR5th 197—§ 14

State v. Erwin., 1976 WL 190854 (Ohio Ct. App. 8th Dist. Cuyahoga County 1976)

19 ALR6th 697—§ 4

State v. Escalante, 148 Ariz. 298, 714 P.2d 468 (Ct. App. Div. 1 1986)

31 ALR6th 49—§ 4

State v. Escamilla, 193 Neb. 503, 227 N.W.2d 852 (1975)

40 ALR6th 1—§ 4, 11

State v. Escherivel, 113 Ariz. 300, 552 P.2d 1194 (1976)

19 ALR6th 115—§ 4

State v. Escobar, 764 S.W.2d 570 (Tex. App. Houston 1st Dist. 1989)

109 ALR5th 99—§ 3

State v. Escobedo, 404 So. 2d 760 (Fla. Dist. Ct. App. 3d Dist. 1981)

108 ALR5th 593—§ 11

State v. Eshuk, 347 So. 2d 704 (Fla. App. D3 1977)

18 ALR5th 1—§ 16

State v. Eskola, 1991 WL 182807 (Tenn. Crim. App. 1991)

93 ALR5th 1—§ 7

State v. Esler, 553 N.W.2d 61 (Minn. Ct. App. 1996)

92 ALR5th 35—§ 7

State v. Esparza, 1990 WL 7966 (Ohio Ct. App. 3d Dist. Defiance County 1990)

65 ALR5th 407—§ 2, 3, 11

State v. Esparza, 1999 WL 155955 (Ohio Ct. App. 3d Dist. Defiance County 1999)

125 ALR5th 357—§ 7

7 ALR6th 233—§ 12

State v. Espe, 2012 WL 4328611 (Minn. Ct. App. 2012)

101 ALR6th 545—§ 4

State v. Esposito, 235 Conn. 802, 670 A.2d 301 (1996)

81 ALR5th 563—§ 3, 7

10 ALR6th 463—§ 3, 4

24 ALR6th 1—§ 21

State v. Esprinal, 488 So. 2d 228 (La. Ct. App. 4th Cir. 1986)

21 ALR6th 771—§ 12

State v. Esquivel, 71 Wash. App. 868, 863 P.2d 113 (Div. 3 1993)

108 ALR5th 593—§ 11, 37

State v. Esslinger, 357 N.W.2d 525 (S.D. 1984)

29 ALR5th 59—§ 7, 14, 20

State v. Esteen, 846 So. 2d 167 (La. Ct. App. 5th Cir. 2003)

103 ALR6th 247—§ 11

State v. Estep, 117 Wash. App. 1023, 2003 WL 21359472 (Div. 3 2003)

38 ALR6th 97—§ 32

State v. Estep, 753 N.E.2d 22 (Ind. Ct. App. 2001)

78 ALR6th 297—§ 47, 49, 53

State v. Estepp, 1997 WL 736501 (Ohio Ct. App. 2d Dist. Montgomery County 1997)

31 ALR6th 465—§ 3, 11, 14, 24, 27, 32

State v. Ester, 1990 WL 252213 (Ohio Ct. App. 3d Dist. Van Wert County 1990)

99 ALR6th 295—§ 19

State v. Estes, 131 Or. App. 188, 883 P.2d 1335 (1994)

70 ALR6th 361—§ 28

State v. Estes, 185 N.C. 752, 117 S.E. 581 (1923)

66 ALR5th 397—§ 3, 10

State v. Estes, 418 A.2d 1108 (Me. 1980)

39 ALR5th 283—§ 2, 4

State v. Estes, 1993 WL 19085 (Ohio Ct. App. 12th Dist. Preble County 1993)

59 ALR5th 1—§ 3, 6

State v. Estes, 2005-Ohio-5478, 2005 WL 2626194 (Ohio Ct. App. 12th Dist. Preble County 2005)

29 ALR6th 1—§ 10

State v. Estlick, 24 Or. App. 117, 544 P.2d 596 (1976)

34 ALR5th 125—§ 13

State v. Estrada, 26 Conn. App. 641, 603 A.2d 1179 (1992)

5 ALR5th 243—§ 6, 7

State v. Estrada, 78 Wash. App. 381, 896 P.2d 1307 (Div. 3 1995)

105 ALR5th 529—§ 12

State v. Estrada, 187 Ariz. 490, 930 P.2d 1004 (Ct. App. Div. 1 1996)

37 ALR6th 357—§ 49

State v. Estrado, 170 Ga. App. 889, 318 S.E.2d 505 (1984)

114 ALR5th 173—§ 8

State v. Estrella, 2004 WL 1375835 (Haw. 2004)

78 ALR6th 1—§ 37

State v. Esway, 1993 WL 385341 (Ohio Ct. App. 5th Dist.Stark County 1993)

59 ALR5th 1—§ 2, 3, 5, 6

State v. Etchison, 188 Neb. 134, 195 N.W.2d 498 (1972)

26 ALR5th 1—§ 3

State v. Etherage, 277 S.C. 523, 290 S.E.2d 413 (1982)

66 ALR5th 397—§ 6, 10

State v. Etienne, 103 Conn. App. 544, 930 A.2d 726 (2007)

81 ALR6th 505—§ 32

State v. Etzel, 1998 WL 865672 (Minn. Ct. App. 1998)

69 ALR6th 579—§ 8, 18

State v. Eubanks, 355 N.W.2d 57 (Iowa 1984)

114 ALR5th 173—§ 7

State v. Euclid Fish Co., 32 Ohio Ops. 2d 85, 95 Ohio L. Abs. 1, 198 N.E.2d 776 (App. Cuyahoga Co. 1964)

50 ALR5th 703—§ 6

State v. Eudy, 163 N.C. App. 612, 594 S.E.2d 257 (2004)

33 ALR6th 91—§ 40

State v. Eugene, 340 N.W.2d 18 (N.D. 1983)

82 ALR5th 359—§ 2, 3
83 ALR5th 277—§ 2, 9, 11, 27
84 ALR5th 487—§ 2, 19, 25
53 ALR6th 81—§ 5, 11
56 ALR6th 185—§ 8

State v. Euresti, 797 S.W.2d 296 (Tex. App. Corpus Christi 1990)

104 ALR5th 229—§ 9
4 ALR6th 113—§ 17
101 ALR6th 1—§ 4, 19

State v. Eutzy, 184 Neb. 755, 172 N.W.2d 94 (1969)

15 ALR6th 173—§ 41

State v. Evans, 28 Ohio App. 2d 265, 57 Ohio Op. 2d 381, 276 N.E.2d 665 (10th Dist. Franklin County 1971)

108 ALR5th 593—§ 50

State v. Evans, 45 Haw. 622, 372 P.2d 365 (1962)

65 ALR5th 407—§ 7, 11

State v. Evans, 63 Ohio St. 3d 231, 586 N.E.2d 1042 (1992)

20 ALR5th 177—§ 3, 7

State v. Evans, 67 Ohio St. 3d 405, 618 N.E.2d 162 (1993)

50 ALR5th 581—§ 5, 7

State v. Evans, 73 N.C. App. 214, 326 S.E.2d 303 (1985)

72 ALR5th 1—§ 10, 30

State v. Evans, 80 Wash. App. 806, 911 P.2d 1344 (Div. 1 1996)

113 ALR5th 597—§ 8

State v. Evans, 109 Or. 503, 221 P. 822 (1924)

104 ALR5th 357—§ 8

State v. Evans, 110 Or. App. 46, 822 P.2d 1198 (1991)

113 ALR5th 517—§ 4

State v. Evans, 115 Kan. 538, 224 P. 492 (1924)

81 ALR5th 563—§ 3, 5

State v. Evans, 129 Wash. App. 211, 118 P.3d 419 (Div. 2 2005)

26 ALR6th 511—§ 42
73 ALR6th 49—§ 8

State v. Evans, 144 Ohio App. 3d 539, 760 N.E.2d 909 (1st Dist. Hamilton County 2001)

35 ALR6th 127—§ 20

State v. Evans, 181 Wis. 2d 978, 512 N.W.2d 259 (Ct. App. 1994)

92 ALR5th 35—§ 22

State v. Evans, 193 N.J. Super. 560, 475 A.2d 97 (Law Div. 1984)

68 ALR5th 299—§ 4, 6

State v. Evans, 203 Conn. 212, 523 A.2d 1306 (1987)

124 ALR5th 1—§ 4

State v. Evans, 212 Neb. 476, 323 N.W.2d 106 (1982)

39 ALR6th 257—§ 19
40 ALR6th 1—§ 19

State v. Evans, 218 Neb. 849, 359 N.W.2d 790 (1984)

79 ALR5th 419—§ 12

State v. Evans, 225 Ga. App. 402, 484 S.E.2d 70 (1997)

124 ALR5th 509—§ 5

State v. Evans, 238 Wis. 2d 411, 2000 WI App 178, 617 N.W.2d 220 (Ct. App. 2000)

38 ALR6th 439—§ 3

State v. Evans, 242 P.3d 220 (Kan. Ct. App. 2010)

For assistance, call 1-800-328-4880

CASES CITED IN ALR5TH AND 6TH

63 ALR6th 351—§ 3
State v. Evans, 261 Mont. 508, 862 P.2d
417 (1993)
65 ALR6th 537—§ 44
State v. Evans, 270 Kan. 585, 17 P.3d
340 (2001)
3 ALR6th 543—§ 9
State v. Evans, 304 So. 2d 338 (La.
1974)
55 ALR5th 125—§ 8
State v. Evans, 311 N.W.2d 481 (Minn.
1981)
73 ALR5th 383—§ 3
State v. Evans, 354 S.C. 579, 582 S.E.2d
407 (2003)
29 ALR6th 1—§ 9
State v. Evans, 439 S.W.2d 170 (Mo.
1969)
31 ALR6th 465—§ 4, 7, 10, 28
State v. Evans, 439 S.W.2d 170 (Mo.
1969).
31 ALR6th 465—§ 3
State v. Evans, 692 So. 2d 216 (Fla. Dist.
Ct. App. 4th Dist. 1997)
35 ALR6th 497—§ 3, 35
State v. Evans, 692 So. 2d 305 (Fla. Dist.
Ct. App. 4th Dist. 1997)
57 ALR6th 83—§ 4
State v. Evans, 745 S.W.2d 880 (Tenn.
Crim. App. 1987)
64 ALR5th 671—§ 8
State v. Evans, 815 S.W.2d 503 (Tenn.
1991)
27 ALR6th 491—§ 5
State v. Evans, 944 P.2d 1120 (Wyo.
1997)
69 ALR6th 579—§ 4
State v. Evans, 1986 WL 5601 (Ohio Ct.
App. 8th Dist. Cuyahoga County
1986)
19 ALR6th 697—§ 4
State v. Evans, 1993 WL 460555 (Tenn.
Crim. App. 1993)
72 ALR5th 403—§ 15
State v. Evans, 1998 WL 550770 (Minn.
Ct. App. 1998)
47 ALR6th 107—§ 24

State v. Evans, 2005 WL 3369912 (N.J.
Super. Ct. App. Div. 2005)
26 ALR6th 511—§ 17
State v. Evans, 2008-Ohio-2032, 2008
WL 1903921 (Ohio Ct. App. 8th
Dist. Cuyahoga County 2008)
78 ALR6th 297—§ 38
State v. Evans, No. 40604 (March 27,
1980, Ct. App. Ohio, 8th App. Dist.
Cuyahoga Co.)
39 ALR5th 283—§ 14, 67
State v. Evans, Slip Op. No. CA86-09-
130 (Ohio App. Butler Co. 1987)
38 ALR5th 433—§ 14
State v. Evenson, 35 S.W.3d 486 (Mo.
Ct. App. S.D. 2000)
68 ALR5th 343—§ 3
State v. Everage, 124 S.W.3d 11 (Mo.
Ct. App. W.D. 2004)
3 ALR6th 543—§ 8
State v. Everett, 157 N.W.2d 144 (Iowa
1968)
56 ALR6th 323—§ 5
State v. Everhardt, 326 N.C. 777, 392
S.E.2d 391 (1990)
5 ALR5th 243—§ 5
44 ALR5th 651—§ 5
State v. Everly, 150 W. Va. 423, 146
S.E.2d 705 (1966)
93 ALR5th 493—§ 3
State v. Everly, 2000 WL 1637 (Ohio Ct.
App. 5th Dist. Stark County 1999)
78 ALR5th 489—§ 10
State v. Everson, 229 Kan. 540, 626 P.2d
1189 (1981)
99 ALR6th 113—§ 11
State v. Everson, 474 N.W.2d 695 (N.D.
1991)
74 ALR5th 319—§ 5, 7 to 9
82 ALR5th 103—§ 5
State v. Everson, 2003 WL 22952715
(Tenn. Ct. App. 2003)
57 ALR6th 163—§ 39
State v. Everybodytalksabout, 131
Wash. App. 227, 126 P.3d 87 (Div.
1 2006)
38 ALR6th 97—§ 25

For assistance, call 1-800-328-4880

685

State v. Everybodytalksabout, 161 Wash. 2d 702, 166 P.3d 693 (2007)
38 ALR6th 97—§ 25
State v. Evjue, 253 Wis. 146, 33 N.W.2d 305, 13 A.L.R.2d 1201 (1948)
40 ALR5th 787—§ 3
State v. Ewing, 81 Haw. 156, 914 P.2d 549 (Ct. App. 1996)
122 ALR5th 593—§ 8
70 ALR6th 513—§ 5
71 ALR6th 471—§ 5
State v. Ewing, 102 Wash. App. 349, 7 P.3d 835 (Div. 1 2000)
92 ALR5th 35—§ 25
State v. Ewing, 221 Neb. 462, 378 N.W.2d 158 (1985)
87 ALR5th 597—§ 7, 8
State v. Exnicious, 223 Mo. 61, 122 S.W. 730 (1909)
5 ALR6th 1—§ 60
State v. Expunged Record (No.) 249,044, 881 So. 2d 104 (La. 2004)
69 ALR6th 1—§ 25
State v. Exum, 213 N.C. 16, 195 S.E. 7 (1938)
73 ALR5th 615—§ 3, 7
State v. Exum, 1991 WL 44137 (Conn. Super. Ct. 1991)
85 ALR5th 1—§ 2, 49
6 ALR6th 533—§ 22
State v. Eyer, 74 Ohio App. 3d 361, 598 N.E.2d 1242 (Hamilton Co. 1991)
51 ALR5th 375—§ 7, 10
State v. Eyle, 236 Or. 199, 388 P.2d 110, 9 A.L.R.3d 628 (1963)
78 ALR5th 567—§ 6
State v. Ezell, 81 Wash. App. 1033, 1996 WL 227502 (Div. 1 1996)
7 ALR6th 233—§ 9
State v. Faafiti, 54 Hawaii 637, 513 P.2d 697 (1973)
32 ALR5th 149—§ 4, 30, 33
State v. Faber, 264 Neb. 198, 647 N.W.2d 67 (2002)
6 ALR6th 533—§ 3, 22
State v. Fabritz, 276 Md. 416, 348 A.2d 275 (1975)

118 ALR5th 253—§ 16
State v. Faciane, 233 La. 1028, 99 So. 2d 333 (1957)
16 ALR6th 329—§ 4
24 ALR6th 591—§ 4
State v. Fadden, 397 N.W.2d 2 (Minn. Ct. App. 1986)
102 ALR5th 525—§ 13
State v. Fader, 358 N.W.2d 42 (Minn. 1984)
15 ALR5th 391—§ 39
92 ALR5th 35—§ 14
State v. Faehnrich, 359 N.W.2d 895 (S.D. 1984)
102 ALR5th 447—§ 14
State v. Fagan, 78 N.M. 618, 435 P.2d 771 (Ct. App. 1967)
34 ALR6th 1—§ 12
State v. Fagan, 798 N.W.2d 736 (Iowa Ct. App. 2011)
70 ALR6th 361—§ 7
State v. Fagan, 857 So. 2d 320 (Fla. Dist. Ct. App. 2d Dist. 2003)
125 ALR5th 537—§ 34
68 ALR6th 527—§ 37
State v. Fagan, 2002 WL 1842415 (Iowa Ct. App. 2002)
70 ALR6th 361—§ 5
71 ALR6th 335—§ 5
State v. Fageroos, 531 N.W.2d 199 (Minn. 1995)
32 ALR6th 171—§ 15, 22
33 ALR6th 1—§ 23
State v. Fahlk, 246 Neb. 834, 524 N.W.2d 39 (1994)
57 ALR6th 445—§ 3
State v. Fain, 116 Idaho 82, 774 P.2d 252 (1989)
27 ALR6th 183—§ 3, 15
State v. Fair, 28 Utah 2d 242, 501 P.2d 107 (1972)
99 ALR6th 295—§ 9
State v. Fair, 209 S.C. 439, 40 S.E.2d 634 (1946)
89 ALR6th 565—§ 14

State v. Fair, 1993 WL 215442 (Ohio Ct. App. 8th Dist. Cuyahoga County 1993)
99 ALR6th 295—§ 9
State v. Fair, 1999 WL 1045074 (Tenn. Crim. App. 1999)
27 ALR6th 183—§ 40
State v. Fair, 2002-Ohio-5561, 2002 WL 31319117 (Ohio Ct. App. 8th Dist. Cuyahoga County 2002)
72 ALR6th 1—§ 6
State v. Fair, 2011-Ohio-3330, 2011 WL 2584234 (Ohio Ct. App. 2d Dist. Montgomery County 2011)
81 ALR6th 505—§ 30
State v. Fairbanks North Star Borough, 736 P.2d 1140 (Alaska 1987)
82 ALR6th 497—§ 7
State v. Fairrow, 1987 WL 17704 (Ohio Ct. App. 4th Dist. Ross County 1987)
99 ALR6th 295—§ 9
State v. Falbo, 190 Wis. 2d 328, 526 N.W.2d 814 (Ct. App. 1994)
67 ALR5th 361—§ 3, 8
State v. Falcon, 87 P.3d 993 (Kan. Ct. App. 2004)
26 ALR6th 511—§ 25, 29
State v. Falcone, 383 So. 2d 1243 (La. 1980)
105 ALR5th 529—§ 14
State v. Falconer, 426 N.W.2d 10 (N.D. 1988)
50 ALR5th 703—§ 3
State v. Fallon, 100 Nev. 509, 685 P.2d 1385, 26 BNA WH Cas. 1554, 114 CCH LC ¶ 56202 (1984)
7 ALR5th 400—§ 3, 7, 9
State v. Falocco, 730 So. 2d 765 (Fla. Dist. Ct. App. 5th Dist. 1999)
113 ALR5th 597—§ 8
State v. Fan, 445 N.W.2d 243 (Minn. App. 1989)
42 ALR5th 291—§ 3, 4, 10
State v. Fancher, 169 Ariz. 266, 818 P.2d 251, 96 Ariz. Adv. Rep. 118 (App. 1991)
15 ALR5th 391—§ 11

State v. Fanelle, 385 N.J. Super. 518, 897 A.2d 1104 (App. Div. 2006)
50 ALR6th 455—§ 32
59 ALR6th 311—§ 10
State v. Fanelle, 404 N.J. Super. 180, 960 A.2d 825, 59 A.L.R.6th 747 (Law Div. 2008)
59 ALR6th 311—§ 8
State v. Faragi, 127 N.H. 1, 498 A.2d 723 (1985)
72 ALR6th 1—§ 6
State v. Farber, 1 Neb. App. 460, 498 N.W.2d 797 (1993)
58 ALR6th 499—§ 83
79 ALR6th 1—§ 15, 19, 65
State v. Faretra, 330 N.J. Super. 527, 750 A.2d 166 (App. Div. 2000)
64 ALR5th 637—§ 3
State v. Farias-Estrada, 203 Or. App. 474, 124 P.3d 1289 (2005)
26 ALR6th 511—§ 50
State v. Farkes, 71 Or. App. 155, 691 P.2d 489 (1984)
1 ALR6th 549—§ 22, 25
State v. Farlow, 336 N.C. 534, 444 S.E.2d 913 (1994)
73 ALR5th 383—§ 6, 38
State v. Farmer, 116 Wash. 2d 414, 805 P.2d 200, 13 A.L.R.5th 1070 (1991)
13 ALR5th 628—§ 3, 12
42 ALR5th 291—§ 4, 10, 24
87 ALR5th 631—§ 11
State v. Farmer, 158 N.C. App. 699, 582 S.E.2d 352 (2003)
102 ALR6th 279—§ 25
State v. Farmer, 191 W. Va. 372, 445 S.E.2d 759 (1994)
39 ALR5th 283—§ 4, 77
State v. Farmer, 407 N.W.2d 821 (S.D. 1987)
20 ALR5th 398—§ 12, 13
State v. Farmer, 812 P.2d 858 (Wash. 1991)
42 ALR5th 291—§ 11
State v. Farmer, 1976 WL 189250 (Ohio Ct. App. 2d Dist. Montgomery County 1976)

99 ALR6th 295—§ 15

State v. Farmer, 1992 WL 52577 (Ohio Ct. App. 11th Dist. Ashtabula County 1992)

69 ALR6th 207—§ 9, 10, 18

State v. Farmer, 1992 WL 52578 (Ohio Ct. App. 11th Dist. Ashtabula County 1992)

69 ALR6th 207—§ 9, 10, 18

State v. Farmer, 1992 WL 52579 (Ohio Ct. App. 11th Dist. Ashtabula County 1992)

69 ALR6th 207—§ 9, 10, 18

State v. Farmer, 1992 WL 52580 (Ohio Ct. App. 11th Dist. Ashtabula County 1992)

69 ALR6th 207—§ 9, 10, 18

State v. Farmer, 1992 WL 52581 (Ohio Ct. App. 11th Dist. Ashtabula County 1992)

69 ALR6th 207—§ 9, 10, 18

State v. Farmer, 1993 WL 247907 (Tenn. Crim. App. 1993)

16 ALR6th 329—§ 15
24 ALR6th 591—§ 10

State v. Farmers Union Grain Co., 80 Wash. App. 287, 908 P.2d 386 (1996)

22 ALR5th 327—§ 77.5

State v. Farnan, 1998 WL 403985 (Wash. Ct. App. Div. 1 1998)

73 ALR5th 383—§ 4

State v. Farner, 66 S.W.3d 188 (Tenn. 2001)

111 ALR5th 529—§ 2, 3, 6
89 ALR6th 565—§ 19, 21

State v. Farner, 2000 WL 872488 (Tenn. Crim. App. 2000)

111 ALR5th 529—§ 2, 6

State v. Farnsworth, 30 Utah 2d 435, 519 P.2d 244 (1974)

37 ALR6th 357—§ 4

State v. Farr, 1992 WL 41284 (Ohio Ct. App. 9th Dist. Summit County 1992)

88 ALR5th 121—§ 2

State v. Farrar, 149 N.C. App. 490, 562 S.E.2d 470 (2002)

3 ALR6th 543—§ 8

State v. Farrell, 209 N.W.2d 103 (Iowa 1973)

31 ALR6th 333—§ 9

State v. Farrell, 223 N.W.2d 270 (Iowa 1974)

31 ALR6th 333—§ 9

State v. Farrell, 1999 WL 812249 (Ohio Ct. App. 2d Dist. Miami County 1999)

38 ALR6th 97—§ 28

State v. Farris, 53 So. 3d 537 (La. Ct. App. 3d Cir. 2010)

103 ALR6th 507—§ 9

State v. Farris, 420 A.2d 928 (Me. 1980)

59 ALR5th 1—§ 4 to 6

State v. Farris, 585 S.W.2d 303 (Mo. Ct. App. W.D. 1979)

70 ALR5th 587—§ 3, 19

State v. Farrugia, 393 So. 2d 614 (Fla. Dist. Ct. App. 1st Dist. 1981)

106 ALR5th 397—§ 4

State v. Farthing, 331 N.J. Super. 58, 751 A.2d 123 (App. Div. 2000)

27 ALR6th 183—§ 31

State v. Fasching, 453 N.W.2d 761 (N.D. 1990)

109 ALR5th 611—§ 2, 3
34 ALR6th 1—§ 11

State v. Fassler, 108 Ariz. 586, 503 P.2d 807 (1972)

62 ALR5th 1—§ 3
122 ALR5th 439—§ 6
55 ALR6th 157—§ 33

State v. Fattorusso, 228 So. 2d 630 (Fla. App. D3 1969)

3 ALR5th 237—§ 3, 8, 12

State v. Faucette, 326 N.C. 676, 392 S.E.2d 71 (1990)

57 ALR5th 141—§ 2, 3

State v. Faulkner, 175 Mo. 546, 75 S.W. 116 (1903)

9 ALR6th 363—§ 43

State v. Faulkner, 1993 WL 125452 (Ohio Ct. App. 2d Dist. Clark County 1993)

43 ALR6th 475—§ 6

State v. Fausel, 295 Conn. 785, 993 A.2d 455 (2010)
  58 ALR6th 499—§ 6
State v. Faust, 254 N.C. 101, 118 S.E.2d 769, 96 A.L.R.2d 1422 (1961)
  54 ALR6th 429—§ 11
State v. Fautenberry, 72 Ohio St. 3d 435, 650 N.E.2d 878 (1995)
  79 ALR5th 33—§ 13, 39, 40
State v. Fauver, 1 Haw. App. 3, 612 P.2d 119 (1980)
  58 ALR6th 499—§ 65
State v. Favoroso, 2007 WL 1814124 (N.J. Super. Ct. App. Div. 2007)
  33 ALR6th 373—§ 17
State v. Favors, 482 N.W.2d 226 (Minn. Ct. App. 1992)
  71 ALR5th 1—§ 59
State v. Fay, 127 N.J.L. 77, 21 A.2d 607 (N.J. Sup. Ct. 1941)
  5 ALR6th 1—§ 63
State v. Fay, 488 N.W.2d 322 (Minn. Ct. App. 1992)
  28 ALR6th 505—§ 8
  59 ALR6th 311—§ 12, 28
State v. Fearing, 30 Md. App. 134, 351 A.2d 896 (1976)
  13 ALR5th 1—§ 2, 20, 23
State v. Fearing, 304 N.C. 471, 284 S.E.2d 487 (1981)
  26 ALR5th 1—§ 3
State v. Fearn, 345 So. 2d 468 (La. 1977)
  62 ALR6th 413—§ 28, 32
State v. Fears, 69 Or. App. 606, 688 P.2d 88 (1984)
  86 ALR5th 59—§ 4, 6
State v. Fears, 86 Ohio St. 3d 329, 1999-Ohio-111, 715 N.E.2d 136 (1999)
  27 ALR6th 183—§ 6
State v. Fears, 1999 WL 1032592 (Ohio Ct. App. 1st Dist. Hamilton County 1999)
  21 ALR6th 1—§ 4
State v. Feaster, 156 N.J. 1, 716 A.2d 395 (1998)
  55 ALR6th 157—§ 5, 77, 99

State v. Featherman, 133 Ariz. 340, 651 P.2d 868 (App. 1982)
  24 ALR5th 465—§ 4, 14, 101 to 103, 107 to 109
State v. Fedak, 9 Haw. App. 98, 825 P.2d 1068 (1992)
  74 ALR5th 319—§ 5, 6, 10
State v. Federici, 179 Conn. 46, 425 A.2d 916 (1979)
  103 ALR6th 347—§ 16
State v. Federico, 103 N.J. 169, 510 A.2d 1147 (1986)
  39 ALR5th 283—§ 4
State v. Fee, 135 Idaho 857, 26 P.3d 40 (Ct. App. 2001)
  115 ALR5th 477—§ 3
  58 ALR6th 499—§ 61
State v. Feemster, 628 S.W.2d 367 (Mo. Ct. App. E.D. 1982)
  103 ALR5th 463—§ 3
State v. Feet, 481 So. 2d 667 (La. Ct. App. 1st Cir. 1985)
  54 ALR6th 429—§ 9
State v. Feintuch, 150 N.J. Super. 414, 375 A.2d 1223 (1977)
  26 ALR5th 1—§ 3, 5
State v. Fekete, 120 N.M. 290, 901 P.2d 708 (1995)
  35 ALR6th 127—§ 5
  45 ALR6th 337—§ 14
State v. Feld, 155 Ariz. 88, 745 P.2d 146, R.I.C.O. Bus. Disp. Guide (CCH) ¶ 7094 (Ct. App. Div. 1 1987)
  58 ALR6th 385—§ 28, 38
State v. Feldman, 254 N.J. Super. 754, 604 A.2d 242 (Law Div. 1992)
  110 ALR5th 213—§ 1
State v. Felger, 19 Or. App. 39, 526 P.2d 611 (1974)
  99 ALR6th 397—§ 17
State v. Feliciano, 901 A.2d 631 (R.I. 2006)
  97 ALR6th 567—§ 3, 8, 9
State v. Felix, 83 P.3d 1270 (Kan. Ct. App. 2004)
  26 ALR6th 511—§ 25

State v. Felix, 410 N.W.2d 398 (Minn. Ct. App. 1987)

73 ALR5th 383—§ 27

State v. Felker, 819 N.E.2d 870 (Ind. Ct. App. 2004)

15 ALR6th 515—§ 17

State v. Fellman, 187 Neb. 767, 193 N.W.2d 775, 50 A.L.R.3d 543 (1972)

79 ALR6th 125—§ 9

State v. Fellows, 84 Wash. App. 1088, 1997 WL 43666 (Div. 1 1997)

73 ALR6th 49—§ 41

State v. Fellows, 588 S.W.2d 211 (Mo. Ct. App. W.D. 1979)

70 ALR5th 587—§ 3

State v. Fellows, 1997 WL 43666 (Wash. Ct. App. Div. 1 1997)

59 ALR5th 615—§ 6, 9

State v. Fellows, 1997 WL 272378 (Ohio Ct. App. 8th Dist. Cuyahoga County 1997)

92 ALR6th 171—§ 4

State v. Felmet, 302 N.C. 173, 273 S.E.2d 708 (1981)

52 ALR5th 195—§ 4

State v. Felson, 299 N.W.2d 918 (Minn. 1980)

41 ALR5th 171—§ 108, 114

State v. Feltes, 51 Iowa 495, 1 N.W. 755 (1879)

82 ALR5th 591—§ 7

State v. Felton, 110 Wis. 2d 485, 329 N.W.2d 161 (1983)

11 ALR5th 871—§ 5

State v. Felton, 204 Wis. 2d 110, 552 N.W.2d 898 (Ct. App. 1996)

90 ALR5th 453—§ 53

State v. Felton, 283 N.C. 368, 196 S.E.2d 239 (1973)

86 ALR5th 59—§ 6

State v. Felton, 330 N.C. 619, 412 S.E.2d 344 (1992)

97 ALR6th 567—§ 3, 5, 9

State v. Felton, 579 S.W.2d 636 (Mo. Ct. App. E.D. 1979)

93 ALR5th 527—§ 20

State v. Feltrop, 803 S.W.2d 1, 11 A.L.R.5th 1111 (Mo. 1991)

11 ALR5th 871—§ 7

83 ALR6th 255—§ 17

State v. Fenn, 41 So. 3d 544 (La. Ct. App. 2d Cir. 2010)

79 ALR6th 1—§ 21, 47

State v. Fenner, 263 N.C. 694, 140 S.E.2d 349 (1965)

66 ALR5th 397—§ 6

State v. Fenney, 448 N.W.2d 54 (Minn. 1989)

22 ALR5th 1—§ 2

State v. Fenton, 19 Ariz. App. 274, 506 P.2d 665 (Div. 2 1973)

103 ALR6th 137—§ 4

State v. Ferdinand, 1979 WL 206795 (Ohio Ct. App. 4th Dist. Scioto County 1979)

99 ALR6th 295—§ 16

State v. Ferdinando, 298 N.C. 737, 260 S.E.2d 423 (1979)

70 ALR6th 361—§ 5

State v. Ferebee, 177 N.C. App. 785, 630 S.E.2d 460 (2006)

30 ALR6th 1—§ 4, 7

State v. Ferebee, 266 N.C. 606, 146 S.E.2d 666 (1966)

59 ALR5th 135—§ 4, 5, 15

State v. Ferebee, 529 S.E.2d 686 (N.C. Ct. App. 2000)

29 ALR5th 487—§ 11

State v. Fergerstrom, 106 Haw. 43, 101 P.3d 652 (Ct. App. 2004)

18 ALR6th 775—§ 5

State v. Ferguson, 2 S.W.3d 912 (Tenn. 1999)

40 ALR5th 113—§ 3, 4

24 ALR6th 1—§ 33

State v. Ferguson, 20 S.W.3d 485 (Mo. 2000)

78 ALR5th 197—§ 3

125 ALR5th 497—§ 4

24 ALR6th 1—§ 51

State v. Ferguson, 41 Ohio App. 3d 306, 535 N.E.2d 708 (10th Dist. Franklin County 1987)

71 ALR6th 335—§ 15
State v. Ferguson, 71 Ohio App. 3d 342, 594 N.E.2d 23 (12th Dist. Butler County 1991)

72 ALR6th 1—§ 4
State v. Ferguson, 76 Wash. App. 560, 886 P.2d 1164 (Div. 1 1995)

57 ALR6th 83—§ 5
State v. Ferguson, 96 Ohio App. 297, 54 Ohio Op. 310, 121 N.E.2d 684 (2d Dist. Franklin County 1954)

102 ALR5th 525—§ 55
State v. Ferguson, 120 Ohio St. 3d 7, 2008-Ohio-4824, 896 N.E.2d 110 (2008)

63 ALR6th 351—§ 3
State v. Ferguson, 138 Wis. 2d 528, 406 N.W.2d 171 (Ct. App. 1987)

35 ALR6th 497—§ 16, 21
State v. Ferguson, 153 Wis. 2d 776, 452 N.W.2d 587 (App. 1989)

7 ALR5th 73—§ 10
State v. Ferguson, 165 Ariz. 275, 798 P.2d 413 (Ct. App. Div. 1 1990)

15 ALR5th 391—§ 13
92 ALR5th 35—§ 7
State v. Ferguson, 244 Wis. 2d 17, 2001 WI App 102, 629 N.W.2d 788 (Ct. App. 2001)

58 ALR6th 499—§ 15
State v. Ferguson, 261 N.C. 558, 135 S.E.2d 626 (1964)

5 ALR5th 243—§ 55
State v. Ferguson, 358 So. 2d 1214 (La. 1978)

65 ALR5th 407—§ 3, 11
State v. Ferguson, 391 N.W.2d 172 (N.D. 1986)

17 ALR5th 851—§ 4
State v. Ferguson, 395 So. 2d 1182 (Fla. App. D4 1981)

46 ALR5th 523—§ 9
State v. Ferguson, 1995 WL 862128 (Del. Super. Ct. 1995)

56 ALR5th 385—§ 2 to 4
State v. Ferguson, 2003-Ohio-866, 2003 WL 548360 (Ohio Ct. App. 3d Dist. Union County 2003)

33 ALR6th 407—§ 5
State v. Fernandez, 89 Wash. App. 292, 948 P.2d 872 (Div. 1 1997)

24 ALR5th 428—§ 4, 19
State v. Fernandez, 712 So. 2d 485 (La. 1998)

34 ALR6th 1—§ 16
State v. Fernando-Granados, 268 Neb. 290, 682 N.W.2d 266 (2004)

49 ALR6th 343—§ 3, 11
State v. Fernando R., 103 Conn. App. 808, 930 A.2d 78 (2007)

28 ALR6th 505—§ 14
State v. Fernane, 185 Ariz. 222, 914 P.2d 1314 (Ct. App. Div. 2 1995)

19 ALR6th 115—§ 4
24 ALR6th 591—§ 4
State v. Fernow, 354 N.W.2d 438 (Minn. 1984)

24 ALR5th 132—§ 5, 7
State v. Ferrara, 176 Conn. 508, 408 A.2d 265 (1979)

12 ALR6th 267—§ 5
State v. Ferrari, 141 N.J. Super. 67, 357 A.2d 286 (App. Div. 1976)

18 ALR6th 1—§ 5, 20
State v. Ferreira, 8 Hawaii App. 1, 791 P.2d 407 (1990)

26 ALR5th 603—§ 4
State v. Ferreira, 152 Ariz. 289, 731 P.2d 1233 (Ct. App. Div. 2 1986)

124 ALR5th 1—§ 5
State v. Ferrell, 41 Or. App. 51, 596 P.2d 1011 (1979)

55 ALR6th 513—§ 5
State v. Ferrell, 191 Conn. 37, 463 A.2d 573, 44 A.L.R.4th 831 (1983)

51 ALR5th 603—§ 3
124 ALR5th 1—§ 3
State v. Ferrell, 399 S.E.2d 834 (W. Va. 1990)

39 ALR5th 283—§ 4, 77
State v. Ferrell, 741 S.W.2d 712 (Mo. App. 1987)

48 ALR5th 555—§ 4
State v. Ferrette, 18 Ohio St. 3d 106, 480 N.E.2d 399 (1985)

51 ALR6th 219—§ 4
State v. Ferrier, 136 Wash. 2d 103, 960 P.2d 927 (1998)
15 ALR6th 515—§ 33, 34
State v. Ferrigno, 5 Conn. Cir. Ct. 468, 256 A.2d 795 (1969)
27 ALR6th 491—§ 4
State v. Ferris, 623 So. 2d 752 (Fla. Dist. Ct. App. 2d Dist. 1993)
67 ALR5th 361—§ 3, 6
State v. Ferris, 1998 WL 568608 (Ohio Ct. App. 12th Dist. Warren County 1998)
78 ALR5th 489—§ 3, 6
State v. Ferrise, 269 N.W.2d 888 (Minn. 1978)
92 ALR6th 171—§ 4
State v. Ferro, 64 Wash. App. 181, 824 P.2d 500 (Div. 3 1992)
60 ALR5th 1—§ 2, 8
State v. Fertig, 143 N.J. 115, 668 A.2d 1076 (1996)
16 ALR5th 841—§ 3
State v. Fertterer, 255 Mont. 73, 841 P.2d 467 (1992)
15 ALR5th 391—§ 11, 53
92 ALR5th 35—§ 21
State v. Fett, 414 N.W.2d 783 (Minn. Ct. App. 1987)
73 ALR5th 383—§ 3
State v. Fetterly, 137 Idaho 729, 52 P.3d 874 (2002)
110 ALR5th 1—§ 19
State v. Fetterly, 254 Or. 47, 456 P.2d 996 (1969)
72 ALR5th 607—§ 3
State v. Fettis, 136 Ariz. 58, 664 P.2d 208 (1983)
59 ALR5th 135—§ 3, 8
State v. Fick, 204 Kan. 422, 464 P.2d 271 (1970)
108 ALR5th 593—§ 37
State v. Field, 132 N.H. 760, 571 A.2d 1276 (1990)
92 ALR6th 1—§ 3
State v. Fielder, 210 Mo. 188, 109 S.W. 580 (1908)

5 ALR6th 1—§ 62
State v. Fielder, 1997 WL 638280 (Ohio Ct. App. 3d Dist. Union County 1997)
78 ALR5th 489—§ 10
State v. Fielding, 135 Iowa 255, 112 N.W. 539 (1907)
24 ALR5th 465—§ 40
State v. Fielding, 862 So. 2d 420 (La. Ct. App. 2d Cir. 2003)
99 ALR6th 397—§ 5
State v. Fields, 8 Tenn. 137, Mart. & Yer. 137, 1827 WL 637 (Ct. Err. & App. 1827)
102 ALR5th 525—§ 22
State v. Fields, 31 Conn. App. 312, 624 A.2d 1165 (1993)
102 ALR6th 365—§ 13
State v. Fields, 67 Haw. 268, 686 P.2d 1379 (1984)
99 ALR5th 557—§ 9, 10, 12
State v. Fields, 77 N.J. 282, 390 A.2d 574 (1978)
43 ALR5th 777—§ 3
State v. Fields, 115 Haw. 503, 168 P.3d 955 (2007)
30 ALR6th 1—§ 3, 4
State v. Fields, 127 Idaho 904, 908 P.2d 1211 (1995)
72 ALR5th 403—§ 12
State v. Fields, 128 Wash. App. 1037, 2005 WL 1622314 (Div. 2 2005)
73 ALR6th 49—§ 50
State v. Fields, 191 Or. App. 127, 79 P.3d 915 (2003)
125 ALR5th 537—§ 36
State v. Fields, 294 N.W.2d 404 (N.D. 1980)
30 ALR6th 103—§ 8, 12, 19, 25, 34
State v. Fields, 434 S.W.2d 507 (Mo. 1968)
81 ALR5th 563—§ 3, 5, 8, 9
State v. Fields, 602 So. 2d 981 (Fla. Dist. Ct. App. 3d Dist. 1992)
113 ALR5th 597—§ 8
State v. Fields, 1991 WL 35747 (Tenn. Crim. App. 1991)

102 ALR6th 279—§ 6, 14
State v. Fields, 1991 WL 262888 (Ohio Ct. App. 9th Dist. Lorain County 1991)
98 ALR6th 455—§ 24
State v. Fields, 1992 WL 41912 (Ohio Ct. App. 8th Dist. Cuyahoga County 1992)
19 ALR6th 697—§ 4
State v. Fields, 2002-Ohio-4451, 2002 WL 1988273 (Ohio Ct. App. 1st Dist. Hamilton County 2002)
4 ALR6th 577—§ 6
State v. Fields, 2003 ND 81, 662 N.W.2d 242 (N.D. 2003)
12 ALR6th 553—§ 11, 24
State v. Fierro, 107 Ariz. 479, 489 P.2d 713 (1971)
87 ALR5th 181—§ 5
55 ALR6th 157—§ 26
State v. Fierro, 124 Ariz. 182, 603 P.2d 74 (1979)
50 ALR5th 467—§ 9
State v. Figaroa, 3 Haw. App. 377, 650 P.2d 1373 (1982)
18 ALR6th 1—§ 2, 5, 37
State v. Figueroa, 122 Ariz. 190, 593 P.2d 940 (Ct. App. Div. 1 1979)
119 ALR5th 275—§ 7
State v. Figueroa, 212 N.J. Super. 343, 515 A.2d 242 (App. Div. 1986)
30 ALR6th 103—§ 42
State v. Figueroa, Slip Op. 51587 (Ohio App. Cuyahoga Co. 1987)
38 ALR5th 433—§ 3
State v. Figured, 116 N.C. App. 1, 446 S.E.2d 838 (1994)
38 ALR5th 433—§ 5, 7
State v. File, No. 41724 (November 18, 1980, Ct. App. Ohio, 8th App. Dist. Cuyahoga Co.)
39 ALR5th 283—§ 14, 76
State v. Filiaggi, 86 Ohio St. 3d 230, 1999-Ohio-99, 714 N.E.2d 867 (1999)
71 ALR6th 625—§ 40
State v. Filiaggi, 86 Ohio St. 3d 230, 1999 WL 562106 (1999)

72 ALR5th 403—§ 15
State v. Fillmore, 187 Ariz. 174, 927 P.2d 1303 (Ct. App. Div. 1 1996)
71 ALR6th 1—§ 4
State v. Fimbres, 222 Ariz. 293, 213 P.3d 1020 (Ct. App. Div. 2 2009)
68 ALR6th 527—§ 42
87 ALR6th 1—§ 41
State v. Final Exit Network, Inc., 41 Media L. Rep. (BNA) 2549, 2013 WL 5418170 (Minn. Ct. App. 2013)
96 ALR6th 475—§ 3, 9
State v. Finbraaten, 363 N.W.2d 473 (Minn. Ct. App. 1985)
73 ALR5th 383—§ 3
State v. Finch, 68 P.3d 123 (Ariz. 2003)
110 ALR5th 1—§ 18
State v. Finch, 137 Wash. 2d 792, 975 P.2d 967 (1999)
56 ALR5th 385—§ 3
State v. Finch, 153 Vt. 216, 569 A.2d 494 (1989)
21 ALR6th 771—§ 4
State v. Finch, 674 N.W.2d 682 (Iowa Ct. App. 2003)
92 ALR6th 171—§ 8
State v. Finch, 1995 WL 334350 (Tenn. Crim. App. 1995)
83 ALR5th 277—§ 9
84 ALR5th 487—§ 21
State v. Finder, 12 S.D. 423, 81 N.W. 959 (1900)
45 ALR5th 591—§ 11
State v. Findley, 1983 WL 4837 (Ohio Ct. App. 2d Dist. Montgomery County 1983)
116 ALR5th 373—§ 3, 6
State v. Findley, 1995 WL 105313 (Tenn. Crim. App. 1995)
64 ALR5th 637—§ 3
State v. Finehout, 136 Ariz. 226, 665 P.2d 570 (1983)
124 ALR5th 1—§ 5
State v. Finfrock, 1998 WL 726478 (Ohio Ct. App. 2d Dist. Montgomery County 1998)
29 ALR6th 237—§ 24

State v. Fingers, 564 S.W.2d 579 (Mo. Ct. App. 1978)

67 ALR6th 341—§ 7

State v. Fink, 92 N.C. App. 523, 375 S.E.2d 303 (1989)

115 ALR5th 403—§ 5

State v. Fink, 557 So. 2d 129 (Fla. Dist. Ct. App. 3d Dist. 1990)

113 ALR5th 597—§ 8

State v. Finlayson, 956 P.2d 283 (Utah Ct. App. 1998)

39 ALR5th 283—§ 41, 47

State v. Finlayson, 2000 UT 10, 994 P.2d 1243 (Utah 2000)

39 ALR5th 283—§ 4, 43

State v. Finley, 85 Ariz. 327, 338 P.2d 790 (1959)

86 ALR5th 59—§ 4

State v. Finley, 118 N.C. 1162, 24 S.E. 495 (1896)

16 ALR6th 329—§ 6

24 ALR6th 591—§ 6

State v. Finley, 136 S.W.3d 823 (Mo. Ct. App. E.D. 2004)

52 ALR6th 1—§ 5

State v. Finley, 219 W. Va. 747, 639 S.E.2d 839 (2006)

99 ALR6th 295—§ 22

State v. Finley, 273 Kan. 237, 42 P.3d 723 (2002)

55 ALR6th 391—§ 22

State v. Finley, 277 S.C. 548, 290 S.E.2d 808 (1982)

51 ALR6th 1—§ 20

State v. Finley, 1991 WL 130401 (Tenn. Crim. App. 1991)

57 ALR5th 141—§ 12

State v. Finnegan, 232 Neb. 75, 439 N.W.2d 496 (1989)

99 ALR5th 557—§ 3

State v. Finnegan, 1998 WL 401809 (Ohio Ct. App. 5th Dist. Licking County 1998)

84 ALR6th 293—§ 31

State v. Finney, 141 Kan. 12, 40 P.2d 411 (1935)

103 ALR6th 35—§ 25

State v. Finney, 1982 WL 5188 (Ohio Ct. App. 9th Dist. Summit County 1982)

51 ALR6th 219—§ 6

State v. Finster, 985 S.W.2d 881 (Mo. Ct. App. S.D. 1999)

45 ALR5th 591—§ 3

State v. Fiocchi, 17 Conn. App. 326, 553 A.2d 181 (1989)

28 ALR6th 505—§ 9

State v. Fioravanti, 46 N.J. 109, 215 A.2d 16 (1965)

29 ALR5th 59—§ 7, 47, 62

State v. First Nat. Bank, 629 P.2d 78 (Alaska 1981)

18 ALR5th 307—§ 3, 7, 35

State v. First Nat'l Bank, 273 Ala. 379, 141 So. 2d 196 (1962)

33 ALR5th 509—§ 11

State v. Fischer, 140 N.W.2d 192 (Iowa 1966)

89 ALR6th 565—§ 13

State v. Fischer, 270 S.C. 402, 242 S.E.2d 437 (1978)

26 ALR5th 378—§ 7

State v. Fischer, 1999 WL 1068064 (Ohio Ct. App. 8th Dist. Cuyahoga County 1999)

78 ALR5th 489—§ 6

State v. Fischer, 2010-Ohio-6238, 2010 WL 5349851 (Ohio 2010)

64 ALR6th 1—§ 19

State v. Fish, 102 N.M. 775, 701 P.2d 374 (App. 1985)

28 ALR5th 754—§ 2, 6

State v. Fish, 782 So. 2d 1087 (La. Ct. App. 5th Cir. 2001)

7 ALR5th 263—§ 5

State v. Fisher, 32 Or. App. 465, 574 P.2d 354 (1978)

99 ALR5th 557—§ 10

State v. Fisher, 96 Wash. 2d 962, 639 P.2d 743 (1982)

112 ALR5th 429—§ 13

State v. Fisher, 108 Wash. 2d 419, 739 P.2d 683 (1987)

73 ALR5th 383—§ 5, 6

State v. Fisher, 123 W. Va. 745, 18 S.E.2d 649 (1941)

97 ALR5th 293—§ 3, 5

State v. Fisher, 132 Wash. App. 26, 130 P.3d 382 (Div. 1 2006)

33 ALR6th 293—§ 5

State v. Fisher, 141 Ariz. 227, 686 P.2d 750 (1984)

58 ALR6th 499—§ 26, 54

State v. Fisher, 156 N.J. 494, 721 A.2d 291 (1998)

71 ALR6th 1—§ 16

State v. Fisher, 158 N.C. App. 133, 580 S.E.2d 405 (2003)

38 ALR6th 97—§ 17, 19

State v. Fisher, 226 Ariz. 563, 250 P.3d 1192, 79 A.L.R.6th 665 (2011)

79 ALR6th 1—§ 8, 11, 42, 84

State v. Fisher, 257 Kan. 65, 891 P.2d 1065 (1995)

39 ALR5th 283—§ 4, 18

State v. Fisher, 285 Wis. 2d 433, 2005 WI App 175, 702 N.W.2d 56 (Ct. App. 2005)

46 ALR6th 241—§ 11, 25, 27

State v. Fisher, 305 N.J. Super. 216, 701 A.2d 1314 (App. Div. 1997)

105 ALR5th 529—§ 31

State v. Fisher, 336 N.C. 684, 445 S.E.2d 866 (1994)

79 ALR5th 33—§ 68

State v. Fisher, 351 N.W.2d 798 (Iowa 1984)

71 ALR5th 1—§ 2, 6

State v. Fisher, 380 So. 2d 1340 (La. 1980)

28 ALR6th 505—§ 9

State v. Fisher, 570 So. 2d 546 (La. App. 4th Cir. 1990)

7 ALR5th 263—§ 7

State v. Fisher, 591 So. 2d 1049 (Fla. Dist. Ct. App. 5th Dist. 1991)

62 ALR5th 1—§ 3, 15

State v. Fisher, 669 So. 2d 460 (La. Ct. App. 1st Cir. 1995)

88 ALR5th 121—§ 2

State v. Fisher, 670 S.W.2d 232 (Tenn. Crim. App. 1983)

86 ALR5th 59—§ 5

State v. Fisher, 700 So. 2d 1253 (Fla. Dist. Ct. App. 4th Dist. 1997)

113 ALR5th 597—§ 8

State v. Fisher, 901 A.2d 120 (Del. 2006)

39 ALR6th 577—§ 10

State v. Fisher, 1987 WL 11673 (Ohio Ct. App. 8th Dist. Cuyahoga County 1987)

78 ALR5th 567—§ 3

State v. Fisher, 1996 WL 659471 (Del. Super. Ct. 1996)

107 ALR5th 311—§ 9

State v. Fisher, 2002 WL 1425389 (Minn. Ct. App. 2002)

106 ALR5th 377—§ 3, 4

State v. Fisher, 2006 WI 44, 290 Wis. 2d 121, 714 N.W.2d 495 (2006)

33 ALR6th 407—§ 6

State v. Fisher, 2007-Ohio-4820, 2007 WL 2713852 (Ohio Ct. App. 5th Dist. Stark County 2007)

67 ALR6th 531—§ 29

State v. Fisk, 165 Vt. 260, 682 A.2d 937 (1996)

9 ALR6th 633—§ 5, 13

10 ALR6th 265—§ 4

State v. Fitanides, 139 N.H. 425, 655 A.2d 411 (1995)

48 ALR5th 659—§ 7, 17

State v. Fitch, 65 Nev. 668, 200 P.2d 991 (1948)

24 ALR6th 747—§ 3

State v. Fitch, 255 Neb. 108, 582 N.W.2d 342 (1998)

41 ALR5th 171—§ 23, 122

State v. Fitzgerald, 14 Or. App. 361, 513 P.2d 817 (1973)

54 ALR5th 141—§ 3, 10

State v. Fitzgerald, 19 Or. App. 860, 530 P.2d 553 (1974)

61 ALR5th 1—§ 3, 12

State v. Fitzgerald, 39 Wash. App. 652, 694 P.2d 1117 (1985)

38 ALR5th 433—§ 11, 19

State v. Fitzgerald, 63 So. 3d 75 (Fla. 2d DCA 2011)

92 ALR6th 295—§ 8, 9, 14
96 ALR6th 355—§ 6, 19, 36, 37

State v. Fitzgerald, 130 Mo. 407, 32 S.W. 1113 (1895)

10 ALR5th 700—§ 5

State v. Fitzgerald, 562 N.W.2d 288 (Minn. 1997)

58 ALR6th 499—§ 94

State v. Fitzgerald, 778 S.W.2d 689 (Mo. App. 1989)

5 ALR5th 243—§ 2, 13

State v. Fitzgerald, 2002-Ohio-3914, 2002 WL 1770487 (Ohio Ct. App. 2d Dist. Greene County 2002)

71 ALR6th 1—§ 14

State v. Fitzgerald, 2006-Ohio-6575, 2006 WL 3634586 (Ohio Ct. App. 8th Dist. Cuyahoga County 2006)

33 ALR6th 91—§ 45

State v. Fitzgerald, 2007 WL 461314 (N.J. Super. Ct. App. Div. 2007)

26 ALR6th 511—§ 4

State v. Fitzgibbon, 114 Or. App. 581, 836 P.2d 154 (1992)

11 ALR6th 237—§ 3, 8

State v. Fitzpatrick, 5 Wash. App. 661, 491 P.2d 262 (Div. 2 1971)

105 ALR5th 499—§ 4

State v. Fitzpatrick, 76 Ohio App. 3d 149, 601 N.E.2d 160 (8th Dist. Cuyahoga County 1991)

92 ALR5th 35—§ 2, 21

State v. Fitzpatrick, 186 Mont. 187, 606 P.2d 1343 (1980)

3 ALR6th 269—§ 23

State v. Fitzpatrick, 193 S.W.3d 280 (Mo. Ct. App. W.D. 2006)

38 ALR6th 97—§ 27

State v. Fitzpatrick, 211 Mont. 341, 684 P.2d 1112 (1984)

21 ALR6th 1—§ 6
63 ALR6th 1—§ 8, 46

State v. Fitzpatrick, 464 So. 2d 1185, 10 FLW 141 (Fla. 1985)

42 ALR5th 581—§ 4

State v. Fitzpatrick, 1994 WL 380992 (Del. Super. Ct. 1994)

47 ALR6th 423—§ 3

State v. Fitzpatrick, 2004-Ohio-5615, 2004 WL 2367987 (Ohio Ct. App. 1st Dist. Hamilton County 2004)

21 ALR6th 1—§ 4
71 ALR6th 625—§ 12

State v. Fitzsimmons, 93 Wash. 2d 436, 610 P.2d 893, 18 A.L.R.4th 690 (1980)

109 ALR5th 611—§ 3

State v. Fixley, 118 Kan. 1, 233 P. 796 (1925)

81 ALR5th 563—§ 3, 8

State v. Flagg, 154 N.H. 690, 918 A.2d 1286 (2007)

55 ALR6th 391—§ 24

State v. Flagg, 760 So. 2d 522 (La. Ct. App. 5th Cir. 2000)

17 ALR6th 327—§ 7

State v. Flaherty, 23 N.D. 313, 136 N.W. 76 (1912)

120 ALR5th 125—§ 2, 3, 5, 8
121 ALR5th 1—§ 2
48 ALR6th 181—§ 4

State v. Flanagan, 2003 MT 123, 316 Mont. 1, 68 P.3d 796 (2003)

46 ALR6th 241—§ 6

State v. Fleck, 763 N.W.2d 39 (Minn. Ct. App. 2009)

92 ALR6th 295—§ 7

State v. Fleck, 777 N.W.2d 233 (Minn. 2010)

92 ALR6th 295—§ 8, 14, 19, 25
93 ALR6th 207—§ 17, 31
94 ALR6th 191—§ 4
95 ALR6th 1—§ 5
96 ALR6th 355—§ 5, 21, 36, 52, 60

State v. Flegel, 485 N.W.2d 210 (S.D. 1992)

58 ALR6th 499—§ 87

State v. Fleming, 52 N.C. App. 563, 279 S.E.2d 29 (1981)

108 ALR5th 593—§ 50

State v. Fleming, 75 Wash. App. 270, 877 P.2d 243 (1994)

15 ALR5th 391—§ 7

State v. Fleming, 125 N.H. 238, 480 A.2d 107 (1984)

15 ALR5th 391—§ 31

State v. Fleming, 159 Or. App. 565, 979 P.2d 771 (1999)

42 ALR5th 291—§ 7

State v. Fleming, 181 Wis. 2d 546, 510 N.W.2d 837 (Ct. App. 1993)

121 ALR5th 551—§ 2, 5, 12

State v. Fleming, 223 Neb. 169, 388 N.W.2d 497 (1986)

84 ALR5th 487—§ 20

State v. Fleming, 254 S.C. 415, 175 S.E.2d 624 (1970)

36 ALR5th 255—§ 32

State v. Fleming, 574 So. 2d 486 (La. Ct. App. 4th Cir. 1991)

16 ALR6th 329—§ 4

24 ALR6th 591—§ 4, 6, 14

State v. Fleming, 2001-Ohio-1497, 2001 WL 871397 (Ohio Ct. App. 2d Dist. Montgomery County 2001)

3 ALR6th 543—§ 9

State v. Fleming, 2005 WI App 254, 288 Wis. 2d 460, 706 N.W.2d 703 (Ct. App. 2005)

84 ALR6th 293—§ 33

State v. Flemming, 1 Neb. App. 12, 487 N.W.2d 564 (1992)

41 ALR5th 171—§ 26

113 ALR5th 517—§ 3

State v. Flemming, 19 S.W.3d 195 (Tenn. 2000)

19 ALR5th 823—§ 3

67 ALR6th 103—§ 8

State v. Flemming, 133 Wash. App. 1001, 2006 WL 1401642 (Div. 2 2006)

26 ALR6th 511—§ 26

State v. Flemming, 409 A.2d 220 (Me. 1979)

54 ALR5th 141—§ 11

State v. Flenoid, 838 S.W.2d 462 (Mo. App. 1992)

41 ALR5th 171—§ 132

State v. Flenoy, 1983 WL 3079 (Ohio Ct. App. 8th Dist.Cuyahoga County 1983)

57 ALR5th 141—§ 11

State v. Flenoy, 1993 WL 497082 (Ohio Ct. App. 8th Dist. Cuyahoga County 1993)

99 ALR6th 295—§ 19

State v. Fleshman, 1992 WL 52582 (Ohio Ct. App. 11th Dist. Ashtabula County 1992)

69 ALR6th 207—§ 9, 10, 18

State v. Fletcher, 24 Or. 295, 33 P. 575 (1893)

11 ALR5th 831—§ 5, 6, 13

State v. Fletcher, 26 Ohio St. 2d 221, 55 Ohio Op. 2d 464, 271 N.E.2d 567 (1971)

97 ALR5th 201—§ 3

State v. Fletcher, 197 Wis. 2d 118, 541 N.W.2d 839 (Ct. App. 1995)

88 ALR5th 121—§ 28

State v. Fletcher, 279 N.C. 85, 181 S.E.2d 405 (1971)

29 ALR6th 1—§ 18

State v. Fletcher, 288 A.2d 92 (Me. 1972)

103 ALR6th 347—§ 9, 14

State v. Fletcher, 341 So. 2d 340 (La. 1976)

62 ALR5th 121—§ 6

State v. Fletcher, 709 S.W.2d 924 (Mo. Ct. App. S.D. 1986)

103 ALR6th 507—§ 33

State v. Fletcher, 789 S.W.2d 565 (Tenn. Crim. App. 1990)

85 ALR5th 1—§ 26

State v. Fletcher, 1999 WL 417829 (Conn. Super. Ct. 1999)

17 ALR6th 327—§ 7

State v. Fletcher, No. 52906 (November 25, 1987, Ct. App. Ohio, 8th App. Dist. Cuyahoga Co.)

39 ALR5th 283—§ 14, 57

State v. Flett, 40 Wash. App. 277, 699 P.2d 774 (Div. 3 1985)

57 ALR5th 141—§ 7

State v. Flieger, 91 Wash. App. 236, 955 P.2d 872 (Div. 3 1998)

71 ALR6th 625—§ 6, 10, 11, 30

State v. Flint, 4 Wash. App. 545, 483 P.2d 170 (1971)

29 ALR5th 59—§ 7, 29

State v. Flint, 171 W. Va. 676, 301 S.E.2d 765 (1983)

85 ALR5th 547—§ 7

State v. Flint, 222 P.3d 1019 (Kan. Ct. App. 2010)

64 ALR6th 131—§ 26

State v. Flood, 301 So. 2d 637 (La. 1974)

77 ALR5th 201—§ 3, 10, 14

78 ALR5th 1—§ 13, 41

State v. Floody, 481 N.W.2d 242 (S.D. 1992)

83 ALR5th 541—§ 3, 4

85 ALR5th 595—§ 5

State v. Flora, 68 Wash. App. 802, 845 P.2d 1355 (Div. 1 1992)

84 ALR6th 89—§ 9

State v. Floray, 715 A.2d 855 (Del. Super. Ct. 1997)

85 ALR5th 595—§ 4

90 ALR5th 453—§ 7

State v. Florczak, 76 Wash. App. 55, 882 P.2d 199 (1994)

38 ALR5th 433—§ 7

State v. Florence, 306 Minn. 442, 239 N.W.2d 892 (1976)

49 ALR5th 639—§ 4

State v. Florence, 2005-Ohio-4508, 2005 WL 2083079 (Ohio Ct. App. 2d Dist. Montgomery County 2005)

7 ALR6th 233—§ 9

30 ALR6th 1—§ 4, 7

State v. Flores, 134 Wash. App. 1024, 2006 WL 2130668 (Div. 3 2006)

26 ALR6th 511—§ 35

State v. Flores, 170 Wis. 2d 272, 488 N.W.2d 116 (Ct. App. 1992)

71 ALR6th 249—§ 8

State v. Flores, 207 Or. App. 49, 139 P.3d 974 (2006)

26 ALR6th 511—§ 27

State v. Flores, 218 Ariz. 407, 188 P.3d 706 (Ct. App. Div. 1 2008)

75 ALR6th 541—§ 3, 7

State v. Flores, 714 A.2d 581 (R.I. 1998)

36 ALR5th 161—§ 27

State v. Flores, 1989 WL 62931 (Ohio App. 4 Dist. 1989)

54 ALR5th 141—§ 10

State v. Flores, 1998 M.T. 328, 292 Mont. 255, 974 P.2d 124 (1998)

5 ALR5th 243—§ 35

State v. Flores, 1999 WL 126705 (Ariz. Ct. App. Div. 1 1999)

68 ALR5th 343—§ 3, 16

State v. Flores, 2005 WI App 233, 287 Wis. 2d 827, 705 N.W.2d 905 (Ct. App. 2005)

80 ALR6th 239—§ 3, 17

State v. Florian, 108 Ohio Misc. 2d 32, 738 N.E.2d 901 (Mun. Ct. 2000)

84 ALR6th 293—§ 16

State v. Flors, 38 Ohio App. 3d 133, 528 N.E.2d 950 (8th Dist.Cuyahoga County 1987)

57 ALR5th 141—§ 11

State v. Flournoy, 535 N.W.2d 354 (Minn. 1995)

60 ALR5th 39—§ 3 to 5, 7, 8, 11, 13

State v. Flowers, 86 P.3d 1025 (Kan. Ct. App. 2004)

37 ALR6th 357—§ 59

State v. Flowers, 100 N.C. App. 58, 394 S.E.2d 296 (1990)

73 ALR5th 383—§ 3

State v. Flowers, 316 A.2d 564 (Del. Super. Ct. 1973)

51 ALR5th 603—§ 2

State v. Flowers, 347 N.C. 1, 489 S.E.2d 391 (1997)

83 ALR6th 255—§ 9

State v. Flowers, 2009-Ohio-4876, 2009 WL 2963757 (Ohio Ct. App. 8th Dist. Cuyahoga County 2009)

99 ALR6th 295—§ 13

State v. Floyd, 116 N.H. 632, 365 A.2d 738 (1976)

61 ALR5th 1—§ 4, 14

State v. Floyd, 253 Conn. 700, 756 A.2d
799 (2000)
12 ALR6th 267—§ 8
State v. Floyd, 510 So. 2d 1180 (Fla.
Dist. Ct. App. 4th Dist. 1987)
47 ALR6th 107—§ 23, 44
State v. Floyd, 847 S.W.2d 97 (Mo. Ct.
App. W.D. 1992)
9 ALR6th 1—§ 17
32 ALR6th 1—§ 5
State v. Floyd, 1978 WL 215819 (Ohio
Ct. App. 11th Dist. Trumbull
County 1978)
42 ALR6th 237—§ 13
State v. Floyd, 2006 WL 2059285 (N.J.
Super. Ct. App. Div. 2006)
62 ALR6th 413—§ 35
State v. Fluellen, 626 S.W.2d 299 (Tenn.
Crim. App. 1981)
83 ALR5th 277—§ 11
State v. Flye, 201 Neb. 115, 266 N.W.2d
237 (1978)
70 ALR5th 1—§ 8
State v. Flying Horse, 455 N.W.2d 605
(S.D. 1990)
37 ALR5th 703—§ 3
State v. Flynn, 107 Idaho 206, 687 P.2d
596 (App. 1984)
6 ALR5th 733—§ 2, 4, 16
State v. Flynn, 109 Ariz. 545, 514 P.2d
466 (1973)
55 ALR5th 423—§ 3
State v. Flynn, 123 N.H. 457, 464 A.2d
268, 43 A.L.R.4th 1145 (1983)
33 ALR5th 453—§ 2, 11
State v. Fodor, 179 Ariz. 442, 880 P.2d
662 (Ct. App. Div. 1 1994)
9 ALR6th 363—§ 46
State v. Foell, 512 N.W.2d 809 (Iowa Ct.
App. 1993)
29 ALR6th 1—§ 10
State v. Fogarty, 128 N.J. 59, 607 A.2d
624 (1992)
18 ALR5th 1—§ 39
State v. Fogarty, 187 Mont. 393, 610
P.2d 140 (1980)
99 ALR5th 557—§ 10

State v. Foisy, 384 A.2d 42 (Me. 1978)
92 ALR6th 1—§ 3
State v. Folck, 325 N.W.2d 368 (Iowa
1982)
39 ALR5th 283—§ 10, 58
State v. Foley, 153 Wis. 2d 748, 451
N.W.2d 796 (App. 1989)
15 ALR5th 391—§ 45
State v. Foley, 448 So. 2d 731 (La. Ct.
App. 5th Cir. 1984)
124 ALR5th 1—§ 3
State v. Folk, 74 Ohio App. 3d 468, 599
N.E.2d 334 (2d Dist. Montgomery
County 1991)
67 ALR5th 361—§ 2 to 4, 6, 11
State v. Folk, 238 Ga. App. 206, 521
S.E.2d 194 (1999)
114 ALR5th 173—§ 2, 8, 9
State v. Folkens, 281 N.W.2d 1 (Iowa
1979)
68 ALR5th 343—§ 3, 5
State v. Follansbee, 2009 WL 2263304
(Ariz. Ct. App. Div. 1 2009)
98 ALR6th 455—§ 6
State v. Fong Loon, 29 Idaho 248, 158
P. 233 (1916)
97 ALR6th 567—§ 4, 10
State v. Fonseca, 124 Ohio App. 3d 231,
705 N.E.2d 1278 (11th Dist. Lake
County 1997)
32 ALR5th 149—§ 4, 26
State v. Fonseca, 670 A.2d 1237 (R.I.
1996)
29 ALR5th 487—§ 3
State v. Fontaine, 711 A.2d 667 (Vt.
1998)
15 ALR5th 391—§ 33
State v. Fonte, 2005 WI 77, 281 Wis. 2d
654, 698 N.W.2d 594 (2005)
47 ALR6th 107—§ 5, 45, 54
State v. Fontenette, 1991 WL 184324
(Ohio Ct. App. 8th Dist. Cuyahoga
County 1991)
77 ALR5th 201—§ 21
78 ALR5th 1—§ 21
State v. Fontenot, 356 So. 2d 1385 (La.
1978)

4 ALR5th 1—§ 2, 4, 10
State v. Forrester, 130 Or. App. 459, 882
P.2d 1124 (1994)
92 ALR5th 35—§ 23
State v. Forrester, 134 Ariz. 444, 657
P.2d 432 (Ct. App. Div. 1 1982)
68 ALR6th 527—§ 4
State v. Forrester, 135 Wash. App. 195,
143 P.3d 880 (Div. 2 2006)
26 ALR6th 511—§ 41
State v. Forrester, 1998 WL 46653 (Ohio
Ct. App. 2d Dist. Greene County
1998)
65 ALR5th 407—§ 3
State v. Forshey, 182 W. Va. 87, 386
S.E.2d 15 (1989)
67 ALR6th 531—§ 17, 19, 21, 23, 33
State v. Forsyth, 20 Or. App. 624, 533
P.2d 176 (1975)
93 ALR5th 327—§ 32
State v. Forsyth, 560 P.2d 337 (Utah
1977)
31 ALR6th 49—§ 4
State v. Forsyth, 2004 ME 116, 859 A.2d
163 (Me. 2004)
58 ALR6th 215—§ 4
State v. Fort, 1990 WL 61716 (Ohio Ct.
App. 8th Dist.Cuyahoga County
1990)
57 ALR5th 141—§ 2, 9
State v. Fort, 2014-Ohio-3412, 17
N.E.3d 1172 (Ohio Ct. App. 8th
Dist. Cuyahoga County 2014)
101 ALR6th 1—§ 31
State v. Forte, 360 N.C. 427, 629 S.E.2d
137 (2006)
30 ALR6th 1—§ 4, 7
State v. Fortenberry, 307 So. 2d 296 (La.
1975)
36 ALR5th 255—§ 4
70 ALR5th 587—§ 3
State v. Fortier, 756 So. 2d 455 (La. Ct.
App. 4th Cir. 2000)
71 ALR6th 1—§ 5
State v. Fortin, 124 Idaho 323, 859 P.2d
359 (App. 1993)
15 ALR5th 391—§ 15

State v. Fortin, 178 N.J. 540, 843 A.2d
974 (2004)
1 ALR6th 657—§ 5
State v. Fortin, 632 A.2d 437 (Me. 1993)
84 ALR6th 293—§ 35
State v. Fortino, 837 So. 2d 684 (La. Ct.
App. 5th Cir. 2002)
11 ALR6th 237—§ 13
State v. Fortman, 1998 WL 135811
(Ohio Ct. App. 2d Dist. Montgom-
ery County 1998)
78 ALR5th 489—§ 3
State v. Fortner, 387 S.E.2d 812 (W. Va.
1989)
39 ALR5th 283—§ 4, 67
State v. Fortt, 2002 WL 387224 (Del.
Super. Ct. 2002)
71 ALR6th 1—§ 5
State v. Fortune in Motion, Inc., 214
Wis. 2d 148, 570 N.W.2d 875 (Ct.
App. 1997)
48 ALR6th 511—§ 24
State v. Fortuny, 42 P.3d 1147 (Alaska
Ct. App. 2002)
46 ALR6th 63—§ 3, 8
State v. Forty Three Thousand Dollars
And No Cents ($43,000.00) In Cas-
hier's Checks, 214 W. Va. 650, 591
S.E.2d 208 (2003)
34 ALR6th 539—§ 9
State v. Forty Three Thousand Dollars
And No Cents ($43,000.00) In Cas-
hier's Checks, 214 W. Va. 650, 591
S.E.2d 208 (2003)
101 ALR6th 1—§ 3, 7, 16, 30, 32, 36
State v. Fossett, 253 Ga. App. 791, 560
S.E.2d 351 (2002)
106 ALR5th 397—§ 4
State v. Fossett, 253 Ga. App. 791, 560
S.E.2d 351, 114 A.L.R.5th 739
(2002)
114 ALR5th 235—§ 11
State v. Foster, 45 Conn. App. 369, 696
A.2d 1003 (1997)
29 ALR5th 59—§ 62
State v. Foster, 81 Wash. App. 508, 915
P.2d 567 (Div. 1 1996)
87 ALR5th 631—§ 24

State v. Foster, 107 Or. App. 481, 812
P.2d 440 (1991)
  70 ALR6th 361—§ 9
State v. Foster, 109 Ohio St. 3d 1, 2006-
Ohio-856, 845 N.E.2d 470 (2006)
  26 ALR6th 511—§ 18 to 20, 35
State v. Foster, 158 N.C. App. 313, 580
S.E.2d 431 (2003)
  34 ALR6th 1—§ 10
State v. Foster, 164 La. 813, 114 So. 696
(1927)
  23 ALR6th 1—§ 15
State v. Foster, 198 Kan. 52, 422 P.2d
964 (1967)
  76 ALR5th 1—§ 23
State v. Foster, 230 Neb. 607, 433
N.W.2d 167 (1988)
  5 ALR5th 243—§ 2, 62
State v. Foster, 258 Conn. 501, 782 A.2d
98 (2001)
  92 ALR6th 1—§ 3, 9
State v. Foster, 284 N.C. 259, 200 S.E.2d
782 (1973)
  116 ALR5th 373—§ 3, 11
State v. Foster, 288 Or. 649, 607 P.2d
173 (1980)
  124 ALR5th 1—§ 5
State v. Foster, 290 Kan. 696, 233 P.3d
265, 103 A.L.R.6th 651 (2010)
  103 ALR6th 35—§ 4, 6
State v. Foster, 437 So. 2d 309 (La. Ct.
App. 2d Cir. 1983)
  9 ALR6th 1—§ 17
State v. Foster, 490 S.W.2d 659 (Mo. Ct.
App. 1973)
  36 ALR5th 255—§ 2
  78 ALR5th 1—§ 31
State v. Foster, 562 So. 2d 808 (Fla. 5th
DCA 1990)
  81 ALR6th 505—§ 32
State v. Foster, 631 S.W.2d 672 (Mo. Ct.
App. E.D. 1982)
  102 ALR5th 447—§ 21
State v. Foster, 674 So. 2d 747 (Fla. Dist.
Ct. App. 1st Dist. 1996)
  109 ALR5th 275—§ 4, 9

State v. Foster, 838 S.W.2d 60 (Mo. Ct.
App. E.D. 1992)
  42 ALR5th 291—§ 10, 15, 25
  79 ALR5th 419—§ 9
  37 ALR6th 357—§ 9, 10, 71
State v. Foster, 1997 ND 8, 560 N.W.2d
194 (N.D. 1997)
  37 ALR6th 357—§ 46, 52
State v. Foster, 1999 -NMSC- 007, 126
N.M. 646, 974 P.2d 140 (1999)
  28 ALR5th 754—§ 5
State v. Foster, 2006-Ohio-1567, 2006
WL 825268 (Ohio Ct. App. 1st Dist.
Hamilton County 2006)
  26 ALR6th 511—§ 18
State v. Foster, 2010 WL 4226991 (Del.
Super. Ct. 2010)
  97 ALR6th 263—§ 4
State v. Foulds, 127 NJL 336, 23 A.2d
895 (1941)
  11 ALR5th 497—§ 4
State v. Fourchy, 106 La. 743, 31 So.
325 (1901)
  63 ALR6th 1—§ 59
State v. Foureman, 68 Ohio App. 3d 162,
587 N.E.2d 925 (12th Dist. Preble
County 1990)
  15 ALR6th 375—§ 18
State v. Fouse, 120 Wis. 2d 471, 355
N.W.2d 366 (App. 1984)
  1 ALR5th 317—§ 3
State v. Foust, 105 Ohio St. 3d 137,
2004-Ohio-7006, 823 N.E.2d 836
(2004)
  38 ALR6th 439—§ 9
State v. Foust, 2005-Ohio-5331, 2005
WL 2462048 (Ohio Ct. App. 8th
Dist. Cuyahoga County 2005)
  21 ALR6th 1—§ 4
State v. Fowler, 22 N.C. App. 144, 205
S.E.2d 749 (1974)
  6 ALR5th 733—§ 2, 4, 14, 15, 30
State v. Fowler, 59 Mont. 356, 197 P.
847 (1921)
  42 ALR5th 547—§ 3
State v. Fowler, 79 R.I. 16, 83 A.2d 67
(1951)
  26 ALR6th 145—§ 4

State v. Fowler, 101 Ariz. 561, 422 P.2d 125 (1967)
   53 ALR6th 81—§ 4
State v. Fowler, 106 Idaho 3, 674 P.2d 432 (App. 1983)
   41 ALR5th 171—§ 7, 10, 14, 18, 20
State v. Fowler, 106 Idaho 3, 674 P.2d 432 (Ct. App. 1983)
   35 ALR6th 497—§ 21, 37
State v. Fowler, 117 W. Va. 761, 188 S.E. 137 (1936)
   29 ALR5th 59—§ 3, 18
State v. Fowler, 131 Wash. App. 1026, 2006 WL 226717 (Div. 2 2006)
   26 ALR6th 511—§ 25
State v. Fowler, 145 Wash. 2d 400, 38 P.3d 335 (2002)
   106 ALR5th 377—§ 3
   113 ALR5th 597—§ 8
State v. Fowler, 172 N.C. 905, 90 S.E. 408 (1916)
   55 ALR5th 125—§ 12, 14, 24
State v. Fowler, 248 N.W.2d 511 (Iowa 1976)
   24 ALR5th 465—§ 2, 14, 42, 43
State v. Fowler, 353 N.C. 599, 548 S.E.2d 684 (2001)
   27 ALR6th 183—§ 10, 35
State v. Fowler, 2005 WI App 41, 279 Wis. 2d 459, 694 N.W.2d 446 (Ct. App. 2005)
   78 ALR6th 417—§ 39
State v. Fowlkes, 169 N.J. 387, 778 A.2d 422 (2001)
   26 ALR6th 511—§ 17
State v. Fowlkes, 634 So. 2d 953 (La. Ct. App. 2d Cir. 1994)
   32 ALR6th 1—§ 4
   81 ALR6th 505—§ 69
State v. Fox, 130 Idaho 385, 941 P.2d 357 (Ct. App. 1997)
   85 ALR5th 187—§ 9
State v. Fox, 165 Or. App. 289, 995 P.2d 1193 (2000)
   105 ALR5th 529—§ 1
State v. Fox, 1999 WL 181248 (Ohio Ct. App. 3d Dist. Wyandot County 1999)

   87 ALR5th 693—§ 3
State v. Foy, 176 Ariz. 166, 859 P.2d 789, 147 Ariz. Adv. Rep. 91 (App. 1993)
   15 ALR5th 391—§ 45
State v. Foye, 100 N.M. 385, 671 P.2d 46 (Ct. App. 1983)
   32 ALR6th 385—§ 4
State v. Fraction, 2007 WL 92661 (Minn. Ct. App. 2007)
   26 ALR6th 511—§ 4
State v. Fraise, 350 So. 2d 154 (La. 1977)
   62 ALR5th 121—§ 6
State v. Fraley, 499 So. 2d 1304 (La. Ct. App. 4th Cir. 1986)
   125 ALR5th 537—§ 40
State v. Frame, 45 Or. App. 723, 609 P.2d 830 (1980)
   65 ALR5th 407—§ 3
State v. Frampton, 737 P.2d 183, 2 U.S.P.Q.2d 1835, 72 A.L.R.4th 1045 (Utah 1987)
   63 ALR6th 303—§ 5, 13
State v. France, 2004 WL 1606987 (Tenn. Crim. App. 2004)
   26 ALR6th 511—§ 22
State v. Francis, 145 Wash. App. 1046, 2008 WL 2791985 (Div. 1 2008)
   78 ALR6th 1—§ 28, 40, 42
State v. Francis, 152 S.C. 17, 149 S.E. 348, 70 A.L.R. 1133 (1929)
   16 ALR6th 329—§ 7
   24 ALR6th 591—§ 6
State v. Francis, 152 Vt. 628, 568 A.2d 389 (1989)
   68 ALR5th 299—§ 4
State v. Francis, 403 So. 2d 680 (La. 1981)
   117 ALR5th 1—§ 4
State v. Francisco, 790 S.W.2d 543 (Tenn. Crim. App. 1989)
   18 ALR6th 1—§ 5, 34
State v. Francis D., 75 Conn. App. 1, 815 A.2d 191 (2003)
   39 ALR6th 257—§ 4
State v. Francois, 650 So. 2d 1131 (Fla. Dist. Ct. App. 3d Dist. 1995)

113 ALR5th 597—§ 8
State v. Francum, 39 N.C. App. 429, 250 S.E.2d 705 (1979)
54 ALR6th 429—§ 20
State v. Frank, 2 Ohio App. 3d 392, 2 Ohio B.R. 466, 442 N.E.2d 469 (Hamilton Co. 1981)
52 ALR5th 655—§ 3
State v. Frank, 60 Idaho 774, 97 P.2d 410 (1939)
24 ALR5th 465—§ 3, 107
State v. Frank, 133 Idaho 364, 986 P.2d 1030 (Ct. App. 1999)
34 ALR6th 1—§ 9
State v. Frank, 298 N.W.2d 324 (Iowa 1980)
55 ALR6th 157—§ 111
State v. Frank, 344 So. 2d 1039 (La. 1977)
11 ALR6th 237—§ 12, 13
State v. Frank, 549 So. 2d 401 (La. Ct. App. 3d Cir. 1989)
79 ALR5th 419—§ 10
State v. Frank, 804 So. 2d 828 (La. Ct. App. 4th Cir. 2001)
1 ALR6th 371—§ 4
State v. Frankel, 179 N.J. 586, 847 A.2d 561 (2004)
58 ALR6th 499—§ 44
State v. Franklin, 62 Ohio St. 3d 118, 580 N.E.2d 1 (1991)
37 ALR5th 515—§ 3
State v. Franklin, 76 So. 3d 423 (La. 2011)
93 ALR6th 275—§ 3
State v. Franklin, 97 Ohio St. 3d 1, 2002-Ohio-5304, 776 N.E.2d 26 (2002)
3 ALR6th 543—§ 12
State v. Franklin, 167 Kan. 706, 208 P.2d 195 (1949)
54 ALR6th 429—§ 20
98 ALR6th 455—§ 17
State v. Franklin, 263 La. 344, 268 So. 2d 249 (1972)
20 ALR6th 479—§ 7
State v. Franklin, 267 S.C. 240, 226 S.E.2d 896 (1976)

93 ALR5th 327—§ 19
State v. Franklin, 281 Md. 51, 375 A.2d 1116 (1977)
42 ALR6th 237—§ 8
State v. Franklin, 353 So. 2d 1315 (La. 1977)
17 ALR6th 327—§ 21
State v. Franklin, 463 A.2d 749 (Me. 1983)
9 ALR6th 1—§ 17
State v. Franklin, 478 A.2d 1107 (Me. 1984)
53 ALR6th 81—§ 9
State v. Franklin, 501 So. 2d 881 (La. App. 5th Cir. 1987)
7 ALR5th 263—§ 7
State v. Franklin, 648 So. 2d 962 (La. Ct. App. 5th Cir. 1994)
72 ALR5th 109—§ 2, 7
78 ALR5th 197—§ 2
79 ALR5th 419—§ 2
80 ALR5th 55—§ 2
95 ALR5th 125—§ 2
State v. Franklin, 735 P.2d 34 (Utah 1987)
97 ALR5th 201—§ 6
State v. Franklin, 841 S.W.2d 639 (Mo. 1992)
35 ALR6th 497—§ 3, 27
101 ALR6th 299—§ 3
State v. Franklin, 858 So. 2d 68 (La. Ct. App. 5th Cir. 2003)
32 ALR6th 1—§ 5
State v. Franklin, 919 S.W.2d 362 (Tenn. Crim. App. 1995)
105 ALR5th 499—§ 4
State v. Franklin, 1989 WL 85134 (Ohio Ct. App. 8th Dist. Cuyahoga County 1989)
88 ALR5th 121—§ 19, 27, 33
State v. Franklin, 1997 WL 83772 (Tenn.Crim.App., Feb 28, 1997)
60 ALR5th 75—§ 12
State v. Franklin, 2002-Ohio-2370, 2002 WL 1000415 (Ohio Ct. App. 2d Dist. Montgomery County 2002)
21 ALR6th 1—§ 4

State v. Franks, 38 Tex. 640, 1873 WL 7481 (1873)

   5 ALR6th 1—§ 35

State v. Franz, 166 Wis. 32, 163 N.W. 191 (1917)

   124 ALR5th 203—§ 11

State v. Frasher, 164 W. Va. 572, 265 S.E.2d 43 (1980)

   22 ALR5th 1—§ 34, 60

   57 ALR6th 445—§ 43

State v. Frasier, 914 S.W.2d 467 (Tenn. 1996)

   109 ALR5th 611—§ 4

State v. Frasure, 2004 MT 305, 323 Mont. 479, 100 P.3d 1013 (2004)

   72 ALR6th 1—§ 4

State v. Frasure, 2008-Ohio-1504, 2008 WL 835820 (Ohio Ct. App. 11th Dist. Ashtabula County 2008)

   56 ALR6th 185—§ 37

State v. Fraternal Order of Eagles, Aerie 2347, 99 Ohio Misc. 2d 33, 715 N.E.2d 630 (County Ct. 1999)

   85 ALR5th 547—§ 7

State v. Frazier, 39 Conn. App. 369, 665 A.2d 142 (1995)

   43 ALR5th 1—§ 8

State v. Frazier, 58 Ohio St. 2d 253, 12 Ohio Ops. 3d 263, 389 N.E.2d 1118 (1979)

   39 ALR5th 283—§ 14

State v. Frazier, 73 Ohio St. 3d 323, 652 N.E.2d 1000 (1995)

   57 ALR5th 141—§ 3

State v. Frazier, 99 Wash. 2d 180, 661 P.2d 126 (1983)

   65 ALR6th 537—§ 4

State v. Frazier, 115 Ohio St. 3d 139, 2007-Ohio-5048, 873 N.E.2d 1263 (2007)

   38 ALR6th 439—§ 4

State v. Frazier, 245 Or. 4, 418 P.2d 841 (1966)

   55 ALR5th 125—§ 12, 20, 22

State v. Frazier, 357 So. 2d 522 (La. 1978)

   88 ALR5th 429—§ 6

State v. Frazier, 631 N.W.2d 432 (Minn. Ct. App. 2001)

   58 ALR6th 385—§ 7

State v. Frazier, 2010-Ohio-4440, 2010 WL 3641344 (Ohio Ct. App. 10th Dist. Franklin County 2010)

   79 ALR6th 125—§ 8

State v. Frear, 142 Wis. 320, 125 N.W. 961 (1910)

   120 ALR5th 125—§ 2, 10

   121 ALR5th 1—§ 2, 30, 58

State v. Frederick, 2010-Ohio-2005, 2010 WL 1818891 (Ohio Ct. App. 6th Dist. Lucas County 2010)

   64 ALR6th 1—§ 9

State v. Frederick, 2010 WL 2901802 (Idaho 2010)

   56 ALR6th 1—§ 6, 38

State v. Fredette, 411 A.2d 65 (Me. 1979)

   33 ALR5th 453—§ 4, 11

State v. Fredette, 462 A.2d 17, 40 A.L.R.4th 498 (Me. 1983)

   103 ALR6th 137—§ 15

State v. Free, 493 So. 2d 781 (La. Ct. App. 2d Cir. 1986)

   95 ALR5th 471—§ 2, 7, 9

State v. Free, 643 So. 2d 767 (La. App. 2d Cir. 1994)

   42 ALR5th 291—§ 10

State v. Freedman, 2009 WL 936847 (Ariz. Ct. App. Div. 1 2009)

   93 ALR6th 275—§ 18

State v. Freedom From Religion Foundation, Inc., 898 P.2d 1013 (Colo. 1995)

   107 ALR5th 1—§ 3, 7, 9, 10, 18, 21

   26 ALR6th 145—§ 3

State v. Freedom of Information Commission, 184 Conn. 102, 441 A.2d 53, 7 Media L. Rep. (BNA) 1830 (1981)

   5 ALR6th 327—§ 6

   8 ALR6th 117—§ 23

State v. Freeman, 33 So. 3d 222 (La. Ct. App. 2d Cir. 2010)

   55 ALR6th 1—§ 29

State v. Freeman, 70 Haw. 434, 774 P.2d 888 (1989)
68 ALR6th 527—§ 45

State v. Freeman, 143 Kan. 315, 55 P.2d 362 (1936)
51 ALR6th 359—§ 19, 32

State v. Freeman, 146 N.C. 615, 60 S.E. 986 (1908)
81 ALR5th 563—§ 3

State v. Freeman, 174 Ariz. 303, 848 P.2d 882, 134 Ariz. Adv. Rep. 15 (App. 1993)
15 ALR5th 391—§ 45

State v. Freeman, 267 Neb. 737, 677 N.W.2d 164 (2004)
103 ALR6th 507—§ 31

State v. Freeman, 542 So. 2d 483 (Fla. Dist. Ct. App. 2d Dist. 1989)
72 ALR5th 1—§ 2, 29

State v. Freeman, 653 So. 2d 801 (La. Ct. App. 3d Cir. 1995)
9 ALR6th 1—§ 17

State v. Freeman, 667 S.W.2d 443 (Mo. App. 1984)
29 ALR5th 59—§ 7

State v. Freeman, 680 N.W.2d 378 (Iowa Ct. App. 2004)
71 ALR6th 1—§ 12

State v. Freeman, 796 So. 2d 574 (Fla. Dist. Ct. App. 2d Dist. 2001)
43 ALR6th 475—§ 8

State v. Freeman, 1995 WL 447664 (Ohio Ct. App. 7th Dist.Harrison County 1995)
57 ALR5th 141—§ 13

State v. Freeman, 2010 WL 293184 (La. Ct. App. 2d Cir. 2010)
55 ALR6th 1—§ 8, 14

State v. Freese, 166 N.W.2d 785 (Iowa 1969)
68 ALR5th 343—§ 3, 8

State v. Freeze, 1995 WL 125657 (Ohio Ct. App. 9th Dist. Medina County 1995)
34 ALR6th 1—§ 10

State v. Fremgen, 914 P.2d 1244 (Alaska 1996)
46 ALR5th 499—§ 4

State v. French, 47 Mo. App. 474, 1892 WL 1475 (1892)
97 ALR5th 537—§ 10

State v. French, 132 P.3d 501 (Kan. Ct. App. 2006)
30 ALR6th 373—§ 10

State v. French, 139 Vt. 320, 428 A.2d 1087 (1981)
39 ALR5th 283—§ 2, 4

State v. French, 166 Ariz. 247, 801 P.2d 482 (Ct. App. Div. 1 1990)
92 ALR5th 35—§ 30

State v. French, 203 N.C. 632, 166 S.E. 747 (1932)
55 ALR6th 157—§ 43

State v. French, 342 N.C. 863, 467 S.E.2d 412 (1996)
37 ALR5th 515—§ 11

State v. French, 400 N.W.2d 111 (Minn. App. 1987)
29 ALR5th 59—§ 6, 11

State v. Frest, 4 Del. 558, 4 Harr. 558, 1844 WL 1119 (Ct. of Oyer & Terminer 1844)
5 ALR6th 1—§ 41

State v. Frey, 178 Wis. 2d 729, 505 N.W.2d 786 (Ct. App. 1993)
67 ALR6th 103—§ 3, 6

State v. Frey, 441 N.W.2d 668 (N.D. 1989)
7 ALR5th 758—§ 13

State v. Freyer, 330 Mo. 62, 48 S.W.2d 894 (1932)
81 ALR5th 563—§ 3, 5, 8, 9

State v. Fricke, 13 Ohio App. 3d 331, 13 Ohio B.R. 409, 469 N.E.2d 1035 (Hamilton Co. 1984)
23 ALR5th 672—§ 9

State v. Fricks, 188 Ga. App. 869, 374 S.E.2d 749 (1988)
56 ALR6th 323—§ 11

State v. Friedlander, 2008-Ohio-2812, 2008 WL 2350893 (Ohio Ct. App. 8th Dist. Cuyahoga County 2008)
43 ALR6th 475—§ 6

State v. Friedlander, 2009-Ohio-3370, 2009 WL 1965450 (Ohio Ct. App. 8th Dist. Cuyahoga County 2009)

99 ALR6th 295—§ 13

State v. Friedli, 118 Wash. App. 1044, 2003 WL 22173063 (Div. 1 2003)

15 ALR6th 515—§ 4

45 ALR6th 643—§ 15

State v. Friedman, 98 NJL 577, 120 A. 8 (1922)

29 ALR5th 59—§ 62

State v. Friedman, 98 N.J.L. 577, 120 A. 8 (N.J. Sup. Ct. 1922)

57 ALR6th 445—§ 15

State v. Friedman, 412 S.W.2d 171 (Mo. 1967)

107 ALR5th 567—§ 12

State v. Friel, 508 A.2d 123 (Me. 1986)

6 ALR6th 533—§ 17

State v. Friel, 1996 WL 339847 (Wash. Ct. App. Div. 3 1996)

106 ALR5th 397—§ 4

State v. Friend, 385 N.W.2d 313 (Minn. App. 1986)

7 ALR5th 263—§ 4

State v. Friend, 493 N.W.2d 540 (Minn. 1992)

37 ALR5th 515—§ 2, 4, 11

State v. Frierson, 302 So. 2d 605 (La. 1974)

68 ALR5th 343—§ 3, 5

State v. Frierson, No. 40811 (December 25, 1990, Ct. App. Ohio, 8th App. Dist. Cuyahoga Co.)

39 ALR5th 283—§ 14, 62

State v. Frieze, 3 Neb. App. 263, 525 N.W.2d 646 (1994)

88 ALR5th 121—§ 14, 22, 25, 36

42 ALR6th 237—§ 4

State v. Friley, 2006-Ohio-230, 2006 WL 164417 (Ohio Ct. App. 10th Dist. Franklin County 2006)

29 ALR6th 237—§ 24

State v. Frink, 42 Or. App. 171, 600 P.2d 456 (1979)

58 ALR6th 499—§ 8

State v. Frinks, 284 N.C. 472, 201 S.E.2d 858 (1974)

80 ALR5th 255—§ 5, 17, 26, 32

State v. Frisby, 161 W. Va. 734, 245 S.E.2d 622 (1978)

116 ALR5th 479—§ 3

State v. Frischenmeyer, 201 P.3d 1 (Kan. Ct. App. 2009)

62 ALR6th 413—§ 46

State v. Frith, 747 So. 2d 1269 (La. Ct. App. 2d Cir. 1999)

103 ALR6th 507—§ 6, 22

State v. Fritsch, 351 N.C. 373, 526 S.E.2d 451 (2000)

118 ALR5th 253—§ 1

State v. Fritz, 27 La. Ann. 689, 1875 WL 7219 (1875)

97 ALR5th 537—§ 44

State v. Fritz, 204 Conn. 156, 527 A.2d 1157 (1987)

13 ALR5th 1—§ 2

19 ALR6th 577—§ 3

State v. Fritz, 2006-Ohio-2920, 2006 WL 1580046 (Ohio Ct. App. 6th Dist. Lucas County 2006)

18 ALR6th 97—§ 8

State v. Frizzell, 207 Kan. 393, 485 P.2d 160 (1971)

56 ALR6th 323—§ 8, 13

State v. Frodert, 84 Wash. App. 20, 924 P.2d 933, R.I.C.O. Bus. Disp. Guide (CCH) ¶ 9198 (Div. 2 1996)

58 ALR6th 385—§ 43, 48 to 52

State v. Froggatt, 1997 WL 219780 (Wash. Ct. App. Div. 2 1997)

71 ALR5th 637—§ 7

State v. Frogge, 359 N.C. 228, 607 S.E.2d 627 (2005)

102 ALR6th 417—§ 9

State v. Froneberger, 81 N.C. App. 398, 344 S.E.2d 344 (1986)

15 ALR5th 391—§ 27

92 ALR5th 35—§ 30

State v. Fronier, 103 N.H. 152, 167 A.2d 56 (1961)

76 ALR5th 1—§ 5

State v. Fronning, 186 Neb. 463, 183 N.W.2d 920 (1971)

3 ALR6th 269—§ 7

State v. Frost, 242 N.J. Super. 601, 577 A.2d 1282 (App. Div. 1990)

57 ALR5th 315—§ 2, 3, 8, 12

State v. Frost, 564 A.2d 70 (Me. 1989)

5 ALR5th 243—§ 2, 21

State v. Frost, 727 So. 2d 417 (La. 1998)

79 ALR5th 33—§ 28

State v. Frost, 2005 MT 165N, 327 Mont. 538, 115 P.3d 221 (2005)

97 ALR6th 263—§ 30

State v. Fry, 61 Hawaii 226, 602 P.2d 13 (1979)

22 ALR5th 660—§ 6, 8

59 ALR5th 135—§ 5

State v. Fry, 142 Wash. App. 456, 174 P.3d 1258 (Div. 3 2008)

50 ALR6th 353—§ 7, 20

State v. Frye, 26 Wash. App. 276, 613 P.2d 152 (1980)

43 ALR5th 1—§ 13

State v. Frye, 341 N.C. 470, 461 S.E.2d 664 (1995)

77 ALR5th 201—§ 3

79 ALR5th 33—§ 67

83 ALR6th 465—§ 4, 18

State v. Frye, 2007-Ohio-6941, 2007 WL 4485730 (Ohio Ct. App. 11th Dist. Ashtabula County 2007)

58 ALR6th 215—§ 11

State v. Fryer, 243 N.W.2d 1 (Iowa 1976)

71 ALR6th 335—§ 13

State v. Fryer, 496 N.W.2d 54 (S.D. 1993)

15 ALR5th 391—§ 5

92 ALR5th 35—§ 25

State v. Fudge, 42 S.W.3d 226 (Tex. App. Austin 2001)

84 ALR6th 293—§ 7, 43

State v. Fuente, 871 S.W.2d 438 (Mo. 1994)

114 ALR5th 173—§ 7

State v. Fuessenich, 50 Conn. App. 187, 717 A.2d 801 (1998)

92 ALR6th 1—§ 3

State v. Fugate, 332 Or. 195, 26 P.3d 802 (Or. Jun 08, 2001)

91 ALR5th 343—§ 8

State v. Fugate, 1998 WL 729221 (Ohio Ct. App. 4th Dist. Washington County 1998)

88 ALR5th 121—§ 3, 14, 22, 26, 28

State v. Fuger, 170 Mont. 442, 554 P.2d 1338 (1976)

5 ALR5th 243—§ 2, 59

State v. Fugitt, 2001 WL 127299 (Ohio Ct. App. 6th Dist. Huron County 2001)

70 ALR6th 1—§ 11

State v. Fuhriman, 137 Idaho 741, 52 P.3d 886 (Ct. App. 2002)

9 ALR6th 541—§ 3, 32

State v. Fuhs, 265 N.J. Super. 188, 625 A.2d 1151 (App. Div. 1993)

59 ALR5th 615—§ 4

62 ALR6th 413—§ 43

State v. Fukusaku, 85 Haw. 462, 946 P.2d 32 (1997)

54 ALR6th 429—§ 5, 7, 11, 13, 20

State v. Fukusaku, 85 Haw. 462, 946 P.2d 32 (Haw. 1997)

20 ALR5th 398—§ 6.5

82 ALR5th 67—§ 3, 5, 9

90 ALR5th 453—§ 45

State v. Fulcher, 294 N.C. 503, 243 S.E.2d 338 (1978)

39 ALR5th 283—§ 4, 56

State v. Fulks, 83 S.D. 433, 160 N.W.2d 418 (1968)

46 ALR5th 499—§ 3

State v. Fulks, 1997 ND 143, 566 N.W.2d 418 (N.D. 1997)

37 ALR6th 357—§ 53, 67

State v. Fullager, 1999 WL 547461 (Ohio Ct. App. 5th Dist. Ashland County 1999)

78 ALR5th 489—§ 3, 10

State v. Fuller, 56 Conn. App. 592, 744 A.2d 931 (2000)

93 ALR5th 683—§ 3

State v. Fuller, 144 Vt. 485, 479 A.2d 173 (1984)

45 ALR5th 591—§ 14

State v. Fuller, 158 Or. App. 501, 976 P.2d 1137 (1999)

68 ALR5th 343—§ 17

State v. Fuller, 166 N.C. App. 548, 603 S.E.2d 569 (2004)
25 ALR6th 379—§ 11

State v. Fuller, 204 Neb. 196, 281 N.W.2d 749 (1979)
38 ALR6th 97—§ 28

State v. Fuller, 278 S.C. 393, 296 S.E.2d 871 (1982)
17 ALR5th 125—§ 3

State v. Fuller, 308 Md. 547, 520 A.2d 1315 (1987)
70 ALR5th 533—§ 6

State v. Fuller, 1987 WL 13850 (Ohio Ct. App. 8th Dist.Cuyahoga County 1987)
57 ALR5th 141—§ 11

State v. Fuller, 1997 WL 15401 (Conn. Super. Ct. 1997)
101 ALR6th 331—§ 21

State v. Fuller, 1999 WL 74129 (Or. Ct. App. 1999)
68 ALR5th 343—§ 3, 4, 17

State v. Fullerton, 1993 WL 236679 (Tenn. Crim. App. 1993)
76 ALR5th 1—§ 6, 11

State v. Fullwood, 193 Conn. 238, 476 A.2d 550 (1984)
102 ALR6th 365—§ 24

State v. Fullwood, 274 S.C. 60, 262 S.E.2d 10 (1979)
53 ALR6th 81—§ 4

State v. Fulminante, 161 Ariz. 237, 778 P.2d 602 (1988)
57 ALR5th 141—§ 7
38 ALR6th 97—§ 29

State v. Fulminante, 193 Ariz. 485, 975 P.2d 75 (1999)
91 ALR5th 343—§ 3, 16
38 ALR6th 97—§ 29

State v. Fulston, 325 N.J. Super. 184, 738 A.2d 380 (App. Div. 1999)
22 ALR5th 1—§ 3

State v. Fulton, 337 So. 2d 866 (La. 1976)
51 ALR6th 359—§ 28

State v. Fulton, 777 So. 2d 1134 (Fla. Dist. Ct. App. 4th Dist. 2001)
113 ALR5th 597—§ 8

State v. Fulton, 1998 WL 188532 (Tenn. Crim. App. 1998)
3 ALR6th 269—§ 25

State v. Fulton, 2003-Ohio-5432, 2003 WL 22326575 (Ohio Ct. App. 12th Dist. Clermont County 2003)
10 ALR6th 463—§ 4, 8

State v. Fults, 98 S.W.3d 877 (Mo. Ct. App. E.D. 2003)
72 ALR6th 227—§ 24

State v. Fung, 907 P.2d 1192, 279 Utah Adv. Rep. 24 (Utah App. 1995)
32 ALR5th 149—§ 50 to 52

State v. Fungone, 134 N.J. Super. 531, 342 A.2d 236 (1975)
14 ALR5th 89—§ 8, 11

State v. Fuqua, 1994 WL 469307 (Tenn. Crim. App. 1994)
119 ALR5th 379—§ 7

State v. Furgerson, 781 So. 2d 1268 (La. Ct. App. 2d Cir. 2001)
19 ALR6th 115—§ 4, 9

State v. Fusco, 136 N.C. App. 268, 523 S.E.2d 741 (1999)
95 ALR5th 229—§ 9

State v. Fussell, 299 S.C. 162, 383 S.E.2d 1 (1989)
15 ALR5th 391—§ 7

State v. Fussell, 941 So. 2d 109 (La. Ct. App. 3d Cir. 2006)
83 ALR6th 465—§ 13

State v. Futch, 123 Or. App. 176, 860 P.2d 264 (1993)
90 ALR5th 453—§ 19
93 ALR6th 275—§ 20

State v. Futo, 990 S.W.2d 7 (Mo. Ct. App. E.D. 1999)
55 ALR6th 157—§ 51

State v. Futrall, 123 Ohio St. 3d 498, 2009-Ohio-5590, 918 N.E.2d 497 (2009)
69 ALR6th 1—§ 33
70 ALR6th 1—§ 5

State v. F. W. Fitch Co., 236 Iowa 208, 17 N.W.2d 380 (1945)
31 ALR5th 171—§ 20

State v. Fye, 97 Wash. App. 1086, 1999 WL 1033555 (Div. 1 1999)
106 ALR5th 397—§ 4

State v. Gabbard, 129 Or. App. 122, 877 P.2d 1217 (1994)
60 ALR5th 1—§ 11
45 ALR6th 643—§ 15

State v. Gabino, 302 Wis. 2d 260, 2007 WI App 138, 732 N.W.2d 863 (Ct. App. 2007)
35 ALR6th 127—§ 22

State v. Gabriel, 1994 WL 718675 (Ohio Ct. App. 7th Dist. Mahoning County 1994)
88 ALR5th 121—§ 13

State v. Gabriella, 163 Iowa 297, 144 N.W. 9 (1913)
50 ALR5th 467—§ 3, 6, 9

State v. Gachot, 609 So. 2d 269 (La. App. 3d Cir. 1992)
22 ALR5th 787—§ 3

State v. Gaddy, 118 Ariz. 594, 578 P.2d 1023 (App. 1978)
12 ALR5th 909—§ 5

State v. Gaddy, 313 Ark. 677, 858 S.W.2d 81 (1993)
9 ALR6th 541—§ 18

State v. Gadreault, 758 A.2d 781 (Vt. 2000)
6 ALR5th 733—§ 16

State v. Gadsden, 245 N.J. Super. 93, 584 A.2d 265 (1990)
27 ALR5th 593—§ 2

State v. Gaebler, 2002-Ohio-2077, 2002 WL 737096 (Ohio Ct. App. 11th Dist. Geauga County 2002)
69 ALR6th 1—§ 29

State v. Gaede, 128 N.M. 559, 2000 -NMCA- 004, 994 P.2d 1177 (Ct. App. 1999)
97 ALR5th 293—§ 3, 17

State v. Gaefe, 2002-Ohio-4995, 2002 WL 31108240 (Ohio Ct. App. 12th Dist. Clinton County 2002)
23 ALR6th 307—§ 44

State v. Gage, 302 N.W.2d 793 (S.D. 1981)
3 ALR6th 269—§ 24

State v. Gagliano, 231 Neb. 911, 438 N.W.2d 783 (1989)
66 ALR5th 135—§ 13

State v. Gagne, 22 N.C. App. 615, 207 S.E.2d 384 (1974)
85 ALR5th 1—§ 33

State v. Gagne, 349 A.2d 193 (Me. 1975)
98 ALR6th 455—§ 19
99 ALR6th 113—§ 8
102 ALR6th 279—§ 14

State v. Gagnon, 18 Conn. App. 694, 561 A.2d 129 (1989)
55 ALR6th 157—§ 14

State v. Gagnon, 139 N.H. 175, 651 A.2d 5 (1994)
9 ALR6th 1—§ 18

State v. Gagnon, 151 Me. 501, 121 A.2d 345 (1956)
76 ALR5th 1—§ 8

State v. Gail, 713 N.W.2d 851 (Minn. 2006)
94 ALR6th 579—§ 1

State v. Gainer, 227 Kan. 670, 608 P.2d 968 (1980)
24 ALR5th 132—§ 2, 5, 6, 8, 14

State v. Gainer, 2004-Ohio-2393, 2004 WL 1067498 (Ohio Ct. App. 8th Dist. Cuyahoga County 2004)
33 ALR6th 407—§ 4

State v. Gaines, 64 Ohio App. 3d 230, 580 N.E.2d 1158 (12th Dist. Clinton County 1990)
68 ALR6th 115—§ 3 to 5, 18, 20, 22 to 24

State v. Gaines, 64 Ohio App. 3d 230, 580 N.E.2d 1158 (Clinton Co. 1990)
6 ALR5th 733—§ 6, 20, 21

State v. Gaines, 82 Ohio App. 3d 467, 612 N.E.2d 749 (12th Dist. Clinton County 1992)
68 ALR6th 115—§ 18

State v. Gaines, 84 Wash. App. 1117, 1997 WL 87101 (Div. 2 1997)
88 ALR5th 121—§ 3, 10, 36

State v. Gaines, 122 Wash. 2d 502, 859 P.2d 36 (1993)
113 ALR5th 597—§ 8

State v. Gaines, 283 N.C. 33, 194 S.E.2d 839 (1973)

22 ALR5th 1—§ 10, 33

State v. Gainey, 32 N.C. App. 682, 233 S.E.2d 671 (1977)

78 ALR5th 1—§ 25

State v. Gainey, 84 N.C. App. 107, 351 S.E.2d 819 (1987)

7 ALR5th 73—§ 2, 5

State v. Gain, No. 435 (October 14, 1981, Ct. App. Ohio, 4th App. Dist. Pickaway Co.)

39 ALR5th 283—§ 14, 56, 60

State v. Gairns, 20 Wash. App. 159, 579 P.2d 386 (Div. 1 1978)

104 ALR5th 357—§ 8

State v. Gaitan, 27 Ariz. App. 718, 558 P.2d 746 (Div. 1 1976)

103 ALR5th 463—§ 3

State v. Gaitan, 2002-NMSC-007, 131 N.M. 758, 42 P.3d 1207 (2002)

3 ALR6th 543—§ 11

State v. Gaitan, 2012 WL 612311 (N.J. 2012)

74 ALR6th 373—§ 23

State v. Gaitor, 1996 WL 488786 (Ohio Ct. App. 5th Dist. Stark County 1996)

19 ALR6th 697—§ 25

State v. Galbraith, 723 S.W.2d 55 (Mo. Ct. App. W.D. 1986)

53 ALR6th 81—§ 5

State v. Galbreath, 69 Wash. 2d 664, 419 P.2d 800 (1966)

71 ALR6th 283—§ 13, 23, 26

State v. Galbreath, 525 N.W.2d 424 (Iowa 1994)

57 ALR6th 445—§ 2, 3, 29

State v. Gale, 35 Or. App. 3, 580 P.2d 1036 (1978)

22 ALR5th 660—§ 9, 11

State v. Gale, 105 Or. App. 489, 805 P.2d 158 (1991)

113 ALR5th 517—§ 7

State v. Gales, 143 Ohio App. 3d 55, 757 N.E.2d 390, 113 A.L.R.5th 745 (8th Dist. Cuyahoga County 2001)

113 ALR5th 517—§ 11

State v. Gales, 240 N.C. 319, 82 S.E.2d 80 (1954)

24 ALR5th 465—§ 33 to 35, 39, 86 to 88, 90

State v. Gales, 265 Neb. 598, 658 N.W.2d 604 (2003)

110 ALR5th 1—§ 19

State v. Galindo, 278 Neb. 599, 774 N.W.2d 190 (2009)

63 ALR6th 1—§ 4, 5, 8, 38

State v. Gall, 1992 WL 217999 (Ohio Ct. App. 11th Dist. Trumbull County 1992)

51 ALR6th 1—§ 19

State v. Gallagher, 97 Ariz. 1, 396 P.2d 241 (1964)

102 ALR6th 279—§ 31

State v. Gallagher, 100 N.M. 697, 675 P.2d 429 (Ct. App. 1984)

99 ALR5th 557—§ 3, 12

State v. Gallagher, 102 N.H. 335, 156 A.2d 765, 77 A.L.R.2d 1167 (1959)

52 ALR5th 655—§ 2

State v. Gallagher, 150 Vt. 341, 554 A.2d 221 (1988)

38 ALR5th 433—§ 11

State v. Gallagher, 286 N.J. Super. 1, 668 A.2d 55 (App. Div. 1995)

55 ALR5th 423—§ 13

State v. Gallant, 307 Or. 152, 764 P.2d 920 (1988)

84 ALR5th 487—§ 22

State v. Gallegos, 88 N.M. 487, 542 P.2d 832 (Ct. App. 1975)

117 ALR5th 1—§ 4

State v. Gallegos, 92 N.M. 370, 588 P.2d 1045 (App. 1978)

57 ALR5th 141—§ 7

State v. Gallegos, 92 N.M. 370, 588 P.2d 1045 (Ct. App. 1978)

66 ALR6th 83—§ 16

State v. Gallegos, 109 N.M. 55, 781 P.2d 783 (Ct. App. 1989)

68 ALR6th 527—§ 37

State v. Gallegos, 967 P.2d 973 (Utah Ct. App. 1998)

71 ALR6th 1—§ 16

State v. Gallegos, 2009 UT 42, 220 P.3d 136 (Utah 2009)

55 ALR6th 513—§ 6

State v. Galli, 967 P.2d 930 (Utah 1998)

92 ALR5th 35—§ 7

State v. Galliano, 696 So. 2d 1043 (La. Ct. App. 1st Cir. 1997)

73 ALR5th 383—§ 29

State v. Galligo, 1996 SD 83, 551 N.W.2d 303 (S.D. 1996)

92 ALR5th 35—§ 25

State v. Gallion, 1992 WL 52583 (Ohio Ct. App. 11th Dist. Ashtabula County 1992)

69 ALR6th 207—§ 9, 10, 18

State v. Gallo, 76 So. 3d 407 (Fla. 2d DCA 2011)

76 ALR6th 1—§ 9, 10

State v. Gallo, 279 So. 2d 71 (Fla. Dist. Ct. App. 2d Dist. 1973)

103 ALR5th 463—§ 8

State v. Galloway, 16 Kan. App. 2d 54, 817 P.2d 1124 (1991)

19 ALR6th 697—§ 4

State v. Galloway, 235 Kan. 70, 680 P.2d 268 (1984)

23 ALR5th 672—§ 3

23 ALR6th 1—§ 15

State v. Galloway, 551 So. 2d 701 (La. App. 1st Cir. 1989)

5 ALR5th 243—§ 61

State v. Galloway, 1990 WL 199902 (Tenn. Crim. App. 1990)

73 ALR5th 383—§ 3

State v. Galloway, 2002-Ohio-4358, 2002 WL 1964827 (Ohio Ct. App. 11th Dist. Lake County 2002)

71 ALR6th 1—§ 5

State v. Gallup, 236 Ga. App. 321, 512 S.E.2d 66 (1999)

64 ALR5th 637—§ 5

State v. Gallup, 500 N.W.2d 437 (Iowa 1993)

12 ALR5th 89—§ 5, 7

State v. Galmore, 994 S.W.2d 120 (Tenn. 1999)

83 ALR5th 277—§ 11

State v. Galusha, 164 Vt. 91, 665 A.2d 595, 87 A.L.R.5th 819 (1995)

87 ALR5th 715—§ 3

State v. Galvan, 108 Ariz. 212, 495 P.2d 442 (1972)

34 ALR5th 125—§ 3

State v. Galvan, 532 N.W.2d 210 (Minn. 1995)

45 ALR5th 1—§ 3, 5, 12, 23, 30

State v. Galvan, 795 S.W.2d 113 (Mo. Ct. App. S.D. 1990)

37 ALR6th 357—§ 3, 43, 56, 67, 71

State v. Galvez, 214 Ariz. 154, 150 P.3d 241 (Ct. App. Div. 1 2006)

70 ALR6th 361—§ 18

71 ALR6th 335—§ 10

State v. Gama, 2009 WL 1362040 (Ariz. Ct. App. Div. 2 2009)

55 ALR6th 1—§ 10

State v. Gamble, 20 Kan. App. 2d 684, 891 P.2d 472 (1995)

69 ALR6th 1—§ 23

State v. Gamble, 211 W. Va. 125, 563 S.E.2d 790 (2001)

70 ALR6th 361—§ 19

State v. Gamble, 2000 WL 45718 (Tenn. Crim. App. 2000)

78 ALR5th 567—§ 5

State v. Gambrell, 274 S.C. 587, 266 S.E.2d 78 (1980)

102 ALR5th 327—§ 5

State v. Gambrell, 814 P.2d 1136 (Utah Ct. App. 1991)

105 ALR5th 499—§ 4

State v. Gambutti, 36 N.J. Super. 219, 115 A.2d 136 (App. Div. 1955)

39 ALR6th 257—§ 8

State v. Gammill, 2 Kan. App. 2d 627, 585 P.2d 1074 (1978)

101 ALR5th 187—§ 10

State v. Ganaway, 2008-Ohio-1629, 2008 WL 885836 (Ohio Ct. App. 8th Dist. Cuyahoga County 2008)

99 ALR6th 295—§ 19

State v. Gandy, 2006-Ohio-6282, 2006 WL 3457692 (Ohio Ct. App. 1st Dist. Hamilton County 2006)

99 ALR6th 295—§ 9, 19

State v. Gangl, 1998 WL 799165 (Minn. Ct. App. 1998)

84 ALR6th 293—§ 38

State v. Gann, 36 Wash. App. 516, 675 P.2d 1261 (Div. 1 1984)

78 ALR6th 417—§ 42

State v. Gant, 216 Ariz. 1, 162 P.3d 640 (2007)

46 ALR6th 495—§ 6
55 ALR6th 1—§ 41

State v. Gantt, 161 N.C. App. 265, 588 S.E.2d 893 (2003)

35 ALR6th 127—§ 5

State v. Gantt, 504 S.W.2d 295 (Mo. Ct. App. 1973)

108 ALR5th 593—§ 34

State v. Gapen, 104 Ohio St. 3d 358, 2004-Ohio-6548, 819 N.E.2d 1047 (2004)

83 ALR6th 255—§ 23

State v. Garantine, 527 So. 2d 1144 (La. Ct. App. 1st Cir. 1988)

103 ALR5th 463—§ 11

State v. Garay, 102 P.3d 503 (Kan. Ct. App. 2004)

26 ALR6th 511—§ 25

State v. Garber, 156 Vt. 637, 587 A.2d 404 (1991)

92 ALR6th 295—§ 7, 30
95 ALR6th 1—§ 11, 25

State v. Garber, 197 Kan. 567, 419 P.2d 896 (1966)

70 ALR5th 169—§ 3, 25

State v. Garber, 249 Neb. 648, 545 N.W.2d 75 (1996)

66 ALR6th 351—§ 5

State v. Garberding, 245 Mont. 356, 801 P.2d 583 (1990)

73 ALR6th 49—§ 4

State v. Garbin, 325 N.J. Super. 521, 739 A.2d 1016 (App. Div. 1999)

58 ALR6th 499—§ 6

State v. Garbutt, 173 Vt. 277, 790 A.2d 444 (2001)

68 ALR6th 607—§ 10

State v. Garceau, 536 A.2d 1129 (Me. 1988)

7 ALR5th 73—§ 11

State v. Garcell, 363 N.C. 10, 678 S.E.2d 618 (2009)

83 ALR6th 255—§ 15

State v. Garcia, 7 Conn. App. 354, 508 A.2d 824 (1986)

109 ALR5th 99—§ 8

State v. Garcia, 25 S.W.3d 908 (Tex. App. Houston 14th Dist. 2000)

84 ALR6th 293—§ 7, 43

State v. Garcia, 32 Ohio App. 3d 38, 513 N.E.2d 1350 (9th Dist. Lorain County 1986)

122 ALR5th 439—§ 4

State v. Garcia, 43 N.M. 242, 89 P.2d 619 (1939)

32 ALR5th 149—§ 5, 74

State v. Garcia, 57 Wash. App. 927, 791 P.2d 244 (Div. 1 1990)

79 ALR5th 419—§ 6, 7, 9, 10

State v. Garcia, 63 Wash. App. 868, 824 P.2d 1220 (Div. 3 1992)

106 ALR5th 397—§ 6

State v. Garcia, 77 Haw. 461, 887 P.2d 671 (Haw. Ct. App. 1995)

85 ALR5th 1—§ 2, 18, 22, 24, 44

State v. Garcia, 90 N.M. 577, 566 P.2d 426 (Ct. App. 1977)

113 ALR5th 517—§ 10

State v. Garcia, 94 N.M. 583, 613 P.2d 725 (App. 1980)

44 ALR5th 651—§ 2, 3

State v. Garcia, 108 Conn. App. 533, 949 A.2d 499 (2008)

101 ALR6th 1—§ 3

State v. Garcia, 116 N.M. 87, 860 P.2d 217 (Ct. App. 1993)

85 ALR5th 261—§ 4

State v. Garcia, 131 N.J. 67, 618 A.2d 326 (1993)

67 ALR5th 149—§ 3, 5

State v. Garcia, 135 N.M. 595, 2004-NMCA-066, 92 P.3d 41 (Ct. App. 2004)

97 ALR6th 653—§ 9

State v. Garcia, 138 Ariz. 211, 673 P.2d 955 (App. 1983)

 5 ALR5th 243—§ 5, 36

 45 ALR5th 531—§ 3

State v. Garcia, 138 Ariz. 211, 673 P.2d 955 (Ct. App. Div. 2 1983)

 103 ALR6th 507—§ 23

State v. Garcia, 156 Ariz. 381, 752 P.2d 34 (Ct. App. Div. 1 1987)

 33 ALR6th 91—§ 37

State v. Garcia, 187 Ariz. 527, 931 P.2d 427 (Ct. App. Div. 2 1996)

 87 ALR5th 361—§ 19

State v. Garcia, 233 Kan. 589, 664 P.2d 1343 (1983)

 124 ALR5th 1—§ 5

 81 ALR6th 505—§ 4

State v. Garcia, 243 Kan. 662, 763 P.2d 585 (1988)

 49 ALR6th 343—§ 4

State v. Garcia, 288 Or. 413, 605 P.2d 671 (1980)

 39 ALR5th 283—§ 4, 57

State v. Garcia, 358 N.C. 382, 597 S.E.2d 724 (2004)

 32 ALR6th 1—§ 9

State v. Garcia, 374 So. 2d 601 (Fla. Dist. Ct. App. 3d Dist. 1979)

 122 ALR5th 439—§ 3

State v. Garcia, 500 N.E.2d 158 (Ind. 1986)

 74 ALR5th 319—§ 5, 6, 9, 11

 116 ALR5th 479—§ 5

State v. Garcia, 519 So. 2d 788 (La. Ct. App. 1st Cir. 1987)

 114 ALR5th 173—§ 7

State v. Garcia, 528 So. 2d 76, 13 FLW 1594 (Fla. App. D2 1988)

 15 ALR5th 39—§ 4

State v. Garcia, 616 N.W.2d 594 (Iowa 2000)

 50 ALR5th 467—§ 9

State v. Garcia, 823 S.W.2d 793 (Tex. App. San Antonio 1992)

 20 ALR6th 161—§ 3

 21 ALR6th 425—§ 3, 5

 23 ALR6th 573—§ 3

State v. Garcia, 866 P.2d 5 (Utah Ct. App. 1993)

 92 ALR5th 35—§ 22

State v. Garcia, 866 P.2d 5, 228 Utah Adv. Rep. 13 (Utah App. 1993)

 15 ALR5th 391—§ 32

State v. Garcia, 1997 ND 60, 561 N.W.2d 599 (N.D. 1997)

 32 ALR6th 171—§ 4, 18, 21

 33 ALR6th 1—§ 6, 20

State v. Garcia, 1997 N.D. 60, 561 N.W.2d 599 (N.D. 1997)

 89 ALR5th 629—§ 9, 11

State v. Garcia, 2001 WL 723241 (Ohio Ct. App. 8th Dist. Cuyahoga County 2001)

 70 ALR6th 1—§ 5

State v. Garcia, 2002 WL 242358 (Tenn. Crim. App. 2002)

 8 ALR6th 265—§ 12

State v. Garcia, 2005 WL 697521 (Tenn. Crim. App. 2005)

 26 ALR6th 511—§ 47

State v. Garcia, 2008 WL 4182863 (Ariz. Ct. App. Div. 1 2008)

 57 ALR6th 445—§ 20

State v. Garcia, 2009 UT App 384, 2009 WL 4987849 (Utah Ct. App. 2009)

 84 ALR6th 427—§ 4

State v. Garcia, 2009 WL 6567152 (N.M. Ct. App. 2009)

 92 ALR6th 295—§ 8, 12

 96 ALR6th 355—§ 9, 31

State v. Garcia, 2010-Ohio-5780, 2010 WL 4867609 (Ohio Ct. App. 8th Dist. Cuyahoga County 2010)

 71 ALR6th 1—§ 4

State v. Garcia, 2011-NMSC-003, 149 N.M. 185, 246 P.3d 1057 (2011)

 69 ALR6th 579—§ 11

State v. Garcia-Contreras, 191 Ariz. 144, 953 P.2d 536 (1998)

 99 ALR6th 295—§ 7

State v. Garcia-Hernandez, 67 Wash. App. 492, 837 P.2d 624 (Div. 1 1992)

 85 ALR5th 1—§ 27

For assistance, call 1-800-328-4880

State v. Garcia-Lorenzo, 110 N.C. App. 319, 430 S.E.2d 290 (1993)
30 ALR6th 103—§ 5

State v. Garcia-Trujillo, 89 Wash. App. 203, 948 P.2d 390 (Div. 1 1997)
97 ALR6th 567—§ 2, 4, 10

State v. Gard, 358 N.W.2d 463 (Minn. Ct. App. 1984)
34 ALR6th 1—§ 8

State v. Gardas, 108 Wis. 2d 785, 324 N.W.2d 833 (1982)
48 ALR5th 659—§ 32

State v. Gardiner, 127 Idaho 156, 898 P.2d 615 (Ct. App. 1995)
92 ALR5th 35—§ 25, 26
93 ALR5th 327—§ 4, 7, 9, 22, 28, 29

State v. Gardner, 2 NCA 233, 498 N.W.2d 605 (Neb. Ct. App. 1993)
22 ALR5th 1—§ 61

State v. Gardner, 16 Or. App. 464, 518 P.2d 1341 (1974)
7 ALR5th 758—§ 14

State v. Gardner, 28 Wash. App. 721, 626 P.2d 56 (Div. 1 1981)
9 ALR6th 1—§ 8

State v. Gardner, 91 N.M. 302, 573 P.2d 236 (Ct. App. 1977)
24 ALR6th 747—§ 37

State v. Gardner, 95 N.M. 171, 619 P.2d 847 (Ct. App. 1980)
99 ALR5th 557—§ 12

State v. Gardner, 201 N.C. 123, 159 S.E. 8 (1931)
19 ALR6th 577—§ 7

State v. Gardner, 328 N.W.2d 159 (Minn. 1983)
73 ALR5th 383—§ 18

State v. Gardner, 606 S.W.2d 236 (Mo. Ct. App. W.D. 1980)
67 ALR5th 637—§ 5, 7

State v. Gardner, 616 A.2d 1124 (R.I. 1992)
72 ALR5th 529—§ 7

State v. Gardner, 649 So. 2d 519 (La. App. 3d Cir. 1994)
42 ALR5th 581—§ 5

State v. Gardner, 651 So. 2d 282 (La. 1995)
42 ALR5th 581—§ 5

State v. Gardner, 685 S.E.2d 115 (N.C. Ct. App. 2009)
57 ALR6th 1—§ 4

State v. Gardner, 789 P.2d 273 (Utah 1989)
42 ALR6th 237—§ 8

State v. Gardner, 789 P.2d 273, 101 Utah Adv. Rep. 3 (Utah 1989)
26 ALR5th 603—§ 4

State v. Gardner, 947 P.2d 630, 62 A.L.R.5th 757 (Utah 1997)
62 ALR5th 121—§ 9

State v. Gardner, 955 S.W.2d 819 (Mo. Ct. App. E.D. 1997)
74 ALR5th 643—§ 3

State v. Garfole, 76 N.J. 445, 388 A.2d 587 (1978)
22 ALR5th 1—§ 4, 8, 15, 24, 31, 32, 36, 45 to 47

State v. Garfole, 80 N.J. 350, 403 A.2d 888 (1979)
22 ALR5th 1—§ 4, 48

State v. Gargare, 88 NJL 389, 95 A. 625 (1915)
29 ALR5th 59—§ 38

State v. Gargus, 855 So. 2d 587 (Ala. Crim. App. 2003)
114 ALR5th 173—§ 8

State v. Garibay, 838 S.W.2d 268 (Tex. App. El Paso 1992)
96 ALR5th 327—§ 3

State v. Garland, 270 N.J. Super. 31, 636 A.2d 541 (App. Div. 1994)
58 ALR6th 499—§ 48

State v. Garland, 617 S.W.2d 176 (Tenn. Crim. 1981)
29 ALR5th 59—§ 58

State v. Garland, 617 S.W.2d 176 (Tenn. Crim. App. 1981)
23 ALR6th 1—§ 3, 7, 17

State v. Garlepied, 454 So. 2d 1147 (La. Ct. App. 4th Cir. 1984)
33 ALR6th 407—§ 40

State v. Garnenez, 2014 WL 6473490 (N.M. Ct. App. 2014)

102 ALR6th 279—§ 16
State v. Garner, 74 Ohio St. 3d 49, 1995-Ohio-168, 656 N.E.2d 623 (1995)
93 ALR6th 391—§ 23
102 ALR6th 365—§ 23
State v. Garner, 115 Ariz. 579, 566 P.2d 1055 (App. 1977)
15 ALR5th 391—§ 2, 5
State v. Garner, 136 N.C. App. 1, 523 S.E.2d 689 (1999)
83 ALR5th 541—§ 3
State v. Garner, 340 N.C. 573, 459 S.E.2d 718 (1995)
79 ALR5th 33—§ 72
State v. Garner, 621 So. 2d 1203 (La. Ct. App. 4th Cir. 1993)
32 ALR6th 1—§ 10
State v. Garner, 2002 WL 484969 (Minn. Ct. App. 2002)
69 ALR6th 579—§ 8, 18
State v. Garnett, 488 N.W.2d 695 (S.D. 1992)
92 ALR5th 35—§ 2, 21
State v. Garnica, 145 Wash. App. 1026, 2008 WL 2582492 (Div. 1 2008)
103 ALR6th 507—§ 8, 14
State v. Garren, 117 N.C. App. 393, 451 S.E.2d 315 (1994)
122 ALR5th 593—§ 2, 8, 16
State v. Garretson, 313 N.J. Super. 348, 712 A.2d 1226 (App. Div. 1998)
100 ALR5th 67—§ 14, 17, 19
State v. Garrett, 29 Or. App. 505, 564 P.2d 726 (1977)
45 ALR6th 435—§ 8
State v. Garrett, 76 Wash. App. 719, 887 P.2d 488 (1995)
38 ALR5th 433—§ 19
State v. Garrett, 181 N.C. App. 150, 639 S.E.2d 453 (2007)
99 ALR6th 295—§ 5
State v. Garrett, 182 W. Va. 166, 386 S.E.2d 823 (1989)
70 ALR5th 1—§ 8
72 ALR5th 109—§ 5
95 ALR5th 125—§ 3

State v. Garrett, 281 Or. 281, 574 P.2d 639 (1978)
6 ALR5th 733—§ 7, 16
State v. Garrett, 567 S.E.2d 523 (S.C. Ct. App. 2002)
100 ALR5th 67—§ 43
State v. Garrett, 682 S.W.2d 153 (Mo. Ct. App. S.D. 1984)
85 ALR5th 187—§ 9
State v. Garrett, 2001 WI App 240, 248 Wis. 2d 61, 635 N.W.2d 615 (Ct. App. 2001)
79 ALR6th 1—§ 38, 61
State v. Garrett, 2004-Ohio-2231, 2004 WL 943862 (Ohio Ct. App. 5th Dist. Richland County 2004)
99 ALR6th 295—§ 16
State v. Garris, 603 So. 2d 277 (La. Ct. App. 2d Cir. 1992)
17 ALR6th 757—§ 4
State v. Garrison, 16 Or. App. 588, 519 P.2d 1295 (1974)
90 ALR5th 225—§ 8
124 ALR5th 1—§ 4
State v. Garrison, 25 Ariz. App. 470, 544 P.2d 687 (Div. 1 1976)
70 ALR5th 533—§ 8
State v. Garrison, 118 Wash. 2d 870, 827 P.2d 1388 (1992)
80 ALR6th 239—§ 3, 20
State v. Garrison, 120 Ariz. 255, 585 P.2d 563 (1978)
1 ALR6th 657—§ 4
29 ALR6th 1—§ 10
State v. Garrison, 128 P.3d 741 (Alaska Ct. App. 2006)
28 ALR6th 505—§ 9
State v. Garrison, 911 So. 2d 346, 202 Ed. Law Rep. 443 (La. Ct. App. 2d Cir. 2005)
78 ALR6th 213—§ 4
State v. Garst, 970 So. 2d 1138 (La. Ct. App. 5th Cir. 2007)
77 ALR6th 197—§ 3, 14
State v. Gartland, 149 N.J. 456, 694 A.2d 564 (1997)
58 ALR5th 749—§ 8, 10
67 ALR5th 637—§ 2, 4, 7

State v. Gartland, 330 N.W.2d 881 (Minn. 1983)
84 ALR6th 427—§ 8

State v. Gartrell, 171 Mo. 489, 71 S.W. 1045 (1903)
101 ALR6th 499—§ 14

State v. Garvey, 42 Conn. 232, 1875 WL 1892 (1875)
103 ALR6th 137—§ 14

State v. Garvey, 283 N.W.2d 153 (N.D. 1979)
112 ALR5th 621—§ 5

State v. Gary F., 189 W. Va. 523, 432 S.E.2d 793 (1993)
37 ALR5th 703—§ 4

State v. Gary L. Benefiel, 1997 WL 117784 (Idaho Ct. App. 1997)
56 ALR6th 323—§ 7

State v. Garza, 21 Or. App. 807, 537 P.2d 114 (1975)
6 ALR6th 533—§ 20

State v. Garza, 104 Or. App. 350, 801 P.2d 860 (1990)
97 ALR6th 653—§ 14

State v. Garza, 112 Wash. App. 312, 48 P.3d 385 (Div. 1 2002)
19 ALR6th 697—§ 5, 17

State v. Garza, 150 Wash. 2d 360, 77 P.3d 347 (2003)
19 ALR6th 697—§ 5, 17
57 ALR6th 313—§ 2

State v. Garza, 239 Neb. 98, 474 N.W.2d 246 (1991)
23 ALR6th 307—§ 42

State v. Garza, 242 Neb. 573, 496 N.W.2d 448 (1993)
12 ALR5th 89—§ 5, 10

State v. Garza, 337 N.W.2d 823 (S.D. 1983)
38 ALR5th 433—§ 3

State v. Gasaway, 1998 WL 131536 (Tenn. Crim. App. 1998)
73 ALR5th 383—§ 5

State v. Gaskin, 412 So. 2d 1007 (La. 1982)
16 ALR6th 329—§ 4
24 ALR6th 591—§ 4, 14

State v. Gaspar, 8 Haw. App. 317, 801 P.2d 30 (1990)
19 ALR6th 115—§ 6, 8, 14

State v. Gaspard, 625 So. 2d 368 (La. Ct. App. 3d Cir. 1993)
66 ALR5th 397—§ 8

State v. Gasparico, 694 A.2d 1204 (R.I. 1997)
27 ALR6th 183—§ 8

State v. Gasser, 29 Ohio App. 3d 115, 29 Ohio B.R. 131, 504 N.E.2d 73 (Wayne Co. 1985)
2 ALR5th 725—§ 13

State v. Gaston, 110 Ohio App. 3d 835, 675 N.E.2d 526 (11th Dist. Lake County 1996)
34 ALR6th 1—§ 5

State v. Gates, 25 Ariz. App. 241, 542 P.2d 822 (Div. 1 1975)
95 ALR5th 229—§ 2, 13, 31

State v. Gates, 65 N.C. App. 277, 309 S.E.2d 498 (1983)
37 ALR5th 319—§ 6

State v. Gates, 118 Ariz. 357, 576 P.2d 1357 (1978)
71 ALR6th 283—§ 6

State v. Gates, 182 Ariz. 459, 897 P.2d 1345, 174 Ariz. Adv. Rep. 30 (App. 1994)
42 ALR5th 291—§ 25

State v. Gates, 306 N.J. Super. 322, 703 A.2d 696 (Law Div. 1997)
50 ALR5th 703—§ 38
45 ALR6th 643—§ 18

State v. Gatewood, 2009-Ohio-5610, 2009 WL 3403167 (Ohio Ct. App. 2d Dist. Clark County 2009)
99 ALR6th 295—§ 12

State v. Gatien, 87 Ohio Misc. 2d 5, 688 N.E.2d 54 (Mun. Ct. 1997)
17 ALR6th 757—§ 5

State v. Gatone, 698 A.2d 230 (R.I. 1997)
86 ALR5th 463—§ 3, 9
102 ALR6th 365—§ 21

State v. Gatson, 2009 WL 2767199 (Mich. Ct. App. 2009)
64 ALR6th 131—§ 5

State v. Gattis, 1996 WL 769328 (Del. Super. Ct. 1996)

15 ALR6th 319—§ 3, 6, 8, 11

State v. Gattling, 95 N.J. Super. 103, 230 A.2d 157 (1967)

45 ALR5th 591—§ 15

State v. Gaudet, 638 So. 2d 1216 (La. Ct. App. 1st Cir. 1994)

90 ALR5th 453—§ 12

State v. Gaudin, 152 Me. 13, 120 A.2d 823 (1956)

50 ALR5th 703—§ 9

State v. Gaughran, 260 N.J. Super. 283, 615 A.2d 1293 (Law Div. 1992)

49 ALR5th 639—§ 2, 4

State v. Gaularpp, 144 Minn. 86, 174 N.W. 445 (1919)

5 ALR5th 243—§ 62

State v. Gauldin, 44 N.C. App. 19, 259 S.E.2d 779 (1979)

114 ALR5th 173—§ 10

State v. Gause, 1993 WL 140445 (Ohio Ct. App. 9th Dist.Lorain County 1993)

57 ALR5th 141—§ 7

State v. Gauthier, 854 So. 2d 910 (La. Ct. App. 3d Cir. 2003)

4 ALR6th 113—§ 15

State v. Gave, 77 Wash. App. 333, 890 P.2d 1088 (Div. 2 1995)

60 ALR5th 1—§ 8, 11

45 ALR6th 643—§ 9

State v. Gavin, 51 Ohio App. 2d 49, 5 Ohio Op. 3d 168, 365 N.E.2d 1263 (8th Dist.Cuyahoga County 1977)

55 ALR5th 125—§ 3, 8

State v. Gavin, 328 N.W.2d 501 (Iowa 1983)

83 ALR5th 277—§ 24

State v. Gawron, 112 Idaho 841, 736 P.2d 1295 (1987)

99 ALR5th 557—§ 3, 15

State v. Gaxiola, 550 P.2d 1298 (Utah 1976)

16 ALR6th 329—§ 4

24 ALR6th 591—§ 4

State v. Gay, 19 S.C.L. 364, 1 Hill (S.C.) 364, 1833 WL 1681 (Ct. App. 1833)

57 ALR6th 445—§ 10

State v. Gay, 2010 WL 2089658 (N.J. Super. Ct. App. Div. 2010)

99 ALR6th 295—§ 16

State v. Gayden, 1985 WL 7377 (Ohio Ct. App. 3d Dist. Allen County 1985)

20 ALR6th 479—§ 14

State v. Gaynor, 119 N.J.L. 582, 197 A. 360 (N.J. Ct. Err. & App. 1938)

58 ALR6th 385—§ 4

State v. G.E.A., 2009 WL 2498202 (Minn. Ct. App. 2009)

69 ALR6th 1—§ 21

State v. Geasley, 85 Ohio App. 3d 360, 619 N.E.2d 1086 (9th Dist. Summit County 1993)

81 ALR6th 505—§ 39

State v. Gebeck, 635 N.W.2d 385 (Minn. Ct. App. 2001)

106 ALR5th 377—§ 4

State v. Gedarro, 19 Wash. App. 826, 579 P.2d 949 (Div. 2 1978)

9 ALR6th 177—§ 42

State v. Gedutis, 163 Vt. 591, 653 A.2d 761 (1994)

52 ALR5th 559—§ 5

State v. Gee, 92 N.C. 756 (1885)

11 ALR5th 831—§ 4, 13

State v. Gee, 262 S.C. 373, 204 S.E.2d 727 (1974)

33 ALR6th 1—§ 4

State v. Gehring, 127 Wash. App. 1024, 2005 WL 1097805 (Div. 2 2005)

73 ALR6th 49—§ 3, 12

State v. Gehrke, 474 N.W.2d 722 (S.D. 1991)

7 ALR5th 263—§ 7

State v. Geiger, 2003-Ohio-4060, 2003 WL 21757704 (Ohio Ct. App. 8th Dist. Cuyahoga County 2003)

70 ALR6th 1—§ 14

State v. Geisler, 22 Conn. App. 142, 576 A.2d 1283 (1990)

119 ALR5th 379—§ 8

58 ALR6th 499—§ 87

State v. Geisler, 222 Conn. 672, 610 A.2d 1225 (1992)

19 ALR5th 470—§ 3, 9
State v. Gell, 151 N.C. App. 599, 2002 WL 1542925 (2002)

40 ALR6th 463—§ 5
State v. Gella, 92 Haw. 135, 988 P.2d 200 (1999)

20 ALR6th 479—§ 3
State v. Gelormino, 24 Conn. App. 563, 590 A.2d 480 (1991)

5 ALR5th 243—§ 58
State v. Gemler, 176 Vt. 257, 2004 VT 3, 844 A.2d 757 (2004)

45 ALR6th 337—§ 9
State v. Gengler, 1993 WL 332450 (Ohio App. Portage Co. 1993)

52 ALR5th 655—§ 3
State v. Gennett, 6 Ohio Misc. 176, 35 Ohio Op. 2d 368, 217 N.E.2d 275 (Mun. Ct. 1966)

6 ALR6th 533—§ 20
State v. Genovesi, 871 P.2d 547 (Utah Ct. App. 1994)

65 ALR5th 407—§ 3
State v. Genovesi, 909 P.2d 916 (Utah Ct. App. 1995)

58 ALR6th 499—§ 33
State v. Genre, 2006 ND 77, 712 N.W.2d 624 (N.D. 2006)

55 ALR6th 513—§ 8 to 10
State v. Gentile, 515 N.W.2d 16 (Iowa 1994)

45 ALR5th 531—§ 7
State v. Gentry, 61 Ohio Misc. 2d 31, 573 N.E.2d 220 (Mun. Ct. 1990)

47 ALR6th 107—§ 11
State v. Gentry, 125 Wash. 2d 570, 888 P.2d 1105 (1995)

79 ALR5th 33—§ 2, 6, 7, 9, 14, 15, 25, 42, 53
38 ALR6th 439—§ 12
83 ALR6th 255—§ 3, 20
State v. George, 50 Ohio App. 2d 297, 4 Ohio Op. 3d 259, 362 N.E.2d 1223 (10th Dist. Franklin County 1975)

28 ALR6th 281—§ 8, 12, 13
State v. George, 67 Wash. App. 217, 834 P.2d 664 (Div. 1 1992)

73 ALR5th 383—§ 3

State v. George, 109 N.H. 531, 257 A.2d 19 (1969)

33 ALR5th 571—§ 3
State v. George, 110 Wash. App. 1070, 2002 WL 453589 (Div. 1 2002)

106 ALR5th 397—§ 4
State v. George, 127 Idaho 693, 905 P.2d 626 (1995)

66 ALR5th 397—§ 16
State v. George, 185 W. Va. 539, 408 S.E.2d 291 (1991)

6 ALR6th 533—§ 21
34 ALR6th 1—§ 12
State v. George, 219 Mont. 377, 711 P.2d 1379 (1986)

7 ALR5th 73—§ 2, 8
State v. George, 250 Ark. 968, 470 S.W.2d 593 (1971)

97 ALR5th 537—§ 26
State v. George, 271 N.C. 438, 156 S.E.2d 845 (1967)

70 ALR6th 361—§ 5, 29, 31
State v. George, 323 S.C. 496, 476 S.E.2d 903 (1996)

70 ALR5th 587—§ 17
State v. George, 331 S.C. 342, 503 S.E.2d 168 (1998)

110 ALR5th 329—§ 5, 6
State v. George, 717 S.W.2d 857 (Mo. App. 1986)

42 ALR5th 291—§ 25
State v. George, 1997 WL 110007 (Tenn. Crim. App. 1997)

73 ALR5th 383—§ 5
State v. George, 2002-Ohio-4205, 2002 WL 1881159 (Ohio Ct. App. 5th Dist. Richland County 2002)

69 ALR6th 1—§ 29
State v. Georgeoff, 163 Ariz. 434, 788 P.2d 1185 (1990)

9 ALR6th 541—§ 29
State v. Gerard, 57 Wis. 2d 611, 205 N.W.2d 374 (1973)

87 ALR6th 109—§ 66
State v. Gerchow, 36 So. 3d 304 (La. Ct. App. 1st Cir. 2010)

69 ALR6th 1—§ 27

State v. Gerhardt, 161 Ariz. 410, 778
P.2d 1306 (Ct. App. Div. 1 1989)
24 ALR6th 1—§ 38
State v. Gerlaugh, 134 Ariz. 164, 654
P.2d 800 (1982)
33 ALR5th 571—§ 3
State v. Gerling, 76 Ohio App. 3d 576,
602 N.E.2d 734 (1st Dist. Hamilton
County 1991)
102 ALR5th 525—§ 13
47 ALR6th 107—§ 11, 12
State v. Germaine, 152 Vt. 106, 564
A.2d 604 (1989)
70 ALR5th 533—§ 3
State v. Germane, 971 A.2d 555 (R.I.
2009)
63 ALR6th 351—§ 3
64 ALR6th 1—§ 7, 12
65 ALR6th 1—§ 4
State v. Germann, 2007 WL 218767
(N.J. Super. Ct. App. Div. 2007)
57 ALR6th 313—§ 6
State v. Gersin, 76 Ohio St. 3d 491, 668
N.E.2d 486 (1996)
87 ALR5th 693—§ 3
State v. Gersin, 1994 WL 652622 (Ohio
Ct. App. 11th Dist. Lake County
1994)
90 ALR5th 453—§ 17
State v. Gertrude, 309 N.J. Super. 354,
707 A.2d 178 (App. Div. 1998)
99 ALR6th 295—§ 12
State v. Gertsch, 2000 WL 1779003
(Idaho Ct. App. 2000)
89 ALR5th 629—§ 5
State v. Gertz, 918 P.2d 1056, 204 Ariz.
Adv. Rep. 45 (Ariz. App. 1995)
29 ALR5th 1—§ 3
State v. Gervais, 394 A.2d 1183 (Me.
1978)
57 ALR5th 141—§ 13
State v. Gesinger, 1997 SD 6, 559
N.W.2d 549 (S.D. 1997)
34 ALR6th 1—§ 10
State v. Gessler, 142 Ariz. 379, 690 P.2d
98 (App. 1984)
18 ALR5th 1—§ 2, 4

State v. Gethers, 585 So. 2d 1140 (Fla.
Dist. Ct. App. 4th Dist. 1991)
70 ALR5th 461—§ 2, 3
State v. Getsinger, 27 Or. App. 339, 556
P.2d 147 (1976)
92 ALR5th 35—§ 25
State v. Gettel, 404 N.W.2d 902 (Minn.
Ct. App. 1987)
73 ALR5th 383—§ 28, 29, 31
State v. Gettier, 438 N.W.2d 1 (Iowa
1989)
72 ALR5th 529—§ 16
State v. Gettling, 2010 UT 17, 2010 WL
841282 (Utah 2010)
55 ALR6th 1—§ 30
State v. Getty, 55 Wash. App. 152, 777
P.2d 1 (Div. 1 1989)
71 ALR5th 1—§ 48
State v. Gevrez, 61 Ariz. 296, 148 P.2d
829 (1944)
82 ALR6th 373—§ 20
98 ALR6th 455—§ 4, 31
State v. Geyer, 194 Conn. 1, 480 A.2d
489 (1984)
37 ALR5th 319—§ 7
State v. Ghan, 721 S.W.2d 128 (Mo.
App. 1986)
5 ALR5th 243—§ 48
State v. Ghuste, 117 N.H. 943, 379 A.2d
1264 (1977)
26 ALR5th 1—§ 4
State v. Ghylin, 250 N.W.2d 252 (N.D.
1977)
52 ALR5th 655—§ 8
92 ALR6th 295—§ 8, 12
93 ALR6th 207—§ 9
95 ALR6th 1—§ 29
State v. Giallombardo, 29 Ohio App. 3d
279, 504 N.E.2d 1202 (11th Dist.
Portage County 1986)
51 ALR6th 219—§ 4
State v. Gianetti, 38 Conn. L. Rptr. 524,
2005 WL 407638 (Conn. Super. Ct.
2005)
69 ALR6th 317—§ 3
State v. Gibbons, 305 N.W.2d 331
(Minn. 1981)

9 ALR5th 369—§ 6

State v. Gibbons, 418 A.2d 830 (R.I. 1980)

39 ALR5th 283—§ 4

78 ALR5th 1—§ 25

State v. Gibbs, 126 N.H. 347, 492 A.2d 1367 (1985)

37 ALR5th 703—§ 5

93 ALR5th 527—§ 3

State v. Gibbs, 244 Mont. 251, 797 P.2d 928 (1990)

50 ALR5th 703—§ 23

State v. Gibbs, 254 Conn. 578, 758 A.2d 327 (2000)

94 ALR5th 537—§ 5

State v. Gibler, 2001-Ohio-1925, 2000 WL 1344545 (Ohio Ct. App. 3d Dist. Defiance County 2000)

80 ALR6th 239—§ 9, 11

State v. Gibson, 15 N.J. 384, 105 A.2d 1, 42 A.L.R.2d 1461 (1954)

72 ALR5th 529—§ 6

State v. Gibson, 17 P.3d 635 (Wash. Ct. App. Div. 2 2001)

11 ALR5th 52—§ 13

State v. Gibson, 32 Wash. App. 217, 646 P.2d 786 (Div. 1 1982)

78 ALR5th 197—§ 14

State v. Gibson, 38 Or. App. 593, 590 P.2d 797 (1979)

22 ALR5th 660—§ 10, 13

State v. Gibson, 104 Wash. App. 792, 17 P.3d 635 (Div. 2 2001)

58 ALR6th 499—§ 12

State v. Gibson, 126 Idaho 256, 881 P.2d 551 (App. 1994)

52 ALR5th 655—§ 6

State v. Gibson, 126 N.J. Super. 25, 312 A.2d 662 (App. Div. 1973)

7 ALR6th 169—§ 20

State v. Gibson, 144 Or. App. 523, 928 P.2d 344 (1996)

65 ALR6th 359—§ 8

State v. Gibson, 152 Wash. App. 945, 219 P.3d 964 (Div. 2 2009)

55 ALR6th 1—§ 3, 10

State v. Gibson, 186 W. Va. 465, 413 S.E.2d 120 (1991)

72 ALR5th 403—§ 3

State v. Gibson, 228 Neb. 455, 422 N.W.2d 570 (1988)

28 ALR6th 505—§ 7, 18

State v. Gibson, 391 So. 2d 421 (La. 1980)

18 ALR6th 1—§ 2

State v. Gibson, 623 S.W.2d 93 (Mo. Ct. App. W.D. 1981)

124 ALR5th 1—§ 5

State v. Gibson, 856 S.W.2d 78 (Mo. App. 1993)

45 ALR5th 1—§ 4, 10, 11, 18, 30

State v. Gibson, 973 S.W.2d 231 (Tenn. Crim. App. 1997)

82 ALR6th 373—§ 9, 17

State v. Gibson, 2000 WL 222011 (Ohio Ct. App. 5th Dist. Richland County 2000)

78 ALR5th 489—§ 10

State v. Gibson, 2002 MT 87N, 310 Mont. 538, 52 P.3d 402 (2002)

63 ALR6th 351—§ 3

State v. Gibson, 2002-Ohio-3153, 2002 WL 1357282 (Ohio Ct. App. 11th Dist. Trumbull County 2002)

31 ALR6th 49—§ 4

State v. Gibson, 2003 WL 22080792 (Tenn. Crim. App. 2003)

84 ALR6th 293—§ 33

State v. Gibson, 2004 WL 2827000 (Tenn. Crim. App. 2004)

63 ALR6th 351—§ 3

State v. Gibson, 2010-Ohio-3447, 2010 WL 2891512 (Ohio Ct. App. 2d Dist. Champaign County 2010)

64 ALR6th 1—§ 19

State v. Giddens, 335 Md. 205, 642 A.2d 870, 37 A.L.R.5th 783 (1994)

37 ALR5th 319—§ 6

State v. Giddens, 681 S.E.2d 504 (N.C. Ct. App. 2009)

57 ALR6th 1—§ 4

State v. Giddens, 2002-Ohio-6148, 2002 WL 31525379 (Ohio Ct. App. 3d Dist. Allen County 2002)

CASES CITED IN ALR5th and ALR6th

71 ALR6th 1—§ 5

State v. Giddings, 216 Kan. 14, 531 P.2d 445 (1975)

108 ALR5th 593—§ 24, 38

State v. Gideon, 257 Kan. 591, 894 P.2d 850 (1995)

79 ALR5th 33—§ 27, 39, 40

State v. Gieffels, 554 P.2d 460 (Alaska 1976)

49 ALR5th 639—§ 4

State v. Gifford, 2008 WL 1813105 (Tenn. Crim. App. 2008)

69 ALR6th 1—§ 22

State v. Giffrow, 127 N.W. 1009 (Iowa 1910)

103 ALR6th 35—§ 16

State v. Giguere, 184 Conn. 400, 439 A.2d 1040 (1981)

22 ALR5th 1—§ 8, 17, 39, 58

State v. Gilbert, 24 Kan. App. 2d 159, 942 P.2d 660 (1997)

11 ALR5th 52—§ 12

State v. Gilbert, 273 S.C. 690, 258 S.E.2d 890 (1979)

10 ALR5th 700—§ 16

State v. Gilbert, 354 So. 2d 508 (La. 1978)

6 ALR6th 533—§ 17

State v. Gilbert, 2009-Ohio-5528, 921 N.E.2d 1126 (Ohio Ct. App. 2d Dist. Clark County 2009)

55 ALR6th 1—§ 6, 40

State v. Gilberto L., 292 Conn. 226, 972 A.2d 205 (2009)

65 ALR6th 537—§ 46, 50, 52

State v. Gilbertson, 95 Wis. 2d 102, 288 N.W.2d 877 (App. 1980)

33 ALR5th 453—§ 5, 8

State v. Gilbertson, 1996 WL 706845 (Minn. Ct. App. 1996)

84 ALR6th 293—§ 22

State v. Gilchrest, 25 Wash. App. 427, 607 P.2d 1243 (Div. 1 1980)

78 ALR6th 417—§ 4, 16

State v. Gilchrest, 37 Wash. App. 531, 681 P.2d 865 (Div. 1 1984)

70 ALR6th 361—§ 8

State v. Gilcreast, 2003-Ohio-7177, 2003 WL 23094873 (Ohio Ct. App. 9th Dist. Summit County 2003)

23 ALR6th 307—§ 40

State v. Gilcrist, 91 Wash. 2d 603, 590 P.2d 809 (1979)

99 ALR6th 295—§ 5

State v. Gilder, 223 Kan. 220, 574 P.2d 196 (1977)

99 ALR6th 295—§ 5

State v. Giles, 239 Md. 458, 212 A.2d 101 (1965)

101 ALR5th 187—§ 8

State v. Giles, 669 A.2d 192 (Me. 1996)

47 ALR6th 107—§ 26

State v. Giles, 697 So. 2d 699 (La. Ct. App. 2d Cir. 1997)

104 ALR5th 229—§ 6
115 ALR5th 403—§ 6, 8
116 ALR5th 325—§ 10
101 ALR6th 1—§ 14, 19, 31, 37

State v. Giles, 2006 WL 3813679 (La. Ct. App. 1st Cir. 2006)

32 ALR6th 1—§ 5

State v. Gilfesis, 148 N.J. Super. 369, 372 A.2d 680 (1977)

32 ALR5th 659—§ 2, 3

State v. Gilham, 97 Mo. App. 296, 70 S.W. 943 (1902)

97 ALR5th 537—§ 25

State v. Gill, 26 Kan. App. 2d 127, 980 P.2d 591 (1999)

59 ALR5th 135—§ 5

State v. Gill, 70 Ohio St. 3d 150, 637 N.E.2d 897 (1994)

52 ALR5th 655—§ 3

State v. Gill, 173 Ga. App. 848, 328 S.E.2d 561 (1985)

23 ALR6th 307—§ 29

State v. Gill, 243 Or. 621, 415 P.2d 166 (1966)

99 ALR6th 113—§ 11

State v. Gill, 488 So. 2d 765 (La. App. 3d Cir. 1986)

2 ALR5th 725—§ 13

State v. Gillard, 40 Ohio St. 3d 226, 533 N.E.2d 272 (1988)

10 ALR5th 700—§ 33
State v. Gille, 2009 OK CIV APP 96, 227 P.3d 1117 (Div. 3 2009)
69 ALR6th 1—§ 23
State v. Gillen, 266 Wis. 2d 693, 2003 WI App 162, 667 N.W.2d 377 (Ct. App. 2003)
121 ALR5th 551—§ 6, 13
State v. Gilles, 173 Wis. 2d 101, 496 N.W.2d 133 (Ct. App. 1992)
112 ALR5th 621—§ 3, 7
State v. Gillespie, 18 Wash. App. 313, 569 P.2d 1174 (Div. 2 1977)
65 ALR5th 407—§ 3, 7, 8, 11, 16
State v. Gillespie, 41 Wash. App. 640, 705 P.2d 808 (Div. 1 1985)
57 ALR6th 445—§ 22
State v. Gillespie, 100 N.J. Super. 71, 241 A.2d 239, 29 A.L.R.3d 927 (1968)
52 ALR5th 655—§ 3
State v. Gillespie, 203 N.J. Super. 417, 497 A.2d 232 (1984)
7 ALR5th 263—§ 7
State v. Gillespie, 445 N.W.2d 661 (S.D. 1989)
5 ALR5th 243—§ 58
State v. Gillespie, 486 So. 2d 984 (La. Ct. App. 2d Cir. 1986)
89 ALR6th 565—§ 12, 29, 31, 33
State v. Gillespie, 503 N.W.2d 612 (Iowa Ct. App. 1993)
113 ALR5th 517—§ 5
State v. Gillespie, 530 N.W.2d 446, 67 A.L.R.5th 713 (Iowa 1995)
67 ALR5th 361—§ 5
State v. Gilliam, 81 Wash. 186, 142 P. 470 (1914)
116 ALR5th 1—§ 18
State v. Gilliam, 748 So. 2d 622 (La. Ct. App. 4th Cir. 1999)
124 ALR5th 1—§ 4
State v. Gillies, 135 Ariz. 500, 662 P.2d 1007 (1983)
84 ALR5th 487—§ 21
State v. Gillies, 142 Ariz. 564, 691 P.2d 655 (1984)

70 ALR5th 647—§ 5
87 ALR6th 1—§ 41
State v. Gillingham, 2010-Ohio-379, 2010 WL 405446 (Ohio Ct. App. 2d Dist. Montgomery County 2010)
64 ALR6th 1—§ 9
State v. Gillison, 2011 WL 6101 (N.J. Super. Ct. App. Div. 2011)
99 ALR6th 295—§ 13
State v. Gillispie, 790 S.W.2d 519 (Mo. Ct. App. S.D. 1990)
105 ALR5th 529—§ 12
State v. Gillord, 653 So. 2d 810 (La. Ct. App. 3d Cir. 1995)
73 ALR5th 383—§ 5
State v. Gilman, 110 R.I. 207, 291 A.2d 425 (1972)
34 ALR5th 125—§ 25, 31
State v. Gilmartin, 535 N.W.2d 650 (Minn. Ct. App. 1995)
69 ALR6th 579—§ 8, 23
State v. Gilmore, 103 N.J. 508, 511 A.2d 1150 (1986)
47 ALR5th 259—§ 2
63 ALR5th 375—§ 2, 5, 6
State v. Gilmore, 529 So. 2d 859 (La. Ct. App. 4th Cir. 1988)
104 ALR5th 357—§ 3
54 ALR6th 429—§ 5, 9, 25
State v. Gilmore, 658 So. 2d 629 (Fla. Dist. Ct. App. 2d Dist. 1995)
113 ALR5th 597—§ 8
State v. Gilmore, 661 S.W.2d 519 (Mo. 1983)
20 ALR5th 177—§ 11
State v. Gilmore, 727 S.W.2d 469 (Mo. Ct. App. E.D. 1987)
105 ALR5th 529—§ 13
State v. Gilmour, 522 N.W.2d 595 (Iowa 1994)
42 ALR5th 291—§ 10, 11, 21, 36
State v. Gilpin, 132 Idaho 643, 977 P.2d 905 (Ct. App. 1999)
76 ALR5th 1—§ 2, 3
77 ALR5th 201—§ 2
78 ALR5th 1—§ 2
79 ALR5th 237—§ 2

State v. Gilroy, 313 N.W.2d 513 (Iowa 1981)
  62 ALR5th 629—§ 4, 5
State v. Gils, 216 Wis. 2d 383, 576 N.W.2d 89 (Ct. App. 1998)
  68 ALR5th 343—§ 3
State v. Gilson, 800 So. 2d 727 (Fla. Dist. Ct. App. 5th Dist. 2001)
  113 ALR5th 597—§ 8
State v. Gilyard, 979 S.W.2d 138 (Mo. 1998)
  86 ALR5th 59—§ 6
State v. Gimbrone, 2011-Ohio-632, 2011 WL 486508 (Ohio Ct. App. 2d Dist. Montgomery County 2011)
  64 ALR6th 1—§ 19
State v. Ginardi, 111 N.J. Super. 435, 268 A.2d 534, 42 A.L.R.3d 1198 (1970)
  23 ALR5th 672—§ 2, 3
  39 ALR5th 283—§ 4, 62
State v. Ginn, 128 Wash. App. 872, 117 P.3d 1155 (Div. 2 2005)
  50 ALR6th 353—§ 19, 21, 28
State v. Ginorio, 619 So. 2d 790 (La. App. 4th Cir. 1993)
  45 ALR5th 1—§ 4, 6, 10, 17, 29
State v. Ginyard, 122 N.C. App. 25, 468 S.E.2d 525 (1996)
  102 ALR5th 447—§ 16
State v. Gionfriddo, 154 Conn. 90, 221 A.2d 851 (1966)
  104 ALR5th 357—§ 3
State v. Giordano, 2004 WL 1463052 (Conn. Super. Ct. 2004)
  52 ALR6th 1—§ 30
  53 ALR6th 1—§ 7
State v. Giorgetti, 868 So. 2d 512 (Fla. 2004)
  33 ALR6th 91—§ 36
State v. Gipson, 2012-Ohio-515, 2012 WL 432851 (Ohio Ct. App. 6th Dist. Erie County 2012)
  94 ALR6th 579—§ 6
State v. Gist, 358 N.W.2d 664 (Minn. 1984)
  73 ALR5th 383—§ 24

State v. Giustra, 1994 WL 564659 (Wis App)
  50 ALR5th 581—§ 7, 9, 20
State v. Givens, 217 Wis. 2d 180, 580 N.W.2d 340 (Ct. App. 1998)
  18 ALR5th 1—§ 11
State v. Givens, 356 N.W.2d 58 (Minn. Ct. App. 1984)
  37 ALR6th 357—§ 21
State v. Givens, 544 N.W.2d 774 (Minn. 1996)
  73 ALR5th 383—§ 3
State v. Givens, 750 So. 2d 242 (La. Ct. App. 4th Cir. 1999)
  83 ALR6th 465—§ 5, 13
State v. Givens, 776 So. 2d 443, 88 A.L.R.5th 707 (La. 2001)
  88 ALR5th 67—§ 3
State v. Givens, 917 S.W.2d 215 (Mo. App. 1996)
  45 ALR5th 1—§ 3, 5, 11, 18
State v. Givens, 917 S.W.2d 215 (Mo. Ct. App. W.D. 1996)
  2 ALR6th 551—§ 4
State v. Glacken, 13 Ohio Misc. 2d 17, 469 N.E.2d 95 (Mun. Ct. 1984)
  112 ALR5th 621—§ 3
State v. Gladden, 279 N.C. 566, 184 S.E.2d 249 (1971)
  28 ALR6th 505—§ 9
State v. Gladney, 577 So. 2d 1179 (La. Ct. App. 2d Cir. 1991)
  57 ALR5th 141—§ 12
State v. Gladstone, 78 Wash. 2d 306, 474 P.2d 274, 42 A.L.R.3d 1061 (1970)
  34 ALR5th 125—§ 5, 8
State v. Glas, 147 Wash. 2d 410, 54 P.3d 147 (2002)
  120 ALR5th 337—§ 2, 3, 6
State v. Glaser, 93 Md. App. 579, 613 A.2d 1011 (1992)
  84 ALR6th 427—§ 12
State v. Glasper, 506 So. 2d 480 (Fla. Dist. Ct. App. 4th Dist. 1987)
  106 ALR5th 377—§ 3
  113 ALR5th 597—§ 8

State v. Glass, 9 Ohio Misc. 2d 10, 9 Ohio B.R. 240, 458 N.E.2d 1302 (1983)

41 ALR5th 171—§ 58, 92, 94, 104, 108

State v. Glassel, 211 Ariz. 33, 116 P.3d 1193 (2005)

21 ALR6th 1—§ 4

State v. Glauvitz, 1998 WL 422230 (Minn. Ct. App. 1998)

34 ALR6th 1—§ 10

State v. Gleason, 80 N.M. 382, 456 P.2d 215 (App. 1969)

29 ALR5th 59—§ 34, 79, 88

State v. Gleason, 123 Idaho 62, 844 P.2d 691 (1992)

90 ALR5th 453—§ 8

State v. Gleason, 130 Idaho 586, 944 P.2d 721 (Ct. App. 1997)

34 ALR6th 1—§ 12

State v. Gledhill, 67 N.J. 565, 342 A.2d 161 (1975)

108 ALR5th 593—§ 15
80 ALR6th 599—§ 5

State v. Glenn, 47 Conn. App. 706, 707 A.2d 736 (1998)

73 ALR6th 49—§ 54

State v. Glenn, 86 Wash. App. 40, 935 P.2d 679 (Div. 1 1997)

62 ALR6th 259—§ 3, 4, 8

State v. Glenn, 251 Conn. 567, 740 A.2d 856 (1999)

73 ALR6th 49—§ 3

State v. Glenn, 333 N.C. 296, 425 S.E.2d 688 (1993)

57 ALR5th 141—§ 3

State v. Glenner, 513 A.2d 1361 (Me. 1986)

29 ALR6th 1—§ 10

State v. Glens Falls Ins. Co., 125 Ariz. 328, 609 P.2d 598 (App. 1980)

14 ALR5th 695—§ 19

State v. Glidden, 127 N.H. 359, 499 A.2d 1349 (1985)

72 ALR5th 109—§ 4, 5

State v. Globe Communications Corp., 648 So. 2d 110 (Fla. 1994)

40 ALR5th 787—§ 3

State v. Glosson, 441 So. 2d 1178 (Fla. App. D1 1983)

18 ALR5th 1—§ 14

State v. Glosson, 462 So. 2d 108 2, 10 FLW 56 (Fla. 1985)

18 ALR5th 1—§ 24

State v. Glosson, 462 So. 2d 1082, 10 FLW 56 (Fla. 1985)

18 ALR5th 1—§ 12, 14

State v. Glover, 52 Ohio App. 2d 35, 6 Ohio Op. 3d 20, 367 N.E.2d 1202 (10th Dist.Franklin County 1976)

65 ALR5th 623—§ 3

State v. Glover, 212 Neb. 713, 325 N.W.2d 155 (1982)

78 ALR6th 417—§ 3

State v. Glover, 270 N.C. 319, 154 S.E.2d 305, 23 A.L.R.3d 492 (1967)

26 ALR5th 1—§ 3, 28, 42

State v. Glover, 1988 WL 130693 (Ohio Ct. App. 4th Dist. Gallia County 1988)

57 ALR6th 83—§ 6

State v. Glover, 2002-Ohio-6035, 2002 WL 31465952 (Ohio Ct. App. 9th Dist. Summit County 2002)

23 ALR6th 307—§ 38

State v. Glowacki, 131 Ohio App. 3d 640, 723 N.E.2d 193 (6th Dist. Wood County 1999)

23 ALR6th 307—§ 9, 15, 34

State v. Glynn, 38 Kan. App. 2d 437, 166 P.3d 1075 (2007)

93 ALR6th 275—§ 13
103 ALR6th 507—§ 26

State v. Glynn, 653 So. 2d 1288 (La. Ct. App. 1st Cir. 1995)

104 ALR5th 357—§ 3
54 ALR6th 429—§ 20

State v. Glynn, 1998 WL 150359 (Ohio Ct. App. 9th Dist. Medina County 1998)

78 ALR5th 489—§ 3

State v. Goad, 692 S.W.2d 32 (Tenn. Crim. App. 1985)

83 ALR5th 277—§ 11

State v. Gobern, 423 A.2d 1177 (R.I. 1981)

CASES CITED IN ALR5th and ALR6th

69 ALR6th 1—§ 21, 23
State v. Goble, 1998 WL 67673 (Ohio Ct. App. 3d Dist. Defiance County 1998)

78 ALR5th 489—§ 10
State v. Gocken, 71 Wash. App. 267, 857 P.2d 1074 (Div. 1 1993)

58 ALR6th 499—§ 52, 97
State v. Godbolt, 1999 WL 254370 (Ohio Ct. App. 5th Dist. Licking County 1999)

125 ALR5th 357—§ 6
State v. Godbolt, 2004-Ohio-317, 2004 WL 117608 (Ohio Ct. App. 5th Dist. Licking County 2004)

99 ALR6th 295—§ 9, 19
State v. Godfrey, 131 N.J. Super. 168, 329 A.2d 75 (App. Div. 1974)

32 ALR6th 1—§ 8
State v. Godfrey, 131 Vt. 629, 313 A.2d 390 (1973)

15 ALR5th 391—§ 50
State v. Godfrey, 137 Vt. 159, 400 A.2d 1026 (1979)

92 ALR6th 295—§ 7, 13
93 ALR6th 207—§ 6, 14, 18, 26
96 ALR6th 355—§ 24, 37, 54
State v. Godfrey, 476 So. 2d 1174 (La. Ct. App. 3d Cir. 1985)

85 ALR5th 547—§ 8
State v. Godsey, 60 S.W.3d 759 (Tenn. 2001)

69 ALR6th 579—§ 4
State v. Godsey, 272 Wis. 406, 75 N.W.2d 572 (1956)

29 ALR5th 59—§ 3, 14
State v. Godsoe, 106 Ariz. 461, 478 P.2d 85 (1970)

45 ALR5th 591—§ 14
State v. Godwin, 121 Idaho 491, 826 P.2d 452, 19 A.L.R.5th 1069 (1992)

19 ALR5th 884—§ 5
State v. Goebel, 2007 ND 4, 725 N.W.2d 578 (N.D. 2007)

69 ALR6th 579—§ 4
State v. Goehring, 2007-Ohio-5886, 2007 WL 3227386 (Ohio Ct. App. 6th Dist. Ottawa County 2007)

48 ALR6th 135—§ 9
State v. Goeman, 126 Wash. App. 1015, 2005 WL 519047 (Div. 1 2005)

26 ALR6th 511—§ 4, 25, 33
State v. Goens, 2003-Ohio-5402, 2003 WL 22318584 (Ohio Ct. App. 2d Dist. Montgomery County 2003)

33 ALR6th 407—§ 5
State v. Goering, 193 Kan. 307, 392 P.2d 930 (1964)

66 ALR5th 397—§ 3, 4, 6
State v. Goerner, 1999 WL 1100140 (Ohio Ct. App. 1st Dist. Hamilton County 1999)

35 ALR6th 361—§ 21
State v. Goettel, 117 Ariz. 287, 572 P.2d 115 (Ct. App. Div. 1 1977)

99 ALR5th 557—§ 3, 10
State v. Goetz, 7 Or. App. 515, 491 P.2d 220 (1971)

4 ALR5th 1—§ 21, 24
State v. Goetz, 187 Kan. 117, 353 P.2d 816 (1960)

37 ALR6th 357—§ 59
State v. Goff, 64 S.D. 80, 264 N.W. 665 (1936)

119 ALR5th 275—§ 13
State v. Goff, 82 Ohio St. 3d 123, 1998-Ohio-369, 694 N.E.2d 916 (1998)

83 ALR6th 255—§ 22
State v. Goff, 129 S.W.3d 857 (Mo. 2004)

103 ALR6th 347—§ 9, 10
State v. Goff, 449 S.W.2d 591 (Mo. 1970)

101 ALR5th 351—§ 14
State v. Goffstein, 342 Mo. 499, 116 S.W.2d 65 (1938)

29 ALR5th 59—§ 7, 40
State v. Goforth, 65 N.C. App. 302, 309 S.E.2d 488 (1983)

114 ALR5th 235—§ 11
State v. Gogg, 561 N.W.2d 360 (Iowa 1997)

113 ALR5th 517—§ 3
State v. Goham, 187 Neb. 34, 187 N.W.2d 305 (1971)

39 ALR5th 283—§ 3

State v. Goines, 16 Ohio App. 3d 168, 474 N.E.2d 1219 (2d Dist. Clark County 1984)

116 ALR5th 479—§ 5

State v. Goins, 24 N.C. App. 468, 211 S.E.2d 481 (1975)

11 ALR5th 497—§ 3, 9

State v. Goins, 1996 WL 438891 (Tenn. Crim. App. 1996)

57 ALR5th 141—§ 9

State v. Gokey, 154 Vt. 129, 574 A.2d 766 (1990)

38 ALR5th 433—§ 5

State v. Goldberg, 161 Kan. 174, 166 P.2d 664 (1946)

116 ALR5th 149—§ 12

State v. Goldberg, 819 So. 2d 123 (Ala. Crim. App. 2001)

33 ALR6th 91—§ 15

State v. Golden, 171 Ga. App. 27, 318 S.E.2d 693 (1984)

74 ALR5th 319—§ 5, 8, 9

State v. Golden, 175 W. Va. 551, 336 S.E.2d 198 (1985)

40 ALR6th 1—§ 4

State v. Golden, 177 Ohio App. 3d 771, 2008-Ohio-3227, 896 N.E.2d 170 (3d Dist. Paulding County 2008)

51 ALR6th 1—§ 20, 24

State v. Goldman, 95 N.J. Super. 50, 229 A.2d 818 (1967)

45 ALR5th 591—§ 15

State v. Goldsmith, 112 Ariz. 399, 542 P.2d 1098 (1975)

36 ALR5th 255—§ 33

State v. Gollehon, 262 Mont. 293, 864 P.2d 1257 (1993)

55 ALR6th 391—§ 5

State v. Golly, 2008-Ohio-447, 2008 WL 323152 (Ohio Ct. App. 8th Dist. Cuyahoga County 2008)

97 ALR6th 653—§ 30

State v. Golotta, 178 N.J. 205, 837 A.2d 359 (2003)

84 ALR6th 293—§ 6, 8, 10, 11, 14, 38

State v. Golphin, 352 N.C. 364, 533 S.E.2d 168 (2000)

110 ALR5th 1—§ 2, 11, 15
16 ALR6th 329—§ 4
24 ALR6th 591—§ 6, 14
32 ALR6th 1—§ 7
81 ALR6th 505—§ 28

State v. Golston, 66 Ohio App. 3d 423, 584 N.E.2d 1336 (8th Dist. Cuyahoga County 1990)

104 ALR5th 229—§ 4
34 ALR6th 539—§ 5
101 ALR6th 1—§ 4, 35

State v. Golubov, 2005-Ohio-4938, 2005 WL 2292822 (Ohio Ct. App. 9th Dist. Wayne County 2005)

15 ALR6th 515—§ 4

State v. Gomes, 79 Haw. 32, 897 P.2d 959 (1995)

9 ALR6th 633—§ 4, 13, 24
14 ALR6th 517—§ 8

State v. Gomes, 604 A.2d 1249 (R.I. 1992)

102 ALR6th 365—§ 26

State v. Gomez, 27 Ariz. App. 248, 553 P.2d 1233 (Div. 2 1976)

108 ALR5th 593—§ 29

State v. Gomez, 89 Vt. 490, 96 A. 190 (1915)

32 ALR5th 149—§ 45

State v. Gomez, 101 Idaho 802, 623 P.2d 110 (1980)

113 ALR5th 517—§ 10

State v. Gomez, 107 Or. App. 698, 813 P.2d 567 (1991)

109 ALR5th 99—§ 8

State v. Gomez, 163 S.W.3d 632 (Tenn. 2005)

26 ALR6th 511—§ 22

State v. Gomez, 1997-NMSC-006, 122 N.M. 777, 932 P.2d 1 (1997)

114 ALR5th 173—§ 9

State v. Gomez, 2010 WL 2396934 (Del. Super. Ct. 2010)

82 ALR6th 373—§ 8

State v. Gongora, 866 S.W.2d 172 (Mo. App. 1993)

---

32 ALR5th 149—§ 53

State v. Gonsalves, 108 Haw. 289, 119 P.3d 597, 26 A.L.R.6th 859 (2005)

26 ALR6th 511—§ 7, 11

State v. Gonsalves, 476 A.2d 108 (R.I. 1984)

106 ALR5th 701—§ 4

68 ALR6th 527—§ 13

State v. Gonyer, 1998 WL 352293 (Ohio Ct. App. 6th Dist. Wood County 1998)

78 ALR5th 489—§ 10

State v. Gonzales, 83 Wash. App. 587, 922 P.2d 210 (1996)

37 ALR5th 319—§ 7

State v. Gonzales, 92 Idaho 152, 438 P.2d 897 (1968)

55 ALR5th 125—§ 3, 9

State v. Gonzales, 111 N.M. 590, 808 P.2d 40 (App. 1991)

20 ALR5th 398—§ 10

State v. Gonzales, 117 Idaho 518, 789 P.2d 206 (Ct. App. 1990)

114 ALR5th 173—§ 7

State v. Gonzales, 181 Ariz. 502, 892 P.2d 838 (1995)

79 ALR5th 33—§ 40

91 ALR5th 343—§ 17

42 ALR6th 237—§ 8

State v. Gonzales, 217 Kan. 159, 535 P.2d 988 (1975)

86 ALR5th 59—§ 3, 4

State v. Gonzales, 314 N.W.2d 825 (Minn. 1982)

103 ALR5th 463—§ 5

State v. Gonzales, 604 A.2d 904 (Me. 1992)

49 ALR6th 343—§ 24

State v. Gonzales-Gutierrez, 216 Or. App. 97, 171 P.3d 384 (2007)

97 ALR6th 567—§ 3, 9

State v. Gonzales-Morales, 138 Wash. 2d 374, 979 P.2d 826 (1999)

32 ALR5th 149—§ 4, 85

State v. Gonzalez, 51 Wash. App. 242, 752 P.2d 939 (Div. 3 1988)

72 ALR6th 1—§ 4

State v. Gonzalez, 116 Wash. App. 1001, 2003 WL 723351 (Div. 3 2003)

63 ALR6th 1—§ 5, 36

State v. Gonzalez, 123 N.J. 462, 588 A.2d 816 (1991)

27 ALR5th 593—§ 29

State v. Gonzalez, 126 Wash. App. 1059, 2005 WL 843751 (Div. 3 2005)

22 ALR6th 1—§ 4

State v. Gonzalez, 143 N.H. 693, 738 A.2d 1247 (1999)

117 ALR5th 407—§ 4

State v. Gonzalez, 156 P.3d 674 (Kan. 2007)

26 ALR6th 511—§ 29

State v. Gonzalez, 206 Conn. 213, 537 A.2d 460 (1988)

93 ALR5th 527—§ 2

94 ALR5th 393—§ 2

95 ALR5th 611—§ 2

101 ALR5th 187—§ 2

102 ALR5th 327—§ 2

24 ALR6th 1—§ 3

53 ALR6th 81—§ 3

55 ALR6th 391—§ 3, 5

56 ALR6th 185—§ 3

State v. Gonzalez, 206 Conn. 391, 538 A.2d 210 (1988)

20 ALR5th 398—§ 3, 12, 42, 43

State v. Gonzalez, 272 Conn. 515, 864 A.2d 847 (2005)

40 ALR6th 1—§ 9

State v. Gonzalez, 283 Neb. 1, 807 N.W.2d 759 (2012)

74 ALR6th 373—§ 18

State v. Gonzalez, 467 So. 2d 723 (Fla. Dist. Ct. App. 3d Dist. 1985)

58 ALR6th 439—§ 48

State v. Gonzalez, 822 P.2d 1214 (Utah Ct. App. 1991)

108 ALR5th 593—§ 48

State v. Gonzalez, 853 P.2d 526, 29 A.L.R.5th 747 (Alaska 1993)

29 ALR5th 1—§ 4

State v. Gonzalez-Alaniz, 151 Or. App. 557, 950 P.2d 404 (1997)

27 ALR5th 593—§ 36

For assistance, call 1-800-328-4880

State v. Gonzalez-Faguaga, 266 Neb. 72, 662 N.W.2d 581 (2003)
9 ALR6th 541—§ 3
State v. Gonzalez-Gongora, 673 S.W.2d 811 (Mo. App. 1984)
32 ALR5th 149—§ 3, 54, 55
State v. Gonzalez-Hernandez, 122 Wash. App. 53, 92 P.3d 789 (Div. 2 2004)
97 ALR6th 567—§ 2, 4, 10
State v. Gonzalez-Perez, 997 So. 2d 1 (La. Ct. App. 1st Cir. 2008)
75 ALR6th 541—§ 12
State v. Gonzalez-Valle, 385 So. 2d 681 (Fla. Dist. Ct. App. 3d Dist. 1980)
65 ALR5th 407—§ 5, 11
State v. Gooch, 164 La. 186, 113 So. 812 (1927)
102 ALR5th 525—§ 19
State v. Good, 308 S.C. 313, 417 S.E.2d 643 (Ct. App. 1992)
62 ALR5th 629—§ 13
State v. Goodburn, 1990 WL 125192 (Ohio Ct. App. 5th Dist. Licking County 1990)
47 ALR6th 107—§ 3
State v. Goodchild, 151 Me. 48, 115 A.2d 725 (1955)
52 ALR5th 655—§ 5
State v. Goode, 341 N.C. 513, 461 S.E.2d 631 (1995)
90 ALR5th 453—§ 16
State v. Goode, 1998 WL 404026 (Ohio Ct. App. 2d Dist. Miami County 1998)
78 ALR5th 489—§ 3
State v. Gooden, 16 Ohio App. 3d 153, 474 N.E.2d 1237 (12th Dist. Madison County 1983)
38 ALR6th 97—§ 28
State v. Gooden, 22 Kan. App. 2d 271, 915 P.2d 169 (1996)
28 ALR6th 505—§ 13
State v. Gooding, 1999 MT 249, 296 Mont. 234, 989 P.2d 304 (1999)
93 ALR5th 327—§ 28
State v. Gooding, 1999 MT 249, 989 P.2d 304 (Mont. 1999)

101 ALR5th 619—§ 9
State v. Gooding, 2008-Ohio-5954, 2008 WL 4907546 (Ohio Ct. App. 5th Dist. Coshocton County 2008)
64 ALR6th 1—§ 9
State v. Goodman, 8 Ohio App. 2d 166, 37 Ohio Op. 2d 186, 221 N.E.2d 202 (7th Dist. Columbiana County 1966)
89 ALR6th 565—§ 5, 13, 14, 34
State v. Goodman, 150 Wash. 2d 774, 83 P.3d 410 (2004)
26 ALR6th 511—§ 42
State v. Goodman, 490 S.W.2d 86 (Mo. 1973)
5 ALR5th 243—§ 59
State v. Goodno, 511 A.2d 456 (Me. 1986)
33 ALR6th 407—§ 4
State v. Goodrich, 47 Wash. App. 114, 733 P.2d 1000 (1987)
15 ALR5th 391—§ 5
State v. Goodseal, 220 Kan. 487, 553 P.2d 279 (1976)
9 ALR6th 1—§ 6
State v. Goodson, 101 N.C. App. 665, 401 S.E.2d 118 (1991)
16 ALR6th 329—§ 4
24 ALR6th 591—§ 6, 14
State v. Goodson, 276 S.C. 243, 277 S.E.2d 602 (1981)
93 ALR5th 527—§ 13
State v. Goodson, 316 N.J. Super. 296, 720 A.2d 381 (App. Div. 1998)
50 ALR6th 455—§ 3
State v. Goodson, 943 S.W.2d 239 (Mo. Ct. App. E.D. 1997)
5 ALR5th 243—§ 10
State v. Goodson, 1999 WL 298072 (Ohio Ct. App. 12th Dist. Preble County 1999)
35 ALR6th 127—§ 5
State v. Goodwin, 118 N.H. 862, 395 A.2d 1234 (1978)
39 ALR5th 283—§ 4
State v. Goodwin, 173 N.J. 583, 803 A.2d 102 (2002)
71 ALR6th 1—§ 8

State v. Goodwin, 189 La. 443, 179 So. 591 (1938)
24 ALR5th 465—§ 41, 49
State v. Goodwin, 686 N.W.2d 40 (Minn. Ct. App. 2004)
50 ALR6th 455—§ 36
State v. Goodwin, 1994 WL 202828 (Ohio Ct. App. 3d Dist. Marion County 1994)
91 ALR5th 343—§ 28
State v. Goodwin, 1998 WL 856582 (Wash. Ct. App. Div. 2 1998)
73 ALR5th 383—§ 3
State v. Goodwin, 2000 WL 555232 (Tenn. Crim. App. 2000)
24 ALR6th 1—§ 29
State v. Goracke, 210 Ariz. 20, 106 P.3d 1035, 29 A.L.R.6th 745 (Ct. App. Div. 1 2005)
29 ALR6th 237—§ 2, 4, 11, 17
State v. Gordh, 2000 WL 135886 (Minn. Ct. App. 2000)
85 ALR5th 1—§ 17
State v. Gordius, 544 A.2d 309 (Me. 1988)
87 ALR5th 693—§ 2, 4
State v. Gordon, 9 Ohio App. 3d 184, 458 N.E.2d 1277 (1st Dist. Hamilton County 1983)
66 ALR5th 397—§ 8
87 ALR5th 597—§ 18
State v. Gordon, 23 Or. App. 587, 543 P.2d 321 (1975)
68 ALR5th 343—§ 3, 14
State v. Gordon, 142 La. 913, 77 So. 789 (1918)
54 ALR6th 429—§ 20
State v. Gordon, 146 N.H. 324, 781 A.2d 976 (2001)
20 ALR6th 561—§ 3, 8, 9, 15, 26
State v. Gordon, 148 N.H. 681, 815 A.2d 379 (2002)
20 ALR6th 561—§ 9, 11, 22
State v. Gordon, 148 N.H. 710, 815 A.2d 392 (2002)
20 ALR6th 561—§ 9, 23
State v. Gordon, 161 Ariz. 308, 778 P.2d 1204 (1989)

67 ALR6th 103—§ 3
State v. Gordon, 161 Ariz. 308, 778 P.2d 1204, 39 Ariz. Adv. Rep. 13 (1989)
39 ALR5th 283—§ 3, 40
State v. Gordon, 218 Wis. 2d 168, 578 N.W.2d 210 (Ct. App. 1998)
84 ALR6th 293—§ 41
State v. Gordon, 221 Kan. 253, 559 P.2d 312 (1977)
18 ALR6th 1—§ 17, 30
State v. Gordon, 387 A.2d 611 (Me. 1978)
9 ALR6th 1—§ 6
State v. Gordon, 645 So. 2d 140 (Fla. Dist. Ct. App. 3d Dist. 1994)
113 ALR5th 597—§ 8
State v. Gordon, 646 So. 2d 995 (La. Ct. App. 1st Cir. 1994)
123 ALR5th 179—§ 8, 9
State v. Gordon, 646 So. 2d 1005 (La. Ct. App. 1st Cir. 1994)
1 ALR6th 371—§ 6
State v. Gordon, 952 S.W.2d 817 (Tenn. 1997)
38 ALR5th 433—§ 21
State v. Gordon Sees The Ground, Jr., 2009 MT 375N, 354 Mont. 391, 222 P.3d 644 (2009)
92 ALR6th 295—§ 12
95 ALR6th 1—§ 4, 18
State v. Gore, 131 Ohio App. 3d 197, 722 N.E.2d 125 (7th Dist. Mahoning County 1999)
39 ALR5th 283—§ 31
State v. Gore, 143 Wash. 2d 288, 21 P.3d 262 (2001)
90 ALR5th 453—§ 43
74 ALR6th 69—§ 12
93 ALR6th 275—§ 25
State v. Gore, 152 Kan. 551, 106 P.2d 704, 131 A.L.R. 1108 (1940)
85 ALR5th 187—§ 8
State v. Goree, 11 Neb. App. 685, 659 N.W.2d 344 (2003)
105 ALR5th 529—§ 13, 30
State v. Goree, 151 Or. App. 621, 950 P.2d 919 (1997)

48 ALR5th 555—§ 3
20 ALR6th 479—§ 3
38 ALR6th 97—§ 25
State v. Gorham, 121 Or. App. 347, 854 P.2d 971 (1993)
60 ALR5th 1—§ 9, 11
45 ALR6th 643—§ 13
State v. Gormon, 584 S.W.2d 420 (Mo. App. 1979)
39 ALR5th 283—§ 4, 60
State v. Gorneault, 2007 ME 49, 918 A.2d 1207 (Me. 2007)
78 ALR6th 213—§ 3
State v. Gortarez, 141 Ariz. 254, 686 P.2d 1224 (1984)
95 ALR5th 471—§ 2, 4
State v. Gosa, 263 N.J. Super. 527, 623 A.2d 301 (1993)
45 ALR5th 1—§ 2, 5, 10, 17, 30
State v. Goseland, 256 Kan. 729, 887 P.2d 1109 (1994)
22 ALR5th 660—§ 6, 15
32 ALR6th 1—§ 7
State v. Goslin, 2009-Ohio-3487, 2009 WL 2056073 (Ohio Ct. App. 5th Dist. Fairfield County 2009)
84 ALR6th 293—§ 3
State v. Gosnell, 62 S.W.3d 740 (Tenn. Crim. App. 2001)
24 ALR6th 591—§ 10
32 ALR6th 1—§ 11
State v. Goss, 85 Fair Empl. Prac. Cas. (BNA) 1012, 2001 WL 423142 (Ark. 2001)
51 ALR5th 1—§ 11
State v. Goss, 995 S.W.2d 617 (Tenn. Crim. App. 1998)
38 ALR6th 97—§ 13
State v. Goss, 2007 WL 2200284 (Tenn. Crim. App. 2007)
58 ALR6th 215—§ 7, 10
State v. Gosselin, 122 Wis. 2d 776, 362 N.W.2d 448 (Ct. App. 1984)
47 ALR6th 107—§ 71
State v. Gosser, 50 N.J. 438, 236 A.2d 377 (1967)
28 ALR6th 505—§ 9

58 ALR6th 499—§ 16
State v. Gossett, 11 Wash. App. 864, 527 P.2d 91 (1974)
45 ALR5th 591—§ 3, 9, 12
State v. Gough, 35 Ohio App. 3d 81, 519 N.E.2d 842 (5th Dist. Licking County 1986)
12 ALR6th 553—§ 5, 11, 26
State v. Gould, 56 Wis. 2d 808, 202 N.W.2d 903 (1973)
5 ALR5th 243—§ 2, 58
State v. Gould, 216 Mont. 455, 704 P.2d 20 (1985)
33 ALR5th 571—§ 3
9 ALR6th 1—§ 17
State v. Gould, 271 Kan. 394, 23 P.3d 801 (2001)
26 ALR6th 511—§ 14
State v. Govan, 320 S.C. 392, 465 S.E.2d 574 (Ct. App. 1995)
23 ALR6th 1—§ 19
State v. Govan, 439 S.E.2d 263 (S.C. 1993)
47 ALR5th 259—§ 4
State v. Gove, 148 Wis. 2d 936, 437 N.W.2d 218 (1989)
121 ALR5th 551—§ 13
State v. Gove, 2009-Ohio-3463, 2009 WL 2054143 (Ohio Ct. App. 8th Dist. Cuyahoga County 2009)
56 ALR6th 1—§ 18
State v. Gowdy, 64 Ohio Misc. 2d 38, 639 N.E.2d 878 (CP 1994)
18 ALR5th 542—§ 3
State v. Gowen, 150 N.H. 286, 837 A.2d 297 (2003)
84 ALR6th 293—§ 19, 41
State v. Gowin, 99 Idaho 195, 579 P.2d 692 (1978)
22 ALR5th 660—§ 8, 12, 20
State v. Goyet, 120 Vt. 12, 132 A.2d 623 (1957)
116 ALR5th 373—§ 3, 11
State v. Goyette, 407 A.2d 1104 (Me. 1979)
50 ALR5th 703—§ 3, 15
State (E.L.) v. G.P.N., 321 N.J. Super. 172, 728 A.2d 316 (App. Div. 1999)

91 ALR6th 435—§ 112

State v. Grace, 61 Wash. App. 787, 812 P.2d 865 (1991)

34 ALR5th 125—§ 15

State v. Grace, 107 Haw. 133, 111 P.3d 28 (Ct. App. 2005)

30 ALR6th 1—§ 3, 6

State v. Grady, 38 N.C. App. 152, 247 S.E.2d 624 (1978)

53 ALR6th 81—§ 9

State v. Grady, 691 S.W.2d 301 (Mo. Ct. App. E.D. 1985)

80 ALR6th 599—§ 5

State v. Graf, 114 Or. App. 275, 835 P.2d 934 (1992)

29 ALR5th 1—§ 2, 4

State v. Graf, 316 Or. 544, 853 P.2d 277 (1993)

29 ALR5th 1—§ 2

State v. Graffam, 202 La. 869, 13 So. 2d 249 (1943)

96 ALR5th 523—§ 4

State v. Graffius, 74 Wash. App. 23, 871 P.2d 1115 (Div. 1 1994)

62 ALR5th 1—§ 2, 4, 15
15 ALR6th 515—§ 4

State v. Gragg, 143 Idaho 74, 137 P.3d 461 (Ct. App. 2005)

33 ALR6th 91—§ 6
63 ALR6th 351—§ 3

State v. Graham, 4 Conn. Cir. Ct. 50, 225 A.2d 205 (App. Div. 1966)

57 ALR6th 445—§ 43

State v. Graham, 35 N.C. App. 700, 242 S.E.2d 512 (1978)

11 ALR5th 497—§ 5, 9, 17, 24

State v. Graham, 68 Wash. App. 878, 846 P.2d 578 (1993)

27 ALR5th 593—§ 6, 26

State v. Graham, 118 N.C. App. 231, 454 S.E.2d 878 (1995)

40 ALR5th 113—§ 3

State v. Graham, 130 Wash. 2d 711, 927 P.2d 227, 65 A.L.R.5th 773 (1996)

65 ALR5th 623—§ 9

State v. Graham, 134 N.M. 613, 2003-NMCA-127, 81 P.3d 556 (Ct. App. 2003)

23 ALR6th 307—§ 38
72 ALR6th 1—§ 6

State v. Graham, 161 Tenn. 557, 30 S.W.2d 274 (1930)

97 ALR5th 537—§ 31

State v. Graham, 184 Neb. 635, 171 N.W.2d 62 (1969)

124 ALR5th 1—§ 5

State v. Graham, 186 Conn. 437, 441 A.2d 857 (1982)

34 ALR6th 1—§ 9

State v. Graham, 200 Conn. 9, 509 A.2d 493 (1986)

3 ALR6th 269—§ 18

State v. Graham, 272 Kan. 2, 30 P.3d 310 (2001)

21 ALR6th 771—§ 4

State v. Graham, 273 Kan. 844, 46 P.3d 1177 (2002)

26 ALR6th 511—§ 3, 25

State v. Graham, 410 N.W.2d 395 (Minn. Ct. App. 1987)

73 ALR5th 383—§ 13

State v. Graham, 422 So. 2d 123 (La. 1982)

9 ALR5th 369—§ 2
77 ALR6th 251—§ 5

State v. Graham, 571 So. 2d 1267 (Ala. Crim. App. 1990)

103 ALR5th 463—§ 3

State v. Graham, 2002 MT 237, 311 Mont. 500, 57 P.3d 54 (2002)

97 ALR6th 263—§ 3, 11

State v. Graham, 2011 WL 336989 (N.J. Super. Ct. App. Div. 2011)

74 ALR6th 373—§ 13

State v. Granberry, 484 S.W.2d 295 (Mo. 1972)

51 ALR6th 219—§ 4

State v. Granberry, 530 S.W.2d 714 (Mo. Ct. App. 1975)

101 ALR6th 331—§ 16

State v. Grandmaison, 327 A.2d 868 (Me. 1974)

---

68 ALR5th 343—§ 3

State v. Grandy, 306 S.C. 224, 411 S.E.2d 207 (1991)

2 ALR6th 551—§ 7

State v. Granger, 982 So. 2d 779 (La. 2008)

69 ALR6th 1—§ 23

State v. Grannis, 183 Ariz. 52, 900 P.2d 1 (1995)

16 ALR6th 329—§ 4

24 ALR6th 591—§ 4, 12

State v. Grant, 2 Conn. Cir. Ct. 156, 196 A.2d 815 (App. Div. 1963)

66 ALR5th 397—§ 12, 17

State v. Grant, 40 N.C. App. 58, 252 S.E.2d 98 (1979)

99 ALR5th 557—§ 10

State v. Grant, 44 Or. App. 671, 606 P.2d 1166 (1980)

42 ALR5th 547—§ 6

State v. Grant, 67 Ohio St. 3d 465, 620 N.E.2d 50 (1993)

85 ALR5th 187—§ 2

State v. Grant, 208 N.C. App. 283, 702 S.E.2d 554 (2010)

103 ALR6th 507—§ 12, 28

State v. Grant, 221 Mont. 122, 717 P.2d 562 (1986)

79 ALR5th 237—§ 11

State v. Grant, 227 Mont. 181, 738 P.2d 106 (1987)

70 ALR6th 361—§ 5, 29

State v. Grant, 242 Neb. 364, 495 N.W.2d 253 (1993)

2 ALR6th 551—§ 5

State v. Grant, 279 N.C. 337, 182 S.E.2d 400 (1971)

55 ALR5th 125—§ 12, 14, 25

State v. Grant, 286 Conn. 499, 944 A.2d 947 (2008)

72 ALR6th 437—§ 11, 15

State v. Grant, 295 So. 2d 168 (La. 1973)

45 ALR5th 531—§ 7, 9

State v. Grant, 571 A.2d 1203 (Me. 1990)

124 ALR5th 1—§ 5

State v. Grant, 769 So. 2d 1180 (La. 2000)

99 ALR6th 295—§ 6

State v. Grant, 832 S.W.2d 624 (Tex. App. Houston 14th Dist. 1992)

117 ALR5th 407—§ 4

State v. Grant, 1993 WL 63376 (Ohio Ct. App. 8th Dist.Cuyahoga County 1993)

57 ALR5th 141—§ 4

State v. Grant, 2007-Ohio-1460, 2007 WL 926398 (Ohio Ct. App. 8th Dist. Cuyahoga County 2007)

32 ALR6th 171—§ 6, 16, 18, 21

33 ALR6th 1—§ 8

State v. Grant, 2008 ME 14, 939 A.2d 93 (Me. 2008)

30 ALR6th 103—§ 10

State v. Grantham, 224 S.C. 41, 77 S.E.2d 291 (1953)

67 ALR5th 637—§ 5, 7

State v. Grasa, 1996 WL 307237 (Ohio App. Butler Co. 1996)

57 ALR5th 141—§ 3

State v. Grasser, 60 Wash. 2d 343, 374 P.2d 149 (1962)

119 ALR5th 275—§ 14

State v. Grate, 2009-Ohio-4452, 2009 WL 2710100 (Ohio Ct. App. 11th Dist. Trumbull County 2009)

63 ALR6th 351—§ 3

State v. Grauberger, 1999 WL 153747 (Minn. Ct. App. 1999)

73 ALR5th 383—§ 29

State v. Graver, 2006-Ohio-5110, 2006 WL 2790301 (Ohio Ct. App. 6th Dist. Fulton County 2006)

26 ALR6th 511—§ 19

State v. Graves, 73 Or. App. 172, 697 P.2d 1384 (1985)

1 ALR6th 549—§ 9

State v. Graves, 119 N.M. 89, 888 P.2d 971 (1994)

43 ALR5th 1—§ 14

State v. Graves, 150 Or. App. 437, 947 P.2d 209 (1997)

11 ALR5th 218—§ 4

State v. Graves, 246 La. 460, 165 So. 2d
285 (1964)
105 ALR5th 529—§ 16
State v. Graves, 269 S.C. 356, 237
S.E.2d 584 (1977)
93 ALR6th 207—§ 26
96 ALR6th 355—§ 24, 37
State v. Graves, 272 Mont. 451, 901
P.2d 549 (1995)
92 ALR5th 35—§ 21, 28
125 ALR5th 357—§ 7
7 ALR6th 233—§ 12
65 ALR6th 537—§ 44
State v. Graves, 352 Mo. 1102, 182
S.W.2d 46 (1944)
63 ALR6th 1—§ 5, 44
State v. Graves, 798 So. 2d 1090 (La. Ct.
App. 3d Cir. 2001)
19 ALR6th 697—§ 14
State v. Graves, 901 P.2d 549 (Mont
1995)
15 ALR5th 391—§ 39
State v. Graves, 2003-Ohio-2359, 2003
WL 21040652 (Ohio Ct. App. 6th
Dist. Lucas County 2003)
26 ALR6th 511—§ 35
43 ALR6th 475—§ 24
State v. Graves, 2005 WL 1683501
(Tenn. Crim. App. 2005)
26 ALR6th 511—§ 22
State v. Gravin, 44 Ohio App. 2d 303,
73 Ohio Op. 2d 365, 338 N.E.2d
539 (7th Dist. Columbiana County
1974)
99 ALR6th 295—§ 10
State v. Grawien, 123 Wis. 2d 428, 367
N.W.2d 816 (App. 1985)
19 ALR5th 470—§ 3, 12
State v. Grawien, 123 Wis. 2d 428, 367
N.W.2d 816 (Ct. App. 1985)
62 ALR6th 413—§ 41
State v. Gray, 3 Wash. App. 146, 473
P.2d 189 (Div. 1 1970)
56 ALR6th 323—§ 5
State v. Gray, 60 Ohio App. 2d 418, 14
Ohio Op. 3d 432, 399 N.E.2d 131
(1st Dist. Hamilton County 1979)
111 ALR5th 239—§ 5

State v. Gray, 62 Ohio St. 3d 514, 584
N.E.2d 710 (1992)
70 ALR5th 461—§ 2, 3
State v. Gray, 63 Conn. App. 151, 772
A.2d 747 (2001)
71 ALR6th 1—§ 11
State v. Gray, 87 Wash. App. 1051, 1997
WL 537861 (Div. 1 1997)
58 ALR6th 499—§ 40, 109
State v. Gray, 129 Idaho 784, 932 P.2d
907 (Ct. App. 1997)
57 ALR5th 141—§ 3
55 ALR6th 157—§ 109
State v. Gray, 151 Wash. App. 1001,
2009 WL 1919016 (Div. 1 2009)
72 ALR6th 227—§ 58
State v. Gray, 172 Mo. 430, 72 S.W. 698
(1903)
98 ALR6th 455—§ 29
State v. Gray, 189 Kan. 398, 369 P.2d
330 (1962)
59 ALR5th 1—§ 4, 6
State v. Gray, 204 W. Va. 248, 511
S.E.2d 873 (1998)
27 ALR6th 183—§ 16
State v. Gray, 221 Conn. 713, 607 A.2d
391 (1992)
85 ALR5th 187—§ 7
State v. Gray, 268 N.C. 69, 150 S.E.2d 1
(1966)
28 ALR6th 505—§ 29
State v. Gray, 285 Ga. App. 124, 645
S.E.2d 598 (2007)
78 ALR6th 297—§ 80
State v. Gray, 291 So. 2d 390 (La. 1974)
100 ALR6th 535—§ 3
State v. Gray, 292 N.C. 270, 233 S.E.2d
905 (1977)
103 ALR6th 507—§ 11, 29
State v. Gray, 347 N.C. 143, 491 S.E.2d
538 (1997)
24 ALR5th 465—§ 14, 42
38 ALR5th 433—§ 28
38 ALR6th 97—§ 13
State v. Gray, 491 S.E.2d 538 (N.C.
1997)
57 ALR5th 141—§ 3, 7

State v. Gray, 761 S.W.2d 240 (Mo. Ct. App. S.D. 1988)
99 ALR6th 295—§ 21
State v. Gray, 887 S.W.2d 369 (Mo. 1994)
47 ALR5th 259—§ 3, 21
79 ALR5th 33—§ 42, 48
State v. Gray, 960 S.W.2d 598 (Tenn. Crim. App. 1997)
73 ALR5th 383—§ 29
State v. Gray, 1992 WL 12642 (Ohio App. Clermont Co. 1992)
52 ALR5th 655—§ 3
State v. Gray, 1998 WL 211791 (Tenn. Crim. App. 1998)
73 ALR5th 383—§ 4, 23
State v. Gray, 2000 ME 145, 755 A.2d 540 (Me. 2000)
84 ALR5th 487—§ 19
State v. Gray, 2002-Ohio-3419, 2002 WL 1453823 (Ohio Ct. App. 8th Dist. Cuyahoga County 2002)
71 ALR6th 1—§ 5
State v. Graybeard, 93 Haw. 513
72 ALR5th 403—§ 3
State v. Grayson, 154 Wash. 2d 333, 111 P.3d 1183 (2005)
26 ALR6th 511—§ 8
State v. Grayson, 336 S.W.3d 138 (Mo. 2011)
84 ALR6th 293—§ 13, 34
State v. Grba, 196 Iowa 241, 194 N.W. 250 (1923)
81 ALR5th 563—§ 3
State v. Greason, 106 Or. App. 529, 809 P.2d 695 (1991)
47 ALR6th 107—§ 29, 40
State v. Greatens, 2007 WI App 138, 302 Wis. 2d 263, 732 N.W.2d 864 (Ct. App. 2007)
84 ALR6th 293—§ 30
State v. Greathouse, 627 S.W.2d 592 (Mo. 1982)
26 ALR6th 451—§ 10
State v. Grecinger, 569 N.W.2d 189 (Minn. 1997)
57 ALR5th 315—§ 2, 3, 6, 7, 9, 11

58 ALR5th 749—§ 6
State v. Greco, 57 Wash. App. 196, 787 P.2d 940 (1990)
42 ALR5th 581—§ 7
State v. Green, 29 N.C. App. 574, 225 S.E.2d 170 (1976)
92 ALR5th 35—§ 15
State v. Green, 32 Or. App. 471, 574 P.2d 356 (1978)
86 ALR5th 59—§ 8
State v. Green, 36 Ohio Misc. 140, 65 Ohio Op. 2d 192, 303 N.E.2d 917 (C.P. 1973)
61 ALR5th 1—§ 2, 3, 7
76 ALR5th 563—§ 4, 5
State v. Green, 55 Conn. App. 706, 740 A.2d 450 (1999)
39 ALR5th 283—§ 40
State v. Green, 76 N.C. App. 642, 334 S.E.2d 263 (1985)
81 ALR5th 563—§ 3, 6
State v. Green, 90 Ohio St. 3d 352, 738 N.E.2d 1208 (2000)
72 ALR5th 403—§ 19
State v. Green, 91 Wash. 2d 431, 588 P.2d 1370 (1979)
32 ALR6th 1—§ 11
State v. Green, 94 Wash. 2d 216, 616 P.2d 628 (1980)
39 ALR5th 283—§ 4, 77
State v. Green, 129 N.C. App. 539, 500 S.E.2d 452 (1998)
32 ALR6th 1—§ 11
State v. Green, 129 N.J. Super. 157, 322 A.2d 495 (1974)
31 ALR5th 704—§ 3
State v. Green, 170 N.J. Super. 292, 406 A.2d 310 (App. Div. 1979)
57 ALR6th 445—§ 7
State v. Green, 194 Conn. 258, 480 A.2d 526 (1984)
93 ALR5th 527—§ 4
State v. Green, 207 Conn. 1, 540 A.2d 659 (1988)
32 ALR6th 1—§ 10
State v. Green, 210 La. 157, 26 So. 2d 487 (1946)

81 ALR5th 563—§ 3, 8
State v. Green, 232 Kan. 116, 652 P.2d
697 (1982)
**24 ALR5th 465—§ 6, 7, 14, 55, 57,
58, 61, 65, 77 to 79**
58 ALR5th 749—§ 7
State v. Green, 245 Kan. 398, 781 P.2d
678 (1989)
64 ALR5th 671—§ 4
State v. Green, 254 Iowa 1379, 121
N.W.2d 89, 95 A.L.R.2d 810 (1963)
85 ALR5th 187—§ 6, 17
State v. Green, 282 So. 2d 461 (La.
1973)
9 ALR6th 1—§ 17
State v. Green, 305 N.C. 463, 290 S.E.2d
625 (1982)
1 ALR6th 657—§ 6
State v. Green, 321 N.C. 594, 365 S.E.2d
587 (1988)
16 ALR6th 329—§ 4
24 ALR6th 591—§ 6, 14
State v. Green, 336 N.C. 142, 443 S.E.2d
14 (1994)
83 ALR6th 255—§ 15
State v. Green, 448 So. 2d 782 (La. Ct.
App. 2d Cir. 1984)
24 ALR6th 1—§ 7
State v. Green, 470 S.W.2d 565 (Mo.
1971)
54 ALR5th 141—§ 3, 4, 7, 9
State v. Green, 476 So. 2d 859 (La. Ct.
App. 2d Cir. 1985)
97 ALR5th 201—§ 3
State v. Green, 484 So. 2d 698 (La. Ct.
App. 1st Cir. 1985)
93 ALR5th 527—§ 20
State v. Green, 598 So. 2d 624 (La. Ct.
App. 3d Cir. 1992)
15 ALR6th 515—§ 6
State v. Green, 613 S.W.2d 229 (Tenn.
Crim. 1980)
55 ALR5th 125—§ 3
State v. Green, 634 So. 2d 503 (La. App.
4th Cir. 1994)
47 ALR5th 259—§ 2
State v. Green, 651 So. 2d 435 (La. Ct.
App. 3d Cir. 1995)

98 ALR6th 455—§ 33
State v. Green, 660 So. 2d 935 (La. Ct.
App. 4th Cir. 1995)
99 ALR6th 295—§ 8
State v. Green, 674 S.W.2d 615 (Mo. Ct.
App. E.D. 1984)
99 ALR6th 295—§ 5, 9
State v. Green, 747 So. 2d 1007 (Fla.
Dist. Ct. App. 3d Dist. 1999)
2 ALR5th 725—§ 13
State v. Green, 810 P.2d 1023 (Alaska
App. 1991)
49 ALR5th 639—§ 4
State v. Green, 960 So. 2d 1270 (La. Ct.
App. 2d Cir. 2007)
34 ALR6th 539—§ 5
101 ALR6th 1—§ 31
State v. Green, 995 S.W.2d 591 (Tenn.
Crim. App. 1998)
14 ALR5th 89—§ 6
State v. Green, 997 So. 2d 42 (La. Ct.
App. 5th Cir. 2008)
69 ALR6th 1—§ 23
State v. Green, 1992 WL 229510 (Ohio
Ct. App. 10th Dist. Franklin County
1992)
19 ALR6th 697—§ 3, 12
State v. Green, 1992 WL 354591 (Ohio
Ct. App. 8th Dist. Cuyahoga County
1992)
99 ALR6th 295—§ 13
State v. Green, 1999 WL 770491 (Ohio
Ct. App. 5th Dist. Licking County
1999)
78 ALR5th 489—§ 10
State v. Green, 2000 WI App 47, 233
Wis. 2d 275, 610 N.W.2d 230 (Ct.
App. 2000)
84 ALR6th 293—§ 40
State v. Green, 2004 UT 76, 99 P.3d 820
(Utah 2004)
22 ALR6th 1—§ 4, 8
State v. Greenawalt, 128 Ariz. 150, 624
P.2d 828 (1981)
63 ALR6th 1—§ 33
93 ALR6th 391—§ 23
State v. Greenberg, 4 Kan. App. 2d 403,
607 P.2d 530 (1980)

11 ALR6th 237—§ 11

30 ALR6th 103—§ 34

State v. Greenberg, 564 So. 2d 1176 (Fla. Dist. Ct. App. 3d Dist. 1990)

69 ALR6th 1—§ 27

State v. Greene, 5 Kan. App. 2d 698, 623 P.2d 933 (1981)

3 ALR5th 521—§ 7

State v. Greene, 12 N.C. App. 687, 184 S.E.2d 523 (1971)

108 ALR5th 593—§ 54

State v. Greene, 67 N.C. App. 703, 314 S.E.2d 262 (1984)

5 ALR5th 243—§ 61

State v. Greene, 74 N.C. App. 21, 328 S.E.2d 1 (1985)

28 ALR6th 505—§ 37

State v. Greene, 172 Wis. 2d 43, 492 N.W.2d 181 (Ct. App. 1992)

85 ALR5th 1—§ 17, 20, 45

State v. Greene, 289 N.C. 578, 223 S.E.2d 365 (1976)

57 ALR6th 445—§ 3, 59

State v. Greene, 324 N.C. 1, 376 S.E.2d 430 (1989)

57 ALR5th 141—§ 7

State v. Greene, 332 N.C. 565, 422 S.E.2d 730 (1992)

32 ALR6th 1—§ 10

State v. Greene, 335 N.C. 548, 438 S.E.2d 743 (1994)

83 ALR5th 541—§ 3

State v. Greene, 929 S.W.2d 376 (Tenn. Crim. App. 1995)

57 ALR6th 83—§ 5

State v. Greene, 1997 WL 358810 (Ohio Ct. App. 10th Dist. Franklin County 1997)

78 ALR6th 297—§ 17, 38, 75

State v. Greene, 2003-Ohio-2832, 2003 WL 21267245 (Ohio Ct. App. 10th Dist. Franklin County 2003)

33 ALR6th 407—§ 4, 5

State v. Greenhaw, 553 S.W.2d 318 (Mo. Ct. App. 1977)

101 ALR6th 331—§ 21

State v. Greenleaf, 591 N.W.2d 488 (Minn. 1999)

20 ALR5th 398—§ 13.5

24 ALR6th 591—§ 5, 12

32 ALR6th 1—§ 5

103 ALR6th 35—§ 7

State v. Greeno, 2003-Ohio-3687, 2003 WL 21585167 (Ohio Ct. App. 3d Dist. Seneca County 2003)

29 ALR6th 1—§ 3, 17

State v. Greensweight, 2008 MT 185, 343 Mont. 474, 187 P.3d 613 (2008)

46 ALR6th 241—§ 17

State v. Greenwald, 446 A.2d 44 (Me. 1982)

57 ALR6th 445—§ 3, 21

State v. Greenwald, 454 A.2d 827 (Me. 1982)

7 ALR5th 73—§ 6

State v. Greenwalt, 2001 WL 46310 (Ohio Ct. App. 5th Dist. Tuscarawas County 2001)

51 ALR6th 139—§ 6

State v. Greenway, 170 Ariz. 155, 823 P.2d 22 (1991)

20 ALR5th 177—§ 3, 7

79 ALR5th 33—§ 9

State v. Greenwood, 115 S.W.3d 527 (Tenn. Crim. App. 2003)

119 ALR5th 379—§ 2, 7, 10

State v. Greenwood, 301 N.C. 705, 273 S.E.2d 438 (1981)

114 ALR5th 173—§ 9

State v. Greenwood, 665 N.E.2d 579 (Ind. 1996)

71 ALR6th 335—§ 13, 24

State v. Greenwood, 2004-Ohio-2737, 2004 WL 1178730 (Ohio Ct. App. 2d Dist. Montgomery County 2004)

55 ALR6th 391—§ 21

State v. Greer, 26 Or. App. 605, 553 P.2d 1087 (1976)

70 ALR6th 1—§ 15

State v. Greer, 39 Ohio St. 3d 236, 530 N.E.2d 382 (1988)

57 ALR5th 141—§ 3, 4

68 ALR5th 343—§ 3

State v. Greer, 163 Kan. 592, 184 P.2d 991 (1947)

24 ALR6th 747—§ 47

State v. Greer, 313 S.W.2d 711 (Mo. 1958)
119 ALR5th 275—§ 2

State v. Greer, 1995 WL 238929 (Ohio Ct. App. 1st Dist. Hamilton County 1995)
43 ALR6th 475—§ 8

State v. Greer, 2009-Ohio-4228, 2009 WL 2574160 (Ohio Ct. App. 8th Dist. Cuyahoga County 2009)
99 ALR6th 113—§ 21

State v. Greeson, 2007 MT 23, 336 Mont. 1, 152 P.3d 695 (2007)
46 ALR6th 241—§ 10

State v. Greever, 878 P.2d 838 (Kan. App. 1994)
7 ALR5th 263—§ 7

State v. Gregoire, 249 La. 890, 192 So. 2d 114 (1966)
55 ALR5th 125—§ 19

State v. Gregorio, 186 N.J. Super. 138, 451 A.2d 980 (Law Div. 1982)
24 ALR6th 255—§ 6, 8, 14

State v. Gregory, 78 N.C. App. 565, 338 S.E.2d 110 (1985)
38 ALR5th 433—§ 9, 11

State v. Gregory, 149 Or. App. 769, 945 P.2d 593 (1997)
92 ALR5th 35—§ 16

State v. Gregory, 198 S.C. 98, 16 S.E.2d 532 (1941)
22 ALR5th 1—§ 34, 45, 55

State v. Gregory, 340 N.C. 365, 459 S.E.2d 638 (1995)
79 ALR5th 33—§ 68, 72
83 ALR6th 255—§ 15

State v. Gregory, 348 N.C. 203, 499 S.E.2d 753 (1998)
38 ALR6th 97—§ 10

State v. Gregory, 862 S.W.2d 574 (Tenn. Crim. 1993)
39 ALR5th 283—§ 4, 41

State v. Gregory, 2005 WL 3194482 (Del. Super. Ct. 2005)
29 ALR6th 237—§ 5, 24

State v. Greiman, 344 N.W.2d 249 (Iowa 1984)
39 ALR5th 283—§ 2, 10, 45

State v. Greiman, 2000 WL 1520217 (Iowa Ct. App. 2000)
69 ALR6th 579—§ 4
71 ALR6th 1—§ 14

State v. Greime, 97 N.C. App. 409, 388 S.E.2d 594 (1990)
85 ALR5th 187—§ 9

State v. Greiner, 518 N.W.2d 636 (Minn. App. 1994)
24 ALR5th 132—§ 7

State v. Grell, 205 Ariz. 57, 66 P.3d 1234 (2003)
122 ALR5th 145—§ 7, 12, 15 to 17, 22

State v. Gremillion, 542 So. 2d 1074 (La. 1989)
111 ALR5th 1—§ 5, 8, 26

State v. Grenier, 55 Conn. App. 630, 739 A.2d 751 (1999)
101 ALR5th 187—§ 8
39 ALR6th 257—§ 4

State v. Grenier, 2002 WL 31111771 (Del. Super. Ct. 2002)
119 ALR5th 379—§ 7

State v. Grenz, 243 N.W.2d 375 (N.D. 1976)
74 ALR5th 453—§ 3, 5

State v. Gress, 1998 WL 321014 (Ohio Ct. App. 2d Dist. Montgomery County 1998)
78 ALR6th 599—§ 4, 8

State v. Gresser, 657 N.W.2d 875, 118 A.L.R.5th 747 (Minn. Ct. App. 2003)
118 ALR5th 347—§ 5, 6

State v. Griatzky, 587 A.2d 234 (Me. 1991)
52 ALR6th 125—§ 25, 44

State v. Grib, 152 Wash. App. 885, 218 P.3d 644 (Div. 3 2009)
55 ALR6th 1—§ 3, 6

State v. Grice, 515 N.W.2d 20 (Iowa 1994)
4 ALR6th 577—§ 11

State v. Grider, 144 Ohio App. 3d 323, 760 N.E.2d 40 (8th Dist. Cuyahoga County 2001)

64 ALR6th 1—§ 7
State v. Grier, 70 N.C. App. 40, 318 S.E.2d 889 (1984)

5 ALR5th 243—§ 7, 11
State v. Grier, 129 Ariz. 279, 630 P.2d 575 (App. 1981)

23 ALR5th 672—§ 3
State v. Grier, 307 N.C. 628, 300 S.E.2d 351 (1983)

77 ALR5th 201—§ 3
State v. Grier, 2005-Ohio-716, 2005 WL 418031 (Ohio Ct. App. 9th Dist. Summit County 2005)

17 ALR6th 327—§ 14
State v. Grierson, 96 N.H. 36, 69 A.2d 851 (1949)

67 ALR5th 637—§ 3, 8
State v. Griest, 2000 WL 64254 (Ariz. Ct. App. Div. 1 2000)

78 ALR5th 567—§ 3
State v. Griffey, 241 S.W.3d 700 (Tex. App. Austin 2007)

84 ALR6th 293—§ 16
State v. Griffey, 457 N.W.2d 13 (Iowa Ct. App. 1990)

84 ALR5th 487—§ 21
State v. Griffin, 100 N.M. 75, 665 P.2d 1166 (Ct. App. 1983)

92 ALR5th 35—§ 30
State v. Griffin, 126 Wash. App. 700, 109 P.3d 870 (Div. 1 2005)

26 ALR6th 511—§ 4
State v. Griffin, 126 Wis. 2d 183, 376 N.W.2d 62 (App. 1985)

19 ALR5th 470—§ 3
State v. Griffin, 152 Vt. 41, 563 A.2d 642 (1989)

95 ALR6th 1—§ 26
96 ALR6th 355—§ 9, 37
State v. Griffin, 170 Wis. 2d 732, 492 N.W.2d 190 (Ct. App. 1992)

1 ALR6th 549—§ 16
State v. Griffin, 202 S.W.3d 670 (Mo. Ct. App. W.D. 2006)

30 ALR6th 1—§ 4
State v. Griffin, 386 N.W.2d 792 (Minn. Ct. App. 1986)

113 ALR5th 597—§ 8
State v. Griffin, 564 N.W.2d 370 (Iowa 1997)

57 ALR5th 315—§ 3, 8, 11
State v. Griffin, 834 N.W.2d 688 (Minn. 2013)

94 ALR6th 579—§ 2, 7
State v. Griffin, 848 S.W.2d 464 (Mo. 1993)

79 ALR5th 33—§ 63
38 ALR6th 97—§ 5
96 ALR6th 269—§ 32
State v. Griffin, 914 S.W.2d 564 (Tenn. Crim. App. 1995)

74 ALR5th 453—§ 6
State v. Griffin, 2004-Ohio-2155, 2004 WL 906086 (Ohio Ct. App. 8th Dist. Cuyahoga County 2004)

72 ALR6th 1—§ 4
State v. Griffin, 2009 WL 4642604 (Tenn. Crim. App. 2009)

69 ALR6th 579—§ 4
State v. Griffin, No. 52124 (May 14, 1987, Ct. App. Ohio, 8th App. Dist. Cuyahoga Co.)

39 ALR5th 283—§ 14, 41
State v. Griffith, 61 Wash. App. 35, 808 P.2d 1171 (Div. 3 1991)

17 ALR6th 327—§ 12
State v. Griffith, 236 Wis. 2d 48

66 ALR5th 397—§ 8
State v. Griffith, 1995 WL 663389 (Neb. Ct. App. 1995)

76 ALR5th 1—§ 18
State v. Griffith, 1996 WL 586780 (Ohio Ct. App. 12th Dist. Butler County 1996)

67 ALR6th 103—§ 4, 5, 10, 15
State v. Griffith, 2000 WI 72, 236 Wis. 2d 48, 613 N.W.2d 72 (2000)

92 ALR6th 171—§ 11
State v. Griffon, 448 So. 2d 1287 (La. 1984)

16 ALR5th 390—§ 3
State v. Grigsby, 2001 WL 585685 (Ohio Ct. App. 2d Dist. Montgomery County 2001)

3 ALR6th 543—§ 10

State v. Grijalva, 85 N.M. 127, 509 P.2d 894 (App. 1973)
4 ALR5th 1—§ 2, 4

State v. Grilli, 304 Minn. 80, 230 N.W.2d 445 (1975)
18 ALR5th 1—§ 3
34 ALR5th 125—§ 6

State v. Grillo, 23 Conn. App. 50, 578 A.2d 677 (1990)
55 ALR6th 391—§ 23

State v. Grim, 854 S.W.2d 403 (Mo. 1993)
47 ALR5th 259—§ 2
110 ALR5th 213—§ 2

State v. Grimes, 111 Wash. App. 544, 46 P.3d 801 (Div. 1 2002)
57 ALR6th 445—§ 36

State v. Grimes, 1992 WL 80764 (Ohio Ct. App. 2d Dist. Champaign County 1992)
9 ALR6th 541—§ 13

State v. Grimes, 1999 MT 145, 295 Mont. 22, 982 P.2d 1037 (1999)
55 ALR6th 513—§ 14

State v. Grindstaff, 77 N.C. App. 467, 335 S.E.2d 208 (1985)
65 ALR5th 407—§ 3, 20

State v. Grisby, 97 Wash. 2d 493, 647 P.2d 6 (1982)
16 ALR6th 329—§ 4
19 ALR6th 115—§ 4
24 ALR6th 591—§ 9

State v. Grisby, 867 S.W.2d 270 (Mo. Ct. App. E.D. 1993)
105 ALR5th 529—§ 13

State v. Grissom, 251 Kan. 851, 840 P.2d 1142 (1992)
7 ALR5th 263—§ 7
33 ALR5th 571—§ 3
65 ALR6th 359—§ 9
69 ALR6th 579—§ 4

State v. Grissom, 956 S.W.2d 514 (Tenn. Crim. App. 1997)
15 ALR5th 391—§ 16

State v. Grissom, 1993 WL 64276 (Tenn. Crim. App. 1993)
76 ALR5th 1—§ 20

State v. Grissom, 1996 WL 218213 (Tenn. Crim. App. 1996)
73 ALR5th 383—§ 5

State v. Grissom, 2000 WL 1595699 (Ohio Ct. App. 6th Dist. Erie County 2000)
99 ALR6th 295—§ 13

State v. Grittman, 203 Or. App. 120, 125 P.3d 20 (2005)
26 ALR6th 511—§ 27

State v. Groce, 983 P.2d 217 (Idaho Ct. App. 1999)
4 ALR5th 1—§ 19

State v. Grogan, 786 So. 2d 862 (La. Ct. App. 3d Cir. 2001)
9 ALR6th 633—§ 5
15 ALR6th 173—§ 41

State v. Groh, 226 Wis. 2d 563, 596 N.W.2d 502, 1999 WL 233416 (Ct. App. 1999)
119 ALR5th 379—§ 2

State v. Grooms, 126 N.C. App. 88, 483 S.E.2d 445 (1997)
116 ALR5th 479—§ 5

State v. Grooms, 359 N.W.2d 901 (S.D. 1984)
112 ALR5th 621—§ 3

State v. Grooms, 1991 WL 249447 (Ohio Ct. App. 5th Dist. Stark County 1991)
81 ALR6th 505—§ 17

State v. Gropp, 1998 WL 162853 (Ohio Ct. App. 9th Dist. Lorain County 1998)
78 ALR5th 489—§ 3

State v. Grose, 982 S.W.2d 349 (Tenn. Crim. App. 1997)
50 ALR5th 467—§ 9

State v. Gross, 134 Md. App. 528, 760 A.2d 725 (2000)
38 ALR6th 439—§ 13

State v. Gross, 225 N.J. Super. 28, 541 A.2d 714 (App. Div. 1988)
107 ALR5th 567—§ 19

State v. Gross, 1999 WL 333233 (Ohio Ct. App. 5th Dist. Muskingum County 1999)
79 ALR6th 1—§ 41, 49, 66

For assistance, call 1-800-328-4880

State v. Grossberg, 1998 WL 117975 (Del. Super. Ct. 1998)
62 ALR5th 629—§ 4
State v. Grossi, 2003 UT App 181, 72 P.3d 686 (Utah Ct. App. 2003)
79 ALR6th 1—§ 8, 20, 42, 44
State v. Groth, 144 Vt. 585, 481 A.2d 26 (1984)
88 ALR5th 121—§ 2
State v. Grover, 193 Or. App. 165, 90 P.3d 8 (2004)
28 ALR6th 505—§ 32
State v. Grover, 518 A.2d 1039 (Me. 1986)
84 ALR5th 487—§ 21
State v. Groves, 239 Neb. 660, 477 N.W.2d 789 (1991)
103 ALR5th 463—§ 3
113 ALR5th 517—§ 3
State v. Groves, 311 So. 2d 230 (La. 1975)
36 ALR5th 255—§ 7
State v. Groves, 2005 WL 2007213 (Neb. Ct. App. 2005)
33 ALR6th 91—§ 31
State v. Grubb, 1981 WL 3438 (Ohio Ct. App. 10th Dist. Franklin County 1981)
71 ALR6th 335—§ 13
State v. Grubb, 2010-Ohio-1265, 2010 WL 1175234 (Ohio Ct. App. 3d Dist. Defiance County 2010)
55 ALR6th 1—§ 6
State v. Grube, 126 Idaho 377, 883 P.2d 1069 (1994)
92 ALR6th 549—§ 44
State v. Gruber, 150 Wash. 66, 272 P. 89 (1928)
11 ALR5th 497—§ 3, 5, 8 to 10, 16, 31
State v. Gruen, 218 Wis. 2d 581, 582 N.W.2d 728 (Ct. App. 1998)
34 ALR6th 1—§ 12
State v. Grumbles, 104 N.C. App. 766, 411 S.E.2d 407 (1991)
67 ALR6th 103—§ 5, 10, 12
State v. Grun, 175 Wis. 2d 624, 502 N.W.2d 283 (Ct. App. 1993)
85 ALR5th 1—§ 2
State v. Grunow, 199 N.J. Super. 241, 488 A.2d 1098 (1985)
37 ALR5th 515—§ 17
State v. Grzelak, 215 Wis. 2d 577, 573 N.W.2d 538 (Ct. App. 1997)
70 ALR6th 361—§ 10
State v. Guajardo, 135 N.H. 401, 605 A.2d 217 (1992)
32 ALR6th 171—§ 8, 9, 15, 16, 19, 21
33 ALR6th 1—§ 20
State v. Guay, 162 N.H. 375, 33 A.3d 1166, 98 A.L.R.6th 761 (2011)
98 ALR6th 455—§ 16, 17
State v. Guayante, 99 Or. App. 649, 783 P.2d 1030 (1989)
13 ALR5th 628—§ 12
State v. Gubitosi, 43 Conn. App. 448, 683 A.2d 419 (1996)
50 ALR5th 581—§ 7, 12
State v. Guerin, 2001 WL 169978 (Minn. Ct. App. 2001)
113 ALR5th 597—§ 5
State v. Guernsey, 104 Haw. 70, 85 P.3d 177 (2004)
84 ALR6th 293—§ 35
State v. Guerra, 93 N.J. 146, 459 A.2d 1159 (1983)
114 ALR5th 173—§ 7
State v. Guerra, 132 Conn. App. 62, 31 A.3d 68 (2011)
74 ALR6th 373—§ 21
State v. Guerra-Reyna, 201 Wis. 2d 751, 549 N.W.2d 779 (App. 1996)
20 ALR5th 398—§ 6.5, 31, 65
State v. Guerrero, 58 Ariz. 421, 120 P.2d 798 (1942)
99 ALR6th 113—§ 17
State v. Guerrero, 134 Or. App. 619, 896 P.2d 14 (1995)
15 ALR5th 391—§ 28
State v. Guerrero, 2011-Ohio-6530, 2011 WL 6382535 (Ohio Ct. App. 12th Dist. Butler County 2011)
74 ALR6th 373—§ 9
State v. Guerrero, 2011 WL 2306078 (Tenn. Crim. App. 2011)

99 ALR6th 295—§ 21

State v. Guerrero-Melchor, 132 Wash. App. 1038, 2006 WL 1064329 (Div. 1 2006)

26 ALR6th 511—§ 25

State v. Guerro, 126 N.M. 699

32 ALR5th 149—§ 15

State v. Guess, 39 Conn. App. 224, 665 A.2d 126 (1995)

16 ALR6th 329—§ 4

24 ALR6th 591—§ 4, 12

State v. Guess, 44 Conn. App. 790, 692 A.2d 849 (1997)

50 ALR5th 467—§ 6

State v. Guest, 583 P.2d 836 (Alaska 1978)

46 ALR5th 499—§ 2, 4

State v. Guevara, 349 N.C. 243, 506 S.E.2d 711 (1998)

79 ALR5th 33—§ 63

State v. Guffey, 39 S.D. 84, 163 N.W. 679 (1917)

10 ALR5th 700—§ 9, 40

State v. Guffey, 649 So. 2d 1169 (La. Ct. App. 3d Cir. 1995)

9 ALR6th 633—§ 5

9 ALR6th 693—§ 23

13 ALR6th 603—§ 41

State v. Guggenmos, 350 Or. 243, 253 P.3d 1042 (2011)

78 ALR6th 297—§ 21, 38, 42

State v. Guice, 645 So. 2d 1193 (La. Ct. App. 2d Cir. 1994)

12 ALR6th 267—§ 5

State v. Guidroz, 721 So. 2d 480 (La. Ct. App. 5th Cir. 1998)

42 ALR5th 581—§ 16

State v. Guidry, 105 Haw. 222, 96 P.3d 242 (2004)

63 ALR6th 351—§ 3

State v. Guidry, 496 So. 2d 650 (La. Ct. App. 1st Cir. 1986)

51 ALR6th 219—§ 4

State v. Guidry, 647 So. 2d 502 (La. Ct. App. 3d Cir. 1994)

90 ALR5th 453—§ 12

State v. Guillet, 3 Conn. Cir. 380, 215 A.2d 685 (1965)

52 ALR5th 655—§ 4

State v. Guillory, 21 So. 3d 945 (La. 2009)

56 ALR6th 1—§ 18

State v. Guillory, 526 So. 2d 1164 (La. Ct. App. 3d Cir. 1988)

38 ALR6th 97—§ 25

State v. Guillory, 544 So. 2d 643 (La. App. 3d Cir. 1989)

10 ALR5th 700—§ 10

State v. Guillory, 715 So. 2d 400 (La. Ct. App. 3d Cir. 1998)

9 ALR6th 1—§ 17

State v. Guin, 1995 WL 51655 (Ohio Ct. App. 3d Dist. Allen County 1995)

99 ALR6th 295—§ 9

State v. Guinn, 42 Ohio St. 3d 92, 537 N.E.2d 656 (1989)

48 ALR6th 511—§ 6, 19

State v. Guirlando, 509 So. 2d 172 (La. App. 1st Cir. 1987)

14 ALR5th 913—§ 2, 3

State v. Guiton, 51 La. Ann 155, 24 So. 784 (1899)

34 ALR5th 723—§ 4

State v. Guizzotti, 60 Wash. App. 289, 803 P.2d 808 (1991)

3 ALR5th 784—§ 10

State v. Guizzotti, 60 Wash. App. 289, 803 P.2d 808 (Div. 2 1991)

7 ALR6th 233—§ 5

State v. Gulbankian, 54 Wis. 2d 599, 196 N.W.2d 730 (1972)

80 ALR5th 597—§ 2, 15, 18

State v. Gulbrandson, 184 Ariz. 46, 906 P.2d 579 (1995)

72 ALR5th 403—§ 10, 15

79 ALR5th 33—§ 9, 40

State v. Gulledge, 257 Kan. 915, 896 P.2d 378 (1995)

12 ALR5th 89—§ 4

State v. Gullett, 418 So. 2d 406 (Fla. Dist. Ct. App. 2d Dist. 1982)

114 ALR5th 173—§ 9

State v. Gullette, 121 Mo. 447, 26 S.W. 354 (1894)

108 ALR5th 593—§ 8

State v. Gulley, 2006-Ohio-2023, 2006 WL 1064062 (Ohio Ct. App. 12th Dist. Clermont County 2006)

71 ALR6th 625—§ 12, 29

State v. Gullings, 244 Or. 173, 416 P.2d 311 (1966)

37 ALR5th 703—§ 5

State v. Guloy, 104 Wash. 2d 412, 705 P.2d 1182, cert den 475 U.S. 1020, 89 L. Ed. 2d 321

14 ALR5th 89—§ 8

State v. Gumphrey, 296 Wis. 2d 421, 2006 WI App 194, 722 N.W.2d 401 (Ct. App. 2006)

62 ALR6th 161—§ 27

State v. Gundel, 56 Conn. App. 805, 746 A.2d 204 (2000)

9 ALR6th 633—§ 5, 37

15 ALR6th 173—§ 39

State v. Gunderson, 74 Wash. 2d 226, 444 P.2d 156 (1968)

15 ALR5th 391—§ 30

92 ALR5th 35—§ 15

84 ALR6th 427—§ 26

State v. Gundlach, 112 Ohio App. 471, 15 Ohio Op. 2d 192, 174 N.E.2d 267 (9th Dist. Medina County 1960)

89 ALR6th 565—§ 10, 13, 29, 31, 33

State v. Gunn, 29 Kan. App. 2d 337, 26 P.3d 710 (2001)

23 ALR6th 307—§ 42

State v. Gunn, 1998 WL 453845 (Ohio Ct. App. 2d Dist. Montgomery County 1998)

70 ALR5th 533—§ 6

State v. Gunnoe, 179 W. Va. 808, 374 S.E.2d 716 (1988)

124 ALR5th 1—§ 4

State v. Gunter, 132 Ariz. 64, 643 P.2d 1034 (Ct. App. Div. 1 1982)

19 ALR6th 411—§ 13

State v. Gunter, 231 N.J. Super. 34, 554 A.2d 1356 (App. Div. 1989)

93 ALR5th 527—§ 4

State v. Gunther, 1985 WL 17720 (Ohio Ct. App. 11th Dist. Trumbull County 1985)

19 ALR6th 697—§ 4

State v. Gurda, 209 Wis. 63, 243 N.W. 317 (1932)

73 ALR5th 223—§ 12

State v. Gurican, 576 So. 2d 709 (Fla. 1991)

105 ALR5th 529—§ 15

State v. Gurley, 919 S.W.2d 635 (Tenn. Crim. App. 1995)

58 ALR5th 749—§ 11

State v. Gurley, 2001 WL 709087 (Ohio Ct. App. 6th Dist. Huron County 2001)

3 ALR6th 543—§ 9

State v. Gurrola, 121 N.M. 34, 908 P.2d 264 (App. 1995)

19 ALR5th 470—§ 3

State v. Gurule, 2013-NMSC-025, 303 P.3d 838 (N.M. 2013)

94 ALR6th 525—§ 9

State v. Gutberlet, 346 N.W.2d 639 (Minn. 1984)

124 ALR5th 1—§ 4

State v. Guthmiller, 499 N.W.2d 590 (N.D. 1993)

84 ALR6th 293—§ 33

State v. Guthrie, 90 Me. 448, 38 A. 368 (1897)

67 ALR5th 361—§ 5

State v. Guthrie, 205 W. Va. 326, 518 S.E.2d 83 (1999)

35 ALR6th 127—§ 5

State v. Guthrie, 2001 SD 61, 627 N.W.2d 401 (S.D. 2001)

27 ALR6th 491—§ 4

State v. Guthrie, 2001 S.D. 61, 2001 WL 521939 (S.D. 2001)

55 ALR5th 125—§ 12

84 ALR5th 1—§ 7.5, 10

90 ALR5th 453—§ 22

State v. Gutierrez, 5 S.W.3d 641 (Tenn. 1999)

73 ALR5th 383—§ 31

State v. Gutierrez, 95 Ohio App. 3d 414, 642 N.E.2d 674 (9th Dist. Lorain County 1994)
23 ALR6th 307—§ 44

State v. Gutierrez, 112 N.M. 774, 819 P.2d 1332 (App. 1991)
19 ALR5th 470—§ 3, 12

State v. Gutierrez, 116 N.M. 431, 863 P.2d 1052 (1993)
2 ALR6th 169—§ 4

State v. Gutierrez, 863 P.2d 1052 (N.M. 1993)
19 ALR5th 470—§ 12

State v. Gutierrez, 2011 WL 559153 (N.J. Super. Ct. App. Div. 2011)
74 ALR6th 373—§ 3

State v. Gutierrez Barajas, 153 Ariz. 511, 738 P.2d 786 (1987)
42 ALR5th 547—§ 5

State v. Gutman, 670 P.2d 1166 (Alaska Ct. App. 1983)
67 ALR5th 361—§ 2 to 4, 8

State v. Guy, 172 Wis. 2d 86, 492 N.W.2d 311 (1992)
33 ALR5th 453—§ 4
50 ALR5th 581—§ 2, 3, 6 to 9, 14, 20

State v. Guy, 1994 WL 605598 (Ohio Ct. App. 9th Dist. Summit County 1994)
89 ALR5th 539—§ 5

State v. Guzek, 322 Or. 245, 906 P.2d 272 (1995)
79 ALR5th 33—§ 9, 42, 52

State v. Guziar, 680 N.E.2d 553 (Ind. Ct. App. 1997)
98 ALR6th 93—§ 33

State v. Guzman, 122 Idaho 981, 842 P.2d 660 (1992)
19 ALR5th 470—§ 3, 12
73 ALR6th 49—§ 4

State v. Guzman, 164 Or. App. 90, 990 P.2d 370 (1999)
99 ALR5th 557—§ 9

State v. Guzman, 199 Wis. 2d 127, 545 N.W.2d 521 (Ct. App. 1995)
57 ALR5th 315—§ 3, 8, 11

State v. Guzman, 240 S.W.3d 362 (Tex. App. Austin 2007)
89 ALR6th 565—§ 32

State v. Guzman, 665 So. 2d 512 (La. Ct. App. 5th Cir. 1995)
73 ALR5th 383—§ 5

State v. Guzman, 888 P.2d 466 (N.M. 1995)
20 ALR5th 398—§ 3, 34, 38

State v. Guzman-Balbuena, 126 Wash. App. 1002, 2005 WL 420259 (Div. 2 2005)
26 ALR6th 511—§ 45

State v. Guzman-Gomez, 13 Neb. App. 235, 690 N.W.2d 804 (2005)
30 ALR6th 103—§ 34, 43

State v. Gwaltney, 31 N.C. App. 240, 228 S.E.2d 764 (1976)
30 ALR6th 103—§ 34

State v. Gyamfi, 110 Wash. App. 1005, 2002 WL 80903 (Div. 1 2002)
7 ALR6th 233—§ 5

State v. Gyles, 313 So. 2d 799 (La. 1975)
64 ALR5th 671—§ 4

State v. Gyngard, 333 S.W.2d 73, 90 A.L.R.2d 639 (Mo. 1960)
54 ALR6th 429—§ 29

State v. H.A., 716 N.W.2d 360 (Minn. Ct. App. 2006)
68 ALR6th 1—§ 10

State v. Haack, 220 Mont. 141, 713 P.2d 1001 (1986)
57 ALR6th 445—§ 11

State v. Haas, 142 La. 271, 76 So. 710 (1917)
5 ALR6th 1—§ 32

State v. Haas, 244 Wis. 2d 289, 2001 WI App 121, 628 N.W.2d 438 (Ct. App. 2001)
5 ALR6th 385—§ 4

State v. Haas, 279 Neb. 812, 782 N.W.2d 584 (2010)
72 ALR6th 227—§ 59

State v. Haas, 2005-Ohio-4350, 2005 WL 2007886 (Ohio Ct. App. 6th Dist. Lucas County 2005)
69 ALR6th 1—§ 3, 24

70 ALR6th 1—§ 3

State v. Habbena, 372 N.W.2d 450 (S.D. 1985)

19 ALR5th 470—§ 3, 5, 14

41 ALR5th 171—§ 13, 16, 18, 68

State v. Haberla, 39 Wis. 2d 334, 159 N.W.2d 11 (1968)

80 ALR5th 597—§ 15, 18

State v. Haberstroh, 119 Nev. 173, 69 P.3d 676 (2003)

21 ALR6th 1—§ 4

State v. Hablutzel, 1988 WL 125019 (Ohio Ct. App. 1st Dist. Hamilton County 1988)

17 ALR6th 327—§ 6

State v. Hackbarth, 256 Wis. 545, 41 N.W.2d 594 (1950)

125 ALR5th 537—§ 1

State v. Hacker, 158 W. Va. 182, 209 S.E.2d 569 (1974)

61 ALR5th 1—§ 12

68 ALR5th 343—§ 3

State v. Hackett, 944 So. 2d 399 (Fla. Dist. Ct. App. 4th Dist. 2006)

55 ALR6th 513—§ 4

State v. Hackman, 189 Ariz. 505, 943 P.2d 865 (Ct. App. Div. 1 1997)

14 ALR5th 913—§ 6

State v. Hackwith, 1995 WL 640769 (Neb. Ct. App. 1995)

84 ALR6th 293—§ 31

State v. Haddenham, 110 N.M. 149, 793 P.2d 279 (Ct. App. 1990)

65 ALR6th 329—§ 4, 7

State v. Haddix, 93 Ohio App. 3d 470, 638 N.E.2d 1096, R.I.C.O. Bus. Disp. Guide (CCH) ¶ 8685 (12th Dist. Preble County 1994)

89 ALR5th 629—§ 12

State v. Haddix, 566 S.W.2d 266 (Mo. App. 1978)

54 ALR5th 141—§ 3, 4, 9

State v. Hadinger, 61 Ohio App. 3d 820, 573 N.E.2d 1191 (10th Dist. Franklin County 1991)

71 ALR5th 285—§ 2, 4

State v. Hadlock, No. 49995 (November 12, 1986, Ct. App. Ohio, 8th App. Dist. Cuyahoga Co.)

39 ALR5th 283—§ 14

State v. Hadsell, 129 Or. App. 171, 878 P.2d 444 (1994)

71 ALR5th 1—§ 59

State v. Haendiges, 1998 WL 103349 (Ohio Ct. App. 9th Dist. Lorain County 1998)

85 ALR5th 595—§ 3

State v. Hafeli, 715 S.W.2d 524 (Mo. Ct. App. E.D. 1986)

67 ALR5th 637—§ 5, 8

State v. Haffner, 140 Wash. App. 1004, 2007 WL 2258815 (Div. 2 2007)

69 ALR6th 579—§ 4

State v. Hafle, 52 Ohio App. 2d 9, 6 Ohio Ops. 3d 5, 367 N.E.2d 1226 (Clinton Co. 1977)

6 ALR5th 733—§ 7, 16

State v. Haga, 954 P.2d 1284 (Utah Ct. App. 1998)

92 ALR5th 35—§ 25

State v. Hagaman, 133 Wis. 2d 381, 395 N.W.2d 617 (Ct. App. 1986)

76 ALR5th 597—§ 2, 3

State v. Hagan, 47 Idaho 315, 274 P. 628 (1929)

55 ALR5th 125—§ 3, 11

State v. Hagan, 99 N.J. Super. 249, 239 A.2d 262 (App. Div. 1968)

68 ALR5th 343—§ 3, 5

State v. Hage, 258 Mont. 498, 853 P.2d 1251 (1993)

36 ALR5th 255—§ 24

State v. Hage, 1997 ND 175, 568 N.W.2d 741 (N.D. 1997)

113 ALR5th 517—§ 6

State v. Hagen, 91 Iowa 510, 60 N.W. 108 (1894)

75 ALR6th 311—§ 56

State v. Hagen, 181 Wis. 2d 934, 512 N.W.2d 180 (Ct. App. 1994)

97 ALR5th 201—§ 3

State v. Hagen, 283 Mont. 156, 939 P.2d 994 (1997)

92 ALR6th 295—§ 12

---

93 ALR6th 207—§ 28

96 ALR6th 355—§ 6

State v. Hagen, 317 N.W.2d 701 (Minn. 1982)

73 ALR5th 383—§ 5, 31

State v. Hagen, 361 N.W.2d 407 (Minn. Ct. App. 1985)

28 ALR6th 505—§ 7, 16

State v. Hagen, 391 N.W.2d 888, 75 A.L.R.4th 887 (Minn. Ct. App. 1986)

40 ALR6th 1—§ 33

State v. Hagerman, 685 S.E.2d 153 (N.C. Ct. App. 2009)

57 ALR6th 1—§ 10

State v. Hagerman Water Right Owners, Inc. (HWRO), 130 Idaho 718, 947 P.2d 391 (1997)

106 ALR5th 523—§ 4, 44

State v. Haggard, 89 Idaho 217, 404 P.2d 580 (1965)

55 ALR5th 125—§ 3, 7

State v. Haggard, 146 Idaho 37, 190 P.3d 193 (Ct. App. 2008)

63 ALR6th 1—§ 5, 11, 36, 38, 42, 55

State v. Haggarty, 20 Wash. App. 335, 579 P.2d 1031 (Div. 3 1978)

85 ALR5th 1—§ 33, 42

55 ALR6th 391—§ 21

State v. Hagstrom, 67 Ohio App. 3d 388, 587 N.E.2d 324 (1st Dist. Hamilton County 1990)

70 ALR6th 1—§ 5

State v. Hagstrom, 1999 WL 527785 (Ohio Ct. App. 12th Dist. Butler County 1999)

17 ALR6th 327—§ 4

State v. Hague, 707 N.W.2d 337 (Iowa Ct. App. 2005)

58 ALR6th 439—§ 24

State v. Hahn, 37 S.W.3d 344 (Mo. Ct. App. W.D. 2000)

3 ALR6th 543—§ 10

State v. Hahn, 100 Wash. App. 391, 996 P.2d 1125 (Div. 2 2000)

92 ALR5th 35—§ 20

State v. Hahn, 660 N.E.2d 606 (Ind. App. 1996)

54 ALR5th 575—§ 31

State v. Haibeck, 2004 ND 163, 685 N.W.2d 512 (N.D. 2004)

20 ALR6th 479—§ 3

34 ALR6th 1—§ 11

State v. Haibeck, 2006 ND 100, 714 N.W.2d 52 (N.D. 2006)

55 ALR6th 391—§ 21

State v. Haight, 2 Conn. Cir. 79, 194 A.2d 718 (1963)

52 ALR5th 655—§ 3

State v. Haigler, 334 S.C. 623, 515 S.E.2d 88 (1999)

15 ALR6th 319—§ 4

State v. Haines, 35 Or. 379, 58 P. 39 (1899)

102 ALR5th 525—§ 33

State v. Haines, 543 So. 2d 1278 (Fla. Dist. Ct. App. 5th Dist. 1989)

64 ALR5th 637—§ 3

State v. Haines, 545 N.E.2d 834 (Ind. App. 1989)

13 ALR5th 628—§ 6, 9

State v. Haines, 774 N.E.2d 984 (Ind. Ct. App. 2002)

109 ALR5th 99—§ 10

State v. Haines, 2010-Ohio-1123, 2010 WL 1041446 (Ohio Ct. App. 2d Dist. Montgomery County 2010)

64 ALR6th 1—§ 7

State v. Hair, 161 N.C. App. 742, 590 S.E.2d 24 (2003)

27 ALR6th 183—§ 35

State v. Hairiston, 33 Conn. Supp. 183, 369 A.2d 255 (1976)

34 ALR5th 125—§ 9

State v. Hairston, 67 Ohio App. 3d 341, 586 N.E.2d 1200 (Cuyahoga Co. 1990)

38 ALR5th 433—§ 30

State v. Hairston, 123 N.C. App. 753, 475 S.E.2d 242 (1996)

77 ALR5th 201—§ 3

38 ALR6th 439—§ 8

State v. Hairston, 133 Idaho 496, 988 P.2d 1170 (1999)

83 ALR6th 465—§ 8, 56

State v. Haislip, 237 Kan. 461, 701 P.2d 909 (1985)

16 ALR5th 841—§ 4

State v. Haith, 7 N.C. App. 552, 172 S.E.2d 912 (1970)

5 ALR5th 243—§ 50, 51

State v. Hakimi, 124 Wash. App. 15, 98 P.3d 809 (Div. 1 2004)

82 ALR6th 373—§ 4, 7, 14, 17

State v. Halahan, 108 Ohio App. 3d 33, 669 N.E.2d 883 (11th Dist. Portage County 1995)

84 ALR6th 293—§ 32

State v. Halczyszak, 1990 WL 32605 (Ohio Ct. App. 8th Dist. Cuyahoga County 1990)

107 ALR5th 567—§ 10

State v. Hale, 45 Hawaii 269, 367 P.2d 81 (1961)

33 ALR5th 571—§ 3

State v. Hale, 94 Wash. App. 46, 971 P.2d 88 (Div. 2 1999)

46 ALR6th 63—§ 7

State v. Hale, 119 Ohio St. 3d 118, 2008-Ohio-3426, 892 N.E.2d 864 (2008)

81 ALR6th 505—§ 4

State v. Hale, 453 N.W.2d 704 (Minn. 1990)

81 ALR6th 505—§ 61

State v. Hale, 2005-Ohio-7080, 2005 WL 3642690 (Ohio Ct. App. 7th Dist. Monroe County 2005)

77 ALR6th 393—§ 54, 96

State v. Hales, 344 N.C. 419, 474 S.E.2d 328 (1996)

85 ALR5th 187—§ 2, 7, 8, 12

State v. Haley, 64 Or. App. 209, 667 P.2d 560 (1983)

7 ALR5th 73—§ 1 to 3

State v. Haley, 687 P.2d 305 (Alaska 1984)

75 ALR5th 619—§ 4

State v. Haley, 2003 WL 1207972 (Neb. Ct. App. 2003)

58 ALR6th 215—§ 20

State v. Haliski, 273 N.J. Super. 157, 641 A.2d 549 (App. Div. 1994)

7 ALR5th 263—§ 7

State v. Halk, 49 Mont. 173, 141 P. 149 (1914)

50 ALR5th 467—§ 3, 5, 6, 9

State v. Hall, 3 Ohio N.P. 125, 4 Ohio Dec. 147 (C.P. 1896)

81 ALR5th 563—§ 3

State v. Hall, 12 Ariz. App. 147, 468 P.2d 598 (Div. 1 1970)

58 ALR6th 439—§ 3

State v. Hall, 22 Wash. App. 862, 593 P.2d 554 (Div. 2 1979)

93 ALR5th 527—§ 15

State v. Hall, 40 Wash. App. 162, 697 P.2d 597 (Div. 1 1985)

102 ALR6th 365—§ 26

State v. Hall, 53 Wash. App. 296, 766 P.2d 512 (Div. 3 1989)

112 ALR5th 429—§ 10

State v. Hall, 66 Hawaii 300, 660 P.2d 33 (1983)

49 ALR5th 639—§ 4

State v. Hall, 66 Ohio Misc. 2d 80, 643 N.E.2d 190 (Mun Ct. 1994)

61 ALR5th 1—§ 3, 5

State v. Hall, 85 N.C. App. 447, 355 S.E.2d 250 (1987)

55 ALR6th 157—§ 114

State v. Hall, 93 N.C. App. 236, 377 S.E.2d 280 (1989)

94 ALR5th 393—§ 9

State v. Hall, 103 Wis. 2d 125, 307 N.W.2d 289 (1981)

32 ALR6th 385—§ 5

State v. Hall, 107 N.M. 17, 751 P.2d 701 (App. 1987)

20 ALR5th 398—§ 47

State v. Hall, 111 Idaho 827, 727 P.2d 1255 (Ct. App. 1986)

35 ALR6th 127—§ 5

State v. Hall, 136 Ariz. 219, 665 P.2d 101 (Ct. App. Div. 1 1983)

72 ALR5th 529—§ 19

State v. Hall, 168 Vt. 327, 719 A.2d 435 (1998)

62 ALR6th 413—§ 52

State v. Hall, 171 W. Va. 212, 298 S.E.2d 246 (1982)

29 ALR5th 59—§ 3, 29

State v. Hall, 174 W. Va. 599, 328 S.E.2d 206 (1985)

9 ALR6th 1—§ 17

State v. Hall, 174 W. Va. 787, 329 S.E.2d 860 (1985)

24 ALR6th 1—§ 20

State v. Hall, 176 Neb. 295, 125 N.W.2d 918 (1964)

20 ALR5th 177—§ 3, 9

State v. Hall, 187 So. 2d 861 (Miss. 1966)

70 ALR5th 587—§ 3

State v. Hall, 196 Wis. 2d 850, 540 N.W.2d 219 (App. 1995)

12 ALR5th 89—§ 4, 5

27 ALR5th 593—§ 7

State v. Hall, 204 Ariz. 442, 65 P.3d 90 (2003)

65 ALR6th 359—§ 3, 9

State v. Hall, 214 Wis. 2d 592, 571 N.W.2d 925 (Ct. App. 1997)

64 ALR5th 637—§ 3

State v. Hall, 225 Iowa 1316, 283 N.W. 414 (1939)

9 ALR6th 1—§ 7

State v. Hall, 235 N.W.2d 702 (Iowa 1975)

49 ALR5th 639—§ 4

State v. Hall, 246 Kan. 728, 793 P.2d 737 (1990)

84 ALR5th 487—§ 3

State v. Hall, 253 N.J. Super. 84, 600 A.2d 1248 (Law Div. 1990)

28 ALR6th 505—§ 6, 32

State v. Hall, 264 N.C. 559, 142 S.E.2d 177 (1965)

65 ALR5th 407—§ 3, 16

State v. Hall, 280 S.C. 74, 310 S.E.2d 429 (1983)

39 ALR5th 283—§ 3

State v. Hall, 297 N.W.2d 80 (Iowa 1980)

9 ALR5th 369—§ 2, 5, 7, 9, 14, 17, 20

State v. Hall, 330 N.C. 808, 412 S.E.2d 883 (1992)

85 ALR5th 595—§ 8

State v. Hall, 353 N.W.2d 37 (S.D. 1984)

34 ALR6th 1—§ 12

57 ALR6th 83—§ 11

92 ALR6th 295—§ 12

93 ALR6th 207—§ 6, 28

96 ALR6th 355—§ 9, 37

State v. Hall, 537 So. 2d 171 (Fla. Dist. Ct. App. 1st Dist. 1989)

57 ALR6th 83—§ 10

State v. Hall, 555 So. 2d 495 (La. Ct. App. 4th Cir. 1989)

17 ALR6th 327—§ 11

State v. Hall, 958 S.W.2d 679 (Tenn. 1997)

83 ALR6th 255—§ 17

State v. Hall, 1980 WL 353151 (Ohio Ct. App. 1st Dist. Hamilton County 1980)

42 ALR6th 237—§ 8

State v. Hall, 1990 WL 188417 (Ohio Ct. App. 9th Dist. Wayne County 1990)

84 ALR6th 293—§ 31

State v. Hall, 2005 WL 428292 (Tenn. Crim. App. 2005)

26 ALR6th 511—§ 25, 27

State v. Hallam, 175 Mont. 492, 575 P.2d 55 (1978)

85 ALR5th 187—§ 15

State v. Halla-Poe, 468 N.W.2d 570 (Minn. Ct. App. 1991)

58 ALR6th 499—§ 15

State v. Halleck, 308 N.W.2d 56 (Iowa 1981)

49 ALR5th 619—§ 2, 6

State v. Hall, No. 78 (October 16, 1979, Ct. App. Ohio, 7th App. Dist. Mahoning Co.)

39 ALR5th 283—§ 14, 44

State v. Halloway, 256 Kan. 449, 886 P.2d 831 (1994)

39 ALR5th 283—§ 4, 67

State v. Halsell, 2009-Ohio-4166, 2009 WL 2517137 (Ohio Ct. App. 9th Dist. Summit County 2009)

99 ALR6th 295—§ 21

State v. Halsen, 111 Wash. 2d 121, 757 P.2d 531 (1988)
15 ALR5th 391—§ 25

State v. Halsey, 232 Neb. 658, 441 N.W.2d 877 (1989)
65 ALR6th 537—§ 44

State v. Halsey, 329 N.J. Super. 553, 748 A.2d 634 (App. Div. 2000)
125 ALR5th 497—§ 3

State v. Halstead, 414 A.2d 1138 (R.I. 1980)
33 ALR5th 571—§ 3

State v. Halverson, 21 Wash. App. 35, 584 P.2d 408 (1978)
43 ALR5th 1—§ 13

State v. Halverson, 277 N.W.2d 723 (S.D. 1979)
50 ALR5th 703—§ 39
18 ALR6th 519—§ 4

State v. Halverson, 362 N.W.2d 501 (Iowa 1985)
67 ALR6th 209—§ 43

State v. Halvorsen, 30 Wash. App. 772, 638 P.2d 124 (Div. 2 1981)
77 ALR6th 393—§ 57

State v. Halvorson, 346 N.W.2d 704 (N.D. 1984)
7 ALR5th 758—§ 8
57 ALR5th 141—§ 11
28 ALR6th 505—§ 31

State v. Halyard, 274 S.C. 397, 264 S.E.2d 841 (1980)
88 ALR5th 121—§ 2, 3, 36

State v. Ham, 39 Wash. App. 7, 691 P.2d 239 (1984)
6 ALR5th 733—§ 2, 5, 24, 26

State v. Ham, 39 Wash. App. 7, 691 P.2d 239 (Div. 1 1984)
69 ALR6th 207—§ 5

State v. Ham, 113 Idaho 405, 744 P.2d 133 (App. 1987)
55 ALR5th 125—§ 3, 6, 7

State v. Ham, 910 P.2d 433 (Ct. App. Utah, 1996)
99 ALR5th 557—§ 9

State v. Ham, 2009-Ohio-3822, 2009 WL 2370908 (Ohio Ct. App. 3d Dist. Wyandot County 2009)
70 ALR6th 329—§ 18

State v. Hamblin, 1990 WL 14547 (Tenn. Crim. App. 1990)
68 ALR6th 527—§ 37

State v. Hambrick, 65 Wyo. 1, 196 P.2d 661 (1948)
104 ALR5th 357—§ 3, 9
54 ALR6th 429—§ 20

State v. Hambrick, 177 W. Va. 26, 350 S.E.2d 537 (1986)
68 ALR5th 343—§ 3, 10

State v. Hamdan, 264 Wis. 2d 433, 2003 WI 113, 665 N.W.2d 785 (2003)
33 ALR6th 407—§ 8

State v. Hamdan, 2003 WI 113, 264 Wis. 2d 433, 665 N.W.2d 785 (2003)
33 ALR6th 407—§ 6

State v. Hamel, 634 A.2d 1272 (Me. 1993)
35 ALR6th 497—§ 24, 38

State v. Hamer, 188 Conn. 562, 452 A.2d 313 (1982)
39 ALR6th 257—§ 42

State v. Hamilton, 20 N.D. 592, 129 N.W. 916 (1910)
120 ALR5th 125—§ 2
121 ALR5th 1—§ 2

State v. Hamilton, 42 La. Ann. 1204, 8 So. 304 (1890)
97 ALR6th 567—§ 3, 9

State v. Hamilton, 75 Ohio St. 3d 636, 1996-Ohio-440, 665 N.E.2d 669 (1996)
70 ALR6th 1—§ 3

State v. Hamilton, 120 Wis. 2d 532, 356 N.W.2d 169 (1984)
66 ALR5th 397—§ 16

State v. Hamilton, 125 N.C. App. 396, 481 S.E.2d 98 (1997)
92 ALR6th 171—§ 18

State v. Hamilton, 142 Ariz. 91, 688 P.2d 983 (1984)
70 ALR5th 1—§ 6

State v. Hamilton, 172 S.C. 453, 174 S.E. 396 (1934)

State v. Hammond, 251 Kan. 501, 837
P.2d 816 (1992)
39 ALR5th 283—§ 4, 22, 23, 32

State v. Hammonds, 616 S.W.2d 890
(Tenn. Crim. App. 1981)
94 ALR5th 393—§ 13

State v. Hammons, 737 S.W.2d 549
(Tenn. Crim. 1987)
31 ALR5th 704—§ 3

State v. Hammontree, 363 So. 2d 1364
(La. 1978)
9 ALR6th 1—§ 17
84 ALR6th 427—§ 21, 26

State v. Hamons, 248 Kan. 51, 805 P.2d
6 (1991)
11 ALR5th 831—§ 7, 8

State v. Hampton, 50 S.W.3d 298 (Mo.
Ct. App. S.D. 2001)
1 ALR6th 549—§ 3
7 ALR6th 169—§ 3
8 ALR6th 265—§ 3

State v. Hampton, 59 Or. App. 512, 651
P.2d 744 (1982)
11 ALR5th 52—§ 11

State v. Hampton, 61 N.J. 250, 294 A.2d
23 (1972)
39 ALR5th 283—§ 4, 81

State v. Hampton, 201 Wis. 2d 661, 549
N.W.2d 756 (App. 1996)
59 ALR5th 1—§ 2, 4, 6

State v. Hampton, 207 Wis. 2d 369, 558
N.W.2d 884 (1996 Ct. App)
55 ALR5th 449—§ 3, 4

State v. Hampton, 213 Ariz. 167, 140
P.3d 950 (2006)
21 ALR6th 1—§ 4

State v. Hampton, 275 S.W.2d 356 (Mo.
1955)
57 ALR6th 445—§ 46

State v. Hampton, 959 S.W.2d 444 (Mo.
1997)
70 ALR5th 587—§ 18

State v. Hampton, 1997 WL 177441
(Wash. Ct. App. Div. 1 1997)
73 ALR5th 383—§ 25

State v. Hamrick, 160 W. Va. 673, 236
S.E.2d 247 (1977)
29 ALR6th 1—§ 17

State v. Hamsley, 672 S.W.2d 437
(Tenn. Crim. 1984)
24 ALR5th 132—§ 5, 12

State v. Hanania, 715 So. 2d 984 (Fla.
Dist. Ct. App. 2d Dist. 1998)
43 ALR6th 475—§ 6

State v. Hancharik, 1992 WL 52597
(Ohio Ct. App. 11th Dist. Ashtabula
County 1992)
69 ALR6th 207—§ 9, 10, 18

State v. Hancock, 44 Wash. App. 297,
721 P.2d 1006 (1986)
29 ALR5th 59—§ 58, 76

State v. Handeland, 221 Wis. 2d 597,
586 N.W.2d 699 (Ct. App. 1998)
45 ALR6th 643—§ 9

State v. Handfield, 115 N.H. 628, 348
A.2d 352 (1975)
109 ALR5th 611—§ 3

State v. Handley, 115 Wash. 2d 275, 796
P.2d 1266 (1990)
73 ALR5th 383—§ 4, 8

State v. Handley, 453 So. 2d 1242 (La.
Ct. App. 1st Cir. 1984)
103 ALR6th 507—§ 12

State v. Handley, 1999 WL 55682 (Ohio
Ct. App. 12th Dist. Clermont
County 1999)
84 ALR6th 293—§ 31

State v. Handy, 27 Wash. 469, 67 P.
1094 (1902)
105 ALR5th 529—§ 11

State v. Haney, 70 Ohio App. 3d 135,
590 N.E.2d 445 (10th Dist. Franklin
County 1991)
70 ALR6th 1—§ 5

State v. Haney, 1999 WL 1054840 (Ohio
Ct. App. 10th Dist. Franklin County
1999)
70 ALR6th 1—§ 5

State v. Hankerson, 2005 UT 47, 122
P.3d 561 (Utah 2005)
37 ALR6th 357—§ 57, 67, 68

State v. Hankerson, 2005 UT App 388,
122 P.3d 684 (Utah Ct. App. 2005)
37 ALR6th 357—§ 68

CASES CITED IN ALR5th and ALR6th

State v. Hankins, 232 Neb. 608, 441
   N.W.2d 854 (1989)
   9 ALR5th 369—§ 2
State v. Hanley, 363 N.W.2d 735 (Minn.
   1985)
   68 ALR5th 343—§ 3
State v. Hanley, 802 N.E.2d 956 (Ind.
   Ct. App. 2004)
   15 ALR6th 515—§ 3
State v. Hann, 173 Ohio App. 3d 716,
   2007-Ohio-6201, 880 N.E.2d 148
   (8th Dist. Cuyahoga County 2007)
   69 ALR6th 1—§ 10
State v. Hanna, 123 Wash. 2d 704, 871
   P.2d 135 (1994)
   40 ALR5th 113—§ 3
State v. Hanna, 901 So. 2d 201 (Fla.
   Dist. Ct. App. 5th Dist. 2005)
   20 ALR6th 161—§ 3
   21 ALR6th 425—§ 3
State v. Hanna, 2001-Ohio-8623, 2002
   WL 4529 (Ohio Ct. App. 12th Dist.
   Warren County 2001)
   21 ALR6th 1—§ 4
State v. Hannagan, 559 P.2d 1059
   (Alaska 1977)
   65 ALR6th 537—§ 49, 51, 53, 59
State v. Hannah, 126 Ariz. 575, 617 P.2d
   527 (1980)
   7 ALR5th 263—§ 2, 7
State v. Hannah, 1990 WL 129316 (Ohio
   Ct. App. 2d Dist. Greene County
   1990)
   84 ALR6th 293—§ 27
State v. Hanners, 235 S.W.3d 609 (Tenn.
   Crim. App. 2007)
   70 ALR6th 1—§ 25
State v. Hanning, 296 S.W.3d 44 (Tenn.
   2009)
   84 ALR6th 293—§ 21, 27
State v. Hannon, 703 N.W.2d 498
   (Minn. 2005)
   30 ALR6th 1—§ 4
State v. Hannuksela, 452 N.W.2d 668
   (Minn. 1990)
   23 ALR6th 1—§ 3, 4, 15

State v. Hansbro, 2002-Ohio-2922, 2002
   WL 1332297 (Ohio Ct. App. 2d
   Dist. Clark County 2002)
   29 ALR6th 237—§ 4, 9, 24
State v. Hansen, 27 N.C. App. 459, 219
   S.E.2d 641 (1975)
   43 ALR5th 1—§ 12
State v. Hansen, 122 Wash. 2d 712, 862
   P.2d 117 (1993)
   9 ALR6th 363—§ 41
State v. Hansen, 125 Idaho 927, 877
   P.2d 898 (1994)
   58 ALR6th 385—§ 33
State v. Hansen, 138 Idaho 791, 69 P.3d
   1052 (2003)
   28 ALR6th 505—§ 7, 9
State v. Hansen, 146 Ariz. 226, 705 P.2d
   466 (App. 1985)
   **32 ALR5th 149—§ 4, 8, 15, 18, 36,
   71, 80, 81**
State v. Hansen, 187 Mont. 91, 608 P.2d
   1083 (1980)
   86 ALR5th 59—§ 4
State v. Hansen, 243 Wis. 2d 328, 2001
   WI 53, 627 N.W.2d 195 (2001)
   97 ALR5th 201—§ 7
State v. Hansen, 286 Minn. 4, 174
   N.W.2d 697 (1970)
   85 ALR5th 187—§ 7
State v. Hansen, 732 P.2d 127 (Utah
   1987)
   112 ALR5th 429—§ 3
State v. Hansen, 877 P.2d 898 (Idaho
   1994)
   15 ALR5th 391—§ 32
State v. Hansen, 2009 WI App 99, 312
   Wis. 2d 813, 754 N.W.2d 255 (Ct.
   App. 2008)
   84 ALR6th 293—§ 19
State v. Hanson, 46 Wash. App. 656,
   731 P.2d 1140 (Div. 1 1987)
   102 ALR6th 365—§ 15
State v. Hanson, 97 Haw. 71, 34 P.3d 1
   (2001)
   125 ALR5th 281—§ 12
State v. Hanson, 100 Wis. 2d 549, 302
   N.W.2d 452 (1981)
   78 ALR6th 417—§ 8

State v. Hanson, 136 Wis. 2d 195, 401
N.W.2d 771 (1987)
96 ALR5th 327—§ 3
State v. Hanson, 138 Wash. App. 322,
157 P.3d 438 (Div. 3 2007)
50 ALR6th 353—§ 22
State v. Hanson, 201 Iowa 579, 207
N.W. 769 (1926)
10 ALR5th 1—§ 29, 31, 37
19 ALR6th 577—§ 7
State v. Hanson, 210 Iowa 773, 231
N.W. 428 (1930)
88 ALR6th 533—§ 11
State v. Hanson, 342 A.2d 300 (Me.
1975)
29 ALR5th 1—§ 3
State v. Hanson, 355 N.W.2d 328 (Minn.
Ct. App. 1984)
111 ALR5th 239—§ 6
State v. Hanson, 405 N.W.2d 467 (Minn.
Ct. App. 1987)
15 ALR5th 391—§ 30
73 ALR5th 383—§ 21
92 ALR5th 35—§ 13
State v. Hanson, 725 So. 2d 514 (La. Ct.
App. 4th Cir. 1998)
90 ALR5th 1—§ 31
State v. Hanson, 938 So. 2d 1147 (La.
Ct. App. 2d Cir. 2006)
103 ALR6th 507—§ 4
State v. Harden, 206 Kan. 365, 480 P.2d
53 (1971)
9 ALR6th 1—§ 8
State v. Harden, 938 So. 2d 480 (Fla.
2006)
79 ALR6th 125—§ 30
State v. Hardges, 2008-Ohio-5567, 2008
WL 4724692 (Ohio Ct. App. 9th
Dist. Summit County 2008)
65 ALR6th 1—§ 8
State v. Hardimon, 310 N.W.2d 564
(Minn. 1981)
20 ALR6th 479—§ 11, 14
24 ALR6th 747—§ 38
State v. Hardin, 90 Nev. 10, 518 P.2d
151 (1974)
61 ALR5th 1—§ 3, 5

State v. Hardin, 212 Neb. 774, 326
N.W.2d 38 (1982)
38 ALR5th 433—§ 38
State v. Hardin, 271 Ark. 606, 609
S.W.2d 64 (1980)
56 ALR6th 185—§ 39
State v. Hardin, 359 N.W.2d 185 (Iowa
1984)
39 ALR5th 283—§ 10, 45
State v. Harding, 196 Md. App. 384, 9
A.3d 547 (2010)
79 ALR6th 631—§ 2
State v. Harding, 399 A.2d 575 (Me.
1979)
102 ALR6th 279—§ 14
State v. Hardison, 326 N.C. 646, 392
S.E.2d 364 (1990)
36 ALR5th 255—§ 32
55 ALR6th 157—§ 114
State v. Hardnick, 1996 WL 748274
(Ohio Ct. App. 2d Dist. Clark
County 1996)
110 ALR5th 329—§ 6
State v. Hardstone Brick Co. of Little
Falls, 172 Minn. 328, 215 N.W. 186
(1927)
58 ALR5th 293—§ 2, 3
State v. Hardwick, 1 Conn. App. 609,
475 A.2d 315 (1984)
81 ALR5th 563—§ 3, 7
State v. Hardwick, 127 Or. App. 132,
871 P.2d 505 (1994)
15 ALR5th 391—§ 11
State v. Hardwick, 144 Wis. 2d 54, 422
N.W.2d 922 (Ct. App. 1988)
121 ALR5th 551—§ 13
State v. Hardy, 133 Wash. 2d 701, 946
P.2d 1175 (1997)
82 ALR5th 359—§ 2
83 ALR5th 277—§ 2
84 ALR5th 487—§ 2, 3
State v. Hardy, 174 La. 458, 141 So. 27
(1932)
97 ALR5th 293—§ 16
State v. Hardy, 230 Ariz. 281, 283 P.3d
12 (2012)
99 ALR6th 295—§ 21

State v. Hardy, 293 N.C. 105, 235 S.E.2d 828 (1977)
83 ALR6th 465—§ 55

State v. Hardy, 339 N.C. 207, 451 S.E.2d 600 (1994)
57 ALR5th 141—§ 3, 7

State v. Hardy, 501 A.2d 815 (Me. 1985)
15 ALR5th 391—§ 4
92 ALR5th 35—§ 25

State v. Hardy, 540 S.E.2d 334 (N.C. 2000)
20 ALR5th 398—§ 11, 42
63 ALR5th 375—§ 5

State v. Hardy, 568 S.W.2d 86 (Mo. Ct. App. 1978)
78 ALR5th 1—§ 21

State v. Hardy, 651 A.2d 322 (Me. 1994)
1 ALR6th 549—§ 8

State v. Harge, 94 N.M. 11, 606 P.2d 1105 (Ct. App. 1979)
29 ALR6th 1—§ 10

State v. Harge, 606 P.2d 1105 (N.M. App. 1979)
49 ALR5th 639—§ 4

State v. Hargis, 5 Kan. App. 2d 608, 620 P.2d 1181 (1980)
15 ALR5th 391—§ 20

State v. Hargrave, 411 So. 2d 1058 (La. 1982)
84 ALR6th 427—§ 5

State v. Hargrave, 631 So. 2d 1208 (La. App. 5th Cir. 1994)
51 ALR5th 425—§ 3, 10

State v. Hargrove, 138 Idaho 632, 67 P.3d 111 (Ct. App. 2003)
87 ALR6th 1—§ 42

State v. Hargrove, 273 Kan. 314, 45 P.3d 376 (2002)
51 ALR6th 1—§ 15
53 ALR6th 1—§ 7

State v. Harig, 118 Wash. App. 1013, 2003 WL 21958588 (Div. 1 2003)
30 ALR6th 373—§ 12

State v. Hariott, 210 S.C. 290, 42 S.E.2d 385 (1947)
67 ALR6th 103—§ 5

State v. Harker, 8 Neb. App. 663, 600 N.W.2d 488 (1999)
29 ALR5th 702—§ 11

State v. Harkey, 213 Wis. 2d 484, 570 N.W.2d 910 (Ct. App. 1997)
82 ALR6th 373—§ 7

State v. Harkness, 196 Wash. 234, 82 P.2d 541 (1938)
13 ALR5th 1—§ 2

State v. Harlow, 176 W. Va. 559, 346 S.E.2d 350 (1986)
9 ALR6th 633—§ 13
15 ALR6th 173—§ 25

State v. Harm, 200 N.W.2d 387 (N.D. 1972)
2 ALR5th 725—§ 3

State v. Harman, 132 Ohio App. 3d 348, 724 N.E.2d 1247 (7th Dist. Mahoning County 1999)
53 ALR6th 305—§ 19

State v. Harman, 174 W. Va. 731, 329 S.E.2d 98 (1985)
37 ALR5th 703—§ 5

State v. Harmer, 141 P.3d 1199 (Kan. Ct. App. 2006)
26 ALR6th 511—§ 25

State v. Harmon, 448 So. 2d 264 (La. Ct. App. 3d Cir. 1984)
79 ALR5th 237—§ 11

State v. Harms, 137 Idaho 891, 55 P.3d 884 (Ct. App. 2002)
81 ALR6th 505—§ 51

State v. Harms, 233 Neb. 882, 449 N.W.2d 1 (1989)
67 ALR6th 531—§ 36

State v. Harner, 153 Wash. 2d 228, 103 P.3d 738 (2004)
78 ALR6th 1—§ 4

State v. Harness, 280 S.W.2d 11 (Mo. 1955)
64 ALR5th 671—§ 10

State v. Harnisch, 114 Nev. 225, 954 P.2d 1180 (1998)
11 ALR5th 52—§ 4

State v. Harnish, 560 A.2d 5 (Me. 1989)
11 ALR5th 831—§ 5, 6
94 ALR5th 393—§ 13

For assistance, call 1-800-328-4880

State v. Harold, 74 Ariz. 210, 246 P.2d 178 (1952)

52 ALR5th 655—§ 3

State v. Harp, 43 Wash. App. 340, 717 P.2d 282 (Div. 2 1986)

73 ALR5th 383—§ 32

State v. Harp, 48 Or. App. 185, 616 P.2d 564 (1980)

59 ALR5th 615—§ 3, 4, 12

State v. Harper, 2 Neb. App. 220, 508 N.W.2d 584 (1993)

51 ALR6th 1—§ 24

State v. Harper, 35 Wash. App. 855, 670 P.2d 296 (Div. 2 1983)

82 ALR6th 373—§ 14

State v. Harper, 62 Wash. App. 69, 813 P.2d 593 (Div. 1 1991)

113 ALR5th 597—§ 8

State v. Harper, 64 Wash. App. 283, 823 P.2d 1137 (Div. 2 1992)

79 ALR5th 419—§ 9

State v. Harper, 72 N.C. App. 471, 325 S.E.2d 30 (1985)

118 ALR5th 253—§ 16

State v. Harper, 82 N.C. App. 398, 346 S.E.2d 223 (1986)

9 ALR6th 1—§ 17

State v. Harper, 95 Wis. 2d 737, 291 N.W.2d 660 (Ct. App. 1980)

68 ALR6th 527—§ 45

State v. Harper, 95 Wis. 2d 737, 291 N.W.2d 660(Ct. App. 1980)

80 ALR6th 599—§ 6

State v. Harper, 214 Neb. 911, 336 N.W.2d 597 (1983)

72 ALR5th 109—§ 5

State v. Harper, 430 So. 2d 627 (La. 1983)

124 ALR5th 1—§ 4

State v. Harper, 660 So. 2d 537 (La. Ct. App. 2d Cir. 1995)

76 ALR5th 563—§ 2, 4, 5
62 ALR6th 413—§ 2

State v. Harper, 753 S.W.2d 360 (Tenn. Crim. App. 1987)

68 ALR5th 343—§ 5

State v. Harper, 778 S.W.2d 836 (Mo. App. 1989)

56 ALR5th 385—§ 5

State v. Harper, 1991 WL 166069 (Del. Super. Ct. 1991)

85 ALR5th 1—§ 24

State v. Harper, 2000 WL 727502 (Conn. Super. Ct. 2000)

55 ALR6th 513—§ 3
56 ALR6th 323—§ 3, 9, 11
57 ALR6th 83—§ 3
58 ALR6th 215—§ 3
81 ALR6th 505—§ 3

State v. Harper, 2006 MT 259, 334 Mont. 138, 144 P.3d 826 (2006)

26 ALR6th 511—§ 4

State v. Harr, 81 Ohio App. 3d 244, 610 N.E.2d 1049 (Medina Co. 1992)

7 ALR5th 73—§ 5

State v. Harrell, 1992 WL 55444 (Ohio Ct. App. 10th Dist. Franklin County 1992)

74 ALR5th 453—§ 3, 5

State v. Harrell, 2007 WL 595885 (Tenn. Crim. App. 2007)

27 ALR6th 183—§ 35

State v. Harrell Ranch, Ltd., 268 S.W.3d 247 (Tex. App. Austin 2008)

49 ALR6th 205—§ 44

State v. Harriman, 434 So. 2d 551 (La. Ct. App. 2d Cir. 1983)

124 ALR5th 1—§ 3

State v. Harriman, 469 So. 2d 298 (La. Ct. App. 2d Cir. 1985)

79 ALR5th 237—§ 11

State v. Harrington, 78 N.C. App. 39, 336 S.E.2d 852 (1985)

46 ALR6th 241—§ 14

State v. Harrington, 171 N.C. App. 17, 614 S.E.2d 337, 19 A.L.R.6th 835 (2005)

19 ALR6th 1—§ 12
19 ALR6th 115—§ 5, 9, 13

State v. Harrington, 349 N.W.2d 758 (Iowa 1984)

11 ALR5th 831—§ 11

State v. Harrington, 534 S.W.2d 44 (Mo. 1976)

---

90 ALR6th 385—§ 19
State v. Harrington, 990 P.2d 144 (Idaho Ct. App. 1999)

7 ALR5th 263—§ 4
State v. Harris, 4 Conn. Cir. Ct. 534, 236 A.2d 479 (App. Div. 1967)

66 ALR5th 397—§ 4, 9, 10
State v. Harris, 10 Conn. App. 217, 522 A.2d 323 (1987)

55 ALR5th 125—§ 13, 14, 22
State v. Harris, 12 Wash. App. 381, 529 P.2d 1138 (Div. 2 1974)

103 ALR6th 35—§ 7, 15
State v. Harris, 12 Wash. App. 481, 530 P.2d 646 (Div. 1 1975)

85 ALR5th 1—§ 17, 50
State v. Harris, 25 Or. App. 71, 547 P.2d 1394 (1976)

81 ALR5th 563—§ 3, 5, 8
State v. Harris, 32 Conn. App. 831, 632 A.2d 50 (1993)

77 ALR6th 251—§ 5
State v. Harris, 36 Wash. App. 746, 677 P.2d 202 (1984)

39 ALR5th 283—§ 4
State v. Harris, 40 Or. App. 317, 594 P.2d 1318 (1979)

33 ALR6th 407—§ 53, 54
State v. Harris, 46 Conn. App. 216, 700 A.2d 1161 (1997)

28 ALR6th 505—§ 31
State v. Harris, 49 Conn. App. 121, 714 A.2d 12 (1998)

70 ALR6th 361—§ 19, 31
State v. Harris, 70 N.J. 586, 362 A.2d 32 (1976)

15 ALR5th 391—§ 50
92 ALR5th 35—§ 10
State v. Harris, 78 N.J. Super. 232, 188 A.2d 215 (1963)

29 ALR5th 59—§ 89
State v. Harris, 89 Ohio App. 3d 147, 623 N.E.2d 1240 (Cuyahoga Co. 1993)

27 ALR5th 593—§ 6
State v. Harris, 98 N.J. Super. 502, 237 A.2d 887 (App. Div. 1968)

68 ALR5th 549—§ 3
State v. Harris, 102 Wash. 2d 148, 685 P.2d 584 (1984)

84 ALR5th 487—§ 25
State v. Harris, 106 Wash. 2d 784, 725 P.2d 975 (1986)

29 ALR6th 1—§ 18
State v. Harris, 108 S.W.3d 127 (Mo. Ct. App. E.D. 2003)

37 ALR6th 357—§ 19
State v. Harris, 133 S.W.3d 523 (Mo. Ct. App. E.D. 2004)

103 ALR6th 507—§ 14
State v. Harris, 149 N.C. 513, 62 S.E. 1090 (1908)

34 ALR5th 723—§ 4
State v. Harris, 153 Iowa 592, 133 N.W. 1078 (1912)

22 ALR5th 1—§ 57
State v. Harris, 154 Wash. App. 87, 224 P.3d 830, 55 A.L.R.6th 663 (Div. 2 2010)

55 ALR6th 1—§ 6, 30, 31, 39, 40
State v. Harris, 156 N.J. 122, 716 A.2d 458 (1998)

55 ALR6th 157—§ 92, 101
State v. Harris, 159 Or. App. 553, 980 P.2d 1132 (1999)

58 ALR6th 385—§ 20
State v. Harris, 167 Or. App. 360, 5 P.3d 1113 (2000)

89 ALR5th 629—§ 8
State v. Harris, 171 N.C. App. 127, 613 S.E.2d 701 (2005)

33 ALR6th 91—§ 18, 40
State v. Harris, 186 Vt. 225, 2009 VT 73, 980 A.2d 785 (2009)

65 ALR6th 537—§ 39
State v. Harris, 189 N.C. App. 49, 657 S.E.2d 701 (2008)

67 ALR6th 103—§ 5
State v. Harris, 194 Neb. 74, 230 N.W.2d 203 (1975)

50 ALR5th 467—§ 2, 3
State v. Harris, 199 Wis. 2d 227, 544 N.W.2d 545, 90 A.L.R. 5th 733 (1996)

90 ALR5th 225—§ 4
State v. Harris, 212 S.C. 124, 46 S.E.2d 682 (1948)

102 ALR6th 279—§ 11
State v. Harris, 244 Neb. 289, 505 N.W.2d 724 (1993)

64 ALR5th 741—§ 3
State v. Harris, 247 Mont. 405, 808 P.2d 453 (1991)

38 ALR5th 433—§ 16, 29
65 ALR6th 537—§ 67
State v. Harris, 284 Neb. 214, 817 N.W.2d 258 (2012)

93 ALR6th 1—§ 38
State v. Harris, 297 So. 2d 431 (La. 1974)

70 ALR5th 587—§ 5
State v. Harris, 333 N.W.2d 873 (Minn. 1983)

65 ALR6th 537—§ 34, 72
State v. Harris, 338 N.C. 211, 449 S.E.2d 462 (1994)

38 ALR5th 433—§ 38
State v. Harris, 342 S.C. 191, 535 S.E.2d 652 (Ct. App. 2000)

97 ALR5th 201—§ 6
State v. Harris, 407 N.W.2d 456 (Minn. Ct. App. 1987)

93 ALR5th 527—§ 11
State v. Harris, 510 So. 2d 439 (La. App. 1st Cir. 1987)

7 ALR5th 263—§ 5, 7
State v. Harris, 535 S.E.2d 614 (N.C. Ct. App. 2000)

39 ALR5th 283—§ 66, 67
86 ALR5th 59—§ 4
State v. Harris, 540 So. 2d 1226 (La. Ct. App. 3d Cir. 1989)

81 ALR5th 563—§ 7
State v. Harris, 589 N.W.2d 782 (Minn. 1999)

111 ALR5th 239—§ 4
State v. Harris, 594 S.W.2d 658 (Mo. Ct. App. S.D. 1980)

9 ALR6th 1—§ 17
State v. Harris, 642 A.2d 1242 (Del. Super. Ct. 1993)

55 ALR5th 125—§ 3, 7
State v. Harris, 649 So. 2d 796 (La. Ct. App. 2d Cir. 1995)

103 ALR6th 507—§ 27
State v. Harris, 657 S.E.2d 701 (N.C. Ct. App. 2008)

30 ALR6th 1—§ 3
State v. Harris, 671 P.2d 175 (Utah 1983)

62 ALR6th 413—§ 40
State v. Harris, 702 N.E.2d 722 (Ind. Ct. App. 1998)

26 ALR5th 378—§ 11
State v. Harris, 765 So. 2d 432 (La. Ct. App. 4th Cir. 2000)

5 ALR5th 243—§ 49
State v. Harris, 868 S.W.2d 203 (Mo. Ct. App. W.D. 1994)

99 ALR6th 295—§ 8, 19
State v. Harris, 882 S.W.2d 730 (Mo. App. 1994)

47 ALR5th 259—§ 10, 13
State v. Harris, 1981 WL 5729 (Ohio Ct. App. 6th Dist. Lucas County 1981)

111 ALR5th 239—§ 3
State v. Harris, 1992 WL 317447 (Ohio Ct. App. 2d Dist. Montgomery County 1992)

34 ALR6th 1—§ 10
State v. Harris, 1994 WL 164185 (Ohio Ct. App. 1st Dist. Hamilton County 1994)

78 ALR6th 297—§ 80
State v. Harris, 1994 WL 678476 (Minn. Ct. App. 1994)

24 ALR6th 747—§ 42
State v. Harris, 1995 WL 136870 (Tenn. Crim. App. 1995)

103 ALR6th 507—§ 8
State v. Harris, 2002-Ohio-5141, 2002 WL 31159437 (Ohio Ct. App. 12th Dist. Clermont County 2002)

38 ALR6th 97—§ 18
State v. Harris, 2002 WL 31015975 (Iowa Ct. App. 2002)

17 ALR6th 327—§ 14

State v. Harris, 2005-Ohio-399, 2005 WL 272985 (Ohio Ct. App. 8th Dist. Cuyahoga County 2005)

17 ALR6th 327—§ 8

State v. Harris, 2005-Ohio-921, 2005 WL 501602 (Ohio Ct. App. 6th Dist. Erie County 2005)

29 ALR6th 237—§ 4, 9, 21

State v. Harris, 2005-Ohio-4935, 2005 WL 2293089 (Ohio Ct. App. 9th Dist. Summit County 2005)

23 ALR6th 307—§ 35

State v. Harris, 2005 WL 419082 (Tenn. Crim. App. 2005)

26 ALR6th 511—§ 25, 47

State v. Harris, 2008 WL 4368209 (Ariz. Ct. App. Div. 1 2008)

62 ALR6th 161—§ 6

State v. Harris, 2010-Ohio-4127, 2010 WL 3443173 (Ohio Ct. App. 10th Dist. Franklin County 2010)

64 ALR6th 1—§ 45

State v. Harrison, 81 N.M. 324, 466 P.2d 890 (Ct. App. 1970)

65 ALR5th 407—§ 12

State v. Harrison, 111 Ariz. 508, 533 P.2d 1143 (1975)

114 ALR5th 173—§ 9

State v. Harrison, 115 N.M. 73, 1992-NMCA-139, 846 P.2d 1082 (Ct. App. 1992)

92 ALR6th 295—§ 8, 25
93 ALR6th 207—§ 6, 26
96 ALR6th 355—§ 24, 37

State v. Harrison, 145 N.C. 408, 59 S.E. 867 (1907)

101 ALR6th 499—§ 15

State v. Harrison, 148 Wash. 2d 550, 61 P.3d 1104 (2003)

9 ALR6th 541—§ 3, 11

State v. Harrison, 149 La. 83, 88 So. 696 (1921)

81 ALR5th 563—§ 3

State v. Harrison, 184 N.C. 762, 114 S.E. 830 (1922)

97 ALR5th 201—§ 3

State v. Harrison, 473 N.W.2d 242 (Iowa App. 1991)

7 ALR5th 73—§ 8

State v. Harrison, 505 So. 2d 783 (La. Ct. App. 2d Cir. 1987)

108 ALR5th 593—§ 33

State v. Harrison, 601 P.2d 922 (Utah 1979)

34 ALR5th 125—§ 19

State v. Harrison, 805 P.2d 769 (Utah Ct. App. 1991)

20 ALR5th 398—§ 3, 10, 60
70 ALR5th 587—§ 22

State v. Harrison, 1978 WL 216973 (Ohio Ct. App. 10th Dist. Franklin County 1978)

35 ALR6th 127—§ 22

State v. Harrison, 1995 WL 479588 (Minn. Ct. App. 1995)

73 ALR5th 383—§ 5

State v. Harrison, 2001 UT 33, 2001 WL 403185 (Utah 2001)

91 ALR5th 343—§ 19

State v. Harrison, 2007-Ohio-7078, 2007 WL 4554974 (Ohio Ct. App. 12th Dist. Madison County 2007)

34 ALR6th 253—§ 5, 13

State v. Harrison, 2013-Ohio-1235, 2013 WL 1286149 (Ohio Ct. App. 2d Dist. Montgomery County 2013)

97 ALR6th 653—§ 29

State v. Harrod, 65 P.3d 948 (Ariz. 2003)

110 ALR5th 1—§ 19

State v. Harrod, 200 Ariz. 309, 26 P.3d 492 (2001)

10 ALR6th 463—§ 4
23 ALR6th 1—§ 15

State v. Harry, 741 S.W.2d 743 (Mo. Ct. App. E.D. 1987)

111 ALR5th 1—§ 35

State v. Hart, 2 Conn. Cir. Ct. 27, 193 A.2d 903 (App. Div. 1963)

89 ALR6th 565—§ 14, 34

State v. Hart, 66 Idaho 217, 157 P.2d 72 (1945)

33 ALR6th 407—§ 5

State v. Hart, 100 Idaho 137, 594 P.2d 647 (1979)

103 ALR5th 463—§ 3

State v. Hart, 105 Haw. 251, 96 P.3d 271 (2004)

33 ALR6th 91—§ 4, 7

State v. Hart, 110 Ariz. 232, 517 P.2d 94 (1973)

58 ALR6th 439—§ 46

State v. Hart, 110 Ohio App. 3d 250, 673 N.E.2d 992, 1996 WL 156725 (3d Dist. Defiance County 1996)

46 ALR5th 499—§ 3

State v. Hart, 191 Mont. 375, 625 P.2d 21 (1981)

3 ALR6th 269—§ 17

State v. Hart, 209 Iowa 119, 227 N.W. 650 (1929)

42 ALR5th 547—§ 6

State v. Hart, 299 Or. 128, 699 P.2d 1113 (1985)

15 ALR5th 391—§ 5

State v. Hart, 391 N.W.2d 677 (S.D. 1986)

23 ALR6th 1—§ 15

State v. Hart, 467 So. 2d 1366 (La. Ct. App. 5th Cir. 1985)

65 ALR6th 537—§ 44

State v. Harte, 395 N.J. Super. 162, 928 A.2d 157 (Law Div. 2006)

34 ALR6th 253—§ 13

State v. Hartfield, 9 Kan. App. 2d 156, 676 P.2d 141 (1984)

19 ALR6th 697—§ 10

State v. Hartford, 213 Or. App. 331, 161 P.3d 331 (2007)

69 ALR6th 1—§ 13

State v. Hartley, 307 S.C. 239, 414 S.E.2d 182 (Ct. App. 1992)

65 ALR6th 537—§ 34, 72

State v. Hartley, 326 N.W.2d 226 (S.D. 1982)

24 ALR6th 1—§ 42

State v. Hartman, 27 Kan. App. 2d 98, 998 P.2d 128 (2000)

37 ALR6th 357—§ 69, 72

State v. Hartman, 93 Ohio St. 3d 274, 2001-Ohio-1580, 754 N.E.2d 1150 (2001)

110 ALR5th 213—§ 5

State v. Hartman, 344 N.C. 445, 476 S.E.2d 328 (1996)

73 ALR5th 383—§ 4, 8, 31

State v. Hartrampf, 118 Or. App. 237, 847 P.2d 856 (1993)

69 ALR6th 207—§ 9, 12

State v. Harts, 7 S.W.3d 78 (Tenn. Crim. App. 1999)

29 ALR6th 1—§ 4

State v. Hartshorn, 175 W. Va. 274, 332 S.E.2d 574 (1985)

103 ALR6th 507—§ 23

State v. Hartup, 126 Ohio App. 3d 768, 711 N.E.2d 315 (8th Dist. Cuyahoga County 1998)

69 ALR6th 1—§ 27

State v. Hartwig, 112 Idaho 370, 732 P.2d 339 (Ct. App. 1987)

58 ALR6th 215—§ 5

State v. Hartzog, 575 So. 2d 1328 (Fla. Dist. Ct. App. 1st Dist. 1991)

65 ALR5th 623—§ 7

State v. Harut, 372 N.W.2d 363 (Minn. App. 1985)

43 ALR5th 1—§ 13

State v. Harvell, 45 N.C. App. 243, 262 S.E.2d 850 (1980)

119 ALR5th 275—§ 8

State v. Harvey, 151 N.J. 117, 699 A.2d 596 (1997)

90 ALR5th 453—§ 49

State v. Harvey, 164 Wash. App. 1027, 2011 WL 5027464 (Div. 1 2011)

101 ALR6th 331—§ 10

State v. Harvey, 184 Mont. 423, 603 P.2d 661 (1979)

3 ALR6th 269—§ 33

State v. Harvey, 547 N.W.2d 706 (Minn. App. 1996)

15 ALR5th 391—§ 50

State v. Harvey, 649 So. 2d 783 (La. Ct. App. 2d Cir. 1995)

111 ALR5th 529—§ 7

State v. Harvill, 860 So. 2d 999 (Fla. Dist. Ct. App. 5th Dist. 2003)

69 ALR6th 1—§ 5

State v. Harville, 1994 WL 697969
(Tenn. Crim. App. 1994)
73 ALR5th 383—§ 20
State v. Harwell, 515 N.W.2d 105
(Minn. Ct. App. 1994)
15 ALR5th 391—§ 31
92 ALR5th 35—§ 2, 28
State v. Harwood, 45 Or. App. 931, 609
P.2d 1312 (1980)
49 ALR5th 639—§ 4
111 ALR5th 239—§ 9
State v. Harwood, 94 Idaho 615, 495
P.2d 160 (1972)
95 ALR5th 611—§ 3
State v. Hasan, 205 Conn. 485, 534 A.2d
877, 71 A.L.R.4th 1137 (1987)
90 ALR5th 453—§ 6
State v. Hasfal, 106 Conn. App. 199, 941
A.2d 387, 45 A.L.R.6th 791 (2008)
45 ALR6th 337—§ 2, 15
State v. Hashimoto, 46 Haw. 183, 377
P.2d 728 (1962)
55 ALR6th 157—§ 112
State v. Hashman, 46 Wash. App. 211,
729 P.2d 651 (Div. 2 1986)
114 ALR5th 235—§ 7
State v. Haskell, 2001 ME 154, 784 A.2d
4 (Me. 2001)
63 ALR6th 351—§ 3
State v. Haskell, 2004 WL 765014 (Me.
Super. Ct. 2004)
101 ALR6th 545—§ 5
State v. Haskett, 827 P.2d 83 (Kan. App.
1992)
12 ALR5th 89—§ 2
State v. Haskins, 131 N.J. 643, 622 A.2d
867 (1993)
27 ALR5th 593—§ 2, 25
State v. Haskins, 139 Wis. 2d 257, 407
N.W.2d 309 (Ct. App. 1987)
70 ALR5th 1—§ 5
State v. Haskins, 188 Conn. 432, 450
A.2d 828 (1982)
70 ALR5th 587—§ 13
97 ALR5th 201—§ 3
State v. Haskins, 255 Mont. 202, 841
P.2d 542 (1992)

18 ALR5th 1—§ 16
State v. Hass, 114 Idaho 554, 758 P.2d
713 (App. 1988)
52 ALR5th 559—§ 3, 6, 10
State v. Hassel, 280 Wis. 2d 637, 2005
WI App 80, 696 N.W.2d 270 (Ct.
App. 2005)
28 ALR6th 505—§ 9
State v. Hassey, 9 Ohio App. 3d 231, 9
Ohio B.R. 403, 459 N.E.2d 573
(Franklin Co. 1983)
37 ALR5th 1—§ 4
State v. Hasson, 153 Or. App. 527, 958
P.2d 183 (1998)
7 ALR6th 233—§ 5
State v. Hastings, 118 Idaho 854, 801
P.2d 563, 1 A.L.R.5th 1207 (1990)
1 ALR5th 938—§ 2, 3
50 ALR6th 353—§ 52
State v. Hastings, 2007 MT 294, 340
Mont. 1, 171 P.3d 726 (2007)
38 ALR6th 1—§ 18, 28
State v. Hatcher, 303 Mo. 13, 259 S.W.
467 (1924)
52 ALR5th 655—§ 3
State v. Hatcher, 372 So. 2d 1024 (La.
1979)
86 ALR5th 59—§ 6
State v. Hatfield, 65 Wash. 550, 118 P.
735 (1911)
108 ALR5th 593—§ 31, 36
State v. Hatfield, 75 Iowa 592, 39 N.W.
910 (1888)
54 ALR6th 429—§ 13, 29
State v. Hatfield, 169 W. Va. 191, 286
S.E.2d 402 (1982)
53 ALR6th 81—§ 7
State v. Hatfield, 213 Kan. 832, 518 P.2d
389 (1974)
66 ALR5th 397—§ 12
State v. Hatfield, 218 Neb. 470, 356
N.W.2d 872 (1984)
42 ALR5th 581—§ 16
State v. Hatfield, 2003 WL 535930
(Tenn. Crim. App. 2003)
119 ALR5th 379—§ 7
State v. Hathaway, 269 S.W.2d 57, 46
A.L.R.2d 942 (Mo. 1954)

99 ALR6th 113—§ 4
State v. Hathaway, 379 N.W.2d 498 (Minn. 1985)
16 ALR6th 329—§ 4
24 ALR6th 591—§ 5, 12
State v. Hatter, 414 N.W.2d 333 (Iowa 1987)
39 ALR5th 283—§ 10, 62
State v. Hatton, 116 Ariz. 142, 568 P.2d 1040 (1977)
28 ALR6th 505—§ 9
State v. Hatton, 240 Mo. App. 1244, 228 S.W.2d 10 (1950)
6 ALR5th 733—§ 2, 3, 15
State v. Hatton, 2002 WL 1424418 (Minn. Ct. App. 2002)
106 ALR5th 377—§ 3
State v. Hauan, 361 N.W.2d 336 (Iowa Ct. App. 1984)
66 ALR5th 397—§ 16
State v. Hauck, 1992 WL 75832 (Tenn. Crim)
51 ALR5th 603—§ 2
State v. Hauck, 2000 WL 123702 (Neb. Ct. App. 2000)
7 ALR6th 233—§ 5
State v. Haug, 237 Kan. 390, 699 P.2d 535 (1985)
69 ALR6th 1—§ 23
State v. Haulk, 38 N.C. App. 357, 247 S.E.2d 798 (1978)
8 ALR5th 775—§ 2
State v. Haun, 695 S.W.2d 546 (Tenn. Crim. App. 1985)
72 ALR5th 529—§ 2, 7
State v. Hauptmann, 115 N.J.L. 412, 180 A. 809 (N.J. Ct. Err. & App. 1935)
101 ALR6th 499—§ 18
103 ALR6th 35—§ 25
State v. Hauser, 19 Wash. App. 506, 576 P.2d 420 (Div. 3 1978)
35 ALR6th 497—§ 9, 31, 37
State v. Hauser, 183 N.C. 769, 111 S.E. 349 (1922)
29 ALR5th 59—§ 26
State v. Hauser, 342 N.C. 382, 464 S.E.2d 443 (1995)

62 ALR5th 1—§ 4, 11, 15
State v. Hausler, 101 N.M. 143, 679 P.2d 811 (1984)
41 ALR5th 171—§ 12, 26, 66, 68, 90, 116
State v. Havas, 95 Nev. 706, 601 P.2d 1197 (1979)
55 ALR6th 391—§ 6
State v. Haverluk, 2000 ND 178, 617 N.W.2d 652 (N.D. 2000)
92 ALR6th 295—§ 13
96 ALR6th 355—§ 6, 7, 9
State v. Havlat, 222 Neb. 554, 385 N.W.2d 436 (1986)
45 ALR6th 643—§ 18
State v. Hawkins, 27 Wash. App. 78, 615 P.2d 1327 (Div. 2 1980)
29 ALR6th 1—§ 9
State v. Hawkins, 39 P.3d 1126 (Alaska Ct. App. 2002)
33 ALR6th 91—§ 33
63 ALR6th 351—§ 3
State v. Hawkins, 53 Wash. App. 598, 769 P.2d 856 (Div. 2 1989)
57 ALR5th 141—§ 11
73 ALR5th 383—§ 3
State v. Hawkins, 104 P.3d 1024 (Kan. Ct. App. 2005)
67 ALR6th 531—§ 26
State v. Hawkins, 131 Idaho 396, 958 P.2d 22 (Ct. App. 1998)
40 ALR5th 113—§ 4
55 ALR5th 125—§ 14
94 ALR5th 393—§ 3
State v. Hawkins, 187 Ga. App. 826, 371 S.E.2d 668 (1988)
43 ALR5th 1—§ 13
State v. Hawkins, 203 N.W.2d 555 (Iowa 1973)
78 ALR5th 567—§ 5
State v. Hawkins, 214 N.C. 326, 199 S.E. 284 (1938)
24 ALR5th 465—§ 4, 9, 41
State v. Hawkins, 260 N.W.2d 150 (Minn. 1977)
11 ALR5th 831—§ 2, 5
State v. Hawkins, 316 N.J. Super. 74, 719 A.2d 689 (App. Div. 1998)

99 ALR6th 295—§ 13, 19

State v. Hawkins, 422 So. 2d 1155 (La. 1982)

66 ALR5th 397—§ 21

State v. Hawkins, 688 So. 2d 473 (La. 1997)

93 ALR5th 527—§ 7, 9

State v. Hawkins, 740 So. 2d 768 (La. Ct. App. 5th Cir. 1999)

39 ALR5th 283—§ 60

State v. Hawkins, 766 N.E.2d 749 (Ind. Ct. App. 2002)

114 ALR5th 173—§ 2, 3, 7

State v. Hawkins, 1996 WL 488830 (Ohio App. 5 Dist.)

50 ALR5th 581—§ 9, 11, 20

State v. Hawks, 114 N.J. 359, 554 A.2d 1330 (1989)

7 ALR5th 263—§ 2, 5, 7

State v. Hawley, 54 N.C.App. 293, 283 S.E.2d 387 (1981)

81 ALR5th 563—§ 3, 5

State v. Hawley, 63 Conn. 47, 27 A. 417 (1893)

11 ALR5th 831—§ 5, 6

State v. Hawley, 229 N.C. 167, 48 S.E.2d 35 (1948)

10 ALR5th 700—§ 2, 35, 38

State v. Haws, 869 P.2d 849 (Okla. Crim. 1994)

52 ALR5th 655—§ 9

State v. Hawse, 2009 WL 1650190 (N.J. Super. Ct. App. Div. 2009)

55 ALR6th 1—§ 8, 29

State v. Hawthorne, 176 Conn. 367, 407 A.2d 1001 (1978)

99 ALR6th 295—§ 9

State v. Hawthorne, 523 S.W.2d 332 (Mo. Ct. App. 1975)

119 ALR5th 275—§ 2

State v. Hawthorne, 573 So. 2d 330, 16 FLW D 29, 15 A.L.R.5th 1075 (Fla. 1991)

15 ALR5th 391—§ 45

State v. Hay, 51 Wash. 576, 99 P. 748 (1909)

51 ALR6th 359—§ 13

State v. Hayden, 90 Wash. App. 100, 950 P.2d 1024 (Div. 1 1998)

110 ALR5th 213—§ 2, 5

State v. Hayden, 707 So. 2d 1360 (La. Ct. App. 5th Cir. 1998)

125 ALR5th 537—§ 1

State v. Hayden, 2005-Ohio-4025, 2005 WL 1846521 (Ohio Ct. App. 2d Dist. Montgomery County 2005)

72 ALR6th 227—§ 49

State v. Hayes, 20 Conn. App. 737, 570 A.2d 716 (1990)

22 ALR5th 1—§ 2, 13

State v. Hayes, 88 Mo. 344, 1885 WL 8041 (1885)

97 ALR5th 537—§ 48

State v. Hayes, 94 Nev. 366, 580 P.2d 122 (1978)

69 ALR6th 1—§ 23

State v. Hayes, 99 Or. App. 322, 781 P.2d 1251 (1989)

4 ALR5th 1—§ 4

State v. Hayes, 170 Vt. 618, 752 A.2d 16 (2000)

18 ALR6th 1—§ 3, 5, 15

State v. Hayes, 190 S.W.3d 665 (Tenn. Crim. App. 2005)

92 ALR6th 1—§ 4, 9

State v. Hayes, 196 Wis. 2d 753, 540 N.W.2d 1 (App. 1995)

43 ALR5th 1—§ 13

State v. Hayes, 273 N.C. 712, 161 S.E.2d 185 (1968)

57 ALR6th 83—§ 9

State v. Hayes, 291 N.C. 293, 230 S.E.2d 146 (1976)

45 ALR5th 1—§ 5, 12, 23, 30

State v. Hayes, 532 N.W.2d 472 (Iowa Ct. App. 1995)

89 ALR5th 629—§ 8

State v. Hayes, 535 N.W.2d 715 (Neb. App. 1995)

50 ALR5th 581—§ 5, 19

State v. Hayes, 561 So. 2d 184 (La. Ct. App. 5th Cir. 1990)

88 ALR5th 121—§ 3, 35

State v. Hayes, 597 S.W.2d 242 (Mo. Ct. App. S.D. 1980)
58 ALR6th 439—§ 14

State v. Hayes, 899 S.W.2d 175 (Tenn. Crim. App. 1995)
73 ALR5th 383—§ 5

State v. Hayes, 1995 WL 347869 (Ohio Ct. App. 10th Dist. Franklin County 1995)
17 ALR6th 327—§ 40

State v. Hayes, 1997 WL 430808 (Ohio Ct. App. 4th Dist. Meigs County 1997)
46 ALR6th 241—§ 17

State v. Hayes, 2004 WL 2185934 (Tenn. Crim. App. 2004)
80 ALR6th 599—§ 8

State v. Hayes, 2005 WL 1252694 (Tenn. Crim. App. 2005)
26 ALR6th 511—§ 22, 25

State v. Hayes, 2005 WL 2007205 (Tenn. Crim. App. 2005)
67 ALR6th 531—§ 26, 36

State v. Hayford, 412 A.2d 987 (Me. 1980)
41 ALR5th 171—§ 10, 58, 60

State v. Haynes, 16 Wash. App. 778, 559 P.2d 583 (Div. 2 1977)
55 ALR6th 391—§ 21

State v. Haynes, 192 Neb. 445, 222 N.W.2d 358 (1974)
117 ALR5th 513—§ 16

State v. Haynes, 288 Or. 59, 602 P.2d 272 (1979)
96 ALR5th 327—§ 2 to 4, 6

State v. Haynes, 514 So. 2d 1206 (La. Ct. App. 2d Cir. 1987)
75 ALR5th 295—§ 21

State v. Haynes, 720 S.W.2d 76 (Tenn. Crim. 1986)
8 ALR5th 775—§ 9

State v. Haynes, 720 S.W.2d 76 (Tenn. Crim. App. 1986)
124 ALR5th 1—§ 5

State v. Haynes, 725 N.W.2d 524 (Minn. 2007)
65 ALR6th 537—§ 7

State v. Hays, 155 Or. App. 41, 964 P.2d 1042 (1998)
118 ALR5th 253—§ 18, 19

State v. Hays, 1997 WL 430856 (Ohio Ct. App. 6th Dist. Ottawa County 1997)
47 ALR6th 107—§ 22, 24

State v. Hayward, 116 Conn. App. 511, 976 A.2d 791 (2009)
67 ALR6th 103—§ 4

State v. Hayward, 327 Or. 397, 963 P.2d 667 (1998)
18 ALR5th 804—§ 8

State v. Haywood, 38 Wash. App. 117, 684 P.2d 1337 (Div. 3 1984)
113 ALR5th 517—§ 14

State v. Haywood, 297 N.C. 686, 256 S.E.2d 715 (1979)
29 ALR5th 59—§ 3, 18

State v. Hazelton, 330 A.2d 919 (Me. 1975)
9 ALR6th 1—§ 17

State v. Hazelwood, 866 P.2d 827 (Alaska 1993)
29 ALR5th 1—§ 4

State v. Hazzard, 43 Wash. App. 335, 716 P.2d 977 (Div. 3 1986)
92 ALR6th 295—§ 36

State v. Hazzard, 139 Wash. 487, 247 P. 957, 47 A.L.R. 538 (1926)
97 ALR5th 293—§ 2

State v. Head, 79 N.C. App. 1, 338 S.E.2d 908 (1986)
65 ALR6th 359—§ 9

State v. Head, 561 N.W.2d 182 (Minn. Ct. App. 1997)
84 ALR5th 487—§ 33

State v. Headley, 18 S.W.2d 37 (Mo. 1929)
54 ALR6th 429—§ 27

State v. Heads, 370 So. 2d 564 (La. 1979)
98 ALR6th 455—§ 22

State v. Heald, 443 A.2d 954 (Me. 1982)
54 ALR5th 141—§ 4, 8, 10

State v. Heard, 246 Miss. 774, 151 So. 2d 417 (1963)

CASES CITED IN ALR5th and ALR6th

31 ALR6th 523—§ 46, 57

State v. Hearn, 89 N.C. App. 103, 365 S.E.2d 206 (1988)

67 ALR5th 637—§ 5, 11

State v. Hearns, 2005 WL 3005701 (N.J. Super. Ct. App. Div. 2005)

26 ALR6th 511—§ 17

State v. Heartfield, 196 Ariz. 407, 998 P.2d 1080 (Ct. App. Div. 2 2000)

91 ALR5th 343—§ 34

State v. Heath, 21 Kan. App. 2d 410, 901 P.2d 29 (1995)

91 ALR5th 343—§ 32

State v. Heath, 75 Or. App. 425, 706 P.2d 598 (1985)

15 ALR5th 391—§ 14

State v. Heath, 237 Mo. 255, 141 S.W. 26 (1911)

54 ALR6th 429—§ 17

State v. Heath, 264 Kan. 557, 957 P.2d 449 (1998)

57 ALR5th 315—§ 8, 11
90 ALR5th 453—§ 33
29 ALR6th 1—§ 8

State v. Heath, 316 N.C. 337, 341 S.E.2d 565 (1986)

72 ALR5th 529—§ 16

State v. Heath, 513 So. 2d 493 (La. App. 2d Cir. 1987)

16 ALR5th 390—§ 2, 3

State v. Heath, 513 So. 2d 493 (La. Ct. App. 2d Cir. 1987)

79 ALR6th 125—§ 13

State v. Heath, 685 N.W.2d 48 (Minn. Ct. App. 2004)

26 ALR6th 511—§ 50
55 ALR6th 391—§ 22

State v. Heath, 2000 M.T. 94, 999 P.2d 324 (Mont. 2000)

50 ALR5th 581—§ 17, 19

State v. Heather, 498 S.W.2d 300 (Mo. Ct. App. 1973)

9 ALR6th 1—§ 10

State v. Heaton, 23 W. Va. 773, 1883 WL 3307 (1883)

57 ALR6th 445—§ 58

State v. Heaton, 108 Ohio App. 3d 38, 669 N.E.2d 885 (12th Dist. Clermont County 1995)

69 ALR6th 1—§ 27

State v. Heaton, 958 P.2d 911 (Utah 1998)

37 ALR6th 357—§ 55, 56, 71

State v. Heaton, 1987 WL 6171 (Ohio Ct. App. 9th Dist. Lorain County 1987)

6 ALR6th 533—§ 17

State v. Hebert, 480 A.2d 742 (Me. 1984)

38 ALR5th 433—§ 3

State v. Hebert, 697 So. 2d 1040 (La. Ct. App. 1st Cir. 1997)

6 ALR6th 533—§ 21

State v. Hecht, 116 Wis. 2d 605, 342 N.W.2d 721 (1984)

34 ALR5th 125—§ 3, 24

State v. Heck, 560 So. 2d 611 (La. Ct. App. 4th Cir. 1990)

56 ALR6th 185—§ 6

State v. Heckel, 122 Wash. App. 60, 93 P.3d 189 (Div. 1 2004)

10 ALR6th 1—§ 12
16 ALR6th 767—§ 42

State v. Heckel, 143 Wash. 2d 824, 24 P.3d 404, 98 A.L.R.5th 703 (2001)

98 ALR5th 167—§ 7

State v. Hecker, 1994 WL 386086 (Ohio Ct. App. 4th Dist. Pickaway County 1994)

99 ALR6th 295—§ 16

State v. Heckman, 993 So. 2d 1004 (Fla. 2d DCA 2007)

76 ALR6th 1—§ 19

State v. Hedding, 122 Vt. 379, 172 A.2d 599 (1961)

104 ALR5th 357—§ 7

State v. Heddings, 2008 MT 402, 347 Mont. 169, 198 P.3d 242 (2008)

46 ALR6th 241—§ 12

State v. Heden, 719 N.W.2d 689 (Minn. 2006)

28 ALR6th 505—§ 9

State v. Hedge, 59 Conn. App. 272, 756 A.2d 319 (2000)

12 ALR6th 553—§ 20

State v. Hedgecoe, 106 N.C. App. 157, 415 S.E.2d 777 (1992)

23 ALR6th 307—§ 32

State v. Hedger, 115 Idaho 598, 768 P.2d 1331 (1989)

93 ALR5th 327—§ 7, 28

State v. Hedger, 248 Kan. 815, 811 P.2d 1170 (1991)

24 ALR5th 465—§ 10, 40

37 ALR5th 515—§ 7, 22

State v. Hedges, 8 P.3d 1259 (Kan. 2000)

78 ALR5th 197—§ 13

State v. Hedin, 67 Wash. 2d 542, 408 P.2d 245 (1965)

5 ALR5th 243—§ 60

State v. Hedley, 593 A.2d 576 (Del. Super. Ct. 1990)

58 ALR6th 499—§ 82

78 ALR6th 297—§ 17, 69

State v. Hefa, 73 Wash. App. 865, 871 P.2d 1093 (1994)

15 ALR5th 391—§ 7

State v. Hefner, 199 N.C. 778, 155 S.E. 879 (1930)

5 ALR5th 243—§ 62

State v. Hegg, 1995 WL 118927 (Minn. Ct. App. 1995)

106 ALR5th 377—§ 3

State v. Hegg, 1998 MT 100, 288 Mont. 254, 956 P.2d 754 (1998)

104 ALR5th 229—§ 3, 6, 17

115 ALR5th 403—§ 5

4 ALR6th 113—§ 44

101 ALR6th 1—§ 29

State v. Hegna, 216 Wis. 2d 384, 576 N.W.2d 89 (Ct. App. 1998)

70 ALR5th 533—§ 7

State v. Hegyi, 185 N.J. Super. 229, 447 A.2d 1369 (Law Div. 1982)

68 ALR5th 299—§ 4, 6

State v. Heidt, 20 N.D. 357, 127 N.W. 72 (1910)

97 ALR5th 537—§ 43

State v. Heikkinen, 94 Or. App. 472, 765 P.2d 1252 (1988)

115 ALR5th 477—§ 3

State v. Heimlich, 2008 WL 2938826 (Tex. App. Austin 2008)

53 ALR6th 305—§ 21

State v. Heisdorffer, 164 N.W.2d 173 (Iowa 1969)

109 ALR5th 611—§ 3

State v. Heisdorffer, 171 N.W.2d 513 (Iowa 1969)

52 ALR5th 655—§ 5

State v. Heiskell, 129 Wash. 2d 113, 916 P.2d 366 (1996)

36 ALR5th 161—§ 6

37 ALR6th 55—§ 14

39 ALR6th 577—§ 4

93 ALR6th 1—§ 43

State v. Helfrich, 183 Mont. 484, 600 P.2d 816 (1979)

19 ALR5th 470—§ 6

State v. Helgoth, 691 S.W.2d 281 (Mo. 1985)

42 ALR5th 291—§ 3, 4, 10, 25

State v. Helker, 88 N.M. 650, 545 P.2d 1028 (Ct. App. 1975)

78 ALR5th 197—§ 13, 14

State v. Hellems, 13 S.W.3d 302 (Mo. Ct. App. E.D. 2000)

37 ALR6th 357—§ 46, 47

State v. Heller, 4 Conn. Cir. Ct. 174, 228 A.2d 815 (App. Div. 1966)

90 ALR5th 225—§ 9

State v. Heller, 2010 WI App 19, 323 Wis. 2d 279, 779 N.W.2d 725 (Ct. App. 2009)

84 ALR6th 293—§ 31

State v. Helm, 504 N.W.2d 142 (Iowa Ct. App. 1993)

110 ALR5th 213—§ 2

State v. Helmer, 203 Ariz. 309, 53 P.3d 1153 (Ct. App. Div. 1 2002)

33 ALR6th 91—§ 6

63 ALR6th 351—§ 3

State v. Helms, 348 N.C. 578, 504 S.E.2d 293 (1998)

90 ALR5th 453—§ 16

State v. Helms, 1994 WL 43862 (Minn. Ct. App. 1994)

73 ALR5th 383—§ 5

State v. Helton, 1993 WL 46464 (Ohio Ct. App. 3d Dist. Logan County 1993)
67 ALR6th 531—§ 15, 27

State v. Helvenston, R.M. Charlt. 48 (Ga. Super. Ct. 1820)
93 ALR5th 493—§ 7, 12

State v. Hemby, 264 Kan. 542, 957 P.2d 428 (1998)
36 ALR5th 161—§ 3
63 ALR6th 351—§ 3

State v. Hemme, 15 Kan. App. 2d 198, 806 P.2d 472 (1991)
109 ALR5th 99—§ 11

State v. Hemmer, 3 Neb. App. 769, 531 N.W.2d 559 (1995)
93 ALR5th 683—§ 3

State v. Hemmer, 2000-Ohio-1842, 2000 WL 681651 (Ohio Ct. App. 3d Dist. Logan County 2000)
55 ALR6th 513—§ 8

State v. Hemmingsen, 2007 WL 1129573 (Wash. Ct. App. Div. 2 2007)
26 ALR6th 511—§ 41

State v. Hemond, 178 Vt. 470, 868 A.2d 734 (2005)
27 ALR6th 183—§ 4

State v. Hempele, 120 N.J. 182, 576 A.2d 793 (1990)
62 ALR5th 1—§ 2 to 5, 9, 11 to 15
18 ALR6th 1—§ 2

State v. Hendershott, 131 Or. App. 531, 887 P.2d 351 (1994)
56 ALR6th 185—§ 39

State v. Henderson, 35 Kan. App. 2d 241, 129 P.3d 646 (2006)
30 ALR6th 1—§ 5

State v. Henderson, 64 N.C. App. 536, 307 S.E.2d 846 (1983)
8 ALR5th 713—§ 10

State v. Henderson, 97 Wash. App. 1051, 1999 WL 791077 (Div. 1 1999)
99 ALR6th 295—§ 19

State v. Henderson, 99 Wash. App. 369, 993 P.2d 928 (Div. 2 2000)
9 ALR6th 541—§ 29

State v. Henderson, 100 N.M. 260, 669 P.2d 736 (Ct. App. 1983)
116 ALR5th 373—§ 3, 6

State v. Henderson, 114 Idaho 293, 756 P.2d 1057 (1988)
19 ALR5th 470—§ 3
74 ALR5th 319—§ 2, 3, 12

State v. Henderson, 116 Ariz. 310, 569 P.2d 252 (App. 1977)
55 ALR5th 423—§ 3

State v. Henderson, 116 Ariz. 310, 569 P.2d 252 (Ct. App. Div. 1 1977)
103 ALR6th 137—§ 7

State v. Henderson, 116 N.M. 541, 865 P.2d 1185 (Ct. App. 1993)
95 ALR5th 229—§ 24

State v. Henderson, 149 Ariz. 254, 717 P.2d 933 (App. 1986)
15 ALR5th 391—§ 22

State v. Henderson, 160 P.3d 776 (Kan. 2007)
30 ALR6th 1—§ 3, 6

State v. Henderson, 166 Miss. 530, 146 So. 456 (1933)
10 ALR5th 139—§ 3, 4

State v. Henderson, 182 Or. 147, 184 P.2d 392 (1947)
11 ALR5th 497—§ 3, 16, 19

State v. Henderson, 226 Kan. 726, 603 P.2d 613 (1979)
10 ALR5th 700—§ 27

State v. Henderson, 243 La. 233, 142 So. 2d 407 (1962)
45 ALR5th 591—§ 14, 15

State v. Henderson, 245 Wis. 2d 345, 2001 WI 97, 629 N.W.2d 613 (2001)
50 ALR6th 455—§ 10, 17, 23, 24, 30

State v. Henderson, 271 Ga. 264, 517 S.E.2d 61 (1999)
14 ALR5th 913—§ 3

State v. Henderson, 277 Neb. 240, 762 N.W.2d 1, 105 Fair Empl. Prac. Cas. (BNA) 1121, 28 I.E.R. Cas. (BNA) 1377, 185 L.R.R.M. (BNA) 3291, 157 Lab. Cas. (CCH) ¶ 60762 (2009)
46 ALR6th 495—§ 32

State v. Henderson, 286 S.C. 465, 334 S.E.2d 519 (Ct. App. 1985)
124 ALR5th 1—§ 5

State v. Henderson, 298 S.C. 331, 380 S.E.2d 817 (1989)
54 ALR5th 141—§ 3 to 5, 8

State v. Henderson, 355 N.W.2d 484 (Minn. App. 1984)
36 ALR5th 255—§ 33
59 ALR5th 1—§ 4 to 6

State v. Henderson, 382 N.W.2d 275 (Minn. Ct. App. 1986)
59 ALR5th 1—§ 4 to 6

State v. Henderson, 435 N.W.2d 394 (Iowa Ct. App. 1988)
62 ALR5th 1—§ 3, 15
92 ALR5th 35—§ 6

State v. Henderson, 537 N.W.2d 763 (Iowa 1995)
71 ALR5th 1—§ 58

State v. Henderson, 623 S.W.2d 638 (Tenn. Crim. 1981)
44 ALR5th 651—§ 4

State v. Henderson, 648 So. 2d 974 (La. Ct. App. 5th Cir. 1994)
11 ALR6th 237—§ 13

State v. Henderson, 892 A.2d 1061 (Del. 2006)
47 ALR6th 423—§ 4

State v. Henderson, 1998 -NMSC- 018, 125 N.M. 434, 963 P.2d 511 (1998)
104 ALR5th 357—§ 7
54 ALR6th 429—§ 6, 12

State v. Henderson, 2002 WL 537042 (Tenn. Crim. App. 2002)
3 ALR6th 543—§ 8

State v. Henderson, 2003-Ohio-1470, 2003 WL 1524508 (Ohio Ct. App. 9th Dist. Lorain County 2003)
23 ALR6th 307—§ 44

State v. Henderson, 2003-Ohio-6522, 2003 WL 22880800 (Ohio Ct. App. 2d Dist. Montgomery County 2003)
71 ALR6th 1—§ 5

State v. Henderson, 2004 WL 1833936 (Minn. Ct. App. 2004)
26 ALR6th 511—§ 50

State v. Henderson, 2011-1384 La. App. 1 Cir. 2/10/12, 2012 WL 602408 (La. Ct. App. 1st Cir. 2012)
84 ALR6th 293—§ 27

State v. Hendon, No. 40656 (January 25, 1980, Ct. App. Ohio, 8th App. Dist. Cuyahoga Co.)
39 ALR5th 283—§ 14, 47

State v. Hendren, 311 N.W.2d 61 (Iowa 1981)
19 ALR6th 697—§ 18

State v. Hendrick, 164 N.W.2d 57 (N.D. 1969)
99 ALR6th 295—§ 21

State v. Hendricks, 25 Wash. App. 775, 610 P.2d 940 (Div. 2 1980)
17 ALR6th 327—§ 30

State v. Hendricks, 586 N.W.2d 413 (Minn. Ct. App. 1998)
92 ALR6th 295—§ 14, 19
95 ALR6th 1—§ 5, 7, 32
96 ALR6th 355—§ 5, 26, 36, 64

State v. Hendricks, 697 N.W.2d 129 (Iowa Ct. App. 2005)
33 ALR6th 91—§ 44

State v. Hendrickson, 81 Wash. App. 397, 914 P.2d 1194 (Div. 1 1996)
58 ALR5th 749—§ 4

State v. Hendrickson, 113 Wash. App. 1009, 2002 WL 1832903 (Div. 1 2002)
125 ALR5th 537—§ 8, 49, 53

State v. Hendrickson, 129 Wash. 2d 61, 917 P.2d 563 (1996)
62 ALR5th 1—§ 2

State v. Hendrickson, 2002 WL 1072072 (Iowa Ct. App. 2002)
72 ALR6th 1—§ 6

State v. Hendrix, 221 Ga. App. 331, 471 S.E.2d 277 (1996)
32 ALR6th 1—§ 10

State v. Hendrix, 314 Or. 170, 838 P.2d 566 (1992)
22 ALR5th 261—§ 2, 10

State v. Hendrix, 454 S.W.2d 40 (Mo. 1970)
98 ALR6th 455—§ 5

For assistance, call 1-800-328-4880

State v. Hennenfent, 490 N.W.2d 299
(Iowa 1992)
  92 ALR5th 35—§ 25
State v. Hennessey, 75 P.3d 769 (Kan.
Ct. App. 2003)
  97 ALR6th 653—§ 13
State v. Hennessey, 80 Wash. App. 190,
907 P.2d 331 (1995)
  27 ALR5th 593—§ 25
State v. Hennessy, 1995 WL 296062
(Minn. Ct. App. 1995)
  101 ALR6th 331—§ 12
State v. Hennigan, 404 So. 2d 222 (La.
1981)
  28 ALR6th 505—§ 9
State v. Henning, 289 Kan. 136, 209
P.3d 711 (2009)
  56 ALR6th 1—§ 3, 7, 40
State v. Hennings, 129 Wash. 2d 512,
919 P.2d 580 (1996)
  63 ALR6th 1—§ 5, 46
State v. Hennon, 314 N.W.2d 405 (Iowa
1982)
  112 ALR5th 429—§ 13
State v. Hennum, 441 N.W.2d 793
(Minn. 1989)
  58 ALR5th 749—§ 9
  113 ALR5th 597—§ 6
State v. Henretta, 2009 WL 1025828
(Tenn. Crim. App. 2009)
  53 ALR6th 1—§ 7
State v. Henrich, 268 Mont. 258, 886
P.2d 402 (1994)
  65 ALR6th 537—§ 67
State v. Henricks, 1998 WL 811569
(Minn. Ct. App. 1998)
  7 ALR6th 233—§ 6
State v. Henry, 31 N.C. 463 (1849)
  17 ALR5th 125—§ 3, 5, 8
State v. Henry, 37 Ohio App. 3d 3, 523
N.E.2d 877 (Wood Co. 1987)
  39 ALR5th 283—§ 14, 60
State v. Henry, 57 N.C. App. 168, 290
S.E.2d 775 (1982)
  55 ALR6th 157—§ 98
State v. Henry, 72 Conn. App. 640, 805
A.2d 823 (2002)

  16 ALR6th 329—§ 4
  24 ALR6th 591—§ 4, 12
State v. Henry, 101 N.M. 277, 681 P.2d
62 (Ct. App. 1984)
  72 ALR5th 403—§ 15
State v. Henry, 116 Or. App. 138, 840
P.2d 1335 (1992)
  4 ALR5th 1—§ 5, 20
State v. Henry, 119 Wash. App. 1035,
2003 WL 22839815 (Div. 1 2003)
  26 ALR6th 511—§ 25
State v. Henry, 133 N.J. 104, 627 A.2d
125 (1993)
  50 ALR6th 1—§ 4
State v. Henry, 189 Ariz. 542, 944 P.2d
57 (1997)
  71 ALR6th 625—§ 18, 29, 37
State v. Henry, 191 Ariz. 283, 955 P.2d
39 (Ct. App. Div. 1 1997)
  20 ALR5th 398—§ 26
State v. Henry, 196 La. 217, 198 So. 910
(1940)
  101 ALR6th 499—§ 4
  102 ALR6th 279—§ 28
State v. Henry, 224 Ariz. 164, 228 P.3d
900 (Ct. App. Div. 2 2010)
  63 ALR6th 351—§ 3
State v. Henry, 263 Kan. 118, 947 P.2d
1020 (1997)
  101 ALR6th 331—§ 12
State v. Henry, 266 Wis. 2d 1059, 2003
WI App 188, 668 N.W.2d 562 (Ct.
App. 2003)
  33 ALR6th 407—§ 5
State v. Henry, 329 S.C. 266, 495 S.E.2d
463 (Ct. App. 1997)
  72 ALR5th 529—§ 15
State v. Henry, 440 So. 2d 872 (La. Ct.
App. 2d Cir. 1983)
  76 ALR5th 563—§ 4, 5
State v. Henry, 733 S.W.2d 127 (Tenn.
Crim. 1987)
  26 ALR5th 765—§ 6, 13, 19, 22
State v. Henry, 1999 WL 92939 (Tenn.
Crim. App. 1999)
  7 ALR6th 233—§ 5

State v. Henry, 2009-Ohio-1138, 2009 WL 653051 (Ohio Ct. App. 11th Dist. Lake County 2009)
71 ALR6th 1—§ 5
State v. Henry H.C., 1997 WL 148619 (Wash. Ct. App. Div. 3 1997)
73 ALR5th 383—§ 5
State v. Hensley, 29 N.C. App. 8, 222 S.E.2d 716 (1976)
5 ALR5th 243—§ 58
State v. Hensley, 90 N.C. App. 245, 368 S.E.2d 208 (1988)
5 ALR5th 243—§ 6
State v. Hensley, 137 Ariz. 80, 669 P.2d 58 (1983)
124 ALR5th 1—§ 5
State v. Hensley, 219 Kan. 826, 549 P.2d 874 (1976)
16 ALR6th 329—§ 4
24 ALR6th 591—§ 4, 15
State v. Hensley, 661 N.E.2d 1246 (Ind. Ct. App. 1996)
76 ALR6th 31—§ 14
State v. Hensley, 770 S.W.2d 730 (Mo. App. 1989)
50 ALR5th 581—§ 2
State v. Henson, 23 Or. App. 234, 541 P.2d 1085 (1975)
57 ALR6th 83—§ 5
State v. Henson, 27 Ohio App. 3d 275, 27 Ohio B.R. 319, 500 N.E.2d 899 (Cuyahoga Co. 1985)
13 ALR5th 872—§ 2, 19
State v. Henson, 91 W. Va. 701, 114 S.E. 273 (1922)
97 ALR5th 201—§ 3
State v. Herbest, 551 A.2d 442 (Me. 1988)
28 ALR6th 245—§ 6
State v. Herbst, 2 Conn. Cir. 236, 197 A.2d 550 (1963)
26 ALR5th 1—§ 4, 10
State v. Herbst, 395 N.W.2d 399 (Minn. App. 1986)
19 ALR5th 470—§ 3, 12
State v. Heredia, 172 Wis. 2d 479, 493 N.W.2d 404 (App. 1992)

12 ALR5th 89—§ 5, 7, 8
State v. Hereford, 518 So. 2d 515 (La. Ct. App. 3d Cir. 1987)
93 ALR5th 327—§ 7, 20
101 ALR5th 619—§ 3
State v. Herem, 384 N.W.2d 880 (Minn. 1986)
34 ALR6th 1—§ 10
State v. Herfel, 49 Wis. 2d 513, 182 N.W.2d 232 (1971)
45 ALR5th 591—§ 14
State v. Herhal, 307 A.2d 553 (Del. Super. 1973)
41 ALR5th 171—§ 6, 12
State v. Heritage, 152 Wash. 2d 210, 95 P.3d 345 (2004)
51 ALR6th 219—§ 4
State v. Herman, 280 S.W.2d 44 (Mo. 1955)
33 ALR5th 571—§ 5
State v. Herman, 1994 WL 587482 (Ohio Ct. App. 11th Dist. Ashtabula County 1994)
67 ALR6th 209—§ 34
State v. Hermann, 164 Wis. 2d 269, 474 N.W.2d 906 (App. 1991)
27 ALR5th 593—§ 3, 8, 9, 13, 31
State v. Hermann, 283 S.W.2d 617 (Mo. 1955)
75 ALR5th 295—§ 7
State v. Hermanson, 1998 WL 463321 (Minn. Ct. App. 1998)
30 ALR6th 483—§ 39
State v. Hermes, 273 Mont. 446, 904 P.2d 587 (1995)
28 ALR6th 505—§ 15
State v. Hermsdorf, 135 N.H. 360, 605 A.2d 1045, 16 A.L.R.5th 1035 (1992)
16 ALR5th 390—§ 3
State v. Hernandez, 4 Ariz. App. 451, 421 P.2d 533 (Div. 2 1966)
108 ALR5th 593—§ 27
State v. Hernandez, 96 Ariz. 28, 391 P.2d 586 (1964)
9 ALR5th 464—§ 5, 10
State v. Hernandez, 104 N.M. 268, 720 P.2d 303 (Ct. App. 1986)

7 ALR6th 169—§ 8
State v. Hernandez, 115 N.M. 6, 846 P.2d 312 (1993)
37 ALR5th 515—§ 4, 11
State v. Hernandez, 120 Idaho 785, 820 P.2d 380 (App. 1991)
32 ALR5th 149—§ 4, 5, 29, 32
State v. Hernandez, 120 Idaho 785, 820 P.2d 380 (Ct. App. 1991)
97 ALR6th 567—§ 3, 9
State v. Hernandez, 121 Idaho 114, 822 P.2d 1011 (Ct. App. 1991)
15 ALR5th 391—§ 32
92 ALR5th 35—§ 2, 21
State v. Hernandez, 132 P.3d 501 (Kan. Ct. App. 2006)
71 ALR6th 625—§ 21, 29
State v. Hernandez, 163 N.J. Super. 283, 394 A.2d 883 (App. Div. 1978)
41 ALR6th 295—§ 9
State v. Hernandez, 170 Ariz. 301, 823 P.2d 1309 (1991)
20 ALR5th 398—§ 2, 3, 31, 36, 50, 52, 53, 62
47 ALR5th 259—§ 2
State v. Hernandez, 199 Or. App. 566, 113 P.3d 437 (2005)
26 ALR6th 511—§ 27
State v. Hernandez, 213 Mont. 221, 689 P.2d 1261 (1984)
29 ALR5th 59—§ 3, 79, 89
State v. Hernandez, 268 Neb. 934, 689 N.W.2d 579 (2004)
73 ALR6th 1—§ 5
State v. Hernandez, 706 So. 2d 66 (Fla. Dist. Ct. App. 2d Dist. 1998)
122 ALR5th 439—§ 4
State v. Hernandez, 815 So. 2d 126 (La. Ct. App. 5th Cir. 2002)
106 ALR5th 377—§ 3
State v. Hernandez, 2001-Ohio-4086, 2001 WL 1403104 (Ohio Ct. App. 10th Dist. Franklin County 2001)
34 ALR6th 1—§ 5
State v. Hernandez, 2005-Ohio-6101, 2005 WL 3073371 (Ohio Ct. App. 10th Dist. Franklin County 2005)
69 ALR6th 1—§ 29

State v. Hernandez, 2006-Ohio-1207, 2006 WL 648856 (Ohio Ct. App. 10th Dist. Franklin County 2006)
26 ALR6th 511—§ 19
State v. Hernandez, 2007-Ohio-5190, 2007 WL 2821659 (Ohio Ct. App. 12th Dist. Preble County 2007)
58 ALR6th 215—§ 20
State v. Hernandez-Mercado, 124 Wash. 2d 368, 879 P.2d 283 (1994)
65 ALR6th 329—§ 4, 8
75 ALR6th 541—§ 13
State v. Herred, 332 Ark. 241, 964 S.W.2d 391 (1998)
41 ALR5th 171—§ 56
State v. Herren, 212 Neb. 706, 325 N.W.2d 151 (1982)
79 ALR5th 419—§ 9
State v. Herren, 2010 SD 101, 792 N.W.2d 551 (S.D. 2010)
84 ALR6th 293—§ 35
State v. Herrera, 49 Or. App. 1075, 621 P.2d 1209 (1980)
29 ALR6th 1—§ 10
State v. Herrera, 92 N.M. 7, 582 P.2d 384 (App. 1978)
28 ALR5th 754—§ 7
State v. Herrera, 365 So. 2d 399 (Fla. Dist. Ct. App. 3d Dist. 1978)
55 ALR6th 391—§ 21
State v. Herrera, 385 N.J. Super. 486, 897 A.2d 1085 (App. Div. 2006)
99 ALR6th 295—§ 14
State v. Herrera, 601 P.2d 75 (N.M. App. 1979)
49 ALR5th 639—§ 4
State v. Herrera-Rodriguez, 164 Ariz. 49, 790 P.2d 747 (App. 1989)
40 ALR5th 113—§ 3
State v. Herrera-Sorrosa, 154 Or. App. 28, 959 P.2d 619 (1998)
19 ALR5th 470—§ 4
State v. Herrick, 1997 N.D. 155, 567 N.W.2d 336 (N.D. 1997)
62 ALR5th 1—§ 15
State v. Herrick, 1999 ND 1, 588 N.W.2d 847 (N.D. 1999)

2 ALR6th 169—§ 3, 5
50 ALR6th 455—§ 6
State v. Herriges, 95 Wash. App. 1037, 1999 WL 293932 (Div. 1 1999)
73 ALR6th 49—§ 11
State v. Herrin, 562 So. 2d 1 (La. Ct. App. 1st Cir. 1990)
81 ALR6th 505—§ 12
State v. Herring, 210 Conn. 78, 554 A.2d 686 (1989)
70 ALR6th 361—§ 19, 29
State v. Herring, 322 N.C. 733, 370 S.E.2d 363 (1988)
103 ALR6th 507—§ 14
State v. Herring, 1999 WL 61064 (Ohio Ct. App. 7th Dist. Mahoning County 1999)
16 ALR6th 329—§ 15
19 ALR6th 115—§ 5
24 ALR6th 591—§ 6, 10
State v. Herring, No. 9257 (November 21, 1979, Ct. App. Ohio, 9th App. Dist. Summit Co.)
39 ALR5th 283—§ 14, 56
State v. Herrmann, 2002 SD 119, 652 N.W.2d 725 (S.D. 2002)
84 ALR6th 293—§ 31
State v. Herrod, 754 S.W.2d 627 (Tenn. Crim. App. 1988)
103 ALR6th 507—§ 4
State v. Herron, 53 S.W.3d 843 (Tex. App. Fort Worth 2001)
69 ALR6th 1—§ 13
State v. Hersch, 445 N.W.2d 626 (N.D. 1989)
24 ALR5th 132—§ 6, 8
State v. Hertwig, 124 Wash. App. 1036, 2004 WL 2861757 (Div. 2 2004)
15 ALR6th 515—§ 33
State v. Hervey, 70 Or. App. 547, 689 P.2d 1322 (1984)
56 ALR6th 323—§ 7, 9, 11
State v. Herwitz, 109 Wash. 153, 186 P. 290 (1919)
54 ALR6th 429—§ 22
State v. Herzog, 125 Or. App. 10, 864 P.2d 1362 (1993)

86 ALR5th 59—§ 5, 6
State v. Heslar, 257 Ind. 307, 274 N.E.2d 261 (1971)
22 ALR5th 327—§ 3
State v. Hess, 9 Ariz. App. 29, 449 P.2d 46 (1969)
85 ALR5th 187—§ 9
51 ALR6th 219—§ 4
State v. Hess, 261 Neb. 368, 622 N.W.2d 891 (2001)
29 ALR6th 237—§ 5, 21
State v. Hesse, 195 Mo. App. 616, 187 S.W. 571 (1916)
13 ALR5th 1—§ 25, 44
State v. Hesse, 281 N.W.2d 491 (Minn. 1979)
40 ALR6th 1—§ 33
State v. Hessner, 124 Wash. App. 1031, 2004 WL 2849691 (Div. 2 2004)
30 ALR6th 373—§ 7
State v. Hester, 45 Ohio St. 2d 71, 74 Ohio Op. 2d 156, 341 N.E.2d 304 (1976)
78 ALR5th 197—§ 4
State v. Hester, 245 N.J. Super. 75, 584 A.2d 256 (App. Div. 1990)
74 ALR5th 319—§ 13
State v. Hester, 324 S.W.3d 1 (Tenn. 2010)
83 ALR6th 465—§ 4, 19
State v. Hester, 343 N.C. 266, 470 S.E.2d 25 (1996)
54 ALR6th 429—§ 7
State v. Hester, 2012 WL 5364690 (Del. Super. Ct. 2012)
99 ALR6th 295—§ 9
State v. Hett, 31 Wash. App. 849, 644 P.2d 1187 (Div. 3 1982)
112 ALR5th 429—§ 3
State v. Hetzko, 283 So. 2d 49 (Fla. Dist. Ct. App. 4th Dist. 1973)
58 ALR6th 499—§ 4
State v. Hewes, 558 A.2d 696 (Me. 1989)
30 ALR6th 103—§ 3, 6, 13, 22
32 ALR6th 1—§ 10, 11

State v. Hewes, 589 A.2d 460 (Me. 1991)

32 ALR6th 1—§ 10

State v. Hewett, 158 N.C. 627, 74 S.E. 356 (1912)

93 ALR5th 683—§ 4

State v. Hewey, 622 A.2d 1151 (Me. 1993)

28 ALR6th 505—§ 11

State v. Hewitt, 259 S.W. 773 (Mo. 1924)

24 ALR6th 747—§ 17, 18

State v. Hewitt, 2001 WL 22486 (Ohio Ct. App. 9th Dist. Lorain County 2001)

87 ALR5th 693—§ 4

State v. Hewlette, 2009-Ohio-4798, 2009 WL 2918989 (Ohio Ct. App. 9th Dist. Wayne County 2009)

67 ALR6th 395—§ 9, 22

State v. Heyer, 962 S.W.2d 401 (Mo. Ct. App. E.D. 1998)

82 ALR5th 103—§ 5

35 ALR6th 127—§ 5

State v. Heyn, 155 Wis. 2d 621, 456 N.W.2d 157 (1990)

15 ALR5th 391—§ 7

44 ALR6th 301—§ 3

State v. Hickam, 71 Or. App. 471, 692 P.2d 672 (1984)

32 ALR6th 1—§ 11

State v. Hickerson, 66 S.W.3d 787 (Mo. Ct. App. S.D. 2002)

105 ALR5th 529—§ 30

State v. Hickman, 119 Idaho 366, 806 P.2d 959 (Ct. App. 1991)

43 ALR6th 475—§ 16

State v. Hickman, 335 N.J. Super. 623, 763 A.2d 330 (App. Div. 2000)

56 ALR6th 323—§ 5

State v. Hickman, 2002-Ohio-3406, 2002 WL 1453759 (Ohio Ct. App. 9th Dist. Summit County 2002)

38 ALR6th 439—§ 4, 5

State v. Hicks, 3 So. 3d 539 (La. Ct. App. 5th Cir. 2008)

79 ALR6th 1—§ 32

State v. Hicks, 11 Kan. App. 2d 76, 714 P.2d 105 (1986)

108 ALR5th 593—§ 35

State v. Hicks, 55 S.W.3d 515 (Tenn. 2001)

116 ALR5th 479—§ 3, 5

State v. Hicks, 61 Wash. App. 923, 812 P.2d 893 (Div. 3 1991)

73 ALR5th 383—§ 2, 3, 28

State v. Hicks, 77 Wash. App. 1, 888 P.2d 1235 (Div. 3 1995)

73 ALR5th 383—§ 5

State v. Hicks, 330 S.C. 207, 499 S.E.2d 209 (1998)

47 ALR5th 259—§ 9

State v. Hicks, 333 N.C. 467, 428 S.E.2d 167 (1993)

32 ALR6th 1—§ 10

State v. Hicks, 395 So. 2d 790 (La. 1981)

53 ALR6th 81—§ 5

State v. Hicks, 495 A.2d 765 (Me. 1985)

65 ALR6th 359—§ 2, 8

State v. Hicks, 607 So. 2d 937 (La. App. 2nd Cir. 1992)

57 ALR5th 141—§ 13

State v. Hicks, 607 So. 2d 937 (La. Ct. App. 2d Cir. 1992)

9 ALR6th 1—§ 10

State v. Hicks, 722 S.W.2d 650 (Mo. App. 1987)

55 ALR5th 125—§ 16, 23

State v. Hicks, 1998 WL 226463 (Ohio Ct. App. 1st Dist. Hamilton County 1998)

78 ALR5th 489—§ 3

State v. Hicks, 2003-Ohio-5526, 2003 WL 22359645 (Ohio Ct. App. 2d Dist. Montgomery County 2003)

33 ALR6th 407—§ 5

State v. Hicks, 2011-Ohio-1184, 2011 WL 862186 (Ohio Ct. App. 7th Dist. Jefferson County 2011)

86 ALR6th 321—§ 6

State v. Hickson, 630 So. 2d 172 (Fla. 1993)

58 ALR5th 749—§ 9

State v. Hidri, 2010 WL 3670962 (Conn. Super. Ct. 2010)

73 ALR6th 49—§ 54

State v. Higby, 26 Wash. App. 457, 613 P.2d 1192 (Div. 2 1980)

112 ALR5th 429—§ 6

State v. Higgenbotham, 264 Kan. 593, 957 P.2d 416 (1998)

39 ALR5th 283—§ 50

State v. Higgin, 257 Minn. 46, 99 N.W.2d 902 (1959)

108 ALR5th 593—§ 27

State v. Higginbotham, 101 Wis. 2d 87, 303 N.W.2d 637 (1981)

78 ALR6th 417—§ 24

State v. Higginbotham, 110 Wis. 2d 393, 329 N.W.2d 250 (Ct. App. 1982)

78 ALR6th 417—§ 42, 69

State v. Higginbotham, 917 P.2d 545 (Utah 1996)

20 ALR5th 398—§ 33.5

State v. Higgins, 422 N.W.2d 277 (Minn. App. 1988)

22 ALR5th 1—§ 5, 14

State v. Higgins, 2002 WL 31016491 (Iowa Ct. App. 2002)

43 ALR6th 475—§ 26

State v. Higgins, 2004 ND 115, 680 N.W.2d 645 (N.D. 2004)

47 ALR6th 107—§ 7, 15, 24

State v. Higgs, 1992 WL 281348 (Ohio Ct. App. 9th Dist.Summit County 1992)

57 ALR5th 141—§ 3

State v. High, 116 La. 79, 40 So. 538 (1906)

102 ALR6th 279—§ 29

State v. High Elk, 298 N.W.2d 87 (S.D. 1980)

55 ALR6th 157—§ 76

State v. Hightower, 231 S.W. 566 (Mo. 1921)

98 ALR6th 455—§ 29

State v. Hightower, 272 So. 2d 363 (La. 1973)

114 ALR5th 235—§ 3

State v. Hightower, 661 A.2d 948 (R.I. 1995)

37 ALR5th 515—§ 17

State v. Hightower, 2005-Ohio-3857, 2005 WL 1793522 (Ohio Ct. App. 8th Dist. Cuyahoga County 2005)

72 ALR6th 227—§ 48

State v. Hiivala, 86 Wash. App. 1066, 1997 WL 345189 (Div. 2 1997)

63 ALR6th 1—§ 5

State v. Hilbert, 145 Ohio App. 3d 824, 764 N.E.2d 1064 (8th Dist. Cuyahoga County 2001)

69 ALR6th 1—§ 4

State v. Hileman, 125 Ohio App. 3d 526, 708 N.E.2d 1078 (12th Dist. Butler County 1998)

45 ALR6th 435—§ 9

State v. Hiles, 1999 WL 3880 (Ohio Ct. App. 5th Dist. Delaware County 1998)

41 ALR6th 141—§ 7

State v. Hill, 11 Ariz. App. 230, 463 P.2d 125 (Div. 2 1969)

66 ALR5th 397—§ 4, 6, 22

State v. Hill, 16 Kan. App. 2d 280, 823 P.2d 201 (1991)

4 ALR5th 1—§ 7, 19

23 ALR6th 307—§ 27

State v. Hill, 58 Conn. App. 797, 755 A.2d 919 (2000)

39 ALR5th 283—§ 57

State v. Hill, 64 Ohio St. 3d 313, 595 N.E.2d 884 (1992)

20 ALR5th 177—§ 3, 9

79 ALR5th 33—§ 39, 41

State v. Hill, 64 Ohio St. 3d 313, 1992-Ohio-43, 595 N.E.2d 884 (1992)

1 ALR6th 657—§ 4

State v. Hill, 104 Ariz. 238, 450 P.2d 696 (1969)

86 ALR5th 59—§ 4, 6

State v. Hill, 110 N.J. Super. 370, 265 A.2d 820 (App. Div. 1970)

85 ALR5th 471—§ 4

State v. Hill, 121 N.J. 150, 578 A.2d 370 (1990)

39 ALR6th 257—§ 23, 27, 38, 42

State v. Hill, 123 Wash. 2d 641, 870 P.2d 313 (1994)
51 ALR5th 375—§ 7, 12

State v. Hill, 127 Ohio App. 3d 441, 713 N.E.2d 73 (2d Dist. Montgomery County 1998)
55 ALR5th 125—§ 12

State v. Hill, 135 Wash. App. 1021, 2006 WL 3056408 (Div. 1 2006)
38 ALR6th 97—§ 26

State v. Hill, 136 Ohio App. 3d 636, 737 N.E.2d 577 (5th Dist. Fairfield County 2000)
60 ALR5th 39—§ 11, 14

State v. Hill, 155 N.J. 270, 714 A.2d 311 (1998)
92 ALR5th 35—§ 21

State v. Hill, 160 Ohio App. 3d 324, 2005-Ohio-1501, 827 N.E.2d 351 (8th Dist. Cuyahoga County 2005)
30 ALR6th 1—§ 3, 5, 6

State v. Hill, 170 Mont. 71, 550 P.2d 390 (1976)
45 ALR5th 1—§ 5, 7, 12, 23

State v. Hill, 201 Wis. 2d 816, 549 N.W.2d 286 (Ct. App. 1996)
84 ALR6th 293—§ 38

State v. Hill, 204 Neb. 743, 285 N.W.2d 229 (1979)
9 ALR6th 693—§ 22
10 ALR6th 265—§ 10
12 ALR6th 389—§ 17
13 ALR6th 603—§ 40

State v. Hill, 211 Kan. 239, 505 P.2d 704 (1973)
28 ALR6th 505—§ 29

State v. Hill, 211 Kan. 287, 507 P.2d 342 (1973)
70 ALR5th 587—§ 3

State v. Hill, 214 Neb. 865, 336 N.W.2d 325 (1983)
15 ALR6th 173—§ 52

State v. Hill, 223 N.C. 711, 28 S.E.2d 100 (1943)
41 ALR5th 1—§ 3, 4, 8

State v. Hill, 256 N.W.2d 279 (Minn. 1977)
99 ALR6th 295—§ 5

State v. Hill, 277 N.C. 547, 178 S.E.2d 462 (1971)
109 ALR5th 611—§ 3

State v. Hill, 361 S.C. 297, 604 S.E.2d 696 (2004)
20 ALR6th 479—§ 3, 12, 14
100 ALR6th 535—§ 3

State v. Hill, 465 N.W.2d 309 (Iowa App. 1990)
43 ALR5th 1—§ 8, 13

State v. Hill, 534 S.E.2d 606 (N.C. Ct. App. 2000)
39 ALR5th 283—§ 31

State v. Hill, 546 So. 2d 212 (La. Ct. App. 4th Cir. 1989)
109 ALR5th 99—§ 3

State v. Hill, 638 So. 2d 1376 (Ala. Crim. App. 1993)
51 ALR6th 1—§ 23
52 ALR6th 1—§ 31

State v. Hill, 688 N.E.2d 1280 (Ind. Ct. App. 1997)
88 ALR5th 121—§ 7, 36

State v. Hill, 698 So. 2d 647 (Fla. Dist. Ct. App. 5th Dist. 1997)
113 ALR5th 597—§ 8

State v. Hill, 742 A.2d 605 (N.J. Super. Ct. App. Div. 1999)
7 ALR5th 263—§ 7

State v. Hill, 742 So. 2d 690 (La. Ct. App. 5th Cir. 1999)
93 ALR6th 275—§ 3

State v. Hill, 808 S.W.2d 882 (Mo. Ct. App. E.D. 1991)
70 ALR5th 587—§ 25

State v. Hill, 875 S.W.2d 278 (Tenn. Crim. App. 1993)
70 ALR6th 361—§ 5, 19

State v. Hill, 996 S.W.2d 544 (Mo. Ct. App. W.D. 1999)
6 ALR5th 733—§ 15

State v. Hill, 1993 WL 492698 (Tenn. Crim. App. 1993)
83 ALR5th 277—§ 15
84 ALR5th 487—§ 3

State v. Hill, 1999 WL 39483 (Wash. Ct. App. Div. 2 1999)

73 ALR5th 383—§ 6

State v. Hill, 2000 WL 1780217 (Ohio Ct. App. 10th Dist. Franklin County 2000)

11 ALR6th 237—§ 10

State v. Hill, 2005 WL 2126834 (Minn. Ct. App. 2005)

26 ALR6th 511—§ 4, 26, 35

State v. Hill, 2006 WL 1229137 (Minn. Ct. App. 2006)

18 ALR6th 97—§ 35

State v. Hill, 2009 UT App 254, 2009 WL 2902525 (Utah Ct. App. 2009)

55 ALR6th 1—§ 21

State v. Hill, 2011 WL 1535515 (Ariz. Ct. App. Div. 1 2011)

70 ALR6th 361—§ 18

State v. Hilleshiem, 291 N.W.2d 314 (Iowa 1980)

74 ALR5th 319—§ 7, 10
116 ALR5th 479—§ 2

State v. Hilliard, 89 Ariz. 129, 359 P.2d 66 (1961)

55 ALR6th 157—§ 33

State v. Hilliker, 117 Vt. 569, 97 A.2d 119 (1953)

50 ALR5th 703—§ 15

State v. Hills, 124 Ariz. 491, 605 P.2d 893 (1980)

50 ALR5th 467—§ 6

State v. Hills, 259 La. 436, 250 So. 2d 394 (1971)

86 ALR5th 59—§ 3

State v. Hills, 283 So. 2d 220 (La. 1973)

58 ALR6th 499—§ 47

State v. Hill, Slip Opinion No. C-74035 (Ohio App. Hamilton Co. 1974)

41 ALR5th 171—§ 6, 16, 68

State v. Hilpipre, 242 N.W.2d 306 (Iowa 1976)

32 ALR6th 1—§ 10

State v. Hilpipre, 395 N.W.2d 899 (Iowa App. 1986)

5 ALR5th 243—§ 2

State v. Himel, 260 La. 949, 257 So. 2d 670 (1972)

51 ALR6th 219—§ 4

State v. Hince, 540 N.W.2d 820 (Minn. 1995)

32 ALR6th 1—§ 11

State v. Hinchey, 181 Ariz. 307, 890 P.2d 602 (1995)

21 ALR6th 1—§ 4

State v. Hinckley, 13 Kan. App. 2d 417, 770 P.2d 497 (1989)

15 ALR5th 391—§ 7

State v. Hiner, 988 S.W.2d 697 (Tenn. Crim. App. 1998)

52 ALR5th 655—§ 6
18 ALR6th 519—§ 20

State v. Hines, 87 Wash. App. 98, 941 P.2d 9 (Div. 3 1997)

112 ALR5th 621—§ 3, 5

State v. Hines, 286 N.C. 377, 211 S.E.2d 201 (1975)

10 ALR5th 700—§ 35

State v. Hines, 314 N.C. 522, 335 S.E.2d 6 (1985)

73 ALR5th 383—§ 3

State v. Hines, 343 N.W.2d 869 (Minn. Ct. App. 1984)

73 ALR5th 383—§ 3

State v. Hines, 354 N.W.2d 91 (Minn. App. 1984)

29 ALR5th 59—§ 58, 76, 79, 86, 89

State v. Hines, 465 So. 2d 958 (La. Ct. App. 2d Cir. 1985)

50 ALR5th 703—§ 2, 15
66 ALR5th 397—§ 21, 23

State v. Hines, 2011 WL 5966910 (Tenn. Crim. App. 2011)

98 ALR6th 455—§ 26

State v. Hines, 2012 WL 246396 (N.J. Super. Ct. App. Div. 2012)

78 ALR6th 297—§ 37

State v. Hinkel, 365 N.W.2d 774 (Minn. 1985)

43 ALR5th 1—§ 13

State v. Hinkhouse, 139 Or. App. 446, 912 P.2d 921 (1996)

13 ALR5th 628—§ 9, 10.5

State v. Hinkle, 1996 WL 494873 (Ohio Ct. App. 11th Dist. Portage County 1996)

85 ALR5th 187—§ 12, 15

State v. Hinnant, 131 N.C. App. 591, 508 S.E.2d 537 (1998)

38 ALR5th 433—§ 5

State v. Hinners, 471 N.W.2d 841 (Iowa 1991)

9 ALR6th 541—§ 32

State v. Hinton, 196 Conn. 289, 493 A.2d 837 (1985)

102 ALR6th 365—§ 15

State v. Hinton, 361 N.C. 207, 639 S.E.2d 437 (2007)

67 ALR6th 103—§ 6, 8

State v. Hintz, 2001 WI App 121, 244 Wis. 2d 287, 628 N.W.2d 437 (Ct. App. 2001)

84 ALR6th 293—§ 38

State v. Hinze, 1987 WL 12458 (Ohio Ct. App. 4th Dist. Scioto County 1987)

118 ALR5th 385—§ 4, 11

State v. Hipps, 348 N.C. 377, 501 S.E.2d 625 (1998)

57 ALR5th 141—§ 3

State v. Hirsch, 129 Ohio App. 3d 294, 717 N.E.2d 789 (1st Dist. Hamilton County 1998)

24 ALR6th 747—§ 30

State v. Hirsch, 338 Or. 622, 114 P.3d 1104 (2005)

33 ALR6th 407—§ 38
85 ALR6th 641—§ 6

State v. Hirschfield, 987 P.2d 99 (Wash. Ct. App. Div. 1 1999)

71 ALR5th 637—§ 8

State v. Hirtle, 47 R.I. 371, 133 A. 444 (1926)

54 ALR6th 429—§ 18

State v. Hitch, 23 Ohio Misc. 2d 29, 491 N.E.2d 1147 (County Ct. 1985)

17 ALR6th 327—§ 13

State v. Hitchcock, 87 Ariz. 277, 350 P.2d 681 (1960)

102 ALR6th 279—§ 29

State v. Hitchcock, 228 Minn. 335, 37 N.W.2d 378 (1949)

2 ALR6th 1—§ 8

State v. Hitchcock, 2009-Ohio-4447, 2009 WL 2710126 (Ohio Ct. App. 11th Dist. Lake County 2009)

64 ALR6th 1—§ 9

State v. Hite, 3 Wash. App. 9, 472 P.2d 600 (1970)

29 ALR5th 59—§ 7

State v. Hitopoulus, 279 S.C. 549, 309 S.E.2d 747 (1983)

66 ALR6th 83—§ 10

State v. Hitt, 273 Kan. 224, 42 P.3d 732 (2002)

26 ALR6th 511—§ 29

State v. Hix, 132 W. Va. 516, 54 S.E.2d 198 (1949)

68 ALR5th 13—§ 3, 9, 12, 39, 41

State v. Hizel, 179 Neb. 661, 139 N.W.2d 832 (1966)

9 ALR6th 1—§ 3

State v. Hjelmstad, 535 N.W.2d 663 (Minn. Ct. App. 1995)

84 ALR6th 293—§ 22

State v. Hlavaty, 871 S.W.2d 600 (Mo. App. 1994)

20 ALR5th 398—§ 55.5, 65

State v. Hoaglin, 8 Ohio Ops. 2d 464, 83 Ohio L. Abs. 37, 160 N.E.2d 440 (Mun Ct. 1959)

50 ALR5th 703—§ 7

State v. Hoak, 316 Wis. 2d 355, 2009 WI App 21, 763 N.W.2d 247 (Ct. App. 2008)

74 ALR6th 69—§ 15

State v. Hoang, 94 Haw. 271, 12 P.3d 371 (Haw. Ct. App. 2000)

72 ALR5th 403—§ 3

State v. Hobbs, 168 W. Va. 13, 282 S.E.2d 258 (1981)

55 ALR6th 157—§ 4, 45

State v. Hobbs, 2007 WL 2840434 (Neb. Ct. App. 2007)

56 ALR6th 323—§ 11

State v. Hobley, 752 So. 2d 771 (La. 1999)

101 ALR5th 187—§ 7

State v. Hobson, 234 Kan. 133, 671 P.2d 1365 (1983)

57 ALR5th 141—§ 9, 10

State v. Hobson, 648 A.2d 1369 (R.I. 1994)

29 ALR6th 1—§ 10

State v. Hobus, 535 N.W.2d 728 (N.D. 1995)

43 ALR6th 475—§ 6

State v. Hochstein, 623 N.W.2d 617 (Minn. Ct. App. 2001)

113 ALR5th 517—§ 3

State v. Hockenhull, 525 A.2d 926 (R.I. 1987)

58 ALR6th 499—§ 101

State v. Hockings, 29 Or. App. 139, 562 P.2d 587 (1977)

94 ALR5th 393—§ 5

State v. Hockman, 1984 WL 6151 (Ohio Ct. App. 9th Dist. Summit County 1984)

85 ALR5th 1—§ 36

State v. Hodge, 5 Wash. App. 639, 490 P.2d 126 (Div. 2 1971)

113 ALR5th 517—§ 8

State v. Hodge, 118 N.C. App. 655, 456 S.E.2d 855 (1995)

94 ALR5th 393—§ 12

State v. Hodge, 131 Ariz. 63, 638 P.2d 730 (App. 1981)

54 ALR5th 141—§ 6

State v. Hodge, 223 P.3d 837 (Kan. Ct. App. 2010)

94 ALR6th 525—§ 20

State v. Hodge, 225 Neb. 94, 402 N.W.2d 867 (1987)

114 ALR5th 235—§ 8
99 ALR6th 397—§ 17

State v. Hodge, 248 Conn. 207, 726 A.2d 531 (1999)

15 ALR6th 319—§ 6

State v. Hodge, 457 So. 2d 152 (La. Ct. App. 2d Cir. 1984)

16 ALR6th 329—§ 5
24 ALR6th 591—§ 4, 14

State v. Hodge, 880 So. 2d 983 (La. Ct. App. 2d Cir. 2004)

69 ALR6th 1—§ 23

State v. Hodge, 2000 WL 1533917 (Ohio Ct. App. 9th Dist. Lorain County 2000)

78 ALR5th 489—§ 10.5

State v. Hodges, 7 S.W.3d 609 (Tenn. Crim. App. 1998)

118 ALR5th 253—§ 16

State v. Hodges, 70 Wash. App. 621, 855 P.2d 291 (Div. 1 1993)

106 ALR5th 377—§ 4

State v. Hodges, 107 Ohio App. 3d 578, 669 N.E.2d 256 (3d Dist. Seneca County 1995)

102 ALR5th 327—§ 3

State v. Hodges, 287 N.W.2d 413 (Minn. 1979)

61 ALR5th 1—§ 3, 14

State v. Hodges, 384 N.W.2d 175 (Minn. Ct. App. 1986)

73 ALR5th 383—§ 3
3 ALR6th 269—§ 24

State v. Hodges, 595 So. 2d 929 (Fla. 1992)

57 ALR5th 141—§ 7

State v. Hodges, 695 S.W.2d 171 (Tenn. 1985)

18 ALR6th 775—§ 3

State v. Hodges, 705 S.W.2d 585 (Mo. Ct. App. S.D. 1986)

112 ALR5th 429—§ 13

State v. Hodges, 944 S.W.2d 346 (Tenn. 1997)

83 ALR6th 255—§ 2, 19

State v. Hodgman, 257 N.W.2d 313 (Minn. 1977)

123 ALR5th 179—§ 3

State v. Hodgson, 512 N.W.2d 95 (Minn. 1994)

1 ALR6th 657—§ 4

State v. Hodsdon, 289 A.2d 635 (Del. Super. Ct. 1972)

31 ALR6th 333—§ 10

State v. Hodson, 907 P.2d 1155 (Utah 1995)

64 ALR5th 741—§ 3

State v. Hoebel, 256 Wis. 549, 41 N.W.2d 865 (1950)

35 ALR6th 1—§ 7, 9, 19

State v. Hoehne, 78 Or. App. 479, 717 P.2d 237 (1986)

---

46 ALR5th 499—§ 5
State v. Hoenscheid, 374 N.W.2d 128 (S.D. 1985)

58 ALR6th 215—§ 6, 7
State v. Hoeplinger, 9 Conn. App. 147, 517 A.2d 632 (1986)

24 ALR5th 465—§ 14, 115, 116
State v. Hoeplinger, 206 Conn. 278, 537 A.2d 1010 (1988)

29 ALR6th 1—§ 9
State v. Hoey, 2005 WL 3742268 (N.J. Super. Ct. App. Div. 2006)

57 ALR6th 83—§ 12
State v. Hofer, 512 N.W.2d 482 (S.D. 1994)

90 ALR5th 453—§ 22
State v. Hoffler, 174 Conn. 452, 389 A.2d 1257 (1978)

103 ALR6th 347—§ 15
State v. Hoffman, 1 N.C.A. 370, 1992 WL 90032 (1992)

78 ALR5th 567—§ 5
State v. Hoffman, 15 Or. App. 524, 516 P.2d 84 (1973)

6 ALR6th 533—§ 16
State v. Hoffman, 106 Wis. 2d 185, 316 N.W.2d 143 (App. 1982)

33 ALR5th 453—§ 6
State v. Hoffman, 116 Idaho 689, 778 P.2d 811 (Ct. App. 1989)

72 ALR5th 403—§ 10
State v. Hoffman, 116 Wash. 2d 51, 804 P.2d 577 (1991)

16 ALR6th 329—§ 11
19 ALR6th 115—§ 4
24 ALR6th 591—§ 9, 13
State v. Hoffman, 123 Idaho 638, 851 P.2d 934 (1993)

79 ALR5th 33—§ 11, 62
State v. Hoffman, 196 Mont. 268, 639 P.2d 507 (1982)

118 ALR5th 253—§ 16
State v. Hoffman, 224 Neb. 830, 401 N.W.2d 683 (1987)

9 ALR6th 633—§ 13, 25
13 ALR6th 603—§ 10, 40

State v. Hoffman, 290 N.J. Super. 588, 676 A.2d 565 (App. Div. 1996)

102 ALR5th 327—§ 7
State v. Hoffman, 745 So. 2d 985 (Fla. Dist. Ct. App. 2d Dist. 1999)

113 ALR5th 597—§ 4
State v. Hoffman, 768 So. 2d 542 (La. 2000)

31 ALR5th 704—§ 7
State v. Hoffman, 2003 MT 26, 314 Mont. 155, 64 P.3d 1013 (2003)

9 ALR6th 1—§ 17
State v. Hoffman, 2009 WL 1752241 (Minn. Ct. App. 2009)

92 ALR6th 171—§ 5
State v. Hoffner, 102 Ohio St. 3d 358, 2004-Ohio-3430, 811 N.E.2d 48 (2004)

29 ALR6th 1—§ 10
State v. Hoffpauir, 355 So. 2d 929 (La. 1978)

9 ALR6th 1—§ 7
State v. Hofmann, 895 S.W.2d 108 (Mo. Ct. App. W.D. 1995)

1 ALR6th 549—§ 16
State v. Hogan, 117 La. 863, 42 So. 352 (1906)

96 ALR5th 523—§ 5
State v. Hogan, 144 N.J. 216, 676 A.2d 533, 49 A.L.R.5th 863 (1996)

49 ALR5th 639—§ 2, 4
State v. Hogan, 297 Minn. 430, 212 N.W.2d 664 (1973)

30 ALR6th 103—§ 58
State v. Hogan, 748 S.W.2d 766 (Mo. Ct. App. E.D. 1988)

65 ALR6th 537—§ 4
State v. Hogg, 118 N.H. 262, 385 A.2d 844 (1978)

97 ALR5th 201—§ 3, 4
State v. Hogg, 2013 WL 1619392 (Tenn. Crim. App. 2013)

94 ALR6th 525—§ 9
State v. Hohensee, 650 S.W.2d 268 (Mo. App. 1982)

18 ALR5th 1—§ 2, 3, 22, 24, 35

For assistance, call 1-800-328-4880

State v. Hohler, 543 A.2d 364, 15 Media
L. R. 1611 (Me. 1988)
60 ALR5th 75—§ 6

State v. Hohman, 136 Vt. 341, 392 A.2d
935 (1978)
32 ALR6th 1—§ 10

State v. Hoimes, 214 N.J. Super. 195,
518 A.2d 773 (App. Div. 1986)
71 ALR6th 335—§ 10, 12

State v. Hoke, 72 Wash. App. 869, 866
P.2d 670 (Div. 1 1994)
69 ALR6th 275—§ 11, 12, 20

State v. Hokenson, 96 Idaho 283, 527
P.2d 487 (1974)
7 ALR5th 758—§ 10

State v. Holbron, 65 Haw. 152, 648 P.2d
194 (1982)
62 ALR6th 413—§ 39

State v. Holbron, 65 Hawaii 152, 648
P.2d 194 (1982)
59 ALR5th 615—§ 3, 4, 12

State v. Holbrook, 274 S.C. 4, 260
S.E.2d 181 (1979)
51 ALR6th 1—§ 19

State v. Holbrook, 2009 WL 406818
(Del. Super. Ct. 2009)
99 ALR6th 295—§ 8

State v. Holcomb, 178 W. Va. 455, 360
S.E.2d 232 (1987)
70 ALR5th 533—§ 4

State v. Holcomb, 627 So. 2d 127, 18
FLW D 2539 (Fla. App. D5 1993)
29 ALR5th 59—§ 34

State v. Holcomb, 956 S.W.2d 286, 64
A.L.R.5th 901 (Mo. Ct. App. W.D.
1997)
64 ALR5th 671—§ 3, 4

State v. Holcombe, 187 S.W.3d 496
(Tex. Crim. App. 2006)
26 ALR6th 659—§ 42

State v. Holcombe, 2004 WL 869074
(Tex. App. Fort Worth 2004)
122 ALR5th 593—§ 8, 9

State v. Holden, 126 Idaho 755, 890 P.2d
341 (Ct. App. 1995)
93 ALR5th 527—§ 11

State v. Holden, 964 P.2d 318 (Utah Ct.
App. 1998)
40 ALR5th 113—§ 3
91 ALR5th 585—§ 6

State v. Holder, 76 Miss. 158, 23 So. 643
(1898)
87 ALR6th 633—§ 8

State v. Holder, 176 N.C. App. 408, 626
S.E.2d 876 (2006)
26 ALR6th 511—§ 27

State v. Holder, 331 N.C. 462, 418
S.E.2d 197 (1992)
57 ALR5th 141—§ 3
79 ALR5th 33—§ 73

State v. Holder, 1999 WL 61055 (Tenn.
Crim. App. 1999)
73 ALR5th 383—§ 5

State v. Holderness, 293 N.W.2d 226
(Iowa 1980)
116 ALR5th 373—§ 3, 12

State v. Holderness, 301 N.W.2d 733
(Iowa 1981)
39 ALR5th 283—§ 10, 59

State v. Holdren, 2003-Ohio-6789, 2003
WL 22950039 (Ohio Ct. App. 5th
Dist. Licking County 2003)
70 ALR6th 1—§ 5

State v. Holdren, 2004-Ohio-3439, 2004
WL 1465744 (Ohio Ct. App. 5th
Dist. Licking County 2004)
70 ALR6th 1—§ 5

State v. Holecek, 260 Neb. 976, 621
N.W.2d 100 (2000)
92 ALR5th 35—§ 25

State v. Holesapple, 92 W. Va. 645, 115
S.E. 794 (1923)
97 ALR5th 201—§ 3

State v. Holguin, 870 P.2d 407, 138
Ariz. Adv. Rep. 5 (Ariz. App. 1993)
15 ALR5th 391—§ 15

State v. Holland, 30 Wash. App. 366,
635 P.2d 142 (1981)
37 ALR5th 703—§ 3

State v. Holland, 81 P.3d 1275 (Kan. Ct.
App. 2004)
122 ALR5th 439—§ 3

State v. Holland, 141 Kan. 307, 40 P.2d
469 (1935)

107 ALR5th 567—§ 10

State v. Holland, 147 Ariz. 453, 711 P.2d 592 (1985)

96 ALR5th 327—§ 3

State v. Holland, 261 S.C. 488, 201 S.E.2d 118 (1973)

16 ALR6th 329—§ 7

24 ALR6th 591—§ 6

State v. Holland, 328 N.J. Super. 1, 744 A.2d 656 (App. Div. 2000)

122 ALR5th 439—§ 7

79 ALR6th 1—§ 40

State v. Holland, 544 So. 2d 461 (La. Ct. App. 2d Cir. 1989)

57 ALR5th 141—§ 11

State v. Holland, 1997 ME 42, 691 A.2d 196 (Me. 1997)

82 ALR6th 317—§ 4

State v. Holland, 2002-Ohio-2927, 2002 WL 1332500 (Ohio Ct. App. 2d Dist. Montgomery County 2002)

73 ALR6th 1—§ 7

State v. Holland Plastics Co., 111 Wis. 2d 497, 331 N.W.2d 320 (1983)

33 ALR5th 1—§ 10

State v. Holle, 202 Kan. 592, 451 P.2d 237 (1969)

68 ALR6th 527—§ 37

State v. Holleman, 2008 WL 3919361 (Ariz. Ct. App. Div. 2 2008)

99 ALR6th 295—§ 13

State v. Hollenback, 212 Ariz. 12, 126 P.3d 159 (Ct. App. Div. 2 2005)

35 ALR6th 361—§ 16, 20

State v. Hollensbe, 720 S.W.2d 14 (Mo. App. 1986)

5 ALR5th 243—§ 6

State v. Holley, 82 Md. App. 381, 571 A.2d 892 (1990)

70 ALR6th 361—§ 7

State v. Holliday, 745 N.W.2d 556 (Minn. 2008)

30 ALR6th 1—§ 3

State v. Hollie, 416 So. 2d 542 (La. 1982)

6 ALR5th 733—§ 2, 12

State v. Hollingsworth, 78 N.C. App. 578, 337 S.E.2d 674 (1985)

38 ALR5th 433—§ 31

State v. Hollingsworth, 160 Wis. 2d 883, 467 N.W.2d 555 (App. 1991)

54 ALR5th 575—§ 14

State v. Hollingsworth, 1994 WL 142491 (Ohio Ct. App. 12th Dist. Warren County 1994)

84 ALR6th 293—§ 33

State v. Hollins, 310 N.W.2d 216 (Iowa 1981)

7 ALR5th 263—§ 4

State v. Hollins, 2002 WL 863310 (Minn. Ct. App. 2002)

34 ALR6th 1—§ 9

State v. Hollis, 98 Ohio App. 3d 549, 649 N.E.2d 11 (11th Dist. Lake County 1994)

111 ALR5th 239—§ 6, 11

State v. Hollis, 214 Wis. 2d 591, 571 N.W.2d 924 (Ct. App. 1997)

99 ALR6th 295—§ 5

State v. Hollman, 232 S.C. 489, 102 S.E.2d 873 (1958)

70 ALR5th 587—§ 3

State v. Hollobaugh, 297 A.2d 395 (Del. Super. Ct. 1972)

52 ALR5th 655—§ 2, 5

State v. Holloman, 240 Kan. 589, 731 P.2d 294 (1987)

39 ALR5th 283—§ 4, 66

State v. Holloran, 140 N.H. 563, 669 A.2d 800 (1995)

92 ALR6th 295—§ 12

96 ALR6th 355—§ 9, 25, 37

State v. Holloway, 38 Ohio St. 3d 239, 527 N.E.2d 831 (1988)

20 ALR5th 177—§ 3, 8, 10

State v. Holloway, 129 Ohio App. 3d 790, 719 N.E.2d 70 (10th Dist. Franklin County 1998)

47 ALR5th 259—§ 4

State v. Holloway, 274 So. 2d 699 (La. 1973)

55 ALR6th 157—§ 33

State v. Holloway, 877 S.W.2d 692 (Mo. App. 1994)

For assistance, call 1-800-328-4880

20 ALR5th 398—§ 29
47 ALR5th 259—§ 2, 3, 13, 21
State v. Holloway, 886 S.W.2d 482 (Tex. App. Houston 1st Dist. 1994)
75 ALR5th 295—§ 32
State v. Holloway, 992 S.W.2d 886 (Mo. Ct. App. S.D. 1999)
66 ALR5th 397—§ 12
State v. Holloway, 2003-Ohio-3298, 2003 WL 21455103 (Ohio Ct. App. 10th Dist. Franklin County 2003)
7 ALR6th 233—§ 6
State v. Holloway, 2005-Ohio-4277, 2005 WL 1983960 (Ohio Ct. App. 10th Dist. Franklin County 2005)
26 ALR6th 511—§ 35
State v. Holloway, 2005 WL 2363041 (N.J. Super. Ct. App. Div. 2005)
79 ALR6th 1—§ 13, 55
State v. Holly, 350 N.W.2d 387 (Minn. Ct. App. 1984)
55 ALR6th 157—§ 4, 69
State v. Holly, 2009-NMSC-004, 145 N.M. 513, 201 P.3d 844, 55 A.L.R.6th 687 (2009)
55 ALR6th 157—§ 4, 21, 93
State v. Holm, 67 Wyo. 360, 224 P.2d 500 (1950)
39 ALR6th 257—§ 23, 26, 42
40 ALR6th 1—§ 6, 11
State v. Holm, 195 Ariz. 42, 985 P.2d 527 (Ct. App. Div. 2 1998)
57 ALR6th 313—§ 8
State v. Holm, 2006 UT 31, 137 P.3d 726, 22 A.L.R.6th 665 (Utah 2006)
22 ALR6th 1—§ 4, 6, 8 to 11
26 ALR6th 659—§ 40
State v. Holman, 58 Wash. 2d 754, 364 P.2d 921 (1961)
29 ALR5th 59—§ 7
State v. Holman, 109 Idaho 382, 707 P.2d 493 (App. 1985)
41 ALR5th 171—§ 2, 26, 58, 72
State v. Holman, 221 Neb. 730, 380 N.W.2d 304 (1986)
56 ALR6th 323—§ 8
State v. Holman, 229 Neb. 57, 424 N.W.2d 627 (1988)

41 ALR5th 171—§ 12
State v. Holman, 353 N.C. 174, 540 S.E.2d 18 (2000)
110 ALR5th 1—§ 3, 11, 14, 15
State v. Holmberg, 194 Neb. 337, 231 N.W.2d 672 (1975)
114 ALR5th 173—§ 7
State v. Holmberg, 449 N.W.2d 376 (Iowa 1989)
15 ALR5th 391—§ 9
State v. Holmberg, 545 N.W.2d 65 (Minn. Ct. App. 1996)
20 ALR6th 161—§ 3
21 ALR6th 425—§ 3
23 ALR6th 573—§ 11
State v. Holmberg, 1991 WL 156631 (Minn. Ct. App. 1991)
73 ALR5th 383—§ 5
State v. Holmes, 30 Ohio St. 3d 20, 506 N.E.2d 204 (1987)
3 ALR6th 269—§ 5, 8
State v. Holmes, 77 Ohio App. 3d 582, 602 N.E.2d 1197 (11th Dist. Ashtabula County 1991)
27 ALR6th 183—§ 15, 17, 33
State v. Holmes, 106 Wis. 2d 31, 315 N.W.2d 703 (1982)
91 ALR5th 437—§ 3
State v. Holmes, 107 Wash. App. 1019, 2001 WL 828515 (Div. 1 2001)
26 ALR6th 511—§ 25
State v. Holmes, 108 Wash. App. 511, 31 P.3d 716 (Div. 1 2001)
15 ALR6th 515—§ 33
State v. Holmes, 142 N.C. App. 614, 544 S.E.2d 18, 7 A.L.R.6th 773 (2001)
7 ALR6th 135—§ 21
7 ALR6th 169—§ 5
State v. Holmes, 221 Neb. 629, 379 N.W.2d 765 (1986)
92 ALR5th 35—§ 22
State v. Holmes, 278 Kan. 603, 102 P.3d 406 (2004)
9 ALR6th 1—§ 17
State v. Holmes, 330 N.C. 826, 412 S.E.2d 660 (1992)
23 ALR6th 1—§ 5, 16

State v. Holmes, 497 So. 2d 5 (La. App. 4th Cir. 1986)
7 ALR5th 263—§ 5
State v. Holmes, 622 S.W.2d 358 (Mo. App. 1981)
39 ALR5th 283—§ 4, 31
State v. Holmes, 643 S.W.2d 282 (Mo. Ct. App. W.D. 1982)
37 ALR6th 357—§ 29
State v. Holmes, 995 S.W.2d 135 (Tenn. Crim. App. 1998)
39 ALR5th 283—§ 75
97 ALR5th 201—§ 3
State v. Holmgren, 229 Wis. 2d 358, 599 N.W.2d 876 (Ct. App. 1999)
15 ALR5th 391—§ 45
State v. Holsclaw, 42 N.C. App. 696, 257 S.E.2d 650 (1979)
50 ALR5th 467—§ 9
State v. Holsinger, 115 Ariz. 271, 564 P.2d 1238 (1977)
12 ALR6th 267—§ 4
State v. Holstead, 354 So. 2d 493 (La. 1977)
42 ALR5th 291—§ 10
State v. Holstine, 260 Mont. 310, 860 P.2d 110 (1993)
106 ALR5th 397—§ 4
State v. Holston, 518 S.E.2d 216 (N.C. Ct. App. 1999)
38 ALR5th 433—§ 41
State v. Holt, 56 Wash. App. 99, 783 P.2d 87 (1989)
13 ALR5th 567—§ 3
State v. Holt, 119 Ohio Misc. 2d 1, 2002-Ohio-3345, 772 N.E.2d 203 (Mun. Ct. 2002)
28 ALR6th 505—§ 9
State v. Holt, 132 Ohio App. 3d 601, 725 N.E.2d 1155 (1st Dist. Hamilton County 1997)
12 ALR6th 267—§ 13
38 ALR6th 97—§ 28
State v. Holt, 255 Kan. 416, 874 P.2d 1183 (1994)
91 ALR5th 343—§ 14
State v. Holt, 603 S.W.2d 698 (Mo. App. 1980)

42 ALR5th 581—§ 16
State v. Holt, 695 S.W.2d 474 (Mo. Ct. App. E.D. 1985)
103 ALR6th 347—§ 6, 13
State v. Holt, 1997 WL 677985 (Ohio Ct. App. 10th Dist. Franklin County 1997)
92 ALR6th 171—§ 4
State v. Holt, 2006 MT 151, 332 Mont. 426, 139 P.3d 819 (2006)
46 ALR6th 241—§ 10
State v. Holt, 2010 UT App 138, 233 P.3d 828 (Utah Ct. App. 2010)
63 ALR6th 351—§ 3
State v. Holtan, 205 Neb. 314, 287 N.W.2d 671 (1980)
72 ALR5th 109—§ 5
State v. Holtcamp, 614 S.W.2d 389, 20 A.L.R.4th 813 (Tenn. Crim. App. 1980)
84 ALR5th 487—§ 22
State v. Holton, 2008 WL 482543 (N.J. Super. Ct. App. Div. 2008)
69 ALR6th 579—§ 11
State v. Holway, 2002 SD 50, 644 N.W.2d 624, 23 A.L.R.6th 879 (S.D. 2002)
23 ALR6th 307—§ 5, 8, 26, 35
State v. Holyoak, 49 Wash. App. 691, 745 P.2d 515 (Div. 3 1987)
73 ALR5th 383—§ 6, 8
State v. Homan, 89 Ohio St. 3d 421, 2000-Ohio-212, 732 N.E.2d 952 (2000)
117 ALR5th 491—§ 2
State v. Home Ins. Co. of New York, 59 Neb. 524, 81 N.W. 443 (1900)
88 ALR6th 533—§ 11
State v. Homeside Lending, Inc., 175 Vt. 239, 2003 VT 17, 826 A.2d 997 (2003)
50 ALR6th 281—§ 9
60 ALR6th 295—§ 34
State v. Honaker, 193 W. Va. 51, 454 S.E.2d 96 (1994)
32 ALR6th 1—§ 9
State v. Honda, 387 So. 2d 219 (Ala. Civ. App. 1980)

107 ALR5th 567—§ 10

State v. Honey, 2005 MT 107, 327 Mont. 49, 112 P.3d 983 (2005)

29 ALR6th 1—§ 18

58 ALR6th 439—§ 21

State v. Hong, 62 Haw. 83, 611 P.2d 595 (1980)

58 ALR6th 215—§ 19

State v. Honig, 78 Mo. 249 (1883)

29 ALR5th 59—§ 7

State v. Honomichl, 410 N.W.2d 544 (S.D. 1987)

16 ALR6th 329—§ 11

24 ALR6th 591—§ 9, 13

State v. Honore, 31 So. 3d 485 (La. Ct. App. 5th Cir. 2010)

66 ALR6th 83—§ 5

State v. Honore, 564 So. 2d 345 (La. App. 5th Cir. 1990)

13 ALR5th 567—§ 3, 4

State v. Ho'o, 99 N.M. 140, 654 P.2d 1040 (Ct. App. 1982)

24 ALR6th 747—§ 30

State v. Hood, 133 Wash. App. 1045, 2006 WL 1918737 (Div. 2 2006)

103 ALR6th 507—§ 33

State v. Hood, 242 Kan. 115, 744 P.2d 816 (1987)

39 ALR5th 283—§ 4, 23, 41

State v. Hooghe, 2005-Ohio-5620, 2005 WL 2713542 (Ohio Ct. App. 12th Dist. Warren County 2005)

78 ALR6th 599—§ 10

State v. Hookfin, 602 So. 2d 757 (La. Ct. App. 4th Cir. 1992)

87 ALR5th 597—§ 13

State v. Hookom, 474 N.W.2d 624 (Minn. Ct. App. 1991)

124 ALR5th 1—§ 5

State v. Hooks, 30 Conn. App. 232, 619 A.2d 1151 (1993)

5 ALR5th 243—§ 6, 7

State v. Hooks, 2006-Ohio-1272, 2006 WL 689041 (Ohio Ct. App. 12th Dist. Butler County 2006)

26 ALR6th 511—§ 19

State v. Hooper, 10 Ohio App. 2d 229, 39 Ohio Op. 2d 435, 227 N.E.2d 414 (7th Dist. Monroe County 1966)

89 ALR6th 565—§ 5

State v. Hooper, 25 Ohio St. 2d 59, 54 Ohio Op. 2d 194, 267 N.E.2d 285 (1971)

89 ALR6th 565—§ 13

State v. Hooper, 100 Wash. App. 179, 997 P.2d 936 (Div. 1 2000)

73 ALR5th 383—§ 16

State v. Hooper, 176 P.3d 911 (Idaho 2007)

30 ALR6th 1—§ 6

State v. Hoopii, 68 Hawaii 246, 710 P.2d 1193 (1985)

39 ALR5th 283—§ 70

State v. Hoosier, 2005 WL 2256101 (Tenn. Crim. App. 2005)

26 ALR6th 511—§ 22

State v. Hoover, 138 Idaho 414, 64 P.3d 340 (Ct. App. 2003)

3 ALR6th 269—§ 25

State v. Hopkins, 113 Wash. App. 954, 55 P.3d 691 (Div. 3 2002)

79 ALR6th 1—§ 8, 44

State v. Hopkins, 134 Wash. App. 780, 142 P.3d 1104 (Div. 2 2006)

30 ALR6th 1—§ 4

State v. Hopkins, 192 W. Va. 483, 453 S.E.2d 317 (1994)

51 ALR6th 219—§ 4

State v. Hopkins, 196 Wis. 2d 36, 538 N.W.2d 543 (1995)

15 ALR5th 391—§ 41

State v. Hopkins, 267 Wis. 2d 277, 2003 WI App 201, 670 N.W.2d 557 (Ct. App. 2003)

33 ALR6th 407—§ 6

34 ALR6th 1—§ 11

State v. Hopkins, 500 S.W.2d 264 (Mo. App. 1973)

45 ALR5th 531—§ 3

State v. Hopkins, 526 A.2d 945 (Me. 1987)

92 ALR5th 35—§ 10

For assistance, call 1-800-328-4880

State v. Hopkins, 573 S.W.2d 744 (Mo. Ct. App. 1978)
97 ALR5th 537—§ 69
State v. Hopkins, 626 So. 2d 820 (La. Ct. App. 2d Cir. 1993)
98 ALR6th 455—§ 22
State v. Hopkins, 692 So. 2d 538 (La. Ct. App. 3d Cir. 1997)
5 ALR5th 243—§ 45
State v. Hopkins, 2003 WI App 22, 259 Wis. 2d 933, 657 N.W.2d 439 (Ct. App. 2002)
99 ALR6th 295—§ 5
State v. Hopkirk, 84 Mo. 278, 1884 WL 9553 (1884)
96 ALR5th 523—§ 5
State v. Hopper, 2009-Ohio-2711, 2009 WL 1623105 (Ohio Ct. App. 8th Dist. Cuyahoga County 2009)
55 ALR6th 1—§ 7, 28
State v. Hopson, 112 Ariz. 497, 543 P.2d 1126 (1975)
70 ALR5th 533—§ 8
State v. Hopson, 144 P.3d 782 (Kan. Ct. App. 2006)
26 ALR6th 511—§ 25
State v. Hopson, 2013 WL 6499536 (Ariz. Ct. App. Div. 2 2013)
97 ALR6th 263—§ 11
State v. Horan, 21 Wis. 2d 66, 123 N.W.2d 488, 98 A.L.R.2d 1227 (1963)
80 ALR5th 597—§ 2, 15
State v. Horn, 8 Hawaii App. 167, 796 P.2d 503 (1990)
26 ALR5th 603—§ 4
State v. Horn, 15 Kan. App. 2d 365, 808 P.2d 438 (1991)
43 ALR5th 1—§ 13
State v. Horn, 58 Hawaii 252, 566 P.2d 1378 (1977)
54 ALR5th 141—§ 3 to 5, 10
State v. Horn, 101 Idaho 192, 610 P.2d 551 (1980)
39 ALR5th 283—§ 4, 33
State v. Horn, 126 Wis. 2d 447, 377 N.W.2d 176 (App. 1985)
3 ALR5th 521—§ 4, 5

State v. Horn, 278 Kan. 24, 91 P.3d 517 (2004)
3 ALR6th 543—§ 12
State v. Horn, 1991 WL 230170 (Minn. Ct. App. 1991)
73 ALR5th 383—§ 5
State v. Hornback, 73 Wash. App. 738, 871 P.2d 1075 (Div. 1 1994)
60 ALR5th 1—§ 8
45 ALR6th 643—§ 11
State v. Hornbeak, 221 Kan. 397, 559 P.2d 385 (1977)
93 ALR5th 527—§ 20
State v. Horne, 209 N.C. 725, 184 S.E. 470 (1935)
24 ALR5th 465—§ 60
State v. Horne, 215 Kan. 448, 524 P.2d 697 (1974)
36 ALR5th 255—§ 29
State v. Horne, 282 S.C. 444, 319 S.E.2d 703 (1984)
64 ALR5th 671—§ 3
State v. Horne, 376 N.J. Super. 201, 869 A.2d 955 (App. Div. 2005)
57 ALR6th 313—§ 8
State v. Horne, 622 S.W.2d 956 (Mo. 1981)
33 ALR6th 407—§ 55, 56
State v. Horner, 310 N.C. 274, 311 S.E.2d 281 (1984)
101 ALR6th 299—§ 4
State v. Horner, 1994 WL 45869 (Ohio App. Ashland Co. 1994)
52 ALR5th 655—§ 3
State v. Horngren, 238 Wis. 2d 347, 2000 WI App 177, 617 N.W.2d 508 (Ct. App. 2000)
58 ALR6th 499—§ 41
State v. Horngren, 2000 WI App 177, 238 Wis. 2d 347, 617 N.W.2d 508 (Ct. App. 2000)
79 ALR6th 1—§ 21, 86
State v. Horsey, 676 S.W.2d 847 (Mo. Ct. App. S.D. 1984)
113 ALR5th 517—§ 6
99 ALR6th 113—§ 4
State v. Horsley, 169 Or. App. 438

26 ALR5th 603—§ 3, 6
State v. Horstman, 829 S.W.2d 903 (Tex. App. Fort Worth 1992)
89 ALR5th 629—§ 9, 11
State v. Hortman, 207 Neb. 393, 299 N.W.2d 187 (1980)
73 ALR5th 383—§ 22
State v. Horton, 28 So. 3d 370 (La. Ct. App. 5th Cir. 2009)
56 ALR6th 185—§ 39
State v. Horton, 86 Or. App. 199, 738 P.2d 609 (1987)
97 ALR6th 653—§ 29
State v. Horton, 136 Wash. App. 29, 146 P.3d 1227 (Div. 3 2006)
71 ALR6th 1—§ 4
State v. Horton, 207 N.J. Super. 555, 504 A.2d 801 (Law Div. 1985)
103 ALR5th 463—§ 3
State v. Horton, 2001 MT 100, 25 P.3d 886 (Mont. 2001)
92 ALR5th 35—§ 18
State v. Horty, 122 Wash. App. 1047, 2004 WL 1689764 (Div. 3 2004)
78 ALR6th 297—§ 46, 63
State v. Horwedel, 66 Or. App. 400, 674 P.2d 623 (1984)
113 ALR5th 517—§ 8
State v. Hoskins, 14 P.3d 997 (Ariz. 2000)
22 ALR5th 1—§ 3
State v. Hoskins, 36 N.C. App. 92, 242 S.E.2d 900 (1978)
104 ALR5th 357—§ 6
54 ALR6th 429—§ 11
State v. Hoskins, 65 P.3d 953 (Ariz. 2003)
110 ALR5th 1—§ 18
State v. Hoskins, 199 Ariz. 127, 14 P.3d 997 (2000)
110 ALR5th 1—§ 2, 20
State v. Hoskins, 292 Minn. 111, 193 N.W.2d 802 (1972)
96 ALR5th 523—§ 3
30 ALR6th 103—§ 7, 16, 26

State v. Hoskins, 2002-Ohio-3451, 2002 WL 1453811 (Ohio Ct. App. 8th Dist. Cuyahoga County 2002)
92 ALR6th 171—§ 18
State v. Hoskinson, 1999 WL 254409 (Ohio Ct. App. 5th Dist. Licking County 1999)
78 ALR5th 489—§ 10
State v. Hosto-Worthy, 877 S.W.2d 150 (Mo. Ct. App. E.D. 1994)
28 ALR6th 505—§ 8
State v. Hosty, 944 So. 2d 255 (Fla. 2006)
30 ALR6th 1—§ 3, 6
State v. Hoth, 50 Conn. App. 77, 718 A.2d 28 (1998)
58 ALR6th 499—§ 52
State v. Hotoph, 750 So. 2d 1036 (La. Ct. App. 5th Cir. 1999)
101 ALR5th 187—§ 8
State v. Houchin, 149 Mont. 503, 428 P.2d 971 (1967)
23 ALR6th 1—§ 15
State v. Hough, 48 Ohio App. 2d 304, 2 Ohio Op. 3d 282, 357 N.E.2d 412 (1st Dist. Hamilton County 1976)
55 ALR6th 157—§ 117
State v. Houghton, 165 Wash. 220, 4 P.2d 1110 (1931)
114 ALR5th 1—§ 16, 18, 24, 30, 31
State v. Houghton, 272 N.W.2d 788, 2 A.L.R.4th 318 (S.D. 1978)
86 ALR5th 59—§ 3 to 5
State v. Houle, 1998 M.T. 235, 966 P.2d 147 (Mont. 1998)
5 ALR5th 243—§ 19
State v. Houlf, 27 Ariz. App. 633, 557 P.2d 565 (Div. 2 1976)
114 ALR5th 173—§ 9
State v. House, 260 Or. 138, 489 P.2d 381 (1971)
118 ALR5th 253—§ 11
State v. House, 340 N.C. 187, 456 S.E.2d 292 (1995)
37 ALR5th 515—§ 11
State v. House, 481 A.2d 1129 (Me. 1984)
56 ALR6th 185—§ 37

State v. House, 1991 WL 42587 (Minn. Ct. App. 1991)
73 ALR5th 383—§ 29

State v. House, 2001 WL 1243934 (Ohio Ct. App. 8th Dist. Cuyahoga County 2001)
27 ALR6th 183—§ 17, 40

State v. House, 2007 WI 79, 302 Wis. 2d 1, 734 N.W.2d 140 (2007)
87 ALR6th 1—§ 31

State v. Houser, 122 Wis. 534, 100 N.W. 964 (1904)
28 ALR6th 175—§ 13

State v. Houser, 234 Neb. 310, 450 N.W.2d 697 (1990)
32 ALR6th 1—§ 8

State v. Houser, 241 Neb. 525, 490 N.W.2d 168 (1992)
32 ALR6th 1—§ 8

State v. Houser, 364 So. 2d 823 (Fla. Dist. Ct. App. 2d Dist. 1978)
103 ALR5th 463—§ 3

State v. Housler, 193 S.W.3d 476 (Tenn. 2006)
20 ALR6th 479—§ 3

State v. Houston, 197 W. Va. 215, 475 S.E.2d 307 (1996)
18 ALR5th 1—§ 3

State v. Houston, 211 N.W.2d 598 (Iowa 1973)
29 ALR5th 59—§ 6, 10

State v. Houston, 328 S.W.3d 867 (Tenn. Crim. App. 2010)
103 ALR6th 137—§ 15, 19

State v. Houston, 702 N.W.2d 268 (Minn. 2005)
26 ALR6th 511—§ 3

State v. Houston, 2000 UT App 242, 9 P.3d 188 (Utah Ct. App. 2000)
92 ALR5th 35—§ 3

State v. Houston, 2000 WL 1793088 (Tenn. Crim. App. 2000)
110 ALR5th 329—§ 5, 6

State v. Houston, 2002-Ohio-329, 2002 WL 199903 (Ohio Ct. App. 8th Dist. Cuyahoga County 2002)
69 ALR6th 1—§ 10

State v. Houston Lighting & Power Co., 609 S.W.2d 263 (Tex. Civ. App. Corpus Christi 1980)
114 ALR5th 561—§ 13

State v. Hout, 2003-Ohio-5088, 2003 WL 22213598 (Ohio Ct. App. 1st Dist. Hamilton County 2003)
24 ALR6th 1—§ 21

State v. Houx, 109 Mo. 654, 19 S.W. 35 (1892)
46 ALR5th 499—§ 3

State v. Hovater, 37 Or. App. 557, 588 P.2d 56 (1978)
99 ALR5th 557—§ 3, 12

State v. Howard, 56 N.C. App. 41, 286 S.E.2d 853 (1982)
68 ALR5th 343—§ 3

State v. Howard, 163 Ariz. 47, 785 P.2d 1235, 44 Ariz. Adv. Rep. 47 (App. 1989)
15 ALR5th 391—§ 30

State v. Howard, 168 Ariz. 458, 815 P.2d 5, 91 Ariz. Adv. Rep. 52 (App. 1991)
15 ALR5th 391—§ 2, 5

State v. Howard, 172 S.W.3d 190 (Tex. App. Dallas 2005)
20 ALR6th 161—§ 4
23 ALR6th 573—§ 14

State v. Howard, 224 Kan. 208, 579 P.2d 702 (1978)
36 ALR5th 255—§ 24

State v. Howard, 243 Kan. 699, 763 P.2d 607 (1988)
39 ALR5th 283—§ 4, 41

State v. Howard, 246 Wis. 2d 475, 2001 WI App 137, 630 N.W.2d 244 (Ct. App. 2001)
9 ALR6th 541—§ 3, 13

State v. Howard, 264 Wis. 2d 893, 2003 WI App 111, 664 N.W.2d 127 (Ct. App. 2003)
9 ALR6th 541—§ 13

State v. Howard, 273 Wis. 2d 785, 2004 WI App 109, 680 N.W.2d 832 (Ct. App. 2004)
48 ALR6th 135—§ 5

State v. Howard, 295 S.C. 462, 369 S.E.2d 132 (1988)
19 ALR5th 351—§ 10

State v. Howard, 383 S.W.2d 701 (Mo. 1964)
55 ALR6th 157—§ 105

State v. Howard, 405 A.2d 206 (Me. 1979)
38 ALR5th 433—§ 47

State v. Howard, 443 So. 2d 632 (La. Ct. App. 3d Cir. 1983)
29 ALR6th 1—§ 4

State v. Howard, 449 S.W.2d 662 (Mo. 1970)
55 ALR6th 157—§ 94

State v. Howard, 588 A.2d 1203 (Me. 1991)
19 ALR6th 697—§ 4

State v. Howard, 624 So. 2d 1277 (La. App. 3d Cir. 1993)
5 ALR5th 243—§ 6, 10

State v. Howard, 626 So. 2d 459 (La. App. 3d Cir. 1993)
9 ALR5th 369—§ 15

State v. Howard, 1987 WL 17620 (Ohio Ct. App. 2d Dist. Clark County 1987)
19 ALR6th 697—§ 14

State v. Howard, 1990 WL 51765 (Tenn. Crim. App. 1990)
73 ALR5th 383—§ 5

State v. Howard, 1999 WL 129459 (Ohio Ct. App. 2d Dist. Clark County 1999)
95 ALR6th 1—§ 10, 28

State v. Howard, 2003-Ohio-5128, 2003 WL 22228699 (Ohio Ct. App. 3d Dist. Seneca County 2003)
33 ALR6th 407—§ 73

State v. Howe, 116 Wash. 2d 466, 805 P.2d 806, 17 A.L.R.5th 881 (1991)
17 ALR5th 111—§ 2 to 4

State v. Howe, 136 Vt. 53, 386 A.2d 1125 (1978)
1 ALR6th 657—§ 4

State v. Howe, 182 N.W.2d 658 (N.D. 1970)
41 ALR5th 171—§ 6, 12, 68, 75, 95, 110

State v. Howe, 1998 WL 226469 (Ohio Ct. App. 1st Dist. Hamilton County 1998)
78 ALR5th 489—§ 3

State v. Howell, 93 Or. App. 551, 763 P.2d 179 (1988)
112 ALR5th 429—§ 12

State v. Howell, 126 Wash. App. 1056, 2005 WL 827424 (Div. 1 2005)
47 ALR6th 107—§ 58

State v. Howell, 141 Wis. 2d 58, 414 N.W.2d 54 (Ct. App. 1987)
87 ALR5th 597—§ 5

State v. Howell, 223 Kan. 282, 573 P.2d 1003 (1977)
32 ALR6th 385—§ 5

State v. Howell, 354 N.W.2d 196 (S.D. 1984)
29 ALR5th 59—§ 14

State v. Howell, 1996 WL 55651 (Tenn. Cr App. 1996)
57 ALR5th 141—§ 3

State v. Howell, 2004-Ohio-2423, 2004 WL 1077527 (Ohio Ct. App. 2d Dist. Montgomery County 2004)
56 ALR6th 185—§ 39

State v. Howell, 2009-Ohio-3985, 2009 WL 2457035 (Ohio Ct. App. 5th Dist. Richland County 2009)
64 ALR6th 1—§ 7, 9, 11

State v. Howerton, 691 S.W.2d 516 (Mo. App. 1985)
5 ALR5th 243—§ 50

State v. Howland, 66 Wash. App. 586, 832 P.2d 1339 (1992)
22 ALR5th 1—§ 20

State v. Howland, 119 N.H. 413, 402 A.2d 188 (1979)
7 ALR5th 758—§ 17

State v. Howland, 124 Wash. App. 1023, 2004 WL 2667381 (Div. 3 2004)
70 ALR6th 361—§ 32

State v. Hoye, 635 So. 2d 1289 (La. Ct. App. 4th Cir. 1994)
97 ALR6th 653—§ 30

State v. Hoyle, 122 R.I. 45, 404 A.2d 69 (1979)
98 ALR6th 455—§ 12

State v. Hoyle, 325 N.C. 232, 382 S.E.2d 752 (1989)
28 ALR6th 505—§ 8

State v. Hoyt, 21 Wis. 2d 284, 128 N.W.2d 645 (1964)
58 ALR6th 499—§ 24

State v. Hoyt, 47 Conn. 518 (1880)
51 ALR5th 603—§ 3, 14

State v. Hoyt, 84 N.H. 38, 146 A. 170 (1929)
70 ALR5th 169—§ 8, 30

State v. H. Samuels Co., Inc., 60 Wis. 2d 631, 211 N.W.2d 417 (1973)
103 ALR5th 157—§ 3, 11

State v. Hubbard, 37 Wash. App. 137, 679 P.2d 391 (Div. 1 1984)
38 ALR6th 97—§ 19

State v. Hubbard, 103 Wash. 2d 570, 693 P.2d 718 (1985)
38 ALR6th 97—§ 19

State v. Hubbard, 150 Ohio App. 3d 623, 2002-Ohio-6904, 782 N.E.2d 674 (7th Dist. Jefferson County 2002)
3 ALR6th 269—§ 5, 8, 13, 28

State v. Hubbard, 328 So. 2d 465 (Fla. App. D2 1976)
34 ALR5th 125—§ 8

State v. Hubbard, 708 So. 2d 1099 (La. Ct. App. 5th Cir. 1998)
104 ALR5th 357—§ 3
54 ALR6th 429—§ 5, 22, 25, 26

State v. Hubbard, 861 P.2d 1053 (Utah Ct. App. 1993)
78 ALR6th 599—§ 4, 18

State v. Hubbard, 1993 WL 293323 (Ohio Ct. App. 1st Dist. Hamilton County 1993)
5 ALR6th 1—§ 51, 57, 61

State v. Hubbard, 2009-Ohio-5817, 2009 WL 3647082 (Ohio Ct. App. 8th Dist. Cuyahoga County 2009)
77 ALR6th 251—§ 5

State v. Hubbel, 286 Mont. 200, 951 P.2d 971 (1997)
76 ALR5th 563—§ 3

State v. Hubbel, 951 P.2d 971 (Mont. 1997)
60 ALR5th 1—§ 4

State v. Hubbs, 261 La. 173, 259 So. 2d 53 (1972)
65 ALR5th 407—§ 3, 16

State v. Hubbs, 268 N.W.2d 188 (Iowa 1978)
119 ALR5th 275—§ 13

State v. Huber, 10 Kan. App. 2d 560, 704 P.2d 1004 (1985)
19 ALR5th 470—§ 3, 12

State v. Huber, 555 N.W.2d 791 (N.D. 1996)
92 ALR6th 295—§ 3, 8, 9
96 ALR6th 355—§ 3

State v. Hubert, 2002 WL 47208 (Minn. Ct. App. 2002)
113 ALR5th 597—§ 3

State v. Huckabee, 41 Conn. App. 565, 677 A.2d 452 (1996)
5 ALR5th 243—§ 7

State v. Huckabee, 166 N.C. App. 281, 603 S.E.2d 169 (2004)
15 ALR6th 515—§ 2
79 ALR6th 1—§ 41

State v. Huckins, 66 Wash. App. 213, 836 P.2d 230 (1992)
42 ALR5th 291—§ 4, 10

State v. Hucks, 323 N.C. 574, 374 S.E.2d 240 (1988)
83 ALR6th 465—§ 4, 18, 21, 23, 68, 78

State v. Huddleston, 80 Wash. App. 916, 912 P.2d 1068 (1996)
5 ALR5th 243—§ 50, 51

State v. Huddleston, 412 A.2d 1148, 8 A.L.R.4th 113 (Del. Super. Ct. 1980)
20 ALR6th 161—§ 3, 4
21 ALR6th 425—§ 3
23 ALR6th 573—§ 4, 10

State v. Hudgins, 188 Wis. 2d 605, 526 N.W.2d 280 (App. 1994)
37 ALR5th 515—§ 24

State v. Hudgins, 400 So. 2d 889 (La. 1981)

18 ALR6th 1—§ 32
State v. Hudson, 11 N.C. App. 712, 182 S.E.2d 198 (1971)

68 ALR6th 527—§ 3
State v. Hudson, 56 N.C. App. 172, 288 S.E.2d 383 (1982)

55 ALR6th 391—§ 17
State v. Hudson, 111 N.H. 25, 274 A.2d 878 (1971)

72 ALR5th 1—§ 7
State v. Hudson, 124 Wash. 2d 107, 874 P.2d 160 (1994)

50 ALR5th 581—§ 2, 5, 7, 8
State v. Hudson, 137 P.3d 1093 (Kan. Ct. App. 2006)

26 ALR6th 511—§ 25
State v. Hudson, 253 La. 992, 221 So. 2d 484 (1969)

16 ALR6th 329—§ 4
24 ALR6th 591—§ 4
State v. Hudson, 281 N.W.2d 870 (Minn. 1979)

117 ALR5th 513—§ 31
State v. Hudson, 289 Wis. 2d 218, 2006 WI App 20, 709 N.W.2d 111 (Ct. App. 2005)

34 ALR6th 1—§ 9
State v. Hudson, 336 S.C. 237, 519 S.E.2d 577 (Ct. App. 1999)

36 ALR5th 161—§ 3
State v. Hudson, 345 N.C. 729, 483 S.E.2d 436 (1997)

47 ALR6th 107—§ 3
State v. Hudson, 358 Mo. 424, 215 S.W.2d 441 (1948)

104 ALR5th 357—§ 8
54 ALR6th 429—§ 13
State v. Hudson, 404 So. 2d 460 (La. 1981)

55 ALR5th 125—§ 3, 7
State v. Hudson, 470 A.2d 786 (Me. 1984)

15 ALR5th 391—§ 12
45 ALR6th 435—§ 3, 5, 17, 26, 33
State v. Hudson, 793 S.W.2d 872 (Mo. Ct. App. E.D. 1990)

108 ALR5th 593—§ 38

80 ALR6th 599—§ 8
State v. Hudson, 950 S.W.2d 543 (Mo. Ct. App. W.D. 1997)

54 ALR6th 429—§ 5, 9, 11
State v. Hudson, 1999 WL 333102 (Ohio Ct. App. 5th Dist. Coshocton County 1999)

85 ALR5th 187—§ 2, 10, 18
State v. Hudson, 2005 MT 142, 327 Mont. 286, 114 P.3d 210 (2005)

92 ALR6th 295—§ 12, 25
93 ALR6th 207—§ 26
94 ALR6th 191—§ 4
96 ALR6th 355—§ 24, 37
State v. Hudson County News Co., 35 N.J. 284, 173 A.2d 20 (1961)

13 ALR5th 567—§ 4
State v. Hudspeth, 22 Wash. App. 292, 593 P.2d 548 (Div. 2 1978)

93 ALR5th 527—§ 6
State v. Hudspeth, 1986 WL 3746 (Ohio Ct. App. 1st Dist. Hamilton County 1986)

70 ALR6th 361—§ 9
State v. Huerstel, 206 Ariz. 93, 75 P.3d 698 (2003)

42 ALR6th 237—§ 8
State v. Huerta, 285 Mont. 245, 947 P.2d 483 (1997)

38 ALR5th 433—§ 31
State v. Huertas, 51 Ohio St. 3d 22, 553 N.E.2d 1058 (1990)

16 ALR5th 152—§ 8
State v. Huff, 14 N.J. 240, 102 A.2d 8 (1954)

72 ALR5th 529—§ 2
State v. Huff, 33 Wash. App. 304, 654 P.2d 1211 (Div. 3 1982)

112 ALR5th 429—§ 13
State v. Huff, 125 N.M. 254, 1998-NMCA-075, 960 P.2d 342 (Ct. App. 1998)

110 ALR5th 329—§ 7
State v. Huff, 282 Neb. 78, 802 N.W.2d 77 (2011)

101 ALR6th 331—§ 9, 10
State v. Huff, 325 N.C. 1, 381 S.E.2d 635 (1989)

72 ALR5th 109—§ 3

State v. Huff, 392 So. 2d 1046 (La. 1980)

9 ALR6th 1—§ 4

State v. Huff, 654 P.2d 1211 (Wash. App. 1982)

43 ALR5th 1—§ 11

State v. Huff, 1999 WL 402222 (Ohio Ct. App. 4th Dist. Highland County 1999)

17 ALR6th 327—§ 34

State v. Huffman, 20 Ohio App. 2d 263, 49 Ohio Ops. 2d 357, 253 N.E.2d 812 (Hancock Co. 1969)

38 ALR5th 357—§ 15

State v. Huffman, 89 Mont. 194, 296 P. 789 (1931)

29 ALR5th 59—§ 3, 42

State v. Huffman, 542 N.W.2d 718 (N.D. 1996)

65 ALR5th 407—§ 2 to 4, 18

State v. Huffman, 607 S.W.2d 702 (Mo. Ct. App. E.D. 1980)

70 ALR5th 587—§ 8

State v. Hufford, 186 Wis. 2d 461, 522 N.W.2d 26 (App. 1994)

15 ALR5th 391—§ 16

State v. Huggins, 186 Neb. 704, 185 N.W.2d 849 (1971)

103 ALR6th 347—§ 26

State v. Huggins, 502 So. 2d 482 (Fla. Dist. Ct. App. 2d Dist. 1987)

11 ALR6th 237—§ 18

State v. Huggins, 659 P.2d 613 (Alaska Ct. App. 1982)

112 ALR5th 621—§ 3

State v. Hughbanks, 159 Ohio App. 3d 257, 2004-Ohio-6429, 823 N.E.2d 544 (1st Dist. Hamilton County 2004)

122 ALR5th 145—§ 17, 22

State v. Hughbanks, 2003-Ohio-187, 2003 WL 131937 (Ohio Ct. App. 1st Dist. Hamilton County 2003)

21 ALR6th 1—§ 4

State v. Hughes, 2 Conn. Cir. Ct. 75, 194 A.2d 722 (App. Div. 1963)

89 ALR6th 565—§ 13, 27, 35, 37

State v. Hughes, 20 Or. App. 493, 532 P.2d 818 (1975)

106 ALR5th 397—§ 10

State v. Hughes, 96 N.M. 606, 633 P.2d 714 (App. 1981)

7 ALR5th 263—§ 7

State v. Hughes, 106 Wash. 2d 176, 721 P.2d 902 (1986)

59 ALR5th 1—§ 4 to 6

State v. Hughes, 108 N.M. 143, 767 P.2d 382 (Ct. App. 1988)

89 ALR5th 629—§ 3

State v. Hughes, 114 N.C. App. 742, 443 S.E.2d 76 (1994)

38 ALR5th 433—§ 11

State v. Hughes, 189 Ariz. 62, 938 P.2d 457 (1997)

27 ALR6th 183—§ 40

State v. Hughes, 192 Ga. App. 46, 384 S.E.2d 682 (1989)

56 ALR6th 323—§ 4

State v. Hughes, 193 Ariz. 72, 969 P.2d 1184 (1998)

11 ALR5th 1—§ 17

State v. Hughes, 215 N.J. Super. 295, 521 A.2d 1295 (App. Div. 1986)

70 ALR5th 587—§ 13

State v. Hughes, 233 Wis. 2d 280, 2000 WI 24, 607 N.W.2d 621 (2000)

122 ALR5th 439—§ 3

State v. Hughes, 246 Kan. 607, 792 P.2d 1023 (1990)

94 ALR5th 497—§ 2, 6, 7

State v. Hughes, 336 S.C. 585, 521 S.E.2d 500 (1999)

79 ALR5th 33—§ 17

38 ALR6th 97—§ 29

98 ALR6th 455—§ 11

State v. Hughes, 587 So. 2d 31 (La. App. 2d Cir. 1991)

42 ALR5th 581—§ 7

State v. Hughes, 687 S.E.2d 710 (N.C. Ct. App. 2009)

57 ALR6th 1—§ 4, 18

State v. Hughes, 702 S.W.2d 864 (Mo. App. 1985)

50 ALR5th 703—§ 9

State v. Hughes, 944 S.W.2d 247 (Mo. Ct. App. W.D. 1997)
70 ALR5th 587—§ 25

State v. Hughes, 1988 WL 132698 (Tenn. Crim. App. 1988)
73 ALR5th 383—§ 20

State v. Hughes, 1992 WL 52473 (Ohio Ct. App. 2d Dist. Miami County 1992)
58 ALR6th 385—§ 20

State v. Hughes, 1998 WL 301730 (Tenn. Crim. App. 1998)
73 ALR5th 383—§ 6, 32

State v. Hughes, 1999 ND 24, 589 N.W.2d 912 (N.D. 1999)
50 ALR6th 455—§ 37

State v. Hughey, 2000 WL 313308 (S.C. 2000)
79 ALR5th 33—§ 28

State v. Hulbert, 265 Mont. 317, 877 P.2d 25 (1994)
112 ALR5th 429—§ 2, 10
114 ALR5th 235—§ 2

State v. Hulbert, 481 N.W.2d 329 (Iowa 1992)
40 ALR5th 113—§ 3
102 ALR5th 327—§ 8
24 ALR6th 1—§ 19

State v. Hulett, 595 S.W.2d 767 (Mo. Ct. App. W.D. 1980)
70 ALR5th 587—§ 19

State v. Hull, 68 Or. App. 817, 683 P.2d 157 (1984)
15 ALR5th 391—§ 45
92 ALR5th 35—§ 7

State v. Hull, 133 Ohio App. 3d 401, 728 N.E.2d 414 (12th Dist. Clermont County 1999)
5 ALR6th 1—§ 7, 23

State v. Hull, 158 Mont. 6, 487 P.2d 1314 (1971)
4 ALR5th 1—§ 4, 5

State v. Hullaby, 641 So. 2d 1094 (La. Ct. App. 2d Cir. 1994)
99 ALR6th 295—§ 5

State v. Hullum, 664 S.W.2d 314 (Tenn. Crim. App. 1983)

4 ALR6th 577—§ 4

State v. Hulsey, 3 Or. App. 64, 471 P.2d 812 (1970)
26 ALR5th 1—§ 3, 6

State v. Hults, 9 Wash. App. 297, 513 P.2d 89 (1973)
45 ALR5th 1—§ 3, 5, 12, 23

State v. Human, 56 Ohio Misc. 5, 10 Ohio Op. 3d 164, 381 N.E.2d 969 (Mun. Ct. 1978)
102 ALR5th 525—§ 5

State v. Human Rights Com'n, 178 Ill. App. 3d 1033, 128 Ill. Dec. 141, 534 N.E.2d 161 (4th Dist. 1989)
93 ALR5th 47—§ 3
94 ALR5th 1—§ 3

State v. Hummel, 483 N.W.2d 68 (Minn. 1992)
37 ALR5th 515—§ 19
55 ALR5th 125—§ 3

State v. Hummell, 228 N.W.2d 77 (Iowa 1975)
50 ALR5th 467—§ 5

State v. Hummert, 188 Ariz. 119, 933 P.2d 1187 (1997)
90 ALR5th 453—§ 28

State v. Humphrey, 22 Conn. Supp. 317, 1 Conn. Cir. 1, 171 A.2d 201 (1961)
26 ALR5th 1—§ 4

State v. Humphrey, 23 Ariz. App. 204, 531 P.2d 1142 (Div. 1 1975)
9 ALR6th 1—§ 20

State v. Humphrey, 129 N.H. 654, 531 A.2d 329 (1987)
102 ALR6th 365—§ 32

State v. Humphrey, 217 Kan. 352, 537 P.2d 155 (1975)
1 ALR6th 549—§ 8

State v. Humphrey, 2003-Ohio-3401, 2003 WL 21487780 (Ohio Ct. App. 2d Dist. Clark County 2003)
19 ALR6th 115—§ 3, 5, 9, 10

State v. Humphreys, 54 N.J. 406, 255 A.2d 273 (1969)
4 ALR5th 1—§ 4, 7, 11
68 ALR5th 299—§ 4

State v. Humphreys, 163 Tenn. 20, 40 S.W.2d 405 (1931)

27 ALR6th 403—§ 15

State v. Humphries, 79 Ohio App. 3d 589, 607 N.E.2d 921 (Clermont Co. 1992)

38 ALR5th 433—§ 25

State v. Humphries, 2008-Ohio-388, 2008 WL 307712 (Ohio Ct. App. 5th Dist. Stark County 2008)

102 ALR6th 279—§ 33

State v. Hund, 76 Or. App. 89, 708 P.2d 621 (1985)

3 ALR5th 521—§ 16

State v. Hundley, 236 Kan. 461, 693 P.2d 475 (1985)

58 ALR5th 749—§ 6

State v. Hungerford, 84 Wis. 2d 236, 267 N.W.2d 258 (1978)

78 ALR6th 417—§ 51, 58

State v. Hungerford, 142 N.H. 110, 697 A.2d 916 (1997)

90 ALR5th 453—§ 48

State v. Hunley, 2013-Ohio-628, 2013 WL 684234 (Ohio Ct. App. 6th Dist. Lucas County 2013)

99 ALR6th 295—§ 15

State v. Hunotte, 69 Wash. App. 670, 851 P.2d 694 (1993)

15 ALR5th 391—§ 11, 45

State v. Hunsaker, 74 Wash. App. 38, 873 P.2d 540 (1994)

6 ALR5th 242—§ 24

State v. Hunsaker, 2004 UT App 339, 2004 WL 2188951 (Utah Ct. App. 2004)

33 ALR6th 373—§ 5, 8

State v. Hunt, 3 Wash. App. 754, 477 P.2d 645 (Div. 3 1970)

84 ALR6th 427—§ 21

State v. Hunt, 8 Ariz. App. 514, 447 P.2d 896 (1968)

28 ALR6th 505—§ 9

State v. Hunt, 25 N.J. 514, 138 A.2d 1 (1958)

66 ALR6th 83—§ 10

State v. Hunt, 53 Wis. 2d 734, 193 N.W.2d 858 (1972)

65 ALR6th 537—§ 4

State v. Hunt, 72 N.C. App. 59, 323 S.E.2d 490 (1984)

24 ALR5th 465—§ 42, 48

State v. Hunt, 100 N.C. App. 43, 394 S.E.2d 221 (1990)

5 ALR5th 243—§ 48

State v. Hunt, 115 N.J. 330, 558 A.2d 1259 (1989)

41 ALR6th 295—§ 9

State v. Hunt, 184 N.J. Super. 304, 445 A.2d 1186 (Law Div. 1981)

24 ALR6th 1—§ 4

State v. Hunt, 270 Kan. 203, 14 P.3d 430 (2000)

3 ALR6th 543—§ 5

State v. Hunt, 297 N.C. 258, 254 S.E.2d 591 (1979)

78 ALR5th 1—§ 36

State v. Hunt, 297 N.C. 447, 255 S.E.2d 182 (1979)

116 ALR5th 373—§ 3, 11

State v. Hunt, 305 N.C. 238, 287 S.E.2d 818 (1982)

73 ALR5th 615—§ 3, 7

State v. Hunt, 324 N.C. 343, 378 S.E.2d 754 (1989)

3 ALR6th 269—§ 22

State v. Hunt, 339 N.C. 622, 457 S.E.2d 276 (1994)

79 ALR5th 33—§ 63

State v. Hunt, 345 N.C. 720, 483 S.E.2d 417 (1997)

53 ALR6th 81—§ 5

55 ALR6th 391—§ 5

State v. Hunt, 357 N.C. 257, 582 S.E.2d 593 (2003)

83 ALR6th 465—§ 18

State v. Hunt, 357 N.C. 454, 591 S.E.2d 502 (2003)

21 ALR6th 1—§ 2, 22

State v. Hunt, 630 S.W.2d 211 (Mo. App. 1982)

3 ALR5th 521—§ 6

State v. Hunt, 660 S.W.2d 513 (Tenn. Crim. 1983)

13 ALR5th 567—§ 3 to 5

State v. Hunt, 665 S.W.2d 751 (Tenn. Crim. App. 1984)
109 ALR5th 99—§ 8

State v. Hunt, 781 P.2d 473 (Utah Ct. App. 1989)
117 ALR5th 513—§ 27

State v. Hunt, 797 So. 2d 138 (La. Ct. App. 2d Cir. 2001)
95 ALR5th 125—§ 3

State v. Hunt, 1988 WL 125300 (Minn. Ct. App. 1988)
56 ALR6th 323—§ 7, 9

State v. Hunt, 2003 WL 21657380 (N.C. 2003)
110 ALR5th 1—§ 8

State v. Hunt, 2010-Ohio-1126, 2010 WL 1042271 (Ohio Ct. App. 2d Dist. Montgomery County 2010)
64 ALR6th 1—§ 9, 11

State v. Hunter, 88 Wash. App. 1018, 1997 WL 701321 (Div. 1 1997)
90 ALR5th 453—§ 43
10 ALR6th 463—§ 4, 6

State v. Hunter, 98 Ohio App. 3d 632, 649 N.E.2d 289 (Cuyahoga Co. 1994)
50 ALR5th 581—§ 7 to 9, 14, 19

State v. Hunter, 107 N.C. App. 402, 420 S.E.2d 700 (1992)
19 ALR5th 470—§ 3

State v. Hunter, 143 N.C. 607, 56 S.E. 547 (1907)
81 ALR5th 563—§ 3

State v. Hunter, 147 Wash. App. 177, 195 P.3d 556 (Div. 1 2008)
64 ALR6th 131—§ 3, 5, 13, 39

State v. Hunter, 241 Conn. 165, 694 A.2d 1317 (1997)
90 ALR5th 453—§ 6
10 ALR6th 463—§ 8
103 ALR6th 247—§ 18

State v. Hunter, 315 N.C. 371, 338 S.E.2d 99 (1986)
15 ALR5th 391—§ 5

State v. Hunter, 586 So. 2d 319, 16 FLW S. 588 (Fla. 1991)
15 ALR5th 39—§ 4

State v. Hunter, 619 S.W.2d 883 (Mo. Ct. App. W.D. 1981)
18 ALR5th 1—§ 12, 13, 20

State v. Hunter, 831 P.2d 1033, 185 Utah Adv. Rep. 13 (Utah App. 1992)
70 ALR5th 587—§ 13

State v. Hunter, 840 S.W.2d 850 (Mo. 1992)
31 ALR5th 229—§ 26, 32, 38

State v. Hunter, 2008 MT 395, 347 Mont. 155, 197 P.3d 998 (2008)
79 ALR5th 33—§ 40

State v. Huntington, 132 Wis. 2d 25, 390 N.W.2d 74 (App. 1986)
46 ALR6th 241—§ 3, 5

State v. Huntington, 216 Wis. 2d 671, 575 N.W.2d 268 (1998)
15 ALR5th 391—§ 45

State v. Huntley, 473 A.2d 859 (Me. 1984)
85 ALR5th 595—§ 3

State v. Huntley, 676 A.2d 501 (Me. 1996)
23 ALR6th 307—§ 4

State v. Huntley, 777 A.2d 249 (Del. Super. Ct. 2000)
19 ALR6th 411—§ 4

State v. Hunt, No. 10632 (November 24, 1982, Ct. App. Ohio, 9th App. Dist. Summit Co.)
92 ALR6th 171—§ 5

State v. Huntsman, 115 Utah 283, 204 P.2d 448 (1949)
39 ALR5th 283—§ 14, 54, 68

State v. Huntsman, 2002-Ohio-6017, 2002 WL 31458234 (Ohio Ct. App. 5th Dist. Stark County 2002)
42 ALR5th 291—§ 34

State v. Huot, 170 Conn. 463, 365 A.2d 1144 (1976)
70 ALR6th 1—§ 5

State v. Hupe, 205 Wis. 2d 114, 555 N.W.2d 411 (Ct. App. 1996)
29 ALR5th 59—§ 8

State v. Hurbean, 23 Ohio App. 2d 119, 52 Ohio Op. 2d 152, 261 N.E.2d 290 (5th Dist. Stark County 1970)
84 ALR6th 293—§ 15

76 ALR5th 597—§ 8

State v. Hurd, 74 Ohio App. 3d 94, 598 N.E.2d 72 (11th Dist. Portage County 1991)

35 ALR6th 361—§ 20

State v. Hurd, 520 S.W.2d 158 (Mo. Ct. App. 1975)

101 ALR5th 187—§ 16

State v. Hurlbert, 351 Mont. 316, 211 P.3d 869, 2009 MT 221 (2009)

56 ALR6th 323—§ 4

State v. Hurley, 207 Neb. 321, 299 N.W.2d 152 (1980)

121 ALR5th 551—§ 13

State v. Hurley, 876 S.W.2d 57 (Tenn. 1993)

51 ALR5th 603—§ 2, 8, 14

State v. Hursey, 176 Ariz. 330, 861 P.2d 615, 150 Ariz. Adv. Rep. 11, 42 A.L.R.5th 933 (1993)

42 ALR5th 581—§ 5, 19, 23

State v. Hurt, 107 Wash. App. 816, 27 P.3d 1276 (Div. 3 2001)

29 ALR6th 237—§ 20, 24

State v. Huse, 842 S.W.2d 579 (Mo. Ct. App. S.D. 1992)

28 ALR6th 505—§ 9

State v. Huseth, 375 N.W.2d 846 (Minn. Ct. App. 1985)

18 ALR6th 1—§ 4

State v. Huskey, 66 S.W.3d 905 (Tenn. Crim. App. 2001)

103 ALR6th 137—§ 15

State v. Huss, 666 N.W.2d 152 (Iowa 2003)

52 ALR6th 567—§ 24

State v. Hussong, 739 N.W.2d 922 (Minn. Ct. App. 2007)

47 ALR6th 107—§ 22, 23

State v. Hutcherson, 25 Kan. App. 2d 501, 968 P.2d 1109 (1998)

2 ALR6th 551—§ 15

State v. Hutchings, 950 P.2d 425 (Utah Ct. App. 1997)

89 ALR5th 629—§ 5

State v. Hutchings, 2003 UT App 409, 2003 WL 22827560 (Utah Ct. App. 2003)

92 ALR6th 295—§ 19

95 ALR6th 1—§ 10

96 ALR6th 355—§ 6, 21, 26, 36, 37, 49, 53, 60

State v. Hutchins, 73 Wash. App. 211, 868 P.2d 196 (Div. 3 1994)

1 ALR6th 549—§ 16

State v. Hutchins, 149 La. 1077, 90 So. 410 (1922)

54 ALR6th 429—§ 11

State v. Hutchins, 214 Or. App. 260, 164 P.3d 318 (2007)

38 ALR6th 97—§ 8

State v. Hutchins, 502 So. 2d 606 (La. App. 3d Cir. 1987)

34 ALR5th 125—§ 20

State v. Hutchins, 636 So. 2d 552, 19 FLW D 1027 (Fla. App. D2 1994)

11 ALR5th 52—§ 9, 10

State v. Hutchinson, 99 N.M. 616, 661 P.2d 1315 (1983)

28 ALR5th 754—§ 7

State v. Hutchinson, 176 W. Va. 172, 342 S.E.2d 138 (1986)

90 ALR5th 225—§ 3

State v. Hutchinson, 458 S.W.2d 553 (Mo. 1970)

72 ALR5th 403—§ 19

State v. Hutchinson, 819 So. 2d 324 (La. 2002)

124 ALR5th 1—§ 4

State v. Hutchison, 56 Wash. App. 863, 785 P.2d 1154 (1990)

11 ALR5th 52—§ 5

State v. Hutchison, 898 S.W.2d 161 (Tenn. 1994)

57 ALR5th 141—§ 5, 7

State v. Hutsell, 120 Wash. 2d 913, 845 P.2d 1325 (1993)

113 ALR5th 597—§ 8

State v. Hutzler, 2003-Ohio-7193, 2003 WL 23095156 (Ohio Ct. App. 9th Dist. Summit County 2003)

29 ALR6th 1—§ 18

State v. Hutzler, 2012-Ohio-6107, 2012 WL 6697466 (Ohio Ct. App. 9th Dist. Summit County 2012)

97 ALR6th 263—§ 17

State v. Huynh, 49 Wash. App. 192, 742 P.2d 160 (Div. 1 1987)

28 ALR6th 505—§ 9

97 ALR6th 567—§ 4, 10

State v. Huynh, 519 N.W.2d 191, R.I.C.O. Bus. Disp. Guide (CCH) ¶ 8611 (Minn. 1994)

89 ALR5th 629—§ 3, 5, 6, 8

State v. Hyatt, 355 N.C. 642, 566 S.E.2d 61 (2002)

124 ALR5th 1—§ 4

State v. Hyde, 26 Ohio App. 2d 32, 55 Ohio Op. 2d 52, 268 N.E.2d 820 (9th Dist. Summit County 1971)

58 ALR6th 499—§ 47

State v. Hyde, 186 Ariz. 252, 921 P.2d 655 (1996)

82 ALR5th 591—§ 9

State v. Hyde, 898 P.2d 71 (Idaho App. 1995)

22 ALR5th 660—§ 6, 11

State v. Hyem, 630 P.2d 202 (Mont 1981)

19 ALR5th 470—§ 6

State v. Hygh, 711 P.2d 264 (Utah 1985)

116 ALR5th 373—§ 3

State v. Hyleman, 89 N.C. App. 424, 366 S.E.2d 530 (1988)

104 ALR5th 165—§ 6, 11

3 ALR6th 269—§ 25

23 ALR6th 307—§ 38

State v. Hyslop, 93 Wash. App. 1038, 1998 WL 886950 (Div. 1 1998)

58 ALR6th 499—§ 8, 11, 12

State v. Iacona, 2001 -Ohio- 1292, 93 Ohio St. 3d 83, 752 N.E.2d 937 (2001)

101 ALR5th 187—§ 11

State v. Iaukea, 56 Haw. 343, 537 P.2d 724 (1975)

86 ALR5th 59—§ 4, 6

State v. I.B., 227 N.J. Super. 362, 547 A.2d 707 (App. Div. 1988)

68 ALR5th 299—§ 7

State v. Ibarra, 74 P.3d 594 (Kan. Ct. App. 2003)

8 ALR6th 265—§ 18

State v. Ibarra, 74 P.3d 594, 2003 WL 21981945 (Kan. Ct. App. 2003)

115 ALR5th 477—§ 5

State v. Ibarra, 864 P.2d 302 (N.M. App. 1993)

5 ALR5th 243—§ 56

State v. Ibarra-Bucanegra, 88 Wash. App. 1001, 1997 WL 288606 (Div. 1 1997)

58 ALR6th 499—§ 31

State v. Ibrahim, 862 A.2d 787 (R.I. 2004)

55 ALR6th 391—§ 7

State v. Ice, 343 Or. 248, 170 P.3d 1049 (2007)

46 ALR6th 495—§ 31

State v. Iglesias, 185 Wis. 2d 118, 517 N.W.2d 175, 42 A.L.R.5th 909 (1994)

42 ALR5th 547—§ 2, 7

State v. Ignot, 701 So. 2d 1001 (La. Ct. App. 2d Cir. 1997)

7 ALR5th 263—§ 6

State v. Igou, 2005 ND 16, 691 N.W.2d 213 (N.D. 2005)

33 ALR6th 91—§ 45

State v. Ikharo, 2011-Ohio-2746, 2011 WL 2201193 (Ohio Ct. App. 10th Dist. Franklin County 2011)

74 ALR6th 373—§ 18

State v. Ildefonso, 262 Neb. 672, 634 N.W.2d 252 (2001)

72 ALR6th 437—§ 4

State v. Iles, 79 Or. App. 586, 719 P.2d 519 (1986)

92 ALR5th 35—§ 22

State v. Illig, 237 Neb. 598, 467 N.W.2d 375 (1991)

58 ALR6th 499—§ 23, 101

State v. Imme, 285 Wis. 2d 805, 2005 WI App 176, 701 N.W.2d 653 (Ct. App. 2005)

62 ALR6th 413—§ 22, 24, 26, 28, 36

State v. Immelt, 150 Wash. App. 681, 208 P.3d 1256 (Div. 1 2009)

70 ALR6th 513—§ 3

State v. Immelt, 2011 WL 5084574 (Wash. 2011)

71 ALR6th 471—§ 3
State v. Industrial Commission of Ohio, 58 Ohio St. 2d 268, 12 Ohio Op. 3d 271, 389 N.E.2d 1126 (1979)

31 ALR6th 199—§ 7
State v. Industrial Commission of Ohio, 1979 WL 209263 (Ohio Ct. App. 10th Dist. Franklin County 1979)

31 ALR6th 199—§ 3
State v. Industrial Commission of Ohio, 1980 WL 353225 (Ohio Ct. App. 10th Dist. Franklin County 1980)

31 ALR6th 199—§ 46
State v. Industrial Commission of Ohio, 1981 WL 3680 (Ohio Ct. App. 10th Dist. Franklin County 1981)

31 ALR6th 199—§ 82
State v. Industrial Commission of Ohio, 1982 WL 4588 (Ohio Ct. App. 10th Dist. Franklin County 1982)

31 ALR6th 199—§ 47
State v. Industrial Commission of Ohio, 1983 WL 3370 (Ohio Ct. App. 10th Dist. Franklin County 1983)

31 ALR6th 199—§ 60
State v. Industrial Commission of Ohio, and Mid America Exposition, Inc, 1985 WL 10079 (Ohio Ct. App. 10th Dist. Franklin County 1985)

31 ALR6th 199—§ 65
State v. Industrial Comm., No. 83AP-1212 (Ohio App. Franklin Co. 1984)

14 ALR5th 1—§ 14
State v. Ing, 53 Haw. 466, 497 P.2d 575 (1972)

111 ALR5th 1—§ 3, 5, 27
State v. Ingel, 18 Md. App. 514, 308 A.2d 223 (1973)

5 ALR6th 423—§ 5
State v. Inger, 292 N.W.2d 119 (Iowa 1980)

50 ALR5th 467—§ 9
State v. Ingersoll, 1994 WL 615127 (Minn. App. Nov 8, 1994)

51 ALR5th 375—§ 4, 8
State v. Ingham, 26 Wash. App. 45, 612 P.2d 801 (1980)

39 ALR5th 283—§ 4, 67

State v. Ingle, 64 Wash. 2d 491, 392 P.2d 442 (1964)

54 ALR6th 429—§ 27
State v. Ingle, 336 N.C. 617, 445 S.E.2d 880 (1994)

79 ALR5th 33—§ 68
State v. Ingleright, 782 S.W.2d 147 (Mo. Ct. App. S.D. 1990)

23 ALR6th 307—§ 44
State v. Ingram, 104 Or. App. 389, 802 P.2d 656 (1990)

43 ALR5th 1—§ 13, 14
109 ALR5th 99—§ 5
State v. Ingram, 196 N.J. 23, 951 A.2d 1000, 57 A.L.R.6th 753 (2008)

57 ALR6th 313—§ 7, 8
State v. Ingram, 198 Kan. 517, 426 P.2d 98 (1967)

55 ALR6th 391—§ 5
State v. Ingram, 251 Or. 324, 445 P.2d 503 (1968)

113 ALR5th 517—§ 10
State v. Ingram, 427 N.E.2d 444 (Ind. 1981)

62 ALR5th 537—§ 3
State v. Ingram, 688 So. 2d 657 (La. Ct. App. 2d Cir. 1997)

103 ALR6th 507—§ 4
State v. Ingram, 1995 WL 146095 (Tenn. Crim. App. 1995)

68 ALR6th 527—§ 37
State v. Ingram, 1997 WL 65524 (Minn. Ct. App. 1997)

73 ALR5th 383—§ 23, 57
State v. Ingram, 2007 WL 2188699 (N.J. Super. Ct. App. Div. 2007)

57 ALR6th 313—§ 8
State v. Ingram, 2008 WL 5135539 (Minn. Ct. App. 2008)

103 ALR6th 347—§ 13
State v. Inman, 39 N.C. App. 366, 249 S.E.2d 884 (1979)

85 ALR5th 547—§ 8
State v. Inman, 151 Ariz. 413, 728 P.2d 283 (Ct. App. Div. 1 1986)

124 ALR5th 1—§ 4
State v. Inman, 350 A.2d 582 (Me. 1976)

35 ALR6th 127—§ 5

State v. Inman, 578 S.W.2d 336 (Mo. App. 1979)

29 ALR5th 59—§ 12

State v. Inman, 692 N.W.2d 76 (Minn. 2005)

69 ALR6th 579—§ 3, 4, 15

State v. Inman, 1982 WL 5552 (Ohio Ct. App. 5th Dist. Stark County 1982)

58 ALR6th 215—§ 12

State v. Inman, 1993 WL 483321 (Tenn. Crim. App. 1993)

24 ALR6th 1—§ 21

State v. Innis, 433 A.2d 646 (R.I. 1981)

39 ALR5th 283—§ 4, 33, 77

State v. Insabella, 190 N.J. Super. 544, 464 A.2d 1165 (1983)

15 ALR5th 391—§ 3

State v. International Trade Club, Inc., 351 So. 2d 895 (Ala. Civ. App. 1977)

61 ALR6th 61—§ 3

State v. Intogna, 101 Ariz. 275, 419 P.2d 59 (1966)

28 ALR6th 505—§ 8

State v. Inzitari, 76 Conn. App. 450, 819 A.2d 898 (2003)

55 ALR6th 157—§ 105

State v. Irala, 68 Conn. App. 499, 792 A.2d 109 (2002)

9 ALR6th 633—§ 3, 5, 6, 24

9 ALR6th 693—§ 3

10 ALR6th 265—§ 3, 6

12 ALR6th 389—§ 3

13 ALR6th 603—§ 3, 37

14 ALR6th 517—§ 3

15 ALR6th 173—§ 3, 4, 11, 46

State v. Irby, 138 Wash. App. 1022, 2007 WL 1229394 (Div. 3 2007)

71 ALR6th 625—§ 3, 22, 29

State v. Irby, 254 S.W.3d 181 (Mo. Ct. App. E.D. 2008)

65 ALR6th 537—§ 24, 73

State v. Irby, Slip Op. C.A. No. E-83-44 (Ohio App. Erie Co. 1984)

38 ALR5th 433—§ 44

State v. Irebaria, 55 Haw. 353, 519 P.2d 1246 (1974)

32 ALR6th 385—§ 5

State v. Ireland, 22 Utah 2d 17, 447 P.2d 375 (1968)

67 ALR6th 103—§ 4

State v. Ireland, 773 P.2d 1375 (Utah 1989)

57 ALR5th 141—§ 13

State v. Ireland, 1998 ME 35, 706 A.2d 597 (Me. 1998)

114 ALR5th 173—§ 6

State v. Irick, 291 N.C. 480, 231 S.E.2d 833 (1977)

81 ALR5th 563—§ 3, 5

State v. Irick, 762 S.W.2d 121 (Tenn. 1988)

83 ALR6th 255—§ 9

State v. Irick, 861 S.W.2d 375 (Tenn. Crim. 1993)

15 ALR5th 391—§ 5, 30

State v. Irizarry-Romero, 1996 WL 488542 (Ohio Ct. App. 5th Dist. Licking County 1996)

82 ALR6th 373—§ 7

State v. Irshaad, 2002 WL 378196 (Minn. Ct. App. 2002)

71 ALR6th 625—§ 18, 22

State v. Irving, 24 Wash. App. 370, 601 P.2d 954 (Div. 2 1979)

86 ALR5th 59—§ 6

State v. Irwin, 43 Wash. App. 553, 718 P.2d 826 (1986)

59 ALR5th 615—§ 3, 4, 9

State v. Irwin, 191 Neb. 169, 214 N.W.2d 595 (1974)

78 ALR6th 417—§ 5

State v. Irwin, 304 N.C. 93, 282 S.E.2d 439 (1981)

39 ALR5th 283—§ 4, 17

State v. Irwin, 2010 ND 132, 785 N.W.2d 245 (N.D. 2010)

63 ALR6th 1—§ 66

State v. Isa, 850 S.W.2d 876 (Mo. 1993)

32 ALR6th 1—§ 11

State v. Isaac, 722 So. 2d 353 (La. Ct. App. 2d Cir. 1998)

104 ALR5th 229—§ 6
116 ALR5th 325—§ 3
4 ALR6th 113—§ 24, 28
34 ALR6th 539—§ 8
101 ALR6th 1—§ 21, 23, 40
State v. Isaacs, 658 So. 2d 29 (La. Ct. App. 5th Cir. 1995)
68 ALR5th 343—§ 2, 3, 6
State v. Isaiah, 874 S.W.2d 429 (Mo. Ct. App. W.D. 1994)
29 ALR6th 1—§ 10
State v. Isenberg, 393 N.W.2d 13 (Minn. App. 1986)
42 ALR5th 547—§ 3
State v. Iser, 2006-Ohio-3225, 2006 WL 1726498 (Ohio Ct. App. 11th Dist. Trumbull County 2006)
26 ALR6th 511—§ 19
State v. Isikoff, 223 Neb. 679, 392 N.W.2d 783 (1986)
43 ALR6th 475—§ 24
State v. Isola, 98 Wash. App. 1017, 1999 WL 1081269 (Div. 1 1999)
74 ALR6th 69—§ 6
State v. Ison, 1980 WL 353212 (Ohio Ct. App. 1st Dist. Clermont County 1980)
30 ALR6th 103—§ 21, 42, 43, 48
State v. Isreal, 86 Ohio App. 3d 696, 621 N.E.2d 793 (Butler Co. 1993)
27 ALR5th 593—§ 19, 24, 25
State v. Issa, 2001-Ohio-3910, 2001 WL 1635592 (Ohio Ct. App. 1st Dist. Hamilton County 2001)
21 ALR6th 1—§ 4
State v. Italiano, 132 N.J. Super. 1, 331 A.2d 289 (App. Div. 1975)
69 ALR6th 1—§ 23
State v. Ito, 90 Haw. 225, 978 P.2d 191 (Haw. Ct. App. 1999)
90 ALR5th 453—§ 45
State v. Itzkovitch, 49 La. Ann. 366, 21 So. 544 (1897)
16 ALR6th 219—§ 18, 20, 23, 30, 36, 37
State v. Iversen, 224 Wis. 2d 644, 590 N.W.2d 282 (Ct. App. 1999)
83 ALR5th 497—§ 2

State v. Iverson, 187 N.W.2d 1 (N.D. 1971)
41 ALR5th 171—§ 9, 12, 16, 95, 98, 108, 114, 122, 134
81 ALR5th 563—§ 3
State v. Iverson, 269 N.W.2d 390 (S.D. 1978)
117 ALR5th 513—§ 21
State v. Iverson, 396 N.W.2d 599 (Minn. Ct. App. 1986)
57 ALR5th 141—§ 7
State v. Iverson, 664 N.W.2d 346 (Minn. 2003)
33 ALR6th 91—§ 22
State v. Iverson, 1998 WL 799183 (Minn. Ct. App. 1998)
73 ALR5th 383—§ 28
State v. Ives, 37 Conn. App. 40, 654 A.2d 789 (1995)
6 ALR6th 533—§ 21
80 ALR6th 239—§ 13
State v. Ivie, 136 Wash. 2d 173, 961 P.2d 941 (1998)
97 ALR5th 201—§ 7
State v. Ivory, 124 N.J. 582, 592 A.2d 205 (1991)
27 ALR5th 593—§ 20, 32
State v. Ivory, 578 S.W.2d 62 (Mo. Ct. App. 1978)
97 ALR5th 201—§ 3
State v. Izaguirre, 272 N.J. Super. 51, 639 A.2d 343 (1994)
32 ALR5th 149—§ 63
State v. Izzo, 623 A.2d 1277 (Me. 1993)
55 ALR6th 513—§ 5
State v. Jack, 167 Mont. 456, 539 P.2d 726 (1975)
31 ALR6th 523—§ 45
State v. Jackmon, 55 Wash. App. 562, 778 P.2d 1079 (Div. 1 1989)
73 ALR5th 383—§ 20
State v. Jacks, 63 Ohio App. 3d 200, 578 N.E.2d 512 (8th Dist. Cuyahoga County 1989)
98 ALR6th 455—§ 16
State v. Jackson, 32 Conn. App. 724, 630 A.2d 164 (1993)

125 ALR5th 537—§ 1
State v. Jackson, 56 Conn. App. 264, 742 A.2d 812 (2000)

29 ALR5th 487—§ 3, 12
State v. Jackson, 70 N.C. App. 782, 321 S.E.2d 169 (1984)

73 ALR5th 383—§ 5
State v. Jackson, 70 Wash. 2d 498, 424 P.2d 313 (1967)

5 ALR5th 243—§ 48
State v. Jackson, 73 Conn. App. 338, 808 A.2d 388 (2002)

24 ALR6th 591—§ 12
State v. Jackson, 77 N.C. App. 832, 336 S.E.2d 437 (1985)

93 ALR5th 327—§ 3, 4, 9, 25, 27
State v. Jackson, 86 Conn. App. 803, 862 A.2d 880 (2005)

39 ALR6th 257—§ 41
State v. Jackson, 92 Ohio St. 3d 436, 2001-Ohio-1266, 751 N.E.2d 946 (2001)

3 ALR6th 269—§ 5, 8
State v. Jackson, 101 Ariz. 399, 420 P.2d 270 (1966)

78 ALR5th 567—§ 8
State v. Jackson, 113 P.3d 834 (Kan. Ct. App. 2005)

37 ALR6th 357—§ 3, 23, 25, 72
State v. Jackson, 113 Wash. App. 762, 54 P.3d 739 (Div. 2 2002)

7 ALR6th 233—§ 9
State v. Jackson, 117 Ariz. 120, 571 P.2d 266 (1977)

41 ALR5th 171—§ 17, 19, 72
State v. Jackson, 126 N.C. App. 129, 484 S.E.2d 405 (1997)

57 ALR5th 141—§ 7
State v. Jackson, 139 Ariz. 213, 677 P.2d 1321 (App. 1983)

4 ALR5th 1—§ 2, 17, 37
State v. Jackson, 150 Wash. 2d 251, 76 P.3d 217, 5 A.L.R.6th 685 (2003)

5 ALR6th 385—§ 2, 4
State v. Jackson, 155 S.W.3d 849 (Mo. Ct. App. W.D. 2005)

37 ALR6th 357—§ 70

125 ALR5th 537—§ 1

State v. Jackson, 170 Ariz. 89, 821 P.2d 1374 (Ct. App. Div. 2 1991)

77 ALR5th 201—§ 21
78 ALR5th 1—§ 40
State v. Jackson, 201 Kan. 795, 443 P.2d 279 (1968)

36 ALR5th 255—§ 11, 30
State v. Jackson, 210 N.W.2d 537 (Iowa 1973)

61 ALR5th 1—§ 3, 5
State v. Jackson, 217 Neb. 363, 348 N.W.2d 876 (1984)

3 ALR6th 269—§ 9, 24
State v. Jackson, 219 P.3d 491 (Kan. Ct. App. 2009)

87 ALR6th 1—§ 41
State v. Jackson, 223 N.W.2d 229 (Iowa 1974)

50 ALR5th 467—§ 7
State v. Jackson, 238 Kan. 793, 714 P.2d 1368 (1986)

39 ALR5th 283—§ 4, 72
State v. Jackson, 269 Ga. 308, 496 S.E.2d 912 (1998)

36 ALR6th 475—§ 18
State v. Jackson, 276 N.J. Super. 626, 648 A.2d 738 (App. Div. 1994)

50 ALR5th 581—§ 9, 19
State v. Jackson, 301 S.C. 49, 389 S.E.2d 654 (1990)

57 ALR6th 313—§ 4
State v. Jackson, 308 N.C. 549, 304 S.E.2d 134 (1983)

32 ALR6th 1—§ 11
State v. Jackson, 309 N.C. 26, 305 S.E.2d 703 (1983)

39 ALR5th 283—§ 4, 31
State v. Jackson, 315 S.C. 219, 433 S.E.2d 19 (Ct. App. 1993)

57 ALR6th 445—§ 38
State v. Jackson, 316 Wis. 2d 412, 2009 WI App 27, 763 N.W.2d 559 (Ct. App. 2009)

69 ALR6th 579—§ 5
State v. Jackson, 320 N.C. 452, 358 S.E.2d 679 (1987)

38 ALR5th 433—§ 11, 12

State v. Jackson, 340 N.C. 301, 457 S.E.2d 862 (1995)
   57 ALR5th 141—§ 11

State v. Jackson, 348 N.C. 52, 497 S.E.2d 409 (1998)
   32 ALR6th 1—§ 8

State v. Jackson, 362 So. 2d 1082 (La. 1978)
   32 ALR6th 1—§ 11

State v. Jackson, 370 N.W.2d 72 (Minn. Ct. App. 1985)
   73 ALR5th 383—§ 36

State v. Jackson, 387 N.W.2d 623 (Iowa Ct. App. 1986)
   9 ALR6th 1—§ 17

State v. Jackson, 419 So. 2d 837 (La. 1982)
   118 ALR5th 253—§ 16

State v. Jackson, 452 So. 2d 1250 (La. Ct. App. 2d Cir. 1984)
   9 ALR6th 1—§ 15

State v. Jackson, 506 S.W.2d 424 (Mo. 1974)
   99 ALR6th 113—§ 21

State v. Jackson, 525 A.2d 215 (Me. 1987)
   57 ALR5th 141—§ 13

State v. Jackson, 584 So. 2d 266 (La. Ct. App. 1st Cir. 1991)
   99 ALR6th 295—§ 21

State v. Jackson, 594 S.W.2d 377 (Mo. App. 1980)
   29 ALR5th 59—§ 7, 26, 39

State v. Jackson, 601 N.W.2d 354 (Iowa 1999)
   13 ALR5th 872—§ 21

State v. Jackson, 658 So. 2d 722 (La. Ct. App. 2d Cir. 1995)
   73 ALR5th 383—§ 5

State v. Jackson, 677 So. 2d 938 (Fla. Dist. Ct. App. 2d Dist. 1996)
   89 ALR5th 629—§ 5

State v. Jackson, 684 So. 2d 1046 (La. App. 1996)
   50 ALR5th 581—§ 16

State v. Jackson, 692 So. 2d 659 (La. Ct. App. 3d Cir. 1997)

   68 ALR5th 343—§ 3

State v. Jackson, 697 S.W.2d 366 (Tenn. Crim. App. 1985)
   39 ALR5th 283—§ 4
   93 ALR5th 683—§ 4

State v. Jackson, 703 S.W.2d 23 (Mo. App. 1985)
   39 ALR5th 283—§ 4, 54

State v. Jackson, 703 S.W.2d 30 (Mo. App. 1985)
   39 ALR5th 283—§ 4, 55

State v. Jackson, 764 So. 2d 64 (La. 2000)
   116 ALR5th 479—§ 2, 5

State v. Jackson, 794 S.W.2d 344 (Mo. Ct. App. S.D. 1990)
   12 ALR6th 267—§ 5

State v. Jackson, 873 P.2d 1166, 237 Utah Adv. Rep. 38 (Utah App. 1994)
   51 ALR5th 375—§ 7, 10

State v. Jackson, 880 So. 2d 841 (La. Ct. App. 5th Cir. 2004)
   16 ALR6th 329—§ 4
   24 ALR6th 591—§ 4, 14

State v. Jackson, 928 S.W.2d 894 (Mo. Ct. App. E.D. 1996)
   105 ALR5th 529—§ 13

State v. Jackson, 937 P.2d 545 (Utah Ct. App. 1997)
   62 ALR5th 1—§ 3, 4, 11, 12, 15
   114 ALR5th 235—§ 9

State v. Jackson, 1998 WL 120281 (Tenn. Crim. App. 1998)
   73 ALR5th 383—§ 22

State v. Jackson, 1999 WL 1101898 (Minn. Ct. App. 1999)
   92 ALR6th 171—§ 16

State v. Jackson, 2002-Ohio-3330, 2002 WL 1379001 (Ohio Ct. App. 10th Dist. Franklin County 2002)
   102 ALR6th 417—§ 88

State v. Jackson, 2005-Ohio-6143, 2005 WL 3081110 (Ohio Ct. App. 2d Dist. Champaign County 2005)
   23 ALR6th 307—§ 33

State v. Jackson, 2005 WL 839299 (Tenn. Crim. App. 2005)

26 ALR6th 511—§ 27

State v. Jackson, 2005 WL 3429738 (N.J. Super. Ct. App. Div. 2005)

26 ALR6th 511—§ 17

State v. Jackson, 2006-Ohio-2210, 2006 WL 1174452 (Ohio Ct. App. 8th Dist. Cuyahoga County 2006)

26 ALR6th 511—§ 33

State v. Jackson, 2006-Ohio-2651, 2006 WL 1459757 (Ohio Ct. App. 11th Dist. Trumbull County 2006)

21 ALR6th 1—§ 4

State v. Jackson, 2007-Ohio-6932, 2007 WL 4481412 (Ohio Ct. App. 11th Dist. Trumbull County 2007)

62 ALR6th 161—§ 14

State v. Jackson, 2010 WL 2650924 (N.C. Ct. App. 2010)

57 ALR6th 1—§ 23

State v. Jackson, 2013 WI App 73, 348 Wis. 2d 263, 831 N.W.2d 824 (Ct. App. 2013)

94 ALR6th 525—§ 9

State v. Jackson, No. 5132 (June 4, 1980, Ct. App. Ohio, 5th App. Dist. Stark Co.)

39 ALR5th 283—§ 14, 60, 63

State v. Jackson, No. 10634 (November 4, 1982, Ct. App. Ohio, 9th App. Dist. Summit Co.)

39 ALR5th 283—§ 14, 67

State v. Jacob, 65 Conn. App. 486, 783 A.2d 69 (2001)

40 ALR6th 1—§ 10

State v. Jacobi, 115 Wash. App. 1010, 2003 WL 141253 (Div. 2 2003)

42 ALR6th 237—§ 8

State v. Jacobs, 10 P.3d 127 (N.M. 2000)

39 ALR5th 283—§ 59

State v. Jacobs, 18 Ariz. App. 471, 503 P.2d 826 (1972)

13 ALR5th 1—§ 27

State v. Jacobs, 26 S.D. 183, 128 N.W. 162 (1910)

11 ALR5th 497—§ 7

State v. Jacobs, 30 Conn. App. 340, 620 A.2d 198 (1993)

92 ALR6th 1—§ 3

State v. Jacobs, 34 Or. App. 755, 579 P.2d 881 (1978)

8 ALR5th 775—§ 2, 7

State v. Jacobs, 55 Or. App. 406, 637 P.2d 1377, Blue Sky L. Rep. (CCH) ¶ 71713 (1981)

58 ALR5th 293—§ 7

State v. Jacobs, 61 N.C. App. 610, 301 S.E.2d 429 (1983)

26 ALR5th 603—§ 3
67 ALR6th 103—§ 5, 10

State v. Jacobs, 93 Ariz. 336, 380 P.2d 998 (1963)

39 ALR5th 283—§ 3

State v. Jacobs, 101 Wash. App. 80, 2 P.3d 974 (Div. 2 2000)

58 ALR6th 499—§ 31

State v. Jacobs, 194 Conn. 119, 479 A.2d 226 (1984)

50 ALR5th 467—§ 5 to 7, 9

State v. Jacobs, 195 La. 281, 196 So. 347 (1940)

108 ALR5th 593—§ 52

State v. Jacobs, 229 Conn. 385, 641 A.2d 1351 (1994)

92 ALR6th 1—§ 3

State v. Jacobs, 251 Iowa 314, 100 N.W.2d 601 (1960)

102 ALR5th 525—§ 22

State v. Jacobs, 371 So. 2d 801 (La. 1979)

54 ALR5th 141—§ 3, 4, 6

State v. Jacobs, 437 So. 2d 166 (Fla. Dist. Ct. App. 5th Dist. 1983)

41 ALR5th 171—§ 13, 82, 121, 133
62 ALR5th 1—§ 2

State v. Jacobs, 607 N.W.2d 679 (Iowa 2000)

121 ALR5th 551—§ 8, 14

State v. Jacobs, 1993 WL 319625 (Ohio App. Hamilton Co. 1993)

52 ALR5th 655—§ 3

State v. Jacobs, 1995 WL 324066 (Ohio Ct. App. 9th Dist. Summit County 1995)

17 ALR6th 327—§ 7

State v. Jacobs, 2000-NMSC-026, 129 N.M. 448, 10 P.3d 127 (2000)

---

78 ALR6th 297—§ 74
State v. Jacobsen, 78 Wash. 2d 491, 477
P.2d 1 (1970)
84 ALR6th 427—§ 21
State v. Jacobsen, 95 Wash. App. 967,
977 P.2d 1250 (Div. 2 1999)
73 ALR5th 383—§ 6
101 ALR6th 545—§ 5
State v. Jacobson, 22 Ariz. App. 260,
526 P.2d 784 (1974)
13 ALR5th 118—§ 7, 10, 15
State v. Jacobson, 36 Wash. App. 446,
674 P.2d 1255 (Div. 1 1983)
71 ALR5th 1—§ 48
State v. Jacobson, 74 Wash. App. 715,
876 P.2d 916 (Div. 1 1994)
57 ALR6th 445—§ 4
State v. Jacobson, 338 N.W.2d 648
(N.D. 1983)
92 ALR6th 295—§ 3
96 ALR6th 355—§ 3
State v. Jacobson, 459 So. 2d 1285 (La.
Ct. App. 1st Cir. 1984)
95 ALR5th 229—§ 16
State v. Jacobus, 205 Wis. 2d 112, 555
N.W.2d 410 (Ct. App. 1996)
110 ALR5th 329—§ 7
20 ALR6th 479—§ 3, 11
State v. Jacoby, 260 N.W.2d 828 (Iowa
1977)
67 ALR5th 637—§ 5, 7
State v. Jacques, 2 Kan. App. 2d 277,
579 P.2d 146 (1978)
27 ALR6th 491—§ 3
State v. Jacques, 225 Kan. 38, 587 P.2d
861 (1978)
64 ALR5th 741—§ 3
113 ALR5th 517—§ 8
State v. Jacumin, 778 S.W.2d 430 (Tenn.
1989)
67 ALR5th 361—§ 3
State v. Jaeger, 240 Mo. 1, 144 S.W. 103
(1912)
56 ALR5th 171—§ 10, 15, 29
State v. Jaeger, 1999 UT 1, 973 P.2d 404
(Utah 1999)
38 ALR5th 433—§ 48

State v. Jaggers, 71 N.J.L. 281, 58 A.
1014 (N.J. Ct. Err. & App. 1904)
73 ALR5th 615—§ 3, 7
State v. Jagodinsky, 209 Wis. 2d 577,
563 N.W.2d 188 (Ct. App. 1997)
88 ALR5th 67—§ 3
15 ALR6th 319—§ 4, 5
State v. Jagusch, 212 Wis. 2d 643, 570
N.W.2d 63 (Ct. App. 1997)
70 ALR5th 491—§ 4
State v. Jaime, 4 Conn. Cir. Ct. 530, 236
A.2d 474 (App. Div. 1967)
66 ALR5th 397—§ 19
State v. Jakeway, 221 Kan. 142, 558
P.2d 113 (1976)
68 ALR5th 343—§ 3, 5
State v. Jalbert, 537 A.2d 593 (Me. 1988)
28 ALR6th 505—§ 9
State v. Jalo, 72 Or. App. 479, 696 P.2d
14 (1985)
46 ALR5th 499—§ 5
State v. James, 6 Neb. App. 444, 573
N.W.2d 816 (1998)
105 ALR5th 499—§ 4
9 ALR6th 633—§ 13
10 ALR6th 265—§ 13
15 ALR6th 173—§ 13
State v. James, 10 Ariz. App. 394, 459
P.2d 121 (1969)
41 ALR5th 171—§ 17
State v. James, 35 Wash. App. 351, 666
P.2d 943 (Div. 3 1983)
9 ALR6th 541—§ 3
State v. James, 41 Ohio App. 2d 147, 70
Ohio Op. 2d 314, 324 N.E.2d 301
(3d Dist. Allen County 1974)
89 ALR6th 565—§ 33
State v. James, 87 Md. App. 39, 589
A.2d 81 (1991)
114 ALR5th 173—§ 6
State v. James, 96 N.J.L. 132, 114 A.
553, 16 A.L.R. 1141 (N.J. Ct. Err.
& App. 1921)
70 ALR5th 587—§ 3
State v. James, 135 P.3d 766 (Kan. 2006)
26 ALR6th 511—§ 25

State v. James, 144 N.J. 538, 677 A.2d 734 (1996)
27 ALR6th 183—§ 4

State v. James, 148 Idaho 574, 225 P.3d 1169 (2010)
58 ALR6th 215—§ 12

State v. James, 159 Or. App. 502, 978 P.2d 415 (1999)
107 ALR5th 697—§ 5

State v. James, 186 W. Va. 173, 411 S.E.2d 692 (1991)
12 ALR6th 267—§ 5

State v. James, 217 Kan. 96, 535 P.2d 991 (1975)
87 ALR5th 181—§ 5

State v. James, 237 Conn. 390, 678 A.2d 1338 (1996)
20 ALR6th 479—§ 3
69 ALR6th 579—§ 4

State v. James, 276 Kan. 737, 79 P.3d 169, 31 A.L.R.6th 745 (2003)
31 ALR6th 465—§ 11, 18

State v. James, 285 Wis. 2d 783, 2005 WI App 188, 703 N.W.2d 727 (Ct. App. 2005)
30 ALR6th 1—§ 4

State v. James, 321 N.C. 676, 365 S.E.2d 579 (1988)
5 ALR5th 243—§ 2, 6

State v. James, 447 So. 2d 580 (La. Ct. App. 3d Cir. 1984)
124 ALR5th 1—§ 5

State v. James, 484 N.W.2d 799 (Minn. App. 1992)
18 ALR5th 1—§ 4

State v. James, 581 So. 2d 349 (La. Ct. App. 4th Cir. 1991)
114 ALR5th 235—§ 3

State v. James, 755 So. 2d 995 (La. Ct. App. 4th Cir. 2000)
18 ALR6th 1—§ 27
71 ALR6th 1—§ 18

State v. James, 788 So. 2d 23 (La. Ct. App. 4th Cir. 2000)
78 ALR6th 297—§ 68

State v. James, 848 S.W.2d 258 (Tex. App. Beaumont 1993)
103 ALR5th 463—§ 2, 5

State v. James, 902 S.W.2d 911, 23 Media L. R. 2560 (Tenn. 1995)
39 ALR5th 103—§ 61

State v. James, 963 P.2d 1080 (Alaska Ct. App. 1998)
65 ALR5th 407—§ 14

State v. James, 1998 WL 832185 (Ohio Ct. App. 10th Dist. Franklin County 1998)
99 ALR6th 295—§ 13

State v. James, 1999 WL 76815 (Ohio Ct. App. 2d Dist. Clark County 1999)
88 ALR5th 121—§ 10, 24, 36

State v. Jameson, 1998 WL 193489 (Ohio Ct. App. 9th Dist. Lorain County 1998)
78 ALR5th 489—§ 3

State v. Jamgochian, 109 R.I. 17, 279 A.2d 923 (1971)
72 ALR5th 1—§ 3

State v. Jamiolkoski, 272 N.J. Super. 326, 639 A.2d 1144 (App. Div. 1994)
15 ALR5th 391—§ 21

State v. Jamison, 93 Wash. 2d 794, 613 P.2d 776 (1980)
74 ALR5th 643—§ 3

State v. Jamison, 482 N.W.2d 409 (Iowa 1992)
43 ALR5th 1—§ 13

State v. Jamison, 2008-Ohio-2472, 2008 WL 2571783 (Ohio Ct. App. 5th Dist. Muskingum County 2008)
99 ALR6th 295—§ 9, 13

State v. Janda, 397 N.W.2d 59 (N.D. 1986)
38 ALR5th 433—§ 28, 48, 53

State v. Janes, 121 Wash. 2d 220, 850 P.2d 495 (1993)
22 ALR5th 787—§ 1 to 3

State v. Janisch, 290 N.W.2d 473 (S.D. 1980)
5 ALR5th 243—§ 39, 62

State v. Janise, 116 Ariz. 557, 570 P.2d 499 (1977)
46 ALR6th 241—§ 31, 34

State v. Janklow, 2005 SD 25, 693 N.W.2d 685 (S.D. 2005)
17 ALR6th 757—§ 7

State v. Jankowski, 1995 WL 686121 (Tenn. Crim. App. 1995)
90 ALR5th 453—§ 23

State v. Jannetta, 355 N.W.2d 189 (Minn. Ct. App. 1984)
111 ALR5th 239—§ 10

State v. Jansen, 1999 WL 285384 (Ohio Ct. App. 8th Dist. Cuyahoga County 1999)
88 ALR5th 121—§ 3, 35

State v. Janson, 964 S.W.2d 552 (Mo. Ct. App. S.D. 1998)
105 ALR5th 529—§ 13

State v. Janssen, 219 Wis. 2d 362, 580 N.W.2d 260 (1998)
31 ALR6th 333—§ 14

State v. Janto, 92 Haw. 19, 986 P.2d 306 (1999)
9 ALR6th 1—§ 6

State v. Januszewski, 182 Conn. 142, 438 A.2d 679 (1980)
34 ALR6th 1—§ 12

State v. Janz, 358 N.W.2d 547 (Iowa 1984)
15 ALR5th 391—§ 22

State v. Jaques, 428 N.W.2d 260 (S.D. 1988)
16 ALR6th 329—§ 7
24 ALR6th 591—§ 9, 13

State v. Jarman, 1999 UT App 269, 987 P.2d 1284 (Utah Ct. App. 1999)
92 ALR6th 1—§ 3, 9

State v. Jarman, 2000 WL 1717535 (Tenn. Crim. App. 2000)
97 ALR6th 653—§ 26

State v. Jaroslowski, 30 Del. 108, 7 Boyce 108, 103 A. 657 (Ct. of Oyer & Terminer 1918)
119 ALR5th 275—§ 2, 4

State v. Jarrells, 2000-Ohio-1634, 2000 WL 141259 (Ohio Ct. App. 3d Dist. Auglaize County 2000)
43 ALR6th 475—§ 16

State v. Jarrett, 530 So. 2d 1089 (Fla. Dist. Ct. App. 5th Dist. 1988)
114 ALR5th 173—§ 7

State v. Jarvis, 145 Vt. 8, 482 A.2d 65 (1984)
52 ALR5th 655—§ 4

State v. Jarvis, 146 Vt. 636, 509 A.2d 1005 (1986)
15 ALR5th 391—§ 26
91 ALR5th 343—§ 33

State v. Jarvis, 172 W. Va. 706, 310 S.E.2d 467 (1983)
66 ALR5th 397—§ 21

State v. Jarvis, 199 W. Va. 38, 483 S.E.2d 38 (1996)
77 ALR5th 201—§ 10

State v. Jarvis, 201 Kan. 678, 443 P.2d 272 (1968)
108 ALR5th 593—§ 49

State v. Jarvis, 649 N.W.2d 186 (Minn. Ct. App. 2002)
69 ALR6th 579—§ 8, 16

State v. Jarzembski, 1996 WL 402012 (Ohio Ct. App. 6th Dist. Fulton County 1996)
93 ALR5th 1—§ 7

State v. Jason, 820 So. 2d 1286 (La. Ct. App. 3d Cir. 2002)
125 ALR5th 497—§ 4

State v. Jason B., 47 Conn. App. 68, 702 A.2d 895 (1997)
18 ALR5th 856—§ 3, 6

State v. Jasuilewicz, 205 N.J. Super. 558, 501 A.2d 583 (App. Div. 1985)
55 ALR6th 157—§ 61

State v. Javier M., 2001-NMSC-030, 131 N.M. 1, 33 P.3d 1 (2001)
28 ALR6th 505—§ 41

State v. Jay, 724 S.W.2d 293 (Mo. App. 1987)
18 ALR5th 1—§ 16

State v. Jaynes, 35 Conn. App. 541, 645 A.2d 1060 (1994)
3 ALR5th 963—§ 3, 7, 10, 12

State v. Jaynes, 36 Conn. App. 417, 650 A.2d 1261 (1994)
95 ALR5th 611—§ 3

State v. Jaynes, 353 N.C. 534, 549 S.E.2d 179 (2001)

83 ALR6th 255—§ 15
State v. Jay, Slip Op. No. 10238 (Ohio App. Summit Co. 1981)
38 ALR5th 433—§ 44
State v. J.B., 309 Ark. 70, 827 S.W.2d 144 (1992)
102 ALR5th 525—§ 55
State v. J.B., 643 So. 2d 402 (La. App. 3d Cir. 1994)
15 ALR5th 391—§ 39
State v. J.B., 2005 WL 2447881 (N.J. Super. Ct. App. Div. 2005)
40 ALR6th 1—§ 23
State v. J.C.E., 235 Mont. 264, 767 P.2d 309 (1988)
38 ALR5th 433—§ 13, 16, 24
State v. J.D., 701 N.E.2d 908 (Ind. Ct. App. 1998)
18 ALR5th 856—§ 4
State v. J.D.O., 993 So. 2d 80 (Fla. 2d DCA 2008)
100 ALR6th 535—§ 3
State v. J.D.W., 910 P.2d 1242 (Utah App. 1995)
9 ALR5th 464—§ 8
State v. Jean, 310 N.C. 157, 311 S.E.2d 266 (1984)
103 ALR6th 507—§ 16
State v. Jeandell, CRIM. A. 89-06-0089, 1992 WL 21398 (Del. Super. Jan. 21, 1992)
99 ALR6th 295—§ 19
State v. Jeff, 761 So. 2d 574 (La. Ct. App. 1st Cir. 1999)
83 ALR5th 541—§ 5
State v. Jeffers, 116 Ariz. 192, 568 P.2d 1090 (Ct. App. Div. 2 1977)
99 ALR5th 557—§ 2, 10, 17
State v. Jeffers, 135 Ariz. 404, 661 P.2d 1105 (1983)
38 ALR5th 433—§ 13, 33
99 ALR6th 295—§ 13
State v. Jefferson, 391 S.W.2d 885 (Mo. 1965)
4 ALR5th 1—§ 4, 5
State v. Jefferson, 413 N.J. Super. 344, 994 A.2d 1067 (App. Div. 2010)

79 ALR6th 1—§ 46
State v. Jefferson, 529 S.W.2d 674 (Tenn. 1975)
70 ALR5th 587—§ 25
54 ALR6th 429—§ 27
State v. Jefferson, 938 S.W.2d 1 (Tenn. Crim. App. 1996)
24 ALR6th 1—§ 28
55 ALR6th 391—§ 5
State v. Jefferson, 2000 WL 502737 (Ohio Ct. App. 5th Dist. Stark County 2000)
125 ALR5th 357—§ 4
7 ALR6th 233—§ 5
State v. Jefferson, 2005 WL 3947950 (N.J. Super. Ct. App. Div. 2006)
40 ALR6th 1—§ 31
State v. Jefferson, 2007 WL 1181006 (Wash. Ct. App. Div. 1 2007)
26 ALR6th 511—§ 26
State v. Jeffords, 121 S.C. 443, 114 S.E. 415 (1922)
16 ALR6th 329—§ 7
State v. Jeffrey, 77 Wash. App. 222, 889 P.2d 956 (Div. 3 1995)
88 ALR5th 121—§ 3, 27
State v. Jeffrey, 220 Conn. 698, 601 A.2d 993 (1991)
102 ALR5th 447—§ 22
State v. Jeffries, 42 Wash. App. 142, 709 P.2d 819 (Div. 3 1985)
15 ALR5th 391—§ 5
92 ALR5th 35—§ 20
State v. Jeffries, 2001 WL 285620 (Ohio Ct. App. 8th Dist. Cuyahoga County 2001)
11 ALR6th 237—§ 16
State v. Jelks, 2008 WI App 148, 314 Wis. 2d 260, 757 N.W.2d 850 (Ct. App. 2008)
78 ALR6th 417—§ 5
State v. Jelliffe, 5 Ohio Misc. 2d 20, 449 N.E.2d 810 (Mun. Ct. 1982)
66 ALR5th 397—§ 24
State v. Jells, 53 Ohio St. 3d 22, 559 N.E.2d 464 (1990)
39 ALR5th 283—§ 14

State v. Jeney, 163 Ariz. 293, 787 P.2d 1089 (Ct. App. Div. 1 1989)
32 ALR6th 1—§ 7

State v. Jenkins, 15 Ohio St. 3d 164, 15 Ohio B.R. 311, 473 N.E.2d 264 (1984)
39 ALR5th 283—§ 14

State v. Jenkins, 15 S.W.3d 914 (Tenn. Crim. App. 1999)
27 ALR5th 593—§ 12

State v. Jenkins, 35 Conn. Supp. 516, 394 A.2d 204 (Super. Ct. Appellate Sess. 1977)
70 ALR6th 1—§ 19

State v. Jenkins, 82 Conn. App. 111, 842 A.2d 1148 (2004)
79 ALR6th 631—§ 4

State v. Jenkins, 82 Conn. App. 802, 847 A.2d 1044 (2004)
124 ALR5th 1—§ 5

State v. Jenkins, 93 Haw. 87, 997 P.2d 13 (2000)
53 ALR6th 81—§ 7
55 ALR6th 391—§ 9, 15, 21

State v. Jenkins, 100 Wash. App. 85, 995 P.2d 1268 (Div. 2 2000)
36 ALR5th 161—§ 12, 27
33 ALR6th 91—§ 3, 10, 22

State v. Jenkins, 104 Ohio App. 3d 265, 661 N.E.2d 806 (1st Dist. Hamilton County 1995)
15 ALR6th 515—§ 1

State v. Jenkins, 115 N.C. App. 520, 445 S.E.2d 622, 45 A.L.R.5th 885 (1994)
45 ALR5th 531—§ 3, 7

State v. Jenkins, 134 La. 185, 63 So. 869 (1913)
11 ALR5th 831—§ 7, 8
22 ALR5th 1—§ 40

State v. Jenkins, 176 W. Va. 652, 346 S.E.2d 802 (1986)
54 ALR6th 429—§ 11

State v. Jenkins, 191 W. Va. 87, 443 S.E.2d 244 (1994)
82 ALR5th 359—§ 3, 5
84 ALR5th 487—§ 24, 25, 29

State v. Jenkins, 257 Ga. 741, 363 S.E.2d 551 (1988)
124 ALR5th 1—§ 5

State v. Jenkins, 321 N.J. Super. 124, 728 A.2d 293 (App. Div. 1999)
100 ALR5th 67—§ 27, 30

State v. Jenkins, 340 So. 2d 157 (La. 1976)
65 ALR5th 407—§ 3
16 ALR6th 329—§ 4
24 ALR6th 591—§ 4, 14

State v. Jenkins, 778 S.W.2d 815 (Mo. Ct. App. E.D. 1989)
72 ALR6th 141—§ 7, 18

State v. Jenkins, 782 N.W.2d 211 (Minn. 2010)
101 ALR6th 331—§ 12

State v. Jenkins, 845 S.W.2d 787 (Tenn. Crim. App. 1992)
65 ALR6th 537—§ 13

State v. Jenkins, 910 So. 2d 934 (Fla. 2d DCA 2005)
94 ALR6th 525—§ 19

State v. Jenkins, 946 S.W.2d 12 (Mo. Ct. App. S.D. 1997)
47 ALR6th 107—§ 42

State v. Jenkins, 1995 WL 634356 (Ohio Ct. App. 2d Dist. Montgomery County 1995)
43 ALR6th 475—§ 8

State v. Jenkins, 1996 WL 662429 (Tenn. Crim. App. 1996)
73 ALR5th 383—§ 29

State v. Jenkins, 1998 WL 917806 (Tenn. Crim. App. 1998)
84 ALR6th 293—§ 21, 33

State v. Jenkins, 2000 WL 288658 (Ohio Ct. App. 7th Dist. Harrison County 2000)
24 ALR6th 1—§ 52

State v. Jenkins, 2005-Ohio-3092, 2005 WL 1423431 (Ohio Ct. App. 11th Dist. Lake County 2005)
38 ALR6th 97—§ 10

State v. Jenkins, 2005 WL 1812827 (Tenn. Crim. App. 2005)
26 ALR6th 511—§ 22

State v. Jenkins, 2005 WL 2447847 (N.J. Super. Ct. App. Div. 2005)
26 ALR6th 511—§ 6, 25

State v. Jenkins, 2007-Ohio-4227, 2007 WL 2351003 (Ohio Ct. App. 11th Dist. Trumbull County 2007)
102 ALR6th 279—§ 7

State v. Jenkins, 2009-Ohio-235, 2009 WL 147654 (Ohio Ct. App. 8th Dist. Cuyahoga County 2009)
71 ALR6th 1—§ 4

State v. Jenner, 434 N.W.2d 76 (S.D. 1988)
16 ALR6th 329—§ 12
24 ALR6th 591—§ 9, 13

State v. Jenner, 451 N.W.2d 710 (S.D. 1990)
29 ALR6th 1—§ 10

State v. Jennette, 706 S.W.2d 614 (Tenn. 1986)
45 ALR6th 643—§ 4

State v. Jennings, 111 Wash. App. 54, 44 P.3d 1 (Div. 2 2002)
71 ALR6th 625—§ 3, 29

State v. Jennings, 130 S.W.3d 43 (Tenn. 2004)
69 ALR6th 1—§ 21

State v. Jennings, 195 Neb. 434, 238 N.W.2d 477 (1976)
4 ALR5th 1—§ 19

State v. Jennings, 333 N.C. 579, 430 S.E.2d 188 (1993)
79 ALR5th 33—§ 13, 63

State v. Jennings, 335 S.C. 82, 515 S.E.2d 107 (Ct. App. 1999)
88 ALR5th 121—§ 3, 10, 32

State v. Jennings, 461 A.2d 361 (R.I. 1983)
58 ALR6th 499—§ 100

State v. Jennings, 555 P.2d 248 (Alaska 1976)
24 ALR5th 200—§ 8

State v. Jennings, 815 S.W.2d 434 (Mo. Ct. App. E.D. 1991)
65 ALR6th 537—§ 24

State v. Jennings, 875 P.2d 566 (Utah Ct. App. 1994)
9 ALR6th 633—§ 14
13 ALR6th 603—§ 20

State v. Jennings, 1991 WL 106100 (Tenn. Crim. App. 1991)
73 ALR5th 383—§ 5

State v. Jensen, 69 Haw. 534, 750 P.2d 932 (1988)
62 ALR6th 413—§ 4, 39

State v. Jensen, 86 Minn. 19, 89 N.W. 1126 (1902)
120 ALR5th 125—§ 2
121 ALR5th 1—§ 2

State v. Jensen, 109 Conn. App. 617, 952 A.2d 95 (2008)
84 ALR6th 293—§ 4, 15, 33

State v. Jensen, 124 N.M. 726
15 ALR5th 391—§ 16

State v. Jensen, 136 Wash. App. 1033, 2007 WL 25473 (Div. 2 2007)
103 ALR6th 347—§ 20

State v. Jensen, 151 Minn. 174, 186 N.W. 581 (1922)
54 ALR6th 429—§ 14

State v. Jensen, 178 Iowa 1098, 160 N.W. 832 (1917)
12 ALR5th 909—§ 4

State v. Jensen, 189 N.W.2d 919 (Iowa 1971)
6 ALR6th 533—§ 11

State v. Jensen, 226 Neb. 40, 409 N.W.2d 319 (1987)
42 ALR5th 291—§ 23

State v. Jensen, 269 Neb. 213, 691 N.W.2d 139 (2005)
5 ALR6th 1—§ 3

State v. Jensen, 269 Neb. 213, 691 N.W.2d 139, 2005 WL 119814 (2005)
5 ALR6th 1—§ 41

State v. Jensen, 313 Or. 587, 837 P.2d 525 (1992)
38 ALR5th 433—§ 14

State v. Jensen, 333 N.W.2d 686 (N.D. 1983)
63 ALR6th 1—§ 55

State v. Jensen, 482 N.W.2d 238 (Minn. Ct. App. 1992)

119 ALR5th 379—§ 3
State v. Jensen, 818 P.2d 551 (Utah 1991)

70 ALR6th 361—§ 29
State v. Jensen, 1998 S.D. 52, 579 N.W.2d 613 (S.D. 1998)

66 ALR5th 135—§ 38
State v. Jensen, 2011 WL 67967 (Minn. Ct. App. 2011)

84 ALR6th 293—§ 17
State v. Jerde, 93 Wash. App. 774, 970 P.2d 781 (Div. 2 1999)

9 ALR6th 541—§ 24
State v. Jerome, 1996 WL 255878 (Ohio Ct. App. 3d Dist. Marion County 1996)

85 ALR5th 595—§ 9
State v. Jerry C.O. (In the Interest of Jerry O.), 1997 WL 3329 (Wis App)

50 ALR5th 581—§ 7, 9, 16, 22
State v. Jesson, 142 Wash. App. 852, 177 P.3d 139 (Div. 3 2008)

45 ALR6th 643—§ 14
State v. Jessup, 31 Wash. App. 304, 641 P.2d 1185 (1982)

18 ALR5th 1—§ 28
State v. Jester, 68 N.J. 87, 342 A.2d 850 (1975)

45 ALR5th 1—§ 5, 10, 21
State v. Jester, 1999 WL 103713 (Tenn. Crim. App. 1999)

73 ALR5th 383—§ 56
State v. Jeter, 160 Wis. 2d 333, 466 N.W.2d 211 (App. 1991)

43 ALR5th 1—§ 13
State v. Jeter, 326 N.C. 457, 389 S.E.2d 805 (1990)

86 ALR5th 59—§ 5
State v. Jeudis, 62 Conn. App. 787, 772 A.2d 715 (2001)

32 ALR5th 149—§ 4, 30, 34
State v. Jeustiniano, 172 Conn. 275, 374 A.2d 209 (1977)

5 ALR5th 243—§ 2, 29, 30, 35
State v. Jewell, 1995 WL 381631 (Tenn. Crim. App. 1995)

73 ALR5th 383—§ 5

State v. Jewett, 146 Vt. 221, 500 A.2d 233 (1985)

31 ALR5th 229—§ 2
State v. Jewett, 148 Vt. 324, 532 A.2d 958 (1987)

19 ALR5th 470—§ 3, 4
State v. J.G., 261 N.J. Super. 409, 619 A.2d 232 (1993)

51 ALR5th 603—§ 2
State v. J.G., 2008 WL 2600713 (N.J. Super. Ct. App. Div. 2008)

69 ALR6th 579—§ 4
State v. J.H., 898 So. 2d 240, 197 Ed. Law Rep. 941 (Fla. Dist. Ct. App. 4th Dist. 2005)

59 ALR6th 393—§ 10
State v. Ji, 251 Kan. 3, 832 P.2d 1176 (1992)

94 ALR5th 537—§ 5
83 ALR6th 465—§ 3
State v. Jiles, 258 Iowa 1324, 142 N.W.2d 451 (1966)

11 ALR5th 497—§ 3
State v. Jim, 13 Neb. App. 112, 688 N.W.2d 895 (2004)

35 ALR6th 127—§ 5
State v. Jim, 765 P.2d 195 (N.M. App. 1988)

20 ALR5th 398—§ 8
State v. Jimenez, 165 Ariz. 444, 799 P.2d 785, 67 Ariz. Adv. Rep. 3 (1990)

20 ALR5th 177—§ 3, 9, 10
State v. Jimenez, 729 A.2d 693 (R.I. 1999)

18 ALR6th 1—§ 5, 36
State v. Jimenez, 828 S.W.2d 455 (Tex. App. El Paso 1992)

31 ALR6th 333—§ 10
State v. Jimenez, 2011 WL 5573832 (N.J. Super. Ct. App. Div. 2011)

72 ALR6th 437—§ 11, 13
74 ALR6th 69—§ 13, 25
State v. Jiminez, 89 N.M. 652, 556 P.2d 60 (App. 1976)

44 ALR5th 651—§ 2, 3
State v. Jiminez, 761 P.2d 577 (Utah Ct. App. 1988)

24 ALR6th 1—§ 39, 40

State v. Jiminez, 2008-Ohio-1601, 2008 WL 867733 (Ohio Ct. App. 2d Dist. Montgomery County 2008)

49 ALR6th 343—§ 14, 17

State v. J.J., 397 N.J. Super. 91, 935 A.2d 1252 (App. Div. 2007)

41 ALR6th 141—§ 6

State v. J.K., 2011-Ohio-5675, 2011 WL 5299296 (Ohio Ct. App. 8th Dist. Cuyahoga County 2011)

70 ALR6th 1—§ 4

State v. J.M., 824 So. 2d 105 (Fla. 2002)

38 ALR6th 1—§ 14, 18

State v. Joas, 2006 WI App 194, 296 Wis. 2d 421, 722 N.W.2d 401 (Ct. App. 2006)

84 ALR6th 293—§ 33

State v. Jock, 404 A.2d 518 (Del. Super. Ct. 1979)

29 ALR6th 1—§ 12

State v. John, 60 Wis. 2d 730, 211 N.W.2d 463 (1973)

105 ALR5th 529—§ 2, 31

State v. John G., 80 Conn. App. 714, 837 A.2d 829 (2004)

39 ALR6th 257—§ 35, 46
40 ALR6th 1—§ 9

State v. Johnican, 830 S.W.2d 215 (Tex. App. Houston 14th Dist. 1992)

87 ALR5th 361—§ 3, 10

State v. John L. Bradley, 1999 WL 824616 (Ohio Ct. App. 3d Dist. Logan County 1999)

78 ALR5th 489—§ 6, 9

State v. Johnlouis, 22 So. 3d 1150 (La. Ct. App. 3d Cir. 2009)

56 ALR6th 1—§ 19, 32

State v. Johns, 34 S.W.3d 93 (Mo. 2000)

110 ALR5th 1—§ 25

State v. Johns, 90 Ohio App. 3d 456, 629 N.E.2d 1069 (9th Dist. Wayne County 1993)

97 ALR6th 653—§ 26

State v. Johns, 185 Neb. 590, 177 N.W.2d 580 (1970)

124 ALR5th 1—§ 3

State v. Johns, 209 La. 244, 24 So. 2d 462 (1945)

9 ALR6th 363—§ 45

State v. Johns, 679 S.W.2d 253 (Mo. 1984)

55 ALR5th 125—§ 3, 7

State v. Johnson, 4 Neb. App. 776, 551 N.W.2d 742 (1996)

70 ALR5th 1—§ 2, 3, 5
72 ALR5th 109—§ 3
95 ALR5th 125—§ 2

State v. Johnson, 5 N.C. App. 469, 168 S.E.2d 709 (1969)

74 ALR5th 453—§ 3

State v. Johnson, 10 Ohio App. 3d 14, 460 N.E.2d 625 (10th Dist. Franklin County 1983)

82 ALR5th 359—§ 4
84 ALR5th 487—§ 21, 25

State v. Johnson, 14 Conn. App. 586, 543 A.2d 740 (1988)

19 ALR5th 823—§ 4, 12, 14
24 ALR6th 1—§ 47

State v. Johnson, 14 Wash. App. 225, 540 P.2d 435 (1975)

29 ALR5th 59—§ 7, 45

State v. Johnson, 16 Wash. App. 899, 559 P.2d 1380 (1977)

55 ALR5th 125—§ 12, 14, 25

State v. Johnson, 22 Conn. App. 40, 576 A.2d 171 (1990)

19 ALR5th 470—§ 12

State v. Johnson, 23 N.J. Super. 304, 93 A.2d 27 (App. Div. 1952)

9 ALR6th 1—§ 10

State v. Johnson, 23 Wash. 2d 751, 162 P.2d 440 (1945)

5 ALR5th 243—§ 59

State v. Johnson, 26 Conn. App. 433, 602 A.2d 36 (1992)

103 ALR6th 507—§ 12

State v. Johnson, 28 So. 3d 1125 (La. Ct. App. 5th Cir. 2009)

72 ALR6th 1—§ 18

State v. Johnson, 32 Ohio St. 3d 109, 512 N.E.2d 652 (1987)

43 ALR5th 777—§ 4

State v. Johnson, 35 Wash. App. 380, 666 P.2d 950 (Div. 1 1983)
   83 ALR5th 277—§ 11
   84 ALR5th 487—§ 23
State v. Johnson, 42 Wash. App. 425, 712 P.2d 301 (Div. 2 1985)
   84 ALR5th 487—§ 3, 19
State v. Johnson, 44 Conn. App. 125, 688 A.2d 867 (1997)
   45 ALR5th 591—§ 3
State v. Johnson, 44 S.C. 556, 21 S.E. 806 (1895)
   105 ALR5th 529—§ 11
State v. Johnson, 48 Wash. App. 681, 739 P.2d 1209 (Div. 1 1987)
   26 ALR6th 451—§ 11
State v. Johnson, 50 Conn. App. 46, 717 A.2d 786 (1998)
   70 ALR5th 533—§ 3
State v. Johnson, 55 Wash. 2d 594, 349 P.2d 227 (1960)
   45 ALR5th 591—§ 3
State v. Johnson, 56 Ohio St. 2d 35, 10 Ohio Ops. 3d 78, 381 N.E.2d 637 (1978)
   50 ALR5th 467—§ 3, 9
State v. Johnson, 59 Wash. App. 867, 802 P.2d 137 (Div. 3 1990)
   1 ALR6th 549—§ 7
   2 ALR6th 551—§ 5
State v. Johnson, 60 N.C. App. 369, 299 S.E.2d 237 (1983)
   55 ALR6th 391—§ 21
State v. Johnson, 60 Ohio App. 2d 45, 14 Ohio Ops. 3d 24, 395 N.E.2d 368 (Hamilton Co. 1977)
   50 ALR5th 467—§ 9
State v. Johnson, 61 N.C. 186 (1867)
   17 ALR5th 125—§ 5
State v. Johnson, 64 S.D. 162, 265 N.W. 599 (1936)
   19 ALR5th 351—§ 9, 18
State v. Johnson, 68 Hawaii 292, 711 P.2d 1295 (1985)
   15 ALR5th 391—§ 45
State v. Johnson, 69 Wash. App. 189, 847 P.2d 960 (1993)

   15 ALR5th 391—§ 16, 45
State v. Johnson, 75 Wash. App. 692, 879 P.2d 984 (Div. 2 1994)
   60 ALR5th 1—§ 8
   78 ALR5th 309—§ 2, 8
   45 ALR6th 643—§ 20
State v. Johnson, 79 Wash. App. 776, 904 P.2d 1188 (Div. 3 1995)
   106 ALR5th 397—§ 4
State v. Johnson, 80 Wash. 522, 141 P. 1040 (1914)
   57 ALR6th 445—§ 26
State v. Johnson, 85 N.M. 465, 513 P.2d 399 (App. 1973)
   55 ALR5th 125—§ 12, 13, 18, 22
State v. Johnson, 87 Minn. 221, 91 N.W. 604 (1902)
   120 ALR5th 125—§ 2
State v. Johnson, 87 Minn. 221, 91 N.W. 840 (1902)
   121 ALR5th 1—§ 2
State v. Johnson, 88 Ohio St. 3d 95, 723 N.E.2d 1054 (2000)
   39 ALR5th 283—§ 20, 37
State v. Johnson, 90 Wash. App. 54, 950 P.2d 981 (Div. 2 1998)
   84 ALR5th 487—§ 31
State v. Johnson, 92 Wash. 2d 671, 600 P.2d 1249 (1979)
   39 ALR5th 283—§ 4, 48, 67
   79 ALR5th 419—§ 9
State v. Johnson, 94 Wash. App. 882, 974 P.2d 855 (Div. 1 1999)
   85 ALR5th 1—§ 44
State v. Johnson, 96 Idaho 727, 536 P.2d 295, 96 A.L.R.3d 1163 (1975)
   85 ALR5th 187—§ 3, 15
State v. Johnson, 96 Wash. 2d 926, 639 P.2d 1332 (1982)
   56 ALR5th 385—§ 6
State v. Johnson, 99 N.M. 682, 662 P.2d 1349 (1983)
   57 ALR5th 141—§ 13
State v. Johnson, 102 Fla. 19, 135 So. 816 (1931)
   107 ALR5th 1—§ 2

State v. Johnson, 104 Wash. App. 409,
16 P.3d 680 (Div. 2 2001)
58 ALR6th 499—§ 31

State v. Johnson, 105 N.M. 63, 728 P.2d
473, R.I.C.O. Bus. Disp. Guide
(CCH) ¶ 6441 (Ct. App. 1986)
58 ALR6th 385—§ 24, 36

State v. Johnson, 105 Wash. 2d 92, 711
P.2d 1017 (1986)
105 ALR5th 529—§ 8

State v. Johnson, 110 Idaho 516, 716
P.2d 1288 (1986)
19 ALR5th 470—§ 3, 12
61 ALR5th 1—§ 2, 3, 7

State v. Johnson, 112 Ariz. 17, 536 P.2d
1035 (1975)
100 ALR6th 535—§ 3

State v. Johnson, 112 Ohio St. 3d 210,
2006-Ohio-6404, 858 N.E.2d 1144
(2006)
71 ALR6th 625—§ 29

State v. Johnson, 116 La. 856, 41 So.
117 (1906)
16 ALR6th 329—§ 6
19 ALR6th 115—§ 9
24 ALR6th 591—§ 4, 14

State v. Johnson, 119 R.I. 749, 383 A.2d
1012 (1978)
29 ALR6th 1—§ 10

State v. Johnson, 120 N.J. 263, 576 A.2d
834 (1990)
9 ALR5th 369—§ 2, 17

State v. Johnson, 124 N.C. App. 462,
478 S.E.2d 16 (1996)
104 ALR5th 229—§ 3, 4

State v. Johnson, 124 Wash. 2d 57, 873
P.2d 514 (1994)
102 ALR6th 279—§ 20

State v. Johnson, 127 N.J. 458, 606 A.2d
315 (1992)
18 ALR5th 1—§ 4

State v. Johnson, 128 N.C. App. 361,
496 S.E.2d 805 (1998)
99 ALR6th 295—§ 5

State v. Johnson, 130 Wash. App. 1005,
2005 WL 2672046 (Div. 3 2005)
19 ALR6th 697—§ 4

State v. Johnson, 131 Idaho 808, 964
P.2d 675 (Ct. App. 1998)
87 ALR5th 631—§ 21

State v. Johnson, 131 N.J. Super. 252,
329 A.2d 560 (App. Div. 1974)
9 ALR6th 633—§ 4
13 ALR6th 603—§ 27, 41

State v. Johnson, 132 Ariz. 5, 643 P.2d
708 (Ct. App. Div. 1 1981)
83 ALR5th 277—§ 9

State v. Johnson, 133 Wis. 2d 207, 395
N.W.2d 176 (1986)
70 ALR5th 1—§ 2, 8

State v. Johnson, 134 W. Va. 357, 59
S.E.2d 485 (1950)
66 ALR5th 397—§ 4, 25

State v. Johnson, 141 La. 775, 75 So.
678 (1917)
98 ALR6th 455—§ 29

State v. Johnson, 141 Wash. 324, 251 P.
589 (1926)
54 ALR6th 429—§ 13

State v. Johnson, 143 Md. App. 173, 794
A.2d 654 (2002)
95 ALR5th 125—§ 3

State v. Johnson, 147 Ariz. 395, 710
P.2d 1050 (1985)
99 ALR6th 295—§ 21

State v. Johnson, 147 P.3d 163 (Kan. Ct.
App. 2006)
99 ALR6th 295—§ 5

State v. Johnson, 159 N.J. Super. 26, 386
A.2d 1339 (1978)
45 ALR5th 531—§ 6

State v. Johnson, 161 N.C. App. 68, 587
S.E.2d 445 (2003)
78 ALR6th 297—§ 37

State v. Johnson, 167 N.J. Super. 64, 400
A.2d 516 (1979)
13 ALR5th 118—§ 2

State v. Johnson, 167 Wash. App. 1041,
2012 WL 1392954 (Div. 1 2012)
98 ALR6th 455—§ 3
99 ALR6th 113—§ 3
101 ALR6th 499—§ 3
102 ALR6th 279—§ 3, 5
103 ALR6th 35—§ 3

State v. Johnson, 168 N.J. 608, 775 A.2d 1273 (2001)

50 ALR6th 455—§ 2, 5, 7, 9, 11, 34

State v. Johnson, 169 N.C. App. 301, 610 S.E.2d 739 (2005)

63 ALR6th 1—§ 5, 17, 36, 42, 44

State v. Johnson, 171 Ariz. 39, 827 P.2d 1134, 108 Ariz. Adv. Rep. 23 (App. 1992)

45 ALR5th 767—§ 16

State v. Johnson, 185 Conn. 163, 440 A.2d 858 (1981)

39 ALR5th 283—§ 3, 45

State v. Johnson, 186 Ariz. 329, 922 P.2d 294 (1996)

90 ALR5th 453—§ 28

State v. Johnson, 186 Or. App. 186, 62 P.3d 861 (2003)

106 ALR5th 397—§ 3

State v. Johnson, 188 N.J. Super. 416, 457 A.2d 1175 (App. Div. 1982)

51 ALR6th 1—§ 20
52 ALR6th 1—§ 3
53 ALR6th 1—§ 3

State v. Johnson, 188 Wis. 2d 80, 524 N.W.2d 648 (Ct. App. 1994)

55 ALR6th 513—§ 12

State v. Johnson, 195 Wash. 545, 81 P.2d 529 (1938)

10 ALR5th 700—§ 15, 30

State v. Johnson, 199 Mont. 211, 646 P.2d 507 (1982)

57 ALR6th 445—§ 49

State v. Johnson, 213 S.C. 241, 49 S.E.2d 6 (1948)

57 ALR6th 313—§ 4

State v. Johnson, 217 Ariz. 58, 170 P.3d 667 (Ct. App. Div. 2 2007)

46 ALR6th 495—§ 6

State v. Johnson, 219 Conn. 557, 594 A.2d 933 (1991)

109 ALR5th 99—§ 3

State v. Johnson, 221 Mont. 503, 719 P.2d 1248 (1986)

109 ALR5th 611—§ 3

State v. Johnson, 227 Conn. 534, 630 A.2d 1059 (1993)

26 ALR5th 1—§ 4

State v. Johnson, 237 Wis. 2d 696, 2000 WI App 143, 616 N.W.2d 923 (Ct. App. 2000)

27 ALR6th 183—§ 38

State v. Johnson, 243 Neb. 758, 502 N.W.2d 477 (1993)

43 ALR5th 1—§ 12
72 ALR6th 1—§ 17

State v. Johnson, 253 Kan. 356, 856 P.2d 134 (1993)

78 ALR6th 297—§ 37, 47

State v. Johnson, 254 N.W.2d 114 (S.D. 1977)

4 ALR5th 1—§ 19

State v. Johnson, 261 Neb. 1001, 627 N.W.2d 753 (2001)

1 ALR6th 549—§ 7

State v. Johnson, 267 Ga. 305, 477 S.E.2d 579 (1996)

103 ALR6th 137—§ 16

State v. Johnson, 268 N.W.2d 613 (S.D. 1978)

9 ALR5th 464—§ 3, 11

State v. Johnson, 269 N.J. Super. 276, 635 A.2d 527 (App. Div. 1993)

52 ALR6th 1—§ 3

State v. Johnson, 274 N.J. Super. 137, 643 A.2d 631 (App. Div. 1994)

19 ALR6th 115—§ 4, 7, 10

State v. Johnson, 278 S.C. 668, 301 S.E.2d 138 (1983)

71 ALR6th 335—§ 5

State v. Johnson, 298 N.C. 47, 257 S.E.2d 597 (1979)

83 ALR6th 465—§ 50

State v. Johnson, 298 N.C. 355, 259 S.E.2d 752 (1979)

83 ALR6th 465—§ 12, 50

State v. Johnson, 300 N.W.2d 4 (Minn. 1980)

86 ALR5th 59—§ 5

State v. Johnson, 301 N.W.2d 625 (N.D. 1981)

69 ALR6th 275—§ 18

State v. Johnson, 306 S.C. 119, 410 S.E.2d 547 (1991)

---

79 ALR5th 33—§ 66, 68
81 ALR5th 563—§ 3
12 ALR6th 267—§ 5
State v. Johnson, 310 So. 2d 600 (La. 1975)
42 ALR5th 581—§ 4
State v. Johnson, 316 S.W.3d 390 (Mo. Ct. App. W.D. 2010)
78 ALR6th 599—§ 8
State v. Johnson, 317 N.C. 343, 346 S.E.2d 596 (1986)
1 ALR6th 657—§ 11
State v. Johnson, 317 N.C. 417, 347 S.E.2d 7 (1986)
86 ALR5th 59—§ 5
State v. Johnson, 318 Mo. 596, 300 S.W. 702 (1927)
19 ALR5th 823—§ 16, 18
State v. Johnson, 318 N.W.2d 417 (Iowa 1982)
119 ALR5th 275—§ 7
State v. Johnson, 319 So. 2d 786 (La. 1975)
55 ALR5th 125—§ 3, 8
State v. Johnson, 327 N.W.2d 580 (Minn. 1982)
73 ALR5th 383—§ 5
State v. Johnson, 334 S.C. 78, 512 S.E.2d 795 (1999)
84 ALR5th 487—§ 22
State v. Johnson, 335 N.C. 509, 438 S.E.2d 722 (1994)
57 ALR6th 445—§ 43
State v. Johnson, 337 N.C. 212, 446 S.E.2d 92 (1994)
39 ALR5th 283—§ 4, 22, 23
State v. Johnson, 340 N.C. 32, 455 S.E.2d 644 (1995)
32 ALR6th 1—§ 11
State v. Johnson, 340 Or. 319, 131 P.3d 173 (2006)
30 ALR6th 1—§ 4, 7
32 ALR6th 1—§ 11
State v. Johnson, 340 P.3d 230 (Wash. Ct. App. Div. 2 2014)
101 ALR6th 545—§ 5

State v. Johnson, 343 So. 2d 155 (La. 1977)
45 ALR5th 531—§ 1
65 ALR5th 407—§ 3, 4, 16
State v. Johnson, 359 N.W.2d 698 (Minn. Ct. App. 1984)
73 ALR5th 383—§ 5
State v. Johnson, 365 N.J. Super. 27, 837 A.2d 1131 (App. Div. 2003)
71 ALR6th 1—§ 4
State v. Johnson, 392 N.W.2d 685 (Minn. Ct. App. 1986)
55 ALR6th 513—§ 8
State v. Johnson, 403 N.W.2d 319 (Minn. Ct. App. 1987)
28 ALR6th 505—§ 7, 11
State v. Johnson, 403 So. 2d 1095 (Fla. Dist. Ct. App. 4th Dist. 1981)
122 ALR5th 439—§ 5
State v. Johnson, 404 So. 2d 239 (La. 1981)
19 ALR6th 115—§ 4, 9, 10
State v. Johnson, 408 So. 2d 1280 (La. 1982)
103 ALR5th 463—§ 3
State v. Johnson, 413 A.2d 931 (Me. 1980)
58 ALR6th 499—§ 97
State v. Johnson, 443 So. 2d 744 (La. Ct. App. 4th Cir. 1983)
93 ALR5th 527—§ 15
State v. Johnson, 463 So. 2d 620 (La. Ct. App. 1st Cir. 1984)
99 ALR6th 295—§ 21
State v. Johnson, 475 So. 2d 394 (La. Ct. App. 1st Cir. 1985)
102 ALR6th 279—§ 5
State v. Johnson, 479 A.2d 1284 (Me. 1984)
27 ALR6th 183—§ 5, 31
State v. Johnson, 483 N.W.2d 109 (Minn. Ct. App. 1992)
19 ALR6th 697—§ 3, 19
State v. Johnson, 485 S.W.2d 106 (Mo. 1972)
88 ALR5th 429—§ 6

State v. Johnson, 509 N.W.2d 681 (S.D. 1993)
1 ALR6th 549—§ 25
State v. Johnson, 529 S.W.2d 658 (Mo. Ct. App. 1975)
125 ALR5th 281—§ 6
State v. Johnson, 531 N.W.2d 275 (N.D. 1995)
114 ALR5th 235—§ 9
State v. Johnson, 534 So. 2d 529 (La. Ct. App. 5th Cir. 1988)
66 ALR5th 397—§ 10, 14
State v. Johnson, 534 So. 2d 1322 (La. Ct. App. 4th Cir. 1988)
103 ALR5th 463—§ 3
State v. Johnson, 539 S.W.2d 493 (Mo. Ct. App. 1976)
68 ALR5th 343—§ 3, 12
79 ALR5th 237—§ 5
State v. Johnson, 549 S.W.2d 627 (Mo. App. 1977)
39 ALR5th 283—§ 4, 59
State v. Johnson, 559 So. 2d 911 (La. Ct. App. 4th Cir. 1990)
54 ALR6th 429—§ 7
State v. Johnson, 561 So. 2d 1139, 15 FLW S. 289, 37 A.L.R.5th 743 (Fla. 1990)
37 ALR5th 1—§ 3
State v. Johnson, 568 N.W.2d 426 (Minn. 1997)
22 ALR5th 1—§ 14, 17, 31, 44
State v. Johnson, 573 So. 2d 127 (Fla. Dist. Ct. App. 4th Dist. 1991)
113 ALR5th 597—§ 8
State v. Johnson, 579 S.W.2d 771 (Mo. Ct. App. S.D. 1979)
65 ALR5th 407—§ 3
State v. Johnson, 580 S.W.2d 254 (Mo. 1979)
29 ALR5th 59—§ 7, 9
State v. Johnson, 595 So. 2d 20, 17 FLW S. 130 (Fla. 1992)
7 ALR5th 263—§ 7
State v. Johnson, 604 So. 2d 685 (La. App. 1st Cir. 1992)
45 ALR5th 531—§ 9

State v. Johnson, 632 S.W.2d 43 (Mo. App. 1982)
36 ALR5th 255—§ 24, 31, 33
State v. Johnson, 632 S.W.2d 506 (Mo. App. 1982)
39 ALR5th 283—§ 4, 54, 60, 67
State v. Johnson, 637 S.W.2d 157 (Mo. App. 1982)
39 ALR5th 283—§ 4, 54, 60, 67
State v. Johnson, 660 So. 2d 942 (La. App. 4th Cir. 1995)
50 ALR5th 581—§ 7, 16, 20
State v. Johnson, 665 So. 2d 1237 (La. App. 2d Cir. 1995)
41 ALR5th 171—§ 52, 54, 85
State v. Johnson, 666 N.W.2d 619 (Iowa Ct. App. 2003)
43 ALR6th 475—§ 22
State v. Johnson, 667 A.2d 523 (R.I. 1995)
104 ALR5th 357—§ 5
54 ALR6th 429—§ 27
State v. Johnson, 672 S.W.2d 160 (Mo. Ct. App. E.D. 1984)
99 ALR6th 113—§ 18
State v. Johnson, 673 S.W.2d 877 (Tenn. Crim. App. 1984)
78 ALR5th 1—§ 22
State v. Johnson, 679 N.W.2d 169 (Minn. Ct. App. 2004)
92 ALR6th 1—§ 5
State v. Johnson, 689 N.W.2d 247 (Minn. Ct. App. 2004)
101 ALR6th 331—§ 12
State v. Johnson, 693 So. 2d 233 (La. Ct. App. 4th Cir. 1997)
99 ALR6th 295—§ 6, 7
State v. Johnson, 695 So. 2d 771 (Fla. 5th DCA 1997)
101 ALR6th 331—§ 10
State v. Johnson, 706 So. 2d 468 (La. Ct. App. 4th Cir. 1997)
38 ALR5th 433—§ 26
State v. Johnson, 716 So. 2d 403, 87 A.L.R.5th 737 (La. Ct. App. 4th Cir. 1998)
87 ALR5th 181—§ 5

State v. Johnson, 720 P.2d 37 (Alaska 1986)

7 ALR5th 758—§ 7

State v. Johnson, 728 So. 2d 901 (La. Ct. App. 5th Cir. 1999)

28 ALR6th 505—§ 11

State v. Johnson, 744 N.W.2d 376 (Minn. 2008)

46 ALR6th 63—§ 3, 11

State v. Johnson, 759 So. 2d 1052 (La. Ct. App. 2d Cir. 2000)

55 ALR5th 423—§ 8.5
102 ALR5th 327—§ 5

State v. Johnson, 764 So. 2d 1113 (La. Ct. App. 4th Cir. 2000)

103 ALR6th 247—§ 13

State v. Johnson, 769 So. 2d 660 (La. Ct. App. 4th Cir. 2000)

41 ALR6th 141—§ 8

State v. Johnson, 770 S.W.2d 263 (Mo. App. 1989)

5 ALR5th 243—§ 2, 58
8 ALR5th 775—§ 5

State v. Johnson, 781 S.W.2d 873 (Tenn. Crim. 1989)

39 ALR5th 283—§ 4

State v. Johnson, 784 P.2d 1135 (Utah 1989)

84 ALR5th 487—§ 13, 21

State v. Johnson, 825 So. 2d 1230 (La. Ct. App. 4th Cir. 2002)

11 ALR6th 237—§ 13

State v. Johnson, 855 S.W.2d 470 (Mo. Ct. App. W.D. 1993)

108 ALR5th 593—§ 20

State v. Johnson, 968 S.W.2d 883 (Tenn. Crim. App. 1997)

15 ALR5th 391—§ 33

State v. Johnson, 980 S.W.2d 414 (Tenn. Crim. App. 1998)

64 ALR5th 637—§ 3

State v. Johnson, 988 S.W.2d 115 (Mo. Ct. App. W.D. 1999)

29 ALR6th 1—§ 8

State v. Johnson, 1987 WL 29567 (Ohio Ct. App. 2d Dist. Montgomery County 1987)

99 ALR6th 295—§ 9

State v. Johnson, 1992 OK CR 72, 877 P.2d 1136 (Okla. Crim. App. 1992)

107 ALR5th 567—§ 3, 11

State v. Johnson, 1992 WL 328492 (Ohio Ct. App. 9th Dist. Summit County 1992)

57 ALR5th 141—§ 2, 3

State v. Johnson, 1994 WL 151103 (Tenn. Crim. App. 1994)

73 ALR5th 383—§ 6

State v. Johnson, 1996 WL 56515 (Minn. Ct. App. 1996)

73 ALR5th 383—§ 5

State v. Johnson, 1996 WL 200623 (Ohio Ct. App. 2d Dist. Montgomery County 1996)

7 ALR6th 233—§ 5

State v. Johnson, 1997 WL 406652 (Minn. Ct. App. 1997)

73 ALR5th 383—§ 20

State v. Johnson, 1997 WL 699694 (Wash. Ct. App. Div. 1 1997)

73 ALR5th 383—§ 4

State v. Johnson, 1998 WL 453768 (Ohio Ct. App. 2d Dist. Montgomery County 1998)

94 ALR5th 393—§ 16

State v. Johnson, 1998 WL 655268 (Ohio Ct. App. 10th Dist. Franklin County 1998)

78 ALR5th 489—§ 3

State v. Johnson, 1998 WL 904917 (Ohio Ct. App. 6th Dist. Lucas County 1998)

78 ALR5th 489—§ 3, 10

State v. Johnson, 1999 ND 33, 590 N.W.2d 192 (N.D. 1999)

37 ALR6th 357—§ 23
50 ALR6th 455—§ 6, 9, 24, 36, 40

State v. Johnson, 2000 WL 1760225 (Ohio Ct. App. 1st Dist. Hamilton County 2000)

21 ALR6th 1—§ 4

State v. Johnson, 2001 -NMSC- 001, 15 P.3d 1233 (N.M. 2000)

52 ALR5th 655—§ 4

State v. Johnson, 2001-NMSC-001, 130 N.M. 6, 15 P.3d 1233 (2000)
92 ALR6th 295—§ 3, 7, 8, 12
93 ALR6th 207—§ 3
95 ALR6th 1—§ 3
State v. Johnson, 2001 WL 316180 (Minn. Ct. App. 2001)
50 ALR6th 455—§ 4, 13, 14, 28, 44
State v. Johnson, 2002-Ohio-6471, 2002 WL 31663503 (Ohio Ct. App. 11th Dist. Ashtabula County 2002)
72 ALR6th 1—§ 4
State v. Johnson, 2005 WL 3487971 (N.J. Super. Ct. App. Div. 2005)
69 ALR6th 1—§ 23
State v. Johnson, 2006-Ohio-7004, 2006 WL 3825219 (Ohio Ct. App. 6th Dist. Ottawa County 2006)
26 ALR6th 511—§ 19
State v. Johnson, 2006 WL 905363 (N.J. 2006)
26 ALR6th 511—§ 17
State v. Johnson, 2006 WL 3218517 (Mo. 2006)
20 ALR6th 479—§ 23
State v. Johnson, 2007 MT 213N, 339 Mont. 537, 169 P.3d 406 (2007)
33 ALR6th 91—§ 19
State v. Johnson, 2009-Ohio-45, 2009 WL 50127 (Ohio Ct. App. 6th Dist. Lucas County 2009)
56 ALR6th 185—§ 39
State v. Johnson, 2010 WL 521028 (Tenn. Crim. App. 2010)
98 ALR6th 455—§ 12
State v. Johnson, 2010 WL 1427279 (N.J. Super. Ct. App. Div. 2010)
98 ALR6th 455—§ 12
State v. Johnson, 2013 WL 5777282 (W. Va. 2013)
102 ALR6th 279—§ 14
State v. Johnson, Slip. Op CA 2361 (Ohio App. Clark Co. 1987)
38 ALR5th 433—§ 55
State v. Johnston, 39 N.C. App. 179, 249 S.E.2d 879 (1978)
29 ALR5th 59—§ 85

State v. Johnston, 64 Ohio App. 3d 238, 580 N.E.2d 1162 (10th Dist.Franklin County 1990)
65 ALR5th 407—§ 7
State v. Johnston, 123 Idaho 222, 846 P.2d 224 (App. 1993)
15 ALR5th 391—§ 45
State v. Johnston, 128 Wash. App. 1043, 2005 WL 1705802 (Div. 2 2005)
26 ALR6th 511—§ 50
State v. Johnston, 133 Wis. 2d 261, 394 N.W.2d 915 (Ct. App. 1986)
23 ALR6th 1—§ 10
State v. Johnston, 143 Wash. App. 1, 177 P.3d 1127 (Div. 3 2007)
56 ALR6th 185—§ 23
State v. Johnston, 150 N.H. 448, 839 A.2d 830 (2004)
15 ALR6th 515—§ 4, 34
State v. Johnston, 154 N.C. App. 500, 572 S.E.2d 438 (2002)
34 ALR6th 1—§ 9
State v. Johnston, 184 Wis. 2d 794, 518 N.W.2d 759 (1994)
50 ALR6th 1—§ 8
State v. Johnston, 193 N.C. App. 247, 666 S.E.2d 891 (2008)
96 ALR6th 355—§ 23
State v. Johnston, 390 N.W.2d 451 (Minn. Ct. App. 1986)
73 ALR5th 383—§ 29
State v. Johnston, 406 N.W.2d 794 (Iowa Ct. App. 1987)
30 ALR6th 103—§ 4, 46
State v. Johnston, 565 So. 2d 262 (Ala. App. 1990)
1 ALR5th 317—§ 4
State v. Johnston, 743 So. 2d 22 (Fla. Dist. Ct. App. 2d Dist. 1999)
79 ALR5th 33—§ 2
State v. Johnston, 957 S.W.2d 734 (Mo. 1997)
78 ALR6th 297—§ 54, 57 to 59
State v. Johnston, 979 S.W.2d 461 (Mo. Ct. App. W.D. 1998)
87 ALR5th 693—§ 2, 4, 5

State v. Johnston, 1986 WL 8798 (Ohio Ct. App. 4th Dist.Hocking County 1986)

57 ALR5th 141—§ 7

State v. Johnston, 2002-Ohio-3295, 2002 WL 1393988 (Ohio Ct. App. 2d Dist. Montgomery County 2002)

3 ALR6th 543—§ 11

State v. Joiner, 20 Ohio N.P. (n.s.) 313, 28 Ohio Dec. 199, 1917 WL 1173 (C.P. 1917)

102 ALR5th 525—§ 79

State v. Joiner, 161 La. 518, 109 So. 51 (1926)

101 ALR6th 499—§ 14

State v. Jola, 409 N.W.2d 17 (Minn. Ct. App. 1987)

15 ALR5th 391—§ 13
92 ALR5th 35—§ 12

State v. Jolivet, 712 P.2d 843, 26 Utah Adv. Rep. 15 (Utah 1986)

39 ALR5th 283—§ 4, 56, 60

State v. Jolla, 384 So. 2d 370 (La. 1980)

28 ALR6th 505—§ 9

State v. Jolley, 312 N.C. 296, 321 S.E.2d 883 (1984)

58 ALR6th 499—§ 21, 98

State v. Jolly, 20 N.C. 108, 3 Dev. & Bat. (Orig. Ed.) 110 (1838)

23 ALR6th 1—§ 4, 16

State v. Joly, 219 Conn. 234, 593 A.2d 96, 16 A.L.R.5th 1093 (1991)

16 ALR5th 841—§ 2, 4

State v. Jones, 2 Kan. App. 2d 38, 573 P.2d 1134 (1978)

58 ALR6th 499—§ 60

State v. Jones, 5 N.J. Misc. 1010, 139 A. 422 (Sup. Ct. 1927)

54 ALR6th 429—§ 5, 7

State v. Jones, 6 Ariz. App. 26, 429 P.2d 518 (1967)

45 ALR5th 591—§ 9

State v. Jones, 11 Kan. App. 2d 428, 724 P.2d 146 (1986)

92 ALR5th 35—§ 2, 21

State v. Jones, 15 S.W.3d 880 (Tenn. Crim. App. 1999)

3 ALR6th 269—§ 9, 22, 27

State v. Jones, 24 Kan. App. 2d 405, 947 P.2d 1030 (1997)

58 ALR6th 499—§ 52

State v. Jones, 27 Kan. App. 2d 476, 5 P.3d 1012 (2000)

92 ALR6th 171—§ 11

State v. Jones, 27 Kan. App. 2d 910, 8 P.3d 1282 (2000)

3 ALR6th 543—§ 4

State v. Jones, 29 S.C. 201, 7 S.E. 296 (1888)

54 ALR6th 429—§ 17

State v. Jones, 33 Wash. App. 275, 653 P.2d 1369 (Div. 1 1982)

59 ALR5th 615—§ 3, 4, 11

State v. Jones, 36 Or. App. 271, 584 P.2d 349 (1978)

99 ALR5th 557—§ 10

State v. Jones, 37 Conn. App. 437, 656 A.2d 696 (1995)

32 ALR6th 1—§ 6
81 ALR6th 505—§ 30

State v. Jones, 37 Ohio St. 2d 21, 66 Ohio Op. 2d 79, 306 N.E.2d 409 (1974)

124 ALR5th 1—§ 3

State v. Jones, 44 Conn. App. 476, 691 A.2d 14 (1997)

69 ALR6th 579—§ 4

State v. Jones, 44 Del. 372, 57 A.2d 109 (Ct. of Oyer & Terminer 1947)

70 ALR5th 587—§ 16

State v. Jones, 45 Or. App. 617, 608 P.2d 1220 (1980)

58 ALR6th 499—§ 48

State v. Jones, 49 Ohio St. 3d 51, 550 N.E.2d 469 (1990)

46 ALR6th 241—§ 10, 19

State v. Jones, 50 Conn. App. 338, 718 A.2d 470 (1998)

40 ALR5th 113—§ 3

State v. Jones, 50 Ohio App. 3d 40, 552 N.E.2d 651 (Lucas Co. 1988)

36 ALR5th 255—§ 5, 8, 33

State v. Jones, 51 Conn. App. 126, 721 A.2d 903 (1998)

90 ALR5th 453—§ 6
23 ALR6th 307—§ 7, 8
State v. Jones, 56 N.C. App. 259, 289
S.E.2d 383 (1982)
79 ALR5th 237—§ 5
State v. Jones, 58 Or. App. 277, 648 P.2d
869 (1982)
6 ALR6th 533—§ 17
State v. Jones, 59 Wash. App. 744, 801
P.2d 263 (Div. 1 1990)
73 ALR5th 383—§ 5
State v. Jones, 72 N.C. App. 610, 325
S.E.2d 309 (1985)
28 ALR6th 505—§ 9
State v. Jones, 72 Ohio App. 3d 522, 595
N.E.2d 485 (6th Dist. Erie County
1991)
109 ALR5th 99—§ 6
State v. Jones, 73 Wyo. 122, 276 P.2d
445 (1954)
96 ALR5th 523—§ 6
State v. Jones, 80 N.C. 415 (1879)
11 ALR5th 831—§ 4, 13
State v. Jones, 82 Or. App. 388, 728 P.2d
100 (1986)
50 ALR5th 703—§ 6
State v. Jones, 83 Ohio App. 3d 723, 615
N.E.2d 713 (2d Dist. Miami County
1992)
1 ALR6th 657—§ 14
State v. Jones, 83 P.3d 1270 (Kan. Ct.
App. 2004)
23 ALR6th 307—§ 40
State v. Jones, 85 Wash. App. 797, 934
P.2d 1224 (Div. 3 1997)
84 ALR6th 293—§ 16
State v. Jones, 88 Ohio St. 3d 430, 727
N.E.2d 886 (2000)
19 ALR5th 470—§ 3
State v. Jones, 89 N.C. App. 584, 367
S.E.2d 139 (1988)
38 ALR5th 433—§ 9, 15
State v. Jones, 91 Ohio St. 3d 335, 2001-
Ohio-57, 744 N.E.2d 1163 (2001)
83 ALR6th 255—§ 23
State v. Jones, 92 Conn. App. 1, 882
A.2d 1277 (2005)

84 ALR6th 427—§ 6
State v. Jones, 93 Wash. App. 166, 968
P.2d 888 (Div. 1 1998)
27 ALR5th 593—§ 32
State v. Jones, 96 N.C. App. 389, 386
S.E.2d 217 (1989)
23 ALR6th 307—§ 14
State v. Jones, 97 N.C. App. 189, 388
S.E.2d 213 (1990)
24 ALR5th 428—§ 2, 18
State v. Jones, 99 N.C. App. 412, 393
S.E.2d 585 (1990)
85 ALR5th 595—§ 2, 9
State v. Jones, 101 Wash. 2d 113, 677
P.2d 131 (1984)
84 ALR5th 487—§ 19
State v. Jones, 105 N.J. Super. 493, 253
A.2d 193 (1969)
29 ALR5th 702—§ 4, 6
State v. Jones, 112 N.C. App. 337, 435
S.E.2d 574 (1993)
28 ALR6th 505—§ 9
State v. Jones, 115 Conn. App. 581, 974
A.2d 72 (2009)
93 ALR6th 275—§ 3, 13
State v. Jones, 115 Idaho 1029, 772 P.2d
236 (Ct. App. 1989)
56 ALR6th 323—§ 5
State v. Jones, 115 Iowa 113, 88 N.W.
196 (1901)
45 ALR5th 591—§ 15
State v. Jones, 130 Wash. 2d 302, 922
P.2d 806 (1996)
73 ALR5th 383—§ 3
90 ALR5th 453—§ 43
State v. Jones, 131 Wash. App. 1021,
2006 WL 182938 (Div. 3 2006)
78 ALR6th 1—§ 15
State v. Jones, 133 N.C. App. 448, 516
S.E.2d 405 (1999)
93 ALR6th 391—§ 8
State v. Jones, 134 So. 3d 1164 (La.
2014)
102 ALR6th 637—§ 2
State v. Jones, 139 Idaho 299, 77 P.3d
988 (Ct. App. 2003)
9 ALR6th 541—§ 3, 11

State v. Jones, 141 Idaho 652, 115 P.3d
743 (2005)
38 ALR6th 1—§ 5
State v. Jones, 149 N.C. App. 977, 563
S.E.2d 308 (2002)
7 ALR6th 169—§ 22, 23
State v. Jones, 159 Wash. 2d 231, 149
P.3d 636 (2006)
26 ALR6th 511—§ 26, 52
State v. Jones, 179 N.J. 377, 846 A.2d
569 (2004)
50 ALR6th 455—§ 8, 26
State v. Jones, 180 Conn. 443, 429 A.2d
936 (1980)
42 ALR5th 581—§ 6, 7
State v. Jones, 181 N.J. Super. 549, 438
A.2d 581, 32 U.C.C. Rep. Serv.
1597 (Law Div. 1981)
105 ALR5th 1—§ 9
State v. Jones, 181 N.J. Super. 549, 438
A.2d 581, 32 U.C.C.R.S. 1597
(1981)
1 ALR5th 317—§ 7
1 ALR5th 346—§ 4, 6
State v. Jones, 187 Kan. 496, 357 P.2d
760, 88 A.L.R.2d 1269 (1960)
59 ALR5th 1—§ 4 to 6
State v. Jones, 188 Ariz. 388, 937 P.2d
310 (1997)
58 ALR6th 499—§ 34
State v. Jones, 188 Wash. 275, 62 P.2d
44 (1936)
54 ALR6th 429—§ 27
State v. Jones, 193 Conn. 70, 475 A.2d
1087 (1984)
55 ALR5th 125—§ 3, 7
State v. Jones, 196 Ga. App. 896, 397
S.E.2d 209 (1990)
2 ALR5th 262—§ 2, 3
State v. Jones, 202 Kan. 31, 446 P.2d
851 (1968)
66 ALR5th 397—§ 5
State v. Jones, 203 Ariz. 1, 49 P.3d 273
(2002)
110 ALR5th 1—§ 19
69 ALR6th 579—§ 4
State v. Jones, 209 P.3d 214 (Kan. Ct.
App. 2009)

63 ALR6th 1—§ 5, 55
State v. Jones, 213 Neb. 1, 328 N.W.2d
166 (1982)
82 ALR5th 67—§ 8
State v. Jones, 215 Tenn. 203, 385
S.W.2d 80 (1964)
11 ALR5th 831—§ 5, 6
State v. Jones, 220 S.W.3d 604 (Tex.
App. Texarkana 2007)
91 ALR6th 435—§ 39
State v. Jones, 222 Kan. 56, 563 P.2d
1021 (1977)
36 ALR5th 255—§ 24, 33
State v. Jones, 229 Kan. 528, 625 P.2d
503 (1981)
6 ALR5th 733—§ 3, 5, 12, 29
State v. Jones, 234 Kan. 1025, 676 P.2d
1281 (1984)
39 ALR5th 283—§ 4, 15, 18
State v. Jones, 246 Kan. 214, 787 P.2d
726 (1990)
29 ALR6th 1—§ 10
State v. Jones, 246 Neb. 673, 522
N.W.2d 414 (1994)
110 ALR5th 329—§ 5, 6
State v. Jones, 256 S.W. 787 (Mo. 1923)
54 ALR6th 429—§ 11
State v. Jones, 257 Wis. 2d 319, 2002
WI App 196, 651 N.W.2d 305 (Ct.
App. 2002)
109 ALR5th 99—§ 12
State v. Jones, 258 N.C. 89, 128 S.E.2d
1 (1962)
5 ALR5th 243—§ 6
State v. Jones, 263 La. 255, 268 So. 2d
216 (1972)
9 ALR6th 1—§ 17
State v. Jones, 263 La. 1012, 270 So. 2d
489 (1972)
98 ALR6th 455—§ 5
State v. Jones, 266 N.W.2d 706 (Minn.
1978)
5 ALR5th 243—§ 62
State v. Jones, 271 N.W.2d 761 (Iowa
1978)
36 ALR5th 255—§ 29, 31

State v. Jones, 273 S.C. 723, 259 S.E.2d
120 (1979)
> **90 ALR5th 453—§ 21**
> **1 ALR6th 657—§ 4**

State v. Jones, 283 Kan. 186, 151 P.3d
22 (2007)
> **32 ALR6th 1—§ 11**

State v. Jones, 289 Minn. 22, 183
N.W.2d 282 (1970)
> **29 ALR5th 59—§ 6, 47**

State v. Jones, 290 N.C. 292, 225 S.E.2d
549 (1976)
> **50 ALR5th 467—§ 7**

State v. Jones, 293 S.C. 54, 358 S.E.2d
701 (1987)
> **47 ALR5th 259—§ 6**

State v. Jones, 296 N.C. 495, 251 S.E.2d
425 (1979)
> **10 ALR5th 700—§ 8**

State v. Jones, 299 N.C. 298, 261 S.E.2d
860 (1980)
> **6 ALR6th 533—§ 21**

State v. Jones, 308 N.J. Super. 15, 705
A.2d 373 (App. Div. 1998)
> **42 ALR6th 237—§ 4**

State v. Jones, 325 S.C. 310, 479 S.E.2d
517 (Ct. App. 1996)
> **98 ALR6th 455—§ 9**

State v. Jones, 327 N.C. 439, 396 S.E.2d
309 (1990)
> **48 ALR5th 555—§ 2**

State v. Jones, 328 N.W.2d 736 (Minn.
1983)
> **73 ALR5th 383—§ 3**

State v. Jones, 332 So. 2d 466 (La. 1976)
> **87 ALR5th 181—§ 4**

State v. Jones, 336 N.C. 229, 443 S.E.2d
48 (1994)
> **79 ALR5th 33—§ 72**

State v. Jones, 337 N.C. 198, 446 S.E.2d
32 (1994)
> **57 ALR5th 141—§ 6**
> **92 ALR6th 549—§ 31, 46**

State v. Jones, 338 Ark. 781, 3 S.W.3d
675 (1999)
> **47 ALR6th 107—§ 35**

State v. Jones, 339 N.C. 114, 451 S.E.2d
826 (1994)
> **38 ALR5th 433—§ 40, 47**

State v. Jones, 342 N.C. 523, 467 S.E.2d
12 (1996)
> **83 ALR5th 541—§ 3**

State v. Jones, 347 N.C. 193, 491 S.E.2d
641 (1997)
> **104 ALR5th 357—§ 3, 6**
> **54 ALR6th 429—§ 9, 11**

State v. Jones, 353 N.C. 159, 538 S.E.2d
917 (2000)
> **84 ALR6th 427—§ 8**

State v. Jones, 357 N.C. 409, 584 S.E.2d
751 (2003)
> **4 ALR6th 577—§ 6**

State v. Jones, 373 So. 2d 1331 (La. Ct.
App. 4th Cir. 1979)
> **82 ALR5th 443—§ 4**
> **83 ALR5th 375—§ 3 to 5**

State v. Jones, 386 So. 2d 1363 (La.
1980)
> **20 ALR6th 479—§ 3**

State v. Jones, 402 N.W.2d 231 (Minn.
Ct. App. 1987)
> **92 ALR5th 35—§ 23**

State v. Jones, 425 So. 2d 178 (Fla. App.
D1 1983)
> **2 ALR5th 262—§ 3**

State v. Jones, 457 A.2d 1116 (Me.
1983)
> **109 ALR5th 611—§ 2, 3**

State v. Jones, 461 So. 2d 97 (Fla. 1984)
> **51 ALR6th 219—§ 4**

State v. Jones, 474 So. 2d 919 (La. 1985)
> **10 ALR5th 700—§ 2, 16, 40**

State v. Jones, 483 So. 2d 433 (Fla.
1986)
> **74 ALR5th 319—§ 5, 6, 8, 9, 11**

State v. Jones, 511 N.W.2d 400 (Iowa
Ct. App. 1993)
> **55 ALR6th 157—§ 4, 84, 110**

State v. Jones, 521 N.W.2d 662 (S.D.
1994)
> **33 ALR6th 353—§ 4**

State v. Jones, 562 So. 2d 740 (Fla. Dist.
Ct. App. 3d Dist. 1990)

---

62 ALR5th 1—§ 2
State v. Jones, 566 N.W.2d 317 (Minn. 1997)
35 ALR6th 127—§ 16
State v. Jones, 593 So. 2d 802 (La. Ct. App. 4th Cir. 1992)
54 ALR6th 429—§ 5, 11
State v. Jones, 625 So. 2d 821, 18 FLW S. 456 (Fla. 1993)
38 ALR5th 433—§ 2, 11
State v. Jones, 637 S.W.2d 337 (Mo. App. 1982)
6 ALR5th 652—§ 2, 8
State v. Jones, 656 P.2d 1012 (Utah 1982)
22 ALR5th 1—§ 5, 7, 32, 33, 44, 59
State v. Jones, 661 S.W.2d 814 (Mo. App. 1983)
36 ALR5th 255—§ 18, 31
State v. Jones, 671 N.W.2d 532 (Iowa Ct. App. 2003)
125 ALR5th 537—§ 49
State v. Jones, 678 So. 2d 1336, 21 FLW D1577 (Fla. App. D5 1996)
29 ALR5th 487—§ 14
State v. Jones, 685 So. 2d 1280 (Fla. 1996)
73 ALR5th 383—§ 39
State v. Jones, 707 So. 2d 975 (La. 1998)
83 ALR6th 465—§ 12, 66
State v. Jones, 726 S.W.2d 400 (Mo. App. 1987)
37 ALR5th 515—§ 4, 26
State v. Jones, 729 N.W.2d 1 (Minn. 2007)
33 ALR6th 91—§ 16, 23
State v. Jones, 735 S.W.2d 803 (Tenn. Crim. App. 1987)
81 ALR5th 563—§ 6
State v. Jones, 765 So. 2d 1191 (La. Ct. App. 2d Cir. 2000)
100 ALR5th 67—§ 43
State v. Jones, 769 So. 2d 28 (La. Ct. App. 4th Cir. 2000)
50 ALR5th 581—§ 7
State v. Jones, 778 So. 2d 1131, 118 A.L.R.5th 739 (La. 2001)

118 ALR5th 253—§ 25
State v. Jones, 822 So. 2d 205 (La. Ct. App. 4th Cir. 2002)
28 ALR6th 505—§ 9
45 ALR6th 337—§ 14
State v. Jones, 979 S.W.2d 171 (Mo. 1998)
54 ALR5th 575—§ 3
91 ALR5th 343—§ 32
83 ALR6th 255—§ 4
State v. Jones, 1994 WL 505120 (Ohio Ct. App. 10th Dist.Franklin County 1994)
59 ALR5th 1—§ 2, 3, 5, 6
State v. Jones, 1994 WL 529397 (Tenn. Crim. App. 1994)
87 ALR5th 693—§ 3
State v. Jones, 1995 WL 763604 (Ohio Ct. App. 1st Dist. Hamilton County 1995)
99 ALR6th 295—§ 13
State v. Jones, 1996 WL 723 (Minn. Ct. App. 1996)
73 ALR5th 383—§ 6, 8
State v. Jones, 1996 WL 571427 (Minn. Ct. App. 1996)
69 ALR6th 579—§ 8, 18
State v. Jones, 1997 WL 275015 (Minn. Ct. App. 1997)
69 ALR6th 579—§ 8, 17
State v. Jones, 1998 WL 267914 (Ohio Ct. App. 4th Dist. Washington County 1998)
78 ALR5th 489—§ 3
State v. Jones, 1998 WL 727344 (Haw. Ct. App. 1998)
72 ALR5th 403—§ 3
State v. Jones, 2001 WL 528021 (Ohio Ct. App. 8th Dist. Cuyahoga County 2001)
43 ALR6th 475—§ 6
State v. Jones, 2002-Ohio-2074, 2002 WL 737074 (Ohio Ct. App. 11th Dist. Ashtabula County 2002)
102 ALR6th 417—§ 78
State v. Jones, 2003-Ohio-219, 2003 WL 139762 (Ohio Ct. App. 6th Dist. Lucas County 2003)

56 ALR6th 185—§ 41
68 ALR6th 115—§ 10 to 12
State v. Jones, 2003-Ohio-1918, 2003 WL 1877664 (Ohio Ct. App. 9th Dist. Summit County 2003)
33 ALR6th 407—§ 5
State v. Jones, 2003 WL 21538435 (Ariz. 2003)
110 ALR5th 1—§ 18
State v. Jones, 2005-Ohio-1494, 2005 WL 730058 (Ohio Ct. App. 8th Dist. Cuyahoga County 2005)
72 ALR6th 1—§ 7
State v. Jones, 2006-Ohio-3239, 2006 WL 1726668 (Ohio Ct. App. 12th Dist. Butler County 2006)
26 ALR6th 511—§ 19
State v. Jones, 2006 WL 1868443 (Tenn. Crim. App. 2006)
26 ALR6th 511—§ 22
State v. Jones, 2008 MT 440, 347 Mont. 512, 199 P.3d 216 (2008)
46 ALR6th 241—§ 18
State v. Jones, 2009 WL 1586815 (Minn. Ct. App. 2009)
71 ALR6th 1—§ 8
State v. Jones, 2009 WL 2951144 (Tenn. Crim. App. 2009)
84 ALR6th 293—§ 10, 23
State v. Jones, 2010-Ohio-2576, 2010 WL 2299128 (Ohio Ct. App. 6th Dist. Lucas County 2010)
99 ALR6th 295—§ 13
State v. Jones, 2010 WL 4074497 (Conn. Super. Ct. 2010)
89 ALR6th 565—§ 11
State v. Jones, 2011-Ohio-1984, 2011 WL 1591285 (Ohio Ct. App. 2d Dist. Montgomery County 2011)
103 ALR6th 347—§ 26
State v. Jones, 2011-Ohio-2063, 2011 WL 1642379 (Ohio Ct. App. 2d Dist. Montgomery County 2011)
79 ALR6th 1—§ 47
State v. Jones, 2012-Ohio-1523, 2012 WL 1142287 (Ohio Ct. App. 4th Dist. Washington County 2012)
84 ALR6th 293—§ 31

State v. Jong Moon Choe, 2008 WL 997052 (N.J. Super. Ct. App. Div. 2008)
69 ALR6th 579—§ 11
State v. Jordan, 75 N.C. App. 637, 331 S.E.2d 232 (1985)
26 ALR5th 1—§ 3, 6, 28, 42
State v. Jordan, 79 Wash. 2d 480, 487 P.2d 617 (1971)
11 ALR5th 52—§ 2, 5, 6
58 ALR6th 499—§ 5
State v. Jordan, 83 Ariz. 248, 320 P.2d 446 (1958)
3 ALR5th 963—§ 6
State v. Jordan, 126 Ariz. 283, 614 P.2d 825 (1980)
93 ALR6th 391—§ 23
State v. Jordan, 128 N.C. App. 469, 495 S.E.2d 732 (1998)
29 ALR6th 1—§ 14
State v. Jordan, 144 Ariz. 240, 697 P.2d 323 (1985)
45 ALR5th 591—§ 18
State v. Jordan, 171 Ariz. 62, 828 P.2d 786, 109 Ariz. Adv. Rep. 48 (Ariz. App. 1992)
20 ALR5th 398—§ 4, 8
State v. Jordan, 193 Kan. 664, 396 P.2d 342 (1964)
102 ALR5th 525—§ 20
State v. Jordan, 201 Wis. 2d 215, 549 N.W.2d 792 (Ct. App. 1996)
72 ALR5th 1—§ 31
State v. Jordan, 277 S.C. 505, 289 S.E.2d 650 (1982)
36 ALR5th 255—§ 27
State v. Jordan, 325 S.W.3d 1 (Tenn. 2010)
69 ALR6th 579—§ 4
State v. Jordan, 665 P.2d 1280 (Utah 1983)
42 ALR5th 291—§ 3 to 6, 10
State v. Jordan, 1995 WL 137033 (Ohio App. 2 Dist.)
50 ALR5th 581—§ 20
State v. Jordan, 2001-Ohio-3988, 2001 WL 1511960 (Ohio Ct. App. 10th Dist. Franklin County 2001)

For assistance, call 1-800-328-4880

17 ALR6th 327—§ 23, 24
State v. Jordan, 2002-Ohio-590, 2002 WL 232879 (Ohio Ct. App. 8th Dist. Cuyahoga County 2002)
71 ALR6th 1—§ 11
State v. Jordan, 2005-Ohio-6064, 2005 WL 3047527 (Ohio Ct. App. 5th Dist. Muskingum County 2005)
26 ALR6th 511—§ 4
71 ALR6th 1—§ 8
State v. Jorden, 134 Ohio App. 3d 131, 730 N.E.2d 447 (1st Dist. Hamilton County 1999)
7 ALR6th 233—§ 5
State v. Jorgensen, 526 N.E.2d 1004 (Ind. App. 1988)
55 ALR5th 125—§ 2, 17, 22
State v. Jorgensen, 785 N.W.2d 708 (Iowa Ct. App. 2009)
71 ALR6th 283—§ 1
State v. Jorgenson, 758 N.W.2d 316 (Minn. Ct. App. 2008)
67 ALR6th 103—§ 10, 15
State v. Josenberger, 17 Kan. App. 2d 167, 836 P.2d 11 (1992)
1 ALR6th 549—§ 8
State v. Joseph, 25 Ohio St. 2d 95, 54 Ohio Op. 2d 228, 267 N.E.2d 125 (1971)
106 ALR5th 397—§ 8
State v. Joseph, 109 Haw. 482, 128 P.3d 795 (2006)
32 ALR6th 1—§ 4
State v. Joseph, 137 La. 52, 68 So. 211 (1915)
87 ALR6th 109—§ 45
State v. Joseph, 543 So. 2d 405 (Fla. Dist. Ct. App. 4th Dist. 1989)
113 ALR5th 597—§ 8
State v. Joseph, 850 So. 2d 1049 (La. Ct. App. 5th Cir. 2003)
117 ALR5th 407—§ 4
State v. Joseph, 1989 WL 90325 (Minn. Ct. App. 1989)
6 ALR6th 533—§ 17
State v. Josephson, 123 Idaho 790, 852 P.2d 1387 (1993)
114 ALR5th 235—§ 10

State v. Josephson, 125 Idaho 119, 867 P.2d 993 (Ct. App. 1993)
99 ALR5th 557—§ 4, 14
State v. Joseph T., 175 W. Va. 598, 336 S.E.2d 728 (1985)
31 ALR5th 229—§ 3, 17, 41, 67
State v. Josey, 290 N.J. Super. 17, 674 A.2d 996 (App. Div. 1996)
17 ALR6th 327—§ 7
State v. Josselyn, 148 N.J. Super. 538, 372 A.2d 1184 (County Ct. 1977)
69 ALR6th 1—§ 35
State v. Joubert, 603 A.2d 861 (Me. 1992)
1 ALR6th 657—§ 4
State v. Journey, 207 Neb. 717, 301 N.W.2d 82 (1981)
71 ALR6th 249—§ 8
State v. Joy, 121 Wash. 2d 333, 851 P.2d 654 (1993)
57 ALR6th 445—§ 28
State v. Joy, 218 Neb. 310, 353 N.W.2d 23 (1984)
124 ALR5th 1—§ 3
State v. Joy, 819 P.2d 108 (Idaho App. 1991)
6 ALR5th 733—§ 3, 12
State v. Joyce, 104 N.C. App. 558, 410 S.E.2d 516 (1991)
39 ALR5th 283—§ 4, 18
State v. Joyce, 243 Conn. 282, 705 A.2d 181 (1997)
53 ALR6th 81—§ 12
State v. Joyce, 1999 WL 693160 (Ohio Ct. App. 3d Dist. Allen County 1999)
78 ALR5th 489—§ 9
State v. Joyner, 225 Conn. 450, 625 A.2d 791 (1993)
72 ALR5th 403—§ 12, 15
State v. Joyner, 286 N.C. 366, 211 S.E.2d 320 (1975)
8 ALR5th 391—§ 2, 3, 5, 7
State v. Joyner, 295 N.C. 55, 243 S.E.2d 367 (1978)
5 ALR5th 243—§ 50

State v. Joyner, 759 S.W.2d 422 (Tenn. Crim. App. 1987)
87 ALR6th 1—§ 6, 7, 11, 29, 41, 46, 57

State v. J.P. Lamb Land Co., 359 N.W.2d 368 (N.D. 1984)
125 ALR5th 147—§ 14

State v. J.P. Lamb Land Co., 401 N.W.2d 713 (N.D. 1987)
125 ALR5th 147—§ 5, 15, 16

State v. J.Q., 130 N.J. 554, 617 A.2d 1196 (1993)
85 ALR5th 595—§ 2, 3, 6, 7

State v. J.R., 120 Wash. App. 1030, 2004 WL 370764 (Div. 1 2004)
7 ALR6th 233—§ 3, 5, 11

State v. J.R.A., 714 N.W.2d 722 (Minn. Ct. App. 2006)
68 ALR6th 1—§ 9
69 ALR6th 1—§ 20

State v. J.R.C., 152 Wis. 2d 89, 447 N.W.2d 540 (Ct. App. 1989)
87 ALR5th 277—§ 8

State v. J-R Distributors, Inc., 82 Wash. 2d 584, 512 P.2d 1049 (1973)
13 ALR5th 567—§ 6

State v. J.S., 70 Wash. App. 659, 855 P.2d 280 (Div. 1 1993)
73 ALR5th 383—§ 5

State v. J.S., 222 N.J. Super. 247, 536 A.2d 769 (App. Div. 1988)
39 ALR6th 257—§ 23, 27, 49
40 ALR6th 1—§ 9

State v. J.T.D., 851 So. 2d 793 (Fla. Dist. Ct. App. 2d Dist. 2003)
59 ALR6th 393—§ 5

State v. Juarez, 120 N.M. 499, 903 P.2d 241 (Ct. App. 1995)
35 ALR6th 127—§ 4

State v. Juarez, 790 P.2d 1045 (N.M. App. 1990)
49 ALR5th 639—§ 4

State v. Juarez-Lopez, 803 N.W.2d 672 (Iowa Ct. App. 2011)
74 ALR6th 373—§ 12

State v. Judd, 147 Wis. 2d 398, 433 N.W.2d 260, R.I.C.O. Bus. Disp. Guide (CCH) ¶ 7101 (Ct. App. 1988)
89 ALR5th 629—§ 5

State v. Jude, 554 N.W.2d 750 (Minn. Ct. App. 1996)
34 ALR6th 643—§ 29

State v. Judge, 275 N.J. Super. 194, 645 A.2d 1224 (App. Div. 1994)
114 ALR5th 173—§ 6
123 ALR5th 179—§ 3, 4

State v. Judge, 315 Mo. 156, 285 S.W. 718 (1926)
5 ALR6th 1—§ 40

State v. Judge of Ninth Judicial Circuit, 13 Ala. 805, 1848 WL 478 (1848)
75 ALR6th 311—§ 27

State v. Judge of Sixth Judicial Dist., 9 La. Ann. 62, 1854 WL 4497 (1854)
97 ALR5th 537—§ 23

State v. Jugger, 217 La. 687, 47 So. 2d 46 (1950)
105 ALR5th 529—§ 12

State v. Julian, 102 Wash. App. 296, 9 P.3d 851 (Div. 3 2000)
46 ALR6th 241—§ 9

State v. Julian, 244 Kan. 101, 765 P.2d 1104 (1988)
37 ALR6th 357—§ 16, 17

State v. Julian, 785 So. 2d 872 (La. Ct. App. 4th Cir. 2001)
50 ALR5th 581—§ 18.6

State v. Julian, 1997 WL 412539 (Tenn. Crim. App. 1997)
73 ALR5th 383—§ 6

State v. Juluke, 374 So. 2d 1259 (La. 1979)
80 ALR6th 599—§ 5

State v. Jumel, 13 La. Ann. 399, 1858 WL 5151 (1858)
33 ALR6th 407—§ 4

State v. Jumpp, 261 N.J. Super. 514, 619 A.2d 602 (1993)
36 ALR5th 255—§ 8, 15

State v. Jung, 19 Ariz. App. 257, 506 P.2d 648 (Div. 2 1973)

112 ALR5th 429—§ 13

State v. Junkin, 123 Ariz. 288, 599 P.2d 244 (App. 1979)

4 ALR5th 1—§ 2, 17, 32, 33

State v. Jurcsek, 247 N.J. Super. 102, 588 A.2d 875 (App. Div. 1991)

102 ALR6th 279—§ 15

103 ALR6th 35—§ 15

State v. Jurek, 52 Ohio App. 3d 30, 556 N.E.2d 1191 (8th Dist. Cuyahoga County 1989)

64 ALR6th 655—§ 17

State v. Jurgensen, 42 Conn. App. 751, 681 A.2d 981 (1996)

57 ALR5th 141—§ 12

State v. Jury, 19 Wash. App. 256, 576 P.2d 1302 (Div. 2 1978)

70 ALR5th 1—§ 2

72 ALR5th 109—§ 2

78 ALR5th 197—§ 5, 15, 18

79 ALR5th 419—§ 2, 8, 11

80 ALR5th 55—§ 2

State v. Just, 184 Mont. 262, 602 P.2d 957 (1979)

57 ALR5th 315—§ 10, 11

State v. Justice, 451 So. 2d 1056 (Fla. App. D2 1984)

2 ALR5th 262—§ 3

State v. Justiniano, 48 Wash. App. 572, 740 P.2d 872 (1987)

38 ALR5th 433—§ 3

State v. Justiniano, 2009 WL 928464 (N.J. Super. Ct. App. Div. 2009)

92 ALR6th 549—§ 29

State v. Justus, 11 Or. 178, 8 P. 337 (1883)

11 ALR5th 497—§ 3, 5, 12

State v. J.V., 132 Wash. App. 533, 132 P.3d 1116 (Div. 1 2006)

78 ALR6th 1—§ 23

State v. J.V.W., 739 So. 2d 173 (Fla. Dist. Ct. App. 2d Dist. 1999)

18 ALR5th 542—§ 5

State v. J.Y., 623 So. 2d 1232 (Fla. Dist. Ct. App. 3d Dist. 1993)

28 ALR6th 505—§ 23

State v. J.Y.M., 711 N.W.2d 139 (Minn. Ct. App. 2006)

69 ALR6th 1—§ 21

State v. Kabayama, 98 N.J. Super. 85, 236 A.2d 164 (App. Div. 1967)

116 ALR5th 479—§ 3, 4

State v. Kabinto, 106 Ariz. 575, 480 P.2d 1 (1971)

32 ALR5th 149—§ 33

State v. Kachanis, 119 R.I. 439, 379 A.2d 915 (1977)

124 ALR5th 1—§ 3

State v. Kachovee, 1999 WL 38994 (Ohio Ct. App. 4th Dist. Scioto County 1999)

99 ALR6th 295—§ 9

State v. Kachovee, 2001-Ohio-2382, 2001 WL 1450840 (Ohio Ct. App. 4th Dist. Scioto County 2001)

99 ALR6th 295—§ 15

State v. Kadivar, 460 So. 2d 391, 9 FLW 2324 (Fla. App. D4 1984)

42 ALR5th 581—§ 2, 12

State v. Kaeff, 2004-Ohio-5288, 2004 WL 2245095 (Ohio Ct. App. 2d Dist. Montgomery County 2004)

67 ALR6th 103—§ 4

State v. Kaempfer, 342 Mo. 1007, 119 S.W.2d 294 (1938)

41 ALR5th 1—§ 3

State v. Kahan, 268 S.C. 240, 233 S.E.2d 293 (1977)

11 ALR5th 497—§ 3, 8

State v. Kahawai, 103 Haw. 462, 83 P.3d 725 (2004)

46 ALR6th 241—§ 19

State v. Kahlon, 172 N.J. Super. 331, 411 A.2d 1178 (App. Div. 1980)

114 ALR5th 173—§ 7

State v. Kailua Auto Wreckers, Inc., 62 Haw. 222, 615 P.2d 730, 10 Envtl. L. Rep. 20951 (1980)

119 ALR5th 205—§ 6

State v. Kalai, 56 Haw. 366, 537 P.2d 8 (1975)

28 ALR6th 505—§ 7, 9

State v. Kalai, 56 Hawaii 366, 537 P.2d 8 (1975)

41 ALR5th 171—§ 12, 55, 77, 103, 106, 108
State v. Kalakosky, 121 Wash. 2d 525, 852 P.2d 1064 (1993)
93 ALR6th 275—§ 4
State v. Kalaola, 120 Haw. 417, 209 P.3d 194 (Ct. App. 2009)
52 ALR6th 125—§ 42
State v. Kaleohano, 99 Haw. 370, 56 P.3d 138 (2002)
56 ALR6th 323—§ 5
State v. Kalk, 234 Wis. 2d 98
42 ALR5th 581—§ 4
State v. Kallenbach, 226 Wis. 2d 563, 596 N.W.2d 502 (Ct. App. 1999)
84 ALR6th 293—§ 32
State v. Kallos, 193 Neb. 113, 225 N.W.2d 553 (1975)
6 ALR6th 533—§ 20
State v. Kalna, 595 S.W.2d 299 (Mo. Ct. App. E.D. 1979)
70 ALR5th 587—§ 13
State v. Kalter, 839 S.W.2d 670 (Mo. Ct. App. E.D. 1992)
28 ALR6th 505—§ 9
State v. Kamai, 184 Ariz. 620, 911 P.2d 626 (Ct. App. Div. 1 1995)
78 ALR5th 567—§ 2, 5, 8
State v. Kaminski, 293 N.W.2d 838 (Minn. 1980)
41 ALR5th 171—§ 86, 94, 95, 107, 108, 126, 130, 136
State v. Kaminski, 2005 WL 3470674 (Conn. Super. Ct. 2005)
74 ALR6th 69—§ 23
State v. Kanamu, 2002 WL 1943738 (Haw. 2002)
121 ALR5th 551—§ 6, 13
State v. Kandies, 342 N.C. 419, 467 S.E.2d 67 (1996)
37 ALR5th 515—§ 4
79 ALR5th 33—§ 67
State v. Kane, 87 Haw. 71, 951 P.2d 934 (1998)
34 ALR6th 1—§ 11
State v. Kane, 586 S.W.2d 812 (Mo. App. 1979)
13 ALR5th 1—§ 2, 47

State v. Kaneakua, 61 Haw. 136, 597 P.2d 590 (1979)
69 ALR6th 207—§ 13, 21
State v. Kaneakua, 61 Hawaii 136, 597 P.2d 590 (1979)
6 ALR5th 733—§ 7, 25
State v. Kang, 866 So. 2d 408 (La. Ct. App. 5th Cir. 2004)
34 ALR6th 1—§ 9
State v. Kang, 2001 WL 1729126 (Del. Super. Ct. 2001)
34 ALR6th 623—§ 4, 7
State v. Kang, 2002 WL 1587852 (Del. Super. Ct. 2002)
84 ALR6th 427—§ 19
State v. Kania, 341 N.W.2d 361 (N.D. 1983)
37 ALR6th 357—§ 43, 46, 53
State v. Kappes, 26 Ariz. App. 567, 550 P.2d 121 (1976)
31 ALR5th 229—§ 5, 8, 32
State v. Karaarslan, 269 N.J. Super. 123, 619 A.2d 1346 (1993)
32 ALR5th 149—§ 4, 45
State v. Karbas, 28 N.C. App. 372, 221 S.E.2d 98 (1976)
76 ALR5th 1—§ 20
State v. Kargar, 679 A.2d 81, 68 A.L.R.5th 751 (Me. 1996)
68 ALR5th 299—§ 2, 3
State v. Karlovetz, 1993 WL 195798 (Ohio Ct. App. 6th Dist. Sandusky County 1993)
32 ALR6th 385—§ 7
State v. Karov, 170 Vt. 650, 756 A.2d 1236 (2000)
35 ALR6th 127—§ 5
State v. Karpenski, 94 Wash. App. 80, 971 P.2d 553 (Div. 2 1999)
71 ALR5th 637—§ 7
90 ALR5th 453—§ 43
State v. Karr, Slip Opinion No. 74AP-296 (Ohio App. Franklin Co. 1974)
41 ALR5th 171—§ 12, 16, 18, 93, 108
State v. Karson, 2010 WL 2977223 (Kan. Ct. App. 2010)
56 ALR6th 1—§ 37

State v. Karussos, 82 Or. App. 248, 728 P.2d 559 (1986)

15 ALR5th 391—§ 39

State v. Kasel, 488 N.W.2d 706 (Iowa 1992)

29 ALR6th 1—§ 7

State v. Kasold, 110 Ariz. 563, 521 P.2d 995 (1974)

111 ALR5th 239—§ 7

State v. Kasparec, 198 Wis. 2d 391, 542 N.W.2d 240 (Ct. App. 1995)

72 ALR5th 403—§ 19

State v. Kasper, 405 N.W.2d 540 (Minn. Ct. App. 1987)

86 ALR5th 59—§ 4

State v. Kasten, 775 So. 2d 992 (Fla. Dist. Ct. App. 3d Dist. 2000)

106 ALR5th 377—§ 6

State v. Kaster, 35 Iowa 221, 1872 WL 372 (1872)

93 ALR5th 621—§ 6, 10, 14

State v. Kasulaitis, 2011-Ohio-852, 2011 WL 683820 (Ohio Ct. App. 8th Dist. Cuyahoga County 2011)

69 ALR6th 1—§ 10

State v. Kasunick, 2009-Ohio-4449, 2009 WL 2710107 (Ohio Ct. App. 11th Dist. Lake County 2009)

63 ALR6th 351—§ 3

64 ALR6th 1—§ 9

State v. Kattaria, 1998 WL 481899 (Minn. Ct. App. 1998)

114 ALR5th 173—§ 7

69 ALR6th 579—§ 8, 27

State v. Kaufman, 265 N.W.2d 610 (Iowa 1978)

112 ALR5th 429—§ 5

State v. Kaufman, 310 N.W.2d 709 (N.D. 1981)

57 ALR6th 445—§ 3, 45

State v. Kay, 129 Idaho 507, 927 P.2d 897 (Ct. App. 1996)

74 ALR6th 69—§ 3, 21

State v. Kay, 164 Wash. 685, 4 P.2d 498 (1931)

84 ALR5th 399—§ 3, 7

State v. Kayer, 194 Ariz. 423, 984 P.2d 31 (1999)

21 ALR6th 1—§ 4

State v. K.D.H., 137 Wash. App. 1063, 2007 WL 1054125 (Div. 2 2007)

33 ALR6th 91—§ 45

37 ALR6th 55—§ 16

38 ALR6th 1—§ 25

State v. Keadle, 51 N.C. App. 660, 277 S.E.2d 456 (1981)

31 ALR5th 229—§ 5, 82

State v. Kearns, 743 S.W.2d 553 (Mo. Ct. App. S.D. 1987)

105 ALR5th 529—§ 13

State v. Keathley, 1986 WL 11486 (Tenn. Crim. App. 1986)

16 ALR6th 329—§ 4

24 ALR6th 591—§ 10

State v. Keating, 202 Mo. 197, 100 S.W. 648 (1907)

5 ALR6th 1—§ 3, 15, 40

State v. Keating, 277 N.J. Super. 141, 649 A.2d 103 (App. Div. 1994)

28 ALR6th 505—§ 7, 16

State v. Keaton, 216 P.3d 731 (Kan. Ct. App. 2009)

55 ALR6th 1—§ 6

State v. Keding, 214 Wis. 2d 363, 571 N.W.2d 450 (Ct. App. 1997)

78 ALR6th 417—§ 70

State v. Kee, 6 P.3d 938 (Kan. Ct. App. 2000)

37 ALR5th 319—§ 5

State v. Kee, 398 A.2d 384 (Me. 1979)

3 ALR5th 521—§ 2, 6

State v. Kee, 956 S.W.2d 298 (Mo. Ct. App. W.D. 1997)

5 ALR5th 243—§ 51

State v. Keehn, 85 Kan. 765, 118 P. 851 (1911)

45 ALR5th 531—§ 3

State v. Keehn, 554 N.W.2d 405 (Minn. Ct. App. 1996)

92 ALR5th 35—§ 20

State v. Keehner, 425 N.W.2d 41 (Iowa 1988)

18 ALR6th 519—§ 4

State v. Keel, 137 Ariz. 532, 672 P.2d 197 (App. 1983)

29 ALR5th 59—§ 3
State v. Keel, 597 So. 2d 250, 17 FLW
S. 129 (Fla. 1992)

7 ALR5th 263—§ 7
State v. Keeler, 238 Kan. 356, 710 P.2d
1279 (1985)

78 ALR5th 567—§ 7
State v. Keeley, 1995 WL 504809 (Tenn.
Crim. App. 1995)

57 ALR5th 141—§ 9
State v. Keen, 926 S.W.2d 727 (Tenn.
1994)

83 ALR6th 255—§ 15
State v. Keen, 1999 WL 254384 (Tenn.
Crim. App. 1999)

39 ALR6th 257—§ 14, 18
State v. Keena, 121 Wash. App. 143, 87
P.3d 1197 (Div. 2 2004)

8 ALR6th 265—§ 15
State v. Keenan, 66 Ohio St. 3d 402, 613
N.E.2d 203 (1993)

3 ALR6th 269—§ 5, 8, 29
State v. Keener, 206 Ariz. 29, 75 P.3d
119 (Ct. App. Div. 1 2003)

4 ALR6th 599—§ 16, 25
State v. Keener, 224 Kan. 100, 577 P.2d
1182 (1978)

52 ALR6th 1—§ 4
State v. Keener, 2006 WL 1931805
(Tenn. Crim. App. 2006)

26 ALR6th 511—§ 22
State v. Keet, 269 Mo. 206, 190 S.W.
573 (1916)

33 ALR6th 407—§ 4, 9
State v. Keeth, 203 S.W.3d 718 (Mo.
App. 2006)

57 ALR6th 83—§ 6
State v. Keeven, 728 S.W.2d 658 (Mo.
Ct. App. E.D. 1987)

28 ALR6th 505—§ 18
State v. Kehn, 50 Ohio St. 2d 11, 4 Ohio
Ops. 3d 74, 361 N.E.2d 1330 (1977)

36 ALR5th 255—§ 29
State v. Keithley, 83 Mont. 177, 271 P.
449 (1928)

29 ALR5th 59—§ 3, 38, 39

State v. Keithley, 227 Neb. 402, 418
N.W.2d 212 (1988)

3 ALR6th 269—§ 25
State v. Keitz, 856 P.2d 685, 216 Utah
Adv. Rep. 19 (Utah App. 1993)

18 ALR5th 1—§ 4, 10, 16
State v. Kekona, 77 Haw. 403, 886 P.2d
740 (1994)

69 ALR6th 579—§ 4
State v. Kekona, 1999 WL 198377
(Wash. Ct. App. Div. 2 1999)

73 ALR5th 383—§ 27
State v. Keliiholokai, 58 Haw. 356, 569
P.2d 891 (1977)

55 ALR6th 157—§ 4, 25
State v. Kell, 303 Or. 89, 734 P.2d 334
(1987)

124 ALR5th 1—§ 5
State v. Keller, 32 Wash. App. 135, 647
P.2d 35 (Div. 1 1982)

86 ALR6th 321—§ 13
91 ALR6th 171—§ 82
State v. Keller, 170 Mont. 372, 553 P.2d
1013 (1976)

76 ALR5th 563—§ 3
State v. Keller, 550 N.W.2d 411 (N.D.
1996)

29 ALR5th 487—§ 12
State v. Keller, 592 So. 2d 1365 (La. Ct.
App. 1st Cir. 1991)

64 ALR5th 671—§ 4, 9
State v. Keller, 870 S.W.2d 255 (Mo. Ct.
App. W.D. 1994)

109 ALR5th 99—§ 8
State v. Keller, 2000 WL 20873 (Ohio
Ct. App. 2d Dist. Montgomery
County 2000)

117 ALR5th 407—§ 4
State v. Keller, 2006 WL 902589 (Ind.
Ct. App. 2006)

15 ALR6th 515—§ 31
State v. Kelley, 52 Wash. App. 581, 762
P.2d 20 (Div. 2 1988)

104 ALR5th 165—§ 9, 11, 14
State v. Kelley, 104 Ariz. 418, 454 P.2d
563 (1969)

4 ALR5th 1—§ 18

State v. Kelley, 163 Vt. 325, 664 A.2d 708 (1995)

73 ALR5th 383—§ 50

State v. Kelley, 229 Conn. 557, 643 A.2d 854 (1994)

39 ALR6th 257—§ 4, 5, 15, 42

State v. Kelley, 460 S.E.2d 368 (S.C. 1995)

37 ALR5th 515—§ 11

State v. Kelley, 683 S.W.2d 1 (Tenn. Crim. App. 1984)

16 ALR6th 329—§ 7

24 ALR6th 591—§ 10

State v. Kelley, 2000 UT 41, 2000 WL 518362 (Utah 2000)

80 ALR5th 55—§ 9

State v. Kelley, 2009 WL 2496838 (N.J. Super. Ct. App. Div. 2009)

65 ALR6th 537—§ 22

State v. Kelling, 108 Idaho 716, 701 P.2d 664 (App. 1985)

8 ALR5th 713—§ 3, 5

State v. Kellogg, 263 N.W.2d 539 (Iowa 1978)

24 ALR5th 465—§ 35

State v. Kellogg, 542 N.W.2d 514 (Iowa 1996)

71 ALR5th 285—§ 2 to 4

State v. Kellough, 1982 WL 3185 (Ohio Ct. App. 12th Dist. Fayette County 1982)

42 ALR6th 237—§ 15

State v. Kelly, 5 Ariz. App. 280, 425 P.2d 850 (1967)

45 ALR5th 591—§ 15

State v. Kelly, 23 Ala. App. 356, 127 So. 797 (1929)

76 ALR5th 485—§ 15

State v. Kelly, 39 N.C. App. 246, 249 S.E.2d 832 (1978)

29 ALR5th 59—§ 3, 32

State v. Kelly, 61 N.J. 283, 294 A.2d 41 (1972)

51 ALR6th 219—§ 4

State v. Kelly, 81 Miss. 1, 32 So. 909 (1902)

57 ALR6th 419—§ 8

State v. Kelly, 93 Ohio App. 3d 257, 638 N.E.2d 153 (Ohio Stark Co. 1994)

36 ALR5th 255—§ 2

State v. Kelly, 97 N.J. 178, 478 A.2d 364 (1984)

58 ALR5th 749—§ 2, 5, 6

State v. Kelly, 99 Ariz. 136, 407 P.2d 95 (1965)

41 ALR5th 171—§ 17

State v. Kelly, 102 Wash. 2d 188, 685 P.2d 564 (1984)

58 ALR5th 749—§ 2

State v. Kelly, 106 Idaho 268, 678 P.2d 60 (App. 1984)

41 ALR5th 171—§ 2, 8, 14

State v. Kelly, 125 N.H. 484, 484 A.2d 1066 (1984)

67 ALR6th 209—§ 41

State v. Kelly, 130 Ariz. 375, 636 P.2d 153 (Ct. App. Div. 2 1981)

6 ALR6th 533—§ 17

State v. Kelly, 213 Kan. 237, 515 P.2d 1030 (1973)

59 ALR5th 135—§ 3, 5, 8

State v. Kelly, 235 Neb. 997, 458 N.W.2d 255 (1990)

15 ALR5th 391—§ 35

State v. Kelly, 256 Conn. 23, 770 A.2d 908 (2001)

39 ALR6th 257—§ 4, 41

63 ALR6th 351—§ 3

State v. Kelly, 256 Conn. 23, 2001 WL 433791 (2001)

90 ALR5th 453—§ 6

State v. Kelly, 284 N.W.2d 236 (Iowa 1979)

55 ALR5th 125—§ 3, 8

State v. Kelly, 435 N.W.2d 807 (Minn. 1989)

28 ALR6th 505—§ 8

42 ALR6th 237—§ 4

State v. Kelly, 439 S.W.2d 487 (Mo. 1969)

32 ALR6th 1—§ 4

State v. Kelly, 519 N.W.2d 202, R.I.C.O. Bus. Disp. Guide (CCH) ¶ 8612 (Minn. 1994)

89 ALR5th 629—§ 5
State v. Kelly, 554 A.2d 632 (R.I. 1989)
38 ALR5th 433—§ 48
State v. Kelly, 718 P.2d 385 (Utah 1986)
103 ALR5th 463—§ 3
28 ALR6th 505—§ 9
State v. Kelly, 1986 WL 10125 (Tenn. Crim. App. 1986)
73 ALR5th 383—§ 5
State v. Kelly, 1999 WL 16796 (Tenn. Crim. App. 1999)
76 ALR5th 1—§ 2, 18
77 ALR5th 201—§ 2
79 ALR5th 237—§ 2
State v. Kelly, 2002-Ohio-5887, 2002 WL 31415032 (Ohio Ct. App. 12th Dist. Warren County 2002)
70 ALR6th 1—§ 5
State v. Kelly, 2004-Ohio-6109, 2004 WL 2635504 (Ohio Ct. App. 8th Dist. Cuyahoga County 2004)
70 ALR6th 1—§ 5
State v. Kelsey, 67 Or. App. 554, 679 P.2d 335 (1984)
125 ALR5th 281—§ 15
State v. Kelsey, 93 Conn. App. 408, 889 A.2d 855 (2006)
53 ALR6th 81—§ 5
56 ALR6th 185—§ 42
State v. Kelsey, 532 P.2d 1001 (Utah 1975)
55 ALR5th 125—§ 3, 7
State v. Kelter, 71 Wash. 2d 52, 426 P.2d 500 (1967)
30 ALR6th 103—§ 25
State v. Kelton, 168 Vt. 629, 724 A.2d 452 (1998)
92 ALR6th 295—§ 7, 13, 22, 25
96 ALR6th 355—§ 9
State v. Kemp, 73 S.D. 458, 44 N.W.2d 214 (1950)
31 ALR6th 523—§ 29, 30, 34
State v. Kemp, 185 Ariz. 52, 912 P.2d 1281 (1996)
38 ALR6th 97—§ 29
State v. Kemp, 429 So. 2d 822 (Fla. Dist. Ct. App. 2d Dist. 1983)

72 ALR5th 1—§ 3
State v. Kempker, 792 S.W.2d 57 (Mo. Ct. App. E.D. 1990)
105 ALR5th 529—§ 12
State v. Kendall, 90 N.M. 236, 561 P.2d 935 (App. 1977)
28 ALR5th 754—§ 7
State v. Kender, 60 Haw. 301, 588 P.2d 447 (1978)
62 ALR6th 413—§ 4, 28, 49
State v. Kender, 60 Hawaii 301, 588 P.2d 447 (1978)
59 ALR5th 615—§ 3, 6, 12
State v. Kendley, 147 Wis. 2d 877, 433 N.W.2d 674 (Ct. App. 1988)
95 ALR5th 471—§ 2, 7
State v. Kendrick, 47 Wash. App. 620, 736 P.2d 1079 (Div. 1 1987)
68 ALR5th 343—§ 3, 13
1 ALR6th 657—§ 6
State v. Kendrick, 2009-Ohio-3876, 2009 WL 2413793 (Ohio Ct. App. 1st Dist. Hamilton County 2009)
68 ALR6th 115—§ 8, 14, 28, 34 to 36
State v. Kendricks, 891 S.W.2d 597 (Tenn. 1994)
39 ALR6th 257—§ 17, 23, 24
40 ALR6th 1—§ 14, 21, 33
State v. Kenimer, 95 P.3d 1042 (Kan. Ct. App. 2004)
26 ALR6th 511—§ 25
State v. Keniston, 21 Kan. App. 2d 818, 908 P.2d 656 (1995)
73 ALR5th 383—§ 3
State v. Kenley, 952 S.W.2d 250 (Mo. 1997)
79 ALR5th 33—§ 65
State v. Kennedy, 68 Or. App. 529, 683 P.2d 116 (1984)
57 ALR6th 83—§ 11
State v. Kennedy, 72 Wash. App. 244, 864 P.2d 410 (Div. 2 1993)
106 ALR5th 397—§ 5
State v. Kennedy, 80 N.M. 152, 452 P.2d 486 (Ct. App. 1969)
65 ALR5th 407—§ 3, 7, 8, 12, 16

State v. Kennedy, 107 Wash. App. 972, 29 P.3d 746 (Div. 2 2001)
15 ALR6th 515—§ 33

State v. Kennedy, 116 Ariz. 566, 570 P.2d 508 (Ct. App. Div. 2 1977)
28 ALR6th 505—§ 11

State v. Kennedy, 139 Idaho 244, 76 P.3d 988, 9 A.L.R.6th 795 (Ct. App. 2003)
9 ALR6th 467—§ 24
9 ALR6th 541—§ 10

State v. Kennedy, 152 N.J. 413, 705 A.2d 757 (1998)
15 ALR5th 391—§ 3

State v. Kennedy, 190 Wis. 2d 253, 528 N.W.2d 9 (App. 1994)
15 ALR5th 391—§ 45

State v. Kennedy, 224 N.W.2d 223, 76 A.L.R.3d 968 (Iowa 1974)
66 ALR6th 351—§ 3, 34
67 ALR6th 209—§ 3, 40

State v. Kennedy, 390 So. 2d 456 (Fla. Dist. Ct. App. 2d Dist. 1980)
107 ALR5th 567—§ 12

State v. Kennedy, 649 S.W.2d 275 (Tenn. Crim. App. 1982)
114 ALR5th 235—§ 6

State v. Kennedy, 698 So. 2d 349 (Fla. Dist. Ct. App. 4th Dist. 1997)
113 ALR5th 597—§ 8

State v. Kennedy, 953 So. 2d 655 (Fla. 1st DCA 2007)
78 ALR6th 297—§ 41, 46

State v. Kennedy, 953 So. 2d 655 (Fla. Dist. Ct. App. 1st Dist. 2007)
45 ALR6th 643—§ 11

State v. Kennedy, 957 So. 2d 757 (La. 2007)
36 ALR6th 681—§ 46
98 ALR6th 455—§ 14
99 ALR6th 113—§ 10

State v. Kennerly, 337 S.C. 617, 524 S.E.2d 837 (1999)
93 ALR5th 493—§ 4, 9

State v. Kenney, 83 Wash. 441, 145 P. 450 (1915)
97 ALR5th 201—§ 3

State v. Kenney, 523 A.2d 853 (R.I. 1987)
46 ALR5th 735—§ 2

State v. Kent, 4 N.D. 577, 62 N.W. 631 (1895)
12 ALR5th 909—§ 8

State v. Kent, 20 Utah 2d 1, 432 P.2d 64 (1967)
61 ALR5th 1—§ 3, 5

State v. Kent, 22 Minn. 41, 1875 WL 3853 (1875)
57 ALR6th 445—§ 11

State v. Kent, 391 N.J. Super. 352, 918 A.2d 626 (App. Div. 2007)
30 ALR6th 1—§ 3, 6

State v. Keough, 18 S.W.3d 175 (Tenn. 2000)
27 ALR6th 183—§ 10, 35

State v. Keperling, 2000 WL 305493 (Del. Super. Ct. 2000)
99 ALR6th 295—§ 9

State v. Kepford, 2004-Ohio-6486, 2004 WL 2785949 (Ohio Ct. App. 3d Dist. Crawford County 2004)
84 ALR6th 293—§ 16

State v. Kerkhove, 423 N.W.2d 160 (S.D. 1988)
24 ALR5th 465—§ 5, 13, 14, 115, 116, 119, 120

State v. Kermoade, 33 Kan. App. 2d 573, 105 P.3d 730 (2005)
15 ALR6th 515—§ 17

State v. Kern, 81 Wash. App. 308, 914 P.2d 114 (Div. 1 1996)
68 ALR5th 549—§ 5, 7
27 ALR6th 491—§ 3

State v. Kern, 2005 MT 44N, 110 P.3d 1056 (Mont. 2005)
69 ALR6th 1—§ 30

State v. Kersey, 903 P.2d 828 (N.M. 1995)
28 ALR5th 754—§ 5, 6

State v. Kessack, 32 N.C. App. 536, 232 S.E.2d 859 (1977)
38 ALR6th 97—§ 27

State v. Kessler, 297 Or. 460, 686 P.2d 345 (1984)
39 ALR5th 283—§ 75

CASES CITED IN ALR5th and ALR6th

State v. Kessler, 470 N.W.2d 536 (Minn. Ct. App. 1991)
103 ALR5th 463—§ 3
State v. Kester, 38 Wash. App. 590, 686 P.2d 1081 (1984)
37 ALR5th 515—§ 10
State v. Kester, 2002 WL 386316 (Del. Super. Ct. 2002)
84 ALR6th 427—§ 4
State v. Ketchum, 97 Haw. 107, 34 P.3d 1006 (2001)
26 ALR6th 451—§ 3
28 ALR6th 505—§ 3, 12
29 ALR6th 1—§ 3
32 ALR6th 1—§ 3
34 ALR6th 1—§ 3
35 ALR6th 127—§ 3
38 ALR6th 97—§ 3
42 ALR6th 237—§ 17, 18
55 ALR6th 513—§ 3
56 ALR6th 323—§ 3
57 ALR6th 83—§ 3
58 ALR6th 215—§ 3
81 ALR6th 505—§ 30
State v. Keyonnie, 91 N.M. 146, 571 P.2d 413 (1977)
24 ALR6th 1—§ 17
State v. Keyonnie, 181 Ariz. 485, 892 P.2d 205 (Ct. App. Div. 1 1995)
109 ALR5th 611—§ 3
State v. Keyonnie, 2007 WL 5209475 (Ariz. Ct. App. Div. 1 2007)
56 ALR6th 323—§ 7, 11
State v. Keys, 331 N.J. Super. 480, 752 A.2d 368 (Law Div. 1998)
78 ALR5th 197—§ 10
State v. K.H., 860 N.E.2d 1284 (Ind. Ct. App. 2007)
39 ALR6th 577—§ 10
State v. Kickapoo Oil, 123 Wis. 2d 542, 367 N.W.2d 243 (Ct. App. 1985)
26 ALR6th 249—§ 6
State v. Kidd, 57 Wash. App. 95, 786 P.2d 847 (Div. 1 1990)
73 ALR5th 383—§ 53
State v. Kidd, 990 S.W.2d 175 (Mo. Ct. App. W.D. 1999)

16 ALR6th 329—§ 11
24 ALR6th 591—§ 9, 13
State v. Kidd, 2005-Ohio-2079, 2005 WL 1009830 (Ohio Ct. App. 11th Dist. Portage County 2005)
69 ALR6th 1—§ 5
State v. Kiefer, 296 Wis. 2d 936, 2006 WI App 223, 724 N.W.2d 274 (Ct. App. 2006)
46 ALR6th 63—§ 7, 9
State v. Kieffer, 207 Wis. 2d 464, 558 N.W.2d 664 (Ct. App. 1996)
55 ALR5th 125—§ 17
State v. Kieffer, 577 N.W.2d 352 (Wis. 1998)
61 ALR5th 1—§ 3
State v. Kiekhefer, 212 Wis. 2d 460, 569 N.W.2d 316 (Ct. App. 1997)
122 ALR5th 439—§ 7
State v. Kielb, 2000 WL 890462 (Minn. Ct. App. 2000)
6 ALR6th 533—§ 22
50 ALR6th 455—§ 9, 24, 36
State v. Kight, 1990 WL 127034 (Ohio App. Jackson Co. 1990)
52 ALR5th 559—§ 7, 12, 14, 17
State v. Kilburn, 1998 WL 142412 (Ohio Ct. App. 12th Dist. Warren County 1998)
70 ALR6th 329—§ 14
State v. Kilby, 679 S.E.2d 430 (N.C. Ct. App. 2009)
57 ALR6th 1—§ 23
State v. Kilby, 763 S.W.2d 389 (Tenn. Crim. 1988)
7 ALR5th 263—§ 4
State v. Kile, 313 N.W.2d 558 (Iowa 1981)
59 ALR5th 1—§ 3, 8
99 ALR6th 295—§ 16
State v. Kilgore, 233 S.C. 6, 103 S.E.2d 321 (1958)
116 ALR5th 149—§ 3
State v. Killebrew, 115 Wis. 2d 243, 340 N.W.2d 470 (1983)
96 ALR6th 269—§ 31
State v. Killebrew, 163 Wis. 2d 525, 472 N.W.2d 247 (Ct. App. 1991)

74 ALR5th 643—§ 3
State v. Killian, 37 N.C. App. 234, 245 S.E.2d 812 (1978)
15 ALR5th 391—§ 7, 27
State v. Killinger, 2009 WL 4017247 (Ariz. Ct. App. Div. 1 2009)
56 ALR6th 323—§ 11
State v. Killion, 95 Kan. 371, 148 P. 643 (1915)
101 ALR6th 499—§ 14
State v. Killion, 483 So. 2d 1281 (La. App. 4th Cir. 1986)
7 ALR5th 263—§ 5
State v. Killion, 2009 WL 1748959 (Tenn. Crim. App. 2009)
68 ALR6th 115—§ 29, 43
State v. Killory, 73 Wis. 2d 400, 243 N.W.2d 475, 99 A.L.R.3d 840 (1976)
102 ALR5th 525—§ 23
State v. Killpack, 276 N.W.2d 368 (Iowa 1979)
79 ALR5th 419—§ 10
19 ALR6th 411—§ 16
State v. Kilmer, 190 W. Va. 617, 439 S.E.2d 881 (1993)
69 ALR6th 579—§ 4
State v. Kilpatrick, 201 Kan. 6, 439 P.2d 99 (1968)
20 ALR5th 177—§ 3, 8
State v. Kiluk, 120 N.H. 1, 410 A.2d 648 (1980)
5 ALR5th 243—§ 61
State v. Kimball, 54 Haw. 83, 503 P.2d 176 (1972)
72 ALR5th 1—§ 15, 32
State v. Kimball, 145 Idaho 542, 181 P.3d 468 (2008)
77 ALR6th 197—§ 17
State v. Kimberley, 103 S.W.3d 850 (Mo. Ct. App. W.D. 2003)
23 ALR6th 307—§ 38
State v. Kimble, 375 So. 2d 924 (La. 1979)
76 ALR5th 563—§ 4, 5
State v. Kimble, 651 So. 2d 1285 (Fla. Dist. Ct. App. 3d Dist. 1995)

113 ALR5th 597—§ 8
State v. Kimble, 1998 WL 65487 (Ohio Ct. App. 8th Dist. Lorain County 1998)
78 ALR5th 489—§ 3
State v. Kimble, 2006-Ohio-6863, 2006 WL 3772223 (Ohio Ct. App. 11th Dist. Trumbull County 2006)
26 ALR6th 511—§ 19, 26
State v. Kimbrell, 320 N.C. 762, 360 S.E.2d 691 (1987)
18 ALR5th 804—§ 2, 3
State v. Kimbro, 197 Conn. 219, 496 A.2d 498 (1985)
19 ALR5th 470—§ 3
74 ALR5th 319—§ 4
State v. Kimbrough, 109 N.J. Super. 57, 262 A.2d 232 (App. Div. 1970)
42 ALR6th 237—§ 8
State v. Kimbrough, 673 So. 2d 1187 (La. Ct. App. 4th Cir. 1996)
28 ALR6th 505—§ 9
State v. Kimmel, 145 Ariz. 581, 703 P.2d 525 (App. 1985)
31 ALR5th 704—§ 16, 18
State v. Kimmel, 202 Kan. 303, 448 P.2d 19 (1968)
59 ALR5th 1—§ 3, 4, 6
State v. Kimmons, 502 N.W.2d 391 (Minn. Ct. App. 1993)
73 ALR5th 383—§ 3
State v. Kinard, 21 Wash. App. 587, 585 P.2d 836 (Div. 3 1978)
55 ALR6th 391—§ 5
State v. Kinard, 2005 WL 2373701 (Del. Super. Ct. 2005)
92 ALR6th 1—§ 3, 9
State v. Kincaid, 83 Ohio App. 3d 341, 614 N.E.2d 1112 (Hocking Co. 1992)
52 ALR5th 655—§ 3
State v. Kincaid, 183 N.C. 709, 110 S.E. 612 (1922)
24 ALR5th 465—§ 74
State v. Kincheloe, 87 N.M. 34, 528 P.2d 893 (Ct. App. 1974)
72 ALR5th 109—§ 3
79 ALR5th 419—§ 4

State v. Kinchen, 290 So. 2d 860 (La. 1974)

99 ALR6th 295—§ 21

State v. Kinder, 22 Mont. 516, 57 P. 94 (1899)

29 ALR5th 59—§ 3

State v. Kinder, 122 S.W.3d 624 (Mo. Ct. App. E.D. 2003)

72 ALR6th 227—§ 34

State v. Kinder, 942 S.W.2d 313 (Mo. 1996)

66 ALR5th 135—§ 43
83 ALR6th 255—§ 15

State v. Kinderman, 271 Minn. 405, 136 N.W.2d 577 (1965)

55 ALR5th 125—§ 3, 7, 8

State v. King, 9 Wash. App. 389, 512 P.2d 771 (1973)

4 ALR5th 1—§ 4

State v. King, 10 Ohio App. 3d 161, 460 N.E.2d 1383 (1st Dist. Hamilton County 1983)

77 ALR6th 251—§ 5

State v. King, 24 Wash. App. 495, 601 P.2d 982 (Div. 2 1979)

78 ALR5th 197—§ 14

State v. King, 42 N.C. App. 210, 256 S.E.2d 247 (1979)

99 ALR5th 557—§ 3

State v. King, 44 N.C. App. 31, 259 S.E.2d 919 (1979)

113 ALR5th 517—§ 13

State v. King, 84 Or. App. 165, 733 P.2d 472 (1987)

51 ALR6th 1—§ 20

State v. King, 95 Wash. App. 1045, 1999 WL 311714 (Div. 3 1999)

99 ALR6th 295—§ 15

State v. King, 99 N.C. App. 283, 393 S.E.2d 152 (1990)

2 ALR6th 551—§ 5

State v. King, 101 Kan. 189, 165 P. 665 (1917)

59 ALR5th 1—§ 4, 6

State v. King, 136 Ohio App. 3d 377, 736 N.E.2d 921 (8th Dist. Cuyahoga County 1999)

50 ALR6th 455—§ 8, 19, 37

State v. King, 140 Ariz. 602, 684 P.2d 174 (Ct. App. Div. 2 1984)

124 ALR5th 1—§ 3

State v. King, 144 La. 430, 80 So. 615 (1919)

81 ALR5th 563—§ 3, 5

State v. King, 188 Neb. 563, 198 N.W.2d 185 (1972)

78 ALR6th 417—§ 5

State v. King, 199 Or. App. 278, 111 P.3d 1146 (2005)

26 ALR6th 179—§ 3, 5, 6, 14, 17

State v. King, 213 Ariz. 632, 146 P.3d 1274 (Ct. App. Div. 2 2006)

30 ALR6th 1—§ 4, 7

State v. King, 215 N.J. Super. 504, 522 A.2d 455 (App. Div. 1987)

97 ALR5th 201—§ 6

State v. King, 215 Wis. 2d 295, 572 N.W.2d 530 (Ct. App. 1997)

70 ALR5th 587—§ 24
15 ALR6th 319—§ 4, 5

State v. King, 248 N.J. Super. 173, 590 A.2d 700 (1991)

27 ALR5th 593—§ 21

State v. King, 268 N.C. 711, 151 S.E.2d 566 (1966)

95 ALR5th 229—§ 19

State v. King, 287 N.C. 645, 215 S.E.2d 540 (1975)

16 ALR6th 329—§ 4

State v. King, 288 Wis. 2d 460, 2005 WI App 254, 706 N.W.2d 702 (Ct. App. 2005)

73 ALR6th 49—§ 37

State v. King, 311 N.C. 603, 320 S.E.2d 1 (1984)

42 ALR6th 237—§ 4

State v. King, 346 N.W.2d 750 (S.D. 1984)

84 ALR5th 487—§ 19

State v. King, 353 N.C. 457, 546 S.E.2d 575 (2001)

110 ALR5th 1—§ 14

State v. King, 367 N.W.2d 599 (Minn. App. 1985)

24 ALR5th 465—§ 61
57 ALR5th 141—§ 9
State v. King, 396 S.E.2d 402, 12 A.L.R.5th 1115 (W. Va. 1990)
12 ALR5th 909—§ 4, 9
State v. King, 492 N.W.2d 211 (Iowa Ct. App. 1992)
9 ALR6th 1—§ 17
State v. King, 518 S.E.2d 663 (W. Va. 1999)
39 ALR5th 283—§ 31
State v. King, 564 S.W.2d 592 (Mo. Ct. App. 1978)
70 ALR5th 587—§ 10
State v. King, 576 N.W.2d 369 (Iowa 1998)
9 ALR6th 541—§ 12
State v. King, 604 P.2d 923 (Utah 1979)
103 ALR6th 507—§ 10, 14
State v. King, 604 So. 2d 661 (La. Ct. App. 1st Cir. 1992)
7 ALR6th 233—§ 5
State v. King, 683 So. 2d 1228 (La. Ct. App. 3d Cir. 1996)
45 ALR5th 1—§ 2, 17
State v. King, 690 N.W.2d 397, 27 A.L.R.6th 657 (Minn. Ct. App. 2005)
27 ALR6th 491—§ 3, 11
State v. King, 707 So. 2d 1374 (La. Ct. App. 3d Cir. 1998)
32 ALR5th 31—§ 7
State v. King, 708 S.W.2d 364 (Mo. App. 1986)
18 ALR5th 1—§ 2, 3, 10, 22
State v. King, 718 S.W.2d 241 (Tenn. 1986)
83 ALR6th 255—§ 17
State v. King, 747 S.W.2d 264 (Mo. Ct. App. E.D. 1988)
5 ALR6th 1—§ 51, 54
State v. King, 799 So. 2d 1241 (La. Ct. App. 3d Cir. 2001)
19 ALR6th 697—§ 14
State v. King, 804 So. 2d 57 (La. Ct. App. 4th Cir. 2001)
99 ALR6th 295—§ 9, 19

State v. King, 1986 WL 15039 (Tenn. Crim. App. 1986)
76 ALR5th 1—§ 2
78 ALR5th 1—§ 2
79 ALR5th 237—§ 2
State v. King, 1991 WL 244483 (Ohio Ct. App. 8th Dist. Cuyahoga County 1991)
17 ALR6th 327—§ 36
State v. King, 1993 WL 497064 (Ohio Ct. App. 8th Dist. Cuyahoga County 1993)
88 ALR5th 121—§ 2
State v. King, 1997 WL 722778 (Ohio Ct. App. 3d Dist. Seneca County 1997)
67 ALR5th 637—§ 5, 7
State v. King, 1998 WL 865751 (Minn. Ct. App. 1998)
8 ALR6th 265—§ 10
State v. King, 1999 WL 1087480 (Ohio Ct. App. 8th Dist. Cuyahoga County 1999)
85 ALR5th 1—§ 21
State v. King, 2005-Ohio-3623, 2005 WL 1670794 (Ohio Ct. App. 12th Dist. Butler County 2005)
93 ALR6th 1—§ 18
State v. King, 2007 WL 326007 (N.J. Super. Ct. App. Div. 2007)
26 ALR6th 511—§ 7
State v. King, 2010 WL 1957373 (N.C. Ct. App. 2010)
57 ALR6th 1—§ 22, 25
State v. Kingsbury, 143 Vt. 20, 460 A.2d 452 (1983)
58 ALR6th 215—§ 8
State v. Kingsley, 252 Kan. 761, 851 P.2d 370 (1993)
37 ALR5th 515—§ 3
State v. Kinkade, 140 Ariz. 91, 680 P.2d 801 (1984)
16 ALR6th 329—§ 5
24 ALR6th 591—§ 4, 12
State v. Kinley, 72 Ohio St. 3d 491, 1995-Ohio-279, 651 N.E.2d 419 (1995)
7 ALR6th 233—§ 15

State v. Kinney, 83 Ohio St. 3d 85, 698 N.E.2d 49 (1998)

43 ALR5th 1—§ 13

State v. Kinsella, 1995 WL 479553 (Minn. Ct. App. 1995)

95 ALR5th 229—§ 3

State v. Kinsey, 20 Wash. App. 299, 579 P.2d 1347 (Div. 3 1978)

7 ALR6th 169—§ 9

State v. Kinsky, 348 N.W.2d 319 (Minn. 1984)

73 ALR5th 383—§ 5

State v. Kinsman, 715 So. 2d 360 (Fla. Dist. Ct. App. 5th Dist. 1998)

113 ALR5th 597—§ 8

State v. Kinstler, 207 Neb. 386, 299 N.W.2d 182 (1980)

78 ALR6th 417—§ 26

State v. Kinstler, 221 Wis. 2d 597, 586 N.W.2d 699 (Ct. App. 1998)

58 ALR6th 499—§ 90

State v. Kipf, 234 Neb. 227, 450 N.W.2d 397 (1990)

36 ALR5th 255—§ 10, 24, 30

State v. Kipi, 72 Hawaii 164, 811 P.2d 815 (1991)

46 ALR5th 735—§ 2

State v. Kirbabas, 232 Ga. App. 474, 502 S.E.2d 314 (1998)

56 ALR6th 323—§ 7

State v. Kirbie, 2008 WL 4602534 (Ariz. Ct. App. Div. 1 2008)

57 ALR6th 1—§ 14

State v. Kirby, 280 Conn. 361, 908 A.2d 506 (2006)

29 ALR6th 1—§ 18
30 ALR6th 1—§ 3, 4, 6, 7

State v. Kircher, 189 Wis. 2d 392, 525 N.W.2d 788 (Ct. App. 1994)

24 ALR6th 1—§ 11

State v. Kirchoff, 156 Vt. 1, 587 A.2d 988 (1991)

45 ALR6th 643—§ 16

State v. Kirkaldie, 179 Mont. 283, 587 P.2d 1298 (1978)

84 ALR6th 427—§ 27

State v. Kirkland, 18 Ohio App. 3d 1, 480 N.E.2d 85 (8th Dist. Cuyahoga County 1984)

19 ALR6th 697—§ 5, 17

State v. Kirkland, 184 Mont. 229, 602 P.2d 586 (1979)

55 ALR6th 157—§ 6, 51

State v. Kirkland, 684 S.W.2d 402 (Mo. App. 1984)

54 ALR5th 141—§ 3, 5, 10

State v. Kirkland, 1997 WL 55936 (Tenn. Crim. App. 1997)

70 ALR5th 647—§ 5
87 ALR6th 1—§ 41

State v. Kirkley, 470 So. 2d 1001 (La. Ct. App. 1st Cir. 1985)

78 ALR5th 1—§ 20, 50, 60, 65

State v. Kirkman, 1998 WL 126255 (Ohio Ct. App. 3d Dist. Marion County 1998)

78 ALR5th 489—§ 10

State v. Kirkpatrick, 45 Or. App. 899, 609 P.2d 433 (1980)

111 ALR5th 239—§ 10

State v. Kirkpatrick, 220 Iowa 974, 263 N.W. 52 (1935)

9 ALR6th 363—§ 40

State v. Kirkpatrick, 320 S.C. 38, 462 S.E.2d 884 (Ct. App. 1995)

1 ALR6th 549—§ 3, 6
7 ALR6th 169—§ 3
8 ALR6th 265—§ 3

State v. Kirksey, 647 S.W.2d 799 (Mo. 1983)

117 ALR5th 513—§ 10

State v. Kirsch, 139 N.H. 647, 662 A.2d 937 (1995)

111 ALR5th 239—§ 11

State v. Kirschbaum, 195 Wis. 2d 11, 535 N.W.2d 462 (Ct. App. 1995)

87 ALR5th 693—§ 3

State v. Kirwin, 137 Wash. App. 387, 153 P.3d 883 (Div. 2 2007)

71 ALR6th 1—§ 8

State v. Kiser, 26 Ariz. App. 106, 546 P.2d 831 (Div. 2 1976)

7 ALR6th 169—§ 8

State v. Kisor, 82 Wash. App. 175, 916 P.2d 978 (Div. 2 1996)
15 ALR5th 391—§ 53
92 ALR5th 35—§ 11, 30

State v. Kissell, 83 Or. App. 630, 732 P.2d 940 (1987)
92 ALR6th 1—§ 8

State v. Kissinger, 599 So. 2d 865 (La. Ct. App. 4th Cir. 1992)
12 ALR6th 267—§ 5

State v. Kissner, 390 N.W.2d 58 (S.D. 1986)
84 ALR6th 293—§ 12, 14, 27

State v. Kistle, 59 N.C. App. 724, 297 S.E.2d 626 (1982)
42 ALR5th 291—§ 2
116 ALR5th 373—§ 3, 8

State v. Kitchen, 207 W. Va. 724, 536 S.E.2d 488 (2000)
39 ALR5th 283—§ 31

State v. Kitchen, 808 P.2d 1127 (Utah Ct. App. 1991)
74 ALR5th 319—§ 6, 11
82 ALR5th 103—§ 3
116 ALR5th 479—§ 5

State v. Kitchen, 1997 ND 241, 572 N.W.2d 106 (N.D. 1997)
45 ALR6th 643—§ 8

State v. Kitchen, 2003-Ohio-5017, 2003 WL 22174602 (Ohio Ct. App. 5th Dist. Ashland County 2003)
71 ALR6th 1—§ 12

State v. Kitchens, 498 N.W.2d 649 (S.D. 1993)
92 ALR6th 295—§ 7, 8, 14, 25
93 ALR6th 207—§ 8, 31
96 ALR6th 355—§ 6, 9, 18, 37, 60

State v. Kittredge, 36 Or. App. 603, 585 P.2d 423 (1978)
112 ALR5th 429—§ 2, 13
114 ALR5th 235—§ 2

State v. Kittrell, 2002 WL 31500759 (Minn. Ct. App. 2002)
51 ALR6th 139—§ 7

State v. Kitzler, 1995 WL 126620 (Ohio Ct. App. 8th Dist. Cuyahoga County 1995)
24 ALR6th 747—§ 34

State v. Kivioja, 225 Wis. 2d 271, 592 N.W.2d 220 (1999)
9 ALR6th 633—§ 13
14 ALR6th 517—§ 7

State v. K.J.B., 2009 WL 672392 (Minn. Ct. App. 2009)
68 ALR6th 1—§ 17

State v. Klafta, 73 Hawaii 109, 831 P.2d 512 (1992)
26 ALR5th 603—§ 4

State v. Klammer, 230 Minn. 372, 41 N.W.2d 451 (1950)
6 ALR5th 733—§ 16

State v. Klattenhoff, 71 Hawaii 598, 801 P.2d 548 (1990)
33 ALR5th 453—§ 4

State v. Klaus, 730 S.W.2d 571 (Mo. App. 1987)
50 ALR5th 467—§ 6

State v. Klauss, 19 Conn. App. 296, 562 A.2d 558 (1989)
58 ALR6th 499—§ 41

State v. Klawitter, 518 N.W.2d 577 (Minn. 1994)
117 ALR5th 491—§ 2, 4

State v. Klawonn, 609 N.W.2d 515 (Iowa 2000)
15 ALR5th 391—§ 30

State v. Klein, 97 Conn. 321, 116 A. 596 (1922)
24 ALR6th 591—§ 4

State v. Klein, 113 Wis. 2d 725, 334 N.W.2d 590 (Ct. App. 1983)
34 ALR6th 1—§ 11

State v. Klein, 574 N.W.2d 347 (Iowa 1998)
18 ALR5th 542—§ 3

State v. Klein, 1985 WL 7095 (Ohio Ct. App. 6th Dist. Wood County 1985)
85 ALR5th 1—§ 15

State v. Kleiner, 1981 WL 3795 (Ohio Ct. App. 11th Dist.Geauga County 1981)
57 ALR5th 141—§ 4

State v. Klem, 438 N.W.2d 798, 17 Media L. Rep. (BNA) 1241 (N.D. 1989)

32 ALR6th 171—§ 5, 22
33 ALR6th 1—§ 21
State v. Klempay, 2011-Ohio-2643, 2011 WL 2175830 (Ohio Ct. App. 7th Dist. Mahoning County 2011)
69 ALR6th 1—§ 28
State v. Kleypas, 272 Kan. 894, 40 P.3d 139 (2001)
83 ALR6th 255—§ 9
State v. Kleypas, 602 S.W.2d 863 (Mo. Ct. App. S.D. 1980)
1 ALR6th 657—§ 4
State v. Kliewer, 210 Kan. 820, 504 P.2d 580 (1972)
66 ALR6th 351—§ 3, 16
67 ALR6th 209—§ 3, 25
State v. Klima, 129 P.3d 582 (Kan. 2006)
26 ALR6th 511—§ 25, 29
State v. Klinger, 96 Wash. App. 619, 980 P.2d 282 (Div. 2 1999)
71 ALR6th 1—§ 4
State v. Klish, 123 Wis. 2d 541, 367 N.W.2d 243 (Ct. App. 1985)
122 ALR5th 439—§ 6
State v. Klosterman, 317 N.W.2d 796 (N.D. 1982)
68 ALR5th 549—§ 3, 6
State v. Kluttz, 9 Conn. App. 686, 521 A.2d 178 (1987)
84 ALR6th 427—§ 16, 17
State v. K.M., 220 N.J. Super. 338, 532 A.2d 254 (App. Div. 1987)
70 ALR6th 1—§ 15
State v. K.M.M., 721 N.W.2d 330 (Minn. Ct. App. 2006)
68 ALR6th 1—§ 10
69 ALR6th 1—§ 20
State v. Knaack, 224 Wis. 2d 645, 590 N.W.2d 283 (Ct. App. 1999)
38 ALR6th 97—§ 28
State v. Knapp, 843 S.W.2d 345 (Mo. 1992)
64 ALR5th 671—§ 7
State v. Knapp, 1991 WL 254275 (Mo. Ct. App. 1991)
64 ALR5th 671—§ 4

State v. Knapp, 2003 WI 121, 265 Wis. 2d 278, 666 N.W.2d 881 (2003)
42 ALR6th 237—§ 8
State v. Knapp, 2011-Ohio-3792, 2011 WL 3300157 (Ohio Ct. App. 10th Dist. Franklin County 2011)
70 ALR6th 1—§ 5
State v. Knauff, 115 Idaho 74, 764 P.2d 441 (Ct. App. 1988)
51 ALR6th 1—§ 19
State v. Knecht, 209 Wis. 2d 600, 568 N.W.2d 37 (Ct. App. 1997)
72 ALR5th 403—§ 19
State v. Knese, 985 S.W.2d 759 (Mo. 1999)
37 ALR5th 515—§ 21
State v. Knies, 125 Wis. 2d 569, 371 N.W.2d 430 (Ct. App. 1985)
33 ALR6th 407—§ 4
State v. Knight, 42 Kan. App. 2d 893, 218 P.3d 1177 (2009)
64 ALR6th 131—§ 2
State v. Knight, 44 Kan. App. 2d 666, 241 P.3d 120 (2010)
64 ALR6th 131—§ 3, 23
State v. Knight, 56 Conn. App. 845, 747 A.2d 13 (2000)
27 ALR5th 593—§ 31, 36
State v. Knight, 63 Haw. 90, 621 P.2d 370 (1980)
59 ALR5th 615—§ 3, 5
State v. Knight, 114 Wash. App. 1050, 2002 WL 31697763 (Div. 1 2002)
16 ALR6th 329—§ 11, 12
24 ALR6th 591—§ 9, 13
State v. Knight, 143 Wis. 2d 408, 421 N.W.2d 847 (1988)
14 ALR5th 89—§ 3
State v. Knight, 145 N.J. 233, 678 A.2d 642 (1996)
12 ALR6th 267—§ 7
State v. Knight, 168 W. Va. 615, 285 S.E.2d 401 (1981)
71 ALR6th 283—§ 7
State v. Knight, 340 N.C. 531, 459 S.E.2d 481 (1995)
80 ALR5th 469—§ 2, 3, 5

State v. Knight, 770 S.W.2d 771 (Tenn. Crim. App. 1988)
43 ALR6th 475—§ 7

State v. Knighton, 436 So. 2d 1141 (La. 1983)
10 ALR5th 700—§ 9, 16

State v. Knoch, 86 Or. App. 15, 738 P.2d 979 (1987)
32 ALR6th 1—§ 5

State v. Knoll, 110 Idaho 678, 718 P.2d 589 (Ct. App. 1986)
119 ALR5th 379—§ 7

State v. Knopik, 2006 WL 1229569 (Minn. Ct. App. 2006)
26 ALR6th 511—§ 26

State v. Knoten, 347 S.C. 296, 555 S.E.2d 391 (2001)
3 ALR6th 543—§ 6

State v. Knott, 132 Idaho 476, 974 P.2d 1105 (1999)
52 ALR5th 655—§ 6

State v. Knotts, 70 S.C. 400, 50 S.E. 9 (1905)
45 ALR5th 591—§ 15

State v. Knotts, 187 W. Va. 795, 421 S.E.2d 917 (1992)
9 ALR5th 102—§ 18

State v. Knowels, 2002 ND 62, 643 N.W.2d 20 (N.D. 2002)
33 ALR6th 91—§ 39

State v. Knowles, 25 Utah 2d 13, 474 P.2d 727 (1970)
92 ALR6th 1—§ 3

State v. Knowles, 275 S.C. 312, 270 S.E.2d 133 (1980)
70 ALR6th 361—§ 9

State v. Knowles, 444 So. 2d 611 (La. 1984)
124 ALR5th 1—§ 5

State v. Knowles, 495 A.2d 335 (Me. 1985)
7 ALR5th 73—§ 2, 4, 5

State v. Knowles, 517 A.2d 1075 (Me. 1986)
7 ALR5th 73—§ 4, 5

State v. Knox, 213 Wis. 2d 318, 570 N.W.2d 599 (Ct. App. 1997)

9 ALR6th 541—§ 3

State v. Knox, 609 So. 2d 803 (La. 1992)
47 ALR5th 259—§ 3, 4

State v. Knuckles, 65 Ohio St. 3d 494, 1992-Ohio-64, 605 N.E.2d 54 (1992)
124 ALR5th 1—§ 5

State v. Knuckles, 196 W. Va. 416, 473 S.E.2d 131 (1996)
17 ALR6th 757—§ 4

State v. Knuckles, 1991 WL 129792 (Ohio Ct. App. 12th Dist.Butler County 1991)
57 ALR5th 141—§ 7

State v. Knuckles, 1995 WL 22713 (Ohio Ct. App. 12th Dist. Butler County 1995)
102 ALR6th 279—§ 11

State v. Knudson, 27 S.D. 400, 131 N.W. 400 (1911)
66 ALR5th 397—§ 3, 9

State v. Knudson, 499 N.W.2d 872 (N.D. 1993)
41 ALR5th 171—§ 2, 9, 12, 16, 17, 55, 63, 68, 72, 85, 108, 122

State v. Knupp, 310 N.W.2d 179 (Iowa 1981)
39 ALR5th 283—§ 10, 60

State v. Knutson, 64 Wash. App. 76, 823 P.2d 513 (1991)
42 ALR5th 291—§ 9

State v. Knutson, 81 Or. App. 353, 725 P.2d 407 (1986)
24 ALR5th 132—§ 5, 7

State v. Knutson, 220 N.W.2d 575 (Iowa 1974)
39 ALR5th 283—§ 10

State v. Knutson, 234 N.W.2d 105 (Iowa 1975)
68 ALR5th 343—§ 3, 10, 13

State v. Knutson 523 N.W.2d 909, 23 Media L. Rep. (BNA) 1056 (Minn. Ct. App. 1994)
60 ALR5th 75—§ 12

State v. Knutson, 1999 WL 430813 (Minn. Ct. App. 1999)
7 ALR6th 233—§ 5

State v. Koberstein, 8 Or. App. 307, 493
P.2d 176 (1972)
85 ALR5th 1—§ 15
State v. Kobow, 466 N.W.2d 747 (Minn.
Ct. App. 1991)
73 ALR5th 383—§ 32
State v. Kobrin Securities, Inc., 111 N.J.
307, 544 A.2d 833 (1988)
37 ALR6th 511—§ 12
State v. Koch, 455 So. 2d 492 (Fla. Dist.
Ct. App. 1st Dist. 1984)
114 ALR5th 173—§ 9
State v. Koch, 2009-Ohio-6998, 2009
WL 5176602 (Ohio Ct. App. 11th
Dist. Lake County 2009)
63 ALR6th 351—§ 3
64 ALR6th 1—§ 9
State v. Kochel, 2008 ND 28, 744
N.W.2d 771 (N.D. 2008)
45 ALR6th 643—§ 8
State v. Kochendorfer, 304 N.W.2d 336
(Minn. 1981)
**41 ALR5th 171—§ 7, 93, 108, 114,
133**
State v. Kociolek, 23 N.J. 400, 129 A.2d
417 (1957)
66 ALR6th 83—§ 10
State v. Kock, 207 Neb. 731, 300
N.W.2d 824 (1981)
84 ALR5th 487—§ 20
State v. Koehler, 107 Ohio Misc. 2d 28,
736 N.E.2d 127 (County Ct. 2000)
76 ALR5th 1—§ 13
State v. Koehler, 448 N.W.2d 886
(Minn. Ct. App. 1989)
72 ALR6th 141—§ 7
State v. Koehling, 381 A.2d 12 (Me.
1978)
50 ALR5th 703—§ 15
State v. Koelling, 1995 WL 125933
(Ohio Ct. App. 10th Dist. Franklin
County 1995)
99 ALR6th 295—§ 19
State v. Koennecke, 274 Or. 169, 545
P.2d 127 (1976)
53 ALR6th 81—§ 7
State v. Koepke, 47 Wash. App. 897,
738 P.2d 295 (1987)

3 ALR5th 784—§ 4, 5
State v. Koerber, 85 Wash. App. 1, 931
P.2d 904 (Div. 1 1996)
71 ALR5th 1—§ 58
State v. Kofines, 33 R.I. 211, 80 A. 432
(1911)
31 ALR6th 523—§ 29
State v. Kohler, 434 So. 2d 1110 (La. Ct.
App. 1st Cir. 1983)
124 ALR5th 1—§ 8
State v. Kohlfuss, 152 Conn. 625, 211
A.2d 143 (1965)
85 ALR5th 547—§ 8
State v. Kolander, 236 Minn. 209, 52
N.W.2d 458 (1952)
84 ALR5th 69—§ 2, 14, 22
85 ALR5th 187—§ 7, 9, 15, 16
State v. Kolia, 116 Haw. 29, 169 P.3d
981 (Ct. App. 2007)
30 ALR6th 103—§ 46
State v. Kolibaba, 2005 WL 3032466
(N.J. Super. Ct. App. Div. 2005)
17 ALR6th 757—§ 4
State v. Kolisch, 185 Or. App. 418, 60
P.3d 576 (2002)
26 ALR6th 179—§ 17
State v. Kolisynk, 49 Wash. App. 890,
746 P.2d 1224 (Div. 1 1987)
83 ALR5th 277—§ 10
State v. Kolla, 672 N.W.2d 1 (Minn. Ct.
App. 2003)
31 ALR6th 523—§ 12
State v. Kollenborn, 304 S.W.2d 855
(Mo. 1957)
119 ALR5th 275—§ 2
State v. Koloske, 100 Wash. 2d 889, 676
P.2d 456 (1984)
105 ALR5th 529—§ 8
State v. Komok, 113 Wash. 2d 810, 783
P.2d 1061 (1989)
83 ALR5th 277—§ 13
State v. Koncaba, 12 Neb. App. 378, 674
N.W.2d 485 (2004)
116 ALR5th 479—§ 5
State v. Konfrst, 251 Neb. 214, 556
N.W.2d 250 (1996)
68 ALR5th 343—§ 3, 16

State v. Kong, 77 Haw. 264, 883 P.2d 686 (Ct. App. 1994)
28 ALR6th 505—§ 10

State v. Konohia, 2005 WL 318634 (Haw. Ct. App. 2005)
7 ALR6th 233—§ 5

State v. Konrath, 218 Wis. 2d 290, 577 N.W.2d 601 (1998)
89 ALR5th 539—§ 3, 5, 8

State v. Kooima, 815 N.W.2d 410 (Iowa Ct. App. 2012)
84 ALR6th 293—§ 21, 27

State v. Kooima, 833 N.W.2d 202 (Iowa 2013)
96 ALR6th 577—§ 7

State v. Kool, 212 N.W.2d 518 (Iowa 1973)
31 ALR6th 333—§ 10, 11

State v. Koome, 84 Wash. 2d 901, 530 P.2d 260 (1975)
77 ALR5th 1—§ 3, 6, 9

State v. Koon, 704 So. 2d 756 (La. 1997)
83 ALR6th 465—§ 19, 79

State v. Koon, 730 So. 2d 503 (La. Ct. App. 2d Cir. 1999)
90 ALR5th 453—§ 12

State v. Koonce, 731 S.W.2d 431 (Mo. Ct. App. E.D. 1987)
102 ALR5th 447—§ 13, 22

State v. Koontz, 145 Wash. 2d 650, 41 P.3d 475 (2002)
65 ALR6th 537—§ 15, 31

State v. Koopmans, 563 N.W.2d 528, 59 A.L.R.5th 781 (Wis 1997)
59 ALR5th 135—§ 3, 6, 15

State v. Kopa, 173 W. Va. 43, 311 S.E.2d 412 (1983)
3 ALR6th 269—§ 9, 22, 25

State v. Koperski, 254 Neb. 624, 578 N.W.2d 837 (1998)
102 ALR5th 447—§ 3, 7

State v. Kopet, 1990 WL 140718 (Minn. Ct. App. 1990)
73 ALR5th 383—§ 28

State v. Koppel, 127 N.H. 286, 499 A.2d 977 (1985)
74 ALR5th 319—§ 3

State v. Koppenhafer, 59 Or. App. 213, 650 P.2d 981 (1982)
109 ALR5th 99—§ 10

State v. Korba, 2009 WL 1025573 (Ariz. Ct. App. Div. 1 2009)
56 ALR6th 185—§ 12, 19, 39

State v. Korbel, 231 Kan. 657, 647 P.2d 1301 (1982)
26 ALR5th 603—§ 4

State v. Kordonowy, 251 Mont. 44, 823 P.2d 854 (1991)
87 ALR5th 181—§ 5

State v. Korf, 201 Neb. 64, 266 N.W.2d 86 (1978)
72 ALR5th 1—§ 29

State v. Korhn, 41 Conn. App. 874, 678 A.2d 492 (1996)
119 ALR5th 379—§ 7

State v. Korich, 130 Wash. 243, 226 P. 1016 (1924)
32 ALR5th 149—§ 29

State v. Korman, 379 So. 2d 1061 (La. 1980)
103 ALR5th 463—§ 3

State v. Kornacki, 2006 WL 2135799 (N.J. Super. Ct. App. Div. 2006)
55 ALR6th 513—§ 8, 10

State v. Kornegay, 313 N.C. 1, 326 S.E.2d 881 (1985)
57 ALR6th 445—§ 23, 59

State v. Kortkamp, 560 N.W.2d 93 (Minn. Ct. App. 1997)
9 ALR6th 541—§ 7

State v. Kosden, 34 So. 3d 521 (La. Ct. App. 2d Cir. 2010)
69 ALR6th 1—§ 10

State v. Koskela, 536 N.W.2d 625 (Minn. 1995)
82 ALR5th 591—§ 9, 10

State v. Koski, 120 N.H. 112, 411 A.2d 1122 (1980)
3 ALR5th 521—§ 6

State v. Koslowski, 130 Wash. App. 1005, 2005 WL 3753136 (Div. 3 2005)
20 ALR6th 479—§ 3

State v. Kosman, 181 Ariz. 487, 892
P.2d 207 (Ct. App. Div. 1 1995)
122 ALR5th 439—§ 3
State v. Koss, 49 Ohio St. 3d 213, 551
N.E.2d 970 (1990)
22 ALR5th 787—§ 3
57 ALR5th 315—§ 2, 4
58 ALR5th 749—§ 6
State v. Kotis, 91 Haw. 319, 984 P.2d 78
(Haw. 1999)
87 ALR5th 277—§ 2, 10
State v. Koton, 157 W. Va. 558, 202
S.E.2d 823 (1974)
29 ALR5th 59—§ 3, 57
State v. Kotwitz, 549 So. 2d 351 (La.
App. 2d Cir. 1989)
18 ALR5th 1—§ 31
State v. Kounelis, 258 N.J. Super. 420,
609 A.2d 1310 (1992)
**32 ALR5th 149—§ 4, 23, 24, 29, 32,
40, 45, 83**
State v. Koveos, 169 Vt. 62, 732 A.2d
722 (1999)
65 ALR6th 537—§ 58
State v. Koziol, 129 Wash. App. 1050,
2005 WL 2502177 (Div. 3 2005)
79 ALR6th 1—§ 4, 7, 32, 34, 41
State v. Koziol, 338 N.W.2d 47 (Minn.
1983)
17 ALR6th 327—§ 12
State v. Kraemer, 156 Wis. 2d 761, 457
N.W.2d 562 (Ct. App. 1990)
74 ALR5th 453—§ 5
State v. Kraimer, 99 Wis. 2d 306, 298
N.W.2d 568 (1980)
58 ALR6th 499—§ 16
State v. Krajewski, 589 So. 2d 254, 16
FLW S. 682 (Fla. 1991)
18 ALR5th 1—§ 12
State v. Krajger, 182 Conn. 497, 438
A.2d 745 (1980)
38 ALR6th 97—§ 12
State v. Kramar, 149 Wis. 2d 767, 440
N.W.2d 317 (1989)
124 ALR5th 1—§ 3
32 ALR6th 1—§ 11
State v. Kramer, 441 N.W.2d 502 (Minn.
App. 1989)

54 ALR5th 575—§ 15
State v. Kramer, 809 S.W.2d 50 (Mo.
App. 1991)
45 ALR5th 591—§ 5, 7
State v. Krammes, 105 N.J. Super. 345,
252 A.2d 223 (App. Div. 1969)
72 ALR5th 607—§ 3
State v. Krantz, 2003-Ohio-4568, 2003
WL 22019766 (Ohio Ct. App. 8th
Dist. Cuyahoga County 2003)
70 ALR6th 1—§ 5
State v. Kraus, 147 N.C. App. 766, 557
S.E.2d 144 (2001)
23 ALR6th 307—§ 42
State v. Krech, 403 N.W.2d 634 (Minn.
1987)
62 ALR5th 1—§ 9, 14
State v. Kreger, 1992 WL 3663 (Minn.
Ct. App. 1992)
17 ALR6th 327—§ 34
State v. Kremer, 307 Minn. 309, 239
N.W.2d 476 (1976)
41 ALR5th 171—§ 2
State v. Krich, 123 N.J.L. 519, 9 A.2d
803 (N.J. Sup. Ct. 1939)
64 ALR6th 655—§ 6
State v. Krieger, 163 Wis. 2d 241, 471
N.W.2d 599 (Ct. App. 1991)
9 ALR6th 633—§ 3
9 ALR6th 693—§ 3
10 ALR6th 265—§ 3
12 ALR6th 389—§ 3
13 ALR6th 603—§ 3
14 ALR6th 517—§ 3
15 ALR6th 173—§ 3
State v. Krieger, 2002 ME 139, 803 A.2d
1026 (Me. 2002)
40 ALR6th 1—§ 4, 5
State v. Kriegh, 23 Kan. App. 2d 935,
937 P.2d 453 (1997)
51 ALR5th 425—§ 3, 4
State v. Kriley, 976 S.W.2d 16 (Mo. Ct.
App. W.D. 1998)
15 ALR6th 515—§ 13
State v. Kristopher G., 201 W. Va. 703,
500 S.E.2d 519 (1997)
15 ALR5th 391—§ 11

State v. Krivitskiy, 70 Ohio App. 3d 293, 590 N.E.2d 1359 (10th Dist. Franklin County 1990)
79 ALR6th 125—§ 4

State v. Krochta, 83 Misc. 2d 129, 372 N.Y.S.2d 397 (Town Ct. 1975)
18 ALR6th 1—§ 5, 9

State v. Krogman, 224 Wis. 2d 645, 590 N.W.2d 283 (Ct. App. 1999)
90 ALR5th 453—§ 53

State v. Krol, 68 N.J. 236 (1975)
43 ALR5th 777—§ 3

State v. Krone, 182 Ariz. 319, 897 P.2d 621 (1995)
1 ALR6th 657—§ 3

State v. Kroner, 49 Ohio App. 3d 133, 551 N.E.2d 212 (1st Dist. Hamilton County 1988)
35 ALR6th 361—§ 7 to 10

State v. Kronich, 160 Wash. 2d 893, 161 P.3d 982 (2007)
30 ALR6th 1—§ 7

State v. Kropp, 1998 WL 165954 (Wash. Ct. App. Div. 2 1998)
68 ALR5th 343—§ 3

State v. Kroupa, 16 Ariz. App. 254, 492 P.2d 750 (Div. 2 1972)
9 ALR6th 1—§ 17

State v. Krowiak, 2005-Ohio-6012, 2005 WL 3029074 (Ohio Ct. App. 8th Dist. Cuyahoga County 2005)
26 ALR6th 511—§ 19

State v. Krueger, 664 So. 2d 26 (Fla. Dist. Ct. App. 3d Dist. 1995)
113 ALR5th 597—§ 3, 8

State v. Krueger, 2008 MT 265, 345 Mont. 147, 190 P.3d 318 (2008)
46 ALR6th 241—§ 19

State v. Kruetz, 229 Wis. 2d 254, 599 N.W.2d 667 (Ct. App. 1999)
84 ALR6th 293—§ 9, 31

State v. Kruger, 926 S.W.2d 486 (Mo. App. 1996)
5 ALR5th 243—§ 10

State v. Krugle, 2002 WL 31883017 (Iowa Ct. App. 2002)
33 ALR6th 91—§ 36

State v. Krummacher, 269 Or. 125, 523 P.2d 1009 (1974)
92 ALR6th 549—§ 38

State v. Kruse, 175 Wis. 2d 89, 499 N.W.2d 185 (Ct. App. 1993)
79 ALR6th 1—§ 38, 62

State v. Kruse, 302 N.W.2d 29 (Minn. 1981)
84 ALR5th 487—§ 19

State v. Kruse, 306 S.W.3d 603, 62 A.L.R.6th 763 (Mo. Ct. App. W.D. 2010)
62 ALR6th 413—§ 4, 18, 30
67 ALR6th 531—§ 4, 13, 36

State v. Kruse, 2006-Ohio-3179, 2006 WL 1718194 (Ohio Ct. App. 6th Dist. Wood County 2006)
26 ALR6th 511—§ 19

State v. Krutowsky, 2003-Ohio-1731, 2003 WL 1759613 (Ohio Ct. App. 8th Dist. Cuyahoga County 2003)
69 ALR6th 1—§ 3
70 ALR6th 1—§ 3

State v. Krzeszowski, 106 Wash. App. 638, 24 P.3d 485 (Div. 1 2001)
85 ALR6th 641—§ 7

State v. Krzywicki, 327 N.W.2d 5 (Minn. 1982)
55 ALR6th 157—§ 62

State v. K.S., 2010 WL 743967 (Fla. Dist. Ct. App. 2d Dist. 2010)
55 ALR6th 1—§ 6

State v. Kuba, 68 Haw. 184, 706 P.2d 1305 (1985)
55 ALR6th 513—§ 5

State v. Kubik, 235 Neb. 612, 456 N.W.2d 487 (1990)
119 ALR5th 379—§ 7

State v. Kuchan, 47 N.M. 209, 139 P.2d 592 (1943)
26 ALR5th 1—§ 3, 29, 33

State v. Kuchera, 114 Wash. App. 1020, 2002 WL 31439839 (Div. 2 2002)
45 ALR6th 643—§ 10

State v. Kueny, 215 N.W.2d 215 (Iowa 1974)
71 ALR6th 283—§ 7, 11

State v. Kugele, 141 Ohio Misc. 2d 20, 2006-Ohio-7275, 868 N.E.2d 759 (Mun. Ct. 2006)
78 ALR6th 599—§ 4, 10

State v. Kuhlman, 722 N.W.2d 1 (Minn. Ct. App. 2006)
26 ALR6th 179—§ 9

State v. Kuhlman, 729 N.W.2d 577 (Minn. 2007)
26 ALR6th 179—§ 9

State v. Kuhlmann, 298 Or. 703, 695 P.2d 571 (1985)
29 ALR5th 1—§ 4

State v. Kuhn, 7 Wash. App. 190, 499 P.2d 49 (Div. 2 1972)
92 ALR6th 1—§ 3, 5, 8

State v. Kuhn, 2003-Ohio-4007, 2003 WL 21731752 (Ohio Ct. App. 7th Dist. Belmont County 2003)
55 ALR6th 513—§ 8

State v. Kuhs, 223 Ariz. 376, 224 P.3d 192 (2010)
98 ALR6th 455—§ 21

State v. Kulseth, 333 N.W.2d 635 (Minn. 1983)
29 ALR6th 1—§ 3, 17
34 ALR6th 1—§ 3
35 ALR6th 127—§ 3
56 ALR6th 323—§ 3

State v. Kummer, 2008 WL 4472610 (Minn. Ct. App. 2008)
47 ALR6th 107—§ 3

State v. Kunkel, 137 Wis. 2d 172, 404 N.W.2d 69 (Ct. App. 1987)
93 ALR5th 327—§ 9
20 ALR6th 479—§ 7

State v. Kunkel, 406 N.W.2d 681 (N.D. 1987)
55 ALR5th 125—§ 3, 5

State v. Kuns, 1990 WL 148065 (Ohio Ct. App. 2d Dist. Montgomery County 1990)
79 ALR6th 1—§ 39, 83

State v. Kuntz, 160 Wis. 2d 722, 467 N.W.2d 531 (1991)
37 ALR5th 319—§ 9

State v. Kuntz, 209 Ariz. 276, 100 P.3d 26 (Ct. App. Div. 1 2004)

34 ALR6th 171—§ 22, 26, 35

State v. Kuone, 243 Kan. 218, 757 P.2d 289 (1988)
71 ALR5th 637—§ 8

State v. Kuperus, 241 Or. App. 605, 251 P.3d 235 (2011)
67 ALR6th 103—§ 23, 26

State v. Kupihea, 98 Haw. 196, 46 P.3d 498 (2002)
23 ALR6th 307—§ 4, 24

State v. Kurszewski, 212 Wis. 2d 638, 570 N.W.2d 61 (Ct. App. 1997)
9 ALR6th 541—§ 15

State v. Kurtz, 46 Or. App. 617, 612 P.2d 749 (1980)
51 ALR5th 375—§ 15

State v. Kurtz, 78 Ariz. 215, 278 P.2d 406 (1954)
65 ALR5th 623—§ 7

State v. Kurtz, 564 S.W.2d 856 (Mo. 1978)
93 ALR5th 327—§ 3, 28, 30

State v. Kurz, 685 N.W.2d 447 (Minn. Ct. App. 2004)
37 ALR6th 357—§ 67

State v. Kurz, 2004 WL 2094536 (Minn. Ct. App. 2004)
37 ALR6th 357—§ 47, 51

State v. Kutska, 222 Wis. 2d 218, 587 N.W.2d 214 (Ct. App. 1998)
111 ALR5th 529—§ 4

State v. Kuykendall, 51 Ohio App. 2d 215, 5 Ohio Ops. 3d 354, 367 N.E.2d 905 (Wayne Co. 1977)
41 ALR5th 171—§ 20, 68

State v. K.V., 821 So. 2d 1127 (Fla. Dist. Ct. App. 4th Dist. 2002)
114 ALR5th 173—§ 9
1 ALR6th 371—§ 4

State v. Kwiatowski, 1989 WL 54373 (Ohio Ct. App. 8th Dist. Cuyahoga County 1989)
6 ALR6th 533—§ 22

State v. Kyger, 787 S.W.2d 13 (Tenn. Crim. App. 1989)
28 ALR6th 505—§ 9

State v. Kyle, 225 S.W. 1012 (Mo. 1920)

104 ALR5th 357—§ 3, 4
54 ALR6th 429—§ 21
State v. Kyles, 513 So. 2d 265 (La. 1987)
62 ALR5th 1—§ 3, 14
State v. Kyseth, 240 N.W.2d 671 (Iowa 1976)
30 ALR6th 103—§ 35
State v. Labanowski, 117 Wash. 2d 405, 816 P.2d 26, 26 A.L.R.5th 874 (1991)
26 ALR5th 603—§ 3, 4
State v. La Barre, 255 Minn. 309, 96 N.W.2d 642 (1959)
22 ALR5th 327—§ 43
State v. La Barre, 292 Minn. 228, 195 N.W.2d 435 (1972)
41 ALR5th 171—§ 2, 39
State v. Labauve, 943 So. 2d 1186 (La. Ct. App. 1st Cir. 2006)
69 ALR6th 1—§ 27
State v. LaBelle, 191 P.3d 362 (Kan. Ct. App. 2008)
67 ALR6th 1—§ 5
State v. LaBelle, 290 Kan. 529, 231 P.3d 1065 (2010)
65 ALR6th 1—§ 26
State v. Labora, 2008-Ohio-3317, 2008 WL 2788288 (Ohio Ct. App. 5th Dist. Licking County 2008)
99 ALR6th 295—§ 15
State v. Labor and Industry Review Com'n, 113 Wis. 2d 107, 334 N.W.2d 279 (Ct. App. 1983)
86 ALR5th 295—§ 4
State v. Laborde, 120 La. 136, 45 So. 38 (1907)
108 ALR5th 593—§ 16
State v. Laborde, 214 La. 644, 38 So. 2d 371 (1948)
85 ALR5th 471—§ 7
State v. Laboy, 270 N.J. Super. 296, 637 A.2d 184 (1994)
33 ALR5th 571—§ 4
State v. Labrecque, 543 A.2d 369 (Me. 1988)
76 ALR5th 1—§ 14
State v. Lacaillade, 131 Vt. 161, 303 A.2d 131 (1973)

28 ALR6th 505—§ 9
State v. Lacayo, 8 So. 3d 385 (Fla. Dist. Ct. App. 3d Dist. 2009)
57 ALR6th 1—§ 20
State v. LaCaze, 759 So. 2d 773 (La. Ct. App. 3d Cir. 1999)
54 ALR6th 429—§ 29
State v. Lacey, 84 Wash. 2d 33, 524 P.2d 1351 (1974)
10 ALR5th 448—§ 6
State v. Lacey, 143 Ariz. 507, 694 P.2d 795 (App. 1984)
41 ALR5th 171—§ 18, 20, 26, 68, 72, 96, 108
State v. Lacey, 1997 WL 593802 (Ohio Ct. App. 3d Dist. Union County 1997)
78 ALR5th 489—§ 10
State v. Lacey, No. 80-C-29, Slip Op., August 14, 1981 (Ohio App. Columbiana Co. 1981)
45 ALR5th 591—§ 9
State v. Lack, 98 N.M. 500, 650 P.2d 22 (App. 1982)
15 ALR5th 391—§ 5
State v. Lackey, 71 N.C. App. 581, 323 S.E.2d 32 (1984)
84 ALR6th 427—§ 25
State v. Lacquey, 117 Ariz. 231, 571 P.2d 1027 (1977)
42 ALR5th 581—§ 9
State v. Lacroute, 134 La. 3, 63 So. 603 (1913)
105 ALR5th 529—§ 11
State v. Lacy, 2001 WI App 146, 246 Wis. 2d 672, 630 N.W.2d 277 (Ct. App. 2001)
93 ALR6th 275—§ 10
State v. Ladd, 308 N.C. 272, 302 S.E.2d 164 (1983)
81 ALR6th 505—§ 52
State v. Ladely, 82 Wash. 2d 172, 509 P.2d 658 (1973)
29 ALR5th 59—§ 7, 22
State v. Ladmer, 775 S.W.2d 6 (Tenn. Crim. 1989)
42 ALR5th 291—§ 34

State v. Ladner, 373 S.C. 103, 644
S.E.2d 684 (2007)
30 ALR6th 1—§ 4, 7
State v. Ladue, 631 A.2d 236 (Vt. 1993)
22 ALR5th 261—§ 2, 5
State v. Ladwig, 434 N.W.2d 594 (S.D.
1989)
119 ALR5th 379—§ 8
State v. Laehn, 186 Wis. 2d 578, 522
N.W.2d 38 (Ct. App. 1994)
84 ALR6th 293—§ 34
State v. Lafata, 614 S.W.2d 27 (Mo. Ct.
App. E.D. 1981)
105 ALR5th 529—§ 11
State v. LaFernier, 37 Wis. 2d 365, 155
N.W.2d 93 (1967)
38 ALR6th 97—§ 18
State v. Lafferty, 749 P.2d 1239, 73 Utah
Adv. Rep. 57 (Utah 1988)
37 ALR5th 515—§ 26
State v. Lafferty, 1998 MT 247, 291
Mont. 157, 967 P.2d 363 (1998)
84 ALR6th 293—§ 13, 14, 30, 34
State v. Laflin, 201 Neb. 824, 272
N.W.2d 376 (1978)
108 ALR5th 593—§ 32
State v. Lafond, 2002 ME 124, 802 A.2d
425 (Me. 2002)
84 ALR6th 293—§ 33
State v. Lafond, 2003 UT App 101, 68
P.3d 1043 (Utah Ct. App. 2003)
92 ALR6th 171—§ 11
State v. La France, 117 N.J. 583, 569
A.2d 1308 (1990)
39 ALR5th 283—§ 4, 22, 40
State v. LaFromboise, 542 N.W.2d 110
(N.D. 1996)
85 ALR5th 1—§ 23
98 ALR5th 305—§ 2
State v. Lagarde, 778 So. 2d 585 (La.
2001)
50 ALR5th 581—§ 17
State v. Lagares, 247 N.J. Super. 392,
589 A.2d 630 (1991)
37 ALR5th 319—§ 7
State v. Lagat, 97 Haw. 492, 40 P.3d 894
(2002)

99 ALR6th 113—§ 10
State v. Lagerquist, 256 S.C. 69, 180
S.E.2d 882 (1971)
55 ALR6th 157—§ 9
State v. LaGrand, 152 Ariz. 483, 733
P.2d 1066 (1987)
70 ALR5th 1—§ 8
State v. Lahurd, 632 So. 2d 1101 (Fla.
Dist. Ct. App. 4th Dist. 1994)
57 ALR6th 445—§ 4
State v. Laik, 62 Wash. App. 734, 815
P.2d 822 (Div. 1 1991)
113 ALR5th 597—§ 8
State v. Laird, 186 Ariz. 203, 920 P.2d
769 (1996)
21 ALR6th 1—§ 4
State v. Laitinen, 77 Wash. 2d 130, 459
P.2d 789 (1969)
72 ALR5th 607—§ 3, 5
State v. Lake, 33 Ohio App. 3d 275, 515
N.E.2d 960 (Franklin Co. 1986)
43 ALR5th 777—§ 3
State v. Lake, 107 Wash. App. 227, 27
P.3d 232 (Div. 2 2001)
9 ALR6th 541—§ 29
State v. Lake, 305 N.C. 143, 286 S.E.2d
541 (1982)
16 ALR6th 329—§ 6
24 ALR6th 591—§ 6, 14
State v. Lakes, 120 Ohio App. 213, 29
Ohio Op. 2d 12, 201 N.E.2d 809
(4th Dist. Adams County 1964)
85 ALR5th 187—§ 4, 9
State v. Lakin, 2006 ME 64, 899 A.2d
777 (Me. 2006)
24 ALR6th 591—§ 10
State v. Lamb, 71 N.J. 545, 366 A.2d
981 (1976)
67 ALR5th 637—§ 5
State v. Lamb, 137 Ga. App. 437, 224
S.E.2d 51 (1976)
31 ALR5th 229—§ 4, 37, 80
State v. Lamb, 168 Vt. 194, 720 A.2d
1101 (1998)
84 ALR6th 293—§ 23, 35
State v. Lamb, 209 Iowa 132, 227 N.W.
830 (1929)

State v. Lance, 48 Or. App. 141, 616 P.2d 546 (1980)
56 ALR6th 185—§ 36

State v. Lance, 222 Mont. 92, 721 P.2d 1258 (1986)
98 ALR5th 445—§ 4

State v. Lance, 1998 WL 57359 (Ohio Ct. App. 1st Dist. Hamilton County 1998)
78 ALR5th 489—§ 4, 6
63 ALR6th 351—§ 3

State v. Lancto, 155 Vt. 168, 582 A.2d 448 (1990)
34 ALR6th 1—§ 12, 16

State v. Land, 104 Wash. App. 1035, 2001 WL 88222 (Div. 2 2001)
27 ALR6th 183—§ 35

State v. Land, 681 S.W.2d 589 (Tenn. Crim. App. 1984)
57 ALR6th 445—§ 15

State v. Landeche, 447 So. 2d 1201 (La. App. 5th Cir. 1984)
52 ALR5th 655—§ 3

State v. Landers, 212 Neb. 48, 321 N.W.2d 418 (1982)
72 ALR5th 109—§ 5

State v. Landis, 2000-Ohio-2016, 2000 WL 33226196 (Ohio Ct. App. 4th Dist. Athens County 2000)
29 ALR6th 237—§ 21

State v. Landrum, 796 So. 2d 94 (La. Ct. App. 2d Cir. 2001)
19 ALR6th 697—§ 4

State v. Landry, 29 Mont. 218, 74 P. 418 (1903)
103 ALR6th 35—§ 21

State v. Landry, 340 So. 2d 150 (La. 1976)
62 ALR5th 121—§ 6

State v. Landry, 428 A.2d 1204 (Me. 1981)
28 ALR5th 459—§ 3

State v. Landry, 557 So. 2d 331 (La. Ct. App. 3d Cir. 1990)
103 ALR5th 463—§ 5

State v. Landry, 588 So. 2d 345 (La. 1991)

92 ALR6th 171—§ 14

State v. Lane, 108 Ohio App. 3d 477, 671 N.E.2d 272 (1st Dist. Hamilton County 1995)
38 ALR6th 439—§ 13

State v. Lane, 154 P.3d 557 (Kan. Ct. App. 2007)
26 ALR6th 511—§ 25, 29

State v. Lane, 271 S.C. 68, 245 S.E.2d 114 (1978)
106 ALR5th 397—§ 4

State v. Lane, 393 N.J. Super. 132, 922 A.2d 828 (App. Div. 2007)
78 ALR6th 297—§ 13, 21, 23

State v. Lane, 414 So. 2d 1223 (La. 1982)
81 ALR6th 505—§ 54

State v. Lane, 649 A.2d 1112 (Me. 1994)
15 ALR5th 391—§ 15
92 ALR5th 35—§ 21

State v. Lane, 673 S.W.2d 874 (Tenn. Crim. App. 1983)
95 ALR6th 1—§ 17

State v. Lane, 791 S.W.2d 947 (Mo. App. 1990)
42 ALR5th 291—§ 9

State v. Lane, 1997 WL 332061 (Tenn. Crim. App. 1997)
73 ALR5th 383—§ 6

State v. Lane, 1998 WL 901739 (Ohio Ct. App. 3d Dist. Marion County 1998)
85 ALR5th 1—§ 15, 23

State v. Lane, 2009 WL 2480730 (Ariz. Ct. App. Div. 2 2009)
94 ALR6th 525—§ 9

State v. Laneesha J., 2010 WL 1817555 (Neb. Ct. App. 2010)
60 ALR6th 193—§ 9

State v. Langan, 6 Neb. App. 739, 577 N.W.2d 752 (1998)
18 ALR6th 519—§ 11

State v. Langan, 410 N.W.2d 149 (N.D. 1987)
2 ALR6th 551—§ 31

State v. Lange, 126 Wis. 2d 513, 376 N.W.2d 868 (App. 1985)

39 ALR5th 283—§ 3

State v. Lange, 158 Wis. 2d 609, 463 N.W.2d 390 (App. 1990)

59 ALR5th 615—§ 3, 12

State v. Lange, 158 Wis. 2d 609, 463 N.W.2d 390 (Ct. App. 1990)

45 ALR6th 643—§ 9

State v. Langford, 95 Mo. 97, 8 S.W. 237 (1888)

50 ALR5th 467—§ 6, 8

State v. Langford, 136 Idaho 334, 33 P.3d 567 (Ct. App. 2001)

30 ALR6th 103—§ 3, 8, 23, 43

State v. Langford, 319 N.C. 332, 354 S.E.2d 518 (1987)

55 ALR6th 157—§ 115

State v. Langland, 42 Wash. App. 287, 711 P.2d 1039 (1985)

7 ALR5th 263—§ 6

State v. Langlet, 283 N.W.2d 330 (Iowa 1979)

40 ALR5th 113—§ 3

76 ALR5th 1—§ 6, 7

State v. Langley, 354 N.W.2d 389 (Minn. 1984)

24 ALR5th 465—§ 12, 115, 118, 120, 122

State v. Langley, 711 So. 2d 651 (La. 1998)

57 ALR5th 141—§ 11

State v. Langlois, 2013-Ohio-5177, 2 N.E.3d 936 (Ohio Ct. App. 6th Dist. Lucas County 2013)

103 ALR6th 247—§ 5

State v. Lanier, 50 N.C. App. 383, 273 S.E.2d 746 (1981)

81 ALR5th 563—§ 3, 5

State v. Lanier, 778 P.2d 9 (Utah 1989)

83 ALR5th 277—§ 9, 11

State v. Lanier, 985 S.W.2d 377 (Mo. Ct. App. E.D. 1999)

5 ALR5th 243—§ 7

State v. Lanier, 1984 WL 5405 (Ohio Ct. App. 2d Dist. Clark County 1984)

99 ALR6th 295—§ 13

State v. Lannert, 889 S.W.2d 131 (Mo. App. 1994)

37 ALR5th 515—§ 3, 10

State v. Lannert, 889 S.W.2d 131 (Mo. Ct. App. E.D. 1994)

32 ALR6th 1—§ 11

State v. Lanzy, 58 Ohio St. 3d 154, 569 N.E.2d 468 (1991)

43 ALR5th 777—§ 4

State v. La Palme, 104 N.H. 97, 179 A.2d 284 (1962)

6 ALR5th 733—§ 16

State v. LaPlaca, 162 N.H. 174, 27 A.3d 719 (2011)

78 ALR6th 1—§ 22, 42

State v. LaPlante, 2011 ME 85, 26 A.3d 337, 78 A.L.R.6th 711 (Me. 2011)

78 ALR6th 213—§ 5

State v. Lapointe, 237 Conn. 694, 678 A.2d 942 (1996)

32 ALR6th 1—§ 11

69 ALR6th 579—§ 4

State v. LaPonsie, 136 Ariz. 73, 664 P.2d 223 (Ct. App. Div. 2 1982)

85 ALR5th 1—§ 24

State v. Lapp, 202 Mont. 327, 658 P.2d 400 (1983)

30 ALR6th 103—§ 8, 25, 34, 48

State v. Lapping, 75 Ohio App. 3d 354, 599 N.E.2d 416 (Trumbull Co. 1991)

6 ALR5th 733—§ 16

State v. Laque, 41 La. Ann 1070, 6 So. 787 (1889)

11 ALR5th 831—§ 5, 6, 20, 21

State v. Lara, 109 N.M. 294, 784 P.2d 1037 (Ct. App. 1989)

84 ALR5th 487—§ 7

State v. Lara, 110 N.M. 507, 797 P.2d 296 (App. 1990)

20 ALR5th 398—§ 2, 10

47 ALR5th 259—§ 2

State v. Lara, 110 N.M. 507, 797 P.2d 296 (Ct. App. 1990)

78 ALR6th 297—§ 41

State v. Laramore, 965 S.W.2d 847 (Mo. Ct. App. E.D. 1998)

37 ALR6th 357—§ 24, 37, 48, 60

State v. Larck, 1986 WL 7902 (Ohio Ct. App. 4th Dist. Ross County 1986)
71 ALR6th 335—§ 17

State v. Larimore, 341 Ark. 397, 17 S.W.3d 87, 101 A.L.R.5th 695 (2000)
101 ALR5th 187—§ 17
24 ALR6th 1—§ 25

State v. La Riviere, 22 Conn. Supp. 385, 1 Conn. Cir. 47, 173 A.2d 900 (1961)
26 ALR5th 1—§ 4, 25

State v. Lark, 163 N.J. 294, 748 A.2d 1103 (2000)
26 ALR5th 378—§ 11

State v. Larkin, 11 Nev. 314, 1876 WL 4565 (1876)
101 ALR6th 499—§ 14

State v. Larkin, 49 N.H. 39 (1869)
29 ALR5th 59—§ 3, 40, 57

State v. Larkins, 79 Wash. 2d 392, 486 P.2d 95 (1971)
4 ALR5th 1—§ 4, 12

State v. Larmond, 244 N.W.2d 233 (Iowa 1976)
45 ALR5th 531—§ 7, 9

State v. Larocco, 794 P.2d 460, 135 Utah Adv. Rep. 16 (Utah 1990)
19 ALR5th 470—§ 3
29 ALR5th 59—§ 78

State v. LaRock, 196 W. Va. 294, 470 S.E.2d 613 (1996)
119 ALR5th 275—§ 7

State v. Larose, 510 So. 2d 732 (La. Ct. App. 4th Cir. 1987)
102 ALR6th 365—§ 20

State v. Larrea, 130 Idaho 290, 939 P.2d 866 (Ct. App. 1997)
105 ALR5th 529—§ 17

State v. Larrimore, 340 N.C. 119, 456 S.E.2d 789 (1995)
45 ALR5th 531—§ 6
79 ALR5th 33—§ 68

State v. Larrinaga, 569 So. 2d 911 (Fla. Dist. Ct. App. 5th Dist. 1990)
102 ALR5th 327—§ 4
24 ALR6th 1—§ 43

State v. Larriva, 178 Ariz. 64, 870 P.2d 1160 (Ct. App. Div. 2 1993)
92 ALR6th 295—§ 13
95 ALR6th 1—§ 10, 35

State v. Larry, 108 Wash. App. 894, 34 P.3d 241 (Div. 2 2001)
19 ALR6th 115—§ 4
24 ALR6th 591—§ 9, 13
27 ALR6th 183—§ 35, 42

State v. Larry, 211 N.J. Super. 221, 511 A.2d 704 (App. Div. 1986)
124 ALR5th 1—§ 4

State v. Larry, 230 Wis. 2d 745, 604 N.W.2d 33 (Ct. App. 1999)
72 ALR6th 437—§ 3, 4

State v. Larry, 2010 UT App 65, 2010 WL 975582 (Utah Ct. App. 2010)
56 ALR6th 1—§ 39

State v. Larsen, 44 Or. App. 643, 606 P.2d 1159 (1980)
39 ALR5th 283—§ 66

State v. Larsen, 578 P.2d 1280 (Utah 1978)
64 ALR5th 671—§ 8

State v. Larsen, 876 P.2d 391 (Utah Ct. App. 1994)
84 ALR5th 487—§ 17

State v. Larson, 94 N.M. 795, 617 P.2d 1310 (1980)
65 ALR5th 407—§ 3

State v. Larson, 119 Wash. App. 1028, 2003 WL 22766043 (Div. 1 2003)
120 ALR5th 337—§ 5

State v. Larson, 132 Wash. App. 1028, 2006 WL 925725 (Div. 2 2006)
103 ALR6th 347—§ 15

State v. Larson, 141 Or. App. 186, 917 P.2d 519 (1996)
57 ALR6th 83—§ 5

State v. Larson, 152 Wis. 2d 88, 447 N.W.2d 539 (Ct. App. 1989)
49 ALR6th 93—§ 3

State v. Larson, 159 Or. App. 34, 977 P.2d 1175 (1999)
76 ALR5th 563—§ 4, 6

State v. Larson, 215 Wis. 2d 155, 572 N.W.2d 127 (Ct. App. 1997)

---

50 ALR6th 455—§ 18
State v. Larson, 240 Mont. 203, 783 P.2d
416 (1989)
57 ALR6th 445—§ 49
State v. Larson, 266 Wis. 2d 236, 2003
WI App 150, 668 N.W.2d 338 (Ct.
App. 2003)
17 ALR6th 327—§ 42
State v. Larson, 346 N.W.2d 199 (Minn.
Ct. App. 1984)
28 ALR6th 505—§ 9
State v. Larson, 379 N.W.2d 165 (Minn.
Ct. App. 1985)
73 ALR5th 383—§ 32
State v. Larson, 393 N.W.2d 238 (Minn.
App. 1986)
15 ALR5th 391—§ 13
State v. Larson, 472 N.W.2d 120 (Minn.
1991)
38 ALR5th 433—§ 5, 10
State v. Larson, 485 N.W.2d 571 (Minn.
Ct. App. 1992)
116 ALR5th 479—§ 5
State v. Larson, 512 N.W.2d 732 (S.D.
1994)
22 ALR5th 1—§ 3, 48
State v. Larson, 605 N.W.2d 706 (Minn.
2000)
121 ALR5th 551—§ 3
State v. Larson, 1998 WL 74263 (Minn.
Ct. App. 1998)
88 ALR5th 121—§ 22, 28
State v. Larson, 2006 WL 618857
(Minn. Ct. App. 2006)
33 ALR6th 91—§ 12, 36
State v. LaRue, 5 Wash. App. 299, 487
P.2d 255, 65 A.L.R.3d 1299 (Div. 1
1971)
108 ALR5th 593—§ 56
State v. LaRue, 19 Wash. App. 841, 578
P.2d 66 (Div. 3 1978)
38 ALR6th 97—§ 30
State v. Lascaris, 37 App. Div. 2d 128,
322 N.Y.S.2d 426 (4th Dep't 1971)
20 ALR5th 534—§ 7
State v. Lashley, 353 N.J. Super. 405,
803 A.2d 139 (App. Div. 2002)

26 ALR6th 511—§ 38
State v. Lasky, 2002 WI App 126, 2002
WL 554523 (Wis. Ct. App. 2002)
97 ALR5th 201—§ 6
State v. Lasnetski, 696 N.W.2d 387
(Minn. Ct. App. 2005)
30 ALR6th 1—§ 4, 7
State v. Lasowski, 4 N.J. Misc. 489, 133
A. 415 (Sup. Ct. 1926)
104 ALR5th 357—§ 4
State v. Lass, 194 Wis. 2d 591, 535
N.W.2d 904 (Ct. App. 1995)
24 ALR6th 1—§ 5
State v. Lassen, 2000 WL 328016 (Iowa
Ct. App. 2000)
114 ALR5th 235—§ 9
State v. Laster, 2007 WL 93169 (N.J.
Super. Ct. App. Div. 2007)
79 ALR6th 1—§ 41
State v. Latham, 30 Wash. App. 776,
638 P.2d 592 (Div. 3 1981)
37 ALR5th 319—§ 4
84 ALR5th 487—§ 3
State v. Latham, 35 Wash. App. 862,
670 P.2d 689 (Div. 1 1983)
83 ALR5th 277—§ 11
State v. Latham, Ohio App. Case No
13-79-5, Slip Opinion (Seneca Co.
1980)
45 ALR5th 1—§ 2, 5, 13, 22, 30
State v. Lathan, 530 S.E.2d 615 (N.C.
Ct. App. 2000)
57 ALR5th 141—§ 4
State v. Lathan, 2000 WL 1005206
(Ohio Ct. App. 6th Dist. Lucas
County 2000)
29 ALR6th 237—§ 24
State v. Latimer, 9 Kan. App. 2d 728,
687 P.2d 648 (1984)
66 ALR5th 397—§ 8
State v. Latimer, 604 N.W.2d 103
(Minn. Ct. App. 1999)
15 ALR5th 391—§ 31
State v. Latimore, 197 N.J. Super. 197,
484 A.2d 702 (App. Div. 1984)
88 ALR5th 121—§ 2, 7, 39
State v. Latimore, 1989 WL 17611
(Minn. Ct. App. 1989)

73 ALR5th 383—§ 3
State v. Latina, 13 Ohio App. 3d 182, 13 Ohio B.R. 229, 468 N.E.2d 1139 (Cuyahoga Co. 1984)
18 ALR5th 1—§ 7, 16
State v. Latiolais, 563 So. 2d 469 (La. Ct. App. 1st Cir. 1990)
9 ALR6th 1—§ 17
State v. LaTray, 2000 MT 262, 302 Mont. 11, 11 P.3d 116 (2000)
92 ALR5th 35—§ 30
State v. Lattanzio, 30 Conn. L. Rptr. 549, 2001 WL 1249640 (Conn. Super. Ct. 2001)
81 ALR6th 257—§ 20
State v. Laturner, 163 P.3d 367 (Kan. Ct. App. 2007)
30 ALR6th 1—§ 3, 6
State v. Lauer, 955 S.W.2d 23 (Mo. Ct. App. S.D. 1997)
5 ALR5th 243—§ 61
State v. Laughlin, 105 Mont. 490, 73 P.2d 718 (1937)
5 ALR5th 243—§ 59
State v. Laughlin, 216 Kan. 54, 530 P.2d 1220 (1975)
83 ALR5th 277—§ 11
State v. Laughlin, 232 Kan. 110, 652 P.2d 690 (1982)
42 ALR5th 581—§ 4
State v. Laureano, 101 Wash. 2d 745, 682 P.2d 889 (1984)
32 ALR5th 149—§ 68
24 ALR6th 1—§ 21
State v. Lauriat, 561 A.2d 496 (Me. 1989)
50 ALR5th 703—§ 31
State v. Laurie, 56 Haw. 664, 548 P.2d 271 (1976)
103 ALR6th 507—§ 22
State v. Laux, 544 S.E.2d 276 (S.C. 2001)
68 ALR5th 343—§ 3
State v. Lavallee, 104 N.H. 443, 189 A.2d 475 (1963)
19 ALR5th 823—§ 15, 17
State v. Lavaris, 106 Wash. 2d 340, 721 P.2d 515 (1986)

3 ALR6th 269—§ 25
State v. Lavastida, 366 N.W.2d 677 (Minn. App. 1985)
32 ALR5th 149—§ 5, 47
State v. Lavazzoli, 434 So. 2d 321 (Fla. 1983)
92 ALR6th 1—§ 8
State v. Laverty, 495 A.2d 831 (Me. 1985)
67 ALR5th 637—§ 6, 11
State v. Lavigne, 675 So. 2d 771 (La. App. 4th Cir. 1996)
50 ALR5th 581—§ 17
State v. Lavora, 195 Wis. 2d 86, 537 N.W.2d 148 (Ct. App. 1995)
76 ALR5th 1—§ 2
77 ALR5th 201—§ 2, 3
78 ALR5th 1—§ 2
79 ALR5th 237—§ 2
State v. Lavoy, 259 N.J. Super. 594, 614 A.2d 1077 (App. Div. 1992)
70 ALR5th 533—§ 2, 4, 11
State v. Lawless, 1998 WL 729233 (Ohio Ct. App. 4th Dist. Washington County 1998)
78 ALR5th 489—§ 3, 10
State v. Lawrence, 196 N.C. 562, 146 S.E. 395 (1929)
73 ALR5th 615—§ 3, 7
State v. Lawrence, 312 N.W.2d 251 (Minn. 1981)
24 ALR5th 132—§ 2, 3, 5, 7
29 ALR5th 59—§ 6, 29, 32
State v. Lawrence, 352 N.C. 1, 530 S.E.2d 807 (2000)
110 ALR5th 1—§ 15
State v. Lawrence, 700 S.W.2d 111 (Mo. Ct. App. E.D. 1985)
86 ALR5th 463—§ 3, 5, 9
State v. Lawrence, 752 So. 2d 934 (La. Ct. App. 4th Cir. 1999)
7 ALR5th 263—§ 4
38 ALR5th 433—§ 3
State v. Lawrence, 849 S.W.2d 761 (Tenn. 1993)
92 ALR6th 295—§ 3, 9, 13, 19
93 ALR6th 207—§ 6, 9, 14, 31

95 ALR6th 1—§ 5, 6

96 ALR6th 355—§ 3, 5, 6, 18, 26, 36, 37, 60

State v. Lawrence, 1988 WL 38127 (Ohio Ct. App. 8th Dist.Cuyahoga County 1988)

57 ALR5th 141—§ 13

State v. Lawrence, 2001 WL 641520 (Minn. Ct. App. 2001)

50 ALR6th 455—§ 20, 34

State v. Lawrentz, 24 Ohio N.P. (n.s.) 603, 1924 WL 2192 (C.P. 1924)

119 ALR5th 275—§ 7

State v. Laws, 262 N.J. Super. 551, 621 A.2d 526 (App. Div. 1993)

67 ALR5th 149—§ 3, 5

State v. Laws, 2001 WL 1617691 (Conn. Super. Ct. 2001)

11 ALR6th 237—§ 12

State v. Lawson, 64 Ohio St. 3d 336, 595 N.E.2d 902 (1992)

39 ALR5th 283—§ 14

95 ALR5th 125—§ 7

State v. Lawson, 144 Ariz. 547, 698 P.2d 1266 (1985)

16 ALR6th 329—§ 4

24 ALR6th 591—§ 4, 12

101 ALR6th 331—§ 17

State v. Lawson, 173 N.C. App. 270, 619 S.E.2d 410 (2005)

67 ALR6th 103—§ 5, 11

State v. Lawson, 256 La. 471, 236 So. 2d 804 (1970)

87 ALR5th 1—§ 15, 32

State v. Lawson, 285 N.C. 320, 204 S.E.2d 843 (1974)

35 ALR6th 127—§ 4

State v. Lawson, 291 S.W.3d 864 (Tenn. 2009)

69 ALR6th 1—§ 21

State v. Lawson, 338 So. 2d 627 (La. 1976)

103 ALR6th 137—§ 15

State v. Lawson, 352 Mo. 1168, 181 S.W.2d 508 (1944)

16 ALR6th 219—§ 35

State v. Lawson, 1989 WL 18948 (Ohio Ct. App. 8th Dist. Cuyahoga County 1989)

107 ALR5th 567—§ 2, 10

State v. Lawson, 2011-Ohio-1255, 2011 WL 941573 (Ohio Ct. App. 10th Dist. Franklin County 2011)

64 ALR6th 1—§ 13

State v. Lawton, 588 So. 2d 72, 16 FLW D 2807 (Fla. App. D4 1991)

18 ALR5th 542—§ 2

State v. Laxton, 78 N.C. 564, 1878 WL 2397 (1878)

98 ALR6th 455—§ 21

State v. Layman, 1999 UT 79, 985 P.2d 911 (Utah 1999)

23 ALR6th 307—§ 45

State v. Layssard, 310 So. 2d 107 (La. 1975)

52 ALR5th 655—§ 3

State v. Lazarone, 130 La. 1, 57 So. 532 (1912)

32 ALR5th 149—§ 51, 63

State v. Lazo, 761 So. 2d 1244 (Fla. Dist. Ct. App. 2d Dist. 2000)

113 ALR5th 597—§ 8

State v. Lazos, 32 Kan. App. 2d 680, 87 P.3d 345 (2004)

63 ALR6th 351—§ 3

State v. Lazzaro, 76 Ohio St. 3d 261, 667 N.E.2d 384 (1996)

66 ALR5th 397—§ 8

87 ALR5th 597—§ 15

State v. L.B., 676 So. 2d 179 (La. Ct. App. 1st Cir. 1996)

69 ALR6th 1—§ 21

State v. Le, 1996 WL 312492 (Wash. Ct. App. Div. 1 1996)

73 ALR5th 383—§ 4, 8

State v. Le, 2000 WL 284425 (Tenn. Crim. App. 2000)

3 ALR6th 543—§ 8

State v. Lea, 499 So. 2d 243 (La. App. 2d Cir. 1986)

7 ALR5th 263—§ 7

State v. Leach, 113 Wash. 2d 735, 782 P.2d 1035 (1989)

68 ALR5th 343—§ 15
State v. Leach, 603 S.E.2d 831 (N.C. Ct. App. 2004)

2 ALR6th 551—§ 9
State v. Leach, 1999 WL 173183 (Ohio Ct. App. 5th Dist. Licking County 1999)

78 ALR5th 489—§ 10
State v. Lead Ind. Assn., Inc., 2001 WL 345830 (R.I. Super. Ct. 2001)

32 ALR6th 261—§ 7
State v. Lead Industries, Ass'n, Inc., 951 A.2d 428, Prod. Liab. Rep. (CCH) ¶ 18031 (R.I. 2008)

49 ALR6th 505—§ 3, 46
State v. Leadinghorse, 192 Neb. 485, 222 N.W.2d 573 (1974)

70 ALR5th 1—§ 7
State v. Leady, 879 S.W.2d 644 (Mo. App. 1994)

42 ALR5th 291—§ 2, 19
State v. Leady, 879 S.W.2d 644 (Mo. Ct. App. W.D. 1994)

37 ALR6th 357—§ 29
State v. Leagea, 673 So. 2d 646 (La. Ct. App. 1st Cir. 1996)

20 ALR5th 398—§ 9
State v. Leak, 5 Ind. 359, 1854 WL 3325 (1854)

101 ALR6th 431—§ 13
State v. Leandry, 151 N.J. Super. 92, 376 A.2d 574 (App. Div. 1977)

58 ALR6th 499—§ 22
State v. Leatherbury, 2003 UT 2, 65 P.3d 1180 (Utah 2003)

37 ALR6th 357—§ 4
State v. Leatherwood, 104 Idaho 100, 656 P.2d 760 (Ct. App. 1982)

24 ALR6th 1—§ 11
State v. Leavitt, 1994 WL 102391 (Ohio Ct. App. 11th Dist. Lake County 1994)

19 ALR6th 697—§ 24
State v. Leazer, 337 N.C. 454, 446 S.E.2d 54 (1994)

37 ALR5th 515—§ 13
State v. LeBlanc, 41 Conn. Supp. 1, 548 A.2d 485 (Super. Ct. 1988)

112 ALR5th 429—§ 17
State v. Le Blanc, 115 Me. 142, 98 A. 119 (1916)

66 ALR5th 397—§ 3, 15
State v. LeBlanc, 862 So. 2d 129 (La. Ct. App. 4th Cir. 2003)

56 ALR6th 185—§ 17
State v. Leblanc, 897 So. 2d 736 (La. Ct. App. 1st Cir. 2004)

26 ALR6th 511—§ 28
State v. Lecarros, 187 Or. App. 105, 66 P.3d 543 (2003)

47 ALR6th 107—§ 28
State v. Le Clair, 425 A.2d 182 (Me. 1981)

22 ALR5th 1—§ 4, 10, 23, 45 to 47, 55, 56
State v. LeCompte, 441 So. 2d 249 (La. Ct. App. 4th Cir. 1983)

97 ALR5th 201—§ 3, 4
State v. LeCoure, 158 Mont. 340, 491 P.2d 1228 (1971)

97 ALR5th 201—§ 3
State v. LeCroy, 461 So. 2d 88 (Fla. 1984)

90 ALR5th 225—§ 4
State v. Ledbetter, 41 Conn. App. 391, 676 A.2d 409 (1996)

38 ALR6th 97—§ 29
State v. Ledbetter, 120 N.C. App. 117, 461 S.E.2d 341 (1995)

109 ALR5th 99—§ 3
State v. Ledder, 31 Or. App. 487, 570 P.2d 994 (1977)

15 ALR5th 391—§ 51
State v. Lederer-Hughes, 688 S.E.2d 119 (N.C. Ct. App. 2009)

57 ALR6th 1—§ 4
State v. Ledet, 298 So. 2d 761 (La. 1974)

36 ALR5th 255—§ 4, 7
State v. Ledet, 792 So. 2d 160 (La. Ct. App. 5th Cir. 2001)

38 ALR6th 439—§ 5
State v. Ledezma, 549 N.W.2d 307 (Iowa App. 1996)

39 ALR5th 283—§ 10

State v. Ledford, 351 S.C. 83, 567 S.E.2d 904 (Ct. App. 2002)
34 ALR6th 1—§ 4

State v. Ledford, 914 So. 2d 1168 (La. Ct. App. 2d Cir. 2005)
78 ALR6th 297—§ 38

State v. Ledger, 175 Wis. 2d 116, 499 N.W.2d 198 (App. 1993)
55 ALR5th 423—§ 10

State v. Ledvina, 71 Wis. 2d 195, 237 N.W.2d 683 (1976)
58 ALR5th 429—§ 2, 7, 8

State v. Lee, 51 Haw. 516, 465 P.2d 573 (1970)
72 ALR5th 607—§ 4, 7

State v. Lee, 53 Ariz. 295, 88 P.2d 996 (1939)
26 ALR5th 1—§ 4, 5

State v. Lee, 73 Ohio Misc. 2d 9, 657 N.E.2d 604 (Mun. Ct. 1995)
71 ALR5th 285—§ 2, 3
7 ALR6th 233—§ 5

State v. Lee, 75 Haw. 80, 856 P.2d 1246 (1993)
23 ALR6th 307—§ 4, 35

State v. Lee, 82 Wash. App. 298, 917 P.2d 159 (1996)
29 ALR5th 487—§ 3, 11

State v. Lee, 117 Idaho 203, 786 P.2d 594 (Ct. App. 1990)
29 ALR6th 237—§ 21

State v. Lee, 128 Ohio App. 3d 710, 716 N.E.2d 751 (1st Dist. Hamilton County 1998)
36 ALR5th 161—§ 6, 11, 16
93 ALR6th 1—§ 15

State v. Lee, 128 Wash. 2d 151, 904 P.2d 1143 (1995)
57 ALR6th 445—§ 38

State v. Lee, 135 Wash. 2d 369, 957 P.2d 741 (1998)
29 ALR5th 487—§ 3, 8, 12

State v. Lee, 166 N.C. 250, 80 S.E. 977 (1914)
54 ALR6th 429—§ 16

State v. Lee, 171 La. 744, 132 So. 219 (1931)
97 ALR5th 293—§ 4

State v. Lee, 177 Conn. 335, 417 A.2d 354 (1979)
39 ALR5th 283—§ 3

State v. Lee, 189 Ariz. 590, 944 P.2d 1204 (1997)
83 ALR6th 465—§ 12, 19, 50

State v. Lee, 189 Ariz. 608, 944 P.2d 1222 (1997)
9 ALR5th 369—§ 3, 8

State v. Lee, 191 Ariz. 542, 959 P.2d 799, 69 A.L.R. 5th 749 (1998)
69 ALR5th 425—§ 2, 4, 5

State v. Lee, 197 Kan. 463, 419 P.2d 927 (1966)
4 ALR6th 577—§ 9

State v. Lee, 211 N.C. 326, 190 S.E. 234 (1937)
81 ALR5th 563—§ 3

State v. Lee, 247 La. 553, 172 So. 2d 678 (1965)
103 ALR5th 463—§ 3

State v. Lee, 282 Mont. 391, 938 P.2d 637 (1997)
84 ALR6th 293—§ 16

State v. Lee, 330 Md. 320, 624 A.2d 492 (1993)
67 ALR5th 361—§ 2, 8

State v. Lee, 335 N.C. 244, 439 S.E.2d 547 (1994)
31 ALR5th 704—§ 8
79 ALR5th 33—§ 17
83 ALR6th 255—§ 22

State v. Lee, 404 A.2d 983 (Me. 1979)
38 ALR5th 433—§ 28

State v. Lee, 439 So. 2d 593 (La. Ct. App. 1st Cir. 1983)
62 ALR6th 413—§ 52

State v. Lee, 494 N.W.2d 475 (Minn. 1992)
32 ALR5th 149—§ 72, 74

State v. Lee, 502 A.2d 332 (R.I. 1985)
57 ALR6th 313—§ 4

State v. Lee, 559 So. 2d 1310 (La. 1990)
57 ALR5th 141—§ 2, 11

State v. Lee, 583 So. 2d 1055, 16 FLW D 1734 (Fla. App. D4 1991)

27 ALR5th 593—§ 17
State v. Lee, 626 S.W.2d 252 (Mo. 1982)
70 ALR6th 361—§ 7
State v. Lee, 654 S.W.2d 876 (Mo. 1983)
55 ALR6th 157—§ 62
State v. Lee, 699 So. 2d 461 (La. Ct. App. 4th Cir. 1997)
99 ALR6th 295—§ 9
State v. Lee, 706 N.W.2d 491 (Minn. 2005)
30 ALR6th 483—§ 39
State v. Lee, 715 So. 2d 582 (La. Ct. App. 3d Cir. 1998)
117 ALR5th 407—§ 4
State v. Lee, 735 So. 2d 715 (La. Ct. App. 4th Cir. 1999)
97 ALR5th 293—§ 3
State v. Lee, 755 So. 2d 1029 (La. Ct. App. 4th Cir. 2000)
4 ALR5th 1—§ 14
State v. Lee, 836 S.W.2d 126 (Tenn. Crim. App. 1991)
85 ALR5th 1—§ 26
State v. Lee, 976 So. 2d 109 (La. 2008)
93 ALR6th 275—§ 5
State v. Lee, 1986 WL 2028 (Ohio Ct. App. 4th Dist.Gallia County 1986)
57 ALR5th 141—§ 5
State v. Lee, 1998 WL 258446 (Ohio Ct. App. 1st Dist. Hamilton County 1998)
78 ALR5th 489—§ 3
State v. Lee, 1998 WL 696905 (Ohio Ct. App. 10th Dist. Franklin County 1998)
97 ALR6th 263—§ 6
State v. Lee, 1999 WL 227394 (Minn. Ct. App. 1999)
69 ALR6th 579—§ 8, 29
State v. Lee, 2002-Ohio-4924, 2002 WL 31087629 (Ohio Ct. App. 8th Dist. Cuyahoga County 2002)
125 ALR5th 497—§ 4
State v. Lee, 2003-Ohio-2737, 2003 WL 21234921 (Ohio Ct. App. 8th Dist. Cuyahoga County 2003)
125 ALR5th 537—§ 2, 39

State v. Lee, 2003-Ohio-4059, 2003 WL 21757505 (Ohio Ct. App. 10th Dist. Franklin County 2003)
24 ALR6th 549—§ 6
State v. Lee, 2005-Ohio-996, 2005 WL 544837 (Ohio Ct. App. 9th Dist. Summit County 2005)
30 ALR6th 1—§ 4, 7
State v. Lee, 2009 WI App 96, 320 Wis. 2d 536, 771 N.W.2d 373 (Ct. App. 2009)
79 ALR6th 1—§ 45
State v. Leeming, 612 So. 2d 308 (La. Ct. App. 5th Cir. 1992)
9 ALR6th 1—§ 22
State v. Leeper, 199 Iowa 432, 200 N.W. 732 (1924)
67 ALR5th 637—§ 5, 7
State v. Leer, 839 N.W.2d 675 (Iowa Ct. App. 2013)
97 ALR6th 653—§ 29
State v. Lefebvre, 91 N.H. 382, 20 A.2d 185 (1941)
6 ALR6th 161—§ 16
State v. Lefever, 91 Ohio App. 3d 301, 632 N.E.2d 589 (Champaign Co. 1993)
42 ALR5th 547—§ 5
State v. Lefevers, 844 N.E.2d 508 (Ind. Ct. App. 2006)
84 ALR6th 293—§ 9, 13, 31
State v. Le Fils, 209 Or. 666, 307 P.2d 1048 (1957)
119 ALR5th 275—§ 2
State v. Lefort, 86 Conn. App. 751, 862 A.2d 875 (2005)
65 ALR6th 537—§ 44
State v. Lefort, 97 P.3d 1072 (Kan. Ct. App. 2004)
15 ALR6th 515—§ 1
State v. Legas, 20 Wash. App. 535, 581 P.2d 172 (Div. 3 1978)
65 ALR5th 407—§ 3
State v. LeGear, 346 N.W.2d 21 (Iowa 1984)
70 ALR5th 1—§ 5
State v. Legendre, 362 So. 2d 570 (La. 1978)

8 ALR5th 775—§ 3
State v. Legendre, 522 So. 2d 1249 (La. App. 4th Cir. 1988)
5 ALR5th 243—§ 58
State v. Leger, 936 So. 2d 108 (La. 2006)
32 ALR6th 1—§ 7
State v. Legg, 207 W. Va. 686, 536 S.E.2d 110 (2000)
18 ALR6th 519—§ 4
State v. Legg, 633 N.W.2d 763 (Iowa 2001)
17 ALR6th 327—§ 12
State v. Legg, 2006 UT App 367, 2006 WL 2578913 (Utah Ct. App. 2006)
37 ALR6th 357—§ 4
State v. Leggett, 363 So. 2d 434 (La. 1978)
99 ALR6th 295—§ 6, 19
State v. Leggett, 2012 WL 1956760 (Ariz. Ct. App. Div. 2 2012)
92 ALR6th 295—§ 19
93 ALR6th 207—§ 13, 28
96 ALR6th 355—§ 5, 26, 36, 49, 53, 62
State v. Legner, 2009-Ohio-3029, 2009 WL 1800213 (Ohio Ct. App. 2d Dist. Montgomery County 2009)
64 ALR6th 1—§ 9, 18
State v. Legnon, 464 So. 2d 910 (La. Ct. App. 4th Cir. 1985)
84 ALR6th 427—§ 10
State v. Lehman, 40 Wash. App. 400, 698 P.2d 606 (Div. 1 1985)
85 ALR5th 1—§ 22, 33
State v. Lehman, 100 Fla. 473, 128 So. 811 (1930)
82 ALR6th 317—§ 3
State v. Lehman, 126 Ariz. 388, 616 P.2d 63 (1980)
57 ALR5th 141—§ 3
State v. Lehman, 1999 ME 124, 736 A.2d 256 (Me. 1999)
84 ALR5th 1—§ 3
State v. Lehr, 67 P.3d 703 (Ariz. 2003)
110 ALR5th 1—§ 19
State v. Lehr, 227 Ariz. 140, 254 P.3d 379 (2011)

71 ALR6th 625—§ 38
State v. Leibhart, 266 Neb. 133, 662 N.W.2d 618 (2003)
103 ALR6th 247—§ 7
State v. Leicht, 124 N.J. Super. 127, 305 A.2d 78 (App. Div. 1973)
57 ALR6th 445—§ 57
State v. Leidholm, 334 N.W.2d 811 (N.D. 1983)
67 ALR5th 637—§ 4, 7
State v. Leigh, 278 N.C. 243, 179 S.E.2d 708 (1971)
66 ALR5th 397—§ 3, 11
State v. Leigh, 580 S.W.2d 536 (Mo. Ct. App. E.D. 1979)
93 ALR5th 527—§ 8
State v. Leigh, 1999 WL 293931 (Wash. Ct. App. Div. 1 1999)
88 ALR5th 121—§ 3, 35
State v. Leighton, 551 A.2d 116 (Me. 1988)
74 ALR5th 319—§ 11, 12
State v. Leisure, 749 S.W.2d 366 (Mo. 1988)
20 ALR5th 177—§ 3, 11
83 ALR6th 255—§ 15
State v. Leisure, 810 S.W.2d 560 (Mo. Ct. App. E.D. 1991)
72 ALR6th 141—§ 8
State v. Leitner, 2002 WI 77, 253 Wis. 2d 449, 646 N.W.2d 341 (2002)
69 ALR6th 1—§ 3, 4
70 ALR6th 1—§ 3
State v. Lejeune, 277 Ga. 749, 594 S.E.2d 637 (2004)
6 ALR6th 533—§ 21
State v. Leleae, 1999 UT App 368, 993 P.2d 232 (Utah Ct. App. 1999)
27 ALR6th 183—§ 35
State v. Lem, 85 Wash. App. 1086, 1997 WL 206777 (Div. 1 1997)
88 ALR5th 121—§ 10, 25, 36
State v. LeMaster, 137 Ariz. 159, 669 P.2d 592 (App. 1983)
59 ALR5th 135—§ 3
State v. LeMay, 2011 MT 323, 363 Mont. 172, 266 P.3d 1278 (2011)

102 ALR6th 621—§ 3

State v. Lemburg, 257 N.W.2d 39 (Iowa 1977)

72 ALR5th 109—§ 6

79 ALR5th 419—§ 12

State v. Leming, 2001 WL 637708 (Tenn. Crim. App. 2001)

100 ALR6th 535—§ 3

State v. Lemler, 2009 SD 86, 774 N.W.2d 272 (S.D. 2009)

69 ALR6th 549—§ 2, 3, 7

State v. Lemme, 104 R.I. 416, 244 A.2d 585 (1968)

26 ALR5th 1—§ 3, 5

State v. Lemmer, 736 N.W.2d 650 (Minn. 2007)

47 ALR6th 107—§ 82

State v. Lemon, 100 Wash. App. 1014, 2000 WL 349765 (Div. 2 2000)

59 ALR6th 393—§ 7

State v. Lemon, 664 So. 2d 1072 (Fla. Dist. Ct. App. 2d Dist. 1995)

113 ALR5th 597—§ 8

State v. Lemonds, 160 N.C. App. 172, 584 S.E.2d 841 (2003)

1 ALR6th 549—§ 4

State v. Lemons, 37 Kan. App. 2d 641, 155 P.3d 732 (2007)

78 ALR6th 297—§ 18, 22, 38, 80

State v. Lemons, No. 2700 (April 21, 1980, Ct. App. Ohio, 11th App. Dist. Trumbull Co.)

39 ALR5th 283—§ 55

State v. Lenahan, 12 Ariz. App. 446, 471 P.2d 748 (Div. 2 1970)

17 ALR6th 327—§ 35

State v. Lender, 266 Minn. 561, 124 N.W.2d 355 (1963)

93 ALR5th 327—§ 6, 7, 18

101 ALR5th 619—§ 9

State v. Lennon, 204 Or. App. 111, 129 P.3d 209 (2006)

26 ALR6th 511—§ 27

State v. Lennon, 427 So. 2d 860 (La. 1983)

7 ALR5th 263—§ 7

State v. Lenoir, 2003-Ohio-2820, 2003 WL 21267227 (Ohio Ct. App. 2d Dist. Montgomery County 2003)

125 ALR5th 357—§ 6

State v. Lentz, 73 Ohio App. 3d 449, 597 N.E.2d 1117 (3d Dist. Seneca County 1991)

35 ALR6th 127—§ 4

State v. Leonard, 157 Ohio App. 3d 653, 2004-Ohio-3323, 813 N.E.2d 50 (1st Dist. Hamilton County 2004)

21 ALR6th 1—§ 4

71 ALR6th 625—§ 4, 5, 12, 26

State v. Leonard, 287 S.C. 462, 339 S.E.2d 159 (Ct. App. 1986)

16 ALR6th 329—§ 7

24 ALR6th 591—§ 6

State v. Leonard, 2007-Ohio-3312, 2007 WL 1874232 (Ohio Ct. App. 1st Dist. Hamilton County 2007)

56 ALR6th 323—§ 7, 9, 11

State v. Leonard, 2007-Ohio-7095, 2007 WL 4562881 (Ohio Ct. App. 1st Dist. Hamilton County 2007)

71 ALR6th 625—§ 23

State v. Leone, 581 A.2d 394 (Me. 1990)

38 ALR5th 433—§ 39

State v. Leonhardt, 1996 WL 539787 (Ohio Ct. App. 1st Dist. Hamilton County 1996)

84 ALR6th 293—§ 27

State v. LePage, 138 Idaho 803, 69 P.3d 1064 (Ct. App. 2003)

125 ALR5th 497—§ 4

State v. LePage, 536 S.W.2d 834 (Mo. Ct. App. 1976)

74 ALR5th 453—§ 6

State v. LePard, 52 Ohio App. 3d 83, 557 N.E.2d 166 (6th Dist. Ottawa County 1989)

47 ALR6th 107—§ 45, 59

State v. Lepri, 1998 WL 242505 (Conn. Super. Ct. 1998)

111 ALR5th 239—§ 4

State v. Leprich, 160 Wis. 2d 472, 465 N.W.2d 844 (Ct. App. 1991)

28 ALR6th 505—§ 9

State v. Lerch, 296 Or. 377, 677 P.2d 678 (1984)

33 ALR5th 571—§ 5

65 ALR6th 359—§ 3

State v. Lerner, 112 R.I. 62, 308 A.2d 324 (1973)

95 ALR6th 219—§ 13

State v. Leroux, 18 Conn. App. 223, 557 A.2d 1271 (1989)

56 ALR6th 185—§ 37

State v. Lescard, 128 N.H. 495, 517 A.2d 1158 (1986)

30 ALR6th 103—§ 5, 46

State v. Lescher, 196 Wis. 2d 645, 539 N.W.2d 336 (Ct. App. 1995)

62 ALR6th 359—§ 17

State v. Lesley, 29 N.C. App. 169, 223 S.E.2d 532 (1976)

52 ALR5th 655—§ 8

State v. Leslie, 136 Ariz. 463, 666 P.2d 1072 (1983)

45 ALR5th 591—§ 15, 18

State v. Leslie, 166 Conn. 393, 349 A.2d 843 (1974)

105 ALR5th 529—§ 11

State v. Leslie, 2011-Ohio-2727, 2011 WL 2225152 (Ohio Ct. App. 4th Dist. Hocking County 2011)

70 ALR6th 329—§ 18

State v. Lesmes, 2008 WL 3875998 (N.J. Super. Ct. App. Div. 2008)

58 ALR6th 439—§ 29

State v. Lessard, 2008 MT 192, 344 Mont. 26, 185 P.3d 1013 (2008)

46 ALR6th 241—§ 20

State v. Letalien, 2009 ME 130, 985 A.2d 4 (Me. 2009)

63 ALR6th 351—§ 4

State v. Letourneau, 33 Kan. App. 2d 585, 106 P.3d 505 (2005)

23 ALR6th 307—§ 44

State v. Letourneau, 146 Vt. 366, 503 A.2d 553 (1985)

50 ALR5th 703—§ 2, 9, 21

State v. Letsche, 2003-Ohio-6942, 2003 WL 22977316 (Ohio Ct. App. 4th Dist. Ross County 2003)

17 ALR6th 327—§ 42

State v. Letterman, 47 Or. App. 1145, 616 P.2d 505, 12 A.L.R.4th 1009 (1980)

97 ALR6th 567—§ 3, 6, 7, 9

State v. Lettice, 221 Wis. 2d 69, 585 N.W.2d 171 (Ct. App. 1998)

121 ALR5th 551—§ 6, 14

State v. Leuch, 198 Wash. 331, 88 P.2d 440 (1939)

11 ALR5th 497—§ 3, 9, 16

State v. Leupp, 96 Wash. App. 324, 980 P.2d 765 (Div. 2 1999)

58 ALR6th 499—§ 28

State v. Leutfaimany, 585 N.W.2d 200 (Iowa 1998)

32 ALR5th 149—§ 30

16 ALR6th 329—§ 4

24 ALR6th 591—§ 4, 12

State v. Leuvoy, 2004-Ohio-2232, 2004 WL 944387 (Ohio Ct. App. 5th Dist. Fairfield County 2004)

30 ALR6th 483—§ 5

State v. Levasseur, 411 So. 2d 295 (Fla. App. D1 1982)

51 ALR5th 375—§ 10

State v. LeVeque, 1993 WL 407255 (Ohio App. Lake Co. 1993)

52 ALR5th 655—§ 3

State v. Levering, 661 S.W.2d 792 (Mo. App. 1983)

3 ALR5th 521—§ 6

State v. Levin, 2007 UT App 65, 156 P.3d 178 (Utah Ct. App. 2007)

57 ALR6th 83—§ 12, 16, 18

State v. Levinson, 71 Haw. 492, 795 P.2d 845 (1990)

70 ALR5th 587—§ 21

State v. Levinson, 71 Hawaii 492, 795 P.2d 845 (1990)

63 ALR5th 375—§ 5

State v. Levitt, 73 S.W.3d 159 (Tenn. Crim. App. 2001)

116 ALR5th 479—§ 3, 5

State v. Levy, 8 Wash. 2d 630, 113 P.2d 306 (1941)

104 ALR5th 357—§ 8

54 ALR6th 429—§ 28

State v. Levy, 156 Wash. 2d 709, 132 P.3d 1076 (2006)

99 ALR6th 295—§ 9

State v. Levy, 2002-Ohio-1434, 2002 WL 1653738 (Ohio Ct. App. 4th Dist. Athens County 2002)

70 ALR6th 1—§ 5

State v. Lewingdon., 1980 WL 354047 (Ohio Ct. App. 5th Dist. Richland County 1980)

101 ALR6th 331—§ 12

State v. Lewis, 24 Misc. 3d 1228(A), 901 N.Y.S.2d 903 (Sup 2009)

69 ALR6th 579—§ 4
78 ALR6th 297—§ 39, 57

State v. Lewis, 27 Kan. App. 2d 380

39 ALR5th 283—§ 21

State v. Lewis, 27 N.C. App. 426, 219 S.E.2d 554 (1975)

5 ALR5th 243—§ 7

State v. Lewis, 49 Or. App. 447, 619 P.2d 684 (1980)

15 ALR5th 391—§ 45

State v. Lewis, 57 Wash. App. 921, 791 P.2d 250 (1990)

15 ALR5th 391—§ 30

State v. Lewis, 60 Conn. App. 219, 759 A.2d 518 (2000)

65 ALR6th 537—§ 3

State v. Lewis, 66 Ohio App. 3d 37, 583 N.E.2d 404 (2d Dist. Greene County 1990)

86 ALR5th 59—§ 3

State v. Lewis, 75 Ohio App. 3d 689, 600 N.E.2d 764 (4th Dist. Ross County 1991)

3 ALR6th 269—§ 5, 8

State v. Lewis, 80 Wash. 532, 141 P. 1025 (1914)

24 ALR5th 465—§ 96

State v. Lewis, 86 S.D. 763, 201 N.W.2d 397 (1972)

55 ALR5th 125—§ 3, 7

State v. Lewis, 94 Haw. 292, 12 P.3d 1233 (Haw. 2000)

72 ALR5th 403—§ 3

State v. Lewis, 104 N.M. 677, 726 P.2d 354 (Ct. App. 1986)

70 ALR5th 1—§ 5
78 ALR5th 197—§ 3, 5, 13
79 ALR5th 419—§ 9, 12

State v. Lewis, 107 Idaho 616, 691 P.2d 1231 (1984)

41 ALR5th 171—§ 14, 18, 20, 26, 72, 97, 120, 121, 136

State v. Lewis, 115 Ariz. 530, 566 P.2d 678 (1977)

64 ALR5th 741—§ 4

State v. Lewis, 144 Idaho 64, 156 P.3d 565 (2007)

69 ALR6th 579—§ 4, 21

State v. Lewis, 156 P.3d 565 (Idaho 2007)

24 ALR6th 1—§ 17

State v. Lewis, 167 Vt. 533, 711 A.2d 669 (1998)

91 ALR5th 343—§ 33
92 ALR5th 35—§ 11

State v. Lewis, 169 Ariz. 4, 816 P.2d 263 (App. 1991)

39 ALR5th 283—§ 3

State v. Lewis, 173 Mont. 1, 565 P.2d 642 (1977)

79 ALR5th 1—§ 11

State v. Lewis, 352 Or. 626, 290 P.3d 288 (2012)

84 ALR6th 427—§ 30

State v. Lewis, 366 So. 2d 1355 (La. 1978)

97 ALR5th 293—§ 8

State v. Lewis, 373 A.2d 603 (Me. 1977)

34 ALR6th 1—§ 12

State v. Lewis, 401 A.2d 645 (Me. 1979)

45 ALR5th 767—§ 8

State v. Lewis, 422 N.W.2d 768 (Minn. Ct. App. 1988)

51 ALR6th 1—§ 25
70 ALR6th 361—§ 35

State v. Lewis, 452 So. 2d 720 (La. Ct. App. 4th Cir. 1984)

78 ALR5th 1—§ 21

State v. Lewis, 573 So. 2d 1282 (La. Ct. App. 4th Cir. 1991)

17 ALR6th 327—§ 7
State v. Lewis, 584 A.2d 622 (Me. 1990)
24 ALR6th 1—§ 27
State v. Lewis, 605 So. 2d 590 (Fla. Dist. Ct. App. 2d Dist. 1992)
109 ALR5th 99—§ 4
27 ALR6th 491—§ 3
State v. Lewis, 633 S.W.2d 110 (Mo. Ct. App. W.D. 1982)
99 ALR6th 295—§ 5, 13
State v. Lewis, 637 S.W.2d 421 (Mo. Ct. App. W.D. 1982)
93 ALR5th 527—§ 6
State v. Lewis, 654 So. 2d 761 (La. Ct. App. 4th Cir. 1995)
90 ALR5th 453—§ 12
38 ALR6th 439—§ 3, 7
State v. Lewis, 675 N.W.2d 516 (Iowa 2004)
62 ALR6th 413—§ 5, 46
State v. Lewis, 711 A.2d 669 (Vt. 1998)
15 ALR5th 391—§ 53
State v. Lewis, 735 S.W.2d 183 (Mo. Ct. App. S.D. 1987)
84 ALR6th 427—§ 18
State v. Lewis, 736 So. 2d 1004 (La. Ct. App. 4th Cir. 1999)
78 ALR5th 1—§ 25
State v. Lewis, 738 So. 2d 1212 (La. Ct. App. 2d Cir. 1999)
84 ALR6th 293—§ 31
State v. Lewis, 755 So. 2d 1025 (La. Ct. App. 4th Cir. 2000)
4 ALR5th 1—§ 14
State v. Lewis, 803 S.W.2d 260 (Tenn. Crim. App. 1990)
39 ALR6th 257—§ 17
State v. Lewis, 892 So. 2d 702 (La. Ct. App. 2d Cir. 2005)
11 ALR6th 237—§ 13
State v. Lewis, 917 S.W.2d 251 (Tenn. Crim. 1995)
15 ALR5th 391—§ 5
State v. Lewis, 1999 WL 797188 (Ohio Ct. App. 3d Dist. Allen County 1999)
78 ALR5th 489—§ 9

State v. Lewis, 2000 WL 1867568 (Ohio Ct. App. 2d Dist. Montgomery County 2000)
31 ALR6th 465—§ 5, 6, 14, 32
State v. Lewis, 2002-Ohio-3950, 2002 WL 1773060 (Ohio Ct. App. 3d Dist. Allen County 2002)
9 ALR6th 541—§ 25
State v. Lewis, 2007 WL 925654 (Idaho 2007)
24 ALR6th 1—§ 14
State v. Lewis, 2008 WL 4216140 (Del. Super. Ct. 2008)
71 ALR6th 1—§ 6
State v. Lewis, 2010 WL 3516881 (N.J. Super. Ct. App. Div. 2010)
69 ALR6th 579—§ 11
State v. Lewis, 2011-Ohio-4137, 2011 WL 3654507 (Ohio Ct. App. 6th Dist. Sandusky County 2011)
99 ALR6th 295—§ 13
State v. Lewis, No. 2942 (June 29, 1984, Ct. App. Ohio, 11th App. Dist. Trumbull Co.)
39 ALR5th 283—§ 14, 38
State v. Lewis, No. 6861 (October 23, 1981, Ct. App. Ohio, 2nd App. Dist. Montgomery Co.)
39 ALR5th 283—§ 14, 21
State v. Lewisohn, 379 A.2d 1192 (Me. 1977)
24 ALR5th 465—§ 2, 4, 14, 42, 45, 48
58 ALR6th 499—§ 18
State v. Leyda, 94 P.3d 397 (Wash. Ct. App. Div. 1 2004)
125 ALR5th 537—§ 7, 15, 24, 30
State v. Leyse, 60 S.D. 384, 244 N.W. 529 (1932)
116 ALR5th 1—§ 59
State v. Libby, 453 A.2d 481 (Me. 1982)
101 ALR6th 331—§ 13
State v. Libby, 546 A.2d 444 (Me. 1988)
55 ALR5th 125—§ 21, 23
State v. Libby, 556 A.2d 1099 (Me. 1989)
6 ALR5th 733—§ 15, 29
92 ALR5th 35—§ 27

45 ALR6th 435—§ 33

State v. Liberty Nat. Bank and Trust Co., 427 N.W.2d 307 (N.D. 1988)

125 ALR5th 147—§ 8, 9

State v. Licea, 707 So. 2d 1155 (Fla. Dist. Ct. App. 2d Dist. 1998)

106 ALR5th 377—§ 5

State v. Licona, 141 So. 3d 333 (La. Ct. App. 5th Cir. 2014)

99 ALR6th 295—§ 21

State v. Lieberman, 222 Neb. 95, 382 N.W.2d 330 (1986)

7 ALR5th 263—§ 7

State v. Lief, 4 Conn. Cir. Ct. 440, 234 A.2d 124 (App. Div. 1967)

57 ALR6th 83—§ 5

State v. Liegakos, 141 Wis. 2d 979, 415 N.W.2d 862 (App. 1987)

36 ALR5th 255—§ 33

State v. Lien, 265 N.W.2d 833 (Minn. 1978)

41 ALR5th 171—§ 7, 9, 42, 93, 100, 107, 108, 114, 121, 123, 133

State v. Lieurance, 844 S.W.2d 81 (Mo. Ct. App. S.D. 1992)

78 ALR6th 417—§ 29

State v. Liezen, 1993 WL 587 (Minn. Ct. App. 1993)

73 ALR5th 383—§ 5

State v. Light, 835 S.W.2d 933 (Mo. Ct. App. E.D. 1992)

99 ALR6th 295—§ 9

State v. Lightfoot, 208 N.J. Super. 475, 506 A.2d 363 (1986)

7 ALR5th 263—§ 7

State v. Lightner, 169 N.C. App. 843, 612 S.E.2d 693 (2005)

99 ALR6th 295—§ 13

State v. Ligouri, 73 N.W.2d 775 (Iowa 1955)

1 ALR6th 657—§ 6

State v. Liland, 2007 WL 174369 (N.J. Super. Ct. App. Div. 2007)

39 ALR6th 577—§ 4

State v. Lilburn, 875 P.2d 1036 (Mont 1994)

17 ALR5th 837—§ 3, 4

State v. Lile, 237 Kan. 210, 699 P.2d 456 (1985)

39 ALR5th 283—§ 4, 67

State v. Liles, 803 So. 2d 125 (La. Ct. App. 5th Cir. 2001)

1 ALR6th 371—§ 6

State v. Lillard, 91 Or. App. 106, 754 P.2d 595 (1988)

113 ALR5th 517—§ 6

State v. Lilleskov, 658 N.W.2d 904 (Minn. Ct. App. 2003)

37 ALR6th 55—§ 8

63 ALR6th 351—§ 3

State v. Lilly, 117 N.C. App. 192, 450 S.E.2d 546 (1994)

103 ALR6th 507—§ 22

State v. Lilly, 278 S.C. 499, 299 S.E.2d 329 (1983)

37 ALR5th 319—§ 4

State v. Lilly, 342 N.C. 409, 464 S.E.2d 42 (1995)

44 ALR5th 651—§ 5

State v. Lima, 546 A.2d 770 (R.I. 1988)

38 ALR5th 433—§ 3, 7

State v. Limarco, 235 P.3d 1267 (Kan. Ct. App. 2010)

74 ALR6th 373—§ 8

State v. Limbrecht, 600 N.W.2d 316 (Iowa 1999)

29 ALR5th 487—§ 11

State v. Limon, 154 P.3d 1184 (Kan. Ct. App. 2007)

30 ALR6th 373—§ 9

State v. Limpus, 128 Ariz. 371, 625 P.2d 960 (App. 1981)

42 ALR5th 291—§ 10, 25

State v. Linam, 93 N.M. 307, 600 P.2d 253 (1979)

7 ALR5th 263—§ 6

State v. Linares, 192 N.J. Super. 391, 470 A.2d 39 (1983)

32 ALR5th 149—§ 4, 45

State v. Lindahl, 309 N.W.2d 763 (Minn. 1981)

86 ALR5th 59—§ 4

State v. Lindberg, 408 N.W.2d 589 (Minn. Ct. App. 1987)

73 ALR5th 383—§ 36
State v. Lindemann, 178 Wis.2d 593, 506 N.W.2d 172 (Ct.App. 1993)
76 ALR5th 597—§ 2, 4
State v. Lindemuth, 56 N.M. 257, 243 P.2d 325 (1952)
90 ALR5th 453—§ 15
State v. Linden, 136 Ariz. 129, 664 P.2d 673 (App. 1983)
39 ALR5th 283—§ 3
State v. Lindermuth, 192 Wis. 2d 767, 532 N.W.2d 471 (App. 1995)
50 ALR5th 581—§ 9
State v. Lindh, 161 Wis. 2d 324, 468 N.W.2d 168, 11 A.L.R.5th 909 (1991)
11 ALR5th 1—§ 21
State v. Lindner, 100 Idaho 37, 592 P.2d 852 (1979)
41 ALR5th 171—§ 7, 10, 14, 16, 18, 24, 72
State v. Lindsay, 18 P.3d 504 (Utah Ct. App. 2000)
37 ALR6th 357—§ 4
State v. Lindsey, 58 N.C. App. 564, 293 S.E.2d 833 (1982)
112 ALR5th 429—§ 7
State v. Lindsey, 194 Wash. 129, 77 P.2d 596 (1938)
45 ALR5th 591—§ 18
State v. Lindsey, 543 So. 2d 886 (La. 1989)
20 ALR5th 177—§ 3, 8
State v. Lindsey, 621 So. 2d 618 (La. Ct. App. 2d Cir. 1993)
12 ALR6th 267—§ 4
State v. Lindsey, 631 So. 2d 486 (La. Ct. App. 4th Cir. 1994)
99 ALR6th 113—§ 18
State v. Lindsey, 632 N.W.2d 652 (Minn. 2001)
92 ALR5th 35—§ 13
State v. Lindsey, 671 So. 2d 1155 (La. Ct. App. 2d Cir. 1996)
93 ALR5th 527—§ 3
State v. Lindsey, 738 So. 2d 974 (Fla. Dist. Ct. App. 5th Dist. 1999)
65 ALR6th 359—§ 6

State v. Lindsey, 868 S.W.2d 114 (Mo. App. 1993)
29 ALR5th 59—§ 7
State v. Lindsey, 1999 WL 1095679 (Tenn. Crim. App. 1999)
65 ALR6th 359—§ 2, 9
State v. Lindsly, 106 Or. App. 459, 808 P.2d 727 (1991)
15 ALR5th 391—§ 9
87 ALR6th 1—§ 53
State v. Lindstedt, 101 Haw. 153, 64 P.3d 282 (Ct. App. 2003)
52 ALR6th 125—§ 7, 14, 44
State v. Lindstrom, 37 Or. App. 513, 588 P.2d 44 (1978)
84 ALR6th 293—§ 41
State v. Lindstrom, 46 Conn. App. 810, 702 A.2d 410 (1997)
39 ALR6th 257—§ 4, 5
State v. Lingle, 209 Neb. 492, 308 N.W.2d 531 (1981)
99 ALR5th 557—§ 14
State v. Link, 25 S.W.3d 136 (Mo. 2000)
78 ALR5th 1—§ 25
State v. Link, 965 S.W.2d 906 (Mo. Ct. App. S.D. 1998)
88 ALR5th 67—§ 6
State v. Linn, 131 Or. App. 487, 885 P.2d 721 (1994)
82 ALR5th 359—§ 2
83 ALR5th 277—§ 2
84 ALR5th 487—§ 2, 21
State v. Linnen, 2009 WL 2365977 (N.J. Super. Ct. App. Div. 2009)
50 ALR6th 455—§ 34
State v. Linner, 77 Ohio Misc. 2d 22, 665 N.E.2d 1180 (Mun. Ct. 1996)
71 ALR5th 285—§ 4
State v. Linsey, 2005 WL 544718 (Tenn. Crim. App. 2005)
26 ALR6th 511—§ 23, 25, 27, 47
State v. Lint, 657 S.W.2d 722 (Mo. App. 1983)
39 ALR5th 283—§ 4, 44
State v. Lint, 657 S.W.2d 722 (Mo. Ct. App. E.D. 1983)
102 ALR5th 447—§ 22

State v. Lint, 665 N.W.2d 440 (Iowa Ct. App. 2003)
81 ALR6th 505—§ 55
State v. Linton, 36 Wash. 2d 67, 216 P.2d 761 (1950)
5 ALR5th 243—§ 2, 38, 45
State v. Linton, 146 Ariz. 184, 704 P.2d 825 (Ct. App. Div. 2 1985)
58 ALR6th 499—§ 26, 57
State v. Linton, 356 N.J. Super. 255, 812 A.2d 382 (App. Div. 2002)
99 ALR6th 397—§ 8
State v. Linville, 2009-Ohio-313, 2009 WL 162061 (Ohio Ct. App. 4th Dist. Ross County 2009)
64 ALR6th 1—§ 7, 9, 11
State v. Lionberg, 533 A.2d 1172 (R.I. 1987)
70 ALR6th 361—§ 32
State v. Lipker, 16 Ohio App. 2d 21, 45 Ohio Op. 2d 34, 241 N.E.2d 171 (4th Dist. Lawrence County 1968)
28 ALR6th 505—§ 29
State v. Lipscomb, 770 So. 2d 29 (La. Ct. App. 4th Cir. 2000)
50 ALR5th 581—§ 7, 17
State v. Liptak, 21 Conn. App. 248, 573 A.2d 323 (1990)
60 ALR5th 1—§ 9
State v. Liquidating Trustees of Republic Petroleum Co., 510 S.W.2d 311 (Tex. 1974)
29 ALR6th 507—§ 16
State v. Lisa, 2011 WL 1434582 (N.J. Super. Ct. App. Div. 2011)
94 ALR6th 525—§ 9
State v. Lisevick, 65 Conn. App. 493, 783 A.2d 73 (2001)
40 ALR6th 1—§ 10
State v. List, 270 N.J. Super. 169, 636 A.2d 1054 (App. Div. 1993)
93 ALR5th 327—§ 7, 9
State v. List, 270 N.J. Super. 252, 636 A.2d 1097 (Law Div. 1990)
99 ALR6th 397—§ 14
State v. Lister, 2 Wash. App. 737, 469 P.2d 597 (Div. 1 1970)
56 ALR6th 323—§ 11

State v. Liston, 28 Tenn. 603, 9 Hum. 603, 1848 WL 1903 (1848)
5 ALR6th 1—§ 34
State v. Liston, 1999 WL 778377 (Ohio Ct. App. 11th Dist. Portage County 1999)
19 ALR6th 697—§ 18
State v. Lite, 592 So. 2d 1202, 17 FLW D 297 (Fla. App. D4 1992)
18 ALR5th 542—§ 2
State v. Litteral, 227 N.C. 527, 43 S.E.2d 84 (1947)
70 ALR5th 587—§ 4
State v. Little, 55 Or. App. 603, 639 P.2d 666 (1982)
39 ALR5th 283—§ 4, 58, 67
State v. Little, 57 Wash. 2d 516, 358 P.2d 120 (1961)
50 ALR5th 467—§ 6
State v. Little, 127 Conn. App. 336, 14 A.3d 1036 (2011)
63 ALR6th 351—§ 3
State v. Little, 127 Conn. App. 336, 2011 WL 781246 (2011)
63 ALR6th 351—§ 3
State v. Little, 228 N.C. 417, 45 S.E.2d 542 (1947)
10 ALR5th 700—§ 35, 40
State v. Little, 421 N.W.2d 172 (Iowa Ct. App. 1988)
32 ALR6th 1—§ 10
State v. Little, 861 S.W.2d 729 (Mo. Ct. App. E.D. 1993)
86 ALR5th 59—§ 3
State v. Little, 1986 WL 13587 (Ohio Ct. App. 8th Dist. Cuyahoga County 1986)
19 ALR6th 697—§ 4
State v. Littlefield, 677 A.2d 1055 (Me. 1996)
84 ALR6th 293—§ 33
State v. Littlejohn, 19 N.C. App. 73, 198 S.E.2d 11 (1973)
14 ALR5th 89—§ 34
State v. Littlejohn, 340 N.C. 750, 459 S.E.2d 629 (1995)
27 ALR6th 183—§ 28, 30

State v. Littleton, 407 So. 2d 1208 (La. 1981)
59 ALR5th 615—§ 3, 4, 9

State v. Livanos, 151 Ariz. 13, 725 P.2d 505 (Ct. App. Div. 1 1986)
29 ALR6th 1—§ 8

State v. Lively, 80 P.3d 1201 (Kan. Ct. App. 2003)
26 ALR6th 511—§ 25

State v. Lively, 921 P.2d 1035, 130 Wash. 2d 1, 65 USLW 2180 (1996)
18 ALR5th 1—§ 15

State v. Livernois, 1997-NMSC-019, 123 N.M. 128, 934 P.2d 1057 (1997)
51 ALR6th 1—§ 20

State v. Livings, 487 So. 2d 475 (La. App. 3d Cir. 1986)
5 ALR5th 243—§ 31, 45

State v. Livings, 664 So. 2d 729 (La. App. 3d Cir. 1995)
50 ALR5th 581—§ 17, 20

State v. Livingston, 35 N.C. App. 163, 241 S.E.2d 136 (1978)
15 ALR5th 391—§ 16

State v. Livingston, 907 S.W.2d 392 (Tenn. 1995)
38 ALR5th 433—§ 11
39 ALR6th 257—§ 3, 14, 18

State v. Livsey, 190 La. 474, 182 So. 576 (1938)
24 ALR6th 591—§ 6

State v. Lizanich, 93 Ohio App. 3d 706, 639 N.E.2d 855 (Franklin Co. 1994)
15 ALR5th 391—§ 53

State v. L.J.P., 637 N.J. Super. 429, 637 A.2d 532 (App. Div. 1994)
51 ALR5th 603—§ 14

State v. L. K. A., 2011 WL 1364435 (Minn. Ct. App. 2011)
68 ALR6th 1—§ 17

State v. Llamas-Villa, 67 Wash. App. 448, 836 P.2d 239 (Div. 1 1992)
104 ALR5th 165—§ 9

State v. Lloyd, 92 Idaho 20, 435 P.2d 797 (1967)
59 ALR5th 615—§ 3, 11

State v. Lloyd, 169 Vt. 643, 740 A.2d 364 (1999)
15 ALR6th 173—§ 41

State v. Lloyd, 337 Mo. 990, 87 S.W.2d 418 (1935)
8 ALR5th 775—§ 6

State v. Lloyd, 354 N.C. 76, 552 S.E.2d 596 (2001)
27 ALR6th 183—§ 14

State v. Lobato, 139 N.M. 431, 2006-NMCA-051, 134 P.3d 122 (Ct. App. 2006)
20 ALR6th 479—§ 3

State v. Lobozzo, 1998 ME 228, 719 A.2d 108 (Me. 1998)
39 ALR5th 283—§ 66

State v. Local 1115 Joint Bd., Nursing Home and Hospital Emp. Division, 56 A.D.2d 310, 392 N.Y.S.2d 884, 95 L.R.R.M. (BNA) 2337, 82 Lab. Cas. (CCH) ¶ 55099 (2d Dep't 1977)
120 ALR5th 351—§ 17

State v. Local No. 2883, American Federation of State, County & Municipal Employees, 463 A.2d 186 (R.I. 1983)
56 ALR5th 757—§ 4

State v. Loce, 267 N.J. Super. 10, 630 A.2d 792 (App. Div. 1993)
3 ALR5th 521—§ 3

State v. Lock, 468 S.W.2d 560 (Tex. Civ. App. Beaumont 1971)
7 ALR5th 113—§ 3, 5

State v. Lock, 839 S.W.2d 436 (Tenn. Crim. App. 1992)
72 ALR6th 141—§ 13

State v. Locke, 149 N.H. 1, 813 A.2d 1182 (2002)
32 ALR6th 1—§ 11

State v. Locke, 771 S.W.2d 132 (Tenn. Crim. App. 1988)
103 ALR6th 507—§ 6, 28

State v. Lockett, 232 Kan. 317, 654 P.2d 433 (1982)
80 ALR6th 239—§ 13, 16

State v. Lockhart, 208 W. Va. 622, 542 S.E.2d 443 (2000)

90 ALR5th 453—§ 26

State v. Lockhart, 298 Conn. 537, 4 A.3d 1176, 69 A.L.R.6th 793 (2010)

69 ALR6th 579—§ 4

State v. Lockhart, 1983 OK CR 76, 664 P.2d 1059 (Okla. Crim. App. 1983)

118 ALR5th 253—§ 18

State v. Lockheed Martin IMS, 2002 WL 99554 (Cal. App. 3d Dist. 2002)

124 ALR5th 375—§ 4

State v. Locklear, 7 N.C. App. 493, 172 S.E.2d 924 (1970)

84 ALR6th 427—§ 21

State v. Locklear, 84 N.C. App. 637, 353 S.E.2d 666 (1987)

31 ALR5th 760—§ 3, 4

State v. Locklear, 138 N.C. App. 549, 531 S.E.2d 853 (2000)

29 ALR6th 1—§ 13

81 ALR6th 505—§ 36

State v. Locklear, 320 N.C. 754, 360 S.E.2d 682 (1987)

57 ALR5th 141—§ 2, 3

State v. Locklear, 322 N.C. 349, 368 S.E.2d 377 (1988)

83 ALR6th 465—§ 4

99 ALR6th 113—§ 4

State v. Locklear, 349 N.C. 118, 505 S.E.2d 277 (1998)

11 ALR5th 497—§ 17

20 ALR5th 398—§ 10, 10.5

State v. Locklear, 363 N.C. 438, 681 S.E.2d 293 (2009)

83 ALR6th 255—§ 30

State v. Lockwood, 160 Vt. 547, 632 A.2d 655 (1993)

99 ALR5th 557—§ 14

State v. Loder, 381 A.2d 290 (Me. 1978)

111 ALR5th 239—§ 2

State v. Lodermeier, 481 N.W.2d 614, 24 A.L.R.5th 810 (S.D. 1992)

24 ALR5th 132—§ 2, 4, 5, 7

29 ALR5th 59—§ 7, 14

60 ALR5th 1—§ 8

State v. Lodge, 42 Wash. App. 380, 711 P.2d 1078 (1985)

42 ALR5th 291—§ 10, 11, 14

State v. Lodge, 2005-Ohio-1908, 2005 WL 937759 (Ohio Ct. App. 2d Dist. Montgomery County 2005)

71 ALR6th 1—§ 8

State v. Loera, 125 Wash. 2d 1005, 886 P.2d 1133 (1994)

68 ALR5th 343—§ 2, 3, 5

State v. Loewen, 97 Wash. 2d 562, 647 P.2d 489 (1982)

11 ALR5th 52—§ 2, 3

State v. Loewen, 199 Wis.2d 123, 545 N.W.2d 519 (Wis. App. 1995)

9 ALR6th 541—§ 10

State v. Loffer, 24 Kan. App. 2d 495, 947 P.2d 458 (1997)

15 ALR5th 391—§ 8

State v. Loftin, 146 N.J. 295, 680 A.2d 677 (1996)

102 ALR6th 279—§ 27

State v. Loftin, 276 S.C. 48, 275 S.E.2d 575 (1981)

61 ALR5th 1—§ 2, 3, 7

State v. Loftis, 1994 WL 315716 (Ohio Ct. App. 11th Dist. Ashtabula County 1994)

81 ALR6th 505—§ 4

State v. Lofton, 528 So. 2d 188 (La. App. 3d Cir. 1988)

45 ALR5th 1—§ 3, 5, 12, 23

State v. Loftus, 1997 SD 131, 573 N.W.2d 167 (S.D. 1997)

38 ALR6th 439—§ 4

State v. Loftus, 1997 S.D. 131, 573 N.W.2d 167 (S.D. 1997)

90 ALR5th 453—§ 22

State v. Logan, 8 Kan. App. 2d 232, 654 P.2d 492 (1982)

66 ALR5th 397—§ 4, 13, 22

State v. Logan, 60 Ohio St. 2d 126, 14 Ohio Ops. 3d 373, 397 N.E.2d 1345 (1979)

39 ALR5th 283—§ 2, 14, 44, 57, 70

State v. Logan, 105 Or. App. 556, 806 P.2d 137 (1991)

38 ALR5th 433—§ 11, 18

State v. Logan, 119 Me. 146, 109 A. 593 (1920)

57 ALR6th 445—§ 61

State v. Logan, 240 Or. App. 554, 248 P.3d 431 (2011)
87 ALR6th 1—§ 36

State v. Logan, 617 S.W.2d 433 (Mo. App. 1981)
55 ALR5th 125—§ 14, 25

State v. Logan, 973 S.W.2d 279 (Tenn. Crim. App. 1998)
66 ALR5th 397—§ 23

State v. Logan, 1988 WL 41132 (Ohio Ct. App. 10th Dist. Franklin County 1988)
19 ALR6th 697—§ 10

State v. Logan, 1997 WL 328020 (Minn. Ct. App. 1997)
73 ALR5th 383—§ 5

State v. Logan, 2002 MT 206, 311 Mont. 239, 53 P.3d 1285 (2002)
117 ALR5th 407—§ 3

State v. Logan, 2003 WL 22413490 (Conn. Super. Ct. 2003)
78 ALR6th 297—§ 42, 69

State v. Loge, 589 N.W.2d 491 (Minn. Ct. App. 1999)
97 ALR6th 653—§ 18

State v. Loge, 608 N.W.2d 152 (Minn. 2000)
97 ALR6th 653—§ 18

State v. Logo, 798 So. 2d 1182 (La. Ct. App. 4th Cir. 2001)
43 ALR6th 355—§ 3, 6

State v. Loh, 275 Mont. 460, 914 P.2d 592 (1996)
28 ALR6th 505—§ 9

State v. Lohnes, 432 N.W.2d 77 (S.D. 1988)
85 ALR5th 547—§ 2, 7

State v. Loins, 26 Kan. App. 2d 624, 993 P.2d 1231 (1999)
23 ALR6th 307—§ 39

State v. Lomak, 1999 WL 138603 (Ohio Ct. App. 10th Dist. Franklin County 1999)
17 ALR6th 327—§ 23

State v. Lomax, 24 Wash. App. 541, 603 P.2d 1267 (Div. 1 1979)
85 ALR5th 1—§ 42

State v. Lombardi, 110 R.I. 776, 298 A.2d 141 (1972)
72 ALR5th 607—§ 3

State v. Lombardo, 52 N.C. App. 316, 278 S.E.2d 318 (1981)
92 ALR6th 1—§ 5

State v. Lombardo, 306 N.C. 594, 295 S.E.2d 399 (1982)
92 ALR6th 1—§ 5

State v. Londagin, 102 S.W.3d 46 (Mo. Ct. App. S.D. 2003)
58 ALR6th 439—§ 25

State v. Lonergan, 505 N.W.2d 349 (Minn. App. 1993)
38 ALR5th 433—§ 3

State v. Long, 49 Ohio App. 3d 1, 550 N.E.2d 522 (1st Dist. Hamilton County 1989)
35 ALR6th 361—§ 7 to 10

State v. Long, 163 Wis. 2d 261, 471 N.W.2d 248 (Ct. App. 1991)
85 ALR5th 1—§ 44

State v. Long, 216 Mont. 65, 700 P.2d 153 (1985)
19 ALR5th 470—§ 3, 6

State v. Long, 216 N.J. Super. 269, 523 A.2d 672 (App. Div. 1987)
43 ALR6th 475—§ 21

State v. Long, 223 Mont. 502, 726 P.2d 1364 (1986)
79 ALR5th 419—§ 9, 12

State v. Long, 250 Iowa 326, 93 N.W.2d 744 (1958)
17 ALR6th 757—§ 4

State v. Long, 336 Mo. 630, 80 S.W.2d 154 (1935)
81 ALR5th 563—§ 3, 8

State v. Long, 544 So. 2d 219 (Fla. Dist. Ct. App. 2d Dist. 1989)
58 ALR6th 385—§ 37

State v. Long, 550 S.W.2d 854 (Mo. App. 1977)
54 ALR5th 575—§ 15

State v. Long, 577 A.2d 765 (Me. 1990)
39 ALR5th 283—§ 4

State v. Long, 1998 WL 74253 (Tenn. Crim. App. 1998)

73 ALR5th 383—§ 6
32 ALR6th 1—§ 10
State v. Longhorn World Championship
Rodeo, Inc., 19 Ohio App. 3d 115,
19 Ohio B.R. 203, 483 N.E.2d 196
(Hamilton Co. 1985)
6 ALR5th 733—§ 15
State v. Longo, 4 Ohio App. 3d 136, 446
N.E.2d 1145 (8th Dist. Cuyahoga
County 1982)
31 ALR6th 49—§ 4
State v. Longo, 608 N.W.2d 471 (Iowa
2000)
114 ALR5th 173—§ 6
State v. Longshore, 141 Wash. 2d 414, 5
P.3d 1256 (2000)
57 ALR6th 445—§ 25
State v. Longstreet, 536 S.W.2d 185
(Mo. Ct. App. 1976)
119 ALR5th 205—§ 6
State v. Loomis, 436 So. 2d 1103 (Fla.
Dist. Ct. App. 4th Dist. 1983)
62 ALR6th 413—§ 39
State v. Loosli, 130 Idaho 398, 941 P.2d
1299 (1997)
20 ALR6th 479—§ 3, 12
29 ALR6th 1—§ 10
State v. Looze, 273 N.W.2d 177 (S.D.
1979)
52 ALR6th 1—§ 22
State v. Lopez, 25 Kan. App. 2d 777,
973 P.2d 802 (1998)
30 ALR6th 373—§ 19
63 ALR6th 351—§ 3
State v. Lopez, 29 Wash. App. 836, 631
P.2d 420 (Div. 1 1981)
97 ALR6th 567—§ 3, 9
State v. Lopez, 74 Wash. App. 264, 872
P.2d 1131 (Div. 1 1994)
42 ALR6th 237—§ 11
State v. Lopez, 79 N.M. 282, 442 P.2d
594 (1968)
30 ALR6th 103—§ 58
State v. Lopez, 79 Wash. App. 755, 904
P.2d 1179 (Div. 3 1995)
62 ALR5th 1—§ 2, 5
State v. Lopez, 80 N.M. 599, 458 P.2d
851 (Ct. App. 1969)

87 ALR5th 181—§ 5
55 ALR6th 157—§ 4
State v. Lopez, 84 N.M. 805, 508 P.2d
1292 (1973)
82 ALR5th 591—§ 9
State v. Lopez, 85 N.M. 742, 516 P.2d
1125 (Ct. App. 1973)
68 ALR6th 527—§ 37
State v. Lopez, 95 Wash. App. 842, 980
P.2d 224 (Div. 3 1999)
38 ALR5th 433—§ 10
State v. Lopez, 107 Idaho 726, 692 P.2d
370 (Ct. App. 1984)
110 ALR5th 329—§ 15
State v. Lopez, 129 N.M. 352, 2000-
NMCA-069, 8 P.3d 154 (Ct. App.
2000)
38 ALR6th 97—§ 29
State v. Lopez, 137 Wash. App. 1064,
2007 WL 1057448 (Div. 3 2007)
73 ALR6th 49—§ 45
State v. Lopez, 173 Ariz. 552, 845 P.2d
478 (Ct. App. Div. 2 1992)
117 ALR5th 1—§ 4
16 ALR6th 329—§ 4
19 ALR6th 115—§ 4, 7, 10
24 ALR6th 591—§ 4, 12
State v. Lopez, 173 Wis. 2d 724, 496
N.W.2d 617 (App. 1992)
20 ALR5th 398—§ 3, 5, 8
State v. Lopez, 174 Ariz. 131, 847 P.2d
1078 (1992)
15 ALR5th 391—§ 31
92 ALR5th 35—§ 26
State v. Lopez, 197 W. Va. 556, 476
S.E.2d 227 (1996)
28 ALR6th 245—§ 10
State v. Lopez, 275 Wis. 2d 878, 2004
WI App 149, 685 N.W.2d 172 (Ct.
App. 2004)
71 ALR6th 625—§ 31
State v. Lopez, 538 N.W.2d 705 (Minn.
Ct. App. 1995)
32 ALR6th 1—§ 11
69 ALR6th 579—§ 8, 23
State v. Lopez, 721 A.2d 837 (R.I. 1998)
20 ALR5th 398—§ 7

State v. Lopez, 872 P.2d 1131 (Wash. App. 1994)
32 ALR5th 149—§ 34
State v. Lopez, 898 S.W.2d 563 (Mo. Ct. App. W.D. 1995)
57 ALR6th 445—§ 58
State v. Lopez, 948 So. 2d 1121 (La. Ct. App. 4th Cir. 2006)
75 ALR6th 541—§ 11
State v. Lopez, 2001 UT App. 123, 24 P.3d 993 (Utah Ct. App. 2001)
39 ALR5th 283—§ 71
State v. Lopez, 2010 WL 3446881 (Ariz. Ct. App. Div. 2 2010)
99 ALR6th 295—§ 8, 13
State v. Loprete, 1992 WL 115371 (Minn. Ct. App. 1992)
73 ALR5th 383—§ 29
State v. Loranger, 250 Wis. 2d 198, 2002 WI App 5, 640 N.W.2d 555 (Ct. App. 2001)
112 ALR5th 429—§ 12
73 ALR6th 49—§ 45
State v. Lord, 286 S.W.2d 737 (Mo. 1956)
83 ALR6th 465—§ 7, 64
State v. Lorefice, 1986 WL 716913 (Del. C.P. 1986)
77 ALR6th 393—§ 76
State v. Lorenz, 59 Ohio App. 3d 17, 570 N.E.2d 285 (Clermont Co. 1988)
42 ALR5th 291—§ 9
State v. Lorenz, 2001 SD 17, 622 N.W.2d 243 (S.D. 2001)
23 ALR6th 1—§ 15
State v. Lorenzi, 2005-Ohio-5718, 2005 WL 2807312 (Ohio Ct. App. 8th Dist. Cuyahoga County 2005)
26 ALR6th 511—§ 19
State v. Lorraine, 66 Ohio St. 3d 414, 613 N.E.2d 212 (1993)
79 ALR5th 33—§ 43
State v. Lorraine, 2005-Ohio-2529, 2005 WL 1208119 (Ohio Ct. App. 11th Dist. Trumbull County 2005)
83 ALR6th 465—§ 19, 70
State v. Losee, 354 N.W.2d 239 (Iowa 1984)

79 ALR5th 419—§ 9
State v. Losieau, 266 N.W.2d 259 (S.D. 1978)
117 ALR5th 513—§ 25
State v. Losson, 262 Mont. 342, 865 P.2d 255 (1993)
57 ALR5th 141—§ 3
State v. Lotegano, 12 N.J. Misc. 49, 169 A. 529 (Sup. Ct. 1933)
54 ALR6th 429—§ 9
State v. Lott, 97 Ohio St. 3d 303, 2002-Ohio-6625, 779 N.E.2d 1011 (2002)
122 ALR5th 145—§ 7, 13, 17
83 ALR6th 465—§ 70
State v. Lott, 255 N.W.2d 105 (Iowa 1977)
34 ALR5th 125—§ 14
State v. Lotter, 255 Neb. 456, 586 N.W.2d 591 (1998)
26 ALR5th 603—§ 6
State v. Lotter, 266 Neb. 758, 669 N.W.2d 438 (2003)
125 ALR5th 497—§ 3
72 ALR6th 227—§ 57
State v. Lottie, 31 Wash. App. 651, 644 P.2d 707 (Div. 1 1982)
78 ALR5th 197—§ 17
79 ALR5th 419—§ 10
State v. Lott, No. 40323 (January 17, 1980, Ct. App. Ohio, 8th App. Dist. Cuyahoga Co.)
39 ALR5th 283—§ 14, 58
State v. Lotton, 527 N.W.2d 840, 51 A.L.R.5th 849 (Minn. App. 1995)
51 ALR5th 425—§ 2, 9
State v. Lotze, 92 Wash. 2d 52, 593 P.2d 811, 13 Env't. Rep. Cas. (BNA) 1123, 5 Media L. Rep. (BNA) 1069 (1979)
51 ALR6th 359—§ 15, 16
State v. Louanis, 79 Vt. 463, 65 A. 532 (1907)
87 ALR5th 715—§ 3
State v. Louchheim, 296 N.C. 314, 250 S.E.2d 630 (1979)
6 ALR6th 533—§ 21
State v. Loucks, 98 Wash. 2d 563, 656 P.2d 480 (1983)

---

81 ALR5th 563—§ 8, 9

State v. Louden, 98 N.J. Super. 134, 236 A.2d 189 (1967)

36 ALR5th 161—§ 20

State v. Louden, 101 Or. App. 367, 790 P.2d 1182 (1990)

15 ALR5th 391—§ 3

State v. Loudon, 857 S.W.2d 878 (Tenn. Crim. App. 1993)

93 ALR5th 1—§ 7

State v. Loughton, 747 P.2d 426 (Utah 1987)

71 ALR5th 637—§ 9

State v. Louis, 97 N.J. Super. 35, 234 A.2d 240 (1967)

45 ALR5th 591—§ 17

State v. Louis, 296 Or. 57, 672 P.2d 708 (1983)

59 ALR5th 615—§ 3, 4, 9

State v. Louis, 682 S.E.2d 248 (N.C. Ct. App. 2009)

55 ALR6th 1—§ 7, 9

State v. Louisiana Toy Co., 483 So. 2d 1264 (La. App. 4th Cir. 1986)

13 ALR5th 567—§ 3

State v. Lounsbery, 74 Wash. 2d 659, 445 P.2d 1017 (1968)

119 ALR5th 275—§ 8, 10

State v. Lounsbury, 178 Iowa 555, 159 N.W. 998 (1916)

12 ALR5th 909—§ 9

State v. Lovato, 118 N.M. 155, 879 P.2d 787 (Ct. App. 1994)

113 ALR5th 517—§ 8

State v. Lovato, 702 P.2d 101 (Utah 1985)

53 ALR6th 81—§ 5

State v. Love, 49 Ohio App. 3d 88, 550 N.E.2d 951 (1st Dist. Hamilton County 1988)

58 ALR6th 499—§ 35

State v. Love, 182 Ariz. 324, 897 P.2d 626 (1995)

92 ALR6th 295—§ 13, 19
93 ALR6th 207—§ 11, 31
96 ALR6th 355—§ 5, 10, 25 to 26, 36, 49, 62

State v. Love, 282 N.J. Super. 590, 660 A.2d 1246 (App. Div. 1995)

103 ALR6th 137—§ 15

State v. Love, 546 S.W.2d 441 (Mo. App. 1976)

22 ALR5th 1—§ 6, 37, 42

State v. Love, 546 S.W.2d 441 (Mo. Ct. App. 1976)

28 ALR6th 505—§ 37
101 ALR6th 331—§ 12

State v. Love, 963 S.W.2d 236 (Mo. Ct. App. W.D. 1997)

39 ALR5th 283—§ 77

State v. Love, 2006-Ohio-1762, 2006 WL 890994 (Ohio Ct. App. 7th Dist. Mahoning County 2006)

16 ALR6th 329—§ 5
24 ALR6th 591—§ 14

State v. Lovejoy, 2000 WL 351171 (Neb. Ct. App. 2000)

96 ALR6th 355—§ 11, 34, 44

State v. Lovelace, 140 Idaho 53, 90 P.3d 278 (2003)

63 ALR6th 1—§ 36

State v. Lovelace, 227 Kan. 348, 607 P.2d 49 (1980)

22 ALR5th 660—§ 11

State v. Lovelace, 812 S.W.2d 446 (Tex. App. Houston (14th Dist.) 1991)

6 ALR5th 711—§ 5

State v. Loveless, 705 N.E.2d 223 (Ind. Ct. App. 1999)

32 ALR5th 659—§ 3

State v. Lovell, 123 Ariz. 482, 600 P.2d 1114 (Ct. App. Div. 2 1978)

21 ALR6th 771—§ 6

State v. Lovell, 2003 WL 22142499 (Tenn. Crim. App. 2003)

78 ALR6th 297—§ 81

State v. Lovely, 451 A.2d 900 (Me. 1982)

80 ALR5th 469—§ 3

State v. Lovett, 3 Vt. 110, 1830 WL 1758 (1830)

87 ALR5th 597—§ 4

State v. Lovin, 339 N.C. 695, 454 S.E.2d 229 (1995)

18 ALR5th 804—§ 4
State v. Loving, 775 N.W.2d 872 (Minn. 2009)
101 ALR6th 331—§ 12
State v. Lowe, 18 Kan. App. 2d 72, 847 P.2d 1334 (1993)
99 ALR6th 295—§ 13
State v. Lowe, 50 Idaho 96, 294 P. 339 (1931)
22 ALR5th 1—§ 34, 56
State v. Lowe, 466 A.2d 866 (Me. 1983)
63 ALR6th 1—§ 44
State v. Lowe, 665 A.2d 740 (N.H. 1995)
38 ALR5th 433—§ 11
State v. Lowe, 1999 WL 194586 (Ohio Ct. App. 9th Dist. Summit County 1999)
78 ALR5th 489—§ 3, 10
State v. Lower, 1999 WL 694856 (Ohio Ct. App. 10th Dist. Franklin County 1999)
78 ALR5th 489—§ 9
State v. Lowery, 15 N.C. App. 596, 190 S.E.2d 282 (1972)
19 ALR5th 823—§ 4, 8, 16, 18
State v. Lowery, 318 N.C. 54, 347 S.E.2d 729 (1986)
16 ALR6th 329—§ 4
24 ALR6th 591—§ 6, 14
State v. Lowman, 82 Ohio App. 3d 831, 613 N.E.2d 692 (12th Dist. Warren County 1992)
71 ALR6th 1—§ 8
State v. Lowmaster, 406 N.W.2d 15 (Minn. App. 1987)
20 ALR5th 398—§ 12, 38
State v. Lownes, 499 N.W.2d 896 (S.D. 1993)
76 ALR5th 1—§ 11
84 ALR6th 293—§ 9, 23
State v. Lowrey, 2004-Ohio-4429, 2004 WL 1879011 (Ohio Ct. App. 5th Dist. Fairfield County 2004)
70 ALR6th 1—§ 4, 23
State v. Lowrie, 12 Wash. App. 155, 528 P.2d 1010 (Div. 3 1974)
85 ALR5th 1—§ 17

State v. Lowrimore, 67 Wash. App. 949, 841 P.2d 779 (1992)
11 ALR5th 52—§ 11
State v. Lowry, 42 W. Va. 205, 24 S.E. 561 (1896)
108 ALR5th 593—§ 49
State v. Lowry, 191 Kan. 701, 383 P.2d 962 (1963)
70 ALR5th 169—§ 25
State v. Lowther, 434 N.W.2d 747 (S.D. 1989)
6 ALR6th 533—§ 3, 21
State v. Loyd, 455 So. 2d 687 (La. Ct. App. 2d Cir. 1984)
9 ALR6th 1—§ 17
State v. Loyd, 530 N.W.2d 708 (Iowa 1995)
74 ALR5th 319—§ 5 to 7, 10
State v. Loyden, 597 So. 2d 156 (La. Ct. App. 3d Cir. 1992)
112 ALR5th 429—§ 13
State v. Loyden, 899 So. 2d 166 (La. Ct. App. 3d Cir. 2005)
33 ALR6th 1—§ 22
State v. Loye, 670 N.W.2d 141 (Iowa 2003)
78 ALR6th 1—§ 13, 26
State v. Loyed, 2004-Ohio-3961, 2004 WL 1688548 (Ohio Ct. App. 8th Dist. Cuyahoga County 2004)
3 ALR6th 543—§ 8
State v. Loza, 71 Ohio St. 3d 61, 641 N.E.2d 1082, 37 A.L.R.5th 841 (1994)
36 ALR5th 255—§ 18
37 ALR5th 515—§ 10
79 ALR5th 33—§ 9, 64
State v. Lozada, 257 N.J. Super. 260, 608 A.2d 407 (App. Div. 1992)
99 ALR6th 113—§ 14
State v. Lozada, 2002-Ohio-1657, 2002 WL 538756 (Ohio Ct. App. 8th Dist. Cuyahoga County 2002)
70 ALR6th 1—§ 5
State v. Lozar, 458 N.W.2d 434 (Minn. App. 1990)
12 ALR5th 89—§ 2

For assistance, call 1-800-328-4880

State v. Lozar, 458 N.W.2d 434 (Minn. Ct. App. 1990)

106 ALR5th 397—§ 4

State v. Lozier, 375 So. 2d 1333 (La. 1979)

17 ALR5th 125—§ 4

State v. L.P., 352 N.J. Super. 369, 800 A.2d 207 (App. Div. 2002)

39 ALR6th 257—§ 19, 26

State v. Lua, 62 Wash. App. 34, 813 P.2d 588 (1991)

27 ALR5th 593—§ 9, 14

State v. Lubbers, 1994 WL 416427 (Ohio Ct. App. 1st Dist. Hamilton County 1994)

47 ALR6th 107—§ 37

State v. Lubotsky, 148 Wis. 2d 435, 434 N.W.2d 859 (App. 1988)

42 ALR5th 291—§ 17, 25

State v. Lucas, 30 N.J. 37, 152 A.2d 50 (1959)

33 ALR5th 571—§ 4

State v. Lucas, 56 Wash. App. 236, 783 P.2d 121 (Div. 1 1989)

99 ALR5th 557—§ 14

State v. Lucas, 63 Conn. App. 263, 775 A.2d 338 (2001)

103 ALR5th 463—§ 7

State v. Lucas, 178 W. Va. 686, 364 S.E.2d 12 (1987)

124 ALR5th 1—§ 4

State v. Lucas, 199 Ariz. 366, 18 P.3d 160 (Ct. App. Div. 1 2001)

15 ALR6th 319—§ 4, 5

State v. Lucas, 201 W. Va. 271, 496 S.E.2d 221 (1997)

15 ALR5th 391—§ 4
92 ALR5th 35—§ 25

State v. Lucas, 385 So. 2d 253 (La. 1980)

70 ALR5th 533—§ 3

State v. Lucas, 762 So. 2d 717 (La. Ct. App. 1st Cir. 2000)

3 ALR5th 963—§ 6

State v. Lucas, 1984 WL 3535 (Ohio Ct. App. 4th Dist. Athens County 1984)

45 ALR6th 643—§ 17

State v. Lucas, 1984 WL 5357 (Ohio Ct. App. 2d Dist. Champaign County 1984)

1 ALR6th 549—§ 8

State v. Lucas, 2005-Ohio-3468, 2005 WL 1580830 (Ohio Ct. App. 5th Dist. Morgan County 2005)

26 ALR6th 511—§ 19

State v. Lucero, 96 N.M. 126, 628 P.2d 696 (Ct. App. 1981)

24 ALR6th 1—§ 5

State v. Lucero, 1998-NMSC-044, 126 N.M. 552, 972 P.2d 1143 (1998)

27 ALR6th 183—§ 35

State v. Lucero, 2004 MT 248, 323 Mont. 42, 97 P.3d 1106 (2004)

46 ALR6th 241—§ 3, 9

State v. Lucht, 1996 WL 422509 (Minn. Ct. App. 1996)

19 ALR6th 697—§ 24

State v. Lucic, 2009-Ohio-5686, 2009 WL 3478508 (Ohio Ct. App. 8th Dist. Cuyahoga County 2009)

55 ALR6th 1—§ 3, 33
71 ALR6th 1—§ 9

State v. Luck, 15 Ohio St. 3d 150, 472 N.E.2d 1097 (1984)

96 ALR5th 327—§ 3

State v. Luck, 353 So. 2d 225, 3 Media L. R. 1571 (La. 1977)

13 ALR5th 567—§ 2, 3

State v. Luckett, 144 Ohio App. 3d 648, 761 N.E.2d 105 (8th Dist. Cuyahoga County 2001)

125 ALR5th 497—§ 4

State v. Luckett, 2010 WL 4075311 (N.J. Super. Ct. App. Div. 2010)

79 ALR6th 1—§ 83

State v. Luckey, 150 Or. 566, 46 P.2d 1042 (1935)

57 ALR6th 445—§ 18, 39

State v. Luckeydoo, 2005-Ohio-3823, 2005 WL 1785101 (Ohio Ct. App. 5th Dist. Licking County 2005)

62 ALR6th 161—§ 9

State v. Luckhardt, 2005 WL 2979319 (Minn. Ct. App. 2005)

26 ALR6th 511—§ 50

State v. Lucy, 2009 WL 4724245 (N.J. Super. Ct. App. Div. 2009)
64 ALR6th 131—§ 8

State v. Ludlow, 28 Utah 2d 434, 503 P.2d 1210 (1972)
66 ALR5th 397—§ 25

State v. Ludtke, 306 N.W.2d 111 (Minn. 1981)
50 ALR5th 581—§ 14, 20

State v. Ludvik, 40 Wash. App. 257, 698 P.2d 1064 (1985)
19 ALR5th 470—§ 3, 14
59 ALR5th 615—§ 3, 4, 6, 9

State v. Ludwig, 18 Wash. App. 50, 566 P.2d 946 (Div. 3 1977)
24 ALR6th 1—§ 17

State v. Ludwig, 423 So. 2d 1073 (La. 1982)
58 ALR6th 499—§ 57

State v. Luellen, 867 S.W.2d 736 (Tenn. Crim. App. 1992)
38 ALR6th 97—§ 30

State v. Luff, 198 N.C. 600, 152 S.E. 791 (1930)
108 ALR5th 593—§ 46

State v. Lukens, 151 Ariz. 502, 729 P.2d 306 (1986)
15 ALR5th 391—§ 45

State v. Luleff, 781 S.W.2d 199 (Mo. Ct. App. E.D. 1989)
111 ALR5th 1—§ 26

State v. Lum, 27 Kan. App. 2d 113, 998 P.2d 137 (2000)
84 ALR5th 1—§ 4

State v. Lumley, 267 Kan. 4, 977 P.2d 914 (1999)
10 ALR6th 463—§ 6
101 ALR6th 545—§ 3

State v. Luna, 91 N.M. 560, 577 P.2d 458 (Ct. App. 1978)
32 ALR6th 1—§ 4

State v. Luna, 211 Neb. 630, 319 N.W.2d 737 (1982)
97 ALR5th 293—§ 4

State v. Luna, 320 N.W.2d 87 (Minn. 1982)
73 ALR5th 383—§ 6

State v. Luna, 378 N.W.2d 229 (S.D. 1985)
71 ALR6th 1—§ 15

State v. Luna, 1994 WL 476031 (Ohio Ct. App. 6th Dist. Huron County 1994)
1 ALR6th 549—§ 25

State v. Luncsford, 428 N.W.2d 314 (Iowa Ct. App. 1988)
102 ALR5th 327—§ 2, 6

State v. Lundahl, 130 Or. App. 385, 882 P.2d 644 (1994)
105 ALR5th 529—§ 15

State v. Lundeen, 297 N.W.2d 232 (Iowa Ct. App. 1980)
71 ALR5th 1—§ 8

State v. Lunderville, 2010 WL 4924943 (N.M. Ct. App. 2010)
84 ALR6th 293—§ 27

State v. Lundin, 91 App. Div. 2d 343, 459 N.Y.S.2d 904 (3d Dep't 1983)
33 ALR5th 1—§ 16

State v. Lung, 70 Wash. 2d 365, 423 P.2d 72 (1967)
65 ALR6th 359—§ 3

State v. Lungsford, 167 N.J. Super. 296, 400 A.2d 843 (App. Div. 1979)
111 ALR5th 1—§ 3, 5, 7, 8, 38

State v. Lunsford, 507 N.W.2d 239 (Minn. Ct. App. 1993)
111 ALR5th 239—§ 10
112 ALR5th 429—§ 17

State v. Luoma, 88 Wash. 2d 28, 558 P.2d 756 (1977)
26 ALR6th 451—§ 8

State v. Lupek, 712 S.E.2d 915 (N.C. Ct. App. 2011)
67 ALR6th 531—§ 4

State v. Lupkovich, 2010 WL 1657561 (N.J. Super. Ct. App. Div. 2010)
92 ALR6th 549—§ 7

State v. Lusher, 708 S.W.2d 188 (Mo. App. 1986)
29 ALR5th 59—§ 7

State v. Lusi, 625 A.2d 1350 (R.I. 1993)
119 ALR5th 379—§ 7, 10, 12

State v. Lussier, 770 N.W.2d 581 (Minn. Ct. App. 2009)
56 ALR6th 1—§ 21

State v. Lussier, 2007 WL 5313372 (Vt. 2007)
92 ALR6th 295—§ 32

State v. Luster, 204 Ga. App. 156, 419 S.E.2d 32 (1992)
70 ALR5th 461—§ 2, 4

State v. Lute, 2000 WL 1729486 (Ohio Ct. App. 9th Dist. Lorain County 2000)
11 ALR6th 237—§ 10

State v. Luttig, 30 Kan. App. 2d 1125, 54 P.3d 974 (2002)
78 ALR6th 297—§ 37, 39, 46

State v. Lutz, 165 N.J. Super. 278, 398 A.2d 115 (App. Div. 1979)
32 ALR6th 1—§ 11

State v. L.W.H., Jr., 2009 WL 1374543 (Minn. Ct. App. 2009)
69 ALR6th 1—§ 4

State v. L.W.J., 717 N.W.2d 451 (Minn. Ct. App. 2006)
68 ALR6th 1—§ 10
69 ALR6th 1—§ 21

State v. Lybarger, 91 Or. App. 316, 754 P.2d 923 (1988)
18 ALR5th 1—§ 5

State v. Lybarger, 165 S.W.3d 180 (Mo. Ct. App. W.D. 2005)
37 ALR6th 357—§ 3

State v. Lyerla, 424 N.W.2d 908 (S.D. 1988)
56 ALR6th 185—§ 39

State v. Lykens, 13 Neb. App. 849, 703 N.W.2d 159 (2005)
29 ALR6th 1—§ 10

State v. Lykins, 1994 WL 240277 (Ohio Ct. App. 6th Dist. Wood County 1994)
34 ALR6th 1—§ 10

State v. Lykken, 484 N.W.2d 869, 39 A.L.R.5th 879 (S.D. 1992)
39 ALR5th 283—§ 4, 40

State v. Lyle, 125 S.C. 406, 118 S.E. 803 (1923)

108 ALR5th 593—§ 50

State v. Lyles, 291 N.J. Super. 517, 677 A.2d 1137 (App. Div. 1996)
39 ALR5th 283—§ 25

State v. Lyles, 308 Md. 129, 517 A.2d 761 (1986)
70 ALR5th 533—§ 3, 6

State v. Lyles, 996 S.W.2d 713 (Mo. Ct. App. E.D. 1999)
39 ALR5th 283—§ 31

State v. Lyles-Gray, 328 S.C. 458, 492 S.E.2d 802 (Ct. App. 1997)
66 ALR5th 397—§ 4

State v. Lyman, 241 Neb. 911, 492 N.W.2d 16 (1992)
72 ALR5th 109—§ 3

State v. Lyman, 776 N.W.2d 865 (Iowa 2010)
100 ALR6th 535—§ 3

State v. Lynch, 94 Or. App. 168, 764 P.2d 957 (1988)
68 ALR5th 343—§ 4, 17

State v. Lynch, 98 Ohio St. 3d 514, 2003-Ohio-2284, 787 N.E.2d 1185 (2003)
122 ALR5th 145—§ 7, 24

State v. Lynch, 119 Or. App. 97, 849 P.2d 556 (1993)
106 ALR5th 397—§ 4

State v. Lynch, 120 Ariz. 584, 587 P.2d 770 (Ct. App. Div. 2 1978)
114 ALR5th 173—§ 7

State v. Lynch, 135 Or. App. 528, 900 P.2d 1042 (1995)
64 ALR5th 637—§ 3

State v. Lynch, 177 N.J. Super. 107, 425 A.2d 696 (App. Div. 1981)
19 ALR6th 697—§ 3, 4

State v. Lynch, 279 N.C. 1, 181 S.E.2d 561 (1971)
104 ALR5th 357—§ 4, 7
54 ALR6th 429—§ 21

State v. Lynch, 327 N.C. 210, 393 S.E.2d 811 (1990)
57 ALR5th 141—§ 3

State v. Lynch, 783 S.W.2d 504 (Mo. App. 1990)

5 ALR5th 243—§ 10
State v. Lynch, 2001-Ohio-3914, 2001 WL 1635760 (Ohio Ct. App. 1st Dist. Hamilton County 2001)

21 ALR6th 1—§ 4
State v. Lynd, 54 Wash. App. 18, 771 P.2d 770 (Div. 1 1989)

58 ALR6th 499—§ 31
State v. Lynn, 1979 WL 208702 (Ohio Ct. App. 1st Dist. Hamilton County 1979)

103 ALR6th 347—§ 7, 26
State v. Lyon, 648 S.W.2d 957 (Tenn. Crim. App. 1982)

23 ALR6th 1—§ 19
State v. Lyons, 83 Ohio App. 3d 525, 615 N.E.2d 310 (2d Dist. Darke County 1992)

78 ALR6th 297—§ 37, 39, 46
State v. Lyons, 152 N.J. Super. 533, 378 A.2d 83 (1977)

32 ALR5th 659—§ 3
State v. Lyons, 159 N.J. Super. 100, 386 A.2d 1378 (1978)

32 ALR5th 659—§ 3
State v. Lyons, 161 Or. App. 355, 985 P.2d 204 (1999)

89 ALR5th 629—§ 8
State v. Lyons, 167 Ga. App. 747, 307 S.E.2d 285 (1983)

62 ALR6th 413—§ 47
State v. Lyons, 324 Or. 256, 924 P.2d 802 (1996)

90 ALR5th 453—§ 19
State v. Lyons, 340 N.C. 646, 459 S.E.2d 770 (1995)

56 ALR6th 185—§ 20
State v. Lyons, 466 A.2d 868 (Me. 1983)

59 ALR5th 1—§ 3, 4, 6
State v. Lyons, 2000 WL 221983 (Ohio Ct. App. 5th Dist. Licking County 2000)

78 ALR5th 489—§ 9
State v. Lyskoski, 47 Wash. 2d 102, 287 P.2d 114 (1955)

54 ALR6th 429—§ 20
State v. Lyszaj, 314 N.C. 256, 333 S.E.2d 288 (1985)

51 ALR6th 1—§ 20
State v. Lytle, 194 Neb. 353, 231 N.W.2d 681 (1975)

50 ALR5th 467—§ 3, 7
State v. Lyttle, 1997 WL 786216 (Ohio Ct. App. 12th Dist. Butler County 1997)

78 ALR5th 489—§ 3
State v. M., 188 N.J. Super. 533, 457 A.2d 1237 (Law Div. 1982)

69 ALR6th 1—§ 22
State v. M., 388 So. 2d 1227 (Fla. 1980)

46 ALR5th 523—§ 3, 9
State v. Mabe, 85 N.C. App. 500, 355 S.E.2d 186 (1987)

92 ALR6th 295—§ 7, 18
93 ALR6th 207—§ 6, 26
96 ALR6th 355—§ 37
State v. Mabe, 306 S.C. 355, 412 S.E.2d 386 (1991)

55 ALR6th 391—§ 21
State v. Mac Cardwell, 133 N.C. App. 496, 516 S.E.2d 388 (1999)

90 ALR5th 453—§ 16
State v. MacDonald, 113 N.H. 725, 313 A.2d 729 (1973)

19 ALR5th 823—§ 15, 17
State v. MacDonald, 253 Kan. 320, 856 P.2d 116 (1993)

114 ALR5th 173—§ 9
State v. MacDonald, 260 N.W.2d 626 (S.D. 1977)

92 ALR6th 295—§ 3
93 ALR6th 207—§ 3
95 ALR6th 1—§ 3
State v. MacDonald, 527 A.2d 758 (Me. 1987)

52 ALR5th 655—§ 3
State v. MacDonald, 598 A.2d 1134 (Del. 1991)

57 ALR5th 141—§ 5
State v. MacDonald, 1998 ME 212, 718 A.2d 195 (Me. 1998)

82 ALR5th 591—§ 3
90 ALR5th 453—§ 13
State v. Mace, 133 Idaho 903, 994 P.2d 1066 (Ct. App. 2000)

---

7 ALR5th 263—§ 4

State v. Mace, 665 S.W.2d 655 (Mo. App. 1984)

5 ALR5th 243—§ 43

State v. MacGillivray, 162 Ariz. 539, 785 P.2d 59 (Ct. App. Div. 1 1989)

79 ALR6th 125—§ 9

State v. Mach, 23 Wash. App. 113, 594 P.2d 1361 (1979)

50 ALR5th 703—§ 35

State v. Machado, 111 N.J. 480, 545 A.2d 174 (1988)

57 ALR5th 141—§ 2, 3

State v. Machholz, 574 N.W.2d 415 (Minn. 1998)

70 ALR6th 513—§ 12

71 ALR6th 471—§ 10

State v. Machia, 38 Conn. Supp. 407, 449 A.2d 1043 (Super Ct. Appellate Sess. 1979)

70 ALR5th 587—§ 5

State v. Machner, 101 Wis. 2d 79, 303 N.W.2d 633 (1981)

78 ALR6th 417—§ 5

State v. Machon, 410 So. 2d 1065 (La. 1982)

108 ALR5th 593—§ 50

State v. MacIntyre, 238 Wis. 406, 298 N.W. 200 (1941)

26 ALR6th 1—§ 7, 11

State v. Mack, 81 N.C. App. 578, 345 S.E.2d 223 (1986)

32 ALR6th 1—§ 7

81 ALR6th 505—§ 28

State v. Mack, 134 Ariz. 89, 654 P.2d 23 (App. 1982)

9 ALR5th 464—§ 7

State v. Mack, 337 Or. 586, 101 P.3d 349 (2004)

30 ALR6th 1—§ 3, 6

State v. MacKenzie, 109 Wash. App. 1004, 2001 WL 1357189 (Div. 1 2001)

80 ALR6th 599—§ 8

State v. Mackey, 638 S.W.2d 830 (Tenn. Crim. 1982)

39 ALR5th 283—§ 4

State v. Mackie, 128 Ohio App. 3d 167, 714 N.E.2d 405 (1st Dist. Hamilton County 1998)

92 ALR6th 295—§ 34

95 ALR6th 1—§ 6, 8, 13, 33

State v. MacKinnon, 1998 MT 78, 288 Mont. 329, 957 P.2d 23 (1998)

93 ALR5th 327—§ 3, 7 to 9

101 ALR5th 619—§ 5

State v. Macklin, 96 Wash. App. 1003, 1999 WL 390962 (Div. 1 1999)

103 ALR6th 347—§ 13

State v. Macklin, 1990 WL 193175 (Ohio Ct. App. 8th Dist. Cuyahoga County 1990)

99 ALR6th 397—§ 8

State v. Mack, No. 42284 (December 24, 1980, Ct. App. Ohio, 8th App. Dist. Cuyahoga Co.)

39 ALR5th 283—§ 14, 28, 71

State v. Maclin, 183 S.W.3d 335 (Tenn. 2006)

30 ALR6th 1—§ 3, 4, 6, 7

State v. MacNab, 334 Or. 469, 51 P.3d 1249 (2002)

63 ALR6th 351—§ 3

State v. Macomber, 7 R.I. 349, 1863 WL 1417 (1863)

5 ALR6th 1—§ 42

State v. Macon, 346 N.C. 109, 484 S.E.2d 538 (1997)

57 ALR5th 141—§ 3

State v. MacPhee, 221 W. Va. 693, 656 S.E.2d 444 (2007)

65 ALR6th 359—§ 5

State v. Madalena, 121 N.M. 63, 908 P.2d 756 (Ct. App. 1995)

74 ALR5th 319—§ 4, 6, 7, 9 to 12

State v. Maddasion, 24 Ariz. App. 492, 539 P.2d 966 (1975)

43 ALR5th 1—§ 3, 8, 13, 15

State v. Madden, 292 N.C. 114, 232 S.E.2d 656 (1977)

16 ALR6th 329—§ 4

24 ALR6th 591—§ 6, 14

State v. Madden, 2010-Ohio-176, 2010 WL 202211 (Ohio Ct. App. 4th Dist. Adams County 2010)

71 ALR6th 1—§ 5
State v. Maddix, 935 S.W.2d 666 (Mo.
Ct. App. W.D. 1996)
71 ALR6th 1—§ 8
State v. Maddox, 27 N.C. App. 58, 217
S.E.2d 765 (1975)
5 ALR5th 243—§ 50
State v. Maddox, 204 Or. App. 421, 129
P.3d 786 (2006)
26 ALR6th 511—§ 27
State v. Maddox, 2008-NMSC-062, 145
N.M. 242, 195 P.3d 1254 (2008)
70 ALR6th 361—§ 29
State v. Madera, 206 Mont. 140, 670
P.2d 552 (1983)
61 ALR5th 1—§ 4, 7
99 ALR6th 397—§ 17
State v. Madera, 210 Conn. 22, 554 A.2d
263 (1989)
9 ALR6th 1—§ 8
State v. Madrid, 74 Idaho 200, 259 P.2d
1044 (1953)
98 ALR6th 455—§ 18
State v. Madrid, 91 N.M. 375, 574 P.2d
594 (Ct. App. 1978)
65 ALR5th 407—§ 3, 4, 7, 8, 16
State v. Madrigal, 87 Ohio St. 3d 378,
2000-Ohio-448, 721 N.E.2d 52
(2000)
72 ALR6th 1—§ 4
State v. Madrigal, 2000 WL 1713874
(Ohio Ct. App. 6th Dist. Lucas
County 2000)
21 ALR6th 1—§ 4
State v. Madry, 93 S.C. 412, 76 S.E. 977
(1913)
45 ALR5th 591—§ 14
State v. Madsen, 125 Ariz. 346, 609 P.2d
1046 (1980)
103 ALR5th 463—§ 9
State v. Madsen, 791 N.W.2d 429 (Iowa
Ct. App. 2010)
69 ALR6th 579—§ 4
State v. Madsen, 2003 WI App 111, 264
Wis. 2d 893, 664 N.W.2d 127 (Ct.
App. 2003)
93 ALR6th 275—§ 10

State v. Maduell, 326 So. 2d 820 (La.
1976)
85 ALR5th 471—§ 7
State v. Maelega, 80 Haw. 172, 907 P.2d
758 (Haw. 1995)
90 ALR5th 453—§ 45
State v. Maelega, 80 Hawaii 172, 907
P.2d 758 (1995)
24 ALR5th 465—§ 3, 14
State v. Magdariaga, 213 Wis. 2d 484,
570 N.W.2d 910 (Ct. App. 1997)
99 ALR6th 295—§ 13
State v. Magee, 517 So. 2d 464 (La. Ct.
App. 1st Cir. 1987)
95 ALR5th 229—§ 26
State v. Magee, 749 So. 2d 874 (La. Ct.
App. 4th Cir. 1999)
4 ALR5th 1—§ 38
State v. Magers, 452 S.W.2d 198 (Mo.
1970)
29 ALR5th 59—§ 7, 14
State v. Maggard, 16 Kan. App. 2d 743,
829 P.2d 591 (1992)
70 ALR6th 361—§ 29
State v. Maggy, 2009-Ohio-3180, 2009
WL 1857292 (Ohio Ct. App. 11th
Dist. Trumbull County 2009)
64 ALR6th 1—§ 7, 9, 11
State v. Magnano, 204 Conn. 259, 528
A.2d 760 (1987)
1 ALR5th 346—§ 8
58 ALR6th 499—§ 97
State v. Magner, 151 N.J. Super. 451,
376 A.2d 1333 (1977)
52 ALR5th 655—§ 3
State v. Magnon, 2008 WL 4866181
(Wis. Ct. App. 2008)
43 ALR6th 475—§ 6
State v. Magnuson, 220 Wis. 2d 468,
583 N.W.2d 843 (Ct. App. 1998)
121 ALR5th 551—§ 2, 13
State v. Magruder, 234 Mont. 492, 765
P.2d 716 (1988)
57 ALR5th 141—§ 7
State v. Maguire, 146 Vt. 49, 498 A.2d
1028 (1985)
109 ALR5th 99—§ 12

State v. Mahaffey, 140 Ohio App. 3d 396, 747 N.E.2d 872 (4th Dist. Jackson County 2000)

43 ALR5th 777—§ 3

State v. Mahaley, 332 N.C. 583, 423 S.E.2d 58 (1992)

32 ALR6th 1—§ 11

State v. Mahan, 971 S.W.2d 307 (Mo. 1998)

76 ALR5th 1—§ 2
77 ALR5th 201—§ 2, 3

State v. Mahaney, 437 A.2d 613 (Me. 1981)

57 ALR5th 141—§ 3

State v. Mahaney, 625 S.W.2d 112, 25 A.L.R.4th 413 (Mo. 1981)

9 ALR6th 1—§ 6

State v. Mahi, 2005 UT App 494, 125 P.3d 103 (Utah Ct. App. 2005)

37 ALR6th 357—§ 42

State v. Mahkuk, 220 Kan. 74, 551 P.2d 869 (1976)

83 ALR5th 277—§ 21
84 ALR5th 487—§ 21, 24
54 ALR6th 429—§ 20

State v. Mahkuk, 736 N.W.2d 675 (Minn. 2007)

33 ALR6th 1—§ 7

State v. Mahkuk, 736 N.W.2d 675, 32 A.L.R.6th 707 (Minn. 2007)

32 ALR6th 1—§ 11
32 ALR6th 171—§ 22

State v. Mahone, 93 Wash. App. 1003, 1998 WL 800185 (Div. 2 1998)

15 ALR6th 515—§ 33

State v. Mahoney, 106 Ariz. 297, 475 P.2d 479 (1970)

122 ALR5th 439—§ 6

State v. Mahoney, 226 N.J. Super. 617, 545 A.2d 235 (App. Div. 1988)

125 ALR5th 281—§ 17

State v. Mahurin, 799 S.W.2d 840 (Mo. 1990)

118 ALR5th 253—§ 4, 10, 16

State v. Mai, 202 N.J. 12, 993 A.2d 1216 (2010)

92 ALR6th 171—§ 3, 18

State v. Mai, 572 N.W.2d 168 (Iowa Ct. App. 1997)

15 ALR5th 391—§ 15

State v. Maiden, 463 So. 2d 848 (La. Ct. App. 2d Cir. 1985)

20 ALR6th 479—§ 12

State v. Maidi, 520 N.W.2d 414 (Minn. App. 1994)

15 ALR5th 391—§ 25

State v. Maidi, 537 N.W.2d 280 (Minn. 1995)

15 ALR5th 391—§ 25

State v. Maier, 423 A.2d 235 (Me. 1980)

57 ALR6th 445—§ 8

State v. Mailman, 2010-NMSC-036, 148 N.M. 702, 242 P.3d 269 (2010)

92 ALR6th 295—§ 10, 17

State v. Mailman, 2010-NMSC-036, 148 N.M. 702, 242 P.3d 269, 95 A.L.R.6th 709 (2010)

94 ALR6th 579—§ 9
95 ALR6th 1—§ 5, 6, 19

State v. Mailo, 69 Haw. 51, 731 P.2d 1264 (1987)

124 ALR5th 1—§ 5

State v. Main, 1994 WL 477751 (Ohio Ct. App. 5th Dist. Stark County 1994)

25 ALR6th 379—§ 10

State v. Main, 1997 WL 414956 (Wash. Ct. App. Div. 3 1997)

73 ALR5th 383—§ 22

State v. Maine State Employees Ass'n, 482 A.2d 461, 121 L.R.R.M. (BNA) 2286 (Me. 1984)

83 ALR6th 143—§ 11

State v. Maiolo, 2003-Ohio-6528, 2003 WL 22887883 (Ohio Ct. App. 2d Dist. Clark County 2003)

71 ALR6th 1—§ 6

State v. Maioriello, 73 Ohio App. 3d 350, 597 N.E.2d 185 (Stark Co. 1992)

26 ALR5th 1—§ 4, 11

State v. Maitland, 2011-Ohio-6244, 2011 WL 6076539 (Ohio Ct. App. 9th Dist. Summit County 2011)

84 ALR6th 293—§ 13, 34

State v. Major, 48 SCL 76 (1866)
29 ALR5th 59—§ 3, 59

State v. Major, 708 So. 2d 813 (La. Ct. App. 4th Cir. 1998)
53 ALR6th 81—§ 9

State v. Makela, 309 N.W.2d 295 (Minn. 1981)
51 ALR6th 219—§ 4

State v. Malarney, 617 So. 2d 739 (Fla. Dist. Ct. App. 4th Dist. 1993)
87 ALR5th 693—§ 3

State v. Malave, 127 N.J. Super. 151, 316 A.2d 706 (1974)
43 ALR5th 1—§ 2, 8

State v. Malbrough, 5 Kan. App. 2d 295, 615 P.2d 165 (1980)
21 ALR5th 275—§ 5

State (Borough of Paramus) v. Malcolm Konner Chevrolet, 226 N.J. Super. 692, 545 A.2d 275 (Law Div. 1988)
103 ALR5th 445—§ 3

State v. Malcom, 58 Del. 1, 203 A.2d 270 (Super Ct. 1964)
51 ALR5th 425—§ 9
55 ALR5th 125—§ 3, 8

State v. Maldonado, 20 Conn. App. 137, 564 A.2d 638 (1989)
88 ALR5th 121—§ 39

State v. Maldonado, 137 N.J. 536, 645 A.2d 1165 (1994)
27 ALR5th 593—§ 29

State v. Maldonado, 176 Mont. 322, 578 P.2d 296 (1978)
71 ALR6th 1—§ 5

State v. Maldonado, 218 Wis. 2d 164, 578 N.W.2d 208 (Ct. App. 1998)
42 ALR6th 237—§ 8

State v. Maletich, 384 N.W.2d 586 (Minn. Ct. App. 1986)
92 ALR6th 295—§ 8, 24
96 ALR6th 355—§ 6

State v. Malhiot, 938 So. 2d 1158 (La. Ct. App. 2d Cir. 2006)
22 ALR6th 533—§ 5

State v. Malick, 457 S.E.2d 482 (W. Va. 1995)
22 ALR5th 1—§ 6

State v. Malik, 552 N.W.2d 730 (Minn. 1996)
34 ALR6th 1—§ 9

State v. Malivao, 105 Haw. 414, 98 P.3d 285 (Ct. App. 2004)
9 ALR6th 633—§ 4, 13
10 ALR6th 265—§ 6

State v. Malkin, 722 P.2d 943 (Alaska 1986)
19 ALR5th 470—§ 3

State v. Mallett, 552 So. 2d 28 (La. App. 3d Cir. 1989)
7 ALR5th 263—§ 4

State v. Mallett, 2003 WL 22901008 (Iowa Ct. App. 2003)
125 ALR5th 537—§ 2, 4

State v. Mallett, 2008-Ohio-2371, 2008 WL 2058640 (Ohio Ct. App. 8th Dist. Cuyahoga County 2008)
71 ALR6th 1—§ 8

State v. Malley, 2003 WL 1215532 (Minn. Ct. App. 2003)
67 ALR6th 531—§ 27

State v. Mallory, 73 Ark. 236, 83 S.W. 955 (1904)
31 ALR6th 523—§ 26

State v. Mallory, 329 N.W.2d 60 (Minn. 1983)
7 ALR5th 263—§ 2, 7

State v. Mallory, 747 S.W.2d 209 (Mo. Ct. App. W.D. 1988)
103 ALR6th 507—§ 33

State v. Malloy, 131 Ariz. 125, 639 P.2d 315 (1981)
82 ALR5th 359—§ 3
83 ALR5th 277—§ 9
84 ALR5th 487—§ 25

State v. Malloy, 309 N.C. 176, 305 S.E.2d 718 (1983)
88 ALR5th 121—§ 39

State v. Malloy, 2004 MT 377, 325 Mont. 86, 103 P.3d 1064 (2004)
46 ALR6th 241—§ 9

State v. Malmquist, 2004 WL 376932 (Minn. Ct. App. 2004)
57 ALR6th 83—§ 11, 19

State v. Malone, 4 Neb. App. 904, 552 N.W.2d 772 (1996)

1 ALR6th 549—§ 15

State v. Malone, 9 Wash. App. 122, 511 P.2d 67 (1973)

2 ALR5th 725—§ 3, 4, 6

State v. Malone, 15 Ohio App. 3d 123, 472 N.E.2d 1122 (9th Dist. Summit County 1984)

39 ALR5th 283—§ 14, 47, 54

70 ALR5th 587—§ 19

State v. Malone, 72 Wash. App. 429, 864 P.2d 990 (1994)

4 ALR5th 1—§ 7

State v. Malone, 90 Wash. App. 1010, 1998 WL 141587 (Div. 1 1998)

88 ALR5th 121—§ 2, 14, 22, 35

State v. Malone, 403 So. 2d 1234 (La. 1981)

99 ALR5th 557—§ 3, 9

State v. Malone, 694 S.W.2d 723 (Mo. 1985)

79 ALR5th 237—§ 3

37 ALR6th 357—§ 54

State v. Malufau, 80 Hawaii 126, 906 P.2d 612 (1995)

5 ALR5th 243—§ 26

State v. Malveaux, 604 S.W.2d 728 (Mo. App. 1980)

36 ALR5th 255—§ 24

State v. Malveo, 609 So. 2d 802 (La. 1992)

47 ALR5th 259—§ 4

State v. Malz, 2004 WL 2340037 (Minn. Ct. App. 2004)

35 ALR6th 127—§ 5

State v. Malzac, 309 Minn. 300, 244 N.W.2d 258 (1976)

9 ALR5th 369—§ 6

State v. Mance, 82 Wash. App. 539, 918 P.2d 527 (Div. 2 1996)

4 ALR6th 599—§ 3, 21

103 ALR6th 347—§ 3, 16

State v. Manchester, 213 Neb. 670, 331 N.W.2d 776 (1983)

24 ALR6th 1—§ 7

27 ALR6th 183—§ 28, 30

State v. Mancinone, 15 Conn. App. 251, 545 A.2d 1131 (1988)

111 ALR5th 239—§ 7

112 ALR5th 429—§ 17

State v. Manes, 961 S.W.2d 889 (Mo. Ct. App. S.D. 1998)

72 ALR5th 403—§ 15

State v. Maness, 321 N.C. 454, 364 S.E.2d 349 (1988)

112 ALR5th 621—§ 5

State v. Mangan, 1999 WL 639246 (Minn. Ct. App. 1999)

80 ALR5th 255—§ 27

State v. Mangen, 1991 WL 216433 (Ohio Ct. App. 2d Dist. Darke County 1991)

54 ALR6th 593—§ 15

State v. Mangino, 108 N.J.L. 475, 156 A. 430 (N.J. Ct. Err. & App. 1931)

97 ALR6th 567—§ 3, 9

State v. Mangrella, 214 N.J. Super. 437, 519 A.2d 926 (1986)

7 ALR5th 263—§ 7

State v. Mangrum, 675 So. 2d 1150 (La. App. 1st Cir. 1996)

50 ALR5th 581—§ 9, 20

State v. Mangum, 30 N.C. App. 311, 226 S.E.2d 852 (1976)

9 ALR6th 1—§ 4

State v. Maniatty, 2003 WL 25745701 (Vt. 2003)

56 ALR6th 323—§ 7

State v. Maniccia, 355 N.W.2d 256 (Iowa Ct. App. 1984)

24 ALR6th 1—§ 6

State v. Manke, 230 Wis. 2d 421, 602 N.W.2d 139 (Ct. App. 1999)

9 ALR6th 633—§ 4, 13, 17, 26

13 ALR6th 603—§ 19, 43

State v. Mankel, 27 Ariz. App. 436, 555 P.2d 1124 (Div. 2 1976)

64 ALR5th 637—§ 5

58 ALR6th 499—§ 39, 97, 107

State v. Manley, 71 Ohio St. 3d 342, 643 N.E.2d 1107 (1994)

27 ALR5th 593—§ 17

State v. Manley, 2002-Ohio-5582, 2002 WL 31323328 (Ohio Ct. App. 3d Dist. Allen County 2002)
3 ALR6th 543—§ 10

State v. Manly, 85 Wash. 2d 120, 530 P.2d 306 (1975)
59 ALR5th 615—§ 3, 4, 6, 10

State v. Mann, 23 S.W.3d 824 (Mo. Ct. App. W.D. 2000)
79 ALR6th 125—§ 3, 8

State v. Mann, 83 Mo. 589 (1884)
11 ALR5th 831—§ 5, 6

State v. Mann, 119 R.I. 720, 382 A.2d 1319 (1978)
13 ALR5th 1—§ 2, 24

State v. Mann, 123 Wis. 2d 375, 367 N.W.2d 209, 79 A.L.R.6th 731 (1985)
79 ALR6th 325—§ 3, 12

State v. Mann, 132 N.J. 410, 625 A.2d 1102 (1993)
73 ALR5th 615—§ 2, 3, 8, 9
39 ALR6th 257—§ 17

State v. Mann, 274 Kan. 670, 56 P.3d 212 (2002)
3 ALR6th 543—§ 8

State v. Mann, 440 So. 2d 406 (Fla. Dist. Ct. App. 4th Dist. 1983)
64 ALR5th 637—§ 4

State v. Mann, 512 N.W.2d 528 (Iowa 1994)
38 ALR5th 433—§ 26

State v. Manning, 74 Ohio App. 3d 19, 598 N.E.2d 25 (9th Dist.Lorain County 1991)
58 ALR5th 749—§ 9

State v. Manning, 146 N.J. Super. 589, 370 A.2d 499 (App. Div. 1977)
66 ALR5th 397—§ 14

State v. Manning, 396 So. 2d 219 (Fla. Dist. Ct. App. 4th Dist. 1981)
85 ALR5th 1—§ 33

State v. Manning, 532 N.W.2d 244 (Minn. App. 1995)
36 ALR5th 161—§ 3

State v. Manning, 532 N.W.2d 244 (Minn. Ct. App. 1995)
63 ALR6th 351—§ 3

State v. Manning, 534 S.E.2d 219 (N.C. Ct. App. 2000)
12 ALR5th 89—§ 4

State v. Manning, 885 So. 2d 1044 (La. 2004)
9 ALR6th 1—§ 17

State v. Manocchio, 743 A.2d 555 (R.I. 2000)
69 ALR6th 1—§ 21
70 ALR6th 1—§ 5

State v. Manos, 237 Ga. App. 699, 516 S.E.2d 548 (1999)
116 ALR5th 479—§ 5

State v. Manry, 56 S.W.3d 806 (Tex. App. Texarkana 2001)
103 ALR5th 463—§ 5

State v. Mansfield, 38 La. Ann. 563, 1886 WL 4360 (1886)
105 ALR5th 529—§ 11

State v. Mantich, 287 Neb. 320, 842 N.W.2d 716 (2014)
102 ALR6th 637—§ 3, 4, 6

State v. Manuel, 213 Wis. 2d 308, 570 N.W.2d 601 (Ct. App. 1997)
80 ALR6th 239—§ 3, 17

State v. Manuel, 229 Ariz. 1, 270 P.3d 828 (2011)
79 ALR6th 1—§ 26, 32, 71

State v. Manuel, 253 La. 195, 217 So. 2d 369 (1968)
9 ALR6th 1—§ 6

State v. Manuel, 408 So. 2d 1235 (La. 1982)
19 ALR6th 115—§ 4, 9, 10
55 ALR6th 157—§ 117

State v. Manuel, 426 So. 2d 140 (La. 1983)
104 ALR5th 229—§ 6

State v. Manussier, 129 Wash. 2d 652, 921 P.2d 473 (1996)
9 ALR6th 177—§ 61
63 ALR6th 1—§ 5, 38

State v. Manzella, 392 So. 2d 403 (La. 1980)
103 ALR5th 463—§ 3

State v. M.A.P., 1996 WL 668127 (Wash. Ct. App. Div. 3 1996)
73 ALR5th 383—§ 5

State v. Maple, 2002-Ohio-1595, 2002 WL 507530 (Ohio Ct. App. 4th Dist. Ross County 2002)
65 ALR6th 537—§ 10

State v. Maravola, 29 Ohio Op. 2d 412, 93 Ohio L. Abs. 341, 198 N.E.2d 88 (Ct. App. 7th Dist. Trumbull County 1963)
89 ALR6th 565—§ 28

State v. Marble, 21 Kan. App. 2d 509, 901 P.2d 521 (1995)
82 ALR5th 359—§ 5
84 ALR5th 487—§ 28

State v. Marbury, 104 Ohio App. 3d 179, 661 N.E.2d 271 (Cuyahoga Co. 1995)
15 ALR5th 391—§ 45

State v. Marbury, 2004-Ohio-1817, 2004 WL 758404 (Ohio Ct. App. 2d Dist. Montgomery County 2004)
7 ALR6th 233—§ 5

State v. Marcal, 388 So. 2d 656 (La. 1980)
42 ALR5th 581—§ 16

State v. Marcel, 67 So. 3d 1223 (Fla. 3d DCA 2011)
77 ALR6th 197—§ 5

State v. Marchand, 31 N.J. 223, 156 A.2d 245, 87 A.L.R.2d 883 (1959)
85 ALR5th 187—§ 21

State v. Marchand, 104 Wash. 2d 434, 706 P.2d 225 (1985)
82 ALR5th 103—§ 3
116 ALR5th 479—§ 5

State v. Marchiani, 336 N.J. Super. 541, 765 A.2d 765 (App. Div. 2001)
63 ALR6th 303—§ 8

State v. Marcial S., 104 Conn. App. 361, 935 A.2d 154 (2007)
40 ALR6th 1—§ 13

State v. Marco, 220 Neb. 96, 368 N.W.2d 470 (1985)
3 ALR6th 269—§ 9, 22, 24

State v. Marconi, 113 N.H. 426, 309 A.2d 505 (1973)
50 ALR5th 703—§ 38

State v. Marcotte, 123 N.H. 245, 459 A.2d 278 (1983)
6 ALR6th 533—§ 21

State v. Marcotte, 124 N.H. 61, 466 A.2d 949 (1983)
112 ALR5th 621—§ 3, 5

State v. Marcotte, 418 A.2d 1118, 8 A.L.R.4th 1059 (Me. 1980)
57 ALR6th 445—§ 35

State v. Marcum, 149 Wash. App. 894, 205 P.3d 969 (Div. 1 2009)
56 ALR6th 323—§ 6

State v. Marcus, 104 Ariz. 231, 450 P.2d 689 (1969)
13 ALR5th 1—§ 25

State v. Marcus, 294 N.J. Super. 267, 683 A.2d 221 (App. Div. 1996)
90 ALR5th 453—§ 49

State v. Marcus, 2002-Ohio-970, 2002 WL 368644 (Ohio Ct. App. 8th Dist. Cuyahoga County 2002)
69 ALR6th 1—§ 29

State v. Maready, 362 N.C. 614, 669 S.E.2d 564 (2008)
84 ALR6th 293—§ 7, 19

State v. Mares, 2014 WY 126, 335 P.3d 487 (Wyo. 2014)
102 ALR6th 637—§ 3, 6

State v. Marhoun, 323 N.W.2d 729 (Minn. 1982)
29 ALR6th 1—§ 10

State v. Mariano, 152 Conn. 85, 203 A.2d 305 (1964)
85 ALR5th 1—§ 44

State v. Marinello, 49 So. 3d 488 (La. Ct. App. 3d Cir. 2010)
94 ALR6th 579—§ 6

State v. Marini, 638 A.2d 507 (R.I. 1994)
33 ALR5th 571—§ 3
29 ALR6th 1—§ 10

State v. Marin Municipal Water Dist., 17 Cal. 2d 699, 111 P.2d 651 (1941)
11 ALR5th 630—§ 4

State v. Marino, 804 So. 2d 47 (La. Ct. App. 4th Cir. 2001)
122 ALR5th 439—§ 3

For assistance, call 1-800-328-4880

State v. Marintorres, 93 Wash. App. 442, 969 P.2d 501 (Div. 2 1999)

32 ALR5th 149—§ 45

State v. Marion, 29 Kan. App. 2d 287, 27 P.3d 924 (2001)

23 ALR6th 307—§ 38

State v. Marion, 126 N.C. App. 58, 483 S.E.2d 447 (1997)

9 ALR6th 1—§ 8

State v. Marise, 2005 WL 589813 (Tenn. Crim. App. 2005)

26 ALR6th 511—§ 25

State v. Mark, 36 Wash. App. 428, 675 P.2d 1250 (1984)

15 ALR5th 391—§ 27

State v. Mark, 120 Haw. 499, 210 P.3d 22 (Ct. App. 2009)

84 ALR6th 89—§ 3

State v. Mark, 2013-1110 La. App. 4 Cir. 7/30/14, 2014 WL 3747597 (La. Ct. App. 4th Cir. 2014)

99 ALR6th 113—§ 11

State v. Marker, 1999 WL 692410 (Ohio Ct. App. 3d Dist. Seneca County 1999)

78 ALR5th 489—§ 9

State v. Markham, 159 Wash. App. 1034, 2011 WL 300186 (Div. 2 2011)

79 ALR6th 1—§ 26, 39

State v. Marko, 36 Ohio App. 2d 114, 65 Ohio Op. 2d 134, 303 N.E.2d 94 (10th Dist. Franklin County 1973)

6 ALR6th 533—§ 21

State v. Marko, 36 Ohio App. 2d 114, 65 Ohio Ops. 2d 134, 303 N.E.2d 94 (Franklin Co. 1973)

41 ALR5th 171—§ 16, 132

State v. Markovitz, 1998 WL 852653 (Ohio Ct. App. 9th Dist. Medina County 1998)

78 ALR5th 489—§ 10

State v. Markowitz, 273 A.D.2d 637, 710 N.Y.S.2d 407 (3d Dep't 2000)

119 ALR5th 205—§ 5

State v. Markowitz, 710 N.Y.S.2d 407 (App. Div. 3d Dep't 2000)

11 ALR5th 388—§ 9

State v. Marks, 29 Conn. L. Rptr. 660, 2000 WL 33298878 (Conn. Super. Ct. 2000)

84 ALR6th 293—§ 38

State v. Marks, 503 So. 2d 32 (La. App. 1st Cir. 1986)

18 ALR5th 1—§ 3

State v. Marks, 758 So. 2d 1131 (Fla. Dist. Ct. App. 4th Dist. 2000)

9 ALR6th 363—§ 3

State v. Marks, 2009-Ohio-3790, 2009 WL 2356812 (Ohio Ct. App. 11th Dist. Ashtabula County 2009)

64 ALR6th 1—§ 9

State v. Markus, 478 N.W.2d 405 (Iowa Ct. App. 1991)

84 ALR6th 293—§ 15, 38

State v. Marler, 428 So. 2d 954 (La. Ct. App. 1st Cir. 1983)

108 ALR5th 593—§ 11

State v. Marley, 54 Haw. 450, 509 P.2d 1095 (1973)

66 ALR5th 135—§ 42

State v. Marley, 54 Hawaii 450, 509 P.2d 1095 (1973)

3 ALR5th 521—§ 10, 21

State v. Marlin, 2005-Ohio-3691, 2005 WL 1705742 (Ohio Ct. App. 8th Dist. Cuyahoga County 2005)

26 ALR6th 511—§ 19

State v. Marlow, 310 N.C. 507, 313 S.E.2d 532 (1984)

16 ALR6th 329—§ 4
24 ALR6th 591—§ 6, 14
54 ALR6th 429—§ 17

State v. Marlow, 1996 WL 84627 (Ohio Ct. App. 9th Dist. Summit County 1996)

17 ALR6th 327—§ 12

State v. Marquart, 123 N.M. 809, 1997-NMCA- 090, 945 P.2d 1027 (Ct. App. 1997)

19 ALR5th 470—§ 3
99 ALR5th 557—§ 3

State v. Marquart, 123 N.M. 809, 1997-NMCA-090, 945 P.2d 1027 (Ct. App. 1997)

92 ALR6th 1—§ 8

State v. Marquez, 124 N.M. 409, 1998-NMCA-010, 951 P.2d 1070 (Ct. App. 1997)

82 ALR6th 373—§ 4, 9

State v. Marquez, 139 Or. App. 379, 912 P.2d 390 (1996)

15 ALR5th 391—§ 9

87 ALR6th 1—§ 55

State v. Marquez-Sosa, 161 Ariz. 500, 779 P.2d 815 (Ct. App. Div. 1 1989)

75 ALR6th 541—§ 16

State v. Marr, 316 N.W.2d 176 (Iowa 1982)

39 ALR5th 283—§ 10, 68

State v. Marra, 222 Conn. 506, 610 A.2d 1113 (1992)

56 ALR6th 185—§ 27, 32

State v. Marra, 295 Conn. 74, 988 A.2d 865 (2010)

72 ALR6th 227—§ 51

State v. Marra, 2008 WL 4925940 (Conn. Super. Ct. 2008)

73 ALR6th 49—§ 58

State v. Marsala, 216 Conn. 150, 579 A.2d 58 (1990)

19 ALR5th 470—§ 3, 12

State v. Marsh, 1 Or. App. 351, 462 P.2d 459 (1969)

11 ALR5th 52—§ 4, 11

State v. Marsh, 16 Kan. App. 2d 377, 823 P.2d 823 (1991)

77 ALR6th 393—§ 31, 78, 80, 82

State v. Marsh, 106 Wash. App. 801, 24 P.3d 1127, 94 A.L.R.5th 753 (Div. 3 2001)

94 ALR5th 537—§ 5

State v. Marsh, 120 Neb. 287, 232 N.W. 99, 72 A.L.R. 285 (1930)

14 ALR6th 543—§ 46

State v. Marsh, 187 Or. App. 47, 66 P.3d 541 (2003)

45 ALR6th 435—§ 12

State v. Marsh, 234 N.C. 101, 66 S.E.2d 684 (1951)

73 ALR5th 615—§ 2, 3, 9

State v. Marsh, 1985 WL 7752 (Ohio Ct. App. 12th Dist. Warren County 1985)

3 ALR6th 269—§ 25

State v. Marsh, 1999 WL 682622 (Ohio Ct. App. 1st Dist. Hamilton County 1999)

84 ALR6th 293—§ 33

State v. Marsh, 2006 WL 2009033 (N.J. Super. Ct. App. Div. 2006)

26 ALR6th 511—§ 25

State v. Marshall, 5 N.C. App. 476, 168 S.E.2d 487 (1969)

5 ALR5th 243—§ 6

State v. Marshall, 45 N.H. 281, 1864 WL 1524 (1864)

5 ALR6th 1—§ 40

State v. Marshall, 60 Ohio App. 2d 371, 14 Ohio Op. 3d 325, 397 N.E.2d 777 (1st Dist. Hamilton County 1979)

69 ALR6th 1—§ 34

State v. Marshall, 88 Wash. App. 1024, 1997 WL 724978 (Div. 2 1997)

88 ALR5th 121—§ 14, 36

State v. Marshall, 94 N.C. App. 20, 380 S.E.2d 360 (1989)

109 ALR5th 99—§ 8

State v. Marshall, 123 N.J. 1, 586 A.2d 85 (1991)

56 ALR6th 185—§ 39

State v. Marshall, 148 N.J. 89, 690 A.2d 1 (1997)

24 ALR6th 1—§ 13

28 ALR6th 505—§ 9

32 ALR6th 1—§ 11

State v. Marshall, 166 Conn. 593, 353 A.2d 756 (1974)

55 ALR6th 157—§ 33

State v. Marshall, 193 Ariz. 547, 975 P.2d 137 (Ct. App. Div. 2 1998)

90 ALR5th 453—§ 28

State v. Marshall, 204 Wis. 2d 279, 554 N.W.2d 685 (Ct. App. 1996)

57 ALR5th 315—§ 11

State v. Marshall, 246 Conn. 799, 717 A.2d 1224 (1998)

39 ALR6th 257—§ 23, 27

State v. Marshall, 410 S.W.3d 663 (Mo. Ct. App. S.D. 2013)

93 ALR6th 275—§ 4

State v. Marshall, 541 N.W.2d 330 (Minn. Ct. App. 1995)
57 ALR6th 445—§ 3, 9

State v. Marshall, 642 N.W.2d 48 (Minn. Ct. App. 2002)
20 ALR6th 479—§ 3, 21

State v. Marshall, 660 So. 2d 819 (La. 1995)
102 ALR5th 327—§ 5

State v. Marshall, 821 S.W.2d 550 (Mo. App. 1991)
6 ALR5th 733—§ 10, 18

State v. Marshall, 1994 WL 47678 (Ohio Ct. App. 2d Dist. Darke County 1994)
88 ALR5th 121—§ 35

State v. Marshall, 2005 WL 1457835 (Tenn. Crim. App. 2005)
26 ALR6th 511—§ 22

State v. Marshall, 2010 WL 286773 (Ariz. Ct. App. Div. 1 2010)
58 ALR6th 499—§ 117
78 ALR6th 297—§ 47

State v. Marshfield, 122 Or. 323, 259 P. 201 (1927)
17 ALR5th 547—§ 30

State v. Martel, 273 Mont. 143, 902 P.2d 14 (1995)
29 ALR5th 487—§ 3

State v. Martellano, 116 Wis. 2d 696, 343 N.W.2d 827 (Ct. App. 1983)
62 ALR6th 259—§ 14

State v. Martens, 90 Ohio App. 3d 338, 629 N.E.2d 462 (3d Dist. Mercer County 1993)
90 ALR5th 453—§ 17

State v. Martens, 521 N.W.2d 768 (Iowa Ct. App. 1994)
100 ALR6th 535—§ 3

State v. Martens, 569 N.W.2d 482 (Iowa 1997)
12 ALR5th 89—§ 22

State v. Martin, 17 P.3d 72 (Alaska Ct. App. 2001)
36 ALR5th 161—§ 16.5
93 ALR6th 1—§ 41

State v. Martin, 21 Ohio St. 3d 91, 21 Ohio B.R. 386, 488 N.E.2d 166 (1986)
26 ALR5th 603—§ 4

State v. Martin, 32 Kan. App. 2d 642, 87 P.3d 337 (2004)
125 ALR5th 537—§ 49

State v. Martin, 33 P.3d 495 (Alaska Ct. App. 2001)
63 ALR6th 351—§ 4

State v. Martin, 38 Conn. App. 731, 663 A.2d 1078 (1995)
39 ALR6th 257—§ 4, 5

State v. Martin, 47 N.C. App. 223, 267 S.E.2d 35 (1980)
39 ALR5th 283—§ 4

State v. Martin, 56 Or. App. 639, 642 P.2d 1196 (1982)
15 ALR5th 391—§ 39
92 ALR5th 35—§ 21

State v. Martin, 59 Ohio St. 212, 52 N.E. 188 (1898)
97 ALR5th 293—§ 4

State v. Martin, 64 Or. App. 469, 668 P.2d 479 (1983)
26 ALR5th 603—§ 4

State v. Martin, 68 N.C. App. 272, 314 S.E.2d 805 (1984)
72 ALR5th 109—§ 4

State v. Martin, 73 Wash. 2d 616, 440 P.2d 429 (1968)
26 ALR5th 1—§ 3, 8, 12, 24

State v. Martin, 77 Conn. App. 778, 825 A.2d 835 (2003)
72 ALR6th 437—§ 5, 8, 11

State v. Martin, 101 N.M. 595, 686 P.2d 937 (1984)
45 ALR5th 531—§ 10
55 ALR6th 391—§ 17

State v. Martin, 102 Haw. 273, 75 P.3d 724 (Ct. App. 2003)
9 ALR6th 633—§ 4, 13
9 ALR6th 693—§ 7, 8, 19, 20
12 ALR6th 389—§ 15
15 ALR6th 173—§ 5, 10

State v. Martin, 137 Wash. 2d 774, 975 P.2d 1020 (1999)

93 ALR5th 327—§ 3, 4, 9
101 ALR5th 619—§ 3
State v. Martin, 154 Wis. 2d 523, 454 N.W.2d 809 (App. 1990)
36 ALR5th 255—§ 29
State v. Martin, 158 Wis. 2d 732, 463 N.W.2d 882 (Ct. App. 1990)
59 ALR6th 311—§ 3
State v. Martin, 182 Vt. 377, 2007 VT 96, 944 A.2d 867, 47 A.L.R.6th 591 (2007)
47 ALR6th 107—§ 3, 11, 57, 78
State v. Martin, 190 Neb. 212, 206 N.W.2d 856 (1973)
29 ALR5th 59—§ 3, 18
State v. Martin, 193 Ind. 120, 139 N.E. 282, 26 A.L.R. 1386 (1923)
11 ALR5th 715—§ 3, 4
State v. Martin, 234 Kan. 548, 673 P.2d 104 (1983)
16 ALR6th 329—§ 5
19 ALR6th 115—§ 7
24 ALR6th 591—§ 4, 12, 15
State v. Martin, 239 Neb. 339, 476 N.W.2d 536 (1991)
63 ALR5th 375—§ 2, 7
State v. Martin, 250 La. 991, 200 So. 2d 871 (1967)
5 ALR6th 1—§ 18, 43
State v. Martin, 252 N.W.2d 438 (Iowa 1977)
13 ALR5th 118—§ 2
State v. Martin, 255 La. 961, 233 So. 2d 898 (1970)
36 ALR5th 255—§ 33
State v. Martin, 261 N.W.2d 341 (Minn. 1977)
61 ALR5th 1—§ 3
68 ALR5th 343—§ 3, 12
State v. Martin, 274 N.W.2d 893 (S.D. 1979)
58 ALR6th 499—§ 17, 97, 98
State v. Martin, 279 Mont. 185, 926 P.2d 1380 (1996)
32 ALR6th 385—§ 5
State v. Martin, 294 N.C. 702, 242 S.E.2d 762 (1978)

29 ALR6th 1—§ 8
State v. Martin, 297 Minn. 470, 212 N.W.2d 847 (1973)
28 ALR6th 505—§ 37
State v. Martin, 376 So. 2d 300 (La. 1979)
65 ALR5th 407—§ 3
State v. Martin, 378 S.C. 113, 662 S.E.2d 406, 70 A.L.R.6th 737 (2008)
70 ALR6th 329—§ 14
State v. Martin, 400 So. 2d 1063 (La. 1981)
98 ALR6th 455—§ 32
State v. Martin, 458 So. 2d 454 (La. 1984)
57 ALR5th 141—§ 2, 3
State v. Martin, 483 So. 2d 1223 (La. Ct. App. 4th Cir. 1986)
88 ALR5th 121—§ 3, 22, 33
State v. Martin, 486 So. 2d 333 (La. Ct. App. 3d Cir. 1986)
72 ALR5th 109—§ 5
State v. Martin, 525 S.W.2d 804 (Mo. Ct. App. 1975)
102 ALR6th 279—§ 13
State v. Martin, 532 P.2d 316 (Alaska 1975)
52 ALR6th 125—§ 14, 45
State v. Martin, 539 So. 2d 1235 (La. 1989)
84 ALR6th 427—§ 8
89 ALR6th 565—§ 29
State v. Martin, 543 N.W.2d 224 (N.D. 1996)
34 ALR6th 1—§ 12
State v. Martin, 551 So. 2d 600 (Fla. Dist. Ct. App. 4th Dist. 1989)
113 ALR5th 597—§ 8
State v. Martin, 553 A.2d 1264 (Me. 1989)
67 ALR6th 531—§ 37
State v. Martin, 562 So. 2d 468 (La. App. 5th Cir. 1990)
3 ALR5th 784—§ 8, 10, 12, 20
State v. Martin, 562 So. 2d 468 (La. Ct. App. 5th Cir. 1990)
7 ALR6th 233—§ 4

State v. Martin, 595 N.W.2d 214 (Minn. Ct. App. 1999)

92 ALR6th 1—§ 5, 9

State v. Martin, 607 So. 2d 775 (La. Ct. App. 1st Cir. 1992)

37 ALR5th 515—§ 9, 19, 22

96 ALR5th 523—§ 3

9 ALR6th 1—§ 10

State v. Martin, 624 So. 2d 448 (La. Ct. App. 4th Cir. 1993)

99 ALR6th 295—§ 19

State v. Martin, 624 S.W.2d 879 (Mo. Ct. App. E.D. 1981)

99 ALR6th 295—§ 5, 10

State v. Martin, 635 So. 2d 1036 (Fla. Dist. Ct. App. 3d Dist. 1994)

65 ALR5th 407—§ 3, 8, 11

State v. Martin, 642 S.W.2d 720 (Tenn. 1982)

83 ALR5th 277—§ 9, 11

84 ALR5th 487—§ 25

State v. Martin, 645 So. 2d 752 (La. App. 5th Cir. 1994)

48 ALR5th 555—§ 3

State v. Martin, 645 So. 2d 752 (La. Ct. App. 5th Cir. 1994)

24 ALR6th 1—§ 51

State v. Martin, 666 S.W.2d 895 (Mo. App. 1984)

11 ALR5th 871—§ 5, 7

State v. Martin, 690 N.W.2d 695 (Iowa Ct. App. 2004)

81 ALR6th 505—§ 8

State v. Martin, 695 N.W.2d 578 (Minn. 2005)

30 ALR6th 1—§ 4

State v. Martin, 719 S.W.2d 522 (Tenn. 1986)

13 ALR5th 567—§ 4

State v. Martin, 761 A.2d 516 (N.H. 2000)

19 ALR5th 470—§ 12

State v. Martin, 765 P.2d 854 (Utah 1988)

51 ALR6th 1—§ 5

72 ALR6th 141—§ 9

State v. Martin, 797 S.W.2d 758 (Mo. Ct. App. E.D. 1990)

98 ALR6th 455—§ 30

99 ALR6th 113—§ 8

State v. Martin, 1996 WL 687028 (Tenn. Crim. App. 1996)

85 ALR5th 471—§ 2, 13

State v. Martin, 2000 WL 1145465 (Ohio Ct. App. 12th Dist. Brown County 2000)

38 ALR6th 439—§ 3, 7

State v. Martin, 2003-Ohio-4058, 2003 WL 21757692 (Ohio Ct. App. 8th Dist. Cuyahoga County 2003)

78 ALR6th 297—§ 58

State v. Martin, 2003 SD 153, 674 N.W.2d 291 (S.D. 2003)

4 ALR6th 1—§ 4

State v. Martin, 2004-Ohio-3027, 2004 WL 1308549 (Ohio Ct. App. 11th Dist. Portage County 2004)

71 ALR6th 1—§ 4

State v. Martin, 2006-Ohio-3226, 2006 WL 1725956 (Ohio Ct. App. 11th Dist. Lake County 2006)

26 ALR6th 511—§ 19

State v. Martin, 2006-Ohio-5263, 2006 WL 2846289 (Ohio Ct. App. 1st Dist. Hamilton County 2006)

26 ALR6th 511—§ 19

State v. Martin, 2007-Ohio-4821, 2007 WL 2713851 (Ohio Ct. App. 5th Dist. Stark County 2007)

67 ALR6th 531—§ 29

State v. Martin, 2011-Ohio-2379, 2011 WL 2021913 (Ohio Ct. App. 9th Dist. Summit County 2011)

78 ALR6th 297—§ 52

State v. Martindale, 88 Wash. App. 1020, 1997 WL 705445 (Div. 3 1997)

15 ALR6th 515—§ 16

State v. Martindale, 2005-Ohio-6437, 2005 WL 3293762 (Ohio Ct. App. 5th Dist. Fairfield County 2005)

58 ALR6th 499—§ 30

State v. Martineau, 148 N.H. 259, 808 A.2d 51 (2002)

90 ALR6th 385—§ 7

State v. Martinez, 15 Ariz. App. 10, 485 P.2d 600 (1971)

4 ALR5th 1—§ 17, 18, 33

State v. Martinez, 20 Kan. App. 2d 824, 893 P.2d 267 (1995)

93 ALR5th 683—§ 3

State v. Martinez, 23 Utah 2d 62, 457 P.2d 613 (1969)

28 ALR6th 505—§ 9

State v. Martinez, 36 Ohio Misc. 29, 65 Ohio Op. 2d 54, 296 N.E.2d 580 (Mun. Ct. 1973)

114 ALR5th 173—§ 6

State v. Martinez, 49 Conn. App. 738, 718 A.2d 22 (1998)

65 ALR5th 407—§ 3

State v. Martinez, 51 Conn. App. 59, 719 A.2d 1213 (1998)

6 ALR6th 533—§ 3, 15

State v. Martinez, 51 Wash. App. 397, 753 P.2d 1011 (1988)

43 ALR5th 1—§ 8, 15

State v. Martinez, 59 Haw. 366, 580 P.2d 1282 (1978)

85 ALR5th 261—§ 3, 5

State v. Martinez, 67 Ariz. 389, 198 P.2d 115 (1948)

86 ALR5th 59—§ 4

State v. Martinez, 78 Wash. App. 870, 899 P.2d 1302 (Div. 2 1995)

71 ALR5th 1—§ 56
92 ALR5th 35—§ 25
56 ALR6th 185—§ 11

State v. Martinez, 86 Wash. App. 1112, 1997 WL 417950 (Div. 2 1997)

20 ALR6th 479—§ 22

State v. Martinez, 89 N.M. 729, 1976-NMCA-103, 557 P.2d 578 (Ct. App. 1976)

99 ALR6th 295—§ 5, 10

State v. Martinez, 98 N.M. 27, 644 P.2d 541 (Ct. App. 1982)

101 ALR5th 187—§ 13

State v. Martinez, 102 Idaho 875, 643 P.2d 555 (Ct. App. 1982)

24 ALR6th 1—§ 5

State v. Martinez, 116 S.W.3d 385 (Tex. App. El Paso 2003)

9 ALR6th 363—§ 47

State v. Martinez, 122 N.M. 476, 1996-NMCA-109, 927 P.2d 31 (Ct. App. 1996)

71 ALR6th 1—§ 11

State v. Martinez, 131 N.M. 254, 2001-NMCA-099, 34 P.3d 643 (Ct. App. 2001)

68 ALR6th 527—§ 5

State v. Martinez, 137 N.M. 432, 2005-NMCA-052, 112 P.3d 293 (Ct. App. 2005)

18 ALR6th 519—§ 19

State v. Martinez, 161 Wash. App. 436, 253 P.3d 445 (Div. 3 2011)

74 ALR6th 373—§ 8

State v. Martinez, 188 Mont. 271, 613 P.2d 974 (1980)

57 ALR5th 141—§ 7

State v. Martinez, 210 Wis. 2d 396, 563 N.W.2d 922 (Ct. App. 1997)

23 ALR6th 307—§ 9

State v. Martinez, 306 Ark. 353, 811 S.W.2d 319 (1991)

41 ALR5th 171—§ 12, 32, 35, 38, 68, 72, 93, 111, 113, 119

State v. Martinez, 407 S.W.3d 669 (Mo. Ct. App. S.D. 2013)

97 ALR6th 567—§ 3, 9

State v. Martinez, 579 N.W.2d 144 (Minn. Ct. App. 1998)

2 ALR6th 169—§ 3, 7
50 ALR6th 455—§ 7, 12, 18, 33

State v. Martinez, 624 A.2d 291 (R.I. 1993)

65 ALR5th 407—§ 3, 19

State v. Martinez, 670 So. 2d 1018 (Fla. Dist. Ct. App. 2d Dist. 1996)

113 ALR5th 597—§ 8

State v. Martinez, 811 P.2d 205 (Utah Ct. App. 1991)

92 ALR6th 1—§ 3

State v. Martinez, 1980-NMSC-066, 94 N.M. 436, 612 P.2d 228 (1980)

103 ALR6th 347—§ 15

State v. Martinez, 1998-NMSC-023, 126 N.M. 39, 966 P.2d 747 (1998)
  46 ALR6th 63—§ 9
State v. Martinez, 2000 UT App. 320, 2000 WL 1707785 (Utah Ct. App. 2000)
  46 ALR5th 499—§ 3
State v. Martinez, 2002 UT App 126, 47 P.3d 115 (Utah Ct. App. 2002)
  102 ALR6th 365—§ 18
State v. Martinez, 2006-Ohio-2002, 2006 WL 1062100 (Ohio Ct. App. 3d Dist. Shelby County 2006)
  62 ALR6th 161—§ 7
State v. Martinez, 2007 WL 3011054 (Conn. Super. Ct. 2007)
  72 ALR6th 227—§ 51
State v. Martini, 104 Or. App. 44, 799 P.2d 184 (1990)
  104 ALR5th 165—§ 15
State v. Martinson, 422 N.W.2d 282 (Minn. Ct. App. 1988)
  29 ALR6th 1—§ 10
State v. Martinson, 671 N.W.2d 887 (Minn. Ct. App. 2003)
  113 ALR5th 597—§ 3
State v. Martinson, 2000 WL 351191 (Neb. Ct. App. 2000)
  96 ALR6th 355—§ 24, 37
State v. Martin V., 102 Conn. App. 381, 926 A.2d 49 (2007)
  39 ALR6th 257—§ 50
State v. Martissa, 18 So. 3d 49 (Fla. Dist. Ct. App. 2d Dist. 2009)
  58 ALR6th 215—§ 20
State v. Marvin, 964 P.2d 313, 79 A.L.R.5th 783 (Utah 1998)
  79 ALR5th 419—§ 9, 10
State v. Marze, 22 N.C. App. 628, 207 S.E.2d 359 (1974)
  81 ALR5th 563—§ 5
State v. Masato Karumai, 101 Utah 592, 126 P.2d 1047 (1942)
  32 ALR5th 149—§ 4, 22, 23, 32
State v. Mascarenas, 86 N.M. 692, 526 P.2d 1285 (App. 1974)
  61 ALR5th 1—§ 4, 5

State v. Masco, 103 N.J. 277, 247 A.2d 136 (1968)
  43 ALR5th 1—§ 13
State v. Mashia, 183 Or. App. 254, 51 P.3d 711 (2002)
  97 ALR6th 653—§ 29
State v. Masino, 94 N.J. 436, 466 A.2d 955 (1983)
  39 ALR5th 283—§ 4, 66, 71
State v. Masnik, 123 N.J.L. 335, 8 A.2d 701 (N.J. Sup. Ct. 1939)
  119 ALR5th 275—§ 2
State v. Mason, 18 N.C. App. 433, 197 S.E.2d 79 (1973)
  118 ALR5th 253—§ 3
State v. Mason, 31 Wash. App. 680, 644 P.2d 710 (1982)
  38 ALR5th 433—§ 52
State v. Mason, 53 Or. App. 811, 633 P.2d 820 (1981)
  32 ALR6th 1—§ 10
State v. Mason, 90 N.J. Super. 464, 218 A.2d 158 (App. Div. 1966)
  51 ALR6th 1—§ 5
  70 ALR6th 361—§ 30
  72 ALR6th 141—§ 4, 6, 11
State v. Mason, 143 Ohio App. 3d 114, 757 N.E.2d 789 (8th Dist. Cuyahoga County 2001)
  87 ALR6th 1—§ 41
State v. Mason, 250 Kan. 393, 827 P.2d 748 (1992)
  39 ALR5th 283—§ 4
State v. Mason, 528 A.2d 1259 (Me. 1987)
  57 ALR5th 141—§ 4, 7
State v. Mason, 1997 WL 211245 (Tenn. Crim. App. 1997)
  87 ALR5th 1—§ 11, 32
State v. Mason, 2005-Ohio-2918, 2005 WL 1385221 (Ohio Ct. App. 12th Dist. Butler County 2005)
  30 ALR6th 103—§ 11, 34
State v. Mason, 2009 WL 1918722 (Minn. Ct. App. 2009)
  69 ALR6th 579—§ 8, 27
State v. Masqua, 210 Kan. 419, 502 P.2d 728 (1972)

86 ALR5th 59—§ 3 to 5, 8
State v. Massa, 95 N.J. Super. 382, 231 A.2d 252 (County Ct. 1967)

70 ALR5th 169—§ 27
State v. Massa, 242 Neb. 70, 493 N.W.2d 175 (1992)

1 ALR6th 549—§ 15
State v. Massaro, 2013 WL 1115018 (Mo. Ct. App. S.D. 2013)

84 ALR6th 293—§ 23
State v. Masse, 1 Conn. Cir. Ct. 381, 24 Conn. Supp. 45, 186 A.2d 553 (App. Div. 1962)

111 ALR5th 1—§ 3, 5, 7, 8, 26
State v. Massee, 132 Idaho 163, 968 P.2d 258 (Ct. App. 1998)

28 ALR6th 505—§ 7, 16
State v. Masselli, 43 N.J. 1, 202 A.2d 415 (1964)

51 ALR6th 1—§ 20
State v. Massenburg, 66 N.C. App. 127, 310 S.E.2d 619 (1984)

7 ALR6th 169—§ 16
State v. Massengill, 1988 WL 29812 (Ohio Ct. App. 9th Dist. Summit County 1988)

6 ALR6th 533—§ 22
State v. Massey, 34 Or. App. 95, 577 P.2d 1364 (1978)

24 ALR6th 747—§ 32, 33, 37
State v. Massey, 98 S.W.3d 105 (Mo. Ct. App. W.D. 2003)

105 ALR5th 529—§ 13
State v. Massey, 106 Or. App. 242, 806 P.2d 193 (1991)

15 ALR5th 391—§ 46
State v. Massey, 316 N.C. 558, 342 S.E.2d 811 (1986)

110 ALR5th 329—§ 5, 14
83 ALR6th 465—§ 12, 52
State v. Massey, 358 Mo. 1108, 219 S.W.2d 326 (1949)

85 ALR5th 471—§ 4
State v. Massey, 492 S.W.2d 48 (Mo. Ct. App. 1973)

108 ALR5th 593—§ 54
State v. Massey, 763 S.W.2d 181 (Mo. Ct. App. W.D. 1988)

77 ALR5th 201—§ 9, 26
78 ALR5th 1—§ 14, 61
State v. Masten, 1989 WL 111983 (Ohio Ct. App. 3d Dist. Hancock County 1989)

65 ALR5th 407—§ 2, 8, 17
State v. Masters, 106 W. Va. 46, 144 S.E. 718 (1928)

26 ALR5th 1—§ 3
State v. Masters, 216 Neb. 304, 343 N.W.2d 744 (1984)

114 ALR5th 173—§ 7
State v. Mastin, 83 Ohio App. 3d 814, 615 N.E.2d 1084 (3d Dist. Auglaize County 1992)

70 ALR6th 1—§ 5
State v. Mastracchio, 546 A.2d 165 (R.I. 1988)

46 ALR5th 735—§ 2
State v. Mastracchio, 605 A.2d 489 (R.I. 1992)

37 ALR5th 703—§ 3
State v. Mastracchio, 721 A.2d 844 (R.I. 1998)

85 ALR5th 1—§ 19
State v. Mastrofine, 551 A.2d 1174 (R.I. 1988)

93 ALR5th 527—§ 4
State v. Mastronardi, 1997 WL 771575 (Ohio Ct. App. 6th Dist. Erie County 1997)

47 ALR6th 107—§ 3, 31, 48, 64, 73
State v. Masuleh, 1999 WL 55496 (Minn. Ct. App. 1999)

73 ALR5th 383—§ 4
State v. Mata, 71 Hawaii 319, 789 P.2d 1122 (1990)

54 ALR5th 575—§ 15
State v. Mata, 230 Wis. 2d 567, 602 N.W.2d 158 (Ct. App. 1999)

1 ALR6th 371—§ 4
State v. Mata, 266 Neb. 668, 668 N.W.2d 448 (2003)

32 ALR6th 1—§ 9
State v. Matafeo, 71 Haw. 183, 787 P.2d 671 (1990)

55 ALR6th 391—§ 5

For assistance, call 1-800-328-4880

State v. Matafeo, 71 Hawaii 183, 787 P.2d 671 (1990)

40 ALR5th 113—§ 4

State v. Matarama, 306 N.J. Super. 6, 703 A.2d 278 (App. Div. 1997)

39 ALR5th 283—§ 25

100 ALR5th 67—§ 11, 44

State v. Mathe, 35 Wash. App. 572, 668 P.2d 599 (Div. 1 1983)

61 ALR5th 1—§ 3, 12

State v. Mathenia, 135 P.3d 766 (Kan. 2006)

26 ALR6th 511—§ 25

State v. Mathers, 64 Vt. 101, 23 A. 590 (1892)

51 ALR5th 603—§ 2, 3, 14

State v. Matheson, 110 N.C. App. 577, 430 S.E.2d 429 (1993)

86 ALR5th 59—§ 4

State v. Matheson, 130 Iowa 440, 103 N.W. 137 (1905)

116 ALR5th 373—§ 3, 9

State v. Mathews, 133 Idaho 300, 986 P.2d 323 (1999)

72 ALR6th 1—§ 18

State v. Mathews, 809 So. 2d 1002 (La. Ct. App. 1st Cir. 2001)

16 ALR6th 329—§ 4

24 ALR6th 591—§ 4, 6, 14

State v. Mathis, 59 Conn. App. 416, 757 A.2d 55 (2000)

27 ALR5th 593—§ 36

State v. Mathis, 293 N.C. 660, 239 S.E.2d 245 (1977)

72 ALR5th 109—§ 5

State v. Mathis, 427 S.W.2d 450 (Mo. 1968)

19 ALR5th 823—§ 16, 18

State v. Mathis, 1993 WL 452038 (Ohio Ct. App. 6th Dist. Lucas County 1993)

35 ALR6th 127—§ 22

State v. Mathis, 2004-Ohio-6749, 2004 WL 2896471 (Ohio Ct. App. 9th Dist. Summit County 2004)

17 ALR6th 327—§ 20

State v. Matias, 51 Haw. 62, 451 P.2d 257 (1969)

68 ALR5th 343—§ 5

State v. Matlock, 289 N.W.2d 625 (Iowa 1980)

35 ALR6th 127—§ 5

State v. Matos, 2004 WI App 88, 272 Wis. 2d 854, 679 N.W.2d 926 (Ct. App. 2004)

95 ALR6th 219—§ 15

State v. Matsamas, 808 P.2d 1048 (Utah 1991)

71 ALR5th 637—§ 7

State v. Matson, 14 Kan. App. 2d 632, 798 P.2d 488 (1990)

12 ALR5th 89—§ 7, 8

State v. Matson, 22 Wash. App. 114, 587 P.2d 540 (1978)

34 ALR5th 125—§ 14

State v. Matson, 120 Or. 666, 253 P. 527 (1927)

54 ALR6th 429—§ 22

State v. Matson, 260 Kan. 366, 921 P.2d 790 (1996)

37 ALR5th 515—§ 3

State v. Matsunaga, 82 Haw. 162, 920 P.2d 376 (Ct. App. 1996)

104 ALR5th 165—§ 5

State v. Matsunami, 1981 WL 9970 (Ohio Ct. App. 1st Dist. Hamilton County 1981)

116 ALR5th 149—§ 11

State v. Matt, 251 Or. 134, 444 P.2d 914 (1968)

9 ALR6th 1—§ 20

State v. Mattachione, 2004-Ohio-6058, 2004 WL 2588390 (Ohio Ct. App. 2d Dist. Greene County 2004)

70 ALR6th 1—§ 5

State v. Mattan, 207 Neb. 679, 300 N.W.2d 810 (1981)

34 ALR6th 1—§ 12

State v. Mattes, 175 Wis. 2d 572, 499 N.W.2d 711, Blue Sky L. Rep. (CCH) ¶ 73822 (Ct. App. 1993)

92 ALR5th 35—§ 7

State v. Mattheson, 407 So. 2d 1150 (La. 1981)

10 ALR5th 700—§ 16

62 ALR5th 1—§ 8, 14

State v. Matthews, 29 Colo. App. 143, 480 P.2d 593 (1971)
14 ALR6th 119—§ 32

State v. Matthews, 80 Ohio App. 3d 409, 609 N.E.2d 574 (8th Dist. Cuyahoga County 1992)
12 ALR6th 267—§ 12

State v. Matthews, 159 Or. App. 580, 978 P.2d 423 (1999)
36 ALR5th 161—§ 3
33 ALR6th 91—§ 6
63 ALR6th 351—§ 3

State v. Matthews, 173 Tenn. 302, 117 S.W.2d 2 (1938)
5 ALR6th 1—§ 16, 31

State v. Matthews, 291 S.C. 339, 353 S.E.2d 444 (1986)
50 ALR5th 467—§ 8, 9

State v. Matthews, 408 So. 2d 1274 (La. 1982)
96 ALR5th 327—§ 3

State v. Matthews, 552 So. 2d 590 (La. Ct. App. 2d Cir. 1989)
109 ALR5th 99—§ 3

State v. Matthews, 654 So. 2d 868 (La. App. 4th Cir. 1995)
50 ALR5th 581—§ 20

State v. Matthews, 720 So. 2d 153 (La. Ct. App. 5th Cir. 1998)
43 ALR6th 475—§ 10

State v. Matthews, 1989 WL 135731 (Del. Super. Ct. 1989)
100 ALR6th 535—§ 3

State v. Matthews, 1996 WL 684328 (Ohio Ct. App. 8th Dist. Cuyahoga County 1996)
68 ALR5th 343—§ 5

State v. Matthews, 2003 ND 108, 665 N.W.2d 28 (N.D. 2003)
58 ALR6th 499—§ 45

State v. Matthews, Slip Op. C.A. No. S-84-24 (Ohio App. Sandusky Co. 1985)
38 ALR5th 433—§ 6

State v. Matthieu, 527 So. 2d 530 (La. App. 3d Cir. 1988)
36 ALR5th 255—§ 7, 31

State v. Matthis, 59 N.C. App. 233, 296 S.E.2d 20 (1982)
70 ALR5th 587—§ 6

State v. Mattila, 77 Or. App. 219, 712 P.2d 832 (1986)
66 ALR5th 397—§ 3, 5, 12

State v. Mattingly, 23 Or. App. 173, 541 P.2d 1063 (1975)
7 ALR5th 758—§ 17

State v. Mattingly, 573 S.W.2d 372 (Mo. Ct. App. 1978)
70 ALR5th 587—§ 3

State v. Mattison, 1995 WL 479635 (Minn. Ct. App. 1995)
84 ALR6th 293—§ 18

State v. Mattix, 2003-Ohio-2383, 2003 WL 21054738 (Ohio Ct. App. 3d Dist. Wyandot County 2003)
89 ALR6th 565—§ 29, 31, 33

State v. Mattox, 13 Ohio App. 3d 52, 13 Ohio B.R. 55, 468 N.E.2d 353 (Champaign Co. 1983)
45 ALR5th 1—§ 3, 7, 8, 22

State v. Mattson, 140 Wis. 2d 24, 409 N.W.2d 138 (App. 1987)
52 ALR5th 655—§ 2, 3, 8

State v. Matulewicz, 101 N.J. 27, 499 A.2d 1363 (1985)
111 ALR5th 1—§ 3, 5, 27

State v. Matute, 2010 WL 4074489 (N.J. Super. Ct. App. Div. 2010)
69 ALR6th 579—§ 11

State v. Maudlin, 416 N.E.2d 477 (Ind. Ct. App. 1st Dist. 1981)
15 ALR6th 1—§ 4, 9, 10, 18

State v. Maugaotega, 107 Haw. 399, 114 P.3d 905 (2005)
26 ALR6th 511—§ 13

State v. Maugeri, 589 So. 2d 896, 16 FLW S. 663 (Fla. 1991)
18 ALR5th 1—§ 12

State v. Maupin, 166 Ariz. 250, 801 P.2d 485 (Ct. App. Div. 1 1990)
92 ALR5th 35—§ 19

State v. Maurer, 15 Ohio St. 3d 239, 15 Ohio B.R. 379, 473 N.E.2d 768 (1984)
39 ALR5th 283—§ 14

State v. Mauro, 149 Ariz. 24, 716 P.2d 393 (1986)
119 ALR5th 275—§ 7

State v. Mauro, 159 Ariz. 186, 766 P.2d 59, 23 Ariz. Adv. Rep. 3 (1988)
57 ALR5th 141—§ 3, 7

State v. Maurstad, 706 N.W.2d 545 (Minn. Ct. App. 2005)
26 ALR6th 511—§ 26

State v. Mauthe, 142 Wis. 2d 620, 419 N.W.2d 279 (Ct. App. 1987)
88 ALR5th 493—§ 4
89 ALR5th 1—§ 5

State v. Max, 1 NCA 1571, 492 N.W.2d 887 (1992)
38 ALR5th 433—§ 11

State v. Maxey, 63 Wash. App. 488, 820 P.2d 515 (Div. 2 1991)
92 ALR6th 295—§ 12
96 ALR6th 355—§ 17

State v. Maxfield, 30 Kan. App. 2d 873, 54 P.3d 500 (2001)
16 ALR6th 329—§ 3
19 ALR6th 115—§ 3
24 ALR6th 591—§ 3

State v. Maxfield, 125 Wash. 2d 378, 886 P.2d 123 (1994)
60 ALR5th 1—§ 8

State v. Maxie, 693 S.W.2d 161 (Mo. App. 1985)
5 ALR5th 243—§ 60

State v. Maximo, 170 Ariz. 94, 821 P.2d 1379 (Ct. App. Div. 2 1991)
55 ALR5th 125—§ 3

State v. Maxon, 110 Wash. 2d 564, 756 P.2d 1297 (1988)
62 ALR5th 629—§ 4

State v. Maxwell, 10 Kan. App. 2d 62, 691 P.2d 1316 (1984)
1 ALR6th 549—§ 8
64 ALR6th 655—§ 18

State v. Maxwell, 50 N.J. Super. 298, 142 A.2d 108 (1958)
5 ALR5th 243—§ 62

State v. Maxwell, 74 Wash. App. 688, 878 P.2d 1220 (Div. 3 1994)
72 ALR5th 607—§ 7

State v. Maxwell, 234 Kan. 393, 672 P.2d 590 (1983)
17 ALR5th 125—§ 3
39 ALR5th 283—§ 4, 22, 23

State v. Maxwell, 647 So. 2d 871 (Fla. Dist. Ct. App. 4th Dist. 1994)
79 ALR5th 33—§ 3, 9, 12, 16, 27

State v. Maxwell, 776 P.2d 836 (Kan. App. 1989)
12 ALR5th 89—§ 5

State v. May, 72 Ohio App. 3d 664, 595 N.E.2d 980 (8th Dist. Cuyahoga County 1991)
70 ALR6th 1—§ 5

State v. May, 93 Idaho 343, 461 P.2d 126 (1969)
108 ALR5th 593—§ 24

State v. May, 292 N.C. 644, 235 S.E.2d 178 (1977)
93 ALR5th 527—§ 6
94 ALR5th 393—§ 13

State v. May, 703 So. 2d 1097 (Fla. Dist. Ct. App. 2d Dist. 1997)
45 ALR5th 591—§ 14

State v. May, 1992 WL 50560 (Tenn. Crim. App. 1992)
101 ALR6th 299—§ 4

State v. May, 1995 WL 23361 (Ohio Ct. App. 4th Dist. Washington County 1995)
88 ALR5th 121—§ 18, 35

State v. May, 2007-Ohio-1428, 2007 WL 914871 (Ohio Ct. App. 4th Dist. Highland County 2007)
58 ALR6th 499—§ 44

State v. May, 2012-Ohio-2766, 2012 WL 2355910 (Ohio Ct. App. 8th Dist. Cuyahoga County 2012)
101 ALR6th 545—§ 5

State v. Maya, 126 N.H. 590, 493 A.2d 1139 (1985)
81 ALR5th 563—§ 2, 6
6 ALR6th 533—§ 15

State v. Mayberry, 248 Kan. 369, 807 P.2d 86 (1991)
101 ALR6th 331—§ 10

State v. Mayberry, 415 N.W.2d 644 (Iowa 1987)

15 ALR5th 391—§ 31
42 ALR5th 465—§ 1
92 ALR5th 35—§ 15
State v. Maycock, 947 P.2d 695 (Utah Ct. App. 1997)
114 ALR5th 173—§ 7
State v. Mayer, 589 So. 2d 1145 (La. Ct. App. 5th Cir. 1991)
57 ALR5th 141—§ 9
93 ALR5th 327—§ 7, 9, 26
State v. Mayes, 251 Mont. 358, 825 P.2d 1196 (1992)
65 ALR6th 537—§ 16
State v. Mayes, 323 N.C. 159, 371 S.E.2d 476 (1988)
59 ALR5th 749—§ 4
State v. Mayfield, 220 S.W.3d 422 (Mo. Ct. App. E.D. 2007)
55 ALR6th 157—§ 4
State v. Mayle, 136 W. Va. 936, 69 S.E.2d 212 (1952)
108 ALR5th 593—§ 57
State v. Mayle, 357 S.E.2d 219 (W. Va. 1987)
3 ALR5th 963—§ 6
State v. Mayle, 2005-Ohio-1346, 2005 WL 678579 (Ohio Ct. App. 7th Dist. Carroll County 2005)
11 ALR6th 237—§ 10, 12
State v. Maynard, 65 N.C. App. 612, 309 S.E.2d 581 (1983)
29 ALR5th 59—§ 76, 84
State v. Maynard, 170 W. Va. 40, 289 S.E.2d 714 (1982)
75 ALR5th 295—§ 25
State v. Mayo, 13 Or. App. 582, 511 P.2d 456 (1973)
5 ALR5th 243—§ 48
State v. Mays, 108 Ohio App. 3d 598, 671 N.E.2d 553 (8th Dist. Cuyahoga County 1996)
79 ALR6th 125—§ 13
State v. Mays, 277 Kan. 359, 85 P.3d 1208 (2004)
16 ALR6th 329—§ 4
19 ALR6th 115—§ 7
24 ALR6th 591—§ 4, 12, 15

State v. Mays, 1987 WL 4724 (Ohio Ct. App. 8th Dist. Cuyahoga County 1987)
19 ALR6th 697—§ 22
State v. Mayse, 97 N.C. App. 559, 389 S.E.2d 585 (1990)
44 ALR5th 651—§ 5
State v. Mays, No. 43190 (October 22, 1981, Ct. App. Ohio, 8th App. Dist. Cuyahoga Co.)
39 ALR5th 283—§ 14
State v. Mayville, 1988 WL 34574 (Ohio Ct. App. 9th Dist. Summit County 1988)
24 ALR6th 747—§ 40
State v. Mazerolle, 614 A.2d 68 (Me. 1992)
72 ALR5th 529—§ 1
State v. Mazon, 2010 WL 5608832 (Ariz. Ct. App. Div. 2 2010)
98 ALR6th 455—§ 26
State v. Mazurek, 237 N.J. Super. 231, 567 A.2d 277 (App. Div. 1989)
74 ALR5th 319—§ 10
State v. Mazzone, 336 Md. 379, 648 A.2d 978 (1994)
51 ALR5th 603—§ 2, 14
State v. M.B.M., 518 N.W.2d 880 (Minn. Ct. App. 1994)
69 ALR6th 1—§ 4
State v. McAdams, 714 P.2d 1236 (Wyo. 1986)
33 ALR6th 407—§ 5
State v. McAfee, slip No. 78AP-757 (Ohio App. Franklin Co. 1979)
36 ALR5th 255—§ 2
State v. McAloon, 40 Me. 133, 1855 WL 1968 (1855)
57 ALR6th 445—§ 50
State v. McAnulty, 491 S.W.2d 259 (Mo. 1973)
29 ALR5th 59—§ 9
State v. McArdle, 91 Or. App. 248, 754 P.2d 918 (1988)
18 ALR5th 1—§ 2, 5
State v. McArthur, 702 So. 2d 1047 (La. Ct. App. 3d Cir. 1997)
20 ALR5th 398—§ 6.5

88 ALR5th 67—§ 3
State v. McArthur, 719 So. 2d 1037 (La. 1998)
86 ALR5th 59—§ 3, 6
State v. McAttee, 2001 WI App 262, 248 Wis. 2d 865, 637 N.W.2d 774 (Ct. App. 2001)
101 ALR6th 331—§ 10
State v. McBarron, 66 N.J.L. 680, 51 A. 146 (N.J. Ct. Err. & App. 1902)
5 ALR6th 1—§ 64
State v. McBlair, 1983 OK CR 144, 670 P.2d 606 (Okla. Crim. App. 1983)
47 ALR6th 107—§ 68
State v. McBride, 19 Mo. 239 (1853)
14 ALR5th 89—§ 10, 16
State v. McBride, 24 Kan. App. 2d 909, 955 P.2d 133 (1998)
12 ALR5th 89—§ 10
State v. McBride, 96 Or. App. 268, 773 P.2d 379 (1989)
106 ALR5th 397—§ 4
State v. McBride, 173 N.C. App. 101, 618 S.E.2d 754 (2005)
23 ALR6th 307—§ 30, 38
26 ALR6th 511—§ 27
State v. McBride, 261 Ga. 60, 401 S.E.2d 484 (1991)
76 ALR5th 563—§ 4, 5
State v. McBride, 666 N.W.2d 351 (Minn. 2003)
1 ALR6th 657—§ 14
State v. McBride, 1999 MT 127, 294 Mont. 461, 982 P.2d 453 (1999)
58 ALR6th 499—§ 84
State v. McCabe, 420 So. 2d 955 (La. 1982)
79 ALR5th 237—§ 11
State v. McCaffrey, 63 Iowa 479, 19 N.W. 331 (1884)
33 ALR6th 353—§ 5
State v. McCague, 314 N.J. Super. 254, 714 A.2d 937 (App. Div. 1998)
68 ALR5th 299—§ 4
23 ALR6th 307—§ 21
State v. McCall, 31 N.C. App. 543, 230 S.E.2d 195 (1976)

84 ALR6th 427—§ 21, 26
State v. McCall, 139 Ariz. 147, 677 P.2d 920 (1983)
16 ALR6th 329—§ 4
24 ALR6th 591—§ 4, 12
State v. McCall, 458 So. 2d 875 (Fla. Dist. Ct. App. 2d Dist. 1984)
64 ALR5th 671—§ 8
State v. McCall, 2005-Ohio-3583, 2005 WL 1653585 (Ohio Ct. App. 8th Dist. Cuyahoga County 2005)
26 ALR6th 511—§ 19
State v. McCall, 2012 WL 1555453 (Ariz. Ct. App. Div. 2 2012)
92 ALR6th 295—§ 3
96 ALR6th 355—§ 3
State v. McCallion, 78 Ohio App. 3d 709, 605 N.E.2d 1289 (11th Dist. Ashtabula County 1992)
69 ALR6th 207—§ 9, 10, 18
State v. McCann, 792 S.W.2d 890 (Mo. Ct. App. E.D. 1990)
78 ALR5th 197—§ 4
State v. McCarter, 91 Wash. 2d 249, 588 P.2d 745 (1978)
78 ALR6th 417—§ 15, 28
State v. McCarthy, 25 Conn. App. 624, 595 A.2d 941 (1991)
4 ALR5th 1—§ 3, 7, 19
State v. McCarthy, 26 Ohio St. 2d 87, 55 Ohio Op. 2d 161, 269 N.E.2d 424 (1971)
65 ALR5th 407—§ 3, 5, 7, 14, 19
State v. McCarthy, 154 Wis. 2d 867, 455 N.W.2d 678 (Ct. App. 1990)
76 ALR5th 1—§ 10
State v. McCarthy, 218 Neb. 246, 353 N.W.2d 14 (1984)
32 ALR6th 1—§ 10
State v. McCarthy, 1999 M.T. 99, 980 P.2d 629 (Mont. 1999)
29 ALR5th 487—§ 7, 11, 12
State v. McCarthy, 2004 MT 312, 324 Mont. 1, 101 P.3d 288 (2004)
19 ALR6th 697—§ 10
State v. McCartney, 65 Or. App. 766, 672 P.2d 1210 (1983)
7 ALR5th 73—§ 2, 7

State v. McCarver, 341 N.C. 364, 462 S.E.2d 25 (1995)

83 ALR6th 255—§ 15

State v. McCaughey, 127 Idaho 669, 904 P.2d 939, 65 A.L.R.5th 745 (1995)

65 ALR5th 407—§ 3, 14, 20

State v. McCauley, 130 W. Va. 401, 43 S.E.2d 454 (1947)

24 ALR6th 747—§ 30

State v. McCave, 282 Neb. 500, 805 N.W.2d 290 (2011)

92 ALR6th 295—§ 3
93 ALR6th 207—§ 3
95 ALR6th 1—§ 3
97 ALR6th 653—§ 20

State v. McCavic, 1999 WL 10242 (Minn. Ct. App. 1999)

69 ALR6th 579—§ 8, 23

State v. McClain, 137 Mo. 307, 38 S.W. 906 (1897)

59 ALR5th 135—§ 3, 4, 10

State v. McClain, 156 Mo. 99, 56 S.W. 731 (1900)

59 ALR5th 135—§ 4, 10

State v. McClain, 171 Conn. 293, 370 A.2d 928 (1976)

117 ALR5th 513—§ 3
72 ALR6th 1—§ 6

State v. McClain, 194 La. 605, 194 So. 563 (1940)

45 ALR5th 591—§ 3

State v. McClain, 248 N.J. Super. 409, 591 A.2d 652 (App. Div. 1991)

58 ALR5th 749—§ 6

State v. McClain, 256 Iowa 175, 125 N.W.2d 764, 4 A.L.R.3d 134 (1964)

50 ALR5th 467—§ 6, 8

State v. McClain, 536 S.W.2d 45 (Mo. Ct. App. 1976)

78 ALR5th 1—§ 25

State v. McClain, 1977 WL 199682 (Ohio Ct. App. 1st Dist. Butler County 1977)

42 ALR6th 237—§ 8

State v. McClain, 1987 WL 6702 (Ohio Ct. App. 12th Dist. Warren County 1987)

107 ALR5th 567—§ 10, 18

State v. McClain, 2006-Ohio-1234, 2006 WL 664960 (Ohio Ct. App. 6th Dist. Wood County 2006)

26 ALR6th 511—§ 19

State v. McClam, 69 Wash. App. 885, 850 P.2d 1377 (Div. 1 1993)

2 ALR6th 551—§ 15

State v. McClamrock, 295 So. 2d 715 (Fla. Dist. Ct. App. 3d Dist. 1974)

90 ALR5th 225—§ 4

State v. McClellan, 125 Ariz. 595, 611 P.2d 948 (Ct. App. Div. 2 1980)

82 ALR5th 359—§ 2
83 ALR5th 277—§ 2
84 ALR5th 487—§ 2

State v. McClellan, 2002-Ohio-5164, 2002 WL 31160074 (Ohio Ct. App. 10th Dist. Franklin County 2002)

30 ALR6th 373—§ 13

State v. McClellan, 2010-Ohio-314, 2010 WL 338205 (Ohio Ct. App. 3d Dist. Allen County 2010)

56 ALR6th 1—§ 9, 32

State v. McClendon, 103 Ariz. 105, 437 P.2d 421, 46 A.L.R.3d 537 (1968)

100 ALR6th 535—§ 3

State v. McClendon, 248 Conn. 572, 730 A.2d 1107 (1999)

90 ALR5th 453—§ 6

State v. McClennon, 2003 WL 21458671 (Tenn. Crim. App. 2003)

27 ALR6th 183—§ 4

State v. McClintic, 731 S.W.2d 853 (Mo. Ct. App. S.D. 1987)

1 ALR6th 549—§ 8

State v. McCloud, 721 So. 2d 1188 (Fla. Dist. Ct. App. 5th Dist. 1998)

113 ALR5th 597—§ 8

State v. McClung, 106 Wash. App. 1018, 2001 WL 528236 (Div. 2 2001)

15 ALR6th 515—§ 33

State v. McClure, 30 Del. 265, 7 Boyce 265, 105 A. 712 (Gen. Sess. 1919)

88 ALR6th 203—§ 49

State v. McClure, 184 W. Va. 418, 400 S.E.2d 853 (1990)

98 ALR6th 455—§ 26

State v. McClure, 504 S.W.2d 664 (Mo. Ct. App. 1974)
    24 ALR6th 747—§ 3, 35, 44
State v. McClurg, 50 Idaho 762, 300 P. 898 (1931)
    24 ALR5th 465—§ 62
State v. McColgan, 631 S.W.2d 151 (Tenn. Crim. App. 1981)
    68 ALR5th 549—§ 3
State v. McColley, 157 N.J. Super. 525, 385 A.2d 264 (1978)
    52 ALR5th 655—§ 3
State v. McCollum, 334 N.C. 208, 433 S.E.2d 144 (1993)
    20 ALR5th 177—§ 3, 10, 12
    47 ALR5th 259—§ 2
    79 ALR5th 33—§ 68, 72
State v. McCollum, 1989 WL 35502 (Ohio Ct. App. 6th Dist.Sandusky County 1989)
    57 ALR5th 141—§ 7
State v. McComb, 111 N.H. 312, 282 A.2d 673 (1971)
    68 ALR5th 343—§ 3
State v. McConnell, 422 So. 2d 74 (Fla. Dist. Ct. App. 2d Dist. 1982)
    62 ALR6th 413—§ 29
State v. McCord, 19 Wash. App. 250, 576 P.2d 892 (Div. 2 1978)
    103 ALR6th 347—§ 5
State v. McCord, 63 Ill. App. 3d 542, 20 Ill. Dec. 257, 379 N.E.2d 1325 (5th Dist. 1978)
    45 ALR5th 1—§ 3, 8, 15
State v. McCord, 140 N.C. App. 634, 538 S.E.2d 633 (2000)
    38 ALR6th 439—§ 4
State v. McCord, 251 Mont. 317, 825 P.2d 194 (1992)
    57 ALR5th 141—§ 11
State v. McCormick, 147 P.3d 1090 (Kan. 2006)
    26 ALR6th 511—§ 25
State v. McCormick, 152 Wash. App. 536, 216 P.3d 475 (Div. 2 2009)
    55 ALR6th 1—§ 6, 30, 31, 40
    56 ALR6th 1—§ 43, 44

State v. McCormick, 584 S.W.2d 821 (Tenn. Crim. App. 1979)
    112 ALR5th 429—§ 13
State v. McCormick, 778 S.W.2d 48 (Tenn. 1989)
    28 ALR6th 505—§ 9
State v. McCowan, 226 Kan. 752, 602 P.2d 1363 (1979)
    37 ALR6th 357—§ 69
State v. McCoy, 45 N.C. App. 686, 263 S.E.2d 801 (1980)
    99 ALR5th 557—§ 3, 12
State v. McCoy, 79 N.C. App. 273, 339 S.E.2d 419 (1986)
    29 ALR5th 59—§ 58, 76
    57 ALR6th 445—§ 43
State v. McCoy, 89 N.C. 466, 1883 WL 2552 (1883)
    57 ALR6th 445—§ 11
State v. McCoy, 94 Ohio App. 165, 51 Ohio Op. 334, 114 N.E.2d 624 (4th Dist. Scioto County 1953)
    102 ALR5th 525—§ 56
State v. McCoy, 100 N.C. App. 574, 397 S.E.2d 355 (1990)
    109 ALR5th 99—§ 4
State v. McCoy, 111 Mo. 517, 20 S.W. 240 (1892)
    11 ALR5th 831—§ 13
State v. McCoy, 320 N.C. 581, 359 S.E.2d 764 (1987)
    110 ALR5th 329—§ 6
State v. McCoy, 400 N.W.2d 807 (Minn. Ct. App. 1987)
    85 ALR5th 595—§ 3
State v. McCoy, 647 S.W.2d 862 (Mo. App. 1983)
    29 ALR5th 59—§ 7, 9, 12
State v. McCoy, 647 S.W.2d 862 (Mo. Ct. App. E.D. 1983)
    57 ALR6th 445—§ 49
State v. McCoy, 742 N.W.2d 593 (Iowa 2007)
    53 ALR6th 305—§ 18
State v. McCoy, 1992 WL 185684 (Ohio Ct. App. 12th Dist. Butler County 1992)

CASES CITED IN ALR5th and ALR6th

99 ALR6th 295—§ 21
State v. McCoy, 1998 WL 526734 (Ohio Ct. App. 6th Dist. Lucas County 1998)
35 ALR6th 497—§ 23
State v. McCoy, 2001 WL 1386196 (Ohio Ct. App. 1st Dist. 2001)
26 ALR6th 511—§ 35
State v. McCoy, 2004-Ohio-6726, 2004 WL 2896356 (Ohio Ct. App. 10th Dist. Franklin County 2004)
70 ALR6th 1—§ 5
State v. McCoy, 2006-Ohio-3930, 2006 WL 2141616 (Ohio Ct. App. 5th Dist. Delaware County 2006)
26 ALR6th 511—§ 19
State v. McCracken, 218 W. Va. 190, 624 S.E.2d 537 (2005)
29 ALR6th 1—§ 10
State v. McCracken, 2003 WL 1618082 (Tenn. Crim. App. 2003)
16 ALR6th 329—§ 15
24 ALR6th 591—§ 10
State v. McCrady, 152 Kan. 566, 106 P.2d 696 (1940)
99 ALR6th 113—§ 10
102 ALR6th 279—§ 6
State v. McCraney, 2003 WL 21998487 (Tenn. Crim. App. 2003)
117 ALR5th 407—§ 3
State v. McCrary, 2002-Ohio-396, 2002 WL 125760 (Ohio Ct. App. 2d Dist. Montgomery County 2002)
32 ALR6th 1—§ 11
State v. McCrary, 2009-Ohio-4390, 2009 WL 2674327 (Ohio Ct. App. 1st Dist. Hamilton County 2009)
72 ALR6th 1—§ 4
State v. McCravey, 692 S.E.2d 409 (N.C. Ct. App. 2010)
57 ALR6th 1—§ 7, 22
State v. McCray, 15 Wash. App. 810, 551 P.2d 1376 (1976)
33 ALR5th 453—§ 5, 8
State v. McCray, 189 Iowa 1239, 179 N.W. 627 (1920)
45 ALR5th 591—§ 4

State v. McCray, 312 N.C. 519, 324 S.E.2d 606 (1985)
42 ALR6th 237—§ 8
State v. McCray, 517 So. 2d 474 (La. Ct. App. 1st Cir. 1987)
57 ALR6th 445—§ 39
State v. McCray, 2006 WL 2567483 (Tenn. Crim. App. 2006)
99 ALR6th 113—§ 9, 19, 22, 24
102 ALR6th 279—§ 13
State v. McCrea, 2005-Ohio-4918, 2005 WL 2277232 (Ohio Ct. App. 12th Dist. Warren County 2005)
69 ALR6th 1—§ 27
State v. McCready, 234 Wis. 2d 110, 2000 WI App 68, 608 N.W.2d 762 (Ct. App. 2000)
121 ALR5th 551—§ 13
State v. McCree, 2011-Ohio-4114, 2011 WL 3652755 (Ohio Ct. App. 5th Dist. Richland County 2011)
99 ALR6th 295—§ 16
State v. McCrimmon, 89 N.C. App. 525, 366 S.E.2d 572 (1988)
27 ALR6th 183—§ 41
State v. McCrone, 63 Ohio App. 3d 831, 580 N.E.2d 468 (9th Dist. Lorain County 1989)
66 ALR5th 397—§ 16
State v. McCuin, 167 Ariz. 447, 808 P.2d 332, 77 Ariz. Adv. Rep. 33 (App. 1991)
36 ALR5th 161—§ 3
State v. McCuin, 171 Ariz. 171, 829 P.2d 1217 (1992)
63 ALR6th 351—§ 3
State v. McCuin, 171 Ariz. 171, 829 P.2d 1217, 111 Ariz. Adv. Rep. 23 (1992)
36 ALR5th 161—§ 3
State v. McCuistion, 275 P.3d 1092, 78 A.L.R.6th 747 (Wash. 2012)
78 ALR6th 417—§ 16, 25
State v. McCullers, 77 N.C. App. 433, 335 S.E.2d 348 (1985)
7 ALR5th 263—§ 7
State v. McCulley, 5 Conn. App. 612, 501 A.2d 392 (1985)

5 ALR5th 243—§ 33
State v. McCulley, 782 S.W.2d 733 (Mo. Ct. App. E.D. 1989)

75 ALR5th 295—§ 30
State v. McCulley, 1994 WL 164013 (Ohio App. 8 Dist.)

50 ALR5th 581—§ 7, 9, 16, 20, 22
State v. McCullough, 56 Wash. App. 655, 784 P.2d 566 (1990)

48 ALR5th 555—§ 4
State v. McCullough, 566 So. 2d 635 (La. Ct. App. 5th Cir. 1990)

112 ALR5th 621—§ 3
State v. McCully, 310 So. 2d 833 (La. 1975)

36 ALR5th 255—§ 7
65 ALR6th 537—§ 17
State v. McCulty, 2002-Ohio-1742, 2002 WL 570252 (Ohio Ct. App. 9th Dist. Wayne County 2002)

73 ALR6th 1—§ 7
State v. McCurdy, 257 So. 2d 92 (Fla. 2d DCA 1972)

80 ALR6th 599—§ 5
State v. McCurley, 2004 WL 2827857 (Del. Super. Ct. 2004)

103 ALR6th 247—§ 16, 19
State v. McCurry, 5 Neb. App. 526, 561 N.W.2d 244 (1997)

34 ALR6th 1—§ 12
State v. McCutcheon, 495 So. 2d 931 (Fla. Dist. Ct. App. 4th Dist. 1986)

24 ALR6th 1—§ 51
State v. McDade, 44 Or. App. 269, 605 P.2d 752 (1980)

124 ALR5th 1—§ 3
State v. McDaniel, 20 Kan. App. 2d 883, 893 P.2d 290 (1995)

9 ALR6th 541—§ 3, 15
State v. McDaniel, 37 Wash. App. 768, 683 P.2d 231 (1984)

38 ALR5th 433—§ 3
State v. McDaniel, 127 Ariz. 13, 617 P.2d 1129 (1980)

45 ALR5th 591—§ 15, 18
State v. McDaniel, 272 N.C. 556, 158 S.E.2d 874 (1968)

38 ALR6th 97—§ 28
State v. McDaniel, 274 N.C. 574, 164 S.E.2d 469 (1968)

38 ALR6th 97—§ 28
State v. McDaniel, 763 P.2d 16 (Kan. 1988)

39 ALR5th 283—§ 4, 40, 41
State v. McDaniels, 114 Wash. App. 1046, 2002 WL 31648777 (Div. 1 2002)

27 ALR6th 183—§ 10, 17
State v. McDaniels, 668 S.W.2d 230 (Mo. Ct. App. E.D. 1984)

86 ALR5th 59—§ 5
State v. McDaniels, 1993 WL 215388 (Ohio Ct. App. 8th Dist.Cuyahoga County 1993)

57 ALR5th 141—§ 13
State v. McDermitt, 406 So. 2d 195 (La. 1981)

16 ALR5th 390—§ 2, 3
State v. McDermott, 72 Ohio St. 3d 570, 651 N.E.2d 985 (1995)

51 ALR5th 603—§ 4
State v. McDermott, 79 Ohio App. 3d 772, 607 N.E.2d 1164 (1992)

51 ALR5th 603—§ 2
State v. McDermott, 2002-Ohio-6982, 2002 WL 31819660 (Ohio Ct. App. 5th Dist. Stark County 2002)

23 ALR6th 307—§ 45
State v. McDew, 1995 WL 160894 (Ohio Ct. App. 5th Dist. Tuscarawas County 1995)

81 ALR6th 505—§ 17
State v. McDonald, 29 Kan. App. 2d 6, 26 P.3d 69 (2001)

9 ALR6th 541—§ 15
State v. McDonald, 92 N.J. Super. 448, 224 A.2d 18 (1966)

4 ALR5th 1—§ 4
State v. McDonald, 164 Miss. 405, 145 So. 508, 86 A.L.R. 290 (1933)

10 ALR6th 31—§ 35
State v. McDonald, 168 Or. App. 452, 7 P.3d 617 (2000)

58 ALR6th 499—§ 9

State v. McDonald, 190 N.W.2d 402 (Iowa 1971)

26 ALR5th 1—§ 3, 43

State v. McDonald, 253 Or. 533, 456 P.2d 80 (1969)

113 ALR5th 517—§ 8

State v. McDonald, 421 N.W.2d 492 (S.D. 1988)

119 ALR5th 379—§ 8

State v. McDonald, 690 So. 2d 1317 (Fla. Dist. Ct. App. 2d Dist. 1997)

68 ALR6th 527—§ 46

State v. McDonald, 826 So. 2d 1081 (Fla. Dist. Ct. App. 4th Dist. 2002)

35 ALR6th 497—§ 23

State v. McDonald, 872 P.2d 627 (Alaska App. 1994)

49 ALR5th 639—§ 4
57 ALR5th 141—§ 5, 11

State v. McDonald, 872 P.2d 627 (Alaska Ct. App. 1994)

117 ALR5th 1—§ 4
65 ALR6th 359—§ 9

State v. McDonald, 1998-NMSC-034, 126 N.M. 44, 966 P.2d 752 (1998)

38 ALR6th 439—§ 4

State v. McDonald, 2000 WL 504113 (Ohio Ct. App. 8th Dist. Cuyahoga County 2000)

3 ALR6th 543—§ 6

State v. McDonough, 468 A.2d 977, 15 Ed. Law Rep. 268 (Me. 1983)

70 ALR5th 169—§ 8

State v. McDougald, 2004-Ohio-4512, 2004 WL 1908314 (Ohio Ct. App. 2d Dist. Miami County 2004)

45 ALR6th 337—§ 6

State v. McDowell, 301 N.C. 279, 271 S.E.2d 286 (1980)

83 ALR6th 465—§ 12, 44

State v. McDowell, 329 N.C. 363, 407 S.E.2d 200 (1991)

68 ALR5th 343—§ 3
83 ALR6th 465—§ 4, 18, 79

State v. McDowell, 824 A.2d 948 (Del. Super. Ct. 2003)

72 ALR6th 141—§ 7

State v. McDowell, 832 S.W.2d 333 (Mo. Ct. App. E.D. 1992)

102 ALR6th 279—§ 7

State v. McDuell, 1989 WL 16962 (Del. Super. Ct. 1989)

62 ALR6th 413—§ 28

State v. McDuffie, 106 N.M. 120, 739 P.2d 989 (Ct. App. 1987)

33 ALR6th 407—§ 47, 48

State v. McElfresh, 1999 WL 547876 (Ohio Ct. App. 5th Dist. Licking County 1999)

87 ALR5th 693—§ 5

State v. McElrath, 322 N.C. 1, 366 S.E.2d 442 (1988)

57 ALR5th 141—§ 5

State v. McElreavy, 157 Vt. 18, 595 A.2d 1332 (1991)

34 ALR6th 1—§ 12

State v. McElroy, 189 Neb. 376, 202 N.W.2d 752 (1972)

4 ALR5th 1—§ 2, 19

State v. McElvain, 228 S.W.3d 592 (Mo. Ct. App. W.D. 2007)

55 ALR6th 391—§ 22

State v. McEwan, 265 N.W.2d 818 (Minn. 1978)

39 ALR5th 283—§ 3

State v. McFadden, 25 Conn. App. 171, 593 A.2d 979 (1991)

19 ALR5th 823—§ 12

State v. McFadden, 216 S.W.3d 673 (Mo. 2007)

36 ALR6th 681—§ 32

State v. McFadden, 318 S.C. 404, 458 S.E.2d 61 (Ct. App. 1995)

38 ALR6th 439—§ 4

State v. McFadden, 320 N.W.2d 608 (Iowa 1982)

89 ALR6th 565—§ 27

State v. McFadden, 476 So. 2d 413 (La. App. 2d Cir. 1985)

9 ALR5th 369—§ 2

State v. McFadden, 1990 WL 105437 (Ohio Ct. App. 4th Dist. Washington County 1990)

57 ALR5th 141—§ 7

State v. McFall, 675 So. 2d 1333 (Ala. Crim. App. 1994)
85 ALR5th 1—§ 29

State v. McFall, 866 S.W.2d 915 (Mo. App. 1993)
7 ALR5th 263—§ 7
33 ALR5th 571—§ 5

State v. McFarland, 88 Idaho 527, 401 P.2d 824 (1965)
76 ALR5th 1—§ 3

State v. McFarland, 125 Idaho 876, 876 P.2d 158 (App. 1994)
22 ALR5th 660—§ 15

State v. McFerron, 890 S.W.2d 764 (Mo. Ct. App. E.D. 1995)
31 ALR6th 49—§ 4

State v. McGacken, 2010 WL 910258 (N.J. Super. Ct. App. Div. 2010)
58 ALR6th 499—§ 47

State v. McGann, 126 N.H. 316, 493 A.2d 452 (1985)
70 ALR6th 361—§ 31

State v. McGarrity, 139 La. 430, 71 So. 730 (1916)
97 ALR5th 537—§ 10

State v. McGeary, 129 N.J. Super. 219, 322 A.2d 830, 77 A.L.R.3d 106 (App. Div. 1974)
111 ALR5th 1—§ 3, 5, 9, 27

State v. McGee, 52 Wis. 2d 736, 190 N.W.2d 893 (1971)
102 ALR6th 365—§ 21

State v. McGee, 60 N.C. App. 658, 299 S.E.2d 796 (1983)
15 ALR5th 39—§ 4

State v. McGee, 88 Wash. App. 1004, 1997 WL 666052 (Div. 1 1997)
42 ALR6th 237—§ 4

State v. McGee, 122 Wash. 2d 783, 864 P.2d 912 (1993)
27 ALR5th 593—§ 32

State v. McGee, 341 Mo. 151, 106 S.W.2d 480 (1937)
41 ALR5th 1—§ 3

State v. McGee, 682 N.W.2d 82 (Iowa Ct. App. 2004)
43 ALR6th 475—§ 22

48 ALR6th 135—§ 12

State v. McGee, 757 So. 2d 50 (La. Ct. App. 4th Cir. 2000)
34 ALR5th 125—§ 16

State v. McGhee, 58 Ohio L. Abs. 377, 96 N.E.2d 419 (Ct. App. 7th Dist. Mahoning County 1949)
24 ALR6th 747—§ 45

State v. McGill, 213 Ariz. 147, 140 P.3d 930 (2006)
21 ALR6th 1—§ 4

State v. McGill, 536 N.W.2d 89 (S.D. 1995)
29 ALR5th 487—§ 3, 12

State v. McGill, 556 P.2d 39 (N.M. App. 1976)
49 ALR5th 639—§ 4

State v. McGinnis, 2 Neb. App. 77, 507 N.W.2d 46 (1993)
15 ALR5th 391—§ 5

State v. McGinnis, 56 Or. 163, 108 P. 132 (1910)
54 ALR6th 429—§ 18

State v. McGinnis, 90 Ohio App. 3d 479, 629 N.E.2d 1084 (4th Dist. Scioto County 1993)
70 ALR6th 1—§ 4

State v. McGinnis, 142 P.3d 338 (Kan. Ct. App. 2006)
87 ALR6th 1—§ 62

State v. McGivney, 36 Or. App. 885, 585 P.2d 767 (1978)
99 ALR5th 557—§ 10

State v. McGlone, 59 Ohio St. 3d 122, 570 N.E.2d 1115 (1991)
52 ALR5th 655—§ 3

State v. McGloster, 303 So. 2d 739 (La. 1974)
70 ALR5th 587—§ 5

State v. McGlothin, 1993 WL 102496 (Ohio Ct. App. 6th Dist. Erie County 1993)
43 ALR6th 475—§ 18

State v. McGonigal, 89 Idaho 177, 403 P.2d 745 (1965)
119 ALR5th 275—§ 13

State v. McGovern, 43 Conn. L. Rptr. 841, 2007 WL 2363718 (Conn. Super. Ct. 2007)
75 ALR6th 181—§ 22
State v. McGovern, 77 Wis. 2d 203, 252 N.W.2d 365 (1977)
68 ALR5th 343—§ 3
State v. McGowan, 541 A.2d 1301 (Me. 1988)
4 ALR5th 1—§ 4, 7, 17
State v. McGowan, 950 S.W.2d 273 (Mo. Ct. App. S.D. 1997)
1 ALR6th 549—§ 32
State v. McGrane, 733 N.W.2d 671 (Iowa 2007)
78 ALR6th 297—§ 3, 6, 30, 42, 51
State v. McGrath, 749 P.2d 631 (Utah 1988)
89 ALR5th 629—§ 3, 8
State v. McGrath, 2010-Ohio-4477, 2010 WL 3721970 (Ohio Ct. App. 8th Dist. Cuyahoga County 2010)
99 ALR6th 295—§ 13
State v. McGraw, 140 W. Va. 547, 85 S.E.2d 849 (1955)
29 ALR5th 59—§ 3
State v. McGraw, 366 So. 2d 1278 (La. 1978)
16 ALR6th 329—§ 6
19 ALR6th 115—§ 4, 9
24 ALR6th 591—§ 4, 6, 14
State v. McGraw, 529 S.E.2d 493 (N.C. Ct. App. 2000)
38 ALR5th 433—§ 10
State v. McGregor, 2008-Ohio-5743, 2008 WL 4814082 (Ohio Ct. App. 8th Dist. Cuyahoga County 2008)
69 ALR6th 1—§ 10
State v. McGrew, 515 N.W.2d 36 (Iowa 1994)
39 ALR5th 283—§ 10, 40
State v. McGriff, 109 Ohio App. 3d 668, 672 N.E.2d 1074 (3d Dist. Logan County 1996)
79 ALR6th 125—§ 10
State v. McGriff, 2006 WL 1515831 (Del. Super. Ct. 2006)
30 ALR6th 1—§ 4

State v. McGuire, 16 Ariz. App. 346, 493 P.2d 513 (1972)
4 ALR5th 1—§ 2, 17, 35
State v. McGuire, 110 N.M. 304, 795 P.2d 996 (1990)
28 ALR5th 754—§ 7
State v. McGuire, 193 Mo. 215, 91 S.W. 939 (1906)
57 ALR6th 445—§ 49
State v. McGuire, 1994 WL 700082 (Ohio Ct. App. 9th Dist. Summit County 1994)
84 ALR5th 1—§ 7
State v. McGuy, 841 A.2d 1109 (R.I. 2003)
3 ALR6th 543—§ 8
State v. McHone, 334 N.C. 627, 435 S.E.2d 296 (1993)
57 ALR5th 141—§ 3
State v. McHorse, 85 N.M. 753, 517 P.2d 75 (Ct. App. 1973)
60 ALR6th 175—§ 5
State v. McHugh, 161 Vt. 574, 635 A.2d 1200 (1993)
70 ALR6th 513—§ 6
71 ALR6th 471—§ 4
State v. McHugh, 630 So. 2d 1259 (La. 1994)
50 ALR5th 703—§ 35
State v. McIlraith, 2009 WL 113269 (Minn. Ct. App. 2009)
47 ALR6th 107—§ 43
State v. McIlrath, 110 Wash. App. 1044, 2002 WL 339415 (Div. 1 2002)
35 ALR6th 497—§ 23
State v. McInnes, 153 So. 2d 854 (Fla. Dist. Ct. App. 1st Dist. 1963)
87 ALR5th 715—§ 3
State v. McIntire, 46 N.C. 1, 1 Jones 1, 1853 WL 1430 (1853)
101 ALR6th 431—§ 13
State v. McIntosh, 333 S.W.2d 51 (Mo. 1960)
41 ALR5th 171—§ 13
State v. McIntosh, 655 S.W.2d 83 (Mo. Ct. App. E.D. 1983)
108 ALR5th 593—§ 41

State v. Mcintosh, 1983 WL 4277 (Ohio Ct. App. 12th Dist. Butler County 1983)
81 ALR5th 1—§ 3
State v. McIntosh, 1989 WL 8471 (Ohio Ct. App. 12th Dist. Warren County 1989)
95 ALR5th 611—§ 5
State v. McIntosh, 2000 WL 558167 (Minn. Ct. App. 2000)
7 ALR6th 233—§ 3, 5
State v. McIntosh, 2005-Ohio-1152, 2005 WL 615645 (Ohio Ct. App. 10th Dist. Franklin County 2005)
48 ALR6th 135—§ 3
State v. McIntosh, 2005 WL 729145 (Tenn. Crim. App. 2005)
26 ALR6th 511—§ 22, 23, 25, 27
State v. McIntyre, 13 N.C. App. 479, 186 S.E.2d 207 (1972)
1 ALR6th 549—§ 25
State v. McIntyre, 123 Or. App. 436, 860 P.2d 299 (1993)
60 ALR5th 1—§ 5
State v. McIntyre, 242 Conn. 318, 699 A.2d 911 (1997)
12 ALR6th 267—§ 12
State v. McIntyre, 1992 WL 125251 (Ohio Ct. App. 9th Dist. Summit County 1992)
19 ALR6th 697—§ 4, 20
State v. McIver, 176 N.C. 718, 96 S.E. 902 (1918)
81 ALR5th 563—§ 3, 5
State v. McIver, 201 Conn. 559, 518 A.2d 1368 (1986)
55 ALR6th 391—§ 7
State v. McKague, 143 Wash. App. 531, 178 P.3d 1035 (Div. 2 2008)
67 ALR6th 531—§ 36
State v. McKay, 154 Wash. App. 1010, 2010 WL 95095 (Div. 2 2010)
56 ALR6th 1—§ 22
State v. McKee, 89 Or. App. 94, 747 P.2d 395 (1987)
33 ALR5th 453—§ 7, 10
State v. McKee, 181 Wis. 2d 354, 510 N.W.2d 807 (Ct. App. 1993)

78 ALR5th 309—§ 4
State v. McKee, 253 Neb. 100, 568 N.W.2d 559 (1997)
62 ALR6th 359—§ 4
State v. McKee, 312 N.W.2d 907, 25 A.L.R.4th 1201 (Iowa 1981)
103 ALR6th 507—§ 22
State v. McKeehan, 91 Idaho 808, 430 P.2d 886 (1967)
5 ALR5th 243—§ 2, 61
19 ALR5th 823—§ 15, 17
State v. McKelvey, 142 N.J. Super. 259, 361 A.2d 96 (1976)
52 ALR5th 655—§ 3
State v. McKenna, 89 Wash. App. 1019, 1998 WL 17687 (Div. 3 1998)
90 ALR5th 453—§ 43
State v. McKenna, 188 Conn. 671, 453 A.2d 435 (1982)
97 ALR5th 201—§ 3
State v. McKenney, 459 A.2d 1093 (Me. 1983)
57 ALR5th 141—§ 12
State v. McKenzie, 532 N.W.2d 210 (Minn. 1995)
60 ALR5th 39—§ 4 to 8, 11, 13
State v. McKenzie, 576 N.E.2d 1258 (Ind. App. 1991)
5 ALR5th 875—§ 23
State v. McKenzie-Adams, 281 Conn. 486, 915 A.2d 822 (2007)
39 ALR6th 257—§ 11, 34, 41
State v. McKeown, 23 Wash. App. 582, 596 P.2d 1100 (1979)
34 ALR5th 125—§ 14
State v. McKercher, 2006-Ohio-1772, 2006 WL 903595 (Ohio Ct. App. 3d Dist. Allen County 2006)
26 ALR6th 511—§ 19
State v. McKessor, 246 Kan. 1, 785 P.2d 1332 (1990)
39 ALR5th 283—§ 4, 18
State v. McKichan, 219 Neb. 560, 364 N.W.2d 47 (1985)
42 ALR5th 547—§ 4
State v. McKim, 98 Wash. 2d 111, 653 P.2d 1040 (1982)

88 ALR5th 121—§ 32

State v. McKimmey, 10 Neb. App. 595, 634 N.W.2d 817 (2001)

8 ALR6th 265—§ 29

State v. McKinley, 7 Ohio App. 3d 255, 7 Ohio B.R. 335, 455 N.E.2d 503 (Cuyahoga Co. 1982)

45 ALR5th 591—§ 2 to 5

State v. McKinney, 36 N.C. App. 614, 244 S.E.2d 455 (1978)

115 ALR5th 403—§ 5

101 ALR6th 1—§ 4

State v. McKinney, 50 Wash. App. 56, 747 P.2d 1113 (Div. 1 1987)

119 ALR5th 275—§ 8, 11

State v. McKinney, 88 W. Va. 400, 106 S.E. 894 (1921)

81 ALR5th 563—§ 3, 5

State v. McKinney, 108 Ariz. 436, 501 P.2d 378 (1972)

9 ALR5th 464—§ 3, 4, 7, 11

State v. McKinney, 112 Ohio Misc. 2d 30, 750 N.E.2d 1237 (C.P. 2000)

4 ALR6th 1—§ 10

State v. McKinney, 153 N.C. App. 369, 570 S.E.2d 238 (2002)

34 ALR6th 1—§ 10

State v. McKinney, 185 Ariz. 567, 917 P.2d 1214 (1996)

21 ALR6th 1—§ 4

State v. McKinney, 194 N.C. App. 374, 671 S.E.2d 596 (2008)

99 ALR6th 397—§ 17

State v. McKinney, 221 Kan. 691, 561 P.2d 432 (1977)

72 ALR5th 403—§ 15, 19

State v. McKinney, 605 S.W.2d 842 (Tenn. Crim. App. 1980)

76 ALR5th 1—§ 13

State v. McKinney, 743 N.W.2d 550 (Iowa 2008)

88 ALR6th 203—§ 27, 78, 79

State v. McKinney, 886 S.W.2d 302 (Tex. App. Houston (1st Dist.) 1994)

15 ALR5th 119—§ 5

State v. McKinney, 1998 WL 517864 (Ohio Ct. App. 5th Dist. Tuscarawas County 1998)

68 ALR5th 343—§ 3

State v. McKinney, 2004-Ohio-5518, 2004 WL 2334318 (Ohio Ct. App. 3d Dist. Defiance County 2004)

24 ALR6th 1—§ 11, 33

State v. McKinney, 2008-Ohio-3256, 2008 WL 2582860 (Ohio Ct. App. 11th Dist. Trumbull County 2008)

38 ALR6th 439—§ 4

State v. McKinney, 2008-Ohio-6522, 2008 WL 5196451 (Ohio Ct. App. 10th Dist. Franklin County 2008)

79 ALR6th 125—§ 4

State v. McKinnon, 88 Wash. 2d 75, 558 P.2d 781 (1977)

31 ALR5th 229—§ 17, 29, 38, 43

State v. McKinnon, 306 N.C. 288, 293 S.E.2d 118 (1982)

111 ALR5th 239—§ 4

6 ALR6th 533—§ 17

State v. McKinsey, 116 Wash. 2d 911, 810 P.2d 907 (1991)

83 ALR5th 277—§ 13

84 ALR5th 487—§ 25

State v. McKitrick, 1990 WL 11452 (Ohio Ct. App. 3d Dist. Union County 1990)

57 ALR6th 83—§ 12

State v. McKnight, 107 Ohio St. 3d 101, 2005-Ohio-6046, 837 N.E.2d 315 (2005)

102 ALR6th 279—§ 22, 27

State v. McKnight, 511 N.W.2d 389 (Iowa 1994)

22 ALR5th 261—§ 4, 6

State v. McKnight, 2001 WL 698150 (Ohio Ct. App. 5th Dist. Richland County 2001)

43 ALR6th 475—§ 21

State v. McKone, 146 P.3d 709 (Kan. Ct. App. 2006)

97 ALR6th 653—§ 17

State v. McKown, 475 N.W.2d 63 (Minn. 1991)

118 ALR5th 253—§ 18, 19

State v. McKoy, 323 N.C. 1, 372 S.E.2d 12 (1988)

10 ALR5th 700—§ 3, 8, 17

State v. McLain, 238 Neb. 225, 469 N.W.2d 539 (1991)

15 ALR5th 391—§ 5

State v. McLain, 367 A.2d 213 (Me. 1976)

28 ALR6th 505—§ 9

State v. McLam, 82 N.M. 242, 478 P.2d 570 (Ct. App. 1970)

58 ALR6th 439—§ 4

State v. McLam, 103 Wash. App. 1054, 2000 WL 1867635 (Div. 2 2000)

7 ALR6th 233—§ 3, 5

State v. McLaren, 135 Vt. 291, 376 A.2d 34 (1977)

28 ALR5th 754—§ 5

State v. McLaren, 763 So. 2d 1171 (Fla. Dist. Ct. App. 4th Dist. 2000)

113 ALR5th 597—§ 8

State v. McLaughlin, 226 W. Va. 229, 700 S.E.2d 289 (2010)

69 ALR6th 415—§ 43

State v. McLaughlin, 265 S.W.3d 257 (Mo. 2008)

46 ALR6th 495—§ 31

State v. McLaughlin, 310 N.J. Super. 242, 708 A.2d 716 (App. Div. 1998)

32 ALR6th 1—§ 11

State v. McLaughlin, 341 N.C. 426, 462 S.E.2d 1 (1995)

79 ALR5th 33—§ 9, 63

State v. McLaurin, 320 N.C. 143, 357 S.E.2d 636 (1987)

23 ALR6th 307—§ 39

State v. McLean, 294 N.C. 623, 242 S.E.2d 814 (1978)

24 ALR6th 747—§ 30

32 ALR6th 1—§ 5

State v. McLellan, 56 N.C. App. 101, 286 S.E.2d 873 (1982)

32 ALR5th 149—§ 29

State v. McLellan, 144 N.H. 602, 744 A.2d 611 (1999)

91 ALR5th 585—§ 9

18 ALR6th 1—§ 2, 5, 30

State v. McLemore, 343 N.C. 240, 479 S.E.2d 2 (1996)

57 ALR5th 141—§ 4

State v. McLemore, 2000 WL 422368 (Ohio Ct. App. 9th Dist. Lorain County 2000)

99 ALR6th 295—§ 13

State v. McLemore, 2012-Ohio-521, 968 N.E.2d 612 (Ohio Ct. App. 2d Dist. Montgomery County 2012)

78 ALR6th 297—§ 69

State v. McLeod, 196 N.C. 542, 146 S.E. 409 (1929)

81 ALR5th 563—§ 3, 5

State v. McLeod, 271 So. 2d 45 (La. 1972)

70 ALR5th 587—§ 3

State v. McLerran, 122 Wash. App. 1022, 2004 WL 1535642 (Div. 3 2004)

26 ALR6th 511—§ 42

State v. McLoughlin, 139 Ariz. 481, 679 P.2d 504 (1984)

24 ALR6th 1—§ 13

State v. McMahan, 131 Kan. 257, 291 P. 745 (1930)

102 ALR6th 279—§ 32

State v. McMahan, 650 S.W.2d 383 (Tenn. Crim. App. 1983)

17 ALR6th 327—§ 3

State v. McMahan, 1994 WL 521228 (Tenn. Crim. App. 1994)

76 ALR5th 485—§ 3

State v. McMahan, 1994 WL 677430 (Tenn. Crim. App. 1994)

76 ALR5th 485—§ 3

State v. McMahan, 1999 WL 177590 (Tenn. Crim. App. 1999)

73 ALR5th 383—§ 4, 12

State v. McMahon, 1998 OK CIV APP 103, 959 P.2d 607 (Div. 4 1998)

69 ALR6th 1—§ 21

State v. McMains, 95 Okla. Crim. 176, 241 P.2d 976 (1952)

35 ALR5th 757—§ 3

State v. McMann, 4 Neb. App. 243, 541 N.W.2d 418 (1995)

15 ALR5th 391—§ 35

State v. McMaster, 259 Or. 291, 486
P.2d 567 (1971)
1 ALR5th 469—§ 7
State v. McMasters, 815 S.W.2d 116
(Mo. Ct. App. E.D. 1991)
87 ALR5th 597—§ 5
State v. McMillan, 94 N.C. 945, 1886
WL 1024 (1886)
105 ALR5th 529—§ 21
State v. McMillan, 553 So. 2d 385 (Fla.
Dist. Ct. App. 4th Dist. 1989)
125 ALR5th 281—§ 11
State v. McMilliam, 243 N.C. 775, 92
S.E.2d 205 (1956)
92 ALR6th 1—§ 5
State v. McMillin, 23 Kan. App. 2d 100,
927 P.2d 949 (1996)
117 ALR5th 407—§ 4
State v. McMillin, 783 S.W.2d 82 (Mo.
1990)
83 ALR6th 255—§ 27
State v. McMinn, 144 N.H. 34, 737 A.2d
1093 (1999)
112 ALR5th 429—§ 7
State v. McMullen, 302 Ark. 252, 789
S.W.2d 715 (1990)
97 ALR5th 201—§ 6
State v. McMurphy, 291 Or. 782, 635
P.2d 372 (1981)
75 ALR5th 619—§ 4
State v. McMurrin, 690 N.W.2d 700
(Iowa Ct. App. 2004)
33 ALR6th 91—§ 46
State v. McMurry, 184 Ariz. 447, 909
P.2d 1084 (Ct. App. Div. 1 1995)
108 ALR5th 593—§ 33
State v. McMurtrey, 151 Ariz. 105, 726
P.2d 202 (1986)
11 ALR6th 237—§ 12
State v. McNamara, 212 N.J. Super. 102,
514 A.2d 63 (App. Div. 1986)
85 ALR5th 471—§ 4
State v. McNaughton, 924 S.W.2d 517
(Mo. App. 1996)
40 ALR5th 113—§ 3
State v. McNaughton, 924 S.W.2d 517
(Mo. Ct. App. W.D. 1996)

114 ALR5th 173—§ 7
55 ALR6th 391—§ 7
State v. McNeal, 95 Wis. 2d 63, 288
N.W.2d 874 (App. 1980)
26 ALR5th 603—§ 3
State v. McNeal, 162 W. Va. 550, 251
S.E.2d 484 (1978)
32 ALR6th 1—§ 4
State v. McNeal, 2000 OK CR 13, 6 P.3d
1055 (Okla. Crim. App. 2000)
117 ALR5th 407—§ 3
State v. McNeal, 2002-Ohio-2981, 2002
WL 1376177 (Ohio Ct. App. 3d
Dist. Allen County 2002)
125 ALR5th 357—§ 2, 6
State v. McNeely, 358 S.W.3d 65 (Mo.
2012)
86 ALR6th 577—§ 8
State v. McNeil, 46 N.C. App. 533, 265
S.E.2d 416 (1980)
36 ALR5th 255—§ 24
State v. McNeil, 164 Vt. 129, 665 A.2d
51 (1995)
52 ALR5th 655—§ 4
State v. McNeil, 362 So. 2d 93 (Fla. 1st
DCA 1978)
103 ALR6th 137—§ 3
State v. McNeil, 445 S.E.2d 461 (S.C.
App. 1994)
29 ALR5th 59—§ 3, 33
State v. McNeil, 753 So. 2d 938 (La. Ct.
App. 4th Cir. 2000)
41 ALR6th 295—§ 11
State v. McNeill, 33 N.C. App. 317, 235
S.E.2d 274 (1977)
68 ALR5th 343—§ 3, 5
State v. McNeill, 83 Ohio St. 3d 438,
700 N.E.2d 596 (1998)
79 ALR5th 33—§ 52
State v. McNeill, 349 N.C. 634, 509
S.E.2d 415 (1998)
29 ALR6th 1—§ 10
State v. McNeilly, 2006 WL 3498043
(Tenn. Crim. App. 2006)
57 ALR6th 83—§ 9
State v. McNicol, 554 P.2d 203 (Utah
1976)

---

79 ALR5th 419—§ 10

State v. McNutt, 124 Wash. App. 344, 101 P.3d 422 (Div. 1 2004)

56 ALR6th 647—§ 6

State v. McPhail, 116 N.H. 440, 362 A.2d 199 (1976)

63 ALR6th 1—§ 10, 36

State v. McPhee, 58 Conn. App. 501, 755 A.2d 893 (2000)

82 ALR6th 373—§ 6, 9, 16

State v. McPherson, 114 Minn. 498, 131 N.W. 645 (1911)

67 ALR5th 637—§ 5, 11

State v. McPherson, 250 Or. 601, 444 P.2d 5 (1968)

29 ALR5th 59—§ 3

State v. McPherson, 630 So. 2d 935 (La. Ct. App. 4th Cir. 1993)

24 ALR6th 1—§ 11

State v. McPherson, 882 S.W.2d 365 (Tenn. Crim. App. 1994)

102 ALR5th 447—§ 11, 22
103 ALR6th 507—§ 8, 14

State v. McQueen, 295 N.C. 96, 244 S.E.2d 414 (1978)

53 ALR6th 1—§ 5
71 ALR6th 335—§ 10

State v. McQuillen, 147 Vt. 386, 518 A.2d 25 (1986)

119 ALR5th 379—§ 8

State v. McRae, 110 N.C. App. 643, 430 S.E.2d 434 (1993)

4 ALR5th 1—§ 38

State v. McRae, 371 N.W.2d 66 (Minn. Ct. App. 1985)

87 ALR5th 181—§ 4

State v. McRae, 494 N.W.2d 252 (Minn. 1992)

32 ALR6th 171—§ 7, 22
33 ALR6th 1—§ 23

State v. McReynolds, 176 P.3d 616 (Wash. Ct. App. Div. 3 2008)

35 ALR6th 361—§ 21

State v. McReynolds, 574 S.W.2d 450 (Mo. Ct. App. 1978)

70 ALR5th 587—§ 3

State v. McSheehan, 137 N.H. 180, 624 A.2d 560 (1993)

27 ALR6th 183—§ 32

State v. McSorley, 128 Wash. App. 598, 116 P.3d 431 (Div. 2 2005)

35 ALR6th 361—§ 19, 21, 23

State v. McVay, 131 Ariz. 369, 641 P.2d 857 (1982)

22 ALR5th 660—§ 15

State v. McVay, 279 N.C. 428, 183 S.E.2d 652 (1971)

55 ALR6th 157—§ 26

State v. McVay, 2000 SD 72, 612 N.W.2d 572 (S.D. 2000)

92 ALR5th 35—§ 2, 7

State v. McWhite, 73 Ohio App. 3d 323, 597 N.E.2d 168 (Lucas Co. 1991)

38 ALR5th 433—§ 10, 11

State v. McWhorter, 138 N.M. 580, 2005-NMCA-133, 124 P.3d 215 (Ct. App. 2005)

23 ALR6th 307—§ 18

State v. McWilliams, 283 P.3d 187 (Kan. 2012)

79 ALR6th 125—§ 5

State v. M.D., 2011-Ohio-1804, 2011 WL 1419629 (Ohio Ct. App. 8th Dist. Cuyahoga County 2011)

70 ALR6th 1—§ 4

State v. Mead, 67 Wash. App. 486, 836 P.2d 257 (1992)

15 ALR5th 391—§ 13

State v. Mead, 100 N.M. 27, 665 P.2d 289 (Ct. App. 1983)

16 ALR6th 329—§ 12
24 ALR6th 591—§ 9, 13

State v. Mead, 318 N.W.2d 440 (Iowa 1982)

39 ALR5th 283—§ 10, 71

State v. Mead, 544 A.2d 1146 (R.I. 1988)

29 ALR6th 1—§ 10

State v. Meade, 80 Ohio St. 3d 419, 1997-Ohio-332, 687 N.E.2d 278 (1997)

19 ALR6th 697—§ 3

State v. Meade, 2010-Ohio-2435, 2010 WL 2184890 (Ohio Ct. App. 12th Dist. Brown County 2010)
65 ALR6th 1—§ 35

State v. Meador, 674 So. 2d 826 (Fla. Dist. Ct. App. 4th Dist. 1996)
90 ALR5th 453—§ 31

State v. Meador, 1992 WL 9521 (Tenn. Crim. App. 1992)
57 ALR5th 141—§ 11

State v. Meadows, 28 Ohio St. 3d 43, 28 Ohio B.R. 146, 503 N.E.2d 697 (1986)
42 ALR5th 291—§ 6

State v. Meadows, 272 N.C. 327, 158 S.E.2d 638 (1968)
28 ALR6th 505—§ 11

State v. Meadows, 745 S.W.2d 886 (Tenn. Crim. App. 1987)
109 ALR5th 99—§ 3

State v. Mealy, 2010 WL 175623 (Del. C.P. 2010)
92 ALR6th 295—§ 7, 19
93 ALR6th 207—§ 13, 25
95 ALR6th 1—§ 5
96 ALR6th 355—§ 5, 25, 26, 36, 37, 49, 63

State v. Meanor, 863 S.W.2d 884 (Mo. 1993)
23 ALR6th 307—§ 44

State v. Means, 213 Or. App. 268, 160 P.3d 1001 (2007)
68 ALR6th 527—§ 44

State v. Means, 547 N.W.2d 615 (Iowa Ct. App. 1996)
101 ALR5th 351—§ 13

State v. Mears, 588 S.W.2d 519 (Mo. Ct. App. S.D. 1979)
70 ALR5th 587—§ 8

State v. Mease, 842 S.W.2d 98 (Mo. 1992)
37 ALR5th 515—§ 26

State v. Mebane, 106 N.C. App. 516, 418 S.E.2d 245 (1992)
39 ALR5th 283—§ 4, 46

State v. Mecham, 173 Ariz. 474, 844 P.2d 641, 122 Ariz. Adv. Rep. 78 (App. 1992)

23 ALR5th 241—§ 45

State v. Mecham, 2000 UT App. 247, 9 P.3d 777 (Utah Ct. App. 2000)
39 ALR5th 283—§ 30

State v. Mechler, 123 S.W.3d 449 (Tex. App. Houston 14th Dist. 2003)
119 ALR5th 379—§ 7, 10

State v. Mechling, 219 W. Va. 366, 633 S.E.2d 311 (2006)
30 ALR6th 1—§ 3, 6, 7

State v. Meckelson, 133 Wash. App. 431, 135 P.3d 991 (Div. 3 2006)
71 ALR6th 1—§ 4

State v. Medders, 153 Ga. App. 680, 266 S.E.2d 331 (1980)
122 ALR5th 439—§ 4

State v. Medibus-Helpmobile, Inc., 481 N.W.2d 86 (Minn. Ct. App. 1992)
79 ALR6th 125—§ 5

State v. Medina, 161 N.C. App. 541, 589 S.E.2d 751 (2003)
3 ALR6th 543—§ 12

State v. Medina, 172 Ariz. 287, 836 P.2d 997, 106 Ariz. Adv. Rep. 59 (App. 1992)
20 ALR5th 398—§ 2, 9, 12, 34, 53

State v. Medina, 189 Neb. 765, 204 N.W.2d 785 (1973)
85 ALR5th 187—§ 5

State v. Medina, 193 Ariz. 504, 975 P.2d 94 (1999)
85 ALR5th 547—§ 8

State v. Medina, 201 N.J. Super. 565, 493 A.2d 623 (1985)
9 ALR5th 464—§ 3 to 5

State v. Medina, 228 Conn. 281, 636 A.2d 351 (1994)
28 ALR6th 505—§ 31

State v. Medley, 400 S.W.2d 87 (Mo. 1966)
61 ALR5th 1—§ 14

State v. Medlin, 333 N.C. 280, 426 S.E.2d 402 (1993)
32 ALR6th 1—§ 5

State v. Medlin, 355 Mo. 564, 197 S.W.2d 626 (1946)
50 ALR5th 467—§ 3 to 5

State v. Medlock, 297 So. 2d 190 (La. 1974)
19 ALR6th 115—§ 4, 9, 10
State v. Medrano, 123 Idaho 114, 844 P.2d 1364 (Ct. App. 1992)
32 ALR6th 1—§ 11
State v. Medrano, 173 Ariz. 393, 844 P.2d 560, 128 Ariz. Adv. Rep. 23 (1992)
20 ALR5th 177—§ 3, 6
State v. Medrano, 285 Mont. 69, 945 P.2d 937 (1997)
5 ALR5th 243—§ 27
State v. Meeker, 128 Wash. App. 1023, 2005 WL 1540807 (Div. 2 2005)
80 ALR6th 239—§ 3, 22
State v. Meekins, 326 N.C. 689, 392 S.E.2d 346 (1990)
57 ALR5th 141—§ 3
State v. Meeks, 118 P.3d 177 (Kan. Ct. App. 2005)
26 ALR6th 511—§ 25
State v. Meeks, 552 So. 2d 328, 14 FLW 2706 (Fla. App. D3 1989)
45 ALR5th 1—§ 5, 11, 18
State v. Meeks, 867 S.W.2d 361 (Tenn. Crim. 1993)
39 ALR5th 283—§ 4, 37
State v. Meemken, 597 N.W.2d 582 (Minn. Ct. App. 1999)
65 ALR6th 537—§ 23
State v. Meints, 212 Neb. 410, 322 N.W.2d 809 (1982)
50 ALR5th 467—§ 4, 9
State v. Meis, 217 Neb. 770, 351 N.W.2d 79 (1984)
42 ALR6th 237—§ 4
State v. Meister, 60 Or. 469, 120 P. 406 (1912)
104 ALR5th 357—§ 9
54 ALR6th 429—§ 20
State v. Meister, 866 S.W.2d 485 (Mo. Ct. App. W. D. 1993)
104 ALR5th 229—§ 12
State v. Meister, 866 S.W.2d 485 (Mo. Ct. App. W.D. 1993)
4 ALR6th 113—§ 6

State v. Mejia, 233 Conn. 215 (1995)
36 ALR5th 255—§ 8, 14
State v. Melanson, 140 N.H. 199, 665 A.2d 338 (1995)
84 ALR6th 293—§ 25, 27
State v. Melcher, 15 Ariz. App. 157, 487 P.2d 3 (Div. 2 1971)
89 ALR6th 565—§ 21
State v. Melcher, 1995 WL 87491 (Neb. Ct. App. 1995)
35 ALR6th 497—§ 21, 35
State v. Melchert-Dinkel, 816 N.W.2d 703 (Minn. Ct. App. 2012)
96 ALR6th 475—§ 4
State v. Melchert-Dinkel, 844 N.W.2d 13, 42 Media L. Rep. (BNA) 1555, 96 A.L.R.6th 755 (Minn. 2014)
96 ALR6th 475—§ 3, 7, 64
State v. Melchoir, 1999 WL 148464 (Ohio Ct. App. 8th Dist. Cuyahoga County 1999)
78 ALR5th 489—§ 3, 10
63 ALR6th 351—§ 3
State v. Mele, 103 N.J. Super. 353, 247 A.2d 176 (County Ct. 1968)
72 ALR5th 607—§ 3, 4
State v. Melemai, 64 Haw. 479, 643 P.2d 541 (1982)
57 ALR6th 83—§ 17
State v. Melendez, 168 Ariz. 275, 812 P.2d 1093, 80 Ariz. Adv. Rep. 46 (App. 1991)
14 ALR5th 913—§ 3
State v. Melendrez, 81 Wash. App. 1003, 1996 WL 146718 (Div. 1 1996)
4 ALR6th 599—§ 16
State v. Melendrez, 91 N.M. 259, 572 P.2d 1267 (Ct. App. 1977)
82 ALR5th 359—§ 3
84 ALR5th 487—§ 22
State v. Melick, 131 Wash. App. 835, 129 P.3d 816 (Div. 1 2006)
78 ALR6th 1—§ 18
State v. Melin, 428 N.W.2d 227, 48 Ed. Law Rep. 977 (N.D. 1988)
70 ALR5th 169—§ 11
State v. Mell, 39 Kan. App. 2d 471, 182 P.3d 1 (2008)

62 ALR6th 413—§ 5, 6, 43
State v. Mellett, 642 N.W.2d 779 (Minn. Ct. App. 2002)

58 ALR6th 215—§ 5
State v. Mellon, 905 A.2d 138 (Del. Fam. Ct. 2006)

38 ALR6th 1—§ 15
State v. Mellor, 73 Utah 104, 272 P. 635 (1928)

59 ALR5th 1—§ 4 to 6
State v. Melloy, 398 N.E.2d 1382 (Ind. Ct. App. 1st Dist. 1980)

15 ALR6th 1—§ 4, 9, 10, 14
State v. Melot, 108 Ariz. 527, 502 P.2d 1346 (1972)

28 ALR6th 505—§ 14
State v. Melson, 638 S.W.2d 342 (Tenn. 1982)

9 ALR5th 369—§ 2, 6, 9, 11
State v. Melton, 141 Ohio App. 3d 713, 753 N.E.2d 241 (1st Dist. Hamilton County 2001)

7 ALR6th 233—§ 5
State v. Melton, 239 Neb. 506, 476 N.W.2d 842 (1991)

30 ALR6th 103—§ 3, 29, 34
32 ALR6th 1—§ 11
State v. Melton, 239 Neb. 790, 478 N.W.2d 341 (1992)

29 ALR6th 1—§ 8
State v. Melton, 296 So. 2d 280 (La. 1974)

94 ALR5th 393—§ 13
State v. Melton, 456 So. 2d 192 (La. Ct. App. 4th Cir. 1984)

9 ALR6th 1—§ 17
State v. Melvern, 32 Wash. 7, 72 P. 489 (1903)

11 ALR5th 497—§ 2, 5
State v. Melvin, 32 N.C. App. 772, 233 S.E.2d 636 (1977)

68 ALR5th 343—§ 3, 12
State v. Melvin, 132 N.H. 308, 564 A.2d 458 (1989)

93 ALR5th 327—§ 28
State v. Melvin, 390 A.2d 1024 (Me. 1978)

42 ALR6th 237—§ 5
State v. Melvin, 913 S.W.2d 195 (Tenn. Crim. App. 1995)

73 ALR5th 383—§ 6, 19
State v. Menard, 844 So. 2d 1117 (La. Ct. App. 3d Cir. 2003)

9 ALR6th 363—§ 51
State v. Mendez, 56 Wash. App. 458, 784 P.2d 168 (1989)

32 ALR5th 149—§ 4, 5, 15, 22, 23, 29, 35
State v. Mendez, 88 Wash. App. 785, 947 P.2d 256 (1997)

66 ALR5th 397—§ 17, 21
State v. Mendez, 129 P.3d 582 (Kan. 2006)

26 ALR6th 511—§ 25
State v. Mendez, 137 Wash. 2d 208, 970 P.2d 722 (1999)

92 ALR6th 171—§ 24
State v. Mendez, 144 P.3d 81 (Kan. Ct. App. 2006)

26 ALR6th 511—§ 25
State v. Mendez, 157 Wis. 2d 289, 459 N.W.2d 578 (Ct. App. 1990)

121 ALR5th 551—§ 13
State v. Mendez, 308 Or. 9, 774 P.2d 1082 (1989)

57 ALR5th 141—§ 7
State v. Mendibles, 25 Ariz. App. 392, 543 P.2d 1149 (1975)

5 ALR5th 243—§ 62
State v. Mendibles, 129 Ariz. 124, 629 P.2d 91 (App. 1981)

22 ALR5th 660—§ 6, 12
State v. Mendoza, 96 Wis. 2d 106, 291 N.W.2d 478 (1980)

42 ALR6th 237—§ 12
State v. Mendoza, 104 Ariz. 395, 454 P.2d 140 (1969)

85 ALR5th 1—§ 16
State v. Mendoza, 109 Ariz. 445, 511 P.2d 627 (1973)

34 ALR5th 125—§ 3
State v. Mendoza, 227 Wis. 2d 838, 596 N.W.2d 736 (1999)

75 ALR5th 295—§ 22

State v. Mendoza, 2002 WL 31756969 (Iowa Ct. App. 2002)

26 ALR6th 511—§ 43
43 ALR6th 475—§ 6, 26

State v. Mendoza, 2006 WL 280596 (N.J. Super. Ct. App. Div. 2006)

26 ALR6th 511—§ 17

State v. Mendoza, 2011 WL 709751 (N.J. Super. Ct. App. Div. 2011)

65 ALR6th 537—§ 21, 22

State v. Mendoza-Lazaro, 211 Or. App. 349, 155 P.3d 63 (2007)

30 ALR6th 1—§ 3, 6

State v. Menne, 380 So. 2d 14 (La. 1980)

29 ALR6th 1—§ 9

State v. Mentola, 691 S.W.2d 420 (Mo. App. 1985)

5 ALR5th 243—§ 19

State v. Menz, 75 Wash. App. 351, 880 P.2d 48 (Div. 2 1994)

58 ALR6th 499—§ 30

State v. Meola, 1998 WL 729589 (Wash. Ct. App. Div. 1 1998)

73 ALR5th 383—§ 5

State v. Mercadante, 2004-Ohio-3593, 2004 WL 1516841 (Ohio Ct. App. 8th Dist. Cuyahoga County 2004)

58 ALR6th 215—§ 7

State v. Mercado, 166 Vt. 632, 699 A.2d 50 (1997)

7 ALR6th 169—§ 8

State v. Mercer, 2 N.C. App. 152, 162 S.E.2d 563 (1968)

24 ALR6th 747—§ 17

State v. Mercer, 101 Wis. 2d 731, 306 N.W.2d 306 (Ct. App. 1981)

31 ALR6th 465—§ 23, 31

State v. Merchant, 791 S.W.2d 840 (Mo. Ct. App. W.D. 1990)

95 ALR5th 125—§ 5

State v. Mercy, 55 Wash. 2d 530, 348 P.2d 978 (1960)

57 ALR6th 445—§ 7

State v. Meredith, 236 Kan. 866, 696 P.2d 403 (1985)

46 ALR6th 63—§ 3

State v. Meredith, 337 Or. 299, 96 P.3d 342 (2004)

5 ALR6th 385—§ 4

State v. Meredith, 400 So. 2d 580 (La. 1981)

9 ALR6th 1—§ 17
28 ALR6th 505—§ 9

State v. Meredith, 2008 WL 942616 (Minn. Ct. App. 2008)

51 ALR6th 139—§ 5

State v. Merino, 81 Haw. 198, 915 P.2d 672 (1996)

9 ALR6th 633—§ 4, 13, 24, 31
10 ALR6th 265—§ 5, 13
12 ALR6th 389—§ 13
13 ALR6th 603—§ 27

State v. Mermis, 105 Wash. App. 738, 20 P.3d 1044, 44 U.C.C. Rep. Serv. 2d 446 (Div. 1 2001)

57 ALR6th 445—§ 7

State v. Merriam, 264 Conn. 617, 835 A.2d 895 (2003)

55 ALR6th 157—§ 65

State v. Merrick, 219 S.W.3d 281 (Mo. Ct. App. S.D. 2007)

37 ALR6th 357—§ 3, 25, 41, 48

State v. Merrifield, 180 Kan. 267, 303 P.2d 155 (1956)

66 ALR5th 397—§ 3, 4, 13

State v. Merrill, 52 S.D. 129, 216 N.W. 874 (1927)

66 ALR5th 397—§ 3, 4, 11

State v. Merrill, 136 Ariz. 300, 665 P.2d 1022 (Ct. App. Div. 1 1983)

92 ALR5th 35—§ 17, 25

State v. Merrill, 252 Neb. 510, 563 N.W.2d 340, 60 A.L.R.5th 755 (1997)

60 ALR5th 1—§ 8

State v. Merrill, 428 N.W.2d 361 (Minn. 1988)

9 ALR5th 369—§ 6

State v. Merrill, 450 N.W.2d 318 (Minn. 1990)

64 ALR5th 671—§ 12 to 14

State v. Merritt, 23 Conn. L. Rptr. 215, 1998 WL 867267 (Conn. Super. Ct. 1998)

92 ALR6th 1—§ 3

State v. Merritt, 143 N.H. 714, 738 A.2d 343 (1999)

68 ALR6th 527—§ 38

State v. Merritt, 519 So. 2d 36 (Fla. Dist. Ct. App. 3d Dist. 1987)

125 ALR5th 281—§ 9

State v. Mershon, 2011 WL 1598779 (N.J. Super. Ct. App. Div. 2011)

70 ALR6th 361—§ 18, 19

State v. Merski, 113 N.H. 323, 307 A.2d 825 (1973)

72 ALR5th 607—§ 4

State v. Merwin, 131 Idaho 642, 962 P.2d 1026 (1998)

90 ALR5th 453—§ 8

State v. Mesa, 520 So. 2d 328 (Fla. Dist. Ct. App. 3d Dist. 1988)

113 ALR5th 597—§ 8

State v. Meshaw, 246 N.C. 205, 98 S.E.2d 13 (1957)

29 ALR5th 59—§ 58

State v. Messer, 2009-Ohio-312, 2009 WL 162058 (Ohio Ct. App. 4th Dist. Ross County 2009)

64 ALR6th 1—§ 7, 9, 11

State v. Messervy, 258 S.C. 110, 187 S.E.2d 524 (1972)

90 ALR6th 385—§ 5

State v. Messina, 1984 WL 3624 (Ohio Ct. App. 8th Dist. Cuyahoga County 1984)

88 ALR5th 121—§ 12, 36

State v. Messinger, 8 Wash. App. 829, 509 P.2d 382 (Div. 3 1973)

12 ALR6th 267—§ 13

State v. Messino, 325 Mo. 743, 30 S.W.2d 750 (1930)

45 ALR5th 591—§ 14

State v. Messner, 246 Wis. 2d 669, 2001 WI App 146, 630 N.W.2d 275 (Ct. App. 2001)

34 ALR6th 1—§ 10

State v. Metcalf, 60 Ohio App. 2d 212, 14 Ohio Ops. 3d 186, 396 N.E.2d 786 (Tuscarawas Co. 1977)

1 ALR5th 938—§ 2, 5, 6

State v. Methfessel, 718 S.W.2d 534 (Mo. App. 1986)

5 ALR5th 243—§ 31

State v. Metje, 269 S.W.2d 128 (Mo. Ct. App. 1954)

95 ALR5th 229—§ 2, 6

State v. Metlin, 467 So. 2d 876 (La. App. 3d Cir. 1985)

15 ALR5th 391—§ 13

State v. Metoyer, 427 So. 2d 93 (La. Ct. App. 3d Cir. 1983)

63 ALR6th 1—§ 53

State v. Metoyer, 612 So. 2d 755 (La. App. 5th Cir. 1992)

7 ALR5th 263—§ 4

State v. Mettenbrink, 3 Neb. App. 7, 520 N.W.2d 780 (1994)

15 ALR5th 391—§ 53

State v. Metz, 131 Or. App. 706, 887 P.2d 795 (1994)

79 ALR5th 33—§ 9, 52

State v. Metz, 162 Or. App. 448, 986 P.2d 714 (1999)

79 ALR5th 33—§ 3

State v. Metz, 422 N.W.2d 754 (Minn. Ct. App. 1988)

64 ALR5th 637—§ 3

State v. Metzger, 199 Neb. 186, 256 N.W.2d 691 (1977)

108 ALR5th 593—§ 53

State v. Metzner, 244 N.W.2d 215 (N.D. 1976)

117 ALR5th 513—§ 5, 12
28 ALR6th 505—§ 14

State v. Meunier, 115 Wis. 2d 696, 339 N.W.2d 367 (Ct. App. 1983)

103 ALR6th 347—§ 13

State v. Meunier, 126 Vt. 176, 224 A.2d 922 (1966)

28 ALR6th 505—§ 9

State v. Meyer, 120 Or. App. 319, 852 P.2d 879 (1993)

42 ALR5th 291—§ 4, 10

State v. Meyer, 128 Wis. 2d 556, 381 N.W.2d 620 (App. 1985)

45 ALR5th 591—§ 15

For assistance, call 1-800-328-4880

State v. Meyer, 216 Wis. 2d 729, 576 N.W.2d 260 (1998)
67 ALR5th 361—§ 3, 6
85 ALR5th 1—§ 22
State v. Meyer, 283 Or. 449, 583 P.2d 553 (1978)
45 ALR5th 767—§ 2, 9
State v. Meyer, 1998 SD 122, 587 N.W.2d 719 (S.D. 1998)
78 ALR6th 297—§ 45
State v. Meyer, 2004 MT 272, 323 Mont. 173, 99 P.3d 185 (2004)
6 ALR6th 533—§ 19
State v. Meyers, 21 Utah 2d 110, 441 P.2d 510 (1968)
35 ALR6th 127—§ 5
State v. Meyers, 223 Neb. 773, 393 N.W.2d 533 (1986)
29 ALR6th 1—§ 10
State v. Meyers, 748 So. 2d 554 (La. Ct. App. 4th Cir. 1999)
12 ALR6th 267—§ 5
State v. Meyers, 1984 WL 3306 (Ohio Ct. App. 12th Dist.Warren County 1984)
57 ALR5th 141—§ 7, 13
State v. Meza, 2005-Ohio-1221, 2005 WL 635028 (Ohio Ct. App. 6th Dist. Lucas County 2005)
24 ALR6th 1—§ 31
State v. Meza, 2006 MT 210, 333 Mont. 305, 143 P.3d 422 (2006)
71 ALR6th 1—§ 8
State v. Michael, 141 W. Va. 1, 87 S.E.2d 595 (1955)
76 ALR5th 1—§ 8
State v. Michael G., 106 N.M. 644, 748 P.2d 17 (App. 1987)
31 ALR5th 229—§ 10, 17, 43
State v. Michael J.B., 187 Wis. 2d 295, 523 N.W.2d 209 (Ct. App. 1994)
87 ALR5th 277—§ 8
State v. Michael M., 2001 ME 92, 772 A.2d 1179 (Me. 2001)
31 ALR5th 229—§ 17, 28
State v. Michaels, 136 N.J. 299, 642 A.2d 1372, 91 Ed. Law Rep. 1034 (1994)

87 ALR5th 693—§ 3
State v. Michaels, 264 N.J. Super. 579, 625 A.2d 489, 83 Ed. Law Rep. 239 (App. Div. 1993)
45 ALR5th 531—§ 7
85 ALR5th 595—§ 7
65 ALR6th 537—§ 19, 20
State v. Michaels, 543 S.W.2d 245 (Mo. Ct. App. 1976)
55 ALR6th 157—§ 106, 115
State v. Michaud, 1998 ME 251, 724 A.2d 1222 (Me. 1998)
30 ALR6th 103—§ 19
State v. Micheliche, 220 N.J. Super. 532, 533 A.2d 41 (App. Div. 1987)
32 ALR6th 1—§ 10
State v. Michels, 141 Wis. 2d 81, 414 N.W.2d 311 (Ct. App. 1987)
119 ALR5th 275—§ 7, 11
121 ALR5th 551—§ 13
State v. Michels, 726 So. 2d 449 (La. Ct. App. 5th Cir. 1999)
124 ALR5th 657—§ 4, 8
State v. Michielli, 132 Wash. 2d 229, 937 P.2d 587, 71 A.L.R.5th 705 (1997)
71 ALR5th 1—§ 49
State v. Mickelson, 18 Or. App. 647, 526 P.2d 583 (1974)
12 ALR6th 553—§ 13, 24
State v. Mickey, 2003-Ohio-6878, 2003 WL 22966889 (Ohio Ct. App. 8th Dist. Cuyahoga County 2003)
78 ALR6th 297—§ 40
State v. Mickle, 199 Iowa 704, 202 N.W. 549 (1925)
64 ALR6th 655—§ 15
State v. Miday, 263 N.C. 747, 140 S.E.2d 325 (1965)
94 ALR5th 613—§ 3, 8
State v. Middaugh, 12 Or. App. 589, 507 P.2d 42 (1973)
65 ALR5th 407—§ 3, 8, 17
State v. Middlebrooks, 840 S.W.2d 317 (Tenn. 1992)
57 ALR5th 141—§ 11
101 ALR5th 187—§ 9

State v. Middlebrooks, 995 S.W.2d 550 (Tenn. 1999)
79 ALR5th 33—§ 71

State v. Middlebrooks, 1998 WL 13819 (Tenn. Crim. App. 1998)
72 ALR5th 529—§ 6

State v. Middleham, 62 Iowa 150, 17 N.W. 446 (1883)
23 ALR6th 1—§ 26

State v. Middleton, 135 Wis. 2d 297, 399 N.W.2d 917 (Ct. App. 1986)
96 ALR5th 327—§ 3
124 ALR5th 1—§ 3
101 ALR6th 331—§ 14

State v. Middleton, 220 W. Va. 89, 640 S.E.2d 152 (2006)
29 ALR6th 1—§ 8

State v. Middleton, 266 S.C. 251, 222 S.E.2d 763 (1976)
55 ALR5th 125—§ 3, 7

State v. Middleton, 294 Or. 427, 657 P.2d 1215 (1983)
57 ALR5th 315—§ 2

State v. Middleton, 295 S.C. 318, 368 S.E.2d 457 (1988)
20 ALR5th 177—§ 3, 10

State v. Middleton, 299 N.J. Super. 22, 690 A.2d 623 (App. Div. 1997)
65 ALR6th 537—§ 43

State v. Middleton, 854 S.W.2d 504 (Mo. Ct. App. W.D. 1993)
25 ALR6th 379—§ 31, 38

State v. Middleton, 995 S.W.2d 443 (Mo. 1999)
37 ALR5th 515—§ 5
79 ALR5th 33—§ 47, 53
83 ALR6th 255—§ 15

State v. Middleton, No. 51545 (January 15, 1987, Ct. App. Ohio, 8th App. Dist. Cuyahoga Co.)
39 ALR5th 283—§ 14, 42

State v. Midgett, 2004 SD 57, 680 N.W.2d 288 (S.D. 2004)
27 ALR6th 183—§ 4

State v. Midland Equities of New York, Inc., 117 Misc. 2d 203, 458 N.Y.S.2d 126 (Sup 1982)

32 ALR6th 531—§ 10

State v. Midwest Pride IV, Inc., 131 Ohio App. 3d 1, 721 N.E.2d 458 (12th Dist. Fayette County 1998)
59 ALR5th 749—§ 4

State v. Miebach, 52 Or. App. 709, 629 P.2d 1312 (1981)
51 ALR6th 1—§ 24
70 ALR6th 361—§ 29
72 ALR6th 141—§ 9, 12

State v. Mier, 147 N.J. Super. 17, 370 A.2d 515 (App. Div. 1977)
67 ALR5th 361—§ 2 to 4, 6

State v. Mierz, 127 Wash. 2d 460, 901 P.2d 286, 50 A.L.R.5th 921 (1995)
50 ALR5th 703—§ 14, 27

State v. Migliore, 2009 WL 2408378 (N.J. Super. Ct. App. Div. 2009)
58 ALR6th 499—§ 38
78 ALR6th 297—§ 83

State v. Migliorino, 150 Wis. 2d 513, 442 N.W.2d 36 (1989)
3 ALR5th 521—§ 4, 5

State v. Mignano, 1990 WL 18129 (Ohio Ct. App. 9th Dist.Summit County 1990)
61 ALR5th 1—§ 14

State v. Miguel, 209 Ariz. 338, 101 P.3d 214 (Ct. App. Div. 1 2004)
27 ALR6th 491—§ 4

State v. Migues, 194 La. 1081, 195 So. 545 (1940)
111 ALR5th 491—§ 3, 9

State v. Mihill, 394 A.2d 1179 (Me. 1978)
19 ALR6th 697—§ 8

State v. Mikolinski, 56 Conn. App. 252, 742 A.2d 1264 (1999)
74 ALR5th 319—§ 6

State v. Mikulewicz, 462 A.2d 497 (Me. 1983)
28 ALR6th 505—§ 8

State v. Mikusch, 138 Ill. 2d 242, 149 Ill. Dec. 704, 562 N.E.2d 168, 59 BNA FEP Cas. 424, 55 CCH EPD ¶ 40511 (1990)
51 ALR5th 1—§ 8

State v. Milano, 297 N.C. 485, 256 S.E.2d 154 (1979)

117 ALR5th 513—§ 29

State v. Milby, 26 Wash. 661, 67 P. 362 (1901)

5 ALR6th 1—§ 69

State v. Milek, 82 Or. App. 88, 727 P.2d 164 (1986)

124 ALR5th 1—§ 4

State v. Miles, 77 Wash. 2d 593, 464 P.2d 723 (1970)

5 ALR5th 243—§ 2, 45, 48

State v. Miles, 87 N.J. Super. 571, 210 A.2d 236 (Law Div. 1965)

78 ALR6th 417—§ 4

State v. Miles, 101 S.W.3d 180 (Tex. App. Dallas 2003)

71 ALR6th 335—§ 10

State v. Miles, 197 Or. App. 86, 104 P.3d 604 (2005)

50 ALR6th 353—§ 15, 42

State v. Miles, 203 Kan. 707, 457 P.2d 166 (1969)

84 ALR6th 427—§ 4

State v. Miles, 339 So. 2d 735 (La. 1976)

62 ALR5th 121—§ 6

State v. Milette, 1998 WL 388354 (R.I. Super. Ct. 1998)

92 ALR6th 171—§ 18

State v. Milk, 519 N.W.2d 313, 37 A.L.R.5th 895 (S.D. 1994)

37 ALR5th 703—§ 3

State v. Milk Handlers & Processors Ass'n, Inc., 52 Misc. 2d 658, 276 N.Y.S.2d 803 (Sup 1967)

120 ALR5th 351—§ 12

State v. Milkie, 306 Wis. 2d 849, 2008 WI App 1, 743 N.W.2d 167 (Ct. App. 2007)

45 ALR6th 337—§ 21

State v. Millan, 151 Wash. App. 492, 212 P.3d 603 (Div. 2 2009)

56 ALR6th 1—§ 43, 44

State v. Millan, 290 Conn. 816, 966 A.2d 699 (2009)

67 ALR6th 103—§ 4

State v. Miller, 16 Ariz. App. 92, 491 P.2d 481 (1971)

5 ALR5th 243—§ 19

State v. Miller, 43 Ohio App. 3d 44, 539 N.E.2d 693 (Medina Co. 1988)

38 ALR5th 433—§ 2, 3, 15

State v. Miller, 43 Or. App. 421, 602 P.2d 1141 (1979)

85 ALR5th 1—§ 17

State v. Miller, 44 Ohio App. 3d 42, 541 N.E.2d 105 (6th Dist. Wood County 1988)

80 ALR5th 55—§ 3
72 ALR6th 1—§ 4

State v. Miller, 54 Haw. 1, 54 Haw. 55, 501 P.2d 363 (1972)

92 ALR5th 593—§ 3, 5, 7, 10, 11
71 ALR6th 283—§ 5

State v. Miller, 61 N.C. App. 1, 300 S.E.2d 431 (1983)

85 ALR5th 187—§ 9

State v. Miller, 67 N.J. 229, 337 A.2d 36 (1975)

42 ALR6th 237—§ 14

State v. Miller, 77 N.C. App. 436, 335 S.E.2d 187 (1985)

48 ALR5th 473—§ 8

State v. Miller, 77 Ohio App. 3d 305, 602 N.E.2d 296 (8th Dist. Cuyahoga County 1991)

61 ALR5th 1—§ 3, 5

State v. Miller, 105 Ohio App. 3d 679, 664 N.E.2d 1309 (4th Dist. Washington County 1995)

71 ALR5th 285—§ 3

State v. Miller, 111 Kan. 231, 206 P. 744, 22 A.L.R. 788 (1922)

35 ALR5th 757—§ 3

State v. Miller, 112 Ariz. 95, 537 P.2d 965 (1975)

103 ALR6th 347—§ 13

State v. Miller, 117 Ohio App. 3d 750, 691 N.E.2d 703 (11th Dist. Lake County 1997)

68 ALR5th 343—§ 3, 4

State v. Miller, 122 Ohio App. 3d 111, 701 N.E.2d 390 (3d Dist. Marion County 1997)

11 ALR6th 237—§ 13
State v. Miller, 131 Idaho 186, 953 P.2d
626 (Ct. App. 1998)
19 ALR6th 697—§ 12
State v. Miller, 141 Wash. App. 1026,
2007 WL 3347833 (Div. 1 2007)
69 ALR6th 579—§ 4
State v. Miller, 147 P.3d 163 (Kan. Ct.
App. 2006)
34 ALR6th 1—§ 8
State v. Miller, 159 N.J. Super. 552, 388
A.2d 993 (1978)
55 ALR5th 125—§ 12, 20, 22
State v. Miller, 164 La. 191, 113 So. 813
(1927)
102 ALR5th 525—§ 19
State v. Miller, 164 La. 192, 113 So. 814
(1927)
102 ALR5th 525—§ 19
State v. Miller, 197 W. Va. 588, 476
S.E.2d 535 (1996)
80 ALR5th 469—§ 3, 5
State v. Miller, 202 Conn. 463, 522 A.2d
249 (1987)
5 ALR5th 243—§ 61
State v. Miller, 204 N.W.2d 834 (Iowa
1973)
52 ALR5th 655—§ 2, 5
State v. Miller, 205 N.J. 109, 13 A.3d
873, 65 A.L.R.6th 809 (2011)
65 ALR6th 537—§ 28
State v. Miller, 208 Or. App. 424, 144
P.3d 1052 (2006)
30 ALR6th 1—§ 3, 6
State v. Miller, 226 Neb. 576, 412
N.W.2d 849 (1987)
94 ALR6th 191—§ 6
96 ALR6th 355—§ 60
State v. Miller, 227 Conn. 363, 630 A.2d
1315 (1993)
74 ALR5th 319—§ 4
State v. Miller, 260 S.C. 1, 193 S.E.2d
802 (1972)
55 ALR5th 125—§ 7
State v. Miller, 277 N.J. Super. 122, 649
A.2d 94 (App. Div. 1994)
71 ALR6th 335—§ 21, 26

State v. Miller, 298 Ga. App. 584, 680
S.E.2d 627 (2009)
56 ALR6th 185—§ 16
State v. Miller, 300 Or. 203, 709 P.2d
225 (1985)
58 ALR6th 499—§ 17
State v. Miller, 308 N.W.2d 4 (Iowa
1981)
26 ALR5th 1—§ 3
State v. Miller, 313 N.W.2d 460 (S.D.
1981)
54 ALR5th 141—§ 3, 10
State v. Miller, 330 N.C. 56, 408 S.E.2d
846 (1991)
3 ALR6th 269—§ 5, 13, 22
State v. Miller, 331 Wis. 2d 732, 2011
WI App 34, 797 N.W.2d 528 (Ct.
App. 2011)
71 ALR6th 625—§ 6, 14, 29
State v. Miller, 336 S.E.2d 910 (W. Va.
1985)
39 ALR5th 283—§ 2, 4, 59
State v. Miller, 342 N.J. Super. 474, 777
A.2d 348, 123 A.L.R.5th 673 (App.
Div. 2001)
123 ALR5th 221—§ 2, 3
State v. Miller, 364 Mo. 320, 261 S.W.2d
103 (1953)
54 ALR6th 429—§ 11
State v. Miller, 477 S.E.2d 915 (N.C.
1996)
57 ALR5th 141—§ 7
State v. Miller, 486 S.W.2d 435 (Mo.
1972)
11 ALR5th 52—§ 2, 5, 6
State v. Miller, 495 So. 2d 422 (La. Ct.
App. 3d Cir. 1986)
103 ALR5th 463—§ 3
State v. Miller, 510 N.W.2d 638 (N.D.
1994)
84 ALR6th 293—§ 3
State v. Miller, 525 N.W.2d 576 (Minn.
Ct. App. 1994)
37 ALR6th 357—§ 41, 43, 44, 46 to
48, 55, 59, 76
State v. Miller, 555 So. 2d 391 (Fla. Dist.
Ct. App. 3d Dist. 1989)
119 ALR5th 379—§ 7, 10

State v. Miller, 573 N.W.2d 661 (Minn. 1998)
29 ALR6th 1—§ 10
69 ALR6th 579—§ 8, 18, 27
State v. Miller, 645 A.2d 1140 (Me. 1994)
92 ALR5th 35—§ 2
State v. Miller, 659 N.W.2d 275 (Minn. Ct. App. 2003)
34 ALR6th 1—§ 9
State v. Miller, 670 So. 2d 420 (La. Ct. App. 3d Cir. 1996)
88 ALR5th 67—§ 6
State v. Miller, 687 S.E.2d 710 (N.C. Ct. App. 2009)
57 ALR6th 1—§ 3, 4
State v. Miller, 815 S.W.2d 28 (Mo. Ct. App. E.D. 1991)
114 ALR5th 235—§ 8
State v. Miller, 1994 WL 246072 (Minn. App)
50 ALR5th 581—§ 7
State v. Miller, 1996 WL 17313 (Ohio Ct. App. 8th Dist. Cuyahoga County 1996)
88 ALR5th 121—§ 22, 28
State v. Miller, 1997 WL 593811 (Tenn. Crim. App. 1997)
73 ALR5th 383—§ 6
State v. Miller, 1998 M.T. 177, 290 Mont. 97, 966 P.2d 721 (1998)
36 ALR5th 161—§ 9.5
State v. Miller, 1999 WL 153777 (Minn. Ct. App. 1999)
76 ALR5th 1—§ 7, 9
State v. Miller, 1999 WL 797189 (Ohio Ct. App. 3d Dist. Allen County 1999)
78 ALR5th 489—§ 9
State v. Miller, 2000 WL 1273467 (Ohio Ct. App. 4th Dist. Ross County 2000)
29 ALR6th 237—§ 24
State v. Miller, 2000 WL 1867404 (Ohio Ct. App. 6th Dist. Lucas County 2000)
7 ALR6th 233—§ 9

State v. Miller, 2001 WL 333818 (Wash. Ct. App. Div. 2 2001)
87 ALR5th 631—§ 18
State v. Miller, 2002-Ohio-3296, 2002 WL 1392587 (Ohio Ct. App. 1st Dist. Hamilton County 2002)
99 ALR6th 295—§ 8
State v. Miller, 2002 WL 31425221 (Iowa Ct. App. 2002)
43 ALR6th 475—§ 20
State v. Miller, 2004 WI App 117, 2004 WL 1057765 (Wis. Ct. App. 2004)
121 ALR5th 551—§ 6, 8, 9, 14
State v. Miller, 2005 ME 84, 875 A.2d 694 (Me. 2005)
26 ALR6th 511—§ 3, 4, 49
State v. Miller, 2013-Ohio-1185, 2013 WL 1281897 (Ohio Ct. App. 8th Dist. Cuyahoga County 2013)
99 ALR6th 295—§ 13
State v. Miller, 2013-Ohio-1651, 2013 WL 1787565 (Ohio Ct. App. 8th Dist. Cuyahoga County 2013)
99 ALR6th 295—§ 13
State v. Millett, 272 N.J. Super. 68, 639 A.2d 352 (App. Div. 1994)
51 ALR6th 1—§ 18
State v. Millican, 158 N.C. 617, 74 S.E. 107 (1912)
22 ALR5th 1—§ 4, 23, 32, 35
State v. Milligan, 1991 WL 162982 (Minn. Ct. App. 1991)
73 ALR5th 383—§ 5, 22
State v. Millington, 377 So. 2d 685 (Fla. 1979)
50 ALR5th 703—§ 28
State v. Mills, 76 Or. App. 301, 710 P.2d 148 (1985)
42 ALR6th 237—§ 8
State v. Mills, 98 Wash. App. 1013, 1999 WL 1054768 (Div. 1 1999)
111 ALR5th 239—§ 8
State v. Mills, 109 P.3d 1290 (Kan. Ct. App. 2005)
37 ALR6th 357—§ 71
State v. Mills, 117 Idaho 534, 789 P.2d 530 (App. 1990)
54 ALR5th 141—§ 3 to 6

State v. Mills, 199 Neb. 295, 258
N.W.2d 628 (1977)
108 ALR5th 593—§ 41
State v. Mills, 219 W. Va. 28, 631 S.E.2d
586 (2005)
55 ALR6th 157—§ 4, 50, 110
State v. Mills, 332 N.C. 392, 420 S.E.2d
114 (1992)
82 ALR5th 67—§ 11
State v. Mills, 562 N.W.2d 276 (Minn.
1997)
27 ALR6th 183—§ 4
State v. Mills, 1985 WL 4562 (Tenn.
Crim. App. 1985)
73 ALR5th 383—§ 3
State v. Mills, 2004-Ohio-267, 2004 WL
103348 (Ohio Ct. App. 2d Dist.
Greene County 2004)
4 ALR6th 1—§ 10
State v. Millsaps, 30 S.W.3d 364 (Tenn.
Crim. App. 2000)
32 ALR5th 149—§ 51
State v. Milner, 206 Conn. 512, 539
A.2d 80 (1988)
111 ALR5th 1—§ 5, 7, 8, 26
State v. Milosevich, 131 Or. App. 51,
883 P.2d 898 (1994)
106 ALR5th 397—§ 4
State v. Milosh, 5 N.J. Misc. 120, 135
A. 658 (1927)
32 ALR5th 149—§ 29, 33
State v. Milton, 2011-Ohio-4773, 2011
WL 4377924 (Ohio Ct. App. 9th
Dist. Summit County 2011)
79 ALR6th 1—§ 29, 34
State v. Milum, 197 Conn. 602, 500
A.2d 555 (1985)
5 ALR5th 243—§ 5
102 ALR5th 327—§ 9
24 ALR6th 1—§ 19
State v. Milum, 213 Kan. 581, 516 P.2d
984 (1973)
54 ALR5th 141—§ 3, 8
State v. Mims, 9 Wash. App. 213, 511
P.2d 1383 (Div. 3 1973)
55 ALR6th 157—§ 89, 96

State v. Mims, 2006-Ohio-862, 2006
WL 456766 (Ohio Ct. App. 6th Dist.
Ottawa County 2006)
62 ALR6th 413—§ 38
State v. Mincey, 130 Ariz. 389, 636 P.2d
637 (1981)
58 ALR6th 499—§ 24, 97, 113
State v. Mincy, 838 P.2d 648 (Utah Ct.
App. 1992)
29 ALR6th 1—§ 10
State v. Miner, 556 N.W.2d 578 (Minn.
Ct. App. 1996)
17 ALR5th 837—§ 3
State v. Mingo, 77 N.J. 576, 392 A.2d
590 (1978)
66 ALR6th 83—§ 14
State v. Mingua, 42 Ohio App. 2d 35, 71
Ohio Op. 2d 234, 327 N.E.2d 791
(10th Dist. Franklin County 1974)
21 ALR6th 771—§ 5
State v. Minkel, 89 S.D. 144, 230
N.W.2d 233 (1975)
26 ALR5th 1—§ 3, 27, 33
State v. Minnick, 15 Iowa 123, 1863 WL
109 (1863)
5 ALR6th 1—§ 29, 40
State v. Minnick, 413 So. 2d 168 (Fla.
Dist. Ct. App. 2d Dist. 1982)
70 ALR6th 361—§ 31
State v. Minor, 80 Conn. App. 87, 832
A.2d 697 (2003)
39 ALR6th 257—§ 3
40 ALR6th 1—§ 27
State v. Minor, 556 S.W.2d 35 (Mo.
1977)
70 ALR5th 587—§ 3
State v. Minshall, 227 Neb. 210, 416
N.W.2d 585 (1987)
9 ALR6th 633—§ 13
13 ALR6th 603—§ 9
State v. Minshall, 1993 WL 472887
(Ohio Ct. App. 4th Dist. Meigs
County 1993)
9 ALR6th 541—§ 8
State v. Minson, 791 S.W.2d 868 (Mo.
Ct. App. E.D. 1990)
1 ALR6th 549—§ 8, 10

State v. Miracle, 2002-Ohio-4480, 2002 WL 2005685 (Ohio Ct. App. 12th Dist. Butler County 2002)
71 ALR6th 1—§ 22

State v. Miramon, 2007 WL 5578361 (Ariz. Ct. App. Div. 2 2007)
98 ALR6th 455—§ 12

State v. Miranda, 56 Conn. App. 298, 742 A.2d 1276 (2000)
118 ALR5th 253—§ 16

State v. Miranda, 245 Conn. 209, 715 A.2d 680 (1998)
118 ALR5th 253—§ 3, 5
97 ALR6th 539—§ 4

State v. Miranda, 260 Conn. 93, 794 A.2d 506 (2002)
118 ALR5th 253—§ 16

State v. Miranda, 274 Conn. 727, 878 A.2d 1118 (2005)
97 ALR6th 539—§ 4

State v. Miranda, 672 N.W.2d 753 (Iowa 2003)
28 ALR6th 505—§ 12

State v. Mireles, 619 N.W.2d 558 (Minn. Ct. App. 2000)
58 ALR6th 385—§ 3

State v. Mireles, 904 S.W.2d 885 (Tex. App. Corpus Christi 1995)
51 ALR5th 603—§ 4, 14
23 ALR6th 1—§ 15

State v. Mirquet, 914 P.2d 1144 (Utah 1996)
34 ALR6th 1—§ 11

State v. Mische, 448 N.W.2d 412 (N.D. 1989)
2 ALR5th 725—§ 13
12 ALR6th 553—§ 25

State v. Misenheimer, 304 N.C. 108, 282 S.E.2d 791 (1981)
95 ALR5th 125—§ 3

State v. Misiorski, 250 Conn. 280, 738 A.2d 595 (1999)
78 ALR5th 489—§ 14

State v. Miskell, 748 So. 2d 409 (La. 1999)
85 ALR5th 1—§ 50
50 ALR6th 455—§ 7, 14, 17, 45

State v. Miskimens, 22 Ohio Misc. 2d 43, 490 N.E.2d 931 (C.P. 1984)
118 ALR5th 253—§ 18, 19

State v. Miskolczi, 123 N.H. 626, 465 A.2d 919 (1983)
55 ALR6th 391—§ 23, 24

State v. Misner, 16 P.3d 953 (Idaho Ct. App. 2000)
68 ALR5th 343—§ 3

State v. Misner, 410 N.W.2d 216 (Iowa 1987)
39 ALR5th 283—§ 2, 10, 71, 78
45 ALR5th 591—§ 2, 5

State v. Missio, 105 Tenn. 218, 58 S.W. 216 (1900)
57 ALR6th 445—§ 57

State v. Missouri, 337 S.C. 548, 524 S.E.2d 394 (1999)
73 ALR6th 49—§ 53

State v. Missouri State Treasurer, 130 S.W.3d 742 (Mo. Ct. App. E.D. 2004)
29 ALR6th 507—§ 15

State v. Mister, 213 Wis. 2d 485, 570 N.W.2d 911 (Ct. App. 1997)
99 ALR6th 295—§ 19

State v. Mistler, 1985 WL 9329 (Ohio Ct. App. 1st Dist. Hamilton County 1985)
123 ALR5th 221—§ 8

State v. Miszak, 69 Wash. App. 426, 848 P.2d 1329 (1993)
15 ALR5th 391—§ 45

State v. Mitchell, 3 Blackf. 229, 1833 WL 2617 (Ind. 1833)
33 ALR6th 407—§ 18

State v. Mitchell, 22 N.C. App. 663, 207 S.E.2d 263 (1974)
99 ALR5th 557—§ 3, 13

State v. Mitchell, 32 Ohio App. 2d 16, 61 Ohio Op. 2d 9, 288 N.E.2d 216 (10th Dist. Franklin County 1972)
31 ALR6th 333—§ 7, 9, 11

State v. Mitchell, 49 So. 3d 958 (La. Ct. App. 4th Cir. 2010)
63 ALR6th 351—§ 3

State v. Mitchell, 54 Conn. App. 361, 738 A.2d 188 (1999)

CASES CITED IN ALR5th and ALR6th

39 ALR6th 257—§ 47, 48
State v. Mitchell, 55 Wash. 513, 104 P.
791 (1909)

120 ALR5th 125—§ 8
State v. Mitchell, 60 Ohio App. 3d 106,
574 N.E.2d 573 (Cuyahoga Co.
1989)

39 ALR5th 283—§ 14, 57
State v. Mitchell, 62 N.C. App. 21, 302
S.E.2d 265 (1983)

50 ALR5th 467—§ 6, 9
State v. Mitchell, 86 N.M. 343, 524 P.2d
206 (App. 1974)

29 ALR5th 59—§ 19, 34
State v. Mitchell, 103 Wis. 2d 692, 310
N.W.2d 652 (Ct. App. 1981)

28 ALR6th 245—§ 8
State v. Mitchell, 104 N.C. App. 514,
410 S.E.2d 211 (1991)

24 ALR5th 428—§ 18
State v. Mitchell, 112 P.3d 256 (Kan.
2005)

26 ALR6th 511—§ 25
State v. Mitchell, 113 N.H. 542, 311
A.2d 134 (1973)

35 ALR6th 127—§ 5
State v. Mitchell, 117 Ohio App. 3d 703,
691 N.E.2d 354 (8th Dist. Cuyahoga
County 1997)

11 ALR6th 237—§ 4, 9
71 ALR6th 1—§ 5
State v. Mitchell, 117 Wash. 2d 521, 817
P.2d 398 (1991)

84 ALR5th 487—§ 25
State v. Mitchell, 124 N.H. 210, 470
A.2d 885 (1983)

93 ALR5th 527—§ 18
State v. Mitchell, 128 Wash. App. 1054,
2005 WL 1796957 (Div. 3 2005)

26 ALR6th 511—§ 48
State v. Mitchell, 144 P.3d 758 (Kan.
2006)

26 ALR6th 511—§ 25
State v. Mitchell, 154 N.C. App. 186,
571 S.E.2d 640 (2002)

116 ALR5th 479—§ 5
State v. Mitchell, 169 Wis. 2d 153, 485
N.W.2d 807 (1992)

22 ALR5th 261—§ 2
State v. Mitchell, 233 P.3d 767 (Kan. Ct.
App. 2010)

62 ALR6th 161—§ 14
State v. Mitchell, 261 S.C. 452, 200
S.E.2d 448 (1973)

104 ALR5th 357—§ 8
54 ALR6th 429—§ 7
State v. Mitchell, 269 Kan. 349, 7 P.3d
1135 (2000)

3 ALR6th 543—§ 8
State v. Mitchell, 282 Minn. 113, 163
N.W.2d 310 (1968)

30 ALR6th 103—§ 26, 34
State v. Mitchell, 336 N.C. 22, 442
S.E.2d 24, 31 A.L.R.5th 965 (1994)

31 ALR5th 760—§ 7
State v. Mitchell, 368 So. 2d 591 (Fla.
1979)

24 ALR6th 1—§ 9
State v. Mitchell, 390 A.2d 495 (Me.
1978)

68 ALR5th 343—§ 3
32 ALR6th 1—§ 11
State v. Mitchell, 450 N.W.2d 828 (Iowa
1990)

73 ALR5th 615—§ 3, 7
State v. Mitchell, 476 So. 2d 825 (La.
Ct. App. 5th Cir. 1985)

84 ALR6th 427—§ 19
State v. Mitchell, 553 So. 2d 915 (La.
Ct. App. 4th Cir. 1989)

99 ALR6th 295—§ 9
State v. Mitchell, 611 S.W.2d 211 (Mo.
1981)

42 ALR6th 237—§ 9
State v. Mitchell, 652 So. 2d 473, 20
FLW D753 (Fla. App. D2 1995)

48 ALR5th 659—§ 7, 17, 18
State v. Mitchell, 659 S.W.2d 4 (Mo.
App. 1983)

11 ALR5th 218—§ 2, 3
State v. Mitchell, 711 N.W.2d 733 (Iowa
Ct. App. 2006)

103 ALR6th 35—§ 7
State v. Mitchell, 751 S.W.2d 65 (Mo.
Ct. App. E.D. 1988)

For assistance, call 1-800-328-4880

99 ALR6th 113—§ 18
State v. Mitchell, 784 P.2d 365 (Kan. 1989)
39 ALR5th 283—§ 4, 41
State v. Mitchell, 847 S.W.2d 185 (Mo. Ct. App. E.D. 1993)
104 ALR5th 357—§ 3, 4, 6
54 ALR6th 429—§ 5, 7, 11, 20
State v. Mitchell, 997 P.2d 373 (Wash. Ct. App. Div. 1 2000)
72 ALR5th 529—§ 7
State v. Mitchell, 1975 WL 182741 (Ohio Ct. App. 8th Dist. Cuyahoga County 1975)
99 ALR6th 295—§ 19
State v. Mitchell, 1995 WL 678624 (Ohio Ct. App. 9th Dist. Summit County 1995)
111 ALR5th 239—§ 3
State v. Mitchell, 1996 WL 366249 (Neb. Ct. App. 1996)
62 ALR6th 413—§ 38
State v. Mitchell, 1998 ME 128, 712 A.2d 1033 (Me. 1998)
116 ALR5th 313—§ 3
State v. Mitchell, 1998 WL 964580 (Ohio Ct. App. 11th Dist. Portage County 1998)
38 ALR6th 439—§ 9, 10
State v. Mitchell, 2005-Ohio-3896, 2005 WL 1799289 (Ohio Ct. App. 11th Dist. Lake County 2005)
26 ALR6th 511—§ 19
State v. Mitchell, 2009 WI App 21, 316 Wis. 2d 355, 763 N.W.2d 247 (Ct. App. 2008)
78 ALR6th 297—§ 81
State v. Mitchell, 2011 WL 726113 (Conn. Super. Ct. 2011)
69 ALR6th 579—§ 4
State v. Mitjans, 408 N.W.2d 824 (Minn. 1987)
32 ALR5th 149—§ 3, 5, 72, 74
73 ALR5th 383—§ 21
49 ALR6th 343—§ 8
97 ALR6th 567—§ 3, 5, 9
State v. Mitsuda, 86 Haw. 37, 947 P.2d 349 (Haw. 1997)

7 ALR5th 263—§ 7
State v. Mittle, 120 S.C. 526, 113 S.E. 335 (1922)
70 ALR5th 587—§ 3
State v. Mitts, 608 S.W.2d 131 (Mo. App. 1980)
6 ALR5th 733—§ 2, 5, 16
State v. Mix, 239 Mont. 351, 781 P.2d 751 (1989)
9 ALR5th 369—§ 13, 17
State v. Mixion, 110 N.C. App. 138, 429 S.E.2d 363 (1993)
24 ALR5th 465—§ 25, 26
57 ALR5th 141—§ 2, 3
State v. Mixon, 251 Ga. App. 168, 554 S.E.2d 196 (2001)
78 ALR6th 297—§ 38, 80
State v. Mixon, 275 S.C. 575, 274 S.E.2d 406 (1981)
24 ALR6th 1—§ 18
State v. Miyahira, 6 Hawaii App. 320, 721 P.2d 718 (1986)
26 ALR5th 603—§ 4
State v. Miyahira, 98 Haw. 287, 47 P.3d 754 (Ct. App. 2002)
102 ALR5th 525—§ 44
State v. Miyasaki, 62 Hawaii 269, 614 P.2d 915 (1980)
29 ALR5th 1—§ 4
State v. Mizanskey, 901 S.W.2d 95 (Mo. Ct. App. W.D. 1995)
1 ALR6th 549—§ 3, 15
7 ALR6th 169—§ 3
8 ALR6th 265—§ 3
State v. Mizell, 2008-Ohio-4907, 2008 WL 4367552 (Ohio Ct. App. 1st Dist. Hamilton County 2008)
71 ALR6th 625—§ 3, 20, 31
State v. M.J., 21 FLW D1517 (Fla. App. D2 1996)
50 ALR5th 581—§ 10, 17
State v. M.K.O., 833 So. 2d 1265 (La. Ct. App. 2d Cir. 2002)
70 ALR6th 1—§ 14
State v. M.L., 253 N.J. Super. 13, 600 A.2d 1211 (App. Div. 1991)
32 ALR6th 1—§ 5

State v. M.L.A., 785 N.W.2d 763, 68
A.L.R.6th 673 (Minn. Ct. App.
2010)
68 ALR6th 1—§ 17

State v. Mlo, 335 N.C. 353, 440 S.E.2d
98 (1994)
56 ALR6th 185—§ 39
97 ALR6th 567—§ 3, 9

State v. M. M., 407 So. 2d 987, 2 Ed.
Law Rep. 314 (Fla. Dist. Ct. App.
4th Dist. 1981)
70 ALR5th 169—§ 25

State v. Moberg, 85 Wash. App. 1081,
1997 WL 206072 (Div. 2 1997)
39 ALR6th 577—§ 4

State v. Moberly, 121 Mo. 604, 26 S.W.
364 (1894)
45 ALR5th 591—§ 20

State v. Mock, 80 Or. App. 365, 722
P.2d 42 (1986)
71 ALR5th 1—§ 60

State v. Modern Recycling, Inc., 558
N.W.2d 770 (Minn. Ct. App. 1997)
119 ALR5th 205—§ 3

State v. Modest, 88 Wash. App. 239, 944
P.2d 417 (Div. 3 1997)
119 ALR5th 275—§ 8, 11

State v. Moe, 50 N.J. 386, 235 A.2d 678
(1967)
13 ALR6th 603—§ 8
14 ALR6th 517—§ 19

State v. Moe, 56 Wash. 2d 111, 351 P.2d
120 (1960)
55 ALR6th 157—§ 30

State v. Moe, 498 N.W.2d 755 (Minn.
Ct. App. 1993)
92 ALR6th 295—§ 30
95 ALR6th 1—§ 4, 34
96 ALR6th 355—§ 9, 24, 37

State v. Moe, 1998 ND 137, 581 N.W.2d
468 (N.D. 1998)
37 ALR6th 357—§ 10
71 ALR6th 335—§ 5

State v. Moederndorfer, 141 Wis. 2d
823, 416 N.W.2d 627 (Ct. App.
1987)
9 ALR6th 541—§ 3

State v. Moehlenbrock, 1996 WL
523780 (Minn. Ct. App. 1996)
67 ALR6th 209—§ 25, 40

State v. Moeller, 178 Conn. 67, 420
A.2d 1153 (1979)
97 ALR5th 201—§ 3

State v. Moeller, 229 Or. App. 306, 211
P.3d 364 (2009)
81 ALR6th 505—§ 15

State v. Moeller, 388 N.W.2d 872 (S.D.
1986)
18 ALR5th 1—§ 2, 3

State v. Moeller, 548 N.W.2d 156 (S.D.
1996)
90 ALR5th 453—§ 22

State v. Moeller, 1996 SD 60, 548
N.W.2d 465 (S.D. 1996)
38 ALR6th 439—§ 7

State v. Moen, 309 Or. 45, 786 P.2d 111
(1990)
38 ALR5th 433—§ 11, 16, 18, 31
21 ALR6th 1—§ 4

State v. Moerman, 182 Ariz. 255, 895
P.2d 1018 (Ct. App. Div. 1 1994)
33 ALR6th 407—§ 5

State v. Moffatt, 2009 WL 1643432
(Tenn. Crim. App. 2009)
92 ALR6th 171—§ 14

State v. Mogan, 627 A.2d 527 (Me.
1993)
1 ALR6th 549—§ 8

State v. Mohajerin, 226 Ariz. 103, 244
P.3d 107 (Ct. App. Div. 2 2010)
70 ALR6th 1—§ 9

State v. Moise, 522 So. 2d 1023 (Fla.
Dist. Ct. App. 5th Dist. 1988)
109 ALR5th 99—§ 5

State v. Moity, 245 La. 546, 159 So. 2d
149 (1963)
44 ALR5th 193—§ 15

State v. Moley, 171 Wis. 2d 207, 490
N.W.2d 764 (Ct. App. 1992)
112 ALR5th 429—§ 12

State v. Molina, 101 N.M. 146, 679 P.2d
814 (1984)
41 ALR5th 171—§ 68

State v. Molinario, 530 So. 2d 665 (La.
Ct. App. 4th Cir. 1988)
11 ALR6th 237—§ 6, 12
State v. Molitoni, 6 Hawaii App. 77, 711
P.2d 1303 (1985)
39 ALR5th 283—§ 4, 70
State v. Mollica, 217 N.J. Super. 95, 524
A.2d 1303 (1987)
19 ALR5th 470—§ 3
State v. Mollicone, 654 A.2d 311 (R.I.
1995)
108 ALR5th 593—§ 44
State v. Molnar, 81 N.J. 475, 410 A.2d
37 (1980)
18 ALR5th 1—§ 32
State v. Monaghan, 116 Idaho 972, 783
P.2d 311 (Ct. App. 1989)
87 ALR5th 1—§ 6, 14, 19, 31
State v. Monay, 85 Haw. 282, 943 P.2d
908 (Haw. 1997)
85 ALR5th 1—§ 22, 24
State v. Mondo, 325 N.W.2d 201 (N.D.
1982)
111 ALR5th 239—§ 2
State v. Mondragon, 107 N.M. 421, 759
P.2d 1003 (Ct. App. 1988)
97 ALR5th 293—§ 2, 3
State v. Mongold, 62 Ohio Misc. 2d 178,
594 N.E.2d 183 (C.P. 1991)
15 ALR6th 375—§ 26
State v. Monick, 125 Ariz. 593, 611 P.2d
946 (Ct. App. Div. 1 1980)
92 ALR5th 35—§ 7
State v. Moning, 2002-Ohio-5097, 2002
WL 31127751 (Ohio Ct. App. 1st
Dist. Hamilton County 2002)
76 ALR6th 289—§ 5
77 ALR6th 543—§ 19
State v. Moniz, 92 Haw. 472, 992 P.2d
741 (Ct. App. 1999)
23 ALR6th 307—§ 39
State v. Monk, 63 N.C. App. 512, 305
S.E.2d 755 (1983)
38 ALR6th 97—§ 13
State v. Monk, 511 S.E.2d 332 (N.C. Ct.
App. 1999)
13 ALR5th 628—§ 7, 9, 10.5

State v. Monk & Associates, Inc., 57
Ala. App. 303, 328 So. 2d 306 (Civ.
App. 1976)
69 ALR5th 477—§ 21
State v. Monosso, 103 Wis. 2d 368, 308
N.W.2d 891 (App. 1981)
15 ALR5th 391—§ 4
State v. Monroe, 101 Idaho 251, 611
P.2d 1036 (1980)
58 ALR6th 499—§ 19
State v. Monroe, 103 Idaho 129, 645
P.2d 363 (1982)
124 ALR5th 1—§ 5
State v. Monroe, 123 Wash. App. 1042,
2004 WL 2335219 (Div. 3 2004)
78 ALR6th 1—§ 51
State v. Monroe, 397 So. 2d 1258 (La.
1981)
10 ALR5th 700—§ 16, 17
State v. Monroe, 508 So. 2d 910 (La. Ct.
App. 4th Cir. 1987)
62 ALR6th 259—§ 8, 13
State v. Monroe, 2000 WL 1358093
(Ohio Ct. App. 10th Dist. Franklin
County 2000)
3 ALR6th 543—§ 8
State v. Monschke, 133 Wash. App. 313,
135 P.3d 966 (Div. 2 2006)
71 ALR6th 625—§ 21, 29
State v. Montague, 671 P.2d 187 (Utah
1983)
7 ALR5th 263—§ 5
State v. Montalbo, 73 Haw. 130, 828
P.2d 1274 (1992)
90 ALR5th 453—§ 45
State v. Montalvo, 324 N.W.2d 650
(Minn. 1982)
32 ALR5th 149—§ 94
State v. Montana, 489 So. 2d 348 (La.
Ct. App. 4th Cir. 1986)
19 ALR6th 115—§ 4, 9, 10
State v. Montano, 18 Kan. App. 2d 502,
855 P.2d 979 (1993)
32 ALR5th 149—§ 5, 82, 93, 96
State v. Montano, 95 N.M. 233, 620 P.2d
887 (Ct. App. 1980)
32 ALR6th 1—§ 11

State v. Montano, 126 N.M. 609
8 ALR5th 775—§ 10

State v. Montegut, 618 So. 2d 883 (La. Ct. App. 4th Cir. 1993)
7 ALR6th 169—§ 11, 14

State v. Monteith, 4 Or. App. 90, 477 P.2d 224 (1970)
114 ALR5th 235—§ 4

State v. Montes, 21 P.3d 592 (Kan. Ct. App. 2001)
39 ALR5th 283—§ 65

State v. Montes, 92 Ohio App. 3d 539, 636 N.E.2d 378 (Cuyahoga Co. 1993)
15 ALR5th 391—§ 45

State v. Montgomery, 34 Kan. App. 2d 549, 122 P.3d 392 (2005)
97 ALR6th 653—§ 9

State v. Montgomery, 50 Or. App. 381, 624 P.2d 151 (1981)
39 ALR5th 283—§ 4, 71

State v. Montgomery, 115 Ariz. 583, 566 P.2d 1329 (1977)
99 ALR5th 557—§ 2, 3, 10, 12, 17, 20

State v. Montgomery, 117 Wis. 2d 782, 343 N.W.2d 830 (App. 1983)
31 ALR5th 229—§ 13, 17, 77

State v. Montgomery, 159 Ohio App. 3d 752, 2005-Ohio-1018, 825 N.E.2d 250 (1st Dist. Hamilton County 2005)
26 ALR6th 511—§ 19, 30

State v. Montgomery, 223 S.W.2d 463 (Mo. 1949)
97 ALR5th 293—§ 3, 11
54 ALR6th 429—§ 11

State v. Montgomery, 291 N.C. 91, 229 S.E.2d 572 (1976)
78 ALR5th 1—§ 21

State v. Montgomery, 665 So. 2d 101 (La. Ct. App. 4th Cir. 1995)
64 ALR5th 741—§ 5

State v. Montgomery, 974 P.2d 904 (Wash. Ct. App. Div. 1 1999)
71 ALR5th 637—§ 3

State v. Montgomery, 2000 WL 331798 (Ohio Ct. App. 2d Dist. Clark County 2000)
81 ALR6th 505—§ 17

State v. Montgomery, 2003-Ohio-5332, 2003 WL 22287990 (Ohio Ct. App. 2d Dist. Greene County 2003)
33 ALR6th 407—§ 5

State v. Montgomery, 2007 UT App 24, 2007 WL 274758 (Utah Ct. App. 2007)
27 ALR6th 183—§ 31

State v. Montgomery, 2010 MT 193, 357 Mont. 348, 239 P.3d 929 (2010)
97 ALR6th 263—§ 4

State v. Montijo, 320 N.J. Super. 483, 727 A.2d 533 (Law Div. 1998)
93 ALR5th 527—§ 15

State v. Montoya, 91 N.M. 752, 580 P.2d 973 (Ct. App. 1978)
78 ALR5th 1—§ 65

State v. Montoya, 93 N.M. 84, 596 P.2d 527 (Ct. App. 1979)
70 ALR5th 533—§ 11

State v. Montoya-Franco, 250 Or. App. 665, 282 P.3d 939, 97 A.L.R.6th 817 (2012)
97 ALR6th 567—§ 3, 9, 12

State v. Moody, 214 Conn. 616, 573 A.2d 716 (1990)
82 ALR5th 67—§ 3

State v. Moody, 393 So. 2d 1212 (La. 1981)
13 ALR5th 1—§ 2, 46

State v. Moody, 1984 WL 7879 (Ohio Ct. App. 6th Dist. Lucas County 1984)
71 ALR6th 335—§ 13

State v. Moody, 2009-Ohio-47, 2009 WL 50122 (Ohio Ct. App. 6th Dist. Lucas County 2009)
64 ALR6th 1—§ 7, 9, 11

State v. Moomey, 581 S.W.2d 899 (Mo. Ct. App. E.D. 1979)
62 ALR6th 413—§ 3
67 ALR6th 531—§ 3
69 ALR6th 275—§ 3

State v. Moon, 44 Ohio App. 2d 275, 73 Ohio Op. 2d 298, 337 N.E.2d 794 (2d Dist. Montgomery County 1975)
99 ALR6th 295—§ 13, 19

State v. Moon, 602 S.W.2d 828 (Mo. Ct. App. W.D. 1980)
70 ALR5th 1—§ 11
72 ALR5th 109—§ 10

State v. Mooney, 218 Conn. 85, 588 A.2d 145 (1991)
66 ALR5th 373—§ 1, 4
101 ALR5th 187—§ 9

State v. Moore, 2 Neb. App. 206, 508 N.W.2d 305 (1993)
41 ALR5th 171—§ 7, 8, 12, 19, 68, 79, 93, 108, 114, 120, 133

State v. Moore, 3 Neb. App. 909, 535 N.W.2d 417 (1995)
85 ALR5th 1—§ 16, 26

State v. Moore, 4 Neb. App. 564, 547 N.W.2d 159 (1996)
11 ALR6th 237—§ 4, 8

State v. Moore, 13 Ohio App. 3d 226, 13 Ohio B.R. 278, 468 N.E.2d 920 (Franklin Co. 1983)
39 ALR5th 283—§ 14, 54

State v. Moore, 23 P.3d 815 (Kan. 2001)
5 ALR5th 243—§ 46

State v. Moore, 29 Wash. App. 354, 628 P.2d 522 (Div. 1 1981)
83 ALR5th 277—§ 11

State v. Moore, 33 Wash. App. 55, 651 P.2d 765 (Div. 1 1982)
83 ALR5th 277—§ 11

State v. Moore, 37 N.C. App. 729, 247 S.E.2d 250 (1978)
99 ALR5th 557—§ 10

State v. Moore, 39 Kan. App. 2d 568, 181 P.3d 1258 (2008)
56 ALR6th 323—§ 7, 9, 11

State v. Moore, 62 Hawaii 301, 614 P.2d 931 (1980)
28 ALR5th 459—§ 2, 4, 6

State v. Moore, 90 Ohio St. 3d 47, 2000-Ohio-10, 734 N.E.2d 804 (2000)
114 ALR5th 173—§ 7

State v. Moore, 90 Ohio St. 3d 47, 2000-Ohio-10, 734 N.E.2d 804, 123 A.L.R.5th 661 (2000)
123 ALR5th 179—§ 7, 11

State v. Moore, 90 Wash. App. 1046, 1998 WL 236489 (Div. 1 1998)
85 ALR5th 1—§ 27

State v. Moore, 94 N.C. App. 55, 379 S.E.2d 858 (1989)
9 ALR6th 1—§ 17

State v. Moore, 105 N.J. Super. 567, 253 A.2d 579 (1969)
46 ALR5th 499—§ 3

State v. Moore, 106 R.I. 92, 256 A.2d 197 (1969)
36 ALR5th 255—§ 24

State v. Moore, 122 N.J. 420, 585 A.2d 864 (1991)
9 ALR5th 369—§ 2, 3, 15

State v. Moore, 127 Wis. 2d 566, 379 N.W.2d 902 (Ct. App. 1985)
99 ALR6th 295—§ 16

State v. Moore, 128 S.W.3d 115 (Mo. Ct. App. E.D. 2003)
84 ALR6th 427—§ 19, 21

State v. Moore, 129 N.C. 494, 39 S.E. 626 (1901)
81 ALR5th 563—§ 5

State v. Moore, 135 N.M. 210, 2004-NMCA-035, 86 P.3d 635 (Ct. App. 2004)
41 ALR6th 141—§ 7

State v. Moore, 143 Iowa 240, 121 N.W. 1052 (1909)
97 ALR5th 201—§ 3

State v. Moore, 165 Ohio App. 3d 538, 2006-Ohio-114, 847 N.E.2d 452 (4th Dist. Pike County 2006)
53 ALR6th 305—§ 10

State v. Moore, 169 N.C. App. 458, 612 S.E.2d 446 (2005)
99 ALR6th 295—§ 9

State v. Moore, 178 N.J. Super. 417, 429 A.2d 397 (App. Div. 1981)
79 ALR5th 419—§ 10

State v. Moore, 186 W. Va. 23, 409 S.E.2d 490 (1990)
3 ALR6th 269—§ 9, 22

State v. Moore, 250 Neb. 805, 553 N.W.2d 120 (1996)

93 ALR6th 391—§ 20

State v. Moore, 254 N.J. Super. 295, 603 A.2d 513 (1992)

31 ALR5th 229—§ 3, 11, 17, 42, 62

State v. Moore, 260 N.J. Super. 12, 614 A.2d 1360 (1992)

19 ALR5th 470—§ 12

State v. Moore, 262 N.C. 431, 137 S.E.2d 812 (1964)

85 ALR5th 187—§ 7, 8

State v. Moore, 268 Mont. 20, 885 P.2d 457 (1994)

90 ALR5th 453—§ 14
35 ALR6th 127—§ 5
38 ALR6th 439—§ 3, 12
65 ALR6th 359—§ 9

State v. Moore, 273 N.C. 132, 159 S.E.2d 314 (1968)

14 ALR5th 89—§ 34

State v. Moore, 275 N.C. 198, 166 S.E.2d 652 (1969)

24 ALR5th 465—§ 33 to 35, 39

State v. Moore, 276 N.C. 142, 171 S.E.2d 453 (1970)

24 ALR5th 465—§ 33 to 35, 39

State v. Moore, 278 So. 2d 781 (La. 1972)

86 ALR5th 59—§ 3 to 5, 8

State v. Moore, 330 N.J. Super. 535, 750 A.2d 171 (App. Div. 2000)

78 ALR5th 567—§ 7

State v. Moore, 414 So. 2d 340 (La. 1982)

10 ALR5th 700—§ 4, 16

State v. Moore, 438 N.W.2d 101 (Minn. 1989)

49 ALR5th 639—§ 4
72 ALR6th 437—§ 6

State v. Moore, 458 N.W.2d 90, 9 A.L.R.5th 1058 (Minn. 1990)

9 ALR5th 369—§ 2, 6, 7, 13, 14

State v. Moore, 500 N.W.2d 75 (Iowa 1993)

15 ALR5th 391—§ 32

State v. Moore, 511 S.E.2d 22 (N.C. Ct. App. 1999)

10 ALR5th 538—§ 7

State v. Moore, 521 P.2d 556 (Utah 1974)

37 ALR6th 357—§ 8, 41, 44

State v. Moore, 566 S.E.2d 713 (N.C. Ct. App. 2002)

103 ALR5th 463—§ 9

State v. Moore, 568 So. 2d 612 (La. Ct. App. 4th Cir. 1990)

58 ALR5th 749—§ 2

State v. Moore, 577 A.2d 348 (Me. 1990)

7 ALR5th 73—§ 2, 8

State v. Moore, 609 N.W.2d 502 (Iowa 2000)

18 ALR6th 519—§ 4

State v. Moore, 614 P.2d 931 (Hawaii 1980)

28 ALR5th 459—§ 8

State v. Moore, 640 So. 2d 561 (La. App. 3d Cir. 1994)

47 ALR5th 259—§ 14

State v. Moore, 678 N.E.2d 1258 (Ind. 1997)

72 ALR5th 109—§ 4

State v. Moore, 690 S.W.2d 453 (Mo. Ct. App. E.D. 1985)

119 ALR5th 275—§ 2

State v. Moore, 703 S.W.2d 183 (Tenn. Crim. App. 1985)

88 ALR5th 121—§ 27

State v. Moore, 722 So. 2d 112 (La. Ct. App. 3d Cir. 1998)

39 ALR5th 1—§ 5

State v. Moore, 744 S.W.2d 479 (Mo. Ct. App. S.D. 1988)

124 ALR5th 1—§ 5

State v. Moore, 774 S.W.2d 590 (Tenn. 1989)

70 ALR6th 361—§ 19
72 ALR6th 141—§ 9

State v. Moore, 782 P.2d 497, 120 Utah Adv. Rep. 10 (Utah 1989)

27 ALR5th 593—§ 5, 6, 8, 10, 11

State v. Moore, 788 P.2d 525, 126 Utah Adv. Rep. 11 (Utah App. 1990)

42 ALR5th 291—§ 34

State v. Moore, 847 So. 2d 53 (La. Ct. App. 3d Cir. 2003)

33 ALR6th 91—§ 30

63 ALR6th 351—§ 3

State v. Moore, 1987 WL 9948 (Ohio Ct. App. 5th Dist. Delaware County 1987)

47 ALR6th 107—§ 45

State v. Moore, 1995 WL 539382 (Neb. Ct. App. 1995)

24 ALR6th 1—§ 40

State v. Moore, 2001 WL 1083717 (Minn. Ct. App. 2001)

114 ALR5th 173—§ 9

State v. Moore, 2003-Ohio-5409, 2003 WL 22318832 (Ohio Ct. App. 2d Dist. Montgomery County 2003)

33 ALR6th 407—§ 5

State v. Moore, 2006-Ohio-305, 2006 WL 202756 (Ohio Ct. App. 8th Dist. Cuyahoga County 2006)

26 ALR6th 511—§ 18

State v. Moore, 2006-Ohio-4556, 2006 WL 2536207 (Ohio Ct. App. 12th Dist. Butler County 2006)

26 ALR6th 511—§ 19

State v. Moore, 2007 ND 7, 725 N.W.2d 910, 37 A.L.R.6th 753 (N.D. 2007)

37 ALR6th 357—§ 3, 46, 55

State v. Moore, 2009-Ohio-5927, 2009 WL 3721009 (Ohio Ct. App. 12th Dist. Preble County 2009)

56 ALR6th 1—§ 29

State v. Moore, 2009 UT App 128, 210 P.3d 967 (Utah Ct. App. 2009)

96 ALR6th 269—§ 53

State v. Moorehart, 2009-Ohio-2844, 2009 WL 1677840 (Ohio Ct. App. 5th Dist. Fairfield County 2009)

63 ALR6th 1—§ 5, 42, 46

69 ALR6th 1—§ 29

State v. Moorehead, 811 S.W.2d 425 (Mo. App. 1991)

3 ALR5th 784—§ 6, 20

State v. Moore, No. 10108 (December 23, 1981, Ct. App. Ohio, 9th App. Dist. Summit Co.)

39 ALR5th 283—§ 14, 33

State v. Moorhead, 308 N.W.2d 60 (Iowa 1981)

70 ALR5th 169—§ 15, 17

State v. Moorman, 82 N.C. App. 594, 347 S.E.2d 857 (1986)

104 ALR5th 357—§ 9

54 ALR6th 429—§ 20

State v. Moorman, 505 N.W.2d 593 (Minn. 1993)

86 ALR5th 59—§ 2, 4, 5

87 ALR5th 181—§ 2

88 ALR5th 429—§ 2

State v. Moosey, 504 A.2d 1001 (R.I. 1986)

51 ALR6th 1—§ 18

70 ALR6th 361—§ 19

State v. Mootispaw, 23 Ohio App. 3d 142, 492 N.E.2d 169 (12th Dist. Fayette County 1985)

87 ALR5th 597—§ 12

State v. Mora, 110 Wash. App. 850, 43 P.3d 38 (Div. 3 2002)

57 ALR6th 445—§ 36, 38

State v. Mora, 307 So. 2d 317 (La. 1975)

31 ALR5th 229—§ 3, 17, 23, 77

State v. Mora, 618 A.2d 1275 (R.I. 1993)

32 ALR5th 149—§ 52, 74, 77

State v. Morahan, 23 Del. 494, 77 A. 488 (1895)

50 ALR5th 467—§ 6

State v. Morales, 32 Ohio St. 3d 252, 513 N.E.2d 267 (1987)

98 ALR6th 455—§ 18

State v. Morales, 39 Conn. App. 617, 667 A.2d 68 (1995)

40 ALR5th 113—§ 4

State v. Morales, 53 Wash. App. 681, 769 P.2d 878 (1989)

20 ALR5th 398—§ 20, 25, 26

State v. Morales, 78 Conn. App. 25, 826 A.2d 217 (2003)

97 ALR6th 567—§ 3, 5, 9

State v. Morales, 129 N.M. 141, 2000-NMCA-046, 2 P.3d 878 (Ct. App. 2000)

108 ALR5th 593—§ 56

For assistance, call 1-800-328-4880

State v. Morales, 170 Ariz. 360, 824
P.2d 756 (Ct. App. Div. 2 1991)
76 ALR5th 1—§ 6

State v. Morales, 173 Wash. 2d 560, 269
P.3d 263 (2012)
97 ALR6th 567—§ 4, 10

State v. Morales, 224 N.J. Super. 72, 539
A.2d 769 (1987)
27 ALR5th 593—§ 6, 7, 12

State v. Morales, 232 Conn. 707, 657
A.2d 585, 40 A.L.R.5th 845 (1995)
40 ALR5th 113—§ 4

State v. Morales, 844 S.W.2d 885 (Tex.
App. Austin 1992)
24 ALR6th 1—§ 17

State v. Morales, 2008 WL 2651980
(Ariz. Ct. App. Div. 2 2008)
58 ALR6th 215—§ 12

State v. Morales, 2009 WL 1658480
(N.J. Super. Ct. App. Div. 2009)
65 ALR6th 537—§ 25, 73, 74

State v. Moralevitz, 70 Ohio App. 2d 20,
24 Ohio Ops. 3d 16, 433 N.E.2d
1280 (Cuyahoga Co. 1980)
39 ALR5th 283—§ 14

State v. Moran, 99 Conn. 115, 121 A.
277, 36 A.L.R. 862 (1923)
118 ALR5th 253—§ 3

State v. Moran, 162 Ariz. 524, 784 P.2d
730 (Ct. App. Div. 1 1989)
70 ALR5th 647—§ 6
87 ALR6th 1—§ 42

State v. Moran, 232 Ariz. 528, 307 P.3d
95 (Ct. App. Div. 2 2013)
92 ALR6th 295—§ 19

State v. Moran, 451 So. 2d 48 (La. Ct.
App. 4th Cir. 1984)
28 ALR6th 505—§ 9

State v. Moran, 2001 WL 32849 (Ala.
Crim. App. 2001)
67 ALR5th 361—§ 4

State v. Moran, 2003 SD 14, 657 N.W.2d
319 (S.D. 2003)
56 ALR6th 185—§ 39

State v. Morato, 2000 SD 149, 619
N.W.2d 655 (S.D. 2000)
34 ALR6th 1—§ 12

State v. Morawe, 122 N.M. 489, 1996-
NMCA-110, 927 P.2d 44 (Ct. App.
1996)
71 ALR6th 335—§ 10

State v. Mordecai, 68 N.C. 207 (1873)
17 ALR5th 125—§ 3, 7

State v. Mordowanec, 259 Conn. 94, 788
A.2d 48 (2002)
106 ALR5th 397—§ 4

State v. Moreau, 35 Wash. App. 688,
669 P.2d 483 (1983)
15 ALR5th 391—§ 16

State v. Moreau, 35 Wash. App. 688,
669 P.2d 483 (Div. 3 1983)
57 ALR6th 445—§ 21

State v. Moreau, 113 N.H. 303, 306 A.2d
764 (1973)
104 ALR5th 165—§ 8
114 ALR5th 235—§ 4

State v. Moreau, 287 N.J. Super. 179,
670 A.2d 608 (Law Div. 1995)
71 ALR6th 335—§ 4

State v. Moreau, 2005 WL 2513074
(N.J. Super. Ct. App. Div. 2005)
26 ALR6th 511—§ 28

State v. Morehouse, 851 S.W.2d 714
(Mo. Ct. App. W.D. 1993)
37 ALR6th 357—§ 71

State v. Morel, 253 N.J. Super. 470, 602
A.2d 285 (1992)
13 ALR5th 118—§ 7

State v. Morel, 676 A.2d 1347 (R.I.
1996)
90 ALR5th 453—§ 20

State v. Moreland, 2002-Ohio-1745,
2002 WL 570253 (Ohio Ct. App.
9th Dist. Lorain County 2002)
70 ALR6th 361—§ 32

State v. Moreno, 27 Ariz. App. 460, 556
P.2d 14 (1976)
55 ALR5th 125—§ 3, 6, 7

State v. Moreno, 27 Ariz. App. 460, 556
P.2d 14 (Div. 1 1976)
28 ALR6th 505—§ 7, 9

State v. Moreno, 92 Ariz. 116, 374 P.2d
872 (1962)
4 ALR5th 1—§ 2, 17, 32, 32 to 34

State v. Moreno, 128 Ariz. 257, 625 P.2d
320 (1981)
79 ALR5th 419—§ 7
State v. Moreno, 228 Neb. 210, 422
N.W.2d 56 (1988)
5 ALR5th 243—§ 59
State v. Moreno, 2010 WL 1960801
(N.C. Ct. App. 2010)
57 ALR6th 1—§ 22
State v. Moreno, 2010 WL 2450776
(Ariz. Ct. App. Div. 1 2010)
79 ALR6th 1—§ 43
State v. Morgan, 8 Wash. App. 189, 504
P.2d 1195 (1973)
15 ALR5th 391—§ 5
State v. Morgan, 55 Ohio App. 3d 182,
563 N.E.2d 307 (3d Dist. Mercer
County 1988)
85 ALR5th 1—§ 37
State v. Morgan, 80 Ohio App. 3d 150,
608 N.E.2d 1114 (Franklin Co.
1992)
39 ALR5th 283—§ 14, 41
State v. Morgan, 118 N.C. App. 461, 455
S.E.2d 490 (1995)
12 ALR5th 89—§ 4
State v. Morgan, 120 Ariz. 2, 583 P.2d
889 (1978)
103 ALR5th 463—§ 3
State v. Morgan, 144 Mo. App. 35, 128
S.W. 839 (1910)
56 ALR5th 171—§ 4, 5, 29
State v. Morgan, 147 La. 205, 84 So. 589
(1920)
51 ALR5th 603—§ 2
State v. Morgan, 196 Mo. 177, 95 S.W.
402 (1906)
93 ALR5th 327—§ 3, 4, 8, 9
State v. Morgan, 198 Mont. 391, 646
P.2d 1177 (1982)
15 ALR5th 391—§ 30
92 ALR5th 35—§ 2, 7
State v. Morgan, 206 Neb. 818, 295
N.W.2d 285 (1980)
99 ALR5th 557—§ 3, 12
State v. Morgan, 207 Kan. 581, 485 P.2d
1371 (1971)

86 ALR5th 59—§ 3 to 5, 8
87 ALR5th 181—§ 3
State v. Morgan, 222 Kan. 149, 563 P.2d
1056 (1977)
67 ALR5th 361—§ 5
109 ALR5th 99—§ 4
27 ALR6th 491—§ 3
State v. Morgan, 231 Kan. 472, 646 P.2d
1064 (1982)
99 ALR6th 295—§ 21
State v. Morgan, 254 Wis. 2d 602, 2002
WI App 124, 648 N.W.2d 23 (Ct.
App. 2002)
34 ALR6th 1—§ 9
State v. Morgan, 287 Minn. 406, 178
N.W.2d 697 (1970)
4 ALR5th 1—§ 4
State v. Morgan, 326 S.C. 503, 485
S.E.2d 112 (Ct. App. 1997)
90 ALR5th 453—§ 21
State v. Morgan, 359 N.C. 131, 604
S.E.2d 886 (2004)
83 ALR6th 255—§ 4
State v. Morgan, 541 S.W.2d 385 (Tenn.
1976)
83 ALR5th 277—§ 9, 11, 28
84 ALR5th 487—§ 22, 23, 25
State v. Morgan, 559 N.W.2d 603 (Iowa
1997)
70 ALR5th 587—§ 15
State v. Morgan, 592 S.W.2d 796 (Mo.
1980)
56 ALR5th 385—§ 5
State v. Morgan, 985 P.2d 1022 (Alaska
Ct. App. 1999)
68 ALR6th 527—§ 7
State v. Morganherring, 350 N.C. 701,
517 S.E.2d 622 (1999)
95 ALR5th 125—§ 3
State v. Morgavi, 58 Wash. App. 733,
794 P.2d 1289 (Div. 2 1990)
64 ALR5th 637—§ 4
State v. Morgen, 127 Idaho 798, 907
P.2d 116 (Ct. App. 1995)
19 ALR6th 697—§ 4
State v. Morgensen, 148 Wash. App. 81,
197 P.3d 715 (Div. 2 2008)

65 ALR6th 537—§ 15

State v. Moriarty, 87 Or. App. 465, 742 P.2d 704 (1987)

    15 ALR5th 391—§ 31
    92 ALR5th 35—§ 13

State v. Moriarty, 133 N.J. Super. 563, 338 A.2d 14 (1975)

    43 ALR5th 1—§ 8

State v. Moriarty, 566 N.W.2d 866 (Iowa 1997)

    123 ALR5th 179—§ 6, 11

State v. Morical, 182 Minn. 368, 234 N.W. 453 (1931)

    102 ALR5th 525—§ 65

State v. Morin, 1999 WL 710887 (Minn. Ct. App. 1999)

    32 ALR6th 171—§ 8, 18, 21
    33 ALR6th 1—§ 22

State v. Morley, 5 N.J. Misc. 987, 139 A. 392 (1927)

    41 ALR5th 171—§ 14, 66, 107, 108

State v. Morley, 134 Wash. 2d 588, 952 P.2d 167 (1998)

    11 ALR5th 218—§ 4, 10, 11

State v. Morrell, 803 P.2d 292 (Utah Ct. App. 1990)

    82 ALR5th 359—§ 2
    83 ALR5th 277—§ 2, 11
    84 ALR5th 487—§ 2
    111 ALR5th 1—§ 26
    112 ALR5th 621—§ 5

State v. Morrill, 42 Conn. App. 669, 681 A.2d 369 (1996)

    74 ALR5th 643—§ 3

State v. Morrill, 205 Conn. 560, 534 A.2d 1165 (1987)

    35 ALR6th 497—§ 7, 9, 23

State v. Morris, 2 Neb. App. 887, 518 N.W.2d 664, 43 A.L.R.5th 885 (1994)

    43 ALR5th 777—§ 4

State v. Morris, 3 Neb. App. 835, 533 N.W.2d 110 (1995)

    37 ALR5th 515—§ 4, 11

State v. Morris, 27 Kan. App. 2d 155, 999 P.2d 283 (2000)

    19 ALR5th 470—§ 12

State v. Morris, 55 Ohio St. 2d 101, 9 Ohio Op. 3d 92, 378 N.E.2d 708 (1978)

    101 ALR6th 431—§ 16

State v. Morris, 64 N.C. App. 595, 307 S.E.2d 783 (1983)

    5 ALR5th 243—§ 51

State v. Morris, 87 Wash. App. 654, 943 P.2d 329 (Div. 1 1997)

    73 ALR5th 383—§ 52

State v. Morris, 98 N.J.L. 621, 121 A. 290 (N.J. Sup. Ct. 1923)

    85 ALR5th 187—§ 21

State v. Morris, 101 Idaho 120, 609 P.2d 652 (1980)

    71 ALR6th 249—§ 8

State v. Morris, 107 Wis. 2d 738, 321 N.W.2d 364 (Ct. App. 1982)

    101 ALR6th 331—§ 21

State v. Morris, 109 N.M. 726, 790 P.2d 523, 60 Ed. Law Rep. 206 (Ct. App. 1990)

    92 ALR5th 35—§ 12

State v. Morris, 114 Wash. 700, 194 P. 898 (1921)

    48 ALR6th 181—§ 4

State v. Morris, 157 Ohio App. 3d 395, 2004-Ohio-2870, 811 N.E.2d 577 (1st Dist. Hamilton County 2004)

    98 ALR6th 455—§ 3
    99 ALR6th 113—§ 3
    101 ALR6th 499—§ 3
    102 ALR6th 279—§ 3
    103 ALR6th 35—§ 3

State v. Morris, 173 Ariz. 14, 839 P.2d 434 (Ct. App. Div. 1 1992)

    15 ALR5th 391—§ 40
    92 ALR5th 35—§ 25

State v. Morris, 208 S.W.2d 701 (Tex. Civ. App. Waco 1948)

    101 ALR6th 431—§ 11

State v. Morris, 242 N.J. Super. 532, 577 A.2d 852 (1990)

    54 ALR5th 141—§ 3, 7

State v. Morris, 272 N.W.2d 35 (Minn. 1978)

    18 ALR5th 1—§ 28

State v. Morris, 281 Minn. 119, 160
N.W.2d 715 (1968)
39 ALR5th 283—§ 3
State v. Morris, 340 So. 2d 195 (La.
1976)
55 ALR5th 125—§ 3, 7
State v. Morris, 522 S.W.2d 93 (Mo. Ct.
App. 1975)
103 ALR6th 347—§ 20
State v. Morris, 644 N.W.2d 114 (Minn.
Ct. App. 2002)
120 ALR5th 337—§ 6
State v. Morris, 662 S.W.2d 884 (Mo.
Ct. App. S.D. 1983)
101 ALR6th 331—§ 12
State v. Morris, 668 P.2d 857 (Alaska
Ct. App. 1983)
67 ALR5th 361—§ 3, 4, 9
State v. Morris, 669 So. 2d 1271 (La. Ct.
App. 4th Cir. 1996)
16 ALR6th 329—§ 4
24 ALR6th 591—§ 4, 14
State v. Morris, 680 A.2d 90, 62
A.L.R.5th 729 (Vt. 1996)
62 ALR5th 1—§ 2, 3, 13, 15
State v. Morris, 1975 WL 181685 (Ohio
Ct. App. 1st Dist. Hamilton County
1975)
63 ALR6th 1—§ 36
State v. Morris, 1986 WL 12861 (Ohio
Ct. App. 8th Dist.Cuyahoga County
1986)
57 ALR5th 141—§ 11
State v. Morris, 2005-Ohio-6025, 2005
WL 3030482 (Ohio Ct. App. 8th
Dist. Cuyahoga County 2005)
43 ALR6th 475—§ 10
State v. Morris, 2009-Ohio-6033, 2009
WL 3807159 (Ohio Ct. App. 11th
Dist. Trumbull County 2009)
64 ALR6th 131—§ 7
State v. Morrison, 46 Kan. 679, 27 P.
133 (1891)
66 ALR5th 397—§ 6, 9, 10
State v. Morrison, 85 N.C. App. 511,
355 S.E.2d 182 (1987)
86 ALR5th 59—§ 4

State v. Morrison, 121 Wash. App. 1037,
2004 WL 1045933 (Div. 1 2004)
8 ALR6th 265—§ 16
State v. Morrison, 243 Neb. 469, 500
N.W.2d 547 (1993)
67 ALR5th 361—§ 2 to 4, 6
State v. Morrison, 310 N.W.2d 135
(Minn. 1981)
86 ALR5th 59—§ 6
State v. Morrison, 437 N.W.2d 422
(Minn. Ct. App. 1989)
73 ALR5th 383—§ 5, 32
State v. Morrison, 1992 WL 125260
(Ohio Ct. App. 10th Dist. Franklin
County 1992)
72 ALR5th 403—§ 19
State v. Morrison, 1997 WL 691442
(Tex. App. Dallas 1997)
65 ALR5th 407—§ 3
State v. Morrison, 2004-Ohio-5724,
2004 WL 2421875 (Ohio Ct. App.
4th Dist. Highland County 2004)
71 ALR6th 1—§ 11
State v. Morrissey, 216 Conn. 185, 577
A.2d 1060 (1990)
19 ALR5th 470—§ 3, 12
State v. Morrissey, 1994 WL 44403
(Ohio Ct. App. 1st Dist. Hamilton
County 1994)
47 ALR6th 107—§ 22, 30, 31
State v. Morrow, 530 S.W.2d 60 (Tenn.
1975)
57 ALR6th 445—§ 43
State v. Morrow, 535 S.W.2d 539 (Mo.
Ct. App. 1976)
66 ALR5th 135—§ 35
State v. Morrow, 683 S.E.2d 754 (N.C.
Ct. App. 2009)
57 ALR6th 1—§ 3, 4, 24 to 26
State v. Morrow, 778 S.W.2d 63 (Tenn.
Crim. App. 1989)
46 ALR6th 63—§ 9
State v. Morrow, 787 S.W.2d 821 (Mo.
Ct. App. W.D. 1990)
105 ALR5th 529—§ 13
State v. Morrow, 968 S.W.2d 100 (Mo.
1998)
79 ALR5th 33—§ 2, 17

State v. Morse, 54 N.J. 32, 252 A.2d 723 (1969)

36 ALR5th 161—§ 20, 25, 26
33 ALR6th 91—§ 27, 28

State v. Morsman, 394 So. 2d 408 (Fla. 1981)

62 ALR6th 413—§ 17, 28

State v. Mortimer, 135 N.J. 517, 641 A.2d 257 (1994)

22 ALR5th 261—§ 3 to 6

State v. Mortley, 532 N.W.2d 498 (Iowa Ct. App. 1995)

32 ALR6th 1—§ 10

State v. Morton, 142 Me. 254, 49 A.2d 907 (1946)

50 ALR5th 703—§ 15

State v. Morton, 155 N.J. 383, 715 A.2d 228 (1998)

24 ALR6th 1—§ 17

State v. Morton, 684 S.W.2d 601 (Mo. Ct. App. S.D. 1985)

1 ALR6th 549—§ 8, 10

State v. Morwitzer, 2001 WL 293621 (Iowa Ct. App. 2001)

26 ALR6th 511—§ 7, 28

State v. Mosby, 595 So. 2d 1135 (La. 1992)

22 ALR5th 1—§ 5, 11, 13, 15, 22, 30, 33, 39, 44, 45, 48, 50, 52

State v. Mosby, 639 S.W.2d 672 (Tenn. Crim. App.1982)

86 ALR5th 463—§ 5

State v. Moscone, 171 Conn. 500, 370 A.2d 1030 (1976)

124 ALR5th 1—§ 3

State v. Moseley, 122 S.C. 62, 114 S.E. 866 (1922)

97 ALR5th 201—§ 3

State v. Moseley, 263 Ga. 680, 436 S.E.2d 632, Prod. Liab. Rep. (CCH) ¶ 13844 (1993)

16 ALR5th 129—§ 3

State v. Moseley, 336 N.C. 710, 445 S.E.2d 906 (1994)

82 ALR5th 67—§ 3, 9

State v. Moseley, 338 N.C. 1, 449 S.E.2d 412 (1994)

79 ALR5th 33—§ 65

State v. Moser, 445 So. 2d 696 (Fla. Dist. Ct. App. 2d Dist. 1984)

52 ALR6th 1—§ 4

State v. Moses, 145 Wash. 2d 370, 37 P.3d 1216 (2002)

116 ALR5th 313—§ 4

State v. Moses, 149 N.C. 581, 151 N.C. 737, 63 S.E. 68 (1908)

105 ALR5th 529—§ 11

State v. Moses, 159 Vt. 294, 618 A.2d 478 (1992)

99 ALR5th 557—§ 14

State v. Moses, 480 So. 2d 146 (Fla. Dist. Ct. App. 2d Dist. 1985)

58 ALR6th 499—§ 8

State v. Moses, 655 So. 2d 779 (La. Ct. App. 4th Cir. 1995)

51 ALR6th 359—§ 28

State v. Moses, 2004-Ohio-4943, 2004 WL 2260571 (Ohio Ct. App. 5th Dist. Stark County 2004)

23 ALR6th 307—§ 38

State v. Mosher, 46 S.D. 336, 192 N.W. 756 (1923)

29 ALR5th 59—§ 7, 40

State v. Mosher, 221 Wis. 2d 203, 584 N.W.2d 553 (Ct. App. 1998)

29 ALR6th 1—§ 5

State v. Mosher, No. 6-101, Slip Op., July 25, 1977 (Ohio App. Lake Co. 1977)

45 ALR5th 591—§ 15

State v. Mosier, 888 S.W.2d 781 (Tenn. Crim. App. 1994)

32 ALR6th 1—§ 10

State v. Mosley, 84 Wash. 2d 608, 528 P.2d 986 (1974)

105 ALR5th 529—§ 11

State v. Moss, 172 Wis. 2d 110, 492 N.W.2d 627 (1992)

85 ALR5th 1—§ 18

State v. Moss, 180 W. Va. 363, 376 S.E.2d 569 (1988)

53 ALR6th 1—§ 14
55 ALR6th 157—§ 4, 88, 110

State v. Moss, 262 N.W.2d 422 (Minn. 1978)

For assistance, call 1-800-328-4880

98 ALR6th 455—§ 14

State v. Moss, 648 So. 2d 206 (Fla. Dist. Ct. App. 3d Dist. 1994)

67 ALR5th 149—§ 3, 5

State v. Moss, 2003-Ohio-6053, 2003 WL 22672018 (Ohio Ct. App. 5th Dist. Stark County 2003)

90 ALR6th 385—§ 8

State v. Moss, 2005 WL 2849158 (N.J. Super. Ct. App. Div. 2005)

26 ALR6th 511—§ 17, 25, 28

State v. Motschenbacher, 163 Or. App. 202, 986 P.2d 1246 (1999)

15 ALR5th 391—§ 5, 15

State v. Motsinger, 200 Or. App. 713, 117 P.3d 313 (2005)

26 ALR6th 511—§ 27

State v. Motsinger, 728 S.W.2d 633 (Mo. Ct. App. E.D. 1987)

31 ALR6th 49—§ 4

State v. Motsko, 261 N.W.2d 860 (N.D. 1977)

39 ALR5th 283—§ 71

State v. Motta, 66 Hawaii 254, 659 P.2d 745 (1983)

23 ALR5th 672—§ 3

State v. Motyka, 2001 WL 100406 (R.I. Super. Ct. 2001)

38 ALR6th 439—§ 12

State v. Moultrie, 271 S.C. 526, 248 S.E.2d 486 (1978)

61 ALR5th 1—§ 3

State v. Mounce, 859 S.W.2d 319 (Tenn. 1993)

103 ALR6th 137—§ 15

State v. Mounsey, 31 Wash. App. 511, 643 P.2d 892 (Div. 3 1982)

55 ALR6th 391—§ 16

State v. Mount, 2003 MT 275, 317 Mont. 481, 78 P.3d 829 (2003)

33 ALR6th 91—§ 6

63 ALR6th 351—§ 3

State v. Mountford, 171 Vt. 487, 769 A.2d 639 (2000)

58 ALR6th 499—§ 2, 95

State v. Mountjoy, 82 Mont. 594, 268 P. 558 (1928)

14 ALR6th 543—§ 46

State v. Mourey, 64 Ohio St. 3d 482, 1992-Ohio-32, 597 N.E.2d 101 (1992)

70 ALR6th 361—§ 19

State v. Moves Camp, 286 N.W.2d 333 (S.D. 1979)

102 ALR5th 327—§ 11

24 ALR6th 1—§ 13, 19, 21

State v. Moya, 138 Ariz. 7, 672 P.2d 959 (Ct. App. Div. 1 1983)

124 ALR5th 1—§ 5

State v. Moyer, 37 Or. App. 477, 587 P.2d 1054 (1978)

5 ALR5th 243—§ 50

State v. Mudgett, 531 S.W.2d 275 (Mo. 1975)

124 ALR5th 1—§ 5

State v. Mueller, 201 Wis. 2d 121, 549 N.W.2d 455, Blue Sky L. Rep. (CCH) ¶ 74113, R.I.C.O. Bus. Disp. Guide (CCH) ¶ 9013 (Ct. App. 1996)

89 ALR5th 629—§ 12

State v. Mueller, 202 Iowa 1067, 208 N.W. 360 (1926)

103 ALR6th 35—§ 6

State v. Mughni, 33 Ohio St. 3d 65, 514 N.E.2d 870 (1987)

39 ALR5th 283—§ 14

State v. Muhammad, 145 N.J. 23, 678 A.2d 164 (1996)

79 ALR5th 33—§ 2, 3, 5, 6, 10, 11, 14, 23, 25

State v. Muhammad, 359 N.J. Super. 361, 820 A.2d 70 (App. Div. 2003)

65 ALR6th 537—§ 28

State v. Muir, 67 Wash. App. 149, 835 P.2d 1049 (Div. 1 1992)

64 ALR5th 637—§ 3

58 ALR6th 499—§ 80

State v. Mulalley, 126 Ariz. 278, 614 P.2d 820 (1980)

54 ALR5th 141—§ 10

State v. Muldrow, 10 Ohio Misc. 2d 11, 460 N.E.2d 1177 (Mun. Ct. 1983)

66 ALR5th 397—§ 25

State v. Muldrow, 156 Wash. App. 1039, 2010 WL 2505602 (Div. 2 2010)
62 ALR6th 161—§ 21
State v. Mulholand, 1992 WL 174698 (Ohio Ct. App. 4th Dist. Gallia County 1992)
84 ALR6th 293—§ 31
State v. Mulholland, 111 R.I. 154, 300 A.2d 271 (1973)
108 ALR5th 593—§ 35
State v. Mulholland, 132 Or. App. 399, 888 P.2d 594 (1995)
19 ALR5th 470—§ 15
State v. Mullen, 577 N.W.2d 505 (Minn. 1998)
29 ALR5th 487—§ 11
State v. Muller, 365 So. 2d 464 (La. 1978)
95 ALR5th 229—§ 34
State v. Mullins, 128 Wash. App. 633, 116 P.3d 441 (Div. 2 2005)
50 ALR6th 353—§ 26, 29, 30
State v. Mullins, 1999 WL 228819 (Tenn. Crim. App. 1999)
73 ALR5th 383—§ 5
19 ALR6th 697—§ 16
State v. Mullins, 2005-Ohio-2193, 2005 WL 1048123 (Ohio Ct. App. 8th Dist. Cuyahoga County 2005)
70 ALR6th 1—§ 5
State v. Mullins, No. 6400 (March 28, 1980, Ct. App. Ohio, 2nd App. Dist. Montgomery Co.)
39 ALR5th 283—§ 14, 19
State v. Mulroy, 152 Minn. 423, 189 N.W. 441 (1922)
104 ALR5th 357—§ 7
54 ALR6th 429—§ 18
State v. Mulvey, 3 Conn. Cir. 297, 213 A.2d 228 (1965)
26 ALR5th 1—§ 4
State v. Mumbaugh, 107 Ariz. 589, 491 P.2d 443 (1971)
29 ALR6th 1—§ 10
State v. Mumley, 153 Vt. 304, 571 A.2d 44 (1989)
72 ALR5th 403—§ 12, 15

State v. Mummey, 264 Mont. 272, 871 P.2d 868 (1994)
19 ALR5th 823—§ 16, 18
State v. Munce, 1992 WL 186542 (Tenn. Crim. App. 1992)
103 ALR6th 137—§ 15
State v. Muncy, 2007-Ohio-1675, 2007 WL 1057007 (Ohio Ct. App. 2d Dist. Montgomery County 2007)
35 ALR6th 127—§ 3
42 ALR6th 237—§ 8
State v. Munday Enterprises, 824 S.W.2d 643 (Tex. App. Austin 1992)
7 ALR5th 113—§ 3
State v. Munday Enters., 868 S.W.2d 319 (Tex. 1993)
15 ALR5th 821—§ 6
State v. Mundell, 8 Hawaii App. 610, 822 P.2d 23 (1991)
51 ALR5th 375—§ 3, 5
State v. Mundell, 8 Haw. App. 610, 822 P.2d 23 (1991)
23 ALR6th 307—§ 40
State v. Mundy, 87 So. 3d 300 (La. Ct. App. 3d Cir. 2012)
101 ALR6th 331—§ 3, 20
State v. Muneer, 733 So. 2d 26 (La. Ct. App. 5th Cir. 1999)
6 ALR5th 733—§ 15
State v. Muniz, Ohio App. Case No L-77-134, Slip Opinion (Lucas Co. 1979)
45 ALR5th 1—§ 2, 5, 6, 12, 23
State v. Munn, 56 S.W.3d 486 (Tenn. 2001)
83 ALR6th 255—§ 33
State v. Munn, 2008 WL 4977361 (Minn. Ct. App. 2008)
92 ALR6th 1—§ 5
State v. Munoz, 233 Conn. 106, 659 A.2d 683 (1995)
32 ALR5th 149—§ 10, 34
State v. Munoz, 233 P.3d 52 (Idaho 2010)
58 ALR6th 215—§ 12
State v. Munoz, 575 So. 2d 848 (La. App. 5th Cir. 1991)

19 ALR5th 823—§ 2, 9, 11
State v. Munoz, 1998-NMSC-048, 126 N.M. 535, 972 P.2d 847 (1998)
34 ALR6th 1—§ 10
State v. Munoz, 2001 MT 85, 305 Mont. 139, 23 P.3d 922 (2001)
9 ALR6th 541—§ 5
State v. Munoz, 2010 WL 919151 (Idaho 2010)
55 ALR6th 513—§ 10
State v. Munsey, 1997 WL 122239 (Tenn. Crim. App. 1997)
73 ALR5th 383—§ 3
93 ALR5th 527—§ 20
State v. Munson, 594 N.W.2d 128 (Minn. 1999)
69 ALR6th 579—§ 8, 32
State v. Munson, 714 S.W.2d 515 (Mo. 1986)
23 ALR6th 307—§ 35
State v. Munson, 1994 OK CR 77, 886 P.2d 999 (Okla. Crim. App. 1994)
93 ALR5th 527—§ 15, 16
State v. Munson, 2007 MT 222, 339 Mont. 68, 169 P.3d 364 (2007)
28 ALR6th 505—§ 8
State v. Murchison, 541 N.W.2d 435 (N.D. 1995)
37 ALR6th 357—§ 69
State v. Murdock, 690 S.E.2d 558 (N.C. Ct. App. 2010)
57 ALR6th 1—§ 4, 12, 18
State v. Murillo, 81 Wash. App. 1048, 1996 WL 269947 (Div. 3 1996)
122 ALR5th 439—§ 2
State v. Murillo, 240 Wis. 2d 666
60 ALR5th 39—§ 5, 7
State v. Murillo, 349 N.C. 573, 509 S.E.2d 752 (1998)
24 ALR5th 465—§ 12, 23, 73
State v. Murnahan, 117 Ohio App. 3d 71, 689 N.E.2d 1021 (2d Dist. Clark County 1996)
70 ALR5th 1—§ 8, 9
State v. Murphy, 7 Ohio Misc. 2d 1, 453 N.E.2d 1304 (Mun. Ct. 1983)
119 ALR5th 379—§ 8

State v. Murphy, 46 La. Ann. 415, 14 So. 920 (1894)
108 ALR5th 593—§ 5
State v. Murphy, 99 Idaho 511, 584 P.2d 1236 (1978)
90 ALR6th 385—§ 7
State v. Murphy, 117 Ariz. 57, 570 P.2d 1070 (1977)
4 ALR5th 1—§ 17, 21
State v. Murphy, 157 S.W.3d 773 (Mo. Ct. App. W.D. 2005)
37 ALR6th 357—§ 3, 21
State v. Murphy, 270 Kan. 804, 19 P.3d 80 (2001)
106 ALR5th 377—§ 3
State v. Murphy, 292 Mo. 275, 237 S.W. 529 (1922)
101 ALR6th 499—§ 15
State v. Murphy, 321 N.C. 738, 365 S.E.2d 615 (1988)
37 ALR5th 515—§ 2, 19
State v. Murphy, 341 Mo. 1229, 111 S.W.2d 132 (1937)
54 ALR6th 429—§ 11
State v. Murphy, 345 Mo. 358, 133 S.W.2d 398 (1939)
97 ALR5th 293—§ 3, 5
State v. Murphy, 431 A.2d 58 (Me. 1981)
15 ALR5th 391—§ 7, 45
State v. Murphy, 463 So. 2d 812 (La. Ct. App. 2d Cir. 1985)
99 ALR6th 295—§ 5
State v. Murphy, 465 So. 2d 811 (La. Ct. App. 2d Cir. 1985)
58 ALR6th 499—§ 21, 103
State v. Murphy, 496 A.2d 623 (Me. 1985)
72 ALR5th 529—§ 11
State v. Murphy, 592 S.W.2d 727 (Mo. 1979)
78 ALR5th 197—§ 10
State v. Murphy, 674 P.2d 1220 (Utah 1983)
23 ALR6th 307—§ 34
State v. Murphy, 2002 WL 1315415 (Neb. Ct. App. 2002)

---

23 ALR6th 679—§ 3, 5

State v. Murphy., 2004 ME 118, 861 A.2d 657 (Me. 2004)

78 ALR6th 1—§ 14

State v. Murr, 443 N.W.2d 833 (Minn. Ct. App. 1989)

81 ALR6th 505—§ 42

State v. Murray, 10 Wash. App. 23, 516 P.2d 517 (1973)

34 ALR5th 125—§ 13

State v. Murray, 63 Haw. 12, 621 P.2d 334 (1980)

92 ALR5th 35—§ 20

State v. Murray, 110 Wash. 2d 706, 757 P.2d 487 (1988)

92 ALR6th 1—§ 8

State v. Murray, 162 Ariz. 211, 782 P.2d 329, 30 Ariz. Adv. Rep. 42 (App. 1989)

4 ALR5th 1—§ 18

State v. Murray, 180 W. Va. 41, 375 S.E.2d 405 (1988)

40 ALR6th 1—§ 31

State v. Murray, 184 Ariz. 9, 906 P.2d 542 (1995)

20 ALR5th 398—§ 9, 24.5, 42.5
90 ALR5th 453—§ 28
16 ALR6th 329—§ 4
24 ALR6th 591—§ 4, 12

State v. Murray, 375 So. 2d 80 (La. 1979)

80 ALR5th 469—§ 3, 5

State v. Murray, 529 N.W.2d 453 (Minn. Ct. App. 1995)

92 ALR5th 35—§ 22

State v. Murray, 539 N.W.2d 368 (Iowa 1995)

96 ALR6th 355—§ 24

State v. Murray, 546 So. 2d 944 (La. Ct. App. 3d Cir. 1989)

20 ALR6th 479—§ 3, 13

State v. Murray, 604 A.2d 903 (Me. 1992)

33 ALR5th 453—§ 6

State v. Murray, 796 P.2d 849 (Alaska Ct. App. 1990)

34 ALR6th 1—§ 8

State v. Murray, 947 P.2d 591 (Okla. Crim. App. 1997)

29 ALR5th 59—§ 29

State v. Murrell, 33 S.C. 83, 11 S.E. 682 (1890)

105 ALR5th 529—§ 11

State v. Murrell, 41 S.C. 549, 19 S.E. 692 (1894)

105 ALR5th 529—§ 11

State v. Murvin, 304 N.C. 523, 284 S.E.2d 289 (1981)

67 ALR6th 341—§ 13, 18

State v. Musack, 254 Iowa 104, 116 N.W.2d 523 (1962)

104 ALR5th 357—§ 6
54 ALR6th 429—§ 7, 9

State v. Muscari, 174 Vt. 101, 807 A.2d 407 (2002)

7 ALR6th 233—§ 5

State v. Muscatello, 57 Ohio App. 2d 231, 11 Ohio Ops. 3d 320, 387 N.E.2d 627 (Cuyahoga Co. 1977)

26 ALR5th 603—§ 4

State v. Muschkat, 706 So. 2d 429 (La. 1998)

72 ALR5th 1—§ 8

State v. Musgrave, 1998 WL 818067 (Ohio Ct. App. 5th Dist. Stark County 1998)

63 ALR6th 351—§ 3

State v. Musick, 101 Mo. 260, 14 S.W. 212 (1890)

54 ALR6th 429—§ 20

State v. Musselwhite, 59 N.C. App. 477, 297 S.E.2d 181 (1982)

5 ALR5th 243—§ 49

State v. Musser, 721 N.W.2d 734 (Iowa 2006)

73 ALR6th 281—§ 12

State v. Musser, 2009-Ohio-4979, 2009 WL 3043966 (Ohio Ct. App. 4th Dist. Ross County 2009)

64 ALR6th 1—§ 9

State v. Mussman, 526 S.W.2d 62 (Mo. Ct. App. 1975)

9 ALR6th 1—§ 19

State v. Mutschler, 204 Ariz. 520, 65 P.3d 469 (Ct. App. Div. 1 2003)

For assistance, call 1-800-328-4880

20 ALR6th 161—§ 3
23 ALR6th 573—§ 13
State v. Muzik, 379 N.W.2d 599 (Minn. Ct. App. 1985)
74 ALR5th 319—§ 3
State v. Mwangi, 2007 WL 2780573 (N.J. Super. Ct. App. Div. 2007)
84 ALR6th 293—§ 21
State v. Myers, 6 Or. App. 219, 487 P.2d 663 (1971)
28 ALR6th 505—§ 4, 8
State v. Myers, 7 N.J. 465, 81 A.2d 710, 25 A.L.R.2d 1171 (1951)
24 ALR5th 465—§ 8, 103, 117
State v. Myers, 19 N.C. App. 311, 198 S.E.2d 438 (1973)
29 ALR5th 59—§ 66, 89
State v. Myers, 59 Ariz. 200, 125 P.2d 441 (1942)
50 ALR5th 467—§ 6
State v. Myers, 61 N.C. App. 554, 301 S.E.2d 401 (1983)
45 ALR5th 1—§ 3, 6, 8, 26
State v. Myers, 82 N.C. App. 299, 346 S.E.2d 273 (1986)
97 ALR5th 201—§ 3
State v. Myers, 82 Ohio L. Abs. 216, 164 N.E.2d 585 (Ct. App. 10th Dist. Franklin County 1959)
76 ALR5th 1—§ 20
State v. Myers, 87 Ohio App. 3d 92, 621 N.E.2d 881 (Medina Co. 1993)
6 ALR5th 733—§ 7, 18
State v. Myers, 102 Wash. 2d 548, 689 P.2d 38 (1984)
85 ALR5th 1—§ 18
State v. Myers, 118 Idaho 608, 798 P.2d 453 (Ct. App. 1990)
58 ALR6th 215—§ 11
State v. Myers, 230 Kan. 697, 640 P.2d 1245, 32 A.L.R.4th 1169 (1982)
51 ALR5th 603—§ 3, 14
State v. Myers, 239 N.J. Super. 158, 570 A.2d 1260 (App. Div. 1990)
58 ALR5th 749—§ 9
State v. Myers, 248 S.W.3d 19 (Mo. Ct. App. E.D. 2008)

30 ALR6th 1—§ 7
State v. Myers, 258 Neb. 300, 603 N.W.2d 378 (1999)
26 ALR5th 603—§ 6
State v. Myers, 260 Kan. 669, 923 P.2d 1024 (1996)
78 ALR5th 489—§ 3
63 ALR6th 351—§ 3
State v. Myers, 301 S.C. 251, 391 S.E.2d 551 (1990)
9 ALR5th 369—§ 2, 11, 18
State v. Myers, 359 N.W.2d 604 (Minn. 1984)
85 ALR5th 595—§ 3
State v. Myers, 382 N.W.2d 91 (Iowa 1986)
85 ALR5th 595—§ 3
State v. Myers, 459 S.E.2d 304 (S.C. 1995)
14 ALR5th 89—§ 11
State v. Myers, 490 So. 2d 700 (La. Ct. App. 2d Cir. 1986)
78 ALR6th 599—§ 4, 8
State v. Myers, 515 So. 2d 333 (Fla. Dist. Ct. App. 3d Dist. 1987)
113 ALR5th 597—§ 3
State v. Myers, 584 So. 2d 242 (La. Ct. App. 5th Cir. 1991)
16 ALR6th 329—§ 4
24 ALR6th 591—§ 4, 6, 14
State v. Myers, 753 So. 2d 921 (La. Ct. App. 4th Cir. 2000)
41 ALR6th 141—§ 8
State v. Myers, 764 S.W.2d 214 (Tenn. Crim. App. 1988)
85 ALR5th 595—§ 8
State v. Myers, 923 P.2d 1024 (Kan. 1996)
36 ALR5th 161—§ 3
State v. Myers, 1992 WL 297626 (Tenn. Crim. App. 1992)
73 ALR5th 383—§ 5
State v. Myers, 2003-Ohio-2936, 2003 WL 21321402 (Ohio Ct. App. 3d Dist. Marion County 2003)
58 ALR6th 499—§ 44, 45

For assistance, call 1-800-328-4880

State v. Myers, 2006 ND 242, 724 N.W.2d 168 (N.D. 2006)
23 ALR6th 307—§ 42

State v. Myers, 2007 WL 2026822 (N.J. Super. Ct. App. Div. 2007)
79 ALR6th 1—§ 69

State v. Myers, 2009-Ohio-5629, 2009 WL 3403967 (Ohio Ct. App. 2d Dist. Montgomery County 2009)
71 ALR6th 1—§ 5

State v. Myers, Ohio App. Case No CA84-01-001, Slip opinion (Preble Co. 1984)
45 ALR5th 1—§ 2 to 4, 8, 22, 29

State v. Myers, Slip Op. No. 12018 (Ohio App. Summit Co. 1985)
38 ALR5th 433—§ 3, 8, 14

State v. Myhre, 2001 SD 109, 633 N.W.2d 186 (S.D. 2001)
57 ALR6th 83—§ 17

State v. Myrick, 102 Wash. 2d 506, 688 P.2d 151 (1984)
45 ALR6th 643—§ 4

State v. Myrick, 228 Kan. 406, 616 P.2d 1066 (1980)
16 ALR6th 329—§ 4
24 ALR6th 591—§ 4, 15

State v. Myrick, 436 A.2d 379 (Me. 1981)
63 ALR6th 1—§ 44

State v. Naas, 409 So. 2d 535 (La. 1981)
36 ALR5th 255—§ 29, 31

State v. Nab, 113 Idaho 168, 742 P.2d 423 (Ct. App. 1987)
103 ALR6th 137—§ 4

State v. Nabarro, 55 Hawaii 583, 525 P.2d 573 (1974)
51 ALR5th 375—§ 3, 5

State v. Nadeau, 395 So. 2d 182 (Fla. Dist. Ct. App. 3d Dist. 1980)
125 ALR5th 281—§ 4

State v. Nadeem, 284 Neb. 513, 822 N.W.2d 372 (2012)
95 ALR6th 219—§ 15

State v. Nagel, 458 N.W.2d 10 (Iowa Ct. App. 1990)
102 ALR6th 365—§ 18, 32

State v. Naicker, 144 Wash. App. 1029, 2008 WL 2025838 (Div. 1 2008)
65 ALR6th 537—§ 4, 22

State v. Nail, 963 S.W.2d 761 (Tenn. Crim. App. 1997)
51 ALR5th 747—§ 3

State v. Nails, 255 La. 1070, 234 So. 2d 184 (1970)
83 ALR6th 465—§ 64

State v. Naisbitt, 827 P.2d 969 (Utah Ct. App. 1992)
114 ALR5th 173—§ 7

State v. Nakdimen, 735 S.W.2d 799 (Tenn. Crim. App. 1987)
32 ALR6th 1—§ 10

State v. Nance, 202 N.C. App. 772, 691 S.E.2d 768 (2010)
98 ALR6th 455—§ 9

State v. Nance, 533 N.W.2d 557 (Iowa 1995)
57 ALR5th 141—§ 3
3 ALR6th 269—§ 25

State v. Naone, 92 Haw. 289, 990 P.2d 1171 (Ct. App. 1999)
101 ALR6th 545—§ 5

State v. Napier, 2005-Ohio-3738, 2005 WL 1707021 (Ohio Ct. App. 2d Dist. Montgomery County 2005)
71 ALR6th 1—§ 4

State v. Napoli, 119 Wash. App. 1067, 2003 WL 23019945 (Div. 1 2003)
1 ALR6th 549—§ 20

State v. Napulou, 85 Haw. 49, 936 P.2d 1297 (Haw. Ct. App. 1997)
3 ALR5th 963—§ 6, 7

State v. Narcisse, 426 So. 2d 118 (La. 1983)
68 ALR5th 343—§ 3
9 ALR6th 1—§ 7

State v. Narcisse, 791 So. 2d 149 (La. Ct. App. 5th Cir. 2001)
79 ALR6th 1—§ 64

State v. Nash, 104 S.W.3d 495 (Tenn. 2003)
1 ALR6th 549—§ 18

State v. Nash, 119 N.H. 728, 407 A.2d 365 (1979)

124 ALR5th 1—§ 5
State v. Nash, 279 Ga. 646, 619 S.E.2d 684 (2005)

81 ALR6th 505—§ 27
State v. Nash, 2005 WL 3059427 (Tenn. Crim. App. 2005)

26 ALR6th 511—§ 22
State v. Nason, 20 Wash. App. 433, 579 P.2d 366 (Div. 2 1978)

105 ALR5th 529—§ 8
State v. Nason, 433 A.2d 424 (Me. 1981)

4 ALR5th 1—§ 17
State v. Nason, 498 A.2d 252 (Me. 1985)

84 ALR5th 487—§ 21
State v. Natale, 184 N.J. 458, 878 A.2d 724 (2005)

26 ALR6th 511—§ 17, 28
State v. Nation, 85 N.M. 291, 511 P.2d 777 (Ct. App. 1973)

108 ALR5th 593—§ 11
State v. National Advertising Co., 409 A.2d 1277 (Me. 1979)

8 ALR5th 391—§ 3, 5
State v. Nations, 676 S.W.2d 282 (Mo. App. 1984)

42 ALR5th 291—§ 2
State v. Natividad, 111 Ariz. 191, 526 P.2d 730 (1974)

32 ALR5th 149—§ 4, 22, 23, 28, 29, 45
State v. Naujoks, 637 N.W.2d 101 (Iowa 2001)

17 ALR6th 327—§ 31
State v. Nava, 2011 WL 6306628 (Minn. Ct. App. 2011)

74 ALR6th 373—§ 18
State v. Navarrete, 221 Neb. 171, 376 N.W.2d 8 (1985)

46 ALR5th 499—§ 3
State v. Navy, 370 S.C. 398, 635 S.E.2d 549 (Ct. App. 2006)

32 ALR6th 1—§ 10
State v. Nayee, 2007 WL 1931336 (N.J. Super. Ct. App. Div. 2007)

99 ALR6th 295—§ 19
State v. Naylor, 474 N.W.2d 314, 18 A.L.R.5th 1066 (Minn. 1991)

18 ALR5th 804—§ 4, 6
State v. Nazar, 675 So. 2d 780 (La. Ct. App. 4th Cir. 1996)

93 ALR5th 683—§ 4
State v. Nazarian, 2004-Ohio-5448, 2004 WL 2293071 (Ohio Ct. App. 9th Dist. Medina County 2004)

58 ALR6th 499—§ 47
State v. Neace, 2006-Ohio-3072, 2006 WL 1669134 (Ohio Ct. App. 3d Dist. Mercer County 2006)

47 ALR6th 107—§ 3
State v. Neace, 2010 WL 4812912 (Ariz. Ct. App. Div. 2 2010)

92 ALR6th 171—§ 4
State v. Neal, 476 S.W.2d 547 (Mo. 1972)

57 ALR6th 83—§ 6
State v. Neal, 682 S.W.2d 860 (Mo. Ct. App. E.D. 1984)

56 ALR6th 323—§ 5
State v. Neal, 979 S.W.2d 223 (Mo. Ct. App. S.D. 1998)

95 ALR6th 1—§ 29
96 ALR6th 355—§ 6, 20, 45
State v. Neal, 1996 WL 28765 (Ohio Ct. App. 10th Dist.Franklin County 1996)

80 ALR5th 469—§ 3, 5
State v. Neal, 1998 WL 1034638 (Tenn. Crim. App. 1998)

73 ALR5th 383—§ 26
State v. Neal, 2005-Ohio-6699, 2005 WL 3475738 (Ohio Ct. App. 5th Dist. Delaware County 2005)

70 ALR6th 361—§ 31
State v. Nealy, 419 So. 2d 336 (Fla. 1982)

92 ALR6th 1—§ 8
State v. Nearhood, 2 Neb. App. 915, 518 N.W.2d 165 (1994)

71 ALR6th 335—§ 5
State v. Neatherlin, 141 N.M. 328, 2007-NMCA-035, 154 P.3d 703 (Ct. App. 2007)

67 ALR6th 103—§ 24, 25
State v. Neave, 117 Wis. 2d 359, 344 N.W.2d 181 (1984)

CASES CITED IN ALR5th and ALR6th

32 ALR5th 149—§ 2, 4, 10, 23 to 26, 28, 29, 45

State v. Nebeker, 657 P.2d 1359 (Utah 1983)

93 ALR5th 527—§ 6

State v. Necaise, 466 So. 2d 660 (La. Ct. App. 5th Cir. 1985)

58 ALR5th 749—§ 6

State v. Nece, 206 N.J. Super. 118, 501 A.2d 1049 (Law Div. 1985)

109 ALR5th 611—§ 3

State v. Ned, 326 So. 2d 477 (La. 1976)

26 ALR6th 451—§ 6

State v. Needs, 99 Idaho 883, 591 P.2d 130 (1979)

24 ALR5th 465—§ 24, 25, 28, 42, 43, 46, 52, 53, 56, 72, 73, 76, 101, 102, 105, 115, 116, 119

37 ALR5th 515—§ 6

State v. Neel, 81 S.W.3d 86 (Mo. Ct. App. W.D. 2002)

23 ALR6th 307—§ 47

State v. Neeley, 91 Ohio Misc. 2d 26, 696 N.E.2d 1123 (Mun. Ct. 1997)

34 ALR6th 1—§ 12

State v. Neeley, 271 S.C. 33, 244 S.E.2d 522 (1978)

29 ALR6th 1—§ 10

State v. Neeley, 748 P.2d 1091 (Utah 1988)

85 ALR5th 471—§ 7

State v. Neeley, 1989 WL 85090 (Ohio Ct. App. 12th Dist. Preble County 1989)

53 ALR6th 305—§ 44

State v. Neely, 261 Iowa 1107, 156 N.W.2d 840 (1968)

65 ALR5th 407—§ 3

State v. Neely, 979 S.W.2d 552 (Mo. Ct. App. S.D. 1998)

19 ALR5th 351—§ 18

State v. Neely, 2002-Ohio-7146, 2002 WL 31859454 (Ohio Ct. App. 12th Dist. Madison County 2002)

99 ALR6th 295—§ 13

State v. Neese, 691 So. 2d 291 (La. Ct. App. 1st Cir. 1997)

9 ALR6th 1—§ 12

State v. Neff, 169 Kan. 116, 218 P.2d 248 (1950)

70 ALR5th 587—§ 5

State v. Neftzer, 62 Ohio Misc. 2d 384, 598 N.E.2d 938 (Mun. Ct. 1992)

66 ALR5th 397—§ 12

State v. Negolfka, Slip Op., No. 52905 (Ohio App. Cuyahoga Co. 1987)

38 ALR5th 433—§ 3, 7, 8

State v. Nehls, 111 Wis. 2d 594, 331 N.W.2d 603 (Ct. App. 1983)

65 ALR5th 407—§ 3

State v. Neiburg, 86 Vt. 392, 85 A. 769 (1913)

23 ALR6th 1—§ 17

State v. Neidenbach, 73 Or. App. 476, 698 P.2d 1040 (1985)

92 ALR6th 1—§ 8

State v. Neider, 94 Mo. 79, 6 S.W. 708 (1888)

97 ALR5th 537—§ 64

State v. Neil, 457 So. 2d 481 (Fla. 1984)

47 ALR5th 259—§ 2

63 ALR5th 375—§ 5, 6

88 ALR5th 67—§ 6, 11

State v. Neill, 244 N.C. 252, 93 S.E.2d 155 (1956)

29 ALR5th 59—§ 3, 8

State v. Nekolite, 2014 SD 55, 2014 WL 3748299 (S.D. 2014)

96 ALR6th 355—§ 46

State v. Nelson, 23 Conn. App. 215, 579 A.2d 1104 (1990)

9 ALR6th 541—§ 21

State v. Nelson, 36 Wash. 126, 78 P. 790 (1904)

57 ALR6th 445—§ 17

State v. Nelson, 63 Wash. 2d 188, 386 P.2d 142 (1963)

83 ALR5th 277—§ 13

57 ALR6th 445—§ 49

State v. Nelson, 69 Haw. 461, 748 P.2d 365 (1987)

124 ALR5th 1—§ 5

20 ALR6th 479—§ 16, 17, 24

42 ALR6th 237—§ 17

For assistance, call 1-800-328-4880

940

State v. Nelson, 74 Wash. App. 380, 874
P.2d 170 (1994)

33 ALR5th 571—§ 3

State v. Nelson, 108 Wash. 2d 491, 740
P.2d 835 (1987)

106 ALR5th 377—§ 3

State v. Nelson, 129 Ariz. 582, 633 P.2d
391 (1981)

24 ALR6th 1—§ 13

State v. Nelson, 131 Idaho 210, 953 P.2d
650 (Ct. App. 1998)

38 ALR5th 433—§ 3
39 ALR5th 283—§ 47
78 ALR5th 1—§ 58, 65

State v. Nelson, 133 Wash. 30, 233 P.
12 (1925)

54 ALR6th 429—§ 13

State v. Nelson, 138 Wis. 2d 418, 406
N.W.2d 385 (1987)

38 ALR5th 433—§ 2, 13, 33

State v. Nelson, 145 Minn. 123, 176
N.W. 164 (1920)

40 ALR6th 99—§ 69

State v. Nelson, 150 N.H. 569, 842 A.2d
83, 70 U.S.P.Q.2d 1254 (2004)

57 ALR6th 445—§ 35

State v. Nelson, 152 Wash. App. 755,
219 P.3d 100, 68 A.L.R.6th 685
(Div. 3 2009)

68 ALR6th 115—§ 8

State v. Nelson, 157 Ariz. 187, 755 P.2d
1175 (Ct. App. Div. 2 1988)

51 ALR6th 1—§ 24
52 ALR6th 1—§ 30

State v. Nelson, 161 N.H. 58, 8 A.3d 40
(2010)

70 ALR6th 361—§ 31, 32

State v. Nelson, 172 Mont. 65, 560 P.2d
897 (1977)

112 ALR5th 621—§ 7

State v. Nelson, 173 N.J. 417, 803 A.2d
1 (2002)

111 ALR5th 491—§ 8

State v. Nelson, 178 N.W.2d 434 (Iowa
1970)

71 ALR6th 283—§ 25

State v. Nelson, 189 W. Va. 778, 434
S.E.2d 697 (1993)

18 ALR6th 1—§ 3, 5, 40

State v. Nelson, 191 Wis. 2d 829, 532
N.W.2d 146 (Ct. App. 1995)

62 ALR6th 359—§ 18

State v. Nelson, 208 Ariz. 5, 90 P.3d 206
(Ct. App. Div. 1 2004)

18 ALR6th 519—§ 19

State v. Nelson, 223 Kan. 572, 575 P.2d
547 (1978)

39 ALR5th 283—§ 4

State v. Nelson, 249 Kan. 689, 822 P.2d
53 (1991)

18 ALR5th 1—§ 17

State v. Nelson, 250 S.C. 6, 156 S.E.2d
341 (1967)

55 ALR5th 423—§ 3

State v. Nelson, 255 N.J. Super. 270, 604
A.2d 999 (Law Div. 1992)

37 ALR6th 511—§ 3, 7, 13

State v. Nelson, 261 La. 153, 259 So. 2d
46 (1972)

65 ALR5th 407—§ 3, 16

State v. Nelson, 298 N.C. 573, 260
S.E.2d 629 (1979)

19 ALR6th 115—§ 5
24 ALR6th 591—§ 6

State v. Nelson, 318 N.J. Super. 242, 723
A.2d 627 (App. Div. 1999)

3 ALR6th 269—§ 5, 13

State v. Nelson, 329 N.W.2d 827 (Minn.
1983)

113 ALR5th 597—§ 8

State v. Nelson, 330 N.J. Super. 206, 749
A.2d 380 (App. Div. 2000)

101 ALR5th 187—§ 9

State v. Nelson, 347 So. 2d 749 (Fla.
App. D4 1977)

41 ALR5th 171—§ 13, 54, 58, 82

State v. Nelson, 354 So. 2d 540 (La.
1978)

64 ALR5th 741—§ 5

State v. Nelson, 381 So. 2d 477 (La.
1980)

113 ALR5th 517—§ 11

State v. Nelson, 399 N.W.2d 629 (Minn. Ct. App. 1987)
24 ALR6th 1—§ 33

State v. Nelson, 459 So. 2d 510 (La. 1984)
9 ALR6th 1—§ 15

State v. Nelson, 499 N.W.2d 512 (Minn. App. 1993)
38 ALR5th 357—§ 5

State v. Nelson, 562 So. 2d 1076 (La. Ct. App. 4th Cir. 1990)
93 ALR5th 527—§ 20
94 ALR5th 393—§ 12

State v. Nelson, 587 So. 2d 176 (La. App. 4th Cir. 1991)
27 ALR5th 540—§ 3, 10

State v. Nelson, 715 So. 2d 1045 (Fla. Dist. Ct. App. 4th Dist. 1998)
113 ALR5th 597—§ 8

State v. Nelson, 780 So. 2d 91 (Fla. Dist. Ct. App. 4th Dist. 2000)
113 ALR5th 597—§ 8

State v. Nelson, 1996 WL 757184 (Alaska Ct. App. 1996)
79 ALR5th 1—§ 14

State v. Nelson, 1998 ME 183, 714 A.2d 832 (Me. 1998)
57 ALR6th 445—§ 8

State v. Nelson, 2000 WL 1369865 (Ohio Ct. App. 8th Dist. Cuyahoga County 2000)
125 ALR5th 497—§ 3

State v. Nelson, 2001 MT 236, 307 Mont. 34, 36 P.3d 405 (2001)
92 ALR6th 295—§ 38

State v. Nelson, 2002 WL 15693 (Minn. Ct. App. 2002)
50 ALR6th 455—§ 23, 24

State v. Nelson, 2003-Ohio-3219, 2003 WL 21419298 (Ohio Ct. App. 8th Dist. Cuyahoga County 2003)
72 ALR6th 1—§ 6

State v. Nelson, 2007 UT App 34, 157 P.3d 329 (Utah Ct. App. 2007)
23 ALR6th 307—§ 33

State v. Nelson, 2008 WL 4539255 (Vt. 2008)
46 ALR6th 63—§ 11

State v. Nelson, 2011 WL 1642638 (Tenn. Crim. App. 2011)
70 ALR6th 329—§ 18

State v. Nelson, Slip Op (March 21, 1985, Kan. App)
11 ALR5th 52—§ 9

State v. Nelson-Waggoner, 2000 UT 59, 6 P.3d 1120 (Utah 2000)
86 ALR5th 59—§ 6

State v. Nemesh, 228 N.J. Super. 597, 550 A.2d 757 (App. Div. 1988)
57 ALR6th 83—§ 9

State v. Nemeth, 82 Ohio St. 3d 202, 694 N.E.2d 1332 (1998)
22 ALR5th 787—§ 3

State v. Nemeth, 130 N.M. 261, 2001-NMCA-029, 23 P.3d 936 (Ct. App. 2001)
58 ALR6th 499—§ 41

State v. Nemeth, 1997 WL 150649 (Ohio Ct. App. 7th Dist.Jefferson County 1997)
58 ALR5th 749—§ 6

State v. Nemitz, 105 Wash. App. 205, 19 P.3d 480 (Div. 3 2001)
94 ALR5th 537—§ 5

State v. Nemitz, 1998 WL 453693 (Ohio Ct. App. 1st Dist. Hamilton County 1998)
78 ALR5th 489—§ 3

State v. Nesbit, 978 S.W.2d 872 (Tenn. 1998)
18 ALR5th 804—§ 4
79 ALR5th 33—§ 7

State v. Nesbitt, 1984 WL 4579 (Ohio Ct. App. 8th Dist. Cuyahoga County 1984)
29 ALR6th 237—§ 4, 9

State v. Neslund, 50 Wash. App. 531, 749 P.2d 725 (Div. 1 1988)
65 ALR6th 359—§ 3

State v. Nesmith, 690 S.E.2d 769 (N.C. Ct. App. 2010)
57 ALR6th 1—§ 23

State v. Ness, 75 S.D. 373, 65 N.W.2d 923 (1954)
101 ALR6th 499—§ 18

103 ALR6th 35—§ 25

State v. Ness, 294 Or. 8, 653 P.2d 548 (1982)

41 ALR5th 171—§ 8, 55, 88, 114, 120, 136

State v. Nethercutt, 48 Wash. 105, 92 P. 938 (1907)

87 ALR5th 715—§ 4

State v. Netherland, 2008-Ohio-7007, 2008 WL 5451339 (Ohio Ct. App. 4th Dist. Ross County 2008)

64 ALR6th 1—§ 7, 9, 11

State v. Netherton, 133 Kan. 685, 3 P.2d 495 (1931)

81 ALR5th 563—§ 3, 5

State v. Netter, 118 Wash. App. 1003, 2003 WL 21907626 (Div. 1 2003)

125 ALR5th 537—§ 2, 54

State v. Nettles, 287 Or. 131, 597 P.2d 1243 (1979)

19 ALR5th 470—§ 5

92 ALR6th 1—§ 8

State v. Nettleton, 233 Mont. 308, 760 P.2d 733 (1988)

23 ALR6th 1—§ 15

State v. Netz, 1996 WL 81514 (Minn. Ct. App. 1996)

69 ALR6th 579—§ 8, 17

State v. Neubauer, 2 Conn. Cir. Ct. 169, 197 A.2d 93 (App. Div. 1963)

66 ALR5th 397—§ 3, 4, 10

State v. Neubauer, 68 Or. App. 885, 683 P.2d 136 (1984)

7 ALR5th 73—§ 3

State v. Neufeld, 260 Kan. 930, 926 P.2d 1325 (1996)

24 ALR6th 255—§ 5, 7, 13

State v. Neulander, 173 N.J. 193, 801 A.2d 255, 30 Media L. Rep. (BNA) 2281 (2002)

95 ALR6th 219—§ 12

State v. Neuman, 179 W. Va. 580, 371 S.E.2d 77 (1988)

72 ALR5th 403—§ 3

State v. Neuzil, 589 N.W.2d 708 (Iowa 1999)

29 ALR5th 487—§ 7, 11, 14

State v. Nevada Power Co., 80 Nev. 131, 390 P.2d 50 (1964)

90 ALR5th 547—§ 16, 19, 21

State v. Nevarez, 148 N.M. 820, 2010-NMCA-049, 242 P.3d 387 (Ct. App. 2010)

97 ALR6th 653—§ 10

State v. Nevels, 571 S.W.2d 736 (Mo. Ct. App. 1978)

70 ALR5th 587—§ 3

State v. Nevels, 712 S.W.2d 688 (Mo. Ct. App. W.D. 1986)

68 ALR5th 343—§ 3, 5

State v. Nevens, 197 N.J. Super. 531, 485 A.2d 345 (Law Div. 1984)

68 ALR5th 299—§ 3 to 5

State v. Nevers, 621 So. 2d 1108 (La. App. 1st Cir. 1993)

7 ALR5th 263—§ 4

State v. Neville, 293 N.W.2d 37 (Minn. 1980)

12 ALR6th 553—§ 9, 20

State v. Nevills, 530 S.W.2d 52 (Mo. Ct. App. 1975)

54 ALR6th 429—§ 11

State v. New, 2006-Ohio-2965, 2006 WL 1629613 (Ohio Ct. App. 10th Dist. Franklin County 2006)

62 ALR6th 413—§ 2

State v. Newby, 97 Or. App. 598, 777 P.2d 994 (1989)

38 ALR5th 433—§ 11

State v. New Chue Her, 510 N.W.2d 218 (Minn. App. 1994)

32 ALR5th 149—§ 54, 56, 72 to 74

State v. Newcomb, 934 S.W.2d 608 (Mo. Ct. App. E.D. 1996)

38 ALR6th 439—§ 13

State v. Newcome, 62 Ohio App. 3d 619, 577 N.E.2d 125 (Cuyahoga Co. 1989)

19 ALR5th 351—§ 9

State v. Newcomer, 48 Wash. App. 83, 737 P.2d 1285 (Div. 3 1987)

51 ALR6th 1—§ 3, 10

State v. Newell, 141 N.H. 199, 679 A.2d 1142 (1996)

83 ALR5th 277—§ 29, 34

State v. Newell, 212 Ariz. 389, 132 P.3d 833, 20 A.L.R.6th 839 (2006)
20 ALR6th 411—§ 21
20 ALR6th 479—§ 3, 11, 12
State v. Newell, 226 Kan. 295, 597 P.2d 1104 (1979)
7 ALR6th 169—§ 12
State v. Newell, 1990 WL 193357 (Ohio Ct. App. 8th Dist. Cuyahoga County 1990)
24 ALR6th 1—§ 13
State v. New England Health Care Employees Union Dist., Loc. 1199, 2003 WL 1874769 (Conn. Super. Ct. 2003)
112 ALR5th 263—§ 2, 57
State v. Newhouse, 147 Wash. App. 1039, 2008 WL 4998492 (Div. 2 2008)
45 ALR6th 643—§ 19
State v. Newkirk, 201 Wis. 2d 217, 549 N.W.2d 793 (Ct. App. 1996)
84 ALR6th 293—§ 27
State v. Newman, 12 Or. App. 266, 506 P.2d 523 (1973)
85 ALR5th 1—§ 2, 10
State v. Newman, 113 Or. App. 102, 832 P.2d 47 (1992)
73 ALR5th 383—§ 26, 32
State v. Newman, 132 N.J. 159, 623 A.2d 1355 (1993)
15 ALR5th 391—§ 32
92 ALR5th 35—§ 22
State v. Newman, 162 Mont. 450, 513 P.2d 258 (1973)
24 ALR5th 465—§ 87
State v. Newman, 235 Kan. 29, 680 P.2d 257 (1984)
23 ALR6th 1—§ 15
State v. Newman, 242 Mont. 315, 790 P.2d 971 (1990)
38 ALR5th 433—§ 6
57 ALR5th 141—§ 13
State v. Newman, 283 So. 2d 756 (La. 1973)
99 ALR6th 113—§ 10
State v. Newman, 292 Or. 216, 637 P.2d 143 (1981)

11 ALR5th 52—§ 9
State v. Newman, 308 N.C. 231, 302 S.E.2d 174 (1983)
39 ALR5th 283—§ 4, 66
State v. Newman, 326 N.W.2d 788 (Iowa 1982)
39 ALR5th 283—§ 10, 59, 67
State v. Newman, 605 S.W.2d 781 (Mo. 1980)
12 ALR5th 909—§ 5, 7, 10
State v. Newman, 750 So. 2d 252 (La. Ct. App. 5th Cir. 1999)
7 ALR5th 263—§ 7
State v. Newman, 1988 WL 56341 (Minn. Ct. App. 1988)
73 ALR5th 383—§ 31
State v. Newman, 1991 WL 131674 (Ohio Ct. App. 9th Dist. Summit County 1991)
15 ALR6th 375—§ 25
State v. Newnam, 409 N.W.2d 79 (N.D. 1987)
29 ALR6th 1—§ 10
State v. Newsome, 544 So. 2d 82 (La. Ct. App. 3d Cir. 1989)
6 ALR6th 533—§ 11
State v. Newsome, No. 6933 (August 7, 1981, Ct. App. Ohio, 2nd App. Dist. Montgomery Co.)
39 ALR5th 283—§ 14, 63, 67
State v. Newstead, 280 S.W.2d 6 (Mo. 1955)
104 ALR5th 357—§ 8
54 ALR6th 429—§ 29
State v. Newstrom, 371 N.W.2d 525, 26 Ed. Law Rep. 1203 (Minn. 1985)
70 ALR5th 169—§ 17
State v. Newton, 44 Iowa 45 (1876)
46 ALR5th 499—§ 3
State v. Newton, 82 N.C. App. 555, 347 S.E.2d 81 (1986)
98 ALR6th 455—§ 16
State v. Newton, 109 Wash. 2d 69, 743 P.2d 254 (1987)
82 ALR5th 359—§ 2, 6
83 ALR5th 277—§ 2, 10
84 ALR5th 487—§ 2, 21

State v. Newton, 227 Ga. App. 394, 489 S.E.2d 147 (1997)
113 ALR5th 517—§ 5
State v. Newton, 291 Or. 788, 636 P.2d 393 (1981)
109 ALR5th 611—§ 3, 6
State v. Newton, 682 P.2d 295 (Utah 1984)
90 ALR5th 225—§ 5
State v. Next Door Cinema Corp., 255 Kan. 112, 587 P.2d 326 (1978)
13 ALR5th 567—§ 4, 5
State v. Neyland, 139 Ohio St. 3d 353, 2014-Ohio-1914, 12 N.E.3d 1112 (2014)
99 ALR6th 295—§ 19
State v. Nez, 130 Idaho 950, 950 P.2d 1289 (Ct. App. 1997)
70 ALR5th 533—§ 3, 4
State v. Ng, 104 Wash. 2d 763, 713 P.2d 63 (1985)
121 ALR5th 551—§ 6, 15
State v. N.G.K., 770 N.W.2d 177 (Minn. Ct. App. 2009)
68 ALR6th 1—§ 9, 16
State v. Nguyen, 68 Wash. App. 906, 847 P.2d 936 (Div. 1 1993)
73 ALR5th 383—§ 4, 40, 42
State v. Nguyen, 94 P.3d 737 (Kan. Ct. App. 2004)
69 ALR6th 1—§ 5
State v. Nguyen, 251 Kan. 69, 833 P.2d 937 (1992)
49 ALR6th 343—§ 4
53 ALR6th 81—§ 7, 9
State v. Nguyen, 281 Kan. 702, 133 P.3d 1259 (2006)
49 ALR6th 343—§ 5, 24
97 ALR6th 567—§ 3, 9
State v. Nguyen, 672 So. 2d 988 (La. Ct. App. 5th Cir. 1996)
11 ALR6th 237—§ 13
State v. Nguyen, 707 So. 2d 66 (La. Ct. App. 4th Cir. 1998)
28 ALR6th 505—§ 7, 16
State v. Nguyen, 878 P.2d 1183, 244 Utah Adv. Rep. 36 (Utah App. 1994)

33 ALR5th 571—§ 3
State v. Nguyen, 880 S.W.2d 627 (Mo. App. 1994)
5 ALR5th 243—§ 7
State v. Nguyen, 2003 WI App 111, 264 Wis. 2d 895, 664 N.W.2d 128 (Ct. App. 2003)
84 ALR6th 293—§ 16
State v. Niblock, 230 Kan. 156, 631 P.2d 661 (1981)
103 ALR6th 347—§ 15
State v. Nicely, 39 Ohio St. 3d 147, 529 N.E.2d 1236 (1988)
65 ALR6th 359—§ 9
State v. Nicholas, 34 Wash. App. 775, 663 P.2d 1356 (Div. 1 1983)
81 ALR5th 563—§ 8
State v. Nicholas, 182 W. Va. 199, 387 S.E.2d 104 (1989)
1 ALR6th 549—§ 10
State v. Nicholas, 491 So. 2d 711 (La. App. 4th Cir. 1986)
7 ALR5th 263—§ 7
State v. Nicholas, 652 So. 2d 666 (La. App. 1st Cir. 1995)
41 ALR5th 171—§ 3, 7, 8, 10, 93, 94, 100, 116, 121, 122, 133
State v. Nicholas, 958 So. 2d 682 (La. Ct. App. 5th Cir. 2007)
78 ALR6th 297—§ 21
State v. Nicholas, 1998 WL 166436 (Ohio Ct. App. 12th Dist. Warren County 1998)
78 ALR5th 489—§ 3, 6
State v. Nicholas H., 131 N.H. 569, 560 A.2d 1156 (1989)
37 ALR5th 703—§ 4
State v. Nichols, 20 Wash. App. 462, 581 P.2d 1371 (Div. 3 1978)
58 ALR6th 499—§ 28
State v. Nichols, 50 Wash. 508, 97 P. 728 (1908)
120 ALR5th 125—§ 2, 3
121 ALR5th 1—§ 2, 16
State v. Nichols, 161 Wash. 2d 1, 162 P.3d 1122 (2007)
71 ALR6th 1—§ 8

State v. Nichols, 201 Ariz. 234, 33 P.3d 1172 (Ct. App. Div. 2 2001)
26 ALR6th 511—§ 46

State v. Nichols, 207 S.W.3d 215 (Mo. Ct. App. S.D. 2006)
37 ALR6th 357—§ 2, 48, 50, 67

State v. Nichols, 225 Ga. App. 609, 484 S.E.2d 507 (1997)
17 ALR6th 327—§ 12

State v. Nichols, 225 Mont. 438, 734 P.2d 170 (1987)
16 ALR5th 152—§ 5

State v. Nichols, 321 N.C. 616, 365 S.E.2d 561, 75 A.L.R.4th 179 (1988)
12 ALR6th 267—§ 8

State v. Nichols, 325 S.C. 111, 481 S.E.2d 118 (1997)
90 ALR6th 385—§ 5

State v. Nichols, 690 N.W.2d 463 (Iowa Ct. App. 2004)
71 ALR6th 1—§ 14

State v. Nichols, 1995 WL 755957 (Tenn. Crim. App. 1995)
102 ALR5th 327—§ 11
24 ALR6th 1—§ 19

State v. Nichols, 1999 MT 212, 295 Mont. 489, 986 P.2d 1093 (1999)
97 ALR6th 263—§ 27

State v. Nicholson, 19 Or. App. 226, 527 P.2d 140 (1974)
124 ALR5th 1—§ 4

State v. Nicholson, 174 Wis. 2d 542, 497 N.W.2d 791 (Ct. App. 1993)
103 ALR5th 463—§ 3

State v. Nicholson, 196 Wis. 2d 373, 539 N.W.2d 135 (Ct. App. 1995)
72 ALR5th 1—§ 29

State v. Nicholson, 1998 WL 820915 (Ohio Ct. App. 12th Dist. Warren County 1998)
78 ALR5th 489—§ 3, 10

State v. Nicholson, 2005 WL 4143037 (N.J. Super. Ct. App. Div. 2006)
39 ALR6th 257—§ 47

State v. Nickelson, 2003 WL 22952740 (Minn. Ct. App. 2003)

101 ALR6th 331—§ 10

State v. Nickerson, 120 N.H. 821, 424 A.2d 190 (1980)
52 ALR6th 125—§ 13, 47

State v. Nicolaus, 340 So. 2d 296 (La. 1976)
99 ALR6th 295—§ 5

State v. Niedermeyer, 48 Or. App. 665, 617 P.2d 911 (1980)
17 ALR6th 327—§ 12

State v. Niel, 640 So. 2d 588 (La. Ct. App. 3d Cir. 1994)
114 ALR5th 235—§ 8

State v. Niel, 671 So. 2d 1111 (La. Ct. App. 3d Cir. 1996)
78 ALR5th 309—§ 5, 6

State v. Nields, 93 Ohio St. 3d 6, 2001-Ohio-1291, 752 N.E.2d 859 (2001)
58 ALR6th 499—§ 17

State v. Niemczyk, 31 Wash. App. 803, 644 P.2d 759 (1982)
54 ALR5th 141—§ 5, 9, 11

State v. Niemeyer, 55 Conn. App. 447, 740 A.2d 416 (1999)
39 ALR5th 283—§ 71
57 ALR5th 315—§ 9
58 ALR5th 749—§ 6

State v. Niese, 1992 WL 2411 (Ohio App. 1992)
57 ALR6th 83—§ 6

State v. Nieto, 101 Ohio St. 409, 130 N.E. 663 (1920)
33 ALR6th 407—§ 5, 6

State v. Nieto, 2000-NMSC-031, 129 N.M. 688, 12 P.3d 442 (2000)
32 ALR6th 1—§ 11

State v. Nieuhaus, 217 Mo. 332, 117 S.W. 73 (1909)
5 ALR5th 243—§ 62

State v. Nieuwenhuis, 146 Ariz. 477, 706 P.2d 1244 (Ct. App. Div. 2 1985)
92 ALR6th 1—§ 6

State v. Nieves, 1997 WL 89213 (Ohio Ct. App. 9th Dist. Lorain County 1997)
58 ALR6th 385—§ 32

State v. Nightengale, 818 So. 2d 819 (La. Ct. App. 2d Cir. 2002)
12 ALR6th 267—§ 5

State v. Nile, 566 A.2d 1087 (Me. 1989)
57 ALR5th 141—§ 2, 7

State v. Niles, 47 Vt. 82, 1874 WL 6599 (1874)
33 ALR6th 353—§ 4

State v. Nilson, 854 P.2d 1029 (Utah Ct. App. 1993)
103 ALR6th 137—§ 3

State v. Nimely, 2002-Ohio-725, 2002 WL 228790 (Ohio Ct. App. 5th Dist. Ashland County 2002)
92 ALR6th 171—§ 18

State v. Ninci, 262 Kan. 21, 936 P.2d 1364 (1997)
29 ALR6th 1—§ 10

State v. Nine, 315 So. 2d 667 (La. 1975)
69 ALR6th 275—§ 34

State v. Nine (9) Sav. Accounts, 535 So. 2d 1097 (La. Ct. App. 2d Cir. 1988)
4 ALR6th 113—§ 4, 6, 8, 12, 14, 16, 22
101 ALR6th 1—§ 34

State v. Nine (9) Sav. Accounts, 540 So. 2d 1055 (La. Ct. App. 2d Cir. 1989)
104 ALR5th 229—§ 6
4 ALR6th 113—§ 4, 6, 16, 17, 19, 22
101 ALR6th 1—§ 16, 30, 34, 46

State v. Nineteen Thousand Two Hundred & Thirty Eight Dollars ($19,238.00) in United States Currency, 157 Ariz. 178, 755 P.2d 1166 (App. 1987)
1 ALR5th 346—§ 4, 5

State v. Nineteen Thousand Two Hundred and Thirty-Eight Dollars ($19,238.00) In U.S. Currency, 157 Ariz. 178, 755 P.2d 1166 (Ct. App. Div. 1 1987)
105 ALR5th 1—§ 4

State v. Nishina, 175 N.J. 502, 816 A.2d 153 (2003)
114 ALR5th 173—§ 8, 12

State v. Nitcher, 720 N.W.2d 547 (Iowa 2006)
71 ALR6th 1—§ 5

State v. Nitenson, 1992 WL 226325 (Ohio Ct. App. 4th Dist. Highland County 1992)
81 ALR6th 505—§ 6

State v. Nival, 42 Conn. App. 307, 678 A.2d 1008 (1996)
5 ALR5th 243—§ 48

State v. Nix, 236 Or. App. 32, 237 P.3d 842 (2010)
62 ALR6th 161—§ 6

State v. Nix, 327 So. 2d 301 (La. 1975)
23 ALR5th 672—§ 4
45 ALR5th 531—§ 3, 9

State v. Nixon, 13 Conn. App. 824, 538 A.2d 1064 (1988)
5 ALR5th 243—§ 6

State v. Nixon, 117 N.C. App. 141, 450 S.E.2d 562 (1994)
57 ALR5th 141—§ 3

State v. N.L.S., 98 Wash. App. 1052, 2000 WL 4161 (Div. 1 2000)
9 ALR6th 541—§ 23

State v. Noble, 126 Ariz. 41, 612 P.2d 497 (1980)
84 ALR5th 487—§ 30

State v. Noble, 152 Ariz. 284, 731 P.2d 1228 (1987)
39 ALR5th 283—§ 3

State v. Noble, 167 Ariz. 440, 808 P.2d 325, 75 Ariz. Adv. Rep. 61 (App. 1990)
36 ALR5th 161—§ 3

State v. Noble, 171 Ariz. 171, 829 P.2d 1217 (1992)
37 ALR6th 55—§ 8
63 ALR6th 351—§ 3

State v. Noble, 171 Ariz. 171, 829 P.2d 1217, 111 Ariz. Adv. Rep. 17 (1992)
36 ALR5th 161—§ 3

State v. Noble, 179 Ga. App. 785, 347 S.E.2d 722 (1986)
84 ALR6th 293—§ 41

State v. Nobles, 106 Ohio App. 3d 246, 665 N.E.2d 1137 (Montgomery Co. 1995)
31 ALR5th 704—§ 7

State v. Nobles, 107 N.C. App. 627, 422 S.E.2d 78 (1992)
50 ALR5th 703—§ 37

State v. Nobles, 122 Idaho 470, 835 P.2d 1281 (1992)
42 ALR6th 237—§ 8

State v. Nobles, 329 N.C. 239, 404 S.E.2d 668 (1991)
73 ALR5th 383—§ 5, 43

State v. Nobles, 350 N.C. 483, 515 S.E.2d 885 (1999)
98 ALR6th 455—§ 16

State v. Nobles, No. 46323 (October 13, 1983, Ct. App. Ohio, 8th App. Dist. Cuyahoga Co.)
39 ALR5th 283—§ 14, 60

State v. Noel, 157 N.J. 141, 723 A.2d 602 (1999)
90 ALR5th 453—§ 49
92 ALR6th 549—§ 32, 39, 43, 47

State v. Noel, 303 N.J. Super. 435, 697 A.2d 157 (App. Div. 1997)
92 ALR6th 549—§ 32

State v. Noggle, 140 Ohio App. 3d 733, 2000-Ohio-1927, 749 N.E.2d 309 (3d Dist. Crawford County 2000)
26 ALR6th 451—§ 10

State v. No Heart, 353 N.W.2d 43 (S.D. 1984)
24 ALR6th 591—§ 9, 13

State v. Nokes, 192 Neb. 844, 224 N.W.2d 776 (1975)
71 ALR6th 1—§ 11

State v. Nolan, 98 Wash. App. 75, 988 P.2d 473 (Div. 1 1999)
105 ALR5th 499—§ 4

State v. Nolan, 168 Mo. 446, 68 S.W. 346 (1902)
5 ALR6th 1—§ 62

State v. Nolan, 283 Neb. 50, 807 N.W.2d 520 (2012)
71 ALR6th 1—§ 11

State v. Nolan, 503 So. 2d 1186 (La. Ct. App. 3d Cir. 1987)
97 ALR5th 293—§ 3, 8
110 ALR5th 329—§ 6

State v. Nolan, 808 S.W.2d 556 (Tex. App. Austin 1991)

116 ALR5th 479—§ 5

State v. Noll, 171 Neb. 831, 108 N.W.2d 108 (1961)
78 ALR6th 417—§ 49, 58

State v. Nollner, 749 P.2d 905 (Alaska App. 1988)
38 ALR5th 433—§ 11

State v. No Neck, 458 N.W.2d 364 (S.D. 1990)
15 ALR5th 391—§ 7
92 ALR5th 35—§ 19

State v. Nonnemacher, 2002 MT 238N, 313 Mont. 419, 63 P.3d 512 (2002)
46 ALR6th 241—§ 10

State v. Norberg, 423 N.W.2d 733 (Minn. Ct. App. 1988)
29 ALR6th 1—§ 10

State v. Nordby, 106 Wash. 2d 514, 723 P.2d 1117 (1986)
73 ALR5th 383—§ 41, 52, 54

State v. Nordlund, 113 Wash. App. 171, 53 P.3d 520 (Div. 2 2002)
73 ALR6th 1—§ 5

State v. Nordstrom, 2000 WL 1577069 (Minn. Ct. App. 2000)
43 ALR6th 475—§ 6

State v. Norfolk, 2005-Ohio-336, 2005 WL 225306 (Ohio Ct. App. 10th Dist. Franklin County 2005)
69 ALR6th 1—§ 16

State v. Norgren, 136 N.H. 399, 616 A.2d 505 (1992)
82 ALR5th 359—§ 2
83 ALR5th 277—§ 2, 14, 29, 33
84 ALR5th 487—§ 2

State v. Noriega, 6 Ariz. App. 428, 433 P.2d 281 (1967)
28 ALR6th 505—§ 9

State v. Norman, 7 Ohio App. 3d 17, 453 N.E.2d 1257 (5th Dist. Delaware County 1982)
3 ALR6th 269—§ 5, 8, 13

State v. Norman, 16 Utah 457, 52 P. 986 (1898)
97 ALR5th 201—§ 3

State v. Norman, 61 Wash. App. 16, 808 P.2d 1159 (Div. 3 1991)

118 ALR5th 253—§ 3, 16, 18
State v. Norman, 76 N.C. App. 623, 334 S.E.2d 247 (1985)
34 ALR5th 125—§ 27
State v. Norman, 153 N.C. 591, 68 S.E. 917 (1910)
81 ALR5th 563—§ 3
State v. Norman, 162 Wash. App. 1039, 2011 WL 2674909 (Div. 1 2011)
101 ALR6th 499—§ 14
State v. Norman, 203 Or. App. 1, 125 P.3d 15 (2005)
30 ALR6th 1—§ 4, 7
State v. Norman, 586 S.W.2d 45 (Mo. App. 1979)
29 ALR5th 59—§ 7, 17
State v. Norman, 2009-Ohio-5458, 2009 WL 3261258 (Ohio Ct. App. 4th Dist. Ross County 2009)
93 ALR6th 275—§ 4
State v. Norring, 2009 WL 2432300 (Minn. Ct. App. 2009)
56 ALR6th 1—§ 11, 32
State v. Norris, 47 S.W.3d 457 (Tenn. Crim. App. 2000)
114 ALR5th 235—§ 8
State v. Norris, 210 Kan. 457, 502 P.2d 817 (1972)
37 ALR6th 357—§ 35
State v. Norris, 212 Mont. 427, 689 P.2d 243 (1984)
86 ALR5th 59—§ 3 to 5
State v. Norris, 244 Kan. 326, 768 P.2d 296 (1989)
9 ALR6th 1—§ 8
State v. Norris, 352 So. 2d 875 (Fla. Dist. Ct. App. 3d Dist. 1977)
23 ALR6th 1—§ 15
State v. Norris, 428 N.W.2d 61 (Minn. 1988)
9 ALR5th 369—§ 6
84 ALR5th 487—§ 13
State v. Norris, 724 So. 2d 630 (Fla. Dist. Ct. App. 5th Dist. 1998)
113 ALR5th 597—§ 8
State v. Norris, 1999 WL 1000034 (Ohio Ct. App. 2d Dist. Montgomery County 1999)

17 ALR6th 327—§ 33
State v. Norris, 2001 UT 104, 48 P.3d 872, 6 A.L.R.6th 749 (Utah 2001)
6 ALR6th 533—§ 11
State v. Norris-Romine, 134 Or. App. 204, 894 P.2d 1221 (1995)
29 ALR5th 487—§ 4
State v. North Dakota Ed. Ass'n, 262 N.W.2d 731, 4 A.L.R.4th 724 (N.D. 1978)
53 ALR6th 491—§ 22
State v. North Fla. Women's Health And Counseling Ser., 2001 WL 111037 (Fla. Dist. Ct. App. 1st Dist. 2001)
77 ALR5th 1—§ 4
State v. Northover, 133 Idaho 655, 991 P.3d 380 (Ct. App. 1999)
78 ALR6th 297—§ 5, 32
State v. Northup, 120 Wash. App. 1019, 2004 WL 295159 (Div. 1 2004)
86 ALR6th 321—§ 13
State v. Norton, 7 S.W.3d 459 (Mo. Ct. App. E.D. 1999)
37 ALR6th 357—§ 72
State v. Norton, 11 P.3d 494 (Idaho Ct. App. 2000)
39 ALR5th 283—§ 39
State v. Norton, 277 Kan. 432, 85 P.3d 686 (2004)
26 ALR6th 511—§ 29
State v. Norton, 328 N.W.2d 142 (Minn. 1982)
73 ALR5th 383—§ 5
State v. Norton, 899 S.W.2d 303 (Tex. App. Houston 14th Dist. 1995)
18 ALR6th 519—§ 10
State v. Norush, 97 N.M. 660, 642 P.2d 1119 (App. 1982)
54 ALR5th 141—§ 3
State v. Norwood, 8 S.W.3d 242 (Mo. Ct. App. W.D. 1999)
5 ALR5th 243—§ 31
State v. Nosic, 1999 WL 99073 (Ohio Ct. App. 5th Dist. Stark County 1999)
78 ALR5th 489—§ 3, 10
State v. Novacek, 178 Wis. 2d 592, 506 N.W.2d 171 (Ct. App. 1993)

85 ALR6th 641—§ 5

State v. Novak, 338 N.W.2d 637 (N.D. 1983)

52 ALR5th 655—§ 2, 5, 8

State v. Novak, 1991 WL 37946 (Ohio Ct. App. 4th Dist.Gallia County 1991)

57 ALR5th 141—§ 13

State v. Novak, 2009-Ohio-6220, 2009 WL 4173580 (Ohio Ct. App. 8th Dist. Cuyahoga County 2009)

70 ALR6th 1—§ 5

State v. Novembrino, 105 N.J. 95, 519 A.2d 820 (1987)

19 ALR5th 470—§ 3, 12

State v. Novicky, 2008 WL 1747805 (Minn. Ct. App. 2008)

62 ALR6th 161—§ 28

State v. Novosel, 120 N.H. 176, 412 A.2d 739 (1980)

55 ALR6th 157—§ 6, 65

State v. Nowden, 2007-Ohio-2914, 2007 WL 1705112 (Ohio Ct. App. 8th Dist. Cuyahoga County 2007)

70 ALR6th 1—§ 5

State v. Nowells, 135 Iowa 53, 109 N.W. 1016 (1906)

11 ALR5th 497—§ 3, 6, 8, 16, 19

State v. Noyes, 36 Conn. 80, 1869 WL 948 (1869)

97 ALR6th 567—§ 4, 10

State v. N.R.O., 2007 WL 2032924 (N.J. Super. Ct. App. Div. 2007)

69 ALR6th 1—§ 25

State v. Nucaro, 614 N.W.2d 856 (Iowa Ct. App. 2000)

71 ALR6th 1—§ 7

State v. Nuckolls, 606 So. 2d 1205 (Fla. Dist. Ct. App. 5th Dist. 1992)

66 ALR6th 351—§ 12

State v. Nuckolls, 617 So. 2d 724 (Fla. Dist. Ct. App. 5th Dist. 1993)

84 ALR5th 1—§ 3

67 ALR6th 209—§ 48

State v. Nuckols, 1 Wash. App. 189, 459 P.2d 979 (Div. 1 1969)

28 ALR6th 505—§ 29

State v. Nunez, 93 Conn. App. 818, 890 A.2d 636 (2006)

102 ALR6th 365—§ 8, 32

State v. Nunez, 162 Vt. 615, 647 A.2d 1007 (1994)

93 ALR5th 327—§ 7, 9

State v. Nunez-Martinez, 90 Wash. App. 250, 951 P.2d 823 (Div. 2 1998)

27 ALR5th 593—§ 21

State v. Nunez-Valdez, 200 N.J. 129, 975 A.2d 418 (2009)

74 ALR6th 373—§ 2, 5, 12, 22

State v. Nunn, 110 Or. App. 96, 821 P.2d 431 (1991)

68 ALR6th 527—§ 45

80 ALR6th 599—§ 6

State v. Nuss, 235 Neb. 107, 454 N.W.2d 482 (1990)

24 ALR5th 132—§ 4, 8

State v. Nutley, 24 Wis. 2d 527, 129 N.W.2d 155 (1964)

16 ALR6th 329—§ 4

24 ALR6th 591—§ 4

State v. N.W., 329 N.J. Super. 326, 747 A.2d 819 (App. Div. 2000)

69 ALR6th 1—§ 26

State v. Nye, 551 A.2d 844 (Me. 1988)

57 ALR5th 141—§ 7

State v. Nygaard, 447 N.W.2d 267 (N.D. 1989)

26 ALR5th 1—§ 3

State v. Oakes, 157 Vt. 171, 598 A.2d 119 (1991)

19 ALR5th 470—§ 3, 12

State v. Oakes, 193 Or. App. 341, 89 P.3d 1274 (2004)

18 ALR6th 519—§ 19

State v. Oakley, 227 S.W.3d 58 (Tex. 2007)

53 ALR6th 305—§ 2, 40, 45

State v. Oatney, 335 Or. 276, 66 P.3d 475 (2003)

110 ALR5th 1—§ 14

State v. Ober, 122 Wash. App. 1028, 2004 WL 1562346 (Div. 2 2004)

79 ALR6th 1—§ 81

For assistance, call 1-800-328-4880

State v. Oberlander, 149 Wis. 2d 132, 438 N.W.2d 580 (1989)

22 ALR5th 1—§ 13, 15, 17, 35

State v. Oborne, 99 Ohio App. 3d 577, 651 N.E.2d 453 (Montgomery Co. 1994)

50 ALR5th 581—§ 13

State v. O'Brien, 95 Wash. App. 1069, 1999 WL 359190 (Div. 3 1999)

103 ALR6th 507—§ 20, 22

State v. O'Brien, 96 Or. App. 498, 774 P.2d 1109 (1989)

15 ALR5th 391—§ 45

State v. O'Brien, 106 Vt. 97, 170 A. 98 (1934)

97 ALR5th 201—§ 3

State v. O'Brien, 132 N.H. 587, 567 A.2d 582 (1989)

7 ALR5th 73—§ 2, 3

State v. O'Brien, 214 Wis. 2d 327, 572 N.W.2d 870 (Ct. App. 1997)

51 ALR5th 375—§ 7

State v. O'Brien, 223 Wis. 2d 303, 588 N.W.2d 8 (1999)

104 ALR5th 165—§ 2

State v. O'Brien, 262 Or. 30, 496 P.2d 191 (1972)

4 ALR5th 1—§ 2, 24

State v. O'Brien, 369 N.W.2d 525 (Minn. 1985)

73 ALR5th 383—§ 6

State v. O'Brien, 429 N.W.2d 293 (Minn. Ct. App. 1988)

113 ALR5th 597—§ 5

State v. O'Brien, 459 N.W.2d 131 (Minn. Ct. App. 1990)

15 ALR5th 391—§ 37
92 ALR5th 35—§ 16

State v. O'Brien, 784 S.W.2d 187 (Mo. App. 1989)

3 ALR5th 521—§ 2, 3

State v. O'Bryan, 96 Idaho 548, 531 P.2d 1193 (1975)

45 ALR5th 1—§ 5, 12, 23
61 ALR5th 1—§ 4, 14
106 ALR5th 397—§ 4

State v. O'Bryant, 219 Ga. App. 862, 467 S.E.2d 342 (1996)

60 ALR5th 1—§ 6

State v. O.C., 748 So. 2d 945 (Fla. 1999)

58 ALR6th 385—§ 6

State v. O'Cain, 108 Wash. App. 542, 31 P.3d 733 (Div. 1 2001)

12 ALR6th 553—§ 3, 10, 11, 26

State v. O'Campo, 103 Idaho 62, 644 P.2d 985 (Ct. App. 1982)

67 ALR5th 361—§ 2, 4

State v. Occhino, 572 N.W.2d 316 (Minn. App. 1997)

66 ALR5th 397—§ 4, 9

State v. Ochoa, 131 Ariz. 175, 639 P.2d 365 (Ct. App. Div. 2 1981)

103 ALR6th 347—§ 13

State v. Ochoa, 314 N.J. Super. 168, 714 A.2d 349 (App. Div. 1998)

69 ALR6th 1—§ 33

State v. Ochoa, 576 So. 2d 854, 16 FLW D 757 (Fla. App. D3 1991)

38 ALR5th 433—§ 3

State v. O'Connell, 179 Wis. 2d 598, 508 N.W.2d 23, R.I.C.O. Bus. Disp. Guide (CCH) ¶ 8673 (Ct. App. 1993)

89 ALR5th 629—§ 4
58 ALR6th 385—§ 20

State v. O'Connell, 275 N.W.2d 197 (Iowa 1979)

24 ALR5th 465—§ 2, 14, 108, 112

State v. O'Connor, 39 Wash. App. 113, 692 P.2d 208 (Div. 1 1984)

80 ALR6th 239—§ 11

State v. O'Connor, 42 N.J. 502, 201 A.2d 705 (1964)

45 ALR5th 531—§ 6

State v. O'Connor, 76 N.J. Super. 246, 184 A.2d 83 (County Ct. 1962)

89 ALR6th 565—§ 13

State v. Odam, 40 Or. App. 551, 595 P.2d 1277 (1979)

50 ALR5th 703—§ 38
18 ALR6th 519—§ 5

State v. O'Daniels, 911 So. 2d 247 (Fla. Dist. Ct. App. 3d Dist. 2005)

70 ALR6th 513—§ 4
71 ALR6th 471—§ 4
State v. Odegaard, 165 N.W.2d 677 (N.D. 1969)
72 ALR5th 607—§ 3 to 5
State v. Odom, 99 N.C. App. 265, 393 S.E.2d 146 (1990)
57 ALR6th 445—§ 45
State v. Odom, 554 So. 2d 1281 (La. Ct. App. 1st Cir. 1989)
95 ALR5th 229—§ 25
State v. Odom, 845 S.W.2d 600 (Mo. Ct. App. E.D. 1992)
105 ALR5th 529—§ 13
State v. Odom, 878 So. 2d 582 (La. Ct. App. 1st Cir. 2004)
99 ALR6th 295—§ 5, 21
State v. Odom, 928 S.W.2d 18 (Tenn. 1996)
69 ALR6th 579—§ 4
State v. Odom, 2002 WL 31322532 (Tenn. Crim. App. 2002)
110 ALR5th 1—§ 3, 8, 15, 20
State v. O'Donnell, 117 N.J. 210, 564 A.2d 1202 (1989)
73 ALR5th 383—§ 60
State v. O'Donnell, 176 Iowa 337, 157 N.W. 870 (1916)
24 ALR5th 465—§ 14, 88
State v. O'Donnell, 280 Minn. 213, 158 N.W.2d 699 (1968)
55 ALR6th 157—§ 111
State v. O'Donnell, 495 A.2d 798 (Me. 1985)
15 ALR5th 391—§ 2
92 ALR5th 35—§ 3, 7
State v. O'Dorle, 738 So. 2d 987 (Fla. Dist. Ct. App. 2d Dist. 1999)
113 ALR5th 597—§ 8
State v. O'Driscoll, 65 Or. App. 362, 671 P.2d 752 (1983)
41 ALR5th 171—§ 8, 12, 66, 88, 116, 135
State v. Odum, 1995 WL 599010 (Tenn. Crim. App. 1995)
99 ALR6th 295—§ 9
State v. Ogar, 229 N.J. Super. 459, 551 A.2d 1037 (1989)

27 ALR5th 593—§ 32, 34
State v. Ogden, 168 Or. App. 249
57 ALR5th 315—§ 11
State v. Ogden, 391 So. 2d 434 (La. 1980)
109 ALR5th 99—§ 8
State v. Ogden, 2011-Ohio-1589, 2011 WL 1215801 (Ohio Ct. App. 10th Dist. Franklin County 2011)
64 ALR6th 1—§ 13
State v. Oglesbee, 24 Wash. App. 769, 603 P.2d 1275 (Div. 3 1979)
57 ALR6th 445—§ 28
State v. Ogletree, 2006-Ohio-4316, 2006 WL 2390255 (Ohio Ct. App. 11th Dist. Portage County 2006)
68 ALR6th 115—§ 9, 11, 14
State v. O'Grady, 19 N.J. Misc. 559, 21 A.2d 864 (1941)
52 ALR5th 655—§ 3
State v. O'Herron, 153 N.J. Super. 570, 380 A.2d 728 (App. Div. 1977)
62 ALR6th 413—§ 30
State v. Ohio Civil Service Employees Ass'n, Local 11, AFSCME, AFL-CIO, 1992 WL 131843 (Ohio Ct. App. 10th Dist. Franklin County 1992)
66 ALR5th 611—§ 9
State v. Ohio Stove Co., 154 Ohio St. 27, 42 Ohio Op. 117, 93 N.E.2d 291 (1950)
31 ALR6th 199—§ 2
State v. Ohler, 219 Neb. 840, 366 N.W.2d 771 (1985)
66 ALR5th 135—§ 13
State v. Ohlson, 131 Wash. App. 71, 125 P.3d 990 (Div. 2 2005)
30 ALR6th 1—§ 4, 7
State v. Ohmer, 162 Ohio App. 3d 150, 2005-Ohio-3487, 832 N.E.2d 1243 (1st Dist. Hamilton County 2005)
33 ALR6th 91—§ 21
State v. Ohnstad, 359 N.W.2d 827 (N.D. 1984)
55 ALR6th 157—§ 115
State v. O'Hora, 12 N.C. App. 250, 182 S.E.2d 823 (1971)

For assistance, call 1-800-328-4880

28 ALR6th 505—§ 11

State v. Oiler, 1987 WL 11252 (Ohio Ct. App. 7th Dist. Columbiana County 1987)

99 ALR6th 295—§ 9

State v. Oinas, 125 Wis. 2d 487, 373 N.W.2d 463 (Ct. App. 1985)

94 ALR5th 393—§ 7

State v. Ojiearontor, 2004 WL 5581864 (Vt. 2004)

82 ALR6th 373—§ 3

State v. Ojile, 2012-Ohio-6015, 2012 WL 6674405 (Ohio Ct. App. 1st Dist. Hamilton County 2012)

103 ALR6th 347—§ 13

State v. Okada, 113 Haw. 363, 152 P.3d 535 (Ct. App. 2007)

34 ALR6th 623—§ 8

State v. Okanogan County, 153 Wash. 399, 280 P. 31, 67 A.L.R. 668 (1929)

35 ALR6th 1—§ 27, 29

State v. O'Kelley, 117 Ariz. 34, 570 P.2d 805 (Ct. App. Div. 2 1977)

66 ALR5th 397—§ 4

State v. O'Kelly, 98 N.C. App. 265, 390 S.E.2d 717 (1990)

106 ALR5th 397—§ 5

State v. O'Kelly, 211 N.W.2d 589 (Iowa 1973)

45 ALR5th 531—§ 9

State v. O'Key, 321 Or. 285, 899 P.2d 663 (1995)

90 ALR5th 453—§ 19

State v. Okuda, 71 Haw. 434, 795 P.2d 1 (1990)

68 ALR5th 299—§ 4
87 ALR5th 597—§ 17

State v. Okumura, 58 Haw. 425, 570 P.2d 848 (1977)

19 ALR6th 697—§ 15

State v. Okumura, 78 Haw. 383, 894 P.2d 80 (Haw. 1995)

24 ALR6th 1—§ 42

State v. Okumura, 78 Hawaii 383, 894 P.2d 80 (1995)

40 ALR5th 113—§ 4

State v. Olague, 156 Wash. App. 1004, 2010 WL 1981830 (Div. 1 2010)

94 ALR6th 525—§ 7

State v. Oland, 1 Or. App. 272, 461 P.2d 277 (1969)

54 ALR6th 429—§ 18

State v. Olan Mills, Incorporated of Tenn., 258 Ala. 303, 63 So. 2d 796 (1952)

89 ALR5th 493—§ 12

State v. Oldenbaugh, 2010-268 La. 12/6/11, 2011 WL 6034516 (La. 2011)

71 ALR6th 625—§ 28

State v. Olderman, 44 Ohio App. 2d 130, 73 Ohio Op. 2d 129, 336 N.E.2d 442 (8th Dist. Cuyahoga County 1975)

95 ALR5th 471—§ 3

State v. Olds, 831 S.W.2d 713 (Mo. App. 1992)

39 ALR5th 283—§ 4, 68

State v. Olesen, 443 N.W.2d 8 (S.D. 1989)

38 ALR5th 433—§ 3

State v. Olin, 143 Wash. App. 1053, 2008 WL 933503 (Div. 2 2008)

80 ALR6th 239—§ 6

State v. Olinghouse, 605 S.W.2d 58 (Mo. 1980)

99 ALR6th 113—§ 18

State v. Oliva, 144 La. 51, 80 So. 195 (1918)

88 ALR6th 203—§ 60

State v. Olivarez, 1999 WL 262158 (Ohio Ct. App. 11th Dist. Lake County 1999)

9 ALR6th 541—§ 32

State v. Olivas, 10 Ariz. App. 285, 458 P.2d 379 (1969)

9 ALR6th 1—§ 6

State v. Olivas, 122 Wash. 2d 73, 856 P.2d 1076 (1993)

76 ALR5th 239—§ 4, 16, 17

State v. Olive, 47 Wash. App. 147, 734 P.2d 36 (Div. 2 1987)

73 ALR5th 383—§ 6

State v. Oliver, 2 Ohio App. 2d 224, 31 Ohio Op. 2d 342, 207 N.E.2d 571 (8th Dist. Cuyahoga County 1965)
52 ALR6th 125—§ 46

State v. Oliver, 85 N.C. App. 1, 354 S.E.2d 527 (1987)
38 ALR5th 433—§ 21

State v. Oliver, 101 Ohio App. 3d 587, 656 N.E.2d 348, 72 A.L.R.5th 757 (8th Dist. Cuyahoga County 1995)
72 ALR5th 403—§ 17

State v. Oliver, 183 Ga. App. 92, 357 S.E.2d 889 (1987)
61 ALR5th 1—§ 2, 3, 9

State v. Oliver, 210 N.C. App. 609, 709 S.E.2d 503 (2011)
102 ALR6th 279—§ 30

State v. Oliver, 293 S.W.3d 437 (Mo. 2009)
94 ALR6th 525—§ 7

State v. Oliver, 682 So. 2d 301 (La. Ct. App. 4th Cir. 1996)
102 ALR5th 327—§ 2, 4, 5, 7

State v. Oliver, 775 S.W.2d 308 (Mo. Ct. App. E.D. 1989)
16 ALR6th 329—§ 11
24 ALR6th 591—§ 9, 13

State v. Oliver, 791 S.W.2d 782 (Mo. Ct. App. E.D. 1990)
16 ALR6th 329—§ 11
19 ALR6th 115—§ 6
24 ALR6th 591—§ 9, 13

State v. Oliver, 874 So. 2d 365 (La. Ct. App. 2d Cir. 2004)
69 ALR6th 1—§ 23

State v. Oliver, 1986 WL 3537 (Tenn. Crim. App. 1986)
99 ALR6th 295—§ 16

State v. Olivera, 344 N.J. Super. 583, 782 A.2d 988 (App. Div. 2001)
35 ALR6th 361—§ 16

State v. Oliviera, 534 A.2d 867 (R.I. 1987)
70 ALR5th 587—§ 21

State v. Olkon, 299 N.W.2d 89 (Minn. 1980)
49 ALR5th 639—§ 4

84 ALR5th 487—§ 13

State v. Oller, 851 S.W.2d 841 (Tenn. Crim. App. 1992)
98 ALR6th 455—§ 17

State v. O'Loughlin, 270 N.J. Super. 472, 637 A.2d 553 (App. Div. 1994)
30 ALR6th 103—§ 13, 18, 33, 52

State v. Olsen, 99 Wis. 2d 572, 299 N.W.2d 632 (App. 1980)
3 ALR5th 521—§ 2, 6, 8

State v. Olsen, 359 N.W.2d 67 (Minn. Ct. App. 1984)
57 ALR5th 141—§ 7

State v. Olsen, 496 So. 2d 1260 (La. App. 5th Cir. 1986)
15 ALR5th 391—§ 45

State v. Olsen, 540 N.W.2d 149 (N.D. 1995)
37 ALR6th 357—§ 48, 56

State v. Olsen, 618 N.W.2d 346 (Iowa 2000)
89 ALR5th 629—§ 1

State v. Olsen, 745 So. 2d 454 (Fla. Dist. Ct. App. 5th Dist. 1999)
18 ALR6th 1—§ 2, 21

State v. Olson, 8 Conn. App. 188, 511 A.2d 379 (1986)
90 ALR5th 619—§ 26

State v. Olson, 34 Or. App. 511, 579 P.2d 277 (1978)
85 ALR5th 1—§ 17

State v. Olson, 47 Wash. App. 514, 735 P.2d 1362 (Div. 1 1987)
87 ALR6th 1—§ 42

State v. Olson, 58 Minn. 431, 59 N.W. 1038 (1894)
102 ALR5th 525—§ 17

State v. Olson, 73 Wash. App. 348, 869 P.2d 110 (Div. 2 1994)
106 ALR5th 397—§ 4

State v. Olson, 74 Wash. App. 126, 872 P.2d 64 (Div. 1 1994)
106 ALR5th 397—§ 4

State v. Olson, 91 Or. App. 290, 754 P.2d 626 (1988)
15 ALR5th 391—§ 45

State v. Olson, 105 Wis. 2d 763, 318 N.W.2d 22 (Ct. App. 1981)

58 ALR6th 499—§ 68

State v. Olson, 134 Ariz. 114, 654 P.2d 48 (Ct. App. Div. 1 1982)

35 ALR6th 497—§ 13, 21

State v. Olson, 140 P.3d 452 (Kan. Ct. App. 2006)

26 ALR6th 511—§ 25

State v. Olson, 180 Mont. 151, 589 P.2d 663 (1979)

106 ALR5th 397—§ 8

State v. Olson, 255 Wis. 2d 835, 2002 WI App 134, 646 N.W.2d 856 (Ct. App. 2002)

73 ALR6th 49—§ 8, 19

State v. Olson, 356 N.W.2d 110 (N.D. 1984)

26 ALR5th 1—§ 3

State v. Olson, 361 N.W.2d 899 (Minn. App. 1985)

18 ALR5th 1—§ 25

State v. Olson, 436 N.W.2d 817 (Minn. Ct. App. 1989)

73 ALR5th 383—§ 5

State v. Olson, 459 N.W.2d 711 (Minn. Ct. App. 1990)

73 ALR5th 383—§ 5
29 ALR6th 1—§ 10

State v. Olson, 560 S.W.2d 71 (Mo. Ct. App. 1977)

70 ALR5th 587—§ 3

State v. Olson, 972 S.W.2d 359 (Mo. Ct. App. E.D. 1998)

82 ALR5th 103—§ 5

State v. Olson, 1993 WL 121248 (Minn. Ct. App. 1993)

67 ALR6th 103—§ 5, 10

State v. Olson, 2002 MT 211, 311 Mont. 270, 55 P.3d 935 (2002)

78 ALR6th 297—§ 4, 26, 31, 33, 34, 40

State v. Olson, 2002 WL 1363800 (Minn. Ct. App. 2002)

113 ALR5th 597—§ 3

State v. Ommundson, 1999 MT 16, 293 Mont. 133, 974 P.2d 620 (1999)

46 ALR6th 241—§ 6, 9, 10, 20

State v. Ondecker, 1990 WL 125478 (Ohio Ct. App. 5th Dist. Stark County 1990)

58 ALR6th 215—§ 7

State v. One 1967 Ford Mustang, 266 Md. 275, 292 A.2d 64 (1972)

1 ALR5th 375—§ 3

State v. One 1972 Lincoln Continental Vin, 295 N.W.2d 343 (S.D. 1980)

1 ALR5th 375—§ 3, 4
6 ALR5th 652—§ 2, 3, 6

State v. One 1972 Pontiac Grand Prix, 90 S.D. 455, 242 N.W.2d 660 (1976)

1 ALR5th 375—§ 3, 4
6 ALR5th 652—§ 2 to 5, 11

State v. One 1976 Chevrolet Van, 19 Conn. App. 195, 562 A.2d 62, 6 A.L.R.5th 1169 (1989)

6 ALR5th 711—§ 3

State v. One 1976 Pontiac Firebird, 168 N.J. Super. 168, 402 A.2d 254, 26 U.C.C.R.S. 1306 (1979)

1 ALR5th 317—§ 7

State v. One 1977 Dodge Van, 165 N.J. Super. 113, 397 A.2d 733 (1979)

1 ALR5th 317—§ 7

State v. One 1978 Chevrolet Corvette, 8 Kan. App. 2d 747, 667 P.2d 893 (1983)

1 ALR5th 317—§ 6

State v. One 1978 Ford Van, Serial No. E11HBCC1893, Pennsylvania Registration ERM-125, 218 N.J. Super. 374, 527 A.2d 935 (App. Div. 1987)

104 ALR5th 229—§ 4, 5, 16
4 ALR6th 113—§ 11
101 ALR6th 1—§ 8

State v. One (1) 1979 Chevrolet Camaro Z-28, 202 N.J. Super. 222, 494 A.2d 816 (1985)

6 ALR5th 652—§ 2, 7

State v. One (1) 1979 Chevrolet Camaro Z-28 Bearing New Jersey Registration 447-UAB, 202 N.J. Super. 222, 494 A.2d 816 (App. Div. 1985)

115 ALR5th 403—§ 9
4 ALR6th 113—§ 14

For assistance, call 1-800-328-4880

101 ALR6th 1—§ 3, 7, 46

State v. One 1979 Pontiac Trans Am, 771 P.2d 682, 104 Utah Adv. Rep. 29, 10 U.C.C.R.S.2d 189, 1 A.L.R.5th 1047 (Utah App. 1989)

1 ALR5th 317—§ 3

State v. One 1981 BMW Auto., 15 Conn. App. 589, 546 A.2d 879 (1988)

6 ALR6th 533—§ 21

State v. One 1982 Silver Honda Motorcycle, 735 P.2d 392, 55 Utah Adv. Rep. 46 (Utah App. 1987)

6 ALR5th 652—§ 2, 13

State v. One 1983 Black Toyota Pickup, 415 N.W.2d 511 (S.D. 1987)

1 ALR5th 375—§ 3

6 ALR5th 652—§ 2, 3

State v. One 1983 Pontiac (Joe Arave), 717 P.2d 1338, 32 Utah Adv. Rep. 18 (Utah 1986)

6 ALR5th 652—§ 2, 7, 13

State v. One (1) 1986 Nissan Auto., 792 S.W.2d 577 (Tex. App. El Paso 1990)

6 ALR5th 711—§ 5

State v. One 1987 Toyota Pickup, 233 Neb. 670, 447 N.W.2d 243 (1989)

1 ALR5th 346—§ 4, 11

State v. One 1988 Chevrolet Camaro, 164 Utah Adv. Rep. 25 (Utah 1991)

1 ALR5th 375—§ 3

State v. One 1988 Chevrolet Camaro, 813 P.2d 1186, 164 Utah Adv. Rep. 25 (Utah 1991)

6 ALR5th 652—§ 11

State v. One 1988 Nissan Pickup, 804 S.W.2d 957 (Tex. App. Tyler 1991)

6 ALR5th 711—§ 5

State v. O'Neal, 190 N.J. 601, 921 A.2d 1079 (2007)

71 ALR6th 1—§ 5

State v. O'Neal, 718 S.W.2d 498 (Mo. 1986)

99 ALR6th 295—§ 16

State v. O'Neal, 2004-Ohio-2862, 2004 WL 1232539 (Ohio Ct. App. 8th Dist. Cuyahoga County 2004)

71 ALR6th 1—§ 6

State v. O'Neal, No. 42331 (December 24, 1980, Ct. App. Ohio, 8th App. Dist. Cuyahoga Co.)

39 ALR5th 283—§ 14, 28

State v. One Blue Corvette, 1999 ME 98, 732 A.2d 856 (Me. 1999)

89 ALR5th 539—§ 9

State v. One Certain Conveyance 1978 Dodge Magnum, etc., 334 N.W.2d 724 (Iowa 1983)

1 ALR5th 317—§ 6

State v. One Certain Conveyance, etc., 207 N.W.2d 547 (Iowa 1973)

1 ALR5th 317—§ 4

State v. One House, 346 N.J. Super. 247, 787 A.2d 905 (App. Div. 2001)

124 ALR5th 509—§ 6

State v. O'Neil, 51 Kan. 651, 33 P. 287 (1893)

24 ALR5th 465—§ 86, 88, 93, 95

State v. O'Neil, 172 Ariz. 180, 836 P.2d 393 (Ct. App. Div. 2 1991)

91 ALR5th 343—§ 22

State v. O'Neill, 91 Wash. App. 978, 967 P.2d 985 (Div. 1 1998)

18 ALR5th 1—§ 31

State v. O'Neill, 208 Mont. 386, 679 P.2d 760 (1984)

106 ALR5th 397—§ 4

109 ALR5th 99—§ 12

State v. O'Neill, 825 S.W.2d 376 (Mo. App. 1992)

42 ALR5th 581—§ 4

State v. One (1) Porsche 2-Door, 526 P.2d 917 (Utah 1974)

1 ALR5th 375—§ 4

6 ALR5th 652—§ 2, 4, 12

State v. One Studebaker Automobile, Engine No. 27824, 50 S.D. 408, 210 N.W. 194 (1926)

102 ALR5th 525—§ 71

State v. One Thousand Two Hundred Sixty-Seven Dollars, 2006 OK 15, 131 P.3d 116 (Okla. 2006)

34 ALR6th 539—§ 6

State v. One Uzi Semi-Automatic 9mm Gun, 589 A.2d 31 (Me. 1991)

1 ALR5th 346—§ 4 to 6

For assistance, call 1-800-328-4880

State v. Onezime, 811 So. 2d 1033 (La. Ct. App. 5th Cir. 2002)

96 ALR5th 327—§ 4

State v. Onorato, 762 A.2d 858 (Vt. 2000)

73 ALR5th 615—§ 3

State v. Ontai, 84 Haw. 56, 929 P.2d 69, R.I.C.O. Bus. Disp. Guide (CCH) ¶ 9171 (Haw. 1996)

89 ALR5th 629—§ 3

State v. Onuskanich, 86 Or. App. 454, 739 P.2d 1062 (1987)

28 ALR6th 505—§ 5, 9

State v. Oody, 823 S.W.2d 554 (Tenn. Crim. App. 1991)

104 ALR5th 357—§ 6

State v. Oquist, 327 N.W.2d 587 (Minn. 1982)

62 ALR5th 1—§ 2, 3, 15

State v. Orange, 22 N.C. App. 220, 206 S.E.2d 377 (1974)

52 ALR6th 125—§ 44

State v. Orban, 1981 WL 3559 (Ohio Ct. App. 10th Dist. Franklin County 1981)

31 ALR6th 199—§ 48

State v. Ordonez, 395 So. 2d 778 (La. 1981)

58 ALR6th 439—§ 42
68 ALR6th 607—§ 18

State v. Ordonez-Villanueva, 138 Or. App. 236, 908 P.2d 333 (1995)

85 ALR5th 1—§ 50

State v. Ordway, 619 A.2d 819 (R.I. 1992)

67 ALR5th 637—§ 4, 7

State v. Orelup, 492 N.W.2d 101 (S.D. 1992)

38 ALR5th 433—§ 3, 6

State v. Oren, 162 Vt. 331, 647 A.2d 1009 (1994)

66 ALR5th 397—§ 6

State v. Orfi, 511 N.W.2d 464 (Minn. Ct. App. 1994)

93 ALR5th 327—§ 4, 6, 7, 16, 22, 28, 30

State v. Orgeron, 620 So. 2d 312 (La. App. 5th Cir. 1993)

44 ALR5th 651—§ 5

State v. Orlando, 2006 WL 2206056 (Tenn. Crim. App. 2006)

55 ALR6th 391—§ 5

State v. Orosco, 199 Neb. 532, 260 N.W.2d 303 (1977)

93 ALR6th 207—§ 14, 18, 26
96 ALR6th 355—§ 24, 37, 54, 60

State v. Orozco, 202 N.W.2d 344 (Iowa 1972)

42 ALR5th 581—§ 3

State v. Orr, 26 Ohio App. 3d 24, 498 N.E.2d 181 (11th Dist. Trumbull County 1985)

45 ALR6th 435—§ 9, 17, 26

State v. Orr, 93 N.J. Super. 140, 225 A.2d 157 (1966)

36 ALR5th 161—§ 25, 26

State v. Orr, 93 N.J. Super. 140, 225 A.2d 157 (App. Div. 1966)

33 ALR6th 91—§ 27, 28

State v. Orr, 304 S.C. 185, 403 S.E.2d 623 (1991)

72 ALR5th 403—§ 3

State v. Orr, 694 S.W.2d 297 (Tenn. 1985)

2 ALR5th 725—§ 5

State v. Orris, 2008-Ohio-5008, 2008 WL 4408596 (Ohio Ct. App. 5th Dist. Delaware County 2008)

71 ALR6th 1—§ 8

State v. Orso, 789 S.W.2d 177 (Mo. Ct. App. E.D. 1990)

58 ALR6th 499—§ 52

State v. Orta, 231 Wis. 2d 782, 2000 WI 4, 604 N.W.2d 543 (2000)

85 ALR5th 1—§ 21

State v. Ortega, 77 N.M. 312, 422 P.2d 353 (1966)

5 ALR5th 243—§ 54

State v. Ortega, 112 N.M. 554, 817 P.2d 1196 (1991)

28 ALR5th 754—§ 6

State v. Ortega, 2008-NMCA-001, 175 P.3d 929 (N.M. Ct. App. 2007)

30 ALR6th 1—§ 3

State v. Ortez, 178 N.C. App. 236, 631 S.E.2d 188 (2006)

32 ALR6th 1—§ 4
49 ALR6th 343—§ 9, 24
State v. Orth, 79 Ohio St. 130, 86 N.E. 476 (1908)
119 ALR5th 275—§ 9
State v. Orth, 178 W. Va. 303, 359 S.E.2d 136
65 ALR5th 623—§ 3
State v. Ortiz, 4 Hawaii App. 143, 662 P.2d 517 (1983)
50 ALR5th 581—§ 3
State v. Ortiz, 67 Hawaii 181, 683 P.2d 822 (1984)
50 ALR5th 581—§ 3
State v. Ortiz, 88 N.M. 370, 540 P.2d 850 (App. 1975)
57 ALR5th 141—§ 11
State v. Ortiz, 92 N.M. 166, 584 P.2d 1306 (App. 1978)
17 ALR5th 125—§ 3, 5
State v. Ortiz, 93 Haw. 399
54 ALR5th 141—§ 3
State v. Ortiz, 113 Wash. 2d 32, 774 P.2d 1229 (1989)
105 ALR5th 529—§ 7
State v. Ortiz, 119 Wash. 2d 294, 831 P.2d 1060 (1992)
22 ALR5th 1—§ 4, 13, 23, 31, 36, 44
40 ALR5th 113—§ 3
State v. Ortiz, 158 Ariz. 528, 764 P.2d 13, 20 Ariz. Adv. Rep. 5 (1988)
7 ALR5th 758—§ 13
State v. Ortiz, 169 Conn. 642, 363 A.2d 1091 (1975)
34 ALR5th 125—§ 31
State v. Ortiz, 185 Ohio App. 3d 733, 2010-Ohio-38, 925 N.E.2d 662 (9th Dist. Lorain County 2010)
65 ALR6th 1—§ 19
State v. Ortiz, 198 Conn. 220, 502 A.2d 400 (1985)
90 ALR5th 453—§ 6
1 ALR6th 657—§ 4
State v. Ortiz, 252 Conn. 533, 747 A.2d 487 (2000)
16 ALR6th 329—§ 4
24 ALR6th 591—§ 4, 12

State v. Ortiz, 257 Neb. 784, 600 N.W.2d 805 (1999)
117 ALR5th 407—§ 3
State v. Ortiz, 766 N.W.2d 244 (Iowa 2009)
49 ALR6th 343—§ 25
State v. Ortiz, 824 A.2d 473 (R.I. 2003)
101 ALR6th 331—§ 12
State v. Orttel, 2011 WL 6015353 (Minn. Ct. App. 2011)
81 ALR6th 257—§ 5
State v. Osakalumi, 194 W. Va. 758, 461 S.E.2d 504 (1995)
56 ALR6th 185—§ 13
State v. Osakalumi, 461 S.E.2d 504 (W. Va. 1995)
40 ALR5th 113—§ 2, 4
State v. Osalde, 116 Wash. App. 1039, 2003 WL 1875588 (Div. 2 2003)
19 ALR6th 115—§ 4
24 ALR6th 591—§ 9, 13
State v. Osborn, 59 Wash. App. 1, 795 P.2d 1174 (Div. 1 1990)
39 ALR6th 257—§ 18
40 ALR6th 1—§ 4
State v. Osborn, 63 Ohio Misc. 17, 16 Ohio Op. 3d 88, 17 Ohio Op. 3d 341, 409 N.E.2d 1077 (County Ct. 1980)
60 ALR5th 1—§ 2, 8
State v. Osborn, 102 Idaho 405, 631 P.2d 187 (1981)
21 ALR6th 1—§ 19
State v. Osborn, 263 Ark. 554, 566 S.W.2d 139 (1978)
122 ALR5th 439—§ 7
State v. Osborn, 455 N.W.2d 292 (Iowa App. 1990)
39 ALR5th 283—§ 10, 31, 77
State v. Osborn, 717 So. 2d 1110 (Fla. Dist. Ct. App. 5th Dist. 1998)
113 ALR5th 597—§ 3
State v. Osborne, 130 Idaho 365, 941 P.2d 337 (Ct. App. 1997)
32 ALR6th 1—§ 11
State v. Osborne, 715 N.W.2d 436 (Minn. 2006)

26 ALR6th 511—§ 45

State v. Osborne, 1986 WL 6681 (Ohio Ct. App. 10th Dist. Franklin County 1986)

111 ALR5th 239—§ 3

State v. Osborne, 1989 WL 155189 (Ohio Ct. App. 6th Dist. Huron County 1989)

77 ALR5th 201—§ 10

State v. Osborne-Bell, 1990 WL 98217 (Ohio Ct. App. 12th Dist. Clinton County 1990)

68 ALR6th 115—§ 4, 5, 20, 22 to 24

State v. Osburn, 9 Ohio App. 3d 343, 460 N.E.2d 314 (9th Dist. Medina County 1983)

72 ALR5th 109—§ 4

State v. Osier, 1999 ND 28, 590 N.W.2d 205 (N.D. 1999)

55 ALR6th 157—§ 24

State v. Osley, 2005-Ohio-5263, 2005 WL 2415941 (Ohio Ct. App. 6th Dist. Fulton County 2005)

26 ALR6th 511—§ 19

State v. Osmus, 73 Wyo. 183, 276 P.2d 469 (1954)

118 ALR5th 253—§ 7

State v. Osoba, 234 Kan. 443, 672 P.2d 1098 (1983)

7 ALR5th 263—§ 7

State v. Ospina, 81 Ohio App. 3d 644, 611 N.E.2d 989 (10th Dist. Franklin County 1992)

32 ALR6th 1—§ 6

State v. Ossey, 446 So. 2d 280 (La. 1984)

37 ALR5th 1—§ 3

State v. Osteen, 216 Mont. 258, 700 P.2d 188 (1985)

28 ALR6th 505—§ 8

State v. Ostrander, 383 N.W.2d 723 (Minn. Ct. App. 1986)

73 ALR5th 383—§ 3

State v. Ostreicher, 31 Conn. L. Rptr. 630, 2002 WL 450393 (Conn. Super. Ct. 2002)

101 ALR6th 545—§ 5, 13

State v. Othoudt, 482 N.W.2d 218 (Minn. 1992)

58 ALR6th 499—§ 87

State v. Otis, 487 N.W.2d 928 (Minn. App. 1992)

43 ALR5th 1—§ 13

State v. Otis, 2009 WL 2436648 (Wash. Ct. App. Div. 2 2009)

50 ALR6th 353—§ 22

State v. Otness, 986 P.2d 890 (Alaska Ct. App. 1999)

33 ALR6th 91—§ 49

State v. O'Toole, 1992 WL 308531 (Ohio Ct. App. 9th Dist. Lorain County 1992)

87 ALR5th 1—§ 9, 10, 21, 25, 32

State v. Ott, 167 Ariz. 420, 808 P.2d 305 (Ct. App. Div. 1 1990)

37 ALR6th 511—§ 7, 8, 10, 14, 26

State v. Otte, 2008 WL 763130 (Minn. Ct. App. 2008)

47 ALR6th 107—§ 20

State v. Ottman, 4 Ohio N.P. 195, 6 Ohio Dec. 265, 1897 WL 785 (C.P. 1897)

63 ALR6th 1—§ 60

State v. Otto, 50 Conn. App. 1, 717 A.2d 775 (1998)

27 ALR5th 593—§ 4

State v. Otto, 184 Neb. 597, 169 N.W.2d 612 (1969)

87 ALR5th 1—§ 10, 33

State v. Ottwell, 239 Mont. 150, 779 P.2d 500 (1989)

57 ALR5th 141—§ 9

State v. Ouellette, 34 Conn. Supp. 649, 382 A.2d 1005 (1977)

7 ALR5th 73—§ 3

State v. Ouellette, 190 Conn. 84, 459 A.2d 1005 (1983)

39 ALR6th 257—§ 20, 42
40 ALR6th 1—§ 41

State v. Ousley, 312 Minn. 546, 254 N.W.2d 73 (1977)

28 ALR6th 505—§ 9

State v. Ouzts, 777 So. 2d 1286 (La. Ct. App. 2d Cir. 2001)

9 ALR6th 1—§ 17

State v. Ovadal, 234 Wis. 2d 526, 2000 WI App 94, 611 N.W.2d 471 (Ct. App. 2000)
70 ALR6th 513—§ 5
71 ALR6th 471—§ 11
State v. Overby, 265 Ala. 39, 89 So. 2d 525 (1956)
21 ALR5th 812—§ 6
State v. Overby, 1999 ND 47, 590 N.W.2d 703 (N.D. 1999)
123 ALR5th 179—§ 4, 10
State v. Overholt, 77 Ohio App. 3d 111, 601 N.E.2d 116 (Auglaize Co. 1991)
15 ALR5th 391—§ 39
State v. Overholt, 2005 WL 123483 (Tenn. Crim. App. 2005)
26 ALR6th 511—§ 8, 22
State v. Overmann, 220 N.W.2d 914 (Iowa 1974)
9 ALR5th 464—§ 4, 11
State v. Oveross, 18 Or. App. 300, 525 P.2d 176 (1974)
99 ALR6th 113—§ 16
State v. Overstreet, 551 S.W.2d 621 (Mo. 1977)
30 ALR6th 103—§ 58
State v. Overton, 60 N.C. App. 1, 298 S.E.2d 695 (1982)
32 ALR5th 149—§ 32
97 ALR5th 201—§ 6
7 ALR6th 169—§ 26
7 ALR6th 487—§ 28
State v. Overton, 279 Kan. 547, 112 P.3d 244 (2005)
102 ALR6th 279—§ 29
State v. Overton, 2000 WL 543227 (Ohio Ct. App. 6th Dist. Lucas County 2000)
98 ALR6th 455—§ 30
State v. Overvold, 64 Wash. App. 440, 825 P.2d 729 (Div. 1 1992)
73 ALR5th 383—§ 5
State v. Owen, 1 Neb. App. 1060, 510 N.W.2d 503 (1993)
38 ALR6th 97—§ 29
State v. Owen, 7 Neb. App. 153, 580 N.W.2d 566 (1998)

66 ALR5th 397—§ 3
State v. Owen, 7 Neb.App. 153, 580 N.W.2d 566 (1998)
66 ALR5th 397—§ 4
State v. Owen, 24 N.C. App. 598, 211 S.E.2d 830 (1975)
39 ALR5th 283—§ 4
State v. Owen, 130 N.C. App. 505, 503 S.E.2d 426, 79 A.L.R.5th 747 (1998)
79 ALR5th 237—§ 5
State v. Owen, 216 S.W.3d 227 (Mo. Ct. App. W.D. 2007)
69 ALR6th 1—§ 25
State v. Owen, 516 S.E.2d 159 (N.C. Ct. App. 1999)
57 ALR5th 315—§ 9, 12
State v. Owen, 869 S.W.2d 310 (Mo. Ct. App. S.D. 1994)
23 ALR6th 307—§ 31, 44
State v. Owens, 38 Conn. App. 801, 663 A.2d 1094 (1995)
102 ALR6th 365—§ 12, 31
State v. Owens, 51 Ohio App. 2d 132, 5 Ohio Op. 3d 290, 366 N.E.2d 1367 (9th Dist. Summit County 1975)
4 ALR6th 577—§ 7
State v. Owens, 65 N.C. App. 107, 308 S.E.2d 494 (1983)
5 ALR5th 243—§ 6
State v. Owens, 78 Wash. App. 897, 899 P.2d 833 (1995)
38 ALR5th 433—§ 3
State v. Owens, 102 N.J. Super. 187, 245 A.2d 736 (App. Div. 1968)
58 ALR6th 499—§ 32
State v. Owens, 112 Iowa 403, 84 N.W. 529 (1900)
42 ALR5th 547—§ 5, 6
State v. Owens, 121 Ohio App. 3d 34, 698 N.E.2d 1030 (2d Dist. Montgomery County 1997)
29 ALR6th 237—§ 4, 6, 9, 21, 24
State v. Owens, 148 Wis. 2d 922, 436 N.W.2d 869 (1989)
20 ALR6th 479—§ 3
State v. Owens, 248 Kan. 273, 807 P.2d 101 (1991)

100 ALR6th 535—§ 3
State v. Owens, 352 S.E.2d 474 (S.C. 1987)
33 ALR5th 571—§ 4
State v. Owens, 567 So. 2d 806 (La. Ct. App. 3d Cir. 1990)
57 ALR5th 141—§ 11
State v. Owens, 820 S.W.2d 757 (Tenn. Crim. App. 1991)
118 ALR5th 253—§ 12, 17
State v. Owens, 2000 WL 1232426 (Ohio Ct. App. 6th Dist. Wood County 2000)
43 ALR6th 475—§ 3, 14
State v. Owens, 2002-Ohio-4485, 2002 WL 2005699 (Ohio Ct. App. 12th Dist. Clermont County 2002)
70 ALR6th 361—§ 4, 19
State v. Owens, 2002 SD 42, 643 N.W.2d 735 (S.D. 2002)
65 ALR6th 537—§ 68
State v. Owsley, 959 S.W.2d 789 (Mo. 1997)
37 ALR6th 357—§ 67
State v. Oxendine, 2010 WL 3001210 (N.C. Ct. App. 2010)
57 ALR6th 1—§ 22, 23
State v. Oyler, 92 Idaho 43, 436 P.2d 709 (1968)
46 ALR6th 241—§ 35
State v. Paben, 990 So. 2d 123 (La. Ct. App. 2d Cir. 2008)
71 ALR6th 1—§ 11
State v. Pace, 51 N.C. App. 79, 275 S.E.2d 254 (1981)
86 ALR5th 59—§ 6
State v. Pace, 316 S.C. 71, 447 S.E.2d 186 (1994)
104 ALR5th 357—§ 3, 7
54 ALR6th 429—§ 6
State v. Pace, 527 P.2d 658 (Utah 1974)
59 ALR5th 1—§ 3, 4, 6
State v. Pacheco, 121 Ariz. 88, 588 P.2d 830 (1978)
117 ALR5th 513—§ 12
State v. Pacheco, 481 A.2d 1009 (R.I. 1984)

101 ALR6th 331—§ 12
State v. Pacific Far East Line, Inc., 261 Cal. App. 2d 609, 68 Cal. Rptr. 67, 1968 A.M.C. 1243 (1st Dist. 1968)
29 ALR6th 507—§ 9, 70
State v. Pacific Indem. Co., 63 Cal. App. 4th 1535, 75 Cal. Rptr. 2d 69 (2d Dist. 1998)
106 ALR5th 523—§ 26
State v. Packard, 184 Conn. 258, 439 A.2d 983 (1981)
23 ALR5th 672—§ 3, 6
55 ALR5th 423—§ 3
State v. Packard, 389 So. 2d 56 (La. 1980)
55 ALR5th 125—§ 3, 4, 7
State v. Packingham, 748 S.E.2d 146 (N.C. Ct. App. 2013)
89 ALR6th 261—§ 22, 30
State v. Padavich, 536 N.W.2d 743 (Iowa 1995)
67 ALR5th 361—§ 5
112 ALR5th 429—§ 7, 12
State v. Padberg, 723 S.W.2d 43 (Mo. Ct. App. E.D. 1986)
99 ALR6th 113—§ 18
State v. Padgett, 300 N.W.2d 145 (Iowa 1981)
23 ALR5th 672—§ 3
State v. Padgett, 557 S.W.2d 731 (Mo. App. 1977)
4 ALR5th 1—§ 2
State v. Padilla, 66 N.M. 289, 347 P.2d 312, 78 A.L.R.2d 908 (1959)
72 ALR5th 529—§ 6
State v. Padilla, 106 Ariz. 230, 474 P.2d 821 (1970)
39 ALR5th 283—§ 3
State v. Padilla, 125 N.M. 665, 1998-NMCA-088, 964 P.2d 829 (Ct. App. 1998)
41 ALR6th 295—§ 9
State v. Paduani, 307 N.J. Super. 134, 704 A.2d 582 (App. Div. 1998)
31 ALR5th 704—§ 15, 16
State v. Pagan, 378 N.J. Super. 549, 876 A.2d 812 (App. Div. 2005)
26 ALR6th 511—§ 28

State v. Page, 23 N.C. App. 539, 209 S.E.2d 379 (1974)
105 ALR5th 529—§ 9

State v. Page, 115 Ariz. 131, 564 P.2d 82 (Ct. App. Div. 1 1976)
99 ALR5th 557—§ 10, 12

State v. Page, 129 Or. App. 558, 879 P.2d 903 (1994)
50 ALR5th 703—§ 10

State v. Page, 130 Wash. App. 1028, 2005 WL 3150580 (Div. 1 2005)
26 ALR6th 511—§ 26, 33

State v. Page, 197 Or. App. 72, 104 P.3d 616 (2005)
30 ALR6th 1—§ 3, 6

State v. Page, 251 La. 810, 206 So. 2d 503 (1968)
16 ALR6th 329—§ 4
24 ALR6th 591—§ 4

State v. Page, 449 So. 2d 813 (Fla. 1984)
84 ALR5th 487—§ 20, 21

State v. Paglino, 319 S.W.2d 613 (Mo. 1958)
85 ALR5th 187—§ 7, 8

State v. Paige, 2005 WL 3357984 (N.J. Super. Ct. App. Div. 2005)
26 ALR6th 511—§ 17

State v. Paige, 2013 WL 2477265 (W. Va. 2013)
99 ALR6th 113—§ 16

State v. Pailon, 590 A.2d 858 (R.I. 1991)
86 ALR5th 463—§ 2, 3, 5

State v. Paine, 69 Wash. App. 873, 850 P.2d 1369 (Div. 1 1993)
113 ALR5th 597—§ 8

State v. Painter, 229 Neb. 278, 426 N.W.2d 513 (1988)
70 ALR5th 1—§ 6

State v. Painter, 265 N.C. 277, 144 S.E.2d 6 (1965)
96 ALR5th 523—§ 5

State v. Painter, 329 Mo. 314, 44 S.W.2d 79 (1931)
73 ALR5th 615—§ 3, 6, 7

State v. Painter, 1994 WL 118985 (Ohio Ct. App. 12th Dist. Clinton County 1994)
1 ALR6th 371—§ 6

State v. Pakulak, 75 Or. App. 418, 706 P.2d 595 (1985)
39 ALR5th 283—§ 4, 18

State v. Palabay, 9 Haw. App. 414, 844 P.2d 1 (1992)
82 ALR6th 373—§ 5, 6, 10, 15, 19

State v. Palacio, 2009-3 La. App. 1 Cir. 10/23/09, 2009 WL 3453930 (La. Ct. App. 1st Cir. 2009)
75 ALR6th 541—§ 12

State v. Paleo, 5 P.3d 276 (Ariz. Ct. App. Div. 1 2000)
20 ALR5th 398—§ 3, 60

State v. Palisbo, 93 Haw. 344
20 ALR5th 398—§ 6.5, 43, 48.5

State v. Palkimas, 153 Conn. 555, 219 A.2d 220 (1966)
29 ALR5th 59—§ 3, 8

State v. Pallotolo, 1996 WL 24702 (Conn. Super. Ct. 1996)
52 ALR6th 567—§ 23

State v. Palm, 299 N.W.2d 740 (Minn. 1980)
28 ALR6th 505—§ 9

State v. Palma, 1998 WL 226453 (Ohio Ct. App. 1st Dist. Hamilton County 1998)
78 ALR5th 489—§ 3

State v. Palmer, 37 Kan. App. 2d 819, 158 P.3d 363 (2007)
30 ALR6th 1—§ 4

State v. Palmer, 45 Del. 308, 72 A.2d 442 (Gen Sess 1950)
54 ALR5th 141—§ 3 to 8

State v. Palmer, 80 Ohio St. 3d 543, 687 N.E.2d 685 (1997)
31 ALR5th 704—§ 16, 18

State v. Palmer, 109 Wash. App. 1051, 2001 WL 1632639 (Div. 2 2001)
7 ALR6th 233—§ 5

State v. Palmer, 125 N.M. 86, 1998 -NMCA- 052, 957 P.2d 71 (Ct. App. 1998)
15 ALR5th 391—§ 39
92 ALR5th 35—§ 16

State v. Palmer, 178 N.C. 822, 101 S.E. 506 (1919)

81 ALR5th 563—§ 3
State v. Palmer, 257 Neb. 702, 600 N.W.2d 756 (1999)

63 ALR6th 1—§ 5, 12, 15, 42
State v. Palmer, 262 Kan. 745, 942 P.2d 19 (1997)

46 ALR6th 63—§ 11
State v. Palmer, 291 Minn. 302, 191 N.W.2d 188 (1971)

28 ALR5th 459—§ 3
State v. Palmer, 334 N.C. 104, 431 S.E.2d 172 (1993)

57 ALR5th 141—§ 7
State v. Palmer, 447 So. 2d 1159 (La. Ct. App. 3d Cir. 1984)

22 ALR6th 533—§ 3, 5
54 ALR6th 429—§ 7
State v. Palmer, 706 So. 2d 156 (La. Ct. App. 1st Cir. 1997)

73 ALR5th 383—§ 9
State v. Palmer, 777 P.2d 521 (Utah Ct. App. 1989)

29 ALR6th 237—§ 21
State v. Palmer, 822 S.W.2d 536 (Mo. App. 1992)

26 ALR5th 1—§ 4, 26
State v. Palmquist, 2003 WL 22398395 (Tenn. Crim. App. 2003)

116 ALR5th 479—§ 5
State v. Palms, 592 S.W.2d 236 (Mo. Ct. App. W.D. 1979)

65 ALR5th 623—§ 5
State v. Palomarez, 134 Ariz. 486, 657 P.2d 899 (App. 1982)

7 ALR5th 758—§ 3, 4
State v. Palubicki, 700 N.W.2d 476, 23 A.L.R.6th 835 (Minn. 2005)

23 ALR6th 1—§ 15, 30, 38
State v. Pam, 98 Wash. 2d 748, 659 P.2d 454 (1983)

83 ALR5th 277—§ 11
State v. Pamperien, 156 Or. App. 153, 967 P.2d 503 (1998)

18 ALR6th 519—§ 19
State v. Pancake, 2003-Ohio-1567, 2003 WL 1596975 (Ohio Ct. App. 2d Dist. Montgomery County 2003)

120 ALR5th 337—§ 2
State v. Pancoast, 5 N.D. 516, 67 N.W. 1052 (1896)

54 ALR6th 429—§ 27
State v. Pandeli, 65 P.3d 950 (Ariz. 2003)

110 ALR5th 1—§ 18
State v. Pando, 122 N.M. 167, 1996-NMCA-078, 921 P.2d 1285 (Ct. App. 1996)

75 ALR6th 541—§ 15
State v. Pando, 284 Ga. App. 70, 643 S.E.2d 342 (2007)

78 ALR6th 297—§ 40
State v. Pang, 132 Wash. 2d 852, 940 P.2d 1293 (1997)

20 ALR6th 561—§ 5, 6, 8 to 11, 13, 18
State v. Pankey, 202 Neb. 595, 276 N.W.2d 233 (1979)

39 ALR5th 283—§ 3
State v. Pannier, 1999 WL 1216327 (Minn. Ct. App. 1999)

119 ALR5th 275—§ 11
State v. Panter, 536 S.W.2d 481 (Mo. Ct. App. 1976)

66 ALR6th 83—§ 5
State v. Panther, 99 Or. App. 184, 781 P.2d 407 (1989)

15 ALR5th 391—§ 32
State v. Panzera, 139 N.H. 235, 652 A.2d 136 (1994)

98 ALR5th 445—§ 4
State v. Panzino, 583 So. 2d 1059 (Fla. Dist. Ct. App. 5th Dist. 1991)

74 ALR6th 69—§ 9
State v. Paone, 290 N.J. Super. 494, 676 A.2d 159 (App. Div. 1996)

15 ALR5th 391—§ 53
State v. Papamilitiadis, 2011 WL 2373305 (N.J. Super. Ct. App. Div. 2011)

74 ALR6th 373—§ 5
State v. Paquette, 151 Vt. 631, 563 A.2d 632 (1989)

52 ALR5th 655—§ 4
State v. Para, 120 Ariz. 26, 583 P.2d 1346 (App. 1978)

---

29 ALR5th 59—§ 30
State v. Paradise, 213 Conn. 388, 567 A.2d 1221 (1990)
11 ALR5th 1—§ 25
72 ALR5th 403—§ 12, 15
State v. Pardee, 1992 WL 52705 (Ohio Ct. App. 11th Dist. Ashtabula County 1992)
69 ALR6th 207—§ 9, 10, 18
State v. Pardo, 2012 WL 1569814 (N.J. Super. Ct. App. Div. 2012)
99 ALR6th 113—§ 13
State v. Parent, 110 Nev. 114, 867 P.2d 1143 (1994)
67 ALR5th 361—§ 2 to 4, 9
State v. Pargeon, 64 Ohio App. 3d 679, 582 N.E.2d 665 (5th Dist.Licking County 1991)
57 ALR5th 315—§ 2, 4, 8 to 11
State v. Pari, 546 A.2d 175 (R.I. 1988)
87 ALR5th 597—§ 9
State v. Paris, 2000-Ohio-1886, 2000 WL 799090 (Ohio Ct. App. 3d Dist. Auglaize County 2000)
41 ALR6th 141—§ 5
State v. Parish, 79 Idaho 75, 310 P.2d 1082 (1957)
26 ALR5th 1—§ 3, 6
State v. Parish, 216 P.3d 191 (Kan. Ct. App. 2009)
84 ALR6th 293—§ 8, 29, 41
State v. Parish, 937 S.W.2d 745 (Mo. Ct. App. S.D. 1997)
82 ALR5th 103—§ 5
State v. Park, 55 Haw. 610, 525 P.2d 586 (1974)
68 ALR5th 299—§ 4
State v. Park, 321 Wis. 2d 477, 2009 WI App 141, 774 N.W.2d 476 (Ct. App. 2009)
74 ALR6th 69—§ 16
State v. Park, 322 Mo. 69, 16 S.W.2d 30 (1929)
57 ALR6th 445—§ 47
State v. Park, 810 P.2d 456 (Utah Ct. App. 1991)
74 ALR5th 319—§ 5
82 ALR5th 103—§ 3

116 ALR5th 479—§ 5
State v. Parker, 7 N.C. App. 191, 171 S.E.2d 665 (1970)
5 ALR5th 243—§ 48
State v. Parker, 31 Ohio App. 3d 128, 31 Ohio B.R. 215, 508 N.E.2d 978 (Montgomery Co. 1986)
39 ALR5th 283—§ 14
State v. Parker, 59 N.C. App. 600, 297 S.E.2d 766 (1982)
34 ALR6th 1—§ 12
State v. Parker, 66 Ohio Misc. 2d 1, 642 N.E.2d 66 (Mun. Ct. 1994)
105 ALR5th 499—§ 4
State v. Parker, 81 N.C. App. 443, 344 S.E.2d 330 (1986)
39 ALR5th 283—§ 4, 31
State v. Parker, 116 Ariz. 3, 567 P.2d 319 (1977)
53 ALR6th 81—§ 7, 9
55 ALR6th 391—§ 7
State v. Parker, 227 La. 916, 80 So. 2d 863 (1955)
111 ALR5th 491—§ 3
State v. Parker, 233 Mo. App. 1037, 128 S.W.2d 288 (1939)
95 ALR5th 229—§ 24
State v. Parker, 350 N.C. 411, 516 S.E.2d 106 (1999)
83 ALR6th 465—§ 18
State v. Parker, 399 So. 2d 24 (Fla. Dist. Ct. App. 3d Dist. 1981)
62 ALR6th 413—§ 13, 28
State v. Parker, 595 So. 2d 765 (La. App. 4th Cir. 1992)
34 ALR5th 125—§ 20
State v. Parker, 622 So. 2d 791 (La. App. 4th Cir. 1993)
50 ALR5th 581—§ 5, 15
State v. Parker, 733 So. 2d 1074 (Fla. Dist. Ct. App. 5th Dist. 1999)
113 ALR5th 597—§ 8
State v. Parker, 836 S.W.2d 930 (Mo. 1992)
47 ALR5th 259—§ 2
State v. Parker, 886 S.W.2d 908 (Mo. 1994)

79 ALR5th 33—§ 47, 53
83 ALR6th 255—§ 15
State v. Parker, 890 S.W.2d 312 (Mo. Ct. App. S.D. 1994)
37 ALR6th 357—§ 3, 5, 17, 23, 25, 33
State v. Parker, 936 P.2d 1118 (Utah Ct. App. 1997)
29 ALR6th 237—§ 21
State v. Parker, 1997 WL 195922 (Tenn. Crim. App. 1997)
7 ALR6th 233—§ 5
State v. Parker, 2002-Ohio-2688, 2002 WL 1301556 (Ohio Ct. App. 6th Dist. Sandusky County 2002)
56 ALR6th 185—§ 19
State v. Parker, No. 9579 (April 14, 1986, Ct. App. Ohio, 2nd App. Dist. Montgomery Co.)
39 ALR5th 283—§ 14, 22
State v. Parkinson, 128 Idaho 29, 909 P.2d 647 (Ct. App. 1996)
90 ALR5th 453—§ 8
State v. Parkinson, 144 Idaho 825, 172 P.3d 1100 (2007)
69 ALR6th 1—§ 21
State v. Parks, 211 Ariz. 19, 116 P.3d 631 (Ct. App. Div. 1 2005)
30 ALR6th 1—§ 3, 6
State v. Parks, 265 Kan. 644, 962 P.2d 486 (1998)
91 ALR5th 343—§ 27
State v. Parks, 273 Ga. App. 682, 616 S.E.2d 456 (2005)
32 ALR6th 1—§ 11
State v. Parks, 1995 WL 418758 (Ohio App. 2 Dist.)
50 ALR5th 581—§ 14, 19
State v. Parmar, 255 Neb. 356, 586 N.W.2d 279 (1998)
29 ALR6th 237—§ 5, 21, 25
State v. Parmenter, 74 Wash. 2d 343, 444 P.2d 680 (1968)
118 ALR5th 253—§ 11, 16
State v. Parowski, 2012 WL 1139066 (Conn. Super. Ct. 2012)
75 ALR6th 443—§ 12
80 ALR6th 239—§ 9

State v. Parr, 65 N.C. App. 415, 308 S.E.2d 881 (1983)
71 ALR6th 335—§ 13
State v. Parr, 182 Wis. 2d 349, 513 N.W.2d 647 (Ct. App. 1994)
87 ALR5th 631—§ 21
State v. Parr, 534 S.E.2d 23 (W. Va. 2000)
22 ALR5th 1—§ 3
State v. Parras, 44 Or. App. 475, 606 P.2d 656 (1980)
32 ALR6th 1—§ 11
35 ALR6th 127—§ 5
State v. Parretti, 1995 WL 269889 (Del. Super. Ct. 1995)
20 ALR6th 561—§ 13, 18
State v. Parris, 219 Conn. 283, 592 A.2d 943 (1991)
39 ALR6th 257—§ 20, 38, 41, 42
40 ALR6th 1—§ 41
State v. Parrish, 205 Kan. 178, 468 P.2d 143 (1970)
85 ALR5th 187—§ 15
State v. Parrish, 598 S.W.2d 840 (Tenn. Crim. App. 1980)
102 ALR5th 525—§ 27
State v. Parrish, 616 So. 2d 1135 (Fla. Dist. Ct. App. 3d Dist. 1993)
113 ALR5th 597—§ 8
State v. Parrott, 102 Or. App. 677, 795 P.2d 1093 (1990)
15 ALR5th 391—§ 15
State v. Parsons, 28 Conn. App. 91, 612 A.2d 73 (1992)
42 ALR5th 291—§ 17
State v. Parsons, 70 Ariz. 399, 222 P.2d 637 (1950)
78 ALR5th 567—§ 8
State v. Parsons, 213 Neb. 349, 328 N.W.2d 795 (1983)
32 ALR6th 1—§ 11
State v. Parsons, 513 S.W.2d 430 (Mo. 1974)
37 ALR5th 515—§ 6
State v. Parsons, 569 So. 2d 437 (Fla. 1990)
18 ALR6th 519—§ 7

State v. Parsons, 1996 WL 665004 (Ohio App. Greene Co. 1996)
52 ALR5th 559—§ 2, 4, 7, 12 to 14, 17

State v. Parsons, 1997 WL 34414 (Tenn. Crim. App. 1997)
73 ALR5th 383—§ 6

State v. Parsons, 2005 ME 69, 874 A.2d 875 (Me. 2005)
27 ALR6th 183—§ 5, 9, 31

State v. Partanen, 67 Ohio App. 248, 21 Ohio Op. 231, 36 N.E.2d 422 (7th Dist. Lake County 1940)
97 ALR5th 537—§ 23

State v. Partlow, 321 N.W.2d 886 (Minn. 1982)
73 ALR5th 383—§ 5

State v. Parton, 251 N.J. Super. 230, 597 A.2d 1088 (App. Div. 1991)
81 ALR5th 563—§ 3, 5, 8

State v. Parton, 303 N.C. 55, 277 S.E.2d 410 (1981)
9 ALR6th 1—§ 8

State v. Parton, 817 S.W.2d 28 (Tenn. Crim. App. 1991)
85 ALR5th 547—§ 8

State v. Pascal, 108 Wash. 2d 125, 736 P.2d 1065 (1987)
58 ALR5th 749—§ 12
113 ALR5th 597—§ 6

State v. Paschal, 358 So. 2d 73 (Fla. Dist. Ct. App. 1st Dist. 1978)
28 ALR6th 505—§ 9

State v. Paschall, 22 Or. App. 236, 538 P.2d 366 (1975)
12 ALR6th 553—§ 20

State v. Pasicznyk, 1997 WL 79501 (Wash. Ct. App. Div. 3 1997)
73 ALR5th 383—§ 5

State v. Pasqua, 157 Ohio App. 3d 427, 2004-Ohio-2992, 811 N.E.2d 601 (1st Dist. Hamilton County 2004)
34 ALR6th 171—§ 27

State v. Passaic County Agr. Soc., 54 NJL 260, 23 A. 680 (1892)
8 ALR5th 653—§ 3

State v. Passante, 225 N.J. Super. 439, 542 A.2d 952, R.I.C.O. Bus. Disp. Guide (CCH) ¶ 6999 (Law Div. 1987)
58 ALR6th 385—§ 20, 23

State v. Passarelli, 130 Ariz. 360, 636 P.2d 138 (Ct. App. Div. 2 1981)
27 ALR6th 183—§ 28, 30

State v. Passerin, 449 A.2d 192 (Del. 1982)
61 ALR5th 1—§ 14

State v. Pastet, 169 Conn. 13, 363 A.2d 41 (1975)
111 ALR5th 491—§ 3

State v. Pastorini, 222 Ga. App. 316, 474 S.E.2d 122 (1996)
57 ALR6th 83—§ 5

State v. Pastorini, 226 Ga. App. 260, 486 S.E.2d 399 (1997)
57 ALR6th 83—§ 5

State v. Pastrana, 94 Wash. App. 463, 972 P.2d 557 (Div. 2 1999)
7 ALR5th 758—§ 4

State v. Patch, 470 So. 2d 585 (La. App. 1st Cir. 1985)
22 ALR5th 1—§ 5, 13, 22, 40, 45, 47, 53, 54

State v. Patel, 160 Ariz. 86, 770 P.2d 390 (Ct. App. Div. 1 1989)
75 ALR6th 541—§ 14

State v. Paterno, 309 N.W.2d 420 (Iowa 1981)
114 ALR5th 235—§ 9

State v. Patillo, 262 Ga. 259, 417 S.E.2d 139 (1992)
20 ALR5th 177—§ 4

State v. Patin, 842 So. 2d 322 (La. 2003)
63 ALR6th 351—§ 3

State v. Patino, 177 Wis. 2d 348, 502 N.W.2d 601 (Ct. App. 1993)
97 ALR6th 567—§ 3, 5, 9

State v. Patricella, 109 Ariz. 393, 510 P.2d 39 (1973)
55 ALR5th 125—§ 16, 26

State v. Patrick, 42 Conn. App. 640, 681 A.2d 380 (1996)
27 ALR5th 593—§ 7, 31

State v. Patrick, 87 Or. App. 430, 742 P.2d 690 (1987)
55 ALR5th 125—§ 4, 7

State v. Patrick, 255 S.C. 130, 177 S.E.2d 545 (1970)
11 ALR5th 52—§ 7

State v. Patscheck, 2000 -NMCA- 062, 6 P.3d 498 (N.M. Ct. App. 2000)
84 ALR5th 1—§ 7

State v. Pattee, 2001 WL 467903 (Tenn. Crim. App. 2001)
3 ALR6th 543—§ 9

State v. Patten, 89 P.3d 662 (Kan. Ct. App. 2004)
8 ALR6th 265—§ 18

State v. Patten, 134 N.H. 319, 591 A.2d 1329 (1991)
105 ALR5th 529—§ 11

State v. Patten, 416 N.W.2d 168, 6 U.C.C. Rep. Serv. 2d 386 (Minn. Ct. App. 1987)
89 ALR5th 319—§ 8, 23

State v. Patterson, 25 Kan. App. 2d 245, 963 P.2d 436 (1998)
30 ALR6th 373—§ 19

State v. Patterson, 37 Wash. App. 275, 679 P.2d 416 (Div. 1 1984)
112 ALR5th 429—§ 13
12 ALR6th 553—§ 6, 22, 36

State v. Patterson, 139 N.M. 322, 2006-NMCA-037, 131 P.3d 1286 (Ct. App. 2006)
97 ALR6th 653—§ 31

State v. Patterson, 145 N.H. 462, 764 A.2d 901 (2000)
69 ALR6th 1—§ 13

State v. Patterson, 200 Kan. 176, 434 P.2d 808 (1967)
24 ALR5th 465—§ 42, 43

State v. Patterson, 243 Kan. 262, 755 P.2d 551 (1988)
39 ALR5th 283—§ 4, 77

State v. Patterson, 273 S.C. 361, 256 S.E.2d 417 (1979)
70 ALR6th 361—§ 30

State v. Patterson, 284 N.C. 190, 200 S.E.2d 16 (1973)
24 ALR5th 465—§ 24 to 26, 30

State v. Patterson, 332 N.C. 409, 420 S.E.2d 98, 23 A.L.R.5th 917 (1992)
23 ALR5th 672—§ 3, 6

State v. Patterson, 367 S.C. 219, 625 S.E.2d 239 (Ct. App. 2006)
27 ALR6th 183—§ 5, 31

State v. Patterson, 582 A.2d 1204 (Me. 1990)
74 ALR5th 319—§ 13

State v. Patterson, 624 S.W.2d 11 (Mo. 1981)
33 ALR6th 407—§ 56

State v. Patterson, 758 So. 2d 955 (La. Ct. App. 4th Cir. 2000)
66 ALR5th 397—§ 25

State v. Patterson, 824 S.W.2d 117 (Mo. App. 1992)
4 ALR5th 1—§ 7

State v. Patterson, 849 S.W.2d 153 (Mo. Ct. App. W.D. 1993)
108 ALR5th 593—§ 20

State v. Patterson, 966 S.W.2d 435 (Tenn. Crim. App. 1997)
23 ALR6th 307—§ 38

State v. Patterson, 1985 WL 7109 (Ohio Ct. App. 6th Dist. Lucas County 1985)
27 ALR6th 183—§ 6, 35

State v. Patterson, 1998 WL 720733 (Ohio Ct. App. 4th Dist. Washington County 1998)
78 ALR5th 489—§ 3

State v. Pattie, 42 S.W.3d 825 (Mo. Ct. App. E.D. 2001)
111 ALR5th 239—§ 9

State v. Patton, 133 N.J. 389, 627 A.2d 1112 (1993)
29 ALR5th 1—§ 2

State v. Patton, 167 Wash. 2d 379, 219 P.3d 651 (2009)
55 ALR6th 1—§ 31, 39
56 ALR6th 1—§ 24

State v. Patton, 201 Or. App. 509, 119 P.3d 250 (2005)
46 ALR6th 241—§ 19

State v. Patton, 1997 WL 593792 (Ohio Ct. App. 3d Dist. Union County 1997)

78 ALR5th 489—§ 10

State v. Patzer, 382 N.W.2d 631, 30 Ed. Law Rep. 1265 (N.D. 1986)

70 ALR5th 169—§ 11

State v. Paul, 82 N.M. 791, 487 P.2d 493 (App. 1971)

21 ALR5th 275—§ 5

State v. Paul, 225 Neb. 432, 405 N.W.2d 608 (1987)

41 ALR5th 171—§ 20, 26, 72

State v. Paul, 548 N.W.2d 260 (Minn. 1996)

17 ALR6th 327—§ 12

State v. Paul, 579 So. 2d 303 (Fla. Dist. Ct. App. 4th Dist. 1991)

18 ALR6th 519—§ 7

State v. Paul, 2002-Ohio-591, 2002 WL 228848 (Ohio Ct. App. 8th Dist. Cuyahoga County 2002)

11 ALR6th 237—§ 12, 13

State v. Pauley, 8 Ohio App. 3d 354, 457 N.E.2d 864 (8th Dist. Cuyahoga County 1982)

33 ALR6th 407—§ 31, 33, 34

State v. Paulk, 842 So. 2d 212 (Fla. Dist. Ct. App. 3d Dist. 2003)

113 ALR5th 597—§ 8

State v. Pavin, 202 N.J. Super. 255, 494 A.2d 834, 55 A.L.R.4th 323 (App. Div. 1985)

9 ALR6th 363—§ 14

State v. Pavlick, 2000 WL 1442 (Ohio Ct. App. 5th Dist. Holmes County 1999)

78 ALR5th 489—§ 9

State v. Pavlovich, 1989 WL 949 (Ohio Ct. App. 11th Dist. Lake County 1989)

99 ALR6th 295—§ 16

State v. Pavlovich, 1989 WL 65439 (Ohio Ct. App. 11th Dist. Lake County 1989)

99 ALR6th 295—§ 13

State v. Pavone, 104 N.C. App. 442, 410 S.E.2d 1 (1991)

1 ALR6th 549—§ 16
2 ALR6th 551—§ 16
11 ALR6th 237—§ 3, 11

State v. Pawlaczyk, 1991 WL 209914 (Ohio App. 7 Dist. 1991)

54 ALR5th 141—§ 3, 8

State v. Paxton, 201 Kan. 353, 440 P.2d 650 (1968)

11 ALR5th 218—§ 3, 8

State v. Paxton, 1992 WL 100410 (Ohio App. Perry Co. 1992)

52 ALR5th 655—§ 3

State v. Payan, 15 Ariz. App. 128, 486 P.2d 808 (1971)

4 ALR5th 1—§ 17, 33

State v. Payan, 277 Neb. 663, 765 N.W.2d 192, 51 A.L.R.6th 573 (2009)

51 ALR6th 139—§ 2, 3, 10, 12

State v. Payne, 45 Wash. App. 528, 726 P.2d 997 (Div. 2 1986)

73 ALR5th 383—§ 8

State v. Payne, 54 Wash. App. 240, 773 P.2d 122 (Div. 3 1989)

112 ALR5th 429—§ 10

State v. Payne, 58 Wash. App. 215, 795 P.2d 134 (Div. 1 1990)

73 ALR5th 383—§ 41, 63

State v. Payne, 96 N.M. 347, 630 P.2d 299 (N.M. App. 1981)

49 ALR5th 639—§ 4

State v. Payne, 104 Ohio App. 3d 364, 662 N.E.2d 60 (12th Dist. Clermont County 1995)

60 ALR5th 1—§ 4
62 ALR5th 1—§ 2, 4, 13, 15

State v. Payne, 149 S.W.3d 20 (Tenn. 2004)

29 ALR6th 1—§ 9

State v. Payne, 150 Or. App. 469, 946 P.2d 353 (1997)

112 ALR5th 429—§ 8

State v. Payne, 219 Conn. 93, 591 A.2d 1246 (1991)

22 ALR5th 1—§ 2, 6, 13, 40

State v. Payne, 327 N.C. 194, 394 S.E.2d 158 (1990)

57 ALR5th 141—§ 6, 7

State v. Payne, 337 N.C. 505, 448 S.E.2d 93 (1994)

83 ALR6th 255—§ 19

State v. Payne, 633 So. 2d 701 (La. App. 1st Cir. 1993)

36 ALR5th 161—§ 3

State v. Payne, 657 So. 2d 531 (La. App. 4th Cir. 1995)

47 ALR5th 259—§ 2

State v. Payne, 777 So. 2d 555 (La. Ct. App. 5th Cir. 2000)

55 ALR5th 423—§ 8.5

State v. Payne, 791 S.W.2d 10 (Tenn. 1990)

37 ALR5th 515—§ 2, 26

State v. Payne, 833 So. 2d 927 (La. 2002)

124 ALR5th 1—§ 5

State v. Payne, 943 S.W.2d 338 (Mo. Ct. App. E.D. 1997)

77 ALR5th 201—§ 13

State v. Payne, 1991 WL 168609 (Tenn. Crim. App. 1991)

78 ALR5th 567—§ 5

State v. Payne, No. 49603 (October 24, 1985, Ct. App. Ohio, 8th App. Dist. Cuyahoga Co.)

39 ALR5th 283—§ 14, 66

State v. Paz, 31 Or. App. 851, 572 P.2d 1036 (1977)

32 ALR6th 1—§ 10

State v. Paz, 111 Wash. App. 1048, 2002 WL 1008999 (Div. 1 2002)

12 ALR6th 553—§ 14, 18

State v. Peabody, 25 R.I. 178, 55 A. 323 (1903)

90 ALR6th 385—§ 7

State v. Peabody, 611 A.2d 826 (R.I. 1992)

100 ALR6th 535—§ 3

State v. Peacock, 725 S.W.2d 87 (Mo. Ct. App. S.D. 1987)

102 ALR6th 279—§ 5

State v. Pearce, 156 Ariz. 287, 751 P.2d 603, 2 Ariz. Adv. Rep. 55 (App. 1988)

15 ALR5th 391—§ 45

State v. Pearce, 994 So. 2d 1094 (Fla. 2008)

102 ALR6th 417—§ 5

State v. Pea River Elec. Cooperative, 434 So. 2d 785 (Ala. Civ. App. 1983)

58 ALR5th 187—§ 34

State v. Pearsall, 156 Wash. App. 357, 231 P.3d 849 (Div. 2 2010)

71 ALR6th 1—§ 8

State v. Pearson, 15 Utah 2d 353, 393 P.2d 390 (1964)

54 ALR5th 141—§ 3, 10

State v. Pearson, 83 Or. App. 624, 732 P.2d 937 (1987)

58 ALR6th 499—§ 94

State v. Pearson, 114 Ohio App. 3d 168, 682 N.E.2d 1086 (3d Dist. Seneca County 1996)

86 ALR5th 59—§ 5

State v. Pearson, 130 Ohio App. 3d 577, 720 N.E.2d 924 (3d Dist. Seneca County 1998)

93 ALR6th 275—§ 7

State v. Pearson, 140 Ariz. 95, 680 P.2d 805 (1984)

16 ALR6th 329—§ 5

24 ALR6th 591—§ 4, 12

State v. Pearson, 220 Neb. 183, 368 N.W.2d 804 (1985)

43 ALR6th 475—§ 21

State v. Pearson, 234 Kan. 906, 678 P.2d 605 (1984)

65 ALR5th 407—§ 3

State v. Pearson, 288 N.C. 34, 215 S.E.2d 598 (1975)

36 ALR5th 255—§ 17

State v. Pearson, 318 N.J. Super. 123, 723 A.2d 84 (App. Div. 1999)

32 ALR6th 1—§ 10

State v. Pearson, 479 N.W.2d 401 (Minn. Ct. App. 1991)

73 ALR5th 383—§ 5

State v. Pearson, 1986 WL 1071 (Ohio Ct. App. 8th Dist. Cuyahoga County 1986)

88 ALR5th 121—§ 35

State v. Pearson, 2004-Ohio-1451, 2004
WL 583895 (Ohio Ct. App. 8th Dist.
Cuyahoga County 2004)
65 ALR6th 1—§ 5, 11, 21
State v. Pearson, 2006-Ohio-5585, 2006
WL 3030787 (Ohio Ct. App. 2d
Dist. Montgomery County 2006)
65 ALR6th 537—§ 10, 13
State v. Pearson, 2011-Ohio-245, 2011
WL 192640 (Ohio Ct. App. 2d Dist.
Montgomery County 2011)
64 ALR6th 1—§ 19
State v. Pearson-Anderson, 136 Idaho
847, 41 P.3d 275 (Ct. App. 2001)
58 ALR6th 499—§ 44
State v. Pearson, No. 83 (September 4,
1985, Ct. App. Ohio, 7th App. Dist.
Mahoning Co.)
39 ALR5th 283—§ 14
State v. Pease, 222 Mont. 455, 724 P.2d
153 (1986)
6 ALR6th 533—§ 21
State v. Peat, 790 S.W.2d 547 (Tenn.
Crim. App. 1990)
98 ALR6th 455—§ 29
State v. Peavyhouse, 1996 WL 129840
(Tenn. Crim. App. 1996)
83 ALR5th 541—§ 2, 3
State v. Peay, 321 S.C. 405, 468 S.E.2d
669 (Ct. App. 1996)
2 ALR6th 551—§ 7, 11
State v. Pebria, 85 Haw. 171, 938 P.2d
1190 (Ct. App. 1997)
31 ALR6th 465—§ 4, 17
State v. Pecha, 225 Neb. 673, 407
N.W.2d 760 (1987)
43 ALR5th 1—§ 11
State v. Peck, 143 Wis. 2d 624, 422
N.W.2d 160 (Ct. App. 1988)
59 ALR5th 615—§ 3, 6, 12
1 ALR6th 549—§ 20
State v. Peck, 652 S.W.2d 244 (Mo. Ct.
App. S.D. 1983)
105 ALR5th 529—§ 11
State v. Peck, 1984 WL 14001 (Ohio Ct.
App. 8th Dist. Cuyahoga County
1984)
78 ALR5th 567—§ 7

State v. Peck, 1991 WL 154534 (Tenn.
Crim. App. 1991)
59 ALR5th 1—§ 3 to 6
State v. Peck, 1999 WL 409715 (Wash.
Ct. App. Div. 1 1999)
73 ALR5th 383—§ 6
State v. Peckham, 255 Kan. 310, 875
P.2d 257 (1994)
84 ALR5th 487—§ 3
State v. Pedersen, 3 NCA 279 (Neb.
1993)
38 ALR5th 433—§ 3
State v. Pederson, 1992 WL 358733
(Minn. Ct. App. 1992)
73 ALR5th 383—§ 5
State v. Pedreira, 1987 WL 25712 (Ohio
Ct. App. 8th Dist.Cuyahoga County
1987)
57 ALR5th 141—§ 8
State v. Peebles, 337 Mo. 973, 87
S.W.2d 167 (1935)
108 ALR5th 593—§ 11
State v. Peele, 196 N.C. App. 668, 675
S.E.2d 682 (2009)
84 ALR6th 293—§ 13, 18, 34
State v. Peele, 298 S.C. 63, 378 S.E.2d
254 (1989)
58 ALR6th 215—§ 5
State v. Peeples, 94 Ohio App. 3d 34, 94
Ohio App. 3d 34., 640 N.E.2d 208
(4th Dist. Pickaway County 1994)
83 ALR5th 541—§ 5
State v. Peeples, 94 Ohio App. 3d 34,
640 N.E.2d 208 (4th Dist. Pickaway
County 1994)
38 ALR6th 97—§ 17
State v. Pegues, 203 Wis. 2d 270, 551
N.W.2d 869 (Ct. App. 1996)
98 ALR6th 455—§ 6
State v. Pejsa, 75 Wash. App. 139, 876
P.2d 963 (Div. 2 1994)
28 ALR6th 505—§ 29
State v. Pelham, 328 N.J. Super. 631,
746 A.2d 557 (Law Div. 1998)
49 ALR5th 639—§ 4
State v. Pellegrino, 194 Conn. 279, 480
A.2d 537 (1984)
96 ALR5th 523—§ 3

State v. Pelletier, 149 N.H. 243, 818
A.2d 292 (2003)
23 ALR6th 1—§ 18

State v. Pelletier, 2005-Ohio-1914, 2005
WL 941002 (Ohio Ct. App. 3d Dist.
Allen County 2005)
26 ALR6th 511—§ 19

State v. Pellicci, 133 N.H. 523, 580 A.2d
710 (1990)
117 ALR5th 407—§ 4

State v. Peltier, 249 Kan. 415, 819 P.2d
628 (1991)
42 ALR5th 291—§ 25

State v. Pelton, 197 Neb. 412, 249
N.W.2d 484 (1977)
19 ALR6th 115—§ 5, 10

State v. Pelton, 801 P.2d 184, 147 Utah
Adv. Rep. 36 (Utah App. 1990)
34 ALR5th 125—§ 18

State v. Pemberthy, 224 N.J. Super. 280,
540 A.2d 227 (1988)
20 ALR5th 398—§ 39

State v. Pena, 2005-Ohio-6103, 2005
WL 3073368 (Ohio Ct. App. 10th
Dist. Franklin County 2005)
26 ALR6th 511—§ 18, 35

State v. Penalber, 386 N.J. Super. 1, 898
A2d 538 (App. Div. 2006)
50 ALR6th 1—§ 8

State v. Penas, 200 Neb. 387, 263
N.W.2d 835 (1978)
17 ALR6th 327—§ 12

State v. Pendergrass, 1997 WL 760724
(Tenn. Crim. App. 1997)
73 ALR5th 383—§ 6

State v. Pendry, 1987 WL 860827 (Del.
C.P. 1987)
92 ALR6th 295—§ 13, 19
93 ALR6th 207—§ 14, 20
94 ALR6th 191—§ 4
96 ALR6th 355—§ 5, 6, 24, 53

State v. Penland, 343 N.C. 634, 472
S.E.2d 734 (1996)
33 ALR6th 353—§ 3, 5

State v. Penley, 284 N.C. 247, 200
S.E.2d 1 (1973)
55 ALR5th 125—§ 3

State v. Penman, 964 P.2d 1157 (Utah
Ct. App. 1998)
95 ALR5th 611—§ 3

State v. Penn, 52 Ohio App. 2d 315, 6
Ohio Op. 3d 357, 369 N.E.2d 1229
(1st Dist. Hamilton County 1977)
70 ALR6th 1—§ 4, 5

State v. Pennell, 54 N.C. App. 252, 283
S.E.2d 397 (1981)
94 ALR5th 393—§ 5

State v. Pennell, 584 A.2d 513 (Del.
Super. 1989)
37 ALR5th 515—§ 2, 6

State v. Pennell, 1989 WL 167445 (Del.
Super. Ct. 1989)
95 ALR6th 219—§ 13

State v. Pennewell, 23 Wash. App. 777,
598 P.2d 748 (Div. 2 1979)
55 ALR6th 391—§ 7

State v. Penney, 2002 WL 31235997
(Me. Super. Ct. 2002)
45 ALR6th 337—§ 13

State v. Pennington, 154 N.J. 344, 712
A.2d 1133 (1998)
11 ALR6th 237—§ 12

State v. Pennington, 162 Vt. 621, 649
A.2d 513 (1994)
21 ALR6th 771—§ 4

State v. Pennison, 763 So. 2d 671 (La.
Ct. App. 1st Cir. 1999)
27 ALR5th 593—§ 36

State v. Penny, 224 Wis. 2d 642, 590
N.W.2d 281 (Ct. App. 1999)
99 ALR6th 295—§ 13

State v. Pennzoil Co., 752 P.2d 975, 100
OGR 359 (Wyo. 1988)
57 ALR5th 753—§ 3

State v. Pentacost, 2000 WL 895590
(Ohio Ct. App. 11th Dist. Trumbull
County 2000)
70 ALR6th 1—§ 4

State v. Pentecost, 64 Wash. App. 656,
825 P.2d 365 (Div. 3 1992)
66 ALR5th 373—§ 4

State v. Peoples, 227 Kan. 127, 605 P.2d
135 (1980)
1 ALR6th 657—§ 4, 6, 11, 14

State v. Peoples, 2007-Ohio-1379, 2007 WL 886720 (Ohio Ct. App. 11th Dist. Lake County 2007)
26 ALR6th 511—§ 19

State v. Pepper, 103 R.I. 310, 237 A.2d 330 (1968)
24 ALR5th 465—§ 8, 117

State v. Peppers, 690 S.E.2d 770 (N.C. Ct. App. 2010)
57 ALR6th 1—§ 11, 18

State v. Perbix, 331 N.W.2d 14 (N.D. 1983)
99 ALR5th 557—§ 2, 10

State v. Perdue, 320 N.C. 51, 357 S.E.2d 345 (1987)
96 ALR5th 523—§ 3

State v. Perea, 142 Ariz. 352, 690 P.2d 71 (1984)
1 ALR6th 657—§ 6
29 ALR6th 1—§ 10

State v. Pereira, 72 Conn. App. 107, 806 A.2d 51 (2002)
40 ALR6th 1—§ 32

State v. Peres-Ochoa, 97 Wash. App. 1073, 1999 WL 982299 (Div. 2 1999)
7 ALR6th 233—§ 15

State v. Perez, 33 Wash. App. 258, 654 P.2d 708 (Div. 2 1982)
31 ALR6th 49—§ 10

State v. Perez, 72 Ohio App. 3d 468, 594 N.E.2d 1041 (10th Dist. Franklin County 1991)
3 ALR6th 269—§ 5, 8, 29

State v. Perez, 78 Conn. App. 610, 828 A.2d 626 (2003)
124 ALR5th 1—§ 8
51 ALR6th 1—§ 20

State v. Perez, 92 Wash. App. 1, 963 P.2d 881 (Div. 1 1998)
109 ALR5th 99—§ 3

State v. Perez, 95 N.M. 262, 620 P.2d 1287 (1980)
14 ALR5th 89—§ 34
55 ALR6th 157—§ 115

State v. Perez, 99 Idaho 181, 579 P.2d 127 (1978)
117 ALR5th 513—§ 5

State v. Perez, 152 Wash. App. 1013, 2009 WL 2938344 (Div. 1 2009)
77 ALR6th 251—§ 3

State v. Perez, 177 N.J. 540, 832 A.2d 303 (2003)
35 ALR6th 361—§ 20

State v. Perez, 183 P.3d 860 (Kan. Ct. App. 2008)
63 ALR6th 351—§ 3

State v. Perez, 340 Or. 310, 131 P.3d 168 (2006)
26 ALR6th 511—§ 36

State v. Perez, 397 N.W.2d 916 (Minn. Ct. App. 1986)
83 ALR5th 277—§ 11

State v. Perez, 404 N.W.2d 834 (Minn. App. 1987)
32 ALR5th 149—§ 5, 29, 32, 93

State v. Perez, 438 So. 2d 436 (Fla. App. D3 1983)
15 ALR5th 39—§ 4, 9

State v. Perez, 745 So. 2d 166 (La. Ct. App. 4th Cir. 1999)
62 ALR6th 259—§ 13

State v. Perez, 906 S.W.2d 558 (Tex. App. San Antonio 1995)
12 ALR5th 89—§ 4

State v. Perez., 1980 WL 354347 (Ohio Ct. App. 8th Dist. Cuyahoga County 1980)
70 ALR6th 361—§ 4

State v. Perez, 2000 WL 1420341 (Ohio Ct. App. 9th Dist. Medina County 2000)
19 ALR6th 697—§ 25

State v. Perez, 2006 WL 2062130 (R.I. Super. Ct. 2006)
65 ALR6th 1—§ 4

State v. Pergande, 146 Wis. 2d 233, 430 N.W.2d 364 (App. 1988)
24 ALR5th 132—§ 4

State v. Perique, 340 So. 2d 1369 (La. 1976)
24 ALR6th 1—§ 13

State v. Perkins, 42 Vt. 399, 1869 WL 2695 (1869)
5 ALR6th 1—§ 23, 46

State v. Perkins, 92 S.W.2d 634 (Mo. 1936)
54 ALR6th 429—§ 13

State v. Perkins, 93 Ohio App. 3d 672, 639 N.E.2d 833 (Ohio App. Cuyahoga Co. 1994)
39 ALR5th 283—§ 14, 31

State v. Perkins, 108 Wash. 2d 212, 737 P.2d 250 (1987)
36 ALR5th 161—§ 9
41 ALR6th 141—§ 7

State v. Perkins, 204 Wis. 2d 275, 554 N.W.2d 683 (Ct. App. 1996)
90 ALR5th 453—§ 53

State v. Perkins, 271 Conn. 218, 856 A.2d 917 (2004)
84 ALR6th 427—§ 4

State v. Perkins, 277 A.2d 501 (Me. 1971)
85 ALR5th 547—§ 7

State v. Perkins, 378 S.C. 57, 661 S.E.2d 366 (2008)
78 ALR6th 1—§ 27, 55

State v. Perkins, 380 S.W.2d 433 (Mo. 1964)
104 ALR5th 357—§ 9
54 ALR6th 429—§ 27

State v. Perkins, 444 N.W.2d 34 (S.D. 1989)
29 ALR6th 1—§ 10

State v. Perkins, 650 S.W.2d 339 (Mo. Ct. App. E.D. 1983)
1 ALR6th 549—§ 8

State v. Perkins, 774 S.W.2d 484 (Mo. Ct. App. E.D. 1989)
38 ALR6th 97—§ 19

State v. Perkins, 2004 WL 1172894 (Del. Super. Ct. 2004)
7 ALR6th 487—§ 32

State v. Perkins, 2009-Ohio-2404, 2009 WL 1424100 (Ohio Ct. App. 5th Dist. Coshocton County 2009)
64 ALR6th 1—§ 7, 9, 11

State v. Perlstein, 206 N.J. Super. 246, 502 A.2d 81 (App. Div. 1985)
66 ALR5th 397—§ 16, 17

State v. Pero, 370 N.J. Super. 203, 851 A.2d 41 (App. Div. 2004)
72 ALR6th 141—§ 9

State v. Perovich, 2001 SD 96, 632 N.W.2d 12 (S.D. 2001)
82 ALR6th 373—§ 7
99 ALR6th 113—§ 4, 10

State v. Perrett, 86 Wash. App. 312, 936 P.2d 426 (Div. 2 1997)
84 ALR5th 487—§ 22

State v. Perrigo, 10 Kan. App. 2d 651, 708 P.2d 987 (1985)
32 ALR5th 149—§ 29

State v. Perry, 5 Ariz. App. 315, 426 P.2d 415 (1967)
5 ALR5th 243—§ 2, 60

State v. Perry, 13 S.W.3d 724 (Tenn. Crim. App. 1999)
9 ALR6th 1—§ 17
35 ALR6th 127—§ 4

State v. Perry, 16 La. Ann 444 (1862)
11 ALR5th 831—§ 20, 21

State v. Perry, 52 N.C. App. 48, 278 S.E.2d 273 (1981)
29 ALR5th 59—§ 58

State v. Perry, 83 Ohio St. 3d 41, 1998-Ohio-422, 697 N.E.2d 624, 48 U.S.P.Q.2d 1125 (1998)
76 ALR6th 289—§ 3, 4
77 ALR6th 543—§ 3, 18

State v. Perry, 116 Ariz. 40, 567 P.2d 786 (App. 1977)
39 ALR5th 283—§ 3, 58, 60

State v. Perry, 116 Ariz. 40, 567 P.2d 786 (Ct. App. Div. 2 1977)
32 ALR6th 385—§ 3

State v. Perry, 124 N.J. 128, 590 A.2d 624 (1991)
99 ALR6th 397—§ 8

State v. Perry, 139 Idaho 520, 81 P.3d 1230 (2003)
10 ALR6th 463—§ 3, 4, 6, 8

State v. Perry, 149 La. 1065, 90 So. 406 (1921)
101 ALR6th 499—§ 15

State v. Perry, 196 Minn. 481, 265 N.W. 302 (1936)
113 ALR5th 1—§ 4, 8, 14

State v. Perry, 268 Neb. 179, 681 N.W.2d 729 (2004)
72 ALR6th 1—§ 6

State v. Perry, 291 N.C. 586, 231 S.E.2d 262 (1977)
103 ALR6th 507—§ 4, 18

State v. Perry, 298 N.C. 502, 259 S.E.2d 496 (1979)
34 ALR6th 1—§ 8
58 ALR6th 439—§ 21

State v. Perry, 305 N.C. 225, 287 S.E.2d 810 (1982)
29 ALR5th 59—§ 3, 76

State v. Perry, 336 Or. 49, 77 P.3d 313 (2003)
33 ALR6th 407—§ 43 to 45

State v. Perry, 420 So. 2d 139 (La. 1982)
70 ALR5th 587—§ 6, 17

State v. Perry, 502 So. 2d 543 (La. 1986)
111 ALR5th 491—§ 3, 4
58 ALR6th 499—§ 20

State v. Perry, 552 A.2d 545 (Me. 1989)
57 ALR5th 141—§ 13

State v. Perry, 610 So. 2d 746 (La. 1992)
111 ALR5th 491—§ 3, 7

State v. Perry, 720 So. 2d 345 (La. Ct. App. 4th Cir. 1998)
19 ALR5th 470—§ 12

State v. Perry, 820 S.W.2d 570 (Mo. Ct. App. E.D. 1991)
72 ALR5th 109—§ 6

State v. Perry, 954 S.W.2d 554 (Mo. Ct. App. S.D. 1997)
26 ALR6th 451—§ 6

State v. Perry, 1996 WL 577653 (Ohio Ct. App. 9th Dist. Summit County 1996)
35 ALR6th 127—§ 5

State v. Perry, 2003-Ohio-6344, 2003 WL 22805880 (Ohio Ct. App. 8th Dist. Cuyahoga County 2003)
41 ALR6th 141—§ 5, 7

State v. Perry, 2005-Ohio-27, 2005 WL 23357 (Ohio Ct. App. 8th Dist. Cuyahoga County 2005)
26 ALR6th 511—§ 19, 33

State v. Perryman, 2004-Ohio-1120, 2004 WL 443394 (Ohio Ct. App. 8th Dist. Cuyahoga County 2004)
1 ALR6th 371—§ 4

State v. Perry, No. 42998 (April 9, 1981, Ct. App. Ohio, 8th App. Dist. Cuyahoga Co.)
39 ALR5th 283—§ 14, 66

State v. Petary, 790 S.W.2d 243 (Mo. 1990)
83 ALR6th 255—§ 2, 17

State v. Pete, 117 Wash. App. 1026, 2003 WL 21387208 (Div. 1 2003)
35 ALR6th 127—§ 5

State v. Peterman, 32 Ind. App. 665, 70 N.E. 550 (Div. 1 1904)
70 ALR5th 169—§ 25

State v. Peters, 12 Ohio App. 2d 83, 41 Ohio Op. 2d 160, 231 N.E.2d 91 (10th Dist. Franklin County 1967)
28 ALR6th 505—§ 4, 8

State v. Peters, 12 Ohio App. 2d 83, 41 Ohio Ops. 2d 160, 231 N.E.2d 91 (Franklin Co. 1967)
24 ALR5th 428—§ 19

State v. Peters, 39 Or. App. 109, 591 P.2d 761 (1979)
24 ALR6th 1—§ 21

State v. Peters, 49 Or. App. 653, 619 P.2d 1360 (1980)
7 ALR5th 73—§ 9

State v. Peters, 123 N.M. 667, 1997-NMCA- 084, 944 P.2d 896 (Ct. App. 1997)
77 ALR5th 201—§ 4, 6
78 ALR5th 1—§ 37

State v. Peters, 189 Ariz. 216, 941 P.2d 228 (1997)
122 ALR5th 439—§ 9
125 ALR5th 281—§ 15

State v. Peters, 192 Wis. 2d 674, 534 N.W.2d 867 (Ct. App. 1995)
90 ALR5th 453—§ 53
38 ALR6th 439—§ 7

State v. Peters, 237 Wis. 2d 741, 2000 WI App 154, 615 N.W.2d 655 (Ct. App. 2000)
115 ALR5th 509—§ 3, 9

State v. Peters, 244 Wis. 2d 470, 2001 WI 74, 628 N.W.2d 797 (2001)
115 ALR5th 509—§ 3, 9

State v. Peters, 261 Neb. 416, 622 N.W.2d 918 (2001)
50 ALR6th 455—§ 23, 24, 36

State v. Peters, 263 Wis. 2d 475, 2003 WI 88, 665 N.W.2d 171, 125 A.L.R.5th 775 (2003)
125 ALR5th 537—§ 2, 3

State v. Peters, 274 Minn. 309, 143 N.W.2d 832 (1966)
5 ALR5th 243—§ 10, 53

State v. Peters, 302 So. 2d 888 (La. 1974)
70 ALR5th 587—§ 3

State v. Peters, 401 So. 2d 838 (Fla. App. D2 1981)
6 ALR5th 652—§ 2, 5, 8

State v. Peters, 546 So. 2d 829 (La. Ct. App. 1st Cir. 1989)
5 ALR6th 385—§ 4

State v. Peters, 582 S.W.2d 323 (Mo. Ct. App. W.D. 1979)
70 ALR5th 587—§ 3

State v. Peters, 695 S.W.2d 140 (Mo. Ct. App. W.D. 1985)
17 ALR6th 327—§ 40

State v. Peters, 731 S.W.2d 480 (Mo. App. 1987)
5 ALR5th 243—§ 51

State v. Peterschick, 126 Wash. App. 1001, 2005 WL 420284 (Div. 2 2005)
56 ALR6th 647—§ 8, 20

State v. Petersen, 16 Neb. App. 339, 744 N.W.2d 266 (2008)
33 ALR6th 373—§ 17
40 ALR6th 355—§ 4

State v. Petersen, 270 Or. 166, 526 P.2d 1008 (1974)
89 ALR6th 565—§ 14

State v. Petersilie, 334 N.C. 169, 432 S.E.2d 832 (1993)
51 ALR6th 359—§ 3, 27

State v. Peterson, 3 Or. App. 17, 469 P.2d 40 (1970)

State v. Peterson, 20 Ariz. App. 296, 512 P.2d 600 (Div. 1 1973)
113 ALR5th 517—§ 6

State v. Peterson, 24 N.C. App. 404, 210 S.E.2d 883 (1975)
72 ALR5th 529—§ 13

State v. Peterson, 25 Kan. App. 2d 354, 964 P.2d 695, 73 A.L.R.5th 789 (1998)
73 ALR5th 383—§ 3

State v. Peterson, 26 Or. App. 471, 552 P.2d 1320 (1976)
68 ALR6th 527—§ 37

State v. Peterson, 30 S.W.3d 209 (Mo. Ct. App. W.D. 2000)
37 ALR6th 357—§ 19

State v. Peterson, 133 Idaho 44, 981 P.2d 1154 (Ct. App. 1999)
80 ALR6th 239—§ 6, 9

State v. Peterson, 137 Idaho 255, 47 P.3d 378 (Ct. App. 2002)
51 ALR6th 1—§ 5

State v. Peterson, 154 N.C. App. 515, 571 S.E.2d 883 (2002)
11 ALR6th 237—§ 3, 11

State v. Peterson, 171 Ariz. 333, 830 P.2d 854 (Ct. App. Div. 1 1991)
103 ALR6th 347—§ 25

State v. Peterson, 173 Ohio App. 3d 575, 2007-Ohio-5667, 879 N.E.2d 806 (2d Dist. Montgomery County 2007)
69 ALR6th 275—§ 8, 32

State v. Peterson, 219 N.W.2d 665 (Iowa 1974)
90 ALR5th 225—§ 5

State v. Peterson, 236 Mont. 247, 769 P.2d 1221 (1989)
93 ALR6th 207—§ 6, 9, 31
96 ALR6th 355—§ 10, 18, 37

State v. Peterson, 265 Kan. 732, 962 P.2d 1076 (1998)
2 ALR5th 725—§ 12

State v. Peterson, 273 Ga. 657, 543 S.E.2d 692 (2001)
58 ALR6th 499—§ 34

State v. Peterson, 364 N.J. Super. 387, 836 A.2d 821 (App. Div. 2003)
125 ALR5th 497—§ 4
72 ALR6th 227—§ 23, 50
State v. Peterson, 490 N.W.2d 53 (Iowa 1992)
27 ALR5th 593—§ 7, 19
State v. Peterson, 525 S.W.2d 599 (Mo. App. 1975)
55 ALR5th 125—§ 3, 6, 7
State v. Peterson, 535 N.W.2d 689 (Minn. App. 1995)
42 ALR5th 291—§ 10, 36
State v. Peterson, 663 N.W.2d 417 (Iowa 2003)
38 ALR6th 97—§ 18
State v. Peterson, 739 So. 2d 561 (Fla. 1999)
35 ALR6th 497—§ 3, 12, 35, 37
State v. Peterson, 868 So. 2d 786 (La. Ct. App. 1st Cir. 2003)
32 ALR6th 1—§ 9
State v. Peterson, 1995 WL 467532 (Neb. Ct. App. 1995)
43 ALR6th 475—§ 21
State v. Peterson, 2002 UT App 53, 42 P.3d 1258 (Utah Ct. App. 2002)
37 ALR6th 357—§ 67
State v. Peterson, 2009-Ohio-5088, 2009 WL 3087315 (Ohio Ct. App. 10th Dist. Franklin County 2009)
55 ALR6th 1—§ 19, 29
State v. Petitjean, 140 Ohio App. 3d 517, 748 N.E.2d 133 (2d Dist. Miami County 2000)
29 ALR6th 1—§ 10
State v. Petkus, 110 N.H. 394, 269 A.2d 123 (1970)
109 ALR5th 611—§ 3
State v. Petrae, 35 So. 3d 1012 (Fla. Dist. Ct. App. 5th Dist. 2010)
57 ALR6th 1—§ 33
State v. Petree, 568 S.W.2d 546 (Mo. Ct. App. 1978)
101 ALR5th 187—§ 7
State v. Petrello, 251 N.J. Super. 476, 598 A.2d 927 (1991)

7 ALR5th 263—§ 7
State v. Petrice, 183 W. Va. 695, 398 S.E.2d 521 (1990)
57 ALR6th 445—§ 43
State v. Petrie, 60 Or. App. 351, 653 P.2d 1015 (1982)
15 ALR5th 391—§ 39
State v. Petrie, 2009 WL 3337626 (Iowa Ct. App. 2009)
55 ALR6th 1—§ 3, 4, 22
State v. Petro, 592 So. 2d 254, 16 FLW D 2398 (Fla. App. D2 1991)
18 ALR5th 1—§ 13
State v. Petrou, 13 Ohio App. 3d 456, 469 N.E.2d 974 (9th Dist. Summit County 1984)
70 ALR6th 1—§ 5
State v. Petruccelli, 743 A.2d 1062 (Vt. 1999)
5 ALR5th 243—§ 47
State v. Petrucelli, 37 N.J. Super. 1, 116 A.2d 721 (App. Div. 1955)
55 ALR6th 157—§ 26
State v. Petry, 524 N.E.2d 1293 (Ind. Ct. App. 2d Dist. 1988)
71 ALR5th 637—§ 11
State v. Petta, 354 So. 2d 563 (La. 1978)
103 ALR5th 463—§ 3
State v. Pettaway, 2010-Ohio-2798, 2010 WL 2474364 (Ohio Ct. App. 6th Dist. Lucas County 2010)
78 ALR6th 297—§ 37, 81
State v. Petterson, 780 S.W.2d 675 (Mo. Ct. App. W.D. 1989)
24 ALR6th 1—§ 17
State v. Petti, 142 N.J. Super. 283, 361 A.2d 108 (App. Div. 1976)
69 ALR6th 1—§ 23
State v. Pettiford, 60 N.C. App. 92, 298 S.E.2d 389 (1982)
5 ALR5th 243—§ 6
State v. Pettigrew, 116 N.M. 135, 860 P.2d 777 (App. 1993)
5 ALR5th 243—§ 61
State v. Pettis, 63 Me. 124, 1873 WL 3121 (1873)
57 ALR6th 445—§ 49

State v. Pettis, 333 N.W.2d 717 (S.D. 1983)
16 ALR5th 855—§ 2
State v. Pettis, 748 S.W.2d 793 (Mo. App. 1988)
5 ALR5th 243—§ 49
State v. Pettit, 73 Or. App. 510, 698 P.2d 1049 (1985)
15 ALR5th 391—§ 32
92 ALR5th 35—§ 22
State v. Pettit, 194 Ariz. 192, 979 P.2d 5 (Ct. App. Div. 1 1998)
55 ALR6th 513—§ 12
State v. Pettit, 2005-Ohio-5202, 2005 WL 2401630 (Ohio Ct. App. 8th Dist. Cuyahoga County 2005)
23 ALR6th 307—§ 44
State v. Pettry, 1990 WL 119162 (Ohio Ct. App. 4th Dist. Jackson County 1990)
103 ALR6th 347—§ 20
State v. Pettus, 89 Wash. App. 688, 951 P.2d 284 (Div. 2 1998)
7 ALR5th 758—§ 6, 8, 17
State v. Petty, 48 Wash. App. 615, 740 P.2d 879 (Div. 1 1987)
112 ALR5th 429—§ 9
28 ALR6th 505—§ 6, 8
State v. Petty, 138 Wash. App. 1054, 2007 WL 1536940 (Div. 3 2007)
79 ALR6th 1—§ 44, 82
State v. Petty, 201 Wis. 2d 337, 548 N.W.2d 817 (1996)
121 ALR5th 551—§ 5, 6, 8, 9, 14
State v. Peyrani, 93 S.W.3d 384 (Tex. App. Houston 14th Dist. 2002)
62 ALR6th 413—§ 38
State v. Peyton, 234 Mo. 517, 137 S.W. 979 (1911)
5 ALR6th 1—§ 15, 31
State v. Pfeifer, 42 Wash. App. 459, 711 P.2d 1100 (Div. 1 1985)
84 ALR5th 487—§ 18
State v. Pfleiderer, 8 S.W.3d 249 (Mo. Ct. App. W.D. 1999)
92 ALR6th 171—§ 14
State v. Phalen, 192 W. Va. 267, 452 S.E.2d 70 (1994)

108 ALR5th 593—§ 10, 20
State v. Pham, 75 Wash. App. 626, 879 P.2d 321 (1994)
32 ALR5th 149—§ 53
State v. Pham, 281 Kan. 1227, 136 P.3d 919 (2006)
49 ALR6th 343—§ 4
State v. Phares, 2009 WL 6763584 (N.M. Ct. App. 2009)
69 ALR6th 579—§ 10, 27
State v. Pharris, 846 P.2d 454, 204 Utah Adv. Rep. 39 (Utah App. 1993)
20 ALR5th 398—§ 2, 5, 10
47 ALR5th 259—§ 2
State v. Phathammavong, 860 P.2d 1001 (Utah Ct. App. 1993)
37 ALR6th 357—§ 42, 53
State v. Pheil, 152 Wis. 2d 523, 449 N.W.2d 858 (Ct. App. 1989)
26 ALR6th 451—§ 6
State v. Phelps, 8 Or. App. 198, 493 P.2d 1059 (1972)
4 ALR5th 1—§ 21
State v. Phelps, 24 Or. App. 329, 545 P.2d 901 (1976)
9 ALR6th 363—§ 45
State v. Phelps, 75 Ohio App.3d 573, 600 N.E.2d 329 (Ohio App. 1 Dist., Hamilton County, 1991)
111 ALR5th 491—§ 3
State v. Phelps, 118 Wash. App. 740, 77 P.3d 678 (Div. 2 2003)
50 ALR6th 353—§ 24
State v. Phelps, 197 W. Va. 713, 478 S.E.2d 563 (1996)
83 ALR6th 465—§ 5, 13, 62
State v. Phelps, 241 Neb. 707, 490 N.W.2d 676 (1992)
48 ALR5th 555—§ 2
State v. Phelps, 273 Neb. 36, 727 N.W.2d 224 (2007)
72 ALR6th 227—§ 57
State v. Phelps, 358 N.C. 142, 592 S.E.2d 687 (2004)
38 ALR6th 97—§ 31
State v. Phelps, 782 P.2d 196, 120 Utah Adv. Rep. 36 (Utah App. 1989)

12 ALR5th 89—§ 2
State v. Philbrick, 436 A.2d 844 (Me. 1981)
9 ALR5th 369—§ 3, 5, 7, 15, 17
57 ALR5th 141—§ 7
30 ALR6th 103—§ 3, 6, 13, 22
32 ALR6th 1—§ 11
State v. Philbrick, 481 A.2d 488 (Me. 1984)
56 ALR6th 185—§ 39
State v. Philip Morris Inc., 30 A.D.3d 26, 813 N.Y.S.2d 71 (1st Dep't 2006)
25 ALR6th 435—§ 44
State v. Philip Morris, Inc., 179 Misc. 2d 435, 686 N.Y.S.2d 564 (Sup 1998)
25 ALR6th 435—§ 2
State v. Philip Morris Inc., 263 A.D.2d 400, 693 N.Y.S.2d 36 (1st Dep't 1999)
25 ALR6th 435—§ 2
State v. Philip Morris, Inc., 2005 WL 2081763 (Conn. Super. Ct. 2005)
25 ALR6th 435—§ 44
State v. Philip Morris USA Inc., 359 N.C. 763, 618 S.E.2d 219 (2005)
25 ALR6th 435—§ 2
State v. Philip Morris USA, Inc., 2006 WL 3490937 (N.C. Super. Ct. 2006)
25 ALR6th 435—§ 2, 44
State v. Philip Morris USA, Inc., 2006 WL 3690892 (Del. Ch. 2006)
25 ALR6th 435—§ 44
State v. Philip Morris USA, Inc., 2007 WL 1138472 (Del. 2007)
25 ALR6th 435—§ 44
State v. Phillip Morris, Inc., 279 Conn. 785, 905 A.2d 42 (2006)
25 ALR6th 435—§ 44
State v. Phillips, 7 Or. App. 41, 489 P.2d 987 (1971)
84 ALR6th 427—§ 4
State v. Phillips, 27 La. Ann. 663, 1875 WL 7340 (1875)
97 ALR5th 537—§ 23
State v. Phillips, 37 N.C. App. 202, 245 S.E.2d 587 (1978)

32 ALR6th 1—§ 9
State v. Phillips, 38 Del. 24, 187 A. 721 (Ct. of Oyer & Terminer 1936)
67 ALR5th 637—§ 5, 11
State v. Phillips, 59 Wash. 252, 109 P. 1047 (1910)
104 ALR5th 357—§ 3, 4
54 ALR6th 429—§ 21
State v. Phillips, 67 P.3d 1228 (Ariz. 2003)
110 ALR5th 1—§ 18
State v. Phillips, 74 Ohio St. 3d 72, 1995-Ohio-171, 656 N.E.2d 643 (1995)
115 ALR5th 509—§ 3, 10
State v. Phillips, 94 Wash. App. 313, 972 P.2d 932 (Div. 3 1999)
101 ALR5th 351—§ 8
State v. Phillips, 140 Vt. 210, 436 A.2d 746 (1981)
103 ALR6th 347—§ 19
State v. Phillips, 151 N.C. App. 185, 565 S.E.2d 697 (2002)
110 ALR5th 1—§ 15
State v. Phillips, 176 Minn. 472, 223 N.W. 912 (1929)
17 ALR5th 547—§ 30
25 ALR5th 391—§ 87
State v. Phillips, 194 W. Va. 569, 461 S.E.2d 75 (1995)
57 ALR5th 141—§ 2, 6
State v. Phillips, 202 Ariz. 427, 46 P.3d 1048 (2002)
41 ALR6th 295—§ 8
State v. Phillips, 228 N.C. 595, 46 S.E.2d 720 (1948)
11 ALR5th 497—§ 3, 16
State v. Phillips, 328 N.C. 1, 399 S.E.2d 293 (1991)
101 ALR5th 187—§ 4, 6, 8, 9
State v. Phillips, 470 P.2d 266 (Alaska 1970)
15 ALR6th 1—§ 4, 10, 18
State v. Phillips, 489 N.W.2d 613 (S.D. 1992)
124 ALR5th 1—§ 5

State v. Phillips, 520 S.E.2d 670 (W. Va. 1999)

    65 ALR5th 623—§ 3

State v. Phillips, 610 N.W.2d 840 (Iowa 2000)

    63 ALR6th 1—§ 5, 55

State v. Phillips, 691 S.E.2d 104 (N.C. Ct. App. 2010)

    57 ALR6th 1—§ 22, 23

State v. Phillips, 809 So. 2d 467 (La. Ct. App. 3d Cir. 2002)

    97 ALR5th 201—§ 3

State v. Phillips, 940 S.W.2d 512 (Mo. 1997)

    70 ALR5th 1—§ 4, 5

    24 ALR6th 1—§ 20

State v. Phillips, 1998 WL 290233 (Ohio Ct. App. 6th Dist. Lucas County 1998)

    93 ALR5th 683—§ 4

State v. Phillips, 2002-Ohio-823, 2002 WL 274637 (Ohio Ct. App. 9th Dist. Summit County 2002)

    21 ALR6th 1—§ 4

State v. Phillips, 2003 WL 1875213 (Neb. Ct. App. 2003)

    114 ALR5th 173—§ 3, 7

State v. Phillips, 2010 WL 1333390 (Tenn. Crim. App. 2010)

    89 ALR6th 565—§ 15

State v. Phillips, 2011-Ohio-475, 2011 WL 345992 (Ohio Ct. App. 8th Dist. Cuyahoga County 2011)

    64 ALR6th 1—§ 9

State v. Philpott, 882 S.W.2d 394 (Tenn. Crim. App. 1994)

    83 ALR5th 277—§ 15

State v. Phinis, 199 Kan. 472, 430 P.2d 251 (1967)

    28 ALR6th 505—§ 34

    29 ALR6th 1—§ 9

State v. Phinney, 117 N.H. 145, 370 A.2d 1153 (1977)

    20 ALR6th 479—§ 3

State v. Phinney, 235 Neb. 486, 455 N.W.2d 795 (1990)

    74 ALR5th 453—§ 2, 5

State v. Phipps, 331 N.C. 427, 418 S.E.2d 178 (1992)

    83 ALR5th 541—§ 3

    32 ALR6th 1—§ 11

State v. Piccus, 1988 WL 32145 (Ohio Ct. App. 8th Dist. Cuyahoga County 1988)

    65 ALR5th 407—§ 3, 5, 11

State v. Piche, 74 Wash. 2d 9, 442 P.2d 632 (1968)

    37 ALR5th 703—§ 3

State v. Pichler, 355 So. 2d 1302 (La. 1978)

    59 ALR5th 1—§ 5, 6

State v. Pichon, 15 Kan. App. 2d 527, 811 P.2d 517 (1991)

    54 ALR5th 141—§ 3 to 5, 10

State v. Pickar, 1993 WL 99456 (Minn. Ct. App. 1993)

    103 ALR6th 347—§ 13

State v. Pickens, 335 N.C. 717, 440 S.E.2d 552 (1994)

    16 ALR6th 329—§ 5

    24 ALR6th 591—§ 6

State v. Pickens, 558 N.W.2d 396 (Iowa 1997)

    37 ALR6th 55—§ 8

    63 ALR6th 351—§ 3

State v. Pickens, 2014-Ohio-5445

    102 ALR6th 417—§ 11

State v. Pickering, 88 S.D. 548, 225 N.W.2d 98 (1975)

    29 ALR5th 59—§ 7, 20

State v. Pickering, 432 So. 2d 1067 (La. Ct. App. 3d Cir. 1983)

    66 ALR5th 397—§ 22

State v. Pickering, 491 A.2d 560 (Me. 1985)

    76 ALR5th 1—§ 5

State v. Pickett, 95 Wash. App. 475, 975 P.2d 584 (Div. 1 1999)

    36 ALR5th 161—§ 27

    33 ALR6th 91—§ 22

State v. Pickett, 121 Ariz. 142, 589 P.2d 16 (1978)

    39 ALR5th 283—§ 3, 61

State v. Pickles, 28 Conn. App. 283, 610 A.2d 716 (1992)

84 ALR6th 427—§ 4

State v. Pickles, 46 N.J. 542, 218 A.2d 609 (1966)

118 ALR5th 253—§ 16

State v. Picklesimer, 1996 WL 599425 (Ohio Ct. App. 4th Dist. Pickaway County 1996)

90 ALR5th 453—§ 17

State v. Pickney, 714 So. 2d 854 (La. Ct. App. 3d Cir. 1998)

55 ALR5th 423—§ 3

State v. Pieger, 42 Conn. App. 460, 680 A.2d 1001 (1996)

33 ALR5th 571—§ 3

State v. Piepenburg, 602 P.2d 702 (Utah 1979)

13 ALR5th 567—§ 3

State v. Pierce, 14 Utah 2d 177, 380 P.2d 725 (1963)

17 ALR5th 125—§ 3

State v. Pierce, 69 Conn. App. 516, 794 A.2d 1123 (2002)

51 ALR6th 139—§ 6

State v. Pierce, 92 P.3d 613 (Kan. Ct. App. 2004)

28 ALR6th 505—§ 9

State v. Pierce, 107 Idaho 96, 685 P.2d 837 (App. 1984)

37 ALR5th 319—§ 4

State v. Pierce, 134 N.C. App. 149, 516 S.E.2d 916 (1999)

93 ALR5th 493—§ 5

State v. Pierce, 137 Idaho 296, 47 P.3d 1266 (Ct. App. 2002)

59 ALR6th 311—§ 18, 19

State v. Pierce, 153 Or. App. 569, 962 P.2d 35, R.I.C.O. Bus. Disp. Guide (CCH) ¶ 9497 (1998)

89 ALR5th 629—§ 5, 8

State v. Pierce, 188 N.J. 155, 902 A.2d 1195 (2006)

26 ALR6th 511—§ 28

State v. Pierce, 204 Neb. 433, 283 N.W.2d 6 (1979)

7 ALR5th 263—§ 3

State v. Pierce, 266 Ga. App. 233, 596 S.E.2d 725 (2004)

55 ALR6th 513—§ 8

State v. Pierce, 269 Conn. 442, 849 A.2d 375 (2004)

51 ALR6th 139—§ 6

State v. Pierce, 2002-Ohio-652, 2002 WL 337727 (Ohio Ct. App. 8th Dist. Cuyahoga County 2002)

70 ALR6th 361—§ 24

State v. Pierce, 2006 ME 75, 899 A.2d 801 (Me. 2006)

34 ALR6th 539—§ 4

101 ALR6th 1—§ 30

State v. Pierce, 2007-Ohio-2364, 2007 WL 1430197 (Ohio Ct. App. 2d Dist. Montgomery County 2007)

34 ALR6th 1—§ 8

State v. Pierre, 125 So. 3d 403 (La. 2013)

97 ALR6th 263—§ 13

State v. Pierre, 208 Mont. 430, 678 P.2d 650 (1984)

6 ALR6th 533—§ 19

State v. Pierre, 572 P.2d 1338 (Utah 1977)

16 ALR6th 329—§ 4

24 ALR6th 591—§ 4

State v. Pierro, 355 N.J. Super. 109, 809 A.2d 804 (App. Div. 2002)

32 ALR6th 385—§ 4

State v. Pierson, 201 Conn. 211, 514 A.2d 724 (1986)

46 ALR5th 499—§ 3

State v. Pierson, 239 Neb. 350, 476 N.W.2d 544 (1991)

33 ALR6th 407—§ 3, 11, 12

State v. Pierson, 554 N.W.2d 555 (Iowa Ct. App. 1996)

29 ALR6th 1—§ 10

State v. Pierson, 1997 WL 600589 (Minn. Ct. App. 1997)

103 ALR6th 347—§ 10

State v. Pierson, 2000 UT App. 274, 12 P.3d 103 (Utah Ct. App. 2000)

39 ALR5th 283—§ 4, 30

State v. Pierstorff, 213 Wis. 2d 486, 570 N.W.2d 912 (Ct. App. 1997)

117 ALR5th 491—§ 2, 5

State v. Pies, 140 Ohio App. 3d 535, 748 N.E.2d 146 (1st Dist. Hamilton County 2000)

34 ALR6th 1—§ 9

State v. Pietranton, 137 W. Va. 477, 72 S.E.2d 617 (1952)

57 ALR6th 445—§ 39

State v. Pietraszewski, 283 N.W.2d 887 (Minn. 1979)

45 ALR5th 767—§ 15

State v. Piette, 16 Conn. Supp. 357 (1949)

52 ALR5th 655—§ 3

State v. Piggott, 1985 WL 6569 (Ohio Ct. App. 4th Dist. Washington County 1985)

32 ALR6th 385—§ 7

State v. Pike, 118 Wash. 2d 585, 826 P.2d 152 (1992)

57 ALR6th 445—§ 3, 18

State v. Pike, 134 N.H. 690, 597 A.2d 1071 (1991)

4 ALR5th 1—§ 7, 19

State v. Pike, 139 N.C. App. 96, 532 S.E.2d 543 (2000)

47 ALR6th 107—§ 22

State v. Pike, 143 Vt. 283, 465 A.2d 1348 (1983)

60 ALR5th 1—§ 8

State v. Pike, 253 Ga. 304, 320 S.E.2d 355 (1984)

99 ALR6th 295—§ 5, 19

State v. Pike, 312 Mo. 27, 278 S.W. 725 (1925)

52 ALR5th 655—§ 3

State v. Piland, 58 N.C. App. 95, 293 S.E.2d 278 (1982)

1 ALR5th 938—§ 3

13 ALR5th 1—§ 12

50 ALR6th 353—§ 44

State v. Pilcher, 472 N.W.2d 327 (Minn. 1991)

69 ALR6th 579—§ 8

State v. Pilgram, 2005 WL 602380 (Tenn. Crim. App. 2005)

54 ALR6th 593—§ 12

State v. Pillar, 359 N.J. Super. 249, 820 A.2d 1 (App. Div. 2003)

39 ALR6th 257—§ 26

State v. Pillow, 1997 WL 271487 (Ohio Ct. App. 2d Dist. Greene County 1997)

63 ALR6th 1—§ 53

State v. Pilot, 1998 WL 297511 (Minn. Ct. App. 1998)

68 ALR5th 343—§ 3

State v. Piluso, 2009 WL 3488693 (N.J. Super. Ct. App. Div. 2009)

69 ALR6th 1—§ 27

State v. Pina, 49 Ohio App. 2d 394, 3 Ohio Ops. 3d 457, 361 N.E.2d 262 (Clark Co. 1975)

32 ALR5th 149—§ 3, 4, 15, 71, 72, 81, 82

State v. Pina, 94 Ariz. 243, 383 P.2d 167 (1963)

65 ALR5th 407—§ 11

State v. Pinardville Athletic Club, 134 N.H. 462, 594 A.2d 1284 (1991)

55 ALR6th 157—§ 101

State v. Pinero, 70 Hawaii 509, 778 P.2d 704 (1989)

26 ALR5th 603—§ 4

State v. Pingitore, 1996 WL 456020 (Wash. Ct. App. Div. 1 1996)

101 ALR6th 545—§ 5

State v. Pink, 236 Kan. 715, 696 P.2d 358 (1985)

39 ALR5th 283—§ 4, 18

State v. Pink, 648 N.W.2d 107 (Iowa 2002)

17 ALR6th 327—§ 42

State v. Pinkham, 141 N.H. 188, 679 A.2d 589 (1996)

60 ALR5th 1—§ 8

State v. Pinkston, 333 S.W.2d 63 (Mo. 1960)

104 ALR5th 357—§ 7, 8

54 ALR6th 429—§ 9

State v. Pinney, 2009 WL 2427967 (Vt. 2009)

58 ALR6th 215—§ 7

State v. Pintner, 2010-Ohio-818, 2010 WL 759218 (Ohio Ct. App. 9th Dist. Lorain County 2010)
69 ALR6th 1—§ 27
State v. Piper, 103 Kan. 794, 176 P. 626 (1918)
76 ALR5th 485—§ 3, 5
State v. Piper, 1997 WL 596507 (Wash. Ct. App. Div. 2 1997)
73 ALR5th 383—§ 27
State v. Piper, 2006 SD 1, 709 N.W.2d 783 (S.D. 2006)
21 ALR6th 1—§ 4
State v. Pipkins, 628 So. 2d 1242 (La. Ct. App. 3d Cir. 1993)
57 ALR5th 141—§ 4
State v. Pippin, 496 N.W.2d 50 (N.D. 1993)
15 ALR5th 391—§ 13
State v. Pires, 55 Wis. 2d 597, 201 N.W.2d 153 (1972)
58 ALR6th 499—§ 4, 100
State v. Pirtle, 127 Wash. 2d 628, 904 P.2d 245 (1995)
79 ALR5th 33—§ 51
State v. Pirtle, 652 S.W.2d 272 (Mo. App. 1983)
7 ALR5th 263—§ 6
State v. Pirtle, 2011 WI App 89, 334 Wis. 2d 211, 799 N.W.2d 492 (Ct. App. 2011)
102 ALR6th 279—§ 30
State v. Pisciotta, 968 S.W.2d 185 (Mo. Ct. App. W.D. 1998)
57 ALR5th 315—§ 4
58 ALR5th 749—§ 6
State v. Pisio, 119 N.M. 252, 889 P.2d 860 (App. 1994)
28 ALR5th 754—§ 5
State v. Pitman, 427 N.W.2d 337 (N.D. 1988)
34 ALR6th 1—§ 5
State v. Pitre, 506 So. 2d 930 (La. Ct. App. 1st Cir. 1987)
9 ALR6th 633—§ 5
14 ALR6th 517—§ 6
State v. Pitt, 209 Or. App. 270, 147 P.3d 940 (2006)

30 ALR6th 1—§ 3, 6
State v. Pitt, 2004 WL 2382156 (Minn. Ct. App. 2004)
78 ALR6th 599—§ 5
State v. Pittman, 209 Conn. 596, 553 A.2d 155 (1989)
32 ALR6th 1—§ 5
State v. Pittman, 332 N.C. 244, 420 S.E.2d 437 (1992)
31 ALR5th 704—§ 8
State v. Pittman, 731 S.W.2d 43 (Mo. App. 1987)
12 ALR5th 909—§ 5
State v. Pitts, 282 S.W.2d 561 (Mo. 1955)
97 ALR5th 293—§ 3, 10
State v. Pitts, 936 So. 2d 1111 (Fla. Dist. Ct. App. 2d Dist. 2006)
20 ALR6th 479—§ 18
29 ALR6th 1—§ 10
State v. Pitts, 2002-Ohio-6291, 2002 WL 31557381 (Ohio Ct. App. 9th Dist. Summit County 2002)
26 ALR6th 511—§ 35
State v. Pitts, 2003-Ohio-1740, 2003 WL 1786467 (Ohio Ct. App. 1st Dist. Hamilton County 2003)
69 ALR6th 1—§ 29
State v. Pitts, 2005-Ohio-5896, 2005 WL 2931967 (Ohio Ct. App. 3d Dist. Allen County 2005)
26 ALR6th 511—§ 19
State v. Pius, 118 N.J.L. 212, 192 A. 89 (N.J. Sup. Ct. 1937)
58 ALR6th 385—§ 4
State v. Pizel, 1999 UT App 270, 987 P.2d 1288 (Utah Ct. App. 1999)
92 ALR6th 1—§ 3, 9
State v. Pizzuto, 119 Idaho 742, 810 P.2d 680 (1991)
83 ALR6th 465—§ 12
State v. P.J. M., 2010 WL 3220138 (Minn. Ct. App. 2010)
69 ALR6th 1—§ 33
State v. P.L., 369 N.J. Super. 291, 848 A.2d 861 (App. Div. 2004)
70 ALR6th 1—§ 16

State v. Placke, 786 So. 2d 889 (La. Ct. App. 2d Cir. 2001)
98 ALR5th 353—§ 6

State v. Placzkiewicz, 2001 MT 254, 307 Mont. 189, 36 P.3d 934 (2001)
97 ALR6th 263—§ 11

State v. Plager, 2004 WL 144122 (Iowa Ct. App. 2004)
34 ALR6th 1—§ 8

State v. Plant, 28 Or. App. 771, 561 P.2d 647 (1977)
58 ALR6th 499—§ 4

State v. Plant, 236 Neb. 317, 461 N.W.2d 253 (1990)
58 ALR6th 499—§ 34

State v. Plant, 532 S.W.2d 900 (Mo. Ct. App. 1976)
51 ALR6th 1—§ 18
72 ALR6th 141—§ 7

State v. Plante, 651 A.2d 1239 (R.I. 1994)
39 ALR5th 283—§ 4, 64

State v. Plantz, 155 W. Va. 24, 180 S.E.2d 614 (1971)
55 ALR5th 125—§ 12, 15, 23

State v. Plath, 277 S.C. 126, 284 S.E.2d 221 (1981)
39 ALR5th 283—§ 3

State v. Platt, 130 Ariz. 570, 637 P.2d 1073 (Ct. App. Div. 2 1981)
62 ALR6th 413—§ 29

State v. Plaut, 124 N.H. 813, 474 A.2d 587 (1984)
5 ALR5th 243—§ 62

State v. Pleasant, 38 Wash. App. 78, 684 P.2d 761 (1984)
18 ALR5th 1—§ 2, 3

State v. Plemons, 216 P.3d 191 (Kan. Ct. App. 2009)
80 ALR6th 599—§ 9

State v. Pless, 1994 WL 530880 (Ohio Ct. App. 8th Dist.Cuyahoga County 1994)
57 ALR5th 141—§ 3

State v. Plotner, 283 Mo. 83, 222 S.W. 767 (1920)
108 ALR5th 593—§ 4

State v. Plowman, 314 Or. 157, 838 P.2d 558 (1992)
22 ALR5th 261—§ 2, 4, 6, 10

State v. Plude, 30 Conn. App. 527, 621 A.2d 1342 (1993)
46 ALR5th 499—§ 2, 3

State v. Pluim, 233 Wis. 2d 274, 2000 WI App 47, 610 N.W.2d 229 (Ct. App. 2000)
73 ALR6th 49—§ 6, 8

State v. Plumley, 368 S.E.2d 726 (W. Va. 1988)
39 ALR5th 283—§ 4, 75

State v. Plumley, 384 S.E.2d 130 (W. Va. 1989)
17 ALR5th 125—§ 3

State v. Plunkett, 62 Nev. 258, 149 P.2d 101 (1944)
73 ALR5th 615—§ 3, 6, 7

State v. P.M.J., 93 Wash. App. 1044, 1998 WL 898803 (Div. 1 1998)
9 ALR6th 541—§ 24

State v. Poag, 159 N.C. App. 312, 583 S.E.2d 661 (2003)
11 ALR6th 237—§ 10

State v. Pobcyn, 1980 WL 354992 (Ohio Ct. App. 8th Dist. Cuyahoga County 1980)
18 ALR6th 1—§ 25

State v. Poblete, 260 P.3d 1102 (Ariz. Ct. App. Div. 2 2011)
74 ALR6th 373—§ 23

State v. Pockert, 53 Wash. App. 491, 768 P.2d 504 (Div. 3 1989)
54 ALR6th 429—§ 18

State v. Podell, 189 Wis. 457, 207 N.W. 709 (1926)
3 ALR6th 49—§ 17

State v. Podzimek, 2010 SD 17, 779 N.W.2d 407 (S.D. 2010)
57 ALR6th 445—§ 41

State v. Poe, 271 Neb. 858, 717 N.W.2d 463 (2006)
72 ALR6th 227—§ 57

State v. Poehnelt, 150 Ariz. 136, 722 P.2d 304 (Ct. App. Div. 2 1985)
72 ALR5th 109—§ 4, 5

State v. Poellinger, 153 Wis. 2d 493, 451 N.W.2d 752 (1990)

6 ALR5th 733—§ 15

State v. Poganski, 257 N.W.2d 578 (Minn. 1977)

24 ALR6th 1—§ 9

State v. Pogue, 2005 WL 1315773 (Tenn. Crim. App. 2005)

26 ALR6th 511—§ 22

State v. Pohlable, 1998 WL 281337 (Ohio Ct. App. 12th Dist. Butler County 1998)

78 ALR5th 489—§ 3

State v. Poirier, 1997 ME 86, 694 A.2d 448 (Me. 1997)

78 ALR5th 1—§ 51

State v. Poissant, 2009-Ohio-4235, 2009 WL 2579574 (Ohio Ct. App. 5th Dist. Fairfield County 2009)

63 ALR6th 351—§ 3

State v. Poitra, 206 Or. App. 207, 136 P.3d 87 (2006)

30 ALR6th 1—§ 3, 6

State v. Poitra, 2010 ND 137, 785 N.W.2d 225 (N.D. 2010)

93 ALR6th 275—§ 12

State v. Pokini, 57 Haw. 17, 548 P.2d 1397 (1976)

104 ALR5th 357—§ 4

State v. Pokorny, 458 A.2d 1212 (Me. 1983)

9 ALR6th 633—§ 4, 5

13 ALR6th 603—§ 6

State v. Polan, 78 Ariz. 253, 278 P.2d 432 (1954)

11 ALR5th 497—§ 3, 30

State v. Polanco, 658 So. 2d 1123, 102 Ed. Law Rep. 1238 (Fla. Dist. Ct. App. 3d Dist. 1995)

59 ALR6th 393—§ 10

State v. Poland, 132 Ariz. 269, 645 P.2d 784 (1982)

97 ALR5th 201—§ 3, 6

State v. Polen, 1998 WL 404207 (Ohio Ct. App. 7th Dist. Carroll County 1998)

29 ALR6th 237—§ 4, 8, 9

State v. Polhamus, 62 Ohio L. Abs. 113, 106 N.E.2d 646 (Ct. App. 2d Dist. Miami County 1951)

39 ALR6th 257—§ 37

State v. Poling, 207 W. Va. 299, 531 S.E.2d 678 (2000)

1 ALR5th 938—§ 3

State v. Poling, 1992 WL 38447 (Ohio Ct. App. 4th Dist. Hocking County 1992)

78 ALR6th 599—§ 11

State v. Politte, 136 Ariz. 117, 664 P.2d 661 (Ct. App. Div. 2 1982)

19 ALR6th 115—§ 4, 7, 10

State v. Polk, 119 Ohio App. 3d 638, 695 N.E.2d 1224 (3d Dist. Auglaize County 1997)

15 ALR5th 391—§ 45

State v. Polk, 376 So. 2d 151 (La. 1979)

62 ALR5th 121—§ 7

State v. Polk, 864 S.W.2d 1 (Mo. Ct. App. W.D. 1993)

1 ALR6th 549—§ 20

State v. Pollard, 80 Wash. App. 60, 906 P.2d 976 (1995)

22 ALR5th 261—§ 4, 10

State v. Pollard, 556 So. 2d 1145, 15 FLW 3 (Fla. App. D2 1989)

45 ALR5th 767—§ 15

State v. Pollard, 886 N.E.2d 69 (Ind. Ct. App. 2008)

40 ALR6th 419—§ 18

State v. Pollard, 908 N.E.2d 1145 (Ind. 2009)

63 ALR6th 351—§ 4

State v. Pollard, 941 S.W.2d 831 (Mo. Ct. App. W.D. 1997)

18 ALR5th 1—§ 3

State v. Polley, 34 S.D. 565, 138 N.W. 300 (1912)

27 ALR6th 403—§ 5, 20

State v. Pollman, 109 Kan. 791, 201 P. 1101 (1921)

108 ALR5th 593—§ 16

State v. Pollnow, 141 Wis. 2d 980, 415 N.W.2d 863 (Ct. App. 1987)

85 ALR5th 1—§ 16

State v. Pollock, 22 N.C. App. 214, 206
S.E.2d 382 (1974)
32 ALR6th 1—§ 4
35 ALR6th 127—§ 4
State v. Pollock, 105 Mo. App. 273, 79
S.W. 980 (1904)
57 ALR6th 445—§ 48
State v. Pollock, 914 S.W.2d 1 (Mo.
App. 1995)
50 ALR5th 703—§ 7
State v. Polyascko, 224 Neb. 272, 397
N.W.2d 633 (1986)
39 ALR6th 257—§ 37
State v. Polzin, 197 Wash. 612, 85 P.2d
1057 (1939)
57 ALR6th 445—§ 20
State v. Pomeroy, 30 Or. 16, 46 P. 797
(1896)
29 ALR5th 59—§ 46
State v. Pometti, 12 N.J. 446, 97 A.2d
399 (1953)
9 ALR6th 633—§ 11
15 ALR6th 173—§ 44
State v. Pona, 926 A.2d 592 (R.I. 2007)
72 ALR6th 437—§ 3, 6
State v. Ponce, 1996 WL 589267 (Ohio
Ct. App. 10th Dist. Franklin County
1996)
101 ALR5th 187—§ 5, 6
State v. Poncelet, 187 Mont. 528, 610
P.2d 698 (1980)
66 ALR5th 135—§ 41
State v. Pond, 131 S.W.3d 792 (Mo.
2004)
1 ALR6th 549—§ 8, 25
State v. Pondexter, 225 Kan. 425, 590
P.2d 1074 (1979)
82 ALR6th 317—§ 3, 14
State v. Pontbriand, 178 Vt. 120, 878
A.2d 227 (2005)
20 ALR6th 479—§ 3
State v. Pontbriand, 178 Vt. 120, 878
A.2d 227, 25 A.L.R.6th 763 (2005)
**25 ALR6th 379—§ 3, 6, 13, 17, 21,
34**
State v. Pontelandolfo, 227 N.J. Super.
419, 547 A.2d 738 (Law Div. 1988)

107 ALR5th 567—§ 9
State v. Pontery, 19 N.J. 457, 117 A.2d
473 (1955)
67 ALR5th 637—§ 3, 7
State v. Pontier, 95 Idaho 707, 518 P.2d
969 (1974)
62 ALR6th 413—§ 39
State v. Pool, 98 N.M. 704, 652 P.2d 254
(Ct. App. 1982)
122 ALR5th 439—§ 3
State v. Poole, 131 Wis. 2d 359, 394
N.W.2d 909 (Ct. App. 1986)
9 ALR6th 541—§ 17
State v. Poole, 197 N.C. App. 630, 680
S.E.2d 270 (2009)
68 ALR6th 115—§ 3
State v. Poole, 945 S.W.2d 93 (Tenn.
1997)
73 ALR5th 383—§ 3
State v. Pooler, 255 N.W.2d 328 (Iowa
1977)
18 ALR5th 1—§ 2, 22
State v. Pope, 6 Conn. Cir. Ct. 712, 313
A.2d 84 (App. Div. 1972)
84 ALR6th 427—§ 3
State v. Pope, 110 Mo. App. 520, 85
S.W. 633 (1905)
97 ALR5th 537—§ 38
State v. Pope, 163 N.C. App. 486, 593
S.E.2d 813 (2004)
55 ALR6th 157—§ 114
State v. Pope, 190 Neb. 689, 211 N.W.2d
923 (1973)
97 ALR5th 201—§ 3
State v. Pope, 603 N.W.2d 749 (Wis. Ct.
App. 1999)
85 ALR5th 1—§ 46
State v. Pope, 2003 MT 330, 318 Mont.
383, 80 P.3d 1232 (2003)
125 ALR5th 497—§ 4
97 ALR6th 263—§ 3, 16
State v. Pope, 2010-Ohio-1749, 2010
WL 1610935 (Ohio Ct. App. 8th
Dist. Cuyahoga County 2010)
92 ALR6th 171—§ 18
State v. Poplin, 56 N.C. App. 304, 289
S.E.2d 124 (1982)

34 ALR5th 125—§ 3, 8
State v. Poppe, 131 Or. App. 14, 883
P.2d 905 (1994)
45 ALR6th 643—§ 9
State v. Porras, 125 Ariz. 490, 610 P.2d
1051 (App. 1980)
26 ALR5th 1—§ 3
State v. Port Clinton Fish Co., 43 Ohio
St. 3d 93, 538 N.E.2d 1055 (1989)
50 ALR5th 703—§ 33
State v. Porter, 5 Wash. App. 460, 488
P.2d 773 (Div. 2 1971)
68 ALR5th 343—§ 3
State v. Porter, 41 La. Ann. 402, 6 So.
337 (1889)
105 ALR5th 529—§ 11
State v. Porter, 94 P.3d 737 (Kan. Ct.
App. 2004)
26 ALR6th 511—§ 25
State v. Porter, 112 Wash. App. 1038,
2002 WL 1505638 (Div. 1 2002)
1 ALR6th 549—§ 7
State v. Porter, 130 Idaho 772, 948 P.2d
127 (1997)
72 ALR6th 1—§ 7
83 ALR6th 465—§ 12, 43, 50
State v. Porter, 143 Mont. 528, 391 P.2d
704 (1964)
24 ALR6th 747—§ 17, 18, 28, 40
State v. Porter, 150 Wash. 2d 732, 82
P.3d 234 (2004)
2 ALR6th 551—§ 11
State v. Porter, 228 Kan. 345, 615 P.2d
146 (1980)
59 ALR5th 1—§ 3, 5, 6
State v. Porter, 235 Neb. 476, 455
N.W.2d 787 (1990)
82 ALR5th 359—§ 2
83 ALR5th 277—§ 2
84 ALR5th 487—§ 2
State v. Porter, 241 Conn. 57, 698 A.2d
739 (1997)
90 ALR5th 453—§ 6
10 ALR6th 463—§ 4, 8
103 ALR6th 247—§ 18
State v. Porter, 303 N.C. 680, 281 S.E.2d
377 (1981)

81 ALR5th 563—§ 5
State v. Porter, 312 Or. 112, 817 P.2d
1306 (1991)
97 ALR6th 653—§ 30
State v. Porter, 326 N.C. 489, 391 S.E.2d
144 (1990)
**20 ALR5th 398—§ 12, 14, 20, 26,
38, 49, 50, 64**
State v. Porter, 587 A.2d 188 (Del.
Super. 1990)
57 ALR5th 141—§ 3
State v. Porter, 615 So. 2d 1073 (La. Ct.
App. 4th Cir. 1993)
85 ALR5th 547—§ 8
State v. Porter, 659 So. 2d 328 (Fla. Dist.
Ct. App. 3d Dist. 1995)
113 ALR5th 597—§ 8
State v. Porter, 755 S.W.2d 3 (Mo. Ct.
App. W.D. 1988)
115 ALR5th 509—§ 9
State v. Porter, 940 S.W.2d 391 (Tex.
App. Austin 1997)
61 ALR5th 1—§ 5
State v. Porter, 1992 WL 15972 (Ohio
Ct. App. 9th Dist. Summit County
1992)
99 ALR6th 295—§ 13
State v. Porter, 2012 WI App 97, 820
N.W.2d 156 (Wis. Ct. App. 2012)
92 ALR6th 171—§ 16
State v. Porter, Slip Op. No. 45-CA-82
(Ohio App. Fairfield Co. 1983)
38 ALR5th 433—§ 19
State v. Portes, 840 A.2d 1131 (R.I.
2004)
58 ALR6th 499—§ 63
State v. Portigue, 125 N.H. 338, 480
A.2d 896 (1984)
31 ALR6th 465—§ 3, 11, 15, 33
State v. Portigue, 125 N.H. 352, 481
A.2d 534 (1984)
29 ALR6th 1—§ 10
31 ALR6th 465—§ 11, 21, 31, 33
State v. Portis, 187 Ariz. 336, 929 P.2d
687 (Ct. App. Div. 1 1996)
21 ALR6th 771—§ 23
State v. Posenjak, 127 Wash. App. 41,
111 P.3d 1206 (Div. 3 2005)

For assistance, call 1-800-328-4880

28 ALR6th 505—§ 9

State v. Post, 118 Wash. 2d 596, 826 P.2d 172 (1992)

38 ALR6th 97—§ 29

State v. Post, 197 Wis. 2d 279, 541 N.W.2d 115 (1995)

87 ALR6th 633—§ 7

State v. Post, 286 N.W.2d 195 (Iowa 1979)

36 ALR5th 255—§ 30

State v. Posta, 37 Ohio App. 3d 144, 524 N.E.2d 920 (8th Dist. Cuyahoga County 1988)

9 ALR6th 633—§ 4

13 ALR6th 603—§ 40

State v. Postell, 735 So. 2d 782 (La. Ct. App. 4th Cir. 1999)

4 ALR5th 1—§ 14

State v. Poster, 892 So. 2d 1071 (Fla. Dist. Ct. App. 2d Dist. 2004)

58 ALR6th 215—§ 12

State v. Posthuma, 204 Wis. 2d 108, 552 N.W.2d 897 (Ct. App. 1996)

85 ALR5th 595—§ 3

State v. Poteet, 692 P.2d 760 (Utah 1984)

5 ALR5th 243—§ 61

State v. Potskowski, 298 N.Y. 299, 83 N.E.2d 125 (1948)

5 ALR5th 243—§ 51

State v. Potter, 72 S.W.3d 307 (Mo. Ct. App. S.D. 2002)

104 ALR5th 165—§ 16

State v. Potter, 109 Idaho 967, 712 P.2d 668 (Ct. App. 1985)

115 ALR5th 509—§ 2

State v. Potter, 148 Vt. 53, 529 A.2d 163 (1987)

104 ALR5th 165—§ 12

State v. Potter, 197 W. Va. 734, 478 S.E.2d 742 (1996)

93 ALR5th 327—§ 3, 4, 6 to 8, 29

101 ALR5th 619—§ 2

State v. Potter, 747 S.W.2d 300 (Mo. Ct. App. S.D. 1988)

71 ALR5th 637—§ 7

State v. Potter, 1998 WL 748722 (Ohio Ct. App. 2d Dist. Montgomery County 1998)

34 ALR6th 1—§ 10

State v. Pottios, 564 A.2d 64 (Me. 1989)

5 ALR5th 243—§ 58

State v. Potts, 93 Wash. App. 82, 969 P.2d 494 (Div. 3 1998)

40 ALR5th 113—§ 4

State v. Potts, 132 Idaho 865, 979 P.2d 1223 (Ct. App. 1999)

9 ALR6th 541—§ 29

State v. Potts, 205 Kan. 42, 468 P.2d 74 (1970)

55 ALR6th 157—§ 7, 26

State v. Potts, 2006-Ohio-2100, 2006 WL 1118930 (Ohio Ct. App. 5th Dist. Richland County 2006)

71 ALR6th 625—§ 3

State v. Pough, 2002-Ohio-6927, 2002 WL 31813100 (Ohio Ct. App. 11th Dist. Trumbull County 2002)

71 ALR6th 1—§ 12

State v. Poulin, 620 N.W.2d 287 (Iowa 2000)

73 ALR6th 1—§ 5

State v. Poulson, 150 Or. App. 164, 945 P.2d 1084 (1997)

113 ALR5th 517—§ 6

State v. Pounds, 176 Wis. 2d 315, 500 N.W.2d 373 (Ct. App. 1993)

34 ALR6th 1—§ 9

State v. Powasnik, 918 P.2d 146, 291 Utah Adv. Rep. 24 (Utah App. 1996)

27 ALR5th 593—§ 35

State v. Powell, 45 Kan. App. 2d 1090, 257 P.3d 1244 (2011)

93 ALR6th 275—§ 13

State v. Powell, 49 Ohio St. 3d 255, 552 N.E.2d 191 (1990)

20 ALR5th 177—§ 3, 8 to 10

39 ALR5th 283—§ 14, 47

State v. Powell, 55 Or. App. 27, 637 P.2d 174 (1981)

109 ALR5th 611—§ 3

State v. Powell, 55 S.W.2d 334 (Mo. Ct. App. 1932)

54 ALR6th 429—§ 9

State v. Powell, 96 N.M. 569, 632 P.2d 1207 (Ct. App. 1981)

113 ALR5th 517—§ 7

State v. Powell, 126 Wash. 2d 244, 893 P.2d 615 (1995)

24 ALR5th 465—§ 107, 108, 115, 116

57 ALR5th 141—§ 6

State v. Powell, 162 Wash. App. 1071, 2011 WL 3330171 (Div. 2 2011)

103 ALR6th 347—§ 4

State v. Powell, 182 N.J. Super. 386, 440 A.2d 1377 (1981)

29 ALR5th 59—§ 7

State v. Powell, 274 Kan. 618, 56 P.3d 189 (2002)

55 ALR6th 157—§ 7, 76

71 ALR6th 625—§ 10, 22, 36

State v. Powell, 318 S.W.3d 297 (Mo. Ct. App. W.D. 2010)

82 ALR6th 373—§ 4, 9

State v. Powell, 336 N.C. 762, 446 S.E.2d 26 (1994)

90 ALR5th 619—§ 2

State v. Powell, 340 N.C. 674, 459 S.E.2d 219 (1995)

102 ALR6th 279—§ 25

State v. Powell, 438 So. 2d 1306 (La. Ct. App. 3d Cir. 1983)

103 ALR6th 507—§ 27

State v. Powell, 585 S.W.2d 302 (Mo. Ct. App. W.D. 1979)

70 ALR5th 587—§ 19

State v. Powell, 591 A.2d 1306 (Me. 1991)

74 ALR5th 319—§ 14

State v. Powell, 598 So. 2d 454 (La. App. 2d Cir. 1992)

9 ALR5th 369—§ 3, 14, 19

State v. Powell, 640 A.2d 209 (Me. 1994)

28 ALR6th 505—§ 9

State v. Powell, 696 So. 2d 789 (Fla. Dist. Ct. App. 2d Dist. 1997)

113 ALR5th 597—§ 3

State v. Powell, 793 S.W.2d 505 (Mo. Ct. App. E.D. 1990)

18 ALR5th 804—§ 4, 10, 16, 19

72 ALR5th 109—§ 4

State v. Powell, 798 S.W.2d 709 (Mo. 1990)

20 ALR5th 177—§ 3

State v. Powell, 971 S.W.2d 577 (Tex. App. Dallas 1998)

70 ALR6th 361—§ 31

71 ALR6th 335—§ 10

State v. Powell, 998 So. 2d 531 (Fla. 2008)

46 ALR6th 495—§ 13

State v. Powell, 1999 WL 333303 (Ohio Ct. App. 5th Dist. Stark County 1999)

78 ALR5th 489—§ 3, 10

State v. Powell, 2000 WL 621137 (Tenn. Crim. App. 2000)

34 ALR6th 1—§ 10

State v. Powers, 78 Wash. App. 264, 896 P.2d 754 (Div. 3 1995)

106 ALR5th 377—§ 4

State v. Powers, 100 Idaho 614, 603 P.2d 569 (1979)

22 ALR5th 660—§ 6, 11

State v. Powers, 331 S.C. 37, 501 S.E.2d 116 (1998)

79 ALR5th 33—§ 52

State v. Powers, 654 N.W.2d 667 (Minn. 2003)

16 ALR6th 329—§ 4

24 ALR6th 591—§ 5, 12

State v. Powers, 2002-Ohio-6672, 2002 WL 31730985 (Ohio Ct. App. 5th Dist. Fairfield County 2002)

69 ALR6th 1—§ 3

70 ALR6th 1—§ 3

State v. Prade, 126 Ohio St. 3d 27, 2010-Ohio-1842, 930 N.E.2d 287 (2010)

72 ALR6th 227—§ 32, 48

State v. Prade, 139 Ohio App. 3d 676, 745 N.E.2d 475 (9th Dist. Summit County 2000)

1 ALR6th 657—§ 14

State v. Prasertphong, 206 Ariz. 70, 75 P.3d 675 (2003)

27 ALR6th 183—§ 31

41 ALR6th 295—§ 8

State v. Prasertphong, 210 Ariz. 496, 114 P.3d 828 (2005)
  27 ALR6th 183—§ 31
  41 ALR6th 295—§ 8
State v. Prater, 958 P.2d 1110 (Alaska Ct. App. 1998)
  84 ALR6th 293—§ 3, 6
State v. Prater, 1999 WL 74548 (Tenn. Crim. App. 1999)
  89 ALR5th 539—§ 14
State v. Prater, 2002-Ohio-4487, 2002 WL 2005708 (Ohio Ct. App. 12th Dist. Warren County 2002)
  113 ALR5th 517—§ 22
State v. Pratt, 114 Kan. 660, 220 P. 505, 34 A.L.R. 189 (1923)
  117 ALR5th 1—§ 4
State v. Pratt, 284 Md. 516, 398 A.2d 421 (1979)
  66 ALR6th 83—§ 10
State v. Pratt, 309 Or. 205, 785 P.2d 350 (1990)
  101 ALR6th 331—§ 21
State v. Pratt, 754 So. 2d 355 (La. Ct. App. 2d Cir. 2000)
  39 ALR5th 283—§ 62
  98 ALR6th 455—§ 8
State v. Pratt, 1988 WL 100481 (Minn. Ct. App. 1988)
  73 ALR5th 383—§ 5
State v. Pratt, 2000 WL 1281217 (Ohio Ct. App. 4th Dist. Pickaway County 2000)
  56 ALR6th 323—§ 7
State v. Prawitt, 2011 UT App 261, 262 P.3d 1203 (Utah Ct. App. 2011)
  92 ALR6th 295—§ 19
  93 ALR6th 207—§ 6, 9
  95 ALR6th 1—§ 5
  96 ALR6th 355—§ 6, 26, 36, 37, 49, 60
State v. Predka, 555 N.W.2d 202 (Iowa 1996)
  114 ALR5th 173—§ 6
State v. Preferred Acci. Ins. Co., 149 So. 2d 632 (La. App. 1st Cir. 1963)
  44 ALR5th 683—§ 17

State v. Prendergast, 103 Haw. 451, 83 P.3d 714 (2004)
  84 ALR6th 293—§ 8, 25
State v. Prentice, 170 N.C. App. 593, 613 S.E.2d 498 (2005)
  52 ALR6th 1—§ 5
  53 ALR6th 1—§ 5
State v. Prentiss, 669 N.W.2d 260 (Iowa Ct. App. 2003)
  124 ALR5th 1—§ 5
State v. Presgraves, 174 W. Va. 683, 328 S.E.2d 699 (1985)
  34 ALR5th 125—§ 10
State v. Presgraves, 1993 WL 218384 (Ohio App. Perry Co. 1993)
  52 ALR5th 655—§ 3
State v. Presidential Women's Center, 707 So. 2d 1145 (Fla. Dist. Ct. App. 4th Dist. 1998)
  119 ALR5th 315—§ 4, 10
State v. Presley, 300 Minn. 556, 220 N.W.2d 486 (1974)
  40 ALR6th 1—§ 33
State v. Presley, 364 N.W.2d 420 (Minn. Ct. App. 1985)
  73 ALR5th 383—§ 5
State v. Presley, 758 So. 2d 308, 93 A.L.R.5th 795 (La. Ct. App. 3d Cir. 2000)
  93 ALR5th 683—§ 4
State v. Presley, 2003-Ohio-6069, 2003 WL 22681425 (Ohio Ct. App. 10th Dist. Franklin County 2003)
  82 ALR6th 373—§ 9, 16
State v. Prestegard, 108 Wash. App. 14, 28 P.3d 817 (Div. 2 2001)
  33 ALR6th 91—§ 10, 45
State v. Preston, 38 Wis. 2d 582, 157 N.W.2d 615 (1968)
  25 ALR6th 1—§ 3
  26 ALR6th 1—§ 3, 25
State v. Preston, 41 Kan. App. 2d 981, 207 P.3d 1081 (2009)
  56 ALR6th 1—§ 29
State v. Preston, 66 Wash. App. 494, 832 P.2d 513 (1992)
  18 ALR5th 542—§ 5

State v. Preston, 142 Ohio App. 3d 619, 756 N.E.2d 705 (12th Dist. Butler County 2001)
89 ALR6th 565—§ 28, 30, 32, 34
State v. Preston, 150 Vt. 511, 555 A.2d 360 (1988)
124 ALR5th 1—§ 4
State v. Preston, 411 A.2d 402 (Me. 1980)
34 ALR6th 1—§ 7
State v. Prestwich, 110 Idaho 966, 719 P.2d 1226 (App. 1986)
41 ALR5th 171—§ 6, 10
State v. Prestwich, 116 Idaho 959, 783 P.2d 298 (1989)
19 ALR5th 470—§ 12
State v. Prevette, 317 N.C. 148, 345 S.E.2d 159 (1986)
39 ALR5th 283—§ 4, 77
State v. Prevo, 178 N.C. 740, 101 S.E. 370 (1919)
56 ALR5th 171—§ 5, 10, 28
State v. Prewitt, 136 Idaho 547, 38 P.3d 126 (Ct. App. 2001)
15 ALR6th 515—§ 4, 22
79 ALR6th 1—§ 69
State v. Pribil, 224 Neb. 28, 395 N.W.2d 543 (1986)
5 ALR5th 243—§ 57
State v. Price, 60 Ohio St. 2d 136, 14 Ohio Ops. 3d 379, 398 N.E.2d 772 (1979)
39 ALR5th 283—§ 14, 66
State v. Price, 88 Wash. App. 1021, 1997 WL 704912 (Div. 3 1997)
15 ALR6th 515—§ 16
State v. Price, 118 N.C. App. 212, 454 S.E.2d 820 (1995)
3 ALR6th 269—§ 25
State v. Price, 123 Ariz. 197, 598 P.2d 1016 (App. 1979)
34 ALR5th 125—§ 9
State v. Price, 165 Ohio App. 3d 198, 2006-Ohio-180, 845 N.E.2d 559 (1st Dist. Hamilton County 2006)
72 ALR6th 227—§ 40
State v. Price, 165 S.W.3d 568 (Mo. Ct. App. S.D. 2005)

24 ALR6th 549—§ 4, 6
State v. Price, 202 Neb. 308, 275 N.W.2d 82 (1979)
3 ALR6th 269—§ 22
State v. Price, 215 Kan. 718, 529 P.2d 85 (1974)
83 ALR5th 277—§ 9, 11
84 ALR5th 487—§ 24, 25
State v. Price, 252 Neb. 365, 562 N.W.2d 340 (1997)
110 ALR5th 329—§ 6
State v. Price, 454 S.E.2d 820 (N.C. App. 1995)
15 ALR5th 391—§ 5
State v. Price, 476 So. 2d 989 (La. App. 1st Cir. 1985)
55 ALR5th 125—§ 3, 12, 21, 22
State v. Price, 772 S.W.2d 9 (Mo. App. 1989)
6 ALR5th 733—§ 4, 18
State v. Prickett, 217 Minn. 629, 15 N.W.2d 95 (1944)
50 ALR5th 703—§ 16
State v. Pride, 1 S.W.3d 494 (Mo. Ct. App. W.D. 1999)
108 ALR5th 593—§ 41
64 ALR6th 655—§ 7, 9
State v. Priest, 2002-Ohio-6787, 2002 WL 31761682 (Ohio Ct. App. 2d Dist. Montgomery County 2002)
31 ALR6th 49—§ 4
State v. Prieto, 172 Ariz. 298, 836 P.2d 1008 (Ct. App. Div. 1 1992)
92 ALR5th 35—§ 20
State v. Prim, 201 Neb. 279, 267 N.W.2d 193 (1978)
9 ALR6th 1—§ 22
State v. Prince, 39 N.C. App. 685, 251 S.E.2d 631 (1979)
29 ALR5th 59—§ 3, 14, 19
State v. Prince, 52 Ohio Misc. 93, 6 Ohio Op. 3d 265, 369 N.E.2d 823 (C.P. 1977)
6 ALR6th 533—§ 11
State v. Prince, 93 Or. App. 106, 760 P.2d 1356 (1988)
112 ALR5th 429—§ 12

State v. Prince, 126 N.M. 547
  66 ALR5th 397—§ 17
State v. Prince, 140 N.J. Super. 418, 356 A.2d 428 (App. Div. 1976)
  105 ALR5th 529—§ 31
State v. Prince, 160 Ariz. 268, 772 P.2d 1121, 32 Ariz. Adv. Rep. 12 (1989)
  57 ALR5th 141—§ 5
State v. Prince, 176 Wis. 2d 510, 502 N.W.2d 617 (Ct. App. 1993)
  58 ALR6th 215—§ 12
State v. Prince, 335 S.C. 466, 517 S.E.2d 229 (Ct. App. 1999)
  29 ALR5th 487—§ 11.5
State v. Prince, 1988 WL 23027 (Tenn. Crim. App. 1988)
  103 ALR6th 507—§ 8
State v. Prior, 662 A.2d 225 (Me. 1995)
  47 ALR6th 107—§ 3
State v. Pritchard, 79 Wash. App. 14, 900 P.2d 560 (Div. 2 1995)
  74 ALR5th 453—§ 6
State v. Pritchard, No. 53238 (December 24, 1987, Ct. App. Ohio, 8th App. Dist. Cuyahoga Co.)
  39 ALR5th 283—§ 14, 47
State v. Pritchett, 12 Wash. App. 673, 530 P.2d 1348 (1975)
  13 ALR5th 118—§ 7
State v. Pritchett, 621 S.W.2d 127 (Tenn. 1981)
  65 ALR5th 407—§ 3, 11, 12, 17
State v. Pritzlaff, 441 N.W.2d 756 (Wis. Ct. App. 1989)
  56 ALR6th 323—§ 11
State v. Prober, 98 Wis. 2d 345, 297 N.W.2d 1 (1980)
  11 ALR5th 52—§ 2, 10
State v. Probst, 247 Kan. 196, 795 P.2d 393 (1990)
  113 ALR5th 517—§ 7
State v. Prociv, 417 N.W.2d 840 (N.D. 1988)
  6 ALR5th 733—§ 10, 16
State v. Procter, 51 Ohio App. 2d 151, 5 Ohio Ops. 3d 309, 367 N.E.2d 908 (Scioto Co. 1977)

  54 ALR5th 141—§ 3, 9, 10
State v. Proctor, 16 Wash. App. 865, 559 P.2d 1363 (Div. 1 1977)
  92 ALR6th 1—§ 5, 8
State v. Proctor, 94 Or. App. 720, 767 P.2d 453 (1989)
  9 ALR5th 369—§ 2, 3, 9
State v. Proctor, 2000 WL 1251969 (Ohio Ct. App. 12th Dist. Butler County 2000)
  29 ALR6th 237—§ 24
State v. Proffitt, 1995 WL 579218 (Minn. Ct. App. 1995)
  69 ALR6th 579—§ 8, 14, 28
State v. Profit, 323 N.W.2d 34 (Minn. 1982)
  73 ALR5th 383—§ 5
State v. Profit, 591 N.W.2d 451 (Minn. 1999)
  121 ALR5th 551—§ 3, 5, 6, 9, 12
State v. Progressive Farmer Co., 257 Ala. 564, 60 So. 2d 144 (1952)
  89 ALR5th 493—§ 14
State v. Progue, 243 La. 337, 144 So. 2d 352 (1962)
  16 ALR6th 329—§ 4
  24 ALR6th 591—§ 4
State v. Prokaeva, 2003 WL 453345 (Minn. Ct. App. 2003)
  34 ALR6th 1—§ 12
State v. Property Seized From Jorge L. Rios, 478 N.W.2d 870 (Iowa Ct. App. 1991)
  104 ALR5th 229—§ 4
  115 ALR5th 403—§ 5
  4 ALR6th 113—§ 7, 23, 37
  34 ALR6th 539—§ 5
  101 ALR6th 1—§ 9, 16, 40
State v. Property Seized from Terrance Martin, 37 So. 3d 1021 (La. Ct. App. 1st Cir. 2010)
  101 ALR6th 1—§ 21
State v. Propotnik, 2008 WL 434580 (Minn. Ct. App. 2008)
  81 ALR6th 505—§ 65
State v. Prosper, 21 Kan. App. 2d 956, 910 P.2d 859 (1996)
  27 ALR5th 593—§ 7, 23

State v. Prosper, 260 Kan. 743, 926 P.2d 231 (1996)

27 ALR5th 593—§ 22, 23, 31

State v. Prosser, 2003-Ohio-5516, 2003 WL 22358564 (Ohio Ct. App. 1st Dist. Hamilton County 2003)

69 ALR6th 1—§ 30

State v. Provencher, 119 N.H. 756, 407 A.2d 369 (1979)

52 ALR5th 655—§ 9

State v. Provoid, 110 N.J. Super. 547, 266 A.2d 307 (App. Div. 1970)

67 ALR5th 637—§ 3, 11

State v. Provost, 490 N.W.2d 93 (Minn. 1992)

35 ALR6th 127—§ 3, 22

State v. Prowell, 834 S.W.2d 852 (Mo. App. 1992)

27 ALR5th 593—§ 7, 8, 12

State v. Prudden, 212 N.J. Super. 608, 515 A.2d 1260 (App. Div. 1986)

29 ALR6th 1—§ 18

State v. Prudden, 515 A.2d 1260 (N.J. Super. AD 1986)

57 ALR5th 141—§ 3

State v. Prude, 76 Miss. 543, 24 So. 871 (1899)

64 ALR5th 671—§ 17

State v. Prudhomme, 532 So. 2d 234 (La. App. 3d Cir. 1988)

34 ALR5th 125—§ 19

State v. Prudhomme, 532 So. 2d 234 (La. Ct. App. 3d Cir. 1988)

19 ALR6th 115—§ 4, 9, 10

State v. Pruett, 144 Mo. 92, 45 S.W. 1114 (1898)

34 ALR5th 723—§ 3

State v. Pruett, 788 S.W.2d 559 (Tenn. 1990)

52 ALR5th 655—§ 2

State v. Pruitt, 97 Ohio App. 3d 258, 646 N.E.2d 547 (11th Dist. Trumbull County 1994)

103 ALR5th 463—§ 5

State v. Pruitt, 145 Wash. App. 784, 187 P.3d 326 (Div. 1 2008)

78 ALR6th 1—§ 3

State v. Pruitt, 449 So. 2d 154 (La. Ct. App. 4th Cir. 1984)

66 ALR5th 135—§ 39

State v. Pruitt, 479 S.W.2d 785 (Mo. 1972)

55 ALR5th 125—§ 7
101 ALR6th 331—§ 12

State v. Pruitt, 777 P.2d 277 (Kan. 1989)

39 ALR5th 283—§ 4, 41

State v. Prunchak, 2007-Ohio-3272, 2007 WL 1848831 (Ohio Ct. App. 8th Dist. Cuyahoga County 2007)

51 ALR6th 139—§ 7

State v. Prunier, 28 Conn. App. 612, 613 A.2d 311 (1992)

22 ALR5th 1—§ 4, 10, 26, 29, 33, 42

State v. Pruser, 127 N.J.L. 97, 21 A.2d 641 (N.J. Sup. Ct. 1941)

5 ALR6th 1—§ 40

State v. Pruss, 145 Idaho 623, 181 P.3d 1231 (2008)

67 ALR6th 531—§ 39

State v. Prutting, 40 Conn. App. 151, 669 A.2d 1228 (1996)

99 ALR6th 295—§ 13

State v. Przeradski, 5 Hawaii App. 29, 677 P.2d 471 (1984)

51 ALR5th 375—§ 3, 5

State v. Public Utility Com'n of Texas, 246 S.W.3d 324 (Tex. App. Austin 2008)

80 ALR6th 1—§ 2, 12, 18, 23, 24, 36, 38 to 41, 61, 62, 71, 91

State v. Public Utility Com'n of Texas, 344 S.W.3d 349 (Tex. 2011)

80 ALR6th 1—§ 12, 16, 18, 36, 38, 67

State v. Puckett, 691 S.W.2d 491 (Mo. App. 1985)

42 ALR5th 581—§ 5

State v. Puente-Gomez, 121 Idaho 702, 827 P.2d 715 (App. 1992)

32 ALR5th 149—§ 5, 50, 52, 54, 56, 58, 73

State v. Pugh, 55 Or. App. 305, 637 P.2d 1325 (1981)

87 ALR5th 597—§ 15

For assistance, call 1-800-328-4880

State v. Pugh, 2010 WI App 46, 324 Wis. 2d 307, 784 N.W.2d 183 (Ct. App. 2010)

81 ALR6th 505—§ 8

State v. Pugliese, 122 N.H. 1141, 455 A.2d 1018 (1982)

55 ALR6th 157—§ 6, 24

State v. Pugliese, 129 N.H. 442, 529 A.2d 925 (1987)

84 ALR5th 487—§ 11

State v. Pulgini, 374 A.2d 822 (Del. 1977)

6 ALR6th 533—§ 17

State v. Pulis, 579 S.W.2d 395 (Mo. Ct. App. S.D. 1979)

57 ALR6th 445—§ 3, 45, 49

State v. Pulizzi, 1997 WL 22596 (Ohio Ct. App. 9th Dist. Summit County 1997)

1 ALR6th 549—§ 24

State v. Pullen, 811 S.W.2d 463 (Mo. Ct. App. E.D. 1991)

70 ALR5th 587—§ 21

State v. Pulphus, 465 A.2d 153 (R.I. 1983)

116 ALR5th 373—§ 3, 5

State v. Purcell, 18 P.3d 113 (Ariz. Ct. App. Div. 1 2001)

63 ALR5th 375—§ 5

State v. Purcell, 336 A.2d 223 (Del. Super. Ct. 1975)

92 ALR6th 295—§ 3, 13
93 ALR6th 207—§ 3
96 ALR6th 355—§ 3

State v. Purdie, 93 N.C. App. 269, 377 S.E.2d 789 (1989)

42 ALR6th 237—§ 8

State v. Purdy, 228 Kan. 264, 615 P.2d 131 (1980)

124 ALR5th 1—§ 5

State v. Purdy, 491 N.W.2d 402 (N.D. 1992)

66 ALR5th 397—§ 4, 25

State v. Puris, 152 Wash. App. 1060, 2009 WL 3723052 (Div. 1 2009)

55 ALR6th 1—§ 31

State v. Purknow, 1992 WL 52706 (Ohio Ct. App. 11th Dist. Ashtabula County 1992)

69 ALR6th 207—§ 9, 10, 18

State v. Purnell, 310 N.J. Super. 407, 708 A.2d 1196 (App. Div. 1998)

29 ALR6th 1—§ 10

State v. Purnell, 394 N.J. Super. 28, 925 A.2d 71 (App. Div. 2007)

99 ALR6th 295—§ 13, 14

State v. Purse, 17 Ariz. App. 174, 496 P.2d 600 (Div. 2 1972)

68 ALR5th 343—§ 3, 17

State v. Purser, 828 P.2d 515, 182 Utah Adv. Rep. 28 (Utah App. 1992)

41 ALR5th 171—§ 2, 13, 16 to 18, 31, 32, 68, 91

State v. Pursifull, 751 P.2d 825 (Utah Ct. App. 1988)

58 ALR6th 499—§ 23

State v. Pursley, 238 Kan. 253, 710 P.2d 1231 (1985)

38 ALR6th 97—§ 28

State v. Purvis, 249 Or. 404, 438 P.2d 1002 (1968)

62 ALR5th 1—§ 6, 14

State v. Purvis, 525 S.W.2d 590 (Mo. Ct. App. 1975)

85 ALR5th 187—§ 9

State v. Purvis, 2006-Ohio-1555, 2006 WL 826349 (Ohio Ct. App. 9th Dist. Medina County 2006)

23 ALR6th 1—§ 15

State v. Putman, 28 N.C. App. 70, 220 S.E.2d 176 (1975)

61 ALR5th 1—§ 4, 8

State v. Putnam, 31 Wash. App. 156, 639 P.2d 858 (1982)

18 ALR5th 1—§ 28

State v. Putt, 955 S.W.2d 640 (Tenn. Crim. App. 1997)

85 ALR5th 261—§ 3, 13, 14

State v. Putzke, 7 Ohio App. 2d 18, 36 Ohio Ops. 2d 67, 218 N.E.2d 627 (Ottawa Co. 1966)

50 ALR5th 703—§ 38

State v. Pye, 282 Ga. 796, 653 S.E.2d 450 (2007)

For assistance, call 1-800-328-4880

32 ALR6th 1—§ 10
State v. Pyle, 155 Or. App. 74, 963 P.2d 721 (1998)

24 ALR5th 465—§ 11, 25
State v. Quabner, 119 Wash. App. 1014, 2003 WL 22700728 (Div. 2 2003)

7 ALR6th 233—§ 5
State v. Qualey, 138 Or. App. 74, 906 P.2d 835 (1995)

11 ALR6th 237—§ 11
46 ALR6th 241—§ 19
State v. Quantex Microsystems, Inc., 809 So. 2d 246 (La. Ct. App. 1st Cir. 2001)

30 ALR6th 341—§ 3
State v. Quarles, 89 Wash. App. 1019, 1998 WL 17683 (Div. 3 1998)

63 ALR6th 1—§ 5
State v. Quarles, 504 A.2d 473 (R.I. 1986)

67 ALR5th 637—§ 4, 8
State v. Quartman, 2007-Ohio-329, 2007 WL 196536 (Ohio Ct. App. 2d Dist. Montgomery County 2007)

78 ALR6th 297—§ 41
State v. Quatrevingt, 670 So. 2d 197 (La. 1996)

90 ALR5th 453—§ 12
State v. Quatro, 44 N.J. Super. 120, 129 A.2d 741 (1957)

29 ALR5th 59—§ 62
State v. Quatsling, 125 Ariz. 255, 609 P.2d 70 (Ct. App. Div. 2 1980)

31 ALR6th 49—§ 10
State v. Quattrocchi, 681 A.2d 879 (R.I. 1996)

90 ALR5th 453—§ 20
State v. Quattrocchi, 1999 WL 284882 (R.I. Super. Ct. 1999)

90 ALR5th 453—§ 20
State v. Queen, 73 Wash. 2d 706, 440 P.2d 461 (1968)

19 ALR5th 351—§ 12
State v. Quelnan, 70 Hawaii 194, 767 P.2d 243 (1989)

52 ALR5th 559—§ 4, 6, 16
State v. Quesnel, 79 Haw. 185, 900 P.2d 182 (Haw. Ct. App. 1995)

85 ALR5th 1—§ 22, 50
State v. Quest, 772 So. 2d 772 (La. Ct. App. 5th Cir. 2000)

19 ALR6th 115—§ 4, 9, 10
State v. Quick, 149 N.C. App. 669, 562 S.E.2d 607 (2002)

1 ALR6th 549—§ 3, 5, 23, 25
7 ALR6th 169—§ 3
8 ALR6th 265—§ 3
State v. Quigg, 72 Wash. App. 828, 866 P.2d 655 (Div. 3 1994)

73 ALR5th 383—§ 5
State v. Quigley, 2005-Ohio-5276, 2005 WL 2416564 (Ohio Ct. App. 11th Dist. Geauga County 2005)

24 ALR6th 549—§ 6
State v. Quillin, 49 Wash. App. 155, 741 P.2d 589 (Div. 3 1987)

65 ALR6th 359—§ 3
State v. Quinlan, 921 A.2d 96 (R.I. 2007)

92 ALR6th 171—§ 4
State v. Quinn, 43 Wash. App. 696, 719 P.2d 936 (Div. 3 1986)

79 ALR6th 125—§ 5, 8
State v. Quinn, 64 Md. App. 668, 498 A.2d 676 (1985)

124 ALR5th 1—§ 4
State v. Quinn, 288 So. 2d 605 (La. 1974)

62 ALR5th 121—§ 6
State v. Quinn, 717 S.W.2d 262 (Mo. App. 1986)

5 ALR5th 243—§ 7
State v. Quinn, 2010 WL 4117188 (N.J. Super. Ct. App. Div. 2010)

78 ALR6th 213—§ 3
State v. Quinnam, 367 A.2d 1032 (Me. 1977)

72 ALR5th 607—§ 3, 4, 6, 10, 11
State v. Quinones, 105 Ariz. 380, 465 P.2d 360 (1970)

4 ALR5th 1—§ 17, 32, 33, 35
State v. Quinones, 168 Ohio App. 3d 425, 2006-Ohio-4096, 860 N.E.2d 793 (8th Dist. Cuyahoga County 2006)

70 ALR6th 361—§ 19

---

71 ALR6th 335—§ 11

State v. Quintero Morelos, 133 Wash. App. 591, 137 P.3d 114 (Div. 3 2006)

75 ALR6th 541—§ 18

State v. Quintero-Negrete, 266 P.3d 1253 (Kan. Ct. App. 2012)

97 ALR6th 653—§ 14

State v. Quiroz, 107 Wash. 2d 791, 733 P.2d 963 (1987)

101 ALR5th 351—§ 7

State v. Ra, 158 Wash. App. 1033, 2010 WL 4539446 (Div. 2 2010)

99 ALR6th 113—§ 13, 16

State v. Rabas, 2001 WI App 58, 241 Wis. 2d 572, 624 N.W.2d 421 (Ct. App. 2001)

84 ALR6th 293—§ 4, 15, 43

State v. Rabb, 920 So. 2d 1175 (Fla. Dist. Ct. App. 4th Dist. 2006)

26 ALR6th 659—§ 17

State v. Rabon, 115 Ariz. 45, 563 P.2d 300 (App. 1977)

39 ALR5th 283—§ 3

State v. Raborn, 771 So. 2d 877 (La. Ct. App. 2d Cir. 2000)

104 ALR5th 165—§ 6

State v. Rack, 318 S.W.2d 211 (Mo. 1958)

54 ALR6th 429—§ 7, 20

State v. Rackis, 333 N.J. Super. 332, 755 A.2d 649 (App. Div. 2000)

65 ALR6th 329—§ 4

State v. Radcliffe, 228 Neb. 868, 424 N.W.2d 608 (1988)

40 ALR6th 317—§ 5

State v. Radcliffe, 483 So. 2d 95 (Fla. Dist. Ct. App. 5th Dist. 1986)

68 ALR5th 343—§ 2, 3, 7

State v. Radford, 2007 WL 831739 (Wash. Ct. App. Div. 2 2007)

26 ALR6th 511—§ 26

State v. Radmacher, 127 Wash. App. 1037, 2005 WL 1303549 (Div. 1 2005)

15 ALR6th 515—§ 34

State v. Radzvilowicz, 47 Conn. App. 1, 703 A.2d 767 (1997)

57 ALR6th 445—§ 3, 10, 23

State v. Rael, 127 N.M. 347, 1999 -NMCA- 068, 981 P.2d 280 (Ct. App. 1999)

89 ALR5th 629—§ 3, 5, 8

State v. Ragan, 22 Wash. App. 591, 593 P.2d 815 (Div. 2 1979)

40 ALR6th 1—§ 10

State v. Ragland, 4 Conn. Cir. 424, 233 A.2d 698 (1967)

7 ALR5th 73—§ 10

State v. Ragland, 836 N.W.2d 107 (Iowa 2013)

102 ALR6th 637—§ 4, 6

State v. Rahman, 23 Ohio St. 3d 146, 492 N.E.2d 401 (1986)

119 ALR5th 275—§ 7

State v. Rahman, 199 W. Va. 144, 483 S.E.2d 273 (1996)

82 ALR5th 359—§ 3

84 ALR5th 487—§ 22

State v. Rainer, 502 N.W.2d 784 (Minn. 1993)

57 ALR5th 141—§ 8

State v. Raines, 55 Wash. App. 459, 778 P.2d 538 (Div. 1 1989)

58 ALR6th 499—§ 32

State v. Raines, 118 S.W.3d 205 (Mo. Ct. App. W.D. 2003)

103 ALR6th 507—§ 8, 19, 20

State v. Raines, 882 S.W.2d 376 (Tenn. Crim. App. 1994)

73 ALR5th 383—§ 8

State v. Rainey, 233 Kan. 13, 660 P.2d 544 (1983)

3 ALR5th 784—§ 2

State v. Rainey, 722 So. 2d 1097 (La. Ct. App. 5th Cir. 1998)

19 ALR5th 823—§ 11

State v. Rains, 574 N.W.2d 904 (Iowa 1998)

95 ALR6th 641—§ 8

State v. Raj, 368 N.W.2d 14 (Minn. Ct. App. 1985)

90 ALR5th 225—§ 4

124 ALR5th 1—§ 5

State v. Raleigh, 2007-Ohio-5515, 2007 WL 2994237 (Ohio Ct. App. 5th Dist. Licking County 2007)
56 ALR6th 323—§ 7

State v. Ralph, 85 Wash. App. 82, 930 P.2d 1235 (Div. 3 1997)
57 ALR6th 445—§ 50

State v. Ramage, 51 Nev. 82, 269 P. 489 (1928)
108 ALR5th 593—§ 24

State v. Ramage, 2000 WL 228249 (Ohio Ct. App. 4th Dist. Highland County 2000)
29 ALR6th 237—§ 21

State v. Ramey, 129 Ohio App. 3d 409, 717 N.E.2d 1153 (1st Dist. Hamilton County 1998)
84 ALR6th 293—§ 4, 15, 43

State v. Ramirez, 49 Wash. App. 814, 746 P.2d 344 (Div. 3 1987)
122 ALR5th 439—§ 7

State v. Ramirez, 62 Wash. App. 301, 814 P.2d 227 (1991)
34 ALR5th 125—§ 14

State v. Ramirez, 79 N.M. 475, 444 P.2d 986 (1968)
50 ALR5th 467—§ 7

State v. Ramirez, 101 Conn. App. 283, 921 A.2d 702 (2007)
30 ALR6th 1—§ 3, 6

State v. Ramirez, 122 Idaho 830, 839 P.2d 1244 (App. 1992)
26 ALR5th 1—§ 4, 28

State v. Ramirez, 122 Wash. App. 1044, 2004 WL 1664241 (Div. 3 2004)
69 ALR6th 207—§ 29

State v. Ramirez, 135 Ohio App. 3d 89, 732 N.E.2d 1065 (11th Dist. Lake County 1999)
49 ALR6th 343—§ 12

State v. Ramirez, 142 Ariz. 171, 688 P.2d 1063 (App. 1984)
37 ALR5th 515—§ 4

State v. Ramirez, 246 Wis. 2d 802, 2001 WI App 158, 633 N.W.2d 656 (Ct. App. 2001)
125 ALR5th 537—§ 2, 3, 20, 25

State v. Ramirez, 535 N.W.2d 847 (S.D. 1995)
34 ALR6th 1—§ 10

State v. Ramirez, 814 P.2d 1131 (Utah Ct. App. 1991)
17 ALR6th 327—§ 14

State v. Ramold, 2 Neb. App. 545, 511 N.W.2d 789 (1994)
68 ALR5th 343—§ 3

State v. Ramos, 226 N.J. Super. 339, 544 A.2d 408 (App. Div. 1988)
39 ALR6th 257—§ 49

State v. Ramos, 574 A.2d 1213 (R.I. 1990)
20 ALR5th 398—§ 3, 14

State v. Ramos, 608 So. 2d 830, 17 FLW D 1895 (Fla. App. D3 1992)
18 ALR5th 1—§ 14, 22, 40

State v. Ramos, 993 So. 2d 281 (La. Ct. App. 1st Cir. 2008)
75 ALR6th 541—§ 12

State v. Ramos, 1994 WL 246138 (Ohio Ct. App. 9th Dist. Lorain County 1994)
31 ALR6th 49—§ 4

State v. Ramsey, 5 Wash. App. 361, 486 P.2d 1109 (Div. 1 1971)
53 ALR6th 81—§ 7, 9
55 ALR6th 391—§ 21

State v. Ramsey, 665 S.W.2d 72 (Mo. Ct. App. S.D. 1984)
58 ALR6th 499—§ 52

State v. Ramsey, 782 P.2d 480 (Utah 1989)
71 ALR5th 637—§ 6

State v. Ramsey, 903 S.W.2d 709 (Tenn. Crim. App. 1995)
84 ALR6th 427—§ 6

State v. Rancourt, 435 A.2d 1095 (Me. 1981)
57 ALR5th 141—§ 2, 5

State v. Rand, 166 Or. 396, 112 P.2d 1034 (1941)
54 ALR6th 429—§ 20

State v. Rand, 430 A.2d 808 (Me. 1981)
6 ALR6th 533—§ 15

State v. Rand, 2014 MT 19N, 2014 WL 223234 (Mont. 2014)
92 ALR6th 295—§ 25
93 ALR6th 207—§ 6
State v. Randall, 116 Ariz. 371, 569 P.2d 313 (Ct. App. Div. 1 1977)
122 ALR5th 439—§ 9
State v. Randall, 141 Ohio App. 3d 160, 750 N.E.2d 615 (11th Dist. Lake County 2001)
93 ALR6th 1—§ 15
State v. Randall, 669 So. 2d 223 (Ala. Crim. App. 1995)
29 ALR5th 487—§ 3
State v. Randle, 484 N.W.2d 220 (Iowa App. 1992)
51 ALR5th 603—§ 4
State v. Randle, 555 N.W.2d 666 (Iowa 1996)
109 ALR5th 99—§ 3
State v. Randleman, 108 Ohio App. 3d 468, 671 N.E.2d 267 (3d Dist. Seneca County 1995)
92 ALR6th 171—§ 4
State v. Randlett, 2009-Ohio-112, 2009 WL 81325 (Ohio Ct. App. 4th Dist. Ross County 2009)
64 ALR6th 1—§ 9
State v. Rando, 848 So. 2d 19 (La. Ct. App. 4th Cir. 2003)
6 ALR6th 533—§ 17
State v. Randolph, 12 Wash. App. 138, 528 P.2d 1008 (1974)
46 ALR5th 499—§ 3
State v. Randolph, 130 P.3d 593 (Kan. Ct. App. 2006)
23 ALR6th 307—§ 38
State v. Randolph, 337 So. 2d 498 (La. 1976)
103 ALR6th 347—§ 13
State v. Randolph, 698 S.W.2d 535 (Mo. Ct. App. E.D. 1985)
97 ALR6th 567—§ 3, 5, 9
State v. Rangel, 12 Ariz. App. 172, 468 P.2d 623 (Div. 1 1970)
85 ALR5th 1—§ 2, 15
State v. Rangel, 328 Or. 294, 977 P.2d 379 (1999)

29 ALR5th 487—§ 3
State v. Rangeloff, 1998 ND 135, 580 N.W.2d 593 (N.D. 1998)
112 ALR5th 429—§ 7
114 ALR5th 235—§ 5
73 ALR6th 49—§ 14
State v. Ranieri, 586 A.2d 1094 (R.I. 1991)
93 ALR5th 527—§ 8
State v. Rankin, 151 Wash. 2d 689, 92 P.3d 202 (2004)
92 ALR6th 171—§ 12
State v. Rankin, 2006-Ohio-2571, 2006 WL 1428914 (Ohio Ct. App. 8th Dist. Cuyahoga County 2006)
26 ALR6th 511—§ 19
State v. Rankin, 2007-Ohio-4844, 2007 WL 2729802 (Ohio Ct. App. 8th Dist. Cuyahoga County 2007)
79 ALR6th 1—§ 37
State v. Ransom, 239 Kan. 594, 722 P.2d 540 (1986)
39 ALR5th 283—§ 4, 66
State v. Ransom, 268 Kan. 653, 999 P.2d 272 (2000)
74 ALR5th 453—§ 6
State v. Ransome, 342 N.C. 847, 467 S.E.2d 404, 57 A.L.R.5th 809 (1996)
57 ALR5th 141—§ 2, 4
State v. Ransome, 392 So. 2d 490 (La. App. 1st Cir. 1980)
10 ALR5th 448—§ 6
State v. Rapozo, 1 Haw. App. 255, 617 P.2d 1235 (1980)
79 ALR5th 419—§ 10
State v. Rappaport, 211 Md. 523, 128 A.2d 270 (1957)
5 ALR6th 1—§ 30
10 ALR6th 31—§ 55
State v. Rardon, 2002 MT 345, 313 Mont. 321, 61 P.3d 132 (2002)
9 ALR6th 541—§ 23
State v. Rasco, 239 Mo. 535, 144 S.W. 449 (1912)
81 ALR5th 563—§ 3
54 ALR6th 429—§ 20
101 ALR6th 499—§ 15

State v. Rash, 34 N.C. 382 (1851)
   24 ALR5th 465—§ 117, 120
State v. Rash, 458 So. 2d 1201 (Fla. Dist. Ct. App. 5th Dist. 1984)
   72 ALR5th 1—§ 3
State v. Rasmussen, 113 Wash. App. 1057, 2002 WL 31295326 (Div. 2 2002)
   101 ALR6th 331—§ 3, 26
State v. Rasmussen, 213 N.W.2d 661 (Iowa 1973)
   60 ALR6th 175—§ 4
State v. Rasmussen, 225 Conn. 55, 621 A.2d 728 (1993)
   32 ALR6th 1—§ 11
State v. Rasor, 319 N.C. 577, 356 S.E.2d 328 (1987)
   16 ALR6th 329—§ 4
   24 ALR6th 591—§ 6, 14
State v. Rassmussen, 92 Idaho 731, 449 P.2d 837 (1969)
   32 ALR6th 1—§ 7
   81 ALR6th 505—§ 17
State v. Rastopsoff, 659 P.2d 630 (Alaska App. 1983)
   7 ALR5th 263—§ 7
State v. Raszick, 1994 WL 728339 (Ohio Ct. App. 5th Dist. Stark County 1994)
   17 ALR6th 327—§ 12
State v. Ratcliff, 95 Ohio App. 3d 199, 642 N.E.2d 31 (5th Dist. Ashland County 1994)
   34 ALR6th 1—§ 10
State v. Ratleff, 2005-Ohio-957, 2005 WL 517343 (Ohio Ct. App. 3d Dist. Logan County 2005)
   26 ALR6th 511—§ 19
State v. Ratley, 16 Kan. App. 2d 589, 827 P.2d 78 (1992)
   65 ALR5th 407—§ 2 to 4, 16, 20
   99 ALR6th 397—§ 15
State v. Rattler, 503 So. 2d 168 (La. Ct. App. 4th Cir. 1987)
   99 ALR6th 295—§ 10, 13
State v. Rattler, 532 So. 2d 852 (La. Ct. App. 4th Cir. 1988)
   109 ALR5th 99—§ 8

   111 ALR5th 239—§ 2
State v. Raudebaugh, 124 Idaho 758, 864 P.2d 596 (1993)
   26 ALR5th 603—§ 3
State v. Raudebaugh, 864 P.2d 596 (Idaho 1993)
   9 ALR5th 369—§ 14
State v. Rawls, 552 So. 2d 764 (La. Ct. App. 1st Cir. 1989)
   68 ALR5th 343—§ 2, 3, 16
State v. Ray, 36 Or. App. 367, 584 P.2d 362 (1978)
   9 ALR6th 363—§ 40
State v. Ray, 41 Or. App. 763, 598 P.2d 1293 (1979)
   92 ALR6th 1—§ 8
State v. Ray, 102 Ohio App. 395, 2 Ohio Ops. 2d 415, 143 N.E.2d 484 (Ross Co. 1956)
   12 ALR5th 909—§ 3
State v. Ray, 116 Wash.2d 531, 806 P.2d 1220 (1991)
   83 ALR5th 277—§ 10
State v. Ray, 116 Wash. 2d 531, 806 P.2d 1220 (1991)
   83 ALR5th 277—§ 10, 13
   84 ALR5th 487—§ 21, 24, 25
State v. Ray, 123 Ariz. 175, 598 P.2d 994 (Ct. App. Div. 1 1978)
   103 ALR6th 347—§ 20
State v. Ray, 191 Neb. 702, 217 N.W.2d 176 (1974)
   108 ALR5th 593—§ 51
State v. Ray, 209 Ariz. 429, 104 P.3d 160 (Ct. App. Div. 2 2004)
   33 ALR6th 91—§ 29
State v. Ray, 229 N.C. 40, 47 S.E.2d 494 (1948)
   26 ALR5th 1—§ 3
State v. Ray, 310 S.C. 431, 427 S.E.2d 171 (1993)
   72 ALR5th 403—§ 3
State v. Ray, 880 S.W.2d 700 (Tenn. Crim. App. 1993)
   57 ALR5th 141—§ 10
State v. Ray, 1998 WL 142377 (Ohio Ct. App. 12th Dist. Butler County 1998)

78 ALR5th 489—§ 3
State v. Ray, 2005-Ohio-4251, 2005 WL 1950992 (Ohio Ct. App. 10th Dist. Franklin County 2005)
70 ALR6th 1—§ 5
State v. Rayfield, 357 S.C. 497, 593 S.E.2d 486 (Ct. App. 2004)
15 ALR6th 319—§ 4
State v. Rayfield, 752 S.E.2d 745 (N.C. Ct. App. 2014)
94 ALR6th 525—§ 21
101 ALR6th 299—§ 4
State v. Raymer, 786 S.W.2d 15 (Tex. App. Dallas 1990)
113 ALR5th 517—§ 17
State v. Raymo, 419 So. 2d 858 (La. 1982)
108 ALR5th 593—§ 31
State v. Raymond, 21 Ariz. App. 116, 516 P.2d 58 (Div. 2 1973)
114 ALR5th 173—§ 9
State v. Raymond, 30 Conn. App. 606, 621 A.2d 755 (1993)
93 ALR5th 683—§ 3
State v. Raymond, 305 Minn. 160, 232 N.W.2d 879 (1975)
29 ALR6th 1—§ 10
State v. Raymond, 446 A.2d 743 (R.I. 1982)
70 ALR5th 587—§ 13
State v. Raymond, 447 So. 2d 51 (La. Ct. App. 1st Cir. 1984)
33 ALR6th 1—§ 8, 12
State v. Raynor, 128 N.C. App. 244, 495 S.E.2d 176 (1998)
39 ALR5th 283—§ 23
State v. Raywalt, 436 N.W.2d 234 (N.D. 1989)
23 ALR6th 307—§ 4, 20
State v. Raywalt, 444 N.W.2d 688 (N.D. 1989)
99 ALR5th 557—§ 20
State v. R.B., 92 Wash. App. 1054, 1998 WL 729678 (Div. 1 1998)
59 ALR6th 393—§ 10
State v. R.B. "J" C., 2004 MT 254, 323 Mont. 62, 97 P.3d 1116, 22 A.L.R.6th 833 (2004)

22 ALR6th 533—§ 3, 4, 57
State v. R.D.S., 2011 WL 1642628 (Minn. Ct. App. 2011)
69 ALR6th 1—§ 5
State v. Re, 1977 WL 182028 (Del. Super. Ct. 1977)
100 ALR6th 535—§ 3
State v. Read, 965 S.W.2d 74 (Tex. App. Austin 1998)
75 ALR5th 295—§ 9, 26
State v. Read, 1979 WL 207622 (Ohio Ct. App. 9th Dist. Summit County 1979)
103 ALR6th 347—§ 20
State v. Ready, 132 Or. App. 422, 888 P.2d 603 (1995)
42 ALR5th 291—§ 7
State v. Ready, 148 Or. App. 149, 939 P.2d 117 (1997)
51 ALR5th 425—§ 3
State v. Ready, 251 S.W.2d 680 (Mo. 1952)
70 ALR5th 587—§ 3
State v. Real Property at 633 East 640 North, Orem, Utah, 2000 UT 17, 994 P.2d 1254 (Utah 2000)
6 ALR5th 652—§ 17
State v. Real Property at East North, Orem, Utah, 2000 UT 17, 994 P.2d 1254 (Utah 2000)
124 ALR5th 509—§ 5
State v. Ream, 223 S.W.3d 874 (Mo. Ct. App. S.D. 2007)
81 ALR6th 505—§ 40
State v. Reams, 284 Mont. 448, 945 P.2d 52 (1997)
69 ALR6th 1—§ 20
State v. Reasonover, 714 S.W.2d 706 (Mo. Ct. App. E.D. 1986)
29 ALR6th 1—§ 10
State v. Reavis, 19 N.C. App. 497, 199 S.E.2d 139 (1973)
85 ALR5th 187—§ 12
State v. Reavley, 2003 MT 298, 318 Mont. 150, 79 P.3d 270 (2003)
20 ALR6th 479—§ 3, 25
29 ALR6th 1—§ 10

State v. R.E.B., 385 N.J. Super. 72, 895 A.2d 1224 (App. Div. 2006)
  39 ALR6th 257—§ 47

State v. Rebeterano, 681 P.2d 1265 (Utah 1984)
  65 ALR6th 359—§ 10

State v. Rechnitz, 20 Mont. 488, 52 P. 264 (1898)
  29 ALR5th 59—§ 3

State v. Recor, 150 Vt. 40, 549 A.2d 1382 (1988)
  38 ALR5th 433—§ 2, 5

State v. Redcrow, 1999 MT 95, 294 Mont. 252, 980 P.2d 622 (1999)
  97 ALR6th 263—§ 32

State v. Reddick, 76 N.J. Super. 347, 184 A.2d 652 (App. Div. 1962)
  103 ALR6th 137—§ 15

State v. Redding, 2007 UT App 350, 172 P.3d 319 (Utah Ct. App. 2007)
  84 ALR6th 427—§ 4, 16

State v. Reddish, 181 N.J. 553, 859 A.2d 1173 (2004)
  65 ALR6th 359—§ 5

State v. Reddish, 2009-Ohio-3643, 2009 WL 2197049 (Ohio Ct. App. 2d Dist. Montgomery County 2009)
  64 ALR6th 1—§ 7

State v. Redepenning, 2000 WL 145332 (Ohio Ct. App. 1st Dist. Hamilton County 2000)
  78 ALR5th 489—§ 9

State v. Red Feather, 205 Neb. 734, 289 N.W.2d 768 (1980)
  38 ALR5th 433—§ 2, 3

State v. Redfield, 95 Wash. App. 1001, 1999 WL 218453 (Div. 3 1999)
  35 ALR6th 361—§ 15, 20, 22

State v. Red Fox, 446 N.W.2d 69 (S.D. 1989)
  78 ALR5th 567—§ 9

State v. Redic, 392 So. 2d 451 (La. 1980)
  29 ALR6th 1—§ 10

State v. Rediker, 214 Minn. 470, 8 N.W.2d 527 (1943)
  24 ALR5th 465—§ 109, 111

State v. Redinger, 64 N.J. 41, 312 A.2d 129 (1973)
  18 ALR5th 1—§ 32

State v. Red Kettle, 239 Neb. 317, 476 N.W.2d 220 (1991)
  29 ALR5th 59—§ 22

State v. Redman, 183 Ind. 332, 109 N.E. 184 (1915)
  10 ALR5th 139—§ 12

State v. Redman, 916 S.W.2d 787 (Mo. 1996)
  71 ALR5th 637—§ 7
  88 ALR5th 67—§ 7

State v. Red Paint, 311 N.W.2d 182 (N.D. 1981)
  101 ALR5th 619—§ 9

State v. Redpath, 668 S.W.2d 99 (Mo. Ct. App. W.D. 1984)
  5 ALR6th 1—§ 51

State v. Ree, 331 N.W.2d 557 (S.D. 1983)
  112 ALR5th 621—§ 3, 10

State v. Reeb, 331 N.C. 159, 415 S.E.2d 362 (1992)
  16 ALR6th 329—§ 4
  24 ALR6th 591—§ 6, 14

State v. Reed, 5 Conn. Cir. 69, 241 A.2d 875 (1967)
  48 ALR5th 473—§ 8, 10
  52 ALR5th 221—§ 2

State v. Reed, 52 Or. 377, 97 P. 627 (1908)
  5 ALR6th 1—§ 63

State v. Reed, 65 Ohio St. 2d 117, 19 Ohio Op. 3d 311, 418 N.E.2d 1359 (1981)
  3 ALR6th 269—§ 5

State v. Reed, 75 S.D. 282, 63 N.W.2d 792 (1954)
  50 ALR5th 703—§ 15

State v. Reed, 77 Haw. 72, 881 P.2d 1218 (1994)
  43 ALR6th 475—§ 10

State v. Reed, 101 Or. App. 277, 790 P.2d 551 (1990)
  8 ALR5th 775—§ 1, 3, 5

State v. Reed, 173 Or. App. 185, 21 P.3d 137 (2001)
71 ALR5th 637—§ 3, 11

State v. Reed, 182 N.C. App. 109, 641 S.E.2d 320 (2007)
62 ALR6th 413—§ 44

State v. Reed, 205 Neb. 45, 286 N.W.2d 111 (1979)
54 ALR5th 141—§ 3 to 5, 8

State v. Reed, 232 A.2d 81 (Me. 1967)
102 ALR6th 279—§ 7

State v. Reed, 248 Kan. 506, 809 P.2d 553 (1991)
9 ALR6th 633—§ 14
10 ALR6th 265—§ 13, 14, 16
13 ALR6th 603—§ 41

State v. Reed, 313 N.W.2d 788 (S.D. 1981)
39 ALR5th 283—§ 4, 66

State v. Reed, 618 N.W.2d 327 (Iowa 2000)
58 ALR6th 385—§ 20

State v. Reed, 640 S.W.2d 188 (Mo. Ct. App. W.D. 1982)
54 ALR6th 429—§ 11, 29
84 ALR6th 427—§ 27

State v. Reed, 658 So. 2d 774 (La. Ct. App. 2d Cir. 1995)
1 ALR6th 493—§ 14, 35

State v. Reed, 712 So. 2d 458 (Fla. Dist. Ct. App. 5th Dist. 1998)
122 ALR5th 439—§ 4

State v. Reed, 1992 WL 52708 (Ohio Ct. App. 11th Dist. Ashtabula County 1992)
69 ALR6th 207—§ 9, 10, 18

State v. Reed, 1994 WL 258636 (Ohio Ct. App. 8th Dist. Cuyahoga County 1994)
67 ALR5th 637—§ 5, 8

State v. Reed, 1999-Ohio-910, 1999 WL 966131 (Ohio Ct. App. 3d Dist. Hancock County 1999)
7 ALR6th 233—§ 5

State v. Reed, 2002-Ohio-680, 2002 WL 243281 (Ohio Ct. App. 10th Dist. Franklin County 2002)
71 ALR6th 1—§ 5

State v. Reed, 2004-Ohio-1881, 2004 WL 786435 (Ohio Ct. App. 9th Dist. Summit County 2004)
65 ALR6th 1—§ 18

State v. Reed, 2005-Ohio-6251, 2005 WL 3150170 (Ohio Ct. App. 10th Dist. Franklin County 2005)
69 ALR6th 1—§ 16

State v. Reed, 2009 WI App 174, 322 Wis. 2d 572, 776 N.W.2d 287 (Ct. App. 2009)
99 ALR6th 295—§ 13

State v. Reed, 2013 WL 6123155 (Tenn. Crim. App. 2013)
101 ALR6th 331—§ 12

State v. Reedeker, 534 P.2d 1240 (Utah 1975)
15 ALR5th 391—§ 45

State v. Reeder, 105 N.C. App. 343, 413 S.E.2d 580 (1992)
38 ALR5th 433—§ 3

State v. Reeder, 249 Neb. 207, 543 N.W.2d 429 (1996)
109 ALR5th 99—§ 12

State v. Reedy, 44 Kan. 190, 24 P. 66 (1890)
34 ALR5th 723—§ 4

State v. Reenstierna, 101 N.H. 286, 140 A.2d 572 (1958)
76 ALR5th 1—§ 23

State v. Reese, 250 La. 151, 194 So. 2d 729 (1967)
70 ALR5th 587—§ 3

State v. Reese, 272 N.W.2d 863 (Iowa 1978)
54 ALR5th 141—§ 2 to 5, 9, 10

State v. Reese, 795 S.W.2d 69 (Mo. 1990)
83 ALR6th 255—§ 15, 17

State v. Reese, 2008-Ohio-2512, 2008 WL 2571864 (Ohio Ct. App. 5th Dist. Richland County 2008)
99 ALR6th 295—§ 15

State v. Reese, 2010 ME 30, 991 A.2d 806 (Me. 2010)
81 ALR6th 505—§ 6

State v. Reeter, 848 S.W.2d 560 (Mo. Ct. App. W.D. 1993)

85 ALR5th 547—§ 2, 6

State v. Reeves, 62 N.C. App. 219, 302 S.E.2d 658 (1983)

57 ALR6th 445—§ 2, 45

State v. Reeves, 150 La. 950, 91 So. 403 (1922)

24 ALR6th 747—§ 17

State v. Reeves, 234 Kan. 250, 671 P.2d 553 (1983)

110 ALR5th 329—§ 5

State v. Reeves, 264 Ark. 622, 574 S.W.2d 647 (1978)

24 ALR5th 132—§ 4, 7

29 ALR5th 59—§ 7

State v. Reeves, 337 N.C. 700, 448 S.E.2d 802 (1994)

79 ALR5th 33—§ 28, 42

State v. Reeves, 488 So. 2d 670 (Fla. Dist. Ct. App. 4th Dist. 1986)

114 ALR5th 173—§ 7

State v. Reevey, 159 N.J. Super. 130, 387 A.2d 381 (App. Div. 1978)

59 ALR5th 1—§ 3, 6

State v. Regan, 28 Wash. App. 680, 625 P.2d 741 (1981)

39 ALR5th 283—§ 4, 67

State v. Regan, 564 So. 2d 1208, 15 FLW D 1938 (Fla. App. D2 1990)

27 ALR5th 593—§ 28, 31

State v. Reger, 148 N.M. 342, 2010-NMCA-056, 236 P.3d 654 (Ct. App. 2010)

92 ALR6th 295—§ 8

96 ALR6th 355—§ 36, 46

State v. Reger, Slip Op. C.A. Nos. 12378, 12384 (Ohio App. Summit Co. 1986)

38 ALR5th 433—§ 8

State v. Reha, 12 Neb. App. 767, 686 N.W.2d 80 (2004)

1 ALR6th 371—§ 4

State v. Rehling, 2008 WL 5057709 (Minn. Ct. App. 2008)

99 ALR6th 397—§ 6

State v. Rehn, 117 Wash. App. 142, 69 P.3d 379 (Div. 3 2003)

58 ALR6th 215—§ 12

State v. Reichenbach, 153 Wash. 2d 126, 101 P.3d 80 (2004)

71 ALR6th 1—§ 4

State v. Reid, 1 Ala. 612, 1840 WL 229 (1840)

33 ALR6th 407—§ 5

State v. Reid, 79 Ohio L. Abs. 475, 156 N.E.2d 510 (Mun. Ct. 1958)

87 ALR5th 1—§ 14

State v. Reid, 91 S.W.3d 247 (Tenn. 2002)

6 ALR6th 533—§ 21

93 ALR6th 391—§ 29

State v. Reid, 98 Wash. App. 152, 988 P.2d 1038 (Div. 2 1999)

92 ALR6th 295—§ 36

State v. Reid, 151 N.C. App. 420, 566 S.E.2d 186 (2002)

2 ALR6th 551—§ 9

State v. Reid, 254 Conn. 540, 757 A.2d 482 (2000)

90 ALR5th 453—§ 6

State v. Reid, 319 Or. 65, 872 P.2d 416, 43 A.L.R.5th 803 (1994)

43 ALR5th 1—§ 13

State v. Reid, 334 N.C. 551, 434 S.E.2d 193 (1993)

42 ALR5th 581—§ 3

State v. Reidhead, 146 Ariz. 314, 705 P.2d 1365 (App. 1985)

38 ALR5th 433—§ 11, 18

State v. Reiman, 284 N.W.2d 860 (S.D. 1979)

39 ALR5th 283—§ 4, 52, 72

State v. Reimann, 19 Kan. App. 2d 431, 870 P.2d 1346 (1994)

28 ALR6th 505—§ 9

State v. Rein, 136 Or. App. 316, 901 P.2d 982 (1995)

122 ALR5th 439—§ 7

State v. Rein, 324 Or. 178, 923 P.2d 639 (1996)

106 ALR5th 397—§ 4

State v. Reiner, 2003 MT 243, 317 Mont. 304, 77 P.3d 210 (2003)

84 ALR6th 293—§ 16

State v. Reinhold, 123 Ariz. 50, 597 P.2d 532 (1979)
28 ALR6th 505—§ 29

State v. Reinier, 628 N.W.2d 460 (Iowa 2001)
15 ALR6th 515—§ 13, 29

State v. Reinke, 702 N.W.2d 308 (Minn. Ct. App. 2005)
77 ALR6th 393—§ 11, 91, 102

State v. Reinschmidt, 984 S.W.2d 189 (Mo. Ct. App. S.D. 1998)
45 ALR5th 1—§ 13, 22

State v. Reis, 430 A.2d 749 (R.I. 1981)
24 ALR5th 428—§ 2, 6, 7
31 ALR5th 760—§ 6, 7

State v. Reisler, 194 N.W.2d 230 (N.D. 1972)
51 ALR6th 359—§ 38

State v. Reitenbaugh, 392 N.W.2d 486 (Iowa 1986)
112 ALR5th 621—§ 3, 5

State v. Reiter, 601 N.W.2d 372 (Iowa 1999)
33 ALR6th 91—§ 20, 37

State v. Reitz, 75 Or. App. 82, 705 P.2d 762 (1985)
84 ALR5th 487—§ 22

State v. Rellihan, 662 S.W.2d 535 (Mo. Ct. App. W.D. 1983)
42 ALR6th 237—§ 9

State v. Remacle, 386 N.W.2d 38 (S.D. 1986)
92 ALR6th 295—§ 3
96 ALR6th 355—§ 3, 9

State v. Remboldt, 64 Wash. App. 505, 827 P.2d 282 (Div. 3 1992)
106 ALR5th 397—§ 4

State v. Rempel, 114 Wash. 2d 77, 785 P.2d 1134 (1990)
105 ALR5th 529—§ 8

State v. Renard, 50 La. Ann. 662, 23 So. 894 (1898)
98 ALR6th 455—§ 21

State v. Rendahl, 58 Or. App. 688, 650 P.2d 128 (1982)
39 ALR5th 283—§ 4, 18

State v. Rendfrey, 2013 WL 6081707 (N.J. Super. Ct. App. Div. 2013)
94 ALR6th 579—§ 4

State v. Renick, 33 Or. 584, 56 P. 275 (1899)
125 ALR5th 537—§ 1

State v. Rentfrow, 15 Wash. App. 837, 552 P.2d 202 (Div. 1 1976)
66 ALR6th 351—§ 6
67 ALR6th 209—§ 40

State v. Rentschler, 444 S.W.2d 453 (Mo. 1969)
54 ALR5th 141—§ 9, 10

State v. Rentz, 2006 UT App 365, 2006 WL 2578911 (Utah Ct. App. 2006)
92 ALR6th 1—§ 3, 9

State v. Repetti, 60 Conn. App. 614, 760 A.2d 964 (2000)
46 ALR6th 241—§ 40

State v. Repp, 117 Wis. 2d 143, 342 N.W.2d 771 (Ct. App. 1983)
58 ALR6th 499—§ 53

State v. Resh, 124 Ohio App. 3d 694, 707 N.E.2d 531 (11th Dist. Portage County 1997)
12 ALR6th 267—§ 14

State v. Resler, 209 Neb. 249, 306 N.W.2d 918 (1981)
58 ALR6th 499—§ 22

State v. Resnick, 287 Minn. 168, 177 N.W.2d 418 (1970)
4 ALR5th 1—§ 4, 21

State v. Respass, 256 Conn. 164, 770 A.2d 471 (2001)
109 ALR5th 99—§ 10
113 ALR5th 517—§ 10

State v. Reuben, 126 Ariz. 108, 612 P.2d 1071 (Ct. App. Div. 1 1980)
114 ALR5th 173—§ 7

State v. Revels, 153 N.C. App. 163, 569 S.E.2d 15 (2002)
98 ALR6th 455—§ 33

State v. Revenaugh, 133 Idaho 774, 992 P.2d 769 (1999)
78 ALR6th 297—§ 17, 37, 79

State v. Revere, 572 So. 2d 117 (La. Ct. App. 1st Cir. 1990)

27 ALR6th 491—§ 3
State v. Rewis, 722 So. 2d 863 (Fla. 5th DCA 1998)

84 ALR6th 293—§ 20
State v. Rexrode, 536 So. 2d 671 (La. App. 3d Cir. 1988)

34 ALR5th 125—§ 3, 17
State v. Reyes, 5 Hawaii App. 651, 706 P.2d 1326 (1985)

26 ALR5th 603—§ 4
State v. Reyes, 50 N.J. 454, 236 A.2d 385 (1967)

24 ALR6th 747—§ 17, 21
State v. Reyes, 132 N.M. 576, 52 P.3d 948

71 ALR6th 249—§ 8
State v. Reyes, 163 Ariz. 488, 788 P.2d 1239, 50 Ariz. Adv. Rep. 45 (App. 1989)

20 ALR5th 398—§ 3, 20, 34, 40, 42, 53
State v. Reyes, 207 N.J. Super. 126, 504 A.2d 43 (App. Div. 1986)

21 ALR6th 771—§ 4
State v. Reyes, 671 A.2d 1236 (R.I. 1996)

88 ALR5th 121—§ 7, 36
State v. Reyes, 989 So. 2d 770 (La. Ct. App. 1st Cir. 2008)

75 ALR6th 541—§ 12
State v. Reyes, 2010 WL 909200 (N.J. Super. Ct. App. Div. 2010)

57 ALR6th 313—§ 7
State v. Reyes, No. 46888 (December 15, 1983, Ct. App. Ohio, 8th App. Dist. Cuyahoga Co.)

39 ALR5th 283—§ 14, 49
State v. Reynaga, 643 So. 2d 431 (La. Ct. App. 3d Cir. 1994)

114 ALR5th 173—§ 7
State v. Reynaga, 2000 -NMCA- 053, 5 P.3d 579 (N.M. Ct. App. 2000)

85 ALR5th 1—§ 19
State v. Reynolds, 7 Ariz. App. 48, 436 P.2d 142 (1968)

28 ALR6th 505—§ 29
State v. Reynolds, 11 Ariz. App. 532, 466 P.2d 405 (Div. 1 1970)

103 ALR5th 463—§ 5
State v. Reynolds, 41 N.J. 163, 195 A.2d 449, 1 A.L.R.3d 1438 (1963)

93 ALR5th 527—§ 2
94 ALR5th 393—§ 2
95 ALR5th 611—§ 2
101 ALR5th 187—§ 2
102 ALR5th 327—§ 2
12 ALR6th 267—§ 3
24 ALR6th 1—§ 3
53 ALR6th 81—§ 3, 5
55 ALR6th 391—§ 3
56 ALR6th 185—§ 3
State v. Reynolds, 80 Ohio St. 3d 670, 687 N.E.2d 1358 (1998)

38 ALR5th 433—§ 26
39 ALR5th 283—§ 14, 22
79 ALR5th 33—§ 2
State v. Reynolds, 93 N.C. App. 552, 378 S.E.2d 557 (1989)

38 ALR5th 433—§ 11
State v. Reynolds, 101 Conn. 224, 125 A. 636 (1924)

19 ALR5th 470—§ 3
State v. Reynolds, 124 N.J. 559, 592 A.2d 194 (1991)

24 ALR6th 1—§ 13
State v. Reynolds, 140 Kan. 269, 36 P.2d 323 (1934)

103 ALR6th 137—§ 4
State v. Reynolds, 171 Ariz. 678, 832 P.2d 695 (Ct. App. Div. 1 1992)

92 ALR5th 35—§ 25
State v. Reynolds, 186 Ohio App. 3d 1, 2009-Ohio-5532, 926 N.E.2d 315 (2d Dist. Montgomery County 2009)

72 ALR6th 227—§ 27, 39, 48
State v. Reynolds, 218 Neb. 753, 359 N.W.2d 93 (1984)

53 ALR6th 1—§ 11
70 ALR6th 361—§ 18
State v. Reynolds, 229 Or. 167, 366 P.2d 524 (1961)

26 ALR5th 1—§ 3, 6
State v. Reynolds, 250 N.W.2d 434 (Iowa 1977)

29 ALR5th 59—§ 2

State v. Reynolds, 264 Conn. 1, 836
A.2d 224 (2003)

21 ALR6th 1—§ 4

State v. Reynolds, 298 N.C. 380, 259
S.E.2d 843 (1979)

34 ALR6th 1—§ 12

State v. Reynolds, 813 S.W.2d 324 (Mo.
Ct. App. E.D. 1991)

72 ALR6th 141—§ 9

State v. Reynolds, 819 S.W.2d 322 (Mo.
1991)

56 ALR5th 385—§ 2, 5

State v. Reynolds, 1988 WL 119390
(Tenn. Crim. App. 1988)

59 ALR5th 1—§ 3 to 6

State v. Reynolds, 2005 WL 2240905
(Tenn. Crim. App. 2005)

15 ALR6th 515—§ 17

State v. Reynua, 807 N.W.2d 473 (Minn.
Ct. App. 2011)

75 ALR6th 541—§ 22

State v. Rheaume, 176 Vt. 413, 2004 VT
35, 853 A.2d 1259 (2004)

81 ALR6th 505—§ 35

State v. Rheaume, 179 Vt. 39, 889 A.2d
711, 28 A.L.R.6th 715 (2005)

28 ALR6th 245—§ 6, 21

State v. Rheaume, 889 A.2d 711 (Vt.
2005)

18 ALR6th 1—§ 2

State v. Rhinehart, 68 N.C. App. 615,
316 S.E.2d 118 (1984)

102 ALR5th 447—§ 16

State v. Rhiner, 662 N.W.2d 373 (Iowa
Ct. App. 2003)

55 ALR6th 391—§ 22
56 ALR6th 185—§ 39

State v. Rhines, 1996 S.D. 55, 548
N.W.2d 415 (S.D. 1996)

20 ALR5th 398—§ 46
79 ALR5th 33—§ 9, 10, 15, 42, 53

State v. Rhoades, 119 Idaho 594, 809
P.2d 455 (1991)

85 ALR5th 547—§ 7

State v. Rhoades, 2007 WI App 19, 298
Wis. 2d 552, 727 N.W.2d 375 (Ct.
App. 2006)

84 ALR6th 293—§ 15, 21, 27

State v. Rhoda, 206 N.J. Super. 584, 503
A.2d 364 (1986)

15 ALR5th 391—§ 45

State v. Rhode, 988 P.2d 685 (Idaho
1999)

45 ALR5th 1—§ 19

State v. Rhode Island Alliance of Social
Service Employees, Local 580,
SEIU, 693 A.2d 1043 (R.I. 1997)

60 ALR5th 669—§ 6

State v. Rhode Island Employment Sec.
Alliance, Local 401, SEIU, AFL-
CIO, 840 A.2d 1093, 174 L.R.R.M.
(BNA) 2220 (R.I. 2003)

14 ALR6th 491—§ 3

State v. Rhoden, 1987 WL 9444 (Tenn.
Crim. App. 1987)

73 ALR5th 383—§ 5

State v. Rhodes, 92 Wash. 2d 755, 600
P.2d 1264 (1979)

101 ALR5th 351—§ 13

State v. Rhodes, 149 N.C. App. 974, 563
S.E.2d 100 (2002)

4 ALR6th 577—§ 4

State v. Rhodes, 627 N.W.2d 74 (Minn.
2001)

93 ALR5th 327—§ 4
67 ALR6th 341—§ 5

State v. Rhodes, 788 P.2d 1380 (Okla.
Crim. 1990)

50 ALR5th 581—§ 2

State v. Rhodes, 1995 WL 425046
(Tenn. Crim. App. 1995)

73 ALR5th 383—§ 8, 29

State v. Rhodes, 2006-Ohio-2401, 2006
WL 1312522 (Ohio Ct. App. 12th
Dist. Butler County 2006)

26 ALR6th 511—§ 19

State v. Rhome, 120 N.C. App. 278, 462
S.E.2d 656 (1995)

57 ALR6th 445—§ 44

State v. Ribalta, 277 N.J. Super. 277,
649 A.2d 862 (App. Div. 1994)

67 ALR5th 149—§ 3, 5

State v. Ribovich, 1987 WL 14438 (Ohio Ct. App. 9th Dist. Medina County 1987)
107 ALR5th 567—§ 10

State v. Ricard, 751 So. 2d 393 (La. Ct. App. 4th Cir. 2000)
99 ALR6th 295—§ 5

State v. Riccard, 142 N.C. App. 298, 542 S.E.2d 320 (2001)
3 ALR6th 269—§ 10, 25

State v. Ricci, 144 N.H. 241, 739 A.2d 404 (1999)
17 ALR6th 327—§ 12

State v. Ricci, 472 A.2d 291 (R.I. 1984)
68 ALR5th 549—§ 3

State v. Rice, 103 Ohio App. 3d 388, 659 N.E.2d 826 (10th Dist. Franklin County 1995)
89 ALR5th 629—§ 12

State v. Rice, 109 Idaho 985, 712 P.2d 686 (App. 1985)
19 ALR5th 470—§ 12

State v. Rice, 110 Wash. 2d 577, 757 P.2d 889 (1988)
111 ALR5th 491—§ 3, 4, 9

State v. Rice, 214 Neb. 518, 335 N.W.2d 269 (1983)
3 ALR5th 784—§ 2

State v. Rice, 261 Kan. 567, 932 P.2d 981 (1997)
65 ALR6th 359—§ 8

State v. Rice, 626 P.2d 104 (Alaska 1981)
50 ALR5th 703—§ 6

State v. Rice, 626 So. 2d 515 (La. App. 3d Cir. 1993)
47 ALR5th 259—§ 2

State v. Rice, 1998 WL 473889 (Tenn. Crim. App. 1998)
73 ALR5th 383—§ 3

State v. Rice, 2003-Ohio-557, 2003 WL 253698 (Ohio Ct. App. 8th Dist. Cuyahoga County 2003)
114 ALR5th 173—§ 7

State v. Rice, 2004-Ohio-697, 2004 WL 292083 (Ohio Ct. App. 12th Dist. Butler County 2004)
3 ALR6th 543—§ 8

State v. Rice, 2009-Ohio-6999, 2009 WL 5176603 (Ohio Ct. App. 11th Dist. Lake County 2009)
64 ALR6th 1—§ 9

State v. Rice Mohawk U.S. Const. Co., Ltd., 692 N.Y.S.2d 43 (App. Div. 1st Dep't 1999)
59 ALR5th 733—§ 4

State v. Rich, 87 N.C. App. 380, 361 S.E.2d 321 (1987)
24 ALR5th 428—§ 18

State v. Rich, 87 Ohio App. 3d 194, 621 N.E.2d 1352, R.I.C.O. Bus. Disp. Guide (CCH) ¶ 8671 (9th Dist. Wayne County 1993)
89 ALR5th 629—§ 8

State v. Rich, 305 N.W.2d 739 (Iowa 1981)
39 ALR5th 283—§ 10, 52

State v. Rich, 417 N.W.2d 868 (S.D. 1988)
5 ALR5th 243—§ 51

State v. Rich, 2006 UT App 233, 138 P.3d 597 (Utah Ct. App. 2006)
37 ALR6th 357—§ 22, 57

State v. Richard, 108 Nev. 626, 836 P.2d 622 (1992)
72 ALR5th 1—§ 3

State v. Richard, 298 S.W.3d 529 (Mo. 2009)
64 ALR6th 131—§ 2, 3, 7

State v. Richard, 798 S.W.2d 468 (Mo. Ct. App. S.D. 1990)
24 ALR6th 1—§ 9

State v. Richard, 2000 WL 1281254 (Ohio Ct. App. 8th Dist. Cuyahoga County 2000)
85 ALR5th 1—§ 21

State v. Richards, 27 Wash. App. 703, 621 P.2d 165 (1980)
29 ALR5th 59—§ 7, 32

State v. Richards, 97 Wash. 587, 167 P. 47 (1917)
9 ALR6th 363—§ 44

State v. Richards, 118 Wis. 2d 414, 347 N.W.2d 906 (App. 1984)
5 ALR5th 243—§ 62

State v. Richards, 136 Wash. 2d 361, 962 P.2d 118 (1998)
  85 ALR5th 1—§ 21, 37
State v. Richards, 155 N.J. Super. 106, 382 A.2d 407 (App. Div. 1978)
  67 ALR5th 361—§ 3
State v. Richards, 166 Ariz. 576, 804 P.2d 109 (Ct. App. Div. 2 1990)
  1 ALR6th 657—§ 4
State v. Richards, 182 W. Va. 664, 391 S.E.2d 354 (1990)
  23 ALR6th 1—§ 28
State v. Richards, 285 Mont. 322, 948 P.2d 240 (1997)
  15 ALR5th 391—§ 5
State v. Richards, 487 So. 2d 98, 11 FLW 965 (Fla. App. D4 1986)
  51 ALR5th 375—§ 7, 10
State v. Richards, 552 N.W.2d 197 (Minn. 1996)
  38 ALR5th 433—§ 35
  57 ALR5th 141—§ 5
State v. Richards, 1997 WL 404067 (Wash. Ct. App. Div. 2 1997)
  73 ALR5th 383—§ 8
State v. Richardson, 47 S.C. 166, 25 S.E. 220 (1896)
  103 ALR6th 137—§ 3, 4
State v. Richardson, 80 Hawaii 1, 904 P.2d 886 (1995)
  41 ALR5th 171—§ 7, 12, 55, 61, 63, 81
State v. Richardson, 105 Wash. App. 19, 19 P.3d 431 (Div. 1 2001)
  11 ALR6th 237—§ 11
State v. Richardson, 112 N.C. App. 58, 434 S.E.2d 657 (1993)
  85 ALR5th 595—§ 3, 5
State v. Richardson, 114 N.M. 725, 845 P.2d 819
  71 ALR6th 249—§ 8
State v. Richardson, 139 Wash. App. 1038, 2007 WL 1885080 (Div. 1 2007)
  38 ALR6th 1—§ 24
State v. Richardson, 175 Ariz. 336, 857 P.2d 388 (Ct. App. Div. 1 1993)
  9 ALR6th 633—§ 15

13 ALR6th 603—§ 20
State v. Richardson, 189 Wis. 2d 418, 525 N.W.2d 378 (Ct. App. 1994)
  58 ALR5th 749—§ 6
State v. Richardson, 197 Wash. 157, 84 P.2d 699 (1938)
  50 ALR5th 467—§ 5, 6
State v. Richardson, 258 La. 62, 245 So. 2d 357 (1971)
  15 ALR5th 391—§ 45
State v. Richardson, 285 A.2d 842, 3 Envt. Rep. Cas. 1866 (Me. 1972)
  50 ALR5th 703—§ 28
State v. Richardson, 328 N.C. 505, 402 S.E.2d 401 (1991)
  22 ALR5th 1—§ 3, 5, 13, 16, 19, 41
State v. Richardson, 434 S.E.2d 657 (N.C. App. 1993)
  38 ALR5th 433—§ 2, 10
State v. Richardson, 529 So. 2d 1301 (La. App. 3d Cir. 1988)
  31 ALR5th 704—§ 4
State v. Richardson, 923 S.W.2d 301 (Mo. 1996)
  70 ALR5th 1—§ 4, 6
  79 ALR5th 419—§ 10
  83 ALR6th 255—§ 15
State v. Richardson, 963 So. 2d 267 (Fla. 2d DCA 2007)
  103 ALR6th 247—§ 9
State v. Richey, 195 La. 319, 196 So. 545 (1940)
  75 ALR5th 295—§ 31
State v. Richmond, 250 Kan. 375, 827 P.2d 743 (1992)
  39 ALR5th 283—§ 4, 41
State v. Richmond, 258 Kan. 449, 904 P.2d 974 (1995)
  39 ALR5th 283—§ 4, 23
State v. Richmond, 347 N.C. 412, 495 S.E.2d 677 (1998)
  103 ALR6th 507—§ 4, 28
State v. Richmond, 590 N.W.2d 33 (Iowa 1999)
  93 ALR5th 327—§ 4
State v. Richmond, 602 N.W.2d 647 (Minn. Ct. App. 1999)

66 ALR5th 397—§ 16
State v. Richter, 235 Wis. 2d 524
64 ALR5th 637—§ 3, 4
State v. Richter, 235 Wis. 2d 524, 2000
WI 58, 612 N.W.2d 29 (2000)
17 ALR6th 327—§ 30
State v. Rickabaugh, 361 N.W.2d 623
(S.D. 1985)
66 ALR6th 83—§ 16
State v. Rickard, 420 So. 2d 303 (Fla.
1982)
62 ALR6th 413—§ 28
State v. Ricketts, 981 S.W.2d 657 (Mo.
Ct. App. W.D. 1998)
85 ALR5th 1—§ 21
State v. Rickman, 178 Wis. 2d 315, 504
N.W.2d 874 (Ct. App. 1993)
65 ALR6th 359—§ 6
State v. Rico, 741 So. 2d 774 (La. Ct.
App. 3d Cir. 1999)
29 ALR5th 487—§ 11, 13
State v. Riddick, 315 N.C. 749, 340
S.E.2d 55 (1986)
85 ALR5th 187—§ 6
State v. Riddle, 149 Or. App. 141, 941
P.2d 1079 (1997)
109 ALR5th 611—§ 3
State v. Riddle, 168 W. Va. 429, 285
S.E.2d 359, 1 Ed. Law Rep. 1008
(1981)
70 ALR5th 169—§ 3, 14, 17
State v. Riddle, 330 Or. 471, 8 P.3d 980
(2000)
66 ALR6th 83—§ 20
State v. Rideau, 376 So. 2d 1251 (La.
1979)
70 ALR5th 533—§ 11
State v. Ridenbaugh, 1999 WL 436769
(Ohio Ct. App. 5th Dist. Licking
County 1999)
78 ALR5th 489—§ 3, 6, 10
State v. Ridgeway, 66 Ohio App. 3d 270,
583 N.E.2d 1123 (Cuyahoga Co.
1990)
39 ALR5th 283—§ 14, 45
State v. Ridgway, 57 Wash. App. 915,
790 P.2d 1263 (1990)

60 ALR5th 1—§ 5
State v. Ridley, 1997 WL 714786
(Wash. Ct. App. Div. 1 1997)
73 ALR5th 383—§ 5
State v. Riechmann, 777 So. 2d 342 (Fla.
2000)
80 ALR5th 55—§ 8
83 ALR6th 465—§ 33
State v. Rieger, 96 Wash. 2d 546, 637
P.2d 236 (1981)
88 ALR5th 121—§ 39
State v. Rieger, 270 Neb. 904, 708
N.W.2d 630 (2006)
72 ALR6th 141—§ 15
State v. Riera, 276 N.C. 361, 172 S.E.2d
535 (1970)
45 ALR5th 1—§ 5, 9, 16
State v. Rife, 215 Neb. 132, 337 N.W.2d
724 (1983)
37 ALR5th 515—§ 7
State v. Riffle, 131 Ariz. 65, 638 P.2d
732 (Ct. App. Div. 2 1981)
31 ALR6th 465—§ 14, 18, 24, 25, 32
State v. Riggins, 68 Ohio App. 2d 1, 22
Ohio Op. 3d 1, 426 N.E.2d 504 (8th
Dist. Cuyahoga County 1980)
74 ALR5th 453—§ 5
State v. Riggins, 138 N.J. Super. 497,
351 A.2d 406 (1976)
43 ALR5th 1—§ 13
State v. Riggins, 180 Or. App. 525, 44
P.3d 615 (2002)
101 ALR5th 351—§ 8, 9
State v. Riggs, 189 Ariz. 327, 942 P.2d
1159 (1997)
91 ALR5th 343—§ 23
State v. Rigual, 49 Conn. App. 420, 714
A.2d 707 (1998)
20 ALR5th 398—§ 6.5
State v. Riker, 123 Wash. 2d 351, 869
P.2d 43 (1994)
90 ALR5th 453—§ 43
State v. Riley, 1 Conn. Cir. Ct. 523, 24
Conn. Supp. 235, 189 A.2d 518
(App. Div. 1962)
78 ALR5th 1—§ 10
State v. Riley, 28 N.J. 188, 145 A.2d 601
(1958)

5 ALR5th 243—§ 2, 62
State v. Riley, 34 Wash. App. 529, 663 P.2d 145 (Div. 3 1983)
6 ALR6th 533—§ 15
State v. Riley, 83 Idaho 346, 362 P.2d 1075 (1961)
119 ALR5th 275—§ 13
State v. Riley, 121 Wash. 2d 22, 846 P.2d 1365 (1993)
4 ALR6th 1—§ 10, 12
87 ALR6th 1—§ 41, 42, 61
State v. Riley, 125 P.3d 1089 (Kan. Ct. App. 2006), unpublished
35 ALR6th 497—§ 37
State v. Riley, 147 Md. App. 113, 807 A.2d 797 (2002)
50 ALR6th 455—§ 4
State v. Riley, 154 Wash. App. 433, 225 P.3d 462 (Div. 1 2010)
55 ALR6th 1—§ 30, 31
State v. Riley, 166 Wis. 2d 299, 479 N.W.2d 234 (App. 1991)
12 ALR5th 89—§ 4
State v. Riley, 196 Ariz. 40, 992 P.2d 1135 (Ct. App. Div. 2 1999)
92 ALR6th 171—§ 18
State v. Riley, 201 W. Va. 708, 500 S.E.2d 524 (1997)
58 ALR5th 749—§ 6
State v. Riley, 230 Wis. 2d 745, 604 N.W.2d 33 (Ct. App. 1999)
27 ALR6th 183—§ 35
State v. Riley, 412 N.J. Super. 162, 988 A.2d 1252 (Law Div. 2009)
87 ALR6th 1—§ 6, 42
State v. Riley, 568 N.W.2d 518 (Minn. 1997)
101 ALR6th 331—§ 12
State v. Riley, 587 So. 2d 130 (La. App. 2d Cir. 1991)
45 ALR5th 1—§ 5, 6, 10, 17
State v. Riley, 1997 WL 771227 (W. Va. 1997)
58 ALR5th 749—§ 6
State v. Riley, 2004-Ohio-4880, 2004 WL 2050521 (Ohio Ct. App. 9th Dist. Summit County 2004)

23 ALR6th 307—§ 38
State v. Riley, 2010 WL 427118 (Wash. Ct. App. Div. 1 2010)
55 ALR6th 1—§ 40
State v. Rimmasch, 775 P.2d 388 (Utah 1989)
90 ALR5th 453—§ 51
24 ALR6th 549—§ 8
State v. Rimmer, 250 S.W.3d 12 (Tenn. 2008)
83 ALR6th 255—§ 12
State v. Rinehart, 152 Wash. App. 1026, 2009 WL 2999177 (Div. 3 2009)
56 ALR6th 1—§ 4
State v. Rinehart, 262 Mont. 204, 864 P.2d 1219 (1993)
112 ALR5th 429—§ 12
State v. Rinehart, 2005 WL 1432223 (Minn. Ct. App. 2005)
26 ALR6th 511—§ 32, 44
State v. Ring, 131 Ariz. 374, 641 P.2d 862 (1982)
39 ALR5th 283—§ 3
72 ALR5th 109—§ 4
State v. Ring, 200 Ariz. 267, 25 P.3d 1139 (2001)
110 ALR5th 1—§ 3, 10, 11, 20
State v. Ring, 2001 WL 201819 (Tenn. Crim. App. 2001)
91 ALR5th 343—§ 32
State v. Ringquist, 433 N.W.2d 207 (N.D. 1988)
112 ALR5th 429—§ 6
State v. Riofta, 166 Wash. 2d 358, 209 P.3d 467 (2009)
72 ALR6th 227—§ 53
State v. Rios, 75 Ohio App. 3d 288, 599 N.E.2d 374 (8th Dist. Cuyahoga County 1991)
70 ALR5th 491—§ 5, 7, 8
State v. Rios, 112 Ariz. 143, 539 P.2d 900 (1975)
32 ALR5th 149—§ 4, 25, 26, 32, 40, 45, 52, 66
State v. Rios, 237 Neb. 232, 465 N.W.2d 611 (1991)
15 ALR5th 391—§ 32
92 ALR5th 35—§ 22

State v. Ripley, 548 N.W.2d 24 (N.D. 1996)
37 ALR6th 357—§ 43, 65
State v. Ripperger, 514 N.W.2d 740 (Iowa App. 1994)
39 ALR5th 283—§ 2, 10, 43
55 ALR5th 423—§ 4
State v. Rippie, 419 So. 2d 1087 (Fla. 1982)
67 ALR5th 637—§ 3, 7
State v. Rippy, 2008-Ohio-6680, 2008 WL 5266097 (Ohio Ct. App. 10th Dist. Franklin County 2008)
71 ALR6th 1—§ 5
State v. Riser, 704 So. 2d 946 (La. Ct. App. 2d Cir. 1997)
85 ALR6th 641—§ 12
State v. Rising, 223 N.C. 747, 28 S.E.2d 221 (1943)
18 ALR6th 509—§ 5
State v. Riske, 152 Wis. 2d 260, 448 N.W.2d 260 (Ct. App. 1989)
76 ALR5th 485—§ 9
State v. Ristau, 305 N.W.2d 499 (Iowa 1981)
70 ALR6th 361—§ 40
State v. Ristau, 340 N.W.2d 273 (Iowa 1983)
39 ALR5th 283—§ 10, 58
State v. Ritchie, 126 Wash. 2d 388, 894 P.2d 1308 (1995)
73 ALR5th 383—§ 3, 5
State v. Ritchie, 174 Ohio App. 3d 582, 2007-Ohio-6577, 883 N.E.2d 1092 (5th Dist. Ashland County 2007)
69 ALR6th 1—§ 5
State v. Ritchie, 1997 WL 164323 (Ohio Ct. App. 9th Dist. Lorain County 1997)
85 ALR5th 595—§ 3
State v. Ritchie, 2000 WL 1209276 (Ohio Ct. App. 2d Dist. Miami County 2000)
69 ALR6th 275—§ 19, 21, 33
State v. Ritt, 599 N.W.2d 802 (Minn. 1999)
57 ALR5th 315—§ 3, 7
85 ALR5th 187—§ 15

State v. Rittenberry, 2001 WL 1464556 (Tenn. Crim. App. 2001)
1 ALR6th 549—§ 7
State v. Rittenhouse, 239 Wis. 2d 592, 2000 WI App 256, 620 N.W.2d 481 (Ct. App. 2000)
119 ALR5th 1—§ 3
State v. Ritts, 94 Wash. App. 784, 973 P.2d 493 (Div. 3 1999)
87 ALR5th 1—§ 6
State v. Ritze, 154 Ohio App. 3d 133, 2003-Ohio-4580, 796 N.E.2d 566 (1st Dist. Hamilton County 2003)
56 ALR6th 185—§ 19
State v. Rivas, 99 Or. App. 23, 781 P.2d 364 (1989)
68 ALR5th 343—§ 3
State v. Rivas, 2011 WL 650388 (N.J. Super. Ct. App. Div. 2011)
99 ALR6th 113—§ 11, 14
State v. Rivenburgh, 11 Utah 2d 95, 355 P.2d 689 (1960)
16 ALR6th 329—§ 4
24 ALR6th 591—§ 4
State v. Rivera, 62 Haw. 120, 612 P.2d 526 (1980)
72 ALR5th 109—§ 5
State v. Rivera, 94 Ariz. 45, 381 P.2d 584 (1963)
97 ALR6th 567—§ 3, 9
State v. Rivera, 106 Haw. 146, 102 P.3d 1044 (2004)
26 ALR6th 511—§ 13
State v. Rivera, 124 N.M. 211, 1997-NMCA-102, 947 P.2d 168 (Ct. App. 1997)
93 ALR6th 207—§ 17
96 ALR6th 355—§ 52
State v. Rivera, 152 Ariz. 507, 733 P.2d 1090 (1987)
9 ALR6th 1—§ 8
State v. Rivera, 207 Ariz. 69, 83 P.3d 69 (Ct. App. Div. 2 2004)
92 ALR6th 295—§ 3, 7, 19
94 ALR6th 191—§ 7
96 ALR6th 355—§ 3
State v. Rivera, 223 Conn. 41, 612 A.2d 749 (1992)

65 ALR6th 537—§ 40

State v. Rivera, 497 N.W.2d 878, 81 Ed. Law Rep. 1064 (Iowa 1993)

70 ALR5th 169—§ 13

State v. Rivera, 804 S.W.2d 141 (Tex. App. Corpus Christi 1990)

6 ALR5th 711—§ 5

State v. Rivera, 2007 WL 924003 (N.J. Super. Ct. App. Div. 2007)

26 ALR6th 511—§ 25, 27

State v. Rivera-Carrillo, 2002-Ohio-1013, 2002 WL 371950 (Ohio Ct. App. 12th Dist. Butler County 2002)

97 ALR6th 567—§ 3, 9

State v. Rivers, 93 Wash. App. 1059, 1999 WL 18047 (Div. 1 1999)

81 ALR6th 505—§ 6

State v. Riviera Beach, 397 So. 2d 685 (Fla. 1981)

53 ALR5th 1—§ 17

State v. Rizo, 463 So. 2d 1165 (Fla. Dist. Ct. App. 3d Dist. 1984)

32 ALR6th 1—§ 10

State v. Rizzo, 69 N.J. 28, 350 A.2d 225 (1975)

6 ALR5th 242—§ 9

State v. Rizzo, 303 Conn. 71, 31 A.3d 1094 (2011)

93 ALR6th 391—§ 20

State v. Rizzo, 2005 WL 1805676 (Conn. Super. Ct. 2005)

69 ALR6th 579—§ 4

State v. R.J. Reynolds Tobacco Co., 304 A.D.2d 379, 761 N.Y.S.2d 596 (1st Dep't 2003)

25 ALR6th 435—§ 48

State v. R.N., 597 So. 2d 862, 17 FLW D 865 (Fla. App. D5 1992)

18 ALR5th 542—§ 5

State v. Roach, 8 Ohio App. 3d 42, 455 N.E.2d 1328 (12th Dist. Warren County 1982)

12 ALR6th 553—§ 22

58 ALR6th 499—§ 15

State v. Roach, 141 N.H. 64, 677 A.2d 157 (1996)

50 ALR5th 581—§ 6

State v. Roach, 146 N.J. 208, 680 A.2d 634 (1996)

121 ALR5th 551—§ 15

State v. Roach, 322 So. 2d 222 (La. 1975)

104 ALR5th 165—§ 11

28 ALR6th 505—§ 7, 9, 16

State v. Roach, 1989 WL 22815 (Tenn. Crim. App. 1989)

1 ALR6th 549—§ 16

State v. Roache, 148 N.H. 45, 803 A.2d 572 (2002)

32 ALR6th 1—§ 11

State v. Roadenbaugh, 234 Kan. 474, 673 P.2d 1166 (1983)

79 ALR5th 237—§ 7

State v. Roan, 532 N.W.2d 563 (Minn. 1995)

24 ALR6th 1—§ 21

69 ALR6th 579—§ 9

State v. Roark, 229 S.W.3d 216 (Mo. Ct. App. W.D. 2007)

84 ALR6th 293—§ 9, 24, 34

State v. Robbins, 35 Wash. 2d 389, 213 P.2d 310 (1950)

23 ALR6th 1—§ 4, 16

State v. Robbins, 272 Kan. 158, 32 P.3d 171 (2001)

70 ALR6th 361—§ 19

State v. Robbins, 275 N.C. 537, 169 S.E.2d 858 (1969)

58 ALR6th 499—§ 6

State v. Roberson, 78 Wash. App. 600, 897 P.2d 443 (Div. 3 1995)

72 ALR6th 141—§ 6

State v. Roberson, 179 Wis. 2d 502, 508 N.W.2d 75 (Ct. App. 1993)

99 ALR6th 295—§ 9

State v. Roberson, 246 N.J. Super. 597, 588 A.2d 434 (1991)

45 ALR5th 1—§ 5

State v. Roberson, 664 So. 2d 687 (La. Ct. App. 3d Cir. 1995)

117 ALR5th 513—§ 28

State v. Roberti, 293 Or. 59, 644 P.2d 1104 (1982)

55 ALR6th 513—§ 8

State v. Roberti, 298 Or. 412, 693 P.2d 27 (1984)
55 ALR6th 513—§ 8
State v. Roberts, 8 S.W.3d 124 (Mo. Ct. App. W.D. 1999)
6 ALR5th 733—§ 14
State v. Roberts, 18 N.C. App. 388, 197 S.E.2d 54 (1973)
39 ALR5th 283—§ 4
State v. Roberts, 25 Ariz. App. 572, 545 P.2d 83 (1976)
14 ALR5th 89—§ 10, 19, 25, 26, 28
State v. Roberts, 62 Ohio St. 2d 94, 403 N.E.2d 971 (Ohio 1980)
2 ALR5th 725—§ 13
State v. Roberts, 62 Ohio St. 2d 170, 16 Ohio Op. 3d 201, 405 N.E.2d 247 (1980)
32 ALR6th 385—§ 4
State v. Roberts, 62 Ohio St. 2d 170, 16 Ohio Ops. 3d 201, 405 N.E.2d 247 (1980)
39 ALR5th 283—§ 14
State v. Roberts, 97 Or. App. 217, 775 P.2d 342 (1989)
38 ALR5th 433—§ 31
State v. Roberts, 102 Ohio App. 3d 514, 657 N.E.2d 547 (9th Dist. Medina County 1995)
104 ALR5th 229—§ 4
115 ALR5th 403—§ 8
4 ALR6th 113—§ 13, 29, 40
34 ALR6th 539—§ 7
101 ALR6th 1—§ 4
State v. Roberts, 120 Wash. App. 1024, 2004 WL 309173 (Div. 3 2004)
7 ALR6th 233—§ 5
State v. Roberts, 136 N.H. 731, 622 A.2d 1225 (1993)
38 ALR5th 433—§ 32, 35
State v. Roberts, 142 Wash. 2d 471, 14 P.3d 713 (2000)
90 ALR5th 453—§ 43
State v. Roberts, 160 Vt. 385, 631 A.2d 835 (1993)
99 ALR6th 397—§ 17
State v. Roberts, 202 Wis. 2d 651, 551 N.W.2d 64 (Ct. App. 1996)
72 ALR5th 403—§ 10
State v. Roberts, 227 Neb. 489, 418 N.W.2d 246, 44 Ed. Law Rep. 681 (1988)
79 ALR5th 1—§ 14
State v. Roberts, 255 Ark. 183, 499 S.W.2d 600 (1973)
28 ALR5th 107—§ 4
State v. Roberts, 273 Ga. 514, 543 S.E.2d 725 (2001)
20 ALR6th 479—§ 22
State v. Roberts, 286 N.C. 265, 210 S.E.2d 396 (1974)
39 ALR5th 283—§ 4
State v. Roberts, 293 N.C. 1, 235 S.E.2d 203 (1977)
103 ALR6th 507—§ 16
State v. Roberts, 331 So. 2d 11 (La. 1976)
86 ALR5th 463—§ 14
State v. Roberts, 384 N.W.2d 688 (S.D. 1986)
12 ALR5th 89—§ 5, 7
State v. Roberts, 434 A.2d 257 (R.I. 1981)
35 ALR6th 497—§ 29
State v. Roberts, 522 S.E.2d 130 (N.C. Ct. App. 1999)
18 ALR5th 1—§ 41
State v. Roberts, 568 So. 2d 1017 (La. 1990)
76 ALR5th 485—§ 3, 4, 17
State v. Roberts, 709 S.W.2d 857 (Mo. 1986)
10 ALR5th 700—§ 34
State v. Roberts, 841 A.2d 175 (R.I. 2003)
56 ALR6th 185—§ 39
State v. Roberts, 948 S.W.2d 577 (Mo. 1997)
83 ALR6th 255—§ 15
State v. Roberts, 957 S.W.2d 449 (Mo. Ct. App. W.D. 1997)
78 ALR6th 297—§ 4, 25, 27, 28
State v. Roberts, 2001 WL 490014 (Ohio Ct. App. 9th Dist. Summit County 2001)

84 ALR6th 293—§ 17

State v. Roberts, 2003 WL 21766240 (Tenn. Crim. App. 2003)

7 ALR6th 233—§ 5

State v. Roberts, 2003 WL 21947259 (Kan. Ct. App. 2003)

26 ALR6th 511—§ 25, 29

State v. Roberts, 2004 WL 2715316 (Tenn. Crim. App. 2004)

26 ALR6th 511—§ 25, 27

State v. Roberts, 2009-Ohio-2977, 2009 WL 1763867 (Ohio Ct. App. 5th Dist. Coshocton County 2009)

64 ALR6th 1—§ 7, 9, 11

State v. Robertson, 51 La. Ann. 159, 24 So. 774 (1899)

105 ALR5th 529—§ 11

State v. Robertson, 86 N.C. 628, 1882 WL 2839 (1882)

54 ALR6th 429—§ 13

State v. Robertson, 108 R.I. 656, 278 A.2d 842 (1971)

72 ALR5th 529—§ 11

State v. Robertson, 111 Ariz. 427, 531 P.2d 1134 (1975)

41 ALR5th 171—§ 68

State v. Robertson, 182 S.W.3d 747 (Mo. Ct. App. W.D. 2006)

52 ALR6th 1—§ 16

State v. Robertson, 328 S.W.2d 576 (Mo. 1959)

99 ALR6th 113—§ 4

State v. Robertson, 386 So. 2d 906 (La. 1980)

29 ALR5th 59—§ 58, 67, 86

State v. Robertson, 615 So. 2d 1036 (La. App. 1st Cir. 1993)

7 ALR5th 263—§ 4

State v. Robertson, 2001 WL 481955 (Minn. Ct. App. 2001)

47 ALR6th 107—§ 23

State v. Robertson, 2009 WL 81291 (Del. Super. Ct. 2009)

71 ALR6th 1—§ 22

State v. Robidoux, 125 N.H. 169, 480 A.2d 67 (1984)

99 ALR6th 295—§ 13

State v. Robinette, 124 N.C. App. 212, 476 S.E.2d 387 (1996)

52 ALR5th 655—§ 8

State v. Robinette, 652 So. 2d 926 (Fla. App. D1 1995)

42 ALR5th 291—§ 34

State v. Robington, 137 Conn. 140, 75 A.2d 394 (1950)

57 ALR6th 445—§ 2, 7

State v. Robinson, 30 Del. 106, 7 Boyce 106, 103 A. 657 (Gen. Sess. 1918)

57 ALR6th 445—§ 49

State v. Robinson, 33 Kan. App. 2d 773, 109 P.3d 185 (2005)

30 ALR6th 1—§ 4

State v. Robinson, 44 Wash. App. 611, 722 P.2d 1379 (1986)

38 ALR5th 433—§ 3, 6

State v. Robinson, 52 La. Ann. 541, 27 So. 129 (1900)

98 ALR6th 455—§ 17

State v. Robinson, 79 Hawaii 468, 903 P.2d 1289 (1995)

57 ALR5th 141—§ 6

State v. Robinson, 89 Wash. App. 530, 953 P.2d 97 (Div. 1 1997)

72 ALR5th 403—§ 11, 12

State v. Robinson, 103 Ohio App. 3d 490, 659 N.E.2d 1292 (1st Dist. Hamilton County 1995)

122 ALR5th 439—§ 7

State v. Robinson, 108 Ariz. 596, 503 P.2d 817 (1972)

34 ALR5th 125—§ 3, 15

State v. Robinson, 118 Kan. 775, 236 P. 647 (1925)

105 ALR5th 1—§ 3, 24

State v. Robinson, 129 P.3d 663 (Kan. Ct. App. 2006)

26 ALR6th 511—§ 25

State v. Robinson, 130 Wash. App. 1038, 2005 WL 3164202 (Div. 2 2005)

27 ALR6th 183—§ 15, 33

State v. Robinson, 132 So. 2d 156 (Fla. 1961)

102 ALR5th 525—§ 72

State v. Robinson, 141 Wis. 2d 979, 415 N.W.2d 862 (Ct. App. 1987)
73 ALR5th 383—§ 9
State v. Robinson, 143 Idaho 306, 142 P.3d 729 (2006)
77 ALR6th 197—§ 10
State v. Robinson, 148 N.C. App. 422, 560 S.E.2d 154 (2002)
106 ALR5th 397—§ 4
State v. Robinson, 153 Ariz. 191, 735 P.2d 801 (1987)
38 ALR5th 433—§ 3, 7, 13, 24
71 ALR5th 637—§ 5
State v. Robinson, 174 Conn. 604, 392 A.2d 475 (1978)
5 ALR5th 243—§ 60
State v. Robinson, 180 W. Va. 400, 376 S.E.2d 606 (1988)
72 ALR5th 403—§ 3
23 ALR6th 1—§ 5, 16
State v. Robinson, 181 N.C. 516, 106 S.E. 155 (1921)
81 ALR5th 563—§ 3, 5
State v. Robinson, 229 Kan. 301, 624 P.2d 964 (1981)
84 ALR5th 487—§ 3
State v. Robinson, 233 Neb. 729, 448 N.W.2d 386 (1989)
65 ALR5th 407—§ 3
State v. Robinson, 237 Conn. 238, 676 A.2d 384 (1996)
20 ALR5th 398—§ 6.5
State v. Robinson, 251 A.2d 552 (Del. 1969)
97 ALR5th 293—§ 3
State v. Robinson, 288 N.W.2d 337 (Iowa 1980)
6 ALR5th 652—§ 2, 3
State v. Robinson, 330 N.C. 1, 409 S.E.2d 288 (1991)
20 ALR5th 177—§ 3, 5
State v. Robinson, 335 S.C. 620, 518 S.E.2d 269 (Ct. App. 1999)
87 ALR6th 1—§ 12, 41
State v. Robinson, 336 N.C. 78, 443 S.E.2d 306 (1994)
83 ALR6th 255—§ 15, 17

State v. Robinson, 339 N.C. 263, 451 S.E.2d 196 (1994)
79 ALR5th 33—§ 70
State v. Robinson, 346 N.C. 586, 488 S.E.2d 174 (1997)
53 ALR6th 81—§ 7
55 ALR6th 391—§ 17
State v. Robinson, 371 N.W.2d 624 (Minn. App. 1985)
43 ALR5th 1—§ 13
State v. Robinson, 388 N.W.2d 43 (Minn. App. 1986)
7 ALR5th 263—§ 4
State v. Robinson, 399 N.J. Super. 400, 944 A.2d 718 (App. Div. 2008)
59 ALR6th 311—§ 4
State v. Robinson, 411 S.E.2d 678 (S.C. App. 1991)
4 ALR5th 1—§ 15
State v. Robinson, 421 So. 2d 229 (La. 1982)
10 ALR5th 700—§ 2, 16
State v. Robinson, 426 S.E.2d 317 (S.C. 1992)
4 ALR5th 1—§ 4, 7, 15
State v. Robinson, 427 N.W.2d 217 (Minn. 1988)
9 ALR5th 369—§ 2, 6
124 ALR5th 1—§ 5
69 ALR6th 579—§ 8
State v. Robinson, 471 So. 2d 1035 (La. Ct. App. 1st Cir. 1985)
71 ALR6th 1—§ 5
State v. Robinson, 484 S.W.2d 186 (Mo. 1972)
70 ALR5th 587—§ 8
State v. Robinson, 496 A.2d 1067 (Me. 1985)
33 ALR6th 353—§ 4
State v. Robinson, 517 N.W.2d 336 (Minn. 1994)
45 ALR5th 1—§ 2, 6, 11, 18, 30
State v. Robinson, 543 S.E.2d 249 (S.C. Ct. App. 2001)
4 ALR5th 1—§ 7
State v. Robinson, 552 So. 2d 943 (Fla. Dist. Ct. App. 4th Dist. 1989)

93 ALR5th 527—§ 3
State v. Robinson, 565 So. 2d 730 (Fla. Dist. Ct. App. 2d Dist. 1990)
85 ALR5th 1—§ 24
State v. Robinson, 572 N.W.2d 720 (Minn. 1997)
87 ALR5th 1—§ 6, 11, 32
State v. Robinson, 618 N.W.2d 306, 147 Ed. Law Rep. 1076 (Iowa 2000)
13 ALR5th 567—§ 4, 10
42 ALR5th 291—§ 29
State v. Robinson, 634 So. 2d 1274 (La. App. 3rd Cir. 1994)
57 ALR5th 141—§ 9
State v. Robinson, 635 So. 2d 130, 19 FLW D 820 (Fla. App. D3 1994)
9 ALR5th 464—§ 3, 4
State v. Robinson, 672 S.W.2d 743 (Mo. App. 1984)
5 ALR5th 243—§ 17
State v. Robinson, 723 So. 2d 350 (Fla. Dist. Ct. App. 2d Dist. 1998)
113 ALR5th 597—§ 8
State v. Robinson, 752 S.W.2d 949 (Mo. App. 1988)
29 ALR5th 59—§ 7, 9, 12
State v. Robinson, 971 S.W.2d 30 (Tenn. Crim. App. 1997)
73 ALR5th 383—§ 29
State v. Robinson, 989 A.2d 965 (R.I. 2010)
69 ALR6th 579—§ 4
State v. Robinson, 1994 WL 684483 (Del. Super. Ct. 1994)
16 ALR6th 329—§ 5
24 ALR6th 591—§ 6, 12
State v. Robinson, 1996 WL 575978 (Ohio App. 5 Dist.)
50 ALR5th 581—§ 5, 7
State v. Robinson, 2003-Ohio-4027, 2003 WL 21743495 (Ohio Ct. App. 5th Dist. Stark County 2003)
23 ALR6th 307—§ 40
State v. Robinson, 2003 WL 649115 (Tenn. Crim. App. 2003)
27 ALR6th 183—§ 29

State v. Robinson, 2003 WL 21946735 (Tenn. Crim. App. 2003)
21 ALR6th 1—§ 4
State v. Robinson, 2004-Ohio-5984, 2004 WL 2538826 (Ohio Ct. App. 2d Dist. Greene County 2004)
46 ALR6th 241—§ 19
State v. Robinson, 2006 WL 1096638 (N.J. Super. Ct. App. Div. 2006)
26 ALR6th 511—§ 17
State v. Robinson, 2007 WL 4531718 (N.J. Super. Ct. App. Div. 2007)
92 ALR6th 549—§ 26
State v. Robinson, 2008-Ohio-216, 2008 WL 192154 (Ohio Ct. App. 8th Dist. Cuyahoga County 2008)
69 ALR6th 1—§ 10
State v. Robison, 281 Mont. 64, 931 P.2d 706 (1997)
92 ALR6th 295—§ 12
94 ALR6th 191—§ 4
State v. Robison, 1986 WL 11935 (Ohio Ct. App. 4th Dist. Pickaway County 1986)
57 ALR5th 141—§ 7
State v. Robison, Slip Op. No. 85 CA 12 (Ohio App. Pickaway Co. 1986)
38 ALR5th 433—§ 13
State v. Robledo, 116 Ariz. 346, 569 P.2d 288 (Ct. App. Div. 1 1977)
99 ALR5th 557—§ 2, 3
92 ALR6th 1—§ 3
State v. Robledo-Kinney, 615 N.W.2d 25 (Minn. 2000)
27 ALR6th 183—§ 31
State v. Robles, 88 Ariz. 253, 355 P.2d 895 (1960)
5 ALR6th 1—§ 19
State v. Robles, 157 Wis. 2d 55, 458 N.W.2d 818 (Ct. App. 1990)
97 ALR6th 567—§ 2, 3, 5, 9
State v. Robles, 171 Ariz. 441, 831 P.2d 440 (Ct. App. Div. 2 1992)
84 ALR6th 293—§ 27
State v. Robles, 182 Ariz. 268, 895 P.2d 1031 (Ct. App. Div. 2 1995)
19 ALR6th 115—§ 4, 7, 10
State v. Roby, 246 So. 2d 566 (Fla. 1971)

34 ALR5th 125—§ 8
State v. Roche, Inc., 2 Neb. App. 445, 511 N.W.2d 195 (1994)
15 ALR5th 391—§ 45
State v. Rochelle, 877 So. 2d 250 (La. Ct. App. 2d Cir. 2004)
21 ALR6th 771—§ 5
State v. Rocheville, 310 S.C. 20, 425 S.E.2d 32 (1993)
79 ALR5th 33—§ 42, 53
State v. Rochon, 393 So. 2d 1224 (La. 1981)
88 ALR5th 429—§ 6
State v. Rock, 92 Wis. 2d 554, 285 N.W.2d 739 (1979)
19 ALR6th 411—§ 13
State v. Rocker, 52 Haw. 336, 475 P.2d 684 (1970)
92 ALR5th 593—§ 3, 5, 7, 10, 11
95 ALR5th 229—§ 4
State v. Rockhold, 243 N.W.2d 846 (Iowa 1976)
114 ALR5th 235—§ 4
State v. Rockholt, 96 N.J. 570, 476 A.2d 1236, 52 A.L.R.4th 757 (1984)
9 ALR5th 464—§ 3, 4, 9
State v. Rodarte, 173 Ariz. 331, 842 P.2d 1344, 122 Ariz. Adv. Rep. 110 (App. 1992)
47 ALR5th 259—§ 2
State v. Rodarte, 842 P.2d 1344, 122 Ariz. Adv. Rep. 110 (Ariz. App. 1992)
20 ALR5th 398—§ 2, 12, 21, 26, 28, 29, 36, 49, 53
State v. Rodas, 2007 WL 581854 (N.J. Super. Ct. App. Div. 2007)
28 ALR6th 505—§ 10
32 ALR6th 1—§ 4
State v. Roderick, 704 So. 2d 49, R.I.C.O. Bus. Disp. Guide (CCH) ¶ 9326 (Miss. 1997)
58 ALR6th 385—§ 35
State v. Roders, 125 Wis. 2d 572, 373 N.W.2d 85 (Ct. App. 1985)
99 ALR6th 113—§ 10
State v. Rodgers, 119 Idaho 1047, 812 P.2d 1208 (1991)

9 ALR5th 369—§ 2, 3, 5, 11, 12
90 ALR5th 453—§ 8
State v. Rodgers, 119 Idaho 1066, 812 P.2d 1227 (App. 1990)
9 ALR5th 369—§ 2
State v. Rodgers, 641 S.W.2d 83 (Mo. 1982)
103 ALR6th 507—§ 34
State v. Rodia, 132 NJL 199, 39 A.2d 484, 156 A.L.R. 523 (1944)
24 ALR5th 465—§ 61
State v. Rodman, 173 Mo. 681, 73 S.W. 605 (1903)
10 ALR5th 700—§ 18
State v. Rodrigue, 409 So. 2d 556 (La. 1982)
35 ALR6th 127—§ 4
State v. Rodrigues, 68 Hawaii 124, 706 P.2d 1293 (1985)
7 ALR5th 263—§ 3, 4
State v. Rodriguez, 48 Wash. App. 815, 740 P.2d 904 (Div. 1 1987)
1 ALR6th 549—§ 7, 8
State v. Rodriguez, 65 Wash. App. 409, 828 P.2d 636 (1992)
55 ALR5th 125—§ 3, 8
62 ALR5th 1—§ 2, 9, 15
State v. Rodriguez, 88 Or. App. 429, 745 P.2d 811 (1987)
15 ALR5th 391—§ 15
State v. Rodriguez, 101 Wash. App. 1016, 2000 WL 788243 (Div. 1 2000)
73 ALR6th 49—§ 19
State v. Rodriguez, 110 Ohio App. 307, 13 Ohio Ops. 2d 79, 169 N.E.2d 444 (Fulton Co. 1959)
32 ALR5th 149—§ 71, 76
State v. Rodriguez, 111 N.C. App. 141, 431 S.E.2d 788 (1993)
9 ALR6th 541—§ 18
State v. Rodriguez, 137 Ariz. 168, 669 P.2d 601 (Ct. App. Div. 2 1983)
9 ALR6th 1—§ 17
State v. Rodriguez, 138 Wash. App. 1047, 2007 WL 1464435 (Div. 1 2007)
33 ALR6th 91—§ 45

State v. Rodriguez, 186 Ariz. 240, 921
P.2d 643 (1996)
90 ALR5th 453—§ 28
10 ALR6th 463—§ 4
32 ALR6th 1—§ 8
83 ALR6th 465—§ 4
State v. Rodriguez, 200 Ariz. 105, 23
P.3d 100 (Ct. App. Div. 2 2001)
26 ALR6th 511—§ 8, 25
State v. Rodriguez, 225 N.J. Super. 466,
542 A.2d 966 (1988)
27 ALR5th 593—§ 5, 9, 10, 14
State v. Rodriguez, 231 Wis. 2d 719,
2000 WI App 1, 605 N.W.2d 663
(Ct. App. 1999)
49 ALR6th 343—§ 4, 20
State v. Rodriguez, 247 Wis. 2d 734,
2001 WI App 206, 634 N.W.2d 844
(Ct. App. 2001)
17 ALR6th 327—§ 22
State v. Rodriguez, 254 Kan. 768, 869
P.2d 631 (1994)
37 ALR6th 357—§ 3
State v. Rodriguez, 272 Neb. 930, 726
N.W.2d 157 (2007)
29 ALR6th 1—§ 11
State v. Rodriguez, 317 Or. 27, 854 P.2d
399 (1993)
75 ALR6th 541—§ 21
State v. Rodriguez, 454 N.W.2d 726
(N.D. 1990)
4 ALR6th 599—§ 12, 22
State v. Rodriguez, 476 So. 2d 503 (La.
App. 1st Cir. 1985)
32 ALR5th 149—§ 22, 23, 32
42 ALR5th 291—§ 30
State v. Rodriguez, 505 N.W.2d 373
(Minn. Ct. App. 1993)
73 ALR5th 383—§ 3
State v. Rodriguez, 559 S.E.2d 435 (Ga.
2002)
101 ALR5th 351—§ 8
State v. Rodriguez, 569 So. 2d 5 (La.
App. 3d Cir. 1990)
45 ALR5th 1—§ 4, 7, 10, 17
State v. Rodriguez, 635 So. 2d 391 (La.
App. 4th Cir. 1994)

32 ALR5th 149—§ 77
State v. Rodriguez, 656 A.2d 262 (Del.
Super. Ct. 1993)
79 ALR5th 33—§ 12
State v. Rodriguez, 785 So. 2d 759 (Fla.
Dist. Ct. App. 3d Dist. 2001)
29 ALR6th 1—§ 10
State v. Rodriguez, 877 S.W.2d 106
(Mo. 1994)
116 ALR5th 479—§ 5
State v. Rodriguez, 985 S.W.2d 83 (Tex.
1999)
1 ALR5th 163—§ 15
State v. Rodriguez, 986 S.W.2d 326
(Tex. App. El Paso 1999)
29 ALR6th 1—§ 3, 5
34 ALR6th 1—§ 3
35 ALR6th 127—§ 3
56 ALR6th 323—§ 3
57 ALR6th 83—§ 3
58 ALR6th 215—§ 3
81 ALR6th 505—§ 3
State v. Rodriguez, 1991 WL 32287
(Tenn. Crim. App. 1991)
68 ALR6th 527—§ 37
State v. Rodriguez, 2003 WL 25745963
(Vt. 2003)
67 ALR6th 103—§ 4
State v. Rodriguez, 2005 WL 1669493
(Minn. Ct. App. 2005)
26 ALR6th 511—§ 32
State v. Rodriguez, 2010-Ohio-1944,
2010 WL 1756881 (Ohio Ct. App.
12th Dist. Preble County 2010)
71 ALR6th 1—§ 12
State v. Rodriguez, 2010 WL 2889565
(Ariz. Ct. App. Div. 1 2010)
71 ALR6th 625—§ 10, 11
State v. Rodriguez-Castillo, 345 Or. 39,
188 P.3d 268 (2008)
97 ALR6th 567—§ 4, 10
State v. Roebuck, 530 So. 2d 1242 (La.
Ct. App. 4th Cir. 1988)
109 ALR5th 99—§ 8
State v. Roenfeldt, 241 Neb. 30, 486
N.W.2d 197 (1992)
38 ALR5th 433—§ 3

State v. Roff, 70 Wash. 2d 606, 424 P.2d 643 (1967)
61 ALR5th 1—§ 4, 5

State v. Roger M., 121 N.H. 19, 424 A.2d 1139 (1981)
69 ALR6th 1—§ 22

State v. Rogers, 4 Ariz. App. 198, 419 P.2d 102 (1966)
54 ALR6th 429—§ 25

State v. Rogers, 17 Ohio St. 3d 174, 17 Ohio B.R. 414, 478 N.E.2d 984 (1985)
20 ALR5th 177—§ 3, 9, 11
39 ALR5th 283—§ 14

State v. Rogers, 28 Ohio St. 3d 427, 28 Ohio B.R. 480, 504 N.E.2d 52 (1986)
10 ALR5th 700—§ 23, 31

State v. Rogers, 30 Wash. App. 653, 638 P.2d 89 (1981)
15 ALR5th 391—§ 13

State v. Rogers, 40 Md. App. 573, 392 A.2d 1186 (1978)
46 ALR5th 523—§ 6, 7

State v. Rogers, 90 N.J. 187, 447 A.2d 537 (1982)
105 ALR5th 529—§ 11

State v. Rogers, 90 N.M. 604, 566 P.2d 1142 (1977)
97 ALR5th 201—§ 3, 4

State v. Rogers, 100 N.M. 517, 673 P.2d 142 (Ct. App. 1983)
59 ALR5th 615—§ 4, 9

State v. Rogers, 102 Or. App. 424, 794 P.2d 1245 (1990)
32 ALR5th 31—§ 3

State v. Rogers, 109 N.C. App. 491, 428 S.E.2d 220 (1993)
38 ALR5th 433—§ 5, 9, 11

State v. Rogers, 111 Wash. App. 1020, 2002 WL 737489 (Div. 2 2002)
58 ALR6th 499—§ 61

State v. Rogers, 112 Wash. 2d 180, 770 P.2d 180 (1989)
113 ALR5th 597—§ 3

State v. Rogers, 112 Wash. App. 1013, 2002 WL 1320260 (Div. 1 2002)

101 ALR6th 545—§ 5

State v. Rogers, 116 N.M. 217, 861 P.2d 258 (Ct. App. 1993)
85 ALR5th 1—§ 26

State v. Rogers, 124 N.J. 113, 590 A.2d 234 (1991)
73 ALR5th 383—§ 20

State v. Rogers, 138 La. 867, 70 So. 863 (1915)
54 ALR6th 429—§ 7

State v. Rogers, 144 Idaho 738, 170 P.3d 881 (2007)
78 ALR6th 1—§ 27, 29, 43

State v. Rogers, 150 La. 1080, 91 So. 518 (1922)
105 ALR5th 529—§ 11

State v. Rogers, 152 Wis. 2d 407, 449 N.W.2d 338 (Ct. App. 1989)
1 ALR6th 549—§ 16

State v. Rogers, 153 N.C. App. 203, 569 S.E.2d 657 (2002)
67 ALR6th 103—§ 5, 10, 12

State v. Rogers, 161 Vt. 236, 638 A.2d 569 (1993)
62 ALR6th 413—§ 42

State v. Rogers, 199 Conn. 453, 508 A.2d 11 (1986)
86 ALR5th 59—§ 4, 5

State v. Rogers, 248 Or. 354, 434 P.2d 338 (1967)
29 ALR5th 59—§ 3, 29

State v. Rogers, 573 S.W.2d 710 (Mo. Ct. App. 1978)
62 ALR6th 1—§ 10
58 ALR6th 499—§ 115

State v. Rogers, 604 S.E.2d 368 (N.C. Ct. App. 2004)
3 ALR6th 543—§ 8

State v. Rogers, 757 So. 2d 655 (La. Ct. App. 1st Cir. 1999)
99 ALR6th 295—§ 16

State v. Rogers, 825 S.W.2d 49 (Mo. App. 1992)
63 ALR5th 375—§ 4

State v. Rogers, 825 S.W.2d 49 (Mo. Ct. App. W.D. 1992)
78 ALR6th 297—§ 43

State v. Rogers, 1999 M.T. 305, 297 Mont. 188, 992 P.2d 229 (1999)
86 ALR5th 59—§ 3

State v. Rogers, 2001 WL 98553 (Iowa Ct. App. 2001)
30 ALR6th 483—§ 43

State v. Rogers, 2005-Ohio-3117, 2005 WL 1460407 (Ohio Ct. App. 9th Dist. Summit County 2005)
23 ALR6th 307—§ 38

State v. Rogers, 2005-Ohio-5358, 2005 WL 2471693 (Ohio Ct. App. 6th Dist. Huron County 2005)
92 ALR6th 171—§ 4

State v. Rogers, 2005 WL 1848480 (Tenn. Crim. App. 2005)
26 ALR6th 511—§ 22

State v. Rogers, 2014 WI App 24, 352 Wis. 2d 755, 843 N.W.2d 711 (Ct. App. 2014)
101 ALR6th 417—§ 8

State v. Rogers, 2014 WL 1327649 (Tenn. Crim. App. 2014)
96 ALR6th 355—§ 45

State v. Rogowski, 130 Ariz. 99, 634 P.2d 387 (1981)
29 ALR5th 59—§ 79, 89

State v. Rogus, 2006 WL 2347802 (Minn. Ct. App. 2006)
56 ALR6th 323—§ 7, 9

State v. Rohm, 609 N.W.2d 504 (Iowa 2000)
15 ALR5th 391—§ 30

State v. Rohman, 261 S.W.2d 69 (Mo. 1953)
54 ALR6th 429—§ 11, 20

State v. Rohrbach, 93 Or. App. 608, 763 P.2d 196 (1988)
65 ALR5th 407—§ 2 to 4, 9, 16

State v. Rohrer, 317 N.W.2d 700 (Minn. 1982)
73 ALR5th 383—§ 5

State v. Rohrich, 132 Wash. 2d 472, 939 P.2d 697 (1997)
71 ALR5th 637—§ 3

State v. Rojano, 519 S.W.2d 42 (Mo. Ct. App. 1975)
55 ALR6th 157—§ 62, 111

State v. Rojas, 64 Ohio St. 3d 131, 592 N.E.2d 1376 (1992)
20 ALR5th 177—§ 3

State v. Rojas, 128 P.3d 442 (Kan. Ct. App. 2006)
26 ALR6th 511—§ 25

State v. Rojas, 177 Ariz. 454, 868 P.2d 1037 (Ct. App. Div. 1 1993)
85 ALR5th 595—§ 3

State v. Rojas-Tapia, 151 Idaho 479, 259 P.3d 625 (Ct. App. 2011)
79 ALR6th 1—§ 8, 81

State v. Rojo, 1999 -NMSC- 001, 126 N.M. 438, 971 P.2d 829 (1998)
28 ALR5th 754—§ 8

State v. Roland, 88 N.C. App. 19, 362 S.E.2d 800 (1987)
59 ALR5th 749—§ 4

State v. Roland, 577 So. 2d 680, 16 FLW D 869 (Fla. App. D4 1991)
27 ALR5th 593—§ 16, 17

State v. Rolen, 662 So. 2d 446 (La. 1995)
97 ALR5th 293—§ 4

State v. Rolerson, 593 A.2d 220 (Me. 1991)
41 ALR6th 295—§ 5, 7

State v. Rolland, 861 S.W.2d 840 (Tenn. Crim. 1992)
39 ALR5th 283—§ 4

State v. Roller, 2004 WL 1686607 (Tenn. Crim. App. 2004)
18 ALR6th 613—§ 4

State v. Rollf, 40 Or. App. 535, 595 P.2d 1377 (1979)
56 ALR6th 185—§ 8

State v. Rollie, 585 S.W.2d 78 (Mo. Ct. App. W.D. 1979)
98 ALR5th 445—§ 4

State v. Rollie M., 41 Wash. App. 55, 701 P.2d 1123 (1985)
43 ALR5th 1—§ 11

State v. Rollins, 20 Conn. App. 27, 564 A.2d 318 (1989)
38 ALR6th 97—§ 14

State v. Rollins, 129 N.H. 684, 533 A.2d 331 (1987)
90 ALR6th 385—§ 7

State v. Rollins, 141 Vt. 105, 444 A.2d 884 (1982)

119 ALR5th 379—§ 5

State v. Rollins, 188 S.W.3d 553 (Tenn. 2006)

69 ALR6th 579—§ 4

State v. Rollins, 605 S.W.2d 828 (Tenn. Crim. 1980)

39 ALR5th 283—§ 4

State v. Rollins, 658 S.E.2d 43 (N.C. Ct. App. 2008)

32 ALR6th 1—§ 10

State v. Rollins, 749 So. 2d 890 (La. Ct. App. 2d Cir. 1999)

79 ALR6th 125—§ 4, 13

State v. Rollins, 2006-Ohio-1879, 2006 WL 988510 (Ohio Ct. App. 3d Dist. Paulding County 2006)

72 ALR6th 1—§ 4

State v. Rolon, 257 Conn. 156, 777 A.2d 604 (2001)

40 ALR6th 1—§ 31

State v. Romain, 1999 MT 161, 295 Mont. 152, 983 P.2d 322 (1999)

45 ALR6th 643—§ 16

State v. Roman, 70 Haw. 351, 772 P.2d 113 (1989)

29 ALR6th 1—§ 3, 7

34 ALR6th 1—§ 3

35 ALR6th 127—§ 3

State v. Roman, 224 Conn. 63, 616 A.2d 266 (1992)

32 ALR5th 149—§ 4, 71, 72

State v. Romans, 452 So. 2d 655 (Fla. App. D2 1984)

2 ALR5th 262—§ 3

State v. Rome, 239 Wis. 2d 491, 2000 WI App 243, 620 N.W.2d 225 (Ct. App. 2000)

58 ALR6th 499—§ 32

State v. Romeo, 542 N.W.2d 543, 49 A.L.R.5th 847 (Iowa 1996)

49 ALR5th 619—§ 2, 3

24 ALR6th 1—§ 21

State v. Romero, 59 Conn. App. 469, 757 A.2d 643 (2000)

39 ALR6th 257—§ 4

State v. Romero, 61 Ariz. 249, 148 P.2d 357 (1944)

19 ALR5th 823—§ 15, 17

State v. Romero, 103 N.M. 532, 710 P.2d 99 (Ct. App. 1985)

95 ALR5th 229—§ 24

State v. Romero, 279 Mont. 58, 926 P.2d 717 (1996)

18 ALR5th 1—§ 35

State v. Romero, 574 So. 2d 330 (La. 1990)

79 ALR6th 125—§ 5, 15, 16

State v. Romero, 2007-1810 La. App. 1 Cir. 2/27/08, 2008 WL 508647 (La. Ct. App. 1st Cir. 2008)

75 ALR6th 541—§ 12

State v. Romers, 159 Ariz. 271, 766 P.2d 623 (Ct. App. Div. 1 1988)

9 ALR6th 633—§ 15, 24

10 ALR6th 265—§ 15

State v. Romig, 73 Or. App. 780, 700 P.2d 293 (1985)

58 ALR6th 385—§ 20

State v. Romine, 166 W. Va. 135, 272 S.E.2d 680 (1980)

62 ALR5th 121—§ 6

State v. Romo, 66 Ariz. 174, 185 P.2d 757 (1947)

78 ALR5th 1—§ 25

State v. Romonto, 190 Neb. 825, 212 N.W.2d 641 (1973)

114 ALR5th 173—§ 6

State v. Romos, 787 N.W.2d 480 (Iowa Ct. App. 2010)

74 ALR6th 373—§ 13

State v. Ronek, 176 N.W.2d 153, 41 A.L.R.3d 1329 (Iowa 1970)

123 ALR5th 411—§ 7

90 ALR6th 385—§ 7

State v. Ronngren, 356 N.W.2d 903 (N.D. 1984)

104 ALR5th 229—§ 4, 5

4 ALR6th 113—§ 14

101 ALR6th 1—§ 7

State v. Ronngren, 361 N.W.2d 224 (N.D. 1985)

62 ALR5th 1—§ 11, 15

85 ALR5th 1—§ 2, 15

State v. Ronquillo, 89 Wash. App. 1037, 1998 WL 87641 (Div. 1 1998)

16 ALR6th 329—§ 4

19 ALR6th 115—§ 4

24 ALR6th 591—§ 9, 13

State v. Rood, 18 Wash. App. 740, 573 P.2d 1325 (Div. 2 1977)

103 ALR5th 463—§ 3

State v. Rood, 188 W. Va. 39, 422 S.E.2d 516 (1992)

99 ALR6th 295—§ 19

State v. Rook, 174 S.C. 225, 177 S.E. 143 (1934)

16 ALR6th 329—§ 7

24 ALR6th 591—§ 6

State v. Rooks, 109 Wash. App. 1009, 2001 WL 1407636 (Div. 2 2001)

82 ALR6th 373—§ 3

State v. Root, 9 P.3d 214 (Wash. 2000)

42 ALR5th 291—§ 25

State v. Root, 193 Ariz. 442, 973 P.2d 1203 (Ct. App. Div. 1 1998)

119 ALR5th 379—§ 3

State v. Root, 202 Or. App. 491, 123 P.3d 281 (2005)

50 ALR6th 353—§ 13

State v. Roper, 34 Or. App. 273, 578 P.2d 479 (1978)

4 ALR6th 577—§ 11

State v. Roper, 378 N.J. Super. 236, 875 A.2d 954 (App. Div. 2005)

71 ALR6th 1—§ 5

State v. Rorvik, 224 Mont. 104, 728 P.2d 419 (1986)

32 ALR6th 1—§ 9

State v. Rosa, 47 Ohio App. 3d 172, 547 N.E.2d 1232 (Cuyahoga Co. 1988)

32 ALR5th 149—§ 54, 56

State v. Rosa, 575 A.2d 727 (Me. 1990)

38 ALR5th 433—§ 26

State v. Rosales, 2002-Ohio-6132, 2002 WL 31516389 (Ohio Ct. App. 4th Dist. Ross County 2002)

29 ALR6th 1—§ 10

State v. Rosales-Gonzales, 59 Wash. App. 583, 799 P.2d 756 (Div. 3 1990)

105 ALR5th 529—§ 7

State v. Rosario, 93 N.C. App. 627, 379 S.E.2d 434 (1989)

18 ALR5th 1—§ 17

24 ALR5th 428—§ 7, 16

State v. Rosario, 195 Ariz. 264, 987 P.2d 226 (Ct. App. Div. 1 1999)

29 ALR6th 237—§ 4, 8, 11

State v. Rosario, 238 Conn. 380, 680 A.2d 237 (1996)

113 ALR5th 517—§ 8

State v. Rosario, 2007 WL 412631 (N.J. Super. Ct. App. Div. 2007)

26 ALR6th 511—§ 17

State v. Rosas, 108 Or. App. 28, 813 P.2d 77 (1991)

92 ALR5th 35—§ 19

State v. Rosch, 146 Wash. App. 1050, 2008 WL 4120052 (Div. 1 2008)

64 ALR6th 131—§ 3, 5

85 ALR6th 641—§ 5

State v. Roscoe, 145 Ariz. 212, 700 P.2d 1312 (1984)

81 ALR5th 563—§ 3

State v. Roscoe, 185 Ariz. 68, 912 P.2d 1297 (1996)

91 ALR5th 343—§ 3, 6, 12

State v. Rose, 7 Wash. App. 176, 498 P.2d 897 (Div. 2 1972)

55 ALR6th 157—§ 45

State v. Rose, 41 N.J. Super. 434, 125 A.2d 351 (1956)

29 ALR5th 59—§ 62

State v. Rose, 45 Or. App. 879, 609 P.2d 875 (1980)

15 ALR5th 391—§ 2

92 ALR5th 35—§ 2, 12

State v. Rose, 53 N.C. App. 608, 281 S.E.2d 404 (1981)

51 ALR6th 1—§ 5

State v. Rose, 75 Wash. App. 28, 876 P.2d 925 (Div. 1 1994)

61 ALR5th 1—§ 3, 11

State v. Rose, 79 N.M. 277, 442 P.2d
589 (1968)
  55 ALR6th 157—§ 4
State v. Rose, 112 Conn. App. 324, 963
A.2d 68 (2009)
  99 ALR6th 295—§ 7
State v. Rose, 112 R.I. 402, 311 A.2d
281 (1973)
  26 ALR5th 1—§ 4, 26
State v. Rose, 168 Conn. 623, 362 A.2d
813 (1975)
  113 ALR5th 517—§ 9
State v. Rose, 249 S.W.2d 324 (Mo.
1952)
  24 ALR6th 747—§ 36 to 38
  54 ALR6th 429—§ 7
State v. Rose, 305 Conn. 594, 46 A.3d
146, 99 A.L.R.6th 765 (2012)
  99 ALR6th 295—§ 2, 7, 17, 18, 37
State v. Rose, 335 N.C. 301, 439 S.E.2d
518 (1994)
  83 ALR6th 255—§ 19, 26
State v. Rose, 804 S.W.2d 816 (Mo. Ct.
App. E.D. 1991)
  72 ALR5th 109—§ 5
State v. Rose, 1988 WL 91317 (Ohio Ct.
App. 3d Dist. Union County 1988)
  57 ALR6th 83—§ 12
State v. Rose, 2007 WL 3036834 (Idaho
2007)
  30 ALR6th 1—§ 4
State v. Roseberry, 210 Ariz. 360, 111
P.3d 402 (2005)
  21 ALR6th 1—§ 4
State v. Roseberry, 222 Kan. 715, 567
P.2d 883 (1977)
  45 ALR5th 767—§ 15
State v. Roseboro, 1990 WL 277237
(Conn. Super. Ct. 1990)
  18 ALR6th 1—§ 5, 24
State v. Rosebrook, 1988 WL 87139
(Ohio Ct. App. 3d Dist. Marion
County 1988)
  107 ALR5th 567—§ 3, 10, 12
State v. Rosebrook, 1991 WL 216869
(Ohio Ct. App. 3d Dist. Union
County 1991)

  107 ALR5th 567—§ 3
State v. Rosen, 72 Wis. 2d 200, 240
N.W.2d 168 (1976)
  6 ALR5th 711—§ 2, 6
  43 ALR5th 545—§ 8
State v. Rosen, 1992 WL 145317 (Minn.
Ct. App. 1992)
  79 ALR5th 1—§ 14
State v. Rosenberg, 144 N.J. Super. 326,
365 A.2d 486 (1976)
  13 ALR5th 567—§ 4
State v. Rosencrans, 128 N.H. 399, 514
A.2d 817 (1986)
  104 ALR5th 357—§ 6
  54 ALR6th 429—§ 27
State v. Rosencrantz, 110 Idaho 124, 714
P.2d 93 (App. 1986)
  57 ALR5th 141—§ 3
State v. Rosenfeld, 93 Wis. 2d 325, 286
N.W.2d 596 (1980)
  31 ALR5th 704—§ 13
State v. Rosenstiel, 473 N.W.2d 59
(Iowa 1991)
  52 ALR5th 655—§ 2, 5
  97 ALR6th 653—§ 20
State v. Roskom, 2007 WL 432989
(Tenn. Crim. App. 2007)
  33 ALR6th 91—§ 46
State v. Rosof, 180 Ga. App. 637, 350
S.E.2d 36 (1986)
  125 ALR5th 281—§ 4
State v. Ross, 42 Wash. App. 806, 714
P.2d 703 (1986)
  3 ALR5th 784—§ 3, 10
State v. Ross, 42 Wash. App. 806, 714
P.2d 703 (Div. 1 1986)
  7 ALR6th 233—§ 5
State v. Ross, 46 N.C. App. 338, 264
S.E.2d 742 (1980)
  78 ALR5th 567—§ 5
State v. Ross, 47 S.D. 188, 197 N.W.
234 (1924)
  104 ALR5th 357—§ 5
State v. Ross, 49 S.W.3d 833 (Tenn.
2001)
  23 ALR6th 307—§ 31, 42

For assistance, call 1-800-328-4880

State v. Ross, 66 Or. App. 504, 674 P.2d 85 (1984)
26 ALR5th 603—§ 4

State v. Ross, 71 Wash. App. 556, 861 P.2d 473 (Div. 2 1993)
73 ALR5th 383—§ 42

State v. Ross, 100 Tenn. 303, 45 S.W. 673 (1898)
42 ALR5th 547—§ 6

State v. Ross, 104 N.M. 23, 715 P.2d 471, Blue Sky L. Rep. (CCH) ¶ 72394 (Ct. App. 1986)
3 ALR6th 269—§ 19, 26

State v. Ross, 130 Vt. 235, 290 A.2d 38 (1972)
78 ALR5th 1—§ 5

State v. Ross, 183 Neb. 1, 157 N.W.2d 860 (1968)
30 ALR6th 103—§ 13

State v. Ross, 230 Conn. 183, 646 A.2d 1318 (1994)
29 ALR6th 1—§ 10

State v. Ross, 275 N.C. 550, 169 S.E.2d 875 (1969)
79 ALR5th 237—§ 3

State v. Ross, 329 Ark. 1, 945 S.W.2d 374 (1997)
30 ALR6th 483—§ 17, 30

State v. Ross, 343 So. 2d 722 (La.1977)
62 ALR5th 121—§ 6

State v. Ross, 451 N.W.2d 231 (Minn. Ct. App. 1990)
65 ALR6th 537—§ 22, 27

State v. Ross, 491 N.W.2d 658 (Minn. 1992)
83 ALR5th 277—§ 9, 11

State v. Ross, 515 S.E.2d 252 (N.C. Ct. App. 1999)
39 ALR5th 283—§ 23

State v. Ross, 674 So. 2d 489 (La. Ct. App. 1st Cir. 1996)
20 ALR5th 398—§ 23

State v. Ross, 704 So. 2d 920 (La. Ct. App. 4th Cir. 1997)
24 ALR6th 1—§ 51

State v. Ross, 782 P.2d 529 (Utah Ct. App. 1989)
84 ALR5th 487—§ 19

State v. Ross, 923 S.W.2d 354 (Mo. App. 1996)
13 ALR5th 628—§ 21

State v. Ross, 965 So. 2d 610 (La. Ct. App. 2d Cir. 2007)
30 ALR6th 103—§ 58

State v. Ross, 1991 WL 13734 (Ohio App. Jackson Co. 1991)
52 ALR5th 559—§ 4, 7

State v. Ross, 1991 WL 13734 (Ohio Ct. App. 4th Dist. Jackson County 1991)
46 ALR6th 241—§ 15

State v. Ross, 2002-Ohio-6084, 2002 WL 31492312 (Ohio Ct. App. 2d Dist. Montgomery County 2002)
55 ALR6th 391—§ 21

State v. Ross, 2012-Ohio-2433, 2012 WL 1971136 (Ohio Ct. App. 7th Dist. Mahoning County 2012)
83 ALR6th 465—§ 55

State v. Rossano, 2011 WL 2671921 (N.J. Super. Ct. App. Div. 2011)
68 ALR6th 527—§ 39

State v. Rosse, 478 N.W.2d 482 (Minn. 1991)
57 ALR6th 83—§ 19

State v. Rossi, 273 So. 2d 265 (La. 1973)
20 ALR5th 398—§ 6

State v. Rossier, 175 Conn. 204, 397 A.2d 110 (1978)
5 ALR5th 243—§ 5

State v. Rossier, 672 A.2d 455 (R.I. 1996)
38 ALR5th 433—§ 26

State v. Rossiter, 2004-Ohio-4727, 2004 WL 1969399 (Ohio Ct. App. 9th Dist. Wayne County 2004)
72 ALR6th 227—§ 11

State v. Rotenberry, 54 N.C. App. 504, 284 S.E.2d 197 (1981)
5 ALR5th 243—§ 2

State v. Roth, 269 N.W.2d 808 (S.D. 1978)
113 ALR5th 517—§ 5

State v. Roth, 827 P.2d 255 (Utah Ct. App. 1992)

84 ALR6th 293—§ 17, 37
State v. Roth, 2004 ND 23, 674 N.W.2d
495 (N.D. 2004)
50 ALR6th 455—§ 37
State v. Rothenberg, 195 Conn. 253, 487
A.2d 545 (1985)
102 ALR5th 447—§ 22
State v. Rothwell, 125 P.3d 1089 (Kan.
Ct. App. 2006)
37 ALR6th 357—§ 54, 59
State v. Rotko, 116 Wash. App. 230, 67
P.3d 1098 (Div. 2 2003)
31 ALR6th 465—§ 11, 22
State v. Roubique, 421 So. 2d 859 (La.
1982)
45 ALR6th 643—§ 10
State v. Rought, 221 N.J. Super. 42, 533
A.2d 419 (Law Div. 1987)
46 ALR6th 63—§ 8
State v. Roughton, 132 Ohio App. 3d
268, 724 N.E.2d 1193 (6th Dist.
Wood County 1999)
94 ALR5th 393—§ 12
State v. Roughton, 689 S.E.2d 246 (N.C.
Ct. App. 2009)
57 ALR6th 1—§ 23
State v. Roundtree, 1992 WL 356386
(Ohio Ct. App. 8th Dist. Cuyahoga
County 1992)
88 ALR5th 121—§ 2, 14, 26, 28
State v. Rounsville, 136 Idaho 869, 42
P.3d 100 (Ct. App. 2002)
73 ALR6th 49—§ 21
State v. Rouse, 53 Ohio App. 3d 48, 557
N.E.2d 1227 (10th Dist. Franklin
County 1988)
17 ALR6th 327—§ 12
State v. Rousseau, 1991 WL 75247
(Minn. Ct. App. 1991)
73 ALR5th 383—§ 5
State v. Roussel, 381 So. 2d 796 (La.
1980)
78 ALR5th 1—§ 20
State v. Routh, 30 Or. App. 901, 568
P.2d 704 (1977)
1 ALR6th 657—§ 4
State v. Routhier, 137 Ariz. 90, 669 P.2d
68 (1983)

124 ALR5th 1—§ 5
State v. Roux, 487 So. 2d 1226 (La. Ct.
App. 3d Cir. 1986)
72 ALR5th 529—§ 11
State v. Rowe, 68 Ohio App. 3d 595, 589
N.E.2d 394 (10th Dist. Franklin
County 1990)
124 ALR5th 1—§ 5
State v. Rowe, 68 Ohio App. 3d 595, 589
N.E.2d 394 (Ohio App. 1990)
48 ALR5th 555—§ 2
State v. Rowe, 104 Iowa 323, 73 N.W.
833 (1898)
20 ALR6th 561—§ 20
State v. Rowe, 155 N.C. 436, 71 S.E.
332 (1911)
104 ALR5th 357—§ 6
State v. Rowe, 210 Neb. 419, 315
N.W.2d 250 (1982)
38 ALR5th 433—§ 41
State v. Rowe, 397 A.2d 558 (Me. 1979)
84 ALR5th 487—§ 19
State v. Rowe, 422 So. 2d 75 (Fla. Dist.
Ct. App. 2d Dist. 1982)
62 ALR6th 413—§ 38, 42
State v. Rowe, 806 P.2d 730, 154 Utah
Adv. Rep. 12 (Utah App. 1991)
41 ALR5th 171—§ 23, 38, 68, 73
State v. Rowe, 806 S.W.2d 122 (Mo. Ct.
App. E.D. 1991)
9 ALR6th 1—§ 17
State v. Rowe, 850 P.2d 427, 196 Utah
Adv. Rep. 14 (Utah 1992)
**41 ALR5th 171—§ 8, 91, 103, 108,
114, 120, 128, 134**
State v. Rowe, 2001-Ohio-8625, 2001
WL 1887770 (Ohio Ct. App. 1st
Dist. Hamilton County 2001)
38 ALR6th 439—§ 12
State v. Rowell, 121 N.M. 111, 908 P.2d
1379, 70 A.L.R.5th 819 (1995)
70 ALR5th 647—§ 4, 6
87 ALR6th 1—§ 25, 42
State v. Rowell, 256 Kan. 200, 883 P.2d
1184 (1994)
72 ALR5th 403—§ 11

State v. Rowland, 263 N.C. 353, 139 S.E.2d 661, 18 A.L.R.3d 1212 (1965)
81 ALR5th 563—§ 3, 5, 8, 9

State v. Rowsey, 343 N.C. 603, 472 S.E.2d 903 (1996)
73 ALR5th 383—§ 42

State v. Roy, 214 Neb. 204, 333 N.W.2d 398 (1983)
82 ALR5th 359—§ 5
84 ALR5th 487—§ 24

State v. Roy, 458 So. 2d 1040 (La. Ct. App. 3d Cir. 1984)
95 ALR5th 229—§ 26

State v. Roy, 944 So. 2d 403 (Fla. Dist. Ct. App. 3d Dist. 2006)
62 ALR6th 413—§ 38

State v. Royal, 234 Kan. 218, 670 P.2d 1337 (1983)
39 ALR5th 283—§ 4

State v. Royster, 590 N.W.2d 82 (Minn. 1999)
88 ALR5th 121—§ 27

State v. Royster, 1998 WL 351413 (Ohio Ct. App. 5th Dist. Stark County 1998)
4 ALR6th 599—§ 11
35 ALR6th 497—§ 29

State v. Rozier, 69 N.C. App. 38, 316 S.E.2d 893 (1984)
19 ALR6th 115—§ 10

State v. Rozier, 2006 WL 1601784 (Minn. Ct. App. 2006)
26 ALR6th 511—§ 44

State v. R.P.H., 173 Wash. 2d 199, 265 P.3d 890 (2011)
85 ALR6th 641—§ 11

State v. Ruan, 419 N.W.2d 734 (Iowa Ct. App. 1987)
84 ALR5th 487—§ 21

State v. Ruane, 912 S.W.2d 766 (Tenn. Cr App. 1995)
57 ALR5th 141—§ 2, 4

State v. Rubenstein, 40 Ohio App. 3d 57, 531 N.E.2d 732 (8th Dist. Cuyahoga County 1987)
70 ALR5th 1—§ 8

State v. Rubey, 2000 ND 119, 611 N.W.2d 888 (N.D. 2000)
33 ALR6th 91—§ 19

State v. Rubio, 131 N.M. 479, 2002-NMCA-007, 39 P.3d 144, 109 A.L.R.5th 747 (Ct. App. 2002)
109 ALR5th 99—§ 2, 8
113 ALR5th 517—§ 2

State v. Rubio, 967 So. 2d 768, R.I.C.O. Bus. Disp. Guide (CCH) ¶ 11327 (Fla. 2007)
79 ALR6th 125—§ 30

State v. Rubio, 1991 WL 261843 (Tenn. Crim. App. 1991)
99 ALR6th 295—§ 13

State v. Ruby, 149 Ohio App. 3d 541, 2002-Ohio-5381, 778 N.E.2d 101 (2d Dist. Champaign County 2002)
23 ALR6th 307—§ 44

State v. Rucker, 267 Kan. 816, 987 P.2d 1080 (1999)
29 ALR5th 487—§ 3

State v. Rucker, 847 S.W.2d 512 (Tenn. Crim. 1992)
38 ALR5th 433—§ 6, 7, 14, 22

State v. Rudd, 60 N.C. App. 425, 299 S.E.2d 251 (1983)
104 ALR5th 357—§ 4
54 ALR6th 429—§ 21

State v. Rudd, 871 S.W.2d 530 (Tex. App. Dallas 1994)
24 ALR6th 1—§ 38

State v. Ruddle, 170 W. Va. 669, 295 S.E.2d 909 (1982)
1 ALR6th 549—§ 8

State v. Rudolph, 332 So. 2d 806 (La. 1976)
86 ALR5th 463—§ 9

State v. Rudy, 105 Wash. 2d 921, 719 P.2d 550 (1986)
97 ALR5th 201—§ 6

State v. Ruebke, 240 Kan. 493, 731 P.2d 842 (1987)
37 ALR5th 515—§ 3, 10

State v. Rueckert, 221 Kan. 727, 561 P.2d 850 (1977)
50 ALR5th 467—§ 4, 9

CASES CITED IN ALR5th and ALR6th

State v. Ruesch, 214 Wis. 2d 548, 571
N.W.2d 898 (Ct. App. 1997)
29 ALR5th 487—§ 3, 7
State v. Ruesga, 851 P.2d 1229, 211
Utah Adv. Rep. 48 (Utah App.
1993)
32 ALR5th 149—§ 22, 23, 36
State v. Ruess, 118 Idaho 707, 800 P.2d
103 (Ct. App. 1990)
112 ALR5th 429—§ 9
State v. Rufener, 401 N.W.2d 740 (S.D.
1987)
3 ALR6th 269—§ 24
State v. Ruff, 252 Kan. 625, 847 P.2d
1258 (1993)
45 ALR5th 591—§ 15
State v. Ruff, 256 S.W.3d 55 (Mo. 2008)
72 ALR6th 227—§ 23
State v. Ruffin, 206 Conn. 678, 539 A.2d
144 (1988)
11 ALR5th 831—§ 11, 18
State v. Rufus, 338 Ark. 305, 993
S.W.2d 490 (1999)
73 ALR6th 49—§ 3, 26, 66
State v. Rugebregt, 965 P.2d 518 (Utah
Ct. App. 1998)
24 ALR6th 549—§ 8
State v. Rugon, 355 So. 2d 876 (La.
1977)
69 ALR6th 1—§ 22
State v. Ruiz, 94 N.M. 771, 617 P.2d 160
(App. 1980)
38 ALR5th 433—§ 40
State v. Ruiz, 213 Wis. 2d 200, 570
N.W.2d 556 (Ct. App. 1997)
67 ALR5th 361—§ 3, 4, 6
State v. Ruiz, 243 Ga. App. 337, 531
S.E.2d 418 (2000)
116 ALR5th 479—§ 5
State v. Ruiz, 243 Ga. App. 337, 2000
WL 283681 (2000)
82 ALR5th 103—§ 6
State v. Ruiz, 843 P.2d 1044, 204 Utah
Adv. Rep. 11 (Utah App. 1992)
41 ALR5th 171—§ 17, 19, 33, 68
State v. Ruiz, 909 So. 2d 986 (Fla. Dist.
Ct. App. 5th Dist. 2005)

33 ALR6th 373—§ 11
State v. Ruiz, 1998 WL 436557 (Ariz.
Ct. App. Div. 1 1998)
72 ALR5th 403—§ 15, 19
State v. Ruiz-Martinez, 173 Or. App.
202, 21 P.3d 147 (2001)
20 ALR5th 398—§ 21
State v. Rulon, 935 S.W.2d 723 (Mo. Ct.
App. E.D. 1996)
80 ALR5th 469—§ 3, 5
State v. Rumley, 194 Mont. 506, 634
P.2d 446 (1981)
84 ALR6th 427—§ 4
State v. Rummel, 2007 WL 1309607
(Kan. Ct. App. 2007)
26 ALR6th 511—§ 25
State v. Rumore, 28 Conn. App. 402,
613 A.2d 1328 (1992)
5 ALR5th 243—§ 31, 62
39 ALR6th 257—§ 42
State v. Runkles, 174 Conn. 405, 389
A.2d 730 (1978)
35 ALR6th 497—§ 29, 35
State v. Runningeagle, 176 Ariz. 59, 859
P.2d 169 (1993)
16 ALR6th 329—§ 4
24 ALR6th 591—§ 4, 12
State v. Runyon, 144 P.3d 782 (Kan. Ct.
App. 2006)
26 ALR6th 511—§ 25
State v. Runyon, 2007-Ohio-590, 2007
WL 438302 (Ohio Ct. App. 12th
Dist. Butler County 2007)
99 ALR6th 295—§ 13
State v. Ruona, 133 Mont. 243, 321 P.2d
615 (1958)
92 ALR6th 295—§ 4, 7, 12
93 ALR6th 207—§ 6
State v. Rupe, 101 Wash. 2d 664, 683
P.2d 571 (1984)
3 ALR5th 784—§ 13, 14
21 ALR6th 1—§ 5
State v. Rupe, 226 Kan. 474, 601 P.2d
675 (1979)
24 ALR5th 465—§ 4, 13, 14, 43
State v. Rupert, 649 A.2d 1013 (R.I.
1994)

93 ALR5th 527—§ 4
State v. Rupnick, 280 Kan. 720, 125 P.3d 541 (2005)
58 ALR6th 439—§ 32
87 ALR6th 1—§ 6, 34, 38
State v. Rupp, 120 Ariz. 490, 586 P.2d 1302 (Ct. App. Div. 1 1978)
50 ALR5th 467—§ 8
99 ALR5th 557—§ 20
118 ALR5th 253—§ 16
State v. Ruscoe, 212 Conn. 223, 563 A.2d 267 (1989)
85 ALR5th 1—§ 25
23 ALR6th 307—§ 38
State v. Rusher, 468 A.2d 1008 (Me. 1983)
9 ALR6th 1—§ 17
State v. Rushing, 935 S.W.2d 30 (Mo. 1996)
50 ALR5th 581—§ 3, 11
State v. Rushing, 1996 WL 133233 (Mo. App. ED)
50 ALR5th 581—§ 3, 7, 9, 11, 20
State v. Rush, Ohio App. Case Nos. 3809, 3818, Slip Opinion (Lorain Co. 1985)
45 ALR5th 1—§ 3, 8, 22
State v. Rushton, 151 Ohio App. 3d 654, 2003-Ohio-692, 785 N.E.2d 492 (7th Dist. Mahoning County 2003)
58 ALR6th 385—§ 3, 8
State v. Rushton, 172 Ariz. 454, 837 P.2d 1189 (App. 1992)
38 ALR5th 433—§ 23
State v. Rushton, 264 Mont. 248, 870 P.2d 1355 (1994)
28 ALR6th 505—§ 15
State v. Rusin, 153 Vt. 36, 568 A.2d 403 (1989)
33 ALR6th 1—§ 12, 18, 20
State v. Rusos, 127 Wash. 65, 219 P. 843 (1923)
32 ALR5th 149—§ 22, 23
State v. Russell, 5 Wis. 2d 196, 92 N.W.2d 210 (1958)
96 ALR5th 523—§ 3
State v. Russell, 29 Conn. App. 59, 612 A.2d 809 (1992)

93 ALR5th 683—§ 3
State v. Russell, 47 Wash. App. 848, 737 P.2d 698 (1987)
1 ALR5th 938—§ 2, 6
State v. Russell, 69 Wash. App. 237, 848 P.2d 743 (Div. 2 1993)
73 ALR5th 383—§ 5
State v. Russell, 76 N.W. 653 (Iowa 1898)
66 ALR5th 397—§ 5
State v. Russell, 83 Wis. 330, 53 N.W. 441 (1892)
51 ALR5th 603—§ 2, 12
State v. Russell, 92 N.C. App. 639, 376 S.E.2d 458 (1989)
55 ALR5th 125—§ 3, 7
State v. Russell, 118 Or. App. 652, 848 P.2d 657 (1993)
58 ALR6th 499—§ 4
State v. Russell, 127 Ohio App. 3d 414, 713 N.E.2d 56 (9th Dist. Summit County 1998)
58 ALR6th 499—§ 54, 56
State v. Russell, 127 Wash. App. 1048, 2005 WL 1301493 (Div. 1 2005)
26 ALR6th 511—§ 4, 25
State v. Russell, 508 N.W.2d 697 (Iowa 1993)
32 ALR5th 659—§ 7
State v. Russell, 571 A.2d 229 (Me. 1990)
87 ALR5th 693—§ 4
State v. Russell, 726 So. 2d 444 (La. Ct. App. 5th Cir. 1999)
19 ALR6th 697—§ 4
State v. Russell, 781 N.W.2d 303 (Iowa Ct. App. 2010)
101 ALR6th 417—§ 8
State v. Russell, 878 P.2d 212 (Idaho App. 1994)
15 ALR5th 391—§ 7
State v. Russell, 882 P.2d 747 (Wash. 1994)
22 ALR5th 1—§ 31
State v. Russell, 1995 WL 635742 (Tenn. Crim. App. 1995)
57 ALR5th 141—§ 2, 9

State v. Russell, 1998 WL 357546 (Ohio Ct. App. 4th Dist. Athens County 1998)

85 ALR5th 1—§ 49

State v. Russell, 1999 WL 107778 (Minn. Ct. App. 1999)

50 ALR6th 455—§ 14, 17, 40

State v. Russell, 2009 WL 2151098 (Minn. Ct. App. 2009)

93 ALR6th 275—§ 18

State v. Russette, 2008 MT 413, 347 Mont. 285, 198 P.3d 791 (2008)

46 ALR6th 241—§ 3, 39

State v. Russo, 62 Conn. App. 129, 2000 WL 33191336 (2001)

90 ALR5th 453—§ 6

State v. Russo, 67 Haw. 126, 681 P.2d 553 (1984)

28 ALR6th 505—§ 8

State v. Russo, 68 Or. App. 760, 683 P.2d 163 (1984)

60 ALR5th 1—§ 4
67 ALR6th 531—§ 4

State v. Russo, 155 Ohio St. 341, 44 Ohio Ops. 317, 98 N.E.2d 830 (1951)

61 ALR5th 375—§ 9

State v. Russo, 213 N.J. Super. 219, 516 A.2d 1161 (Law Div. 1986)

110 ALR5th 329—§ 13

State v. Russo, 243 N.J. Super. 383, 579 A.2d 834 (1990)

37 ALR5th 515—§ 23

State v. Russo, 328 N.J. Super. 181, 745 A.2d 540 (App. Div. 2000)

10 ALR5th 538—§ 5, 7, 17

State v. Russo, 333 N.J. Super. 119, 754 A.2d 623 (App. Div. 2000)

93 ALR5th 527—§ 18

State v. Russo, 700 A.2d 161 (Del. Super. Ct. 1996)

79 ALR5th 419—§ 7, 10

State v. Rust, 208 Neb. 320, 303 N.W.2d 490 (1981)

72 ALR5th 109—§ 4

State v. Rust, 481 N.W.2d 610 (S.D. 1992)

15 ALR5th 391—§ 16

State v. Ruth, 98 Idaho 879, 574 P.2d 1357 (1978)

79 ALR5th 419—§ 4

State v. Ruthardt, 680 A.2d 349 (Del. Super. Ct. 1996)

90 ALR5th 453—§ 7

State v. Rutledge, 37 Wash. 523, 79 P. 1123 (1905)

41 ALR5th 1—§ 3, 5

State v. Rutledge, 205 Ariz. 7, 66 P.3d 50 (2003)

21 ALR6th 1—§ 4

State v. Rutledge, 232 S.C. 223, 101 S.E.2d 289, 67 A.L.R.2d 747 (1957)

29 ALR5th 59—§ 3, 38, 85

State v. Rutten, 73 Idaho 25, 245 P.2d 778 (1952)

104 ALR5th 357—§ 9
54 ALR6th 429—§ 20

State v. Rutter, 93 S.W.3d 714 (Mo. 2002)

78 ALR6th 297—§ 55

State v. Ruttman, 1999 S.D. 112, 598 N.W.2d 910 (S.D. 1999)

15 ALR5th 391—§ 53

State v. Rutzinski, 2001 WI 22, 241 Wis. 2d 729, 623 N.W.2d 516 (2001)

84 ALR6th 293—§ 8, 14, 25

State v. Ruud, 90 N.M. 647, 567 P.2d 496 (Ct. App. 1977)

116 ALR5th 479—§ 3

State v. Ruvido, 137 Me. 102, 15 A.2d 293 (1940)

31 ALR6th 523—§ 27, 56

State v. Ruybal, 408 A.2d 1284 (Me. 1979)

45 ALR5th 591—§ 2, 14

State v. Ruzicka, 202 Neb. 257, 274 N.W.2d 873 (1979)

114 ALR5th 173—§ 3, 7

State v. R.W., 104 N.J. 14, 514 A.2d 1287 (1986)

45 ALR5th 531—§ 8

State v. R.W., 200 N.J. Super. 560, 491 A.2d 1304 (1985)

45 ALR5th 531—§ 8

State v. Ryan, 48 Conn. App. 148, 709
A.2d 21 (1998)

37 ALR5th 319—§ 6

State v. Ryan, 103 Wash. 2d 165, 691
P.2d 197 (1984)

71 ALR5th 637—§ 7

State v. Ryan, 113 R.I. 343, 321 A.2d 92
(1974)

31 ALR6th 465—§ 14

State v. Ryan, 139 N.M. 354, 2006-
NMCA-044, 132 P.3d 1040 (Ct.
App. 2006)

18 ALR6th 1—§ 5, 12, 29, 30, 33

State v. Ryan, 176 Wis. 2d 513, 502
N.W.2d 618 (Ct. App. 1993)

72 ALR5th 403—§ 15

State v. Ryan, 182 Mont. 130, 595 P.2d
1146 (1979)

28 ALR6th 505—§ 7, 11, 13

State v. Ryan, 229 Mont. 7, 744 P.2d
1242 (1987)

92 ALR6th 295—§ 12
93 ALR6th 207—§ 26
96 ALR6th 355—§ 24, 60

State v. Ryan, 233 Neb. 74, 444 N.W.2d
610 (1989)

45 ALR5th 531—§ 3, 9
83 ALR6th 465—§ 4

State v. Ryan, 248 Neb. 405, 534
N.W.2d 766 (1995)

72 ALR5th 109—§ 9

State v. Ryan, 501 N.W.2d 516 (Iowa
1993)

12 ALR5th 89—§ 5, 8

State v. Rybolt, 133 Ariz. 276, 650 P.2d
1258 (App. 1982)

7 ALR5th 263—§ 4

State v. Rydberg, 519 N.W.2d 306 (N.D.
1994)

62 ALR5th 1—§ 3, 4, 11, 12, 15

State v. Ryder, 196 N.C. App. 56, 674
S.E.2d 805 (2009)

67 ALR6th 103—§ 8

State v. Rydeski, 214 Wis. 2d 101, 571
N.W.2d 417 (Ct. App. 1997)

28 ALR5th 459—§ 3

State v. Rye, 2 Wash. App. 920, 471
P.2d 96 (Div. 1 1970)

65 ALR5th 407—§ 2 to 4, 15, 16

State v. Ryea, 153 Vt. 451, 571 A.2d 674
(1990)

60 ALR5th 1—§ 8

State v. Ryks, 2009 WL 1515516 (Minn.
Ct. App. 2009)

64 ALR6th 131—§ 2

State v. Rymer, 241 Wis. 2d 50, 2001
WI App 31, 622 N.W.2d 770 (Ct.
App. 2000)

91 ALR5th 343—§ 2, 37

State v. Ryon, 2005-NMSC-005, 137
N.M. 174, 108 P.3d 1032 (2005)

58 ALR6th 499—§ 41, 74

State v. Ryyth, 2001 SD 50, 626 N.W.2d
290, 2001 WL 392660 (S.D. 2001)

92 ALR5th 35—§ 19

State v. S., 90 Wis. 2d 613, 280 N.W.2d
356 (App. 1979)

29 ALR5th 1—§ 2, 3

State v. S.A., 290 N.J. Super. 240, 675
A.2d 678 (App. Div. 1996)

65 ALR6th 329—§ 10

State v. Saah, 67 Ohio App. 3d 86, 585
N.E.2d 999 (Cuyahoga Co. 1990)

32 ALR5th 149—§ 5, 29, 32, 33

State v. Sabater, 3 Kan. App. 2d 692,
601 P.2d 11 (1979)

4 ALR5th 1—§ 4, 7

State v. Sabetta, 672 A.2d 451 (R.I.
1996)

26 ALR5th 1—§ 4

State v. Sabetta, 680 A.2d 927 (R.I.
1996)

37 ALR5th 515—§ 11
104 ALR5th 357—§ 8
54 ALR6th 429—§ 27

State v. Sabia, 1 Conn. App. 315, 471
A.2d 673 (1984)

1 ALR5th 346—§ 8

State v. Sabin, 79 Wis. 2d 302, 255
N.W.2d 320 (1977)

23 ALR6th 1—§ 15, 16

State v. Sabo, 86 N.J. Super. 508, 207
A.2d 340 (App. Div. 1965)

---

108 ALR5th 593—§ 35

State v. Sabo, 108 Ohio St. 200, 1 Ohio
L. Abs. 468, 140 N.E. 499 (1923)

41 ALR5th 171—§ 16, 58, 72

State v. Sabo, 2007 ND 193, 742 N.W.2d
812, 67 A.L.R.6th 659 (N.D. 2007)

67 ALR6th 209—§ 21

State v. Sabol, 2010-Ohio-993, 2010
WL 892111 (Ohio Ct. App. 2d Dist.
Montgomery County 2010)

64 ALR6th 1—§ 7

State v. Sachs, 264 S.C. 541, 216 S.E.2d
501 (1975)

67 ALR5th 361—§ 3, 6

State v. Sack, 210 Or. 552, 300 P.2d 427
(1957)

24 ALR5th 465—§ 123

State v. Saddler, 538 So. 2d 1073 (La.
Ct. App. 3d Cir. 1989)

99 ALR6th 295—§ 21

State v. Sadler, 85 Or. App. 134, 735
P.2d 1267 (1987)

30 ALR6th 103—§ 19

State v. Sadler, 147 Wash. App. 97, 193
P.3d 1108 (Div. 2 2008)

78 ALR6th 297—§ 29, 46, 48

State v. Sadowsky, 2008 MT 405, 347
Mont. 192, 197 P.3d 1018 (2008)

46 ALR6th 241—§ 3, 13

State v. Saecker, 196 Wis. 2d 646, 539
N.W.2d 336 (Ct. App. 1995)

125 ALR5th 497—§ 4

State v. Sage, 31 Ohio St. 3d 173, 510
N.E.2d 343 (1987)

57 ALR5th 141—§ 2, 6

State v. Sage, 977 S.W.2d 65 (Mo. Ct.
App. W.D. 1998)

20 ALR5th 398—§ 3

State v. Sager, 169 N.J. Super. 38, 404
A.2d 52 (Law Div. 1979)

114 ALR5th 235—§ 11

State v. Sager, 600 S.W.2d 541 (Mo. Ct.
App. W.D. 1980)

1 ALR6th 657—§ 4

State v. Saharath, 355 N.W.2d 312
(Minn. Ct. App. 1984)

73 ALR5th 383—§ 3

State v. Sahlie, 277 N.W.2d 591 (S.D.
1979)

83 ALR5th 541—§ 3

State v. Sahr, 470 N.W.2d 185 (N.D.
1991)

3 ALR5th 521—§ 3

State v. Sailo, 910 S.W.2d 184 (Tex.
App. Fort Worth 1995)

84 ALR6th 293—§ 19, 41

State v. Sainz, 18 Ariz. App. 358, 501
P.2d 1199 (Div. 2 1972)

58 ALR6th 499—§ 26

State v. Sainz, 23 Wash. App. 532, 596
P.2d 1090 (Div. 3 1979)

85 ALR5th 1—§ 33

State v. Saiz, 427 N.W.2d 825 (S.D.
1988)

19 ALR5th 470—§ 3, 12

State v. Sakellson, 379 N.W.2d 779
(N.D. 1985)

85 ALR5th 1—§ 11

State v. Sakobie, 165 N.C. App. 447,
598 S.E.2d 615 (2004)

63 ALR6th 351—§ 3

State v. Salame, 24 N.C. App. 1, 210
S.E.2d 77 (1974)

18 ALR5th 1—§ 2, 3

State v. Salas, 92 Conn. App. 541, 885
A.2d 1258 (2005)

12 ALR6th 389—§ 9

State v. Salas, 237 Neb. 546, 466
N.W.2d 790 (1991)

117 ALR5th 513—§ 3

State v. Salas, 289 Kan. 245, 210 P.3d
635 (2009)

72 ALR6th 227—§ 6

State v. Salata, 859 S.W.2d 728 (Mo.
App. 1993)

42 ALR5th 291—§ 4, 10, 25

State v. Salazar, 79 N.M. 592, 446 P.2d
644 (1968)

74 ALR5th 453—§ 3
101 ALR5th 351—§ 2

State v. Salazar, 98 N.M. 70, 644 P.2d
1059 (Ct. App. 1982)

68 ALR6th 527—§ 45

State v. Salazar, 146 Ariz. 540, 707 P.2d 944 (1985)
95 ALR5th 125—§ 7

State v. Salazar, 182 Ariz. 604, 898 P.2d 982, 192 Ariz. Adv. Rep. 37 (App. 1995)
54 ALR5th 575—§ 29

State v. Salazar, 504 N.W.2d 774 (Minn. 1993)
38 ALR5th 433—§ 7

State v. Salazar, 1997-NMSC-044, 123 N.M. 778, 945 P.2d 996 (1997)
9 ALR6th 1—§ 17

State v. Salazar, 2000 WL 1269662 (Wash. Ct. App. Div. 3 2000)
85 ALR5th 1—§ 21

State v. Salcido-Corral, 262 Kan. 392, 940 P.2d 11 (1997)
73 ALR5th 383—§ 5
49 ALR6th 343—§ 20

State v. Saldana, 310 Minn. 249, 246 N.W.2d 37 (1976)
32 ALR5th 149—§ 29, 34

State v. Saldano, 36 Wash. App. 344, 675 P.2d 1231 (Div. 1 1984)
83 ALR5th 277—§ 11

State v. Salenas, 112 N.M. 268, 814 P.2d 136 (App. 1991)
18 ALR5th 1—§ 14

State v. Salgado, 164 Wash. App. 1029, 2011 WL 5084687 (Div. 3 2011)
93 ALR6th 275—§ 5

State v. Salim, 2003-Ohio-2024, 2003 WL 1916756 (Ohio Ct. App. 8th Dist. Cuyahoga County 2003)
69 ALR6th 1—§ 10, 29

State v. Salinas, 87 Wash. 2d 112, 549 P.2d 712 (1976)
5 ALR5th 243—§ 62

State v. Salinas, 134 Idaho 362, 2 P.3d 747 (Ct. App. 2000)
17 ALR6th 327—§ 32

State v. Salisbury, 330 S.C. 250, 498 S.E.2d 655 (Ct. App. 1998)
56 ALR6th 323—§ 7

State v. Salit, 613 P.2d 245 (Alaska 1980)
125 ALR5th 281—§ 5

State v. Sallee, 624 S.W.2d 184 (Mo. Ct. App. S.D. 1981)
70 ALR6th 361—§ 31

State v. Salley, 514 A.2d 465 (Me. 1986)
41 ALR5th 171—§ 10, 16, 18, 20

State v. Salley, 601 So. 2d 309 (Fla. Dist. Ct. App. 4th Dist. 1992)
113 ALR5th 597—§ 8

State v. Sallie, 81 Ohio St. 3d 673, 693 N.E.2d 267 (1998)
11 ALR5th 871—§ 5
58 ALR5th 749—§ 6

State v. Sallis, 574 N.W.2d 15 (Iowa 1998)
81 ALR6th 505—§ 6

State v. Salmon, 279 S.C. 344, 306 S.E.2d 620 (1983)
69 ALR6th 1—§ 21

State v. Salmons, 203 W. Va. 561, 509 S.E.2d 842, 80 A.L.R.5th 741 (1998)
72 ALR5th 403—§ 3
80 ALR5th 469—§ 3, 5

State v. Salmons, 1996 WL 331136 (Neb. Ct. App. 1996)
9 ALR6th 541—§ 10

State v. Salmons, 2004-Ohio-3773, 2004 WL 1587069 (Ohio Ct. App. 2d Dist. Champaign County 2004)
46 ALR6th 241—§ 44

State v. Salois, 235 Mont. 276, 766 P.2d 1306 (1988)
23 ALR6th 307—§ 38

State v. Saloka, 1990 WL 52632 (Minn. Ct. App. 1990)
101 ALR6th 331—§ 10

State v. Salony, 528 So. 2d 404 (Fla. Dist. Ct. App. 3d Dist. 1988)
113 ALR5th 597—§ 8

State v. Salsbury, 129 Idaho 307, 924 P.2d 208, 24 Media L. R. 2454 (1996)
60 ALR5th 75—§ 7, 9

State v. Saltarelli, 98 Wash. 2d 358, 655 P.2d 697 (1982)
86 ALR5th 59—§ 3, 6

State v. Salters, 273 S.C. 501, 257 S.E.2d 502 (1979)

55 ALR6th 157—§ 4, 29

State v. Saltzer, 20 Ohio App. 3d 277, 485 N.E.2d 831 (8th Dist. Cuyahoga County 1985)

70 ALR6th 1—§ 5

State v. Saltzman, 194 Neb. 525, 233 N.W.2d 914 (1975)

42 ALR5th 581—§ 13

State v. Saltzman, 224 Neb. 74, 395 N.W.2d 530 (1986)

29 ALR6th 1—§ 10

State v. Salvatore, 57 Conn. App. 396, 749 A.2d 71 (2000)

73 ALR6th 49—§ 10, 43, 55

State v. Salvatore, No. 49519 (September 26, 1985, Ct. App. Ohio, 8th App. Dist. Cuyahoga Co.)

39 ALR5th 283—§ 14, 47

State v. Saly, 90 Wash. App. 1050, 1998 WL 246676 (Div. 2 1998)

88 ALR5th 121—§ 22, 35

State v. Salyers, 239 Neb. 1002, 480 N.W.2d 173 (1992)

46 ALR6th 241—§ 16

State v. Salzman, 139 Ariz. 521, 679 P.2d 544 (Ct. App. Div. 2 1984)

119 ALR5th 275—§ 8

State v. Sam, 478 So. 2d 769 (La. Ct. App. 3d Cir. 1985)

53 ALR6th 81—§ 5

State v. Samaha, 180 Conn. 565, 430 A.2d 1290 (1980)

39 ALR5th 283—§ 3

State v. Samonte, 83 Haw. 507, 928 P.2d 1, 60 A.L.R.5th 765 (Haw. 1996)

60 ALR5th 39—§ 2 to 9, 11, 13

State v. Samples, 2005 MT 210, 328 Mont. 242, 119 P.3d 1191 (2005)

33 ALR6th 91—§ 6

State v. Sampson, 36 Ohio App. 3d 166, 521 N.E.2d 1149 (10th Dist. Franklin County 1987)

56 ALR6th 185—§ 29

State v. Sampson, 167 Or. App. 489, 6 P.3d 543 (2000)

117 ALR5th 491—§ 2, 3

State v. Sampson, 362 Md. 438, 765 A.2d 629 (2001)

62 ALR5th 1—§ 3

State v. Sampson, 669 A.2d 1326 (Me. 1996)

84 ALR6th 293—§ 27, 29

State v. Sams, 676 So. 2d 1045 (Fla. 5th DCA 1996)

101 ALR6th 331—§ 10

State v. Samuel, 243 S.W.3d 592 (Tenn. Crim. App. 2007)

103 ALR6th 507—§ 14

State v. Samuel, 1991 WL 76061 (Ohio Ct. App. 8th Dist. Cuyahoga County 1991)

78 ALR5th 567—§ 9

State v. Samuels, 273 Conn. 541, 871 A.2d 1005 (2005)

39 ALR6th 257—§ 34, 35

State v. Sanchez, 17 P.3d 1275 (Wash. Ct. App. Div. 3 2001)

27 ALR5th 593—§ 36

State v. Sanchez, 22 Ohio App. 2d 145, 51 Ohio Op. 2d 292, 259 N.E.2d 139 (3d Dist. Defiance County 1970)

102 ALR5th 525—§ 39

State v. Sanchez, 39 So. 3d 834 (La. Ct. App. 1st Cir. 2010)

75 ALR6th 541—§ 12

State v. Sanchez, 48 Kan. App. 2d 608, 296 P.3d 1133, 94 A.L.R.6th 671 (2013)

94 ALR6th 111—§ 19

94 ALR6th 191—§ 7

State v. Sanchez, 72 Wash. App. 821, 867 P.2d 638 (1994)

20 ALR5th 398—§ 42, 65

State v. Sanchez, 73 Wash. App. 486, 869 P.2d 1133 (Div. 3 1994)

15 ALR5th 391—§ 46

92 ALR5th 35—§ 25

State v. Sanchez, 74 Wash. App. 763, 875 P.2d 712 (Div. 3 1994)

105 ALR5th 499—§ 4

State v. Sanchez, 87 N.M. 256, 531 P.2d 1229 (App. 1975)

7 ALR5th 263—§ 6

State v. Sanchez, 90 N.M. 61, 559 P.2d 849 (Ct. App. 1976)
105 ALR5th 529—§ 17

State v. Sanchez, 98 N.M. 781, 652 P.2d 1232 (Ct. App. 1982)
76 ALR5th 1—§ 6

State v. Sanchez, 120 N.M. 247, 901 P.2d 178 (1995)
80 ALR5th 55—§ 8

State v. Sanchez, 122 Wash. App. 579, 94 P.3d 384 (Div. 3 2004)
99 ALR6th 295—§ 9, 15

State v. Sanchez, 126 N.M. 559, 1999-NMCA-004, 972 P.2d 1150 (Ct. App. 1998)
55 ALR6th 391—§ 21

State v. Sanchez, 128 Ariz. 525, 627 P.2d 676 (1981)
85 ALR5th 1—§ 4

State v. Sanchez, 130 Ariz. 295, 635 P.2d 1217 (App. 1981)
31 ALR5th 704—§ 16, 18

State v. Sanchez, 131 N.M. 355, 2001-NMCA-109, 36 P.3d 446 (Ct. App. 2001)
56 ALR6th 323—§ 13

State v. Sanchez, 136 Or. App. 329, 901 P.2d 978 (1995)
71 ALR5th 1—§ 38

State v. Sanchez, 179 N.J. 409, 846 A.2d 588 (2004)
50 ALR6th 455—§ 26

State v. Sanchez, 192 Ariz. 454, 967 P.2d 129 (Ct. App. Div. 2 1998)
40 ALR5th 113—§ 3

State v. Sanchez, 224 N.J. Super. 231, 540 A.2d 201 (App. Div. 1988)
16 ALR6th 329—§ 7
24 ALR6th 591—§ 6
28 ALR6th 505—§ 5, 9

State v. Sanchez, 856 S.W.2d 166 (Tex. Crim. App. 1993)
116 ALR5th 479—§ 5

State v. Sanchez, 1994 WL 258667 (Ohio Ct. App. 8th Dist. Cuyahoga County 1994)
58 ALR6th 385—§ 20

State v. Sanchez, 2007 WL 1687529 (N.J. Super. Ct. App. Div. 2007)
35 ALR6th 361—§ 20

State v. Sanchez, 2010 WL 4451851 (Wash. Ct. App. Div. 3 2010)
62 ALR6th 161—§ 11

State v. Sanchez-Acosta, 110 Wash. App. 1030, 2002 WL 242766 (Div. 2 2002)
49 ALR6th 343—§ 20

State v. Sanchez-Cazares, 276 Kan. 451, 78 P.3d 55 (2003)
19 ALR6th 411—§ 16

State v. Sanchez-Diaz, 683 N.W.2d 824 (Minn. 2004)
49 ALR6th 343—§ 5, 29

State v. Sandberg, 392 N.W.2d 298 (Minn. Ct. App. 1986)
40 ALR6th 1—§ 33

State v. Sandefer, 79 Wash. App. 178, 900 P.2d 1132 (Div. 1 1995)
11 ALR6th 237—§ 10, 12

State v. Sanders, 8 Wash. App. 306, 506 P.2d 892 (Div. 2 1973)
58 ALR6th 499—§ 6

State v. Sanders, 35 Or. App. 503, 582 P.2d 22 (1978)
78 ALR6th 417—§ 5

State v. Sanders, 66 Wash. App. 878, 833 P.2d 452 (Div. 1 1992)
119 ALR5th 275—§ 8, 10

State v. Sanders, 75 P.3d 769 (Kan. Ct. App. 2003)
26 ALR6th 511—§ 25

State v. Sanders, 92 Ohio St. 3d 245, 2001-Ohio-189, 750 N.E.2d 90 (2001)
104 ALR5th 357—§ 6

State v. Sanders, 95 N.C. App. 56, 381 S.E.2d 827 (1989)
9 ALR5th 464—§ 3, 10

State v. Sanders, 112 N.C. App. 477, 435 S.E.2d 842 (1993)
50 ALR5th 581—§ 7, 20
82 ALR5th 103—§ 5
116 ALR5th 479—§ 5

State v. Sanders, 117 N.M. 452, 872 P.2d 870 (1994)

27 ALR6th 183—§ 15, 33

State v. Sanders, 130 Ohio App. 3d 789, 721 N.E.2d 433 (11th Dist. Ashtabula County 1998)

112 ALR5th 621—§ 3, 5

24 ALR6th 1—§ 14

State v. Sanders, 135 P.3d 766 (Kan. 2006)

26 ALR6th 511—§ 25

State v. Sanders, 155 Ga. App. 274, 270 S.E.2d 850 (1980)

103 ALR5th 463—§ 8

State v. Sanders, 223 Kan. 550, 575 P.2d 533 (1978)

5 ALR5th 243—§ 58

State v. Sanders, 225 Kan. 147, 587 P.2d 893 (1978)

110 ALR5th 329—§ 5

State v. Sanders, 251 S.C. 431, 163 S.E.2d 220 (1968)

90 ALR5th 225—§ 9

State v. Sanders, 263 Kan. 317, 949 P.2d 1084 (1997)

20 ALR5th 398—§ 5, 33.5, 35, 42.5

State v. Sanders, 272 Kan. 445, 33 P.3d 596 (2001)

20 ALR6th 479—§ 3

State v. Sanders, 357 So. 2d 492 (La. 1978)

33 ALR6th 407—§ 35

State v. Sanders, 463 So. 2d 1022 (La. App. 3d Cir. 1985)

55 ALR5th 125—§ 9

State v. Sanders, 539 So. 2d 114 (La. App. 2d Cir. 1989)

59 ALR5th 1—§ 3, 6

State v. Sanders, 728 So. 2d 777 (Fla. Dist. Ct. App. 2d Dist. 1999)

113 ALR5th 597—§ 8

State v. Sanders, 775 N.W.2d 883 (Minn. 2009)

69 ALR6th 579—§ 8, 15

State v. Sanders, 784 So. 2d 19 (La. Ct. App. 5th Cir. 2001)

7 ALR5th 263—§ 5

State v. Sanders, 842 S.W.2d 257 (Tenn. Crim. 1992)

39 ALR5th 283—§ 4, 15

State v. Sanders, 1992 WL 52709 (Ohio Ct. App. 11th Dist. Ashtabula County 1992)

69 ALR6th 207—§ 9, 10, 18

State v. Sanders, 1992 WL 52710 (Ohio Ct. App. 11th Dist. Ashtabula County 1992)

69 ALR6th 207—§ 9, 10, 18

State v. Sanders, 1992 WL 52712 (Ohio Ct. App. 11th Dist. Ashtabula County 1992)

69 ALR6th 207—§ 9, 10, 18

State v. Sanders, 2000 WI App 161, 238 Wis. 2d 94, 617 N.W.2d 677 (Ct. App. 2000)

99 ALR6th 295—§ 16

State v. Sanders, 2000 WL 1006574 (Ohio Ct. App. 2d Dist. Montgomery County 2000)

3 ALR6th 543—§ 8

State v. Sanders, 2004-Ohio-5629, 2004 WL 2376014 (Ohio Ct. App. 11th Dist. Portage County 2004)

50 ALR6th 455—§ 14

State v. Sanders, 2005-Ohio-6350, 2005 WL 3219584 (Ohio Ct. App. 8th Dist. Cuyahoga County 2005)

30 ALR6th 1—§ 4, 5

State v. Sanders, 2008 WI 85, 311 Wis. 2d 257, 752 N.W.2d 713 (2008)

78 ALR6th 297—§ 7, 58

State v. Sanderson, 898 P.2d 483, 187 Ariz. Adv. Rep. 41 (Ariz. App. 1995)

20 ALR5th 398—§ 5, 14, 35, 36, 49

State v. Sanderson, 1995 WL 567060 (Tenn. Crim. App. 1995)

73 ALR5th 383—§ 4, 8

State v. Sandford, 1994 WL 463846 (Ohio App. 8 Dist.)

50 ALR5th 581—§ 5, 7, 20

State v. Sandifer, 359 So. 2d 990 (La. 1978)

80 ALR6th 599—§ 8

State v. Sandiford, 149 La. 933, 90 So. 261 (1921)

54 ALR6th 429—§ 20

State v. Sandles, 740 S.W.2d 169 (Mo. 1987)

37 ALR5th 515—§ 26

State v. Sandlin, 61 N.C. App. 421, 300 S.E.2d 893 (1983)

32 ALR5th 149—§ 62
83 ALR6th 465—§ 10

State v. Sandlin, 86 Ohio St. 3d 165, 1999-Ohio-147, 712 N.E.2d 740 (1999)

70 ALR6th 1—§ 5

State v. Sandlin, No. 346 (April 9, 1980, Ct. App. Ohio, 1st App. Dist. Warren Co.)

39 ALR5th 283—§ 14, 67

State v. Sandman, 4 Utah 2d 69, 286 P.2d 1060 (1955)

66 ALR5th 397—§ 4, 15, 23

State v. Sandoval, 92 Idaho 853, 452 P.2d 350 (1969)

30 ALR6th 103—§ 8, 31, 34, 39

State v. Sandoval, 92 N.M. 476, 590 P.2d 175 (Ct. App. 1979)

114 ALR5th 173—§ 3, 5

State v. Sandoval, 99 N.M. 173, 655 P.2d 1017 (1982)

55 ALR6th 157—§ 4, 93

State v. Sandoval, 105 N.M. 696, 736 P.2d 501 (App. 1987)

20 ALR5th 398—§ 7, 60

State v. Sandoval, 171 Wash. 2d 163, 249 P.3d 1015, 74 A.L.R.6th 733 (2011)

74 ALR6th 373—§ 3, 8

State v. Sandoval, 842 S.W.2d 782 (Tex. App. Corpus Christi 1992)

49 ALR5th 639—§ 3

State v. Sandoval-Tena, 71 P.3d 1055 (Idaho 2003)

112 ALR5th 621—§ 5

State v. Sandstrom, 225 Kan. 717, 595 P.2d 324 (1979)

110 ALR5th 329—§ 5
19 ALR6th 697—§ 25

State v. Sandstrom, 273 Kan. 558, 44 P.3d 434 (2002)

69 ALR6th 1—§ 5

State v. Sandy, 6 Ohio App. 3d 37, 452 N.E.2d 515 (5th Dist.Ashland County 1982)

55 ALR5th 125—§ 3

State v. Sanford, 660 So. 2d 555 (La. Ct. App. 2d Cir. 1995)

73 ALR5th 383—§ 5
98 ALR6th 455—§ 30

State v. Sanner, 655 S.W.2d 868 (Mo. Ct. App. S.D. 1983)

101 ALR6th 331—§ 21

State v. Santanna, 153 Ariz. 147, 735 P.2d 757 (1987)

79 ALR5th 419—§ 10

State v. Santeramo, 1994 WL 455628 (Minn. Ct. App. 1994)

1 ALR6th 549—§ 8

State v. Santiago, 53 Haw. 254, 492 P.2d 657 (1971)

42 ALR6th 237—§ 17, 18

State v. Santiago, 103 Conn. App. 406, 931 A.2d 298 (2007)

30 ALR6th 1—§ 3

State v. Santiago, 206 Wis. 2d 3, 556 N.W.2d 687 (1996)

49 ALR6th 343—§ 3, 16

State v. Santiago, 245 Conn. 301, 715 A.2d 1 (1998)

49 ALR6th 343—§ 26

State v. Santiago, 250 N.J. Super. 30, 593 A.2d 357, 19 Media L. R. 1214 (1991)

60 ALR5th 75—§ 2, 15

State v. Santiago, 253 N.J. Super. 197, 601 A.2d 714 (1991)

27 ALR5th 593—§ 5, 7, 9

State v. Santos, 101 N.J. Super. 98, 243 A.2d 274 (App. Div. 1968)

64 ALR5th 741—§ 5

State v. Santos, 122 R.I. 799, 413 A.2d 58 (1980)

86 ALR5th 59—§ 3, 8

State v. Santos, 2012 WL 1581999 (N.J. 2012)

74 ALR6th 373—§ 23

State v. Sapp, 207 W. Va. 606, 535 S.E.2d 205 (2000)

3 ALR6th 543—§ 8

State v. Sapp, 1995 WL 491390 (Ohio Ct. App. 10th Dist.Franklin County 1995)

59 ALR5th 1—§ 2, 5, 6

State v. Sapsford, 22 Ohio App. 3d 1, 488 N.E.2d 218 (9th Dist. Summit County 1983)

1 ALR6th 657—§ 13

State v. Sarabia, 118 Wis. 2d 655, 348 N.W.2d 527 (1984)

95 ALR5th 611—§ 6

State v. Saraceno, 15 Conn. App. 222, 545 A.2d 1116 (1988)

39 ALR6th 257—§ 20

State v. Sarandria, 2004 WL 1430314 (Haw. 2004)

56 ALR6th 323—§ 5

State v. Sarbaum, 270 Mont. 176, 890 P.2d 1284 (1995)

114 ALR5th 235—§ 8

State v. Sardo, 112 Ariz. 509, 543 P.2d 1138 (1975)

35 ALR6th 497—§ 21

State v. Sargent, 40 Wash. App. 340, 698 P.2d 598 (1985)

24 ALR5th 465—§ 63

State v. Sargent, 111 Wash. 2d 641, 762 P.2d 1127 (1988)

38 ALR6th 97—§ 18

State v. Sargent, 617 So. 2d 1115, 18 FLW D 1188 (Fla. App. D5 1993)

18 ALR5th 1—§ 12

State v. Sargent, 702 S.W.2d 877 (Mo. Ct. App. E.D. 1985)

56 ALR6th 185—§ 6, 39

State v. Sargent, 738 A.2d 351 (N.H. 1999)

87 ALR5th 693—§ 3

State v. Sargent, 1998 WL 103008 (Ohio Ct. App. 12th Dist.Butler County 1998)

63 ALR5th 331—§ 8, 19

State v. Sarinske, 91 Wis. 2d 14, 280 N.W.2d 725 (1979)

23 ALR6th 1—§ 15, 19

State v. Sarrio, 875 So. 2d 898 (La. Ct. App. 5th Cir. 2004)

11 ALR6th 237—§ 18

State v. Sarto, 195 N.J. Super. 565, 481 A.2d 281 (App. Div. 1984)

114 ALR5th 173—§ 7

State v. Sarvis, 265 S.C. 144, 217 S.E.2d 38 (1975)

76 ALR5th 1—§ 3

State v. Sasak, 178 Ariz. 182, 871 P.2d 729 (Ct. App. Div. 1 1993)

85 ALR5th 471—§ 3

State v. Sass, 181 Wis. 2d 1003, 513 N.W.2d 707 (Wis App. 1994)

51 ALR5th 603—§ 8

State v. Sassoon, 240 Ga. 745, 242 S.E.2d 121 (1978)

52 ALR6th 1—§ 18

53 ALR6th 1—§ 5

State v. Satter, 1996 SD 9, 543 N.W.2d 249 (S.D. 1996)

38 ALR6th 97—§ 28

State v. Satter, 2009 SD 35, 766 N.W.2d 153 (S.D. 2009)

84 ALR6th 293—§ 7, 19, 41

State v. Satterfield, 3 Kan. App. 2d 212, 592 P.2d 135 (1979)

9 ALR5th 369—§ 2, 8, 12

State v. Sattler, 1996 WL 270932 (Wash. Ct. App. Div. 1 1996)

73 ALR5th 383—§ 3

State v. Sauber, 125 Wash. App. 1041, 2005 WL 352100 (Div. 1 2005)

26 ALR6th 511—§ 45

State v. Saucedo-Duran, 1994 WL 373318 (Minn. Ct. App. 1994)

17 ALR6th 327—§ 42

State v. Sauer, 217 Minn. 591, 15 N.W.2d 17 (1944)

32 ALR5th 149—§ 52

State v. Saul, 434 N.W.2d 572 (N.D. 1989)

92 ALR6th 295—§ 7

95 ALR6th 1—§ 7, 28

State v. Saulino, 29 Ohio Misc. 25, 58 Ohio Op. 2d 21, 277 N.E.2d 580 (Mun. Ct. 1971)

31 ALR6th 333—§ 9

State v. Sauls, 356 N.W.2d 516 (Iowa 1984)
16 ALR6th 329—§ 5
24 ALR6th 591—§ 4, 12
State v. Saunders, 68 Iowa 370, 27 N.W. 455 (1886)
108 ALR5th 593—§ 49
State v. Saunders, 91 Wash. App. 575, 958 P.2d 364 (Div. 2 1998)
37 ALR5th 319—§ 5
State v. Saunders, 97 P.3d 1072 (Kan. Ct. App. 2004)
30 ALR6th 373—§ 15
State v. Saunders, 102 Ariz. 565, 435 P.2d 39 (1967)
34 ALR6th 1—§ 11
State v. Saunders, 103 Or. App. 488, 799 P.2d 159 (1990)
50 ALR5th 703—§ 37, 38
State v. Saunders, 267 Conn. 363, 838 A.2d 186 (2004)
103 ALR6th 137—§ 1, 11, 13
State v. Saunders, 886 P.2d 496 (Okla. Crim. 1994)
29 ALR5th 487—§ 3
State v. Saunders, 2000 WL 739455 (Tenn. Crim. App. 2000)
84 ALR6th 427—§ 10
State v. Saunders, No. 78 (October 4, 1978, Ct. App. Ohio, 2nd App. Dist. Miami Co.)
39 ALR5th 283—§ 14, 41
State v. Sauter, 120 Ariz. 222, 585 P.2d 242 (1978)
50 ALR5th 467—§ 6, 9
State v. Sauter, 125 Mont. 109, 232 P.2d 731 (1951)
86 ALR5th 59—§ 8
State v. Sautter, 1989 WL 90630 (Ohio Ct. App. 6th Dist.Lucas County 1989)
62 ALR5th 1—§ 4
State v. Sauve, 164 Vt. 134, 666 A.2d 1164 (1995)
71 ALR5th 1—§ 40
State v. Savage, 30 Ohio St. 3d 1, 30 Ohio B.R. 11, 506 N.E.2d 196 (1987)

51 ALR5th 603—§ 2
State v. Savage, 37 Del. 509, 186 A. 738 (Gen. Sess. 1936)
57 ALR6th 445—§ 49
State v. Savage, 115 N.M. 250, 849 P.2d 1073 (Ct. App. 1992)
43 ALR6th 475—§ 21
State v. Savage, 120 N.J. 594, 577 A.2d 455 (1990)
72 ALR5th 109—§ 6
72 ALR5th 403—§ 2, 11
79 ALR5th 419—§ 6, 12
State v. Savage, 161 Conn. 445, 290 A.2d 221 (1971)
98 ALR6th 455—§ 17
State v. Savage, 208 Or. App. 472, 144 P.3d 1063 (2006)
26 ALR6th 511—§ 50
State v. Savage, 522 S.W.2d 144 (Mo. Ct. App. 1975)
71 ALR6th 335—§ 12
State v. Savage, 575 So. 2d 478 (La. Ct. App. 3d Cir. 1991)
110 ALR5th 329—§ 5
State v. Savage, 2000 WL 1369926 (Ohio Ct. App. 2d Dist. Clark County 2000)
108 ALR5th 593—§ 49
State v. Savant, 146 Ariz. 306, 705 P.2d 1357 (App. 1985)
57 ALR5th 141—§ 12
State v. Savario, 721 So. 2d 1084 (La. Ct. App. 1st Cir. 1998)
73 ALR5th 383—§ 5
State v. Saver, 295 Minn. 581, 205 N.W.2d 508 (1973)
41 ALR5th 171—§ 34
State v. Savino, 567 So. 2d 892, 15 FLW S. 518 (Fla. 1990)
22 ALR5th 1—§ 14, 29, 38, 45, 46
State v. Savo, 150 Vt. 610, 556 A.2d 54 (1987)
85 ALR5th 547—§ 8
State v. Savre, 129 Iowa 122, 105 N.W. 387 (1905)
5 ALR6th 1—§ 25, 40

CASES CITED IN ALR5th and ALR6th

State v. Sawicki, 173 Conn. 389, 377
A.2d 1103 (1977)
5 ALR5th 243—§ 59
State v. Sawyer, 96 Wash. App. 1074,
1999 WL 619075 (Div. 1 1999)
16 ALR6th 329—§ 11
24 ALR6th 591—§ 9, 13
State v. Sawyer, 96 Wash. App. 1074,
1999 WL 619078 (Div. 1 1999)
38 ALR6th 97—§ 29
State v. Sawyer, 174 Mont. 512, 571
P.2d 1131 (1977)
19 ALR5th 470—§ 6
State v. Sawyer, 227 Conn. 566, 630
A.2d 1064 (1993)
26 ALR5th 603—§ 3
State v. Sawyer, 346 So. 2d 1071 (Fla.
Dist. Ct. App. 3d Dist. 1977)
72 ALR5th 1—§ 8, 31
State v. Sax, 139 N.J. Super. 157, 353
A.2d 113 (1976)
29 ALR5th 702—§ 5 to 7, 11
State v. Saxon, 226 N.J. Super. 653, 545
A.2d 255 (1988)
54 ALR5th 141—§ 5, 7, 9
State v. Saxon, 261 S.C. 523, 201 S.E.2d
114 (1973)
9 ALR6th 1—§ 17
State v. Saxton, 2003 MT 105, 315
Mont. 315, 68 P.3d 721 (2003)
58 ALR6th 499—§ 28
State v. Sayers, 199 Mont. 228, 648 P.2d
291 (1982)
19 ALR5th 470—§ 6
State v. Sayers, 211 Neb. 555, 319
N.W.2d 438, 31 A.L.R.4th 666
(1982)
57 ALR6th 313—§ 6
State v. Sayler, 36 Wash. App. 230, 673
P.2d 870 (Div. 2 1983)
95 ALR5th 229—§ 24, 25
State v. Sayler, 443 N.W.2d 915 (N.D.
1989)
31 ALR6th 49—§ 4
State v. Sayles, 579 S.W.2d 748 (Mo.
App. 1979)
55 ALR5th 125—§ 3, 8

State v. Sayles, 662 N.W.2d 1 (Iowa
2003)
111 ALR5th 529—§ 5
State v. Saylor, 163 P.3d 385 (Kan. Ct.
App. 2007)
78 ALR6th 297—§ 18, 22, 69
State v. Saylor, 1991 WL 117038 (Tenn.
Crim. App. 1991)
98 ALR6th 455—§ 17
State v. S.B., 758 So. 2d 1253 (Fla. Dist.
Ct. App. 4th Dist. 2000)
55 ALR5th 125—§ 3
State v. Sbrilli, 136 N.J.L. 66, 54 A.2d
221 (N.J. Sup. Ct. 1947)
24 ALR6th 747—§ 17
State v. Scalara, 2010 WL 1039278
(Wash. Ct. App. Div. 2 2010)
55 ALR6th 1—§ 6
State v. Scales, 518 N.W.2d 587 (Minn.
1994)
**69 ALR6th 579—§ 3, 8, 9, 14 to 18,
23, 24, 27 to 29, 31, 32, 34, 35**
State v. Scales, 655 So. 2d 1326 (La.
1995)
79 ALR5th 33—§ 2, 52, 71
State v. Scammicca, 1999 WL 333179
(Ohio Ct. App. 5th Dist. Licking
County 1999)
78 ALR5th 489—§ 10
State v. Scarboro, 110 N.C. 232, 14 S.E.
737 (1892)
48 ALR6th 181—§ 4
State v. Scarborough, 1991 WL 241961
(Ohio Ct. App. 12th Dist. Warren
County 1991)
33 ALR6th 353—§ 5
State v. Scarborough, 1998 WL 204928
(Ohio Ct. App. 12th Dist. Warren
County 1998)
78 ALR5th 489—§ 3
State v. Scarbury, 2003-Ohio-6483,
2003 WL 22861737 (Ohio Ct. App.
5th Dist. Knox County 2003)
33 ALR6th 407—§ 4
State v. Scarlet, 800 So. 2d 220 (Fla.
2001)
92 ALR6th 1—§ 3, 8, 10

State v. Scarpiello, 40 Conn. App. 189, 670 A.2d 856 (1996)

45 ALR5th 531—§ 3, 11

State v. Schaaf, 169 Ariz. 323, 819 P.2d 909 (1991)

51 ALR6th 1—§ 20

70 ALR6th 361—§ 31

State v. Schaar, No. 40034 (January 17, 1980, Ct. App. Ohio, 8th App. Dist. Cuyahoga Co.)

39 ALR5th 283—§ 14, 32, 61

State v. Schackart, 190 Ariz. 238, 947 P.2d 315 (1997)

21 ALR6th 1—§ 4

State v. Schad, 129 Ariz. 557, 633 P.2d 366 (1981)

68 ALR5th 343—§ 3, 17

State v. Schaefer, 704 So. 2d 300 (La. Ct. App. 5th Cir. 1997)

39 ALR5th 283—§ 81

100 ALR5th 67—§ 2, 11, 43

State v. Schaeffer, 129 Wis. 459, 109 N.W. 522 (1906)

32 ALR5th 57—§ 3, 4

State v. Schaeffer, 450 N.W.2d 754 (N.D. 1990)

6 ALR5th 733—§ 16

State v. Schael, 131 Wis. 2d 405, 388 N.W.2d 641 (Ct. App. 1986)

79 ALR5th 419—§ 10

State v. Schafer, 5 Conn. Cir. Ct. 669, 260 A.2d 623 (App. Div. 1969)

104 ALR5th 357—§ 6

54 ALR6th 429—§ 11

State v. Schaffel, 4 Conn. Cir. Ct. 234, 229 A.2d 552 (App. Div. 1966)

65 ALR5th 407—§ 3

68 ALR5th 343—§ 3

State v. Schaffer, 113 Ohio App. 125, 17 Ohio Op. 2d 114, 177 N.E.2d 534 (4th Dist. Lawrence County 1960)

67 ALR6th 103—§ 4

State v. Schaffer, 114 Or. App. 328, 835 P.2d 134 (1992)

57 ALR6th 83—§ 5

State v. Schaffer, 133 Idaho 126, 982 P.2d 961 (Ct. App. 1999)

67 ALR6th 531—§ 36

79 ALR6th 1—§ 4, 23

State v. Schaffer, 202 Ariz. 592, 48 P.3d 1202 (Ct. App. Div. 1 2002)

67 ALR6th 103—§ 3, 17

State v. Schaffer, 354 S.W.2d 829 (Mo. 1962)

99 ALR6th 113—§ 10

State v. Schaffer, 1997 WL 576376 (Ohio Ct. App. 9th Dist. Wayne County 1997)

93 ALR5th 1—§ 7

State v. Schaller, 199 Wis. 2d 23, 544 N.W.2d 247 (Ct. App. 1995)

57 ALR5th 315—§ 3

State v. Schambow, 176 Wis. 2d 286, 500 N.W.2d 362 (Ct. App. 1993)

30 ALR6th 103—§ 8, 45, 58

State v. Schamburge, 344 So. 2d 997 (La. 1977)

7 ALR5th 263—§ 5

State v. Schares, 548 N.W.2d 894 (Iowa 1996)

92 ALR5th 35—§ 25

State v. Scharf, 288 Or. 451, 288 Or. 621, 605 P.2d 690 (1980)

109 ALR5th 611—§ 3

State v. Scharmer, 501 N.W.2d 620 (Minn. 1993)

81 ALR5th 563—§ 8, 9

State v. Schatz-Sousa, 89 Wash. App. 1062, 1998 WL 130093 (Div. 1 1998)

90 ALR5th 453—§ 43

10 ALR6th 463—§ 4

State v. Schau, 1983 WL 6704 (Ohio Ct. App. 7th Dist. Belmont County 1983)

85 ALR5th 1—§ 17

State v. Schauenberg, 197 Iowa 445, 197 N.W. 295 (1924)

37 ALR6th 511—§ 14

State v. Schectman, 291 So. 2d 259 (Fla. Dist. Ct. App. 4th Dist. 1974)

6 ALR6th 533—§ 19

State v. Scheer, 49 Or. App. 937, 620 P.2d 973 (1980)

112 ALR5th 429—§ 2, 13

114 ALR5th 235—§ 2
State v. Scheetz, 286 Mont. 41, 950 P.2d 722 (1997)
117 ALR5th 407—§ 4
State v. Scheibelhoffer, 1999 WL 476106 (Ohio Ct. App. 11th Dist. Lake County 1999)
124 ALR5th 509—§ 6
State v. Scheidemann, 252 Or. 70, 448 P.2d 358 (1968)
114 ALR5th 235—§ 4
State v. Schell, 492 So. 2d 169 (La. App. 1st Cir. 1986)
54 ALR5th 141—§ 2 to 5, 8, 10
State v. Schenectady Chemicals, Inc., 117 Misc. 2d 960, 459 N.Y.S.2d 971, 13 ELR 20550 (1983)
6 ALR5th 883—§ 2, 7
State v. Schenker, 2007-Ohio-3732, 2007 WL 2110922 (Ohio Ct. App. 5th Dist. Tuscarawas County 2007)
65 ALR6th 537—§ 12, 55, 60, 71
State v. Scherzer, 301 N.J. Super. 363, 694 A.2d 196 (App. Div. 1997)
49 ALR5th 639—§ 4
57 ALR5th 141—§ 7
59 ALR5th 1—§ 6
80 ALR5th 55—§ 3
39 ALR6th 257—§ 3
40 ALR6th 1—§ 9
State v. Schexnayder, 685 So. 2d 357 (La. Ct. App. 5th Cir. 1996)
56 ALR6th 185—§ 39
State v. Schiele, 2004 ND 53, 676 N.W.2d 813 (N.D. 2004)
33 ALR6th 373—§ 17
State v. Schilleman, 125 Ariz. 294, 609 P.2d 564 (1980)
94 ALR5th 393—§ 5
State v. Schimpf, 782 S.W.2d 186 (Tenn. Crim. App. 1989)
85 ALR5th 595—§ 2, 6
State v. Schimpf, 1999 WL 173601 (Ohio Ct. App. 5th Dist. Licking County 1999)
78 ALR5th 489—§ 10
State v. Schirmer, 104 N.C. App. 472, 409 S.E.2d 704 (1991)

71 ALR6th 335—§ 10
State v. Schirmer, 646 So. 2d 890 (La. 1994)
5 ALR6th 1—§ 5, 8, 10
51 ALR6th 359—§ 36
65 ALR6th 441—§ 7
70 ALR6th 513—§ 12
State v. Schlaefli, 117 Ariz. 1, 570 P.2d 772 (1977)
99 ALR6th 295—§ 9
State v. Schlagel, 490 S.W.2d 81 (Mo. 1973)
55 ALR6th 157—§ 30, 33
State v. Schlangen, 2009 WL 5088758 (Minn. Ct. App. 2009)
56 ALR6th 1—§ 8
State v. Schlapper, 2010 WL 1443277 (Wis. Ct. App. 2010)
55 ALR6th 1—§ 7, 20
State v. Schleeper, 806 S.W.2d 459 (Mo. Ct. App. E.D. 1991)
105 ALR5th 529—§ 2, 4
State v. Schleigh, 210 Or. 155, 310 P.2d 341 (1957)
82 ALR5th 591—§ 2, 6, 8
State v. Schliep, 2000 WL 821493 (Minn. Ct. App. 2000)
63 ALR6th 1—§ 36
State v. Schlittenhardt, 147 N.W.2d 118 (N.D. 1966)
31 ALR5th 704—§ 15
State v. Schloegel, 319 Wis. 2d 741, 2009 WI App 85, 769 N.W.2d 130, 246 Ed. Law Rep. 1003, 59 A.L.R.6th 759 (Ct. App. 2009)
59 ALR6th 393—§ 7
State v. Schloredt, 97 Wash. App. 789, 987 P.2d 647 (Div. 1 1999)
113 ALR5th 597—§ 3
68 ALR6th 527—§ 11
State v. Schlosser, 79 Ohio St. 3d 329, 681 N.E.2d 911 (1997)
89 ALR5th 629—§ 3, 12
State v. Schlosser, 202 N.W.2d 136 (N.D. 1972)
99 ALR5th 557—§ 3, 12
92 ALR6th 1—§ 3

State v. Schmadeka, 136 Idaho 595, 38
P.3d 633, 114 A.L.R.5th 729 (Ct.
App. 2001)
114 ALR5th 173—§ 2, 7, 11
State v. Schmaling, 198 Wis. 2d 756,
543 N.W.2d 555 (Ct. App. 1995)
92 ALR5th 35—§ 2, 19
State v. Schmaling, 198 Wis. 2d 757,
543 N.W.2d 555 (App. 1995)
15 ALR5th 391—§ 30
State v. Schmeets, 278 N.W.2d 401
(N.D. 1979)
41 ALR5th 171—§ 58
State v. Schmid, 84 N.J. 535, 423 A.2d
615 (1980)
52 ALR5th 195—§ 3
State v. Schmid, 487 N.W.2d 539 (Minn.
Ct. App. 1992)
102 ALR5th 327—§ 11
24 ALR6th 1—§ 19
State v. Schmidt, 5 Neb. App. 653, 562
N.W.2d 859 (1997)
40 ALR5th 113—§ 3
56 ALR6th 185—§ 39
State v. Schmidt, 29 Ohio St. 3d 32, 505
N.E.2d 627, 38 Ed. Law Rep. 1137
(1987)
70 ALR5th 169—§ 8
State v. Schmidt, 48 Wash. App. 639,
740 P.2d 351 (Div. 3 1987)
85 ALR5th 1—§ 2, 22, 27
State v. Schmidt, 84 Haw. 191, 932 P.2d
328 (Ct. App. 1997)
70 ALR6th 361—§ 19, 31, 32
State v. Schmidt, 138 Wis. 53, 119 N.W.
647 (1909)
32 ALR5th 57—§ 3
State v. Schmidt, 141 Wash. 660, 252 P.
118 (1927)
54 ALR6th 429—§ 9
State v. Schmidt, 143 Wash. 2d 658, 23
P.3d 462 (2001)
63 ALR6th 351—§ 3
State v. Schmidt, 163 La. 512, 112 So.
400 (1927)
111 ALR5th 491—§ 3
State v. Schmidt, 213 Neb. 126, 327
N.W.2d 624 (1982)

39 ALR5th 283—§ 3
State v. Schmidt, 239 Iowa 440, 30
N.W.2d 473 (1948)
57 ALR6th 445—§ 22
State v. Schmidt, 558 So. 2d 255 (La.
App. 5th Cir. 1990)
15 ALR5th 391—§ 30
State v. Schmidt, 699 So. 2d 448 (La. Ct.
App. 3d Cir. 1997)
90 ALR5th 453—§ 12
State v. Schmidt, 805 S.W.2d 25 (Tex.
App. Austin 1991)
7 ALR5th 113—§ 2 to 5
State v. Schmidt, 860 S.W.2d 396 (Mo.
Ct. App. E.D. 1993)
37 ALR6th 357—§ 68
State v. Schmidt, 867 S.W.2d 769 (Tex.
1993)
7 ALR5th 113—§ 5
State v. Schmidt, 2000 WL 1027370
(Iowa Ct. App. 2000)
85 ALR5th 1—§ 21
State v. Schmidt, 2008 ME 151, 957
A.2d 80 (Me. 2008)
57 ALR6th 445—§ 20
State v. Schmidt, 2008 WL 4602135
(Tex. App. Fort Worth 2008)
84 ALR6th 293—§ 32
State v. Schmidt, 2010 WL 695692
(Minn. Ct. App. 2010)
72 ALR6th 141—§ 16
State v. Schmidtbauer, 2001 WL 290281
(Minn. Ct. App. 2000)
73 ALR6th 49—§ 6
State v. Schmitt, 110 Or. App. 374, 822
P.2d 159 (1991)
65 ALR5th 407—§ 3
State v. Schmitt, 144 Idaho 768, 171
P.3d 259 (Ct. App. 2007)
97 ALR6th 653—§ 20
State v. Schmitt, 1999 WL 211819
(Wash. Ct. App. Div. 3 1999)
73 ALR5th 383—§ 3
State v. Schmitt, 2001 ND 57, 623
N.W.2d 409 (N.D. 2001)
112 ALR5th 429—§ 7

State v. Schmitz, 369 N.W.2d 579 (Minn. Ct. App. 1985)

84 ALR6th 293—§ 41

State v. Schmuck, 121 Wash. 2d 373, 850 P.2d 1332 (1993)

18 ALR6th 519—§ 19

State v. Schneider, 36 Wash. App. 237, 673 P.2d 200 (1983)

56 ALR5th 385—§ 4

State v. Schneider, 126 Idaho 624, 888 P.2d 798 (Ct. App. 1995)

105 ALR5th 529—§ 21

State v. Schneider, 401 So. 2d 865 (Fla. Dist. Ct. App. 3d Dist. 1981)

114 ALR5th 173—§ 9

State v. Schneider, 402 N.W.2d 779 (Minn. 1987)

66 ALR6th 83—§ 11

State v. Schneider, 597 N.W.2d 889 (Minn. 1999)

103 ALR6th 247—§ 9

State v. Schneider, 981 So. 2d 107 (La. Ct. App. 3d Cir. 2008)

68 ALR6th 115—§ 3, 9, 11, 43, 62

State v. Schneiderhan, 261 Mont. 161, 862 P.2d 37 (1993)

71 ALR5th 1—§ 35

State v. Schnelle, 7 S.W.3d 447 (Mo. Ct. App. W.D. 1999)

5 ALR5th 243—§ 34, 45

State v. Schneller, 199 La. 811, 7 So. 2d 66 (1942)

24 ALR5th 132—§ 3, 9

State v. Schnick, 819 S.W.2d 330 (Mo. 1991)

30 ALR6th 103—§ 19

State v. Schnipper, 1984 WL 4126 (Ohio Ct. App. 2d Dist.Montgomery County 1984)

57 ALR5th 141—§ 9

State v. Schnorr, 346 N.W.2d 380 (Minn. Ct. App. 1984)

103 ALR5th 463—§ 5

State v. Schoenbneelt, 171 Conn. 119, 368 A.2d 117 (1976)

103 ALR6th 347—§ 10

State v. Schoendaller, 176 Mont. 376, 578 P.2d 730 (1978)

114 ALR5th 173—§ 10

State v. Schoene, 10 Or. App. 390, 499 P.2d 834 (1972)

29 ALR5th 59—§ 59, 84, 85

State v. Schoening, 770 So. 2d 762 (La. 2000)

91 ALR5th 343—§ 3

State v. Schoening, 807 So. 2d 252 (La. Ct. App. 3d Cir. 2000)

9 ALR6th 1—§ 17

State v. Schofill, 63 Haw. 77, 621 P.2d 364 (1980)

68 ALR5th 299—§ 4

State v. Scholes, 2008 ND 146, 753 N.W.2d 377, 74 A.L.R.6th 633 (N.D. 2008)

74 ALR6th 69—§ 3, 8

State v. Scholl, 2004 SD 85, 684 N.W.2d 83 (S.D. 2004)

84 ALR6th 293—§ 10, 11, 25, 38

State v. Scholten, 445 N.W.2d 30 (S.D. 1989)

5 ALR5th 243—§ 57

State v. Schoonmaker, 249 Neb. 330, 543 N.W.2d 194 (1996)

117 ALR5th 513—§ 22

State v. Schoonover, 99 P.3d 1152 (Kan. Ct. App. 2004)

8 ALR6th 265—§ 17, 18

State v. Schoonover, 281 Kan. 453, 133 P.3d 48 (2006)

23 ALR6th 307—§ 27

State v. Schotl, 289 Minn. 175, 182 N.W.2d 878 (1971)

55 ALR5th 125—§ 3, 6, 7

State v. Schott, 222 Neb. 456, 384 N.W.2d 620 (1986)

6 ALR5th 733—§ 7, 16

State v. Schrader, 135 Wash. 650, 238 P. 617 (1925)

105 ALR5th 529—§ 16

State v. Schrader, 196 Neb. 632, 244 N.W.2d 498 (1976)

67 ALR6th 531—§ 37

State v. Schrader, 1999 WL 436731 (Ohio Ct. App. 5th Dist. Coshocton County 1999)
78 ALR5th 489—§ 3, 10
State v. Schrag, 21 Or. App. 655, 536 P.2d 461 (1975)
64 ALR5th 637—§ 3
State v. Schreck, 226 Neb. 172, 409 N.W.2d 624 (1987)
5 ALR5th 243—§ 15
State v. Schrein, 244 Neb. 136, 504 N.W.2d 827 (1993)
27 ALR6th 183—§ 31
State v. Schreuder, 726 P.2d 1215, 39 Utah Adv. Rep. 46 (Utah 1986)
38 ALR5th 433—§ 43
State v. Schrier, 300 N.W.2d 305 (Iowa 1981)
103 ALR6th 507—§ 14
State v. Schroeder, 62 Or. App. 331, 661 P.2d 111 (1983)
111 ALR5th 239—§ 3
6 ALR6th 533—§ 22
State v. Schroeder, 67 Wash. App. 110, 834 P.2d 105 (Div. 2 1992)
82 ALR5th 359—§ 6
83 ALR5th 277—§ 10
State v. Schroeder, 109 Wash. App. 30, 32 P.3d 1022 (Div. 2 2001)
58 ALR6th 499—§ 24, 115
State v. Schroeder, 149 Vt. 163, 540 A.2d 647 (1987)
21 ALR6th 771—§ 4
State v. Schroeder, 201 Kan. 811, 443 P.2d 284 (1968)
97 ALR5th 537—§ 47
State v. Schroeder, 401 N.W.2d 671 (Minn. Ct. App. 1987)
73 ALR5th 383—§ 31
State v. Schroeder, 560 N.W.2d 739 (Minn. Ct. App. 1997)
35 ALR6th 127—§ 15
69 ALR6th 579—§ 8, 27
State v. Schubkegel, 261 S.W.2d 933 (Mo. 1953)
54 ALR6th 429—§ 11

State v. Schuette, 223 Neb. 777, 393 N.W.2d 718 (1986)
5 ALR5th 243—§ 49
State v. Schuette, 423 N.W.2d 104 (Minn. Ct. App. 1988)
97 ALR6th 653—§ 29
State v. Schuler, 243 N.W.2d 367 (N.D. 1976)
92 ALR6th 295—§ 8
95 ALR6th 1—§ 15, 29
96 ALR6th 355—§ 9, 37
State v. Schuler, 1997 WL 76337 (Minn. Ct. App. 1997)
77 ALR6th 393—§ 11, 91
State v. Schuller, 280 Md. 305, 372 A.2d 1076 (1977)
113 ALR5th 1—§ 3, 10
State v. Schuller, 1992 WL 80713 (Ohio App. Clinton Co. 1992)
52 ALR5th 655—§ 3
State v. Schult, 2001 WL 195179 (Iowa Ct. App. 2001)
106 ALR5th 397—§ 5
113 ALR5th 517—§ 5
State v. Schultz, 1 Ohio Misc. 81, 30 Ohio Op. 2d 420, 205 N.E.2d 126 (Mun. Ct. 1964)
89 ALR6th 565—§ 4, 5
State v. Schultz, 23 Ohio App. 3d 130, 23 Ohio B.R. 242, 491 N.E.2d 735 (Franklin Co. 1985)
51 ALR5th 375—§ 11
State v. Schultz, 135 Wis. 644, 114 N.W. 505 (1908)
87 ALR5th 715—§ 4
State v. Schultz, 140 Ariz. 222, 681 P.2d 374 (1984)
79 ALR5th 419—§ 7
State v. Schultz, 141 N.H. 101, 677 A.2d 675 (1996)
7 ALR5th 758—§ 13
State v. Schultz, 146 Wash. App. 1057, 2008 WL 4216255 (Div. 2 2008)
58 ALR6th 499—§ 30
State v. Schultz, 148 Wis. 2d 370, 435 N.W.2d 305 (Ct. App. 1988)
72 ALR5th 109—§ 3

State v. Schultz, 245 N.W.2d 316 (Iowa 1976)

42 ALR5th 547—§ 6

State v. Schultz, 252 Kan. 819, 850 P.2d 818, 33 A.L.R.5th 835 (1993)

33 ALR5th 453—§ 2, 4

State v. Schultz, 271 N.W.2d 836 (Minn. 1978)

114 ALR5th 173—§ 7

State v. Schultz, 388 So. 2d 1326 (Fla. Dist. Ct. App. 4th Dist. 180)

62 ALR5th 1—§ 3, 14

State v. Schultz, 676 N.W.2d 337 (Minn. Ct. App. 2004)

68 ALR6th 1—§ 10

State v. Schultz, 1983 WL 4749 (Ohio Ct. App. 8th Dist. Cuyahoga County 1983)

38 ALR6th 97—§ 29

State v. Schultz, 1990 WL 96772 (Minn. Ct. App. 1990)

35 ALR6th 127—§ 4

State v. Schulze, 116 Wash. 2d 154, 804 P.2d 566 (1991)

109 ALR5th 611—§ 3

State v. Schumacher, 214 Kan. 1, 519 P.2d 1116 (1974)

32 ALR6th 531—§ 6, 39

State v. Schumacher, 1990 WL 42273 (Ohio Ct. App. 4th Dist. Gallia County 1990)

92 ALR6th 295—§ 8, 15
96 ALR6th 355—§ 4, 37

State v. Schur, 217 Kan. 741, 538 P.2d 689 (1975)

122 ALR5th 439—§ 7

State v. Schussler, 1999 WL 451118 (Minn. Ct. App. 1999)

47 ALR6th 107—§ 20

State v. Schuster, 273 Kan. 989, 46 P.3d 1140 (2002)

34 ALR6th 623—§ 5

State v. Schwab, 95 Or. App. 593, 771 P.2d 277 (1989)

99 ALR5th 557—§ 4, 9

State v. Schwab, 103 Wash. 2d 542, 693 P.2d 108 (1985)

63 ALR5th 1—§ 13

State v. Schwab, 119 Ohio App. 3d 463, 695 N.E.2d 801 (12th Dist. Butler County 1997)

29 ALR5th 487—§ 3, 11, 12

State v. Schwalk, 430 N.W.2d 317 (N.D. 1988)

92 ALR6th 295—§ 4, 7
93 ALR6th 207—§ 6

State v. Schwartz, 173 Or. App. 301, 21 P.3d 1128 (2001)

87 ALR6th 1—§ 6, 36, 41, 52

State v. Schwartz, 188 Ariz. 313, 935 P.2d 891 (Ct. App. Div. 1 1996)

89 ALR5th 629—§ 5

State v. Schwartz, 467 N.W.2d 240 (Iowa 1991)

29 ALR6th 1—§ 10

State v. Schwartz, 2005-Ohio-3171, 2005 WL 1490100 (Ohio Ct. App. 1st Dist. Hamilton County 2005)

69 ALR6th 1—§ 7

State v. Schweigert, 118 P.3d 177 (Kan. Ct. App. 2005)

30 ALR6th 373—§ 18

State v. Schwein, 2000 M.T. 371, 16 P.3d 373 (Mont. 2000)

52 ALR5th 655—§ 6

State v. Schweitzer, 533 N.W.2d 156 (S.D. 1995)

90 ALR5th 453—§ 22

State v. Schwender, 2007 WL 2103851 (Minn. Ct. App. 2007)

69 ALR6th 579—§ 8, 29

State v. Schyhart, 199 S.W. 205 (Mo. 1917)

22 ALR5th 1—§ 14

State v. Scigliano, 120 Ariz. 6, 583 P.2d 893 (1978)

68 ALR5th 549—§ 3, 6, 7

State v. Scoby, 536 So. 2d 615 (La. Ct. App. 1st Cir. 1988)

9 ALR6th 1—§ 17

State v. Scott, 17 Ariz. App. 183, 496 P.2d 609 (Div. 2 1972)

96 ALR6th 269—§ 31

State v. Scott, 21 Wash. App. 113, 584 P.2d 423 (1978)

---

51 ALR5th 375—§ 14
State v. Scott, 33 S.W.3d 746 (Tenn. 2000)
90 ALR5th 453—§ 23
State v. Scott, 61 Ohio St. 2d 155, 15 Ohio Op. 3d 182, 400 N.E.2d 375 (1980)
65 ALR5th 407—§ 3, 19
State v. Scott, 70 Kan. 692, 79 P. 126 (1905)
105 ALR5th 529—§ 11
State v. Scott, 72 Wash. App. 207, 866 P.2d 1258 (Div. 1 1993)
73 ALR5th 383—§ 3
State v. Scott, 82 Or. App. 645, 729 P.2d 585 (1986)
51 ALR5th 425—§ 3, 5, 6
State v. Scott, 87 Haw. 80, 951 P.2d 1243 (Haw. 1998)
67 ALR5th 361—§ 5
State v. Scott, 92 Ohio St. 3d 1, 2001-Ohio-148, 748 N.E.2d 11, 111 A.L.R.5th 777 (2001)
111 ALR5th 491—§ 2 to 4
State v. Scott, 95 Wash. App. 1064, 1999 WL 350690 (Div. 1 1999)
51 ALR6th 219—§ 4
State v. Scott, 96 Or. App. 451, 773 P.2d 394 (1989)
15 ALR6th 375—§ 4
State v. Scott, 99 Minn. 145, 108 N.W. 828 (1906)
120 ALR5th 125—§ 2
121 ALR5th 1—§ 2, 9, 16
State v. Scott, 101 Ohio St. 3d 31, 2004-Ohio-10, 800 N.E.2d 1133 (2004)
122 ALR5th 145—§ 24
98 ALR6th 455—§ 11
State v. Scott, 117 Kan. 303, 235 P. 380 (1924)
22 ALR5th 1—§ 61
State v. Scott, 118 Ariz. 383, 576 P.2d 1383 (Ct. App. Div. 2 1978)
71 ALR6th 1—§ 5
State v. Scott, 123 La. 1085, 49 So. 715 (1909)
66 ALR5th 397—§ 4, 13

State v. Scott, 131 Wash. App. 1036, 2006 WL 322360 (Div. 1 2006)
41 ALR6th 141—§ 7
63 ALR6th 351—§ 3
State v. Scott, 200 Neb. 265, 263 N.W.2d 659 (1978)
99 ALR6th 113—§ 5
State v. Scott, 214 Mo. 257, 113 S.W. 1069 (1908)
5 ALR6th 1—§ 61
State v. Scott, 230 Kan. 564, 639 P.2d 1131 (1982)
9 ALR5th 193—§ 9, 28, 36
State v. Scott, 265 Kan. 1, 961 P.2d 667 (1998)
78 ALR5th 489—§ 8
30 ALR6th 373—§ 5
37 ALR6th 55—§ 11
State v. Scott, 286 Kan. 54, 183 P.3d 801 (2008)
83 ALR6th 255—§ 2, 5, 8, 16, 18
State v. Scott, 331 N.C. 39, 413 S.E.2d 787 (1992)
86 ALR5th 59—§ 2, 6
88 ALR5th 429—§ 2
State v. Scott, 343 N.C. 313, 471 S.E.2d 605 (1996)
57 ALR5th 141—§ 3
58 ALR6th 499—§ 52, 56
78 ALR6th 297—§ 86
State v. Scott, 400 So. 2d 627 (La. 1981)
118 ALR5th 253—§ 16, 25
State v. Scott, 518 N.W.2d 347 (Iowa 1994)
50 ALR5th 581—§ 5, 6, 14
55 ALR6th 513—§ 5
State v. Scott, 525 S.W.2d 410 (Mo. Ct. App. 1975)
68 ALR6th 527—§ 37
State v. Scott, 619 N.W.2d 371 (Iowa 2000)
19 ALR5th 470—§ 15
State v. Scott, 649 S.W.2d 559 (Mo. Ct. App. W.D. 1983)
102 ALR5th 447—§ 9
State v. Scott, 693 So. 2d 86 (Fla. Dist. Ct. App. 2d Dist. 1997)

113 ALR5th 597—§ 8

State v. Scott, 774 So. 2d 794 (Fla. Dist. Ct. App. 3d Dist. 2000)

68 ALR5th 343—§ 3

State v. Scott, 786 So. 2d 606 (Fla. Dist. Ct. App. 5th Dist. 2001)

45 ALR6th 337—§ 9

State v. Scott, 2001 WL 846037 (Tenn. Crim. App. 2001)

68 ALR6th 115—§ 8, 17, 31

State v. Scott, 2003-Ohio-2797, 2003 WL 21255964 (Ohio Ct. App. 6th Dist. Sandusky County 2003)

72 ALR6th 1—§ 4

State v. Scott, 2006-Ohio-257, 2006 WL 173171 (Ohio Ct. App. 5th Dist. Stark County 2006)

21 ALR6th 1—§ 4

State v. Scott, 2006-Ohio-4016, 2006 WL 2219220 (Ohio Ct. App. 2d Dist. Montgomery County 2006)

27 ALR6th 183—§ 15

State v. Scott, 2006-Ohio-6390, 2006 WL 3506321 (Ohio Ct. App. 5th Dist. Morgan County 2006)

26 ALR6th 511—§ 19

State v. Scott, 2007-Ohio-6258, 2007 WL 4166246 (Ohio Ct. App. 7th Dist. Mahoning County 2007)

32 ALR6th 171—§ 16, 21
33 ALR6th 1—§ 6

State v. Scott, 2007-Ohio-6258, 2007 WL 4166246 (Ohio Ct.App. 7th Dist. Mahoning County 2007)

32 ALR6th 171—§ 20

State v. Scott, C.A. No. L-76-161, Slip Op., December 30, 1976 (Ohio App. Lucas Co. 1976)

45 ALR5th 591—§ 5

State v. Scovell, 54 Or. App. 391, 635 P.2d 7 (1981)

39 ALR5th 283—§ 4, 15, 24

State v. Scovill, 144 N.H. 409, 743 A.2d 303 (1999)

27 ALR6th 183—§ 15, 32

State v. Scramuzza, 408 So. 2d 1316 (La. 1982)

103 ALR5th 463—§ 6

State v. Scribner, 72 Conn. App. 736, 805 A.2d 812 (2002)

84 ALR6th 427—§ 27

State v. Scroggins, 110 Idaho 380, 716 P.2d 1152 (1985)

41 ALR6th 295—§ 9

State v. Scrotsky, 39 N.J. 410, 189 A.2d 23 (1963)

61 ALR5th 1—§ 3, 7

State v. Scruggs, 136 Ohio App. 3d 631, 737 N.E.2d 574 (2d Dist. Montgomery County 2000)

29 ALR5th 487—§ 5, 13

State v. Scruggs, 192 La. 297, 187 So. 673 (1939)

105 ALR5th 529—§ 11

State v. Scuderi, 2004 UT App 464, 2004 WL 2821676 (Utah Ct. App. 2004)

37 ALR6th 357—§ 55, 56

State v. Scussel, 117 N.M. 241, 871 P.2d 5 (Ct. App. 1994)

119 ALR5th 379—§ 2

State v. Seadin, 181 Mont. 294, 593 P.2d 451 (1979)

70 ALR6th 361—§ 37
71 ALR6th 335—§ 11
72 ALR6th 141—§ 10

State v. Seagull, 26 Wash. App. 58, 613 P.2d 528 (Div. 2 1980)

67 ALR6th 531—§ 34

State v. Seagull, 95 Wash. 2d 898, 632 P.2d 44 (1981)

69 ALR6th 275—§ 34

State v. Seale, 853 P.2d 862 (Utah 1993)

72 ALR5th 109—§ 9

State v. Seals, 684 So. 2d 368 (La. 1996)

20 ALR5th 398—§ 9

State v. Seals, 735 S.W.2d 849 (Tenn. Crim. App. 1987)

73 ALR5th 383—§ 3

State v. Seaman, 236 Mont. 466, 771 P.2d 950 (1989)

113 ALR5th 517—§ 10

State v. Seamen's Club, 1997 ME 70, 691 A.2d 1248 (Me. 1997)

50 ALR5th 703—§ 28

For assistance, call 1-800-328-4880

State v. Searles, 141 N.H. 224, 680 A.2d
612, 57 A.L.R.5th 819 (1996)

57 ALR5th 315—§ 3, 9, 11

State v. Searles, 635 A.2d 940 (Me.
1993)

54 ALR5th 141—§ 3, 4, 10

State v. Sears, 202 Ga. App. 352, 414
S.E.2d 494, 102-247 Fulton County
D R 13B (1991)

7 ALR5th 263—§ 7

State v. Sears, 298 So. 2d 814 (La. 1974)

79 ALR5th 237—§ 3

9 ALR6th 1—§ 22

State v. Sears, 553 P.2d 907 (Alaska
1976)

92 ALR6th 1—§ 4 to 5

State v. Seaton, 817 S.W.2d 535, 88
A.L.R.5th 743 (Mo. Ct. App. E.D.
1991)

88 ALR5th 429—§ 4

State v. Seavey, 147 N.H. 304, 789 A.2d
621 (2001)

58 ALR6th 499—§ 87

State v. Sebastian, 243 Conn. 115, 701
A.2d 13 (1997)

9 ALR6th 177—§ 66

State v. Seckman, 124 W. Va. 740, 22
S.E.2d 374 (1942)

86 ALR5th 59—§ 4

State v. Second Judicial Dist. Court, 86
Nev. 531, 471 P.2d 224 (1970)

13 ALR5th 118—§ 7, 10

State v. Secrist, 244 Wis. 2d 201, 589
N.W.2d 387 (1999)

114 ALR5th 173—§ 9

State v. Sederburg, 25 S.W.3d 172 (Mo.
Ct. App. S.D. 2000)

37 ALR6th 357—§ 16, 48, 76

State v. See, 2008 WL 3834770 (Minn.
Ct. App. 2008)

71 ALR6th 1—§ 12

State v. Seeber, 2005 WL 406210 (Minn.
Ct. App. 2005)

30 ALR6th 483—§ 5, 16

State v. Seeger, 725 S.W.2d 39 (Mo.
App. 1986)

26 ALR5th 1—§ 4, 34, 42

State v. Seenes, 212 W. Va. 353, 572
S.E.2d 876 (2002)

70 ALR6th 361—§ 19, 30

State v. Seering, 701 N.W.2d 655 (Iowa
2005)

25 ALR6th 227—§ 5, 10, 20, 24

63 ALR6th 351—§ 3

State v. Seery, 95 Iowa 652, 64 N.W.
631 (1895)

66 ALR5th 397—§ 5

State v. Seevanhsa, 495 N.W.2d 354
(Iowa Ct. App. 1992)

85 ALR5th 595—§ 3

State v. Seffens, 1992 WL 75831 (Tenn.
Crim. App. 1992)

73 ALR5th 615—§ 3, 5

State v. Seger, 532 A.2d 1013 (Me.
1987)

22 ALR5th 1—§ 4, 10, 15, 30, 31, 40

State v. Segers, 355 So. 2d 238 (La.
1978)

106 ALR5th 397—§ 4

114 ALR5th 235—§ 9

State v. Sego, 2006 WL 3734664 (Del.
C.P. 2006)

45 ALR6th 435—§ 3

State v. Segotta, 100 N.M. 18, 665 P.2d
280 (Ct. App. 1983)

16 ALR6th 329—§ 12

24 ALR6th 591—§ 9, 13

State v. Seiber, 56 Ohio St. 3d 4, 564
N.E.2d 408 (1990)

72 ALR5th 109—§ 5

State v. Seibers, 1989 WL 71008 (Tenn.
Crim. App. 1989)

84 ALR6th 293—§ 18

State v. Seibert, 103 S.W.3d 295 (Mo.
Ct. App. S.D. 2003)

30 ALR6th 103—§ 3, 25, 27

State v. Seidt, 805 S.W.2d 737 (Mo. Ct.
App. W.D. 1991)

78 ALR6th 417—§ 71

State v. Seige, 2009 WL 659198 (Conn.
Super. Ct. 2009)

47 ALR6th 107—§ 37, 39

State v. Self, 130 W. Va. 515, 44 S.E.2d
582 (1947)

59 ALR5th 135—§ 4, 16
State v. Self, 353 So. 2d 1282 (La. 1977)
84 ALR6th 427—§ 20
State v. Self, 492 So. 2d 319 (Ala. Crim. App. 1986)
107 ALR5th 567—§ 10, 11
State v. Selland, 54 Wash. App. 122, 772 P.2d 534 (1989)
15 ALR5th 391—§ 11
State v. Sellars, 331 N.J. Super. 110, 751 A.2d 151 (App. Div. 2000)
59 ALR5th 135—§ 8
State v. Sellers, 76 Or. App. 552, 709 P.2d 768 (1985)
15 ALR5th 391—§ 46
State v. Sells, 1988 WL 116335 (Ohio Ct. App. 2d Dist. Champaign County 1988)
99 ALR6th 295—§ 13
State v. Sells, 1991 WL 355090 (Ohio Ct. App. 3d Dist.Logan County 1991)
57 ALR5th 141—§ 12
State v. Selmon, 343 So. 2d 720 (La. 1977)
97 ALR5th 293—§ 4, 8
State v. Selph, 625 S.W.2d 285 (Tenn. Crim. 1981)
45 ALR5th 1—§ 3, 6, 8, 26
State v. Seltzer, 629 S.W.2d 458 (Mo. App. 1981)
29 ALR5th 59—§ 34
State v. Selvy, 72 S.W.3d 219 (Mo. Ct. App. E.D. 2002)
105 ALR5th 529—§ 20
State v. Seminary, 165 La. 67, 115 So. 370 (1927)
54 ALR6th 429—§ 3
State v. Senegal, 333 So. 2d 924 (La. 1976)
5 ALR6th 1—§ 69
State v. Sengxay, 80 Wash. App. 11, 906 P.2d 368 (1995)
32 ALR5th 149—§ 4, 56
State v. Senko, 457 A.2d 824 (Me. 1983)
32 ALR5th 659—§ 3

State v. Senn, 32 S.C. 392, 11 S.E. 292 (1890)
24 ALR5th 465—§ 96
103 ALR6th 137—§ 3
State v. Senquiz, 68 Conn. App. 571, 793 A.2d 1095 (2002)
39 ALR6th 257—§ 46
40 ALR6th 1—§ 5, 27
State v. Sephus, 32 S.W.3d 369 (Tex. App. Waco 2000)
52 ALR6th 1—§ 3, 4, 31
53 ALR6th 1—§ 3
State v. Sepulvado, 655 So. 2d 623 (La. Ct. App. 2d Cir. 1995)
73 ALR5th 383—§ 5
State v. Sequeira, 93 Haw. 34, 995 P.2d 335 (Haw. Ct. App. 2000)
15 ALR5th 391—§ 32
92 ALR5th 35—§ 22
State v. Sequin, 9 Haw. App. 551, 851 P.2d 926 (1993)
88 ALR5th 121—§ 2, 7
State v. Sereg, 229 Iowa 1105, 296 N.W. 231 (1941)
45 ALR5th 591—§ 9
State v. Serna, 163 Ariz. 260, 787 P.2d 1056 (1990)
55 ALR6th 391—§ 5
State v. Serna, 176 Ariz. 267, 860 P.2d 1320, 139 Ariz. Adv. Rep. 29 (App. 1993)
31 ALR5th 229—§ 2, 3, 17, 52, 58, 69
State v. Sero, 82 N.M. 17, 474 P.2d 503 (Ct. App. 1970)
104 ALR5th 165—§ 5
State v. Sero, 153 Wash. App. 1001, 2009 WL 3756735 (Div. 2 2009)
56 ALR6th 1—§ 14, 22
State v. Serrano, 95 Wash. App. 700, 977 P.2d 47 (Div. 3 1999)
32 ALR5th 149—§ 53
State v. Serret, 198 N.J. Super. 21, 486 A.2d 345 (App. Div. 1984)
53 ALR6th 81—§ 12
State v. Sessoms, 187 N.J. Super. 625, 455 A.2d 595 (Law Div. 1982)
97 ALR5th 201—§ 6, 7

For assistance, call 1-800-328-4880

State v. Setters, 2001 MT 101, 25 P.3d 893 (Mont. 2001)

92 ALR5th 35—§ 19

State v. Setzer, 42 N.C. App. 98, 256 S.E.2d 485 (1979)

34 ALR6th 1—§ 12

State v. Sevelin, 204 Wis. 2d 127, 554 N.W.2d 521 (Ct. App. 1996)

46 ALR6th 63—§ 3, 8

State v. Seventeen Thousand Five Hundred Dollars ($17,500) Cash, 609 So. 2d 978 (La. Ct. App. 4th Cir. 1992)

34 ALR6th 539—§ 6

State v. Seven Thousand Dollars, 136 N.J. 223, 642 A.2d 967 (1994)

104 ALR5th 229—§ 4, 5

115 ALR5th 403—§ 8

116 ALR5th 325—§ 3

4 ALR6th 113—§ 29

34 ALR6th 539—§ 9

101 ALR6th 1—§ 29, 51, 59

State v. Seventy-Seven Thousand Fourteen & No/100 ($77,014.00) Dollars, 607 So. 2d 576 (La. Ct. App. 3d Cir. 1992)

34 ALR6th 539—§ 5, 9

State v. Seventy-Seven Thousand Fourteen & No/100 ($77,014.00) Dollars, 607 So. 2d 576 (La. Ct. App. 3d Cir. 1992)

104 ALR5th 229—§ 6

116 ALR5th 325—§ 3

4 ALR6th 113—§ 5, 23, 25

101 ALR6th 1—§ 31, 45

State v. Seventy-Three Thousand One Hundred Thirty Dollars United States Currency, 2001 UT 67, 31 P.3d 514 (Utah 2001)

104 ALR5th 229—§ 4, 15

116 ALR5th 325—§ 3

101 ALR6th 1—§ 41

State v. Severance, 108 N.H. 404, 237 A.2d 683 (1968)

116 ALR5th 479—§ 6

State v. Severino, 56 Haw. 378, 537 P.2d 1187 (1975)

109 ALR5th 611—§ 5

State v. Sewell, 38 Conn. App. 20, 658 A.2d 598 (1995)

5 ALR5th 243—§ 53, 56

State v. Sexton, 176 Ariz. 171, 859 P.2d 794, 148 Ariz. Adv. Rep. 19 (App. 1993)

15 ALR5th 391—§ 40

State v. Sexton, 336 N.C. 321, 444 S.E.2d 879 (1994)

79 ALR5th 33—§ 13, 42, 63, 68

State v. Sexton, 2002-Ohio-3617, 2002 WL 1542676 (Ohio Ct. App. 10th Dist. Franklin County 2002)

56 ALR6th 185—§ 10

State v. Seyferth, 134 Wis. 2d 354, 397 N.W.2d 666 (App. 1986)

41 ALR5th 171—§ 2, 87, 120, 124, 134

State v. Seymour, 140 N.H. 736, 673 A.2d 786 (1996)

37 ALR5th 515—§ 11

State v. Seymour, No. 1136 (August 20, 1986, Ct. App. Ohio, 4th App. Dist. Ross Co.)

39 ALR5th 283—§ 14, 66

State v. Sfameni, 113 R.I. 150, 318 A.2d 460 (1974)

9 ALR6th 633—§ 4, 5

12 ALR6th 389—§ 7

13 ALR6th 603—§ 41

15 ALR6th 173—§ 41

State v. S.H., 75 Wash. App. 1, 877 P.2d 205 (Div. 1 1994)

73 ALR5th 383—§ 6, 27, 28

State v. Shabazz, 400 N.J. Super. 203, 946 A.2d 626 (2005)

40 ALR6th 595—§ 3

State v. Shade, 172 P.3d 1222 (Kan. Ct. App. 2007)

56 ALR6th 323—§ 7

State v. Shaffer, 223 Kan. 244, 574 P.2d 205 (1977)

50 ALR5th 467—§ 8, 9

State v. Shaffer, 227 Mont. 221, 738 P.2d 491 (1987)

84 ALR6th 293—§ 31

CASES CITED IN ALR5th and ALR6th

State v. Shaffer, 2006-Ohio-4939, 2006 WL 2714946 (Ohio Ct. App. 11th Dist. Portage County 2006)
26 ALR6th 511—§ 19
State v. Shaffer, 2010-Ohio-1744, 2010 WL 1610753 (Ohio Ct. App. 8th Dist. Cuyahoga County 2010)
78 ALR6th 297—§ 76
State v. Shafranek, 576 N.W.2d 115 (Iowa 1998)
97 ALR5th 201—§ 2 to 4, 6
State v. Shahan, 335 A.2d 277 (Del. Super. Ct. 1975)
57 ALR6th 445—§ 3, 8
State v. Shaheen, 81 N.H. 194, 123 A. 223 (1924)
104 ALR5th 357—§ 8
State v. Shakoor, 2003-Ohio-5140, 2003 WL 22231582 (Ohio Ct. App. 7th Dist. Mahoning County 2003)
3 ALR6th 543—§ 2, 9
State v. Shambley, 281 Neb. 317, 795 N.W.2d 884, 78 A.L.R.6th 655 (2011)
78 ALR6th 1—§ 27, 29, 39, 42, 52
State v. Shanahan, 404 A.2d 975 (Me. 1979)
28 ALR6th 505—§ 9
State v. Shandola, 120 Wash. App. 1005, 2004 WL 194380 (Div. 2 2004)
27 ALR6th 183—§ 42
State v. Shaney, 361 N.W.2d 921 (Minn. Ct. App. 1985)
73 ALR5th 383—§ 5
State v. Shankle, 7 N.C. App. 564, 172 S.E.2d 904 (1970)
5 ALR5th 243—§ 6
State v. Shankle, 58 Or. App. 134, 647 P.2d 959 (1982)
116 ALR5th 479—§ 5
State v. Shanklin, 16 N.C. App. 712, 193 S.E.2d 341 (1972)
6 ALR6th 533—§ 15
State v. Shanks, 178 Ind. 330, 99 N.E. 481 (1912)
5 ALR6th 1—§ 33
State v. Shannahan, 69 Wash. App. 512, 849 P.2d 1239 (1993)

15 ALR5th 391—§ 33
State v. Shannon, 77 Wash. App. 379, 892 P.2d 757 (1995)
27 ALR5th 593—§ 18
State v. Shannon, 472 So. 2d 286 (La. App. 1st Cir. 1985)
19 ALR5th 470—§ 2, 3, 12
State v. Shannon, 795 S.W.2d 426 (Mo. Ct. App. E.D. 1990)
108 ALR5th 593—§ 27
State v. Shannon, 892 S.W.2d 761 (Mo. App. 1995)
18 ALR5th 1—§ 3, 10
State v. Shape, 517 N.W.2d 650 (S.D. 1994)
83 ALR6th 465—§ 13, 67
State v. Sharkey, 821 S.W.2d 544 (Mo. Ct. App. E.D. 1991)
84 ALR6th 229—§ 7
State v. Sharon H., 429 A.2d 1321 (Del. Super. Ct. 1981)
103 ALR5th 255—§ 25
State v. Sharp, 104 Idaho 691, 662 P.2d 1135 (1983)
34 ALR5th 125—§ 14
State v. Sharp, 180 Wis. 2d 640, 511 N.W.2d 316 (Ct. App. 1993)
27 ALR6th 183—§ 4
State v. Sharp, 193 Ariz. 414, 973 P.2d 1171 (1999)
21 ALR6th 1—§ 4
58 ALR6th 499—§ 5, 53
State v. Sharp, 217 Mont. 40, 702 P.2d 959 (1985)
84 ALR6th 293—§ 33
State v. Sharpe, 174 Ohio App. 3d 498, 2008-Ohio-267, 882 N.E.2d 960 (2d Dist. Clark County 2008)
78 ALR6th 297—§ 11, 40, 69
State v. Sharpe, 178 Wis. 2d 313, 504 N.W.2d 873 (Ct. App. 1993)
46 ALR6th 63—§ 4
State v. Sharpe, 195 Conn. 651, 491 A.2d 345 (1985)
111 ALR5th 1—§ 3, 8
State v. Sharpe, 239 S.C. 258, 122 S.E.2d 622 (1961)

83 ALR6th 465—§ 6, 74
State v. Sharpley, 2009 WL 406797 (Del. Super. Ct. 2009)
84 ALR6th 427—§ 5
State v. Sharp, No. 43262 (June 18, 1981, Ct. App. Ohio, 8th App. Dist. Cuyahoga Co.)
39 ALR5th 283—§ 14, 41
State v. Shatney, 572 A.2d 872 (R.I. 1990)
70 ALR6th 361—§ 29
State v. Shatto, 285 N.W.2d 492 (Minn. 1979)
84 ALR6th 427—§ 26
State v. Shattuck, 55 Wash. App. 131, 776 P.2d 1001 (Div. 1 1989)
109 ALR5th 611—§ 4
State v. Shattuck, 704 N.W.2d 131 (Minn. 2005)
26 ALR6th 511—§ 16
State v. Shaver, 233 Mont. 438, 760 P.2d 1230 (1988)
15 ALR5th 391—§ 39
State v. Shaw, 65 Ohio App. 3d 821, 585 N.E.2d 515 (Clark Co. 1990)
26 ALR5th 603—§ 4
State v. Shaw, 75 Wash. 326, 135 P. 20 (1913)
24 ALR6th 747—§ 31
State v. Shaw, 89 Vt. 121, 94 A. 434 (1915)
23 ALR6th 1—§ 17
State v. Shaw, 98 N.M. 580, 651 P.2d 115 (Ct. App. 1982)
70 ALR6th 361—§ 33
State v. Shaw, 185 Conn. 372, 441 A.2d 561 (1981)
24 ALR6th 1—§ 21
State v. Shaw, 328 S.C. 454, 492 S.E.2d 402 (Ct. App. 1997)
84 ALR5th 487—§ 22
State v. Shaw, 2009 WL 1362270 (Ariz. Ct. App. Div. 2 2009)
56 ALR6th 1—§ 4, 33
State v. Shawley, 334 Mo. 352, 67 S.W.2d 74 (1933)
79 ALR5th 237—§ 4

State v. Shea, 58 S.D. 210, 235 N.W. 648 (1931)
54 ALR6th 429—§ 29
State v. Sheahan, 1988 WL 32105 (Ohio Ct. App. 8th Dist. Cuyahoga County 1988)
43 ALR6th 475—§ 6
State v. Shearin, 170 N.C. App. 222, 612 S.E.2d 371 (2005)
92 ALR6th 171—§ 20
State v. Shears, 68 Wis. 2d 217, 229 N.W.2d 103 (1975)
16 ALR6th 329—§ 7
24 ALR6th 591—§ 4
State v. Shears, 260 Kan. 823, 925 P.2d 1136 (1996)
15 ALR6th 173—§ 47, 50
State v. Shed, 828 So. 2d 124 (La. Ct. App. 2d Cir. 2002)
15 ALR6th 515—§ 14
State v. Shedd, 10 N.C. App. 139, 177 S.E.2d 723 (1970)
65 ALR5th 407—§ 3, 16
State v. Shedd, 274 N.C. 95, 161 S.E.2d 477 (1968)
36 ALR5th 255—§ 17, 33
State v. Shedrick, 61 Ohio St. 3d 331, 574 N.E.2d 1065 (1991)
86 ALR5th 59—§ 5
State v. Sheedy, 124 N.H. 738, 474 A.2d 1042 (1984)
33 ALR5th 453—§ 7, 11
State v. Sheehan, 72 Ohio Misc. 2d 58, 656 N.E.2d 746 (Mun. Ct. 1995)
84 ALR6th 293—§ 34
State v. Sheeley, 63 Nev. 88, 162 P.2d 96 (1945)
29 ALR5th 59—§ 56
State v. Sheeran, 441 A.2d 235 (Del. Super. Ct. 1981)
97 ALR5th 201—§ 3
State v. Sheets, 48 Wash. 2d 65, 290 P.2d 974 (1955)
22 ALR5th 327—§ 55
State v. Sheets, 112 Ohio App. 3d 1, 677 N.E.2d 818 (4th Dist. Highland County 1996)

---

70 ALR6th 329—§ 14
State v. Sheets, 197 Wis. 2d 119, 541
N.W.2d 839 (Ct. App. 1995)

15 ALR6th 375—§ 24
State v. Sheets, 291 N.W.2d 35 (Iowa
1980)

53 ALR6th 81—§ 7
State v. Sheets, 2005-Ohio-803, 2005
WL 435149 (Ohio Ct. App. 4th Dist.
Athens County 2005)

97 ALR6th 263—§ 7
State v. Shehan, 242 Kan. 127, 744 P.2d
824 (1987)

37 ALR5th 515—§ 10
State v. Shelbrick, 33 N.J. Super. 7, 109
A.2d 17 (1954)

29 ALR5th 59—§ 62, 65, 88
State v. Shelby, 90 Mo. 302, 2 S.W. 468
(1886)

33 ALR6th 407—§ 4, 9
State v. Shelley, 628 S.W.2d 436 (Tenn.
Crim. App. 1981)

68 ALR6th 527—§ 30, 37
State v. Shelli, 675 S.W.2d 79 (Mo. App.
1984)

45 ALR5th 1—§ 5, 12, 23, 28
State v. Shelton, 182 N.C. App. 530, 642
S.E.2d 548 (2007)

57 ALR6th 83—§ 12, 16
State v. Shelton, 320 S.W.3d 186 (Mo.
Ct. App. E.D. 2010)

69 ALR6th 1—§ 12
State v. Shelton, 554 P.2d 404 (Alaska
1976)

**41 ALR5th 171—§ 2, 12, 22, 58, 90,
108**
State v. Shelton, 871 S.W.2d 598 (Mo.
App. 1994)

47 ALR5th 259—§ 2
State v. Shepard, 13 Ohio App. 3d 389,
13 Ohio B.R. 473, 469 N.E.2d 1040
(1984)

43 ALR5th 777—§ 4
State v. Shepard, 158 N.H. 743, 973
A.2d 318 (2009)

84 ALR6th 427—§ 7
State v. Shepard, 955 P.2d 352 (Utah Ct.
App. 1998)

92 ALR6th 171—§ 4
State v. Shepardson, 194 Neb. 673, 235
N.W.2d 218 (1975)

56 ALR6th 323—§ 3, 9, 11
State v. Shepcaro, 45 Ohio App. 2d 293,
74 Ohio Ops. 2d 437, 344 N.E.2d
352 (Franklin Co. 1975)

41 ALR5th 171—§ 68, 93, 120, 133
State v. Shephard, 53 Wash. App. 194,
766 P.2d 467 (Div. 3 1988)

73 ALR5th 383—§ 32
State v. Shephard, 248 Ga. App. 433,
546 S.E.2d 823 (2001)

58 ALR6th 499—§ 87
State v. Shephard, 255 Iowa 1218, 124
N.W.2d 712 (1963)

65 ALR5th 407—§ 3, 11
State v. Shepherd, 21 Or. App. 52, 533
P.2d 353 (1975)

71 ALR5th 1—§ 59
State v. Shepherd, 110 Wash. App. 544,
41 P.3d 1235 (Div. 3 2002)

50 ALR6th 353—§ 17, 27
State v. Shepherd, 902 S.W.2d 895
(Tenn.,1995)

79 ALR5th 33—§ 7
81 ALR5th 563—§ 3
State v. Shepherd, 1999 UT App. 305,
989 P.2d 503, Blue Sky L. Rep.
(CCH) ¶ 74194 (Utah Ct. App.
1999)

47 ALR5th 259—§ 9
88 ALR5th 67—§ 5
State v. Shepler, 141 Ariz. 43, 684 P.2d
924 (App. 1984)

42 ALR5th 291—§ 25
State v. Sheppard, 100 Ohio App. 345,
60 Ohio Op. 298, 128 N.E.2d 471
(8th Dist. Cuyahoga County 1955)

54 ALR6th 429—§ 9
State v. Sheppard, 172 W. Va. 656, 310
S.E.2d 173 (1983)

90 ALR5th 225—§ 3
State v. Sheppard, 325 N.W.2d 911
(Iowa Ct. App. 1982)

28 ALR6th 245—§ 7
State v. Sheppard, 679 So. 2d 899 (La.
1996)

72 ALR5th 109—§ 3

State v. Sherburne, 571 A.2d 1181, 87 A.L.R.4th 965 (Me. 1990)

50 ALR5th 703—§ 3, 15, 27

State v. Sheridan, 230 Neb. 979, 434 N.W.2d 338 (1989)

40 ALR6th 1—§ 9

State v. Sheriff, 190 Mont. 131, 619 P.2d 181 (1980)

27 ALR6th 183—§ 35

State v. Sherman, 66 Or. App. 144, 672 P.2d 1370 (1983)

28 ALR6th 505—§ 9

State v. Sherman, 106 Iowa 684 (1898)

46 ALR5th 499—§ 3

State v. Sherman, 266 S.W.3d 395 (Tenn. 2008)

97 ALR6th 539—§ 3, 4

State v. Sherman, 1998 WL 852566 (Ohio Ct. App. 1st Dist. Hamilton County 1998)

81 ALR6th 505—§ 5

State v. Sherratt, 2009 WL 2569267 (Utah Ct. App. 2009)

97 ALR6th 263—§ 3

State v. Sherrick, 98 Ariz. 46, 402 P.2d 1 (1965)

41 ALR5th 171—§ 17

State v. Sherrill, 247 Ga. App. 708, 545 S.E.2d 110 (2001)

74 ALR5th 319—§ 5

State v. Sherwood, 5 Conn. Cir. Ct. 583, 258 A.2d 558 (App. Div. 1969)

66 ALR5th 397—§ 19

State v. Sherwood, 25 Conn. App. 725, 596 A.2d 470 (1991)

53 ALR6th 81—§ 5, 7, 9
55 ALR6th 391—§ 5

State v. Sherwood, 341 N.W.2d 574 (Minn. Ct. App. 1983)

106 ALR5th 377—§ 3

State v. Sherwood, 352 N.W.2d 831 (Minn. Ct. App. 1984)

6 ALR6th 533—§ 15

State v. Shewfelt, 948 P.2d 470 (Alaska 1997)

65 ALR6th 537—§ 48, 53

State v. Shields, 308 Conn. 678, 69 A.3d 293 (2013)

101 ALR6th 299—§ 11

State v. Shields, 593 A.2d 986 (Del. Super. Ct. 1990)

70 ALR5th 1—§ 3

State v. Shields, 2002-Ohio-1777, 2002 WL 471986 (Ohio Ct. App. 2d Dist. Montgomery County 2002)

11 ALR6th 237—§ 10, 12

State v. Shields, 2007 WL 1828875 (Conn. Super. Ct. 2007)

101 ALR6th 299—§ 11

State v. Shifflett, 1993 WL 372233 (Ohio Ct. App. 2d Dist. Montgomery County 1993)

107 ALR5th 567—§ 11, 18

State v. Shifflett, 1994 WL 37277 (Ohio Ct. App. 2d Dist. Montgomery County 1994)

107 ALR5th 567—§ 2, 18

State v. Shilling, 440 So. 2d 110 (La. 1983)

16 ALR6th 329—§ 4
24 ALR6th 591—§ 14

State v. Shillow, 602 So. 2d 28 (La. App. 3d Cir. 1992)

27 ALR5th 593—§ 2, 12, 24

State v. Shimon, 182 N.W.2d 113 (Iowa 1970)

89 ALR6th 565—§ 17, 21

State v. Shine, 173 N.C. App. 699, 619 S.E.2d 895 (2005)

26 ALR6th 511—§ 27

State v. Shineman, 94 Wash. App. 57, 971 P.2d 94 (Div. 2 1999)

9 ALR6th 541—§ 3

State v. Shingaki, 65 Hawaii 116, 648 P.2d 190, 8 Media L. R. 2111 (1982)

42 ALR5th 291—§ 3, 5

State v. Shingleton, 2013-Ohio-3943, 2013 WL 5172952 (Ohio Ct. App. 2d Dist. Montgomery County 2013)

102 ALR6th 637—§ 7

State v. Shipley, 94 Ohio App. 3d 771, 641 N.E.2d 822 (5th Dist. Licking County 1994)

67 ALR6th 341—§ 10

State v. Shipley, 94 Ohio App. 3d 771, 641 N.E.2d 822 (Licking Co. 1994)
51 ALR5th 603—§ 2, 4, 14
State v. Shipley, 1984 WL 3451 (Ohio Ct. App. 12th Dist. Butler County 1984)
30 ALR6th 103—§ 48
State v. Shipman, 77 N.C. App. 650, 335 S.E.2d 912 (1985)
108 ALR5th 593—§ 36
State v. Shipp, 155 N.C. App. 294, 573 S.E.2d 721 (2002)
32 ALR6th 385—§ 4
State v. Shipp, 712 So. 2d 230 (La. Ct. App. 2d Cir. 1998)
103 ALR6th 507—§ 18
State v. Shire, 850 S.W.2d 923 (Mo. Ct. App. S.D. 1993)
67 ALR6th 341—§ 9
State v. Shirley, 10 So. 3d 224 (La. 2009)
57 ALR6th 83—§ 5
State v. Shirley, 117 Ariz. 105, 570 P.2d 1278 (Ct. App. Div. 2 1977)
92 ALR6th 1—§ 3
State v. Shirley M., 136 Ohio App. 3d 753, 737 N.E.2d 1013 (8th Dist. Cuyahoga County 2000)
69 ALR6th 1—§ 36
State v. Shively, 268 Kan. 573, 999 P.2d 952 (2000)
10 ALR6th 463—§ 4
State v. Shively, 268 Kan. 589, 999 P.2d 259 (2000)
50 ALR6th 455—§ 10, 15
State v. Shively, 999 P.2d 259 (Kan. 2000)
85 ALR5th 1—§ 48
State v. Shlionsky, 184 Ariz. 631, 911 P.2d 637 (Ct. App. Div. 2 1996)
70 ALR5th 533—§ 7
State v. Shoemaker, 334 N.C. 252, 432 S.E.2d 314 (1993)
57 ALR5th 141—§ 6
State v. Shoemaker, 801 N.W.2d 378 (Iowa Ct. App. 2011)
92 ALR6th 1—§ 3

State v. Shoen, 578 N.W.2d 708 (Minn. 1998)
32 ALR6th 1—§ 11
State v. Shondel, 22 Utah 2d 343, 453 P.2d 146 (1969)
33 ALR6th 373—§ 8
State v. Shook, 1992 WL 213877 (Ohio Ct. App. 10th Dist. Franklin County 1992)
102 ALR6th 279—§ 29
State v. Short, 327 S.C. 329, 489 S.E.2d 209 (Ct. App. 1997)
47 ALR5th 259—§ 22
State v. Short, 958 So. 2d 93 (La. Ct. App. 3d Cir. 2007)
98 ALR6th 455—§ 12
State v. Short, 2000 WL 210412 (Iowa Ct. App. 2000)
84 ALR6th 293—§ 33
State v. Short, 2005-Ohio-4578, 2005 WL 2100969 (Ohio Ct. App. 8th Dist. Cuyahoga County 2005)
26 ALR6th 511—§ 18
43 ALR6th 475—§ 6
State v. Short, 2010-Ohio-1526, 2010 WL 1270320 (Ohio Ct. App. 12th Dist. Warren County 2010)
99 ALR6th 295—§ 13
State v. Shorter, 814 So. 2d 1117 (Fla. Dist. Ct. App. 4th Dist. 2002)
113 ALR5th 597—§ 3, 8
State v. Shorter, 1995 WL 147064 (Minn. Ct. App. 1995)
73 ALR5th 383—§ 23, 31
State v. Shouse, 268 Mo. 199, 186 S.W. 1064 (1916)
118 ALR5th 253—§ 9
State v. Showalter, 134 Or. App. 34, 894 P.2d 504 (1995)
104 ALR5th 165—§ 13
State v. Showalter, 427 N.W.2d 166 (Iowa 1988)
67 ALR6th 531—§ 28
State v. Showcase Products, Inc., 501 So. 2d 11 (Fla. Dist. Ct. App. 4th Dist. 1986)
6 ALR6th 533—§ 22
18 ALR6th 1—§ 5, 9

State v. Shriner, 751 N.W.2d 538 (Minn. 2008)

46 ALR6th 495—§ 6

State v. Shropshire, 1996 WL 189931 (Tenn. Crim. App. 1996)

43 ALR6th 475—§ 6

State v. Shubert, 102 N.C. App. 419, 402 S.E.2d 642 (1991)

19 ALR5th 823—§ 2, 4, 8

67 ALR6th 103—§ 10

State v. Shuck, 34 Wash. App. 456, 661 P.2d 1020 (1983)

42 ALR5th 291—§ 4

State v. Shuck, 953 S.W.2d 662, 70 A.L.R.5th 743 (Tenn. 1997)

70 ALR5th 491—§ 2, 3, 8

State v. Shuffelen, 150 Wash. App. 244, 208 P.3d 1167 (Div. 1 2009)

56 ALR6th 323—§ 11

State v. Shuler, 344 S.C. 604, 545 S.E.2d 805 (2001)

3 ALR6th 543—§ 2

15 ALR6th 319—§ 4

State v. Shull, 331 N.W.2d 284 (S.D. 1983)

50 ALR5th 703—§ 10, 15

State v. Shult, 380 N.W.2d 352 (S.D. 1986)

84 ALR5th 487—§ 20

State v. Shults, 169 Mont. 33, 544 P.2d 817 (1976)

78 ALR5th 567—§ 7

State v. Shultz, 138 Wash. 2d 638, 980 P.2d 1265 (1999)

63 ALR6th 1—§ 5, 53

State v. Shultz, 177 Iowa 321, 158 N.W. 539 (1916)

119 ALR5th 275—§ 13

State v. Shultz, 1994 WL 101512 (Ohio Ct. App. 2d Dist. Miami County 1994)

111 ALR5th 239—§ 2

State v. Shuman, 639 P.2d 155 (Utah 1981)

28 ALR6th 505—§ 9

32 ALR6th 1—§ 11

State v. Shumate, 629 S.W.2d 379 (Mo. App. 1981)

23 ALR5th 672—§ 4

State v. Shumway, 124 Or. App. 131, 861 P.2d 384 (1993)

84 ALR6th 293—§ 43

State v. Shumway, 137 Ariz. 585, 672 P.2d 929 (1983)

84 ALR6th 427—§ 26

State v. Shupper, 263 S.C. 53, 207 S.E.2d 799 (1974)

41 ALR5th 171—§ 85, 86, 108

State v. Sibbett, 145 Wash. App. 1042, 2008 WL 2738602 (Div. 3 2008)

79 ALR6th 1—§ 32, 33

State v. Sibert, 135 Wash. App. 1025, 2006 WL 3026124 (Div. 2 2006)

26 ALR6th 511—§ 25, 33, 41

State v. Sibley, 411 S.W.2d 187 (Mo. 1967)

24 ALR6th 747—§ 30

State v. Sickels, 275 N.W.2d 809 (Minn. 1979)

25 ALR6th 379—§ 3, 8

State v. Sickles, 655 A.2d 1254 (Me. 1995)

38 ALR5th 433—§ 19

State v. Siddall, 103 Me. 144, 68 A. 634 (1907)

9 ALR6th 633—§ 5

13 ALR6th 603—§ 5

State v. Sidney, Slip Opinion No. 981 (Ohio App. Erie Co. 1975)

41 ALR5th 171—§ 30

State v. Sidoti, 134 N.J. Super. 426, 341 A.2d 670 (1975)

51 ALR5th 603—§ 2

State v. Sidway, 139 Vt. 480, 431 A.2d 1237 (1981)

26 ALR5th 1—§ 3, 26

State v. Siegal, 281 Mont. 250, 934 P.2d 176 (1997)

59 ALR5th 615—§ 7

78 ALR5th 309—§ 8

114 ALR5th 235—§ 8

45 ALR6th 643—§ 19

State v. Siegel, 679 So. 2d 1201 (Fla. Dist. Ct. App. 5th Dist. 1996)
62 ALR5th 1—§ 3
78 ALR5th 309—§ 6

State v. Siemer, 454 N.W.2d 857 (Iowa 1990)
39 ALR5th 283—§ 10, 74

State v. Siering, 35 Conn. App. 173, 644 A.2d 958 (1994)
33 ALR6th 353—§ 3, 4

State v. Sierra, 2011 WL 5166493 (Ariz. Ct. App. Div. 2 2011)
95 ALR6th 1—§ 5

State v. Sievers, 2 Neb. App. 463, 511 N.W.2d 205 (1994)
99 ALR5th 557—§ 12, 15

State v. Sieyes, 168 Wash. 2d 276, 225 P.3d 995 (2010)
64 ALR6th 131—§ 14

State v. Siferd, 151 Ohio App. 3d 103, 2002-Ohio-6801, 783 N.E.2d 591 (3d Dist. Hancock County 2002)
58 ALR6th 385—§ 33

State v. Sigarroa, 269 Wis. 2d 234, 2004 WI App 16, 674 N.W.2d 894 (Ct. App. 2003)
45 ALR6th 643—§ 11

State v. Sigman, 118 Wash. 2d 442, 826 P.2d 144, 24 A.L.R.5th 856 (1992)
24 ALR5th 428—§ 2, 4, 9

State v. Sigro, 1995 WL 13556 (Ariz. App. Div. 1)
50 ALR5th 581—§ 5, 7, 10

State v. Siirila, 292 Minn. 1, 193 N.W.2d 467 (1971)
4 ALR5th 1—§ 4, 11, 21
43 ALR5th 1—§ 7

State v. Silcox, 694 S.W.2d 755 (Mo. App. 1985)
37 ALR5th 319—§ 9

State v. Siler, 116 Ohio St. 3d 39, 2007-Ohio-5637, 876 N.E.2d 534 (2007)
30 ALR6th 1—§ 6
36 ALR6th 681—§ 13

State v. Siler, 164 Ohio App. 3d 680, 2005-Ohio-6591, 843 N.E.2d 863 (5th Dist. Ashland County 2005)
30 ALR6th 1—§ 6

State v. Siler, 310 N.C. 731, 314 S.E.2d 547 (1984)
2 ALR6th 551—§ 4, 29

State v. Silhan, 297 N.C. 660, 256 S.E.2d 702 (1979)
39 ALR5th 283—§ 4, 60

State v. Siliski, 238 S.W.3d 338 (Tenn. Crim. App. 2007)
77 ALR6th 393—§ 75, 90

State v. Siliski, 2006 WL 1931814 (Tenn. Crim. App. 2006)
70 ALR6th 329—§ 16

State v. Siliski, 2006 WL 2742345 (Tenn. Crim. App. 2006)
77 ALR6th 393—§ 82

State v. Silva, 53 Hawaii 232, 491 P.2d 1216 (1971)
46 ALR5th 499—§ 3

State v. Silva, 106 Idaho 14, 674 P.2d 443 (Ct. App. 1983)
29 ALR6th 1—§ 10

State v. Silva, 110 R.I. 290, 292 A.2d 228 (1972)
29 ALR5th 59—§ 3

State v. Silva, 864 P.2d 583 (Hawaii 1993)
5 ALR5th 243—§ 34, 59, 61

State v. Silva, 1976 WL 188456 (Ohio Ct. App. 6th Dist. Lucas County 1976)
38 ALR6th 97—§ 18

State v. Silva, 2003-Ohio-4275, 2003 WL 21919878 (Ohio Ct. App. 5th Dist. Stark County 2003)
125 ALR5th 537—§ 49, 51

State v. Silva-Baltazar, 125 Wash. 2d 472, 886 P.2d 138 (1994)
27 ALR5th 593—§ 26

State v. Silvaz, 2003 UT App 32, 2003 WL 21297270 (Utah Ct. App. 2003)
33 ALR6th 373—§ 8

State v. Silver, 314 S.C. 483, 431 S.E.2d 250 (1993)
56 ALR6th 323—§ 7

State v. Silver, 737 P.2d 1221 (Okla. Crim. 1987)
3 ALR5th 963—§ 6

State v. Silvers, 255 Neb. 702, 587 N.W.2d 325 (1998)

71 ALR6th 1—§ 10

State v. Silvestrini, 2009 WL 233370 (Minn. Ct. App. 2009)

101 ALR6th 331—§ 13

103 ALR6th 347—§ 14

State v. Silvey, 894 S.W.2d 662 (Mo. 1995)

71 ALR5th 637—§ 7

State v. Simants, 182 Neb. 491, 155 N.W.2d 788 (1968)

18 ALR5th 856—§ 3

State v. Simbach, 742 So. 2d 365 (Fla. Dist. Ct. App. 2d Dist. 1999)

6 ALR5th 733—§ 5

State v. Simko, 71 Ohio St. 3d 483, 644 N.E.2d 345 (1994)

57 ALR5th 141—§ 2, 3

State v. Simmerman, No. 11252 (December 25, 1990, Ct. App. Ohio, 9th App. Dist. Summit Co.)

39 ALR5th 283—§ 14, 67

State v. Simmington, 235 N.C. 612, 70 S.E.2d 842 (1952)

15 ALR5th 391—§ 33

State v. Simmons, 36 N.C. App. 354, 244 S.E.2d 168 (1978)

6 ALR5th 733—§ 2, 4, 12, 28

State v. Simmons, 65 N.C. App. 294, 309 S.E.2d 493 (1983)

19 ALR6th 115—§ 5, 9, 11

State v. Simmons, 99 So. 3d 28 (La. 2012)

102 ALR6th 637—§ 7

State v. Simmons, 114 R.I. 16, 327 A.2d 843, 74 A.L.R.3d 1251 (1974)

87 ALR5th 715—§ 4

State v. Simmons, 117 Ark. 159, 174 S.W. 238 (1915)

5 ALR6th 1—§ 32

State v. Simmons, 131 P.3d 1280 (Kan. Ct. App. 2006)

26 ALR6th 511—§ 25

State v. Simmons, 190 Vt. 141, 2011 VT 69, 27 A.3d 1065 (2011)

88 ALR6th 319—§ 15, 16, 37

State v. Simmons, 191 N.C. App. 224, 662 S.E.2d 559 (2008)

99 ALR6th 113—§ 11, 14

State v. Simmons, 267 S.C. 479, 229 S.E.2d 597 (1976)

104 ALR5th 357—§ 3, 8

State v. Simmons, 331 N.J. Super. 512, 752 A.2d 724 (App. Div. 2000)

71 ALR5th 1—§ 30

State v. Simmons, 357 So. 2d 517 (La. 1978)

62 ALR5th 121—§ 6

State v. Simmons, 381 So. 2d 803 (La. 1980)

16 ALR6th 329—§ 4

24 ALR6th 591—§ 14

State v. Simmons, 422 So. 2d 138 (La. 1982)

7 ALR5th 263—§ 7

State v. Simmons, 435 A.2d 1090 (Me. 1981)

35 ALR6th 127—§ 22

State v. Simmons, 454 N.W.2d 866 (Iowa 1990)

39 ALR5th 283—§ 10, 74

State v. Simmons, 573 P.2d 341 (Utah 1977)

57 ALR6th 445—§ 3, 49

State v. Simmons, 751 So. 2d 85 (Mo. App. 1988)

5 ALR5th 243—§ 11

State v. Simmons, 866 P.2d 614, 230 Utah Adv. Rep. 22 (Utah App. 1993)

41 ALR5th 171—§ 4, 8, 13, 17, 23, 38, 68, 93, 114, 120, 133

State v. Simmons, 939 S.W.2d 487 (Mo. Ct. App. W.D. 1997)

99 ALR6th 295—§ 13

State v. Simmons, 955 S.W.2d 729 (Mo. 1997)

70 ALR5th 1—§ 4, 5

State v. Simmons, 955 S.W.2d 752 (Mo. 1997)

72 ALR5th 109—§ 5

79 ALR5th 33—§ 7, 8, 17

102 ALR6th 417—§ 100

State v. Simmons, 1995 WL 754071 (Ohio Ct. App. 4th Dist. Scioto County 1995)
99 ALR6th 295—§ 5
State v. Simmons, 2001 WL 950082 (Minn. Ct. App. 2001)
84 ALR6th 293—§ 22
State v. Simmons, 2006-Ohio-4751, 2006 WL 2639382 (Ohio Ct. App. 8th Dist. Cuyahoga County 2006)
26 ALR6th 511—§ 19
State v. Simmons, 2008-Ohio-4747, 2008 WL 4278333 (Ohio Ct. App. 2d Dist. Montgomery County 2008)
68 ALR6th 115—§ 17
State v. Simms, 9 Ohio App. 3d 302, 459 N.E.2d 1316 (10th Dist. Franklin County 1983)
66 ALR5th 135—§ 44
State v. Simms, 10 Wash. App. 75, 516 P.2d 1088 (Div. 2 1973)
92 ALR6th 1—§ 3, 8
State v. Simms, 201 Conn. 395, 518 A.2d 35 (1986)
101 ALR5th 187—§ 9
State v. Simms, 1999 WL 797175 (Ohio Ct. App. 3d Dist. Allen County 1999)
78 ALR5th 489—§ 9
State v. Simnick, 17 Neb. App. 766, 771 N.W.2d 196 (2009)
51 ALR6th 139—§ 12
State v. Simnick, 279 Neb. 499, 779 N.W.2d 335 (2010)
63 ALR6th 351—§ 4
State v. Simon, 87 Ohio St. 3d 531, 2000-Ohio-474, 721 N.E.2d 1041 (2000)
69 ALR6th 1—§ 23
State v. Simon, 131 La. 520, 59 So. 975 (1912)
24 ALR5th 465—§ 43
State v. Simon, 297 N.W.2d 206, 23 A.L.R.4th 583 (Iowa 1980)
98 ALR5th 445—§ 4
State v. Simon, 635 S.W.2d 498 (Tenn. 1982)
83 ALR6th 465—§ 27

State v. Simon, 1988 WL 63538 (Tenn. Crim. App. 1988)
83 ALR6th 465—§ 27
State v. Simon, 1992 WL 127137 (Ohio App. Perry Co. 1992)
52 ALR5th 655—§ 3
State v. Simonette, 881 P.2d 963 (Utah Ct. App. 1994)
15 ALR5th 391—§ 39
92 ALR5th 35—§ 7
State v. Simons, 172 Wash. 438, 20 P.2d 844 (1933)
54 ALR6th 429—§ 3
State v. Simonsen, 319 Or. 510, 878 P.2d 409 (1994)
96 ALR5th 327—§ 3
State v. Simpson, 9 Hawaii App. 165, 827 P.2d 1156 (1992)
7 ALR5th 263—§ 4
State v. Simpson, 32 Nev. 138, 104 P. 244 (1909)
57 ALR6th 445—§ 58
State v. Simpson, 112 Idaho 644, 734 P.2d 669 (Ct. App. 1987)
78 ALR6th 599—§ 5
State v. Simpson, 114 Wash. App. 1073, 2002 WL 31863322 (Div. 1 2002)
81 ALR6th 505—§ 24
State v. Simpson, 118 Wis. 2d 454, 347 N.W.2d 920 (App. 1984)
39 ALR5th 283—§ 3, 63
State v. Simpson, 185 Wis. 2d 772, 519 N.W.2d 662 (Ct. App. 1994)
72 ALR5th 403—§ 10, 19
State v. Simpson, 200 Wis. 2d 798, 548 N.W.2d 105 (Ct. App. 1996)
9 ALR6th 633—§ 13, 52
14 ALR6th 517—§ 12
State v. Simpson, 202 N.C. App. 586, 691 S.E.2d 132 (2010)
99 ALR6th 295—§ 16
State v. Simpson, 245 Or. App. 152, 261 P.3d 90 (2011)
84 ALR6th 293—§ 7, 8, 12, 14, 15
State v. Simpson, 247 La. 883, 175 So. 2d 255 (1965)
54 ALR6th 429—§ 7

State v. Simpson, 297 N.C. 399, 255 S.E.2d 147 (1979)
    9 ALR5th 369—§ 2, 7
State v. Simpson, 325 S.C. 37, 479 S.E.2d 57 (1996)
    79 ALR5th 33—§ 42, 52
State v. Simpson, 341 N.C. 316, 462 S.E.2d 191 (1995)
    83 ALR6th 255—§ 15
State v. Simpson, 629 So. 2d 468 (La. Ct. App. 3d Cir. 1993)
    68 ALR5th 343—§ 3, 5
State v. Simpson, 836 S.W.2d 75 (Mo. Ct. App. S.D. 1992)
    105 ALR5th 529—§ 27
State v. Simpson, 946 P.2d 890 (Alaska Ct. App. 1997)
    18 ALR5th 1—§ 41
State v. Simpson, 1994 WL 587896 (Ohio Ct. App. 11th Dist. Lake County 1994)
    57 ALR5th 141—§ 9
State v. Simpson, 2002-Ohio-3717, 2002 WL 1625559 (Ohio Ct. App. 10th Dist. Franklin County 2002)
    38 ALR6th 97—§ 27
State v. Simpson, 2009 MT 43, 349 Mont. 275, 203 P.3d 791 (2009)
    46 ALR6th 241—§ 20
State v. Sims, 67 Wash. App. 50, 834 P.2d 78 (Div. 1 1992)
    45 ALR5th 591—§ 15
    73 ALR5th 383—§ 3
State v. Sims, 75 N.J. 337, 382 A.2d 638 (1978)
    43 ALR5th 1—§ 13
State v. Sims, 77 Wash. App. 236, 890 P.2d 521 (1995)
    38 ALR5th 433—§ 31, 34
State v. Sims, 127 Ohio App. 3d 603, 713 N.E.2d 513 (2d Dist. Montgomery County 1998)
    28 ALR6th 505—§ 32
State v. Sims, 213 N.C. 590, 197 S.E. 176 (1938)
    70 ALR5th 587—§ 5
State v. Sims, 357 So. 2d 1095 (La. 1978)

69 ALR6th 1—§ 22
State v. Sims, 526 N.W.2d 201 (Minn. 1994)
    83 ALR5th 277—§ 11
    84 ALR5th 487—§ 13, 22
State v. Sims, 808 P.2d 141 (Utah Ct. App. 1991)
    82 ALR5th 103—§ 3, 6
State v. Sims, 2005-Ohio-6226, 2005 WL 3117205 (Ohio Ct. App. 1st Dist. Hamilton County 2005)
    26 ALR6th 511—§ 26
State v. Sims, 2010-NMSC-027, 148 N.M. 330, 236 P.3d 642 (2010)
    92 ALR6th 295—§ 10, 17
State v. Sims, 2010-NMSC-027, 148 N.M. 330, 236 P.3d 642, 93 A.L.R.6th 647 (2010)
    93 ALR6th 123—§ 108
    93 ALR6th 207—§ 11
    96 ALR6th 355—§ 5, 11, 26, 36, 49, 62
State v. Sinacore, 151 N.J. Super. 106, 376 A.2d 580 (1977)
    13 ALR5th 118—§ 7
State v. Sinclair, 301 N.C. 193, 270 S.E.2d 418 (1980)
    9 ALR6th 693—§ 17
State v. Sinclair, 2004-Ohio-1242, 2004 WL 527921 (Ohio Ct. App. 8th Dist. Cuyahoga County 2004)
    26 ALR6th 511—§ 35
State v. Sinderson, 455 S.W.2d 486 (Mo. 1970)
    101 ALR5th 351—§ 14
State v. Singerman, 115 Ohio App. 3d 273, 685 N.E.2d 279 (2d Dist. Montgomery County 1996)
    24 ALR6th 1—§ 6
State v. Singh, 59 Conn. App. 638, 757 A.2d 1175 (2000)
    85 ALR5th 187—§ 18
State v. Singh, 124 Wash. App. 1023, 2004 WL 2699921 (Div. 1 2004)
    68 ALR6th 607—§ 10
State v. Singh, 126 Wash. App. 1012, 2005 WL 603062 (Div. 1 2005)
    26 ALR6th 511—§ 45

State v. Singletary, 73 N.C. App. 612, 327 S.E.2d 11 (1985)
   66 ALR5th 397—§ 6, 13
State v. Singleton, 66 Ariz. 49, 182 P.2d 920 (1947)
   104 ALR5th 357—§ 7
State v. Singleton, 102 N.M. 66, 691 P.2d 67 (App. 1984)
   39 ALR5th 283—§ 3, 67
State v. Singleton, 174 Conn. 112, 384 A.2d 334 (1977)
   30 ALR6th 103—§ 5
State v. Singleton, 288 Or. 89, 602 P.2d 1059 (1979)
   124 ALR5th 1—§ 3
State v. Singleton, 460 S.E.2d 573 (S.C. 1995)
   32 ALR5th 659—§ 3
State v. Singleton, 689 S.E.2d 562 (N.C. Ct. App. 2010)
   57 ALR6th 1—§ 3, 22, 30
State v. Singleton, 801 So. 2d 1150 (La. Ct. App. 4th Cir. 2001)
   100 ALR5th 67—§ 44
State v. Sings, 35 N.C. App. 1, 240 S.E.2d 471 (1978)
   9 ALR6th 1—§ 6
State v. Sinks, 168 Wis. 2d 245, 483 N.W.2d 286 (Ct. App. 1992)
   124 ALR5th 657—§ 2, 4, 8
State v. Sinnott, 163 N.C. App. 268, 593 S.E.2d 439 (2004)
   88 ALR6th 203—§ 12, 53
State v. Sinsel, 249 Neb. 369, 543 N.W.2d 457 (1996)
   18 ALR6th 1—§ 5, 27
State v. Siqueiros, 121 Ariz. 465, 591 P.2d 557 (Ct. App. Div. 2 1978)
   58 ALR6th 499—§ 115
State v. Sirek, 374 N.W.2d 481 (Minn. Ct. App. 1985)
   73 ALR5th 383—§ 3
State v. Sirmay, 40 Utah 525, 122 P. 748 (1912)
   9 ALR6th 1—§ 7
State v. Sisneros, 137 Ariz. 323, 670 P.2d 721 (1983)

State v. Sisson, 2008 WL 162825 (Del. Super. Ct. 2008)
   74 ALR6th 69—§ 16
State v. Sisti, 62 N.J. Super. 84, 162 A.2d 297 (1960)
   52 ALR5th 655—§ 3, 5
State v. Sistrunk, 57 Wash. App. 210, 787 P.2d 937 (Div. 3 1990)
   97 ALR6th 653—§ 30
State v. Sites, 20 W. Va. 13, 1882 WL 3495 (1882)
   105 ALR5th 529—§ 11
State v. Sitting Crow, 428 N.W.2d 268 (S.D. 1988)
   16 ALR6th 329—§ 7
   24 ALR6th 591—§ 9, 13
State v. Sivri, 46 Conn. App. 578, 700 A.2d 96 (1997)
   26 ALR5th 603—§ 6
State v. Sivri, 231 Conn. 115, 646 A.2d 169 (1994)
   6 ALR6th 533—§ 15
State v. Six, 805 S.W.2d 159 (Mo. 1991)
   80 ALR5th 55—§ 4
   83 ALR6th 255—§ 17
State v. Six Hundred Seventy Six Dollars $676 U.S. Currency Seized from Branch, 719 So. 2d 154 (La. Ct. App. 2d Cir. 1998)
   104 ALR5th 229—§ 12
   101 ALR6th 1—§ 7
State v. Skaggs, 120 Ariz. 467, 586 P.2d 1279 (1978)
   80 ALR5th 469—§ 3, 5
State v. Skaggs, 2006-Ohio-1476, 2006 WL 772027 (Ohio Ct. App. 10th Dist. Franklin County 2006)
   67 ALR6th 395—§ 8 to 10
State v. Skanes, 212 Or. App. 169, 2007 WL 1139448 (2007)
   26 ALR6th 511—§ 26, 31
State v. Skatzes, 2003-Ohio-516, 2003 WL 24196406 (Ohio Ct. App. 2d Dist. Montgomery County 2003)
   21 ALR6th 1—§ 4

State v. Skau, 2008 WI App 51, 309 Wis. 2d 236, 747 N.W.2d 528 (Ct. App. 2008)

84 ALR6th 293—§ 38

State v. Skelton, 77 S.W.3d 791 (Tenn. Crim. App. 2001)

103 ALR6th 137—§ 15, 19

State v. Skidmore, 755 So. 2d 647 (Fla. Dist. Ct. App. 4th Dist. 1999)

113 ALR5th 597—§ 3

State v. Skiffer, 253 La. 405, 218 So. 2d 313 (1969)

35 ALR6th 127—§ 4

State v. Skillings, 98 N.H. 203, 97 A.2d 202 (1953)

93 ALR5th 683—§ 3

State v. Skinner, 3 Wash. App. 367, 475 P.2d 129 (1970)

22 ALR5th 660—§ 2

State v. Skinner, 110 Ariz. 135, 515 P.2d 880 (1973)

3 ALR6th 269—§ 23

State v. Skinner, 122 Wash. App. 1011, 2004 WL 1444882 (Div. 1 2004)

58 ALR6th 215—§ 12

State v. Skinner, 132 Conn. 163, 43 A.2d 76 (1945)

34 ALR5th 723—§ 3

State v. Skinner, 210 Kan. 354, 503 P.2d 168 (1972)

56 ALR5th 783—§ 4

State v. Skinner, 450 N.W.2d 648 (Minn. Ct. App. 1990)

73 ALR5th 383—§ 6, 28, 31

State v. Skinner, 632 A.2d 82 (Del. 1993)

70 ALR6th 1—§ 22
86 ALR6th 321—§ 13
91 ALR6th 171—§ 84

State v. Skinner, 1995 WL 237045 (Ohio Ct. App. 11th Dist.Lake County 1995)

59 ALR5th 1—§ 2, 5

State v. Skipper, 737 So. 2d 872 (La. Ct. App. 4th Cir. 1999)

39 ALR5th 283—§ 58

State v. Skipper, 906 So. 2d 399 (La. 2005)

26 ALR6th 511—§ 3

State v. Skjonsby, 319 N.W.2d 764 (N.D. 1982)

49 ALR5th 639—§ 4

State v. Skolar, 692 So. 2d 309 (Fla. Dist. Ct. App. 5th Dist. 1997)

125 ALR5th 357—§ 9
7 ALR6th 233—§ 18

State v. Skripick, 1987 WL 18439 (Ohio Ct. App. 6th Dist. Lucas County 1987)

84 ALR6th 293—§ 40

State v. Slade, 116 N.H. 436, 362 A.2d 194 (1976)

58 ALR6th 499—§ 25, 115

State v. Slade, 167 Wis. 2d 487, 482 N.W.2d 669 (Ct. App. 1992)

57 ALR5th 315—§ 3, 12

State v. Slade, 168 Wis. 2d 358, 485 N.W.2d 839 (Ct. App. 1992)

57 ALR5th 315—§ 3, 12

State v. Sladeck, 132 Ohio App. 3d 86, 724 N.E.2d 488 (1st Dist. Hamilton County 1998)

64 ALR5th 637—§ 3

State v. Slagle, 65 Ohio St. 3d 597, 605 N.E.2d 916 (1992)

79 ALR5th 33—§ 65
9 ALR6th 1—§ 17

State v. Slaid, 614 So. 2d 1326 (La. App. 3d Cir. 1993)

54 ALR5th 141—§ 3 to 5, 9, 10

State v. Slater, 133 Idaho 882, 994 P.2d 625 (Ct. App. 1999)

28 ALR6th 505—§ 7, 9
78 ALR6th 297—§ 3, 7, 36, 50
79 ALR6th 1—§ 3

State v. Slater, 136 Idaho 293, 32 P.3d 685 (Ct. App. 2001)

99 ALR6th 295—§ 21

State v. Slater, 267 Kan. 694, 986 P.2d 1038 (1999)

84 ALR6th 293—§ 4, 8, 35

State v. Slatko, 432 So. 2d 635 (Fla. Dist. Ct. App. 3d Dist. 1983)

62 ALR5th 1—§ 4, 15

State v. Slattery, 56 Wash. App. 820, 787 P.2d 932 (1990)

---

31 ALR5th 229—§ 3, 17, 43, 62, 65, 67
State v. Slaughter, 451 So. 2d 59 (La. Ct. App. 4th Cir. 1984)
107 ALR5th 567—§ 2, 11
State v. Sledge, 2010 WL 2651633 (N.C. Ct. App. 2010)
57 ALR6th 1—§ 22
State v. Sleppy, 213 P.3d 447 (Kan. Ct. App. 2009)
55 ALR6th 1—§ 6
State v. S.L.H., 755 N.W.2d 271 (Minn. 2008)
68 ALR6th 1—§ 9, 14, 17
State v. Slider, 70 Ohio App. 2d 283, 24 Ohio Ops. 3d 387, 437 N.E.2d 5 (Franklin Co. 1980)
29 ALR5th 59—§ 7
State v. Slighte, 157 Wash. App. 618, 238 P.3d 83 (Div. 2 2010)
72 ALR6th 1—§ 6
State v. Sloan, 316 N.C. 714, 343 S.E.2d 527 (1986)
78 ALR5th 1—§ 29
State v. Sloan, 912 S.W.2d 592 (Mo. Ct. App. E.D. 1995)
87 ALR5th 693—§ 3
State v. Sloane, 111 N.J. 293, 544 A.2d 826 (1988)
5 ALR5th 243—§ 49
State v. Slobodian, 120 N.J. Super. 68, 293 A.2d 399 (App. Div. 1972)
42 ALR6th 237—§ 13
State v. Slocum, 132 Vt. 476, 321 A.2d 51 (1974)
28 ALR6th 505—§ 5, 14
State v. Slowe, 728 P.2d 110 (Utah 1985)
67 ALR5th 361—§ 3, 4, 7
State v. Slowikowski, 307 Or. 19, 761 P.2d 1315 (1988)
106 ALR5th 397—§ 4
117 ALR5th 407—§ 4
State v. Sly, 58 Wash. App. 740, 794 P.2d 1316 (Div. 1 1990)
73 ALR5th 383—§ 8, 40
State v. Sly, 459 So. 2d 479 (Fla. 2d DCA 1984)

103 ALR6th 137—§ 15
State v. Slyter, 242 P.3d 1281 (Kan. Ct. App. 2010)
92 ALR6th 295—§ 3
93 ALR6th 207—§ 3
94 ALR6th 191—§ 3
State v. Smagula, 133 N.H. 600, 578 A.2d 1215 (1990)
93 ALR5th 527—§ 3
State v. Small, 1 Conn. App. 584, 474 A.2d 460 (1984)
102 ALR6th 365—§ 19
State v. Small, 156 Me. 10, 157 A.2d 874 (1960)
57 ALR6th 445—§ 50
State v. Small, 162 Ohio App. 3d 375, 2005-Ohio-3813, 833 N.E.2d 774 (10th Dist. Franklin County 2005)
33 ALR6th 91—§ 4
State v. Small, 693 So. 2d 180 (La. Ct. App. 2d Cir. 1997)
78 ALR5th 1—§ 14
38 ALR6th 439—§ 5
State v. Small, 829 P.2d 129 (Utah Ct. App. 1992)
82 ALR5th 103—§ 3
116 ALR5th 479—§ 2
State v. Smalley, 138 Ga. App. 747, 227 S.E.2d 488 (1976)
118 ALR5th 213—§ 10
State v. Smalley, 2007 WL 4107175 (Conn. Super. Ct. 2007)
67 ALR6th 531—§ 36
State v. Smalls, 111 A.D.2d 38, 488 N.Y.S.2d 712 (1985)
49 ALR5th 639—§ 4
State v. Smarr, 121 N.C. 669, 28 S.E. 549 (1897)
22 ALR5th 1—§ 8, 23, 35
State v. Smart, 2009 MT 1, 348 Mont. 274, 201 P.3d 123 (2009)
46 ALR6th 241—§ 19
101 ALR6th 545—§ 5
State v. Smead, 1989 WL 10247 (Ohio Ct. App. 2d Dist. Montgomery County 1989)
78 ALR5th 567—§ 5

State v. Smeen, 147 N.J. Super. 229, 371
A.2d 93 (App. Div. 1977)
46 ALR6th 63—§ 7
State v. Smelter, 36 Wash. App. 439,
674 P.2d 690 (Div. 1 1984)
92 ALR6th 295—§ 3, 8 to 9, 12
95 ALR6th 1—§ 6, 8, 10, 21
96 ALR6th 355—§ 3
State v. S.M.H., 76 Wash. App. 550, 887
P.2d 903 (Div. 1 1995)
38 ALR6th 1—§ 15
State v. S. M. H. (In re S.M.H.), 76
Wash. App. 550, 887 P. 2d 903
(1995)
36 ALR5th 161—§ 24
State v. Smigelski, 1995 WL 358480
(Ohio Ct. App. 6th Dist. Lucas
County 1995)
18 ALR6th 519—§ 21
State v. Smiley, 529 So. 2d 349 (Fla.
Dist. Ct. App. 1st Dist. 1988)
70 ALR6th 361—§ 21
State v. Smith, 3 Ohio App. 3d 115, 444
N.E.2d 85 (8th Dist. Cuyahoga
County 1981)
72 ALR5th 109—§ 10
State v. Smith, 4 N.C. App. 261, 166
S.E.2d 473 (1969)
57 ALR6th 445—§ 54
State v. Smith, 5 S.W.3d 595 (Mo. Ct.
App. E.D. 1999)
70 ALR5th 587—§ 24
State v. Smith, 8 Ohio Misc. 148, 37
Ohio Op. 2d 220, 221 N.E.2d 627
(Mun. Ct. 1966)
89 ALR6th 565—§ 5, 33
State v. Smith, 10 Or. App. 557, 500
P.2d 1217 (1972)
114 ALR5th 173—§ 9
State v. Smith, 11 La. Ann. 633, 1856
WL 4793 (1856)
33 ALR6th 407—§ 4
State v. Smith, 12 Ariz. App. 272, 469
P.2d 838 (Div. 1 1970)
9 ALR6th 1—§ 8
State v. Smith, 15 Wash. App. 103, 547
P.2d 299 (Div. 1 1976)
9 ALR6th 1—§ 6

State v. Smith, 15 Wash. App. 716, 552
P.2d 1059 (1976)
**41 ALR5th 171—§ 3, 120, 122, 124,
135**
State v. Smith, 16 Kan. App. 2d 478, 825
P.2d 541 (1992)
110 ALR5th 329—§ 4
State v. Smith, 21 Neb. 311, 488 N.W.2d
33 (1992)
57 ALR5th 141—§ 7
State v. Smith, 21 Or. App. 270, 534
P.2d 1180 (1975)
7 ALR5th 758—§ 9
State v. Smith, 32 N.M. 191, 252 P. 1003
(1927)
108 ALR5th 593—§ 50
State v. Smith, 32 S.W.3d 532 (Mo.
2000)
42 ALR5th 581—§ 16
State v. Smith, 34 Kan. App. 2d 368, 119
P.3d 679 (2005)
72 ALR6th 227—§ 11, 57
State v. Smith, 34 N.C. App. 671, 239
S.E.2d 610 (1977)
85 ALR5th 187—§ 15
State v. Smith, 35 Conn. App. 51, 644
A.2d 923 (1994)
65 ALR6th 537—§ 40
State v. Smith, 38 P.3d 1149 (Alaska
2002)
34 ALR6th 1—§ 8
State v. Smith, 39 Ohio App. 2d 190, 68
Ohio Op. 2d 379, 316 N.E.2d 902
(1st Dist. Hamilton County 1974)
7 ALR6th 169—§ 11
State v. Smith, 39 Wash. App. 642, 694
P.2d 660 (Div. 1 1984)
103 ALR5th 463—§ 11
73 ALR6th 49—§ 23
State v. Smith, 40 Or. App. 91, 594 P.2d
860 (1979)
7 ALR6th 169—§ 18
State v. Smith, 42 Wash. App. 399, 711
P.2d 372 (Div. 1 1985)
15 ALR5th 391—§ 7
92 ALR5th 35—§ 25
State v. Smith, 51 Or. App. 223, 625
P.2d 1321 (1981)

50 ALR5th 703—§ 4
State v. Smith, 55 Wis. 2d 451, 198 N.W.2d 588 (1972)

78 ALR6th 417—§ 42
State v. Smith, 56 Wash. App. 909, 786 P.2d 320 (Div. 3 1990)

84 ALR5th 487—§ 20
State v. Smith, 58 N.J. 202, 276 A.2d 369 (1971)

18 ALR5th 542—§ 2, 3
State v. Smith, 60 Or. App. 139, 652 P.2d 882 (1982)

99 ALR5th 557—§ 15
State v. Smith, 60 Wash. App. 592, 805 P.2d 256 (Div. 1 1991)

111 ALR5th 239—§ 11
State v. Smith, 64 Or. App. 588, 669 P.2d 368 (1983)

71 ALR6th 335—§ 8
State v. Smith, 66 Or. App. 374, 675 P.2d 1060 (1984)

98 ALR5th 445—§ 3
State v. Smith, 72 Or. App. 130, 694 P.2d 1013 (1985)

19 ALR5th 470—§ 3
State v. Smith, 80 Ohio St. 3d 89, 684 N.E.2d 668 (1997)

79 ALR5th 419—§ 10, 13
State v. Smith, 80 Ohio St. 3d 89, 1997-Ohio-355, 684 N.E.2d 668 (1997)

7 ALR6th 233—§ 9
69 ALR6th 579—§ 4
State v. Smith, 82 Wash. App. 327, 917 P.2d 1108 (1996)

38 ALR5th 433—§ 26
State v. Smith, 88 Wash. App. 1026, 1997 WL 709419 (Div. 2 1997)

85 ALR5th 1—§ 15
State v. Smith, 91 Haw. 450, 984 P.2d 1276 (Haw. Ct. App. 1999)

93 ALR5th 683—§ 3
State v. Smith, 93 Wash. App. 45, 966 P.2d 411 (Div. 2 1998)

79 ALR5th 1—§ 2, 6
State v. Smith, 99 N.C. App. 184, 392 S.E.2d 625 (1990)

15 ALR5th 391—§ 30

State v. Smith, 100 N.M. 352, 670 P.2d 963 (App. 1983)

29 ALR5th 59—§ 3, 31
State v. Smith, 101 Or. 127, 199 P. 194, 16 A.L.R. 1220 (1921)

97 ALR5th 201—§ 3
State v. Smith, 101 S.C. 293, 85 S.E. 958 (1915)

34 ALR5th 723—§ 4
State v. Smith, 101 Wash. App. 1027, 2000 WL 816847 (Div. 2 2000)

43 ALR6th 475—§ 21
State v. Smith, 108 Ohio App. 3d 663, 671 N.E.2d 594 (4th Dist. Gallia County 1996)

66 ALR5th 397—§ 9
State v. Smith, 110 Ariz. 221, 517 P.2d 83 (1973)

35 ALR6th 497—§ 14, 29
State v. Smith, 115 N.M. 749, 858 P.2d 416 (Ct. App. 1993)

52 ALR6th 1—§ 3, 34
70 ALR6th 361—§ 38
71 ALR6th 335—§ 10
State v. Smith, 115 Ohio App. 3d 419, 685 N.E.2d 595 (3d Dist. Auglaize County 1996)

70 ALR5th 1—§ 6
State v. Smith, 116 Idaho 553, 777 P.2d 1226 (App. 1989)

7 ALR5th 263—§ 4
State v. Smith, 119 Wash. 2d 385, 831 P.2d 1082 (1992)

15 ALR5th 391—§ 7
State v. Smith, 120 Idaho 77, 813 P.2d 888 (1991)

12 ALR5th 89—§ 5
State v. Smith, 121 Idaho 20, 822 P.2d 539 (Ct. App. 1991)

92 ALR6th 295—§ 3
96 ALR6th 355—§ 3
State v. Smith, 122 Ariz. 58, 593 P.2d 281 (1979)

6 ALR6th 533—§ 21
State v. Smith, 123 Ohio App. 3d 48, 702 N.E.2d 1245 (2d Dist. Montgomery County 1997)

29 ALR6th 237—§ 24

State v. Smith, 124 N.C. App. 565, 478
S.E.2d 237 (1996)
67 ALR5th 361—§ 3, 4, 7, 12

State v. Smith, 124 Ohio St. 3d 163,
2009-Ohio-6426, 920 N.E.2d 949
(2009)
62 ALR6th 161—§ 6

State v. Smith, 124 Ohio St. 3d 163,
2009-Ohio-6426, 920 N.E.2d 949,
62 A.L.R.6th 677 (2009)
62 ALR6th 161—§ 7
66 ALR6th 635—§ 5

State v. Smith, 126 Ohio App. 3d 193,
709 N.E.2d 1245 (7th Dist. Mahoning County 1998)
29 ALR5th 487—§ 3, 5, 7, 11, 12

State v. Smith, 129 Ariz. 28, 628 P.2d
65 (App. 1981)
16 ALR5th 855—§ 2

State v. Smith, 130 Wash. 2d 215, 922
P.2d 811 (1996)
40 ALR5th 113—§ 3

State v. Smith, 131 Wis. 2d 220, 388
N.W.2d 601 (1986)
17 ALR6th 327—§ 27

State v. Smith, 134 N.J. 599, 637 A.2d
158 (1994)
92 ALR6th 171—§ 3, 18

State v. Smith, 135 N.C. App. 649, 522
S.E.2d 321 (1999)
55 ALR6th 157—§ 15

State v. Smith, 137 Wash. App. 262, 153
P.3d 199 (Div. 3 2007)
78 ALR6th 297—§ 41

State v. Smith, 138 Ariz. 79, 673 P.2d
17 (1983)
41 ALR6th 295—§ 8

State v. Smith, 139 Ohio App. 3d 398,
744 N.E.2d 201 (8th Dist. Cuyahoga
County 2000)
125 ALR5th 537—§ 27

State v. Smith, 154 Vt. 645, 577 A.2d
279 (1990)
84 ALR6th 293—§ 31

State v. Smith, 155 N.C. App. 500, 573
S.E.2d 618 (2002)
99 ALR6th 295—§ 9

State v. Smith, 156 Ariz. 518, 753 P.2d
1174 (App. 1987)
42 ALR5th 291—§ 2, 6, 32

State v. Smith, 157 S.W.3d 687 (Mo. Ct.
App. W.D. 2004)
55 ALR6th 391—§ 22

State v. Smith, 160 N.C. App. 107, 584
S.E.2d 830 (2003)
32 ALR6th 1—§ 5

State v. Smith, 162 Wash. App. 1071,
2011 WL 3276661 (Div. 3 2011)
73 ALR6th 49—§ 8

State v. Smith, 168 Mont. 93, 541 P.2d
351 (1975)
42 ALR6th 237—§ 13

State v. Smith, 173 Kan. 807, 252 P.2d
917 (1953)
85 ALR5th 187—§ 6, 7, 9

State v. Smith, 174 Wash. App. 1036,
2013 WL 1490143 (Div. 2 2013)
101 ALR6th 545—§ 11

State v. Smith, 178 N.W.2d 329 (Iowa
1970)
61 ALR5th 1—§ 3, 5

State v. Smith, 183 Wis. 2d 431, 516
N.W.2d 20 (Ct. App. 1994)
99 ALR6th 295—§ 16

State v. Smith, 186 N.C. App. 57, 650
S.E.2d 29 (2007)
67 ALR6th 103—§ 15

State v. Smith, 186 W. Va. 33, 410
S.E.2d 269 (1991)
71 ALR6th 1—§ 4

State v. Smith, 190 W. Va. 374, 438
S.E.2d 554 (1993)
114 ALR5th 173—§ 8

State v. Smith, 193 Ariz. 452, 974 P.2d
431 (1999)
20 ALR5th 177—§ 11
32 ALR6th 1—§ 5

State v. Smith, 195 N.J. Super. 468, 480
A.2d 236 (Law Div. 1984)
68 ALR5th 299—§ 3

State v. Smith, 197 Ariz. 333, 4 P.3d 388
(Ct. App. Div. 2 1999)
28 ALR6th 505—§ 9

State v. Smith, 197 Wash. 363, 85 P.2d 651 (1938)

   50 ALR5th 703—§ 10

State v. Smith, 198 W. Va. 441, 481 S.E.2d 747 (1996)

   58 ALR5th 749—§ 4

State v. Smith, 200 Conn. 465, 512 A.2d 189 (1986)

   102 ALR6th 365—§ 2

State v. Smith, 200 S.C. 188, 20 S.E.2d 726 (1942)

   24 ALR5th 465—§ 23

State v. Smith, 202 Neb. 501, 276 N.W.2d 104 (1979)

   57 ALR5th 141—§ 4

State v. Smith, 203 Ariz. 75, 50 P.3d 825 (2002)

   110 ALR5th 1—§ 19

State v. Smith, 207 Wis. 2d 258, 558 N.W.2d 379 (1997)

   9 ALR6th 541—§ 10

State v. Smith, 210 Conn. 132, 554 A.2d 713 (1989)

   102 ALR5th 447—§ 5, 6

State v. Smith, 210 N.J. Super. 43, 509 A.2d 206 (1986)

   39 ALR5th 283—§ 4

State v. Smith, 215 Ariz. 221, 159 P.3d 531 (2007)

   36 ALR6th 681—§ 46

State v. Smith, 216 Kan. 265, 530 P.2d 1215 (1975)

   86 ALR5th 59—§ 3, 6

State v. Smith, 222 S.W. 455 (Mo. 1920)

   78 ALR5th 1—§ 33

State v. Smith, 224 Kan. 662, 585 P.2d 1006 (1978)

   39 ALR5th 283—§ 4, 15

State v. Smith, 243 La. 656, 146 So. 2d 152 (1962)

   52 ALR6th 125—§ 37

State v. Smith, 245 Kan. 381, 781 P.2d 666 (1989)

   101 ALR5th 187—§ 7

State v. Smith, 253 Or. 280, 453 P.2d 942 (1969)

   57 ALR6th 445—§ 58

State v. Smith, 254 Kan. 144, 864 P.2d 709 (1993)

   58 ALR5th 749—§ 4

State v. Smith, 259 La. 515, 250 So. 2d 724 (1971)

   86 ALR5th 59—§ 3

State v. Smith, 262 N.J. Super. 487, 621 A.2d 493 (1993)

   13 ALR5th 628—§ 5, 9

State v. Smith, 269 N.J. Super. 86, 634 A.2d 576 (App. Div. 1993)

   49 ALR5th 639—§ 4

State v. Smith, 271 Kan. 666, 24 P.3d 727 (2001)

   3 ALR6th 543—§ 10

   12 ALR6th 267—§ 8

State v. Smith, 272 N.W.2d 859 (Iowa 1978)

   78 ALR5th 1—§ 12

State v. Smith, 276 Mont. 434, 916 P.2d 773 (1996)

   11 ALR6th 237—§ 13

State v. Smith, 277 A.2d 481 (Me. 1971)

   101 ALR6th 299—§ 4

   103 ALR6th 347—§ 9, 13

State v. Smith, 297 Or. 339, 683 P.2d 1370 (1984)

   68 ALR5th 343—§ 14

State v. Smith, 301 N.C. 695, 272 S.E.2d 852 (1981)

   16 ALR6th 329—§ 4

   24 ALR6th 591—§ 6

State v. Smith, 307 N.J. Super. 1, 704 A.2d 73 (App. Div. 1997)

   20 ALR6th 479—§ 3

State v. Smith, 315 N.C. 76, 337 S.E.2d 833 (1985)

   38 ALR5th 433—§ 9, 10, 17

State v. Smith, 316 Md. 223, 557 A.2d 1343 (1989)

   70 ALR6th 361—§ 13

State v. Smith, 326 S.C. 39, 482 S.E.2d 777 (1997)

   76 ALR5th 1—§ 10

State v. Smith, 327 Or. 366, 963 P.2d 642 (1998)

   19 ALR5th 470—§ 15

117 ALR5th 407—§ 4
State v. Smith, 338 S.C. 66, 525 S.E.2d
263 (Ct. App. 1999)
59 ALR5th 1—§ 6
State v. Smith, 340 So. 2d 247 (La. 1976)
45 ALR6th 337—§ 23
State v. Smith, 342 N.C. 407, 464 S.E.2d
45 (1995)
79 ALR6th 631—§ 4
State v. Smith, 344 N.W.2d 505 (S.D.
1984)
103 ALR5th 463—§ 3
State v. Smith, 346 N.C. 794, 488 S.E.2d
210 (1997)
15 ALR6th 515—§ 2, 27
State v. Smith, 352 N.C. 531, 532 S.E.2d
773 (2000)
94 ALR5th 537—§ 5
110 ALR5th 1—§ 15
110 ALR5th 329—§ 13
State v. Smith, 352 So. 2d 216 (La. 1977)
66 ALR5th 397—§ 8, 12
State v. Smith, 354 Mo. 1088, 193
S.W.2d 499 (1946)
57 ALR6th 445—§ 27
State v. Smith, 359 S.C. 481, 597 S.E.2d
888 (Ct. App. 2004)
16 ALR6th 329—§ 7
24 ALR6th 591—§ 6, 14
State v. Smith, 359 So. 2d 160 (La. 1978)
97 ALR5th 201—§ 3
State v. Smith, 381 A.2d 1117 (Me.
1978)
6 ALR6th 533—§ 20
State v. Smith, 384 A.2d 687 (Me. 1978)
23 ALR6th 1—§ 15
State v. Smith, 397 So. 2d 1326 (La.
1981)
103 ALR5th 463—§ 3
State v. Smith, 400 So. 2d 587 (La. 1981)
79 ALR5th 237—§ 9
State v. Smith, 407 So. 2d 652 (La. 1981)
34 ALR6th 1—§ 10
State v. Smith, 448 N.W.2d 550 (Minn.
Ct. App. 1989)
73 ALR6th 49—§ 17
State v. Smith, 467 S.W.2d 6 (Mo. 1971)

70 ALR5th 587—§ 19
State v. Smith, 470 So. 2d 128 (La. Ct.
App. 4th Cir. 1985)
16 ALR6th 329—§ 4
24 ALR6th 591—§ 4, 14
State v. Smith, 476 N.W.2d 511, 19
A.L.R.5th 951 (Minn. 1991)
19 ALR5th 351—§ 11
State v. Smith, 489 So. 2d 255 (La. Ct.
App. 5th Cir. 1986)
119 ALR5th 275—§ 8
State v. Smith, 496 So. 2d 195, 11 FLW
2160 (Fla. App. D3 1986)
50 ALR5th 467—§ 5
State v. Smith, 504 So. 2d 1070 (La. Ct.
App. 1st Cir. 1987)
102 ALR5th 327—§ 6
State v. Smith, 540 S.W.2d 189 (Mo. Ct.
App. 1976)
40 ALR6th 1—§ 28
State v. Smith, 543 So. 2d 555 (La. Ct.
App. 4th Cir. 1989)
70 ALR5th 587—§ 25
State v. Smith, 563 S.W.2d 162 (Mo. Ct.
App. 1978)
85 ALR5th 671—§ 8
State v. Smith, 578 So. 2d 1374 (Ala.
App. 1991)
6 ALR5th 652—§ 6
State v. Smith, 578 So. 2d 1374 (Ala.
Civ. App. 1991)
104 ALR5th 229—§ 7
115 ALR5th 403—§ 9
State v. Smith, 584 So. 2d 145 (Fla. 2d
DCA 1991)
97 ALR6th 653—§ 5
State v. Smith, 595 S.W.2d 764 (Mo. Ct.
App. W.D. 1980)
70 ALR5th 587—§ 8
State v. Smith, 604 N.W.2d 662 (Iowa
2000)
36 ALR5th 161—§ 27
33 ALR6th 91—§ 20
State v. Smith, 614 So. 2d 778 (La. App.
2d Cir. 1993)
18 ALR5th 1—§ 4

State v. Smith, 615 A.2d 1162 (Me. 1992)
18 ALR5th 1—§ 36
State v. Smith, 619 N.W.2d 766 (Minn. Ct. App. 2000)
88 ALR5th 121—§ 34
State v. Smith, 626 S.W.2d 256 (Mo. App. 1981)
39 ALR5th 283—§ 54, 60, 67
State v. Smith, 638 N.E.2d 1353 (Ind. Ct. App. 1994)
84 ALR6th 293—§ 40
State v. Smith, 649 So. 2d 145 (La. Ct. App. 2d Cir. 1995)
73 ALR5th 383—§ 5
State v. Smith, 651 So. 2d 890 (La. App. 2d Cir. 1995)
3 ALR5th 963—§ 4
State v. Smith, 674 P.2d 562 (Okla. Crim. App. 1984)
74 ALR5th 319—§ 3
State v. Smith, 686 S.W.2d 543 (Mo. Ct. App. S.D. 1985)
37 ALR6th 357—§ 3
State v. Smith, 687 S.E.2d 525 (N.C. Ct. App. 2010)
57 ALR6th 1—§ 25
State v. Smith, 688 S.W.2d 813 (Mo. Ct. App. S.D. 1985)
1 ALR6th 549—§ 25
State v. Smith, 715 So. 2d 925 (Ala. Crim. App. 1998)
29 ALR6th 1—§ 10
State v. Smith, 734 So. 2d 826 (La. Ct. App. 4th Cir. 1999)
34 ALR5th 125—§ 6
State v. Smith, 735 S.W.2d 795 (Mo. Ct. App. E.D. 1987)
70 ALR6th 1—§ 17
State v. Smith, 747 S.W.2d 678 (Mo. Ct. App. S.D. 1988)
38 ALR6th 97—§ 28
State v. Smith, 755 S.W.2d 757 (Tenn. 1988)
83 ALR6th 465—§ 53
State v. Smith, 756 S.W.2d 493 (Mo. 1988)

83 ALR6th 255—§ 15
State v. Smith, 793 So. 2d 1199 (La. 2001)
103 ALR6th 35—§ 19
State v. Smith, 815 S.W.2d 74 (Mo. Ct. App. E.D. 1991)
105 ALR5th 529—§ 13
State v. Smith, 849 S.W.2d 209 (Mo. Ct. App. E.D. 1993)
37 ALR6th 357—§ 3, 9, 10
State v. Smith, 850 S.W.2d 934 (Mo. Ct. App. S.D. 1993)
65 ALR5th 407—§ 3, 16
State v. Smith, 857 S.W.2d 1 (Tenn. 1993)
83 ALR5th 541—§ 3, 4
State v. Smith, 867 S.W.2d 343 (Tenn. Crim. App. 1993)
97 ALR5th 537—§ 62
State v. Smith, 868 S.W.2d 561 (Tenn. 1993)
57 ALR5th 141—§ 7
72 ALR5th 529—§ 6
103 ALR5th 463—§ 3
7 ALR6th 233—§ 4
29 ALR6th 1—§ 10
State v. Smith, 891 S.W.2d 922 (Tenn. Crim. 1994)
44 ALR5th 651—§ 5
State v. Smith, 891 S.W.2d 922 (Tenn. Crim. App. 1994)
103 ALR6th 507—§ 22
State v. Smith, 898 S.W.2d 742 (Tenn. Crim. 1994)
15 ALR5th 391—§ 4
State v. Smith, 906 S.W.2d 6 (Tenn. Crim. App. 1995)
85 ALR5th 471—§ 7
State v. Smith, 909 P.2d 236 (Utah 1995)
73 ALR5th 383—§ 5
38 ALR6th 439—§ 13
State v. Smith, 910 S.W.2d 457 (Tenn. Crim. App. 1995)
73 ALR5th 383—§ 6
State v. Smith, 936 So. 2d 255 (La. Ct. App. 2d Cir. 2006)
24 ALR6th 1—§ 21

State v. Smith, 944 S.W.2d 901 (Mo. 1997)

    9 ALR6th 1—§ 12

State v. Smith, 966 S.W.2d 1 (Mo. Ct. App. W.D. 1997)

    68 ALR5th 343—§ 3, 12, 17

State v. Smith, 972 S.W.2d 476, 107 A.L.R.5th 791 (Mo. Ct. App. W.D. 1998)

    107 ALR5th 567—§ 10

State v. Smith, 993 So. 2d 659 (La. Ct. App. 5th Cir. 2008)

    41 ALR6th 141—§ 8

State v. Smith, 993 S.W.2d 6 (Tenn. 1999)

    79 ALR5th 33—§ 9, 52

State v. Smith, 1975 WL 181349 (Ohio Ct. App. 10th Dist. Franklin County 1975)

    99 ALR6th 295—§ 13

State v. Smith, 1986 WL 8196 (Ohio Ct. App. 9th Dist. Lorain County 1986)

    99 ALR6th 295—§ 13

State v. Smith, 1989 WL 61052 (Ohio Ct. App. 9th Dist. Summit County 1989)

    53 ALR6th 305—§ 44

State v. Smith, 1993 WL 536068 (Ohio Ct. App. 8th Dist. Cuyahoga County 1993)

    72 ALR5th 1—§ 29

State v. Smith, 1994 WL 50665 (Ohio Ct. App. 8th Dist. Cuyahoga County 1994)

    99 ALR6th 295—§ 13

State v. Smith, 1994 WL 361851 (Tenn. Crim. App. 1994)

    90 ALR5th 453—§ 23

State v. Smith, 1995 WL 84021 (Tenn. Crim. App. 1995)

    99 ALR6th 295—§ 16

State v. Smith, 1996 WL 27908 (Ohio Ct. App. 9th Dist.Lorain County 1996)

    57 ALR5th 141—§ 7

State v. Smith, 1996 WL 239823 (Ohio Ct. App. 2d Dist. Miami County 1996)

    25 ALR6th 379—§ 3, 6, 13, 16, 25, 32

State v. Smith, 1996 WL 738113 (Neb. App)

    50 ALR5th 581—§ 7

State v. Smith, 1997 WL 304418 (Ohio Ct. App. 10th Dist. Franklin County 1997)

    58 ALR6th 439—§ 9

State v. Smith, 1997 WL 476828 (Ohio Ct. App. 8th Dist. Cuyahoga County 1997)

    99 ALR6th 113—§ 21

State v. Smith, 1998 SD 6, 573 N.W.2d 515 (S.D. 1998)

    9 ALR6th 1—§ 17

State v. Smith, 1998 WL 470495 (Ohio Ct. App. 4th Dist. Hocking County 1998)

    63 ALR6th 351—§ 3

State v. Smith, 1998 WL 566806 (Minn. Ct. App. 1998)

    73 ALR5th 383—§ 21

State v. Smith, 1999 N.D. 9, 589 N.W.2d 546 (N.D. 1999)

    99 ALR5th 557—§ 9

State v. Smith, 1999 WL 34821 (Ohio Ct. App. 2d Dist. Montgomery County 1999)

    29 ALR6th 237—§ 21

State v. Smith, 1999 WL 357359 (N.J. 1999)

    71 ALR5th 637—§ 3

State v. Smith, 2000 WL 263405 (Ohio Ct. App. 8th Dist. Cuyahoga County 2000)

    78 ALR5th 489—§ 9

State v. Smith, 2001 WL 283390 (Conn. Super. Ct. 2001)

    81 ALR6th 257—§ 20

State v. Smith, 2002-Ohio-1729, 2002 WL 553705 (Ohio Ct. App. 12th Dist. Butler County 2002)

    35 ALR6th 361—§ 20

State v. Smith, 2002 WL 31819041 (Minn. Ct. App. 2002)

    81 ALR6th 505—§ 68

State v. Smith, 2003-Ohio-5524, 2003 WL 22369273 (Ohio Ct. App. 4th Dist. Ross County 2003)
1 ALR6th 657—§ 4

State v. Smith, 2004 MT 16N, 320 Mont. 528, 87 P.3d 1042 (2004)
46 ALR6th 241—§ 10

State v. Smith, 2004-Ohio-2388, 2004 WL 1059504 (Ohio Ct. App. 5th Dist. Stark County 2004)
70 ALR6th 1—§ 5

State v. Smith, 2004-Ohio-6668, 2004 WL 2849057 (Ohio Ct. App. 3d Dist. Marion County 2004)
70 ALR6th 1—§ 5

State v. Smith, 2005-Ohio-4910, 2005 WL 2268252 (Ohio Ct. App. 4th Dist. Washington County 2005)
26 ALR6th 511—§ 19

State v. Smith, 2006-820 La. App. 1 Cir. 12/28/06, 2006 WL 3804657 (La. Ct. App. 1st Cir. 2006)
26 ALR6th 511—§ 51

State v. Smith, 2006-Ohio-2365, 2006 WL 1305087 (Ohio Ct. App. 2d Dist. Montgomery County 2006)
99 ALR6th 295—§ 13

State v. Smith, 2006-Ohio-4541, 2006 WL 2532304 (Ohio Ct. App. 11th Dist. Lake County 2006)
26 ALR6th 511—§ 19

State v. Smith, 2006 WI 74, 291 Wis. 2d 569, 716 N.W.2d 482 (2006)
26 ALR6th 659—§ 37

State v. Smith, 2007-Ohio-2873, 2007 WL 1674086 (Ohio Ct. App. 10th Dist. Franklin County 2007)
70 ALR6th 1—§ 4

State v. Smith, 2007-Ohio-3786, 2007 WL 2141593 (Ohio Ct. App. 1st Dist. Hamilton County 2007)
79 ALR6th 1—§ 76

State v. Smith, 2007-Ohio-7055, 2007 WL 4554459 (Ohio Ct. App. 9th Dist. Summit County 2007)
69 ALR6th 1—§ 10

State v. Smith, 2009-Ohio-2380, 2009 WL 1423965 (Ohio Ct. App. 8th Dist. Cuyahoga County 2009)
69 ALR6th 1—§ 5

State v. Smith, 2009 WL 4251070 (N.J. Super. Ct. App. Div. 2009)
79 ALR6th 125—§ 4

State v. Smith, 2010 WI 16, 323 Wis. 2d 377, 780 N.W.2d 90 (2010)
93 ALR6th 1—§ 21

State v. Smith, 2010 WL 2977965 (Tenn. Crim. App. 2010)
77 ALR6th 197—§ 4

State v. Smith, 2010 WL 3000016 (Minn. Ct. App. 2010)
71 ALR6th 625—§ 15, 24

State v. Smith, 2010 WL 3466998, 699 S.E.2d 140 (2010)
63 ALR6th 351—§ 3

State v. Smith, 2011-Ohio-6872, 2011 WL 6938328 (Ohio Ct. App. 5th Dist. Stark County 2011)
79 ALR6th 1—§ 80

State v. Smith Armstrong Norris, 1981 WL 6315 (Ohio Ct. App. 5th Dist. Licking County 1981)
68 ALR6th 115—§ 4, 5, 20, 22 to 24

State v. Smith, No. 38318 (August 16, 1979, Ct. App. Ohio, 8th App. Dist. Cuyahoga Co.)
39 ALR5th 283—§ 14, 70

State v. Smolen, 4 Conn. Cir. Ct. 385, 232 A.2d 339 (App. Div. 1967)
116 ALR5th 479—§ 4

State v. Smoot, 97 Or. App. 255, 775 P.2d 344 (1989)
33 ALR6th 407—§ 26

State v. Smotherman, 1997 WL 770981 (Ohio Ct. App. 10th Dist. Franklin County 1997)
99 ALR6th 295—§ 13

State v. Smothers, 1987 WL 11317 (Tenn. Crim. App. 1987)
103 ALR6th 507—§ 8

State v. Snapp, 153 Wash. App. 485, 219 P.3d 971 (Div. 2 2009)
55 ALR6th 1—§ 9, 39, 40

State v. Sneed, 63 Ohio St. 3d 3, 584
N.E.2d 1160 (1992)
68 ALR5th 343—§ 3, 5
State v. Sneed, 327 N.C. 266, 393 S.E.2d
531 (1990)
57 ALR5th 141—§ 12
State v. Sneed, 571 So. 2d 735 (La. Ct.
App. 2d Cir. 1990)
16 ALR6th 329—§ 4
24 ALR6th 591—§ 4, 14
State v. Sneeden, 108 N.C. App. 506,
424 S.E.2d 449 (1993)
86 ALR5th 59—§ 3, 4, 6
State v. Snell, 46 Wash. 327, 89 P. 931
(1907)
87 ALR6th 109—§ 61
State v. Snell, 142 N.M. 452, 2007-
NMCA-113, 166 P.3d 1106 (Ct.
App. 2007)
34 ALR6th 1—§ 9
46 ALR6th 495—§ 13
State v. Snell, 177 Neb. 396, 128 N.W.2d
823 (1964)
26 ALR5th 1—§ 3
State v. Snell, 892 A.2d 108 (R.I. 2006)
99 ALR6th 295—§ 10
State v. Snell, 950 S.W.2d 108 (Tex.
App. El Paso 1997)
29 ALR6th 507—§ 11, 47
State v. Snelling, 266 Kan. 986, 975
P.2d 259 (1999)
36 ALR5th 161—§ 27
State v. Snider, 81 W. Va. 522, 94 S.E.
981 (1918)
50 ALR5th 467—§ 6, 8
State v. Snider, 197 Neb. 317, 248
N.W.2d 342 (1977)
22 ALR5th 660—§ 6, 9
State v. Snider, 616 S.W.2d 133 (Mo.
App. 1981)
36 ALR5th 255—§ 24, 31
State v. Snipes, 71 N.C. App. 206, 321
S.E.2d 559 (1984)
57 ALR6th 445—§ 8
State v. Snodgrass, 117 Ariz. 107, 570
P.2d 1280 (Ct. App. Div. 1 1977)
66 ALR5th 397—§ 4, 10

State v. Snodgrass, 121 Ariz. 409, 590
P.2d 948 (Ct. App. Div. 1 1979)
66 ALR5th 397—§ 10
State v. Snodgrass, 346 N.W.2d 472
(Iowa 1984)
16 ALR6th 329—§ 4
24 ALR6th 591—§ 4, 12
State v. Snover, 88 P.3d 807 (Kan. Ct.
App. 2004)
26 ALR6th 511—§ 29
State v. Snow, 513 A.2d 274 (Me. 1986)
9 ALR6th 1—§ 8
State v. Snow, 527 A.2d 750 (Me. 1987)
50 ALR5th 703—§ 15
State v. Snowden, 138 Ariz. 402, 675
P.2d 289 (App. 1983)
3 ALR5th 784—§ 2
State v. Snyder, 12 Ariz. App. 142, 468
P.2d 593 (1970)
41 ALR5th 171—§ 17, 68
State v. Snyder, 84 Wash. 485, 147 P.
38 (1915)
23 ALR6th 1—§ 15
State v. Snyder, 256 La. 601, 237 So. 2d
392 (1970)
42 ALR5th 581—§ 15
State v. Snyder, 747 P.2d 417 (Utah
1987)
92 ALR5th 35—§ 7
State v. Snyder, 860 P.2d 351 (Utah Ct.
App. 1993)
38 ALR6th 97—§ 28
State v. Snyder, 942 So. 2d 484 (La.
2006)
26 ALR6th 659—§ 37
36 ALR6th 681—§ 32
State v. Snyder, 2000 WL 504110 (Ohio
Ct. App. 8th Dist. Cuyahoga County
2000)
70 ALR6th 1—§ 5
State v. Soares, 648 A.2d 804 (R.I. 1994)
92 ALR6th 171—§ 4
State v. Sobel, 363 So. 2d 324 (Fla.
1978)
24 ALR6th 1—§ 9
State v. Sobie, 343 So. 2d 73 (Fla. Dist.
Ct. App. 3d Dist. 1977)

69 ALR6th 1—§ 4

State v. Socolof, 28 Wash. App. 407, 623 P.2d 733 (Div. 1 1981)

81 ALR5th 563—§ 3

State v. Sodders, 130 Ariz. 23, 633 P.2d 432 (App. 1981)

7 ALR5th 758—§ 13

State v. Soderholm, 68 Wash. App. 363, 842 P.2d 1039 (1993)

15 ALR5th 391—§ 21

State v. Soderquist, 63 Wash. App. 144, 816 P.2d 1264 (Div. 3 1991)

73 ALR5th 383—§ 14

State v. Soders, 106 Ariz. 79, 471 P.2d 275 (1970)

39 ALR5th 283—§ 3

State v. Soen, 132 Or. App. 377, 888 P.2d 583 (1995)

28 ALR6th 505—§ 9

State v. Solarski, 374 N.J. Super. 176, 863 A.2d 1095 (App. Div. 2005)

47 ALR6th 107—§ 74

State v. Solberg, 66 Wash. App. 66, 831 P.2d 754 (Div. 1 1992)

106 ALR5th 397—§ 4

State v. Soldi, 145 N.H. 571, 765 A.2d 1048 (2000)

3 ALR6th 269—§ 4, 25

State v. Solem, 301 Minn. 282, 222 N.W.2d 98 (1974)

48 ALR6th 511—§ 7, 19

State v. Soles, 119 N.C. App. 375, 459 S.E.2d 4 (1995)

29 ALR6th 1—§ 10

State v. Solfest, 212 Wis. 2d 644, 570 N.W.2d 64 (Ct. App. 1997)

68 ALR6th 527—§ 37

State v. Solis, 2009 WL 6593953 (N.M. Ct. App. 2009)

68 ALR6th 115—§ 8

State v. Sollars, 706 S.W.2d 485 (Mo. Ct. App. W.D. 1986)

107 ALR5th 567—§ 10, 12

State v. Sollars, 747 S.W.2d 134 (Mo. 1988)

107 ALR5th 567—§ 3

State v. Solly, 1984 WL 14435 (Ohio Ct. App. 6th Dist. Lucas County 1984)

34 ALR6th 1—§ 12

State v. Solman, 131 Conn. App. 846, 29 A.3d 183 (2011)

72 ALR6th 227—§ 37

State v. Solomon, 5 Wash. App. 412, 487 P.2d 643 (Div. 1 1971)

57 ALR6th 445—§ 59

State v. Solomon, 128 Vt. 197, 260 A.2d 377 (1969)

72 ALR5th 607—§ 3

State v. Solomon, 257 Kan. 212, 891 P.2d 407 (1995)

9 ALR6th 633—§ 18

State v. Soloway, 603 S.W.2d 688 (Mo. Ct. App. S.D. 1980)

37 ALR6th 357—§ 21
71 ALR6th 335—§ 5

State v. Somerlot, 209 W. Va. 125, 544 S.E.2d 52 (2000)

71 ALR6th 335—§ 13

State v. Somerville, 21 Me. 14, 1842 WL 1143 (1842)

57 ALR6th 445—§ 49

State v. Somma, 215 N.J. Super. 142, 521 A.2d 386 (1986)

2 ALR5th 725—§ 13

State v. Sommerfield, 2006-Ohio-1420, 2006 WL 758747 (Ohio Ct. App. 3d Dist. Union County 2006)

33 ALR6th 91—§ 10

State v. Sommerset, 21 N.C. App. 272, 204 S.E.2d 206 (1974)

39 ALR5th 283—§ 4

State v. Sonka, 893 S.W.2d 388 (Mo. App. 1995)

42 ALR5th 581—§ 12

State v. Sonko, 1996 WL 267749 (Ohio Ct. App. 9th Dist.Lorain County 1996)

57 ALR5th 315—§ 4

State v. Sonneland, 80 Wash. 2d 343, 494 P.2d 469 (1972)

71 ALR5th 1—§ 14

State v. Sonnenberg, 2005 WL 3664050 (Minn. Ct. App. 2006)

27 ALR6th 183—§ 6, 32

State v. Sonnenfeld, 114 Nev. 631, 958 P.2d 1215 (1998)

84 ALR6th 293—§ 27

State v. Sonner, 253 Mo. 440, 161 S.W. 723 (1913)

64 ALR5th 671—§ 17

State v. Sonnier, 422 S.W.3d 521 (Mo. Ct. App. E.D. 2014)

99 ALR6th 295—§ 5

State v. Sonnier, 773 S.W.2d 60 (Tex. App. Houston 1st Dist. 1989)

84 ALR6th 427—§ 4

State v. Sood, 47 Kan. App. 2d 1098, 283 P.3d 224 (2012)

87 ALR6th 1—§ 33, 41

State v. Sorakrai, 543 So. 2d 294, 14 FLW 1069 (Fla. App. D2 1989)

42 ALR5th 291—§ 36

State v. Sorbel, 124 Idaho 275, 858 P.2d 814 (Ct. App. 1993)

85 ALR5th 1—§ 23

State v. Sorenson, 143 Wis. 2d 226, 421 N.W.2d 77 (1988)

38 ALR5th 433—§ 11

State v. Sorenson, 152 Wis. 2d 471, 449 N.W.2d 280 (App. 1989)

38 ALR5th 433—§ 3

State v. Sorenson, 430 N.W.2d 231 (Minn. Ct. App. 1988)

45 ALR6th 643—§ 18

State v. Sorge, 249 N.J. Super. 144, 591 A.2d 1382 (Law Div. 1991)

68 ALR5th 299—§ 3

State v. Soriano, 68 Or. App. 642, 684 P.2d 1220 (1984)

29 ALR5th 1—§ 2, 4

State v. Soriano, 107 N.J. Super. 286, 258 A.2d 140 (1968)

45 ALR5th 531—§ 2, 6

State v. Soriano, 298 Or. 392, 693 P.2d 26 (1984)

29 ALR5th 1—§ 4

State v. Sorich, 226 Neb. 547, 412 N.W.2d 484 (1987)

99 ALR6th 295—§ 16

State v. Sorino, 108 Haw. 162, 118 P.3d 645 (2005)

10 ALR6th 265—§ 6

State v. Sorrell, 120 N.H. 472, 416 A.2d 1375 (1980)

68 ALR5th 343—§ 3

State v. Sorrell, 152 Vt. 543, 568 A.2d 376 (1989)

5 ALR5th 243—§ 47

State v. Sorrell, 656 So. 2d 1045 (La. Ct. App. 5th Cir. 1995)

63 ALR6th 351—§ 3

State v. Sorrels, 33 N.C. App. 374, 235 S.E.2d 70 (1977)

98 ALR6th 455—§ 17

State v. Sosnoskie, 2009-Ohio-2327, 2009 WL 1393338 (Ohio Ct. App. 2d Dist. Montgomery County 2009)

53 ALR6th 81—§ 13

State v. Sotelo, 197 Neb. 334, 248 N.W.2d 767 (1977)

1 ALR6th 549—§ 16

State v. Soto, 45 Wash. App. 839, 727 P.2d 999 (1986)

45 ALR5th 591—§ 15

State v. Soto, 241 N.J. Super. 476, 575 A.2d 501 (1990)

27 ALR5th 593—§ 29

State v. Soto, 378 N.W.2d 625 (Minn. 1985)

64 ALR5th 671—§ 8

State v. Soto-Fong, 187 Ariz. 186, 928 P.2d 610 (1996)

11 ALR5th 831—§ 5

State v. Soucy, 139 N.H. 349, 653 A.2d 561 (1995)

50 ALR5th 467—§ 2, 9

State v. Souder, 1997 WL 619806 (Ohio Ct. App. 3d Dist. Union County 1997)

78 ALR5th 489—§ 10

State v. Sound Sleeper, 2010 SD 71, 787 N.W.2d 787 (S.D. 2010)

97 ALR6th 653—§ 29

State v. Sour Mountain Realty, Inc., 276 A.D.2d 8, 714 N.Y.S.2d 78, 31 Envtl. L. Rep. 20167 (2d Dep't 2000)

CASES CITED IN ALR5th and ALR6th

44 ALR6th 325—§ 11, 12
State v. Sours, 633 S.W.2d 255 (Mo. App. 1982)
29 ALR5th 59—§ 7, 12, 34, 39, 40
State v. Sousa, 151 N.H. 297, 855 A.2d 1284 (2004)
84 ALR6th 293—§ 8, 10, 11, 14
State v. South, 285 S.C. 529, 331 S.E.2d 775 (1985)
36 ALR5th 255—§ 18
State v. South, 885 P.2d 795 (Utah Ct. App. 1994)
122 ALR5th 439—§ 7
State v. Southerland, 316 S.C. 377, 447 S.E.2d 862 (1994)
79 ALR5th 33—§ 42
State v. Southern, 304 N.W.2d 329 (Minn. 1981)
28 ALR6th 505—§ 9
State v. Southern, 1999 M.T. 94, 294 Mont. 225, 980 P.2d 3 (1999)
90 ALR5th 453—§ 14
State v. Southern, 2004 WL 2659056 (Tenn. Crim. App. 2004)
26 ALR6th 511—§ 25, 27
State v. Southern Bell Tel. & Tel. Co., 204 Tenn. 207, 319 S.W.2d 90 (1958)
122 ALR5th 337—§ 14
State v. Southern Elec. Generating Co., 274 Ala. 668, 151 So. 2d 216 (1963)
58 ALR5th 187—§ 2, 24
State v. Southern Kraft Corporation, 243 Ala. 223, 8 So. 2d 886 (1942)
89 ALR5th 493—§ 11
State v. Souto, 578 N.W.2d 744 (Minn. 1998)
113 ALR5th 517—§ 7
State v. S.P., 49 Wash. App. 45, 746 P.2d 813 (1987)
18 ALR5th 856—§ 5
State v. Spadafore, 159 W. Va. 236, 220 S.E.2d 655 (1975)
3 ALR6th 269—§ 22
State v. Spadoni, 137 Wash. 684, 243 P. 854 (1926)
104 ALR5th 357—§ 4

State v. Spain, 3 N.C. App. 266, 164 S.E.2d 486 (1968)
119 ALR5th 275—§ 8
State v. Spain, 76 Ohio App. 3d 643, 602 N.E.2d 775 (3d Dist. Union County 1992)
32 ALR6th 1—§ 4
State v. Span, 819 P.2d 329 (Utah 1991)
85 ALR5th 187—§ 6, 7
State v. Spangler, 92 Wash. 636, 159 P. 810 (1916)
24 ALR5th 465—§ 48
State v. Sparen, 29 Conn. L. Rptr. 302, 2001 WL 206078 (Conn. Super. Ct. 2001)
84 ALR6th 293—§ 39
State v. Sparks, 641 S.E.2d 339 (N.C. Ct. App. 2007)
33 ALR6th 91—§ 11
State v. Sparks, 657 S.E.2d 655 (N.C. 2008)
33 ALR6th 91—§ 11
State v. Sparr, 13 Neb. App. 144, 688 N.W.2d 913 (2004)
92 ALR6th 171—§ 4
State v. Spates, 129 P.3d 125 (Kan. Ct. App. 2006)
37 ALR6th 357—§ 10
State v. Spates, 588 So. 2d 398 (La. App. 2d Cir. 1991)
4 ALR5th 1—§ 38
State v. Spates, 588 So. 2d 398 (La. Ct. App. 2d Cir. 1991)
23 ALR6th 307—§ 3
State v. Spates, 2006-Ohio-1564, 2006 WL 826083 (Ohio Ct. App. 8th Dist. Cuyahoga County 2006)
26 ALR6th 511—§ 19
State v. Spath, 1998 ND 133, 581 N.W.2d 123 (N.D. 1998)
11 ALR6th 237—§ 10
State v. Spaulding, 313 N.W.2d 878 (Iowa 1981)
119 ALR5th 275—§ 8
State v. Spaulding, 2002-Ohio-4935, 2002 WL 31094752 (Ohio Ct. App. 1st Dist. Hamilton County 2002)
34 ALR6th 1—§ 9

38 ALR6th 97—§ 4

State v. Spearin, 477 A.2d 1147 (Me. 1984)

85 ALR5th 187—§ 6, 9, 14

State v. Spears, 184 Ariz. 277, 908 P.2d 1062 (1996)

15 ALR5th 391—§ 31

59 ALR5th 1—§ 2

92 ALR5th 35—§ 13

State v. Spears, 223 Or. App. 675, 196 P.3d 1037 (2008)

87 ALR6th 1—§ 41

State v. Spears, 246 Kan. 283, 788 P.2d 261 (1990)

51 ALR5th 603—§ 4, 8, 14

State v. Spears, 570 So. 2d 888 (Ala. Crim. App. 1990)

58 ALR6th 499—§ 97

State v. Spears, 1999 WL 144064 (Ohio Ct. App. 4th Dist. Hocking County 1999)

29 ALR6th 237—§ 21

State v. Spears, 1999 WL 239272 (Wash. Ct. App. Div. 2 1999)

73 ALR5th 383—§ 3

State v. Speck, 1996 WL 141726 (Tenn. Crim. App. 1996)

73 ALR5th 383—§ 5

State v. Speers, 17 Conn. App. 587, 554 A.2d 769 (1989)

81 ALR6th 257—§ 3, 13

State v. Speese, 191 Wis. 2d 205, 528 N.W.2d 63 (App. 1995)

51 ALR5th 603—§ 2, 4, 11

State v. Speith, 244 Mont. 392, 797 P.2d 221 (1990)

76 ALR5th 485—§ 3, 17

State v. Spell, 461 So. 2d 654 (La. App. 1st Cir. 1984)

15 ALR5th 391—§ 5

State v. Speller, 86 N.C. 697, 1882 WL 2858 (1882)

33 ALR6th 407—§ 9

State v. Spellman, 40 N.C. App. 591, 253 S.E.2d 320 (1979)

5 ALR5th 243—§ 48

State v. Spellman, 562 So. 2d 455 (La. 1990)

99 ALR6th 295—§ 3, 7, 14

State v. Spence, 182 W. Va. 472, 388 S.E.2d 498 (1989)

102 ALR6th 365—§ 10, 22

State v. Spencer, 9 Wash. App. 95, 510 P.2d 833 (Div. 3 1973)

113 ALR5th 517—§ 21

State v. Spencer, 48 Conn. L. Rptr. 80, 2009 WL 2357696 (Conn. Super. Ct. 2009)

77 ALR6th 197—§ 14

State v. Spencer, 149 N.H. 622, 826 A.2d 546 (2003)

29 ALR6th 1—§ 9

State v. Spencer, 268 Conn. 575, 848 A.2d 1183 (2004)

79 ALR6th 1—§ 3, 11, 16, 18, 27, 42, 44

State v. Spencer, 305 Or. 59, 750 P.2d 147 (1988)

109 ALR5th 611—§ 3

State v. Spencer, 319 Ark. 454, 892 S.W.2d 484 (1995)

29 ALR6th 1—§ 10

State v. Spencer, 414 N.W.2d 528 (Minn. Ct. App. 1987)

51 ALR6th 219—§ 4

State v. Spencer, 631 So. 2d 1363 (La. App. 5th Cir. 1994)

47 ALR5th 259—§ 2, 13, 15

State v. Spencer, 663 So. 2d 271 (La. Ct. App. 3d Cir. 1995)

90 ALR5th 453—§ 12

State v. Spencer, 1998 WL 293824 (Wash. Ct. App. Div. 2 1998)

73 ALR5th 383—§ 5

State v. Speonk Fuel Inc., 710 N.Y.S.2d 652 (App. Div. 3d Dep't 2000)

5 ALR5th 1—§ 17

State v. Sperry, 47 Ohio Misc. 1, 72 Ohio Op. 2d 296, 1 Ohio Op. 3d 180, 351 N.E.2d 807 (C.P. 1974)

17 ALR6th 327—§ 34

State v. Speyer, 67 Vt. 502, 32 A. 476 (1895)

93 ALR5th 621—§ 3

State v. Spicer, 3 Or. App. 120, 473 P.2d 147 (1970)

85 ALR5th 1—§ 37

State v. Spicer, 254 Or. 68, 456 P.2d 965 (1969)

114 ALR5th 235—§ 3

State v. Spicer, 1998 WL 12660 (Wash. Ct. App. Div. 3 1998)

71 ALR5th 637—§ 3

State v. Spicer, 1999 WL 458771 (Del. Super. Ct. 1999)

37 ALR6th 511—§ 10, 13, 21

State v. Spicer, 2005-Ohio-4302, 2005 WL 1993933 (Ohio Ct. App. 1st Dist. Hamilton County 2005)

70 ALR6th 1—§ 5

State v. Spidel, 10 Neb. App. 605, 634 N.W.2d 825 (2001)

74 ALR6th 69—§ 3, 5

State v. Spiegel, 111 Iowa 701, 83 N.W. 722 (1900)

20 ALR6th 561—§ 20

State v. Spikes, 202 Or. App. 229, 120 P.3d 1258 (2005)

26 ALR6th 511—§ 36

State v. Spillane, 54 Conn. App. 201, 737 A.2d 479 (1999)

40 ALR5th 113—§ 4

State v. Spillers, 105 La. 163, 29 So. 480 (1900)

101 ALR6th 499—§ 15

State v. Spilton, 315 S.W.3d 350 (Mo. 2010)

79 ALR6th 125—§ 5, 24, 26

State v. Spinks, 79 Ohio App. 3d 720, 607 N.E.2d 1130 (8th Dist. Cuyahoga County 1992)

112 ALR5th 621—§ 7
19 ALR6th 697—§ 18

State v. Spinks, 136 N.C. App. 153, 523 S.E.2d 129 (1999)

3 ALR6th 269—§ 9, 24

State v. Spino, 143 Or. App. 619, 925 P.2d 101 (1996)

92 ALR5th 35—§ 28

State v. Spirko, 59 Ohio St. 3d 1, 570 N.E.2d 229 (1991)

10 ALR5th 700—§ 30
31 ALR5th 704—§ 16

State v. Spitz, 650 So. 2d 271 (La. App. 1st Cir. 1994)

7 ALR5th 263—§ 3

State v. Spivak, 130 Or. App. 153, 880 P.2d 964 (1994)

69 ALR6th 1—§ 33

State v. Spivey, 81 Ohio St. 3d 405, 1998-Ohio-437, 692 N.E.2d 151 (1998)

9 ALR6th 633—§ 4, 5
14 ALR6th 517—§ 5

State v. Spivey, 151 N.C. 676, 65 S.E. 995 (1909)

81 ALR5th 563—§ 3

State v. Spivey, 675 So. 2d 1335 (Ala. Crim. App. 1994)

103 ALR5th 463—§ 3

State v. Spivey, 755 S.W.2d 361 (Mo. Ct. App. E.D. 1988)

97 ALR6th 567—§ 3, 9

State v. Spoke Committee, University Center, Grand Forks, 270 N.W.2d 339 (N.D. 1978)

105 ALR5th 1—§ 24

State v. Spooner, 520 So. 2d 336 (La. 1988)

104 ALR5th 229—§ 6
115 ALR5th 403—§ 8
4 ALR6th 113—§ 25
34 ALR6th 539—§ 5

State v. Spotted Hawk, 22 Mont. 33, 55 P. 1026 (1899)

24 ALR6th 747—§ 3

State v. Spradlin, 187 Ohio App. 3d 767, 2010-Ohio-2140, 933 N.E.2d 1131 (2d Dist. Montgomery County 2010)

79 ALR6th 1—§ 43

State v. Spraggin, 71 Wis. 2d 604, 239 N.W.2d 297 (1976)

55 ALR6th 157—§ 62

State v. Spraggins, 839 S.W.2d 599 (Mo. App. 1992)

4 ALR5th 1—§ 38, 39

State v. Spraggins, 2005-Ohio-5977, 2005 WL 3007132 (Ohio Ct. App. 8th Dist. Cuyahoga County 2005)
26 ALR6th 511—§ 19

State v. Sprague, 86 A.3d 700 (N.H. 2014)
98 ALR6th 455—§ 19

State v. Sprague, 105 N.H. 355, 200 A.2d 206 (1964)
88 ALR6th 203—§ 51

State v. Sprague, 146 N.H. 334, 771 A.2d 583 (2001)
70 ALR6th 361—§ 31

State v. Sprague, 166 N.H. 29, 86 A.3d 700 (2014)
102 ALR6th 279—§ 16

State v. Spratt, 31 S.W.3d 587 (Tenn. Crim. App. 2000)
38 ALR5th 433—§ 31
47 ALR5th 259—§ 4, 11
38 ALR6th 439—§ 4

State v. Spratt, 120 R.I. 192, 386 A.2d 1094 (1978)
92 ALR6th 1—§ 3

State v. Spratt, 126 Ariz. 184, 613 P.2d 848 (App. 1980)
59 ALR5th 1—§ 5, 6

State v. Sprecher, 2000 SD 17, 606 N.W.2d 138 (S.D. 2000)
92 ALR5th 35—§ 10

State v. Spreitz, 190 Ariz. 129, 945 P.2d 1260 (1997)
21 ALR6th 1—§ 4

State v. Sprester, 26 S.W.3d 603 (Mo. Ct. App. S.D. 2000)
105 ALR5th 529—§ 13

State v. Springer, 133 N.H. 223, 574 A.2d 1381 (1990)
92 ALR5th 35—§ 25

State v. Springer, 135 Ohio App. 3d 767, 735 N.E.2d 914 (7th Dist. Jefferson County 1999)
32 ALR6th 1—§ 11

State v. Springer, 965 So. 2d 270 (Fla. Dist. Ct. App. 5th Dist. 2007)
40 ALR6th 419—§ 26

State v. Springfielt, 1997 WL 627606 (Wash. Ct. App. Div. 2 1997)
73 ALR5th 383—§ 5

State v. Springmier, 559 N.E.2d 319 (Ind. Ct. App. 1990)
84 ALR6th 293—§ 38

State v. Springs, 33 N.C. App. 61, 234 S.E.2d 193 (1977)
5 ALR5th 243—§ 11

State v. Springs, 1999 WL 148369 (Ohio Ct. App. 7th Dist. Mahoning County 1999)
29 ALR6th 237—§ 24

State v. Sproling, 752 S.W.2d 884 (Mo. App. 1988)
56 ALR5th 385—§ 5

State v. Spruill, 338 N.C. 612, 452 S.E.2d 279 (1994)
45 ALR5th 531—§ 3
79 ALR5th 33—§ 63

State v. Spry, 126 W. Va. 781, 30 S.E.2d 88 (1944)
105 ALR5th 529—§ 11

State v. Spurgeon, 904 P.2d 220 (Utah Ct. App. 1995)
123 ALR5th 179—§ 2, 4, 10

State v. Spurling, 385 So. 2d 672 (Fla. Dist. Ct. App. 2d Dist. 1980)
72 ALR5th 1—§ 29

State v. Spurlock, 874 S.W.2d 602 (Tenn. Crim. App. 1993)
24 ALR6th 1—§ 20, 44

State v. Squire, 888 P.2d 1102, 254 Utah Adv. Rep. 37 (Utah App. 1994)
37 ALR5th 319—§ 3

State v. Srey, 400 N.W.2d 722 (Minn. 1987)
15 ALR5th 391—§ 21

State v. S.R.W., 2010 WL 3220144 (Minn. Ct. App. 2010)
69 ALR6th 1—§ 20

State v. Staab, 430 So. 2d 54 (La. 1983)
98 ALR5th 445—§ 6

State v. Staats, 658 N.W.2d 207 (Minn. 2003)
28 ALR6th 505—§ 18

State v. Stacey, 2009-Ohio-3816, 2009 WL 2356888 (Ohio Ct. App. 3d Dist. Seneca County 2009)

CASES CITED IN ALR5th and ALR6th

64 ALR6th 1—§ 9, 45

State v. Stachler, 58 Hawaii 412, 570 P.2d 1323 (1977)

59 ALR5th 615—§ 3, 7, 12

State v. Stackhouse, 2007 WL 3196145 (N.J. Super. Ct. App. Div. 2007)

69 ALR6th 579—§ 11

State v. Stacy, 1998 WL 226466 (Ohio Ct. App. 1st Dist. Hamilton County 1998)

78 ALR5th 489—§ 3

State v. Staeheli, 102 Wash. 2d 305, 685 P.2d 591 (1984)

109 ALR5th 611—§ 6

State v. Stafford, 158 Ohio App. 3d 509, 2004-Ohio-3893, 817 N.E.2d 411 (1st Dist. Hamilton County 2004)

11 ALR6th 237—§ 4, 11

34 ALR6th 1—§ 9

State v. Stafford, 208 Mont. 324, 678 P.2d 644 (1984)

26 ALR5th 1—§ 3, 34, 35

State v. Stafford, 213 Kan. 152, 515 P.2d 769 (1973)

16 ALR5th 152—§ 12

State v. Stafford, 317 N.C. 568, 346 S.E.2d 463 (1986)

38 ALR5th 433—§ 11, 19

State v. Stafford, 340 N.W.2d 669 (Minn. 1983)

5 ALR5th 243—§ 21

State v. Stafford, 593 So. 2d 496, 17 FLW S. 62 (Fla. 1992)

22 ALR5th 660—§ 11

State v. Stafford, 845 P.2d 894 (Okla. Crim. 1992)

41 ALR5th 171—§ 9, 12, 107

State v. Stafford, 1997 WL 118113 (Minn. Ct. App. 1997)

37 ALR6th 357—§ 59

State v. Stafford, 2002-Ohio-5243, 2002 WL 31170127 (Ohio Ct. App. 7th Dist. Noble County 2002)

46 ALR6th 63—§ 16

State v. Stager, 329 N.C. 278, 406 S.E.2d 876 (1991)

57 ALR5th 141—§ 3, 7

State v. Stagno, 739 P.2d 198 (Alaska Ct. App. 1987)

89 ALR5th 539—§ 12

State v. Stahl, 111 Ohio St. 3d 186, 2006-Ohio-5482, 855 N.E.2d 834 (2006)

30 ALR6th 1—§ 4, 7

State v. Stakes, 227 Kan. 711, 608 P.2d 997 (1980)

27 ALR6th 1—§ 23

State v. Stakes, 235 Kan. 539, 680 P.2d 306 (1984)

27 ALR6th 1—§ 23

State v. Stalder, 630 So. 2d 1072, 19 FLW S. 56 (Fla. 1994)

22 ALR5th 261—§ 6

State v. Staley, 1 Fulton County D. Rep. 1450, 2001 WL 360730 (Ga. Ct. App. 2001)

84 ALR5th 1—§ 13.5

State v. Stalheim, 275 Or. 683, 552 P.2d 829, 79 A.L.R.3d 969 (1976)

15 ALR5th 391—§ 39

92 ALR5th 35—§ 2, 17

State v. Stallings, 89 Ohio St. 3d 280, 731 N.E.2d 159 (2000)

26 ALR5th 603—§ 4

State v. Stallings, 107 N.C. App. 241, 419 S.E.2d 586 (1992)

85 ALR5th 595—§ 7, 8

State v. Stallings, 150 Ohio App. 3d 5, 2002-Ohio-5942, 778 N.E.2d 1110 (9th Dist. Summit County 2002)

58 ALR6th 385—§ 3, 8, 10

State v. Stallings, 253 S.C. 451, 171 S.E.2d 588 (1969)

70 ALR5th 587—§ 3

State v. Stallings, 316 N.C. 535, 342 S.E.2d 519 (1986)

15 ALR5th 391—§ 32

92 ALR5th 35—§ 22

State v. Stallings, 334 Mo. 1, 64 S.W.2d 643 (1933)

24 ALR5th 465—§ 14, 49

State v. Stallworth, 645 So. 2d 323 (Ala. Crim. App. 1994)

4 ALR6th 599—§ 12, 27

State v. St. Amant, 536 A.2d 897 (R.I. 1988)

98 ALR6th 455—§ 22

State v. Stamm, 616 N.E.2d 377 (Ind. Ct. App. 2d Dist. 1993)

119 ALR5th 379—§ 8

State v. Stamper, 615 So. 2d 1359 (La. Ct. App. 2d Cir. 1993)

73 ALR5th 383—§ 6, 31

State v. Stanfield, 1 S.W.2d 834 (Mo. 1927)

54 ALR6th 429—§ 13

State v. Stanfield, 105 Wis. 2d 553, 314 N.W.2d 339 (1982)

6 ALR5th 733—§ 10, 14, 15

State v. Stankevicius, 3 Conn. Cir. Ct. 580, 222 A.2d 356 (App. Div. 1966)

103 ALR6th 137—§ 4, 6

State v. Stanley, 110 N.C. App. 87, 429 S.E.2d 349 (1993)

73 ALR5th 383—§ 21

State v. Stanley, 167 Ariz. 519, 809 P.2d 944 (1991)

32 ALR6th 1—§ 9

State v. Stanley, 167 Ariz. 519, 809 P.2d 944, 81 Ariz. Adv. Rep. 3, 82 Ariz. Adv. Rep. 3 (1991)

55 ALR5th 125—§ 18, 26

State v. Stanley, 1993 WL 112551 (Ohio App. Washington Co. 1993)

52 ALR5th 655—§ 3

State v. Stanley, 1997 WL 789965 (Tenn. Crim. App. 1997)

30 ALR6th 413—§ 13, 16

State v. Stanley, 2001 -NMSC- 037, 131 N.M. 368, 37 P.3d 85 (2001)

103 ALR5th 463—§ 8

State v. Stanley, 2008-Ohio-4840, 2008 WL 4335676 (Ohio Ct. App. 9th Dist. Summit County 2008)

84 ALR6th 293—§ 33

State v. Stanphill, 53 Wash. App. 623, 769 P.2d 861 (Div. 3 1989)

117 ALR5th 407—§ 4

State v. Stanphill, 206 Kan. 612, 481 P.2d 998 (1971)

70 ALR5th 587—§ 3

State v. Stanton, 68 Wash. App. 855, 845 P.2d 1365 (Div. 2 1993)

57 ALR6th 445—§ 7

State v. Stanton, 611 A.2d 29 (Del. Super. Ct. 1991)

70 ALR6th 361—§ 9

State v. Stape, 2009-Ohio-420, 2009 WL 242358 (Ohio Ct. App. 2d Dist. Montgomery County 2009)

41 ALR6th 141—§ 5

State v. Staples, 88 Ohio App. 3d 359, 623 N.E.2d 1313 (Allen Co. 1993)

27 ALR5th 593—§ 25

State v. Staples, 126 Minn. 396, 148 N.W. 283 (1914)

118 ALR5th 253—§ 3

State v. Staples, 354 A.2d 771 (Me. 1976)

19 ALR6th 697—§ 2, 6, 9, 19

57 ALR6th 313—§ 4, 6

State v. Stapleton, 638 S.W.2d 850 (Tenn. Crim. App. 1982)

32 ALR6th 1—§ 11

State v. Star, 10 P.3d 37 (Kan. Ct. App. 2000)

27 ALR5th 593—§ 20

State v. Starcher, 1992 WL 52599 (Ohio Ct. App. 11th Dist. Ashtabula County 1992)

69 ALR6th 207—§ 9, 10, 18

State v. Starfield, 481 N.W.2d 834 (Minn. 1992)

92 ALR6th 295—§ 7 to 9, 19, 25, 30, 33, 35

94 ALR6th 191—§ 4

95 ALR6th 1—§ 5, 7, 11, 23, 29

96 ALR6th 355—§ 5, 36, 49, 53, 61

State v. Stark, 66 Wash. App. 423, 832 P.2d 109 (1992)

12 ALR5th 149—§ 12, 17

13 ALR5th 628—§ 4, 10, 12

State v. Stark, 109 Wash. App. 1007, 2001 WL 1357191 (Div. 1 2001)

56 ALR6th 647—§ 18

State v. Starke, 81 Wis. 2d 399, 260 N.W.2d 739 (1978)

33 ALR5th 453—§ 4, 7

State v. Starkey, 437 N.W.2d 573 (Iowa 1989)

92 ALR5th 35—§ 6

State v. Starkey, 536 S.W.2d 858 (Mo. Ct. App. 1976)

29 ALR6th 1—§ 8

State v. Starks, 658 S.W.2d 544 (Tenn. Crim. App. 1983)

114 ALR5th 235—§ 5

State v. Starnes, 396 N.W.2d 676 (Minn. App. 1986)

34 ALR5th 125—§ 3, 8

State v. Starnes, 1995 WL 415230 (Tenn. Crim. App. 1995)

57 ALR5th 141—§ 2, 13

State v. Starr, 676 S.W.2d 311 (Mo. App. 1984)

11 ALR5th 497—§ 3, 28

State v. Starr Enterprises, Inc., 226 Kan. 288, 597 P.2d 1098 (1979)

13 ALR5th 567—§ 4, 5

State v. Starrish, 86 Wash. 2d 200, 544 P.2d 1 (1975)

71 ALR5th 1—§ 64

State v. Starzinger, 179 N.W.2d 761 (Iowa 1970)

22 ALR5th 327—§ 25, 28, 33

State v. Statczar, 228 Mont. 446, 743 P.2d 606 (1987)

51 ALR5th 603—§ 2, 4, 8

State v. State Board of Examiners, 74 Mont. 1, 238 P. 316 (1925)

82 ALR6th 497—§ 38

State v. Staten, 172 N.C. App. 673, 616 S.E.2d 650 (2005)

67 ALR6th 103—§ 8

State v. Staton, 1991 WL 35224 (Ohio Ct. App. 2d Dist. Greene County 1991)

62 ALR6th 413—§ 38

State v. Staudacher, 1991 WL 144784 (Minn. Ct. App. 1991)

113 ALR5th 597—§ 3

State v. Stayer, 706 P.2d 611 (Utah 1985)

92 ALR5th 35—§ 25

State v. Stayer, 2006-Ohio-2780, 2006 WL 1519982 (Ohio Ct. App. 3d Dist. Defiance County 2006)

26 ALR6th 511—§ 19

State v. St. Cloud, 465 N.W.2d 177 (S.D. 1991)

39 ALR5th 283—§ 4, 55
121 ALR5th 551—§ 2, 5, 8, 11, 14

State v. Steadman, 152 Wis. 2d 293, 448 N.W.2d 267 (App. 1989)

42 ALR5th 291—§ 18

State v. Stearns, 7 Ohio App. 3d 11, 454 N.E.2d 139 (8th Dist. Cuyahoga County 1982)

3 ALR6th 269—§ 5, 8, 13, 28

State v. Stearns, 130 N.H. 475, 547 A.2d 672 (1988)

33 ALR5th 453—§ 7, 11

State v. Stearns, 240 Ga. App. 806, 524 S.E.2d 554 (1999)

74 ALR5th 319—§ 6, 8

State v. Stebbings, 90 Wash. App. 1031, 1998 WL 184933 (Div. 1 1998)

79 ALR6th 1—§ 34

State v. Stebbins, 47 Wash. App. 482, 735 P.2d 1353 (Div. 1 1987)

103 ALR6th 347—§ 13

State v. Steele, 33 Or. App. 491, 577 P.2d 524 (1978)

39 ALR5th 283—§ 4, 64

State v. Steele, 100 N.M. 492, 672 P.2d 665 (App. 1983)

15 ALR5th 391—§ 22

State v. Steele, 178 W. Va. 330, 359 S.E.2d 558 (1987)

58 ALR5th 749—§ 3

State v. Steele, 189 Wis. 2d 493, 527 N.W.2d 400 (Ct. App. 1994)

84 ALR6th 293—§ 15

State v. Steele, 1993 WL 415836 (Tenn. Crim. App. 1993)

73 ALR5th 383—§ 8, 16

State v. Steele, 2001 WL 721806 (Ohio Ct. App. 10th Dist. Franklin County 2001)

3 ALR6th 543—§ 12
83 ALR6th 465—§ 19, 42, 48

State v. Steele, 2004-Ohio-4628, 2004 WL 1944832 (Ohio Ct. App. 8th Dist. Cuyahoga County 2004)
3 ALR6th 543—§ 8
State v. Steele, 2005-Ohio-943, 2005 WL 516526 (Ohio Ct. App. 12th Dist. Butler County 2005)
34 ALR6th 253—§ 13, 17
72 ALR6th 1—§ 4
State v. Steelman, 16 S.W.3d 483 (Tex. App. Eastland 2000)
19 ALR5th 470—§ 15
122 ALR5th 439—§ 7
State v. Steelman, 93 S.W.3d 102 (Tex. Crim. App. 2002)
122 ALR5th 439—§ 7
State v. Steelman, 126 Ariz. 19, 612 P.2d 475 (1980)
7 ALR5th 263—§ 7
State v. Steely, 327 Mo. 16, 33 S.W.2d 938 (1930)
81 ALR5th 563—§ 3, 5, 10
State v. Steen, 138 Wash. App. 1028, 2007 WL 1248436 (Div. 2 2007)
71 ALR6th 283—§ 26
State v. Steen, 164 Wash. App. 789, 265 P.3d 901 (Div. 2 2011)
73 ALR6th 281—§ 34
State v. Steen, 1994 WL 322963 (Ohio App. Vinton Co. 1994)
52 ALR5th 559—§ 7, 13, 14
State v. Steen, 2004 ND 228, 690 N.W.2d 239 (N.D. 2004)
72 ALR6th 1—§ 7
State v. Steer, 128 N.H. 490, 517 A.2d 797 (1986)
42 ALR5th 291—§ 14, 29
State v. Steeves, 29 Or. 85, 43 P. 947 (1896)
26 ALR5th 603—§ 4
State v. Stefan, 313 Wis. 2d 831, 2008 WI App 135, 756 N.W.2d 809 (Ct. App. 2008)
69 ALR6th 579—§ 6
State v. Stefani, 139 N.M. 719, 2006-NMCA-073, 137 P.3d 659 (Ct. App. 2006)
23 ALR6th 307—§ 40

State v. Steffen, 31 Ohio St. 3d 111, 509 N.E.2d 383 (1987)
57 ALR5th 141—§ 2, 7
State v. Steffen, 1985 WL 4301 (Ohio Ct. App. 1st Dist.Hamilton County 1985)
57 ALR5th 141—§ 7
State v. Steffes, 500 N.W.2d 608 (N.D. 1993)
24 ALR6th 1—§ 14
State v. Steffy, 173 Ariz. 90, 839 P.2d 1135 (Ct. App. Div. 1 1992)
92 ALR5th 35—§ 2, 6, 25
State v. Stegmann, 286 N.C. 638, 213 S.E.2d 262 (1975)
62 ALR5th 121—§ 3
86 ALR5th 59—§ 5, 8
State v. Stehlin, 312 S.W.2d 838 (Mo. 1958)
99 ALR6th 113—§ 10
State v. Steiger, 134 Ariz. 268, 655 P.2d 808 (Ct. App. Div. 1 1982)
18 ALR6th 1—§ 5, 27
67 ALR6th 531—§ 27
State v. Steimel, 921 A.2d 378 (N.H. 2007)
30 ALR6th 103—§ 21, 32, 43, 51
State v. Stein, 203 Kan. 638, 456 P.2d 1 (1969)
31 ALR5th 229—§ 2, 31, 40
State v. Stein, 1989 WL 78500 (Ohio Ct. App. 8th Dist. Cuyahoga County 1989)
19 ALR6th 697—§ 25
State v. Steinbach, 101 Wash. 2d 460, 679 P.2d 369 (1984)
17 ALR5th 111—§ 2 to 4
State v. Steinbach, 575 N.W.2d 193, 1998 N.D. 18 (N.D. 1998)
66 ALR5th 397—§ 8, 23, 25
State v. Steinbuch, 514 N.W.2d 793 (Minn. 1994)
57 ALR5th 141—§ 6
State v. Steineman, 2004-Ohio-6188, 2004 WL 2649784 (Ohio Ct. App. 3d Dist. Logan County 2004)
58 ALR6th 499—§ 30

State v. Steingraber, 296 N.W.2d 543 (S.D. 1980)
85 ALR5th 1—§ 9, 10
State v. Steinhaus, 405 N.W.2d 270 (Minn. Ct. App. 1987)
73 ALR5th 383—§ 5
State v. Steinman, 79 Ohio App. 3d 246, 607 N.E.2d 67 (2d Dist. Montgomery County 1992)
67 ALR6th 209—§ 40, 52, 54
State v. Steltzer, 288 N.W.2d 557 (Iowa 1980)
80 ALR5th 55—§ 3
State v. Ste. Marie, 97-168 La. App. 3 Cir. 4/18/1, 2001 WL 388947 (La. Ct. App. 3d Cir. 2001)
85 ALR5th 595—§ 6
State v. Ste. Marie, 770 So. 2d 315 (La. 2000)
102 ALR5th 327—§ 10
24 ALR6th 1—§ 43
State v. Stember, 565 So. 2d 725 (Fla. Dist. Ct. App. 4th Dist. 1990)
18 ALR6th 519—§ 7
State v. Stenger, 111 Wash. 2d 516, 760 P.2d 357 (1988)
42 ALR5th 581—§ 4, 17
State v. Stenger, 158 P.3d 375 (Kan. Ct. App. 2007)
30 ALR6th 373—§ 17
51 ALR6th 139—§ 3, 6
State v. Stenson, 132 Wash. 2d 668, 940 P.2d 1239 (1997)
82 ALR5th 67—§ 3
State v. Stephani, 369 N.W.2d 540 (Minn. Ct. App. 1985)
53 ALR6th 81—§ 5
State v. Stephens, 32 Tex. 155, 1869 WL 4786 (1869)
57 ALR6th 445—§ 38
State v. Stephens, 57 Ohio App. 2d 229, 11 Ohio Op. 3d 301, 387 N.E.2d 252 (1st Dist. Hamilton County 1978)
66 ALR5th 397—§ 3, 8
State v. Stephens, 110 N.M. 525, 797 P.2d 314 (App. 1990)
29 ALR5th 59—§ 3, 22, 32

State v. Stephens, 191 La. 111, 184 So. 559 (1938)
75 ALR5th 295—§ 31
State v. Stephens, 507 S.W.2d 18 (Mo. 1974)
9 ALR6th 1—§ 17
State v. Stephens, 699 S.W.2d 106 (Mo. App. 1985)
22 ALR5th 1—§ 5, 42
State v. Stephenson, 85 S.C. 247, 67 S.E. 239 (1910)
67 ALR5th 637—§ 3
State v. Stephenson, 310 Minn. 229, 245 N.W.2d 621 (1976)
41 ALR5th 171—§ 6, 12, 137
State v. Stephenson, 706 So. 2d 604 (La. Ct. App. 2d Cir. 1998)
15 ALR5th 391—§ 53
State v. Stephenson, 878 S.W.2d 530 (Tenn. 1994)
96 ALR5th 327—§ 3
State v. Stepherson, 15 S.W.3d 898 (Tenn. Crim. App. 1999)
109 ALR5th 99—§ 11
State v. Stepney, 88 Wash. App. 1050, 1997 WL 765710 (Div. 2 1997)
39 ALR6th 577—§ 4
State v. Sterling, 15 Or. App. 425, 516 P.2d 87 (1973)
87 ALR5th 181—§ 5
State v. Sterling, 131 So. 3d 295 (La. Ct. App. 5th Cir. 2013)
102 ALR6th 279—§ 16
State v. Sterling, 759 So. 2d 60 (La. 2000)
103 ALR5th 463—§ 3
State v. Stern, 197 N.J. Super. 49, 484 A.2d 38 (App. Div. 1984)
68 ALR5th 299—§ 4
State v. Stern, 210 Minn. 107, 297 N.W. 321 (1941)
97 ALR5th 293—§ 3, 9
State v. Sterner, 124 Or. App. 439, 862 P.2d 1321 (1993)
105 ALR5th 529—§ 8
State v. Stessman, 460 N.W.2d 461 (Iowa 1990)

92 ALR5th 35—§ 30

State v. Steven G.B., 204 Wis. 2d 108, 552 N.W.2d 897 (Ct. App. 1996)

10 ALR6th 463—§ 4, 8

State v. Stevens, 26 Kan. App. 2d 606, 992 P.2d 1244 (1999)

54 ALR6th 99—§ 49

State v. Stevens, 26 Wis. 2d 451, 132 N.W.2d 502 (1965)

55 ALR6th 157—§ 94

State v. Stevens, 35 Wash. App. 68, 665 P.2d 426 (Div. 1 1983)

99 ALR6th 295—§ 13

State v. Stevens, 36 Kan. App. 2d 323, 138 P.3d 1262 (2006)

57 ALR6th 83—§ 11

State v. Stevens, 58 Wash. App. 478, 794 P.2d 38 (Div. 1 1990)

73 ALR5th 383—§ 5

State v. Stevens, 65 Ohio Misc. 4, 19 Ohio Ops. 3d 29, 413 N.E.2d 862 (1979)

24 ALR5th 132—§ 4, 14

29 ALR5th 59—§ 7, 31

State v. Stevens, 94 N.C. App. 194, 379 S.E.2d 863 (1989)

78 ALR5th 567—§ 3

State v. Stevens, 121 N.H. 287, 428 A.2d 1241 (1981)

102 ALR5th 525—§ 21

State v. Stevens, 123 Wis. 2d 303, 367 N.W.2d 788 (1985)

62 ALR5th 1—§ 2, 5

State v. Stevens, 126 Idaho 822, 892 P.2d 889 (1995)

103 ALR6th 137—§ 11, 12

State v. Stevens, 137 Vt. 473, 408 A.2d 622 (1979)

78 ALR5th 1—§ 51

State v. Stevens, 154 Vt. 614, 580 A.2d 493 (1990)

92 ALR6th 295—§ 13

94 ALR6th 191—§ 4

95 ALR6th 1—§ 11, 32

96 ALR6th 355—§ 24, 45, 53, 60

State v. Stevens, 181 Wis. 2d 410, 511 N.W.2d 591 (1994)

28 ALR6th 505—§ 6, 8

81 ALR6th 505—§ 6, 7

State v. Stevens, 213 Wis. 2d 324, 570 N.W.2d 593 (Ct. App. 1997)

50 ALR6th 455—§ 18

State v. Stevens, 285 Kan. 307, 172 P.3d 570 (2007)

57 ALR6th 83—§ 11

State v. Stevens, 311 Or. 119, 806 P.2d 92 (1991)

28 ALR6th 505—§ 9

58 ALR6th 499—§ 49

State v. Stevens, 328 Or. 116, 970 P.2d 215 (1998)

57 ALR5th 315—§ 9

State v. Stevens, 574 So. 2d 197 (Fla. 1st DCA 1991)

101 ALR6th 331—§ 13

State v. Stevens, 580 N.W.2d 75 (Minn. Ct. App. 1998)

62 ALR5th 629—§ 3, 6, 7

State v. Stevens, 672 So. 2d 986 (La. App. 5th Cir. 1996)

50 ALR5th 581—§ 7, 15, 20

State v. Stevens, 992 P.2d 1244 (Kan. Ct. App. 1999)

36 ALR5th 161—§ 13

State v. Stevenson, 55 Wash. App. 725, 780 P.2d 873 (Div. 2 1989)

56 ALR6th 185—§ 13

58 ALR6th 499—§ 98, 111

State v. Stevenson, 81 N.C. App. 409, 344 S.E.2d 334 (1986)

67 ALR5th 637—§ 5, 11

State v. Stevenson, 89 Ark. 31, 116 S.W. 202 (1909)

97 ALR5th 537—§ 23

State v. Stevenson, 236 Wis. 2d 86, 2000 WI 71, 613 N.W.2d 90 (2000)

120 ALR5th 337—§ 3

State v. Stevenson, 323 So. 2d 762 (La. 1975)

69 ALR6th 579—§ 4

State v. Stevenson, 523 S.W.2d 349 (Mo. Ct. App. 1975)

124 ALR5th 1—§ 4

State v. Stevenson, 589 S.W.2d 44 (Mo. Ct. App. E.D. 1979)
104 ALR5th 165—§ 7

State v. Stevenson, 707 So. 2d 902 (Fla. Dist. Ct. App. 2d Dist. 1998)
62 ALR5th 1—§ 15
109 ALR5th 99—§ 10

State v. Stevenson, 784 S.W.2d 143 (Tex. App. Fort Worth 1990)
28 ALR6th 505—§ 10

State v. Stevenson, 958 S.W.2d 824 (Tex. Crim. App. 1997)
57 ALR6th 83—§ 9

State v. Stevenson, 993 S.W.2d 857 (Tex. App. Fort Worth 1999)
57 ALR6th 83—§ 9

State v. Stevenson, 1996 WL 255894 (Ohio Ct. App. 9th Dist. Wayne County 1996)
77 ALR6th 393—§ 75, 77

State v. Stevenson, 2011 WL 4444478 (N.J. Super. Ct. App. Div. 2011)
93 ALR6th 275—§ 7

State v. Steward, 9 Or. App. 35, 496 P.2d 40 (1972)
4 ALR5th 1—§ 21

State v. Steward, 52 Wash. App. 413, 760 P.2d 939 (1988)
15 ALR5th 391—§ 46

State v. Steward, 734 S.W.2d 821 (Mo. 1987)
50 ALR5th 467—§ 5

State v. Stewart, 6 Or. App. 264, 487 P.2d 899 (1971)
54 ALR6th 1—§ 14

State v. Stewart, 17 S.W.3d 162 (Mo. Ct. App. E.D. 2000)
2 ALR6th 551—§ 4

State v. Stewart, 38 Ohio L. Abs. 543, 50 N.E.2d 910 (Ct. App. 2d Dist. Franklin County 1943)
102 ALR5th 525—§ 14

State v. Stewart, 75 Ohio App. 3d 141, 598 N.E.2d 1275 (11th Dist. Ashtabula County 1991)
102 ALR6th 279—§ 32

State v. Stewart, 75 Ohio App. 3d 141, 598 N.E.2d 1275 (11th Dist.Ashtabula County 1991)
57 ALR5th 141—§ 4

State v. Stewart, 96 N.J. 596, 477 A.2d 300 (1984)
88 ALR5th 121—§ 7, 36

State v. Stewart, 96 Wash. App. 1040, 1999 WL 499437 (Div. 3 1999)
88 ALR5th 121—§ 2, 22, 31

State v. Stewart, 135 P.3d 219 (Kan. Ct. App. 2006)
37 ALR6th 357—§ 33, 72

State v. Stewart, 142 Wash. App. 1040, 2008 WL 199836 (Div. 3 2008)
69 ALR6th 579—§ 4

State v. Stewart, 219 Kan. 523, 548 P.2d 787 (1976)
55 ALR6th 157—§ 30, 45, 51

State v. Stewart, 266 Mont. 525, 881 P.2d 629 (1994)
70 ALR6th 361—§ 29

State v. Stewart, 278 S.C. 296, 295 S.E.2d 627, 29 A.L.R.4th 649 (1982)
102 ALR6th 279—§ 4
103 ALR6th 35—§ 24

State v. Stewart, 368 Md. 26, 791 A.2d 143 (2002)
26 ALR6th 511—§ 28

State v. Stewart, 452 So. 2d 186 (La. App. 4th Cir. 1984)
34 ALR5th 125—§ 31

State v. Stewart, 615 S.W.2d 600 (Mo. App. 1981)
39 ALR5th 283—§ 4, 63

State v. Stewart, 643 N.W.2d 281, 111 A.L.R.5th 791 (Minn. 2002)
111 ALR5th 529—§ 2, 3, 7

State v. Stewart, 648 So. 2d 15 (La. Ct. App. 4th Cir. 1994)
27 ALR6th 491—§ 3

State v. Stewart, 691 S.E.2d 767 (N.C. Ct. App. 2010)
57 ALR6th 1—§ 4, 22, 27

State v. Stewart, 749 So. 2d 555 (Fla. Dist. Ct. App. 2d Dist. 2000)

113 ALR5th 597—§ 3
State v. Stewart, 1993 WL 532630 (Tenn. Crim. App. 1993)
73 ALR5th 383—§ 5
State v. Stewart, 1994 WL 664938 (Minn. Ct. App. 1994)
73 ALR6th 49—§ 39
State v. Stewart, 2006-Ohio-813, 2006 WL 440153 (Ohio Ct. App. 8th Dist. Cuyahoga County 2006)
71 ALR6th 1—§ 11
State v. Stewart, 2007 WL 4171128 (Wash. Ct. App. Div. 3 2007)
33 ALR6th 91—§ 45
State v. Stewart, 2010 WL 3293920 (Tenn. Crim. App. 2010)
78 ALR6th 1—§ 3
State v. Stewart, No. 44331 (October 7, 1982, Ct. App. Ohio, 8th App. Dist. Cuyahoga Co.)
39 ALR5th 283—§ 14, 55
State v. Stewart, Slip Opinion Nos. 42144, 42145, 42146 (Ohio App. Cuyahoga Co. 1980)
41 ALR5th 171—§ 24, 27, 68
State v. St. Fleur, 2009 WL 2567987 (N.J. Super. Ct. App. Div. 2009)
71 ALR6th 1—§ 6
State v. St. Francis, 151 Vt. 384, 563 A.2d 249 (1989)
56 ALR5th 783—§ 3
State v. St. Hilaire, 97 Or. App. 108, 775 P.2d 876 (1989)
85 ALR5th 595—§ 9
State v. Stich, 399 N.W.2d 198 (Minn. Ct. App. 1987)
78 ALR6th 599—§ 6
84 ALR6th 293—§ 19
State v. Stickles, 1985 WL 10321 (Ohio Ct. App. 10th Dist. Franklin County 1985)
54 ALR6th 593—§ 12
State v. Stiff, 117 Kan. 243, 118 Kan. 208, 234 P. 700 (1924)
103 ALR6th 137—§ 4
State v. Stiff, 177 W. Va. 241, 351 S.E.2d 428 (1986)
102 ALR6th 365—§ 16

State v. Stiffler, 117 Idaho 405, 788 P.2d 220 (1990)
46 ALR5th 499—§ 3
State v. Stigger, 2006 WL 2194507 (N.J. Super. Ct. App. Div. 2006)
26 ALR6th 511—§ 50
State v. Stigler, 2007 WL 3152768 (Minn. Ct. App. 2007)
67 ALR6th 103—§ 7, 10, 12
State v. Stiles, 233 N.J. Super. 299, 558 A.2d 1333 (App. Div. 1989)
71 ALR6th 335—§ 10, 13
State v. Stiles, 2008 MT 390, 347 Mont. 95, 197 P.3d 966 (2008)
46 ALR6th 241—§ 20
State v. Stilley, 416 So. 2d 928 (La. 1982)
72 ALR5th 1—§ 18
5 ALR6th 1—§ 8, 10
State v. Stilling, 770 P.2d 137 (Utah 1989)
51 ALR6th 1—§ 15, 18
53 ALR6th 1—§ 5
State v. Stills, 642 So. 2d 316 (La. Ct. App. 4th Cir. 1994)
84 ALR5th 399—§ 3, 7
State v. Stills, 1998-NMSC-009, 125 N.M. 66, 957 P.2d 51 (1998)
56 ALR6th 185—§ 10
State v. Stillwell, 114 Kan. 808, 220 P. 1058 (1923)
90 ALR5th 619—§ 27
State v. Stimage, 2005 WL 3108225 (N.J. Super. Ct. App. Div. 2005)
26 ALR6th 511—§ 17
State v. Stines, 683 S.E.2d 411 (N.C. Ct. App. 2009)
57 ALR6th 1—§ 4, 6
State v. Stingley, 10 Iowa 488, 1860 WL 209 (1860)
97 ALR5th 537—§ 47
State v. Stinson, 134 Wash. App. 1043, 2006 WL 2375031 (Div. 3 2006)
26 ALR6th 511—§ 26
State v. Stinson, 134 Wis. 2d 224, 397 N.W.2d 136 (Ct. App. 1986)
1 ALR6th 657—§ 3, 14

For assistance, call 1-800-328-4880

State v. Stinson, 146 Ariz. 89, 703 P.2d 1238 (App. 1985)
18 ALR5th 1—§ 4, 6

State v. Stinson, 424 A.2d 327 (Me. 1981)
15 ALR5th 391—§ 11

State v. Stinson, 472 A.2d 416 (Me. 1984)
38 ALR5th 433—§ 45

State v. Stirba, 972 P.2d 918 (Utah Ct. App. 1998)
15 ALR5th 391—§ 45

State v. Stites, 5 Utah 2d 101, 297 P.2d 227 (1956)
57 ALR6th 445—§ 23

State v. Stith, 660 S.W.2d 419 (Mo. Ct. App. S.D. 1983)
55 ALR6th 157—§ 15

State v. St. John, 94 Mo. App. 229, 68 S.W. 374 (1902)
51 ALR5th 603—§ 2, 8, 14

State v. St. Louis, 128 Conn. App. 703, 18 A.3d 648 (2011)
72 ALR6th 437—§ 11

State v. Stockman, 2009-Ohio-266, 2009 WL 154258 (Ohio Ct. App. 6th Dist. Lucas County 2009)
64 ALR6th 1—§ 9, 19

State v. Stockton, 13 N.C. App. 287, 185 S.E.2d 459 (1971)
59 ALR5th 135—§ 4, 14

State v. Stockton, 85 Ariz. 153, 333 P.2d 735 (1958)
6 ALR5th 733—§ 25
69 ALR6th 207—§ 22

State v. Stockton, 105 Or. App. 162, 803 P.2d 1227 (1991)
15 ALR5th 391—§ 8

State v. Stoddard, 206 Conn. 157, 537 A.2d 446 (1988)
96 ALR5th 327—§ 2, 3

State v. Stoddard, 909 S.W.2d 454 (Tenn. Crim. App. 1994)
18 ALR6th 1—§ 5, 34

State v. Stoffer, 2011-Ohio-5133, 2011 WL 4579182 (Ohio Ct. App. 7th Dist. Columbiana County 2011)
94 ALR6th 525—§ 7

State v. Stojetz, 84 Ohio St. 3d 452, 705 N.E.2d 329 (1999)
79 ALR5th 33—§ 40

State v. Stokely, 842 S.W.2d 77 (Mo. 1992)
46 ALR5th 499—§ 3

State v. Stokes, 215 Kan. 5, 523 P.2d 364 (1974)
24 ALR6th 747—§ 21

State v. Stokes, 345 S.C. 368, 548 S.E.2d 202 (2001)
27 ALR6th 183—§ 28, 30

State v. Stokes, 1997 WL 764815 (Ohio Ct. App. 8th Dist. Cuyahoga County 1997)
38 ALR6th 439—§ 9

State v. Stoller, 107 Utah 429, 154 P.2d 649 (1945)
24 ALR6th 747—§ 17, 18

State v. Stolte, 991 S.W.2d 336 (Tex. App. Fort Worth 1999)
84 ALR6th 293—§ 8, 38

State v. Stonaker, 149 Or. App. 728, 945 P.2d 573 (1997)
7 ALR6th 233—§ 3, 5

State v. Stone, 69 Ohio App. 3d 383, 590 N.E.2d 1283 (Lorain Co. 1990)
29 ALR5th 59—§ 73

State v. Stone, 104 Ariz. 339, 452 P.2d 513 (1969)
112 ALR5th 621—§ 3, 5, 6

State v. Stone, 114 N.H. 114, 316 A.2d 196 (1974)
34 ALR5th 125—§ 9

State v. Stone, 170 Vt. 496, 756 A.2d 785 (2000)
92 ALR6th 171—§ 21

State v. Stone, 397 A.2d 989 (Me. 1979)
96 ALR5th 327—§ 3

State v. Stone, 467 N.W.2d 905 (S.D. 1991)
24 ALR5th 428—§ 2, 3

State v. Stone, 756 A.2d 785 (Vt. 2000)
66 ALR5th 397—§ 25

State v. Stone, 926 S.W.2d 895 (Mo. Ct. App. W.D. 1996)

50 ALR5th 703—§ 27

State v. Stone, 2005 WI App 111, 283 Wis. 2d 510, 698 N.W.2d 133 (Ct. App. 2005)

84 ALR6th 293—§ 9, 33

State v. Stone, 2008-Ohio-2615, 2008 WL 2230649 (Ohio Ct. App. 11th Dist. Portage County 2008)

56 ALR6th 323—§ 7, 11

State v. Stonecipher (In re R.L.S.), 879 P.2d 1258 (Okla. App. 1994)

20 ALR5th 700—§ 5

40 ALR5th 227—§ 57

State v. Stoneman, 132 Or. App. 137, 888 P.2d 39 (1994)

42 ALR5th 291—§ 7

State v. Stoneman, 323 Or. 536, 920 P.2d 535 (1996)

42 ALR5th 291—§ 17, 25, 37

State v. Stoops, 4 Kan. App. 2d 130, 603 P.2d 221 (1979)

42 ALR6th 237—§ 8

State v. Storer, 2005-Ohio-1919, 2005 WL 941017 (Ohio Ct. App. 3d Dist. Auglaize County 2005)

33 ALR6th 91—§ 31

State v. Storey, 40 S.W.3d 898 (Mo. 2001)

110 ALR5th 1—§ 2

State v. Storey, 901 S.W.2d 886 (Mo. 1995)

79 ALR5th 33—§ 65, 72

State v. Storey, 1998 ME 161, 713 A.2d 331 (Me. 1998)

50 ALR5th 581—§ 19

State v. Storm, 125 Mont. 346, 238 P.2d 1161 (1951)

81 ALR5th 563—§ 4

State v. Storms, 112 R.I. 454, 311 A.2d 567 (1973)

54 ALR5th 575—§ 4

State v. Story, 608 S.W.2d 599 (Tenn. Crim. App. 1980)

90 ALR5th 225—§ 7

124 ALR5th 1—§ 5

State v. Story, 646 S.W.2d 68 (Mo. 1983)

1 ALR6th 549—§ 10

State v. Stott, 171 N.J. 343, 794 A.2d 120 (2002)

25 ALR6th 379—§ 12, 15, 20, 36

28 ALR6th 245—§ 4

State v. Stott, 243 Neb. 967, 503 N.W.2d 822 (1993)

43 ALR5th 1—§ 4

67 ALR5th 361—§ 2 to 4, 8

State v. Stouffer, 28 Ohio App. 2d 229, 57 Ohio Op. 2d 342, 276 N.E.2d 651 (10th Dist. Franklin County 1971)

72 ALR5th 607—§ 3, 5

State v. Stouffer, 352 Md. 97, 721 A.2d 207 (1998)

39 ALR5th 283—§ 71

State v. Stough, 148 Or. App. 353, 939 P.2d 652 (1997)

71 ALR5th 1—§ 17

State v. Stout, 958 S.W.2d 32 (Mo. Ct. App. E.D. 1997)

6 ALR5th 733—§ 15

State v. Stover, 14 Or. App. 559, 513 P.2d 537 (1973)

119 ALR5th 275—§ 7

State v. Stowe, 2010-Ohio-4646, 2010 WL 3784701 (Ohio Ct. App. 5th Dist. Delaware County 2010)

70 ALR6th 361—§ 24

State v. Stowers, 81 Ohio St. 3d 260, 690 N.E.2d 881 (1998)

85 ALR5th 595—§ 4

State v. St. Pierre, 17 Conn. App. 100, 549 A.2d 1090 (1988)

52 ALR5th 655—§ 2, 9

State v. Stragisher, 2004-Ohio-6797, 2004 WL 2913250 (Ohio Ct. App. 7th Dist. Columbiana County 2004)

35 ALR6th 127—§ 5

State v. Strahan, 325 So. 2d 231 (La. 1975)

71 ALR6th 1—§ 6

72 ALR6th 1—§ 6

State v. Strain, 885 P.2d 810 (Utah Ct. App. 1994)

92 ALR6th 549—§ 23

CASES CITED IN ALR5th and ALR6th

State v. Strait, Ohio App. Case No
81AP-218, Slip Opinion (Franklin
Co. 1981)
45 ALR5th 1—§ 5, 10, 25, 29

State v. Strandberg, 223 Mont. 132, 724
P.2d 710 (1986)
54 ALR5th 141—§ 3 to 5, 10

State v. Strandy, 49 Wash. App. 537,
745 P.2d 43 (1987)
37 ALR5th 515—§ 2, 3, 10

State v. Strange, 772 S.W.2d 440 (Tenn.
Crim. App. 1989)
90 ALR5th 225—§ 3

State v. Stratton, 99 Or. App. 538, 783
P.2d 41 (1989)
15 ALR5th 391—§ 15

State v. Strausberg, 895 P.2d 831 (Utah
Ct. App. 1995)
57 ALR6th 83—§ 11

State v. Strauss, 20 P.3d 1022 (Wash. Ct.
App. Div. 1 2001)
90 ALR5th 453—§ 43

State v. Strauss, 779 S.W.2d 591 (Mo.
Ct. App. E.D. 1989)
55 ALR6th 157—§ 4, 8

State v. Strawser, 10 Ohio Misc. 2d 21,
461 N.E.2d 330 (C.P. 1983)
29 ALR6th 1—§ 10

State v. Streath, 73 N.C. App. 546, 327
S.E.2d 240 (1985)
95 ALR5th 229—§ 19

State v. Strecker, 230 Kan. 602, 641
P.2d 379 (1982)
68 ALR5th 343—§ 3

State v. Streekstra, 2010 WI App 19, 323
Wis. 2d 279, 779 N.W.2d 725 (Ct.
App. 2009)
84 ALR6th 293—§ 33

State v. Streeper, 113 Idaho 662, 747
P.2d 71 (1987)
81 ALR5th 563—§ 3, 5

State v. Streeter, 2 Storey 358, 52 Del.
358, 158 A.2d 284 (Del. 1960)
46 ALR5th 735—§ 2

State v. Streich, 163 Vt. 331, 658 A.2d
38 (1995)
90 ALR5th 453—§ 25

State v. Stribley, 532 N.W.2d 170 (Iowa
Ct. App. 1995)
85 ALR5th 595—§ 8

State v. Strickland, 20 N.C. App. 470,
201 S.E.2d 501 (1974)
29 ALR5th 59—§ 3, 8, 19

State v. Strickland, 36 Or. App. 119, 584
P.2d 310 (1978)
39 ALR5th 283—§ 4, 63

State v. Strickland, 243 Conn. 339, 703
A.2d 109, 70 A.L.R.5th 771 (1997)
70 ALR5th 533—§ 2, 3

State v. Strickland, 532 S.W.2d 912
(Tenn. 1975)
37 ALR5th 703—§ 3, 5

State v. Strickland, 683 So. 2d 218 (La.
1996)
62 ALR5th 1—§ 14
88 ALR5th 67—§ 10

State v. Strickland, 2008 WL 1699447
(N.J. Super. Ct. App. Div. 2008)
99 ALR6th 295—§ 7

State v. Strickland, 2009-Ohio-5424,
2009 WL 3255305 (Ohio Ct. App.
11th Dist. Lake County 2009)
63 ALR6th 351—§ 4

State v. Stricklin, 2009 WL 2433142
(Tenn. Crim. App. 2009)
65 ALR6th 537—§ 34

State v. Stringer, 49 Or. App. 51, 618
P.2d 1309 (1980)
84 ALR6th 427—§ 20

State v. Stringer, 258 Ga. 605, 372
S.E.2d 426 (1988)
103 ALR6th 347—§ 3, 25

State v. Stringer, 271 Mont. 367, 897
P.2d 1063 (1995)
57 ALR5th 315—§ 2, 3, 10, 11

State v. Stringer, 291 Or. 527, 633 P.2d
770 (1981)
84 ALR6th 427—§ 20

State v. Stringer, 2009-Ohio-909, 2009
WL 499313 (Ohio Ct. App. 9th Dist.
Medina County 2009)
70 ALR6th 1—§ 4

State v. Stringfellow, 126 La. 720, 52
So. 1002 (1910)

For assistance, call 1-800-328-4880

49 ALR5th 619—§ 2, 3
State v. Stripling, 354 So. 2d 1297 (La. 1978)

62 ALR5th 121—§ 6
State v. Strode, 116 Wash. App. 1001, 2003 WL 723363 (Div. 3 2003)

15 ALR6th 515—§ 33, 34
State v. Strohm, 75 Wash. App. 301, 879 P.2d 962 (Div. 1 1994)

89 ALR5th 629—§ 10
State v. Stromberg, 783 P.2d 54 (Utah Ct. App. 1989)

112 ALR5th 429—§ 17
State v. Stromberg, 783 P.2d 54, 121 Utah Adv. Rep. 22 (Utah App. 1989)

27 ALR5th 593—§ 5
State v. Strome, 26 Ohio N.P. (n.s.) 406, 1926 WL 2505 (C.P. 1926)

119 ALR5th 275—§ 7, 10
State v. Strommen, 411 N.W.2d 540 (Minn. Ct. App. 1987)

73 ALR5th 383—§ 5
State v. Strong, 153 Mo. 548, 55 S.W. 78 (1900)

50 ALR5th 467—§ 6, 8, 9
State v. Strong, 484 S.W.2d 657 (Mo. 1972)

79 ALR5th 237—§ 3
State v. Strong, 1991 WL 65095 (Tenn. Crim. App. 1991)

73 ALR5th 383—§ 3
State v. Strother, 606 So. 2d 891 (La. Ct. App. 2d Cir. 1992)

73 ALR5th 383—§ 4
State v. Stroud, 200 Neb. 27, 261 N.W.2d 777 (1978)

22 ALR5th 660—§ 6
State v. Stroud, 438 So. 2d 1172 (La. Ct. App. 3d Cir. 1983)

112 ALR5th 429—§ 13
State v. Stroud, 1995 WL 600004 (Ohio App. 2 Dist.)

50 ALR5th 581—§ 7
State v. Stroud, 1999 WL 980627 (Ohio Ct. App. 8th Dist. Cuyahoga County 1999)

17 ALR6th 327—§ 35
State v. Strouth, 620 S.W.2d 467 (Tenn. 1981)

70 ALR5th 587—§ 20
State v. Strozier, 172 Ohio App. 3d 780, 2007-Ohio-4575, 876 N.E.2d 1304 (2d Dist. Montgomery County 2007)

58 ALR6th 215—§ 11
State v. Strubhar, 82 Or. App. 560, 728 P.2d 928 (1986)

112 ALR5th 429—§ 5
State v. Strutt, 4 Conn. Cir. Ct. 501, 236 A.2d 357 (App. Div. 1967)

32 ALR6th 1—§ 4
State v. Strutton, 62 Ohio App. 3d 248, 575 N.E.2d 466 (2d Dist. Montgomery County 1988)

19 ALR6th 411—§ 10
State v. Stuart, 192 W. Va. 428, 452 S.E.2d 886 (1994)

84 ALR6th 293—§ 33
State v. Stuart, 2005 WI 47, 279 Wis. 2d 659, 695 N.W.2d 259 (2005)

30 ALR6th 1—§ 3, 6
State v. Stuart, 2008 WL 4572654 (Ariz. Ct. App. Div. 2 2008)

56 ALR6th 323—§ 11
State v. Stubblefield, 249 Neb. 436, 543 N.W.2d 743 (1996)

12 ALR5th 89—§ 4
State v. Stubbs, 270 Mont. 364, 892 P.2d 547 (1995)

50 ALR5th 581—§ 7
State v. Stubby, 146 P.3d 709 (Kan. Ct. App. 2006)

26 ALR6th 511—§ 25
State v. Stuck, 434 N.W.2d 43 (S.D. 1988)

51 ALR5th 603—§ 2
State v. Stuckey, 174 W. Va. 236, 324 S.E.2d 379 (1984)

21 ALR6th 771—§ 5
State v. Studer, 1990 WL 52492 (Ohio Ct. App. 5th Dist. Stark County 1990)

58 ALR6th 215—§ 12

State v. Stuhr, 58 Wash. App. 660, 794 P.2d 1297 (Div. 2 1990)
   73 ALR5th 383—§ 3
State v. Stuit, 176 Mont. 84, 576 P.2d 264 (1978)
   54 ALR5th 141—§ 3 to 6, 10
State v. Stukenborg, 21 Ohio Op. 2d 378, 89 Ohio L. Abs. 539, 185 N.E.2d 133 (C.P. 1962)
   89 ALR6th 565—§ 10, 31
State v. Stumm, 312 N.W.2d 248 (Minn. 1981)
   73 ALR5th 383—§ 5
State v. Stupi, 231 N.J. Super. 284, 555 A.2d 681 (App. Div. 1989)
   17 ALR6th 327—§ 37
   79 ALR6th 1—§ 69
State v. Sturdivant, 304 N.C. 293, 283 S.E.2d 719 (1981)
   39 ALR5th 283—§ 4, 54
State v. Sturkie, 91 N.C. App. 249, 371 S.E.2d 288 (1988)
   55 ALR5th 125—§ 12, 14, 26
State v. Sturm, 2010-Ohio-336, 2009 WL 5670403 (Ohio Ct. App. 5th Dist. Stark County 2009)
   64 ALR6th 1—§ 7, 9
State v. Stuthman, 2 Neb. App. 317, 509 N.W.2d 410 (1993)
   15 ALR5th 391—§ 53
State v. Stutliff, 97 Idaho 523, 547 P.2d 1128 (1976)
   119 ALR5th 379—§ 7, 10
State v. Stutsman, 566 So. 2d 880 (Fla. Dist. Ct. App. 3d Dist. 1990)
   113 ALR5th 597—§ 8
State v. Stutts, 723 S.W.2d 594 (Mo. App. 1987)
   10 ALR5th 700—§ 31
State v. Styers, 177 Ariz. 104, 865 P.2d 765, 154 Ariz. Adv. Rep. 32 (1993)
   39 ALR5th 283—§ 3
State v. Styles, 93 N.C. App. 596, 379 S.E.2d 255 (1989)
   73 ALR5th 383—§ 3
   81 ALR5th 563—§ 3
State v. Styles, 166 Vt. 615, 693 A.2d 734 (1997)

21 ALR6th 771—§ 31
State v. St. Yves, 2000 ME 97, 751 A.2d 1018 (Me. 2000)
   58 ALR6th 499—§ 49
State v. Suarez, 510 So. 2d 643 (Fla. Dist. Ct. App. 2d Dist. 1987)
   13 ALR6th 603—§ 32
State v. Suarez, 2008 WL 834323 (N.J. Super. Ct. App. Div. 2008)
   79 ALR6th 1—§ 39
State v. Suazo (In re Suazo), 117 N.M. 784, 877 P.2d 1088 (1994)
   28 ALR5th 459—§ 4 to 6, 11
State v. Sublet, 150 N.M. 378, 2011-NMCA-075, 258 P.3d 1170 (Ct. App. 2011)
   79 ALR6th 1—§ 22, 62
State v. Sucharew, 205 Ariz. 16, 66 P.3d 59 (Ct. App. Div. 1 2003)
   67 ALR6th 341—§ 6
State v. Suddith, 379 Md. 425, 842 A.2d 716 (2004)
   23 ALR6th 307—§ 44
State v. Suel, 2003-Ohio-3299, 2003 WL 21455276 (Ohio Ct. App. 10th Dist. Franklin County 2003)
   70 ALR6th 1—§ 5
State v. Suero, 721 A.2d 426 (R.I. 1998)
   39 ALR5th 283—§ 60
State v. Suffredini, 224 Neb. 220, 397 N.W.2d 51 (1986)
   9 ALR6th 633—§ 5, 13
   9 ALR6th 693—§ 16, 18, 21
   13 ALR6th 603—§ 22
   15 ALR6th 173—§ 8
State v. Suggs, 13 Or. App. 484, 511 P.2d 405 (1973)
   124 ALR5th 1—§ 4
State v. Sugimoto, 62 Haw. 259, 614 P.2d 386 (1980)
   29 ALR6th 1—§ 10
State v. Suits, 73 Wis. 2d 352, 243 N.W.2d 206 (1976)
   19 ALR6th 115—§ 4
State v. Sullivan, 24 Or. App. 99, 544 P.2d 616 (1976)
   15 ALR5th 391—§ 39

State v. Sullivan, 49 S.W.3d 800 (Mo. Ct. App. W.D. 2001)
35 ALR6th 497—§ 21

State v. Sullivan, 60 Wash. 2d 214, 373 P.2d 474 (1962)
51 ALR5th 603—§ 2, 4

State v. Sullivan, 69 P.3d 1006 (Ariz. Ct. App. Div. 1 2003)
108 ALR5th 593—§ 5.5, 43

State v. Sullivan, 87 P.3d 993 (Kan. Ct. App. 2004)
8 ALR6th 265—§ 16

State v. Sullivan, 94 P.3d 737 (Kan. Ct. App. 2004)
26 ALR6th 511—§ 25

State v. Sullivan, 95 Fla. 191, 116 So. 255 (1928)
102 ALR5th 525—§ 19

State v. Sullivan, 123 Wash. App. 1005, 2004 WL 1879843 (Div. 2 2004)
38 ALR6th 1—§ 26

State v. Sullivan, 197 Mont. 395, 642 P.2d 1008 (1982)
46 ALR6th 241—§ 34

State v. Sullivan, 267 S.C. 610, 230 S.E.2d 621 (1976)
106 ALR5th 397—§ 4

State v. Sullivan, 377 S.W.2d 839 (Tex. Civ. App. Austin 1964)
60 ALR5th 459—§ 2, 26

State v. Sully, 219 Kan. 222, 547 P.2d 344 (1976)
16 ALR6th 329—§ 4
19 ALR6th 115—§ 7
24 ALR6th 591—§ 4, 12, 15

State v. Sumerlin, 139 Or. App. 579, 913 P.2d 340 (1996)
113 ALR5th 431—§ 2

State v. Sumler, 395 So. 2d 766 (La. 1981)
31 ALR6th 465—§ 14, 22

State v. Summerlin, 138 Ariz. 426, 675 P.2d 686 (1983)
65 ALR5th 407—§ 3

State v. Summers, 52 Wash. App. 767, 764 P.2d 250 (1988)
55 ALR5th 125—§ 2, 3, 7, 12, 14, 22

State v. Summers, 60 Wash. 2d 702, 375 P.2d 143 (1962)
15 ALR5th 391—§ 30
92 ALR5th 35—§ 30

State v. Summers, 92 N.C. App. 453, 374 S.E.2d 631 (1988)
38 ALR5th 433—§ 3

State v. Summers, 276 S.C. 11, 274 S.E.2d 427 (1981)
65 ALR6th 537—§ 40

State v. Summers, 440 So. 2d 911 (La. Ct. App. 2d Cir. 1983)
122 ALR5th 439—§ 7

State v. Summers, 692 S.W.2d 439 (Tenn. Crim. 1985)
13 ALR5th 567—§ 3

State v. Summers, 2002-Ohio-5284, 2002 WL 31185794 (Ohio Ct. App. 5th Dist. Morgan County 2002)
71 ALR6th 1—§ 14

State v. Summers, 2008 WL 4613664 (Tenn. Crim. App. 2008)
55 ALR6th 513—§ 8

State v. S.U.N., 2011 WL 4008315 (Minn. Ct. App. 2011)
68 ALR6th 1—§ 17

State v. Sundberg, 349 Or. 608, 247 P.3d 1213 (2011)
95 ALR6th 219—§ 3, 14

State v. Sunford, 244 Mont. 411, 796 P.2d 1084 (1990)
18 ALR6th 519—§ 12

State v. Superior Court (Bolduc), 83 Cal. App. 4th 597, 99 Cal. Rptr. 2d 735 (2d Dist. 2000)
25 ALR6th 435—§ 7

State v. Superior Court, 104 Ariz. 440, 454 P.2d 982 (1969)
46 ALR5th 499—§ 3

State v. Superior Court, 111 Ariz. 130, 524 P.2d 951 (1974)
27 ALR5th 174—§ 3, 4, 27

State v. Superior Court In and For County of Maricopa, 186 Ariz. 363, 922 P.2d 927 (Ct. App. Div. 1 1996)
91 ALR5th 343—§ 12

State v. Superior Court In and For County of Maricopa, 187 Ariz. 411, 930 P.2d 488 (Ct. App. Div. 1 1996)
87 ALR5th 631—§ 3

State v. Superior Court In and For Greenlee County, 153 Ariz. 119, 735 P.2d 149 (Ct. App. Div. 2 1987)
92 ALR6th 295—§ 7, 19, 25

State v. Superior Court In and For Pima County, 143 Ariz. 45, 691 P.2d 1073 (1984)
74 ALR5th 319—§ 8, 11

State v. Superior Court of County of Cochise, 149 Ariz. 269, 718 P.2d 171, 60 ALR4th 1103 (1986)
117 ALR5th 491—§ 2

State v. Superior Court of King County, 35 Wash. 303, 77 P. 382 (1904)
44 ALR6th 259—§ 21

State v. Superior Court of Pima County, 7 Ariz. App. 170, 436 P.2d 948 (1968)
74 ALR5th 453—§ 5

State v. Superior Court of Pima County, 155 Ariz. 403, 747 P.2d 564 (Ct. App. Div. 2 1986)
76 ALR5th 597—§ 2, 4

State v. Superior Court of Pima County, 155 Ariz. 408, 747 P.2d 569 (1987)
76 ALR5th 597—§ 2

State v. Superior Court of Skagit County, 159 Wash. 277, 292 P. 1011 (1930)
120 ALR5th 229—§ 7, 14

State v. Superior Court of Washington for King County, 113 Wash. 54, 193 P. 226 (1920)
48 ALR6th 181—§ 4, 10

State v. Supinski, 779 S.W.2d 258 (Mo. App. 1989)
56 ALR5th 385—§ 5

State v. Supinski, 779 S.W.2d 258 (Mo. Ct. App. W.D. 1989)
107 ALR5th 567—§ 10, 13

State v. Surma, 263 Wis. 388, 57 N.W.2d 370 (1953)
6 ALR5th 733—§ 2, 15, 31

State v. Surritte, 35 S.W.3d 873, 105 A.L.R.5th 781 (Mo. Ct. App. W.D. 2001)
105 ALR5th 529—§ 13

State v. Suskey, 2009 WL 6667960 (N.M. Ct. App. 2009)
84 ALR6th 293—§ 29

State v. Susser, 1992 WL 41834 (Ohio Ct. App. 2d Dist. Montgomery County 1992)
23 ALR6th 307—§ 26

State v. Sussmann, 374 So. 2d 1256 (La. 1979)
21 ALR6th 771—§ 7

State v. Sutherland, 15 P.3d 1051 (Wash. Ct. App. Div. 2 2001)
26 ALR5th 1—§ 4

State v. Sutherland, 92 Ohio App. 3d 840, 637 N.E.2d 366 (Auglaize Co. 1994)
50 ALR5th 581—§ 7

State v. Sutorius, 122 Ohio App. 3d 1, 701 N.E.2d 1 (1st Dist. Hamilton County 1997)
57 ALR5th 141—§ 3

State v. Sutphin, 466 S.E.2d 402 (W. Va. 1995)
57 ALR5th 141—§ 9

State v. Sutten, 2002 WL 762655 (Minn. Ct. App. 2002)
84 ALR6th 293—§ 28

State v. Suttles, 287 Or. 15, 597 P.2d 786 (1979)
119 ALR5th 275—§ 8, 10

State v. Suttles, 1987 WL 17248 (Tenn. Crim. App. 1987)
32 ALR6th 171—§ 3, 6
33 ALR6th 1—§ 3, 19, 20

State v. Suttles, 1999 WL 817205 (Tenn. Ct. App. 1999)
21 ALR6th 1—§ 4

State v. Sutton, 27 Ariz. App. 134, 551 P.2d 583 (Div. 1 1976)
80 ALR6th 599—§ 6

State v. Sutton, 167 N.C. App. 242, 605 S.E.2d 483 (2004)
55 ALR6th 513—§ 5

For assistance, call 1-800-328-4880

State v. Sutton, 258 Ga. 382, 369 S.E.2d 249 (1988)
76 ALR5th 563—§ 4, 5
State v. Sutton, 494 So. 2d 1371 (La. Ct. App. 2d Cir. 1986)
92 ALR6th 1—§ 5
State v. Sutton, 1998 WL 301733 (Tenn. Crim. App. 1998)
73 ALR5th 383—§ 3, 4
State v. Sutton, 2002-Ohio-6901, 2002 WL 31813086 (Ohio Ct. App. 7th Dist. Mahoning County 2002)
79 ALR6th 1—§ 41
State v. Sutton, 2005 WL 924294 (Tenn. Crim. App. 2005)
26 ALR6th 511—§ 35
State v. Sveum, 220 Wis. 2d 396, 584 N.W.2d 137 (Ct. App. 1998)
29 ALR5th 487—§ 5, 12
State v. Svoboda, 220 La. 260, 56 So. 2d 416 (1951)
13 ALR5th 118—§ 2, 14
State v. Swader, 72 Or. App. 593, 697 P.2d 557 (1985)
29 ALR6th 1—§ 10
State v. Swafford, 20 Kan. App. 2d 563, 890 P.2d 368 (1995)
27 ALR5th 593—§ 31
State v. Swaggerty, 15 Or. App. 343, 515 P.2d 952 (1973)
39 ALR5th 283—§ 4, 56
State v. Swain, 10 Wash. App. 885, 520 P.2d 950 (1974)
34 ALR5th 125—§ 3
State v. Swain, 92 N.C. App. 240, 374 S.E.2d 173 (1988)
88 ALR6th 203—§ 58
State v. Swain, 269 N.W.2d 707 (Minn. 1978)
82 ALR5th 67—§ 6
27 ALR6th 491—§ 3
State v. Swan, 51 Ohio App. 3d 141, 554 N.E.2d 1374 (Williams Co. 1988)
15 ALR5th 391—§ 5
State v. Swan, 114 Wash. 2d 613, 790 P.2d 610 (1990)
71 ALR5th 637—§ 7

87 ALR5th 693—§ 4
State v. Swaney, 2000 WL 1471068 (Ohio Ct. App. 9th Dist. Lorain County 2000)
78 ALR5th 489—§ 10.5
State v. Swank, 2008-Ohio-6059, 2008 WL 4964659 (Ohio Ct. App. 11th Dist. Lake County 2008)
64 ALR6th 1—§ 7
State v. Swansen, 201 P.3d 2 (Kan. Ct. App. 2009)
62 ALR6th 413—§ 46
State v. Swanson, 28 Wash. App. 759, 626 P.2d 527 (Div. 1 1981)
100 ALR6th 535—§ 3
State v. Swanson, 228 N.W.2d 101 (Iowa 1975)
29 ALR6th 1—§ 10
State v. Swanson, 680 S.W.2d 487 (Tenn. Crim. App. 1984)
94 ALR5th 393—§ 13
State v. Swanson, 1994 WL 114337 (Neb. Ct. App. 1994)
34 ALR6th 1—§ 12
State v. Swanson, 1999 WL 592237 (Tenn. Crim. App. 1999)
46 ALR6th 63—§ 14
State v. Swartz, 601 N.W.2d 348 (Iowa 1999)
63 ALR6th 1—§ 10, 53
State v. Swavola, 840 P.2d 1238 (N.M. App. 1992)
11 ALR5th 871—§ 6, 7
State v. Sway, 15 Ohio St. 3d 112, 15 Ohio B.R. 265, 472 N.E.2d 1065 (1984)
13 ALR5th 1—§ 25, 30
State v. Swearingen, 131 Ohio App. 3d 124, 721 N.E.2d 1097 (3d Dist. Marion County 1999)
109 ALR5th 99—§ 10
State v. Sweat, 221 S.C. 270, 70 S.E.2d 234 (1952)
29 ALR5th 59—§ 3, 56
State v. Sweatt, 333 N.C. 407, 427 S.E.2d 112 (1993)
30 ALR6th 103—§ 17, 58

State v. Sweatt, 427 A.2d 940 (Me. 1981)
18 ALR6th 1—§ 5, 31
State v. Sweeney, 33 Minn. 23, 21 N.W. 847 (1884)
102 ALR5th 525—§ 63
State v. Sweeney, 701 S.W.2d 420 (Mo. 1985)
19 ALR5th 470—§ 12
67 ALR5th 361—§ 11
State v. Sweet, 93 Or. App. 642, 763 P.2d 739 (1988)
7 ALR5th 73—§ 2, 8
State v. Sweet, 101 Kan. 746, 168 P. 1112 (1917)
81 ALR5th 563—§ 3
State v. Sweet, 138 Wash. 2d 466, 980 P.2d 1223 (1999)
73 ALR5th 383—§ 32
State v. Sweet, 1998 M.T. 30, 287 Mont. 336, 954 P.2d 1133 (1998)
40 ALR5th 113—§ 3
State v. Sweetin, 134 Kan. 663, 8 P.2d 397 (1932)
45 ALR5th 591—§ 15
State v. Swenningson, 297 N.W.2d 405 (N.D. 1980)
55 ALR5th 125—§ 3, 6, 7
State v. Swenson, 59 Wash. App. 586, 799 P.2d 1188 (Div. 1 1990)
58 ALR6th 499—§ 80
State v. Swenson, 62 Wash. 2d 259, 382 P.2d 614 (1963)
99 ALR6th 113—§ 10
State v. Swett, 158 Or. App. 28, 972 P.2d 909 (1999)
71 ALR5th 1—§ 41
State v. Swett, 1998 ME 76, 709 A.2d 729 (Me. 1998)
56 ALR6th 323—§ 7, 9
State v. Swick, 1992 WL 147398 (Ohio Ct. App. 5th Dist. Licking County 1992)
103 ALR6th 347—§ 10
State v. Swift, 173 Wis. 2d 870, 496 N.W.2d 713, CCH Blue Sky L. Rep. ¶ 73806, RICO Bus Disp Guide (CCH) ¶ 8226 (App. 1993)

33 ALR5th 453—§ 4, 6
State v. Swift, 232 Ga. 535, 207 S.E.2d 459 (1974)
82 ALR5th 103—§ 5
116 ALR5th 479—§ 7
State v. Swiger, 175 W. Va. 578, 336 S.E.2d 541 (1985)
70 ALR5th 1—§ 9
State v. Swinburne, 116 Ariz. 403, 569 P.2d 833 (1977)
42 ALR6th 237—§ 5
State v. Swindell, 271 S.W.2d 533 (Mo. 1954)
99 ALR6th 113—§ 10
State v. Swingler, 632 S.W.2d 267 (Mo. Ct. App. E.D. 1982)
30 ALR6th 103—§ 26, 34, 58
State v. Swink, 2000 UT App 262, 11 P.3d 299 (Utah Ct. App. 2000)
38 ALR6th 97—§ 3, 5
State v. Swinney, 280 Kan. 768, 127 P.3d 261 (2006)
67 ALR6th 531—§ 6, 37
State v. Swinney, 1989 WL 86260 (Ohio Ct. App. 4th Dist. Pickaway County 1989)
38 ALR6th 97—§ 16
State v. Swinson, 940 S.W.2d 552 (Mo. Ct. App. S.D. 1997)
92 ALR6th 295—§ 12, 24
96 ALR6th 355—§ 12
State v. Swinton, 268 Conn. 781, 847 A.2d 921 (2004)
1 ALR6th 657—§ 6, 10
State v. Swires, 1988 WL 99184 (Ohio Ct. App. 9th Dist. Wayne County 1988)
4 ALR6th 599—§ 13
State v. Swise, 100 N.M. 256, 669 P.2d 732 (1983)
58 ALR6th 439—§ 29
State v. Switchenko, 3 Conn. Cir. 511, 217 A.2d 484 (1965)
52 ALR5th 655—§ 2, 4
State v. Switzer, 22 Ohio St. 2d 47, 51 Ohio Ops. 2d 69, 257 N.E.2d 908 (1970)
50 ALR5th 703—§ 31

State v. Sword, 68 Haw. 343, 713 P.2d 432 (1986)

79 ALR6th 125—§ 32

State v. Sword, 229 Mont. 370, 747 P.2d 206 (1987)

97 ALR5th 201—§ 7

State v. Sykes, 35 Kan. App. 2d 517, 132 P.3d 485 (2006)

26 ALR6th 511—§ 25

State v. Sykes, 194 Mont. 14, 663 P.2d 691 (1983)

19 ALR5th 470—§ 6

State v. Sykes, 412 N.W.2d 578 (Iowa 1987)

35 ALR6th 497—§ 23, 37

State v. Sylvester, 118 Wash. App. 1020, 2003 WL 21964885 (Div. 2 2003)

125 ALR5th 537—§ 25

State v. Symonds, 57 Me. 148, 1869 WL 2220 (1869)

10 ALR6th 31—§ 2

State v. Syriani, 333 N.C. 350, 428 S.E.2d 118 (1993)

24 ALR5th 465—§ 7, 14, 52 to 57, 59, 60, 62 to 69

83 ALR6th 255—§ 9

State v. Syrotchen, 61 Wash. App. 261, 810 P.2d 64 (Div. 1 1991)

51 ALR6th 1—§ 20, 28

State v. Sysinger, 25 S.D. 110, 125 N.W. 879 (1910)

51 ALR5th 603—§ 2, 3, 14

State v. Szabo, 166 Conn. 289, 348 A.2d 588 (1974)

57 ALR6th 83—§ 5

State v. Szarek, 433 A.2d 193 (R.I. 1981)

26 ALR5th 1—§ 4, 29 to 31, 33

State v. Szarkowitz, 157 Wis. 2d 740, 460 N.W.2d 819 (Ct. App. 1990)

92 ALR5th 35—§ 7

State v. Szemple, 135 N.J. 406, 640 A.2d 817 (1994)

51 ALR5th 603—§ 2, 3, 14

93 ALR5th 327—§ 7, 32

101 ALR5th 619—§ 3, 5

State v. $2,434.00 Cash, 461 N.W.2d 346 (Iowa Ct. App. 1990)

4 ALR6th 113—§ 11

State v. $10,000 Seized from Mary Patrick, 562 N.W.2d 192 (Iowa Ct. App. 1997)

4 ALR6th 113—§ 12, 18, 37, 39

State v. $29,177.00 U.S. Currency, 638 So. 2d 653 (La. Ct. App. 3d Cir. 1994)

4 ALR6th 113—§ 19, 31, 40

State v. $36,560.00 in U.S. Currency, 289 N.J. Super. 237, 673 A.2d 810 (App. Div. 1996)

4 ALR6th 113—§ 20

State v. Tabasko, 22 Ohio St. 2d 36, 51 Ohio Ops. 2d 64, 257 N.E.2d 744 (1970)

24 ALR5th 428—§ 2, 11

State v. Tabler, 178 Ind. App. 31, 381 N.E.2d 502 (1978)

5 ALR5th 875—§ 3

State v. Tabor, 678 S.W.2d 45 (Tenn. 1984)

6 ALR5th 733—§ 2, 6, 26

69 ALR6th 207—§ 9

State v. Tackett, 2007-Ohio-556, 2007 WL 428182 (Ohio Ct. App. 5th Dist. Licking County 2007)

71 ALR6th 625—§ 18

State v. Tackitt, 2003 MT 81, 315 Mont. 59, 67 P.3d 295, 117 A.L.R.5th 743 (2003)

117 ALR5th 407—§ 3

State v. Taffaro, 2007 WL 737803 (N.J. Super. Ct. App. Div. 2007)

40 ALR6th 355—§ 9

State v. Tafoya, 105 N.M. 117, 729 P.2d 1371 (Ct. App. 1986)

59 ALR5th 1—§ 3, 6

State v. Tages, 10 Ariz. App. 127, 457 P.2d 289 (1969)

66 ALR5th 397—§ 4, 9

State v. Taggart, 7 Or. App. 479, 491 P.2d 1187 (1971)

61 ALR5th 1—§ 3, 7

State v. Taggart, 14 Or. App. 408, 512 P.2d 1359 (1973)

61 ALR5th 1—§ 4, 5

State v. Tague, 188 Kan. 462, 363 P.2d 454 (1961)

97 ALR5th 293—§ 3

State v. Talarico, 2003 SD 41, 661 N.W.2d 11 (S.D. 2003)

19 ALR6th 697—§ 10

23 ALR6th 1—§ 15

State v. Talbert, 873 S.W.2d 321 (Mo. App. 1994)

37 ALR5th 1—§ 2

State v. Talbot, 24 Or. App. 379, 545 P.2d 599 (1976)

39 ALR5th 283—§ 4

State v. Talbot, 71 N.J. 160, 364 A.2d 9 (1976)

9 ALR5th 464—§ 5, 9

18 ALR5th 1—§ 4

State v. Talbot, 792 P.2d 489 (Utah Ct. App. 1990)

74 ALR5th 319—§ 14

State v. Taliaferro, 2 Ohio App. 3d 405, 442 N.E.2d 481 (10th Dist. Franklin County 1981)

82 ALR5th 359—§ 4

84 ALR5th 487—§ 19, 21, 25

State v. Tallchief, 84 P.3d 636 (Kan. Ct. App. 2004)

31 ALR6th 49—§ 4

State v. Tallent, 1991 WL 43554 (Tenn. Crim. App. 1991)

76 ALR5th 1—§ 20

State v. Talley, 14 Wash. App. 484, 543 P.2d 348 (1975)

61 ALR5th 1—§ 4, 8

State v. Talley, 18 Ohio St. 3d 152, 18 Ohio B.R. 210, 480 N.E.2d 439 (1985)

39 ALR5th 283—§ 14

State v. Talley, 103 N.M. 33, 702 P.2d 353 (Ct. App. 1985)

78 ALR5th 197—§ 14

State v. Talley, 110 N.C. App. 180, 429 S.E.2d 604 (1993)

6 ALR5th 733—§ 4, 16

State v. Talley, 122 Wash. 2d 192, 858 P.2d 217 (1993)

22 ALR5th 261—§ 2, 4 to 7

State v. Talley, 573 So. 2d 1192 (La. App. 4th Cir. 1991)

7 ALR5th 263—§ 7

State v. Talley, 2006 WL 2947435 (Tenn. Crim. App. 2006)

84 ALR6th 229—§ 14

State v. Tamez, 506 So. 2d 531 (La. App. 1st Cir. 1987)

32 ALR5th 149—§ 15, 50, 51, 54, 59, 69, 71

State v. Tamplin, 126 Ariz. 175, 613 P.2d 839 (Ct. App. Div. 2 1980)

80 ALR5th 55—§ 6

State v. Tamplin, 146 Ariz. 377, 706 P.2d 389 (Ct. App. Div. 2 1985)

42 ALR6th 237—§ 15

State v. Tanaka, 67 Haw. 658, 701 P.2d 1274 (1985)

62 ALR5th 1—§ 4, 15

State v. Tanguay, 388 A.2d 913 (Me. 1978)

34 ALR6th 1—§ 12

State v. Tankersley, 191 Ariz. 359, 956 P.2d 486 (1998)

90 ALR5th 453—§ 28

1 ALR6th 657—§ 15

State v. Tanley, 172 Minn. 372, 215 N.W. 514 (1927)

98 ALR6th 455—§ 12

State v. Tanner, 54 Wash. 2d 535, 341 P.2d 869 (1959)

119 ALR5th 275—§ 2

State v. Tanner, 90 Ohio App. 3d 761, 630 N.E.2d 751 (Franklin Co. 1993)

57 ALR5th 141—§ 12

State v. Tanner, 224 La. 374, 69 So. 2d 505 (1953)

85 ALR5th 547—§ 6

State v. Tanner, 304 Or. 312, 745 P.2d 757 (1987)

19 ALR5th 470—§ 2, 3

State v. Tanner, 534 So. 2d 535, 9 U.S.P.Q.2d 1898 (La. Ct. App. 5th Cir. 1988)

87 ALR6th 1—§ 41

State v. Tanner, 534 So. 2d 535, 9 U.S.P.Q.2d (BNA) 1898 (La. Ct. App. 5th Cir. 1988)

84 ALR5th 1—§ 3, 7

State v. Tanner, 1995 WL 116682 (Ohio Ct. App. 4 Dist. Ross County 1995)

60 ALR5th 1—§ 6

State v. Tannyhill, 90 Kan. 598, 135 P. 674 (1913)

66 ALR5th 397—§ 23

State v. Tapia, 89 N.M. 221, 549 P.2d 636 (App. 1976)

29 ALR5th 59—§ 19, 24, 79

State v. Tapia, 113 N.J. Super. 322, 273 A.2d 769 (1971)

51 ALR5th 603—§ 2, 8

State v. Tapia, 113 N.J. Super. 322, 273 A.2d 769 (App. Div. 1971)

66 ALR6th 83—§ 4

State v. Taplin, 36 Wash. App. 664, 676 P.2d 504 (Div. 1 1984)

64 ALR5th 741—§ 4

State v. Tapp, 136 Idaho 354, 33 P.3d 828 (Ct. App. 2001)

20 ALR6th 479—§ 12

State v. Tapp, 353 So. 2d 265 (La. 1977)

64 ALR5th 741—§ 3, 4

State v. Tapp, 788 So. 2d 1215 (La. Ct. App. 4th Cir. 2001)

34 ALR6th 1—§ 10

State v. Tapply, 124 N.H. 318, 470 A.2d 900 (1983)

124 ALR5th 1—§ 5

State v. Tarango, 105 N.M. 592, 734 P.2d 1275 (Ct. App. 1987)

52 ALR6th 1—§ 34
70 ALR6th 361—§ 5
71 ALR6th 335—§ 5, 8, 13

State v. Tarantino, 587 A.2d 1095 (Me. 1991)

19 ALR5th 470—§ 3

State v. Taravella, 2003-Ohio-4880, 2003 WL 22120272 (Ohio Ct. App. 7th Dist. Harrison County 2003)

3 ALR6th 543—§ 10

State v. Tardiff, 117 N.H. 53, 369 A.2d 182 (1977)

52 ALR5th 655—§ 2, 4

State v. Tarnavsky, 84 Wash. App. 1056, 1996 WL 742400 (Div. 3 1996)

70 ALR6th 329—§ 13, 15

State v. Tarrance, 252 La. 396, 211 So. 2d 304 (1968)

28 ALR6th 505—§ 34

State v. Tarver, 137 N.M. 115, 2005-NMCA-030, 108 P.3d 1 (Ct. App. 2005)

56 ALR6th 553—§ 18

State v. Tarver, 272 N.J. Super. 414, 640 A.2d 314 (App. Div. 1994)

27 ALR5th 593—§ 17, 35

State v. Tarver, 2005-Ohio-3119, 2005 WL 1463240 (Ohio Ct. App. 5th Dist. Stark County 2005)

30 ALR6th 1—§ 4, 5

State v. Tarvis, 465 A.2d 164 (R.I. 1983)

16 ALR6th 329—§ 11
24 ALR6th 591—§ 9

State v. Tarwid, 147 Wis. 2d 95, 433 N.W.2d 255 (Ct. App. 1988)

55 ALR6th 391—§ 21

State v. Tasker, 469 A.2d 1254 (Me. 1984)

6 ALR5th 733—§ 7, 17

State v. Tassone, 431 A.2d 1217 (R.I. 1981)

76 ALR5th 485—§ 15

State v. Tata, Ohio App. Case No 1134, Slip Opinion (Greene Co. 1981)

45 ALR5th 1—§ 2, 5, 6, 8, 26, 27

State v. Tate, 102 N.J. 64, 505 A.2d 941 (1986)

1 ALR5th 938—§ 3
50 ALR6th 353—§ 48

State v. Tate, 130 So. 3d 829, 102 A.L.R.6th 865 (La. 2013)

102 ALR6th 637—§ 3, 5, 7, 8

State v. Tate, 196 Mont. 248, 639 P.2d 1149 (1982)

11 ALR6th 237—§ 4, 8

State v. Tate, 341 N.W.2d 63 (Iowa App. 1983)

18 ALR5th 804—§ 2, 6

State v. Tate, 407 So. 2d 1131 (La. 1981)

112 ALR5th 429—§ 3

State v. Tate, 407 So. 2d 1133 (La. 1981)

6 ALR6th 533—§ 21

State v. Tate, 582 S.W.2d 329 (Mo. Ct. App. W.D. 1979)
70 ALR5th 587—§ 3

State v. Tate, 653 S.E.2d 892 (N.C. Ct. App. 2007)
30 ALR6th 1—§ 7

State v. Tate, 657 So. 2d 567 (La. Ct. App. 4th Cir. 1995)
19 ALR6th 115—§ 4, 9, 11

State v. Tate, 682 N.W.2d 169, 18 A.L.R.6th 895 (Minn. Ct. App. 2004)
18 ALR6th 629—§ 34
18 ALR6th 775—§ 4

State v. Tate, 851 So. 2d 921 (La. 2003)
122 ALR5th 145—§ 9, 23

State v. Tate, 1989 WL 102503 (Tenn. Crim. App. 1989)
73 ALR5th 383—§ 3

State v. Tatro, 2009-Ohio-2968, 2009 WL 1744492 (Ohio Ct. App. 5th Dist. Coshocton County 2009)
64 ALR6th 1—§ 7, 9, 11

State v. Tatum, 2008 WL 2601390 (Del. Super. Ct. 2008)
71 ALR6th 1—§ 12

State v. Taua, 98 Haw. 426, 49 P.3d 1227 (2002)
117 ALR5th 407—§ 4

State v. Tavares, 63 Hawaii 509, 630 P.2d 633 (1981)
7 ALR5th 263—§ 3, 4

State v. Tavares, 110 Haw. 283, 132 P.3d 851 (2006)
58 ALR6th 215—§ 17

State v. Tavares, 364 N.J. Super. 496, 837 A.2d 398 (App. Div. 2003)
50 ALR6th 455—§ 15, 34

State v. Tavera, 2011 WL 675921 (Tenn. Crim. App. 2011)
70 ALR6th 1—§ 25

State v. Taveras, 2009 WL 1887150 (N.J. Super. Ct. App. Div. 2009)
57 ALR6th 313—§ 6

State v. Taylor, 2 P.3d 674 (Ariz. Ct. App. Div. 2 1999)
71 ALR5th 637—§ 5

State v. Taylor, 8 N.C. App. 544, 174 S.E.2d 872 (1970)
26 ALR5th 765—§ 23

State v. Taylor, 18 S.W.3d 366 (Mo. 2000)
79 ALR5th 33—§ 56

State v. Taylor, 27 Ariz. App. 140, 551 P.2d 589 (Div. 1 1976)
80 ALR6th 599—§ 6

State v. Taylor, 27 Kan. App. 2d 62, 998 P.2d 123 (2000)
65 ALR6th 1—§ 26

State v. Taylor, 28 Conn. Supp. 19, 246 A.2d 898 (Super. Ct. 1968)
112 ALR5th 429—§ 15

State v. Taylor, 30 S.D. 304, 138 N.W. 372 (1912)
102 ALR5th 227—§ 6

State v. Taylor, 31 Or. App. 135, 571 P.2d 508 (1977)
6 ALR6th 533—§ 19

State v. Taylor, 38 N.J. Super. 6, 118 A.2d 36 (App. Div. 1955)
66 ALR5th 397—§ 14
52 ALR6th 125—§ 18, 44

State v. Taylor, 46 So. 3d 504 (Ala. Crim. App. 2010)
92 ALR6th 171—§ 4

State v. Taylor, 51 Ohio App. 3d 173, 555 N.E.2d 649 (8th Dist. Cuyahoga County 1988)
51 ALR6th 1—§ 3, 19
70 ALR6th 361—§ 3

State v. Taylor, 59 Or. App. 396, 650 P.2d 1090 (1982)
58 ALR6th 215—§ 4

State v. Taylor, 60 Wis. 2d 506, 210 N.W.2d 873 (1973)
103 ALR6th 347—§ 16

State v. Taylor, 63 Conn. App. 386, 776 A.2d 1154 (2001)
51 ALR6th 1—§ 5

State v. Taylor, 67 Wash. App. 350, 835 P.2d 245 (1992)
36 ALR5th 161—§ 3

State v. Taylor, 67 Wash. App. 350, 835 P.2d 245 (Div. 1 1992)

63 ALR6th 351—§ 3
State v. Taylor, 80 N.J. 353, 403 A.2d 889 (1979)
9 ALR6th 633—§ 4, 11
15 ALR6th 173—§ 36
State v. Taylor, 86 Wash. App. 442, 936 P.2d 1218 (Div. 1 1997)
15 ALR5th 391—§ 50
State v. Taylor, 90 Wash. App. 312, 950 P.2d 526 (Div. 2 1998)
39 ALR5th 283—§ 71
State v. Taylor, 101 Wash. 148, 172 P. 217 (1918)
90 ALR6th 385—§ 2
State v. Taylor, 104 N.M. 88, 717 P.2d 64 (Ct. App. 1986)
92 ALR5th 35—§ 22
State v. Taylor, 106 Ohio App. 3d 741, 667 N.E.2d 60 (Montgomery Co. 1995)
37 ALR5th 1—§ 3
State v. Taylor, 109 Wash. 2d 438, 745 P.2d 510 (1987)
26 ALR5th 603—§ 4
State v. Taylor, 112 Ariz. 68, 537 P.2d 938 (1975)
85 ALR5th 187—§ 12, 15
29 ALR6th 1—§ 10
State v. Taylor, 118 N.H. 855, 395 A.2d 505 (1978)
81 ALR5th 563—§ 3, 5, 8, 10
State v. Taylor, 123 S.W.3d 924 (Mo. Ct. App. S.D. 2004)
3 ALR6th 543—§ 6
State v. Taylor, 128 N.C. App. 394, 496 S.E.2d 811 (1998)
121 ALR5th 551—§ 2, 6, 12
State v. Taylor, 132 N.H. 314, 566 A.2d 172 (1989)
119 ALR5th 379—§ 7
State v. Taylor, 134 S.W.3d 21 (Mo. 2004)
122 ALR5th 145—§ 3
83 ALR6th 255—§ 1, 12, 15, 22
State v. Taylor, 135 P.3d 766 (Kan. 2006)
26 ALR6th 511—§ 25

State v. Taylor, 142 N.H. 6, 694 A.2d 977 (1997)
88 ALR5th 67—§ 5
State v. Taylor, 144 Ohio App. 3d 255, 759 N.E.2d 1281 (2d Dist. Darke County 2001)
58 ALR6th 499—§ 51
State v. Taylor, 163 Mont. 106, 515 P.2d 695 (1973)
119 ALR5th 275—§ 7
State v. Taylor, 173 La. 1010, 139 So. 463 (1931)
16 ALR6th 329—§ 4
24 ALR6th 591—§ 4, 14
State v. Taylor, 174 Ohio App. 3d 477, 2007-Ohio-7066, 882 N.E.2d 945 (1st Dist. Hamilton County 2007)
35 ALR6th 497—§ 37
State v. Taylor, 178 N.C. App. 395, 632 S.E.2d 218 (2006)
34 ALR6th 253—§ 7
State v. Taylor, 196 Conn. 225, 492 A.2d 155 (1985)
57 ALR6th 445—§ 3, 49
State v. Taylor, 203 Mont. 284, 661 P.2d 33 (1983)
92 ALR6th 295—§ 12
93 ALR6th 207—§ 6
95 ALR6th 1—§ 4, 30
96 ALR6th 355—§ 37
State v. Taylor, 231 Kan. 171, 642 P.2d 989 (1982)
32 ALR6th 1—§ 11
State v. Taylor, 234 Kan. 401, 673 P.2d 1140 (1983)
29 ALR6th 1—§ 10
State v. Taylor, 249 Or. 268, 437 P.2d 853 (1968)
57 ALR6th 83—§ 5
State v. Taylor, 266 S.W.3d 553 (Tex. App. Tyler 2008)
69 ALR6th 1—§ 9
State v. Taylor, 290 Minn. 515, 187 N.W.2d 129 (1971)
86 ALR5th 59—§ 3, 4
State v. Taylor, 293 Mo. 210, 238 S.W. 489 (1922)

24 ALR6th 747—§ 17, 18
State v. Taylor, 303 So. 2d 169 (La. 1974)
55 ALR5th 125—§ 3, 9
State v. Taylor, 332 N.C. 372, 420 S.E.2d 414 (1992)
57 ALR5th 141—§ 5, 7
State v. Taylor, 333 S.C. 159, 508 S.E.2d 870 (1998)
27 ALR6th 183—§ 32
State v. Taylor, 337 N.C. 597, 447 S.E.2d 360 (1994)
81 ALR5th 563—§ 3
State v. Taylor, 344 N.C. 31, 473 S.E.2d 596 (1996)
54 ALR6th 429—§ 9
State v. Taylor, 347 So. 2d 172 (La. 1977)
7 ALR5th 263—§ 5
70 ALR5th 587—§ 3, 6
State v. Taylor, 356 Mo. 1216, 205 S.W.2d 734 (1947)
70 ALR5th 587—§ 3
State v. Taylor, 422 So. 2d 109 (La. 1982)
94 ALR5th 393—§ 5
State v. Taylor, 456 S.W.2d 9 (Mo. 1970)
101 ALR5th 351—§ 14
State v. Taylor, 468 So. 2d 617 (La. Ct. App. 2d Cir. 1985)
65 ALR5th 407—§ 3
76 ALR5th 563—§ 4, 5
101 ALR6th 331—§ 22, 25
State v. Taylor, 482 So. 2d 578 (Fla. Dist. Ct. App. 5th Dist. 1986)
106 ALR5th 377—§ 3
State v. Taylor, 485 So. 2d 117 (La. App. 2d Cir. 1986)
19 ALR5th 823—§ 2, 9, 11
State v. Taylor, 486 S.W.2d 239 (Mo. 1972)
111 ALR5th 1—§ 3, 5, 7, 27
State v. Taylor, 501 So. 2d 816 (La. Ct. App. 4th Cir. 1986)
4 ALR6th 599—§ 13

State v. Taylor, 506 N.W.2d 767 (Iowa 1993)
15 ALR5th 391—§ 45
State v. Taylor, 510 So. 2d 849 (Ala. App. 1986)
41 ALR5th 171—§ 2, 14
State v. Taylor, 538 P.2d 310 (Utah 1975)
37 ALR6th 357—§ 37, 41
State v. Taylor, 562 A.2d 445 (R.I. 1989)
39 ALR5th 283—§ 4, 54
State v. Taylor, 570 P.2d 697 (Utah 1977)
29 ALR5th 59—§ 7
State v. Taylor, 621 A.2d 1252 (R.I. 1993)
4 ALR6th 599—§ 5, 21
State v. Taylor, 650 N.W.2d 190 (Minn. 2002)
125 ALR5th 357—§ 9
7 ALR6th 233—§ 17
State v. Taylor, 661 A.2d 665 (Me. 1995)
39 ALR5th 283—§ 4, 66
State v. Taylor, 669 So. 2d 364 (La. 1996)
79 ALR5th 33—§ 25, 42, 52, 59, 63
State v. Taylor, 688 So. 2d 1262 (La. Ct. App. 3d Cir. 1997)
57 ALR5th 141—§ 12
State v. Taylor, 701 So. 2d 766 (La. Ct. App. 4th Cir. 1997)
55 ALR6th 391—§ 21
State v. Taylor, 729 S.W.2d 483 (Mo. Ct. App. W.D. 1987)
70 ALR6th 361—§ 28
State v. Taylor, 735 S.W.2d 412 (Mo. Ct. App. S.D. 1987)
85 ALR5th 547—§ 7, 8
State v. Taylor, 757 So. 2d 63 (La. Ct. App. 5th Cir. 2000)
85 ALR5th 1—§ 29
State v. Taylor, 771 S.W.2d 387 (Tenn. 1989)
99 ALR6th 295—§ 8
State v. Taylor, 818 P.2d 561, 169 Utah Adv. Rep. 62 (Utah App. 1991)
12 ALR5th 89—§ 2

State v. Taylor, 850 So. 2d 5 (La. Ct. App. 4th Cir. 2003)

7 ALR6th 233—§ 9

State v. Taylor, 993 S.W.2d 33 (Tenn. 1999)

83 ALR5th 277—§ 9

State v. Taylor, 1983 WL 5896 (Ohio Ct. App. 8th Dist.Cuyahoga County 1983)

57 ALR5th 141—§ 12

State v. Taylor, 1990 WL 50751 (Tenn. Crim. App. 1990)

73 ALR5th 383—§ 3

State v. Taylor, 1991 WL 205649 (Ohio Ct. App. 8th Dist.Cuyahoga County 1991)

57 ALR5th 141—§ 3

State v. Taylor, 1995 WL 356761 (Conn. Super. Ct. 1995)

79 ALR6th 325—§ 3, 6, 7

State v. Taylor, 1998 WL 849324 (Tenn. Crim. App. 1998)

79 ALR5th 237—§ 3, 11

State v. Taylor, 1999 WL 965445 (Ohio Ct. App. 12th Dist. Clermont County 1999)

85 ALR5th 1—§ 24

State v. Taylor, 2003-Ohio-6963, 2003 WL 22994561 (Ohio Ct. App. 11th Dist. Geauga County 2003)

65 ALR6th 1—§ 18

State v. Taylor, 2006-Ohio-6813, 2006 WL 3759554 (Ohio Ct. App. 2d Dist. Miami County 2006)

34 ALR6th 253—§ 3, 13

State v. Taylor, 2008 WL 624913 (Tenn. Crim. App. 2008)

99 ALR6th 295—§ 13

State v. Taylor, 2009-Ohio-6496, 2009 WL 4727835 (Ohio Ct. App. 6th Dist. Huron County 2009)

71 ALR6th 1—§ 5

State v. Taylor, No. 42117 (December 11, 1980, Ct. App. Ohio, 8th App. Dist. Cuyahoga Co.)

39 ALR5th 283—§ 14, 71

State v. Tayse, 2013-Ohio-5801, 2013 WL 6870033 (Ohio Ct. App. 9th Dist. Summit County 2013)

97 ALR6th 263—§ 7

State v. T.B.D., 656 So. 2d 479, 20 FLW S. 274 (Fla. 1995)

22 ALR5th 261—§ 4, 6

State v. Teague, 175 S.W.3d 167 (Mo. Ct. App. S.D. 2005)

37 ALR6th 357—§ 52, 76

State v. Teague, 645 S.W.2d 392 (Tenn. 1983)

37 ALR5th 515—§ 2, 3

State v. Teague, 1992 WL 331038 (Tenn. Crim. App. 1992)

113 ALR5th 517—§ 18

State v. Teal, 624 S.W.2d 122 (Mo. App. 1981)

5 ALR5th 243—§ 48

State v. Teamer, 82 Ohio St. 3d 490, 696 N.E.2d 1049 (1998)

4 ALR5th 1—§ 7

State v. Teasley, 82 N.C. App. 150, 346 S.E.2d 227 (1986)

115 ALR5th 403—§ 5
34 ALR6th 539—§ 5

State v. Teasley, 1993 WL 481403 (Tenn. Crim. App. 1993)

73 ALR5th 383—§ 3

State v. Tedder, 62 N.C. App. 12, 302 S.E.2d 318 (1983)

15 ALR5th 391—§ 16

State v. Tedder, 169 N.C. App. 446, 610 S.E.2d 774 (2005)

17 ALR6th 757—§ 4

State v. Tedford, 195 Ga. App. 372, 393 S.E.2d 502 (1990)

6 ALR6th 533—§ 22

State v. Teel, 103 N.M. 684, 712 P.2d 792 (Ct. App. 1985)

23 ALR6th 1—§ 14, 15, 24

State v. Teeter, 85 N.C. App. 624, 355 S.E.2d 804 (1987)

24 ALR6th 549—§ 4

State v. Teeter, 239 Mo. 475, 144 S.W. 445 (1912)

104 ALR5th 357—§ 7

State v. Teets, 2008 MT 130, 343 Mont. 73, 183 P.3d 45 (2008)
46 ALR6th 241—§ 5

State v. T.E.H., 91 Wash. App. 908, 960 P.2d 441 (Div. 1 1998)
18 ALR5th 856—§ 5

State v. Teigen, 381 N.W.2d 529 (Minn. Ct. App. 1986)
84 ALR6th 293—§ 32

State v. Teitle, 117 Vt. 190, 90 A.2d 562 (1952)
84 ALR5th 69—§ 17
85 ALR5th 187—§ 12

State v. Telfair, 637 S.W.2d 179 (Mo. Ct. App. E.D. 1982)
103 ALR6th 347—§ 6, 13

State v. Telford, 420 N.J. Super. 465, 22 A.3d 43 (App. Div. 2011)
74 ALR6th 373—§ 5

State v. Telford, 940 P.2d 522 (Utah Ct. App. 1997)
16 ALR6th 329—§ 6
24 ALR6th 591—§ 4, 12

State v. Tella, 113 R.I. 303, 321 A.2d 87 (1974)
6 ALR6th 533—§ 10, 20

State v. Teller Native Corp., 904 P.2d 847 (Alaska 1995)
107 ALR5th 311—§ 2, 3
109 ALR5th 421—§ 12

State v. Tellez, 6 Ariz. App. 251, 431 P.2d 691, 25 A.L.R.3d 1063 (1967)
55 ALR6th 513—§ 5

State v. Tellier, 526 A.2d 941 (Me. 1987)
82 ALR5th 591—§ 2, 8

State v. Tellington, 2005-Ohio-470, 2005 WL 293518 (Ohio Ct. App. 9th Dist. Summit County 2005)
45 ALR6th 337—§ 32

State v. Temple, 65 Hawaii 261, 650 P.2d 1358 (1982)
24 ALR5th 132—§ 4, 7
29 ALR5th 59—§ 7, 31

State v. Temple, 302 N.C. 1, 273 S.E.2d 273 (1981)
1 ALR6th 657—§ 4

State v. Templeton, 22 Or. App. 322, 538 P.2d 950 (1975)
34 ALR5th 125—§ 13

State v. Tenerelli, 583 N.W.2d 1 (Minn. Ct. App. 1998)
15 ALR5th 391—§ 5

State v. Tenerelli, 598 N.W.2d 668 (Minn. 1999)
15 ALR5th 391—§ 5

State v. Tenley, 179 W. Va. 209, 366 S.E.2d 657 (1988)
124 ALR5th 1—§ 4

State v. Tennant, 173 W. Va. 627, 319 S.E.2d 395 (1984)
26 ALR5th 1—§ 3, 50

State v. Tennant, 262 La. 941, 265 So. 2d 230 (1972)
99 ALR6th 295—§ 5

State v. Tenney, 143 Vt. 213, 464 A.2d 747 (1983)
50 ALR5th 703—§ 15

State v. Tenney, 1997 WL 224970 (Ohio Ct. App. 6th Dist. Lucas County 1997)
84 ALR6th 293—§ 18

State v. Tenney, 2003 ME 100, 828 A.2d 755 (Me. 2003)
19 ALR6th 697—§ 3, 4

State v. Tensley, 249 N.W.2d 659 (Iowa 1977)
66 ALR6th 83—§ 11

State v. Teran, 71 Wash. App. 668, 862 P.2d 137 (Div. 3 1993)
49 ALR6th 343—§ 9

State v. Terline, 23 R.I. 530, 51 A. 204 (1902)
97 ALR6th 567—§ 4, 10

State v. Ternaku, 156 N.J. Super. 30, 383 A.2d 437 (App. Div. 1978)
70 ALR6th 361—§ 19

State v. Ternes, 92 Ohio Misc.2d 76, 700 N.E.2d 435 (Ohio Mun. 1998)
66 ALR5th 397—§ 21

State v. Terrazas, 162 Ariz. 357, 783 P.2d 803 (Ct. App. Div. 1 1989)
97 ALR6th 567—§ 3, 9

State v. Terrell, 156 Ariz. 499, 753 P.2d
189 (Ct. App. Div. 2 1988)
82 ALR5th 359—§ 3
84 ALR5th 487—§ 25

State v. Terrell, 283 N.W.2d 529 (Minn.
1979)
58 ALR6th 499—§ 18

State v. Terrell, 1981 WL 3816 (Ohio
Ct. App. 1st Dist. Hamilton County
1981)
99 ALR6th 295—§ 10

State v. Terrill, 241 N.W.2d 16 (Iowa
1976)
86 ALR5th 59—§ 5

State v. Terrovona, 105 Wash. 2d 632,
716 P.2d 295 (1986)
57 ALR5th 141—§ 5

State v. Terry, 239 Wis. 2d 519
2 ALR5th 262—§ 3, 6

State v. Terry, 333 Or. 163, 37 P.3d 157
(2001)
110 ALR5th 1—§ 3, 14
32 ALR6th 1—§ 11

State v. Teter, 633 S.W.2d 417 (Mo.
App. 1982)
26 ALR5th 1—§ 4, 25, 29

State v. Tettamble, 450 S.W.2d 191
(Mo. 1970)
45 ALR5th 591—§ 15

State v. Tetzlaff, 75 Wash. 2d 649, 453
P.2d 638 (1969)
38 ALR6th 97—§ 28

State v. Tetzner, 221 Wis. 2d 598, 586
N.W.2d 699 (Ct. App. 1998)
56 ALR6th 185—§ 39

State v. Teuber, 19 Wash. App. 651, 577
P.2d 147 (Div. 1 1978)
24 ALR6th 1—§ 13

State v. Texas Elec. Service Co., 488
S.W.2d 878 (Tex. Civ. App. Fort
Worth 1972)
29 ALR6th 507—§ 27, 52, 61

State v. Texel, 230 Neb. 810, 433
N.W.2d 541 (1989)
62 ALR5th 1—§ 3

State v. Texter, 896 A.2d 40 (R.I. 2006)
92 ALR6th 1—§ 3

State v. T.G., 800 So. 2d 204 (Fla. 2001)
101 ALR5th 351—§ 9

State v. Thackston, 289 Ga. 412, 716
S.E.2d 517 (2011)
92 ALR6th 1—§ 3, 9

State v. Thackston, 289 Ga. 412, 716
S.E.2d 517, 92 A.L.R.6th 645
(2011)
91 ALR6th 435—§ 153

State v. Thaggard, 527 N.W.2d 804
(Minn. 1995)
69 ALR6th 579—§ 8

State v. Thames, 316 Wis. 2d 357, 2009
WI App 21, 763 N.W.2d 249 (Ct.
App. 2008)
56 ALR6th 185—§ 39

State v. Thames, 599 N.W.2d 122
(Minn. 1999)
3 ALR6th 269—§ 25

State v. Tharp, 27 Wash. App. 198, 616
P.2d 693 (1980)
37 ALR5th 515—§ 3

State v. Tharpe, 726 S.W.2d 896 (Tenn.
1987)
29 ALR5th 59—§ 3, 9

State v. Theis, 2003-Ohio-1968, 2003
WL 1901343 (Ohio Ct. App. 8th
Dist. Cuyahoga County 2003)
19 ALR6th 411—§ 26

State v. Theison, 709 P.2d 307 (Utah
1985)
69 ALR6th 1—§ 5

State v. Theoferlius D., 93 Conn. App.
88, 888 A.2d 118 (2006)
33 ALR6th 91—§ 29

State v. Theroff, 33 Wash. App. 741, 657
P.2d 800 (Div. 3 1983)
92 ALR5th 35—§ 27

State v. Therriault, 485 A.2d 986 (Me.
1984)
111 ALR5th 1—§ 2, 3, 7, 38

State v. Therrien, 117 Conn. App. 256,
978 A.2d 556 (2009)
72 ALR6th 437—§ 21

State v. Theuring, 46 Ohio App. 3d 152,
546 N.E.2d 436 (Hamilton Co.
1988)
15 ALR5th 391—§ 30

State v. Thibeault, 621 A.2d 418 (Me. 1993)
27 ALR6th 183—§ 5, 24, 34
State v. Thibodeau, 317 A.2d 172 (Me. 1974)
29 ALR5th 59—§ 3
68 ALR5th 343—§ 3
State v. Thibodeau, 496 A.2d 635 (Me. 1985)
28 ALR6th 505—§ 18
34 ALR6th 1—§ 9
State v. Thibodeaux, 48 La. Ann. 600, 19 So. 680 (1896)
105 ALR5th 529—§ 24
State v. Thibodeaux, 315 So. 2d 769 (La. 1975)
19 ALR6th 115—§ 4, 9, 11
24 ALR6th 591—§ 6, 14
State v. Thibodeaux, 341 N.C. 53, 459 S.E.2d 501 (1995)
69 ALR6th 579—§ 4
State v. Thien Duc Le, 743 S.W.2d 199 (Tenn. Crim. 1987)
32 ALR5th 149—§ 4, 29, 32
State v. Thill, 474 N.W.2d 86 (S.D. 1991)
74 ALR5th 319—§ 7, 13
State v. Thom, 615 So. 2d 355 (La. App. 5th Cir. 1993)
38 ALR5th 433—§ 28, 48
State v. Thom, 615 So. 2d 355 (La. Ct. App. 5th Cir. 1993)
103 ALR6th 507—§ 20, 31
State v. Thomas, 6 Neb. App. 510, 574 N.W.2d 542 (1998)
15 ALR5th 391—§ 32
92 ALR5th 35—§ 22
State v. Thomas, 12 P.3d 420 (Kan. Ct. App. 2000)
14 ALR5th 913—§ 6
State v. Thomas, 13 Ohio App. 3d 211, 13 Ohio B.R. 261, 468 N.E.2d 763 (Summit Co. 1983)
22 ALR5th 787—§ 3
State v. Thomas, 20 N.C. App. 255, 201 S.E.2d 201 (1973)
4 ALR5th 1—§ 4, 10

State v. Thomas, 22 N.C. App. 206, 206 S.E.2d 390 (1974)
30 ALR6th 103—§ 34
State v. Thomas, 28 Kan. App. 2d 70, 12 P.3d 420, 122 A.L.R.5th 765 (2000)
122 ALR5th 439—§ 4
State v. Thomas, 28 N.C. App. 495, 221 S.E.2d 749 (1976)
52 ALR6th 125—§ 44
State v. Thomas, 29 Del. 195, 6 Boyce 195, 97 A. 869 (Gen. Sess. 1916)
108 ALR5th 593—§ 46
State v. Thomas, 33 Or. App. 69, 575 P.2d 171 (1978)
99 ALR5th 557—§ 10
State v. Thomas, 40 Ohio St. 3d 213, 533 N.E.2d 286 (1988)
26 ALR5th 603—§ 4
State v. Thomas, 57 Wash. App. 403, 788 P.2d 24 (Div. 3 1990)
73 ALR5th 383—§ 41, 54
State v. Thomas, 61 Ohio St. 2d 254, 15 Ohio Ops. 3d 262, 400 N.E.2d 897 (1980)
39 ALR5th 283—§ 14
State v. Thomas, 63 Ohio App. 3d 501, 579 N.E.2d 290 (10th Dist. Franklin County 1991)
38 ALR6th 439—§ 11
State v. Thomas, 65 N.C. App. 539, 309 S.E.2d 564 (1983)
34 ALR5th 125—§ 8, 14
State v. Thomas, 66 Ohio St. 2d 518, 20 Ohio Op. 3d 424, 423 N.E.2d 137 (1981)
22 ALR5th 787—§ 3
58 ALR5th 749—§ 6
State v. Thomas, 68 Wash. App. 268, 843 P.2d 540 (1992)
27 ALR5th 593—§ 8, 25, 32
State v. Thomas, 77 Ohio St. 3d 323, 673 N.E.2d 1339, 67 A.L.R.5th 781 (1997)
58 ALR5th 749—§ 8, 10
67 ALR5th 637—§ 2, 5, 8
State v. Thomas, 82 P.3d 531 (Kan. Ct. App. 2004)
9 ALR6th 363—§ 37

State v. Thomas, 97 Ohio St. 3d 309, 2002-Ohio-6624, 779 N.E.2d 1017 (2002)
122 ALR5th 145—§ 7, 24

State v. Thomas, 103 N.C. App. 264, 405 S.E.2d 214 (1991)
3 ALR5th 521—§ 3

State v. Thomas, 104 Ariz. 408, 454 P.2d 153 (1969)
58 ALR6th 215—§ 12

State v. Thomas, 110 Ariz. 106, 515 P.2d 851 (1973)
88 ALR5th 429—§ 3

State v. Thomas, 121 Wash. 2d 504, 851 P.2d 673 (1993)
27 ALR6th 491—§ 3

State v. Thomas, 128 Wash. 2d 553, 910 P.2d 475 (1996)
72 ALR5th 403—§ 11 to 13, 15

State v. Thomas, 128 Wis. 2d 93, 381 N.W.2d 567 (App. 1985)
28 ALR5th 754—§ 7

State v. Thomas, 132 N.J. 247, 624 A.2d 975, 27 A.L.R.5th 887 (1993)
27 ALR5th 593—§ 21

State v. Thomas, 132 P.3d 958 (Kan. 2006)
26 ALR6th 511—§ 25

State v. Thomas, 135 Iowa 717, 109 N.W. 900 (1906)
103 ALR6th 35—§ 17, 20

State v. Thomas, 138 Wash. 2d 630, 980 P.2d 1275 (1999)
30 ALR6th 373—§ 13

State v. Thomas, 139 Or. App. 308 (1996)
39 ALR5th 283—§ 4, 41

State v. Thomas, 157 W. Va. 640, 203 S.E.2d 445 (1974)
117 ALR5th 513—§ 4
71 ALR6th 1—§ 4

State v. Thomas, 188 N.J. 137, 902 A.2d 1185 (2006)
26 ALR6th 511—§ 17, 28

State v. Thomas, 210 Neb. 298, 314 N.W.2d 15 (1981)
5 ALR5th 243—§ 2, 33

State v. Thomas, 220 Kan. 104, 551 P.2d 873 (1976)
83 ALR5th 277—§ 11

State v. Thomas, 224 La. 431, 69 So. 2d 738 (1953)
19 ALR6th 115—§ 10

State v. Thomas, 224 N.J. Super. 221, 540 A.2d 196 (1988)
55 ALR5th 125—§ 18, 23

State v. Thomas, 236 Neb. 553, 462 N.W.2d 862 (1990)
66 ALR5th 135—§ 13

State v. Thomas, 256 N.J. Super. 563, 607 A.2d 997 (1992)
27 ALR5th 593—§ 21, 29

State v. Thomas, 275 N.W.2d 211 (Iowa 1979)
51 ALR6th 1—§ 5
53 ALR6th 1—§ 5
71 ALR6th 335—§ 10

State v. Thomas, 280 Kan. 526, 124 P.3d 48, 17 A.L.R.6th 813 (2005)
17 ALR6th 159—§ 71
17 ALR6th 327—§ 7

State v. Thomas, 287 S.C. 411, 339 S.E.2d 129 (1986)
10 ALR5th 700—§ 10

State v. Thomas, 319 So. 2d 789 (La. 1975)
41 ALR6th 295—§ 15

State v. Thomas, 325 Md. 160, 599 A.2d 1171 (1992)
66 ALR6th 83—§ 10

State v. Thomas, 325 So. 2d 593 (La. 1976)
99 ALR6th 295—§ 5, 10

State v. Thomas, 332 N.C. 544, 423 S.E.2d 75 (1992)
103 ALR6th 507—§ 4, 28

State v. Thomas, 350 N.C. 315, 514 S.E.2d 486 (1999)
39 ALR5th 283—§ 25

State v. Thomas, 392 N.J. Super. 169, 920 A.2d 142 (App. Div. 2007)
26 ALR6th 511—§ 31

State v. Thomas, 420 N.W.2d 747 (N.D. 1988)

52 ALR5th 655—§ 8
State v. Thomas, 439 So. 2d 629 (La. Ct. App. 1st Cir. 1983)

103 ALR6th 507—§ 4
State v. Thomas, 536 S.W.2d 529 (Mo. Ct. App. 1976)

81 ALR5th 563—§ 3
State v. Thomas, 540 N.W.2d 658 (Iowa 1995)

43 ALR5th 1—§ 13
State v. Thomas, 570 So. 2d 1023 (Fla. Dist. Ct. App. 3d Dist. 1990)

125 ALR5th 497—§ 4
State v. Thomas, 596 S.W.2d 409 (Mo. 1980)

70 ALR5th 587—§ 8, 10
State v. Thomas, 598 N.W.2d 389 (Minn. Ct. App. 1999)

68 ALR5th 343—§ 17
State v. Thomas, 625 S.W.2d 115 (Mo. 1981)

70 ALR5th 1—§ 9
State v. Thomas, 637 So. 2d 1272 (La. Ct. App. 4th Cir. 1994)

102 ALR5th 327—§ 7
State v. Thomas, 659 N.W.2d 217 (Iowa 2003)

78 ALR6th 1—§ 12, 60
State v. Thomas, 791 S.W.2d 861 (Mo. Ct. App. E.D. 1990)

104 ALR5th 357—§ 8
54 ALR6th 429—§ 29
State v. Thomas, 818 S.W.2d 350 (Tenn. Crim. 1991)

51 ALR5th 375—§ 3 to 6
State v. Thomas, 818 S.W.2d 350 (Tenn. Crim. App. 1991)

109 ALR5th 99—§ 9
State v. Thomas, 843 So. 2d 834 (Ala. Crim. App. 2002)

30 ALR6th 103—§ 21, 25, 47
State v. Thomas, 926 So. 2d 578 (La. Ct. App. 4th Cir. 2006)

77 ALR6th 197—§ 13
State v. Thomas, 972 S.W.2d 309 (Mo. Ct. App. W.D. 1998)

37 ALR6th 357—§ 33
State v. Thomas, 1990 WL 29286 (Tenn. Crim. App. 1990)

93 ALR5th 527—§ 4
State v. Thomas, 1993 WL 293636 (Ohio Ct. App. 4th Dist. Lawrence County 1993)

52 ALR6th 567—§ 23
State v. Thomas, 1994 WL 24330 (Ohio Ct. App. 6th Dist. Lucas County 1994)

18 ALR6th 519—§ 4
State v. Thomas, 1998 WL 195953 (Tenn. Crim. App. 1998)

73 ALR5th 383—§ 3
State v. Thomas, 1999 UT 2, 974 P.2d 269 (Utah 1999)

71 ALR5th 637—§ 8, 9
State v. Thomas, 1999 WL 43311 (Ohio Ct. App. 8th Dist. Cuyahoga County 1999)

78 ALR5th 489—§ 3, 10
State v. Thomas, 2004 WI App 115, 274 Wis. 2d 513, 683 N.W.2d 497 (Ct. App. 2004)

85 ALR6th 641—§ 3, 6, 8
State v. Thomas, 2006-Ohio-3779, 2006 WL 2042826 (Ohio Ct. App. 12th Dist. Butler County 2006)

26 ALR6th 511—§ 19
State v. Thomas, 2006 WL 521426 (Tenn. Crim. App. 2006)

51 ALR6th 1—§ 15
State v. Thomas, 2006 WL 2547084 (N.J. Super. Ct. App. Div. 2006)

26 ALR6th 511—§ 17
State v. Thomas, 2007 WL 1119289 (N.J. Super. Ct. App. Div. 2007)

26 ALR6th 511—§ 7, 31
State v. Thomas, 2008 WL 4193391 (Ariz. Ct. App. Div. 2 2008)

63 ALR6th 1—§ 55
State v. Thomas, 2009-Ohio-3461, 2009 WL 2054145 (Ohio Ct. App. 8th Dist. Cuyahoga County 2009)

55 ALR6th 1—§ 3, 6, 32
State v. Thomas, 2010-Ohio-3534, 2010 WL 2990724 (Ohio Ct. App. 2d Dist. Montgomery County 2010)

For assistance, call 1-800-328-4880

72 ALR6th 227—§ 26
State v. Thomas, 2010-Ohio-4627, 2010 WL 3766757 (Ohio Ct. App. 5th Dist. Richland County 2010)
78 ALR6th 297—§ 50, 55
State v. Thomason, 2000 WL 298695 (Tenn. Crim. App. 2000)
91 ALR5th 343—§ 15
82 ALR6th 373—§ 17
State v. Thompkins, 891 So. 2d 1151, 10 A.L.R.6th 785 (Fla. Dist. Ct. App. 4th Dist. 2005)
10 ALR6th 375—§ 17
10 ALR6th 463—§ 8
State v. Thompson, 10 Ariz. App. 301, 458 P.2d 395 (Div. 2 1969)
96 ALR5th 523—§ 5
State v. Thompson, 17 Wash. App. 639, 564 P.2d 820 (1977)
55 ALR5th 125—§ 3
State v. Thompson, 64 N.C. App. 485, 307 S.E.2d 838 (1983)
124 ALR5th 1—§ 3
State v. Thompson, 69 Wash. App. 436, 848 P.2d 1317 (Div. 1 1993)
71 ALR6th 1—§ 5
State v. Thompson, 71 Conn. App. 8, 799 A.2d 1126 (2002)
39 ALR6th 257—§ 4
State v. Thompson, 72 Ohio Misc. 2d 39, 655 N.E.2d 835 (C.P. 1995)
17 ALR6th 327—§ 22
State v. Thompson, 73 Wash. App. 122, 867 P.2d 691 (Div. 2 1994)
42 ALR6th 237—§ 8
State v. Thompson, 73 Wash. App. 654, 870 P.2d 1022 (Div. 1 1994)
65 ALR6th 359—§ 3
State v. Thompson, 95 N.C. 596, 1886 WL 1154 (1886)
57 ALR6th 445—§ 30
State v. Thompson, 95 Wash. 2d 888, 632 P.2d 50 (1981)
82 ALR5th 359—§ 2
83 ALR5th 277—§ 2
84 ALR5th 487—§ 2
State v. Thompson, 97 Wash. App. 1038, 1999 WL 730912 (Div. 1 1999)

16 ALR6th 329—§ 11
24 ALR6th 591—§ 9, 13
State v. Thompson, 110 N.C. App. 217, 429 S.E.2d 590 (1993)
86 ALR5th 463—§ 9
State v. Thompson, 110 Ohio Misc. 2d 139, 745 N.E.2d 1159 (C.P. 2000)
111 ALR5th 239—§ 8
State v. Thompson, 127 Ohio App. 3d 511, 713 N.E.2d 456 (8th Dist. Cuyahoga County 1998)
39 ALR5th 283—§ 41
State v. Thompson, 129 N.C. App. 13, 497 S.E.2d 126 (1998)
39 ALR5th 283—§ 18
State v. Thompson, 132 N.H. 730, 571 A.2d 266 (1990)
50 ALR6th 455—§ 34
State v. Thompson, 133 N.J. Super. 180, 336 A.2d 11 (App. Div. 1975)
53 ALR6th 1—§ 11
State v. Thompson, 138 Or. App. 247, 908 P.2d 329 (1995)
15 ALR5th 391—§ 45
State v. Thompson, 146 Ariz. 552, 707 P.2d 956 (App. 1985)
38 ALR5th 433—§ 18, 19
State v. Thompson, 146 Ariz. 552, 707 P.2d 956 (Ct. App. Div. 2 1985)
28 ALR6th 505—§ 9
State v. Thompson, 155 Wash. App. 294, 229 P.3d 901 (Div. 1 2010)
72 ALR6th 227—§ 52
State v. Thompson, 169 Ariz. 471, 820 P.2d 335, 98 Ariz. Adv. Rep. 53 (App. 1991)
38 ALR5th 433—§ 23
State v. Thompson, 176 W. Va. 300, 342 S.E.2d 268 (1986)
1 ALR6th 549—§ 8
State v. Thompson, 194 Ariz. 295, 981 P.2d 595, 108 A.L.R.5th 859 (Ct. App. Div. 1 1999)
108 ALR5th 593—§ 20
State v. Thompson, 196 Neb. 55, 241 N.W.2d 511 (1976)
59 ALR5th 615—§ 6, 9

State v. Thompson, 221 Kan. 165, 558
P.2d 1079 (1976)
> **63 ALR6th 1—§ 5, 53**

State v. Thompson, 222 Wis. 2d 179,
585 N.W.2d 905 (Ct. App. 1998)
> **28 ALR6th 245—§ 6**

State v. Thompson, 244 Neb. 189, 505
N.W.2d 673 (1993)
> **4 ALR5th 1—§ 7**
> **64 ALR5th 741—§ 3**

State v. Thompson, 244 Neb. 375, 507
N.W.2d 253 (1993)
> **27 ALR6th 183—§ 35**

State v. Thompson, 263 Mont. 17, 865
P.2d 1125 (1993)
> **38 ALR5th 433—§ 11**

State v. Thompson, 278 S.C. 1, 292
S.E.2d 581 (1982)
> **98 ALR6th 455—§ 11**

State v. Thompson, 284 Ga. App. 744,
644 S.E.2d 889 (2007)
> **70 ALR6th 361—§ 17**

State v. Thompson, 290 N.C. 431, 226
S.E.2d 487 (1976)
> **86 ALR5th 59—§ 5**

State v. Thompson, 295 N.W.2d 8 (S.D.
1980)
> **84 ALR6th 293—§ 31**

State v. Thompson, 301 So. 2d 317 (La.
1974)
> **70 ALR5th 587—§ 5**

State v. Thompson, 306 N.W.2d 841
(Minn. 1981)
> **108 ALR5th 593—§ 19**

State v. Thompson, 328 N.C. 477, 402
S.E.2d 386 (1991)
> **73 ALR5th 383—§ 4, 28**

State v. Thompson, 329 S.C. 72, 495
S.E.2d 437 (1998)
> **66 ALR6th 83—§ 10**

State v. Thompson, 332 N.C. 204, 420
S.E.2d 395 (1992)
> **27 ALR6th 183—§ 10, 35**
> **32 ALR6th 1—§ 5**

State v. Thompson, 353 So. 2d 235 (La.
1977)
> **42 ALR5th 581—§ 11**

State v. Thompson, 354 So. 2d 513 (La.
1978)
> **6 ALR6th 533—§ 12**

State v. Thompson, 396 S.W.2d 697
(Mo. 1965)
> **95 ALR5th 611—§ 3**
> **53 ALR6th 81—§ 8**

State v. Thompson, 427 N.W.2d 266
(Minn. Ct. App. 1988)
> **65 ALR5th 407—§ 3 to 5, 15**

State v. Thompson, 428 S.W.2d 742
(Mo. 1968)
> **57 ALR6th 445—§ 46**

State v. Thompson, 503 A.2d 689 (Me.
1986)
> **77 ALR5th 201—§ 9**

State v. Thompson, 570 So. 2d 1144
(Fla. Dist. Ct. App. 4th Dist. 1990)
> **113 ALR5th 597—§ 8**

State v. Thompson, 687 N.E.2d 225
(Ind. Ct. App. 1997)
> **71 ALR6th 335—§ 22**

State v. Thompson, 751 P.2d 805,
R.I.C.O. Bus. Disp. Guide (CCH)
¶ 6895, 1988-1 Trade Cas. (CCH)
¶ 67925 (Utah Ct. App. 1988)
> **58 ALR6th 385—§ 20, 26**

State v. Thompson, 751 P.2d 805,
R.I.C.O. Bus. Disp. Guide (CCH)
¶ 6895, 1988-1 Trade Cas. (CCH)
¶ 67925 (Utah Ct. App. 1988)
> **58 ALR6th 385—§ 39**

State v. Thompson, 768 S.W.2d 239
(Tenn. 1989)
> **70 ALR5th 587—§ 13**

State v. Thompson, 810 P.2d 415, 157
Utah Adv. Rep. 6, 1991-1 CCH
Trade Cases ¶ 69396 (Utah 1991)
> **33 ALR5th 453—§ 3**

State v. Thompson, 820 S.W.2d 591
(Mo. Ct. App. E.D. 1991)
> **67 ALR6th 531—§ 25**

State v. Thompson, 894 So. 2d 1268 (La.
Ct. App. 2d Cir. 2005)
> **71 ALR6th 1—§ 5**

State v. Thompson, 1992 WL 95875
(Minn. Ct. App. 1992)
> **73 ALR5th 383—§ 29, 62**

For assistance, call 1-800-328-4880

State v. Thompson, 1997 SD 15, 560 N.W.2d 535 (S.D. 1997)
29 ALR6th 1—§ 10

State v. Thompson, 1997 WL 607485 (Tenn. Crim. App. 1997)
72 ALR5th 403—§ 15

State v. Thompson, 1998 WL 221052 (Tenn. Crim. App. 1998)
89 ALR5th 539—§ 12

State v. Thompson, 1999 WL 254417 (Ohio Ct. App. 5th Dist. Licking County 1999)
78 ALR5th 489—§ 10

State v. Thompson, 2001 MT 119, 305 Mont. 342, 28 P.3d 1068 (2001)
102 ALR5th 327—§ 4

State v. Thompson, 2001 WL 912715 (Tenn. Crim. App. 2001)
16 ALR6th 329—§ 15
24 ALR6th 591—§ 10

State v. Thompson, 2006-Ohio-2004, 2006 WL 1062015 (Ohio Ct. App. 3d Dist. Allen County 2006)
26 ALR6th 511—§ 19

State v. Thompson, 2011 WL 2535519 (Wis. Ct. App. 2011)
69 ALR6th 1—§ 15

State v. Thompson, 2012 WL 581293 (Wash. 2012)
72 ALR6th 227—§ 33, 52

State v. Thompson, 2014-Ohio-4751, 2014 WL 5483952 (Ohio 2014)
102 ALR6th 417—§ 23

State v. Thomson, 109 N.H. 205, 247 A.2d 179 (1968)
70 ALR5th 587—§ 3

State v. Thomson, 123 Wash. 2d 877, 872 P.2d 1097 (1994)
19 ALR6th 697—§ 2, 4, 5

State v. Thorne, 43 Wash. 2d 47, 260 P.2d 331 (1953)
51 ALR5th 603—§ 3

State v. Thorne, 129 Wash. 2d 736, 921 P.2d 514 (1996)
63 ALR6th 1—§ 5, 36

State v. Thornton, 119 Wash. 2d 578, 835 P.2d 216 (1992)

119 ALR5th 275—§ 14

State v. Thornton, 172 Ariz. 449, 837 P.2d 1184 (Ct. App. Div. 1 1992)
109 ALR5th 611—§ 4

State v. Thornton, 187 Ariz. 325, 929 P.2d 676 (1996)
52 ALR6th 1—§ 7

State v. Thornton, 453 A.2d 489 (Me. 1982)
45 ALR6th 643—§ 15

State v. Thornton, 621 So. 2d 173 (La. App. 4th Cir. 1993)
50 ALR5th 581—§ 2

State v. Thornton, 651 S.W.2d 164 (Mo. App. 1983)
7 ALR5th 263—§ 6

State v. Thornton, 930 S.W.2d 54 (Mo. Ct. App. S.D. 1996)
105 ALR5th 529—§ 13

State v. Thornton, 1991 WL 221942 (Ohio Ct. App. 8th Dist. Cuyahoga County 1991)
88 ALR5th 121—§ 3, 22, 27

State v. Thornton, 2005-Ohio-3744, 2005 WL 1714208 (Ohio Ct. App. 2d Dist. Montgomery County 2005)
19 ALR6th 697—§ 4

State v. Thorpe, 94 N.C. App. 270, 380 S.E.2d 777 (1989)
24 ALR5th 428—§ 2, 11

State v. Thorpe, 326 N.C. 451, 390 S.E.2d 311 (1990)
34 ALR5th 125—§ 4, 21

State v. Thorsness, 165 Mont. 321, 528 P.2d 692 (1974)
92 ALR6th 1—§ 3

State v. Thorson, 302 So. 2d 578 (La. 1974)
85 ALR5th 1—§ 44

State v. Three Thousand Sixty Seven Dollars and Sixty-Five Cents ($3,067.65) in U.S. Currency, 4 Neb. App. 443, 545 N.W.2d 129 (1996)
34 ALR6th 539—§ 4, 6, 8, 10

State v. Three Thousand Sixty Seven Dollars and Sixty-Five Cents ($3,067.65) in U.S. Currency, 4 Neb. App. 443, 545 N.W.2d 129 (1996)

104 ALR5th 229—§ 3
115 ALR5th 403—§ 8
116 ALR5th 325—§ 3
4 ALR6th 113—§ 16
101 ALR6th 1—§ 7, 23

State v. Thresher, 350 S.W.2d 1 (Mo. 1961)

9 ALR6th 1—§ 17

State v. Thrift, 440 S.E.2d 341 (S.C. 1994)

29 ALR5th 1—§ 2, 4

State v. Throm, 178 Wis. 2d 317, 504 N.W.2d 875 (Ct. App. 1993)

35 ALR6th 497—§ 13, 23

State v. Thrower, 62 Ohio App. 3d 359, 575 N.E.2d 863 (9th Dist. Summit County 1989)

89 ALR5th 629—§ 8, 12
58 ALR6th 385—§ 20, 21, 45

State v. Thucos, 390 So. 2d 1281 (La. 1980)

32 ALR5th 149—§ 22, 23, 32
124 ALR5th 1—§ 5

State v. Thunder, 2010 SD 3, 777 N.W.2d 373 (S.D. 2010)

62 ALR6th 161—§ 17

State v. Thunder Hawk, 212 Neb. 350, 322 N.W.2d 669 (1982)

30 ALR6th 103—§ 6, 24, 46

State v. Thurlow, 152 Idaho 256, 269 P.3d 813, 83 A.L.R.6th 765 (Ct. App. 2011)

83 ALR6th 465—§ 4, 5, 13, 29, 62

State v. Thurmer, 348 N.W.2d 776 (Minn. Ct. App. 1984)

92 ALR6th 295—§ 8
93 ALR6th 207—§ 6, 14, 20, 28
94 ALR6th 191—§ 4
96 ALR6th 355—§ 9, 37, 53, 60

State v. Thurmon, 1996 WL 594085 (Tenn. Crim. App. 1996)

76 ALR5th 1—§ 5, 17

State v. Thursby, 245 S.W.2d 859 (Mo. 1952)

54 ALR6th 429—§ 5

State v. Thurston, 735 S.W.2d 108 (Mo. App. 1987)

5 ALR5th 243—§ 11

State v. Thyfault, 121 N.J. Super. 487, 297 A.2d 873 (County Ct. 1972)

125 ALR5th 537—§ 1

State v. Tia, 196 Wis. 2d 645, 539 N.W.2d 336 (Ct. App. 1995)

7 ALR6th 233—§ 19

State v. Tibbet, 96 Or. App. 116, 771 P.2d 654 (1989)

84 ALR6th 293—§ 42

State v. Tibbetts, 92 Ohio St. 3d 146, 2001-Ohio-132, 749 N.E.2d 226 (2001)

71 ALR6th 1—§ 6
72 ALR6th 1—§ 6

State v. Tibbetts, 2001 WL 303234 (Ohio Ct. App. 1st Dist. Hamilton County 2001)

21 ALR6th 1—§ 4

State v. Tibiatowski, 590 N.W.2d 305 (Minn. 1999)

38 ALR6th 97—§ 29
81 ALR6th 505—§ 28

State v. Tiche, 33 Conn. Supp. 51, 360 A.2d 135 (Super. Ct. 1976)

97 ALR5th 201—§ 3

State v. Tichnell, 306 Md. 428, 509 A.2d 1179 (1986)

79 ALR5th 419—§ 9

State v. Tichon, 102 Ohio App. 3d 758, 658 N.E.2d 16 (Summit Co. 1995)

29 ALR5th 487—§ 11

State v. Tidmore, 604 S.W.2d 879 (Tenn. Crim. App. 1980)

57 ALR6th 313—§ 7

State v. Tidwell, 888 S.W.2d 736 (Mo. Ct. App. S.D. 1994)

58 ALR6th 499—§ 19, 97, 106

State v. Tidyman, 54 Or. App. 640, 635 P.2d 1355 (1981)

111 ALR5th 239—§ 8

State v. Tierney, 584 S.W.2d 618 (Mo. App. 1979)

For assistance, call 1-800-328-4880

34 ALR5th 125—§ 8
State v. Tierney, 584 S.W.2d 618 (Mo. Ct. App. W.D. 1979)
8 ALR6th 265—§ 8
State v. Tiessen, 354 N.W.2d 473 (Minn. Ct. App. 1984)
78 ALR5th 197—§ 4
State v. Tilford, 41 Or. App. 433, 599 P.2d 1144 (1979)
88 ALR5th 121—§ 28
State v. Tiller, 168 W.Va. 522, 285 S.E.2d 371 (1981)
57 ALR6th 313—§ 2
State v. Tillett, 119 Wash. App. 1013, 2003 WL 23221519 (Div. 3 2003)
19 ALR6th 115—§ 4, 7, 10
State v. Tillett, 173 Ind. 133, 89 N.E. 589 (1909)
57 ALR6th 445—§ 59
State v. Tilley, 99 569 La. 7/6/, 2000 WL 900583 (La. 2000)
79 ALR5th 33—§ 56
State v. Tilson, 619 S.W.2d 544 (Tenn. Crim. 1981)
29 ALR5th 59—§ 18
State v. Tilt, 2004 UT App 395, 101 P.3d 838 (Utah Ct. App. 2004)
69 ALR6th 579—§ 4
State v. Timas, 82 Haw. 499, 923 P.2d 916 (Ct. App. 1996)
43 ALR6th 475—§ 16
State v. Timberlake, 2006 WL 1932969 (N.J. Super. Ct. App. Div. 2006)
26 ALR6th 511—§ 17
State v. Timley, 25 Kan. App. 2d 779, 975 P.2d 264 (1998)
34 ALR6th 1—§ 10
State v. Timley, 255 Kan. 286, 875 P.2d 242 (1994)
88 ALR5th 67—§ 5
State v. Timmendequas, 161 N.J. 515, 737 A.2d 55 (1999)
91 ALR5th 343—§ 37
1 ALR6th 657—§ 4
28 ALR6th 505—§ 9
State v. Timmons, 574 S.W.2d 950 (Mo. Ct. App. 1978)

68 ALR5th 343—§ 3, 10
State v. Timperley, 1999 SD 75, 599 N.W.2d 866 (S.D. 1999)
41 ALR6th 141—§ 7
State v. Tim S., 41 Wash. App. 60, 701 P.2d 1120 (Div. 3 1985)
42 ALR6th 237—§ 9
State v. Tinch, 84 Ohio App. 3d 111, 616 N.E.2d 529 (Warren Co. 1992)
39 ALR5th 283—§ 14
State v. Tindal, 50 Wash. App. 401, 748 P.2d 695 (1988)
15 ALR5th 391—§ 45
State v. Tindall, 213 S.C. 484, 50 S.E.2d 188 (1948)
29 ALR5th 59—§ 3, 56
State v. Tinker, 2005-Ohio-2289, 2005 WL 1109686 (Ohio Ct. App. 10th Dist. Franklin County 2005)
70 ALR6th 1—§ 5
State v. Tinkham, 143 N.H. 73, 719 A.2d 580 (1998)
31 ALR5th 229—§ 28, 68, 69, 72
State v. Tinklenberg, 292 Minn. 271, 194 N.W.2d 590 (1972)
84 ALR6th 427—§ 14, 21
State v. Tippecanoe County Court, 432 N.E.2d 1377 (Ind. 1982)
42 ALR5th 581—§ 4, 5, 17
State v. Tippett, 624 N.W.2d 176 (Iowa 2001)
34 ALR6th 171—§ 17
State v. Tipton, 206 Neb. 731, 294 N.W.2d 869 (1980)
101 ALR6th 299—§ 4
State v. Tirado, 358 N.C. 551, 599 S.E.2d 515 (2004)
83 ALR6th 255—§ 9
State v. Tirone, 64 N.J. 222, 314 A.2d 601 (1974)
39 ALR6th 257—§ 47, 49
State v. Tiscareno, 190 Ariz. 542, 950 P.2d 1163 (Ct. App. Div. 1 1997)
5 ALR5th 243—§ 21
State v. Tischer, 2010 WI App 33, 323 Wis. 2d 823, 781 N.W.2d 551 (Ct. App. 2010)

84 ALR6th 293—§ 18, 34
State v. Tischio, 107 N.J. 504, 527 A.2d 388 (1987)
119 ALR5th 379—§ 6, 11
State v. Tisdale, 2003-Ohio-4209, 2003 WL 21862348 (Ohio Ct. App. 2d Dist. Montgomery County 2003)
24 ALR6th 1—§ 5
State v. Tisius, 92 S.W.3d 751 (Mo. 2002)
110 ALR5th 1—§ 3, 15
State v. Tito, 616 So. 2d 39, 18 FLW S. 206 (Fla. 1993)
7 ALR5th 263—§ 7
22 ALR5th 660—§ 11
State v. T.L.W., 457 So. 2d 566 (Fla. Dist. Ct. App. 2d Dist. 1984)
55 ALR6th 391—§ 21
State v. T.M., 2009 WL 1472589 (N.J. Super. Ct. App. Div. 2009)
94 ALR6th 525—§ 8
State v. T.M.B, 590 N.W.2d 809 (Minn. Ct. App. 1999)
68 ALR6th 1—§ 17
State v. Toca, 141 So. 3d 265 (La. 2014)
102 ALR6th 637—§ 7
State v. Toca, 769 So. 2d 665 (La. Ct. App. 4th Cir. 2000)
45 ALR5th 1—§ 11, 18
State v. Tocco, 156 Ariz. 116, 750 P.2d 874 (1988)
58 ALR6th 385—§ 20
State v. Toce, 6 Conn. Cir. Ct. 192, 269 A.2d 421 (App. Div. 1969)
85 ALR5th 547—§ 7
State v. Toda, 1998 WL 526732 (Ohio Ct. App. 6th Dist. Wood County 1998)
78 ALR5th 489—§ 10
State v. Today's Bookstore, 86 Ohio App. 3d 810, 621 N.E.2d 1283 (Montgomery Co. 1993)
51 ALR5th 603—§ 2, 4, 11, 14
State v. Todd, 24 Kan. App. 2d 796, 954 P.2d 1 (1998)
38 ALR5th 433—§ 31
State v. Todd, 70 S.W.3d 509 (Mo. Ct. App. W.D. 2002)

23 ALR6th 307—§ 40
State v. Todd, 78 Wash. 2d 362, 474 P.2d 542 (1970)
16 ALR6th 329—§ 4
State v. Todd, 468 N.W.2d 462 (Iowa 1991)
6 ALR5th 733—§ 2, 25
69 ALR6th 207—§ 7
State v. Todd, 2012 WL 2150859 (Tenn. Crim. App. 2012)
98 ALR6th 455—§ 6
State v. Toffolio, 349 So. 2d 174 (Fla. Dist. Ct. App. 1st Dist. 1977)
114 ALR5th 173—§ 9
State v. Tokar, 918 S.W.2d 753 (Mo. 1996)
83 ALR6th 255—§ 25
State v. Tolbert, 223 Neb. 794, 394 N.W.2d 288 (1986)
22 ALR5th 660—§ 11, 13, 17
State v. Tolbert, 716 So. 2d 949 (La. Ct. App. 2d Cir. 1998)
37 ALR5th 515—§ 3
State v. Toliver, 304 S.C. 298, 403 S.E.2d 676 (App. 1991)
27 ALR5th 593—§ 32
State v. Tollefson, 2000 WL 1182828 (Minn. Ct. App. 2000)
69 ALR6th 579—§ 8, 14
State v. Tolliver, 33 Ohio App. 3d 110, 514 N.E.2d 922 (5th Dist. Guernsey County 1986)
82 ALR5th 359—§ 4
84 ALR5th 487—§ 21, 25
State v. Tolliver, 268 Neb. 920, 689 N.W.2d 567 (2004)
38 ALR6th 439—§ 12
State v. Tolliver, 839 S.W.2d 296 (Mo. 1992)
103 ALR6th 137—§ 15, 18
State v. Tolliver, 2004-Ohio-1603, 2004 WL 625683 (Ohio Ct. App. 10th Dist. Franklin County 2004)
124 ALR5th 1—§ 5
State v. Tolonen, 280 Wis. 2d 557, 2005 WI App 59, 694 N.W.2d 509 (Ct. App. 2005)
16 ALR6th 329—§ 4

For assistance, call 1-800-328-4880

24 ALR6th 591—§ 4, 12
State v. Tomasko, 242 Conn. 505, 700 A.2d 28 (1997)
24 ALR6th 1—§ 18
State v. Tomassi, 137 Conn. 113, 75 A.2d 67 (1950)
50 ALR5th 467—§ 6, 8
State v. Tomasso, 49 Conn. Supp. 327, 878 A.2d 413, 38 Conn. L. Rptr. 304 (Super. Ct. 2004)
37 ALR6th 511—§ 3, 13, 45, 51
State v. Tomes, 118 Idaho 952, 801 P.2d 1303 (Ct. App. 1990)
78 ALR5th 567—§ 5
State v. Tomlin, 609 N.W.2d 282 (Minn. Ct. App. 2000)
66 ALR5th 397—§ 8
State v. Tomlin, 622 N.W.2d 546 (Minn. 2001)
66 ALR5th 397—§ 25
State v. Tomlin, 864 S.W.2d 364 (Mo. App. 1993)
39 ALR5th 283—§ 4, 55
State v. Tomlinson, 98 N.M. 337, 648 P.2d 795 (App. 1982)
28 ALR5th 754—§ 8
State v. Tompkins, 1996 WL 612855 (Ohio Ct. App. 2d Dist. Clark County 1996)
42 ALR6th 237—§ 8
State v. Toney, 215 Ga. App. 64, 449 S.E.2d 892 (1994)
111 ALR5th 239—§ 3
State v. Toney, 537 S.W.2d 586 (Mo. Ct. App. 1976)
55 ALR5th 125—§ 12
State v. Tookes, 67 Hawaii 608, 699 P.2d 983 (1985)
18 ALR5th 1—§ 28
State v. Topete, 221 Neb. 771, 380 N.W.2d 635 (1986)
32 ALR5th 149—§ 5, 29
State v. Toppi, 275 A.2d 805 (Me. 1971)
84 ALR5th 487—§ 19
State v. Topping, 248 N.J. Super. 86, 590 A.2d 252 (App. Div. 1991)
92 ALR5th 35—§ 2, 22

State v. Torgerson, 57 N.D. 152, 220 N.W. 834 (1928)
14 ALR6th 543—§ 46
State v. Torkelson, 404 N.W.2d 352 (Minn. Ct. App. 1987)
101 ALR5th 187—§ 11
State v. Torline, 215 Kan. 539, 527 P.2d 994 (1974)
87 ALR5th 597—§ 2, 10, 13
State v. Toro, 62 Conn. App. 635, 772 A.2d 648 (2001)
100 ALR5th 67—§ 22
State v. Toro, 229 N.J. Super. 215, 551 A.2d 170 (App. Div. 1988)
55 ALR6th 513—§ 14
State v. Torres, 21 Conn. App. 568, 575 A.2d 702 (1990)
28 ALR6th 505—§ 18
29 ALR6th 1—§ 16
State v. Torres, 60 Conn. App. 562, 761 A.2d 766 (2000)
39 ALR6th 257—§ 4
State v. Torres, 82 S.W.3d 236 (Tenn. 2002)
27 ALR6th 183—§ 34
State v. Torres, 85 Conn. App. 303, 858 A.2d 776 (2004)
32 ALR6th 1—§ 11
State v. Torres, 86 Md. App. 560, 587 A.2d 582 (1991)
52 ALR6th 1—§ 28
State v. Torres, 121 N.H. 828, 435 A.2d 527 (1981)
7 ALR5th 758—§ 13
State v. Torres, 122 Haw. 2, 222 P.3d 409, 65 A.L.R.6th 735 (Ct. App. 2009)
65 ALR6th 359—§ 5
101 ALR6th 331—§ 9, 12
State v. Torres, 130 N.H. 340, 540 A.2d 1217 (1988)
28 ALR6th 505—§ 8
38 ALR6th 97—§ 18
State v. Torres, 135 P.3d 766 (Kan. 2006)
26 ALR6th 511—§ 25

State v. Torres, 137 N.M. 607, 2005-NMCA-070, 113 P.3d 877 (Ct. App. 2005)
71 ALR6th 1—§ 11

State v. Torres, 162 Ariz. 70, 781 P.2d 47 (Ct. App. Div. 1 1989)
94 ALR5th 393—§ 7

State v. Torres, 201 Or. App. 275, 118 P.3d 268 (2005)
58 ALR6th 499—§ 39

State v. Torres, 254 Neb. 91, 574 N.W.2d 153 (1998)
36 ALR5th 161—§ 27

State v. Torres, 322 N.C. 440, 368 S.E.2d 609 (1988)
32 ALR5th 149—§ 29, 50, 52, 62

State v. Torres, 330 N.C. 517, 412 S.E.2d 20 (1992)
73 ALR5th 383—§ 29
124 ALR5th 1—§ 5

State v. Torres, 524 A.2d 1120 (R.I. 1987)
103 ALR6th 137—§ 19

State v. Torres, 1999 -NMSC- 010, 127 N.M. 20, 976 P.2d 20 (1999)
90 ALR5th 453—§ 15

State v. Torrez, 112 Ariz. 525, 544 P.2d 207 (1975)
113 ALR5th 517—§ 10

State v. Toste, 178 Conn. 626, 424 A.2d 293 (1979)
66 ALR6th 83—§ 10

State v. Tostenson, 2002 WL 15786 (Minn. Ct. App. 2002)
106 ALR5th 377—§ 3

State v. Touchet, 642 So. 2d 1213 (La. 1994)
83 ALR5th 541—§ 3

State v. Tourtillott, 289 Or. 845, 618 P.2d 423 (1980)
116 ALR5th 479—§ 5

State v. Tourville, 295 S.W.2d 1 (Mo. 1956)
11 ALR5th 497—§ 25

State v. Towe, 246 Ga. App. 808, 541 S.E.2d 423 (2000)
6 ALR6th 533—§ 17

State v. Tower, 84 Me. 444, 24 A. 898 (1892)
31 ALR6th 523—§ 29

State v. Tower, 267 Mont. 63, 881 P.2d 1317 (1994)
34 ALR5th 125—§ 9

State v. Towery, 186 Ariz. 168, 920 P.2d 290 (1996)
121 ALR5th 551—§ 2, 7 to 9, 14

State v. Towle, 125 Ariz. 397, 609 P.2d 1097 (Ct. App. Div. 2 1980)
92 ALR6th 1—§ 3

State v. Townley, 149 Minn. 5, 182 N.W. 773, 17 A.L.R. 253 (1921)
54 ALR6th 429—§ 11

State v. Townsend, 105 Wash. App. 622, 20 P.3d 1027 (Div. 3 2001)
92 ALR5th 15—§ 2

State v. Townsend, 124 Idaho 881, 865 P.2d 972 (1993)
26 ALR5th 603—§ 3
67 ALR6th 103—§ 3, 4

State v. Townsend, 186 W. Va. 283, 412 S.E.2d 477 (1991)
104 ALR5th 165—§ 14

State v. Townsend, 307 Wis. 2d 694, 2008 WI App 20, 746 N.W.2d 493 (Ct. App. 2008)
69 ALR6th 579—§ 5

State v. Townsend, 2001-Ohio-1485, 2001 WL 959186 (Ohio Ct. App. 2d Dist. Montgomery County 2001)
26 ALR6th 511—§ 35

State v. Township of Lyndhurst, 278 N.J. Super. 192, 650 A.2d 840 (Ch. Div. 1994)
24 ALR6th 255—§ 5, 11, 17

State v. Townsley, 1 West. L.J. 260, 1 Ohio Dec. Rep. 36, 1843 WL 2582 (Ohio C.P. 1843)
5 ALR6th 1—§ 34

State v. T.P., 835 So. 2d 1277 (Fla. Dist. Ct. App. 4th Dist. 2003)
114 ALR5th 173—§ 9
123 ALR5th 179—§ 3

State v. Trackwell, 235 Neb. 845, 458 N.W.2d 181, 14 U.C.C.R.S.2d 331 (1990)

25 ALR5th 696—§ 33, 45
State v. Tracy, 158 Wash. 2d 683, 147 P.3d 559 (2006)
50 ALR6th 353—§ 14
State v. Tracy, 482 N.W.2d 675 (Iowa 1992)
38 ALR5th 433—§ 11
State v. Tracy, 1999 WL 254442 (Ohio Ct. App. 5th Dist. Licking County 1999)
78 ALR5th 489—§ 10
State v. Traffic Tel. Workers' Federation of N. J., 2 N.J. 335, 66 A.2d 616, 24 L.R.R.M. (BNA) 2071, 16 Lab. Cas. (CCH) ¶ 65162, 9 A.L.R.2d 854 (1949)
63 ALR6th 1—§ 61
State v. Trafton, 425 A.2d 1320 (Me. 1981)
84 ALR5th 487—§ 24
State v. Trahan, 229 Neb. 683, 428 N.W.2d 619 (1988)
62 ALR5th 1—§ 4, 15
46 ALR6th 241—§ 11
State v. Trahan, 752 So. 2d 921 (La. Ct. App. 4th Cir. 1999)
15 ALR5th 391—§ 30
State v. Trail, 328 S.E.2d 671 (W. Va. 1985)
39 ALR5th 283—§ 4, 66
State v. Trainor, 83 Haw. 250, 925 P.2d 818 (1996)
15 ALR6th 515—§ 1
State v. Tramantano, 28 Conn. Supp. 325, 260 A.2d 128 (1969)
43 ALR5th 1—§ 7
State v. Trammel, 1999 WL 22884 (Ohio Ct. App. 2d Dist. Montgomery County 1999)
45 ALR6th 643—§ 20
State v. Trammell, 240 Neb. 724, 484 N.W.2d 263 (1992)
55 ALR6th 391—§ 24
State v. Trammer, 2005-Ohio-3852, 2005 WL 1793511 (Ohio Ct. App. 8th Dist. Cuyahoga County 2005)
23 ALR6th 307—§ 31
71 ALR6th 1—§ 8

State v. Tran, 1995 WL 564817 (Minn. Ct. App. 1995)
73 ALR5th 383—§ 5
State v. Transon, 186 Ariz. 482, 924 P.2d 486 (Ct. App. Div. 1 1996)
96 ALR5th 327—§ 3
State v. Tranter, 2001 WL 290192 (Ohio Ct. App. 12th Dist. Clermont County 2001)
92 ALR6th 1—§ 3
State v. Trapp, 34 Ohio Misc. 2d 32, 518 N.E.2d 617 (C.P. 1987)
53 ALR6th 305—§ 3
State v. Trapper, 48 N.C. App. 481, 269 S.E.2d 680 (1980)
104 ALR5th 165—§ 12
106 ALR5th 397—§ 4
State v. Traster, 610 So. 2d 572 (Fla. Dist. Ct. App. 4th Dist. 1992)
113 ALR5th 597—§ 8
State v. Trasvina, 16 Wash. App. 519, 557 P.2d 368 (Div. 1 1976)
103 ALR5th 463—§ 3
112 ALR5th 429—§ 13
State v. Travatello, 24 N.C. App. 511, 211 S.E.2d 467 (1975)
104 ALR5th 165—§ 12
State v. Travis, 250 Or. 213, 441 P.2d 597 (1968)
35 ALR6th 127—§ 22
State v. Trawitzki, 238 Wis. 2d 795
29 ALR5th 59—§ 74
State v. Trax, 179 Or. App. 193, 39 P.3d 887 (2002)
114 ALR5th 235—§ 8
State v. Traxler, 583 N.W.2d 556 (Minn. 1998)
45 ALR5th 1—§ 15
State v. Traylor, 467 So. 2d 875 (La. App. 2d Cir. 1985)
1 ALR5th 317—§ 7
State v. Traylor, 723 So. 2d 497 (La. Ct. App. 2d Cir. 1998)
50 ALR5th 581—§ 3, 7
State v. Traywick, 72 Ohio App. 3d 674, 595 N.E.2d 986 (Cuyahoga Co. 1991)

---

43 ALR5th 777—§ 2, 4
State v. T.R.D., 286 Conn. 191, 2008 WL 726287 (2008)

33 ALR6th 91—§ 5, 38, 40
State v. Treadway, 28 Utah 2d 160, 499 P.2d 846 (1972)

41 ALR5th 171—§ 23
State v. Treece, 129 N.C. App. 93, 497 S.E.2d 124 (1998)

70 ALR6th 361—§ 19
State v. Tremblay, 118 Wash. App. 1055, 2003 WL 22236043 (Div. 2 2003)

8 ALR6th 265—§ 26
State v. Tremmel, 644 So. 2d 102 (Fla. App. D2 1994)

29 ALR5th 487—§ 3
State v. Trenidad, 23 Wash. App. 418, 595 P.2d 957 (Div. 3 1979)

12 ALR6th 553—§ 3, 5, 11, 26
State v. Trepagnier, 744 So. 2d 181 (La. Ct. App. 4th Cir. 1999)

5 ALR5th 243—§ 10
State v. Trepanier, 71 Wash. App. 372, 858 P.2d 511 (Div. 1 1993)

83 ALR5th 277—§ 13
State v. Trepanier, 204 Wis. 2d 505, 555 N.W.2d 394 (Ct. App. 1996)

76 ALR5th 239—§ 4
State v. Trevino, 10 Wash. App. 89, 516 P.2d 779 (1973)

32 ALR5th 149—§ 29, 33
State v. Trevino, 132 Idaho 888, 980 P.2d 552 (1999)

90 ALR5th 453—§ 8
10 ALR6th 463—§ 4, 8
State v. Trevino, 230 Neb. 494, 432 N.W.2d 503 (1988)

5 ALR5th 243—§ 10
State v. Tribbet, 415 So. 2d 182 (La. 1982)

93 ALR5th 527—§ 3
State v. Tribble, 1985 WL 4928 (Ohio Ct. App. 2d Dist. Montgomery County 1985)

6 ALR6th 533—§ 15
State v. Tribblet, 96 Wash. App. 662, 980 P.2d 794 (Div. 1 1999)

92 ALR5th 35—§ 20
State v. Tribou, 488 A.2d 472 (Me. 1985)

9 ALR6th 1—§ 17
State v. Trickel, 16 Wash. App. 18, 553 P.2d 139 (Div. 2 1976)

55 ALR6th 157—§ 39
State v. Trigon, Inc., 657 N.W.2d 441, 19 O.S.H. Cas. (BNA) 2175 (Iowa 2003)

58 ALR6th 439—§ 28
State v. Trimble, 122 Ohio St. 3d 297, 2009-Ohio-2961, 911 N.E.2d 242 (2009)

102 ALR6th 279—§ 12
103 ALR6th 35—§ 7
State v. Trimble, 371 N.W.2d 921 (Minn. Ct. App. 1985)

55 ALR6th 391—§ 16
State v. Trine, 236 Conn. 216, 673 A.2d 1098 (1996)

50 ALR5th 581—§ 3, 5, 7, 10, 14, 20
State v. Triplett, 187 W. Va. 760, 421 S.E.2d 511 (1992)

36 ALR5th 255—§ 8
State v. Tripp, 84 Conn. 640, 81 A. 247 (1911)

77 ALR6th 393—§ 55
State v. Tripp, 168 N.C. 150, 83 S.E. 630 (1914)

102 ALR5th 525—§ 67
State v. Troen, 100 Or. App. 442, 786 P.2d 751 (1990)

3 ALR5th 521—§ 2, 13
State v. Troglin, 2002 WL 385800 (Tenn. Crim. App. 2002)

38 ALR6th 97—§ 17
State v. Troisi, 124 Ohio St. 3d 404, 2010-Ohio-275, 922 N.E.2d 957, 93 U.S.P.Q.2d 1800 (2010)

63 ALR6th 303—§ 13
State v. Trombley, 136 Vt. 333, 388 A.2d 433 (1978)

50 ALR5th 703—§ 9
State v. Tronchin, 223 N.J. Super. 586, 539 A.2d 330 (1988)

39 ALR5th 283—§ 2

For assistance, call 1-800-328-4880

State v. Trost, 244 N.W.2d 556 (Iowa 1976)
3 ALR6th 269—§ 9, 19
State v. Trostle, 951 P.2d 869 (Ariz. 1997)
20 ALR5th 398—§ 3, 24, 52
39 ALR5th 283—§ 31
State v. Troupe, 237 Conn. 284, 677 A.2d 917 (1996)
39 ALR6th 257—§ 3, 4, 20, 27, 42, 50
40 ALR6th 1—§ 2, 5, 9, 10, 27, 31, 41
State v. Troupe, 891 S.W.2d 808 (Mo. 1995)
105 ALR5th 529—§ 13
State v. Trowbridge, 2013-Ohio-1749, 2013 WL 1857143 (Ohio Ct. App. 1st Dist. Hamilton County 2013)
99 ALR6th 295—§ 9, 13
State v. Trower, 2001 SD 72, 629 N.W.2d 594 (S.D. 2001)
63 ALR6th 351—§ 4
State v. Troyer, 910 P.2d 1182 (Utah 1995)
42 ALR6th 237—§ 8
State v. Trucott, 145 Vt. 274, 487 A.2d 149 (1984)
52 ALR5th 655—§ 2, 4
92 ALR6th 295—§ 3, 4, 7, 13
93 ALR6th 207—§ 3, 6, 28
95 ALR6th 1—§ 3
96 ALR6th 355—§ 9
State v. Trudell, 243 Kan. 29, 755 P.2d 511 (1988)
64 ALR5th 671—§ 8
State v. Trudelle, 142 N.M. 18, 2007-NMCA-066, 162 P.3d 173 (Ct. App. 2007)
78 ALR6th 297—§ 22, 40, 80
State v. True, 438 A.2d 460 (Me. 1981)
38 ALR5th 433—§ 26, 31
State v. Truesdale, 301 S.C. 546, 393 S.E.2d 168 (1990)
20 ALR6th 479—§ 3
State v. Trujillo, 95 N.M. 535, 624 P.2d 44 (1981)
104 ALR5th 165—§ 14

42 ALR6th 237—§ 5
State v. Trujillo, 117 Utah 237, 214 P.2d 626 (1950)
32 ALR5th 149—§ 29, 71
State v. Trujillo, 153 Wash. App. 454, 222 P.3d 129 (Div. 3 2009)
71 ALR6th 1—§ 5
State v. Trujillo, 656 P.2d 403 (Utah 1982)
37 ALR6th 357—§ 54
State v. Trujillo, 869 S.W.2d 844 (Mo. App. 1994)
36 ALR5th 255—§ 24
State v. Trujillo, 869 S.W.2d 844 (Mo. Ct. App. W.D. 1994)
57 ALR6th 83—§ 11
State v. Truman, 115 Ariz. 145, 564 P.2d 96 (App. 1977)
13 ALR5th 118—§ 7
State v. Trumble, 113 Idaho 835, 748 P.2d 826 (Ct. App. 1987)
24 ALR6th 1—§ 38
State v. Trummer, 114 Ohio App. 3d 456, 683 N.E.2d 392 (7th Dist.Columbiana County 1996)
26 ALR5th 603—§ 4
State v. Trunfio, 58 N.J. Super. 445, 156 A.2d 486 (App. Div. 1959)
57 ALR6th 445—§ 57
State v. Truster, 334 S.W.2d 104 (Mo. 1960)
11 ALR5th 497—§ 3, 5, 8
State v. Tryon, 431 N.W.2d 11 (Iowa Ct. App. 1988)
39 ALR5th 283—§ 10, 41
79 ALR5th 419—§ 9, 10
State v. Tschen, 2004-Ohio-991, 2004 WL 396357 (Ohio Ct. App. 8th Dist. Cuyahoga County 2004)
69 ALR6th 1—§ 10
State v. T.T., 594 So. 2d 839 (Fla. Dist. Ct. App. 5th Dist. 1992)
114 ALR5th 173—§ 12
122 ALR5th 439—§ 4
State v. Tuck, 127 Wash. App. 1008, 2005 WL 950688 (Div. 2 2005)
38 ALR6th 1—§ 13

State v. Tuck, 173 N.C. App. 61, 618 S.E.2d 265 (2005)
20 ALR6th 479—§ 3

State v. Tucker, 68 P.3d 110 (Ariz. 2003)
110 ALR5th 1—§ 19

State v. Tucker, 81 Ohio St. 3d 431, 1998-Ohio-438, 692 N.E.2d 171 (1998)
38 ALR6th 97—§ 27

State v. Tucker, 118 Ariz. 76, 574 P.2d 1295 (1978)
68 ALR5th 343—§ 4, 5, 17

State v. Tucker, 131 N.H. 526, 557 A.2d 270 (1989)
30 ALR6th 103—§ 8, 19, 26, 43, 48

State v. Tucker, 157 Ariz. 433, 759 P.2d 579 (1988)
94 ALR5th 393—§ 5

State v. Tucker, 242 Ga. App. 3, 528 S.E.2d 523 (2000)
104 ALR5th 229—§ 12
115 ALR5th 403—§ 3, 8
101 ALR6th 1—§ 7

State v. Tucker, 264 N.J. Super. 549, 625 A.2d 34 (App. Div. 1993)
85 ALR5th 471—§ 10

State v. Tucker, 317 N.C. 532, 346 S.E.2d 417 (1986)
39 ALR5th 283—§ 4, 66

State v. Tucker, 376 S.C. 412, 656 S.E.2d 403 (Ct. App. 2008)
52 ALR6th 1—§ 3, 32
53 ALR6th 1—§ 3

State v. Tucker, 1987 WL 8032 (Ohio Ct. App. 2d Dist. Darke County 1987)
72 ALR6th 141—§ 12

State v. Tuesno, 408 So. 2d 1269 (La. 1982)
22 ALR5th 1—§ 40, 54, 58, 59

State v. Tuesno, 456 So. 2d 186 (La. Ct. App. 4th Cir. 1984)
11 ALR6th 237—§ 12, 13

State v. Tull, 240 Md. 49, 212 A.2d 729 (1965)
72 ALR5th 529—§ 3

State v. Tully, 150 N.J. Super. 516, 376 A.2d 194 (App. Div. 1977)
69 ALR6th 1—§ 5

State v. Tully, 198 Wash. 605, 89 P.2d 517 (1939)
33 ALR6th 407—§ 21

State v. Tumblin, 868 So. 2d 902 (La. Ct. App. 5th Cir. 2004)
69 ALR6th 1—§ 5

State v. Tunell, 51 Wash. App. 274, 753 P.2d 543 (Div. 1 1988)
73 ALR5th 383—§ 5

State v. Tuomi, 2003 WI App 22, 259 Wis. 2d 935, 657 N.W.2d 440 (Ct. App. 2002)
84 ALR6th 293—§ 16, 34

State v. Tupko, 161 Conn. 20, 282 A.2d 911 (1971)
13 ALR6th 603—§ 44

State v. Turbeville, 235 Kan. 993, 686 P.2d 138 (1984)
39 ALR5th 283—§ 4, 71, 72

State v. Turecek, 456 N.W.2d 219 (Iowa 1990)
3 ALR6th 269—§ 9

State v. Turgeon, 165 Vt. 28, 676 A.2d 339 (1996)
11 ALR6th 237—§ 3, 15

State v. Turkowski, 2002 WL 47197 (Minn. Ct. App. 2002)
47 ALR6th 107—§ 22

State v. Turley, 442 S.W.2d 75 (Mo. 1969)
37 ALR6th 357—§ 8, 25

State v. Turley, 518 S.W.2d 207 (Mo. Ct. App. 1974)
97 ALR5th 201—§ 3

State v. Turmelle, 132 N.H. 148, 562 A.2d 196 (1989)
19 ALR5th 470—§ 3

State v. Turnbeaugh, 110 Idaho 11, 713 P.2d 447 (Ct. App. 1985)
112 ALR5th 429—§ 7

State v. Turnbough, 388 S.W.2d 781 (Mo. 1965)
85 ALR5th 187—§ 7, 9

State v. Turnbow, 99 Or. 270, 195 P. 569 (1921)
    85 ALR5th 471—§ 4

State v. Turnbull, 766 N.W.2d 78 (Minn. Ct. App. 2009)
    64 ALR6th 131—§ 2, 3

State v. Turner, 13 N.C. App. 603, 186 S.E.2d 681 (1972)
    89 ALR6th 565—§ 13, 25

State v. Turner, 22 Kan. App. 2d 564, 919 P.2d 370 (1996)
    15 ALR5th 391—§ 21
    22 ALR5th 660—§ 17

State v. Turner, 35 Wash. App. 192, 665 P.2d 923 (Div. 1 1983)
    83 ALR5th 277—§ 11

State v. Turner, 42 Wash. App. 242, 711 P.2d 353 (1985)
    1 ALR5th 938—§ 4, 6

State v. Turner, 59 N.D. 229, 229 N.W. 7 (1930)
    54 ALR6th 429—§ 11

State v. Turner, 103 N.C. App. 331, 406 S.E.2d 147 (1991)
    73 ALR5th 383—§ 22

State v. Turner, 117 N.C. App. 457, 451 S.E.2d 19 (1994)
    52 ALR5th 655—§ 8

State v. Turner, 142 Ariz. 138, 688 P.2d 1030 (Ct. App. Div. 2 1984)
    99 ALR5th 557—§ 2, 12

State v. Turner, 143 Wash. App. 1058, 2008 WL 1701845 (Div. 1 2008)
    103 ALR6th 347—§ 3, 20

State v. Turner, 145 Wash. App. 899, 187 P.3d 835 (Div. 1 2008)
    69 ALR6th 579—§ 4

State v. Turner, 153 Or. App. 66, 956 P.2d 215 (1998)
    16 ALR6th 329—§ 16
    24 ALR6th 591—§ 11

State v. Turner, 246 N.J. Super. 22, 586 A.2d 850 (1991)
    5 ALR5th 243—§ 48

State v. Turner, 252 Conn. 714, 751 A.2d 372 (2000)
    24 ALR6th 591—§ 4

State v. Turner, 257 Kan. 19, 891 P.2d 317 (1995)
    92 ALR6th 1—§ 6

State v. Turner, 259 Kan. 864, 915 P.2d 753 (1996)
    92 ALR6th 1—§ 6

State v. Turner, 265 Mont. 337, 877 P.2d 978 (1994)
    55 ALR6th 391—§ 5

State v. Turner, 267 Conn. 414, 838 A.2d 947 (2004)
    29 ALR6th 1—§ 10

State v. Turner, 320 S.W.2d 579 (Mo. 1959)
    54 ALR6th 429—§ 29

State v. Turner, 330 N.C. 249, 410 S.E.2d 847 (1991)
    98 ALR6th 455—§ 32

State v. Turner, 337 So. 2d 1090 (La. 1976)
    6 ALR6th 533—§ 11

State v. Turner, 371 S.C. 595, 641 S.E.2d 436 (2007)
    34 ALR6th 1—§ 10

State v. Turner, 382 N.W.2d 252 (Minn. Ct. App. 1986)
    67 ALR5th 431—§ 4, 12

State v. Turner, 550 N.W.2d 622 (Minn. 1996)
    60 ALR5th 75—§ 3, 6, 12

State v. Turner, 633 S.W.2d 421 (Mo. Ct. App. W.D. 1982)
    1 ALR6th 657—§ 4

State v. Turner, 716 S.W.2d 462 (Mo. Ct. App. E.D. 1986)
    58 ALR6th 499—§ 19

State v. Turner, 721 So. 2d 962 (La. Ct. App. 2d Cir. 1998)
    88 ALR5th 121—§ 3, 28

State v. Turner, 859 So. 2d 911 (La. Ct. App. 2d Cir. 2003)
    102 ALR6th 279—§ 32

State v. Turner, 879 S.W.2d 819 (Tenn. 1994)
    70 ALR5th 587—§ 21

State v. Turner, 1982 WL 8721 (Ohio Ct. App. 1st Dist. Hamilton County 1982)
88 ALR5th 121—§ 36
58 ALR6th 215—§ 20
State v. Turner, 2000 M.T. 270, 12 P.3d 934 (Mont. 2000)
72 ALR5th 109—§ 3, 6
State v. Turner, 2003 WL 22848972 (Tenn. Crim. App. 2003)
125 ALR5th 537—§ 18, 39
State v. Turner, No. 59866 (December 12, 1985, Ct. App. Ohio, 1st App. Dist. Cuyahoga Co.)
39 ALR5th 283—§ 14, 39
State v. Turpin, 2003-Ohio-4955, 2003 WL 22146531 (Ohio Ct. App. 8th Dist. Cuyahoga County 2003)
29 ALR6th 1—§ 10
State v. Tushoski, 199 Wis. 2d 125, 545 N.W.2d 520 (Ct. App. 1995)
84 ALR6th 293—§ 23
State v. Tuttle, 16 Utah 2d 288, 399 P.2d 580 (1965)
55 ALR5th 125—§ 3, 7
State v. Tuttle, 713 P.2d 703 (Utah 1985)
105 ALR5th 529—§ 25
State v. Tuttle, 730 P.2d 630, 42 Utah Adv. Rep. 8 (Utah 1986)
54 ALR5th 141—§ 3 to 5, 10
State v. Tuttle, 2002 SD 94, 650 N.W.2d 20 (S.D. 2002)
20 ALR6th 479—§ 3
State v. Tweed, 491 N.W.2d 412 (N.D. 1992)
7 ALR5th 758—§ 4, 15, 17
State v. Tweedie, 444 A.2d 855 (R.I. 1982)
6 ALR5th 733—§ 2, 13
State v. Twitty, 18 Ohio App. 2d 15, 47 Ohio Op. 2d 14, 246 N.E.2d 556 (10th Dist. Franklin County 1969)
55 ALR6th 513—§ 5
State v. Two Bulls, 1996 SD 53, 547 N.W.2d 764 (S.D. 1996)
84 ALR6th 427—§ 19, 21
State v. Twohig, 238 Neb. 92, 469 N.W.2d 344 (1991)

34 ALR6th 1—§ 11
State v. Tyes, 1983 WL 2999 (Ohio Ct. App. 8th Dist. Cuyahoga County 1983)
34 ALR6th 1—§ 5
42 ALR6th 237—§ 4
State v. Tyes, No. 48447 (January 17, 1985, Ct. App. Ohio, 8th App. Dist. Cuyahoga Co.)
39 ALR5th 283—§ 14, 66
State v. Tykwinski, 170 Ariz. 365, 824 P.2d 761 (Ct. App. Div. 1 1991)
74 ALR5th 319—§ 5, 6, 10
State v. Tyler, 50 Ohio St. 3d 24, 553 N.E.2d 576 (1990)
70 ALR5th 1—§ 6
3 ALR6th 269—§ 25
State v. Tyler, 103 S.W.3d 245 (Mo. Ct. App. E.D. 2003)
72 ALR6th 227—§ 44
State v. Tyler, 138 P.3d 417 (Kan. Ct. App. 2006)
23 ALR6th 307—§ 38
State v. Tyler, 138 Wash. App. 120, 155 P.3d 1002 (Div. 3 2007)
30 ALR6th 1—§ 3, 6
State v. Tyler, 251 Kan. 616, 840 P.2d 413 (1992)
55 ALR6th 157—§ 117
State v. Tyler, 306 S.W.2d 452 (Mo. 1957)
98 ALR6th 455—§ 24
99 ALR6th 113—§ 10
State v. Tyler, 342 So. 2d 574 (La. 1977)
101 ALR5th 187—§ 9
State v. Tyler, 587 S.W.2d 918 (Mo. Ct. App. W.D. 1979)
42 ALR5th 581—§ 12
98 ALR5th 445—§ 3
State v. Tyler, 598 S.W.2d 798 (Tenn. Crim. App. 1980)
58 ALR6th 499—§ 24, 101
State v. Tyler, 622 S.W.2d 379 (Mo. Ct. App. E.D. 1981)
86 ALR5th 463—§ 8
State v. Tyler, 723 So. 2d 939 (La. 1998)
47 ALR5th 259—§ 15

State v. Tyler, 749 So. 2d 767 (La. Ct. App. 4th Cir. 1999)
97 ALR6th 653—§ 31
State v. Tyler, 1988 WL 13188 (Ohio Ct. App. 8th Dist.Cuyahoga County 1988)
57 ALR5th 141—§ 12
State v. Tyner, 273 S.C. 646, 258 S.E.2d 559 (1979)
10 ALR5th 700—§ 16
20 ALR5th 177—§ 3
State v. Tyree, 1998 WL 135132 (Tenn. Crim. App. 1998)
73 ALR5th 383—§ 3
State v. Tyren, 91 Ohio Misc. 2d 67, 697 N.E.2d 293 (C.P. 1998)
71 ALR5th 1—§ 55
State v. Tyrrell, 60 Haw. 17, 586 P.2d 1028 (1978)
70 ALR5th 1—§ 6, 8
78 ALR5th 197—§ 14
State v. Tyrrell, 137 Wash. App. 1006, 2007 WL 430422 (Div. 2 2007)
78 ALR6th 1—§ 16
State v. Tyrrell, 2007 WL 430422 (Wash. Ct. App. Div. 2 2007)
26 ALR6th 511—§ 52
State v. Tyson, 56 Or. App. 777, 643 P.2d 396 (1982)
30 ALR6th 103—§ 19, 26, 58
State v. Tyson, 2003 WL 141127 (Tenn. Crim. App. 2003)
3 ALR6th 543—§ 6
State v. Tzintzun-Jimenez, 72 Wash. App. 852, 866 P.2d 667 (1994)
50 ALR5th 581—§ 7, 9, 14, 20
State v. Udstuen, 345 N.W.2d 766 (Minn. 1984)
73 ALR5th 383—§ 5
State v. Ugarte, 176 La. 54, 145 So. 266 (1932)
29 ALR5th 59—§ 3, 19
State v. Uhler, 61 Ohio Misc. 37, 14 Ohio Op. 3d 158, 15 Ohio Op. 3d 457, 402 N.E.2d 556 (C.P. 1979)
89 ALR6th 565—§ 14
State v. Uhthoff, 45 Wash. App. 261, 724 P.2d 1103 (Div. 1 1986)

102 ALR5th 525—§ 72
State v. Ulesky, 54 N.J. 26, 252 A.2d 720 (1969)
36 ALR5th 161—§ 17
State v. Ulin, 113 Ariz. 141, 548 P.2d 19 (1976)
50 ALR5th 467—§ 2, 7, 8
State v. Ulis, 91 Ohio App. 3d 656, 633 N.E.2d 562 (Lucas Co. 1993)
38 ALR5th 433—§ 13
State v. Ulm, 326 N.W.2d 159 (Minn. 1982)
28 ALR6th 505—§ 9
State v. Ulmer, 21 Ariz. App. 378, 519 P.2d 867 (Div. 1 1974)
80 ALR6th 599—§ 5
State v. Ulmer, 182 Ohio App. 3d 96, 2009-Ohio-1737, 911 N.E.2d 942 (6th Dist. Lucas County 2009)
63 ALR6th 351—§ 3
State v. Ulrey, 41 Kan. App. 2d 1052, 208 P.3d 317 (2009)
92 ALR6th 171—§ 4
State v. Ulrich, 17 Ohio App. 3d 182, 478 N.E.2d 812 (6th Dist. Wood County 1984)
119 ALR5th 379—§ 7
State v. Ulrich, 265 N.J. Super. 569, 628 A.2d 368 (App. Div. 1993)
67 ALR5th 361—§ 2 to 4
State v. Ulvestad, 414 N.W.2d 737 (Minn. App. 1987)
15 ALR5th 391—§ 44
State v. Ulvestad, 414 N.W.2d 737 (Minn. Ct. App. 1987)
66 ALR6th 351—§ 25, 64
67 ALR6th 209—§ 21
State v. Underdahl, 607 N.W.2d 786 (Minn. Ct. App. 2000)
38 ALR6th 97—§ 3, 29
State v. Underwood, 84 N.C. App. 408, 352 S.E.2d 898 (1987)
73 ALR5th 383—§ 28
State v. Underwood, 134 N.C. App. 533, 518 S.E.2d 231 (1999)
90 ALR5th 453—§ 16
State v. Underwood, 286 N.J. Super. 129, 668 A.2d 447 (App. Div. 1995)

27 ALR6th 183—§ 45
State v. Underwood, 669 S.W.2d 700 (Tenn. Crim. App. 1984)
28 ALR6th 505—§ 9
State v. Underwood, Slip Op (April 28, 1982, Ohio App. 12th Dist, Clermont Co.)
11 ALR5th 52—§ 6
State v. Unger, 103 N.J.L. 18, 134 A. 886 (N.J. Sup. Ct. 1926)
24 ALR6th 747—§ 17
State v. Ungerer, 1996 WL 362804 (Ohio Ct. App. 5th Dist. Ashland County 1996)
87 ALR5th 693—§ 3
State v. University of Alaska, 624 P.2d 807 (Alaska 1981)
10 ALR5th 448—§ 6
State v. Unnamed Defendant, 150 Wis. 2d 352, 441 N.W.2d 696 (1989)
90 ALR6th 385—§ 7
State v. Upchurch, 510 So. 2d 112 (La. Ct. App. 3d Cir. 1987)
12 ALR6th 553—§ 22, 36
State v. Upright, 72 N.C. App. 94, 323 S.E.2d 479 (1984)
16 ALR6th 329—§ 4
24 ALR6th 591—§ 6, 14
State v. Upton, 167 N.W.2d 625 (Iowa 1969)
29 ALR5th 59—§ 29, 40
State v. Urann, 128 Wash. App. 1054, 2005 WL 1796958 (Div. 3 2005)
26 ALR6th 511—§ 8
State v. Urbach, 83 Or. App. 39, 730 P.2d 571 (1986)
109 ALR5th 99—§ 2
113 ALR5th 517—§ 2, 3
State v. Urban, 2002-Ohio-1438, 2002 WL 464980 (Ohio Ct. App. 10th Dist. Franklin County 2002)
79 ALR6th 125—§ 4, 14
State v. Urbanek, 177 N.W.2d 14 (Iowa 1970)
31 ALR5th 171—§ 3, 8, 32
State v. Urena, 899 A.2d 1281 (R.I. 2006)
35 ALR6th 127—§ 5

State v. Uriarte, 194 Ariz. 275, 981 P.2d 575 (Ct. App. Div. 1 1998)
91 ALR5th 343—§ 16
State v. Urias, 8 Ariz. App. 319, 446 P.2d 18 (1968)
4 ALR5th 1—§ 17, 34
State v. Urick, No. 45682 (June 9, 1983, Ct. App. Ohio, 8th App. Dist. Cuyahoga Co.)
39 ALR5th 283—§ 14, 56
State v. Urquhart, 105 Idaho 92, 665 P.2d 1102 (App. 1983)
54 ALR5th 141—§ 3 to 5, 10
State v. Usher, 26 Or. App. 489, 552 P.2d 1345 (1976)
15 ALR5th 391—§ 39
State v. Ussery, 106 N.C. App. 371, 416 S.E.2d 610 (1992)
27 ALR5th 593—§ 24
State v. U. S. Steel Corp., 281 Ala. 553, 206 So. 2d 358 (1968)
89 ALR5th 493—§ 8
State v. Ustaszewski, 2006-Ohio-329, 2006 WL 205104 (Ohio Ct. App. 6th Dist. Lucas County 2006)
72 ALR6th 227—§ 41
State v. Ute, 1993 WL 218375 (Ohio Ct. App. 5th Dist. Richland County 1993)
84 ALR6th 293—§ 33
State v. Utterback, 240 Neb. 981, 485 N.W.2d 760 (1992)
73 ALR6th 49—§ 20
State v. Utvick, 2004 ND 36, 675 N.W.2d 387 (N.D. 2004)
2 ALR6th 169—§ 3, 5
50 ALR6th 455—§ 6, 15
State v. Vaccaro, 91 Wash. App. 1044, 1998 WL 375109 (Div. 1 1998)
90 ALR5th 453—§ 43
State v. Vaccaro, 142 N.J. Super. 167, 361 A.2d 47 (1976)
13 ALR5th 1—§ 2 to 4, 20, 25
State v. Vader, 114 N.J. Super. 260, 276 A.2d 151 (App. Div. 1971)
99 ALR6th 397—§ 10
State v. Vainio, 2001 MT 220, 306 Mont. 439, 35 P.3d 948 (2001)

79 ALR6th 125—§ 3, 9

State v. Vakas, 242 Kan. 103, 744 P.2d 812 (1987)

13 ALR5th 1—§ 2

State v. Valdez, 5 Neb. App. 506, 562 N.W.2d 64 (1997)

109 ALR5th 99—§ 12

State v. Valdez, 23 Ariz. App. 518, 534 P.2d 449 (Div. 2 1975)

86 ALR5th 59—§ 4

State v. Valdez, 91 N.M. 567, 577 P.2d 465 (App. 1978)

43 ALR5th 1—§ 2

State v. Valdez, 95 N.M. 70, 618 P.2d 1234 (1980)

64 ALR6th 655—§ 18

State v. Valdez, 111 N.M. 438, 806 P.2d 578 (Ct. App. 1990)

78 ALR6th 297—§ 22, 80

State v. Valdez, 115 Ariz. 1, 562 P.2d 1368 (App. 1977)

4 ALR5th 1—§ 17, 21

State v. Valdez, 167 Wash. 2d 761, 224 P.3d 751 (2009)

55 ALR6th 1—§ 6, 31, 39

State v. Valdez, 182 Ariz. 165, 894 P.2d 708, 181 Ariz. Adv. Rep. 7 (App. 1994)

42 ALR5th 291—§ 9, 25

State v. Valdez, 2003 UT App 314, 78 P.3d 627 (Utah Ct. App. 2003)

125 ALR5th 537—§ 15

State v. Vale, 650 So. 2d 379 (La. Ct. App. 5th Cir. 1995)

19 ALR6th 115—§ 4, 9, 10

State v. Vale, 2005-Ohio-3725, 2005 WL 1706999 (Ohio Ct. App. 8th Dist. Cuyahoga County 2005)

69 ALR6th 1—§ 29

State v. Valencia, 132 Ariz. 248, 645 P.2d 239 (1982)

45 ALR5th 591—§ 18

State v. Valencia, 205 Neb. 719, 290 N.W.2d 181 (1980)

33 ALR6th 407—§ 3, 11, 13

State v. Valencia Olaya, 105 N.M. 690, 736 P.2d 495 (Ct. App. 1987)

116 ALR5th 479—§ 5

State v. Valentin, 105 N.J. 14, 519 A.2d 322 (1987)

87 ALR5th 597—§ 2, 13

State v. Valentine, 74 Ohio App. 3d 110, 598 N.E.2d 82 (4th Dist. Lawrence County 1991)

85 ALR5th 1—§ 17, 24

State v. Valentine, 100 Wash. App. 1058, 2000 WL 628996 (Div. 1 2000)

78 ALR6th 1—§ 37

State v. Valentine, 132 Wash. 2d 1, 935 P.2d 1294 (1997)

18 ALR5th 1—§ 41

State v. Valentine, 260 Kan. 431, 921 P.2d 770 (1996)

5 ALR5th 243—§ 9

State v. Valentine, 264 Or. 54, 504 P.2d 84 (1972)

85 ALR5th 1—§ 10

State v. Valentine, 364 So. 2d 595 (La. 1978)

62 ALR5th 121—§ 6

State v. Valento, 405 N.W.2d 914 (Minn. App. 1987)

41 ALR5th 171—§ 12, 114

State v. Valenzuela, 3 Ariz. App. 278, 413 P.2d 788 (1966)

85 ALR5th 1—§ 18

State v. Valenzuela, 94 N.M. 340, 610 P.2d 744 (1980)

7 ALR5th 263—§ 6

State v. Valenzuela, 116 Ariz. 61, 567 P.2d 1190 (1977)

21 ALR6th 771—§ 22

State v. Valenzuela, 130 N.H. 175, 536 A.2d 1252 (1987)

41 ALR5th 171—§ 6, 137

State v. Valeriani, 101 N.J. Super. 396, 244 A.2d 510 (1968)

26 ALR5th 1—§ 4

State v. Valeu, 257 Iowa 867, 134 N.W.2d 911 (1965)

52 ALR5th 655—§ 5

State v. Vallejos, 122 N.M. 318, 924 P.2d 727 (App. 1996)

18 ALR5th 1—§ 4
State v. Valley, 149 Wash. App. 1003, 2009 WL 449084 (Div. 2 2009)

71 ALR6th 1—§ 5
State v. Valley, 252 Mont. 489, 830 P.2d 1255 (1992)

112 ALR5th 429—§ 7, 12
State v. Valverde, 128 Idaho 237, 912 P.2d 124 (Ct. App. 1996)

7 ALR6th 233—§ 5
State v. Vanacker, 759 S.W.2d 391 (Mo. Ct. App. S.D. 1988)

82 ALR5th 103—§ 5
State v. Van Ackeren, 194 Neb. 650, 235 N.W.2d 210 (1975)

68 ALR5th 343—§ 3, 16
State v. Van Ackeren, 200 Neb. 812, 265 N.W.2d 675 (1978)

68 ALR5th 343—§ 3
State v. Van Adams, 194 Ariz. 408, 984 P.2d 16 (1999)

21 ALR6th 1—§ 4
State v. Vanassche, 566 A.2d 1077 (Me. 1989)

78 ALR5th 1—§ 51
State v. Vanatter, 869 S.W.2d 754 (Mo. 1994)

22 ALR5th 261—§ 6
State v. Van Beek, 1999 ND 53, 591 N.W.2d 112 (N.D. 1999)

2 ALR6th 169—§ 3, 5
50 ALR6th 455—§ 6, 8, 9, 15, 19
State v. Van Buren, 101 Wash. App. 206, 2 P.3d 991 (Div. 2 2000)

9 ALR6th 541—§ 24
State v. Van Buren, 112 Wash. App. 585, 49 P.3d 966 (Div. 2 2002)

9 ALR6th 541—§ 24
State v. Van Camp, 6 Conn. Cir. Ct. 609, 281 A.2d 584 (App. Div. 1971)

31 ALR6th 333—§ 7, 11, 13
State v. Vance, 53 Or. App. 290, 631 P.2d 843 (1981)

97 ALR6th 653—§ 27
State v. Vance, 61 Haw. 291, 602 P.2d 933 (1979)

68 ALR5th 299—§ 4

State v. Vance, 61 Hawaii 291, 602 P.2d 933 (1979)

4 ALR5th 1—§ 3, 6, 7
State v. Vance, 119 Vt. 268, 125 A.2d 800 (1956)

6 ALR5th 733—§ 10, 16
State v. Vance, 199 Wis. 2d 526, 546 N.W.2d 580 (Ct. App. 1996)

84 ALR6th 293—§ 21
State v. Vance, 392 N.W.2d 679 (Minn. App. 1986)

3 ALR5th 784—§ 14
State v. Vance, 633 S.W.2d 442 (Mo. Ct. App. W.D. 1982)

111 ALR5th 1—§ 8, 26
State v. Vance, 2007 WL 4395710 (Wash. Ct. App. Div. 2 2007)

33 ALR6th 91—§ 51
State v. Vance, Slip Opinion No. 76AP-662 (Ohio App. Franklin Co. 1977)

41 ALR5th 171—§ 66, 91, 108
State v. Vancleave, 163 Or. App. 252, 989 P.2d 473 (1999)

15 ALR5th 391—§ 5
State v. VanDemortel, 224 Wis. 2d 643, 590 N.W.2d 282 (Ct. App. 1999)

76 ALR5th 1—§ 7, 10
State v. Vanderbilt, 1992 WL 69650 (Tenn. Crim. App. 1992)

73 ALR5th 383—§ 5
State v. Vanderhorst, 257 S.C. 114, 184 S.E.2d 540 (1971)

55 ALR6th 157—§ 17
State v. Vanderpool, 39 Ohio St. 273, 1883 WL 178 (1883)

20 ALR6th 561—§ 16
State v. Vanderpool, 99 Wash. App. 709, 995 P.2d 104 (Div. 3 2000)

33 ALR6th 91—§ 36
State v. Vandersall, 2003-Ohio-6380, 2003 WL 22830599 (Ohio Ct. App. 6th Dist. Lucas County 2003)

35 ALR6th 361—§ 20
State v. Vandersommen, 2008 WL 4902386 (Ariz. Ct. App. Div. 2 2008)

71 ALR6th 1—§ 5

State v. Vanderveer, 285 N.J. Super. 475, 667 A.2d 382 (App. Div. 1995)
122 ALR5th 439—§ 4

State v. Vandervort, 276 Kan. 164, 72 P.3d 925 (2003)
29 ALR6th 1—§ 10

State v. Vandeveer, 23 Ariz. App. 331, 533 P.2d 91 (Div. 1 1975)
81 ALR6th 505—§ 54

State v. Vandeventer, 746 S.W.2d 658 (Mo. App. 1988)
42 ALR5th 291—§ 30

State v. Vandiver, 19 Kan. App. 2d 786, 876 P.2d 205 (1994)
122 ALR5th 439—§ 8

State v. Vandiver, 257 Kan. 53, 891 P.2d 350 (1995)
122 ALR5th 439—§ 8

State v. Van Doren, 657 S.W.2d 708 (Mo. Ct. App. E.D. 1983)
39 ALR6th 257—§ 17

State v. Van Dort, 502 P.2d 453 (Alaska 1972)
57 ALR6th 419—§ 8

State v. VanDusen, 166 Vt. 240, 691 A.2d 1053 (1997)
91 ALR5th 343—§ 33

State v. Van Dyken, 242 Mont. 415, 791 P.2d 1350 (1990)
26 ALR5th 603—§ 3
38 ALR5th 433—§ 38

State v. Van Dyne, 26 Ohio App. 3d 95, 498 N.E.2d 221 (10th Dist. Franklin County 1985)
97 ALR6th 653—§ 3

State v. Vane, 105 Wash. 170, 177 P. 728 (1919)
41 ALR5th 1—§ 5

State v. Van Egdom, 292 N.W.2d 586 (S.D. 1980)
72 ALR5th 109—§ 6

State v. Van Egmond, 206 Neb. 331, 293 N.W.2d 72 (1980)
66 ALR5th 397—§ 10, 12, 25

State v. Vangen, 72 Wash. 2d 548, 433 P.2d 691 (1967)
80 ALR6th 599—§ 8

State v. Van Gorden, 326 N.W.2d 633 (Minn. 1982)
73 ALR5th 383—§ 3

State v. Van Haele, 199 Mont. 522, 649 P.2d 1311 (1982)
19 ALR5th 470—§ 6

State v. Vanhorn, 2000 WL 234557 (Ohio Ct. App. 6th Dist. Lucas County 2000)
41 ALR6th 295—§ 4, 6

State v. Van Laarhoven, 90 Wis. 2d 67, 279 N.W.2d 488 (App. 1979)
29 ALR5th 702—§ 2, 3

State v. Van Laarhoven, 90 Wis. 2d 67, 279 N.W.2d 488 (Ct. App. 1979)
82 ALR6th 317—§ 12, 13

State v. Van Matre, 777 P.2d 459 (Utah 1989)
71 ALR5th 637—§ 3

State v. Vann, 162 N.C. 534, 77 S.E. 295 (1913)
103 ALR6th 35—§ 7

State v. Van Natta, 805 S.W.2d 40 (Tex. App. Fort Worth 1991)
74 ALR5th 319—§ 8, 12

State v. Vanness, 99 Or. App. 120, 781 P.2d 391 (1989)
84 ALR6th 293—§ 15

State v. Van Orman, 642 S.W.2d 636 (Mo. 1982)
103 ALR6th 507—§ 22

State v. Vanover, 721 A.2d 430 (R.I. 1998)
40 ALR5th 113—§ 4

State v. Vanover, 2002 WL 984368 (Iowa Ct. App. 2002)
99 ALR6th 295—§ 13, 16

State v. Van Pham, 234 Kan. 649, 675 P.2d 848 (1984)
32 ALR5th 149—§ 3, 5, 29, 51, 52, 65, 74
16 ALR6th 329—§ 4
19 ALR6th 115—§ 7
24 ALR6th 591—§ 4, 12, 15

State v. Van Rees, 246 N.W.2d 339 (Iowa 1976)
24 ALR6th 1—§ 21

State v. Van Sickle, 90 Ohio App. 3d 301, 629 N.E.2d 39 (Franklin Co. 1993)

37 ALR5th 515—§ 8, 9, 25

State v. Vanstory, 84 N.C. App. 535, 353 S.E.2d 236 (1987)

73 ALR5th 383—§ 5

State v. Van Straten, 140 Wis. 2d 306, 409 N.W.2d 448 (Ct. App. 1987)

80 ALR5th 469—§ 3, 5

State v. Van Tassel, 103 Iowa 6, 72 N.W. 497 (1897)

78 ALR5th 1—§ 33

State v. Van Tassel, 2009 WL 1684072 (Minn. Ct. App. 2009)

84 ALR6th 427—§ 5

State v. Van Tran, 864 S.W.2d 465 (Tenn. 1993)

32 ALR5th 149—§ 51, 52
37 ALR5th 515—§ 2, 3
83 ALR6th 255—§ 22

State v. VanWagner, 504 N.W.2d 746 (Minn. 1993)

34 ALR6th 1—§ 10

State v. Van Walchren, 112 Or. App. 240, 828 P.2d 1044 (1992)

26 ALR5th 1—§ 3

State v. Van Wert, 294 Minn. 464, 199 N.W.2d 514 (1972)

41 ALR5th 171—§ 31, 41
27 ALR6th 491—§ 3

State v. Van Winkle, 254 Kan. 214, 864 P.2d 729 (1993)

18 ALR5th 1—§ 4

State v. Varela, 178 Ariz. 319, 873 P.2d 657 (Ct. App. Div. 1 1993)

85 ALR5th 595—§ 8

State v. Varela, 636 So. 2d 559, 19 FLW D 1006 (Fla. App. D5 1994)

46 ALR5th 523—§ 9

State v. Vargas, 420 A.2d 809 (R.I. 1980)

3 ALR6th 269—§ 5, 13

State v. Vargas, 424 S.W.2d 416 (Tex. 1968)

53 ALR6th 305—§ 47

State v. Vargovich, 113 Idaho 354, 743 P.2d 1007 (Ct. App. 1987)

6 ALR6th 533—§ 19

State v. Vargus, 118 R.I. 113, 373 A.2d 150 (1977)

34 ALR6th 1—§ 11

State v. Varlese, 171 N.J. Super. 347, 409 A.2d 285 (App. Div. 1979)

55 ALR6th 157—§ 45

State v. Varnell, 137 Wash. App. 925, 155 P.3d 971 (Div. 2 2007)

78 ALR6th 1—§ 28, 32, 42, 58

State v. Varner, 2003-Ohio-719, 2003 WL 357526 (Ohio Ct. App. 9th Dist. Summit County 2003)

23 ALR6th 307—§ 38

State v. Varner, Docket No. C-1790874 (Nov 19, 1980, Ohio App. Hamilton Co.)

18 ALR5th 1—§ 28

State v. Varricchio, 176 Conn. 445, 408 A.2d 239 (1979)

89 ALR6th 565—§ 3, 17

State v. Varszegi, 236 Conn. 266, 673 A.2d 90, 54 A.L.R.5th 775 (1996)

54 ALR5th 141—§ 3 to 6, 10

State v. Vashon, 123 Me. 412, 123 A. 511 (1924)

102 ALR5th 525—§ 20

State v. Vasquez, 48 Conn. App. 130, 708 A.2d 976 (1998)

7 ALR6th 169—§ 23

State v. Vasquez, 80 Wash. App. 5, 906 P.2d 351 (1995)

27 ALR5th 593—§ 17

State v. Vasquez, 101 Utah 444, 121 P.2d 903, 140 A.L.R. 755 (1942)

32 ALR5th 149—§ 4, 25, 26, 32, 33

State v. Vasquez, 374 N.J. Super. 252, 864 A.2d 409 (App. Div. 2005)

26 ALR6th 511—§ 28

State v. Vass, 191 Conn. 604, 469 A.2d 767 (1983)

39 ALR5th 283—§ 3
102 ALR6th 365—§ 28

State v. Vaster, 99 Wash. 2d 44, 659 P.2d 528 (1983)

40 ALR5th 113—§ 3
State v. Vater, 1996 WL 280772 (Wash. Ct. App. Div. 1 1996)
73 ALR5th 383—§ 27
State v. Vaughan, 136 Mo. App. 645, 118 S.W. 1186 (1909)
51 ALR5th 603—§ 2
State v. Vaughan, 144 S.W.3d 391 (Tenn. Crim. App. 2003)
27 ALR6th 183—§ 6, 32
State v. Vaughan, 1997 WL 605082 (Ohio Ct. App. 3d Dist. Union County 1997)
78 ALR5th 489—§ 10
State v. Vaughn, 29 S.W.3d 33 (Tenn. Crim. App. 1998)
72 ALR5th 607—§ 3, 9, 10
State v. Vaughn, 106 Ohio App. 3d 775, 667 N.E.2d 82 (12th Dist. Butler County 1995)
76 ALR5th 485—§ 19
State v. Vaughn, 199 Conn. 557, 508 A.2d 430 (1986)
102 ALR6th 365—§ 18
State v. Vaughn, 296 N.C. 167, 250 S.E.2d 210 (1978)
51 ALR6th 1—§ 20, 24
71 ALR6th 335—§ 12
State v. Vaughn, 2007 MT 164, 338 Mont. 97, 164 P.3d 873 (2007)
71 ALR6th 1—§ 22
State v. Vaught, 56 Ohio St. 2d 93, 10 Ohio Op. 3d 224, 382 N.E.2d 213 (1978)
84 ALR6th 427—§ 3, 5
State v. Vawter, 33 N.C. App. 131, 234 S.E.2d 438 (1977)
39 ALR5th 283—§ 4
State v. V.C., 600 So. 2d 1280, 76 Ed. Law Rep. 270 (Fla. Dist. Ct. App. 3d Dist. 1992)
59 ALR6th 393—§ 3
State v. V.E., 2007 WL 1556094 (N.J. Super. Ct. App. Div. 2007)
39 ALR6th 257—§ 36
State v. Veach, 224 Tenn. 412, 456 S.W.2d 650 (1970)
29 ALR5th 59—§ 3, 29

State v. Vedder, 668 S.W.2d 639 (Mo. App. 1984)
7 ALR5th 73—§ 11
State v. Vega, 38 Conn. Supp. 313, 444 A.2d 927 (Super. Ct. Appellate Sess. 1982)
95 ALR5th 229—§ 2, 25
State v. Vega, 200 N.J. Super. 448, 491 A.2d 797 (Law Div. 1984)
109 ALR5th 611—§ 3
56 ALR6th 323—§ 7, 11
State v. Vega-Bonilla, 1996 WL 737533 (Ohio Ct. App. 4th Dist. Washington County 1996)
55 ALR6th 513—§ 8
State v. Veillon, 105 La. 411, 29 So. 883 (1901)
104 ALR5th 357—§ 4
54 ALR6th 429—§ 9
State v. Veiman, 249 Neb. 875, 546 N.W.2d 785 (1996)
35 ALR6th 127—§ 12
State v. Vela, 100 Wash. 2d 636, 673 P.2d 185 (1983)
26 ALR5th 1—§ 3
State v. Velarde, 67 N.M. 224, 354 P.2d 522 (1960)
86 ALR5th 59—§ 8
State v. Velarde, 734 P.2d 440 (Utah 1986)
16 ALR6th 329—§ 4
24 ALR6th 591—§ 4, 12
State v. Velarde, 734 P.2d 449, 47 Utah Adv. Rep. 8 (Utah 1986)
50 ALR5th 467—§ 6, 9
State v. Velasco-Felix, 2010 WL 3057246 (Ariz. Ct. App. Div. 1 2010)
73 ALR6th 49—§ 58
State v. Velasquez, 641 P.2d 115 (Utah 1982)
37 ALR6th 357—§ 67
State v. Velasquez, 1999 ND 217, 602 N.W.2d 693 (N.D. 1999)
92 ALR5th 35—§ 22
State v. Velasquez, 1999 N.D. 217, 602 N.W.2d 693 (N.D. 1999)
15 ALR5th 391—§ 32

State v. Veley, 37 Or. App. 235, 586 P.2d 1130 (1978)
111 ALR5th 239—§ 6

State v. Velez, 17 Conn. App. 186, 551 A.2d 421 (1988)
39 ALR6th 257—§ 42

State v. Velez, 329 N.J. Super. 128, 746 A.2d 1073 (App. Div. 2000)
125 ALR5th 497—§ 3

State v. Velez, 588 So. 2d 116 (La. Ct. App. 3d Cir. 1991)
101 ALR5th 187—§ 6
16 ALR6th 329—§ 4
24 ALR6th 591—§ 4, 14

State v. Velez, 1995 WL 264544 (Ohio App. 8 Dist.)
50 ALR5th 581—§ 8, 16, 20

State v. Velishek, 410 N.W.2d 893 (Minn. Ct. App. 1987)
112 ALR5th 429—§ 10

State v. Veluzat, 578 A.2d 93 (R.I. 1990)
38 ALR5th 433—§ 11, 19

State v. Vending Mach. Corp. of America, 1935 OK 1138, 174 Okla. 603, 51 P.2d 724, 103 A.L.R. 391 (1935)
66 ALR6th 315—§ 21

State v. Venegas, 137 Ariz. 171, 669 P.2d 604 (Ct. App. Div. 1 1983)
84 ALR6th 427—§ 8

State v. Venman, 151 Vt. 561, 564 A.2d 574 (1989)
79 ALR6th 125—§ 3, 5

State v. Vennard, 159 Conn. 385, 270 A.2d 837 (1970)
51 ALR5th 603—§ 3

State v. Vento, 533 A.2d 1161 (R.I. 1987)
73 ALR5th 615—§ 2, 7

State v. Ventre, 811 A.2d 1178 (R.I. 2002)
3 ALR6th 543—§ 6

State v. Ventris, 285 Kan. 595, 176 P.3d 920 (2008)
46 ALR6th 495—§ 13

State v. Ventry, 439 So. 2d 1144 (La. Ct. App. 4th Cir. 1983)
103 ALR5th 463—§ 3

State v. Ventura, 101 Ohio Misc. 2d 15, 720 N.E.2d 1024 (C.P. 1999)
60 ALR5th 75—§ 12

State v. Ventura, 353 N.J. Super. 251, 802 A.2d 545 (App. Div. 2002)
50 ALR6th 455—§ 33, 35
59 ALR6th 311—§ 1

State v. Ventura, 2005-Ohio-5048, 2005 WL 2335317 (Ohio Ct. App. 12th Dist. Butler County 2005)
69 ALR6th 1—§ 29

State v. Venus, 2006 WL 758312 (N.J. Super. Ct. App. Div. 2006)
18 ALR6th 519—§ 8

State v. Vera, 159 Ariz. 237, 766 P.2d 110, 19 Ariz. Adv. Rep. 5 (App. 1988)
15 ALR5th 391—§ 4

State v. Verdolini, 76 Conn. App. 466, 819 A.2d 901 (2003)
21 ALR6th 771—§ 4

State v. Verdone, 114 R.I. 613, 337 A.2d 804 (1975)
85 ALR5th 547—§ 8

State v. Vergilio, 261 N.J. Super. 648, 619 A.2d 671 (1993)
45 ALR5th 531—§ 6

State v. Verhagen, 86 Wis. 2d 262, 272 N.W.2d 105 (Ct. App. 1978)
65 ALR5th 407—§ 3, 4, 13, 20

State v. Verikokidis, 925 P.2d 1255 (Utah 1996)
105 ALR5th 529—§ 11

State v. Verive, 128 Ariz. 570, 627 P.2d 721 (Ariz. App. 1981)
49 ALR5th 639—§ 2, 4

State v. Vermillion, 66 Wash. App. 332, 832 P.2d 95 (Div. 3 1992)
73 ALR5th 383—§ 42

State v. Vermilya, 395 N.W.2d 151 (N.D. 1986)
99 ALR5th 557—§ 9

State v. Vermuele, 160 Ariz. 295, 772 P.2d 1148 (Ct. App. Div. 2 1989)
92 ALR6th 295—§ 13, 19
96 ALR6th 355—§ 9

State v. Vernon, 116 N.M. 737, 867 P.2d 407 (N.M. 1993)

28 ALR5th 754—§ 2, 5, 8
39 ALR5th 283—§ 77
State v. Vernon, 251 La. 1099, 208 So. 2d 690 (1968)
70 ALR5th 587—§ 3
State v. Vernon, 2009-Ohio-3937, 2009 WL 2426138 (Ohio Ct. App. 11th Dist. Lake County 2009)
63 ALR6th 351—§ 3
64 ALR6th 1—§ 9
State v. Verona, 93 NJL 389, 108 A. 250 (1919)
29 ALR5th 59—§ 62
State v. Verrecchia, 880 A.2d 89 (R.I. 2005)
80 ALR6th 239—§ 3, 9
State v. Verrill, 120 Me. 41, 112 A. 673 (1921)
26 ALR5th 1—§ 4
State v. Verrinder, 161 Vt. 250, 637 A.2d 1382 (1993)
57 ALR5th 141—§ 9
57 ALR5th 315—§ 11
State v. Versnel, 98 P.3d 672 (Kan. Ct. App. 2004)
26 ALR6th 511—§ 25
State v. Vert, 39 N.C. App. 26, 249 S.E.2d 476 (1978)
39 ALR5th 283—§ 4, 18
State v. Vessichio, 197 Conn. 644, 500 A.2d 1311 (1985)
2 ALR6th 551—§ 16
State v. Vestal, 740 S.W.2d 378 (Mo. Ct. App. E.D. 1987)
68 ALR6th 527—§ 37
State v. Veverka, 271 N.W.2d 744 (Iowa 1978)
79 ALR5th 419—§ 7
State v. Via, 146 Ariz. 108, 704 P.2d 238 (1985)
57 ALR5th 141—§ 5
State v. Vialpando, 2004 UT App 95, 89 P.3d 209 (Utah Ct. App. 2004)
92 ALR6th 295—§ 8, 13, 19, 25
96 ALR6th 355—§ 6, 26, 36, 49, 60
State v. Viatical Services, Inc., 741 So. 2d 560 (Fla. Dist. Ct. App. 4th Dist. 1999)

28 ALR6th 281—§ 3, 19
State v. Vicars, 207 Neb. 325, 299 N.W.2d 421 (1980)
104 ALR5th 165—§ 12
119 ALR5th 275—§ 8
67 ALR6th 531—§ 4, 36
State v. Vick, 130 N.C. App. 207, 502 S.E.2d 871 (1998)
85 ALR5th 1—§ 25
State v. Vick, 502 S.E.2d 871 (N.C. Ct. App. 1998)
67 ALR5th 637—§ 5
State v. Vick, 1998 ND 214, 587 N.W.2d 567 (N.D. 1998)
92 ALR5th 35—§ 25
State v. Vickers, 129 Ariz. 506, 633 P.2d 315 (1981)
42 ALR6th 237—§ 8
State v. Vickers, 138 Ariz. 450, 675 P.2d 710 (1983)
85 ALR5th 547—§ 8
State v. Vickers, 159 Ariz. 532, 768 P.2d 1177 (1989)
38 ALR6th 97—§ 29
State v. Vickers, 180 Ariz. 521, 885 P.2d 1086, 179 Ariz. Adv. Rep. 3 (1994)
40 ALR5th 113—§ 3
State v. Vickers, 184 N.C. 676, 114 S.E. 168 (1922)
76 ALR5th 485—§ 3, 7
State v. Victor, 235 Neb. 770, 457 N.W.2d 431 (1990)
32 ALR6th 1—§ 11
State v. Victor O., 301 Conn. 163, 20 A.3d 669, 84 A.L.R.6th 701 (2011)
84 ALR6th 263—§ 5
State v. Victorsen, 627 N.W.2d 655 (Minn. Ct. App. 2001)
69 ALR6th 579—§ 8, 34
State v. Victory Fireworks, Inc., 602 N.W.2d 128 (Wis. Ct. App. 1999)
48 ALR5th 659—§ 34
State v. Vidor, 75 Wash. 2d 607, 452 P.2d 961 (1969)
55 ALR5th 125—§ 3, 7
State v. Vietor, 261 N.W.2d 828 (Iowa 1978)

---

109 ALR5th 611—§ 3, 4, 6
State v. Vigh, 871 P.2d 1030 (Utah Ct. App. 1994)

112 ALR5th 429—§ 4, 7
State v. Vigh, 871 P.2d 1030, 234 Utah Adv. Rep. 44 (Utah App. 1994)

4 ALR5th 1—§ 4, 14
27 ALR5th 593—§ 23
State v. Vigil, 97 N.M. 749, 643 P.2d 618 (Ct. App. 1982)

21 ALR6th 771—§ 7, 10
State v. Vigil, 110 N.M. 254, 794 P.2d 728 (1990)

11 ALR5th 871—§ 7
State v. Vigliano, 50 N.J. 51, 232 A.2d 129 (1967)

101 ALR5th 187—§ 9
State v. Viles, 702 P.2d 1175 (Utah 1985)

37 ALR6th 357—§ 25
State v. Villa, 179 Ariz. 486, 880 P.2d 706, 159 Ariz. Adv. Rep. 22 (App. 1994)

33 ALR5th 571—§ 3
State v. Villalobos, 1994 WL 71363 (Minn. Ct. App. 1994)

73 ALR5th 383—§ 21
State v. Villalovo, 481 So. 2d 1303 (Fla. Dist. Ct. App. 3d Dist. 1986)

113 ALR5th 597—§ 4
State v. Villanueva, 2005 MT 192, 328 Mont. 135, 118 P.3d 179 (2005)

34 ALR6th 171—§ 34
State v. Villa-Perez, 835 S.W.2d 897 (Mo. 1992)

114 ALR5th 173—§ 7
State v. Villarreal, 857 P.2d 949 (Utah Ct. App. 1993)

80 ALR5th 55—§ 12
State v. Villegas-Varela, 132 Or. App. 112, 887 P.2d 809 (1994)

84 ALR6th 293—§ 16, 30
State v. Villella, 266 Ga. App. 499, 597 S.E.2d 563 (2004)

15 ALR6th 375—§ 19
State v. Villeza, 85 Haw. 258, 942 P.2d 522 (Haw. 1997)

60 ALR5th 39—§ 3
State v. Vinal, 198 Conn. 644, 504 A.2d 1364 (1986)

16 ALR6th 329—§ 5
19 ALR6th 115—§ 5
24 ALR6th 591—§ 4, 12
State v. Vince, 305 So. 2d 916 (La. 1974)

87 ALR5th 181—§ 5
State v. Vincent, 25 Conn. Supp. 96, 197 A.2d 79 (Super. Ct. 1961)

103 ALR6th 137—§ 4
State v. Vincent, 229 Conn. 164, 640 A.2d 94 (1994)

6 ALR6th 533—§ 21
State v. Vincent, 258 Kan. 694, 908 P.2d 619 (1995)

16 ALR6th 329—§ 4
19 ALR6th 115—§ 7
24 ALR6th 591—§ 4, 12, 15
State v. Vincent, 845 P.2d 254, 202 Utah Adv. Rep. 31 (Utah App. 1992)

26 ALR5th 765—§ 4, 6, 7, 9 to 12, 16, 17, 19, 20, 22
State v. Vincent, 883 P.2d 278, 250 Utah Adv. Rep. 5 (Utah 1994)

26 ALR5th 765—§ 4, 9, 10, 12, 20, 23
State v. Vincent, 1990 WL 74295 (Del. Super. Ct. 1990)

61 ALR5th 1—§ 3, 14
State v. Vincent, 2000 WL 221991 (Ohio Ct. App. 5th Dist. Stark County 2000)

78 ALR5th 489—§ 10
State v. Vincik, 398 N.W.2d 788 (Iowa 1987)

96 ALR5th 523—§ 4
State v. Vincik, 436 N.W.2d 350 (Iowa 1989)

58 ALR6th 499—§ 3, 21, 98, 101
State v. Vinegra, 73 N.J. 484, 376 A.2d 150 (1977)

29 ALR5th 1—§ 2
State v. Vines, 71 Conn. App. 751, 804 A.2d 877 (2002)

65 ALR6th 537—§ 58, 61
State v. Vines, 268 Conn. 239, 842 A.2d 1086 (2004)

65 ALR6th 537—§ 61
State v. Vineyard, 497 S.W.2d 821 (Mo. Ct. App. 1973)
55 ALR6th 157—§ 76, 111
State v. Vining, 2 Wash. App. 802, 472 P.2d 564, 53 A.L.R.3d 390 (Div. 2 1970)
29 ALR6th 1—§ 9
State v. Vinson, 298 So. 2d 505 (Fla. App. D2 1974)
13 ALR5th 1—§ 35
State v. Vinson, 833 S.W.2d 399 (Mo. Ct. App. E.D. 1992)
99 ALR6th 113—§ 22
State v. Vinyard, 50 Wash. App. 888, 751 P.2d 339 (1988)
15 ALR5th 391—§ 25
State v. Violett, 79 S.D. 292, 111 N.W.2d 598 (1961)
99 ALR6th 113—§ 8, 18
State v. Visser, 188 Wash. 179, 61 P.2d 1284 (1936)
50 ALR5th 703—§ 15
State v. Vistell, 1985 WL 10647 (Ohio Ct. App. 9th Dist. Summit County 1985)
19 ALR6th 697—§ 4
State v. Vital, 505 So. 2d 1006 (La. Ct. App. 3d Cir. 1987)
1 ALR6th 657—§ 14
State v. Vitale, 23 Ariz. App. 37, 530 P.2d 394 (Div. 2 1975)
67 ALR5th 361—§ 2, 4, 7
State v. Vitale, 96 Ohio App. 3d 695, 645 N.E.2d 1277 (8th Dist. Cuyahoga County 1994)
57 ALR6th 445—§ 18
State v. Vitanza, 1992 WL 190586 (Ohio Ct. App. 11th Dist. Lake County 1992)
17 ALR6th 327—§ 38
State v. Vitiello, 377 N.J. Super. 452, 873 A.2d 591 (App. Div. 2005)
90 ALR6th 385—§ 5
State v. VJW, 37 Wash. App. 428, 680 P.2d 1068 (Div. 1 1984)
72 ALR5th 1—§ 10, 30

State v. Vlacil, 645 P.2d 677, 28 A.L.R.4th 1086 (Utah 1982)
75 ALR6th 541—§ 13
State v. Vliet, 95 Haw. 94, 19 P.3d 42 (2001)
119 ALR5th 379—§ 3
State v. Voelkel, 2 Conn. Cir. 459, 202 A.2d 250 (1964)
6 ALR5th 733—§ 2, 4, 12
State v. Voelkers, 547 N.W.2d 625 (Iowa App. 1996)
45 ALR5th 591—§ 7
State v. Voeller, 356 N.W.2d 115 (N.D. 1984)
55 ALR6th 157—§ 96
State v. Vogel, 428 N.W.2d 272 (S.D. 1988)
59 ALR5th 615—§ 3, 4, 6, 7, 10
State v. Vogel, 2005-Ohio-5757, 2005 WL 2840641 (Ohio Ct. App. 3d Dist. Crawford County 2005)
26 ALR6th 511—§ 19
State v. Vogele, 2004 WL 2284197 (Conn. Super. Ct. 2004)
58 ALR6th 215—§ 7, 10
State v. Vogt, 685 S.E.2d 23 (N.C. Ct. App. 2009)
57 ALR6th 1—§ 4, 18
State v. Vogt, 2001 WL 709233 (N.J. Super. Ct. App. Div. 2001)
67 ALR5th 431—§ 4
State v. Voigt, 2007 ND 100, 734 N.W.2d 787 (N.D. 2007)
103 ALR6th 137—§ 19
State v. Volberding, 30 Utah 2d 257, 516 P.2d 359 (1973)
57 ALR6th 445—§ 49
State v. Volk, 220 N.W.2d 607 (Iowa 1974)
89 ALR6th 565—§ 6, 12, 27
State v. Volk, 421 N.W.2d 360 (Minn. Ct. App. 1988)
73 ALR5th 383—§ 2, 60
State v. Volpe, 38 Ohio St. 3d 191, 527 N.E.2d 818 (1988)
38 ALR6th 1—§ 13

State v. Volquardts, 540 So. 2d 497 (La. Ct. App. 1st Cir. 1989)
57 ALR5th 141—§ 6
State v. Voltz, 626 S.W.2d 291 (Tenn. Crim. App. 1981)
9 ALR6th 1—§ 20
State v. Vonhof, 51 Wash. App. 33, 751 P.2d 1221 (Div. 3 1988)
106 ALR5th 397—§ 4
State v. Vosika, 83 Or. App. 298, 731 P.2d 449 (1987)
38 ALR5th 433—§ 11
State v. Votava, 149 Wash. 2d 178, 66 P.3d 1050 (2003)
92 ALR6th 295—§ 8, 9, 13, 36
93 ALR6th 207—§ 10
State v. Votta, 299 S.W.3d 130, 71 A.L.R.6th 755 (Tex. Crim. App. 2009)
70 ALR6th 361—§ 22
71 ALR6th 335—§ 12
State v. Voyles, 823 S.W.2d 143 (Mo. Ct. App. E.D. 1992)
105 ALR5th 529—§ 12
State v. Vreeland, 53 N.J. Super. 169, 147 A.2d 49 (1958)
52 ALR5th 655—§ 3
State v. Vriezema, 62 Wash. App. 437, 814 P.2d 248 (Div. 1 1991)
97 ALR6th 653—§ 29
State v. Vroman, 1997 WL 193168 (Ohio Ct. App. 4th Dist. Ross County 1997)
29 ALR6th 237—§ 4, 9, 24
State v. Vu, 307 Or. 419, 770 P.2d 577 (1989)
42 ALR6th 237—§ 4
State v. Vue, 606 N.W.2d 719 (Minn. Ct. App. 2000)
57 ALR5th 315—§ 9, 12
State v. Vue, 1992 WL 153093 (Minn. Ct. App. 1992)
73 ALR5th 383—§ 3
State v. Vuin, 89 Ohio L. Abs. 193, 185 N.E.2d 506 (C.P. 1962)
85 ALR5th 1—§ 32
State v. Vumback, 68 Conn. App. 313, 791 A.2d 569 (2002)

39 ALR6th 257—§ 32
40 ALR6th 1—§ 10
State v. Wacaser, 794 S.W.2d 190 (Mo. 1990)
42 ALR5th 581—§ 7
83 ALR6th 255—§ 15
State v. Wachholtz, 131 Idaho 74, 952 P.2d 396 (Ct. App. 1998)
71 ALR6th 625—§ 40
State v. Wacker, 317 Or. 419, 856 P.2d 1029 (1993)
59 ALR5th 615—§ 3, 4, 11
91 ALR5th 585—§ 12
State v. Waddell, 282 N.C. 431, 194 S.E.2d 19 (1973)
62 ALR5th 121—§ 6
93 ALR6th 391—§ 12
State v. Waddell, 351 N.C. 413, 527 S.E.2d 644 (2000)
38 ALR5th 433—§ 5
State v. Waddell, 504 S.E.2d 84 (N.C. Ct. App. 1998)
38 ALR5th 433—§ 5
State v. Waddles, 336 So. 2d 810 (La. 1976)
87 ALR5th 181—§ 5
State v. Waddy, 63 Ohio St. 3d 424, 588 N.E.2d 819 (1992)
72 ALR6th 437—§ 20
State v. Wade, 7 Neb. App. 169, 581 N.W.2d 906 (1998)
22 ALR5th 1—§ 7
State v. Wade, 40 N.J. 27, 190 A.2d 657 (1963)
96 ALR5th 523—§ 3
State v. Wade, 95 S.C. 387, 79 S.E. 106 (1913)
16 ALR6th 329—§ 4, 7
State v. Wade, 105 Nev. 206, 772 P.2d 1291 (1989)
70 ALR6th 361—§ 7
State v. Wade, 136 N.H. 750, 622 A.2d 832 (1993)
38 ALR5th 433—§ 3
State v. Wade, 224 N.C. 760, 32 S.E.2d 314 (1944)
46 ALR5th 499—§ 3

State v. Wade, 467 N.W.2d 283 (Iowa 1991)
   7 ALR5th 263—§ 7
State v. Wade, 544 So. 2d 1028 (Fla. Dist. Ct. App. 2d Dist. 1989)
   68 ALR5th 549—§ 3
   84 ALR5th 1—§ 8
State v. Wade, 635 S.W.2d 51 (Mo. Ct. App. W.D. 1982)
   93 ALR5th 527—§ 4
State v. Wade, 815 S.W.2d 489 (Mo. Ct. App. S.D. 1991)
   108 ALR5th 593—§ 46
State v. Wade, 2010 WL 5543880 (Ohio Ct. App. 10th Dist. Franklin County 2010)
   63 ALR6th 351—§ 3
State v. Wadlow, 93 Md. App. 260, 611 A.2d 1091 (1992)
   30 ALR5th 121—§ 6
State v. Wagenman, 2003 UT App 146, 71 P.3d 184 (Utah Ct. App. 2003)
   37 ALR6th 357—§ 48, 56
State v. Wages, 87 Ohio App. 3d 780, 623 N.E.2d 193 (Ohio App. Cuyahoga County 1993)
   57 ALR5th 141—§ 3
State v. Wagner, 36 Wash. App. 286, 673 P.2d 638 (Div. 1 1983)
   81 ALR5th 563—§ 3
State v. Wagner, 46 Or. App. 9, 610 P.2d 301 (1980)
   99 ALR5th 557—§ 10
State v. Wagner, 92 Wash. App. 1030, 1998 WL 642488 (Div. 1 1998)
   110 ALR5th 213—§ 2
State v. Wagner, 484 N.W.2d 212 (Iowa App. 1992)
   18 ALR5th 525—§ 3
State v. Wagner, 596 N.W.2d 83 (Iowa 1999)
   54 ALR6th 1—§ 5
State v. Wagner, 2011 WL 1466465 (Minn. Ct. App. 2011)
   89 ALR6th 565—§ 13
State v. Wagoner, 126 N.M. 9, 1998-NMCA-124, 966 P.2d 176, 1998 WL 560375 (Ct. App. 1998)

   122 ALR5th 439—§ 7
State v. Wagoner, 683 S.E.2d 391 (N.C. Ct. App. 2009)
   57 ALR6th 1—§ 3, 4, 8, 12, 18
State v. Wagstaff, 202 S.C. 443, 25 S.E.2d 484 (1943)
   99 ALR6th 113—§ 7
State v. Wagster, 361 So. 2d 849 (La. 1978)
   55 ALR5th 125—§ 3, 9, 10
State v. Wahl, 365 N.J. Super. 356, 839 A.2d 120 (App. Div. 2004)
   65 ALR6th 329—§ 4, 10
State v. Wahl, 450 N.W.2d 710 (N.D. 1990)
   67 ALR5th 361—§ 3
State v. Wahle, 298 N.W.2d 795 (S.D. 1980)
   16 ALR5th 152—§ 3, 9
State v. Waiau, 60 Haw. 93, 588 P.2d 412 (1978)
   9 ALR6th 541—§ 10
State v. Waibel, 89 Ohio App. 3d 522, 625 N.E.2d 637 (9th Dist. Medina County 1993)
   34 ALR6th 1—§ 10
State v. Waiblinger, 1998 WL 464944 (Wash. Ct. App. Div. 3 1998)
   73 ALR5th 383—§ 6, 8
State v. Waidelich, 140 Idaho 622, 97 P.3d 489 (Ct. App. 2004)
   44 ALR6th 301—§ 5
State v. Waino, 611 N.W.2d 575 (Minn. Ct. App. 2000)
   5 ALR5th 243—§ 22
State v. Wainwright, 18 Kan. App. 2d 449, 856 P.2d 163 (1993)
   81 ALR5th 563—§ 3, 5, 8
State v. Waite, 13 Ohio App. 3d 379, 469 N.E.2d 965 (9th Dist. Wayne County 1984)
   112 ALR5th 621—§ 3
State v. Waite, 27 Ohio App. 2d 187, 56 Ohio Op. 2d 350, 273 N.E.2d 343 (9th Dist. Medina County 1971)
   89 ALR6th 565—§ 4, 12
State v. Waite, 803 P.2d 1279, 150 Utah Adv. Rep. 16 (Utah App. 1990)

CASES CITED IN ALR5th and ALR6th

33 ALR5th 453—§ 9, 10
State v. Waits, 185 Neb. 780, 178
N.W.2d 774 (1970)
67 ALR5th 361—§ 3, 6
State v. Wakefield, 267 Kan. 116, 977
P.2d 941 (1999)
85 ALR5th 1—§ 23
103 ALR5th 463—§ 3
10 ALR6th 463—§ 4
State v. Wakefield, 682 S.W.2d 136
(Mo. Ct. App. S.D. 1984)
107 ALR5th 567—§ 12
108 ALR5th 593—§ 11
State v. Wakefield, 712 S.W.2d 442
(Mo. Ct. App. S.D. 1986)
107 ALR5th 567—§ 12
State v. Wakeford, 1998 MT 16, 287
Mont. 220, 953 P.2d 1065 (1998)
58 ALR6th 499—§ 41
State v. Walberg, 109 Wis. 2d 96, 325
N.W.2d 687 (1982)
54 ALR5th 575—§ 11
State v. Walden, 183 Ariz. 595, 905 P.2d
974 (1995)
7 ALR6th 233—§ 5
State v. Walden, 1993 WL 114610
(Tenn. Crim. App. 1993)
57 ALR5th 141—§ 6
State v. Walden, 2004 WL 2319761
(Tenn. Crim. App. 2004)
26 ALR6th 511—§ 25
State v. Waldenburg, 9 Wash. App. 529,
513 P.2d 577 (Div. 3 1973)
67 ALR6th 209—§ 25, 26, 40
State v. Walder, 952 So. 2d 21 (La. Ct.
App. 1st Cir. 2006)
45 ALR6th 435—§ 4, 20, 21
State v. Walder, 965 So. 2d 865 (La.
2007)
45 ALR6th 435—§ 20, 21
State v. Walder, 1997 WL 87088 (Ohio
Ct. App. 3d Dist. Allen County
1997)
111 ALR5th 239—§ 8
State v. Walder, 2009-716 La. App. 1
Cir. 9/11/09, 2009 WL 3162220
(La. Ct. App. 1st Cir. 2009)

70 ALR6th 329—§ 18
State v. Waldon, 287 N.W.2d 628
(Minn. 1979)
78 ALR6th 417—§ 28
State v. Waldroup, 100 Ohio App. 3d
508, 654 N.E.2d 390 (12th Dist.
Preble County 1995)
117 ALR5th 407—§ 4
State v. Waldrup, 2011 WL 5008420
(Kan. Ct. App. 2011)
**70 ALR6th 361—§ 3.5, 29.2, 29.3,
30, 31**
State v. Waldschmidt, 12 Kan. App. 2d
284, 740 P.2d 617 (1987)
62 ALR6th 413—§ 22, 26, 38
State v. Waleczek, 90 Wash. 2d 746, 585
P.2d 797 (1978)
119 ALR5th 275—§ 8, 11
State v. Walen, 563 N.W.2d 742 (Minn.
1997)
72 ALR5th 403—§ 2, 10
State v. Walker, 11 Wash. App. 84, 521
P.2d 215 (1974)
18 ALR5th 1—§ 3
State v. Walker, 13 Wash. App. 545, 536
P.2d 657 (Div. 1 1975)
101 ALR5th 187—§ 7
State v. Walker, 19 Or. App. 420, 528
P.2d 113 (1974)
31 ALR5th 229—§ 3
State v. Walker, 29 S.W.3d 885 (Tenn.
Crim. App. 1999)
37 ALR5th 319—§ 5, 7
State v. Walker, 40 Wash. App. 658, 700
P.2d 1168 (Div. 2 1985)
58 ALR5th 749—§ 6
State v. Walker, 53 Ohio St. 2d 192, 7
Ohio Op. 3d 368, 374 N.E.2d 132
(1978)
111 ALR5th 1—§ 27
State v. Walker, 58 Or. App. 607, 649
P.2d 624 (1982)
72 ALR5th 529—§ 7
State v. Walker, 82 Wash. 2d 851, 514
P.2d 919 (1973)
34 ALR5th 125—§ 2, 9
State v. Walker, 84 N.C. App. 540, 353
S.E.2d 245 (1987)

39 ALR5th 283—§ 4, 61
State v. Walker, 87 Wash. App. 1079, 1997 WL 599169 (Div. 1 1997)
101 ALR6th 331—§ 13
State v. Walker, 90 Conn. App. 737, 881 A.2d 406 (2005)
26 ALR6th 511—§ 8, 35
State v. Walker, 90 Ohio App. 3d 352, 629 N.E.2d 471 (3d Dist. Marion County 1993)
28 ALR6th 505—§ 9
State v. Walker, 107 Idaho 308, 688 P.2d 1213 (Ct. App. 1984)
85 ALR5th 1—§ 33
State v. Walker, 125 N.M. 603, 1998 -NMCA- 117, 964 P.2d 164 (Ct. App. 1998)
68 ALR5th 343—§ 3, 12
State v. Walker, 129 Wash. App. 258, 118 P.3d 935 (Div. 1 2005)
30 ALR6th 1—§ 3, 4, 6, 7
State v. Walker, 136 Wash. 2d 678, 965 P.2d 1079 (1998)
65 ALR5th 407—§ 3, 9
State v. Walker, 144 P.3d 758 (Kan. 2006)
26 ALR6th 511—§ 25
State v. Walker, 154 Wis. 2d 158, 453 N.W.2d 127 (1990)
22 ALR5th 1—§ 4, 11, 15, 23, 30, 33, 39, 40, 54
47 ALR5th 259—§ 2
62 ALR6th 413—§ 5, 38
State v. Walker, 164 Ohio App. 3d 114, 2005-Ohio-5592, 841 N.E.2d 376 (2d Dist. Greene County 2005)
45 ALR6th 435—§ 3, 12
70 ALR6th 329—§ 14
State v. Walker, 181 Ariz. 475, 891 P.2d 942 (Ct. App. Div. 1 1995)
69 ALR5th 425—§ 4, 5
State v. Walker, 204 Ga. App. 1, 418 S.E.2d 384 (1992)
29 ALR6th 1—§ 10
State v. Walker, 216 N.J. Super. 39, 522 A.2d 1021 (1987)
44 ALR5th 651—§ 3

State v. Walker, 236 N.W.2d 292 (Iowa 1975)
6 ALR5th 733—§ 2, 16
State v. Walker, 252 Kan. 279, 845 P.2d 1 (1993)
45 ALR5th 531—§ 3
9 ALR6th 1—§ 17
State v. Walker, 332 N.C. 520, 422 S.E.2d 716 (1992)
57 ALR5th 141—§ 7
State v. Walker, 432 So. 2d 1057 (La. Ct. App. 3d Cir. 1983)
97 ALR5th 293—§ 8
State v. Walker, 503 So. 2d 866 (Ala. Civ. App. 1987)
104 ALR5th 229—§ 7
115 ALR5th 403—§ 5
4 ALR6th 113—§ 17, 23, 29
101 ALR6th 1—§ 14, 29
State v. Walker, 506 N.W.2d 430 (Iowa 1993)
58 ALR6th 385—§ 3, 8, 18
State v. Walker, 659 S.W.2d 349 (Mo. App. 1983)
29 ALR5th 59—§ 7, 39, 62, 75, 79, 84, 89
State v. Walker, 731 So. 2d 98 (Fla. Dist. Ct. App. 4th Dist. 1999)
113 ALR5th 597—§ 3
State v. Walker, 795 S.W.2d 628 (Mo. Ct. App. E.D. 1990)
37 ALR6th 357—§ 64
State v. Walker, 905 S.W.2d 554 (Tenn. 1995)
76 ALR5th 485—§ 4, 9, 20
State v. Walker, 965 P.2d 1079 (Wash. 1998)
65 ALR5th 407—§ 3, 9, 11
State v. Walker, 1996 WL 589116 (Minn. Ct. App. 1996)
69 ALR6th 579—§ 8, 32
State v. Walker, 2001 WL 1782885 (Ohio Ct. App. 5th Dist. Stark County 2001)
7 ALR6th 233—§ 5
State v. Walker, 2002 WL 31749974 (Wis. Ct. App. 2002)
106 ALR5th 397—§ 4

State v. Walker, 2006-Ohio-4018, 2006 WL 2252966 (Ohio Ct. App. 2d Dist. Greene County 2006)
45 ALR6th 435—§ 12

State v. Walker, 2006-Ohio-6488, 2006 WL 3544742 (Ohio Ct. App. 3d Dist. Seneca County 2006)
26 ALR6th 511—§ 19

State v. Walker, 2006 WL 3434628 (N.J. Super. Ct. App. Div. 2006)
26 ALR6th 511—§ 17

State v. Walker, 2007 WI App 216, 305 Wis. 2d 656, 739 N.W.2d 492 (Ct. App. 2007)
84 ALR6th 293—§ 34

State v. Walker, No. 49037 (May 9, 1985, Ct. App. Ohio, 8th App. Dist. Cuyahoga Co.)
39 ALR5th 283—§ 14, 29

State v. Wall, 36 N.J. 216, 176 A.2d 8 (1961)
9 ALR6th 633—§ 5
13 ALR6th 603—§ 34

State v. Wall, 46 Wash. App. 218, 729 P.2d 656 (Div. 1 1986)
73 ALR5th 383—§ 41, 63, 64

State v. Wall, 49 N.C. App. 678, 272 S.E.2d 152 (1980)
32 ALR5th 31—§ 3

State v. Wall, 52 Wash. App. 665, 763 P.2d 462 (Div. 3 1988)
56 ALR6th 185—§ 13

State v. Wall, 87 N.C. App. 621, 361 S.E.2d 900 (1987)
73 ALR5th 383—§ 5

State v. Wall, 126 N.J. Super. 594, 316 A.2d 28 (1974)
22 ALR5th 660—§ 6, 9

State v. Wall, 206 Kan. 760, 482 P.2d 41 (1971)
26 ALR5th 1—§ 3, 14

State v. Wall, 457 So. 2d 1225 (La. Ct. App. 1st Cir. 1984)
124 ALR5th 1—§ 5

State v. Wallace, 29 Or. App. 429, 563 P.2d 1237 (1977)
122 ALR5th 439—§ 4

State v. Wallace, 71 N.C. App. 681, 323 S.E.2d 403 (1984)
4 ALR6th 577—§ 9

State v. Wallace, 84 Wash. App. 1049, 1996 WL 734631 (Div. 1 1996)
103 ALR6th 507—§ 16, 30, 33

State v. Wallace, 105 Haw. 131, 94 P.3d 1275 (2004)
124 ALR5th 1—§ 5

State v. Wallace, 111 N.C. App. 581, 433 S.E.2d 238 (1993)
78 ALR6th 297—§ 42, 47, 51

State v. Wallace, 162 N.C. 622, 78 S.E. 1 (1913)
51 ALR5th 603—§ 2, 3, 14

State v. Wallace, 166 Ohio App. 3d 845, 2006-Ohio-2477, 853 N.E.2d 704 (1st Dist. Hamilton County 2006)
94 ALR6th 191—§ 7

State v. Wallace, 181 Conn. 237, 435 A.2d 20 (1980)
81 ALR5th 563—§ 3

State v. Wallace, 351 N.C. 481, 528 S.E.2d 326 (2000)
110 ALR5th 1—§ 14

State v. Wallace, 545 N.W.2d 674 (Minn. Ct. App. 1996)
92 ALR5th 35—§ 22

State v. Wallace, 611 S.W.2d 251 (Mo. App. 1980)
55 ALR5th 125—§ 3

State v. Wallace, 2006 WL 16315 (Tenn. Crim. App. 2006)
26 ALR6th 511—§ 22

State v. Wallace, 2009 WL 1139120 (N.J. Super. Ct. App. Div. 2009)
79 ALR6th 1—§ 55

State v. Wallace, 2011 WL 2552640 (Del. Super. Ct. 2011)
78 ALR6th 297—§ 37, 77

State v. Wallace, No. 40401 (January 25, 1980, Ct. App. Ohio, 8th App. Dist. Cuyahoga Co.)
39 ALR5th 283—§ 14, 44

State v. Wallace, State v. Wallace, 313 N.J. Super. 435, 712 A.2d 1270 (App. Div. 1998)
66 ALR5th 397—§ 21

For assistance, call 1-800-328-4880

State v. Wallen, 114 Ariz. 355, 560 P.2d 1262 (App. 1977)
45 ALR5th 591—§ 2, 3
State v. Wallen, 2010-Ohio-480, 2010 WL 529864 (Ohio Ct. App. 3d Dist. Marion County 2010)
77 ALR6th 393—§ 18, 34
State v. Waller, 80 N.M. 380, 456 P.2d 213 (Ct. App. 1969)
89 ALR6th 565—§ 21, 23
State v. Waller, 2009 WL 230493 (Tenn. Crim. App. 2009)
101 ALR6th 545—§ 4
State v. Waller, 2010 WL 3947498 (Tenn. Crim. App. 2010)
70 ALR6th 1—§ 25
State v. Walley, 2004 WL 2255255 (Tenn. Crim. App. 2004)
26 ALR6th 511—§ 25
State v. Walls, 342 N.C. 1, 463 S.E.2d 738 (1995)
79 ALR5th 33—§ 63, 66
State v. Walls, 348 S.C. 26, 558 S.E.2d 524 (2002)
63 ALR6th 351—§ 3
State v. Walls, 1997 WL 20346 (Minn. Ct. App. 1997)
7 ALR6th 233—§ 11
State v. Walls, 1997 WL 258463 (Wash. Ct. App. Div. 1 1997)
73 ALR5th 383—§ 22, 58
State v. Wallway, 72 Wash. App. 407, 865 P.2d 531 (Div. 2 1994)
27 ALR6th 491—§ 3
State v. Wal-Mart Stores, Inc., 207 A.D.2d 150, 621 N.Y.S.2d 158, 10 I.E.R. Cas. (BNA) 255, 66 Empl. Prac. Dec. (CCH) ¶ 43435 (3d Dep't 1995)
71 ALR5th 257—§ 10
123 ALR5th 411—§ 62
State v. Walmsley, 216 Neb. 336, 344 N.W.2d 450 (1984)
62 ALR6th 413—§ 42
State v. Walsh, 66 Ohio App. 2d 85, 20 Ohio Op. 3d 178, 420 N.E.2d 1013, Blue Sky L. Rep. (CCH) ¶ 71631 (10th Dist. Franklin County 1979)

State v. Walsh, 73 Ohio Op. 2d 498 (C.P. 1975)
66 ALR5th 135—§ 37
70 ALR6th 1—§ 5
State v. Walsh, 103 Or. App. 517, 798 P.2d 262 (1990)
84 ALR6th 293—§ 3
State v. Walsh, 203 Mo. 605, 102 S.W. 513 (1907)
5 ALR6th 1—§ 45
State v. Walshire, 634 N.W.2d 625 (Iowa 2001)
84 ALR6th 293—§ 9, 14, 38
State v. Walsson, 1996 WL 227479 (Ohio Ct. App. 12th Dist. Clermont County 1996)
79 ALR6th 1—§ 43
State v. Walston, 67 N.C. App. 110, 312 S.E.2d 676 (1984)
125 ALR5th 537—§ 32, 33
State v. Walten, 241 N.J. Super. 529, 575 A.2d 529 (1990)
26 ALR5th 1—§ 4
State v. Walter, 36 Or. App. 303, 584 P.2d 356 (1978)
89 ALR6th 565—§ 13
State v. Walter, 178 Wis. 2d 317, 504 N.W.2d 875 (Ct. App. 1993)
27 ALR6th 183—§ 16, 18
State v. Walter, 615 So. 2d 1023 (La. App. 1st Cir. 1993)
7 ALR5th 263—§ 6
State v. Walters, 8 Kan. App. 2d 237, 655 P.2d 947 (1982)
103 ALR6th 347—§ 8, 13
State v. Walters, 94 Conn. App. 297, 891 A.2d 1003 (2006)
34 ALR6th 1—§ 10
State v. Walters, 120 Idaho 46, 813 P.2d 857 (1990)
85 ALR5th 187—§ 3, 4
State v. Walters, 230 Neb. 539, 432 N.W.2d 528 (1988)
103 ALR5th 463—§ 8
State v. Walters, 440 So. 2d 115 (La. 1983)
95 ALR5th 229—§ 3

For assistance, call 1-800-328-4880

State v. Walters, 2008-Ohio-1466, 2008
WL 836407 (Ohio Ct. App. 9th Dist.
Summit County 2008)
78 ALR6th 297—§ 3, 53
State v. Walthers, 2003 WL 21961467
(Minn. Ct. App. 2003)
69 ALR6th 1—§ 20
State v. Walton, 41 Conn. App. 831, 678
A.2d 986 (1996)
29 ALR6th 1—§ 10
State v. Walton, 41 S.W.3d 75 (Tenn.
2001)
34 ALR6th 1—§ 9
81 ALR6th 505—§ 53
State v. Walton, 64 Wash. App. 410, 824
P.2d 533 (Div. 3 1992)
32 ALR6th 1—§ 7
81 ALR6th 505—§ 33
State v. Walton, 133 Ariz. 282, 650 P.2d
1264 (App. 1982)
7 ALR5th 758—§ 3, 4
State v. Walton, 227 Conn. 32, 630 A.2d
990 (1993)
19 ALR6th 115—§ 5, 7, 10
State v. Walton, 256 Kan. 484, 885 P.2d
1255 (1994)
9 ALR6th 633—§ 14
14 ALR6th 517—§ 10
15 ALR6th 173—§ 11
State v. Walton, 734 S.W.2d 502 (Mo.
1987)
70 ALR6th 361—§ 19
State v. Walton, 899 S.W.2d 915 (Mo.
Ct. App. W.D. 1995)
79 ALR5th 419—§ 18
State v. Walton, 1990 WL 16528 (Ohio
Ct. App. 3d Dist. Wyandot County
1990)
99 ALR6th 295—§ 13
State v. Walz, 88 S.D. 262, 218 N.W.2d
480 (1974)
76 ALR5th 1—§ 20
State v. Wanczyk, 196 N.J. Super. 397,
482 A.2d 964 (Law Div. 1984)
81 ALR5th 563—§ 3, 5
State v. Wandle, 75 Or. App. 746, 707
P.2d 1281 (1985)

32 ALR6th 1—§ 11
State v. Wanlass, 953 P.2d 1147 (Utah
Ct. App. 1998)
15 ALR6th 173—§ 23
State v. Wanrow, 39 Or. App. 13, 591
P.2d 751 (1979)
92 ALR5th 35—§ 23
State v. Wanta, 224 Wis. 2d 679, 592
N.W.2d 645 (Ct. App. 1999)
15 ALR5th 391—§ 17.5
State v. Warbington, 129 Ohio App. 3d
568, 718 N.E.2d 516 (10th Dist.
Franklin County 1998)
15 ALR5th 391—§ 21
State v. Ward, 15 Ohio St. 3d 355, 474
N.E.2d 300 (1984)
112 ALR5th 621—§ 3
State v. Ward, 16 Or. App. 556, 519 P.2d
1269 (1974)
122 ALR5th 439—§ 6
1 ALR6th 371—§ 6
State v. Ward, 20 Kan. App. 2d 238, 886
P.2d 890 (1994)
38 ALR6th 1—§ 15
State v. Ward, 49 Wash. App. 427, 743
P.2d 853 (Div. 1 1987)
113 ALR5th 597—§ 8
State v. Ward, 61 Vt. 153, 17 A. 483
(1889)
12 ALR5th 909—§ 4
State v. Ward, 62 Hawaii 509, 617 P.2d
568 (1980)
59 ALR5th 615—§ 3, 5, 6, 10
State v. Ward, 85 Ohio App. 3d 378, 619
N.E.2d 1097 (Summit Co. 1993)
42 ALR5th 291—§ 25
State v. Ward, 92 Ohio App. 3d 631, 637
N.E.2d 16 (Hamilton Co. 1993)
27 ALR5th 593—§ 5, 6, 9, 10
State v. Ward, 92 Ohio App. 179, 49
Ohio Op. 312, 109 N.E.2d 488 (2d
Dist. Montgomery County 1952)
119 ALR5th 275—§ 9
State v. Ward, 105 Wash. App. 1027,
2001 WL 287472 (Div. 1 2001)
7 ALR6th 233—§ 6
State v. Ward, 123 Wash. 2d 488, 869
P.2d 1062 (1994)

36 ALR5th 161—§ 3, 6, 9
33 ALR6th 91—§ 6, 9
41 ALR6th 141—§ 5, 7
63 ALR6th 351—§ 3
93 ALR6th 1—§ 17
State v. Ward, 130 Ohio App. 3d 551, 720 N.E.2d 603 (8th Dist. Cuyahoga County 1999)
36 ALR5th 161—§ 13
78 ALR5th 489—§ 6, 7
State v. Ward, 135 Idaho 68, 14 P.3d 388 (Ct. App. 2000)
24 ALR6th 1—§ 31
State v. Ward, 231 Wis. 2d 723, 2000 WI 3, 604 N.W.2d 517 (2000)
85 ALR5th 1—§ 21
State v. Ward, 286 N.C. 304, 210 S.E.2d 407 (1974)
36 ALR5th 255—§ 27, 28, 30
State v. Ward, 337 Mo. 425, 85 S.W.2d 1 (1935)
87 ALR5th 181—§ 7
83 ALR6th 465—§ 65
State v. Ward, 338 N.C. 64, 449 S.E.2d 709 (1994)
79 ALR5th 33—§ 63
98 ALR6th 455—§ 5
State v. Ward, 354 N.C. 231, 555 S.E.2d 251 (2001)
95 ALR6th 219—§ 18
State v. Ward, 624 A.2d 485 (Me. 1993)
41 ALR5th 171—§ 16, 18, 20
State v. Ward, 1985 WL 11128 (Ohio Ct. App. 4th Dist. Vinton County 1985)
57 ALR5th 141—§ 7
State v. Ward, 1995 WL 434240 (Ohio Ct. App. 5th Dist. Richland County 1995)
24 ALR6th 591—§ 14
State v. Ward, 2000 WL 1370993 (Ohio Ct. App. 12th Dist. Clermont County 2000)
51 ALR6th 1—§ 24
State v. Ward, 2004 WL 1413925 (Tenn. Crim. App. 2004)
103 ALR6th 507—§ 4

State v. Ward, 2005-Ohio-3036, 2005 WL 1413242 (Ohio Ct. App. 1st Dist. Hamilton County 2005)
26 ALR6th 511—§ 7, 19
State v. Ward, 2009-Ohio-4192, 2009 WL 2568414 (Ohio Ct. App. 8th Dist. Cuyahoga County 2009)
67 ALR6th 209—§ 25
State v. Ward, 2011 WI App 151, 337 Wis. 2d 655, 807 N.W.2d 23 (Ct. App. 2011)
93 ALR6th 275—§ 30
State v. Wardell, 2005 MT 252, 329 Mont. 9, 122 P.3d 443 (2005)
33 ALR6th 91—§ 7, 11
State v. Warden, 80 Wash. App. 448, 909 P.2d 941 (Div. 1 1996)
73 ALR5th 383—§ 3
State v. Wardle, 137 Idaho 808, 53 P.3d 1227 (Ct. App. 2002)
4 ALR6th 1—§ 10, 15
46 ALR6th 241—§ 12
State v. Wardwell, 158 Me. 307, 183 A.2d 896 (1962)
76 ALR5th 1—§ 2
77 ALR5th 201—§ 2, 10
79 ALR5th 237—§ 2
85 ALR5th 187—§ 9
State v. Ware, 63 Ohio St. 2d 84, 17 Ohio Ops. 3d 51, 406 N.E.2d 1112 (1980)
39 ALR5th 283—§ 14, 47
State v. Ware, 118 N.M. 319, 881 P.2d 679 (1994)
53 ALR6th 81—§ 13
State v. Ware, 1997 WL 30346 (Tenn. Crim. App. 1997)
73 ALR5th 383—§ 3
State v. Ware, 2008-Ohio-2038, 2008 WL 1903993 (Ohio Ct. App. 8th Dist. Cuyahoga County 2008)
56 ALR6th 323—§ 11
State v. Warfield, 184 Wis. 56, 198 N.W. 854 (1924)
61 ALR5th 1—§ 3, 12
State v. Warlick, 179 La. 997, 155 So. 460 (1934)
98 ALR6th 455—§ 17

CASES CITED IN ALR5th and ALR6th

State v. Warmbrun, 277 N.J. Super. 51,
648 A.2d 1153 (App. Div. 1994)
9 ALR6th 1—§ 17
State v. Warndahl, 436 N.W.2d 770
(Minn. 1989)
124 ALR5th 1—§ 5
State v. Warner, 55 Ohio St. 3d 31, 564
N.E.2d 18 (1990)
15 ALR5th 391—§ 43
State v. Warner, 93 Kan. 378, 144 P. 220
(1914)
101 ALR6th 499—§ 15
State v. Warner, 181 Or. App. 622, 47
P.3d 497 (2002)
30 ALR6th 103—§ 21
State v. Warner, 626 A.2d 205 (R.I.
1993)
39 ALR5th 283—§ 2, 4, 69
State v. Warner, 649 S.W.2d 580 (Tenn.
1983)
85 ALR5th 471—§ 7
State v. Warner, 760 N.W.2d 209 (Iowa
Ct. App. 2008)
75 ALR6th 181—§ 18
State v. Warner, 762 So. 2d 507 (Fla.
2000)
11 ALR6th 237—§ 4, 8
State v. Warner, 788 P.2d 1041, 129
Utah Adv. Rep. 21 (Utah App.
1990)
4 ALR5th 1—§ 19
State v. Warner, 1992 WL 267460 (Ohio
App. Portage Co. 1992)
52 ALR5th 655—§ 3
State v. Warness, 77 Wash. App. 636,
893 P.2d 665 (Div. 1 1995)
1 ALR6th 657—§ 4
State v. Warnimont, 2004-Ohio-5516,
2004 WL 2334280 (Ohio Ct. App.
3d Dist. Putnam County 2004)
46 ALR6th 63—§ 11
State v. Warrell, 41 Ohio App. 3d 286,
534 N.E.2d 1237 (9th Dist. Medina
County 1987)
34 ALR6th 1—§ 12
State v. Warren, 67 Ohio App. 3d 789,
588 N.E.2d 905 (6th Dist. Lucas
County 1990)

3 ALR6th 269—§ 5, 14
State v. Warren, 78 S.W.3d 797 (Mo. Ct.
App. S.D. 2002)
47 ALR6th 107—§ 27
State v. Warren, 88 Or. App. 462, 745
P.2d 822 (1987)
3 ALR6th 269—§ 4, 22, 25
State v. Warren, 100 Conn. App. 407,
919 A.2d 465 (2007)
30 ALR6th 1—§ 4
State v. Warren, 109 Mo. 430, 19 S.W.
191 (1892)
108 ALR5th 593—§ 28
State v. Warren, 121 Ariz. 306, 589 P.2d
1338 (Ct. App. Div. 2 1978)
106 ALR5th 397—§ 4
State v. Warren, 122 N.C. App. 738, 471
S.E.2d 667 (1996)
39 ALR5th 283—§ 18
State v. Warren, 125 Ohio App. 3d 298,
708 N.E.2d 288 (8th Dist. Cuyahoga
County 1998)
11 ALR6th 237—§ 11
State v. Warren, 348 N.C. 80, 499 S.E.2d
431 (1998)
36 ALR5th 255—§ 8
State v. Warren, 629 So. 2d 1014 (Fla.
Dist. Ct. App. 4th Dist. 1993)
106 ALR5th 377—§ 4
State v. Warren, 1980 WL 351175 (Ohio
Ct. App. 6th Dist. Lucas County
1980)
99 ALR6th 295—§ 21
State v. Warren, 1991 WL 156521 (Ohio
App. Hocking Co. 1991)
52 ALR5th 655—§ 3
State v. Warren, 1992 WL 394872 (Ohio
Ct. App. 10th Dist. Franklin County
1992)
88 ALR5th 121—§ 2
State v. Warrington, 884 S.W.2d 711
(Mo. Ct. App. S.D. 1994)
1 ALR6th 549—§ 25
State v. Warsame, 735 N.W.2d 684
(Minn. 2007)
30 ALR6th 1—§ 7
State v. Warshow, 138 Vt. 22, 410 A.2d
1000 (1979)

CASES CITED IN ALR5TH AND 6TH

3 ALR5th 521—§ 6
State v. Wasava, 1999 WL 169461 (Wash. Ct. App. Div. 1 1999)

73 ALR5th 383—§ 3
State v. Wash, 39 Or. App. 447, 592 P.2d 1035 (1979)

22 ALR5th 660—§ 11
State v. Washatka, 2004-Ohio-5384, 2004 WL 2252048 (Ohio Ct. App. 8th Dist. Cuyahoga County 2004)

26 ALR6th 511—§ 19
State v. Washburn, 34 Conn. App. 557, 642 A.2d 70 (1994)

63 ALR6th 1—§ 16, 66
State v. Washington, 17 Ariz. App. 207, 496 P.2d 633 (1972)

4 ALR5th 1—§ 2, 17, 33
State v. Washington, 34 Wash. App. 410, 661 P.2d 605 (Div. 1 1983)

19 ALR6th 697—§ 4, 5
State v. Washington, 86 N.C. App. 235, 357 S.E.2d 419 (1987)

55 ALR5th 125—§ 3 to 6, 10, 11
67 ALR6th 531—§ 16, 19, 21, 23, 27
State v. Washington, 126 Ohio App. 3d 264, 710 N.E.2d 307 (2d Dist. Montgomery County 1998)

87 ALR6th 1—§ 41
State v. Washington, 131 N.C. App. 156, 506 S.E.2d 283 (1998)

72 ALR5th 529—§ 16
State v. Washington, 134 Wis. 2d 108, 396 N.W.2d 156 (1986)

50 ALR5th 581—§ 8, 9, 20
State v. Washington, 142 Ohio App. 3d 268, 755 N.E.2d 422 (8th Dist. Cuyahoga County 2001)

32 ALR6th 171—§ 5, 22
33 ALR6th 1—§ 5
State v. Washington, 142 Wis. 2d 630, 419 N.W.2d 275 (Ct. App. 1987)

121 ALR5th 551—§ 6, 13
State v. Washington, 165 N.J. Super. 149, 397 A.2d 1101 (App. Div. 1979)

55 ALR6th 391—§ 12, 21, 23
State v. Washington, 226 Kan. 768, 602 P.2d 1377 (1979)

101 ALR6th 299—§ 6
State v. Washington, 272 So. 2d 355 (La. 1973)

70 ALR5th 587—§ 3
86 ALR5th 59—§ 3
State v. Washington, 330 N.C. 188, 410 S.E.2d 55 (1991)

34 ALR6th 1—§ 9
State v. Washington, 364 So. 2d 958 (La. 1978)

37 ALR5th 1—§ 3
State v. Washington, 386 So. 2d 1368 (La. 1980)

22 ALR5th 1—§ 56
State v. Washington, 407 So. 2d 1138 (La. 1981)

55 ALR5th 125—§ 3
State v. Washington, 549 S.W.2d 547 (Mo. Ct. App. 1977)

6 ALR6th 533—§ 5
State v. Washington, 605 So. 2d 720 (La. Ct. App. 2d Cir. 1992)

88 ALR5th 121—§ 2, 3, 26, 36
State v. Washington, 670 So. 2d 1255 (La. Ct. App. 5th Cir. 1996)

100 ALR5th 67—§ 8, 11
State v. Washington, 931 So. 2d 1120 (La. Ct. App. 4th Cir. 2006)

26 ALR6th 511—§ 28
State v. Washington, 1995 WL 373531 (Ohio Ct. App. 10th Dist. Franklin County 1995)

99 ALR6th 295—§ 15
State v. Washington, 2000 WL 33115698 (Del. Super. Ct. 2000)

125 ALR5th 497—§ 3
State v. Washington, 2002-Ohio-5834, 2002 WL 31401558 (Ohio Ct. App. 8th Dist. Cuyahoga County 2002)

72 ALR6th 1—§ 6
State v. Washington, 2006-Ohio-7000, 2006 WL 3825237 (Ohio Ct. App. 6th Dist. Fulton County 2006)

26 ALR6th 511—§ 19
State v. Wasson, 54 Wash. App. 156, 772 P.2d 1039 (Div. 3 1989)

93 ALR5th 527—§ 22

For assistance, call 1-800-328-4880

State v. Wasson, 125 N.M. 656, 1998-NMCA-087, 964 P.2d 820 (Ct. App. 1998)

108 ALR5th 593—§ 12, 15

State v. Wasson, 299 S.C. 508, 386 S.E.2d 255 (1989)

55 ALR6th 157—§ 110, 114

State v. Wasson, 602 N.W.2d 247 (Minn. Ct. App. 1999)

50 ALR5th 581—§ 3

State v. Wasson, 615 N.W.2d 316 (Minn. 2000)

50 ALR6th 455—§ 3, 6, 8, 12, 19, 36

State v. Waterhouse, 30 Or. App. 269, 567 P.2d 551 (1977)

54 ALR5th 141—§ 10

State v. Waterhouse, 513 A.2d 862 (Me. 1986)

18 ALR5th 804—§ 2, 4, 6, 8, 11

State v. Waterman, 190 N.W.2d 809 (Iowa 1971)

31 ALR6th 333—§ 7, 9, 11

State v. Waterman, 215 Neb. 768, 340 N.W.2d 438 (1983)

121 ALR5th 551—§ 13

State v. Waterman, 264 Conn. 484, 825 A.2d 63 (2003)

51 ALR6th 139—§ 6

State v. Waters, 515 N.W.2d 562 (Iowa Ct. App. 1994)

102 ALR5th 327—§ 8

24 ALR6th 1—§ 43

State v. Waters, 2007 WL 1098120 (Del. Super. Ct. 2007)

92 ALR6th 1—§ 3

State v. Watkins, 2 Ohio App. 3d 402, 442 N.E.2d 478 (10th Dist. Franklin County 1981)

112 ALR5th 621—§ 7

State v. Watkins, 14 Conn. App. 67, 540 A.2d 76 (1988)

22 ALR5th 1—§ 2, 5, 11, 33, 44

State v. Watkins, 61 Wash. App. 552, 811 P.2d 953 (Div. 1 1991)

83 ALR5th 277—§ 10

State v. Watkins, 96 Ohio App. 3d 195, 644 N.E.2d 1049 (Hamilton Co. 1994)

15 ALR5th 391—§ 5

State v. Watkins, 126 Ariz. 293, 614 P.2d 835 (1980)

7 ALR5th 758—§ 14, 22

State v. Watkins, 156 Mont. 456, 481 P.2d 689 (1971)

29 ALR5th 59—§ 12

State v. Watkins, 227 Neb. 677, 419 N.W.2d 660 (1988)

3 ALR6th 269—§ 10

State v. Watkins, 316 N.W.2d 627 (S.D. 1981)

54 ALR5th 141—§ 3, 11

State v. Watkins, 621 So. 2d 157 (La. App. 4th Cir. 1993)

55 ALR5th 125—§ 3, 7

State v. Watkins, 1988 WL 100606 (Minn. Ct. App. 1988)

73 ALR5th 383—§ 22

State v. Watkins, 1997 WL 396215 (Minn. Ct. App. 1997)

73 ALR5th 383—§ 5

State v. Watkins, 1997 WL 766462 (Tenn. Crim. App. 1997)

4 ALR6th 577—§ 9

State v. Watkins, 2005-Ohio-2359, 2005 WL 1131576 (Ohio Ct. App. 3d Dist. Allen County 2005)

26 ALR6th 511—§ 25

State v. Watkins, 2005 WL 351240 (Tenn. Crim. App. 2005)

26 ALR6th 511—§ 25

State v. Watkins, No. 10252 (October 26, 1987, Ct. App. Ohio, 2nd App. Dist. Montgomery Co.)

39 ALR5th 283—§ 14, 73

State v. Watkins, No. 48469 (January 24, 1985, Ct. App. Ohio, 8th App. Dist. Cuyahoga Co.)

39 ALR5th 283—§ 14, 63

State v. Watson, 7 Ariz. App. 81, 436 P.2d 175 (1967)

5 ALR5th 875—§ 4, 34, 43

State v. Watson, 65 Me. 74, 1876 WL 4091 (1876)

85 ALR5th 187—§ 8, 10

State v. Watson, 71 Hawaii 258, 787 P.2d 691 (1990)

63 ALR5th 375—§ 7
State v. Watts, 2007-Ohio-221, 2007 WL 136311 (Ohio Ct. App. 12th Dist. 2007)
32 ALR6th 1—§ 11
State v. Waverly Cent. School Dist., 28 App. Div. 2d 628, 280 N.Y.S.2d 505 (3d Dep't 1967)
11 ALR5th 630—§ 2
State v. Way, 38 S.C. 333, 17 S.E. 39 (1893)
104 ALR5th 357—§ 6
54 ALR6th 429—§ 17
State v. Way, 297 N.C. 293, 254 S.E.2d 760 (1979)
33 ALR6th 353—§ 3
State v. Waz, 240 Conn. 365, 692 A.2d 1217 (1997)
117 ALR5th 407—§ 4
State v. W.B., 205 N.J. 588, 17 A.3d 187 (2011)
65 ALR6th 537—§ 21
State v. Weakley, 627 S.E.2d 315 (N.C. Ct. App. 2006)
23 ALR6th 307—§ 38
State v. Wear, 15 Ohio App. 3d 77, 15 Ohio B.R. 106, 472 N.E.2d 778 (Clermont Co. 1984)
6 ALR5th 733—§ 6, 23, 25, 26
State v. Wear, 15 Ohio App. 3d 77, 472 N.E.2d 778 (12th Dist. Clermont County 1984)
69 ALR6th 207—§ 9, 10, 18, 19
State v. Wear, 214 P.3d 1226 (Kan. Ct. App. 2009)
55 ALR6th 1—§ 6
State v. Weasler, 230 Wis. 2d 747, 604 N.W.2d 34 (Ct. App. 1999)
62 ALR6th 413—§ 39
State v. Weatherspoon, 1998 ND 148, 583 N.W.2d 391 (N.D. 1998)
27 ALR6th 183—§ 13
State v. Weaver, 57 Iowa 730, 11 N.W. 675 (1882)
11 ALR5th 831—§ 23, 24
State v. Weaver, 123 N.C. App. 276, 473 S.E.2d 362 (1996)
39 ALR5th 283—§ 30

State v. Weaver, 195 Mont. 481, 637 P.2d 23 (1981)
55 ALR6th 157—§ 6, 28
State v. Weaver, 319 Or. 212, 874 P.2d 1322 (1994)
76 ALR5th 563—§ 4 to 6
State v. Weaver, 382 S.E.2d 327 (W. Va. 1989)
39 ALR5th 283—§ 4, 66
State v. Weaver, 405 N.W.2d 852 (Iowa 1987)
92 ALR6th 295—§ 23
95 ALR6th 1—§ 4, 26
96 ALR6th 355—§ 24
State v. Weaver, 733 N.W.2d 793 (Minn. Ct. App. 2007)
30 ALR6th 1—§ 3, 6
State v. Weaver, 912 S.W.2d 499 (Mo. 1995)
15 ALR6th 319—§ 11
24 ALR6th 1—§ 11
83 ALR6th 255—§ 17
State v. Weaver, 1995 WL 314672 (Ohio Ct. App. 9th Dist. Lorain County 1995)
57 ALR5th 141—§ 7
State v. Weaver, 1997 WL 823965 (Ohio Ct. App. 9th Dist. Lorain County 1997)
90 ALR5th 453—§ 17
10 ALR6th 463—§ 6
State v. Weaver, 1998 WL 485571 (Tenn. Crim. App. 1998)
84 ALR6th 293—§ 25
State v. Webb, 36 N.D. 235, 162 N.W. 358 (1917)
97 ALR5th 293—§ 3
State v. Webb, 64 Wash. App. 480, 824 P.2d 1257 (Div. 1 1992)
57 ALR6th 445—§ 12
State v. Webb, 70 Ohio St. 3d 325, 1994-Ohio-425, 638 N.E.2d 1023 (1994)
93 ALR6th 391—§ 28
State v. Webb, 76 Idaho 162, 279 P.2d 634 (1955)
76 ALR5th 1—§ 8
State v. Webb, 78 Ariz. 8, 274 P.2d 338 (1954)

92 ALR6th 295—§ 7 to 9, 23
93 ALR6th 207—§ 6, 26
96 ALR6th 355—§ 24, 37
State v. Webb, 87 N.C. 558, 1882 WL
2993 (1882)
57 ALR6th 445—§ 10
State v. Webb, 123 P.3d 212 (Kan. Ct.
App. 2005)
34 ALR6th 1—§ 10
State v. Webb, 130 Idaho 462, 943 P.2d
52 (1997)
45 ALR6th 643—§ 17
State v. Webb, 130 S.W.3d 799 (Tenn.
Crim. App. 2003)
45 ALR6th 435—§ 5, 17
77 ALR6th 393—§ 75, 93
State v. Webb, 151 Vt. 200, 559 A.2d
658 (1989)
92 ALR5th 35—§ 25
State v. Webb, 164 Ariz. 348, 793 P.2d
105, 51 Ariz. Adv. Rep. 44 (App.
1990)
3 ALR5th 784—§ 5
State v. Webb, 193 Ga. App. 2, 386
S.E.2d 891 (1989)
82 ALR5th 103—§ 5
State v. Webb, 238 Conn. 389, 680 A.2d
147 (1996)
59 ALR5th 1—§ 3, 4, 6
85 ALR5th 547—§ 8
State v. Webb, 239 Iowa 693, 31 N.W.2d
337 (1948)
33 ALR5th 571—§ 5
State v. Webb, 252 Conn. 128, 750 A.2d
448 (2000)
21 ALR6th 1—§ 4, 10, 13, 15
State v. Webb, 307 So. 2d 582 (La. 1975)
70 ALR5th 587—§ 3
State v. Webb, 311 So. 2d 190 (Fla. App.
D2 1975)
24 ALR5th 132—§ 5, 8
State v. Webb, 324 Or. 380, 927 P.2d 79
(1996)
102 ALR5th 525—§ 65
State v. Webb, 373 Ark. 65, 281 S.W.3d
273 (2008)
70 ALR6th 1—§ 5

State v. Webb, 424 So. 2d 233 (La. 1982)
16 ALR6th 329—§ 5
24 ALR6th 591—§ 4, 14
State v. Webb, 493 N.W.2d 868 (Iowa
App. 1992)
2 ALR5th 725—§ 13, 15
State v. Webb, 516 N.W.2d 824 (Iowa
1994)
57 ALR6th 313—§ 5
State v. Webb, 544 S.W.2d 53 (Mo.
App. 1976)
29 ALR5th 59—§ 39
State v. Webb, 824 S.W.2d 464 (Mo. Ct.
App. S.D. 1992)
67 ALR5th 361—§ 3
4 ALR6th 599—§ 14, 28
State v. Webb, 1999 WL 693162 (Ohio
Ct. App. 3d Dist. Allen County
1999)
78 ALR5th 489—§ 9
State v. Webb, 2010-Ohio-5743, 2010
WL 4887407 (Ohio Ct. App. 2d
Dist. Montgomery County 2010)
69 ALR6th 1—§ 29
State v. Webb, 2011 WL 6260447 (N.J.
Super. Ct. App. Div. 2011)
78 ALR6th 297—§ 44, 48
State v. Webber, 112 Mont. 284, 116
P.2d 679, 136 A.L.R. 1077 (1941)
29 ALR5th 59—§ 3, 38, 39
State v. Webber, 292 N.W.2d 5 (Minn.
1980)
86 ALR5th 463—§ 10
State v. Weber, 137 N.H. 193, 624 A.2d
967 (1993)
32 ALR6th 171—§ 9, 15
33 ALR6th 1—§ 23
State v. Weber, 139 So. 3d 519 (La.
2014)
101 ALR6th 331—§ 10
State v. Weber, 172 Or. App. 704, 19
P.3d 378 (2001)
26 ALR6th 179—§ 3, 5
State v. Weber, 266 Wis. 2d 1060, 2003
WI App 188, 668 N.W.2d 562 (Ct.
App. 2003)
38 ALR6th 97—§ 5

For assistance, call 1-800-328-4880

State v. Weber, 1995 WL 238940 (Minn. Ct. App. 1995)

45 ALR6th 435—§ 31, 32

State v. Weber, 2003 WI App 188, 266 Wis. 2d 1060, 668 N.W.2d 562 (Ct. App. 2003)

81 ALR6th 505—§ 33

State v. Webster, 127 Wash. App. 1056, 2005 WL 1335518 (Div. 3 2005)

71 ALR6th 625—§ 17, 20

State v. Webster, 170 Ariz. 372, 824 P.2d 768 (Ct. App. Div. 2 1991)

92 ALR6th 171—§ 23

State v. Weddell, 410 N.W.2d 553 (S.D. 1987)

16 ALR6th 329—§ 11

24 ALR6th 591—§ 9, 13

State v. Weedon, 342 So. 2d 642 (La. 1977)

57 ALR5th 141—§ 2, 6

State v. Weeks, 270 Mont. 63, 891 P.2d 477 (1995)

77 ALR5th 201—§ 11, 14

90 ALR5th 453—§ 14

State v. Weeks, 335 So. 2d 274 (Fla. 1976)

13 ALR5th 1—§ 3

State v. Weeks, 1992 WL 54269 (Ohio Ct. App. 11th Dist. Ashtabula County 1992)

69 ALR6th 207—§ 9, 10, 18

State v. Weeks, 2000 ME 171, 761 A.2d 44 (Me. 2000)

42 ALR5th 291—§ 10

State v. Weems, 1996 WL 417652 (Tenn. Crim. App. 1996)

57 ALR5th 141—§ 2, 5

State v. Wees, 138 Idaho 119, 58 P.3d 103 (Ct. App. 2002)

40 ALR6th 463—§ 3

State v. Weese, 67 Wash. App. 259, 834 P.2d 1099 (1992)

18 ALR5th 542—§ 5

State v. Wegmann, 2008-Ohio-622, 2008 WL 434981 (Ohio Ct. App. 3d Dist. Allen County 2008)

34 ALR6th 253—§ 14

State v. Weidenhof, 205 Conn. 262, 533 A.2d 545 (1987)

23 ALR5th 672—§ 6

State v. Weidner, 235 Wis. 2d 306, 2000 WI 52, 611 N.W.2d 684 (2000)

98 ALR5th 167—§ 8

State v. Weigel, 194 N.J. Super. 451, 477 A.2d 372 (1984)

77 ALR5th 523—§ 7

State v. Weigel, 194 N.J. Super. 451, 477 A.2d 372 (App. Div. 1984)

108 ALR5th 593—§ 15

State v. Weigel, 228 Kan. 194, 612 P.2d 636 (1980)

17 ALR5th 851—§ 2

39 ALR5th 283—§ 4, 18

State v. Weigold, 281 Minn. 73, 160 N.W.2d 577 (1968)

40 ALR6th 1—§ 33

State v. Weiker, 279 N.W.2d 683 (S.D. 1979)

6 ALR6th 533—§ 15

State v. Weiker, 342 N.W.2d 7 (S.D. 1983)

113 ALR5th 517—§ 20

State v. Weimer, 2005-Ohio-2361, 2005 WL 1131773 (Ohio Ct. App. 11th Dist. Trumbull County 2005)

46 ALR6th 241—§ 14, 25

State v. Weinberg, 215 Conn. 231, 575 A.2d 1003 (1990)

72 ALR6th 437—§ 4

State v. Weinberg, 364 So. 2d 964 (La. 1978)

113 ALR5th 517—§ 3

State v. Weinberger, 204 Mont. 278, 665 P.2d 202 (1983)

57 ALR5th 141—§ 12

State v. Weind, 50 Ohio St. 2d 224, 4 Ohio Op. 3d 413, 364 N.E.2d 224 (1977)

65 ALR6th 537—§ 14

State v. Weinstein, 224 N.C. 645, 31 S.E.2d 920, 156 A.L.R. 625 (1944)

57 ALR6th 445—§ 32

State v. Weir, 506 S.W.2d 437 (Mo. 1974)

---

39 ALR5th 283—§ 2

State v. Weis, 246 Kan. 694, 792 P.2d 989 (1990)

124 ALR5th 1—§ 3

State v. Weis, 285 Mont. 41, 945 P.2d 900 (1997)

52 ALR5th 655—§ 4

State v. Weisbrode, 653 A.2d 411 (Me. 1995)

39 ALR6th 257—§ 19
40 ALR6th 1—§ 29

State v. Weisenbarger, 2002-Ohio-291, 2002 WL 104618 (Ohio Ct. App. 12th Dist. Preble County 2002)

23 ALR6th 307—§ 44

State v. Weisman, 121 Wis. 2d 701, 361 N.W.2d 311 (Ct. App. 1984)

63 ALR6th 1—§ 66

State v. Weiss, 155 Vt. 558, 587 A.2d 73 (1991)

41 ALR5th 171—§ 12, 26, 63

State v. Weiss, 935 So. 2d 110 (Fla. Dist. Ct. App. 4th Dist. 2006)

32 ALR6th 1—§ 10

State v. Weitzman, 121 N.H. 83, 427 A.2d 3 (1981)

3 ALR5th 521—§ 6

State v. Welch, 21 Minn. 22, 1874 WL 3749 (1874)

5 ALR6th 1—§ 46

State v. Welch, 37 Wis. 196 (1875)

66 ALR5th 397—§ 6, 11, 23

State v. Welch, 69 N.C. App. 668, 318 S.E.2d 4 (1984)

39 ALR5th 283—§ 4, 58

State v. Welch, 135 Vt. 316, 376 A.2d 351 (1977)

109 ALR5th 611—§ 3

State v. Welch, 368 So. 2d 965 (La. 1979)

62 ALR5th 121—§ 6

State v. Welch, 441 A.2d 539 (R.I. 1982)

24 ALR5th 428—§ 6, 7

State v. Welch, 448 So. 2d 705 (La. Ct. App. 1st Cir. 1984)

101 ALR5th 619—§ 5
20 ALR6th 479—§ 12, 15

State v. Welch, 755 S.W.2d 624 (Mo. Ct. App. W.D. 1988)

74 ALR5th 319—§ 7 to 10

State v. Welch, 1999 WL 142823 (Wash. Ct. App. Div. 2 1999)

73 ALR5th 383—§ 3

State v. Welch, 2005 WL 357902 (Tenn. Crim. App. 2005)

26 ALR6th 511—§ 25

State v. Welch, 2006-Ohio-6684, 2006 WL 3702650 (Ohio Ct. App. 3d Dist. Wyandot County 2006)

26 ALR6th 511—§ 19

State v. Welcome, 458 So. 2d 1235 (La. 1983)

20 ALR5th 177—§ 3, 10

State v. Weldele, 2003 MT 117, 315 Mont. 452, 69 P.3d 1162 (2003)

69 ALR6th 1—§ 30

State v. Welker, 37 Wash. App. 628, 683 P.2d 1110 (Div. 2 1984)

81 ALR5th 563—§ 3, 7

State v. Welker, 127 Wash. App. 222, 110 P.3d 1167 (Div. 2 2005)

70 ALR6th 361—§ 14

State v. Welker, 178 W. Va. 47, 357 S.E.2d 240 (1987)

22 ALR5th 1—§ 61
38 ALR5th 433—§ 50

State v. Weller, 76 Wash. App. 165, 884 P.2d 610 (Div. 3 1994)

106 ALR5th 397—§ 4

State v. Weller, 225 N.J. Super. 274, 542 A.2d 55 (Law Div. 1986)

111 ALR5th 1—§ 3, 5, 7, 27
112 ALR5th 621—§ 3, 5

State v. Weller, 590 So. 2d 923 (Fla. 1991)

2 ALR6th 551—§ 29

State v. Weller, 644 A.2d 839, 33 A.L.R.5th 889 (Vt. 1994)

33 ALR5th 571—§ 3

State v. Wellington., 1979 WL 209664 (Ohio Ct. App. 5th Dist. Richland County 1979)

81 ALR6th 505—§ 4

State v. Wellington, 1981 WL 6168 (Ohio Ct. App. 5th Dist. Richland County 1981)
42 ALR6th 237—§ 8

State v. Wellner, 318 N.W.2d 324 (S.D. 1982)
18 ALR6th 1—§ 5, 22, 26

State v. Wells, 18 Kan. App. 2d 735, 861 P.2d 828 (1993)
15 ALR5th 391—§ 5

State v. Wells, 92 Neb. 337, 138 N.W. 165 (1912)
121 ALR5th 1—§ 55

State v. Wells, 110 Ohio App. 3d 275, 673 N.E.2d 1008 (10th Dist. Franklin County 1996)
51 ALR6th 1—§ 15
71 ALR6th 335—§ 16

State v. Wells, 195 Wis. 551, 218 N.W. 811 (1928)
108 ALR5th 593—§ 28

State v. Wells, 276 N.W.2d 679 (N.D. 1979)
22 ALR5th 660—§ 6, 8, 13

State v. Wells, 336 N.J. Super. 139, 763 A.2d 1279 (Law Div. 2000)
4 ALR5th 1—§ 32
68 ALR5th 299—§ 5.5

State v. Wells, 516 So. 2d 74 (Fla. Dist. Ct. App. 5th Dist. 1987)
114 ALR5th 173—§ 9, 12

State v. Wells, 638 N.W.2d 456 (Minn. Ct. App. 2002)
70 ALR6th 361—§ 19, 32

State v. Wells, 965 So. 2d 834 (Fla. 4th DCA 2007)
89 ALR6th 565—§ 9

State v. Wells, 2009-Ohio-1305, 2009 WL 737664 (Ohio Ct. App. 12th Dist. Warren County 2009)
99 ALR6th 295—§ 13

State v. Welsh, 26 Kan. App. 2d 362, 988 P.2d 261 (1999)
51 ALR6th 219—§ 4

State v. Welsh, 371 So. 2d 1314 (La. 1979)
112 ALR5th 429—§ 13

State v. Wembley, 728 N.W.2d 243 (Minn. 2007)
65 ALR6th 537—§ 58

State v. Wemyss, 2006 WL 9518 (Minn. Ct. App. 2006)
33 ALR6th 91—§ 36

State v. Wendler, 83 Idaho 213, 360 P.2d 697 (1961)
54 ALR6th 429—§ 22

State v. Wenger, 1999 -NMCA- 092, 985 P.2d 1205 (N.M. Ct. App. 1999)
52 ALR5th 655—§ 4

State v. Wengren, 889 P.2d 96 (Idaho App. 1995)
12 ALR5th 89—§ 4

State v. Weniger, 1989 WL 120275 (Minn. Ct. App. 1989)
125 ALR5th 281—§ 15

State v. Wening, 81 Ohio App. 174, 36 Ohio Op. 487, 77 N.E.2d 724 (6th Dist. Lucas County 1947)
102 ALR5th 525—§ 22

State v. Wentling, 1987 WL 9943 (Ohio Ct. App. 5th Dist. Stark County 1987)
57 ALR5th 141—§ 13

State v. Wentz, 805 P.2d 962 (Alaska 1991)
73 ALR5th 383—§ 15, 17

State v. Wentzel, 1998 WL 842057 (Tenn. Crim. App. 1998)
73 ALR5th 383—§ 3

State v. Werder, 112 Or. App. 179, 828 P.2d 474 (1992)
19 ALR5th 823—§ 2, 9, 11

State v. Were, 2009-Ohio-4494, 2009 WL 2768021 (Ohio Ct. App. 1st Dist. Hamilton County 2009)
71 ALR6th 625—§ 29, 34

State v. Werling, 234 Iowa 1109, 13 N.W.2d 318 (1944)
76 ALR5th 1—§ 20

State v. Werner, 9 S.W.3d 590 (Mo. 2000)
26 ALR6th 451—§ 7

State v. Werner, 302 Md. 550, 489 A.2d 1119 (1985)
39 ALR6th 257—§ 18

State v. Werner, 725 N.W.2d 767 (Minn. Ct. App. 2007)
55 ALR6th 513—§ 8
State v. Werner, 831 A.2d 183 (R.I. 2003)
70 ALR6th 361—§ 31
State v. Werner, 851 A.2d 1093 (R.I. 2004)
10 ALR6th 463—§ 3, 4, 6, 8
State v. Werner, 2003 UT App 268, 76 P.3d 204 (Utah Ct. App. 2003)
20 ALR6th 479—§ 3
State v. Werneth, 101 Idaho 241, 611 P.2d 1026 (1980)
103 ALR6th 137—§ 11
State v. Werowinski, 179 Or. App. 522, 40 P.3d 545 (2002)
34 ALR6th 1—§ 10
State v. Werry, 6 Wash. App. 540, 494 P.2d 1002 (Div. 2 1972)
28 ALR6th 505—§ 7, 14
State v. Wesco, Inc., 911 A.2d 281 (Vt. 2006)
27 ALR6th 565—§ 7
State v. Wesley, 2009 WI App 99, 312 Wis. 2d 812, 754 N.W.2d 254 (Ct. App. 2008)
79 ALR6th 1—§ 37
State v. Wessendorf, 777 P.2d 523, 113 Utah Adv. Rep. 37 (Utah App. 1989)
50 ALR5th 467—§ 6
State v. Wessinger, 736 So. 2d 162 (La. 1999)
79 ALR5th 33—§ 28
110 ALR5th 329—§ 6
98 ALR6th 455—§ 13, 14
State v. West, 1 Or. App. 41, 458 P.2d 706 (1969)
84 ALR6th 427—§ 6
State v. West, 20 Idaho 387, 118 P. 773 (1911)
102 ALR5th 525—§ 65
State v. West, 164 Vt. 192, 667 A.2d 540 (1995)
71 ALR5th 285—§ 3
State v. West, 176 Ariz. 432, 862 P.2d 192, 149 Ariz. Adv. Rep. 5 (1993)

45 ALR5th 531—§ 3, 9
State v. West, 185 Wis. 2d 68, 517 N.W.2d 482 (1994)
51 ALR5th 425—§ 2
68 ALR5th 343—§ 2 to 4, 12
State v. West, 223 Neb. 241, 388 N.W.2d 823 (1986)
58 ALR6th 499—§ 21
State v. West, 260 N.W.2d 215 (S.D. 1977)
97 ALR5th 201—§ 3, 4, 7
State v. West, 262 So. 2d 457 (Fla. Dist. Ct. App. 4th Dist. 1972)
108 ALR5th 593—§ 41
State v. West, 317 N.C. 219, 345 S.E.2d 186 (1986)
93 ALR5th 327—§ 3, 7, 9, 28
28 ALR6th 505—§ 16
State v. West, 475 A.2d 1141 (Me. 1984)
99 ALR6th 113—§ 10
State v. West, 553 So. 2d 945 (La. Ct. App. 4th Cir. 1989)
101 ALR5th 187—§ 5
State v. West, 561 So. 2d 808 (La. App. 2d Cir. 1990)
12 ALR5th 909—§ 12
State v. West, 767 S.W.2d 387 (Tenn. 1989)
11 ALR5th 831—§ 4
State v. West, 866 S.W.2d 150 (Mo. App. 1993)
47 ALR5th 259—§ 2, 3, 12 to 14
State v. West, 2006-Ohio-5834, 2006 WL 3159354 (Ohio Ct. App. 3d Dist. Auglaize County 2006)
63 ALR6th 1—§ 5, 38, 66
State v. West, 2010-Ohio-1786, 2010 WL 1632316 (Ohio Ct. App. 2d Dist. Montgomery County 2010)
57 ALR6th 83—§ 6
State v. West, 2013-Ohio-96, 2013 WL 177625 (Ohio Ct. App. 8th Dist. Cuyahoga County 2013)
101 ALR6th 1—§ 37
State v. Westbrooks, 345 N.C. 43, 478 S.E.2d 483 (1996)
57 ALR5th 141—§ 7

State v. Westcott, 121 S.W.3d 543 (Mo. Ct. App. W.D. 2003)
72 ALR6th 227—§ 44

State v. Westeen, 591 N.W.2d 203 (Iowa 1999)
24 ALR5th 428—§ 7, 11

State v. Westenskow, 109 Wash. App. 1072, 2002 WL 26289 (Div. 3 2002)
96 ALR6th 355—§ 24, 37, 55

State v. Wester, 71 N.C. App. 321, 322 S.E.2d 421 (1984)
5 ALR5th 243—§ 61

State v. Westerman, 945 P.2d 695 (Utah Ct. App. 1997)
15 ALR5th 391—§ 15
92 ALR5th 35—§ 25

State v. Westerman, 971 S.W.2d 932 (Mo. Ct. App. W.D. 1998)
5 ALR5th 243—§ 45

State v. Westfall, 46 Ohio St. 2d 31, 75 Ohio Op. 2d 97, 346 N.E.2d 282 (1976)
29 ALR6th 237—§ 4, 6, 9, 21

State v. Westlund, 302 Or. 225, 729 P.2d 541 (1986)
18 ALR5th 1—§ 39

State v. Weston, 66 Wash. App. 140, 831 P.2d 771 (Div. 1 1992)
72 ALR6th 413—§ 6

State v. Weston, 202 S.W.2d 50 (Mo. 1947)
52 ALR5th 655—§ 3

State v. Weston, 367 S.C. 279, 625 S.E.2d 641 (2006)
65 ALR6th 359—§ 9

State v. Westry, 15 N.C. App. 1, 189 S.E.2d 618 (1972)
99 ALR6th 295—§ 13

State v. Westside Fish Co., 31 Or. App. 299, 570 P.2d 401 (1977)
50 ALR5th 703—§ 37

State v. Wetherell, 259 Neb. 341, 609 N.W.2d 672 (2000)
9 ALR6th 633—§ 5, 13, 25
9 ALR6th 693—§ 18
13 ALR6th 603—§ 31
15 ALR6th 173—§ 31

State v. Wetzel, 7 Haw. App. 532, 782 P.2d 891 (1989)
119 ALR5th 379—§ 7

State v. Wetzel, 868 P.2d 64 (Utah 1993)
57 ALR5th 141—§ 3

State v. Weygandt, 20 Wash. App. 599, 581 P.2d 1376 (Div. 1 1978)
56 ALR6th 185—§ 10

State v. Whalen, 214 W. Va. 299, 588 S.E.2d 677 (2003)
30 ALR6th 373—§ 8, 19
41 ALR6th 141—§ 8
63 ALR6th 351—§ 3

State v. Whalen, 234 Mo. 539, 137 S.W. 881 (1911)
5 ALR6th 1—§ 40

State v. Whaley, 389 N.W.2d 919 (Minn. App. 1986)
5 ALR5th 243—§ 45, 59

State v. Whalon, 1 Wash. App. 785, 464 P.2d 730 (Div. 2 1970)
87 ALR5th 181—§ 5
104 ALR5th 357—§ 6, 8

State v. Whatman, 1992 WL 365304 (Ohio Ct. App. 6th Dist. Sandusky County 1992)
97 ALR6th 539—§ 4

State v. Wheadon, 779 S.W.2d 708 (Mo. App. 1989)
5 ALR5th 243—§ 2, 21

State v. Wheat, 471 So. 2d 1027 (La. Ct. App. 1st Cir. 1985)
84 ALR6th 427—§ 4, 21

State v. Wheat, 2002 WI App 153, 256 Wis. 2d 270, 647 N.W.2d 441 (Ct. App. 2002)
92 ALR6th 1—§ 3, 9

State v. Wheel, 587 A.2d 933 (Vt. 1990)
18 ALR5th 1—§ 32

State v. Wheeler, 70 N.C. App. 191, 319 S.E.2d 631 (1984)
17 ALR5th 125—§ 3
73 ALR5th 383—§ 3

State v. Wheeler, 108 Wash. 2d 230, 737 P.2d 1005 (1987)
57 ALR6th 313—§ 5
81 ALR6th 505—§ 43

State v. Wheeler, 123 W. Va. 279, 14 S.E.2d 677 (1941)
11 ALR5th 218—§ 3

State v. Wheeler, 126 Wash. App. 1026, 2005 WL 583401 (Div. 1 2005)
38 ALR6th 1—§ 5

State v. Wheeler, 195 Kan. 184, 403 P.2d 1015 (1965)
45 ALR5th 531—§ 3

State v. Wheeler, 266 Wis. 2d 1059, 2003 WI App 188, 668 N.W.2d 562 (Ct. App. 2003)
33 ALR6th 407—§ 5

State v. Wheeler, 496 A.2d 1382 (R.I. 1985)
90 ALR5th 453—§ 20
95 ALR5th 471—§ 7, 18

State v. Wheeler, 845 S.W.2d 678 (Mo. App. 1993)
27 ALR5th 593—§ 6, 7, 12

State v. Wheeler, 845 S.W.2d 678 (Mo. Ct. App. E.D. 1993)
110 ALR5th 329—§ 6, 13

State v. Wheelock, 218 Iowa 178, 254 N.W. 313 (1934)
103 ALR6th 35—§ 25

State v. Whelan, 728 So. 2d 807 (Fla. Dist. Ct. App. 3d Dist. 1999)
58 ALR6th 215—§ 5

State v. Wherry, 188 Wis. 2d 605, 526 N.W.2d 280 (Ct. App. 1994)
99 ALR6th 295—§ 20, 21

State v. Whetstone, 30 Wash. 2d 301, 191 P.2d 818 (1948)
54 ALR6th 429—§ 20

State v. Whetzel, 200 W. Va. 45, 488 S.E.2d 45 (1997)
15 ALR5th 391—§ 4

State v. Whipple, 143 Minn. 403, 173 N.W. 801 (1919)
13 ALR5th 1—§ 28

State v. Whipple, 2001 M.T. 16, 19 P.3d 228 (Mont. 2001)
38 ALR5th 433—§ 3

State v. Whisenant, 127 Ohio App. 3d 75, 711 N.E.2d 1016 (11th Dist. Portage County 1998)

28 ALR6th 505—§ 26

State v. Whisler, 2008 MT 276, 345 Mont. 292, 190 P.3d 1098 (2008)
79 ALR6th 1—§ 39, 49

State v. Whisman, 33 Or. App. 147, 575 P.2d 1005 (1978)
54 ALR5th 141—§ 3, 9, 10

State v. Whistler, 127 P.3d 341 (Kan. 2006)
26 ALR6th 511—§ 25

State v. Whitaker, 132 Wash. App. 1033, 2006 WL 1000074 (Div. 1 2006)
30 ALR6th 1—§ 7
36 ALR6th 681—§ 13

State v. Whitaker, 133 Wash. App. 199, 135 P.3d 923 (Div. 1 2006)
30 ALR6th 1—§ 7

State v. Whitaker, 228 N.C. 352, 45 S.E.2d 860 (1947)
105 ALR5th 243—§ 4

State v. Whitaker, 260 Kan. 85, 917 P.2d 859 (1996)
5 ALR5th 243—§ 7

State v. Whitaker, 364 N.C. 404, 700 S.E.2d 215 (2010)
64 ALR6th 131—§ 5

State v. Whitaker, 364 N.C. 404, 700 S.E.2d 215, 63 A.L.R.6th 755 (2010)
63 ALR6th 1—§ 5, 11, 36, 44, 46, 53

State v. Whitaker, 689 S.E.2d 395 (N.C. Ct. App. 2009)
64 ALR6th 131—§ 3, 5, 6

State v. White, 2 Neb. App. 106, 507 N.W.2d 654 (1993)
38 ALR5th 433—§ 27

State v. White, 10 Wash. 611, 39 P. 160 (1895)
54 ALR6th 429—§ 21

State v. White, 26 Ariz. App. 505, 549 P.2d 600 (Div. 1 1976)
125 ALR5th 281—§ 2, 4, 12

State v. White, 27 N.C. App. 198, 218 S.E.2d 493 (1975)
29 ALR5th 59—§ 3

State v. White, 28 S.W.3d 391 (Mo. Ct. App. W.D. 2000)

27 ALR5th 593—§ 25, 30, 31.5, 36
State v. White, 76 Conn. App. 509, 819 A.2d 932 (2003)
9 ALR6th 633—§ 5, 24, 39
13 ALR6th 603—§ 44
14 ALR6th 517—§ 7
State v. White, 76 Wash. App. 801, 888 P.2d 169 (Div. 1 1995)
4 ALR6th 599—§ 13
State v. White, 81 S.W.3d 561 (Mo. Ct. App. W.D. 2002)
105 ALR5th 529—§ 20
State v. White, 85 Ohio St. 3d 433, 709 N.E.2d 140 (1999)
70 ALR5th 1—§ 9, 11
79 ALR5th 33—§ 9
State v. White, 87 N.C. App. 311, 361 S.E.2d 301 (1987)
24 ALR5th 132—§ 3
State v. White, 96 Or. App. 713, 773 P.2d 824 (1989)
29 ALR5th 1—§ 4
State v. White, 101 N.C. App. 593, 401 S.E.2d 106 (1991)
86 ALR5th 59—§ 5
State v. White, 104 N.C. App. 165, 408 S.E.2d 871 (1991)
2 ALR6th 551—§ 16
State v. White, 105 N.H. 159, 196 A.2d 33 (1963)
5 ALR5th 243—§ 59
State v. White, 106 Wash. App. 1010, 2001 WL 479178 (Div. 1 2001)
7 ALR6th 233—§ 5, 11
State v. White, 110 Ohio App. 3d 347, 674 N.E.2d 405 (1996)
50 ALR5th 581—§ 7, 24
State v. White, 112 Wis. 2d 178, 332 N.W.2d 756, 10 Ed. Law Rep. 795 (1983)
70 ALR5th 169—§ 16
State v. White, 118 Ariz. 47, 574 P.2d 840 (Ct. App. Div. 1 1977)
122 ALR5th 439—§ 5
State v. White, 126 Mo. 591, 29 S.W. 591 (1895)
57 ALR6th 445—§ 27

State v. White, 131 Ohio App. 3d 587, 723 N.E.2d 158 (10th Dist. Franklin County 1998)
36 ALR5th 161—§ 3, 6, 12, 16
63 ALR6th 351—§ 3
93 ALR6th 1—§ 41
State v. White, 142 N.C. App. 201, 542 S.E.2d 265 (2001)
93 ALR5th 683—§ 4
State v. White, 149 P.3d 547 (Kan. Ct. App. 2007)
37 ALR6th 357—§ 3
State v. White, 162 N.C. App. 183, 590 S.E.2d 448 (2004)
63 ALR6th 351—§ 3
State v. White, 164 N.H. 418, 58 A.3d 643 (2012)
89 ALR6th 261—§ 29, 45
State v. White, 169 Conn. 223, 363 A.2d 143 (1975)
21 ALR6th 771—§ 10
State v. White, 172 Vt. 493, 782 A.2d 1187 (2001)
110 ALR5th 213—§ 2
State v. White, 175 Ohio App. 3d 302, 2008-Ohio-657, 886 N.E.2d 904 (9th Dist. Summit County 2008)
78 ALR6th 297—§ 38
State v. White, 195 S.W. 994 (Mo. 1917)
81 ALR5th 563—§ 3
State v. White, 227 N.J. Super. 443, 547 A.2d 1131 (App. Div. 1988)
101 ALR5th 187—§ 10
State v. White, 234 Kan. 340, 673 P.2d 1106 (1983)
70 ALR6th 361—§ 5
State v. White, 237 Mo. 208, 140 S.W. 896 (1911)
5 ALR6th 1—§ 44
State v. White, 244 Neb. 577, 508 N.W.2d 554 (1993)
78 ALR5th 567—§ 10
State v. White, 264 N.C. 600, 142 S.E.2d 153 (1965)
99 ALR5th 557—§ 13
92 ALR6th 1—§ 3

State v. White, 270 N.C. 78, 153 S.E.2d 774 (1967)

  5 ALR5th 243—§ 48

State v. White, 272 Neb. 421, 722 N.W.2d 343 (2006)

  57 ALR6th 445—§ 34

State v. White, 274 Neb. 419, 740 N.W.2d 801 (2007)

  72 ALR6th 227—§ 56

State v. White, 275 Kan. 580, 67 P.3d 138 (2003)

  16 ALR6th 329—§ 4
  19 ALR6th 115—§ 7
  24 ALR6th 591—§ 4, 12, 15

State v. White, 286 N.C. 395, 211 S.E.2d 445 (1975)

  10 ALR5th 700—§ 3, 35, 38 to 40, 42

State v. White, 319 N.W.2d 213 (Iowa 1982)

  33 ALR5th 571—§ 5

State v. White, 321 So. 2d 491 (La. 1975)

  79 ALR5th 237—§ 6

State v. White, 340 N.C. 264, 457 S.E.2d 841 (1995)

  83 ALR5th 541—§ 3, 6

State v. White, 348 S.C. 532, 560 S.E.2d 420 (2002)

  67 ALR6th 395—§ 11, 14, 15, 29

State v. White, 363 Mo. 83, 248 S.W.2d 841 (1952)

  86 ALR5th 637—§ 5

State v. White, 369 N.W.2d 301 (Minn. Ct. App. 1985)

  103 ALR6th 137—§ 14, 18

State v. White, 399 So. 2d 172 (La. 1981)

  31 ALR6th 465—§ 14, 22
  58 ALR6th 499—§ 24, 101

State v. White, 464 N.W.2d 585 (Minn. App. 1990)

  42 ALR5th 291—§ 3, 10, 37

State v. White, 504 N.W.2d 211 (Minn. 1993)

  109 ALR5th 611—§ 2, 3

State v. White, 533 N.E.2d 1273 (Ind. Ct. App. 4th Dist. 1989)

  108 ALR5th 593—§ 18

State v. White, 538 N.W.2d 237 (S.D. 1995)

  87 ALR5th 181—§ 3, 4, 6

State v. White, 595 S.W.2d 777 (Mo. Ct. App. W.D. 1980)

  70 ALR5th 587—§ 3

State v. White, 649 S.W.2d 598 (Tenn. Crim. App. 1982)

  73 ALR5th 615—§ 3, 15

State v. White, 674 N.W.2d 683 (Iowa Ct. App. 2003)

  34 ALR6th 1—§ 10

State v. White, 706 S.W.2d 498 (Mo. Ct. App. W.D. 1986)

  37 ALR6th 357—§ 23, 25

State v. White, 715 So. 2d 714 (La. Ct. App. 5th Cir. 1998)

  45 ALR5th 1—§ 11

State v. White, 728 S.W.2d 564 (Mo. Ct. App. W.D. 1987)

  37 ALR6th 357—§ 41, 53

State v. White, 738 S.W.2d 590 (Mo. App. 1987)

  5 ALR5th 243—§ 8

State v. White, 755 So. 2d 830 (Fla. Dist. Ct. App. 5th Dist. 2000)

  113 ALR5th 597—§ 8

State v. White, 770 S.W.2d 357 (Mo. Ct. App. E.D. 1989)

  90 ALR5th 225—§ 4

State v. White, 842 So. 2d 257 (Fla. Dist. Ct. App. 1st Dist. 2003)

  113 ALR5th 597—§ 8

State v. White, 851 P.2d 1195, 210 Utah Adv. Rep. 59 (Utah App. 1993)

  41 ALR5th 171—§ 13, 68

State v. White, 1986 WL 6048 (Ohio Ct. App. 4th Dist. Athens County 1986)

  30 ALR6th 103—§ 24, 46, 57

State v. White, 1990 WL 20067 (Ohio Ct. App. 3d Dist. Marion County 1990)

  99 ALR6th 397—§ 17

State v. White, 1995 WL 336977 (Tenn. Crim. App)

  50 ALR5th 581—§ 7, 9, 13, 22

State v. White, 1999 WL 1000000 (Ohio Ct. App. 2d Dist. Miami County 1999)
  78 ALR5th 489—§ 9
State v. White, 2002-Ohio-262, 2002 WL 63294 (Ohio Ct. App. 2d Dist. Montgomery County 2002)
  55 ALR6th 513—§ 10
State v. White, 2004 MT 103, 321 Mont. 45, 88 P.3d 1258, 14 A.L.R.6th 855 (2004)
  9 ALR6th 633—§ 14
  14 ALR6th 491—§ 7
  14 ALR6th 517—§ 6
State v. White, 2006-Ohio-4746, 2006 WL 2627429 (Ohio Ct. App. 5th Dist. Morgan County 2006)
  26 ALR6th 511—§ 20
State v. White, 2009-Ohio-5557, 2009 WL 3389156 (Ohio Ct. App. 8th Dist. Cuyahoga County 2009)
  56 ALR6th 1—§ 19, 32
State v. Whiteman, 2003-Ohio-2229, 2003 WL 21000988 (Ohio Ct. App. 11th Dist. Portage County 2003)
  9 ALR6th 541—§ 18
State v. White Oak Co., LLC, 13 A.D.3d 435, 787 N.Y.S.2d 333 (2d Dep't 2004)
  44 ALR6th 325—§ 12
State v. Whitesell, 13 P.3d 887 (Kan. 2000)
  29 ALR5th 487—§ 14
State v. Whiteshield, 91 N.M. 96, 570 P.2d 927 (Ct. App. 1977)
  79 ALR5th 419—§ 4
State v. Whiteside, 2000 WL 1455271 (Ohio Ct. App. 10th Dist. Franklin County 2000)
  97 ALR5th 201—§ 3
State v. Whitfield, 75 Conn. App. 201, 815 A.2d 233 (2003)
  39 ALR6th 257—§ 42
  40 ALR6th 1—§ 5
State v. Whitfield, 107 S.W.3d 253 (Mo. 2003)
  110 ALR5th 1—§ 18

State v. Whitfield, 315 N.W.2d 753 (Iowa 1982)
  39 ALR5th 283—§ 10
State v. Whitfield, 444 So. 2d 1154 (Fla. Dist. Ct. App. 2d Dist. 1984)
  28 ALR6th 505—§ 11, 34
State v. Whitfield, 837 S.W.2d 503 (Mo. 1992)
  70 ALR5th 587—§ 17, 18
  24 ALR6th 1—§ 45
State v. Whitfield, 2003 WL 21386284 (Mo. 2003)
  110 ALR5th 1—§ 18
State v. Whiting, 493 So. 2d 286 (La. App. 2d Cir. 1986)
  6 ALR5th 652—§ 2, 3
State v. Whitley, 53 Conn. App. 414, 730 A.2d 1212 (1999)
  24 ALR6th 549—§ 6
State v. Whitley, 128 N.M. 403, 1999-NMCA-155, 993 P.2d 117 (Ct. App. 1999)
  112 ALR5th 429—§ 3
State v. Whitlow, 285 Mont. 430, 949 P.2d 239 (1997)
  27 ALR6th 183—§ 15, 33
State v. Whitman, 788 S.W.2d 328 (Mo. App. 1990)
  59 ALR5th 1—§ 3, 4, 6
State v. Whitman, 2001 WI App 121, 244 Wis. 2d 286, 628 N.W.2d 439 (Ct. App. 2001)
  99 ALR6th 295—§ 5, 16
State v. Whitman, 2003 WI App 1, 259 Wis. 2d 482, 655 N.W.2d 547 (Ct. App. 2002)
  99 ALR6th 295—§ 13
State v. Whitney, 81 Haw. 99, 912 P.2d 596 (Ct. App. 1996)
  95 ALR5th 229—§ 2, 27
State v. Whitney, 96 Wash. 2d 578, 637 P.2d 956 (1981)
  14 ALR5th 89—§ 6
State v. Whitney, 151 Ariz. 113, 726 P.2d 210 (Ct. App. Div. 1 1985)
  92 ALR5th 35—§ 2, 7
State v. Whitney, 2012 ME 105, 2012 WL 3191988 (Me. 2012)

For assistance, call 1-800-328-4880

78 ALR6th 213—§ 5
State v. Whitney-Biggs, 147 Or. App. 509, 936 P.2d 1047 (1997)
58 ALR5th 749—§ 2, 7
State v. Whitsel, 339 N.W.2d 149 (Iowa 1983)
124 ALR5th 1—§ 5
State v. Whitsell, 262 La. 165, 262 So. 2d 509 (1972)
86 ALR5th 59—§ 3
State v. Whitt, 184 W. Va. 340, 400 S.E.2d 584 (1990)
32 ALR6th 1—§ 9
State v. Whitt, 404 So. 2d 254 (La. 1981)
16 ALR6th 329—§ 4
24 ALR6th 591—§ 4, 14
State v. Whitt, 2011-Ohio-3022, 2011 WL 2447416 (Ohio Ct. App. 5th Dist. Coshocton County 2011)
93 ALR6th 275—§ 3, 9
State v. Whittaker, 568 N.W.2d 440 (Minn. 1997)
22 ALR5th 1—§ 3, 17, 31, 41, 44
State v. Whitted, 14 N.C. App. 62, 187 S.E.2d 391 (1972)
5 ALR5th 243—§ 11
State v. Whitted, 99 N.C. App. 502, 393 S.E.2d 590 (1990)
33 ALR5th 453—§ 9
State v. Whitted, 112 N.C. App. 640, 436 S.E.2d 275 (1993)
50 ALR5th 581—§ 9, 16, 20
State v. Whittemore, 166 Wis. 2d 127, 479 N.W.2d 566 (Ct. App. 1991)
70 ALR6th 361—§ 19
State v. Whittemore, 390 A.2d 1046 (Me. 1978)
1 ALR6th 549—§ 8
State v. Whittenmeir, 725 S.W.2d 686 (Tenn. Crim. App. 1986)
73 ALR5th 383—§ 29
State v. Whittier, 21 Me. 341 (1842)
14 ALR5th 89—§ 6, 10, 14
State v. Whittington, 318 N.C. 114, 347 S.E.2d 403 (1986)
39 ALR5th 283—§ 4, 52

State v. Whittington, 2013 WL 820413 (Tex. App. San Antonio 2013)
84 ALR6th 293—§ 15
State v. Whittle, 156 Ariz. 405, 752 P.2d 494, 2 Ariz. Adv. Rep. 3 (1988)
7 ALR5th 758—§ 13
State v. Whitton, 770 So. 2d 844 (La. Ct. App. 4th Cir. 2000)
73 ALR5th 581—§ 5
State v. Whittsette, 1997 WL 67764 (Ohio Ct. App. 8th Dist. Cuyahoga County 1997)
19 ALR6th 697—§ 6
State v. Whitworth, 126 Mo. 573, 29 S.W. 595 (1895)
54 ALR6th 429—§ 3, 13
State v. Whorley, 720 So. 2d 282 (Fla. Dist. Ct. App. 2d Dist. 1998)
31 ALR5th 229—§ 17, 42, 68
State v. Whyte, 133 N.J. 481, 628 A.2d 287 (1993)
88 ALR5th 121—§ 8, 36
State v. Whyte, 2005-Ohio-4057, 2005 WL 1864143 (Ohio Ct. App. 12th Dist. Butler County 2005)
26 ALR6th 511—§ 19
State v. Wickenhauser, 309 S.C. 377, 423 S.E.2d 344 (1992)
46 ALR6th 241—§ 22
State v. Wickham, 1988 WL 35646 (Minn. Ct. App. 1988)
73 ALR5th 383—§ 29
State v. Wickizer, 859 S.W.2d 873 (Mo. Ct. App. W.D. 1993)
103 ALR6th 247—§ 9
State v. Wickline, 399 S.E.2d 42 (W. Va. 1990)
11 ALR5th 871—§ 3
State v. Wickstrom, 405 N.W.2d 1 (Minn. Ct. App. 1987)
50 ALR5th 467—§ 6
73 ALR5th 383—§ 9
State v. Widdicombe, 130 Mont. 325, 301 P.2d 1116 (1956)
50 ALR5th 703—§ 17
State v. Widdison, 2000 UT App 185, 4 P.3d 100 (Utah Ct. App. 2000)

CASES CITED IN ALR5th and ALR6th

119 ALR5th 275—§ 11
State v. Wideman, 165 Ariz. 364, 798 P.2d 1373 (Ct. App. Div. 1 1990)
15 ALR5th 391—§ 31
92 ALR5th 35—§ 13
State v. Widmer-Baum, 653 N.W.2d 351 (Iowa 2002)
53 ALR6th 1—§ 4
72 ALR6th 141—§ 6
State v. Wiedenheft, 136 Idaho 14, 27 P.3d 873 (Ct. App. 2001)
58 ALR6th 499—§ 31
State v. Wiegand, 645 N.W.2d 125 (Minn. 2002)
117 ALR5th 407—§ 3
State v. Wier, 22 Or. App. 549, 540 P.2d 394 (1975)
67 ALR6th 103—§ 4
State v. Wies, 128 Wash. App. 1051, 2005 WL 1727056 (Div. 1 2005)
15 ALR6th 515—§ 34
State v. Wiese, 342 N.W.2d 858 (Iowa 1984)
46 ALR6th 63—§ 9
State v. Wiezorek, 786 N.W.2d 520 (Iowa Ct. App. 2010)
92 ALR6th 295—§ 3, 7, 8
93 ALR6th 207—§ 3, 6, 26
95 ALR6th 1—§ 3
State v. Wig, 30 Kan. App. 2d 1078, 55 P.3d 354 (2002)
23 ALR6th 307—§ 31
State v. Wiggett, 75 Or. App. 474, 707 P.2d 101 (1985)
5 ALR5th 243—§ 62
State v. Wiggins, 7 Conn. App. 95, 507 A.2d 518 (1986)
59 ALR5th 1—§ 2, 3, 5, 6
State v. Wiggins, 171 N.C. 813, 89 S.E. 58 (1916)
81 ALR5th 563—§ 3
State v. Wiggins, 334 N.C. 18, 431 S.E.2d 755 (1993)
32 ALR6th 1—§ 11
State v. Wiggins, 360 S.W.2d 716 (Mo. 1962)
97 ALR5th 293—§ 3, 10

State v. Wiggins, 729 S.W.2d 291 (Tenn. App. 1987)
37 ALR5th 319—§ 10
State v. Wigglesworth, 186 Or. App. 374, 63 P.3d 1185 (2003)
33 ALR6th 91—§ 10
State v. Wight, 765 P.2d 12 (Utah Ct. App. 1988)
83 ALR5th 277—§ 11
84 ALR5th 487—§ 19, 21
State v. Wika, 464 N.W.2d 630 (S.D. 1991)
31 ALR6th 49—§ 6
State v. Wilbur, 115 R.I. 7, 339 A.2d 730 (1975)
85 ALR5th 187—§ 9
State v. Wilburn, 66 Tenn. 57, 1872 WL 4248 (1872)
33 ALR6th 407—§ 22
State v. Wilburn, 2000 WL 1439 (Ohio Ct. App. 5th Dist. Holmes County 1999)
78 ALR5th 489—§ 10
State v. Wilcox, 16 Ohio App. 3d 273, 475 N.E.2d 516 (11th Dist. Trumbull County 1984)
70 ALR5th 1—§ 8
State v. Wilcox, 44 Or. App. 173, 605 P.2d 721 (1980)
92 ALR6th 1—§ 8
State v. Wilcox, 131 N.C. 707, 42 S.E. 536 (1902)
101 ALR6th 499—§ 15
State v. Wilcox, 254 Conn. 441, 758 A.2d 824 (2000)
102 ALR5th 327—§ 6
State v. Wilcox, 1992 WL 292289 (Ohio Ct. App. 8th Dist. Cuyahoga County 1992)
88 ALR5th 121—§ 19, 28
State v. Wilcoxon, 639 So. 2d 385 (La. Ct. App. 2d Cir. 1994)
84 ALR6th 427—§ 17
State v. Wild, 266 Mont. 331, 880 P.2d 840 (1994)
55 ALR6th 391—§ 5
State v. Wilder, 4 Wash. App. 850, 486 P.2d 319 (1971)

State v. Wilkins, 2003 WL 1028310 (Tex. App. San Antonio 2003)
55 ALR6th 513—§ 12
State v. Wilkinson, 176 Conn. 451, 408 A.2d 232 (1979)
89 ALR6th 565—§ 6, 20
State v. Wilkinson, 269 Kan. 603, 9 P.3d 1 (2000)
36 ALR5th 161—§ 3, 19
63 ALR6th 351—§ 3
State v. Wilkinson, 344 N.C. 198, 474 S.E.2d 375 (1996)
1 ALR6th 657—§ 14
State v. Wilkinson, 861 S.W.2d 746 (Mo. Ct. App. S.D. 1993)
124 ALR5th 1—§ 3
State v. Wilkinson, 2000 WL 992105 (Kan. 2000)
78 ALR5th 489—§ 16
State v. Wilks, 117 Wis. 2d 495, 345 N.W.2d 498 (Ct. App. 1984)
72 ALR5th 1—§ 3
State v. Will, 131 Or. App. 498, 885 P.2d 715 (1994)
51 ALR5th 425—§ 5
58 ALR6th 499—§ 99
State v. Willard, 139 N.H. 568, 660 A.2d 1086 (1995)
92 ALR6th 295—§ 12
93 ALR6th 207—§ 4, 11
State v. Willard, 351 N.W.2d 516 (Iowa 1984)
84 ALR5th 487—§ 21
State v. Wille, 185 Wis. 2d 673, 518 N.W.2d 325 (Ct. App. 1994)
101 ALR6th 331—§ 12
State v. Wille, 615 So. 2d 328 (La. 1993)
85 ALR5th 471—§ 6
State v. Willers, 794 S.W.2d 315 (Mo. App. 1990)
4 ALR5th 1—§ 2, 4, 5, 7
30 ALR5th 121—§ 2
State v. Willette, 421 N.W.2d 342 (Minn. Ct. App. 1988)
119 ALR5th 275—§ 11
State v. Willey, 363 A.2d 739 (Me. 1976)

114 ALR5th 235—§ 4
State v. William, 199 Or. App. 191, 110 P.3d 1114 (2005)
30 ALR6th 1—§ 4, 7
State v. William, 248 Kan. 389, 807 P.2d 1292 (1991)
32 ALR6th 1—§ 11
State v. William C., 71 Conn. App. 47, 801 A.2d 823 (2002)
101 ALR5th 187—§ 7
State v. William C., 103 Conn. App. 508, 930 A.2d 753 (2007)
39 ALR6th 257—§ 41
State v. Williamitis, 2006-Ohio-2904, 2006 WL 1574844 (Ohio Ct. App. 2d Dist. Montgomery County 2006)
43 ALR6th 475—§ 6
State v. Williams, 2 Ohio App. 3d 289, 441 N.E.2d 832 (9th Dist. Lorain County 1981)
79 ALR5th 237—§ 11
State v. Williams, 4 Ohio St. 3d 53, 446 N.E.2d 444 (1983)
90 ALR5th 453—§ 17
95 ALR5th 471—§ 3, 7, 18
State v. Williams, 4 Wash. App. 908, 484 P.2d 1167 (Div. 1 1971)
118 ALR5th 253—§ 3, 5, 12, 16, 18
State v. Williams, 6 Ohio St. 3d 281, 452 N.E.2d 1323 (1983)
124 ALR5th 1—§ 5
State v. Williams, 7 Ohio N.P. 562, 5 Ohio Dec. 545, 1897 WL 749 (C.P. 1897)
97 ALR5th 293—§ 4
State v. Williams, 9 S.W.3d 3 (Mo. Ct. App. W.D. 1999)
109 ALR5th 99—§ 2, 7
112 ALR5th 429—§ 2
113 ALR5th 517—§ 2
114 ALR5th 235—§ 2
4 ALR6th 599—§ 24, 29
State v. Williams, 14 W. Va. 851, 1878 WL 3794 (1878)
97 ALR5th 537—§ 24
State v. Williams, 16 Wash. App. 868, 560 P.2d 1160 (Div. 2 1977)
64 ALR5th 741—§ 4

State v. Williams, 18 Kan. App. 2d 424,
856 P.2d 158 (1993)
46 ALR6th 63—§ 3
State v. Williams, 28 Kan. App. 2d 97,
11 P.3d 1187 (2000)
93 ALR5th 493—§ 4
State v. Williams, 31 N.C. App. 111, 228
S.E.2d 668 (1976)
5 ALR5th 243—§ 6
State v. Williams, 33 N.C. App. 397, 235
S.E.2d 86 (1977)
59 ALR5th 1—§ 4, 6
State v. Williams, 38 Ohio St. 3d 346,
528 N.E.2d 910 (1988)
10 ALR5th 700—§ 31
State v. Williams, 47 N.C. App. 205, 266
S.E.2d 705 (1980)
61 ALR5th 1—§ 4, 8
State v. Williams, 59 N.J. 493, 284 A.2d
172 (1971)
38 ALR6th 97—§ 29
State v. Williams, 62 Wash. App. 748,
815 P.2d 825 (1991)
4 ALR5th 1—§ 7
State v. Williams, 64 Wash. 2d 842, 394
P.2d 693 (1964)
15 ALR5th 821—§ 8
State v. Williams, 65 Conn. App. 59,
782 A.2d 149 (2001)
28 ALR6th 505—§ 11
State v. Williams, 65 Conn. App. 449,
783 A.2d 53 (2001)
40 ALR6th 1—§ 10
State v. Williams, 65 N.C. App. 373, 309
S.E.2d 266 (1983)
29 ALR5th 59—§ 32
State v. Williams, 70 Wash. App. 567,
853 P.2d 1388 (1993)
27 ALR5th 593—§ 2
State v. Williams, 74 N.C. App. 574, 328
S.E.2d 775 (1985)
73 ALR5th 383—§ 3
State v. Williams, 75 Ohio App. 3d 102,
598 N.E.2d 1250, 1991 WL 352666,
59 A.L.R.5th 899 (10th
Dist.Franklin County 1991)
59 ALR5th 749—§ 3

State v. Williams, 79 Ohio St. 3d 459,
683 N.E.2d 1126 (1997)
71 ALR5th 285—§ 2, 3
State v. Williams, 80 Ohio App. 3d 648,
610 N.E.2d 545 (Lorain Co. 1992)
36 ALR5th 255—§ 8, 13, 15, 17, 30
State v. Williams, 84 N.J. 217, 417 A.2d
1046 (1980)
18 ALR6th 1—§ 5, 12, 16, 33
State v. Williams, 84 Ohio App. 3d 129,
616 N.E.2d 540 (12th Dist. Clermont County 1992)
66 ALR5th 397—§ 13, 17
State v. Williams, 86 Wash. App. 1056,
1997 WL 335541 (Div. 2 1997)
7 ALR6th 233—§ 5
State v. Williams, 88 Ohio St. 3d 513,
728 N.E.2d 342 (2000)
78 ALR5th 489—§ 6, 7
State v. Williams, 88 Ohio St. 3d 513,
2000-Ohio-428, 728 N.E.2d 342
(2000)
37 ALR6th 55—§ 9
64 ALR6th 1—§ 11, 15, 16
State v. Williams, 93 Wash. App. 340,
968 P.2d 26 (Div. 2 1998)
50 ALR6th 353—§ 47
State v. Williams, 94 Ohio App. 249, 51
Ohio Ops. 414, 115 N.E.2d 36
(1952)
50 ALR5th 703—§ 6
State v. Williams, 94 Ohio Misc. 2d 113,
703 N.E.2d 1284 (C.P. 1998)
90 ALR5th 453—§ 17
State v. Williams, 97 Fla. 159, 120 So.
310 (1929)
75 ALR6th 311—§ 18, 29
State v. Williams, 97 N.J. Super. 573,
235 A.2d 684 (County Ct. 1967)
32 ALR6th 1—§ 5
State v. Williams, 97 Wash. App. 257,
983 P.2d 687 (Div. 1 1999)
46 ALR6th 241—§ 43
State v. Williams, 97 Wash. App. 1002,
1999 WL 639461 (Div. 1 1999)
16 ALR6th 329—§ 11
24 ALR6th 591—§ 9, 13

State v. Williams, 99 Ohio St. 3d 493, 2003-Ohio-4396, 794 N.E.2d 27 (2003)
29 ALR6th 1—§ 10

State v. Williams, 108 So. 3d 255 (La. Ct. App. 4th Cir. 2013)
102 ALR6th 637—§ 7

State v. Williams, 111 Ariz. 222, 526 P.2d 1244 (1974)
39 ALR5th 283—§ 3

State v. Williams, 111 Ariz. 511, 533 P.2d 1146 (1975)
86 ALR5th 59—§ 8

State v. Williams, 113 P.3d 834 (Kan. Ct. App. 2005)
56 ALR6th 323—§ 5

State v. Williams, 115 Ohio App. 3d 24, 684 N.E.2d 358 (11th Dist. Trumbull County 1996)
27 ALR6th 183—§ 45

State v. Williams, 116 N.C. App. 225, 447 S.E.2d 817 (1994)
79 ALR5th 33—§ 62
58 ALR6th 499—§ 23, 98

State v. Williams, 120 S.W.3d 294 (Mo. Ct. App. W.D. 2003)
37 ALR6th 357—§ 25

State v. Williams, 121 Ariz. 213, 589 P.2d 456 (Ct. App. Div. 2 1978)
99 ALR6th 113—§ 11

State v. Williams, 122 Ariz. 146, 593 P.2d 896 (1979)
19 ALR5th 351—§ 10
98 ALR5th 445—§ 4

State v. Williams, 126 Ohio Misc. 2d 47, 2003-Ohio-7294, 802 N.E.2d 195 (Mun. Ct. 2003)
24 ALR6th 1—§ 14, 32

State v. Williams, 127 N.C. App. 464, 490 S.E.2d 583 (1997)
22 ALR6th 533—§ 11

State v. Williams, 127 Wash. 658, 221 P. 289 (1923)
42 ALR5th 547—§ 4

State v. Williams, 131 Ariz. 211, 639 P.2d 1036 (1982)
2 ALR5th 262—§ 3

State v. Williams, 131 Or. App. 85, 883 P.2d 918 (1994)
73 ALR5th 383—§ 3

State v. Williams, 133 Ariz. 220, 650 P.2d 1202 (1982)
11 ALR5th 831—§ 5, 6

State v. Williams, 137 Wash. 2d 746, 975 P.2d 963 (1999)
72 ALR5th 403—§ 11

State v. Williams, 137 Wash. App. 736, 154 P.3d 322 (Div. 2 2007)
30 ALR6th 1—§ 4

State v. Williams, 145 N.C. App. 472, 552 S.E.2d 174 (2001)
78 ALR6th 297—§ 52

State v. Williams, 148 N.M. 160, 2010-NMCA-030, 231 P.3d 616 (Ct. App. 2010)
79 ALR6th 631—§ 3, 4

State v. Williams, 148 Ohio App. 3d 473, 2002-Ohio-3777, 773 N.E.2d 1107 (10th Dist. Franklin County 2002)
58 ALR6th 385—§ 3, 8

State v. Williams, 149 Ohio App. 3d 434, 2002-Ohio-4831, 777 N.E.2d 892 (6th Dist. Lucas County 2002)
21 ALR6th 1—§ 4

State v. Williams, 150 P.3d 926 (Kan. Ct. App. 2007)
26 ALR6th 511—§ 25

State v. Williams, 155 Wash. App. 1014, 2010 WL 1223116 (Div. 2 2010)
55 ALR6th 1—§ 31

State v. Williams, 157 Ohio App. 3d 374, 2004-Ohio-2857, 811 N.E.2d 561 (8th Dist. Cuyahoga County 2004)
29 ALR6th 237—§ 24

State v. Williams, 159 Wash. App. 298, 244 P.3d 1018, 102 A.L.R.6th 755 (Div. 1 2011)
102 ALR6th 279—§ 25, 27, 29

State v. Williams, 160 W. Va. 19, 230 S.E.2d 742 (1976)
55 ALR6th 157—§ 4, 113

State v. Williams, 168 Ariz. 367, 813 P.2d 1376 (Ct. App. Div. 1 1991)

76 ALR5th 1—§ 20
State v. Williams, 172 W. Va. 295, 305
    S.E.2d 251 (1983)
55 ALR6th 157—§ 110, 112, 115
State v. Williams, 182 Ariz. 548, 898
    P.2d 497 (Ct. App. Div. 1 1995)
103 ALR6th 347—§ 15
State v. Williams, 183 Ariz. 368, 904
    P.2d 437 (1995)
79 ALR5th 33—§ 9, 40
State v. Williams, 184 N.J. 432, 877
    A.2d 1258 (2005)
32 ALR6th 285—§ 14, 28
State v. Williams, 190 N.C. App. 173,
    660 S.E.2d 200 (2008)
57 ALR6th 1—§ 32
State v. Williams, 190 W. Va. 538, 438
    S.E.2d 881 (1993)
69 ALR6th 579—§ 4
State v. Williams, 191 Or. App. 270, 81
    P.3d 743 (2003)
114 ALR5th 235—§ 6
State v. Williams, 197 N.J. Super. 127,
    484 A.2d 331 (1984)
5 ALR5th 243—§ 2
State v. Williams, 203 Conn. 159, 523
    A.2d 1284 (1987)
93 ALR5th 527—§ 4
State v. Williams, 203 Neb. 649, 279
    N.W.2d 847 (1979)
72 ALR5th 1—§ 29
State v. Williams, 205 Neb. 56, 287
    N.W.2d 18 (1979)
87 ALR5th 181—§ 3
State v. Williams, 208 So. 2d 172 (Miss.
    1968)
9 ALR6th 1—§ 5
State v. Williams, 212 Ga. App. 164,
    441 S.E.2d 501 (1994)
64 ALR5th 637—§ 4
58 ALR6th 499—§ 80
State v. Williams, 212 Neb. 860, 326
    N.W.2d 678 (1982)
82 ALR5th 359—§ 3, 5
84 ALR5th 487—§ 24
State v. Williams, 214 N.J. Super. 12,
    518 A.2d 234 (1986)

**22 ALR5th 1—§ 4, 5, 13, 15, 22, 31,
    45 to 47, 53**
State v. Williams, 217 N.W.2d 573
    (Iowa 1974)
12 ALR5th 909—§ 8
State v. Williams, 220 Ga. App. 100,
    469 S.E.2d 261, 96 Fulton County
    D R 570 (1996)
50 ALR5th 581—§ 7
State v. Williams, 224 Kan. 468, 580
    P.2d 1341 (1978)
39 ALR5th 283—§ 4
State v. Williams, 224 Neb. 114, 396
    N.W.2d 114 (1986)
3 ALR6th 269—§ 22
State v. Williams, 225 Ga. App. 736,
    484 S.E.2d 775 (1997)
84 ALR6th 293—§ 36
State v. Williams, 226 Kan. 82, 595 P.2d
    1104 (1979)
98 ALR5th 445—§ 4
State v. Williams, 226 Kan. 688, 602
    P.2d 1332 (1979)
39 ALR5th 283—§ 4, 22, 40
State v. Williams, 235 Kan. 485, 681
    P.2d 660 (1984)
3 ALR5th 784—§ 14, 16
State v. Williams, 239 Neb. 985, 480
    N.W.2d 390 (1992)
79 ALR5th 33—§ 42
State v. Williams, 239 N.J. Super. 620,
    571 A.2d 1358 (App. Div. 1990)
67 ALR5th 149—§ 5
State v. Williams, 243 Neb. 959, 503
    N.W.2d 561 (1993)
1 ALR6th 549—§ 15
2 ALR6th 551—§ 5
State v. Williams, 250 La. 64, 193 So.
    2d 787 (1967)
19 ALR6th 115—§ 4, 9, 10
State v. Williams, 253 Neb. 619, 573
    N.W.2d 106 (1997)
51 ALR6th 1—§ 15
State v. Williams, 259 Kan. 432, 913
    P.2d 587 (1996)
12 ALR6th 389—§ 11
State v. Williams, 263 N.C. 800, 140
    S.E.2d 529 (1965)

105 ALR5th 529—§ 26

State v. Williams, 268 Kan. 1, 988 P.2d 722 (1999)

12 ALR6th 267—§ 6

State v. Williams, 271 So. 2d 857 (La. 1973)

42 ALR6th 237—§ 8

State v. Williams, 275 Ga. App. 612, 621 S.E.2d 581 (2005)

50 ALR6th 455—§ 7

State v. Williams, 278 Md. 180, 361 A.2d 122 (1976)

72 ALR5th 529—§ 5

State v. Williams, 286 N.C. 422, 212 S.E.2d 113 (1975)

62 ALR5th 121—§ 3

State v. Williams, 288 N.C. 680, 220 S.E.2d 558 (1975)

79 ALR5th 237—§ 10

State v. Williams, 289 N.J. Super. 611, 674 A.2d 643 (App. Div. 1996)

100 ALR5th 67—§ 6, 27, 29, 40, 44

State v. Williams, 297 S.C. 290, 376 S.E.2d 773 (1989)

76 ALR5th 1—§ 3, 9

State v. Williams, 297 S.C. 404, 377 S.E.2d 308 (1989)

113 ALR5th 517—§ 18

State v. Williams, 301 S.C. 369, 392 S.E.2d 181 (1990)

76 ALR5th 1—§ 5, 11, 20

State v. Williams, 301 So. 2d 587 (La. 1974)

70 ALR5th 587—§ 3

State v. Williams, 304 N.C. 394, 284 S.E.2d 437 (1981)

83 ALR6th 465—§ 12, 58

State v. Williams, 308 N.C. 339, 302 S.E.2d 441 (1983)

39 ALR5th 283—§ 4

State v. Williams, 308 N.C. 357, 302 S.E.2d 438 (1983)

39 ALR5th 283—§ 41

State v. Williams, 326 So. 2d 815 (La. 1976)

97 ALR5th 293—§ 4, 8

State v. Williams, 329 P.3d 400, 101 A.L.R.6th 663 (Kan. 2014)

101 ALR6th 417—§ 3 to 5, 26

State v. Williams, 338 So. 2d 672 (La. 1976)

12 ALR6th 267—§ 8

State v. Williams, 339 N.C. 1, 452 S.E.2d 245 (1994)

31 ALR5th 704—§ 4

State v. Williams, 341 N.C. 1, 459 S.E.2d 208 (1995)

3 ALR6th 269—§ 5, 13

State v. Williams, 353 So. 2d 1299 (La. 1977)

76 ALR5th 563—§ 4, 5

State v. Williams, 355 N.C. 501, 565 S.E.2d 609 (2002)

110 ALR5th 1—§ 15

State v. Williams, 358 So. 2d 943 (La. 1978)

33 ALR6th 407—§ 36, 37

State v. Williams, 359 So. 2d 115 (La. 1978)

29 ALR5th 59—§ 3, 9

State v. Williams, 377 N.J. Super. 130, 871 A.2d 744 (App. Div. 2005)

39 ALR6th 257—§ 47

State v. Williams, 388 A.2d 500 (Me. 1978)

9 ALR5th 369—§ 5
95 ALR5th 471—§ 7

State v. Williams, 389 So. 2d 384 (La. 1980)

106 ALR5th 701—§ 3
68 ALR6th 527—§ 37

State v. Williams, 392 Md. 194, 896 A.2d 973 (2006)

101 ALR6th 331—§ 3

State v. Williams, 395 A.2d 1158 (Me. 1978)

57 ALR5th 141—§ 3

State v. Williams, 445 So. 2d 1171 (La. 1984)

9 ALR5th 369—§ 14

State v. Williams, 458 So. 2d 1315 (La. Ct. App. 1st Cir. 1984)

102 ALR5th 327—§ 3

24 ALR6th 1—§ 19, 21
State v. Williams, 471 So. 2d 255 (La. App. 1st Cir. 1985)
45 ALR5th 1—§ 5, 7, 12, 23
State v. Williams, 471 So. 2d 255 (La. Ct. App. 1st Cir. 1985)
55 ALR6th 391—§ 21
State v. Williams, 478 So. 2d 983 (La. Ct. App. 4th Cir. 1985)
93 ALR5th 527—§ 24
24 ALR6th 1—§ 21
State v. Williams, 500 So. 2d 811 (La. Ct. App. 1st Cir. 1986)
104 ALR5th 357—§ 8
54 ALR6th 429—§ 20
State v. Williams, 517 So. 2d 1268 (La. Ct. App. 4th Cir. 1987)
85 ALR5th 471—§ 7
State v. Williams, 525 N.W.2d 538 (Minn. 1994)
69 ALR5th 425—§ 4 to 6
69 ALR6th 579—§ 8
State v. Williams, 535 N.W.2d 277 (Minn. 1995)
26 ALR6th 451—§ 7
69 ALR6th 579—§ 9
State v. Williams, 536 S.W.2d 947 (Mo. App. 1976)
55 ALR5th 125—§ 9
State v. Williams, 577 S.W.2d 59 (Mo. App. 1978)
55 ALR5th 125—§ 12, 21, 22
59 ALR5th 1—§ 4, 7
State v. Williams, 593 N.W.2d 227 (Minn. 1999)
22 ALR5th 1—§ 49
State v. Williams, 593 So. 2d 753 (La. App. 5th Cir. 1992)
29 ALR5th 59—§ 55
State v. Williams, 594 So. 2d 476 (La. Ct. App. 4th Cir. 1992)
99 ALR6th 295—§ 10
State v. Williams, 595 S.W.2d 378 (Mo. Ct. App. W.D. 1980)
70 ALR5th 587—§ 4
State v. Williams, 602 So. 2d 318 (La. Ct. App. 1st Cir. 1992)

9 ALR6th 1—§ 17
State v. Williams, 635 S.W.2d 55 (Mo. App. 1982)
29 ALR5th 59—§ 7
State v. Williams, 682 So. 2d 1245 (Fla. Dist. Ct. App. 5th Dist. 1996)
113 ALR5th 597—§ 8
State v. Williams, 688 So. 2d 1343 (La. Ct. App. 3d Cir. 1997)
103 ALR5th 463—§ 3
State v. Williams, 689 S.E.2d 412 (N.C. Ct. App. 2009)
67 ALR6th 103—§ 5, 10
State v. Williams, 689 So. 2d 1233 (Fla. Dist. Ct. App. 2d Dist. 1997)
92 ALR5th 35—§ 25
State v. Williams, 693 So. 2d 870 (La. Ct. App. 3d Cir. 1997)
19 ALR6th 697—§ 8
State v. Williams, 695 N.W.2d 23 (Iowa 2005)
30 ALR6th 1—§ 4, 5
State v. Williams, 696 S.W.2d 809 (Mo. Ct. App. W.D. 1985)
102 ALR5th 447—§ 10, 13
State v. Williams, 708 So. 2d 703 (La. 1998)
79 ALR5th 33—§ 25, 52
State v. Williams, 729 So. 2d 1080 (La. Ct. App. 1st Cir. 1999)
27 ALR5th 593—§ 8, 28, 31
State v. Williams, 739 So. 2d 717 (Fla. Dist. Ct. App. 5th Dist. 1999)
114 ALR5th 173—§ 7
State v. Williams, 740 S.W.2d 244 (Mo. App. 1987)
5 ALR5th 243—§ 51
State v. Williams, 747 So. 2d 1256 (La. Ct. App. 2d Cir. 1999)
83 ALR6th 465—§ 5, 64
State v. Williams, 747 S.W.2d 635 (Mo. Ct. App. W.D. 1988)
85 ALR5th 547—§ 8
State v. Williams, 752 S.W.2d 454 (Mo. Ct. App. W.D. 1988)
93 ALR6th 207—§ 6, 14, 18, 28
96 ALR6th 355—§ 9, 55

State v. Williams, 768 S.W.2d 714 (Tenn. Crim. App. 1988)
73 ALR5th 383—§ 5

State v. Williams, 784 S.W.2d 309 (Mo. App. 1990)
5 ALR5th 243—§ 48

State v. Williams, 787 S.W.2d 308 (Mo. Ct. App. E.D. 1990)
58 ALR5th 749—§ 2, 3

State v. Williams, 788 So. 2d 515 (La. Ct. App. 4th Cir. 2001)
109 ALR5th 99—§ 10

State v. Williams, 831 So. 2d 835 (La. 2002)
122 ALR5th 145—§ 3, 7, 9, 11, 13, 16, 17, 22

State v. Williams, 839 So. 2d 1095 (La. Ct. App. 3d Cir. 2003)
41 ALR6th 141—§ 8

State v. Williams, 839 S.W.2d 732 (Mo. Ct. App. S.D. 1992)
71 ALR6th 1—§ 8

State v. Williams, 858 So. 2d 878 (La. Ct. App. 2d Cir. 2003)
114 ALR5th 173—§ 7

State v. Williams, 860 S.W.2d 364 (Mo. App. 1993)
39 ALR5th 283—§ 4, 62

State v. Williams, 870 So. 2d 938 (Fla. Dist. Ct. App. 5th Dist. 2004)
113 ALR5th 597—§ 4

State v. Williams, 898 P.2d 497, 192 Ariz. Adv. Rep. 27 (Ariz. App. 1995)
20 ALR5th 398—§ 5, 12, 20, 65

State v. Williams, 932 So. 2d 693 (La. Ct. App. 4th Cir. 2006)
26 ALR6th 511—§ 28

State v. Williams, 938 S.W.2d 456 (Tex. Crim. App. 1997)
51 ALR6th 1—§ 5
52 ALR6th 1—§ 3

State v. Williams, 941 N.E.2d 565 (Ind. Ct. App. 2011)
78 ALR6th 297—§ 41

State v. Williams, 1990 WL 88784 (Ohio Ct. App. 3d Dist. Hardin County 1990)
54 ALR6th 593—§ 11

State v. Williams, 1992 WL 9531 (Ohio App. Clermont Co. 1992)
52 ALR5th 655—§ 3

State v. Williams, 1993 WL 489748 (Ohio Ct. App. 8th Dist. Cuyahoga County 1993)
85 ALR5th 471—§ 7

State v. Williams, 1995 WL 34810 (Minn. Ct. App. 1995)
73 ALR5th 383—§ 21

State v. Williams, 1995 WL 248530 (Ohio Ct. App. 8th Dist. Cuyahoga County 1995)
67 ALR5th 637—§ 5, 8

State v. Williams, 1996 WL 653819 (Tenn. Crim. App. 1996)
7 ALR6th 233—§ 4

State v. Williams, 1996 WL 666725 (Ohio Ct. App. 3d Dist. Allen County 1996)
20 ALR6th 479—§ 3, 23

State v. Williams, 1999 WL 10256 (Minn. Ct. App. 1999)
73 ALR5th 383—§ 28

State v. Williams, 1999 WL 76633 (Ohio Ct. App. 11th Dist. Lake County 1999)
78 ALR5th 489—§ 9

State v. Williams, 2000 WL 426562 (Ohio Ct. App. 8th Dist. Cuyahoga County 2000)
122 ALR5th 439—§ 7

State v. Williams, 2000 WL 977297 (R.I. Super. Ct. 2000)
63 ALR6th 351—§ 3

State v. Williams, 2002 WL 47185 (Minn. Ct. App. 2002)
113 ALR5th 597—§ 4, 6

State v. Williams, 2003-Ohio-6342, 2003 WL 22805741 (Ohio Ct. App. 8th Dist. Cuyahoga County 2003)
3 ALR6th 543—§ 12

State v. Williams, 2004-Ohio-4316, 2004 WL 1836731 (Ohio Ct. App. 9th Dist. Summit County 2004)
23 ALR6th 307—§ 38

State v. Williams, 2004 WL 1661219
(Minn. Ct. App. 2004)
34 ALR6th 1—§ 10

State v. Williams, 2005 WL 1475313
(Tenn. Crim. App. 2005)
55 ALR6th 513—§ 8

State v. Williams, 2005 WL 2877986
(N.J. Super. Ct. App. Div. 2005)
12 ALR6th 553—§ 20

State v. Williams, 2005 WL 4044580
(N.J. Super. Ct. App. Div. 2006)
26 ALR6th 511—§ 26

State v. Williams, 2006-Ohio-1939,
2006 WL 1029767 (Ohio Ct. App.
8th Dist. Cuyahoga County 2006)
26 ALR6th 511—§ 19

State v. Williams, 2008-Ohio-6195,
2008 WL 5052748 (Ohio Ct. App.
12th Dist. Warren County 2008)
63 ALR6th 351—§ 3
64 ALR6th 1—§ 7, 9, 11

State v. Williams, 2009 WI App 95, 320
Wis. 2d 484, 769 N.W.2d 878 (Ct.
App. 2009)
101 ALR6th 331—§ 12

State v. Williams, 2010-Ohio-901, 2010
WL 866130 (Ohio Ct. App. 8th Dist.
Cuyahoga County 2010)
62 ALR6th 161—§ 7

State v. Williams, 2010-Ohio-1523,
2010 WL 1274229 (Ohio Ct. App.
12th Dist. Clinton County 2010)
55 ALR6th 1—§ 14

State v. Williams, 2010-Ohio-4520,
2010 WL 3722895 (Ohio Ct. App.
10th Dist. Franklin County 2010)
70 ALR6th 1—§ 5

State v. Williams, 2010 WL 10387 (Wis.
Ct. App. 2010)
55 ALR6th 1—§ 26

State v. Williams, 2010 WL 153976
(Minn. Ct. App. 2010)
64 ALR6th 131—§ 2

State v. Williams, 2010 WL 1223116
(Wash. Ct. App. Div. 2 2010)
55 ALR6th 1—§ 30, 39

State v. Williams, 2011-NMSC-026,
149 N.M. 729, 255 P.3d 307, 79
A.L.R.6th 795 (2011)
79 ALR6th 631—§ 3, 4

State v. Williams, 2011 WL 5395634
(N.M. Ct. App. 2011)
79 ALR6th 631—§ 3, 4

State v. Williams, 2012 WL 1836101
(N.J. Super. Ct. App. Div. 2012)
99 ALR6th 295—§ 16

State v. Williams, 2013-Ohio-1905,
2013 WL 1932817 (Ohio Ct. App.
8th Dist. Cuyahoga County 2013)
97 ALR6th 263—§ 20

State v. Williams, No. 81 (March 19,
1984, Ct. App. Ohio, 7th App. Dist.
Mahoning Co.)
39 ALR5th 283—§ 14, 31, 65

State v. Williams, No. 41378 (May 22,
1990, Ct. App. Ohio, 8th App. Dist.
Cuyahoga Co.)
39 ALR5th 283—§ 14, 58

State v. Williams, No. 51100 (November
13, 1990, Ct. App. Ohio, 8th App.
Dist. Cuyahoga Co.)
39 ALR5th 283—§ 14, 46

State v. Williamson, 10 Ohio St. 2d 195,
39 Ohio Op. 2d 231, 226 N.E.2d
735 (1967)
**29 ALR6th 237—§ 4, 6, 8, 9, 19, 21,
24**

State v. Williamson, 78 N.M. 751, 438
P.2d 161 (1968)
55 ALR5th 125—§ 3, 9

State v. Williamson, 145 La. 9, 81 So.
737 (1919)
98 ALR6th 455—§ 13

State v. Williamson, 206 Conn. 685, 539
A.2d 561 (1988)
39 ALR5th 283—§ 3
99 ALR6th 295—§ 5

State v. Williamson, 214 Or. App. 281,
164 P.3d 315 (2007)
50 ALR6th 353—§ 41

State v. Williamson, 349 N.W.2d 645
(S.D. 1984)
42 ALR6th 237—§ 8

State v. Williamson, 668 S.W.2d 597 (Mo. App. 1984)
  26 ALR5th 1—§ 4, 35
State v. Williamson, 805 So. 2d 1235 (La. Ct. App. 2d Cir. 2002)
  110 ALR5th 329—§ 7
State v. Williamson, 1986 WL 1669 (Tenn. Crim. App. 1986)
  73 ALR5th 383—§ 5
State v. Willian, 423 N.E.2d 668 (Ind. Ct. App. 1st Dist. 1981)
  15 ALR6th 1—§ 4, 9, 10, 18
State v. Willie, 410 So. 2d 1019 (La. 1982)
  10 ALR5th 700—§ 9, 16
  38 ALR6th 97—§ 29
State v. Williquette, 190 Wis. 2d 678, 526 N.W.2d 144 (1995)
  14 ALR5th 89—§ 26, 32
State v. Williquette, 385 N.W.2d 145 (Wis 1986)
  53 ALR5th 499—§ 2
State v. Willis, 61 N.C. App. 23, 300 S.E.2d 420 (1983)
  7 ALR6th 169—§ 8
State v. Willis, 64 Wash. App. 634, 825 P.2d 357 (Div. 3 1992)
  38 ALR6th 97—§ 12
State v. Willis, 98 N.M. 771, 652 P.2d 1222 (Ct. App. 1982)
  64 ALR5th 671—§ 8
State v. Willis, 128 Mo. App. 214, 106 S.W. 584 (1907)
  13 ALR5th 1—§ 44
State v. Willis, 145 Vt. 459, 494 A.2d 108 (1985)
  28 ALR6th 505—§ 11
State v. Willis, 364 N.W.2d 498 (Minn. App. 1985)
  22 ALR5th 1—§ 3, 4, 45, 48
State v. Willis, 1994 WL 693912 (Ohio Ct. App. 4th Dist. Lawrence County 1994)
  34 ALR6th 1—§ 12
State v. Willis, 2003 ME 55, 820 A.2d 1216 (Me. 2003)
  9 ALR6th 633—§ 5, 7

State v. Willis, 2004 UT 93, 100 P.3d 1218 (Utah 2004)
  85 ALR6th 641—§ 5
State v. Willits, 96 Ariz. 184, 393 P.2d 274 (1964)
  40 ALR5th 113—§ 3
State v. Willner, 199 S.W. 126 (Mo. 1917)
  29 ALR5th 59—§ 7
State v. Willoughby, 81 Ohio App. 3d 562, 611 N.E.2d 937 (6th Dist. Lucas County 1992)
  58 ALR6th 499—§ 26
State v. Willoughby, 83 Haw. 496, 927 P.2d 1379 (Ct. App. 1996)
  51 ALR6th 1—§ 18
State v. Willoughby, 507 A.2d 1060 (Me. 1986)
  73 ALR5th 581—§ 2, 6
  82 ALR5th 591—§ 13
State v. Willoughby, 532 A.2d 1020 (Me. 1987)
  62 ALR5th 629—§ 4, 14
State v. Wills, 70 Minn. 403, 73 N.W. 177 (1897)
  108 ALR5th 593—§ 52
State v. Wills, 120 Ohio App. 3d 320, 697 N.E.2d 1072 (8th Dist. Cuyahoga County 1997)
  102 ALR6th 365—§ 20, 26
State v. Wills, 524 N.W.2d 507 (Minn. App. 1994)
  51 ALR5th 375—§ 4, 11
State v. Wills, 1989 WL 109332 (Minn. Ct. App. 1989)
  59 ALR5th 615—§ 11
State v. Willstead, 248 Wis. 240, 21 N.W.2d 271 (1946)
  19 ALR6th 577—§ 6
State v. Wilmore, 10 Ariz. App. 443, 459 P.2d 531 (Div. 2 1969)
  57 ALR6th 445—§ 45
State v. Wilshusen, 116 Wash. App. 1032, 2003 WL 1824881 (Div. 1 2003)
  16 ALR6th 329—§ 12
  24 ALR6th 591—§ 9, 13

State v. Wilson, 6 Kan. App. 2d 302, 627
P.2d 1185 (1981)
7 ALR5th 263—§ 6
State v. Wilson, 20 Or. App. 553, 532
P.2d 825 (1975)
40 ALR6th 1—§ 4, 12
State v. Wilson, 22 Utah 2d 361, 453
P.2d 158 (1969)
37 ALR6th 357—§ 75
State v. Wilson, 25 Ariz. App. 49, 540
P.2d 1268 (1975)
**41 ALR5th 171—§ 2, 30, 58, 76,
105, 107, 108**
State v. Wilson, 41 Wash. App. 397, 704
P.2d 1217 (Div. 3 1985)
1 ALR6th 549—§ 7
State v. Wilson, 56 So. 3d 375 (La. Ct.
App. 5th Cir. 2010)
67 ALR6th 531—§ 27
99 ALR6th 397—§ 8
State v. Wilson, 57 Ohio App. 2d 11, 11
Ohio Op. 3d 8, 384 N.E.2d 1300
(1st Dist. Hamilton County 1978)
99 ALR6th 295—§ 13
State v. Wilson, 73 Ohio St. 3d 40, 652
N.E.2d 196 (1995)
74 ALR5th 453—§ 5
State v. Wilson, 74 Ohio St. 3d 381, 659
N.E.2d 292 (1996)
79 ALR5th 33—§ 53
State v. Wilson, 77 Ohio App. 3d 718,
603 N.E.2d 305 (8th Dist. Cuyahoga
County 1991)
23 ALR6th 307—§ 13
State v. Wilson, 79 Wash. App. 1060,
907 P.2d 1211 (1995)
26 ALR5th 1—§ 3
State v. Wilson, 83 Or. App. 616, 733
P.2d 54 (1987)
113 ALR5th 517—§ 3
State v. Wilson, 83 Wash. App. 546, 922
P.2d 188 (1996)
37 ALR5th 319—§ 6, 7
State v. Wilson, 94 P.3d 737 (Kan. Ct.
App. 2004)
26 ALR6th 511—§ 25
State v. Wilson, 95 Wash. 2d 828, 631
P.2d 362 (1981)

34 ALR5th 125—§ 3, 14
State v. Wilson, 100 Wash. App. 44, 995
P.2d 1260 (Div. 3 2000)
15 ALR5th 391—§ 45
State v. Wilson, 109 N.M. 541, 787 P.2d
821 (1990)
24 ALR6th 747—§ 44
State v. Wilson, 109 Wash. App. 1054,
2001 WL 1640739 (Div. 2 2001)
71 ALR6th 625—§ 10, 19, 28, 29
State v. Wilson, 111 Or. App. 147, 826
P.2d 1010 (1992)
73 ALR5th 383—§ 5
State v. Wilson, 112 N.C. App. 777, 437
S.E.2d 387 (1993)
50 ALR5th 581—§ 5 to 7, 9, 16, 19
State v. Wilson, 113 Ariz. 363, 555 P.2d
321 (1976)
102 ALR6th 279—§ 32
State v. Wilson, 116 N.M. 793, 867 P.2d
1175 (1994)
20 ALR5th 398—§ 10, 13, 20
State v. Wilson, 120 Or. App. 382, 852
P.2d 910 (1993)
113 ALR5th 517—§ 7
State v. Wilson, 121 Or. App. 460, 855
P.2d 657 (1993)
38 ALR5th 433—§ 18
State v. Wilson, 140 P.3d 452 (Kan. Ct.
App. 2006)
62 ALR6th 413—§ 34
State v. Wilson, 142 N.M. 737, 2007-
NMCA-111, 169 P.3d 1184 (Ct.
App. 2007)
34 ALR6th 1—§ 9
State v. Wilson, 164 S.W.3d 355 (Tenn.
Crim. App. 2003)
27 ALR6th 183—§ 4
State v. Wilson, 165 N.J. 657, 762 A.2d
647 (2000)
65 ALR6th 537—§ 36, 40
State v. Wilson, 169 S.W.3d 870 (Mo.
Ct. App. W.D. 2005)
35 ALR6th 127—§ 4
State v. Wilson, 173 N.C. App. 758, 620
S.E.2d 321 (2005)
62 ALR6th 161—§ 9

State v. Wilson, 179 Wis. 2d 660, 508 N.W.2d 44 (Ct. App. 1993)
72 ALR5th 403—§ 10, 19

State v. Wilson, 180 Conn. 481, 429 A.2d 931 (1980)
81 ALR5th 563—§ 3, 5

State v. Wilson, 218 Or. 575, 346 P.2d 115, 79 A.L.R.2d 587 (1959)
93 ALR5th 683—§ 3

State v. Wilson, 229 Wis. 2d 256, 600 N.W.2d 14 (Ct. App. 1999)
62 ALR6th 413—§ 14, 22, 26, 30, 44

State v. Wilson, 257 Ga. App. 120, 570 S.E.2d 409 (2002)
29 ALR6th 1—§ 9

State v. Wilson, 274 S.C. 352, 264 S.E.2d 414 (1980)
15 ALR5th 391—§ 20

State v. Wilson, 296 N.C. 298, 250 S.E.2d 621, 99 A.L.R.3d 115 (1979)
39 ALR5th 283—§ 4, 59

State v. Wilson, 322 N.C. 117, 367 S.E.2d 589 (1988)
39 ALR5th 283—§ 77

State v. Wilson, 335 N.J. Super. 359, 762 A.2d 660 (App. Div. 1999)
65 ALR6th 537—§ 36, 40
98 ALR6th 455—§ 33

State v. Wilson, 340 N.C. 720, 459 S.E.2d 192 (1995)
9 ALR6th 1—§ 8

State v. Wilson, 354 N.C. 493, 556 S.E.2d 272 (2001)
83 ALR6th 465—§ 4, 18

State v. Wilson, 464 So. 2d 667, 10 FLW 602 (Fla. App. D2 1985)
6 ALR5th 733—§ 16

State v. Wilson, 520 So. 2d 864 (La. Ct. App. 3d Cir. 1987)
1 ALR6th 371—§ 4

State v. Wilson, 523 So. 2d 178 (Fla. Dist. Ct. App. 3d Dist. 1988)
113 ALR5th 597—§ 8

State v. Wilson, 535 N.W.2d 597 (Minn. 1995)
69 ALR6th 579—§ 9

State v. Wilson, 539 N.W.2d 241 (Minn. 1995)
113 ALR5th 597—§ 3

State v. Wilson, 613 So. 2d 234 (La. App. 1st Cir. 1992)
15 ALR5th 391—§ 30

State v. Wilson, 632 So. 2d 861 (La. App. 2d Cir. 1994)
47 ALR5th 259—§ 2, 21

State v. Wilson, 660 So. 2d 571 (La. Ct. App. 2d Cir. 1995)
73 ALR5th 383—§ 3

State v. Wilson, 679 So. 2d 963 (La. Ct. App. 2d Cir. 1996)
101 ALR5th 187—§ 7

State v. Wilson, 685 So. 2d 1063 (La. 1996)
62 ALR5th 121—§ 8

State v. Wilson, 747 So. 2d 1051 (Fla. Dist. Ct. App. 5th Dist. 2000)
28 ALR6th 505—§ 14

State v. Wilson, 826 S.W.2d 79 (Mo. Ct. App. E.D. 1992)
102 ALR6th 279—§ 16
103 ALR6th 35—§ 16

State v. Wilson, 1993 WL 79626 (Tenn. Crim. App. 1993)
73 ALR5th 383—§ 5

State v. Wilson, 1993 WL 434580 (Ohio Ct. App. 6th Dist. Lucas County 1993)
84 ALR6th 293—§ 17

State v. Wilson, 2000 S.D. 133, 618 N.W.2d 513 (S.D. 2000)
19 ALR5th 470—§ 12

State v. Wilson, 2001 WL 845749 (Del. Super. Ct. 2001)
69 ALR6th 275—§ 15, 24, 26

State v. Wilson, 2002 WL 378191 (Minn. Ct. App. 2002)
37 ALR6th 357—§ 59

State v. Wilson, 2002 WL 31259461 (Tenn. Crim. App. 2002)
3 ALR6th 543—§ 8

State v. Wilson, 2004-Ohio-1566, 2004 WL 614790 (Ohio Ct. App. 5th Dist. Stark County 2004)

24 ALR6th 1—§ 33

State v. Wilson, 2005-Ohio-5959, 2005 WL 2995130 (Ohio Ct. App. 5th Dist. Stark County 2005)

71 ALR6th 1—§ 6

State v. Wilson, 2006 WL 1044943 (N.J. Super. Ct. App. Div. 2006)

50 ALR6th 455—§ 24

State v. Wilson, 2007-Ohio-6581, 2007 WL 4305715 (Ohio Ct. App. 2d Dist. Montgomery County 2007)

78 ALR6th 213—§ 5

State v. Wilson, 2009-Ohio-2744, 2009 WL 1636604 (Ohio Ct. App. 2d Dist. Clark County 2009)

71 ALR6th 1—§ 8

State v. Wilson, 2013 WL 3148279 (Tenn. Crim. App. 2013)

101 ALR6th 331—§ 12

State v. Wilson, Slip Op. No. 52031 (Ohio App. Cuyahoga Co. 1987)

38 ALR5th 433—§ 10, 16, 17

State v. Wimberly, 246 Kan. 200, 787 P.2d 729 (1990)

11 ALR5th 218—§ 3, 8

State v. Wimberly, 467 N.W.2d 499 (S.D. 1991)

77 ALR5th 201—§ 9

State v. Wimberly, 618 So. 2d 908 (La. App. 1st Cir. 1993)

22 ALR5th 660—§ 6, 8

State v. Wimbs, 74 Wash. App. 511, 874 P.2d 193 (1994)

27 ALR5th 593—§ 5, 6, 23, 32, 35

State v. Wimby, 119 La. 139, 43 So. 984 (1907)

98 ALR6th 455—§ 13

State v. Winborn, 472 So. 2d 117 (La. Ct. App. 5th Cir. 1985)

9 ALR6th 1—§ 17

State v. Winchell, 363 N.W.2d 747 (Minn. 1985)

73 ALR5th 383—§ 5

State v. Winchester, No. 52636 (August 27, 1987, Ct. App. Ohio, 8th App. Dist. Cuyahoga Co.)

39 ALR5th 283—§ 14, 45, 60

State v. Windham, 57 N.C. App. 571, 291 S.E.2d 876 (1982)

112 ALR5th 429—§ 6

State v. Windsor, 205 N.J. Super. 450, 501 A.2d 194 (1985)

7 ALR5th 263—§ 7

State v. Windy City Fireworks, Inc., 600 N.E.2d 555 (Ind. App. 1992)

48 ALR5th 659—§ 32, 34

State v. Wine, 787 S.W.2d 31 (Tenn. Crim. App. 1989)

67 ALR5th 361—§ 2 to 4, 6

State v. Winfield, 1987 WL 7981 (Tenn. Crim. App. 1987)

114 ALR5th 173—§ 7

State v. Winfrey, 359 So. 2d 73 (La. 1978)

64 ALR5th 741—§ 3

State v. Wingate, 668 So. 2d 1324 (La. App. 1st Cir. 1996)

50 ALR5th 703—§ 5, 27, 29

State v. Wingerd, 40 Ohio App. 2d 236, 69 Ohio Ops. 2d 217, 318 N.E.2d 866 (Athens Co. 1974)

31 ALR5th 229—§ 31

State v. Winkel, 2008 MT 89, 342 Mont. 267, 182 P.3d 54 (2008)

46 ALR6th 241—§ 15

State v. Winkler, 552 N.W.2d 347 (N.D. 1996)

60 ALR5th 1—§ 8

28 ALR6th 505—§ 18

72 ALR6th 437—§ 17

State v. Winship, 2004-Ohio-6360, 2004 WL 2715906 (Ohio Ct. App. 10th Dist. Franklin County 2004)

70 ALR6th 1—§ 5

State v. Winslow, 97 N.C. App. 551, 389 S.E.2d 436 (1990)

19 ALR6th 115—§ 5, 9, 10

State v. Winslow, 274 Neb. 427, 740 N.W.2d 794 (2007)

72 ALR6th 227—§ 11, 56

State v. Winslow, 389 S.E.2d 436, 97 N.C. App. 551

2 ALR6th 551—§ 5

State v. Winstead, 150 N.H. 244, 836 A.2d 775 (2003)

92 ALR6th 295—§ 12
93 ALR6th 207—§ 4, 26
96 ALR6th 355—§ 24, 37
State v. Winston, 47 N.C. App. 363, 267 S.E.2d 43 (1980)
22 ALR5th 1—§ 12, 38
State v. Winter, 146 Ariz. 461, 706 P.2d 1228 (Ct. App. Div. 1 1985)
78 ALR5th 567—§ 5
State v. Winter, 238 Kan. 530, 712 P.2d 1228 (1986)
56 ALR6th 185—§ 34
State v. Winters, 16 Utah 2d 139, 396 P.2d 872 (1964)
4 ALR5th 1—§ 2
State v. Winthrop, 43 Iowa 519 (1876)
64 ALR5th 671—§ 2
State v. Winton, 148 N.M. 75, 2010-NMCA-020, 229 P.3d 1247 (Ct. App. 2009)
59 ALR6th 311—§ 18, 19
State v. Winton, 153 Ariz. 302, 736 P.2d 386 (Ct. App. Div. 1 1987)
87 ALR6th 1—§ 23
State v. Winward, 909 P.2d 909 (Utah Ct. App. 1995)
108 ALR5th 593—§ 9
State v. Wisconsin Motor Carriers Ass'n, Inc., 1980-81 Trade Cas. (CCH) ¶ 63739, 1981 WL 11450 (Wis. Cir. Ct. 1981)
94 ALR5th 455—§ 24
State v. Wise, 150 Or. App. 449, 946 P.2d 363 (1997)
15 ALR5th 391—§ 45
State v. Wise, 178 N.C. App. 154, 630 S.E.2d 732 (2006)
33 ALR6th 91—§ 45
State v. Wise, 202 Or. App. 661, 123 P.3d 370 (2005)
26 ALR6th 511—§ 27
State v. Wise, 284 A.2d 292 (Del. 1971)
43 ALR5th 1—§ 13
State v. Wise, 326 N.C. 421, 390 S.E.2d 142 (1990)
101 ALR5th 187—§ 5

State v. Wise, 434 So. 2d 1308 (La. Ct. App. 3d Cir. 1983)
113 ALR5th 517—§ 6
State v. Wise, 603 So. 2d 61 (Fla. 2d DCA 1992)
78 ALR6th 599—§ 5, 13
State v. Wise, 644 So. 2d 230 (La. Ct. App. 4th Cir. 1994)
99 ALR6th 295—§ 9
State v. Wise, 879 S.W.2d 494 (Mo. 1994)
79 ALR5th 33—§ 7, 9, 63
9 ALR6th 1—§ 17
24 ALR6th 1—§ 35, 45
83 ALR6th 255—§ 13, 15, 26
State v. Wisinger, 618 So. 2d 923 (La. Ct. App. 1st Cir. 1993)
78 ALR5th 197—§ 14
State v. Wisnewski, 134 Wis. 497, 114 N.W. 1113 (1908)
42 ALR5th 547—§ 6
State v. Wisniewski, 2007 WL 5209492 (Ariz. Ct. App. Div. 1 2007)
92 ALR6th 295—§ 19
96 ALR6th 355—§ 6, 37
State v. Wisowaty, 137 N.H. 298, 627 A.2d 572 (1993)
72 ALR5th 109—§ 10
State v. Wisser Co., 170 App. Div. 2d 918, 566 N.Y.S.2d 747 (3d Dep't 1991)
11 ALR5th 388—§ 9
State v. Wissing, 66 Wash. App. 745, 833 P.2d 424 (1992)
42 ALR5th 291—§ 22, 25
State v. Wissink, 172 N.C. App. 829, 617 S.E.2d 319 (2005)
26 ALR6th 511—§ 27
State v. Witherbee, 79 Or. App. 36, 717 P.2d 661 (1986)
33 ALR6th 407—§ 12, 14
State v. Witherbee, 131 Wash. App. 1012, 2006 WL 122212 (Div. 2 2006)
26 ALR6th 511—§ 4
State v. Witherington, 702 So. 2d 263 (Fla. Dist. Ct. App. 5th Dist. 1997)

State v. Wolford., 1978 WL 218310 (Ohio Ct. App. 8th Dist. Cuyahoga County 1978)
19 ALR6th 697—§ 4

State v. Wolfs, 119 Or. App. 262, 850 P.2d 1139 (1993)
7 ALR6th 233—§ 9

State v. Wolfson, 2003-Ohio-4440, 2003 WL 21995244 (Ohio Ct. App. 4th Dist. Lawrence County 2003)
9 ALR6th 541—§ 3

State v. Woll, 35 Wash. App. 560, 668 P.2d 610 (Div. 2 1983)
71 ALR5th 1—§ 47

State v. Wolland, 902 So. 2d 278 (Fla. 3d DCA 2005)
79 ALR6th 125—§ 30

State v. Wolske, 143 Wis. 2d 175, 420 N.W.2d 60 (Ct. App. 1988)
47 ALR6th 107—§ 5, 17, 77

State v. Womack, 145 N.J. 576, 679 A.2d 606 (1996)
49 ALR5th 639—§ 4

State v. Womack, 967 P.2d 536 (Utah Ct. App. 1998)
67 ALR5th 361—§ 3, 4, 6

State v. Wommack, 770 So. 2d 365 (La. Ct. App. 3d Cir. 2000)
1 ALR6th 657—§ 4, 14

State v. Wonders, 23 Kan. App. 2d 287, 929 P.2d 792 (1996)
50 ALR5th 581—§ 2, 3, 5 to 7, 9, 14, 20

State v. Wonders, 263 Kan. 582, 952 P.2d 1351 (1998)
50 ALR5th 581—§ 14

State v. Wong, 68 Hawaii 221, 708 P.2d 825 (1985)
59 ALR5th 615—§ 3, 11

State v. Wong, 138 N.H. 56, 635 A.2d 470 (1993)
75 ALR5th 295—§ 11

State v. Woo, 84 Wash. 2d 472, 527 P.2d 271 (1974)
90 ALR5th 453—§ 43

State v. Wood, 52 Wash. App. 159, 758 P.2d 530 (Div. 1 1988)
119 ALR5th 275—§ 11

State v. Wood, 67 Or. App. 218, 678 P.2d 1238 (1984)
57 ALR5th 141—§ 12

State v. Wood, 71 Or. App. 126, 691 P.2d 116 (1984)
50 ALR5th 703—§ 17, 27

State v. Wood, 89 Wash. 2d 97, 569 P.2d 1148 (1977)
2 ALR5th 301—§ 2, 4
2 ALR5th 337—§ 4

State v. Wood, 112 Iowa 411, 84 N.W. 520 (1900)
50 ALR5th 467—§ 6, 8

State v. Wood, 112 Or. App. 61, 827 P.2d 924 (1992)
28 ALR6th 505—§ 11

State v. Wood, 114 Or. App. 601, 836 P.2d 176 (1992)
104 ALR5th 165—§ 4

State v. Wood, 118 Kan. 58, 233 P. 1029 (1925)
45 ALR5th 591—§ 6

State v. Wood, 128 S.W.3d 913 (Mo. Ct. App. W.D. 2004)
20 ALR6th 479—§ 3, 5

State v. Wood, 180 Ariz. 53, 881 P.2d 1158 (1994)
57 ALR5th 141—§ 3, 6

State v. Wood, 195 Neb. 353, 238 N.W.2d 226 (1976)
114 ALR5th 173—§ 7

State v. Wood, 204 Wis. 2d 111, 552 N.W.2d 898 (Ct. App. 1996)
79 ALR6th 1—§ 39

State v. Wood, 230 Kan. 477, 638 P.2d 908 (1982)
24 ALR5th 465—§ 16, 34

State v. Wood, 457 So. 2d 206 (La. App. 2d Cir. 1984)
19 ALR5th 470—§ 3, 12

State v. Wood, 607 S.E.2d 57 (S.C. 2004)
3 ALR6th 543—§ 5

State v. Wood, 868 P.2d 70 (Utah 1993)
34 ALR6th 1—§ 12

For assistance, call 1-800-328-4880

State v. Wood, 2010-Ohio-884, 2010 WL 781174 (Ohio Ct. App. 5th Dist. Stark County 2010)
65 ALR6th 1—§ 13

State v. Wood, 2010-Ohio-2759, 2010 WL 2413615 (Ohio Ct. App. 5th Dist. Stark County 2010)
65 ALR6th 1—§ 4

State v. Woo Dak San, 1930-NMSC-019, 35 N.M. 105, 290 P. 322 (1930)
103 ALR6th 137—§ 15

State v. Woodall, 16 Ohio Misc. 226, 45 Ohio Op. 2d 179, 241 N.E.2d 755 (C.P. 1968)
57 ALR6th 83—§ 5

State v. Woodall, 32 Wash. App. 407, 647 P.2d 1051 (Div. 3 1982)
85 ALR5th 1—§ 27

State v. Woodall, 155 Ariz. 1, 744 P.2d 732 (App. 1987)
7 ALR5th 758—§ 11

State v. Woodall, 162 Ariz. 591, 785 P.2d 111, 50 Ariz. Adv. Rep. 65 (App. 1989)
48 ALR5th 473—§ 13

State v. Woodall, 385 S.E.2d 253 (W. Va. 1989)
39 ALR5th 283—§ 4, 62

State v. Woodard, 11 Conn. App. 499, 528 A.2d 404 (1987)
5 ALR5th 243—§ 2, 7

State v. Woodard, 365 N.C. 334, 210 N.C. App. 725, 709 S.E.2d 430 (2011)
99 ALR6th 295—§ 9

State v. Woodard, 2010-Ohio-2949, 2010 WL 2557715 (Ohio Ct. App. 11th Dist. Ashtabula County 2010)
92 ALR6th 171—§ 4

State v. Woodard, 2013 ME 36, 68 A.3d 1250 (Me. 2013)
94 ALR6th 239—§ 3, 93, 105

State v. Woodbridge, 153 Ohio App. 3d 121, 2003-Ohio-2931, 791 N.E.2d 1035 (7th Dist. Mahoning County 2003)
58 ALR6th 385—§ 3, 5

State v. Woodburn, 1999 WL 167848 (Ohio Ct. App. 7th Dist. Columbiana County 1999)
78 ALR5th 489—§ 3, 6, 9, 10

State v. Woodbury, 2004 WL 1771480 (Tex. App. Corpus Christi 2004)
78 ALR6th 297—§ 38, 40

State v. Woodcock, 407 N.W.2d 603 (Iowa 1987)
111 ALR5th 239—§ 9

State v. Woodcox, 2004 WL 28193 (Cal. App. 3d Dist. 2004)
62 ALR6th 413—§ 30

State v. Woodfield, 62 Or. App. 69, 659 P.2d 1006 (1983)
22 ALR5th 1—§ 2, 42

State v. Woodland, 768 S.W.2d 617 (Mo. App. 1989)
39 ALR5th 283—§ 4, 51

State v. Woodman, 122 Ohio App. 3d 774, 702 N.E.2d 974 (10th Dist. Franklin County 1997)
63 ALR6th 1—§ 5, 11, 55

State v. Woodman, 125 N.H. 381, 480 A.2d 169 (1984)
56 ALR6th 185—§ 44

State v. Woodrome, 768 S.W.2d 149 (Mo. Ct. App. W.D. 1989)
37 ALR6th 357—§ 20

State v. Woodrow, 58 W. Va. 527, 52 S.E. 545 (1905)
119 ALR5th 275—§ 2

State v. Woods, 8 Ohio App. 3d 56, 455 N.E.2d 1289 (8th Dist. Cuyahoga County 1982)
19 ALR6th 697—§ 6

State v. Woods, 20 Ohio Misc. 2d 1, 484 N.E.2d 773 (C.P. 1984)
70 ALR5th 491—§ 3, 7, 8

State v. Woods, 23 Conn. App. 615, 583 A.2d 639 (1990)
54 ALR5th 141—§ 3 to 5, 10

State v. Woods, 63 Wash. App. 588, 821 P.2d 1235 (1991)
17 ALR5th 111—§ 2, 4

State v. Woods, 130 N.H. 721, 546 A.2d 1073 (1988)
38 ALR5th 433—§ 3

State v. Woods, 136 N.C. App. 386, 524 S.E.2d 363 (2000)
58 ALR6th 499—§ 39, 112

State v. Woods, 170 Wis. 2d 736, 492 N.W.2d 192 (Ct. App. 1992)
81 ALR6th 505—§ 54

State v. Woods, 179 Kan. 601, 296 P.2d 1114 (1956)
99 ALR6th 295—§ 21

State v. Woods, 214 Kan. 739, 522 P.2d 967 (1974)
1 ALR6th 549—§ 8

State v. Woods, 283 Mont. 359, 942 P.2d 88 (1997)
38 ALR6th 97—§ 27

State v. Woods, 283 So. 2d 753 (La. 1973)
42 ALR5th 581—§ 2, 3, 19

State v. Woods, 293 N.C. 58, 235 S.E.2d 47 (1977)
55 ALR6th 157—§ 8

State v. Woods, 435 So. 2d 1137 (La. Ct. App. 1st Cir. 1983)
9 ALR6th 1—§ 17

State v. Woods, 524 S.E.2d 363 (N.C. Ct. App. 2000)
64 ALR5th 637—§ 3

State v. Woods, 654 A.2d 960 (N.H. 1995)
15 ALR5th 391—§ 5

State v. Woods, 806 S.W.2d 205 (Tenn. Crim. App. 1990)
51 ALR5th 425—§ 2
55 ALR5th 125—§ 2, 12, 15, 22
68 ALR5th 343—§ 2
79 ALR5th 237—§ 11

State v. Woods, 812 S.W.2d 267 (Mo. Ct. App. S.D. 1991)
105 ALR5th 529—§ 13

State v. Woods, 861 S.W.2d 326 (Mo. Ct. App. S.D. 1993)
68 ALR5th 343—§ 3, 12
117 ALR5th 513—§ 5

State v. Woods, 1996 WL 430874 (Ohio App. 2 Dist.)
50 ALR5th 581—§ 7, 9, 16, 20

State v. Woods, 1997 WL 602963 (Ohio Ct. App. 1st Dist. Hamilton County 1997)
58 ALR6th 385—§ 20

State v. Woodward, 69 Wyo. 262, 240 P.2d 1157 (1952)
5 ALR5th 243—§ 58

State v. Woodward, 121 N.M. 1, 908 P.2d 231 (1995)
24 ALR5th 465—§ 107, 108, 111
38 ALR5th 433—§ 31

State v. Woodward, 408 N.W.2d 927 (Minn. Ct. App. 1987)
92 ALR6th 295—§ 14
95 ALR6th 1—§ 7, 23
96 ALR6th 355—§ 24, 45, 60

State v. Woodward, 617 A.2d 542 (Me. 1992)
27 ALR6th 183—§ 34, 35

State v. Woodward, 2011 WL 4407565 (N.J. Super. Ct. App. Div. 2011)
78 ALR6th 1—§ 8

State v. Woodward, A13-0703, 2014 WL 2921837 (Minn. Ct. App. June 30, 2014)
99 ALR6th 295—§ 5

State v. Woody, 48 Wash. App. 772, 742 P.2d 133 (Div. 3 1987)
73 ALR5th 383—§ 5

State v. Woody, 699 S.W.2d 517 (Mo. Ct. App. S.D. 1985)
1 ALR6th 549—§ 8, 10

State v. Woody, 1996 WL 243880 (Ohio App. 5 Dist.)
50 ALR5th 581—§ 7

State v. Woody, 1999 WL 743601 (Del. Super. Ct. 1999)
62 ALR6th 413—§ 29

State v. Woodyard, 414 N.W.2d 654 (Iowa App. 1987)
11 ALR5th 1—§ 9

State v. Wooley, 523 So. 2d 883 (La. Ct. App. 4th Cir. 1988)
67 ALR6th 341—§ 11, 19

State v. Woolf, 120 Idaho 21, 813 P.2d 360 (Ct. App. 1991)
92 ALR6th 295—§ 11, 25

93 ALR6th 207—§ 6, 7, 9
96 ALR6th 355—§ 23, 35
State v. Woolridge, 224 Kan. 480, 580
P.2d 1350 (1978)
84 ALR5th 487—§ 10
State v. Woolverton, 35 Kan. App. 2d
478, 131 P.3d 1253 (2006)
26 ALR6th 451—§ 3
38 ALR6th 97—§ 3
56 ALR6th 323—§ 3
81 ALR6th 505—§ 3
State v. Woolverton, 159 P.3d 985 (Kan.
2007)
29 ALR6th 1—§ 3
State v. Woolverton, 159 P.3d 985, 28
A.L.R.6th 825 (Kan. 2007)
28 ALR6th 505—§ 7, 11
State v. Woolverton, 284 Kan. 59, 159
P.3d 985, 28 A.L.R.6th 825 (2007)
32 ALR6th 1—§ 3
57 ALR6th 83—§ 3
State v. Wooten, 20 N.C. App. 499, 201
S.E.2d 696 (1974)
45 ALR5th 1—§ 5
State v. Wooten, 55 N.C. App. 530, 286
S.E.2d 635 (1982)
7 ALR6th 169—§ 11
State v. Wooten, 135 N.J. Super. 6, 342
A.2d 549 (1975)
39 ALR5th 283—§ 4, 7
State v. Wooten, 194 N.C. App. 524, 669
S.E.2d 749 (2008)
57 ALR6th 1—§ 16, 28
State v. Wooten, 344 N.C. 316, 474
S.E.2d 360 (1996)
83 ALR6th 255—§ 15
State v. Wooten, 2003-Ohio-7159, 2003
WL 23024520 (Ohio Ct. App. 10th
Dist. Franklin County 2003)
46 ALR6th 241—§ 20
State v. Woo Won Choi, 55 Wash. App.
895, 781 P.2d 505 (Div. 1 1989)
32 ALR5th 149—§ 4, 5, 24 to 29, 32,
33
79 ALR5th 419—§ 10
State v. Wopschall, 2009 WL 975571
(Ariz. Ct. App. Div. 2 2009)
97 ALR6th 263—§ 11

State v. Woratzeck, 134 Ariz. 452, 657
P.2d 865 (1982)
65 ALR5th 407—§ 3
State v. Word, 80 N.M. 377, 456 P.2d
210 (Ct. App. 1969)
124 ALR5th 1—§ 4, 7
State v. Words, 226 Kan. 59, 596 P.2d
129 (1979)
39 ALR5th 283—§ 4, 28
State v. Workman, 126 Ohio App. 3d
422, 710 N.E.2d 744 (5th Dist. Stark
County 1998)
5 ALR6th 1—§ 3, 7, 12, 23, 61
65 ALR6th 441—§ 3
State v. Workman, 344 N.C. 482, 476
S.E.2d 301 (1996)
16 ALR6th 329—§ 4
24 ALR6th 591—§ 6, 14
State v. Workman, 852 P.2d 981, 212
Utah Adv. Rep. 3 (Utah 1993)
42 ALR5th 291—§ 16, 22, 25
State v. Workman, 1992 WL 54307
(Ohio Ct. App. 11th Dist. Ashtabula
County 1992)
69 ALR6th 207—§ 9, 10, 18
State v. Worland, 20 Wash. App. 559,
582 P.2d 539 (Div. 2 1978)
113 ALR5th 517—§ 8
State v. Worley, 265 S.C. 551, 220
S.E.2d 242 (1975)
54 ALR5th 141—§ 2 to 6, 8
State v. Worley, 369 S.E.2d 706 (W. Va.
1988)
55 ALR5th 125—§ 3, 7
State v. Worm, 268 Neb. 74, 680 N.W.2d
151 (2004)
63 ALR6th 351—§ 3
64 ALR6th 1—§ 7, 9
State v. Worrell, 233 Kan. 968, 666 P.2d
703 (1983)
18 ALR6th 1—§ 5, 30
State v. Worsley, 336 N.C. 268, 443
S.E.2d 68 (1994)
65 ALR5th 407—§ 3, 16
State v. Worth, 37 Wash. App. 889, 683
P.2d 622 (1984)
43 ALR5th 1—§ 2

State v. Worth, 217 Kan. 393, 537 P.2d 191 (1975)

97 ALR5th 201—§ 6

State v. Wortham, 63 Ariz. 148, 160 P.2d 352 (1945)

97 ALR5th 201—§ 7

State v. Worthen, 550 So. 2d 399 (La. Ct. App. 3d Cir. 1989)

1 ALR6th 657—§ 14

99 ALR6th 113—§ 6, 11, 14

State v. Worthington, 8 S.W.3d 83 (Mo. 1999)

79 ALR5th 33—§ 62

State v. Worthington, 970 P.2d 714 (Utah Ct. App. 1998)

28 ALR6th 505—§ 9

State v. Worthon, 585 S.W.2d 143 (Mo. App. 1979)

55 ALR5th 125—§ 3

State v. Worthy, 583 N.W.2d 270 (Minn. 1998)

19 ALR6th 697—§ 3, 10

State v. Wotnoske, 177 Wis. 2d 621, 503 N.W.2d 22 (Ct. App. 1993)

62 ALR6th 413—§ 32, 44

State v. Wragge, 1994 WL 258494 (Neb. Ct. App. 1994)

63 ALR6th 351—§ 3

State v. Wraggs, 496 S.W.2d 38 (Mo. App. 1973)

19 ALR5th 823—§ 16, 18

State v. Wray, 2011 WL 1045116 (N.J. Super. Ct. App. Div. 2011)

74 ALR6th 373—§ 12

State v. Wright, 7 Kan. App. 2d 631, 646 P.2d 1128 (1982)

22 ALR5th 660—§ 2

State v. Wright, 12 Wash. App. 585, 530 P.2d 704 (Div. 1 1975)

24 ALR6th 747—§ 49

State v. Wright, 58 Conn. App. 136, 752 A.2d 1147 (2000)

122 ALR5th 439—§ 6

State v. Wright, 78 Wash. App. 93, 896 P.2d 713 (1995)

20 ALR5th 398—§ 3, 65

State v. Wright, 115 Idaho 1043, 772 P.2d 250 (Ct. App. 1989)

67 ALR5th 361—§ 2 to 4, 6

State v. Wright, 120 S.W.3d 792 (Mo. Ct. App. W.D. 2003)

9 ALR6th 541—§ 18

State v. Wright, 125 Ariz. 36, 607 P.2d 19 (Ct. App. Div. 2 1979)

58 ALR6th 499—§ 15

State v. Wright, 131 Ariz. 578, 643 P.2d 23 (Ct. App. Div. 2 1982)

85 ALR5th 1—§ 37

State v. Wright, 137 Ohio App. 3d 737, 739 N.E.2d 1172 (11th Dist. Lake County 2000)

46 ALR6th 241—§ 26, 28

State v. Wright, 145 Wash. App. 1045, 2008 WL 2791860 (Div. 1 2008)

69 ALR6th 579—§ 4

State v. Wright, 151 N.C. App. 493, 566 S.E.2d 151 (2002)

7 ALR6th 233—§ 9

State v. Wright, 154 Vt. 512, 581 A.2d 720 (1989)

26 ALR5th 603—§ 4

23 ALR6th 1—§ 10, 15

State v. Wright, 161 Ariz. 394, 778 P.2d 1290 (Ct. App. Div. 1 1989)

28 ALR6th 505—§ 22

State v. Wright, 184 N.C. App. 464, 646 S.E.2d 625 (2007)

38 ALR6th 97—§ 3, 19

State v. Wright, 193 Neb. 91, 225 N.W.2d 425 (1975)

72 ALR5th 109—§ 5

State v. Wright, 198 Conn. 273, 502 A.2d 911 (1986)

7 ALR5th 263—§ 2, 6

State v. Wright, 203 Kan. 54, 453 P.2d 1 (1969)

59 ALR5th 1—§ 3, 6

State v. Wright, 204 Ga. App. 382, 419 S.E.2d 334 (1992)

79 ALR6th 1—§ 52

State v. Wright, 271 S.C. 534, 248 S.E.2d 490 (1978)

104 ALR5th 357—§ 3

---

54 ALR6th 429—§ 17, 26
State v. Wright, 323 Or. 8, 913 P.2d 321 (1996)

99 ALR6th 113—§ 8
State v. Wright, 378 N.W.2d 727 (Iowa Ct. App. 1985)

62 ALR5th 629—§ 14
State v. Wright, 426 N.W.2d 3 (N.D. 1988)

76 ALR5th 1—§ 12
State v. Wright, 441 So. 2d 1301 (La. Ct. App. 1st Cir. 1983)

55 ALR6th 391—§ 5
103 ALR6th 35—§ 7
State v. Wright, 456 N.W.2d 661 (Iowa 1990)

37 ALR5th 703—§ 4
State v. Wright, 509 So. 2d 784 (La. App. 5th Cir. 1987)

7 ALR5th 263—§ 7
State v. Wright, 549 A.2d 1128 (Me. 1988)

50 ALR5th 703—§ 10
State v. Wright, 598 So. 2d 493 (La. App. 2d Cir. 1992)

11 ALR5th 218—§ 6, 18
State v. Wright, 632 S.W.2d 296 (Mo. Ct. App. E.D. 1982)

99 ALR6th 295—§ 5, 13
State v. Wright, 664 So. 2d 712 (La. App. 3d Cir. 1995)

27 ALR5th 593—§ 35
State v. Wright, 726 N.W.2d 464 (Minn. 2007)

30 ALR6th 1—§ 3, 4, 6, 7
State v. Wright, 745 P.2d 447 (Utah 1987)

37 ALR6th 357—§ 4, 23, 25
State v. Wright, 751 S.W.2d 48 (Mo. 1988)

71 ALR5th 637—§ 4, 7
State v. Wright, 763 S.W.2d 167 (Mo. Ct. App. W.D. 1988)

105 ALR5th 529—§ 13
State v. Wright, 779 N.W.2d 494 (Iowa Ct. App. 2010)

94 ALR6th 579—§ 1

State v. Wright, 1987 WL 11672 (Ohio Ct. App. 8th Dist. Cuyahoga County 1987)

103 ALR6th 347—§ 23
State v. Wright, 1997 WL 13729 (Tenn. Crim. App. 1997)

67 ALR5th 361—§ 3, 4, 10
State v. Wright, 1998 WL 305504 (Conn. Super. Ct. 1998)

62 ALR5th 1—§ 4, 15
State v. Wright, 1999 UT App 86, 977 P.2d 505 (Utah Ct. App. 1999)

114 ALR5th 173—§ 7, 11
State v. Wright, 2009-Ohio-6773, 2009 WL 4936377 (Ohio Ct. App. 10th Dist. Franklin County 2009)

71 ALR6th 1—§ 8
State v. Wright, 2012 WL 1400932 (Del. Super. Ct. 2012)

97 ALR6th 263—§ 28, 29
State v. Wrisley, 138 Or. App. 344, 909 P.2d 877 (1995)

88 ALR5th 121—§ 25, 36
State v. Wrobel, 3 Conn. Cir. 57, 207 A.2d 280 (1964)

6 ALR5th 733—§ 2, 14, 28, 31
State v. Wry, 591 So. 2d 774 (La. Ct. App. 2d Cir. 1991)

70 ALR5th 1—§ 8
State v. Wrzesien, 135 Wash. App. 1040, 2006 WL 3201048 (Div. 2 2006)

26 ALR6th 511—§ 41
State v. Wrzesinski, 2006 MT 263, 334 Mont. 157, 145 P.3d 985 (2006)

56 ALR6th 323—§ 7, 11
State v. Wuensch, 1989 WL 69735 (Ohio Ct. App. 9th Dist. Medina County 1989)

67 ALR6th 531—§ 25, 29
State v. Wussler, 139 Ariz. 428, 679 P.2d 74 (1984)

26 ALR5th 603—§ 3
16 ALR6th 329—§ 4
24 ALR6th 591—§ 4, 12
State v. W. U. Tel. Co., 12 N.J. 468, 97 A.2d 480 (1953)

54 ALR6th 429—§ 20

State v. Wyant, 64 Ohio St. 3d 566, 597
N.E.2d 450 (1992)
22 ALR5th 261—§ 6
State v. Wyant, 68 Ohio St. 3d 162, 624
N.E.2d 722 (1994)
22 ALR5th 261—§ 6
State v. Wyant, 174 W. Va. 567, 328
S.E.2d 174 (1985)
82 ALR5th 67—§ 3
32 ALR6th 1—§ 11
State v. Wyatt, 198 W. Va. 530, 482
S.E.2d 147 (1996)
90 ALR5th 453—§ 26
118 ALR5th 253—§ 5
State v. Wyatt, 234 Neb. 349, 451
N.W.2d 84 (1990)
7 ALR5th 263—§ 6
State v. Wyatt, 327 So. 2d 401 (La.
1976)
68 ALR5th 343—§ 3, 12
17 ALR6th 327—§ 23
State v. Wyatt, 2002-Ohio-4479, 2002
WL 2005770 (Ohio Ct. App. 4th
Dist. Pike County 2002)
3 ALR6th 269—§ 5, 8, 13, 28
State v. Wyche, 518 A.2d 907 (R.I.
1986)
101 ALR5th 187—§ 11
State v. Wyer, 2003-Ohio-6926, 2003
WL 22976573 (Ohio Ct. App. 8th
Dist. Cuyahoga County 2003)
70 ALR6th 361—§ 36
State v. Wyman, 59 Vt. 527, 8 A. 900
(1887)
34 ALR5th 723—§ 4
State v. Wyman, 97 Idaho 486, 547 P.2d
531 (1976)
9 ALR6th 1—§ 17
State v. Wynn, 623 So. 2d 848 (Fla. Dist.
Ct. App. 2d Dist. 1993)
1 ALR6th 371—§ 4
State v. Wynn, 1999 WL 1080698 (Ohio
Ct. App. 10th Dist. Franklin County
1999)
78 ALR5th 489—§ 9
State v. Wynne, 108 N.M. 134, 767 P.2d
373 (Ct. App. 1988)
89 ALR5th 629—§ 3

State v. Wynter, 19 Conn. App. 654, 564
A.2d 296 (1989)
96 ALR5th 523—§ 3
State v. Wyrick, 35 N.C. App. 352, 241
S.E.2d 355 (1978)
107 ALR5th 567—§ 16
State v. Xie, 62 Ohio St. 3d 521, 584
N.E.2d 715 (1992)
31 ALR6th 49—§ 10
State v. Yackley, 43 Ohio St. 3d 181,
539 N.E.2d 1118 (1989)
70 ALR6th 1—§ 5
State v. Yaden, 118 Ohio App. 3d 410,
692 N.E.2d 1097, 71 A.L.R.5th 749
(1st Dist. Hamilton County 1997)
71 ALR5th 285—§ 2, 4
State v. Yadon, 179 Wis. 2d 852, 514
N.W.2d 725 (Ct. App. 1993)
58 ALR6th 499—§ 7
State v. Yaeger, 2007 WI App 110, 730
N.W.2d 461 (Wis. Ct. App. 2007)
29 ALR6th 1—§ 10
State v. Yager, 139 Idaho 680, 85 P.3d
656 (2004)
20 ALR6th 479—§ 3
State v. Yahya, 2011-Ohio-6090, 2011
WL 5868794 (Ohio Ct. App. 10th
Dist. Franklin County 2011)
74 ALR6th 373—§ 8
State v. Yakey, 43 Wash. 15, 85 P. 990
(1906)
90 ALR6th 385—§ 2, 7
State v. Yamashiro, 817 P.2d 123 (Ha-
waii App. 1991)
5 ALR5th 243—§ 15, 19, 34, 44
State v. Yananokwiak, 65 N.C. App.
513, 309 S.E.2d 560 (1983)
17 ALR6th 327—§ 34
State v. Yancey, 6 SCL 237 (1812)
14 ALR5th 89—§ 10, 16
State v. Yanez, 469 N.W.2d 452 (Minn.
Ct. App. 1991)
73 ALR5th 383—§ 26
State v. Yanez, 716 A.2d 759 (R.I. 1998)
46 ALR5th 499—§ 3
State v. Yang, 201 Wis. 2d 725, 549
N.W.2d 769 (App. 1996)

32 ALR5th 149—§ 26, 32

State v. Yang, 627 N.W.2d 666 (Minn. Ct. App. 2001)

32 ALR5th 149—§ 22

State v. Yang, 2001 WL 379134 (Minn. Ct. App. 2001)

19 ALR6th 697—§ 3, 19

State v. Yang, 2002 WL 1363911 (Minn. Ct. App. 2002)

92 ALR6th 171—§ 14

State v. Yanowitz, 67 Ohio App. 2d 141, 21 Ohio Op. 3d 445, 426 N.E.2d 190 (8th Dist. Cuyahoga County 1980)

109 ALR5th 99—§ 8

State v. Yant, 376 N.W.2d 487 (Minn. Ct. App. 1985)

59 ALR5th 1—§ 2, 5, 6

State v. Yarbrough, 1991 WL 4469 (Tenn. Crim. App. 1991)

73 ALR5th 383—§ 5

State v. Yardley, 267 Kan. 37, 978 P.2d 886 (1999)

10 ALR5th 700—§ 31

State v. Yaritz, 287 N.W.2d 13 (Minn. 1979)

27 ALR6th 491—§ 3

State v. Yarrell, 172 N.C. App. 135, 616 S.E.2d 258 (2005)

67 ALR6th 103—§ 5, 10, 14

State v. Yates, 166 Ohio App. 3d 19, 2006-Ohio-1424, 848 N.E.2d 917 (2d Dist. Greene County 2006)

71 ALR6th 1—§ 13

State v. Yates, 350 So. 2d 1169 (La. 1977)

99 ALR6th 295—§ 5

State v. Yates, 357 So. 2d 541 (La. 1978)

51 ALR6th 219—§ 4

State v. Yates, 589 S.E.2d 902 (N.C. Ct. App. 2004)

122 ALR5th 439—§ 4

State v. Yazzie, 67 Wyo. 256, 218 P.2d 482 (1950)

70 ALR5th 587—§ 3

State v. Ybarra, 102 Idaho 573, 634 P.2d 435 (1981)

32 ALR6th 1—§ 9

State v. Ybarra, 156 Ariz. 275, 751 P.2d 591 (App. 1987)

4 ALR5th 1—§ 17, 32

State v. Ybarra, 386 S.W.2d 384 (Mo. 1965)

46 ALR5th 499—§ 3

State v. Yearwood, 178 N.C. 813, 101 S.E. 513 (1919)

81 ALR5th 563—§ 3, 5, 8

State v. Yee, 129 N.H. 155, 523 A.2d 116, 25 Env't. Rep. Cas. (BNA) 1798 (1987)

122 ALR5th 593—§ 10

State v. Yellock, 106 N.C. App. 704, 418 S.E.2d 256 (1992)

39 ALR5th 283—§ 46

State v. Yelverton, 334 N.C. 532, 434 S.E.2d 183 (1993)

87 ALR5th 181—§ 4, 8

State v. Yeoman, 24 Kan. App. 2d 639, 951 P.2d 964 (1997)

12 ALR5th 89—§ 4

State v. Yerkey, 2001-Ohio-1792, 2001 WL 1468914 (Ohio Ct. App. 5th Dist. Stark County 2001)

78 ALR6th 297—§ 52

State v. Yirga, 2002-Ohio-2832, 2002 WL 1299860 (Ohio Ct. App. 3d Dist. Wyandot County 2002)

96 ALR6th 269—§ 14

State v. Yoder, 96 Idaho 651, 534 P.2d 771 (1975)

103 ALR5th 463—§ 3

State v. Yoder, 935 P.2d 534 (Utah Ct. App. 1997)

58 ALR6th 499—§ 49

State v. Yoder, 1991 WL 82868 (Ohio Ct. App. 3d Dist. Paulding County 1991)

72 ALR5th 1—§ 33

State v. Yodprasit, 564 N.W.2d 383, 74 A.L.R.5th 775 (Iowa 1997)

74 ALR5th 453—§ 2, 3, 5

State v. Yorczyk, 167 Conn. 434, 356 A.2d 169 (1974)

6 ALR5th 733—§ 2, 16

State v. York, 11 Wash. App. 137, 521 P.2d 950 (Div. 3 1974)

61 ALR5th 1—§ 3, 5

State v. York, 66 Ohio App. 3d 149, 583 N.E.2d 1046 (12th Dist. Warren County 1990)

51 ALR6th 1—§ 24

52 ALR6th 1—§ 34

70 ALR6th 361—§ 32

State v. York, 115 Ohio App. 3d 245, 685 N.E.2d 261 (4th Dist. Jackson County 1996)

112 ALR5th 621—§ 3, 7

State v. York, 122 Ohio App. 3d 226, 701 N.E.2d 463 (11th Dist. Lake County 1997)

67 ALR6th 531—§ 12, 23, 28

State v. York, 159 Wash. App. 1026, 2011 WL 103555 (Div. 3 2011)

101 ALR6th 545—§ 5

State v. York, 159 Wis. 2d 215, 464 N.W.2d 36 (Ct. App. 1990)

58 ALR6th 499—§ 52

State v. York, 511 S.W.2d 758 (Mo. 1974)

71 ALR6th 335—§ 10

State v. Yoshida, 44 Haw. 352, 354 P.2d 986 (1960)

65 ALR6th 359—§ 5

State v. Yoshino, 50 Haw. 287, 439 P.2d 666 (1968)

16 ALR6th 329—§ 8

24 ALR6th 591—§ 7

State v. Yost, 232 Kan. 370, 654 P.2d 458 (1982)

92 ALR5th 35—§ 30

State v. Yost, 235 Neb. 325, 455 N.W.2d 162 (1990)

15 ALR5th 391—§ 4

State v. Yost, 2005-Ohio-3138, 2005 WL 1484023 (Ohio Ct. App. 8th Dist. Cuyahoga County 2005)

26 ALR6th 511—§ 19

State v. Youlten, 151 Ohio App. 3d 518, 2003-Ohio-430, 784 N.E.2d 768 (8th Dist. Cuyahoga County 2003)

84 ALR6th 263—§ 9

State v. Young, 15 Wash. App. 581, 550 P.2d 689 (Div. 1 1976)

64 ALR5th 741—§ 4

State v. Young, 20 N.C. App. 316, 201 S.E.2d 370 (1973)

4 ALR5th 1—§ 4, 10

State v. Young, 37 Ohio St. 3d 249, 525 N.E.2d 1363 (1988)

42 ALR5th 291—§ 3, 4, 10, 24

111 ALR5th 239—§ 6

State v. Young, 50 Ohio App. 3d 17, 552 N.E.2d 226 (4th Dist. Athens County 1988)

87 ALR5th 1—§ 14

State v. Young, 62 Ohio St. 2d 370, 16 Ohio Op. 3d 416, 406 N.E.2d 499 (1980)

58 ALR6th 385—§ 20

State v. Young, 62 Wash. App. 895, 802 P.2d 829 (Div. 1 1991)

111 ALR5th 239—§ 9

State v. Young, 63 Wash. App. 324, 818 P.2d 1375 (Div. 2 1991)

15 ALR5th 391—§ 30

92 ALR5th 35—§ 18

State v. Young, 83 Wash. 2d 937, 523 P.2d 934 (1974)

79 ALR5th 1—§ 8

State v. Young, 95 N.J. Super. 535, 231 A.2d 857 (1967)

52 ALR5th 655—§ 3

State v. Young, 107 Idaho 671, 691 P.2d 1286 (Ct. App. 1984)

45 ALR6th 643—§ 13

State v. Young, 108 Or. App. 196, 816 P.2d 612 (1991)

112 ALR5th 429—§ 8

State v. Young, 112 Ariz. 361, 542 P.2d 20 (1975)

36 ALR5th 161—§ 9

41 ALR6th 141—§ 7

State v. Young, 117 N.M. 688, 875 P.2d 1119 (Ct. App. 1994)

9 ALR6th 1—§ 11

State v. Young, 119 Or. App. 470, 851 P.2d 626 (1993)

15 ALR5th 391—§ 45

State v. Young, 123 Wash. 2d 173, 867 P.2d 593 (1994)
  78 ALR5th 309—§ 7, 8
State v. Young, 131 S.C. 94, 126 S.E. 445 (1924)
  101 ALR6th 499—§ 18
  103 ALR6th 35—§ 16, 19, 25
State v. Young, 135 Ariz. 437, 661 P.2d 1138 (Ct. App. Div. 1 1982)
  18 ALR6th 1—§ 5, 8, 29
State v. Young, 140 N.C. App. 1, 535 S.E.2d 380 (2000)
  33 ALR6th 91—§ 37
State v. Young, 183 P.3d 860 (Kan. Ct. App. 2008)
  51 ALR6th 139—§ 6
State v. Young, 185 N.E.2d 33 (Ohio 1962)
  43 ALR5th 1—§ 10
State v. Young, 185 Wis. 2d 918, 520 N.W.2d 291 (Ct. App. 1994)
  67 ALR6th 531—§ 29
State v. Young, 212 Wis. 2d 417, 569 N.W.2d 84 (Ct. App. 1997)
  37 ALR5th 1—§ 4
State v. Young, 223 Ariz. 447, 224 P.3d 944 (Ct. App. Div. 1 2010)
  87 ALR6th 1—§ 42
State v. Young, 234 Ga. 488, 216 S.E.2d 586 (1975)
  31 ALR5th 229—§ 3, 17, 80
State v. Young, 303 A.2d 113 (Me. 1973)
  116 ALR5th 373—§ 3, 16
State v. Young, 312 N.C. 669, 325 S.E.2d 181 (1985)
  17 ALR5th 125—§ 3
State v. Young, 406 S.E.2d 758, 13 A.L.R.5th 899 (W. Va. 1991)
  13 ALR5th 1—§ 2, 35, 37, 49, 50
State v. Young, 427 S.W.2d 510 (Mo. 1968)
  4 ALR5th 1—§ 14
State v. Young, 469 So. 2d 1014 (La. Ct. App. 1st Cir. 1985)
  9 ALR6th 1—§ 17

State v. Young, 472 So. 2d 297 (La. Ct. App. 1st Cir. 1985)
  33 ALR6th 407—§ 4
State v. Young, 560 A.2d 1095 (Me. 1989)
  58 ALR6th 439—§ 4
State v. Young, 618 So. 2d 1149 (La. Ct. App. 2d Cir. 1993)
  23 ALR6th 307—§ 39
State v. Young, 695 S.W.2d 882 (Mo. 1985)
  6 ALR5th 733—§ 26
  69 ALR6th 207—§ 10
State v. Young, 701 S.W.2d 429 (Mo. 1985)
  83 ALR6th 255—§ 15
State v. Young, 701 S.W.2d 490 (Mo. Ct. App. E.D. 1985)
  103 ALR6th 347—§ 13
State v. Young, 712 So. 2d 273 (La. Ct. App. 1st Cir. 1998)
  29 ALR5th 487—§ 13
State v. Young, 853 P.2d 327 (Utah 1993)
  110 ALR5th 329—§ 4, 5
  55 ALR6th 157—§ 4, 36
State v. Young, 1987 WL 13693 (Ohio Ct. App. 6th Dist. Lucas County 1987)
  17 ALR6th 327—§ 37
State v. Young, 1996 WL 571366 (Ohio Ct. App. 12th Dist. Brown County 1996)
  57 ALR6th 83—§ 6
State v. Young, 1997 WL 43676 (Wash. Ct. App. Div. 1 1997)
  73 ALR5th 383—§ 9, 57
State v. Young, 1998 WL 258466 (Tenn. Crim. App. 1998)
  90 ALR5th 453—§ 23
State v. Young, 1999 WL 1179574 (Tenn. Crim. App. 1999)
  97 ALR6th 653—§ 26
State v. Young, 2004-Ohio-5896, 2004 WL 2504393 (Ohio Ct. App. 6th Dist. Erie County 2004)
  72 ALR6th 1—§ 4

State v. Young, 2007 MT 323, 340 Mont. 153, 174 P.3d 460 (2007)
46 ALR6th 241—§ 9

State v. Young, 2011-Ohio-4875, 2011 WL 4424839 (Ohio Ct. App. 2d Dist. Montgomery County 2011)
78 ALR6th 297—§ 21, 39, 57, 79

State v. Youngblood, 173 Ariz. 502, 844 P.2d 1152, 129 Ariz. Adv. Rep. 11, 131 Ariz. Adv. Rep. 3 (1993)
40 ALR5th 113—§ 2, 3

State v. Youngblood, 217 W. Va. 535, 618 S.E.2d 544 (2005)
71 ALR6th 625—§ 10, 23

State v. Yow, 2010 WL 1957478 (N.C. Ct. App. 2010)
57 ALR6th 1—§ 4, 10, 26

State v. Yrigolla, 38 Kan. App. 2d 1029, 175 P.3d 276 (2008)
69 ALR6th 1—§ 13

State v. Yuen, 105 Haw. 251, 96 P.3d 271 (2004)
93 ALR6th 1—§ 5

State v. Yun, 2001 WL 1082354 (Ohio Ct. App. 5th Dist. Stark County 2001)
7 ALR6th 233—§ 9

State v. Yurch, 37 Conn. App. 72, 654 A.2d 1246 (1995)
108 ALR5th 593—§ 23

State v. Zabrinas, 24 P.3d 77 (Kan. 2001)
42 ALR5th 291—§ 17

State v. Zaccadelli, 472 A.2d 928 (Me. 1984)
41 ALR5th 171—§ 10, 16, 26

State v. Zaccardi, 280 Minn. 291, 159 N.W.2d 108 (1968)
39 ALR6th 257—§ 19
40 ALR6th 1—§ 33

State v. Zackery, 31 Ohio App. 3d 264, 31 Ohio B.R. 549, 511 N.E.2d 135 (Hamilton Co. 1987)
8 ALR5th 775—§ 2

State v. Zadoyan, 290 N.J. Super. 280, 675 A.2d 698 (App. Div. 1996)
100 ALR5th 67—§ 23

State v. Zaehringer, 325 N.W.2d 754 (Iowa 1982)

37 ALR5th 319—§ 5

State v. Zaerr, 110 Ariz. 585, 521 P.2d 1131 (1974)
94 ALR5th 393—§ 5

State v. Zahl, 259 N.J. Super. 372, 613 A.2d 508 (Law Div. 1992)
68 ALR5th 299—§ 5

State v. Zahner, 545 N.W.2d 337 (Iowa Ct. App. 1996)
86 ALR5th 463—§ 3, 7

State v. Zahniser, 2000 WL 492072 (Ohio Ct. App. 5th Dist. Ashland County 2000)
43 ALR6th 475—§ 21

State v. Zaldivar, 34 So. 3d 76 (Fla. 3d DCA 2010)
92 ALR6th 171—§ 4

State v. Zambrano, 2011 WL 1660697 (N.J. Super. Ct. App. Div. 2011)
74 ALR6th 373—§ 5

State v. Zamechek, 110 Wash. App. 1048, 2002 WL 339366 (Div. 1 2002)
15 ALR6th 515—§ 4

State v. Zamora, 63 Wash. App. 220, 817 P.2d 880 (1991)
27 ALR5th 593—§ 2

State v. Zamora, 114 Ariz. 75, 559 P.2d 195 (Ct. App. Div. 1 1976)
114 ALR5th 173—§ 7

State v. Zamora, 129 Idaho 817, 933 P.2d 106 (1997)
85 ALR5th 471—§ 7

State v. Zamora, 137 N.M. 301, 2005-NMCA-039, 110 P.3d 517 (Ct. App. 2005)
79 ALR6th 1—§ 62

State v. Zamora, 247 Kan. 684, 803 P.2d 568 (1990)
39 ALR5th 283—§ 4, 46

State v. Zancauske, 804 S.W.2d 851 (Mo. Ct. App. S.D. 1991)
29 ALR6th 1—§ 9

State v. Zander, 2004 WL 2857501 (Minn. Ct. App. 2004)
44 ALR6th 325—§ 14

State v. Zanelli, 212 Wis. 2d 358, 569 N.W.2d 301 (Ct. App. 1997)

36 ALR5th 161—§ 9.5
State v. Zanger, 572 So. 2d 1379, 16 FLW D 29 (Fla. 1991)
29 ALR5th 59—§ 5, 86
State v. Zangrilli, 440 A.2d 710 (R.I. 1982)
67 ALR6th 103—§ 5, 10, 14
State v. Zanker, 179 Minn. 355, 229 N.W. 311 (1930)
113 ALR5th 1—§ 4, 8, 14
State v. Zapata, 713 So. 2d 1152 (La. Ct. App. 5th Cir. 1998)
68 ALR5th 343—§ 3, 16
State v. Zaragoza, 221 Ariz. 49, 209 P.3d 629 (2009)
92 ALR6th 295—§ 20, 25
96 ALR6th 355—§ 5, 26, 36, 49, 62
State v. Zarasua, 1 N.C.A. 1187, 1992 WL 196804 (1992)
27 ALR6th 183—§ 15, 28, 30
State v. Zarick, 227 Conn. 207, 630 A.2d 565 (1993)
42 ALR5th 291—§ 3
State v. Zaritz, 235 Neb. 599, 456 N.W.2d 479 (1990)
84 ALR5th 487—§ 4
State v. Zarm, 302 Wis. 2d 261, 2007 WI App 138, 732 N.W.2d 863 (Ct. App. 2007)
69 ALR6th 579—§ 5
State v. Zarrilli, 216 N.J. Super. 231, 523 A.2d 284 (Law Div. 1987)
68 ALR5th 299—§ 3, 5
State v. Zaruba, 306 N.W.2d 772 (Iowa 1981)
92 ALR5th 35—§ 22
State v. Zavala, 136 Ariz. 356, 666 P.2d 456 (1983)
92 ALR6th 295—§ 3, 13
93 ALR6th 207—§ 4, 7, 24
96 ALR6th 355—§ 3, 12, 24
State v. Zavala, 259 N.J. Super. 235, 611 A.2d 1169 (1992)
20 ALR5th 398—§ 2, 3, 10, 12, 34, 42
47 ALR5th 259—§ 2
State v. Zawistowski, 339 So. 2d 315 (Fla. Dist. Ct. App. 1st Dist. 1976)

70 ALR6th 1—§ 18
State v. Zebroski, 2001 WL 1079010 (Del. Super. Ct. 2001)
110 ALR5th 1—§ 3, 20
State v. Zeciri, 43 P.3d 169 (Alaska Ct. App. 2002)
58 ALR6th 1—§ 5
State v. Zeien, 505 N.W.2d 498 (Iowa 1993)
57 ALR6th 445—§ 12
State v. Zeiglar, 690 S.E.2d 768 (N.C. Ct. App. 2010)
57 ALR6th 1—§ 3
State v. Zeigler, 77 P.3d 1009 (Kan. Ct. App. 2003)
26 ALR6th 511—§ 25
State v. Zektzer, 13 Wash. App. 24, 533 P.2d 399 (Div. 1 1975)
72 ALR5th 607—§ 3
State v. Zelinka, 130 Or. App. 464, 882 P.2d 624 (1994)
28 ALR6th 505—§ 9
45 ALR6th 337—§ 33
State v. Zenquis, 131 N.J. 84, 618 A.2d 335 (1993)
67 ALR5th 149—§ 3, 6
State v. Zepeda, 2012 WL 566907 (Ariz. Ct. App. Div. 2 2012)
95 ALR6th 1—§ 10, 28
State v. Zeta Chi Fraternity, 142 N.H. 16, 696 A.2d 530, 119 Ed. Law Rep. 1019 (1997)
99 ALR5th 557—§ 3, 10, 13
State v. Zgodava, 384 N.W.2d 522 (Minn. Ct. App. 1986)
24 ALR6th 747—§ 36
State v. Zhu, 21 Kan. App. 2d 914, 909 P.2d 679 (1996)
29 ALR5th 487—§ 12
State v. Zibell, 32 Wash. App. 158, 646 P.2d 154 (Div. 1 1982)
83 ALR5th 277—§ 11
84 ALR5th 487—§ 25
State v. Zichko, 129 Idaho 259, 923 P.2d 966 (1996)
33 ALR6th 91—§ 9, 10, 33, 49
93 ALR6th 1—§ 36

State v. Ziegler, 19 Wash. App. 119, 575 P.2d 723 (1978)
9 ALR5th 464—§ 4, 10
State v. Ziegler, 226 N.J. Super. 504, 544 A.2d 914 (Law Div. 1988)
68 ALR5th 299—§ 4, 7
State v. Ziegler, 637 So. 2d 109 (La. 1994)
18 ALR6th 1—§ 5
State v. Ziemann, 14 Neb. App. 117, 705 N.W.2d 59 (2005)
45 ALR6th 435—§ 3, 4, 12, 16, 30
State v. Ziepfel, 107 Ohio App. 3d 646, 669 N.E.2d 299 (1st Dist. Hamilton County 1995)
89 ALR5th 539—§ 4
State v. Zimmelman, 62 N.J. 279, 301 A.2d 129 (1973)
31 ALR6th 333—§ 14
State v. Zimmer, 166 Wis. 2d 3, 480 N.W.2d 569 (Ct. App. 1991)
70 ALR6th 329—§ 16
State v. Zimmerman, 23 N.C. App. 396, 209 S.E.2d 350 (1974)
1 ALR6th 549—§ 16
State v. Zimmerman, 37 Or. App. 163, 586 P.2d 377 (1978)
92 ALR5th 35—§ 7
State v. Zimmerman, 121 Idaho 971, 829 P.2d 861 (1992)
38 ALR5th 433—§ 2, 5
State v. Zimmerman, 175 Mont. 179, 573 P.2d 174 (1977)
97 ALR5th 201—§ 7
State v. Zimmerman, 251 Kan. 54, 833 P.2d 925 (1992)
39 ALR5th 283—§ 4, 41
55 ALR6th 157—§ 7, 26, 30
State v. Zimmerman, 529 N.W.2d 171, 55 A.L.R.5th 805 (N.D. 1995)
55 ALR5th 125—§ 3, 11
State v. Zimmerman, 823 S.W.2d 220 (Tenn. Crim. 1991)
11 ALR5th 871—§ 4, 6, 7
State v. Zimmerman, 1989 WL 145160 (Ohio Ct. App. 3d Dist. Auglaize County 1989)

67 ALR6th 209—§ 21
State v. Zindros, 189 Conn. 228, 456 A.2d 288 (1983)
61 ALR5th 1—§ 3, 14
State v. Zink, 519 N.W.2d 581 (N.D. 1994)
76 ALR5th 1—§ 4
State v. Zinkiewicz, 67 Ohio App. 3d 99, 585 N.E.2d 1007 (2d Dist. Montgomery County 1990)
111 ALR5th 239—§ 2, 6
State v. Zinkiewicz, 67 Ohio App. 3d 99, 585 N.E.2d 1007 (Montgomery Co. 1990)
42 ALR5th 291—§ 4
State v. Zinmeister, 27 Ohio App. 3d 313, 501 N.E.2d 59 (8th Dist. Cuyahoga County 1985)
6 ALR6th 533—§ 11
State v. Zinsli, 156 Or. App. 245, 966 P.2d 1200 (1998)
40 ALR5th 113—§ 4
24 ALR6th 1—§ 32
State v. Zirkle, 1997 WL 567938 (Ohio Ct. App. 4th Dist. Meigs County 1997)
24 ALR6th 1—§ 28
State v. Zito, 2006 MT 211, 333 Mont. 312, 143 P.3d 108 (2006)
28 ALR6th 505—§ 7, 9
State v. Zobel, 81 S.D. 260, 134 N.W.2d 101 (1965)
118 ALR5th 253—§ 3
State v. Zobel, 192 Neb. 480, 222 N.W.2d 570 (1974)
18 ALR5th 804—§ 2
State v. Zobel, 1997 WL 220295 (Ohio Ct. App. 5th Dist. Tuscarawas County 1997)
19 ALR6th 697—§ 21
State v. Zonge, 973 S.W.2d 250 (Tenn. Crim. App. 1997)
99 ALR6th 295—§ 13
State v. Zucconi, 50 N.J. 361, 235 A.2d 193 (1967)
28 ALR6th 505—§ 9
30 ALR6th 103—§ 42

State v. Zugg, 2007 WL 1413133 (Kan. Ct. App. 2007)
26 ALR6th 511—§ 25

State v. Zumalt, 202 Kan. 595, 451 P.2d 253 (1969)
97 ALR5th 293—§ 3, 7

State v. Zuniga, 237 Kan. 788, 703 P.2d 805 (1985)
49 ALR6th 343—§ 4

State Acci. Ins. Fund v. Holston, 63 Or. App. 348, 663 P.2d 795 (1983)
36 ALR5th 225—§ 3

State Acci. Ins. Fund Corp. v. Luhrs, 63 Or. App. 78, 663 P.2d 418 (1983)
14 ALR5th 1—§ 10

State Acc. Ins. Fund Corp. v. Anderson, 94 Or. App. 11, 764 P.2d 924 (1988)
82 ALR5th 149—§ 63

State Acc. Ins. Fund Corp. v. Griffith, 66 Or. App. 709, 675 P.2d 1092 (1984)
113 ALR5th 115—§ 10, 18, 27, 31, 63

State Acc. Ins. Fund Corp. v. Lucas, 94 Or. App. 132, 764 P.2d 235 (1988)
82 ALR5th 149—§ 2, 22, 23, 37, 54, 64

State Acc. Ins. Fund Corp. v. Mitchell, 63 Or. App. 488, 664 P.2d 1134 (1983)
113 ALR5th 115—§ 10, 32, 33, 52

State Acc. Ins. Fund Corp. v. Noffsinger, 80 Or. App. 640, 723 P.2d 358 (1986)
10 ALR5th 245—§ 23
82 ALR5th 149—§ 2, 5, 15, 20, 22, 24, 64
83 ALR5th 103—§ 18, 26
84 ALR5th 249—§ 40
113 ALR5th 115—§ 1, 2, 10, 14, 31, 32, 35, 53

State Acc. Ins. Fund Corp. v. Reel, 303 Or. 210, 735 P.2d 364 (1987)
42 ALR6th 61—§ 7

State Acc. Ins. Fund Corp. v. Shilling, 66 Or. App. 600, 675 P.2d 1081 (1984)
113 ALR5th 115—§ 10, 18, 27, 47, 54

State Acc. Ins. Fund Corp. v. Varner, 89 Or. App. 421, 749 P.2d 606 (1988)
82 ALR5th 149—§ 22, 31, 37, 52, 54

State Administrative Bd. of Election Laws v. Board of Sup'rs of Elections of Baltimore City, 342 Md. 586, 679 A.2d 96 (1996)
51 ALR6th 287—§ 3

State Agency of Dev. & Community Affairs, Dep't of Hous. & Community Affairs v. Bisson, 161 Vt. 8, 632 A.2d 34 (1993)
43 ALR5th 705—§ 3, 5, 25

State Analysis, Inc. v. American Financial Services Assoc., 621 F. Supp. 2d 309 (E.D. Va. 2009)
76 ALR6th 289—§ 4
77 ALR6th 543—§ 18
87 ALR6th 1—§ 21

State Attorney, Fourth Judicial Circuit of Florida, Office of v. Parrotino, 628 So. 2d 1097 (Fla. 1993)
90 ALR5th 273—§ 8, 10

State Auditor, State Office of v. Minnesota Ass'n of Professional Employees, 504 N.W.2d 751, 144 L.R.R.M. (BNA) 2102 (Minn. 1993)
112 ALR5th 263—§ 64

State Auto. Ins. Co. v. Rowland, 221 Tenn. 421, 427 S.W.2d 30 (1968)
51 ALR5th 701—§ 9

State Auto Ins. Companies v. McClamroch, 129 N.C. App. 214, 497 S.E.2d 439 (1998)
113 ALR5th 1—§ 12

State Auto Ins. Companies v. Summy, 234 F.3d 131 (3d Cir. 2000)
89 ALR5th 1—§ 21

State Auto. Mut. Ins. Co. v. American Re-Insurance Co., 748 F. Supp. 556 (S.D. Ohio 1990)
85 ALR6th 531—§ 13

State Auto. Mut. Ins. Co. v. Dolosich, 135 Ohio App. 3d 601, 735 N.E.2d 38 (8th Dist. Cuyahoga County 1999)
35 ALR5th 375—§ 63

For assistance, call 1-800-328-4880

State Auto. Mut. Ins. Co. v. Ellis, 700
S.W.2d 801 (Ky. App. 1985)
25 ALR5th 60—§ 4

State Auto Mut. Ins. Co. v. McIntyre,
652 F. Supp. 1177 (N.D. Ala. 1987)
60 ALR5th 239—§ 12

State Auto. Mut. Ins. Co. v. Rowe, 28
Ohio St. 3d 143, 502 N.E.2d 1008
(1986)
77 ALR5th 319—§ 7
78 ALR5th 341—§ 4

State Auto. Mut. Ins. Co. v. Skeens, 661
F. Supp. 1109 (S.D. W. Va. 1987)
66 ALR5th 269—§ 9

State Auto. Mut. Ins. Co. v. Spray, 547
F.2d 397 (7th Cir. 1977)
110 ALR5th 465—§ 2, 10

State Auto. Mut. Ins. Co. v. Trautwein,
414 S.W.2d 587, 23 A.L.R.3d 1254
(Ky. 1967)
56 ALR5th 407—§ 3, 4

State Auto. Mut. Ins. Co. v. Youler, 396
S.E.2d 737 (W. Va. 1990)
40 ALR5th 603—§ 9

State Auto Property and Cas. Ins. Co. v.
Eastern Data Systems, Inc., 587
F.3d 226 (4th Cir. 2009)
69 ALR6th 415—§ 54

State Bank & Trust of Kenmare v.
Brekke, 1999 ND 212, 602 N.W.2d
681 (N.D. 1999)
98 ALR5th 665—§ 3

State Bank of Brooten v. American Nat.
Bank of Little Falls, 266 N.W.2d
496, 23 U.C.C. Rep. Serv. (CBC)
935, 97 A.L.R.3d 706 (Minn. 1978)
77 ALR5th 429—§ 3

State Bank of Dodge City v. McKibben,
146 Kan. 341, 70 P.2d 1 (1937)
20 ALR5th 229—§ 3, 5, 6, 32

State Bank of Fisk v. Omega Electronics, Inc., 634 S.W.2d 234, 34
U.C.C.R.S. 934 (Mo. App. 1982)
61 ALR5th 525—§ 13

State Bank of Indiana v. Bell, 5 Blackf
127 (Ind. 1839)
8 ALR5th 653—§ 3

State Bank of Standish v. Curry, 190
Mich. App. 616, 476 N.W.2d 635,
16 U.C.C.R.S.2d 32 (1991)
18 ALR5th 307—§ 5, 15, 32, 33

State Bank of Standish v. Curry, 442
Mich. 76, 500 N.W.2d 104 (1993)
18 ALR5th 307—§ 3, 4, 6, 33

State Bank of Townsend v. Maryann's,
Inc., 204 Mont. 21, 664 P.2d 295
(1983)
18 ALR5th 307—§ 2

State Bar v. Cramer, 399 Mich. 116, 249
N.W.2d 1 (1976)
32 ALR6th 531—§ 14
40 ALR6th 463—§ 20

State Bar Asso. v. Connecticut Bank &
Trust Co., 20 Conn. Supp. 248, 131
A.2d 646 (1957)
8 ALR5th 653—§ 3

State Bar of Ariz. v. Arizona Land Title
& Trust Co., 90 Ariz. 76, 366 P.2d
1, 87 Ohio L. Abs. 418 (1961)
25 ALR6th 323—§ 4
40 ALR6th 463—§ 17

State Bar of Ariz. v. Arizona Land Title
& Trust Co., 91 Ariz. 293, 371 P.2d
1020 (1962)
40 ALR6th 463—§ 17

State Bar of Michigan v. Galloway, 124
Mich. App. 271, 335 N.W.2d 475
(1983)
8 ALR5th 653—§ 7

State Bar of Montana v. Krivec, 193
Mont. 477, 632 P.2d 707 (1981)
35 ALR6th 1—§ 7, 9, 11, 25

State Bar of Texas v. Sutherland, 766
S.W.2d 340 (Tex. App. El Paso
1989)
63 ALR6th 1—§ 5, 60

State Bldg. Comm'n, State ex rel. v.
Moore, 155 W. Va. 212, 184 S.E.2d
94 (1971)
36 ALR5th 657—§ 13

State by Abrams v. Magley, 105 App.
Div. 2d 208, 484 N.Y.S.2d 251 (3d
Dep't 1984)
43 ALR5th 705—§ 2

For assistance, call 1-800-328-4880

State, By and Through Albemarle Child Support Enforcement Agency ex rel. George v. Bray, 130 N.C. App. 552, 503 S.E.2d 686 (1998)

90 ALR5th 1—§ 26, 41, 44, 47

18 ALR6th 97—§ 16, 19, 21, 26, 33

State By and Through Dep't of Revenue ex rel. Sorenson v. Roske, 229 Mont. 151, 745 P.2d 365 (1987)

58 ALR5th 669—§ 5, 12

State By and Through Div. of Consumer Protection v. Rio Vista Oil, Ltd., 786 P.2d 1343, 1990-1 Trade Cas. (CCH) ¶ 68943 (Utah 1990)

26 ALR6th 249—§ 4

State By and Through Indiana State Highway Commission v. Fair, 423 N.E.2d 738 (Ind. Ct. App. 1st Dist. 1981)

15 ALR6th 1—§ 4, 5, 9, 10, 19

State By and Through State Highway Commission v. Oregon-Washington Lumber Co., 24 Or. App. 187, 544 P.2d 1058 (1976)

85 ALR5th 671—§ 5

State By and Through State Highway Commission v. Superbilt Mfg. Co., 204 Or. 393, 281 P.2d 707 (1955)

107 ALR5th 311—§ 13

109 ALR5th 421—§ 12

State By and Through Town of South Carthage, Tenn. v. Barrett, 840 S.W.2d 895 (Tenn. 1992)

102 ALR5th 525—§ 27

State, by Atty. Gen. v. Minimum Rate Pricing, Inc., 1998 WL 428810 (Minn. Dist. Ct. 1998)

77 ALR6th 1—§ 15

State by Beaulieu v. Independent Sch. Dist. No. 624, 533 N.W.2d 393, 68 BNA FEP Cas. 257 (Minn. 1995)

51 ALR5th 1—§ 8

State by Commissioner of Transp. v. Hess Realty Corp., 226 N.J. Super. 256, 543 A.2d 1050 (1988)

22 ALR5th 327—§ 25

State by Commissioner of Transp. v. Monmouth Hills, Inc., 110 N.J. Super. 449, 266 A.2d 133 (1970)

15 ALR5th 821—§ 2, 9, 10

State by Commissioner of Transp. v. Stulman, 136 N.J. Super. 148, 345 A.2d 329 (1975)

7 ALR5th 113—§ 6

State by Commissioner of Transp. v. Van Nortwick, 260 N.J. Super. 555, 617 A.2d 284 (1992)

15 ALR5th 821—§ 11

State, by Com'r of Transp. v. Sun Oil Co., 160 N.J. Super. 513, 390 A.2d 661 (Law Div. 1978)

49 ALR6th 205—§ 4, 18

State by Cooper v. French, 460 N.W.2d 2 (Minn. 1990)

10 ALR6th 513—§ 6

State by Cooper v. Hennepin County, 441 N.W.2d 106, 1 A.D. Cas. (BNA) 1490, 51 Fair Empl. Prac. Cas. (BNA) 166, 51 Empl. Prac. Dec. (CCH) ¶ 39383 (Minn. 1989)

77 ALR5th 595—§ 2, 8

102 ALR5th 1—§ 5, 7

State by Cooper v. Moorhead State University, 455 N.W.2d 79, 60 Ed. Law Rep. 602, 69 Fair Empl. Prac. Cas. (BNA) 455 (Minn. Ct. App. 1990)

81 ALR5th 367—§ 46

14 ALR6th 417—§ 8

State by Cooper v. Mower County Social Services, 434 N.W.2d 494, 69 Fair Empl. Prac. Cas. (BNA) 517 (Minn. Ct. App. 1989)

14 ALR6th 417—§ 8

State by Department of Highways v. Helehan, 189 Mont. 339, 615 P.2d 925 (1980)

10 ALR5th 448—§ 6

State by Department of Highways v. Olsen, 166 Mont. 139, 531 P.2d 1330 (1975)

10 ALR5th 448—§ 2, 6

State by Department of Highways v. Schumacher, 180 Mont. 329, 590 P.2d 1110 (1979)

10 ALR5th 448—§ 6

State by Furman v. Amsted Industries, 48 N.J. 544, 226 A.2d 715 (1967)

29 ALR6th 507—§ 14, 18

State by Furman v. Jefferson Lake Sulphur Co., 36 N.J. 577, 178 A.2d 329 (1962)

29 ALR6th 507—§ 10, 64

State by Humphrey v. Alpine Air Products, Inc., 490 N.W.2d 888, 1992-2 CCH Trade Cases ¶ 69966 (Minn. App. 1992)

54 ALR5th 631—§ 4

State by Humphrey v. Granite Gate Resorts, Inc., 568 N.W.2d 715 (Minn. Ct. App. 1997)

81 ALR5th 41—§ 4

State by Johnson v. Sports & Health Club, Inc., 392 N.W.2d 329, 41 CCH EPD ¶ 36617 (Minn. App. 1986)

37 ALR5th 349—§ 3, 15, 20, 21, 24

State by Kobayashi v. Midkiff, 49 Haw. 252, 413 P.2d 249 (1966)

85 ALR5th 471—§ 4

State by Lord v. First Nat. Bank of St. Paul, 313 N.W.2d 390 (Minn. 1981)

29 ALR6th 507—§ 9

State by McClure v. Sports & Health Club, Inc., 370 N.W.2d 844, 37 BNA FEP Cas. 1463, 37 CCH EPD ¶ 35227 (Minn. 1985)

37 ALR5th 349—§ 3, 15, 20, 21, 23, 24

State, by Minnesota State Ethical Practices Bd. v. Red Lake DFL Committee, 303 N.W.2d 54 (Minn. 1981)

51 ALR6th 359—§ 5

State by Mondale v. Independent School Dist., 266 Minn. 85, 123 N.W.2d 121 (1963)

29 ALR5th 36—§ 3

State by Parsons v. U. S. Steel Corp., 22 N.J. 341, 126 A.2d 168, 31 Lab. Cas. (CCH) ¶ 70253 (1956)

29 ALR6th 507—§ 18, 24, 70

State by Richman v. F. W. Woolworth Co., 45 N.J. Super. 259, 132 A.2d 550 (Ch. Div. 1957)

29 ALR6th 507—§ 64

State by Richman v. Sperry & Hutchinson Co., 56 N.J. Super. 589, 153 A.2d 691 (App. Div. 1959)

29 ALR6th 507—§ 18

State, by Rochester Ass'n of Neighborhoods v. City of Rochester, 268 N.W.2d 885 (Minn. 1978)

73 ALR5th 223—§ 9

State by State Highway Comm'r v. Cooper, 24 N.J. 261, 131 A.2d 756 (1957)

29 ALR5th 36—§ 3

State by State Highway Comm'r v. Union County Park Com., 89 N.J. Super. 202, 214 A.2d 446 (1965)

49 ALR5th 769—§ 2, 10

State, by State Road Commission v. Sanders, 125 W. Va. 143, 23 S.E.2d 113 (1942)

111 ALR5th 313—§ 12

State by Washington Wildlife Preservation, Inc. v. State, 329 N.W.2d 543 (Minn. 1983)

111 ALR5th 313—§ 17

State by Welfare Div. of Dep't of Health, Welfare & Rehabilitation v. Capital Convalescent Ctr., 92 Nev. 147, 547 P.2d 677 (1976)

45 ALR5th 109—§ 16

State by Woyke v. Tonka Corp., 420 N.W.2d 624 (Minn. App. 1988)

6 ALR5th 162—§ 2, 5, 8

25 ALR5th 568—§ 9

State, Child Support Enforcement Div. v. Bromley, 987 P.2d 183 (Alaska 1999)

90 ALR5th 1—§ 40, 50

State, City of Crystal v. A.J.H., 2009 WL 3735988 (Minn. Ct. App. 2009)

68 ALR6th 1—§ 9

State, City of Crystal v. S.D.G., 2009 WL 1684456 (Minn. Ct. App. 2009)

68 ALR6th 1—§ 17

State, City of Falcon Heights v. Pazder-
ski, 352 N.W.2d 85 (Minn. Ct. App.
1984)

92 ALR6th 295—§ 8, 26

93 ALR6th 207—§ 12, 14, 16, 28

State/City of Hamilton v. Breedlove,
1994 WL 327593 (Ohio Ct. App.
12th Dist. Butler County 1994)

87 ALR5th 1—§ 10, 19, 21, 31

State, City of Maple Grove v. Horner,
617 N.W.2d 452 (Minn. Ct. App.
2000)

69 ALR6th 1—§ 20, 22

State College Motor Inn, Inc. v. Mer-
hige, 25 Pa. D. & C.3d 43, 1982 WL
335 (C.P. 1982)

52 ALR6th 271—§ 21

State Commercial Fisheries Entry
Com'n v. Carlson, 65 P.3d 851
(Alaska 2003)

31 ALR6th 523—§ 11

State, Commissioner of v. Seibert, 220
Wis. 2d 308, 582 N.W.2d 745 (Ct.
App. 1998)

78 ALR6th 417—§ 71

State, Commitment of v. Seibert, 220
Wis. 2d 308, 582 N.W.2d 745 (Ct.
App. 1998)

87 ALR5th 277—§ 28

State Committee of Independence Party
of New York v. Berman, 294 F.
Supp. 2d 518 (S.D. N.Y. 2003)

120 ALR5th 125—§ 9

State, Commonwealth of v. Smith, 454
Pa. Super. 489, 685 A.2d 1030
(1996)

50 ALR5th 581—§ 7

State Compensation Fund v. Yazzie, 25
Ariz. App. 89, 541 P.2d 415 (Div. 1
1975)

100 ALR5th 567—§ 9

State Compensation Ins. Fund v. Bankers Indem. Ins. Co., 106 F.2d 368
(C.C.A. 9th Cir. 1939)

57 ALR5th 591—§ 5

State Compensation Ins. Fund v. Commercial Union Ins. Co., 631 P.2d
1168 (Colo. App. 1981)

33 ALR5th 587—§ 5

State Compensation Ins. Fund v. Gulf
Ins. Co., 628 P.2d 182 (Colo. App.
1981)

33 ALR5th 587—§ 5

State Compensation Ins. Fund v. Industrial Acc. Commission of Cal., 194
Cal. 28, 227 P. 168 (1924)

42 ALR6th 61—§ 13

State Compensation Ins. Fund v. Industrial Com'n of Colo., 98 Colo. 563,
58 P.2d 759 (1936)

42 ALR6th 61—§ 9

State Compensation Ins. Fund v. Riley,
9 Cal. 2d 126, 69 P.2d 985, 111
A.L.R. 1503 (1937)

65 ALR5th 1—§ 6, 7, 24, 34

State Compensation Ins. Fund v. Superior Court of Siskiyou County, 237
Cal. App. 2d 416, 46 Cal. Rptr. 891
(3d Dist. 1965)

13 ALR5th 289—§ 2, 14

State Compensation Ins. Fund v. Walter,
143 Colo. 549, 354 P.2d 591 (1960)

4 ALR5th 585—§ 3, 16, 19

State Compensation Ins. Fund v. Work-
ers' Comp. Appeals Bd., 133 Cal.
App. 3d 643, 184 Cal. Rptr. 111, 47
Cal. Comp. Cas. (MB) 729 (5th
Dist. 1982)

42 ALR6th 61—§ 29

State Compensation Ins. Fund v. Workers' Compensation Appeals Board,
59 Cal. App. 3d 647, 130 Cal. Rptr.
831 (2d Dist. 1976)

8 ALR5th 798—§ 3

State Compensation Ins. Fund v. WPS,
Inc., 70 Cal. App. 4th 644, 82 Cal.
Rptr. 2d 799 (2d Dist. 1999)

51 ALR5th 603—§ 4, 11

State Comp. Ins. Fund v. Superior Court,
91 Cal. App. 4th 1080, 111 Cal.
Rptr. 2d 284, 66 Cal. Comp. Cas.
(MB) 1061 (2d Dist. 2001)

9 ALR6th 363—§ 15

State Comp. Ins. Fund v. Workers' Comp. Appeals Bd., 69 Cal. Comp. Cas. (MB) 342, 2004 WL 759308 (App. 5th Dist. 2004)
41 ALR6th 207—§ 6

State, Com'r of Human Services v. A. B. C., 2011 WL 68616 (Minn. Ct. App. 2011)
68 ALR6th 1—§ 14

State Conservation Dep't v. Seaman, 396 Mich. 299, 240 N.W.2d 206 (1976)
50 ALR5th 703—§ 35, 38

State Contracting & Engineering Corp. v. Condotte America, Inc., 197 Fed. Appx. 915 (Fed. Cir. 2006)
49 ALR6th 505—§ 17

State Court Adm'r, Office of v. Background Information Services, Inc., 994 P.2d 420 (Colo. 1999)
27 ALR6th 403—§ 22

State DCS ex rel. State of AK v. Anderson, 189 Or. App. 162, 74 P.3d 1149 (2003)
18 ALR6th 97—§ 24, 43

State Dental Council & Examining Bd. v. Pollock, 457 Pa. 264, 318 A.2d 910 (1974)
10 ALR5th 1—§ 2, 3

State, Dept. of Revenue v. Modern Trailer Sales, Inc., 175 Colo. 296, 486 P.2d 1064 (1971)
38 ALR6th 255—§ 26

State Div. Of Family And Youth Services v. V.S., 2002 WL 1004097 (Alaska 2002)
61 ALR6th 521—§ 32

State, Div. of Hotels/Restaurants, Div. of Risk Management v. Cole, 664 So. 2d 291 (Fla. Dist. Ct. App. 1st Dist. 1995)
13 ALR6th 209—§ 4, 14, 16
39 ALR6th 445—§ 41

State Div. of Human Rights on Complaint of Cottongim v. Onondaga County Sheriff's Dept., 71 N.Y.2d 623, 528 N.Y.S.2d 802, 524 N.E.2d 123, 59 Fair Empl. Prac. Cas. (BNA) 1444, 47 Empl. Prac. Dec. (CCH) ¶ 38311 (1988)
14 ALR6th 417—§ 8

State Div. of Human Rights on Complaint of Cottongim v. Onondaga County Sheriff's Dept., 127 A.D.2d 986, 513 N.Y.S.2d 68, 59 Fair Empl. Prac. Cas. (BNA) 1443 (4th Dep't 1987)
14 ALR6th 417—§ 8

State Emp. Bargaining Agent Coalition v. Rowland, 718 F.3d 126, 195 L.R.R.M. (BNA) 2925 (2d Cir. 2013)
96 ALR6th 577—§ 11

State Employees' Unions, In re, 587 A.2d 919, 136 L.R.R.M. (BNA) 2885 (R.I. 1991)
82 ALR6th 497—§ 24, 77

State, Employment Sec. Dept. v. Evans, 111 Nev. 1118, 901 P.2d 156 (1995)
18 ALR6th 195—§ 3

State Ethics Com'n v. Evans, 382 Md. 370, 855 A.2d 364 (2004)
35 ALR6th 1—§ 18, 20, 24

State ex inf. Heath v. Tankar Gas, 250 Wis. 218, 26 N.W.2d 647 (1947)
26 ALR6th 249—§ 16

State ex rel. v. American Sur. Co. of New York, 22 Tenn. App. 197, 120 S.W.2d 967 (1938)
73 ALR6th 571—§ 71

State ex rel. v. Caldwell, 21 Tenn. App. 396, 111 S.W.2d 377 (1937)
23 ALR6th 1—§ 22

State ex rel. Armstrong v. Davey, 130 Ohio St. 160, 4 Ohio Op. 38, 198 N.E. 180 (1935)
62 ALR6th 143—§ 6, 10

State ex rel., Bullock v. Philip Morris, Inc., 2009 MT 261, 352 Mont. 30, 217 P.3d 475 (2009)
56 ALR6th 679—§ 2

State ex rel. Bunker Resource Recycling and Reclamation, Inc. v. Mehan, 782 S.W.2d 381, 30 Env't. Rep. Cas. (BNA) 2055 (Mo. 1990)

63 ALR6th 1—§ 4, 11, 15, 17, 37, 45, 62

State ex rel. Byrd v. Chadwick, 956 S.W.2d 369 (Mo. Ct. App. W.D. 1997)

60 ALR6th 295—§ 33

State ex rel. Carroll v. Simmons, 61 Wash. 2d 146, 377 P.2d 421 (1962)

63 ALR6th 1—§ 60

State ex rel. C.D., 2008 UT App 477, 200 P.3d 194 (Utah Ct. App. 2008)

61 ALR6th 521—§ 5, 11, 31

State ex rel. Clark v. Smith, 104 Mo. 661, 16 S.W. 503 (1891)

60 ALR6th 481—§ 4, 33

State ex rel. Corbin v. Superior Court In and For County of Maricopa, 159 Ariz. 307, 767 P.2d 30 (Ct. App. Div. 1 1988)

57 ALR6th 445—§ 14

State ex rel. Davis v. Kivett, 180 Tenn. 598, 177 S.W.2d 551 (1944)

60 ALR6th 481—§ 4

State ex rel. Ferrara v. Neill, 165 S.W.3d 539 (Mo. Ct. App. E.D. 2005)

59 ALR6th 161—§ 4, 41
60 ALR6th 193—§ 15

State ex rel. Groppi v. Leslie, 44 Wis. 2d 282, 171 N.W.2d 192 (1969)

63 ALR6th 1—§ 36

State ex rel. Hager v. Oakley, 154 W. Va. 528, 177 S.E.2d 585 (1970)

60 ALR6th 481—§ 4, 31

State ex rel. Hoover v. Smith, 198 W. Va. 507, 482 S.E.2d 124 (1997)

65 ALR6th 295—§ 5

State ex rel. Janda v. Janda, 2005 WL 3526568 (Neb. Ct. App. 2005)

59 ALR6th 161—§ 17, 30, 35

State ex rel. J.S.B. v. Hvass, 2006 WL 1148090 (Minn. Ct. App. 2006)

63 ALR6th 351—§ 3

State ex rel. Kutil v. Blake, 223 W. Va. 711, 679 S.E.2d 310 (2009)

61 ALR6th 1—§ 12, 17

State ex rel. Lance v. District Court of Thirteenth Judicial Dist., In and For Yellowstone County, 168 Mont. 297, 542 P.2d 1211 (1975)

60 ALR6th 175—§ 5

State ex rel. Martinez v. Cuyahoga Cty. Bd. of Elections, 2006-Ohio-1665, 2006 WL 847211 (Ohio Ct. App. 8th Dist. Cuyahoga County 2006)

60 ALR6th 481—§ 4, 7

State ex rel. Matz v. Brown, 37 Ohio St. 3d 279, 525 N.E.2d 805 (1988)

63 ALR6th 1—§ 5, 20, 64

State ex rel. McDulin v. Indus. Comm., 89 Ohio St. 3d 390, 2000-Ohio-205, 732 N.E.2d 367 (2000)

63 ALR6th 187—§ 33

State ex rel. McIntyre v. Board of Election Com'rs of City of Milwaukee, 273 Wis. 395, 78 N.W.2d 752 (1956)

60 ALR6th 481—§ 4, 25, 43

State ex rel. Meyer v. Woodbury, 321 Mo. 275, 10 S.W.2d 524 (1928)

56 ALR6th 523—§ 9

State ex rel. Nagin v. Celebrezze, 63 Ohio St. 2d 323, 17 Ohio Op. 3d 391, 410 N.E.2d 762 (1980)

59 ALR6th 111—§ 20

State ex rel. Numrich v. City of Mequon Bd. of Zoning Appeals, 242 Wis. 2d 677, 2001 WI App 88, 626 N.W.2d 366 (Ct. App. 2001)

64 ALR6th 601—§ 25

State ex rel. Olivieri v. State, 779 So. 2d 735 (La. 2001)

63 ALR6th 351—§ 3

State ex rel. Osborne v. Cook, 185 Or. App. 317, 59 P.3d 531 (2002)

56 ALR6th 553—§ 44

State ex rel. O'Sullivan v. Swanson, 127 Neb. 806, 257 N.W. 255 (1934)

59 ALR6th 111—§ 18, 25

State ex rel. Oviatt v. Knowles, 236 Ind. 517, 141 N.E.2d 854 (1957)

60 ALR6th 481—§ 4, 46

For assistance, call 1-800-328-4880

State ex rel. Pemberton v. Superior Court of Whatcom County, 196 Wash. 468, 83 P.2d 345 (1938)
60 ALR6th 481—§ 24

State ex rel. P.F.B., 2008 UT App 271, 191 P.3d 49 (Utah Ct. App. 2008)
57 ALR6th 163—§ 37

State ex rel. Quick-Ruben v. Verharen, 136 Wash. 2d 888, 969 P.2d 64 (1998)
60 ALR6th 481—§ 21

State ex rel. Roberts v. Acropolis McLoughlin, Inc., 150 Or. App. 180, 945 P.2d 647, 5 Wage & Hour Cas. 2d (BNA) 920 (1997)
61 ALR6th 61—§ 17

State ex rel. Roberts v. Bomareto Enterprises, Inc., 153 Or. App. 183, 956 P.2d 254, 4 Wage & Hour Cas. 2d (BNA) 902 (1998)
61 ALR6th 61—§ 17

State ex rel. Roberts v. Wall, 2007 WL 1482386 (Tenn. Ct. App. 2007)
60 ALR6th 193—§ 33

State ex rel. Smoleski v. County Court of Hancock County, 153 W. Va. 21, 166 S.E.2d 777 (1969)
60 ALR6th 481—§ 4, 30, 44

State ex rel. Staley v. Wayne County Court, 137 W. Va. 431, 73 S.E.2d 827 (1952)
60 ALR6th 481—§ 4, 31

State ex rel. Stoll v. Logan Cty. Bd. of Elections, 117 Ohio St. 3d 76, 2008-Ohio-333, 881 N.E.2d 1214 (2008)
60 ALR6th 481—§ 4

State ex rel. Tayr Kilaab al Ghashiyah (Khan) v. Sullivan, 235 Wis. 2d 260, 2000 WI App 109, 613 N.W.2d 203 (Ct. App. 2000)
63 ALR6th 1—§ 5, 53

State ex rel. Thornburg v. Tavern and Other Bldgs. and Lots at 1907 N. Main St., Kannapolis, N.C., 96 N.C. App. 84, 384 S.E.2d 585 (1989)
58 ALR6th 385—§ 53

State ex rel. Webster v. Webster, 196 Or. 532, 250 P.2d 403 (1952)

State ex rel. Willke v. Taft, 107 Ohio St. 3d 1, 2005-Ohio-5303, 836 N.E.2d 536 (2005)
60 ALR6th 481—§ 4

State Farm Auto. Ins. Co. v. Alexander, 62 Ohio St. 3d 397, 583 N.E.2d 309 (1992)
33 ALR5th 121—§ 8

State Farm Auto. Ins. Co. v. Blanco, 208 A.D.2d 933, 617 N.Y.S.2d 898 (2d Dep't 1994)
16 ALR6th 491—§ 7

State Farm Auto. Ins. Co. v. Cabuzzi, 123 N.H. 451, 462 A.2d 129 (1983)
55 ALR5th 747—§ 3

State Farm Auto. Ins. Co. v. Chatham Development, Corp., 1995 WL 347836 (Ohio Ct. App. 10th Dist. Franklin County 1995)
104 ALR6th 1—§ 19

State Farm Auto. Ins. Co. v. Hafley, 1991 WL 46696 (Tenn. Ct. App. 1991)
57 ALR5th 141—§ 2, 15

State Farm Auto. Ins. Co. v. Kiehne, 97 N.M. 470, 641 P.2d 501 (1982)
33 ALR5th 121—§ 2, 7, 36

State Farm Auto. Ins. Co. v. Morris, 612 So. 2d 440 (Ala. 1993)
6 ALR5th 297—§ 7

State Farm Automobile Insurance Co. v. Greer, 777 P.2d 941, 55 Ed. Law Rep. 316 (Okla. 1989)
58 ALR5th 511—§ 3

State Farm Automobile Insurance Company v. Barth, 579 So. 2d 154 (Fla. App. D5 1991)
42 ALR5th 727—§ 2, 3

State Farm Cas. v. Black & Decker, 2002-Ohio-5821, 2002 WL 31398693 (Ohio Ct. App. 8th Dist. Cuyahoga County 2002)
122 ALR5th 515—§ 4

State Farm Fire and Cas. Co. v. All Elec., Inc., 99 Nev. 222, 660 P.2d 995 (1983)
5 ALR6th 497—§ 8 to 10

State Farm Fire and Cas. Co. v. Bongen, 925 P.2d 1042 (Alaska 1996)

37 ALR6th 657—§ 4, 7, 10

State Farm Fire & Cas. Co. v. Burkhardt, 96 F. Supp. 2d 1343 (M.D. Ala. 2000)

35 ALR5th 375—§ 49

97 ALR5th 473—§ 3, 16

State Farm Fire & Cas. Co. v. Caley, 936 S.W.2d 250 (Mo. Ct. App. W.D. 1997)

8 ALR5th 254—§ 5

State Farm Fire and Cas. Co. v. Darsie, 161 N.C. App. 542, 589 S.E.2d 391 (2003)

23 ALR6th 697—§ 11

State Farm Fire and Cas. Co. v. Davis, 612 So. 2d 458 (Ala. 1993)

94 ALR5th 567—§ 2

State Farm Fire and Cas. Co. v. Dayco Products, Inc., 19 A.D.3d 923, 798 N.Y.S.2d 159 (3d Dep't 2005)

104 ALR6th 97—§ 9

State Farm Fire & Cas. Co. v. Gandy, 925 S.W.2d 696 (Tex. 1996)

22 ALR5th 483—§ 3

State Farm Fire & Cas. Co. v. Gibson Products of Sulphur, 346 So. 2d 1287 (La. Ct. App. 3d Cir. 1977)

3 ALR6th 355—§ 15

State Farm Fire & Cas. Co. v. Glass, 421 So. 2d 759 (Fla. Dist. Ct. App. 4th Dist. 1982)

103 ALR5th 1—§ 4

State Farm Fire and Cas. Co. v. Groff, 2011 WL 3937317 (E.D. Okla. 2011)

90 ALR6th 635—§ 25

State Farm Fire & Cas. Co. v. Gros, 818 S.W.2d 908 (Tex. App. Austin 1991)

117 ALR5th 155—§ 6, 11

State Farm Fire & Cas. Co. v. Guest, 203 Ga. App. 711, 417 S.E.2d 419 (1992)

79 ALR5th 289—§ 13, 14

State Farm Fire & Cas. Co. v. Housing Authority of Crisfield, 1995 WL 131295 (D. Md. 1995)

98 ALR5th 1—§ 3, 4

State Farm Fire and Cas. Co. v. Jones, 329 Ill. App. 3d 219, 263 Ill. Dec. 724, 768 N.E.2d 805 (2d Dist. 2002)

17 ALR6th 1—§ 10

State Farm Fire and Cas. Co. v. Keenan, 953 F. Supp. 103 (E.D. Pa. 1997)

110 ALR5th 465—§ 2, 19

State Farm Fire & Cas. Co. v. Lambert, 291 Ala. 645, 285 So. 2d 917 (1973)

78 ALR5th 341—§ 3

State Farm Fire and Cas. Co. v. Martin, 872 F.2d 319 (9th Cir. 1989)

37 ALR6th 657—§ 5

State Farm Fire & Cas. Co. v. Middleton, 65 F. Supp. 2d 1240 (M.D. Ala. 1999)

35 ALR5th 375—§ 31

State Farm Fire and Cas. Co. v. Otto, 106 F.3d 279 (9th Cir. 1997)

75 ALR6th 235—§ 4, 22

State Farm Fire and Cas. Co. v. Pacific Rent-All, Inc., 90 Haw. 315, 978 P.2d 753 (1999)

125 ALR5th 1—§ 4

State Farm Fire and Cas. Co. v. Plutsky, 848 F.2d 199 (9th Cir. 1988)

97 ALR5th 473—§ 3, 13

State Farm Fire and Cas. Co. v. Sawyer, 522 So. 2d 248 (Ala. 1988)

84 ALR5th 69—§ 21

State Farm Fire & Cas. Co. v. Slade, 747 So. 2d 293 (Ala. 1999)

37 ALR6th 657—§ 4, 10

State Farm Fire & Cas. Co. v. Sundance Development Corp., 2003 UT App 367, 78 P.3d 995, 485 Utah Adv. Rep. 32, 2003 WL 22410626 (Utah Ct. App. 2003)

122 ALR5th 1—§ 9

State Farm Fire and Cas. Co. v. Super City, Inc., 125 Mich. App. 65, 335 N.W.2d 714 (1983)

17 ALR6th 1—§ 19

State Farm Fire & Cas. Co. v. T.B. ex rel. Bruce, 762 N.E.2d 1227 (Ind. 2002)

120 ALR5th 559—§ 10

State Farm Fire and Cas. Co. v. Vaughan, 968 S.W.2d 931 (Tex. 1998)

35 ALR5th 375—§ 10

State Farm Fire and Cas. Co. v. Weiss, 194 P.3d 1063, 50 A.L.R.6th 593 (Colo. App. 2008)

50 ALR6th 53—§ 3 to 5

64 ALR6th 473—§ 8

State Farm Fire & Cas. Co. v. Westchester Inv. Co., 721 F. Supp. 1165 (C.D. Cal. 1989)

97 ALR5th 473—§ 13, 14

State Farm Fire and Cas. Co. v. Yapejian, 152 Ill. 2d 533, 178 Ill. Dec. 745, 605 N.E.2d 539 (1992)

103 ALR5th 1—§ 4, 6

State Farm Fire & Cas. Co., State ex rel. v. Madden, 192 W. Va. 155, 451 S.E.2d 721 (1994)

105 ALR5th 1—§ 23

State Farm Fire & Casualty Co. v. Century Indemnity Co., 59 Cal. App. 4th 648, 69 Cal. Rptr. 2d 403 (6th Dist. 1997)

94 ALR5th 567—§ 2, 4

State Farm Fire & Casualty Co. v. Drasin, 152 Cal. App. 3d 864, 199 Cal. Rptr. 749 (2d Dist. 1984)

35 ALR5th 375—§ 3, 17

State Farm Fire & Casualty Co. v. Eddy, 218 Cal. App. 3d 958, 267 Cal. Rptr. 379 (6th Dist. 1990)

8 ALR5th 254—§ 5, 10, 13

State Farm Fire & Casualty Co. v. Ezrin, 764 F. Supp. 153 (N.D. Cal. 1991)

8 ALR5th 254—§ 10

State Farm Fire & Casualty Co. v. Friend, 478 So. 2d 1198, 10 FLW 2681 (Fla. App. D4 1985)

35 ALR5th 375—§ 8, 19

State Farm Fire & Casualty Co. v. Geary, 699 F. Supp. 756 (N.D. Cal. 1987)

35 ALR5th 375—§ 3, 31

State Farm Fire & Casualty Co. v. Helminiak, 74 Ohio Misc. 2d 91, 659 N.E.2d 385 (CP Ct. 1995)

58 ALR5th 483—§ 3, 5

State Farm Fire & Casualty Co. v. Hiermer, 720 F. Supp. 1310 (S.D. Ohio 1988)

8 ALR5th 254—§ 3, 8, 11

35 ALR5th 375—§ 3, 49, 100

State Farm Fire & Casualty Co. v. Hornback, 217 Kan. 17, 535 P.2d 441 (1975)

9 ALR5th 102—§ 3

State Farm Fire & Casualty Co. v. Irene S., 138 App. Div. 2d 589, 526 N.Y.S.2d 171 (2d Dep't 1988)

8 ALR5th 254—§ 10

State Farm Fire & Casualty Co. v. Jioras, 24 Cal. App. 4th 1619, 29 Cal. Rptr. 2d 840, 94 C.D.O.S. 3364, 94 Daily Journal DAR 6326 (4th Dist. 1994)

35 ALR5th 375—§ 2, 57

State Farm Fire & Casualty Co. v. Moore, 103 Ill. App. 3d 250, 58 Ill. Dec. 609, 430 N.E.2d 641 (2d Dist. 1981)

35 ALR5th 375—§ 3, 11, 71, 75, 77

State Farm Fire & Casualty Co. v. National Union Fire Ins. Co., 87 Ill. App. 2d 15, 230 N.E.2d 513 (2d Dist. 1967)

35 ALR5th 375—§ 83, 96

State Farm Fire & Casualty Co. v. Palma, 555 So. 2d 836, 15 FLW S. 29 (Fla. 1990)

23 ALR5th 241—§ 2, 15

State Farm Fire & Casualty Co. v. Palma, 585 So. 2d 329, 16 FLW D 1979 (Fla. App. D4 1991)

23 ALR5th 241—§ 2

State Farm Fire & Casualty Co. v. Pickard, 849 F.2d 1220 (CA9 Nev. 1988)

8 ALR5th 254—§ 9, 12

State Farm Fire & Casualty Co. v. Ponder, 469 So. 2d 1262 (Ala. 1985)

1 ALR5th 817—§ 14

State Farm Fire & Casualty Co. v. Reed, 826 S.W.2d 659 (Tex. App. Houston (14th Dist.) 1992)
35 ALR5th 375—§ 10

State Farm Fire & Casualty Co. v. Reed, 873 S.W.2d 698, 35 A.L.R.5th 895 (Tex. 1993)
35 ALR5th 375—§ 64, 74, 76

State Farm Fire & Casualty Co. v. Simmons, 857 S.W.2d 126 (Tex. App. Beaumont 1993)
14 ALR5th 242—§ 12

State Farm Fire & Casualty Co. v. Simpson, 477 So. 2d 242 (Miss. 1985)
6 ALR5th 297—§ 6, 19, 35, 49

State Farm Fire & Casualty Co. v. Smith, 907 F.2d 900 (CA9 Nev. 1990)
8 ALR5th 254—§ 10

State Farm Fire & Casualty Co. v. Stinnett, 71 Ill. App. 3d 217, 27 Ill. Dec. 604, 389 N.E.2d 668 (5th Dist. 1979)
35 ALR5th 375—§ 60, 107

State Farm Fire & Casualty Co. v. Stockton, 295 Ark. 560, 750 S.W.2d 945 (1988)
23 ALR5th 241—§ 11

State Farm Fire & Casualty Co. v. Superior Court, 54 Cal. App. 4th 625, 62 Cal. Rptr. 2d 834 (2d Dist. 1997)
9 ALR6th 363—§ 14

State Farm Fire & Casualty Co. v. Superior Court, 215 Cal. App. 3d 1435, 264 Cal. Rptr. 269 (4th Dist. 1989)
30 ALR5th 170—§ 4

State Farm Fire & Casualty Co. v. Tan, 691 F. Supp. 1271 (S.D. Cal. 1988)
16 ALR5th 412—§ 35, 37

State Farm Fire & Casualty Co. v. Thomas, 756 F. Supp. 440 (N.D. Cal. 1991)
8 ALR5th 254—§ 7, 13

State Farm Fire & Casualty Co. v. Von Der Lieth, 54 Cal. 3d 1123, 2 Cal. Rptr. 2d 183, 820 P.2d 285, 91 Daily Journal DAR 15465, 30 A.L.R.5th 786 (1991)
30 ALR5th 170—§ 4, 40, 79, 84

State Farm Fire & Casualty Ins. Co. v. Miceli, 164 Ill. App. 3d 874, 115 Ill. Dec. 832, 518 N.E.2d 357 (1st Dist. 1987)
1 ALR5th 817—§ 13
16 ALR5th 412—§ 39

State Farm Fire & Casualty Ins. Co. v. Walker, 157 Wis. 2d 459, 459 N.W.2d 605 (App. 1990)
16 ALR5th 412—§ 2

State Farm General Ins. Co. v. JT's Frames, Inc., 181 Cal. App. 4th 429, 104 Cal. Rptr. 3d 573 (2d Dist. 2010)
77 ALR6th 1—§ 8

State Farm General Ins. Co. v. Lawlis, 773 S.W.2d 948 (Tex. App. Beaumont 1989)
16 ALR5th 412—§ 11

State Farm General Ins. Co. v. Wood, 1 S.W.3d 658 (Tenn. Ct. App. 1999)
4 ALR5th 117—§ 5

State Farm Gen. Ins. Co. v. Oliver, 658 F. Supp. 1546 (N.D. Ala. 1987)
4 ALR5th 117—§ 2, 3

State Farm Ins. Co. v. American Mfrs. Mut. Ins. Co., 843 P.2d 1210 (Alaska 1992)
23 ALR5th 241—§ 11

State Farm Ins. Co. v. Bullock, 316 Pa. Super. 475, 463 A.2d 463 (1983)
103 ALR5th 1—§ 3

State Farm Ins. Co. v. Chase, 2002 WL 47796 (Minn. Ct. App. 2002)
121 ALR5th 157—§ 17

State Farm Ins. Companies v. Junction Diagnostic Radiology, P.A., 2000 WL 34510270 (N.J. Super. Ct. Law Div. 2000)
69 ALR6th 317—§ 43

State Farm Life Ins. Co. v. Bass, 605 So. 2d 908 (Fla. Dist. Ct. App. 3d Dist. 1992)
118 ALR5th 91—§ 19

State Farm Lloyds v. Kessler, 932 S.W.2d 732 (Tex. App. Fort Worth 1996)
58 ALR5th 483—§ 5

State Farm Lloyds v. Nicolau, 951 S.W.2d 444 (Tex. 1997)

115 ALR5th 589—§ 4

State Farm Mut. Auto. Ins. Co. (Callisto), Matter of, 255 A.D.2d 876, 680 N.Y.S.2d 39 (4th Dep't 1998)

16 ALR6th 491—§ 4

State Farm Mut. Auto. Ins. Co., Petition of, 708 So. 2d 1282 (La. Ct. App. 5th Cir. 1998)

12 ALR5th 577—§ 12

State Farm Mut. Auto. Ins. Co. v. Abramowicz, 386 A.2d 670 (Del. 1978)

77 ALR5th 319—§ 3

78 ALR5th 341—§ 5

State Farm Mut. Auto. Ins. Co. v. Alfarone, 62 A.D.2d 1034, 404 N.Y.S.2d 35 (2d Dep't 1978)

103 ALR5th 1—§ 3

State Farm Mut. Auto. Ins. Co. v. Allstate Ins. Co., 684 S.W.2d 283 (Ky. Ct. App. 1984)

125 ALR5th 1—§ 38

State Farm Mut. Auto. Ins. Co. v. Asuncion, 42 F.3d 1402 (9th Cir. 1994)

16 ALR6th 491—§ 20

State Farm Mut. Auto. Ins. Co. v. Automobile Underwriters, Inc., 371 F.2d 999 (7th Cir. 1967)

110 ALR5th 465—§ 3

State Farm Mut. Auto. Ins. Co. v. Avena, 133 A.D.2d 159, 518 N.Y.S.2d 678 (2d Dep't 1987)

103 ALR5th 1—§ 6

State Farm Mut. Auto. Ins. Co. v. Ballard, 2002-NMSC-030, 132 N.M. 696, 54 P.3d 537 (2002)

110 ALR5th 465—§ 5

State Farm Mut. Auto. Ins. Co. v. Bass, 231 Ga. 269, 201 S.E.2d 444 (1973)

123 ALR5th 259—§ 3

State Farm Mut. Auto. Ins. Co. v. Berg, 70 Or. App. 410, 689 P.2d 959 (1984)

6 ALR5th 297—§ 7

State Farm Mut. Auto. Ins. Co. v. Bermudez, 111 A.D.2d 858, 490 N.Y.S.2d 595 (2d Dep't 1985)

111 ALR5th 1—§ 3

State Farm Mut. Auto. Ins. Co. v. Blystra, 883 F. Supp. 583 (D.C. N.M. 1995)

41 ALR5th 91—§ 3

State Farm Mut. Auto. Ins. Co. v. Board of Regents, 226 Ga. 310, 174 S.E.2d 920 (1970)

33 ALR5th 587—§ 5

State Farm Mut. Auto. Ins. Co. v. Bowers, 255 Va. 581, 500 S.E.2d 212 (1998)

65 ALR5th 649—§ 5

State Farm Mut. Auto. Ins. Co. v. Brown, 48 Ark. App. 136, 892 S.W.2d 519 (1995)

115 ALR5th 589—§ 5

State Farm Mut. Auto. Ins. Co. v. Brudnock, 151 Ariz. 268, 727 P.2d 321 (1986)

77 ALR5th 319—§ 3

78 ALR5th 341—§ 3

State Farm Mut. Auto. Ins. Co. v. Cahoon, 287 Ala. 462, 252 So. 2d 619 (1971)

31 ALR5th 116—§ 5

33 ALR5th 587—§ 5

State Farm Mut. Auto. Ins. Co. v. Calcutt, 340 S.C. 231, 530 S.E.2d 896 (Ct. App. 2000)

31 ALR5th 116—§ 3

State Farm Mut. Auto. Ins. Co. v. Carlson, 130 Ga. App. 27, 202 S.E.2d 213 (1973)

77 ALR5th 319—§ 2

79 ALR5th 289—§ 2, 7

State Farm Mut. Auto. Ins. Co. v. Casualty Reciprocal Exchange, 600 So. 2d 106 (La. App. 2d Cir. 1992)

25 ALR5th 60—§ 5, 8

State Farm Mut. Auto. Ins. Co. v. Clark, 544 So. 2d 1141 (Fla. Dist. Ct. App. 4th Dist. 1989)

102 ALR5th 647—§ 21

State Farm Mut. Auto. Ins. Co. v. Clyde, 920 P.2d 1183 (Utah 1996)

84 ALR5th 687—§ 2, 5

State Farm Mut. Auto. Ins. Co. v. Collins, 75 Ga.App. 335, 43 S.E.2d 277 (1947)

63 ALR5th 427—§ 2

State Farm Mut. Auto. Ins. Co. v. Continental Cas. Co., 264 Wis. 493, 59 N.W.2d 425 (1953)

17 ALR6th 1—§ 24

State Farm Mut. Auto. Ins. Co. v. Crane, 217 Cal. App. 3d 1127, 266 Cal. Rptr. 422 (3d Dist. 1990)

23 ALR5th 75—§ 2, 5

State Farm Mut. Auto. Ins. Co. v. Davis, 122 Cal. App. 3d Supp. 23, 176 Cal. Rptr. 517 (App. Dep't Super. Ct. 1981)

125 ALR5th 1—§ 15

State Farm Mut. Auto. Ins. Co. v. Davis, 937 F.2d 1415 (9th Cir. 1991)

110 ALR5th 465—§ 2, 26

State Farm Mut. Auto. Ins. Co. v. Davis, 937 F.2d 1415 (CA9 Cal. 1991)

41 ALR5th 91—§ 3

State Farm Mut. Auto. Ins. Co. v. Drury, 222 Ga. App. 196, 474 S.E.2d 64 (1996)

116 ALR5th 247—§ 4

State Farm Mut. Auto Ins. Co. v. Dyer, 19 F.3d 514 (CA10 Wyo. 1994)

43 ALR5th 149—§ 3, 15

State Farm Mut. Auto. Ins. Co. v. Elkins, 451 S.W.2d 528 (Tex. Civ. App. Tyler 1970)

125 ALR5th 1—§ 5

State Farm Mut. Auto. Ins. Co. v. Estep, 873 N.E.2d 1021 (Ind. 2007)

64 ALR6th 473—§ 3, 17

State Farm Mut. Auto. Ins. Co. v. Fee, 1990 WL 191938 (E.D. Pa.1990)

103 ALR5th 1—§ 4

State Farm Mut. Auto. Ins. Co. v. Fernandez, 767 F.2d 1299 (9th Cir. 1985)

103 ALR5th 1—§ 11

State Farm Mut. Auto. Ins. Co. v. Ford Motor Co., 736 So. 2d 384 (Miss. Ct. App. 1999)

47 ALR5th 677—§ 4

State Farm Mut. Auto. Ins. Co. v. Ganz, 119 So. 2d 319 (Fla. 3d DCA 1960)

97 ALR6th 567—§ 4, 12

State Farm Mut. Auto. Ins. Co. v. Gazaway, 152 Ga. App. 716, 263 S.E.2d 693 (1979)

66 ALR5th 269—§ 8

State Farm Mut. Auto. Ins. Co. v. Gengelbach, 664 F. Supp. 1275 (W.D. Mo. 1987)

35 ALR5th 375—§ 69, 118

State Farm Mut. Auto. Ins. Co. v. George Hyman Const. Co., 306 Ill. App. 3d 874, 240 Ill. Dec. 62, 715 N.E.2d 749 (4th Dist. 1999)

100 ALR5th 481—§ 3

State Farm Mut. Auto. Ins. Co. v. Gillette, 251 Wis. 2d 561, 2002 WI 31, 641 N.W.2d 662 (2002)

110 ALR5th 465—§ 31

State Farm Mut. Auto. Ins. Co. v. Graham, 860 P.2d 566 (Colo. App. 1993)

33 ALR5th 121—§ 38

State Farm Mut. Auto. Ins. Co. v. Guleserian, 28 Cal. App. 3d 397, 104 Cal. Rptr. 683 (2d Dist. 1972)

103 ALR5th 1—§ 3

State Farm Mut. Auto. Ins. Co. v. Harper, 125 Ga. App. 696, 188 S.E.2d 813 (1972)

123 ALR5th 259—§ 4

State Farm Mut. Auto. Ins. Co. v. Holland, 324 N.C. 466, 380 S.E.2d 100 (1989)

46 ALR5th 557—§ 6

State Farm Mut. Auto. Ins. Co. v. Hollingsworth, 668 F. Supp. 1476 (D.C. Wyo 1987)

43 ALR5th 149—§ 18

State Farm Mut. Auto. Ins. Co. v. Jenkins, 370 So. 2d 1201 (Fla. App. D1 1979)

40 ALR5th 603—§ 9

State Farm Mut. Auto. Ins. Co. v. Jinks, 203 Ga. App. 176, 416 S.E.2d 539 (1992)

123 ALR5th 259—§ 6

State Farm Mut. Auto. Ins. Co. v. Johnson, 72 Wash. App. 580, 871 P.2d 1066 (Div. 1 1994)

66 ALR5th 269—§ 6

State Farm Mut. Auto. Ins. Co. v. Karasek, 22 Ariz. App. 87, 523 P.2d 1324 (1974)

31 ALR5th 116—§ 5

33 ALR5th 587—§ 5

State Farm Mut. Auto. Ins. Co. v. K.A.W., 575 So. 2d 630 (Fla. 1991)

72 ALR6th 563—§ 20, 29

State Farm Mut. Auto. Ins. Co. v. Kentucky School Bd. Ins. Trust, 851 F. Supp. 835, 91 Ed. Law Rep. 968 (E.D. Ky. 1994)

80 ALR6th 389—§ 3

State Farm Mut. Auto. Ins. Co. v. Kuehling, 475 So. 2d 1159 (Miss. 1985)

40 ALR5th 603—§ 4

State Farm Mut. Auto. Ins. Co. v. Kujawa, 782 So. 2d 1003 (Fla. Dist. Ct. App. 4th Dist. 2001)

2 ALR6th 279—§ 28

State Farm Mut. Auto. Ins. Co. v. La-Sage, 262 Ark. 631, 559 S.W.2d 702 (1978)

79 ALR5th 289—§ 5

State Farm Mut. Auto. Ins. Co. v. Levinson, 438 N.W.2d 110 (Minn. App. 1989)

2 ALR5th 922—§ 7

State Farm Mut. Auto. Ins. Co. v. Malmberg, 639 So. 2d 615 (Fla. 1994)

2 ALR6th 279—§ 4

State Farm Mut. Auto. Ins. Co. v. Maloney, 111 A.D.2d 917, 490 N.Y.S.2d 815 (2d Dep't 1985)

16 ALR6th 491—§ 8

State Farm Mut. Auto. Ins. Co. v. Marko, 695 So. 2d 874 (Fla. Dist. Ct. App. 2d Dist. 1997)

119 ALR5th 121—§ 3

121 ALR5th 325—§ 3

State Farm Mut. Auto. Ins. Co. v. Martinez-Lozano, 916 F. Supp. 996, 131 Lab. Cas. (CCH) ¶ 33386 (E.D. Cal. 1996)

110 ALR5th 465—§ 2, 12

State Farm Mut. Auto. Ins. Co. v. Maryland Auto. Ins. Fund, 277 Md. 602, 356 A.2d 560 (1976)

78 ALR5th 341—§ 3

State Farm Mut. Auto. Ins. Co. v. Matlock, 446 S.W.2d 81 (Tex. Civ. App. Texarkana 1969)

77 ALR5th 319—§ 3

State Farm Mut. Auto. Ins. Co. v. Matlock, 462 S.W.2d 277 (Tex. 1970)

77 ALR5th 319—§ 3

State Farm Mut. Auto. Ins. Co. v. McMillan, 925 P.2d 785 (Colo. 1996)

86 ALR6th 321—§ 9, 10, 12 to 13

87 ALR6th 197—§ 40, 62

91 ALR6th 171—§ 41, 43

State Farm Mut. Auto. Ins. Co. v. Mitchell, 553 S.W.2d 691 (Ky. 1977)

77 ALR5th 319—§ 10

State Farm Mut. Auto. Ins. Co. v. Moore, 597 So. 2d 805, 17 FLW D 175 (Fla. App. D2 1992)

23 ALR5th 241—§ 11

State Farm Mut. Auto. Ins. Co. v. Murphy, 263 Ill. App. 3d 100, 200 Ill. Dec. 194, 635 N.E.2d 533 (1st Dist. 1994)

31 ALR5th 116—§ 3, 6, 7

State Farm Mut. Auto. Ins. Co. v. Norman, 191 W. Va. 498, 446 S.E.2d 720 (1994)

79 ALR5th 289—§ 14

State Farm Mut. Auto Ins. Co. v. North River Ins. Co., 288 S.C. 374, 342 S.E.2d 627 (App. 1986)

43 ALR5th 149—§ 3

State Farm Mut. Auto. Ins. Co. v. Northwestern Nat. Ins. Co., 912 P.2d 983 (Utah 1996)

125 ALR5th 1—§ 41

State Farm Mut. Auto. Ins. Co. v. Novotny, 657 So. 2d 1210 (Fla. Dist. Ct. App. 5th Dist. 1995)

For assistance, call 1-800-328-4880

7 ALR6th 563—§ 5
21 ALR6th 671—§ 5
State Farm Mut. Auto. Ins. Co. v. Partridge, 10 Cal. 3d 94, 109 Cal. Rptr. 811, 514 P.2d 123 (1973)
30 ALR5th 170—§ 4
State Farm Mut. Auto. Ins. Co. v. Peninsula Ins. Co., 585 A.2d 1313 (Del. Super. 1988)
25 ALR5th 60—§ 2
State Farm Mut. Auto. Ins. Co. v. Penland, 668 So. 2d 200 (Fla. Dist. Ct. App. 4th Dist. 1995)
62 ALR5th 537—§ 4
State Farm Mut. Auto. Ins. Co. v. Pharr, 305 Ark. 459, 808 S.W.2d 769 (1991)
23 ALR5th 1—§ 20
State Farm Mut. Auto. Ins. Co. v. Pichay, 834 F. Supp. 329 (D.C. Hawaii 1993)
41 ALR5th 91—§ 3
State Farm Mut. Auto. Ins. Co. v. Pierce, 182 Neb. 805, 157 N.W.2d 399 (1968)
33 ALR5th 121—§ 2, 11, 18
State Farm Mut. Auto. Ins. Co. v. Raglan, 164 Misc. 2d 790, 626 N.Y.S.2d 356 (Sup. 1995)
40 ALR5th 603—§ 4
State Farm Mut. Auto. Ins. Co. v. Ramsey, 295 S.C. 349, 368 S.E.2d 477 (Ct. App. 1988)
96 ALR5th 107—§ 6
State Farm Mut. Auto. Ins. Co. v. Reynolds, 676 F. Supp. 106 (W.D. Va. 1987)
6 ALR5th 883—§ 5, 6, 8
17 ALR6th 1—§ 12
State Farm Mut. Auto. Ins. Co. v. Robinson, 129 Idaho 447, 926 P.2d 631 (1996)
110 ALR5th 465—§ 2, 20
State Farm Mut. Auto. Ins. Co. v. Roe, 226 Mich. App. 258, 573 N.W.2d 628 (1997)
43 ALR5th 149—§ 3, 5, 8, 10, 17

State Farm Mut. Auto. Ins. Co. v. Rutkin, 199 So. 2d 705 (Fla. 1967)
103 ALR5th 1—§ 2
State Farm Mut. Auto. Ins. Co. v. Selders, 187 Neb. 342, 190 N.W.2d 789 (1971)
66 ALR5th 269—§ 3
State Farm Mut. Auto. Ins. Co. v. Self, 93 F.2d 139 (C.C.A. 5th Cir. 1937)
57 ALR5th 591—§ 5
State Farm Mut. Auto. Ins. Co. v. Sellers, 2012 WL 1110105 (N.D. Ind. 2012)
75 ALR6th 235—§ 25
State Farm Mut. Auto. Ins. Co. v. Sewell, 223 Ga. 31, 153 S.E.2d 432 (1967)
100 ALR5th 293—§ 6
State Farm Mut. Auto. Ins. Co. v. Smalley Transport Co., 696 So. 2d 522 (Fla. Dist. Ct. App. 3d Dist. 1997)
125 ALR5th 1—§ 9
State Farm Mut. Auto. Ins. Co. v. Smith, 129 Misc. 2d 828, 494 N.Y.S.2d 647 (Sup. Ct. 1985)
79 ALR5th 289—§ 11
State Farm Mut. Auto. Ins. Co. v. Smith, 197 Ill. 2d 369, 259 Ill. Dec. 18, 757 N.E.2d 881 (2001)
123 ALR5th 259—§ 4
State Farm Mut. Auto. Ins. Co. v. Smith, 281 S.C. 209, 314 S.E.2d 333 (1984)
82 ALR6th 497—§ 28
State Farm Mut. Auto. Ins. Co. v. Smith, 565 So. 2d 751 (Fla. Dist. Ct. App. 5th Dist. 1990)
62 ALR5th 537—§ 4
State Farm Mut. Auto. Ins. Co. v. Spinola, 374 F.2d 873 (5th Cir. 1967)
79 ALR5th 289—§ 7
State Farm Mut. Auto. Ins. Co. v. Spotten, 610 N.E.2d 299 (Ind. Ct. App. 3d Dist. 1993)
41 ALR5th 91—§ 3
79 ALR5th 289—§ 18
State Farm Mut. Auto. Ins. Co. v. Staff, 26 Ill. App. 3d 217, 325 N.E.2d 1 (4th Dist. 1975)

For assistance, call 1-800-328-4880

CASES CITED IN ALR5th and ALR6th

43 ALR5th 149—§ 11, 17
State Farm Mut. Auto. Ins. Co. v. Stanford, 728 F. Supp. 363 (E.D. Pa. 1990)

103 ALR5th 1—§ 4
State Farm Mut. Auto. Ins. Co. v. State, 124 N.J. 32, 590 A.2d 191 (1991)

63 ALR6th 1—§ 46
State Farm Mut. Auto. Ins. Co. v. Stein, 886 P.2d 326 (Colo. Ct. App. 1994)

103 ALR5th 1—§ 13
State Farm Mut. Auto. Ins. Co. v. Superior Court, 23 Cal. App. 4th 1297, 28 Cal. Rptr. 2d 711 (2d Dist. 1994)

103 ALR5th 1—§ 23
State Farm Mut. Auto. Ins. Co. v. Szwec, 36 A.D.2d 863, 321 N.Y.S.2d 800 (2d Dep't 1971)

103 ALR5th 1—§ 5
State Farm Mut. Auto. Ins. Co. v. Thomas, 316 Ark. 345, 871 S.W.2d 571 (1994)

116 ALR5th 247—§ 7
State Farm Mut. Auto. Ins. Co. v. Valencia, 120 N.M. 662, 905 P.2d 202 (App. 1995)

40 ALR5th 603—§ 10
State Farm Mut. Auto. Ins. Co. v. Vaughn, 253 Ga. App. 217, 558 S.E.2d 769, 161 Ed. Law Rep. 1045 (2002)

80 ALR6th 389—§ 6
State Farm Mut. Auto. Ins. Co. v. Wallace, 743 So. 2d 448 (Ala. 1999)

23 ALR5th 75—§ 3
State Farm Mut. Auto. Ins. Co. v. Washington, 641 A.2d 449 (Del. Sup. 1994)

33 ALR5th 121—§ 7
State Farm Mut. Auto. Ins. Co. v. Wee, 196 N.W.2d 54 (N.D. 1971)

125 ALR5th 1—§ 40
State Farm Mut. Auto. Ins. Co. v. Weiford, 831 P.2d 1264 (Alaska 1992)

115 ALR5th 589—§ 3
State Farm Mut. Auto. Ins. Co. v. Worrell, 1991 WL 133644 (E.D. Pa.1991)

103 ALR5th 1—§ 20
State Farm Mut. Auto. Ins. Co. v. Wrap-On Co., 626 So. 2d 874 (La. App. 3d Cir. 1993)

29 ALR5th 534—§ 13, 33
State Farm Mut. Auto. Ins. Co. v. W.R. Grace & Co., 834 F. Supp. 1046 (C.D. Ill. 1992)

81 ALR5th 483—§ 5
24 ALR6th 497—§ 7
State Farm Mut. Auto. Ins. Co. v. W.R. Grace & Co., 834 F. Supp. 1052 (C.D. Ill. 1993)

5 ALR6th 497—§ 11
State Farm Mut. Auto. Ins. Co. v. W.R. Grace & Company-Conn., 24 F.3d 955, Prod. Liab. Rep. (CCH) ¶ 13994 (7th Cir. 1994)

122 ALR5th 1—§ 37
5 ALR6th 497—§ 3
State Farm Mut. Auto. Ins. Co. v. Wright, 245 Ga. App. 493, 538 S.E.2d 147 (2000)

125 ALR5th 1—§ 5
State Farm Mut. Auto. Ins. Co. v. Yang, 35 Cal. App. 4th 563, 41 Cal. Rptr. 2d 210 (5th Dist. 1995)

41 ALR5th 91—§ 4
79 ALR5th 289—§ 18
State Farm Mut. Auto. Ins. Co. v. Zubiate, 808 S.W.2d 590 (Tex. App. El Paso 1991)

14 ALR5th 242—§ 12
State Farm Mut. Auto. Owners Co. v. Venia, 1989 WL 135304 (Ohio Ct. App. 6th Dist.Lucas County 1989)

58 ALR5th 511—§ 3
State Farm Mut. Ins. Co. v. Blevins, 49 Ohio St. 3d 165, 551 N.E.2d 955 (1990)

103 ALR5th 1—§ 40
State Farm Mut. Ins. Co. v. Del Pizzo, 185 A.D.2d 352, 586 N.Y.S.2d 310 (2d Dep't 1992)

16 ALR6th 491—§ 4, 8
State Farm Mut. Ins. Co. v. Donath, 164 A.D.2d 889, 559 N.Y.S.2d 567 (2d Dep't 1990)

State Highway Com. v. Stadler, 158 Kan. 289, 148 P.2d 296 (1944)
31 ALR5th 171—§ 2, 11, 12, 20

State Highway Commission v. Demarest, 263 Or. 590, 503 P.2d 682 (1972)
107 ALR5th 311—§ 10
109 ALR5th 421—§ 2 to 4, 12 to 14

State Highway Commission v. Earl, 82 S.D. 139, 143 N.W.2d 88 (1966)
66 ALR6th 83—§ 18

State Highway Commission v. Moore, 204 Kan. 502, 464 P.2d 188 (1970)
49 ALR6th 205—§ 23

State Highway Commission v. Southern Union Gas Co., 65 N.M. 84, 332 P.2d 1007, 75 A.L.R.2d 408 (1958)
122 ALR5th 337—§ 14

State Highway Commission, State ex rel. v. Steinkraus, 76 N.M. 617, 417 P.2d 431 (1966)
66 ALR6th 83—§ 18

State Highway Commission, State ex rel. v. Wally Hutter Oil Co., 467 S.W.2d 279 (Mo. Ct. App. 1971)
107 ALR5th 311—§ 6, 9

State Highway Comm'n v. West Great Falls Flood Control & Drainage Dist., 155 Mont. 157, 468 P.2d 753 (1970)
36 ALR5th 657—§ 7

State Highway Com'n of Wyoming v. Brasel & Sims Const. Co., Inc., 688 P.2d 871 (Wyo. 1984)
124 ALR5th 375—§ 3, 5, 8, 11

State Highway Com'n, State ex rel. v. Union Electric Co. of Missouri, 142 S.W.2d 1099 (Mo. Ct. App. 1940)
122 ALR5th 337—§ 16

State Highway Comr. v. Howard, 213 Va. 731, 195 S.E.2d 880 (1973)
15 ALR5th 821—§ 2, 11

State Highway Com., State ex rel. v. Beaty, 505 S.W.2d 147 (Mo. App. 1974)
31 ALR5th 171—§ 10

State Highway Com., State ex rel. v. Grants, 69 N.M. 145, 364 P.2d 853 (1961)
11 ALR5th 630—§ 12

State Highway Com., State ex rel. v. Lavasek, 73 N.M. 33, 385 P.2d 361 (1963)
7 ALR5th 113—§ 6

State Highway Com., State ex rel. v. St. Charles County Associates, 698 S.W.2d 34 (Mo. App. 1985)
22 ALR5th 327—§ 58

State Highway Dep't v. Hinson, 517 S.W.2d 308 (Tex. Civ. App. Corpus Christi 1974)
62 ALR5th 537—§ 3

State Highway Dept., State ex rel. v. 62.96247 Acres of Land, More or Less, in New Castle Hundred, New Castle County, 57 Del. 40, 193 A.2d 799 (Super. Ct. 1963)
66 ALR6th 83—§ 17

State Highway Dep't, State ex rel. v. Hidalgo Area Development Corp., 94 N.M. 63, 607 P.2d 601 (1980)
61 ALR5th 739—§ 2, 3, 7

State Hosp., State ex rel. v. Hintz, 281 N.W.2d 564 (N.D. 1979)
49 ALR5th 1—§ 10

State, Indiana Dept. of Revenue v. Adams, 762 N.E.2d 728 (Ind. 2002)
105 ALR5th 1—§ 3, 14

State, Indiana State Highway Com. v. Speidel, 181 Ind. App. 448, 392 N.E.2d 1172 (1979)
3 ALR5th 1—§ 3, 4, 9

State Indus. Acc. Commission v. Eggiman, 172 Or. 19, 139 P.2d 565 (1943)
40 ALR6th 99—§ 28

State Indus. Ins. System v. Buckley, 100 Nev. 376, 682 P.2d 1387 (1984)
109 ALR5th 161—§ 4, 7, 8

State Indus. Ins. System v. Jesch, 101 Nev. 690, 709 P.2d 172 (1985)
100 ALR5th 567—§ 9

State Indus. Ins. System v. Lodge, 107 Nev. 867, 822 P.2d 664 (1991)

100 ALR5th 567—§ 9

State Industrial Ins. System v. Woodall, 106 Nev. 653, 799 P.2d 552 (1990)

16 ALR5th 191—§ 2, 17

State in Interest of C., In re, 121 N.J. Super. 108, 296 A.2d 102 (1972)

31 ALR5th 229—§ 3, 17, 46, 77

State in Interest of C.V. v. T.V., 499 So. 2d 159 (La. App. 2d Cir. 1986)

53 ALR5th 499—§ 5

State in Interest of D.A.C., 933 P.2d 993 (Utah Ct. App. 1997)

63 ALR6th 429—§ 3

State in Interest of HLD v. CDM, 563 So. 2d 360 (La. App. 3d Cir. 1990)

53 ALR5th 499—§ 2, 5

State in Interest of L.L.Z. v. M.Y.S., 620 So. 2d 1309 (La. 1993)

20 ALR5th 534—§ 14

State in Interest of M.W.H. v. Aguilar, 794 P.2d 27 (Utah Ct. App. 1990)

61 ALR5th 151—§ 8

State, In re v. S.D.K., 2008-Ohio-3515, 2008 WL 2732180 (Ohio Ct. App. 12th Dist. Warren County 2008)

89 ALR6th 565—§ 17, 27, 29, 31, 33

State Ins. Co. v. Maackens, 38 NJL 564 (1876)

16 ALR5th 412—§ 14

State Ins. Fund v. Hamblin, 31 Misc. 2d 977, 222 N.Y.S.2d 732 (Sup 1961)

114 ALR5th 561—§ 20

State Ins. Fund v. Industrial Commission, 15 Utah 2d 363, 393 P.2d 397 (1964)

42 ALR6th 61—§ 4

State Ins. Fund v. Industrial Commission, 16 Utah 2d 269, 399 P.2d 208 (1965)

86 ALR5th 295—§ 3

State Ins. Fund, State ex rel. v. Bone, 344 P.2d 562 (Okla. 1959)

21 ALR5th 82—§ 3, 22

State in the Interest of S.C. v. D.N.C., 639 So. 2d 426 (La. App. 2d Cir. 1994)

20 ALR5th 534—§ 14

State in the Interest of Travers v. Travers, 665 So. 2d 625 (La. App. 2d Cir. 1995)

57 ALR5th 389—§ 16

State, Labor Dept. v. America's Cup, 11 Conn. L. Rptr. 379, 1994 WL 162415 (Conn. Super. Ct. 1994)

61 ALR6th 61—§ 7, 11

State, Lake Minnetonka Conservation District v. Horner, 617 N.W.2d 789 (Minn. 2000)

47 ALR6th 107—§ 22, 32, 33

State Legislature—1982, In re Apportionment of, 413 Mich. 96, 321 N.W.2d 565 (1982)

114 ALR5th 311—§ 2 to 4

State Licensing Board for Healing Arts v. Alabama Board of Podiatry, 287 Ala. 132, 249 So. 2d 611 (1971)

10 ALR5th 1—§ 3

State Line Fishing & Hunting Club, Inc. v. City of Waskom, Tex., 754 F. Supp. 1104, 21 Envtl. L. Rep. 21095 (E.D. Tex. 1991)

92 ALR5th 517—§ 10

State, MCS City of Kettering v. West, 1995 WL 371095 (Ohio Ct. App. 2d Dist. Montgomery County 1995)

56 ALR6th 323—§ 7, 11

State Med. Bd. of Ohio v. Murray, 66 Ohio St. 3d 527, 1993-Ohio-14, 613 N.E.2d 636 (1993)

65 ALR6th 295—§ 12

State, Michigan State Treasurer v. Turner, 110 Mich. App. 228, 312 N.W.2d 418 (1981)

13 ALR5th 872—§ 16

Stat EMS, LLC v. Emergency M.E.D. Stat, LLC, 2008 WL 1733375 (Mich. Ct. App. 2008)

43 ALR6th 611—§ 9, 46

State Mut. Auto. Ins. Co. v. Mercado, 70 A.D.2d 513, 415 N.Y.S.2d 864 (1st Dep't 1979)

103 ALR5th 1—§ 6, 9

State Mut. Cyclone Ins. Co. v. Abbott, 52 Mich. App. 103, 216 N.W.2d 606 (1974)

35 ALR5th 375—§ 2, 3, 7, 30, 69, 96

State Mut. Ins. Co. v. Russell, 185 Mich. App. 521, 462 N.W.2d 785 (1990)

35 ALR5th 375—§ 3, 7, 13, 69, 82

Staten v. Ohio Exterminating Co., Inc., 123 Ohio App. 3d 526, 704 N.E.2d 621 (10th Dist. Franklin County 1997)

13 ALR5th 217—§ 11

Staten v. State, 140 Ga. 110, 78 S.E. 766 (1913)

105 ALR5th 529—§ 11

Staten v. Steel, 222 Or. App. 17, 191 P.3d 778 (2008)

54 ALR6th 99—§ 35

Staten v. Superior Court, 45 Cal. App. 4th 1628, 53 Cal. Rptr. 2d 657 (1st Dist. 1996)

66 ALR5th 135—§ 21

State, New York State Dept. of Agriculture and Markets (Public Employees Federation Inc.), In re, 277 A.D.2d 564, 715 N.Y.S.2d 101, 166 L.R.R.M. (BNA) 2126 (3d Dep't 2000)

112 ALR5th 263—§ 75

State, o/b/o Genessee County v. Christenson, 1999 WL 1071564 (Ohio Ct. App. 5th Dist. Delaware County 1999)

90 ALR5th 1—§ 32

State Office for Services to Children and Families, State ex rel. v. Armijo, 151 Or. App. 666, 950 P.2d 357 (1997)

20 ALR5th 534—§ 3

State Office for Services to Children and Families, State ex rel. v. Chapman, 169 Or. App. 168

1 ALR5th 469—§ 17

State Office for Services to Children and Families, State ex rel. v. Chapman, 169 Or. App. 168, 8 P.3d 243 (2000)

12 ALR6th 417—§ 6

State Office for Services to Children and Families, State ex rel. v. Hammons, 170 Or. App. 287, 12 P.3d 983 (2000)

1 ALR5th 469—§ 14

State Office for Services to Children and Families, State ex rel. v. Klamath Tribe, 170 Or. App. 106, 11 P.3d 701, 89 A.L.R.5th 699 (2000)

89 ALR5th 195—§ 3

State Office for Services to Children and Families, State ex rel. v. Mellor, 181 Or. App. 468, 47 P.3d 19 (2002)

12 ALR6th 417—§ 14

State Office for Services to Children and Families, State ex rel. v. Mendez, 162 Or. App. 601, 986 P.2d 670 (1999)

1 ALR5th 469—§ 12

State Office for Services to Children and Families, State ex rel. v. Stillman, 167 Or. App. 446

20 ALR5th 534—§ 3

State, Office of Attorney General, Dept. of Legal Affairs v. Commerce Commercial Leasing, LLC, 946 So. 2d 1253 (Fla. Dist. Ct. App. 1st Dist. 2007)

48 ALR6th 511—§ 21

State, Office of Health Care Access v. Housatonic Valley Radiology Associates, P.C., 2009 WL 1424662 (Conn. Super. Ct. 2009)

63 ALR6th 1—§ 5, 17, 37, 47

State, Office of State Attorney for Thirteenth Judicial Circuit v. Powell, 586 So. 2d 1180 (Fla. Dist. Ct. App. 2d Dist. 1991)

90 ALR5th 273—§ 3, 4, 10, 11

State on Behalf of Dunn v. Wiegand, 2 Neb. App. 580, 512 N.W.2d 419 (1994)

86 ALR5th 637—§ 3

State on Behalf of Hendrix v. Waters, 89 Wash. App. 921, 951 P.2d 317 (Div. 1 1998)

20 ALR5th 534—§ 12

State on Behalf of Joseph F. v. Rial, 251 Neb. 1, 554 N.W.2d 769 (1996)

77 ALR5th 201—§ 4

State on Behalf of Matchett v. Dunkle,
244 Neb. 639, 508 N.W.2d 580
(1993)

87 ALR5th 361—§ 9

State, on Inf. of Taylor v. Salary Pur-
chasing Co., 358 Mo. 1022, 218
S.W.2d 571 (1949)

73 ALR6th 571—§ 47, 55

State Personnel Bd. v. Lloyd, 752 P.2d
559, 3 BNA IER Cas. 297 (Colo.
1988)

45 ALR5th 173—§ 4

State Planning, Department of v. Mayor
and Council of City of Hagerstown,
288 Md. 9, 415 A.2d 296 (1980)

47 ALR6th 439—§ 3, 11

State Press Co. v. Willett, 219 Ark. 850,
245 S.W.2d 403 (1952)

12 ALR5th 195—§ 48

State Public Bldg. Asbestos Litigation,
In re, 193 W. Va. 119, 454 S.E.2d
413 (1994)

112 ALR5th 113—§ 29

State Public Works Board, State ex rel.
v. Los Angeles, 256 Cal. App. 2d
930, 64 Cal. Rptr. 476 (2d Dist.
1967)

49 ALR5th 769—§ 2, 11

State Racing Com. v. Robertson, 111
Ohio App. 435, 14 Ohio Ops. 2d
456, 172 N.E.2d 628 (Franklin Co.
1960)

59 ALR5th 203—§ 62

State Racing Comm'n v. McManus, 82
N.M. 108, 476 P.2d 767 (1970)

59 ALR5th 203—§ 27

State Real Estate Com. v. Carroll, 39 Pa.
D. & C.2d 768 (1966)

7 ALR5th 474—§ 90, 166

State Real Estate Com. v. Farkas, 1 Pa.
Cmwlth. 134, 274 A.2d 238 (1971)

7 ALR5th 474—§ 84, 90, 93, 155

State Real Estate Com. v. Harris, 184 Pa.
Super. 667, 136 A.2d 849 (1957)

7 ALR5th 474—§ 46

State Real Estate Com. v. Miller, 21 Pa.
Cmwlth. 483, 346 A.2d 861 (1975)

7 ALR5th 474—§ 22, 72

State Real Estate Com. v. O'Data, 1 Pa.
Cmwlth. 286, 274 A.2d 232 (1971)

7 ALR5th 474—§ 147

State Real Estate Com. v. Roberts, 441
Pa. 159, 271 A.2d 246 (1970)

7 ALR5th 474—§ 160

State Real Estate Com. v. Tice, 200 Pa.
Super. 553, 190 A.2d 188 (1963)

7 ALR5th 474—§ 23

State Real Estate Com. v. Vogel, 21 Pa.
D. & C.2d 797 (1960)

7 ALR5th 474—§ 155

State Real Estate Comm. v. Schnabel, 67
Dauph County 155 (Pa. 1944)

7 ALR5th 474—§ 62

State Real Estate Commission v. Felix,
383 So. 2d 941 (Fla. Dist. Ct. App.
1st Dist. 1980)

112 ALR5th 509—§ 18

13 ALR6th 209—§ 28

39 ALR6th 445—§ 43

State Road Commission v. Utah Power
& Light Co., 10 Utah 2d 333, 353
P.2d 171 (1960)

122 ALR5th 337—§ 14

States v. R.D. Werner Co., Inc., 799 P.2d
427, Prod. Liab. Rep. (CCH)
¶ 12624 (Colo. Ct. App. 1990)

81 ALR5th 245—§ 5

State's Attorney, Cook County, In re
Petition of, 179 Conn. 102, 425
A.2d 588 (1979)

33 ALR5th 453—§ 3

State Sav. Bank v. Hosmer, 95 Mich.
100, 54 N.W. 632 (1893)

20 ALR5th 229—§ 32

States Shingle Co. v. Kaufman, 227 Cal.
App. 2d 830, 39 Cal. Rptr. 196 (3d
Dist. 1964)

104 ALR6th 1—§ 17

States S. S. Co. v. Aetna Ins. Co., 59
B.R. 314, 1985 AMC 2749 (F. N.D.
Cal. 1985)

30 ALR5th 170—§ 50

State Statutes or Ordinances Requiring
Persons Previously Convicted of
Crime to Register with Authorities
as Applied to Juvenile Offenders-

Expungement, Stay or Deferral, Exceptions, Exemptions, and Waiver, 39 A.L.R.6th 577

77 ALR6th 197—§ 1

State Stove Mfg. Co. v. Hodges, 189 So. 2d 113 (Miss. 1966)

5 ALR5th 875—§ 48

State Street Auto Sales, Inc., In re, 81 B.R. 215, 5 U.C.C. Rep. Serv. 2d 1342 (Bankr. D. Mass. 1988)

58 ALR6th 289—§ 2, 26

State Street Bank & Trust Co. v. D'Amario, 368 Mass. 542, 333 N.E.2d 407 (1975)

36 ALR5th 395—§ 4

State Street Bank & Trust Co. v. Mutual Life Ins. Co. of New York, 811 F. Supp. 915 (S.D. N.Y. 1993)

117 ALR5th 155—§ 10

State Street Bank & Trust Co. v. Strawser, 908 F. Supp. 249, 30 U.C.C. Rep. Serv. 2d (CBC) 477 (M.D. Pa. 1995)

89 ALR5th 577—§ 11

State Street Trust Co. v. Ernst, 278 N.Y. 104, 15 N.E.2d 416, 120 A.L.R. 1250 (1938)

48 ALR5th 389—§ 4

State, Support Enforcement Services v. Beasley, 801 So. 2d 515 (La. Ct. App. 3d Cir. 2001)

18 ALR6th 97—§ 38

State Tax Commission v. Board of Education of Holton, 146 Kan. 722, 73 P.2d 49, 115 A.L.R. 1401 (1937)

69 ALR5th 477—§ 2, 20

State Tax Comm'n v. Oliver's Laundry & Dry Cleaning Co., 19 Ariz. App. 442, 508 P.2d 107 (1973)

33 ALR5th 509—§ 2, 18

State Teachers Retirement Bd. v. Board of Tax Appeals, 177 Ohio St. 61, 29 Ohio Op. 2d 187, 202 N.E.2d 418 (1964)

114 ALR5th 561—§ 15

State Teachers Retirement Bd. v. Kinney, 68 Ohio St. 2d 195, 22 Ohio Op. 3d 434, 429 N.E.2d 1069, 1 Ed. Law Rep. 1265 (1981)

114 ALR5th 561—§ 16

State Teachers Retirement System of Ohio, Board of v. Cuyahoga Falls City School Dist. Bd. of Educ., 26 Ohio App. 3d 45, 498 N.E.2d 167, 35 Ed. Law Rep. 266 (9th Dist.Summit County 1985)

56 ALR5th 493—§ 18

State, Through Dept. of Culture, Recreation and Tourism v. Aetna Cas. and Sur. Co., 700 So. 2d 1303 (La. Ct. App. 4th Cir. 1997)

115 ALR5th 589—§ 3

State Through Dep't of Health and Human Resources in Interest of Lymuel v. Duvigneaud, 704 So. 2d 398 (La. Ct. App. 4th Cir. 1997)

87 ALR5th 361—§ 6, 27

State, Through Dept. of Highways v. Bougere, 363 So. 2d 228 (La. Ct. App. 4th Cir. 1978)

49 ALR6th 205—§ 18, 33, 54

State Through Dept. of Highways v. Cefalu, 233 So. 2d 273 (La. Ct. App. 1st Cir. 1970)

49 ALR6th 205—§ 5, 18, 51, 54

State Through Dept. of Highways v. Davis, 149 So. 2d 164 (La. Ct. App. 3d Cir. 1963)

49 ALR6th 205—§ 23

State Through Dept. of Highways v. Hayward, 243 La. 1036, 150 So. 2d 6 (1963)

49 ALR6th 205—§ 23

State, Through Dept. of Highways v. Lutcher & Moore Cypress Lumber Co., Ltd., 364 So. 2d 134 (La. Ct. App. 4th Cir. 1978)

49 ALR6th 205—§ 18, 33, 41, 54

State Through Dept. of Highways v. New Orleans & N. E. R. Co., 194 So. 2d 429 (La. Ct. App. 1st Cir. 1966)

49 ALR6th 205—§ 23

State Through Dept. of Highways v. Neyrey, 186 So. 2d 705 (La. Ct. App. 4th Cir. 1966)

49 ALR6th 205—§ 54

State Through Dept. of Highways v. Ponder, 140 So. 2d 426 (La. Ct. App. 1st Cir. 1962)

49 ALR6th 205—§ 23

State Through Dep't of Social Services, Office of Family Support in Interest of Seals v. Seals, 701 So. 2d 746 (La. Ct. App. 4th Cir. 1997)

39 ALR5th 1—§ 6

State Through DHHR in Interest of Dubroc v. Cole, 460 So. 2d 100 (La. Ct. App. 3d Cir. 1984)

86 ALR5th 637—§ 2, 3

State, to Use of Henning's Heirs v. Keller, 79 Tenn. 399, 1883 WL 3729 (1883)

117 ALR5th 23—§ 6, 20

State, Tp. of Pennsauken v. Schad, 160 N.J. 156, 733 A.2d 1159 (1999)

20 ALR6th 161—§ 3

23 ALR6th 573—§ 11

State Treasurer v. Cuellar, 190 Mich. app 464, 476 N.W.2d 644 (1991)

13 ALR5th 872—§ 20

State Treasurer v. Ulysses Apartments, Inc., 232 App. Div. 393, 250 N.Y.S. 190 (1931)

61 ALR5th 375—§ 5, 7, 14

State Treasurer v. Wilson, 132 Mich. App. 648, 347 N.W.2d 770 (1984)

13 ALR5th 872—§ 2

State Treasurer v. Wilson, 150 Mich. App. 78, 388 N.W.2d 312 (1986)

13 ALR5th 872—§ 7, 8

State Treasurer v. Wilson, 423 Mich. 138, 377 N.W.2d 703 (1985)

13 ALR5th 872—§ 4, 15, 18

State Treasurer on behalf of Department of Corrections v. Brown, 125 Mich. App. 620, 337 N.W.2d 23 (1983)

13 ALR5th 872—§ 6, 11

State Troopers Fraternal Ass'n of New Jersey, Inc. v. State, 149 N.J. 38, 692 A.2d 519, 156 L.R.R.M. (BNA) 2824 (1997)

34 ALR6th 327—§ 6

State Unauthorized Practice of Law Committee v. Paul Mason & Associates, Inc., 46 F.3d 469, 26 Bankr. Ct. Dec. (CRR) 927, Bankr. L. Rep. (CCH) ¶ 76380 (5th Cir. 1995)

32 ALR6th 531—§ 3, 8, 19, 27, 34, 40

State University of New York at Albany v. State Human Rights Appeal Bd., 81 A.D.2d 688, 438 N.Y.S.2d 643, 37 Fair Empl. Prac. Cas. (BNA) 1806, 26 Empl. Prac. Dec. (CCH) ¶ 32056 (3d Dep't 1981)

94 ALR5th 1—§ 4, 11

State upon Information of Reardon v. Mueller, 388 S.W.2d 53 (Mo. Ct. App. 1965)

74 ALR6th 209—§ 3, 18

State use of Miles v. Brainin, 224 Md. 156, 167 A.2d 117, 88 A.L.R.2d 1178 (1961)

43 ALR5th 87—§ 8

State use of Palmer Supply Co. v. Walsh & Co., 575 P.2d 1213, 24 CCF ¶ 82266 (Alaska 1978)

23 ALR5th 241—§ 9

State use of Parr v. Board of County Comrs., 207 Md. 91, 113 A.2d 397 (1955)

23 ALR5th 1—§ 2, 13

State use of Standard Supply Co. v. Vance Plumbing & Electric Co., 195 N.C. 629, 143 S.E. 248 (1928)

54 ALR5th 649—§ 3, 4

Statewide Grievance Committee v. Goldstein, 1996 WL 753092 (Conn. Super. Ct. 1996)

32 ALR6th 531—§ 39

Statewide Grievance Committee v. Griffin, 1996 WL 219601 (Conn. Super. Ct. 1996)

43 ALR6th 163—§ 19

Statewide Grievance Committee v. Hochberg, 25 Conn. L. Rptr. 212, 1999 WL 566865 (Conn. Super. Ct. 1999)

43 ALR6th 163—§ 20

Statewide Grievance Committee v. Patton, 15 Conn. L. Rptr. 124, 1995 WL 569416 (Conn. Super. Ct. 1995)

32 ALR6th 531—§ 39

Statewide Grievance Committee v. Patton, 239 Conn. 251, 683 A.2d 1359 (1996)

32 ALR6th 531—§ 39

Statewide Grievance Committee v. Sablone, 1994 WL 62264 (Conn. Super. Ct. 1994)

43 ALR6th 163—§ 3, 16
44 ALR6th 75—§ 3
45 ALR6th 175—§ 3

Statewide Grievance Committee v. Tartaglia, 2003 WL 22904558 (Conn. Super. Ct. 2003)

45 ALR6th 175—§ 26

Statewide Grievance Committee v. Zadora, 62 Conn. App. 828, 772 A.2d 681 (2001)

40 ALR6th 463—§ 3, 20

Statewide Roofing, Inc. v. Eastern Suffolk Bd. of Co-op. Educational Services, 173 Misc. 2d 514, 661 N.Y.S.2d 922, 120 Ed. Law Rep. 1134 (Sup. Ct. 1997)

49 ALR5th 747—§ 3

State-William Partnership v. Gale, 169 Mich. App. 170, 425 N.W.2d 756 (1988)

8 ALR5th 312—§ 3

State Workmen's Ins. Fund v. Workmen's Compensation Appeal Bd., 677 A.2d 892 (Pa. Cmwlth. 1996)

14 ALR5th 1—§ 10

State Y.M.C.A. v. Industrial Commission, 235 Wis. 161, 292 N.W. 324 (1940)

11 ALR6th 351—§ 27, 29

Statham v. Domyan, 153 Ill. App. 3d 1003, 106 Ill. Dec. 813, 506 N.E.2d 613 (5th Dist. 1987)

40 ALR5th 697—§ 5, 7, 13, 23

Statham v. State, 41 Ga. 507 (1871)

66 ALR5th 397—§ 4

Static Control Components, Inc. v. Lexmark Intern., Inc., 697 F.3d 387, 104 U.S.P.Q.2d 1352, 2012-2 Trade Cas. (CCH) ¶ 78027 (6th Cir. 2012)

86 ALR6th 577—§ 6
96 ALR6th 577—§ 4

Station v. W.C.A.B. (Pittsburgh Steelers Sports Inc.), 147 Pa. Commw. 512, 608 A.2d 625 (1992)

112 ALR5th 365—§ 9

Stations West, LLC v. Pinnacle Bank of OR, 338 Fed. Appx. 658 (9th Cir. 2009)

81 ALR6th 161—§ 5
82 ALR6th 43—§ 13

Statler v. Catalano, 167 Ill. App. 3d 397, 118 Ill. Dec. 283, 521 N.E.2d 565 (5th Dist. 1988)

14 ALR5th 242—§ 3, 23
25 ALR5th 568—§ 48

Statler v. Dodson, 195 W. Va. 646, 466 S.E.2d 497 (1995)

56 ALR5th 1—§ 3

Statler v. International Broth. of Elec. Workers Local Union 71, 51 Ohio St. 2d 36, 5 Ohio Op. 3d 20, 364 N.E.2d 874, 95 L.R.R.M. (BNA) 3139, 82 Lab. Cas. (CCH) ¶ 10035 (1977)

110 ALR5th 111—§ 6

Statler v. State, 2005 WL 1745434 (Tex. App. Corpus Christi 2005)

68 ALR6th 527—§ 37

Statler Hotels v. Herbert Rosenthal Jewelry Corp., 351 S.W.2d 579 (Tex. Civ. App. Dallas 1961)

112 ALR5th 621—§ 9

Statom v. Lumbermans Mutual Casualty Company, 431 N.Y.S.2d 875 (Sup. 1980)

43 ALR5th 545—§ 12

Staton v. BAC Home Loans Servicing, L.P., 2012 WL 1624296 (D. Or. 2012)

86 ALR6th 411—§ 5

Staton v. BAC Home Loans Servicing, LP, 2014 WL 1803376 (D. Or. 2014)

104 ALR6th 485—§ 5

Staton v. Boeing Co., 327 F.3d 938, 55 Fed. R. Serv. 3d 1299 (9th Cir. 2003)

60 ALR6th 295—§ 42, 61

Staton v. Parke, 12 F.3d 214 (6th Cir. 1993)

98 ALR6th 455—§ 16

Staton v. Russell, 565 S.E.2d 103 (N.C. Ct. App. 2002)

20 ALR6th 211—§ 4, 14, 41

Staton v. State, 164 Ga. App. 464, 297 S.E.2d 375 (1982)

62 ALR6th 413—§ 33

Staton v. Staton, 467 So. 2d 1236 (La. Ct. App. 2d Cir. 1985)

59 ALR6th 433—§ 47

Statser v. Chickasaw Lumber Co., 327 P.2d 686 (Okla. 1958)

46 ALR5th 1—§ 22

Statz v. McWaters, 726 So. 2d 660 (Ala. Civ. App. 1998)

6 ALR5th 1—§ 12

Staub v. Breg, Inc., 2012 WL 1078335 (D. Ariz. 2012)

90 ALR6th 75—§ 3, 10, 12, 19, 21, 24, 27, 44

Staub v. Proctor Hosp., 130 S. Ct. 2089, 176 L. Ed. 2d 720 (2010)

56 ALR6th 679—§ 4

Staub v. Proctor Hosp., 131 S. Ct. 1186, 179 L. Ed. 2d 144, 111 Fair Empl. Prac. Cas. (BNA) 993, 190 L.R.R.M. (BNA) 2257, 94 Empl. Prac. Dec. (CCH) ¶ 44114, 160 Lab. Cas. (CCH) ¶ 10350 (2011)

66 ALR6th 635—§ 4

Staub v. Proctor Hosp., 560 F.3d 647, 186 L.R.R.M. (BNA) 2001, 92 Empl. Prac. Dec. (CCH) ¶ 43723, 157 Lab. Cas. (CCH) ¶ 11213 (7th Cir. 2009)

56 ALR6th 679—§ 4
66 ALR6th 635—§ 4

Staubach v. Cities Service Oil Co., 127 N.J.L. 577, 24 A.2d 193 (N.J. Sup. Ct. 1942)

41 ALR6th 207—§ 28

Stauber v. City of New York, 2004 WL 1593870 (S.D. N.Y. 2004)

46 ALR6th 465—§ 3, 6, 8

Staubes v. City of Folly Beach, 339 S.C. 406, 529 S.E.2d 543 (2000)

24 ALR5th 200—§ 9

Staudacher v. Staudacher, 310 Minn. 189, 246 N.W.2d 34 (1976)

53 ALR5th 375—§ 14

Staudt v. State, 616 So. 2d 600 (Fla. Dist. Ct. App. 4th Dist. 1993)

15 ALR5th 391—§ 52
92 ALR5th 35—§ 2, 21

Stauffacher v. State, 299 So. 2d 188 (Miss. 1974)

105 ALR5th 529—§ 11

Stauffer, In re Conduct of, 327 Or. 44, 956 P.2d 967 (1998)

26 ALR6th 1—§ 7

Stauffer v. Isaly Dairy Co., 4 Ohio App. 2d 15, 33 Ohio Op. 2d 44, 211 N.E.2d 72 (7th Dist. Mahoning County 1965)

98 ALR6th 93—§ 18

Stauffer v. Stauffer, 379 So. 2d 922 (Miss. 1980)

17 ALR5th 366—§ 32

Stauffer v. Zavaris, 37 F.3d 1495 (10th Cir. 1994)

94 ALR5th 393—§ 7

Stauffer Chemical Co. v. Buckalew, 456 So. 2d 778 (Ala. 1984)

15 ALR5th 119—§ 3, 5, 15, 21, 32, 33, 51, 53, 59, 74, 93

Stauffer Chemical Co. v. Keysor-Century Corp., 541 F. Supp. 239 (D.C. Del. 1982)

23 ALR5th 744—§ 7

Stauffer Communications, Inc. v. Mitchell, 246 Kan. 492, 789 P.2d 1153, 17 Media L. R. 1739 (1990)

39 ALR5th 103—§ 2, 55

St. Augustine, City of v. Brooks, 55 So. 2d 96 (Fla. 1951)

81 ALR6th 363—§ 5

St. Augustine, City of v. Middleton, 147 Fla. 529, 3 So. 2d 153 (1941)

114 ALR5th 561—§ 9

St. Augustine Pools, Inc. v. James M. Barker, Inc., 687 So. 2d 957 (Fla. Dist. Ct. App. 5th Dist. 1997)

100 ALR5th 481—§ 10, 11

Stauhs v. Board of Review, Division of Employment Sec., Dep't of Labor and Industry, 93 N.J. Super. 451, 226 A.2d 182 (App. Div. 1967)

68 ALR5th 13—§ 2, 9, 13, 18, 31, 39

75 ALR5th 339—§ 6, 7

Staunch v. Continental Airlines, Inc., 129 S. Ct. 223, 172 L. Ed. 2d 143, 104 Fair Empl. Prac. Cas. (BNA) 736, 14 Wage & Hour Cas. 2d (BNA) 128 (2008)

46 ALR6th 495—§ 32

Staunch v. Continental Airlines, Inc., 511 F.3d 625, 102 Fair Empl. Prac. Cas. (BNA) 820, 13 Wage & Hour Cas. 2d (BNA) 175, 90 Empl. Prac. Dec. (CCH) ¶ 43071, 155 Lab. Cas. (CCH) ¶ 35384 (6th Cir. 2008)

46 ALR6th 495—§ 32

Staunton Coal Co. v. Fischer, 119 Ill. App. 284, 1905 WL 1876 (4th Dist. 1905)

76 ALR6th 31—§ 11

Staunton, Commonwealth ex rel. v. Austin, 209 Pa. Super. 187, 223 A.2d 892 (1966)

53 ALR5th 375—§ 39

Stauth v. National Union Fire Ins. Co. of Pittsburgh, 185 F.3d 875 (10th Cir. 1999)

22 ALR6th 113—§ 67

Staver v. Staver, 217 N.J. Super. 541, 526 A.2d 290 (Ch. Div. 1987)

36 ALR6th 1—§ 18

Stavinoha v. Stavinoha, 126 S.W.3d 604 (Tex. App. Houston 14th Dist. 2004)

81 ALR6th 655—§ 4

Stavis v. Carney, 12 Mass. L. Rptr. 3, 2000 WL 1170090 (Mass. Super. Ct. 2000)

91 ALR6th 435—§ 11, 45

Stavitz v. New York, 98 App. Div. 2d 529, 471 N.Y.S.2d 272 (1st Dep't 1984)

36 ALR5th 1—§ 3

Stavros v. Office of Legislative Research and General Counsel, 2000 UT 63, 15 P.3d 1013 (Utah 2000)

94 ALR5th 537—§ 3

Stawicki v. Israel, 778 F.2d 380 (7th Cir. 1985)

20 ALR6th 479—§ 18

Stayberg v. Henderson, 277 Minn. 16, 151 N.W.2d 290 (1967)

31 ALR5th 572—§ 17

Stayinfront, Inc. v. Tobin, 2006 WL 3228033 (D.N.J. 2006)

26 ALR6th 287—§ 27

Stayton v. Smith & Nephew Richards, Inc., 1993 WL 459929 (E.D. La. 1993)

57 ALR5th 1—§ 6

St. Casimir Church v. Frankiewicz, 563 N.E.2d 1331 (Ind. App. 1990)

8 ALR5th 1—§ 7, 48, 51

St. Catherine Hosp. of Garden City v. Rodriguez, 25 Kan. App. 2d 763, 971 P.2d 754, 15 I.E.R. Cas. (BNA) 699 (1998)

16 ALR6th 1—§ 8

St. Catherine's Church Corp. v. Technical Planning Associates, Inc., 9 Conn. App. 682, 520 A.2d 1298 (1987)

46 ALR5th 1—§ 8

St. Charles County v. City of O'Fallon, 972 S.W.2d 327 (Mo. Ct. App. E.D. 1998)

17 ALR5th 195—§ 4

St. Charles County v. Director of Revenue, 961 S.W.2d 44 (Mo. 1998)

1 ALR6th 1—§ 9

St. Charles, State ex rel. County of v. City of St. Peters, 876 S.W.2d 46 (Mo. Ct. App. W.D. 1994)

CASES CITED IN ALR5TH AND 6TH

44 ALR6th 259—§ 14
St. Charles, State ex rel. County of v.
Mehan, 854 S.W.2d 531 (Mo. Ct.
App. W.D. 1993)
44 ALR6th 259—§ 14
St. Christopher-Ottilie ex rel. Ricarte
Angel C. v. Awilda C., 632
N.Y.S.2d 222 (App. Div. 2d Dep't
1995)
20 ALR5th 534—§ 14
St. Clair v. B & L Paving Co., 270 Pa.
Super. 277, 411 A.2d 525 (1979)
75 ALR5th 413—§ 2, 3, 49
St. Clair v. Caldwell & Riddle, 72 Ala.
527 (1882)
19 ALR5th 622—§ 7, 11, 16
St. Clair v. Com., 140 S.W.3d 510 (Ky.
2004)
56 ALR6th 185—§ 39
65 ALR6th 537—§ 29
St. Clair v. Com., 174 S.W.3d 474 (Ky.
2005)
93 ALR6th 391—§ 16
St. Clair v. Faulkner, 305 N.W.2d 441
(Iowa 1981)
67 ALR5th 1—§ 18
78 ALR5th 465—§ 4
St. Clair v. First Nat. Bank of Ingleside,
422 S.W.2d 558 (Tex. Civ. App.
Corpus Christi 1967)
106 ALR5th 475—§ 5
St. Clair v. General Motors Corp., 10 F.
Supp. 2d 523, 41 Fed. R. Serv. 3d
(LCP) 1105 (M.D.N.C. 1998)
39 ALR5th 267—§ 4, 5
St. Clair v. Johnny's Oyster & Shrimp,
Inc., 76 F. Supp. 2d 773, 2000
A.M.C. 769, 53 Fed. R. Evid. Serv.
1 (S.D. Tex. 1999)
34 ALR6th 253—§ 12
St. Clair v. State, 575 So. 2d 243, 16
FLW D 434 (Fla. App. D2 1991)
34 ALR5th 125—§ 14, 25
St. Clair, People ex rel. v. Davis, 143
A.D. 579, 127 N.Y.S. 1072 (2d
Dep't 1911)
102 ALR5th 525—§ 44

St. Cloud Nat. Bank & Trust Co. v. Brut-
ger, 488 N.W.2d 852 (Minn. Ct.
App. 1992)
102 ALR5th 253—§ 3, 6
St. Croix, Ltd. v. Bath Tp., 118 Ohio
App. 3d 438, 693 N.E.2d 297, 139
O.G.R. 363 (9th Dist. Summit
County 1997)
84 ALR6th 133—§ 15
Std. Fed. Bank v. Staff, 168 Ohio App.
3d 14, 2006-Ohio-3601, 857 N.E.2d
1245 (1st Dist. Hamilton County
2006)
86 ALR6th 321—§ 11, 12
88 ALR6th 385—§ 21
Stead v. F. E. Myers Co., Div. of McNeil
Corp., 785 F. Supp. 56 (D.C. Vt.
1990)
17 ALR5th 327—§ 2
Steadman v. Halland, 197 Mont. 45, 641
P.2d 448 (1982)
114 ALR5th 1—§ 21
Steadman v. Sinclair, 223 A.D.2d 392,
636 N.Y.S.2d 325 (1st Dep't 1996)
83 ALR5th 1—§ 10
Steadman v. South Central Bell Tel. Co.,
362 So. 2d 1144 (La. Ct. App. 2d
Cir. 1978)
125 ALR5th 457—§ 4
Steadman v. Steadman, 36 Wash. App.
77, 671 P.2d 808 (1983)
5 ALR5th 550—§ 17
Steakhouse, Inc. v. City of Raleigh,
N.C., 166 F.3d 634 (4th Cir. 1999)
10 ALR5th 538—§ 9
Steaks Unlimited v. Deaner, 623 F.2d
264, 6 Media L. R. 1129, 30 FR
Serv. 2d 550 (CA3 Pa. 1980)
**19 ALR5th 1—§ 2, 11, 140, 148,
149, 153, 157, 159**
60 ALR5th 75—§ 16, 17
Steaks Unlimited, Inc. v. Deaner, 623
F.2d 264, 6 Media L. Rep. (BNA)
1129, 30 Fed. R. Serv. 2d 550 (3d
Cir. 1980)
42 ALR6th 353—§ 26

Steamfitters Local Union No. 420 Welfare Fund v. Philip Morris, Inc., 171 F.3d 912, 23 Employee Benefits Cas. (BNA) 1141, R.I.C.O. Bus. Disp. Guide (CCH) ¶ 9672 (3d Cir. 1999)

36 ALR5th 541—§ 15, 23.5

Stearn & Co., L.L.C. v. U.S., 499 F. Supp. 2d 899, Unempl. Ins. Rep. (CCH) ¶ 14098C, 2007-2 U.S. Tax Cas. (CCH) ¶ 50676, 100 A.F.T.R.2d 2007-5039 (E.D. Mich. 2007)

47 ALR6th 1—§ 41

Stearns, In re Marriage of, 88 Ohio App. 3d 264, 623 N.E.2d 711 (10th Dist. Franklin County 1993)

123 ALR5th 565—§ 7, 10, 12, 14, 21, 29, 30
124 ALR5th 441—§ 7
1 ALR6th 493—§ 4, 5, 18
2 ALR6th 439—§ 42
3 ALR6th 641—§ 16, 27

Stearns v. Allen, 183 Mass. 404, 67 N.E. 349 (1903)

15 ALR5th 1—§ 8

Stearns v. Commission of Public Docks, 246 Or. 36, 423 P.2d 748, 55 Lab. Cas. (CCH) ¶ 51639 (1967)

110 ALR5th 111—§ 21

Stearns v. Los Angeles County, 275 Cal. App. 2d 134, 79 Cal. Rptr. 757 (2d Dist. 1969)

97 ALR5th 419—§ 14

Stearns v. NCR Corp., 297 F.3d 706, 28 Employee Benefits Cas. (BNA) 1769 (8th Cir. 2002)

74 ALR6th 267—§ 8

Stearns v. Stearns, 284 S.C. 459, 327 S.E.2d 343 (1985)

102 ALR5th 395—§ 14

Stearns v. Williams, 72 Idaho 276, 240 P.2d 833 (1952)

58 ALR5th 387—§ 6

Stearns Airpoort Equipment Co., Inc. v. Revolving Media, Ltd., 1996 WL 722073 (N.D. Tex. 1996)

79 ALR5th 587—§ 3, 5, 8

Stearns Co., Ltd. v. U.S., 34 Fed. Cl. 264 (1995)

66 ALR5th 135—§ 17

Steates, In re, 260 A.D.2d 839, 688 N.Y.S.2d 759 (3d Dep't 1999)

121 ALR5th 467—§ 9

Stebane Nash Co. v. Campbellsport Mut. Ins. Co., 27 Wis. 2d 112, 133 N.W.2d 737, 16 A.L.R.3d 760 (1965)

37 ALR5th 41—§ 5

Stebbins v. Concord Wrigley Drugs, Inc., 164 Mich. App. 204, 416 N.W.2d 381 (1987)

44 ALR5th 393—§ 12

Stebbins v. County of Crawford, 92 Pa. 289, 1879 WL 11670 (1879)

98 ALR5th 353—§ 7

Stebbins v. Gonzales, 3 Cal. App. 4th 1138, 5 Cal. Rptr. 2d 88, 72 Ed. Law Rep. 926 (3d Dist. 1992)

106 ALR5th 523—§ 23

Stebbins v. Stebbins, 121 N.H. 1060, 438 A.2d 295 (1981)

14 ALR5th 557—§ 6

Stebens v. K-Mart Corp., 99 N.M. 720, 663 P.2d 379 (Ct. App. 1983)

61 ALR5th 375—§ 2, 10

Steber v. Norris, 188 Wis. 366, 206 N.W. 173, 43 A.L.R. 501 (1925)

118 ALR5th 513—§ 6, 10

Steblein v. Bernard, 6 Misc. 3d 1033(A), 800 N.Y.S.2d 357 (Sup 2005)

59 ALR6th 433—§ 59

Stebley v. Litton Loan Servicing, LLP, 202 Cal. App. 4th 522, 134 Cal. Rptr. 3d 604 (3d Dist. 2011)

81 ALR6th 161—§ 5

Stebok v. American General Life & Acci. Ins. Co., 715 F. Supp. 711, 29 BNA WH Cas. 442, 115 CCH LC ¶ 56219 (W.D. Pa. 1989)

18 ALR5th 577—§ 26

Steck v. Com., Unemployment Compensation Bd. of Review, 78 Pa. Commw. 514, 467 A.2d 1378 (1983)

25 ALR6th 101—§ 10, 11

Steckal v. Haughton Elevator Co., Inc., 59 N.Y.2d 628, 463 N.Y.S.2d 186, 449 N.E.2d 1264 (1983)
   117 ALR5th 267—§ 11

Steckel v. Blafas, 549 So. 2d 1211 (Fla. Dist. Ct. App. 4th Dist. 1989)
   67 ALR5th 1—§ 22

Steckelberg v. Randolph, 448 N.W.2d 458 (Iowa 1989)
   11 ALR5th 88—§ 4

Steckler v. Steckler, 293 S.W.2d 129 (Mo. Ct. App. 1956)
   108 ALR5th 359—§ 9
   119 ALR5th 445—§ 8, 10

Steckler v. Steckler, 519 N.W.2d 23 (N.D. 1994)
   59 ALR6th 433—§ 79

Steckler v. Steckler, 921 So. 2d 740 (Fla. Dist. Ct. App. 5th Dist. 2006)
   53 ALR6th 419—§ 48, 56
   59 ALR6th 161—§ 15

Steckler v. U.S., 98-1 U.S. Tax Cas. (CCH) ¶ 50219, 81 A.F.T.R.2d 98-1049, 1998 WL 28235 (E.D. La. 1998)
   93 ALR5th 1—§ 2, 4, 9

Stecyk v. Bell Helicopter Textron, Inc., Prod. Liab. Rep. (CCH) ¶ 14576, 1996 WL 153555 (E.D. Pa. 1996)
   72 ALR5th 299—§ 2, 38, 46

Steczo v. Steczo, 135 Ariz. 199, 659 P.2d 1344 (Ct. App. Div. 1 1983)
   59 ALR6th 433—§ 55

Stedman v. Rome, 88 Hun. 279, 34 N.Y.S. 737 (1895)
   57 ALR5th 689—§ 16

St. Edwards' College v. Morris, 82 Tex. 1, 17 S.W. 512 (1891)
   114 ALR5th 561—§ 19

Stedwell v. City of Chicago, 297 Ill. 486, 130 N.E. 729, 17 A.L.R. 829 (1921)
   111 ALR5th 579—§ 21

Steed v. Cuevas, 24 Ariz. App. 547, 540 P.2d 166 (Div. 1 1975)
   112 ALR5th 621—§ 6

Steed v. Dodgen, 85 F. Supp. 956 (W.D. Tex. 1949)
   31 ALR6th 523—§ 11

Steed v. McKenzie, 344 So. 2d 689 (La. Ct. App. 1st Cir. 1977)
   82 ALR5th 443—§ 4
   83 ALR5th 375—§ 4, 5

Steed v. St. Paul's United Methodist Church, 728 So. 2d 931 (La. Ct. App. 2d Cir. 1999)
   108 ALR5th 495—§ 2, 9
   109 ALR5th 541—§ 9

Steedley v. Snowden, 138 Ga. App. 155, 225 S.E.2d 703 (1976)
   3 ALR5th 1—§ 3, 21

Steed Mortg. Co. v. Arthur, 37 Md. App. 592, 378 A.2d 690 (1977)
   20 ALR5th 229—§ 4 to 6, 17, 30

Steeg v. Baskin Family Camps, Inc., 124 S.W.3d 633 (Tex. App. Austin 2003)
   79 ALR6th 487—§ 7, 35

Steege v. Board of Appeals, 26 Mass. App. 970, 527 N.E.2d 1176 (1988)
   38 ALR5th 357—§ 3, 7

Steel & Wire Corp. v. Thyssen Inc., 20 U.C.C. Rep. Serv. 892 (E.D. Mich. 1976)
   89 ALR5th 319—§ 23

Steelcase Inc. v. Haworth, Inc., 954 F. Supp. 1195, 43 U.S.P.Q.2d 1041 (W.D. Mich. 1997)
   85 ALR6th 1—§ 29

Steel Cities Chemical Co. v. Jenkins, 17 Ala. App. 221, 84 So. 408 (1919)
   25 ALR5th 568—§ 36

Steel Co. v. Citizens for a Better Environment, 523 U.S. 83, 118 S. Ct. 1003, 140 L. Ed. 2d 210, 46 Env't. Rep. Cas. (BNA) 1097, 28 Envtl. L. Rep. 20434 (1998)
   90 ALR6th 385—§ 2

Steele, In re, 22 F. Cas. 1202, No. 13346 (W.D. Tenn. 1879)
   44 ALR6th 481—§ 8

Steele, In re, 30 A.D.3d 92, 812 N.Y.S.2d 640 (2d Dep't 2006)
   45 ALR6th 175—§ 26

Steele, In re, 914 A.2d 679 (D.C. 2007)
   44 ALR6th 75—§ 10

Steele, In re Estate of, 85 A.D.3d 1375, 925 N.Y.S.2d 250 (3d Dep' 2011)
74 ALR6th 549—§ 13

Steele, Matter of Marriage of, 92 Or. App. 532, 759 P.2d 304 (1988)
38 ALR6th 313—§ 5

Steele, Petition of, 262 Mont. 481, 865 P.2d 285 (1993)
108 ALR5th 289—§ 2, 12

Steele v. Atlanta Maternal Fetal Medicine, P.C., 271 Ga. App. 622, 610 S.E.2d 546 (2005)
124 ALR5th 623—§ 3, 7

Steele v. Auburn Vocational School Dist., 104 Ohio App. 3d 204, 661 N.E.2d 767, 107 Ed. Law Rep. 273 (11th Dist. Lake County 1994)
85 ALR5th 301—§ 18

Steele v. Beard, 830 F. Supp. 2d 49 (W.D. Pa. 2011)
83 ALR6th 255—§ 16

Steele v. Cingular Wireless LLC, 2007 WL 2456104 (Cal. App. 1st Dist. 2007)
36 ALR6th 443—§ 10

Steele v. City of Boston, 128 Mass. 583, 1880 WL 10755 (1880)
29 ALR6th 369—§ 39

Steele v. Collagen Corp., 54 Cal. App. 4th 1474, 63 Cal. Rptr. 2d 879, Prod. Liab. Rep. (CCH) ¶ 14955 (3d Dist. 1997)
23 ALR6th 223—§ 3

Steele v. Collins, 2009-Ohio-4836, 2009 WL 2941541 (Ohio Ct. App. 10th Dist. Franklin County 2009)
96 ALR6th 269—§ 10

Steele v. Darner, 124 Mo. App. 338, 103 S.W. 582 (1907)
25 ALR5th 391—§ 63

Steele v. Drummond, 275 U.S. 199, 48 S. Ct. 53, 72 L. Ed. 238 (1927)
35 ALR6th 1—§ 27

Steele v. Eaton, 130 Vt. 1, 285 A.2d 749 (1971)
13 ALR5th 289—§ 7, 18

Steele v. Fairview General Hosp., 1992 WL 333158 (Ohio Ct. App. 8th Dist. Cuyahoga County 1992)
93 ALR6th 123—§ 36

Steele v. Fairview General Hosp., 1992 WL 333158 (Ohio Ct. App. 8th Dist.Cuyahoga County 1992)
57 ALR5th 141—§ 14

Steele v. Federal Bureau of Prisons, 355 F.3d 1204 (10th Cir. 2003)
22 ALR6th 19—§ 3

Steele v. First Nat'l Bank, 1992 WL 123818 (D.C. Kan. 1992)
51 ALR5th 603—§ 5, 11, 14

Steele v. Gann, 197 Ark. 480, 123 S.W.2d 520, 120 A.L.R. 754 (1939)
76 ALR6th 31—§ 49

Steele v. Honea, 261 Ga. 644, 409 S.E.2d 652, 19 Media L. Rep. (BNA) 1605 (1991)
114 ALR5th 1—§ 11

Steele v. Houston, 603 S.W.2d 786 (Tex. 1980)
23 ALR5th 834—§ 3

Steele v. Isikoff, 130 F. Supp. 2d 23, 28 Media L. Rep. (BNA) 2630 (D.D.C. 2000)
98 ALR5th 353—§ 4

Steele v. Jensen Instrument Co., 59 Cal. App. 4th 326, 69 Cal. Rptr. 2d 135 (2d Dist. 1997)
119 ALR5th 121—§ 4
2 ALR6th 279—§ 10, 15

Steele v. Kehoe, 747 So. 2d 931 (Fla. 1999)
4 ALR5th 273—§ 6.5
13 ALR6th 1—§ 4

Steele v. Kerrigan, 148 N.J. 1, 689 A.2d 685 (1997)
54 ALR5th 379—§ 3

Steele v. Queen City Broadcasting Co., 54 Wash. 2d 402, 341 P.2d 499 (1959)
88 ALR5th 641—§ 3, 7

Steele v. Rosehill Cemetery Co., 294 Ill. App. 568, 14 N.E.2d 241 (1938)
54 ALR5th 681—§ 1

Steele v. Rosenfeld, LLC, 936 So. 2d 488 (Ala. 2005)

43 ALR6th 611—§ 66

Steele v. Spokesman-Review, 138 Idaho 249, 61 P.3d 606, 31 Media L. Rep. (BNA) 1412 (2002)

22 ALR6th 553—§ 16

Steele v. State, 213 Miss. 739, 57 So. 2d 574 (1952)

29 ALR5th 59—§ 3, 43, 85

Steele v. State, 216 Ga. App. 276, 454 S.E.2d 590 (1995)

16 ALR6th 329—§ 6

24 ALR6th 591—§ 6

Steele v. State, 537 So. 2d 711 (Fla. Dist. Ct. App. 5th Dist. 1989)

66 ALR5th 397—§ 8

Steele v. State, 561 So. 2d 638 (Fla. Dist. Ct. App. 1st Dist. 1990)

23 ALR6th 307—§ 31

Steele v. Statesman Ins. Co., 530 Pa. 190, 607 A.2d 742 (1992)

30 ALR5th 170—§ 85

Steele v. Steele, 250 Ga. 101, 296 S.E.2d 570 (1982)

20 ALR5th 700—§ 54

Steele v. Steele, 732 So. 2d 546 (La. Ct. App. 5th Cir. 1999)

9 ALR5th 321—§ 6

12 ALR5th 546—§ 4

Steele v. Town of Allenstown, 124 N.H. 487, 471 A.2d 1179 (1984)

90 ALR5th 547—§ 9

Steele v. Turner Broadcasting System, Inc., 607 F. Supp. 2d 258 (D. Mass. 2009)

76 ALR6th 289—§ 4

77 ALR6th 543—§ 18

Steele v. U.S., 267 U.S. 498, 45 S. Ct. 414, 69 L. Ed. 757 (1925)

103 ALR5th 463—§ 2, 3

Steele v. U.S., 440 F. Supp. 266 (D.C. Neb. 1977)

29 ALR5th 59—§ 57, 77, 88, 89

Steele v. Woods, 327 S.W.2d 187 (Mo. 1959)

108 ALR5th 385—§ 8

Steele, People ex rel. v. French, 10 N.Y.S. 792 (Gen. Term 1890)

19 ALR6th 217—§ 53

Steele-Smith Dry Goods Co. v. Blythe, 208 Ala. 288, 94 So. 281 (1922)

2 ALR5th 1—§ 53

Steele, Texas Emp. Ins. Ass'n, Intervenor v. Wiedemann Mach. Co., 280 F.2d 380 (3d Cir. 1960)

64 ALR5th 119—§ 3

Steel Hill Dev., Inc. v. Sanbornton, 469 F.2d 956, 3 ELR 20018 (CA1 N.H. 1972)

1 ALR5th 622—§ 17, 19, 26

Steelman v. Mallory, 110 Idaho 510, 716 P.2d 1282 (1986)

10 ALR6th 293—§ 4, 14

39 ALR6th 1—§ 10, 13

Steelman v. State, 486 N.E.2d 523 (Ind. 1985)

7 ALR5th 263—§ 6

70 ALR6th 361—§ 29

71 ALR6th 335—§ 8

Steelman v. State, 602 N.E.2d 152 (Ind. App. 1992)

7 ALR5th 263—§ 6

27 ALR5th 593—§ 7, 10, 23, 25, 31

Steelmet, Inc. v. Caribe Towing Corp., 842 F.2d 1237 (CA11 Fla. 1988)

23 ALR5th 75—§ 3

Steel Products Co. v. Millers Nat'l Ins. Co., 209 N.W.2d 32 (Iowa 1973)

37 ALR5th 41—§ 3, 8, 32, 48, 53

Steel Sales Corp. v. Industrial Commission, 293 Ill. 435, 127 N.E. 698, 14 A.L.R. 274 (1920)

80 ALR5th 417—§ 3

Steelstone Industries, Inc. v. McCrum, 2001 ME 171, 785 A.2d 1256, 27 Employee Benefits Cas. (BNA) 1638, 113 A.L.R.5th 739 (Me. 2001)

113 ALR5th 487—§ 5, 12

Steelvest, Inc. v. Scansteel Service Center, Inc., 807 S.W.2d 476 (Ky. 1991)

9 ALR6th 363—§ 4

Steen v. County Council of Sussex County, 576 A.2d 642 (Del. Ch. 1989)

55 ALR6th 635—§ 10

Steen v. Scheel, 46 Neb. 252, 64 N.W. 957 (1895)

13 ALR5th 169—§ 7

Steen v. Those Underwriters at Lloyds, London Signatory to Policy No. E0100191, 442 N.W.2d 158 (Minn. Ct. App. 1989)

16 ALR6th 491—§ 9

Steenblock v. Elkhorn Township Bd., 245 Neb. 722, 515 N.W.2d 128, 33 A.L.R.5th 933 (1994)

33 ALR5th 731—§ 2, 6, 9

34 ALR5th 591—§ 2

35 ALR5th 113—§ 2

Steenhuis v. Holland, 217 Ala. 105, 115 So. 2 (1927)

6 ALR5th 883—§ 23

Steenmeyer Corp. v. Mortenson-Neal, 731 P.2d 1221 (Alaska 1987)

23 ALR5th 241—§ 47

Steere, In re, 217 Kan. 276, 536 P.2d 54 (1975)

49 ALR6th 505—§ 22, 50

Steere v. Cupp, 226 Kan. 566, 602 P.2d 1267, 5 Media L. R. 2046 (1979)

19 ALR5th 1—§ 40, 65, 105, 110

Steere v. Tiffany, 13 R.I. 568 (1882)

62 ALR5th 219—§ 34

Steering Committee v. Exxon Mobil Corp., 461 F.3d 598 (5th Cir. 2006)

57 ALR6th 383—§ 12

Steering Committee v. U.S., 6 F.3d 572, 64 A.L.R.5th 831 (9th Cir. 1993)

64 ALR5th 235—§ 2, 3, 9

Steese v. State, 114 Nev. 479, 960 P.2d 321 (1998)

40 ALR5th 113—§ 3

55 ALR6th 391—§ 7, 13

Steese v. State, 170 Tex. Crim. 269, 340 S.W.2d 49 (1960)

105 ALR5th 529—§ 24

Steeves v. Sinclair, 56 App. Div. 448, 67 N.Y.S. 776 (1900)

46 ALR5th 1—§ 16

Steeves v. U.S., 294 F. Supp. 446 (D.S.C. 1968)

7 ALR6th 1—§ 14

Stefan v. Chrysler Corp., 472 F. Supp. 262 (D.C. Md. 1979)

6 ALR5th 883—§ 5

Stefani v. Baird & Warner, Inc., 157 Ill. App. 3d 167, 109 Ill. Dec. 444, 510 N.E.2d 65 (1st Dist. 1987)

71 ALR5th 491—§ 51

Stefani v. Bhagat, 149 Mich. App. 431, 386 N.W.2d 203 (1986)

24 ALR5th 1—§ 27, 28

Stefania v. McNiff, 49 Misc. 2d 480, 267 N.Y.S.2d 854 (Sup. Ct. 1966)

12 ALR5th 195—§ 50

94 ALR5th 149—§ 3, 6, 8

Stefaniak v. HSBC Bank USA, N.A., 2008 WL 7630102 (W.D. N.Y. 2008)

60 ALR6th 295—§ 58

Stefan Jewelers, Inc. v. Electro-Protective Corp., 161 Ga. App. 385, 288 S.E.2d 667 (1982)

36 ALR6th 305—§ 9

Stefano v. Smith, 705 F. Supp. 733 (D. Conn. 1989)

17 ALR6th 1—§ 25

Stefano & Associates, Inc. v. Global Lending Group, Inc., 2008-Ohio-177, 2008 WL 186638 (Ohio Ct. App. 9th Dist. Summit County 2008)

77 ALR6th 1—§ 21, 49, 118

Stefanoff v. State, 78 S.W.3d 496 (Tex. App. Austin 2002)

50 ALR6th 353—§ 47

Stefanski v. R.A. Zehetner & Assocs., 855 F. Supp. 1030, 65 BNA FEP Cas. 539 (E.D. Wis 1994)

51 ALR5th 163—§ 5

Steffan v. Aspin, 8 F.3d 57, 87 Ed. Law Rep. 32, 63 Fair Empl. Prac. Cas. (BNA) 300, 63 Empl. Prac. Dec. (CCH) ¶ 42668 (D.C. Cir. 1993)

96 ALR5th 391—§ 8

Steffan v. Cheney, 780 F. Supp. 1, 72 Ed. Law Rep. 84 (D.D.C. 1991)

For assistance, call 1-800-328-4880

96 ALR5th 391—§ 8
Steffan v. Perry, 41 F.3d 677, 96 Ed. Law Rep. 32, 69 Fair Empl. Prac. Cas. (BNA) 245 (D.C. Cir. 1994)
96 ALR5th 391—§ 3, 8, 9
Steffen v. Steffen, 527 So. 2d 967 (Fla. Dist. Ct. App. 1st Dist. 1988)
59 ALR6th 433—§ 44
Steffens v. Fisher, 161 Mo. App. 386, 143 S.W. 1101 (1912)
25 ALR5th 391—§ 4, 5
Steffens v. Keeler, 200 Mich. App. 179, 503 N.W.2d 675 (1993)
93 ALR5th 621—§ 18
8 ALR6th 465—§ 18
Steffens v. Peterson, 503 N.W.2d 254 (S.D. 1993)
47 ALR5th 129—§ 11, 16
Steffens v. Proehl, 171 N.W.2d 297 (Iowa 1969)
42 ALR6th 545—§ 3, 8, 18, 20, 21
43 ALR6th 375—§ 3, 4, 11, 36
Steffenson v. Carrara, 59 A.D.2d 786, 398 N.Y.S.2d 743 (2d Dep't 1977)
69 ALR5th 1—§ 3, 6
Steffes v. Ford Motor Co., 239 Mich. 501, 214 N.W. 953 (1927)
41 ALR6th 207—§ 17
Steffes v. Thurmer, 2008 WL 1969753 (E.D. Wis. 2008)
48 ALR6th 135—§ 16
Steffy v. Com., Unemployment Compensation Bd. of Review, 499 Pa. 367, 453 A.2d 591 (1982)
68 ALR5th 13—§ 19, 23
Stefl v. Medtronic, Inc., 916 S.W.2d 879, Prod. Liab. Rep. (CCH) ¶ 14550 (Mo. Ct. App. E.D. 1996)
88 ALR6th 1—§ 2, 7, 15, 26, 60
Stef Shipping Corp. v. Norris Grain Co., 209 F. Supp. 249 (S.D. N.Y. 1962)
67 ALR5th 179—§ 5
Stegall, In re, 2007 WL 1125635 (Bankr. S.D. Iowa 2007)
44 ALR6th 481—§ 44
Stegall v. Audette, 2005 WL 2038545 (E.D. Mich. 2005)
65 ALR6th 93—§ 21

Stegall v. J & J Exterminating, 651 So. 2d 400 (La. Ct. App. 3d Cir. 1995)
79 ALR5th 201—§ 10, 14
Stegall v. Ohio State Med. Bd., 92 Ohio App. 3d 389, 635 N.E.2d 1291 (10th Dist. Franklin County 1993)
19 ALR6th 577—§ 10, 12
Stegall v. State Farm Mut. Auto. Ins. Co., 702 So. 2d 66 (La. Ct. App. 2d Cir. 1997)
50 ALR5th 1—§ 4
Stegall v. Wilson, 416 S.W.2d 658 (Mo. Ct. App. 1967)
111 ALR5th 1—§ 5, 9, 12, 13
Stegall v. WTWV, Inc., 609 So. 2d 348, 20 Media L. Rep. (BNA) 1280 (Miss. 1992)
42 ALR6th 353—§ 27
Stegemann, In re, 206 B.R. 176, 37 Collier Bankr. Cas. 2d (MB) 902 (Bankr. C.D. Ill. 1997)
32 ALR6th 531—§ 14
Stegemoller v. ACandS, Inc., 767 N.E.2d 974 (Ind. 2002)
33 ALR6th 325—§ 3
Ste. Genevieve School dist. v. Board of Aldermen of City of Ste. Genevieve, 2001 WL 586532 (Mo. Ct. App. E.D. 2001)
115 ALR5th 563—§ 3
Steger v. Steger, 728 S.W.2d 651 (Mo. Ct. App. E.D. 1987)
120 ALR5th 229—§ 7, 22
Steglich v. Guerrero, 437 So. 2d 209 (Fla. Dist. Ct. App. 3d Dist. 1983)
58 ALR5th 669—§ 12, 20
Stegmaier v. State, 863 S.W.2d 924 (Mo. App. 1993)
22 ALR5th 261—§ 6
Stegmeier v. St. Elizabeth Hosp., 239 N.J. Super. 475, 571 A.2d 1006 (App. Div. 1990)
95 ALR6th 85—§ 65
Stegmiller v. H. P. E., Inc., 81 Ill. App. 3d 1144, 37 Ill. Dec. 63, 401 N.E.2d 1156 (1st Dist. 1980)
102 ALR5th 99—§ 6

Stehl v. Brown's Sporting Goods, Inc., 236 Ill. App. 3d 976, 177 Ill. Dec. 267, 603 N.E.2d 48 (3d Dist. 1992)
117 ALR5th 155—§ 10

Stehl v. Dose, 83 Ill. App. 3d 440, 38 Ill. Dec. 697, 403 N.E.2d 1301 (3d Dist. 1980)
11 ALR5th 127—§ 12, 29

Stehouwer v. Lewis, 249 Mich. 76, 227 N.W. 759, 74 A.L.R. 844 (1929)
9 ALR5th 102—§ 22

Stehr v. State, 92 Neb. 755, 139 N.W. 676 (1913)
118 ALR5th 253—§ 3, 16, 20
97 ALR6th 539—§ 7

Stehwein v. Olcott, 78 N.M. 95, 428 P.2d 634 (1967)
21 ALR5th 82—§ 3, 11

Steichman v. Hurst, 2 Ill. App. 3d 415, 275 N.E.2d 679 (2d Dist. 1971)
11 ALR5th 127—§ 21, 45

Steiden v. Kroger Co., 483 S.W.2d 146 (Ky. 1972)
44 ALR5th 525—§ 7

Steier v. Batavia Park Dist., 283 Ill. App. 3d 968, 219 Ill. Dec. 327, 670 N.E.2d 1215 (2d Dist. 1996)
118 ALR5th 347—§ 11, 14, 15

Steiger v. Superior Court for Maricopa County, 112 Ariz. 1, 536 P.2d 689 (1975)
24 ALR6th 255—§ 4, 10, 16

Steigerwaldt v. Town of King, 199 Wis. 2d 525, 546 N.W.2d 580 (Ct. App. 1996)
13 ALR6th 721—§ 4

Steigler v. Anderson, 360 F. Supp. 1286 (D. Del. 1973)
28 ALR6th 505—§ 34

Steigler v. Anderson, 496 F.2d 793 (3d Cir. 1974)
28 ALR6th 505—§ 34
29 ALR6th 1—§ 8
58 ALR6th 499—§ 60

Steigler v. Insurance Co. of North America, 306 A.2d 742 (Del. 1973)
37 ALR6th 511—§ 43

Steigler v. Superior Court In and For New Castle County, 252 A.2d 300 (Del. 1969)
28 ALR6th 505—§ 34

Steimel v. Incorporated Village of Rockville Centre, 965 F. Supp. 366 (E.D.N.Y. 1997)
64 ALR5th 519—§ 7, 17

Stein, Matter of, 108 N.M. 734, 779 P.2d 111 (1989)
45 ALR6th 175—§ 14

Stein v. American Residential Management, Inc., 781 S.W.2d 385 (Tex. App. Houston (14th Dist.) 1989)
22 ALR5th 483—§ 3

Stein v. Asheville City Bd. Of Educ., 360 N.C. 321, 626 S.E.2d 263, 206 Ed. Law Rep. 735 (2006)
80 ALR6th 469—§ 36, 48

Stein v. Chase Home Finance, LLC, 662 F.3d 976 (8th Cir. 2011)
86 ALR6th 411—§ 5

Stein v. Com., Dep't of Transp., 144 Pa. Commw. 105, 601 A.2d 384, 72 Ed. Law Rep. 242 (1991)
72 ALR5th 469—§ 18

Stein v. Dahm, 96 Ala. 481, 11 So. 597 (1892)
62 ALR5th 219—§ 54

Stein v. Drake, 116 Cal. App. 2d 779, 254 P.2d 613 (2d Dist. 1953)
75 ALR5th 595—§ 3

Stein v. Feldmann, 85 Ill. App. 3d 973, 41 Ill. Dec. 270, 407 N.E.2d 768 (1st Dist. 1980)
26 ALR5th 107—§ 8
60 ALR5th 669—§ 8

Stein v. Frank, 575 S.W.2d 399 (Tex. Civ. App. Dallas 1978)
85 ALR5th 547—§ 3

Stein v. Geonerco, Inc., 105 Wash. App. 41, 17 P.3d 1266 (Div. 1 2001)
13 ALR6th 145—§ 5, 9

Stein v. Glaser, 5 N.J. Tax 373 (1983)
2 ALR6th 1—§ 74

Stein v. Insurance Corp. of America, 566 So. 2d 1114 (La. App. 1990)
7 ALR5th 1—§ 11, 14

43 ALR5th 87—§ 2, 3, 14

Stein v. Insurance Corp. of America, 569 So2d 984 (La. 1990)

7 ALR5th 1—§ 11, 14

Stein v. International Ins. Co., 217 Cal. App. 3d 609, 266 Cal. Rptr. 72 (4th Dist. 1990)

92 ALR5th 273—§ 6

Stein v. Katz, 213 Conn. 282, 567 A.2d 1183 (1989)

5 ALR6th 133—§ 7

Stein v. Lebowitz-Pine View Hotel, Inc., 111 App. Div. 2d 572, 489 N.Y.S.2d 635 (3d Dep't 1985)

55 ALR5th 463—§ 3

Stein v. Lyon, 91 App. Div. 593, 87 N.Y.S. 125 (2d Dep't 1904)

25 ALR5th 123—§ 9, 18

Stein v. McGraw-Hill, Inc., 782 F. Supp. 207, 61 Fair Empl. Prac. Cas. (BNA) 841, 61 Empl. Prac. Dec. (CCH) ¶ 42305 (S.D. N.Y. 1992)

85 ALR6th 323—§ 94

Stein v. Overlook Joint Venture, 246 Md. 75, 227 A.2d 226 (1967)

6 ALR6th 1—§ 3

15 ALR6th 1—§ 4, 9, 10

Stein v. Penatello, 185 A.D.2d 976, 587 N.Y.S.2d 37 (2d Dep't 1992)

62 ALR5th 537—§ 4

Stein v. Pennsylvania Dock & Warehouse Co., 10 N.J. Misc. 568, 159 A. 683 (1932)

46 ALR5th 1—§ 27

Stein v. Shaw, 6 N.J. 525, 79 A.2d 310 (1951)

59 ALR5th 693—§ 2, 4

Stein v. Smith, 358 Md. 670, 751 A.2d 504 (2000)

104 ALR6th 1—§ 19

Stein v. Soyer, 43 U.S.P.Q.2d (BNA) 1479, 1997 WL 104967 (S.D. N.Y. 1997)

80 ALR5th 487—§ 2

Stein v. Sprint Corp., 22 F. Supp. 2d 1210 (D. Kan. 1998)

115 ALR5th 709—§ 3

Stein v. State, 632 So. 2d 1361 (Fla. 1994)

79 ALR5th 33—§ 63

Stein v. Stein, 184 Misc. 2d 276, 707 N.Y.S.2d 754 (Sup. Ct. 1999)

4 ALR5th 403—§ 5

38 ALR5th 69—§ 5

Stein v. Stein, 789 S.W.2d 87 (Mo. App. 1990)

9 ALR5th 568—§ 15

Stein v. Trager, 36 Misc. 2d 227, 232 N.Y.S.2d 362 (Sup 1962)

7 ALR6th 135—§ 5

Stein v. Trans World Airlines, Inc., 25 App. Div. 2d 732, 268 N.Y.S.2d 752 (1st Dep't 1966)

10 ALR5th 371—§ 3, 4, 17

14 ALR5th 662—§ 2, 6

Steinauer v. Sarpy County, 217 Neb. 830, 353 N.W.2d 715 (1984)

50 ALR5th 1—§ 4, 12

51 ALR5th 467—§ 2, 6

52 ALR5th 1—§ 2

Steinbach, Matter of, 228 A.D.2d 88, 651 N.Y.S.2d 523 (1st Dep't 1997)

45 ALR6th 175—§ 7, 23, 25

Steinbach v. Barfield, 428 So. 2d 915 (La. Ct. App. 1st Cir. 1983)

95 ALR6th 541—§ 29

Steinbach v. Gustafson, 177 Wis. 2d 178, 502 N.W.2d 156 (Ct. App. 1993)

86 ALR6th 321—§ 4

Steinbach v. Northwestern Nat. Life Ins. Co., 728 F. Supp. 1389, 51 BNA FEP Cas. 701, 4 BNA IER Cas. 1816, 52 CCH EPD ¶ 39568 (D.C. Minn. 1989)

21 ALR5th 1—§ 3

Steinbach v. Northwestern Nat. Life Ins. Co., 728 F. Supp. 1389, 51 Fair Empl. Prac. Cas. (BNA) 701, 4 I.E.R. Cas. (BNA) 1816, 52 Empl. Prac. Dec. (CCH) ¶ 39568 (D. Minn. 1989)

52 ALR6th 271—§ 4

Steinbauer Assoc., Inc. v. Smith, 599 So. 2d 746, 17 FLW D 1396 (Fla. App. D3 1992)

5 ALR5th 875—§ 20

Steinbeck v. Com., 862 S.W.2d 912 (Ky. Ct. App. 1993)

74 ALR5th 319—§ 5, 6, 13

Steinbeck v. Philip Stenger Sons, Inc., 46 Ohio App. 2d 22, 75 Ohio Ops. 2d 25, 345 N.E.2d 633 (Hamilton Co. 1975)

14 ALR5th 242—§ 20

Steinberg, In re, 197 Cal. App. 2d 264, 17 Cal. Rptr. 431 (5th Dist. 1961)

75 ALR6th 311—§ 13, 22, 26, 28

Steinberg, In re, 448 Mass. 1024, 863 N.E.2d 928 (2007)

44 ALR6th 75—§ 26

Steinberg, In re, 720 A.2d 900 (D.C. 1998)

45 ALR6th 175—§ 5, 7, 11, 19

Steinberg, In re, 953 A.2d 306 (D.C. 2008)

44 ALR6th 75—§ 4

Steinberg v. Abatecola, 2003 WL 22753603 (Cal. App. 4th Dist. 2003)

45 ALR6th 493—§ 30, 32, 38

Steinberg v. Bloom, 5 N.Y.S.2d 774 (Sup. App. T 1938)

2 ALR5th 1—§ 6

Steinberg v. Carey, 470 F. Supp. 471, CCH Fed Secur L. Rep. ¶ 96840 (S.D. N.Y. 1979)

23 ALR5th 241—§ 2, 18

Steinberg v. Chicago Medical School, 69 Ill. 2d 320, 13 Ill. Dec. 699, 371 N.E.2d 634 (1977)

63 ALR5th 1—§ 17

Steinberg v. Commonwealth, Unemployment Compensation Board of Review, 34 Pa. Cmwlth. 294, 383 A.2d 1284 (1978)

46 ALR5th 659—§ 13

Steinberg v. District of Columbia, 901 F. Supp. 2d 63 (D.D.C. 2012)

89 ALR6th 1—§ 89

Steinberg v. Dunseth, 276 Ill. App. 3d 1038, 213 Ill. Dec. 218, 658 N.E.2d 1239 (4th Dist. 1995)

100 ALR6th 139—§ 39

Steinberg v. Ford Motor Co., 72 Mich. App. 520, 250 N.W.2d 115 (1976)

48 ALR5th 1—§ 2, 13

Steinberg v. Hoshijo, 88 Haw. 10, 960 P.2d 1218, 73 Empl. Prac. Dec. (CCH) ¶ 45445 (Haw. 1998)

83 ALR5th 1—§ 5

93 ALR5th 47—§ 3

Steinberg v. Indemnity Ins. Co., 364 F.2d 266 (CA5 La. 1966)

19 ALR5th 563—§ 29

Steinberg v. Mendel Rosenzweig Fine Furs, Inc., 9 Misc. 2d 611, 167 N.Y.S.2d 685 (Sup 1957)

120 ALR5th 351—§ 6

Steinberg v. South Dakota Dep't of Military and Veterans Affairs, 2000 S.D. 36, 607 N.W.2d 596 (S.D. 2000)

4 ALR5th 585—§ 16

Steinberg v. Steinberg, 1982 WL 2446 (Ohio Ct. App. 8th Dist. Cuyahoga County 1982)

81 ALR6th 1—§ 16

Steinberg v. Thomas, 659 F. Supp. 789 (D. Colo. 1987)

7 ALR6th 563—§ 5

Steinbrenner v. Commissioner of Public Safety, 413 N.W.2d 557 (Minn. Ct. App. 1987)

17 ALR6th 327—§ 12

Stein-Brief Group, Inc. v. Home Indem. Co., 65 Cal. App. 4th 364, 76 Cal. Rptr. 2d 3 (4th Dist. 1998)

97 ALR5th 473—§ 3, 18

Steinbrunner v. Turner Funeral Home, Inc., 2002 WL 14088 (Tenn. Ct. App. 2002)

97 ALR5th 419—§ 14

Steinbugler, Application of, 297 N.Y. 713, 77 N.E.2d 16 (1947)

8 ALR6th 1—§ 32

Steinburg v. Chesterfield County Planning Com'n, 527 F.3d 377 (4th Cir. 2008)

---

70 ALR6th 513—§ 11

71 ALR6th 471—§ 11

Steineke v. Share Health Plan, 246 Neb.
374, 518 N.W.2d 904, 56 A.L.R.5th
929 (1994)

51 ALR5th 271—§ 4

56 ALR5th 737—§ 3

Steiner, In re, 2006 WL 3333085 (Mich.
Ct. App. 2006)

27 ALR6th 323—§ 5

Steiner, In re Marriage of, 89 Cal. App.
3d 363, 152 Cal. Rptr. 612 (5th Dist.
1979)

5 ALR5th 550—§ 3

40 ALR5th 227—§ 17, 31, 39

67 ALR5th 1—§ 3, 25

Steiner v. City of Lebanon, 40 Ohio
App. 2d 219, 69 Ohio Op. 2d 207,
318 N.E.2d 853 (1st Dist. Warren
County 1973)

54 ALR6th 201—§ 22, 29, 44

Steiner v. Dacio, 2001-Ohio-1777, 2001
WL 1450980 (Ohio Ct. App. 5th
Dist. Tuscarawas County 2001)

95 ALR6th 541—§ 30, 60, 61

Steiner v. Enright, 237 A.D.2d 899, 654
N.Y.S.2d 515 (4th Dep't 1997)

50 ALR5th 1—§ 14

Steiner v. Fruehauf Corp., 121 F.R.D.
304 (E.D. Mich. 1988)

23 ALR5th 241—§ 21

Steiner v. Hercules, Inc., 835 F. Supp.
771 (D.C. Del. 1993)

23 ALR5th 241—§ 20

Steiner v. Jones, 677 N.Y.S.2d 124
(App. Div. 1st Dep't 1998)

30 ALR5th 571—§ 62

Steiner v. Southmark Corp., 739 F.
Supp. 1087 (N.D. Tex. 1990)

48 ALR5th 389—§ 3

Steiner v. Steiner, 179 Ariz. 606, 880
P.2d 1152 (Ariz. App. 1994)

46 ALR5th 735—§ 3

Steiner v. Steiner, 788 So. 2d 771 (Miss.
2001)

59 ALR6th 433—§ 78

Steiner v. Steiner, 1995 WL 416941
(Ohio Ct. App. 4th Dist. Scioto
County 1995)

110 ALR5th 371—§ 6

Steiner Corp. v. American Dist. Tele-
graph, 106 Idaho 787, 683 P.2d 435
(1984)

36 ALR6th 305—§ 4

Steiner Corp. v. Benninghoff, 5 F. Supp.
2d 1117 (D. Nev. 1998)

16 ALR6th 693—§ 17

Steinfeld, Re, 79 B.R. 78 (F. BC M.D.
Fla. 1987)

14 ALR5th 242—§ 53

Steinfeld v. Foote-Goldman Proctologic
Medical Group, Inc., 50 Cal. App.
4th 1542, 58 Cal. Rptr. 2d 371 (2d
Dist. 1996)

125 ALR5th 193—§ 9, 10

Steinfeld v. Foote-Goldman Proctologic
Medical Group, Inc., 60 Cal. App.
4th 13, 70 Cal. Rptr. 2d 41 (2d Dist.
1997)

2 ALR6th 279—§ 19

Steingart v. White, 198 Cal. App. 3d
406, 243 Cal. Rptr. 678 (2d Dist.
1988)

14 ALR6th 301—§ 6, 20

Steingut v. Guaranty Trust Co. of N.Y.,
58 F. Supp. 623 (S.D. N.Y. 1944)

108 ALR5th 189—§ 12

Steinhaeufel v. Reliance Ins. Cos., 495
S.W.2d 463 (Mo. App. 1973)

31 ALR5th 116—§ 6

Steinhardt v. Batt, 753 So. 2d 928 (La.
Ct. App. 4th Cir. 2000)

74 ALR6th 209—§ 15

Steinhaus v. American Home Products
Corp., 795 N.Y.S.2d 41 (App. Div.
1st Dep't 2005)

125 ALR5th 357—§ 10

Steinhauser v. Steinhauser, 2000 WL
486618 (Neb. Ct. App. 2000)

36 ALR6th 1—§ 6, 13, 32

Steinhilber v. Alphonse, 68 N.Y.2d 283,
508 N.Y.S.2d 901, 501 N.E.2d 550,
1 I.E.R. Cas. (BNA) 1212, 123
L.R.R.M. (BNA) 2937, 13 Media L.

Rep. (BNA) 1562, 65 A.L.R.4th 987 (1986)

94 ALR5th 149—§ 5

Steinhoff v. Fisch, 847 P.2d 191 (Colo. App. 1992)

39 ALR5th 33—§ 8

Steinhorst v. H. C. Prange Co., 48 Wis. 2d 679, 180 N.W.2d 525 (1970)

1 ALR6th 297—§ 3, 4, 6, 8, 10, 17

Steinhour v. Ohio State University, 62 Ohio App. 3d 704, 577 N.E.2d 413 (Franklin Co. 1989)

57 ALR5th 477—§ 42

Steinhouse v. Herman Miller, Inc., 443 Pa. Super. 395, 661 A.2d 1379 (1995)

3 ALR6th 355—§ 10

Steinitz v. Motor Vehicle Acc. Indemnification Corp., 33 Misc. 2d 228, 225 N.Y.S.2d 147 (Sup. Ct. 1962)

103 ALR5th 1—§ 3

Steinkamp v. Caremark, 3 S.W.3d 191 (Tex. App. El Paso 1999)

31 ALR5th 1—§ 19

Steinke, In re, 2 Cal. App. 3d 569, 82 Cal. Rptr. 789 (1st Dist. 1969)

95 ALR5th 229—§ 15

Steinke v. Bell, 32 N.J. Super. 67, 107 A.2d 825 (App. Div. 1954)

11 ALR6th 695—§ 8

Steinke v. City of Andover, 525 N.W.2d 173 (Minn. 1994)

98 ALR6th 231—§ 44, 47

Steinke v. Palladium Amusement Co., 28 S.W.2d 440 (Mo. App. 1930)

38 ALR5th 107—§ 9

Steinke v. Player, 145 F.3d 1325, 1998 WL 230828 (4th Cir. 1998)

96 ALR5th 107—§ 6

Steinke v. Steinke, 126 Wis. 2d 372, 376 N.W.2d 839 (1985)

102 ALR5th 395—§ 4

Steinke, State ex rel. v. Lautenbaugh, 263 Neb. 652, 642 N.W.2d 132 (2002)

9 ALR6th 177—§ 5, 9

Steinkuehler v. State, 507 N.W.2d 716 (Iowa Ct. App. 1993)

78 ALR5th 197—§ 2, 10, 14

Steinle v. Workmen's Compensation Appeal Bd., 38 Pa. Commw. 241, 393 A.2d 503 (1978)

107 ALR5th 441—§ 28
109 ALR5th 161—§ 7
112 ALR5th 509—§ 18
122 ALR5th 653—§ 4
20 ALR6th 641—§ 26
39 ALR6th 445—§ 8

Steinman v. Baltimore Antiseptic Steam Laundry Co., 109 Md. 62, 71 A. 517 (1908)

13 ALR5th 217—§ 6

Steinman v. Di Roberts, 23 App. Div. 2d 693, 257 N.Y.S.2d 695 (2d Dep't 1965)

54 ALR5th 443—§ 15

Steinman v. John Hall Tailoring Co., 99 Kan. 699, 163 P. 452 (1917)

75 ALR5th 1—§ 7, 13, 14

Steinman v. Steinman, 80 App. Div. 2d 892, 436 N.Y.S.2d 901 (2d Dep't 1981)

5 ALR5th 550—§ 5

Steinmann v. Administrator, Unemployment Compensation Act, 25 Conn. Supp. 445, 207 A.2d 65 (Super Ct. 1964)

68 ALR5th 13—§ 9, 39, 40

Steinmann v. Silverman, 14 N.Y.2d 243, 251 N.Y.S.2d 1, 200 N.E.2d 192 (1964)

119 ALR5th 519—§ 6, 9

Steinmetz v. Caldor, Inc., 170 A.D.2d 935, 566 N.Y.S.2d 766 (3d Dep't 1991)

1 ALR6th 297—§ 26

Steinmetz v. Kern, 375 Ill. 616, 32 N.E.2d 151 (1941)

24 ALR6th 399—§ 8, 17

Steinmetz v. Klabunde, 261 Minn. 487, 113 N.W.2d 444 (1962)

40 ALR6th 99—§ 65

Steinmetz v. Saathoff, 84 S.W.2d 437 (Mo. App. 1935)

27 ALR5th 174—§ 68

Steinway v. Village of Pontoon Beach, 2008 WL 2704897 (S.D. Ill. 2008)
45 ALR6th 1—§ 21, 23

Steinwehr v. State, 37 Tenn. 586, 5 Sneed 586, 1858 WL 2801 (1858)
5 ALR6th 1—§ 36, 46

Steiny & Co., Inc. v. J.A. Jones Const. Co., 2002 WL 596800 (Cal. App. 4th Dist. 2002)
124 ALR5th 375—§ 3, 5

Steinzeig v. Mechanics & Traders Ins. Co., 297 S.W.2d 778 (Mo. App. 1957)
22 ALR5th 579—§ 7, 23

Steirer by Steirer v. Bethlehem Area School Dist., 987 F.2d 989, 81 Ed. Law Rep. 734 (3d Cir. 1993)
73 ALR6th 281—§ 6
88 ALR6th 203—§ 11, 24, 52

Steketee v. Lintz, Williams & Rothberg, 38 Cal. 3d 46, 210 Cal. Rptr. 781, 694 P.2d 1153 (1985)
71 ALR5th 307—§ 4, 17, 20, 22
14 ALR6th 301—§ 6

Stelco Industries, Inc. v. Cohen, 182 Conn. 561, 438 A.2d 759, 31 U.C.C. Rep. Serv. 86 (1980)
89 ALR5th 319—§ 7

St. Elizabeth's Hosp. v. State Bd. of Professional Medical Conduct, 174 A.D.2d 225, 579 N.Y.S.2d 457 (3d Dep't 1992)
65 ALR6th 295—§ 26

Stell, Re, 56 Wash. App. 356, 783 P.2d 615 (1989)
15 ALR5th 692—§ 8, 12

Stell v. Caylor, 223 So. 2d 423 (La. App. 3d Cir. 1969)
11 ALR5th 715—§ 2, 9, 20

Stell v. Firestone Tire & Rubber Co., 306 F. Supp. 17 (W.D. N.C. 1969)
48 ALR5th 1—§ 2
93 ALR5th 103—§ 2

Stell v. Jay Hales Development Co., 11 Cal. App. 4th 1214, 15 Cal. Rptr. 2d 220 (2d Dist. 1992)
118 ALR5th 91—§ 16

Stell v. State, 2013 WL 3947179 (Tex. App. Dallas 2013)
99 ALR6th 295—§ 13

Stell v. Townsends California Glace Fruits, Inc., 138 Cal. App. Supp. 777, 28 P.2d 1077 (1934)
2 ALR5th 1—§ 2, 49

Stella v. DePaul Community Health Center, Inc., 642 F.2d 258 (8th Cir. 1981)
75 ALR5th 1—§ 3

Stella Jewelry Mfg. v. Naviga Belgamar ex rel. Penem Int'l, 885 F. Supp. 84 (S.D. N.Y. 1995)
22 ALR5th 579—§ 21

Stellakis v. Hasbrouck, 112 N.J.L. 184, 170 A. 31 (N.J. Sup. Ct. 1934)
104 ALR6th 97—§ 3

Steller v. Pennsylvania Securities Com'n, 877 A.2d 518, Blue Sky L. Rep. (CCH) ¶ 74545 (Pa. Commw. Ct. 2005)
28 ALR6th 281—§ 14, 27

Steller v. Steller, 97 N.J. Super. 493, 235 A.2d 476, 31 A.L.R.3d 526 (1967)
48 ALR5th 473—§ 8
52 ALR5th 221—§ 3, 20

Stelloh v. Cottage 83, 52 Ill. App. 2d 168, 201 N.E.2d 672 (1st Dist. 1964)
43 ALR5th 207—§ 6, 34, 36

Stelluti v. Casapenn Enterprises, LLC, 203 N.J. 286, 1 A.3d 678, 61 A.L.R.6th 659 (2010)
61 ALR6th 147—§ 3, 4, 8, 9

Stellwagen v. Clum, 245 U.S. 605, 38 S. Ct. 215, 62 L. Ed. 507 (1918)
77 ALR6th 273—§ 6

Stelly v. State, 1994 WL 400302 (Tex. App. Houston 1st Dist. 1994)
68 ALR6th 527—§ 37

Stelly v. Waggoner Estates, 355 So. 2d 12 (La. App. 1st Cir. 1977)
1 ALR5th 132—§ 19

Stelmack v. Glen Alden Coal Co., 339 Pa. 410, 14 A.2d 127 (1940)
98 ALR5th 353—§ 8

Stelter v. Calvert, 456 S.W.2d 202 (Tex. Civ. App. Austin 1970)
14 ALR6th 119—§ 88

Steltz v. City of Wausau, 88 Wis. 618, 60 N.W. 1054 (1894)
54 ALR6th 201—§ 48

Stem, Ex parte, 571 So. 2d 1112, 13 U.C.C.R.S.2d 1070 (Ala)
38 ALR5th 191—§ 2, 9

Ste-Marie v. State, 32 S.W.3d 446 (Tex. App. Houston 14th Dist. 2000)
78 ALR6th 599—§ 11

Stemen v. Coffman, 92 Mich. App. 595, 285 N.W.2d 305 (1979)
24 ALR5th 200—§ 3, 54

Stemley v. Downtown Medical Bldg., Inc., 762 S.W.2d 43 (Mo. 1988)
100 ALR5th 409—§ 13

Stemme v. Stemme, 351 S.W.2d 823 (Mo. Ct. App. 1961)
119 ALR5th 445—§ 5, 8, 20

Stemmer v. Kline, 128 N.J.L. 455, 26 A.2d 489 (N.J. Ct. Err. & App. 1942)
72 ALR5th 529—§ 20

Stemmer v. Scottish Union & National Ins. Co., 33 Or. 65, 53 P. 498 (1898)
63 ALR5th 675—§ 3

Stemmler v. City of Pittsburgh, 287 Pa. 365, 135 A. 100, 49 A.L.R. 1227 (1926)
12 ALR6th 645—§ 50, 53

Stemmler v. Randolph & C. R. Co., 169 N.C. 46, 85 S.E. 21 (1915)
25 ALR5th 391—§ 20

Stemmler v. State, 32 App. Div. 2d 861, 301 N.Y.S.2d 403 (3d Dep't 1969)
38 ALR5th 107—§ 4

Stemple v. Dobson, 400 S.E.2d 561, 8 A.L.R.5th 957 (W. Va. 1990)
8 ALR5th 312—§ 4

Stemple v. Maryland Cas. Co., 2005 WL 3489510 (D. Kan. 2005)
69 ALR6th 415—§ 10, 17, 54

Stempler v. Stempler, 143 A.D.2d 410, 532 N.Y.S.2d 550 (2d Dep't 1988)
4 ALR5th 403—§ 3, 5

7 ALR6th 411—§ 12, 43

Stemplewski v. Suntrust Mortg., Inc., 2010 WL 2179152 (N.D. Cal. 2010)
86 ALR6th 411—§ 5

Stenberg v. Carhart, 120 S. Ct. 2597 (U.S. 2000)
76 ALR5th 637—§ 3 to 5

Stenberg v. Carhart, 2000 WL 825889 (U.S. June 28, 2000)
76 ALR5th 637—§ 1 to 6

Stenberg v. Liennemann, 20 Mont. 457, 52 P. 84 (1898)
46 ALR5th 1—§ 22

Stenberg, State ex rel. v. Moore, 258 Neb. 738, 605 N.W.2d 440 (2000)
73 ALR6th 281—§ 31

Stenbock v. Hartford Fire Ins. Co., 217 F.3d 846 (9th Cir. 2000)
98 ALR5th 1—§ 19

Stender v. Stender, 181 Mich. 648, 148 N.W. 255 (1914)
31 ALR5th 499—§ 3, 15

Stender v. Vincent, 92 Haw. 355, 992 P.2d 50 (2000)
102 ALR5th 99—§ 4

Stene v. Hillgren, 78 S.D. 1, 98 N.W.2d 156 (1959)
12 ALR5th 195—§ 4, 10

Stenehjem v. Kyn Jin Cho, 631 P.2d 482 (Alaska 1981)
13 ALR5th 684—§ 2

Stenehjem, State ex rel. v. FreeEats.com, Inc., 2006 ND 84, 712 N.W.2d 828 (N.D. 2006)
26 ALR6th 659—§ 57
77 ALR6th 1—§ 13, 15

Stenerson, Matter of Marriage of, 30 Or. App. 61, 566 P.2d 205 (1977)
124 ALR5th 441—§ 3, 4, 8

Stengel v. Columbus, 737 F. Supp. 1460 (S.D. Ohio 1989)
36 ALR5th 1—§ 2, 17, 19, 23

Stengel v. Medtronic Inc., 704 F.3d 1224, Prod. Liab. Rep. (CCH) ¶ 18981 (9th Cir. 2013)
90 ALR6th 75—§ 1

Stenger v. Genesys Regional Medical Center, 2005 WL 2372145 (Mich. Ct. App. 2005)
92 ALR6th 379—§ 28

Stenhouse v. Winn Dixie Stores, Inc., 147 Ga. App. 473, 249 S.E.2d 276 (1978)
40 ALR5th 135—§ 2, 15, 17
1 ALR6th 297—§ 17

Stennis v. Rekkas, 233 Ill. App. 3d 813, 175 Ill. Dec. 45, 599 N.E.2d 1059 (1st Dist. 1992)
4 ALR5th 210—§ 5, 12

Stenovich v. Wachtell, Lipton, Rosen & Katz, 195 Misc. 2d 99, 756 N.Y.S.2d 367 (Sup 2003)
47 ALR6th 255—§ 15

Stenquist, In re Marriage of, 145 Cal. App. 3d 430, 193 Cal. Rptr. 587 (4th Dist. 1983)
59 ALR6th 433—§ 78

Stenrich Group v. Jemmott, 251 Va. 186, 467 S.E.2d 795, 17 BNA OSHC 1573 (1996)
14 ALR5th 1—§ 3

Stenshoel, In re Marriage of, 72 Wash. App. 800, 866 P.2d 635 (1993)
10 ALR5th 191—§ 4, 5

Stenson v. McLaughlin, 2001 DNH 159, 2001 WL 1033614 (D.N.H. 2001)
53 ALR6th 491—§ 22
73 ALR6th 281—§ 31

Stensrud v. Szabo Contracting Co., Inc., 16 Nat'l Disability Law Rep. ¶ 73, 1999 WL 592110 (N.D. Ill. 1999)
99 ALR5th 65—§ 9

Stensto v. Sunset Memorial Park, Inc., 759 S.W.2d 261, 1988-2 CCH Trade Cases ¶ 68213 (Mo. App. 1988)
54 ALR5th 681—§ 2, 21

Stensvad v. Miners and Merchants Bank of Roundup, 196 Mont. 193, 640 P.2d 1303 (1982)
81 ALR6th 161—§ 4
82 ALR6th 43—§ 8

Stenzel v. Dell, Inc., 2005 ME 37, 870 A.2d 133 (Me. 2005)
13 ALR6th 145—§ 9, 17

Stenzler v. Commerdinger, 50 Misc. 2d 235, 269 N.Y.S.2d 865 (1966)
2 ALR5th 553—§ 47

Steo v. Cucuzza, 624 N.Y.S.2d 203 (App. Div. 2d Dep't 1995)
9 ALR5th 321—§ 11

Stepakoff v. Kantar, 393 Mass. 836, 473 N.E.2d 1131 (1985)
81 ALR5th 167—§ 9

Stepanek v. Rinker Materials Corp., 697 So. 2d 200 (Fla. Dist. Ct. App. 1st Dist. 1997)
22 ALR6th 329—§ 13, 28

Stepanek v. Roth, 418 So. 2d 74 (Miss. 1982)
25 ALR5th 233—§ 14

Stepdesign, Inc. v. Research Media, Inc., 442 F. Supp. 32, 200 U.S.P.Q. 77 (S.D. N.Y. 1977)
76 ALR6th 289—§ 7

Stepek v. Doe, 392 Ill. App. 3d 739, 331 Ill. Dec. 246, 910 N.E.2d 655 (1st Dist. 2009)
53 ALR6th 569—§ 11

S. Tepfer & Sons, Inc. v. Zschaler, 25 A.D.2d 786, 269 N.Y.S.2d 552 (2d Dep't 1966)
24 ALR6th 399—§ 18

Stephan v. Allstate Ins. Co., 26 Ariz. App. 367, 548 P.2d 1179, 80 A.L.R.3d 1173 (Div. 1 1976)
63 ALR5th 427—§ 2, 15

Stephan v. Apartment Hotels, 1938 OK 149, 182 Okla. 274, 77 P.2d 539 (1938)
99 ALR5th 141—§ 3, 6

Stephan v. Lynch, 136 Vt. 226, 388 A.2d 376 (1978)
18 ALR5th 525—§ 3

Stephan v. Marlin Firearms Co., 353 F.2d 819 (2d Cir. 1965)
47 ALR5th 395—§ 14
96 ALR5th 239—§ 15

Stephan v. Sears Roebuck & Co., 110 N.H. 248, 266 A.2d 855, 7 U.C.C. Rep. Serv. 1318 (1970)
4 ALR6th 401—§ 4, 6

Stephan v. State, 205 Ga. App. 241, 422 S.E.2d 25, 92 Fulton County D R 1664 (1992)

18 ALR5th 804—§ 2, 4, 8

Stephan v. State, 711 P.2d 1156 (Alaska 1985)

69 ALR6th 579—§ 8, 23, 30

Stephanie, In re, 456 A.2d 268 (R.I. 1983)

116 ALR5th 559—§ 6

Stephanie, In re, 660 A.2d 260 (R.I. 1995)

122 ALR5th 385—§ 15

Stephan, State ex rel. v. Carlin, 230 Kan. 252, 631 P.2d 668 (1981)

87 ALR6th 633—§ 8

Stephan, State ex rel. v. GAF Corp., 242 Kan. 152, 747 P.2d 1326 (1987)

3 ALR5th 851—§ 9
14 ALR5th 242—§ 36
47 ALR5th 395—§ 15

Stephan, State ex rel. v. Kansas House of Representatives, 236 Kan. 45, 687 P.2d 622 (1984)

24 ALR6th 255—§ 5, 11, 13

Stephan, State ex rel. v. Williams, 246 Kan. 681, 793 P.2d 234 (1990)

32 ALR6th 531—§ 33

Stephen, Matter of, 239 A.D.2d 963, 659 N.Y.S.2d 588 (4th Dep't 1997)

61 ALR5th 151—§ 5, 15

Stephen v. City of Lincoln, 209 Neb. 792, 311 N.W.2d 889 (1981)

87 ALR5th 1—§ 10, 18, 20, 31

Stephen v. Commissioner of Social Sec., 386 F. Supp. 2d 1257, 106 Soc. Sec. Rep. Serv. 529 (M.D. Fla. 2005)

17 ALR6th 593—§ 3, 5, 7

Stephen v. MacKinnon, 7 Mass. L. Rptr. 241, 1997 WL 426972 (Mass. Super. Ct. 1997)

85 ALR5th 261—§ 3, 4, 6

Stephen v. Maximum Sec. & Investigations, Inc., 2000 WL 1774849 (S.D. N.Y. 2000)

103 ALR5th 557—§ 5

Stephen v. Zivnostenska Banka, Nat. Corp., 3 N.Y.2d 862, 166 N.Y.S.2d 309, 145 N.E.2d 24 (1957)

108 ALR5th 189—§ 12

Stephen & Hayes Const., Inc. v. Meadowbrook Homes, Inc., 988 F. Supp. 1194, 45 U.S.P.Q.2d 1939 (N.D. Ill. 1998)

76 ALR6th 289—§ 4, 5
77 ALR6th 543—§ 6, 11

Stephen C., In re, 170 App. Div. 2d 1035, 566 N.Y.S.2d 178 (4th Dep't 1991)

61 ALR5th 151—§ 10

Stephen Equip. Co. v. Baca, 703 P.2d 1332 (Colo. App. 1985)

57 ALR5th 141—§ 21

Stephen K. v. Roni L., 105 Cal. App. 3d 640, 164 Cal. Rptr. 618, 31 A.L.R.4th 383 (2d Dist. 1980)

2 ALR5th 301—§ 3
2 ALR5th 337—§ 3

Stephen L.H. v. Sherry L.H., 195 W. Va. 384, 465 S.E.2d 841 (1995)

1 ALR5th 776—§ 11

Stephens, In re, 149 B.R. 414 (Bankr. E.D. Tex. 1992)

89 ALR5th 577—§ 14

Stephens, In re, 851 N.E.2d 1256 (Ind. 2006)

25 ALR6th 1—§ 38

Stephens, In re Marriage of, 184 Cal. App. 3d 616, 229 Cal. Rptr. 238 (5th Dist. 1986)

59 ALR6th 433—§ 61

Stephens, Matter of, 98 Misc. 2d 137, 413 N.Y.S.2d 591 (Fam. Ct. 1979)

71 ALR5th 1—§ 3

Stephens v. A-Able Rents Co., 101 Ohio App. 3d 20, 654 N.E.2d 1315 (8th Dist. Cuyahoga County 1995)

96 ALR5th 485—§ 15

Stephens v. Alabama State Docks Terminal Ry., 723 So. 2d 83 (Ala. Civ. App. 1998)

79 ALR6th 377—§ 5

Stephens v. Allied Mut. Ins. Co., 182 Neb. 562, 156 N.W.2d 133, 26 A.L.R.3d 873 (1968)
31 ALR5th 116—§ 5
40 ALR5th 603—§ 4
Stephens v. American Home Assur. Co., 811 F. Supp. 937 (S.D. N.Y. 1993)
39 ALR6th 391—§ 9
Stephens v. American Home Assur. Co., 1995 WL 230333, 23 Media L. Rep. 1769 (S.D. N.Y., Apr 17, 1995)
60 ALR5th 75—§ 16
Stephens v. Berry, 249 Cal. App. 2d 474, 57 Cal. Rptr. 505 (1st Dist. 1967)
97 ALR6th 375—§ 19
Stephens v. Bongart, 15 N.J. Misc. 80, 189 A. 131 (Juv. & Dom. Rel. Ct. 1937)
70 ALR5th 169—§ 5, 27
Stephens v. Carter, 246 N.C. 318, 98 S.E.2d 311 (1957)
107 ALR5th 311—§ 5
Stephens v. City of Butler, Ala., 509 F. Supp. 2d 1098 (S.D. Ala. 2007)
45 ALR6th 1—§ 25, 32
52 ALR6th 623—§ 12
Stephens v. City of Topeka, Kan., 33 F. Supp. 2d 947, 77 Empl. Prac. Dec. (CCH) ¶ 46272 (D. Kan. 1999)
105 ALR5th 499—§ 4
Stephens v. Clairmont Center, Inc., 230 Ga. App. 793, 498 S.E.2d 307 (1998)
31 ALR5th 550—§ 9
43 ALR5th 207—§ 5, 76, 82
Stephens v. Coldwell Banker Commercial Group, Inc., 199 Cal. App. 3d 1394, 245 Cal. Rptr. 606, 54 Fair Empl. Prac. Cas. (BNA) 1102 (1st Dist. 1988)
51 ALR5th 1—§ 5
81 ALR5th 367—§ 34
Stephens v. Collison, 256 Ill. 238, 99 N.E. 914 (1912)
23 ALR6th 1—§ 31
Stephens v. Costello, 55 F. Supp. 2d 163 (W.D. N.Y. 1999)
12 ALR6th 267—§ 10

Stephens v. Creel, 429 So. 2d 278 (Ala. 1983)
33 ALR5th 1—§ 16
Stephens v. Crestview Cadillac, Inc., 64 Ohio App. 3d 129, 580 N.E.2d 842 (10th Dist. Franklin County 1989)
67 ALR6th 209—§ 40
Stephens v. Denison, 64 S.W.3d 297 (Ky. Ct. App. 2001)
11 ALR6th 1—§ 4, 11
12 ALR6th 1—§ 4, 18
Stephens v. Denison, 150 S.W.3d 80 (Ky. Ct. App. 2004)
60 ALR6th 1—§ 88
Stephens v. Dover Elevator Co., 109 Ga. App. 112, 135 S.E.2d 593 (1964)
115 ALR5th 1—§ 14
Stephens v. Ely, 162 N.Y. 79, 56 N.E. 499 (1900)
109 ALR5th 421—§ 3, 8
Stephens v. Equitable Life Assur. Society of U.S., 850 So. 2d 78 (Miss. 2003)
61 ALR6th 239—§ 33
Stephens v. Fourth Judicial Dist. Court, 2006 MT 21, 331 Mont. 40, 128 P.3d 1026 (2006)
52 ALR6th 433—§ 8, 11
Stephens v. Fourth Judicial Dist. Court, 2006 MT 21, 331 Mont. 40, 128 P.3d 1026 (Mont. 2006)
57 ALR6th 163—§ 4, 7, 16, 41, 42
Stephens v. G.D. Searle & Co., 602 F. Supp. 379, 40 U.C.C. Rep. Serv. 441 (E.D. Mich. 1985)
54 ALR5th 1—§ 3 to 5, 9
57 ALR5th 1—§ 5, 30
93 ALR5th 103—§ 12
83 ALR6th 1—§ 31, 48
Stephens v. Geoghegan, 702 So. 2d 517 (Fla. Dist. Ct. App. 2d Dist. 1997)
100 ALR5th 341—§ 3, 8
Stephens v. Gillispie, 126 Wash. App. 375, 108 P.3d 1230 (Div. 3 2005)
9 ALR6th 363—§ 16
Stephens v. Guffey, 409 S.W.2d 62 (Mo. 1966)
26 ALR5th 401—§ 14, 27

Stephens v. Henderson, 741 P.2d 952, 63 Utah Adv. Rep. 10 (Utah 1987)
38 ALR5th 107—§ 4

Stephens v. John Hancock Mut. Life Ins. Co., 12 N.J. Super. 537, 79 A.2d 903, 28 BNA LRRM 2542 (1951)
5 ALR5th 422—§ 3

Stephens v. Jones, 710 S.W.2d 38 (Tenn. App. 1984)
3 ALR5th 1—§ 3, 4, 11

Stephens v. Lever Bros. Co., 155 S.W.2d 540, 4 CCH LC ¶ 60713 (Mo. App. 1941)
14 ALR5th 242—§ 47

Stephens v. LPP Mortgage, Ltd., 316 S.W.3d 742 (Tex. App. Austin 2010)
86 ALR6th 411—§ 3

Stephens v. Mayor, Etc., of Albany, 84 Ga. 630, 11 S.E. 150 (1890)
56 ALR6th 523—§ 7

Stephens v. Miami Copper Co., 59 Ariz. 528, 130 P.2d 507 (1942)
26 ALR5th 127—§ 7

Stephens v. Natchitoches Parish School Board, 110 So. 2d 156 (La. App. 2d Cir. 1959)
27 ALR5th 174—§ 68

Stephens v. Parkview Hosp., Inc., 745 N.E.2d 262 (Ind. Ct. App. 2001)
16 ALR5th 262—§ 31

Stephens v. Pattou, 208 A.D. 63, 203 N.Y.S. 40 (1st Dep't 1924)
52 ALR6th 271—§ 6

Stephens v. Petrino, 350 Ark. 268, 86 S.W.3d 836 (2002)
95 ALR6th 85—§ 65

Stephens v. Schadler, 182 Ky. 833, 207 S.W. 704 (1919)
3 ALR5th 237—§ 19, 20

Stephens v. Shelbyville Central Schools, 162 Ind. App. 229, 318 N.E.2d 590 (1st Dist. 1974)
66 ALR5th 1—§ 2, 21

Stephens v. Snyder Clinic Ass'n, 230 Kan. 115, 631 P.2d 222 (1981)
5 ALR6th 133—§ 4, 14
14 ALR6th 301—§ 15

Stephens v. Southern Pacific Co., 109 Cal. 86, 41 P. 783 (1895)
25 ALR5th 391—§ 101

Stephens v. Sponholz, 674 N.Y.S.2d 244 (App. Div. 4th Dep't 1998)
8 ALR5th 312—§ 4

Stephens v. State, 43 So. 3d 709 (Fla. 1st DCA 2010)
78 ALR6th 417—§ 41

Stephens v. State, 97 S.W. 483 (Tex. Crim. App. 1906)
54 ALR6th 429—§ 26, 29

Stephens v. State, 247 Ga. App. 719, 545 S.E.2d 325 (2001)
6 ALR5th 733—§ 15
68 ALR6th 115—§ 29, 40

Stephens v. State, 276 S.W.3d 148 (Tex. App. Amarillo 2008)
103 ALR6th 247—§ 19

Stephens v. State, 290 Ark. 440, 720 S.W.2d 301 (1986)
91 ALR5th 343—§ 4

Stephens v. State, 369 N.W.2d 603 (Minn. Ct. App. 1985)
73 ALR5th 383—§ 6

Stephens v. State, 541 N.E.2d 280 (Ind. 1989)
72 ALR5th 109—§ 5, 6

Stephens v. State, 675 So. 2d 73 (Ala. Crim. App. 1995)
27 ALR5th 593—§ 28

Stephens v. State, 774 P.2d 60 (Wyo. 1989)
38 ALR5th 433—§ 11, 16, 24

Stephens v. State Dept. of Revenue, Motor Vehicle Div., 671 P.2d 1348 (Colo. Ct. App. 1983)
109 ALR5th 611—§ 6

Stephens v. State Farm Mut. Auto. Ins. Co., 508 F.2d 1363 (5th Cir. 1975)
16 ALR6th 491—§ 4

Stephens v. State of Cal., 28 F.3d 108 (9th Cir. 1994)
72 ALR5th 403—§ 15

Stephens v. Stearns, 106 Idaho 249, 678 P.2d 41 (1984)
70 ALR5th 261—§ 2

74 ALR5th 523—§ 2, 6, 38
75 ALR5th 413—§ 2
Stephens v. Stephens, 181 Ky. 480, 205 S.W. 573 (1918)
3 ALR5th 394—§ 6, 7, 21
Stephens v. Stephens, 407 N.W.2d 468 (Minn. App. 1987)
11 ALR5th 259—§ 30
Stephens v. Stephens, 472 So. 2d 1071 (Ala. Civ. App. 1985)
49 ALR5th 441—§ 21
Stephens v. Stephens, 646 N.E.2d 682 (Ind. App. 1995)
20 ALR5th 700—§ 20
Stephens v. Stephens, 1993 WL 50867 (Ohio Ct. App. 10th Dist. Franklin County 1993)
59 ALR6th 433—§ 74
Stephens v. Tate, 147 Ga. App. 366, 249 S.E.2d 92 (1978)
2 ALR5th 553—§ 48
Stephens v. Toomey, 51 Cal. 2d 864, 338 P.2d 182 (1959)
10 ALR6th 31—§ 54
Stephens v. Town of Jonesboro, 642 So. 2d 274 (La. App. 2d Cir. 1994)
48 ALR5th 129—§ 14
50 ALR5th 1—§ 9
Stephens v. U.S., 14 F. Supp. 2d 1322 (N.D. Ga. 1998)
71 ALR6th 1—§ 8
Stephens v. U.S., 83 A.F.T.R.2d 99-1756, 1999 WL 256233 (E.D. Cal. 1999)
2 ALR6th 195—§ 16
Stephens v. Wayne County Concealed Weapons Licensing Bd., 2012 WL 2865783 (Mich. Ct. App. 2012)
91 ALR6th 435—§ 22, 29, 151
Stephens v. West Virginia College of Graduate Studies, 203 W. Va. 81, 506 S.E.2d 336 (1998)
9 ALR5th 321—§ 5
11 ALR5th 588—§ 4
Stephens v. Yeomans, 327 F. Supp. 1182 (D.N.J. 1970)
10 ALR6th 31—§ 20

Stephens & Rankin, Inc. v. Hartnett, 160 App. Div. 2d 1201, 555 N.Y.S.2d 208, 29 BNA WH Cas. 1309, 116 CCH LC ¶ 56405 (3d Dep't 1990)
5 ALR5th 470—§ 3
Stephens Industries, Inc. v. Haskins & Sells, 438 F.2d 357 (CA10 Colo. 1971)
48 ALR5th 389—§ 3, 5, 7
Stephenson, In re Marriage of, 39 Cal. App. 4th 71, 46 Cal. Rptr. 2d 8 (4th Dist. 1995)
36 ALR6th 1—§ 6, 12, 15, 26
Stephenson v. 30 Fifth Ave., Inc., 1 App. Div. 2d 469, 151 N.Y.S.2d 37 (1956)
42 ALR5th 53—§ 32
Stephenson v. Barringer, 758 F. Supp. 657 (D.C. Kan. 1991)
8 ALR5th 653—§ 3
Stephenson v. Bartlett, 357 N.C. 301, 582 S.E.2d 247, 2003 WL 21657178 (2003)
114 ALR5th 311—§ 7
Stephenson v. Capano Development, Inc., 462 A.2d 1069 (Del. 1983)
117 ALR5th 155—§ 10
Stephenson v. City of Fort Smith, 71 Ark. App. 190, 36 S.W.3d 754 (2000)
93 ALR6th 207—§ 24, 30
96 ALR6th 355—§ 8, 22
Stephenson v. City of Palm Springs, 52 Cal. 2d 407, 340 P.2d 1009, 44 L.R.R.M. (BNA) 2371, 37 Lab. Cas. (CCH) ¶ 65596 (1959)
105 ALR5th 243—§ 10
Stephenson v. Davenport Community School Dist., 110 F.3d 1303, 117 Ed. Law Rep. 443 (8th Cir. 1997)
58 ALR5th 1—§ 42, 55
Stephenson v. Dow Chemical Co., 129 S. Ct. 1523, 173 L. Ed. 2d 667 (2009)
46 ALR6th 495—§ 40
Stephenson v. Furnas Elec. Co., 522 N.W.2d 828 (Iowa 1994)
14 ALR5th 1—§ 3

Stephenson v. Hammons, 308 P.2d 317
(Okla. 1957)
48 ALR5th 473—§ 5, 6

Stephenson v. Holiday Rambler Corp.,
709 So. 2d 139 (Fla. Dist. Ct. App.
4th Dist. 1998)
119 ALR5th 121—§ 3, 6
2 ALR6th 279—§ 15

Stephenson v. Honeywell Intern., Inc.,
669 F. Supp. 2d 1259 (D. Kan.
2009)
69 ALR6th 415—§ 59

Stephenson v. Litton Sys., Inc., 97 Ohio
App. 3d 125, 646 N.E.2d 259, 10
I.E.R. Cas. (BNA) 759 (2d Dist.
Montgomery County 1994)
104 ALR5th 1—§ 3

Stephenson v. Martin, 259 N.W.2d 467
(Minn. 1977)
125 ALR5th 1—§ 10

Stephenson v. Oatman, 71 Tenn. 462
(1879)
67 ALR5th 179—§ 9

Stephenson v. Perlitz, 537 S.W.2d 287
(Tex. Civ. App. Beaumont 1976)
25 ALR5th 123—§ 9

Stephenson v. Redd, 21 Va. Cir. 302,
1990 WL 751302 (1990)
75 ALR6th 109—§ 3

Stephenson v. Samford Zoning Bd.,
1999 WL 370527 (Conn. Super. Ct.
1999)
73 ALR5th 223—§ 8

Stephenson v. State, 334 Ark. 520, 975
S.W.2d 830 (1998)
23 ALR6th 307—§ 42

Stephenson v. State, 494 S.W.2d 900
(Tex. Crim. 1973)
55 ALR5th 125—§ 3

Stephenson v. State, 606 A.2d 740 (Del.
Sup. 1992)
31 ALR5th 704—§ 5, 15, 16

Stephenson v. State, 801 So. 2d 34 (Ala.
Crim. App. 2000)
70 ALR6th 361—§ 34

Stephenson v. State, 864 N.E.2d 1022
(Ind. 2007)
71 ALR6th 625—§ 28

Stephenson v. State St. Bank & Trust
Co., 924 F. Supp. 1258 (D.C. Mass.
1996)
17 ALR5th 1—§ 3, 4

Stephenson v. Stephenson, 58 Va. Cir.
410, 2002 WL 507769 (2002)
16 ALR6th 693—§ 11

Stephenson v. Stephenson, 847 So. 2d
175 (La. Ct. App. 2d Cir. 2003)
26 ALR6th 331—§ 26

Stephenson v. Stewart, 285 S.W. 908
(Tex. Civ. App. 1926)
31 ALR5th 572—§ 9

Stephenson v. Velasquez, 141 Fed.
Appx. 301 (5th Cir. 2005)
89 ALR6th 1—§ 100

Stephenson v. Wilson, 619 F.3d 664 (7th
Cir. 2010)
71 ALR6th 625—§ 3, 26, 31

Stephens, State ex rel. v. Henson, 772
S.W.2d 706 (Mo. Ct. App. S.D.
1989)
99 ALR6th 1—§ 11

Stephen Sussna Associates v. Randolph
Tp. in Morris County, 122 N.J.
Super. 458, 300 A.2d 857 (App.
Div. 1973)
119 ALR5th 121—§ 2, 3

Stephen W., In re, 221 Cal. App. 3d 629,
271 Cal. Rptr. 319 (3d Dist. 1990)
20 ALR5th 534—§ 4

Stephen W. Brown Radiology Associates v. Gowers, 157 Ga. App. 770,
278 S.E.2d 653 (1981)
96 ALR6th 503—§ 76

Stepheny v. State, 570 S.W.2d 356
(Tenn. Crim. App. 1978)
39 ALR6th 257—§ 37

Stepherson v. State, 225 Ga. App. 219,
483 S.E.2d 631 (1997)
66 ALR5th 397—§ 4

Stephfon W., In re, 191 W. Va. 20, 442
S.E.2d 717 (1994)
37 ALR5th 703—§ 3, 5

Stephl v. Moore, 94 Fla. 313, 114 So.
455 (1927)
25 ALR5th 123—§ 10

Stephney v. State, 564 So. 2d 1246 (Fla. Dist. Ct. App. 3d Dist. 1990)
11 ALR6th 237—§ 4, 8, 12

Stepic v. Penton Media, Inc., 2000 WL 1867399 (Ohio Ct. App. 8th Dist. Cuyahoga County 2000)
94 ALR5th 1—§ 21, 24

Stepnes v. Tennessen, 2006 WL 2375645 (D. Minn. 2006)
86 ALR6th 173—§ 8

Stepp v. Black, 14 Tenn. App. 153 (1931)
12 ALR5th 195—§ 43 to 45

Stepp v. Ford Motor Credit Co., 623 F. Supp. 583, 1986-1 CCH Trade Cases ¶ 66937 (E.D. Wis 1985)
52 ALR5th 613—§ 3

Steppe v. Farber, 205 Wis. 80, 236 N.W. 530 (1931)
34 ALR5th 651—§ 2, 10

Steppe v. State, 193 So. 2d 617 (Fla. Dist. Ct. App. 3d Dist. 1967)
79 ALR5th 1—§ 12

Step Plan Services, Inc. v. Koresko, 12 A.3d 401 (Pa. Super. Ct. 2010)
104 ALR6th 303—§ 10

Steppler v. Board of Adjustment of Radnor Tp., 5 Pa. D. & C.2d 8 (C.P. 1955)
63 ALR5th 607—§ 10

Stepps v. State, 242 Ark. 587, 414 S.W.2d 620 (1967)
53 ALR6th 81—§ 5

Steppuhn v. Chicago, G. W. R. Co., 199 Mo. App. 571, 204 S.W. 579 (1918)
12 ALR5th 195—§ 42

Step-Saver Data Systems, Inc. v. Wyse Technology, 939 F.2d 91, 15 U.C.C. Rep. Serv. 2d 1 (3d Cir. 1991)
106 ALR5th 309—§ 4

Step Saver, Inc. v. Glacier Salt, Inc., 2005 WL 1389581 (Minn. Ct. App. 2005)
85 ALR6th 1—§ 28

Stepsay, In re, 15 Cal. 2d 71, 98 P.2d 489 (1940)
8 ALR6th 1—§ 17

Steptoe v. Auto-Owners Ins. Co., 210 Ga. App. 756, 437 S.E.2d 626 (1993)
116 ALR5th 247—§ 2
123 ALR5th 259—§ 2

Steptoe v. State, 1994 WL 222217 (Tex. App. Houston 14th Dist. 1994)
68 ALR6th 527—§ 37

Sterbenz v. Attina, 205 F. Supp. 2d 65 (E.D. N.Y. 2002)
101 ALR5th 61—§ 18

Sterbenz v. Sterbenz, 2004-Ohio-4577, 2004 WL 1933196 (Ohio Ct. App. 9th Dist. Summit County 2004)
39 ALR6th 205—§ 4

Sterchi Bros. Stores v. Podhouser, 61 Ga. App. 184, 6 S.E.2d 92 (1939)
104 ALR6th 97—§ 3

Stergios v. Forest Place Homeowner's Asso., 651 S.W.2d 396 (Tex. App. Dallas 1983)
25 ALR5th 233—§ 2, 25

Sterling v. Archambault, 138 Colo. 222, 332 P.2d 994 (1958)
10 ALR6th 31—§ 37

Sterling v. Audubon Ins. Co., 452 So. 2d 709 (La. App. 3d Cir. 1984)
56 ALR5th 407—§ 2

Sterling v. City of Oakland, 208 Cal. App. 2d 1, 24 Cal. Rptr. 696 (1st Dist. 1962)
68 ALR6th 1—§ 4

Sterling v. Contemporary Development Co., 1996 WL 367704 (Conn. Super. Ct. 1996)
104 ALR6th 1—§ 30

Sterling v. Gil Soucy Trucking, Ltd., 146 N.C. App. 173, 552 S.E.2d 674 (2001)
17 ALR6th 1—§ 27

Sterling v. H.P. Hood, Inc., 1 Wage & Hour Cas. 2d (BNA) 1567, 127 Lab. Cas. (CCH) ¶ 33058, 1993 WL 379431 (N.D. N.Y. 1993)
103 ALR5th 557—§ 5

Sterling v. Keidan, 162 Mich. App. 88, 412 N.W.2d 255 (1987)
51 ALR5th 603—§ 2

Sterling v. Miller, 2 A.D.2d 900, 157 N.Y.S.2d 145 (2d Dep't 1956)
11 ALR6th 587—§ 8

Sterling v. Orleans Parish School Bd., 679 So. 2d 167 (La. Ct. App. 4th Cir. 1996)
79 ALR5th 201—§ 15

Sterling v. Rust Communications, 113 S.W.3d 279, 31 Media L. Rep. (BNA) 2558 (Mo. Ct. App. E.D. 2003)
22 ALR6th 553—§ 16, 18, 23

Sterling v. Smith, 200 Pa. Super. 544, 189 A.2d 889 (1963)
18 ALR5th 230—§ 16

Sterling v. State, 421 So. 2d 1375 (Ala. Crim. App. 1982)
114 ALR5th 173—§ 9
123 ALR5th 179—§ 2, 4, 9

Sterling v. State, 814 S.W.2d 261 (Tex. App. Austin 1991)
23 ALR6th 1—§ 4, 15, 19

Sterling v. State, 2002 WL 31840756 (Tex. App. Amarillo 2002)
58 ALR6th 215—§ 7

Sterling v. Tenet, 416 F.3d 338, 96 Fair Empl. Prac. Cas. (BNA) 225, 86 Empl. Prac. Dec. (CCH) ¶ 42040 (4th Cir. 2005)
23 ALR6th 521—§ 2, 16

Sterling v. Upjohn Healthcare Services, Inc., 299 Ark. 278, 772 S.W.2d 329, 4 I.E.R. Cas. (BNA) 920 (1989)
7 ALR6th 563—§ 5

Sterling v. U.S. Agencies Cas. Co., Inc., 818 So. 2d 1053 (La. Ct. App. 4th Cir. 2002)
115 ALR5th 589—§ 8

Sterling v. Velsicol Chem. Corp., 855 F.2d 1188, 26 Fed. Rules Evid. Serv. 1037, 11 FR Serv. 3d 213, 19 ELR 20404 (CA6 Tenn. 1988)
6 ALR5th 162—§ 8
50 ALR5th 1—§ 12
51 ALR5th 467—§ 7
52 ALR5th 1—§ 4

Sterling v. Velsicol Chemical Corp., 647 F. Supp. 303, 24 Envt. Rep. Cas. 2017, 17 ELR 20081 (W.D. Tenn. 1986)
25 ALR5th 568—§ 5, 22

Sterling v. Williams, 2003 WL 174801 (Tenn. Ct. App. 2003)
21 ALR6th 577—§ 20

Sterling Boat Co., Inc. v. Arizona Marine, Inc., 134 Ariz. 55, 653 P.2d 703, 35 U.C.C. Rep. Serv. 1272 (Ct. App. Div. 1 1982)
58 ALR6th 289—§ 26

Sterling Builders, Inc. v. United Nat. Ins. Co., 79 Cal. App. 4th 105, 93 Cal. Rptr. 2d 697 (4th Dist. 2000)
97 ALR5th 473—§ 3, 19

Sterling Cheek v. Chubb & Son, Inc., 70 A.D.2d 622, 416 N.Y.S.2d 313 (2d Dep't 1979)
67 ALR5th 179—§ 8

Sterling Cotton Mills, Inc. v. Vaughan, 24 N.C. App. 696, 212 S.E.2d 199 (1975)
25 ALR5th 123—§ 3

Sterling Drug, Inc. v. Cornish, 370 F.2d 82 (CA8 Mo. 1966)
57 ALR5th 1—§ 3, 27

Sterling Drug, Inc. v. Oxford, 294 Ark. 239, 743 S.W.2d 380, 3 I.E.R. Cas. (BNA) 1060 (1988)
105 ALR5th 351—§ 3, 4, 12

Sterling Drug, Inc. v. Yarrow, 408 F.2d 978 (CA8 S.D. 1969)
57 ALR5th 1—§ 27

Sterling Elec. & Furniture Co. v. Peterson, 409 Pa. 435, 187 A.2d 285 (1963)
91 ALR5th 485—§ 6

Sterling Nat. Bank as Assignee of NorVergence, Inc. v. Eastern Shipping Worldwide, Inc., 35 A.D.3d 222, 826 N.Y.S.2d 235 (1st Dep't 2006)
39 ALR6th 629—§ 4

Sterling Sav. Bank v. Air Wisconsin Airlines Corp., 492 F. Supp. 2d 1256, 63 U.C.C. Rep. Serv. 2d 565 (E.D. Wash. 2007)

62 ALR6th 1—§ 9, 49

Sterling's Service v. Maughan, 635 P.2d 96 (Utah 1981)

79 ALR6th 211—§ 24

Sterling Steel Treating, Inc., Re, 94 B.R. 924, 18 BCD 1108, 21 CBC2d 126 (F. BC ED Mich. 1989)

8 ALR5th 312—§ 9, 13

Sterling Stores Co. v. Martin, 238 Ark. 1041, 386 S.W.2d 711 (1965)

6 ALR6th 1—§ 46, 51

Stern, Application of, 285 N.Y. 239, 33 N.E.2d 689, 133 A.L.R. 1332 (1941)

38 ALR5th 69—§ 3, 4

Stern, Matter of, 90 A.D.2d 338, 457 N.Y.S.2d 67 (1st Dep't 1982)

26 ALR6th 1—§ 26

Stern, Matter of, 92 N.J. 611, 458 A.2d 1279 (1983)

102 ALR5th 253—§ 10

Stern v. Ambach, 128 App. Div. 2d 232, 516 N.Y.S.2d 319 (3d Dep't 1987)

10 ALR5th 1—§ 28

Stern v. American States Ins. Co., 2003 WL 1611291 (Cal. App. 2d Dist. 2003)

45 ALR6th 493—§ 3, 4, 11, 23, 30, 32, 46, 52, 60

Stern v. Bluestone, 12 N.Y.3d 873, 883 N.Y.S.2d 782, 911 N.E.2d 844 (2009)

77 ALR6th 1—§ 101

Stern v. Bluestone, 47 A.D.3d 576, 850 N.Y.S.2d 90 (1st Dep't 2008)

77 ALR6th 1—§ 65

Stern v. Calzado, 163 App. Div. 2d 299, 557 N.Y.S.2d 156 (2d Dep't 1990)

48 ALR5th 129—§ 14

Stern v. Cincinnati Ins. Co., 252 Va. 307, 477 S.E.2d 517 (1996)

80 ALR6th 389—§ 17, 19

Stern v. Connecticut Medical Examining Bd., 208 Conn. 492, 545 A.2d 1080 (1988)

19 ALR6th 577—§ 3, 13

Stern v. Cosby, 645 F. Supp. 2d 258, 37 Media L. Rep. (BNA) 2288, 54 A.L.R.6th 725 (S.D. N.Y. 2009)

54 ALR6th 165—§ 7, 14

Stern v. Daniel, 47 Wash. 96, 91 P. 552 (1907)

71 ALR6th 249—§ 11

Stern v. Delphi Internet Services Corp., 165 Misc. 2d 21, 626 N.Y.S.2d 694, 23 Media L. Rep. (BNA) 1789 (Sup 1995)

54 ALR6th 99—§ 19, 21, 34, 36

Stern v. Great Plains Federal Sav. & Loan Asso., 778 P.2d 933 (Okla. App. 1989)

31 ALR5th 664—§ 7

Stern v. Hausberg, 22 A.D.2d 669, 253 N.Y.S.2d 447 (1st Dep't 1964)

17 ALR6th 159—§ 43

Stern v. Insurance Co. of North America, 62 N.J. 582, 303 A.2d 883 (1973)

35 ALR5th 375—§ 18

Stern v. Lanng, 106 La. 738, 31 So. 303 (1901)

30 ALR5th 571—§ 57

Stern v. Marshall, 131 S. Ct. 2594, 180 L. Ed. 2d 475, 55 Bankr. Ct. Dec. (CRR) 1, 65 Collier Bankr. Cas. 2d (MB) 827, Bankr. L. Rep. (CCH) ¶ 82032 (2011)

96 ALR6th 577—§ 8

Stern v. New Haven Community Schools, 529 F. Supp. 31 (E.D. Mich. 1981)

31 ALR5th 229—§ 16

Stern v. Roux, 2010 WL 1050302 (Ariz. Ct. App. Div. 1 2010)

57 ALR6th 163—§ 11, 12, 16, 42
60 ALR6th 193—§ 8
66 ALR6th 269—§ 16

Stern v. State, 128 A.D.2d 926, 512 N.Y.S.2d 580 (3d Dep't 1987)

48 ALR6th 243—§ 19

Stern v. State, 739 So. 2d 1203 (Fla. Dist. Ct. App. 4th Dist. 1999)

63 ALR6th 303—§ 18, 20

Stern v. Stern, 40 Ill. App. 2d 374, 188 N.E.2d 97 (1st Dist. 1963)

124 ALR5th 203—§ 10, 14

Stern v. Stern, 66 N.J. 340, 331 A.2d 257, 74 A.L.R.3d 613 (1975)

9 ALR5th 568—§ 14

3 ALR6th 447—§ 6, 12

Stern v. Stern, 67 App. Div. 2d 253, 415 N.Y.S.2d 225 (1st Dep't 1979)

17 ALR5th 366—§ 12

Stern v. Stern, 273 A.D.2d 298, 708 N.Y.S.2d 707 (2d Dep't 2000)

123 ALR5th 565—§ 7, 24

Stern v. Stern, 636 So. 2d 735, 18 FLW D 2590 (Fla. App. D4 1993)

30 ALR5th 139—§ 3

Stern v. Stern, 708 N.Y.S.2d 707 (App. Div. 2d Dep't 2000)

17 ALR5th 366—§ 11

Stern v. Taft, 49 Ohio App. 2d 405, 3 Ohio Op. 3d 463, 361 N.E.2d 279 (1st Dist. Hamilton County 1976)

75 ALR5th 1—§ 10

Stern v. Tarrant County Hospital Dist., 778 F.2d 1052 (CA5 Tex. 1985)

28 ALR5th 107—§ 21

Stern v. Unemployment Compensation Board of Review, 194 Pa. Super. 405, 168 A.2d 605 (1961)

23 ALR5th 176—§ 13

Stern v. Wisconsin Dept. of Revenue, 63 Wis. 2d 506, 217 N.W.2d 326 (1974)

2 ALR6th 1—§ 8

Stern v. Zamudio, 780 So. 2d 155 (Fla. Dist. Ct. App. 2d Dist. 2001)

125 ALR5th 193—§ 6

Stern & Son, Inc. v. Gary Joint Venture, 530 N.E.2d 306 (Ind. App. 1988)

46 ALR5th 1—§ 25

Sternbach v. Cornell University, 162 A.D.2d 922, 558 N.Y.S.2d 252, 61 Ed. Law Rep. 1068 (3d Dep't 1990)

75 ALR5th 413—§ 5, 11, 17, 44

Sternberg v. Hill, 269 A.D.2d 730, 711 N.Y.S.2d 512 (3d Dep't 2000)

14 ALR6th 543—§ 15

Sternberg v. Johnston, 131 S. Ct. 102, 178 L. Ed. 2d 29 (2010)

66 ALR6th 635—§ 8

Sternberg v. Johnston, 595 F.3d 937, Bankr. L. Rep. (CCH) ¶ 81682 (9th Cir. 2010)

66 ALR6th 635—§ 8

Sternberg v. New York Water Service Corp., 155 A.D.2d 658, 548 N.Y.S.2d 247, 10 U.C.C. Rep. Serv. 2d 732 (2d Dep't 1989)

97 ALR6th 1—§ 2, 26

Sternberg v. State Bar of Mich., 384 Mich. 588, 185 N.W.2d 395 (1971)

37 ALR6th 511—§ 12

Sternberg v. Sternberg, 203 Ga. 298, 46 S.E.2d 349 (1948)

32 ALR5th 673—§ 3

Sternberg Dredging Co. v. Sternberg's Estate, 351 Ill. App. (abstract) 514, 115 N.E.2d 557 (1953)

23 ALR5th 744—§ 5

Sternberger v. Marathon Oil Co., 257 Kan. 315, 894 P.2d 788, 132 O.G.R. 65 (1995)

99 ALR5th 415—§ 3

50 ALR6th 281—§ 28

Sternemann v. Langs, 93 App. Div. 2d 819, 460 N.Y.S.2d 614 (2d Dep't 1983)

51 ALR5th 467—§ 11, 15

Stern Enters. v. Plaza Theaters I & II, 105 Ohio App. 3d 601, 664 N.E.2d 981 (Portage Co. 1995)

14 ALR5th 242—§ 27

Sterner v. Freed, 391 Pa. Super. 254, 570 A.2d 1079 (1990)

111 ALR5th 313—§ 3

Sterner Aero AB v. Page Airmotive, Inc., 499 F.2d 709, 14 U.C.C.R.S. 1080 (CA10 Okla. 1974)

9 ALR5th 1—§ 14

Sternfels v. Metropolitan S. R. Co., 73 App. Div. 494, 77 N.Y.S. 309 (1902)

42 ALR5th 465—§ 3

Sterngass v. Town of Woodbury, 433 F. Supp. 2d 351 (S.D. N.Y. 2006)

68 ALR6th 229—§ 8
Sternheim v. Andrew Jackson Hotel
Operating Co., 42 Tenn. App. 613,
305 S.W.2d 249 (1957)
6 ALR6th 1—§ 3, 31, 33
Sternheim v. Silver Bell of Roslyn, Inc.,
66 Misc. 2d 726, 321 N.Y.S.2d 965,
9 U.C.C. Rep. Serv. 465 (City Ct.
1971)
44 ALR6th 441—§ 8
Sternoff Metals Corp. v. Vertecs Corp.,
39 Wash. App. 333, 693 P.2d 175
(1984)
42 ALR5th 199—§ 3, 6
Sterrett v. Hartzell, 640 N.E.2d 74, 94
Ed. Law Rep. 460 (Ind. Ct. App. 1st
Dist. 1994)
112 ALR5th 185—§ 4, 8
120 ALR5th 229—§ 7, 18
Sterrett v. Sterrett, 45 Ala. App. 375,
231 So. 2d 152 (Civ App. 1970)
53 ALR5th 375—§ 43
Sterry v. State, 959 S.W.2d 249 (Tex.
App. Dallas 1997)
22 ALR5th 261—§ 10
Stetser v. TAP Pharmaceutical Products,
Inc., 165 N.C. App. 1, 598 S.E.2d
570, 2004-1 Trade Cas. (CCH)
¶ 74464 (2004)
50 ALR6th 281—§ 3, 29
Stetson, Appeal of, 138 N.H. 293, 639
A.2d 245 (1994)
112 ALR5th 509—§ 17
13 ALR6th 209—§ 3, 14
39 ALR6th 445—§ 22
Stetson v. Feringa, 114 A.D.3d 1089,
981 N.Y.S.2d 207 (3d Dep't 2014)
96 ALR6th 103—§ 4
100 ALR6th 1—§ 38
Stetson-Post Mill Co. v. Brown, 21
Wash. 619, 59 P. 507 (1899)
46 ALR5th 1—§ 27, 47
Stetter v. reliable Silk Mfg. Co., 15 Pa.
D. & C. 18, 1930 WL 4681 (C.P.
1930)
103 ALR5th 157—§ 4, 11
Stettner v. Graubard, 82 Misc. 2d 132,
368 N.Y.S.2d 683 (Town Ct. 1975)

61 ALR5th 635—§ 6, 11, 21
Stetz v. American Casualty Co., 368 So.
2d 912 (Fla. App. D3 1979)
6 ALR5th 297—§ 18, 34
Stetz v. Skaggs Drug Ctrs., 114 N.M.
465, 840 P.2d 612 (App. 1992)
48 ALR5th 129—§ 12, 15, 20
Stetzer, People ex rel. v. Rawson, 61
Barb. 619, 1872 WL 9570 (N.Y.
Gen. Term 1872)
102 ALR5th 525—§ 23
Steuart Petroleum Co. v. Board of
County Comm'rs, 276 Md. 435, 347
A.2d 854 (1975)
38 ALR5th 737—§ 3
Steuben, Application of, 97 N.Y.S.2d
613 (Sup. Ct. 1950)
66 ALR5th 611—§ 3
Steuben Contracting, Inc. v. Employers
Ins. of Wausau, 975 F. Supp. 479
(W.D. N.Y. 1997)
98 ALR5th 193—§ 12
105 ALR5th 95—§ 18
Steuben Place Recreation Corp. v.
McGuiness, 15 Misc. 3d 1114(A),
839 N.Y.S.2d 437 (City Ct. 2007)
48 ALR6th 223—§ 2, 6
Steudle v. Territory, 19 Okla. 492, 91 P.
1024 (1907)
14 ALR5th 89—§ 25, 26, 32
Steuerwald v. Munn, 90 N.J. Eq. 474,
107 A. 796 (1919)
4 ALR5th 772—§ 5
Steve v. State, 875 P.2d 110 (Alaska
App. 1994)
46 ALR5th 499—§ 2, 4
Steve B.D., In re, 112 Idaho 22, 730 P.2d
942 (1986)
61 ALR5th 151—§ 11
Steve Foley Cadillac/Hanley Dawson v.
Industrial Com'n, 283 Ill. App. 3d
607, 219 Ill. Dec. 207, 670 N.E.2d
885 (1st Dist. 1996)
107 ALR5th 441—§ 14
109 ALR5th 161—§ 19
20 ALR6th 641—§ 10
Steve H. v. Wendy S., 67 Cal. Rptr. 2d
90 (App. 2d Dist. 1997)

110 ALR5th 371—§ 4
Steven, In re, 510 A.2d 955 (R.I. 1986)
46 ALR5th 523—§ 5, 11
Steven A. v. Susan B., 2003 WL 1985795 (Cal. App. 6th Dist. 2003)
123 ALR5th 565—§ 25
Steven C., In re, 169 Wis. 2d 727, 486 N.W.2d 572 (App. 1992)
40 ALR5th 227—§ 3, 43
Steven-Daniels Corp. v. Commercial Nat. Bank, 673 S.W.2d 651, 39 U.C.C. Rep. Serv. 553 (Tex. App. Dallas 1984)
91 ALR5th 89—§ 4
Steven E., In re, 229 Cal. App. 3d 1162, 280 Cal. Rptr. 540, 91 C.D.O.S. 3155, 91 Daily Journal DAR 5210 (2d Dist. 1991)
46 ALR5th 523—§ 2, 8
Steven F. v. Anaheim Union High School Dist., 112 Cal. App. 4th 904, 6 Cal. Rptr. 3d 105, 182 Ed. Law Rep. 565 (4th Dist. 2003)
123 ALR5th 411—§ 11
Steven G. v. Christine W., 151 Misc. 2d 99, 571 N.Y.S.2d 669 (Fam. Ct. 1991)
58 ALR5th 669—§ 3, 13
Steven G. by Robert G. v. Herget, 178 Wis. 2d 674, 505 N.W.2d 422 (Ct. App. 1993)
60 ALR5th 239—§ 4
Steven Greenberg Photography v. Matt Garrett's of Brockton, Inc., 816 F. Supp. 46 (D.C. Mass. 1992)
23 ALR5th 241—§ 33
Steven J. S., In re, 183 Wis. 2d 347, 515 N.W.2d 719 (Wis App. 1994)
28 ALR5th 46—§ 3, 6, 8
Steven Operating, Inc. v. Home State Sav., 105 F.R.D. 7 (S.D. Ohio 1984)
18 ALR5th 307—§ 2
Steven R. J. v. Nancy J., 117 Misc. 2d 725, 459 N.Y.S.2d 249 (Fam Ct. 1983)
46 ALR5th 735—§ 2, 9
Stevens, In Interest of, 669 A.2d 33 (Del. 1995)

61 ALR5th 151—§ 2, 8
Stevens, In re, 119 Cal. App. 4th 1228, 120 Cal. App. 4th 881H, 15 Cal. Rptr. 3d 168 (2d Dist. 2004)
4 ALR6th 1—§ 11
Stevens, In re, 130 F.3d 1027, Bankr. L. Rep. (CCH) ¶ 77587 (11th Cir. 1997)
47 ALR6th 347—§ 7
Stevens, In re Commitment of, 345 Ill. App. 3d 1050, 281 Ill. Dec. 415, 803 N.E.2d 1036 (4th Dist. 2004)
20 ALR6th 607—§ 5
Stevens, In re Commitment of, 2011 WL 691855 (Minn. Ct. App. 2011)
78 ALR6th 417—§ 5
Stevens, Matter of Estate of, 675 N.Y.S.2d 182 (App. Div. 3d Dep't 1998)
56 ALR5th 1—§ 3
Stevens v. Anderson, 75 Ariz. 331, 256 P.2d 712 (1953)
69 ALR5th 219—§ 3, 7
Stevens v. Anderson, 393 A.2d 158 (Me. 1978)
111 ALR5th 313—§ 3
Stevens v. Bechtel Constr. Corp., 655 So. 2d 423 (La. App. 4th Cir. 1995)
12 ALR5th 658—§ 33
Stevens v. Berger, 428 F. Supp. 896 (E.D.N.Y. 1977)
93 ALR5th 1—§ 3, 8
Stevens v. Bispham, 316 Or. 221, 851 P.2d 556 (1993)
12 ALR6th 1—§ 4, 5
Stevens v. Bow Mills Methodist Church, 111 N.H. 340, 283 A.2d 488 (1971)
8 ALR5th 1—§ 6, 32, 48
Stevens v. Bronx Cross County Medical Group, P.C., 256 A.D.2d 165, 681 N.Y.S.2d 531 (1st Dep't 1998)
48 ALR5th 129—§ 12
Stevens v. Burnham, 62 Neb. 672, 87 N.W. 546 (1901)
46 ALR5th 1—§ 9
109 ALR5th 421—§ 5
Stevens v. Buss, 128 S. Ct. 2423 (U.S. 2008)

36 ALR6th 681—§ 13

Stevens v. Cincinnati Ins. Co., 2002 WL 984631 (Iowa Ct. App. 2002)

22 ALR6th 113—§ 16

Stevens v. City of Glendale, 125 Cal. App. 3d 986, 178 Cal. Rptr. 367 (2d Dist. 1981)

106 ALR5th 523—§ 36

Stevens v. City of New York, 2013 WL 81327 (S.D. N.Y. 2013)

89 ALR6th 1—§ 55

Stevens v. Commonwealth, 124 Ky. 32, 30 Ky. L. Rptr. 290, 98 S.W. 284 (1906)

98 ALR6th 455—§ 19

Stevens v. Commonwealth, 1995 WL 748632 (Va. Ct. App. 1995)

107 ALR5th 567—§ 10

Stevens v. Com., Unemployment Compensation Bd. of Review, 81 Pa. Commw. 239, 473 A.2d 254 (1984)

25 ALR6th 101—§ 4

Stevens v. Equidyne Extractive Industries 1980, Petro/Coal Program 1, 694 F. Supp. 1057, CCH Fed Secur L. Rep. ¶ 93959 (S.D. N.Y. 1988)

7 ALR5th 852—§ 8, 33

Stevens v. Equidyne Extractive Industries 1980, Petro/Coal Program 1, 694 F. Supp. 1057, Fed. Sec. L. Rep. (CCH) ¶ 93959 (S.D. N.Y. 1988)

11 ALR6th 1—§ 4

Stevens v. Essex Fells Country Club, 136 N.J.L. 656, 57 A.2d 469 (N.J. Sup. Ct. 1948)

11 ALR6th 351—§ 29

Stevens v. First Interstate Bank of California, 167 Or. App. 280, 999 P.2d 551 (2000)

125 ALR5th 537—§ 1

Stevens v. Fleming, 116 Idaho 523, 777 P.2d 1196 (1989)

46 ALR5th 479—§ 2

Stevens v. Friedman, 58 W. Va. 78, 51 S.E. 132 (1905)

12 ALR5th 195—§ 3, 10

Stevens v. Hartford Acc. and Indem. Co., 29 Conn. App. 378, 615 A.2d 507 (1992)

84 ALR5th 399—§ 3, 12, 20

Stevens v. Hartford Acc. and Indem. Co., 39 Conn. App. 429, 664 A.2d 826 (1995)

84 ALR5th 399—§ 12

103 ALR5th 1—§ 3, 8

Stevens v. Horton, 161 Or. App. 454, 984 P.2d 868 (1999)

4 ALR5th 273—§ 3

Stevens v. Hunt, 646 F.2d 1168 (6th Cir. 1981)

90 ALR6th 235—§ 43

Stevens v. Inhabitants of Lincoln, 114 Mass. 476, 1874 WL 9459 (1874)

81 ALR6th 363—§ 21

Stevens v. Inland Waters, Inc., 220 Mich. App. 212, 559 N.W.2d 61, 6 A.D. Cas. (BNA) 490 (1996)

102 ALR5th 1—§ 5, 7

Stevens v. Iowa Newspapers, Inc., 711 N.W.2d 732, 34 Media L. Rep. (BNA) 1430 (Iowa Ct. App. 2006)

22 ALR6th 553—§ 16, 20, 32

Stevens v. Jeffrey Allen Corp., 131 Ohio App. 3d 298, 722 N.E.2d 533 (1st Dist. Hamilton County 1997)

15 ALR5th 119—§ 5

Stevens v. Kirby, 86 A.D.2d 391, 450 N.Y.S.2d 607 (4th Dep't 1982)

111 ALR5th 1—§ 3, 6, 8, 9

Stevens v. Lake, 615 So. 2d 1177 (Miss. 1993)

67 ALR5th 587—§ 2
87 ALR5th 473—§ 4, 14
11 ALR6th 1—§ 3, 4, 9
12 ALR6th 1—§ 3
13 ALR6th 1—§ 3
14 ALR6th 1—§ 3
15 ALR6th 427—§ 3

Stevens v. Lawyers Mut. Liability Ins. Co. of North Carolina, 789 F.2d 1056, 4 Fed. R. Serv. 3d 1151 (4th Cir. 1986)

92 ALR5th 273—§ 13

Steven S. v. Mary S., 277 Neb. 124, 760 N.W.2d 28 (2009)
100 ALR6th 1—§ 20
Stevens v. McBride, 489 F.3d 883 (7th Cir. 2007)
36 ALR6th 681—§ 13
71 ALR6th 625—§ 29
Stevens v. Metropolitan Transp. Authority Police Dept., 293 F. Supp. 2d 415 (S.D. N.Y. 2003)
65 ALR6th 93—§ 30
Stevens v. Moore, 211 S.C. 498, 46 S.E.2d 73 (1948)
27 ALR5th 174—§ 61, 63
Stevens v. Mt. Vernon Fire Ins. Co., 395 So. 2d 1206 (Fla. App. D3 1981)
5 ALR5th 875—§ 48
Stevens v. Murphy, 69 Wash. 2d 939, 421 P.2d 668 (1966)
118 ALR5th 513—§ 3
Stevens v. Muse, 562 So. 2d 852 (Fla. Dist. Ct. App. 4th Dist. 1990)
69 ALR5th 219—§ 7, 8
Stevens v. National Educ. Centers, Inc., 990 S.W.2d 374 (Tex. App. Houston 14th Dist. 1999)
86 ALR5th 397—§ 9
Stevens v. Owens-Corning Fiberglas Corp., 49 Cal. App. 4th 1645, 57 Cal. Rptr. 2d 525, 96 C.D.O.S. 7619, 96 Daily Journal DAR 12527, CCH Prod. Liab. Rep. ¶ 14753 (1st Dist. 1996)
12 ALR5th 195—§ 19
Stevens v. Owens-Corning Fiberglas Corp., 49 Cal. App. 4th 1645, 57 Cal. Rptr. 2d 525, Prod. Liab. Rep. (CCH) ¶ 14753 (1st Dist. 1996)
24 ALR6th 497—§ 17
Stevens v. Parke, Davis & Co., 9 Cal. 3d 51, 107 Cal. Rptr. 45, 507 P.2d 653, 94 A.L.R.3d 1059 (1973)
57 ALR5th 1—§ 3, 21 to 23, 26, 27
Stevens v. People, 796 P.2d 946 (Colo. 1990)
71 ALR5th 637—§ 11
Stevens v. Richardson, 755 P.2d 389 (Alaska 1988)
23 ALR5th 241—§ 22
Stevens v. Rock Springs Nat. Bank, 577 P.2d 1374 (Wyo. 1978)
79 ALR6th 211—§ 35
Stevens v. Rogers, 16 Utah 105, 51 P. 261 (1897)
67 ALR5th 587—§ 4
Stevens v. Roman Catholic Bishop, 49 Cal. App. 3d 877, 123 Cal. Rptr. 171 (5th Dist. 1975)
27 ALR5th 174—§ 3, 47
Stevens v. Sadiq, 176 Ill. App. 3d 333, 125 Ill. Dec. 750, 530 N.E.2d 1159 (4th Dist. 1988)
42 ALR5th 1—§ 10
Stevens v. Security Pacific Mortg. Corp., 53 Wash. App. 507, 768 P.2d 1007 (Div.1 1989)
100 ALR5th 409—§ 2
Stevens v. Smolka, 11 App. Div. 2d 896, 202 N.Y.S.2d 783 (1960)
38 ALR5th 357—§ 3
Stevens v. Snyder, 874 S.W.2d 241 (Tex. App. Dallas 1994)
43 ALR5th 545—§ 2
Stevens v. Stanford, 766 So. 2d 849 (Ala. Civ. App. 1999)
111 ALR5th 1—§ 3, 5, 8, 13
Stevens v. State, 26 Ohio App. 53, 5 Ohio L. Abs. 691, 159 N.E. 834 (4th Dist. Lawrence County 1927)
105 ALR5th 529—§ 25
Stevens v. State, 27 Tex. App. 461, 11 S.W. 459 (1889)
5 ALR5th 243—§ 48
Stevens v. State, 34 Md. App. 164, 366 A.2d 414 (1976)
2 ALR5th 262—§ 3
Stevens v. State, 93 Ga. 307, 20 S.E. 331 (1893)
102 ALR6th 279—§ 5
Stevens v. State, 176 Ga. App. 583, 336 S.E.2d 846 (1985)
5 ALR5th 243—§ 50
Stevens v. State, 210 Ga. App. 355, 436 S.E.2d 82, 93 Fulton County D R 3499 (1993)
34 ALR5th 125—§ 3, 8

Stevens v. State, 267 Ind. 541, 372 N.E.2d 165 (1978)

24 ALR6th 1—§ 17

Stevens v. State, 443 P.2d 600 (Alaska 1968)

58 ALR6th 499—§ 98

Stevens v. State, 458 So. 2d 726 (Miss. 1984)

9 ALR6th 1—§ 6

Stevens v. State, 592 So. 2d 758 (Fla. App. D5 1992)

7 ALR5th 263—§ 4

Stevens v. State, 667 S.W.2d 534 (Tex. Crim. App. 1984)

68 ALR5th 343—§ 12

Stevens v. State, 691 N.E.2d 412 (Ind. 1997)

79 ALR5th 33—§ 2

Stevens v. State, 717 So. 2d 311 (Miss. 1998)

16 ALR6th 329—§ 5
24 ALR6th 591—§ 4, 14

Stevens v. State, 770 N.E.2d 739 (Ind. 2002)

71 ALR6th 625—§ 28, 37

Stevens v. State, 770 S.W.2d 496 (Mo. Ct. App. E.D. 1989)

31 ALR6th 49—§ 4

Stevens v. State, 806 So. 2d 1031, 119 A.L.R.5th 695 (Miss. 2001)

119 ALR5th 275—§ 7, 11

Stevens v. State, 823 So. 2d 319 (Fla. Dist. Ct. App. 2d Dist. 2002)

21 ALR6th 771—§ 5

Stevens v. State, 900 S.W.2d 348 (Tex. App. Texarkana 1995)

40 ALR5th 113—§ 4

Stevens v. State, 938 S.W.2d 517 (Tex. App. Fort Worth 1997)

15 ALR6th 173—§ 27

Stevens v. State, 2001 WL 518323 (Ark. Ct. App. 2001)

25 ALR6th 379—§ 3, 13

Stevens v. Steak n Shake, Inc., 35 F. Supp. 2d 882 (M.D. Fla. 1998)

103 ALR6th 1—§ 9

Stevens v. Stevens, 23 Ohio St. 3d 115, 492 N.E.2d 131 (1986)

3 ALR6th 447—§ 4, 9

Stevens v. Stevens, 177 N.J. Super. 167, 425 A.2d 1081 (1981)

16 ALR5th 650—§ 7, 9, 14

Stevens v. Stevens, 184 Neb. 370, 167 N.W.2d 761 (1969)

49 ALR5th 441—§ 12

Stevens v. Stevens, 266 Mich. 446, 254 N.W. 162 (1934)

32 ALR5th 673—§ 4

Stevens v. Stevens, 412 S.E.2d 257 (W. Va. 1991)

17 ALR5th 143—§ 5, 6

Stevens v. Stevens, 476 So. 2d 883 (La. Ct. App. 2d Cir. 1985)

59 ALR6th 433—§ 63

Stevens v. Stevens, 505 S.E.2d 674 (W. Va. 1998)

10 ALR5th 191—§ 7
17 ALR5th 366—§ 9

Stevens v. Stover, 727 F. Supp. 668 (D.D.C. 1990)

101 ALR5th 515—§ 15

Stevens v. Superior Court, 28 Cal. App. 3d 1, 104 Cal. Rptr. 369 (2d Dist. 1972)

88 ALR5th 545—§ 6, 25

Stevens v. Superior Court, 180 Cal. App. 3d 605, 225 Cal. Rptr. 624 (2d Dist. 1986)

35 ALR5th 145—§ 40

Stevens v. Thielen, 394 N.W.2d 834 (Minn. App. 1986)

54 ALR5th 313—§ 18

Stevens v. Tillman, 568 F. Supp. 289, 36 BNA FEP Cas. 1232 (N.D. Ill. 1983)

19 ALR5th 1—§ 90
44 ALR5th 193—§ 30

Stevens v. Villacorta, 2006 WL 822100 (M.D. Fla. 2006)

89 ALR6th 1—§ 117

Stevens v. Wells Fargo Bank, N.A., 2012 WL 5951087 (N.D. Tex. 2012)

86 ALR6th 411—§ 5

Stevens v. Winthrop South Nassau University Health System, Inc., 89 A.D.3d 835, 932 N.Y.S.2d 514, 273 Ed. Law Rep. 391 (2d Dep't 2011)
95 ALR6th 85—§ 7, 13

Stevens v. Wood Sawmill, Inc., 426 N.W.2d 13 (S.D. 1988)
21 ALR5th 82—§ 3, 23

Stevens v. Wright Contracting Co., 92 Ga. App. 373, 88 S.E.2d 511 (1955)
9 ALR5th 102—§ 9, 12, 13

Stevens County Social Service Dep't ex rel. Banken v. Banken, 403 N.W.2d 693 (Minn. App. 1987)
28 ALR5th 46—§ 11, 12

Stevensen v. Goodson, 924 P.2d 339 (Utah 1996)
85 ALR5th 353—§ 15

Stevens, Estate of v. C.I.R., T.C. Memo. 2000-53, T.C.M. (RIA) ¶ 2000-053, 79 T.C.M. (CCH) 1519 (2000)
16 ALR6th 693—§ 12

Stevens Ford, Inc. v. BZ Results, LLC, 2006 WL 3114366 (Conn. Super. Ct. 2006)
32 ALR6th 419—§ 3

Stevenson, In re, 167 Mont. 220, 538 P.2d 5 (1975)
37 ALR5th 703—§ 3

Stevenson v. Ada County Sheriff, 972 F.2d 1343 (9th Cir. 1992)
89 ALR6th 1—§ 118

Stevenson v. Board of Education, 426 F.2d 1154 (CA5 Ga. 1970)
58 ALR5th 1—§ 50

Stevenson v. Brodt, 2010 WL 4068727 (Minn. Ct. App. 2010)
91 ALR6th 1—§ 7, 9

Stevenson v. Clark Regional Medical Center, Inc., 2010 WL 5018517 (Ky. Ct. App. 2010)
97 ALR6th 83—§ 49, 60

Stevenson v. County Officers Electoral Bd., 58 Ill. App. 3d 24, 15 Ill. Dec. 571, 373 N.E.2d 1043 (3d Dist. 1978)
14 ALR6th 543—§ 3, 38

Stevenson v. Four Winds Travel, Inc., 462 F.2d 899, 20 A.L.R. Fed 1 (CA5 Fla. 1972)
2 ALR5th 396—§ 2, 3, 25

Stevenson v. Lavalco, Inc., 669 So. 2d 608 (La. Ct. App. 2d Cir. 1996)
7 ALR6th 563—§ 5

Stevenson v. McMillan, 250 Iowa 737, 95 N.W.2d 719 (1959)
34 ALR5th 57—§ 2, 3, 5

Stevenson v. Nauton, 71 Ill. App. 3d 831, 28 Ill. Dec. 71, 390 N.E.2d 53 (1st Dist. 1979)
30 ALR5th 571—§ 7, 9, 26

Stevenson v. Northington, 204 N.C. 690, 169 S.E. 622 (1933)
67 ALR6th 437—§ 6, 12

Stevenson v. Robinson, 37 So. 2d 568 (Miss. 1948)
33 ALR5th 205—§ 11

Stevenson v. Spivey, 132 Va. 115, 110 S.E. 367, 21 A.L.R. 1276 (1922)
119 ALR5th 519—§ 5, 9

Stevenson v. State, 137 Misc. 2d 313, 520 N.Y.S.2d 492 (Ct. Cl. 1987)
53 ALR6th 305—§ 25

Stevenson v. State, 709 A.2d 619 (Del. 1998)
16 ALR6th 329—§ 4
24 ALR6th 591—§ 6, 12

Stevenson v. State Bd. of Medical Examiners, 10 Cal. App. 3d 433, 88 Cal. Rptr. 815 (3d Dist. 1970)
65 ALR6th 295—§ 12

Stevenson v. State Farm Indem. Co., 311 N.J. Super. 363, 709 A.2d 1359 (App. Div. 1998)
42 ALR5th 727—§ 4

Stevenson v. Stevenson, 452 So. 2d 869 (Ala. Civ. App. 1984)
21 ALR5th 396—§ 11, 19, 53
73 ALR5th 185—§ 3

Stevenson v. Sullivan, 190 Neb. 295, 207 N.W.2d 680 (1973)
109 ALR5th 611—§ 6

Stevenson v. Superior Court, 16 Cal. 4th 880, 66 Cal. Rptr. 2d 888, 941 P.2d 1157, 74 Fair Empl. Prac. Cas. (BNA) 1623, 13 I.E.R. Cas. (BNA) 321, 72 Empl. Prac. Dec. (CCH) ¶ 45272 (1997)
105 ALR5th 351—§ 3 to 5

Stevenson v. Thornburgh, 1991 WL 17713 (D. Kan. 1991)
54 ALR6th 1—§ 14

Stevenson v. Williamson, 547 F. Supp. 2d 544 (M.D. La. 2008)
37 ALR6th 137—§ 4

Stevenson v. Winn-Dixie Atlanta, 211 Ga. App. 572, 440 S.E.2d 465, 93 Fulton County D R 4548, CCH Prod. Liab. Rep. ¶ 13822 (1993)
2 ALR5th 1—§ 31

Stevenson v. Woodward, 3 Cal. App. 754, 86 P. 990 (1906)
46 ALR5th 1—§ 27

Stevenson v. Yates, 183 Ky. 196, 208 S.W. 820 (1919)
2 ALR5th 769—§ 3

Stevenson ex rel. Stevenson v. Martin County Bd. of Educ., 3 Fed. Appx. 25, 151 Ed. Law Rep. 446 (4th Cir. 2001)
98 ALR6th 599—§ 39, 50, 67

Stevenson, State, to Use of v. Reigart, 1 Gill 1, 1843 WL 2171 (Md. 1843)
98 ALR5th 353—§ 7

Stevens Point, City of v. Pliska, 151 Wis. 2d 783, 151 Wis. 2d 784, 447 N.W.2d 394 (Ct. App. 1989)
86 ALR6th 321—§ 12, 13
91 ALR6th 171—§ 97

Stevens Supply Co. v. Stamm, 41 Ga. App. 239, 152 S.E. 602 (1930)
46 ALR5th 1—§ 47

Stever, Re Estate of, 155 Colo. 1, 392 P.2d 286 (1964)
3 ALR5th 394—§ 6, 7, 14

Steverson v. City of Vicksburg, Miss., 900 F. Supp. 1 (S.D. Miss. 1994)
20 ALR6th 161—§ 3, 4
21 ALR6th 425—§ 9, 10
23 ALR6th 573—§ 7, 14

Steverson v. Hospital Authority of Ware County, 129 Ga. App. 510, 199 S.E.2d 881 (1973)
6 ALR5th 534—§ 25, 27, 32

Steveson v. Frolic Footwear, 70 Ark. App. 383, 20 S.W.3d 413 (2000)
14 ALR5th 1—§ 5

Steve Spicer Motors, Inc. v. Gilliam, 19 S.W.3d 153 (Mo. Ct. App. S.D. 2000)
17 ALR6th 1—§ 9

Stevo v. Frasor, 2011 WL 253963 (N.D. Ill. 2011)
86 ALR6th 173—§ 6

Steward v. Folz, 190 Fed. Appx. 476 (7th Cir. 2006)
63 ALR6th 351—§ 3

Steward v. Folz, 2005 WL 2237792 (S.D. Ind. 2005)
93 ALR6th 1—§ 5

Steward v. Goetz, 945 S.W.2d 520 (Mo. Ct. App. E.D. 1997)
60 ALR6th 1—§ 40

Steward v. Magnolia, 134 N.J. Super. 312, 340 A.2d 678 (1975)
36 ALR5th 1—§ 12, 25

Steward v. Poole, 196 Mich. App. 25, 492 N.W.2d 475 (1992)
43 ALR5th 545—§ 46

Steward v. Richardson, 353 F. Supp. 822 (E.D. Mich. 1972)
122 ALR5th 205—§ 3, 10, 38, 45

Steward v. State, 182 Ga. App. 659, 356 S.E.2d 890 (1987)
56 ALR6th 323—§ 11

Steward v. State, 636 N.E.2d 143 (Ind. Ct. App. 1st Dist. 1994)
59 ALR5th 1—§ 4, 6
85 ALR5th 595—§ 2, 3

Steward v. State, 652 N.E.2d 490 (Ind. 1995)
90 ALR5th 453—§ 9

Steward v. Steward, 111 Nev. 295, 890 P.2d 777 (1995)
71 ALR5th 99—§ 3, 6

Steward v. World-Wide Automobiles Corp., 20 Misc. 2d 188, 189 N.Y.S.2d 540 (Sup 1959)

2 ALR6th 387—§ 4

Stewart, Estate of, 122 Cal. App. 3d 625, 176 Cal. Rptr. 142 (4th Dist. 1981)

122 ALR5th 205—§ 26, 51

Stewart, Ex parte, 659 So. 2d 122 (Ala. 1993)

83 ALR6th 255—§ 21

Stewart, In re, 275 A.D.2d 552, 711 N.Y.S.2d 615 (3d Dep't 2000)

25 ALR6th 101—§ 11

Stewart, In re Marriage of, 243 Mont. 180, 793 P.2d 813 (1990)

28 ALR5th 46—§ 9, 10

Stewart, In re Marriage of, 356 N.W.2d 611 (Iowa Ct. App. 1984)

3 ALR6th 447—§ 4, 9

104 ALR6th 181—§ 7

Stewart v. Auto-Owners Ins. Co., 230 Ga. App. 265, 495 S.E.2d 882 (1998)

33 ALR5th 587—§ 4

Stewart v. Bailey, 7 F.3d 384 (4th Cir. 1993)

53 ALR6th 1—§ 7

Stewart v. Barber, 182 Misc. 91, 43 N.Y.S.2d 560 (Sup. Ct. 1943)

1 ALR6th 135—§ 4, 7, 22

Stewart v. Bee-Dee Neon & Signs, Inc., 751 So. 2d 196 (Fla. Dist. Ct. App. 1st Dist. 2000)

6 ALR5th 242—§ 10

Stewart v. Beegun, 126 Ill. App. 2d 120, 261 N.E.2d 491 (1st Dist. 1970)

99 ALR5th 141—§ 15, 17

Stewart v. Blackwell, 356 F. Supp. 2d 791 (N.D. Ohio 2004)

12 ALR6th 523—§ 12

Stewart v. Blackwell, 444 F.3d 843, 2006 FED App. 0143P (6th Cir. 2006)

104 ALR6th 547—§ 11

Stewart v. Blackwell, 473 F.3d 692, 2007 FED App. 0015P (6th Cir. 2007)

104 ALR6th 547—§ 11

Stewart v. Board of Medical Quality Assur., 80 Cal. App. 3d 172, 143 Cal. Rptr. 641 (2d Dist. 1978)

10 ALR5th 1—§ 40

Stewart v. Brown, 546 S.W.2d 204, 21 U.C.C. Rep. Serv. 1250 (Mo. Ct. App. 1977)

86 ALR5th 527—§ 13, 19

Stewart v. Capps, 247 Kan. 549, 802 P.2d 1226 (1990)

31 ALR5th 116—§ 3

40 ALR5th 603—§ 4

Stewart v. Casey, 182 Mont. 185, 595 P.2d 1176 (1979)

10 ALR5th 448—§ 5

Stewart v. Cendant Mobility Services Corp., 2002 WL 442385 (Conn. Super. Ct. 2002)

52 ALR6th 271—§ 6

Stewart v. City of Marshfield, 431 S.W.2d 819 (Mo. Ct. App. 1968)

101 ALR5th 287—§ 3

Stewart v. City of Springfield, 350 Mo. 234, 165 S.W.2d 626 (1942)

92 ALR5th 517—§ 10

Stewart v. Clarke, 2014 WL 2480076 (E.D. Va. 2014)

102 ALR6th 637—§ 5, 12, 13

Stewart v. Coffman, 748 P.2d 579, 73 Utah Adv. Rep. 119 (Utah App. 1988)

50 ALR5th 301—§ 5

Stewart v. Com., 479 S.W.2d 23 (Ky. 1972)

97 ALR5th 293—§ 3, 15

Stewart v. Com., 2008 WL 399626 (Ky. Ct. App. 2008)

78 ALR6th 1—§ 30, 41

Stewart v. Combs, 368 Ark. 121, 243 S.W.3d 294 (2006)

87 ALR6th 495—§ 4, 12, 15, 54, 74, 76

Stewart v. Commonwealth, 2 Ky. L. Rptr. 386, 11 Ky. Op. 138, 1881 WL 7995 (Ky. 1881)

97 ALR5th 293—§ 3

Stewart v. Commonwealth, 245 Va. 222, 427 S.E.2d 394 (1993)

37 ALR5th 515—§ 4

Stewart v. County of Cook, 192 Ill. App. 3d 848, 140 Ill. Dec. 23, 549 N.E.2d 674 (1st Dist. 1989)
57 ALR5th 689—§ 8

Stewart v. Cox, 55 Cal. 2d 857, 13 Cal. Rptr. 521, 362 P.2d 345 (1961)
65 ALR5th 105—§ 28
75 ALR5th 413—§ 3 to 5, 7 to 9, 12, 16, 51

Stewart v. Davis, 149 Tex. 584, 235 S.W.2d 979 (1951)
122 ALR5th 205—§ 3, 41

Stewart v. De Noon, 220 Pa. 154, 69 A. 587 (1908)
17 ALR5th 547—§ 14, 20

Stewart v. District of Columbia Bd. of Zoning Adjustment, 305 A.2d 516, 3 Envtl. L. Rep. 20477 (D.C. 1973)
63 ALR5th 607—§ 10, 11, 14

Stewart v. Dollar Tree, 635 So. 2d 73, 19 FLW D 177 (Fla. App. D1 1994)
46 ALR5th 659—§ 12

Stewart v. Donges, 915 F.2d 572 (10th Cir. 1990)
80 ALR6th 239—§ 3, 4

Stewart v. Dryden Mut. Ins. Co., 156 App. Div. 2d 951, 549 N.Y.S.2d 246 (4th Dep't 1989)
35 ALR5th 375—§ 3, 28

Stewart v. Eden, 2 Cai. R. 150, 1804 WL 814 (N.Y. Sup 1804)
98 ALR5th 353—§ 3

Stewart v. Evans, 2006 MT 102, 332 Mont. 148, 136 P.3d 524 (2006)
59 ALR6th 161—§ 38
60 ALR6th 193—§ 22

Stewart v. Fakhruddin, 2010 WL 2134150 (Tenn. Ct. App. 2010)
80 ALR6th 469—§ 8, 11, 14, 22, 29, 57

Stewart v. Favors, 264 Ga. App. 156, 590 S.E.2d 186 (2003)
22 ALR6th 49—§ 4

Stewart v. Finkelstone, 206 Mass. 28, 92 N.E. 37 (1910)
25 ALR5th 233—§ 2, 19

Stewart v. Florence Nightingale Health Center, 1999 WL 179373 (S.D. N.Y. 1999)
67 ALR6th 437—§ 9, 15, 18

Stewart v. Gamero, 2007 WL 2994635 (Cal. App. 2d Dist. 2007)
97 ALR6th 375—§ 21

Stewart v. Garrett, 65 Md. 289, 4 A. 399 (1886)
74 ALR5th 369—§ 8

Stewart v. Gates, 450 F. Supp. 583 (C.D. Cal. 1978)
98 ALR5th 445—§ 5
6 ALR6th 483—§ 6

Stewart v. Green, 300 So. 2d 899 (Fla. 1974)
43 ALR5th 705—§ 3, 5

Stewart v. Hanover Ins. Co., 416 So. 2d 286 (La. App. 3d Cir. 1982)
26 ALR5th 401—§ 2, 19

Stewart v. Hardie, 978 S.W.2d 203 (Tex. App. Fort Worth 1998)
85 ALR5th 353—§ 2, 11

Stewart v. Haughton Elevator Co., 87 Ohio App. 3d 122, 621 N.E.2d 901 (10th Dist. Franklin County 1993)
117 ALR5th 267—§ 16
122 ALR5th 1—§ 16

Stewart v. Herrington, 2008 WL 3822597 (S.D. Miss. 2008)
89 ALR6th 1—§ 102

Stewart v. Hicks, 182 Ind. App. 308, 395 N.E.2d 308 (1979)
86 ALR6th 321—§ 12
89 ALR6th 409—§ 24

Stewart v. Houston Lighting & Power Co., 998 F. Supp. 746 (S.D. Tex. 1998)
20 ALR6th 1—§ 7

Stewart v. Hutchinson, 120 Mo. App. 32, 96 S.W. 253 (1906)
74 ALR5th 369—§ 10

Stewart v. International Business Machines Corp., 867 F. Supp. 238, 73 Fair Empl. Prac. Cas. (BNA) 421 (S.D. N.Y. 1994)
19 ALR6th 1—§ 7

Stewart v. Inter-Ocean Reinsurance Corp., 260 Ky. 787, 86 S.W.2d 703 (1935)

87 ALR6th 319—§ 47

Stewart v. Iowa C. R. Co., 136 Iowa 182, 113 N.W. 764 (1907)

17 ALR5th 547—§ 38

Stewart v. Jackson, 635 N.E.2d 186 (Ind. Ct. App. 1st Dist. 1994)

81 ALR5th 345—§ 2, 3

Stewart v. Janssen Pharmaceutica, Inc., 780 S.W.2d 910, CCH Prod. Liab. Rep. ¶ 12414 (Tex. App. El Paso 1989)

57 ALR5th 1—§ 3, 26

Stewart v. Johnson, 209 W. Va. 476, 549 S.E.2d 670 (2001)

27 ALR6th 183—§ 45

Stewart v. Jones, 318 Ill. App. 3d 552, 252 Ill. Dec. 358, 742 N.E.2d 896, 117 A.L.R.5th 761 (2d Dist. 2001)

117 ALR5th 441—§ 4

Stewart v. Kennedy, 70 Ohio St. 3d 536, 639 N.E.2d 790 (1994)

9 ALR5th 321—§ 3

Stewart v. Kentucky Lottery Corp., 986 S.W.2d 918 (Ky. Ct. App. 1998)

70 ALR6th 661—§ 7

Stewart v. Kuskin & Rotberg, 106 S.W.2d 1074 (Tex. Civ. App. Texarkana 1937)

75 ALR5th 1—§ 4, 13

Stewart v. Lewis, 292 So. 2d 303 (La. Ct. App. 1st Cir. 1974)

50 ALR6th 95—§ 5, 10

Stewart v. Lopes, 40 Conn. Supp. 354, 499 A.2d 442 (Super. Ct. 1985)

72 ALR6th 141—§ 12

Stewart v. Martin, 353 Mo. 1, 181 S.W.2d 657 (1944)

2 ALR5th 1—§ 62

Stewart v. Martin, 2008 WL 447525 (U.S. 2008)

36 ALR6th 681—§ 21

Stewart v. McGinnis, 5 F.3d 1031, 26 Fed. R. Serv. 3d 1299 (7th Cir. 1993)

89 ALR6th 1—§ 29, 117

Stewart v. McManus, 924 F.2d 138 (8th Cir. 1991)

54 ALR6th 1—§ 7, 8, 23

Stewart v. M.D.F., Inc., 83 F.3d 247, 35 Fed. R. Serv. 3d (LCP) 242 (8th Cir. 1996)

123 ALR5th 1—§ 5

Stewart v. Midani, 525 F. Supp. 843 (N.D. Ga. 1981)

58 ALR5th 613—§ 8, 10
64 ALR6th 249—§ 13

Stewart v. Mortgage Electronic Registration Systems, Inc., 2010 WL 1055131 (D. Or. 2010)

86 ALR6th 411—§ 5

Stewart v. Nation-Wide Check Corp., 279 N.C. 278, 182 S.E.2d 410 (1971)

53 ALR6th 213—§ 4

Stewart v. New York City Health & Hosps. Corp., 616 N.Y.S.2d 499 (App. Div. 1st Dep't 1994)

2 ALR5th 769—§ 4

Stewart v. New York State Div. of Human Rights, 128 App. Div. 2d 625, 512 N.Y.S.2d 877 (2d Dep't 1987)

51 ALR5th 1—§ 7

Stewart v. Olean Medical Group, P.C., 17 A.D.3d 1094, 795 N.Y.S.2d 420 (4th Dep't 2005)

92 ALR6th 379—§ 4, 35, 114

Stewart v. Pantry, Inc., 715 F. Supp. 1361, 4 I.E.R. Cas. (BNA) 526, 124 Lab. Cas. (CCH) P 57266 (W.D. Ky. 1988)

38 ALR6th 541—§ 14

Stewart v. Patrick, 68 N.Y. 450 (1877)

61 ALR5th 739—§ 2, 3, 9

Stewart v. Patrick, 68 N.Y. 450, 1877 WL 11882 (1877)

91 ALR6th 1—§ 46

Stewart v. Paul, Hastings, Janofsky & Walker, LLP, 201 F. Supp. 2d 291, 7 Wage & Hour Cas. 2d (BNA) 1608, 82 Empl. Prac. Dec. (CCH) ¶ 41100, 146 Lab. Cas. (CCH) ¶ 34529 (S.D. N.Y. 2002)

22 ALR6th 49—§ 8, 29

For assistance, call 1-800-328-4880

Stewart v. People, 83 Colo. 289, 264 P. 720 (1928)
50 ALR5th 703—§ 9

Stewart v. People, 161 Colo. 1, 419 P.2d 650, 26 A.L.R.3d 943 (1966)
41 ALR5th 171—§ 66

Stewart v. Presbyterian Hosp. in City of New York, 12 A.D.3d 201, 784 N.Y.S.2d 521 (1st Dep't 2004)
97 ALR6th 83—§ 10

Stewart v. Preston Pipeline Inc., 134 Cal. App. 4th 1565, 36 Cal. Rptr. 3d 901 (6th Dist. 2005)
32 ALR6th 285—§ 30

Stewart v. Price, 718 So. 2d 205 (Fla. 1st DCA 1998)
97 ALR6th 83—§ 5, 102

Stewart v. Progressive American Ins. Co., 595 So. 2d 272 (Fla. Dist. Ct. App. 1st Dist. 1992)
118 ALR5th 91—§ 19
2 ALR6th 279—§ 14, 28

Stewart v. Ragland, 934 F.2d 1033, 91 Daily Journal DAR 6985, 91 Daily Journal DAR 7181 (CA9 Cal. 1991)
52 ALR5th 491—§ 6

Stewart v. Rahr Malting Co., 435 N.W.2d 538 (Minn. 1989)
26 ALR5th 127—§ 2

Stewart v. Riley, 114 W. Va. 578, 172 S.E. 791 (1934)
53 ALR6th 213—§ 4

Stewart v. Rio Vista, 72 Cal. App. 2d 279, 164 P.2d 274 (1945)
53 ALR5th 617—§ 3, 4

Stewart v. Roberts, 132 Ga. App. 700, 209 S.E.2d 119 (1974)
27 ALR5th 174—§ 3, 26

Stewart v. Robinson, 115 F. Supp. 2d 188, 2000 DNH 58, 111 A.L.R.5th 695 (D.N.H. 2000)
111 ALR5th 159—§ 9

Stewart v. Rudner, 349 Mich. 459, 84 N.W.2d 816 (1957)
4 ALR5th 148—§ 12

Stewart v. Rutgers, 930 F. Supp. 1034 (D.C. N.J. 1996)
19 ALR5th 439—§ 3

Stewart v. Sbarro, 142 N.J. Super. 581, 362 A.2d 581 (App. Div. 1976)
60 ALR6th 1—§ 29

Stewart v. Schmieder, 386 So. 2d 1351 (La. 1980)
24 ALR5th 200—§ 24, 25, 49

Stewart v. Schwartz Brothers-Jeffer Memorial Chapel, Inc., 159 Misc. 2d 884, 606 N.Y.S.2d 965 (Sup 1993)
8 ALR6th 339—§ 11

Stewart v. Secor Realty & Inv. Corp., 667 So. 2d 52 (Ala. 1995)
115 ALR5th 251—§ 18

Stewart v. Shannon & Luchs Co., 46 A.2d 863 (Mun. Ct. App. D.C. 1946)
114 ALR5th 443—§ 28

Stewart v. Sieben, Inc., 783 S.W.2d 432 (Mo. Ct. App. E.D. 1989)
88 ALR5th 301—§ 23, 24

Stewart v. Sizemore, 306 S.W.2d 821 (Ky. 1957)
17 ALR5th 547—§ 3

Stewart v. Socony Vacuum Oil Co., 3 App. Div. 2d 582, 163 N.Y.S.2d 22 (3d Dep't 1957)
12 ALR5th 577—§ 2, 11

Stewart v. Stanley, 199 La. 146, 5 So. 2d 531 (1941)
97 ALR5th 537—§ 55

Stewart v. State, 22 S.W.3d 646 (Tex. App. Austin 2000)
84 ALR6th 293—§ 30

Stewart v. State, 37 So. 3d 243 (Fla. 2010)
102 ALR6th 417—§ 104

Stewart v. State, 77 S.W. 791 (Tex. Crim. App. 1903)
105 ALR5th 529—§ 3

Stewart v. State, 92 Wash. 2d 285, 597 P.2d 101 (1979)
15 ALR6th 1—§ 4, 8 to 10, 15

Stewart v. State, 103 S.W.3d 483 (Tex. App. San Antonio 2003)
119 ALR5th 379—§ 8

Stewart v. State, 133 A.D.2d 112, 518 N.Y.S.2d 648 (2d Dep't 1987)
53 ALR6th 305—§ 27

Stewart v. State, 184 Ga. App. 289, 361 S.E.2d 268 (1987)

3 ALR5th 784—§ 16, 20

Stewart v. State, 187 So. 2d 358 (Fla. Dist. Ct. App. 1st Dist. 1966)

78 ALR5th 567—§ 3

Stewart v. State, 377 So. 2d 613 (Miss. 1979)

4 ALR5th 273—§ 35

Stewart v. State, 405 So. 2d 402 (Ala. Crim. App. 1981)

67 ALR6th 103—§ 4

Stewart v. State, 442 N.E.2d 1026 (Ind. 1982)

79 ALR5th 237—§ 5

Stewart v. State, 474 N.E.2d 1010 (Ind. 1985)

102 ALR6th 365—§ 13

Stewart v. State, 489 So. 2d 176 (Fla. Dist. Ct. App. 1st Dist. 1986)

73 ALR5th 383—§ 32

Stewart v. State, 527 P.2d 22 (Okla. Crim. App. 1974)

65 ALR5th 623—§ 4

Stewart v. State, 629 So. 2d 982, 19 FLW D 32 (Fla. App. D5 1993)

15 ALR5th 391—§ 45

Stewart v. State, 652 S.W.2d 496 (Tex. App. Houston 1st Dist. 1983)

97 ALR5th 201—§ 3, 4

Stewart v. State, 680 S.W.2d 513 (Tex. App. Beaumont 1984)

9 ALR6th 633—§ 10
14 ALR6th 517—§ 11

Stewart v. State, 681 S.W.2d 774 (Tex. App. Houston 14th Dist. 1984)

58 ALR6th 499—§ 89

Stewart v. State, 688 N.E.2d 1254 (Ind. 1997)

58 ALR6th 499—§ 4

Stewart v. State, 756 P.2d 900 (Alaska App. 1988)

57 ALR5th 141—§ 12

Stewart v. State, 1915 OK CR 22, 11 Okla. Crim. 400, 146 P. 921 (1915)

101 ALR6th 431—§ 18

Stewart v. State, 1997 WL 524154 (Tex. App. Dallas 1997)

19 ALR6th 697—§ 25
57 ALR6th 313—§ 3

Stewart v. State, 2009-Ohio-4317, 2009 WL 2602216 (Ohio Ct. App. 5th Dist. Richland County 2009)

64 ALR6th 1—§ 7, 9, 11

Stewart v. State, 2010 Ark. App. 9, 373 S.W.3d 387 (2010)

96 ALR6th 355—§ 8, 37

Stewart v. State Farm Mut. Auto. Ins. Co., 341 S.C. 143, 533 S.E.2d 597 (Ct. App. 2000)

96 ALR5th 107—§ 6
99 ALR5th 301—§ 9

Stewart v. Stewart, 83 Or. App. 675, 732 P.2d 951 (1987)

5 ALR5th 550—§ 10
21 ALR5th 396—§ 3, 11, 19, 52

Stewart v. Stewart, 91 Ariz. 356, 372 P.2d 697 (1962)

112 ALR5th 399—§ 4

Stewart v. Stewart, 141 N.C. App. 236, 541 S.E.2d 209 (2000)

39 ALR6th 205—§ 3, 8, 11

Stewart v. Stewart, 354 So. 2d 816 (Ala. App. 1977)

17 ALR5th 366—§ 27, 31

Stewart v. Stewart, 905 S.W.2d 114 (Mo. App. 1995)

21 ALR5th 396—§ 11, 19

Stewart v. Stewart, 1995 WL 765961 (Ohio Ct. App. 2d Dist. Greene County 1995)

36 ALR6th 1—§ 5, 6, 25

Stewart v. Stewart, 2005-Ohio-346, 2005 WL 237330 (Ohio Ct. App. 11th Dist. Portage County 2005)

88 ALR6th 203—§ 84

Stewart v. Sulzer Orthopedics, Inc., 2011 WL 2491593 (N.D. Okla. 2011)

96 ALR6th 1—§ 6

Stewart v. Sumpter, 2005 WL 1653001 (S.D. Tex. 2005)

89 ALR6th 1—§ 99

Stewart v. Sun Sentinel Co., 695 So. 2d 360, 25 Media L. Rep. (BNA) 1763 (Fla. Dist. Ct. App. 4th Dist. 1997)
44 ALR5th 193—§ 25
100 ALR5th 341—§ 3

Stewart v. Superior Court In and For County of Maricopa, 163 Ariz. 227, 787 P.2d 126 (Ct. App. 1989)
62 ALR5th 629—§ 4

Stewart v. Talbott, 58 Colo. 563, 146 P. 771 (1913)
46 ALR5th 1—§ 45

Stewart v. Tasnet, Inc., 718 So. 2d 820 (Fla. Dist. Ct. App. 2d Dist. 1998)
118 ALR5th 91—§ 8
125 ALR5th 193—§ 7

Stewart v. Taylor, 953 F. Supp. 1047 (S.D. Ind. 1997)
51 ALR6th 359—§ 3, 28
53 ALR6th 491—§ 3

Stewart v. TCF Nat. Bank, 2012 WL 6015586 (D. Minn. 2012)
86 ALR6th 411—§ 5

Stewart v. Tessitore, 222 So. 2d 584 (La. App. 4th Cir. 1969)
9 ALR5th 826—§ 3

Stewart v. Texas Lottery Com'n, 975 S.W.2d 732 (Tex. App. Corpus Christi 1998)
48 ALR6th 243—§ 17

Stewart v. Thomas, 64 Kan. 511, 68 P. 70 (1902)
86 ALR5th 527—§ 9

Stewart v. Thomas, 538 F. Supp. 891, 30 Fair Empl. Prac. Cas. (BNA) 1609, 29 Empl. Prac. Dec. (CCH) ¶ 32860 (D.D.C. 1982)
20 ALR6th 1—§ 4

Stewart v. Thomson, 97 Ky. 575, 17 Ky. L. Rptr. 381, 31 S.W. 133 (1895)
20 ALR6th 211—§ 26

Stewart v. Thornburgh, 1991 WL 17715 (D. Kan. 1991)
54 ALR6th 1—§ 14

Stewart v. Todd, 190 Iowa 283, 180 N.W. 146, 20 A.L.R. 1272 (1920)
87 ALR6th 495—§ 67

Stewart v. Town of Waterford, 152 A.D.2d 837, 543 N.Y.S.2d 770 (3d Dep't 1989)
12 ALR6th 645—§ 21

Stewart v. U.S., 151 F.2d 386 (C.C.A. 8th Cir. 1945)
57 ALR6th 445—§ 52

Stewart v. U.S., 668 A.2d 857 (D.C. 1995)
20 ALR6th 479—§ 3

Stewart v. U.S., 716 F.2d 755 (10th Cir. 1982)
11 ALR6th 351—§ 6

Stewart v. U.S., 716 F.2d 755, 35 FR Serv. 2d 868 (CA10 Colo. 1982)
4 ALR5th 443—§ 21

Stewart v. Utah Public Service Com'n, 885 P.2d 759, 156 Pub. Util. Rep. 4th (PUR) 41 (Utah 1994)
106 ALR5th 523—§ 3, 42

Stewart v. Valenta, 361 S.W.2d 910 (Tex. Civ. App. Eastland 1962)
76 ALR5th 337—§ 12

Stewart v. Volkswagen of America, Inc., 81 N.Y.2d 203, 597 N.Y.S.2d 612, 613 N.E.2d 518 (1993)
76 ALR6th 465—§ 22

Stewart v. Vulliet, 888 N.E.2d 761 (Ind. 2008)
57 ALR6th 163—§ 19, 45

Stewart v. Walker, 5 So. 3d 746 (Fla. 4th DCA 2009)
103 ALR6th 461—§ 7

Stewart v. Walls, 534 So. 2d 1033 (Miss. 1988)
4 ALR5th 273—§ 35

Stewart v. Welsh, 142 Tex. 314, 178 S.W.2d 506 (1944)
25 ALR5th 123—§ 2, 10
76 ALR5th 337—§ 14

Stewart v. Wilson, 92 Ga. App. 514, 88 S.E.2d 752 (1955)
23 ALR6th 1—§ 11

Stewart v. Yellow Freight Systems, Inc., 702 F. Supp. 230, 48 BNA FEP Cas. 1257 (E.D. Mo. 1988)
12 ALR5th 508—§ 3

Stewart Abstract Co. v. Judicial Commission of Jefferson County, 131 S.W.2d 686 (Tex. Civ. App. Beaumont 1939)
40 ALR6th 463—§ 16

Stewart & Jasper Orchards v. Salazar, 132 S. Ct. 498, 181 L. Ed. 2d 388 (2011)
76 ALR6th 587—§ 25

Stewart Dry Goods Co. v. Lewis, 294 U.S. 550, 79 L. Ed. 1054, 55 S. Ct. 525 (1935)
21 ALR5th 812—§ 4

Stewart ex rel. Hill v. Kralman, 240 Or. App. 510, 248 P.3d 6 (2011)
98 ALR6th 231—§ 5

Stewart M. Muller Const. Co. v. Clement Ferdinand & Co., 36 A.D.2d 814, 320 N.Y.S.2d 277 (1st Dep't 1971)
31 ALR6th 433—§ 3

Stewart, People ex rel. v. Wilson, 257 App. Div. 555, 13 N.Y.S.2d 749 (1939)
11 ALR5th 218—§ 4, 11

Stewart Select Cars, Inc. v. Moore, 619 So. 2d 1037 (Fla. Dist. Ct. App. 4th Dist. 1993)
119 ALR5th 121—§ 3
121 ALR5th 325—§ 4

Stewart, State ex rel. v. Blair, 356 Mo. 790, 203 S.W.2d 716 (1947)
88 ALR5th 463—§ 5
97 ALR5th 293—§ 4

Stewart, State ex rel. v. Martinez, 2011-NMSC-045, 270 P.3d 96, Unempl. Ins. Rep. (CCH) ¶ 8238, 87 A.L.R.6th 795 (N.M. 2011)
87 ALR6th 495—§ 85
87 ALR6th 633—§ 8

Stewart's Will, Re, 5 N.Y.S. 32 (Sur 1889)
3 ALR5th 590—§ 33

Stewart Tabori & Chang, Inc. v. Stewart, 723 N.Y.S.2d 492 (App. Div. 1st Dep't 2001)
60 ALR5th 669—§ 6

Stewart Tenants Corp. v. Diesel Const. Co., 16 A.D.2d 895, 229 N.Y.S.2d 204 (1st Dep't 1962)
31 ALR6th 433—§ 14

Stewart Title & Trust of Tucson v. Pribbeno, 129 Ariz. 15, 628 P.2d 52 (Ct. App. Div. 2 1981)
75 ALR5th 1—§ 8, 13 to 15

Stewart Title Guaranty Co. v. Cheatham, 764 S.W.2d 315 (Tex. App. Texarkana 1988)
19 ALR5th 786—§ 6

Stewart Title Guaranty Co. v. Hadnot, 101 S.W.3d 642, 4 A.L.R.6th 763 (Tex. App. Houston 1st Dist. 2003)
4 ALR6th 509—§ 8

Stewart Title Guar. Co. v. Aiello, 911 S.W.2d 463 (Tex. App. El Paso 1995)
14 ALR5th 242—§ 12

Stewart Title Guar. Co. v. Greenlands Realty, L.L.C., 58 F. Supp. 2d 370 (D.N.J. 1999)
19 ALR5th 786—§ 8

Stewart Title of California, Inc. v. Fidelity Nat. Title Co., 279 Fed. Appx. 473 (9th Cir. 2008)
76 ALR6th 289—§ 5
77 ALR6th 543—§ 11

Stewart Warner Corp. v. Burns International Secur. Services, Inc., 353 F. Supp. 1387 (N.D. Ill. 1973)
13 ALR5th 217—§ 2, 20, 21

Stewart Warner, Datafax Corp. v. Industrial Commission, 76 Ill. 2d 464, 31 Ill. Dec. 195, 394 N.E.2d 397 (1979)
107 ALR5th 441—§ 6
109 ALR5th 161—§ 9
20 ALR6th 641—§ 23

Steyne, In re, 1998 WL 34020729 (Bankr. D. S.C. 1998)
32 ALR6th 531—§ 33

St. Francis, City of v. Kalan, 188 Wis. 2d 79, 524 N.W.2d 647 (Ct. App. 1994)
86 ALR6th 321—§ 4
88 ALR6th 385—§ 82

St. Francis Hospital Ass'n v. Bowers, 99 Ohio App. 133, 58 Ohio Ops. 248, 131 N.E.2d 624 (Guernsey Co. 1954)

30 ALR5th 494—§ 9

St. Francis Xavier Hosp. v. Ruscon/Abco, 285 S.C. 584, 330 S.E.2d 548 (Ct. App. 1985)

31 ALR6th 433—§ 3

St. Gelais v. Jackson, 769 S.W.2d 249 (Tex. App. Houston 14th Dist. 1988)

2 ALR5th 449—§ 3

64 ALR5th 163—§ 16

St. Gemme v. Tomlin, 118 Ill. App. 3d 766, 74 Ill. Dec. 264, 455 N.E.2d 294 (4th Dist. 1983)

125 ALR5th 403—§ 14

St. George v. Deerfield Beach, 568 So. 2d 931, 15 FLW D 2029 (Fla. App. D4 1990)

16 ALR5th 605—§ 11

St. George Textile Corp. v. Brookside Mills, 85 N.Y.S.2d 621 (Sup. Ct. 1948)

67 ALR5th 179—§ 3

St. Germain v. Dutchess County Agricultural Society, 712 N.Y.S.2d 146 (App. Div. 2d Dep't 2000)

68 ALR5th 599—§ 13.5

St. Germain v. Husqvarna Corp., 544 A.2d 1283, Prod. Liab. Rep. (CCH) ¶ 11881 (Me. 1988)

4 ALR6th 401—§ 3, 5

St. Germain v. Motor Vehicle Acc. Indemnification Corp., 39 Misc. 2d 248, 240 N.Y.S.2d 454 (Sup. Ct. 1963)

103 ALR5th 1—§ 7

St. Germaine v. Pendergast, 411 Mass. 615, 584 N.E.2d 611 (1992)

12 ALR6th 241—§ 6

St. Gregory's Church v. O'Connor, 13 Ariz. App. 421, 477 P.2d 540 (1970)

10 ALR5th 371—§ 3

St. Gregory's Church v. O'Connor, 13 Ariz. App. 421, 477 P.2d 540 (Div. 1 1970)

15 ALR6th 1—§ 4, 10

Stiber v. Director, Div. of Taxation, 9 N.J. Tax 623, 1988 WL 42482 (1988)

2 ALR6th 1—§ 76

Stich v. Oakdale Dental Center, P.C., 120 A.D.2d 794, 501 N.Y.S.2d 529 (3d Dep't 1986)

120 ALR5th 483—§ 9

Stich v. Oakdale Dental Center, P. C., 120 App. Div. 2d 794, 501 N.Y.S.2d 529 (3d Dep't 1986)

11 ALR5th 88—§ 4

Stich v. Stich, 435 N.W.2d 848 (Minn. App. 1989)

11 ALR5th 259—§ 28

Stickel v. Excess Ins. Co. of America, 136 Ohio St. 49, 15 Ohio Op. 570, 23 N.E.2d 839 (1939)

87 ALR6th 319—§ 38

Stickel v. Harris, 196 Cal. App. 3d 575, 242 Cal. Rptr. 88 (1st Dist. 1987)

73 ALR6th 571—§ 36, 38, 79, 84

Stickel v. State, 975 A.2d 780 (Del. 2009)

89 ALR6th 565—§ 15

Stickels v. General Rental Co., 750 F. Supp. 729, 18 Media L. R. 1644, 18 FR Serv. 3d 665 (E.D. Va. 1990)

60 ALR5th 75—§ 7 to 9

Stickle v. Heublein, Inc., 716 F.2d 1550, 219 U.S.P.Q. (BNA) 377, 36 U.C.C. Rep. Serv. 1625 (Fed. Cir. 1983)

89 ALR5th 319—§ 9, 25

Stickle, People ex rel. v. Fay, 14 N.Y.2d 683, 249 N.Y.S.2d 879, 198 N.E.2d 909 (1964)

85 ALR5th 471—§ 7

Stickler v. American Augers, Inc., 303 Ill. App. 3d 689, 236 Ill. Dec. 817, 708 N.E.2d 403 (1st Dist. 1999)

17 ALR6th 1—§ 26, 28

Stickler v. American Augers, Inc., 325 Ill. App. 3d 506, 258 Ill. Dec. 884, 757 N.E.2d 573 (1st Dist. 2001)

17 ALR6th 1—§ 26, 28

For assistance, call 1-800-328-4880

Stickler, U.S. ex rel. v. Tehan, 365 F.2d 199, 37 Ohio Op. 2d 337, 38 Ohio Op. 2d 244 (6th Cir. 1966)

55 ALR6th 157—§ 49

Stickles v. Reichardt, 203 Wis. 579, 234 N.W. 728 (1930)

58 ALR5th 387—§ 3

Stickley v. Baskerville, 281 F. Supp. 2d 851 (W.D. Va. 2003)

19 ALR6th 411—§ 13

Stickney v. Chester County Communications, Ltd., 361 Pa. Super. 166, 522 A.2d 66, 13 Media L. R. 2192 (1987)

44 ALR5th 193—§ 21

Stickney v. City of Saco, 2001 ME 69, 770 A.2d 592 (Me. 2001)

62 ALR5th 219—§ 3, 63

Stickney v. Wesley Medical Center, 244 Kan. 147, 768 P.2d 253 (1989)

11 ALR5th 1—§ 3, 4

Stidham v. Clark, 74 S.W.3d 719 (Ky. 2002)

66 ALR6th 83—§ 3

Stidham v. Commonwealth, 221 Ky. 49, 297 S.W. 929 (1927)

81 ALR5th 563—§ 3, 5

Stidham v. Duncan, 931 S.W.2d 463 (Ky. Ct. App. 1996)

40 ALR6th 99—§ 54

Stidham v. Peace Officer Standards And Training, 265 F.3d 1144, 17 I.E.R. Cas. (BNA) 1747 (10th Cir. 2001)

41 ALR6th 391—§ 14

Stidham v. State, 1 N.E.3d 222 (Ind. Ct. App. 2013)

94 ALR6th 525—§ 9

Stidham v. State, 637 N.E.2d 140 (Ind. 1994)

9 ALR5th 369—§ 15

39 ALR5th 283—§ 3

Stiefel v. Bayly, Martin & Fay, Inc., 242 N.J. Super. 643, 577 A.2d 1303 (1990)

2 ALR5th 922—§ 4, 7

52 ALR5th 451—§ 4

Stiefel v. Illinois Union Insurance Company, 116 Ill.App.3d 73, 72 Ill.Dec. 141, 452 N.E.2d 73 (1983)

92 ALR5th 273—§ 9

Stiegele v. State, 714 P.2d 356 (Alaska App. 1986)

7 ALR5th 758—§ 11

Stiegele v. State, 714 P.2d 356 (Alaska Ct. App. 1986)

55 ALR6th 157—§ 12

Stiehler, Re Estate of, 133 Misc. 2d 253, 506 N.Y.S.2d 845 (1986)

3 ALR5th 590—§ 7, 13

Stiehler v. Public Serv. Com'n, 629 A.2d 1211 (Dist. Col. App. 1993)

58 ALR5th 187—§ 2, 28

Stienback v. Halsey, 115 Cal. App. 2d 213, 251 P.2d 1008 (1953)

44 ALR5th 1—§ 6, 21

Stier, In re Marriage of, 178 Cal. App. 3d 42, 223 Cal. Rptr. 599 (4th Dist. 1986)

59 ALR6th 433—§ 78

Stier v. City of Derby, 119 Conn. 44, 174 A. 332 (1934)

107 ALR5th 441—§ 17

109 ALR5th 161—§ 4, 7, 8

20 ALR6th 641—§ 3, 20

Stier v. People, 2009 WL 4817831 (Cal. App. 1st Dist. 2009)

93 ALR6th 1—§ 35

Stier, Kent & Canady, Inc. v. Jackson, 317 S.C. 179, 452 S.E.2d 606 (Ct. App. 1994)

60 ALR5th 669—§ 6, 8

Stiesberg v. State of Cal., 80 F.3d 353 (9th Cir. 1996)

10 ALR6th 531—§ 5

Stifel v. Butcher, 487 S.W.2d 24 (Mo. 1972)

36 ALR5th 395—§ 3, 10

Stifel, Nicolaus and Co., Inc. v. Francis, 872 S.W.2d 484 (Mo. Ct. App. W.D. 1994)

14 ALR6th 491—§ 5

Stiffarm v. City of Pullman Police Dept., 2006 WL 2263457 (E.D. Wash. 2006)

65 ALR6th 93—§ 19

Stiff by Stiff v. Eastern Illinois Area of Special Educ., 279 Ill. App. 3d 1076, 216 Ill. Dec. 893, 666 N.E.2d 343, 110 Ed. Law Rep. 1167 (4th Dist. 1996)

68 ALR5th 519—§ 5, 9

Stifflear v. Bristol-Myers Squibb Co., 931 P.2d 471, 1996-1 Trade Cas. (CCH) ¶ 71399 (Colo. Ct. App. 1996)

35 ALR6th 245—§ 4, 9, 11, 13

Stigall v. Brown, 2007 WL 1098580 (Cal. App. 3d Dist. 2007)

45 ALR6th 493—§ 4, 30

Stiger v. Hewlett Bay Park, 283 App. Div. 827, 129 N.Y.S.2d 38 (1954)

53 ALR5th 1—§ 27, 38

Stigger v. State, 1997 WL 644974 (Minn. Ct. App. 1997)

65 ALR6th 537—§ 28

Stigger v. State, 2007 WL 2131715 (Tex. App. Texarkana 2007)

70 ALR6th 361—§ 18

71 ALR6th 335—§ 8

Stigler v. Chicago, 48 Ill. 2d 20, 268 N.E.2d 26 (1971)

24 ALR5th 200—§ 20, 22, 24, 26, 29, 54

Stiglich v. Tracks, D.C., Inc., 721 F. Supp. 1386 (D.C. Dist. Col. 1989)

44 ALR5th 91—§ 8, 10

Stiles, Ex parte, 958 S.W.2d 414 (Tex. App. Waco 1997)

102 ALR5th 647—§ 9

70 ALR6th 1—§ 8

Stiles v. Batavia Atomic Horseshoes, Inc., 174 App. Div. 2d 287, 579 N.Y.S.2d 790, CCH Prod. Liab. Rep. ¶ 13171 (4th Dep't 1992)

9 ALR5th 1—§ 3, 5, 8

Stiles v. Chrysler Motors Corp., 89 Ohio App. 3d 256, 624 N.E.2d 238, 149 L.R.R.M. (BNA) 2251 (6th Dist. Lucas County 1993)

94 ALR5th 149—§ 4, 8

Stiles v. Commissioner of Public Safety, 369 N.W.2d 347 (Minn. Ct. App.1985)

76 ALR5th 597—§ 2, 5

Stiles v. Estate of Ryan, 173 Cal. App. 3d 1057, 219 Cal. Rptr. 647 (1st Dist. 1985)

125 ALR5th 193—§ 7

34 ALR6th 431—§ 4, 21

Stiles v. Industrial Commission, 25 Ariz. App. 543, 545 P.2d 54 (Div. 1 1976)

40 ALR6th 99—§ 65

Stiles v. Oklahoma Tax Com'n, 1987 OK 85, 752 P.2d 800 (Okla. 1987)

13 ALR6th 209—§ 18, 24, 48

Stiles v. Panorama Lanes, Inc., 107 Ill. App. 3d 896, 63 Ill. Dec. 503, 438 N.E.2d 241 (5th Dist. 1982)

74 ALR5th 49—§ 4

Stiles v. Skylark Meats, Inc., 231 Neb. 863, 438 N.W.2d 494 (1989)

34 ALR5th 699—§ 2

Stiles v. State, 39 Okla. Crim. 174 (1928)

41 ALR5th 1—§ 7

Stiles v. State, 902 P.2d 1104 (Okla. Crim. 1995)

20 ALR5th 398—§ 3

Still, In re, 393 B.R. 896 (Bankr. C.D. Cal. 2008)

44 ALR6th 225—§ 3, 7, 9 to 11

Still v. Citizens Bank of Drumright, 6 U.C.C.R.S. 813 (Okla. App. 1969)

61 ALR5th 525—§ 15

Still v. Norfolk & W. R. Co., 368 U.S. 35, 7 L. Ed. 103, 82 S. Ct. 148 (1961)

12 ALR5th 658—§ 2

Still v. Still, 96 Ill. App. 2d 320, 238 N.E.2d 613 (1968)

49 ALR5th 441—§ 21

Stiller v. La Porte Hosp., Inc., 570 N.E.2d 99 (Ind. App. 1991)

28 ALR5th 107—§ 3, 5, 13, 16

Stiller v. Leatherman, 646 N.E.2d 701 (Ind. Ct. App. 1995)

95 ALR6th 85—§ 39

Stilley, Re, 66 Ill. 2d 515, 6 Ill. Dec. 873, 363 N.E.2d 820 (1977)

---

20 ALR5th 534—§ 7

Stilley v. Galaza, 120 Fed. Appx. 683 (9th Cir. 2005)

32 ALR6th 1—§ 11

Stillings v. Gorczyk, 2002 WL 34423169 (Vt. 2002)

46 ALR6th 63—§ 15

Stillman, In re Estate of, 88 N.J. Super. 168, 211 A.2d 222 (1965)

36 ALR5th 395—§ 12

Stillman, Matter of, 188 A.D.2d 832, 591 N.Y.S.2d 863 (3d Dep't 1992)

44 ALR6th 75—§ 27

Stillman v. Multi-States Electric, 28 Ark. App. 193, 771 S.W.2d 807 (1989)

12 ALR5th 658—§ 4, 5, 17

Stillman v. Stillman, 80 App. Div. 2d 356, 439 N.Y.S.2d 119 (1st Dep't 1981)

38 ALR5th 69—§ 3

Stillman Pond, Inc. v. Watson, 115 Cal. App. 2d 440, 252 P.2d 717 (1953)

7 ALR5th 474—§ 10, 13, 92, 154, 157

Stills v. Engle, 573 F. Supp. 814 (S.D. Ohio 1983)

72 ALR6th 1—§ 7

Stills v. Mayor, 438 P.2d 477 (Okla. 1968)

33 ALR5th 205—§ 9
34 ALR5th 1—§ 3

Stills v. State, 728 S.W.2d 422 (Tex. App. Eastland 1987)

26 ALR5th 1—§ 3, 28, 29

Stillwagoner v. Travelers Ins. Co., 979 S.W.2d 354 (Tex. App. Tyler 1998)

6 ALR6th 391—§ 5, 14

Stillwater Columbia Asso. v. Shepherd, 727 P.2d 596 (Okla. App. 1986)

62 ALR5th 219—§ 30, 33, 49

Stilp v. Com., 588 Pa. 539, 905 A.2d 918 (2006)

27 ALR6th 403—§ 5

Stiltner v. Beretta U.S.A. Corp., 74 F.3d 1473, 19 Employee Benefits Cas. (BNA) 2568 (4th Cir. 1996)

125 ALR5th 457—§ 4

Stilwell v. Gust, 148 N.C. App. 128, 557 S.E.2d 627 (2001)

119 ALR5th 121—§ 4
2 ALR6th 279—§ 11, 16

Stilz v. Ketelsen, 75 Ind. App. 166, 129 N.E. 31 (1920)

97 ALR5th 537—§ 45

Stimburys v. Stimburys, 1993 WL 12303 (Ohio Ct. App. 8th Dist. Cuyahoga County 1993)

7 ALR6th 411—§ 3, 4, 9, 12, 31

Stimmel v. Shearson, Hammill & Co., 411 F. Supp. 345 (D.C. Or. 1976)

52 ALR5th 491—§ 8

Stimpel v. State Personnel Bd., 6 Cal. App. 3d 206, 85 Cal. Rptr. 797, 2 Fair Empl. Prac. Cas. (BNA) 1125, 2 Fair Empl. Prac. Cas. (BNA) 1127, 2 Empl. Prac. Dec. (CCH) ¶ 10313 (2d Dist. 1970)

107 ALR5th 623—§ 7

Stimpfel v. Fensten & Gelber, 2002 WL 343382 (Cal. App. 2d Dist. 2002)

58 ALR6th 1—§ 5, 34

Stimpson v. Carlson, 11 Cal. App. 4th 1201, 14 Cal. Rptr. 2d 670, 92 C.D.O.S. 10247, 92 Daily Journal DAR 17161, 1993 AMC 1049 (1st Dist. 1992)

55 ALR5th 529—§ 4

Stimpson v. Ford Motor Co., 988 So. 2d 1119, Prod. Liab. Rep. (CCH) ¶ 18063 (Fla. 5th DCA 2008)

76 ALR6th 465—§ 21

Stimpson v. Stimpson, 213 Ga. 235, 98 S.E.2d 559 (1957)

101 ALR6th 455—§ 7

Stimson v. Dunham, Carrigan, Hayden Co., 146 Cal. 281, 79 P. 968 (1905)

4 ALR5th 772—§ 2

Stinchcomb v. Presbyterian Medical Care Corp., 211 N.C. App. 556, 710 S.E.2d 320 (2011)

100 ALR6th 139—§ 9

Stine, In re, 2006-Ohio-6687, 2006 WL 3702673 (Ohio Ct. App. 3d Dist. Hancock County 2006)

49 ALR6th 505—§ 48

Stine v. Continental Cas. Co., 419 Mich. 89, 349 N.W.2d 127 (1984)
105 ALR5th 499—§ 4

Stine v. Continental Casualty Co., 419 Mich. 89, 349 N.W.2d 127 (1984)
14 ALR5th 695—§ 13

Stineman, Application of, 52 Ohio St. 3d 88, 556 N.E.2d 184 (1990)
8 ALR6th 1—§ 35

Stiner v. Dechant, 114 Ohio App. 3d 209, 683 N.E.2d 26 (9th Dist. Lorain County 1996)
75 ALR5th 413—§ 7
98 ALR6th 231—§ 5, 24

Stines v. Otis Elevator Co., 104 Ill. App. 3d 608, 60 Ill. Dec. 399, 432 N.E.2d 1298 (1st Dist. 1982)
13 ALR5th 289—§ 16, 28
115 ALR5th 1—§ 23, 25

Stinky Love, Inc. v. Lacy, 2004 WL 1803273 (Cal. App. 2d Dist. 2004)
47 ALR6th 1—§ 18, 60

Stinnes Corp. v. Kerr-McGee Coal Corp., 309 Ill. App. 3d 707, 243 Ill. Dec. 98, 722 N.E.2d 1167 (5th Dist. 1999)
101 ALR5th 61—§ 13, 14, 40
102 ALR5th 99—§ 8

Stinnes Interoil, Inc. v. Apex Oil Co., 604 F. Supp. 978, 41 U.C.C.R.S. 1293 (S.D. N.Y. 1985)
61 ALR5th 611—§ 4

Stinnett v. Gilchrist, 419 So. 2d 238 (Ala. Civ. App. 1982)
82 ALR5th 389—§ 2

Stinnett v. Williamson County Sheriff's Dept., 858 S.W.2d 573, 75 Fair Empl. Prac. Cas. (BNA) 629 (Tex. App. Austin 1993)
10 ALR6th 531—§ 3

Stinnett by Stinnett v. Sears Roebuck & Co., 201 A.D.2d 362, 607 N.Y.S.2d 646 (1st Dep't 1994)
11 ALR6th 587—§ 16, 25

Stinski v. State, 281 Ga. 783, 642 S.E.2d 1 (2007)
63 ALR6th 1—§ 53

Stinson v. American Sterilizer Co., 570 So. 2d 618, 7 BNA IER Cas. 648 (Ala. 1990)
17 ALR5th 1—§ 3

Stinson v. America's Home Place, Inc., 108 F. Supp. 2d 1278 (M.D. Ala. 2000)
22 ALR6th 49—§ 4

Stinson v. Aultman, Miller & Co., 54 Kan. 537, 38 P. 788 (1895)
87 ALR5th 473—§ 3

Stinson v. Carter, 543 So. 2d 1198 (Ala. Civ. App. 1989)
119 ALR5th 445—§ 6, 8, 10
1 ALR6th 493—§ 4, 6, 25
2 ALR6th 439—§ 39

Stinson v. Clark Equipment Co., 473 N.W.2d 333 (Minn. Ct. App. 1991)
120 ALR5th 559—§ 6, 8
34 ALR6th 431—§ 4, 5, 11, 16, 20, 29, 33, 35

Stinson v. Columbus & Chicago Motor Freight, Inc., 69 Ohio L. Abs. 449, 125 N.E.2d 881 (App. Franklin Co. 1952)
52 ALR5th 655—§ 2

Stinson v. Davis, 20 Ky. L. Rptr. 1942, 50 S.W. 550 (Ky. 1899)
67 ALR5th 179—§ 9

Stinson v. E.I. DuPont De Nemours and Co., 904 S.W.2d 428, Prod. Liab. Rep. (CCH) ¶ 14273 (Mo. Ct. App. W.D. 1995)
15 ALR5th 119—§ 5
69 ALR5th 137—§ 9, 10

Stinson v. Feminist Women's Health Center, Inc., 416 So. 2d 1183 (Fla. Dist. Ct. App. 1st Dist. 1982)
9 ALR6th 285—§ 4

Stinson v. Green, 2008 WL 4062087 (N.D. Tex. 2008)
65 ALR6th 93—§ 22

Stinson v. Physicians Immediate Care, Ltd., 269 Ill. App. 3d 659, 207 Ill. Dec. 96, 646 N.E.2d 930, 10 I.E.R. Cas. (BNA) 756 (2d Dist. 1995)
19 ALR6th 793—§ 8

Stinson v. Sharp, 80 S.W.3d 852 (Mo. Ct. App. S.D. 2002)

85 ALR6th 229—§ 4

Stinson v. State, 256 Ga. App. 902, 569 S.E.2d 858 (2002)

121 ALR5th 551—§ 4, 6, 7

Stinson v. State, 262 Ind. 189, 313 N.E.2d 699 (1974)

24 ALR6th 1—§ 18

Stinson, State ex rel. v. Morgan, 226 Wis. 2d 100, 593 N.W.2d 924 (Ct. App. 1999)

85 ALR6th 229—§ 26

Stipe v. Joseph A. Neyrey General Contractors, Inc., 385 So. 2d 568 (La. Ct. App. 4th Cir. 1980)

5 ALR6th 497—§ 7

Stipp v. Kim, 874 F. Supp. 663 (E.D. Pa. 1995)

64 ALR6th 249—§ 37

Stipp v. State, 371 So. 2d 712 (Fla. Dist. Ct. App. 4th Dist. 1979)

55 ALR6th 391—§ 20

Stires v. Carnival Corp., 243 F. Supp. 2d 1313 (M.D. Fla. 2002)

8 ALR6th 399—§ 10

Stirgus v. Stirgus, 172 Miss. 337, 160 So. 285 (1935)

52 ALR5th 221—§ 3, 7, 28

Stirlen v. Supercuts, Inc., 51 Cal. App. 4th 1519, 60 Cal. Rptr. 2d 138, 12 I.E.R. Cas. (BNA) 684, 12 I.E.R. Cas. (BNA) 1127 (1st Dist. 1997)

60 ALR5th 669—§ 4

Stirman v. Michael Graves Design Group, Inc., 983 So. 2d 626, Prod. Liab. Rep. (CCH) ¶ 17985 (Fla. 3d DCA 2008)

93 ALR6th 463—§ 6, 8, 14

Stirtan v. Blethen, 79 Wash. 10, 139 P. 618 (1914)

35 ALR6th 1—§ 28

Stirton v. Trump, 202 Or. App. 252, 121 P.3d 714 (2005)

70 ALR6th 329—§ 8

Stissi v. Interstate and Ocean Transport Co. of Philadelphia, 765 F.2d 370, 1986 A.M.C. 1032 (2d Cir. 1985)

66 ALR5th 135—§ 20

Stissi v. Interstate & Ocean Transport Co. of Philadelphia, 814 F.2d 848, 1987 A.M.C. 1441 (2d Cir. 1987)

11 ALR6th 587—§ 8

Stites v. Danek Medical, Inc., 1999 WL 1133274 (S.D. Tex. 1999)

81 ALR5th 483—§ 5

Stites v. Sundstrand Heat Transfer, Inc., 660 F. Supp. 1516, 18 ELR 20203 (W.D. Mich. 1987)

6 ALR5th 162—§ 2, 8

Stith v. Com., 2005 WL 41529 (Va. Ct. App. 2005)

81 ALR6th 505—§ 59

Stith v. Stith, 384 So. 2d 317 (Fla. App. D2 1980)

49 ALR5th 441—§ 16

Stith v. Willis, 219 Ga. 62, 131 S.E.2d 620 (1963)

122 ALR5th 205—§ 3, 18

Stitsworth v. Ford Motor Co., 1996 WL 67610 (E.D. Pa. 1996)

82 ALR5th 501—§ 2, 5, 7, 22, 31, 33, 39, 40, 43

Stitt v. Holland Abundant Life Fellowship, 243 Mich. App. 461, 624 N.W.2d 427 (2000)

90 ALR5th 453—§ 35
119 ALR5th 121—§ 3, 6
121 ALR5th 325—§ 7

Stitt v. Holland Abundant Life Fellowship, 462 Mich. 591, 614 N.W.2d 88 (2000)

8 ALR5th 1—§ 6

Stiuso v. City of New York, 228 A.D.2d 663, 645 N.Y.S.2d 314 (2d Dep't 1996)

50 ALR5th 1—§ 13

Stiuso v. City of New York, 645 N.Y.S.2d 314 (App. Div. 2d Dep't 1996)

50 ALR5th 1—§ 13

Stiver v. Parker, 975 F.2d 261 (6th Cir. 1992)

58 ALR6th 1—§ 5, 30

Stivers, In re, 648 N.E.2d 1147 (Ind. 1995)

50 ALR5th 703—§ 27
Stivers v. Department of Employment, 42 Cal. 2d 486, 267 P.2d 792 (1954)

60 ALR5th 459—§ 2, 13
Stivers v. State, 64 Ark. App. 113, 978 S.W.2d 749 (1998)

96 ALR6th 355—§ 45, 60, 61
Stivers v. Stevens, 581 N.E.2d 1253, 122 Lab. Cas. (CCH) ¶ 57025 (Ind. Ct. App. 4th Dist. 1991)

86 ALR5th 397—§ 3, 9
St. James v. JPMorgan Chase Bank, N.A., 2012 WL 3089275 (Cal. App. 4th Dist. 2012)

86 ALR6th 411—§ 5
St. James Const. Corp. v. Long, 677 N.Y.S.2d 381 (App. Div. 2d Dep't 1998)

23 ALR5th 744—§ 8
St. James Plaza v. Notey, 95 A.D.2d 804, 463 N.Y.S.2d 523 (2d Dep't 1983)

24 ALR6th 399—§ 16
St. Jean v. Racal Mortg., 952 F. Supp. 22 (D. Me. 1997)

73 ALR6th 425—§ 24
St. Joe Minerals Corp. v. Workmen's Compensation Appeal Bd. (Margetic), 73 Pa. Cmwlth. 189, 458 A.2d 295 (1983)

3 ALR5th 907—§ 7
St. John v. Archer, 147 S.W.2d 519 (Tex. Civ. App. 1941)

51 ALR5th 747—§ 3, 5
St. John v. Building Trades Council of Reno and Vicinity, 76 Nev. 290, 352 P.2d 820, 46 L.R.R.M. (BNA) 2527, 40 Lab. Cas. (CCH) ¶ 66591 (1960)

105 ALR5th 243—§ 20
St. John v. Com., Unemployment Compensation Bd. of Review, 108 Pa. Commw. 560, 529 A.2d 1218 (1987)

68 ALR5th 13—§ 9, 38
St. John v. McColley, 653 F. Supp. 2d 1155 (D.N.M. 2009)

64 ALR6th 131—§ 36

St. John v. Northwest Trustee Services, Inc., 2011 WL 2009902 (W.D. Wash. 2011)

86 ALR6th 411—§ 5
St. John v. Pope, 901 S.W.2d 420 (Tex. 1995)

51 ALR5th 301—§ 17
St. John v. State, 363 So. 2d 862 (Fla. Dist. Ct. App. 4th Dist. 1978)

35 ALR6th 497—§ 12, 27
St. John v. State, 400 So. 2d 779 (Fla. Dist. Ct. App. 1st Dist. 1981)

62 ALR5th 1—§ 10
St. John v. State, 523 N.E.2d 1353 (Ind. 1988)

12 ALR6th 267—§ 5
St. John v. State of N.C. Parole Com'n, 764 F. Supp. 403, 33 Fed. R. Evid. Serv. (LCP) 1329 (W.D. N.C. 1991)

59 ALR5th 749—§ 4
St. John v. Superior Court In and For Los Angeles County, 178 Cal. App. 2d 794, 3 Cal. Rptr. 535, Blue Sky L. Rep. (CCH) ¶ 70467, 84 A.L.R.2d 415 (2d Dist. 1960)

58 ALR5th 293—§ 6
St. John Mortg. Co., Inc. v. U.S. Fidelity and Guar. Co., 9 U.C.C. Rep. Serv. 2d (CBC) 34 (E.D. Pa. 1988)

62 ALR5th 137—§ 15, 28
St. Johns & H. R. Co. v. Ransom, 33 Fla. 406, 14 So. 892 (1894)

17 ALR5th 547—§ 53
St. Johnsbury Trucking Co., Inc. v. State, 118 N.H. 209, 385 A.2d 215 (1978)

81 ALR6th 97—§ 22
St. Johns County v. Northeast Florida Builders Ass'n, Inc., 583 So. 2d 635, 69 Ed. Law Rep. 636 (Fla. 1991)

16 ALR6th 289—§ 8, 17, 19
St. John's Home of Milwaukee v. Continental Cas. Co., 147 Wis. 2d 764, 434 N.W.2d 112 (Ct. App. 1988)

16 ALR6th 603—§ 13
St. John's Hospital & School of Nursing, Inc. v. Chapman, 434 P.2d 160 (Okla. 1967)

---

20 ALR5th 1—§ 6, 42, 45

St. John's Medical Center, Inc. v. Spradling, 510 S.W.2d 417 (Mo. 1974)

69 ALR5th 477—§ 20

St. John's Mercy Medical Center, State ex rel. v. Hoester, 708 S.W.2d 796 (Mo. Ct. App. E.D. 1986)

69 ALR5th 559—§ 7, 9, 14

St. John's United Church of Christ v. City of Chicago, 502 F.3d 616 (7th Cir. 2007)

36 ALR6th 681—§ 9

St. John's United Church of Christ v. City of Chicago, Ill., 128 S. Ct. 2431 (U.S. 2008)

36 ALR6th 681—§ 9

St. Johnsville, Village of v. Travelers Indem. Co., 93 A.D.2d 932, 462 N.Y.S.2d 317 (3d Dep't 1983)

93 ALR6th 463—§ 7, 25

St. John's Well Child and Family Center v. Schwarzenegger, 50 Cal. 4th 960, 116 Cal. Rptr. 3d 195, 239 P.3d 651 (2010)

87 ALR6th 633—§ 5

St. John Town Bd. v. Lambert, 725 N.E.2d 507 (Ind. Ct. App. 2000)

111 ALR5th 579—§ 16

St. Joseph v. Borg, 1995 WL 768951 (N.D. Cal. 1995)

82 ALR5th 67—§ 3, 8, 9

St. Joseph B. R. Co., State ex rel. v. Shain, 341 Mo. 733, 108 S.W.2d 351 (1937)

14 ALR5th 242—§ 47

St. Joseph, City of v. Levin, 128 Mo. 588, 31 S.W. 101 (1895)

16 ALR6th 219—§ 17, 19

St. Joseph, City of v. Miller, 409 S.W.2d 749 (Mo. Ct. App. 1966)

89 ALR6th 565—§ 14

St. Joseph Equipment v. Massey-Ferguson, Inc., 546 F. Supp. 1245 (W.D. Wis 1982)

52 ALR5th 613—§ 3

St. Joseph Health Center v. Missouri Labor and Indus. Relations Com'n, 768 S.W.2d 123 (Mo. Ct. App. W.D. 1988)

75 ALR5th 339—§ 7

St. Joseph Hospital v. Quinn, 241 Md. 371, 216 A.2d 732, 25 A.L.R.3d 849 (1966)

16 ALR5th 262—§ 37, 42

St. Joseph Iron Co. v. H. K. Halverson & Co., 48 Mo. App. 383 (1892)

16 ALR5th 548—§ 6

St. Joseph Light & Power Co. v. Kaw Valley Tunneling, Inc., 589 S.W.2d 260 (Mo. 1979)

54 ALR6th 201—§ 10

St. Joseph Light & Power Co. v. Zurich Ins. Co., 698 F.2d 1351 (CA8 Mo. 1983)

37 ALR5th 41—§ 12, 27

St. Joseph Mining Co. v. Pettitt, 90 Okla. 242, 216 P. 657 (1923)

26 ALR5th 127—§ 11

St. Joseph School v. Lamm, 288 Ala. 68, 257 So. 2d 318 (1972)

47 ALR5th 1—§ 13

St. Joseph's Hosp. and Medical Center v. Maricopa County, 142 Ariz. 94, 688 P.2d 986 (1984)

113 ALR5th 95—§ 7, 8

St. Jude Medical, Inc., In re, 425 F.3d 1116 (8th Cir. 2005)

50 ALR6th 281—§ 29

St. Jude Medical, Inc. Silzone Heart Valves Products Liability Litigation, In re, 2003 WL 1589527 (D. Minn. 2003)

115 ALR5th 709—§ 3

St-Laurent v. Fiermonti Oldsmobile, 136 N.H. 70, 611 A.2d 638, 19 U.C.C.R.S.2d 460 (1992)

38 ALR5th 191—§ 4, 17

St. Laurent v. Town of Sturbridge, 1990 WL 92470 (D. Mass. 1990)

17 ALR6th 327—§ 3, 12

For assistance, call 1-800-328-4880

St. Lawrence County Dep't of Social Services on behalf of Lori A. W. v. Raymond J. D., 128 Misc. 2d 105, 488 N.Y.S.2d 962 (Fam Ct. 1985)
46 ALR5th 735—§ 2

St. Ledger v. Com., Revenue Cabinet, 942 S.W.2d 893 (Ky. 1997)
1 ALR6th 1—§ 4, 8

St. Leger v. American Fire and Cas. Ins. Co., 870 F. Supp. 641 (E.D. Pa. 1994)
98 ALR5th 193—§ 8
106 ALR5th 1—§ 3

St. Lewis v. Firestone, 130 A.2d 317 (Mun. Ct. App. D.C. 1957)
84 ALR5th 69—§ 5, 11, 17

St. Louis v. Bridgeton, 705 S.W.2d 524 (Mo. App. 1985)
53 ALR5th 1—§ 6, 12, 13, 22, 25, 32

St. Louis v. Klocker, 637 S.W.2d 174 (Mo. App. 1982)
3 ALR5th 521—§ 2, 3

St. Louis v. Rockwell Graphic Systems, Inc., 153 Ill. 2d 1, 178 Ill. Dec. 761, 605 N.E.2d 555 (1992)
122 ALR5th 1—§ 2, 7, 11, 23, 26, 33, 35, 37, 39

St. Louis v. St. Louis Theater Co., 202 Mo. 690, 100 S.W. 627 (1907)
30 ALR5th 549—§ 2

St. Louis & S. F. R. Co. v. Goode, 1914 OK 237, 42 Okla. 784, 142 P. 1185 (1914)
23 ALR6th 1—§ 8

St. Louis & S. F. R. Co. v. Ludlum, 63 Kan. 719, 66 P. 1045 (1901)
17 ALR5th 547—§ 53, 55

St. Louis & S. F. R. Co. v. Madden, 77 Kan. 80, 93 P. 586 (1908)
25 ALR5th 391—§ 82, 91, 93 to 95

St. Louis & S. F. R. Co. v. Richardson, 47 Kan. 517, 28 P. 183 (1891)
17 ALR5th 547—§ 53

St. Louis & S. W. R. Co. v. Ford, 65 Ark. 96, 45 S.W. 55 (1898)
25 ALR5th 391—§ 54, 89

St. Louis, B. & M. R. Co. v. Maddox, 152 S.W. 225 (Tex. Civ. App. 1912)

St. Louis Bank for Sav., FSB v. American Cas. Co. of Reading, Pennsylvania, 927 F.2d 1042 (8th Cir. 1991)
22 ALR6th 113—§ 76
34 ALR6th 345—§ 35

St. Louis, City of v. Burton, 478 S.W.2d 320 (Mo. 1972)
72 ALR5th 1—§ 3, 29

St. Louis, City of v. City of Bridgeton, 806 S.W.2d 717 (Mo. Ct. App. E.D. 1991)
5 ALR6th 327—§ 9
8 ALR6th 117—§ 4

St. Louis, City of v. Gloner, 210 Mo. 502, 109 S.W. 30 (1908)
72 ALR5th 1—§ 7
52 ALR6th 125—§ 5, 49

St. Louis, City of v. Jameson, 972 S.W.2d 302, 87 A.L.R.5th 731 (Mo. Ct. App. E.D. 1998)
87 ALR5th 1—§ 12, 13, 30

St. Louis, City of v. Kiely, 652 S.W.2d 694 (Mo. Ct. App. E.D. 1983)
106 ALR5th 337—§ 3

St. Louis, City of v. Liberman, 547 S.W.2d 452 (Mo. 1977)
16 ALR6th 219—§ 19, 24
88 ALR6th 203—§ 80

St. Louis, City of v. Michigan Underground Storage Tank Financial Assur. Policy Bd., 215 Mich. App. 69, 544 N.W.2d 705 (1996)
11 ALR5th 388—§ 14

St. Louis, City of v. O'Neill Lumber Co., 114 Mo. 74, 21 S.W. 484 (1893)
81 ALR6th 363—§ 4, 20

St. Louis, City of v. Vert, 84 Mo. 204, 1884 WL 9544 (1884)
33 ALR6th 407—§ 18

St. Louis County v. B.A.P., Inc., 18 S.W.3d 397, 28 Media L. Rep. (BNA) 1777 (Mo. Ct. App. E.D. 2000)
10 ALR5th 538—§ 5

St. Louis County v. Champ, 438 S.W.2d 205 (Mo. 1969)

17 ALR5th 195—§ 7, 10
St. Louis County v. Peerless Park, 494 S.W.2d 673 (Mo. App. 1973)

17 ALR5th 195—§ 7
St. Louis County v. Peerless Park, 726 S.W.2d 405 (Mo. App. 1987)

17 ALR5th 195—§ 4, 7, 9, 10
St. Louis Dressed Beef & Provision Co. v. Maryland Casualty Co., 201 U.S. 173, 26 S. Ct. 400, 50 L. Ed. 712 (1906)

16 ALR6th 491—§ 4, 10
St. Louis Fireworks Co. v. Wilson, 5 Tenn. Civ. App. 388, 5 Higgins 388 (1915)

21 ALR6th 81—§ 98
St. Louis Housing Authority v. Lo Duca, 700 S.W.2d 101 (Mo. Ct. App. E.D. 1985)

114 ALR5th 443—§ 41
St. Louis, I. M. & S. P. R. Co. v. Paul, 173 U.S. 404, 43 L. Ed. 746, 19 S. Ct. 419 (1899)

18 ALR5th 577—§ 3, 4
St. Louis, I. M. & S. R. Co. v. Bailey, 87 Ark. 132, 112 S.W. 180 (1908)

18 ALR5th 577—§ 41
St. Louis, I. M. & S. R. Co. v. Broomfield, 83 Ark. 288, 104 S.W. 133 (1907)

18 ALR5th 577—§ 41, 44
St. Louis, I. M. & S. R. Co. v. Bryant, 92 Ark. 425, 122 S.W. 996 (1909)

18 ALR5th 577—§ 49
St. Louis, I. M. & S. R. Co. v. Clements, 82 Ark. 3, 99 S.W. 1106 (1907)

25 ALR5th 391—§ 55
St. Louis, I. M. & S. R. Co. v. Hecht, 38 Ark. 357 (1882)

17 ALR5th 547—§ 65
St. Louis, I. M. & S. R. Co. v. McClerkin, 88 Ark. 277, 114 S.W. 240 (1908)

18 ALR5th 577—§ 9, 41
St. Louis, I. M. & S. R. Co. v. Paul, 64 Ark. 83, 40 S.W. 705 (1897)

18 ALR5th 577—§ 4 to 6

St. Louis, I. M. & S. R. Co. v. Stamps, 84 Ark. 241, 104 S.W. 1114 (1907)

12 ALR5th 195—§ 27
St. Louis, I. M. & S. R. Co. v. Yonley, 53 Ark. 503, 13 S.W. 333 (1890)

25 ALR5th 391—§ 87, 91
St. Louis, I.M. & S. Ry. Co. v. Philpot, 72 Ark. 23, 77 S.W. 901 (1903)

61 ALR5th 635—§ 3, 13, 20
St. Louis Little Rock Hospital, Inc. v. Gaertner, 682 S.W.2d 146 (Mo. App. 1984)

26 ALR5th 628—§ 3

27 ALR5th 76—§ 3, 36

28 ALR5th 1—§ 3
St. Louis Park v. King, 246 Minn. 422, 75 N.W.2d 487 (1956)

56 ALR5th 171—§ 3, 9, 27
St. Louis Park, City of v. Bunkers, 310 Minn. 431, 247 N.W.2d 404 (1976)

109 ALR5th 611—§ 3
St. Louis Rose Co. v. Unemployment Compensation Com., 348 Mo. 1153, 159 S.W. 249 (1941)

60 ALR5th 459—§ 2, 20
St. Louis-San Francisco R. Co. v. Mills, 271 U.S. 344, 70 L. Ed. 979, 46 S. Ct. 520 (1926)

40 ALR5th 1—§ 8
St. Louis-San Francisco Ry. Co. v. Powell, 1963 OK 209, 385 P.2d 465 (Okla. 1963)

15 ALR6th 1—§ 4, 23
St. Louis S. F. R. Co. v. De Voe, 152 Ark. 38, 237 S.W. 433 (1922)

18 ALR5th 577—§ 41
St. Louis S. F. R. Co. v. Kilgore, 366 P.2d 936 (Okla. 1961)

15 ALR5th 119—§ 5
St. Louis S. F. R. Co. v. Pearson, 170 Ark. 842, 281 S.W. 910 (1926)

58 ALR5th 535—§ 3
St. Louis Southwestern Ry. Co. v. Henwood, 157 F.2d 337 (C.C.A. 8th Cir. 1946)

84 ALR5th 399—§ 16

St. Louis Southwestern Ry. Co. v. Jackson, 242 Ark. 858, 416 S.W.2d 273 (1967)
15 ALR6th 1—§ 4, 5, 7 to 10, 22
St. Louis Southwestern Ry. Co. v. Ragland, 304 Ark. 1, 800 S.W.2d 410 (1990)
81 ALR6th 97—§ 26
St. Louis Southwestern Ry. Co. of Texas v. Griffin, 106 Tex. 477, 171 S.W. 703 (1914)
95 ALR5th 1—§ 5
St. Louis Southwestern Ry. Co. of Texas v. Hixon, 104 Tex. 267, 137 S.W. 343 (1911)
95 ALR5th 1—§ 12
St. Louis S. R. Co. v. Adcock, 269 S.W. 144 (Tex. Civ. App. 1924)
17 ALR5th 547—§ 46, 51
St. Louis S. R. Co. v. Anderson, 173 S.W. 908 (Tex. Civ. App. 1914)
17 ALR5th 547—§ 71, 79
St. Louis S. R. Co. v. Brown, 75 Ark. 137, 86 S.W. 994 (1905)
18 ALR5th 577—§ 40
St. Louis S. R. Co. v. Connally, 93 S.W. 206 (Tex. Civ. App. 1906)
17 ALR5th 547—§ 45, 52, 53
St. Louis S. R. Co. v. Garner, 164 S.W. 385 (Tex. Civ. App. 1914)
25 ALR5th 391—§ 54, 56
St. Louis S. R. Co. v. Gentry, 80 S.W. 844 (Tex. Civ. App. 1904)
17 ALR5th 547—§ 53, 81
St. Louis S. R. Co. v. Hagler, 160 Ark. 543, 254 S.W. 1071 (1923)
12 ALR5th 195—§ 12
St. Louis S. R. Co. v. Henderson, 55 Tex. Civ. App. 425, 119 S.W. 891 (1909)
17 ALR5th 547—§ 66
St. Louis S. R. Co. v. Jackson, 242 Ark. 858, 416 S.W.2d 273 (1967)
15 ALR5th 119—§ 5, 6, 15, 25, 26, 29, 31, 59, 61, 63, 70
St. Louis S. R. Co. v. Jones, 138 S.W.2d 577 (Tex. Civ. App. 1940)
17 ALR5th 547—§ 71

St. Louis S. R. Co. v. Ragland, 304 Ark. 1, 800 S.W.2d 410 (1990)
33 ALR5th 509—§ 2, 5
St. Louis S. R. Co. v. Steele, 190 Ark. 662, 80 S.W.2d 623 (1935)
58 ALR5th 535—§ 8
St. Louis S. R. Co. v. Thompson, 108 S.W. 453 (Tex. Civ. App. 1908)
14 ALR5th 242—§ 49
St. Louis S. R. Co. v. Thompson, 192 S.W. 1095 (Tex. Civ. App. 1917)
14 ALR5th 242—§ 49
St. Louis, State ex rel. City of v. Judge of Court of Criminal Correction, Division No. 2., 542 S.W.2d 1 (Mo. Ct. App. 1976)
102 ALR5th 525—§ 12
St. Louis Street Flushing Mach. Co. v. Sanitary Street Flushing Mach. Co., 161 F. 725 (C.C.A. 8th Cir. 1908)
85 ALR6th 1—§ 24, 32
St. Louis S. W. R. Co. v. Knight, 41 S.W. 416 (Tex. Civ. App. 1897)
17 ALR5th 547—§ 54
St. Louis Teachers' Credit Union v. Marsh, 585 S.W.2d 474 (Mo. 1979)
73 ALR6th 571—§ 16, 54
St. Luke Evangelical Lutheran Church, Inc. v. Smith, 74 Md. App. 353, 537 A.2d 1196 (1988)
19 ALR5th 1—§ 96
St. Luke Evangelical Lutheran Church, Inc. v. Smith, 318 Md. 337, 568 A.2d 35 (1990)
109 ALR5th 541—§ 3
St. Luke's Cataract and Laser Institute, P.A. v. Sanderson, 70 Fed. R. Evid. Serv. 174 (M.D. Fla. 2006)
34 ALR6th 253—§ 12
St. Luke's Episcopal Hosp. v. Agbor, 952 S.W.2d 503 (Tex. 1997)
98 ALR5th 533—§ 18
St. Luke's Evangelical Lutheran Church of Country Homes v. Hales, 13 Wash. App. 483, 534 P.2d 1379 (Div. 3 1975)
76 ALR5th 337—§ 13

St. Luke's Hosp. v. Giertz, 458 Mich. 448, 581 N.W.2d 665 (1998)
17 ALR6th 1—§ 19

St. Luke's Hosp. v. Giertz, 1996 WL 33348610 (Mich. Ct. App. 1996)
17 ALR6th 1—§ 19

St. Luke's Hospital v. Consolidated Mut. Ins. Co., 32 Misc. 2d 657, 217 N.Y.S.2d 843 (1961)
16 ALR5th 262—§ 49

St. Luke's Memorial Hospital v. Peterson, 108 Wis. 2d 772, 324 N.W.2d 297 (2d Dist. 1982)
16 ALR5th 262—§ 35

St. Margaret Mercy Healthcare Centers, Inc. v. Ho, 663 N.E.2d 1220 (Ind. Ct. App. 1996)
16 ALR6th 1—§ 30

St. Margaret Seneca Place v. Board of Property Assessment, Appeals & Review, 536 Pa. 478, 640 A.2d 380, 34 A.L.R.5th 845 (1994)
34 ALR5th 529—§ 4

St. Martin v. KFC Corp., 935 F. Supp. 898 (W.D. Ky. 1996)
52 ALR5th 613—§ 3

St. Martin's Press, Inc. v. Carey, 605 F.2d 41, 4 Media L. R. 1968 (CA2 N.Y. 1979)
42 ALR5th 291—§ 3

St. Mary Medical Center, Inc. v. Casko, 639 N.E.2d 312, Prod. Liab. Rep. (CCH) ¶ 14013 (Ind. Ct. App. 3d Dist. 1994)
65 ALR5th 357—§ 7

St. Mary's Area Water Authority v. St. Paul Fire & Marine Ins. Co., 464 F. Supp. 2d 397 (M.D. Pa. 2006)
37 ALR6th 657—§ 6
90 ALR6th 635—§ 9

St. Mary's Byzantine Church v. Mantich, 505 N.E.2d 811 (Ind. App. 1987)
8 ALR5th 1—§ 34, 47

St. Marys, City of v. Huber, 1981 WL 6700 (Ohio Ct. App. 3d Dist. Auglaize County 1981)
102 ALR5th 525—§ 13

St. Marys Foundry Co., State ex rel. v. Industrial Com'n, 78 Ohio St. 3d 521, point1997/point, 1997-Ohio-25, 678 N.E.2d 1390 (1997)
31 ALR6th 199—§ 99

St. Marys Gas Co. v. Brodbeck, 114 Ohio St. 423, 4 Ohio L. Abs. 225, 151 N.E. 323 (1926)
34 ALR5th 1—§ 2, 5, 6

St. Mary's Hosp., Inc. v. Brinson, 685 So. 2d 33 (Fla. Dist. Ct. App. 4th Dist. 1996)
101 ALR5th 61—§ 3, 31

St. Mary's Hosp., Inc. v. Radiology Professional Corp., 205 Ga. App. 121, 421 S.E.2d 731, 92 Fulton County D R 1448 (1992)
28 ALR5th 107—§ 29

St. Mary's Hospital, Inc. v. Phillipe, 769 So. 2d 961 (Fla. 2000)
26 ALR5th 245—§ 30

St. Mary's Indus. School for Boys v. Brown, 45 Md. 310 (1876)
65 ALR5th 1—§ 12

St. Mary's Mill Co. v. Illinois Oil Co., 254 S.W. 735 (Mo. App. 1923)
17 ALR5th 547—§ 4, 20

St. Michael's Orphan Asylum, etc. v. Conneen Const. Co., 115 N.J. Eq. 334, 170 A. 649 (1933)
4 ALR5th 772—§ 93

St. Michelle v. Robinson, 52 Wash. App. 309, 759 P.2d 467 (1988)
9 ALR5th 321—§ 9

STN Enterprises, Inc., In re, 44 B.R. 512 (Bankr. D. Vt. 1984)
44 ALR6th 441—§ 9

Stobaugh v. Norwegian Cruise Line Ltd., 5 S.W.3d 232, 2001 A.M.C. 215 (Tex. App. Houston 14th Dist. 1999)
6 ALR6th 659—§ 4

Stobaugh v. State, 614 P.2d 767 (Alaska 1980)
20 ALR6th 479—§ 3

Stobaugh v. Wallace, 757 F. Supp. 653, 66 Ed. Law Rep. 245 (W.D. Pa. 1990)

70 ALR5th 169—§ 35

Stober v. Lechmere, Inc., 6 Mass. L. Rptr. 676, 1997 WL 211801 (Mass. Super. Ct. 1997)

74 ALR5th 49—§ 2 to 4, 6, 19

Stober v. McCarter, 4 Ohio St. 513, 1855 WL 13 (1855)

23 ALR6th 1—§ 24

Stock v. ADCO General Corp., 96 N.M. 544, 632 P.2d 1182 (Ct. App. 1981)

8 ALR6th 549—§ 6, 10

Stock v. Fife, 13 Mass. App. 75, 430 N.E.2d 845 (1982)

3 ALR5th 1—§ 3, 4, 51

Stock v. Grantham, 125 N.M. 564, 1998-NMCA-081, 964 P.2d 125, 136 Lab. Cas. (CCH) ¶ 58439 (Ct. App. 1998)

7 ALR6th 563—§ 17

Stockard v. State, 391 So. 2d 1065 (Ala. App. 1980)

24 ALR5th 465—§ 2, 41

Stockburger v. Riley, 21 Cal. App. 2d 165, 68 P.2d 741 (3d Dist. 1937)

65 ALR5th 1—§ 2, 34

Stockdale, In re Marriage of, 781 N.W.2d 101 (Iowa Ct. App. 2010)

99 ALR6th 203—§ 32

Stockdale v. Baba, 153 Ohio App. 3d 712, 2003-Ohio-4366, 795 N.E.2d 727 (10th Dist. Franklin County 2003)

30 ALR6th 241—§ 3, 21

Stockdale v. Bird & Son, Inc., 399 Mass. 249, 503 N.E.2d 951 (1987)

96 ALR5th 107—§ 6

99 ALR5th 301—§ 9

Stockdale v. Hughes, 173 A.D.2d 1075, 570 N.Y.S.2d 412 (3d Dep't 1991)

118 ALR5th 1—§ 5

Stocker v. Cataldi, 483 N.E.2d 461 (Ind. Ct. App. 3d Dist. 1985)

91 ALR5th 1—§ 4, 12

Stocker v. Huff, 109 Ind. App. 668, 37 N.E.2d 4 (1941)

25 ALR5th 391—§ 34

Stocker v. Sheehan, 13 A.D.3d 1, 786 N.Y.S.2d 126 (1st Dep't 2004)

59 ALR6th 161—§ 3, 15, 41

60 ALR6th 193—§ 10, 15

Stocker v. Warden, SCI Graterford, 2004 WL 603400 (E.D. Pa. 2004)

31 ALR6th 1—§ 14

Stockett v. Tolin, 791 F. Supp. 1536, 58 Fair Empl. Prac. Cas. (BNA) 1441, 59 Empl. Prac. Dec. (CCH) ¶ 41568, 123 Lab. Cas. (CCH) ¶ 35696 (S.D. Fla. 1992)

12 ALR5th 195—§ 11, 69

81 ALR5th 367—§ 15

Stock Exchanges Options Trading Antitrust Litigation, In re, 2006 WL 3498590 (S.D. N.Y. 2006)

60 ALR6th 295—§ 42, 71

Stockham Pipe Fittings Co. v. Williams, 245 Ala. 570, 18 So. 2d 93 (1943)

80 ALR5th 417—§ 4

41 ALR6th 207—§ 18

Stockheimer v. Carwin Co., 135 N.J.L. 49, 50 A.2d 145 (N.J. Sup. Ct. 1946)

100 ALR5th 567—§ 9

Stockler v. City of Detroit, 885 F.2d 871 (6th Cir. 1989)

89 ALR6th 1—§ 49, 108

Stockman v. J.C. Industries, Inc., 854 S.W.2d 24 (Mo. Ct. App. W.D. 1993)

11 ALR6th 351—§ 3, 11

Stockmen's Livestock Market, Inc. v. Norwest Bank of Sioux City, 135 F.3d 1236 (8th Cir. 1998)

9 ALR5th 63—§ 6

Stocks v. State, 224 Ga. App. 433, 481 S.E.2d 230 (1997)

28 ALR6th 505—§ 31

Stocks v. Stocks, 1998 WL 262634 (Ark. Ct. App. 1998)

109 ALR5th 1—§ 5, 9

Stockstill v. Shell Oil Co., 3 F.3d 868, 8 I.E.R. Cas. (BNA) 1529, 62 Empl. Prac. Dec. (CCH) ¶ 42562 (5th Cir. 1993)

53 ALR6th 213—§ 13

Stockton v. Com., 227 Va. 124, 314 S.E.2d 371 (1984)

85 ALR5th 547—§ 8

Stockton v. Gristedes Supermarkets, Inc., 177 App. Div. 2d 425, 576 N.Y.S.2d 267, 16 U.C.C.R.S.2d 723 (1st Dep't 1991)
45 ALR5th 389—§ 5, 21

Stockton v. Kroger Co., 559 S.W.2d 101 (Tex. Civ. App. Dallas 1977)
123 ALR5th 1—§ 3

Stockton v. Murray, 41 F.3d 920 (4th Cir. 1994)
12 ALR6th 267—§ 8

Stockton v. Oldenburg, 305 Ill. App. 3d 897, 238 Ill. Dec. 1013, 713 N.E.2d 259 (4th Dist. 1999)
40 ALR5th 697—§ 26.5

Stockton v. Silco Constr. Co., 319 Or. 365, 877 P.2d 71 (1994)
5 ALR5th 513—§ 7
7 ALR5th 444—§ 3

Stockton v. State, 509 P.2d 153 (Okla. Crim. 1973)
39 ALR5th 283—§ 3

Stockton v. Tester, 273 S.W.2d 783 (Mo. Ct. App. 1954)
107 ALR5th 311—§ 2, 13

Stockton Kenworth, Inc. v. Mentzer Detroit Diesel, Inc., 101 Nev. 400, 705 P.2d 145, 41 U.C.C. Rep. Serv. 1837 (1985)
118 ALR5th 91—§ 19, 23

Stockton Newspapers, Inc. v. Redevelopment Agency, 171 Cal. App. 3d 95, 214 Cal. Rptr. 561 (3d Dist. 1985)
34 ALR5th 591—§ 14

Stockwell v. Bloomfield State Bank, 174 Ind. App. 307, 367 N.E.2d 42, 22 U.C.C. Rep. Serv. (CBC) 726 (1st Dist. 1977)
61 ALR5th 525—§ 15

Stockwell v. Great Atlantic & Pacific Tea Co., 583 So. 2d 1186 (La. Ct. App. 1st Cir. 1991)
123 ALR5th 1—§ 3

Stockwell v. Marks, 17 Me. 455, 1840 WL 969 (1840)
109 ALR5th 421—§ 3

Stockwell v. Stockwell, 116 Idaho 297, 775 P.2d 611 (1989)
15 ALR5th 692—§ 23, 30

Stockwell v. Township Bd. of White Lake, 22 Mich. 341, 1871 WL 2991 (1871)
28 ALR6th 175—§ 9

Stoddard v. Davidson, 355 Pa. Super. 262, 513 A.2d 419 (1986)
96 ALR5th 107—§ 8
99 ALR5th 301—§ 15

Stoddard v. Edelman, 4 Cal. App. 3d 544, 84 Cal. Rptr. 443 (2d Dist. 1970)
4 ALR6th 263—§ 29

Stoddard v. Lyon, 18 S.D. 207, 99 N.W. 1116 (1904)
86 ALR6th 411—§ 2

Stoddard v. Nelson, 99 Idaho 293, 581 P.2d 339 (1978)
21 ALR5th 82—§ 2, 4

Stoddard v. Quinn, 593 F. Supp. 300 (D. Me. 1984)
59 ALR6th 111—§ 9

Stoddard v. School Dist. No. 1, Lincoln County, Wyo., 590 F.2d 829 (10th Cir. 1979)
123 ALR5th 411—§ 56

Stoddard v. State, 395 Md. 653, 911 A.2d 1245 (2006)
70 ALR6th 1—§ 19

Stoddard v. Wyeth, Inc., 630 F. Supp. 2d 631, 56 A.L.R.6th 761 (E.D. N.C. 2009)
56 ALR6th 161—§ 3, 5, 7

Stoddard, People ex rel. v. Williams, 64 Cal. 87, 27 P. 939 (1883)
56 ALR5th 171—§ 4, 19

Stoddard, Town of v. Northern Sec. Ins. Co., Inc., 718 F. Supp. 1062 (D.N.H. 1989)
97 ALR5th 473—§ 4, 7

Stoecker v. Brush Wellman, Inc., 194 Ariz. 448, 984 P.2d 534 (1999)
16 ALR6th 143—§ 14

For assistance, call 1-800-328-4880

Stoecklein v. Illinois Tool Works, Inc.,
589 F. Supp. 139, 36 Fair Empl.
Prac. Cas. (BNA) 1154, 36 Empl.
Prac. Dec. (CCH) ¶ 34943 (N.D. Ill.
1984)

104 ALR5th 1—§ 3, 5
105 ALR5th 351—§ 3
11 ALR6th 447—§ 7

Stoeey v. Brush, 256 Mass. 101, 152
N.E. 225 (1926)

25 ALR5th 233—§ 12

Stoehr v. City of St. Paul, 54 Minn. 549,
56 N.W. 250 (1893)

54 ALR6th 201—§ 13

Stoelker v. Thornton, 88 Ala. 241, 6 So.
680 (1889)

6 ALR6th 391—§ 5

S. Toepfer, Inc. v. Those Certain Underwriters at Lloyd's, London, 182
App. Div. 2d 481, 582 N.Y.S.2d
183 (1st Dep't 1992)

22 ALR5th 579—§ 38

Stoeppelman v. Hays-Fendler Const.
Co., 437 S.W.2d 143 (Mo. Ct. App.
1968)

24 ALR6th 747—§ 8

Stoeppelman v. Hays-Fendler Constr.
Co., 437 S.W.2d 143 (Mo. App.
1968)

15 ALR5th 119—§ 5, 15, 16, 23

Stoerzinger v. Big v. Supermarkets Inc.,
188 A.D.2d 790, 591 N.Y.S.2d 257
(3d Dep't 1992)

123 ALR5th 1—§ 4

Stoes Bros., Inc. v. Freudenthal, 81 N.M.
61, 463 P.2d 37 (Ct. App. 1969)

8 ALR6th 549—§ 2, 10

Stoesser v. Dunham, 689 N.Y.S.2d 276
(App. Div. 3d Dep't 1999)

53 ALR5th 375—§ 23

Stofer v. Montgomery Ward & Co., 249
F.2d 285 (8th Cir. 1957)

1 ALR6th 297—§ 16

Stoffels v. Harmony Hill Farm, 389 N.J.
Super. 207, 912 A.2d 184 (App.
Div. 2006)

79 ALR6th 487—§ 46, 51

Stofman v. World Marine Underwriters,
Inc., 729 So. 2d 959 (Fla. Dist. Ct.
App. 4th Dist. 1999)

119 ALR5th 121—§ 2, 3, 10
121 ALR5th 325—§ 3
2 ALR6th 279—§ 4
34 ALR6th 431—§ 20

Stogner v. Geis, 397 S.W.2d 494 (Tex.
Civ. App. Tyler 1965)

58 ALR5th 535—§ 19

Stogsdill v. Manor Convalescent Home,
Inc., 35 Ill. App. 3d 634, 343 N.E.2d
589, 83 A.L.R.3d 838 (2d Dist.
1976)

35 ALR5th 145—§ 12
108 ALR5th 385—§ 3

St.-Oharra v. Colucci, 67 A.D.2d 1104,
415 N.Y.S.2d 142 (4th Dep't 1979)

91 ALR6th 435—§ 123

Stoianoff v. Commissioner of Motor
Vehicles, 107 F. Supp. 2d 439 (S.D.
N.Y. 2000)

93 ALR5th 1—§ 2, 5
30 ALR6th 483—§ 3

Stojkovic v. Weller, 802 S.W.2d 152
(Mo. 1991)

33 ALR5th 303—§ 2, 3, 9, 11, 12, 14

Stokeling v. State, 189 Md. App. 653,
985 A.2d 175 (2009)

92 ALR6th 171—§ 16

Stokely v. Owens, 189 Va. 248, 52
S.E.2d 164 (1949)

1 ALR6th 135—§ 8, 39

Stokely-Van Camp, Inc. v. Ferguson,
271 Ala. 120, 122 So. 2d 356 (1959)

2 ALR5th 1—§ 3, 5, 9

Stoker v. Bellemeade, LLC, 272 Ga.
App. 817, 615 S.E.2d 1 (2005)

48 ALR6th 1—§ 27, 88, 110

Stoker v. Elniff, 33 S.W.2d 977 (Mo.
App. 1931)

12 ALR5th 195—§ 66

Stoker v. Jim Marsh American Corp., 91
Nev. 164, 532 P.2d 1031 (1975)

23 ALR5th 241—§ 48

Stoker v. Ogden City, 88 Utah 389, 54
P.2d 849 (1936)

10 ALR5th 371—§ 3

Stoker v. State, 692 N.E.2d 1386 (Ind. Ct. App. 1998)

69 ALR6th 579—§ 4

Stokes, In re Marriage of, 234 Or. App. 566, 228 P.3d 701 (2010)

59 ALR6th 433—§ 68

Stokes, Re Marriage of, 43 Colo. App. 461, 608 P.2d 824 (1979)

3 ALR5th 394—§ 5, 7, 11

Stokes v. Bally's Pacwest, Inc., 113 Wash. App. 442, 54 P.3d 161 (Div. 1 2002)

61 ALR6th 147—§ 14

Stokes v. Bechtel North American Power Corp., 614 F. Supp. 732 (N.D. Cal. 1985)

105 ALR5th 351—§ 3, 5, 12

Stokes v. Berick, 1999 WL 1313668 (Ohio Ct. App. 11th Dist. Lake County 1999)

13 ALR6th 1—§ 4

Stokes v. Board of Directors of La Cav Imp. Co., 654 So. 2d 524 (Miss. 1995)

115 ALR5th 251—§ 38

Stokes v. Board of Review of Indus. Com'n of Utah, 832 P.2d 56 (Utah Ct. App. 1992)

73 ALR5th 1—§ 4, 6

97 ALR5th 1—§ 5

106 ALR5th 111—§ 5

108 ALR5th 1—§ 6

Stokes v. CBS Inc., 25 F. Supp. 2d 992, 27 Media L. Rep. (BNA) 1385 (D. Minn. 1998)

100 ALR5th 341—§ 3

42 ALR6th 353—§ 13

Stokes v. City of Madison, 930 F.2d 1163 (7th Cir. 1991)

80 ALR5th 255—§ 4, 14, 16

122 ALR5th 593—§ 2, 5, 7

Stokes v. Dailey, 97 N.W.2d 676 (N.D. 1959)

19 ALR5th 563—§ 2, 7

30 ALR5th 571—§ 2

47 ALR5th 433—§ 18

108 ALR5th 385—§ 12

Stokes v. First Nat. Bank, 306 S.C. 46, 410 S.E.2d 248 (1991)

97 ALR5th 1—§ 5

106 ALR5th 111—§ 18

108 ALR5th 1—§ 29, 30

Stokes v. Gary Barbera Enterprises, Inc., 2001 PA Super 239, 783 A.2d 296 (2001)

66 ALR6th 351—§ 47

Stokes v. Haynes, 428 S.W.2d 227 (Ky. 1968)

3 ALR5th 146—§ 8

7 ALR5th 1—§ 22

Stokes v. Langley, 348 F. Supp. 2d 606 (M.D.N.C. 2004)

42 ALR6th 237—§ 8

Stokes v. Leung, 651 S.W.2d 704 (Tenn. Ct. App. 1982)

81 ALR5th 167—§ 8

Stokes v. McRae, 247 Ga. 658, 278 S.E.2d 393 (1981)

102 ALR5th 647—§ 21

Stokes v. Meimaris, 111 Ohio App. 3d 176, 675 N.E.2d 1289 (8th Dist. Cuyahoga County 1996)

7 ALR6th 135—§ 4

Stokes v. Oster Development, Inc., 807 So. 2d 987, 101 A.L.R.5th 731 (La. Ct. App. 5th Cir. 2002)

101 ALR5th 447—§ 12, 13

Stokes v. Procunier, 744 F.2d 475 (CA5 Tex. 1984)

7 ALR5th 263—§ 6

Stokes v. Puckett, 972 S.W.2d 921 (Tex. App. Beaumont 1998)

52 ALR5th 1—§ 3

20 ALR6th 1—§ 4

Stokes v. State, 72 Md. App. 673, 532 A.2d 189 (1987)

59 ALR5th 1—§ 2

Stokes v. State, 548 So. 2d 118 (Miss. 1989)

55 ALR5th 125—§ 3, 7

Stokes v. State, 604 So. 2d 836, 17 FLW D 1144 (Fla. App. D1 1992)

43 ALR5th 1—§ 14

Stokes v. State, 738 P.2d 1364 (Okla. Crim. App. 1987)

74 ALR5th 453—§ 2, 5
Stokes v. State, 978 S.W.2d 674 (Tex. App. Eastland 1998)

85 ALR5th 1—§ 49
Stokes v. State, 2006 WL 137227 (Ark. 2006)

29 ALR6th 237—§ 5, 24
Stokes v. Stewart, 774 So. 2d 1215 (La. Ct. App. 1st Cir. 2000)

91 ALR5th 1—§ 3, 4
Stokes v. Stokes, 143 Ariz. 590, 694 P.2d 1204 (App. 1984)

52 ALR5th 221—§ 25
Stokes v. Stokes, 751 P.2d 1363, 16 A.L.R.5th 1085 (Alaska 1988)

16 ALR5th 650—§ 6, 7, 11
Stokes v. Stokes, 1987 OK 56, 738 P.2d 1346 (Okla. 1987)

59 ALR6th 433—§ 61
Stokes v. Town Council of New White-land, Indiana, 2007 WL 1430705 (S.D. Ind. 2007)

89 ALR6th 1—§ 40
Stokes by & Through Stokes v. Tulsa Pub. Sch., 875 P.2d 445 (Okla. App. 1994)

23 ALR5th 1—§ 2, 9
Stokka v. Cass County Elec. Co-op., Inc., 373 N.W.2d 911 (N.D. 1985)

98 ALR6th 231—§ 30
Stokley v. Ryan, 659 F.3d 802 (9th Cir. 2011)

102 ALR6th 417—§ 16
Stokoe v. Upton, 40 Mich. 581, 1879 WL 3089 (1879)

109 ALR5th 421—§ 5
Stokus v. Marsh, 217 Cal. App. 3d 647, 266 Cal. Rptr. 90 (1st Dist. 1990)

10 ALR5th 448—§ 4
Stolarick v. Novak, 401 Pa. Super. 171, 584 A.2d 1034 (1991)

95 ALR5th 533—§ 3
124 ALR5th 203—§ 3, 6, 8
Stolarik v. Hendrick Mfg. Corp., 767 F. Supp. 88 (M.D. Pa. 1991)

4 ALR6th 401—§ 5
Stolba v. Vesci, 909 S.W.2d 706 (Mo. Ct. App. S.D. 1995)

25 ALR5th 123—§ 9
76 ALR5th 337—§ 20
Stolberg v. Stolberg, 538 N.E.2d 1 (Ind. App. 1989)

4 ALR5th 403—§ 3
Stole v. U.S. Steel Corp., 34 Misc. 2d 103, 227 N.Y.S.2d 595 (Sup 1962)

103 ALR5th 339—§ 15, 16
Stoler v. Penn Cent. Transp. Co., 583 F.2d 896, 11 Ohio Op. 3d 316, 3 Fed. R. Evid. Serv. 683 (6th Cir. 1978)

15 ALR6th 1—§ 3
Stoler v. Penn Cent. Transp. Co., 583 F.2d 896, 11 Ohio Op. 3d 316, 3 Fed. R. Evid. Serv. (LCP) 683 (6th Cir. 1978)

66 ALR5th 135—§ 1
Stoleson v. U.S., 708 F.2d 1217 (CA7 Wis. 1983)

6 ALR5th 162—§ 11
Stoll v. Goodnight Corp., 469 So. 2d 1072 (La. App. 2d Cir. 1985)

18 ALR5th 577—§ 43
Stoll v. State, 724 So. 2d 90 (Ala. Crim. App. 1998)

47 ALR6th 107—§ 13
Stoll v. Stoll, 243 Minn. 510, 68 N.W.2d 367 (1955)

53 ALR5th 375—§ 21
Stolle v. Baylor College of Medicine, 981 S.W.2d 709 (Tex. App. Houston 1st Dist. 1998)

100 ALR6th 477—§ 15, 23, 25
Stollenwerk v. Township of Mullica, 316 N.J. Super. 379, 720 A.2d 422 (App. Div. 1998)

16 ALR5th 605—§ 5
Stollenwerk v. Tri-West Healthcare Alliance, 2005 WL 2465906 (D. Ariz. 2005)

50 ALR6th 33—§ 6
Stoller v. Ackerson, 39 A.D.2d 934, 333 N.Y.S.2d 222 (2d Dep't 1972)

14 ALR6th 543—§ 18
Stoller v. College of Medicine, 562 F. Supp. 403, 11 Ed. Law Rep. 185 (M.D. Pa. 1983)

For assistance, call 1-800-328-4880

90 ALR6th 235—§ 43

Stollings, In re, 65 Ohio App. 3d 183, 583 N.E.2d 367 (Hardin Co. 1989)

40 ALR5th 697—§ 5, 9 to 11, 13, 15, 17, 22

Stollsteimer v. Morgan, 39 Pa. D. & C. 270, 1940 WL 2584 (C.P. 1940)

1 ALR6th 135—§ 2, 5

Stoltenberg, State Ex Rel. v. the Industrial Commission of Ohio, 1983 WL 3858 (Ohio Ct. App. 10th Dist. Franklin County 1983)

31 ALR6th 199—§ 47

Stoltman v. Stoltman, 170 Mich. App. 653, 429 N.W.2d 220 (1988)

36 ALR6th 1—§ 26

Stolt-Nielsen S.A. v. AnimalFeeds International Corp., 130 S. Ct. 1758, 176 L. Ed. 2d 605, 93 Empl. Prac. Dec. (CCH) ¶ 43878, 2010-1 Trade Cas. (CCH) ¶ 76982, 2010 A.M.C. 913 (2010)

56 ALR6th 679—§ 2

Stolt-Nielsen SA v. AnimalFeeds Intern. Corp., 548 F.3d 85, 2008-2 Trade Cas. (CCH) ¶ 76355, 2008 A.M.C. 2722 (2d Cir. 2008)

56 ALR6th 679—§ 2

Stoltz v. County of Lancaster, 2011 WL 815709 (E.D. Pa. 2011)

95 ALR6th 341—§ 57

Stoltz v. Friday, 325 Ark. 399, 926 S.W.2d 438 (1996)

67 ALR5th 587—§ 7
11 ALR6th 1—§ 4, 12

Stoltz v. Wilmington Trust Co., 1992 WL 127516 (Del. Ch. 1992)

56 ALR5th 565—§ 49

Stoltzner v. American Motors Jeep Corp. Inc., 127 Ill. App. 3d 816, 82 Ill. Dec. 909, 469 N.E.2d 443, 39 U.C.C. Rep. Serv. (CBC) 907 (1st Dist. 1984)

81 ALR5th 483—§ 3

Stolz v. Bank of America, 15 Cal. App. 4th 217, 19 Cal. Rptr. 2d 19 (3d Dist. 1993)

45 ALR6th 493—§ 32

Stolz v. Board of Regents of University, 4 A.D.2d 361, 165 N.Y.S.2d 179 (3d Dep't 1957)

19 ALR6th 577—§ 4

Stolz v. KSFM 102 FM, 30 Cal. App. 4th 195, 35 Cal. Rptr. 2d 740, 94 C.D.O.S. 8802, 94 Daily Journal DAR 16269, 23 Media L. R. 1233 (3d Dist. 1994)

19 ALR5th 1—§ 37, 176

Stolz v. McKowen, 14 Wash. App. 808, 545 P.2d 584 (1976)

59 ALR5th 733—§ 3

Stolzenburg v. Ford Motor Co., 143 F.3d 402, 76 Fair Empl. Prac. Cas. (BNA) 1244, 73 Empl. Prac. Dec. (CCH) ¶ 45350 (8th Cir. 1998)

81 ALR5th 367—§ 36

Stom, Re Marriage of, 226 N.W.2d 797 (Iowa 1975)

17 ALR5th 366—§ 8

Stomp, Inc. v. NeatO, LLC, 61 F. Supp. 2d 1074 (C.D. Cal. 1999)

81 ALR5th 41—§ 5, 9
106 ALR5th 309—§ 3

Stone, Ex parte, 87 Cal. App. 2d 777, 197 P.2d 847 (3d Dist. 1948)

78 ALR6th 417—§ 4

Stone, In re, 166 B.R. 269 (Bankr. W.D. Pa. 1994)

32 ALR6th 531—§ 39
40 ALR6th 463—§ 18

Stone, In re Marriage of, 274 Mont. 331, 908 P.2d 670 (1995)

59 ALR6th 433—§ 34, 61

Stone, Matter of, 230 A.D.2d 481, 657 N.Y.S.2d 2 (1st Dep't 1997)

25 ALR6th 1—§ 28

Stone, Matter of Compensation of, 57 Or. App. 808, 646 P.2d 668 (1982)

86 ALR5th 295—§ 7

Stone, Re Marriage of, 155 Ill. App. 3d 62, 107 Ill. Dec. 747, 507 N.E.2d 900, 77 A.L.R.4th 661 (4th Dist. 1987)

10 ALR5th 191—§ 5

Stone v. A.L.S. Const. Co., 108 A.D.2d 1036, 485 N.Y.S.2d 605 (3d Dep't 1985)
42 ALR6th 61—§ 12
Stone v. Bayley, 75 Wash. 184, 134 P. 820 (1913)
14 ALR5th 557—§ 9, 10, 15, 25, 27
Stone v. Board of Governance of Pennsylvania Bar, 312 Pa. 576, 168 A. 473, 90 A.L.R. 1109 (1933)
37 ALR6th 511—§ 18
Stone v. Boston & A. R. Co., 171 Mass. 536, 51 N.E. 1 (1898)
17 ALR5th 547—§ 74
Stone v. Burch, 114 Fla. 460, 154 So. 128 (1934)
88 ALR5th 463—§ 2, 4
Stone v. C. I. T. Corp., 122 Pa. Super. 71, 184 A. 674 (1936)
14 ALR5th 242—§ 25
Stone v. City of Paducah, 120 Ky. 322, 27 Ky. L. Rptr. 717, 86 S.W. 531 (1905)
87 ALR6th 109—§ 5, 7, 41
Stone v. City of Pleasanton, 115 Kan. 378, 223 P. 312 (1924)
111 ALR5th 579—§ 22
Stone v. City of Wilton, 331 N.W.2d 398 (Iowa 1983)
4 ALR6th 263—§ 11
Stone v. City of Wylie, 34 S.W.2d 842 (Tex. Comm'n App. 1931)
92 ALR5th 517—§ 4
Stone v. County of Butte, 172 F.3d 58 (9th Cir. 1999)
30 ALR6th 483—§ 5
Stone v. Cupp, 39 Or. App. 473, 592 P.2d 1044 (1979)
9 ALR6th 541—§ 10
Stone v. Damons, 252 Fed. Appx. 581 (5th Cir. 2007)
65 ALR6th 93—§ 20
Stone v. Daviess County Div. of Children and Family Services, 656 N.E.2d 824, 13 A.D.D. 325, 6 A.D. Cas. (BNA) 1483 (Ind. Ct. App. 1995)
119 ALR5th 351—§ 3, 4, 6

Stone v. District of Columbia, 99 U.S. App. D.C. 32, 237 F.2d 28 (1956)
45 ALR5th 173—§ 12
Stone v. Earp, 331 Mich. 606, 50 N.W.2d 172 (1951)
7 ALR5th 143—§ 2
Stone v. Edmondson, 168 Tenn. 698, 80 S.W.2d 665 (1935)
60 ALR6th 481—§ 4
Stone v. Edwards, 35 Tex. 556, 1872 WL 7441 (1872)
85 ALR6th 1—§ 37
Stone v. Essex County Newspapers, Inc., 367 Mass. 849, 330 N.E.2d 161 (1975)
19 ALR5th 1—§ 93, 105, 110
Stone v. Estate of Sigman, 1998 OK CIV APP 173, 970 P.2d 1185 (Div. 4 1998)
99 ALR6th 1—§ 18
Stone v. Foster, 106 Cal. App. 3d 334, 164 Cal. Rptr. 901 (3d Dist. 1980)
19 ALR5th 563—§ 5, 29
Stone v. Frederick L. Hobby Associates II, 2001 WL 861822 (Conn. Super. Ct. 2001)
27 ALR6th 465—§ 4
47 ALR6th 1—§ 50
Stone v. Freezer, 280 App. Div. 103, 111 N.Y.S.2d 710 (1952)
38 ALR5th 69—§ 3, 6
Stone v. FWD Corp., 822 F. Supp. 1211 (D.C. Md. 1993)
53 ALR5th 535—§ 10, 13
Stone v. Graham, 449 U.S. 39, 101 S. Ct. 192, 66 L. Ed. 2d 199 (1980)
107 ALR5th 1—§ 4, 6, 10, 19
Stone v. Hechler, 782 F. Supp. 1116 (N.D. W. Va. 1992)
114 ALR5th 311—§ 6
34 ALR6th 643—§ 32
Stone v. Jacobson, 258 A.D. 300, 16 N.Y.S.2d 504 (4th Dep't 1939)
16 ALR6th 219—§ 44
Stone v. Jeffres, 208 So. 2d 827 (Fla. 1968)
79 ALR5th 201—§ 4, 8, 10, 11

Stone v. Jetmar Properties, LLC, 733 N.W.2d 480, 43 A.L.R.6th 813 (Minn. Ct. App. 2007)
43 ALR6th 611—§ 23, 58

Stone v. Johnston, 167 Mo. App. 456, 151 S.W. 987 (1912)
67 ALR5th 179—§ 3

Stone v. Martin, 85 N.C. App. 410, 355 S.E.2d 255 (1987)
14 ALR5th 242—§ 10

Stone v. Mayflower Sch. Dist., 319 Ark. 771, 894 S.W.2d 881 (1995)
56 ALR5th 493—§ 5

Stone v. McCullion, 27 Ohio App. 3d 112, 500 N.E.2d 326 (1st Dist. Hamilton County 1985)
96 ALR5th 327—§ 3

Stone v. McGregor, 99 Tex. 51, 87 S.W. 334 (1905)
36 ALR6th 387—§ 9

Stone v. Palms West Hosp., 941 So. 2d 514 (Fla. Dist. Ct. App. 4th Dist. 2006)
64 ALR6th 249—§ 13

Stone v. Pamoja House, 111 Fed. Appx. 624 (2d Cir. 2004)
63 ALR6th 1—§ 33

Stone v. Pillsbury, 167 Mass. 332, 45 N.E. 768 (1897)
1 ALR6th 135—§ 5, 18

Stone v. Powell, 428 U.S. 465, 49 L. Ed. 2d 1067, 96 S. Ct. 3037 (1976)
19 ALR5th 470—§ 2

Stone v. Powell, 428 U.S. 465, 96 S. Ct. 3037, 49 L. Ed. 2d 1067 (1976)
11 ALR6th 237—§ 2
92 ALR6th 1—§ 3

Stone v. Puffer-Hubbard Mfg. Co., 187 Minn. 173, 244 N.W. 555 (1932)
104 ALR6th 97—§ 3

Stone v. Rapp, 236 So. 2d 274 (La. App. 4th Cir. 1970)
24 ALR5th 174—§ 5

Stone v. Regents of University of California, 77 Cal. App. 4th 736, 92 Cal. Rptr. 2d 94, 140 Ed. Law Rep. 1012 (4th Dist. 1999)
47 ALR5th 553—§ 22

Stone v. Shea, 113 N.H. 174, 304 A.2d 647 (1973)
92 ALR6th 1—§ 3

Stone v. Smith, Kline & French Laboratories, 731 F.2d 1575 (CA11 Ala. 1984)
57 ALR5th 1—§ 3

Stone v. State, 23 Tenn. 27, 4 Hum. 27 (1843)
59 ALR5th 1—§ 4, 6

Stone v. State, 191 N.C. App. 402, 664 S.E.2d 32, 234 Ed. Law Rep. 1030 (2008)
82 ALR6th 497—§ 16

Stone v. State, 402 So. 2d 1330 (Fla. Dist. Ct. App. 1st Dist. 1981)
62 ALR5th 1—§ 4, 15

Stone v. State, 638 S.W.2d 629 (Tex. App. Houston 1st Dist. 1982)
72 ALR5th 109—§ 5

Stone v. State, 641 So. 2d 293 (Ala. Crim. App. 1993)
76 ALR5th 1—§ 10, 20

Stone v. State, 671 N.E.2d 499 (Ind. App. 1996)
50 ALR5th 581—§ 7

Stone v. State, 705 So. 2d 1316 (Ala. Crim. App. 1996)
116 ALR5th 479—§ 5

Stone v. State, 745 P.2d 1344 (Wyo. 1987)
9 ALR6th 1—§ 10

Stone v. State, 751 S.W.2d 579 (Tex. App. Houston (1st Dist.) 1988)
10 ALR5th 700—§ 2, 11

Stone v. State, 951 S.W.2d 205 (Tex. App. Houston 14th Dist. 1997)
9 ALR6th 633—§ 8, 10

Stone v. Steed, 923 S.W.2d 282 (Ark. App. 1996)
20 ALR5th 534—§ 10

Stone v. St. Joseph's Hosp. of Parkersburg, 208 W. Va. 91, 538 S.E.2d 389, 11 A.D. Cas. (BNA) 213 (2000)
102 ALR5th 1—§ 4

Stone v. Stone, 7 P.3d 887 (Wyo. 2000)
90 ALR5th 1—§ 17

Stone v. Stone, 9 Ohio App. 3d 6, 457 N.E.2d 919 (12th Dist.Warren County 1983)

62 ALR5th 591—§ 3

Stone v. Stone, 16 Wash. 2d 315, 133 P.2d 526 (1943)

124 ALR5th 203—§ 9

Stone v. Stone, 26 So. 3d 1232 (Ala. Civ. App. 2009)

59 ALR6th 433—§ 61

Stone v. Stone, 188 Ark. 622, 67 S.W.2d 189 (1934)

52 ALR5th 221—§ 7, 30

Stone v. Stone, 200 W. Va. 15, 488 S.E.2d 15, 102 A.L.R.5th 751 (1997)

102 ALR5th 395—§ 2, 7, 10

Stone v. Stone, 292 So. 2d 686 (La. 1974)

38 ALR5th 69—§ 5

Stone v. Stone, 636 N.W.2d 594 (Minn. App. 2001)

57 ALR6th 163—§ 39

Stone v. Stone, 725 S.W.2d 145 (Mo. Ct. App. E.D. 1987)

59 ALR6th 433—§ 38

Stone v. Superior Court, 31 Cal. 3d 503, 183 Cal. Rptr. 647, 646 P.2d 809 (1982)

26 ALR5th 603—§ 7

Stone v. United Engineering, a Div. of Wean, Inc., 197 W. Va. 347, 475 S.E.2d 439 (1996)

122 ALR5th 1—§ 2, 35

Stone v. U.S., 408 F.2d 995 (CA5 Fla. 1969)

27 ALR5th 174—§ 102

Stone v. Wall, 734 So. 2d 1038 (Fla. 1999)

103 ALR6th 461—§ 6, 13, 21

Stone v. Welling, 14 Mich. 514 (1866)

13 ALR5th 684—§ 2

Stone v. Williams, 64 N.Y.2d 639, 485 N.Y.S.2d 42, 474 N.E.2d 250 (1984)

60 ALR5th 379—§ 8

Stone v. Williamson, 2007 WL 1135686 (Mich. Ct. App. 2007)

64 ALR6th 249—§ 19

Stone v. Wilton, 331 N.W.2d 398 (Iowa 1983)

38 ALR5th 737—§ 3 to 5

Stone v. Winn Dixie Stores, Inc., 212 Ga. App. 291, 442 S.E.2d 1, 94 Fulton County D R 431 (1994)

40 ALR5th 135—§ 2, 15

Stone v. Wyckoff, 102 N.J. Super. 26, 245 A.2d 215 (App. Div. 1968)

116 ALR5th 1—§ 10, 23, 35, 62 to 64, 67

13 ALR6th 661—§ 23, 35

Stone & Webster Engineering Corp. v. First Nat. Bank & Trust Co. of Greenfield, 345 Mass. 1, 184 N.E.2d 358, 1 U.C.C. Rep. Serv. 195, 99 A.L.R.2d 628 (1962)

91 ALR5th 89—§ 7

104 ALR5th 459—§ 2, 5

Stoneberger v. Davis, 74 S.D. 300, 51 N.W.2d 873 (1952)

46 ALR5th 1—§ 16, 24

107 ALR5th 311—§ 4

Stonebraker v. State, 594 So. 2d 351 (Fla. Dist. Ct. App. 2d Dist. 1992)

46 ALR6th 241—§ 10

Stoneburner v. England, 202 A.2d 652 (Dist. Col. App. 1964)

18 ALR5th 542—§ 8

Stonecipher v. Kornhaus, 623 So. 2d 955 (Miss. 1993)

8 ALR5th 312—§ 8

Stonecipher v. Poplar Bluff R1 School Dist., 205 S.W.3d 326, 28 A.L.R.6th 703 (Mo. Ct. App. S.D. 2006)

28 ALR6th 175—§ 4 to 6, 81

Stonecipher v. Sexton, 54 F.R.D. 435 (D. Kan. 1972)

78 ALR6th 151—§ 7

Stone City Music v. Santillanes, 702 F. Supp. 249 (D. Or. 1988)

37 ALR6th 243—§ 53

Stone City Music v. Santillanes, 702 F. Supp. 249 (D.C. Or. 1988)

23 ALR5th 241—§ 30

Stonecraft, LLC, In re, 322 B.R. 623 (Bankr. S.D. Miss. 2005)

CASES CITED IN ALR5th and ALR6th

49 ALR6th 1—§ 29
Stonehedge Square Ltd. Partnership v. Movie Merchants, Inc., 552 Pa. 412, 715 A.2d 1082 (1998)
75 ALR5th 1—§ 2, 3
Stone Hill Community Ass'n v. Norpel, 492 N.W.2d 409 (Iowa 1992)
115 ALR5th 251—§ 45
51 ALR6th 533—§ 5
Stonehocker v. Cassano, 154 Cal. App. 2d 732, 316 P.2d 717 (2d Dist. 1957)
52 ALR5th 491—§ 7
Stoneking v. Briggs, 254 Cal. App. 2d 563, 62 Cal. Rptr. 249, 56 Lab. Cas. (CCH) ¶ 51766 (1st Dist. 1967)
94 ALR5th 149—§ 2, 5
Stoneking v. Orleans Village, 127 Vt. 161, 243 A.2d 763 (1968)
54 ALR6th 201—§ 11 to 13, 18
Stoneking v. State, 800 P.2d 949 (Alaska Ct. App. 1990)
27 ALR6th 183—§ 19, 35
Stone Machinery Co. v. Kessler, 1 Wash. App. 750, 463 P.2d 651, 7 U.C.C.R.S. 135 (1970)
25 ALR5th 696—§ 28
Stoneman v. Drollinger, 2000 MT 274, 302 Mont. 107, 14 P.3d 12 (2000)
38 ALR6th 313—§ 11
Stoneman v. Drollinger, 2003 MT 25, 314 Mont. 139, 64 P.3d 997 (2003)
100 ALR5th 1—§ 6, 14
Stoneman v. Turner Metal Prods., 2007-Ohio-1719, 2007 WL 1083869 (Ohio Ct. App. 8th Dist. Cuyahoga County 2007)
77 ALR6th 1—§ 96
Stone Mfg. Co. v. NCNB of South Carolina, 308 S.C. 287, 417 S.E.2d 628, 18 U.C.C.R.S.2d 502 (App. 1992)
45 ALR5th 389—§ 26, 32
Stone Mfg. Co. v. South Carolina Employment Sec. Com'n, 219 S.C. 239, 64 S.E.2d 644 (1951)
25 ALR6th 101—§ 5

Stone Mountain Memorial Ass'n v. Zauber, 262 Ga. 661, 424 S.E.2d 279 (1993)
70 ALR6th 513—§ 8
71 ALR6th 471—§ 4
Stone Post Co. v. Corcoran, 80 NJL 549, 77 A. 1031 (1910)
4 ALR5th 772—§ 59
Stoner v. Carr, 97 Idaho 641, 550 P.2d 259 (1976)
76 ALR6th 31—§ 37
Stoner v. Fortson, 359 F. Supp. 579 (N.D. Ga. 1972)
121 ALR5th 1—§ 5
Stoner v. Houston, 265 Ark. 928, 582 S.W.2d 28 (1979)
2 ALR5th 449—§ 3, 4
Stoner v. Nash Finch, Inc., 446 N.W.2d 747, 87 A.L.R.4th 117 (N.D. 1989)
12 ALR5th 195—§ 67
Stoner v. Stehm, 200 Iowa 809, 202 N.W. 530 (1925)
35 ALR6th 1—§ 27, 29
Stoner v. Stoner, 163 Conn. 345, 307 A.2d 146 (1972)
28 ALR5th 46—§ 2, 11, 12, 15, 16
Stoner v. Wilson, 140 Kan. 383, 36 P.2d 999 (1934)
14 ALR5th 242—§ 3, 46
Stoner Creek Stud, Inc. v. Revenue Cabinet Com. of Ky., 746 S.W.2d 73 (Ky. Ct. App. 1987)
113 ALR5th 313—§ 17
Stoneridge Inv. Partners, LLC v. Scientific-Atlanta, 128 S. Ct. 761, 169 L. Ed. 2d 627, Fed. Sec. L. Rep. (CCH) ¶ 94556 (U.S. 2008)
36 ALR6th 681—§ 45
Stoneridge Inv. Partners, LLC v. Scientific-Atlanta, Inc., 127 S. Ct. 1873, 167 L. Ed. 2d 363 (U.S. 2007)
26 ALR6th 659—§ 53
Stoneridge Parkway Partners v. MW Housing Partners III, 153 Cal. App. 4th 1373, 64 Cal. Rptr. 3d 61 (3d Dist. 2007)
73 ALR6th 571—§ 35, 84

Stones v. Sears, Roebuck & Co., 251 Neb. 560, 558 N.W.2d 540, Prod. Liab. Rep. (CCH) ¶ 14861 (1997)
122 ALR5th 515—§ 2, 11

Stoneson Development Corp. v. Superior Court (Coffey), 197 Cal. App. 3d 178, 242 Cal. Rptr. 721, Prod. Liab. Rep. (CCH) ¶ 11660 (1st Dist. 1987)
122 ALR5th 1—§ 7

Stones River Motors, Inc. v. Mid-South Pub. Co., 651 S.W.2d 713 (Tenn. App. 1983)
54 ALR5th 443—§ 11, 19

Stone Street Capital, Inc. v. Bureau of State Lottery, 263 Mich. App. 683, 689 N.W.2d 541 (2004)
48 ALR6th 243—§ 14

Stonewall Ins. Co. v. Asbestos Claims Management Corp., 73 F.3d 1178 (2d Cir. 1995)
49 ALR6th 169—§ 3, 7

Stonewall Ins. Co. v. Asbestos Claims Mgmt. Corp., 73 F.3d 1178 (CA2 N.Y. 1995)
14 ALR5th 695—§ 5

Stonewall Ins. Co. v. City of Palos Verdes Estates, 7 Cal. App. 4th 309, 9 Cal. Rptr. 2d 663, 92 C.D.O.S. 4957, 92 Daily Journal DAR 7831 (2d Dist. 1992)
14 ALR5th 695—§ 7, 19

Stonewall Ins. Co. v. Heter, 438 So. 2d 950 (Fla. App. D4 1983)
2 ALR5th 922—§ 5, 8
52 ALR5th 451—§ 3

Stonewall Ins. Co. v. National Gypsum Co., 1988 WL 96159 (S.D. N.Y. 1988)
104 ALR6th 207—§ 21

Stonewall Ins. Co. v. National Gypsum Co., 1992 WL 123144 (S.D. N.Y. 1992)
89 ALR5th 1—§ 22

Stonewall Surplus Lines Ins. Co. v. Drabek, 835 S.W.2d 708 (Tex. App. Corpus Christi 1992)
50 ALR6th 53—§ 7, 8

Stonewall Union v. City of Columbus, 931 F.2d 1130 (6th Cir. 1991)
80 ALR5th 255—§ 14, 15, 34

Stoney v. MacDougall, 31 N.C. App. 678, 230 S.E.2d 592 (1976)
36 ALR5th 395—§ 12

Stoney Run Co. v. Prudential-LMI Commercial Ins. Co., 47 F.3d 34 (2d Cir. 1995)
98 ALR5th 193—§ 4
106 ALR5th 1—§ 3

Stong v. People, 74 Colo. 283, 220 P. 999 (1923)
87 ALR6th 633—§ 6

St. Onge, Stewart, Johnson and Reens, LLC v. Media Group, Inc., 84 Conn. App. 88, 851 A.2d 1242 (2004)
58 ALR6th 1—§ 5, 68

Stooks v. Foote, 20 App. Div. 622, 46 N.Y.S. 718 (1897)
25 ALR5th 391—§ 34

Stooksbury v. American Nat. Property and Cas. Co., 126 S.W.3d 505 (Tenn. Ct. App. 2003)
116 ALR5th 247—§ 4

Stoops v. Mulhorn, 383 Pa. 132, 117 A.2d 733 (1955)
27 ALR5th 174—§ 64

Stop 35, Inc. v. Haines, 374 Pa. Super. 604, 543 A.2d 1133 (1988)
18 ALR5th 230—§ 3, 7

Stop & Shop Companies, Inc. v. Gilbane Bldg. Co., 364 Mass. 325, 304 N.E.2d 429 (1973)
31 ALR6th 433—§ 5

Stopczynski v. Ford Motor Co., 200 Mich. App. 190, 503 N.W.2d 912 (1993)
7 ALR6th 563—§ 5

Stopczynski v. Governor of State, 92 Mich. App. 191, 285 N.W.2d 62 (1979)
87 ALR6th 633—§ 3

Stopka v. Lesser, 82 Ill. App. 3d 323, 37 Ill. Dec. 779, 402 N.E.2d 781 (1st Dist. 1980)
61 ALR5th 307—§ 6, 9

Stop Olympic Prison v. United States Olympic Committee, 489 F. Supp. 1112, 207 USPQ 237 (S.D. N.Y. 1980)

19 ALR5th 1—§ 179

Stoppel v. Woolner, 4 Ohio Dec. Reprint 489, 2 Cleve LR 252, 4 WL Bull 576, revd without op 8 WL Bull 235, on the authority of 37 OS 194 (1879)

31 ALR5th 572—§ 33

Stopper v. Kantner, 29 Pa. Super. 48, 1905 WL 3785 (1905)

109 ALR5th 421—§ 5, 9, 14

Stop the Beach Renourishment, Inc. v. Florida Dept. of Environmental Protection, 130 S. Ct. 2592, 70 Env't. Rep. Cas. (BNA) 1505 (2010)

56 ALR6th 679—§ 12

Stop Youth Addiction, Inc. v. Lucky Stores, Inc., 17 Cal. 4th 553, 71 Cal. Rptr. 2d 731, 950 P.2d 1086 (1998)

66 ALR6th 315—§ 17

Storace v. Mariano, 35 Conn. Supp. 28, 391 A.2d 1347 (C.P. 1978)

91 ALR6th 435—§ 97

Storage Masters-Chesterfield, L.L.C. v. City of Chesterfield, 27 S.W.3d 862 (Mo. Ct. App. E.D. 2000)

30 ALR5th 549—§ 8

Storage Services v. Oosterbaan, 214 Cal. App. 3d 498, 262 Cal. Rptr. 689 (1st Dist. 1989)

46 ALR6th 185—§ 7, 18

Storar, Matter of, 52 N.Y.2d 363, 438 N.Y.S.2d 266, 420 N.E.2d 64 (1981)

100 ALR6th 477—§ 31

Storch v. Com., State Bd. of Vehicle Mfrs., Dealers and Salespersons, 132 Pa. Commw. 240, 572 A.2d 819 (1990)

67 ALR6th 209—§ 21

Storch v. LaGuardia Medical Group, P.C., 619 N.Y.S.2d 314 (App. Div. 2d Dep't 1994)

47 ALR5th 433—§ 13

Storch v. Storch, 38 App. Div. 2d 904, 329 N.Y.S.2d 474 (1st Dep't 1972)

38 ALR5th 69—§ 4

Stordeur v. Computer Associates Intern., Inc., 995 F. Supp. 94, 81 Fair Empl. Prac. Cas. (BNA) 1347 (E.D.N.Y. 1998)

83 ALR5th 1—§ 3, 10
94 ALR5th 1—§ 3

Storer v. Brown, 415 U.S. 724, 94 S. Ct. 1274, 39 L. Ed. 2d 714 (1974)

120 ALR5th 1—§ 22
121 ALR5th 1—§ 53
34 ALR6th 643—§ 2, 3, 21

Storer v. Tharp, 29 Va. Cir. 286, 1992 WL 885009 (1992)

101 ALR5th 447—§ 7

Storer Broadcasting Co., State ex rel. v. Gorenstein, 131 Wis. 2d 342, 388 N.W.2d 633, 12 Media L. R. 1870 (App. 1986)

16 ALR5th 152—§ 2, 4, 8

Storer Cable Communications v. City of Montgomery, Ala., 806 F. Supp. 1518, 1992-2 Trade Cas. (CCH) ¶ 70031 (M.D. Ala. 1992)

76 ALR6th 289—§ 5
77 ALR6th 543—§ 19

Storey v. Chase Bankcard Services, Inc., 970 F. Supp. 722 (D. Ariz. 1997)

73 ALR5th 1—§ 2, 3, 5, 6
94 ALR5th 1—§ 3

Storey v. Leonas, 904 N.E.2d 229 (Ind. Ct. App. 2009)

58 ALR6th 1—§ 5
60 ALR6th 1—§ 53

Storey v. Poss, 2000 WL 1478565 (Tenn. Ct. App. 2000)

12 ALR6th 1—§ 4, 5
14 ALR6th 1—§ 4

Storey v. State, 830 N.E.2d 1011 (Ind. Ct. App. 2005)

35 ALR6th 127—§ 4

Storey v. United States Fidelity & Guaranty Co., 32 Idaho 388, 183 P. 990 (1919)

5 ALR5th 56—§ 24

Storey v. University of New Mexico Hospital/BCMC, 105 N.M. 205, 730 P.2d 1187 (1986)
16 ALR5th 262—§ 5

Storey v. Westinghouse Elec. Corp., 554 So. 2d 619 (Fla. Dist. Ct. App. 3d Dist. 1989)
115 ALR5th 1—§ 25

Storey & Fawcett v. Nampa & Meridian Irr. Dist., 32 Idaho 713, 187 P. 946 (1920)
81 ALR6th 363—§ 4, 5

Storey's Will, Re, 134 Misc. 791, 236 N.Y.S. 518 (1929)
3 ALR5th 590—§ 15

Storie v. Independent School Dist., No. 13, 834 F. Supp. 2d 1305, 280 Ed. Law Rep. 894 (E.D. Okla. 2011)
90 ALR6th 235—§ 9

Storie v. U.S., 142 F.R.D. 317, 793 F. Supp. 221 (E.D. Mo. 1992)
48 ALR5th 129—§ 8

Storie v. U.S., 793 F. Supp. 221 (E.D. Mo. 1992)
83 ALR5th 589—§ 5
123 ALR5th 1—§ 12

Storjohn v. Fay, 246 Neb. 454, 519 N.W.2d 521 (1994)
21 ALR5th 82—§ 8

Stork v. International Bazaar, Inc., 54 Wash. App. 274, 774 P.2d 22, 57 BNA FEP Cas. 1056 (1989)
51 ALR5th 1—§ 6

Stork v. McKinley, 444 Fed. Appx. 920 (7th Cir. 2011)
89 ALR6th 1—§ 113

Storke v. Penn Mut. Life Ins. Co., 390 Ill. 619, 61 N.E.2d 552 (1945)
76 ALR5th 337—§ 15

Storley v. Armour & Co., 107 F.2d 499 (CA8 N.D. 1939)
25 ALR5th 568—§ 33

Storlie v. Quality Pork Processors, 1995 WL 593022 (Minn. Ct. App. 1995)
102 ALR5th 1—§ 5, 7

Storlien v. Storlien, 386 N.W.2d 812 (Minn. Ct. App. 1986)
95 ALR5th 533—§ 5

124 ALR5th 203—§ 5

Storm v. Golden, 371 Pa. Super. 368, 538 A.2d 61 (1988)
58 ALR6th 1—§ 5
60 ALR6th 1—§ 40

Storm v. Legion Ins. Co., 265 Wis. 2d 169, 2003 WI 120, 665 N.W.2d 353 (2003)
14 ALR6th 301—§ 9

Storm v. Legion Ins. Co., 2003 WI 120, 265 Wis. 2d 169, 665 N.W.2d 353, 23 A.L.R.6th 939 (2003)
23 ALR6th 697—§ 6, 16

Storm v. Storm, 470 P.2d 367 (Wyo. 1970)
38 ALR6th 313—§ 14

Storm & Associates, Ltd. v. Cuculich, 298 Ill. App. 3d 1040, 233 Ill. Dec. 101, 700 N.E.2d 202 (1st Dist. 1998)
56 ALR5th 1—§ 3

Stormans, Inc. v. Selecky, 251 F.R.D. 573 (W.D. Wash. 2008)
41 ALR6th 555—§ 4

Stormans, Inc. v. Selecky, 524 F. Supp. 2d 1245 (W.D. Wash. 2007)
41 ALR6th 555—§ 3, 6

Stormans Inc. v. Selecky, 526 F.3d 406, 103 Fair Empl. Prac. Cas. (BNA) 509, 91 Empl. Prac. Dec. (CCH) ¶ 43177 (9th Cir. 2008)
41 ALR6th 555—§ 5

Stormer v. Alberts Const. Co., 401 Pa. 461, 165 A.2d 87 (1960)
15 ALR6th 1—§ 4, 8

Storm Impact, Inc. v. Software of Month Club, 13 F. Supp. 2d 782, 48 U.S.P.Q.2d (BNA) 1266 (N.D. Ill. 1998)
106 ALR5th 309—§ 3

Storms, Matter of, 170 Mich. App. 713, 428 N.W.2d 751 (1988)
113 ALR5th 349—§ 6

Storms, Re, 170 Mich. App. 713, 428 N.W.2d 751 (1988)
1 ALR5th 469—§ 13

Storms v. Bergsieker, 254 Mont. 130, 835 P.2d 738, 22 A.L.R.5th 942 (1992)
22 ALR5th 800—§ 3

Storms v. Storms, 183 Mich. App. 132, 454 N.W.2d 175 (1990)
38 ALR5th 433—§ 11

Storms v. United States Fidelity & Guaranty Co., 118 N.H. 427, 388 A.2d 578 (1978)
14 ALR5th 695—§ 25

Storms v. Vargas, 256 A.D.2d 458, 682 N.Y.S.2d 404 (2d Dep't 1998)
50 ALR5th 1—§ 10

Storm, State ex rel. v. Hought, 56 N.D. 663, 219 N.W. 213, 58 A.L.R. 186 (1928)
61 ALR5th 375—§ 11

Stornant v. Licari-Packard Grosse Pointe, Inc., 332 Mich. 210, 50 N.W.2d 762 (1952)
4 ALR5th 443—§ 13

Stornanti v. Commonwealth, 389 Mass. 518, 451 N.E.2d 707 (1983)
16 ALR5th 390—§ 2

Stornello v. Department of Corrections, 2013 WL 951174 (Mich. Ct. App. 2013)
85 ALR6th 229—§ 4

Storozuk v. W. A. Butler Co., 3 Ohio Misc. 60, 31 Ohio Ops. 2d 91, 203 N.E.2d 511 (1964)
12 ALR5th 1—§ 27

Storr v. Anderson School, 919 F. Supp. 144, 108 Ed. Law Rep. 267, 72 Fair Empl. Prac. Cas. (BNA) 107 (S.D. N.Y. 1996)
83 ALR5th 1—§ 3, 10

Storr v. Keljik, 178 Minn. 391, 227 N.W. 211 (1929)
45 ALR5th 251—§ 6

Storrer v. Kier Constr. Corp., 129 Idaho 745, 932 P.2d 373 (App. 1997)
60 ALR5th 669—§ 3, 7

Storrs v. Holcomb, 168 Misc. 2d 898, 645 N.Y.S.2d 286 (Sup 1996)
8 ALR6th 339—§ 3

Storrs v. Holcomb, 168 Misc. 2d 898, 645 N.Y.S.2d 286 (Sup. Ct. 1996)
81 ALR5th 1—§ 2, 3, 5, 6, 10

Storrs v. Lutheran Hospitals & Homes Soc., 609 P.2d 24 (Alaska 1980)
28 ALR5th 107—§ 13

Storrs v. State Medical Bd., 664 P.2d 547 (Alaska 1983)
10 ALR5th 1—§ 41
106 ALR5th 523—§ 24

Storrs v. Wills, 170 Ga. App. 179, 316 S.E.2d 758 (1984)
58 ALR6th 1—§ 5

Storthz v. Midland Hills Land Co., 192 Ark. 273, 90 S.W.2d 772 (1936)
76 ALR5th 337—§ 9

Story v. Doris, 110 Ga. 65, 35 S.E. 314 (1900)
36 ALR6th 387—§ 4

Story v. Hammond, 4 Ohio. 376 (1831)
25 ALR5th 568—§ 21

Story v. Lanier, 166 S.W.3d 167 (Tenn. Ct. App. 2004)
70 ALR6th 209—§ 25

Story v. Latto, 702 F. Supp. 708 (N.D. Ill. 1989)
48 ALR5th 1—§ 10

Story v. McCurtain Memorial Medical Management, Inc., 634 P.2d 778 (Okla. App. 1981)
2 ALR5th 286—§ 5
3 ALR5th 146—§ 16

Story v. Perkins, 243 F. 997 (S.D. Ga. 1917)
88 ALR6th 203—§ 76

Story v. Rives, 97 F.2d 182 (App. D.C. 1938)
62 ALR6th 517—§ 54

Story v. State, 53 So. 2d 920 (Fla. 1951)
93 ALR5th 493—§ 9

Story v. State, 326 Ark. 86, 929 S.W.2d 709 (1996)
42 ALR5th 547—§ 5, 6.5

Story & Clark Piano Co. v. Gibbons, 96 Mo. App. 218, 70 S.W. 168 (1902)
5 ALR5th 422—§ 3

Stoskoff v. Wicklund, 49 N.D. 708, 193 N.W. 312 (1922)
43 ALR5th 87—§ 4, 13

Stothfang v. Cincinnati Aluminum Casting Co., 13 Ohio App. 334, 1920 WL 535 (1st Dist. Hamilton County 1920)
103 ALR5th 157—§ 4, 11

Stotlar v. Hester, 92 N.M. 26, 582 P.2d 403 (Ct. App. 1978)
44 ALR6th 1—§ 5, 15, 18

Stotler v. Stotler, 19 Ohio NP NS 369 (1916)
3 ALR5th 394—§ 6, 7

Stott v. City of Manchester, 109 N.H. 59, 242 A.2d 58 (1968)
74 ALR5th 49—§ 73

Stott v. Dvorak, 1994 WL 131131 (Conn. Super. Ct. 1994)
111 ALR5th 313—§ 20

Stott v. State, 1975 OK CR 132, 538 P.2d 1061 (Okla. Crim. App. 1975)
80 ALR5th 469—§ 3, 5

Stotter v. University of Texas at San Antonio, 508 F.3d 812, 26 I.E.R. Cas. (BNA) 1409 (5th Cir. 2007)
32 ALR6th 457—§ 7

Stotter v. University of Texas at San Antonio, 508 F.3d 812, 227 Ed. Law Rep. 569, 26 I.E.R. Cas. (BNA) 1409 (5th Cir. 2007)
89 ALR6th 1—§ 40

Stotter v. Wingo, 794 S.W.2d 50 (Tex. App. San Antonio 1990)
17 ALR6th 159—§ 33

Stottlemire v. Cawood, 213 F. Supp. 897 (D.C. Dist. Col. 1963)
47 ALR5th 433—§ 9
57 ALR5th 1—§ 3

Stotts v. Meyer, 822 S.W.2d 887 (Mo. Ct. App. E.D. 1991)
77 ALR6th 251—§ 4

Stotz, Estate of v. Everson, 1994 WL 702867 (Conn. Super. Ct. 1994)
2 ALR6th 195—§ 9

Stoudemire v. State, 365 So. 2d 376 (Ala. App. 1978)
29 ALR5th 59—§ 3, 52

Stoudemire v. Stoudemire, 248 Mich. App. 325, 639 N.W.2d 274 (2001)
109 ALR5th 1—§ 9

Stouffer v. Commonwealth, DOT, 127 Pa. Cmwlth. 610, 562 A.2d 922 (1989)
46 ALR5th 557—§ 3

Stouffer v. Com., Pennsylvania State Police, 76 Pa. Commw. 397, 464 A.2d 595 (1983)
19 ALR6th 217—§ 3, 55

Stouffer v. Reynolds, 168 F.3d 1155 (10th Cir. 1999)
125 ALR5th 497—§ 3

Stouffer v. State, 2006 OK CR 46, 147 P.3d 245 (Okla. Crim. App. 2006)
30 ALR6th 1—§ 4

Stouffer, U.S. ex rel. v. Com. of Pennsylvania, 374 F. Supp. 702 (M.D. Pa. 1974)
55 ALR6th 157—§ 75, 78

Stough v. Dickmann, 238 Pa. Super. 619, 361 A.2d 639 (1976)
19 ALR5th 622—§ 56

Stough v. State, 62 Haw. 620, 618 P.2d 301 (1980)
71 ALR6th 1—§ 11

Stough v. Young, 185 So. 476 (La. Ct. App. 2d Cir. 1938)
91 ALR5th 1—§ 17

Stoughton v. Mutual of Enumclaw, 61 Wash. App. 365, 810 P.2d 80 (1991)
35 ALR5th 375—§ 3, 10, 30, 70, 76

Stoughton, Town of v. Grieve, 345 Mass. 771, 187 N.E.2d 857 (1963)
77 ALR6th 393—§ 98

Stoumen v. Public Serv. Mut. Ins. Co., 834 F. Supp. 140 (E.D. Pa. 1993)
52 ALR5th 451—§ 3

Stouse v. Excise Board of Coal County, 170 Okla. 9, 38 P.2d 539 (1934)
56 ALR5th 171—§ 4, 18

Stout, Ex parte, 82 Tex. Crim. 183, 198 S.W. 967 (1917)
72 ALR5th 1—§ 3, 4

Stout v. Animal Control Appeals Bd., 1990 WL 10515511 (Alaska 1990)
77 ALR6th 393—§ 83, 85

Stout v. Borg-Warner Corp., 933 F.2d 331, CCH Prod. Liab. Rep. ¶ 12835 (CA5 Tex. 1991)
53 ALR5th 535—§ 3, 5
Stout v. Christian, 593 S.W.2d 146 (Tex. Civ. App. Austin 1980)
111 ALR5th 313—§ 12
Stout v. Christie, Manson & Woods Intern., Inc., 255 A.D.2d 224, 681 N.Y.S.2d 19 (1st Dep't 1998)
27 ALR5th 76—§ 36
Stout v. City of Martin, 395 S.W.2d 591 (Ky. 1965)
101 ALR5th 287—§ 14
Stout v. Com., 44 S.W.3d 781 (Ky. Ct. App. 2000)
37 ALR5th 703—§ 6
Stout v. Cupp, 426 F.2d 881 (9th Cir. 1970)
101 ALR5th 187—§ 8
Stout v. Grand Prairie Independent School Dist., 733 S.W.2d 290 (Tex. App. Dallas 1987)
25 ALR5th 784—§ 2, 5
Stout v. International Business Machines Corp., 798 F. Supp. 998, 60 Fair Empl. Prac. Cas. (BNA) 31, 60 Empl. Prac. Dec. (CCH) ¶ 41940 (S.D. N.Y. 1992)
103 ALR5th 557—§ 5
Stout v. Mitschele, 135 NJL 406, 52 A.2d 422 (1947)
38 ALR5th 357—§ 7, 17
Stout v. Piedmont Wholesale Grocery, 729 S.W.2d 49 (Mo. Ct. App. S.D. 1987)
82 ALR5th 149—§ 2, 57, 64
Stout v. State, 26 Okla. Crim. 390, 224 P. 375 (1924)
13 ALR5th 1—§ 26
Stout v. State, 244 Ark. 676, 426 S.W.2d 800 (1968)
28 ALR6th 505—§ 9
Stout v. Stout, 207 W. Va. 580, 534 S.E.2d 776 (2000)
90 ALR5th 1—§ 20
Stout v. Stout, 610 S.W.2d 380 (Mo. Ct. App. E.D. 1980)

11 ALR6th 125—§ 18, 20
Stout v. West Virginia Office of Ins. Com'r, 2012 WL 5471430 (W. Va. 2012)
99 ALR6th 643—§ 26
Stoutamire, In re, 201 B.R. 592, Bankr. L. Rep. (CCH) ¶ 77141 (Bankr. S.D. Ga. 1996)
64 ALR6th 655—§ 6
Stoute, Re, 55 Wash. 2d 377, 347 P.2d 1068 (1960)
10 ALR5th 1—§ 2, 30
Stoute v. Long, 722 So. 2d 102 (La. Ct. App. 3d Cir. 1998)
49 ALR6th 169—§ 4
Stoute v. U.S., 2011 WL 2037672 (D. Md. 2011)
68 ALR6th 1—§ 15
Stout, State ex rel. v. Rigg, 252 Minn. 503, 90 N.W.2d 910 (1958)
97 ALR5th 293—§ 3, 9
Stovall v. Allums, 2005 WL 2002069 (M.D. Ala. 2005)
52 ALR6th 125—§ 45
Stovall v. Brown Memorial Hosp., 1994 WL 721608 (Ohio Ct. App. 11th Dist. Ashtabula County 1994)
64 ALR6th 249—§ 34
Stovall v. Burns & Roe, 145 F.2d 230, 15 L.R.R.M. (BNA) 628 (C.C.A. 4th Cir. 1944)
94 ALR5th 149—§ 8
Stovall v. Com., 213 Va. 67, 189 S.E.2d 353 (1972)
113 ALR5th 517—§ 14
Stovall v. DaimlerChrysler Motors Corp., 270 Ga. App. 791, 608 S.E.2d 245, Prod. Liab. Rep. (CCH) ¶ 17203 (2004)
76 ALR6th 465—§ 19
Stovall v. Harms, 214 Kan. 835, 522 P.2d 353 (1974)
9 ALR5th 746—§ 3, 12, 21
Stovall v. Sally Salmon Seafood, 84 Or. App. 612, 735 P.2d 18 (1987)
14 ALR5th 1—§ 13
Stovall v. Sally Salmon Seafood, 306 Or. 25, 757 P.2d 410 (1988)

For assistance, call 1-800-328-4880

12 ALR5th 658—§ 4
Stovall v. State, 2004 WL 950047 (Tex. App. Tyler 2004)

117 ALR5th 491—§ 3
Stovall & Co. v. Tate, 124 Ga. App. 605, 184 S.E.2d 834, 9 U.C.C.R.S. 1365 (1971)

50 ALR5th 327—§ 7
Stovall, State ex rel. v. Confimed.com, L.L.C., 272 Kan. 1313, 38 P.3d 707 (2002)

3 ALR6th 1—§ 6
Stovall, State ex rel. v. Cooper, 2001 WL 34117813 (Kan. Dist. Ct. 2001)

48 ALR6th 511—§ 23
Stovall, State ex rel. v. DVM Enterprises, Inc., 275 Kan. 243, 62 P.3d 653, 49 U.C.C. Rep. Serv. 2d 782 (2003)

3 ALR6th 1—§ 6
Stovall, State ex rel. v. Meneley, 271 Kan. 355, 22 P.3d 124 (2001)

37 ALR6th 511—§ 3, 4, 7, 8, 10, 22, 48
Stover, Ex parte, 663 So. 2d 948 (Ala. 1995)

93 ALR6th 463—§ 20, 32
Stover, In re, 65 Cal. App. 622, 224 P. 771 (1st Dist. 1924)

3 ALR6th 49—§ 19
8 ALR6th 1—§ 12
Stover, In re, 278 Kan. 835, 104 P.3d 394 (2005)

46 ALR6th 365—§ 17
Stover v. Aetna Casualty & Surety Co., 658 F. Supp. 156 (S.D. W. Va. 1987)

16 ALR5th 412—§ 7
Stover v. Atchley, 189 Ga. App. 56, 374 S.E.2d 775 (1988)

12 ALR5th 195—§ 10
Stover v. Auto & Home Center, Inc., 1987 WL 20440 (Ohio Ct. App. 6th Dist. Williams County 1987)

66 ALR6th 351—§ 53
Stover v. Ed Miller & Sons, Inc., 194 Neb. 422, 231 N.W.2d 700 (1975)

74 ALR5th 523—§ 3, 20

Stover v. Retirement Bd. of City of St. Clair Shores Firemen and Police Pension under Act 345, Public Acts 1937, 78 Mich. App. 409, 260 N.W.2d 112 (1977)

91 ALR5th 225—§ 5 to 8, 13, 16
Stover v. Robilotto, 716 N.Y.S.2d 146 (App. Div. 3d Dep't 2000)

19 ALR5th 405—§ 3
Stover v. Seitz, 527 S.W.2d 829 (Tex. Civ. App. Waco 1975)

36 ALR5th 395—§ 5
Stover v. State, 621 N.E.2d 664 (Ind. App. 1993)

39 ALR5th 283—§ 3
Stover v. Unemployment Compensation Bd. of Review, 196 Pa. Super. 92, 173 A.2d 678 (1961)

68 ALR5th 13—§ 20
Stovern v. Calmar, 204 Iowa 983, 216 N.W. 112 (1927)

25 ALR5th 568—§ 27
Stovern v. Town of Calmar, 207 Iowa 1126, 224 N.W. 26 (1929)

92 ALR5th 517—§ 6, 11, 13
Stover, People ex rel. v. Stover, 112 App. Div. 2d 519, 490 N.Y.S.2d 925 (3d Dep't 1985)

20 ALR5th 700—§ 54, 59, 63
Stowe v. Bologna, 417 Mass. 199, 629 N.E.2d 304 (1994)

10 ALR5th 448—§ 4
Stowe v. Hopper, 238 Ga. 139, 231 S.E.2d 736 (1977)

70 ALR5th 1—§ 6
Stowe v. Sheriff, 2003 WL 21715341 (D. Me. 2003)

89 ALR6th 1—§ 75
Stowe v. State, 109 Nev. 743, 857 P.2d 15 (1993)

29 ALR5th 59—§ 7, 57, 76, 88
Stowe v. State, 163 Ga. App. 535, 295 S.E.2d 209 (1982)

15 ALR5th 391—§ 45
Stowell v. City of Wichita, Kan., 1995 WL 363413 (D. Kan. 1991)

57 ALR5th 633—§ 3

Stowell v. Cuomo, 52 N.Y.2d 208, 437 N.Y.S.2d 270, 418 N.E.2d 1289 (1981)

7 ALR5th 474—§ 132

Stowers v. Humphrey, 576 So. 2d 138 (Miss. 1991)

21 ALR5th 396—§ 58

Stowers v. Wheat, 78 F.2d 25 (CA5 Fla. 1935)

46 ALR5th 1—§ 21

Stow Mun. Elec. Dept. v. Department of Public Utilities, 426 Mass. 341, 688 N.E.2d 1337 (1997)

80 ALR6th 1—§ 12, 24, 26, 27, 40, 43, 105

Stozenski v. Borough of Forty Fort, Luzerne County, 456 Pa. 5, 317 A.2d 602 (1974)

62 ALR5th 219—§ 25

St. Patrick's Home for Aged and Infirm v. Laticrete Intern., Inc., 696 N.Y.S.2d 117, 39 U.C.C. Rep. Serv. 2d (CBC) 774 (App. Div. 1st Dep't 1999)

49 ALR5th 1—§ 46

St. Patrick's Home for Aged and Infirm v. Laticrete Intern., Inc., 1999 WL 773648 (N.Y. App. Div. 1st Dep't 1999)

81 ALR5th 483—§ 2, 5

St. Paul v. Carlone, 419 N.W.2d 129 (Minn. App. 1988)

10 ALR5th 538—§ 3

St. Paul, City of v. Froysland, 310 Minn. 268, 246 N.W.2d 435 (1976)

69 ALR6th 1—§ 21

St. Paul, City of v. Lytle, 69 Minn. 1, 71 N.W. 703 (1897)

16 ALR6th 219—§ 13, 14, 40, 41

St. Paul, City of v. Various Items of Drug Paraphernalia, 474 N.W.2d 413 (Minn. Ct. App. 1991)

23 ALR6th 307—§ 4, 16

St. Paul Dredging Co. v. State, 259 Minn. 398, 107 N.W.2d 717 (1961)

25 ALR6th 265—§ 6

St. Paul Fire v. Hill, 157 Wis. 2d 505, 460 N.W.2d 447 (App. 1990)

35 ALR5th 375—§ 3, 22, 111

St. Paul Fire and Marine Cas. Ins. Co. v. Chong, 979 F.2d 858 (10th Cir. 1992)

92 ALR5th 273—§ 14

St. Paul Fire & Marine Ins. Co. v. Advanced Interventional Systems, Inc., 21 F.3d 424, 30 U.S.P.Q.2d (BNA) 1494 (4th Cir. 1994)

98 ALR5th 1—§ 11

St. Paul Fire and Marine Ins. Co. v. Albany County School Dist. No. 1, 763 P.2d 1255, 50 Ed. Law Rep. 190 (Wyo. 1988)

94 ALR5th 567—§ 7, 14

St. Paul Fire & Marine Ins. Co. v. Alderman, 216 Ga. App. 777, 455 S.E.2d 852 (1995)

60 ALR5th 239—§ 4

St. Paul Fire & Marine Ins. Co. v. American Home Assur. Co., 444 Mich. 560, 514 N.W.2d 113 (1994)

92 ALR5th 273—§ 16

St. Paul Fire and Marine Ins. Co. v. API, Inc., 2004 WL 2161181 (Minn. Ct. App. 2004)

22 ALR6th 387—§ 6, 44

St. Paul Fire & Marine Ins. Co. v. Asbury, 149 Ariz. 565, 720 P.2d 540 (Ct. App. Div. 2 1986)

60 ALR5th 239—§ 2, 4, 5, 13, 14, 27

St. Paul Fire & Marine Ins. Co. v. Baltimore & O. R. Co., 129 Ohio St. 401, 2 Ohio Ops. 396, 195 N.E. 861 (1935)

17 ALR5th 547—§ 46, 48

St. Paul Fire and Marine Ins. Co. v. Birch, Stewart, Kolasch & Birch, LLP, 233 F. Supp. 2d 171 (D. Mass. 2002)

50 ALR6th 53—§ 4
64 ALR6th 473—§ 15

St. Paul Fire and Marine Ins. Co. v. Birch, Stewart, Kolasch & Birch, LLP., 379 F. Supp. 2d 183 (D. Mass. 2005)

50 ALR6th 53—§ 3, 7, 8
64 ALR6th 473—§ 15

St. Paul Fire and Marine Ins. Co. v. Birch, Stewart, Kolasch & Birch, LLP, 408 F. Supp. 2d 59 (D. Mass. 2006)

64 ALR6th 473—§ 15

St. Paul Fire & Marine Ins. Co. v. Branch Bank & Trust Co., 834 F.2d 416 (CA4 N.C. 1987)

5 ALR5th 132—§ 4, 6, 9, 13, 14

St. Paul Fire & Marine Ins. Co. v. Briggs, 464 N.W.2d 535 (Minn. Ct. App. 1990)

22 ALR6th 113—§ 37
34 ALR6th 345—§ 3, 24

St. Paul Fire and Marine Ins. Co. v. Campbell County School Dist. No. 1, 612 F. Supp. 285, 26 Ed. Law Rep. 628 (D. Wyo. 1985)

94 ALR5th 567—§ 1

St. Paul Fire & Marine Ins. Co. v. Children's Hospital Nat. Medical Center, 670 F. Supp. 393 (D.C. Dist. Col. 1987)

14 ALR5th 695—§ 23

St. Paul Fire & Marine Ins. Co. v. Cohen-Walker, Inc., 171 Ga. App. 542, 320 S.E.2d 385 (1984)

55 ALR5th 681—§ 7

St. Paul Fire & Marine Ins. Co. v. Crosetti Bros., Inc., 256 Or. 576, 475 P.2d 69 (1970)

59 ALR5th 733—§ 3

St. Paul Fire & Marine Ins. Co. v. Davidson, 148 Ga. App. 82, 251 S.E.2d 32 (1978)

13 ALR5th 289—§ 2, 13, 21

St. Paul Fire & Marine Ins. Co. v. Dean, 308 F. Supp. 1378 (W.D. Ark. 1970)

110 ALR5th 465—§ 3

St. Paul Fire & Marine Ins. Co. v. D.H.L., 459 N.W.2d 704 (Minn. 1990)

60 ALR5th 239—§ 3

St. Paul Fire & Marine Ins. Co. v. Edge Memorial Hosp., 584 So. 2d 1316 (Ala. 1991)

18 ALR5th 474—§ 8

St. Paul Fire and Marine Ins. Co. v. Federal Deposit Ins. Corp., 765 F. Supp. 538 (D. Minn. 1991)

14 ALR6th 687—§ 14
22 ALR6th 113—§ 76

St. Paul Fire & Marine Ins. Co. v. Federal Deposit Ins. Corp., 968 F.2d 695 (CA8 Minn. 1992)

21 ALR5th 292—§ 2, 3, 6, 16, 19, 23, 26

St. Paul Fire & Marine Ins. Co. v. General Mut. Ins. Co., 282 Ala. 695, 213 So. 2d 856 (1968)

55 ALR5th 681—§ 6

St. Paul Fire & Marine Ins. Co. v. Getty Oil Co., 1989 OK 139, 782 P.2d 915 (Okla. 1989)

5 ALR6th 497—§ 4, 9 to 11

St. Paul Fire & Marine Ins. Co. v. Goza, 137 Ga. App. 581, 224 S.E.2d 429 (1976)

2 ALR5th 922—§ 5
123 ALR5th 259—§ 4

St. Paul Fire & Marine Ins. Co. v. Guardian Alarm Co. of Michigan, 115 Mich. App. 278, 320 N.W.2d 244 (1982)

36 ALR6th 305—§ 9, 14, 15

St. Paul Fire and Marine Ins. Co. v. Heath Fielding Ind. Broking, Ltd., 1993 WL 187778 (S.D. N.Y. 1993)

39 ALR6th 391—§ 5

St. Paul Fire & Marine Ins. Co. v. Icard, Merrill, Cullis and Timm, P. A., 196 So. 2d 219 (Fla. Dist. Ct. App. 2d Dist. 1967)

92 ALR5th 273—§ 21

St. Paul Fire & Marine Ins. Co. v. Love, 447 N.W.2d 5 (Minn. Ct. App. 1989)

60 ALR5th 239—§ 11

St. Paul Fire & Marine Ins. Co. v. Love, 459 N.W.2d 698 (Minn. 1990)

60 ALR5th 239—§ 3, 4

St. Paul Fire & Marine Ins. Co. v. Mayor's Jewelers of Ft. Lauderdale, Inc., 465 F.2d 317 (CA5 Fla. 1972)

22 ALR5th 579—§ 14

St. Paul Fire & Marine Ins. Co. v. Mc-Cormick & Baxter Creosoting Co., 126 Or. App. 689, 870 P.2d 260 (1994)

48 ALR5th 355—§ 2, 4, 7

St. Paul Fire and Marine Ins. Co. v. Mitchell, 164 Ga. App. 215, 296 S.E.2d 126, 33 A.L.R.4th 1 (1982)

60 ALR5th 239—§ 3, 27

St. Paul Fire & Marine Ins. Co. v. Molton, Allen & Williams Corp., 592 So. 2d 199 (Ala. 1991)

55 ALR5th 681—§ 3, 7, 9

St. Paul Fire & Marine Ins. Co. v. Mori, 486 N.W.2d 803 (Minn. Ct. App. 1992)

60 ALR5th 239—§ 3, 4

St. Paul Fire & Marine Ins. Co. v. Northern Grain Co., 365 F.2d 361 (CA8 S.D. 1966)

18 ALR5th 187—§ 5

St. Paul Fire and Marine Ins. Co. v. Parzen, 569 F. Supp. 753 (E.D. Mich. 1983)

92 ALR5th 273—§ 10, 25

St. Paul Fire & Marine Ins. Co. v. Pearson Const. Co., 547 N.E.2d 853 (Ind. Ct. App. 4th Dist. 1989)

74 ALR5th 523—§ 3, 6, 10, 32

St. Paul Fire & Marine Ins. Co. v. Pennsylvania Mfrs. Ass'n Ins. Co., 1985 WL 4459 (E.D. Pa. 1985)

16 ALR6th 491—§ 4

St. Paul Fire & Marine Ins. Co. v. Powell-Walton-Milward, Inc., 870 S.W.2d 223 (Ky. 1994)

55 ALR5th 681—§ 2, 7

St. Paul Fire & Marine Ins. Co. v. Quintana, 165 Mich. App. 719, 419 N.W.2d 60 (1988)

60 ALR5th 239—§ 4

St. Paul Fire & Marine Ins. Co. v. Roberts, 331 So. 2d 529 (La. App. 1st Cir. 1976)

27 ALR5th 174—§ 3, 4, 32

St. Paul Fire & Marine Ins. Co. v. Sample, 533 So. 2d 1196, 13 FLW 2553 (Fla. App. D2 1988)

23 ALR5th 241—§ 11

St. Paul Fire & Marine Ins. Co. v. Schilling, 520 N.W.2d 884, 43 A.L.R.5th 827 (S.D. 1994)

43 ALR5th 149—§ 13, 15

St. Paul Fire and Marine Ins. Co. v. Shernow, 222 Conn. 823, 610 A.2d 1281 (1992)

60 ALR5th 239—§ 4, 13, 27

St. Paul Fire and Marine Ins. Co. v. Shure, 647 So. 2d 877 (Fla. Dist. Ct. App. 4th Dist. 1994)

17 ALR6th 1—§ 26

St. Paul Fire & Marine Ins. Co. v. S.L. Nusbaum & Co., 227 Va. 407, 316 S.E.2d 734 (1984)

35 ALR5th 83—§ 11

St. Paul Fire & Marine Ins. Co. v. Southern Pacific Co., 30 Cal. App. 140, 157 P. 247 (1916)

25 ALR5th 391—§ 20

St. Paul Fire & Marine Ins. Co. v. Sparrow, 378 N.W.2d 12 (Minn. App. 1985)

43 ALR5th 149—§ 5

St. Paul Fire and Marine Ins. Co. v. Starr, 651 S.W.2d 517 (Mo. Ct. App. W.D. 1983)

92 ALR5th 273—§ 21

St. Paul Fire and Marine Ins. Co. v. State Bank of Salem, 412 N.E.2d 103, 30 U.C.C. Rep. Serv. (CBC) 557 (Ind. Ct. App. 1st Dist. 1980)

77 ALR5th 429—§ 4

St. Paul Fire and Marine Ins. Co. v. Torpoco, 879 S.W.2d 831 (Tenn. 1994)

60 ALR5th 239—§ 4, 13, 27

St. Paul Fire & Marine Ins. Co. v. Updegrave, 33 Wash. App. 653, 656 P.2d 1130, 35 A.L.R.4th 1 (Div. 3 1983)

63 ALR5th 1—§ 10
117 ALR5th 155—§ 8

St. Paul Fire & Marine Ins. Co. v. Valentine, 665 So. 2d 43 (La. App. 1st Cir. 1995)

14 ALR5th 695—§ 4

St. Paul Fire and Marine Ins. Co. v. Warwick Dyeing Corp., 26 F.3d 1195, 38 Env't. Rep. Cas. (BNA) 1976 (1st Cir. 1994)

89 ALR5th 1—§ 6
97 ALR5th 359—§ 4

St. Paul Fire & Marine Ins. Co. v. Wedgewood Realty, Inc., 639 S.W.2d 233 (Mo. App. 1982)

35 ALR5th 83—§ 6

St. Paul Fire & Marine Ins. Co. v. Welsh, 501 So. 2d 54, 12 FLW 221 (Fla. App. D4 1987)

51 ALR5th 603—§ 8

St. Paul Fire & Marine Ins. Co. v. Woolley/Sweeney Hotel No. 5, 545 So. 2d 958 (Fla. Dist. Ct. App. 4th Dist. 1989)

100 ALR5th 481—§ 3

St. Paul Fire & Marine Ins. Co., Inc. v. McCormick & Baxter Creosoting Co., 324 Or. 184, 923 P.2d 1200, 43 Env't. Rep. Cas. (BNA) 1903 (1996)

89 ALR5th 1—§ 10

St. Paul Fire & Marine Insurance Co. v. Gilmore, 168 Ariz. 159, 812 P.2d 977, 87 Ariz. Adv. Rep. 3 (1991)

2 ALR5th 922—§ 4

St. Paul Ins. Co. v. Armas, 173 Ill. App. 3d 669, 123 Ill. Dec. 283, 527 N.E.2d 921 (1st Dist. 1988)

14 ALR5th 695—§ 23

St. Paul Ins. Co. v. Bonded Realty, Inc., 578 S.W.2d 191 (Tex. Civ. App. El Paso 1979)

35 ALR5th 83—§ 4

St. Paul Ins. Co. v. Rutgers Casualty Ins. Co., 232 N.J. Super. 582, 557 A.2d 1052 (1989)

25 ALR5th 60—§ 3, 7

St. Paul Ins. Companies v. Lusis, 6 Wash. App. 205, 492 P.2d 575, 56 A.L.R.3d 687 (Div. 2 1971)

63 ALR5th 675—§ 3

St. Paul Ins. Co. of Bellaire, Texas v. AFIA Worldwide Ins. Co., 937 F.2d 274 (5th Cir. 1991)

50 ALR6th 53—§ 4

St. Paul Ins. Co. of Illinois v. Cromeans, 771 F. Supp. 349 (N.D. Ala. 1991)

60 ALR5th 239—§ 2, 4, 8, 12

St. Paul Medical Center v. Cecil, 842 S.W.2d 808 (Tex. App. Dallas 1992)

6 ALR5th 490—§ 12

St. Paul Mercury Ins. Co. v. Circuit Court of Craighead County, Western Div., 348 Ark. 197, 73 S.W.3d 584 (2002)

100 ALR6th 139—§ 5

St. Paul Mercury Ins. Co. v. Foster, 268 F. Supp. 2d 1035, 31 Employee Benefits Cas. (BNA) 1399 (C.D. Ill. 2003)

22 ALR6th 113—§ 40
34 ALR6th 345—§ 18

St. Paul Mercury Ins. Co. v. JBA Intern., Inc., 2003 WL 22272120 (D. Minn. 2003)

9 ALR6th 467—§ 24

St. Paul Mercury Ins. Co. v. Jeep Corp., 175 Mont. 69, 572 P.2d 204 (1977)

47 ALR5th 677—§ 4

St. Paul Mercury Ins. Co. v. Northern States Power Co., 2005 WL 3529139 (Minn. Ct. App. 2005)

20 ALR6th 211—§ 6

St. Paul Mercury Ins. Co. v. Sugarland Industries, Inc., 406 S.W.2d 778 (Tex. Civ. App. 1966)

18 ALR5th 187—§ 3

St. Paul Surplus Lines Ins. Co. v. 1401 Dixon's, Inc., 582 F. Supp. 865 (E.D. Pa. 1984)

44 ALR5th 91—§ 7, 8, 12

St. Paul Surplus Lines Ins. Co. v. Dal-Worth Tank Co., 917 S.W.2d 29 (Tex. App. Amarillo 1995)

22 ALR5th 483—§ 3, 23

St. Paul Surplus Lines Ins. Co. v. Mentor Corp., 503 N.W.2d 511 (Minn. Ct. App. 1993)

20 ALR6th 211—§ 9, 11

St. Paul Surplus Lines Ins. Co. v. Remley, 2009 WL 2070779 (E.D. Mo. 2009)

50 ALR6th 53—§ 4, 5, 12

St. Peter v. Ampak-Division of Gatewood Products, Inc., 199 W. Va. 365, 484 S.E.2d 481, 7 A.D. Cas. (BNA) 1709 (1997)

83 ALR5th 1—§ 10

St. Petersburg, City of v. Remia, 41 So. 3d 322 (Fla. 2d DCA 2010)

76 ALR6th 543—§ 7

St. Petersburg Yacht Charters, Inc. v. Morgan Yacht, Inc., 457 So. 2d 1028 (Fla. Dist. Ct. App. 2d Dist. 1984)

2 ALR6th 387—§ 4

St. Peter's Catholic Church v. Vannote, 66 N.J. Eq. 78, 56 A. 1037 (1904)

4 ALR5th 772—§ 59

St. Peters, City of v. Hill, 9 S.W.3d 652, 109 A.L.R.5th 799 (Mo. Ct. App. E.D. 1999)

109 ALR5th 421—§ 3, 5, 6, 11

St. Phillips v. O'Donnell, 137 Ill. App. 3d 639, 92 Ill. Dec. 354, 484 N.E.2d 1209 (2d Dist. 1985)

31 ALR5th 550—§ 5

St. Pierre v. Gabel, 351 So. 2d 821 (La. Ct. App. 1st Cir. 1977)

4 ALR6th 401—§ 5, 7

St. Pierre v. Maingot, 2002 WL 31473850 (E.D. La. 2002)

76 ALR6th 465—§ 16

Stracener v. Brown, 345 So. 2d 1282 (La. App. 3d Cir. 1977)

2 ALR5th 811—§ 10, 12, 32

Stracener v. Millers Cas. Ins. Co. of Texas, 682 So. 2d 940 (La. Ct. App. 3d Cir. 1996)

77 ALR5th 319—§ 6

Stracener v. Nynnally Bros. Motor Co., 11 La. App. 541, 121 So. 617 (1929)

47 ALR5th 677—§ 7, 8, 17

Stracener v. United Services Auto. Asso., 777 S.W.2d 378 (Tex. 1989)

40 ALR5th 603—§ 9

Strach v. St. John Hosp. Corp., 160 Mich. App. 251, 408 N.W.2d 441 (1987)

64 ALR6th 249—§ 33

Strachan v. John F. Kennedy Memorial Hosp., 109 N.J. 523, 538 A.2d 346 (1988)

86 ALR5th 693—§ 3, 4, 7
100 ALR6th 477—§ 13, 18

Strachan v. John F. Kennedy Memorial Hosp., 209 N.J. Super. 300, 507 A.2d 718, 58 A.L.R.4th 181 (App. Div. 1986)

96 ALR5th 107—§ 7

Strachan v. Soloff, 157 App. Div. 2d 122, 554 N.Y.S.2d 565 (1st Dep't 1990)

13 ALR5th 118—§ 9, 18

Strachen v. State, 380 So. 2d 487 (Fla. 3d DCA 1980)

78 ALR6th 417—§ 4

Strack v. Great Atlantic & Pac. Tea Co., 35 Wis. 2d 51, 150 N.W.2d 361 (1967)

1 ALR6th 297—§ 8, 10

Strack v. Strack, 12 Wis. 2d 537, 107 N.W.2d 632 (1961)

27 ALR5th 174—§ 26

Straczynski, In re Conservatorship of, 2009 WL 613876 (Cal. App. 4th Dist. 2009)

72 ALR6th 563—§ 15

Strader v. Beneficial Finance Co. of Aurora, 191 Colo. 206, 551 P.2d 720 (1976)

73 ALR6th 425—§ 2, 35, 64, 70

Strader v. Garrison, 611 F.2d 61 (4th Cir. 1979)

31 ALR6th 49—§ 11

Strader v. Union Hall, Inc., 486 F. Supp. 159 (N.D. Ill. 1980)

6 ALR5th 297—§ 3, 9, 33, 39, 40

Stradford v. State, 787 S.W.2d 832 (Mo. Ct. App. E.D. 1990)

105 ALR5th 529—§ 31

Stradinger v. City of Whitewater, 89 Wis. 2d 19, 277 N.W.2d 827 (1979)

86 ALR6th 321—§ 4

Stradling v. Sun American Mortg., 2011 WL 1226102 (D. Utah 2011)
86 ALR6th 411—§ 5

Stradt v. State, 608 N.W.2d 28 (Iowa 2000)
7 ALR5th 263—§ 3

Stradtner v. Cincinnati Reds, Inc., 39 Ohio App. 2d 199, 68 Ohio Op. 2d 384, 316 N.E.2d 924 (1st Dist. Hamilton County 1972)
82 ALR6th 417—§ 11

Strafford Technology, Inc. v. Camcar Div. of Textron, Inc., 147 N.H. 174, 784 A.2d 1198 (2001)
32 ALR6th 419—§ 7

Strahan v. Davis, 872 S.W.2d 828 (Tex. App. Waco 1994)
26 ALR5th 401—§ 3, 7, 32

Strahan v. Gauldin, 756 So. 2d 158 (Fla. Dist. Ct. App. 5th Dist. 2000)
119 ALR5th 121—§ 3, 11
125 ALR5th 193—§ 9

Strahan v. State, 87 Tex. Crim. 324, 221 S.W. 976 (1920)
85 ALR5th 471—§ 2

Strahan v. State, 729 So. 2d 800 (Miss. 1998)
16 ALR6th 329—§ 4
24 ALR6th 591—§ 4, 14

Strahin v. Lantz, 193 W. Va. 285, 456 S.E.2d 12 (1995)
62 ALR5th 219—§ 26, 42

Strahler v. St. Luke's Hosp., 706 S.W.2d 7, 62 A.L.R.4th 735 (Mo. 1986)
71 ALR5th 307—§ 5, 10, 16, 21
1 ALR6th 407—§ 8, 15
76 ALR6th 31—§ 41

Strahlmann v. Anderson, 58 Misc. 2d 963, 297 N.Y.S.2d 47 (J. Ct. 1968)
12 ALR6th 123—§ 5

Strahorn v. Sears, Roebuck & Co., 50 Del. 50, 123 A.2d 107 (Super. Ct. 1956)
63 ALR6th 495—§ 5, 7, 11

Strahorn v. State, 436 So. 2d 447 (Fla. Dist. Ct. App. 2d Dist. 1983)
56 ALR6th 185—§ 39

Strahsburg v. Winn-Dixie Montgomery, Inc., 601 So. 2d 916 (Ala. 1992)
123 ALR5th 1—§ 9

Strain v. Mitchell Mfg. Co., 534 So. 2d 1385, 50 Ed. Law Rep. 1301, Prod. Liab. Rep. (CCH) ¶ 12075 (La. Ct. App. 4th Cir. 1988)
3 ALR6th 355—§ 3, 23

Strain v. Sarafan, 57 App. Div. 2d 525, 393 N.Y.S.2d 572 (1st Dep't 1977)
59 ALR5th 203—§ 48

Strain v. Tennessee Bureau of Investigation, 2009 WL 137210 (Tenn. Ct. App. 2009)
77 ALR6th 197—§ 5

Strain, State ex rel. v. Foster, 272 Or. 464, 537 P.2d 547 (1975)
54 ALR5th 575—§ 25
91 ALR5th 437—§ 4

Strait, Application of, 120 N.J. 477, 577 A.2d 149 (1990)
3 ALR6th 49—§ 3, 13, 16

Strait Shooters, Inc. v. St. Tammany Parish, 2001 WL 1491182 (E.D. La. 2001)
122 ALR5th 593—§ 2

Straka v. Voyles, 69 Utah 123, 252 P. 677 (1927)
12 ALR5th 195—§ 60

Straker v. Metropolitan Transit Authority, 333 F. Supp. 2d 91 (E.D. N.Y. 2004)
95 ALR6th 341—§ 17

Strakos v. Gehring, 360 S.W.2d 787 (Tex. 1962)
75 ALR5th 413—§ 2, 3, 7, 9, 29

Straley v. Calongne Drayage & Storage, Inc., 346 So. 2d 171 (La. 1977)
117 ALR5th 267—§ 21

Stramaglia v. Jenkins, 9 Ill. App. 3d 703, 292 N.E.2d 912 (2d Dist. 1973)
75 ALR6th 311—§ 56

Stranahan v. Fred Meyer, Inc., 153 Or. App. 442, 958 P.2d 854 (1998)
52 ALR5th 195—§ 3

Stranak v. Tomasovic, 309 Ill. App. 177, 32 N.E.2d 994 (4th Dist. 1941)
91 ALR5th 485—§ 6

Strand v. Grinnell Auto. Garage Co., 136 Iowa 68, 113 N.W. 488 (1907)
49 ALR5th 685—§ 3, 10

Strand v. State Dep't of Motor Vehicles, 8 Wash. App. 877, 509 P.2d 999 (Div. 1 1973)
76 ALR5th 597—§ 8

Strand v. Strand, 57 App. Div. 2d 1033, 395 N.Y.S.2d 254 (3d Dep't 1977)
55 ALR5th 647—§ 6

Strand v. U.S. Bank Nat. Ass'n ND, 2005 ND 68, 693 N.W.2d 918 (N.D. 2005)
13 ALR6th 145—§ 3

Strandberg v. Kansas City, 415 S.W.2d 737 (Mo. 1967)
73 ALR5th 223—§ 8
4 ALR6th 263—§ 14

Strandell v. Jackson County, 115 F.R.D. 333, 7 FR Serv. 3d 1191 (S.D. Ill. 1987)
43 ALR5th 545—§ 11

Strandell v. Jackson County, 838 F.2d 884, 9 FR Serv. 3d 752 (CA7 Ill. 1987)
43 ALR5th 545—§ 11

Strandholm v. General Const. Co., 235 Or. 145, 382 P.2d 843 (1963)
75 ALR5th 413—§ 3, 5, 12, 15, 24

Strand Property Corp. v. Municipal Court, 148 Cal. App. 3d 882, 200 Cal. Rptr. 47 (4th Dist. 1983)
10 ALR5th 538—§ 3, 5, 14

Strang v. Lomenzo, 51 App. Div. 2d 729, 379 N.Y.S.2d 132 (2d Dep't 1976)
7 ALR5th 474—§ 189

Strang v. Oregon W. R. & N. Co., 83 Or. 644, 163 P. 1181 (1917)
17 ALR5th 547—§ 62

Strang v. Visa U.S.A., Inc., 2005 WL 1403769 (Wis. Cir. Ct. 2005)
35 ALR6th 245—§ 6, 16

Strange v. Albert Kahn Associates, Inc., 2005 WL 3488280 (Ky. Ct. App. 2005)
47 ALR6th 303—§ 6

Strange v. City of Tuscaloosa, 652 So. 2d 773 (Ala. Crim. App. 1994)
58 ALR6th 499—§ 75

Strange v. Henderson, 223 Ga. App. 218, 477 S.E.2d 330 (1996)
40 ALR6th 231—§ 7

Strange v. State, 530 So. 2d 1336 (Miss. 1988)
41 ALR5th 171—§ 13, 59, 86, 107, 119
122 ALR5th 439—§ 7

Strangi v. Wilson, 223 Miss. 122, 77 So. 2d 697 (1955)
4 ALR5th 772—§ 2

Strangio v. New York Power Authority, 713 N.Y.S.2d 613 (App. Div. 4th Dep't 2000)
26 ALR5th 401—§ 20

Straniere v. Silver, 89 N.Y.2d 825, 653 N.Y.S.2d 270, 675 N.E.2d 1222 (1996)
24 ALR6th 255—§ 5, 11, 13

Strank v. Mercy Hospital of Johnston, 383 Pa. 54, 117 A.2d 697 (1955)
47 ALR5th 1—§ 32

Stransky v. American Isuzu Motors, 829 F. Supp. 788 (E.D. Pa. 1993)
49 ALR5th 1—§ 40, 43, 44

Strasbaugh v. Steward Sanitary Can Co., 127 Md. 632, 96 A. 863 (1916)
23 ALR5th 744—§ 5

Strasberg v. Equitable Life Assur. Soc. of U.S., 277 A.D. 430, 100 N.Y.S.2d 593 (1st Dep't 1950)
100 ALR5th 617—§ 10

Strasburg, In Re Disciplinary Proceedings Against, 154 Wis. 2d 90, 452 N.W.2d 152 (1990)
58 ALR5th 429—§ 6

Strasburg, Matter of Disciplinary Proceedings Against, 154 Wis. 2d 90, 452 N.W.2d 152 (1990)
26 ALR6th 1—§ 7

Strasburg, Matter of Disciplinary Proceedings Against, 217 Wis. 2d 318, 577 N.W.2d 1 (1998)
40 ALR6th 463—§ 27, 30

Strasburger v. Board of Educ., Hardin County Community Unit School Dist. No. 1, 143 F.3d 351, 126 Ed. Law Rep. 577, 13 I.E.R. Cas. (BNA) 1687 (7th Cir. 1998)
89 ALR6th 1—§ 123

Strass v. Civil Service Bd. of City of Sioux Falls, 72 S.D. 341, 34 N.W.2d 218 (1948)
19 ALR6th 217—§ 15

Strasser v. Character and Fitness Committee of Kentucky Office of Bar Admissions, 160 S.W.3d 789, 2005 WL 928727 (Ky. 2005)
8 ALR6th 1—§ 37

Strasser v. Yalamanchi, 783 So. 2d 1087 (Fla. Dist. Ct. App. 4th Dist. 2001)
3 ALR6th 13—§ 8

Strassmann, In re, 18 B.R. 346 (Bankr. E.D. Pa. 1982)
90 ALR6th 385—§ 5

Strassner, In re Marriage of, 895 S.W.2d 614 (Mo. Ct. App. E.D. 1995)
59 ALR6th 433—§ 79, 92

Stratagem Dev. Corp. v. Heron Int'l N.V., 153 F.R.D. 535 (S.D. N.Y. 1994)
51 ALR5th 603—§ 2, 4

Stratakis v. Beauchamp, 268 Md. 643, 304 A.2d 244 (1973)
1 ALR5th 622—§ 12, 19

Strata Marketing, Inc. v. Murphy, 317 Ill. App. 3d 1054, 251 Ill. Dec. 595, 740 N.E.2d 1166, 17 I.E.R. Cas. (BNA) 494 (1st Dist. 2000)
36 ALR6th 537—§ 4, 21

Strata Production Co. v. Mercury Exploration Co., 121 N.M. 622, 916 P.2d 822, 133 O.G.R. 85 (1996)
65 ALR5th 211—§ 2, 3, 7, 41, 48, 51

Stratcap Investments, Inc., In re Petition of, 154 Ohio App. 3d 89, 2003-Ohio-4589, 796 N.E.2d 73 (2d Dist. Clark County 2003)
27 ALR6th 323—§ 8

Strategic Defense Intern., Inc. v. U.S., 745 F. Supp. 2d 1214 (M.D. Fla. 2010)

72 ALR6th 1—§ 18

Stratemeyer v. Lincoln County, 259 Mont. 147, 855 P.2d 506 (1993)
83 ALR5th 103—§ 7, 38
84 ALR5th 249—§ 44

Stratemeyer v. Lincoln County, 276 Mont. 67, 915 P.2d 175 (1996)
83 ALR5th 103—§ 7
84 ALR5th 249—§ 44

Straten, In re, 2010 WL 2868185 (N.J. Super. Ct. App. Div. 2010)
91 ALR6th 435—§ 89

Stratford v. Boland, 306 Pa. Super. 475, 452 A.2d 824 (1982)
31 ALR5th 664—§ 3

Stratford v. Stratford, 631 P.2d 296 (Mont 1981)
9 ALR5th 568—§ 6

Stratford Corp. v. Pacific Mut. Life Ins. Co., 159 Colo. 430, 412 P.2d 233 (1966)
13 ALR5th 684—§ 3, 12, 22

Stratford Homes, Inc. v. Lorusso, 1995 WL 780977 (W.D. N.Y. 1995)
98 ALR5th 1—§ 17

Stratford School Dist. v. Employers Reinsurance Corp., 105 F.3d 45 (1st Cir. 1997)
94 ALR5th 567—§ 13, 15

Stratis v. Eastern Air Lines, Inc., 682 F.2d 406 (CA2 N.Y. 1982)
48 ALR5th 129—§ 4
51 ALR5th 467—§ 3, 9
52 ALR5th 1—§ 8

Stratman v. Brent, 291 Ill. App. 3d 123, 225 Ill. Dec. 448, 683 N.E.2d 951 (2d Dist. 1997)
100 ALR5th 341—§ 7

Stratman v. Hagen, 221 Neb. 157, 376 N.W.2d 3 (1985)
58 ALR5th 669—§ 8

Stratso v. Song, 17 Ohio App. 3d 39, 477 N.E.2d 1176 (10th Dist. Franklin County 1984)
64 ALR6th 249—§ 19

Stratton v. Equitable Bank, N.A., 104 B.R. 713, 11 U.C.C. Rep. Serv. 2d 149 (D. Md. 1989)

91 ALR5th 89—§ 4

Stratton v. Garvey Intern., Inc., 9 Kan. App. 2d 254, 676 P.2d 1290 (1984)

13 ALR6th 355—§ 4, 16

18 ALR6th 629—§ 10, 21

Stratton v. J. J. Newberry Co., 117 Conn. 522, 169 A. 56 (1933)

63 ALR6th 495—§ 16, 43

Stratton v. State, 257 Ga. 593, 362 S.E.2d 47 (1987)

24 ALR5th 465—§ 6, 34, 36, 40

Stratton v. Stratton, 77 Me. 373 (1885)

38 ALR5th 69—§ 3

Stratton v. Stratton's Adm'r, 149 Ky. 473, 149 S.W. 900 (1912)

88 ALR6th 533—§ 11

Stratton v. Wilson, 170 Ky. 61, 185 S.W. 522 (1916)

3 ALR5th 394—§ 26

Stratton Oakmont, Inc. v. Prodigy Services Co., 23 Media L. Rep. (BNA) 1794, 1995 WL 323710 (N.Y. Sup. Ct. 1995)

84 ALR5th 169—§ 2, 4, 5

Straub, In re, 158 F. 375 (N.D. W. Va. 1908)

36 ALR6th 387—§ 8

Straub v. Fisher and Paykel Health Care, 1999 UT 102, 990 P.2d 384, Prod. Liab. Rep. (CCH) ¶ 15694, 90 A.L.R. 5th 721 (Utah 1999)

89 ALR5th 255—§ 5

90 ALR5th 179—§ 4, 11, 13

Straub v. Straub, 209 Mich. App. 77, 530 N.W.2d 125 (1995)

6 ALR6th 229—§ 8, 22

Straub v. Wilson, 7 Ohio Dec. Rep. 358, 2 W.L.B. 158, 1877 WL 5905 (Ohio C.P. 1877)

60 ALR6th 481—§ 4, 30

Straube v. Emanuel Lutheran Charity Bd., 287 Or. 375, 600 P.2d 381 (1979)

28 ALR5th 107—§ 5, 18

Strauch v. Keane, 801 F. Supp. 1271 (S.D. N.Y. 1992)

28 ALR6th 505—§ 9

Strauch v. Strauch, 401 N.W.2d 444 (Minn. App. 1987)

17 ALR5th 143—§ 2, 3

Strauchs v. Hartnett, 1999 WL 262428 (Va. Cir. Ct. 1999)

97 ALR6th 375—§ 6, 16

Strauder v. State of West Virginia, 100 U.S. 303, 25 L. Ed. 664, 1879 WL 16562 (1879)

15 ALR6th 319—§ 2

Strauder v. West Virginia, 100 U.S. 303, 10 Otto. 303, 25 L. Ed. 664 (1880)

47 ALR5th 259—§ 2

Straughan v. Ahmed, 618 So. 2d 1225 (La. Ct. App. 5th Cir. 1993)

92 ALR6th 379—§ 38, 115

Straughan v. Tsouvalos, 246 Md. 242, 228 A.2d 300 (1967)

20 ALR5th 1—§ 7, 41

Straughn v. Camp, 293 So. 2d 689 (Fla. 1974)

114 ALR5th 561—§ 21

Straughn v. State, 2003 WL 21246480 (Ala. Crim. App. 2003)

116 ALR5th 373—§ 2, 3, 14

Straughter v. Cesco, Inc., 262 So. 2d 126 (La. Ct. App. 1st Cir. 1972)

84 ALR5th 249—§ 2, 26

Straughter v. State of California, 108 Cal. App. 3d 412, 169 Cal. Rptr. 471 (3d Dist. 1980)

73 ALR6th 571—§ 66

Straus v. Allstate Ins. Co., 62 Ill. App. 3d 289, 19 Ill. Dec. 433, 378 N.E.2d 1308 (1st Dist. 1978)

63 ALR5th 427—§ 2, 22

Straus v. Anderson, 366 Ill. 426, 9 N.E.2d 205 (1937)

4 ALR5th 693—§ 9, 16

Straus v. Barnett, 140 Pa. 111, 21 A. 253 (1891)

103 ALR5th 157—§ 11, 15

Straus v. Cunningham, 159 A.D. 718, 144 N.Y.S. 1014 (1st Dep't 1913)

98 ALR5th 353—§ 3, 7

Straus v. McDonald, 67 Va. Cir. 116, 2005 WL 832168 (2005)

96 ALR6th 503—§ 41

For assistance, call 1-800-328-4880

Straus-Bodenheimer Co. v. Marshall, 91 S.W.2d 865 (Tex. Civ. App. 1936)

58 ALR5th 535—§ 7, 18

Straus-Frank Co. v. Hughes, 138 Tex. 50, 156 S.W.2d 519 (1941)

58 ALR5th 325—§ 2, 3, 8

Strauss, Claim of, 229 A.D.2d 652, 645 N.Y.S.2d 141 (3d Dep't 1996)

95 ALR5th 329—§ 24

Strauss, Ex parte, 320 Mo. 349, 7 S.W.2d 1000 (1928)

54 ALR5th 743—§ 3

88 ALR5th 463—§ 13, 14

Strauss v. A. L. Randall Co., 144 Cal. App. 3d 514, 194 Cal. Rptr. 520, 37 BNA FEP Cas. 1531, 33 CCH EPD ¶ 34275 (2d Dist. 1983)

51 ALR5th 1—§ 7

Strauss v. A. L. Randall Co., 144 Cal. App. 3d 514, 194 Cal. Rptr. 520, 37 Fair Empl. Prac. Cas. (BNA) 1531, 33 Empl. Prac. Dec. (CCH) ¶ 34275 (2d Dist. 1983)

105 ALR5th 351—§ 3

Strauss v. Biggs, 525 A.2d 992 (Del. Sup. 1987)

12 ALR5th 195—§ 30

35 ALR5th 145—§ 2, 6 to 8

Strauss v. Buckley, 20 Cal. App. 2d 7, 65 P.2d 1352 (1937)

33 ALR5th 303—§ 5

Strauss v. Cilek, 418 N.W.2d 378 (Iowa Ct. App. 1987)

99 ALR5th 445—§ 7

Strauss v. Ginzberg, 218 Minn. 57, 15 N.W.2d 130, 155 A.L.R. 1000 (1944)

76 ALR5th 337—§ 20

119 ALR5th 519—§ 15

Strauss v. Industrial Commission, 73 Ariz. 285, 240 P.2d 550 (1952)

28 ALR6th 1—§ 3, 4, 13, 29, 46, 69

Strauss v. New Amsterdam Cas. Co., 30 Misc. 2d 345, 216 N.Y.S.2d 861 (Mun. Ct. 1961)

92 ALR5th 273—§ 6, 28

Strauss v. Railroad Co., 7 W. Va. 368 (1874)

16 ALR5th 548—§ 4, 5

Strauss v. Schlimm, 144 N.Y.S.2d 229 (Sup. 1955)

63 ALR5th 517—§ 39, 53

Strauss v. Square D Co., 201 Neb. 571, 270 N.W.2d 917 (1978)

68 ALR5th 13—§ 4, 7, 31

Strauss v. State, 131 N.J. Super. 571, 330 A.2d 646 (Law Div. 1974)

75 ALR5th 619—§ 3

Strauss v. Stratojac Corp., 810 F.2d 679, 6 FR Serv. 3d 1336 (CA7 Ind. 1987)

14 ALR5th 242—§ 49

Strauss v. Strauss, 148 Fla. 23, 3 So. 2d 727 (1941)

18 ALR5th 230—§ 7

Strauss v. Superior Court of Los Angeles County, 36 Cal. 2d 396, 224 P.2d 726 (1950)

12 ALR5th 577—§ 2, 9

Strauss v. Turck, 197 Wis. 586, 222 N.W. 811 (1929)

75 ALR5th 1—§ 7, 13, 16

Strauss, Estate of v. Schaeffer, 781 S.W.2d 274 (Mo. App. 1989)

17 ALR5th 366—§ 9

Straver v. Straver, 26 N.J. Misc. 218, 59 A.2d 39 (Ch. 1948)

55 ALR5th 557—§ 9 to 11

Straw v. Chase Revel, Inc., 813 F.2d 356, 13 Media L. R. 2269 (CA11 Ga. 1987)

19 ALR5th 1—§ 50

Strawhacker v. State, 304 Ark. 726, 804 S.W.2d 720 (1991)

55 ALR5th 423—§ 5

Strawhorn v. Strawhorn, 49 Md. App. 649, 435 A.2d 466 (1981)

17 ALR5th 366—§ 10

Strawn v. Canuso, 140 N.J. 43, 657 A.2d 420, 41 A.L.R.5th 859 (1995)

41 ALR5th 157—§ 2, 3

Strawn v. Farmers Ins. Co. of Oregon, 233 Or. App. 401, 226 P.3d 86 (2010)

60 ALR6th 295—§ 37, 67

Strawn Mercantile Co. v. First Nat'l Bank, 279 S.W. 473 (Tex. Civ. App. 1925)
48 ALR5th 473—§ 5, 18

Straws v. Fail, 17 A.D.2d 998, 233 N.Y.S.2d 893 (3d Dep't 1962)
83 ALR5th 103—§ 3
84 ALR5th 249—§ 44

Strawser, In re Adoption of, 36 Ohio App. 3d 232, 522 N.E.2d 1105 (Franklin Co. 1987)
61 ALR5th 151—§ 7

Strawser v. Atkins, 290 F.3d 720 (4th Cir. 2002)
25 ALR6th 435—§ 7

Strawser v. Exxon Co., U.S.A., a Div. of Exxon Corp., 843 P.2d 613 (Wyo. 1992)
57 ALR5th 633—§ 3

Strawser v. Lawton, 126 F. Supp. 2d 994 (S.D. W. Va. 2001)
25 ALR6th 435—§ 7, 68

Strawser v. Wright, 80 Ohio App. 3d 751, 610 N.E.2d 610 (12th Dist. Preble County 1992)
61 ALR5th 635—§ 8
91 ALR5th 545—§ 4

Strayer v. Petry, 3 Pa. D. & C.4th 299, 54 Empl. Prac. Dec. (CCH) ¶ 40184, 1989 WL 223554 (C.P. 1989)
103 ALR5th 557—§ 6

Strayhorn v. Willow Creek Resources, Inc., 161 S.W.3d 716 (Tex. App. Austin 2005)
14 ALR6th 119—§ 72

St. Raymond v. City of New Orleans, 769 So. 2d 562 (La. Ct. App. 4th Cir. 2000)
26 ALR5th 736—§ 4

Straz v. Kansas Bankers Surety Co., 165 F.3d 33 (7th Cir. 1998)
34 ALR6th 345—§ 34

Strazzulla Bros. Co. v. Fargo Real Estate Trust, 152 F.2d 61 (CA1 Mass. 1945)
22 ALR5th 327—§ 25

Stream v. CBK Agronomics, Inc., 79 Misc. 2d 607, 361 N.Y.S.2d 110, 16 U.C.C.R.S. 177 (1974)
23 ALR5th 241—§ 3

Stream v. Sportscar Salon, Ltd., 91 Misc. 2d 99, 397 N.Y.S.2d 677, 22 U.C.C.R.S. 631 (1977)
38 ALR5th 191—§ 2, 14

Streat v. State, 11 Md. App. 543, 275 A.2d 537 (1971)
68 ALR5th 343—§ 3, 4, 10

Streater v. Kelly, 2002 WL 31460697 (Conn. Super. Ct. 2002)
11 ALR6th 1—§ 4, 6

Streater v. State, 119 Md. App. 267, 704 A.2d 541 (1998)
29 ALR5th 487—§ 12

Streber v. Hunter, 221 F.3d 701, 55 Fed. R. Evid. Serv. 376 (5th Cir. 2000)
13 ALR6th 1—§ 4, 5
58 ALR6th 1—§ 3
59 ALR6th 1—§ 3
60 ALR6th 1—§ 3
78 ALR6th 151—§ 11

Streckfus Steamers v. Shuttleworth, 86 F.2d 327 (C.C.A. 4th Cir. 1936)
21 ALR6th 81—§ 72

Street v. Calvert, 541 S.W.2d 576 (Tenn. 1976)
9 ALR5th 826—§ 2, 6

Street v. City of Anniston, 381 So. 2d 26 (Ala. 1980)
5 ALR6th 133—§ 9, 14
14 ALR6th 301—§ 15

Street v. Corrections Corporation of America, 102 F.3d 810, 1996 FED App. 0387P (6th Cir. 1996)
119 ALR5th 1—§ 5, 17

Street v. Darwin Ranch, Inc., 75 F. Supp. 2d 1296 (D. Wyo. 1999)
54 ALR5th 513—§ 5

Street v. Davis, 143 Misc. 2d 983, 542 N.Y.S.2d 968 (Civ Ct. 1989)
42 ALR5th 53—§ 5, 56

Street v. Gerstenslager Co., 103 Ohio App. 3d 156, 658 N.E.2d 1105, 152 BNA LRRM 2851 (Wayne Co. 1995)

51 ALR5th 1—§ 7

Street v. Hedgepath, 607 A.2d 1238, 75 Ed. Law Rep. 336 (D.C. 1992)

97 ALR6th 83—§ 6

Street v. J.C. Bradford & Co., 886 F.2d 1472, CCH Fed Secur L. Rep. ¶ 94768 (CA6 Tenn. 1989)

29 ALR5th 664—§ 2

Street v. National Broadcasting Co., 645 F.2d 1227, 7 Media L. R. 1001 (CA6 Tenn. 1981)

19 ALR5th 1—§ 2, 101

Street v. National Broadcasting Co., 645 F.2d 1227, 7 Media L. Rep. (BNA) 1001 (6th Cir. 1981)

42 ALR6th 353—§ 7

Street v. New York, 394 U.S. 576, 89 S. Ct. 1354, 22 L. Ed. 2d 572 (1969)

31 ALR6th 333—§ 7, 10

Street v. Street, 731 So. 2d 1224 (Ala. Civ. App. 1999)

34 ALR5th 57—§ 3

Street v. Vose, 936 F.2d 38 (1st Cir. 1991)

23 ALR6th 697—§ 8, 14

Street v. Wachovia Mortg., 2013 WL 135376 (D. Ariz. 2013)

86 ALR6th 411—§ 5

Street v. Waddell, 3 S.W.3d 504 (Tenn. Ct. App. 1999)

47 ALR5th 523—§ 4

Street v. Washington Hosp. Center, 558 A.2d 690 (D.C. 1989)

58 ALR5th 613—§ 10
64 ALR6th 249—§ 34
97 ALR6th 83—§ 80

Street Condominium v. Hausner, 245 A.D.2d 209, 666 N.Y.S.2d 619 (1st Dep't 1997)

10 ALR5th 448—§ 9

Street Corp., 707 N.Y.S.2d 630 (App. Div. 1st Dep't 2000)

43 ALR5th 207—§ 21

Streeter v. Executive Jet Management, 2005 WL 4357633 (Conn. Super. Ct. 2005)

103 ALR6th 461—§ 40

Streeter v. Rifton Management, LLC, 38 Conn. L. Rptr. 493, 2004 WL 3130585 (Conn. Super. Ct. 2004)

103 ALR6th 461—§ 40

Streeter v. Young, 583 So. 2d 1339 (Ala. 1991)

4 ALR5th 273—§ 34

Street, In re v. McIlvaine, 1996 WL 361507 (Del. Ch. 1996)

91 ALR6th 1—§ 5

Streetman v. Lasater, 185 S.W. 930 (Tex. Civ. App. 1916)

14 ALR5th 242—§ 26

Streetman v. State, 455 So. 2d 1080, 9 FLW 1910 (Fla. App. D2 1984)

8 ALR5th 775—§ 1

Streets v. M.G.I.C. Mortg. Corp., 177 Ind. App. 184, 378 N.E.2d 915 (1978)

10 ALR5th 448—§ 5
73 ALR6th 425—§ 18, 32, 65, 69

Streetsboro Educ. Ass'n v. Streetsboro City Sch. Dist. Bd. of Educ., 68 Ohio St. 3d 288, 626 N.E.2d 110 (1994)

57 ALR5th 477—§ 33, 49

Stregack v. Moldofsky, 474 So. 2d 206, 10 FLW 316 (Fla. 1985)

3 ALR5th 394—§ 4

St. Regis Apartment Corp. v. Sweitzer, 32 Wis. 2d 426, 145 N.W.2d 711 (1966)

75 ALR5th 1—§ 7

St. Regis Paper Co. v. Brown, 247 Ga. 361, 276 S.E.2d 24 (1981)

99 ALR6th 591—§ 9

St. Regis Paper Co. v. Pellizzeri, 394 So. 2d 234 (Fla. Dist. Ct. App. 1st Dist. 1981)

79 ALR5th 201—§ 10

St. Regis Paper Co. v. Watson, 409 So. 2d 75, 35 A.L.R.4th 532 (Fla. App. D1 1982)

14 ALR5th 242—§ 40

St. Regis Paper Co. v. Watson, 428 So. 2d 243 (Fla. 1983)

14 ALR5th 242—§ 2

Strehlow, In re, 84 B.R. 241 (Bankr. S.D. Fla. 1988)
74 ALR6th 549—§ 10

Strei v. Brooks, 95 Cal. App. 589, 273 P. 145 (1st Dist. 1928)
75 ALR5th 1—§ 3

Streib v. Veigel, 109 Idaho 174, 706 P.2d 63 (1985)
7 ALR5th 852—§ 23, 24

Streicher v. Streicher, 128 Mich. App. 5, 339 N.W.2d 661 (1983)
53 ALR5th 375—§ 14
95 ALR5th 533—§ 5
124 ALR5th 203—§ 5, 7

Streicher v. Tommy's Electric Co., 164 Cal. App. 3d 876, 211 Cal. Rptr. 22 (6th Dist. 1985)
93 ALR6th 463—§ 20, 32

Streifel v. Hansch, 40 Wash. App. 233, 698 P.2d 570 (Div. 3 1985)
13 ALR6th 1—§ 4
15 ALR6th 427—§ 6

Streiff v. City of Milwaukee, 89 Wis. 218, 61 N.W. 770 (1895)
54 ALR6th 201—§ 44

Streight v. Estate of Streight, 226 Or. 386, 360 P.2d 304 (1961)
14 ALR5th 557—§ 6, 15

Streips v. LTV Corp., 216 A.D.2d 923, 629 N.Y.S.2d 132 (4th Dep't 1995)
52 ALR6th 271—§ 21

Streisand v. West, 304 A.D.2d 650, 757 N.Y.S.2d 600 (2d Dep't 2003)
92 ALR6th 379—§ 7

Streit v. American Drug Stores, Inc., 2003 WL 932396 (Cal. App. 2d Dist. 2003)
100 ALR6th 139—§ 49

Streitweiser v. Middlesex Mut. Assur. Co., 219 Conn. 371, 593 A.2d 498 (1991)
77 ALR5th 319—§ 3
78 ALR5th 341—§ 3
79 ALR5th 289—§ 15

Strelov v. Hertz Corp., 171 A.D.2d 420, 566 N.Y.S.2d 646 (1st Dep't 1991)
121 ALR5th 157—§ 4

Strenke v. Hogner, 287 Wis. 2d 135, 2005 WI App 194, 704 N.W.2d 309 (Ct. App. 2005)
26 ALR6th 659—§ 7

Stress-Care, Inc. v. W.C.A.B., 62 Cal. Comp. Cas. (MB) 907, 1997 WL 697073 (App. 2d Dist. 1997)
112 ALR5th 399—§ 12

Stresscon International, Inc. v. Ralph Merritt Development Corp., 368 So. 2d 384 (Fla. App. D3 1979)
3 ALR5th 237—§ 20

Stretch v. State Board of Medical Examiners, 88 NJL 92, 95 A. 623 (1915)
32 ALR5th 57—§ 3

Strezinski v. City of Greensboro, 187 N.C. App. 703, 654 S.E.2d 263 (2007)
99 ALR6th 643—§ 18

Stribling v. Chicago Housing Authority, 34 Ill. App. 3d 551, 340 N.E.2d 47 (1st Dist. 1975)
43 ALR5th 207—§ 4, 5, 22, 25, 29, 36, 45, 47

Stribling v. Jolley, 241 Mo. App. 1123, 253 S.W.2d 519 (1952)
28 ALR5th 107—§ 21

Stribling Motor Co. v. Smith, 195 Miss. 547, 15 So. 2d 364 (1943)
27 ALR5th 764—§ 3

Strick Corp. v. Strickland, 162 F. Supp. 2d 372 (E.D. Pa. 2001)
96 ALR5th 1—§ 4

Stricker v. Stricker, 474 So. 2d 1146 (Ala. Civ. App. 1985)
71 ALR5th 99—§ 6

Stricker v. Swift Bros. Const. Co., 260 N.W.2d 500, 97 L.R.R.M. (BNA) 2367, 83 Lab. Cas. (CCH) ¶ 10494 (S.D. 1977)
105 ALR5th 243—§ 18
110 ALR5th 111—§ 4

Strickland, Ex parte, 724 S.W.2d 132 (Tex. App. Eastland 1987)
32 ALR5th 31—§ 3

Strickland, In re, 339 Or. 595, 124 P.3d 1225 (2005)
43 ALR6th 163—§ 3

44 ALR6th 75—§ 3
45 ALR6th 175—§ 3
Strickland, Re Estate of, 181 Neb. 478, 149 N.W.2d 344 (1967)
3 ALR5th 394—§ 6 to 8
Strickland v. American Pitch Pine Export Co., 224 La. 949, 71 So. 2d 338 (1954)
11 ALR5th 715—§ 9, 41, 45
Strickland v. Bowater, Inc., 472 S.E.2d 635 (S.C. App. 1996)
63 ALR5th 163—§ 3, 9
Strickland v. Communications and Cable of Chicago, Inc., 304 Ill. App. 3d 679, 237 Ill. Dec. 632, 710 N.E.2d 55, 15 I.E.R. Cas. (BNA) 854 (1st Dist. 1999)
13 ALR5th 217—§ 4
Strickland v. Dyer, 192 Ark. 462, 92 S.W.2d 206 (1936)
6 ALR6th 391—§ 5
Strickland v. Fowler, 499 So. 2d 199, Prod. Liab. Rep. (CCH) ¶ 11353 (La. Ct. App. 2d Cir. 1986)
88 ALR5th 1—§ 3, 5
Strickland v. Hospital Authority of Albany/Dougherty County, 241 Ga. App. 1, 525 S.E.2d 724 (1999)
38 ALR6th 399—§ 3, 4
Strickland v. Montgomery Lumber Co., 171 N.C. 755, 88 S.E. 340 (1916)
17 ALR5th 547—§ 9
Strickland v. Moskos, 131 S.C. 247, 127 S.E. 265 (1925)
12 ALR5th 195—§ 3, 13
Strickland v. National Gypsum Co., 348 So. 2d 497 (Ala. Civ. App. 1977)
112 ALR5th 509—§ 18
122 ALR5th 653—§ 2
13 ALR6th 209—§ 12, 14, 41
39 ALR6th 445—§ 41
Strickland v. Osborn, 333 So. 2d 582 (Ala. App. 1976)
15 ALR5th 692—§ 35
Strickland v. Perruccio, 5 Conn. Cir. 142, 246 A.2d 810 (1968)
50 ALR5th 417—§ 6, 10

Strickland v. Ports Petroleum Co., Inc., 256 Ga. 669, 353 S.E.2d 17, 1987-1 Trade Cas. (CCH) ¶ 67456 (1987)
26 ALR6th 249—§ 5
Strickland v. Prudential Ins. Co. of America, 278 S.C. 82, 292 S.E.2d 301 (1982)
116 ALR5th 247—§ 5
Strickland v. Roberts, 382 So. 2d 1338 (Fla. App. D5 1980)
34 ALR5th 77—§ 4, 9
Strickland v. Royal Lubricant Co., Inc., 911 F. Supp. 1460, Prod. Liab. Rep. (CCH) ¶ 14608 (M.D. Ala. 1995)
53 ALR5th 535—§ 3, 5
72 ALR5th 299—§ 2, 14, 38
Strickland v. State, 16 Ga. App. 234, 85 S.E. 83 (1915)
14 ALR5th 89—§ 22
Strickland v. State, 156 Ga. App. 475, 274 S.E.2d 823 (1980)
45 ALR5th 591—§ 2, 15
Strickland v. State, 164 Ga. App. 845, 297 S.E.2d 491 (1982)
24 ALR5th 465—§ 9, 115, 117
Strickland v. State, 221 Ga. App. 516, 471 S.E.2d 576 (1996)
58 ALR6th 499—§ 13
Strickland v. State, 270 Ga. App. 187, 605 S.E.2d 890 (2004)
78 ALR6th 213—§ 3
Strickland v. State, 923 S.W.2d 617 (Tex. App. Houston (1st Dist.) 1995)
50 ALR5th 581—§ 3, 5, 9
Strickland v. State Farm Ins. Companies, 607 So. 2d 769 (La. Ct. App. 1st Cir. 1992)
66 ALR5th 269—§ 7
Strickland v. Strickland, 285 Ala. 693, 235 So. 2d 833 (1970)
95 ALR5th 533—§ 5
124 ALR5th 203—§ 5
Strickland v. Strickland, 297 S.C. 248, 376 S.E.2d 268 (1989)
38 ALR6th 313—§ 5
Strickland v. Strickland, 470 N.W.2d 832 (S.D. 1991)

9 ALR5th 568—§ 9
Strickland v. Transamerica Ins. Co., 481 F.2d 138 (CA5 La. 1973)
1 ALR5th 132—§ 10
Strickland v. Trust Co. of Georgia, 230 Ga. 714, 198 S.E.2d 668 (1973)
31 ALR5th 499—§ 2, 3
Strickland v. University of Scranton, 700 A.2d 979, 121 Ed. Law Rep. 251 (Pa. Super. Ct. 1997)
38 ALR6th 541—§ 29
79 ALR6th 377—§ 41, 42
Strickland v. Warden, Southern Ohio Correctional Inst., 2010 WL 4919753 (S.D. Ohio 2010)
103 ALR6th 137—§ 8
Strickland v. Washington, 466 U.S. 668, 104 S. Ct. 2052, 80 L. Ed. 2d 674 (1984)
8 ALR5th 713—§ 3, 5, 8, 11
11 ALR5th 871—§ 3
70 ALR5th 1—§ 2, 4, 7, 8, 11
72 ALR5th 109—§ 2 to 7, 10
78 ALR5th 197—§ 2 to 7, 9 to 11, 13 to 15
79 ALR5th 419—§ 2 to 4, 6, 7, 9, 10, 12, 13, 18, 21
80 ALR5th 55—§ 2 to 6, 8, 12
95 ALR5th 125—§ 2 to 5, 7 to 9
117 ALR5th 513—§ 3 to 5, 7, 8, 10, 19, 22, 23
19 ALR6th 411—§ 2
31 ALR6th 49—§ 3 to 8, 10 to 12, 14, 15
56 ALR6th 679—§ 16
62 ALR6th 259—§ 3, 6, 8, 13
66 ALR6th 635—§ 22
71 ALR6th 1—§ 2, 5 to 9, 11, 12, 14 to 20, 22
72 ALR6th 1—§ 2, 4, 7, 9 to 12, 14, 18
72 ALR6th 141—§ 16
73 ALR6th 1—§ 2, 5 to 7, 9
74 ALR6th 373—§ 2 to 13, 15, 17 to 23
83 ALR6th 465—§ 27
92 ALR6th 549—§ 24, 27, 29
99 ALR6th 295—§ 1

102 ALR6th 417—§ 1 to 3, 11, 15 to 17, 24 to 25, 28, 31, 34 to 37, 39, 40, 42, 43, 45, 51, 53, 55, 62, 69, 77, 79, 80, 89, 92, 98, 99, 101, 106, 111, 112
103 ALR6th 247—§ 1, 2, 5 to 9, 11 to 19, 21, 24
Strickland v. Winterville, 130 Ga. App. 425, 203 S.E.2d 706 (1973)
9 ALR5th 102—§ 6, 22
Stricklin v. Investors Syndicate Life Ins. & Annuity Co., 391 F. Supp. 246 (W.D. Okla. 1975)
73 ALR6th 425—§ 20
73 ALR6th 571—§ 61
Stricklin v. Stricklin, 456 So. 2d 809 (Ala. App. 1984)
49 ALR5th 441—§ 20
Strid, In re Disciplinary Action Against, 551 N.W.2d 212 (Minn. 1996)
27 ALR6th 1—§ 33
Stride v. 120 West Madison Bldg. Corp., 132 Ill. App. 3d 601, 87 Ill. Dec. 790, 477 N.E.2d 1318 (1st Dist. 1985)
13 ALR5th 169—§ 2
Striegler, In Interest of, 915 S.W.2d 629 (Tex. App. Amarillo 1996)
76 ALR5th 191—§ 3
Strignano ex rel. Strignano v. Jamaica Hosp., 181 Misc. 2d 155, 694 N.Y.S.2d 857 (Sup 1999)
1 ALR6th 407—§ 11, 15
Strignano ex rel. Strignano v. Jamaica Hosp., 181 Misc. 2d 155, 694 N.Y.S.2d 857 (Sup. Ct. 1999)
71 ALR5th 307—§ 14, 18
Striker v. Commonwealth, Horse Racing Com., 34 Pa. Cmwlth. 373, 383 A.2d 967 (1978)
59 ALR5th 203—§ 21, 62
Striker v. Nakamura, 50 Hawaii 590, 446 P.2d 35 (1968)
5 ALR5th 875—§ 23
Strimple, Commonwealth ex rel. v. von Wiederhold (1954) 4 Bucks Co LR 171
124 ALR5th 203—§ 4, 6

Stringer v. Com., 956 S.W.2d 883 (Ky. 1997)

38 ALR5th 433—§ 5

90 ALR5th 453—§ 11

Stringer v. Estate of Jasaitis, 146 Ill. App. 3d 270, 100 Ill. Dec. 131, 496 N.E.2d 1196 (1st Dist. 1986)

99 ALR6th 1—§ 11

Stringer v. Fireman's Fund Ins. Co., 622 So. 2d 145, 18 FLW D 1753 (Fla. App. D3 1993)

16 ALR5th 412—§ 5

Stringer v. Jackson, 862 F.2d 1108 (CA5 Miss. 1988)

10 ALR5th 700—§ 17

Stringer v. Jackson, 2009 WL 3753746 (S.D. Fla. 2009)

89 ALR6th 1—§ 118

Stringer v. Rowe, 616 F.2d 993 (7th Cir. 1980)

65 ALR6th 93—§ 58

Stringer v. Sheffield, 451 So. 2d 320 (Ala. Civ. App. 1984)

112 ALR5th 185—§ 4, 10

119 ALR5th 445—§ 6, 13

124 ALR5th 441—§ 3, 7, 8, 12

2 ALR6th 439—§ 41

Stringer v. State, 108 Nev. 413, 836 P.2d 609 (1992)

20 ALR6th 479—§ 3

Stringer v. State, 109 Tex. Crim. 497, 5 S.W.2d 526 (1928)

102 ALR5th 447—§ 22

Stringer v. State, 783 So. 2d 1153 (Fla. Dist. Ct. App. 4th Dist. 2001)

39 ALR5th 283—§ 3

Stringer Constr. Co. v. La Grange State Bank, 148 Ill. App. 3d 621, 102 Ill. Dec. 168, 499 N.E.2d 948 (1st Dist. 1984)

13 ALR5th 465—§ 15

56 ALR5th 565—§ 47

Stringer, State ex rel. v. Quigg, 91 Fla. 197, 107 So. 409 (1926)

13 ALR5th 118—§ 7, 10

Stringfellow v. State Farm Life Ins. Co., 743 So. 2d 439 (Ala. 1999)

61 ALR6th 239—§ 11

Stringfellow's of New York, Ltd. v. City of New York, 91 N.Y.2d 382, 671 N.Y.S.2d 406, 694 N.E.2d 407 (1998)

10 ALR5th 538—§ 3, 7, 28

Stringfellow's of New York, Ltd. v. City of New York, 171 Misc. 2d 376, 653 N.Y.S.2d 801 (Sup. Ct. 1996)

10 ALR5th 538—§ 10

Stringfield v. City of Hackensack, 68 N.J. Super. 38, 171 A.2d 361 (App. Div. 1961)

74 ALR5th 49—§ 73

Striplin v. State, 499 P.2d 446 (Okla. Crim. 1972)

9 ALR5th 464—§ 4, 11

Stripling v. Godfrey, 143 Ga. App. 742, 240 S.E.2d 145 (1977)

91 ALR5th 1—§ 10

Stripling v. Literary Guild of America, Inc., 5 Media L. R. 1958 (W.D. Tex. 1979)

19 ALR5th 1—§ 72

Stripling v. New England Sav. Bank, 1993 WL 137552 (Conn. Super. Ct. 1993)

119 ALR5th 121—§ 3

2 ALR6th 279—§ 20

Stripling v. State, 47 Tex. Crim. 117, 80 S.W. 376 (1904)

54 ALR6th 429—§ 11

Strite Governor Pulley Co. v. Lyons, 129 Minn. 372, 152 N.W. 765 (1915)

19 ALR5th 622—§ 2

Stritt v. State Accident Insurance Fund, 37 Or. App. 893, 588 P.2d 136 (1978)

36 ALR5th 225—§ 3, 6

Strobel v. City of Cincinnati, 32 Ohio App. 333, 168 N.E. 543 (1st Dist. Hamilton County 1929)

12 ALR6th 645—§ 44, 54

Strobel v. Garrison, 255 Or. 16, 464 P.2d 688 (1970)

15 ALR5th 1—§ 9

Strobel v. Park, 292 Pa. 200, 140 A. 877, 57 A.L.R. 253 (1927)

100 ALR5th 409—§ 2

Stroble v. Anderson, 587 F.2d 830 (6th Cir. 1978)
51 ALR6th 1—§ 19

Strocher, Re Marriage of, 95 Ill. App. 3d 339, 50 Ill. Dec. 908, 420 N.E.2d 225 (4th Dist. 1981)
15 ALR5th 692—§ 17

St. Rock v. Gagnon, 342 Mass. 722, 175 N.E.2d 361 (1961)
60 ALR5th 379—§ 7

Strock v. Pressnell, 38 Ohio St. 3d 207, 527 N.E.2d 1235, 75 A.L.R.4th 729 (1988)
5 ALR5th 530—§ 3 to 5, 8
99 ALR5th 445—§ 3, 4
101 ALR5th 1—§ 5, 8

Strock v. Southern Farm Bureau Cas. Ins. Co., 998 F.2d 1010 (4th Cir. 1993)
111 ALR5th 529—§ 5

Strode v. Com., 301 Ky. 676, 192 S.W.2d 963 (1946)
24 ALR6th 747—§ 30

Strode v. Meyer Bros. Drug Co., 101 Mo. App. 627, 74 S.W. 379 (1903)
6 ALR6th 391—§ 5, 11, 14, 17, 21

Strode v. Silverman, 209 S.W.2d 415 (Tex. Civ. App. Waco 1948)
82 ALR5th 443—§ 4

Stroehmann Bakeries, Inc. v. Local 776, Intern. Broth. of Teamsters, 969 F.2d 1436, 59 Fair Empl. Prac. Cas. (BNA) 249, 140 L.R.R.M. (BNA) 2625, 59 Empl. Prac. Dec. (CCH) ¶ 41620, 122 Lab. Cas. (CCH) ¶ 10252 (3d Cir. 1992)
66 ALR5th 611—§ 10

Stroemer v. Van Orsdel, 74 Neb. 132, 107 N.W. 125 (1906)
35 ALR6th 1—§ 29

Strogov v. Attorney General of State of N.Y, 191 F.3d 188 (2d Cir. 1999)
79 ALR6th 125—§ 5, 8, 24

Stroh v. Alaska State Housing Authority, 459 P.2d 480 (Alaska 1968)
107 ALR5th 311—§ 14

Stroh v. American Recreation & Mobile Home Corp., 35 Colo. App. 196, 530 P.2d 989, 16 U.C.C.R.S. 726 (1975)
38 ALR5th 191—§ 3, 40

Stroh v. General Motors Corp., 213 A.D.2d 267, 623 N.Y.S.2d 873 (1st Dep' 1995)
67 ALR6th 341—§ 8

Stroh v. Omni Arabians, Inc., 131 Md. App. 178, 748 A.2d 1015 (2000)
73 ALR6th 571—§ 47, 69

Stroh v. Rhoads, 188 Or. 563, 217 P.2d 245 (1950)
6 ALR5th 534—§ 8

Stroh Corp. v. K & S. Development Corp., 247 N.W.2d 750 (Iowa 1976)
46 ALR5th 1—§ 2, 24

Stroh Corp. v. K & S Development Corp., 247 N.W.2d 750 (Iowa 1976)
88 ALR6th 533—§ 19

Strohkorb v. U.S., 268 F. Supp. 526 (E.D. Va. 1967)
27 ALR5th 174—§ 103

Strohmeyer v. International Broth. of Painters and Allied Trades, 989 F. Supp. 455, 76 Fair Empl. Prac. Cas. (BNA) 359 (W.D. N.Y. 1997)
51 ALR5th 1—§ 7

Stroh Oil Co. v. Office of State Fire Marshal, 281 Ill. App. 3d 121, 216 Ill. Dec. 480, 665 N.E.2d 540 (4th Dist. 1996)
11 ALR5th 388—§ 3

Stroik v. State, 671 A.2d 1335 (Del. 1996)
89 ALR5th 629—§ 3, 8, 10

Stroka v. United Airlines, 364 N.J. Super. 333, 835 A.2d 1247 (App. Div. 2003)
20 ALR6th 729—§ 6

Stroker v. Rubin, 1994 WL 719694 (E.D. Pa)
51 ALR5th 271—§ 3

Strokes v. Unemployment Compensation Board of Review, 29 Pa. Cmwlth. 584, 372 A.2d 485 (1977)
15 ALR5th 653—§ 2, 10

Strom v. Erie County Pistol Permit Dept., 6 A.D.3d 1110, 776 N.Y.S.2d 685 (4th Dep't 2004)

91 ALR6th 435—§ 76, 115

Strom v. Lindstrom, 201 Minn. 226, 275 N.W. 833 (1937)

60 ALR6th 481—§ 4, 25

Stroman, In re, 78 B.R. 785 (Bankr. D. S.C. 1987)

46 ALR6th 401—§ 7

Stroman v. Williams, 291 S.C. 376, 353 S.E.2d 704 (Ct. App. 1987)

65 ALR5th 591—§ 3

Stromback v. New Line Cinema, 384 F.3d 283, 72 U.S.P.Q.2d 1545, Fed. Sec. L. Rep. (CCH) ¶ 28878, 2004 FED App. 0314P (6th Cir. 2004)

76 ALR6th 289—§ 2, 4, 5
77 ALR6th 543—§ 2, 10, 12, 15

Stromberg v. French, 60 N.D. 750, 236 N.W. 477 (1931)

58 ALR5th 1—§ 44

Stromberg v. Moore, 170 S.W.3d 26 (Mo. Ct. App. E.D. 2005)

88 ALR6th 533—§ 19

Stromberg v. Oyster Bay, 140 Misc. 2d 295, 530 N.Y.S.2d 476 (1988)

24 ALR5th 200—§ 2

Stromberg v. Rubenstein, 19 Misc. 647, 44 N.Y.S. 405 (1897)

44 ALR5th 1—§ 15, 16

Stromberg-Carlson Corp. v. Bank Melli Iran, 467 F. Supp. 530 (S.D. N.Y. 1979)

56 ALR5th 565—§ 21

Stromberg Hatchery v. Iowa Employment Secur. Com., 239 Iowa 1047, 33 N.W.2d 498 (1948)

60 ALR5th 459—§ 2, 18

Stromberg Metal Works, Inc. v. University Of Maryland, 382 Md. 151, 854 A.2d 1220 (2004)

5 ALR6th 327—§ 3, 5

Stromberg's v. Victor Gruen and Associates, 384 F.2d 163 (10th Cir. 1967)

75 ALR5th 413—§ 5, 13, 48

Stromberg Sheet Metal Works, Inc. v. U.S. Fidelity & Guar. Co., 71 Va. Cir. 122, 2006 WL 1994544 (2006)

81 ALR6th 363—§ 4

Strong, Re, 61 Ohio Misc. 2d 244, 577 N.E.2d 163 (1988)

15 ALR5th 391—§ 30

Strong v. Abner, 268 Ky. 502, 105 S.W.2d 599 (1937)

9 ALR6th 363—§ 28

Strong v. Baker, 2008 WL 859086 (Tenn. Ct. App. 2008)

58 ALR6th 1—§ 5, 21, 65
59 ALR6th 1—§ 4, 16
60 ALR6th 1—§ 72

Strong v. Beroujon, 18 Ala. 168 (1850)

67 ALR5th 179—§ 11

Strong v. Chmielewski, 77 A.D.2d 952, 431 N.Y.S.2d 121 (2d Dep't 1980)

121 ALR5th 1—§ 36

Strong v. C.I.R., Inc., 184 Wis. 2d 619, 516 N.W.2d 719, 2 BNA WH Cas. 2d 452 (1994)

5 ALR5th 513—§ 7
7 ALR5th 444—§ 3

Strong v. C.I.R., Inc., 184 Wis. 2d 619, 516 N.W.2d 719, 2 Wage & Hour Cas. 2d (BNA) 452, 128 Lab. Cas. (CCH) ¶ 57718 (1994)

104 ALR6th 1—§ 3

Strong v. Gilster Mary Lee Corp., 23 S.W.3d 234 (Mo. Ct. App. E.D. 2000)

8 ALR5th 653—§ 3

Strong v. Henra Realty Corp., 89 A.D.2d 829, 453 N.Y.S.2d 192 (1st Dep't 1982)

100 ALR5th 409—§ 9

Strong v. Kansas Parole Bd., 115 P.3d 794 (Kan. Ct. App. 2005)

75 ALR6th 181—§ 8

Strong v. Laubach, 2004 OK 21, 89 P.3d 1066 (Okla. 2004)

69 ALR6th 415—§ 43

Strong v. Oakwood Hosp. Corp., 118 Mich. App. 395, 325 N.W.2d 435 (1982)

24 ALR5th 1—§ 3

64 ALR5th 475—§ 5

Strong v. Oklahoma Publishing Co., 899 P.2d 1185 (Okla. App. 1995)

44 ALR5th 193—§ 29, 43

Strong v. Owens, 91 Cal. App. 2d 336, 205 P.2d 48 (2d Dist. 1949)

58 ALR5th 669—§ 3

Strong v. Phoenix Ins. Co., 62 Mo. 289, 1876 WL 9721 (1876)

87 ALR6th 319—§ 3

Strong v. Pontiac General Hospital, 117 Mich. App. 143, 323 N.W.2d 629 (1982)

24 ALR5th 1—§ 3

Strong v. Shefveland, 249 Minn. 59, 81 N.W.2d 247 (1957)

8 ALR5th 1—§ 36

Strong v. Stalder, 2008 WL 294814 (E.D. La. 2008)

89 ALR6th 1—§ 115

Strong v. State, 25 Ill. Ct. Cl. 231, 1965 WL 6440 (Ill. Ct. Cl. 1965)

53 ALR6th 305—§ 21

Strong v. State, 246 Ga. 612, 272 S.E.2d 281 (1980)

13 ALR5th 1—§ 2

Strong v. State, 599 So. 2d 264 (Fla. Dist. Ct. App. 2d Dist. 1992)

46 ALR6th 241—§ 24

Strong v. State, 805 S.W.2d 478 (Tex. App. Tyler 1990)

89 ALR5th 629—§ 9 to 11

58 ALR5th 385—§ 20

Strong v. State, 947 So. 2d 552 (Fla. Dist. Ct. App. 3d Dist. 2006)

40 ALR6th 1—§ 31

Strong v. Strong, 66 Mass. 135, 12 Cush. 135 (1853)

67 ALR5th 179—§ 3

Strong v. Stryker Corp., 2010 WL 4967876 (D. Minn. 2010)

90 ALR6th 75—§ 4, 10, 14, 39, 41

Strong v. Telectronics Pacing Systems, Inc., 78 F.3d 256, Prod. Liab. Rep. (CCH) ¶ 14532, 1996 FED App. 0091P (6th Cir. 1996)

23 ALR6th 223—§ 3

Strong v. Telectronics Pacing Systems, Inc., 891 F. Supp. 401, Prod. Liab. Rep. (CCH) ¶ 14369 (W.D. Mich. 1994)

23 ALR6th 223—§ 24, 25

Strong v. Trosclair, 423 So. 2d 13 (La. Ct. App. 1st Cir. 1982)

71 ALR5th 99—§ 2, 3, 6

Strong v. Williams, 154 Mont. 65, 460 P.2d 90 (1969)

26 ALR5th 401—§ 8, 10

Strong Delivery Ministry Asso. v. Board of Appeals, 543 F.2d 32 (CA7 Ill. 1976)

8 ALR5th 653—§ 3

Strongman v. Idaho Potato Com'n, 129 Idaho 766, 932 P.2d 889, 70 Empl. Prac. Dec. (CCH) ¶ 44706 (1997)

93 ALR5th 47—§ 4

Strong, Marriage of v. Strong, 2000 M.T. 178, 8 P.3d 763 (Mont. 2000)

52 ALR5th 221—§ 7

Strong, Marriage of v. Strong, 2000 MT 178, 300 Mont. 331, 8 P.3d 763 (2000)

59 ALR6th 433—§ 19, 79

Strongsville v. Waiwood, 62 Ohio App. 3d 521, 577 N.E.2d 63 (Cuyahoga Co. 1989)

42 ALR5th 581—§ 12

Strong's Will, In re, 47 Misc. 2d 1069, 264 N.Y.S.2d 84 (1965)

36 ALR5th 395—§ 12, 23

Strong's Will, In re, 171 Misc. 445, 12 N.Y.S.2d 544 (1939)

56 ALR5th 133—§ 4

Stroop v. Day, 896 P.2d 439 (Mont 1995)

11 ALR5th 127—§ 23, 36

Stroop v. Rutherford County, 567 S.W.2d 753 (Tenn. 1978)

1 ALR6th 229—§ 28

Strother v. Alabama Farm Bureau Mut. Casualty Co., 474 So. 2d 85 (Ala. 1985)

6 ALR5th 297—§ 40, 45

Strother v. Capitol Bankers Life Ins. Co., 68 Wash. App. 224, 842 P.2d 504 (Div. 1 1992)

117 ALR5th 155—§ 12

Strother v. District of Columbia, 372 A.2d 1291 (D.C. 1977)

94 ALR6th 111—§ 11

Strother v. Herold, 230 Neb. 801, 433 N.W.2d 535, 3 A.L.R.5th 999 (1989)

3 ALR5th 1—§ 3, 47, 59

Strother v. Kennedy, 106 Ga. App. 381, 127 S.E.2d 25 (1962)

122 ALR5th 205—§ 3, 41

Strother v. Pacific Gas & Electric Co., 94 Cal. App. 2d 525, 211 P.2d 624 (1949)

49 ALR5th 659—§ 9

Strother v. State, 587 So. 2d 1243 (Ala. Crim. App. 1991)

47 ALR5th 259—§ 10

Strother v. State, 677 So. 2d 962 (Fla. Dist. Ct. App. 1st Dist. 1996)

15 ALR6th 173—§ 19

Stroud v. Cincinnati Ins. Co., 1992 WL 63296 (Ohio App. 1 Dist.)

52 ALR5th 451—§ 3

Stroud v. Dorr-Oliver, Inc., 112 Ariz. 403, 542 P.2d 1102 (1975)

3 ALR5th 851—§ 17, 18

Stroud v. Golson, 741 So. 2d 182 (La. Ct. App. 2d Cir. 1999)

57 ALR5th 141—§ 14
94 ALR6th 431—§ 57

Stroud v. Hennepin County Medical Center, 544 N.W.2d 42 (Minn. Ct. App. 1996)

64 ALR5th 163—§ 3, 9, 14

Stroud v. Liberty Mut. Ins. Co., 429 So. 2d 492 (La. App. 3d Cir. 1983)

33 ALR5th 587—§ 4

Stroud v. Motor Vehicle Acci. Indemnification Corp., 17 App. Div. 2d 616, 231 N.Y.S.2d 18 (1st Dep't 1962)

56 ALR5th 757—§ 3

Stroud v. Motor Vehicle Acc. Indemnification Corp., 17 A.D.2d 616, 231 N.Y.S.2d 18 (1st Dep't 1962)

103 ALR5th 1—§ 4

Stroud v. Ryan, 297 Ark. 472, 763 S.W.2d 76 (1989)

87 ALR5th 473—§ 15
11 ALR6th 1—§ 4, 6, 10

Stroud v. State, 246 Ga. 717, 273 S.E.2d 155 (1980)

86 ALR5th 463—§ 9

Stroud v. State, 787 N.E.2d 430 (Ind. Ct. App. 2003)

55 ALR6th 157—§ 95

Stroud v. Stroud, 9 S.W.3d 579 (Ky. Ct. App. 1999)

102 ALR6th 153—§ 24

Stroud v. VBFSB Holding Corp., 917 S.W.2d 75 (Tex. App. San Antonio 1996)

19 ALR5th 439—§ 5

Stroud v. Ward, 169 Mich. App. 1, 425 N.W.2d 490 (1988)

12 ALR6th 1—§ 16

Stroudsburg Area School Dist. v. Kelly, 701 A.2d 1000, 122 Ed. Law Rep. 206 (Pa. Commw. Ct. 1997)

28 ALR6th 175—§ 11

Strouf v. Strouf, 176 Mont. 406, 578 P.2d 746 (1978)

5 ALR5th 550—§ 28
6 ALR5th 69—§ 6

Strough v. State, 501 So. 2d 488 (Ala. Crim. App. 1986)

15 ALR5th 391—§ 39
92 ALR5th 35—§ 16

Strougo v. BEA Associates, 199 F.R.D. 515 (S.D. N.Y. 2001)

47 ALR6th 255—§ 7

Strougo ex rel. Brazilian Equity Fund, Inc. v. Bassini, 258 F. Supp. 2d 254, Fed. Sec. L. Rep. (CCH) ¶ 92410 (S.D. N.Y. 2003)

60 ALR6th 295—§ 6, 71

Strougo on Behalf of Brazilian Equity Fund, Inc. v. Bassini, 1 F. Supp. 2d 268 (S.D. N.Y. 1998)

43 ALR6th 1—§ 15

Stroup, In re Marriage of, 2003 WL 21061366 (Cal. App. 4th Dist. 2003)

59 ALR6th 433—§ 47

Stroup v. Johnson, 539 S.W.2d 711 (Mo. App. 1976)

62 ALR5th 219—§ 36

Stroupe v. Eller, 262 N.C. 573, 138 S.E.2d 240 (1964)

78 ALR6th 229—§ 4

Strouse, In re, 23 F. Cas. 261 No. 13548 (D. Nev. 1871)

105 ALR5th 1—§ 3

Strouse v. City of Los Angeles Dept. of Airports, 2004 WL 501036 (Cal. App. 2d Dist. 2004)

19 ALR6th 217—§ 5

Strouse v. Olson, 397 N.W.2d 651 (S.D. 1986)

71 ALR5th 99—§ 3, 6

Strout v. Albanese, 178 F.3d 57, 135 Ed. Law Rep. 398 (1st Cir. 1999)

78 ALR5th 133—§ 14 to 18

Strout v. Central Maine Medical Center, 2014 ME 77, 2014 WL 2579624 (Me. 2014)

97 ALR6th 519—§ 7

Strout Realty, Inc. v. Henry, 758 S.W.2d 197 (Mo. Ct. App. S.D. 1988)

86 ALR5th 527—§ 9

Stro-Wold Farms v. Finnell, 211 Ill. App. 3d 113, 155 Ill. Dec. 545, 569 N.E.2d 1156 (1st Dist. 1991)

6 ALR5th 883—§ 12

Stro-Wold Farms v. Finnell, 211 Ill. App. 3d 113, 155 Ill. Dec. 545, 569 N.E.2d 1156 (4th Dist. 1991)

17 ALR6th 1—§ 11

Strozier v. State, 277 Ga. 78, 586 S.E.2d 309 (2003)

99 ALR6th 295—§ 21

Strozinsky v. School Dist. of Brown Deer, 237 Wis. 2d 19, 2000 WI 97, 614 N.W.2d 443, 146 Ed. Law Rep. 470, 16 I.E.R. Cas. (BNA) 879 (2000)

104 ALR5th 1—§ 3, 4, 13

Strubble v. United Services Auto. Asso., 35 Cal. App. 3d 498, 110 Cal. Rptr. 828 (2d Dist. 1973)

30 ALR5th 170—§ 2, 84

Strube v. U.S., 206 F. Supp. 2d 677 (E.D. Pa. 2002)

72 ALR6th 1—§ 7

Strubhart v. Perry Memorial Hosp. Trust Authority, 1995 OK 10, 903 P.2d 263 (Okla. 1995)

98 ALR5th 533—§ 3

Struble v. Lacks Industries, Inc., 157 Mich. App. 169, 403 N.W.2d 71, 107 CCH LC ¶ 55801 (1986)

53 ALR5th 219—§ 3, 11

Struchynski v. Decker, 194 N.W.2d 741, 68 Lab. Cas. (CCH) ¶ 52825 (N.D. 1972)

86 ALR6th 321—§ 11

91 ALR6th 171—§ 11

Struck v. Everett, 17 Wash. 2d 218, 135 P.2d 67 (1943)

57 ALR5th 477—§ 31

Struckman v. Board of Trustees, 38 Cal. App. 2d 373, 101 P.2d 151 (1940)

57 ALR5th 477—§ 19

Struckman v. Burns, 205 Conn. 542, 534 A.2d 888 (1987)

118 ALR5th 91—§ 10, 28

Struck, State ex rel. v. Struck, 526 N.W.2d 500 (S.D. 1995)

57 ALR5th 389—§ 2, 4

Structural Building Products Corp. v. Business Ins. Agency, Inc., 281 A.D.2d 617, 722 N.Y.S.2d 559 (2d Dep't 2001)

98 ALR5th 1—§ 20

Structural Building Products Corp. v. Business Ins. Agency, Inc., 722 N.Y.S.2d 559 (App. Div. 2d Dep't 2001)

60 ALR5th 165—§ 4, 14

Structural Components Int., Inc. v. City Of Charlotte, 154 N.C. App. 119, 573 S.E.2d 166 (2002)

26 ALR6th 179—§ 3

Structurals Northwest, Ltd. v. Fifth & Park Place, Inc., 33 Wash. App. 710, 658 P.2d 679 (1983)

10 ALR5th 448—§ 8

23 ALR5th 241—§ 9

Structural Steel Fabricators, Inc. v. City of Orange, 234 Cal. App. 3d 1206, 286 Cal. Rptr. 24 (4th Dist. 1991)
81 ALR6th 363—§ 4

Structured Asset Funding, LLC v. Taylor, 14 Misc. 3d 1230(A), 2007 WL 446608 (N.Y. Sup 2007)
27 ALR6th 323—§ 22

Struebing v. American Ins. Co., 197 Wis. 487, 222 N.W. 831 (1928)
16 ALR5th 412—§ 34

Struett v. Arlington Trust Co., 23 Mass. App. Ct. 152, 499 N.E.2d 845 (1986)
86 ALR6th 321—§ 11
91 ALR6th 171—§ 21

Struges v. Hy-Vee Employee Benefit Plan & Trust, 991 F.2d 479 (CA8 S.D. 1993)
23 ALR5th 241—§ 37

Struhar v. City of Cleveland, 7 F. Supp. 2d 948, 46 Env't. Rep. Cas. (BNA) 2019, 28 Envtl. L. Rep. 21572 (N.D. Ohio 1998)
17 ALR5th 327—§ 15

Strujan v. AOL, 12 Misc. 3d 1160(A), 819 N.Y.S.2d 213 (N.Y. City Civ. Ct. 2006)
84 ALR6th 589—§ 4

Strum v. Strum, 22 Ill. App. 3d 147, 317 N.E.2d 59 (4th Dist. 1974)
120 ALR5th 229—§ 3, 7, 22

Strumph v. Schering Corp., 133 N.J. 33, 626 A.2d 1090, CCH Prod. Liab. Rep. ¶ 13547 (1993)
57 ALR5th 1—§ 26

Strumph v. Schering Corp., 256 N.J. Super. 309, 606 A.2d 1140, CCH Prod. Liab. Rep. ¶ 13289 (1992)
57 ALR5th 1—§ 3

Strumsky v. State, 69 P.3d 499 (Alaska Ct. App. 2003)
27 ALR6th 183—§ 19

Struna v. Convenient Food Mart, 160 Ohio App. 3d 655, 2005-Ohio-1861, 828 N.E.2d 647 (8th Dist. Cuyahoga County 2005)
48 ALR6th 243—§ 5, 10

Struna v. Harleen, Inc., 2003-Ohio-3713, 2003 WL 21640892 (Ohio Ct. Cl. 2003)
48 ALR6th 243—§ 5, 10

Strunck, In re Marriage of, 212 Ill. App. 3d 76, 155 Ill. Dec. 781, 570 N.E.2d 1 (5th Dist. 1991)
59 ALR6th 433—§ 20

Strunk v. Keller, 75 Pa. Super. 462, 1921 WL 2101 (1921)
40 ALR6th 99—§ 29

Strunk v. Public Employees Retirement Bd., 338 Or. 145, 108 P.3d 1058 (2005)
27 ALR6th 403—§ 6

Strunk v. Strunk, 445 S.W.2d 145, 35 A.L.R.3d 683 (Ky. 1969)
4 ALR5th 1000—§ 2, 3

Strunk, Commonwealth ex rel. v. Cummins, 258 Pa. Super. 326, 392 A.2d 817 (1978)
15 ALR5th 692—§ 10, 25

Strussion v. Akron Beacon Journal Pub. Co., 2002-Ohio-3200, 30 Media L. Rep. (BNA) 1948, 2002 WL 1371166 (Ohio Ct. App. 9th Dist. Summit County 2002)
22 ALR6th 553—§ 21, 36

Struthers, Matter of, 179 Ariz. 216, 877 P.2d 789 (1994)
27 ALR6th 1—§ 19

Struthers, City of v. Clay, 13 Ohio L. Abs. 97, 1932 WL 1804 (Ct. App. 7th Dist. Mahoning County 1932)
57 ALR6th 355—§ 3

Strutz v. Hall, 308 F. Supp. 2d 767 (E.D. Mich. 2004)
65 ALR6th 93—§ 17

Stryczek v. Methodist Hospitals, Inc., 694 N.E.2d 1186 (Ind. Ct. App. 1998)
24 ALR6th 549—§ 15

Stryker v. Rasch, 57 Wyo. 34, 112 P.2d 570, 136 A.L.R. 770 (1941)
86 ALR6th 411—§ 2

Stryker v. State Farm Mut. Auto. Ins. Co., 74 Ill. 2d 507, 24 Ill. Dec. 832, 386 N.E.2d 36 (1978)

31 ALR5th 116—§ 3

Stryker v. Welch, 128 Kan. 632, 279 P. 25 (1929)

60 ALR6th 481—§ 24

Strzelczyk v. Jett, 264 Mont. 153, 870 P.2d 730 (1994)

43 ALR5th 87—§ 14

Strzelecki v. Johns-Manville Products Corp., 65 N.J. 314, 322 A.2d 168 (1974)

11 ALR6th 351—§ 25

STS Land Associates, L.P. v. City of Hollywood by City Com'n, 585 So. 2d 1170 (Fla. Dist. Ct. App. 4th Dist. 1991)

63 ALR5th 607—§ 12

St. Stephen's Club v. Youngstown Metropolitan Housing Authority, 160 Ohio St. 194, 52 Ohio Ops. 3, 115 N.E.2d 385 (1953)

53 ALR5th 1—§ 26, 34

S.T.T., In re, 2003 UT App 439, 83 P.3d 398 (Utah Ct. App. 2003)

86 ALR6th 321—§ 4

90 ALR6th 451—§ 110

S.T.T., In re Estate of, 2006 UT 46, 144 P.3d 1083 (Utah 2006)

86 ALR6th 1—§ 18, 19

St. Tammany Inv. Properties, Inc. v. Cairns, 425 So. 2d 252 (La. App. 1st Cir. 1982)

45 ALR5th 251—§ 17

St. Tammany Parish Tax Collector v. Barnesandnoble.Com, 481 F. Supp. 2d 575, 30 A.L.R.6th 683 (E.D. La. 2007)

30 ALR6th 341—§ 4, 32

St. Thomas-St. John Hotel & Tourism Ass'n, Inc. v. Government of U.S. Virgin Islands, 218 F.3d 232, 16 I.E.R. Cas. (BNA) 779, 164 L.R.R.M. (BNA) 2705, 141 Lab. Cas. (CCH) ¶ 58964 (3d Cir. 2000)

108 ALR5th 253—§ 2

110 ALR5th 111—§ 2

St. Thomas—St. John Hotel & Tourism Ass'n, Inc. v. Government of U.S. Virgin Islands, 218 F.3d 232, 16 I.E.R. Cas. (BNA) 779, 164 L.R.R.M. (BNA) 2705, 141 Lab. Cas. (CCH) ¶ 58964 (3d Cir. 2000)

120 ALR5th 351—§ 2

Stuard v. Porter, 79 Ohio St. 1, 6 Ohiolr 516, 85 N.E. 1062 (1908)

58 ALR5th 535—§ 5

Stuart, In re, 942 A.2d 1118 (D.C. 2008)

44 ALR6th 75—§ 27

Stuart, In re Marriage of, 141 Ill. App. 3d 314, 95 Ill. Dec. 770, 490 N.E.2d 243 (5th Dist. 1986)

26 ALR6th 331—§ 26

Stuart, Matter of Marriage of, 107 Or. App. 549, 813 P.2d 49 (1991)

3 ALR6th 447—§ 4, 5, 7

Stuart v. American Cyanamid Co., 158 F.3d 622 (2d Cir. 1998)

30 ALR5th 1—§ 24

98 ALR6th 417—§ 4

Stuart v. American States Ins. Co., 134 Wash. 2d 814, 953 P.2d 462 (1998)

35 ALR5th 375—§ 3, 15

Stuart v. Beech Aircraft Corp., 753 F. Supp. 317 (D. Kan. 1990)

93 ALR5th 269—§ 3, 7

Stuart v. Brookline, 587 N.E.2d 1384 (Mass. 1992)

50 ALR5th 1—§ 4

51 ALR5th 467—§ 5

52 ALR5th 1—§ 3, 9

Stuart v. Chawney, 454 Mich. 200, 560 N.W.2d 336 (1997)

115 ALR5th 251—§ 21

Stuart v. Danka Corp., 986 F. Supp. 741 (E.D. N.Y. 1997)

10 ALR6th 375—§ 7

Stuart v. Doyle, 95 Conn. 732, 112 A. 653 (1921)

27 ALR5th 174—§ 83

Stuart v. Hawley, 22 Barb. 619 (N.Y. 1856)

25 ALR5th 391—§ 3, 5

Stuart v. Huff, 2011 WL 6330668 (M.D. N.C. 2011)

73 ALR6th 281—§ 9

Stuart v. Kansas City, 102 Kan. 307, 102 Kan. 563, 171 P. 913 (1918)

41 ALR6th 207—§ 21

Stuart v. Kleck, 129 F.2d 400 (CA9 Ariz. 1942)

60 ALR5th 459—§ 2, 4, 5, 16

Stuart v. New City Diner, 758 So. 2d 345 (La. Ct. App. 4th Cir. 2000)

14 ALR5th 1—§ 4, 5

Stuart v. Porcello, 193 A.D.2d 311, 603 N.Y.S.2d 597, 22 Media L. Rep. (BNA) 1700 (3d Dep't 1993)

94 ALR5th 149—§ 8

Stuart v. Porcello, 193 App. Div. 2d 311, 603 N.Y.S.2d 597 (3d Dep't 1993)

44 ALR5th 193—§ 20, 36, 49

Stuart v. Radioshack Corp., 2010 WL 3155645 (N.D. Cal. 2010)

60 ALR6th 295—§ 13

Stuart v. Secrest, 170 N.W.2d 878 (N.D. 1969)

11 ALR6th 587—§ 20

Stuart v. State, 127 Idaho 806, 907 P.2d 783 (1995)

24 ALR6th 1—§ 4

Stuart v. State, 267 Ga. App. 463, 600 S.E.2d 629 (2004)

11 ALR6th 237—§ 13
68 ALR6th 527—§ 37

Stuart v. State, 561 S.W.2d 181 (Tex. Crim. App. 1978)

86 ALR5th 59—§ 6

Stuart v. State, Div. for Children and Youth Services, 134 N.H. 702, 597 A.2d 1076 (1991)

8 ALR6th 339—§ 19

Stuart v. Stuart, 46 Ark. App. 259, 878 S.W.2d 785 (1994)

119 ALR5th 445—§ 19
7 ALR6th 411—§ 17, 43

Stuart v. Stuart, 143 Wis. 2d 347, 421 N.W.2d 505 (1988)

4 ALR5th 972—§ 4, 5
110 ALR5th 371—§ 6

Stuart v. Stuart, 516 So. 2d 1277 (La. Ct. App. 2d Cir. 1987)

5 ALR5th 550—§ 9
5 ALR5th 788—§ 2, 5, 7, 14, 16
21 ALR5th 396—§ 2, 3, 11, 19, 61
80 ALR5th 117—§ 2

Stuart v. Tarrant County Child Welfare Unit, 677 S.W.2d 273 (Tex. App. Fort Worth 1984)

6 ALR6th 161—§ 21

Stuart v. Tomasino, 148 A.D.2d 370, 539 N.Y.S.2d 327 (1st Dep't 1989)

37 ALR6th 511—§ 4, 34, 50

Stuart & Henley v. Ford, 5 Ohio C.D. 260 (Ohio Cir. Ct. 1896)

75 ALR5th 1—§ 10

Stuart Becker & Co., P.C. v. Steven Kessler Motor Cars, Inc., 135 Misc. 2d 1069, 517 N.Y.S.2d 692 (Sup. Ct. 1987)

88 ALR5th 301—§ 9

Stuart S., In re, 104 Cal. App. 4th 203, 127 Cal. Rptr. 2d 856 (3d Dist. 2002)

10 ALR6th 173—§ 35

Stubaus v. Whitman, 339 N.J. Super. 38, 770 A.2d 1222, 153 Ed. Law Rep. 681 (App. Div. 2001)

110 ALR5th 293—§ 3
115 ALR5th 563—§ 3

Stubblefield, Ex parte, 412 S.W.2d 63 (Tex. Crim. App. 1966)

85 ALR5th 471—§ 7

Stubblefield v. Commonwealth, 10 Va. App. 343, 392 S.E.2d 197 (1990)

32 ALR5th 149—§ 5, 29, 72, 76

Stubblefield v. Dong My Ha, 10 Pa. D. & C.3d 751 (1978)

16 ALR5th 650—§ 6
21 ALR5th 396—§ 3, 9, 18, 21, 30

Stubblefield v. Imbler, 33 Or. 446, 54 P. 198 (1898)

12 ALR6th 123—§ 4

Stubblefield Construction Co. v. City of San Bernardino, 32 Cal. App. 4th 687, 38 Cal. Rptr. 2d 413 (4th Dist. 1995)

38 ALR5th 737—§ 3

Stubbs v. Bank of America, 844 F. Supp. 2d 1267 (N.D. Ga. 2012)

---

81 ALR6th 161—§ 4

82 ALR6th 43—§ 12

Stubbs v. Copper Mountain, 862 P.2d 978 (Colo. App. 1993)

22 ALR5th 483—§ 22, 25

Stubbs v. Hemmert, 567 P.2d 168 (Utah 1977)

10 ALR5th 448—§ 5

Stubbs v. North Memorial Medical Center, 448 N.W.2d 78, 17 Media L. Rep. (BNA) 1090 (Minn. Ct. App. 1989)

87 ALR5th 277—§ 2

Stubbs v. Nutter, 2010 WL 3421015 (E.D. Pa. 2010)

95 ALR6th 341—§ 3

Stubbs v. Ortega, 977 S.W.2d 718 (Tex. App. Fort Worth 1998)

32 ALR5th 673—§ 3

Stubbs v. Panek, 829 S.W.2d 544 (Mo. App. 1992)

43 ALR5th 207—§ 5, 23, 24, 52

Stubbs v. State, 811 So. 2d 384 (Miss. Ct. App. 2001)

73 ALR6th 1—§ 5

Stubbs v. State, 845 So. 2d 656, 1 A.L.R.6th 819 (Miss. 2003)

1 ALR6th 657—§ 4

Stubbs v. Stuart, 469 S.W.2d 311 (Tex. Civ. App. Houston 14th Dist. 1971)

75 ALR5th 1—§ 3

Stubbs v. Weathersby, 320 Or. 620, 892 P.2d 991 (1995)

82 ALR5th 443—§ 4, 5

83 ALR5th 375—§ 11

84 ALR5th 191—§ 7

Stubbs v. Webb, 28 Ohio St. 3d 300, 503 N.E.2d 745 (1986)

5 ALR6th 133—§ 12

Stubbs v. Whiting, 22 Va. 322, 1 Rand. 322, 1823 WL 987 (1823)

87 ALR6th 495—§ 27

Stuber, Claim of, 253 A.D.2d 972, 677 N.Y.S.2d 824 (3d Dep't 1998)

25 ALR6th 101—§ 4

Stuber, State ex rel. v. Industrial Commission of Ohio, 127 Ohio St. 325, 188 N.E. 526 (1933)

31 ALR6th 199—§ 15, 74, 75

Stubley v. Allison Realty Co., 124 App. Div. 162, 108 N.Y.S. 759 (1908)

24 ALR5th 200—§ 20, 54

Stubli v. Big D Intern. Trucks, Inc., 107 Nev. 309, 810 P.2d 785 (1991)

121 ALR5th 157—§ 5

Stuborn Ltd. Partnership v. Bernstein, 245 F. Supp. 2d 312 (D. Mass. 2003)

64 ALR6th 365—§ 3

Stucchio v. Huffstetler, 720 So. 2d 288 (Fla. Dist. Ct. App. 5th Dist. 1998)

67 ALR6th 437—§ 14

Stucci v. City of St. Paul, 403 N.W.2d 850 (Minn. App. 1987)

38 ALR5th 107—§ 12

Stuchell v. Mortland, 8 Wash. App. 884, 509 P.2d 770 (Div. 1 1973)

109 ALR5th 421—§ 6

Stucke v. Thomas Chevrolet, Cadillac, 1999 WL 486947 (Minn. Ct. App. 1999)

83 ALR5th 1—§ 13, 15

Stucker v. McMains, 71 Cal. App. 2d 35, 161 P.2d 997 (2d Dist. 1945)

87 ALR5th 1—§ 10, 12, 21

Stucker v. Summit County, 870 P.2d 283, 233 Utah Adv. Rep. 11 (Utah App. 1994)

38 ALR5th 737—§ 2, 3

Stuckert v. Brownlee, 138 Ill. App. 3d 788, 93 Ill. Dec. 294, 486 N.E.2d 395 (2d Dist. 1985)

6 ALR6th 229—§ 8, 24, 26

Stuckey's Carriage Inn v. Phillips, 122 Ga. App. 681, 178 S.E.2d 543 (1970)

15 ALR5th 119—§ 3, 5, 32, 85

Stuckman v. Kosciusko County Bd. of Zoning Appeals, 506 N.E.2d 1079 (Ind. 1987)

116 ALR5th 373—§ 3, 10

Stuckwish v. Hagan Corp., 316 Pa. 513, 175 A. 381 (1934)

16 ALR5th 1—§ 2, 13

For assistance, call 1-800-328-4880

Stuczynski v. Stuczynski, 238 Neb. 368, 471 N.W.2d 122, 17 A.L.R.5th 944 (1991)

17 ALR5th 143—§ 2, 3, 6, 8, 9
49 ALR5th 441—§ 2

Studard v. Department of Transp., 219 Ga. App. 643, 466 S.E.2d 236, 96 Fulton County D R 84 (1995)

15 ALR5th 119—§ 5

Studdard v. South Cent. Bell Tel. Co., 356 So. 2d 139 (Ala. 1978)

28 ALR5th 603—§ 5, 9, 11

Studebaker v. Nettie's Flower Garden, Inc., 842 S.W.2d 227 (Mo. App. 1992)

27 ALR5th 174—§ 3, 4, 39

Studebaker-Worthington Leasing, Corp. v. New Concepts Realty, Inc., 14 Misc. 3d 1233(A), 836 N.Y.S.2d 503 (Dist. Ct. 2007)

39 ALR6th 629—§ 4

Studebaker Worthington Leasing Corp. v. Texas Shutters Corp., 243 S.W.3d 737 (Tex. App. Houston 14th Dist. 2007)

39 ALR6th 629—§ 4

Student Coalition for Peace v. Lower Merion School Dist. Bd. of School Directors, 776 F.2d 431, 28 Ed. Law Rep. 388 (3d Cir. 1985)

70 ALR6th 513—§ 17
71 ALR6th 471—§ 7

Student Doe v. Com. of Pa., 593 F. Supp. 54, 20 Ed. Law Rep. 540 (E.D. Pa. 1984)

115 ALR5th 183—§ 3, 4, 7, 18

Student Finance Corp., In re, 335 B.R. 539 (D. Del. 2005)

23 ALR6th 457—§ 5, 7, 10, 25

Student Roe by Roe v. Com. of Pa., 638 F. Supp. 929, 33 Ed. Law Rep. 1132 (E.D. Pa. 1986)

115 ALR5th 183—§ 2 to 4, 7, 13, 18

Students Against Apartheid Coalition v. O'Neil, 660 F. Supp. 333, 40 Ed. Law Rep. 167 (W.D. Va. 1987)

70 ALR6th 513—§ 16
71 ALR6th 471—§ 12

Studer v. Seneca County Humane Society, 2000-Ohio-1823, 2000 WL 566738 (Ohio Ct. App. 3d Dist. Seneca County 2000)

70 ALR6th 329—§ 14

Studivent v. Huskey, 2013 WL 690022 (M.D. N.C. 2013)

95 ALR6th 341—§ 22

Studley v. School Dist. No. 38 of Hall County, 210 Neb. 669, 316 N.W.2d 603, 2 Ed. Law Rep. 1162 (1982)

68 ALR5th 663—§ 4

Studley Box & Lumber Co. v. National Fire Ins. Co., 85 N.H. 96, 154 A. 337 (1931)

37 ALR5th 41—§ 18, 20, 31, 40

Studstill v. Borg Warner Leasing, a Div. of Borg Warner Acceptance Corp., 806 F.2d 1005, 50 Fair Empl. Prac. Cas. (BNA) 427, 42 Empl. Prac. Dec. (CCH) ¶ 36759, 6 Fed. R. Serv. 3d 834 (11th Cir. 1986)

20 ALR6th 1—§ 5

Studt v. Studt, 443 N.W.2d 639 (S.D. 1989)

28 ALR5th 46—§ 11

Studwell Inc. v. Korean Exchange Bank, 55 Cal. App. 4th 1185, 64 Cal. Rptr. 2d 538 (2d Dist. 1997)

56 ALR5th 565—§ 49

Study v. U.S., 2010 WL 1257655 (N.D. Fla. 2010)

95 ALR6th 341—§ 41

Studyvin, In re Marriage of, 779 S.W.2d 338 (Mo. Ct. App. S.D. 1989)

3 ALR6th 447—§ 4, 7

Stuebgen v. State, 547 S.W.2d 29 (Tex. Crim. App. 1977)

108 ALR5th 593—§ 39

Stueck v. G. C. Murphy Co., 107 Conn. 656, 142 A. 301 (1928)

62 ALR5th 219—§ 18, 27

Stuehrenberg v. State, 420 N.E.2d 1329 (Ind. Ct. App. 1981)

43 ALR6th 475—§ 4

Stuempges v. Parke, Davis & Co., 297 N.W.2d 252, 24 A.L.R.4th 132 (Minn. 1980)

12 ALR5th 195—§ 3
14 ALR5th 242—§ 49
52 ALR6th 271—§ 4
Stueve v. American Honda Motors Co., 457 F. Supp. 740 (D.C. Kan. 1978)
6 ALR5th 883—§ 21
Stueve v. Commissioner of Revenue, 1991 WL 10079 (Minn. Tax Ct. 1991)
118 ALR5th 597—§ 13
Stufflebean v. State, 986 S.W.2d 189 (Mo. Ct. App. W.D. 1999)
31 ALR6th 49—§ 4
Stufflebean v. Stufflebean, 941 S.W.2d 844 (Mo. Ct. App. W.D. 1997)
76 ALR5th 191—§ 3
Stufflebeem v. Adelsbach, 135 Cal. 221, 67 P. 140 (1901)
62 ALR5th 219—§ 54
Stuhr v. Barkwill, 215 Or. 285, 332 P.2d 603 (1958)
30 ALR5th 571—§ 30
Stukas v. Streiter, 83 A.D.3d 18, 918 N.Y.S.2d 176 (2d Dep't 2011)
92 ALR6th 379—§ 19, 33
Stukey, In re Estate of, 2004 MT 279, 323 Mont. 241, 100 P.3d 114 (2004)
32 ALR6th 285—§ 24
Stulce v. Stulce, 961 So. 2d 173 (Ala. Civ. App. 2007)
52 ALR6th 433—§ 14
57 ALR6th 163—§ 43
Stull, Ex parte, 280 S.E.2d 209 (S.C. 1981)
40 ALR5th 697—§ 4
Stull, In re Estate of, 8 Neb. App. 301, 593 N.W.2d 18 (1999)
56 ALR5th 107—§ 6
Stull v. American States Ins. Co., 963 F. Supp. 492 (D. Md. 1997)
105 ALR5th 95—§ 18
Stull v. Baker, 410 F. Supp. 1326, CCH Fed Secur L. Rep. ¶ 95466 (S.D. N.Y. 1976)
23 ALR5th 241—§ 19
Stull v. First American Title Ins. Co., 2000 ME 21, 745 A.2d 975 (Me. 2000)

6 ALR5th 297—§ 49
Stull v. Hoke, 326 Or. 72, 948 P.2d 722 (1997)
29 ALR6th 237—§ 14, 26, 29
Stull v. School Board, 459 F.2d 339 (CA3 Pa. 1972)
58 ALR5th 1—§ 5, 9, 10, 25, 26
Stuller v. Price, 2004-Ohio-4416, 2004 WL 1879014 (Ohio Ct. App. 10th Dist. Franklin County 2004)
64 ALR6th 249—§ 32
Stults, In re, 644 N.E.2d 1239 (Ind. 1994)
1 ALR5th 874—§ 6, 9
Stults v. Conoco, Inc., 76 F.3d 651, 70 Fair Empl. Prac. Cas. (BNA) 732, 67 Empl. Prac. Dec. (CCH) ¶ 43925 (5th Cir. 1996)
83 ALR5th 1—§ 5
Stultz v. Stultz, 644 N.E.2d 589 (Ind. App. 1994)
34 ALR5th 447—§ 3, 9
Stumler v. Ferry-Morse Seed Co., 644 F.2d 667, 30 U.C.C. Rep. Serv. (CBC) 1590 (7th Cir. 1981)
81 ALR5th 483—§ 5
Stump v. 209 E. 56th St. Corp., 622 N.Y.S.2d 517 (N.Y. App. Div. 1st Dep't 1995)
12 ALR5th 577—§ 11
Stump v. Ashland, Inc., 201 W. Va. 541, 499 S.E.2d 41 (1997)
96 ALR5th 107—§ 7
99 ALR5th 301—§ 4
Stump v. Crawford & Co., 726 F. Supp. 228 (N.D. Ind. 1989)
11 ALR5th 88—§ 3
Stump v. Follmer Trucking Co., 448 Pa. 313, 292 A.2d 294 (1972)
107 ALR5th 441—§ 2, 11
109 ALR5th 161—§ 4, 10, 12, 13
20 ALR6th 641—§ 20
Stump v. Gates, 777 F. Supp. 808 (D. Colo. 1991)
101 ALR5th 515—§ 6
Stump v. Norfolk Shipbuilding & Dry Dock Corp., 187 Va. 932, 48 S.E.2d 209 (1948)

---

3 ALR5th 907—§ 2, 4
Stump v. Wal-Mart Stores, Inc., 942 F. Supp. 347 (E.D. Ky. 1996)
21 ALR6th 671—§ 5
Stumpf v. Continental Casualty Co., 102 Or. App. 302, 794 P.2d 1228 (1990)
23 ALR5th 241—§ 16
Stumpf v. Eidemiller, 94 Or. App. 576, 767 P.2d 77 (1989)
20 ALR5th 229—§ 3, 30
Stumpf v. Lau, 108 Nev. 826, 839 P.2d 120 (1992)
112 ALR5th 1—§ 8
Stumpf v. State, 749 P.2d 880 (Alaska Ct. App. 1988)
27 ALR6th 183—§ 20
Stumpf v. Stumpf, 613 So. 2d 683 (La. App. 5th Cir. 1993)
51 ALR5th 603—§ 8
Stundon v. Stadnik, 469 P.2d 16 (Wyo. 1970)
30 ALR5th 571—§ 2, 21, 38, 40, 45, 51
Stunkard, In re Adoption of, 380 Pa. Super. 107, 551 A.2d 253 (1988)
61 ALR5th 151—§ 11
Stunkel v. Hanley Landscape, Inc., 633 So. 2d 117 (Fla. Dist. Ct. App. 4th Dist. 1994)
119 ALR5th 121—§ 3, 6
Stunkel v. Price Elec. Co-op., 229 Wis. 2d 664, 599 N.W.2d 919 (Ct. App. 1999)
91 ALR5th 517—§ 3, 6
Stuntz, State ex rel. v. Chisholm, 196 Minn. 285, 264 N.W. 798 (1936)
17 ALR5th 195—§ 11
Stupek v. Wyle Laboratories Corp., 327 Or. 433, 963 P.2d 678, 14 I.E.R. Cas. (BNA) 670, 136 Lab. Cas. (CCH) ¶ 58465 (1998)
19 ALR5th 439—§ 8
Stupka v. Peoples Cab Co., 437 Pa. 509, 264 A.2d 373 (1970)
101 ALR5th 61—§ 1
Sturbridge, Town of v. McDowell, 35 Mass. App. 924, 624 N.E.2d 114 (1993)

38 ALR5th 357—§ 8
Sturbridge, Town of v. McDowell, 35 Mass. App. Ct. 924, 624 N.E.2d 114 (1993)
77 ALR6th 393—§ 98, 99, 103
Sturbridge, Town of v. Tantasqua Regional School Dist., 22 Mass. L. Rptr. 68, 2006 WL 4114307 (Mass. Super. Ct. 2006)
76 ALR6th 543—§ 14
Sturdza v. United Arab Emirates, 281 F.3d 1287, 62 U.S.P.Q.2d 1071 (D.C. Cir. 2002)
76 ALR6th 289—§ 5
77 ALR6th 543—§ 13
Sturgenegger v. Taylor, 4 S.C.L. 480, 2 Brev. 480 (S.C. 1811)
69 ALR5th 645—§ 4
Sturgeon v. Avon Products, Inc., 571 F.2d 5, 16 BNA FEP Cas. 1082, 16 CCH EPD ¶ 8139 (CA7 Ind. 1978)
51 ALR5th 1—§ 8
Sturgeon v. Bratton, 174 Cal. App. 4th 1407, 95 Cal. Rptr. 3d 718 (2d Dist. 2009)
75 ALR6th 541—§ 27
Sturgeon v. Clark, 69 N.M. 132, 364 P.2d 757 (1961)
26 ALR5th 401—§ 8, 34
Sturgeon v. Com., 2009 WL 2901227 (Ky. Ct. App. 2009)
63 ALR6th 351—§ 3
Sturgeon v. Commissioner of Public Safety, 350 N.W.2d 487 (Minn. Ct. App. 1984)
96 ALR5th 327—§ 3
Sturgeon v. Quarterman, 615 F. Supp. 2d 546 (S.D. Tex. 2009)
103 ALR6th 247—§ 3, 24
Sturgeon v. Retherford Publications, Inc., 1999 OK CIV APP 78, 987 P.2d 1218, 28 Media L. Rep. (BNA) 1144 (Okla. Civ. App. Div. 4 1999)
94 ALR5th 455—§ 8
Sturgeon v. Sturgeon, 849 S.W.2d 171 (Mo. App. 1993)
9 ALR5th 568—§ 11
28 ALR5th 46—§ 11, 16

Sturges v. Charles L. Harney, Inc., 165 Cal. App. 2d 306, 331 P.2d 1072 (1st Dist. 1958)
25 ALR5th 568—§ 51

Sturges v. Chilmark, 380 Mass. 246, 402 N.E.2d 1346 (1980)
2 ALR5th 553—§ 23, 63

Sturges v. Crowninshield, 17 U.S. 122, 4 L. Ed. 529, 1819 WL 2136 (1819)
77 ALR6th 273—§ 4

Sturgill v. M & M, Inc., 329 A.2d 360 (Del. 1974)
61 ALR6th 61—§ 3

Sturgill v. M & M, Inc., 329 A.2d 360 (Del. Sup. 1974)
16 ALR5th 191—§ 2, 9

Sturgill, Estate of v. United Services Auto. Ass'n, 84 Wash. App. 877, 930 P.2d 945 (Div. 3 1997)
66 ALR5th 269—§ 7

Sturgis, Matter of, 242 A.D.2d 831, 661 N.Y.S.2d 887 (3d Dep't 1997)
43 ALR6th 163—§ 26

Sturgis v. City of Rock Hill, 112 S.C. 485, 100 S.E. 163 (1919)
92 ALR5th 517—§ 11, 13

Sturgis v. District of Columbia Dep't of Employment Services, 629 A.2d 547 (D.C. 1993)
97 ALR5th 1—§ 5

Sturgis v. District of Columbia Dept. of Employment Services, 629 A.2d 547 (D.C. 1993)
106 ALR5th 111—§ 5, 14, 18, 24, 29, 39, 40
108 ALR5th 1—§ 2, 48

Sturgis v. Kansas C. R. Co., 228 S.W. 861 (Mo. App. 1921)
12 ALR5th 195—§ 10

Sturgis v. Robbins, 62 Me. 289 (1874)
25 ALR5th 391—§ 87

Sturgis Sav. & Loan Ass'n v. Italian Village, Inc., 81 Mich. App. 577, 265 N.W.2d 755 (1978)
10 ALR5th 448—§ 8

Sturiano v. Brooks, 523 So. 2d 1126 (Fla. 1988)
110 ALR5th 465—§ 4

Sturkie v. Commonwealth Life Ins. Co., 180 S.C. 177, 185 S.E. 541 (1936)
14 ALR5th 242—§ 34

Sturlaugson v. Renville Farmers Lumber Co., 295 Minn. 334, 204 N.W.2d 430 (1973)
26 ALR5th 401—§ 4, 24

Sturm v. Boker, 150 U.S. 312, 14 S. Ct. 99, 37 L. Ed. 1093 (1893)
58 ALR6th 289—§ 2

Sturm v. Feifer, 186 N.J. Super. 329, 452 A.2d 686 (1982)
12 ALR5th 577—§ 11

Sturm v. Green, 398 P.2d 799 (Okla. 1965)
7 ALR5th 1—§ 4, 33

Sturm v. Muens, 224 S.W.3d 758 (Tex. App. Houston 14th Dist. 2007)
73 ALR6th 571—§ 7, 11, 42

Sturm v. Simpson's Garment Co., 271 Wis. 587, 74 N.W.2d 137 (1956)
123 ALR5th 1—§ 6, 13

Sturm v. Sturm, 1992 WL 95871 (Minn. Ct. App. 1992)
80 ALR5th 487—§ 2, 3

Sturm, Ruger & Co. v. Day, 615 P.2d 621 (Alaska 1980)
12 ALR5th 195—§ 20

Sturm, Ruger & Co., Inc. v. Bloyd, 586 S.W.2d 19 (Ky. 1979)
96 ALR5th 239—§ 6

Sturm, Ruger & Co., Inc. v. Day, 594 P.2d 38 (Alaska 1979)
96 ALR5th 239—§ 4

Sturpe v. Unemployment Compensation Bd. of Review, 823 A.2d 239, 25 A.L.R.6th 635 (Pa. Commw. Ct. 2003)
25 ALR6th 101—§ 5, 60

Sturrock v. Louisiana State Racing Com., 437 So. 2d 357 (La. App. 4th Cir. 1983)
59 ALR5th 203—§ 14

Sturtevant v. Broome County, 188 A.D.2d 893, 591 N.Y.S.2d 631 (3d Dep't 1992)
107 ALR5th 441—§ 2, 20
109 ALR5th 161—§ 9, 19

20 ALR6th 641—§ 22

Stuski v. Lauer, 548 Pa. 338, 697 A.2d 235 (1997)

14 ALR6th 543—§ 16

Stutes v. Rossclaire Constr., Inc., 575 So. 2d 466 (La. App. 3d Cir. 1991)

11 ALR5th 715—§ 14, 36, 41, 56

23 ALR5th 241—§ 2, 40, 42

Stuthman v. Stuthman, 245 Neb. 846, 515 N.W.2d 781 (1994)

13 ALR5th 169—§ 3

Stuto v. Corning Glass Works, Prod. Liab. Rep. (CCH) ¶ 12585, 1990 WL 105615 (D. Mass. 1990)

93 ALR5th 103—§ 12, 14

Stutts v. Duke Power Co., 47 N.C. App. 76, 266 S.E.2d 861 (1980)

52 ALR6th 271—§ 19

Stutts v. Ford Motor Co., 574 F. Supp. 100 (M.D. Tenn. 1983)

30 ALR5th 1—§ 3, 7

Stutts v. Swaim, 30 N.C. App. 611, 228 S.E.2d 750 (1976)

73 ALR5th 223—§ 11

Stutz, In re Marriage of, 126 Cal. App. 3d 1038, 179 Cal. Rptr. 312 (3d Dist. 1981)

123 ALR5th 565—§ 9, 25

Stutz v. State, 979 N.E.2d 1076 (Ind. Ct. App. 2012)

99 ALR6th 295—§ 21

Stutz v. Stutz, 2005 WL 2016828 (Tenn. Ct. App. 2005)

77 ALR6th 293—§ 11, 47

Stutzman v. West Des Moines Ob/Gyn, P.C., 2013 WL 5745829 (Iowa Ct. App. 2013)

92 ALR6th 379—§ 36

Stutzman Feed Service, Inc. v. Todd & Sargent, Inc., 336 F. Supp. 417, 1972 CCH Trade Cases ¶ 73854 (S.D. Iowa 1972)

23 ALR5th 744—§ 5

Stuyvesant Fuel Service Corp. v. 99-105 3rd Avenue Realty LLC, 192 Misc. 2d 104, 745 N.Y.S.2d 680 (N.Y. City Civ. Ct. 2002)

47 ALR6th 1—§ 8

Stuyvesant Ins. Co. v. Jacksonville Oil Mill, 10 F.2d 54 (CA6 Tenn. 1926)

37 ALR5th 41—§ 4

Stuyvesant Ins. Co. v. Square D. Co., 399 So. 2d 1102 (Fla. 3d DCA 1981)

76 ALR6th 31—§ 9

St. Vincent's Hosp. and Medical Center of New York v. Division of Human Rights of Executive Dept. of State of N.Y., 553 F. Supp. 375, 37 Fair Empl. Prac. Cas. (BNA) 1724 (S.D. N.Y. 1982)

103 ALR5th 557—§ 2

St. Vladimir's Ukranian Orthodox Church v. Fun Bun, Inc., 3 Pa. Commw. 394, 283 A.2d 308 (1971)

73 ALR5th 223—§ 8

Styck v. Karnes, 462 N.E.2d 1327 (1984 Ind. App)

15 ALR5th 692—§ 4

Styers, In re Marriage of, 124 Wash. App. 1021, 2004 WL 2669339 (Div. 2 2004)

86 ALR6th 321—§ 12

90 ALR6th 451—§ 83

Styles v. Ceranski, 916 P.2d 1164, 207 Ariz. Adv. Rep. 24 (Ariz. App. 1996)

43 ALR5th 87—§ 13

Styles v. Com., 507 S.W.2d 487 (Ky. 1974)

17 ALR6th 327—§ 23

Styles v. State, 118 Ga. App. 445, 164 S.E.2d 156 (1968)

50 ALR5th 467—§ 8

Styles v. State, 279 Ga. 134, 610 S.E.2d 23 (2005)

16 ALR6th 329—§ 4

24 ALR6th 591—§ 6

Styles v. Village of Newport, 76 Vt. 154, 56 A. 662 (1904)

114 ALR5th 561—§ 12

Stella Stylianou v. St. Luke's/Roosevelt Hosp. Center, 902 F. Supp. 54, 67 Empl. Prac. Dec. (CCH) ¶ 43995 (S.D. N.Y. 1995)

11 ALR6th 447—§ 6

Suan v. State, 511 So. 2d 144 (Miss. 1987)

31 ALR5th 704—§ 15

Suarez v. Commissioner of Internal Revenue, 58 T.C. 792, 1972 WL 2560 (1972)

105 ALR5th 1—§ 3, 14

Suarez v. Mashantucket Pequot Gaming Enterprise, 2011 WL 4852521 (Mash. Pequot Tribal Ct. 2011)

76 ALR6th 395—§ 10

Suarez v. New York, 186 App. Div. 2d 415, 589 N.Y.S.2d 10 (1st Dep't 1992)

50 ALR5th 1—§ 3, 12

52 ALR5th 1—§ 8

Suarez v. State, 377 So. 2d 769 (Fla. App. D3 1979)

52 ALR5th 559—§ 4, 6

Suarez v. State, 481 So. 2d 1201, 11 FLW 1 (Fla. 1985)

32 ALR5th 149—§ 4, 28, 72, 89, 91

Suarez v. Town of Ogden Dunes, Ind., 581 F.3d 591, 81 A.L.R.6th 741 (7th Cir. 2009)

81 ALR6th 257—§ 16

Suarez v. U.S., 309 F.2d 709 (CA5 Fla. 1962)

32 ALR5th 149—§ 22, 23, 33

Suarez Matos v. Ashford Presbyterian Community Hosp., 4 F.3d 47, 37 Fed. Rules Evid. Serv. 874 (CA1 Puerto Rico 1993)

42 ALR5th 1—§ 9

Suarez Matos v. Ashford Presbyterian Community Hosp., Inc., 4 F.3d 47, 37 Fed. R. Evid. Serv. 874 (1st Cir. 1993)

93 ALR6th 123—§ 48, 66

Suarez-Negrete v. Trotta, 47 Conn. App. 517, 705 A.2d 215 (1998)

119 ALR5th 121—§ 3, 11

Suarez Ortega v. Pujals de Suarez, 465 So. 2d 607, 10 FLW 744 (Fla. App. D3 1985)

5 ALR5th 550—§ 37

5 ALR5th 788—§ 4

Suastez v. Plastic Dress-Up Co., 31 Cal. 3d 774, 183 Cal. Rptr. 846, 647 P.2d 122, 3 EBC 2429, 25 BNA WH Cas. 1040, 94 CCH LC ¶ 55356, 33 A.L.R.4th 254 (1982)

18 ALR5th 577—§ 27

Subaru of America, Matter of, 141 Misc. 2d 41, 532 N.Y.S.2d 617 (Sup. Ct. 1988)

82 ALR5th 501—§ 5, 12

88 ALR5th 301—§ 14

Subaru of America, Inc. v. Peters, 256 Va. 43, 500 S.E.2d 803 (1998)

63 ALR5th 1—§ 5

88 ALR5th 301—§ 13, 20

Subbe-Hirt v. Baccigalupi, 94 F.3d 111, 11 I.E.R. Cas. (BNA) 1793, 132 Lab. Cas. (CCH) ¶ 58187 (3d Cir. 1996)

20 ALR6th 1—§ 4

Subel, Ex parte, 541 So. 2d 15 (Ala. 1989)

105 ALR5th 529—§ 12

Suber v. Bulloch County Bd. of Educ., 722 F. Supp. 736, 56 Ed. Law Rep. 947, 52 Fair Empl. Prac. Cas. (BNA) 735, 5 I.E.R. Cas. (BNA) 1697, 52 Empl. Prac. Dec. (CCH) ¶ 39678 (S.D. Ga. 1989)

7 ALR6th 563—§ 9

Suber v. Chrysler Corp., 104 F.3d 578 (3d Cir. 1997)

82 ALR5th 501—§ 2, 5

88 ALR5th 301—§ 37

Suber v. Fountain, 151 Ga. App. 283, 259 S.E.2d 685 (1979)

14 ALR5th 242—§ 3, 18

Suber v. State, 176 Ga. 525, 168 S.E. 585 (1933)

88 ALR5th 429—§ 3

Sublette v. Board of Education, 664 F. Supp. 265 (W.D. Ky. 1987)

57 ALR5th 477—§ 42

Sublette County Rural Health Care Dist. v. Miley, 942 P.2d 1101 (Wyo. 1997)

5 ALR6th 327—§ 3, 8, 9, 13

8 ALR6th 117—§ 14

Sublimity Ins. Co. v. Shaw, 127 Idaho 707, 905 P.2d 640 (1995)
40 ALR5th 603—§ 9

Subpoena Duces Tecum Served on Willkie Farr & Gallagher, In re, 1997 WL 118369 (S.D. N.Y. 1997)
66 ALR6th 83—§ 7

Subpoena Duces Tecum to America On-line, Inc., In re, 52 Va. Cir. 26, 2000 WL 1210372 (2000)
120 ALR5th 195—§ 3, 6

Subpoena Duces Tecum to Ayala, In re, 162 Misc. 2d 108, 616 N.Y.S.2d 575 (Sup. 1994)
60 ALR5th 75—§ 12 to 14

Subpoenas to News Media Petitioners, In re, 240 Mich. App. 369, 613 N.W.2d 342, 28 Media L. Rep. (BNA) 1662 (2000)
60 ALR5th 75—§ 12

Subramani v. Bruno Machinery Corp., 289 A.D.2d 167, 736 N.Y.S.2d 315 (1st Dep't 2001)
92 ALR5th 227—§ 4
18 ALR6th 629—§ 10

Subramaniam v. Beal, 2013 WL 5462339 (D. Or. 2013)
104 ALR6th 485—§ 3, 5

Subramanian v. Health Foundation Support Services of South Florida, Inc., 732 So. 2d 442 (Fla. Dist. Ct. App. 3d Dist. 1999)
112 ALR5th 47—§ 5

Subuh v. State, 732 So. 2d 40 (Fla. Dist. Ct. App. 2d Dist. 1999)
23 ALR6th 307—§ 36

Suburban Cable TV Co., Inc. v. Com., 131 Pa. Commw. 368, 570 A.2d 601 (1990)
23 ALR6th 165—§ 3, 5, 33, 34

Suburban Hosp., Inc. v. Kirson, 128 Md. App. 533, 739 A.2d 875 (1999)
80 ALR5th 417—§ 4

Suburban Janitorial Services v. Clarke American, 72 Wash. App. 302, 863 P.2d 1377 (Div. 1 1993)
86 ALR6th 321—§ 5, 11
89 ALR6th 409—§ 13

Suburban Propane Gas Corp. v. Papen, 245 A.2d 795 (Del. Sup. 1968)
34 ALR5th 1—§ 3, 5

Suburban Sanitation Service, Inc. v. Millstein, 19 Conn. App. 283, 562 A.2d 551 (1989)
50 ALR5th 417—§ 6

Suburban Trust Co. v. Waller, 44 Md. App. 335, 408 A.2d 758 (1979)
33 ALR5th 453—§ 2

Suburban Video, Inc. v. City of Dela-field, 694 F. Supp. 585 (E.D. Wis. 1988)
20 ALR6th 161—§ 3
21 ALR6th 425—§ 3
23 ALR6th 573—§ 17

Suburbia Gardens Nursery, Inc. v. County of St. Louis, 377 S.W.2d 266 (Mo. 1964)
38 ALR5th 357—§ 4, 17

Subway Restaurants, Inc. v. Kessler, 273 Kan. 969, 46 P.3d 1113 (2002)
86 ALR6th 321—§ 4, 7
91 ALR6th 171—§ 102, 103

Succession of—see name of party

Sucesores de Abarca, Inc., In re, 862 F.2d 394 (1st Cir. 1988)
107 ALR5th 311—§ 3

Such v. Bank of State, 121 F. 202 (CCD N.Y. 1903)
56 ALR5th 1—§ 3

Suchodolski v. Michigan Consol. Gas Co., 412 Mich. 692, 316 N.W.2d 710, 115 BNA LRRM 4449, 99 CCH LC ¶ 55416 (1982)
52 ALR5th 405—§ 4, 5

Suchodolski v. Michigan Consol. Gas Co., 412 Mich. 692, 316 N.W.2d 710, 115 L.R.R.M. (BNA) 4449, 99 Lab. Cas. (CCH) ¶ 55416 (1982)
105 ALR5th 351—§ 3

Suchomajcz v. Hummel Chemical Co., Newark, New Jersey, 524 F.2d 19 (3d Cir. 1975)
21 ALR6th 81—§ 52, 55, 58, 59

Suchomel v. Suburban Life Newspapers, Inc., 40 Ill. 2d 32, 240 N.E.2d 1 (1968)

44 ALR5th 193—§ 21
Suchta v. Robinett, 596 P.2d 1380 (Wyo. 1979)
18 ALR5th 474—§ 9, 10
Suckle v. Madison General Hospital, 362 F. Supp. 1196 (W.D. Wis 1973)
28 ALR5th 107—§ 5, 41
Suckle v. Madison General Hospital, 499 F.2d 1364 (CA7 Wis. 1974)
28 ALR5th 107—§ 13
Sudamax Industria E Comercio De Cigaros, Ltda v. Buttes & Ashes, Inc., 2007 WL 1035144 (W.D. Ky. 2007)
25 ALR6th 435—§ 69
Sudan v. Sudan, 2003 WL 1884208 (Tex. App. Houston 14th Dist. 2003)
110 ALR5th 371—§ 14
Sudan, Republic of v. Rux, 127 S. Ct. 1325, 167 L. Ed. 2d 78 (U.S. 2007)
26 ALR6th 659—§ 36
Suddarth v. Slane, 539 F. Supp. 612 (W.D. Va. 1982)
123 ALR5th 411—§ 7, 8, 53, 57, 59
Sudderth v. White, 621 S.W.2d 33 (Ky. Ct. App. 1981)
94 ALR6th 111—§ 11
Suddith v. University of Southern Mississippi, 2007 WL 2178048 (Miss. Ct. App. 2007)
32 ALR6th 457—§ 7
Sudduth v. Howard, 646 So. 2d 664 (Ala. 1994)
79 ALR5th 587—§ 3, 6, 8
Sudduth v. Mowdy, 991 So. 2d 1241 (Miss. Ct. App. 2008)
99 ALR6th 203—§ 16, 24
Sudduth v. State, Dep't of Transp. & Dev., 619 So. 2d 618 (La. App. 3d Cir. 1993)
10 ALR5th 371—§ 5
Sude v. Commonwealth, Unemployment Compensation Board of Review, 43 Pa. Cmwlth. 533, 402 A.2d 1122 (1979)
33 ALR5th 643—§ 7, 10
Sudeith v. City of St. Paul, 210 Minn. 321, 298 N.W. 46 (1941)

80 ALR5th 417—§ 3
Sudenga Industries, Inc. v. Fulton Performance Products, Inc., 894 F. Supp. 1235, 29 U.C.C. Rep. Serv. 2d (CBC) 140 (N.D. Iowa 1995)
81 ALR5th 483—§ 5
Sudler v. State, 611 A.2d 945 (Del. Sup. 1992)
31 ALR5th 704—§ 6, 18
Sudol v. Rudy Papa Motors, 175 N.J. Super. 238, 417 A.2d 1133, 29 U.C.C.R.S. 1290 (Dist. Ct. 1980)
47 ALR5th 677—§ 2
Sue & Sam Mfg. Co. v. United Protective Alarm Systems, Inc., 119 A.D.2d 664, 501 N.Y.S.2d 102 (2d Dep't 1986)
36 ALR6th 305—§ 20
Sue Davidson, P.C. v. Naranjo, 904 P.2d 354 (Wyo. 1995)
49 ALR5th 595—§ 3
Sue-Haven Farms, Inc. v. Levine, 49 App. Div. 2d 294, 374 N.Y.S.2d 413 (3d Dep't 1975)
60 ALR5th 459—§ 2, 10, 17
Suess v. Lee Sapp Leasing, Inc., 229 Neb. 755, 428 N.W.2d 899, 28 BNA WH Cas. 1629 (1988)
11 ALR5th 715—§ 25, 41
S.U. ex rel. Feldman v. Youth Care of Utah, Inc., 345 F. Supp. 2d 1269 (D. Utah 2004)
88 ALR6th 203—§ 39
Suffield Development Associates Ltd. Partnership v. National Loan Investors, L.P., 97 Conn. App. 541, 905 A.2d 1214 (2006)
70 ALR6th 209—§ 45
Suffolk County Dep't of Social Servs. ex rel. Anthony G. v. Anthony G., 222 App. Div. 2d 593, 636 N.Y.S.2d 636 (2d Dep't 1995)
46 ALR5th 735—§ 2
Suffolk Federal Credit Union v. Cumis Ins. Soc., Inc., 270 F.R.D. 141 (E.D. N.Y. 2010)
104 ALR6th 207—§ 4

Suffolk Housing Services v. Brookhaven, 91 Misc. 2d 80, 397 N.Y.S.2d 302 (1977)
1 ALR5th 622—§ 3

Suffolk Outdoor Advertising Co. v. Southampton, 60 N.Y.2d 70, 468 N.Y.S.2d 450, 455 N.E.2d 1245 (1983)
8 ALR5th 391—§ 3, 5

Suffolk Roadways, Inc. v. Minuse, 56 Misc. 2d 6, 287 N.Y.S.2d 965 (1968)
53 ALR5th 287—§ 3, 4, 7, 10, 11

Sufka v. Barney, 2008 WL 2787715 (D. Minn. 2008)
68 ALR6th 389—§ 3, 8, 15, 17, 21, 22

Suflas v. Cleveland Wrecking Co., 218 F. Supp. 289 (E.D. Pa. 1963)
14 ALR5th 242—§ 4

Sufrin v. Hosier, 896 F. Supp. 766 (N.D. Ill. 1995)
11 ALR6th 587—§ 7, 8

Sugar v. State Through Collector of Revenue, 243 La. 217, 142 So. 2d 401 (1962)
2 ALR6th 1—§ 67

Sugar Creek, City of v. Reese, 969 S.W.2d 888 (Mo. Ct. App. W.D. 1998)
8 ALR5th 391—§ 3

Sugarhouse Realty, Inc., In re, 192 B.R. 355 (E.D. Pa. 1996)
8 ALR5th 312—§ 10

Sugarland Industries, Inc. v. Thomas, 420 A.2d 142 (Del. Sup. 1980)
10 ALR5th 448—§ 3
23 ALR5th 241—§ 21

Sugarloaf Mining Co. Permit No. P-272-M-CO, In re, 310 Ark. 772, 840 S.W.2d 172, 19 U.C.C.R.S.2d 565 (1992)
56 ALR5th 565—§ 47

Sugarloaf Township School Dist. v. Conyngham Borough, 79 Pa. D & C. 36 (1950)
17 ALR5th 195—§ 32, 36, 38

Sugarman v. RCA Corp., 639 F. Supp. 780 (M.D. Pa. 1985)
21 ALR6th 671—§ 5
38 ALR6th 541—§ 9

Sugarman v. State Bar, 51 Cal. 3d 609, 274 Cal. Rptr. 246, 798 P.2d 843 (1990)
9 ALR5th 193—§ 17, 18, 22, 24

Sugarman v. Sugarman, 797 F.2d 3 (1st Cir. 1986)
10 ALR6th 293—§ 6, 9

Sugarman v. Township of Teaneck, 272 N.J. Super. 162, 639 A.2d 402 (App. Div. 1994)
4 ALR6th 263—§ 19

Sugarman v. Village of Chester, 192 F. Supp. 2d 282 (S.D. N.Y. 2002)
51 ALR6th 359—§ 3, 16
53 ALR6th 491—§ 3

Sugg v. Morris, 392 P.2d 313 (Alaska 1964)
69 ALR5th 219—§ 3

Suggs v. Capital Cities/ABC, Inc., 52 BNA FEP Cas. 1842, 54 CCH EPD ¶ 40195 (F. S.D. N.Y.1990)
28 ALR5th 1—§ 20

Suggs v. Norris, 88 N.C. App. 539, 364 S.E.2d 159 (1988)
69 ALR5th 219—§ 7 to 9

Suggs v. State, 87 Md. App. 250, 589 A.2d 551 (1991)
104 ALR5th 357—§ 7, 8
54 ALR6th 429—§ 6, 8, 20, 28

Suggs v. State, 923 So. 2d 419 (Fla. 2005)
21 ALR6th 1—§ 4

Suggs v. State Farm Fire & Casualty Co., 833 F.2d 883, 24 Fed. Rules Evid. Serv. 78, cert den 486 U.S. 1007, 100 L. Ed. 2d 196 (CA10 N.M. 1987)
7 ALR5th 143—§ 5

Suggs v. Veridian Trident, 2002 WL 192859 (Cal. App. 2d Dist. 2002)
17 ALR6th 563—§ 5, 7

Suggs, U.S. ex rel. v. LaVallee, 422 F. Supp. 1042 (S.D.N.Y. 1976)
101 ALR5th 187—§ 7

Sugrue v. Champion, 128 Conn. 574, 24 A.2d 890 (1942)

26 ALR5th 127—§ 11

Sugrue v. Janssen, 713 S.W.2d 44 (Mo. Ct. App. E.D. 1986)

41 ALR6th 1—§ 8

Suhn v. Breg, Inc., 2010 WL 5301043 (D.S.D. 2010)

90 ALR6th 75—§ 16, 24, 44

Suhor v. Gooch, 244 F. 361 (CA4 Va. 1917)

3 ALR5th 394—§ 7, 14

Suhor v. Medina, 421 So2d 271 (La. App. 4 Cir. 1982)

58 ALR5th 613—§ 8

Suhr v. Metcalfe, 33 Cal. App. 59, 164 P. 407 (1917)

4 ALR5th 772—§ 3, 4, 20

Suhre v. Haywood County, 55 F. Supp. 2d 384 (W.D. N.C. 1999)

107 ALR5th 1—§ 3, 8, 10, 18, 21

Suhre v. Jefferson Parish School Bd., 601 So. 2d 718 (La. App. 5th Cir. 1992)

48 ALR5th 129—§ 8

Suhre v. Jefferson Parish School Bd., 601 So. 2d 718 (La. Ct. App. 5th Cir. 1992)

7 ALR6th 1—§ 2, 11, 19

Suid v. Newsweek Magazine, 503 F. Supp. 146, 211 U.S.P.Q. 898 (D.D.C. 1980)

76 ALR6th 289—§ 4

77 ALR6th 543—§ 12

Suing v. Catton, 118 Ill. App. 2d 468, 254 N.E.2d 806 (3d Dist. 1970)

104 ALR5th 331—§ 5

Suire v. Patin's Tire Service, Inc., 251 So. 2d 182 (La. App. 3d Cir. 1971)

27 ALR5th 174—§ 85

Suitor, State ex rel. v. Stremel, 968 S.W.2d 221 (Mo. Ct. App. S.D. 1998)

37 ALR6th 357—§ 21

71 ALR6th 335—§ 11

Suits v. State, 143 Idaho 160, 139 P.3d 762, 43 A.L.R.6th 803 (Ct. App. 2006)

43 ALR6th 475—§ 8

Sukala v. Heritage Mut. Ins. Co., 240 Wis. 2d 65

31 ALR5th 116—§ 3

Sukala v. Heritage Mut. Ins. Co., 2005 WI 83, 282 Wis. 2d 46, 698 N.W.2d 610 (2005)

86 ALR6th 321—§ 4, 13

91 ALR6th 171—§ 3, 45

Sukert v. State, 325 So. 2d 439 (Fla. App. D3 1976)

52 ALR5th 559—§ 4, 13

Sukhu, In re, 107 B.R. 729 (Bankr. N.D. Cal. 1989)

36 ALR6th 387—§ 10

Sukljian v. Charles Ross & Son Co., 69 N.Y.2d 89, 511 N.Y.S.2d 821, 503 N.E.2d 1358, CCH Prod. Liab. Rep. ¶ 11292 (1986)

9 ALR5th 1—§ 8

Sukljian v. Charles Ross & Son Co., 116 App. Div. 2d 9, 499 N.Y.S.2d 466, CCH Prod. Liab. Rep. ¶ 10930 (3d Dep't 1986)

9 ALR5th 1—§ 5, 8, 11, 12

Sukut-Coulson, Inc. v. Allied Canon Co., 85 Cal. App. 3d 648, 149 Cal. Rptr. 711 (2d Dist. 1978)

81 ALR6th 363—§ 4

Sulat v. Board of Review, 176 N.J. Super. 584, 424 A.2d 451 (1980)

33 ALR5th 643—§ 12

Sulecki v. Southeast Nat. Bank, 358 Pa. Super. 132, 516 A.2d 1217 (1986)

12 ALR5th 195—§ 52

14 ALR5th 242—§ 4, 6, 43

Sulesky v. U.S., 545 F. Supp. 426 (S.D. W. Va. 1982)

51 ALR5th 467—§ 16

52 ALR5th 1—§ 8

Sulfuric Acid Antitrust Litigation, In re, 235 F.R.D. 407, 2006-1 Trade Cas. (CCH) ¶ 75315 (N.D. Ill. 2006)

26 ALR6th 287—§ 24, 25

Sulkis v. Zane, 208 Kan. 800, 494 P.2d 1233 (1972)

112 ALR5th 621—§ 8

Sulkow v. Stern, 767 N.Y.S.2d 557 (App. Term 2003)

114 ALR5th 443—§ 4

Sulkow v. Stern, 2003 N.Y. Slip Op. 23745, 2003 WL 22056678 (N.Y. App. Term 2003)

114 ALR5th 443—§ 4

Sulkowska v. City of New York, 129 F. Supp. 2d 274 (S.D. N.Y. 2001)

12 ALR5th 195—§ 5, 7

Sullenger v. Setco Northwest, Inc., 74 Or. App. 345, 702 P.2d 1139 (1985)

51 ALR5th 301—§ 17, 19

Sullenger v. State, 79 Tex. Crim. 98, 182 S.W. 1140 (1916)

117 ALR5th 1—§ 4

Sullens v. Carroll, 446 F.2d 1392 (CA5 Fla. 1971)

4 ALR5th 273—§ 6

Sullinger, In re Marriage of, 2002 WL 31794153 (Cal. App. 4th Dist. 2002)

77 ALR6th 293—§ 33, 51, 59

Sullins v. Allstate Ins. Co., 340 Md. 503, 667 A.2d 617 (1995)

48 ALR5th 355—§ 2

Sullins v. American Medical Response of Oklahoma, Inc., 2001 OK 20, 23 P.3d 259 (Okla. 2001)

69 ALR6th 415—§ 43

Sullins v. Third & Catalina Constr. Partnership, 124 Ariz. 114, 602 P.2d 495 (App. 1979)

15 ALR5th 119—§ 5, 32, 35

Sullivan, In re, 43 A.D.3d 1270, 843 N.Y.S.2d 693 (3d Dep't 2007)

45 ALR6th 175—§ 24

Sullivan, In re, 64 S.D. 165, 265 N.W. 601 (1936)

40 ALR6th 463—§ 26

Sullivan, In re, 83 B.R. 623 (BC S.D. Iowa 1988)

52 ALR5th 221—§ 12, 13

Sullivan, In re, 103 B.R. 792, 9 U.C.C. Rep. Serv. 2d 552 (Bankr. N.D. Miss. 1989)

58 ALR6th 289—§ 6

Sullivan, In re, 143 Cal. 462, 77 P. 153 (1904)

84 ALR5th 399—§ 3, 5, 14

Sullivan, In re, 494 S.W.2d 329 (Mo. 1973)

25 ALR6th 1—§ 6

Sullivan, In re, 694 N.Y.S.2d 529 (App. Div. 3d Dep't 1999)

9 ALR5th 193—§ 7

Sullivan, In re Marriage of, 37 Cal. 3d 762, 209 Cal. Rptr. 354, 691 P.2d 1020 (1984)

4 ALR5th 403—§ 2, 3, 5

Sullivan, In re Marriage of, 134 Cal. App. 3d 634, 184 Cal. Rptr. 796 (4th Dist. 1982)

4 ALR5th 403—§ 3, 5

Sullivan, Matter of, 192 A.D.2d 866, 596 N.Y.S.2d 567 (3d Dep't 1993)

43 ALR6th 163—§ 53

Sullivan, Matter of, 678 N.Y.S.2d 169 (App. Div. 3d Dep't 1998)

9 ALR5th 193—§ 5

Sullivan v. Abraham & Straus, Inc., 75 N.Y.S.2d 221 (App. Term 1947)

63 ALR6th 495—§ 75

Sullivan v. Ajax Navigation Corp., 881 F. Supp. 906, 1995 A.M.C. 2407 (S.D. N.Y. 1995)

82 ALR6th 175—§ 25

Sullivan v. Allegheny Ford Truck Sales, Inc., 283 Pa. Super. 351, 423 A.2d 1292 (1980)

47 ALR5th 677—§ 5, 11, 18

Sullivan v. Analysis & Technology, Inc., 2000 WL 1825395 (Conn. Super. Ct. 2000)

105 ALR5th 351—§ 3, 9, 12

Sullivan v. Askew, 348 So. 2d 312 (Fla. 1977)

101 ALR6th 431—§ 3

Sullivan v. Aslanides, 374 N.J. Super. 68, 863 A.2d 409 (App. Div. 2005)

15 ALR6th 427—§ 27

Sullivan v. Barra, 22 Cal. App. 2d 20, 70 P.2d 495 (1937)

27 ALR5th 174—§ 63

Sullivan v. Barrett, 510 So. 2d 982 (Fla. Dist. Ct. App. 4th Dist. 1987)
16 ALR6th 1—§ 28

Sullivan v. Birmingham Fire Ins. Co., 185 So. 2d 336 (La. App. 4th Cir. 1966)
8 ALR5th 1—§ 18, 29, 33, 46

Sullivan v. Board of Com'rs of Oak Lawn Park Dist., 318 Ill. App. 3d 1067, 252 Ill. Dec. 901, 743 N.E.2d 1057, 1 A.L.R.6th 757 (1st Dist. 2001)
1 ALR6th 229—§ 7, 16, 33

Sullivan v. Bonafonte, 172 Conn. 612, 376 A.2d 69 (1977)
58 ALR5th 669—§ 4, 11

Sullivan v. Bond, 91 App. D.C. 99, 198 F.2d 529 (1952)
3 ALR5th 590—§ 17

Sullivan v. Boston Gas Co., 414 Mass. 129, 605 N.E.2d 805 (1993)
96 ALR5th 107—§ 6

Sullivan v. Carberry, 67 Me. 531, 1877 WL 4160 (1877)
109 ALR5th 421—§ 3

Sullivan v. Central Bank of the South, 601 So. 2d 985 (Ala. 1992)
86 ALR5th 527—§ 13

Sullivan v. City of Augusta, 511 F.3d 16 (1st Cir. 2007)
46 ALR6th 495—§ 37
70 ALR6th 513—§ 12
71 ALR6th 471—§ 6

Sullivan v. City of Augusta, Me., 129 S. Ct. 112, 172 L. Ed. 2d 35 (2008)
46 ALR6th 495—§ 37

Sullivan v. Cloud, 62 Ohio App. 462, 16 Ohio Ops. 152, 30 Ohio L. Abs. 266, 24 N.E.2d 625 (Hamilton Co. 1939)
5 ALR5th 422—§ 7

Sullivan v. Commissioner of Public Safety, 1995 WL 479570 (Minn. Ct. App. 1995)
69 ALR6th 579—§ 8, 23

Sullivan v. Commonwealth, 93 Pa. 284 (1880)
11 ALR5th 497—§ 6

Sullivan v. Commonwealth Edison Co., 115 Ill. App. 3d 560, 71 Ill. Dec. 312, 450 N.E.2d 1191 (1st Dist. 1983)
58 ALR5th 187—§ 2, 28, 54

Sullivan v. Conway, 157 F.3d 1092, 160 L.R.R.M. (BNA) 2080, 136 Lab. Cas. (CCH) ¶ 10253 (7th Cir. 1998)
52 ALR6th 271—§ 11

Sullivan v. Conway, 959 F. Supp. 877, 155 L.R.R.M. (BNA) 2099 (N.D. Ill. 1997)
105 ALR5th 351—§ 3

Sullivan v. CUNA Mut. Ins. Society, 649 F.3d 553 (7th Cir. 2011)
74 ALR6th 267—§ 8

Sullivan v. Daily Mirror, 232 A.D. 507, 250 N.Y.S. 420 (1st Dep't 1931)
52 ALR6th 271—§ 6

Sullivan v. Davis, 454 S.E.2d 907 (S.C. App. 1995)
5 ALR5th 875—§ 23, 32

Sullivan v. Delaware & H. Canal Co., 72 Vt. 353, 47 A. 1084 (1900)
10 ALR5th 371—§ 11

Sullivan v. Demas, 124 Vt. 397, 205 A.2d 818 (1964)
107 ALR5th 311—§ 4

Sullivan v. DeRamcy, 2010 WL 2331181 (E.D. Tex. 2010)
89 ALR6th 1—§ 55

Sullivan v. Doe, 159 Mont. 50, 495 P.2d 193 (1972)
31 ALR5th 116—§ 5

Sullivan v. Easco Corp., 662 F. Supp. 1396, 8 EBC 2108 (D.C. Md. 1987)
23 ALR5th 241—§ 2, 42

Sullivan v. First Presbyterian Church, 260 Iowa 1373, 152 N.W.2d 628 (1967)
8 ALR5th 1—§ 6, 11, 47

Sullivan v. Ford Motor Co., Prod. Liab. Rep. (CCH) ¶ 15789, 2000 WL 343777 (S.D. N.Y. 2000)
89 ALR5th 255—§ 5
90 ALR5th 179—§ 3
98 ALR5th 609—§ 5 to 7

For assistance, call 1-800-328-4880

Sullivan v. Fox, 189 Cal. App. 3d 673, 235 Cal. Rptr. 5 (1st Dist. 1987)

66 ALR5th 135—§ 32

Sullivan v. Grasso, 292 F. Supp. 411 (D. Conn. 1968)

75 ALR6th 311—§ 29

Sullivan v. Griffin Health Services Corp., 2 Conn. L. Rptr. 510, 135 L.R.R.M. (BNA) 2665, 1990 WL 283704 (Conn. Super. Ct. 1990)

120 ALR5th 351—§ 17

Sullivan v. Henry, 160 Ga. App. 791, 287 S.E.2d 652 (1982)

93 ALR6th 123—§ 75

Sullivan v. H. P. Hood & Sons, Inc., 341 Mass. 216, 168 N.E.2d 80 (1960)

50 ALR5th 327—§ 3

Sullivan v. Hurley, 167 Misc. 2d 534, 635 N.Y.S.2d 437 (Sup. 1995)

60 ALR5th 75—§ 12, 13

Sullivan v. I.N.S., 772 F.2d 609 (9th Cir. 1985)

8 ALR6th 339—§ 18

Sullivan v. Invacare Corp., 23 Misc. 3d 1136(A), 889 N.Y.S.2d 884 (Sup 2009)

54 ALR6th 619—§ 28

Sullivan v. Joy Mfg. Co., 70 N.Y.2d 806, 523 N.Y.S.2d 427, 517 N.E.2d 1313 (1987)

92 ALR5th 227—§ 7

Sullivan v. Knick, 38 Va. App. 773, 568 S.E.2d 430 (2002)

96 ALR6th 103—§ 5

Sullivan v. Kuykendall, 82 Ky. 483, 6 Ky. L. Rptr. 481, 1885 WL 5740 (1885)

97 ALR6th 567—§ 3, 11

Sullivan v. Laman, 150 Colo. 542, 375 P.2d 92 (1962)

21 ALR5th 82—§ 4

Sullivan v. Lockhart, 958 F.2d 823 (8th Cir. 1992)

12 ALR6th 267—§ 5

Sullivan v. Manhattan Market Co., 251 Mass. 395, 146 N.E. 673 (1925)

1 ALR5th 1—§ 3

Sullivan v. Massachusetts Mut. Life Ins. Co., 802 F. Supp. 716, 7 BNA IER Cas. 1414, CCH Fed Secur L. Rep. ¶ 97299 (D.C. Conn. 1992)

52 ALR5th 405—§ 4, 13

Sullivan v. Massachusetts Mut. Life Ins. Co., 802 F. Supp. 716, 7 I.E.R. Cas. (BNA) 1414, Fed. Sec. L. Rep. (CCH) ¶ 97299 (D. Conn. 1992)

104 ALR5th 1—§ 4

105 ALR5th 351—§ 3, 4, 6, 11

Sullivan v. Matt, 130 Cal. App. 2d 134, 278 P.2d 499 (2d Dist. 1955)

12 ALR5th 195—§ 3, 12

Sullivan v. McCallum, 231 So. 2d 801 (Miss. 1970)

25 ALR5th 233—§ 3

Sullivan v. McGaw, 134 Ill. App. 3d 455, 89 Ill. Dec. 540, 480 N.E.2d 1283 (2d Dist. 1985)

40 ALR5th 697—§ 22

Sullivan v. Meade Independent School Dist. No. 101, 530 F.2d 799 (8th Cir. 1976)

123 ALR5th 411—§ 39, 40

Sullivan v. Methodist Hospitals of Dallas, 699 S.W.2d 265, 76 A.L.R.4th 1112 (Tex. App. Corpus Christi 1985)

6 ALR5th 534—§ 4, 7

Sullivan v. Michigan Dept. of Corrections, 2008 WL 5411657 (E.D. Mich. 2008)

89 ALR6th 1—§ 77

Sullivan v. Mitchell, 750 So. 2d 1173 (La. Ct. App. 5th Cir. 2000)

5 ALR5th 788—§ 22

20 ALR5th 700—§ 7

Sullivan v. Morrow, 504 S.W.2d 767 (Tenn. App. 1973)

12 ALR5th 195—§ 12

Sullivan v. Municipal Court of Roxbury Dist., 322 Mass. 566, 78 N.E.2d 618 (1948)

19 ALR6th 217—§ 55

Sullivan v. Municipality of Anchorage, 577 P.2d 1070 (Alaska 1978)

76 ALR5th 1—§ 22

Sullivan v. Naturalis, Inc., 5 F.3d 1410, 28 U.S.P.Q.2d 1618 (11th Cir. 1993)

76 ALR6th 289—§ 6

Sullivan v. Owens, 2011 WL 2409311 (Tex. App. Eastland 2011)

85 ALR6th 229—§ 20

Sullivan v. Paycor, Inc., 2013 WL 2286069 (W.D. Ky. 2013)

92 ALR6th 121—§ 4

Sullivan v. Price, 368 So. 2d 614 (Fla. App. D1 1979)

20 ALR5th 1—§ 43, 60

Sullivan v. Price, 386 So. 2d 241 (Fla. 1980)

20 ALR5th 1—§ 5, 43, 52

Sullivan v. Quick, 465 So. 2d 254 (La. App. 3d Cir. 1985)

50 ALR5th 1—§ 7, 9

Sullivan v. R.E. Bean Constr. Co., 147 Vt. 310, 515 A.2d 1063 (1986)

16 ALR5th 548—§ 13

Sullivan v. Regan, 206 A.D.2d 788, 615 N.Y.S.2d 117 (3d Dep't 1994)

57 ALR6th 445—§ 39

Sullivan v. Reilly, 12 Mass. L. Rptr. 184, 2000 WL 776414 (Mass. Super. Ct. 2000)

19 ALR6th 335—§ 4

Sullivan v. Rilling, 1994 WL 684767 (N.D. Ill. 1994)

79 ALR5th 587—§ 5 to 8

Sullivan v. Ringland, 117 N.H. 596, 376 A.2d 130 (1977)

85 ALR6th 429—§ 4

Sullivan v. Rooney, 404 Mass. 160, 533 N.E.2d 1372 (1989)

69 ALR5th 219—§ 3

Sullivan v. Rowan Companies, Inc., 952 F.2d 141, Prod. Liab. Rep. (CCH) ¶ 13036, 34 Fed. R. Evid. Serv. 1161 (5th Cir. 1992)

93 ALR5th 103—§ 26

Sullivan v. Sapp, 866 So. 2d 28 (Fla. 2004)

86 ALR6th 1—§ 8

Sullivan v. Securities Inv. Co. of St. Louis, 1972 OK 43, 508 P.2d 1077 (Okla. 1972)

73 ALR6th 571—§ 55, 59

Sullivan v. Shaw, 6 F. Supp. 112 (S.D. Cal. 1934)

80 ALR5th 255—§ 3, 39, 43

Sullivan v. Sirop, 74 A.D.3d 1326, 905 N.Y.S.2d 240 (2d Dep't 2010)

64 ALR6th 249—§ 20

Sullivan v. State, 132 Md. App. 682, 753 A.2d 601 (2000)

50 ALR5th 581—§ 8, 18.5

Sullivan v. State, 213 Miss. 14, 56 So. 2d 93 (1952)

54 ALR6th 429—§ 9

Sullivan v. State, 572 S.W.2d 778 (Tex. Civ. App. El Paso 1978)

10 ALR5th 139—§ 2, 6, 9

Sullivan v. State, 585 N.W.2d 782 (Minn. 1998)

29 ALR6th 1—§ 10

Sullivan v. State, 636 A.2d 931 (Del. 1994)

79 ALR5th 33—§ 57, 72

Sullivan v. State, 651 So. 2d 1138 (Ala. Crim. App. 1994)

112 ALR5th 429—§ 13

Sullivan v. State, 716 P.2d 684 (Okla. Crim. App. 1986)

65 ALR5th 407—§ 3, 16

Sullivan v. State, 742 So. 2d 202 (Ala. Crim. App. 1999)

37 ALR5th 319—§ 10

82 ALR5th 359—§ 3

84 ALR5th 487—§ 3

Sullivan v. State, 1986 OK CR 39, 716 P.2d 684 (Okla. Crim. App. 1986)

99 ALR6th 397—§ 15

Sullivan v. State of Ala., 666 F.2d 478 (11th Cir. 1982)

29 ALR6th 1—§ 10

Sullivan v. State of N.J., Div. of Gaming Enforcement, 602 F. Supp. 1216 (D.N.J. 1985)

95 ALR6th 341—§ 64

Sullivan v. Sullivan, 87 App. Div. 2d 42, 451 N.Y.S.2d 851 (3d Dep't 1982)

5 ALR5th 550—§ 17

Sullivan v. Sullivan, 98 Ill. App. 3d 928, 54 Ill. Dec. 207, 424 N.E.2d 957 (3d Dist. 1981)

36 ALR5th 527—§ 3

Sullivan v. Sullivan, 141 Conn. 235, 104 A.2d 898 (1954)

124 ALR5th 203—§ 10

Sullivan v. Sullivan, 159 S.W.3d 529 (Mo. Ct. App. W.D. 2005)

3 ALR6th 447—§ 6

Sullivan v. Sullivan, 175 Mich. App. 508, 438 N.W.2d 309 (1989)

3 ALR6th 447—§ 6, 22

Sullivan v. Sullivan, 223 Neb. 273, 388 N.W.2d 516 (1986)

38 ALR6th 313—§ 11

Sullivan v. Sullivan, 736 So. 2d 103 (Fla. Dist. Ct. App. 4th Dist. 1999)

20 ALR5th 534—§ 10

53 ALR5th 375—§ 20

Sullivan v. Sullivan, 2004 UT App 485, 105 P.3d 963 (Utah Ct. App. 2004)

57 ALR6th 163—§ 40

Sullivan v. Syracuse, 77 Hun. 440, 29 N.Y.S. 105 (1894)

57 ALR5th 689—§ 17

Sullivan v. Texas Dept. of Public Safety, 93 S.W.3d 149 (Tex. App. Beaumont 2002)

91 ALR6th 435—§ 58

Sullivan v. Thomas Organization, P.C., 88 Mich. App. 77, 276 N.W.2d 522 (1979)

31 ALR5th 664—§ 8

Sullivan v. Thompson, 30 Cal. App. 2d 675, 87 P.2d 62 (1939)

27 ALR5th 174—§ 3, 4, 39

Sullivan v. Town of Acton, 38 Mass. App. Ct. 113, 645 N.E.2d 700 (1995)

73 ALR5th 223—§ 2, 5, 13

Sullivan v. U.S., 428 F. Supp. 79, 22 Fair Empl. Prac. Cas. (BNA) 1137 (E.D. Wis. 1977)

82 ALR5th 149—§ 3, 64

97 ALR5th 1—§ 3

108 ALR5th 1—§ 19

Sullivan v. Valley City Park Dist., 1997 WL 33135312 (D.N.D. 1997)

28 ALR6th 175—§ 12

Sullivan v. Wickwire, 476 N.W.2d 69 (Iowa 1991)

57 ALR6th 355—§ 10, 11

Sullivan v. Woods, 5 Ariz. 196, 50 P. 113 (1897)

5 ALR5th 422—§ 3, 4

Sullivan v. Worley Companies, 2012-95 La. App. 1 Cir. 12/21/12, 2012 WL 6677786 (La. Ct. App. 1st Cir. 2012)

102 ALR6th 1—§ 54 to 57, 61, 63

Sullivan v. Worley Companies Worley Catastrophe Services, L.L.C., 2012-1140 La. App. 1 Cir. 12/21/12, 2012 WL 6681799 (La. Ct. App. 1st Cir. 2012)

102 ALR6th 1—§ 15

Sullivan v. Young Bros. & Co., Inc., 91 F.3d 242, Prod. Liab. Rep. (CCH) ¶ 14703, 35 Fed. R. Serv. 3d 5, 30 U.C.C. Rep. Serv. 2d 121 (1st Cir. 1996)

50 ALR5th 327—§ 7, 10

89 ALR5th 319—§ 25

Sullivan v. Zimmer, Inc., 2007 WL 1342559 (D. Neb. 2007)

89 ALR6th 337—§ 5

Sullivan v. Zoning Bd. of Adjustment, 83 Pa. Cmwlth. 228, 478 A.2d 912 (1984)

8 ALR5th 391—§ 3

Sullivan & Langston Co. v. Richardson, 169 Ill. App. 578 (1912)

46 ALR5th 1—§ 45

Sullivan County v. Edward L. Nezelek Inc., 42 N.Y.2d 123, 397 N.Y.S.2d 371, 366 N.E.2d 72 (1977)

31 ALR6th 433—§ 7, 9

Sullivan, County of v. State, 137 App. Div. 2d 165, 528 N.Y.S.2d 227 (3d Dep't 1988)

11 ALR5th 630—§ 8

Sullivan Industries, Inc. v. Double Seal Glass Co., 192 Mich. App. 333, 480 N.W.2d 623, CCH Prod. Liab. Rep. ¶ 13141, 17 U.C.C.R.S.2d 61 (1991)
43 ALR5th 545—§ 40

Sullivan, People ex rel. v. Waldo, 159 A.D. 303, 144 N.Y.S. 250 (2d Dep't 1913)
19 ALR6th 217—§ 29

Sullivan's Wholesale Drug Co., Inc. v. Faryl's Pharmacy, Inc., 214 Ill. App. 3d 1073, 158 Ill. Dec. 185, 573 N.E.2d 1370 (5th Dist. 1991)
63 ALR5th 1—§ 14
117 ALR5th 155—§ 12

Sullo v. Cinco Star, Inc., 755 So. 2d 822 (Fla. Dist. Ct. App. 5th Dist. 2000)
48 ALR5th 473—§ 18

Sulls v. Director of Revenue, 819 S.W.2d 782 (Mo. App. 1991)
23 ALR5th 108—§ 3

Sulpho-Saline Bath Co. v. Allen, 66 Neb. 295, 92 N.W. 354 (1902)
54 ALR5th 393—§ 3, 6

Sulser v. Country Mut. Ins. Co., 147 Ill. 2d 548, 169 Ill. Dec. 254, 591 N.E.2d 427 (1992)
31 ALR5th 116—§ 3

Sultan v. Safeco Surplus Lines Ins., 444 Fed. Appx. 376 (11th Cir. 2011)
96 ALR6th 125—§ 22

Suluki v. State, 302 Ga. App. 735, 691 S.E.2d 626 (2010)
72 ALR6th 1—§ 5

Sulzer Hip Prosthesis and Knee Prosthesis Liability Litigation, In re, 455 F. Supp. 2d 709 (N.D. Ohio 2006)
23 ALR6th 223—§ 3

Suman v. Superior Court, 39 Cal. App. 4th 1309, 46 Cal. Rptr. 2d 507 (2d Dist. 1995)
88 ALR5th 301—§ 4

Sumdum v. State, 612 P.2d 1018 (Alaska 1980)
61 ALR5th 1—§ 4, 5

Sumerell, In re, 194 B.R. 818 (Bankr. E.D. Tenn. 1996)
46 ALR6th 401—§ 8

Sumerlin v. Cox, 344 S.W.2d 742 (Tex. Civ. App. Eastland 1961)
1 ALR6th 135—§ 7, 38

Sumida v. Pacific Auto. Ins. Co., 51 Cal. App. 2d 472, 125 P.2d 87 (1942)
57 ALR5th 591—§ 5

Sumien v. CareFlite, 34 I.E.R. Cas. (BNA) 77, 2012 WL 2579525 (Tex. App. Fort Worth 2012)
103 ALR6th 19—§ 4

Summa Four, Inc. v. AT & T Wireless Services, Inc., 994 F. Supp. 575 (D. Del. 1998)
85 ALR6th 1—§ 57

Summe v. Judicial Retirement and Removal Com'n, 947 S.W.2d 42 (Ky. 1997)
51 ALR6th 359—§ 26

Summer v. Board of Corrections of State of Idaho, 2005 WL 1458738 (D. Idaho 2005)
63 ALR6th 1—§ 33

Summer v. Land & Leisure, Inc., 571 F. Supp. 380, CCH Fed Secur L. Rep. ¶ 99489 (S.D. Fla. 1983)
7 ALR5th 852—§ 37

Summer Communications, Inc. v. Three A's Holding, LLC, 175 F.3d 1008 (2d Cir. 1999)
44 ALR6th 441—§ 8

Summerfield v. Pringle, 65 Idaho 300, 144 P.2d 214 (1943)
12 ALR5th 195—§ 43

Summerfield v. Superior Court, 144 Ariz. 467, 698 P.2d 712 (1985)
43 ALR5th 87—§ 14

Summerhill v. State, 436 So. 2d 2 (Ala. App. 1983)
7 ALR5th 263—§ 5, 7

Summerlin v. Johnson, 176 Ga. App. 336, 335 S.E.2d 879 (1985)
6 ALR5th 242—§ 10, 22

Summerlin v. Schriro, 427 F.3d 623 (9th Cir. 2005)
102 ALR6th 417—§ 7

Summerlin v. State, 7 Ark. App. 10, 643 S.W.2d 582 (1982)
24 ALR6th 747—§ 39

Summerlin v. State, 296 Ark. 347, 756 S.W.2d 908 (1988)

39 ALR5th 283—§ 4, 66

Summerlin v. State, 607 S.W.2d 495 (Tenn. Crim. App. 1980)

31 ALR6th 49—§ 4

Summerour v. Cartrett, 220 Ga. 31, 136 S.E.2d 724 (1964)

10 ALR5th 139—§ 6, 12

Summers, In re, 987 P.2d 153 (Wyo. 1999)

97 ALR5th 1—§ 2, 4, 14
106 ALR5th 111—§ 2, 34
108 ALR5th 1—§ 2, 29

Summers v. Alliance Mut. Casualty Co., 210 Kan. 57, 499 P.2d 1067 (1972)

9 ALR5th 826—§ 9

Summers v. Bransford-Hinds Bldg. Co., 383 S.W.2d 947 (Tex. Civ. App. Eastland 1964)

33 ALR5th 1—§ 17

Summers v. Burdick, 191 Cal. App. 2d 464, 13 Cal. Rptr. 68 (1st Dist. 1961)

111 ALR5th 1—§ 4, 10

Summers v. City of Raymond, Miss., 105 F. Supp. 2d 549 (S.D. Miss. 2000)

86 ALR6th 173—§ 6

Summers v. City of Rochester, 60 A.D.3d 1271, 875 N.Y.S.2d 658 (4th Dep't 2009)

43 ALR6th 611—§ 55

Summers v. Dretke, 431 F.3d 861 (5th Cir. 2005)

22 ALR6th 19—§ 7

Summers v. Gatson, 205 W. Va. 198, 517 S.E.2d 295 (1999)

18 ALR6th 195—§ 33
57 ALR6th 445—§ 6

Summers v. Giant Food Stores, Inc., 1999 PA Super 314, 743 A.2d 498 (Pa. Super. Ct. 1999)

44 ALR5th 525—§ 5

Summers v. Grant Park Baptist Church, 243 Or. 362, 413 P.2d 611 (1966)

8 ALR5th 1—§ 17, 29, 38

Summers v. Hallam Cooley Enterprises, 56 Cal. App. 2d 112, 132 P.2d 60 (4th Dist. 1942)

36 ALR6th 387—§ 10

Summers v. Harrison Constr., 298 S.C. 451, 381 S.E.2d 493 (App. 1989)

24 ALR5th 200—§ 24, 28

Summers v. Keller, 152 Mo. App. 626, 133 S.W. 1180 (1911)

14 ALR5th 242—§ 24

Summers v. Middleton & Rutlinger, P.S.C., 214 F. Supp. 2d 751, 82 Empl. Prac. Dec. (CCH) ¶ 41118, 146 Lab. Cas. (CCH) ¶ 34547 (W.D. Ky. 2002)

102 ALR5th 1—§ 3.5, 5, 7

Summers v. Milwaukie Union High School Dist. No. 5, Clackamas County, 4 Or. App. 596, 481 P.2d 369 (1971)

66 ALR5th 1—§ 16

Summers v. Montgomery Elevator Co., 243 Kan. 393, 757 P.2d 1255 (1988)

117 ALR5th 267—§ 3

Summers v. Northern Illinois Gas Co., 117 Ill. App. 2d 125, 253 N.E.2d 881 (1st Dist. 1969)

34 ALR5th 1—§ 4, 6

Summers v. PennyMac Corp., 2012 WL 5944943 (N.D. Tex. 2012)

86 ALR6th 411—§ 5

Summers v. Quarterman, 127 S. Ct. 353 (U.S. 2006)

22 ALR6th 19—§ 7

Summers v. Sears, Roebuck & Co., 549 F. Supp. 1157, 33 BNA FEP Cas. 508, 115 BNA LRRM 4812, 30 CCH EPD ¶ 33148, 117 CCH LC ¶ 56480 (E.D. Mich. 1982)

17 ALR5th 1—§ 4

Summers v. Slivinsky, 141 Ohio App. 3d 82, 749 N.E.2d 854 (7th Dist. Jefferson County 2001)

25 ALR5th 784—§ 3

Summers v. State, 33 Ala. App. 358, 36 So. 2d 571 (1947)

87 ALR5th 181—§ 4

Summers v. State, 41 Md. App. 489, 397 A.2d 286 (1979)

45 ALR5th 591—§ 2, 15

Summers v. State, 148 P.3d 778 (Nev. 2006)

30 ALR6th 1—§ 4

Summers v. State, 263 Ga. App. 338, 587 S.E.2d 768 (2003)

125 ALR5th 537—§ 2, 20

Summers v. State, 726 S.W.2d 479 (Mo. Ct. App. S.D. 1987)

117 ALR5th 513—§ 5

Summers v. State, 845 S.W.2d 440 (Tex. App. Eastland 1992)

42 ALR5th 291—§ 25

Summers v. State, 1999 WL 173977 (Tenn. Crim. App. 1999)

70 ALR5th 1—§ 5

Summers v. State Farm Mut. Auto. Ins. Co., 864 F.2d 700 (CA10 Utah 1988)

34 ALR5th 699—§ 2, 3

Summers v. Tarpley, 208 S.W. 266 (Mo. Ct. App. 1919)

108 ALR5th 385—§ 8

Summers v. Texas, 519 U.S. 826, 117 S. Ct. 89, 136 L. Ed. 2d 45 (1996)

22 ALR6th 19—§ 7

Summers v. Texas Dept. of Criminal Justice, 2006 WL 3040948 (5th Cir. 2006)

22 ALR6th 19—§ 7

Summers v. Tice, 33 Cal. 2d 80, 199 P.2d 1, 5 A.L.R.2d 91 (1948)

63 ALR5th 195—§ 2, 3, 7

Summers v. Union Electric Co., 565 S.W.2d 677 (Mo. App. 1978)

46 ALR5th 423—§ 3, 16, 19, 20

Summers v. U.S., 11 F.2d 583 (CA4 Va. 1926)

14 ALR5th 89—§ 6, 20

Summers v. Welltech, Inc., 935 S.W.2d 228, CCH Blue Sky L. Rep. ¶ 74137 (Tex. App. Houston (1st Dist.) 1996)

52 ALR5th 491—§ 5

Summers ex rel. Dawson v. St. Andrew's Episcopal School, Inc., 759 So. 2d 1203, 145 Ed. Law Rep. 830 (Miss. 2000)

86 ALR5th 1—§ 15
96 ALR5th 107—§ 8
99 ALR5th 301—§ 13

Summers Hardware & Supply Co. v. Steele, 794 S.W.2d 358 (Tenn. App. 1990)

59 ALR5th 733—§ 3

Summers-Horton v. Horton, 1989 WL 29421 (Ohio Ct. App. 10th Dist. Franklin County 1989)

80 ALR5th 487—§ 3, 10

Summer T., In re, 2002 WL 31547030 (Cal. App. 2d Dist. 2002)

53 ALR6th 419—§ 41, 49

Summerville v. City of New York, 257 A.D.2d 566, 683 N.Y.S.2d 579 (2d Dep't 1999)

36 ALR5th 1—§ 7

Summerville v. Lipsig, 270 A.D.2d 213, 704 N.Y.S.2d 598 (1st Dep't 2000)

9 ALR6th 285—§ 15, 16

Summerville v. State Highway Com., 139 Kan. 530, 32 P.2d 224 (1934)

1 ALR5th 163—§ 2, 24

Summerville v. Warden, State Prison, 229 Conn. 397, 641 A.2d 1356 (1994)

97 ALR6th 263—§ 13

Summey v. Lacy, 42 Colo. App. 1, 588 P.2d 892 (1978)

6 ALR5th 883—§ 7

Summit Associates, Inc. v. Liberty Mut. Fire Ins. Co., 229 N.J. Super. 56, 550 A.2d 1235 (App. Div. 1988)

88 ALR5th 493—§ 6
89 ALR5th 1—§ 14

Summit Bank v. Panos, 570 N.E.2d 960 (Ind. Ct. App. 4th Dist. 1991)

81 ALR5th 167—§ 8

Summit Lodging, LLC v. Jones, Spitz, Moorhead, Baird & Albergotti, P.A., 176 N.C. App. 697, 627 S.E.2d 259 (2006)

78 ALR6th 151—§ 28

Summit Ltd. v. Levy, 111 F.R.D. 40 (S.D. N.Y. 1986)

66 ALR6th 83—§ 7

Summit Medical Associates, P.C. v. James, 984 F. Supp. 1404 (M.D. Ala. 1998)

76 ALR5th 637—§ 4, 5

77 ALR5th 1—§ 12

5 ALR6th 423—§ 7

Summit Medical Associates, P.C. v. Pryor, 180 F.3d 1326 (11th Cir. 1999)

76 ALR5th 637—§ 4, 6

Summit Medical Associates, P.C. v. Siegelman, 130 F. Supp. 2d 1307 (M.D. Ala. 2001)

76 ALR5th 637—§ 4

Summit Medical Center of Alabama, Inc. v. Riley, 274 F. Supp. 2d 1262 (M.D. Ala. 2003)

73 ALR6th 281—§ 10

Summit Medical Center of Alabama, Inc. v. Riley, 274 F. Supp. 2d 1262, 2003 WL 21757343 (M.D. Ala. 2003)

119 ALR5th 315—§ 4

Summit Medical Center of Alabama, Inc. v. Riley, 284 F. Supp. 2d 1350 (M.D. Ala. 2003)

119 ALR5th 315—§ 4

Summit Medical Center of Alabama, Inc. v. Riley, 318 F. Supp. 2d 1109 (M.D. Ala. 2003)

119 ALR5th 315—§ 7

Summit Medical Center of Alabama, Inc. v. Siegelman, 227 F. Supp. 2d 1194, 119 A.L.R.5th 747 (M.D. Ala. 2002)

119 ALR5th 315—§ 3, 5, 8, 9

Summit Pool Supplies, Inc. v. Price, 461 So. 2d 272, 10 FLW 11 (Fla. App. D5 1985)

8 ALR5th 653—§ 3

Summit Properties, Inc. v. Public Service Co. of New Mexico, 138 N.M. 208, 2005-NMCA-090, 118 P.3d 716 (Ct. App. 2005)

104 ALR6th 303—§ 17

Summit Staffing Polk County, Inc., In re, 305 B.R. 347 (Bankr. M.D. Fla. 2003)

28 ALR6th 461—§ 6

Summitt by Boyd v. Roberts, 903 S.W.2d 631, 102 Ed. Law Rep. 883 (Mo. Ct. App. W.D. 1995)

72 ALR5th 469—§ 2

Summit Tp. Taxpayers Ass'n v. Summit Tp. Bd. of Sup'rs, 49 Pa. Commw. 459, 411 A.2d 1263 (1980)

47 ALR6th 439—§ 10

Summit Trust Services, Inc. v. Snyder, 936 P.2d 623 (Colo. App. 1997)

100 ALR6th 281—§ 28

Summitville Tiles, Inc. v. Jackson, 1988 WL 122836 (Ohio Ct. App. 7th Dist. Columbiana County 1988)

110 ALR5th 111—§ 8

Summum v. Callaghan, 130 F.3d 906 (10th Cir. 1997)

107 ALR5th 1—§ 3, 8, 16

70 ALR6th 513—§ 10

71 ALR6th 471—§ 6

Summum v. City of Ogden, 297 F.3d 995 (10th Cir. 2002)

107 ALR5th 1—§ 4, 5, 16, 21

70 ALR6th 513—§ 10

71 ALR6th 471—§ 8

Summum v. Duchesne City, 482 F.3d 1263 (10th Cir. 2007)

46 ALR6th 495—§ 10

Summum v. Pleasant Grove City, 483 F.3d 1044 (10th Cir. 2007)

36 ALR6th 681—§ 9

46 ALR6th 495—§ 10

Sumner, In re, 762 A.2d 528 (D.C. 2000)

45 ALR6th 175—§ 6, 16, 18

Sumner v. Biomet, Inc., 434 Fed. Appx. 834 (11th Cir. 2011)

96 ALR6th 1—§ 47

Sumner v. Coe, 40 Or. App. 815, 596 P.2d 617 (1979)

4 ALR5th 443—§ 7

Sumner v. Fel-Air, Inc., 680 P.2d 1109 (Alaska 1984)

37 ALR5th 459—§ 2

38 ALR5th 191—§ 6

Sumner v. Glover, 2008 WL 2873672 (M.D. Ala. 2008)
65 ALR6th 93—§ 66

Sumner v. Michelin North America, Inc., 966 F. Supp. 1567, 24 A.D.D. 1124, 7 A.D. Cas. (BNA) 439 (M.D. Ala. 1997)
99 ALR5th 65—§ 9

Sumner v. Reicheniker, 9 Kan. 320, 1872 WL 630 (1872)
24 ALR6th 399—§ 17

Sumner v. U.S., 794 F. Supp. 1358 (M.D. Tenn. 1992)
50 ALR5th 1—§ 4, 6
51 ALR5th 467—§ 5
52 ALR5th 1—§ 3, 9

Sumner v. Utley, 7 Conn. 257, 1828 WL 76 (1828)
16 ALR6th 1—§ 6, 12

Sumnicht v. Toyota Motor Sales, U.S.A., Inc., 121 Wis. 2d 338, 360 N.W.2d 2 (1984)
73 ALR5th 75—§ 3, 5, 8

Sumnicht, By and Through Sumnicht v. Sackman, 968 S.W.2d 171 (Mo. Ct. App. W.D. 1998)
99 ALR5th 203—§ 8

Sumowicz v. Kelly, 14 A.D.3d 407, 787 N.Y.S.2d 654 (1st Dep't 2005)
91 ALR6th 435—§ 138

Sumpter, In re, 171 B.R. 835, CCH Bankr L. Rptr. ¶ 76104 (BC N.D. Ill. 1994)
14 ALR5th 242—§ 53

Sumrall v. Navistar Financial Corp., 818 S.W.2d 548 (Tex. App. Beaumont 1991)
85 ALR5th 353—§ 36

Sumrall v. Russell, 255 S.W. 239 (Tex. Civ. App. 1923)
46 ALR5th 1—§ 23, 47

Sumter v. Sumter, 280 S.C. 94, 311 S.E.2d 88 (App. 1984)
17 ALR5th 366—§ 8

Sumter Police Dep't, City of v. One (1) Blue Mazda Truck VIN No. JM2UF1132N0294812, 330 S.C. 371, 498 S.E.2d 894 (Ct. App. 1998)

89 ALR5th 539—§ 13

Sun v. Stewart, 242 F.3d 383 (9th Cir. 2000)
70 ALR6th 361—§ 32

Sun Alliance Ins. Co. v. Soto, 836 F.2d 834 (CA3 V.I. 1988)
35 ALR5th 375—§ 3, 57

Sunbeam Television Corp. v. Columbia Broadcasting System, Inc., 694 F. Supp. 889 (S.D. Fla. 1988)
37 ALR5th 645—§ 3, 5

Sunbelt Grain WKS, LLC, In re, 406 B.R. 918, 51 Bankr. Ct. Dec. (CRR) 242 (Bankr. D. Kan. 2009)
48 ALR6th 475—§ 15

Sunbow Industries, Inc. v. London, 58 N.C. App. 751, 294 S.E.2d 409 (1982)
11 ALR6th 1—§ 4, 9

Sunbreaker Condominium Ass'n v. Travelers Ins. Co., 79 Wash. App. 368, 901 P.2d 1079 (1995)
30 ALR5th 170—§ 77, 126.5

SunBridge Healthcare Corp. v. Penny, 160 S.W.3d 230 (Tex. App. Texarkana 2005)
24 ALR6th 549—§ 22

Sun Coal Co. v. State Industrial Com., 84 Okla. 164, 203 P. 1042 (1922)
26 ALR5th 127—§ 11

Sun Co., Inc. v. Petroleum Underground Storage Tank Release Comp. Bd., 133 Ohio App. 3d 449, 728 N.E.2d 447 (6th Dist. Lucas County 1999)
11 ALR5th 388—§ 14

Sundahl v. State, 154 Neb. 550, 48 N.W.2d 689 (1951)
55 ALR6th 157—§ 115
102 ALR6th 279—§ 7

Sundance v. Municipal Court, 192 Cal. App. 3d 268, 237 Cal. Rptr. 269 (2d Dist. 1987)
106 ALR5th 523—§ 37

Sundance Hills Homeowners Asso. v. Board of County Comrs., 188 Colo. 321, 534 P.2d 1212 (1975)
1 ALR5th 622—§ 17, 29

For assistance, call 1-800-328-4880

Sundaram v. Novello, 53 A.D.3d 804, 861 N.Y.S.2d 822 (3d Dep't 2008)
65 ALR6th 295—§ 14
Sunday v. State, 755 S.W.2d 500 (Tex. App. Beaumont 1988)
85 ALR5th 471—§ 5, 7
Sunday v. Stratton Corp., 136 Vt. 293, 390 A.2d 398 (1978)
39 ALR5th 103—§ 5
Sundberg v. Boeing Airplane Co., 52 Wash. 2d 734, 328 P.2d 692 (1958)
16 ALR5th 548—§ 4
Sundberg v. Lampert Lumber Co., 390 N.W.2d 352 (Minn. Ct. App. 1986)
111 ALR5th 207—§ 4, 13
Sundberg v. State, 636 P.2d 619 (Alaska App. 1981)
29 ALR5th 59—§ 7, 58, 84
Sundby, State ex rel. v. Adamany, 71 Wis. 2d 118, 237 N.W.2d 910 (1976)
87 ALR6th 633—§ 7
Sundell v. Town of New London, 119 N.H. 839, 409 A.2d 1315 (1979)
92 ALR5th 517—§ 7
101 ALR5th 287—§ 7, 8
Sundene v. Koppenhoefer, 343 Ill. App. 164, 98 N.E.2d 538 (1951)
52 ALR5th 155—§ 5, 8, 10
Sunderhaus, In re Adoption of, 63 Ohio St. 3d 127, 585 N.E.2d 418 (1992)
61 ALR5th 151—§ 7
Sunderland & Saunders v. Hibbard, 97 Neb. 21, 149 N.W. 57 (1914)
74 ALR5th 369—§ 8
Sunderman v. Agarwal, 322 Ill. App. 3d 900, 255 Ill. Dec. 895, 750 N.E.2d 1280 (2d Dist. 2001)
94 ALR6th 431—§ 25
Sundet v. Olin Mathieson Chemical Corp., 179 Neb. 587, 139 N.W.2d 368 (1966)
96 ALR5th 239—§ 26
Sundheim v. Beaver County Bldg. & Loan Ass'n, 140 Pa. Super. 529, 14 A.2d 349 (1940)
56 ALR5th 1—§ 5

Sundheim v. Board of County Comm'rs, 904 P.2d 1337 (Colo. App. 1995)
59 ALR5th 615—§ 12
Sundland v. Korfund Co., 260 A.D. 80, 20 N.Y.S.2d 819 (1st Dep't 1940)
24 ALR6th 399—§ 17
Sundowner Mfg. Co. v. Kinman, 536 S.W.2d 642 (Tex. Civ. App. - Texarkana 1976)
61 ALR5th 473—§ 3
Sundown, Inc. v. Pearson Real Estate Co., Inc., 8 P.3d 324 (Wyo. 2000)
8 ALR5th 312—§ 3
Sundquist Homes, Inc. v. County of Snohomish, 276 F. Supp. 2d 1123, 181 Ed. Law Rep. 159 (W.D. Wash. 2003)
1 ALR6th 229—§ 3, 27
16 ALR6th 289—§ 26
Sundstrom v. McDonnell Douglas Corp., 816 F. Supp. 577, 93 Daily Journal DAR 6105 (N.D. Cal. 1992)
53 ALR5th 535—§ 3 to 8
Sun Elec. Corp. v. St. Paul Fire and Marine Ins. Co., 1995 WL 270230 (N.D. Ill. 1995)
98 ALR5th 1—§ 6, 23
Sunenblick v. Harrell, 145 F.R.D. 314, 25 Fed. R. Serv. 3d 646 (S.D. N.Y. 1993)
114 ALR5th 129—§ 7
Sunenblick v. Harrell, 895 F. Supp. 616, 38 U.S.P.Q.2d (BNA) 1716 (S.D. N.Y. 1995)
114 ALR5th 129—§ 3, 9
Suneson v. Holloway Const. Co., 337 Ark. 571, 992 S.W.2d 79 (1999)
75 ALR5th 413—§ 3
Sunflower Elec. Co-op., Inc. v. Tomlinson Oil Co., Inc., 7 Kan. App. 2d 131, 638 P.2d 963, 32 U.C.C. Rep. Serv. 1462 (1981)
104 ALR6th 303—§ 11
Sunflower Electric Cooperative, Inc. v. Tomlinson Oil Co., 7 Kan. App. 2d 131, 638 P.2d 963, 32 U.C.C.R.S. 1462 (1981)
55 ALR5th 1—§ 41

CASES CITED IN ALR5th and ALR6th

Sunflower Electric Power Corporation v. Clyde Bergemann, Inc., 2005 WL 1842754 (D. Kan. 2005)

94 ALR6th 1—§ 5, 6, 13, 24, 52

Sunflower Pipeline Co. v. State Corp. Com., 5 Kan. App. 2d 715, 624 P.2d 466 (1981)

41 ALR5th 783—§ 3

Sung v. Commissioner of Revenue Services, 44 Conn. Supp. 461, 691 A.2d 41, 16 Conn. L. Rptr. 256 (Super. Tax 1996)

118 ALR5th 597—§ 21

Sung v. Hong, 678 N.Y.S.2d 116 (App. Div. 2d Dep't 1998)

60 ALR5th 165—§ 14

Sunga v. Lee, 13 Ill. App. 2d 76, 141 N.E.2d 63 (1st Dist. 1957)

61 ALR5th 707—§ 25

Sung Park v. Indiana University School of Dentistry, 692 F.3d 828, 284 Ed. Law Rep. 21 (7th Cir. 2012)

90 ALR6th 235—§ 54, 70

Sun Hill Industries, Inc. v. Kraftsman Group, Inc., 27 Conn. App. 688, 610 A.2d 684, 20 U.C.C. Rep. Serv. 2d 147 (1992)

89 ALR5th 319—§ 22

Suniland Toys & Juvenile Furniture, Inc. v. Karns, 148 So. 2d 523 (Fla. 1963)

11 ALR6th 351—§ 19

Sun Ins. Office v. Hohenstein, 128 Misc. 870, 220 N.Y.S. 386 (Mun. Ct. 1927)

125 ALR5th 1—§ 5

Sun Ins. Office, Ltd. v. Clay, 133 So. 2d 735 (Fla. 1961)

30 ALR5th 170—§ 2, 3, 66.5
56 ALR5th 407—§ 16

Sun Ins. Office, Ltd. v. Neff, 1991 WL 22279 (E.D. Pa. 1991)

103 ALR5th 1—§ 13

Sun Intern. Bahamas, Ltd. v. Wagner, 758 So. 2d 1190 (Fla. Dist. Ct. App. 3d Dist. 2000)

14 ALR5th 242—§ 54

Sunior v. Sunior, 20 Ohio App. 476, 3 Ohio L. Abs. 293, 152 N.E. 729 (6th Dist. Lucas County 1925)

122 ALR5th 205—§ 3, 10

Sunja S., Re, 175 App. Div. 2d 132, 571 N.Y.S.2d 826 (2d Dep't 1991)

1 ALR5th 469—§ 15

Sunkett v. Misci, 183 F. Supp. 2d 691, 87 Fair Empl. Prac. Cas. (BNA) 1742 (D.N.J. 2002)

13 ALR6th 499—§ 10, 21, 22

Sunkist Soft Drinks, Inc. v. Sunkist Growers, Inc., 10 F.3d 753 (11th Cir. 1993)

64 ALR5th 475—§ 2
67 ALR5th 179—§ 5
22 ALR6th 387—§ 7, 12, 30, 50

Sunlake Apartment Residents v. Tonti Dev. Corp., 522 So. 2d 1298 (La. App. 5th Cir. 1988)

24 ALR5th 200—§ 5

Sunlake Apartment Residents v. Tonti Dev. Corp., 602 So. 2d 22 (La. App. 5th Cir. 1992)

24 ALR5th 200—§ 24, 49, 50

Sun Life Assur. Co. of Canada v. Berck, 770 F. Supp. 2d 728 (D. Del. 2011)

91 ALR6th 327—§ 5, 13

Sunlight Carbon Co. v. St. Louis & S. F. R. Co., 15 F.2d 802 (CA8 Okla. 1926)

17 ALR5th 547—§ 38, 53

Sunlight Distribution, Inc. v. Bank of Communications, 1995 WL 46636 (S.D. N.Y. 1995)

56 ALR5th 565—§ 14, 58, 60

Sunlight Electric Supply Co. v. McKee, 226 Cal. App. 2d 47, 37 Cal. Rptr. 782 (4th Dist. 1964)

4 ALR5th 772—§ 2

Sun Mut. Ins. Co. v. Geo. Seeligson & Co., 59 Tex. 3 (1883)

20 ALR5th 229—§ 17, 30

Sunnen Products Co. v. Travelers Cas. & Sur. Co. of America, 2010 WL 743633 (E.D. Mo. 2010)

104 ALR6th 207—§ 4

Sun 'N Lake of Sebring Imp. Dist. v. McIntyre, 800 So. 2d 715, 114 A.L.R.5th 815 (Fla. Dist. Ct. App. 2d Dist. 2001)

114 ALR5th 561—§ 4

Sun 'n Sand, Inc. v. United California Bank, 21 Cal. 3d 671, 148 Cal. Rptr. 329, 582 P.2d 920, 24 U.C.C. Rep. Serv. (CBC) 667, 21 U.C.C. Rep. Serv. 2d (CBC) 1003 (1978)

45 ALR5th 389—§ 2, 3, 23, 28
77 ALR5th 429—§ 3

Sunny Farms, Ltd. v. North Codorus Tp., 81 Pa. Commw. 371, 474 A.2d 56 (1984)

47 ALR6th 439—§ 9

Sunnyland Foods, Inc. v. Catrett, 395 So. 2d 1005 (Ala. App. 1980)

3 ALR5th 907—§ 8

Sunny Ridge Enterprises, Inc. v. Fireman's Fund Ins. Co., Inc., 132 F. Supp. 2d 525 (E.D. Ky. 2001)

89 ALR5th 1—§ 9
98 ALR5th 193—§ 21
105 ALR5th 95—§ 11

Sunny Ridge Manor, In re Appeal of, 106 Idaho 98, 675 P.2d 813 (1984)

34 ALR5th 529—§ 7

Sunny Slope Water Co. v. Pasadena, 1 Cal. 2d 87, 33 P.2d 672 (1934)

53 ALR5th 1—§ 6

Sunnyvale v. Dallas County Board of School Trustees, 283 S.W.2d 296 (Tex. Civ. App. Dallas 1955)

17 ALR5th 195—§ 31

Sunnyvale, Town of v. Mayhew, 905 S.W.2d 234 (Tex. App. Dallas 1994)

1 ALR5th 622—§ 17

Sunny Wood Convalescent Home, Inc. v. ZBA of Town of Norwich, 4 Conn. L. Rptr. 488, 1991 WL 172845 (Conn. Super. Ct. 1991)

4 ALR6th 263—§ 5

Sun Oil Co. v. Clifton, 16 N.J. Super. 265, 84 A.2d 555 (1951)

38 ALR5th 737—§ 3, 11

Sun Oil Co. v. Upper Arlington, 55 Ohio App. 2d 27, 9 Ohio Ops. 3d 196, 379 N.E.2d 266 (Franklin Co. 1977)

8 ALR5th 391—§ 3

Sun Oil Co. v. Wortman, 486 U.S. 717, 108 S. Ct. 2117, 100 L. Ed. 2d 743 (1988)

50 ALR6th 281—§ 25, 28

Sun Protection Factory, Inc. v. Tender Corp., 68 Fed. R. Evid. Serv. 590 (M.D. Fla. 2005)

34 ALR6th 253—§ 12

Sun Pub. Co. v. Mecklenburg News, Inc., 594 F. Supp. 1512, 1985-1 CCH Trade Cases ¶ 66509 (E.D. Va. 1984)

23 ALR5th 241—§ 23

Sunray Oil Corp. v. Sharpe, 209 F.2d 937 (CA5 Tex. 1954)

25 ALR5th 568—§ 17

Sun Ref. & Mktg. Co. v. Crosby Valve & Gage Co., 68 Ohio St. 3d 397, 627 N.E.2d 552, CCH Prod. Liab. Rep. ¶ 13888, 23 U.C.C.R.S.2d 759 (1994)

49 ALR5th 1—§ 48

Sunridge Development Corp. v. RB & G Engineering, Inc., 2010 UT 6, 230 P.3d 1000 (Utah 2010)

61 ALR6th 445—§ 11

Sunrise v. Broward County, 473 So. 2d 1387, 10 FLW 2000 (Fla. App. D4 1985)

17 ALR5th 195—§ 4, 9

Sunrise Acres, Inc. v. Ford-Wehmeyer, Inc., 598 S.W.2d 916 (Tex. Civ. App. Waco 1980)

23 ALR5th 241—§ 9

Sunrise Hosp. v. Eighth Judicial Dist. Court, 866 P.2d 1143 (Nev 1994)

12 ALR5th 577—§ 6

Sunrise Properties, Inc. v. Bacon, Wilson, Ratner, Cohen, Salvage, Fialky & Fitzgerald, P.C., 425 Mass. 63, 679 N.E.2d 540 (1997)

92 ALR5th 273—§ 7, 12

Sunrise Sav. & Loan Ass'n v. Mariner's Cay Development Corp., 295 S.C. 208, 367 S.E.2d 696 (1988)

61 ALR5th 525—§ 5

Sunrizon Homes, Inc. v. American Guar. Inv. Corp., 1988 OK 145, 782 P.2d 103, 7 U.C.C. Rep. Serv. 2d (CBC) 796 (Okla. 1988)

77 ALR5th 523—§ 3

Sunseri v. Board of Medical Examiners, 224 Cal. App. 2d 309, 36 Cal. Rptr. 553 (1st Dist. 1964)

19 ALR6th 577—§ 10

Sunset Acres Motel, Inc. v. Jacobs, 336 S.W.2d 473 (Mo. 1960)

46 ALR6th 185—§ 7

Sunset Bay Assoc., Re, 944 F.2d 1503, 91 C.D.O.S. 7627, 91 Daily Journal DAR 11691, 26 CBC2d 572 (CA9 Cal. 1991)

13 ALR5th 684—§ 9, 13, 24

Sunset Ins. Co. v. Gomila, 834 So. 2d 654 (La. Ct. App. 5th Cir. 2002)

58 ALR6th 1—§ 5, 19

Sunset Invest., Ltd. v. Sargent, 52 N.C. App. 284, 278 S.E.2d 558, 31 U.C.C.R.S. 1436 (1981)

56 ALR5th 565—§ 17

Sunset Park Redevelopment Comm. v. Bowery Sav. Bank, 161 Misc. 2d 344, 613 N.Y.S.2d 563, 24 U.C.C.R.S.2d 985 (Sup. 1994)

45 ALR5th 389—§ 33

Sunset Park Redevelopment Committee, Inc. v. Bowery Sav. Bank, 161 Misc. 2d 344, 613 N.Y.S.2d 563, 24 U.C.C. Rep. Serv. 2d 985 (Sup 1994)

104 ALR5th 459—§ 7

Sunset Park Redevelopment Committee, Inc. v. Bowery Sav. Bank, 224 A.D.2d 608, 639 N.Y.S.2d 418, 31 U.C.C. Rep. Serv. 2d 184 (2d Dep't 1996)

45 ALR5th 389—§ 11
104 ALR5th 459—§ 7

Sunshine v. Morgan, 39 Misc. 778, 81 N.Y.S. 278 (1902)

46 ALR5th 1—§ 47

Sunshine v. Sunshine, 30 Colo. App. 67, 488 P.2d 1131 (1971)

84 ALR5th 399—§ 3, 4

Sunshine Investments, Inc. v. Brooks, 642 So. 2d 408, 130 Lab. Cas. (CCH) ¶ 57881 (Ala. 1994)

53 ALR6th 213—§ 8

Sunshine Jr. Stores, Inc. v. State, Dep't of Environmental Regulation, 556 So. 2d 1177, 15 FLW 307 (Fla. App. D1 1990)

11 ALR5th 388—§ 7

Sunshine Secur. & Detective Agency v. Wells Fargo Armored Services Corp., 496 So. 2d 246, 11 FLW 2266 (Fla. App. D3 1986)

13 ALR5th 217—§ 14

Sunshine Sportswear & Electronics, Inc. v. WSOC Television, Inc., 738 F. Supp. 1499, 16 Media L. R. 2273 (D.C. S.C. 1989)

19 ALR5th 1—§ 2, 12, 135, 153

Sunshine Sportswear & Electronics, Inc. v. WSOC Television, Inc., 738 F. Supp. 1499, 16 Media L. Rep. (BNA) 2273 (D.S.C. 1989)

13 ALR6th 111—§ 4, 15
42 ALR6th 353—§ 26

Sun Shipbuilding & Dry Dock Co. v. Unemployment Compensation Bd. of Review, 169 Pa. Super. 393, 82 A.2d 58 (1951)

95 ALR5th 329—§ 8

Sun Shipbuilding & Dry Dock Co. v. Unemployment Compensation Bd. of Review, 358 Pa. 224, 56 A.2d 254 (1948)

25 ALR6th 101—§ 4

Sun Shipbuilding & Dry Dock Co. v. Unemployment Compensation Board of Review, 358 Pa. 224, 56 A.2d 254 (1948)

45 ALR5th 715—§ 5

Sunstate Equip. Corp. v. Industrial Comm'n, 135 Ariz. 477, 662 P.2d 152 (App. 1983)

33 ALR5th 587—§ 5

For assistance, call 1-800-328-4880

Sun State Services, Inc. v. Florida Unemployment Appeals Com'n, 503 So. 2d 373 (Fla. Dist. Ct. App. 1st Dist. 1987)
26 ALR6th 111—§ 8

Suntech Processing Systems, L.L.C. v. Sun Communications, Inc., 1998 WL 767672 (Tex. App. Dallas 1998)
49 ALR6th 1—§ 27, 56, 59 to 62, 81

Suntech Processing Systems, L.L.C. v. Sun Communications, Inc., 2000 WL 1780236 (Tex. App. Dallas 2000)
48 ALR6th 1—§ 69, 72, 103

Suntide Inn Motel, In re, 563 P.2d 125 (Okla. 1977)
53 ALR5th 1—§ 4, 25, 41

SunTrust Bank, Nashville v. Johnson, 46 S.W.3d 216 (Tenn. Ct. App. 2000)
38 ALR6th 255—§ 8, 13

Sun Valley Water Beds of Utah, Inc. v. Herm Hughes & Son, Inc., 782 P.2d 188 (Utah 1989)
5 ALR6th 497—§ 4, 5

Sunwest Bank, N.A. v. Miller's Performance Warehouse, 112 N.M. 492, 816 P.2d 1114, 27 A.L.R.5th 949 (1991)
27 ALR5th 764—§ 6

Sup v. Cervenka, 331 Ill. 459, 163 N.E. 396 (1928)
91 ALR5th 225—§ 3

Super, Ex parte, 76 Tex. Crim. 415, 175 S.W. 697 (1915)
19 ALR5th 351—§ 6

Superb Video v. County of Kenosha, 195 Wis. 2d 715, 537 N.W.2d 25 (Ct. App. 1995)
20 ALR6th 161—§ 3
21 ALR6th 425—§ 5
23 ALR6th 573—§ 17

Super Chief Credit Union v. McCoy, 3 Kan. App. 2d 25, 595 P.2d 346 (1978)
98 ALR5th 353—§ 3, 7

Super Discount Mkts. v. Coney, 210 Ga. App. 659, 436 S.E.2d 803, 93 Fulton County D R 3840 (1993)
20 ALR5th 1—§ 4, 14

Super Flea Market of Chattanooga, Inc. v. Olsen, 677 S.W.2d 449 (Tenn. 1984)
88 ALR6th 203—§ 54

Superformance Intern., Inc. v. Hartford Cas. Ins. Co., 2002 WL 1159618 (E.D. Va. 2002)
98 ALR5th 1—§ 12, 22

Superguide Corp. v. Kegan, 987 F. Supp. 481, 44 U.S.P.Q.2d (BNA) 1770 (W.D. N.C. 1997)
81 ALR5th 41—§ 5, 10

Superhighway Consulting, Inc. v. Techwave, Inc., 1999 WL 1044870 (N.D. Ill. 1999)
34 ALR6th 253—§ 5

Superhype Pub., Inc. v. Vasiliou, 838 F. Supp. 1220 (S.D. Ohio 1993)
37 ALR6th 243—§ 12, 19, 53, 57, 59

Superintendent v. Grover, 76 Mass. App. Ct. 1117, 922 N.E.2d 863 (2010)
91 ALR6th 435—§ 68, 130

Superintendent, Massachusetts Correctional Institution, Walpole v. Hill, 472 U.S. 445, 105 S. Ct. 2768, 86 L. Ed. 2d 356 (1985)
96 ALR6th 269—§ 2

Superintendent of Ins. v. Baker & Hostetler, 668 F. Supp. 1054 (N.D. Ohio 1987)
44 ALR5th 683—§ 20

Superintendent of Ins. v. International Equipment Leasing, Inc., 247 N.J. Super. 119, 588 A.2d 883 (1991)
44 ALR5th 683—§ 21

Superior Asphalt & Concrete Co. v. Department of Labor and Industries, 19 Wash. App. 800, 578 P.2d 59 (Div. 3 1978)
28 ALR6th 1—§ 3, 14, 18, 30, 40, 79

Superior Bank FSB v. Golding, 152 Ill. 2d 480, 178 Ill. Dec. 720, 605 N.E.2d 514 (1992)
13 ALR6th 1—§ 4, 5

Superior Bank, F.S.B. v. Tandem Nat. Mortg., Inc., 197 F. Supp. 2d 298 (D. Md. 2000)

44 ALR6th 1—§ 8, 15, 21, 22

Superior Beverage/Glass Container Consol. Pretrial, Re, 133 F.R.D. 119, 1991-1 CCH Trade Cases ¶ 69405 (N.D. Ill. 1990)

23 ALR5th 241—§ 26

Superior Clay Corp. v. Clay Sewer Pipe Ass'n, 5 Ohio Misc. 247, 34 Ohio Op. 2d 492, 215 N.E.2d 437, 149 U.S.P.Q. 313 (C.P. 1963)

85 ALR6th 1—§ 29

Superior Coal Co. v. Industrial Com., 326 Ill. 584, 158 N.E. 209, 54 A.L.R. 634 (1927)

3 ALR5th 907—§ 3

Superior Const. Co., Inc. v. Brock, 445 F.3d 1334, 2006 A.M.C. 1038, 66 A.L.R.6th 717 (11th Cir. 2006)

66 ALR6th 185—§ 6

Superior Consultant Co., Inc. v. Bailey, 2000 WL 1279161 (E.D. Mich. 2000)

36 ALR6th 537—§ 6, 9

Superior Consulting Co., Inc. v. Walling, 851 F. Supp. 839 (E.D. Mich. 1994)

79 ALR5th 587—§ 4

Superior Court v. Ricketts, 153 Md. App. 281, 836 A.2d 707 (2003)

18 ALR6th 97—§ 31

Superior Derrick Services, Inc. v. Anderson, 831 S.W.2d 868, 18 U.C.C. Rep. Serv. 2d (CBC) 706 (Tex. App. Houston 14th Dist. 1992)

61 ALR5th 611—§ 2, 3

Superior Distributing Co., State ex rel. v. Davis, 132 Ohio St. 308, 8 Ohio Op. 70, 7 N.E.2d 652 (1937)

116 ALR5th 149—§ 13

Superior Equipment Co., Inc. v. Maryland Cas. Co., 986 S.W.2d 477 (Mo. Ct. App. E.D. 1998)

14 ALR5th 695—§ 5

110 ALR5th 465—§ 21

Superior Essex Cable v. Price, 2004 WL 2634169 (Ky. Ct. App. 2004)

99 ALR6th 643—§ 17

Superior Farm Management, L.L.C. v. Montgomery, 270 Ga. 615, 513 S.E.2d 215, 93 A.L.R.5th 789 (1999)

93 ALR5th 621—§ 5

Superior Foundry, Inc., State ex rel. v. Industrial Commission, 168 Ohio St. 537, 7 Ohio Op. 2d 419, 156 N.E.2d 742 (1959)

86 ALR5th 295—§ 7

Superior Ice & Coal Co. v. Belger Cartage Service, Inc., 337 S.W.2d 897 (Mo. 1960)

84 ALR5th 69—§ 5, 7

Superior Ins. Co. v. Superior Court of Los Angeles County, 37 Cal. 2d 749, 235 P.2d 833 (1951)

12 ALR5th 577—§ 5

Superior Mortg. Co. v. Division of Real Estate, 164 Cal. App. 2d 783, 331 P.2d 462 (2d Dist. 1958)

7 ALR5th 474—§ 38

Superior Oil Co. v. City of Port Arthur, 628 S.W.2d 94 (Tex. App. Beaumont 1981)

9 ALR6th 177—§ 46

Superior Steel, Inc. v. Bituminous Cas. Corp., 415 So. 2d 354 (La. Ct. App. 1st Cir. 1982)

49 ALR6th 169—§ 7

Superior Trucks, Inc. v. Allen, 664 S.W.2d 136 (Tex. App. Houston 1st Dist. 1983)

63 ALR5th 1—§ 5

Superior Woolen Co. Tailors v. M. Samuels & Co., 219 Ky. 539, 293 S.W. 1078 (1927)

75 ALR5th 1—§ 5, 17

Supermarkets Operating Co. v. Arkwright Mut. Ins. Co., 257 F. Supp. 273 (E.D. Pa. 1966)

37 ALR5th 41—§ 3, 34, 36 to 38

Superskate, Inc. v. Nolen by Miller, 641 So. 2d 231, 38 A.L.R.5th 855 (Ala. 1994)

For assistance, call 1-800-328-4880

38 ALR5th 107—§ 5

SuperTurf, Inc. v. Monsanto Co., 660 F.2d 1275, 1981-2 CCH Trade Cases ¶ 64316, 32 FR Serv. 2d 1300 (CA8 Mo. 1981)

2 ALR5th 449—§ 3, 4

Supervalu, Inc. v. W.C.A.B. (Pettinato), 727 A.2d 1174 (Pa. Commw. Ct. 1999)

97 ALR5th 1—§ 4

106 ALR5th 111—§ 19

108 ALR5th 1—§ 29

Super Valu Stores, Inc. v. D-Mart Food Stores, Inc., 146 Wis. 2d 568, 431 N.W.2d 721 (App. 1988)

52 ALR5th 613—§ 3

Supervisor of Assessments of Baltimore City v. Har Sinai West Corp., 95 Md. App. 631, 622 A.2d 786 (1993)

90 ALR5th 547—§ 10

Supervisors, Board of v. Allman, 215 Va. 434, 211 S.E.2d 48 (1975)

1 ALR5th 622—§ 17

Supervisors, Board of v. Centre Hills Country Club, 18 Pa. Cmwlth. 40, 333 A.2d 822 (1975)

2 ALR5th 553—§ 88

Supervisors, Board of v. Cities Service Oil Co., 213 Va. 359, 193 S.E.2d 1 (1972)

38 ALR5th 737—§ 3, 8

Supervisors, Board of v. Medical Structures, Inc., 213 Va. 355, 192 S.E.2d 799 (1972)

38 ALR5th 737—§ 3

Supervisors, Board of v. Miller, 170 N.W.2d 358 (Iowa 1969)

8 ALR5th 391—§ 3, 7

Supervisors, Board of v. Paaske, 250 Iowa 1293, 98 N.W.2d 827 (1959)

1 ALR5th 622—§ 20

38 ALR5th 737—§ 3

Supervisors, Board of v. Williams, 216 Va. 49, 216 S.E.2d 33 (1975)

1 ALR5th 622—§ 17

Supervisors for Louisiana State University Agricultural and Mechanical College, In re v. Smack Apparel Co., 550 F.3d 465, 239 Ed. Law Rep. 874, 89 U.S.P.Q.2d 1338 (5th Cir. 2008)

46 ALR6th 495—§ 52

Supervisors of County of Boone v. Rainbow Gardens, 14 Ill. 2d 504, 153 N.E.2d 16 (1958)

56 ALR5th 171—§ 3, 7, 16

Supervisors of Fairfax County, Board of v. Lukinson, 214 Va. 239, 198 S.E.2d 603 (1973)

22 ALR6th 295—§ 5, 7

Supik v. Bodie, Nagle, Dolina, Smith & Hobbs, P.A, 152 Md. App. 698, 834 A.2d 170 (2003)

14 ALR6th 1—§ 10

Supinski v. W.C.A.B. (School Dist. of Philadelphia), 133 Pa. Commw. 631, 577 A.2d 944, 61 Ed. Law Rep. 1283 (1990)

82 ALR5th 149—§ 2, 36, 37, 65

Supplies for Industry, Inc. v. Christensen, 135 Ariz. 107, 659 P.2d 660 (App. 1983)

12 ALR5th 847—§ 10, 12, 14

Support of Rockman, Re, 217 Mont. 498, 705 P.2d 590 (1985)

11 ALR5th 259—§ 8, 10, 34

Suppus v. Bradley, 101 N.Y.S.2d 557 (Sup 1950)

88 ALR6th 203—§ 19, 67

SupraLife Intern. v. Whiting, 2005 WL 246748 (Cal. App. 4th Dist. 2005)

22 ALR6th 387—§ 37

Supreme Bumpers, Inc., State ex rel. v. Indus. Comm., 98 Ohio St. 3d 134, 2002-Ohio-7089, 781 N.E.2d 170 (2002)

31 ALR6th 199—§ 52

Supreme Council C. K. A. v. Fidelity & C. Co., 63 F. 48 (CA6 Tenn. 1894)

5 ALR5th 132—§ 4, 5, 19

Supreme Council of Royal Arcanum v. State Tax Commission, 358 Mass. 111, 260 N.E.2d 822 (1970)

69 ALR5th 477—§ 15

Supreme Court of Indiana, Matter of Contempt of the, 673 N.E.2d 755 (Ind. 1996)

40 ALR6th 463—§ 26

Supreme Lodge of Mystic Workers of the World v. Jones, 113 Ill. App. 241, 1903 WL 3483 (3d Dist. 1903)

23 ALR6th 1—§ 8

Supreme Oil Co. v. Metropolitan Transp. Authority, 1997 WL 607544 (S.D. N.Y. 1997)

107 ALR5th 311—§ 10

Supreme Video, Inc. v. Schauz, 808 F. Supp. 1380 (E.D. Wis. 1992)

74 ALR6th 69—§ 3, 25

Sup'rs of Fairfax County, Board of v. DeGroff Enterprises, Inc., 214 Va. 235, 198 S.E.2d 600, 62 A.L.R.3d 874 (1973)

22 ALR6th 295—§ 5, 7

Sup'rs of Fairfax County, VA, Board of v. U.S. Home Corp., 18 Va. Cir. 181, 1989 WL 646518 (1989)

32 ALR6th 261—§ 4, 6

Sup'rs of Henrico County, Board of v. Fralin and Waldron, Inc., 222 Va. 218, 278 S.E.2d 859 (1981)

73 ALR5th 223—§ 13

Sup'rs of Jefferson County, Board of v. Board of Sup'rs of Milwaukee County, 20 Wis. 139, 1865 WL 826 (1865)

27 ALR6th 403—§ 11

Sup'rs of Loudoun County, Board of v. Pumphrey, 221 Va. 205, 269 S.E.2d 361 (1980)

94 ALR6th 239—§ 44

Sup'rs of Lower Gwynedd Tp., Board of v. West, 47 Pa. Commw. 646, 409 A.2d 465 (1979)

19 ALR6th 217—§ 27

Sup'rs of Palmyra Tp., Board of v. Lakeside Resort Enterprises, LP, 127 S. Ct. 1170 (U.S. 2007)

26 ALR6th 659—§ 12

Sur v. Glidden-Durkee, a div. of S. C. M. Corp., 681 F.2d 490 (7th Cir. 1982)

63 ALR5th 427—§ 2, 3, 27

Surabian v. Surabian, 362 Mass. 342, 285 N.E.2d 909 (1972)

47 ALR5th 129—§ 7

Surace v. Danna, 248 N.Y. 18, 161 N.E. 315 (1928)

48 ALR5th 473—§ 5, 18

Surace v. Wainwright, 637 F. Supp. 460 (S.D. Fla. 1986)

9 ALR6th 1—§ 10

Suran v. Lustic Shoe Store, 14 Ohio L. Abs. 590 (Ct. App. 7th Dist. Mahoning County 1933)

123 ALR5th 1—§ 8

Surdi v. Dallmer, 18 Misc. 2d 218, 185 N.Y.S.2d 988 (Sup 1959)

106 ALR5th 475—§ 6

Sureeporn Roll v. State, 473 N.E.2d 161 (Ind. App. 1985)

45 ALR5th 767—§ 15

Surety Mortg., Inc. v. Equitable Mortg. Resources, Inc., 534 So. 2d 780, 13 FLW 2549 (Fla. App. D2 1988)

5 ALR5th 875—§ 4, 20, 34

Surety Sav. & Loan Ass'n v. State Department of Transp. Division of Highways, 54 Wis. 2d 438, 195 N.W.2d 464 (1972)

93 ALR6th 363—§ 3, 4, 8

Surety Sav. & Loan Co. v. Kanzig, 53 Ohio St. 2d 108, 7 Ohio Op. 3d 187, 372 N.E.2d 602, 23 U.C.C. Rep. Serv. 804 (1978)

35 ALR6th 437—§ 13

Surfside v. Morrison Assurance Co., 394 So. 2d 530 (Fla. App. D3 1981)

35 ALR5th 731—§ 9

Surfside, Town of v. Higgenbotham, 733 So. 2d 1040 (Fla. Dist. Ct. App. 3d Dist. 1999)

19 ALR6th 217—§ 16

Surget v. Arighi, 19 Miss. 87 (1848)

43 ALR5th 207—§ 17, 61

Surgi v. Otis Elevator Co., 541 So. 2d 297 (La. App. 5th Cir. 1989)

100 ALR5th 409—§ 2

Surgi v. Otis Elevator Co., 541 So. 2d 297 (La. Ct. App. 5th Cir. 1989)

99 ALR5th 141—§ 11, 29

115 ALR5th 1—§ 29

117 ALR5th 267—§ 4

Surgical Design Corp. v. Correa, 284 A.D.2d 528, 727 N.Y.S.2d 462 (2d Dep't 2001)

9 ALR6th 363—§ 20

Surgical Design Corp. v. Correa, 799 N.Y.S.2d 584 (App. Div. 2d Dep't 2005)

9 ALR6th 363—§ 10

Surgical Laser Technologies v. Commonwealth, Dep't of Revenue, 156 Pa. Cmwlth. 48, 626 A.2d 664 (1993)

33 ALR5th 509—§ 23

Surgidev Corp. v. Eye Technology, Inc., 648 F. Supp. 661 (D. Minn. 1986)

36 ALR6th 537—§ 4, 7

Surgin Surgical Instrumentation, Inc. v. Truck Ins. Exchange, 76 Cal. Rptr. 2d 303 (App. 4th Dist. 1998)

98 ALR5th 1—§ 11

Suria v. Shiffman, 67 N.Y.2d 87, 499 N.Y.S.2d 913, 490 N.E.2d 832 (1986)

9 ALR5th 746—§ 16

28 ALR5th 497—§ 4, 7

108 ALR5th 385—§ 11

Surianello v. State, 92 Nev. 492, 553 P.2d 942 (1976)

18 ALR5th 804—§ 6, 8

Suriano v. Sears, Roebuck & Co., 117 Wash. App. 819, 72 P.3d 1097 (Div. 3 2003)

1 ALR6th 297—§ 14

Suriano, State ex rel. v. Gaughan, 198 W. Va. 339, 480 S.E.2d 548 (1996)

19 ALR5th 1—§ 38, 110

Surina v. Lucey, 168 Cal. App. 3d 539, 214 Cal. Rptr. 509 (2d Dist. 1985)

103 ALR6th 461—§ 22

Surinach v. Pesquera De Busquets, 460 F. Supp. 121 (D.C. Puerto Rico 1978)

8 ALR5th 875—§ 3

Surinach v. Pesquera De Busquets, 604 F.2d 73 (CA1 Puerto Rico 1979)

8 ALR5th 875—§ 3, 4

Suring State Bank v. Giese, 210 Wis. 489, 246 N.W. 556, 85 A.L.R. 1477 (1933)

4 ALR5th 693—§ 2, 3, 5, 14, 17, 19

Surini v. Adamowicz, 200 App. Div. 2d 737, 607 N.Y.S.2d 113 (2d Dep't 1994)

43 ALR5th 207—§ 79

Suritz v. Kelner, 155 So. 2d 831 (Fla. Dist. Ct. App. 3d Dist. 1963)

58 ALR6th 1—§ 33

Surmacz v. Department of Public Welfare, 148 Pa. Commw. 585, 612 A.2d 566 (1992)

37 ALR6th 137—§ 16

Surman v. Merrill, Lynch, Pierce, Fenner & Smith, 733 F.2d 59, Blue Sky L. Rep. (CCH) ¶ 71968, Fed. Sec. L. Rep. (CCH) ¶ 91443 (8th Cir. 1984)

22 ALR6th 49—§ 4

Suroviec v. Mitchell, 347 Pa. Super. 399, 500 A.2d 894 (1985)

69 ALR5th 1—§ 3, 5

Surprenant v. Massachusetts Turnpike Authority, 768 F. Supp. 2d 312 (D. Mass. 2011)

83 ALR6th 399—§ 2, 3

Surprenant v. Massachusetts Turnpike Authority, 2010 WL 785306 (D. Mass. 2010)

83 ALR6th 399—§ 3, 4

Surratt v. Surratt, 85 Ark. App. 267, 148 S.W.3d 761 (2004)

59 ALR6th 433—§ 61

Surrency v. Harbison, 489 So. 2d 1097 (Ala. 1986)

14 ALR5th 242—§ 4

Surrey v. Lumbermens Mut. Cas. Co., 384 Mass. 171, 424 N.E.2d 234 (1981)

77 ALR5th 319—§ 3

78 ALR5th 341—§ 5

Surrey v. TrueBeginnings, 168 Cal. App. 4th 414, 85 Cal. Rptr. 3d 443 (4th Dist. 2008)

48 ALR6th 351—§ 3

Surrick v. Zoning Hearing Bd., 476 Pa. 182, 382 A.2d 105 (1977)

1 ALR5th 622—§ 17, 33

Surry v. Starkey, 115 N.H. 31, 332 A.2d 172 (1975)

8 ALR5th 391—§ 3

Suruda v. Jersey City Bd. of Education, 167 N.J. Super. 331, 400 A.2d 860 (1979)

47 ALR5th 553—§ 27

Survance v. State, 465 N.E.2d 1076 (Ind. 1984)

97 ALR5th 537—§ 83

Susag v. City of Lake Forest, 94 Cal. App. 4th 1401, 115 Cal. Rptr. 2d 269 (4th Dist. 2002)

65 ALR6th 93—§ 15

Susan, Adoption of, 416 Mass. 1003, 619 N.E.2d 323 (1993)

27 ALR5th 54—§ 3

61 ALR6th 1—§ 7, 16

Susan G v. Bane, 199 A.D.2d 804, 605 N.Y.S.2d 522 (3d Dep't 1993)

36 ALR6th 475—§ 13

Susan GG v. James HH, 244 A.D.2d 731, 664 N.Y.S.2d 657 (3d Dep't 1997)

1 ALR5th 776—§ 10

Susan I. Sheperdson v. Local Union No. 401 of International Association of Bridge Structural and Ornamental Workers and International Association of Bridge Structural and Ornamental Ironworkers Washington, D.C., 32 Phila. Co. Rptr. 267, 1995 WL 1316024 (Pa. C.P. 1995)

20 ALR6th 1—§ 5

Susan L. v. Steven L., 273 Neb. 24, 729 N.W.2d 35 (2007)

53 ALR6th 419—§ 45

66 ALR6th 269—§ 10, 22

Susan M. v. New York Law School, 76 N.Y.2d 241, 557 N.Y.S.2d 297, 556 N.E.2d 1104 (1990)

47 ALR5th 1—§ 19, 32

Susan N. v. Wilson School Dist., 70 F.3d 751, 13 A.D.D. 879, 105 Ed. Law Rep. 23 (3d Cir. 1995)

115 ALR5th 183—§ 3

Susan T., Conservatorship of, 8 Cal. 4th 1005, 36 Cal. Rptr. 2d 40, 884 P.2d 988 (1994)

105 ALR5th 1—§ 3, 17

Susemiehl v. Red River Lumber Co., 306 Ill. App. 430, 28 N.E.2d 743 (1940)

27 ALR5th 174—§ 55

Susens v. State, 1992 WL 178590 (Tex. App. Dallas 1992)

35 ALR6th 127—§ 5

Susilo v. Wells Fargo Bank, N.A., 796 F. Supp. 2d 1177 (C.D. Cal. 2011)

81 ALR6th 161—§ 4

82 ALR6th 43—§ 4

Suska v. Unemployment Compensation Bd. of Review, 166 Pa. Super. 293, 70 A.2d 397 (1950)

68 ALR5th 13—§ 11, 39

Susman v. City of New Orleans, 727 So. 2d 1190 (La. Ct. App. 4th Cir. 1999)

50 ALR5th 1—§ 11

52 ALR5th 1—§ 8

Susman v. Exchange Nat. Bank of Colorado Springs, 117 Colo. 12, 183 P.2d 571 (1947)

86 ALR5th 527—§ 15, 18, 19

Susnik v. Western Indem. Co., 14 Kan. App. 2d 421, 795 P.2d 71 (1989)

35 ALR5th 375—§ 3, 13, 70, 80, 83

Suson, In re, 2003 WL 22434753 (Tex. App. Corpus Christi 2003)

116 ALR5th 1—§ 3

Susor v. Indian Shores, 4 Fla. Supp. 2d 37 (6th Cir. Ct. 1983)

1 ALR5th 622—§ 17, 19

Suspension of Attorney Jo Ann Fulton, In re, 445 F. Supp. 2d 1325 (D. Wyo. 2006)

44 ALR6th 75—§ 6

Suspension of Driver's License of Smith, In re, 115 Idaho 808, 770 P.2d 817 (App. 1989)

28 ALR5th 459—§ 4, 5, 8
Suspension of Haldeman, 18 Pa. D. &
C.3d 623, 1981 WL 879 (C.P. 1981)
19 ALR6th 217—§ 49
Susquehanna Patriot Commercial Leasing Co., Inc. v. Holper Industries,
Inc., 2007 PA Super 173, 928 A.2d
278 (2007)
39 ALR6th 629—§ 2, 4
Susquehanna Power Co. v. State Tax
Commission of Md., 283 U.S. 291,
51 S. Ct. 434, 75 L. Ed. 1042 (1931)
90 ALR5th 547—§ 8
Suss v. American Soc. for Prevention of
Cruelty to Animals, 823 F. Supp.
181 (S.D. N.Y. 1993)
98 ALR5th 305—§ 3, 19
58 ALR6th 499—§ 91
Sussan v. Nova Southeastern University,
723 So. 2d 933, 131 Ed. Law Rep.
1176, 138 Lab. Cas. (CCH) ¶ 58613
(Fla. Dist. Ct. App. 4th Dist. 1999)
13 ALR6th 499—§ 12
Susser v. Carvel Corp., 206 F. Supp. 636
(S.D. NY)
52 ALR5th 613—§ 2
Susser v. City of New York, 97 Misc. 2d
984, 413 N.Y.S.2d 83 (City Civ. Ct.
1979)
90 ALR5th 273—§ 3, 4, 15
Sussex v. Snyder, 307 Mich. 30, 11
N.W.2d 314 (1943)
86 ALR5th 527—§ 7
Sussman v. American Broadcasting
Companies, Inc., 971 F. Supp. 432
(C.D. Cal. 1997)
101 ALR5th 61—§ 27
Sussman v. Florida East Coast Properties, Inc., 557 So. 2d 74, 15 FLW D
210 (Fla. App. D3 1990)
27 ALR5th 174—§ 3, 4, 8
Sussman v. Grado, 192 Misc. 2d 628,
746 N.Y.S.2d 548 (Dist. Ct. 2002)
109 ALR5th 275—§ 2, 6
Sussman v. New York City Health and
Hospitals Corp., 10 Nat'l Disability
Law Rep. P. 132, 1997 WL 334964
(S.D. N.Y. 1997)

64 ALR5th 519—§ 16
82 ALR5th 1—§ 8
Sussman v. Overlook Hospital Asso., 95
N.J. Super. 418, 231 A.2d 389
(1967)
28 ALR5th 107—§ 3
Sussman v. Porter, 137 F. 161 (C.C.D.
N.J. 1905)
35 ALR6th 1—§ 28, 30
Susswein, In re, 18 A.D.3d 1091, 795
N.Y.S.2d 413 (3d Dep't 2005)
37 ALR6th 243—§ 58
Susswein (Nationwide Ins. Co.), Matter
of, 204 A.D.2d 849, 611 N.Y.S.2d
960 (3d Dep't 1994)
103 ALR5th 1—§ 2, 29
Suste v. Sterr, 135 Ill. App. 3d 652, 90
Ill. Dec. 477, 482 N.E.2d 184 (3d
Dist. 1985)
98 ALR6th 93—§ 53
Suster v. Arkansas Dep't of Human Services, 314 Ark. 92, 858 S.W.2d 122
(1993)
71 ALR5th 99—§ 3, 7
Sustrik, Ex parte, 721 S.W.2d 592 (Tex.
App. Fort Worth 1986)
32 ALR5th 31—§ 3
Sutch's Estate, In re, 201 Pa. 305, 50 A.
943 (1902)
98 ALR5th 353—§ 3, 7
Sutcliffe v. Ft. Dodge Gas & Electric
Co., 218 Iowa 1386, 257 N.W. 406
(1934)
34 ALR5th 1—§ 2, 5
Sutcliffe v. Iowa State Traveling Men's
Ass'n, 119 Iowa 220, 93 N.W. 90
(1903)
23 ALR6th 1—§ 15, 26, 30
Sutcliffe's Estate, In re, 7 Fiduc Rep. 564
(Pa. Orphans' Ct. 1957)
56 ALR5th 133—§ 3
Suter v. Carnival Corp., 2007 A.M.C.
2564, 2007 WL 4662144 (S.D. Fla.
2007)
81 ALR6th 235—§ 6, 10
Suter v. City of Lafayette, 57 Cal. App.
4th 1109, 67 Cal. Rptr. 2d 420 (1st
Dist. 1997)

106 ALR5th 523—§ 7, 10
19 ALR6th 335—§ 5, 7, 8, 18, 19
Suter v. Goedert, 396 B.R. 535, 60 Collier Bankr. Cas. 2d (MB) 1444 (D. Nev. 2008)
99 ALR6th 481—§ 51
Suter v. Harsco Corp., 403 S.E.2d 751, 122 CCH LC ¶ 57055, 6 BNA IER Cas. 756, 17 A.L.R.5th 863 (W. Va. 1991)
17 ALR5th 1—§ 8
Suter v. San Angelo Foundry & Mach. Co., 81 N.J. 150, 406 A.2d 140 (1979)
86 ALR5th 215—§ 8, 18
Sutera v. Board of Firearms, 8 Conn. L. Rptr. 200, 1993 WL 12126 (Conn. Super. Ct. 1993)
91 ALR6th 435—§ 5, 39
Sutera v. Estate of Washton, 34 Conn. L. Rptr. 388, 2003 WL 1478788 (Conn. Super. Ct. 2003)
11 ALR6th 1—§ 4, 15
Sutera v. Transportation Sec. Admin., 708 F. Supp. 2d 304, 30 I.E.R. Cas. (BNA) 1188 (E.D. N.Y. 2010)
95 ALR6th 341—§ 6
Sutherland v. Auch Inter-Borough Transit Co., 366 F. Supp. 127 (E.D. Pa. 1973)
7 ALR6th 1—§ 35
Sutherland v. Caballero, 759 S.W.2d 945 (Tex. 1988)
13 ALR6th 1—§ 4
Sutherland v. Cobern, 843 S.W.2d 127 (Tex. App. Texarkana 1992)
59 ALR6th 433—§ 88
Sutherland v. County of Nassau, 151 App. Div. 2d 468, 542 N.Y.S.2d 258 (2d Dep't 1989)
4 ALR5th 210—§ 12
5 ALR5th 875—§ 4
Sutherland v. Department of Labor and Industries, 4 Wash. App. 333, 481 P.2d 453 (Div. 3 1971)
112 ALR5th 509—§ 18
122 ALR5th 653—§ 6
13 ALR6th 209—§ 27, 30

39 ALR6th 445—§ 35
Sutherland v. Glens Falls Ins. Co., 493 So. 2d 87 (Fla. Dist. Ct. App. 4th Dist. 1986)
66 ALR5th 269—§ 6
Sutherland v. Gross, 105 Nev. 192, 772 P.2d 1287 (1989)
102 ALR5th 647—§ 12
Sutherland v. Guthrie, 86 W. Va. 208, 103 S.E. 298 (1920)
24 ALR6th 399—§ 8, 17
Sutherland v. Hurin, 185 Mont. 544, 605 P.2d 1133 (1980)
86 ALR5th 637—§ 3
Sutherland v. Nationwide Gen. Ins. Co., 96 Ohio App. 3d 793, 645 N.E.2d 1338 (10th Dist. Franklin County 1994)
81 ALR5th 367—§ 34
14 ALR6th 417—§ 10
Sutherland v. Nationwide Gen. Ins. Co., 102 Ohio App. 3d 297, 657 N.E.2d 281 (10th Dist. Franklin County 1995)
106 ALR5th 523—§ 14
Sutherland v. NN Investors Life Ins. Co., Inc., 897 F.2d 593 (1st Cir. 1990)
100 ALR5th 617—§ 9
Sutherland v. Standard Life & Acc. Ins. Co., 87 Iowa 505, 54 N.W. 453 (1893)
100 ALR5th 617—§ 11
Sutherland v. State, 2003 WL 22725268 (Tex. App. Fort Worth 2003)
69 ALR6th 1—§ 13
Sutherland v. Sutherland, 61 Ohio App. 3d 154, 572 N.E.2d 215 (10th Dist. Franklin County 1989)
72 ALR6th 413—§ 3
Sutherland v. Sutherland, 192 Va. 764, 66 S.E.2d 537 (1951)
61 ALR5th 707—§ 22
Sutherland v. Time Saver Stores, Inc., 428 So. 2d 972 (La. Ct. App. 1st Cir. 1983)
84 ALR5th 249—§ 2
Sutherlin v. Fenenga, 111 N.M. 767, 810 P.2d 353 (App. 1991)

For assistance, call 1-800-328-4880

35 ALR5th 145—§ 9
63 ALR5th 285—§ 2, 5
Sutherlin v. Grant, 99 Idaho 864, 590
P.2d 1010 (1979)
40 ALR6th 99—§ 22
Sutherlin v. Independent School Dist.
No. 40 of Nowata County, Okla.,
960 F. Supp. 2d 1254, 301 Ed. Law
Rep. 379 (N.D. Okla. 2013)
**98 ALR6th 599—§ 11, 12, 14, 43,
54, 59, 83, 96**
Sutherlin v. State, 136 Neb. 809, 287
N.W. 614 (1939)
108 ALR5th 593—§ 46
Sutkowski v. Director, Div. of Taxation,
312 N.J. Super. 465, 712 A.2d 229
(App. Div. 1998)
118 ALR5th 597—§ 33
Sutkowski v. Universal Marion Corp., 5
Ill. App. 3d 313, 281 N.E.2d 749
(3d Dist. 1972)
64 ALR5th 119—§ 3
Sutler v. Palmetto Elec. Co-op., Inc., 325
S.C. 465, 481 S.E.2d 179, 12 I.E.R.
Cas. (BNA) 827 (Ct. App. 1997)
90 ALR5th 687—§ 3 to 5
Sutliff v. Gilbert, 8 Ohio. 405 (1838)
19 ALR5th 622—§ 33, 37, 40, 47
Sutlive v. Hackney, 164 Ga. App. 740,
297 S.E.2d 515 (1982)
28 ALR5th 497—§ 2
Sutowski v. Eli Lilly & Co., 82 Ohio St.
3d 347, 696 N.E.2d 187 (1998)
63 ALR5th 195—§ 4
Sutphen v. Benthian, 165 N.J. Super. 79,
397 A.2d 709 (App. Div. 1979)
66 ALR5th 1—§ 43
Sutphen v. Town of North Hempstead,
30 N.Y.S. 128 (Gen. Term 1894)
12 ALR6th 645—§ 38
Suts v. Chicago & N. W. R. Co., 203
Wis. 532, 234 N.W. 715 (1930)
17 ALR5th 547—§ 36, 38
Sutter v. General Petroleum Corp., 28
Cal. 2d 525, 170 P.2d 898, 167
A.L.R. 271 (1946)
10 ALR6th 293—§ 7, 11

Sutter v. Oxford Health Plans LLC, 675
F.3d 215, 162 Lab. Cas. (CCH) P
10527 (3d Cir. 2012)
86 ALR6th 577—§ 5
Sutter v. Payne, 337 Ark. 330, 989
S.W.2d 887 (1999)
102 ALR5th 647—§ 14
Sutter Sensible Planning, Inc. v. Board
of Supervisors, 122 Cal. App. 3d
813, 176 Cal. Rptr. 342 (3d Dist.
1981)
34 ALR5th 591—§ 2, 16
35 ALR5th 113—§ 2
Suttle v. Bailey, 68 N.M. 283, 361 P.2d
325 (1961)
119 ALR5th 519—§ 12, 23
Suttle v. State, 565 So. 2d 1197 (Ala.
Crim. App. 1990)
76 ALR5th 1—§ 6
Suttles v. Florida Real Estate Com., 139
Fla. 210, 190 So. 433 (1939)
7 ALR5th 474—§ 189
Suttles v. Florida Real Estate Com., 152
Fla. 432, 12 So. 2d 176 (1943)
7 ALR5th 474—§ 29, 56
Sutton, In re Marriage of, 233 S.W.3d
786 (Mo. Ct. App. E.D. 2007)
100 ALR6th 1—§ 24
Sutton, Matter of, 1996 WL 659002
(Del. Super. Ct. 1996)
9 ALR6th 363—§ 42
Sutton v. Anderson, 176 Neb. 543, 126
N.W.2d 836 (1964)
60 ALR6th 481—§ 4, 40
Sutton v. Bell, 683 F. Supp. 2d 640 (E.D.
Tenn. 2010)
102 ALR6th 417—§ 11
Sutton v. Calhoun, 593 F.2d 127 (CA10
Okla. 1979)
42 ALR5th 1—§ 3
Sutton v. Civil Service Com'n, 91 Ill. 2d
404, 63 Ill. Dec. 409, 438 N.E.2d
147 (1982)
19 ALR6th 217—§ 26
Sutton v. Commonwealth, 623 S.W.2d
879 (Ky. 1981)
29 ALR5th 59—§ 6, 23, 31, 56

Sutton v. Duplessis, 584 So. 2d 362, 69
   Ed. Law Rep. 968 (La. Ct. App. 4th
   Cir. 1991)
   72 ALR5th 469—§ 14

Sutton v. East Metro Clean N Press Inc.,
   2009 WL 3735878 (Minn. Ct. App.
   2009)
   80 ALR6th 635—§ 12

Sutton v. Flores, 2010 WL 2006243
   (Ariz. Ct. App. Div. 2 2010)
   57 ALR6th 163—§ 11

Sutton v. Frost, 432 A.2d 1311 (Me.
   1981)
   107 ALR5th 311—§ 4

Sutton v. Herbert, 39 F. Supp. 2d 335
   (S.D. N.Y. 1999)
   24 ALR5th 465—§ 3

Sutton v. Inland Const. Co., 144 Neb.
   721, 14 N.W.2d 387 (1943)
   27 ALR5th 174—§ 30

Sutton v. Mytich, 197 Ill. App. 3d 672,
   144 Ill. Dec. 196, 555 N.E.2d 93 (3d
   Dist. 1990)
   10 ALR5th 828—§ 11

Sutton v. Overcash, 251 Ill. App. 3d 737,
   191 Ill. Dec. 230, 623 N.E.2d 820
   (3d Dist. 1993)
   7 ALR6th 563—§ 4

Sutton v. Sanders, 556 N.E.2d 1362
   (Ind. Ct. App. 1st Dist. 1990)
   91 ALR5th 1—§ 15

Sutton v. Sanders, 556 N.E.2d 1362
   (Ind. Ct. App. 1990)
   97 ALR6th 375—§ 6

Sutton v. Schwartz, 808 S.W.2d 15 (Mo.
   Ct. App. E.D. 1991)
   119 ALR5th 445—§ 8, 14
   120 ALR5th 229—§ 7, 14
   2 ALR6th 439—§ 4, 17, 45

Sutton v. Schwartz, 860 S.W.2d 833
   (Mo. Ct. App. E.D. 1993)
   55 ALR5th 557—§ 13

Sutton v. Snyder, 2005-Ohio-5603, 2005
   WL 2709568 (Ohio Ct. App. 11th
   Dist. Trumbull County 2005)
   14 ALR6th 1—§ 4

Sutton v. Southwest Forest Industries,
   Inc., 643 F. Supp. 662 (D.C. Kan.
   1986)
   14 ALR5th 242—§ 7

Sutton v. State, 190 Ga. App. 56, 378
   S.E.2d 491 (1989)
   15 ALR5th 391—§ 45

Sutton v. State, 191 Ark. 186, 84 S.W.2d
   373 (1935)
   108 ALR5th 593—§ 18

Sutton v. State, 197 Ark. 686, 122
   S.W.2d 617 (1938)
   119 ALR5th 275—§ 13

Sutton v. State, 419 S.W.2d 857 (Tex.
   Crim. App. 1967)
   28 ALR6th 505—§ 9

Sutton v. Subaru of America, Inc., 771
   F. Supp. 321 (D. Kan. 1991)
   56 ALR5th 1—§ 3

Sutton v. Sutton, 359 So. 2d 392 (Ala.
   Civ. App. 1978)
   119 ALR5th 445—§ 6, 10
   124 ALR5th 441—§ 3, 16

Sutton v. Sutton, 1991 WL 16234 (Tenn.
   Ct. App. 1991)
   112 ALR5th 185—§ 4, 8

Sutton v. Sutton, 2000 WL 15051 (Neb.
   Ct. App. 2000)
   102 ALR5th 395—§ 6

Sutton v. Tanger, 115 Cal. App. 267, 1
   P.2d 521 (1st Dist. 1931)
   103 ALR5th 339—§ 3

Sutton v. Tennessee Civil Service Com.,
   779 S.W.2d 788 (Tenn. 1989)
   57 ALR5th 477—§ 30

Sutton v. United Airlines, Inc., 119 S.
   Ct. 2139, 144 L. Ed. 2d 450, 9 A.D.
   Cas. (BNA) 673 (U.S. 1999)
   77 ALR5th 595—§ 2

Sutton v. United Air Lines, Inc., 130
   F.3d 893, 7 A.D. Cas. (BNA) 1167
   (10th Cir. 1997)
   77 ALR5th 595—§ 2

Sutton v. United Air Lines, Inc., 527
   U.S. 471, 119 S. Ct. 2139, 144 L.
   Ed. 2d 450, 9 A.D. Cas. (BNA) 673
   (1999)
   102 ALR5th 1—§ 7

Sutton v. Ward, 92 N.C. App. 215, 374 S.E.2d 277 (1988)
42 ALR6th 545—§ 6, 18, 20
43 ALR6th 375—§ 4, 15, 46
Sutton v. Winn Dixie Stores, Inc., 233 Ga. App. 424, 504 S.E.2d 245 (1998)
123 ALR5th 1—§ 2, 3
Sutton and Widner, In re, 85 Wash. App. 487, 933 P.2d 1069 (Div. 3 1997)
69 ALR5th 219—§ 6
Sutton's Steel & Supply, Inc. v. Bellsouth Mobility, Inc., 776 So. 2d 589 (La. Ct. App. 3d Cir. 2000)
13 ALR6th 145—§ 8
Sutton Steel & Supply, Inc. v. BellSouth Mobility, Inc., 971 So. 2d 1257 (La. Ct. App. 3d Cir. 2007)
50 ALR6th 281—§ 27
Suvada v. White Motor Co., 32 Ill. 2d 612, 210 N.E.2d 182, 2 U.C.C. Rep. Serv. (CBC) 762 (1965)
73 ALR5th 75—§ 3
75 ALR5th 413—§ 12
Suzore v. Rutherford, 35 Tenn. App. 678, 251 S.W.2d 129 (1952)
12 ALR5th 195—§ 4 to 6, 8
Suzuki v. Eli Lilly and Co., 2002 WL 258263 (Cal. App. 2d Dist. 2002)
80 ALR6th 469—§ 22, 29, 55
Suzuki v. Hitachi Global Storage Technologies, Inc., 2010 WL 956896 (N.D. Cal. 2010)
60 ALR6th 295—§ 42, 52
S.V., In re, 2008 WL 5390905 (Cal. App. 2d Dist. 2008)
52 ALR6th 433—§ 31
53 ALR6th 419—§ 4, 44, 52
Svea Fire & Life Ins. Co. v. Spokane, P. & S. R. Co., 175 Wash. 622, 28 P.2d 266 (1933)
17 ALR5th 547—§ 36
Svejcara v. Whitman, 82 N.M. 739, 487 P.2d 167 (App. 1971)
33 ALR5th 303—§ 3, 5, 12, 15
Svendsen v. County of Riverside, 2003 WL 133463 (Cal. App. 4th Dist. 2003)

14 ALR6th 119—§ 4
Svenska Finans Intern. BV v. Scolaro, Shulman, Cohen, Lawler & Burstein, P.C., 37 F. Supp. 2d 178 (N.D. N.Y. 1999)
76 ALR6th 31—§ 26
Svenson v. Engelke, 211 Cal. 500, 296 P. 281 (1931)
50 ALR5th 703—§ 16
Sventek v. Vincent, 2009 WL 1684665 (W.D. Pa. 2009)
73 ALR6th 1—§ 5
Svestka v. First Nat'l Bank in Stuttgart, 602 S.W.2d 604, 29 U.C.C.R.S. 1111 (Ark. 1980)
61 ALR5th 525—§ 4
Svet v. Mayfield, 56 Ohio App. 3d 17, 564 N.E.2d 735 (9th Dist. Summit County 1989)
86 ALR5th 295—§ 20
SVG Lithography Systems, Inc. v. Ultratech Stepper, Inc., 334 F. Supp. 2d 21 (D. Mass. 2004)
85 ALR6th 1—§ 29
Svidlow v. State, 90 Tex. Crim. 510, 236 S.W. 101 (1921)
5 ALR5th 243—§ 58
Sviland v. South Carolina Employment Sec. Com., 300 S.C. 305, 387 S.E.2d 688 (App. 1989)
41 ALR5th 123—§ 5, 15
Svistunoff v. Svistunoff, 108 Cal. App. 2d 638, 239 P.2d 650 (1952)
5 ALR5th 422—§ 3, 4
S. Volpe & Co., Inc. v. Board of Appeals of Wareham, 4 Mass. App. Ct. 357, 348 N.E.2d 807 (1976)
63 ALR5th 607—§ 7
Svrcek v. Rosenberg, 203 Md. App. 705, 40 A.3d 494, 77 U.C.C. Rep. Serv. 2d 218 (2012)
86 ALR6th 411—§ 5
S.W., In Interest of, 127 Idaho 513, 903 P.2d 102 (Ct. App. 1995)
57 ALR5th 141—§ 2, 22
S.W., In re, 148 Cal. App. 4th 1501, 56 Cal. Rptr. 3d 665 (5th Dist. 2007)
52 ALR6th 433—§ 25

57 ALR6th 163—§ 42, 48
S.W., In re, 428 N.W.2d 521 (S.D. 1988)
38 ALR5th 433—§ 3, 19
S.W., In re, 670 N.W.2d 433 (Iowa App. 2003)
116 ALR5th 559—§ 3
S.W. v. Duncan, 2001 OK 39, 24 P.3d 846 (Okla. 2001)
82 ALR5th 389—§ 3
100 ALR5th 1—§ 8, 12
59 ALR6th 161—§ 12, 43
60 ALR6th 193—§ 31
S.W. v. Spring Lake Park School Dist. No. 16, 580 N.W.2d 19, 127 Ed. Law Rep. 422 (Minn. 1998)
100 ALR6th 563—§ 41
Swaaley v. U.S., 180 Ct. Cl. 1, 376 F.2d 857 (1967)
44 ALR5th 193—§ 6
Swacker v. Pennroad Corp., 30 Del. Ch. 495, 57 A.2d 63 (1947)
11 ALR6th 587—§ 24
Swackhammer v. State, 808 P.2d 219 (Wyo. 1991)
21 ALR6th 771—§ 9
Swaczyk v. Detroit Edison Co., 207 Mich. 494, 174 N.W. 197 (1919)
95 ALR5th 29—§ 3
Swaffar v. State, 258 S.W.3d 254 (Tex. App. Fort Worth 2008)
84 ALR6th 293—§ 18
Swafford v. Bank of America Corp., 2005 WL 3078631 (S.D.Tex. 2005)
11 ALR6th 447—§ 6
Swafford v. Globe American Casualty Co., 187 Ga. App. 730, 371 S.E.2d 180 (1988)
40 ALR5th 603—§ 10
Swafford v. Lafleur, 576 So. 2d 57 (La. App. 1st Cir. 1990)
55 ALR5th 681—§ 6
Swafford v. Wortman, 2 F. Supp. 2d 1429 (D. Kan. 1998)
14 ALR6th 301—§ 4, 13, 19
Swage v. Inn Philadelphia, 72 Fair Empl. Prac. Cas. (BNA) 438, 68 Empl. Prac. Dec. (CCH) ¶ 44153, 1996 WL 368316 (E.D. Pa. 1996)

73 ALR5th 1—§ 3, 5, 6
Swager v. Peterson, 49 Idaho 785, 291 P. 1049 (1930)
80 ALR5th 533—§ 5
Swagger v. City of Crystal, 379 N.W.2d 183 (Minn. Ct. App. 1985)
82 ALR6th 417—§ 4, 15
Swagger v. State, 228 Ark. 51, 305 S.W.2d 682 (1957)
55 ALR6th 157—§ 74, 105
Swaggerty v. Petersen, 280 Or. 739, 572 P.2d 1309 (1977)
25 ALR5th 123—§ 9, 27, 29, 40
25 ALR5th 233—§ 12
Swagler v. Sheridan, 2011 WL 2635937 (D. Md. 2011)
101 ALR6th 207—§ 4, 15, 16
Swagler v. Sheridan, 2011 WL 2746649 (D. Md. 2011)
70 ALR6th 513—§ 4
71 ALR6th 471—§ 10
Swagman v. Swift & Co., 7 Mich. App. 608, 152 N.W.2d 562 (1967)
52 ALR6th 271—§ 7
Swaim v. State, 257 Ark. 166, 514 S.W.2d 706 (1974)
43 ALR6th 475—§ 15
Swaim v. Westchester Academy, 208 F. Supp. 2d 579, 167 Ed. Law Rep. 141 (M.D. N.C. 2002)
11 ALR6th 447—§ 11
Swain v. Alabama, 380 U.S. 202, 13 L. Ed. 2d 759, 85 S. Ct. 824 (1965)
20 ALR5th 398—§ 2
47 ALR5th 259—§ 2
63 ALR5th 375—§ 2, 3
Swain v. Alabama, 380 U.S. 202, 85 S. Ct. 824, 13 L. Ed. 2d 759 (1965)
15 ALR6th 319—§ 2
Swain v. Board of Adjustment, 433 S.W.2d 727 (Tex. Civ. App. Dallas 1968)
8 ALR5th 391—§ 3, 9
Swain v. Curry, 595 So. 2d 168 (Fla. 1st DCA 1992)
92 ALR6th 379—§ 37
Swain v. Oregon State Correctional Inst., 91 Or. App. 584, 756 P.2d 65 (1988)

96 ALR6th 269—§ 12
Swain v. Pressley, 430 U.S. 372, 97 S.
Ct. 1224, 51 L. Ed. 2d 411 (1977)
31 ALR6th 1—§ 7 to 9, 14, 16
Swain v. State, 661 S.W.2d 125 (Tex.
Crim. 1983)
42 ALR5th 291—§ 36
Swain v. Superintendent, Old Colony
Correctional Center, 29 Mass. App.
Ct. 918, 556 N.E.2d 1061 (1990)
78 ALR6th 417—§ 3
Swain v. Swain, 660 So. 2d 1356 (Ala.
Civ. App. 1995)
11 ALR6th 125—§ 4 to 6, 10, 11, 26
Swain v. Thompson, 281 Ga. 30, 635
S.E.2d 779 (2006)
60 ALR6th 481—§ 4, 45
Swain v. Webre, 106 La. 161, 30 So. 331
(1901)
62 ALR5th 219—§ 54
Swain v. Wells, 210 Ga. 394, 80 S.E.2d
321 (1954)
112 ALR5th 185—§ 6, 14
Swait v. University of Nebraska at
Omaha, 2008 WL 5083245 (D. Neb.
2008)
64 ALR6th 131—§ 23
Swaite v. State, 272 Ark. 128, 612
S.W.2d 307 (1981)
7 ALR5th 758—§ 9, 13
Swajian v. General Motors Corp., 559
A.2d 1041, Prod. Liab. Rep. (CCH)
¶ 12166 (R.I. 1989)
62 ALR5th 537—§ 3
Swaka, In re Marriage of, 319 P.3d 69
(Wash. Ct. App. Div. 2 2014)
96 ALR6th 103—§ 3
Swallow v. Emergency Medicine of
Idaho, P.A., 138 Idaho 589, 67 P.3d
68 (2003)
44 ALR6th 391—§ 5
Swallow v. Enterprise Truck Lines, Inc.,
894 S.W.2d 232 (Mo. Ct. App. E.D.
1995)
63 ALR6th 187—§ 23
Swallows v. G. Wendell Weathers,
D.D.S., P.C., 915 S.W.2d 763 (Mo.
1996)

17 ALR6th 159—§ 12, 55
Swallows v. Holden, 812 S.W.2d 552
(Mo. Ct. App. S.D. 1991)
15 ALR6th 241—§ 14
Swamy v. Hodges, 583 So. 2d 1095 (Fla.
Dist. Ct. App. 1st Dist. 1991)
84 ALR5th 619—§ 6
Swan v. Country Mut. Ins. Co., 306 Ill.
App. 3d 958, 240 Ill. Dec. 1, 715
N.E.2d 688 (1st Dist. 1999)
77 ALR5th 319—§ 4
78 ALR5th 341—§ 6
Swan v. Department of Public Safety,
311 So. 2d 498 (La. Ct. App. 4th
Cir. 1975)
109 ALR5th 611—§ 5
Swan v. I.P., Inc., 613 So. 2d 846, CCH
Prod. Liab. Rep. ¶ 13451 (Miss.
1993)
3 ALR5th 851—§ 12, 14, 15
Swan v. Riverbank Canning Co., 81 Cal.
App. 2d 555, 184 P.2d 686 (1947)
5 ALR5th 422—§ 3
Swan v. State, 28 A.3d 362 (Del. 2011)
102 ALR6th 417—§ 69
Swan v. State, 820 A.2d 342 (Del. 2003)
110 ALR5th 1—§ 7
Swan v. Swan, 106 Nev. 464, 796 P.2d
221 (1990)
5 ALR5th 550—§ 38
6 ALR5th 69—§ 6, 10
21 ALR5th 396—§ 21, 26
Swan v. Thompson, 124 Cal. 193, 56 P.
878 (1899)
52 ALR6th 271—§ 8
Swanagan v. Al Piemonte Ford Sales,
Inc., 1995 WL 493480 (N.D. Ill.
1995)
115 ALR5th 709—§ 2
117 ALR5th 155—§ 2, 10
Swanbeck v. Hubbard, 336 Ill. App. 384,
84 N.E.2d 159 (1949)
27 ALR5th 174—§ 68
Swan Crewboats, Inc. v. Phipps, 2002
A.M.C. 2877, 2002 WL 1733647
(E.D. La. 2002)
66 ALR6th 185—§ 16

Swanek v. Hutzel Hospital, 115 Mich.
App. 254, 320 N.W.2d 234 (1982)
2 ALR5th 769—§ 2
3 ALR5th 123—§ 2
4 ALR5th 148—§ 2
4 ALR5th 210—§ 2
6 ALR5th 490—§ 2
6 ALR5th 534—§ 2
7 ALR5th 1—§ 2
Swan, Estate of v. Balan, 956 A.2d 1222
(Del. 2008)
98 ALR6th 1—§ 16
Swaney v. Peden Steel Co., 259 N.C.
531, 131 S.E.2d 601 (1963)
3 ALR5th 851—§ 17
Swanger v. State, 251 Ga. App. 182, 554
S.E.2d 207 (2001)
8 ALR6th 265—§ 3, 7
Swanger v. State, 445 N.W.2d 344 (Iowa
1989)
45 ALR5th 109—§ 5
45 ALR5th 173—§ 5
Swangstu v. Misenhimer, 2002 WL
397004 (Tex. App. El Paso 2002)
94 ALR6th 431—§ 9, 29
Swanier v. State, 473 So. 2d 180 (Miss.
1985)
9 ALR6th 1—§ 12
Swanigan v. American Nat'l Red Cross,
438 S.E.2d 251 (S.C. 1993)
12 ALR5th 1—§ 6
Swanigan v. U.S., 853 A.2d 742 (D.C.
2004)
70 ALR6th 361—§ 7
Swank v. Halivopoulos, 108 N.J. Super.
120, 260 A.2d 240 (1969)
2 ALR5th 811—§ 2, 26
Swank v. Smart, 898 F.2d 1247, 5 I.E.R.
Cas. (BNA) 323 (7th Cir. 1990)
123 ALR5th 411—§ 64
Swank v. Tanner, 2012 WL 1565298
(E.D. La. 2012)
89 ALR6th 1—§ 115
95 ALR6th 341—§ 51
Swanks v. Washington Metropolitan
Area Transit Authority, 116 F.3d
582, 22 A.D.D. 12, 6 A.D. Cas.
(BNA) 1544 (D.C. Cir. 1997)

99 ALR5th 65—§ 9
Swann v. Bowie, 2 Cranch CC 221, F.
Cas. No 13672 (Dist. Col. 1820)
61 ALR5th 635—§ 21
Swann v. City-Parish, 492 So. 2d 1225
(La. App. 1st Cir. 1986)
50 ALR5th 1—§ 4
52 ALR5th 1—§ 8
Swann v. Commonwealth, 247 Va. 222,
441 S.E.2d 195 (1994)
37 ALR5th 515—§ 2, 21
Swann v. Prudential Ins. Co. of America, 95 Md. App. 365, 620 A.2d 989
(1993)
99 ALR5th 141—§ 9, 12
Swann v. State, 412 So. 2d 1253 (Ala.
App. 1982)
7 ALR5th 758—§ 13
Swann v. State, 637 P.2d 888 (Okla.
Crim. App. 1981)
95 ALR5th 229—§ 3
Swann v. United Gas Co., 266 N.C. 132,
146 S.E.2d 17 (1966)
84 ALR5th 69—§ 19
Swann & Weiskopf, Ltd. v. Meed Associates, Inc., 304 Ill. App. 3d 970,
238 Ill. Dec. 292, 711 N.E.2d 395
(1st Dist. 1999)
33 ALR5th 1—§ 16
Swanner v. Anchorage Equal Rights
Com'n, 874 P.2d 274 (Alaska 1994)
10 ALR6th 513—§ 3 to 5
Swanner v. State, 170 Tex. Crim. 591,
342 S.W.2d 577 (1961)
26 ALR5th 1—§ 3, 34, 42
Swannie v. State, 2000 WL 1790085
(Tex. App. Dallas)
117 ALR5th 491—§ 8
Swans v. City of Lansing, 65 F. Supp.
2d 625 (W.D. Mich. 1998)
12 ALR5th 195—§ 35
Swansea v. County of St. Clair, 45 Ill.
App. 3d 184, 4 Ill. Dec. 33, 359
N.E.2d 866 (5th Dist. 1977)
53 ALR5th 1—§ 25, 33
Swansea, Village of v. St. Clair County,
45 Ill. App. 3d 184, 4 Ill. Dec. 33,
359 N.E.2d 866 (5th Dist. 1977)

77 ALR6th 393—§ 59

Swanson, In re Marriage of, 586 N.W.2d 527 (Iowa Ct. App. 1998)

82 ALR5th 389—§ 3

Swanson, Petition of, 403 Mass. 1004, 528 N.E.2d 875 (1988)

78 ALR6th 417—§ 38

Swanson, Re Marriage of, 220 Mont. 490, 716 P.2d 219 (1986)

9 ALR5th 568—§ 15, 16

Swanson v. Board of Police Com'rs of Village of Lake in the Hills, 197 Ill. App. 3d 592, 144 Ill. Dec. 138, 555 N.E.2d 35 (2d Dist. 1990)

19 ALR6th 217—§ 26, 54

72 ALR6th 563—§ 27

Swanson v. City of Chetek, 695 F. Supp. 2d 896 (W.D. Wis. 2010)

86 ALR6th 173—§ 6

Swanson v. City of Chetek, 2013 WL 3018926 (7th Cir. 2013)

86 ALR6th 173—§ 5

Swanson v. City of St. Paul, 526 N.W.2d 366 (Minn. 1995)

112 ALR5th 509—§ 16

122 ALR5th 653—§ 2

13 ALR6th 209—§ 13, 48

39 ALR6th 445—§ 3, 21

Swanson v. Columbia Transit Corp., 311 Minn. 538, 248 N.W.2d 732 (1976)

95 ALR5th 329—§ 4

Swanson v. Department of Public Safety and Corrections, 837 So. 2d 634 (La. Ct. App. 1st Cir. 2002)

85 ALR6th 229—§ 30

Swanson v. EMC Mortg. Corp., 2009 WL 3627925 (E.D. Cal. 2009)

86 ALR6th 411—§ 5

Swanson v. Faulkner, 55 F.3d 956, 19 Employee Benefits Cas. (BNA) 1577 (4th Cir. 1995)

50 ALR6th 281—§ 23

Swanson v. General Paint Co., 361 P.2d 842 (Okla. 1961)

4 ALR5th 443—§ 20

4 ALR5th 585—§ 3, 5, 15

Swanson v. Georgetown Collection, Inc., 1995 WL 72717 (N.D. N.Y. 1995)

114 ALR5th 129—§ 9

Swanson v. Knight, 105 Or. App. 462, 805 P.2d 156 (1991)

91 ALR5th 1—§ 3, 19

Swanson v. Liquid Air Corp., 55 Wash. App. 917, 781 P.2d 900, 5 BNA IER Cas. 318, 117 CCH LC ¶ 56436 (1989)

17 ALR5th 1—§ 3

Swanson v. Liquid Air Corp., 118 Wash. 2d 512, 826 P.2d 664, 7 BNA IER Cas. 366, 125 CCH LC ¶ 57376 (1992)

17 ALR5th 1—§ 5, 9

Swanson v. Minneapolis-Honeywell Regulator Co., 240 Minn. 449, 61 N.W.2d 526 (1953)

2 ALR5th 475—§ 11

Swanson v. Morgan, 2012 WL 297110 (U.S. 2012)

76 ALR6th 587—§ 12, 15, 49

Swanson v. Roehl Transport, Inc., 83 Fed. R. Evid. Serv. 734 (E.D. Tex. 2010)

77 ALR6th 251—§ 5

Swanson v. Roman Catholic Bishop of Portland, 1997 ME 63, 692 A.2d 441 (Me. 1997)

101 ALR5th 1—§ 4

Swanson v. Senior Resource Connection, 254 F. Supp. 2d 945 (S.D. Ohio 2003)

10 ALR6th 375—§ 7

Swanson v. Sheppard, 445 N.W.2d 654, 55 Ed. Law Rep. 1145 (N.D. 1989)

58 ALR6th 1—§ 36

Swanson v. State, 308 Ark. 28, 823 S.W.2d 812 (1992)

38 ALR6th 439—§ 4

Swanson v. State, 335 N.C. 674, 441 S.E.2d 537, 18 Employee Benefits Cas. (BNA) 1303 (1994)

1 ALR6th 1—§ 9

14 ALR6th 119—§ 52

Swanson v. State, 722 S.W.2d 158 (Tex. App. Houston (14th Dist.) 1986)
7 ALR5th 263—§ 6
Swanson v. State Farm Fire & Casualty Co., 349 So. 2d 202 (Fla. App. D4 1977)
22 ALR5th 483—§ 3
Swanson v. St. John's Lutheran Hosp., 182 Mont. 414, 597 P.2d 702 (1979)
34 ALR5th 699—§ 5
Swanson v. Swanson, 137 Neb. 699, 290 N.W. 908 (1939)
53 ALR5th 375—§ 12
Swanson v. Swanson, 464 S.W.2d 225 (Mo. 1971)
49 ALR5th 441—§ 13
Swanson v. University of Hawaii Professional Assembly, 269 F. Supp. 2d 1252, 179 Ed. Law Rep. 694, 172 L.R.R.M. (BNA) 2740 (D. Haw. 2003)
73 ALR6th 281—§ 15
Swanson v. Wesley College, Inc., 402 A.2d 401 (Del. Super. 1979)
47 ALR5th 1—§ 15, 17, 21
Swanson v. Worley, 490 F.3d 894 (11th Cir. 2007)
59 ALR6th 111—§ 4, 8
Swanson By and Through Swanson v. Guthrie Independent School Dist. No. I-L, 135 F.3d 694, 123 Ed. Law Rep. 1087 (10th Cir. 1998)
70 ALR5th 169—§ 20
Swanston v. Swanston, 502 N.W.2d 506 (N.D. 1993)
53 ALR5th 375—§ 5
Swanton v. Brigeois-Ashton, 134 Wash. App. 1067, 2006 WL 2664497 (Div. 1 2006)
34 ALR6th 253—§ 5
Swanton Sav. Bank & Trust Co. v. Tremblay, 113 Vt. 530, 37 A.2d 381 (1944)
86 ALR5th 527—§ 9
Swanton, Village of v. Barker, 2000 WL 1545041 (Ohio Ct. App. 6th Dist. Fulton County 2000)
45 ALR6th 435—§ 9

Swantz v. Colby, 745 N.W.2d 95 (Iowa Ct. App. 2007)
95 ALR6th 541—§ 29
Sward v. Sward, 410 N.W.2d 442 (Minn. Ct. App. 1987)
59 ALR6th 433—§ 3
Swars v. Council of City of Vallejo, 33 Cal. 2d 867, 206 P.2d 355 (1949)
19 ALR6th 217—§ 9
Swartley v. Tredyffrin Easttown School Dist., 287 Pa. Super. 499, 430 A.2d 1001 (1981)
7 ALR6th 1—§ 35
Swartout v. Spokane, 21 Wash. App. 665, 586 P.2d 135 (1978)
21 ALR5th 812—§ 5
Swartz, In re Marriage of, 209 Or. App. 709, 149 P.3d 316 (2006)
36 ALR6th 1—§ 20
Swartz, In re Marriage of, 512 N.W.2d 825 (Iowa Ct. App. 1993)
124 ALR5th 537—§ 4
Swartz, Matter of, 141 Ariz. 266, 686 P.2d 1236 (1984)
25 ALR6th 1—§ 3, 31
26 ALR6th 1—§ 3
27 ALR6th 1—§ 3
Swartz v. Berkshire Life Ins. Co., 2000 WL 1448627 (S.D. N.Y. 2000)
23 ALR6th 697—§ 14
Swartz v. Biben, 87 Pa. Super. 270 (1926)
5 ALR5th 422—§ 3
Swartz v. Bly, 183 N.W.2d 733 (Iowa 1971)
36 ALR6th 387—§ 7
Swartz v. City Mortg., Inc., 2012 WL 5987571 (D. Haw. 2012)
81 ALR6th 161—§ 5
Swartz v. General Elec. Co., 327 Pa. Super. 58, 474 A.2d 1172 (1984)
84 ALR5th 69—§ 3, 21
Swartz v. Illinois Indus. Com'n, 359 Ill. App. 3d 1083, 297 Ill. Dec. 486, 837 N.E.2d 937 (3d Dist. 2005)
13 ALR6th 209—§ 14, 41, 47
Swartz v. Iowa, 2002 WL 32173383 (N.D. Iowa 2002)

63 ALR6th 1—§ 42

Swartz v. McNabb, 830 So. 2d 1093 (La. Ct. App. 3d Cir. 2002)

110 ALR5th 465—§ 12

Swartz v. Schering-Plough Corp., 53 F. Supp. 2d 95 (D. Mass. 1999)

87 ALR6th 1—§ 66

Swartz v. Sears, Roebuck and Co., 264 Ill. App. 3d 254, 201 Ill. Dec. 210, 636 N.E.2d 642 (1st Dist. 1993)

83 ALR5th 589—§ 6

Swartz v. State, 61 S.W.3d 781 (Tex. App. Corpus Christi 2001)

68 ALR6th 527—§ 37

Swartz v. State, 506 N.W.2d 792 (Iowa Ct. App. 1993)

101 ALR5th 187—§ 9

Swartz v. Steele, 42 Ohio App. 2d 1, 71 Ohio Ops. 2d 46, 325 N.E.2d 910 (Cuyahoga Co. 1974)

12 ALR5th 195—§ 45

Swartz v. Sunderland, 403 Pa. 222, 169 A.2d 289 (1961)

17 ALR6th 1—§ 16

Swartz v. Swartz, 43 App. Div. 2d 1012, 349 N.Y.S.2d 1005 (4th Dep't 1973)

46 ALR5th 735—§ 2

Swartz v. Swartz, 49 App. Div. 2d 254, 374 N.Y.S.2d 857 (4th Dep't 1975)

38 ALR5th 69—§ 6

Swartz v. Swartz, 887 S.W.2d 644 (Mo. Ct. App. W.D. 1994)

125 ALR5th 133—§ 4
76 ALR6th 31—§ 9

Swartzbauer v. Lead Industries Ass'n, Inc., 794 F. Supp. 142, Prod. Liab. Rep. (CCH) ¶ 13430 (E.D. Pa. 1992)

63 ALR5th 195—§ 3 to 5, 7
69 ALR5th 137—§ 11

Swartzenberg v. Trivedi, 189 A.D.2d 151, 594 N.Y.S.2d 927 (4th Dep't 1993)

69 ALR5th 559—§ 23

Swartzentruber v. Wee-K Corp., 1997 WL 28537 (Ohio App. 4 Dist. 1997)

54 ALR5th 513—§ 3, 6

Swartzfager, Matter of, 290 Or. 799, 626 P.2d 882 (1981)

113 ALR5th 349—§ 21

Swartzlander v. Forms-Rite Business Forms & Printing Service, Inc., 174 App. Div. 2d 971, 572 N.Y.S.2d 537 (4th Dep't 1991)

27 ALR5th 174—§ 55

Swartzlander v. Hunt Laboratory, Inc., 552 So. 2d 1339 (La. Ct. App. 5th Cir. 1989)

92 ALR6th 379—§ 59

Swartzwelder v. Freeport Coal Co., 131 W. Va. 276, 46 S.E.2d 813 (1948)

8 ALR5th 653—§ 8

Swasey v. Barron, 46 Mass. App. Ct. 127, 703 N.E.2d 1208 (1999)

13 ALR6th 1—§ 4
14 ALR6th 1—§ 10

Swatch v. Treat, 41 Mass. App. Ct. 559, 671 N.E.2d 1004 (1996)

69 ALR5th 559—§ 7

Swate v. Schiffers, 975 S.W.2d 70, 26 Media L. Rep. (BNA) 2258 (Tex. App. San Antonio 1998)

19 ALR5th 1—§ 38
54 ALR6th 165—§ 11

Swate v. Taylor, 12 F.Supp.2d 591 (S.D. Tex. 1998)

68 ALR5th 549—§ 3, 9

Swavely v. Eno, 54 Pa. Super. 82 (1913)

46 ALR5th 581—§ 3
47 ALR5th 1—§ 13

Swaw v. Ortell, 137 Ill. App. 3d 60, 92 Ill. Dec. 49, 484 N.E.2d 780 (1st Dist. 1984)

8 ALR5th 312—§ 11
24 ALR5th 200—§ 24, 41

Swayne v. L.D.S. Social Services, 795 P.2d 637 (Utah 1990)

28 ALR6th 349—§ 36, 37, 39, 41

Swayne v. L.D.S. Social Servs., 795 P.2d 637, 136 Utah Adv. Rep. 18 (Utah 1990)

61 ALR5th 151—§ 12, 14

Swayze v. A.O. Smith Corp., 694 F. Supp. 619, Prod. Liab. Rep. (CCH) ¶ 12028 (E.D. Ark. 1988)

112 ALR5th 113—§ 16
13 ALR6th 355—§ 4, 35
18 ALR6th 629—§ 11

Swayze v. McNeil Laboratories, Inc., 807 F.2d 464, CCH Prod. Liab. Rep. ¶ 11224 (CA5 Miss. 1987)
57 ALR5th 1—§ 3

Swayze v. Swayze, 176 Conn. 323, 408 A.2d 1 (1978)
112 ALR5th 185—§ 4, 8
36 ALR6th 1—§ 32, 33

Sweaney v. District Court In and For Eighteenth Judicial Dist., 713 P.2d 914 (Colo. 1986)
37 ALR6th 357—§ 3
72 ALR6th 141—§ 10

Sweaney v. State, 632 S.W.2d 932 (Tex. App. Fort Worth 1982)
41 ALR5th 1—§ 7

Sweaney v. United Loan & Finance Co., 205 Kan. 66, 468 P.2d 124 (1970)
12 ALR5th 195—§ 12, 42, 52

Sweany v. Walgreen Co., 323 Ill. App. (abstract) 439, 55 N.E.2d 723 (1944)
2 ALR5th 1—§ 68

Swearengen v. Johns, 210 Ark. 119, 194 S.W.2d 445 (1946)
25 ALR5th 391—§ 78

Swearengin v. Evergreen Lawns, 85 Ark. App. 61, 145 S.W.3d 830 (2004)
28 ALR6th 1—§ 3, 14, 18, 22, 33, 79

Swearingen v. Industrial Com'n, 298 Ill. App. 3d 666, 232 Ill. Dec. 790, 699 N.E.2d 237 (5th Dist. 1998)
63 ALR6th 187—§ 12

Swearingen v. Long, 889 F. Supp. 587 (N.D. N.Y. 1995)
6 ALR5th 162—§ 12

Swearingen v. State, 31 Okla. Crim. 66, 237 P. 135 (1925)
54 ALR6th 429—§ 13

Swearingen v. State, 101 S.W.3d 89 (Tex. Crim. App. 2003)
9 ALR6th 363—§ 36
67 ALR6th 341—§ 7

Swearingen Lumber Co. v. Washington School Tp., 125 Iowa 283, 99 N.W. 730 (1904)
16 ALR5th 548—§ 7

Swearingen, State ex rel v. Industrial Com'n of Ohio, 1982 WL 3977 (Ohio Ct. App. 10th Dist. Franklin County 1982)
31 ALR6th 199—§ 47

Swearington v. California Dept. of Corrections and Rehabilitation, 2012 WL 5288812 (E.D. Cal. 2012)
89 ALR6th 1—§ 115

Swearngin v. Sears Roebuck & Co., 376 F.2d 637 (10th Cir. 1967)
93 ALR5th 103—§ 4

Sweat v. Boeder, 2013 UT App 206, 309 P.3d 295 (Utah Ct. App. 2013)
97 ALR6th 375—§ 13

Sweat v. Commonwealth, 29 Ky. LR 1067, 96 S.W. 843 (1906)
41 ALR5th 1—§ 3

Sweat v. Darr, 235 Kan. 570, 684 P.2d 347 (1984)
71 ALR6th 335—§ 8

Sweat v. Fuhriman, 23 Utah 2d 331, 463 P.2d 3 (1969)
9 ALR5th 826—§ 18

Sweat v. Hollister, 37 Cal. App. 4th 603, 43 Cal. Rptr. 2d 399 (4th Dist. 1995)
124 ALR5th 575—§ 21

Sweatland v. Park Corp., 181 A.D.2d 243, 587 N.Y.S.2d 54 (4th Dep't 1992)
92 ALR5th 227—§ 5, 11
109 ALR5th 301—§ 5, 16
112 ALR5th 113—§ 10

Sweatt v. International Development Corp., 242 Ga. App. 753, 531 S.E.2d 192 (2000)
39 ALR5th 33—§ 3

Sweatt v. Jarboe, 167 Ga. App. 267, 305 S.E.2d 923 (1983)
5 ALR5th 422—§ 3

Sweatt v. Norman, 283 S.C. 443, 322 S.E.2d 478 (App. 1984)
50 ALR5th 1—§ 9, 11, 13

For assistance, call 1-800-328-4880

Sweatt v. State, 2003 WL 22243348 (Tenn. Crim. App. 2003)

125 ALR5th 497—§ 3

Sweatt v. Wong, 145 N.C. App. 33, 549 S.E.2d 222 (2001)

110 ALR5th 329—§ 5

Sweazea v. State, 588 S.W.2d 244 (Mo. Ct. App. E.D. 1979)

72 ALR5th 109—§ 6

Sweazie v. Haley, 219 So. 2d 560 (La. App. 3d Cir. 1969)

9 ALR5th 826—§ 25, 29

Sweco, Inc. v. Continental Sulfur and Chemical, 808 S.W.2d 112, 14 U.C.C. Rep. Serv. 2d 1034 (Tex. App. El Paso 1991)

88 ALR6th 1—§ 2, 9, 24, 80

Swedberg v. Battle Creek Mut. Ins. Co., 218 Neb. 447, 356 N.W.2d 456 (1984)

56 ALR5th 407—§ 25

Swedeen v. Swedeen, 270 Minn. 491, 134 N.W.2d 871 (1965)

8 ALR6th 549—§ 11, 15

Swedenberg v. Phillips, 562 So. 2d 170 (Ala. 1990)

8 ALR6th 465—§ 19

Swedenburg v. Kelly, 72 U.S.L.W. 3600, 2004 WL 473703 (U.S. 2004)

116 ALR5th 149—§ 15, 23

Swedenburg v. Kelly, 232 F. Supp. 2d 135 (S.D. N.Y. 2002)

116 ALR5th 149—§ 4, 15

Swedenburg v. Kelly, 358 F.3d 223 (2d Cir. 2004)

116 ALR5th 149—§ 4, 23

Swedenburg v. Kelly, 358 F.3d 223, 2004 WL 254401 (2d Cir. 2004)

116 ALR5th 149—§ 15, 23

Swedenburg v. Kelly, 2000 WL 1264285 (S.D. N.Y. 2000)

116 ALR5th 149—§ 15

Swedish Crucible Steel Co. v. Travelers Indem. Co., 387 F. Supp. 231 (E.D. Mich. 1974)

37 ALR5th 41—§ 8, 16, 18

Sweeden v. Hunting Tubular Threading, Inc., 806 So. 2d 728 (La. Ct. App. 5th Cir. 2001)

22 ALR6th 329—§ 29

Sweeney, In re, 725 A.2d 1013 (D.C. 1999)

43 ALR6th 163—§ 14

Sweeney, In re, 1990 WL 37788 (Ohio Ct. App. 1st Dist. Hamilton County 1990)

87 ALR5th 361—§ 18

Sweeney, Re Estate of, 210 Kan. 216, 500 P.2d 56 (1972)

14 ALR5th 557—§ 6, 9, 11

Sweeney v. Bailey, 7 S.D. 404, 64 N.W. 188 (1895)

27 ALR5th 764—§ 5

Sweeney v. Burns, 34 Conn. Supp. 94, 377 A.2d 338 (C.P. 1977)

10 ALR6th 31—§ 22, 34

Sweeney v. Hartford Acci. & Indem. Co., 136 N.J. Super. 591, 347 A.2d 380 (1975)

31 ALR5th 116—§ 5

Sweeney v. Kerr's Adm'r, 16 Ky. LR 33, 25 S.W. 273 (1894)

53 ALR5th 287—§ 4, 12

Sweeney v. Lebel, 139 Me. 280, 29 A.2d 746 (1943)

44 ALR5th 1—§ 17

Sweeney v. Levy, 67 Pa. D & C. 5 (1948)

13 ALR5th 289—§ 16, 28

Sweeney v. Levy, 67 Pa. D. & C. 5, 1949 WL 3030 (C.P. 1949)

100 ALR5th 409—§ 13
115 ALR5th 1—§ 15

Sweeney v. Mack, 625 So. 2d 15 (Fla. Dist. Ct. App. 5th Dist. 1993)

115 ALR5th 251—§ 6, 56

Sweeney v. McCormick, 159 App. Div. 2d 832, 552 N.Y.S.2d 707 (3d Dep't 1990)

33 ALR5th 303—§ 3, 6, 11, 15, 28

Sweeney v. McLeod, 15 Or. 330, 15 P. 275 (1887)

35 ALR6th 1—§ 28

Sweeney v. Merrill, 38 Kan. 216, 16 P. 454 (1888)

CASES CITED IN ALR5th and ALR6th

25 ALR5th 391—§ 5, 12
Sweeney v. Meyers, 199 Minn. 21, 270 N.W. 906 (1937)
14 ALR5th 242—§ 5, 27
Sweeney v. Prisoners' Legal Servs., 146 App. Div. 2d 1, 538 N.Y.S.2d 370 (3d Dep't 1989)
44 ALR5th 193—§ 25
Sweeney v. State, 486 N.E.2d 651 (Ind. Ct. App. 2d Dist. 1985)
95 ALR5th 229—§ 3
Sweeney v. State, 704 N.E.2d 86 (Ind. 1998)
27 ALR6th 183—§ 35
Sweeney v. State, 768 S.W.2d 253 (Tenn. 1989)
15 ALR6th 1—§ 18
Sweeney v. State Farm Mut. Ins. Co., 419 So. 2d 985 (La. App. 1982)
48 ALR5th 129—§ 17, 18
Sweeney v. Sweeney, 534 A.2d 1290 (Me. 1987)
3 ALR6th 447—§ 6, 8
Sweeney v. Sweeney, 583 So. 2d 398 (Fla. App. D1 1991)
9 ALR5th 568—§ 24
Sweeney v. Sweeney, 1998 WL 635286 (Ohio Ct. App. 10th Dist. Franklin County 1998)
7 ALR6th 411—§ 3, 33
Sweeney v. Tofany, 56 Misc. 2d 291, 288 N.Y.S.2d 649 (1968)
28 ALR5th 459—§ 3
Sweeney v. Tucker, 473 Pa. 493, 375 A.2d 698 (1977)
9 ALR6th 177—§ 19
24 ALR6th 255—§ 6, 12, 18
Sweeney, Cohn, Stahl & Vaccaro v. Kane, 6 A.D.3d 72, 773 N.Y.S.2d 420 (App. Div. 2d Dep't 2004)
2 ALR6th 195—§ 3, 4, 14
Sweeney, Estate of v. Charpentier, 675 A.2d 824 (R.I. 1996)
57 ALR5th 141—§ 18
Sweeney, People ex rel. v. Allman, 315 Ill. App. 133, 42 N.E.2d 115 (1st Dist. 1942)
19 ALR6th 217—§ 16

Sweeny v. Sweeny, 43 Wash. 2d 542, 262 P.2d 207 (1953)
70 ALR5th 377—§ 7
Sweepster, Inc. v. Scio Tp., 225 Mich. App. 497, 571 N.W.2d 553 (1997)
90 ALR5th 547—§ 6
Sweere, State ex rel. v. Crookham, 289 Or. 3, 609 P.2d 361 (1980)
28 ALR5th 664—§ 3
Sweet, Claim of, 212 A.D.2d 845, 622 N.Y.S.2d 139 (3d Dep't 1995)
25 ALR6th 101—§ 21
Sweet, In re Marriage of, 316 Ill. App. 3d 101, 249 Ill. Dec. 212, 735 N.E.2d 1037 (2d Dist. 2000)
28 ALR5th 46—§ 9
Sweet v. Childs, 507 F.2d 675 (5th Cir. 1975)
90 ALR6th 235—§ 21
Sweet v. Clare-Mar Camp, Inc., 38 Ohio App. 3d 6, 526 N.E.2d 74 (Cuyahoga Co. 1987)
33 ALR5th 205—§ 9
Sweet v. Moore, 822 So. 2d 1269 (Fla. 2002)
110 ALR5th 1—§ 2, 9
83 ALR6th 255—§ 9, 25
Sweet v. Myers, 3 S.D. 324, 53 N.W. 187 (1892)
109 ALR5th 421—§ 3
Sweet v. Ringwelski, 362 Mich. 138, 106 N.W.2d 742, 90 A.L.R.2d 1434 (1961)
14 ALR5th 193—§ 5 to 9
Sweet v. Sisters of Providence, 895 P.2d 484 (Alaska 1995)
51 ALR5th 301—§ 2, 3
Sweet v. Sisters of Providence in Washington, 895 P.2d 484 (Alaska 1995)
101 ALR5th 61—§ 3
121 ALR5th 157—§ 10
Sweet v. State, 195 Misc. 494, 89 N.Y.S.2d 506 (1949)
8 ALR5th 177—§ 3
Sweet v. State, 313 So. 2d 130 (Fla. Dist. Ct. App. 2d Dist. 1975)
86 ALR5th 59—§ 5

Sweet v. State, 371 Md. 1, 806 A.2d 265 (2002)
51 ALR6th 139—§ 8

Sweet v. State, 498 N.E.2d 924 (Ind. 1986)
83 ALR5th 277—§ 10

Sweet v. State, 693 So. 2d 644 (Fla. Dist. Ct. App. 4th Dist. 1997)
27 ALR6th 183—§ 34

Sweet v. Stormont Vail Regional Medical Center, 231 Kan. 604, 647 P.2d 1274, 26 BNA WH Cas. 1438, 98 CCH LC ¶ 55395 (1982)
11 ALR5th 715—§ 26

Sweet v. Tigard-Tualatin School Dist. #23J, 124 Fed. Appx. 482 (9th Cir. 2005)
3 ALR6th 153—§ 17

Sweet v. Tigard-Tualatin School Dist. #23J, 124 Fed. Appx. 482, 196 Ed. Law Rep. 474 (9th Cir. 2005)
67 ALR6th 437—§ 15, 18
68 ALR6th 331—§ 22, 26

Sweet v. Trahan, 159 So. 2d 782 (La. App. 3d Cir. 1964)
27 ALR5th 174—§ 3, 93

Sweeten v. State, 2002 WL 980675 (Tex. App. Dallas 2002)
117 ALR5th 491—§ 7

Sweeten, 2002 -Ohio- 2552, In re, 2002 WL 1040229 (Ohio Ct. App. 1st Dist. Hamilton County 2002)
101 ALR5th 351—§ 7

Sweeting v. Hammons, 521 So. 2d 226 (Fla. Dist. Ct. App. 3d Dist. 1988)
109 ALR5th 421—§ 12

Sweetman v. Laredo E.& R. Co., 204 S.W. 701 (Tex. Civ. App. 1918)
40 ALR5th 1—§ 4

Sweetman v. State Elections Enforcement Com'n, 249 Conn. 296, 732 A.2d 144, 136 Ed. Law Rep. 442 (1999)
51 ALR6th 359—§ 35

Sweetman v. State Highway Dept., 137 Mich. App. 14, 357 N.W.2d 783 (1984)
15 ALR6th 1—§ 10, 14

Sweetman v. Town of Cumberland, 117 R.I. 134, 364 A.2d 1277 (1976)
73 ALR5th 223—§ 13

Sweetwood, Application of, 91 N.J. Super. 496, 221 A.2d 543 (App. Div. 1966)
75 ALR6th 311—§ 86

Sweezy v. Collins Northern Ice Co., 171 Mich. 75, 137 N.W. 84 (1912)
45 ALR5th 251—§ 7, 17, 21

Sweezy v. Vallette, 37 R.I. 51, 90 A. 1078 (1914)
62 ALR5th 219—§ 17

Sweigart, Appeal of, 117 Pa. Commw. 84, 544 A.2d 74 (1988)
4 ALR6th 263—§ 14

Sweigart v. Sweigart, 33 Ohio L. Abs. 250, 35 N.E.2d 578 (App. Miami Co. 1940)
52 ALR5th 221—§ 8

Sweitzer v. Sanchez, 80 N.M. 408, 456 P.2d 882 (App. 1969)
12 ALR5th 195—§ 66

Sweitzer v. Wisconsin Dept. of Revenue, 65 Wis. 2d 235, 222 N.W.2d 662 (1974)
2 ALR6th 1—§ 67

Swelbar v. Lahti, 473 N.W.2d 77 (Minn. App. 1991)
46 ALR5th 557—§ 3

Swendra v. Oc-Unk, Inc., 134 App. Div. 2d 905, 522 N.Y.S.2d 64 (4th Dep't 1987)
16 ALR5th 1—§ 33

Swendsen v. Gross, 530 So. 2d 764 (Ala. 1988)
97 ALR6th 83—§ 72

Sweney v. State, 265 Ga. App. 21, 593 S.E.2d 12 (2003)
7 ALR6th 233—§ 9

Swensen, In re Disciplinary Proceedings Against, 2008 WI 113, 754 N.W.2d 499 (Wis. 2008)
44 ALR6th 75—§ 27
45 ALR6th 175—§ 26

Swensen v. Marino, 306 Mass. 582, 29 N.E.2d 15, 130 A.L.R. 763 (1940)
111 ALR5th 313—§ 9

Swenson, In re, 183 Minn. 602, 237 N.W. 589 (1931)

93 ALR5th 327—§ 3, 4, 6 to 9
101 ALR5th 619—§ 3

Swenson v. Aurora, 196 Ill. App. 83 (1915)

53 ALR5th 617—§ 5
57 ALR5th 689—§ 4, 8

Swenson v. Bender, 764 N.W.2d 596 (Minn. Ct. App. 2009)

83 ALR6th 195—§ 4

Swenson v. Chevron Chemical Co., 89 S.D. 497, 234 N.W.2d 38, 18 U.C.C. Rep. Serv. 67 (1975)

84 ALR6th 1—§ 9, 11, 13, 21, 55

Swenson v. Doschadis, 152 Wis. 2d 773, 450 N.W.2d 254 (App. 1989)

38 ALR5th 433—§ 67

Swenson v. Northern Crop Ins., Inc., 498 N.W.2d 174 (N.D. 1993)

20 ALR6th 1—§ 6

Swenson v. Pramstaller, 169 Fed. Appx. 449, 2006 FED App. 0153N (6th Cir. 2006)

68 ALR6th 389—§ 23

Swenson v. Sawoska, 215 Conn. 148, 575 A.2d 206 (1990)

111 ALR5th 1—§ 3, 8, 13

Swenson v. Siskiyou County, 498 Fed. Appx. 719 (9th Cir. 2012)

89 ALR6th 1—§ 46

Swenson v. State, 1974 OK CR 159, 525 P.2d 1395 (Okla. Crim. App. 1974)

1 ALR6th 549—§ 8

Swenson v. Zacher, 264 Minn. 203, 118 N.W.2d 786 (1962)

42 ALR6th 61—§ 4

Swerdfeger v. Krueger, 145 Colo. 180, 358 P.2d 479 (1960)

11 ALR5th 127—§ 2, 4, 37

Swerdlick v. Koch, 721 A.2d 849, 27 Media L. Rep. (BNA) 1801 (R.I. 1998)

96 ALR5th 107—§ 6

Sweren v. Sheehy, 2001 WL 1783076 (Del. Super. Ct. 2001)

2 ALR6th 279—§ 23

34 ALR6th 431—§ 4, 5, 13, 18, 19, 21

Swerine, In re Disciplinary Action Against, 513 N.W.2d 463 (Minn. 1994)

26 ALR6th 1—§ 25

Swersky v. Dreyer and Traub, 219 A.D.2d 321, 643 N.Y.S.2d 33 (1st Dep't 1996)

9 ALR6th 285—§ 13

Swetich v. Smith, 802 P.2d 869 (Wyo. 1990)

47 ALR5th 129—§ 3, 12

Swetman v. Gerace, 349 So. 2d 977 (La. App. 1st Cir. 1977)

33 ALR5th 643—§ 3, 9

Swett v. Gray, 141 Cal. 63, 74 P. 439 (1903)

12 ALR5th 195—§ 3, 44

Swett v. State, 268 A.2d 814 (Me. 1970)

12 ALR6th 267—§ 5

Swfte Intern., Ltd. v. Selective Ins. Co. of America, 1994 WL 827812 (D. Del. 1994)

98 ALR5th 1—§ 12

Swicegood v. Pliva, Inc., 543 F. Supp. 2d 1351 (N.D. Ga. 2008)

56 ALR6th 161—§ 3, 5, 7

Swick v. The New York Times Co., 357 N.J. Super. 371, 815 A.2d 508 (App. Div. 2003)

101 ALR5th 61—§ 3, 22

Swickard v. Wayne County Medical Examiner, 196 Mich. App. 98, 492 N.W.2d 497 (1992)

118 ALR5th 1—§ 4, 7, 11

Swider v. Yeutter, 762 F. Supp. 225, 55 Fair Empl. Prac. Cas. (BNA) 1441, 6 I.E.R. Cas. (BNA) 1469, 61 Empl. Prac. Dec. (CCH) ¶ 42102 (N.D. Ill. 1991)

7 ALR6th 563—§ 8

Swiderski v. Prudential Property and Cas. Ins. Co., 672 S.W.2d 264 (Tex. App. Corpus Christi 1984)

16 ALR6th 491—§ 22

For assistance, call 1-800-328-4880

Swidryk v. St. Michael's Medical Center, 201 N.J. Super. 601, 493 A.2d 641 (1985)

46 ALR5th 581—§ 25

Swieckowski by Swieckowski v. City of Ft. Collins, 934 P.2d 1380 (Colo. 1997)

12 ALR6th 645—§ 23

Swierczek v. Lynch, 237 Neb. 469, 466 N.W.2d 512 (1991)

11 ALR6th 695—§ 42, 58, 59

Swift v. American Home Assurance Co., 22 Wash. App. 777, 591 P.2d 1216 (1979)

55 ALR5th 681—§ 6

Swift v. American Mut. Ins. Co., 399 Mass. 373, 504 N.E.2d 621 (1987)

13 ALR5th 289—§ 3

Swift v. Broyles, 115 Ga. 885, 42 S.E. 277 (1902)

25 ALR5th 568—§ 34

Swift v. Century Ins. Co. of New York, 264 So. 2d 88 (Fla. Dist. Ct. App. 3d Dist. 1972)

66 ALR5th 269—§ 12

Swift v. Daniels, 103 Cal. App. 3d 263, 162 Cal. Rptr. 863 (2d Dist. 1980)

84 ALR5th 399—§ 3, 8, 13

Swift v. Davila, 2009 WL 2588749 (E.D. Wis. 2009)

59 ALR6th 311—§ 4, 5, 13

Swift v. Dickerman, 31 Conn. 285, 1863 WL 763 (1863)

16 ALR6th 1—§ 11

Swift v. Graves, 173 Misc. 1085, 19 N.Y.S.2d 686 (1940)

8 ALR5th 825—§ 8

Swift v. Island County, 87 Wash. 2d 348, 552 P.2d 175, 6 Envtl. L. Rep. 20684 (1976)

106 ALR5th 523—§ 3, 36

Swift v. Kniffen, 706 P.2d 296 (Alaska 1985)

62 ALR5th 219—§ 25

Swift v. Seidler, 988 S.W.2d 860 (Tex. App. San Antonio 1999)

87 ALR5th 473—§ 8

14 ALR6th 1—§ 5

Swift v. State, 509 S.W.2d 586 (Tex. Crim. App. 1974)

68 ALR5th 343—§ 3, 12

Swift v. Swift, 162 App. Div. 2d 784, 557 N.Y.S.2d 695 (3d Dep't 1990)

1 ALR5th 776—§ 2, 12

Swift v. Taxation Division Director, 183 N.J. Super. 378, 443 A.2d 1132 (Tax Ct. 1982)

2 ALR6th 1—§ 22

Swift v. U.S., 649 F. Supp. 596, 42 Fair Empl. Prac. Cas. (BNA) 787, 1 I.E.R. Cas. (BNA) 1248 (D.D.C. 1986)

96 ALR5th 391—§ 32

Swift Aire Lines, Inc., In re, 30 B.R. 490, 10 BCD 290 (BAP9 Cal. 1983)

56 ALR5th 565—§ 14

Swift & Co. v. Blackwell, 84 F.2d 130 (CA4 Va. 1936)

1 ALR5th 1—§ 48

Swift & Co. v. Blades, 502 S.W.2d 513 (Ky. 1973)

26 ALR5th 127—§ 11, 12

Swift & Co. v. Bowling, 293 F. 279 (CA4 W. Va. 1923)

25 ALR5th 391—§ 88, 91

Swift & Co. v. Forbus, 1949 OK 111, 201 Okla. 516, 207 P.2d 251 (1949)

41 ALR6th 207—§ 4

Swift & Co. v. Hawkins, 174 Miss. 253, 164 So. 231 (1935)

1 ALR5th 1—§ 3, 47, 56

Swift & Co. v. Industrial Com., 350 Ill. 413, 183 N.E. 476 (1932)

47 ALR5th 801—§ 3

Swift & Co. v. Mabry, 203 Ark. 818, 159 S.W.2d 61 (1942)

2 ALR5th 1—§ 3

Swift & Co. v. See, 30 Ohio App. 127, 6 Ohio L. Abs. 277, 164 N.E. 432 (6th Dist. Lucas County 1928)

31 ALR6th 199—§ 74

Swift & Co. v. Wells, 201 Va. 213, 110 S.E.2d 203 (1959)

2 ALR5th 1—§ 14

Swift County Bank v. United Farmers Elevators, 366 N.W.2d 606, 40 U.C.C.R.S. 1501 (Minn. App. 1985)
9 ALR5th 708—§ 2, 10

Swift Energy Co., In re, 2004 WL 1172330 (Tex. App. Houston 1st Dist. 2004)
86 ALR6th 519—§ 7

Swift Independent Packing Co. v. District Union Local One, United Food and Commercial Workers Int. Union, AFL-CIO, C.L.C., 575 F. Supp. 912, 115 L.R.R.M. (BNA) 3256, 100 Lab. Cas. (CCH) ¶ 10934 (N.D.N.Y. 1983)
66 ALR5th 611—§ 3

Swift Textiles, Inc. v. Lawson, 135 Ga. App. 799, 219 S.E.2d 167, 18 U.C.C.R.S. 115 (1975)
55 ALR5th 1—§ 2, 6

Swiggum, In re, 267 Minn. 548, 125 N.W.2d 169 (1963)
26 ALR6th 1—§ 6

Swillum v. Empire Gas Transport, Inc., 698 S.W.2d 921 (Mo. App. 1985)
61 ALR5th 375—§ 14

Swimmer v. Janis, 21 Misc. 2d 274, 193 N.Y.S.2d 919 (1959)
42 ALR5th 53—§ 5, 28, 29

Swindall v. Cox Enterprises, Inc., 253 Ga. App. 235, 558 S.E.2d 788, 30 Media L. Rep. (BNA) 1350 (2002)
22 ALR6th 553—§ 16

Swindall v. State Election Bd., 1934 OK 259, 168 Okla. 97, 32 P.2d 691 (1934)
121 ALR5th 1—§ 49

Swindle v. Jack B. Kelly, Inc., 549 So. 2d 21 (Ala. 1989)
94 ALR6th 111—§ 11

Swindle v. Livingston Parish School Bd., 655 F.3d 386, 272 Ed. Law Rep. 779 (5th Cir. 2011)
90 ALR6th 235—§ 6

Swindle v. Livingston Parish School Bd., 2008 WL 5157727 (M.D. La. 2008)
90 ALR6th 235—§ 6

Swindle v. State, 169 Ga. App. 773, 315 S.E.2d 285 (1984)
124 ALR5th 1—§ 5

Swindle v. State, 274 Ga. 668, 558 S.E.2d 385 (2002)
12 ALR6th 267—§ 8

Swinebroad-Denton, Inc. v. Hornback, 744 S.W.2d 429 (Ky. App. 1987)
7 ALR5th 474—§ 151

Swineford v. Nichols, 16 Ohio Op. 2d 432, 87 Ohio L. Abs. 493, 177 N.E.2d 304 (C.P. 1961)
1 ALR6th 135—§ 2 to 4, 11

Swinehart v. Turbin, 1985 WL 1284 (N.D. Ill. 1985)
9 ALR6th 285—§ 4

Swinger v. Bell, 373 S.W.2d 30 (Mo. 1963)
9 ALR5th 102—§ 3

Swinger Realty Corp. v. A. S. Kizner Imports, Inc., 70 Misc. 2d 742, 335 N.Y.S.2d 108 (1972)
42 ALR5th 53—§ 41, 42

Swinney v. State, 529 S.W.2d 70 (Tex. Crim. App. 1975)
65 ALR5th 407—§ 3, 19

Swinney v. State, 828 S.W.2d 254 (Tex. App. Houston (1st Dist.) 1992)
34 ALR5th 125—§ 3, 14

Swinson, In re, 2010 WL 4103547 (Mich. Ct. App. 2010)
61 ALR6th 521—§ 5, 22, 25

Swinton v. City of New York, 785 F. Supp. 2d 3 (E.D. N.Y. 2011)
95 ALR6th 341—§ 38

Swinton v. Safir, 93 N.Y.2d 758, 697 N.Y.S.2d 869, 720 N.E.2d 89, 15 I.E.R. Cas. (BNA) 1528 (1999)
95 ALR6th 341—§ 7, 40

Swire v. Swire, 202 N.J. Super. 289, 494 A.2d 1035 (1985)
20 ALR5th 700—§ 54
40 ALR5th 227—§ 23

Swisher, In re, 179 P.3d 412 (Kan. 2008)
32 ALR6th 531—§ 43

Swisher v. Com., 256 Va. 471, 506 S.E.2d 763 (1998)

29 ALR6th 1—§ 5

Swisher v. Midwest Partitions, Inc., 2000 WL 351167 (Neb. Ct. App. 2000)

40 ALR6th 99—§ 19

Swisher v. Pitz, 2005 PA Super 56, 868 A.2d 1228 (2005)

80 ALR6th 469—§ 22, 29, 31

Swiss Colony, Inc. v. Department of Industry, Labor and Human Relations, 72 Wis. 2d 46, 240 N.W.2d 128 (1976)

97 ALR5th 1—§ 2
106 ALR5th 111—§ 5, 33
108 ALR5th 1—§ 29, 39

Swiss Credit Bank v. Chemical Bank, 422 F. Supp. 1305, 20 U.C.C. Rep. Serv. (CBC) 444 (S.D. N.Y. 1976)

77 ALR5th 429—§ 5

Swiss Reinsurance Am. Corp., Inc. v. Roetzel & Andress, 163 Ohio App. 3d 336, 2005-Ohio-4799, 837 N.E.2d 1215 (9th Dist. Summit County 2005)

50 ALR6th 53—§ 6

Switch Communications Group v. Ballard, 2011 WL 3859725 (D. Nev. 2011)

72 ALR6th 563—§ 9, 15, 25

Switching Systems, Inc. v. C.M. Buck & Associates, Inc., 1997 WL 403667 (N.D. Ill. 1997)

79 ALR5th 587—§ 3, 6

Switka v. City of Youngstown, 2006-Ohio-4617, 2006 WL 2574086 (Ohio Ct. App. 7th Dist. Mahoning County 2006)

44 ALR6th 545—§ 9

Switzer v. Berry, 198 F.3d 1255 (10th Cir. 2000)

27 ALR6th 403—§ 4, 14

Switzer v. City of Tulsa, 598 P.2d 247 (Okla. Crim. App. 1979)

72 ALR5th 1—§ 18

Switzer v. Mercantile Bank of St. Louis, N.A., 932 S.W.2d 893 (Mo. Ct. App. E.D. 1996)

36 ALR5th 395—§ 16

Switzer v. Newton Health Care Corp., 734 F. Supp. 954 (D.C. Kan. 1990)

7 ALR5th 1—§ 16

Switzer v. Rivera, 174 F. Supp. 2d 1097 (D. Nev. 2001)

7 ALR6th 135—§ 3

Switzer v. Sullivan, 1996 WL 52911 (N.D. Ill. 1996)

30 ALR6th 413—§ 13, 14

Switzerland. Lane v. New York Times, 8 Media L. R. 1623 (W.D. Tenn. 1982)

19 ALR5th 1—§ 40

Swogger v. Grimm, 1989 WL 1280 (Ohio Ct. App. 7th Dist. Mahoning County 1989)

36 ALR6th 1—§ 18

Swope, In re Detention of, 343 Ill. App. 3d 152, 277 Ill. Dec. 864, 797 N.E.2d 211 (2d Dist. 2003)

78 ALR6th 417—§ 84

Swope v. Bratton, 541 F. Supp. 99 (W.D. Ark. 1982)

123 ALR5th 411—§ 7, 56

Swope v. Farrar, 66 Ga. App. 52, 17 S.E.2d 92 (1941)

38 ALR5th 107—§ 3

Swope v. Federal Sur. Co., 171 La. 369, 131 So. 50 (1930)

100 ALR5th 617—§ 11

Swope v. General Motors Corp., 445 F. Supp. 1222 (W.D. Mo. 1978)

6 ALR5th 883—§ 2, 26

Swope v. Razzaq, 428 F.3d 1152 (8th Cir. 2005)

96 ALR6th 503—§ 55

Swope v. Siegel-Robert, Inc., 243 F.3d 486 (8th Cir. 2001)

16 ALR6th 693—§ 16

Sword v. NKC Hospitals, Inc., 661 N.E.2d 10 (Ind. Ct. App. 1996)

58 ALR5th 613—§ 10

Sword v. NKC Hospitals, Inc., 714 N.E.2d 142 (Ind. 1999)

64 ALR6th 249—§ 9

Sword v. Sword, 399 Mich. 367, 249 N.W.2d 88 (1976)

32 ALR5th 31—§ 3

Swota v. Eddy Valve Co., 8 A.D.2d 574, 183 N.Y.S.2d 363 (3d Dep't 1959)
86 ALR5th 295—§ 4

Swycaffer v. Swycaffer, 44 Cal. 2d 689, 285 P.2d 1 (1955)
5 ALR5th 863—§ 3, 4

Swygert v. Swygert, 46 N.C. App. 173, 264 S.E.2d 902 (1980)
5 ALR5th 422—§ 3, 4

Swyters v. Motorola Employees Credit Union, 244 Ga. App. 356, 535 S.E.2d 508 (2000)
6 ALR5th 297—§ 12
8 ALR6th 549—§ 13

Syakhasone v. State, 72 Ark. App. 385, 39 S.W.3d 5 (2001)
85 ALR5th 1—§ 28, 50

Sybedon Corp. v. Bank Leumi Trust Co., 22 U.C.C.R.S.2d 1111 (N.Y. Sup. 1994)
45 ALR5th 389—§ 26

Sybedon Corp. v. Bank Leumi Trust Co., 638 N.Y.S.2d 50 (App. Div. 1st Dep't 1996)
45 ALR5th 389—§ 22

Sybedon Corp. v. Bank Leumi Trust Co. of New York, 224 App. Div. 2d 320, 638 N.Y.S.2d 50 (1st Dep't 1996)
45 ALR5th 389—§ 22

Sybenga, In re, 1999 WL 957718 (Ohio Ct. App. 2d Dist. Montgomery County 1999)
18 ALR6th 97—§ 33

Sybersound Records, Inc. v. UAV Corp., 517 F.3d 1137, 86 U.S.P.Q.2d 1065, R.I.C.O. Bus. Disp. Guide (CCH) ¶ 11446, 2008-1 Trade Cas. (CCH) ¶ 76091 (9th Cir. 2008)
76 ALR6th 289—§ 4
77 ALR6th 543—§ 8

Sycamore Preserve Works v. Chicago & N. W. R. Co., 366 Ill. 11, 7 N.E.2d 740, 111 A.L.R. 1133 (1937)
17 ALR5th 547—§ 67, 72

Syck v. State, 130 Ga. App. 50, 202 S.E.2d 464 (1973)
54 ALR5th 141—§ 3, 6

Syczhk v. Szczerbaniewicz, 233 App. Div. 342, 252 N.Y.S. 780 (1931)
49 ALR5th 685—§ 3

Sydenham v. Santiago, 392 So. 2d 357 (Fla. App. D4 1981)
2 ALR5th 369—§ 4

Sydlik v. REEIII, Inc., 195 S.W.3d 329 (Tex. App. Houston 14th Dist. 2006)
61 ALR6th 147—§ 12, 14, 18
76 ALR6th 395—§ 13

Sydnor v. Conseco Financial Servicing Corp., 252 F.3d 302 (4th Cir. 2001)
22 ALR6th 49—§ 3, 4, 13, 20

Sye v. State, 55 Md. App. 356, 468 A.2d 641 (1983)
16 ALR6th 329—§ 9
24 ALR6th 591—§ 8

Syed v. State, 642 S.W.2d 200 (Tex. App. Houston (14th Dist.) 1982)
32 ALR5th 149—§ 5, 33, 70

Syester v. Banta, 257 Iowa 613, 133 N.W.2d 666 (1965)
14 ALR5th 242—§ 40

Syfers v. State, 135 Wash. App. 1006, 2006 WL 2873786 (Div. 1 2006)
29 ALR6th 369—§ 47, 48

Sykes, Estate of, 477 Pa. 254, 383 A.2d 920 (1978)
36 ALR5th 395—§ 3, 5 to 7, 12, 23

Sykes v. McDowell, 786 F.2d 1098 (CA11 Ala. 1986)
12 ALR5th 195—§ 36

Sykes v. Mortgage Electronic Registration Systems, Inc., 2012 WL 914922 (D. Idaho 2012)
86 ALR6th 411—§ 5

Sykes v. Nationwide Ins. Co., 327 Md. 261, 608 A.2d 1242 (1992)
33 ALR5th 121—§ 41

Sykes v. Pioneer Title of Ada County, 2013 WL 458343 (D. Idaho 2013)
86 ALR6th 411—§ 5

Sykes v. Rutgers, State University of New Jersey, 308 N.J. Super. 265, 705 A.2d 1241, 124 Ed. Law Rep. 341 (App. Div. 1998)
74 ALR5th 49—§ 73

For assistance, call 1-800-328-4880

Sykes v. State, 757 So. 2d 997 (Miss. 2000)

29 ALR6th 237—§ 4, 8

Sykes v. Stix, Baer & Fuller Co., 238 S.W.2d 918 (Mo. Ct. App. 1951)

63 ALR6th 495—§ 43, 51

Sykes v. Sykes, 2004 WL 803279 (Cal. App. 2d Dist. 2004)

39 ALR6th 155—§ 16

Sykes v. U.S., 131 S. Ct. 2267 (2011)

66 ALR6th 635—§ 41

Sykes' Will, In re, 53 N.Y.S.2d 442 (Sur 1945)

56 ALR5th 133—§ 4

Sylar v. State, 340 So. 2d 10 (Miss. 1976)

9 ALR5th 464—§ 8, 9, 11

Sylgab Steel & Wire Corp. v. Imoco-Gateway Corp., 62 F.R.D. 454, 182 USPQ 187, 18 FR Serv. 2d 812 (N.D. Ill. 1974)

27 ALR5th 76—§ 9

Sylk v. Rosenberg, 754 So. 2d 836 (Fla. Dist. Ct. App. 3d Dist. 2000)

9 ALR5th 321—§ 10

Sylla v. United States Fidelity & Guaranty Co., 54 Cal. App. 3d 895, 127 Cal. Rptr. 38 (2d Dist. 1976)

14 ALR5th 695—§ 22, 24

Sylling, In re Marriage of, 2002 WL 1038855 (Cal. App. 4th Dist. 2002)

11 ALR6th 125—§ 16

Sylmark Holdings Ltd. v. Silicone Zone Intern. Ltd., 5 Misc. 3d 285, 783 N.Y.S.2d 758 (Sup 2004)

85 ALR6th 1—§ 12

Sylor v. Irwin, 62 Misc. 2d 469, 308 N.Y.S.2d 937 (Sup 1970)

50 ALR6th 95—§ 6

Sylvan v. Sylvan Bros., 225 S.C. 429, 82 S.E.2d 794 (1954)

15 ALR6th 633—§ 3, 13, 15, 28, 34

Sylvane v. Whelan, 506 F. Supp. 1355 (E.D.N.Y. 1981)

92 ALR5th 593—§ 3, 7, 10, 11

Sylvan Glens Homeowners Ass'n v. McFadden, 103 Mich. App. 118, 302 N.W.2d 615 (1981)

83 ALR5th 651—§ 7

81 ALR6th 469—§ 6, 7

Sylvania, City of v. Glass, 1994 WL 39068 (Ohio App. Lucas Co. 1994)

52 ALR5th 559—§ 4

Sylvania Elec. Products v. Barker, 228 F.2d 842 (1st Cir. 1955)

16 ALR6th 143—§ 27

Sylvester, In re, 220 B.R. 89 (B.A.P. 9th Cir. 1998)

99 ALR6th 481—§ 50, 69

Sylvester v. Abdalla, 137 Or. App. 26, 903 P.2d 410 (1995)

60 ALR5th 669—§ 6, 8

Sylvester v. Brockway Motor Truck Corporation, 232 A.D. 364, 250 N.Y.S. 35 (3d Dep't 1931)

103 ALR5th 339—§ 12

Sylvester v. CIGNA Corp., 401 F. Supp. 2d 147 (D. Me. 2005)

60 ALR6th 295—§ 66

Sylvester v. Liberty Life Ins. Co., 42 P.3d 38, 100 A.L.R.5th 793 (Colo. Ct. App. 2001)

100 ALR5th 617—§ 8, 10

Sylvester v. Mentor Corp., 663 So. 2d 176, Prod. Liab. Rep. (CCH) ¶ 14426 (La. Ct. App. 3d Cir. 1995)

23 ALR6th 223—§ 3

Sylvester v. Pennsylvania R. Co., 357 Pa. 213, 53 A.2d 537 (1947)

19 ALR5th 622—§ 2

Sylvester v. Peruso, 286 Pa. Super. 225, 428 A.2d 653 (1981)

42 ALR6th 545—§ 8, 10, 14, 18, 20

43 ALR6th 375—§ 4, 11, 21, 49

Sylvester v. State, 549 N.E.2d 37 (Ind. 1990)

79 ALR5th 237—§ 3

Sylvester v. Unisys Corp., 1999 WL 167725 (E.D. Pa. 1999)

103 ALR5th 557—§ 3

Sylvester Bros. Development Co. v. Great Cent. Ins. Co., 480 N.W.2d 368 (Minn. Ct. App. 1992)

88 ALR5th 493—§ 3

Sylvester Bros. Development Co. v. Great Cent. Ins. Co., 503 N.W.2d 793 (Minn. Ct. App. 1993)
88 ALR5th 493—§ 3
89 ALR5th 1—§ 5
Sylvestre v. Martin, 23 Mass. L. Rptr. 408, 2008 WL 82631 (Mass. Super. Ct. 2008)
69 ALR6th 317—§ 12
Sylvestri v. Warner & Swasey Co., 398 F.2d 598 (2d Cir. 1968)
93 ALR5th 103—§ 11, 12
Sylvia v. Maddox, 2007 WL 2300799 (W.D. N.C. 2007)
65 ALR6th 93—§ 61
Sylvis By and Through Sylvis v. Walling, 248 Neb. 168, 532 N.W.2d 312 (1995)
87 ALR5th 361—§ 9, 24
Symanski v. First Nat. Bank of Danville, 151 Ill. 2d 578, 186 Ill. Dec. 395, 616 N.E.2d 348 (1993)
86 ALR5th 527—§ 6
Symbax, Inc. v. Bingaman, 219 A.D.2d 552, 631 N.Y.S.2d 829 (1st Dep't 1995)
109 ALR5th 301—§ 2
Symcox v. Zuk, 221 Cal. App. 2d 383, 34 Cal. Rptr. 462 (2d Dist. 1963)
39 ALR6th 155—§ 10
Symczyk v. Genesis HealthCare Corp., 656 F.3d 189, 18 Wage & Hour Cas. 2d (BNA) 1, 161 Lab. Cas. (CCH) ¶ 35940, 80 Fed. R. Serv. 3d 1122 (3d Cir. 2011)
76 ALR6th 587—§ 26, 27, 37
Symeonidis v. Paxton Capital Group, Inc., 8 Wage & Hour Cas. 2d (BNA) 48, 2002 WL 1988263 (D. Md. 2002)
105 ALR5th 351—§ 9
Symes Investing Co. v. Wheelock, 55 Colo. 459, 136 P. 65 (1913)
18 ALR5th 437—§ 3
Symetra Life Ins. Co. v. Rapid Settlements Ltd., 2007 WL 114497 (S.D. Tex. 2007)
27 ALR6th 323—§ 31

Symmons v. O'Keeffe, 419 Mass. 288, 644 N.E.2d 631 (1995)
28 ALR5th 1—§ 24
Symonds v. Adler Restaurant Equipment Co., 10 U.C.C. Rep. Serv. 1179 (Okla. Ct. App. 1971)
101 ALR5th 563—§ 6
Symons Corp. v. Quality Concrete Const., Inc., 108 N.C. App. 17, 422 S.E.2d 365 (1992)
58 ALR5th 325—§ 4, 5
Symphony Fabrics Corp. v. Bernson Silk Mills, Inc., 12 N.Y.2d 409, 240 N.Y.S.2d 23, 190 N.E.2d 418 (1963)
31 ALR6th 433—§ 7, 9
Symphony Space, Inc. v. Pergola Properties, Inc., 88 N.Y.2d 466, 646 N.Y.S.2d 641, 669 N.E.2d 799 (1996)
99 ALR6th 591—§ 9
Sympson v. Rogers, 314 S.W.2d 717 (Mo. 1958)
59 ALR5th 693—§ 7
Sympson v. Rogers, 406 S.W.2d 26, 24 A.L.R.3d 1183 (Mo. 1966)
59 ALR5th 693—§ 5, 7
11 ALR6th 587—§ 25
Syms Corp. v. Commissioner of Revenue, 436 Mass. 505, 765 N.E.2d 758 (2002)
11 ALR6th 543—§ 6, 16 to 18, 22, 23
Synacek v. Omaha Cold Storage Terminals, 247 Neb. 244, 526 N.W.2d 91 (1995)
51 ALR5th 1—§ 7
Synanon Foundation, Inc. v. Time, Inc., 5 Media L. R. 1924 (Cal Super 1979)
19 ALR5th 1—§ 96, 163
Syncor Intern. Corp. v. Palmer, 542 S.E.2d 479 (W. Va. 2001)
30 ALR5th 494—§ 9
Syndex Corp. v. Dean, 820 S.W.2d 869, 57 Fair Empl. Prac. Cas. (BNA) 547 (Tex. App. Austin 1991)
38 ALR5th 433—§ 61

94 ALR5th 1—§ 3

Syndicate Bldg. Corp. v. Lorber, 128 A.D.2d 381, 512 N.Y.S.2d 674 (1st Dep't 1987)

75 ALR5th 1—§ 3

Syndicate Clothing Co. v. Garfield, 204 Iowa 159, 214 N.W. 598 (1927)

42 ALR5th 221—§ 24

Synergetics v. Marathon Ranching Co., 701 P.2d 1106 (Utah 1985)

14 ALR5th 242—§ 4, 40

Synergistic Technologies, Inc. v. IDB Mobile Communications, Inc., 871 F. Supp. 24, 35 U.S.P.Q.2d 1823, 27 U.C.C. Rep. Serv. 2d 428 (D.D.C. 1994)

87 ALR6th 1—§ 88

Synergystex Intern., Inc. v. Motorists Mut. Ins. Co., 1994 WL 395626 (Ohio Ct. App. 9th Dist. Medina County 1994)

98 ALR5th 1—§ 18

Synigal v. Jefferson Parish Correctional Center, 2006 WL 3388489 (E.D. La. 2006)

89 ALR6th 1—§ 115

Synnex Corp. v. ADT Sec. Services, Inc., 394 N.J. Super. 577, 928 A.2d 37, 36 A.L.R.6th 853 (App. Div. 2007)

36 ALR6th 305—§ 11

Syno v. Syno, 406 Pa. Super. 218, 594 A.2d 307 (1991)

32 ALR5th 673—§ 3

Synovia G., Re, 163 App. Div. 2d 257, 558 N.Y.S.2d 539 (1st Dep't 1990)

20 ALR5th 534—§ 10

Synowicz v. Mazur, 148 Wis. 2d 952, 438 N.W.2d 596 (App. 1989)

22 ALR5th 464—§ 3

Syntex Agri-Business, Inc., State ex rel. v. Adolf, 700 S.W.2d 886 (Mo. App. 1985)

27 ALR5th 76—§ 34

Syntex Laboratories, Inc. v. Department of Treasury, 188 Mich. App. 383, 470 N.W.2d 665 (1991)

30 ALR5th 494—§ 2, 9

Synthes USA, LLC v. Spinal Kinetics, Inc., 2011 WL 811731 (N.D. Cal. 2011)

86 ALR6th 519—§ 7

Synthroid Marketing Litigation, In re, 110 F. Supp. 2d 676 (N.D. Ill. 2000)

23 ALR5th 241—§ 26

Synthroid Marketing Litigation, In re, 264 F.3d 712, 2001-2 Trade Cas. (CCH) ¶ 73407, 51 Fed. R. Serv. 3d 736 (7th Cir. 2001)

60 ALR6th 295—§ 6, 47

Syntron Bioresearch, Inc. v. Fan, 2002 WL 660446 (Cal. App. 4th Dist. 2002)

85 ALR6th 1—§ 59

Synygy, Inc. v. Scott-Levin, Inc., 51 F. Supp. 2d 570 (E.D. Pa. 1999)

3 ALR6th 153—§ 16

Sypert v. U.S., 559 F. Supp. 546 (D.C. Dist. Col. 1983)

6 ALR5th 162—§ 2, 6

Syphrit v. Turner, 446 So. 2d 626 (Ala. App. 1983)

15 ALR5th 692—§ 10

Sypien v. State Farm Mut. Auto. Ins. Co., 111 Ill. App. 3d 19, 66 Ill. Dec. 780, 443 N.E.2d 706, 36 A.L.R.4th 580 (1st Dist. 1982)

66 ALR5th 269—§ 12

Sypniewski v. Planning and Zoning Comm'n of Town of Seymour, 1990 WL 271546 (Conn. Super. Ct. 1990)

4 ALR6th 263—§ 14

Sypniewski v. Warren Hills Regional Bd. of Educ., 307 F.3d 243, 170 Ed. Law Rep. 83 (3d Cir. 2002)

66 ALR6th 493—§ 5

Syracuse v. Diao, 272 A.D.2d 881, 707 N.Y.S.2d 570 (4th Dep't 2000)

64 ALR6th 249—§ 17

Syracuse Aggregate Corp. v. Weise, 72 App. Div. 2d 254, 424 N.Y.S.2d 556 (4th Dep't 1980)

8 ALR5th 391—§ 3

Syracuse Bros., Inc. v. Darcy, 127 App. Div. 2d 588, 511 N.Y.S.2d 389 (2d Dep't 1987)

---

63 ALR5th 607—§ 8

Syracuse Grade Crossing Com. v. Delaware, L. & W. R. Co., 197 Misc. 192, 97 N.Y.S.2d 279 (1940)

22 ALR5th 327—§ 58

Syracuse Grade Crossing Com. v. M. A. Wellin Oil Co., 268 App. Div. 627, 52 N.Y.S.2d 692 (1944)

7 ALR5th 113—§ 6

Syracuse Grade Crossing Commission v. Delaware, L. & W.R. Co., 197 Misc. 192, 97 N.Y.S.2d 279 (Sup 1940)

111 ALR5th 313—§ 17

Syracuse Supply Co. v. Railway Express Agency, Inc., 45 Misc. 2d 1000, 258 N.Y.S.2d 477 (1965)

25 ALR5th 233—§ 19

Syrcle v. Springer, 239 Ill. App. 3d 148, 179 Ill. Dec. 910, 606 N.E.2d 742 (1992)

21 ALR5th 82—§ 3, 31

Syrek v. California Unemployment Ins. Appeal Board, 54 Cal. 2d 519, 7 Cal. Rptr. 97, 354 P.2d 625 (1960)

41 ALR5th 123—§ 10

Syrian Antiochian Orthodox Archdiocese of New York and All North America v. Palisades Associates, 110 N.J. Super. 34, 264 A.2d 257 (Ch. Div. 1970)

115 ALR5th 251—§ 3, 6

Syrie v. Knoll Intern., 748 F.2d 304 (5th Cir. 1984)

3 ALR6th 355—§ 9

Syrie v. Knoll International, 748 F.2d 304, CCH Prod. Liab. Rep. ¶ 10285 (CA5 Tex. 1984)

47 ALR5th 395—§ 3, 15

Syring v. Tucker, 174 Wis. 2d 787, 498 N.W.2d 370 (1993)

87 ALR5th 631—§ 7, 34, 36

Syrkowski v. Appleyard, 420 Mich. 367, 362 N.W.2d 211 (1985)

77 ALR5th 567—§ 6

Syrowik v. City of Detroit, 119 Mich. App. 343, 326 N.W.2d 507 (1982)

29 ALR6th 369—§ 42, 45, 47

Sysco Food Services, Inc. v. Trapnell, 890 S.W.2d 796, Prod. Liab. Rep. (CCH) ¶ 13943 (Tex. 1994)

2 ALR5th 1—§ 5

Sysco Food Services of Philadelphia v. W.C.A.B. (Sebastiano), 940 A.2d 1270 (Pa. Commw. Ct. 2008)

41 ALR6th 207—§ 21

Sysco Intermountain Food Serv. v. Twin Falls, 109 Idaho 88, 705 P.2d 548 (App. 1985)

45 ALR5th 173—§ 2

Syska v. Montgomery County Bd. of Ed., 45 Md. App. 626, 415 A.2d 301 (1980)

94 ALR5th 613—§ 3, 8

Systematic Recycling, LLC v. City of Detroit, 685 F. Supp. 2d 663 (E.D. Mich. 2010)

68 ALR6th 229—§ 8

Systemized of New England, Inc. v. SCM, Inc., 732 F.2d 1030, 39 U.C.C. Rep. Serv. 387 (1st Cir. 1984)

89 ALR5th 319—§ 23

System One Southeast, Inc. v. Avery Dennison Corp., 704 So. 2d 665 (Fla. Dist. Ct. App. 2d Dist. 1997)

8 ALR5th 653—§ 3

Systems v. ADT Sec. Services, Inc., 2008 WL 682232 (D.N.J. 2008)

36 ALR6th 305—§ 11

Systems Contracting Corp. v. Reeves, 85 Ark. App. 286, 151 S.W.3d 18 (2004)

22 ALR6th 329—§ 24

Systems Design & Management Information, Inc. v. Kansas City Post Office Employees Credit Union, 14 Kan. App. 2d 266, 788 P.2d 878, 11 U.C.C.R.S.2d 775 (1990)

38 ALR5th 1—§ 9

Systems Invest. Corp. v. National Auto. & Casualty Ins. Co., 25 Cal. App. 3d 1057, 102 Cal. Rptr. 378 (2d Dist. 1972)

4 ALR5th 772—§ 91, 109

System Software Associates, Inc. v. Trapp, 1995 WL 506058 (N.D. Ill. 1995)

79 ALR5th 587—§ 3, 7

System Structures, Inc. v. Blair Chevrolet, Inc., 24 A.D.2d 457, 260 N.Y.S.2d 396 (2d Dep't 1965)

31 ALR6th 433—§ 7

Systems XIX, Inc. v. Parker, 30 F. Supp. 2d 1225 (N.D. Cal. 1998)

76 ALR6th 289—§ 4, 5

77 ALR6th 543—§ 6

Syverson, In re Marriage of, 281 Mont. 1, 931 P.2d 691 (1997)

57 ALR5th 389—§ 2

70 ALR5th 377—§ 3

Syvertsen v. Great American Ins. Co., 700 N.Y.S.2d 289 (App. Div. 3d Dep't 1999)

58 ALR5th 483—§ 5

Sywak v. O'Connor Hospital, 199 Cal. App. 3d 423, 244 Cal. Rptr. 753 (6th Dist. 1988)

28 ALR5th 107—§ 14, 16, 18

Syx v. Midfield Volkswagen, Inc., 518 So. 2d 94 (Ala. 1987)

8 ALR6th 549—§ 5, 13, 27

S.Z., In re, 2003 WL 22080216 (Cal. App. 4th Dist. 2003)

59 ALR6th 393—§ 10

S.Z., In re Welfare of, 547 N.W.2d 886 (Minn. 1996)

20 ALR5th 534—§ 6, 17

S.Z., Matter of, 325 N.W.2d 53 (S.D. 1982)

89 ALR5th 195—§ 8

S.Z., Matter of Welfare of, 547 N.W.2d 886 (Minn. 1996)

12 ALR6th 417—§ 7, 9

Szabo v. State, 798 So. 2d 912 (Fla. 2d DCA 2001)

92 ALR6th 1—§ 8

Szaferman, Lakind, Blumstein, Blader & Lehmann, P.C. v. Parise, 2010 WL 624084 (N.J. Super. Ct. App. Div. 2010)

58 ALR6th 1—§ 5

Szaflarski v. Lurie Co., 1991 WL 169356 (N.D. Ill. 1991)

104 ALR5th 1—§ 3, 12

105 ALR5th 351—§ 6

Szajna v. General Motors Corp., 115 Ill. 2d 294, 104 Ill. Dec. 898, 503 N.E.2d 760, 1986-2 CCH Trade Cases ¶ 67381, 2 U.C.C.R.S.2d 1268 (1986)

50 ALR5th 327—§ 2, 4

Szakal v. Akron Rubber Development, 2003-Ohio-6820, 2003 WL 22956437 (Ohio Ct. App. 9th Dist. Summit County 2003)

22 ALR6th 329—§ 23

Szarejko v. Amerling Volkswagen, Inc., 55 App. Div. 2d 801, 390 N.Y.S.2d 266 (3d Dep't 1976)

12 ALR5th 195—§ 64

Szczech v. Chicago City Ry. Co., 157 Ill. App. 150, 1910 WL 2210 (1st Dist. 1910)

97 ALR6th 567—§ 2, 4, 12

Szczepanski v. Cendant Mortg. Services, 873 A.2d 1099 (Del. 2005)

88 ALR6th 385—§ 53

Szczerkowski v. Karmelowicz, 60 Conn. App. 429, 759 A.2d 1050 (2000)

58 ALR5th 669—§ 28

Szczotka v. Snowridge, Inc., 869 F. Supp. 247 (D.C. Vt. 1994)

54 ALR5th 513—§ 3, 5

Szczygiel v. Szczygiel, 153 Misc. 2d 411, 581 N.Y.S.2d 522 (Sup. 1991)

34 ALR5th 447—§ 7

Szefczek v. Hillsborough Beacon, 286 N.J. Super. 247, 668 A.2d 1099 (Law Div. 1995)

77 ALR6th 1—§ 20, 95, 119

Szekely, Matter of, 936 F.2d 897, 24 Collier Bankr. Cas. 2d (MB) 2028, Bankr. L. Rep. (CCH) ¶ 74070 (7th Cir. 1991)

83 ALR6th 605—§ 5

Szelega Enterprises, Inc. v. Town of Vestal, 36 A.D.2d 483, 320 N.Y.S.2d 963 (3d Dep't 1971)

63 ALR5th 607—§ 4, 7

Szelenyi v. Miller, 564 A.2d 768 (Me. 1989)
86 ALR5th 527—§ 13, 14

Szeliga v. Des Plaines, 4 Ill. App. 3d 257, 280 N.E.2d 767 (1st Dist. 1972)
1 ALR5th 622—§ 19

Szeliga v. Szeliga, 2012-Ohio-1973, 2012 WL 1580065 (Ohio Ct. App. 2d Dist. Greene County 2012)
96 ALR6th 103—§ 3

Szemplinski, In re, 134 Misc. 2d 162, 509 N.Y.S.2d 475 (1986)
40 ALR5th 697—§ 16, 22

Szendy, In re, 244 A.D. 49, 278 N.Y.S. 199 (1st Dep't 1935)
40 ALR6th 463—§ 26

Szetela v. Discover Bank, 97 Cal. App. 4th 1094, 118 Cal. Rptr. 2d 862 (4th Dist. 2002)
13 ALR6th 145—§ 3, 4
83 ALR6th 143—§ 5

Szeto v. Louisiana State Bd. of Dentistry, 508 F. Supp. 268 (E.D. La. 1981)
88 ALR6th 627—§ 13

Szewczyk v. State, 7 Md. App. 597, 256 A.2d 713 (1969)
57 ALR6th 445—§ 5, 45

Sziber v. Stout, 419 Mich. 514, 358 N.W.2d 330 (1984)
11 ALR5th 630—§ 6, 8

Szikszay v. Buelow, 107 Misc. 2d 886, 436 N.Y.S.2d 558 (Sup 1981)
5 ALR6th 327—§ 15
8 ALR6th 117—§ 25

Szilagyi v. Bethlehem, 312 Pa. 260, 167 A. 782 (1933)
54 ALR5th 649—§ 3

Szilagyi v. North Florida Hotel Corp., 610 So. 2d 1319 (Fla. Dist. Ct. App. 1st Dist. 1992)
99 ALR5th 141—§ 30

Szilvasy v. Saviers, 70 Ohio App. 34, 24 Ohio Op. 336, 44 N.E.2d 732 (7th Dist. Mahoning County 1942)
76 ALR5th 337—§ 20

Szkorla v. Vecchione, 231 Cal. App. 3d 1541, 283 Cal. Rptr. 219, 91 Daily Journal DAR 8407 (4th Dist. 1991)
28 ALR5th 497—§ 8

Szlafrak v. Donaldson, 149 Ind. App. 200, 271 N.E.2d 170 (1971)
9 ALR5th 826—§ 6

Szlek v. U.S. Bank Nat. Ass'n, 2012 WL 3756941 (N.D. Ga. 2012)
86 ALR6th 411—§ 5

Szlovak v. Holcombe, 2004 WL 553010 (Cal. App. 4th Dist. 2004)
45 ALR6th 493—§ 36

Szmania v. Bank of America Home Loans, Inc., 2011 WL 3841606 (W.D. Wash. 2011)
86 ALR6th 411—§ 5

Szmyd v. Szmyd, 641 P.2d 14 (Alaska 1982)
6 ALR5th 69—§ 5
21 ALR5th 396—§ 4, 11, 19, 22, 26, 57

Sznyter v. Malone, 155 Cal. App. 4th 1152, 66 Cal. Rptr. 3d 633 (4th Dist. 2007)
77 ALR6th 1—§ 65

Szojka v. Unemployment Compensation Bd. of Review, 187 Pa. Super. 643, 146 A.2d 81 (1958)
80 ALR6th 635—§ 12

Szoke v. Zoning Bd. of Adjustment of Borough of Monmouth Beach, 260 N.J. Super. 341, 616 A.2d 942 (App. Div. 1992)
4 ALR6th 263—§ 5

Szopko v. Kinsman Marine Transit Co., 96 Mich. App. 64, 292 N.W.2d 486 (1980)
33 ALR5th 205—§ 5, 30

Szot v. Allstate Ins. Co., 161 F. Supp. 2d 596 (D. Md. 2001)
53 ALR6th 213—§ 5

Szpak v. Szpak, 114 N.J. Eq. 143, 168 A. 386 (1933)
18 ALR5th 230—§ 12

Szrama v. Alumo Products Co., Inc., 118 Misc. 2d 1008, 462 N.Y.S.2d 156 (Sup. Ct. 1983)

81 ALR5th 483—§ 5

Szteinbaum v. Kaes Inversiones y Valores, C.A., 476 So. 2d 247, 10 FLW 2209 (Fla. App. D3 1985)

8 ALR5th 653—§ 3

Sztejn v. Columbia Bristle & Soft Hair Corp., 267 A.D. 94, 44 N.Y.S.2d 497 (1st Dep't 1943)

67 ALR5th 179—§ 3

Sztorc v. Northwest Hosp., 146 Ill. App. 3d 275, 100 Ill. Dec. 135, 496 N.E.2d 1200 (1st Dist. 1986)

64 ALR6th 249—§ 19

Szturm v. Huntington Blizzard Hockey Associates Ltd. Partnership, 205 W. Va. 56, 516 S.E.2d 267, 5 Wage & Hour Cas. 2d (BNA) 711 (1999)

70 ALR6th 209—§ 49

Szuba, In re, 290 A.D.2d 643, 735 N.Y.S.2d 653 (3d Dep't 2002)

44 ALR6th 75—§ 4, 25, 31

Szuchon v. Lehman, 273 F.3d 299 (3d Cir. 2001)

102 ALR6th 279—§ 29

Szukiewicz v. Warden of Maryland Penitentiary, 213 Md. 636, 131 A.2d 390 (1957)

32 ALR5th 149—§ 24, 40

Szymanski, In re, 189 B.R. 5 (N.D. Ill. 1995)

99 ALR6th 481—§ 27

Szymanski v. Boston Mut. Life Ins. Co., 56 Mass. App. Ct. 367, 778 N.E.2d 16 (2002)

61 ALR6th 239—§ 29

Szymanski v. Brown, 221 Mich. App. 423, 562 N.W.2d 212 (1997)

2 ALR6th 279—§ 22

Szymanski v. Halle's Dept. Store, 63 Ohio St. 2d 195, 17 Ohio Op. 3d 120, 407 N.E.2d 502 (1980)

107 ALR5th 441—§ 7

109 ALR5th 161—§ 4

Szymanski v. Szymanski, 188 Iowa 931, 176 N.W. 806 (1920)

52 ALR5th 221—§ 12, 29

Szymczyk v. Signs Now Corp., 168 N.C. App. 182, 606 S.E.2d 728 (2005)

20 ALR6th 211—§ 11, 13, 40

Szymenski v. State, 500 N.E.2d 213 (Ind. Ct. App. 1986)

92 ALR6th 1—§ 4

Szymkowski v. Iowa & Howard Citizens for Better Government, 140 Wis. 2d 860, 409 N.W.2d 670 (Ct. App. 1987)

114 ALR5th 1—§ 31

Szyplinski v. Midwest Mobile Home Supply Co., Inc., 308 Minn. 152, 241 N.W.2d 306 (1976)

1 ALR6th 297—§ 5, 9

ANNOTATION TITLES

1 ALR5th

Liability for injury or death allegedly caused by foreign object in food or food product. **1 ALR5th 1.**

Who is an "executive officer" of insured within meaning of liability insurance policy. **1 ALR5th 132.**

Governmental tort liability for detour accidents. **1 ALR5th 163.**

Liability of hospital, physician, or other medical personnel for death or injury from use of drugs to stimulate labor. **1 ALR5th 243.**

Liability of hospital, physician, or other medical personnel for death or injury to mother or child caused by improper administration of, or failure to administer, anesthesia or tranquilizers, or similar drugs, during labor and delivery. **1 ALR5th 269.**

Effect of forfeiture proceedings under uniform controlled substances act or similar statute on lien against property subject to forfeiture. **1 ALR5th 317.**

Forfeitability of property, under uniform controlled substances act or similar statute, where property or evidence supporting forfeiture was illegally seized. **1 ALR5th 346.**

Application of forfeiture provisions of Uniform Controlled Substances Act or similar statute where drugs were possessed for personal use. **1 ALR5th 375.**

Employer's state-law liability for withdrawing, or substantially altering, job offer for indefinite period before employee actually commences employment. **1 ALR5th 401.**

Products liability of endorser, trade association, certifier, or similar party who expresses approval of product. **1 ALR5th 431.**

Parent's mental deficiency as factor in termination of parental rights—modern status. **1 ALR5th 469.**

Validity of zoning laws setting minimum lot size requirements. **1 ALR5th 622.**

Denial or restriction of visitation rights to parent charged with sexually abusing child. **1 ALR5th 776.**

Construction and effect of property insurance provision permitting recovery of replacement cost of property. **1 ALR5th 817.**

Misconduct involving intoxication as ground for disciplinary action against attorney. **1 ALR5th 874.**

Defense of necessity, duress, or coercion in prosecution for violation of state narcotics laws. **1 ALR5th 938.**

Proper execution of self-proving affidavit as validating or otherwise curing defect in execution of will itself. **1 ALR5th 965.**

2 ALR5th

Liability for injury or death allegedly caused by spoilage, contamination, or other deleterious condition of food or food product. **2 ALR5th 1.**

Liability for injury or death allegedly caused by food product containing object related to, but not intended to be present in, product. **2 ALR5th 189.**

Determination that state failed to prove charges relied upon for revocation of probation as barring subsequent criminal action based on same underlying charges. **2 ALR5th 262.**

Hospital's liability for injury resulting from failure to have sufficient number of nurses on duty. **2 ALR5th 286.**

Sexual partner's tort liability to other partner for fraudulent misrepresentation regarding sterility or use of birth control resulting in pregnancy. **2 ALR5th 301.**

Parent's child support liability as affected by other parent's fraudulent misrepresentation regarding sterility or use of birth control, or refusal to abort pregnancy. **2 ALR5th 337.**

Franchisor's tort liability for injuries allegedly caused by assault or other criminal activity on or near franchise premises. **2 ALR5th 369.**

ANNOTATION TITLES

Liability of travel publication, travel agent, or similar party for personal injury or death of traveler. **2 ALR5th 396.**

Plaintiff's rights to punitive or multiple damages when cause of action renders both available. **2 ALR5th 449.**

Unemployment compensation: eligibility as affected by claimant's refusal to work at particular times or on particular shifts for domestic or family reasons. **2 ALR5th 475.**

Construction and application of zoning laws setting minimum lot size requirements. **2 ALR5th 553.**

Validity, construction, application, and effect of statute requiring conditions, in addition to expiration of time, for reinstatement of suspended or revoked driver's license. **2 ALR5th 725.**

Liability for incorrectly diagnosing existence or nature of pregnancy. **2 ALR5th 769.**

Liability of hospital, physician, or other medical personnel for death or injury to child caused by improper postdelivery diagnosis, care, and representations. **2 ALR5th 811.**

"Excess" or "umbrella" insurance policy as providing coverage for accidents with uninsured or underinsured motorists. **2 ALR5th 922.**

Duty of retail establishment, or its employees, to assist patron choking on food. **2 ALR5th 966.**

3 ALR5th

Modern status of rule imputing motor vehicle driver's negligence to passenger on joint venture theory. **3 ALR5th 1.**

Liability of physician, nurse, or hospital for failure to contact physician or to keep physician sufficiently informed concerning status of mother during pregnancy, labor, and childbirth. **3 ALR5th 123.**

Liability of hospital, physician, or other medical personnel for death or injury to mother or child caused by inadequate attendance or monitoring of patient during and after pregnancy, labor, and delivery. **3 ALR5th 146.**

For assistance, call 1-800-328-4880

ANNOTATION TITLES

Dismissal of state court action for plaintiff's failure or refusal to obey court order relating to pleadings or parties. **3 ALR5th 237.**

Liability of doctor or other health practitioner to third party contracting contagious disease from doctor's patient. **3 ALR5th 370.**

Failure to disclose extent or value of property owned as ground for avoiding premarital contract. **3 ALR5th 394.**

"Choice of evils," necessity, duress, or similar defense to state or local criminal charges based on acts of public protest. **3 ALR5th 521.**

What constitutes contest or attempt to defeat will within provision thereof forfeiting share of contesting beneficiary. **3 ALR5th 590.**

Refusal of medical treatment on religious grounds as affecting right to recover for personal injury or death. **3 ALR5th 721.**

Insured's recovery of uninsured motorist claim against insurer as affecting subsequent recovery against tortfeasors causing injury. **3 ALR5th 746.**

Admissibility of tape recording or transcript of "911" emergency telephone call. **3 ALR5th 784.**

Products liability: roofs and roofing materials. **3 ALR5th 851.**

What amounts to failure or refusal to submit to medical treatment sufficient to bar recovery of workers' compensation. **3 ALR5th 907.**

Threats of violence against juror in criminal trial as ground for mistrial or dismissal of juror. **3 ALR5th 963.**

4 ALR5th

Minimum quantity of drug required to support claim that defendant is guilty of criminal "possession" of drug under state law. **4 ALR5th 1.**

Fire insurance: failure to disclose prior fires affecting insured's property as ground for avoidance of policy. **4 ALR5th 117.**

For assistance, call 1-800-328-4880

1364

Liability of hospital, physician, or other medical personnel for death or injury to mother or child caused by improper choice between, or timing of, vaginal or cesarean delivery. **4 ALR5th 148.**

Liability of hospital, physician, or other medical personnel for death or injury to mother or child caused by improper procedures during vaginal delivery. **4 ALR5th 210.**

Legal malpractice in defense of criminal prosecution. **4 ALR5th 273.**

Divorce: spouse's right to order that other spouse pay expert witness fees. **4 ALR5th 403.**

Workers' compensation: coverage of injury occurring in parking lot provided by employer, while employee was going to or coming from work. **4 ALR5th 443.**

Workers' compensation: coverage of injury occurring between workplace and parking lot provided by employer, while employee is going to or coming from work. **4 ALR5th 585.**

Products liability: prefabricated buildings. **4 ALR5th 667.**

Propriety of setting minimum or "upset price" for sale of property at judicial foreclosure. **4 ALR5th 693.**

Comparative negligence: judgment allocating fault in action against less than all potential defendants as precluding subsequent action against parties not sued in original action. **4 ALR5th 753.**

Construction and effect of statutes requiring construction fundholder to withhold payments upon "stop notice" from subcontractor, materialman, or other person entitled to funds. **4 ALR5th 772.**

Joinder of tort actions between spouses with proceeding for dissolution of marriage. **4 ALR5th 972.**

Propriety of surgically invading incompetent or minor for benefit of third party. **4 ALR5th 1000.**

5 ALR5th

Tort liability for pollution from underground storage tank. **5 ALR5th 1.**

Ratification of attorney's unauthorized compromise of action. **5 ALR5th 56.**

Computation of net "loss" for which fidelity insurer is liable. **5 ALR5th 132.**

Sufficiency of bodily injury to support charge of aggravated assault. **5 ALR5th 243.**

Filing of notice of appeal as affecting jurisdiction of state trial court to consider motion to vacate judgment. **5 ALR5th 422.**

What entities or projects are "public" for purposes of state statutes requiring payment of prevailing wages on public works projects. **5 ALR5th 470.**

Who is "employee," "workman" or the like, of contractor subject to state statute requiring payment of prevailing wages on public works projects. **5 ALR5th 513.**

Liability of church or religious society for sexual misconduct of clergy. **5 ALR5th 530.**

Significant connection jurisdiction of court under § 3(a)(2) of the Uniform Child Custody Jurisdiction Act (UCCJA) and the Parental Kidnapping Prevention Act (PKPA), 28 U.S.C.A. § 1738a(c)(2)(b). **5 ALR5th 550.**

Abandonment and emergency jurisdiction of court under § 3(a)(3) of the Uniform Child Custody Jurisdiction Act (UCCJA) and the Parental Kidnapping Prevention Act (PKPA), 28 U.S.C.A. § 1738a(c)(2)(c). **5 ALR5th 788.**

Authority of court, upon entering default judgment, to make orders for child custody or support which were not specifically requested in pleadings of prevailing party. **5 ALR5th 863.**

Propriety of limiting to issue of damages alone new trial granted on ground of inadequacy of damages—modern cases. **5 ALR5th 875.**

6 ALR5th

Home state jurisdiction of court under § 3(a)(1) of the Uniform Child Custody Jurisdiction Act (UCCJA) or the Parental Kidnapping Prevention Act (PKPA), 28 U.S.C.A.

§ 1738a(c)(2)(a). **6 ALR5th 1.**

Default jurisdiction of court under § 3(a)(4) of the Uniform Child Custody Jurisdiction Act (UCCJA) or the Parental Kidnapping Prevention Act (PKPA), 28 U.S.C.A. § 1738a(c)(2)(d). **6 ALR5th 69.**

Infliction of emotional distress: toxic exposure. **6 ALR5th 162.**

Disqualification of member of law firm as requiring disqualification of entire firm—state cases. **6 ALR5th 242.**

Liability of insurer, or insurance agent or adjuster, for infliction of emotional distress. **6 ALR5th 297.**

Liability of hospital, physician, or other medical personnel for death or injury to mother or child caused by improper treatment during labor. **6 ALR5th 490.**

Liability of hospital, physician, or other medical personnel for death or injury to mother caused by improper postdelivery diagnosis, care, and representations. **6 ALR5th 534.**

Insurer's liability to insurance agent or broker for damages suffered as result of insurer's denial of coverage or refusal to pay policy proceeds to insured. **6 ALR5th 611.**

Forfeitability of property under uniform controlled substances act or similar statute where amount of controlled substance seized is small. **6 ALR5th 652.**

Delay in setting hearing date or in holding hearing as affecting forfeitability under uniform controlled substances act or similar statute. **6 ALR5th 711.**

What constitutes offense of cruelty to animals—modern cases. **6 ALR5th 733.**

Release of one joint tortfeasor as discharging liability of others under Uniform Contribution Among Tortfeasors Act and other statutes expressly governing effect of release. **6 ALR5th 883.**

7 ALR5th

Liability of hospital, physician, or other medical personnel for death or injury to mother or child caused by improper diagnosis and treatment of mother relating to and during pregnancy. **7 ALR5th 1.**

Automobiles: necessity or emergency as defense in prosecution for driving without operator's license or while license is suspended. **7 ALR5th 73.**

Eminent domain: compensability of loss of visibility of owner's property. **7 ALR5th 113.**

Admissibility of polygraph or similar lie detector test results, or willingness to submit to test, on issues of coverage under insurance policy, or insurer's good faith belief that claim was not covered. **7 ALR5th 143.**

Easement, servitude, or covenant as affected by sale for taxes. **7 ALR5th 187.**

Chronological or procedural sequence of former convictions as affecting enhancement of penalty under habitual offender statutes. **7 ALR5th 263.**

What are "prevailing wages," or the like, for purposes of state statute requiring payment of prevailing wages on public works projects. **7 ALR5th 400.**

Employers subject to state statutes requiring payment of prevailing wages on public works projects. **7 ALR5th 444.**

Laws regulating begging, panhandling, or similar activity by poor or homeless persons. **7 ALR5th 455.**

Grounds for revocation or suspension of license of real-estate broker or salesperson. **7 ALR5th 474.**

Validity and construction of "extreme indifference" murder statute. **7 ALR5th 758.**

Purchaser's disbelief in, or nonreliance upon, express warranties made by seller in contract for sale of business as precluding action for breach of express warranties. **7 ALR5th 841.**

Application of statute of limitations to actions for breach of duty in performing services of public accountant. **7 ALR5th 852.**

Right of workers' compensation insurer or employer paying to a workers' compensation fund, on the compensable death of an employee with no dependents, to indemnity or subrogation from proceeds of wrongful death action brought against third-party tortfeasor. **7 ALR5th 969.**

Stakeholder's liability for loss of interpleaded funds after they leave stakeholder's control. **7 ALR5th 976.**

8 ALR5th

Liability for personal injury or death allegedly caused by defect in church premises. **8 ALR5th 1.**

Liability for injury or death from collision with guy wire. **8 ALR5th 177.**

Homeowner's liability insurance coverage of emotional distress allegedly inflicted on third party by insured. **8 ALR5th 254.**

Construction and effect of provision in contract for sale of realty by which purchaser agrees to take property "as is" or in its existing condition. **8 ALR5th 312.**

Validity of provisions for amortization of nonconforming uses. **8 ALR5th 391.**

What constitutes compliance of documents presented with terms of letter of credit so as to require honor of draft under UCC § 5-114. **8 ALR5th 463.**

Propriety and effect of corporation's appearance pro se through agent who is not attorney. **8 ALR5th 653.**

Ineffective assistance of counsel: compulsion, duress, necessity, or "hostage syndrome" defense. **8 ALR5th 713.**

Stationary object or attached fixture as deadly or dangerous weapon for purposes of statute aggravating offenses such as assault, robbery, or homicide. **8 ALR5th 775.**

Workers' compensation: compensability of injury during tryout, employment test, or similar activity designed to determine employability. **8 ALR5th 798.**

Licensing and regulation of practice of physical therapy. **8 ALR5th 825.**

Validity of state statute prohibiting health providers from the practice of waiving patients' obligation to pay health insurance deductibles or copayments, or advertising such practice. **8 ALR5th 855.**

Liability of public or private agency or its employees to prospective adoptive parents in contract or tort for failure to complete arrangement for adoption. **8 ALR5th 860.**

Validity of state or local government regulation requiring private school to report attendance and similar information to government—post-Yoder cases. **8 ALR5th 875.**

9 ALR5th

Products liability: application of strict liability doctrine to seller of used product. **9 ALR5th 1.**

Right to prejudgment interest on punitive or multiple damages awards. **9 ALR5th 63.**

Prospective juror's connection with insurance company as ground for challenge for cause. **9 ALR5th 102.**

Disciplinary action against attorney taking loan from client. **9 ALR5th 193.**

Running of limitations against action for civil damages for sexual abuse of child. **9 ALR5th 321.**

Admissibility, in criminal prosecution, of expert opinion evidence as to "blood splatter" interpretation. **9 ALR5th 369.**

Propriety of telephone testimony or hearings in prison proceedings. **9 ALR5th 451.**

Entrapment as defense to charge of selling or supplying narcotics where government agents supplied narcotics to defendant and purchased them from him. **9 ALR5th 464.**

"Caller ID" System, allowing telephone call recipient to ascertain number of telephone from which call originated, as violation of right to privacy, wiretapping statute, or similar protections. **9 ALR5th 553.**

Divorce and separation: consideration of tax consequences in distribution of marital property. **9 ALR5th 568.**

Equitable estoppel of secured party's right to assert prior, perfected security interest against other secured creditor or subsequent purchaser under article 9 of uniform commercial code. **9 ALR5th 708.**

Joint and several liability of physicians whose independent negligence in treatment of patient causes indivisible injury. **9 ALR5th 746.**

Sufficiency of evidence to raise last clear chance doctrine in cases of automobile collision with pedestrian or bicyclist—modern cases. **9 ALR5th 826.**

Recovery of attorneys' fees and costs of litigation incurred as result of breach of agreement not to sue. **9 ALR5th 933.**

Liability of private operator of "halfway house" or group home housing convicted prisoners before final release for injury to third person caused by inmate. **9 ALR5th 969.**

10 ALR5th

Rights as to notice and hearing in proceeding to revoke or suspend license to practice medicine. **10 ALR5th 1.**

What constitutes conviction within statutory or constitutional provision making conviction of crime ground of disqualification for, removal from, or vacancy in, public office. **10 ALR5th 139.**

Divorce and separation: award of interest on deferred installment payments of marital asset distribution. **10 ALR5th 191.**

Right to workers' compensation for injuries suffered after termination of employment. **10 ALR5th 245.**

What projects involve work subject to state statutes requiring payment of prevailing wages on public works projects. **10 ALR5th 337.**

Employees' private right of action to enforce state statute requiring payment of prevailing wages on public works projects. **10 ALR5th 360.**

Admissibility of evidence of absence of other accidents or injuries at place where injury or damage occurred. **10 ALR5th 371.**

Excessiveness or adequacy of attorneys' fees in matters involving real estate—modern cases. **10 ALR5th 448.**

Validity of ordinances restricting location of "adult entertainment" or sex-oriented businesses. **10 ALR5th 538.**

Admissibility of evidence of polygraph test results, or offer or refusal to take test, in action for malicious prosecution. **10 ALR5th 663.**

Modern status of sudden emergency doctrine. **10 ALR5th 680.**

Prejudicial effect of statement by prosecutor that verdict, recommendation of punishment, or other finding by jury is subject to review or correction by other authorities. **10 ALR5th 700.**

Legal malpractice: negligence or fault of client as defense. **10 ALR5th 828.**

11 ALR5th

Propriety of questioning expert witness regarding specific incidents or allegations of expert's unprofessional conduct or professional negligence. **11 ALR5th 1.**

Lawfulness of search of person or personal effects under medical emergency exception to warrant requirement. **11 ALR5th 52.**

Fraud actions: right to recover for mental or emotional distress. **11 ALR5th 88.**

Intentional provocation, contributory or comparative negligence, or assumption of risk as defense to action for injury by dog. **11 ALR5th 127.**

Use of prior military conviction to establish repeat offender status. **11 ALR5th 218.**

Spouse's right to set off debt owed by other spouse against accrued spousal or child support payments. **11 ALR5th 259.**

State and local government control of pollution from underground storage tanks. **11 ALR5th 388.**

Application of statute of limitations in private tort actions based on injury to persons or property caused by underground flow of contaminants. **11 ALR5th 438.**

Admissibility, in homicide prosecution, of evidence as to tests made to ascertain distance from gun to victim when

---

gun was fired. **11 ALR5th 497.**

Emotional or psychological "blocking" or repression as tolling running of statute of limitations. **11 ALR5th 588.**

Right of one governmental subdivision to sue another such subdivision for damages. **11 ALR5th 630.**

Validity, construction, and effect of state laws requiring payment of wages on resignation of employee immediatley or within specified period. **11 ALR5th 715.**

Admissibility of evidence in homicide case that victim was threatened by one other than defendant. **11 ALR5th 831.**

Ineffective assistance of counsel: battered spouse syndrome as defense to homicide or other criminal offense. **11 ALR5th 871.**

12 ALR5th

Medical malpractice: who are "health care providers," or the like, whose actions fall within statutes specifically governing actions and damages for medical malpractice. **12 ALR5th 1.**

Validity, construction and application of state laws imposing tax or license fee on possession, sale, or the like, of illegal narcotics. **12 ALR5th 89.**

State statutes or regulations expressly governing disclosure of fact that person has tested positive for Human Immunodeficiency Virus (HIV) or Acquired Immunodeficiency Syndrome (AIDS). **12 ALR5th 149.**

Excessiveness or inadequacy of punitive damages awarded in personal injury or death cases. **12 ALR5th 195.**

Right to jury trial in action under state civil rights law. **12 ALR5th 508.**

Posttraumatic syndrome as tolling running of statute of limitations. **12 ALR5th 546.**

Propriety of state court's grant or denial of application for pre-action production or inspection of documents, persons, or other evidence. **12 ALR5th 577.**

Vendor's obligation to disclose to purchaser of land presence of contamination from hazardous substances or wastes. **12 ALR5th 630.**

Eligibility for workers' compensation as affected by claimant's misrepresentation of health or physical condition at time of hiring. **12 ALR5th 658.**

Enforceability, by purchaser or successor of business, of covenant not to compete entered into by predecessor and its employees. **12 ALR5th 847.**

Disqualification or recusal of prosecuting attorney because of relationship with alleged victim or victim's family. **12 ALR5th 909.**

What statute of limitations applies to state law action by public sector employee for breach of union's duty of fair representation. **12 ALR5th 950.**

13 ALR5th

State law criminal liability of licensed physician for prescribing or dispensing drug or similar controlled substance. **13 ALR5th 1.**

Right of extraditee to bail after issuance of governor's warrant and pending final disposition of habeas corpus claim. **13 ALR5th 118.**

What constitutes tenant's holding over of leased premises. **13 ALR5th 169.**

Employer's liability for assault, theft, or similar intentional wrong committed by employee at home or business of customer. **13 ALR5th 217.**

Breach of assumed duty to inspect property as ground for liability to third party. **13 ALR5th 289.**

Jurors as within coverage of workers' compensation acts. **13 ALR5th 444.**

Modification, revocation, or reformation of letter of credit—modern cases. **13 ALR5th 465.**

Obscenity prosecutions: statutory exemption based on dissemination to persons or entities having scientific, educational, or similar justification for possession of such materials. **13 ALR5th 567.**

Common-law strict liability in tort of prior landowner or lessee to subsequent owner for contamination of land with hazardous waste resulting from prior owner's or lessee's abnormally dangerous or ultrahazardous activity. **13 ALR5th 600.**

Transmission or risk of transmission of Human Immunodeficiency Virus (HIV) or Acquired Immunodeficiency Syndrome (AIDS) as basis for prosecution or sentencing in criminal or military discipline case. **13 ALR5th 628.**

Construction mortgagee-lender's duty to protect interest of subordinated purchase-money mortgagee. **13 ALR5th 684.**

Propriety of applying minority discount to value of shares purchased by corporation or its shareholders from minority shareholders. **13 ALR5th 840.**

Validity, construction, and application of state statute requiring inmate to reimburse government for expense of incarceration. **13 ALR5th 872.**

14 ALR5th

Workers' compensation: recovery for carpal tunnel syndrome. **14 ALR5th 1.**

Products liability: lighters and lighter fluid. **14 ALR5th 47.**

Criminal law: propriety of reassembling jury to amend, correct, clarify, or otherwise change verdict after jury has been discharged, or has reached or sealed its verdict and separated. **14 ALR5th 89.**

Motorist's liability for signaling other vehicle or pedestrian to proceed, or to pass signaling vehicle. **14 ALR5th 193.**

Excessiveness or inadequacy of punitive damages in cases not involving personal injury or death. **14 ALR5th 242.**

Employer's liability, under state law, for fraud or misrepresentation inducing employee to take early retirement. **14 ALR5th 537.**

Death of obligor parent as affecting decree for support of child. **14 ALR5th 557.**

Air carrier's liability for injury from condition of airport premises. **14 ALR5th 662.**

Event triggering liability insurance coverage as occurring within period of time covered by liability insurance policy where injury or damage is delayed—modern cases. **14 ALR5th 695.**

Prisoner's rights as to search and seizure under state law or constitution—post-Hudson cases. **14 ALR5th 913.**

Liability of guardian ad litem for infant party to civil suit for negligence in connection with suit. **14 ALR5th 929.**

Recovery under state law of attorney's fees by lay pro se litigant. **14 ALR5th 947.**

15 ALR5th

Validity of birth parent's "blanket" consent to adoption which fails to identify adoptive parents. **15 ALR5th 1.**

Right of criminal defendant to raise entrapment defense based on having dealt with other party who was entrapped. **15 ALR5th 39.**

Rescission or cancellation of insurance policy for insured's misrepresentation or concealment of information concerning Human Immunodeficiency Virus (HIV), Acquired Immunodeficiency Syndrome (AIDS), or related health problems. **15 ALR5th 92.**

Admissibility of evidence of repairs, change of conditions, or precautions taken after accident—modern state cases. **15 ALR5th 119.**

"Unconscionability," under UCC § 2-302, of bank's letter of credit or other financing arrangements. **15 ALR5th 365.**

Liability of contractor who abandons building project before completion for liquidated damages for delay. **15 ALR5th 376.**

Measure and elements of restitution to which victim is entitled under state criminal statute. **15 ALR5th 391.**

Unemployment compensation claimant's eligibility as affected by loss of, or failure to obtain, license, certificate, or similar qualification for continued employment. **15 ALR5th 653.**

Continuity of residence as factor in contest between parent and nonparent for custody of child who has been residing with nonparent—modern status. **15 ALR5th 692.**

For assistance, call 1-800-328-4880

Abutting owner's right to damages for limitation of access caused by traffic regulation. **15 ALR5th 821.**

Laws prohibiting or regulating "escort services," "outcall entertainment," or similar services used to carry on prostitution. **15 ALR5th 900.**

Consorting with, or maintaining social relations with, criminal figure as ground for disciplinary action against judge. **15 ALR5th 923.**

16 ALR5th

Liability of motorbus carrier or driver for death of, or injury to, discharged passenger struck by other vehicle. **16 ALR5th 1.**

Ineffective assistance of counsel: right of attorney to withdraw, as appointed defense counsel, due to self-avowed incompetence. **16 ALR5th 118.**

Validity, construction, and application of statutes requiring that percentage of punitive damages awards be paid directly to state or court-administered fund. **16 ALR5th 129.**

Physician's use of patient's tissues, cells, or bodily substances for medical research or economic purposes. **16 ALR5th 143.**

Exclusion of public and media from voir dire examination of prospective jurors in state criminal case. **16 ALR5th 152.**

Workers' compensation: tips or gratuities as factor in determining amount of compensation. **16 ALR5th 191.**

In-house counsel's right to maintain action for wrongful discharge. **16 ALR5th 239.**

Construction, operation, and effect of statute giving hospital lien against recovery from tortfeasor causing patient's injuries. **16 ALR5th 262.**

Criminal liability of pharmacy or pharmacist for welfare fraud in connection with supplying prescription drugs. **16 ALR5th 390.**

Requirement under property insurance policy that insured submit to examination under oath as to loss. **16 ALR5th 412.**

Garnishment of funds payable under building and construction contract. **16 ALR5th 548.**

Liability for negligence of ambulance attendants, emergency medical technicians, and the like, rendering emergency medical care outside hospital. **16 ALR5th 605.**

Parties' misconduct as ground for declining jurisdiction under § 8 of the Uniform Child Custody Jurisdiction Act (UCCJA). **16 ALR5th 650.**

Sufficiency of evidence that witness in criminal case was hypnotized, for purposes of determining admissibility of testimony given under hypnosis or of hypnotically enhanced testimony. **16 ALR5th 841.**

Forfeiture of homestead based on criminal activity conducted on premises—state cases. **16 ALR5th 855.**

17 ALR5th

Effectiveness of employer's disclaimer of representations in personnel manual or employee handbook altering at-will employment relationship. **17 ALR5th 1.**

Minor's entry into home of parent as sufficient to sustain burglary charge. **17 ALR5th 111.**

Use of fraud or trick as "constructive breaking" for purpose of burglary or breaking and entering offense. **17 ALR5th 125.**

Consideration of obligated spouse's earnings from overtime or "second job" held in addition to regular full-time employment in fixing alimony or child support awards. **17 ALR5th 143.**

Liability of school or school personnel in connection with suicide of student. **17 ALR5th 179.**

Right of one governmental subdivision to challenge annexation proceedings by another such subdivision. **17 ALR5th 195.**

Recovery of damages for expense of medical monitoring to detect or prevent future disease or condition. **17 ALR5th 327.**

Excessiveness or adequacy of attorneys' fees in domestic relations cases. **17 ALR5th 366.**

For assistance, call 1-800-328-4880

Liability of property owner for damages from spread of accidental fire originating on his property. **17 ALR5th 547.**

Validity and construction of statutes or ordinances imposing civil or criminal penalties on alarm system users, installers, or servicers for false alarms. **17 ALR5th 825.**

Validity and construction of statutes prohibiting harassment of hunters, fishermen, or trappers. **17 ALR5th 837.**

Cautionary instructions to jury as to reliability of, or factors to be considered in evaluating, voice identification testimony. **17 ALR5th 851.**

18 ALR5th

Actions by state official involving defendant as constituting "outrageous" conduct violating due process guaranties. **18 ALR5th 1.**

Liability policy coverage for insured's injury to third party's investments, anticipated profits, goodwill, or the like, unaccompanied by physical property damage. **18 ALR5th 187.**

Action for tortious interference with bequest as precluded by will contest remedy. **18 ALR5th 211.**

Validity and effect of one spouse's conveyance to other spouse of interest in property held as estate by the entireties. **18 ALR5th 230.**

Promissory estoppel of lending institution based on promise to lend money. **18 ALR5th 307.**

Landlord's permitting third party to occupy premises rent-free as acceptance of tenant's surrender of premises. **18 ALR5th 437.**

Liability of insurer to insured for settling third-party claim within policy limits resulting in detriment to insured. **18 ALR5th 474.**

Applicability of comparative negligence principles to intentional torts. **18 ALR5th 525.**

Validity and application of statute or regulation authorizing revocation or suspension of driver's license for reason unrelated to use of, or ability to operate, motor vehicle. **18 ALR5th 542.**

Validity, construction, and effect of state laws requiring payment of wages on discharge of employee immediately or within specified period. **18 ALR5th 577.**

Admissibility and prejudicial effect of evidence, in criminal prosecution, of defendant's involvement with witchcraft, satanism, or the like. **18 ALR5th 804.**

Statute protecting minors in a specified age range from rape or other sexual activity as applicable to defendant minor within protected age group. **18 ALR5th 856.**

Attorney malpractice in connection with services related to adoption of child. **18 ALR5th 892.**

Legal malpractice in defense of parents at proceedings to terminate parental rights over dependent or neglected children. **18 ALR5th 902.**

19 ALR5th

Who is "public figure" for purposes of defamation action. **19 ALR5th 1.**

Criminal defendant's representation by person not licensed to practice law as violation of right to counsel. **19 ALR5th 351.**

Landlord's liability for injury or death of tenant's child from lead paint poisoning. **19 ALR5th 405.**

When statute of limitations commences to run as to cause of action for wrongful discharge. **19 ALR5th 439.**

State constitutional requirements as to exclusion of evidence unlawfully seized—post-Leon cases. **19 ALR5th 470.**

What constitutes mental illness or disorder, insanity, or the like, within provision limiting or excluding coverage under health or disability policy. **19 ALR5th 533.**

Malpractice in treatment of skin disease, disorder, blemish, or scar. **19 ALR5th 563.**

Propriety of reassembling jury to amend, correct, clarify, or otherwise change verdict after discharge or separation at conclusion of civil case. **19 ALR5th 622.**

Title insurer's negligent failure to discover and disclose defect as basis for liability in tort. **19 ALR5th 786.**

Kicking as aggravated assault, or assault with dangerous or deadly weapon. **19 ALR5th 823.**

Search and seizure: lawfulness of demand for driver's license, vehicle registration, or proof of insurance pursuant to police stop to assist motorist. **19 ALR5th 884.**

Liability of surety on private bond for statutory penalties imposed for nonpayment. **19 ALR5th 900.**

20 ALR5th

Necessity of expert testimony on issue of permanence of injury and future pain and suffering. **20 ALR5th 1.**

Propriety of imposing capital punishment on mentally retarded individuals. **20 ALR5th 177.**

Sufficiency, as to content, of notice of garnishment required to be served upon garnishee. **20 ALR5th 229.**

Workers' compensation: coverage of employee's injury or death from exposure to the elements—modern cases. **20 ALR5th 346.**

Use of peremptory challenges to exclude ethnic and racial groups, other than black Americans, from criminal jury—post-Batson state cases. **20 ALR5th 398.**

Financing agency's liability to purchaser of new home or structure for consequences of construction defects. **20 ALR5th 499.**

Parent's use of drugs as factor in award of custody of children, visitation rights, or termination of parental rights. **20 ALR5th 534.**

Pre-emption by workers' compensation statute of employee's remedy under state "whistleblower" statute. **20 ALR5th 677.**

Pending proceeding in another state as ground for declining jurisdiction under § 6(a) of the Uniform Child Custody Jurisdiction Act (UCCJA) or the Parental Kidnapping

---

Prevention Act (PKPA), 28 U.S.C.A. § 1738A(g). **20 ALR5th 700.**

21 ALR5th

Pre-emption of wrongful discharge cause of action by civil rights laws. **21 ALR5th 1.**

Instructions on "unavoidable accident," "mere accident," or the like, in motor vehicle cases—modern cases. **21 ALR5th 82.**

Power of court or other public agency to order medical treatment over parental religious objections for child whose life is not immediately endangered. **21 ALR5th 248.**

Who may institute proceedings to revoke probation. **21 ALR5th 275.**

Validity, construction, and effect of "regulatory exclusion" in directors' and officers' liability insurance policy. **21 ALR5th 292.**

Inconvenience of forum as ground for declining jurisdiction under § 7 of the Uniform Child Custody Jurisdiction Act (UCCJA). **21 ALR5th 396.**

Validity of state or local gross receipts tax on gambling. **21 ALR5th 812.**

22 ALR5th

Admissibility of evidence of commission of similar crime by one other than accused. **22 ALR5th 1.**

Workers' compensation: Lyme disease. **22 ALR5th 246.**

Validity, construction, and effect of "hate crimes" statutes, "ethnic intimidation" statutes, or the like. **22 ALR5th 261.**

Validity, construction, and effect of statute or lease provision expressly governing rights and compensation of lessee upon condemnation of leased property. **22 ALR5th 327.**

Applicability of comparative negligence doctrine to actions based on negligent misrepresentation. **22 ALR5th 464.**

Validity and effect of "Mary Carter" or similar agreement setting maximum liability of one cotortfeasor and providing for reduction or extinguishment thereof relative to recovery against nonagreeing cotortfeasor. **22 ALR5th 483.**

Construction and effect of "jeweler's block" policies or provisions contained therein. **22 ALR5th 579.**

Right of convicted defendant or prosecution to receive updated presentence report at sentencing proceedings. **22 ALR5th 660.**

Admissibility of evidence of battered child syndrome on issue of self-defense. **22 ALR5th 787.**

Unjust enrichment of landowner based on adjoining landowner's construction, improvement, or repair of commonly used highway, street, or bridge. **22 ALR5th 800.**

23 ALR5th

Tort liability of public schools and institutions of higher learning for accidents associated with transportation of students. **23 ALR5th 1.**

Liability of insurer for prejudgment interest in excess of policy limits for covered loss. **23 ALR5th 75.**

Admissibility, in motor vehicle license suspension proceedings, of evidence obtained by unlawful search and seizure. **23 ALR5th 108.**

Retaliatory eviction of tenant for reporting landlord's violation of law. **23 ALR5th 140.**

Employee's control or ownership of corporation as precluding receipt of benefits under state unemployment compensation provisions. **23 ALR5th 176.**

Excessiveness or inadequacy of attorney's fees in matters involving commercial and general business activities. **23 ALR5th 241.**

Admissibility in evidence of composite picture or sketch produced by police to identify offender. **23 ALR5th 672.**

Application of statute denying access to courts or invalidating contracts where corporation fails to comply with regulatory statute as affected by compliance after commencement of action. **23 ALR5th 744.**

Uninsured and underinsured motorist coverage: enforceability of policy provision limiting appeals from arbitration. **23 ALR5th 801.**

Right to compensation for real property damaged by law enforcement personnel in course of apprehending suspect. **23 ALR5th 834.**

24 ALR5th

Arbitration of medical malpractice claims. **24 ALR5th 1.**

Possession of stolen property as continuing offense. **24 ALR5th 132.**

Failure to lose weight as basis for reduction of damages in personal injury action. **24 ALR5th 174.**

Municipal liability for negligent performance of building inspector's duties. **24 ALR5th 200.**

Validity and construction of state statutes criminalizing the act of permitting real property to be used in connection with illegal drug activities. **24 ALR5th 428.**

Admissibility of evidence of prior physical acts of spousal abuse committed by defendant accused of murdering spouse or former spouse. **24 ALR5th 465.**

Uninsured or underinsured motorist insurance: validity and construction of policy provision purporting to reduce recovery by amount of social security disability benefits or payments under similar disability benefits law. **24 ALR5th 766.**

Liability of motorist for injury to child on skateboard. **24 ALR5th 780.**

25 ALR5th

Liability of adult assailant's family to third party for physical assault. **25 ALR5th 1.**

Application of automobile insurance "entitlement" exclusion to family member. **25 ALR5th 60.**

Application of "fireman's rule" to preclude recovery by peace officer for injuries inflicted by defendant in resisting arrest. **25 ALR5th 97.**

Waiver of right to enforce restrictive covenant by failure to object to other violations. **25 ALR5th 123.**

Laches or delay in bringing suit as affecting right to enforce restrictive building covenant. **25 ALR5th 233.**

Smoking as basis for reduction of damages in personal injury action. **25 ALR5th 343.**

Liability for spread of fire intentionally set for legitimate purpose. **25 ALR5th 391.**

Nuisance as entitling owner or occupant of real estate to recover damages for personal inconvenience, discomfort, annoyance, anguish, or sickness, distinct from, or in addition to, damages for depreciation in value of property or its use. **25 ALR5th 568.**

Secured transactions: right of secured party to take possession of collateral on default under UCC § 9-503. **25 ALR5th 696.**

Liability of school or school personnel for injury to student resulting from cheerleader activities. **25 ALR5th 784.**

26 ALR5th

Necessity and sufficiency of showing, in criminal prosecution under "hit-and-run" statute, accused's knowledge of accident, injury, or damage. **26 ALR5th 1.**

Validity and construction of agreement between attorney and client to arbitrate disputes arising between them. **26 ALR5th 107.**

Workers' compensation: reopening lump-sum compensation payment. **26 ALR5th 127.**

Validity, construction, and application of state statutory provisions limiting amount of recovery in medical malpractice claims. **26 ALR5th 245.**

Criminal liability for false personation during stop for traffic infraction. **26 ALR5th 378.**

Sufficiency of evidence to prove future medical expenses as result of injury to back, neck, or spine. **26 ALR5th 401.**

When should jury's deliberation proceed from charged offense to lesser-included offense. **26 ALR5th 603.**

Determination of whether a communication is from a corporate client for purposes of the attorney-client privilege—modern cases. **26 ALR5th 628.**

Zoning authority as estopped from revoking legally issued building permit. **26 ALR5th 736.**

Determination of indigency entitling accused in state criminal case to appointment of counsel on appeal. **26 ALR5th 765.**

27 ALR5th

Liability for breach of employment severance agreement. **27 ALR5th 1.**

Adoption of child by same-sex partners. **27 ALR5th 54.**

What corporate communications are entitled to attorney-client privilege—modern cases. **27 ALR5th 76.**

Employer's liability for negligence of employee in driving his or her own automobile. **27 ALR5th 174.**

Loss of income due to incarceration as affecting child support obligation. **27 ALR5th 540.**

Validity, construction, and application of state statutes prohibiting sale or possession of controlled substances within specified distance of schools. **27 ALR5th 593.**

Products liability: failure to provide product warning or instruction in foreign language or to use universally accepted pictographs or symbols. **27 ALR5th 697.**

Liability of secured creditor under the Uniform Commercial Code to third party on ground of unjust enrichment. **27 ALR5th 719.**

Priority between attorney's charging lien against judgment and opposing party's right of setoff against same judgment. **27 ALR5th 764.**

Architectural drawings or illustrations as exempt from sales or use tax. **27 ALR5th 794.**

28 ALR5th

What persons or entities may assert or waive corporation's attorney-client privilege—modern cases. **28 ALR5th 1.**

Treatment of depreciation expenses claimed for tax or accounting purposes in determining ability to pay child or spousal support. **28 ALR5th 46.**

Exclusion of, or discrimination against, physician or surgeon by hospital. **28 ALR5th 107.**

Enforceability of agreement restricting right of attorney to compete with former law firm. **28 ALR5th 420.**

Driving while intoxicated: subsequent consent to sobriety test as affecting initial refusal. **28 ALR5th 459.**

Medical malpractice in connection with breast augmentation, reduction, or reconstruction. **28 ALR5th 497.**

Validity, construction, and application of workers' compensation provisions relating to nonresident alien dependents. **28 ALR5th 547.**

Liability of one excavating on private property for injury to public utility cables, conduits, or the like. **28 ALR5th 603.**

Execution, outside of forum, of guaranty of obligations under contract to be performed within forum state as conferring jurisdiction over nonresident guarantors under "long-arm" statute or rule of forum. **28 ALR5th 664.**

Validity, construction, and application of "hold to service" provision of kidnapping statute. **28 ALR5th 754.**

29 ALR5th

Propriety, under state constitutional provisions, of granting use or transactional immunity for compelled incriminating testimony—post-Kastigar cases. **29 ALR5th 1.**

Measure of damages or compensation in eminent domain as affected by premises being restricted to particular educational, religious, charitable, or noncommercial use. **29 ALR5th 36.**

Participation in larceny or theft as precluding conviction for receiving or concealing the stolen property. **29 ALR5th 59.**

Validity and operation of "step-down" provision of automobile liability policy reducing coverage for permissive users. **29 ALR5th 469.**

For assistance, call 1-800-328-4880

Validity, construction, and application of stalking statutes. **29 ALR5th 487.**

Disciplinary action against attorney for making gift or loan to judge. **29 ALR5th 505.**

Admissibility of government factfinding in products liability actions. **29 ALR5th 534.**

Validity, construction, and application of state or local law prohibiting manufacture, possession, or transfer of "assault weapon". **29 ALR5th 664.**

Profane or obscene language by party, witness, or observer during trial proceedings as basis for contempt citation. **29 ALR5th 702.**

Disqualification of judge as affecting validity of decision in which other nondisqualified judges participated. **29 ALR5th 722.**

30 ALR5th

Validity and construction of statute terminating right of action for product-caused injury at fixed period after manufacture, sale, or delivery of product. **30 ALR5th 1.**

Validity, construction, and application of state "drug kingpin" statutes. **30 ALR5th 121.**

Divorce and separation: workers' compensation benefits as marital property subject to distribution. **30 ALR5th 139.**

Coverage under all-risk insurance. **30 ALR5th 170.**

Sales and use tax exemption for medical supplies. **30 ALR5th 494.**

Validity and construction of zoning regulations relating to illuminated signs. **30 ALR5th 549.**

Ophthalmological malpractice. **30 ALR5th 571.**

Validity, construction, and application of "hazing" statutes. **30 ALR5th 683.**

Scope of provision in liability policy issued to municipal corporation or similar governmental body limiting coverage to injuries arising out of construction, maintenance, or repair work. **30 ALR5th 699.**

Musical sound recording as punishable obscenity. **30 ALR5th 718.**

31 ALR5th

Medical malpractice: negligent catheterization. **31 ALR5th 1.**

Uninsured and underinsured motorist coverage: validity, construction, and effect of policy provision purporting to reduce coverage by amount paid or payable under workers' compensation law. **31 ALR5th 116.**

Measure and elements of damages for injury to bridge. **31 ALR5th 171.**

Search conducted by school official or teacher as violation of Fourth Amendment or equivalent state constitutional provision. **31 ALR5th 229.**

What passes under term "personal property" in will. **31 ALR5th 499.**

Liability of owner or operator of shopping center, or business housed therein, for injury to patron on premises from criminal attack by third party. **31 ALR5th 550.**

Prejudicial effect, in civil case, of communications between court officials or attendants and jurors. **31 ALR5th 572.**

Architect's services as within mechanics' lien statute. **31 ALR5th 664.**

Failure or refusal of state court judge to have record made of bench conference with counsel in criminal proceeding. **31 ALR5th 704.**

Validity, construction, and application of state or local law prohibiting maintenance of vehicle for purpose of keeping or selling controlled substances. **31 ALR5th 760.**

32 ALR5th

Liability of air carrier for injury to passenger caused by fall of object from overhead baggage compartment. **32 ALR5th 1.**

Right to appointment of counsel in contempt proceedings. **32 ALR5th 31.**

False or fraudulent statements or nondisclosures in application for issuance or renewal of license to practice as ground for disciplinary action against, or refusal to license, medical practitioner. **32 ALR5th 57.**

Right of accused to have evidence or court proceedings interpreted, because accused or other participant in proceedings is not proficient in the language used. **32 ALR5th 149.**

Death or injury from taking illegal drugs or narcotics as accidental or result of accidental means within insurance coverage. **32 ALR5th 629.**

Operation of mopeds and motorized recreational two-, three-, and four-wheeled vehicles as within scope of driving while intoxicated statutes. **32 ALR5th 659.**

Power of incompetent spouse's guardian or representative to sue for granting or vacation of divorce or annulment of marriage, or to make compromise or settlement in such suit. **32 ALR5th 673.**

Propriety of attorney's surreptitious sound recording of statements by others who are or may become involved in litigation. **32 ALR5th 715.**

33 ALR5th

Modern status of the application of "discovery rule" to postpone running of limitations against actions relating to breach of building and construction contracts. **33 ALR5th 1.**

Validity, construction, and application of "named driver exclusion" in automobile insurance policy. **33 ALR5th 121.**

Prejudicial effect, in civil case, of communications between judges and jurors. **33 ALR5th 205.**

Intoxication of automobile driver as basis for awarding punitive damages. **33 ALR5th 303.**

Search and seizure of bank records pertaining to customer as violation of customer's rights under state law. **33 ALR5th 453.**

Construction and application of state corporate income tax

---

statutes allowing net operating loss deductions. **33 ALR5th 509.**

Sufficiency of corroboration of confession for purpose of establishing corpus delicti as question of law or fact. **33 ALR5th 571.**

Right of employer or workers' compensation carrier to lien against, or reimbursement out of, uninsured or underinsured motorist proceeds payable to employee injured by third party. **33 ALR5th 587.**

Medical malpractice liability of sports medicine care providers for injury to, or death of, athlete. **33 ALR5th 619.**

Right to unemployment compensation or social security benefits of teacher or other school employee. **33 ALR5th 643.**

Emergency exception under state law making proceedings by public bodies open to the public. **33 ALR5th 731.**

Right of defendant in criminal contempt proceeding to obtain information by deposition. **33 ALR5th 761.**

34 ALR5th

Res ipsa loquitur in gas leak cases. **34 ALR5th 1.**

Age of parent as factor in awarding custody. **34 ALR5th 57.**

Liability for injuries to, or death of, water-skiers. **34 ALR5th 77.**

Criminality of act of directing to, or recommending, source from which illicit drugs may be purchased. **34 ALR5th 125.**

Right to credit on child support payments for social security or other government dependency payments made for benefit of child. **34 ALR5th 447.**

Nursing homes as exempt from property taxation. **34 ALR5th 529.**

Attorney-client exception under state law making proceedings by public bodies open to the public. **34 ALR5th 591.**

Contracts for breeding horses. **34 ALR5th 651.**

After-acquired evidence of employee's misconduct as barring or limiting recovery in action for wrongful discharge. **34 ALR5th 699.**

Sexual intercourse between persons related by half blood as incest. **34 ALR5th 723.**

35 ALR5th

Prejudicial effect of trial judge's remarks, during civil jury trial, disparaging litigants, witnesses, or subject matter of litigation—modern cases. **35 ALR5th 1.**

Real-estate agents' and brokers' professional liability insurance. **35 ALR5th 83.**

Pending or prospective litigation exception under state law making proceedings by public bodies open to the public. **35 ALR5th 113.**

Allowance of punitive damages in medical malpractice action. **35 ALR5th 145.**

Liability for breach of farming lease or contract. **35 ALR5th 285.**

Construction and application of "business pursuits" exclusion provision in general liability policy. **35 ALR5th 375.**

Vicarious liability of attorney for acts of associated counsel. **35 ALR5th 717.**

Construction and application of provision in liability insurance policy excluding coverage for injuries sustained during athletic or sports contest or exhibition. **35 ALR5th 731.**

Support provisions of judicial decree or order as limit of parent's liability for expenses of child. **35 ALR5th 757.**

Insurable interest of foster child or stepchild in life of foster or step parent, or vice versa. **35 ALR5th 781.**

36 ALR5th

Liability of municipal corporation or other governmental entity for injury or death caused by action or inaction of off-duty police officer. **36 ALR5th 1.**

Computer software or printout transactions as subject to state sales or use tax. **36 ALR5th 133.**

State statutes or ordinances requiring persons previously convicted of crime to register with authorities. **36 ALR5th 161.**

Employee's reimbursement for travel expenses incurred in obtaining treatment of work-related injury. **36 ALR5th 225.**

Taking and use of trial notes by jury. **36 ALR5th 255.**

Smoking as factor in child custody and visitation cases. **36 ALR5th 377.**

Adopted child as within class named in testamentary gift. **36 ALR5th 395.**

Full faith and credit "last-in-time" rule as applicable to sister state divorce or custody judgment which is inconsistent with the forum state's earlier judgment. **36 ALR5th 527.**

Products liability: cigarettes and other tobacco products. **36 ALR5th 541.**

What constitutes "construction or maintenance" of highways or roads in constitutional provision or statute allowing disbursements from state road fund for that purpose. **36 ALR5th 657.**

37 ALR5th

Propriety of stop and search by law enforcement officers based solely on drug courier profile. **37 ALR5th 1.**

Business interruption insurance. **37 ALR5th 41.**

Adopted child as within class named in deed or inter vivos trust instrument. **37 ALR5th 237.**

Propriety of using prior conviction for drug dealing to impeach witness in criminal trial. **37 ALR5th 319.**

Judicial construction and application of state legislation prohibiting religious discrimination in employment. **37 ALR5th 349.**

Sales: what constitutes "reasonable grounds for insecurity" justifying demand for adequate assurance of performance under UCC § 2-609. **37 ALR5th 459.**

Admissibility in homicide prosecution of allegedly gruesome or inflammatory visual recording of crime scene. **37 ALR5th 515.**

Existence and nature of cause of action for equitable bill of discovery. **37 ALR5th 645.**

Applicability of rules of evidence to juvenile transfer, waiver, or certification hearings. **37 ALR5th 703.**

38 ALR5th

Validity, construction, and application of computer software licensing agreements. **38 ALR5th 1.**

Liability for discharge of employee from private employment on ground of political views or conduct. **38 ALR5th 39.**

Validity and construction of provisions for arbitration of disputes as to alimony or support payments or child visitation or custody matters. **38 ALR5th 69.**

Liability of owner or operator of skating rink for injury to patron. **38 ALR5th 107.**

What constitutes "substantial impairment" entitling buyer to revoke his acceptance of goods under UCC § 2-608(1). **38 ALR5th 191.**

Construction and application of the terms "agricultural," "farm," "farming," or the like, in zoning regulations. **38 ALR5th 357.**

Admissibility of statements made for purposes of medical diagnosis or treatment as hearsay exception under Rule 803(4) of the Uniform Rules of Evidence. **38 ALR5th 433.**

Presumption or inference, in products liability action based on failure to warn, that user of product would have heeded an adequate warning had one been given. **38 ALR5th 683.**

Activities in preparation for building as establishing valid nonconforming use or vested right to engage in construction for intended use. **38 ALR5th 737.**

39 ALR5th

Decrease in income of obligor spouse following voluntary termination of employment as basis for modification of child support award. **39 ALR5th 1.**

Provision in land contract for liquidated damages upon default of purchaser as affecting right of vendor to maintain action for damages for breach of contract. **39 ALR5th 33.**

Propriety of civil or criminal forfeiture of computer hardware or software. **39 ALR5th 87.**

Propriety of exclusion of press or other media representatives from civil trial. **39 ALR5th 103.**

Products liability: defective motor vehicle air bag systems. **39 ALR5th 267.**

Seizure or detention for purpose of committing rape, robbery, or other offense as constituting separate crime of kidnapping. **39 ALR5th 283.**

Recovery of punitive damages for injuries resulting from transport, handling, and storage of toxic or hazardous substances. **39 ALR5th 763.**

Physicians' and surgeons' liens. **39 ALR5th 787.**

40 ALR5th

Employer's liability to employee or agent for injury or death resulting from assault or criminal attack by third person. **40 ALR5th 1.**

Damages for wrongful termination of franchise other than automobile dealership contracts. **40 ALR5th 57.**

Failure of police to preserve potentially exculpatory evidence as violating criminal defendant's rights under state constitution. **40 ALR5th 113.**

Liability for injury to customer from object projecting into aisle or passageway in store. **40 ALR5th 135.**

Recognition and enforcement of out-of-state custody decree under § 13 of the Uniform Child Custody Jurisdiction Act (UCCJA) or the Parental Kidnapping Prevention Act (PKPA), 28 U.S.C.A. § 1738A(a). **40 ALR5th 227.**

Validity and construction of provision of uninsured or underinsured motorist coverage that damages under the coverage will be reduced by amount of recovery from tortfeasor. **40 ALR5th 603.**

Rights and remedies of parents inter se with respect to the names of their children. **40 ALR5th 697.**

Propriety of publishing identity of sexual assault victim. **40 ALR5th 787.**

Liability for injury to customer or patron from amusement device maintained by store or shopping center for use by customers. **40 ALR5th 807.**

41 ALR5th

Right of defendant in prosecution for perjury to have the "two witnesses, or one witness and corroborating circumstances," rule included in charge to jury—state cases. **41 ALR5th 1.**

Wrongful discharge: employer's liability under state law for discharge of employee based on garnishment order against wages. **41 ALR5th 31.**

Constitutionality, construction, and application of statutes requiring bond or other security in taxpayers' action. **41 ALR5th 47.**

Automobile insurance coverage for drive-by shootings and other incidents involving the intentional discharge of firearms from moving motor vehicles. **41 ALR5th 91.**

Eligibility for unemployment compensation as affected by claimant's voluntary separation or refusal to work alleging that the work is illegal or immoral. **41 ALR5th 123.**

Liability of vendor or real-estate broker for failure to disclose information concerning off-site conditions affecting value of property. **41 ALR5th 157.**

Propriety of execution of search warrant at nighttime. **41 ALR5th 171.**

Collateral source rule: admissibility of evidence of availability to plaintiff of free public special education on issue of amount of damages recoverable from defendant. **41 ALR5th 771.**

Public service commission's implied authority to order refund of public utility revenues. **41 ALR5th 783.**

42 ALR5th

Medical malpractice: physician's admission of negligence as establishing standard of care and breach of that standard. **42 ALR5th 1.**

Contractual jury trial waivers in state civil cases. **42 ALR5th 53.**

What constitutes "dealing" under UCC § 3-305(2), providing that holder in due course takes instrument free from all defenses of any party to instrument with whom holder has not dealt. **42 ALR5th 137.**

Liability of proprietor of store, business, or place of amusement, for injury to one using baby stroller, shopping cart, or the like, furnished by defendant. **42 ALR5th 159.**

Liability of insurance agent or broker for placing insurance with insolvent carrier. **42 ALR5th 199.**

Place where corporation is doing business for purposes of state venue statute. **42 ALR5th 221.**

Validity, construction, and application of state statutes or ordinances regulating sexual performance by child. **42 ALR5th 291.**

Wrongful death damages for loss of expectancy of inheritance from decedent. **42 ALR5th 465.**

Propriety of applying cash bail to payment of fine. **42 ALR5th 547.**

Disqualification of prosecuting attorney in state criminal case on account of relationship with accused. **42 ALR5th 581.**

Products liability: theatrical equipment and props. **42 ALR5th 699.**

No-fault insurance coverage for injury or death of insured occurring during carjacking or attempted carjacking. **42 ALR5th 727.**

43 ALR5th

Sufficiency of description in warrant of person to be searched. **43 ALR5th 1.**

Medical malpractice in connection with diagnosis, care, or treatment of diabetes. **43 ALR5th 87.**

Validity, construction, and application of provision in automobile liability policy excluding from coverage injury to, or death of, employee of insured. **43 ALR5th 149.**

Landlord's liability for failure to protect tenant from criminal acts of third person. **43 ALR5th 207.**

Discharge of mortgage and taking back of new mortgage as affecting lien intervening between old and new mortgages. **43 ALR5th 519.**

Alternative dispute resolution: sanctions for failure to participate in good faith in, or comply with agreement made in, mediation. **43 ALR5th 545.**

Coverage under medical and health insurance plans for services performed by dentists, oral surgeons, and orthodontists. **43 ALR5th 657.**

Validity, construction, and application of mobile home eviction statutes. **43 ALR5th 705.**

Propriety of transferring patient found not guilty by reason of insanity to less restrictive confinement. **43 ALR5th 777.**

Attorney's obligation to share fee award with party representing public interest. **43 ALR5th 793.**

44 ALR5th

Rights in respect of engagement and courtship presents when marriage does not ensue. **44 ALR5th 1.**

Validity, construction, and effect of assault and battery exclusion in liability insurance policy at issue. **44 ALR5th 91.**

Who is "public official" for purposes of defamation action. **44 ALR5th 193.**

Liability of pharmacist who accurately fills prescription for harm resulting to user. **44 ALR5th 393.**

Liability of owner or operator of business premises for injuries from electrically operated door. **44 ALR5th 525.**

For assistance, call 1-800-328-4880

Workers' compensation: law enforcement officer's recovery for injury sustained during exercise or physical recreation activities. **44 ALR5th 569.**

Validity, construction, and application of state statute or law pertaining to telephone solicitation. **44 ALR5th 619.**

Sufficiency of allegations or evidence of victim's mental injury or emotional distress to support charge of aggravated degree of rape, sodomy, or other sexual offense. **44 ALR5th 651.**

Divorce and separation: attorney's contingent fee contracts as marital property subject to distribution. **44 ALR5th 671.**

Validity, construction, and application of Uniform Insurers Liquidation Act. **44 ALR5th 683.**

45 ALR5th

Sufficiency of random sampling of drug or contraband to establish jurisdictional amount required for conviction. **45 ALR5th 1.**

Complaint as satisfying requirement of notice of claim upon states, municipalities, and other political subdivisions. **45 ALR5th 109.**

Persons or entities upon whom notice of injury or claim against state or state agencies may or must be served. **45 ALR5th 173.**

Validity, construction, and application of state statute giving carrier lien on goods for transportation and incidental storage charges. **45 ALR5th 227.**

Measure and elements of damages for lessee's breach of covenant as to repairs. **45 ALR5th 251.**

Construction and effect of "padded payroll" rule of UCC § 3-405. **45 ALR5th 389.**

Gestures, facial expressions, or other nonverbal communication of trial judge in criminal case as ground for relief. **45 ALR5th 531.**

Substitution of judge in state criminal trial. **45 ALR5th 591.**

Unemployment compensation: leaving employment to become self-employed or to go into business for oneself as affecting right to unemployment compensation. **45 ALR5th 715.**

Libel and slander: charging one with breach or nonperformance of contract. **45 ALR5th 739.**

Validity, construction, and application of state statute criminalizing possession of contraband by individual in penal or correctional institution. **45 ALR5th 767.**

46 ALR5th

Landlord's liability to third party for repairs authorized by tenant. **46 ALR5th 1.**

Liability of electric company to one other than employee for injury or death arising from commencement or resumption of service. **46 ALR5th 423.**

Validity, construction, and application of the Uniform Fire Code. **46 ALR5th 479.**

Mistake or lack of information as to victim's age as defense to statutory rape. **46 ALR5th 499.**

Validity, construction, and application of juvenile escape statutes. **46 ALR5th 523.**

Failure to use or misuse of automobile child safety seat or restraint system as affecting recovery for personal injury or death. **46 ALR5th 557.**

Liability of private school or educational institution for breach of contract arising from provision of deficient educational instruction. **46 ALR5th 581.**

Unemployment compensation: leaving employment in pursuit of other employment as affecting right to unemployment compensation. **46 ALR5th 659.**

Family court jurisdiction to hear contract claims. **46 ALR5th 735.**

Propriety of, and liability related to, issuance or enforcement of Do Not Resuscitate (DNR) orders. **46 ALR5th 793.**

Secondary smoke as battery. **46 ALR5th 813.**

Liability of nursing home for violating statutory duty to notify third party concerning patient's medical condition. **46 ALR5th 821.**

47 ALR5th

Liability of private school or educational institution for breach of contract arising from expulsion or suspension of student. **47 ALR5th 1.**

Alimony as affected by recipient spouse's remarriage in absence of controlling specific statute. **47 ALR5th 129.**

Validity, construction, and application of provision in separation agreement affecting distribution or payment of attorneys' fees. **47 ALR5th 207.**

Use of peremptory challenges to exclude Caucasian persons, as a racial group, from criminal jury—post-Batson state cases. **47 ALR5th 259.**

Products liability: Manufacturer's postsale obligation to modify, repair, or recall product. **47 ALR5th 395.**

Malpractice: Physician's liability for injury or death resulting from side effects of drugs intentionally administered to or prescribed for patient. **47 ALR5th 433.**

Alzheimer's disease as affecting testamentary capacity. **47 ALR5th 523.**

What constitutes "vacant land" within meaning of liability or property insurance policy provisions. **47 ALR5th 535.**

Payment of attorneys' services in defending action brought against officials individually as within power or obligation of public body. **47 ALR5th 553.**

Liability on implied warranties in sale of used motor vehicle. **47 ALR5th 677.**

Unemployment compensation: leaving employment in pursuit of education or to attend training as affecting right to unemployment compensation. **47 ALR5th 775.**

Presumption or inference that accidental death of employee engaged in occupation of manufacturing or processing arose out of and in course of employment. **47 ALR5th 801.**

48 ALR5th

Liability under state law for injuries resulting from defective automobile seatbelt, shoulder harness, or restraint system. **48 ALR5th 1.**

Excessiveness or adequacy of damages awarded for injuries to trunk or torso, or internal injuries. **48 ALR5th 129.**

What constitutes "suit" triggering insurer's duty to defend environmental claims—state cases. **48 ALR5th 355.**

Liability of independent accountant to investors or shareholders. **48 ALR5th 389.**

Validity, construction, and effect of statutory exemptions of proceeds of workers' compensation awards. **48 ALR5th 473.**

Coercive conduct by private person as affecting admissibility of confession under state statutes or constitutional provisions—post-Connelly cases. **48 ALR5th 555.**

Malpractice in diagnosis and treatment of male urinary tract and related organs. **48 ALR5th 575.**

Validity, construction, and application of state or local laws regulating the sale, possession, use, or transport of fireworks. **48 ALR5th 659.**

49 ALR5th

Causes of action governed by limitations period in UCC § 2-725. **49 ALR5th 1.**

Excessiveness or inadequacy of lump-sum alimony award. **49 ALR5th 441.**

Alimony or child-support awards as subject to attorneys' liens. **49 ALR5th 595.**

Criminal liability of attorney for tampering with evidence. **49 ALR5th 619.**

Duty of prosecutor to present exculpatory evidence to state grand jury. **49 ALR5th 639.**

Liability of owner of wires, poles, or structures struck by aircraft for resulting injury or damage. **49 ALR5th 659.**

Valuing damages in personal injury actions awarded for gratuitously rendered nursing and medical care. **49 ALR5th 685.**

Reviewability before trial of order denying qualified immunity to defendant sued in state court under 42 U.S.C.A. § 1983. **49 ALR5th 717.**

Authority of state, municipality, or other governmental entity to accept late bids for public works contracts. **49 ALR5th 747.**

Construction and application of rule requiring public use for which property is condemned to be "more necessary" or "higher use" than public use to which property is already appropriated—state takings. **49 ALR5th 769.**

50 ALR5th

Excessiveness or adequacy of damages awarded for injuries to head or brain. **50 ALR5th 1.**

Products liability: recovery for injury or death resulting from intentional inhalation of product's fumes or vapors to produce intoxicating or similar effect. **50 ALR5th 275.**

Admissibility and effect of evidence of professional ethics rules in legal malpractice action. **50 ALR5th 301.**

Third-party beneficiaries of warranties under UCC § 2-318. **50 ALR5th 327.**

Breach of warranty in sale, installation, repair, design, or inspection of septic or sewage disposal systems. **50 ALR5th 417.**

Homicide: liability where death immediately results from treatment or mistreatment of injury inflicted by defendant. **50 ALR5th 467.**

Application of "plain-feel" exception to warrant requirements—state cases. **50 ALR5th 581.**

Amendment of record of judgment in state civil case to correct judicial errors and omissions. **50 ALR5th 653.**

Validity, construction, and application of state wildlife possession laws. **50 ALR5th 703.**

51 ALR5th

Application of state law to age discrimination in employment. **51 ALR5th 1.**

Workers' compensation as precluding employee's suit against employer for sexual harassment in the workplace. **51 ALR5th 163.**

Construction and effect of statutes mandating consideration of, or creating presumptions regarding, domestic violence in awarding custody of children. **51 ALR5th 241.**

Liability of health maintenance organizations (HMOs) for negligence of member physicians. **51 ALR5th 271.**

Malpractice in diagnosis or treatment of meningitis. **51 ALR5th 301.**

Propriety of search of nonoccupant visitor's belongings pursuant to warrant issued for another's premises. **51 ALR5th 375.**

Admissibility of evidence discovered in search of adult defendant's property or residence authorized by defendant's minor child—state cases. **51 ALR5th 425.**

Excessiveness or adequacy of damages awarded for injuries to nerves or nervous system. **51 ALR5th 467.**

Waiver of evidentiary privilege by inadvertent disclosure—state law. **51 ALR5th 603.**

Duty of liability insurer to initiate settlement negotiations. **51 ALR5th 701.**

Power of successor judge taking office during term time to vacate, set aside, or annul judgment entered by his or her predecessor. **51 ALR5th 747.**

52 ALR5th

Excessiveness or adequacy of damages awarded for injuries causing mental or psychological damages. **52 ALR5th 1.**

Liability for injury or damages resulting from operation of vehicle in funeral procession or in procession which is claimed to have such legal status. **52 ALR5th 155.**

Validity, under state constitutions, of private shopping center's prohibition or regulation of political, social, or religious expression or activity. **52 ALR5th 195.**

Enforcement of claim for alimony or support, or for attorneys' fees and costs incurred in connection therewith, against exemptions. **52 ALR5th 221.**

Wrongful discharge based on public policy derived from professional ethics codes. **52 ALR5th 405.**

Requirement that multicoverage umbrella insurance policy offer uninsured- or underinsured-motorist coverage equal to liability limits under umbrella provisions. **52 ALR5th 451.**

Propriety of prophylactic availability programs. **52 ALR5th 477.**

What gives rise to right of rescission under state blue sky laws. **52 ALR5th 491.**

Availability of discovery at probation revocation hearings. **52 ALR5th 559.**

Existence of fiduciary duty between franchisor and franchisee. **52 ALR5th 613.**

Applicability, to operation of motor vehicle on private property, of legislation making drunken driving a criminal offense. **52 ALR5th 655.**

53 ALR5th

Applicability of zoning regulations to governmental projects or activities. **53 ALR5th 1.**

Negligent discharge of employee. **53 ALR5th 219.**

Circumstances under which attorney retains right to compensation notwithstanding voluntary withdrawal from case. **53 ALR5th 287.**

Mental health of contesting parent as factor in award of child custody. **53 ALR5th 375.**

Sufficiency of evidence to establish parent's knowledge or allowance of child's sexual abuse by another under statute permitting termination of parental rights for "allowing" or "knowingly allowing" such abuse to occur. **53 ALR5th 499.**

The government-contractor defense to state products-liability claims. **53 ALR5th 535.**

Sufficiency of notice of claim against local governmental unit as regards identity, name, address, and residence of claimant. **53 ALR5th 617.**

Applicability of waiver or estoppel to preclude claim of nonconformance of documents as ground for dishonor of presentment under letter of credit under UCC § 5-114. **53 ALR5th 667.**

54 ALR5th

Liability of manufacturer or seller for injury or death allegedly caused by use of contraceptive. **54 ALR5th 1.**

Duress, necessity, or conditions of confinement as justification for escape from prison. **54 ALR5th 141.**

Social host's liability for death or injuries incurred by person to whom alcohol was served. **54 ALR5th 313.**

Apportionment of liability between landowners and assailants for injuries to crime victims. **54 ALR5th 379.**

Liability for loss of hat, coat, or other property deposited by customer in place of business. **54 ALR5th 393.**

Defamation: publication of letter to editor in newspaper as actionable. **54 ALR5th 443.**

Validity, construction, and effect of agreement exempting operator of amusement facility from liability for personal injury or death of patron. **54 ALR5th 513.**

Disqualification of judge for bias against counsel for litigant. **54 ALR5th 575.**

Constitutional right to jury trial in cause of action under state unfair or deceptive trade practices law. **54 ALR5th 631.**

State or local government's liability to subcontractors, laborers, or materialmen for failure to require general contractor to post bond. **54 ALR5th 649.**

Validity, construction, and application of statutes or ordinances regulating perpetual-care trust funds of cemeteries and mausoleums. **54 ALR5th 681.**

The propriety of conditioning parole on defendant's not entering specified geographical area. **54 ALR5th 743.**

55 ALR5th

Impracticability of performance of sales contract under UCC § 2-615. **55 ALR5th 1.**

Admissibility of evidence discovered in search of defendant's property or residence authorized by defendant's adult relative other than spouse—state cases. **55 ALR5th 125.**

Admissibility of evidence of voice identification of defendant as affected by allegedly suggestive voice lineup procedures. **55 ALR5th 423.**

Admissibility of threats to defendant made by third parties to support claim of self-defense in criminal prosecution for assault or homicide. **55 ALR5th 449.**

Liability of hotel, motel, resort, or private membership club or association operating swimming pool, for injury or death of guest or member. **55 ALR5th 463.**

Liability of participant in team athletic competition for injury to or death of another participant. **55 ALR5th 529.**

What voluntary acts of child, other than marriage or entry into military service, terminate parent's obligation to support. **55 ALR5th 557.**

Doctrine of forum non conveniens: assumption or denial of jurisdiction of action involving matrimonial dispute. **55 ALR5th 647.**

Insurance agents' and brokers' professional liability insurance. **55 ALR5th 681.**

Validity of territorial restrictions on uninsured/underinsured coverage in automobile insurance policies. **55 ALR5th 747.**

Validity, construction, and effect of state or local cabaret tax. **55 ALR5th 771.**

56 ALR5th

Limitation to quantum meruit recovery, where attorney employed under contingent-fee contract is discharged without cause. **56 ALR5th 1.**

Method of calculating attorneys' fees awarded in common-fund or common-benefit cases—state cases. **56 ALR5th 107.**

Construction, and application of "pay-all-taxes" provision in will, as including liability of nontestamentary property for inheritance and estate taxes. **56 ALR5th 133.**

Propriety of using census data as basis for governmental regulations or activities—state cases. **56 ALR5th 171.**

Validity, construction, and application of concurrent-sentence doctrine—state cases. **56 ALR5th 385.**

What constitutes "vandalism" or "malicious mischief" within meaning of insurance policy specifically extending coverage to losses from such causes. **56 ALR5th 407.**

What constitutes medical or surgical treatment, or the like, within exclusionary clause of accident policy or accidental-death feature of life policy. **56 ALR5th 471.**

Services included in computing period of service for purpose of teachers' seniority, salary, tenure, or retirement benefits. **56 ALR5th 493.**

Validity, construction, and application of the Uniform Customs and Practice for Documentary Credits (UCP). **56 ALR5th 565.**

Liability of third-party health-care payor for injury arising from failure to authorize required treatment. **56 ALR5th 737.**

Participation in arbitration proceedings as waiver of objections to arbitrability under state law. **56 ALR5th 757.**

Disqualification of judge based on property-ownership interest in litigation which consists of more than mere ownership of stock—state cases. **56 ALR5th 783.**

57 ALR5th

Construction and application of learned-intermediary doctrine. **57 ALR5th 1.**

Admissibility of evidence of declarant's then-existing mental, emotional, or physical condition, under Rule 803(3) of Uniform Rules of Evidence and similar formulations. **57 ALR5th 141.**

Admissibility of expert testimony concerning domestic-violence syndromes to assist jury in evaluating victim's testimony or behavior. **57 ALR5th 315.**

Application of child-support guidelines to cases of joint-,

split-, or similar shared-custody arrangements. **57 ALR5th 389.**

Validity, construction, and application of state family-, parental-, or medical-leave acts. **57 ALR5th 477.**

What constitutes use of automobile "to carry persons or property for fee" within exclusion of automobile insurance policy. **57 ALR5th 591.**

Right of attorney to conduct ex parte interviews with former corporate employees. **57 ALR5th 633.**

Sufficiency of notice of claim against local political entity as regards time when accident occurred. **57 ALR5th 689.**

Oil and gas: rights of royalty owners to take-or-pay settlements. **57 ALR5th 753.**

58 ALR5th

Validity of regulation by public-school authorities as to clothes or personal appearance of pupils. **58 ALR5th 1.**

Constitutionality, construction, and application of state and local public-utility-gross-receipts-tax statutes—modern cases. **58 ALR5th 187.**

Investigative authority of administrative agencies in state regulation of securities. **58 ALR5th 293.**

Guaranty as covering renewals, after revocation, of claims within coverage at time of revocation. **58 ALR5th 325.**

Illegality as basis for denying remedy of specific performance for breach of contract. **58 ALR5th 387.**

Engaging in offensive personality as ground for disciplinary action against attorney. **58 ALR5th 429.**

Handling, preparing, presenting, or trying workers'-compensation claims or cases as practice of law. **58 ALR5th 449.**

Negligent misrepresentation as "accident" or "occurrence" warranting insurance coverage. **58 ALR5th 483.**

Validity, construction, and application of exclusion of government vehicles from uninsured-motorist provision. **58 ALR5th 511.**

Venue of wrongful-death action. **58 ALR5th 535.**

Hospital liability as to diagnosis and care of patients in emergency room. **58 ALR5th 613.**

Right of putative father to visitation with child born out of wedlock. **58 ALR5th 669.**

Admissibility of expert or opinion evidence of battered-woman syndrome on issue of self-defense. **58 ALR5th 749.**

59 ALR5th

Inattention of juror from sleepiness or other cause as ground for reversal or new trial. **59 ALR5th 1.**

Voluntary absence of accused when sentence is pronounced. **59 ALR5th 135.**

Automobile insurance: what constitutes "occupying" under owned-vehicle exclusion of uninsured- or underinsured-motorist coverage of automobile insurance policy. **59 ALR5th 191.**

Disciplinary proceedings against horse trainer or jockey. **59 ALR5th 203.**

Products liability: computer hardware and software. **59 ALR5th 461.**

Consideration of obligor's personal-injury recovery or settlement in fixing alimony or child support. **59 ALR5th 489.**

Recovery for emotional distress based on fear of contracting HIV or AIDS. **59 ALR5th 535.**

Observation through binoculars as constituting unreasonable search. **59 ALR5th 615.**

Conveyance or surrender of property as an accord and satisfaction of contract obligation. **59 ALR5th 665.**

Attorney's right to compensation as affected by disbarment or suspension before complete performance. **59 ALR5th 693.**

Indemnitor's liability to indemnitee for attorney's fees and expenses arising out of defense of action alleging indemnitee's negligence. **59 ALR5th 733.**

Admissibility of evidence of public-opinion polls or surveys in obscenity prosecutions on issue whether materials in question are obscene. **59 ALR5th 749.**

60 ALR5th

Search and seizure: reasonable expectation of privacy in driveways. **60 ALR5th 1.**

Propriety of using anonymous juries in state criminal cases. **60 ALR5th 39.**

Reportorial privilege as to nonconfidential news information. **60 ALR5th 75.**

Liability of insurance agent or broker on ground of inadequacy of liability-insurance coverage procured. **60 ALR5th 165.**

Coverage of professional-liability or -indemnity policy for sexual contact with patients by physicians, surgeons, and other healers. **60 ALR5th 239.**

Liability of owner or operator of self-service filling station for injury or death of patron. **60 ALR5th 379.**

Products liability: cement and concrete. **60 ALR5th 413.**

What constitutes "agricultural" or "farm" labor within social-security or unemployment-compensation acts. **60 ALR5th 459.**

Validity and construction of regulations of governing body of condominium or cooperative apartment pertaining to parking. **60 ALR5th 647.**

Awarding attorneys' fees in connection with arbitration. **60 ALR5th 669.**

61 ALR5th

Admissibility of evidence discovered in warrantless search of rental property authorized by lessor of such property—state cases. **61 ALR5th 1.**

Rights of unwed father to obstruct adoption of his child by withholding consent. **61 ALR5th 151.**

Medical-malpractice countersuits. **61 ALR5th 307.**

Violation of employment rule as barring claim for workers' compensation. **61 ALR5th 375.**

Products liability: liability for injury or death allegedly caused by defect in mobile home or trailer. **61 ALR5th 473.**

What constitutes unjustifiable impairment of collateral, discharging parties to a negotiable instrument under UCC § 3-606(1)(b). **61 ALR5th 525.**

Sales: construction and application of UCC § 2-612(2), dealing with rejection of goods under installment contracts. **61 ALR5th 611.**

Damages for killing or injuring dog. **61 ALR5th 635.**

Judicial notice of attorney customs and practices. **61 ALR5th 707.**

Conveyance with reference to tree or similar monument as giving title to center thereof. **61 ALR5th 739.**

62 ALR5th

Searches and seizures: reasonable expectation of privacy in contents of garbage or trash receptacle. **62 ALR5th 1.**

Application of death penalty to nonhomicide cases. **62 ALR5th 121.**

Construction and application of statute-of-frauds provision under UCC § 1-206 governing personal property not otherwise covered. **62 ALR5th 137.**

Policy requiring residence or occupation of dwelling of insured as eliminating coverage when homeowner sells or ceases to occupy premises. **62 ALR5th 189.**

Loss of private easement by nonuse. **62 ALR5th 219.**

Liability of landlord for injury or death occasioned by swimming pool maintained for tenants. **62 ALR5th 475.**

Nonuse of seatbelt as reducing amount of damages recoverable. **62 ALR5th 537.**

Initial award or denial of child custody to homosexual or lesbian parent. **62 ALR5th 591.**

Testimonial privilege for confidential communications between relatives other than husband and wife—state cases. **62 ALR5th 629.**

For assistance, call 1-800-328-4880

Validity, construction, and application of regulations regarding outside employment of governmental employees or officers. **62 ALR5th 671.**

63 ALR5th

Who is a "consumer" entitled to protection of state deceptive trade practice and consumer protection acts. **63 ALR5th 1.**

Compensability of Specially Equipped Van or Vehicle under Workers' Compensation Statutes. **63 ALR5th 163.**

"Concert Of Activity," "Alternate Liability," "Enterprise Liability," Or Similar Theory As Basis For Imposing Liability Upon One Or More Manufacturers Of Defective Uniform Product, In Absence Of Identification Of Manufacturer Of Precise Unit Or Batch Causing Injury. **63 ALR5th 195.**

Propriety of inquiry on voir dire as to juror's attitude toward, or acquaintance with literature dealing with, amount of damage awards. **63 ALR5th 285.**

Admissibility of Ancient Documents as Hearsay Exception Under Rule 803(16) of the Uniform Rules of Evidence. **63 ALR5th 331.**

Use of Peremptory Challenges to Exclude Persons from Criminal Jury Based on Religious Affiliation—Post-Batson State Cases. **63 ALR5th 375.**

Consideration of sales tax in determining value of stolen property or amount of theft. **63 ALR5th 417.**

Waiver or estoppel of insurer on basis of statements or omissions in promotional, illustrative, or explanatory materials given to insured. **63 ALR5th 427.**

Validity and construction of statute or ordinance requiring installation of automatic sprinklers. **63 ALR5th 517.**

Application of zoning regulations to golf courses, swimming pools, tennis courts, or the like. **63 ALR5th 607.**

Setting aside arbitration award on ground of interest or bias of arbitrators—insurance appraisals or arbitrations. **63 ALR5th 675.**

64 ALR5th

Liability of Owner of Private Residential Swimming Pool for Injury or Death Occasioned Thereby. **64 ALR5th 1.**

Products Liability: Admissibility of Evidence of Subsequent Repairs or other Remedial Measures by Third Party other than Defendant. **64 ALR5th 119.**

Waiver of Right to Default Judgment. **64 ALR5th 163.**

Liability of Vendor for Food or Beverage Spilled on Customer. **64 ALR5th 205.**

Death or Injury to Occupant of Airplane from Collision or Near-Collision with another Aircraft. **64 ALR5th 235.**

Liability for Donee's Contraction of Acquired Immune Deficiency Syndrome (AIDS) from Blood Transfusion. **64 ALR5th 333.**

Setting Aside Arbitration Award on Ground of Interest or Bias of Arbitrators—Torts. **64 ALR5th 475.**

Waiver of, or Estoppel to Assert, Failure to Give or Defects in Notice of Claim Against State or Local Political Subdivision—Modern Status. **64 ALR5th 519.**

Belief that Burglary Is in Progress or Has Recently Been Committed as Exigent Circumstance Justifying Warrantless Search of Premises. **64 ALR5th 637.**

Homicide Based on Killing of Unborn Child. **64 ALR5th 671.**

Propriety of Police Action Involving Application of Choke Hold, Constriction of Throat, or the Like to Prevent Accused from Swallowing Evidence—State Cases. **64 ALR5th 741.**

Propriety of Exclusion of Persons From Horseracing Tracks for Reasons Other than Color or Race. **64 ALR5th 769.**

65 ALR5th

Privatization of governmental services by state or local governmental agency. **65 ALR5th 1.**

Products liability: Swimming pools and accessories. **65 ALR5th 105.**

For assistance, call 1-800-328-4880

Propriety of probation condition exposing defendant to public shame or ridicule. **65 ALR5th 187.**

Oil and gas farmout agreements. **65 ALR5th 211.**

Liability of hospital or medical practitioner under doctrine of strict liability in tort, or breach of warranty, for harm caused by drug, medical instrument, or similar device used in treating patient. **65 ALR5th 357.**

Admissibility of evidence discovered in search of defendant's property or residence authorized by defendant's spouse (resident or nonresident)—state cases. **65 ALR5th 407.**

Custodial parent's homosexual or lesbian relationship with third person as justifying modification of child custody order. **65 ALR5th 591.**

Performance of public duty by off-duty police officer acting as private security guard. **65 ALR5th 623.**

When is medical expense "incurred" under policy providing for payment of medical expenses incurred within fixed period of time from date of injury. **65 ALR5th 649.**

66 ALR5th

Tort liability of public schools and institutions of higher learning for accidents occurring in physical education classes. **66 ALR5th 1.**

Prisoner's right to die or refuse medical treatment. **66 ALR5th 111.**

Admissibility of expert testimony regarding questions of domestic law. **66 ALR5th 135.**

Validity, construction, and application of restrictions on use or possession of tobacco products in correctional facilities. **66 ALR5th 237.**

Who is "member" or "resident" of same "family" or "household" within no-fault or uninsured motorist provisions of motor vehicle insurance policy. **66 ALR5th 269.**

Search and seizure: reasonable expectation of privacy in tent or campsite. **66 ALR5th 373.**

What constitutes obstructing or resisting officer, in absence of actual force. **66 ALR5th 397.**

Discovery, in medical malpractice action, of names and medical records of other patients to whom defendant has given treatment similar to that allegedly injuring plaintiff. **66 ALR5th 591.**

Setting aside arbitration award on ground of interest or bias of arbitrator—labor disputes. **66 ALR5th 611.**

67 ALR5th

Significant connection jurisdiction of court to modify foreign child custody decree under § § 3(a)(2) and 14(b) of the Uniform Child Custody Jurisdiction Act (UCCJA) and the Parental Kidnapping Prevention Act (PKPA), 28 U.S.C.A. § § 1738A(c)(2)(b) and 1738A(f)(1). **67 ALR5th 1.**

Police surveillance privilege. **67 ALR5th 149.**

Setting aside arbitration award on ground of interest or bias of arbitrators—commercial, business, or real estate transactions. **67 ALR5th 179.**

Validity of anticipatory search warrants—state cases. **67 ALR5th 361.**

Regulation of exposure of female, but not male, breasts. **67 ALR5th 431.**

When statute of limitations commences to run against promise to pay debt "when able," "when convenient," or the like. **67 ALR5th 479.**

Construction of incontestable clause applicable to disability insurance. **67 ALR5th 513.**

When statute of limitations begins to run upon action against attorney for legal malpractice—deliberate wrongful acts or omissions. **67 ALR5th 587.**

Homicide: duty to retreat where assailant and assailed share the same living quarters. **67 ALR5th 637.**

68 ALR5th

Former employer's or supervisor's tort liability to prospective employer or third person for misrepresentation or nondisclosure in employment reference. **68 ALR5th 1.**

Leaving employment, or unavailability for particular job or duties, because of sickness or disability, as affecting right to unemployment compensation. **68 ALR5th 13.**

Defense of inconsequential or de minimis violation in criminal prosecution. **68 ALR5th 299.**

Admissibility of evidence discovered in search of defendant's property or residence authorized by one, other than relative, who is cotenant or common resident with defendant—state cases. **68 ALR5th 343.**

Tort liability of schools and institutions of higher learning for personal injury suffered during school field trip. **68 ALR5th 519.**

Civilian participation in execution of search warrant as affecting legality of search. **68 ALR5th 549.**

Liability for injury inflicted by horse, dog, or other domestic animal exhibited at show. **68 ALR5th 599.**

Tort liability of public schools and institutions of higher learning for accidents occurring during school athletic events. **68 ALR5th 663.**

69 ALR5th

Grandparents' visitation rights where child's parents are deceased, or where status of parents is unspecified. **69 ALR5th 1.**

Products liability: paints, stains, and similar products. **69 ALR5th 137.**

Property rights arising from relationship of couple cohabiting without marriage. **69 ALR5th 219.**

Physical injury requirement for emotional distress claim based on false positive conclusion on medical test diagnosing disease. **69 ALR5th 411.**

Admissibility of drug courier profile testimony in criminal prosecution. **69 ALR5th 425.**

Exemption of charitable or educational organization from sales or use tax. **69 ALR5th 477.**

Scope and extent of protection from disclosure of medical peer review proceedings relating to claim in medical malpractice action. **69 ALR5th 559.**

Comparative negligence of driver as defense to enhanced injury, crashworthiness, or second collision claim. **69 ALR5th 625.**

Liability for statement or publication charging plaintiff with killing of, cruelty to, or inhumane treatment of animals. **69 ALR5th 645.**

70 ALR5th

Adequacy of defense counsel's representation of criminal client—issues of incompetency. **70 ALR5th 1.**

Validity, construction, and application of statute, regulation, or policy governing home schooling or affecting rights of home-schooled students. **70 ALR5th 169.**

Modern status of rules regarding tort liability of building or construction contractor for injury or damage to third person occurring after completion and acceptance of work; exceptions to "completed and accepted" rule. **70 ALR5th 261.**

Custodial parent's relocation as grounds for change of custody. **70 ALR5th 377.**

Prosecution of mother for prenatal substance abuse based on endangerment of or delivery of controlled substance to child. **70 ALR5th 461.**

Admissibility of expert testimony as to susceptibility of defendant to inducement for purpose of establishing entrapment defense. **70 ALR5th 491.**

Validity and construction of contracts by organizations in business of providing expert witnesses, research assistance, and consultation services to attorneys in specific litigation. **70 ALR5th 513.**

Right and sufficiency of allocution in probation revocation proceeding. **70 ALR5th 533.**

Exclusion of women from grand or trial jury or jury panel in criminal case as violation of constitutional rights of accused or as ground for reversal of conviction—state cases. **70 ALR5th 587.**

Computer fraud. **70 ALR5th 647.**

ANNOTATION TITLES

71 ALR5th

Dismissal of state criminal charge in furtherance of, or in interest of, justice. **71 ALR5th 1.**

Grandparents' visitation rights where child's parents are living. **71 ALR5th 99.**

Wrongful discharge based on employer's fraternization policy. **71 ALR5th 257.**

"Cohabitation" for purposes of domestic violence statutes. **71 ALR5th 285.**

Medical malpractice statutes of limitation minority provisions. **71 ALR5th 307.**

When is instrument "payable on demand or at a definite time" as required to constitute negotiable instrument under §§ 3-104(a)(2), 3-108(a, b) of Uniform Commercial Code. **71 ALR5th 443.**

Liability for tortious interference with prospective contractual relations involving sale of business, stock, or real estate. **71 ALR5th 491.**

Validity, construction, and application of child hearsay statutes. **71 ALR5th 637.**

Sufficient nexus for state to require foreign entity to collect state's compensating, sales, or use tax—post-Complete Auto Transit cases. **71 ALR5th 671.**

72 ALR5th

Validity, construction, and application of loitering statutes and ordinances. **72 ALR5th 1.**

Adequacy of defense counsel's representation of criminal client—pretrial conduct or conduct at unspecified time regarding issues of insanity. **72 ALR5th 109.**

Home state jurisdiction of court to modify foreign child custody decree under §§ 3(a)(1) and 14(a)(2) of Uniform Child Custody Jurisdiction Act (UCCJA) and Parental Kidnapping Prevention Act (PKPA), 28 U.S.C.A. §§ 1738A(c)(2)(A) and 1738A(f)(1). **72 ALR5th 249.**

Products liability: helicopters. **72 ALR5th 299.**

For assistance, call 1-800-328-4880

Requirement that court advise accused of, and make inquiry with respect to, waiver of right to testify. **72 ALR5th 403.**

Tort liability of public schools and institutions of higher learning for injury to student walking to or from school. **72 ALR5th 469.**

Qualification of nonmedical psychologist to testify as to mental condition or competency. **72 ALR5th 529.**

Validity of traffic regulations requiring motorcyclists to wear helmets or other protective headgear. **72 ALR5th 607.**

73 ALR5th

Same-sex sexual harassment under state antidiscrimination laws. **73 ALR5th 1.**

Products liability: consumer expectations test. **73 ALR5th 75.**

Declining jurisdiction to modify prior child custody decree under § 14(a)(1) of Uniform Child Custody Jurisdiction Act (UCCJA) and Parental Kidnapping Prevention Act (PKPA), 28 U.S.C.A. § 1738A(f)(2). **73 ALR5th 185.**

Determination whether zoning or rezoning of particular parcel constitutes illegal spot zoning. **73 ALR5th 223.**

Vulnerability of victim as aggravating factor under state sentencing guidelines. **73 ALR5th 383.**

Admissibility of expert testimony regarding credibility of confession. **73 ALR5th 581.**

Effect of same-sex relationship on right to spousal support. **73 ALR5th 599.**

Admissibility of evidence relating to accused's attempt to commit suicide. **73 ALR5th 615.**

74 ALR5th

"Wrongful adoption" causes of action against adoption agencies where children have or develop mental or physical problems that are misrepresented or not disclosed to adoptive parents. **74 ALR5th 1.**

Liability of owner, operator, or other parties, for personal injuries allegedly resulting from snow or ice on premises of parking lot. **74 ALR5th 49.**

Validity of police roadblocks or checkpoints for purpose of discovery of alcoholic intoxication—post-Sitz cases. **74 ALR5th 319.**

Right to recover money lent for gambling purposes. **74 ALR5th 369.**

Validity of governmental domestic partnership enactment. **74 ALR5th 439.**

Juvenile's guilty or no contest plea in adult court as waiver of defects in transfer or certification proceedings. **74 ALR5th 453.**

Check as evidencing advancement. **74 ALR5th 491.**

Modern status of rules regarding tort liability of building or construction contractor for injury or damage to third person occurring after completion and acceptance of work; "completed and accepted" rule. **74 ALR5th 523.**

Admissibility of lay witness interpretation of surveillance photograph or videotape. **74 ALR5th 643.**

75 ALR5th

Landlord's duty, on tenant's failure to occupy, or abandonment of, premises, to mitigate damages by accepting or procuring another tenant. **75 ALR5th 1.**

Validity, construction, and application of blood shield statutes. **75 ALR5th 229.**

Disqualification or exemption of juror for conviction of, or prosecution for, criminal offense. **75 ALR5th 295.**

Eligibility for unemployment compensation of employee who retires voluntarily. **75 ALR5th 339.**

Modern status of rules regarding tort liability of building or construction contractor for injury or damage to third person occurring after completion and acceptance of work; "foreseeability" or "modern" rule. **75 ALR5th 413.**

What constitutes undertaking or instruction to do any act in addition to payment of money as limitation on definition of negotiable instrument under UCC § 3-104. **75 ALR5th 559.**

Skier's liability for injuries to or death of another person. **75 ALR5th 583.**

Validity and effect under state law of arbitration agreement provision for alternative method of appointment of arbitrator where one party fails or refuses to follow appointment procedure specified in agreement. **75 ALR5th 595.**

Implied cause of action for damages for violation of provisions of state constitutions. **75 ALR5th 619.**

76 ALR5th

Authentication of blood sample taken from human body for purposes of determining blood alcohol content. **76 ALR5th 1.**

Basis for imputing income for purpose of determining child support where obligor spouse is voluntarily unemployed or underemployed. **76 ALR5th 191.**

Validity, construction, and operation of state DNA database statutes. **76 ALR5th 239.**

What constitutes "fixed amount of money" for purposes of [rev] § 3-104 of Uniform Commercial Code providing that negotiable instrument must contain unconditional promise to pay fixed amount of money. **76 ALR5th 289.**

Change in character of neighborhood as affecting validity or enforceability of restrictive covenant. **76 ALR5th 337.**

Effect of delay in taking defendant into custody after conviction and sentence. **76 ALR5th 485.**

Effect of retroactive consent on legality of otherwise unlawful search and seizure. **76 ALR5th 563.**

Mental incapacity as justifying refusal to submit to tests for driving while intoxicated. **76 ALR5th 597.**

Validity, construction, and application of statutory restrictions on partial birth abortions. **76 ALR5th 637.**

77 ALR5th

Validity, construction, and application of statutes requiring parental notification of or consent to minor's abortion. **77 ALR5th 1.**

For assistance, call 1-800-328-4880

Authentication of blood sample taken from human body for purposes other than determining blood alcohol content. **77 ALR5th 201.**

Uninsured motorist indorsement: construction and application of requirement that there be "physical contact" with unidentified or hit-and-run vehicle; "miss-and-run" cases. **77 ALR5th 319.**

When is instrument issued or transferred for "value" under UCC § 3-303. **77 ALR5th 429.**

When is instrument "payable to bearer or to order" as required to constitute negotiable instrument under Article 3 of the Uniform Commercial Code [rev] § § 3-104(a)(1) and 3-109. **77 ALR5th 523.**

Damage action for HIV testing without consent of person tested. **77 ALR5th 541.**

Determination of status as legal or natural parents in contested surrogacy births. **77 ALR5th 567.**

Visual impairment as handicap or disability under state employment discrimination law. **77 ALR5th 595.**

78 ALR5th

Authentication of organic nonblood specimen taken from human body for purposes of analysis. **78 ALR5th 1.**

Validity and construction of school choice programs—post-Lemon v. Kurtzman. **78 ALR5th 133.**

Adequacy of defense counsel's representation of criminal client—conduct occurring at time of trial regarding issues of diminished capacity, intoxication, and unconsciousness. **78 ALR5th 197.**

Permissibility and sufficiency of warrantless use of thermal imager or Forward Looking Infra-Red Radar (F.L.I.R.). **78 ALR5th 309.**

Uninsured motorist indorsement: general issues regarding requirement that there be "physical contact" with unidentified or hit-and-run vehicle. **78 ALR5th 341.**

Abandonment jurisdiction of court under § § 3(a)(3)(i) and 14(a) of Uniform Child Custody Jurisdiction Act and

Parental Kidnapping Prevention Act, 28 U.S.C.A. § § 1738A(c)(2)(C)(i) and 1738A(f), notwithstanding existence of prior valid custody decree rendered by second state. **78 ALR5th 465.**

Validity, construction, and application of state statutes authorizing community notification of release of convicted sex offender. **78 ALR5th 489.**

Validity, construction, and application of statute or regulation governing charter schools. **78 ALR5th 533.**

Joyriding or similar charge as lesser-included offense of larceny or similar charge. **78 ALR5th 567.**

79 ALR5th

Imposition of state or local penalties for threatening to use explosive devices at schools or other buildings. **79 ALR5th 1.**

Victim impact evidence in capital sentencing hearings—post-Payne v. Tennessee. **79 ALR5th 33.**

Workers' compensation: availability, rate, or method of calculation of interest on attorney's fees or penalties. **79 ALR5th 201.**

Authentication of bullets and other inorganic substances removed from human body for purposes of analysis. **79 ALR5th 237.**

Uninsured motorist indorsement: construction and application of requirement that there be "physical contact" with unidentified or hit-and-run vehicle; "hit-and-run" cases. **79 ALR5th 289.**

Civil liability of pharmacists or druggists for failure to warn of potential drug interactions in use of prescription drug. **79 ALR5th 409.**

Adequacy of defense counsel's representation of criminal client—pretrial conduct or conduct at unspecified time regarding issues of diminished capacity, intoxication, and unconsciousness. **79 ALR5th 419.**

Validity, construction, and application of "fiduciary shield" doctrine—modern cases. **79 ALR5th 587.**

Construction and application of limited liability company acts. **79 ALR5th 689.**

80 ALR5th

Child custody and visitation rights arising from same-sex relationship. **80 ALR5th 1.**

Adequacy of defense counsel's representation of criminal client—issues of mental matters concerning persons, other than counsel's client, who are involved in criminal case. **80 ALR5th 55.**

Emergency jurisdiction of court under § § 3(a)(3)(ii) and 14(a) of Uniform Child Custody Jurisdiction Act and Parental Kidnapping Prevention Act, 28 U.S.C.A. § § 1738A(c)(2)(C)(ii) and 1738A(f), to protect interests of child notwithstanding existence of prior, valid custody decree rendered by another state. **80 ALR5th 117.**

Validity, construction, and application of state or local enactments regulating parades. **80 ALR5th 255.**

Employee's injuries sustained in use of employer's restroom as covered by workers' compensation. **80 ALR5th 417.**

Examination and challenge of state case jurors on basis of attitudes toward homosexuality. **80 ALR5th 469.**

Copyright, patent, or other intellectual property as marital property for purposes of alimony, support, or divorce settlement. **80 ALR5th 487.**

Spouse's cause of action for negligent personal injury, or proceeds therefrom, as separate or community property. **80 ALR5th 533.**

Attorneys at law: disciplinary proceedings for drafting instrument such as will or trust under which attorney-drafter or member of attorney's family or law firm is beneficiary, grantee, legatee, or devisee. **80 ALR5th 597.**

81 ALR5th

Marriage between persons of same sex. **81 ALR5th 1.**

Internet Web site activities of nonresident person or corporation as conferring personal jurisdiction under long-arm statutes and due process clause. **81 ALR5th 41.**

Liability of doctor, psychiatrist, or psychologist for failure to take steps to prevent patient's suicide. **81 ALR5th 167.**

Products liability: ladders. **81 ALR5th 245.**

Children's day care use as violation of restrictive covenant. **81 ALR5th 345.**

Availability and scope of punitive damages under state employment discrimination law. **81 ALR5th 367.**

What constitutes warranty explicitly extending to "future performance" for purposes of UCC § 2-725(2). **81 ALR5th 483.**

Evidence of trailing by dogs in criminal cases. **81 ALR5th 563.**

82 ALR5th

Validity, construction, and application of state enactment, order, or regulation expressly prohibiting sexual orientation discrimination. **82 ALR5th 1.**

Admissibility of results of presumptive tests indicating presence of blood on object. **82 ALR5th 67.**

Validity of police roadblocks or checkpoints for purpose of discovery of illegal narcotics violations. **82 ALR5th 103.**

Right to workers' compensation for emotional distress or like injury suffered by claimant as result of sudden emotional stimuli involving personnel action. **82 ALR5th 149.**

Comment Note: What constitutes crime involving 'dishonesty or false statement' under Rule 609(a)(2) of the Uniform Rules of Evidence or similar state rule?—general considerations. **82 ALR5th 359.**

Appealability of interlocutory or pendente lite order for temporary child custody. **82 ALR5th 389.**

Comment Note: Natural parent's indigence as precluding finding that failure to support child waived requirement of consent to adoption—general principles. **82 ALR5th 443.**

Award of attorney's fees under state motor vehicle warranty legislation (lemon laws). **82 ALR5th 501.**

For assistance, call 1-800-328-4880

Admissibility of expert testimony regarding reliability of accused's confession where accused allegedly suffered from mental disorder or defect at time of confession. **82 ALR5th 591.**

83 ALR5th

Individual Liability of Supervisors, Managers, Officers or Co-employees for Discriminatory Actions Under State Civil Rights Act. **83 ALR5th 1.**

Right to Workers' Compensation for Emotional Distress or Like Injury Suffered by Claimant as Result of Sudden Stimuli Involving Nonpersonnel Action—Right to Compensation Under Particular Statutory Provisions and Requisites of, and Factors Affecting, Compensability. **83 ALR5th 103.**

What Constitutes Crime Involving "Dishonesty or False Statement" Under Rule 609(a)(2) of Uniform Rules of Evidence or Similar State Rule—Crimes Involving Violence or Potential for Violence. **83 ALR5th 277.**

Natural Parent's Indigence Resulting from Unemployment or Underemployment as Precluding Finding that Failure to Support Child Waived Requirement of Consent to Adoption. **83 ALR5th 375.**

What Constitutes Private Club or Association Not Otherwise Open to Public that Is Exempt from State Civil Rights Statute. **83 ALR5th 467.**

What Constitutes "Unauthorized Practice of Law" by Out-of-State Counsel. **83 ALR5th 497.**

Right of Indigent Defendant in State Criminal Prosecution to Ex Parte In Camera Hearing on Request for State-Funded Expert Witness. **83 ALR5th 541.**

Comparative Negligence, Contributory Negligence and Assumption of Risk in Action Against Owner of Store, Office, or Similar Place of Business by Invitee Falling on Tracked-In Water or Snow. **83 ALR5th 589.**

What Is "Mobile Home," "House Trailer," "Trailer House," or "Trailer" Within Meaning of Restrictive Covenant. **83 ALR5th 651.**

For assistance, call 1-800-328-4880

ANNOTATION TITLES

84 ALR5th

Validity of Search or Seizure of Computer, Computer Disk, or Computer Peripheral Equipment. **84 ALR5th 1.**

Admissibility of Expert and Opinion Evidence as to Cause or Origin of Fire—Modern Civil Cases. **84 ALR5th 69.**

Liability of Internet Service Provider for Internet or E-mail Defamation. **84 ALR5th 169.**

Natural Parent's Indigence as Precluding Finding that Failure to Support Child Waived Requirement of Consent to Adoption—Factors Other Than Employment Status. **84 ALR5th 191.**

Right to Workers' Compensation for Emotional Distress or Like Injury Suffered by Claimant as Result of Sudden Stimuli Involving Nonpersonnel Action—Compensability Under Particular Circumstances. **84 ALR5th 249.**

Power of Successor or Substituted Judge, in Civil Case, to Render Decision or Enter Judgment on Testimony Heard by Predecessor. **84 ALR5th 399.**

What Constitutes Crime Involving "Dishonesty Or False Statement" Under Rule 609(a)(2) Of The Uniform Rules Of Evidence Or Similar State Rule—Nonviolent Crimes. **84 ALR5th 487.**

Contributory Negligence or Comparative Negligence Based on Failure of Patient to Follow Instructions as Defense in Action Against Physician or Surgeon for Medical Malpractice. **84 ALR5th 619.**

Who, Other Than Parent, May Recover for Loss of Consortium on Death of Minor Child. **84 ALR5th 687.**

85 ALR5th

What Constitutes Compliance with Knock-and-Announce Rule in Search of Private Premises—State Cases. **85 ALR5th 1.**

Admissibility of Expert and Opinion Evidence as to Cause or Origin of Fire in Criminal Prosecution for Arson or Related Offense—Modern Cases. **85 ALR5th 187.**

Federal and State Constitutions as Protecting Prison Visitor Against Unreasonable Searches and Seizures. **85 ALR5th 261.**

Tort Liability of Public Schools and Institutions of Higher Learning for Accident Involving Motor Vehicle Operated by Student. **85 ALR5th 301.**

Judicial Estoppel of Subsequent Action Based on Statements, Positions, or Omissions as to Claim or Interest in Bankruptcy Proceeding. **85 ALR5th 353.**

Prior Representation or Activity as Prosecuting Attorney as Disqualifying Judge from Sitting or Acting in Criminal Case. **85 ALR5th 471.**

Disqualification of Judge for Having Decided Different Case Against Litigant—State Cases. **85 ALR5th 547.**

Admissibility of Expert Testimony on Child Sexual Abuse Accommodation Syndrome (CSAAS) in Criminal Case. **85 ALR5th 595.**

Admissibility in Evidence of Aerial Photographs. **85 ALR5th 671.**

86 ALR5th

Liability, Under State Law Claims, of Public and Private Schools and Institutions of Higher Learning for Teacher's, Other Employee's, or Student's Sexual Relationship with, or Sexual Harassment or Abuse of, Student. **86 ALR5th 1.**

Admissibility, in Rape Case, of Evidence that Accused Raped or Attempted to Rape Person Other Than Prosecutrix—Prior Offenses. **86 ALR5th 59.**

Products Liability: Prudent Manufacturer Test. **86 ALR5th 215.**

When Limitations Period Begins to Run as to Claim for Disability Benefits for Contracting of Disease under Workers' Compensation or Occupational Diseases Act. **86 ALR5th 295.**

Excessiveness or Adequacy of Damages for Wrongful Termination of At-Will Employee Under State Law. **86 ALR5th 397.**

Admissibility of In-Court Identification as Affected by Pretrial Encounter that was not Result of Action by Police, Prosecutors, and the Like. **86 ALR5th 463.**

Joint Bank Account as Subject to Attachment, Garnishment, or Execution by Creditor of One Joint Depositor. **86 ALR5th 527.**

Right of Illegitimate Child to Maintain Action to Determine Paternity. **86 ALR5th 637.**

Civil Liability of Hospital for Negligent Handling, Transportation, and Disposition of Corpse. **86 ALR5th 693.**

87 ALR5th

Construction and Application of Statutory Provision Requiring Motorists to Yield Right-of-Way to Emergency Vehicle. **87 ALR5th 1.**

Admissibility, in Rape Case, of Evidence that Accused Raped or Attempted to Rape Person Other than Prosecutrix—Subsequent Acts. **87 ALR5th 181.**

Right of Husband, Wife, or Other Party to Custody of Frozen Embryo, Pre-embryo, or Pre-zygote in Event of Divorce, Death, or Other Circumstances. **87 ALR5th 253.**

Construction and Application of State Patient Bill of Rights Statutes. **87 ALR5th 277.**

Liability of Father for Retroactive Child Support on Judicial Determination of Paternity. **87 ALR5th 361.**

Attorney Malpractice—Tolling or Other Exceptions to Running of Statute of Limitations. **87 ALR5th 473.**

Defenses to State Obstruction of Justice Charge Relating to Interfering with Criminal Investigation or Judicial Proceeding. **87 ALR5th 597.**

Validity, and Propriety under Circumstances, of Court-Ordered HIV Testing. **87 ALR5th 631.**

Admissibility of Expert Testimony as to Proper Techniques for Interviewing Children or Evaluating Techniques Employed in Particular Case. **87 ALR5th 693.**

Injury to Reputation or Mental Well-Being as Within Penal Extortion Statutes Requiring Threat of "Injury to the Person". **87 ALR5th 715.**

88 ALR5th

Firearm or Ammunition Manufacturer or Seller's Liability for Injuries Caused to Another by Use of Gun in Committing Crime. **88 ALR5th 1.**

Voir Dire Exclusions of Men from State Trial Jury or Jury Panel—Post-J.E.B. v. Alabama ex rel T.B, 511 U.S. 127, Cases. **88 ALR5th 67.**

What Constitutes "Constructive Possession" of Unregistered or Otherwise Prohibited Weapon Under State Law. **88 ALR5th 121.**

Validity, Construction and Effect of State Motor Vehicle Warranty Legislation (Lemon Laws). **88 ALR5th 301.**

Admissibility, in Rape Case, of Evidence that Accused Raped, or Attempted to Rape, Person Other Than Prosecutrix—Offenses Unspecified as to Time. **88 ALR5th 429.**

Revocation of Order Commuting State Criminal Sentence. **88 ALR5th 463.**

Construction of Qualified Pollution Exclusion Clause in Liability Insurance Policy. **88 ALR5th 493.**

Construction and Application of Uniform Foreign Money-Judgments Recognition Act. **88 ALR5th 545.**

Tower or Antenna as Constituting Nuisance. **88 ALR5th 641.**

89 ALR5th

Application of Qualified Pollution Exclusion Clause in Liability Insurance Policy. **89 ALR5th 1.**

Construction and Application of Indian Child Welfare Act of 1978 (ICWA) (25 U.S.C.A. § § 1901 *et seq*) Upon Child Custody Determinations. **89 ALR5th 195.**

Recovery Under State Law for Negligent Infliction of Emotional Distress due to Witnessing Injury to Another Where Bystander Plaintiff Must Suffer Physical Impact or Be in Zone of Danger. **89 ALR5th 255.**

Sufficiency and Timeliness of Buyer's Notice Under UCC § 2-607(3)(a) of Seller's Breach of Warranty. **89 ALR5th 319.**

Items or Materials Exempt From Use Tax as Becoming Component Part or Ingredient of Manufactured or Processed Article. **89 ALR5th 493.**

Validity, Construction, and Application of Statute Permitting Forfeiture of Motor Vehicle for Operation of Vehicle While Intoxicated. **89 ALR5th 539.**

Duress, Incapacity, Illegality, or Similar Defense Rendering Obligation a Nullity as Affecting Enforceability of Negotiable Instrument Against Holder in Due Course Under UCC [rev] § 3-305(a)(1)(ii). **89 ALR5th 577.**

Criminal Prosecutions under State RICO Statutes for Engaging in Organized Criminal Activity. **89 ALR5th 629.**

90 ALR5th

Construction and Application of Uniform Interstate Family Support Act. **90 ALR5th 1.**

Bystander Recovery Under State Law for Emotional Distress from Witnessing Another's Injury in Products Liability Context. **90 ALR5th 179.**

Denial of Accused's Request for Initial Contact with Attorney in Cases Involving Offenses other than Drunk Driving—Cases Focusing on Presence of Inculpatory Evidence other than Statements by Accused and Cases Focusing on Absence of Particular Inculpatory Evidence. **90 ALR5th 225.**

Liability of Municipality or Other Governmental Unit for Failure to Provide Police Protection From Crime. **90 ALR5th 273.**

Post-Daubert Standards for Admissibility of Scientific and Other Expert Evidence in State Courts. **90 ALR5th 453.**

Inclusion of Intangible Asset Values in Tangible Property Tax Assessments. **90 ALR5th 547.**

Keeping of Domestic Animal As Constituting Public or Private Nuisance. **90 ALR5th 619.**

Who are "Public Employers" or "Public Employees" Within the Meaning of State Whistleblower Protection Acts. **90 ALR5th 687.**

For assistance, call 1-800-328-4880

91 ALR5th

Liability Based on Entrusting Automobile to One Who is Intoxicated or Known to be Excessive User of Intoxicants. **91 ALR5th 1.**

Payee's and Drawer's Right of Recovery, in Conversion Under Pre-1990 UCC § 3-419, or Post-1990 UCC § 3-420 [Rev], for Money Paid on Unauthorized Indorsement. **91 ALR5th 89.**

What Constitutes "Salary," "Wages," "Pay," or the Like, Within Pension Law Basing Benefits Thereon. **91 ALR5th 225.**

Validity, Construction, and Application of State Constitutional or Statutory Victims' Bill of Rights. **91 ALR5th 343.**

Laws Governing Judicial Recusal or Disqualification in State Proceeding as Violating Federal or State Constitution. **91 ALR5th 437.**

Vacating or Opening Judgment by Confession on Ground of Fraud, Illegality, or Mistake. **91 ALR5th 485.**

Recovery from Electrical Utility for Personal Injury or Property Damage Resulting from Stray Voltage. **91 ALR5th 517.**

Recovery of Damages for Emotional Distress Due to Treatment of Pets and Animals. **91 ALR5th 545.**

Constitutionality of Secret Video Surveillance. **91 ALR5th 585.**

92 ALR5th

State Regulation of Telephone "Slamming". **92 ALR5th 1.**

Expectation of Privacy in Internet Communications. **92 ALR5th 15.**

Persons or Entities Entitled to Restitution as "Victim" Under State Criminal Restitution Statute. **92 ALR5th 35.**

Liability of Successor Corporation for Injury or Damage Caused by Product Issued by Predecessor, Based on Successor's Independent Duty to Warn Third Party of Danger or Defect. **92 ALR5th 227.**

Lawyers' Professional Liability Insurance. **92 ALR5th 273.**

Right of Indigent Parent to Appointed Counsel in Proceeding for Involuntary Termination of Parental Rights. **92 ALR5th 379.**

Tort Liability Arising from Skydiving, Parachuting, or Parasailing Accident. **92 ALR5th 473.**

Sewage Treatment Plant as Constituting Nuisance. **92 ALR5th 517.**

Nudity as Constituting Nuisance. **92 ALR5th 593.**

93 ALR5th

Free Exercise of Religion as Applied to Individual's Objection to Obtaining or Disclosing Social Security Number. **93 ALR5th 1.**

When is Work Environment Intimidating, Hostile or Offensive, so as to Constitute Sexual Harassment Under State Law. **93 ALR5th 47.**

Products Liability: Statements in Advertisements as Affecting Liability of Manufacturers or Sellers for Injury Caused by Product Other than Tobacco. **93 ALR5th 103.**

Liability Under Common Law for Wrongful or Retaliatory Discharge of At-Will Employee for In-House Complaints or Efforts Relating to Health or Safety. **93 ALR5th 269.**

Subject Matter and Waiver of Privilege Covering Communications to Clergy Member or Spiritual Adviser. **93 ALR5th 327.**

Holding Jurors in Contempt Under State Law. **93 ALR5th 493.**

Failure of State Prosecutor to Disclose Exculpatory Photographic Evidence as Violating Due Process. **93 ALR5th 527.**

Hog Breeding, Confining, or Processing Facility as Constituting Nuisance. **93 ALR5th 621.**

Attempt to Commit Assault as Criminal Offense. **93 ALR5th 683.**

ANNOTATION TITLES

94 ALR5th

When Is Supervisor's or Coemployee's Hostile Environment Sexual Harassment Imputable to Employer Under State Law. **94 ALR5th 1.**

Libel and Slander: Statements Regarding Labor Relations or Disputes. **94 ALR5th 149.**

Establishment and Construction of Requirements Contracts Under § 2-306(1) Of Uniform Commercial Code. **94 ALR5th 247.**

Failure of State Prosecutor to Disclose Fingerprint Evidence as Violating Due Process. **94 ALR5th 393.**

Application of Noerr-Pennington Doctrine by State Courts. **94 ALR5th 455.**

Constitutionality of State Statutes Banning Distribution of Sexual Devices. **94 ALR5th 497.**

"English Only" Requirement for Conduct of Public Affairs. **94 ALR5th 537.**

Educator's Liability Insurance. **94 ALR5th 567.**

Power of Court or Other Public Agency to Order Vaccination over Parental Religious Objection. **94 ALR5th 613.**

95 ALR5th

Validity, Construction, and Operation of State Blacklisting Statutes. **95 ALR5th 1.**

Electrical Utility's Liability to Nonemployee for Personal Injury or Property Damage, Other Than Strict Liability, Resulting from Exposure of Person or Motor Vehicle to Sagging or Downed Power Line. **95 ALR5th 29.**

Adequacy of Defense Counsel's Representation of Criminal Client—Conduct at Trial Regarding Issues of Insanity. **95 ALR5th 125.**

What Constitutes "Public Place" Within Meaning of State Statute or Local Ordinance Prohibiting Indecency or Commission of Sexual Act in Public Place. **95 ALR5th 229.**

Work-Related Inefficiency, Incompetence, or Negligence as "Misconduct" Barring Unemployment Compensation. **95 ALR5th 329.**

Construction and Operation of Twenty-Seventh Amendment to United States Constitution Relating to Congressional Compensation. **95 ALR5th 459.**

Admissibility and Weight of Voice Spectrographic Analysis Evidence. **95 ALR5th 471.**

Religion as Factor in Visitation Cases. **95 ALR5th 533.**

Failure of State Prosecutor to Disclose Exculpatory Ballistic Evidence as Violating Due Process. **95 ALR5th 611.**

96 ALR5th

World Wide Web Domain as Violating State Trademark Protection Statute or State Unfair Trade Practices Act. **96 ALR5th 1.**

Discipline of Attorney for Failure to Comply with Continuing Legal Education Requirements. **96 ALR5th 23.**

Homosexuality as Ground for Divorce. **96 ALR5th 83.**

Recovery Under State Law for Negligent Infliction of Emotional Distress Under Rule of Dillon v. Legg, 68 Cal. 2d 728, 69 Cal. Rptr. 72, 441 P.2d 912 (1968), or Refinements Thereof. **96 ALR5th 107.**

Products Liability: Firearms, Ammunition, and Chemical Weapons. **96 ALR5th 239.**

Denial of, or Interference with, Accused's Right to Have Attorney Initially Contact Accused. **96 ALR5th 327.**

Federal and State Constitutional Provisions as Prohibiting Discrimination in Employment on Basis of Gay, Lesbian, or Bisexual Sexual Orientation or Conduct. **96 ALR5th 391.**

Validity and Operation of Pre-employment Drug Testing—State Cases. **96 ALR5th 485.**

Sufficiency of Showing that Voluntariness of Confession or Admission was Affected by Alcohol or Other Drugs—Drugs or Narcotics Administered as Part of Medical Treatment and Drugs or Intoxicants Administered by the Police. **96 ALR5th 523.**

97 ALR5th

Right to Workers' Compensation for Emotional Distress or

Like Injury Suffered by Claimant as Result of Nonsudden Stimuli—Right to Compensation Under Particular Statutory Provisions. **97 ALR5th 1.**

Validity, Construction, and Application of Road or Transportation Impact Fee Statutes or Ordinances. **97 ALR5th 123.**

Conviction or Acquittal in Federal Court as Bar to Prosecution in State Court for State Offense Based on Same Facts—Modern View. **97 ALR5th 201.**

Pardoned or Expunged Conviction as "Prior Offense" Under State Statute or Regulation Enhancing Punishment for Subsequent Conviction. **97 ALR5th 293.**

What Constitutes "Pollutant," "Contaminant," "Irritant" or "Waste" Within Meaning of Qualified Pollution Exclusion in Liability Insurance Policy. **97 ALR5th 359.**

Civil Liability in Conjunction with Autopsy. **97 ALR5th 419.**

Constitutional Validity of Continuing Legal Education Requirements for Attorneys. **97 ALR5th 457.**

Construction and Application of "Invasion of the Right of Private Occupancy" Clause in Comprehensive General Liability Policy. **97 ALR5th 473.**

Construction and Validity of State Provisions Governing Designation of Substitute, Pro Tempore, or Special Judge. **97 ALR5th 537.**

98 ALR5th

Advertising Injury Insurance. **98 ALR5th 1.**

Validity of State Statutes and Administrative Regulations Regulating Internet Communications Under Commerce Clause and First Amendment of Federal Constitution. **98 ALR5th 167.**

What Constitutes "Pollutant," "Contaminant," "Irritant," or "Waste" Within Meaning of Absolute or Total Pollution Exclusion in Liability Insurance Policy. **98 ALR5th 193.**

Destruction of Property as Violation of Fourth Amendment. **98 ALR5th 305.**

Moral or Natural Obligation as Consideration for Contract. **98 ALR5th 353.**

Sufficiency of Access to Legal Research Facilities Afforded Defendant Confined in State Prison or Local Jail. **98 ALR5th 445.**

Tort Claim for Negligent Credentialing of Physician. **98 ALR5th 533.**

Relationship Between Victim and Plaintiff-Witness as Affecting Right to Recover Under State Law for Negligent Infliction of Emotional Distress Due to Witnessing Injury to Another Where Bystander Plaintiff Is Not Member of Victim's Immediate Family. **98 ALR5th 609.**

Defects in Title Encompassed by Warranty of Special Warranty Deed. **98 ALR5th 665.**

99 ALR5th

Discrimination Against Pregnant Employee as Violation of State Fair Employment Laws. **99 ALR5th 1.**

Judicial Estoppel in Civil Action Arising from Representation or Conduct in Prior Administrative Proceeding. **99 ALR5th 65.**

Liability of Building Owner, Lessee, or Manager for Injury or Death Resulting from Use of Automatic Passenger Elevator. **99 ALR5th 141.**

Immediacy of Observation of Injury as Affecting Right to Recover Damages for Shock or Mental Anguish from Witnessing Injury to Another. **99 ALR5th 301.**

Sufficiency of "At the Well" Language in Oil and Gas Leases to Allocate Costs. **99 ALR5th 415.**

Action for Intentional Infliction of Emotional Distress Against Paramours. **99 ALR5th 445.**

Restrictions on Parent's Child Visitation Rights Based on Parent's Sexual Conduct. **99 ALR5th 475.**

Validity of Requirement That, as Condition of Probation, Defendant Submit to Warrantless Searches. **99 ALR5th 557.**

Divorce Decree or Settlement Agreement as Affecting Divorced Spouse's Right to Recover as Named Beneficiary on Former Spouse's Individual Retirement Account. **99 ALR5th 637.**

100 ALR5th

Construction and Operation of Uniform Child Custody Jurisdiction and Enforcement Act. **100 ALR5th 1.**

Validity, Construction, and Application of State Carjacking Statutes. **100 ALR5th 67.**

Exclusion of Public From State Criminal Trial to Preserve Safety or Confidentiality of Undercover Police Officer Witness. **100 ALR5th 171.**

Loss or Impairment of Vision as Within Meaning of Total Disability Clause. **100 ALR5th 293.**

Immunity of Police or Other Law Enforcement Officer From Liability in Defamation Action. **100 ALR5th 341.**

Right to Contribution or Indemnity on Behalf of Owner, Operator, Maintainer, Repairer, or Installer of Automatic Passenger Elevator in Action by Elevator User. **100 ALR5th 409.**

Enforcement of Arbitration Agreement Contained in Construction Contract by or Against Nonsignatory. **100 ALR5th 481.**

When Time Period Commences as to Claim Under Workers' Compensation or Occupational Diseases Act for Death of Worker Due to Contraction of Disease. **100 ALR5th 567.**

Clause in Life, Accident, or Health Policy Excluding or Limiting Liability in Case of Insured's Use of Intoxicants or Narcotics. **100 ALR5th 617.**

101 ALR5th

Liability of Church or Religious Organization for Negligent Hiring, Retention, or Supervision of Priest, Minister, or Other Clergy Based on Sexual Misconduct. **101 ALR5th 1.**

Negligent Spoliation of Evidence, Interfering with Prospective Civil Action, as Actionable. **101 ALR5th 61.**

Failure of State Prosecutor to Disclose Exculpatory Medical

Reports and Tests as Violating Due Process. **101 ALR5th 187.**

Remedies for Sewage Treatment Plant Alleged or Deemed to Be Nuisance. **101 ALR5th 287.**

Validity and Efficacy of Minor's Waiver of Right to Counsel—Cases Decided Since Application of Gault, 387 U.S. 1, 87 S. Ct. 1428, 18 L. Ed. 2d 527 (1967). **101 ALR5th 351.**

Validity, Construction, and Application of New Home Warranty Acts. **101 ALR5th 447.**

Recovery for Emotional Distress Resulting from Actions of Law Enforcement Officers. **101 ALR5th 515.**

Resale of Goods Under UCC § p§ t2-706. **101 ALR5th 563.**

Who Are "Clergy" or Like Within Privilege Attaching to Communications to Clergy Members or Spiritual Advisers. **101 ALR5th 619.**

102 ALR5th

What Constitutes Substantial Limitation on Major Life Activity of Working for Purposes of State Civil Rights Acts. **102 ALR5th 1.**

Effect of Spoliation of Evidence in Products Liability Action. **102 ALR5th 99.**

Right to Jury Trial in Child Neglect, Child Abuse, or Termination of Parental Rights Proceedings. **102 ALR5th 227.**

Construction and Operation of Attorney's General or Classic Retainer Fee or Salary Contract Under State Law. **102 ALR5th 253.**

Failure of State Prosecutor to Disclose Pretrial Statement Made by Crime Victim as Violating Due Process. **102 ALR5th 327.**

Propriety of Equalizing Income of Spouses Through Alimony Awards. **102 ALR5th 395.**

Defense of Mistake of Fact as to Victim's Consent in Rape Prosecution. **102 ALR5th 447.**

Criminal Jurisdiction of Municipal or Other Local Court. **102 ALR5th 525.**

Imposition of Default Judgment Against Codefendant—Modern Treatment. **102 ALR5th 647.**

103 ALR5th

What Issues Are Arbitrable Under Arbitration Provisions of Uninsured and Underinsured Motorist Insurance. **103 ALR5th 1.**

Vibrations Not Accompanied by Blasting or Explosion as Constituting Nuisance. **103 ALR5th 157.**

Restricting Access to Judicial Records of Concluded Adoption Proceedings. **103 ALR5th 255.**

What Constitutes "Use" or "Operation" Within Statute Making Owner of Motor Vehicle Liable for Negligence in its Use or Operation. **103 ALR5th 339.**

Validity of State Statutory Cap on Punitive Damages. **103 ALR5th 379.**

Challenges to Punch Card Ballots and Punch Card Voting Systems. **103 ALR5th 417.**

Validity, Construction, and Application of Zoning Ordinances Regulating Display of Noncommercial Flags or Banners. **103 ALR5th 445.**

Error, in Either Search Warrant or Application for Warrant, as to Address of Place to be Searched as Rendering Warrant Invalid. **103 ALR5th 463.**

Pursuit of Nonjudicial Remedy for Employment Discrimination as Amounting to Election Against Judicial Remedy. **103 ALR5th 557.**

104 ALR5th

Common-Law Retaliatory Discharge of Employee for Refusing to Perform or Participate in Unlawful or Wrongful Acts. **104 ALR5th 1.**

Search Warrant as Authorizing Search of Structures on Property Other Than Main House or Other Building, or Location Other than Designated Portion of Building. **104 ALR5th 165.**

Burden of Proof and Presumptions in Tracing Currency, Bank Account, or Cash Equivalent to Illegal Drug Trafficking so as to Permit Forfeiture, or Declaration as Contraband, Under State Law. **104 ALR5th 229.**

Insurer's Waiver of Defense of Statute of Limitations. **104 ALR5th 331.**

Nature and Determination of Prejudice Caused by Remarks or Acts of State Trial Judge Criticizing, Rebuking, or Punishing Defense Counsel in Criminal Case as Requiring New Trial or Reversal—Individualized Determinations. **104 ALR5th 357.**

Drawer's Right of Recovery Against Depositary Bank That Accepts Check With Missing Indorsement or in Violation of Restrictive Indorsement. **104 ALR5th 459.**

Admissibility and Effect of Evidence of Electromagnetic Fields Generated by Power Lines, or Public Perception Thereof, in Action to Value Land or to Recover for Personal Injury or Property Damage. **104 ALR5th 503.**

Defamation of Manufacturer, Regarding Product, Other than Through Statement Charging Breach or Nonperformance of Contract. **104 ALR5th 523.**

Right to Credit on Child Support Arrearages for Time Parties Resided Together After Separation or Divorce. **104 ALR5th 605.**

105 ALR5th

Admissibility, in Civil Proceeding, of Evidence Obtained Through Unlawful Search and Seizure. **105 ALR5th 1.**

Construction and Application of Absolute or Total Pollution Exclusion in Liability Insurance Policy—Discharge at or from Waste Disposal, Treatment, or Salvage Facility, Manufacturing Site, Oil, Gas, or Ore-Related Business or Equipment, or Similar Site. **105 ALR5th 95.**

Sexual Conduct or Orientation as Ground for Denial of Admission to Bar. **105 ALR5th 217.**

Validity, Construction, and Application of State Right-to-Work Provisions. **105 ALR5th 243.**

Validity, Construction, and Operation of Municipal Ordinances Proscribing or Restricting Smoking in

Restaurants. **105 ALR5th 333.**

Common-Law Retaliatory Discharge of Employee for Disclosing Unlawful Acts or Other Misconduct of Employer or Fellow Employees. **105 ALR5th 351.**

Precedential Effect of Unpublished Opinions. **105 ALR5th 499.**

Effect of Escape by, or Fugitive Status of, State Criminal Defendant on Availability of Appeal or Other Post-Verdict or Post-Conviction Relief—State Cases. **105 ALR5th 529.**

106 ALR5th

Construction and Application of Absolute or Total Pollution Exclusion Clause in Liability Insurance Policy-Discharge at or from Sites Other than Waste Disposal, Treatment or Salvage Facility, Manufacturing Site, Oil, Gas or Ore Related-Business or Similar Sites. **106 ALR5th 1.**

Right to Workers' Compensation for Emotional Distress or Like Injury Suffered by Claimant as Result of Nonsudden Stimuli—Requisites of, and Factors Affecting, Compensability. **106 ALR5th 111.**

Use of Employer's E-Mail or Internet System as Misconduct Precluding Unemployment Compensation. **106 ALR5th 297.**

Enforceability of "Clickwrap" or "Shrinkwrap" Agreements Common in Computer Software, Hardware, and Internet Transactions. **106 ALR5th 309.**

First Amendment Protection Afforded to Commercial and Home Video Games. **106 ALR5th 337.**

Downward Departure Under State Sentencing Guidelines Based on Extraordinary Family Circumstances. **106 ALR5th 377.**

Odor Detectable by Unaided Person as Furnishing Probable Cause for Search Warrant. **106 ALR5th 397.**

Defamation of Building Contractor or Subcontractor Other than Through Statement Charging Breach or Nonperformance of Contract. **106 ALR5th 475.**

Private Attorney General Doctrine—State Cases. **106 ALR5th 523.**

ANNOTATION TITLES

Successful Negotiation of Commercial Transaction as Element of State Offense of Credit Card Fraud or False Pretense in Use of Credit Card. **106 ALR5th 701.**

107 ALR5th

First Amendment Challenges to Display of Religious Symbols on Public Property. **107 ALR5th 1.**

Falsehoods, Misrepresentations, Impersonations, and Other Irresponsible Conduct as Bearing on Requisite Good Moral Character for Admission to Bar—Conduct Related to Admission to Bar. **107 ALR5th 167.**

Validity of Rules and Regulations Concerning Viewing of Execution of Death Penalty. **107 ALR5th 291.**

What Constitutes Trade Fixture—Modern Cases. **107 ALR5th 311.**

Right to Workers' Compensation for Physical Injury or Illness Suffered by Claimant as Result of Sudden Mental Stimuli—Compensability Under Particular Circumstances. **107 ALR5th 441.**

Applicability of Common-Law Trespass Actions to Electronic Communications. **107 ALR5th 549.**

Criminal Liability, Under State Law, Concerning Illegal Removal or Alteration of Vehicle Identification Number, Including Sale or Possession of Altered Motor Vehicles or Parts. **107 ALR5th 567.**

Necessity of, and What Constitutes, Employer's Reasonable Accommodation of Employee's Religious Preference Under State Law. **107 ALR5th 623.**

Validity, Construction, and Application of State "Buy American" Acts. **107 ALR5th 673.**

Validity, Construction, and Application of Municipal Drug Exclusion Zone. **107 ALR5th 697.**

108 ALR5th

Right to Workers' Compensation for Emotional Distress or Like Injury Suffered by Claimant as Result of Nonsudden Stimuli—Compensability Under Particular

Circumstances. **108 ALR5th 1.**

Validity of State and Local Statutes Allegedly Infringing on Federal Government's Exclusive Power over Foreign Affairs—Nonalien Cases. **108 ALR5th 189.**

Right of Public Defenders to Join Collective Bargaining Unit. **108 ALR5th 241.**

Construction of Garmon Preemption Doctrine by State Courts. **108 ALR5th 253.**

Failure To Pay Creditors as Affecting Applicant's Moral Character for Purposes of Admission to the Bar. **108 ALR5th 289.**

Liability of Cigarette Manufacturers for Punitive Damages. **108 ALR5th 343.**

Right to Credit Against Child Support Arrearages for Time Child Spent in Custody of Noncustodial Parent, Other than for Visitation or Under Court Order, Without Custodial Parent's Approval. **108 ALR5th 359.**

Contributory Negligence, Comparative Negligence, or Assumption of Risk, Other than Failing to Reveal Medical History or Follow Instructions, as Defense in Action Against Physician or Surgeon for Medical Malpractice. **108 ALR5th 385.**

Defamation of Member of Clergy. **108 ALR5th 495.**

Evidence of Intent to Defraud in State Forgery Prosecution. **108 ALR5th 593.**

109 ALR5th

Divorce and Separation: Determination of Whether Proceeds from Personal Injury Settlement or Recovery Constitute Marital Property. **109 ALR5th 1.**

When Are Facts Offered in Support of Search Warrant for Evidence of Sale or Possession of Cocaine so Untimely As to Be Stale—State Cases. **109 ALR5th 99.**

Right to Workers' Compensation for Physical Injury or Illness Suffered by Claimant as Result of Sudden Mental Stimuli—Right to Compensation Under Particular Statutory Provisions and Requisites of, and Factors Affecting,

Compensability. **109 ALR5th 161.**

What Constitutes Unauthorized Practice of Law by Paralegal. **109 ALR5th 275.**

Liability of Successor Corporation for Injury or Damage Caused by Product Issued by Predecessor, Based on Merger or Consolidation of Transferor and Transferee. **109 ALR5th 301.**

Exemplary or Punitive Damages for Pharmacist's Wrongful Conduct in Preparing or Dispensing Medical Prescription—Cases Not Under Consumer Product Safety Act (15 U.S.C.A. § p§ t2072). **109 ALR5th 397.**

Time Within Which Tenant's Right to Remove Trade Fixtures Must Be Exercised. **109 ALR5th 421.**

Defamation of Church Member by Church or Church Official. **109 ALR5th 541.**

Denial of Accused's Request for Initial Contact with Attorney—Drunk Driving Cases. **109 ALR5th 611.**

110 ALR5th

Application of Apprendi v. New Jersey, 530 U.S. 466, 120 S. Ct. 2348, 147 L. Ed. 2d 435 (2000) and Ring v. Arizona, 536 U.S. 584, 122 S. Ct. 2428, 153 L. Ed. 2d 556 (2002) to State Death Penalty Proceedings. **110 ALR5th 1.**

Application of Garmon Preemption Doctrine by State Courts—Construction and Transportation Industries. **110 ALR5th 111.**

Admissibility and Weight of Fingerprint Evidence Obtained or Visualized by Chemical, Laser, and Digitally Enhanced Imaging Processes. **110 ALR5th 213.**

Retirement of Husband as Change of Circumstances Warranting Modification of Divorce Decree—Prospective Retirement. **110 ALR5th 237.**

Satisfaction of Statute of Frauds by E-Mail. **110 ALR5th 277.**

Validity of Public School Funding Systems. **110 ALR5th 293.**

Validity and Application of Computerized Jury Selection Practice or Procedure. **110 ALR5th 329.**

Intentional Infliction of Distress in Marital Context. **110 ALR5th 371.**

Conflict of Laws in Determination of Coverage Under Automobile Liability Insurance Policy. **110 ALR5th 465.**

Parents' Mental Illness or Mental Deficiency as Ground for Termination of Parental Rights—Constitutional Issues. **110 ALR5th 579.**

111 ALR5th

Admissibility in State Court Proceedings of Police Reports as Business Records. **111 ALR5th 1.**

Effect of Appointment of Legal Representative for Person Under Mental Disability on Running of State Statute of Limitations Against Such Person. **111 ALR5th 159.**

When Is Corporation Close, or Closely-Held, Corporation Under Common or Statutory Law. **111 ALR5th 207.**

When Are Facts Offered in Support of Search Warrant for Evidence of Sexual Offense So Untimely As To Be Stale—State Cases. **111 ALR5th 239.**

What Constitutes, and Remedies for, Misuse of Easement. **111 ALR5th 313.**

Validity, Construction, and Application of State Birth-Related Neurological Injury Compensation Programs. **111 ALR5th 459.**

Propriety of Carrying Out Death Sentences Against Mentally Ill Individuals. **111 ALR5th 491.**

Admissibility of Computer-Generated Animation. **111 ALR5th 529.**

Liability of Municipal Corporation or Electric Utility for Injury Resulting from Inoperative, Malfunctioning, or Otherwise Defective Streetlight. **111 ALR5th 579.**

112 ALR5th

Validity, Construction, and Operation of Constitutional and Statutory "Term Limits" Provisions. **112 ALR5th 1.**

Construction of State Offer of Judgment Rule—Issues of Time. **112 ALR5th 47.**

Liability of Successor Corporation for Injury or Damage Caused by Product Issued by Predecessor, Based on Successor's Express or Implied Agreement to Assume Liability or Where Transfer Was Fraudulent, in Bad Faith, or Without Adequate Consideration. **112 ALR5th 113.**

Right to Credit Against Child Support Arrearages for Time Child Lived in Custody of Noncustodial Parent, Other Than for Visitation, Where Custodial Parent's Approval Was Not in Issue or Was Disputed by Parties. **112 ALR5th 185.**

Vacating on Public Policy Grounds Arbitration Awards Reinstating Discharged Employees—State Cases. **112 ALR5th 263.**

Award of Workers' Compensation Benefits to Professional Athletes. **112 ALR5th 365.**

Application of "Fugitive Disentitlement Doctrine" to Civil Matters—State Cases. **112 ALR5th 399.**

When Are Facts Relating to Marijuana, Provided by One Other than Police or Other Law Enforcement Officer, so Untimely as To Be Stale When Offered in Support of Search Warrant for Evidence of Sale or Possession of a Controlled Substance—State Cases. **112 ALR5th 429.**

Right to Workers' Compensation for Physical Injury or Illness Suffered by Claimant as Result of Nonsudden Mental Stimuli—Compensability of Particular Physical Injuries or Illnesses. **112 ALR5th 509.**

Admissibility in State Court Proceedings of Police Reports Under Official Record Exception to Hearsay Rule. **112 ALR5th 621.**

113 ALR5th

Validity, Construction, and Operation of Statute or Regulation Forbidding, Regulating, or Limiting Peaceful Residential Picketing. **113 ALR5th 1.**

Validity, Construction, and Application of State Statutes Limiting or Barring Public Health Care to Indigent Aliens. **113 ALR5th 95.**

Compensability Under Occupational Disease Statutes of Emotional Distress or Like Injury Suffered by Claimant

As Result of Nonsudden Stimuli. **113 ALR5th 115.**

Validity, Construction, and Application of Uniform Veterans' Guardianship Act. **113 ALR5th 283.**

Parts and Supplies Used in Repair As Subject to Sales and Use Taxes. **113 ALR5th 313.**

Parents' Mental Illness or Mental Deficiency As Ground for Termination of Parental Rights—General Considerations. **113 ALR5th 349.**

Validity, Construction, and Application of State Civil and Criminal Elder Abuse Laws. **113 ALR5th 431.**

Individual Retirement Accounts As Exempt from Money Judgments in State Courts. **113 ALR5th 487.**

When Are Facts Relating to Drug Other than Cocaine or Marijuana So Untimely As To Be Stale When Offered in Support of Search Warrant for Evidence of Sale or Possession of Controlled Substance—State Cases. **113 ALR5th 517.**

Downward Departure Under State Sentencing Guidelines Permitting Downward Departure for Defendants with Significantly Reduced Mental Capacity, Including Alcohol or Drug Dependency. **113 ALR5th 597.**

114 ALR5th

Sufficiency of Particular Charges As Affecting Enforceability of Recall Petition. **114 ALR5th 1.**

Reverse Confusion Doctrine Under State Trademark Law. **114 ALR5th 129.**

Validity of Warrantless Search of Motor Vehicle Based on Odor of Marijuana—State Cases. **114 ALR5th 173.**

When Are Facts Relating to Marijuana, Provided by Police or Other Law Enforcement Officer, So Untimely As to Be Stale When Offered in Support of Search Warrant for Evidence of Sale or Possession of Controlled Substance—State Cases. **114 ALR5th 235.**

Exhaustion of Administrative Remedies As Prerequisite to Judicial Action to Compel Disclosure Under State Freedom of Information Acts. **114 ALR5th 283.**

Application of Constitutional "Compactness Requirement" to Redistricting. **114 ALR5th 311.**

State Court Jurisdiction over Congressional Redistricting Disputes. **114 ALR5th 387.**

Toxic Mold in Residences and Other Buildings: Liability and Other Issues. **114 ALR5th 397.**

Effect, As Between Landlord and Tenant, of Lease Clause Restricting Keeping of Pets. **114 ALR5th 443.**

When Is Property Owned by State or Local Governmental Body Put to Public Use So As to Be Eligible for Property Tax Exemption. **114 ALR5th 561.**

115 ALR5th

Liability of Maintainer, Repairer, or Installer of Automatic Passenger Elevator for Injury Resulting from Use of Elevator. **115 ALR5th 1.**

Special Education Requirements of Gifted Students. **115 ALR5th 183.**

Validity and Construction of Restrictive Covenant Requiring Lot Owner To Obtain Approval of Plans for Construction or Renovation. **115 ALR5th 251.**

Evidence Considered in Tracing Currency, Bank Account, or Cash Equivalent to Illegal Drug Trafficking so as to Permit Forfeiture, or Declaration as Contraband, Under State Law—Proximity of Asset to Drugs, Paraphernalia, or Records. **115 ALR5th 403.**

Validity of Warrantless Search Based in Whole or in Part on Odor of Narcotics other than Marijuana, or Chemical Related to Manufacture of such Narcotics. **115 ALR5th 477.**

Constitutional and Statutory Validity of Judicial Videoconferencing. **115 ALR5th 509.**

Procedural Issues Concerning Public School Funding Cases. **115 ALR5th 563.**

What Constitutes Bad Faith on Part of Insurer Rendering It Liable for Statutory Penalty Imposed for Bad Faith in Failure To Pay, or Delay in Paying, Insured's Claim—

For assistance, call 1-800-328-4880

Particular Conduct of Insurer. **115 ALR5th 589.**

Right to Private Action Under State Consumer Protection Act—Equitable Relief Available. **115 ALR5th 709.**

116 ALR5th

Sufficiency of Technical and Procedural Aspects of Recall Petitions. **116 ALR5th 1.**

Interplay Between Twenty-First Amendment and Commerce Clause Concerning State Regulation of Intoxicating Liquors. **116 ALR5th 149.**

Validity, Construction, and Operation of State Religious Freedom Restoration Acts. **116 ALR5th 233.**

What Constitutes Bad Faith on Part of Insurer Rendering it Liable for Statutory Penalty Imposed for Bad Faith in Failure To Pay, or Delay in Paying, Insured's Claim—Particular Grounds for Denial of Claim: Matters Relating to Policy. **116 ALR5th 247.**

Validity of State Prosecution Subsequent to Tribal Court Prosecution. **116 ALR5th 313.**

Evidence Considered in Tracing Currency, Bank Account, or Cash Equivalent to Illegal Drug Trafficking So As To Permit Forfeiture, or Declaration as Contraband, Under State Law—Odor of Drugs. **116 ALR5th 325.**

Construction and Application of Silent Witness Theory. **116 ALR5th 373.**

Construction of State Offer of Judgment Rule—Issues Concerning Revocation and Succession. **116 ALR5th 433.**

Validity of Routine Roadblocks by State or Local Police for Purpose of Discovery of Driver's License, Registration, and Safety Violations. **116 ALR5th 479.**

Parents' Mental Illness or Mental Deficiency as Ground for Termination of Parental Rights—Effect on Parenting Ability and Parental Rights. **116 ALR5th 559.**

117 ALR5th

Prejudical Effect of Juror's Inability to Comprehend English. **117 ALR5th 1.**

ANNOTATION TITLES

Surveyor's Liability for Mistake in, or Misrepresentation as to Accuracy of, Survey of Real Property. **117 ALR5th 23.**

Right to Private Action Under State Consumer Protection Act—Preconditions to Action. **117 ALR5th 155.**

Products Liability: Liability of Manufacturer, Supplier, or Seller of Passenger or Freight Elevator, Hoist, or Elevator Component for Injury or Damage Resulting from Alleged Defect in Elevator or Component. **117 ALR5th 267.**

Parents' Mental Illness or Mental Deficiency as Ground for Termination of Parental Rights—Best Interests Analysis. **117 ALR5th 349.**

Use of Trained Dog to Detect Narcotics or Drugs as Unreasonable Search in Violation of State Constitutions. **117 ALR5th 407.**

Contractual Waiver of Exclusivity of Workers' Compensation Remedy. **117 ALR5th 441.**

Validity, Construction, and Operation of School "Zero Tolerance" Policies Towards Drugs, Alcohol, or Violence. **117 ALR5th 459.**

Vertical Gaze Nystagmus Test: Use in Impaired Driving Prosecution. **117 ALR5th 491.**

Adequacy of Defense Counsel's Representation of Criminal Client Regarding Search and Seizure Issues—Motions and Objections During Trial and Matters Other than Pretrial Motions. **117 ALR5th 513.**

118 ALR5th

Construction and Application of State Freedom of Information Act Provisions Concerning Award of Attorney's Fees and Other Litigation Costs. **118 ALR5th 1.**

Construction of State Offer of Judgment Rule—Sufficiency of Offer and Contract Formation Issues. **118 ALR5th 91.**

First Amendment Protection Afforded to Comic Books, Comic Strips, and Cartoons. **118 ALR5th 213.**

Parents' Criminal Liability for Failure to Provide Medical Attention to Their Children. **118 ALR5th 253.**

Validity, Construction, and Application of State Statutes and Local Ordinances Governing Personal Watercraft Use. **118 ALR5th 347.**

Right to Credit Against Child Support Arrearages for Time Children Spent in Custody of Noncustodial Parent Pursuant to Visitation or Court Order. **118 ALR5th 385.**

Validity Of State Statutes And Regulations Limiting or Restricting Public Funding for Abortions Sought By Indigent Women. **118 ALR5th 463.**

Liability of Parent or Person in Loco Parentis for Personal Tort Against Minor Child—Willful or Malicious Act. **118 ALR5th 513.**

Parents' Mental Illness or Mental Deficiency as Ground for Termination of Parental Rights—Issues Concerning Guardian Ad Litem and Counsel. **118 ALR5th 561.**

State Income Tax Treatment of S Corporations and Their Shareholders. **118 ALR5th 597.**

119 ALR5th

Rights of Prisoners in Private Prisons. **119 ALR5th 1.**

Allowance and Determination of Attorney's Fees Under State Offer of Judgment Rule. **119 ALR5th 121.**

Unauthorized Practice of Law—Real Estate Closings. **119 ALR5th 191.**

"Responsible Corporate Officer" Doctrine or "Responsible Relationship" of Corporate Officer to Corporate Violation of Law. **119 ALR5th 205.**

Competency of One Spouse to Testify Against Other in Prosecution for Offense Against Child of Both or Either or Neither. **119 ALR5th 275.**

Validity of State "Informed Consent" Statutes by Which Providers of Abortions Are Required to Provide Patient Seeking Abortion with Certain Information. **119 ALR5th 315.**

Parents' Mental Illness or Mental Deficiency As Ground for Termination of Parental Rights—Applicability of Americans With Disabilities Act. **119 ALR5th 351.**

For assistance, call 1-800-328-4880

Admissibility and Sufficiency of Extrapolation Evidence in DUI Prosecutions. **119 ALR5th 379.**

Right to Credit on Child-Support Arrearages for Money Given Directly to Child. **119 ALR5th 445.**

When Is Tract Subject to "General Plan of Development" so As to Subject All Parcels in Tract to Restrictive Covenants Included in General Plan. **119 ALR5th 519.**

120 ALR5th

Validity, Construction, and Application of State Statutes Governing "Minor Political Parties". **120 ALR5th 1.**

Constitutionality of Voter Participation Provisions for Primary Elections. **120 ALR5th 125.**

Right of Corporation, Absent Specific Statutory Subpoena Power, to Disclosure of Identity of Anonymous or Pseudonymous Internet User. **120 ALR5th 195.**

Right to Credit Against Child Support Arrearages for Time Child Lived with Noncustodial Parent, Other Than for Visitation or by Court Order, with Approval of Custodial Parent. **120 ALR5th 229.**

Criminal Prosecution of Video or Photographic Voyeurism. **120 ALR5th 337.**

Application of Garmon Preemption Doctrine by State Courts—Industries Other Than Construction and Transportation. **120 ALR5th 351.**

Criticism or Disparagement of Dentist's Character, Competence, or Conduct as Defamation. **120 ALR5th 483.**

Postaccident Conduct by Employer, Employer's Insurer, or Employer's Employees in Relation to Workers' Compensation Claim as Waiving, or Estopping Employer from Asserting, Exclusivity Otherwise Afforded by Workers' Compensation Statute. **120 ALR5th 513.**

State Offer of Judgment Rule—Construction, Operation, and Effect of Acceptance and Resulting Judgment. **120 ALR5th 559.**

121 ALR5th

Constitutionality of Candidate Participation Provisions for

Primary Elections. **121 ALR5th 1.**

Effect of Spoliation of Evidence in Tort Actions Other than Product Liability Actions. **121 ALR5th 157.**

Liability for Conversion and Misappropriation of Genetic Material. **121 ALR5th 315.**

Disallowance of Award Under State Offer of Judgment Rule Due to Lack of Good Faith. **121 ALR5th 325.**

Insurance Agents or Brokers as Professionals or Nonprofessionals for Purposes of Malpractice Statutes of Limitations. **121 ALR5th 365.**

Judicial Estoppel: Representation or Conduct, Other than Mere Participation, in Arbitration Proceeding as Barring Contrary Position in Subsequent Litigation. **121 ALR5th 403.**

Validity of Statutes and Ordinances Restricting Hours of "Adult Entertainment" or Sex-Oriented Businesses. **121 ALR5th 427.**

Unemployment Compensation: Harassment or Other Mistreatment by Coworker as "Good Cause" Justifying Abandonment of Employment. **121 ALR5th 467.**

Application of Workers' Compensation Laws to Illegal Aliens. **121 ALR5th 523.**

Judicial Estoppel in Criminal Prosecution. **121 ALR5th 551.**

122 ALR5th

What Constitutes "Improvement to Real Property" for Purposes of Statute of Repose or Statute of Limitations. **122 ALR5th 1.**

Application of Constitutional Rule of Atkins v. Virginia, 536 U.S. 304, 122 S. Ct. 2242, 153 L. Ed. 2d 335 (2002), that Execution of Mentally Retarded Persons Constitutes "Cruel and Unusual Punishment" in Violation of Eighth Amendment. **122 ALR5th 145.**

Modern Status of Law as to Equitable Adoption or Adoption by Estoppel. **122 ALR5th 205.**

State or Local Governmental Body's Action or Inaction, in Provision of Public Utility Services, Benefiting Private

Company as Constituting Gift of Money, or Pledge of Credit, to Private Party in Violation of State Constitutional Provision. **122 ALR5th 337.**

Parents' Mental Illness or Mental Deficiency as Ground for Termination of Parental Rights-Evidentiary Issues. **122 ALR5th 385.**

Validity of Warrantless Search of Other than Motor Vehicle or Occupant of Vehicle Based on Odor of Marijuana-State Cases. **122 ALR5th 439.**

Products Liability: Household Equipment Relating to Storage, Preparation, Cooking, and Disposal of Food. **122 ALR5th 515.**

Validity of State or Local Enactment Regulating Sound Amplification in Public Area. **122 ALR5th 593.**

Right to Workers' Compensation for Physical Injury or Illness Suffered by Claimant as Result of Nonsudden Mental Stimuli-Right to Compensation Under Particular Statutory Provisions. **122 ALR5th 653.**

123 ALR5th

Liability of Owner of Store, Office, or Similar Place of Business to Invitee Falling on Tracked—In Water or Snow. **123 ALR5th 1.**

Validity of Warrantless Search of Motor Vehicle Driver Based on Odor of Marijuana-State Cases. **123 ALR5th 179.**

Validity of Search Conducted Pursuant to Parole Warrant. **123 ALR5th 221.**

What Constitutes Bad Faith on Part of Insurer Rendering it Liable for Statutory Penalty Imposed for Bad Faith in Failure to Pay, or Delay in Paying, Insured's Claim-Particular Grounds for Denial of Claim: Risks, Causes, and Extent of Loss, Injury, Disability, or Death. **123 ALR5th 259.**

Validity, Construction, and Application of Adequate Public Facilities Statutes or Ordinances. **123 ALR5th 349.**

Construction and Application of Church Autonomy Doctrine. **123 ALR5th 385.**

Federal and State Constitutional Provisions and State Statutes as Prohibiting Employment Discrimination Based on Heterosexual Conduct or Relationship. **123 ALR5th 411.**

Right to Credit on Child Support for Contributions to Housing Costs, Utility Bills, and Other Alleged Household Necessities Made for Child's Benefit While Child is Not Living with Obligor Parent. **123 ALR5th 565.**

124 ALR5th

Denial of Accused's Request for Initial Contact with Attorney in Cases Involving Offenses Other than Drunk Driving-Cases Focusing on Presence of Inculpatory Statements. **124 ALR5th 1.**

Religion as Factor in Child Custody Cases. **124 ALR5th 203.**

"Total Cost Method (or Approach)" and "Modified Total Cost Method (or Approach)" to Proving Damages in State Contract Cases. **124 ALR5th 375.**

Right to Credit on Child Support Arrearages for Gifts to Child. **124 ALR5th 441.**

When Does Forfeiture of Real Property Violate Excessive Fines Clause of Eighth Amendment or State Constitutions-State Cases. **124 ALR5th 509.**

Division of Lottery Proceeds in Divorce Proceedings. **124 ALR5th 537.**

When Is Party Judicially or Equitably Estopped from Asserting Claim for, or Defense to, Award of Attorney's or Other Court Ordered Fees. **124 ALR5th 575.**

Propriety of "Hindsight" Charge in Medical Malpractice Actions. **124 ALR5th 623.**

Dog as Deadly or Dangerous Weapon for Purposes of Statutes Aggravating Offenses Such as Assault and Robbery. **124 ALR5th 657.**

Admissibility of Ion Scan Evidence. **124 ALR5th 691.**

125 ALR5th

Conduct or Inaction by Insurer Constituting Waiver of, or

Creating Estoppel to Assert, Right of Subrogation. **125 ALR5th 1.**

Liability of Parent or Person In Loco Parentis for Personal Tort Against Minor Child-Sexual Abuse. **125 ALR5th 133.**

Validity, Construction, and Application of State Constitutional and Statutory Provisions Regarding Corporate Farming. **125 ALR5th 147.**

Application of State Offer of Judgment Rule-Apportionment Issues in Multiple Party Setting. **125 ALR5th 193.**

Validity of Airport Security Measures. **125 ALR5th 281.**

When Is Hearsay Statement Made to 911 Operator Admissible as "Present Sense Impression" Under Uniform Rules of Evidence 803(1) or Similar State Rule. **125 ALR5th 357.**

Liability of Dentist for Extraction of Teeth-Lack of Informed Consent. **125 ALR5th 403.**

Liability of Employer, Supervisor, or Manager for Intentionally or Recklessly Causing Employee Emotional Distress-Failure to Provide Pension or Disability Benefits. **125 ALR5th 457.**

DNA Evidence as Newly Discovered Evidence Which Will Warrant Grant of New Trial or Other Postconviction Relief in Criminal Case. **125 ALR5th 497.**

Validity, Construction, and Application of State Statutes Relating to Offense of Identity Theft. **125 ALR5th 537.**

1 ALR6th

Validity and Applicability of Statutory Time Limit Concerning Taxpayer's Claim for State Tax Refund. **1 ALR6th 1.**

Construction and Application of "Residential Purposes Only" or Similar Covenant Restriction to Incidental Use of Dwelling for Business, Professional, or Other Purposes. **1 ALR6th 135.**

Voluntary Payment Doctrine as Bar To Recovery of Payment of Generally Unlawful Tax. **1 ALR6th 229.**

Liability of Owner or Operator of Store or Similar Place of Business for Injury Resulting from Defective or Dangerous Shelves, Displays, Racks, Counters, or the Like. **1 ALR6th 297.**

Validity of Warrantless Search of Motor Vehicle Passenger Based on Odor of Marijuana. **1 ALR6th 371.**

Effect of Appointment of Legal Representative for Minor on Running of State Statute of Limitations Against Minor. **1 ALR6th 407.**

Right to Credit on Child Support for Health Insurance, Medical, Dental, and Orthodontic Expenses Paid for Child's Benefit While Child Is Not Living with Obligor Parent. **1 ALR6th 493.**

Propriety of Lesser-Included-Offense Charge in State Prosecution of Narcotics Defendant—Marijuana Cases. **1 ALR6th 549.**

Admissibility and Sufficiency of Bite Mark Evidence as Basis for Identification of Accused. **1 ALR6th 657.**

2 ALR6th

State Income Tax Treatment of Partnerships and Partners. **2 ALR6th 1.**

Application of Leon Good Faith Exception to Exclusionary Rule Where Police Fail to Comply with Knock and Announce Requirement During Execution of Search Warrant. **2 ALR6th 169.**

Acceptance and Application of Reverse Veil-Piercing—Third-Party Claimant. **2 ALR6th 195.**

Application and Construction of State Offer of Judgment Rule—Determining Whether Offeror Is Entitled to Award. **2 ALR6th 279.**

Construction and Application of "Intracorporate Conspiracy Doctrine" as Applied to Corporation and Its Employees—State Cases. **2 ALR6th 387.**

Admissibility and Use of Evidence of Nonuse of Bicycle Helmets. **2 ALR6th 429.**

Right to Credit on Child Support for Contributions to Educational Expenses of Child While Child is Not Living with Obligor Parent. **2 ALR6th 439.**

Propriety of Insurers' Use of Staff Attorneys to Represent Insureds. **2 ALR6th 537.**

Propriety of Lesser-Included-Offense Charge in State Prosecution of Narcotics Defendant—Cocaine Cases. **2 ALR6th 551.**

Criticism and Disparagement of Veterinarian's or Animal Trainer's Competence, or Conduct, as Defamation. **2 ALR6th 657.**

3 ALR6th

State and Federal Regulation of Prescribing Medication Over the Internet. **3 ALR6th 1.**

Electronic Spoliation of Evidence. **3 ALR6th 13.**

Criminal Record as Affecting Applicant's Moral Character for Purposes of Admission to the Bar. **3 ALR6th 49.**

Individual and Corporate Liability for Libel and Slander in Electronic Communications, Including E-mail, Internet and Websites. **3 ALR6th 153.**

Propriety, Under Uniform Rule of Evidence 607, of Impeachment of Party's Own Witness. **3 ALR6th 269.**

Products Liability: Home and Office Furnishings Propriety, Under Uniform Rule of Evidence 607, of Impeachment of Party's Own Witness. **3 ALR6th 355.**

Spouse's Professional Degree or License as Marital Property for Purposes of Alimony, Support, or Property Settlement. **3 ALR6th 447.**

Propriety of Lesser-Included-Offense Charge of Voluntary Manslaughter to Jury in State Murder Prosecution—Twenty-First Century Cases. **3 ALR6th 543.**

Insurance Coverage for Claims of Violations of the Telephone Consumer Protection Act (47 U.S.C.A § 227). **3 ALR6th 625.**

Right to Credit on Child Support for Contributions to Travel Expenses of Child While Child Is Not Living with Obligor Parent. **3 ALR6th 641.**

4 ALR6th

Validity of Condition of Probation, Supervised Release, or

ANNOTATION TITLES

Parole Restricting Computer Use or Internet Access. **4 ALR6th 1.**

Right to Workers' Compensation for Injury Suffered at Worker's Home Where Home is Claimed as "Work Situs". **4 ALR6th 57.**

Evidence Considered in Tracing Currency, Bank Account, or Cash Equivalent to Illegal Drug Trafficking so as to Permit Forfeiture, or Declaration as Contraband, Under State Law—Explanation or Lack Thereof. **4 ALR6th 113.**

Bias or Interest of Administrative Officer Sitting in Zoning Proceeding as Necessitating Disqualification of Officer or Affecting Validity of Zoning Decision. **4 ALR6th 263.**

Products Liability: Mechanical or Chain Saw or Components Thereof. **4 ALR6th 401.**

Estoppel of Insurer to Assert Statute-of-Limitations Defense—Homeowners' Insurers. **4 ALR6th 509.**

Right to Credit on Child Support for Continued Payments to Custodial Parent for Child Who has Reached Majority or Otherwise Become Emancipated. **4 ALR6th 531.**

Robbery: Identification of Victim as Person Named in Indictment or Information. **4 ALR6th 577.**

Application in State Narcotics Cases of Collective Knowledge Doctrine or Fellow Officers' Rule Under Fourth Amendment—Cocaine Cases

Robbery: Identification of Victim as Person Named in Indictment or Information. **4 ALR6th 599.**

5 ALR6th

Validity, Construction, and Application of State Statutory Voting Offenses. **5 ALR6th 1.**

Validity of Medical Malpractice Statutes of Repose. **5 ALR6th 133.**

Construction and Application of Interstate Compact on the Placement of Children. **5 ALR6th 193.**

Child Support Obligations of Former Same-Sex Partners. **5 ALR6th 303.**

What Constitutes Commercial or Financial Information, Exclusive of Trade Secrets, Exempt From Disclosure Under State Freedom of Information Acts—General Rules of Construction. **5 ALR6th 327.**

Fourth Amendment Protections, and Equivalent State Constitutional Protections, as Applied to the Use of GPS Technology, Transponder, or the Like, to Monitor Location and Movement of Motor Vehicle, Aircraft, or Watercraft. **5 ALR6th 385.**

Validity of Statutory Requirement that Abortion Occur in Hospital. **5 ALR6th 423.**

Rights and Liabilities of Unaccredited Law Schools and Their Students. **5 ALR6th 449.**

Validity, Construction, and Application of Governmental or Private Regulation of Breast-Feeding. **5 ALR6th 485.**

Validity, as to Claim Alleging Design or Building Defects, of Statute Imposing Time Limitations Upon Action Against Architect, Engineer, or Builder for Injury or Death Arising out of Defective or Unsafe Condition of Improvement to Real Property. **5 ALR6th 497.**

6 ALR6th

Liability of Building Owner or Operator for Injury Resulting from Nonautomatic Swinging Door. **6 ALR6th 1.**

Determination that Child is Neglected or Dependent, or that Parental Rights Should be Terminated, on Basis that Parent Has Failed to Provide for Child's Education. **6 ALR6th 161.**

Right of Parent to Regain Custody of Child After Temporary Conditional Relinquishment of Custody. **6 ALR6th 229.**

Appropriateness of "Error In Judgment" Charge in Medical Malpractice Actions. **6 ALR6th 311.**

Validity and Application of Uniform Anatomical Gift Act. **6 ALR6th 365.**

Right of Creditor Beneficiary or Assignee of Insurance Policy on Life of Debtor to Excess Proceeds over Amount Owed on Debt. **6 ALR6th 391.**

Moral Character for Admission to Bar—Conduct Unrelated to Admission to Bar. **8 ALR6th 1.**

What Constitutes Commercial or Financial Information, Exclusive of Trade Secrets, Exempt from Disclosure Under State Freedom of Information Acts—Specific Applications. **8 ALR6th 117.**

Propriety of Lesser-Included-Offense Charge in State Prosecution of Narcotics Defendant—Methamphetamine Cases. **8 ALR6th 265.**

Validity of Legal Claim Predicated on Nonmarital Same-Sex Relationship. **8 ALR6th 339.**

Vicarious or Imputed Liability for Intentional Infliction of Emotional Distress—Nonemployee Plaintiffs. **8 ALR6th 399.**

Construction and Application of State Statutory Cap on Punitive Damages in Tort Cases Exclusive of Medical Malpractice Actions. **8 ALR6th 439.**

Validity, Construction, and Application of Right-to-Farm Acts. **8 ALR6th 465.**

Insured's Duty to Read Insurance Policy as Affirmative Defense in Claims Against Insurance Agents and Brokers. **8 ALR6th 549.**

Validity, Construction, and Operation of State Statutes Regulating Issuance of Special or Vanity License Plates. **8 ALR6th 639.**

Validity and Application of Enactment Prohibiting Discrimination by Governmental Contractors on Basis of Sexual Orientation. **8 ALR6th 667.**

9 ALR6th

Sufficiency of Showing that Voluntariness of Confession or Admission Was Affected by Alcohol or Other Drugs—Self-Intoxication. **9 ALR6th 1.**

Construction and Application of Political Question Doctrine by State Courts. **9 ALR6th 177.**

Allowance of Punitive Damages in Action Against Attorney for Malpractice. **9 ALR 6th 285.**

ANNOTATION TITLES

Crime-Fraud Exception to Attorney-Client Privilege in State Courts—Contemplated Crime. **9 ALR6th 363.**

Effect on Child Support Duties and Arrearages of Remarriage of Parents to Each Other. **9 ALR6th 437.**

Construction and Application of Insurance Extended Reporting Endorsements. **9 ALR6th 467.**

Choice of Remedies Where State Prosecutor Has Breached Plea Bargain. **9 ALR6th 541.**

Presentence Withdrawal of Plea of Nolo Contendere or Non Vult Contendere Under State Law—General Principles, Effect of Withdrawal, and Procedural Matters. **9 ALR6th 633.**

Presentence Withdrawal of Plea of Nolo Contendere or Non Vult Contendere Under State Law—Misunderstanding or Lack of Knowledge as to Nature of Charge, and Necessity of Factual Basis for Plea. **9 ALR6th 693.**

10 ALR6th

Validity, Construction, and Application of Federal and State Statutes Regulating Unsolicited E-mail or "Spam". **10 ALR6th 1.**

Validity, Construction, and Application of State Criminal Disenfranchisement Provisions. **10 ALR6th 31.**

Construction and Application by State Courts of the Federal Adoption and Safe Families Act and Its Implementing State Statutes. **10 ALR6th 173.**

Presentence Withdrawal of Plea of Nolo Contendere or Non Vult Contendere Under State Law—Awareness of Collateral Consequences of Plea, and Competency to Enter Plea. **10 ALR6th 265.**

Action in Own Name by Shareholder of Closely Held Corporation. **10 ALR6th 293.**

Liability of Employer, Supervisor, or Manager for Intentionally or Recklessly Causing Employee Emotional Distress—Disability Discrimination. **10 ALR6th 375.**

Admissibility in State Criminal Case of Results of Polygraph (Lie Detector) Test—Post-Daubert Cases. **10 ALR6th 463.**

Landlord's Refusal to Rent to Unmarried Couple as Protected by Landlord's Religious Beliefs. **10 ALR6th 513.**

What Constitutes Activity of Employee Protected Under State Whistleblower Protection Statute Covering Employee's "Report," "Disclosure," "Notification," or the Like of Wrongdoing—Sufficiency of Report. **10 ALR6th 531.**

Enforcement of Arbitration Agreement Contained in Real Estate Contract by or Against Nonsignatory Under State Law. **10 ALR6th 669.**

11 ALR6th

When Statute of Limitations Begins to Run on Action Against Attorney for Malpractice Based upon Negligence—View that Statute Begins to Run from Time of Occurrence of Negligent Act or Omission. **11 ALR6th 1.**

Retirement of Husband as Change of Circumstances Warranting Modification of Divorce Decree—Conventional Retirement at 65 Years of Age or Older. **11 ALR6th 125.**

Propriety of Sentencing Judge's Imposition of Harsher Sentence than Offered in Connection with Plea Bargain Rejected or Withdrawn Plea by Defendant—State Cases. **11 ALR6th 237.**

Application of the "Mutual Benefit" Doctrine to Workers' Compensation Cases. **11 ALR6th 351.**

Liability of Employer, Supervisor, or Manager for Intentionally or Recklessly Causing Employee Emotional Distress—Age Discrimination. **11 ALR6th 447.**

Criminal and Civil Regulation of Paintball Guns. **11 ALR6th 525.**

State Income Tax Treatment of Intangible Holding Companies. **11 ALR6th 543.**

Validity and Enforceability of Express Fee-Splitting Agreements Between Attorneys. **11 ALR6th 587.**

Medical Negligence in Extraction of Tooth, Established Through Lay Testimony or Doctrine of Res Ipsa Loquitur. **11 ALR6th 695.**

ANNOTATION TITLES

12 ALR6th

When Statute of Limitations Begins to Run on Action Against Attorney for Malpractice Based upon Negligence—View that Statute Begins to Run from Time of Occurrence of Sustaining Damage or Injury and Other Theories. **12 ALR6th 1.**

Sufficiency of Description of Terms and Conditions of Lease, or Lease Provision, so as to Comply with Statute of Frauds. **12 ALR6th 123.**

Adult Child's Right of Action for Loss of Parental Consortium. **12 ALR6th 241.**

Failure of State Prosecutor to Disclose Existence of Plea Bargain or Other Deals with Witness as Violating Due Process. **12 ALR6th 267.**

Presentence Withdrawal of Plea of Nolo Contendere or Non Vult Contendere Under State Law—Assertion or Finding of Innocence and Defendant's Knowledge or Waiver of Other Particular Rights at Time of Plea. **12 ALR6th 389.**

Parent's Mental Illness or Mental Deficiency as Ground for Termination of Parental Rights—Issues Concerning Rehabilitative and Reunification Services. **12 ALR6th 417.**

Electronic Voting Systems. **12 ALR6th 523.**

Application in State Narcotics Cases of Collective Knowledge Doctrine or Fellow Officers' Rule Under Fourth Amendment—Drugs Other than Marijuana or Cocaine and Unidentified Drugs. **12 ALR6th 553.**

State and Local Governmental Liability for Injury or Death of Bicyclist Due to Defect or Obstruction in Public Roadway or Sidewalk. **12 ALR6th 645.**

13 ALR6th

When Statute of Limitations Begins to Run on Action Against Attorney for Malpractice Based upon Negligence—View that Statute Begins to Run from Time Client Discovers, or Should Have Discovered, Negligent Act or Omission—Statement of Rule and Application of Rule to Providing Client with Allegedly Negligent Advice or Failing to Advise. **13 ALR6th 1.**

Libel and Slander: Construction and Application of the Neutral Reportage Privilege. **13 ALR6th 111.**

Validity of Arbitration Clause Precluding Class Actions. **13 ALR6th 145.**

Right To Workers' Compensation for Physical Injury or Illness Suffered by Claimant as Result of Nonsudden Mental Stimuli—Requisites of, and Factors Affecting, Compensability. **13 ALR6th 209.**

Liability of Successor Corporation for Injury or Damage Caused by Product Issued by Predecessor, Based on Mere Continuation or Continuity of Enterprise Exceptions to Nonliability. **13 ALR6th 355.**

What Constitutes Activity of Employee, Other than "Reporting" Wrongdoing, Protected Under State Whistleblower Protection Statute. **13 ALR6th 499.**

Presentence Withdrawal of Plea of Nolo Contendere or Non Vult Contendere Under State Law—Particular Circumstances as Constituting Grounds for Withdrawal, Excluding Issues of Knowledge, Factual Basis, Competency, Evidence, Defenses, Sentencing and Punishment, and Ineffective Assistance of Counsel. **13 ALR6th 603.**

Constitutionality of State and Local Recall Provisions. **13 ALR6th 661.**

Allowance of Punitive Damages in State Freedom of Information Actions. **13 ALR6th 721.**

14 ALR6th

When Statute of Limitations Begins to Run on Action Against Attorney for Malpractice Based upon Negligence—View That Statute Begins to Run from Time Client Discovers, or Should Have Discovered, Negligent Act or Omission—Application of Rule to Conduct of Litigation and Delay or Inaction in Conducting Client's Affairs. **14 ALR6th 1.**

Construction and Operation of Statutory Time Limit for Filing Claim for State Tax Refund. **14 ALR6th 119.**

Excessiveness or Inadequacy of Damage Awards Against Drunk Drivers. **14 ALR6th 263.**

What Constitutes Reverse or Majority Race or National Origin Discrimination in Employment Under State Law. **14 ALR6th 277.**

Timeliness of Action Under Medical Malpractice Statute of Repose, Aside from Effect of Fraudulent Concealment of Patient's Cause of Action. **14 ALR6th 301.**

Compensatory Damages Recoverable Under State Law Actions for Employer's Sexual Harassment or Discrimination. **14 ALR6th 417.**

Adoption of Manifest Disregard of Law Standard as Non-statutory Ground to Review Arbitration Awards Governed by Uniform Arbitration Act (UAA). **14 ALR6th 491.**

Presentence Withdrawal of Nolo Contendere or Non Vult Contendere Under State Law—Newly Discovered or Available Evidence, and Possible Defense. **14 ALR6th 517.**

Effect of Irregularities or Defects in Primary Petitions—State Cases. **14 ALR6th 543.**

Construction and Application of Insured vs. Insured Exclusion of Directors and Officers Insurance Policy. **14 ALR6th 687.**

15 ALR6th

Admissibility of Evidence of Prior Accidents or Injuries at Same Place. **15 ALR6th 1.**

Snowboarder's Liability for Injuries to or Death of Another Person. **15 ALR6th 161.**

Presentence Withdrawal of Plea of Nolo Contendere or Non Vult Contendere Under State Law—Sentencing and Punishment Issues; Ineffective Assistance of Counsel. **15 ALR6th 173.**

Assumption of Mortgage on Real Property as Consideration for Conveyance That Is Attacked as Fraudulent. **15 ALR6th 241.**

Adoption and Application of "Tainted" Approach or "Dual Motivation" Analysis in Determining Whether Existence of Single Discriminatory Reason for Peremptory Strike Results in Automatic Baston Violation When Neutral Reasons Also Have Been Articulated. **15 ALR6th 319.**

Validity, Construction, and Application of Ignition Interlock Laws. **15 ALR6th 375.**

When Statute of Limitations Begins to Run on Action Against Attorney for Malpractice Based Upon Negligence—View that Statute Begins to Run from Time Client Discovers, or Should Have Discovered, Negligent Act or Omission—Application of Rule to Property, Estate, Corporate, and Document Cases. **15 ALR6th 427.**

Construction and Application of Rule Permitting Knock and Talk Visits Under Fourth Amendment and State Constitutions. **15 ALR6th 515.**

Right to Workers' Compensation for Injury Suffered by Worker En Route to or from Workers' Home Where Home Is Claimed as "Work Situs". **15 ALR6th 633.**

16 ALR6th

Criticism or Disparagement of Physician's Character, Competence, or Conduct as Defamation. **16 ALR6th 1.**

Validity of State Statutes, Regulations, or other Identification Requirements Restricting or Denying Driver's Licenses to Illegal Aliens. **16 ALR6th 131.**

Recovery for Exposure to Beryllium. **16 ALR6th 143.**

Validity of Statutes, Ordinances, and Regulations Governing Pawn Shops. **16 ALR6th 219.**

Validity, Construction, and Application of School Impact Fee Statutes or Ordinances. **16 ALR6th 289.**

Antagonistic Defenses as Ground for Separate Trials of Codefendants in State Homicide Offenses—Factual Applications. **16 ALR6th 329.**

Conduct or Inaction by Insurer Constituting Waiver of, or Creating Estoppel to Assert, Defense of Consent to Settle Provision Under Insurance Policy. **16 ALR6th 491.**

Liability Insurer's Duty to Defend Action Against Insured After Insurer's Full Performance of its Payment Obligations Under Policy Expressly Providing that Duty to Defend Ends on Payment of Policy Limits. **16 ALR6th 603.**

When Statute of Limitations Begins to Run on Action Against Attorney for Malpractice Based Upon Negligence—View that Statute Begins to Run from Time Client Discovers, or Should Have Discovered, Negligent Act or Omission—Application of Rule to Negligent Misrepresentation, Failure to Supervise Junior Counsel, Conflict of Interest, Billing Disputes, and Unspecified Acts of Negligence. **16 ALR6th 653.**

Use of Marketability Discount in Valuing Closely Held Corporation or Its Stock. **16 ALR6th 693.**

17 ALR6th

Contribution Between Joint Tortfeasors as Affected by Settlement with Injured Party by One or More Tortfeasors. **17 ALR6th 1.**

When Statute of Limitations Begins to Run in Case of Dental Malpractice. **17 ALR6th 159.**

When Is Warrantless Entry of House or Other Building Justified Under "Hot Pursuit" Doctrine. **17 ALR6th 327.**

Liability of Hotel or Motel Operator for Injury to Guest Resulting from Assault by Third Party. **17 ALR6th 453.**

What Constitutes Racial Harassment in Employment Violative of State Civil Rights Acts. **17 ALR6th 563.**

Legal Status of Posthumously Conceived Child of Decedent. **17 ALR6th 593.**

State Corporate Income Taxation of Foreign Dividends. **17 ALR6th 623.**

What Constitutes "Repeated" or "Willful" Violation for Purposes of State Occupational Safety and Health Acts. **17 ALR6th 715.**

Claim of Diabetic Reaction or Hypoglycemia as Defense in Prosecution for Driving While Under Inffluence of Alcohol or Drugs. **17 ALR6th 757.**

18 ALR6th

Employee's Expectation of Privacy in Workplace. **18 ALR6th 1.**

Validity, Construction, and Application of Full Faith and Credit for Child Support Orders Act (FFCCSOA), 28 U.S.C.A. § 1738B - State Cases. **18 ALR6th 97.**

Conduct or Activities of Employees During Off-Duty Hours as Misconduct Barring Unemployment Compensation Benefits. **18 ALR6th 195.**

Medical Negligence in Extraction of Tooth, Established Through Expert Testimony. **18 ALR6th 325.**

Continuance of Case Because of Illness of Expert Witness. **18 ALR6th 509.**

Authority of Public Official, Whose Duties or Functions Generally Do Not Entail Traffic Stops, To Effectuate Traffic Stop of Vehicle. **18 ALR6th 519.**

Admissibility in Evidence, in Civil Action, of Tachograph or Similar Paper or Tape Recording of Speed of Motor Vehicle, Railroad Locomotive, or the Like. **18 ALR6th 613.**

Liability of Successor Corporation for Injury or Damage Caused by Product Issued by Predecessor, Based on "Product Line" Successor Liability. **18 ALR6th 629.**

Wearing of Religious Symbols in Courtroom as Protected by First Amendment. **18 ALR6th 775.**

Validity, Construction, and Operation of State and Municipal Act or Regulation Requiring Notice of Pesticide and Herbicide Use. **18 ALR6th 793.**

19 ALR6th

Liability of Employer, Supervisor, or Manager for Intentionally or Recklessly Causing Employee Emotional Distress—Ethnic, Racial, or Religious Harassment or Discrimination. **19 ALR6th 1.**

Antagonistic Defenses as Ground for Separate Trials of Codefendants in Criminal Case—State Narcotics Offenses. **19 ALR6th 115.**

Nonsexual Misconduct or Irregularity as Amounting to "Conduct Unbecoming an Officer," Justifying Police

Officer's Demotion or Removal or Suspension from Duty. **19 ALR6th 217.**

Validity, Construction, and Application of Municipal Restrictions on Location or Operations of Facilities for Sale or Use of Firearms. **19 ALR6th 335.**

Adequacy of Defense Counsel's Representation of Criminal Client Regarding Guilty Pleas—Coercion or Duress. **19 ALR6th 411.**

Effect of Fraudulent or Negligent Concealment of Patient's Cause of Action on Timeliness of Action Under Medical Malpractice Statute of Repose. **19 ALR6th 475.**

Wrongful or Excessive Prescription of Drugs as Ground for Revocation or Suspension of Physician's or Dentist's License to Practice. **19 ALR6th 577.**

Sufficiency of Showing Defendant's "Voluntary Absence" from Trial for Purposes of State Criminal Procedure Rules or Statutes Authorizing Continuation of Trial Notwithstanding Such Absence. **19 ALR6th 697.**

Liability of Clinical Laboratories for Negligence. **19 ALR6th 793.**

20 ALR6th

Liability of Employer, Supervisor, or Manager for Intentionally or Recklessly Causing Employee Emotional Distress—Sexual Harassment, Sexual Discrimination, or Accusations Concerning Sexual Conduct or Orientation. **20 ALR6th 1.**

Validity of Statutes and Ordinances Regulating Operation of Sexually Oriented Businesses—Legal Issues and Principles. **20 ALR6th 161.**

Propriety Under Circumstances of State Court Injunction Against Nonmatrimonial Action in Court of Sister State. **20 ALR6th 211.**

Propriety of Radio and Television Attorney Advertisements. **20 ALR6th 385.**

Construction and Application of Notice of Claim and Notice of Potential Claims Provisions of Directors' and Officers'

Liability Insurance Policy. **20 ALR6th 411.**

Voluntary Nature of Confession as Affected by Appeal to Religious Beliefs. **20 ALR6th 479.**

Application of Doctrine of Specialty to State Criminal Prosecution of Accused Extradited from Foreign Country. **20 ALR6th 561.**

Admissibility of Actuarial Risk Assessment Testimony in Proceeding to Commit Sex Offender. **20 ALR6th 607.**

Right to Workers' Compensation for Physical Injury or Illness Suffered by Claimant as Result of Sudden Mental Stimuli—Compensability of Particular Injuries and Illnesses. **20 ALR6th 641.**

Recovery of Workers' Compensation for Acts of Terrorism. **20 ALR6th 729.**

21 ALR6th

Substantive Challenges to Propriety of Execution by Lethal Injection in State Capital Proceedings. **21 ALR6th 1.**

Common-Law Liability for Injury Caused by Fireworks or Firecracker. **21 ALR6th 81.**

Restrictions in Federal and State Constitutions Takings Clauses and Eminent Domain Statutes. **21 ALR6th 261.**

"Palimony" Actions for Support Following Termination of Nonmarital Relationships. **21 ALR6th 351.**

Validity of Statutes and Ordinances Regulating Operation of Sexually Oriented Businesses—Types of Businesses Regulated. **21 ALR6th 425.**

Construction and Application of "Tail" Insurance Policies. **21 ALR6th 515.**

Effect of Parent's Military Service Upon Child Custody. **21 ALR6th 577.**

Liability of Employer, Supervisor, or Manager for Intentionally or Recklessly Causing Employee Emotional Distress—Accusation or Implication of Employee's Dishonesty. **21 ALR6th 671.**

Sufficiency of Hearsay Evidence in Probation Revocation Hearings. **21 ALR6th 771.**

ANNOTATION TITLES

22 ALR6th

Validity of Bigamy and Polygamy Statutes and Constitutional Provisions. **22 ALR6th 1.**

Timeliness of Challenge, Under 42 U.S.C.A. § 1983, to Constitutionality of State Executions by Lethal Injection. **22 ALR6th 19.**

Claim of Unconscionability of Contract as Subject to Compulsory Arbitration Clause Contained in Contract. **22 ALR6th 49.**

Construction and Application of Directors and Officers Insurance Policy, Exclusive of Exclusion and Notice of Claim Provisions. **22 ALR6th 113.**

Validity, Construction, and Application of Inclusionary Zoning Ordinances and Programs. **22 ALR6th 295.**

Workers' Compensation: Validity, Construction, and Application of Statutes Providing that Worker Who Suffers Workplace Injury and Subsequently Tests Positive for Alcohol Impairment or Illegal Drug Use Is Not Eligible for Workers' Compensation Benefits. **22 ALR6th 329.**

Application of Equitable Estoppel to Compel Arbitration By or Against Nonsignatory—State Cases. **22 ALR6th 387.**

Cigarette Lighter as Deadly or Dangerous Weapon. **22 ALR6th 533.**

Liability of Newspaper for Libel and Slander—21st Century Cases. **22 ALR6th 553.**

23 ALR6th

"Communications" Within Testimonial Privilege of Confidential Communications Between Husband and Wife as Including Knowledge Derived from Observation by One Spouse of Acts of Other Spouse. **23 ALR6th 1.**

Cable Television Equipment or Services as Subject to Sales or Use Tax. **23 ALR6th 165.**

Products Liability: Cardiac Pacemakers. **23 ALR6th 223.**

Construction and Application of State Drug Paraphernalia Acts. **23 ALR6th 307.**

"Deepening Insolvency" as Cause of Action in Tort. **23 ALR6th 457.**

Invocation and Effect of State Secrets Privilege. **23 ALR6th 521.**

Validity of Statutes and Ordinances Regulating the Operation of Sexually Oriented Businesses—Nature of Regulation. **23 ALR6th 573.**

Validity, Construction, and Application of State Statutes Enhancing Penalty for Sale or Possession of Controlled Substances Within Specified Distance of Playgrounds. **23 ALR6th 679.**

When Is Person, Other than One Claiming Posttraumatic Stress Syndrome or Memory Repression, Within Coverage of Statutory Provision Tolling Running of Limitations Period on Basis of Mental Disability. **23 ALR6th 697.**

24 ALR6th

Failure of State Prosecutor to Disclose Exculpatory Tape Recorded Evidence as Violating Due Process. **24 ALR6th 1.**

Constitutional Validity of State or Local Regulation of Contributions by or to Political Action Committees. **24 ALR6th 179.**

Construction and Application of Federal and State Constitutional and Statutory Speech or Debate Provisions. **24 ALR6th 255.**

Application of "Faithless Servant Doctrine". **24 ALR6th 399.**

Construction and Application of "Public Authority" Defense to Criminal Prosecution of Private Citizen. **24 ALR6th 455.**

Recovery of Punitive Damages for Exposure to Asbestos. **24 ALR6th 497.**

Admissibility of Expert Testimony by Nurses. **24 ALR6th 549.**

Antagonistic Defenses as Ground for Separate Trials of Codefendants in State Homicide Offenses—Applicable

ANNOTATION TITLES

26 ALR6th

Attorney's Charging Excessive Fee as Ground for Disciplinary Action—Estate, Trust, Domestic Relations, and Family Law Matters. **26 ALR6th 1.**

Eligibility for Unemployment Compensation as Affected by Voluntary Resignation Because of Change of Location of Residence Under Statute Conditioning Benefits upon Leaving for "Good Cause Attributable to the Employer". **26 ALR6th 111.**

State Constitutional Challenges to the Display of Religious Symbols on Public Property. **26 ALR6th 145.**

Automated Traffic Enforcement Systems. **26 ALR6th 179.**

State Tax Consequences of Election Under § 338 of Internal Revenue Code (26 U.S.C.A. § 338). **26 ALR6th 219.**

Validity, Construction, and Application of State Statutory Provisions Prohibiting Sale of Gasoline Below Cost. **26 ALR6th 249.**

Application of Attorney-Client Privilege to Electronic Documents. **26 ALR6th 287.**

Parents' Work Schedules and Associated Dependent Care Issues as Factors in Child Custody Determinations. **26 ALR6th 331.**

What Constitutes "Custodial Interrogation" of Juvenile by Police Officer Within Rule of Miranda v. Arizona Requiring that Suspect Be Informed of Federal Constitutional Rights Before Custodial Interrogation—At Police Station or Sheriff's Office. **26 ALR6th 451.**

Application of Apprendi v. New Jersey, 530 U.S. 466, 120 S. Ct. 2348, 147 L. Ed. 2d 435 (2000), and Blakely v. Washington, 542 U.S. 296, 124 S. Ct. 2531, 159 L. Ed. 2d 403, 6 A.L.R. Fed. 2d 619 (2004), to State Controlled Substance Proceedings. **26 ALR6th 511.**

2006 to 2007 A.L.R. United States Supreme Court Review. **26 ALR6th 659.**

27 ALR6th

Attorney's Charging Excessive Fee as Ground for Disciplinary Action—Business and Tax, Employee Benefits and

Termination, Civil Rights, and Other Limited Civil Matters. **27 ALR6th 1.**

Eligibility for Unemployment Compensation as Affected by Voluntary Resignation Because of Change of Location of Residence Under Statute Denying Benefits to Certain Claimants Based on Particular Disqualifying Motive for Move or Unavailability for Work. **27 ALR6th 123.**

Construction and Application of Uniform Rule of Evidence 106, Applying Doctrine of Completeness to Writings and Recorded Statements. **27 ALR6th 183.**

Construction and Application of State Structured Settlement Protection Acts. **27 ALR6th 323.**

Construction and Application of Rule of Necessity in Judicial Actions, Providing that a Judge Is Not Disqualified to Try a Case Because of Personal Interest If Case Cannot Be Heard Otherwise. **27 ALR6th 403.**

Effect of Radon Gas on Real Estate Contracts and Agreements. **27 ALR6th 465.**

Timeliness of Execution of Search Warrant. **27 ALR6th 491.**

Constitutionality of Requiring Presentation of Photographic Identification in Order to Vote. **27 ALR6th 541.**

Discovery of Deleted E-mail and Other Deleted Electronic Records. **27 ALR6th 565.**

28 ALR6th

Right to Workers' Compensation for Injury Suffered by Employee While Driving Employer's Vehicle. **28 ALR6th 1.**

Construction and Application of Rule of Necessity Providing that Administrative or Quasi-judicial Officer Is Not Disqualified to Determine a Matter Because of Bias or Personal Interest if Case Cannot Be Heard Otherwise. **28 ALR6th 175.**

Hospital as Within Constitutional Provision Forbidding Unreasonable Searches and Seizures. **28 ALR6th 245.**

State Regulation of Viatical Life Insurance Programs, Viatical Settlements, and Viatical Investments. **28 ALR6th 281.**

Requirements and Effects of Putative Father Registries. **28 ALR6th 349.**

Validity of Super-Majority Voting Requirements in Constitutional, Statutory, and Other Public Provisions. **28 ALR6th 439.**

Sufficiency and Effectiveness of Designation of Debtor in Financing Statement under Uniform Commercial Code § § 9-503 and 9-506 (Revised 2000). **28 ALR6th 461.**

Constitutional Right of Prisoners to Abortion Services and Facilities. **28 ALR6th 485.**

What Constitutes "Custodial Interrogation" by Police Officer Within Rule of Miranda v. Arizona Requiring That Suspect Be Informed of His or Her Federal Constitutional Rights Before Custodial Interrogation—At Suspect's or Third Party's Residence. **28 ALR6th 505.**

29 ALR6th

What Constitutes "Custodial Interrogation" of Adult by Police Officer Within Rule of Miranda v. Arizona Requiring that Suspect Be Informed of Federal Constitutional Rights Before Custodial Interrogation—At Police Station or Sheriff's Office, Where Defendant Voluntarily Appears or Appears at Request of Law Enforcement Personnel, or Where Unspecified as to Circumstances Upon Which Defendant Is Present. **29 ALR6th 1.**

Discoverability of Metadata. **29 ALR6th 167.**

Rescission of Directors' and Officers' Liability Insurance Policy. **29 ALR6th 189.**

Application of "Prisoner Mailbox Rule" by State Courts under State Statutory and Common Law. **29 ALR6th 237.**

Validity, Construction, and Application of Early Voting Statutes. **29 ALR6th 343.**

Liability of State or Local Governmental Entity for Injury Sustained or Caused by Persons Sledding, Tobogganing, Coasting, or Otherwise Sliding on Snow on Government Land. **29 ALR6th 369.**

State Regulation of Payday Loans. **29 ALR6th 461.**

Backdating Stock Options as Breach of Corporate or Fiduciary Duties. **29 ALR6th 491.**

Validity, Construction, and Application of State Statutes Implementing the Uniform Unclaimed Property Act or its Predecessor—Modern Status. **29 ALR6th 507.**

30 ALR6th

Comment Note: Construction and Application of Supreme Court's Ruling in Crawford v. Washington, 541 U.S. 36, 124 S. Ct. 1354, 158 L. Ed. 2d 177, 63 Fed. R. Evid. Serv. 1077 (2004), with Respect to Confrontation Clause Challenges to Admissibility of Hearsay Statement by Declarant Whom Defendant Had No Opportunity to Cross-Examine. **30 ALR6th 1.**

What Constitutes "Custodial Interrogation" at Hospital by Police Offcer Within Rule of Miranda v. Arizona Requiring that Suspect Be Informed of His or Her Federal Constitutional Rights Before Custodial Interrogation—Suspect Hospital Patient. **30 ALR6th 103.**

Claims for Vicarious and Individual Liability for Infliction of Emotional Distress Derived from Use of Internet and Electronic Communications. **30 ALR6th 241.**

First Amendment Protection Afforded to Web Site Operators. **30 ALR6th 299.**

Validity, Construction, and Application of Sales, Use, and Utility Taxes on Retail Transactions of Internet Sellers and Internet Access Providers. **30 ALR6th 341.**

Validity, Construction, and Application of State Statute Including "Sexually Motivated Offenses" Within Definition of Sex Offense for Purposes of Sentencing or Classification of Defendant as Sex Offender. **30 ALR6th 373.**

Construction and Application of Long-Term Care Insurance Policies. **30 ALR6th 395.**

Service of Process Via Computer or Fax. **30 ALR6th 413.**

Constitutionality of Legislative Prayer Practices. **30 ALR6th 459.**

Validity, Construction, and Application of State Statutes Providing for Revocation of Driver's License for Failure to

Pay Child Support. **30 ALR6th 483.**

31 ALR6th

Construction and Application of Suspension Clause of United States Constitution, U.S. Const. Art. I, § 9, cl. 2. **31 ALR6th 1.**

Adequacy of Defense Counsel's Representation of Criminal Client Regarding Guilty Pleas—Probation, Parole, or Pardon Possibilities. **31 ALR6th 49.**

Validity, Construction, and Application of Provisions of Workers' Compensation Act for Additional Compensation Because of Failure To Comply with Specific Requirement of Statute or Regulation by Public for Protection of Workers. **31 ALR6th 199.**

Validity, and Standing to Challenge Validity, of State Statute Prohibiting Flag Desecration and Misuse. **31 ALR6th 333.**

Validity, Construction, and Application of Exclusion or Inclusion of Religious Uses/Places of Worship in Single' Family Residential Zoning Districts. **31 ALR6th 395.**

Consolidation by State Court of Arbitration Proceedings Brought Under State Law. **31 ALR6th 433.**

What Constitutes "Custodial Interrogation" at Hospital by Police Officer Within Rule of Miranda v. Arizona Requiring That Suspect Be Informed of His Federal Constitutional Rights Before Custodial Interrogation—Suspect Hospital Visitor, Not Patient. **31 ALR6th 465.**

Validity, Construction, and Application of State Statutes Prohibiting, Limiting, or Regulating Fishing or Hunting in State by Nonresidents. **31 ALR6th 523.**

Validity, Construction, and Application of State Statutes Criminalizing Possession of Body Armor by Felon Convicted of Violent Crime. **31 ALR6th 615.**

32 ALR6th

What Constitutes "Custodial Interrogation" of Adult by Police Officer Within Rule of Miranda v. Arizona Requiring that Suspect Be Informed of Federal Constitutional Rights Before Custodial Interrogation—At Police Station or Sheriff's Office, Where Defendant Is Escorted or Accompanied by Law Enforcement Personnel, or Is Otherwise at Station or Office Involuntarily. **32 ALR6th 1.**

Determination of Request for Exclusion of Public from State Criminal Trial in Order to Preserve Safety, Confidentiality, or Well-Being of Witness Who Is Not Undercover Police Officer—Issues of Proof, Consideration of Alternatives, and Scope of Closure. **32 ALR6th 171.**

Construction and Application of "Municipal Cost Recovery Rule," or "Free Public Services Doctrine". **32 ALR6th 261.**

Construction and Application of State Mediation Privilege. **32 ALR6th 285.**

Desire of Accused to Testify on Just One of Multiple Charges as Basis for Severance of Trials. **32 ALR6th 385.**

Permissive or Mandatory Nature of Forum Selection Clauses Under State Law. **32 ALR6th 419.**

Application of Class-of-One Theory of Equal Protection to Public Employment. **32 ALR6th 457.**

Applicability of Insurance Policies to Alleged Bodily Injury Arising from Use of Cellular Telephones. **32 ALR6th 505.**

Matters Constituting Unauthorized Practice of Law in Bankruptcy Proceedings. **32 ALR6th 531.**

33 ALR6th

Basis for Exclusion of Public from State Criminal Trial in Order to Preserve Safety, Confidentiality, or Well-Being of Witness Who Is Not Undercover Police Officer. **33 ALR6th 1.**

Validity, Construction, and Application of State Statutes Imposing Criminal Penalties for Failure to Register as Required Under Sex Offender or Other Criminal Registration Statutes. **33 ALR6th 91.**

Workers' Compensation: Nonathlete Students as Covered Employees. **33 ALR6th 251.**

Preemptive Effect of Uniform Controlled Substances Act Upon Local Ordinances. **33 ALR6th 293.**

Recovery of Computer-Assisted Research Costs as Part of or in Addition to Attorney's Fees Under State Law. **33 ALR6th 305.**

Liability of Property Owners to Persons Who Have Never Been on or Near Their Property for Exposure to Asbestos Carried Home on Household Member's Clothing. **33 ALR6th 325.**

Offense of Rape After Withdrawal of Consent. **33 ALR6th 353.**

Validity, Construction, and Application of State Statutes Prohibiting Child Luring as Applied to Cases Involving Luring of Child by Means of Electronic Communications. **33 ALR6th 373.**

Constitutionality of State Statutes and Local Ordinances Regulating Concealed Weapons. **33 ALR6th 407.**

Validity, Construction, and Application of State Statutory Requirements Concerning Placement of Independent Candidate for President of the United States on Ballot. **33 ALR6th 513.**

34 ALR6th

What Constitutes "Custodial Interrogation" by Police Officer Within Rule of Miranda v. Arizona Requiring that Suspect Be Informed of His or Her Federal Constitutional Rights Before Custodial Interrogation—At Police Vehicle, Where Defendant Outside, but in Immediate Vicinity of, Vehicle, or Where Defendant in Parked or Stationary Law Enforcement Vehicle. **34 ALR6th 1.**

Validity, Construction, and Application of State Statutory Requirement that Person Convicted of Sexual Offense in Other Jurisdiction Register or Be Classified as Sexual Offender in Forum State. **34 ALR6th 171.**

Authentication of Electronically Stored Evidence, Including Text Messages and E-mail. **34 ALR6th 253.**

Increase, or Promise of Increase or Withholding of Increase, of Wages as Unfair Labor Practice Under State Labor

Relations Acts. **34 ALR6th 327.**

Construction and Application of Exclusion Provisions of Directors and Officers Insurance Policy, Exclusive of Regulatory and Insured vs. Insured Exclusions. **34 ALR6th 345.**

Recoverable Costs Under State Offer of Judgment Rule. **34 ALR6th 431.**

Evidence Considered in Tracing Currency, Bank Account, or Cash Equivalent to Illegal Drug Trafficking so as to Permit Forfeiture, or Declaration as Contraband, Under State Law—Amount and Packaging of Money and Drugs. **34 ALR6th 539.**

Validity, Construction, and Application of State "Zero Tolerance" Laws Relating to Underage Drinking and Driving. **34 ALR6th 23.**

Construction and Application of Elections Clause of United States Constitution, U.S. Const. Art. I, § 4, cl.1, and State Constitutional Provisions Concerning Congressional Elections. **34 ALR6th 643.**

35 ALR6th

Validity, Construction, and Application of State and Municipal Enactments Regulating Lobbying and of Lobbying Contracts. **35 ALR6th 1.**

What Constitutes "Custodial Interrogation" by Police Officer Within Rule of Miranda v. Arizona Requiring that Suspect Be Informed of His or Her Federal Constitutional Rights Before Custodial Interrogation—At Police Vehicle, Where Defendant in Moving Vehicle, or Where Unspecified as to Whether Vehicle Moving or Stationary. **35 ALR6th 127.**

Right of Retail Buyer of Price-Fixed Product to Sue Manufacturer on State Antitrust Claim. **35 ALR6th 245.**

Validity, Construction, and Application of State Statutes Prohibiting Child Luring as Applied to Cases Involving Luring of Child by Means of Verbal or Other Nonelectronic Communications. **35 ALR6th 361.**

First Amendment Protection Afforded to Blogs and Bloggers. **35 ALR6th 407.**

Employment of Competitor's Former Employee. **36 ALR6th 537.**

2007 to 2008 ALR United States Supreme Court Review. **36 ALR6th 681.**

37 ALR6th

Construction and Application of State Antitakeover Statutes. **37 ALR6th 1.**

State Statutes or Ordinances Requiring Persons Previously Convicted of Crime to Register with Authorities as Applied to Juvenile Offenders—Constitutional Issues. **37 ALR6th 55.**

What Constitutes Activity of Public or State Employee Protected Under State Whistleblower Protection Statute Covering Employee's "Report," "Disclosure," "Notiffication," or the Like of Wrongdoing—Nature of Activity Reported. **37 ALR6th 137.**

Judicial Decisions Involving ASCAP. **37 ALR6th 243.**

Construction and Application of Uniform Mandatory Disposition of Detainers Act. **37 ALR6th 357.**

Pendency of Criminal Prosecution as Ground for Continuance or Postponement of Civil Action Involving Facts or Transactions upon which Prosecution Is Predicated—State Cases. **37 ALR6th 511.**

Validity, Construction, and Application of Anticoncurrent Causation (ACC) Clauses in Insurance Policies. **37 ALR6th 657.**

38 ALR6th

State Statutes or Ordinances Requiring Persons Previously Convicted of Crime to Register with Authorities as Applied to Juvenile Offenders—Duty to Register, Requirements for Registration, and Procedural Matters. **38 ALR6th 1.**

What Constitutes "Custodial Interrogation" Within Rule of Miranda v. Arizona Requiring that Suspect Be Informed of Federal Constitutional Rights Before Custodial Interrogation—In Jail or Prison. **38 ALR6th 97.**

Recovery of Sales Taxes Paid on Bad Debts. **38 ALR6th 255.**

Inherited Property as Marital or Separate Property in Divorce Action. **38 ALR6th 313.**

Liability of Hospital for Injury Arising from Use of Nondefective Wheelchair. **38 ALR6th 399.**

Qualification as Expert To Testify as to Findings or Results of Scientific Test Concerning DNA Matching. **38 ALR6th 439.**

Liability of Employer, Supervisor, or Manager for Intentionally or Recklessly Causing Employee Emotional Distress—Defamation, Invasion of Privacy, and Employer's Alleged Misuse of Company Procedures. **38 ALR6th 541.**

39 ALR6th

Majority's Fiduciary Obligation to Minority Shareholder of Close Corporation—Breach and Remedy. **39 ALR6th 1.**

Application of Doctrine of Election of Remedies Where One Claim Sounds in Tort and Other Claim Sounds in Contract. **39 ALR6th 155.**

Divorce and Separation: Appreciation in Value of Separate Property During Marriage with Contribution by Either Spouse as Separate or Community Property (Doctrine of "Active Appreciation"). **39 ALR6th 205.**

Application of Common-Law "Fresh Complaint" Doctrine as to Admissibility of Alleged Victim's Disclosure of Sexual Offense—Post-1950 Cases. **39 ALR6th 257.**

Validity and Effect of Retrocessional Reinsurance Agreements. **39 ALR6th 391.**

Right to Workers' Compensation for Physical Injury or Illness Suffered by Claimant as Result of Nonsudden Mental Stimuli—Compensability Under Particular Circumstances. **39 ALR6th 445.**

State Statutes or Ordinances Requiring Persons Previously Convicted of Crime to Register with Authorities as Applied to Juvenile Offenders—Expungement, Stay or

Deferral, Exceptions, Exemptions, and Waiver. **39 ALR6th 577.**

Enforceability of Floating Forum Selection Clauses. **39 ALR6th 629.**

40 ALR6th

Restrictions on Disclosure of Contents of Complaint Alleging Sexual Offense Under Common-Law "Fresh Complaint" Doctrine—Post-1950. **40 ALR6th 1.**

Validity, Construction, and Application of Statutory Provisions Exempting or Otherwise Restricting Farm and Agricultural Workers from Worker's Compensation Coverage. **40 ALR6th 99.**

Defamation by Radio—Actual Malice. **40 ALR6th 231.**

Conversion of Electronic Data, Including Domain Names. **40 ALR6th 295.**

Validity, Construction, and Application of State Statutes Regulating or Proscribing Payment in Connection with Gathering Signatures on Nominating Petitions for Public Office or Initiative Petitions. **40 ALR6th 317.**

Admissibility of Computer Forensic Testimony. **40 ALR6th 355.**

Actions by or Against Individuals or Groups Protesting or Picketing at Funerals. **40 ALR6th 375.**

Validity, Construction, and Application of Statutory and Municipal Enactments and Conditions of Release Prohibiting Sex Offenders from Parks. **40 ALR6th 419.**

Unauthorized Practice of Law as Contempt. **40 ALR6th 463.**

Admissibility of Evidence Taken from Vehicular Event Data Recorders(EDR), Sensing Diagnostic Modules (SDM), or "Black Boxes". **40 ALR6th 595.**

41 ALR6th

Legal Malpractice in Connection with Attorney's Withdrawal as Counsel—Criminal and Business-Related Cases. **41 ALR6th 1.**

ANNOTATION TITLES

Interplay Between 21st Amendment and Sherman Act Concerning State Regulation of Intoxicating Liquors. **41 ALR6th 77.**

Court's Duty to Advise Sex Offender as to Sex Offender Registration Consequences or Other Restrictions Arising from Plea of Guilty, or to Determine that Offender Is Advised Thereof. **41 ALR6th 141.**

Right to Compensation Under State Workers' Compensation Statute for Injuries Sustained During or as Result of Horseplay, Joking, Fooling, or the Like. **41 ALR6th 207.**

Propriety of Use of Multiple Juries at Joint Trial of Multiple Defendants in State Criminal Prosecution. **41 ALR6th 295.**

Validity of State and Local Taxation and Regulation of Voice over Internet Protocol (VoIP) Service. **41 ALR6th 375.**

Application of Stigma-Plus Due Process Claims to Education Context. **41 ALR6th 391.**

Retroactive Application of State Statutes Concerning Asbestos Liability. **41 ALR6th 445.**

Automobile Liability Insurance Policy Exclusion as Applied to Loss or Injury Resulting from Insured's Flight from Police. **41 ALR6th 527.**

Propriety of Pharmacy and Pharmacist's Refusal to Fill Prescription for Contraceptives. **41 ALR6th 555.**

42 ALR6th

Liability Arising from Postponement or Cancellation of Concert. **42 ALR6th 1.**

Injury to Employee as Arising out of or in Course of Employment for Purposes of State Workers' Compensation Statute—Effect of Employer-Provided Living Quarters, Room and Board, or the Like. **42 ALR6th 61.**

Propriety of Using Otherwise Inadmissible Statement, Taken in Violation of Miranda Rule, to Impeach Criminal Defendant's Credibility—State Cases. **42 ALR6th 237.**

Recovery for Nonconsensual Human Medical Experimentation. **42 ALR6th 301.**

ANNOTATION TITLES

Defamation by Television—Actual Malice. **42 ALR6th 353**

Legal Malpractice in Connection with Attorney's Withdrawal as Counsel—Tort, Civil Rights, Family Law, Probate, and Unspecified Cases. **42 ALR6th 463.**

Construction and Application of Exclusive Remedy Rule Under State Workers' Compensation Statutes with Respect to Liability for Injury or Death of Employee as Passenger in Employer-Provided Vehicle—Requisites for, and Factors Affecting, Applicability and Who May Invoke Rule. **42 ALR6th 545.**

43 ALR6th

Circumstances Excusing Demand Upon Board of Directors that is Otherwise Prerequisite to Bringing of Stockholder's Derivative Suit on Behalf of Corporation. **43 ALR6th 1.**

Reciprocal Discipline of Attorneys—Criminal Conduct. **43 ALR6th 163.**

Admissibility of Biomedical Engineer Testimony. **43 ALR6th 327.**

Validity of Search of Cruise Ship Cabin. **43 ALR6th 355.**

Construction and Application of Exclusive Remedy Rule Under State Workers' Compensation Statute With Respect to Liability for Injury or Death of Employee as Passenger in Employer-Provided Vehicle—Against Whom May Rule Be Invoked and Application of Rule to Particular Situations and Employees. **43 ALR6th 375.**

Adequacy of Defense Counsel's Representation of Criminal Client Regarding Entrapment Defense—State Cases. **43 ALR6th 475.**

Construction and Application of Limited Liability Company Acts—Issues Relating to Formation of Limited Liability Company and Addition or Disassociation of Members Thereto. **43 ALR6th 611.**

44 ALR6th

Liability to Third Party for Negligent or Fraudulent Appraisal of Value of Real. **44 ALR6th 1.**

Reciprocal Discipline of Attorneys—Noncriminal Misconduct Towards Clients Not Involving Client Funds. **44 ALR6th 75.**

Construction and Application of State Statutes Governing Mortgage or Foreclosure Consultants and Purchasers. **44 ALR6th 225.**

Validity of Extraterritorial Condemnation by Municipality. **44 ALR6th 259.**

Measure and Elements of Restitution to Which Victim is Entitled Under State Criminal Statute—Payment for Installation of Alarm or Locks or Change of Locks Due to Burglary, Attempted Burglary, or Felonious Breaking and Entering. **44 ALR6th 301.**

Construction and Application of State Endangered Species Acts. **44 ALR6th 325.**

Physician's Liability for Patient's Addiction to or Overdose from Prescription Drugs. **44 ALR6th 391.**

"Sale on Approval" and "Sale or Return" Contracts Under Uniform Commercial Code § 2-326. **44 ALR6th 441.**

Jewelry and Clothing as Within Debtor's Exemptions Under State Statutes. **44 ALR6th 481.**

Exclusive Remedy Provision of State Workers' Compensation Statute as Applied to Injuries Sustained During or as the Result of Horseplay, Joking, Fooling, or the Like. **44 ALR6th 545.**

45 ALR6th

When Does Use of Taser Constitute Violation of Constitutional Rights. **45 ALR6th 1.**

Reciprocal Discipline of Attorneys—Commingling or Other Mishandling of Client Funds. **45 ALR6th 175.**

What Constitutes "Custodial Interrogation" by Police Officer Within Rule of Miranda v. Arizona Requiring that Suspect Be Informed of Federal Constitutional Rights Before Custodial Interrogation—Upon Hotel Property. **45 ALR6th 337.**

Liability of Prescription Drug Manufacturer for Drug User's Suicide or Attempted Suicide. **45 ALR6th 385.**

Propriety, Measure, and Elements of Restitution to Which Victim is Entitled Under State Criminal Statute—Cruelty to, Killing, or Abandonment of, Animals. **45 ALR6th 435.**

Validity, Construction, and Application of State Vexatious Litigant Statutes. **45 ALR6th 493.**

Validity of Search and Reasonable Expectation of Privacy as Affected by No Trespassing or Similar Signage. **45 ALR6th 643.**

46 ALR6th

Construction and Application of Limited Liability Company Acts—Issues Relating to Liability of Limited Liability Company for Acts of Its Members, Managers, Officers, and Agents. **46 ALR6th 1.**

Defendant's Right to Credit for Time Spent in Halfway House, Rehabilitation Center, or Similar Restrictive Environment as Condition of Pretrial Release. **46 ALR6th 63.**

Right of Principal to Recover Punitive Damages for Agent's or Broker's Breach of Duty. **46 ALR6th 185.**

Propriety of Requirement, as Condition of Probation, That Defendant Refrain from Use of Intoxicants. **46 ALR6th 241.**

Liability of Corporations for Climate Change and Weather Conditions. **46 ALR6th 345.**

Disciplining Attorney for Abuse or Misuse of Computer Technology, Including Internet and E-Mail Activities. **46 ALR6th 365.**

Construction and Application of Exemption for Firearms Under State Law. **46 ALR6th 401.**

Regulation of Pre-Paid Stored-Value "Gift Cards". **46 ALR6th 437.**

Validity of Restrictions Imposed During National Political Conventions Impinging Upon Rights to Freedom of Speech and Assembly Under First Amendment. **46 ALR6th 465.**

2008 to 2009 A.L.R. United States Supreme Court Review. **46 ALR6th 495.**

47 ALR6th

Construction and Application of Limited Liability Company Acts—Issues Relating to Personal Liability of Individual Members and Managers of Limited Liability Company as to Third Parties. **47 ALR6th 1.**

Validity, Construction, and Application of Statutes Prohibiting Boating While Intoxicated, Boating While Under the Influence, or the Like. **47 ALR6th 107.**

Construction and Application of Fiduciary Duty Exception to Attorney-Client Privilege. **47 ALR6th 255.**

Necessity and Admissibility of Expert Testimony to Establish Malpractice or Breach of Professional Standard of Care by Architect. **47 ALR6th 303.**

Creation and Perfection of Security Interests in Insurance Proceeds Under Article 9 of Uniform Commercial Code. **47 ALR6th 347.**

Construction and Application of "Automatic Companion Rule" or Person's "Mere Propinquity" to Arrestee to Determine Propriety of Search of Person for Weapons or Firearms. **47 ALR6th 423.**

Right to Intervene in Court Review of Zoning Proceeding. **47 ALR6th 439.**

48 ALR6th

Construction and Application of Limited Liability Company Acts—Issues Relating to Derivative Actions and Actions Between Members of Limited Liability Company. **48 ALR6th 1.**

Prejudicial Effect of Juror Misconduct Arising from Internet Usage. **48 ALR6th 135.**

Validity of Statute Requiring Proof and Disclosure of Information as Condition of Registration to Vote. **48 ALR6th 181.**

Construction and Applicability of State Statutes Governing Health Club Membership Contracts or Fees. **48 ALR6th 223.**

State Lotteries: Actions by Ticketholders or Other Claimants Against State or Contractor for State. **48 ALR6th 243.**

Civil Liability of Internet Dating Services. **48 ALR6th 351.**

Workers' Compensation: Value of Employer-Provided Room, Board, or Clothing as Factor in Determining Basis for or Calculation of Amount of Compensation Under State Workers' Compensation Statute. **48 ALR6th 387.**

What Constitutes "Future Goods" Within Scope of U.C.C. Article 2. 475 Practices Forbidden by State Deceptive Trade Practice and Consumer Protection Acts—Pyramid or Ponzi or Referral Sales Schemes. **48 ALR6th 511.**

49 ALR6th

Construction and Application of Limited Liability Company Acts—Issues Relating to Dissolution and Winding Up of Affairs of Limited Liability Company. **49 ALR6th 1.**

Disqualification or Recusal of Judge Due to Comments at Continuing Legal Education (CLE) Seminar or Other Educational Meetings. **49 ALR6th 93.**

Validity of Adverse Personnel Action or Adverse Action Affecting Student's Academic Standing Based on Internet Posting or Expression, Including Social Networking. **49 ALR6th 115.**

Challenges to Regulation of Balloon Signs or Other Inflated Signs. **49 ALR6th 153.**

Construction and Application of "Sistership" Clause of Products Liability Insurance Policy Excepting from Coverage Cost of Product Recall or Withdrawal of Product from Market. **49 ALR6th 169.**

Elements and Measure of Compensation in Eminent Domain Proceeding for Temporary Taking of Property. **49 ALR6th 205.**

Suppression of Statements Made During Police Interview of Non-English-Speaking Defendant. **49 ALR6th 343.**

Golf Course or Driving Range as Nuisance. **49 ALR6th 477.**

Court Rules and Rules of Professional Conduct Limiting Amount of Contingent Fees or Otherwise Imposing Conditions on Contingent Fee Contracts. **49 ALR6th 505.**

50 ALR6th

Construction and Application of Consent-Once-Removed Doctrine, Permitting Warrantless Entry Into Residence by Law Enforcement Officers for Purposes of Effectuating Arrest or Search Where Confidential Informant or Undercover Officer Enters with Consent and Observes Criminal Activity or Contraband in Plain View. **50 ALR6th 1.**

Liability for Risk of Future Identity Theft. **50 ALR6th 33.**

Right of Insurer to Assert Equitable Subrogation Claim Against Attorney for Insured on Grounds of Professional Malpractice. **50 ALR6th 53.**

Comment Note: Governmental Liability for Failure to Reduce Vegetation Obscuring View at Railroad Crossing or at Street or Highway Intersection. **50 ALR6th 95.**

Validity, Construction, and Application of Arbitration Agreement in Contract for Admission to Nursing Home. **50 ALR6th 187.**

Applicability of State Sales and Use Tax Exemptions for Custom Programs Prepared to Special Order of Customer. **50 ALR6th 261.**

Application of Full Faith and Credit Principles to Class-Action Litigation and Judgments. **50 ALR6th 281.**

Construction and Application of Medical Marijuana Laws and Medical Necessity Defense to Marijuana Laws. **50 ALR6th 353.**

Sufficiency of Showing to Support No-Knock Search Warrant—Cases Decided After Richards v. Wisconsin, 520 U.S. 385, 117 S.Ct. 1416, 137 L. Ed. 2d 615 (1997). **50 ALR6th 455.**

51 ALR6th

Construction and Application of Article IV of Interstate Agreement on Detainers (IAD): Issues Related to "Speedy Trial" Requirement, and Construction of Essential Terms. **51 ALR6th 1.**

Application of Apprendi v. New Jersey, 530 U.S. 466, 120 S. Ct. 2348, 147 L. Ed. 2d 435 (2000), and Blakely v. Washington, 542 U.S. 296, 124 S. Ct. 2531, 159 L. Ed. 2d 403, 6 A.L.R. Fed. 2d 619 (2004), to Sex Offender Registration Statutes. **51 ALR6th 139.**

What Constitutes "Custodial Interrogation" Within Rule of Miranda v. Arizona Requiring That Suspect Be Informed of His Federal Constitutional Rights Before Custodial Interrogation—Private Security Guards, Detectives, or Police. **51 ALR6th 219.**

Validity, Construction, and Application of State Taxes on Revenues and Income from Communications Satellite Services. **51 ALR6th 257.**

Validity of Statute Providing for Purging Voter Registration Lists of Inactive Voters. **51 ALR6th 287.**

Liability of Retailer and Its Affiliate Bank to Credit Card Issuer for Costs Arising out of Breach of Retailer's Computer Security. **51 ALR6th 311.**

Application of Municipal Taxpayer Standing Doctrine. **51 ALR6th 333.**

Constitutionality, Construction, and Application of Statute or Regulatory Action Respecting Political Advertising—Print Media Cases. **51 ALR6th 359.**

Recovery on Insurance Policy When Death Occurs by Autoerotic Asphyxiation. **51 ALR6th 495.**

Restrictive Covenants or Homeowners' Association Regulations Restricting or Prohibiting Flags, Signage, or the Like on Homeowner's Property as Restraint on Free Speech. **51 ALR6th 533.**

52 ALR6th

Construction and Application of Article IV of Interstate Agreement on Detainers (IAD): Issues Related to "Anti-Shuttling" Provision, Dismissal of Action Against Detainee, and Adequacy of Certificate. **52 ALR6th 1.**

Validity, Construction, and Application of State Statutes and Municipal Ordinances Proscribing Failure or Refusal to Obey Police Officer's Order to Move On, or Disperse, on

Street, as Disorderly Conduct. **52 ALR6th 125.**

Statements Reflecting Upon Nongovernmental Employee as Defamation Per Se—Injury to Plaintiff's Business, Trade, Profession, or Office. **52 ALR6th 271.**

Construction and Application of Uniform Child Custody Jurisdiction and Enforcement Act's Significant Connection Jurisdiction Provision. **52 ALR6th 433.**

Extended Commitment of One Committed to Institution as Consequence of Acquittal of Crime on Ground of Insanity. **52 ALR6th 567.**

Liability of Police Officer for Assault and Battery Arising from Use of Stun Gun or Taser Device. **52 ALR6th 623.**

53 ALR6th

Construction and Application of Article IV of Interstate Agreement on Detainers (IAD): Issues Related to Custody, Temporary Custody, Contest as to Legality of Custody, Necessity of Hearing, and Transmittal Orders. **53 ALR6th 1.**

Failure of State Prosecutor to Disclose Exculpatory Physical Evidence as Violating Due Process—Weapons. **53 ALR6th 81.**

Perfection of Security Interests by Possession, Delivery, or Control Under Revised Article 9 of Uniform Commercial Code. **53 ALR6th 159.**

Statements Reflecting upon Nongovernmental Employee as Defamation Per Se—Other than Injury to Plaintiff's Business, Trade, Profession, or Office. **53 ALR6th 213.**

Construction and Application of State Statutes Providing Compensation for Wrongful Conviction and Incarceration. **53 ALR6th 305.**

Construction and Application of Uniform Child Custody Jurisdiction and Enforcement Act's Temporary Emergency Jurisdiction Provision. **53 ALR6th 419.**

Constitutionality, Construction, and Application of Statute or Regulatory Activity Respecting Political Advertising Nonprint Media Cases, or Cases Implicating Both Print and Nonprint Media. **53 ALR6th 491.**

Application of First Amendment's "Ministerial Exception" or "Ecclesiastical Exception" to State Civil Rights Claims. **53 ALR6th 569.**

54 ALR6th

Validity, Construction, and Application of Interstate Corrections Compact and Implementing State Laws-Jurisdictional Issues, Governing Law, and Validity and Applicability of Compact. **54 ALR6th 1.**

Invasion of Privacy by Internet or Website Postings. **54 ALR6th 99.**

Construction and Application of Libel-Proof Doctrine. **54 ALR6th 165.**

Municipal Liability for Damage Resulting from Obstruction or Clogging of Drain or Sewer. **54 ALR6th 201.**

Justification and Correction of Remarks or Acts of State Trial Judge Criticizing, Rebuking, or Punishing Defense Counsel in Criminal Case as Otherwise Requiring New Trial or Reversal. **54 ALR6th 429.**

Construction and Application of Uniform Rule of Evidence 803(17), Providing Hearsay Exception for Market Reports, and Commercial Publications. **54 ALR6th 593.**

Liability of Manufacturer, Distributor, or Seller for Injury Caused by Wheelchair. **54 ALR6th 619.**

Disclosure of Electronic Data Under State Public Records and Freedom of Information Acts. **54 ALR6th 653.**

55 ALR6th

Construction and Application of Supreme Court's Holding in Arizona v. Gant, 129 S. Ct. 1710, 173 L. Ed. 2d 485, 47 A.L.R. Fed. 2d 657 (2009), That Police May Search Vehicle Incident to Recent Occupant's Arrest Only if Arrestee is Within Reaching Distance of Passenger Compartment at Time of Search or it is Reasonable to Believe Vehicle Contains Evidence of Offense—Substantive Traffic Offenses. **55 ALR6th 1.**

Interrogation or Poll of Jurors, During Criminal Trial, as to Whether They Were Exposed to Media Publicity Pertaining to Alleged Crime or Trial. **55 ALR6th 157.**

Failure of State Prosecutor to Disclose Exculpatory Physical Evidence as Violating Due Process—Personal Items Other Than Weapons. **55 ALR6th 391.**

What Constitutes "Custodial Interrogation" by Police Officer Within Rule of Miranda v. Arizona Requiring That Suspect Be Informed of His or Her Federal Constitutional Rights Before Custodial Interrogation—At Nonpolice Vehicle for Traffic Stop, Where Defendant Outside, But in Immediate Vicinity of Vehicle, or Where Unspecified as to Whether Inside or Outside of Nonpolice Vehicle. **55 ALR6th 513.**

Validity of Statute Restricting Voter Registration Solicitations by Third Parties or Organizations. **55 ALR6th 599.**

Zoning Scheme, Plan, or Ordinance as Temporary Taking. **55 ALR6th 635.**

56 ALR6th

Construction and Application of Supreme Court's Holding in Arizona v. Gant, 129 S. Ct. 1710, 173 L. Ed. 2d 485, 47 A.L.R. Fed. 2d 657 (2009), that Police May Search Vehicle Incident to Recent Occupant's Arrest Only if Arrestee Is Within Reaching Distance of Passenger Compartment at Time of Search or It Is Reasonable to Believe Vehicle Contains Evidence of Offense—Pretextual Traffic Offenses and Other Criminal Investigations. **56 ALR6th 1.**

Liability of Name Brand Drug Manufacturer for Injury or Death Resulting from Use of Prescription Drug's Generic Equivalent. **56 ALR6th 161.**

Failure of State Prosecutor to Disclose Exculpatory Physical Evidence as Violating Due Process—Evidence Other Than Weapons or Personal Items. **56 ALR6th 185.**

What Constitutes "Custodial Interrogation" by Police Officer Within Rule of Miranda v. Arizona Requiring That Suspect Be Informed of His or Her Federal Constitutional Rights Before Custodial Interrogation—In Nonpolice

Vehicle for Traffic Stop. **56 ALR6th 323.**

Liability of Manufacturer for Injuries Arising from Use of, or Failure to Use, Stun Gun or Taser Device. **56 ALR6th 467.**

Validity of Statute Limiting Time Period for Voter Registration. **56 ALR6th 523.**

Construction and Application of Interstate Corrections Compact and Implementing State Laws—Equivalency of Conditions and Rights and Responsibilities of Parties. **56 ALR6th 553.**

Validity, Construction, and Application of Overt Act Requirement of State Statutes Providing for Commitment of Sexually Dangerous Persons. **56 ALR6th 647.**

2009 to 2010 A.L.R. United States Supreme Court Review. **56 ALR6th 679.**

57 ALR6th

Validity and Applicability of State Requirement That Person Convicted or Indicted of Sex Offenses Be Subject to Electronic Location Monitoring, Including Use of Satellite or Global Positioning System. **57 ALR6th 1.**

What Constitutes "Custodial Interrogation" by Police Officer Within Rule of Miranda v. Arizona Requiring That Suspect Be Informed of Federal Constitutional Rights Before Custodial Interrogation—At Nonpolice Vehicle for Other Than Traffic Stop. **57 ALR6th 83.**

Construction and Application of Uniform Child Custody Jurisdiction and Enforcement Act's Home State Jurisdiction Provision. **57 ALR6th 163.**

Propriety of Employer's Discharge of or Failure to Hire Employee Due to Employee's Use of Medical Marijuana. **57 ALR6th 285.**

Necessity and Content of Instructions to Jury Respecting Reasons for or Inferences from Accused's Absence from State Criminal Trial. **57 ALR6th 313.**

Liability of State or Municipality for Unsafe Roadway Condition Arising from Rain, Snow, Fog, or Other

Atmospheric Condition, Naturally Occurring or Created by Another. **57 ALR6th 355.**

Propriety and Application of Lone Pine Orders Used to Expedite Claims and Increase Judicial Efficiency in Mass Tort Litigation. **57 ALR6th 383.**

Validity of Residency and Precinct-Specific Requirements of State Voter Registration Statutes. **57 ALR6th 419.**

What is "Property of Another" Within Statute Proscribing Larceny, Theft, or Embezzlement of Property of Another. **57 ALR6th 445.**

58 ALR6th

Admissibility and Necessity of Expert Evidence as to Standards of Practice and Negligence in Malpractice Action Against Attorney—General Principles and Conduct Related to Interaction with Client. **58 ALR6th 1.**

What Constitutes "Custodial Interrogation" by Police Officer Within Rule of Miranda v. Arizona Requiring That Suspect be Informed of Federal Constitutional Rights Before Custodial Interrogation—Where Unspecified as to Precise Location of Roadside Questioning by Law Enforcement Officers. **58 ALR6th 215.**

Consignment Transactions Under Uniform Commercial Code Article 9 on Secured Transactions. **58 ALR6th 289.**

Validity of Criminal State Racketeer Influenced and Corrupt Organizations Acts and Similar Acts Related to Gang Activity and the Like. **58 ALR6th 385.**

What Constitutes "Custodial Interrogation" Within Rule of Miranda v. Arizona Requiring That Suspect be Informed of Federal Constitutional Rights Before Custodial Interrogation—At Suspect's Place of Employment or Business. **58 ALR6th 439.**

Necessity of Rendering Medical Assistance as Circumstance Permitting Warrantless Entry or Search of Building or Premises. **58 ALR6th 499.**

59 ALR6th

Admissibility and Necessity of Expert Evidence as to Standards of Practice and Negligence in Malpractice Action

ANNOTATION TITLES

Against Attorney—Conduct Related to Procedural Issues. **59 ALR6th 1.**

Validity, Construction, and Application of State Requirements for Placement of Independent Candidates for United States Senate on Ballot. **59 ALR6th 111.**

Construction and Application of Uniform Child Custody Jurisdiction and Enforcement Act's Exclusive, Continuing Jurisdiction Provision—No Significant Connection/Substantial Evidence. **59 ALR6th 161.**

Propriety of Execution of No-Knock Search Warrant. **59 ALR6th 311.**

What Constitutes "Custodial Interrogation" Within Rule of Miranda v. Arizona Requiring That Suspect be Informed of Federal Constitutional Rights Before Custodial Interrogation—At School. **59 ALR6th 393.**

Construction and Application of Federal Uniformed Services Former Spouse Protection Act in State Court Divorce Proceedings. **59 ALR6th 433.**

60 ALR6th

Admissibility and Necessity of Expert Evidence as to Standards of Practice and Negligence in Malpractice Action Against Attorney—Conduct Related to Substantive Representation and Transactional Matters. **60 ALR6th 1.**

Preemption of State Regulation of Controlled Substances by Federal Controlled Substances Act. **60 ALR6th 175.**

Construction and Application of Uniform Child Custody Jurisdiction and Enforcement Act's Exclusive, Continuing Jurisdiction Provision—Other Than No Significant Connection/Substantial Evidence. **60 ALR6th 193.**

Propriety of Incentive Awards or Incentive Agreements in Class Actions. **60 ALR6th 295.**

Validity, Construction and Application of State Statutory Limitations Periods Governing Election Contests. **60 ALR6th 481.**

Gender Reassignment or "Sex Change" Surgery as Covered Procedure Under State Medical Assistance Program. **60 ALR6th 627.**

For assistance, call 1-800-328-4880

61 ALR6th

Adoption of Child by Same-Sex Partners. **61 ALR6th 1.**

Tips as Wages for Purposes of State Wage Laws. **61 ALR6th 61.**

Validity, Construction, and Effect of Agreement Exempting Operator of Fitness or Health Club or Gym from Liability for Personal Injury or Death of Patron. **61 ALR6th 147.**

Remedies of Purchasers and Bidders on Internet Auction Web Sites. **61 ALR6th 207.**

Liability of Insurer for Fraud, Misrepresentation, or Deceptive Trade Practices in Connection with Vanishing Premium Life Insurance Policy. **61 ALR6th 239.**

Obligation of Online Travel Companies to Collect and Remit Hotel Occupancy Taxes. **61 ALR6th 387.**

Tort Liability of Project Architect or Engineer for Economic Damages Suffered by Contractor or Subcontractor. **61 ALR6th 445.**

Construction and Application by State Courts of Indian Child Welfare Act of 1978 Requirement of Active Efforts to Provide Remedial Services, 25 U.S.C.A. § 1912(d). **61 ALR6th 521.**

Liability to Spectator at Football Game Who is Injured as Result of Hazards of Game. **61 ALR6th 603.**

62 ALR6th

Construction and Application to Immediate Parties of Uniform Commercial Code Article 4A Governing Funds Transfers. **62 ALR6th 1.**

Construction and Application of Vacancies in House of Representatives Clause of United States Constitution, U.S. Const. Art. I, § 2, cl. 4, and State Provisions Concerning Such Elections. **62 ALR6th 143.**

Validity of Search of Wireless Communication Devices. **62 ALR6th 161.**

Applicability of Valued-Policy Statutes to Flood, Wind, and Hurricane Damage. **62 ALR6th 227.**

For assistance, call 1-800-328-4880

Propriety and Effect of Law Students Acting as Counsel in Court Suit. **62 ALR6th 259.**

Construction and Application of State Constitutional Provisions Concerning Defenses of Assumption of Risk and Contributory Negligence. **62 ALR6th 313.**

Validity, Construction, and Application of State Statutes and Municipal Ordinances or Orders Providing Buffer Zones Around Health Care Facilities That Offer Abortion Services. **62 ALR6th 359.**

Search and Seizure: Reasonable Expectation of Privacy in Backyards. **62 ALR6th 413.**

Construction and Application of U.S. Const. Art. I, § 9, cl. 3, Proscribing Federal Bills of Attainder. **62 ALR6th 517.**

63 ALR6th

Construction and Application of U.S. Const. Art. I, § 10, cl. 1, and State Constitutional Provisions Proscribing State Bills of Attainder. **63 ALR6th 1.**

Workers' Compensation: Value of Expenses Reimbursed by Employer as Factor in Determining Basis for or Calculation of Amount of Compensation Under State Workers' Compensation Statute. **63 ALR6th 187.**

Absolute Immunity for Failing to Disclose Exculpatory Evidence Under 42 U.S.C.A. § 1983 Following Imbler v. Pachtman, 424 U.S. 409, 96 S. Ct. 984, 47 L. Ed. 2d 128 (1976). **63 ALR6th 255.**

Validity, Construction, and Application of State Trademark Counterfeiting Statutes. **63 ALR6th 303.**

Validity of State Sex Offender Registration Laws Under Ex Post Facto Prohibitions. **63 ALR6th 351.**

Validity, Construction, and Application of Placement Preferences of State and Federal Indian Child Welfare Acts. **63 ALR6th 429.**

Liability for Injury on or in Connection with Escalator. **63 ALR6th 495.**

64 ALR6th

Validity, Construction and Application of State Sex Offender

Registration Statutes Concerning Level of Classification—General Principles, Evidentiary Matters, and Assistance of Counsel. **64 ALR6th 1.**

Construction and Application of United States Supreme Court Holdings in District of Columbia v. Heller, 554 U.S. 570, 128 S. Ct. 2783, 171 L. Ed. 2d 637 (2008) and McDonald v. City of Chicago, Ill., 130 S. Ct. 3020, 177 L. Ed. 2d 894 (2010) Respecting Second Amendment Right to Keep and Bear Arms, to State or Local Laws Regulating Firearms or Other Weapons. **64 ALR6th 131.**

Liability of Hospital or Sanitarium for Negligence of Independent Physician or Surgeon—Exception Where Physician Has Ostensible Agency or "Agency by Estoppel". **64 ALR6th 249.**

Application of Anti-SLAPP ("Strategic Lawsuit Against Public Participation") Statutes to Real Estate Development, Land Use, and Zoning Disputes. **64 ALR6th 365.**

Assignability of Claim for Legal Malpractice. **64 ALR6th 473.**

Challenges Under State Law to Wind Energy Facilities and Laws Regulating or Prohibiting Such Facilities. **64 ALR6th 601.**

Applicability of Attorney-Client Privilege to Communications Made in Presence of or Solely to or by Other Attorneys, Coparties, and Their Staff. **64 ALR6th 655.**

65 ALR6th

Validity, Construction, and Application of State Sex Offender Registration Statutes Concerning Level of Classification—Initial Classification Determination. **65 ALR6th 1.**

When Does Use of Pepper Spray, Mace, or Other Similar Chemical Irritants Constitute Violation of Constitutional Rights. **65 ALR6th 93.**

Pretrial Discovery in Disciplinary Proceedings Against Physician. **65 ALR6th 295.**

Preemption of State Regulation of Weapons and Other Laws by Federal Gun Control Act. **65 ALR6th 329.**

Sufficiency of Evidence to Support Homicide Conviction Where No Body Was Produced. **65 ALR6th 359.**

Validity, Construction, and Application of State Statutes Regulating Solicitation or Exit Polling Near Voting Precincts. **65 ALR6th 441.**

Construction and Application of Supreme Court's Holding in Citizens United v. Federal Election Com'n, 130 S. Ct. 876, 175 L. Ed. 2d 753, 187 L.R.R.M. (BNA) 2961, 159 Lab. Cas. (CCH) § p§ t 10166 (2010), That Government May Not Prohibit Independent and Indirect Corporate Expenditures on Political Speech. **65 ALR6th 503.**

Propriety of Audio or Video Playback of Testimony or Statement to Jury. **65 ALR6th 537.**

66 ALR6th

Validity, Construction, and Application of State Sex Offender Registration Statutes Concerning Level of Classification—Claims for Downward Departure. **66 ALR6th 1.**

Applicability of Attorney-Client Privilege to Communications Made in Presence of or Solely to or by Nonattorney Consultants, Professionals, and Similar Contractors. **66 ALR6th 83.**

Construction and Application of "Pennsylvania Rule" in Ship Collisions and Other Maritime Accidents. **66 ALR6th 185.**

Applicability and Application of Uniform Child Custody Jurisdiction and Enforcement Act (UCCJEA) to International Child Custody and Support Actions. **66 ALR6th 269.**

Validity, Construction, and Application of State and Local Laws Providing for Civil Liability for Tobacco Sales or Distribution to Minors. **66 ALR6th 315.**

Validity, Construction and Application of State Laws Concerning, Relating to, or Encompassing Disclosure of and Tampering with Motor Vehicle Odometer—Validity of Statutory Provisions, Construction of Statute and Particular Terms, and Remedies. **66 ALR6th 351.**

Propriety of Prohibition of Display or Wearing of Confederate Flag. 493 Effect of Uniform Commercial Code Article 4A on Attachment, Garnishment, Forfeiture or Other Third-Party Process Against Funds Transfers. **66 ALR6th 567.**

2010 to 2011 A.L.R. United States Supreme Court Review. **66 ALR6th 635.**

67 ALR6th

Validity, Construction, and Application of State Sex Offender Registration Statutes Concerning Level of Classification—Claims Challenging Upward Departure. **67 ALR6th 1.**

Parts of Human Body, other than Feet, as Deadly or Dangerous Weapons or Instrumentalities for Purposes of Statutes Aggravating Offenses such as Assault and Robbery. **67 ALR6th 103.**

Validity, Construction, and Application of State Laws Concerning, Relating to, or Encompassing Disclosure of and Tampering with Motor Vehicle Odometer—Statutes of Limitation, Parties to Action, Evidentiary Matters, and Particular Violations of Statute. **67 ALR6th 209.**

Applicability of Attorney-Client Privilege to Communications Made in Presence of or Solely to or by Family Members or Companion, Confidant, or Friend of Attorneys or Client or Attesting Witnesses for Client's Will. **67 ALR6th 341.**

Regulation of Business of Tattooing. **67 ALR6th 395.**

Defamation of Psychiatrist, Psychologist, or Counselor. **67 ALR6th 437.**

Search and Seizure: Reasonable Expectation of Privacy in Outbuildings. **67 ALR6th 531.**

Validity of Runoff Voting Election Methodology. **67 ALR6th 609.**

Constitutionality of State Laws Regulating Use or Sale of Physician—Identifying Prescription Information for Commercial Purposes. **67 ALR6th 629.**

68 ALR6th

Judicial Expunction of Criminal Record of Convicted Adult in Absence of Authorizing Statute. **68 ALR6th 1.**

Validity, Construction, and Application of Criminal Statutes and Ordinances to Prosecution for Dogfighting. **68 ALR6th 115.**

Class-of-One Equal Protection Claims Based Upon Real Estate Development, Zoning, and Planning. **68 ALR6th 229.**

Construction and Application of Term "Actual Charges" in Supplemental Health Insurance Policy. **68 ALR6th 297.**

Invasion of Privacy by Using or Obtaining E-Mail or Computer Files. **68 ALR6th 331.**

Prison Inmate's Eighth Amendment Rights to Treatment for Sleep Disorders. **68 ALR6th 389.**

Validity, Construction, and Application of 17th Amendment to United States Constitution, Providing for Direct Election of Senators and Filling Vacancies in State's Senatorial Delegation. **68 ALR6th 489.**

Criminal Liability for Unauthorized Use of Credit Card Under State Credit Card Statutes. **68 ALR6th 527.**

What Constitutes "Custodial Interrogation" Within Rule of Miranda v. Arizona Requiring that Suspect Be Informed of His or Her Federal Constitutional Rights Before Custodial Interrogation—At Border or Functional Equivalent of Border. **68 ALR6th 607.**

69 ALR6th

Judicial Expunction of Criminal Record of Convicted Adult Under Statute—General Principles, and Expunction of Criminal Records Under Statutes Providing for Such Relief Where Criminal Proceeding Is Terminated in Favor of Defendant, upon Completion of Probation, upon Suspended Sentence, and Where Expungement Relief Predicated upon Type, and Number, of Offenses. **69 ALR6th 1.**

Validity, Construction, and Application of Statutes and

Ordinances to Prosecution for Cockfighting. **69 ALR6th 207.**

Search and Seizure: Reasonable Expectation of Privacy in Side Yards. **69 ALR6th 275.**

Propriety and Use of Balance Billing in Health Care Context. **69 ALR6th 317.**

Construction and Application of Uniform Certification of Questions of Law Act. **69 ALR6th 415.**

Liability of Organization Sponsoring or Administering Arbitration to Parties Involved in Proceeding. **69 ALR6th 513.**

Admissibility and Use of Secure Continuous Remote Alcohol Monitoring (SCRAM) Devices in Civil and Criminal Proceedings. **69 ALR6th 549.**

Criminal Defendant's Right to Electronic Recordation of Interrogations and Confessions. **69 ALR6th 579.**

70 ALR6th

Judicial Expunction of Criminal Record of Convicted Adult Under Statute-Expunction Under Statutes Addressing "First Offenders" and "Innocent Persons," Where Conviction Was for Minor Drug or Other Offense, Where Indictment Has Not Been Presented Against Accused or Accused Has been Released from Custody, and Where Court Considered Impact of Nolle Prosequi, Partial Dismissal, Pardon, Rehabilitation, and Lesser-Included Offenses. **70 ALR6th 1.**

Propriety of School Policies, and Measures Taken Pursuant to School Policies, Prohibiting the Possession, Display, or Use of Cell Phones in School. **70 ALR6th 145.**

Construction and Application of State Abandoned Newborn Infant Protection Acts. **70 ALR6th 183.**

Construction and Application of Revised Uniform Partnership Act . 209 Challenges to Pre- and Post-Conviction Forfeitures and to Postconviction Restitution Under Animal Cruelty Statutes. **70 ALR6th 329.**

Construction and Application of Article III of Interstate Agreement on Detainers (IAD)—Issues Related to "Speedy

Trial" Requirement, and Construction of Essential Terms. **70 ALR6th 361.**

Constitutionality of Restricting Public Speech in Street, Sidewalk, Park, or Other Public Forum—Characteristics of . **70 ALR6th 513.**

Propriety and Sufficiency of Electronic Filing of Notice of Appeal in State. **70 ALR6th 661.**

71 ALR6th

Adequacy of Defense Counsel's Representation of Criminal Client Regarding Search and Seizure Issues—Pretrial Motions—Suppression Motions Where No Warrant. **71 ALR6th 1.**

Construction and Application of Self-Protection or Self-Defense Exception to Attorney-Client. **71 ALR6th 249.**

Validity of State and Municipal Indecent Exposure Statutes and Ordinances. **71 ALR6th 283.**

Construction and Application of Article III of Interstate Agreement on Detainers (IAD): Issues Related to Certificate, Request by Defendant for Disposition, and "Anti-Shuttling" Provision. **71 ALR6th 335.**

Constitutionality of Restricting Public Speech in Street, Sidewalk, Park, or Other Public Forum—Manner of. **71 ALR6th 471.**

Propriety and Prejudicial Effect of Requiring Defendant to Wear Stun Belt or Shock Belt During Course of State Criminal Trial. **71 ALR6th 625.**

72 ALR6th

Adequacy of Defense Counsel's Representation of Criminal Client Regarding Search and Seizure Issues—Pretrial Motions—Suppression Motions Where Warrant Was Involved. **72 ALR6th 1.**

Construction and Application of Article III of Interstate Agreement on Detainers (IAD): Issues Related To Custody, Duties of Prison Officials, Waiver of Extradition, Escape, Assistance of Counsel, and Necessity of Hearing. **72 ALR6th 141.**

ANNOTATION TITLES

Validity, Construction, and Application of State Statutes and Rules Governing Requests for Postconviction DNA Testing. **72 ALR6th 227.**

Enforcement and Validity of Litigation Funding Agreements. **72 ALR6th 385.**

Entitlement to Attorney's Fees Under Uniform Parentage Act of 1973. **72 ALR6th 413.**

Reverse-Franks Claims, Where Police Arguably Omit Facts from Search or Arrest Warrant Affidavit Material to Finding of Probable Cause with Reckless Disregard for the Truth—Underlying Homicide and Assault Offenses. **72 ALR6th 437.**

Constitutional Challenges to Compelled Speech—General Principles. **72 ALR6th 513.**

Standing of Person, Other than Former Client, to Seek Disqualification of Attorney in Civil Action. **72 ALR6th 563.**

73 ALR6th

Adequacy of Defense Counsel's Representation of Criminal Client Regarding Search and Seizure Issues—Pretrial Motions—Motions Other than for Suppression. **73 ALR6th 1.**

Reverse-Franks Claims, Where Police Arguably Omit Facts from Search or Arrest Warrant Affidavit Material to Finding of Probable Cause with Reckless Disregard for Truth—Underlying Drug Offenses. **73 ALR6th 49.**

Constitutional Challenges to Compelled Speech—Particular Situations or Circumstances. **73 ALR6th 281.**

Regulation of Consumer Loans Under Uniform Consumer Credit Code. **73 ALR6th 425.**

Construction and Application of Usury Provisions in State Constitutions. **73 ALR6th 571.**

Enforceability of Insurance Policy Protective Safeguards Endorsement (PSE). **73 ALR6th 681.**

74 ALR6th

Construction and Application of Uniform Division of Income

for Tax Purposes Act (UDITPA)—Determination of Business Income. **74 ALR6th 1.**

Reverse-Franks Claims, Where Police Arguably Omit Facts from Search or Arrest Warrant Affidavit Material to Finding of Probable Cause with Reckless Disregard for the Truth—Underlying Sexual Offenses. **74 ALR6th 69.**

Validity of Parental Responsibility Statutes and Ordinances Holding Parents Liable for Criminal Acts of Their Children. **74 ALR6th 181.**

Construction and Application of Statutes and Ordinances Concerning Establishment of Residency, as Condition for Running for Municipal Office. **74 ALR6th 209.**

Vested Right of Retiree to Promised Medical Insurance Benefits from Private Employer. **74 ALR6th 267.**

Construction and Application by State Courts of Supreme Court's Ruling in Padilla v. Kentucky, 130 S. Ct. 1473, 176 L. Ed. 2d 284 (2010), That Defense Counsel Has Obligation to Advise Defendant That Entering Guilty Plea Could Result in Deportation. **74 ALR6th 373.**

Liability of Seller for Fraud or Misrepresentation as to Health or Breeding of Puppy or Adult Dog. **74 ALR6th 505.**

Purchase of Annuity by Debtor as Fraud on Creditors. **74 ALR6th 549.**

75 ALR6th

Release or Compromise or Waiver by Parent of Cause of Action for Injuries to Child as Affecting Right of Child. **75 ALR6th 1.**

Construction and Application of Contact Sports Exception to Negligence. **75 ALR6th 109.**

Construction and Application of Interstate Compact for Adult Offender Supervision. **75 ALR6th 181.**

Validity, Construction, and Application of Exhaustion Clause of Underinsured Motorist Coverage Plan. **75 ALR6th 235.**

Challenges to Write-in Ballots and Certification of Write-in Candidates. **75 ALR6th 311.**

Reverse-Franks Claims, Where Police Arguably Omit Facts from Search or Arrest Warrant Affidavit Material to Finding of Probable Cause with Reckless Disregard for Truth—Underlying Weapons Offenses. **75 ALR6th 443.**

Preemption of State Statute, Law, Ordinance, or Policy with Respect to Law Enforcement or Criminal Prosecution as to Aliens. **75 ALR6th 541.**

76 ALR6th

Construction and Application of "Make My Day" and "Stand Your Ground" Statutes. **76 ALR6th 1.**

Validity, and Applicability to Causes of Action, of Statute Shortening Limitation Period or Period of Repose. **76 ALR6th 31.**

Issues Arising in Same Sex Divorce and Dissolution of Same-Sex Civil Unions. **76 ALR6th 257.**

Preemption of State Law Claim by Federal Copyright Act—General Views and Jurisdictional Issues. **76 ALR6th 289.**

Products Liability: Exercise, Fitness, and Related Equipment. **76 ALR6th 395.**

Products Liability: Sudden or Unexpected Acceleration of Motor Vehicle. **76 ALR6th 465.**

Construction and Application of State Prohibitions of Unfunded Mandates. **76 ALR6th 543.**

2011 to 2012 A.L.R. United States Supreme Court Review. **76 ALR6th 587.**

77 ALR6th

Validity, Construction and Application of Telephone Consumer Protection Act (47 U.S.C.A. § 227)—State Cases. **77 ALR6th 1.**

Removal of Adults from State Sex Offender Registries. **77 ALR6th 197.**

Propriety of Juror's Tests or Experiments Outside of Court or Jury Room. **77 ALR6th 251.**

Constitutionality of State Bankruptcy-Specific Exemptions Under Supremacy Clause and Bankruptcy Clause of U.S.

Constitution (U.S. Const., Art. VI, cl. 2 and Art. I, § 8, cl. 4). **77 ALR6th 273.**

Validity of Postnuptial Agreements in Contemplation of Divorce. **77 ALR6th 293.**

State and Local Regulation of Operation of Dog Breeding and Kennel Facilities. **77 ALR6th 393.**

Preemption of State Law Claim by Federal Copyright Act—Nature or Type of Claim Asserted. **77 ALR6th 543.**

78 ALR6th

Due Process Afforded in Drug Court Proceedings. **78 ALR6th 1.**

Automobile Repair Shop's Duty to Provide Customer with Information, Estimates, or Replaced Parts, Under Automobile Repair Consumer Protection Act. **78 ALR6th 97.**

In Personam Jurisdiction, Under Long-Arm Statute, over Nonresident Attorney in Legal Malpractice Action. **78 ALR6th 151.**

Construction and Application of Illinois v. Lidster, 540 U.S. 419, 124 S. Ct. 885, 157 L. Ed. 2d 843 (2004), Governing Validity of Police Roadblock, Checkpoint, or Other Detention of Vehicle for Gathering of Information. **78 ALR6th 213.**

Validity, Construction, and Effect of Statute, Ordinance, or Other Measure Involving Fluoridation of Public Water Supply. **78 ALR6th 229.**

Construction and Application by State Courts of Protective Sweep Doctrine Recognized in Maryland v. Buie, 494 U.S. 325, 110 S. Ct. 1093, 108 L. Ed. 2d 276 (1990)—Warrantless Search of House for Dangerous Persons. **78 ALR6th 297.**

Discharge from Commitment and Supervised Release of Civilly Committed Sex Offender Under State Law. **78 ALR6th 417.**

Permissibility Under Fourth Amendment of Terry Stop to Investigate Completed Misdemeanor. **78 ALR6th 599.**

79 ALR6th

Construction and Application by State Courts of Protective Sweep Doctrine Recognized in Maryland v. Buie, 494 U.S. 325, 110 S. Ct. 1093, 108 L. Ed. 2d 276 (1990)—Warrantless Search of Apartment or Other Non-House Dwelling for Dangerous Persons. **79 ALR6th 1.**

State Criminal Prosecution Against Medical Practitioner for Fraud in Connection with Claims Under Medicaid, Medicare, or Similar Welfare Program for Providing Medical Services. **79 ALR6th 125.**

Regulation of Consumer Credit Sales and Consumer Leases Under Uniform Consumer Credit Code. **79 ALR6th 211.**

Reverse-Franks Claims, Where Police Arguably Omit Facts from Search or Arrest Warrant Affidavit Material to Finding of Probable Cause with Reckless Disregard for Truth—Underlying Vehicular Offenses. **79 ALR6th 325.**

Admissibility of Person's Status as Illegal Alien in Civil Pretrial and Trial Proceedings. **79 ALR6th 351.**

What Constitutes Duress by Employer or Former Employer Vitiating Employee's Release of Employer from Claims Arising out of Employment. **79 ALR6th 377.**

Validity, Construction, and Application of Statutory Exemptions from Liability for Persons Injured by Equine or Equestrian Activities. **79 ALR6th 487.**

Validity of "Reach-In" Searches. **79 ALR6th 631.**

80 ALR6th

Special Commentary: Recovery of "Stranded Costs" by Utilities. **80 ALR6th 1.**

Validity, Construction, and Application of State Greenhouse Gas Reduction Acts and Regulations. **80 ALR6th 203.**

Reverse-Franks Claims, Where Police Arguably Omit Facts from Search or Arrest Warrant Affidavit Material to Finding of Probable Cause with Reckless Disregard for Truth—Underlying Theft and Burglary Offenses. **80 ALR6th 239.**

Construction and Application of Uniform Division of Income for Tax Purposes Act (UDITPA)—Apportionment of Business Income. **80 ALR6th 325.**

Application of Uninsured or Underinsured Motorist or No-Fault Insurance to School Bus Incidents. **80 ALR6th 389.**

Civil Liability of Psychiatrist Arising out of Patient's Violent Conduct Resulting in Injury to or Death of Patient or Third Party Allegedly Caused in Whole or Part by Mental Disorder. **80 ALR6th 469.**

Signing Credit Charge, Credit Sales Slip, or Credit Electronic Point of Sale Terminal, as Forgery. **80 ALR6th 599.**

Unemployment Compensation as Affected by Employer's Relocation or Transfer of Employee from Place of Employment. **80 ALR6th 635.**

81 ALR6th

Application, Recognition, or Consideration of Jewish Law by Courts in United States. **81 ALR6th 1.**

Construction and Application of Uniform Division of Income for Tax Purposes Act (UDITPA)—Availability of Relief from Standard Apportionment Formula and Other Issues. **81 ALR6th 97.**

Recognition of Action for Damages for Wrongful Foreclosure—General Views. **81 ALR6th 161.**

Liability of Cruise Ship Operator for Medical Negligence. **81 ALR6th 235.**

Reverse-Franks Claims, Where Police Arguably Omit Facts from Search or Arrest Warrant Affidavit Material to Finding of Probable Cause with Reckless Disregard for the Truth—Underlying Miscellaneous Offenses. **81 ALR6th 257.**

Subjection of Municipal Property, or Alleged Municipal Property, to Mechanics' Liens. **81 ALR6th 363.**

Validity and Construction of Restrictive Covenant Prohibiting or Governing Outside Storage or Parking of House Trailers, Motor Homes, Campers, Vans, and Like, in Residential Neighborhoods. **81 ALR6th 469.**

Construction and Application of Booking Question Exception to Miranda. **81 ALR6th 505.**

Divorce and Separation: Health Insurance Benefits as Marital Asset. **81 ALR6th 655.**

82 ALR6th

Application, Recognition, or Consideration of Islamic Law by Courts in United States. **82 ALR6th 1.**

Recognition of Action for Damages for Wrongful Foreclosure—Types of Actions. **82 ALR6th 43.**

Liability of Cruise Ship Operator for Injury to or Death of Passengers . **82 ALR6th 175.**

Qualification as Expert to Testify in Legal Malpractice Action. **82 ALR6th 281.**

Propriety of Holding State Courtroom Spectators in Contempt. **82 ALR6th 317.**

Propriety of Allowing Witness to Hold Stuffed Animal, Doll, Toy or Other Comfort Item During Testimony. **82 ALR6th 373.**

Liability to Spectator at Baseball Game Who Is Hit by Ball or Injured as Result of Other Hazards of Game—Failure to Provide or Maintain Sufficient Screening. **82 ALR6th 417.**

Validity, Construction, and Application of State Constitutional and Statutory Balanced Budget Provisions. **82 ALR6th 497.**

83 ALR6th

Statement in Advertisements, Product Brochures or Other Promotional Materials as Constituting "Affirmation of Fact" Giving Rise to Express Warranty Under UCC § 2-313(1)(a). **83 ALR6th 1.**

Construction and Application of Death Knell Doctrine in State Actions. **83 ALR6th 143.**

Claims of Student Plagiarism and Student Claims Arising from Such Allegations. **83 ALR6th 195.**

Validity, Construction, and Application of Pattern and Nonpattern Jury Instructions in State Death Penalty Proceedings. **83 ALR6th 255.**

Validity of Policies or Practices Regarding Highway or Bridge Toll Discounts. **83 ALR6th 399.**

Validity, Construction, and Application of State Statute Forbidding Unfair Trade Practice or Competition by Discriminatory Allowance of Rebates, Commissions, Discounts, or the Like. **83 ALR6th 419.**

Necessity or Propriety of Court's Provision of Cocounsel to Criminal Defendant Who Is Already Represented by Counsel—State Prosecutions. **83 ALR6th 465.**

Homestead Right of Cotenant as Affecting Partition. **83 ALR6th 605.**

84 ALR6th

Statement in Product Packaging, User Manuals, or Other Product Documentation as Constituting "Affirmation of Fact" Giving Rise to Express Warranty Under UCC § 2-313(1)(a). **84 ALR6th 1.**

Criminal and Civil Liability of Civilians and Police Officers Concerning Recording of Police Actions. **84 ALR6th 89.**

Validity of Zoning Regulations Prohibiting or Regulating Removal or Exploitation of Oil and Gas, Including Hydrofracking. **84 ALR6th 133.**

Judicial Removal for Cause and Peremptory Strike Validity Under Batson Against Jurors Based upon Viewing Police Procedural Programs, Live Television Trials, Reality Legal Television, or Other Crime and Legal Based Television Programs. **84 ALR6th 229.**

Fifth Amendment Privilege Against Self-Incrimination as Applied to Compelled Disclosure of Password or Production of Otherwise Encrypted Electronically Stored Data. **84 ALR6th 251.**

Admissibility and Propriety of Use of Abel Assessment for Sexual Interest Test. **84 ALR6th 263.**

Permissibility under Fourth Amendment of Investigatory Traffic Stop Based Solely on Anonymous Tip Reporting Drunk Driving. **84 ALR6th 293.**

Establishment of Negligence Within Meaning of Statute Penalizing Negligent Homicide by Operation of Motor

Vehicle—Speeding or Driving at Unsafe Speed. **84 ALR6th 427.**

Validity and Enforceability of Forum Selection Clauses in Internet Transactions. **84 ALR6th 589.**

85 ALR6th

Jurisdiction of State Court Over Actions Involving Patents. **85 ALR6th 1.**

Validity, Construction, and Application of State Prison Litigation Reform Acts. **85 ALR6th 229.**

Construction and Effect of Severance or Dismissal Pay Provisions of Employment Contract or Collective Labor Agreement. **85 ALR6th 323.**

Action in Replevin for Recovery of Dog or Cat. **85 ALR6th 429.**

Application of Anti-SLAPP ("Strategic Lawsuit Against Public Participation") Statutes to Invasion of Privacy Claims. **85 ALR6th 475.**

Application of Follow the Fortunes Doctrine, Imposing Legal Duty on Reinsurer to Pay its Share of Settlement Made by Reinsured with Original Parties. **85 ALR6th 531.**

Validity of State Gun Control Legislation Under State Constitutional Provisions Securing Right to Bear Arms—Convicted Felons. **85 ALR6th 641.**

86 ALR6th

Validity of Grandparent Visitation Statutes. **86 ALR6th 1.**

Class—of—One Equal Protection Claims Based upon Law Enforcement Actions. **86 ALR6th 173.**

Construction and Application of State Rules of Civil Procedure Authorizing Relief from Final Judgment or Order for "Any Other Reason"—General Principles. **86 ALR6th 321.**

Necessity of Production of Original Note Involved in Mortgage Foreclosure—Twenty—First Century Cases. **86 ALR6th 411.**

Construction and Application of Apex—Deposition Rule. **86 ALR6th 519.**

2012 to 2013 A.L.R. United States Supreme Court Review. **86 ALR6th 577.**

87 ALR6th

Validity, Construction, and Application of State Computer Crime and Fraud Laws. **87 ALR6th 1.**

Application of Section 1 of 13th Amendment to United States Constitution, U.S. Const. Amend. XIII, § 1, Prohibiting Slavery and Involuntary Servitude—Labor Required as Punishment for Crime. **87 ALR6th 109.**

Construction and Application of State Rules of Civil Procedure Authorizing Relief from Final Judgment or Order for "Any Other Reason"—Negligence and Intentional Tort Cases. **87 ALR6th 197.**

Who May Enforce Liability of Reinsurer. **87 ALR6th 319.**

Validity, Construction, and Application of Statutes Directly or Indirectly Proscribing Unauthorized Practice of Law on Internet. **87 ALR6th 479.**

Validity of Postnuptial Agreements in Contemplation of Spouse's Death. **87 ALR6th 495.**

Disapproval by Governor of Bill in Part or Approval with Modifications. **87 ALR6th 633.**

88 ALR6th

Oral Statement as Constituting "Affirmation of Fact" Giving Rise to Express Warranty Under UCC § 2-313(1)(a). **88 ALR6th 1.**

Application of Section 1 of 13th Amendment to United States Constitution, U.S. Const. Amend. XIII, § 1, Prohibiting Slavery and Involuntary Servitude—Labor Required by Law or Force Not as Punishment for Crime. **88 ALR6th 203.**

Expectation of Privacy in and Discovery of Social Networking Web Site Postings and Communications. **88 ALR6th 319.**

Construction and Application of State Rules of Civil Procedure Authorizing Relief from Final Judgment or Order for "Any Other Reason"—Real Estate and Construction—Related Cases. **88 ALR6th 385.**

Doctrine of Election of Remedies as Operating Against Person Not Party to Prior Judicial Proceeding. **88 ALR6th 533.**

Preemption of State Statute, Law, Ordinance, or Policy with Respect to Employment— and Education—Related Issues Involving Aliens. **88 ALR6th 627.**

Liability Arising from Air Shows or Other Aerial Exhibitions for Injury and Death of Spectators and Participants. **88 ALR6th 679.**

89 ALR6th

Construction and Application of Parratt—Hudson Doctrine, Providing That Where Deprivation of Property Interest Is Occasioned by Random and Unauthorized Conduct of State Officials, Procedural Due Process Inquiry Is Limited to Issue of Adequacy of Postdeprivation Remedies Provided by State. **89 ALR6th 1.**

Validity, Construction, and Application of State Sex Offender Statutes Prohibiting Use of Computers and Internet as Conditions of Probation or Sentence. **89 ALR6th 261.**

Liability of Manufacturer or Distributor for Injuries Arising from Allegedly Defective Artificial Knee Devices or Prostheses. **89 ALR6th 337.**

Construction and Application of State Rules of Civil Procedure Authorizing Relief from Final Judgment or Order for "Any Other Reason"—Business—Related, Corporate, and Contract Cases. **89 ALR6th 409.**

Criminal Liability for Street Racing (Drag Racing). **89 ALR6th 565.**

Provision of Hormone Therapy or Sexual Reassignment Surgery to State Inmates with Gender Identity Disorder (GID). **89 ALR6th 701.**

90 ALR6th

Validity, Construction, and Application of State Debt Adjusting Statutes. **90 ALR6th 1.**

Products Liability: Pain Pumps. **90 ALR6th 75.**

School's Violation of Student's Substantive Due Process Rights by Suspending or Expelling Student. **90 ALR6th 235.**

Power of Private Citizen to Institute Criminal Proceedings Without Authorization or Approval by Prosecuting Attorney. **90 ALR6th 385.**

Construction and Application of State Workers' Compensation Laws to Claim for Hearing Loss—Resulting from Single Traumatic Accident or Event. **90 ALR6th 425.**

Construction and Application of State Rules of Civil Procedure Authorizing Relief From Final Judgment or Order for "Any Other Reason"—Probate and Family Law Cases. **90 ALR6th 451.**

Property Damage Insurance: What Constitutes "Contamination" Within Policy Clause Excluding Coverage. **90 ALR6th 635.**

91 ALR6th

Application of Practical Location Doctrine in Establishing Boundary Line. **91 ALR6th 1.**

Construction and Application of State Rules of Civil Procedure Authorizing Relief from Final Judgment or Order for "Any Other Reason"—Employment, Insurance, Workers' Compensation, and Other and Unspecified Cases. **91 ALR6th 171.**

Validity, Construction, and Application of Stranger— Originated Life Insurance Policies. **91 ALR6th 327.**

School's Violation of Parents' Substantive Due Process Rights Due to Their Child's Suspension or Expulsion. **91 ALR6th 365.**

Liability of Law School for Deceptive Acts or Practices, False Advertising, and Otherwise, Based upon Employment Information for Graduates. **91 ALR6th 383.**

Breach of Bailment of Electronic Data. **91 ALR6th 409.**

Liability for Negligence in Hydraulic Fracturing, Hydro— fracturing, or Hydro—fracking. **91 ALR6th 423.**

Judicial Review of State or Local Administrative Order Approving, Denying, or Revoking Permit or License to Carry, Possess, or Own Firearm. **91 ALR6th 435.**

92 ALR6th

Admissibility, in State Probation Revocation Proceedings, of Evidence Obtained Through Illegal Search and Seizure. **92 ALR6th 1.**

Application of State Statutes Regulating Claims of Hostile Work Environment or Sexual Harassment Based on Sexual, Romantic, or Paramour Favoritism. **92 ALR6th 121.**

Liability of Food Manufacturer Based on Statement in Product Labeling or Promotion Relating to, or Inconsistent with Presence of, Trans Fat in Product. **92 ALR6th 141.**

Construction and Application by State Courts of Federal and State Constitutional Standards Governing Police Orders to Passengers in Car Lawfully Pulled over for Traffic Stop. **92 ALR6th 171.**

What Constitutes Driving, Operating, or Being in Control of Motor Vehicle for Purposes of Driving While Intoxicated Statute, Regulation, or Ordinance—Being in Physical Control or Actual Physical Control—General Principles. **92 ALR6th 295.**

Medical Malpractice in Diagnosis and Treatment of Breast Cancer. **92 ALR6th 379.**

Use and Effect of Comparative Bullet Lead Analysis (CBLA) in Criminal Cases. **92 ALR6th 549**

93 ALR6th

Validity of State Sex Offender Registration Laws Under Equal Protection Guarantees. **93 ALR6th 1.**

Medical Malpractice in Diagnosis and Treatment of Cancer of Female Reproductive System. **93 ALR6th 123.**

What Constitutes Driving, Operating, or Being in Control of Motor Vehicle for Purposes of Driving While Intoxicated Statute, Regulation, or Ordinance—Being in Physical

Control or Actual Physical Control—Motorist Sleeping or Unconscious. **93 ALR6th 207.**

Sufficiency of Search Warrant for DNA Sample. **93 ALR6th 275.**

Loss or Impairment of Landowner's Access to Existing Controlled—Access Road or Highway as Compensable Taking Absent Government Condemnation or Occupation of Landowner's Realty. **93 ALR6th 363.**

Application of Fair Warning Requirement of Due Process Clause to State Death Penalty Proceedings Premised upon Retroactive Application of Case Law. **93 ALR6th 391.**

Application of Relation Back Doctrine Permitting Change in Party After Statute of Limitations Has Run in State Court Action—Products Liability Cases. **93 ALR6th 463.**

94 ALR6th

Statement in Contract Proposals, Contract Correspondence, or Contract Itself as Constituting "Affirmation of Fact" Giving Rise to Express Warranty Under U.C.C. § 2-313(1)(a). **94 ALR6th 1.**

Application of Relation Back Doctrine Permitting Change in Party After Statute of Limitations Has Run in State Court Action—Wrongful Death Cases. **94 ALR6th 111.**

What Constitutes Driving, Operating, or Being in Control of Motor Vehicle for Purposes of Driving While Intoxicated Statute, Regulation, or Ordinance—Being in Physical Control or Actual Physical Control—Passengers. **94 ALR6th 191.**

Click Fraud, Automated or Otherwise Invalid Clicks, as Basis for Liability of Internet Advertising and Service Provider to Advertising Party. **94 ALR6th 215.**

Validity, Construction, and Application of Statute or Ordinances Requiring Return Deposits on Soft Drinks, Beer, Water Bottles, or Similar Containers. **94 ALR6th 239.**

Adequacy, Sufficiency, and Effect of Compliance with Requirement of Notice of Claim Under Reinsurance Policies. **94 ALR6th 341.**

Medical Malpractice in Diagnosis and Treatment of Lung Cancer. **94 ALR6th 431.**

Validity of Search of Digital Camera and Associated Memory Cards. **94 ALR6th 525.**

Validity of Use of Cellular Telephone or Tower to Track Prospective, Real Time, or Historical Position of Possessor of Phone Under State Law. **94 ALR6th 579.**

95 ALR6th

What Constitutes Driving, Operating, or Being in Control of Motor Vehicle for Purposes of Driving While Intoxicated Statute or Ordinance—Being in Actual Physical Control—Status of Vehicle. **95 ALR6th 1.**

Validity, Construction, and Application of Browsewrap Agreements. **95 ALR6th 57.**

Application of Relation Back Doctrine Permitting Change in Party After Statute of Limitations Has Run in State Court Action—Medical Malpractice Cases Against Physicians and Other Individual Health Care Providers. **95 ALR6th 85.**

Propriety of Disclosure of State Jurors' Personal Identifying Information. **95 ALR6th 219.**

Application of Stigma—Plus Due Process Claims Other than Education Context. **95 ALR6th 341.**

Liability of Hospice in Tort, in Contract, or Pursuant to Statute, for Maltreatment or Mistreatment of Patient. **95 ALR6th 479.**

Medical Malpractice in Diagnosis and Treatment of Colorectal Cancer. **95 ALR6th 541.**

Requirement for, and Admissibility of, Expert Testimony to Determine Whether Use of Particular Amount of Force in Course of Making Arrest Was Unreasonable. **95 ALR6th 641.**

96 ALR6th

Products Liability: Hip Prostheses. **96 ALR6th 1.**

Availability and Use of Electronic Communication in Child Custody and Visitation Determinations. **96 ALR6th 103.**

Liability for Unfair or Deceptive Practices with Respect to Force-Placed Insurance. **96 ALR6th 125.**

Discrimination on Basis of Person's Transgender or Trans-sexual Status as Violation of State or Local Law. **96 ALR6th 189.**

Propriety of Holding Prisoner in Isolation—State Cases. **96 ALR6th 269.**

What Constitutes Driving, Operating, or Being in Control of Motor Vehicle for Purposes of Driving while Intoxicated Statute or Ordinance—Being in Actual Physical Control—Factors and Circumstances Establishing Actual Physical Control; Miscellaneous Situations. **96 ALR6th 355.**

Validity of Criminalization of Urging or Assisting Suicide Under State Statutes and Common Law. **96 ALR6th 475.**

Medical Malpractice in Diagnosis and Treatment of Cancer of Male Reproductive System. **96 ALR6th 503.**

2013 to 2014 A.L.R. United States Supreme Court Review. **96 ALR6th 577.**

97 ALR6th

Electricity, Gas, or Water Furnished by Public Utility or Alternative Supplier as "Goods" Within Provisions of Uniform Commercial Code, Article 2 on Sales. **97 ALR6th 1.**

Medical Malpractice in Diagnosis and Treatment of Cancer Other than Breast, Lung, Colorectal System, or Reproductive System Cancer. **97 ALR6th 83.**

Actual Innocence Exception to Procedural Bars in State Post-Conviction Proceedings. **97 ALR6th 263.**

Application of Relation Back Doctrine Permitting Change in Party After Statute of Limitations Has Run in State Court Action—Motor Vehicle Accident or Injury Cases: Individual Drivers, Parents, Owners or Lessors, and Passengers. **97 ALR6th 375.**

Admissibility of Evidence of Medical Defendant's Apologetic Statements or the Like as Evidence of Negligence. **97 ALR6th 519.**

Criminal Liability of Nonparent for Failure to Obtain Medical Treatment for Minor Based on Duty of One Acting in

Loco Parentis. **97 ALR6th 539.**

Admissibility of Testimony Concerning Extrajudicial Statements Made to, or in Presence of, Witness Through Interpreter—State Cases. **97 ALR6th 567.**

Validity, Construction, and Application of Open Container Laws. **97 ALR6th 653.**

98 ALR6th

Liability of Physician or Health Care Facility for False Positive Diagnosis of Cancer. **98 ALR6th 1.**

Application of Relation-Back Doctrine Permitting Change in Party After Statute of Limitations Has Run in State Court Action—Motor Vehicle Accident or Injury Cases: Corporations, Municipalities, Insurers, and Employers. **98 ALR6th 93.**

Liability for Injury or Death Resulting from Use or Operation of Snowmobile. **98 ALR6th 231.**

Fraud, Misrepresentation, or Deception as Estopping Reliance on Nonmedical Malpractice Statutes of Repose. **98 ALR6th 417.**

Emotional Manifestations by Victim or Family of Victim During Criminal Trial as Ground for Reversal, New Trial, or Mistrial—Emotional Manifestations by Victim or Relative as Spectator During Particular Trial Phases. **98 ALR6th 455.**

Liability of Public School or School District Under U.S. Constitution for Bullying, Harassment, or Intimidation of Student by Another Student. **98 ALR6th 599.**

99 ALR6th

Application of Relation-Back Doctrine Permitting Change in Party After Statute of Limitations Has Run in State Court Action—Motor Vehicle Accident or Injury Cases: Estates, and Other or Unspecified Parties. **99 ALR6th 1.**

Emotional Manifestations by Victim or Family of Victim During or Immediately Before or After Own Testimony During Criminal Trial as Ground for Reversal, New Trial, or Mistrial. **99 ALR6th 113.**

Sufficiency of Evidence to Modify Existing Joint Legal Custody of Children Pursuant to Consent Order and/or Divorce Judgment—General Principles, Jurisdictional Issues, and General Issues Related to "Best Interests of Child". **99 ALR6th 203.**

Comment Note: Propriety and Prejudicial Effect of Compelling Accused to Wear Prison Clothing at Jury Trial—State Cases. **99 ALR6th 295.**

Search and Seizure: What Constitutes Abandonment of Real Property Within Rule that Search and Seizure of Abandoned Property Is Not Unreasonable. **99 ALR6th 397.**

Validity, Construction, and Application of State Exemption Statutes for Proceeds of Personal Injury or Wrongful Death Lawsuits. **99 ALR6th 481.**

Lease Renewal Provision as Violating Rule Against Perpetuities or Restraints on Alienation. **99 ALR6th 591.**

Validity, Construction, and Application of State Workers' Compensation Laws to Claim for Hearing Loss—Resulting from Long Term Noise Exposure. **99 ALR6th 643.**

100 ALR6th

Sufficiency of Evidence to Modify Existing Joint Legal Custody of Children Pursuant to Consent Order and/or Divorce Judgment—Conduct or Condition of Parents; Evidentiary Issues. **100 ALR6th 1.**

Application of Relation-Back Doctrine Permitting Change in Party After Statute of Limitations Has Run in State Court Action—Medical Malpractice Cases in Actions Involving Hospitals, Clinics, and the Like. **100 ALR6th 139.**

Construction and Application of State Exemptions for Health Aids. **100 ALR6th 251.**

Judicial Remedies for Proceeds and Funds from Ponzi Schemes. **100 ALR6th 281.**

Imprisonment as Constituting Withdrawal from Conspiracy. **100 ALR6th 335.**

Tort Liability for Hazing or Initiation Rituals Associated with Schools, Colleges, or Universities. **100 ALR6th 365.**

Tortious Maintenance or Removal of Life Supports. **100 ALR6th 477.**

Amnesia as Affecting Defendant's Competency to Stand Trial. **100 ALR6th 535.**

Liability of Public or Private Schools or Institutions of Higher Learning, or Personnel Thereof, in Connection with Suicide of Student. **100 ALR6th 563.**

101 ALR6th

Evidence Considered in Tracing Currency, Bank Account, or Cash Equivalent to Illegal Drug Trafficking so as to Permit Forfeiture, or Declaration as Contraband, Under State Law—Factors Other than Proximity, Explanation, Amount, Packaging, and Odor. **101 ALR6th 1.**

Construction and Application of "Integral Participant" Doctrine, Which Defines Level of Actor's Involvement in Constitutional Injury that Will Support Finding of Personal Liability. **101 ALR6th 207.**

Application of Collective Knowledge Doctrine or Fellow Officers' Rule Under Fourth Amendment in Prosecution for Prostitution, Pornography, or Other Sexually Based Offense—State Cases. **101 ALR6th 299.**

Application of Collective Knowledge Doctrine or Fellow Officers' Rule Under Fourth Amendment in Murder, Homicide or Manslaughter Prosecution—State Cases. **101 ALR6th 331.**

Validity, Construction, and Application of State Statutes Proscribing Human Trafficking. **101 ALR6th 417.**

Judicial Investigation of Pardon by Governor. **101 ALR6th 431.**

What Amounts to Habitual Intemperance, Drunkenness, Excessive Drug Use, and the Like Within Statute Relating to Substantive Grounds for Divorce. **101 ALR6th 455.**

Disruptive Conduct of Spectators in Presence of Jury During Criminal Trial as Basis for Reversal, New Trial, or Mistrial—Applause and Cheering by Spectators. **101 ALR6th 499.**

Validity and Application of Therapeutic Polygraph Examinations in Sex Offender Treatment. **101 ALR6th 545.**

102 ALR6th

Major Event Litigation: Deepwater Horizon Incident. **102 ALR6th 1.**

Sufficiency of Evidence to Modify Existing Joint Legal Custody of Children Pursuant to Consent Order and/or Divorce Judgment—Primary Custody, Visitation, Residence, and Relocation. **102 ALR6th 153.**

Disruptive Conduct of Spectators in Presence of Jury During Criminal Trial as Basis for Reversal, New Trial, or Mistrial—Spoken Words. **102 ALR6th 279.**

Criminal Defendant's Age or Height as Factor in Determination of Whether Circumstances of Witness's Identification of Defendant in Photographic Array Shown by Police to Witness Were Impermissibly Suggestive as Matter of Federal Constitutional Law. **102 ALR6th 365.**

Adequacy, Under Strickland Standard, of Defense Counsel's Representation of Client in Sentencing Phase of State Court Death Penalty Case—Investigation of, and Presentation of Evidence Regarding, Client's Brain Damage or Abnormality. **102 ALR6th 417.**

Construction and Application of State Statutory Provisions Prohibiting Racial Profiling. **102 ALR6th 621.**

Retroactive Application, in Postconviction Proceedings, of Constitutional Rule of Miller v. Alabama, 132 S. Ct. 2455, 183 L. Ed. 2d 407 (2012), that Mandatory Life Sentence Without Parole for Those Under Age of 18 at Time of Their Homicide Crimes Violates Eighth Amendment's Prohibition of Cruel and Unusual Punishments. **102 ALR6th 637.**

103 ALR6th

Retail Establishment's Surveillance of or Refusal to Serve Individuals on Basis of Race or Ethnicity, or Other Alleged Instances of Consumer "Racial Profiling," as Infringement of Civil Rights Under State Law. **103 ALR6th 1.**

Adverse Employment Action Taken Against Employee for Social Media Communications. **103 ALR6th 19.**

Disruptive Conduct of Spectators in Presence of Jury During Criminal Trial as Basis for Reversal, New Trial, or Mistrial—Laughter, Crying, and Other Nonverbal Sounds by Spectators. **103 ALR6th 35.**

Evidentiary Issues and Liability Determinations in Products Liability Actions Concerning Baby Products. **103 ALR6th 81.**

What Constitutes Accused's Consent to Court's Discharge of Jury or to Grant of Motion for Mistrial Which Will Constitute Waiver of Former Jeopardy Plea—Silence or Failure to Object or Protest. **103 ALR6th 137.**

Adequacy of Defense Counsel's Representation of Criminal Client—Daubert or Frye Challenge to Expert Witness or Testimony. **103 ALR6th 247.**

Application of Collective Knowledge Doctrine or Fellow Officers' Rule Under Fourth Amendment in Prosecution for Robbery, Burglary, Larceny, or Other Theft Offense—State Cases. **103 ALR6th 347.**

Recognition and Application of Common Law Action for Tortious Interference with Parental Rights. **103 ALR6th 461.**

Sufficiency of Allegations or Evidence of Serious Bodily Injury to Support Charge of Aggravated Degree of Rape, Sodomy, or Other Sexual Abuse. **103 ALR6th 507.**

104 ALR6th

Application of Relation-Back Doctrine Permitting Change in Party After Statute of Limitations Has Run in State Court Action—Construction Cases. **104 ALR6th 1.**

Products Liability: Clothes Washing Machines. **104 ALR6th 97.**

Divorce and Separation: Custody Disputes Concerning Pets. **104 ALR6th 181.**

Discoverability of Communications Between Insurer and Reinsurer. **104 ALR6th 207.**

Construction and Application of Restatement Second, Contracts § 261: Discharge by Supervening

Impracticability. **104 ALR6th 303.**

Action for Damages for Attempted Wrongful Foreclosure. **104 ALR6th 485.**

Application of Equal Protection Principle Recognized in Bush v. Gore, 531 U.S. 98, 121 S. Ct. 525, 148 L. Ed. 2d 388 (2000), to Elections Cases. **104 ALR6th 547.**

ANNOTATION HISTORY TABLE

This table lists annotations in ALR5th through Volume 125 and ALR6th through Volume 104 which have been superseded or supplemented by later annotations.

ALR5th

1 ALR5th 469
§ 3-9, Superseded 110 ALR5th 579
§ 10-13, Superseded 113 ALR5th 349
§ 14-48, Superseded 113 ALR5th 349, 116 ALR5th 559, 117 ALR5th 349, 118 ALR5th 561, 119 ALR5th 351, 122 ALR5th 385, 12 ALR6th 417

1 ALR5th 938
§ 3[a], 3[b], Superseded 50 ALR6th 353

3 ALR5th 784
§ 9, Superseded 125 ALR5th 357
§ 10, Superseded 7 ALR6th 233

5 ALR5th 530
§ 5, 6, Superseded 101 ALR5th 1

6 ALR5th 733
§ 19-22[c], Superseded 68 ALR6th 115
§ 23-26[d], Superseded 69 ALR6th 207

10 ALR5th 245
§ 22, 23, Superseded 82 ALR5th 149, 83 ALR5th 103, 84 ALR5th 249, 97 ALR5th 1, 106 ALR5th 111, 108 ALR5th 1

12 ALR5th 195
§ 19[a]-19[e], Superseded 24 ALR6th 497

14 ALR5th 242
§ 48, Superseded 86 ALR5th 397

15 ALR5th 391
§ 7[k], Superseded 44 ALR6th 301
§ 12[a], 12[b], Superseded 45 ALR6th 435

15 ALR5th 900
Superseded 23 ALR6th 573

17 ALR5th 179
Superseded 100 ALR6th 563

18 ALR5th 542
Superseded 30 ALR6th 483

25 ALR5th 996
Superseded 47 ALR6th 347

27 ALR5th 54
Superseded 61 ALR6th 1

36 ALR5th 133
§§ 3[c], 4[c], Superseded 50 ALR6th 261

36 ALR5th 161
§ 3[a], 3[b], Superseded 63 ALR6th 351
§ 6, Superseded 93 ALR6th 1
§ 9[a], 9[b], Superseded 41 ALR6th 141
§ 19.2, Superseded 64 ALR6th 1, 65 ALR6th 1, 66 ALR6th 1, 67 ALR6th 1
§ 20.5, Superseded 34 ALR6th 171
§ 24, Superseded 37 ALR6th 55, 38 ALR6th 1, 39 ALR6th 577
§ 25[a]-26[g], Superseded 33 ALR6th 91

37 ALR5th 349
§ 11[b], 12[a-f], Superseded 107 ALR5th 623

44 ALR5th 393
§ 13, Superseded 79 ALR5th 409

47 ALR5th 1
§ 8, Superseded 83 ALR6th 195

58 ALR5th 613
§ 10, Superseded 64 ALR6th 249

60 ALR5th 1
§ 11, Superseded 45 ALR6th 643

60 ALR5th 165
§ 6, 7, 8, Superseded 8 ALR6th 549

61 ALR5th 635
§ 8, 22, Superseded 91 ALR5th 545

70 ALR5th 647
Superseded 87 ALR6th 1

79 ALR5th 689
Superseded 43 ALR6th 611, 46 ALR6th 1, 47 ALR6th 1, 48 ALR6th 1, 49 ALR6th 1

81 ALR5th 41
§ 8, Superseded 3 ALR6th 153

84 ALR5th 1
§ 13.7, Superseded 45 ALR Fed 2d 1

89 ALR5th 195
§ 7[a], 7[b], Superseded 63 ALR6th 429
§ 17[a] to 17[c], Superseded 61 ALR6th 521

92 ALR5th 15
§ 4.5, Superseded 88 ALR6th 319

93 ALR5th 47
§ 18, Superseded 92 ALR6th 121

100 ALR5th 1
§ 3.1, Superseded 66 ALR6th 269
§ 3.9 to 4[i], Superseded 57 ALR6th 163
§ 5[a], 5[c], Superseded 52 ALR6th 433
§ 8[a] to 8[c], 8.5, Superseded 59 ALR6th 161, 60 ALR6th 193
§ 10[a] to [e], Superseded 53 ALR6th 419

ALR6th

5 ALR6th 1
§ 65, 66, Superseded 65 ALR6th 441

37 ALR6th 55
§ 13, 14, Superseded 93 ALR6th 1

2005 ALR6th 1
Superseded 101 ALR6th 1